Special Supplement

1975
BRITANNICA
BOOK OF THE YEAR

This issue of the *Britannica Book of the Year* is the first to appear since the publication in February 1974 of the 15th Edition of *Encyclopædia Britannica*. We take the opportunity to address this introductory message to new subscribers and to present two special essays, the first of a series linking the *Book of the Year* with selected subject areas in the *Britannica*.

The basic purpose of the *Book of the Year* is to provide coverage of people, places, and events of prominence during the past calendar year and to review developments in subject areas of wide interest. To a large extent, therefore, the *Book of the Year* updates the *Britannica*. But its usefulness to the *Britannica* owner is greatly increased if the *Book of the Year* also points out the *Britannica*'s more extensive, in-depth coverage of the same subject areas, providing the reader with the background information needed for more complete understanding of events.

In this 1975 issue of the *Book of the Year* we have introduced a code to refer the reader to relevant articles and parts of articles in the Macropædia of the new *Britannica*. It takes the form of numbers and letters set unobtrusively in brackets at the end of articles. This code is based on the system used in the Propædia of the new *Britannica*, which presents both an Outline of Knowledge (on which the overall structure of the new *Britannica* is based) and a Guide to subject coverage and its location in the Macropædia.

Consider, for example, the *Book of the Year* article CHESS. At the end of it, the reference [452.C.3.c.ii] appears. The first three numbers refer to a Section in the Propædia—namely, to Section 452. When you find this in the Propædia (on page 275), turn to subject C.3.c.ii—which is chess (this appears on page 278). Opposite the entry you will discover a reference indicating that there is an article on chess in Volume 4 of the *Britannica*.

The code is intended to lead the reader first to the Propædia, where a subject of interest is shown in its proper place in the Outline of Knowledge and in its broad setting; and then to the Macropædia. Whereas the *Book of the Year* article provides information on major events that occurred in the world of chess during the year under review, the Macropædia article presents a comprehensive account of the history, rules, and strategy of the game. Thus the former updates and complements the latter.

Some subjects treated in the *Book of the Year* may bear a less straightforward relationship to corresponding Macropædia subject matter than does CHESS, and the end-of-article code references may thus be more complex. The reference principle is the same, however, and the code allows the reader to explore the relationship to the full.

There are some *Book of the Year* articles that carry no code references. These include articles on subjects that are presented in the Micropædia rather than in the Macropædia of the *Britannica;* feature articles and special reports; and articles such as those covering disasters or obituaries, which by their nature have no place in the *Britannica* itself.

The relationship between the *Book of the Year* and the *Britannica* is also demonstrated by the two essays that follow, one on *Change and Permanence in the Sciences,* the other on *The Relevance of Philosophy Today.* Their two authors, both eminent scholars as well as contributors to the new *Britannica*, were asked to consider this question: In your opinion, is it likely that the new *Britannica*'s coverage of your special area of knowledge will require revision in the next few years? And if so, to what extent?

Their answers in these essays are comforting from an encyclopaedic point of view. Both suggest that the present *Britannica* coverage of their subject areas will continue to be current for years to come. Perhaps this is not so surprising in the case of philosophy, Professor Bird's field of study. We do not expect rapid change in philosophy and would probably feel that its development is relatively slow—even more so than that of the arts and certainly slower than that of the sciences. And so the coverage of ancient and modern philosophy in the new *Britannica* should stand the test of time for many years to come.

Dr. Lustig's essay may be more surprising. In it, he argues that the real pace of scientific development is also slow, despite the surface ferment that would appear to us to manifest extremely rapid change. Change is rapid indeed in the details of scientific knowledge but, he argues, not in its essential underlying structure. This means that the new *Britannica* will remain current in the sciences as well as in philosophy. It also means that the world around us may not be changing in its fundamental characteristics as fast as it seems to be—and as fast as the pundits tell us it is. It would not be the first time that the pundits were wrong.

CHARLES VAN DOREN

Change and Permanence in the Sciences

by Lawrence K. Lustig

It is often said that science is a cumulative venture, each generation of investigators receiving from its predecessors an array of facts, hypotheses, theories, and natural laws upon which new discoveries or interpretations may be based. The arts, on the other hand, are said to be discontinuous, or noncumulative, each work of individual genius standing by itself. The jazz musician need not base his creativity on that of the classical masters, nor does the novelist depicting street life in the modern ghetto derive much inspiration from the works of Shakespeare. Moreover, it may fairly be said that if Shakespeare or Wagner or van Gogh had never lived, then the works of these masters would not be part of our cultural heritage today. In science, however, the work of comparable figures—Newton, Darwin, or Einstein, for example—would likely have come to pass in any case, in precisely the same guise but filtered through the minds of other individuals.

This is true because literature, music, and painting are imaginative, creative enterprises, whereas science, whatever genius or originality may enter and underpin a brilliant synthesis or interpretation, is, in the final analysis, dependent upon the facts in nature's storehouse. These facts remain, ever present, whether they have to do with the elemental abundance of chemicals in the universe, the evidence of organic evolution, or the laws of gravity, magnetism, and electricity. They simply await a discoverer—if not Einstein then, in due course, another of his kind. But the key to the puzzle ultimately will be found, the advance in scientific knowledge will not be lost because a particular individual has not lived. Truly this represents a substantial difference between the arts and the sciences.

To turn the coin over and search for similarity, let us consider again, but in a different vein, the historical discontinuities said to be present in the arts. Taking music as an example, it is clear that different periods of history and different cultures have provided correspondingly varied musical statements. The linkage of musical form and drama that characterizes Wagner's powerful *Ring* or Prokofiev's vivid *Alexander Nevsky*, the tonality and beauty of the works of such symphonic masters as Beethoven, Brahms, and Tchaikovsky, and the concertos of Mozart and fugues of Bach—each such art form differs dramatically from representative Eastern music, from the work of some modern classical cacophonists, and from

Lawrence K. Lustig, a former university professor and research scientist, served as Senior Editor during preparation of the 15th Edition of the Encyclopædia Britannica. *His editorial responsibility ultimately included Part One, the physical sciences, Part Two, the earth sciences, and Part Seven, technology. He also contributed five scientific articles that appear in the Macropædia and approximately 800 entries for the Micropædia.*

the "rock" or "soul" genre of the 1960s. Looked at in one way, it may be said that in each case a particular kind of musical statement arose, underwent a flowering, and subsequently declined, at least insofar as the number of practitioners is concerned.

The Step-Function Model. Composers of the 1970s produce nothing that resembles the works of Liszt, Haydn, Chopin, or others of a bygone age, despite the fact that knowledge of how to write the kinds of music that flourished in the past has not been lost. If one were to depict graphically the advances in music—or any other art form—that have been made in relation to time, the plot would consist of a series of upward pulses or spurts of great significance, each followed by a level plateau representing the efforts of followers and devotees to enlarge, advance, and embellish the particular statement, style, or format of the art in question. Such a graph is commonly termed a step function, in part because of its resemblance to a staircase. And though the number of upward steps and the lengths of plateaus that depict historical developments may vary from one field to another, it will be argued here that the nature of scientific advance also accords well with the step-function model.

The business of science is, after all, the explanation of myriad natural phenomena and events, to render intelligible the empirical facts of the universe by organizing them within a framework of theoretical concepts and natural laws. Some have chosen to view each great development in science in terms of its historical debt to its predecessors—to those we honour as giants in their fields of endeavour. Hence, the investigations of Gilbert, Faraday, Ampère, Ørsted, and their colleagues may be said to have paved the way for Maxwell's brilliant synthesis of electricity and magnetism, and his predictions concerning electromagnetic wave motion. Darwin's concept of the origin of species and the descent of man similarly can be traced to the observations and data of a number of biologists, some of whom were his contemporaries, others his predecessors. Scientific advance can indeed be viewed as a consolidative effort in this sense. But each great synthesis of previous knowledge has also produced the plateau effect described above: scores of scientists seeking to test any newly discovered law in different environments or under different circumstances, to define or extend the boundaries within which it is operative, or to apply it to some range of phenomena not considered by the original discoverer.

It is this secondary effort, the fallout from the original discovery, that gives rise to the erroneous impression that science is in constant flux and turmoil, with great strides forward signaled by each new article to appear in the scientific journals. Such secondary effort is necessary and commendable and, in fact, it may well provide the basis for some subsequent advance of profound significance. But it should be recognized for what it is: the laws of nature that have been deduced by men are relatively few in number and the vast majority of scientists who have ever lived have spent their energies examining some aspect of the monumental achievements of a relative handful of individuals. No one can foretell the date of the next fundamental discovery in any branch of the sciences, but it is certain that advances of great significance are not common occurrences. The step function is more nearly the true model of progress; the following examples may serve to illustrate this point.

Johannes Kepler and Apollo 11. On July 20, 1969, the success of the Apollo 11 space mission astonished the world. What had once been the sole province of fiction writers became hard reality—men from Earth had left this planet's gravity field, traveled a quarter of a million miles through space, and walked upon our Moon! The magnitude of this accomplishment impressed all, even to the dullest and most jaded among us, and the scientific and technological achievements that made such a feat possible were widely and quite properly acclaimed. Without detracting in any way from this feat, and the engineering ingenuity involved in the design of literally thousands of different flight and support systems, it is fair to say that calculation of a proper orbit and launch trajectory by computer was a basic requirement for the success of this mission. And these calculations in turn depended upon knowledge of the movements of Earth and Moon through space during the period of the Apollo 11 flight. When was this knowledge acquired by mankind?

As any history of science will reveal, the German astronomer Johannes Kepler is principally responsible for elucidating the laws of planetary motion, which in fact bear his name. He was appointed successor to Tycho Brahe as imperial mathematician of the Holy Roman Empire in 1601 and, more importantly, he became the inheritor of Tycho's enormous bank of astronomical data of an empirical nature. Looking backward in time, Kepler may be viewed as the consolidator of scientific facts and hypotheses that had been assembled by Tycho; by Galileo, who was Kepler's contemporary; and certainly by Copernicus, who correctly deduced that the Earth revolves about the Sun. But it was Kepler who demonstrated in 1609 that the orbit of Mars must be an ellipse. Until that time it had been universally believed that the planets were quintessential bodies, manifestations of a fundamental order or harmony in the universe compatible only with perfectly circular orbits about the Sun. The natural laws set forth by Kepler as a consequence of his investigation of Mars and comparable problems were three in number. The first law states that the planets of the solar system follow elliptical paths about the Sun, the latter body occupying one focus of each such ellipse. The second law states that a line joining the position of the Sun and that of any given planet will sweep through equal areas of the orbital ellipse in equal times. And the third law states that the squares of the periods of revolution of any two planets are proportional to the cubes of their mean distances from the Sun; this is sometimes termed the 3/2 rule. If Kepler's laws are considered in relation to the hiatus of knowledge they succeeded then it obviously can be argued that they rep-

resent a great upward surge, or significant scientific advance, in terms of the step-function model of the history of science. Subsequent efforts in this field of inquiry must then be regarded as part of a developmental plateau, during which time interval the laws of planetary motion were enlarged upon or otherwise refined.

The universal genius of Sir Isaac Newton, who was born in the year of Galileo's death, is well known. His discovery of the laws of motion and gravitation represents a separate and discrete pulse of enormous scientific and historic significance. Newton announced in 1687 that the force of attraction between any two bodies varies directly with the product of their masses and inversely with the square of their separation distance, or more formally, that $F = G(m_1 m_2)/r^2$, in which m_1 and m_2 are the masses of the two bodies, r is their separation distance, and G is the universal gravitational constant. But this brilliant observation may also be viewed as merely supplying analytical support for Kepler's observationally derived planetary laws. From this viewpoint, the physical laws involved were simply given a quantitative basis by Newton, and the significant pulse of the step function occurred prior to his contribution, undeniably great though it was.

In a similar vein, more than a score of eminent mathematicians have for two hundred years devoted their attention to solution of the famous n-body problem of celestial mechanics. This problem requires mathematical prediction of the motions and interactions of three or more celestial bodies revolving around each other or around a common centre. All such work may be viewed as derivative from Kepler's original insight. So too, the discovery of the planet Neptune in 1846. This triumph of 19th-century astronomy resulted from observations of perturbations in the calculated orbit of Uranus. The orbital departures were deduced to be attributable to the existence of a previously unknown body which had to have the mass and location of the planet Neptune. Having established that Neptune had to be at a certain place in the night sky, the astronomers pointed their telescopes—and found it. Modern observations of some distant binary star systems involve the same principle; indeed, perturbations in the path of any tracked body are assumed to result from the presence of another body, albeit one invisible to the observer. Save for the advance in mathematical techniques, this work basically is similar to Kepler's conclusion that the Martian orbit had to be elliptical rather than circular.

The advent of high-speed electronic computers made possible the calculation of precise launch trajectories and ballistic flight paths and, as stated earlier, it made possible the Apollo 11 mission and other lunar voyages. But even today, in an era when space probes are used to calculate the gravitational influence of the Earth, Jupiter, and other planets upon the orbital paths of those probes—a form of astronomical experimentation undreamed of in Kepler's day—the scientific advance that occurs in this field rests on a historic plateau. The great spurt upward was marked by the discovery of the laws of planetary motion in 1609.

Dmitry Mendeleyev and Element 106. Chemistry, like astronomy, offers a number of examples that may be used to illustrate the step-function model of scientific advance. Because the history of chemistry is of briefer duration, one cannot reach back quite so far as Kepler's day. Save for this fact, the parallels are clear. In 1974, for example, a dispute arose concerning a report that Soviet scientists had successfully synthesized chemical element 106 for the first time. Leaving aside the question of the validity of this claim, it should be noted that the synthesis of any element, like a trip to the Moon, is a most complex technological and scientific feat. The experimental wizardry employed, however, is dependent ultimately on knowledge of the chemical elements and their properties and, most importantly, on knowledge of the interrelationships that exist among the elements. In this sense, the thesis is undeniable that the modern ferment alluded to here is traceable to a great surge of chemical knowledge in 1869, the year in which Dmitry Mendeleyev set forth the periodic law governing the elements.

Mendeleyev was the 17th child of an impoverished Siberian teacher and was most fortunate to gain access to the universities of St. Petersburg and Heidelberg, where he studied chemistry in the late 1850s. As in the case of Kepler, one can regard Mendeleyev as an inheritor and consolidator of the findings of a number of distinguished predecessors and contemporaries. Clearly relevant is the celebrated work of Lavoisier, who provided the fundamental concept of an element, and of Dalton and Cannizzaro on atomic and molecular weights. And further debt must be acknowledged to several 19th-century chemists who sought the key to the linkage of the elements. Noteworthy in this regard were Döbereiner's investigations of triads—three elements related by the fact that the weight of one was midway between the weights of the other two—and the attempts of de Chancourtois and Newlands to classify the known chemical elements in various ways. It may be said that all such work pointed the way for Mendeleyev's discovery. But construction of his table of elements in 1869, and later refinements, demonstrated for the first time that there is a periodic recurrence of the physical and chemical properties of the elements when they are arrayed in order of increasing atomic weight, or more precisely and in accord with modern findings, when arrayed in order of increasing atomic number (the number of protons in the nucleus of an element).

The importance of Mendeleyev's scheme cannot be overstated. It permitted a rational classification of the chemical elements and the identification of groups of elements with related properties. Moreover, it provided a method for prediction of the existence of elements unknown at that time—by filling in the blank boxes in the columns and rows of the table. And finally, it allowed for the recognition that the properties of the elements are a function of their atomic structure. This last did not emerge until the 20th century, when Lewis provided insight to the relation of valence and chemical bonding, and the efforts of Bohr, Schrödinger, and others gave rise to the totally new field of quantum mechanics.

But in Mendeleyev's time it was clearly perceived that elements aligned in vertical columns of the table formed groups with related properties. Thus, discovery of the first two noble gases, helium and argon, led to prediction of occurrence of the others in the group—neon, krypton, xenon, and radon. We now know that these particular elements exhibit similar properties because their outermost electron shell is filled, hence the valence in each case is zero. For this reason chemical stability is the rule, and they combine with other substances only reluctantly or in special circumstance. Mendeleyev himself predicted the existence of scandium, gallium, and germanium, each of which had not yet been discovered, and he detected errors in the previously determined atomic weights of several elements because they did not fit properly within his scheme.

Mendeleyev could not have foreseen the use of cyclotrons to assault atomic nuclei, the rise of particle physics generally, or the incredible brevity of the half-lives of man-made elements that have been produced. But his tabular array clearly prescribed a single place for each naturally occurring element. Only those elements of ever greater atomic weight and number could remain unknown once the periodic table was filled and, in this sense, he predicted them all. Mendeleyev's discovery of the periodic law formed a cornerstone of modern chemistry. It was a scientific advance of such moment in the history of the discipline that the creation of new elements today can be considered logical and expected events on the 100-year plateau that has followed his contribution to knowledge.

Bragg's Law and the Structure of DNA. Turning now to the life sciences, the topic for discussion must necessarily be molecular biology and the structure of deoxyribonucleic acid, more commonly designated DNA. Few fields of investigation seem so fertile and active today and scientific periodicals are veritably brimful of papers exploring various ramifications of this basic stuff of life.

DNA occurs in the nuclei of living cells, where it provides the genetic pattern of the chromosomes and determines the inherited characteristics of an organism. Considered in detail, the atomic structure of DNA is exceedingly complex. Each molecule consists of two strands or chains of three kinds of essential organic units, namely sugars, phosphates, and nitrogenous bases; and the latter are of four kinds, termed adenine, thymine, cytosine, and guanine. The adenine in one strand is paired with equal amounts of thymine in the second, as are the cytosine and guanine that are present. These complementary bases are held together by hydrogen bonds; for this reason, the two strands of DNA are adjacent to and coiled about each other, giving rise to a configuration resembling a double helix. This has been described as "the spiral staircase of life," and elucidation of the atomic arrangement in the DNA molecule by J. D. Watson and F. H. C. Crick in 1953 subsequently won them a Nobel Prize.

This discovery was of such fundamental significance that the limits of the developmental plateau of knowledge extending into the future cannot yet be foreseen. Fifty, or even one hundred, years from now another generation of scientists still may be engaged in pursuits directly traceable to this enormous advance of scientific knowledge. Indeed, it has been argued by some that the fields of biochemistry and biophysics are the most challenging and exciting of all the natural sciences today for this very reason. And yet, there was another input to the step-function model of advance in the life sciences, one with at least an equal claim to parentage and merit. Like the chemical linkage between element 106 and Mendeleyev's periodic table, structural determinations of all substances stem principally from a great insight of Sir William and Sir Lawrence Bragg, father and son.

There is, as always, some debt to the past and, in the case of the Braggs, mention must be made of Röntgen's discovery of X-rays in 1895, and Max von Laue's announcement in 1912 that crystals could diffract X-rays much like beams of light. Nevertheless, the step function began in 1912 with a series of brilliant experiments by Lawrence Bragg after consultation with his father, who was a physicist and technological innovator of renown. Essentially, the Braggs discovered a crystalline code that was destined to give rise to the fields of X-ray crystallography, solid state physics, and metallurgy—and to determination of the structure of proteins and the double helix of Watson and Crick. They found that a simple but fundamental natural law governed the passage of X-rays through any crystalline substance. Termed the Bragg equation, this law of X-ray diffraction states that $n\lambda = 2d \sin \theta$, in which λ is the wavelength of the incident radiation, θ is the angle of incidence with which the X-rays impinge upon the crystal under consideration, and, most important, d is the interlayer spacing, or distance in angstroms between adjacent layers of atoms within the crystal. It is this latter fact which made possible all subsequent structural investigations—that is, ascertaining the precise locations and arrangements of the atoms or molecules that make up all organic or inorganic substances.

The Braggs were jointly awarded the Nobel Prize for Physics in 1915 and their endeavours generated a vast amount of subsequent research of outstanding merit. At the Cavendish Laboratory in Cambridge where Lawrence Bragg was professor, J. D. Bernal began his important work on the X-ray analysis of organic macromolecules, and it was at this same institution that Max Perutz and John Kendrew studied the two basic proteins myoglobin and hemoglobin by similar methods. They too won a Nobel Prize. And the connecting thread stretched across the plateau of knowledge when Francis Crick came to Cavendish to study under Perutz—and was later joined by Watson. It is therefore not extravagant to argue that once Bragg's law was discovered, all the resulting scientific advance became inevitable. Just as Mendeleyev may be said to have predicted elements still unknown in his day, so too the Braggs would not be surprised at the structural determination of DNA and solution of the genetic riddle by means of X-ray diffraction methods. The true significance of their work cannot be overstated and the entire sequence of discoveries fits easily within the step-function model of scientific advance.

Harry Hess and the New Geology. A final example may be taken from the earth sciences which, like molecular biology, are considered by many to be in the throes of revolutionary change. Each year is witness to the publication of a greater number of papers in the scientific journals, more clamour for space on the programs of national and international scientific meetings, larger and better equipped expeditions to plumb the ocean depths and search the remote parts of the Earth, and an ever increasing need for more financial support. The cause of all this sound and fury was the arrival of a unifying concept termed plate tectonics, within whose framework large numbers of investigators are currently seeking to locate the data of the Earth and its history.

According to this concept, the outermost layer of the Earth consists of six rigid plates of major or continental dimensions, and a larger number of minor ones, all of which are in constant restless motion, abutting at plate boundaries and thus producing a remarkable number of effects. Earthquakes, volcanic phenomena, and mountain building, and their loci in time and space, are each explicable in terms of the concept. Similarly, the relative youthfulness of oceanic sediments, paleomagnetic data from these same rocks, a legion of data requiring the movement of continents through geological time, and such seeming anomalies as the sequential age difference of the several Hawaiian Islands—all these and more are facts consistent with the theory of plate tectonics.

It is clear that the current explosive ferment corresponds, as in previous examples, to the plateau portion of the step-function model. The basic surge involved in this scientific advance in the earth sciences was the notion of seafloor spreading set forth by Harry Hess in the early 1960s. There is again some debt to the past, the German meteorologist Alfred Wegener had argued for continental drift as early as 1912 in order to explain the similarity of coastlines of eastern South America and western Africa. And, indeed, it must be said that L. C. King, A. L. du Toit, and other geologists familiar with Southern Hemisphere data, particularly on the Late Paleozoic glaciation and the distribution of *Glossopteris* flora in southern latitudes, provided strong support for the drift hypothesis. But even the advent of paleomagnetic evidence in the 1950s failed to convince the skeptics, for no suitable geophysical mechanism to accomplish the movements of continents was known at that time.

Into this theoretical vacuum Hess thrust the proposal that the midoceanic ridges—undersea mountain chains that exist in the central parts of each of the major ocean basins—served as loci for the formation of new oceanic crust, the latter spreading outward from the ridges and plunging downward into the Earth's mantle at the boundaries between the ocean basins and adjacent continents. This one brilliant scheme, termed "geopoetry" by some, provided a satisfactory synthesis of all preexisting knowledge in the field, and simultaneously set the stage for an explosion of subsequent investigations. Many notable achievements might be mentioned in this regard, among them the recognition by Vine and Mathews that paleomagnetic patterns and absolute age data were coincident on opposite sides of the ridges, and the actual concept of plate tectonics as set forth by X. Le Pichon in 1968. But all such studies, including recent surveys of mineral wealth in the bottom sediments of the Red Sea—a site of active seafloor spreading which has permitted the influx and concentration of heavy elements from the underlying mantle—were inspired by the scientific input of Hess. All modern research can be construed as an attempt to explore, test, and expand upon his work.

Scientific Advance and Progress. The nature of scientific advance commonly has been considered to be at variance with the nature of artistic advance, because historical discontinuities are the rule in the arts, and not so in the sciences. It has been argued here, however, that examples compatible with the discontinuous or step-function model can readily be drawn from any field of science. Although it is true that each generation of scientists has had the benefit of previous discoveries of facts, theories, and natural laws on which to build, if one looks forward from the point of a new discovery the plateau structure of the overall advancement of knowledge becomes apparent. The consequences of the work of a Kepler, a Mendeleyev, or a Hess make extremely persuasive the notion that the history of science is like a kind of staircase in time. There exist only a few steps upward, but each is of great horizontal extent—long enough to accommodate the efforts of most of the scientists who have ever lived.

True genius in science, therefore—if by genius we mean creative originality—is as rare as it is in the arts. Perhaps it is even rarer. Perhaps there are more musicians the equal of Mozart than chemists the equal of Mendeleyev; more poets the equal of Homer than physicists the equal of Kepler; more painters the equal of Rembrandt than molecular anatomists the equal of the Braggs, Watson, and Crick. In any case, there are few enough members of any of these groups and we should relinquish one of our most commonly held prejudices: "progress" is not to be taken for granted in science, any more than it is to be expected in the arts. Progress is always a surprise, ever a wonder, and truly a marvelous event whenever it occurs.

NOTE TO THE READER
The interested reader of this essay can obtain additional information on the history of science and related matters by recourse to the Propædia. See particularly Part Ten, Division III, in which Section 10/31 treats the history and philosophy of science, and Sections 10/32, 10/33, and 10/34 treat the physical sciences, earth sciences, and biological sciences, respectively. Relevant biographical data may be found in articles in the Macropædia and the Micropædia.

The Relevance of Philosophy Today

by Otto A. Bird

Modern society is facing a crisis of values and few of us seem to know where we stand on major issues of the day. The traditional answers of the past are thought to be irrelevant in our complex world. Take a list at random from your daily newspaper—abortion, open housing, women's liberation, political patronage, homosexuality, welfare programs, hunger in the third world—how many of us know what stand we really should take on these and similar issues? The world has changed, in part because of dramatic advances of science and technology; but no serious thinker can rightly blame them for all the confusion and uncertainty that trouble us. The modern world is nothing more than the end product of choices we have freely made. It is a reflection of self-defined goals, of priorities we have established, and of the relative values we have placed on

Otto A. Bird is University Professor of Arts and Letters at the University of Notre Dame, and Consulting Editor for The Great Ideas Today. During preparation of the 15th Edition of the Encyclopædia Britannica, Dr. Bird served as adviser on philosophy for Part Ten of the Propædia. He also contributed four articles that appear in the Macropædia.

things. Science and technology gave man the ability to leave footprints on the Moon, but neither was involved in the value judgment that space capsules should be built to carry astronauts to outer space. And scientists are now capable of producing life in a test tube. Is this another of man's magnificent accomplishments or does it verge on sacrilege, a horrendous misuse of human knowledge? Such questions clearly involve moral and social values—and values are the proper preserve of philosophy.

If we are to find our way along a darkened path, then philosophy must light the lamp. No other discipline can help us. History can tell us how men acted in the past; it can tell us what goals they sought, and what they valued most; but history cannot tell us whether we should imitate those actions, pursue those same goals, or adopt those values as our own. Science can give us the power to transform the face of the Earth and to extend our domain beyond our planet. But science as such is no more capable than history when it comes to evaluating a proper course of human action. History and science constitute the knowledge of power, but they stand mute in the realm of values. Only the discipline of philosophy can distinguish real from apparent good, inordinate desires from legitimate needs, and the proper order of priorities whenever individual desires (and even legitimate rights) conflict with the common good of society as a whole—a circumstance that is a commonplace today.

Aristotle underscored the role of values in determining the course of human actions in his *Nicomachean Ethics*. He said that the moral conduct of those who value wealth will be determined by monetary values, whereas those who esteem honour will so act as to ensure that honour will be accorded them. This eternal truth suggests that an individual's actions are invariably affected by what he values most. Aristotle's thoughts were expressed well over 2,000 years ago, but they are as valid today as they were in ancient Greece. Because human nature is immutable, modern man can read the great philosophers of the ages and, through them, rediscover the very principles he needs to orientate his life in the 20th century.

Two Basic Intuitions. Although recent developments in philosophy are highly complex and fraught with subtleties, it is neither inaccurate nor exaggerated to claim that they rest upon two central and basic intuitions. The first is that time and change are of decisive importance in human experience and our understanding of it. The second involves language and the realization of its decisive influence upon thought and experience. Both time and language, of course, have concerned philosophers since antiquity, but these ideas have in modern times become the central focus of philosophical speculation.

The linguistic approach to philosophy has been far from beneficial in its effect upon values, however. All too often it has led to trivialization and overspecialization in which words are substituted for substance—we talk about values to the detriment of the way we ought to feel and to act.

Time and change have come to be of critical importance in philosophy during the recent period in which man's daily life has undergone the most profound and dramatic changes in its entire history. Conditions of life during the era of the American founding fathers, for example, were not fundamentally different from those encountered by Plato and Aristotle. Indeed, George Washington and Thomas Jefferson might well have felt more at home in the ancient pagan world than in America of the 1970s. Every activity bearing upon the way we live today has undergone revolutionary change; most radical of all, perhaps, has been the accelerating rate of change itself.

This same period has also been marked by the immense development of two disciplines that are especially time-dependent: history and science, and the kinds of knowledge and ways of learning that support them. Both disciplines, albeit in different ways, have a special concern with the temporal dimension. For history, of course, time past provides its very subject matter, and because time continues to grow, history always has more to do. Science, in a quite different but no less intimate way, is also bound up with time. A certain physicist is said to have remarked, for example, that he never bothered to read anything more than five years old. He thus implied that work more than five years old is already obsolete, given the rate at which research is being developed. Many scientists share this conviction because they believe that scientific advance is a process that absorbs and digests all past achievements, eliminating those that are no longer useful.

Such intense awareness of the import of time could not fail to affect thinking about values. Many have concluded that there are no constant values in human existence, and that every generation, if not indeed each individual, must find or construct them anew. If this state of mind is thought to be the only acceptable one—an attitude now held by many—then philosophy has a great and urgent opportunity: to reaffirm the values that are as unchangeable as human nature itself.

Human Constants. It cannot be denied that philosophy, like history and science, has frequently been infected by the disease of "chronolatry." This has shown up most spectacularly when the discovery of a new method of philosophizing has, supposedly, made it possible to "junk" all prior philosophy, and to set it on "the right path of science." Descartes and Kant are perhaps the most eminent examples of such optimism, but supporters exist in contemporary schools. Yet the history of philosophy itself belies these attempts. Philosophy has never been successful in ridding itself of its past. Although many have attempted to bury it and have even convinced themselves of their success, it has never failed to reappear and again assert its vitality. Men still continue to learn philosophy and to "do" it by studying the thought of Plato and Aristotle as well as that of Descartes and Kant. Philosophy and science stand in a very different relation to their temporal dimensions; *i.e.,* each to its own past and future. For this reason, among others, philosophy is capable of rendering unique service, for one of its primary functions is to establish norms of conduct—objective, immutable human values—to guide our lives in a world of constant change.

It is especially significant that the changes that have occurred in the cultural world were wrought by man. Man is, of course, at any given time and place a product of his culture, but not exclusively so. Culture is not creation ex nihilo. It has to work within the context provided by nature. Thus man remains as much a natural being as a cultural product, and it is constancy, not change, that stands forth as the great and impressive fact. It remains as true today as it was in 1975 B.C., and indeed during every stage of human history about which anything is known, that man is a creature of flesh and bone, that he is born and dies, and that in between he is subject to many needs and demands that arise from the kind of being that he is as he lives out his life in pursuit of happiness. Corresponding to these natural needs are the goods that are capable of satisfying them: such goods as food of a certain kind and quantity so as to provide health and strength; knowledge and understanding; love, friendship, and the respect of his fellows; pleasures of both mind and body; and the means of acquiring and retaining these goods, such as peace in a just and free society. All of these are goods for man. They are now, and they always have been. But not all are equal in value, and the pursuit of one can conflict with that of another. Accordingly, there is need to establish an order of priorities among them.

These, of course, are not the only goods. It is also good, and an action of love, that a man should lay down his life for his friend, even though life itself is such a great good that an eternal life constitutes a still greater good. Indeed, the aspirations of man are so boundless that, whenever measured by the finitude of his possibilities, he appears, on the one hand, as the archetype of the absurd and, on the other, as a creature whose heart cannot find rest anywhere short of the infinite God. It is also true that in any time and under any particular set of conditions man's moral task consists essentially in being a good man rather than in achieving a good life.

Another human constant that needs reaffirmation is that, in the realm of values, knowledge alone is never sufficient. Food and drink are goods that satisfy natural needs and furnish the means to strength and health. Yet an excess no less than a deficiency of them is bad and even can lead to the destruction of the person. In fact, affluence is in some ways worse in this case and harder to remedy than poverty. To remedy malnutrition, one need only obtain the proper food; however difficult that may be in a particular case, it is easier to acquire than virtue. Yet ultimately the only remedy for gluttony and drunkenness is the self-control that is secured by temperance, and this is a quality of character that is not to be had merely for the asking. Merely knowing that temperance is the only remedy is not to be equated with actual acquisition of the virtue. One may know well what ought to be done, even want to do it, and yet fail to do so time after time. At issue in this case, which is typical of all our moral life, is the relation between external goods and the moral character that is requisite for their proper use. As Henri Bergson emphasized a generation ago, before any of the massive energy shortages were upon us, the promise of technology to meet the needs of a decent life for all peoples of the world cannot be kept without reaffirming and strengthening spiritual values; or, as he expressed it, mechanics calls for mysticism.

The Great Concerns. If it is to make a significant contribution to our thinking about values, philosophy must overcome the narrow specialization that has become characteristic of much of its academic pursuit and return to the study of the great concerns of mankind: the problems of life and death, man's welfare and his destiny; all that the ancients referred to as *res magnae* ("the great things").

That such a need is felt by the general public is amply evident from the renewed and widespread interest in religion.

In the world of academe, philosophy has been increasingly fragmented and its traditional function as an over-arching discipline, concerned with the interconnection of problems and solutions given to them by different disciplines, has been lost. Yet, the need to attempt to see things whole, to perceive manifold interrelations, has become increasingly urgent. Philosophy, in embracing the scientific ideal of specialization, has betrayed itself and has run a grave risk of forfeiting any claim upon the attention and respect of a wider world.

The widespread questioning of values has been directed not only at science but at reason itself. The upsurge of interest in the occult, in astrology, in witchcraft, and even in diabolism bears witness to this claim. Although this interest may indicate revulsion against the scientific intellect and its technological applications, and manifest a thirst for something more than these are capable of satisfying, it also lays bare a dangerous confusion. This confusion results from identifying the scientific intellect with reason itself. Science is a work and an achievement of reason, and, indeed, a very great one. But it is by no means the only work of reason. Reason is also at work in all the humanities, achieving knowledge just as valuable as that of science, and, in the matter of values, capable of accomplishing much more.

The world of the humanities is one of fundamental human experience that is open to all men. It is a world of dreams and aspirations, of constant searching for a good and better life; values are a never ceasing concern. It is only within the wider world, with which the humanities are concerned, that science can find its justification and its value. But the justification of science and of reason itself cannot be achieved and reaffirmed unless philosophy again strives for a grand and synoptic view of the way in which all knowledge emanates from the fundamental experience that men have of the natural and human world, one in which all people are born and must die.

NOTE TO THE READER
The interested reader should consult the Propædia of the *Encyclopædia Britannica,* particularly Section 10/51.A.1, which is entitled "Diverse conceptions of philosophy," and Section 10/52.B.3.e: "Philosophy in the 20th century." For detailed discussions of the several schools of modern philosophy, see the subheadings under Section 10/53.A.2. References relating to values, ethics, moral philosophy, obligation, duty, theories of conduct, and the like are provided in Section 10/51.B.6 and 10/53.D. See also the list of major philosophers and references to their biographies in the Macropædia following Section 10/53.

1975 BRITANNICA BOOK OF THE YEAR

ENCYCLOPÆDIA BRITANNICA, INC.

Chicago, Toronto, London, Geneva, Sydney, Tokyo, Manila, Johannesburg, Seoul

THE UNIVERSITY OF CHICAGO

The Britannica Book of the Year is published with the editorial advice
of the faculties of the University of Chicago

Contents

Feature Articles

Chronology of Events

Book of the Year

Special Reports

A World Without Want

by Indira Gandhi

Indira Gandhi has been prime minister of India since 1966. A student of Visva-Bharati University, Bengal, and of Oxford University, Mrs. Gandhi has devoted much of her career to economic planning and social reform. Her concern for the underprivileged of the world is well known and is revealed again in the following article, which sets forth her views on the problem of hunger. Overpopulation, which is considered by many observers to be a dominant factor in the world hunger problem, is treated principally in the Special Report entitled World Population Year.

Two-thirds of the world's peoples are underprivileged, and this despite such breathtaking achievements of science as space travel, instant communication, and the unraveling of the very building blocks of life. Technology has given us the knowledge to supplement or to substitute what has been provided in nature. Yet many hundreds of millions remain undernourished and are denied the minimum clothing, shelter, medical care, and education.

Why does this paradox exist? Natural resources are unevenly distributed, and some countries have acquired tremendous economic power because of their advanced technology. Individual and national self-centredness is to the fore, and there is no feeling of collective responsibility. The world is still at the stage of economic nationalism.

I belong to a generation that spent its childhood and youth (the so-called years of careless rapture!) fighting every inch of the way for our basic human rights as citizens of an ancient and honourable land. It was a hard life, of sacrifice and insecurity, of anger and impatience. Yet the hope in our eyes and our hearts never dimmed, for we were beckoned by the star of freedom, by the bright promise of a world without want and exploitation. Can it be only 27 years ago? Science, the key to the new world for which we longed, has not been allowed to serve those whose need is greatest but has been made to pander to the desire for profits and to narrow national objectives. Far from having provided more, today we face a world beset by dire forecasts of global food inadequacies, where even the richest countries are experiencing shortages of one article or other.

Many countries that are labeled as developing are the very lands where civilization began. Poor today, though rich in their contribution to the story of man, Iraq, Egypt, India, Iran, and China were among the early cradles of intellect and endeavour. Here man first became farmer, plant breeder, and metallurgist. Here he fathomed the mysteries of mathematics and medicine, the movement of stars in the sky and of thoughts in his own mind. The first seers in India arose from among farmers, singing praise of the earth, water, and the sun and celebrating the energy of growing things. From the sun comes rain, they said, and from rain food, and from food all living beings.

Until two hundred years ago, India was regarded as the world's most prosperous country, a magnet for traders, seafarers, and military adventurers. The wealth of Akbar the Mughal is computed at several score times that of the Holy Roman emperor Charles V or Louis XIV of France. Yet in his reign—as in those of the others—the common people lived in poverty. The multitude starved, while nobles lived in splendour. Even in those times there were large irrigation works in countries like China and India, but famines were not unusual. Among countries as within countries, there have always been rich and poor. Military power and looting led to the impoverishment of the vanquished and the enrichment of the victor.

Until the modern idea arose of social engineering for equality, only small and compact societies could avoid unseemly disparities. In earlier times, the larger the extent and efficiency of government, the wider the gap between a small number of rich and the masses of the poor. The Industrial Revolution and the rise of colonialism sharpened international disparities. Even the difference in the life span of people in Western Europe and South Asia is the sequel of Europe's earlier lead in science, for until the beginning of the 19th century, mortality rates were roughly the same in all countries. But the present affluence of the advanced countries is due as much to colonial exploitation as to their mastery over science and modern technology.

The pace of a country's technological advance depends upon the stock of technology it has already accumulated. Any survey of elementary human needs and the means to fulfill them brings out the incongruous coexistence of overabundance and deprivation. In Western Europe and North America, people's chief worry is to restrict their intake of calories, for their average consumption is 22% higher than the energy requirements of the body. Elsewhere, entire nations suffer from malnutrition. For us in India, scarcity is only a missed monsoon away.

The Meaning of Want. The definition of want is not constant. Increasing incomes in a time of transition from one stage of technology to another bring many changes in their train—in habits as well as in the very concept of what is desirable. Additional earnings are only partly spent on more food and other necessities, while the rest go into displaying the signs of new status. To give only one example, in India the rise in the income scale has meant giving up millets for rice and wheat, discarding regional costumes in favour of modern city wear. Need has a psychological no less than an economic connotation.

There are at least three kinds of want: first, a shortage of the essentials of existence, such as minimum nutrition, clothing, and housing; second, the absence of elements, such as education and recreation, that give meaning and purpose to life; and third, the absence of the extras that advertising proclaims as necessary to good living.

The first kind of want in the world: "a shortage of the essentials of existence, such as minimum nutrition, clothing, and housing."

Mahatma Gandhi once said that the hungry see God in the form of bread. Many millions are not yet vouchsafed this grace. The per capita availability of grain in the less developed countries is hardly 200 kg. a year, whereas in developed countries it is close to 1,000 kg. It should be noted that nearly 90% of the consumption of grain in developed countries is indirect, through its conversion into meat and poultry. In 1970 the rich countries used some 375 million metric tons of cereals to feed animals, a quantity greater than the total cereal consumption by human beings and domesticated animals in China and India put together. The noted economist Barbara Ward has computed that, since 1967, the United States has added to its grain-beef conversion rate almost the entire equivalent of India's level of consumption. Meanwhile, according to a UN estimate, the demand for food between 1970 and 1985 will grow by 27% in developed countries and by 72% in developing countries.

A Basic Inequality. The world food problem highlights the contradictions inherent in the massive and continuing injustice in the control of the world's resources—which, we have lately begun to realize, are not unlimited. Land is unevenly distributed. On a per capita basis, the United States and the Soviet Union have close to 0.9 ha. of arable land. Canada has 2 ha. and Australia more than 3 ha. The distribution of other resources—in particular, technology and material inputs—has also been unequal.

Is it not remarkable that, in spite of these disadvantages, developing countries as a group were able to achieve, over the last decade, a growth rate in agricultural production close to that of the industrial countries? But their demands

have grown even faster, due to increases in population and per capita income and changed eating habits. To a great extent, this gap has had to be filled by the transfer of food surpluses, mostly of the rich countries of North America. The U.S. and Canada have controlled a larger share of the world's exportable grain supplies than the Middle East does of the world's oil.

The mechanism of food aid saved farmers in rich countries from the disastrous decline in incomes that surplus production would have caused. For decades these countries restricted acreage and actually paid their farmers not to grow crops! Now the United States has ended restrictions on acreage, but increases in domestic consumption there, and changes in trade patterns and in attitudes toward aid, rule out long-term dependence on North American surpluses. It is urgent that developing countries improve their domestic production. That is the only sure basis for sustained growth in other sectors.

In 1970 technological and other experts had prophesied widespread famine in India, but for us it was a year of plenty, when our new agricultural policy bore abundant fruit and we could accumulate a buffer stock of nine million metric tons of grain. But the year following brought unforeseen events—ten million refugees, a war followed by acute drought. Aid was stalled. Our surplus was depleted, though we managed to get by with marginal imports. Then we were hit by the world financial crisis and the skyrocketing price of oil. In addition, drought has persisted in successive seasons.

The Present Food Crisis. The current worldwide concern over food is a poignant consequence of events since 1972. Drought made itself felt across whole continents, causing production to fall simultaneously in the Soviet Union, China, India, parts of Africa, and Southeast Asia. Total world production of cereals went down by 4%, or more than 30 million metric tons. In such a situation it was natural for food-surplus countries to make the most of their advantage. Grain prices rose to dizzy heights, adding to the already escalating forces of worldwide inflation and compounding the problems of developing countries already staggered by steep increases in the price of oil. In the absence of an international system governing trade in grain, the limited stocks that were available in "surplus" countries were distributed, through bilateral trade, to those who could afford to pay.

India's current balance of payments problem is almost entirely due to the high prices of food, fertilizers, and oil. We are exploring every possibility of substituting other fuels to meet the energy needs of our economy, but what can take the place of food and fertilizer? Fertilizer is in short supply all over the world because of high oil prices and because the demand in developed countries has increased tremendously. I have read that the United States uses three million metric tons of fertilizer just to keep its lawns green. This is more than the entire supply available to India to grow food in 1971.

Africa illustrates the severity of the present food crisis along with the untapped potential for higher production. In the Sahelian zone of Africa, drought conditions have persisted for a number of years. On the same continent, the land-man ratio in several countries is favourable, and there is ample opportunity to develop the land if the tsetse fly and other disease carriers can be controlled. It has been estimated that when this is accomplished an area of nearly seven million square kilometres—larger than the entire agricultural area of the United States—can be brought under cultivation.

World grain stocks have slumped to a precariously low level. In 1961 they totaled 154 million metric tons and, in addition, land deliberately withheld from production represented a potential output of some 70 million metric tons. In 1974 grain stocks were estimated at 89 million metric tons, the equivalent of barely four weeks' consumption, and there is little idle land left in "surplus" countries. The capacity of the world to meet a sudden adverse turn in the weather is thus greatly reduced.

The demand for food may exceed its potential supply for many years to come. According to estimates of the UN Food and Agriculture Organization the world production of cereals, currently about 1,200,000,000 metric tons, will have to increase on an average by 25 million metric tons each year to meet the rising demand. By 1985 developing countries might face a total annual gap of nearly 85 million metric tons of food grains. Nor is this dismal prognosis of a gaping chasm between what is likely to be available and what is needed confined to less developed countries. James J. Needham, chairman of the New York Stock Exchange, has said that in the period 1974–85 capital will fall approximately $650 billion short of U.S. economic requirements.

Three distinct needs must be met:

1. Greater production in developing countries;
2. Assurance of some internationally controlled supplies to meet abnormal shortages that might occur in a bad year; and
3. Generation of adequate purchasing power for developing countries to finance needed imports.

Increasing Food Supplies. The first step is clearly the responsibility of the developing countries themselves. They must set their priorities right and provide for investment in land improvement, use of water, production of fertilizer, and the development of technologies needed to increase food production. In affluent nations, both agriculture and industry use mass-production techniques. Agriculture itself has become an industry in which fewer people cultivate ever increasing areas with the help of machines. With such capital-intensive technology, per capita productivity is high and so are individual incomes. In India, on the other hand, we face a situation where more and more people will have to cultivate progressively smaller areas of land. Unemployment figures in India appear most depressing when employment is calculated in terms of per capita productivity. This is the basis of our poverty. Our most urgent task, therefore, is to augment per hectare productivity through the scientific use of our biological and physical assets.

This goal can be achieved only through widespread involvement of the rural community in scientific methods of farming in which every individual can participate. Unfor-

Drought in India. In the early 1970s the rains bypassed parts of western India and these women must dig for water in a dried-up riverbed. The bridge suggests former days of abundant water in this area.

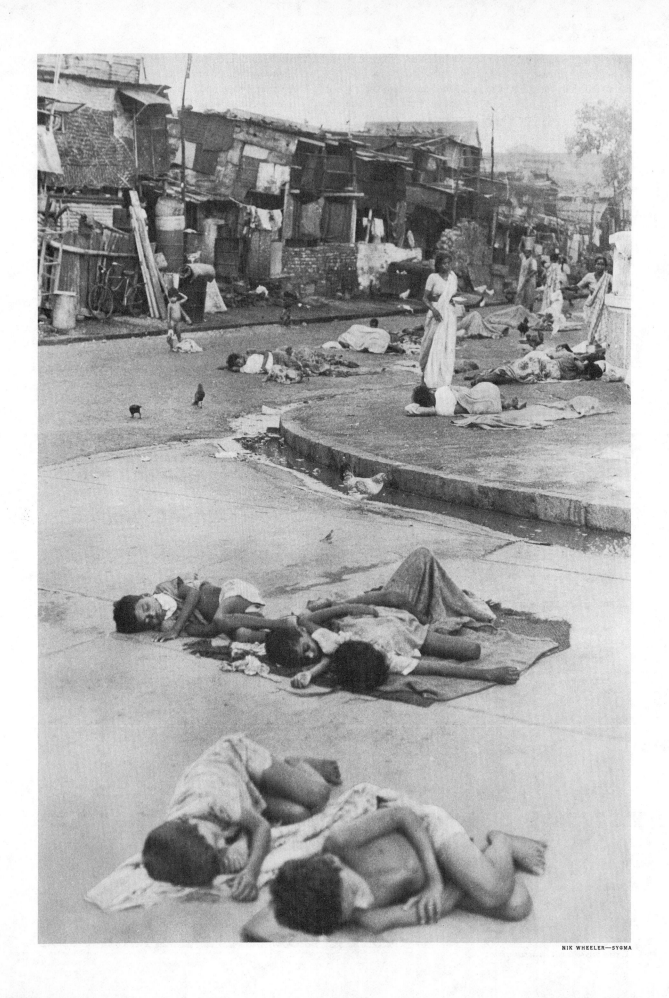

tunately, even in agriculture much of the planning has been based on the model of mass production evolved in affluent countries, without regard to our peculiar circumstances. Experts and technical knowledge are driving forces that push us inexorably. The men and women who may be simple but yet must remain the most concerned and affected by our programs tend to be relegated to the sidelines as somewhat bewildered spectators.

The interest and enthusiasm of farmers and their wives must be aroused, not only in increasing production but in seeing that the grain reaches the market on time. Scientific farming should be part of the all-round development of the village. And women play a very important part in all aspects of village life—economic, political, and cultural. Most developmental processes have bypassed them and have not appreciated their relevance to the achievement of development goals.

India has many sophisticated and large-scale industries, but vast areas and groups of people are untouched by them and the pressure on land continues to be excessive. Life is hard in the rural areas. Therefore, we cannot neglect small-scale industries and village crafts that could be greatly improved by intermediate technology. Far from being incompatible with modernization, intermediate technology is a step in that direction. It is intended to increase efficiency and to lighten drudgery, without alienating people from their environment. In developing societies there will always be room for processes that create work for people where they live, using local materials and without the necessity of imports or high investment.

The indiscriminate adoption of norms and practices from opulent societies has led to a disorientation of values and aesthetic feeling. In their emulation of international vogues, architects in tropical countries sometimes become oblivious even of climatic conditions. It is delightful to sit in an air-conditioned room, but what if this diverts power from essential production in field and factory? Labour-saving methods are welcome when they save time and money, but not when they seal off possible sources of employment. In many branches of engineering, especially agricultural engineering, there should be many-faceted research aimed at developing improvements and methods that will make fuller use of the experience and capability of the local people and of the available materials with which they are familiar. This may well lead to patterns of satisfaction that are different from those of the advanced countries.

The Need for Modern Agricultural Programs. In irrigated areas, employment can be increased through multiple cropping. Scientific dry farming is more useful in semiarid regions. Tropical and subtropical regions are fortunate in having abundant sunlight, and with adequate water and nutrients some crop or other can be grown during all 12 months. The Indicative World Plan prepared by the FAO acknowledges that multiple cropping will have to play a dominant role in increasing employment opportunities and lowering underemployment in the rural areas of the tropics. In the Indo-Gangetic plain of North India we have a large

underground reserve of water. Some of our farmers have developed low-cost devices that can be used to tap this resource, such as tube wells made of bamboo, but if energy—either electric or diesel power—is not available, the wells cannot function. By that much, the opportunities for employment generation provided by multiple cropping will have been diminished.

Mixed farming, combining agriculture and livestock husbandry, has a large potential in irrigated as well as rain-fed areas. It adds to income and employment for farmers with small holdings and for landless labour. But mixed farming should not be introduced without adequate scientific investigation. For example, poultry farming should be encouraged only if there are plenty of food grains, since poultry consume large quantities of maize, sorghum, and other grains. On the other hand, the cow and the buffalo can digest cellulosic material that man cannot utilize. Thus, the relationship between the cow and the human being is complementary and not competitive. In China scavenging animals like pigs have been used effectively in production systems based on recycling principles. The same principles can be adopted for pond fisheries by developing highly productive systems based upon the supply of some waste produce of ducks and pigs. Such high-synergy systems have a multiplier effect on economic growth.

In July and August, eastern India and Bangladesh are often devastated by floods, and the Brahmaputra Valley is chronically flood-prone. Flood control is not always possible, and even when it is possible it involves heavy investment. At present, the main crop in these areas is raised in the flood season, with the result that crops are often destroyed. With the help of surface irrigation and the use of underground water, the flood-free months could be converted into the main cropping season. However, this also requires power.

Modern mechanized agriculture itself has become a major consumer of energy derived from nonrenewable resources. It has been calculated that while India uses 286 kilocalories of energy to produce one kilogram of rice protein, affluent nations use 2,800 kilocalories to produce a kilogram of wheat protein and 65,000 kilocalories to produce one kilogram of beef protein. Obviously, poor countries should take care that their agricultural growth is not entirely dependent on scarce, expensive, and pollution-generating forms of energy.

Developing countries that are not endowed with fossil fuels should try to achieve their agricultural goals by energy conservation and recycling. This is the best way of ensuring growth that does not erode the long-term production potential. For a long time the Indian farmer was skeptical about modern agriculture, but in the last 10 to 12 years he has adopted new methods with great alacrity and has taken to cultivating many new crops. Just as industrialization everywhere has elbowed out traditional rural crafts, so with the advent of modern farming, the farmer is abandoning several excellent traditional practices. He tends to apply more chemical fertilizer than prudence and science would dictate. The farmer should be reeducated to use organic fertilizer—compost and green manure—along with inorganic. In other matters also, what is known and cheap is not necessarily harmful or useless.

"The living conditions of the people of India . . . should be compared not with conditions in the rich countries but with the state of affairs prevailing at the time of our liberation from colonial rule."

The scarcity of pesticides may strike developing countries with even more severity than the fertilizer shortage. Tropical conditions are particularly hospitable to insects. A way out is through pest-management procedures that are locally relevant. These may be based on pest avoidance instead of control, or on taking advantage scientifically of natural enmities within the insect world. Even if pesticides are plentiful, experience shows that insects soon become resistant to them. Farmers should be more judicious in their use of pesticides, learning the value of many insects and the importance of maintaining nature's balance.

Research can never end. Every agroecological milieu has its own problems, and new ones keep appearing. For example, during the southwest monsoon period in India, many soil nutrients are lost because of leaching. This could be minimized by mixing fertilizer with margosa cake, derived from the seeds of the margosa tree. Such local solutions to local problems must be encouraged.

Even affluent countries must now conserve energy, which is becoming scarce and costly. Scientists and technologists have yet to develop commercially feasible methods of harnessing the energy of the sun, wind, and tides, but this work is attracting greater attention and several experiments are under way. Hitherto unused sources of natural power must be developed as quickly as possible to meet the needs of production and to assure remunerative employment to a fast-growing population.

Growth Strategies and Resource Constraint. Human endeavour and organizational change alone will not compensate for deficiencies in natural endowments and the material inputs of modern agriculture. Systems that have used labour as a substitute for capital or technology have not escaped vast food deficits. This is demonstrated by the wide fluctuations in food production in the Soviet Union and China and their resultant recourse to large-scale imports from abroad.

In the last few years, developments in different parts of the world, especially in the matter of food, prompt reflection on the different theories of development that have been propounded from time to time. It has been said that certain forms of government or certain constitutional frameworks promote faster growth than others; that excessive individualism or concern with human rights and legal remedies may act as a brake on economic progress; and that some governments and states can be characterized as "soft states" with little prospect of rapid human improvement. The present economic crisis seems to belie such generalizations. Economic development is a complex process, and the reasons that some economies are growing more rapidly than others cannot be found solely in the forms of government or institutions prevalent in different societies.

Adequacy of resources and their efficient use play an important part in development. There are also random and uncontrollable factors, including the unpredictability of nature. Agricultural production is particularly vulnerable to such forces, and at one time or another almost all countries have to face the consequences of fluctuations in food production on the economy as a whole. Discipline in society is as essential as a determined effort to augment production and secure its equitable distribution. The choice of right priorities and technology is a must; we cannot ignore the fact that resources are limited and the efforts

Death in Africa. The worst drought of the 20th century brought famine, disease, and death to animals and humans alike, in Kenya (left) and Ethiopia (above). The devastation and disaster were even more widespread in West Africa than in East Africa.

of individual countries to achieve self-sufficiency in food must be supported by international action to assist in meeting unforeseen contingencies.

The existence of present deficiencies should not detract from the very considerable progress in agricultural development that has already been achieved in several developing countries, including India. In contrast to the near-stagnation of the decades before India achieved independence in 1947, agricultural production since planning began in the early 1950s has maintained a long-term growth trend of about 3.5% annually. India is thus among the countries in which agricultural growth has been ahead of the growth in population, although not so much ahead as we would have liked. At the beginning of the 1950s, grain

production was around 50 million–55 million metric tons; in the middle 1970s, it is in the neighbourhood of 105 million–110 million metric tons. (*See* Table.) In a matter of two decades, grain production in absolute terms has been doubled. In the early stages, most of the increase came about through the extension of cultivation, but as land became scarcer, reliance had to be placed on increasing productivity per hectare. The advent of new technology in the mid-1960s, including high-yielding varieties of seeds and the massive application of fertilizer, along with a package of improved practices, has led to a significant transformation of agriculture in some parts of India, notably the northwest.

The Green Revolution: a Mixed Picture. For anyone with an adequate understanding of production processes in a country like India, with its widely divergent conditions, there was neither euphoria nor subsequent disenchantment about the so-called Green Revolution. Both attitudes reflect oversimplification and lack of touch with the situation on the ground.

In recent years, there has been a sharp increase in the consumption of chemical fertilizers and pesticides, in minor irrigation, in the spread of improved varieties of seeds, and in the provision of credit and marketing facilities. This tempo of progress must be sustained and extended to other parts of the country. In particular, attention is now being given to dry-farming techniques and to major irrigation schemes, along with intensive area development. The structure of production in rural society is of

Food-Grain Production in India

	1950-51	1971-72
	Grain (in 000,000 metric tons)	
Rice	22.05	43.07
Wheat	6.82	26.41
Maize	2.36	5.10
Millets	8.93	13.04
Other cereals	5.65	6.46
Pulses	9.20	11.09
Total	55.01	105.17
	1950-51	1973-74
Total cropped area	131.9 million ha.	169 million ha.
Gross irrigated area	22,560,000 ha.	45 million ha.
Proportion of irrigated area to total	17%	27%
Use of nitrogenous fertilizer (N content)	55,000 metric tons	1,970,000 metric tons

vital importance, and this is why land reforms are crucial to India's agricultural program.

Planning and Technology. In the last 20 years, two million people have acquired title to land for the first time. Landless labourers are being given house sites and loans to build homes of their own. Ceilings have been placed on the total area that a person or a family can own, and the surplus is being distributed among the landless. There is considerable resistance to this from the bigger landowners, and the implementation of these programs has been rather slow.

Just as, at the international level, the more advanced nations are in a better position to use science and technology for further advancement, so at our national level we find that intensive farming methods and the extension services of the agricultural universities have benefited the comparatively well-off farmer, widening the gap between him and others in the rural community. To correct this imbalance, it is only fair that the new rural rich should contribute to rural uplift, since their prosperity is due to the inputs now available to them. Recently we have launched special programs to help marginal farmers and cultivators in dry areas.

In any drought-stricken area in India, the sudden and total drop in purchasing power is even more serious than the loss of crops. Even if enough food can be moved in from other parts of the country, few can afford to buy it. Hence we are compelled to start public works that will generate some income immediately and enable people to feed themselves rather than subsist on food doles. In 1965–66, when two successive monsoons failed in eastern India, we provided work for three million people. In 1971–72, when the rains bypassed Maharashtra, Gujarat, and Rajasthan in western India, 9.5 million people were employed on relief works. To have averted deaths during droughts of such magnitude is no mean achievement.

The increase in the production of grain and other crops has been uneven because of climatic variations from year to year. Even now, only about 25% of our cultivated area is irrigated. In view of the shortage of funds, investment in irrigation has traditionally been of a protective nature. Only during the last few years has it been possible to provide resources for the full utilization of available water through irrigation systems. With improved water management and assured inputs, especially of fertilizer, it has been estimated that India could double its food production in the next 15 years. Some developing countries have an even higher potential. In the current year it is unlikely that requirements will be met, even though we are giving the highest priority to fertilizer imports.

The world shortage of fertilizer is a major handicap to all developing countries in the medium term. The maldistribution of fertilizer stems partly from variations in natural endowments, but mainly it is a result of the inability of the developing countries to invest adequately in fertilizer production. International action must be initiated to correct this. The world cannot risk the free play of market forces in a commodity like fertilizer, any more than in food supplies. Equitable distribution of the limited fertilizer available in the world should be an integral part of the world food security system.

Ensuring World Food Security. Recent experience also indicates that a world without want cannot come into being unless nations agree among themselves to create an emergency food reserve that can be used in times of need and a world buffer stock of grain that can be used to level out fluctuations in food production and prices.

On the national plane, hardly any country is able to operate a free market system in so basic a commodity as grain. Price support is necessary to protect producers, and some control has to be exercised over stocks and distribution in the interest of the consumer. Difficulties arise partly from the nature of the cycle of agricultural production and partly because of unequal distribution of incomes within each country. They are aggravated in those countries where the demand for food has been rising faster than domestic supplies.

The world must think in terms not of free trade but of arrangements that will ensure the distribution of limited food supplies in accordance with some criterion of need, rather than solely on the basis of purchasing power. Such arrangements may involve an international system of voluntary contributions to a world buffer stock; alternatively, they could take the form of an agreement among nations to maintain a minimum level of stocks for times of scarcity in accordance with internationally agreed rules. They imply national and international action to create adequate and efficient storage capacity and a conscious decision to control consumption when crops are good in order to build adequate stocks for the future. This is especially necessary in the richer countries.

Any system of food security for the world will mean some sacrifices, some curtailment of current consumption on the part of the developed countries. If they substituted direct use of grains, vegetables, and other foods for even one-third of their meat and poultry consumption, enough supplies would be released to make up the potential world deficit in cereals. World demand for grain has gone up not only because of increasing population and improved diets in the less developed countries, but also because of changing consumption patterns within affluent countries. They have the means to pay for what they want and, in the process, the limited resources of the world are wasted and the really needy are deprived. Voluntary restraint or the turning of enlightened enthusiasts to vegetarianism will make hardly any dent. Eating habits and patterns of production must be guided by systematic fiscal and other governmental action in order to influence the relative prices of different products.

Until recently there was no shortage of grain on a global scale; yet from time to time individual countries have faced acute shortages and have lacked the funds to import supplies from other regions. Within the poor countries, the main brunt is borne by the weakest sections of the populace. Thus national policies are as important as international action. The entire philosophy of development—as it affects an individual nation and the world as a whole—has so far concentrated attention on problems of economic growth and of ensuring relative rates of growth that will reduce disparities among developing and developed countries. It is now generally realized that this approach to development is inadequate. The attack on poverty must be more direct, within nations as among nations. Such an approach involves massive redistribution of economic opportunities, not merely transfers from rich to poor through bilateral or international aid programs. It involves devising worldwide arrangements to assure the world's poor that technological progress will not be to their disadvantage, that economic growth will be everywhere accompanied by social justice.

The Overpopulation Question. Underdevelopment, poverty, and hunger are often regarded as consequences of burgeoning population. Many in the affluent lands, reading at their breakfast table of starvation in Africa or Asia, are content to shrug their shoulders and blame it on the increase in numbers.

There is no question but that world population must be contained. Poorer countries have made large outlays on population control; however, the basic problem is one not of money but of personnel, not of methods but of motivation. Couples do not decide on the size of their family in terms of its effect on the per capita income of the nation or on the world's food problem. What concerns them is the

effect on their own standard of living. For educated, well-to-do parents, each new baby makes heavy demands on time and budget. For the really poor, an extra child makes hardly any difference. It may, in fact, be regarded as an earner and a helper.

India has the largest officially sponsored family-planning program of any country, and our birthrate has been coming down, though it varies sharply from state to state. It is lower where per capita incomes are high or where women have more education and wider interests. For the country as a whole, the birthrate has fallen from 41 per 1,000 population to 37 in the last decade, but it is 30 in Kerala and Tamil Nadu, where education has made great headway, and 33 in Punjab, where the increase in agricultural production has been tangible. Family planning cannot be viewed in isolation. It is part of development.

Our increased population is not due entirely to new births. Thanks to our public health programs, which have curbed, although not yet eradicated, several diseases, the life span of the average Indian has risen and the death rate, which was 31 per 1,000 population in the 1930s, is

"For us in India, scarcity is only a missed monsoon away." Rations of rice being distributed in an Indian village.

THOMAS HÖPKER

down to 17 per 1,000. We cannot rest on our laurels, however. We find, for instance, that mosquitoes have reappeared and that the new strain is resistant to insecticides.

Considering the vast number of people involved and the rising cost of modern medicine, we must place greater emphasis on the prevention of disease. Proper nutrition and sanitation are essential. So is education, especially of mothers. Some knowledge of elementary health care could prevent much illness. For example, almost four-fifths of blindness could be prevented by giving babies the vitamins so handily found in leafy vegetables.

We are encouraging a new approach to medical education and organization so that health services are not concentrated around hospitals but reach out to village homes. Indigenous systems of medicine, the Ayurvedic and the Unani, have centuries of experience behind them. To give one example, the Sarpagandha plant has long been known as a cure for ailments of the heart and nervous system, but our modern doctors ignored it until it was rediscovered by the West and given a place in pharmacopoeias under the name reserpine. We have descriptions of caesarean sections and plastic surgery as they were performed in ancient times and of many efficacious rural remedies that should now be investigated scientifically. We have seen how the ancient Chinese practice of acupuncture has suddenly aroused worldwide interest. Even science is not immune to the dictates of dogma!

I wonder if any contemporary society is satisfied with its educational system. The developing countries face special problems, however, for the colonial education structures most of them inherited have proved wholly inadequate for the needs of a developing economy. We read that China has succeeded in overhauling its educational fabric by totally breaking with the past and by cutting itself off from the world for an entire generation. But it is not always possible or even desirable to do this.

In India there has been a phenomenal quantitative growth in education. The school population has increased from around 23 million to nearly 90 million in three decades, and the number of college students from 300,000 to 3 million. Several qualitative changes have also taken place—a new emphasis has been placed on science and engineering and on the building up of scientific research centres and national laboratories, some of which have earned international renown. Still, the large majority of our young people pass through the educational mill without acquiring the vocational skills they need to earn a living or, what is more important, the confidence and intellectual attributes that will enable them to face life.

An open and democratic society grants many rights to the individual; it also expects far more responsibility and maturity from him than an authoritarian society does. The number of our educated unemployed has grown, but many of them are unemployable. Everyone talks of the need for change but most are afraid of it and resist it. We are indeed witnessing a greater demand for vocational training, and more polytechnics and agricultural colleges are being established. We are advised that higher education should be restricted, but this raises a pertinent social question. All these years, opportunities for higher education have been confined to a privileged few. Should its doors be closed just when other classes and sections of the population are able to avail themselves of it?

Experiments in education are being undertaken by individuals and organizations in many countries. I was especially interested to learn of UNESCO's educational work in some countries of Africa. However, the basic issues concerning educational reforms are often clouded over by a preoccupation with unemployment. The sole purpose of education is not to enable young people to get jobs or even to know more, but to help them become better human beings, growing in awareness and compassion so they can grapple with the problems of today and be prepared for the challenges of tomorrow.

In the beginning I referred to the remarkable progress made by science and its demonstrated capacity to fulfill human requirements. How do we harness this creative potential for national and global purposes? Too often, scientific knowledge has been made subservient to national objectives, especially in the realms of energy and metallurgy. In medicine there is a somewhat greater awareness of international responsibility. Certainly a wider pooling of experience and inquiry in the fields of agriculture and nutrition is called for.

A consortium of technical experts drawn from different countries, disciplines, and organizations could ensure that scientific programs are based upon critical action-reaction analyses. There have been reports of changes in the global weather pattern. The variations we have experienced during the past few years are unfortunately to our disadvantage, and the position of the Sahelian zone of Africa is even worse. Thus there is little time to lose in initiating a new style of national scientific endeavour and a type of international cooperation that is designed to eradicate hunger and poverty.

National Interests in a Shrinking World. No country can afford to take a narrow view of its own interests, since it has to live in a world that is closely interlinked. The richer regions cannot abdicate their concern. Prosperity for some cannot be enjoyed in the midst of poverty for most. It is not military confrontation alone that imperils world peace; disparity is an equal danger. As Rabindranath Tagore once wrote, power has to be made secure not only against power but also against weakness. So the quest for an egalitarian society is not merely humanitarian. It is a practical necessity if the world order is to survive.

Perhaps we are still remote from a meaningful system of world taxation and redistribution of wealth through such taxation, but international economic policy must at least aim at securing rapid growth in world income, greater equality of opportunity among the nations of the world, and a worldwide system of economic security, especially food security. In 1974 two major world congresses were held, one dealing with population and the other with food supply. These subjects are of vital importance for most developing countries. It is to be hoped that the congresses provided us with some insight into the thinking of those who have the power to help the less fortunate among their fellow human beings.

Whether one thinks in terms of geography, historical perspective, or cultural patterns, it seems as though Europe and North America have long regarded their two continents as the hub of the world. Formerly, as far as they were concerned, Africa and Asia existed to be used for their purposes—and indeed this was the case for many long years. Colonialism has gone, but their attitude of self-importance continues. Interest is taken in our development, but the criteria they use to assess our progress are those of contemporary trends in the affluent countries; their angle of vision is still based on their interest and global strategy. They ignore the relevance of climate, of geographical compulsion and the forces of history, of centuries of national experience and civilization.

When foreigners visit India, they profess shock at our poverty. They have no idea of the stupendous effort required for a nation of 560 million (with such wide diversity and such different levels of development among regions) just to survive in this fast-changing and highly competitive world—to say nothing of traveling from one age to another as we are trying to do. The living conditions of the people of India and other developing countries should be compared not with conditions in the rich countries but with the state of affairs prevailing at the time of our liberation from colonial rule.

It is easy for rich nations to forget that they too had poverty not so long ago and that pockets of poverty still exist in the heart of their plenty and extravagance. I write this with no thought of complaint or accusation, for I am only too conscious of the fact that a similar situation exists in my own country—and perhaps in other developing countries as well—between town and village. Those who live in cities tend to think that they are India and that the rural areas, where the vast majority of our people live, are on the periphery.

The pattern of growth that we have copied from the advanced countries itself generates dissatisfaction. And disquiet is most marked in those sections whose expectations are the highest, such as the urban, educated middle classes and skilled workers in the more sophisticated industries. In a way, the outlook of such groups is similar to that of the people of rich countries: a feeling that they alone matter and a disinterestedness in the welfare of the huge numbers who live in villages. Unless the minds of people are remolded, infused with comprehension of and compassion for the suffering of the many, progress itself will be unreal.

In the Western world, the political revolution followed the economic revolution, but here they are taking place simultaneously. When a giant heaves itself awake after centuries of sleep, much dust will be raised. When a country is aroused after generations of apathy, many types of evil will come to the surface. Today, our countries are in ferment. We must try to understand the primary forces behind the changes that are shaking our societies, instead of finding fault with the efforts governments are making to solve age-old problems, made vastly more complex by the new problems of growth and by the interaction of global crosscurrents.

I have written mostly about India, for that is where my own experience lies. By and large, similar situations exist in other developing countries although, because of India's greater size and population, every problem here assumes gigantic proportions. Developing countries do need assistance at various levels and in varying degrees, but equally they need deeper understanding of their aspirations and difficulties.

Information Industries in the United States

by Anthony Oettinger and Peter Shapiro

E ach person's five senses receive and transmit to his brain every waking hour countless messages from other persons and objects. Many of these messages apparently cost nothing, and so the information they contain not only is plentiful but also seems cheap. But while information is prodigiously plentiful, much of it is available as a product of information services that are far from cheap. In fact, of every $5 spent in the United States in the early 1970s on goods, services, construction, and new machines, more than $1 was allocated to an information service of some kind.

To illustrate the overall expenditures on information services in 1970, the table below lists the revenues of information-related industries and outlays for tax-supported public institutions. Also included is spending on information services within broader industries. The latter group includes banking and credit card services, insurance, and securities listings.

At first glance, it seems arguable whether the primary outputs of the "processors" in the table, with the clear exception of data processing services, are information services or something else. However, each of these agencies' and services' "production lines" is nothing more than an information-handling process. For example, information processing is a fundamental prerequisite to posting Social Security, Medicare, and medical insurance payments. In 1971 the Social Security Administration was mailing 27

Anthony Oettinger is a professor of applied mathematics at Harvard University and is director of the Program on Information Technologies and Public Policy at that institution. He has written extensively on the subject of information, as developed in this article, and is the author of several books, including Automatic Language Translation and Run, Computer, Run: The Mythology of Educational Innovation.

Peter Shapiro is a former research fellow in the Program on Information Technologies and Public Policy at Harvard and is currently a staff member of the telecommunications group of Arthur D. Little, Inc., Cambridge, Mass. His works include Networking in Cable Television: Analysis of Present Practices and Future Alternatives.

million payments per month to Social Security recipients and their beneficiaries and was also processing $18 million per month in hospital bills.

Similarly, by the early 1970s banks were spending an estimated $4.3 billion per year on processing checks, and banks and other firms were spending another $2.4 billion per year on processing slips and billings for the nation's credit cards. These expenditures are understandable when compared with the numbers of checks and credit-card statements that required handling. In 1970 an estimated 22,500,000,000 checks were written on commercial banks' demand-deposit accounts; the corresponding estimate for credit-card transactions is 4,700,000,000.

The Information Industries. Many of the United States's largest private enterprises and publicly supported institutions have as their sole or primary product a service that involves one or more of the functions of creating, processing, collecting, or communicating information. These enterprises and institutions are best viewed as information industries that serve as society's perceptors, nervous system, and memory. They aggregate and complement actions of individuals both in developing society's assumptions about the way things are and should be and in transmitting such assumptions to successive generations. As discussed above, they consume a large part of the annual GNP, but they also play a significant role in stimulating general economic growth and distributing its benefits. For these reasons, the ways in which these industries perform and develop are of crucial public concern.

Particularly critical issues for the next decade and beyond concern the structure of the information industries

Expenditures for Information Services in the U.S. in 1970
In $000,000,000

Industry, agency, or service	Revenue or outlay
Creators	
Research and development	26.6
Advertising	7.9
Computer programming services	0.8
Authors, playwrights, and poets	no estimate
Processors	
Data processing services	1.4
Social Security Administration	1.0
Legal services	8.5
Banking and credit card services	6.7
Insurance agents	8.2
Securities brokers	3.1
Collectors	
Libraries	2.1
Intelligence community	over 4.0
Data bank information retrieval services	no estimate
Public opinion pollers	no estimate
Communicators	
Education	76.6
Telephone	17.5
Telegraph	0.4
Postal services	7.9
Mobile radio	1.9
Television	2.8
Radio	1.1
Cable television	0.3
Newspapers	7.0
Periodicals	5.2
Book publishing	3.5
Motion pictures	4.5
Theatres	0.1
Agriculture change agents	0.3
Information equipment producers	
Computers and related equipment	6.1
Television and radio sets	4.6
Paper	7.3
Photographic equipment and supplies	4.4
Total	220

Sources: Estimates by Program on Information Technologies and Public Policy, Harvard University, and Arthur D. Little, Inc.; estimates based on U.S. government and industry figures. Double counting not eliminated.

markets, namely, determining which functions should be performed by private and public institutions; privacy versus access to information; and public control over media content. The following paragraphs are devoted to a discussion of these issues.

Structure of Information Industries Markets. Despite their diverse origins, formerly separate industries now are jockeying for control of old and new markets. Long-standing boundaries between them have been broken down by the merging of technologies for processing, storing, and communicating information. Autonomous functioning of the industries is giving way to interdependence and, more traumatically for the institutions concerned, to direct competition. Markets traditionally characterized by stable monopoly and oligopoly structures are now experiencing the challenges of competition.

The effects of technological change are pervasive. For example, printing, once associated with movable, reusable slugs of metal type, increasingly relies on computer-aided composition directly onto photosensitive paper. Some visions of future home delivery of "newspapers" foresee an all-electric operation from the moment the news item leaves the reporter's hand to its delivery via wire, microwave, or laser beam to the television set of the reader, who then has the option of capturing the text permanently through some form of dry-copying or printing technology. The telephone companies and cable television systems will eventually compete with paper boys, delivery trucks, and the post office in the home delivery of locally produced "printed" media. For nonlocal delivery, the post office may face challenges from the telephone companies, new microwave common carriers, and from various domestic satellite systems.

Taking a more futuristic perspective, one can visualize newspapers being someday complemented by, replaced by, or transformed into computerized information retrieval systems. Subscribers will be able to request via their home terminals any items they wish to read. Although much institutional change will be required before such systems are in operation, they are becoming technologically feasible and on a small, highly focused scale some prototypes are already being tested by information scientists. For example, the National Library of Medicine has established a system for computerized searching of its bibliographic files. Called Medical Literature Analysis and Retrieval System (MEDLARS), this system is accessible nationwide through leased telecommunications facilities.

Besides their major impact on printed media, such information retrieval systems would obviously have implications for (or might be transformations of) libraries, data banks, and the electronic media. More important, they would affect the availability of information resources for citizens and organizations; current inadequacies and inequities might be either resolved or exacerbated depending on the rules governing the operations of these systems.

With computers increasingly used as switching devices in communications networks, and with electronic communications facilities becoming intrinsic elements in computer data processing services, the distinction between processing and communications is becoming blurry. As the functions of the two seem to merge, contests loom between the giant data processing industry, dominated by International Business Machines Corp. (IBM), and the equally huge telecommunications industry, dominated by American Telephone and Telegraph Co. (AT & T). The overlap of these industries has already led to an extensive inquiry by the Federal Communications Commission (FCC), but the issue of the proper functions to be performed by carriers and processors remains open. In 1974 IBM agreed to acquire financial control of a prospective domestic satellite enterprise, marking its explicit challenge to telecommunications companies. On another front, computer manufacturers and makers of dry-copying equipment have entered each other's territory. IBM now makes copying machines, and Xerox is producing computers.

Though there are many possible examples of confusion and conflict at the boundaries between information services, there are also some important instances of coordination of operations. The widespread tie-ins of computer and communications services are cases in point. Another is Western Union's "Mailgram" service, which links private-sector electronic transmission with public-sector on-foot transmission. Customers with teleprinters on their premises teletype their messages to Western Union headquarters, while others telephone in their messages; the telegraph company then retransmits the messages to post offices equipped with teleprinters where postal workers remove the messages, place them in envelopes, and put them in the first-class mail stream for next-day delivery. For the telegraph company, "Mailgram" represents a potentially lucrative transformation of its ailing telegram service, and for the Postal Service it may be a first step into the age of electronically delivered mail.

Examples of structural change dislocating traditional roles and practices are particularly evident in two of the communications markets. The first is that in which broadcasters, motion-picture theatres, and telephone companies have in recent times distributed information to, from, and among points within a community; this market is now making room for a potentially highly versatile newcomer, cable television. The second such market involves telecommunications services that heretofore have been the exclusive province of the local telephone company.

Structural upset in the local information distribution market is being created largely by the growth of cable television. Cable TV's first and still primary function has been to receive distant television signals, via microwave and high antennas, and to retransmit these along high-capacity coaxial cable to the sets of local subscribers. Even on this basis, cable television represents competition for local broadcasters in that its subscribers have additional viewing options. But cable's major potential lies in the programming it originates rather than in what it retransmits. It is in this potential that broadcasters and theatre owners foresee danger. They view as the real threat the payment system called pay-cable, which offers to subscribers for a per-program or per-channel charge such fare as movies, sports, and special-interest events. As of 1974 in the U.S. there were more than 3,000 cable television systems serving about eight million subscribers (about 13% of the nation's TV homes), but only 46 of these offered pay-cable. However, pay-cable was growing, causing the National Association of Broadcasters in 1973 to mount a $600,000 publicity campaign against it.

The anxiety of broadcasters derives from the prospect of reduced viewing audiences and, therefore, reduced advertising revenues. In addition, they fear that successful pay-cable operations could outbid them for desirable programming. Theatre owners anticipate fewer box-office customers because motion pictures could be viewed more cheaply and comfortably at home. Motion-picture producers are cautious because much of their current revenue comes from broadcast television, but they are also prepared to see pay-cable develop as an alternate market for movie distribution. Sports promoters have similarly conflicting motivations. These and other factors have led to restrictive regulations from the FCC. For example, between 1966 and 1972 cable television systems were essentially prohibited from importing distant television stations into the nation's largest 100 markets. However, in 1972 there was some easing of the rules to permit some signals to be imported into major markets. Some limitations were: with certain exceptions, movies could not be shown that had been released to theatres more than two, but less than ten years previously; no sports events could be shown that had been televised live, on a non-pay basis, within the preceding two years; and dramatic series with interconnected plots were prohibited.

Expansion of pay-cable could result in eventual replacement of advertiser-supported mass programming by more narrowly focused viewer-supported television programs. Whether this or more modest impacts would be in the public's best interest is a matter of hot debate among the parties; thus far, the "public's" representatives in the government rule-making arenas have been academic and think-tank spokesmen who generally have supported the pay-cable concept.

Cable television eventually also may challenge local telephone systems in providing facilities to businesses and other organizations for high-volume data, voice, or video communications between predesignated offices within a city. Other communications entities in this market would include the Postal Service and, in the future, point-to-point local microwave, laser beam, and optical-fibre systems. Cable's possible role in delivering print media to the home has already been mentioned.

Whether cable television will actually achieve these wonders is still an open question. Financing difficulties, the translating of broadcaster hostility into restrictive regulations, the uncertainties of big-city markets, and the limited goals of cable entrepreneurs have impeded development of this new medium. Nevertheless, preliminary stages of a revolution in the systems for locally distributing information are clearly visible and almost upon us.

With regard to a second major market in which structural changes have dislocated traditional patterns, AT & T has argued that efficient operation of the complex system that links the nation's millions of telephones requires that the Bell System control, and to a large extent provide, all aspects of telecommunications service, from terminal to terminal. In operating its "natural monopoly" service, AT & T has become one of the world's largest private organizations. Along with the several relatively small independent telephone companies, it absorbs each year almost 20% of the capital that all of the corporations in the U.S. raise from outside sources.

Yet, increasingly since 1968, AT & T's monopoly in various segments of its telecommunications market has been breached by the entry of competitive firms. In the six years since the FCC ruled that non-Bell System terminals could be attached to Bell System lines, an industry has developed to provide terminals ranging from decorator telephones to local switchboards. In addition, a series of regulatory decisions beginning in 1969 has helped to enable microwave companies and domestic satellite carriers to provide competitive leased circuits for data, voice, and video communications between cities.

AT & T has relentlessly opposed entry by the new terminals and leased-circuit companies on numerous technological, economic, and social grounds, whereas the prospective entrants, communications users, and the FCC have dwelt upon the benefits that open competition would yield. Innovations in terminals already have blossomed and, in competitive leased-line markets, prices have been cut. AT & T also has responded to competition by developing new leased-line facilities designed for transmission of data to and among computers.

Although revenues from terminals and the leased lines that are at stake total more than $1 billion, representing only a small proportion of the Bell System's overall income, the results of market restructuring in these areas could have wider implications. First, the quantity, quality, and cost of services available to the public have been and may additionally be affected. Also, AT & T's relationships with other businesses, government agencies, and individuals may be altered: the telephone company's relative power may be increased or decreased, and the scope of its role in society broadened or narrowed. If the new entrants fail to gain viable footholds, it will be many years before AT & T's supremacy even in minor telecommunications sectors again is challenged. On the other hand, increased introduction of non-Bell components into the nation's telecommunications system could lead to loss of efficiency in planning for the future by Bell, possibly to Bell's shrugging off that burden altogether, and perhaps to higher rates for residential telephone users.

The issues are complex. All branches of government have been drawn into the fray, including the White House, the courts, the Department of Justice, which instituted an antitrust suit against AT & T in late 1974, the Department of Defense, the Congress, and state public utility commissions as well as the FCC. The public's stake is large, for the reasons described in the previous paragraph, but its best interest remains unclear; at any rate, disinterested representatives of the public have yet to be heard.

Privacy and Access to Information. The main thrust of technological innovation has been to improve the ability of the information industries to process, store, and communicate information. Most would applaud this as a progressive trend. Danger flags have been raised, however, with respect to the implications of these changes for citizens' rights of privacy—their rights to control the dissemination of information about themselves as balanced by the legitimate requirements of law-enforcement agencies, credit, insurance, and other necessary services for improved access to such personal information.

The legal rights to privacy stem from constitutional interpretations and judicial, legislative, executive, and administrative acts at federal and state levels. In general, these date from an 1890 *Harvard Law Review* article by Samuel Warren and Louis Brandeis that cited the dangers of "recent innovations and business methods" (instantaneous photographs and newspaper enterprises). The article called for explicit recognition of the implicitly accepted right of citizens to be let alone. Some states subsequently enacted privacy legislation, and others amended their constitutions to include privacy rights. In 1965 the U.S. Supreme Court held that a "zone of privacy" was created by constitutional guarantees such as the First Amendment on freedom of association, the Fourth against unauthorized search and seizure, and the Fifth against self-incrimination. In 1967 the court included electronic surveillance as violating the Fourth Amendment, except where such surveillance was authorized by judicial order. Congress in 1968 drew boundaries on the ability of government to intercept private messages through wiretapping.

Concern for privacy recently has been revived in view of the widespread development of computerized data banks. Manual record-keeping systems had long existed in government agencies and private companies to keep track of individuals for such purposes as law enforcement, highway safety, national security, or pre-employment checking. But computers made a difference in that they permitted vastly enlarged data storing and processing systems, and they also facilitated access to personal data and the transfer of such data among separate organizations.

The current extent of development of the data bank industry is illustrated by the following figures. The FBI operates a number of law-enforcement record systems. As of the early 1970s its fingerprint file contained nonduplicated print sets of 86 million persons, of which 19 million sets were stored in the criminal section; its "narrative" file held 6 million records produced by criminal, civil, applicant, and special investigations; its "name-index" file contained 56 million cards arranged by name of persons and groups and used as an index to the narrative file.

The FBI files are made available to various law-enforcement jurisdictions throughout the U.S. and are used in FBI reports written on individuals or groups for interested government agencies. An information retrieval service is operated by the FBI to provide data to inquiring police officers on an on-line telecommunications basis. This service, called the National Crime Information Center (NCIC), as of 1974 held 4.5 million items, of which 450,-000 were criminal histories. A separate but similar network, called the National Law Enforcement Teletype System (NLETS), was operated for the states.

Credit bureaus are private data banks that provide information on individuals to such subscribers as department stores, automobile dealers, banks, and local businesses. The largest credit bureau in the early 1970s was TRW Credit Data of Long Beach, Calif. In 1970 this company provided 12 million credit reports to 7,000 subscribers; the reports were based on records held concerning some 30 million individuals. The largest pre-employment and pre-insurance data bank, Retail Credit Co. of Atlanta, Ga., produces more than 35 million reports each year from 45 million files maintained on individuals and businesses.

The link between privacy and freedom appears obvious to many Americans, and threats to privacy implied in data bank operations can cause emotions to run high. However, for an economic system based on credit to function, the U.S. needs credit reporting centres; for the society to combat increasingly sophisticated criminals, law enforcement agencies need prompt, effective, information retrieval systems; and for public service agencies to perform both short-term services and long-run planning, they must have information on the people they serve. The critical questions turn not on the existence of these data banks and information retrieval services but rather on the rules that might prevent abuses of them.

In 1970 the U.S. Congress passed the Fair Credit Reporting Act, which permits individuals to interrogate a data bank and review the accuracy of its records concerning themselves. A report in 1973 out of the U.S. Department of Health, Education, and Welfare (HEW) suggested further legislation to ensure that individuals be able to find out what information is held on them by data banks, to obtain a copy of such information, to contest its accuracy, and to be informed of its uses. As of April 1974, in efforts to codify the HEW report, there were 102 privacy bills pending in the House of Representatives and similar legislation sponsored by 62 lawmakers in the Senate. Some states enacted additional privacy laws: for example, Massachusetts limited the dissemination of criminal offender records to criminal justice agencies and others authorized by specific state or federal statutes. In implementing this law, Massachusetts had authorized, as of March 1974, the disclosure of records to approximately 70 federal and state agencies but had refused the requests of 104 other organizations, including credit bureaus, insurance companies, and executive departments of state and federal governments.

As data bank and information retrieval systems become more inclusive, more interconnected, and more efficient, the issue of privacy will deserve commensurately deepening public attention and concern. The critical questions will require continuing public vigilance: What information on individuals should be collected and how? Should the subjects of the information be informed? How should the information be kept, and with what safeguards? How can it be changed? Who is to be permitted to see it, and for what purposes? How can regulations concerning the operations of data banks be enforced?

Public Control over Media Content. As of 1972 approximately 64 million homes in the U.S. had television sets, daily newspapers had a paid circulation of 111 million, and periodicals a circulation of 410 million. A basic postulate of the U.S. democratic system is that the independent operations of these and other media are checks on the power of government. Freedom from public control over media content was enshrined in the First Amendment to the Constitution: "Congress shall make no law . . . abridging the freedom of speech, or of the press. . . ."

However, 200 years later the process of defining the limits of press freedom continues, both with regard to print media and even more intensively with respect to the major electronic medium, television. This discussion will focus on control-of-content issues as they affect television.

The foothold for state and citizen intervention in television content is that broadcast stations use the electronic spectrum, or airwaves, for which they require licenses from the FCC. Unlike newspapers, therefore, broadcast stations become accountable for their use of a public resource. Citizen groups have fought in the FCC and courts to block renewal of licenses to broadcasters who they claim do not reflect community viewpoints in their programming. Generally, the citizen groups and local stations arrive at compromises on hiring and programming practices before the licensing decision has to be made by the FCC. Broadcasters have lobbied forcefully to extend the licensing period beyond its current three years and thus to reduce their vulnerability to citizen-group pressures; as of 1974 legislation providing for this extension was pending in Congress.

Broadcasters are subject to the Fairness Doctrine, which asserts that they shall present controversial issues and at the same time make a genuine effort to represent fairly the different viewpoints. The doctrine's history has evolved through various FCC rulings and a 1959 amendment to the Communications Act of 1934. Based on a postulated "right of the public to be informed," the doctrine has been applied to news, public affairs, religious, and dramatic programming as well as to liquor advertisements (1946) and cigarette advertisements (1967). The broadcaster's obligation in the case of advertisements was to provide time for counteradvertisements. In 1974 there were several moves to reduce the scope of the doctrine: a U.S. Court of Appeals found that commercials suggesting that Chevron F-310 gasoline reduced air pollution were not subject to Fairness Doctrine constraints, and the FCC adopted a report that rejected as a precedent for future decisions its own prior ruling that cigarette commercials raised a fairness issue.

Broadcasters tend to view the Fairness Doctrine as an abridgment of their First Amendment protection; the public, however, has benefited from it because it has served as a wedge to gain television time to counteract perceived biases in programming. An additional benefit has been to curb excessively one-sided programming on the part of some licensees. On the other hand, the doctrine has also curbed forthright editorializing and controversial programming by broadcasters.

Television programming also has come under scrutiny for its effects on the attitudes and behaviour of children. Research on the effects of televised violence is almost as old as television itself, beginning in the early 1950s, and has roots in previous concerns over violence depicted in motion pictures and in comic books. In 1969 a set of 23 studies costing $1 million was sponsored by the surgeon general of the U.S. at the request of Sen. John Pastore (Dem., R.I.) to explore further the general hypothesis that violence in the media sets examples for violence-prone viewers—that it not only might trigger violent behaviours but also would suggest the most effective ways of doing harm. An advisory committee established to advise the surgeon general on the results of the studies included representatives of broadcasters, the public, and the scientific community. Possibly because of this composition, the com-

mittee's report in 1972 was inconclusive, although it did find an association between the aggressive behaviour of certain children and their television viewing.

Citizen groups have been the active parties seeking to reduce violent content on television; an especially prominent group, Action for Children's Television (ACT), evolved from a meeting of mothers in Boston in 1968. The controversy continues in 1974, as do the presentations on television of violent cartoons and action programming. Citizen groups such as ACT have also worked for changes in child-oriented advertising over television. Several large drug companies in 1972 were induced through ACT pressure to end their advertising of vitamins on children's television. In 1974, under severe pressure from citizens' groups, the Federal Trade Commission, and the FCC, broadcasters imposed on themselves a limit to the number of minutes per hour in children's programs that would be given over to advertising, and banned on such programs the advertising of nonprescription drugs or vitamins.

Control over media content is an issue that has many faces other than the few described here. Recently, for example, there was great concern over intimidation that broadcasters claimed was explicit in the attacks by former U.S. vice-president Spiro Agnew and other White House spokesmen on the television networks and in the several challenges of broadcast station licenses by friends of the Nixon administration. As long as political and social mores continue to evolve, and as long as the First Amendment is taken seriously in the United States as a guarantor of a way of life, the control-over-media-content issues will remain critical and never wholly resolved.

Other Information Industries Issues. How the information services markets are structured, how individual personal privacy can be reconciled with the information needs of crucial social services, and how the constitutionally protected freedom of the press is being modified by efforts of the public to control media content raise critical questions to which this essay has given brief attention. But the information services sector of the economy is enormous, and the huge information industries are inextricably bound up with the fate of the society as a whole. There are many important issues that are not discussed in this essay. One of these is the issue posed in the effective bypassing of a constitutionally mandated copyright law by the use of Xerox copying machines, tape recorders, and cable television. As the U.S. Constitution recognized, creators of information must somehow be rewarded for their efforts so that creativity can be maintained. What should be the formula for providing such rewards in an era of increasingly easy copying and sharing of information through electronic technology?

A second issue concerns society's priorities in allocating its information services dollars: On what kinds of problems should research and development funds be spent? How can the public influence the evolution of information services and the structuring of information markets to redress inadequacy or inequity in the distribution to citizens of information resources? Resolution of all such issues requires at the outset the recognition of common factors in the private and public enterprises here discussed as information industries.

JANUARY

1 *Northern Ireland coalition assumes power*

An executive governing body composed of 15 members of both the Protestant and Roman Catholic factions took office in the beleaguered province of Northern Ireland. The move ended 21 months of direct rule by the British government. Brian Faulkner, Unionist Party leader, was chief of the executive body.

3 *Spain's new premier forms Cabinet*

Carlos Arias Navarro, sworn in as the new premier of Spain on January 2, named his Cabinet and later pledged to allow some political and social liberalization in the country. Arias replaced Luis Carrero Blanco, who was assassinated in December 1973 by members of the Basque separatist group ETA.

4 *United States: President Nixon refuses to comply with subpoenas*

Pres. Richard M. Nixon told the Senate committee investigating Watergate that he would not comply with subpoenas calling for him to surrender hundreds of White House tapes and documents. In a letter to committee chairman Sam J. Ervin, Jr. (Dem., N.C.), Nixon stated: "To produce the material you now seek would unquestionably destroy any vestige of confidentiality of Presidential communications, thereby irreparably impairing the constitutional functions of the office of the Presidency."

New Watergate defense attorney hired

James D. St. Clair was hired by President Nixon to replace J. Fred Buzhardt, Jr., as special counsel to the president in charge of his Watergate defense. Buzhardt was named White House counsel, a post previously held by John W. Dean III.

Attorney general vacancy filled

William B. Saxbe was sworn in as U.S. attorney general. Saxbe, the fourth attorney general to serve in the Nixon administration, filled the vacancy that was created on Oct. 20, 1973, by the resignation of Elliot L. Richardson.

7 *Japanese devaluation*

The Bank of Japan suspended its intervention in support of the yen on foreign exchange markets. A 6.7% de facto devaluation of the yen immediately followed and the British pound and West German mark also suffered declines as the U.S. dollar rose sharply and the price of gold increased.

8 *South Korean President Park cracks down on dissidents*

In a move designed to end growing opposition to the new constitution, South Korean Pres. Park Chung Hee proclaimed two emergency measures and decreed that anyone criticizing the constitution faced up to 15 years' imprisonment.

9 *Developments in the worldwide energy crisis*

The Organization of Petroleum Exporting Countries (OPEC) concluded a three-day meeting in Geneva with the announcement that there would be no change in the price of crude oil prior to April 1.

In the U.S. the White House announced that President Nixon had invited the foreign ministers of major oil-consuming nations to meet in Washington in February to discuss energy problems.

State of emergency continues in the United Kingdom

The government extended the state of emergency in the U.K. for a third month. Slowdowns by coal miners and railroad engineers and reduced oil supplies contributed to the crisis. As the country entered its second week of the three-day workweek, Prime Minister Edward Heath announced the establishment of a Department of Energy. Heath also announced that since the three-day week was instituted on Dec. 31, 1973, the country had saved about 1.5 million tons of coal and reduced electricity consumption by 21%.

15 *Watergate: Report on 18½-minute tape gap*

A panel of experts reported to U.S. District Court Judge John J. Sirica that an 18½-minute gap on a tape of a conversation between President Nixon and former White House aide H. R. Haldeman, surrendered to the court by President Nixon in connection with the Watergate affair, had been caused by at least five separate erasures and rerecordings.

17 *United States: Inflationary trend continues*

The U.S. Department of Commerce reported a slowdown in the growth of the gross national product during the last quarter of 1973, combined with the worst quarterly rise in inflation since 1951. The U.S. Department of Labor reported on January 8 that the wholesale price index had risen 18.2% in 1973.

18 *Suez disengagement agreement signed*

Egypt and Israel signed an agreement to separate their forces along the Suez Canal, ending the conflict that began on Oct. 6, 1973, when Egyptian forces attacked territory in the Sinai Peninsula occupied by Israel since the 1967 Arab-Israeli war. The accord was negotiated by U.S. Secretary of State Henry Kissinger in a series of meetings with Egyptian and Israeli officials. Syria, which had attacked Israeli-held positions in the Golan Heights at the same time Egypt moved in the Sinai, was not a party to the agreement.

Britons face a winter of austerity reminiscent of the World War II years. In Christmas week 1973 storekeepers show determination to make the best of hardship caused by power cuts.

FEBRUARY

19 *Franc devalued*

French Finance Minister Valéry Giscard d'Estaing announced that France would allow the franc to float for six months. The announcement came a day after the meeting of the International Monetary Fund's Committee of 20 in Rome had ended in disagreement over how to deal with the monetary effects of the oil crisis. The decision by France had far-reaching effects and was contrary to the IMF's declaration that "countries must not adopt policies which . . . merely aggravate the problems of other countries."

21 *United States: 93rd Congress convenes in Washington*

The second session of the 93rd U.S. Congress convened in Washington, D.C., facing energy shortages, spiraling prices, unemployment, and possible impeachment of the president. The Senate consisted of 56 Democrats, 43 Republicans, and 1 independent. The House of Representatives was composed of 243 Democrats and 189 Republicans, with three vacancies.

Japanese problems

In a major policy speech to the Diet, Japanese Prime Minister Kakuei Tanaka urged his countrymen to listen to criticism in order to improve their mutual relationships with other countries of the world. The speech followed Tanaka's return from a Southeast Asian tour that had been marred by anti-Japanese demonstrations in Thailand and Indonesia. Domestically, Japan faced serious economic problems, including spiraling prices "fueled by the oil problem" and a high balance of payments deficit.

23 *Sub-Saharan drought worsens*

Addeke H. Boerma, director general of the UN Food and Agriculture Organization (FAO), reported that the severe drought in sub-Saharan Africa had worsened. The nations most severely affected were Chad, Mali, Mauritania, Niger, Senegal, and Upper Volta.

25 *Pullout of Israeli forces along the Suez Canal*

Israeli forces formally began withdrawing along the Suez Canal. Details of the disengagement were drawn up the day before at a meeting of Israeli and Egyptian chiefs at Kilometre 101 on the Cairo-Suez road.

Food riots in India

A number of persons were reported to have died in the state of Gujarat, India, since riots protesting food prices and shortages broke out on January 18. Maharashtra State experienced similar protests earlier in the month.

26 *Koruturk approves coalition Cabinet in Turkey*

Turkish Pres. Fahri Koruturk formally approved the coalition Cabinet formed by Bulent Ecevit, leader of the Republican People's Party. The RPP and the National Salvation Party agreed to form the coalition government on January 15.

Argentine terrorism continues

One day after the Argentine Chamber of Deputies passed a strong antiterrorism bill, 19 bombing attacks against leftist leaders and organizations were reported in various Argentine cities. Pres. Juan Perón had earlier urged strong action against guerrilla terrorists following a bloody gun battle between left-wing guerrillas and soldiers at an army tank garrison in Azul.

27 *Continuing warfare in Syria*

Syrians claimed to have inflicted heavy Israeli casualties in sporadic fighting in the Golan Heights. The U.S. and Egypt continued to put pressure on Syria to enter into negotiations with Israel. Since the 1967 Arab-Israeli war the Israelis controlled the strategically located Golan Heights, which are inside Syrian territory. During the October 1973 war Israel pushed about 15 mi. farther, to within artillery range of the Syrian capital of Damascus.

30 *United States: State of the union address*

Pres. Richard M. Nixon, in his state of the union address, urged an end to consideration of the Watergate affair and promised improvements in the economy and the energy crisis. He also outlined major programs in health care, welfare reform, and mass transit.

Cambodian rebel attacks

Fighting continued between Khmer Rouge insurgents and Cambodian government forces, and Cambodian Pres. Lon Nol declared a six-month state of emergency. Close to 100 civilians had been reported killed since January 23, when rebel attacks began on the capital of Phnom Penh.

FEBRUARY

2 *"Cultural Revolution II"*

In a campaign aimed against the teachings of Confucius and the policies of the late defense minister Lin Piao, China launched what was seen as a new Cultural Revolution. In an article in the Communist Party newspaper, *Jenmin Jih Pao,* the campaign was described as a "war against feudalism, capitalism, and revisionism and a heavy blow to revisionism, imperialism, and reaction. It is a matter of first importance for the whole party, the whole army, and the whole nation." Apparently related to this ideological drive was the announcement in January of a military shake-up.

4 *Record U.S. budget*

President Nixon submitted his proposed budget for fiscal 1975. Calling for $304.4 billion in expenditures, it was the first U.S. budget to surpass $300 billion. On February 1 in his annual economic report to Congress, Nixon indicated a "highly uncertain" outlook for the economy. On the same day wage and price controls, in ef-

fect for most retailers since August 1973, were lifted. Controls remained on food, motor vehicles and parts, and petroleum products.

Hearst kidnapping

Patricia Hearst, the 19-year-old granddaughter of the late newspaper publisher William Randolph Hearst, was kidnapped from her Berkeley, Calif., apartment by a group connected with the radical-terrorist Symbionese Liberation Army.

6 *United States: Impeachment investigation ratified*

By a vote of 410–4 the U.S. House of Representatives approved a resolution ratifying the House Judiciary Committee's presidential impeachment investigation and giving the committee broad subpoena powers.

Arab oil boycott warning

U.S. Secretary of State Henry Kissinger warned Arab countries that their continua-

tion of the embargo on oil to the U.S., in effect since the October 1973 Middle East war, "must be construed as a form of blackmail." The statement was made by Kissinger as U.S. efforts toward negotiating a peace in the Middle East continued.

7 *Grenada declares independence*

After 200 years under British rule, the Caribbean island of Grenada became independent. Prime Minister Eric M. Gairy urged an end to antigovernment demonstrations. These were in protest against Gairy's one-man rule and an unemployment rate of more than 50%. Resulting incidents of violence had swept the island since November 1973.

8 *United States: Skylab splashes down*

Skylab 4, the last scheduled U.S. Skylab mission until the U.S.-Soviet joint endeavour planned for July 1975, splashed down in the Pacific Ocean. The three astronauts aboard the orbiting scientific craft

WIDE WORLD

The Skylab space station in earth orbit, photographed by the Skylab 4 astronauts from the command module. The left-side solar shield was lost when the space station was launched in May 1973.

spent a record 84 days 1 hour 16 minutes in space. Three days earlier an unmanned probe of the planet Venus by Mariner 10 had relayed data that indicated Venus was not closely related to the earth.

10 *Coal miners strike in the United Kingdom*

After rejecting a 16.5% pay raise offered by Prime Minister Edward Heath, British coal miners began a full-scale strike, demanding 30–40% pay increases. The scheduling of the strike, ordered by the National Union of Mineworkers (NUM) after a vote by the miners, had caused Heath to dissolve Parliament and call for a general election to be held February 28, 16 months earlier than required.

11 *Southeast Asian conflicts continue*

Nearly 200 civilians were reported killed at Phnom Penh, Cambodia, in one of the worst rebel shellings in the conflict between Khmer Rouge insurgents and Cambodian government forces. In South Vietnam the Saigon government claimed to have killed 118 Communists in clashes southwest of the city of Pleiku. The exchange of prisoners of war between South Vietnam and the Viet Cong resumed February 8 after a seven-month suspension.

United States: Independent truckers end violence-marked strike

Independent truckers returned to work after accepting an agreement negotiated with the help of Pennsylvania Gov. Milton J. Shapp. A number of violent incidents involving truckers occurred on highways in Illinois, Indiana, Ohio, and Pennsylvania. The truckers were protesting the

55-mph speed limit, which went into effect in January as a fuel-saving measure; reduced fuel supplies; and higher fuel costs. On February 7, after an eight-day strike, the truckers' representatives accepted the administration's proposal, which included a 6% surcharge on freight rates.

13 *U.S.S.R. deports Solzhenitsyn*

The Soviet Union deported dissident novelist Aleksandr Solzhenitsyn and issued a decree stripping him of his citizenship. Solzhenitsyn's family would remain in the U.S.S.R. until he decided on a permanent residence. This was the first forced Soviet expulsion of a major political dissident since 1929, when Joseph Stalin exiled his erstwhile colleague Leon Trotsky.

Washington energy conference

A communiqué issued following a three-day meeting of 13 major oil-consuming nations (Belgium, Canada, Denmark, France, Great Britain, West Germany, Ireland, Italy, Japan, Luxembourg, The Netherlands, Norway, and the U.S.) endorsed a U.S. proposal for cooperation in dealing with the energy crisis. The agreement came despite French Foreign Minister Michel Jobert's vociferous opposition to several key points in the program.

19 *United States: Hearst giveaway plan*

Randolph Hearst announced a plan to give away $2 million worth of food for release of his daughter, Patricia, kidnapped on February 4 by members of the Symbionese Liberation Army. The kidnappers had issued a mandate on February 12 for Hearst to provide $70 worth of food for

every needy person in the state of California, a demand that Hearst said he was unable to meet.

23 *Latin-American conference*

A conference of Western Hemisphere foreign ministers adjourned in Mexico City and issued the "Declaration of Tlatelolco," calling for future conferences but containing few concrete decisions. The three-day conference was attended by U.S. Secretary of State Henry Kissinger and foreign ministers from 24 Latin-American and Caribbean nations.

24 *Islamic nations meet at Lahore*

A three-day meeting of more than 30 Islamic heads of state and government at Lahore, Pak., ended with the issuance of the "Declaration of Lahore," establishing a committee to study ways of assisting less developed Muslim nations hit by high oil prices, while rejecting specific aid measures. The nations also recognized the Palestine Liberation Organization as sole representative of the Palestinians and repeated demands that the Old City of Jerusalem be returned to Arab control. On the first day of the meeting Pakistan officially recognized the nation of Bangladesh (formerly East Pakistan), which had broken away from Pakistani control in 1971.

27 *Syria releases Israeli POW list*

U.S. Secretary of State Henry Kissinger delivered a list of Israeli POWs held by Syria to Israeli Prime Minister Golda Meir in Jerusalem. Kissinger had obtained the list from Syrian Pres. Hafez al-Assad. Israel later announced that receipt of the list fulfilled its conditions for holding disengagement talks with Syria.

Canadian Parliament opens

Newly appointed Gov.-Gen. Jules Léger opened the second session of the 29th Canadian Parliament in Ottawa with a speech in which the government called for a record $22 billion spending program.

28 *U.S. and Egypt resume diplomatic relations*

During a visit to Cairo by U.S. Secretary of State Henry Kissinger it was announced that the U.S. and Egypt were resuming full-scale diplomatic relations. The Egyptian government reported on February 7 that it had begun clearing the Suez Canal of sunken ships and mines and shells in preparation for reopening of the canal, closed since 1967. Israeli troops completed their withdrawal from the western bank of the canal on February 21.

U.K. general elections

The Labour and Conservative parties both failed to gain a majority in Parliament in British elections. Final results gave Labour 301 seats, Conservatives 296, Liberals 14, and others 24.

MARCH

1 *United States: Watergate indictments*

Seven former White House and Nixon campaign officials were indicted, on charges including conspiracy, obstruction of justice, and making false statements to investigators, by the grand jury investigating the Watergate affair. The seven included former attorney general John N. Mitchell and former White House advisers John Ehrlichman and H. R. Haldeman.

2 *Burma: Revolutionary Council dissolved*

In accordance with the provisions of the country's new constitution effective in January, Burmese Prime Minister Ne Win dissolved the ruling Revolutionary Council and turned its powers over to the new People's Assembly. The new constitution established Burma as a socialist republic with one-party rule. The country had been ruled by a military coalition since 1962.

4 *United States: Military expenditure defended*

In a report to Congress defending the fiscal 1975 defense budget, U.S. Secretary of Defense James Schlesinger warned that the U.S. must increase military vigilance against the Soviet Union because "détente is not the only, and in certain circumstances not the primary, policy interest of the U.S.S.R."

EEC offers cooperation with the Arabs

After gaining approval of EEC foreign ministers meeting in Brussels, an offer was made by the EEC to explore the possibilities of long-range economic cooperation with 20 Arab countries.

United Kingdom: Labour government takes over

Harold Wilson, leader of the Labour Party, was appointed as the new British prime minister. Conservative Party leader Edward Heath had resigned as prime minister after failing to win the Liberals' support for a coalition government. Heath sought to form the coalition after his party failed to win a parliamentary majority in the February 28 elections.

5 *Ethiopian unrest*

In response to nationwide unrest that started with rioting in the capital, Addis Ababa, and an army mutiny in Asmara on February 26, Ethiopian Emperor Haile Selassie agreed to call a constitutional convention in an attempt to quiet the disturbances. On February 28 the former Ethiopian ambassador to the UN, Endalkachew Makonnen, was appointed by Selassie to head a new Cabinet.

10 *New Israeli government sworn in*

Prime Minister Golda Meir and her new 22-member coalition Cabinet, including Moshe Dayan as defense minister, were sworn in as the government of Israel. Meir announced the formation of the majority coalition on March 6 after a nine-week government crisis and threats by Dayan that he would resign in response to severe public criticism of the role he allegedly played in the October 1973 war.

11 *United Kingdom: Domestic affairs*

The British government ended the state of emergency that was declared in November 1973 because of fuel shortages. On March 6 the National Union of Mineworkers and the National Coal Board agreed on a settlement of the nationwide miners' strike that would give the miners a 30% overall increase in wages. On March 7 Energy Secretary Eric Varley canceled the three-day workweek.

14 *Kurds seize Iraqi land*

Kurdish rebels, led by Gen. Mustafa al-Barzani, seized a large area on the Iraqi border with Turkey after several days of fighting between the Kurds and Iraqi troops. Iran filed a complaint on March 6 with the UN Security Council concerning alleged Iraqi attacks on the Iranian border. The fighting, which had reportedly been going on sporadically since December 1973, coincided with increased unrest among the Iraqi Kurds, who rejected a plan put forward by the Iraqi government that would give them autonomous status. The Kurds were alleged to have received arms and assistance from Iran.

15 *New Latin-American leaders*

Ernesto Geisel was sworn in as the president of Brazil. Geisel was the fourth military man to hold the office since the armed forces seized power in Brazil in 1964. On March 12 Carlos Andrés Pérez, in his inaugural address as president of Venezuela, promised that he would seek a national consensus for nationalization of U.S. oil interests.

18 *U.S. oil embargo lifted*

At a meeting of the Organization of Petroleum Exporting Countries in Vienna, seven oil-producing nations agreed to lift the embargo on oil shipments to the U.S. Syria and Libya planned to continue the embargo, and Iraq did not attend the meeting. The embargo, imposed in October 1973, remained in effect against Denmark and The Netherlands because, according to Saudi Arabian oil minister Ahmad Zaki al-Yamani, they "have not made clear their position on asking for a full (Israeli) withdrawal from occupied territories."

South Vietnamese fighting worsens

The South Vietnamese government announced that over 400 North Vietnamese and close to 100 government soldiers had been killed in the Central Highlands of

Kurdish artillery in action along the Iraqi-Turkish border during fighting between Kurdish rebels and Iraqi troops.

SVEN SIMON/KATHERINE YOUNG PHOTOGRAPHY

South Vietnam in the worst fighting since the signing of the cease-fire agreement in January 1973.

19 *Food riots in India*

Twenty-two persons were reported to have been killed in Bihar State, India, in several days of rioting over rising food prices and political corruption. The Bihari riots followed the March 15 decision by Prime Minister Indira Gandhi to dissolve the state assembly in Gujarat because of mounting unrest there.

EEC-U.S. relations

President Nixon, in a speech to the National Association of Broadcasters meeting in Houston, Tex., softened his remarks made four days earlier at a question-and-answer session before business executives in Chicago, at which time he accused the EEC and Europe of adhering to a policy of "confrontation and even hostility" with the U.S. Relations between the U.S. and the EEC had been strained earlier in the month when the EEC announced its intention to cooperate with 20 Arab countries. The U.S. State Department protested that the EEC had not consulted with the U.S. before making its Arab cooperation offer.

21 *United States: Watergate grand jury report ruling upheld by Court of Appeals*

The U.S. Court of Appeals upheld U.S. District Court Judge John J. Sirica's ruling that the secret grand jury report on Nixon's possible role in the Watergate affair should be turned over to the House of Representatives for purposes of its impeachment inquiry.

28 *Kissinger talks with leaders in Moscow*

U.S. Secretary of State Henry Kissinger returned to Washington after three days of talks with Soviet leaders in Moscow. A general communiqué issued jointly by the U.S. and Moscow indicated that no substantive progress toward breaking the deadlock in the Geneva strategic arms limitation talks (SALT II) and other matters had been made.

Greek-Turkish relations worsen

Turkish bombers made unauthorized sorties into Greek airspace during a NATO naval exercise, causing Greece to withdraw from the exercise. Relations between the two countries were already strained by arguments over Cyprus and oil rights in the Aegean Sea.

Ceausescu is Romanian president

Romanian Communist Party leader Nicolae Ceausescu was elected to the newly created post of president of Romania. Ion Gheorghe Maurer resigned as premier two days earlier and was replaced by Deputy Premier Manea Manescu.

29 *Indirect negotiations on Israeli-Syrian conflict begin*

Israeli proposals for troop disengagement were submitted by Defense Minister Moshe Dayan to U.S. Secretary of State Henry Kissinger in Washington. This began the first round of indirect negotiations on the Israeli-Syrian conflict.

Solzhenitsyn reunited with family

Exiled Soviet novelist Aleksandr Solzhenitsyn was reunited with his family in Zürich, Switz. Natalya Solzhenitsyn left Moscow with their four sons and her mother to reside in Switzerland, where Solzhenitsyn was expected to apply for political asylum.

APRIL

1 *U.K. seeks renegotiation of EEC terms*

At a meeting of EEC foreign ministers in Luxembourg, U.K. Foreign Secretary James Callaghan warned that Britain wanted major revisions to be made in the terms under which it joined the EEC in January 1973. This position was one of the Labour Party's election promises, ostensibly to better Britain's economic position in the Community. Callaghan stated that it was possible that the question of U.K. withdrawal from the EEC might be put to a popular vote.

2 *French President Pompidou dies in Paris*

Georges Pompidou, Gen. Charles de Gaulle's successor to the French presidency after de Gaulle's resignation in 1969, died in Paris. Alain Poher, president of the Senate, became interim president until elections could be held.

3 *President Nixon agrees to pay delinquent taxes*

Reports issued separately by the Internal Revenue Service and the Congressional Joint Committee on Internal Revenue Taxation indicated that President Nixon owed over $400,000 in back taxes for the period of his first term in office. Nixon agreed to pay $432,787.13 plus interest after their issuance. The congressional committee's findings indicated that he had failed to report five categories of taxable income and claimed six categories of unwarranted deductions.

5 *Coalition government formed in Laos*

A coalition government (the third since 1957) composed of neutralist, rightist, and pro-Communist Pathet Lao was formed in Laos. Prince Souvanna Phouma continued as premier, and Pathet Lao leader Prince Souphanouvong, after 11 years in exile, became head of an advisory body, the National Political Council.

8 *Baseball's Aaron betters Ruth home run record*

Hank Aaron of the Atlanta Braves, in a game in Atlanta, Ga., against the Los Angeles Dodgers, hit his 715th career home run, surpassing Babe Ruth's total of 714. Aaron's total at the conclusion of the 1974 season was 733.

9 *Indian subcontinent accord signed in New Delhi*

India, Pakistan, and Bangladesh signed an agreement in New Delhi, the first indication of an opening of relations and easing of tensions among the three nations since the 1971 Indo-Pakistani war. The agreement provided for release of 195 Pakistani soldiers to be tried for war crimes by Bangladesh, and Pakistan agreed to accept more non-Bengalis from Bangladesh and to repatriate Bengalis in Pakistan.

10 *Golda Meir to resign*

Golda Meir announced her "irrevocable" decision to resign as prime minister of Israel, a post she had held since 1969. She agreed to stay on in a caretaker capacity until a new government was formed or elections were held. Mrs. Meir's resignation, which brought down the month-old coalition government, was prompted by a judicial commission report placing the blame for Israel's military unpreparedness at the beginning of the October 1973 war on the top military command. The so-called Arganat Report cleared Defense Minister Moshe Dayan of responsibility for the bungling but caused deep division in Mrs. Meir's Labour Party.

11 *United States: House committee subpoenas tapes*

After rejecting a White House compromise offer, the House Judiciary Committee, by a vote of 33–3, issued a subpoena ordering President Nixon to turn over tapes and other presidential materials relating to 42 White House conversations. It was reportedly the first subpoena ever served on a president by a House committee. The deadline for compliance was set at April 25.

12 *Qiryat Shemona and retaliation*

Israeli troops raided six villages in Lebanon in retaliation for the April 11 attack by 3 Palestinian guerrillas on Qiryat Shemona, Israel, near the Lebanese border, in which 18 persons were killed.

MAY

HENRI BUREAU—SYGMA

Joyous crowds in Lisbon following the overthrow of the Portuguese government by a military junta in April.

13 *Syria submits troop disengagement plan*

Syrian military intelligence chief Brig. Gen. Hikmat Khalil al-Shihabi submitted his country's plan for troop disengagement with Israel on the Golan Heights in a meeting with U.S. Secretary of State Henry Kissinger in Washington.

18 *Egypt no longer relies exclusively on Soviet aid*

After 18 years of exclusive Egyptian reliance on Soviet military matériel, Pres. Anwar as-Sadat announced that Egypt would begin to seek other sources of arms. Egyptian requests to the U.S.S.R. for supplies had not been acted upon by that country for six months.

19 *Israeli-Syrian air battle*

Syria and Israel fought their first air battle over the Golan Heights since the October 1973 war. Artillery engagements continued on the Golan Heights-Mt. Hermon front, in the wake of Kissinger's receipt of troop disengagement proposals from both countries.

21 *Colombia elects president*

In Colombia's first free presidential election in more than two decades, the people elected Alfonso López Michelsen, candidate of the Liberal Party, with about 55% of the votes.

22 *Yitzhak Rabin chosen to form new Israeli government*

The Central Committee of Israel's ruling Labour Party, by a vote of 298–254, elected Yitzhak Rabin to form a new Cabinet. Rabin had served as chief of staff during the June 1967 war and was ambassador to the U.S. (1968–73).

24 *Vorster's party gains in South African elections*

The Nationalist Party of South African Prime Minister B. J. Vorster increased its parliamentary majority by four seats in national elections, a virtual mandate for Vorster's apartheid policies.

25 *Portuguese coup*

A seven-man junta led by Gen. António de Spínola assumed power in Portugal after dissident army officers seized control of the government in a virtually bloodless coup. Pres. Américo Tomás and Premier Marcello Caetano were deposed in the overthrow. The junta promised to put the country back on its feet, after the demoralizing efforts of the old government to preserve control over the overseas territories of Angola, Mozambique, and Portuguese Guinea (Guinea-Bissau).

28 *Federal jury acquits Mitchell and Stans*

After 26 hours of deliberation spread over four days, a federal district court jury in New York City acquitted former attorney general John N. Mitchell and former commerce secretary Maurice Stans of all charges related to a secret Nixon campaign contribution by financier Robert Vesco.

29 *Nixon to release transcripts*

President Nixon, in a nationwide television address, stated that he planned to release 1,308 pages of edited tape transcripts of Watergate-related White House conversations to the House Judiciary Committee.

30 *United States: President's authority to impose controls ends*

The Economic Stabilization Act of 1970, which gave the president authority to impose mandatory wage and price controls, expired. Only prices in the petroleum industry remained controlled under authority of the 1973 Emergency Petroleum Allocation Act.

MAY

1 *United States: Watergate transcripts published*

U.S. newspapers began publishing installments or excerpts of the White House-edited Watergate tape transcripts released on April 30 by President Nixon. The *Chicago Tribune* managed to get the entire document into most of its morning editions. The Government Printing Office planned to sell copies of the transcripts, as did numerous paperback distributors. The House Judiciary Committee voted to notify President Nixon that his release of the transcripts instead of the actual tapes did not constitute compliance with the committee's subpoena.

6 *West German Chancellor Brandt resigns*

West German Chancellor Willy Brandt submitted his resignation to Pres. Gustav Heinemann. In resigning Brandt took full responsibility for "negligence in connection with the Guillaume spy affair," in which Günter Guillaume, an aide to the chancellor, was discovered to be an East German spy. Heinemann was asked to name Walter Scheel, leader of the Free Democrats (the principal coalition partner of Brandt's Social Democrats), to head a caretaker government until a new chancellor was chosen.

8 *Rail strike in India*

Indian railway workers began a nationwide strike, demanding higher wages and shorter working hours. The strike threatened to cripple India, which relies heavily on railways for production and trade.

9 *United States: Formal impeachment hearings open*

The House Judiciary Committee opened the formal hearings at which it would decide whether or not to recommend that the full House impeach President Nixon. The initial session summarized events leading to the Watergate burglary of June 1972.

Canadian government dissolved

After being defeated on a vote of no confidence in the House of Commons on May 8, the minority Liberal government of Canadian Prime Minister Pierre Trudeau was dissolved, and elections were set for July 8. The vote centred on Parliament's rejection of the government's budget, which was said to deal ineffectively with Canada's rising inflation.

13 *Italians support divorce law*

In a two-day referendum Italian voters overwhelmingly supported retention of the three-year-old law permitting divorce. The vote was considered a blow to the ruling Christian Democrat Party, which wanted the law repealed.

Millions of children face malnutrition

Henry R. Labouisse, executive director of UNICEF, told a UNICEF board meeting that at least 400 million children in less developed countries face severe malnutrition, even starvation, and recommended that the board declare an emergency situation.

14 *101st archbishop of Canterbury named*

The archbishop of York, the Most Rev. Donald Coggan, was named to be the 101st archbishop of Canterbury by Queen Elizabeth II. Coggan was to succeed the Most Rev. Michael Ramsey, retiring at the age of 70, as titular head of the worldwide Anglican Communion.

15 *Spínola assumes Portuguese presidency*

Gen. António de Spínola became provisional president of Portugal and announced the formation of a Cabinet, with Adelino da Palma Carlos as premier; Mário Soares, a socialist who had been exiled under the old military regime, became foreign minister. Meanwhile, guerrilla leaders in the Portuguese African territories of Angola, Portuguese Guinea (Guinea-Bissau), and Mozambique continued their fight for independence from Portugal.

20 Israeli children die in Ma'alot massacre

Three Palestinian guerrillas, after crossing the border from Lebanon, entered the village of Ma'alot, Israel, and took 90 schoolchildren hostage, demanding the release of 20 guerrillas who were being held prisoner in Israel. The Israeli government agreed to concede to the guerrillas' demands but, after a mixup regarding the deadline for release of the prisoners, Israeli troops stormed the school and the ensuing battle left 20 children and the 3 guerrillas dead.

16 *Ma'alot retaliation by Israel*

In the heaviest raids ever carried out by Israeli jets against Lebanon, close to 50 persons were reported killed and over 170 wounded in reprisal for the guerrilla raid on the Israeli village of Ma'alot on May 15.

West German chancellor sworn in

Helmut Schmidt, finance minister in the outgoing Cabinet of Willy Brandt, was sworn in as the chancellor of West Germany. On May 15 the presidential electoral college elected Walter Scheel to succeed retiring Pres. Gustav Heinemann.

17 *Shoot-out between the Symbionese Liberation Army and Los Angeles police*

Six members of the Symbionese Liberation Army, who had kidnapped and claimed to have converted to their cause publishing heiress Patricia Hearst, were killed in a shoot-out with police in Los Angeles. Since Miss Hearst was not found in the charred

UPI COMPIX

President Nixon after his April television address announcing release to the House Judiciary Committee of edited White House tape transcripts, shown at right.

rubble after the shoot-out, she was presumed to be alive, and the FBI subsequently issued a warrant for her arrest.

18 *India explodes nuclear device*

In an underground test in the Rajasthan Desert, India exploded its first nuclear device, thus becoming the sixth nuclear power after the U.S., the U.S.S.R., the U.K., France, and China. In an announcement by the Indian government calling it "a peaceful nuclear explosion experiment," it also was stated that India had "no intention of producing nuclear weapons."

Antiguerrilla operations in Argentina

Argentine federal police began mass arrests in Tucumán Province in a drive against the left-wing People's Revolutionary Party (ERP). Left-wingers in the country had been restless since Pres. Juan Perón's May Day address, which prompted fighting between right- and left-wing Peronistas in the streets of Buenos Aires.

21–22 *Ma'alot reprisals continue*

Reprisal raids for the May 15 attack on Ma'alot were continued by Israeli jets on Palestinian targets in Lebanon. Jerusalem and most of northern Israel were placed on security alert after reports that a group of Palestinian guerrillas had infiltrated across the Lebanese border.

22 *United States: Nixon refuses to release additional tapes*

In a letter to House Judiciary Committee Chairman Peter W. Rodino, Jr. (Dem., N.J.), President Nixon stated that he would not comply with two subpoenas issued by the committee on May 15 for additional tapes and documents related to the Watergate affair and that further subpoenas would be rejected also. On May 21 Rodino issued a statement in which he indicated that President Nixon had learned of the Watergate cover-up earlier than March 21, 1973, as he had previously admitted, and that this had been edited out of the transcripts released April 30.

Israeli soldiers rush to remove Israeli children from a Ma'alot school after the May 15 gun battle between Palestinian guerrillas and Israeli troops, which resulted in the deaths of many children.

N. GUTMAN—SIPA/LIAISON

27 *Valéry Giscard d'Estaing new French president*

Valéry Giscard d'Estaing was sworn in as president of France, after narrowly defeating leftist candidate François Mitterrand in a runoff election May 19. Giscard d'Estaing, finance minister under Georges Pompidou, named Jacques Chirac premier.

28 *Rail strike ends in India*

Union officials ended the 20-day rail strike that had disrupted major Indian cities but did not have the crippling effect that the union leaders had anticipated. The walkout was quashed when the government began mass arrests of railway union leaders and workers.

Yitzhak Rabin forms Israeli Cabinet

Yitzhak Rabin, prime minister-designate of Israel, announced the formation of a new Cabinet to replace the caretaker government of Golda Meir. The new Cabinet consisted of members of the Labour Party, the Independent Liberals, and the Civil Rights List. Notably absent were Moshe Dayan, Abba Eban, and Pinhas Sapir, who had been ranking members in Mrs. Meir's government.

Executive coalition in Northern Ireland falls after five-month rule

Northern Ireland's Executive coalition of Protestants and Roman Catholics collapsed, and the chief of the body, Brian Faulkner, resigned. The demise was brought about by a general strike of the Ulster Workers' Council, a group of Protestant extremists, which had crippled the economy and gained wide public support.

29 *Ulster Workers' Council ends strike in Northern Ireland*

After achieving one of its main objectives, the overthrow of the provincial Executive coalition, the Ulster Workers' Council called off the general strike in Northern Ireland that began May 15. The British government in London immediately imposed a form of direct rule on the province.

Labor government of Whitlam retains narrow majority in Australia

Australian Prime Minister Gough Whitlam formally claimed victory for his Labor Party in the May 18 elections. Final results indicated that Labor obtained 66 seats in the House of Representatives, against 61 for the Liberal-Country Party coalition.

The Senate consisted of 29 seats each for the Labor and Liberal-Country parties, with the balance of power held by one member of the Liberal Movement and an independent.

31 *Israel and Syria sign disengagement agreement*

Israel and Syria formally signed an agreement in Geneva to disengage their forces on the Golan Heights. Agreement was reached May 29 after over a month of intensive negotiation by U.S. Secretary of State Henry Kissinger. It was the first such agreement between the two countries since the armistice of 1948.

Supreme Court to consider tape case

The U.S. Supreme Court granted special Watergate prosecutor Leon Jaworski's plea for prompt consideration of Nixon's refusal on the grounds of executive privilege to turn over 64 White House tapes. On May 20, U.S. District Court Judge John J. Sirica ordered Nixon to comply with Jaworski's subpoena for the tapes, which Jaworski felt were essential to the trial of seven former Nixon aides accused in the Watergate cover-up. The seven men were indicted on March 1.

JUNE

3 *United States: Colson pleads guilty*

Charles W. Colson, formerly one of President Nixon's closest aides, pleaded guilty to a charge that he obstructed justice in the trial of Daniel Ellsberg, which was thrown out of court in 1973 because of government interference. (Ellsberg had been indicted for unauthorized possession of the Pentagon papers in June 1971.) In return for Colson's guilty plea, all other pending charges against him were dropped, and he agreed to testify in other Watergate-related cases.

Israeli coalition wins parliamentary approval

The Israeli Knesset approved Yitzhak Rabin as prime minister by a vote of 61–51 with 5 abstentions.

4 *The U.K. eases EEC demands*

At a meeting of EEC foreign ministers in Luxembourg, British Foreign Secretary James Callaghan presented his country's demands for renegotiation of the terms of its EEC membership. The U.K.'s tone on this occasion was more conciliatory than its April threat to withdraw from the Community if renegotiation failed.

Uganda's Amin accused of creating "reign of terror"

The Geneva-based International Commission of Jurists, after a three-year study, accused Ugandan Pres. Idi Amin of creating a "reign of terror." The group concluded that Uganda had experienced a "total breakdown in the rule of law."

10 *EEC ministers to cooperate with Arabs*

At a meeting in Bonn, W.Ger., the nine foreign ministers of the EEC agreed to pursue their March offer of economic, technical, and cultural cooperation with 20 Arab nations. Progress on the matter had been delayed because of U.S. objections.

11 *Kissinger resignation threat*

Accompanying President Nixon on his trip to the Middle East, U.S. Secretary of State Henry Kissinger held an emotional news

Chinese posters on a wall near Peking's city hall. Left-wing militants charged, among other things, "a serious recurrence of right-wing deviation among the leaders."

conference in Salzburg, Aus., in which he threatened to resign unless his name was cleared of charges that he had participated in illegal wiretaps undertaken by the White House in 1971. The charges, made by unidentified congressional sources, alleged that he had played a more important part in federal wiretapping than he had indicated during the 1973 Senate hearing on his confirmation as secretary of state.

12 *Argentine President Perón agrees to remain in office*

Argentine Pres. Juan Perón withdrew his threat to resign after thousands of Peronistas gathered outside Government House to remonstrate with him. The resignation threat had been made in the wake of rising inflation, shortages, and crippling strikes, as Perón sought full public support for his economic policies.

13 *IMF's Committee of 20 meets in Washington, D.C.*

The International Monetary Fund's Committee of 20 ended its sixth and final meeting with the adoption of interim rules for dealing with international monetary affairs. Final agreement on a permanent solution to the international monetary crisis had eluded the committee since its meetings began in September 1972. Attempts to reach a solution were abandoned in January after soaring world inflation and quadrupled oil prices were added to existing trade and balance of payments problems.

China: Poster war in Peking

Posters denouncing the Municipal Revolutionary Committee, Peking's equivalent of a city council, were put up outside committee offices by private citizens. The posters appeared to be a radical counterattack against reported suppression by conservative officials. They accorded with a directive that was issued on May 18 by the Chinese Communist Party's Central Committee authorizing people to criticize local officials.

14 *Smallpox epidemic hits India*

Between 10,000 and 30,000 persons were reported to have died in India, primarily in Bihar State, in one of the worst smallpox epidemics in recent history.

Independence talks collapse in Guinea

Talks between Portugal and the African Party for the Independence of Guinea and Cape Verde (PAIGC) collapsed, presumably in response to a speech delivered June 11 by Portuguese Pres. António de Spínola. In the speech, which reportedly angered the PAIGC, Spínola offered to let the African territories of Angola, Portuguese Guinea (Guinea-Bissau), and Mozambique decide their own future once "a climate of freedom" and democratic institutions had been established there.

Big Ben screened by smoke from a fire following an IRA bomb explosion at the Houses of Parliament, London.

15 *United States: Supreme Court to consider "unindicted co-conspirator" question*

The U.S. Supreme Court agreed to broaden its consideration of the White House tapes matter and include the question of whether the Watergate grand jury had the right to name President Nixon as an unindicted coconspirator in the Watergate cover-up. The White House on June 5 acknowledged that the grand jury had voted in February to name Nixon as an unindicted co-conspirator. In other Watergate developments, the final report of the panel of electronic experts appointed by the court, submitted to U.S. District Court Judge John J. Sirica on June 4, indicated that the 18½-minute gap on one of the Watergate tapes had been manually produced.

17 *Houses of Parliament bombed*

The Houses of Parliament in London were damaged by a bomb explosion that injured 11 persons. London police blamed the incident on the militant Provisional wing of the Irish Republican Army which opposed, among other things, the presence of British troops in Northern Ireland. British Prime Minister Harold Wilson told the House of Commons June 4 that withdrawal of British troops from Northern Ireland offered "no easy solution" to the Ulster problem.

19 *Nixon concludes Middle East tour*

U.S. Pres. Richard Nixon returned to Washington after a one-week tour that included stops in Egypt, Saudi Arabia, Syria, Israel, and Jordan. In Cairo, Nixon and Egyptian Pres. Anwar as-Sadat signed an agreement of friendship and cooperation with a provision under which the U.S. would provide Egypt with nuclear technology for peaceful purposes. In Syria, Nixon and Pres. Hafez al-Assad announced resumption of diplomatic relations, and in Jerusalem promises of military and economic aid as well as nuclear technology were made to Israel.

20 *Watergate: House committee reveals transcript discrepancies*

A number of House Judiciary Committee staff memoranda were released indicating that the committee's versions of some of President Nixon's Watergate tapes were significantly different from the edited transcripts made public by the White House. The committee's versions suggest that Nixon knew of some elements of the Watergate scandal before the meeting with John W. Dean III on March 21, 1973.

Italian Cabinet resumes operation

Italian Premier Mariano Rumor informed Pres. Giovanni Leone that his Cabinet was functioning again. Leone refused to accept Rumor's resignation, tendered on June 10, and ordered the members of the coalition government to settle their differences. These principally involved methods of dealing with Italy's serious economic crisis.

Third UN Law of the Sea Conference opens

The third UN Conference on the Law of the Sea opened in Caracas, Venezuela, with over 5,000 delegates and observers from 148 nations attending. The ten-week session was to be devoted to drafting an international treaty to govern man's use of the oceans.

23 *Israeli pullout from Syria*

Israeli troops completed their withdrawal from Syrian territory occupied during the October 1973 war. The exchange of prisoners of war between the two countries began June 1, and the first 500 members of the 1,250-man UN Disengagement Observer Force arrived in Qunaytirah, Syria, on June 5.

25 *Israel files complaint against Lebanon*

As antagonism between the Palestinians and Israelis continued, Israel filed a complaint with the UN Security Council charging that Lebanon should be held responsible for the June 24 guerrilla attack on Nahariya, Israel, because it continued to permit terrorist groups to operate freely from Lebanese territory. The latest terrorist attack, and Israel's damaging air attacks on Lebanon June 18–20, in retaliation for the June 13 Palestinian raid on Kibbutz Shamir, brought threats and counterthreats from both sides.

JULY

26 Bank collapse in West Germany

Because of heavy losses incurred in foreign exchange trading, the West German Bankhaus I.D. Herstatt KG, one of the country's largest private banks, was ordered liquidated. It was the first bank to so collapse and the fourth major institution in the world to encounter trouble since the major currencies were allowed to float early in 1973.

NATO countries sign declaration in Brussels

The heads of state of 15 NATO countries, meeting in Brussels, signed a 14-point declaration of principles on Atlantic relations. It included a pledge to improve communication and consultation on matters of common interest. The declaration was agreed upon by the countries' foreign ministers in Ottawa on June 19.

27 Nixon arrives in Moscow for summit talks

U.S. Pres. Richard M. Nixon arrived in Moscow for his third summit meeting with Soviet Communist Party leader Leonid I. Brezhnev. The two leaders pledged a "strengthening of universal peace" and expressed hope that significant progress could be made by the two powers in the control of nuclear weapons.

JULY

1 Argentina's Perón dies

Argentine Pres. Juan Perón died in Buenos Aires and was succeeded by his wife and vice-president, Isabel. Mrs. Perón, who had taken over the duties of the presidency on June 29, was the first woman chief of state in the Americas.

2 Soviet TV network censors U.S. satellite broadcasts

Satellite reports from Moscow by correspondents of three major U.S. TV networks were cut off when the reporters attempted to discuss activities of Soviet dissidents, including the hunger strike of physicist Andrei Sakharov that began June 29. The correspondents were in Moscow to cover President Nixon's visit.

3 Nixon returns from Moscow summit

U.S. Pres. Richard M. Nixon returned to the U.S. following his visit to Moscow and addressed the nation from Limestone, Me. Several agreements on nuclear matters were signed by Nixon and Soviet Communist Party leader Leonid I. Brezhnev, but the summit failed to produce any permanent gains toward limitations on offensive weapons.

7 West Germany is world soccer champion

West Germany won a 2–1 victory over The Netherlands in the World Cup soccer final at Olympic Stadium in Munich. The West Germans would hold the world title at least until 1978, when the next competition would be held in Argentina.

8 United States of America v. Richard M. Nixon

Presidential defense counsel James D. St. Clair and special Watergate prosecutor Leon Jaworski presented oral arguments to the Supreme Court in the cases of United States of America v. Richard M. Nixon and Richard M. Nixon v. United States of America. At issue was the constitutionality of President Nixon's claim of executive privilege in relation to the Watergate tapes and other documents, and whether the grand jury had the right to name the president as an unindicted co-conspirator in the Watergate cover-up.

Israelis retaliate for Nahariya raid

Thirty fishing boats in three southern Lebanese ports were sunk by Israeli naval commandos in retaliation for the June 24 Palestinian attack on Nahariya, Israel. The guerrillas were believed to have gained access to Nahariya by sea from southern Lebanon.

Trudeau regains majority in Canadian elections

The Liberal Party of Canadian Prime Minister Pierre Elliott Trudeau won an absolute majority in the House of Commons in national elections. The elections, which were called in May following the government's defeat in a no-confidence vote against the proposed budget, gave Trudeau the majority he had lost in the 1972 elections.

Assistance for financially troubled banks

Representatives of 11 major central banks, from the U.S., Canada, Japan, and eight Western European nations, agreed in principle to assist financially troubled banks in their respective countries. The agreement stemmed from concern over the collapse of the Herstatt bank in West Germany and reports that other banks were in trouble as the result of losses incurred in foreign exchange trading.

9 U.S. House committee releases transcripts

The House Judiciary Committee produced its own transcripts of eight Watergate-related White House conversations. The House transcripts differed in some major respects from those previously released by the White House. The variations pointed toward greater involvement of President Nixon in the Watergate cover-up.

13 Portugal gets new premier

Army Col. Vasco dos Santos Gonçalves, considered to be a leftist, was named premier by Portuguese Pres. António de Spínola. Gonçalves replaced the centrist Adélino da Palma Carlos, who resigned July 9 after the Council of State refused to grant his Cabinet additional powers. Spínola had dismissed Carlos' two-month-old civilian Cabinet on July 11.

United States: Senate Watergate committee issues final report

After a 17-month investigation, the Senate Select Committee to Investigate the 1972 Presidential Campaign Activities released its final report. The report recapitulated the evidence the committee had uncovered and made 35 recommendations for cleaning up campaign practices and for other legislative changes.

15 Makarios overthrown on Cyprus

Greek officers led the Cypriot National Guard in a coup that ousted Archbishop Makarios III as president of Cyprus. Greek Cypriot newspaper publisher and former guerrilla leader Nikos Sampson was sworn in to succeed him. Initial reports from the troubled island indicated that Makarios had been killed in the fighting, but these proved false, and Makarios eventually escaped to London.

16 Greek-Turkish relations strained

As relations between Turkey and Greece worsened over the Cyprus situation, U.S. Ambassador to Turkey William B. Macomber, Jr., returned to Ankara, ostensibly to aid in efforts to ward off a conflict between the two nations. Macomber had been recalled to Washington for consultations concerning Turkey's July 1 lifting of the ban on opium poppy cultivation.

Political unrest in Japan

Takeo Fukuda, Japanese finance minister, resigned his powerful post in the wake of demands for organizational reform in the ruling Liberal-Democratic Party. The demands were brought on by the party's loss of eight seats in the upper chamber of the country's national legislature, the House of Councillors, in elections on July 7. State Minister Shigeru Hori also resigned July 16, and Deputy Prime Minister Takeo Miki resigned four days earlier.

20–22 Cyprus powderkeg explodes

Turkey, claiming its right to protect the Turkish communities on Cyprus, invaded that island by sea and air at sunrise. Turkish troops gained control of a 16-mi. corridor from the port of Kyrenia to the capital of Nicosia, and fighting erupted along the "Green Line," which separates

The U.S. House Judiciary Committee following its historic vote to recommend impeachment of Pres. Richard M. Nixon.

the Greek and Turkish sectors of the capital. Greece ordered a general mobilization of forces and sent troops to the Turkish border in Thrace. Subsequently, both countries accepted a UN proposal for a cease-fire to become effective July 22. British Foreign Secretary James Callaghan announced that representatives from Turkey, Greece, and Britain would begin talks in Geneva within a few days.

23 Greek military junta resigns; new president for Cyprus

The Greek military junta under the leadership of Brig. Gen. Demetrios Ioannides resigned, and Greek Pres. Phaidon Gizikis summoned former prime minister Konstantinos Karamanlis from his self-imposed exile in Paris to form a new civilian government. In Cyprus Nikos Sampson resigned as president and was succeeded by Glafkos Clerides, speaker of the Cypriot House of Representatives and a moderate. Sampson, a proponent of *enosis,* had failed to gain Cypriot support since taking over the presidency on July 15, and resigned in what he termed "the national interest."

24 United States: Supreme Court rules against Nixon

The Supreme Court ruled 8–0 that claims of executive privilege could not be used to withhold evidence in a criminal trial and that President Nixon must provide the tapes and documents of 64 presidential conversations subpoenaed by Special Prosecutor Leon Jaworski for use in the Watergate cover-up trial. In a statement read by his defense lawyer, James D. St. Clair, Nixon announced that he would comply with the ruling.

27 Portugal promises to free territories

Portuguese Pres. António de Spínola promised to start transferring power immediately to the people of the three African territories of Angola, Mozambique, and Portuguese Guinea (Guinea-Bissau). The three territories had been part of Portugal since 1933.

27–30 United States: House committee recommends impeachment

The House Judiciary Committee recessed after approving three articles recommending that the U.S. House of Representatives impeach President Nixon and seek his removal from office through a Senate trial. The first article, adopted on July 27 by a vote of 27–11, charged President Nixon with obstruction of justice. The second article, charging that President Nixon had failed "repeatedly" to carry out his constitutional oath and duty to uphold the nation's laws, was adopted by a vote of 28–10 on July 29. Nixon's defiance of the committee's subpoenas was cited in the third article, and it was adopted by a vote of 21–17 on July 30. On July 30 the tapes of 20 White House conversations were turned over to U.S. District Court Judge John J. Sirica, the first step by the White House in complying with the Supreme Court's July 24 decision.

30 New cease-fire on Cyprus

Turkey, Greece, and Great Britain signed an agreement in Geneva providing for a standstill cease-fire on Cyprus. The agreement included an expanded peacekeeping role for the United Nations Peacekeeping Force in Cyprus (UNFICYP), and provisions for new talks between the parties aimed at "reestablishing constitutional government" on Cyprus. The three countries are all guarantors of Cyprus' sovereignty under the treaties which granted the island independence in 1960. Fighting had continued on Cyprus despite the UN-sponsored cease-fire of July 22. Further negotiations on political issues were slated to begin in Geneva August 8.

31 Greece charges Turkish violations

Cypriot Pres. Glafkos Clerides charged that Turkey had more than doubled the territory under its control since the July 22 cease-fire and was continuing to expand its bridgehead around Kyrenia despite the provisions of the July 30 cease-fire.

AUGUST

1 Constitution reinstated in Greece

Greek Prime Minister Konstantinos Karamanlis reinstated the 1952 constitution, abolished in 1967 by the military junta. Provisions of the constitution relating to the monarchy were temporarily suspended.

3 Provisional Cabinet approved in Ethiopia

Emperor Haile Selassie approved a new provisional Cabinet in Ethiopia to be headed by Michael Imru. On July 22 Endalkachew Makonnen had been deposed as prime minister by the Military Council for failing to effect their demands for reform. It was announced on August 1 that Makonnen had been arrested.

5 Nixon releases transcripts—admits his complicity

U.S. Pres. Richard M. Nixon released subpoenaed transcripts of three conversations of June 23, 1972, and ordered them turned over to U.S. District Court Judge John J. Sirica. The transcripts showed that six days after the Watergate break-in Nixon had ordered an end to FBI investigation of the matter. In an accompanying statement Nixon said: "At the time, I did not realize the extent of the implications which these conversations might now appear to have. As a result, those arguing my case, as well as those passing judgment on the case, did so with information that was incomplete and in some respects erroneous. This was a serious act of omission for which I take full responsibility and which I deeply regret."

6 United States: Kissinger cleared in wiretap controversy

The Senate Foreign Relations Committee issued a report clearing U.S. Secretary of State Henry Kissinger of responsibility for the wiretapping of 17 officials and newsmen, including some of his subordinates, between 1969 and 1971. Kissinger had threatened in June to resign unless cleared of the charges, which alleged that he had played a greater role in federal wiretaps than he had indicated at his 1973 Senate confirmation hearings.

8 Nixon announces his intention to resign

Three days after his admission of complicity in the Watergate cover-up and amid eroding support evidenced in public statements by an overwhelming number of fellow Republicans as well as Democrats, Pres. Richard M. Nixon announced that he would submit his resignation the following day because he had lost his "political base in Congress."

Cyprus cease-fire talks resume in Geneva

As fighting continued on Cyprus, peace talks between Greece, Turkey, and Great Britain resumed in Geneva in an attempt to establish an effective cease-fire and to resolve the political differences underlying the fighting. Meanwhile, representatives of the three nations and the UN were in Nicosia attempting to establish cease-fire lines in accordance with the July 30 cease-fire declaration.

9 Gerald Ford sworn in as president of the United States of America

Vice-Pres. Gerald R. Ford was sworn in as the 38th president of the United States of America by Chief Justice Warren Burger. Richard M. Nixon's formal resignation was delivered to Secretary of State Henry Kissinger as Nixon was en route from Washington, D.C., to his home in San Clemente, Calif.

14 Cyprus talks break down

The Geneva talks between Greece, Turkey, Great Britain, and Greek Cypriot and Turkish Cypriot leaders broke down when Turkey refused to allow time for Greek and Greek Cypriot consultations on the Turkish plan for a federal system on Cyprus. Within hours Turkish forces unleashed heavy air and ground attacks on Cyprus, as the Turks began using military force to gain the demands they were unable to obtain in Geneva.

16 Turkey declares a unilateral cease-fire

Turkey reached its objective of partitioning Cyprus de facto into Greek Cypriot and Turkish Cypriot areas and declared a unilateral cease-fire. With the northern third of the island under its control Turkey announced that it was willing to resume negotiations in Geneva, a proposal that the Greeks rejected.

19 U.S. ambassador to Cyprus killed in Nicosia

Rodger P. Davies, U.S. ambassador to Cyprus, was shot and killed during an anti-American demonstration at the U.S. embassy in Nicosia. The demonstration was headed by Greek Cypriots who believed that the U.S. had sided with Turkey in the Cyprus situation.

20 Nelson Rockefeller nominated for U.S. vice-presidency

U.S. Pres. Gerald R. Ford announced that he had chosen Nelson Rockefeller, former governor of New York, to be the next vice-president of the United States. In his spirit of "openness and candor" Ford had solicited suggestions for the office from members of Congress, governors, and his personal staff and advisers.

24 New president in India

Fakhruddin Ali Ahmed formally took office as president of India. Ahmed, who had the support of Prime Minister Indira Gandhi, was elected on August 17 to succeed V. V. Giri.

President Nixon and his family bid farewell to the White House staff.

PICTORIAL PARADE

26 *Waldheim effects Cypriot meeting*

UN Secretary-General Kurt Waldheim succeeded in bringing about the first meeting between Cypriot Pres. Glafkos Clerides and Rauf Denktash, the leader of the Turkish community on Cyprus, since the Geneva talks collapsed on August 14. Denktash and Clerides discussed only the refugee problem, avoiding political issues, but agreed to meet once a week thereafter.

Portugal grants independence to Guinea-Bissau

Portugal signed an agreement, effective September 10, granting independence to Portuguese Guinea. The agreement ended

400 years of dominance over the West African territory by Portugal. Negotiations continued with nationalist leaders in Mozambique, another African territory seeking independence from Portugal.

27 *United States: Stock market hits four-year low*

The stock market continued to lose ground, with the Dow Jones industrial average dropping to a four-year low of 671.54 on the New York Stock Exchange.

29–30 *UN conferences end*

The third UN Conference on the Law of the Sea adjourned in Caracas, Venezuela, on August 29 without having reached spe-

cific agreement on any of the matters before it. In Bucharest, Rom., the UN World Population Conference ended with the approval of a "Plan of Action" but no specific goals were agreed upon during the 12-day conference.

31 *West Germany to aid Italy*

West Germany agreed to lend $2 billion to Italy to ease the serious economic crisis in that country. In an interview released on August 24 West German Chancellor Helmut Schmidt had warned the Ford administration that extreme measures taken to curb inflation in the U.S. could seriously disrupt the world economy. Schmidt, the former finance minister, said that deflation in the U.S. economy would eventually spread to world markets.

SEPTEMBER

2 *United States: Federal standards set for private pensions*

President Ford signed into law a pension reform bill. The new law, aimed at protecting the retirement benefits of an estimated 23 million employees from company mismanagement and bankruptcy, will ensure that pensions benefits are paid.

4 *U.S. and East Germany establish diplomatic relations*

The U.S. established formal diplomatic relations with East Germany, the last major Western country to do so since 1971, when the Communist country emerged from isolation on acceding to the four-power Berlin pact. Embassies were to be opened in both countries by early 1975.

5 *Economists meet in Washington, D.C.*

President Ford presided over the first of several meetings scheduled as preliminaries to an economic summit to be held September 27 and 28. Twenty-eight U.S. economists were almost unanimous in concluding that the Federal Reserve Board should ease its tough monetary policy, which they said affected money, credit, interest rates, and, indirectly, the stock market.

8 *President Ford grants Nixon full pardon*

Pursuant to the power conferred upon him by Art. II, sec. 2 of the U.S. Constitution, Pres. Gerald Ford granted a full pardon to former president Richard M. Nixon for all federal crimes he "committed or may have committed or taken part in" while in office. It was announced that an agreement had been made with Nixon whereby he would be given title to his presidential papers and tapes, but that they would be kept intact and available for use in judicial proceedings for three years.

Evel Knievel fails to traverse Snake River Canyon

U.S. stuntman Evel Knievel failed in his highly publicized attempt to cross the Snake River Canyon in Idaho in a steam-propelled rocket. The vehicle parachuted safely to the bottom of the canyon and Knievel was rescued by helicopter.

10 *President Ford's support waning*

A *New York Times* poll indicated that public support for President Ford had dropped sharply as a result of his pardon September 8 of former president Nixon.

12 *Haile Selassie deposed as emperor of Ethiopia*

Haile Selassie I, emperor of Ethiopia since 1930, was peacefully deposed by the ruling Military Council. Crown Prince Asfa Wossen, who had lived in Switzerland since suffering a stroke in 1972, was asked to return as figurehead monarch. Parliament was dissolved and the constitution suspended. Lieut. Gen. Aman Michael Andom was put in charge of the Provisional Military Administrative Council.

Court-ordered busing leads to violence in Boston

Boston public schools opened under a busing plan ordered in June by Federal District Court Judge W. Arthur Garrity to promote integration. A number of schools, mainly in South Boston, were boycotted by white students and there were scattered incidents of violence.

16 *United States: Clemency for Vietnam war deserters and draft evaders*

President Ford signed a proclamation offering conditional clemency to thousands of Vietnam war deserters and draft evaders, in return for an oath of allegiance and up to 24 months of alternative service. The proclamation was received coolly by most of the estimated 7,000 evaders and deserters residing in Canada.

17 *29th UN General Assembly opens*

Abdel-Aziz Bouteflika, foreign minister of Algeria, was unanimously elected president of the 29th General Assembly at its opening session in New York City.

Angry parents opposed to busing rebuke Sen. Edward Kennedy in Boston.

UPI COMPIX

OCTOBER

Japanese terrorists free hostages

French ambassador to The Netherlands Jacques Senard and eight other hostages were freed by the Japanese terrorists who took over the French embassy in The Hague on September 13. The captors, who said they were members of the Japanese Red Army, were demanding the release of an army comrade from a French prison. The terrorists, along with the prisoner, Yutaka Furuya (who had been flown from Paris to The Hague), fled the country in a French airliner.

18 *U.K.: General election announced*

British Prime Minister Harold Wilson called for a general election to be held October 10, the second to be held in 1974. It was the first time in more than 50 years that two general elections had been called in one year in the U.K.

19 *Former president Nixon subpoenaed*

Special Watergate prosecutor Leon Jaworski subpoenaed former U.S. president Richard Nixon to appear as a prosecution witness in the Watergate cover-up trial. The subpoena was served on Nixon at his San Clemente, Calif., estate.

Japanese–South Korean tensions eased

Japanese Prime Minister Kakuei Tanaka sent a letter to South Korean Pres. Park Chung Hee expressing regret that the August 15 assassination attempt on Park had been planned in Japan. Tanaka also extended condolences over the death of Park's wife, who had been killed by the would-be assassin.

19–20 *Hurricane Fifi strikes Honduras*

Hurricane Fifi struck Honduras, killing thousands and leaving millions of dollars worth of devastation in its wake. Tons of relief supplies were sent from all over the world, but a Honduran official estimated that it would be at least two years before the country's economy had recovered fully from the disaster.

20 *United States: New White House press secretary*

Ron Nessen, a National Broadcasting Co. correspondent, was named White House press secretary by Pres. Ford. Ford's first press secretary, Jerald terHorst, had resigned September 8 in protest against the pardon of former president Nixon.

23 *Release of Greek Cypriot and Turkish Cypriot prisoners begins*

The general release of all Greek Cypriot and Turkish Cypriot prisoners began, according to terms of an agreement reached on September 20 by Cypriot Pres. Glafkos Clerides and Turkish Cypriot leader Rauf Denktash. The exchange of sick and wounded prisoners had been completed on September 21.

25 *Nixon being treated for blood clot*

Former president Nixon's personal physician announced that Nixon, who had been hospitalized at Long Beach, Calif., on September 23 for treatment of phlebitis and tests, had a blood clot in his lung, but the situation was "not critical at this time."

28 *White House "summit" on inflation ends*

In a speech ending the two-day national conference on inflation President Ford announced that three decisions had been made to aid in implementing a program to deal with inflation and recession. Specific points of the program were not announced, but there was agreement among most of the participants that cutting the federal budget would not do much very quickly to reduce the rate of inflation.

30 *Canada's 30th Parliament opens*

In the speech from the throne opening Canada's 30th Parliament, the government promised to attack the problem of inflation. In developments earlier this month, Canadian Energy Minister Donald Macdonald had announced a new policy to protect the domestic uranium market and on September 20 Canada had unilaterally raised the price of natural gas exported to the U.S. by 67%.

Portuguese president resigns

Gen. António de Spínola resigned as provisional president of Portugal and was replaced by Gen. Francisco da Costa Gomes, chief of the joint military staff. On September 7 Portuguese Foreign Minister Mário Soares and Frelimo leader Samora Machel signed an agreement whereby the Portuguese African territory of Mozambique would become fully independent on June 25, 1975.

U.S. Senators meet with Castro

Senate Foreign Relations Committee members Jacob Javits (Rep., N.Y.) and Claiborne Pell (Dem., R.I.) returned from a visit to Cuba, which they had undertaken on their own initiative. They had met with Prime Minister Fidel Castro in Havana in an attempt to end the 13-year rift between their respective governments. The Organization of American States, which had instituted sanctions against Cuba in 1964, voted unanimously on September 20 to consider lifting those sanctions.

Repeal of year-round Daylight Saving Time

The U.S. Senate completed action on a measure repealing year-round Daylight Saving Time, which had been instituted on Jan. 6, 1974, as an energy-saving device. Standard Time was to be reinstated during November–February.

OCTOBER

1 *25 years of Communist rule in China*

Fireworks and music and dance performances in Peking's parks marked the 25th anniversary of Communist rule in China. Notably absent was Chairman Mao Tsetung, believed to be too frail to appear on the rostrum of the Gate of Heavenly Peace, where in 1949 he stood to proclaim the birth of the People's Republic of China.

Watergate cover-up trial opens

The Watergate cover-up trial opened in Washington, D.C., before U.S. District Court Judge John J. Sirica. Involving the events that forced the resignation of Richard M. Nixon, the trial had five defendants—former attorney general John N. Mitchell, ex-Nixon aides H. R. Haldeman and John Ehrlichman, Kenneth Parkinson, lawyer for the Committee for the Re-election of the President, and former assistant attorney general Robert C. Mardian.

3 *United States: Dow Jones average falls below 600*

Prices on the New York Stock Exchange dropped for ten consecutive sessions and the Dow Jones industrial average fell below the 600 mark for the first time in almost 12 years, closing at 587.61. On Jan. 11, 1973, the Dow Jones average had peaked at 1,051.7.

4 *Response to the worldwide oil crisis*

After a five-day joint meeting with the World Bank in Washington, D.C., the International Monetary Fund announced that it was drawing up plans for a major new lending operation. Administered by the IMF and funded principally by the oil-producing nations, it would benefit countries in financial disarray because of their difficulties in paying higher prices for needed oil imports.

EEC council of aid ministers agreed on October 3 to contribute $150 million to aid 25 less developed nations that were worst hit by quadrupled oil prices. Under the joint agreement $30 million would go to the

UN emergency fund set up for this purpose and $120 million would go directly to the countries involved.

6 *The German Democratic Republic marks 25 years*

Appearing as guest of honour at a rally in East Berlin celebrating the 25th anniversary of East Germany, Soviet Communist Party leader Leonid I. Brezhnev stated that he is prepared to take additional steps with the U.S. to curb the arms race.

President Ford urges U.S. to "whip inflation now"

U.S. Pres. Gerald Ford presented his anti-inflation program to a joint session of Congress. Proposals included a board to develop national energy policy, a cut in foreign oil imports, a 5% surtax on families earning more than $15,000 annually, and measures to help the depressed housing industry.

9 *Hostages freed in the Dominican Republic*

A U.S. official and six other hostages held by left-wing guerrillas for almost two weeks in the Venezuelan consulate in Santo Domingo were freed after the terrorists accepted a Dominican government offer of safe-conduct to Panama.

10 *Labour Party wins slim majority in United Kingdom*

Prime Minister Harold Wilson and his Labour Party were returned to power in the second general election to be held in Great Britain in 1974. The returns showed Labour with a three-seat majority over the combined strength of Conservatives, Liberals, and other parties in the 635-seat House of Commons.

11 *Brezhnev urges reopening of Middle East talks*

Soviet Communist Party leader Leonid I. Brezhnev urged that Middle East peace talks in Geneva be reconvened at the earliest date, contending that further delay would mean sitting "on a powderkeg which might blow up at any moment." He charged that Israel and "her traditional foreign patrons" were trying to evade the resumption of such negotiations.

14 *Palestine Liberation Organization is recognized by the United Nations*

The UN General Assembly recognized the Palestine Liberation Organization as "the representative of the Palestinian people," and invited the PLO to participate in the assembly's debate on Palestine in November. The vote was 105–4, with 20 abstentions. The four voting against were the U.S., Israel, the Dominican Republic, and Bolivia. Many Western bloc nations, including a few EEC members, voted to extend recognition.

French workers granted unemployment pay

French management and labour leaders agreed to a plan that gives 20 million wage earners in France a guarantee of one year's pay if they are laid off because of bad economic conditions. The agreement, which was supported by the Giscard government, will be financed by a fund to which employers, employees, and eventually the government will contribute.

15 *National Guard is mobilized in Boston*

Massachusetts Gov. Francis Sargent ordered the mobilization of 450 National Guardsmen as racial violence ignited by court-ordered busing continued in Boston's schools. Sargent had asked President Ford to send federal troops to the city, a request that the president refused on the ground that the use of U.S. troops would not be in order until the state's full resources had been exhausted.

Rockefeller requests action

Vice-president-designate Nelson Rockefeller requested "immediate" congressional hearings on his nomination because the issue was "being tried in the press . . . without my having the opportunity to present all the facts." He was referring to continued reports concerning his substantial gifts to former aides and public officials. Under the 25th Amendment to the U.S. Constitution, a majority vote in both houses of Congress must confirm the nomination of the person chosen to fill a vice-presidential vacancy. They act after hearings and votes by the designated congressional committees.

17 *President Ford defends the Nixon pardon*

In what is believed to be the first formal appearance by a president of the United States before a congressional panel, Gerald Ford came before a House subcommittee in an attempt to quash suspicions raised by his unconditional pardon of Richard Nixon. The pardon, Ford said, was granted solely "out of my concern to serve the best interests of my country." He also stated that no "deal" had been made between himself and former president Nixon.

American League's Oakland A's capture World Series

Baseball's Oakland A's beat the Los Angeles Dodgers by a score of 3–2, to win their third consecutive World Series.

18 *U.S.-Soviet trade program*

In an announcement made at the White House, Sen. Henry Jackson (Dem., Wash.) said that President Ford and Congress had formally agreed on a compromise to provide trade benefits to the U.S.S.R. In return, Moscow would relax its stringent emigration policies. U.S. Secretary of State Henry Kissinger said that Moscow had assured him that there would be an end to harassment of would-be Soviet emigrants.

20 *Swiss voters reject deportation referendum*

Voters in Switzerland rejected by a substantial margin a proposal that would have meant deporting one half of the country's 1.1 million foreigners, including 300,000 immigrant workers, by the end of 1977. The proposal lost, with 66% voting against.

Pres. Gerald Ford defends the Nixon pardon before a congressional panel.

PICTORIAL PARADE

UPI COMPIX

King Hussein (left) of Jordan at the Arab summit conference in Rabat, Morocco.

21 *Mexican-U.S. border meeting*

Mexican Pres. Luis Echeverría Álvarez and U.S. Pres. Gerald Ford met on both sides of the Arizona-Mexican border. No formal agreements were signed and Eche-verría, commenting on the recently reported discovery of substantial deposits of oil in southeastern Mexico, called the development very important—considering current world market prices. The implication of his statement was that the U.S. would not receive preferential treatment from Mexico.

23 *Former Greek prime minister Papadopoulos exiled*

Former Greek Prime Minister Georgios Papadopoulos and four other leaders of the 1967 military coup in Greece were arrested and exiled to the Aegean island of Kea, 60 mi. SE of Athens. With the first elections under the democratic regime set for November 17, opponents of Prime Minister Konstantinos Karamanlis had been criticizing him for indecisive action with regard to the former military dictators.

25 *Fanfani fails to form coalition*

After 11 days of negotiation, Amintore Fanfani abandoned his attempt to form a coalition government in Italy. On October 3 Italy's 36th Cabinet since World War II had resigned and Pres. Giovanni Leone had asked Fanfani to form a government. Premier Mariano Rumor remained as head of a caretaker regime.

28 *Arab nations back Arafat and PLO*

At a meeting in Rabat, Morocco, 20 Arab heads of state, including Jordan's King Hussein, unanimously issued a declaration calling for the creation of an independent Palestinian state and recognizing the Palestine Liberation Organization as the "sole legitimate representative of the Palestinian people." The decision was a victory for Yasir Arafat, the PLO leader.

NOVEMBER

5 *Democrats receive mandate in U.S. elections*

The Democratic Party swept toward domination of the 94th Congress, raising their majority to two-thirds in the House of Representatives and three-fifths in the Senate. The Democrats won 27 governorships against 7 for Republicans; an independent was victorious in Maine. In the Senate, Democrats captured formerly Republican-held seats in Colorado, Florida, Kentucky, and Vermont. Nevada was the only state in which the Republicans gained a seat held by a Democratic senator. In the House the Democrats gained 43 seats, to bring their total to 291 against 144 for the Republicans.

6 *State of siege in Argentina*

Argentine Pres. Isabel Perón placed the nation under a state of siege as political assassinations and terrorist attacks continued. She acted after meeting with the three armed forces commanders following the assassinations of the federal police chief and his wife and a former Peronist union official. About 140 persons had died in political violence since the death of her husband on July 1.

8 *National Guardsmen acquitted in Kent State killings*

Eight former Ohio National Guardsmen were acquitted of violating the rights of students at a demonstration at Kent State University on May 4, 1970, in which four students were killed and nine wounded. Chief Judge Frank J. Battisti of the U.S. District Court in Cleveland said that the government prosecutors had not proved "beyond a reasonable doubt" that the guardsmen willfully intended to deprive the students of their civil rights.

10 *Sub-Saharan countries receive needed rain*

The *New York Times* reported that sub-Saharan countries suffering famine as a consequence of severe drought were experiencing a normal autumn rainy season.

12 *UN General Assembly suspends South Africa*

The UN General Assembly voted 91–22 to suspend South Africa's participation in the assembly's current session. The decision did not exclude the nation from membership.

13 *UN debate on Palestine opens*

The UN General Assembly debate on the Palestine question opened with Yasir Arafat, head of the Palestine Liberation Organization, telling the delegates that his organization's goal remained a Palestinian state that would include Muslims, Christians, and Jews.

15 *Government party soundly defeated in Brazil*

In the freest elections to be held in more than ten years, the Brazilian Democratic Movement, the only officially tolerated opposition group in the country, defeated the government party, ARENA, in federal and state elections. The results were seen as a repudiation of the government's economic and social policies and a protest against an estimated 33% inflation rate.

16 *World Food Conference approves new agency*

At the final session of its 11-day meeting in Rome, the World Food Conference approved the formation of a new UN agency (the World Food Council) to supervise programs intended to provide less developed nations with more and better food.

17 *Karamanlis victorious in Greece*

Prime Minister Konstantinos Karamanlis won an overwhelming victory in the first democratic election to be held in Greece since 1964. The New Democracy Party, which Karamanlis founded in September, received about 55% of the vote in the first official returns and it was believed that the party would control almost 200 seats in the 300-member Parliament.

18 *Ford begins East Asian tour*

U.S. Pres. Gerald Ford arrived in Japan, the first stop on an eight-day journey to East Asia. The president defined his travels as both timely and significant as a step toward preserving world peace.

20 *Antitrust action against AT&T*

The Department of Justice filed an antitrust suit in a federal court in Washington, D.C., against the American Telephone and Telegraph Co., the world's largest privately owned corporation. The suit alleged that AT&T held an illegal near-monopoly of the telecommunications business and attempted to force AT&T to divest itself of the Western Electric Co., a manufacturing subsidiary. It would also require that the corporation get out of the long-distance telephone business or dispose of some or all of the 23 wholly or partly owned local Bell telephone companies.

UN Palestine debate continues

In the UN General Assembly debate on the Palestine question, Britain, France, and Italy urged a Middle East settlement that would enable Israel to live peacefully

within its pre-1967 war boundaries. This was the position taken by the EEC and first stated by the West German delegate on November 19. Britain's delegate stressed that the right of Palestine should not infringe or challenge the right of Israel to exist as a state.

22 *Canada reduces U.S. oil allocation*

Canada, the largest single supplier of oil to the U.S., announced that exports of crude oil to the U.S. would be reduced by 100,000 bbl. a day, to 800,000 bbl., effective Jan. 1, 1975. Further reductions were expected and Canada eventually plans to stop exports completely.

UN grants observer status to the PLO

The UN General Assembly approved two resolutions declaring that the Palestinian people have the right to independence and sovereignty, and that the PLO should be granted observer status in UN affairs.

23 *Moro forms Italian Cabinet*

Aldo Moro, Christian Democrat foreign minister in the outgoing Cabinet of Mariano Rumor, formed a minority government of Christian Democrats and Republicans. Pres. Giovanni Leone approved the Cabinet, ending the crisis that began when Rumor's Cabinet resigned on October 3.

24 *Executions in Ethiopia*

Two former prime ministers, the head of the ruling Military Council, and a grandson of Emperor Haile Selassie were among the 60 people whose execution was announced by the military government in Ethiopia. A radio broadcast said the executions were "an act of justice." Most of those executed

The Alem-Bekanye prison compound in Addis Ababa, Eth., site of the November executions.

CAMERAPIX/KEYSTONE

had been arrested during the purge that culminated in the overthrow of Selassie on September 12.

Police charge six in U.K. pub bombings

Police charged six men from Northern Ireland with the bombings of two crowded pubs in Birmingham, Eng., on November 21. Nineteen people were killed and over 100 were wounded in the worst display of anti-British terrorism in over two years.

Brezhnev and Ford reach tentative agreement on nuclear weapons

At a meeting in Vladivostok, U.S.S.R., U.S. Pres. Gerald Ford and Soviet party leader Leonid I. Brezhnev reached tentative agreement to limit their countries' offensive strategic nuclear weapons and delivery vehicles through 1985. U.S. Secretary of State Henry Kissinger called it a breakthrough, but critics termed it meaningless, in the effort to halt the arms race.

26 *Japan's Tanaka announces resignation*

Kakuei Tanaka yielded to pressure that he step down as prime minister of Japan. The move came as a result of accusations that he had used his high political office to amass a considerable personal fortune. The resignation was submitted to the ruling Liberal-Democratic Party, which would choose his successor.

29 *Britain outlaws Irish Republican Army*

In the wake of bombings and other terrorist attacks, the House of Commons approved legislation outlawing the IRA and giving the police unprecedented powers to fight terrorism in Britain. The laws authorized police to search and detain suspected terrorists and to impose restrictions on travel between Ireland and England.

National Assembly legalizes abortion in France

In a historic breakthrough for a predominantly Roman Catholic country, France's National Assembly voted to legalize abortion during the first ten weeks of pregnancy. The vote overturned a 1920 law.

Nixon too ill to testify in Watergate cover-up trial

A court-appointed panel of three physicians informed U.S. District Court Judge John J. Sirica that former president Richard M. Nixon's poor health would not permit his appearance at the cover-up trial in Washington, D.C., until at least Feb. 16, 1975, and that he would not be able to testify by deposition until January 6. Attorneys for the five defendants accused of covering up the June 17, 1972, break-in of Democratic National Committee headquarters in the Watergate complex began presenting their cases November 25.

DECEMBER

2 *U.S. faces triple threat*

In a televised news conference President Ford said that the U.S. faced three challenges—inflation, recession, and an energy crisis. This was the first time he had not given inflation as the first among the nation's woes, and he called on the 93rd Congress to act on his recommendations for $4.6 billion in budgetary reductions. He also asked the legislators to pass emergency measures to curb rising unemployment before adjourning.

3 *Pioneer 11 begins five-year journey to Saturn*

The U.S. space vehicle Pioneer 11 headed toward Saturn after surviving a pass within 26,600 mi. of Jupiter. It gave scientists substantial information on the planet's atmospheric conditions and internal properties, as well as on the moons of Jupiter, one of which exhibited a polar cap. The spacecraft will arrive in the vicinity of Saturn in 1979.

5 *Nixon need not testify*

U.S. District Court Judge John J. Sirica ruled that former president Richard Nixon need not testify in any way—either on the witness stand or by deposition—at the Watergate cover-up trial. Sirica's six-page opinion cited Nixon's poor health and the fact that his testimony's value to the defendants "should not be unrealistically overestimated" as reasons for the ruling.

Takeo Miki, new prime minister of Japan, practices calligraphy at home with his wife, Mutsuko.

Mine workers sign contract in U.S.

United Mine Workers' leaders signed a new three-year labour contract with the coal industry, ending a 24-day miners' strike. Arnold R. Miller, president of the union, said that 56% of the 79,495 members who had exercised their new right to reject or accept their leaders' proposal had voted for the new contract.

7 *Greek Cypriots hail Makarios in Nicosia*

Thousands of enthusiastic Greek Cypriots greeted President Makarios of Cyprus in the capital from which he fled for his life in a coup in July. In a speech delivered from the balcony of the Palace of the Ethnarch, Makarios promised not to accept partition of the island between ethnic Greeks and Turks. Uncertainty over the political fate of the island continued since talks between Greek and Turkish leaders collapsed in August.

9 *Greek Parliament reopens after seven years*

One day after the Greek electorate voted resoundingly to make Greece a republic and eliminate the monarchy that was established in 1832, 300 members of the new Parliament were sworn in. The vote, taken on December 8, ran about 2 to 1 in favour of "uncrowned democracy," as it was designated on the ballot. This meant that King Constantine, who had been in exile since the military coup of 1967, would be stripped of his title.

Takeo Miki new Japanese prime minister

Takeo Miki of the Liberal-Democratic Party was formally elected prime minister by the Japanese Diet. Miki, who has held a long succession of Cabinet posts, including foreign minister and deputy prime minister, succeeded Kakuei Tanaka, who resigned on November 26.

U.K. energy-saving program

The British government announced a mandatory energy-saving program, including lower speed limits on many highways and a maximum temperature of 68° F in most buildings, except homes and hospitals. The program was aimed at reducing energy consumption by 10% as well as expenditures on imported oil, which now total more than $8 billion annually. On December 3 Defense Secretary Roy Mason announced plans to cut defense spending by reducing manpower, ending new programs, and closing overseas bases. The cuts were expected to save about $700 million a year —from a current defense budget of $8.6 billion a year.

10 *Solzhenitsyn claims Nobel Prize*

Aleksandr Solzhenitsyn received the Nobel Prize for Literature that he was unable to claim when it was awarded to him in 1970. The ten winners of the 1974 awards for literature, physiology or medicine, chemistry, physics, and economics also received their prizes at the ceremonies in Stockholm.

Pound reaches new low

Reports that the major oil-exporting nations would stop taking the pound sterling in payment for oil touched off a run on the currency, driving it to its lowest level ever. The Bank of England intervened on foreign exchange markets to support the pound, which fell by 1.15 cents against the dollar to $2.3240.

Mills resigns chairmanship of the House Ways and Means Committee

Rep. Wilbur D. Mills (Dem., Ark.) resigned his position as chairman of the U.S. House of Representatives Ways and Means Committee, a post he had held since 1958. On December 2 Mills's Democratic colleagues in the House divested him of his authority to make committee assignments and the next day agreed without dissent to increase the committee's membership from 25 to 37, further reducing his vast power. Mills had been the subject of ridicule and scorn because of his indiscreet association with strip-tease dancer Fanne Foxe.

11 *Student protest in Burma*

Burmese youths began rioting in Rangoon after troops and policemen removed the body of former UN secretary-general U Thant from a mausoleum that students had built on the university campus. U Thant had died in New York City on November 25. The protest represented resentment against the rule of Burmese Pres. Ne Win who overthrew Premier U Nu, a political mentor of U Thant.

18 *Layoffs increase in the U.S.*

As layoffs in U.S. manufacturing industries increased, General Motors Corp. announced additional layoffs and production cutbacks for the first quarter of 1975. The action reflected one of the sharpest declines in the automotive industry since World War II. By January GM would have 91,000 workers laid off with another 41,000 temporarily laid off. The industry-wide automobile sales decline, down 30%, was expected to continue.

29th session of UN General Assembly recessed

UN General Assembly Pres. Abdel-Aziz Bouteflika of Algeria recessed the 29th session of the assembly. Action taken during the 13-week session included suspending South Africa, thus denying that country the right to participate and vote in the assembly, and granting Yasir Arafat's Palestine Liberation Organization observer status in the body. Bouteflika recessed the body rather than adjourning it so that members could be called back for a Middle East debate without the formality of conducting a poll on reconvening.

19 *Rockefeller becomes 41st vice-president of the U.S.*

Nelson Aldrich Rockefeller was sworn in as vice-president of the United States by Chief Justice Warren E. Burger in a televised ceremony in the Senate chamber, marking the first time that neither the president nor the vice-president had been elected to office. Rockefeller had been confirmed by the House of Representatives by a vote of 287–128.

20 *93rd U.S. Congress adjourns*

The 93rd Congress adjourned after giving approval to a controversial trade reform bill. Much of the Congress' two years were taken up with the Watergate investigation and impeachment proceedings against former president Richard Nixon, but some congressional leaders believed that much of the legislation enacted would prove to be of historic significance.

24 *1975 Holy Year inaugurated.*

Pope Paul VI tapped three times on the Holy Door to St. Peter's Basilica in Rome, which had been walled up since 1950—the last Holy Year of the Roman Catholic Church—and led a procession into the church, inaugurating the 1975 Holy Year.

Christian pilgrims attending midnight mass in the Church of the Nativity in Bethlehem were searched by Israeli security forces because of recent terrorism in Jerusalem and Tel Aviv.

Pope Paul VI at the threshold of the Holy Door on Christmas Eve.

Remains of suburban homes in Darwin, Austr., after the cyclone on Christmas Day.

25 *Darwin airlift begins*

An airlift was begun to evacuate victims of the cyclone that struck Darwin, Austr., on Christmas Day. Ninety percent of the city was destroyed and 47 were killed in what was described as the worst natural catastrophe in Australia's history. Difficulties were exacerbated by Darwin's relative remoteness; relief supplies came principally from Sydney, almost 2,000 mi. away.

28 *Soviets hit U.S. trade bill*

A spokesman from the Kremlin warned that the Soviet Union might reexamine its economic commitments to the U.S., particularly in light of what the Soviets view as discriminatory provisions in the trade reform bill enacted by the U.S. Congress on December 20. The U.S.S.R. charged that Congress violated the 1972 accord providing for equal status between the two countries by attaching qualifications to the bill that linked the U.S. extension of lower import tariffs to a policy of freer Soviet emigration.

29 *Tax cuts proposed to slow recession in U.S.*

A source in the Ford administration said that the president had abandoned his proposal for an anti-inflationary income tax surcharge. Economists were reported to be putting strong pressure on Ford to do the opposite and cut taxes as a stimulus to increase consumer spending and pull the economy out of the worsening recession.

30 *5,000 dead in Pakistani earthquake*

Official reports indicated that nearly 5,000 persons were killed in an earthquake that struck a number of towns in northern Pakistan on December 28. The toll was expected to rise as runners reached regions farther to the north, which had been cut off since the quake.

Brezhnev postpones trip to Middle East

Soviet party leader Leonid I. Brezhnev indefinitely postponed his visit to Egypt, Syria, and Iraq, planned for mid-January 1975. The postponement was seen as a setback for Moscow, which had recently been attempting to increase its influence in bringing about a Middle East peace settlement. Some sources reported that Brezhnev was in ill health, but others saw the "illness" as a diplomatic one.

31 *CIA domestic spying reported*

William E. Colby, director of Central Intelligence for the U.S., reported to President Ford in response to allegations published December 22 in the *New York Times* that the Central Intelligence Agency (CIA) spied on U.S. citizens. In the report Colby told of thousands of files on citizens and of electronic surveillance, break-ins, and mail inspection. Three chairmen of major congressional committees had announced that they would begin extensive hearings into CIA activities when the 94th Congress convened in January.

Cease-fire continues in Northern Ireland

Britain announced the release of a number of political prisoners, buoying hopes for an extension of the holiday cease-fire that had been called by the Irish Republican Army on December 22.

Gold sales legal in U.S. after 41 years

The widely heralded gold rush in the U.S. did not materialize as only a small number of purchases were made on the first day that gold bullion sales were legal in the U.S. Prices fell $5 to $9 an ounce at various trading centres; in London the price fell from $195.25 to $186.50 an ounce.

1974

Advertising

At the beginning of 1974 the advertising industry was, at best, cautiously optimistic about what the coming year held in store. Despite the fact that 1973 had been a good year for the business worldwide, the spectres of inflation, materials shortages, the energy crisis, and continuing pressure on the regulatory front contributed to either cautious optimism or some slight negativism on the part of marketers.

The year 1973 had indeed been a record one for many. In Britain expenditure was up by 23% and only an acute media shortage during the last quarter prevented the figure from going higher. It was also the first year in almost a decade in which the number of people employed by the industry had increased. Although at the close of 1973 there were rumours of massive staff cuts by agencies, most shed their surplus fat by attrition to bring the total employed by agencies at the end of 1974 to 14,000, a drop of 6,000 in eight years. The outlook for the critical last quarter of 1974 was very uncertain, an uncertainty aggravated in Britain by the political upheaval of a second general election within 12 months.

In the U.S., according to an *Advertising Age* survey of major media organizations, advertising volume for 1974 was expected to show a 4.5% gain over the previous year, with an anticipated total for 1974 of $14,245,000,000. Of the ten major media categories covered in the survey only two remained constant in volume compared with the previous year: direct mail and point-of-purchase advertising. Projected national ad volume in newspapers was $1,047,000,000, up 4.7% from 1973. Total ad volume for newspapers, including retail and classified as well as national advertising, was expected to hit $7.8 billion, a gain of 4.5%. Network television estimates showed total network, spot, and local TV ad revenues up 9%, to $4,870,000,000 in 1974. Magazines were slated for a 3% boost in volume for the year, to a total of $1,350,-000,000. Business publications were anticipating a move into the billion-dollar category, with a $1,030,-000,000 ad volume figure, up 5.5% from the previous year. Total network, spot, and local radio advertising was expected to reach $1,330,000,000 for 1974. National outdoor advertising, according to *Advertising Age*'s estimate, would move to $185 million in 1974, an increase of almost 9%. Direct mail and point of purchase held about even, with $4 billion and $2.5 billion respectively.

But despite the dollar volume gains racked up by advertisers, there were some severe distress signs on the horizon as the year drew to a close, and it was runaway inflation that lay at the root of the trouble. Probably the most ominous news from the U.S. in the final quarter of 1974 came from Detroit, where by the end of 1974 sales were off by 35%. But the automakers were not in a mood to pull back on their promotional activities in the wake of the steep slump in sales; instead, they announced plans to spend additional ad dollars in an attempt to reverse the declining sales curve. One way in which a number of advertisers approached the problem of selling in a highly inflationary economy was to institute price/value advertising, stressing that the products advertised at the price shown are a bargain, or a good value.

It was not only on the financial front that the advertising business was threatened. Politicians, legislators, taxmen, and consumer activists were laying siege with increasing vigour. In the U.S., Lewis Engman, chairman of the Federal Trade Commission (FTC), startled the ad community by announcing that he was having the FTC draft guidelines that would outlaw premium offers to children. The hue and cry that followed Engman's announcement apparently gave the FTC chairman second thoughts, and it was announced that the FTC would permit public comment on the issue before any final verdict was reached. The proposed ban on premiums was only part of a much larger picture—the advertising directed to children, particularly the advertising beamed to the younger generation via the country's most ubiquitous babysitter, the television set. Demands on advertisers whose ads are directed primarily to children ranged all the way from those of the strong consumer activist groups who wanted all advertising to children banned to the more moderate voices who wanted more strict time limitations on commercials and advertising of certain products—like over-the-counter drugs—banned from children's programs.

Despite the U.S. surgeon general's report of 1964 and the subsequent banning of cigarette advertising from the airwaves starting in 1971, U.S. sales of cigarettes continued to rise. A study by *Advertising Age* of sales and ad expenditures in 1973 for the top 20 brands showed that even though there was a decline in ad spending for this group of 3.5% in 1973, their sales volume jumped 4.6%. The 1973 outlay was 22.2% less than the $241,093,469 invested in advertising the top 20 cigarette brands in 1970, the year before the broadcast ad ban went into effect. Although the broadcast ban had not affected an upward industry sales volume trend, it had severely hampered the marketing of new brands. But the cigarette makers continued to introduce new brands, or differing versions of established ones. Chesterfield, still among the top 20, though sales had been slipping each year, announced late in 1974 that it was returning to one of its most successful advertising themes: "They satisfy"; the new copy line would read: "They satisfied then. They satisfy now."

Two U.S. airlines found themselves in trouble with both women's liberation groups and some of their own stewardesses and other female employees because of allegedly sexist ad themes. National Airlines, which had brought down the wrath of these same forces in 1973 when it ran ads featuring a photo of a stewardess with the headline reading: "Hi! I'm Debbie. Fly me to (a National Airlines destination city)," decided to start a new version of that campaign, still featuring a photo of a stewardess but with the headline changed to read: "I'm going to fly you like you've never been flown before." Continental Airlines encountered similar opposition when it launched an ad campaign around the theme: "We really move our tail for you." Neither airline indicated it planned any changes.

One of U.S. television's best-known ad personalities was retired from active service in the fall. Josephine the Plumber (actress Jane Withers), after 11 years of scouring the nation's sinks with Comet cleanser, was dropped by Procter & Gamble because the company felt she was losing her effectiveness.

The Committee of Ministers of the Council of Europe was preparing a paper concerned with the control of tobacco and alcohol advertising and measures to curb consumption of these products. The same group was also responsible for the Consumer Protection Charter, which included a provision for

Aden:
see Yemen, People's Democratic Republic of

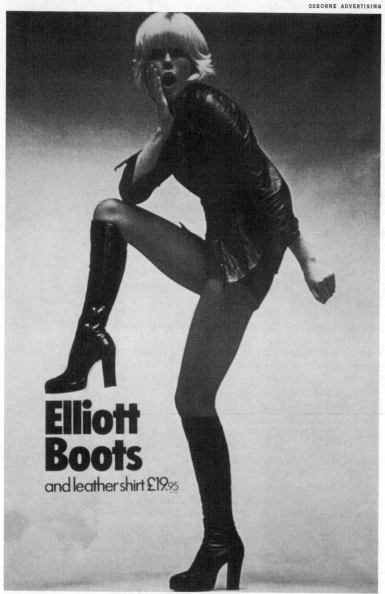

Elliott Boots
and leather shirt £19.95

One of 32 winning entries in the 1974 British Poster Design Awards was the Elliott Boots advertisement.

the interests of advertising, and when the party took over government early in 1974 no time was lost in applying pressure. This included the announcement that in the future service industries would be brought within the jurisdiction of the Fair Trade Act, concerned with restrictive practices that could be construed as operating against the public interest. The government also made it clear that it was not satisfied with the effectiveness of the voluntary control system operated by the advertising industry to prevent and discipline malpractice. Unless this was improved, a tax would be imposed on the industry to finance a statutory control system. In fact, the intention to tax advertising in one form or another had been part of the Labour Party's election manifesto. The advertising industry moved rapidly in self-defense, imposing a levy amounting to 0.1% of all advertising revenue (except TV, which was included in another system) to finance a larger staff for the Advertising Standards Authority, the industry's self-disciplinary watchdog, and also a publicity campaign to tell the public about the work of the authority. The television companies also responded with their own campaign to inform viewers of their existing control system. Subsequently the minister for consumer affairs, Shirley Williams (see BIOGRAPHY), agreed to receive a deputation representing all sides of the advertising industry for a presentation covering the economic and social aspects of advertising.

The defensive moves by the industry in Britain were echoed in other countries, for example, in West Germany where two leading publishing groups, Axel Springer and Heinrich Bauer, each ran campaigns designed to inform the public of the economic and social benefits of advertising. Axel Springer's campaign, prepared by Lintas, the international advertising agency, was offered at no cost to other publishing groups. A third campaign proposed by GWA, the German agency association, was in preparation by the U.S.-based agency Leo Burnett.

In Britain advertisers of tobacco products and alcoholic drinks agreed to accept tighter controls to be administered by the Advertising Standards Authority. These would outlaw drink advertising aimed at young people and any suggestion that smoking improved the quality of life. In addition, it was announced that all cigarette advertisements would be compelled to quote the official tar yield. In Norway advertising of cigarettes was banned altogether. But perhaps the most extreme development took place in The Netherlands, where legislation was to be introduced at the end of the year forbidding advertising that encouraged "increased consumption of confectionery" and decreeing that all advertisements for sweets and chocolates should carry a symbol of a toothbrush.

The industry in Australia was busy setting up its own Advertising Standards Advisory Authority, and the Australian Broadcasting Control Board, following in Canada's footsteps, introduced a tough new directive relating to TV commercials aimed at children. The Japanese, also concerned with self-regulation, established the Japanese Advertising Review Organization (JARO) similar to the Code of Advertising Practices Committee in Britain.

Turning to the agency scene, news that Interpublic, the huge multinational agency, was to acquire Troost International made it the first agency group to top the billion-dollar mark. Interpublic, which already included the McCann-Erickson and Wasey Campbell-Ewald groups, had 1973 billings of $969 million to

corrective advertising. Late in 1973 a Consumers' Consultative Committee was established to "represent consumer interests to the European Commission and to advise the Commission on the formulation and implementation of policies and actions regarding consumer protection and information, either when requested to do so by the Commission or on its own initiative." Included in the draft program were projects to define and establish "criteria for judging whether an advertisement was considered deceptive, misleading or unfair to consumers in any way; by requiring advertisers to justify the validity of claims made by them; and by seeking a way to end quickly any deceptive or unfair campaign." It seemed likely that the International Chamber of Commerce advertising code would be accepted as the general guideline.

There was an interesting precedent when the Commission agreed to reserve three million Community units of account (about $4 million) in order to give help in the form of advertising support to the marketing of beef in EEC countries. This was to take the form of an additional contribution equal to the budget already proposed by member states for this purpose.

The British Labour Party, when in opposition, had issued a Green Paper that was generally hostile to which Troost's European organization would add a further $53 million. J. Walter Thompson, with world billings up from $722 million in 1972 to $845 million in 1973, maintained its lead as the largest single agency. A challenge from Dentsu Advertising Ltd., the vast Japanese conglomerate with 1973 billings of $950 million, was rejected by the other contenders on grounds that the method of computing billings in Japan was so different as to invalidate comparison.

Annual billings of U.S. advertising agencies hit an all-time record of $12.9 billion in 1973, according to *Advertising Age*'s annual survey. This total was billed by 689 agencies, with the top ten agencies billing $5.3 billion. Many of the most striking gains registered by leading U.S. agencies were in the international field, reflecting the trend among U.S. agencies to increase their overseas business. The top ten in billing for 1973 were J. Walter Thompson ($845 million), McCann-Erickson ($680,989,000), Young & Rubicam ($650 million), Leo Burnett Co. ($512,443,000), Ted Bates & Co. ($484,282,500), SSC&B Inc. ($483,494,000), Ogilvy & Mather ($432 million), Batten, Barton, Durstine & Osborn ($428,585,000), D'Arcy-Mac-Manus ($396 million), and Grey Advertising ($352 million).

In West Germany, Lintas, with billings of DM. 250.4 million, just failed to overtake McCann, which had billings of DM. 252.7 million, as the first ranking agency. In France, Havas-Conseil, with Fr. 550 million, retained its lead over Publicis-Conseil's billings of Fr. 445 million. In Italy the agency scene was enlivened by the news that OGD was to combine with Linea SPN, the house agency of ENI, a major state-owned holding company, to give a total billing of 17 million lire, just ahead of McCann-Erickson, currently the largest agency with 1973 turnover of 16,422,000 lire. In Finland, contrary to the general trend, agency turnover was up 14.2% for the first quarter of 1974 over the same period in 1973. Agencies in Finland were charging their clients 14.5% on overdue bills, 2% over the bank rate, which may have contributed to their well-being.

In Britain the agency of Massius Wynne-Williams, with billings of £32 million, overtook Ogilvy Benson Mather (£26 million) to regain its position behind J. Walter Thompson (£41.1 million). Fourth was McCann-Erickson with £25 million, and fifth, Leo Burnett with £23 million.

In Hong Kong a distinguished name in Far East advertising disappeared when Cathay Advertising Ltd. (1973 billings $12.5 million), already an associate of George Patterson of Australia (part of the Ted Bates group), became Ted Bates, Hong Kong.

The media also suffered from the effects of inflation. The price and scarcity of newsprint, and in Britain continuing industrial strife, added to the burden of print media, and in the case of national newspapers in Britain, the ability of several to survive if the trend continued was in question. In June the chairman of the Council of the Royal Society of Arts wrote a letter to *The Times* (London) complaining that the proliferation of advertising billboards at cricket grounds was spoiling his enjoyment of the game. A month later another hallowed British tradition, the Oxford-Cambridge boat race, announced the intention to seek a sponsor, but no doubt the chairman of the RSA would have taken comfort from the decision of West Germany's two television channels, ARD and ZDF, to cancel live transmissions of several major sporting events from Switzerland, Italy, and Austria because of excessive billboard and other advertising within camera range.

In the U.S. the top 100 advertisers raised their total ad and promotion investment in 1973 to $5,680,000,-000, a 7.8% increase, despite a slowdown in ad growth early in the second half of that year, according to the annual tabulation by *Advertising Age*. Nine of the top ten advertisers increased their expenditures in 1973; the tenth, Sears, Roebuck, spent about the same as in 1972. The top ten and their 1973 ad and promotions outlays: Procter & Gamble ($310 million), Sears, Roebuck and Co. ($215 million), General Foods ($180 million), General Motors ($158.4 million), Warner-Lambert ($141,723,000), American Home Products Corp. ($133 million), Bristol-Myers ($132 million), Ford Motor Co. ($127.2 million), Colgate-Palmolive ($120 million), and the U.S. government ($99.2 million). Procter & Gamble, perennial leader of the pack in ad expenditures, had a very sizable increase in 1973—from $275 million the previous year to $310 million. A large part of the increase went into a $15 million introductory campaign for their new Sure aerosol antiperspirant deodorant. Almost as big a boost as Procter & Gamble's was chalked up by the U.S. government, which moved into the top ten by increasing its ad spending from $65,828,000 in 1972 to $99.2 million in 1973. Most of the government increase came from heavy armed forces recruitment advertising and increased outlays for public service campaigns and U.S. Postal Service advertising.

Two more major U.S. advertising agencies that had gone public decided to abandon the venture and return to private ownership in 1974, thus joining Clinton E. Frank Inc., which had reached a similar decision in 1973. McCaffrey & McCall announced in February that it planned to buy back its publicly held shares and seven months later Wells, Rich, Greene made a similar announcement.

(JARLATH JOHN GRAHAM; GEOFFREY DEMPSEY)

See also Consumerism; Industrial Production and Technology; Marketing and Merchandising; Publishing; Telecommunications; Television and Radio.

[534.I; 629.C.4.c]

Afghanistan

A republic in central Asia, Afghanistan is bordered by the U.S.S.R., China, Pakistan, and Iran. Area: 252,000 sq.mi. (652,000 sq.km.). Pop. (1973 est.): 18,293,800, including (1963 est.) Pashtoon 59%; Tadzhik 29%; Uzbek 5%; Hazara 3%. Cap. and largest city: Kabul (pop., 1973 est., 341,000). Language: Dari Persian and Pashto. Religion: Muslim. President in 1974, Sardar Mohammad Daud Khan.

Throughout 1974 Afghanistan continued to suffer from the effects of the shortage of rainfall that had afflicted the northern and central areas during the preceding three years. Many of the affected areas were remote and difficult to reach, lying as they did beyond the main lines of communication and the few good highways laid down by Soviet and U.S. engineers as part of the massive aid programs of their respective countries. President Daud and his Cabinet in Kabul did their best to mount rescue operations with the help of aid from abroad, but in areas where the subsistence level remained low, even in the best of times, deaths from starvation could not be prevented. Inevitably, discontent over the failure of the new republican regime to cope with economic difficulties manifested itself in a number of areas. In the capital

Aerospace Industry: *see* Defense; Industrial Production and Technology; Space Exploration; Transportation

itself, the euphoria that had followed the abolition of the monarchy in 1973 and the attendant hopes for the dawn of a more democratic era began to pass away in the face of the president's masterful rule. Many who had expected an improvement in their position, including members of the armed services and the central bureaucracy, found themselves disappointed.

The leaders of the abortive attempts to overthrow the republican regime in September and December 1973 were executed; those who had followed them were sentenced to long terms of imprisonment. The Kabul press accused Pakistan of fomenting these conspiracies, but no solid evidence for the accusation was forthcoming. In view of Pakistani Prime Minister Z. A. Bhutto's desire for friendly relations with Afghanistan, it was more likely that the conspiracies were the products of domestic discontent.

Further symptoms of this disaffection were manifested during 1974. In the autumn it was announced that another attempt to overthrow the regime had been discovered and quashed; its leader had been executed and 11 participants imprisoned. Shortly afterward there was trouble in Takhar Province, where the Muslim Brotherhood, which disliked President Daud's secularizing policy, was very influential. The government was obliged to take stern action; 70 members of the brotherhood were arrested, along with the governor of the province, the revenue commissioner, and the superintendent of police, and all were brought to trial on charges of plotting against the state.

Nevertheless, the president's personal authority over the central government was never effectively challenged. He commanded the loyalty of the bulk of the armed forces, and their efficiency, thanks to Soviet help in both training and the supply of sophisticated weaponry, was high. The central government was strong enough to enforce its will upon outlying areas should the occasion arise.

The president's firm rule was also manifested in his management of foreign affairs. His close ties with the Soviet Union were not allowed to imperil Afghanistan's cherished and traditional neutrality. He concluded a cooperation agreement with China and formed a new link with Bangladesh, to which he promised assistance. Only with Pakistan were his relations difficult; he continued to support schemes for the creation of an independent Pakhtunistan and a new "Greater Baluchistan" that, if realized, would give Afghanistan a corridor through friendly territory to the coast of the Arabian Sea. His representatives raised these questions at numerous international gatherings, including the Islamic summit held at Lahore, Pak., early in the year, but they received little or no encouragement. However, this in no way diminished Daud's determination to persist with his plans.

(L. F. RUSHBROOK WILLIAMS)

[978.C.2]

African Affairs

Portugal's 400-year-old African empire finally collapsed in 1974 following a military coup in Lisbon in April; this development presaged far-reaching changes in southern Africa. Guinea-Bissau became Africa's 44th independent state (counting the Malagasy Republic) in September; Mozambique was promised its independence for June 1975, but no date was set for Angola's freedom. Apart from a number of small islands, the only dependent states left on the continent were the Spanish Sahara, the French Territory of the Afars and Issas, the British colony of Southern Rhodesia (which had unilaterally declared its independence in 1965), and South West Africa (Namibia). Another momentous event was a military coup in February in the ancient Ethiopian empire which by September ended the long rule of Emperor Haile Selassie I (see BIOGRAPHY) and brought new uncertainty to the Horn of Africa. The continent's worst drought in living memory continued to ravage millions of people, while the dramatic rise in oil prices severely disrupted the economies of all but the eight oil-producing African countries.

Drought and Food. There was little relief from the great drought; when the rains came to some areas, they fell in floods that brought new distress as it became even more difficult to bring in food and medical supplies. In Wallo Province, Ethiopia, where more than three million people were afflicted by famine, locusts followed the rains, bringing further ruin. Apart from Ethiopia the worst-affected region was the Sahel —the sub-Saharan region embracing, as its nucleus, Mali, Upper Volta, Niger, and Chad; these were four of the poorest countries in the world. Altogether, an area of some 5.5 million sq.mi. was affected. The famine was worsened by reduced harvests in a large part of Africa and by the rapid depletion of world food reserves. It was estimated that a total target of one million tons of food would be required to alleviate conditions in the Sahelian countries. (See AGRICULTURE AND FOOD SUPPLIES: Special Report.)

The deterioration in the world food situation was especially marked in Africa, which, as a region, had the poorest record in the less developed world. This was due partly to the drought, partly to an actual decline of agricultural production in 16 countries (2%

down in North Africa, but 5% up in Central Africa), and partly to rising living standards with a resultant increase in demand for food; for example, cereal imports rose by 40% to 7.3 million tons in the decade up to the end of 1973.

Wars and Coups. The three colonial wars in Angola, Mozambique, and Guinea-Bissau had all ended by October after a promise of independence by Portugal. This left four areas of armed conflict. In Eritrea the Eritrean Liberation Front (ELF), with the backing of radical Arab states, continued its fight for the province's independence from Ethiopia. In Chad a mainly Muslim movement continued its rebellion despite the withdrawal of Libyan support and French disengagement from support for the government forces. In Rhodesia the guerrilla challenge by the Zimbabwe African National Union (ZANU) forces grew in violence until the Lusaka negotiations in December. (See *Southern Africa*, below.) In Namibia the South West African People's Organization (SWAPO) maintained its challenge against South Africa, which still refused to comply with UN decisions declaring the former mandated territory independent.

Only one military coup (other than Ethiopia's) occurred during 1974; in Niger, Pres. Hamani Diori was overthrown in April. Promises by military regimes to hand back power to civilians were not fulfilled. In Upper Volta, Gen. Sangoulé Lamizana in February reversed his policy because of the alleged failure of the politicians to face up to their responsibilities; and, more significantly, in Nigeria the federal military government in October canceled its previous promise to surrender power in 1976.

Southern Africa. Mozambique's promised independence under a government to be formed by the successful Front for the Liberation of Mozambique (Frelimo) brought new dangers to its two white-ruled neighbours, Rhodesia and South Africa. For Rhodesia, where Ian Smith's regime had successfully maintained its rebellion against the U.K. since 1966, the dangers were to both economy and security. The Smith regime had in the past depended largely on Mozambique for its easiest access to the sea and as a means of evading the international campaign of sanctions. The anti-Smith guerrilla movement could hope to count on Frelimo's support once the latter took power in 1975. Rhodesia's extensive frontier with Mozambique was also likely to become more vulnerable after the final withdrawal of the Portuguese Army.

For South Africa the changes in Mozambique meant that the republic would have a large neighbour under black rule. The republic had relied heavily on the 100,000 migrant workers from Mozambique to operate its gold mines, and it had counted heavily on the much-needed input of cheap energy from Mozambique's Cabora Bassa hydroelectric project, due to begin operating in 1975. Although South Africa was considerably less vulnerable to the pressures of a hostile neighbour than was Rhodesia, its prime minister, B. J. Vorster, reacted to the announcement of the Portuguese reversal of policy by embarking on a vigorous campaign of détente with black Africa. Through secret diplomacy with the Ivory Coast, Senegal, Malawi, Zambia, Botswana, and Tanzania, he persuaded the Smith regime to enter into an agreement following talks at Lusaka, Zambia, in December. All political prisoners were to be released in Rhodesia as a prelude to a constitutional conference to be held early in 1975. The Africans, on their part, agreed to suspend guerrilla activities. Already faced with growing inter-

UPI COMPIX

national pressures because of its refusal to conform with UN decisions revoking South Africa's mandate over Namibia, the Vorster regime gave positive indications that it might be willing to adopt a more flexible policy toward the future independence of that disputed territory. Meanwhile, there were predictable signs, after the success of the armed struggle against the Portuguese, that the Organization of African Unity (OAU) would intensify support for the guerrilla forces operating in southern Africa.

The Organization of African Unity. The 11th annual summit conference of African heads of state was held in Muqdisho, Somalia's capital, in June. The republic of Guinea-Bissau took its place as the OAU's 42nd member state. The OAU's secretary-general, Nzo Ekangaki, resigned because of internal organizational disputes. He had previously been criticized for engaging Lonrho, the British-based multinational corporation, to survey the effects of higher oil prices on African economies. His successor was William Aurelien Eteki Mboumoua (*see* BIOGRAPHY) from Cameroon, chosen after the two leading contenders—Somalia's foreign minister, Omar Arteh, and Zambia's foreign minister, Vernon Mwaanga—had both failed to win the necessary two-thirds voting majority.

The most important items on the agenda of the summit conference related to formulating a continental approach to negotiations with Portugal for the independence of its colonies; a further mediation effort to resolve the long-standing dispute between Somalia and Ethiopia over their rival frontier claims; and the impact of increased energy costs on African economies. Agreement was reached in February on the establishment of an Arab Bank for Economic Development in Africa (ABEDA) with an initial capital of $200 million. This agreement followed protracted negotiations between the OAU's special Committee of Seven and the Arab League. The OAU summit also endorsed the so-called Yaoundé Declaration adopted by its African Liberation Committee (ALC) in the capital of Cameroon in May; its two main points were a promise of friendship to Portugal on condition that it negotiated the independence of its African colonies only with liberation movements recognized by the OAU, and a firm commitment to increase financial and military support for the liberation movements in Rhodesia, South Africa, and Namibia.

Five African leaders gathered at Yaoundé, Cameroon, to discuss common concerns set forth by the Lake Chad Basin Commission. From left to right are: Presidents Jean-Bédel Bokassa, Central African Republic; Hamani Diori, Niger; Ahmadou Ahidjo, Cameroon; Yakubu Gowon, Nigeria; and N'Garta Tombalbaye of Chad.

Trained militia on review in Mumbue, Angola. These troops were trained by the Portuguese ex-commando at their front as part of the process toward independence in Portuguese Africa.

Intra-African Relations. Harmonizing relations between Arab and non-Arab African countries was a major activity during 1974. All but four of the black African states (Malawi, Swaziland, Lesotho, and Mauritius), having suspended their relations with Israel in 1973, expected that the Arab oil producers would continue supplying oil to them while, for the first time, imposing a total oil embargo on Rhodesia and South Africa. Some African states (notably Ghana and Kenya) adopted critical attitudes toward the Arab states for not doing enough, while others pressed for more generous treatment. In addition to funding ABEDA, the Arab oil producers were also persuaded to set up an Arab Bank for Agricultural and Industrial Development, with an initial capital of $500 million and a technical assistance fund of $15 million; this meant that a total of $715 million would be available in loans to assist, over the next eight years, African and other less developed nations suffering from the increased prices for oil. Somalia followed Mauritania to become the second Muslim, but non-Arab, state to join the Arab League. The Sudan played a leading role in mediating between the African and Arab worlds.

Libya continued its maverick role in pursuit of its Islamic designs. In January it announced an agreement with Tunisia to establish a joint Arab Islamic Republic, but nothing came of the proposal. The Libyan leader, Col. Muammar al-Qaddafi, extended his quarrel with Egypt's Pres. Anwar as-Sadat to the point of an open break, Sadat announcing that he disagreed "100 percent" with Qaddafi's policies. Libyan-Sudan relations improved after a visit by Sudan's Pres. Gaafar Nimeiry to Tripoli. Relations between Libya and Gen. Idi Amin's (*see* BIOGRAPHY) Uganda cooled somewhat during the year, but Qaddafi maintained good relations with Chad, Niger, and Togo. In place of the earlier proposed Egypt-Libya-Sudan-Syria union, an agreement was signed by Egypt and the Sudan in February to establish common institutions for closer cooperation between the two countries.

Somalia, whose president, Maj. Gen. Muhammad Siyad Barrah, became the 1974 chairman of the OAU, played an active role in trying to forge closer links between black Africa and the Arab Middle East. When General Amin once again alleged that Uganda was about to be invaded by Tanzania and Zambia, the Somalis acted as intermediaries, only to find the charges groundless. Somalia failed, however, to make any progress in pressing its border claims against Ethiopia, despite the efforts of the OAU Goodwill Committee chaired by Nigeria's Gen. Yakubu Gowon.

In East Africa, relations between Uganda and its neighbours remained tense, with Kenya adopting a somewhat more critical attitude toward Amin than before. Relations between Kenya and Tanzania (both members of the East African Community) worsened when a trade dispute led the former to close its frontier with Tanzania for a brief period. Tanzania and Zambia maintained their traditional close working relationship; with Zaire they established a firm triple alliance that played an especially active role in trying to restore peace among the warring Angolan liberation movements as a prerequisite for starting negotiations with the Portuguese for Angola's independence.

In northern Africa, Algeria's Pres. Houari Boumédienne (*see* BIOGRAPHY) continued as in 1973 to maintain his important leadership role in relation both to Africa and to the nonaligned world. He discouraged the proposed merger between Tunisia and Libya, and he gave important backing to President Sadat in his conflicts with the Libyans and with the more militant Palestinian leaders.

The French-speaking African community continued to be mainly concerned with the future of the declining Common African and Mauritian Organization (OCAM; *see* below). The Ivory Coast helped to promote a reconciliation between Guinea and France, while OAU mediation was accepted in a frontier dispute between Mali and Upper Volta. Morocco's militant campaign in support of its claim to the Spanish Sahara upset its neighbours, Mauritania and Algeria, both rival claimants to the phosphate-rich semidesert Spanish colony.

External Relations. In the absence of a Middle Eastern settlement, Africa's official policy continued to be largely hostile toward Israel; strong moral support was given to the Palestine Liberation Organization (PLO). Relations between black Africa and the Arab oil-producing states were, however, not free from friction. (See *The Organization of African Unity*, above.) The U.S.S.R., on the whole, maintained a low-profile presence in Africa except in Somalia, which it continued to supply with modern weapons. Egypt's policy of seeking closer relations with the U.S. was combined with a continuingly critical, but still friendly, attitude toward Moscow. Libya, a critic of Soviet Communism, went some way toward establishing better relations with the U.S.S.R. The Soviets continued to provide support for the liberation movements committed to an armed struggle in southern Africa, but their desire to strengthen the presence of their navy in the Mediterranean Sea and Indian Ocean was not welcomed by any African government.

China's policies continued to win more friends on the continent, mainly because of its generous and effective aid programs, support for liberation movements, and careful policy of nonintervention in African affairs. The leaders of two countries previously hostile to China, Pres. Mobutu Sese Seko of Zaire and Pres. Omar Bongo of Gabon, both visited Peking and established cordial relations. As a result of Mobutu's visit, the Chinese agreed to provide 250 military experts to help train Holden Roberto's National Front for the Liberation of Angola (FNLA), whose external headquarters were in Zaire.

While African relations with Britain continued to be generally friendly, they were marked by continuous criticism of British policy toward Rhodesia, South Africa, and Namibia, especially over joint military exercises with South Africa at the Simonstown naval base, Britain's continued use of which was under discussion. U.S. Secretary of State Henry Kissinger's peace efforts in the Middle East found favour in Africa, but the disclosure of the contents of a U.S. policy document, supposedly approved by Kissinger, favouring a more conciliatory attitude toward South Africa, produced predictably angry reactions.

French policy continued to undergo changes as more French-speaking African countries demanded revisions of their special treaty relations with Paris and changes in OCAM. (See *Intra-African Relations*, above.) Senegal joined the growing list of former French colonies that negotiated new treaty relations with Paris; it terminated the previous agreement granting the French title to a military base at Dakar. The French agreed to grant independence to the Comoro Islands, and at the same time announced their intention of moving their naval base from Diego Suarez in Madagascar to a new site in Mayotte in the Comoros. French arms sales to South Africa and its expanding trade with that republic continued to attract criticism from black Africa, but the arms that it supplied and its Middle East policies won France favour among North African Arab states.

Spanish policy in the Sahara brought a threat of armed conflict with Morocco; Spain's offer of a referendum for the colony's mainly nomadic inhabitants to determine their own future failed to placate its African critics. African countries adopted a sharply critical attitude to the developed nations because of their international trading policies, and especially because of the greater costs of industrial exports in the wake of the rise in oil prices. Negotiations to find an acceptable economic relationship between the EEC and the associated and associable states of Africa, the

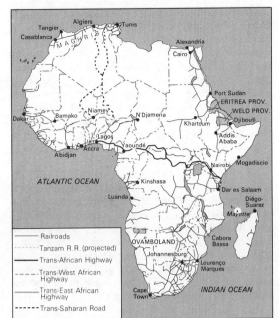

Distribution of overland communication routes in Africa.

Caribbean, and the Pacific continued. (*See* COMMERCIAL AND TRADE POLICIES.)

Economy. The energy crisis, produced by steeply increased oil prices, seriously impaired the continent's economies, except for the eight oil-producing countries (Libya, Algeria, Nigeria, Egypt, Angola, Gabon, Tunisia, and the Congo). The 35 (Guinea-Bissau excluded) non-oil-producing countries were further hit by the resultant increase in the cost of imports from the industrialized nations as well as by the need for increased food imports. (See *Drought and Food*, above.) These developments put a severe strain on the balance of payments problems of the great majority of African countries. For the lucky eight oil producers, total fuel exports were expected to reach 270 million metric tons in 1974, earning them about $12 billion. The additional cost to the rest of the continent was estimated at about $1.3 billion, as compared with about $500 million in 1973.

Africa's overall economic performance continued its disappointing downward trend in 1974. By the end of 1973 the growth rate of the gross domestic product (GDP) had declined to 4.3%, as compared with 4.7% during the 1960s. The share of agriculture in the total output of independent Africa declined from 41.5% in 1960 to 29.7% in 1972 and showed signs of falling even lower. Manufacturing output continued to show a small rise in values in 1973–74 from the 5.7% increase shown in 1972; but this was still short of the minimum 8% target set by the International Development Strategy Plan. By contrast, mineral production and exports continued to rise, with greater attention being given to crude petroleum and mineral exploration. By 1974 about 10% of the world's total petroleum production came from Africa.

The value of independent Africa's exports, at $14,-160,000,000, was 18% higher in 1972 than in 1971. The value of imports in 1972 amounted to $12,387,000,000, an increase of 8.5% over the previous year. The balance of payments of most African countries continued to be characterized by deficits on the current account; the exceptions were the petroleum- and other mineral-exporting countries.

Communications. The major road projects were still the trans-African and the trans-Saharan highways,

TROG—PUNCH/ROTHCO

which would eventually link West Africa to East and North Africa, respectively. Railways continued to be the most important long-distance carriers in terms of bulk volume. The Tanzam railway being built by the Chinese would link landlocked Zambia to Tanzania when finally completed in 1975. Airline traffic continued to increase in 1974, and harbour facilities were considerably improved with greater use of container techniques. The Pan-African Telecommunications Network remained the most important project in this field; when finally completed it would serve 33 countries.

Population. The 1972 estimate put the continent's population at 322 million. Projection studies calculated that the total population would be 457 million in 1980 and 818 million in the year 2000. If no decline in the fertility rate occurred, the population could reach 900 million by the end of the century. The higher birth and mortality rates produced a population structure in which 45% of all Africans were below the age of 15, 52% were between 15 and 65, and only 3% were above 65 years of age.

(COLIN LEGUM)

See also Dependent States; Refugees; articles on the various political units.

[971.D.6; 978.D-E]

ENCYCLOPÆDIA BRITANNICA FILMS. *Africa: Living in Two Worlds* (1970); *Boy of Botswana* (1970); *City Boy of the Ivory Coast* (1970); *A Family of Liberia* (1970); *Two Boys of Ethiopia* (1970); *Youth Builds a Nation in Tanzania* (1970); *Silent Safari* (1972); *Elephant* (1973); *Giraffe* (1973); *Lion* (1973); *Zebra* (1973); *Cheetah* (1973).

Agriculture and Food Supplies

Early hopes for a banner year in agriculture in 1973–74 withered as Asian crops, affected by serious fertilizer shortages and poor weather, failed to materialize and severe drought in the U.S. reduced grain production. This destroyed prospects for a buildup in world grain stocks, which had been drawn down to critically low levels. By fall most estimates indicated that 1974 harvests would be about 2% less than in 1973.

WORLD FOOD SUPPLIES

On the basis of data collected by the Food and Agriculture Organization of the United Nations (FAO), total world food production in 1973 increased 4% from a year earlier to an index of 131 (1961–65 = 100). This provided a 4% increase in per capita supplies in the developed market economies, but re-

duced output in the Near East and Africa held per capita gains in the less developed regions to only 2%. By the end of the summer of 1974, there was little hope that 1973–74 crops would prove sufficient to avert famine in some heavily populated regions of the less developed world. World grain stocks had been lowered to levels that had not obtained for more than 20 years, while population during this period had increased more than 50%. Generally rising affluence had also increased demand.

This was not an overnight development. Several observers had been predicting severe shortages—and even widespread famine—for a decade or more. But several events in 1973–74 brought about a confluence of trends that could no longer be ignored. Production setbacks in the less developed regions and poor grain crops in critical areas of the developed world in 1972–73 combined to lay the groundwork for heavy trading in cereals and animal feedstuffs. Touched off by heavy Soviet purchases and fueled by the accelerating demand for feedstuffs in Western Europe, Japan, and other areas, cereal purchases in the dollar market were given added impetus by currency revaluations. As a result, stocks were reduced to very low levels and prices of cereals and oilseeds skyrocketed. Countries with limited foreign exchange had difficulty obtaining needed supplies. Then, at the turn of the year, the Arab oil embargo and the sharp increase in fuel prices set the stage for energy and fertilizer shortages.

It had been hoped that increased productivity, resulting in large measure from the combination of production inputs known as the Green Revolution, would enable large areas of the less developed world to reach some reasonable degree of self-sufficiency in food. But a shortage of at least one of the key ingredients—fertilizer—halted further adoption of the new high-yield varieties and was, in fact, cited as a principal cause of a production shortfall of some 20 million metric tons of grain in the less developed countries in 1974.

By late September it was clear that 1974–75 crops, affected by adverse weather in parts of North America, South Asia, and China, would not equal the estimated record 1,253,000,000 tons of grain produced in 1973–74. Production of wheat, coarse grains, and rice all fell below 1973–74 levels, and reduced output of soybeans in the U.S. foreclosed the possibility of improved oil meal and vegetable oil supplies. There were indications of increased meat supplies, though high prices continued to restrict demand.

No one could predict with any degree of accuracy the effect of reduced production and stocks on the world's populations. For those in the developed regions, supplies would be adequate, though high prices were forcing some shifts in consumption patterns. The effects would fall hardest on heavily populated South Asia and the drought-beleaguered nations of the African Sahel. At midyear an assessment of the world food situation by the FAO indicated that 20 to 25% of the populations in the Far East, the Near East, and Africa suffered from "significant undernutrition." In early July UN Secretary-General Kurt Waldheim warned that the "sheer survival of millions" depended on sustained relief measures by the international community. Later in the month Norman E. Borlaug, winner of the Nobel Peace Prize in 1970 for his contribution to the development of high-yield grains, forecast that from 10 million to 50 million people in India would starve to death unless massive food aid was forthcoming.

Table I. Indexes of Food and Agricultural Production
Average 1961–65 = 100

Region	Total agricultural production			Per capita food production		
	1973*	1972	1969–71	1973*	1972	1969–71
Developed market economies†	126	122	118	114	112	110
Western Europe	123	120	118	115	113	112
North America	121	118	112	112	110	108
Oceania	127	120	122	116	108	109
Eastern Europe and the U.S.S.R.	144	133	128	131	122	120
Less developed market economies†	130	125	122	101	99	102
Latin America	131	126	122	100	100	102
Near East (excluding Israel)	131	138	125	99	107	103
Far East (excluding China and Japan)	132	121	122	103	96	103
Africa (excluding South Africa)	122	126	121	95	101	102
World	129	124	121	108	105	106

*Preliminary.
†Including countries in other regions not specified.
Source: Food and Agriculture Organization of the United Nations, *Monthly Bulletin of Agricultural Statistics* (March 1974).

Concern over the world food situation culminated in a World Food Conference, held in Rome in November under the aegis of the FAO. Despite the pleas of several less developed nations, little in the way of immediate action to relieve famine emerged from the 12-day conference. However, the delegates did agree in principle to several long-term recommendations, including establishment of an agricultural development fund, originally proposed by a group of Arab countries. Subject to approval by the UN General Assembly, a World Food Council was to be established which would coordinate a three-year program to deliver ten million tons of grain per year to needy countries over three years, a permanent grain stockpile to meet emergency conditions, and an early warning system to monitor crop conditions and provide advance notice of possible famine. The UN body, however, was to have a purely coordinating role, and details of the projects were to be worked out later.

Differences within the U.S. government reemerged among members of the U.S. delegation to the conference. Some urged an increase in food aid for humanitarian reasons or believed, with U.S. Secretary of State Henry Kissinger, that the national interest dictated a trade-off between U.S. food resources and the resources of the less developed countries, including oil. Others agreed with the Departments of Agriculture and the Treasury that world hunger problems had been exaggerated, that a solution could be achieved through expanded trade and continuation of modest food assistance directed toward improving productivity in the less developed countries, and that a substantial increase in food aid would exacerbate the inflationary spiral. Secretary of Agriculture Earl L. Butz, the head of the U.S. delegation, emphasized that food is "a tool in the kit of American diplomacy."

Consumption, Expenditures, and Prices. The index of per capita food production among the less developed nations rose from 101 (1961–65 = 100) in 1972 to 103 in 1973 and from 115 to 120 in the developed economies. Even so, production reverses and distribution problems left many countries in extremely difficult circumstances. Deaths from famine in the African Sahel were estimated at more than 100,000 in 1973 alone. Drought in Ethiopia affected hundreds of thousands. Poor crops and maldistribu-

**Table II. Food Price Index Changes
in Selected Countries, 1974**

Country and month		Index 1970=100	Percentage change from		
			Previous month	Three months	One year
United States	July	139.7	+0.1	+1.2	+13.9
Canada	July	146.3	+1.0	+5.2	+16.3
Japan	July	157.6	+2.9	+.2	+28.0
United Kingdom	July	163.2	−.4	+2.3	+17.0
Denmark	June	144.4	+.4	+2.3	+9.9
Germany, West	July	124.1	−.6	+.6	+3.6
Italy	July	144.8	+2.3	+4.3	+15.8
Belgium	July	126.0	+2.3	+4.4	+3.5
Netherlands, The	July	128.1	+.5	+1.3	+6.3
France	June	141.1	+.9	+3.7	+13.5
Brazil	July	231.5	+2.3	+5.1	+40.6

Source: U.S. Department of Agriculture, Foreign Agricultural Service, *Foreign Agriculture* (Oct. 7, 1974).

tion set off food riots early in the year in India, and flooding in Pakistan and Bangladesh led to high prices and food shortages. Inflation in most developed economies continued to push food prices to very high levels, creating dissatisfaction and, more seriously, hardship among lower-income consumers.

In the U.S. the index of per capita consumption of all foods was expected to rise about 2% in 1974, to 103.7 (1967 = 100). This represented a return to 1972 levels following a 4% decline in consumption of animal products in 1973. Meat consumption was expected to average 6% more than the 175.7 lb. per capita reported for 1973, and beef consumption, forecast at 115 lb., would be second only to the record 116 lb. of 1972. A decline in consumption of milk and cream was offset by a 7% increase in per capita use of cheese. Cereal grains, fats and oils, and sugar showed little change from 1973, while egg consumption continued its long decline.

Food prices continued to rise. The Consumer Price Index for all food stood at 159.5 (1967 = 100) in the second quarter of 1974, or 15.5% more than a year earlier, and retail food prices were up 16.1%. In late August the U.S. Department of Agriculture (USDA) estimated that retail food prices for all of 1974 could average as much as 17% above 1973. At midyear personal consumption expenditures for food reached an annual rate of nearly $161 billion. Total food expenditures in the first half of 1974 represented 16.6% of disposable personal income, or 15.9% more than in

Tomato plants attain heights of ten feet in plastic-covered greenhouses near Tucson, Ariz. Ideal growth conditions are artificially maintained and tomato yields are four times greater than in open irrigated fields in Arizona and California.

Table III. Survey of Retail Food Prices in Selected Cities, Sept. 4, 1974

In U.S. dollars per pound, converted at current exchange rates

City	Steak, sirloin, boneless	Roast, chuck, boneless	Roast, pork, boneless	Pork chops	Ham, canned	Bacon, sliced pkgd.	Broilers, whole	Eggs, dozen	Butter	Cheese (Cheddar, Edam, Gouda)	Milk, whole quart	Oil, cooking quart	Tomatoes	Onions, yellow	Apples	Oranges, dozen	Bread, white pkgd.
Bonn, W. Ger.	3.37	2.14	3.37	1.87	2.07	3.54	0.71	0.89	1.28	1.47	0.34	1.51	0.27	0.19	0.40	2.25	0.51
Brasília, Braz.	1.15	1.15	2.23	1.86	2.23	2.33	.66	.67	1.18	1.87	.20	1.09	.27	.39	.25	.52	.68
Brussels, Belg.	2.80	1.56	1.36	1.47	3.16	1.47	.86	.87	1.29	1.51	.33	1.49	.37	.11	.21	1.74	.23
Buenos Aires, Arg.*	.83	.42	.47	.43	†	1.20	.49	.75	.98	1.48	.14	.66	.42	.08	.13	.85	.26
Canberra, Austr.	1.99	.97	1.58	1.57	2.51	2.21	1.39	1.27	.99	1.34	.45	1.43	.58	.30	.49	1.43	.57
Copenhagen, Den.	3.97	1.62	†	2.09	2.37	2.16	.92	1.22	1.16	1.40	.31	2.76‡	.73	.43	.52	1.66	.48
London, Eng.	2.73	1.20	.97	1.34	1.34	1.76	.58	.79	.51	.83	.16	1.31	.32	.20	.23	1.55	.34
Mexico City, Mex.	1.23	1.18	1.94	1.45	2.43	1.40	1.36	.88	1.87	1.76	.27	1.31	.18	.14	.35	1.09	.28
Ottawa, Ont.	2.02	1.21	1.75	1.71	1.78	1.39	.84	.82	.90	1.35	.44	1.51	.29	.25	.44	1.00	.44
Paris, France	2.40	1.37	1.74	1.51	2.15	2.84	.84	.42	1.31	1.27	.30	1.63	.20	.18	.45	1.82	.60
Rome, Italy	2.75	1.92	1.58	1.72	1.84	1.43	1.06	.97	1.58	1.10	†	†	.27	.17	.22	1.68	.34
Stockholm, Swed.	4.12	1.72	3.17	2.08	2.67	2.27	1.02	1.18	1.19	1.53	.28	3.68‡	.66	.48	.50	1.54	.68
The Hague, Neth.	3.25	2.09	2.36	1.66	1.66	2.66	.67	.95	1.17	1.17	.28	1.19	.16	.08	.24	1.27	.15
Tokyo, Jap.	15.00	3.60	2.48	2.55	2.68	4.35	†	†	1.22	2.64	.60	.51	†	.19	.92	4.43	.44
Washington, D.C.	2.56	1.32	2.89	1.92	1.34	1.15	.63	.81	.82	1.35	.44	1.17	.50	.21	.38	1.32	.35
Median	2.73	1.37	1.84	1.71	2.19	2.16	.84	.88	1.18	1.40	.31	1.37	.31	.19	.38	1.54	.44

*Government ceiling prices are listed for meat.
†Not available.
‡Not commonly used for cooking.

Source: U.S. Department of Agriculture, Foreign Agricultural Service, *Foreign Agriculture* (Oct. 7, 1974).

1973. The 15.5% rise in food prices between mid-1973 and mid-1974 compared with a 10.7% increase in retail prices of all goods and services in the Consumer Price Index.

Several controversies associated with retail food prices surfaced in 1974. Early in the year leaders of the U.S. baking industry contended that continued exports of wheat could drive the retail price of bread to $1 per loaf, a claim that Secretary of Agriculture Butz labeled "an unresponsible scare tactic." Bread prices in August averaged 39.4 cents per pound, 27.2% more than in August 1973. Late in March congressional hearings were announced to investigate the paradox of low cattle prices and high retail meat prices. It was contended that, despite lower wholesale prices for meat animals, the food industry had not passed savings along to consumers but was using 1974 gains to offset losses and low profits experienced under price controls. In the second quarter retail meat prices declined to about year-earlier levels, but consumers continued to resist buying. In mid-June a USDA official reported that the spread between farm and retail beef prices had grown from 41.3 cents per pound in 1972 to 51.9 cents in April 1974. In the fall some farmers held highly publicized calf slaughters to dramatize their claim that they would lose money if they raised the animals to maturity. High sugar prices were said to be forcing many small, independent bakers out of business late in the year.

Assistance. The acute need for increased food assistance in 1973–74 posed an economic and moral dilemma for the developed nations. Not only was their ability to respond severely taxed because of reduced stocks, but the costs of both food relief and development assistance had been made more punishing by currency revaluations and inflation. Moreover, the continuing disaster in the Sahel and the threat of widespread suffering in the Indian subcontinent presented a challenge of awesome dimensions.

The World Food Program continued to provide relief and to pursue a number of development projects throughout the world. In opening its pledging conference for the 1975–76 biennium in February, one of its officials noted that the rise in commodity prices had reduced the program's effectiveness by 40%. A target of $440 million was set for the 1975–76 biennium, compared with $340 million pledged in 1973–74. Some 49 countries pledged $331 million in commodities and cash. The U.S., the largest donor, pledged $140 million, including $93 million in grains.

Crop losses dimmed the prospect for any substantial increase in U.S. food aid in 1975 beyond the 3.2 million metric tons provided in 1973–74. Resistance to providing additional aid, though unorganized and not widespread, was beginning to be expressed on several levels, including administration officials concerned about inflation and consumer representatives concerned about prices. Even so, Pres. Gerald Ford in late September pledged an increase in the amount of money the U.S. would spend on food for nations in need. Questions were immediately raised as to whether, in light of price increases, the president's pledge implied an increase in volume. In November the president turned down a request by Democratic members of the U.S. delegation to the Rome conference urging that U.S. food aid be increased by one million tons.

Food aid shipments under the major U.S. effort, Public Law 480, or Food for Peace, totaled an estimated $987 million in 1973–74. This was a slight increase in value from a year earlier, but the overall volume of shipments was down about 50%. A higher quantity was shipped under Title I—sales for dollars on long-term credits—while shipments under the program's disaster relief, economic development, and child-feeding provisions were reduced. Shipments of wheat under Public Law 480 fell from about 420,000

Crossing cattle with buffalo, a Tracy, Calif., rancher has developed a herd of 5,000 "beefalos" which thrive on grass and require no feed. Consumer reaction to experimentally marketed beefalo meat in May was generally favourable and it was hoped that the hybrid animal would help solve the problem of rising meat costs.

MARTIN WESTON—NEWSWEEK

tons in 1972–73 to about 173,700 tons. The USDA requested an appropriation of $778,473,000 for 1974–75 Food for Peace operations. Late in September the House Appropriations Committee approved the budget request in its report, which allocated 52% to Title I programs. Although the bill was passed in the House on October 9, the program was criticized by congressmen and others for supplying South Vietnam and Cambodia with large amounts of food that were alleged to have been converted into money for military purposes. In July an amendment to the Foreign Assistance Act provided $150 million for disaster relief and rehabilitation aid to the drought-stricken African nations, Pakistan, and Nicaragua.

Domestic food assistance in the U.S. was estimated at some $5.1 billion in 1973–74, an increase of about 20% from the year earlier. The Food Stamp Program, which subsidized food purchases of low-income persons and families, accounted for approximately $2,-995,367,000, and participation averaged about 14 million persons per month. Direct distribution of farm foods in areas where the Food Stamp Program was not yet operating totaled about $246,037,000. Child nutrition programs were estimated to cost about $1,612,000,000. Late in the year an administration proposal to raise the cost of food stamps to 30% of the recipients' net income was criticized by poor people's groups and some members of Congress.

Marketing and Manufacturing. Of the $132.2 billion spent for food by U.S. consumers in 1973, an estimated $82.3 billion represented the costs of transportation, processing, and marketing. This marked a 5% rise in the "margin" between farm and retail value as compared with a year earlier. By mid-1974 marketing margins had risen 36% above August 1973, the last month of the federal price freeze.

Labour costs, at an estimated $40.3 billion, accounted for 49% of the total marketing bill for U.S. foods in 1973; this was 7.2% more than in 1972. Packaging costs totaling $10 billion were 6% above a year earlier, reflecting sharp increases in the prices of paper and other packaging materials. Rail and transport costs of $6.1 billion were unchanged, as increased transport rates offset the smaller volume of farm goods marketed. Capital costs associated with the processing and marketing of farm foods rose about 6%, to $6.9 billion, and interest rates for long-term credit and commercial and factory building costs increased 0.2 and 6.6%, respectively. Advertising costs for the food industry were reported at $2.3 billion. Corporate profits, before taxes, for the food industry were reported at $4.6 billion, an increase of about 31%. The largest share of the total marketing bill went to the food-processing industry, which accounted for $28.1 billion. Food wholesalers accounted for $11.7 billion of the marketing bill, food retailers for $23.6 billion, and restaurants and other food-service institutions for $18.8 billion.

Sharply increased prices of food processors and retailers brought critical responses from political leaders and consumers in 1974. Generally speaking, the brunt of criticism was borne by food retailers, whose prices continued to increase long after prices received by farmers and wholesalers began to decline. Early in the year, the chairman of the Federal Trade Commission (FTC) announced that a broad investigation was under way to determine if mergers in the food industry had contributed to food price rises. Earlier, the FTC moved to break up the market power of the nation's four largest breakfast cereal companies.

Empty cattle pens at the Chicago-Joliet livestock centre indicate the fluctuations in beef delivery during 1974.

NORTH AMERICA

United States. *Crops.* The 1974 crop year proved disappointing. With strong domestic and world demand for wheat and feed grains, record high net farm income for 1973, and the release of nine million acres formerly set aside under federal programs, early projections for overall production were high. March 1974 planting intentions indicated a drive by U.S. farmers for all-out production, as well as some shifting to high-demand crops such as corn and wheat. However, heavy spring moisture delayed plantings and a long, hot, dry period in the Midwestern and plains states dealt sharp blows to production hopes. Moisture conditions improved in late August and early September, but early frosts further damaged corn and soybean crops. Critical drought conditions also caused sharp declines in per-acre yields, especially for corn, sorghum, wheat, soybeans, and cotton. All-crop production dropped sharply to an indicated index of 110 (1967 = 100), 10 points below a year earlier.

Production of food grains (wheat, rye, and rice) was indicated at 54,109,000 metric tons, up 7% from 51,458,000 tons a year earlier. The total wheat crop, though somewhat smaller than originally hoped, was forecast at 1,780,594,000 bu., 4% above 1973 and 15% more than the 1972 crop. Harvested acreage for all wheat rose 19% to 64,102,000 ac., the largest combined wheat acreage since 1953. Hard red winter wheat accounted for 879,310,000 bu. or slightly more than half the total crop, soft red winter wheat for 288,876,000 bu., durum for 78,014,000 bu., hard red spring wheat for 284,253,000 bu., and white wheat, both winter and spring, for 250,141,000 bu., a 40% increase over 1973. The rye crop was indicated at 19,616,000 bu., compared with 26,398,000 bu. a year earlier. Rice production was estimated at a record 114,808,000 cwt., 24% above the 1973 crop.

Projected production of feed grains (corn, sorghum, oats, and barley) was 20% below a year earlier. Corn for grain was forecast initially at 6,700,000,000 bu., but drought conditions and early frosts reduced this to 4,621,248,000 bu., 18% below the record 1973 crop. Even so, the 1974 harvest was the fourth largest on record. Acreage was up 3% but per acre yield fell from 91.4 bu. in 1973 to 72.5. Sorghum grain production was indicated at 609,272,000 bu., a drastic 35% decline from a year earlier. Oat production was 648,-711,000 bu., compared with 663,860,000 bu. in 1973,

Table IV. U.S. Grain Production and Stocks

Commodity	Beginning stocks*	Production	Utilization†	Ending stocks
Wheat (000,000 bu.)				
1972–73	863	1,545	1,970	439
1973–74 indicated	439	1,711	1,905	249
1974–75 projected	249	1,781	1,813–1,763	218–268
Corn (000,000 bu.)				
1972–73	1,126	5,573	5,991	709
1973–74 indicated	709	5,643	5,925	428
1974–75 projected	428	4,718	4,832–4,812	315–335
Feed grains (000,000 bu.)				
1972–73	48.4	199.9	216.3	32.4
1973–74 indicated	32.4	205.0	217.2	20.5
1974–75 projected	20.5	168.0	176.1–174.9	12.8–14.0
Rice (000,000 cwt.)				
1972–73	11.4	85.4	89.8	5.1
1973–74 indicated	5.1	92.8	86.4	7.8
1974–75 projected	7.8	113.6	102.3–95.3	19.1–26.1
Soybeans (000,000 bu.)				
1972–73	72.0	1,270.6	1,283	60
1973–74 indicated	60.0	1,567.0	1,455	172
1974–75 projected	172.0	1,262.0	1,374	60

*Marketing year begins July 1 for wheat, barley, and oats; August 1 for rice; September 1 for soybeans; and October 1 for corn and sorghum.
†Utilization includes domestic disappearance, exports; for soybeans, crushings, seed, feed, and residual; and for corn and feed grains, food and seed.
Source: U.S. Department of Agriculture, *Agricultural Supply and Demand Estimates* (Oct. 11, 1974).

and barley was forecast at 325,402,000 bu., compared with 1973 production of 424,483,000 bu.

At 102 (1967 = 100), the production index for hay and forage was down 7 points from a year earlier. Production of all hay was estimated at 123,-824,000 short tons, the smallest crop since 1966. Alfalfa hay, comprising more than half the total, fell 9% to 71,601,000 tons. October 1 range and pasture conditions varied from 96 (80 or over = good to excellent) in Kentucky to 47 (35–49 = severe drought) in South Dakota. The 1974 oilseed crop, forecast at 44.4 million tons, was the second largest on record, but it was 18% lower than in 1973. Harvested soybean acreage fell to 52,510,000 from 56,416,000 a year earlier, and per acre yield was cut to 23.7 bu. from 27.8. The total soybean crop was forecast at 1,243,912,000 bu., compared with 1,566,518,000 bu. in 1973. Peanut production, forecast at 3,762,690,000 lb., was slightly above a year earlier. Flaxseed production fell from 16,437,000 bu. to 14,543,000 bu.; total acreage rose but yield declined to 8.4 bu. per ac. from 9.5 bu. in 1973 and 12.1 bu. in 1972.

Indicated production of all sugar crops fell 10 points

Cattle are unable to slake their thirst at this waterless pond in South Dakota. Drought conditions were widespread in several Midwestern states during the year.

WIDE WORLD

below 1973 to an index of 106 (1967 = 100). Sugarbeet production was forecast at 22,394,000 tons, compared with 24,507,000 tons in 1973, and sugarcane was forecast at 25,338,000 tons, 2% below a year earlier. The Louisiana crop was threatened by a hurricane in the fall, but appeared to have recovered.

Cotton prices continued the strong upward trend that began in 1973, and cotton producers responded with an 18% increase in planted acreage. Per acre yield was down substantially, however, and total production, forecast at 12,052,600 bales, was slightly below 1973. Upland cotton accounted for 11,975,300 bales and the longer-staple American-Pima for 77,300 bales.

Tobacco production was forecast at 1,962,643,000 lb., 15% above 1973. Flue-cured production accounted for 1,260,221,000 lb. and burley for 564,435,000 lb., an increase of 25% over the preceding year. Acreage in the burley belt was up 15% and yield was 2,205 lb. per ac., compared with 2,026 lb. a year earlier.

Indications were for moderately larger supplies of processed vegetables for the 1974 marketing season, with primary gains in tomato products and frozen items. Total acreage of seven major processing vegetables was 7% larger than in 1973 and total processing tonnage for eight items (including contract cabbage) was indicated as being up 17%. Tomato tonnage was expected to represent more than 60% of the total.

Sweet potatoes were up 7% to 13,460,000 cwt. Production of dried edible beans was forecast at a record 21,616,000 cwt., compared with 16,886,000 cwt. a year earlier. Dried peas were indicated at 3,461,000 cwt., representing a significant increase over 1973 production of 1,665,000 cwt.

Cold weather during the bloom period lowered the indicated pecan crop to 149,500,000 lb., 46% below the large 1973 crop and 21% less than in 1972. Filbert and walnut production also fell, to 8,850 tons and 141,200 tons, respectively, but almond production, indicated at 180,000 tons, was up substantially. The total deciduous fruit crop was forecast at 10.9 million tons, about the same as in 1973 but almost 30% above the small 1972 crop. At an indicated 6,208,300,-000 lb., the commercial apple crop was well above 1972 levels. Peach production rose, while pears, plums, and prunes, though below 1973, were still above the short 1972 crop. Sweet cherries were down but tart cherry production, at an indicated 127,500 tons, was far above the 1973 crop of 87,020 tons. Grape production was expected to total 4,218,400 tons, about the same as a year earlier; California continued to be the leading producing state with 3.8 million tons. The cranberry harvest was indicated at 2,208,000 bbl.

Indicated citrus production included a total orange crop of 233,750,000 boxes, 8% above the previous season and 4% above the 1972–73 record. California orange production was the largest since 1946–47. Grapefruit declined 8% to 58 million boxes, while the Arizona lemon crop was forecast at a record 5.5 million boxes, 90% above a year earlier. Early tangerine crop forecasts suggested a possible 8% decline.

Livestock. Livestock producers, especially cattle feeders, experienced a generally unfavourable year. During the first two quarters slaughter cattle prices dropped from a high of nearly $50 per hundredweight to around $34–$36. Feed costs remained high, and many of the cattle sold in the depressed slaughter market had been purchased earlier when feeder cattle prices were at record high levels. Summer drought conditions drove feed prices even higher, causing

Table V. Cotton Production of the Principal Producing Countries

In 000 480-lb. bales net

Country	Indicated 1974*	1973	Average 1967–71	Average 1960–64
Argentina	600	542	463	552
Brazil	2,500	2,600	2,890	2,235
China	9,500	10,300	8,960	5,040
Colombia	700	625	565	335
Egypt	2,100	2,248	2,237	2,037
Greece	505	505	465	337
India	5,200	5,500	5,090	4,741
Iran	950	920	672	494
Mexico	1,885	1,470	1,872	2,206
Pakistan	3,100	2,860	2,609	1,656
Peru	405	410	404	632
Spain	260	220	270	427
Sudan	850	1,100	1,061	675
Syria	670	715	681	656
Turkey	2,600	2,356	1,974	1,091
U.S.S.R.	12,000	11,800	9,730	7,370
United States	12,813	12,958	9,813	14,795

*Preliminary.
Source: U.S. Department of Agriculture, Foreign Agricultural Service.

Table VI. Orange (Including Tangerine) Production in Principal Producing Countries

In 000 metric tons

Country	1973*	1972	Average 1960–64
Algeria	448	451	402
Argentina	864	1,032	743
Brazil	3,208	2,560	964
Greece	432	432	274
Israel	1,160	1,076	592
Italy	1,685	1,581	1,099
Japan	3,766	4,056	1,373
Mexico	1,142	1,270	842
Morocco	984	988	555
South Africa	579	539	500
Spain	2,434	2,642	1,835
Turkey	507	563	305
United States	8,985	9,246	5,231

*Preliminary.
Source: U.S. Department of Agriculture, Foreign Agricultural Service.

many feeders to leave feedlot losses unreplaced. Commercial red meat production for the first six months of 1974 totaled 18,400,000,000 lb., 6% above the corresponding period of 1973. The wholesale meat price index rose 1% in the first half of the year and the retail meat price index averaged ten points higher, but the September index of prices received by farmers for meat animals was 29% below a year earlier. A record 127,540,000 head of cattle and calves were on farms and ranches as of Jan. 1, 1974, 6% more than a year earlier. However, the number of cattle on feedlots fell to 10 million head, leaving 90% of the cattle inventory feeding on grass and other roughage. Feedlot placements for the first half of the year were down 21% from a year earlier and the lowest since 1967. Fed cattle slaughter was weak, but increased nonfed steer and heifer slaughter raised the January–June total to 17.3 million head.

The number of milk cows declined for the second successive year. Milk cows on farms totaled 11,149,000 in June, 2.3% below a year earlier, but lower slaughter prices prompted dairy farmers to reduce herd culling. Milk production for the first two quarters fell to 59,300,000,000 lb. Farmers received an average of $7.98 per hundredweight for fluid market milk during August.

Pork production rose 7% in the first half of 1974 to nearly 7,000,000,000 lb., and the increase was expected to continue in the second half. January–June 1974 slaughter totaled 41.2 million head, 4% more than a year earlier, and slaughter hogs averaged six pounds heavier. However, farrowing intentions as of June 1 suggested smaller pork supplies in early 1975. Seasonally large fall pork production and substantially increased supplies of lower-grade beef were expected to keep hog prices comparatively low. The hog-corn ratio for September was only 10.2, compared with 20.4 a year earlier and 23 in 1972, a trend that usually foreshadowed a decrease in production.

The 1974 lamb crop was down 8% to 10,607,000 head, continuing the decline in the U.S. sheep and lamb industry. Sheep and lamb slaughter during the first two quarters amounted to about 4.3 million head, 8% below year-earlier levels. August 15 prices, at $38 per hundredweight, were somewhat stronger than for hogs, cattle, and calves and only slightly lower than for steers and heifers. Despite a predicted 15–17% decline in fall and winter sheep and lamb slaughter, lamb prices were not expected to rise much because of larger beef supplies and lower beef prices.

Egg production continued the downward trend begun in April 1972. January–September output totaled 122.7 million cases, the lowest production for that period since 1966. At midyear there were about 285 million layer hens on farms, compared with 290 million in June 1973. As of August broiler production was well above 1973 levels, but it was expected to decline sharply by the end of the year. Broiler meat output through August at federally inspected slaughter plants totaled 4,781,000,000 lb. The 1974 turkey crop was indicated at a record 132.7 million birds.

Farm Prices, Costs, Income, and Finances. On Oct. 15, 1974, prices received by farmers stood at a composite index of 185 (1967 = 100), compared with 184 a year earlier. Index levels (unadjusted) for all crops showed an increase, from 150 to 228, but there was a sharp drop in prices for livestock and products, from 188 to 155. Dairy products showed the least decline—from 161 to 158—while meat animals fell from 200 to 151, poultry and eggs from 191 to 167, and wool products from 187 to 146.

At 175, the index of prices paid by farmers for commodities and services was 18% above a year earlier. Prices of all production items rose from 153 in October 1973 to 183 a year later. Feeder livestock prices fell nearly 37% in that period, from 190 to 119, while feed costs rose 35 points to an index of 211. The parity ratio, a measure of farmers' purchasing power, fell to 102 in September from 127 a year earlier. In June farmers received about 39% of the consumer's food dollar, compared with 46% in 1973. Realized net income for the second quarter was $23.9 billion, far below the $30.3 billion high in 1973 but substantially above earlier years. Second-quarter farm production expenses were a record high $74.5 billion. Five million workers were employed on U.S. farms at the end of August.

The year was marked by input shortages of varying severity. Under the mandatory fuel allocation program established in 1973, farmers and industries associated with agriculture were to receive gasoline and middle distillate fuels at 100% of need; however, 1974 petroleum prices were expected to average 50% above year-earlier levels. Mid-September indices indicated an 81% increase in fertilizer prices. Until price ceilings on domestically produced fertilizers were lifted in October 1973, U.S. prices were not competitive on the world market and, as exports increased, domestic supplies suffered. Prices soared when ceilings were removed, but they were still sufficiently below world prices to encourage U.S. manufacturers to continue heavy foreign sales. This, together with uncertain supplies of natural gas feedstocks for nitrogen production, transportation problems, especially for phosphates, greater farm demand, and increased use per acre, led to shifting marketing patterns and shortages for many farmers.

Total farm assets as of Jan. 1, 1974, were valued at $478.8 billion, up 23.8% from January 1973; real estate accounted for $325.3 billion. The average value of farmland per acre rose nearly 25% in the year ended March 1, 1974. According to September 1 estimates, farm debt on Jan. 1, 1974, stood at $83,884,-000,000, a 12% increase over the previous year. Mortgage debt accounted for $41,280,000,000 and short-term debt (excluding Commodity Credit Corporation loans) for $42,104,000,000.

Trade and Stocks. U.S. agricultural exports reached record levels in fiscal 1974. Agricultural exports amounted to $21,320,000,000, 65% above the record $12.9 billion of fiscal 1973. At the same time, agricultural imports also rose, to $9.5 billion from $7.3 billion. The leading export was wheat (including products), with an export value of $4,738,000,000. Feed grains (excluding products) accounted for $4,651,-000,000, or double the previous year's sales. Soybean exports amounted to $4.4 billion, compared with $2.3 billion a year earlier. Japan continued to be the leading market with purchases of $3.4 billion. Western Europe bought $6.8 billion of farm commodities; Canada, $1.2 billion; China, $852 million; and the U.S.S.R., $509 million.

By August 1974 export activities had begun to slow and by the end of August, USDA specialists were forecasting a decline of up to 50% in total feed-grain exports. Causes were identified as steadily rising prices for U.S. corn, a lessening of foreign demand because of improved crops in some areas, and strong pressure from consumer groups and others to keep domestic food prices down.

Despite repeated assertions by congressional leaders and administration officials that export controls would not be implemented, several agreements were negotiated during the summer that effectively cut or held back exports of wheat and feed grains. The commissioner of agriculture of the EEC agreed to a temporary 10% cutback in U.S. corn orders; Japanese trade representatives told USDA officials they would need 10% less feed grains during the next fiscal year; and the Soviet Union canceled orders for 13.3 million bu. of wheat. In October the White House unexpectedly requested two major grain exporters to cancel sales of $500 million in wheat and feed grains to the Soviet Union and moved to implement a system of tight supervision over large grain sales.

October 1 stocks of corn were reported at 428 million bu., compared with 709 million in 1973 and 1,126,-000,000 in 1972. For all feed grains, beginning stocks for 1974–75 totaled 20.5 million short tons (32.4 million in 1973–74). Wheat stocks, indicated at 249 million bu. for 1973–74, were expected to drop to 218 million bu. for 1974–75, and carryover stocks of soybeans, reported at 172 million bu. in August, were projected at 60 million bu. by August 1975. Only rice stocks were expected to rise.

Legislation and Administration. To assist hard-pressed livestock producers, Congress enacted the Emergency Livestock Credit Act of 1974, establishing a one-year guaranteed loan program. Individual loans were limited to $250,000 and the total loan debt ceiling to $2 billion. Congress also considered, but failed to pass, legislation to indemnify poultry producers whose flocks were destroyed when federal inspectors detected traces of the chemical dieldrin in some birds.

A bill to extend the Sugar Act for five years failed House passage in June; defeat of the measure meant the end of sugar import quotas and domestic beet and cane production allocation as of Dec. 31, 1974. On November 18, however, the White House announced that the president had imposed an import quota of seven million short tons of sugar for 1975, to be purchased on a first come-first served basis rather than under the country-by-country quota system specified in the Sugar Act. The action made it possible to keep import duties on sugar at current levels. Nevertheless, with the retail price of sugar up from 18 cents a pound in January to 60–65 cents in November and with even higher prices forecast, the government urged Americans to conserve supplies and reduce sugar consumption.

Canada. Early expectations of Canada Agriculture (formerly the federal Department of Agriculture) for a larger wheat crop were set back by unfavourable weather conditions, especially in the Prairie Provinces. The Wheat Board had looked for total production of well over 16 million metric tons, but September 19 estimates were reduced to about 14.2 million tons, some 2 million tons below 1973 levels. With June 30 stocks of only 10.2 million tons, exports were expected to decline to a possible 11.6 million tons. The export picture was also disturbed by labour problems, including an eight-month slowdown, followed by a complete work stoppage in August, by grain handlers in Vancouver, B.C. The accidental closing of the St. Lawrence Seaway cut July–August exports by nearly a million tons. In June negotiations were completed for the sale of 2,030,000 metric tons of wheat to China, bringing total Canadian wheat sales to China in 1974 to 3,050,000 tons.

With 55,000 additional hectares planted, estimated corn production rose to 2,875,000 tons from 2,767,-000, despite a 6% decline in yield. Oat production, forecast at 4,530,000 tons, was down from 5,041,000 tons a year earlier. A new feed grains policy, announced in May, provided for a national market for feed grains, with prices based on supply and demand; a price guarantee to producers for commercial sales to the market not under Wheat Board control; a special reserve stock; and provisions for a delivery quota system to be imposed at the discretion of the board. First official estimates for oilseed crops indicated some increase in rapeseed production, to 54.7 million bu., and a slight decline in flaxseed.

Cattle herds rose 6.1% during the first two quarters of 1974, to a record high 14,978,000 head. Beef cows and heifers were up 7.7 and 8.5%, respectively, and steers were up 18.2%. Canada Agriculture forecast a possible significant increase in cow slaughter, depending on the level of feeder cattle prices and the availability of adequate forage supplies. In April Canada forbade importation of meat and meat animals fed with the growth hormone diethylstilbestrol (DES) after a U.S. Court of Appeals reversed a lower court order banning use of the hormone in feeding U.S. livestock. The hormone, which had been found to cause cancer in laboratory animals, was illegal in Canada. This action effectively prevented the importation of U.S. slaughter cattle and caused live cattle prices to rise sharply. In August Canada agreed to a U.S. proposal whereby animals exported to Canada would be certified as free from exposure to DES. However, this coincided with the imposition of a new import quota system for cattle and beef, to be in effect until Aug. 11, 1975. The quota system was an attempt to

Table VII. Poultry Meat Production in Selected Countries*			
In 000,000 lb.			
Country	1974†	1973	1972	Average 1955–59
Austria	105	109	98	4
Belgium-Luxembourg	244	244	249	95
Canada	1,065	1,043	981	428
Denmark	207	199	188	58
France	1,750	1,723	1,540	511
Germany, West	566	604	575	172
Greece	185	176	183	36
Italy	1,985	1,883	1,812	215
Japan	1,538	1,519	1,368	—
Netherlands, The	690	721	690	96
Poland	385	385	351	109
Spain	765	761	725	—
United Kingdom	1,496	1,483	1,384	455
United States	11,023	10,992	11,104	5,480

*On ready-to-cook basis.
†Preliminary.
Source: U.S. Department of Agriculture, Foreign Agricultural Service.

Table VIII. Egg Production in Specified Countries		
In 000,000 eggs		
Country	1974*	1973	1972
Austria	1,500	1,564	1,542
Belgium-Luxembourg	4,000	3,867	3,950
Canada	5,682	5,540	5,621
Denmark	1,200	1,212	1,227
France	12,700	12,400	11,800
Germany, West	15,000	15,506	16,143
Greece	2,175	2,140	1,919
Italy	11,700	11,564	10,612
Japan	30,000	30,082	29,915
Netherlands, The	4,850	4,701	4,421
Poland	7,650	7,505	7,476
Spain	7,600	7,525	7,440
United Kingdom	14,160	13,800	14,736
United States	65,628	66,551	69,879

*Preliminary.
Source: U.S. Department of Agriculture, Foreign Agricultural Service.

Table IX. Milk Cows and Milk Production in Specified Countries					
	Number of milk cows in 000			Milk production in 000,000 lb.		
Country	1973*	1972	Average 1961–65	1974*	1973*	Average 1961–65
Australia	2,657	2,566	3,190	15,435	15,899	16,308
Austria	1,036	902	1,122	7,240	7,231	6,750
Belgium-Luxembourg	1,076	1,025	1,024	9,215	8,885	8,792
Canada	2,177	2,211	2,930	16,975	16,886	18,504
Denmark	1,156	1,122	1,428	11,000	10,787	11,713
France	7,678	7,500	9,409	67,775	65,170	55,206
Germany, West	5,466	5,442	5,852	47,725	46,883	45,368
Greece	1,096	1,018	434	1,595	1,448	1,050
Ireland	2,104	1,895	1,373	9,480	9,092	6,465
Italy	3,980	3,165	3,448	19,810	19,841	20,508
Japan	909	1,111	717	10,585	10,829	5,976
Netherlands, The	2,100	1,970	1,701	21,925	20,569	15,578
New Zealand	2,190	2,255	2,007	13,936	12,669	13,544
Norway	413	414	567	3,970	3,979	3,638
Sweden	754	740	1,180	6,395	6,592	8,437
Switzerland	888	873	926	7,275	7,252	6,782
United Kingdom	3,993	4,696	4,202	30,435	30,519	24,791
United States	11,419	11,710	16,195	114,500	115,620	125,660

*Preliminary.
Source: U.S. Department of Agriculture, Foreign Agricultural Service.

correct serious problems brought about by a beef carcass grading system instituted in 1972. Indications were that the system caused a sharp increase in demand, a severe decline in the supply of lower-grade animals, and a subsequent rapid rise in imports of slaughter beef from the U.S.

Preliminary estimates showed an inventory of 6,997,999 hogs, compared with 6,944,000 in 1973. The Canadian surplus resulted in large exports to the South St. Paul market, causing prices there to range 3 to 5 cents below other markets in the Corn Belt. A contract for the sale of 150,000 head of market hogs to Japan was executed in early spring. After being in operation slightly more than a year, the Canadian Egg Marketing Agency (CEMA) was accused of a series of irrational decisions, including selling eggs in the U.S. for less than the Canadian price and destruction of nearly 28 million overaged, improperly stored eggs at a time of rising prices and world shortages. CEMA had also been criticized by the Ontario Egg Producers' Marketing Board, which was opposed to heavy egg imports from the United States. On May 8 the government announced a plan to require permits for the importation of eggs and products and turkeys.

LATIN AMERICA

Weather throughout the region was generally favourable in 1973–74, and agricultural production was expected to rise 6% above that of a year earlier. Grain crops, particularly corn and wheat, showed substantial improvement, sugar production continued to expand, the 1974–75 coffee crop was expected to be a third more than the frost-damaged crop of 1973–74, and oilseeds appeared to be maintaining a rising trend. Increased production of coffee and sugar would improve foreign earnings, but higher costs of petroleum and other imports made the task of increasing productivity more difficult.

Mexico. Grains, soybeans, and sugar all registered gains in 1973–74, and the outlook for 1974–75 was for continued improvement. Even so, agricultural output continued to be outpaced by demand, and increased imports of grains and oilseed products contributed to a trade deficit reported to be growing at a rate of 40% per year. The cost of some basic foodstuffs rose by as much as 100%.

The 1974–75 wheat crop was estimated at 2.1 million metric tons, 5% above a year earlier, but imports of about one million tons would still be needed. The

corn harvest rose slightly to 9.5 million tons, and sorghum, an increasingly important livestock feed, rose 15% to 2 million tons. Fertilizer shortages threatened the planned expansion of 1974–75 grain crops, particularly of wheat, which was heavily dependent on fertilizer application. Production of oilseed crops fell 3.7% in 1973–74; cotton and safflower acreage was reduced, and adverse weather affected copra and sesame output. Soybean production rose sharply to an estimated 510,000 tons, but the outlook for continued expansion was clouded by a possible shortage of irrigation water in Sonora. Cotton production, at an estimated 1,550,000 bales (480 lb. net), was about 10% below a year earlier; however, increased production was expected in 1974–75 as farmers switched to cotton

A plant pathologist injects disease organisms into a corn plant at the international centre for agricultural experiments at El Batán, Mex. The goal of such studies is to produce disease-resistant varieties of corn and thus increase crop yield.

COURTESY, CENTRO INTERNACIONAL DE MEJORAMIENTO DE MAIZ Y TRIGO from soybeans. Livestock numbers rose 2% in 1973, and higher domestic prices encouraged a 6% increase in slaughter. Agricultural exports increased about 21% in 1973. Exports of coffee to the U.S. rose 45% as Mexico took advantage of high prices and suspension of quotas under the International Coffee Agreement.

Central America. Agricultural production rose throughout the six-nation region in 1973, and the outlook was for continued expansion in 1974, particularly for cotton and sugar. Corn crops in 1973–74 rose to 1,729,000 metric tons. Rice harvests were up about 8%, with lower production in El Salvador and Panama offset by increased output in Costa Rica. Sugar production rose nearly 7% to 1,093,000 tons. The 1974–75 coffee crop was forecast at 7,850,000 bags (60 kg. each), a 9% increase over 1973–74 crops; only Costa Rica's crop was expected to decline from 1973–74 levels. The 28% increase in cocoa bean production, to 9,100 tons, was attributable to the larger crop in Costa Rica. Cattle numbers rose 3.5% to 10,452,000 head; the Costa Rican herd increased by 9% while the other five countries reported modest gains. Beef production in the region was expected to increase about 5% in 1974, but most governments did not increase export quotas. Panama took the lead in urging Central American countries to raise export taxes on bananas. (*See* PANAMA.)

South America. With excellent soybean, corn, and coffee crops forecast for 1974–75, agricultural output in Brazil was expected to rise 8%, continuing the upward trend of 1973–74. Almost all major crops except coffee and cotton improved in 1973–74, providing most of the country's food needs and contributing to a significant gain in export earnings. The corn harvest rose 8% to an estimated 15 million metric tons, but with domestic demand increased by the fast-growing poultry industry, exports were banned by the government to maintain domestic supplies. Production of

oilseeds, especially soybeans, continued to change the face of Brazil's agriculture. Soybean production in 1973–74 rose to 4.8 million tons; exports reached nearly four million tons of soybeans and meal equivalent; and the outlook for 1974–75 was for a harvest of nearly seven million tons. Cocoa production was forecast at 225,000 tons in 1973–74, a sharp increase from the drought-damaged 1972–73 midcrop. Livestock numbers at the beginning of 1974 were 2 to 3% above a year earlier. In October a 50% decrease in beef exports was decreed for 1974, 1975, and 1976 in order to build up herds. New fertilizer plants were under construction to supplement imports.

The 1973–74 Brazilian coffee crop declined to 14.5 million bags from 24 million as a result of severe frost damage, and reserve stocks were drawn down to fill export orders. However, a harvest of 27 million bags was forecast for 1974–75. Other major producers also expected larger crops, raising prospects for a 1974–75 world coffee crop of 80,053,000 bags, the largest since 1965 and more than 25% above 1973–74. South American production as a whole was estimated at 39,948,-000 bags, an increase of 50%, while production of an estimated 20,299,000 bags in Africa would be about 10% more than in 1973–74. This would increase the exportable supply 35% to approximately 60,145,000 bags, raising the probability of reduced prices.

The International Coffee Agreement had been extended for two years in October 1973, but its operative economic clauses had been dropped and it no longer provided the basis for orderly world trade. Café Mondial Ltd., which had been formed in 1973 by countries representing 85% of world production, announced in early July that it planned to intervene in London and New York markets to prevent a price decline. Following the lead of the Organization of Petroleum Exporting Countries (OPEC), it also announced its intention to strengthen a system for withholding supplies to maintain favourable prices. By early October, Brazil, Colombia, Ivory Coast, and Angola, among others, had announced plans to withhold about 12 million bags from world markets, but the success of this effort was problematical. Coffee prices continued to decline, largely because of large inventories in the U.S., and there were reports that Brazil had indicated a willingness to enter into "special deals" with major roasters. In November seven Latin-American countries, Costa Rica, the Dominican Republic, Guatemala, Honduras, Nicaragua, Mexico, and Venezuela, formed a multinational company, Café Suaves Centrales, S.A. de C.V., to negotiate international coffee prices. Brazil and Colombia participated in the decision to set up the company but would not take an active part in its operations.

Argentine agriculture continued its strong growth, although reports of drought in important producing areas cast some doubt on early forecasts for excellent 1974–75 grain crops. Production of 22,833,000 tons of grains in 1973–74 provided an export surplus of 10,-712,000 tons, and improved oilseed and fruit crops contributed to an estimated 10% increase in overall output in 1974. Beef production in 1973 had declined 2% from 1972, to 2,152,000 tons, but 1974 production was expected to increase by as much as 10%. Beef exports also fell in 1973 as a result of weakened demand in Europe and the government's determination to assure adequate domestic supplies at reasonable prices. In late 1973 the government nationalized the grain trade, making the National Grain Board the exclusive buyer and marketing agent for wheat, corn, and sor-

**Table X. Centrifugal Sugar Production
in Principal Producing Countries**

In 000 metric tons, raw value

Country	1973-74	1972-73	Average 1964-65–1968-69
Argentina	1,650	1,294	991
Australia	2,600	2,900	2,290
Brazil	6,935	6,164	4,356
China	2,630	2,457	1,441
Colombia	832	815	553
Cuba	5,806	5,250	5,163
Czechoslovakia	750	779	942
Denmark	400	342	340
Dominican Republic	1,225	1,143	723
Egypt	650	590	397
France	3,543	3,382	2,128
Germany, East	750	720	650
Germany, West	2,504	2,214	1,921
India	5,000	4,572	3,551
Indonesia	950	890	642
Iran	700	625	351
Italy	1,130	1,283	1,317
Jamaica	383	331	464
Japan	650	647	361
Mauritius	718	686	626
Mexico	2,878	2,770	2,301
Netherlands, The	832	756	656
Pakistan	725	479	404
Peru	940	920	755
Philippines	2,302	2,312	1,559
Poland	1,837	1,829	1,713
Romania	580	577	433
South Africa	1,732	1,915	1,426
Spain	820	851	614
Taiwan	850	780	902
Turkey	725	811	712
United Kingdom	1,168	1,180	969
U.S.S.R.	10,300	8,500	9,930
United States	5,184	5,817	4,968
U.S. dependencies*	250	231	678
Yugoslavia	472	427	436
World total	81,174	76,595	65,219

*Puerto Rico and Virgin Islands of the U.S.
Source: U.S. Department of Agriculture, Foreign Agricultural Service.

**Table XI. Coffee Production (Green)
in Principal Producing Countries**

In 000 bags, 60 kg. each

Country	1974-75*	1973-74	1972-71	Average 1965-66–1969-70
Angola	3,600	3,500	3,750	3,180
Brazil	27,000	14,500	24,000	23,240
Cameroon	1,250	1,300	1,440	1,120
Colombia	9,500	8,700	8,800	8,030
Costa Rica	1,425	1,575	1,335	1,250
Ecuador	1,200	870	1,100	969
El Salvador	2,570	2,070	2,100	2,116
Guatemala	2,300	2,200	2,250	1,812
India	1,750	1,600	1,580	1,209
Indonesia	2,800	2,750	2,700	2,080
Ivory Coast	4,100	3,100	5,050	3,850
Malagasy Republic	1,100	1,000	1,000	904
Mexico	3,500	3,100	3,700	2,895
Peru	900	1,000	1,030	888
Philippines	900	865	850	741
Tanzania	950	600	800	823
Uganda	3,100	3,100	2,850	2,887
Venezuela	1,200	1,150	1,100	807
Zaire	1,235	1,320	1,380	995
Total North America	13,419	12,395	12,933	11,050
Total South America	39,948	26,368	36,190	34,136
Total Africa	20,299	18,330	21,215	17,835
Total Asia and Oceania	6,387	6,094	5,947	4,618
World total	80,053	63,187	76,285	67,640

*Second estimate (September 1974).
Source: U.S. Department of Agriculture, Foreign Agricultural Service.

ghum. It was authorized to make bilateral agreements with foreign buyers, and sales agreements were reported with China and North Korea.

Agriculture in Uruguay and Paraguay continued to reflect stagnant economies. Paraguay's 7% rise in crop production in 1973 was partially offset by reduced output of livestock products. Most crops in the six Andean Group countries (Peru, Bolivia, Chile, Ecuador, Colombia, and Venezuela) showed improvement in 1973–74, and the outlook for 1974–75 was good. Chile's performance was mixed, reflecting uncertainties associated with the agrarian reform policies of the new military government and the failure of official prices to keep up with inflation. Agricultural output rose sharply in Bolivia in 1973 with recovery from adverse weather in the highly populated Altiplano. The wheat, barley, and corn crops improved, and sugar production rose 50%. Output of almost all crops in Peru also rose. Production of red meat in 1973 was down slightly, but lower supplies were partly offset by expansion in poultry. The 15-day-per-month ban on beef sales was continued.

Several factors combined to hold Ecuador's agriculture to a no-growth level in 1973–74. Farmers adopted a "wait and see" attitude toward government measures promising agrarian reform, while excessive rain in the coastal regions and drought and frost in the Sierra severely affected some crops. The agricultural situation was eased by increased petroleum exports to the U.S., which helped pay for imports of wheat, soybeans, and farm machinery. Overall output in Colombia declined in 1973–74, largely because of severe drought and fertilizer shortages. Coffee production rose 10%, however, and the outlook was for a further increase to 9.5 million bags in 1974–75. In Venezuela shortfalls in corn and cotton in 1973 were attributed to drought and floods, but rice, sugar, and sesame showed substantial improvements. Livestock production, which had increased about 5% per year for five years, failed to maintain its momentum, partly because of drought and feed shortages.

Caribbean Countries. Total agricultural output in the Caribbean countries declined slightly in 1973–74, to an index of 116 (1961–65 = 100) from 117 a year earlier. Adverse weather in some countries, together with political and economic difficulties and population increases, reduced per capita food production from an index of 98 in 1972–73 to 95. Most Caribbean countries continued to be heavily dependent on food imports; Cuba was reported to have imported 919,000 metric tons of wheat and wheat flour in 1973, mostly from Canada.

Sugar production throughout the region rose to an estimated 7,750,000 tons (raw value) in 1973–74, an increase of nearly 10% above a year earlier. The Cuban harvest, at 5.8 million tons, was 10.5% larger than in 1972–73, and production of 1,225,000 tons in the Dominican Republic represented a 7% improvement. World sugar production in 1974–75 was expected to rise to about 83.7 million tons (raw value), exceeding the 1973–74 record of an estimated 81,174,000 tons. Increases were expected in South America, Asia, and Oceania, while the outlook for Western Europe and North America was for harvests about equal to those of 1973–74. At the same time, world consumption was expected to reach 81.5 million tons. Prices rose sharply in 1974, from a 1973 average of 9.61 cents per pound to 15.32 cents in January 1974 and 36 cents in New York in early September. High prices were reported to have reduced consumption rates in some countries.

The high world price was also credited with refusal by the U.S. Congress to extend domestic sugar legislation that since the mid-1930s had maintained U.S. prices above world levels, although an overall U.S. import quota for 1975 was later set by the president. Cuba was said to be promoting the formation of an association of sugar-exporting countries patterned after OPEC.

WESTERN EUROPE

At its March 1974 meeting, the EEC agreed to increase farm price support prices by an average of 8.5%; support prices were increased 4–6% for most grains and 15% for hard wheat. The Community did not change the intervention price for butter, which had been plagued by surpluses, but the price for skimmed, powdered milk was raised 19.7%. To protect British consumers from price increases, the British beef support price was raised only 6.3% for 1974, half the increase in other countries. A subsidy on calf and pig production and an increase in the consumer subsidy on butter were to be met by British rather than EEC funds.

Farmers throughout Western Europe were hard hit by inflation. In Italy, where the government controlled prices of such household staples as pasta, bread, sugar, and meat, chronic shortages appeared as producers held back deliveries. Widespread farmers' strikes and protests eventually led to the announcement of an unprecedented midseason increase in price supports. Italian farmhands staged a 24-hour strike for higher pay, sharecroppers held rallies to demand government aid, and cattle breeders and dairy farmers manned border crossings in an effort to stop trains bringing meat and dairy products into the country. In July French farmers demonstrated for a 12.5% increase in prices, a ban on imports of non-EEC food products, and subsidies for fertilizer, fuel oil, and other farm supplies. Argentine meat was dumped at Le Havre, and other shipments of food were dumped and burned. By August French protests had become so disruptive that the agriculture minister threatened to withhold a promised $120 million in farm aid. Farmers in The Netherlands blocked highways with farm machinery, and in mid-September simultaneous demonstrations were held in all nine EEC countries. On September 20 an overall increase of 5% in support prices was announced. West Germany was strongly opposed to the

An outbreak of foot-and-mouth disease in Brittany, France, was brought under control by slaughtering 17,000 animals, principally pigs. It was the first such epidemic in the region in nearly 20 years.

A.F.P./PICTORIAL PARADE

increase, but the disagreement was resolved at a meeting in early October. Earlier, West Germany had succeeded in exempting durum wheat from an EEC plan to raise farm price levels by 8–9%.

Western Europe enjoyed generally favourable weather in 1974, although early fruit crops in some areas were damaged by frost and small grain and row crops in the northern regions suffered from dry conditions from March through June. In the fall west-central France was declared a disaster area because of drought. The worst drought conditions in parts of Britain in 50 years were alleviated by June rain.

Total grain production in Western Europe in 1974–75 was projected at 135.4 million metric tons, compared with 133.2 million tons in 1973–74. Imports were forecast at 37.7 million tons, far below 1973–74 levels of 47.1 million tons, and exports were also expected to fall, from 26 million tons to about 23.4 million tons. Total wheat production rose to 53.2 million tons in 1974. To prevent an outflow of EEC grain, export levies on cereals were increased in August.

Italy reported a good harvest, though there was some dispute among producers and government statisticians on the size of the 1974 grain crop. In September the Central Statistical Institute projected soft wheat production at 6.8 million tons and durum production at 2.7 million tons. The barley and oat crops rose 20.5 and 10%, respectively, but drought conditions cut corn production 10–15%. Although weather and low temperatures delayed late summer cereal harvests in Britain and caused some loss of quality, September projections indicated that wheat production had risen to 5,250,000 tons. Oats and barley were below a year earlier, while corn and rye harvests were projected at the same levels. France forecast an increase in wheat and corn production, but rye, oats, and barley declined. West Germany enjoyed increases of 6% in wheat production, 4% in oat production, 6% for corn, and slight increases for rye and barley. Denmark experienced losses for all grains, while Finland, Norway, and Sweden showed gains.

A serious red meat surplus in Western Europe was expected to continue well into 1975–76. The EEC approved subsidies on beef and veal exports for the first time in December 1973, and on July 16, 1974, the Community banned all imports of beef, veal, and live animals through the end of October. The resulting drop in European imports was expected to have serious implications for other producing nations with beef supply problems of their own. Midyear forecasts for Western Europe showed cattle inventories at 94.1 million head, a 4% increase over 1973, while hog numbers were 24% above the 1965–69 average. Total red meat production for the EEC was expected to increase 7–8% in 1974. At the same time, rising meat prices discouraged consumption, and beef stocks of 250,000 tons by year's end were predicted. By September storage capacity in the EEC was reported to be exhausted.

Western European poultry producers experienced problems of high feed costs, surpluses of competing protein foods, and tight credit in 1974. During the summer DANPO, the largest Danish poultry slaughter cooperative, was taken over by creditors, and one of the largest turkey producers in the U.K. was forced into receivership. In the EEC an effort was made to cut broiler production by 10%, and export subsidies were made available to dispose of surpluses outside the Community. France took advantage of the subsidy by exporting 10,000 tons of broilers to the U.S.S.R.

A serious sugar shortage occurred in England when Commonwealth Sugar Agreement (CSA) countries diverted supplies to world markets to take advantage of higher prices; it was relieved when payments under the CSA were increased. Filbert and almond production rose sharply in Spain and Italy, with Italy's almond crop at twice the 1973 level. Olive oil production in Italy was expected to rise as much as 32%. Spain planted an estimated 45,700 ac. to processing tomatoes, a 12% increase over 1973. The Western European apple crop declined some 19% because of early frost, heavy rain, and low temperatures during the blossoming period.

EASTERN EUROPE AND THE U.S.S.R.

Eastern Europe. Although foreign trade prices within Comecon were frozen through 1975, approximately a third of the members' trade was conducted with nonmembers. Thus Eastern Europe was not isolated from world market prices, and retail prices for gasoline, diesel fuel, coffee, cocoa, fruits, and vegetables were raised in 1974. However, government subsidies absorbed price rises for bread, milk, meat, and sugar. In Yugoslavia, which did not belong to Comecon and had a less tightly regulated economy, retail prices increased 23% during the first seven months of the year. There were indications that the 85% of Yugoslavia's farmland in private ownership was being shifted to a more predominantly collectivized system.

Eastern Europe experienced dry weather conditions from the fall of 1973 until the end of April 1974. Good rainfall occurred during late April and early May, but heavy rains in May, June, and July caused some flooding and delayed the harvest of winter grains and the planting of silage crops. East Germany was the exception; favourable weather prevailed there all year.

The 1974 grain harvest in Eastern Europe was forecast at nearly 87 million metric tons, the level of the previous two years. Preliminary figures showed wheat production at 32.2 million tons, up slightly from 1973 but substantially more than the 1968–72 average. Late reports from Hungary were of a record wheat harvest —larger than the 4.5 million tons of 1973. Rye production, at 10,379,000 tons, was down somewhat from a year earlier. The oat crop also declined, while barley, at 12,765,000 tons, was about the same. Total corn production, at 25,230,000 tons, was well above the 1968–72 average. Feed supplies were low in relation to livestock numbers, however. A good potato crop was expected to dampen demand for grain.

Like other producing nations, the Eastern European countries were caught in a situation of red meat oversupply. Midyear inventories for cattle were reported at 37,636,000 head, nearly 4% over 1973, and hog numbers had risen 3.3% to 154.5 million. Stocks of frozen beef began to build after the Common Market ban on beef and cattle imports went into effect. Eastern European feeders slowed slaughter operations, and shifts to other markets were expected.

U.S.S.R. Plans for 1974 were announced after the December 1973 meeting of the Supreme Soviet. Government capital investment in agriculture was to be 11.6% higher than in 1973, with a major share allocated to land improvements. Funds were also earmarked for the purchase of 64.6 million metric tons of fertilizer, major increases in farm machinery, and construction of new poultry, cattle, and hog units. Gross agricultural production was scheduled to rise 6.4% over the 1973 record.

The Soviet Union enjoyed a generally favourable winter in 1973–74, although the southwestern section was abnormally dry until late April. The area east of the Urals was hot and dry throughout the growing season, and drought took its toll on regional crops. Crop production for 1974 appeared to be approximately 5% below year-earlier levels while livestock production increased 5 to 10%. Thus, overall agricultural production would be somewhat larger than in 1973, although short of the planned 6.4% increase. Total grain production was estimated at about 205 million tons, or 8% below 1973 production, but the quality was expected to be generally good. Wheat production was forecast at 90 million tons, nearly 18% less than the record 1973 crop, and total feed-grain production (barley, oats, and corn) at a record 88 million tons.

Several incidents cast doubts on final figures, however. In accordance with agreements of the U.S.-U.S.S.R. Joint Working Group on Agricultural Economic Research and Information, the U.S. sent a three-man delegation to the Soviet Union in August to gather information on the 1974 grain crop, but its itinerary was rejected. After canceling an order for 13.3 million bu. of U.S. wheat in August, the Soviets entered the market in September to buy 3.4 million tons of wheat and corn. That sale was halted by the U.S. government, but a 2.2 million-ton sale was negotiated in October after the Soviets agreed to receive the grain in staggered shipments and not to buy any additional U.S. grain until the summer of 1975.

The ninth five-year plan (1971–75) had called for massive increases in the Soviet livestock industry, and this effort explained at least part of the unprecedented Soviet grain purchases. Output of livestock products in 1974 was expected to be 5 to 10% above a year earlier. Livestock numbers at the beginning of the year were at record levels for all classes except hogs, and midyear inventories showed 106.2 million head of cattle, compared with 104,006,000 head a year earlier. Meat production was estimated at 14.4 million tons and milk production at 90.8 million tons.

Total oilseed output was forecast at 7 million tons, nearly 6% less than the 1973 record. Soybean production was expected to return to normal levels after the rather poor 1973 crop. Spring coolness apparently reduced sugar-beet and potato crops. Estimated sugar-beet production was down by 3–8% and the potato crop by 7–12%.

AFRICA

Total agricultural production in Africa declined in 1973, from an index of 125 (1961–65 = 100) to 120, and per capita food production fell about 6%. Drought, which had seriously affected the Sahelian region for several years, spread southward and eastward. Dry weather also seriously affected crops in South Africa. All three of Africa's most important export crops—coffee, cotton, and cocoa beans—were smaller in 1973. High prices increased export earnings in several countries, but the gains were generally offset by the equally high prices of imports.

Northern Africa. Agricultural production throughout most of the Maghreb and Libya declined in 1973–74 as a result of adverse weather. Algeria's production of about 1.1 million metric tons of wheat was the smallest since 1966. Morocco's wheat harvest was down 21%, and barley was nearly 50% below a year earlier. Total production in Libya declined an estimated 20%. By contrast, Tunisia did exceptionally well; cereals improved slightly and production of an estimated 140,000 tons of olive oil contributed to a 15% increase in overall agricultural output. On a per

capita basis, food production fell sharply in Morocco, Algeria, and Libya, and rose 14% in Tunisia. The regional outlook was for a 20% increase in 1974–75 cereal crops. Structural changes continued to be made. Algeria continued to redistribute large holdings. Morocco's redistribution of land belonging to foreigners had been completed in 1973.

Agricultural production in Egypt increased 5% in 1973–74, with larger crops of cereals, citrus, sugar, and cotton. An increase in wheat production of nearly 14% was attributed in large measure to adoption of a new variety, Giza 155, a cross between Mexican dwarf varieties and local wheats. Cotton production rose to an estimated 2.4 million bales. The lower volume of cotton shipments in 1973 was offset by higher prices, raising the value of cotton exports above $500 million. At the same time, higher grain prices increased the value of agricultural imports to some $470 million. The U.S. once again became a major supplier of grains to Egypt. Agricultural output in the Sudan in 1973–74 declined from an index of 144 to 132, and per capita food production fell from 110 to 99. Sorghum, millet, peanuts, sugar, and oilseeds all declined, though the important cotton crop rose 22% to 1.1 million bales.

Sub-Sahara. Rain came to the drought-stricken nations of the Sahel in late August and early September 1974, breaking—at least temporarily—the drought that had ravaged the region for over six years. Whether the rains would be sufficient to restore some degree of food self-sufficiency was highly questionable. Some experts thought that relief supplies would be needed for several years. Harvests in Mauritania, Mali, Upper Volta, Niger, Chad, and The Gambia in 1973–74 continued to be as much as 25% below those in 1969–70. Livestock herds were down by at least 25%, and the FAO estimated that over 3.5 million cattle had died in 1973 alone. Conditions in Senegal, at the western terminus of the region, did show a marked improvement, with total 1973–74 production rising to an index of 101 from 73 a year earlier. The millet, sorghum, and rice crops all improved, and the 1973 peanut crop was up 20%. Elsewhere in the region, 1973 peanut crops were reported to be poor; Niger's was less than half the previous year's output of 195,000 metric tons, and Mali's fell to an estimated 100,000 tons from 150,000. (*See* Special Report.)

East Africa. Drought conditions appeared in several East African countries in 1973–74. Ethiopia was most severely hit, but parts of Kenya, Tanzania, and the Malagasy Republic were also affected. Total agricultural production in 1973–74 declined, with only Malawi showing a slight increase. Wheat production in Ethiopia, Kenya, and Tanzania fell to an estimated 1,680,000 metric tons for 1974–75, and Ethiopia's rye harvest was down 6%. However, the important corn crop showed a slight improvement. Corn production in Zambia, Tanzania, Burundi, and Uganda was expected to recover from relatively poor crops in 1973–74. Rice production continued almost unchanged, at an estimated 2,043,000 tons; 1,805,000 tons were accounted for by the Malagasy Republic.

Sugar production throughout the region showed a modest improvement in 1973–74; the estimated output of 1,618,000 tons was about 6% more than in 1972–73. Tea production in 1974 was down about 6%, to 112,500 tons; Kenya's output of an estimated 49,-000 tons was about 15% less than in 1973. East Africa's 1974–75 coffee crop was estimated at 5,017,000 bags, marking a strong recovery from the year before when it had fallen by 15%. Kenya's 1974–75 output,

Circular farms
in the Libyan Desert
employ electrically
controlled irrigation
systems. Up to 1,200 gal.
of water per minute
can be discharged on each
205-ac. disc.

estimated at 1,217,000 bags, was up 16%. Masai tribesmen in Kenya were said to have lost a high percentage of their cattle herds in the 1973–74 drought.

With reduced sisal output in Kenya and Brazil partially offset by increases in Tanzania and Angola, world production declined about 2.6% in 1973–74, to 1,433,000,000 lb. World production of all hard fibres (sisal, henequen, and abaca) was forecast at 2,011,-000,000 lb. for 1974–75, almost equal to the previous crop. Henequen, grown mostly in Mexico, was expected to total 350 million lb., and abaca was forecast at 228 million lb., with the Philippines accounting for 201 million lb. Rapidly rising demand pushed prices upward. In mid-April 1974 Tanzanian-Kenyan sisal prices reached $1,075 per metric ton, compared with $420 a year earlier.

West Africa. About half the 14 nations of the region increased output in 1973–74, but only 5 of the less populous countries raised per capita food production. Drought conditions were reported in the northern parts of Nigeria, Cameroon, Dahomey, Ghana, and Guinea adjacent to the southern reaches of the Sahel. The region's 1973–74 corn crop, estimated at 3,329,000 metric tons, was about 6% above the 1968–72 average, and the forecast of 3,460,000 tons in 1974–75 represented a further increase of about 4%. Nigeria's corn harvest was 12% above a year earlier, but per capita food production in Nigeria declined in 1973 by about 5%. In Ghana, where corn production rose nearly 20% in 1973–74, per capita food production was down nearly 6%. Rice production for the region was estimated at 2,131,000 tons, 5% more than in 1972–73. Production in Zaire rose nearly 30% to an estimated 227,000 tons.

Total sorghum and millet production for the region was estimated at 6.5 million tons, about 10% less than a year earlier; Nigerian production was down 11%, offsetting slight gains in several smaller countries. Cassava and other root crops rose 3% to 55.8 million tons, but peanut production in 1973–74 appeared to be down substantially. Drought reduced peanut crops in Cameroon, Dahomey, Togo, and Ghana, and the important Nigerian crop, estimated at 700,000 tons,

was sharply below the 1972–73 crop of 1,125,000 tons. Reports in February indicated that Nigeria's Northern States Marketing Board was having difficulty purchasing peanuts from local farmers, who were reluctant to sell their crops because of possible food shortages. Some of the crop was also being smuggled into Chad and Niger, where high prices could be obtained.

West African governments continued to encourage agricultural production through a variety of price incentives and development schemes. With technical assistance from the U.S., Israel, and Taiwan, Ghana was constructing a 50-mi. irrigation canal to move water from the Volta Dam to the Accra plains, where intensive vegetable production was planned. Ivory Coast planned to increase cocoa acreage some 320,000 ac. by 1981; a second cocoa-processing plant was being completed and a new factory complex for processing palm oil was opened. Nigeria continued to extend its highway system to improve marketing of farm products.

The 1973–74 cocoa bean harvest in West Africa was indicated at 962,400 tons, about 4% less than in 1972–73. Production was down 13% in Ghana, to an estimated 365,000 tons, and about 11% in Nigeria, where a 235,000-ton crop was forecast. Ivory Coast and Cameroon reported gains. Early estimates for 1974–75 placed total world production at 1,461,300 tons, only slightly more than the 1,451,500 tons of 1973–74. The West African crop was estimated at 1,035,800 tons as weather conditions in September and October cut earlier forecasts of production gains to about 8%, while a reduced Brazilian main crop brought South American production to an estimated 279,100 tons, compared with 353,600 tons a year earlier. Tight supplies and record prices characterized the cocoa market in 1974; prices reached a peak of $1.30 per pound (N.Y. spot "Accra") in May and then dropped to $1.06 by the end of August. High prices were lowering consumption in the major cocoa-using nations. U.S. grindings in January–June 1974 totaled 126,417 tons, compared with 151,275 tons in the first half of 1973; the West German grind was reported to be down 15%; and The Netherlands grind fell 4.5%. The International Cocoa Agreement, which came into force on

June 30, 1973, had little influence in 1974, since cocoa prices throughout the year substantially exceeded the agreement's price range of 23–32 cents.

Southern Africa. Production in South Africa and Rhodesia declined in 1973–74. Drought in the western Transvaal and northwestern Orange Free State damaged corn and sorghum crops, reducing South Africa's total output to an index of 118 from 141 a year earlier, while in Rhodesia the production index fell from 113 to 96. South Africa's corn crop, estimated at 9 million metric tons, was down 18%. The 1.6 million-ton Rhodesian corn crop was 20% below 1972–73, and the Rhodesian wheat harvest declined by the same amount. Wheat production in South Africa fell from 1,835,000 tons to 1,725,000. Sorghum production declined 50% in 1973, to 242,000 tons, and wool production fell for the third consecutive year.

Sugar production in South Africa fell about 9% in 1973–74, to an estimated 1,732,000 tons; with domestic consumption at about 950,000 tons, some 800,000 tons would be available for export, compared with shipments of over a million tons in 1972–73. Additional land was to be planted to sugarcane before the 1975–76 season. Cotton production was estimated at about 78,000 bales in 1973. Tobacco output continued its downward trend, to about 26,600 tons. Deciduous fruit production was seriously affected by drought in 1973, and exports fell 16%. Adverse weather also reduced oilseed production, but generally good grazing conditions increased cattle numbers to about 8.2 million head. A levy of about $15 per ton on fish-meal sales was being used to build up a fund to encourage soybean production.

MIDDLE EAST AND THE INDIAN SUBCONTINENT

Middle East. The 1974 wheat crop in the Middle East fell short of early projections, though most nations reported gains in actual production. Rainfall was sparse during the critical growing months, especially in Turkey and Iran, the region's major producers. Turkey expected a crop of eight million metric tons, the same as a year earlier but nearly one million tons below the 1968–72 average; imports were forecast at 1.5 million tons. Iran predicted an average crop of 3.9 million tons and expected to import 1.3 million tons. Iraq's wheat crop rose to 1.6 million tons, despite unfavourable weather. Israeli wheat production was forecast at 300,000 tons, an impressive gain over the 242,000-ton crop of 1973. Turkey increased its barley production to 3.1 million tons.

Early in the year Turkey announced that its three-year ban on opium poppy production would be lifted. In making the announcement, the government cited loss of employment and income; 100,000 families which had cultivated poppies had been forced to turn to less profitable crops such as wheat, barley, and sugar beets. (*See* DRUG ABUSE.)

Israeli citrus exports were expected to rise to 47 million crates during the winter months, with the bulk of the shipments going to Western Europe. Of the total, 22 million crates were Shamouti oranges, 12.5 million were grapefruit, 10.5 million were Valencia oranges, and the rest were lemons and navel oranges.

Indian Subcontinent. Indian agriculture experienced a devastating year in 1974. Severe drought, shortages, and low farm prices contributed to a production decline of at least 7%, and there were predictions of widespread famine. Farmers found themselves without enough fuel to operate irrigation pumps at full capacity. Fertilizer, desperately needed for growing the new, high-yield varieties of seeds, was scarce and extremely expensive. Fertilizer plants were reported to be running at only 60% of capacity, largely because of fuel shortages.

Workers harvest rice in a lush producing area of Java. Despite bountiful yields, population increases have led to a life of hunger and want for most. The population density is about 2,200 per square mile in this region.

Table XII. World Cocoa Production in Leading Areas*

In 000 metric tons

Area	Forecast 1974-75	1973-74	1972-73	Average 1963-64– 1967-68
World total	1,461.3	1,451.5	1,398.3	1,327.4
North and Central America	92.2	86.0	78.7	77.3
Dominican Republic	38.0	32.0	28.0	30.8
Mexico	30.0	30.0	29.0	20.7
South America	279.1	353.6	242.0	237.2
Brazil	175.0	245.5	158.7	146.1
Ecuador	55.0	62.0	43.0	48.4
Africa	1,035.8	961.8	1,039.6	981.0
Ghana	395.0	355.0	420.0	445.4
Nigeria	230.0	215.0	264.0	241.7
Ivory Coast	220.0	210.0	178.8	131.1
Cameroon	114.0	110.0	106.9	86.2
Asia and Oceania	54.2	50.1	38.0	31.9
Papua New Guinea	30.0	29.0	22.0	20.3

*Crop year, October 1 to September 30.
Source: U.S. Department of Agriculture, Foreign Agricultural Service.

Table XIII. Tea Production in Principal Producing Areas

In 000 metric tons

Area	Forecast 1974	1973*	1972	Average 1965-69
World total†	1,226.5	1,218.7	1,194.1	1,003.2
Asia and Oceania	1,052.7	1,034.7	1,012.6	890.7
Bangladesh	30.0	27.7	23.8	28.5
India	480.0	470.0	455.5	384.6
Indonesia	55.0	54.5	49.8	40.1
Japan	97.0	95.0	94.8	84.1
Sri Lanka	210.0	211.3	213.5	223.1
Taiwan	29.0	28.6	26.2	23.5
Turkey	45.0	43.2	46.5	23.9
U.S.S.R.	75.0	73.0	71.3	56.0
Africa	144.6	152.0	148.8	88.9
Kenya	49.0	56.6	53.3	26.8
Malawi	24.6	23.6	20.7	15.6
Mozambique	18.5	18.8	18.7	13.9
Uganda	20.0	20.4	23.4	12.7
South America	29.2	32.0	32.7	23.6
Argentina	20.0	23.1	24.0	16.5

*Preliminary.
†Excluding China.
Source: U.S. Department of Agriculture, Foreign Agricultural Service.

Potatoes are irradiated
with cobalt-60
in Hokkaido, Japan. Each
container carries 1.4
tons of potatoes
around the radiation
source (centre).
The exposure prevents
germination and rot,
thus permitting long-term
storage.

Early in the year the government abandoned a year-old nationalized wheat distribution program, designed originally to eliminate private traders and to stabilize wheat prices at low levels. Farmers had held back supplies, shortages developed, and the cost of wheat had risen dramatically. Distribution of foodstuffs to cities especially was inadequate, and food riots had erupted throughout the country.

Despite the failure of the nationalization program, fears that lack of government control would result in continuing food price rises seemed well founded. By fall, as rains failed and crop estimates became more gloomy, there were reports of widespread hunger and starvation. Tragically, hunger arose not only from lack of food but from lack of money. In some parts of the country market prices for rice doubled over a two-week period in early September. In October there was some relief as prices for grains, sugar, vegetable oils, and other essential items declined 10 to 20%. This appeared to be the result of strong government measures against smuggling and hoarding and of rainfall in several drought areas. Some economists, however, saw the declines as omens of recession. Massive food aid was needed. In October 1973 the Soviet Union had agreed to lend India two million metric tons of wheat. Beginning in April India purchased 1.8 million tons from other nations, chiefly the U.S., and an agreement providing at least one million tons of U.S. grain was announced in October.

Total food-grain output for July 1973–June 1974 rose significantly, to 103 million tons, but the favourable fall weather of 1973 did not continue into the new year. At 24 million–25 million tons, estimated coarse grain production for 1974–75 would be 10% below a year earlier. Wheat production was also expected to decline, from 24,923,000 tons to 22.5 million, but rice was expected to rise. Estimated 1973–74 production of major oilseeds was up 21% but still short of domestic demand. In March the Ministry of Commerce banned exports of Bengal Deshi cotton for the remainder of the 1973–74 season. Tea production in 1974 was expected to reach a record 480,000 tons.

Severe flooding in Bangladesh in July and August affected 20,000 sq.mi. and devastated the main rice crop. Unless farmers could replant in the fall, losses would reach one million tons or more. Initial estimates were that 80% of the summer crop was destroyed, along with seedlings planted for the main winter crop. Government officials estimated that at least 40% of the annual food output of 12 million tons was lost. Wheat production, forecast at 150,000 tons, was larger than the 90,000-ton 1973 crop but still painfully short of demand. Massive imports were needed to ensure average per capita consumption of 15–16 oz. per day. In October the U.S. agreed to send 100,000 tons of wheat and wheat flour and 50,000 tons of rice under Public Law 480. At least 50,000 tons of wheat had been shipped by year's end.

Government programs in Pakistan designed to encourage rice production appeared to have had some success. September projections for the 1974–75 crop were 3.8 million tons (rough basis), compared with 3.6 million tons in 1973–74. The 1974 wheat crop was projected at eight million tons. Pakistan looked toward self-sufficiency in wheat, though it still expected to import 500,000–700,000 tons to build stocks and to supply ration stores.

FAR EAST

Japan initiated a new program to increase agricultural production, expand grain and oilseed stocks, and expedite the diversification of supply sources. Soft wheat and soybean production were to be increased in order to balance domestic supply and demand for rice and to prevent fallow rice land from being brought back into production. Early indications were that rice land would decline by an additional 850,000 ac. in 1974. Conversion incentive payments were set at $535 per acre for annual crops and $610 per acre for permanent crops. Added to these were direct payments of $157 per ton for soybeans and $126 per ton for wheat, plus high guaranteed prices for both crops. Incentive payments were also scheduled for oats, corn (for silage), clover, and rye.

The northern regions of China experienced heavy rains in the fall of 1973 and an extremely dry winter. Early cold spells affected field operations in central and southern China, and subsequent unstable conditions indicated lower crop production. Weather conditions in most other parts of Asia were generally favourable. The Philippines were an exception, as mid-October typhoons on Luzon caused approximately $18 million damage to rice crops.

Preliminary reports indicated a 1974–75 world rice crop slightly below the year-earlier record of 309.8 million metric tons (paddy). Thailand forecast a decline of about 300,000 tons as a result of drought during the planting season, and Burma expected a decline of about 300,000 tons. Partly offsetting these losses were improved production in northern and eastern Asia, bumper crops in Indonesia, and gains in Sri Lanka. South Vietnam expected some improvement.

In the early fall China announced that its grain production was adequate to feed the nation's 800 million people. Reports varied, but mid-September estimates released in Peking were for a 1974 grain crop of 250 million tons. Late reports indicated a 1974 rice crop of nearly 103 million tons, the same as the 1973 record. Wheat was forecast at 27.7 million tons, a slight decline from 1973 but well above 1972 levels. Nonetheless, large wheat purchases were negotiated with Canada (75 million bu.) and Australia (one million tons). This brought total committed wheat imports for 1974–75 to 5,650,000 tons. During 1973–74 China imported approximately $1 billion in farm products from the U.S. In June it canceled orders for 48 million bu. of U.S. corn and shifted to a purchase of $121 million worth of soybeans.

continued on page 68

World Production and Trade of Principal Grains
In 000 metric tons

	Wheat Production 1961-65 average	Wheat Production 1973	Wheat Imports−/Exports+ 1970-73 average	Barley Production 1961-65 average	Barley Production 1973	Barley Imports−/Exports+ 1970-73 average	Oats Production 1961-65 average	Oats Production 1973	Oats Imports−/Exports+ 1970-73 average	Rye Production 1961-65 average	Rye Production 1973	Rye Imports−/Exports+ 1970-73 average	Corn (Maize) Production 1961-65 average	Corn (Maize) Production 1973	Corn (Maize) Imports−/Exports+ 1970-73 average	Rice Production 1961-65 average	Rice Production 1973	Rice Imports−/Exports+ 1970-73 average
World total	254,302	377,055	−51,840* / +53,333*	99.703	165,505	−11,365* / +11,572*	47,818	56,896	−1,720* / +1,741*	33,833	29,753	−687* / +770*	216,617	312,567	−31,689* / +32,226*	253,065	321,079	−8,065* / +7,861*
EUROPE																		
Austria	704	917	−45 / +3*	563	1,011	−40	322	281	−27	393	430	−2	197	850	−64 / +1*	—	—	−55
Belgium	826	c.900	−1,227 / +261†	485	660	−871† / +145†	389	240	−70* / +5†	120	63	−8† / +4†	2	c.25	−1,452† / +443*†	—	—	−60† / +21†
Bulgaria	2,213	c.3,014	−104‡ / +295*	694	c.1,440	−40*	141	c.70	—	58	c.20	—	1,601	c.2,850	−16* / +237*	36	60§	−2* / +2*
Czechoslovakia	1,779	c.4,300	−1,159*	1,556	c.2,980	−128* / +47*	792	c.670	—	897	c.570	−137*	474	c.690	−370*	—	—	−c.76*
Denmark	535	520	−9 / +77*	3,506	5,450	−182 / +199	713	460	−32 / +14	380	140	−19*	—	—	−255 / +1*	—	—	−12 / +1*
Finland	448	462	−21 / +70*	400	992	−14 / +20*	828	1,169	+92*	141	124	−18	—	—	−14	—	—	−14
France	12,495	17,792	−308 / +4,902	6,594	10,844	−6 / +3,405	2,583	2,203	+159	367	327	−7 / +51	2,760	10,635	−379 / +3,369	120	71	−117 / +9
Germany, East	1,357	c.2,800	−1,984* / +8*	1,291	c.2,500	−415*	850	c.850	—	1,741	c.1,670	−40*	3	27§	−614*	—	—	−40*
Germany, West	4,607	7,134	−2,424 / +736	3,462	6,622	−1,721 / +404	2,185	3,045	−545 / +18	3,028	2,574	−60 / +204	55	573	−3,163 / +186*	—	—	−165 / +28
Greece	1,765	1,738	−3 / +48*	248	856	−3* / +6*	143	102	—	19	c.9§	—	241	656	−330*	87	c.82	−1* / +9*
Hungary	2,020	4,500	−214 / +325*	969	876	−194* / +6*	108	70	−7*	271	176	−23* / +12*	3,350	c.6,000	−64* / +137*	36	c.65	−16*
Ireland	343	215	−144	575	900	−81	357	155	−10	1	c.1§	—	20	c.14§	−211	—	—	−3
Italy	8,857	8,958	−1,522 / +207	276	448	−1,181 / +3*	545	425	−181 / +2*	87	39	−1*	3,633	5,052	−4,646 / +14	612	970	−13 / +345
Netherlands, The	606	725	−1,570 / +495	390	383	−184 / +142	421	134	−90 / +81	312	105	−28 / +40	c.1	10§	−2,897 / +449*	—	—	−67 / +23
Norway	19	12§	−393	440	530	−156 / +2	126	320	−2	3	5§	−58	—	—	−95	—	—	−6
Poland	2,988	c.5,900	−1,455*	1,368	c.3,400	−1,014* / +111*	2,641	c.3,000	+17*	7,466	c.8,300	−76† / +29*	20	c.14§	−294*	—	—	−68*
Portugal	550	489	−235	61	55§	−92*	87	76	—	176	124	−15*	560	533	−603	167	180	−12
Romania	4,321	c.5,300	+166*	415	c.820	−117*	154	c.110	—	95	c.45	—	5,853	c.9,000	−70* / +374*	40	c.63	−42*
Spain	4,365	3,948	−64* / +79	1,959	4,433	−59* / +7*	447	429	−23*	385	269	—	1,101	2,019	−2,254 / +3*	387	378	+53
Sweden	909	1,255	−25 / +271	1,167	1,804	−7*	1,304	1,380	−1* / +291	142	321	−2* / +76	14	c.100§	−35	—	—	−15
Switzerland	355	c.390	−436	102	c.200	−449	40	c.35	−175	52	c.48	−33	14	c.100§	−227	—	—	−22
U.S.S.R.	64,207	109,700	−c.6,900 / +5,037	20,318	c.52,000	−740* / +410*	6,052	c.20,000	−217* / +1,556*	15,093	c.12,000	−13* / +127*	13,122	13,400	−1,428	390	1,770	+12*
United Kingdom	3,520	5,007	−4,391 / +10	6,668	8,993	−831 / +126	1,531	1,087	−15 / +43	21	16	−35	—	—	−3,153 / +11*	—	—	−135 / +2*
Yugoslavia	3,599	4,703	−c.390* / +3*	557	540	−107*	343	275	−13*	169	125	—	5,618	7,800	+130*	23	31§	−16* / +1*
ASIA																		
Burma	38	27§	—	—	—	—	—	—	—	—	—	—	58	c.80§	+12*	7,786	c.8,580	+637*
Cambodia	170		+16*													2,461	953	+117‡
China	c.22,230	c.35,000	−c.5,140	c.14,700	c.19,500	−c.300*	c.1,690	c.2,700	—	—	—	—	c.22,756	c.29,700	−c.580*	c.86,038	c.107,000	−c.8 / +c.885*
India	11,191	24,923	−c.2,180	2,590	2,327	—	—	—	—	—	—	—	4,593	c.6,500	−5*	52,752	c.67,500	−192* / +19*
Indonesia	—	—	−388*	—	—	—	—	—	—	—	—	—	2,804	c.2,500	+c.114*	12,393	c.20,321	−728*
Iran	2,873	c.4,775	−429*	792	c.1,200	−64*	—	—	—	—	—	—	c.16	c.25§	−41*	851	1,500	−c.49*
Iraq	849	957	−378* / +50*	851	c.1,100	+32*	—	—	—	—	—	—	2	c.16§	−2*	137	c.240	−49‡
Japan	1,332	203	−5,022	1,380	216	−990	145	45	−161	2	c.1§	−138	97	29§	−6,212	16,444	15,580	−15 / +546
Korea, South	277	257	−1,551*	1,419	2,110	−144*	—	—	−4*	37	c.16	—	26	54§	−325*	4,809	5,730	−836*
Malaysia	—	—	−340 / +1*	—	—	−6*	—	—	—	—	—	—	c.9	c.13§	−218*	1,141	c.1,940	−291* / +4*
Pakistan	4,152	7,442	−402* / +59†	118	109	—	—	—	—	—	—	—	514	c.700	−3*	1,825	c.3,810	−c.18* / +c.458
Philippines	—	—	−598*	—	—	−2*	—	—	—	—	—	—	1,305	c.2,200	−73*	3,957	5,550	−290*
Syria	1,093	593	−421* / +50*	649	102	−67‡ / +72*	3	3§	—	—	—	—	7	15§	−1*	1	1∥	−48*
Thailand	—	—	−57*	—	—	—	—	—	—	—	—	—	815	c.2,500	−5* / +1,632*	11,267	c.14,200	+1,400
Turkey	8,585	10,082	−445	3,447	2,900	+19*	495	376	—	734	700	—	950	1,040	−3*	222	203§	−6*
Vietnam, South	—	—	−145*	—	—	−c.7*	—	—	—	—	—	—	39	c.35§	−c.93*	5,029	c.6,500	−366*
AFRICA																		
Algeria	1,254	c.1,100	−627*	476	c.450	−c.43*	28	c.30	+2*	—	—	—	5	c.6§	−18* / +130*	7	c.5§	−8*
Egypt	1,459	c.1,840	−c.1,960	137	c.110	−26*	15	c.20§	−1*	—	—	—	1,913	c.2,400	−67*	1,845	c.2,680	+542*
Kenya	122	c.185§	−26* / +25	15	c.20§	—	2	4§	—	—	—	—	c.1,100	c.1,300	−14* / +63	14	30§	−7*
Morocco	1,336	1,897	−474*	1,316	913	−5* / +42*	18	c.17	—	2	c.2§	—	352	221	+3*	20	13§	+3*
South Africa	840	1,607	−47 / +6*	37	36§	−16*	117	103	−1*	11	7	−2*	5,229	4,300	−51 / +1,788	c.2	c.3§	−83 / +2*
Tunisia	446	690	−330* / +4*	145	210	−8* / +3*	6	c.14	—	—	—	—	—	—	−19*	—	—	−2*
NORTH AMERICA																		
Canada	15,364	17,112	+12,434	3,860	10,333	+3,680	6,075	5,041	+172	319	363	+213	1,072	2,767	−492 / +11*	—	—	−60
Mexico	1,549	1,980	−273† / +63‡	175	c.300	−1* / +7*	76	c.35	−17*	—	—	—	7,369	9,500	−317* / +234*	314	c.475	−6* / +4*
United States	33,040	46,576	−15 / +23,076¶	8,676	9,244	−244* / +1,375	13,847	9,636	−30 / +334	828	671	−9 / +236	95,561	143,344	−49 / +20,712¶	3,084	4,210	−32* / +1,708
SOUTH AMERICA																		
Argentina	7,541	6,500	+1,913	679	750	+103	676	515	+160	422	432	+31	4,984	9,700	−1* / +4,681	193	260	+61
Bolivia	48	c.70§	−26*	61	c.65§	—	c.11§	c.11§	—	—	—	—	254	c.260§	—	43	c.75§	
Brazil	574	1,800	−1,817*	26	c.26§	−32*	20	c.28	−23*	17	c.21	—	10,112	c.15,338	−2* / +976*	6,123	c.8,200	−14* / +82*
Chile	1,082	747	−470*	74	107	+12*	89	109	+6‡	7	8	—	206	294	−348*	84	86§	−43*
Colombia	118	79§	−345*	106	c.115	−40*	—	—	−6*	—	—	—	827	c.1,000	−2* / +3*	576	c.1,100	−c.15*
Peru	150	149	−692*	185	c.165	−14*	3	c.1§	—	c.1	c.1§	—	490	c.645	−38*	324	427	+57
Uruguay	465	c.400	−42* / +27*	30	28§	+14*	72	c.59	−1*	—	—	—	148	229	—	67	128§	
Venezuela	1	c.1	−673*	—	—	—	—	—	−10*	—	—	—	477	c.700	−121*	136	c.250	−2* / +20*
OCEANIA																		
Australia	8,222	11,500	+7,071	978	2,132	+1,058	1,172	1,361	+292	11	c.25	—	169	188	−1*	136	316	+146
New Zealand	248	420	−36* / +22*	98	261	−14*	34	49	—	—	—	—	16	135§	—	—	—	−5*

Note: (—) indicates quantity nil or negligible. (c.) indicates provisional or estimated. *1970-72 average. †Belgium-Luxembourg economic union. ‡1970-71 average. §1972. ∥1970. ¶Including foreign aid shipments. ¶1966.

Sources: FAO *Monthly Bulletin of Agricultural Economics and Statistics; FAO Production Yearbook 1972; FAO Trade Yearbook 1972;* Commonwealth Secretariat, *Grain Bulletin, Rice Bulletin.*

(M. C. MacDONALD)

THE SAHEL DROUGHT

By Martin Walker

The great West African drought was a disaster that took the world by surprise. Yet it was no sudden act of God, no overnight buildup of thunderclouds, hurricane, or typhoon, but the result of a long process of ecological rape and political mismanagement that could have been predicted some years before the news first broke in 1973.

It is easier to understand these failings if we remember the remoteness of the Sahel lands where the tragedy began. The Sahel (the name comes from the Arabic word meaning shore) is the boundary between the true desert of the vast Sahara and the beginning of the fertile lands and forests that stretch down to the West African coast. The Sahel, therefore, is essentially an area of marginal land, supporting Tuareg and Fulani nomads with their camels and cattle in the north, and thousands of villages, dependent on subsistence crops of millet, maize, and sorghum, in the south.

The Sahel region stretches from the Atlantic Ocean on the west through Mauritania, Mali, Upper Volta, Niger, and Chad to the very centre of the African continent. Much of Senegal, Ghana, Cameroon, Nigeria, and the Central African Republic is also Sahelian in ecology, and it can be argued that the Ethiopian drought formed the eastern flank of the great dry belt that extended across Africa by 1974. UN Secretary-General Kurt Waldheim estimated in March 1974 that as many as 25 million Africans were directly affected—and this in one of the least densely populated parts of the earth.

Causative Factors. The human roots of the problem go back to 1960, when France began to give independence to its West African colonies. A handful of tiny countries, none economically viable and all more or less dependent on French budgetary and administrative aid, were left with a highly centralized, French-style civil service in a region where slow communications impeded administration. Without census, tax roll, or statistics, the embryonic nations began the daunting task of development.

The first decade of independence began well, with eight years of good rains. International aid provided new wells, brought vaccination programs for the cattle and the nomads, and the growing economies of the coastal nations like Nigeria and Ivory Coast provided ready markets for the expanding herds. In short, the 1960s saw a population explosion among the Sahel's human and animal inhabitants, until in 1968 bad rains served the first warning that the fragile ecological balance of the desert shore could not support so much life. Few cattle died in that year, but around most of the new wells there were great swathes of dead land where the cattle and goats between them had overgrazed until not a tree or bush or blade of grass remained. The governments of the Sahel, meanwhile, were wondering what to do about the "nomad problem." The nomads, culturally different from the settled blacks of the south who dominated politics, had little time for tax collectors and less for the man-made national frontiers that cut across their traditional trading routes. Sporadic guerrilla warfare plagued the Sahel throughout the 1960s.

Martin Walker is a journalist on the staff of The Guardian, *London. He visited the Sahel region in 1973 and 1974 and his reports on conditions south of the Sahara were notable for their clarity and perception.*

Equally shortsighted were the relatively rich neighbours of the Sahel nations, the fast-developing coastal countries of Ivory Coast, Ghana, and Nigeria, who took up to 40% of the young adult males of the Sahel countries and the bulk of their only export—livestock—without ever attempting to integrate their economies. Nomads from Niger have to drive their cattle down the long trail to the slaughterhouses of northern Nigeria, where they are paid in Nigerian money. Since this money cannot be spent in Niger, they buy Nigerian goods (at inflated prices) and smuggle them home. In 1973, according to an estimate of the European Development Fund, two-thirds of Niger's peanut exports had been "imported" from Nigeria.

Flight from the Desert. The greatest tragedy of the Sahel came after the disastrous year of 1972, when almost no rain fell. The vast cattle herds had devoured what little desert pasture there was by December. The herds moved south, to the Niger River and to the Senegal, where they were met by angry peasants whose own crops had failed. By May 1974 the mighty Senegal was salt 250 km. from the sea, so feeble was its flow. The dry riverbeds were choked with the dead cattle of Mauritania (herd loss 70%), Mali (55%), Niger (80%), and Chad (70%). With the dwindling herds came a swelling mass of refugees. The town of Rosso on the Senegal grew from 8,000 to 40,000 within the space of six weeks.

The first warnings of the disaster had reached the UN Food and Agriculture Organization in Rome in October 1972, but there was no effective means of evaluating the scale of the emergency until the herds and refugees began to reach the major centres in early 1973. Nor were the local governments eager to undermine their precarious authority by admitting to the world that their people were starving. By June 1973 the nature of the crisis was beginning to emerge. Between half and two-thirds of the cattle herds were dead, and the bulk of the survivors had trekked far to the south. The nomads who had driven their cattle south had left families and dependents in the north, where at least two million scattered people were in desperate need of food aid. Another million peasants from the marginal villages had fled to the cities and were living in makeshift, disease-prone encampments. Behind them a vast tract of land was now bereft of trees, of desert scrub, of pasture, and of the hardy Sahel vegetation that traditionally held back the desert. In 1973 there were places where the Sahara advanced southward up to 100 km.

The nomads and peasants of the Sahel are a hardy people, accustomed to deprivation and disease. Even in the good years of the 1960s, infant mortality among the Tuareg rarely fell below 50%. But some of the new diseases that came with the refugees led to disaster. In the remote villages of the Aïr Massif, in northern Niger, about half the school-age children perished in a measles outbreak. In Mauritania, in 1974, influenza and chicken pox were the killers. In Chad diphtheria was widespread. When the FAO's regional administrator, Moise Mensah, visited northern Chad in mid-1973, he was asked by local chiefs not to send any vaccine, because diphtheria would bring a faster and more merciful death than starvation.

There will never be any wholly reliable statistics of how many people died in 1973 because of the drought. The Carnegie Endowment report, *Disaster in the Desert,* by two individuals with no first-hand experience of the disaster, estimated the death toll at 100,000. The Sahel countries' own coordinating office placed it at not less than 50,000. The truth probably lies between the two figures, and the toll for 1974 was probably similar. Of greater long-term importance is the effect of malnutrition, which will blight the children who did survive for the rest of their lives. One British journalist reported that the only children he had seen alive in a series of nomad encampments were deformed or suffering from speech and motor impediments.

The immediate result for the Sahel nations was economic disruption, further weakening their already frail economies. Before the drought, Upper Volta had a per capita gross national product of $55, and the inhabitants of Niger had an average annual income of $85. In Niger the decimation of the cattle herds instantly removed that 35% of the tax base which came from the head tax on the nomads' animals. By late 1973 the international oil crisis was adding its own savage financial effects.

International Aid: Difficulties and Delays. When the cattle died in 1973 they were eaten—a major contributory factor in the mixture of luck and muddle that staved off mass starvation. An international airlift of essential supplies was organized from May onward. Pres. Hamani Diori of Niger later pointed out that the cost of the airlift in his own country would have paid for the irrigation of 11,000 ha. of land near the Niger River that could have produced the 110,000 tons of food Niger needed. In Mali the team of three U.S. Hercules transport aircraft expended one ton of aviation fuel for every ton of food they flew to the worst-hit area. In Chad it took 19 tons of aviation fuel to fly in one ton of medical supplies. And the aviation fuel had to compete with food for the available rail transport.

The distribution of the 550,000 tons of food aid donated in 1973 fell into three stages. First, transport to the few overloaded ports of West Africa. In Dakar, Senegal, grain that had arrived in July was still stored on the docks as late as November, soaked and partly ruined by the rainy season. The second stage involved moving the food from the ports to the regional centres. The Dakar–Mali railroad was the vital link, moving up to 10,000 tons a month. But both road and rail transport ceased to be reliable after the rains began to wash out the dirt tracks and undermine the railway lines. The third stage of distribution, from regional centre to famine area and refugee camp, depended on trucks. In the Sahel, UN officials were reporting that the life of a modern truck was about 1,000 hours because of the desert conditions and lack of maintenance facilities.

In September 1973 an FAO investigating committee estimated that 650,000 tons of food would be needed for 1974, which meant that distribution from the ports had to begin in January if all the food was to reach the affected areas before the rains came. The Sahel governments themselves put their food needs at 1.2 million tons. Bureaucratic and budgetary delays at the FAO in Rome and the U.S. Agency for International Development headquarters in Washington meant that 1974 food shipments did not begin to arrive in great quantity until late March. The situation was saved, ironically, by the spread of the drought into Nigeria, where it cut the peanut crop by 60%. This freed the vast Nigerian truck fleet. Over 400 Nigerian trucks were hired by the FAO in early June and used as a nonstop shuttle to the Sahel, moving up to 50,000 tons of food each month.

It was in 1974 that the political whirlwind was reaped. In Niger the social strains of the drought, combined with a political crisis, led to a military coup that overthrew the civilian government of President Diori in April. In Ethiopia the drought brought a sudden acceleration of social unrest and dissatisfaction that led to Emperor Haile Selassie's final downfall in September.

Rehabilitation or Resettlement? Research into climatic changes that had brought on the drought pointed to a long-term, fundamental climatic shift that would render much of the Sahel uninhabitable within two decades. The study, collated at the Massachusetts Institute of Technology, was cited by the U.S. delegate to the July conference of the UN Economic and Social Council. He argued that emergency food aid must continue, but long-term attempts to irrigate or rehabilitate the Sahel would be doomed to failure.

The evidence for this long-term climatic change is not yet conclusive, but it is strong enough to remove the expensive option, urged by the Sahel governments, of a billion-dollar investment in irrigation and restocking of the region. Increasingly, the aid agencies and the Sahel governments are beginning to accept the fact that the nomad way of life may have come to an end. Much of the nomads' economic role in camel-borne trade (particularly of salt) has been taken over by trucks, and the expansion of the desert has significantly reduced the amount of grazing land left to them. If expansion of the Sahara continues then the way of the Tuareg could be doomed and the proud, impoverished nomads forced to become resettled cultivators.

But at least some lessons have been learned. Notice has been served on the third world that rural development must never overstrain the local ecological balance. And the international food agencies, accustomed to providing relief in countries such as India with effective distribution systems, have learned not to send food that will rot before it can be delivered. Above all, in the year when world food reserves fell to an all-time low, the threat of further disaster in the Sahel helped to concentrate the minds of the international community on the need to prepare for what Paul Ehrlich has called "the decade of famine."

Refugees search for wind-scattered grain in the sand at a food distribution site in the Sahel.

A chopper-harvester cuts through a field of sugarcane in Queensland, Austr. The Australian sugar industry, concentrated on the Queensland coast, is almost entirely mechanized.

continued from page 64

Thailand's corn production was forecast at three million tons for 1974–75, a substantial gain over year-earlier levels of 2,350,000 tons. There was speculation that corn might eventually replace rice as Thailand's main agricultural export. Corn production in the Philippines rose to an estimated 2,350,000 tons, but imports of wheat, corn, and rice were expected to rise as domestic needs increased and an effort was made to maintain adequate stock levels. South Korea announced production goals of 458,000 tons of oilseeds for 1974, a 56% increase over 1973.

World production of palm oil in 1974 was forecast at 2.6 million tons (oil equivalent), up 13% from 1973. Philippine copra production, at an estimated 1,120,000 tons (in oil), would account for nearly half the total. Philippine copra and coconut oil exports fell 44% during the first six months of 1974. In August the government moved to create a marketing board to sustain the prevailing price—at 400% above the traditional level—and to maintain the country's predominant market position. However, by late August, Philippine copra prices on European markets fell to a low $630 per ton. Philippine export prices, shipping charges, and export taxes discouraged exporters, and supplies began to increase at a rate of 50,000 tons a month above processing capacity. Indonesia, as the second largest producer of copra, forecast 1974 output at 567,000 tons, 2% more than a year earlier.

Tea production in Sri Lanka totaled 108,421 tons in 1974, 5% below the same period a year earlier. Total production for 1974 was forecast at 210,000 tons, a sharp decline from the 1965–69 average of 223,100 tons. South Korea's mushroom harvest was indicated at 46.3 million lb., a 30% decline from 1973; the loss was blamed on increased production costs. Taiwan's 1973 canned pineapple pack rose 6% to 3.2 million standard cases (45 lb. net); production for 1974 was set at four million cases.

According to midyear estimates, cattle and hog numbers rose in Asian nations in 1974. Late 1973 reports from the New China News Agency described a 4.5-fold increase in hog numbers, from 57.8 million in 1949 to nearly 260 million in 1972. The USDA estimated China's hog numbers at 234,890,000. Japan's June hog inventory stood at 7.8 million, reflecting steadily increasing pork consumption in that country. Japan continued to import pork and pork products, and in May a contract to purchase 150,000 market hogs was negotiated with a Canadian packing company. South Korea appeared to be making progress in developing its dairy industry. The dairy cattle population had grown from 2,000 head in 1965 to 17,000 in 1972, and milk production had risen correspondingly.

OCEANIA

Australia. Recovery from drought marked the 1973–74 crop year. Despite heavy rains and flooding in some areas, crops were as much as 25% above a year earlier and total agricultural output rose 6.6%. The wheat harvest nearly doubled to an estimated 12,045,-000 metric tons, although some 1.8 million tons were reported to be "off-grade" as a result of rain-induced root rot and rust disease. Deliveries of wheat to the Australian Wheat Board totaled 11,067,191 tons, of which approximately 5.4 million tons were exported in the July 1973–June 1974 period. Wheat stocks at the end of June 1974 were estimated at 5.2 million tons, higher than a year earlier but considerably below the 12,299,000 tons held in 1970.

The 1973–74 feed-grains harvests were estimated at 4.8 million tons, a third more than the drought-damaged coarse grains crops of a year earlier. Barley totaled 2,467,000 tons; oats, 1,160,000 tons; and corn, 157,000 tons. Some rust-affected wheat acreages in Victoria and South Australia would probably be planted to barley in 1974–75, and larger barley plantings were expected in Western Australia. The 1973–74 sorghum harvest was estimated at 995,000 tons, but the outlook for 1974–75 was clouded by the large quantity of off-grade wheat available for cattle feed.

Forecasts of livestock numbers in January 1974 were higher than a year earlier. Cattle numbers, at 31.5 million head, were up by 8%; sheep numbers, at 143 million, by 2%; and hogs at 3,250,000, were slightly higher. Total red meat production in 1973 fell slightly to an estimated 2,327,800 tons, although beef and veal production rose 13%. Lamb and mutton continued a three-year decline. U.S. imports of Australian meat fell 7% in the first six months of 1974. In October Australia joined with 11 other meat-exporting countries to protest the EEC ban on beef imports. With the dairy industry facing major overproduction of butterfat, the government established a $42 million adjustment program to encourage whole milk deliveries and diversification.

Table XIV. Production of Meats in Principal Producing Countries
In 000 metric tons, carcass-weight basis

Country	Beef and veal 1973*	1972	Average 1964–68	Pork (excluding lard) 1973*	1972	Average 1964–68	Mutton, lamb, and goat meat 1973*	1972	Average 1964–68
Argentina	2,152.0	2,198.0	2,283.8	300.0	244.0	199.8	135.2	133.7	181.8
Australia	1,493.6	1,320.9	940.6	234.7	211.3	137.8	599.5	865.7	616.6
Belgium-Luxembourg	267.0	267.0	230.2	586.4	538.9	279.0	2.8	2.8	3.0
Brazil	2,450.0	2,020.0	1,517.2	700.6	645.2	532.6	58.4	57.6	54.0
Canada	896.5	897.6	853.0	617.1	631.7	493.8	9.9	9.0	10.6
Colombia	405.6	454.1	360.8	91.7	86.2	68.2	3.7	3.8	3.8
Denmark	185.5	171.0	186.4	772.6	765.8	722.6	0.7	1.1	2.0
France	1,454.0	1,455.0	1,492.8	1,388.0	1,386.0	1,219.0	131.0	132.0	115.4
Germany, West	1,193.0	1,203.0	1,183.4	2,237.0	2,354.0	1,962.0	11.0	11.0	11.6
Italy	710.0	753.0	661.6	552.0	528.0	458.2	41.0	43.0	39.0
Japan	226.0	294.7	179.0	840.0	769.1	448.6	0.7	0.9	1.6
Mexico	642.6	592.5	469.2	388.6	394.7	227.0	54.8	53.0	59.0
Netherlands, The	258.7	268.5	268.8	769.7	743.3	504.6	9.5	10.7	8.6
New Zealand	428.9	421.1	303.6	29.3	42.0	40.6	537.6	563.4	508.0
Poland	536.4	499.9	458.8	1,223.9	1,098.8	874.4	27.6	24.6	24.2
South Africa	542.9	556.9	447.2	98.0	84.5	57.8	108.9	132.9	133.4
Spain	350.0	302.6	211.4	595.0	461.0	357.2	145.0	137.0	131.8
U.S.S.R.	5,487.0	5,363.3	4,182.8	3,515.0	3,768.8	2,804.0	950.0	880.7	969.6
United Kingdom	875.9	908.9	880.4	1,006.9	1,008.9	872.8	235.7	219.5	255.8
United States	9,787.7	10,374.2	9,296.6	5,738.5	6,180.7	5,501.0	232.7	246.3	296.2
Yugoslavia	267.5	260.0	264.4	441.1	454.8	412.0	60.0	60.0	52.8

*Preliminary.
Source: U.S. Department of Agriculture, Foreign Agricultural Service.

Australia's 1974 wool clip produced an estimated 772,000 tons, greasy basis, an increase of 10% from the low production of 1973 but 7% below average. Exports of wool for the 1973–74 season were estimated at 587,269 tons, a decrease from 760,457 tons a year earlier. World wool production in 1973–74 was estimated at 2,611,900 tons, greasy basis, 4.5% above a year earlier but somewhat less than the 1965–69 average. World prices had reached their highest levels in 20 years in the first quarter of 1973, but they subsequently declined as monetary instability and energy shortages reduced mill consumption. The average prices of Australian wools on the world market fell as much as 30% in late 1973 and early 1974, and in the July auctions at Sydney the Australian Wool Corporation, apparently to prevent further erosion, bought a reported 200,000 bales, two-thirds of the first offering from the 1974 clip, presumably at prices equal to or above the intervention price of A$2.50 per kilogram. The corporation subsequently postponed auctions planned for August until further government financial support could be obtained.

New Zealand. Agricultural production declined about 4% in 1973–74. Crop production fell an estimated 3.5%, and livestock output was 3.7% below a year earlier. Grain harvests declined approximately 13%, reflecting the government's emphasis on livestock and livestock products. A low ceiling price on wheat contributed to a smaller harvest, reported at 245,000 metric tons. Barley production continued to decline; 1973–74 production of 208,000 tons was 16% below the 1968–72 average. Production of feed grains increased, however.

Livestock numbers as of Jan. 1, 1974, reflected the effects of drought. Sheep numbers fell slightly to 56.8 million head, and hog numbers, at 409,000 head, were down sharply. Cattle numbers rose slightly to an estimated 9.2 million head. Production of mutton and lamb fell more than 4%, as lower weights and lambing rates prevented sheep farmers from taking advantage of higher prices. Milk production decreased slightly to 13,561,000,000 lb., largely as a result of drought conditions, and dairy exports fell as the world supply situation improved. Wool production in 1974 rose to an estimated 304,500 tons, greasy basis, marking a return to pre-drought levels. Wool exports, estimated at 245,159 tons, were more than 20% below 1972–73.

(HARVEY R. SHERMAN; FRANCES G. ROBBINS)

See also Alcoholic Beverages; Commercial and Trade Policies; Commodity Trade; Cooperatives; Environment; Fisheries; Food Processing; Gardening; Industrial Production and Technology; Prices; United Nations. [451.B.1.c; 534.E; 731; 10/37.C]

ENCYCLOPÆDIA BRITANNICA FILMS. *Problems of Conservation—Soil* (1969); *Problems of Conservation—Our Natural Resources* (1970); *The Farmer in a Changing America* (1973).

Albania

A people's republic in the western Balkan Peninsula, Albania is on the Adriatic Sea, bordered by Greece and Yugoslavia. Area: 11,100 sq.mi. (28,748 sq.km.). Pop. (1973 est.): 2,315,000. Cap. and largest city: Tirana (pop., 1971 est., 174,800). Language: Albanian. Religion: Muslim, Orthodox, Roman Catholic. First secretary of the Albanian (Communist) Party of Labour in 1974, Enver Hoxha; president of the Presidium of the

ALBANIA
Education. (1971–72) Primary, pupils 579,759, teachers 20,555; secondary (including vocational and teacher training), pupils 95,796, teachers 3,030; higher (including Tirana University), students 28,668, teachers 1,153.
Finance. Monetary unit: lek, with (Sept. 16, 1974) an official exchange rate of 4 leks to U.S. $1 (free rate of 10.10 leks = £1 sterling) and a noncommercial (tourist) rate of 10.25 leks to U.S. $1 (free rate of 23.25 leks = £1 sterling). Budget (1970 est.): revenue 5,247,000,000 leks; expenditure 4,937,000,000 leks.
Foreign Trade. (1964) Imports 490.6 million leks; exports 299,620,000 leks. Import sources: China 63%; Czechoslovakia 10%; Poland 8%. Export destinations: China 40%; Czechoslovakia 19%; East Germany 10%; Poland 10%. Main exports: fuels, minerals, and metals (including crude oil, iron ore, chrome ore, and copper chemicals) 54%; foodstuffs (including vegetables, wine, and fruit) 23%; raw materials (including tobacco and wool) 17%.
Transport and Communications. Roads (motorable; 1960) 3,100 km. Motor vehicles in use (1970): passenger *c.* 3,500; commercial (including buses) *c.* 11,200. Railways: (1972) *c.* 201 km.; traffic (1969) 220.4 million passenger-km., freight 230 million net ton-km. Shipping (1973): merchant vessels 100 gross tons and over 57,068. Shipping traffic (1970): goods loaded *c.* 2.1 million metric tons, unloaded *c.* 670,000 metric tons. Telephones (Dec. 1963) 10,150. Radio receivers (Dec. 1972) 170,000. Television receivers (Dec. 1972) 3,000.
Agriculture. Production (in 000; metric tons; 1972; 1971 in parentheses): corn 300 (270); wheat *c.* 250 (*c.* 230); oats *c.* 16 (*c.* 15); cotton, lint *c.* 8 (*c.* 7); sugar, raw value *c.* 19 (*c.* 18); potatoes *c.* 140 (*c.* 140); wine *c.* 10 (*c.* 10); tobacco *c.* 13 (*c.* 13). Livestock (in 000; Dec. 1972): sheep *c.* 1,590; cattle *c.* 444; pigs *c.* 154; goats *c.* 1,300; poultry *c.* 1,800.
Industry. Production (in 000; metric tons; 1972): crude oil 1,569; lignite (1971) 675; petroleum products (1971) 968; chrome ore (oxide content; 1971) 230; iron ore (1970) *c.* 540; copper ore (metal content) 7; cement (1971) 360; electricity (kw-hr.; 1971) 1,104,000.

People's Assembly, Haxhi Leshi; chairman of the Council of Ministers (premier), Mehmet Shehu.

On Nov. 29, 1973, on the occasion of Albania's National Day, the Moscow daily *Pravda*, the chief organ of the Communist Party of the Soviet Union, had published an editorial suggesting that Soviet-Albanian relations should become normal once more. The editorial indicated that the basis for such a relationship could be found in mutual respect for national sovereignty, territorial integrity, nonintervention in domestic affairs, and economic cooperation. Difficulties in Soviet-Albanian relations, which had arisen in December 1961 when Moscow severed diplomatic relations with Tirana, were considered by the Soviet government as short-term passing problems.

This offer to renew Soviet-Albanian diplomatic relations was by no means the first since the rupture of 1961. It was also reiterated on Jan. 16, 1974, when the official Soviet news agency Tass distributed an article from the foreign affairs weekly review *Novoye Vremya* claiming that the time had come to end the abnormal situation existing between the two countries. According to a report from Belgrade, Yugos., Hoxha rejected—as he had on previous occasions—an official Soviet invitation to renew diplomatic relations that was extended at about the same time. He stated that relations between the two countries could be restored to normality only when the people of the Soviet Union reestablished a true Marxist-Leninist regime.

On Oct. 3, 1974, Hoxha announced that Albania wished to establish friendly relations with Yugoslavia and Greece, though not yet with Bulgaria; he indicated that diplomatic relations could also be set up with Great Britain and West Germany, but were out of the question with the U.S. and the U.S.S.R.

Aircraft:
see Defense; Industrial Production and Technology; Transportation

Air Forces:
see Defense

Early in September it was reported that Col. Gen. Beqir Balluku, defense minister since 1953, had been removed from his post. A possible explanation lay in a speech General Balluku had delivered several months earlier in which, contrary to the party line, he had said that the U.S. and the Soviet Union did not represent equal threats to the country. After the election of the new National Assembly in October, Premier Mehmet Shehu took over the job of defense minister. A report from Vienna in May 1974 stated that 80-year-old Monsignor Damian, head of the Albanian Orthodox Church and archbishop of Tirana, had died in November 1973. He had been imprisoned since 1967, when all churches and mosques in Albania were closed in an effort to make Albania the first "atheist state in the world."

On May 21 a bomb exploded in the Albanian embassy in Rome, causing considerable damage but no injuries, and three other bombs were found. In an energetic note of protest delivered to the Italian embassy in Tirana by the Albanian Ministry of Foreign Affairs, the incident was blamed on "fascist provocation" aimed at disturbing relations between the two countries.   (K. M. SMOGORZEWSKI)

[972.B.3]

Alcoholic Beverages

Beer. The prevailing upward trend in world beer production continued even more strongly in 1973, encouraged by particularly good "beer weather" in most of the important beer-producing areas. An increase of 42 million hectolitres (hl.) brought total production to over 730 million hl. (1 hl. = about 26 gal.). Rates of increase throughout the world were: Western Europe 5.6%, Eastern Europe 3.9%, North America 3.6%, Central and South America 12.6%, Africa 15.3%, Australia and Oceania 4.9%.

To judge from data available for the first eight months of 1974, a further rise in the world average rate of increase of at least 5% over the previous year could be expected. While the increase in Western Europe was unlikely to be as marked as in 1973, in North America it was expected to be significantly greater. In the period from January to August 1974, U.S. breweries sold over 5% more beer than in the same period of 1973. On the other hand, in West Germany, the world's second-largest beer producer and the country with the highest average per capita consumption (*see* Table I), the increase was no more than about 0.5% and the market showed increasing signs of saturation. Likewise in Austria, Switzerland, Belgium, and Scandinavia, expansion of the market seemed to have reached the sticking point. Of the southern European wine-producing countries, only Spain showed any impressive rise in beer consumption. France had registered an increase of more than 12% in 1973, but this followed several years of pronounced stagnation. In the U.K. a great increase in output had been recorded in 1973 and also in the first half of 1974, but the rate of increase was expected to slow down gradually thereafter. This left The Netherlands as the EEC member country most likely to continue with above-average expansion rates. There, the rate of beer consumption had doubled since the mid-1960s, when it had been no more than about one-third the level of consumption in neighbouring Belgium.

A marked feature of the situation of the brewing industry in many countries was the combination of increasing production and decreasing profits. Thus, for example, in the first half of 1974 the world's largest brewery, Anheuser-Busch Inc. of St. Louis, Mo., recorded an increase in output of 17% (to some 19.5 million hl.) but a decrease in profits of 16%. To the perennial problem of constantly rising labour costs had been added price increases for raw materials of a magnitude unparalleled for many years. Partly due to the world oil crisis and partly due to other signs of scarcity (most of the shortages being exacerbated by speculation), almost the entire range of brewing and packaging materials had been subject to spectacular rises in cost. For example, in the U.S. alone in the first seven months of 1974 the price of beer cans—in a country where canned beer accounts for 60% of the market—rose by 25–30%.

Table I. Estimated Consumption of Beer in Selected Countries

In litres* per capita of total population

Country	1971	1972	1973
Belgium†	140	140	150
Germany, West	144.41	145.3	146.7
Czechoslovakia	144.7	145.6	145.5
Luxembourg	123.8	124	131.3
Australia‡	125.8	127.3	130
New Zealand	121.4	121	...
Denmark	114.81	108.05	113
Germany, East	104.1	107.3	112.7
United Kingdom	105.7	105.6	112
Austria	101.8	103.7	110.1
Canada§	78.4	83.5	86
Ireland	73.7	76.9	80.2
United States	71.9	73.4	76.4
Switzerland	77.7	73.6	75.8
Netherlands, The	62.36	65.7	73.46
Hungary	60.2	57.3	61.6
Sweden	57.4	57.4	56.6
Finland	49.4	53.8	54.3
France	41.9	40.3	44.5
Spain	35.8	36	42.5
Norway	39.24	41.22	42.02
Venezuela	48	41	41
Bulgaria	37.87	39.51	...
Poland	33.7	35.5	37.8
Japan	29.1	31.9	35.1

*One litre=1.0567 U.S. quarts=0.8799 imperial quart.
†Including so-called "household beer."
‡Years ending June 30.
§Years ending March 31.

Table II. Estimated Consumption of Potable Distilled Spirits in Selected Countries

In litres* of 100% pure spirit per capita of population

Country	1971	1972	1973
Poland	3.5	3.9	4.2
Luxembourg	2.2	2.8	3.3
Germany, East	2.8	2.9	3.2
Spain	3.4	2.9	3.1
United States	2.91	2.95	3.03
Germany, West	3.32	2.93	3.02
Canada†	2.49	2.86	2.96
Hungary	2.9	3.05	2.9
Yugoslavia	2.8	2.8	...
Czechoslovakia	2.34	2.51	2.66
Sweden	2.5	2.65	2.65
Netherlands, The	2.11	2.28	2.55
Iceland	2.41	2.49	2.53
Finland	2.1	2.2	2.5
Surinam	2.5	2.5	...
Austria	2.28	2.36	2.4
France‡	2.23	2.3	2.3
Italy	1.8	1.9	2.2
Switzerland	1.92	2.04	2
Bulgaria	2	2	...
Ireland	1.48	1.69	1.82
Cyprus	1.6	1.8	1.8
Belgium	1.56	1.59	1.75
Norway	1.59	1.66	1.66
Denmark	1.41	1.54	1.53

†Years ending March 31.
‡Including aperitifs.

Table III. Estimated Consumption of Wine in Selected Countries

In litres* per capita of total population

Country	1971	1972	1973
Italy	112.7	110.9	109.3
France†	106.8	106.9	106.4
Portugal	105.7	82.4	88.3
Argentina	85.3	79.7	73.1
Spain	60	63.5	67.9
Chile	44	44	44
Switzerland‡	41.8	44.8	42.7
Luxembourg	40.9	41.5	40.9
Hungary	38.5	38.4	38.5
Greece	40	40	37
Austria	33.2	34	35
Romania	23.1	21.8	32.6
Yugoslavia	26.9	27.1	...
Uruguay	25	25.5	...
Germany, West	20.5	21.8	22.6
Bulgaria	19.3	20	...
Belgium	14.5	15.6	15.3
Czechoslovakia	12.5	13	12
Denmark	6.66	7.48	10.73
South Africa	11.28	9.97	10.72
Australia§	8.7	9	9.9
U.S.S.R.	11.4	11.8	9.1
Netherlands, The	6.23	7.81	8.87
Cyprus	8.2	8.2	8.2
New Zealand	6.84	7.55	...

†Excluding cider (c. 20 litres per capita annually).
‡Excluding cider (c. 6.85 litres per capita 1971–72).
§Years ending June 30.

Source: Produktschap voor Gedistilleerde Dranken, *Hoeveel alcoholhoudende dranken worden er in de wereld gedronken?*

In addition to this the industry in the U.S. had had to face barley prices more than double those of the previous year as a result of a drought in North American barley-producing areas. This was not without its effect on world market prices, which took a sharp upward turn. The international market situation was scarcely more satisfactory for other crops used in the industry, such as rice, corn, and sugar. In Central Europe barley and malt prices rose by up to one-third, although prices in the EEC remained below world prices due to EEC regulations.

The fact that hop requirements could still be met at favourable prices was small comfort since for many brewers this factor now accounted for only 1–2% of costs, and for some less than 1%. The hop content of most beers was progressively decreasing due to three main factors: a trend toward lighter, milder beers; the cultivation of varieties of hop with a higher bitterness content; and the growing use of concentrated hop extracts and powders, which required far smaller quantities and could be stored for years without loss of potency. In the case of additives, regulations such as the U.S. labeling law affected the situation by requiring that they be precisely listed on containers.

(TILMAN SCHMITT)

Spirits. With the notable exception of cognac brandy, spirits enjoyed a good year in 1973–74 despite economic problems in many markets and reduced purchasing power among consumers. A cynical observer might have concluded that bad times were good for the spirits market, at least in Britain, where sales rose appreciably during the gloomy period of the three-day working week toward the end of the 1973–74 winter.

Perhaps the most successful spirit, in terms of volume increase if not in profitability, was Scotch whisky. During the first eight months of 1974 exports at 61,006,224 proof gal. represented an increase of 27% over the corresponding period of 1973. As the result of an increase in the export price of Scotch at the beginning of 1974, the value of those exports rose by 40% to £221,920,099. Because Scotch exports had reached 78,449,664 proof gal., worth £260 million in 1973, 1974 promised to be another record year.

Vodka sales also increased significantly in important spirits markets. Total vodka sales in Britain were estimated at 932,000 proof gal. in 1974, compared with 732,000 proof gal. in the previous year, an increase of 27.3%. Gin sales rose too, but by a modest 4.6% in the U.K. in the January–June period.

A curious fact concerning 1974 spirits sales was that, despite economic troubles in many markets, sales of more expensive "premium" brands of Scotch and American whiskies, gin, and vodka did well, especially in the U.S. market. In contrast to these better selling spirits was cognac brandy, hit by high production costs. Following a 15-year period of expansion during which exports rose to an all-time high of 270,912 hl. of pure alcohol in 1972–73, exports in 1973–74 fell back to 230,440 hl. In the important cognac markets of West Germany and Hong Kong, exports fell by more than 30%. Sales in America, hit since 1964 by an extra duty on all cognac entering the U.S. at a cost of over $9 a U.S. gallon, were expected to improve in 1974 following an agreement to raise the limit to $17. This would just allow the least expensive "three star" cognacs to get through.

(COLIN PARNELL)

Apparent consumption of distilled spirits in the U.S. in 1973 reached a record high of 402.5 million gal., 2.7% above 1972. Per capita annual consumption rose 2.1% to 1.93 gal. Total expenditure for alcoholic beverages for 1973 was $26.9 billion, compared with $25.7 billion in 1972. The U.S. federal excise tax on spirits remained at $10.50 per proof gal. During fiscal 1974, U.S. agents seized 1,813 stills producing illicit spirits, 785 less than in 1973.

Social drinking continued to become more liberalized in 1974. Six more states, making a total of 32, lowered the drinking age below 21; two states lessened or removed the ban on serving liquor on election days.

A total of 821,602,063 gal. of distilled spirits were produced in the U.S. in fiscal 1974, 4.4% less than in 1973. This included production at industrial alcohol plants, some of which was not used for beverages. Whiskey production declined 17.3%, to 92,599,166 tax gal. Brandy increased 76.3%, to 20,559,829 tax gal., and rum decreased 28.9%, to 1,131,195 tax gal.

Total U.S. bottlings rose 0.4% in 1973. Whiskey increased 6.1% to account for 181,572,665 gal., or 53.5% of the total 339,131,702 gal. bottled. Whiskey bottlings by type were: blended whiskey 34.3%, straights 37.5%, blended straights 0.8%, bonded 2.1%, light whiskey 2.2%, and bulk imports 23.1%. Bourbon whiskey continued as the largest selling spirit in the world, sales amounting to 72,002,090 gal. Vodka continued its phenomenal increase, jumping 12% to 70,358,477 gal. Gin increased 0.6%, to 36,944,363 gal. Cordials increased 11.6%, to 31,652,556 gal., and brandy rose 8.9%, to 14,206,861 gal. There were 4,396,780 gal. of rum bottled, an increase of 1.6%.

In Canada public revenue from alcoholic beverage taxes rose 12.8% to Can$1,243,866,000 in fiscal 1973. Consumption of spirits in the same year climbed 8.1% to 31,310,000 imperial gal. Production rose 5.1% to 90,920,000 imperial tax gal.; imports decreased 1.3% to 7,651,000 imperial tax gal.; and exports increased 17.7% to 29,522,000 imperial tax gal. (JULIUS WILE)

Wine. World production of wine in 1974 was estimated at 318 million hl., 37 million hl. below the previous year's all-time record but still above the 1972 production and the average for the years 1967–71. Quantitatively, 1974 was thus an excellent year, despite the fact that weather conditions were not consistently favourable in the main wine-producing countries. Quality, while differing from one country to another, was in general no better than average.

Early wine is subjected to high intensity light in a device called a Weberizer, after its inventor, George Weber. Within seconds the wine acquires a smoother and more mellow taste that otherwise can be achieved only by aging in wine cellars.

BRIAN ALPERT—KEYSTONE

Smaller harvests in Europe, the source of more than 80% of the world's wine, were almost solely responsible for the reduced total production in 1974. However, the two other main wine-producing regions, Argentina and the U.S., with 40 million hl. and 11 million hl., respectively, also produced less.

The French harvest of 73 million hl., while 13% below that of the previous year, was still abundant and well above the average for the previous decade (66 million hl.). The wine was well up to average in quality, with rather low alcoholic content. In the Bordeaux district weather conditions were bad during the harvest, but the wines, although not exceptional, were of quite good quality. In Burgundy, although dry periods followed by overabundant rainfall occurred during growth, the harvest was of good average quality. In Alsace the harvest was below the average of recent years but quality was excellent. In Champagne both quantity and quality were satisfactory.

In Italy too the harvest, at 70 million hl., was down from the previous year, with all regions, but especially the north, experiencing a decline. Quality was better almost everywhere, but strength varied.

In Spain relatively abundant rainfall had a beneficial effect, and despite damage caused by hail and disease the harvest, at 30 million hl., considerably exceeded the average of the five previous years. The West German harvest, which had reached 10.5 million hl. in 1973, fell to 7.5 million hl. in 1974—still appreciably above average.

In the Bordeaux "winegate" affair, 8 of the 18 wine shippers and merchants accused of fraudulently adulterating and mislabeling some 40,000 hl. of wine were convicted on December 18 and received sentences ranging up to the maximum of one year's imprisonment and a fine of Fr. 27,000. (PAUL MAURON)

Approximately 4.2 million tons of grapes were harvested in the U.S. in 1974, well above the 3.2 million-ton average of the previous five years and almost the match of the big 1973 crop. California accounted for 3.8 million tons of the total, roughly 100,000 tons below the state's 1973 harvest. New York, second-largest grape producer, harvested 190,000 tons, a substantial 48% above the previous year's mark. In most areas the weather was nearly ideal, and great hopes were held for many of the wines produced.

By grape classification, the California harvest included 1.2 million tons of wine variety grapes (a new high); just under 2 million tons of raisin varieties, mainly Thompson Seedless; and 600,000 tons of table grapes. California wineries crushed just over 60% (2.3 million tons) of the harvested total. All major U.S. grape areas recorded substantial 1974 vineyard plantings.

During 1974, some wine prices, especially those of the lesser known imported wines, declined slightly, following several years of an upward price trend. Prices of U.S. wines generally held their own, lower costs for grapes being offset by increases in the costs of labour, bottles, and shipping. (IRVING H. MARCUS)

[731.E.8.a–c]

Algeria

A republic on the north coast of Africa, Algeria is bounded by Morocco, Spanish Sahara, Mauritania, Mali, Niger, Libya, and Tunisia. Area: 896,593 sq.mi. (2,322,164 sq.km.). Pop. (1973 est.): 15,772,000. Cap. and largest city: Algiers (département pop., 1970

ALGERIA
Education. (1972–73) Primary, pupils 2,244,844, teachers 51,461; secondary, pupils 278,543, teachers 9,892; vocational, pupils 57,422, teachers 3,391; teacher training, students 7,128, teachers 542; higher (including 3 universities), students 26,522.
Finance. Monetary unit: dinar, with (Sept. 16, 1974) a free rate of 4.02 dinars to U.S. $1 (9.29 dinars = £1 sterling). Gold, SDRs, and foreign exchange, central bank: (June 1974) U.S. $1,859,000,-000; (June 1973) U.S. $433 million. Budget (1972 actual): revenue 9,333,000,000 dinars; expenditure 7,729,000,000 dinars. Money supply: (Dec. 1973) 21,-483,000,000 dinars; (Dec. 1972) 16,746,000,000 dinars.
Foreign Trade. (1973) Imports 9,748,000,000 dinars; exports 7,514,000,000 dinars. Import sources (1972): France 30%; West Germany 13%; Italy 10%; U.S. 7%; U.K. 5%; Belgium-Luxembourg 5%; Spain 5%. Export destinations (1972): France 23%; West Germany 19%; U.S. 8%; Spain 8%; Italy 8%; U.S.S.R. 5%; Belgium-Luxembourg 5%. Main exports (1972): crude oil 79%; wine 6%.
Transport and Communications. Roads (1972) 78,408 km. Motor vehicles in use (1972): passenger 165,022; commercial (including buses) 90,771. Railways: (1971) 3,951 km.; traffic (1972) 1,016,000,000 passenger-km., freight 1,533,000,000 net ton-km. Air traffic (1972): 699 million passenger-km.; freight 4.9 million net ton-km. Shipping (1973): merchant vessels 100 gross tons and over 56; gross tonnage 162,832. Shipping traffic (1971): goods loaded c. 33,472,000 metric tons, unloaded c. 4 million metric tons. Telephones (Dec. 1972) 212,000. Radio licenses (Dec. 1972) 710,000. Television licenses (Dec. 1972) 150,-000.
Agriculture. Production (in 000; metric tons; 1973; 1972 in parentheses): wheat c. 1,100 (1,956); barley c. 450 (720); oats c. 30 (39); potatoes c. 300 (c. 300); dates (1972) c. 110, (1971) c. 110; figs (1972) c. 65, (1971) c. 65; oranges (1972) c. 380, (1971) c. 380; mandarin oranges and tangerines (1972) c. 130, (1971) c. 130; tomatoes c. 152 (c. 150); onions c. 42 (c. 40); tobacco (1972) c. 6, (1971) c. 6; olives c. 150 (c. 120); wine c. 650 (570). Livestock (in 000; Nov. 1972): sheep c. 7,500; goats c. 2,200; cattle c. 870; asses c. 320; horses c. 140; camels c. 185.
Industry. Production (in 000; metric tons; 1972): iron ore (53–55% metal content) 3,660; phosphate rock (1971) 491; crude oil (1973) 51,154; natural gas (cu.m.; 1971) 2,965,000; electricity (kw-hr.; 1971) 2,126,000.

est., 1,839,000). Language: Arabic, Berber, French. Religion: Muslim. President in 1974, Col. Houari Boumédienne.

Celebrating in November 1974 the 20th anniversary of the start of their struggle for independence from the French, Algerians could look with some pride at the leadership President Boumédienne (see BIOGRAPHY) was giving to other new nations, particularly the primary producers, to achieve what they saw as economic rights; at the new authority of their foreign minister, Abdel-Aziz Bouteflika (see BIOGRAPHY), in his role as president of the UN General Assembly; at the evolution of a Palestinian Arab entity along lines long advocated by Algeria's leaders; and at the newly won independence of African territories, in which Algeria had played no small part. If it was still a time of austerity and massive rural underemployment at home, at least the effects of the nation's attempt at an industrial revolution were beginning to be felt.

Early in 1974 President Boumédienne had taken the initiative in calling for a meeting at the UN on raw materials, and in April a special session of the General Assembly was held on this subject, with Boumédienne making the keynote speech. Boumédienne's advice to the primary producers, to nationalize their resources and band together to show their strength in the face of what he saw as the inflexible attitude of the industrialized states, appeared pertinent, if somewhat alarming, economic good sense. Boumédienne nevertheless saw Algeria's role as a catalyst of cooperation between producers and consumers. At the end of October he called for a summit conference of oil producers in face of the mounting financial problems that sharp oil price rises were causing, and the following month he urged the formation of a cartel of iron-ore producers.

In the aftermath of the Arab-Israeli war of October 1973, Algeria continued in 1974 its policy of encouraging Palestinian Arabs to stand united. U.S. Secretary of State Henry Kissinger, on his Middle East peace missions, made a point of calling at Algiers in April and October (although full diplomatic relations with the U.S. were not restored until November), and Algerian policy was vindicated when the Arab summit conference at Rabat, Morocco, in October confirmed the Palestine Liberation Organization (PLO) as sole spokesman for the Palestinian Arabs and when the UN General Assembly in November gave the PLO a hearing. And, with the change in regime in Portugal, Algeria's diplomats were able, too, to play an effective mediatory role in negotiations looking toward independence of the Portuguese territories.

Algeria, which had been in the forefront among the Arabs in its oil policy, both on prices and on state participation, was not slow to catch up with the Persian Gulf oil producers in their moves toward ever higher crude-oil prices. In September 1973 the posted price of Algerian crude had been raised to what then seemed the remarkably high level of $5 a barrel; in January 1974 a posted price of more than $16 a barrel was announced. The ban on supplies to the U.S. was lifted in March and to The Netherlands in June, and production was maintained through 1974 at close to the 1972 and 1973 levels of 50 million tons a year. Proximity to European markets ensured sustained interest in increasing the level of Algerian production, and the French state oil companies, dispossessed of their Saharan interests in 1971, were in the forefront in taking up new exploratory concessions. The expansion of the hydrocarbons industry, particularly the building of new pipelines (one direct to Italy) and the extension of gas liquefaction plants, went ahead, and a contract for the supply of the first 5 in a proposed fleet of 13 gas tankers was, significantly, awarded to a French shipyard. The restoration of good relations with France seemed assured.

The new oil wealth made it possible to introduce in January a budget providing for expenditures one-third higher than in 1973 and then, in May, to announce a four-year plan, revised in light of the increased oil revenues, which envisaged a government investment program of $26 billion from 1974 through 1977. The emphasis of the expenditures would remain on rapid industrialization. While Algeria's industrial revolution continued in full swing, the "agrarian revolution," launched in 1971, was making slower progress. After three years of agrarian reform, it was reported in November that only about 75,000 people had benefited, although in all some two million acres of former state or nationalized land had been converted to cooperative farm management. The third phase of the plan included the afforestation of a 900-mi. belt of land stretching from the Moroccan to the Tunisian border and deep into the Sahara, in order to reclaim the desert, and an attempt to bring an organized livelihood to some 170,000 nomadic herdsmen.

In November President Boumédienne announced that the economic and agrarian revolutions would be followed by a third, "socialist" revolution. Despite his repeated efforts to bring new life into the sole political organization, the National Liberation Front, the front failed to inspire enthusiasm for popular participation in government. In a new attempt to overcome this apathy, Boumédienne intended to form a new "Muslim, not Marxist" socialist party as the vanguard of social change.   (PETER KILNER)

[978.D.2.d]

Andorra

An autonomous principality of Europe, Andorra is in the Pyrenees Mountains between Spain and France. Area: 179 sq.mi. (464 sq.km.). Pop. (1973 est.): 23,-105. Cap.: Andorra la Vella (commune pop., 1973 est., 9,659). Language: Catalan (official), French, Spanish. Religion: predominantly Roman Catholic. Co-princes: the president of the French Republic and the bishop of Urgel, Spain, represented by their *veguers* (provosts) and *batlles* (prosecutors). An elected Council General of 24 members elects the first syndic; in 1974, Julià Reig-Ribó.

Several meetings were held in late 1973 and in February 1974 between the co-princes of Andorra and their representatives. The French official position concerning Andorra had always been that official and diplomatic responsibility for the principality rested with the president of the French Republic, while religious and ecclesiastical control was vested in the bishop of Urgel. The Spanish authorities, including the bishop of Urgel, maintained that the two co-princes were equal in all lay affairs and that any allocation of temporal powers to one co-prince could lead to the domination of Andorra by his state. In fact, the condition of coequality did have great appeal to the Andorran populace.

Although little about the meetings was made public, it appeared that the co-princes had agreed to maintain the status quo and perhaps to cooperate more fully in modernizing the somewhat feudal status of the principality. Thus, a single representative was named to participate in a UNESCO meeting on education; previously both France and Spain had claimed the right to represent Andorra on such occasions.

There were other signs that the jealousy and antagonism that had grown up between the two states might be abating, but certain vague areas of authority remained to cause difficulties. Andorra lacked a constitution in the modern sense, and many of the powers exercised by the princes, as well as by Parliament and the syndic, derived from tradition. Further, there were growing differences between the comparatively modernizing attitudes of the princes and the Andorran segment of the government, which remained inherently conservative.   (ROBERT D. HODGSON)

ANDORRA
Education. (1969–70) Primary, pupils 1,850, teachers 63; secondary, pupils 804, teachers 48.
Finance and Trade. Monetary units: French franc and Spanish peseta. No income tax, death duty, or customs; public treasury is funded by a 3% levy on gasoline and liquor. Foreign trade (1973): imports from France Fr. 347,395,000 (U.S. $74,550,000), from Spain 2,192,961,000 pesetas (U.S. $37,340,-000); exports to France Fr. 9,202,000 (U.S. $1,970,-000), to Spain 36,963,000 pesetas (U.S. $630,000). Tourism (1973) *c.* 4 million visitors.
Communications. Radio receivers (Dec. 1973) 6,000. Television receivers (Dec. 1969) 1,700.
Agriculture. Production: cereals, potatoes, tobacco, wool. Livestock (in 000; 1973): sheep *c.* 25; cattle *c.* 3; horses *c.* 1.

Antarctica

During 1974 Argentina, Australia, Chile, France, Japan, New Zealand, South Africa, the U.K., the U.S.S.R., and the U.S. continued their scientific study of the Antarctic and the surrounding waters from 34 stations in the Antarctic Treaty area and 9 stations on outlying islands.

Three major meetings associated with Antarctica took place in 1974. The Polar Oceans Conference held in Montreal in May passed a number of recommendations about the need for international cooperation in the study of the Southern Ocean, particularly of its living resources. These were endorsed by the meeting of the Intergovernmental Oceanographic Commission's International Coordination Group for the Southern Ocean held in Buenos Aires, Arg., in July.

The 13th meeting of the Scientific Committee on Antarctic Research (SCAR) was held in Jackson Hole, Wyo., September 3–7. Meetings of the SCAR working groups on biology, human biology and medicine, logistics, and upper atmosphere physics were held at the same time. The third SCAR/IUBS (International Union of Biological Sciences) Symposium on Antarctic Biology was held in Washington, D.C., in August.

Scientific Programs. One of the notable scientific achievements of the year was the publication of a map showing, for a large area of the Antarctic, detailed contours of the land lying below the immensely thick ice cover. The result of many years of fruitful cooperation between the U.S. and the U.K. in airborne radio-echo sounding of the ice sheet, the work is an example of the trend toward closer international cooperation on scientific projects that are too big for any one nation to undertake alone. Others are the Dry Valleys Drilling Project (the U.S., New Zealand, and Japan), the International Antarctic Glaciological Project (the U.S., Australia, France, the U.S.S.R., and the U.K.), and the Glaciology of the Antarctic Peninsula Project (Argentina, Chile, the U.K., the U.S., and the U.S.S.R.).

Argentina. An Argentine Air Force Hercules transport aircraft flew from Buenos Aires across the Antarctic continent to Canberra, Austr., and back in December 1973. The flight was part of a study of the feasibility of developing a commercial route between South America and Australia. The flight refueled in the Antarctic at the Vice Comodoro Marambio Station on Seymour Island. Argentina continued a wide range of scientific studies from its seven stations on the South Orkney Islands, the Antarctic Peninsula, and at the southern end of the Weddell Sea. The geophysical program at the last station, Belgrano, was being extended in scope.

Australia. Australia continued scientific investigation from three stations on the continent and one station on Macquarie Island. A helicopter was lost in the southern Prince Charles Mountains in the course of carrying out detailed geologic mapping. Contributions to the International Antarctic Glaciological Project featured prominently and included 40 hours of aerial radio-echo sounding of the Lambert Glacier, a deep-core drilling followed by logging of the bore-hole movement at Casey Station, and the resurvey and extension of a 200-km. line of georeceiver stations southward from the Law Dome. A new biological laboratory was established at Davis Station. An opportunity was taken to visit the huts built by Sir Douglas Mawson at Cape Denison in 1911–14. Some were still there.

Chile. Chile continued to carry out scientific programs at three stations on the Antarctic Peninsula and the South Shetland Islands. Logistic support was provided by two ships and one helicopter. Scientific programs included seismologic studies, geologic surveys, and a varied biological program including seal censuses, soil biology, and research on Antarctic fishes. Chile continued to operate a complete program of meteorological observations.

France. After 25 years of uninterrupted scientific work in this area, Expéditions Polaires Françaises in

A group of penguins enjoy the summer weather near the Argentine Station, Antarctic Peninsula.

1974 completed a wide range of scientific studies from its Dumont d'Urville Station in Adélie Land. Particular attention was paid to the possibility of building an airstrip near the station so that France would be able to participate in the international Antarctic airbus scheme first proposed by the U.S. and now under consideration by SCAR and Antarctic Treaty governments. Considerable civil engineering work was carried out at Dumont d'Urville, including the installation of further freshwater and oil storage tanks. As part of the French contribution to the International Antarctic Glaciological Project a 305-m.-deep ice core was obtained 4 km. from the coast for ice movement and isotopic dating studies.

Japan. Forty members of the 15th Japanese Antarctic Expedition arrived on the icebreaker "Fuji" on January 1. All supplies for Syowa Station had to be transported some 40 mi. over fast ice by helicopter and vehicles. A new laboratory for environmental and biological studies was constructed at Syowa. A party of ten undertook a major glaciologic, geologic, and terrestrial survey traverse in the vicinity of the Yamato Mountains. An important achievement was the resurvey of a 250-km.-long strain grid to show how much the ice had moved since the grid was established in 1970. The expedition had its first fatal accident since 1960 when a member of the "Fuji" crew fell into a crevasse. Japanese scientists participated in the Dry Valley Drilling Project. In October 1973 the Japanese government established the National Institute of Polar Research under the Ministry of Education to be responsible for furthering Japanese polar research, carrying out their Antarctic programs, and organizing postgraduate studies.

New Zealand. A large proportion of the New Zealand program was related to the Dry Valley Drilling Project. Twelve men spent the winter at Scott Base and four at Vanda Station. Two parties from Canterbury University carried out a varied biological research program including a thorough search of the floor of the Taylor Valley for fossilized seals: 60 were found. A Victoria University of Wellington party, led by Janet Crump, undertook a number of geologic investigations. Fieldwork was curtailed by bad weather, heavy snow, and a serious case of carbon monoxide poisoning in the party. The New Zealand Antarctic Society continued to supply caretakers for the huts built at Cape Royds by Sir Ernest Shackleton and at Cape Evans by Capt. R. F. Scott. The warm summer produced many relics of early expeditions that had been hitherto buried in snow and ice both in and outside the huts.

South Africa. South Africa continued to maintain stations on the continent, at Sanae, and on Gough Island and Marion Island. The 15th South African National Antarctic Expedition installed new equipment at Sanae in connection with cosmic ray and whistler programs. A party of six occupied a forward base, Grunehogna, in the Ahlmannryggen some 215 km. S of Sanae. This party engaged in geologic investigations and radio-echo sounding of the ice in the vicinity. Gough Island suffered a severe water shortage in the early part of the year. A radio beacon to assist civil aviation was being installed and a program of biological research has been started.

United Kingdom. The 1973–74 program at six stations included the completion of a five-year preliminary botanical survey of South Georgia, the beginning of a research program on the reindeer of South Georgia, and the completion of the rebuilding of

Halley Bay Station. Because of heavy snowfall in this region, the station has had to be rebuilt three times since it was first established in 1956.

The feasibility of a new air link between Adelaide Island and Halley Bay was established by a two-way flight in February. Good weather enabled rapid progress to be made with topographic and geophysical surveys of Palmer Land. Over 5,000 mi. of airborne magnetometer traverses were completed. An Adélie penguin found in George VI Sound, more than 100 mi. from the nearest open water, was flown to Adelaide Island and released.

In the U.K. a map of Alexander Island at a scale of 1:250,000 was produced using imagery from the U.S. satellite ERTS 1; work was begun on the British Antarctic Survey headquarters in Cambridge and a diploma course in polar studies was established at the Scott Polar Research Institute there.

U.S.S.R. The Soviet Union continued a wide-ranging scientific program at five coastal stations and one inland station manned by a total of 233 scientists and support personnel. The main scientific centre, with 94 men, was Molodezhnaya in Enderby Land. No further attempt was made to establish a seventh permanent station on the Hobbs Coast. The field program concentrated on the Amery Ice Shelf and Lambert Glacier where considerable progress was made in the topographic and geologic survey of this important region. Two surface traverses were made to resupply Vostok station. Soviet fishing fleets were again active in the Southern Ocean catching fish and krill.

United States. Coupled with 39 other projects, the year saw further fieldwork in two major interdisciplinary programs. The dry (*i.e.*, with no glaciers) valleys on the western side of McMurdo Sound present a large number of scientific opportunities and problems in the geologic, glaciologic, and biological history of the Antarctic. The Dry Valley Drilling Project involved 21 U.S., 8 Japanese, and 28 New Zealand scientists and technicians. After an exhaustive study of the environmental effect of drilling in this very sensitive area, judged against the potential scientific value, a New Zealand team drilled six holes in the valleys and three on Ross Island. Among the more startling results was the discovery of viable microorganisms from rock tens of thousands of years old.

The second large-scale program—the Ross Ice Shelf Project—will eventually involve drilling through the floating ice shelf in order to study its regime and the waters beneath it. Work in 1973–74 involved 345 flying hours in a Twin Otter providing data for maps of ice thickness, water thickness, and the depth of the ocean bottom. Forty-seven ice shelf movement stations were established for subsequent measurement.

Marine activities included further drilling of the ocean floor in the Scotia and Bellingshausen seas by the "Glomar Challenger" and biological work from the "Hero" in Antarctic Peninsula waters.

Other Developments. Tourism in the Antarctic increased with the addition of an Argentine cruise ship, the "Cabo San Rocque," to the long-active "Lindblad Explorer." The Australian David Lewis, whose yacht "Ice Bird" had been dismasted the previous year during an attempt to circumnavigate the Antarctic single-handed, started out from the U.S. Palmer Station, where his yacht had spent the winter, and was dismasted again in February 800 mi. SW of Cape Town, which he reached after 25 days under jury rig.

(JOHN ARNFIELD HEAP)

See also Earth Sciences.

Anthropology

Occasional encyclopaedic inventories of anthropology have given way in the last 20 years to more restricted publications in the face of increased specialization and increased publication output by the ever growing numbers of anthropologists. But 1973 saw the publication of the *Handbook of Social and Cultural Anthropology* under the editorship of John J. Honigmann. Although its length surpasses by about one-third the widely acclaimed *Anthropology Today* (a published account of a 1952 symposium attended by anthropologists from all parts of the world), the handbook's 28 chapters cover only half as many topics and only one of anthropology's major subfields is treated. The tendency toward increased specialization can also be seen by considering what the handbook excludes. The two rapidly developing fields of primate behaviour and biological determinants in social behaviour, which link physical with sociocultural anthropology, are not represented. Similarly, the work of those archaeologists attempting to bridge the subfields of prehistory and ethnology was left unsurveyed. Honigmann's remark that the first of these interfaces, and presumably the second, was not included because a sufficient body of substantive findings does not yet exist may be well taken, but this exclusion also indicates the difficulty of integration of the subfields of anthropology because of the increasing development of specialized knowledge. By the same token, it is not difficult to understand the inclusion of some 14 articles on topically defined subjects such as law, warfare, belief systems, economics, politics, pluralism, urbanism, or education. Indeed, anthropology seems to be advancing by the addition of topics to its inventory of subjects rather than by developing paradigms that relate these substantively defined areas or the subfields.

The topical diversification of sociocultural anthropology has itself undergone a noticeable change since the publication of *Anthropology Today,* in which

topics were defined either areally or with respect to institutions. An examination of the program for the 73rd annual meeting of the American Anthropological Association (AAA), held in 1974 in Mexico City, shows the emergence of quite another dimension. Approximately 260 sections (each with several papers) were held, and of these 113 relate to contemporary socioeconomic problems. For example, there were 21 sections on social conflict, class and caste, status differentials, leadership, and various aspects of the politics of groups in dominant-subordinate relationships. Fifteen sections were devoted to modernization, economic development, and other matters relating to the impact of colonialization or industrialization. The status of women (especially in Western society), sex roles, sexual differences in behaviour, and homosexuality were the subject of 13 sessions, while ethnographic studies of Western sociocultural systems, urbanization, various aspects of medical anthropology, ethnic identity, and aging were examined in 43 sections. In this same vein, it is noteworthy that 1974 saw the inauguration of a master's degree program in applied anthropology at the University of South Florida, Tampa. The program aimed at producing graduates with specialties in urban and medical anthropology who can work in nonacademic contexts. This tendency to look inward and to develop research around social issues resulted, in part, from the increased economic and political difficulties of conducting field research in other parts of the world, but also as a product of heightened social awareness and concern developing out of social history in the last decade.

The handbook and the inventory of papers presented at the AAA meeting are also indicative of the broader methodological and theoretical concerns of anthropology. One is the increasing use and sophistication of ecological models in anthropology. The underlying assumption of this approach is that human societies are adaptive systems, and that sociocultural change is the result of selective factors operating on them. This has stimulated considerable research attempting to measure variables such as ca-

An early man site near Pittsburgh, Pa., yields artifacts suggesting habitation as much as 15,000 years ago. Most previous discoveries of such sites have been restricted to the arid parts of the western U.S. because the eastern climate tends to weather and destroy the evidence.

UPI COMPIX

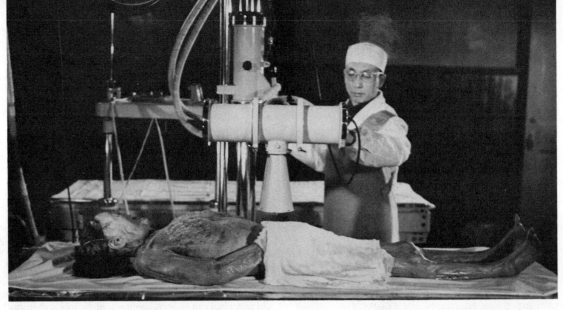

COURTESY, THE PERMANENT MIS-
SION OF THE PEOPLE'S REPUBLIC
OF CHINA TO THE UNITED NA-
TIONS

Chinese technician X-rays
the body of a 2,100-
year-old woman prior
to an autopsy.
The remarkable degree
of preservation
is evident from this
photograph.

loric output, carrying capacity of the land, degree of extractive efficiency of given technological systems, and demographic pressures. This trend has produced no breakthrough, but as more is understood about the operation of variables of this type it should be possible to understand in a more detailed way the conditions under which a society evolves from one type of macrostructure to another.

The systemic approach has also increased the utility of mathematics in anthropology. Although statistics have always played an important role in the discipline, mathematics in the broader sense of a methodological approach utilizing axiomatic models is a more recent introduction. Inclusion of the topic in the handbook and the occurrence of a conference on the subject in 1974 indicate an increasing ability on the part of anthropologists to utilize this approach.

Finally, the handbook contains an article on the methodology of cross-cultural comparison. This method permits drawing an adequate sample of societies for the cross-cultural testing of hypotheses, while moving away from ethnically defined units as the units of comparison.

It is of special interest that some anthropologists have considered the possibility that cross-cultural studies and contact between members of different cultures may not be limited to our planet. A contest was organized by two anthropologists to generate papers on the topic of "Cultural Patterns of Extraterrestrial Communities" for the 1974 AAA meeting. Seven papers were selected for presentation concerning topics such as the problems involved in establishing stable contact with extraterrestrial beings, and speculation concerning their possible modes of organization and communication. Interest in this area was also evidenced by the publication of *Alternative Anthropological Futures: Anthropological Theory and Science Fiction,* a collection of readings in which similar problems are raised by science fiction writers as they imagine what our culture may be like in the future. Constructing and evaluating these efforts help elucidate assumptions made about the nature of organized behaviour and communication.

Two books appeared that represent the continued interest in altered states of consciousness. *Hallucinogens and Shamanism* is a collection of articles dealing with the use of hallucinogenic substances by curers, diviners, and other ritual specialists, and also suggests that their use might account for experiences commonly recounted by European witches. *Religion, Altered*

States of Consciousness and Social Change was also published, but this work is focused on trance and its role in sociocultural change and cross-culturally examines the correlation of certain societal types, generated from trance types, with selected social organizational variables.

Aside from these general trends in sociocultural anthropology, a significant development has taken place in prehistoric studies. Utilizing the fact that certain amino acids change from one type to another at a constant rate in fossil bone, as detected by their differential reaction to polarized light, a biological clock can be constructed for determining the age of fossils within the 5,000–100,000-year age range. This technique was applied to California Paleo-Indian material and the results indicate that man may have been in North America 50,000 years ago. This is the earliest date yet obtained for human fossil material or artifacts from the New World and tends to substantiate speculation that man's arrival there was considerably earlier than conventionally supposed. Comparable dates using other techniques have been established for Paleo-Australian materials as well, suggesting a radiation of modern human forms over a broader area than previously indicated.

(PHILIP L. NEWMAN)

See also Archaeology.
[10/36.B]

Archaeology

Eastern Hemisphere. The smoldering Arab-Israeli dispute and the disorders on Cyprus upset the normal pace of archaeological activities in the eastern Mediterranean regions, but in other respects the 1973–74 season was essentially a good one. Pressure against illicit traffic in antiquities continued. Italian investigators pressed their inquiry into the circumstances surrounding the discovery of a Greek vase acquired for $1 million by New York's Metropolitan Museum of Art in 1972. A near life-size sacred sculpture, stolen from the Kom kingdom of Cameroon in 1966, was returned. Also returned was the head of a figure from a Roman mosaic found at Apamea, Syria, and stolen from Aleppo. In both cases, museum directors had purchased the pieces from dealers.

Two major archaeological salvage efforts, both above new dams on the Euphrates River, were terminated upon completion of the dams. Much had been saved and learned, but much more was lost as the flood pools filled.

The year had its moments of archaeological whimsy. Seventy Greek sailors carrying full-length mirrors lined up on a pier in Athens and focused the sun's rays on a small target boat, in an effort to simulate Archimedes' legendary exploit of setting fire to a Roman fleet. The experiment worked! The East Germans were seeking the return of the famous bust of the Egyptian queen Nefertiti from the West Germans. The Egyptians themselves had sought its return for years. Another of the almost annual pleas for permission to seek the remains of Noah's Ark on Mt. Ararat was made to the Turkish government by so-called archaeologists. No trace having been found so far, a member of an earlier group suggested that the survivors of the biblical flood may have used the timbers from the Ark to build new homes.

Pleistocene Prehistory. A joint U.S.-French-Ethiopian expedition announced the discovery of human bones believed to be three to four million years old near the Awash Valley in Ethiopia. Preliminary dating indicated that these were the oldest human remains found to date and might be 1.5 million years older than those found by Richard Leakey near Lake Rudolf, Kenya, two years earlier. Also in East Africa, Glynn Isaac and Garniss Curtis of the University of California reported finding Acheulean-type hand axes perhaps 1.5 million years old and thus presumably made by the African hominid *Australopithecus*. Formerly, Acheulean-type stone tools were thought to be no older than 500,000 years. In a small cave on the French Riviera, Henry de Lumley recovered tools of the simpler types ("pebble tools") associated with *Australopithecus* in Africa. Most of the long-term programs at Middle and Upper Paleolithic sites in western Europe were continued. Particularly important were the continuing exposures made by André Leroi-Gourhan and M. N. Brézillon at the open-air living site of Pincevent, France, underlining the fact that not all Paleolithic peoples were cave dwellers.

The Near East. Work in more remote districts of the Arab lands was still restricted in most countries. In Egypt a new expedition of the University of Innsbruck, Aus., began work on a late prehistoric site near Gizeh in the Cairo suburbs. Using petrographic analysis, a California group established that the stone of the gigantic colossi of Memnon at Thebes came from a quarry near Cairo. The Oriental Institute of the University of Chicago, marking the 50th year of its epigraphic and architectural survey work in the Luxor area, undertook the detailed recording of the 14th-dynasty battle scenes on the temple walls at Karnak.

A British group undertook the clearance of fortifications at Jawa, a 4th millennium B.C. site in the badlands of northeastern Jordan. In Syria, likewise, most activity took place in the northern and eastern regions. P. Matthiae of the University of Rome completed his tenth campaign at the site of Tell Mardikh south of Aleppo. The site was a large urban settlement, with temples and palaces from the 3rd into the 2nd millennium B.C. with some later occupation as well. Political restrictions inhibited work in classic southern Mesopotamia, though the Oriental Institute's work at ancient Nippur, under McGuire Gibson's direction, did proceed fruitfully. A sequence of temple structures was cleared, and the complete plan of a well-preserved house of the Old Babylonian period was exposed.

The Iranian government's antiquities service was becoming reluctant to grant permission for new excavations, due in part to the pressure of archaeological refugees from the Arab countries. The government's large-scale restorations at Persepolis, the ancient Persian religious capital, proceeded as part of a joint effort with Italian colleagues. The remains of an unknown palace, adjacent to and perhaps earlier than Persepolis itself, were being cleared. The long-range program of the French at Susa continued, under Jean Perrot's direction. In hopes of recovering its missing head, more work was done in the area where the splendid large statue of Darius I was found earlier. A Belgian expedition cleared more undisturbed graves in Luristan, adding to the inventory of the famous group of bronzes, most of which had been known only as individual pieces marketed by illicit dealers. The Joint Iranian Expedition (Chicago and Los Angeles) at Chogha Mish also continued, with work concentrated on 6th- and 4th-millennium B.C. levels. In Soviet Turkmenistan, V. Masson's work at the site of Altyn Tepe yielded strong evidence of contact with 3rd-millennium B.C. Mesopotamia.

Machteld Mellink's detailed annual review of archaeological activities in Turkey again appeared in the *American Journal of Archaeology.* Considerable importance was attached to the interest of Turkish workers in the Pontic (Black Sea) region, one of the archaeologically least known areas of the country. Tahsin Ozguc's long-term work at Kul Tepe continued, with the excavation of the palace area nearing completion. Broad new areas of the Hittite capital of Bogazkoy were exposed by a German expedition under Peter Neve. Nimet Ozguc's work on the city mound of Acemhuyuk encountered burned building ruins and many artifacts. Harald Hauptmann's work at the great mound of Norsuntepe established a long sequence of materials, from the mid-1st millennium well back into the 4th millennium B.C. Several sites along the Mediterranean coast yielded evidence of Mycenaean and Minoan contact.

The Greco-Roman Regions. Mellink's summary also included work on many of the great classical sites in Turkey; Aphrodisias, Ephesus, Knidos, Pergamon, and Sardis were all being worked, and an underwater survey located some 18 ancient ships off Bodrum-Halicarnassus. At Xanthos a French excavator, Henri Metzger, recovered a tablet with an inscription in

Archaeologists examine two bronze Trojan horses discovered in northern Jutland in 10 m. of water. The find dates back to about A.D. 1300, and it is hoped that an entire ship ultimately will be found in sediments farther offshore.

TAGE JENSEN—NORDISK PRESSEFOTO/PICTORIAL PARADE

Greek, Aramaic, and Lycian which he claimed might lead to the decipherment of Lycian. In Greece itself, there was concern that caverns and gullies on the lower slopes of the Acropolis in Athens needed reinforcement. Michael Jameson of the University of Pennsylvania described the clearance and mapping of a drowned Greek temple, in shallow water at Porto Cheli east of Corinth. The late Roman theatre at Stobi, in Macedonia, was being cleared. Some 40 sites were located in a survey on the island of Paros, and a sarcophagus of Phoenician type indicated the wider activities of the Parian marble workshops.

The find of the year in Italy appeared to have been the relocation and beginning clearances of Oplonti, some 10 mi. N of Pompeii. In Rome the ruins of a fine villa with Dionysian frescoes were encountered in probes beneath the Baths of Caracalla. The tomb of a woman containing rich ornaments of gold and silver, opened at Castel di Decimia just south of Rome, dated to the time of Rome's founding.

Later Prehistoric and Historic Europe. Of considerable significance was the appearance of Colin Renfrew's book *Before Civilization: The Radiocarbon Revolution and Prehistoric Europe.* The "revolution" concerned the adjustment of radiocarbon dates to conform with corrections derived from tree ring chronology. Since the adjusted dates are much earlier, Renfrew believed that previous workers had been wrong in concluding that important late prehistoric developments in Europe resulted from diffusion from the Near East. Both provocative and overly facile, the book was certain to affect generalizations concerning later prehistory.

French workers were involved with the clearance of several dozen Gallo-Roman ruins and with some clearly earlier village sites. One group of villages of about 4000 B.C. was investigated along the French stretch of the Moselle River. A rich Bronze Age tomb was discovered in the vicinity of Fribourg, Switz. T. Malinowski of the Poznan Museum excavated an important 1st-millennium B.C. site in Poland, evidently a trading post for the amber trade.

Asia and Africa. Fieldwork in the Transvaal included various surveys for Iron Age sites. In East Africa Desmond Clark of the University of California excavated two Sudanese sites, one with the remains of nomadic pastoralists and the other with early village-type remains. Thurston Shaw of Ibadan (Nigeria) University conducted a survey in the Niger delta.

Limited activities were again allowed in Pakistan. Walter Fairservis' American Museum of Natural History group excavated on a small Harappan site east of Karachi, and George Dales of the University of California worked on another Harappan site, a possible seaport, northwest of Karachi. Finds of Roman and Byzantine coins were noted well up into central Asia, and near Orsk, in the southern Urals, a rich Sarmatian family burial included a golden neck collar bearing the name of the Persian king Artaxerxes. China published a long list of finds, many of which were taken to be the result of salvage clearances.

(ROBERT J. BRAIDWOOD)

Western Hemisphere. Passage of the Moss-Bennett archaeological conservation act by the U.S. Congress and its signing into law by Pres. Richard Nixon in 1974 were welcomed by U.S. archaeologists. The act provided that up to 1% of the cost of a proposed federal construction project, such as a dam, building, or highway, could be used to mitigate any unavoidable adverse effects on archaeological or historic resources.

Charles R. McGimsey III, director of the Arkansas Archaeological Survey and president of the Society for American Archaeology, pointed out that, because the legislation was permissive rather than mandatory, the archaeological profession must play a major role in encouraging its implementation.

Because funds available for archaeological research had steadily declined for several years, the Moss-Bennett bill, as well as other recent environmental protection legislation, provided needed financial backing. Major problems resulted from these funding sources, however, because they elevated the importance of contract or salvage archaeology, often considered a stepchild of the profession because service to agencies had sometimes been emphasized over research. The legislation highlighted the need to integrate protection and preservation of archaeological resources with traditional research objectives.

That protection was needed was made clear by the growing recreational use by off-road vehicle enthusiasts of the 17 million-ac. California Desert. Many fragile archaeological sites, including centuries-old rock sculptures, had been badly damaged or destroyed by such use. The Society for California Archaeology joined the Sierra Club and the Environmental Defense Fund as co-plaintiffs in a suit against the Bureau of Land Management, the federal agency responsible for managing most of the desert portion of California, asking that off-road recreational driving be halted until requirements of the National Environmental Policy Act and federal antiquities legislation had been met.

Archaeological research interests in 1974 centred on the use of models and computer simulation in archaeological inference, statistical manipulation of archaeological data, methods of spatial and locational analysis, and the relationship between social stratification and exchange systems. Replication studies of artifact function and methods of tool manufacture continued to receive emphasis, as did reconstructions of prehistoric diets and environments. Vaughn M. Bryant, Jr., Texas A. & M. University, utilized prehistoric human coprolites (feces) to reconstruct dietary patterns and seasonal site occupancy in southwestern Texas between 800 B.C. and A.D. 500. A dental analysis of three populations representing the Hopewell culture of the Ohio Valley (c. 300 B.C. to A.D. 200) was reported by James Addington, Ohio State Museum, who found that tooth-wear patterns and dental health suggested a diet derived mainly from intensive collecting and hunting.

North America. John A. Eddy, National Center for Atmospheric Research, Boulder, Colo., reported that the alignment of rock cairns making up the Big Horn Medicine Wheel in northern Wyoming showed specific correlations with astronomical phenomena associated with the summer solstice. Eddy suggested that it may have been constructed to predict this event, thus helping to mark the time of the annual Sun Dance of Plains Indian culture. Using changes in the declination of the sun as a guide, he calculated that the rock features were probably constructed about A.D. 1700. A radiocarbon date of more than 10,000 years was reported for human bone and associated obsidian artifacts from a deeply buried site exposed by an eroding stream near Clear Lake, Calif. This was one of the earliest examples of obsidian use in North America.

Mesoamerica. In a review of archaeological work carried out from Michoacán to Sinaloa along the west coast of Mexico, an area peripheral to the major developments of Mesoamerican civilization, Clement

W. Meighan, University of California at Los Angeles, proposed that the region did not enter the sphere of central Mexico until about A.D. 500. Prior to that time, western Mexico was the centre of an indigenous tradition of unknown origin, characterized by large shaft tombs and pottery figurine grave offerings.

A comparison of ancient pollen from Guila Naquitz Cave in Oaxaca, Mex., with modern pollen from the same locality was reported by James Schoenwetter, Arizona State University. Although plants belonging to the preceramic period of cave occupancy, dated about 6000 to 8000 B.C., were identical with modern plants found in the region, different frequency patterns among the species indicated an ancient climate that was cooler but more arid than that of the present day. The analysis also suggested that a maize-like plant was being cultivated at this period.

Stylistic comparisons and X-ray diffraction analysis of paste composition were employed by Evelyn C. Rattray and Marie Farnsworth, University of Missouri, to distinguish imported trade ware from locally manufactured ceramics at Teotihuacán, a step necessary in the delineation of exchange relationships. William A. Haviland, University of Vermont, proposed that stoneworking and monument carving were not the only specialized occupations among the Classic Maya at Tikal, Guatemala; other crafts, including figurine manufacture and work in obsidian, also may have been carried out by specialized craftsmen. Haviland tentatively suggested that they were all members of a single lineage devoted to occupational specialties.

B. L. Turner II, University of Wisconsin, reported on an extensive system of relic agricultural terraces and raised fields in Campeche and Quintana Roo on the Yucatán Peninsula of Mexico. These features indicated that the prehistoric lowland Maya practiced intensive agriculture, in which the frequency of cultivation exceeded the frequency of fallowing, rather than the shifting agriculture with long-term fallowing usually attributed to them.

Central America. Junius Bird, American Museum of Natural History, supervised continuing investigations of Paleoindian materials in the Madden Lake area of the Canal Zone, Panama. Fluted points were recovered, as well as indications of a very early stone tool workshop. Richard W. Magnus, Yale University, continued investigations along the Atlantic coastal zone of central Nicaragua. He conducted the first scientific excavation of an undisturbed site that contained stone statuary characteristic of that region. In El Salvador, Howard Ernest, Harvard University, excavated a Mayan site near San Salvador that was scheduled to be destroyed by construction work.

Andean South America. Manuel A. Landivar, Casa de la Cultura, reported on excavations in the vicinity of Cuenca, in the southern highlands of Ecuador. A complex of Spanish structures, built prior to A.D. 1557, utilized lintels and other stones from Inca buildings. The high quality of the stonework and the quantity of remains suggested that Cuenca had been an important Inca centre.

In Bolivia, Maks Portugal Zamora and Maz Portugal Ortiz, Museo Nacional de Arqueología, investigated the Kallamarka site, located near the Tiwanaku (Tiahuanaco) type-site. Kallamarka was built prior to the founding of Tiwanaku and was characterized by embellished ceremonial structures of novel form and by a diversity of unique ceramic features such as animal effigy jars and human figurines. In Peru, David L. Browman, Washington University, St. Louis, Mo.,

reported research on llama and alpaca pastoralism from the development of the Tiwanaku state to the present day. Initially, the subsistence economy was mainly pastoral and farming was secondary. Later, agriculture replaced pastoralism, though animals continued to be important as beasts of burden.

The fifth year of field studies of the Chan Chan-Moche Valley Project was completed under the direction of Carol J. Mackey, California State University, Northridge, and Michael E. Moseley, Harvard University. Chan Chan, overlooking the sea at the mouth of the Moche River, was the largest pre-Columbian city in South America. Approximately 2,000 archaeological sites had been located in the vicinity of Chan Chan, scattered throughout the Moche Valley from the Pacific Ocean to the Andean foothills.

Southern South America. Jorge Fernández, Mina Aguilar, investigated a large preceramic workshop at Espinazo del Diablo in northwestern Argentina in cooperation with Juan Schobinger and J. R. Bárcena, Universidad Nacional de Cuyo. The site appeared to have been utilized by early hunters between 6000 and 3000 B.C. In the Cuyo region, investigations under the general direction of Mariano Gambier, Centro de Investigaciones Arqueológicas y Museo, continued to produce data on preceramic and protoceramic cultures. A survey to the west of the Ansilta Range resulted in the discovery of a lithic complex believed to represent specialized hunters and to date about 6500 B.C.

In the Patagonian region, a team from Universidad Nacional de Buenos Aires, directed by Marcelo Bórmida and Amalia Sanguinetti de Bórmeda, discovered a rough pebble-tool assemblage on the lower Neuquén River. The assemblage consisted of chopping tools and large flakes and was believed to date about 10,000 B.C. The complex may have been the source for later lithic industries of the region. Also in Patagonia, material found by Augusto Cardich, Universidad Nacional de La Plata, in northern Santa Cruz Province was dated by radiocarbon as earlier than 10,000 B.C.

(DAVID A. FREDRICKSON)

See also Anthropology.

[732.G.8.c; 10/41.B.2.a.ii]

ENCYCLOPÆDIA BRITANNICA FILMS. *Sentinels of Silence (Ruins of Ancient Mexico)* (1973).

Architecture

The energy crisis precipitated by the Middle East war of October 1973 stimulated architects and engineers to examine building methods designed to conserve the maximum amount of energy. The U.S. federal government took the initiative, with the General Services Administration (GSA) publishing *Energy Conservation Design Guidelines for Office Buildings.* In a new Federal Office Building for Manchester, N.H., begun in the spring of 1974, Dubin, Mendel & Bloom, engineering consultants to the GSA, planned to save 35–50% of the average annual energy expenditure for a six-story office block. This saving was made possible by careful analysis of many factors, including the glass-to-wall surface ratio. The information collected was analyzed by computer to determine the most efficient thermal design for the building's exterior. As a result, the glass area was reduced from 50 to 10% of the surface, the south side of the building having large areas of glass to take advantage of the maximum amount of winter sun while on the north wall there were no windows at all. Redundant lighting was lessened by using fewer interior walls, while huge solar collectors on the roof would supply 50% of the energy needs, exclusive of electricity.

Dubin, Mendel & Bloom were also the engineers for another building that utilized solar power: the new administration and research centre for the New York Botanical Gardens at the Mary Flagley Carey Arboretum. The architect was Malcolm B. Wells. Maximum aesthetic effect was derived from the soaring solar collectors crowning the roof like giant sails, while sliding insulated panels for the windows controlled night heat loss. Inside, the emphasis was on task lighting—direct light where it is most needed at any given time—rather than on space lighting common in most office buildings. A further saving in resources was made by using rainwater for such needs as toilet flushing.

Charles W. Moore Associates constructed a unique house in Guilford, Conn., designed to use the sun's energy, the south roof being entirely covered by a solar collector while the walls were used as a reverse thermos bottle, the heated water being stored in the perimeter walls. A science building powered by solar energy was built for the Madeira School, McLean, Va. Designed by Arthur Cotton Moore Associates, the building housed laboratories for chemistry, biology, and physics.

In the U.K., the New General Infirmary and Medical/Dental Schools, to be built by the United Leeds Hospitals, was to have its own generating station using natural gas or oil. The hospital's energy requirements were great enough to make this an economical proposition. Designers of the complex were Building Design Partnership, Preston Group.

Another sign of the times was in the celebration of Expo 74, the world's fair held in Spokane, Wash., where emphasis was placed more on permanent long-term environmental considerations than on spectacular temporary exhibition architecture. The U.S. pavilion was covered by a vast temporary vinyl tent, while the Washington State pavilion was a permanent structure, to be used as an opera house and convention centre. The 100-ac. park formed for the exhibition was to remain.

Educational and Cultural Buildings. At Columbia University in New York City, the projected Sherman Fairchild Center for the Life Sciences by architects Mitchell/Giurgola Associates was to be an eight-story laboratory flanked by Beaux-Arts Classical buildings. The new laboratory will consist of a glass-walled volume, in front of which will float a concrete fenestration screen. There will be two components: a large rectangular space housing laboratory facilities, and a smaller, irregular element housing administrative offices, classrooms, and the like. Separation of laboratory facilities from classrooms was also a feature of the design of the new Agricultural Sciences Building (South) at the University of Kentucky, Lexington, by the Design Environment Group Architects of Louisville, Ky. The structure, of cast-in-place concrete with sandblasted surfaces, had the teaching areas grouped around a plaza at ground level and a research building connected to it by a pedestrian bridge. The building won the 1973 Kentucky Society of Architects Honor Award for Design Excellence.

The new Science Building for the Central Institute of Research of the National University of La Plata, Arg., was designed by architects Baudizzone, Diaz, Erbin, Lestard, Traine and Varas. Again a distinction was made between functional needs of classroom space and laboratory space. The building consisted of a box

with a glazed side and a closed side, the open, sunny side housing classrooms and the dark side the labs. Valuable scientific equipment could thus be kept in a heat-and-light-controlled environment.

In India the new Xavier Technical Institute near Baroda was built on a campus of 12 ac. Architect Hasmukh C. Patel incorporated classrooms, library, dormitories, and other elements into a grid plan with each building and then each group of buildings arranged around a court. Most were only one story high, and emphasis was placed on quality of construction to inspire students at the institute who were training to be craftsmen in mechanical and electrical work.

The new Oxon Run Educational Center in Washington, D.C., was to be the first school in the capital to accommodate both primary and secondary grades. Designed by Lawrence B. Perkins and Philip Will, Jr., it could be used after hours for a variety of community activities. The open plan design incorporated 350,000 sq.ft. on three levels.

An imaginatively planned nursery school at Osaka, Jap., was designed by Takamitsu Azuma, arranged around a courtyard with extensive areas of glass facing onto the courtyard. Using the building was intended to be an educational experience in itself for the children attending the school. Only the primary colours, red, yellow, and blue, were used, and emphasis was on the maximum amount of light and air.

The redesigned scheme for the John F. Kennedy Library at Harvard University was unveiled by architects I. M. Pei and Partners. The new scheme consisted of three elements: the library, an academic building for Harvard, and Commonwealth Park. The scale of the buildings had been reduced, and a new park area created for public use.

In England a new public library for Maidenhead, Berkshire, was designed by Ahrends, Burton & Koralek. On three levels, the structure was a steel space frame clad with red engineering bricks. Large areas of glass were also included.

One of the problems that faced architects Eesley, Lee and Vargo when they designed the Ohio River Museum, Marietta, O., was that the site was subject to heavy and frequent flooding. To overcome this, they raised the building complex 12 ft. off the ground, the elements being linked by open bridges that had large windows only on the side looking out toward the river. Underneath one structure was a large outdoor display area for steamboat artifacts, while mechanical

The new Federal Reserve Bank in Minneapolis, Minn., employs suspension principles in its construction. The above-ground, 11-story element is hung from cables as in bridge design. An additional three stories are underground and are reputed to be fortress-like, for money-handling operations.

English architect Tom Kay won the Eternit Prize for single family dwellings for this house, his own residence, in Camden Town, London.

TOM KAY

services were housed on the roof, out of reach of flood-waters.

The state of Colorado held a competition for a new major public building, the Colorado State Judicial/ Heritage Center complex. The competition was open to all Colorado architects. The winner was Rogers-Nagel-Langhart, whose scheme featured a six-story structure to house judicial functions with a neighbouring low, terraced building forming the Heritage Center.

In Australia the Adelaide Festival Theatre, seating 2,000, was the first stage of a cultural complex that would ultimately include three other theatres. The informal and pragmatic design by Hassell & Partners consisted of a steel frame with ribbed precast concrete cladding.

Commercial and Municipal Buildings. Construction was planned to start in 1974 on a new scheme designed to revitalize the downtown area of Burlington, Vt. Plans prepared by the Office of Mies van der Rohe and Freeman-French-Freeman called for new offices, apartments, shopping facilities, and hotels, with a common parking area. The 17-ac. site, to be called Burlington Square, would feature an all-weather pedestrian mall. A glass-covered arcade 76 ft. high was the focal point of a new plan for downtown Denver, Colo., by Kevin Roche and John Dinkeloo. Four blocks of downtown were to become an integrated area with theatres, shops, and restaurants. Existing buildings would be renovated.

A small fire station on the east side of Seattle, Wash., by architects Hobbs Fukui Associates was the result of the activities of that city's design commission, a body recommending architects for public buildings and making special efforts to choose young firms. The layout of the fire station consisted of two "boxes," one large and one small, for equipment and people. Built of dark brown brick, the station was notable for the geometric masses of its volumes, especially the projecting hose tower. The U.S. Courthouse Annex, Chicago, a 27-story tower providing correctional facilities for prisoners and detainees there on a temporary basis, looked rather like a three-sided IBM card. The building, designed for the GSA by architects Harry Weese & Associates, was due to be completed

in mid-1975. The primary facade motif of 5-in.-wide floor-to-ceiling slit windows of bronze glass gave the building its strange appearance, the narrowness of the windows eliminating the need for bars.

In Paris, designs for the new Australian Embassy by an international team including Harry Seidler & Associates, architects; Marcel Breuer, consulting architect; and structural consultant Pier Luigi Nervi were approved. Two buildings, one the chancery and the other containing 34 residential apartments for diplomats, formed a flattened-out S-curve on an awkward wedge-shaped site in the centre of Paris.

Hyatt Regency, whose hotels in San Francisco and Atlanta, Ga., had attracted much interest, planned to build three more hotels, in Phoenix, Ariz., Dearborn, Mich., and Kansas City, Mo. The Phoenix and Dearborn hotels were designed by Charles Luckman Associates and the Kansas City hotel by Welton Becket and Associates with Horner and Blessing. The 1,000-room Kansas City hotel was to incorporate a 290-ft.-high atrium space. A new building for Trio Industries, manufacturers of architectural metal building products, was designed to use the technology that the company had developed. The structure, to be built at Shelton, Conn., to house administrative, research, and production facilities, was designed by architects Shreve, Lamb & Harmon Associates.

The central office of the Bank of Brazil, Buenos Aires, Arg., was designed by architects Raúl Raña Veloso, Hernán Alvarez, and Samuel Forster. The 21-story glass tower would house bank offices accessible to the public on the two lowest floors.

An office building in boomerang form graced a sloping triangular site in McLean, Va. Designed by Segreti, Stillwell & Hasselman, the two- and three-story elements fitted the land contours of the site. The structure was steel-framed and clad in asbestos wall panels with sealed plastic window bubbles. The world headquarters for Nabisco, Inc., being constructed by the Grad Partnership on a 121-ac. site in Morris County, N.J., was a three-story building of precast gray concrete panels and gray solar glass consisting of two back-to-back U-shapes joined by a skylit interior court.

The headquarters for Indonesia's National Bank in Jakarta would be that country's largest structure. Designed by Daniel, Mann, Johnson & Mendenhall with P. T. Perentjana Daja, the 35-story structure was to be sheathed in reflective glass.

A multi-use building in New York City designed by David Kenneth Specter contained seven different urban functions. The 52-story structure housed a garage, a glass-covered arcade, retail space, a cafe, offices, a club, and apartments.

A 30-story office tower, which would be the tallest building in Portugal, was proposed for Lisbon in a master plan prepared by Emery Roth & Sons in association with Multiplano of Lisbon. Harry Seidler & Associates was the architect for the MLC Centre proposed to be built in Sydney, Austr. It included a 64-story concrete tower to be supported on eight massive columns. The *Financial Times* 1973 Industrial Architecture Award went to Ove Arup Associates for its John Player & Sons cigarette factory in Nottingham, Eng.

Housing. Architect M. F. Grzesik and engineer J. D. Winders designed a housing system for construction above roadways and railways for Siege Systems Ltd. of Great Britain. The design was made up of a series of inverted V-shaped structural concrete frames.

New performing arts building at the University of Akron, Ohio, is said to be one of the world's most versatile. Movable and motorized interior segments, including the ceiling, permit conversion in minutes to accommodate 900 to 3,000 persons.

COURTESY, THE GOODYEAR TIRE & RUBBER CO. AND UNIVERSITY NEWS SERVICE, THE UNIVERSITY OF AKRON

A development of multilevel flats in a 32-story luxury apartment building on Cumballa Hill, Bombay, India, was designed by architect Charles Correa in association with Pravina Mehta. The flats interlocked in such a way as to allow a terrace garden for each apartment, ensuring essential cross ventilation in a hot climate. The construction was of concrete with a central core.

One of the most admired private residences of the year was the Morgan house, Atlantic Beach, Jacksonville, Fla. Designed by architect William Morgan for his own family, the house consisted of two triangular volumes butting together. Windows opened the house toward the ocean, while blind walls on the other three sides ensured privacy. A central stair linked interior spaces. Bleached wood siding laid in a diagonal pattern was used to clad the exterior and was repeated inside.

In the U.K. a new public housing project on Marquess Road, Islington, London, by architects Darbourne & Darke demonstrated the type of housing now favoured by local authorities. The project, maintaining a high density of 200 persons per acre, consisted of low-rise buildings having a maximum height of four or five stories. Built of gray bricks, the development harmonized with the surrounding traditional London terraced houses. An open space for each family was provided in the form of garden courts.

The death of Louis I. Kahn (*see* OBITUARIES) at the age of 73 was mourned by those concerned with architecture around the world. Kahn, whose works combined strict purity of form with a richness of volumes derived from true functional requirements, was credited by the magazine *Architecture Plus* with changing the direction of modern architecture more than anyone else in the past quarter-century.

(SANDRA MILLIKIN)

See also Cities and Urban Affairs; Engineering Projects; Historic Preservation; Housing; Industrial Production and Technology.

[626.A.1–5; 626.C]

Arctic Regions

After years of debate over environmental, social, and economic issues, the trans-Alaska pipeline, one of the most massive development projects ever undertaken in the northern regions, finally got under way in 1974. Similar and even larger resource projects were in the exploration and planning stages in other parts of the North American Arctic. It was clear that the Alaskan experience in resolving issues was affecting the development strategies of industry and government alike.

The U.S. secretary of the interior, Rogers C. B. Morton, issued the long-awaited construction permit for the 789-mi., 48-in. trans-Alaska pipeline on Jan. 23, 1974, more than two months after Pres. Richard Nixon signed legislation authorizing the right-of-way.

Construction work began at the end of April when about 1,200 workers, assigned to remote camps in connection with a winter resupply and camp expansion program, were reassigned to work on the initial phase of the project, a 360-mi.-long road from the Yukon River to the Prudhoe Bay oil fields. The 1974 program included finishing the road by the end of November, thereby allowing the Alyeska Pipeline Service Co. and the contractors to cut down on expensive air shipments for this portion of the route. One of the early problems reported was the high turnover of employees—approximately 15% of the total work force.

In April the U.S. and Canadian governments were asked to approve construction of a $5.7 billion, 2,600-mi. pipeline to carry natural gas from the North Slope of Alaska and the Mackenzie River delta of northern Canada into the major energy-consuming areas of the two countries. The application was filed by the Alaskan Arctic Gas Pipeline Co. and Canadian Arctic Gas Pipeline Ltd. The president of Alaskan Arctic Gas said that, when full capacity was reached, the pipeline would deliver well over 4,000,000,000 cu.ft. of gas a day, or about 6% of current North American demand. Alaskan Arctic Gas would own and operate 200 mi. of the pipeline in Alaska, while Canadian Arctic Gas would own and operate the 2,400 mi. across northern and western Canada.

In August the Alberta Gas Trunk Line Co. announced plans for a smaller, more Canadian-oriented gas pipeline from the Arctic. Alberta Gas had been formed by two competitive Canadian pipeline groups, one sponsored by Alberta Gas Trunk Line and one by TransCanada PipeLines Ltd., after the Canadian government made it clear it would consider only one Arctic pipeline proposal.

Further potential oil and gas resources in the offshore areas of the Canadian Arctic were confirmed in April when Imperial Oil Ltd. announced the discovery of a multizone oil and gas well in the Mackenzie River delta region. The exploratory well was the second drilled by Imperial from a man-made island constructed in the shallow waters of the Beaufort Sea and was the forerunner of more drilling ventures to be conducted, beginning in 1976, from floating vessels in deeper Beaufort Sea waters. The discovery was one of more than 15 separate oil or gas discoveries in the Mackenzie River delta region.

At the same time, the Canadian government and the petroleum industry agreed to embark on a major program of environmental assessment. A group of 18 companies agreed to provide $4.5 million required for 21 separate environmental studies related to the Beaufort Sea. The program was designed to provide the government with sufficient data to assess the environmental impact of oil and gas drilling from ships or floating platforms in the Beaufort Sea area. In 1973 scientists of the Geological Survey of Canada had estimated that

The remote fastness of the Arctic embraces this construction camp along the route of the trans-Alaska pipeline. The Brooks Range is in the background.

there were 6,000,000,000 bbl. of recoverable oil and more than 90 trillion cu.ft. of recoverable natural gas in the Beaufort Sea-Mackenzie delta region.

Early in the year about $130 million in first payments for the settlement of native land claims in Alaska reached the hands of the 12 Alaska Native Corporations. The payments would be made on an annual basis. In April the secretary of the interior withdrew the remaining 15 million ac. of unclassified land in Alaska, signifying an end to homesteading and unreserved public lands in the 49th state. The long-expected move put the acreage into the D-1 category, meaning that federal agencies would study its potential use and designation. Exploration of resources would be permissible, but not extraction of nonmetalliferous minerals. In June the Department of the Interior designated a land area totaling more than 2 million ac. as a national historical landmark. Cape Krusenstern, part of the land bridge believed to have linked Asia and Alaska in prehistoric times, contains evidences of nearly every major cultural period thus far identified in Arctic history.

Self-government for the Canadian Yukon and Northwest Territories moved a step closer when amendments to the acts governing the territories were introduced in Parliament. The main changes proposed in the Yukon Act would increase the number of councillors and would be tied to fluctuations in the population of the territory. An increase in the size of the Northwest Territories council was also proposed, and all 15 councillors would be elected.

The Canadian government announced that it would have an equity interest in a new lead-zinc mine on Baffin Island designed to provide employment opportunities for Eskimo people in the area. Under terms of the agreement, an independent Canadian company based in Calgary, Alta., Nanisivik Mines Ltd., was formed to develop lead-zinc deposits at Strathcona Sound on the northern end of Baffin Island. Nanisivik, which means "place where people find things," would operate the first Canadian mine north of the Arctic Circle.

Some Canadian studies were aimed at the construction of reinforced vessels capable of carrying about 30,000 tons of concentrate through the northern ice. This would lengthen the shipping season in the eastern Arctic from about 10 to more than 20 weeks.

An Eskimo group in the Mackenzie delta launched a ranch-management project with the purchase of a 5,000-animal herd of domesticated reindeer from the Canadian government. The reindeer herd had been brought to Canada from Alaska more than 40 years earlier and had been maintained in the delta region to provide meat and hides for the local population. A grazing reserve of 18,000 sq.mi. in the delta would continue to be used by the new company.

An agreement was concluded delimiting the continental shelf area between the Canadian Arctic Islands and Greenland. Under the 1958 UN Convention on the Continental Shelf, either party could extend its sovereign rights in the area for the purpose of exploration and exploitation of natural resources. The dividing line, stretching some 1,430 nautical miles, was the longest continental-shelf delimitation in the world.

Soviet scientists were reported to have discovered archaeological evidence supporting the theory that ancient Asian tribes migrated to the American continent over what is now the Bering Strait. Nikolai Dikov, head of an expedition to the Kamchatka Peninsula on the Soviet Union's Pacific coast, said his group

had discovered objects, such as beads and belts, that had previously been found only in America.

Preparations were under way for one of the largest Arctic research projects in U.S. history, the Arctic Ice Dynamics Joint Experiment (AIDJEX). Four manned stations and at least ten buoys were to be established in the Beaufort Sea during March and April of 1975. The stations would be maintained continuously for one year.   (KENNETH DE LA BARRE)

Argentina

The federal republic of Argentina occupies the southeastern section of South America and is bounded by Bolivia, Paraguay, Brazil, Uruguay, Chile, and the Atlantic Ocean. It is the second largest Latin-American country, after Brazil, with an area of 1,072,-163 sq.mi. (2,776,889 sq.km.). Pop. (1973 est.): 24,-286,000. Cap. and largest city: Buenos Aires (pop., 1973 est., 2,976,000). Language: Spanish. Religion: mainly Roman Catholic. Presidents in 1974, Juan Domingo Perón and, after July 1, María Estela Martínez de Perón.

Domestic Affairs. Pres. Juan Domingo Perón (*see* OBITUARIES) died on July 1, 1974, after nine months in office, and was succeeded by his wife and vice-president, María Estela Martínez de Perón (*see* BIOGRAPHY). While in exile, from 1955 to 1973, Juan Perón had wooed the left wing of the Peronist movement and supported the most belligerent labour unions. Once returned to power, however, he modified this policy, forming close links with the armed forces and other previously oppositionist right-wing groups and at the same time using his political skill to maintain the respect of the left. Without Perón this situation could not be maintained, and divisions in the government and in the Peronist movement, already present when Perón was alive (as when the police overthrew the Peronist left government of Córdoba Province in February in favour of the Peronist right), were brought into the open. Mrs. Perón failed to retain the close support of any power group. Even the labour unions, traditional bastions of Peronism, offered only nominal support. In a gesture toward the workers who still revered Perón's second wife as a near saint, the president ordered the body of Eva Duarte Perón returned to Argentina. It had been hidden abroad for some 19 years.

Terrorist activity and political violence increased after the death of Perón. As hard-liners in the government threatened to step up their activities against terrorists, especially the illegal ERP (People's Revolutionary Army) and the Montoneros, the latter declared that they were going underground again. A fascist terrorist organization, the Anti-Communist League, conducted reprisals. By November the number of political killings since Perón's death was nearing 150, and on November 6, following the assassination of Alberto Villar, the chief of federal police, the government declared a state of siege.

Foreign Relations. Domestic difficulties clearly preoccupied the new president when she took office, and there was no indication whether she intended to continue Perón's line on foreign policy or, indeed, whether she could do so, since in this field, as in domestic politics, Perón had relied much on his own

Areas:
see Populations and Areas; *see also the individual country articles*

personality. In May the minister of economy led a trade mission to various European countries, including members of the Comecon bloc (the Soviet Union and Communist nations of Eastern Europe). The minister's visit was a success; Argentina was offered lines of credit for the purchase of goods, and at the same time found new markets for its own exports. The U.S.S.R. agreed to participate in one of the largest hydroelectric schemes to be set up in Argentina; Poland was to help with the development of the Río Turbio coal mine; Czechoslovakia with the development of mining, transport, and energy supply; and Hungary with railway and telecommunications projects. In addition to projecting the image of a world statesman, Perón had been anxious to compete with the growing dominance of Brazil in Latin-American affairs. He accordingly tried to forge stronger links with Uruguay, Paraguay, and Peru, and went a long way toward changing the attitudes of other Latin-American states toward Cuba (during 1974 Argentina offered Cuba substantial credits).

The Economy. A gross domestic product growth rate of 6.2% was reported by the government for the first six months of the year, as compared with one of 4.8% in 1973 as a whole and 3.8% in 1972. The satisfactory economic development in 1973 and during the first half of 1974 was due in part to excellent sorghum and corn harvests and to increased industrial production (especially of automobiles, tractors, and farm machinery), and in part to the high level of exports. The external position in 1973 was very strong. An increase of 57.1% in exports to $3,050,000,000 (as a result of high international prices for agricultural products) and one of only 9.7% in imports to $2,090,-000,000 resulted in a record trade surplus of $960 million in 1973, as compared with one of $36 million in 1972. This trend continued in 1974; in the first half of the year exports amounted to $1,549,000,000, and international reserves rose to $2 billion from $1.3 billion in December 1973 and $500 million at the end of 1972. Nevertheless, commodity prices showed signs of weakening, as the government revised downward its forecast of exports for 1974 as a whole to $3.5 billion. In any case, a constricting factor in 1974 was the imposition by the EEC of higher tariff barriers on meat, an important part of Argentina's total exports.

The government achieved a reasonable degree of price stability during 1974—although the underlying causes of inflation were not tackled—largely by

Members of a Peronist youth group march in protest in southern Buenos Aires Province. Although they had helped him return to power, Perón's government imposed various restraints on the leftists during the early part of the year.

squeezing company profits, contributing to a notable decline in private investment. As a result of legislation governing foreign investment passed in November 1973, new foreign investment in the country was very low. Official institutions, however, such as the Inter-American Development Bank, provided large sums for development projects. At the end of 1973 the government published an ambitious long-term development plan. This envisaged a cumulative annual growth rate target for the gross domestic product of 7.8% based on increased productivity, exports, domestic savings, and investment. One objective was to reduce the country's dependence on imported petroleum: although Argentina imported only 15% of its domestic requirements for petroleum, imports of fuel were nevertheless a significant item. The plan, therefore, called for substantial investment in order to increase production of petroleum and derivatives, natural gas, and coal, and for increases in energy from hydroelectric sources; work was already under way on several important hydroelectric projects. In March Perón inaugurated a nuclear plant at Atucha, the first in Latin America, which would use natural uranium from deposits in Mendoza. Work began at the end of May on a second nuclear plant, and a third was in the planning stage.   (FRANCES KIRKHAM)

[974.F.1]

ARGENTINA
Education. (1973) Primary, pupils 3,508,406, teachers 189,456; secondary, pupils 422,652, teachers 59,521; vocational, pupils 703,063, teachers 88,962; higher (including 14 main universities), students 369,168, teaching staff 28,139.
Finance. Monetary unit: peso, with (Sept. 16, 1974) an official rate of 5 pesos to U.S. $1 (free rate of 11.51 pesos = £1 sterling) and a financial rate of 9.98 pesos to U.S. $1 (free rate of 23.03 pesos = £1 sterling). Gold, SDRs, and foreign exchange, central bank: (March 1974) U.S. $1,470,000,000; (March 1973) U.S. $645 million. Budget (1973 actual): revenue 19,085,-000,000 pesos; expenditure 38,660,000,000 pesos. Gross national product: (1970) 93,760,000,000 pesos; (1969) 79,590,000,000 pesos. Money supply: (Dec. 1973) 67,950,000,000 pesos; (Dec. 1972) 33.6 billion pesos. Cost of living (Buenos Aires; 1970 = 100): (April 1974) 386; (April 1973) 344.
Foreign Trade. (1972) Imports 15,630,000,-000 pesos; exports 15,425,000,000 pesos. Import sources: U.S. 20%; West Germany 13%; Brazil 9%; Japan 7%; U.K. 7%; Italy 6%. Export destinations: Italy 13%; West Germany 12%; U.S. 10%; Brazil 10%; U.K. 9%; Chile 8%; France 6%; The Netherlands 6%. Main exports: meat 36%; corn 8%; hides and skins 6%; wheat 5%.
Transport and Communications. Roads (1972) 283,775 km. Motor vehicles in use (1971): passenger 1,680,000; commercial 788,-000. Railways: (1971) 39,546 km.; traffic (1972) 12,183,000,000 passenger-km., freight 12,284,-000,000 net ton-km. Air traffic (1972): 2,963,-000,000 passenger-km.; freight 87.3 million net ton-km. Shipping (1973): merchant vessels 100 gross tons and over 351; gross tonnage 1,452,-552. Shipping traffic (1971): goods loaded 14,-051,000 metric tons, unloaded 10,662,000 metric tons.
Agriculture. Production (in 000; metric tons; 1973; 1972 in parentheses): wheat 6,500 (7,-900); corn 9,700 (5,860); sorghum 5,159 (2,-502); barley 750 (880); oats 515 (566); rye 432 (690); potatoes 1,535 (1,340); sugar, raw value 1,570 (1,303); linseed 320 (330); sunflower seed 800 (828); cotton, lint 125 (87); tomatoes 500 (492); oranges (1972) 743, (1971) 990; apples (1972) 512, (1971) 424; wine 2,200 (1,999); tobacco 74 (74); beef and veal c. 2,090 (2,198); cheese (1972) 200, (1971) 188; wool (1972) 84, (1971) 86; quebracho extract (1972) 96, (1971) 79. Livestock (in 000; June 1973): cattle 55,464; sheep c. 40,000; pigs 4,533; goats (1972) c. 5,250; horses (1972) c. 3,500; chickens (1972) c. 33,000.
Industry. Fuel and power (in 000; metric tons; 1973): crude oil 21,434; natural gas (cu.m.) 6,729,000; coal (1972) 675; electricity (kw-hr.; 1972) 25,319,000. Production (in 000; metric tons; 1972): cement 5,454; crude steel (1973) 2,155; cotton yarn 89; nylon, etc., yarn and fibres 37; passenger cars (including assembly; units) 202; commercial vehicles (including assembly; units) 67.

Art Exhibitions

The growing interest in native arts and crafts was marked during the year by several exhibitions devoted to folk art, the most important being "The Flowering of American Folk Art, 1776–1876," organized by the Whitney Museum of American Art, New York City, and traveling later to Richmond, Va., and the De Young Museum in San Francisco. A few people had been collecting folk art for many years, but it was only recently that collecting such items as American quilts and native paintings had become fashionable. The Whitney exhibition illustrated the full range of American life and was certainly the most definitive of its kind ever held. Among the finest objects shown were the carved items: shop signs, statues, gravestones, figureheads, and weather vanes. Pictures in the exhibition were drawn, painted, or stitched. The Art Institute of Chicago held an exhibition of its entire collection of nearly 160 woven American coverlets, dating from about 1800 to 1900.

A major exhibition devoted to "American Self-Portraits" was organized by the International Exhibitions Foundation of Washington, D.C., and shown at the National Portrait Gallery, Washington, and the Indianapolis (Ind.) Museum of Art. The exhibition, the first of its kind, included 109 works lent by many major museums and private collections and covering three centuries of changing tastes. Among the artists represented were Benjamin West, J. S. Copley, J. M. Whistler, J. S. Sargent, Thomas Eakins, Ben Shahn, and Andy Warhol. "Artists of the Pacific Northwest" was the title of a major show held at the National Collection of Fine Arts, Smithsonian Institution, Washington, D.C. Forty-six artists were represented, including Mark Tobey, Morris Graves, and C. S. Price. A special exhibition of the works of Frederic Remington was held at the Whitney Gallery of Western Art, Cody, Wyo.

In West Germany the Kunstgewerbemuseum, Cologne, held a show entitled "Objects USA" that illustrated the difficulty of defining decorative art when many traditional concepts of art had been overthrown by modern technology. Other exhibitions of works by

American artists included one devoted to Everett Shinn, a member of "The Eight," a group of American painters, also known as the Ashcan School, who were active early in the 20th century. The show was organized by the New Jersey State Museum in cooperation with the Delaware Art Museum and the Munson-Williams-Proctor Institute, Utica, N.Y. The 77 paintings, watercolours, and sketches, lent by 33 public institutions and private collectors, included many examples of Shinn's well-known depictions of the glamorous nightlife of New York. New York life also played an important role in the paintings of Richard Lindner, a German Expressionist who emigrated to that city. An exhibition of his works was seen in Paris, Rotterdam, Neth., Düsseldorf, W.Ger., and Zürich, Switz.

The long-forgotten but recently rediscovered history painter and illustrator Edward Austin Abbey, best known as an illustrator for *Harper's* magazine, was the subject of an exhibition held at the Albany (N.Y.) Institute of History and Art and at the Pennsylvania Academy. The exhibition was assembled by the Yale University Art Gallery, which owned a large collection of Abbey's works. The New York Museum of Modern Art organized a small exhibition of paintings by Gerald Murphy. Better known as a friend of the novelist F. Scott Fitzgerald than as an artist, Murphy and his wife, Sarah, were important figures in the expatriate American community in Paris in the 1920s. Only a few of Murphy's very competent abstract paintings had survived. The exhibition was also seen in San Francisco in the summer.

One of the most pleasant exhibitions in London was "Landscape in Britain *c.* 1750–1850" at the Tate Gallery. The collection illustrated the complexity of ideas behind the rendition of landscape and included works by unknown as well as famous artists. Also in London, the Royal Academy celebrated the centenary of the first Impressionist exhibition, held in Paris on April 15, 1874, with an exhibition entitled "Impressionism —Its Masters, Precursors, and Its Influence in Britain." The 137 paintings and watercolours from public and private collections in Britain included works by the French founders of the movement and by their English followers, notably W. R. Sickert and Wilson Steer. Another major exhibition celebrating the cen-

An observer studies Joan Miró's dramatic creation entitled "The Ski Lesson" at the Grand Palais des Beaux Arts in Paris.

KEYSTONE

tenary, jointly organized by the Louvre and New York City's Metropolitan Museum of Art, drew huge crowds to the Grand Palais in Paris in the fall.

At the Victoria and Albert Museum, an exhibition entitled "Music in the 18th Century" included examples of work by the most celebrated British and French makers of musical instruments. The items were drawn from the museum's own collection as well as from the collection of the Horniman Museum, London, the Conservatoire in Paris, and various private sources. The show was seen at several other British and French museums and also at the Edinburgh Festival. Another exhibition that attracted crowds to the Victoria and Albert commemorated the 150th anniversary of the poet Byron's death and included paintings, manuscripts, and letters as well as such relics as the traveling bed on which Byron died. An exhibition at Somerset House to mark the centenary of Winston Churchill's birth was the first to be held in the newly reopened 18th-century rooms designed by Sir William Chambers.

The Hayward Gallery held a number of worthwhile shows during the year. In April "Vorticism and Its Allies" was devoted to the English group led by Wyndham Lewis and included works by David Bomberg, Henri Gaudier-Brzeska, and Vanessa Bell. The exhibition, which featured a splendid section devoted to catalogs, posters, and the magazine *Blast* published by the group, was indicative of a growing interest in 20th-century British art. The Norwegian Expressionist painter Edvard Munch was the subject of an exhibition at the Hayward Gallery, organized by the Arts Council in collaboration with the Edvard Munch Museum, Oslo; paintings, drawings, watercolours, and prints were obtained from public and private collections in Norway and elsewhere. Munch was also honoured in Paris, where he lived for many years, in a show of 250 items at the Musée d'Art Moderne.

A major retrospective devoted to the English painter Lucian Freud, also at the Hayward Gallery early in the year, illustrated Freud's independent search for factual objectivity in two dimensions. Still another British painter was honoured with a retrospective at the Tate entitled "The Late Richard Dadd." Dadd, though little known, painted pictures of remarkable intensity in a style related to that of the Pre-Raphaelites. After murdering his father in 1843, he was confined for over 40 years to hospital and prison, where he painted some of his finest works.

Major exhibitions in Paris included one devoted to Georges Braque, a pioneer of Cubism. Held at the Orangerie des Tuileries, the show included 140 canvases dating from 1900 to 1963. Another Cubist painter, Juan Gris, was honoured with a large retrospective at the Orangerie—the first such exhibition of his works in Paris. "Pastels et miniatures du XVIIIème siècle" was the title of a delightful exhibition at the Louvre's Pavillon de Flore. Forty pastels, including work by lesser known artists in the medium, captured the delightful spirit of the 18th century, while the 180 exquisite miniatures included portraits, mythological scenes, and topographical subjects.

At the Museum of the Petit Palais, "Treasures of the Equator" featured pre-Columbian art of equatorial South America, covering the period from prehistoric times to the European conquest in 1534. The items were very different from the more familiar pottery and jewelry of ancient Mexico and Peru.

Following the huge international success of the previous year's "Treasures of Chinese Art," further shows were devoted to objects from the Orient and the Middle East. The Boston Museum of Fine Arts held the first exhibition in the U.S. to explore recent archaeological discoveries in China. Entitled "Unearthing China's Past," it included more than 100 works of Chinese art from Western collections, together with photographs of works unearthed since 1949. Some splendid bronzes were included. "Chinese Figure Painting," one of a series of exhibitions held to celebrate the 50th anniversary of the Freer Gallery, Washington, D.C., showed the status achieved by figure painting in China long before landscape was accepted as an independent subject. The Hans Popper Collection of Oriental Art was first seen at the Asian Art Museum of San Francisco and then traveled to Baltimore, Md., Cleveland, O., and Seattle, Wash. The collection, covering the period from the 13th century B.C. to the 14th century A.D., was especially strong in ancient bronzes, Bronze Age artifacts, Buddhist sculptures, ceramics, and Korean celadons. One of the finest collections of Islamic art in the world, the Palevsky-Heeramaneck collection, had been acquired by the Los Angeles County Museum of Art and was shown there in the spring. It covered the period from A.D. 700 to 1900 and included paintings, bronzes, glass, textiles, calligraphy, and ceramics.

Several major exhibitions featured graphic works. Sixteenth-century Italian drawings from the collection of Janos Scholz, a well-known cellist and collector, were shown at the Pierpont Morgan Library, New York City, in January and February. The show had been seen the previous year at the National Gallery, Washington, D.C., where the works were deposited. The drawings, many of which had not previously been displayed together, included works by Raphael, Leonardo, Correggio, and Titian. The complexity of the art of engraving was illustrated by an exhibition at the Wallraf-Richardz Museum, Cologne. Designed to present a panorama of engraving from the origins of the technique to modern times, it included engravings, etchings, coloured lithographs, and silk screen, as well as works achieved by modern photographic processes.

An exhibition of drawings by the 18th-century French painter François Boucher taken from North American collections was shown at the Art Institute of Chicago, having been seen earlier at the National Gallery. A quarter of all Boucher's drawings were in the U.S., and 100 were shown in the exhibition. "One Hundred Master Drawings from New England Private Collections" at the Boston Museum of Fine Arts covered the whole of modern art history from the Italian Renaissance to the present.

A number of exhibitions were devoted to artists who had worked in the 20th century. Works by the colour-field abstractionist Jules Olitski were shown at the Pasadena (Calif.) Museum of Modern Art in a show organized by the Boston Museum of Fine Arts and first seen there. Olitski, who was born in the U.S.S.R. in 1922 and had had a strong influence on younger painters, was best known for his technique of spraying fine layers of acrylic paint onto raw canvases to create soft expanses of colour. A tribute to Le Corbusier at the Musée des Beaux-Arts, Chalon, France, emphasized his paintings rather than his architectural work.

A tribute to the Spanish Surrealist Joan Miró, held at the New York Museum of Modern Art to honour the artist's 81st birthday, was drawn from the museum's own extensive collection, the best Miró collection in the world. It included about 40 paintings, sculptures, and collages, some of which had never before been on public view. An exhibition of works by Belgian Symbolists and Surrealists, organized by the Belgian Ministry of National Education and Culture, was shown at the New York Cultural Center and later at the new Museum of Fine Arts, Houston, Tex. The show featured 120 works by painters working from about 1885 to the present. René Magritte and Paul Delvaux were both well represented.

At the Portsmouth (Eng.) Museum and Art Gallery, a fine show of works by the German Expressionist sculptor Wilhelm Lehmbruck featured sculptures, paintings, and graphics on loan from the Lehmbruck family and the Wilhelm-Lehmbruck-Museum, Duisburg, W.Ger. A selection from the show had previously traveled to Washington, D.C., and Berlin. "Masterpieces of 20th Century Art," the Nordrhein Westfalen collection from Düsseldorf, was seen at the Tate in the autumn. A small exhibition at the National Gallery, London, was hailed as a model for future art exhibitions. "Dutch Townscape Painting," a display of about a dozen items from the gallery's own collection, was seen as an alternative to the kind of large loan exhibition that was increasingly difficult to mount as owners became reluctant to risk lending paintings under current conditions. The show focused on a small idea that could be well illustrated and easily grasped in an entirely satisfactory way.

Two exhibitions focused on aspects of art nouveau: "Jewelry from the Belle-Époque to the Present" at the Palais des Beaux-Arts in Charleroi, Belg., and "Brussels 1900," devoted to art nouveau architecture, at the Architectural Association in London. The latter included 168 photographs and original drawings organized as an archive of the Belle Époque and as a stimulus to protect what remained of this architecture.

Some of the finest art collections in the U.S. were in the possession of universities. "Paintings from Midwestern University Collections," sponsored by a consortium of 11 Midwestern universities, included 42 works encompassing a wide range of subjects and styles. "Ivory Carvings in Early Medieval England— 700–1200," a fascinating Arts Council exhibition at the Victoria and Albert Museum, assembled over 60 carvings in walrus ivory, whalebone, and elephant ivory. To commemorate the centenary of the death of J. M. W. Turner, the Royal Academy mounted a large

exhibition of his works which opened in November and was scheduled to run until March 1975.

(SANDRA MILLIKIN)

See also Museums; Photography.

[612.B; 613.A–B]

ENCYCLOPÆDIA BRITANNICA FILMS. *Henry Moore—The Sculptor* (1969); *Siqueiros—"El Maestro"* (1969); *Richard Hunt—Sculptor* (1970); *Interpretations* (1970); *Textiles and Ornamental Arts of India* (1973).

Art Sales

The 1973–74 art auction season opened with a continuation of the boom conditions of the previous year. At Christie's Croxeth Hall sale in Liverpool in September 1973 a sporting painting by the minor Victorian artist Richard Ansdell brought as much as £89,250 and a Sèvres dinner service, £21,000. This pattern continued through the autumn but the Arab-Israeli war and the oil crisis induced a fit of nerves, and during November–December buyers withdrew on a massive scale. At Christie's major Old Master sale on December 3, 45 out of 133 lots were unsold.

Then from mid-December buyers flooded back into the market, causing a mini-boom in the sales of January and February 1974. The major March sales saw a pronounced cooling down with very selective buying in the upper reaches of the market. By the major summer sales of June and July prices were coming down substantially at the top of the market and many rare treasures remained unsold. The decline in prices was concentrated at the top of the market and in special fields previously particularly favoured by investors; prices in the middle range remained firm.

The market in Impressionist and modern pictures was affected. Earlier in the season many new auction records were established, especially for 20th-century artists. A pink period Picasso gouache, "Jeune Homme au Bouquet," brought $720,000 at Parke-Bernet, New York, in October 1973, but this price was beaten when his Cubist "Femme Assise" made £340,000 at Sotheby's in December. This sale also brought £90,000 for Max Ernst's "Le Toreador." The sale in Paris by a Japanese collector of Paul Delvaux's "Grande Allée" of 1964 for Fr. 950,000 made a dramatic start to the spring sales, and in May 1974 Salvador Dali's "Resurrection of the Flesh" brought $245,000 in New York while a Brancusi bronze, "La Négresse Blonde II," became the most expensive sculpture ever sold at auction ($750,000). But in London in July many major works failed to sell, notably Cézanne's "La Moisson," bought in at £325,500, Picasso's Cubist "Buste de Femme" at £304,500, and Monet's "Les Bords de la Seine à Argenteuil" at £194,250 (compared with a purchase price of £252,000 in 1970).

The speculative spiral in the higher reaches of the Chinese porcelain market also collapsed in the summer of 1974. Previously, an unknown 15th-century blue and white *mei p'ing* reached £135,000 at Phillips, Son & Neale in London in October 1973. Staggering prices at Sotheby's first Hong Kong sale in November included £190,000 for a Hsuan Te bowl that had sold for £35,000 in the London trade less than a year before. In December Christie's sold a damaged underglaze red ewer (14th century) for £168,000. A new level of prices for *famille rose* birds and animals was announced in March 1974 when Helen Glatz, a London dealer, paid £60,000 for a pair of pheasants, £36,000 for a pair of hawks, and £34,000 for a pair of monkeys. On April 2 at Sotheby's the same dealer

An exhibit of Civil War art in New York included this pen and ink drawing of the Battle of Shiloh, April 1862. The collection, valued at $240,000 and "lost" for 60 years in an attic in New Orleans, was acquired by the American Heritage Society.

WIDE WORLD

swept the board paying sensational prices for early blue and white, early monochromes, *famille rose* birds, and the best 17th- and 18th-century Chinese taste pieces; a massive early Ming (*c.* 1400) bottle-shaped vase decorated with a dragon cost her £420,000, the highest auction price ever paid in the applied arts field. But at Christie's Frederick M. Mayer collection sale in June and at Sotheby's on July 10, Mrs. Glatz and a few other key dealers withdrew from the bidding and prices collapsed from April's record levels. It was essentially the prices for ceramics that suffered. Rare works of art brought top prices at the Mayer sale, for example an archaic bronze *fang'i* (wine vessel), £178,500.

A special feature of the season was Sotheby's series of single collection sales where the auctioneers had either guaranteed a minimum outturn or arranged special contract terms. The method antagonized dealers and the sales did not match expectations. Two sales were held from the Jack R. Dick collection of sporting paintings on Oct. 31, 1973, and June 26, 1974; in the first prices were high, up to Sotheby's estimates, with Stubbs's "Goldfinder" at £225,000, Arthur Devis' "Swaine Family" at £136,000, and J. F. Herring's "Great North Road" at £70,000. But in June prices averaged around half Sotheby's estimates and many paintings were unsold.

Another example was the Antonio Santamarina collection of Impressionist paintings sold on April 2. This was complicated by Argentina's efforts to stop the sale, claiming that the paintings had been illegally exported; a rare Toulouse-Lautrec, "Au Cirque Fernando," made £210,000, but Manet's "Isabelle au Manchon" was startlingly cheap at £100,000.

Two collection sales were, however, highly successful. A Canadian collection of English porcelain sold at Sotheby's in November 1973 established new price records for virtually every English factory: Chelsea £32,000, Worcester £20,000, Bow £6,000, etc. The Henri Vever collection of Japanese prints at Sotheby's in March 1974 established a wholly new level of prices for the best prints and drawings: a double portrait by Sharaku at £32,000, a Toyonobu colour print of an actor at £22,000, and a drawing by Hokusai, "The Rape," at £28,000.

In February a major controversy about the sale of church property was touched off in England when the parish church of Broadwater in Sussex sold a funeral helmet which had lodged with them since 1526 for a record £22,000 at Sotheby's. In April a pair of English 17th-century dolls went to a Swiss buyer for £16,000, but following a public appeal they were later acquired by the Victoria and Albert Museum, London. The marvelous Benin bronze flute player was sold in London in July for £185,000.

Book Sales. Book auctions survived the 1973–74 season with no downturn in prices. Indeed, prices continued to rise in almost every book-collecting field, with atlases and natural history colour-plate books in particular mounting in popularity and value.

At Christie's Croxeth Hall sale of September 1973 John Gould's *Birds of Great Britain* and D. G. Elliot's *Family of Pheasants* brought £10,000 each. Samuel Cutis' *Monograph on the Genus Camellia* of 1819 with his *Beauties of Flora* made £14,000 in May, while Gould's *Humming Birds* made £13,000 and his *Birds of Europe*, £11,000. In the same month the full 11-volume Blaeu atlas of 1662 made £25,000.

Among 18th-century books sold in Paris in November two works fetched Fr. 170,000 each: Le Riche de

WIDE WORLD

The Benin bronze figure of a flute player, dating from the 16th century, was sold at Sotheby's in London for £185,000 ($442,150). This was the highest price ever paid for a primitive art work

la Popelinière's *Tableaux des Moeurs du Temps* and a *Représentation des fêtes donnés par la ville de Strasbourg* for Louis XV in 1744—in a superb yellow morocco binding. The following month, also in Paris, a copy of Horace, extensively annotated by Jean Racine, made Fr. 155,000, and the autograph orchestral manuscript of Offenbach's *La Vie Parisienne*, Fr. 82,-000. Musical associations also brought high prices at Sotheby's in March 1974 with a four-volume Italian-German dictionary bearing Mozart's signature inside each cover at £2,500 and a group of autographed letters from Puccini to Mrs. Sybil Seligman at £8,200.

The highlight of the summer sales was the auction of 19 books and 2 manuscripts from the Chatsworth library—a great library formed by successive dukes of Devonshire—at Christie's on June 6. Together they realized £522,900. Included was one of the earliest and finest manuscripts of Chaucer's *The Canterbury Tales*, possibly written for King Henry VII's mother on the occasion of her wedding in about 1450. It went

A. C. COOPER

Part of a luxurious illuminated manuscript of Chaucer's "The Canterbury Tales." The manuscript, thought to have been written about 1450, was sold at Christie's for £90,000 ($216,000) in June.

This handsome Dutch doll's house, dating from about 1860, was part of a collection of dolls and toys sold at Christie's in September. The back of the house opens to reveal five rooms decorated in Neoclassical fashion.

to U.S. dealer Lew David Feldman (House of El Dieff) for £90,000. Top price among the printed books was £60,000 for Cicero's *De Oratore* printed at Subiaco in 1465. The Durandus printed at Mainz by Johann Fust and Peter Schoeffer in 1459 made £48,-000, and Petrarch's *Canzoniere, Sonetti e Trionfi,* Venice, 1470, £40,000.

The following week Sotheby's sold three books by Copernicus from the Harrison D. Horblit library. The first (1543) edition of *De Revolutionibus Orbium Coelestium* reached £44,000; the rarer but less important *De Lateribus et Angulis Triangulorum* of 1542, £7,500; and a second (1566) edition of *De Revolutionibus,* £7,000.

Two notable features of the season's sales in London were the popularity of children's books and juvenilia and new sales of English illustrated books—an offshoot, to some extent, of English picture collecting. William Blake's *Illustrations of the Book of Job* reached £3,200 in December 1973; in January 1974 an autographed manuscript of Edward Lear's *Nonsense Alphabet* made £1,500; and in June some proof pages deleted by Lewis Carroll from *Alice's Adventures Through the Looking Glass,* £1,700. At Sotheby's major sale of English illustrated books in March £2,000 was paid for the printer-designer G. Bottomley's *Frescoes from Buried Temples* of 1928.

(GERALDINE NORMAN)

[613.B.2.b]

Astronomy

X-ray Binary Stars and Black Holes. The study of X-ray binary stars was one of the most active areas in astronomy during the year. X-ray binaries consist of close pairs of stars, one of which has completed its evolution and degenerated into a collapsed state. Meanwhile, the other is losing matter into an accretion disk where it spirals inward onto the collapsed object, becoming enormously hot as it falls and giving rise to the observed X radiation. In favourable circumstances the stars may eclipse each other as they revolve, giving characteristic periods (of a few days) which can be used to search for optical counterparts of the X-ray

sources. Identification candidates were found for about ten objects, and a refined position was determined for Cen X-3, leading to its final identification, from experiments on the Copernicus satellite.

The collapsed star can take a number of forms. First, it may be a white dwarf, which has a mass comparable to that of the sun and a size similar to the earth; such a star is supported by the pressure of degenerate electrons. Second, it may be a neutron star (with degenerate neutron pressure), which represents a further stage of collapse to a size of about 10 km. (1 km. = 0.62 mi.). Third, the star may become a "black hole" in which the mass collapses indefinitely to form an entity from which no light or, indeed, any matter is able to escape. Thus, an observer can know nothing about events going on within a black hole although the star's mass still exists and can exert a gravitational pull on other matter. For stars heavier than about two solar masses the black hole alternative is the only one available, and enormous interest has been focused on finding an X-ray binary with a collapsed object mass heavier than this.

Some binaries can be definitely ruled out. For instance, the X rays from Her X-1 and Cen X-3 have regular pulsation periods of 1.24 and 4.84 sec., respectively, which are probably due to the infalling matter being guided by magnetic fields onto hot spots on the surface of a rotating neutron star. Cyg X-1, however, is a prime candidate. The observed spectral type sets the primary star mass at about 20 times that of the sun, which indicates (with the binary period) that the collapsed object must be at least six solar masses. During the year two other black hole candidates, 2U 1700-37 and 2U 0900-40, were proposed by investigators at the Mount Stromlo Observatory near Canberra, Austr.

An alternative explanation for Cyg X-1 that does not require a black hole has been proposed. It involves a triple-star system, comprising the observed primary, a main sequence B (hot, blue) star, and an X-ray neutron star, of 25, 8, and 1 solar masses, respectively. The two lightest stars could form a close pair revolving around the heaviest, or else the two heaviest could be a close binary with the neutron star in an extended orbit. In either case, the X rays are produced by the accretion of matter onto the collapsed star in the usual way.

Photomosaic of Venus transmitted by Mariner 10 from a distance of about 710,000 km. (440,000 mi.). Cloud patterns reveal the general circulation of the planet's upper atmosphere.

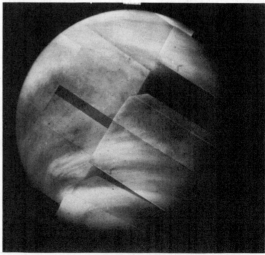

Orion Nebula. The Orion Nebula has long been known as the finest example of a diffuse emission nebula in the sky. More recently it has, with several other such nebulas, been found to be an interesting source of infrared radiation and of molecular lines observed at radio wavelengths. The region is of enormous interest regarding star formation processes and was intensively investigated during the year. New results reported included (1) the detection of dimethyl ether, $(CH_3)_2O$, the largest molecule yet seen in interstellar space, of methylamine, CH_3NH_2, and of the ^{17}O isotope in carbon monoxide; (2) the discovery of a high-velocity hydrogen cloud moving out from the region at 60 km. per sec.; (3) evidence for a magnetic field in the infrared/molecular cloud; and (4) the discovery of an entirely new infrared/molecular cloud located 12' north of the previously known one, and outside the boundary of the optical nebula.

In the infrared the Orion Nebula is a powerful extended source, but it contains a more intense compact infrared nebula (the Kleinmann-Low nebula) embedded in which is a star detectable only in the infrared (the Becklin-Neugebauer object). During the year high-resolution studies of the Kleinmann-Low nebula were made at wavelengths of 5, 10.5, and 21 microns, and four additional compact sources were discovered. (One micron = one-millionth of a metre.)

All these observations forced several workers to propose a new picture for the nebula. It now appears that the well-known optical object is but an ionized protrusion on the side toward the earth of a 1,000-solar mass cloud of neutral gas, dust, and molecules. The ionized gas, driven by pressure gradients in the underlying neutral cloud, is expanding toward the earth and to the southwest.

Observational Aspects of Star Formation. The wealth of new information that has been obtained in infrared and molecular line studies is beginning to form an interesting picture of the processes of star formation in our galaxy. The whole chain of events is not yet clear, but the year's work certainly identified some of the links.

It has been suggested that the infrared/molecular clouds (such as the Kleinmann-Low nebula, *see* above) are in the processes of gravitational collapse and star formation. Such clouds require an internal source of energy to feed their observed radiation, and newly forming stars could provide this. The observed compact infrared sources in the Kleinmann-Low nebula represent such protostars. It also was shown that mass loss from massive, newly formed stars could effectively mask their visual light and make them shine entirely in the infrared (as with the Becklin-Neugebauer object).

Another link in the chain is provided by the Herbig-Haro objects. These are "semistellar," emission-line features appearing in association with dark interstellar clouds. They vary on a time scale of years. Several investigators discovered small infrared sources associated but not spatially coincident with these objects, and detected and measured their optical polarization. Their interpretation is that the Herbig-Haro objects appear when the star-formation cloud disperses sufficiently for the newly formed stars to illuminate parts of it in certain directions, while still remaining obscured to the observer. Thus, these objects are small reflection surfaces providing an indirect view of these stars.

The T Tauri stars represent a still later link in the chain. They too are associated with dark interstellar clouds but are clearly observable as stars at visual wavelengths. They have nebular emission lines superimposed on their stellar spectra, revealing the presence of a circumstellar envelope. In the case of T Tauri itself, there is also an associated nebula extending to 1,500 astronomical units from the star. (An astronomical unit is the distance from the earth to the sun, 150 million km.) Studies of this nebula confirmed a relationship between these stars and the Herbig-Haro objects. It now appears that when the star-formation cloud finally disperses it is as T Tauris that the newly formed stars appear.

Circumstellar Shells. Circumstellar shells of tenuous matter are a feature of several types of star. They have been the subject of much investigation, particularly with infrared techniques but also by other means, including lunar occultations and radio studies.

Late-type supergiants (very large, very cool stars) were among the first studied at infrared wavelengths. It was found that they have excesses of radiation, in the 8–14 micron region and at about 20 microns, which are coincident with characteristic emission features of certain silicate materials. Such excesses have been found in M-type Mira variables, S-type stars, and RV Tauri stars. Many oxygen-rich M supergiants were found to emit the 1,612 MHz radio line from the OH radical as well. The general picture that emerges from these findings is that of a large, cool star with a circumstellar shell composed mostly of silicate grains. This model was further confirmed by observations of a 650-day period, oxygen-rich Mira, IRC + 10011, as it was occulted by the moon.

Among the hotter stars to show evidence of circumstellar matter are the emission-line B stars (Be stars). These objects are thought to be in a state of temporary gravitational collapse following the exhaustion of the nuclear hydrogen fuel in their central regions. During the year there were two studies of these objects, at shorter wavelengths (0.3–3.5 microns) and at longer wavelengths (2.3–19.5 microns). It was concluded that the infrared spectrum is best explained not by particles but by the radiation of electrons as they speed past or are captured by neutral hydrogen atoms. These stars may therefore be envisaged as surrounded by hot (10,000° K) gaseous shells at about four times their radius.

Extragalactic Astronomy. Quasars have the largest red shifts of any astronomical objects, and are thought to represent the most distant and most rapidly receding parts of our expanding universe so far detected. (Red shift is defined as the observed shift in wavelength of a spectral feature divided by the intrinsic wavelength of that feature. It is a measure of the object's velocity of recession from the earth.) Until recently no red shift higher than 3 had been measured, although several quasars had been observed close to that limit. The question had, therefore, arisen as to whether this apparent cutoff represented some distance limit to objects in the universe. An answer has now been given by the discovery of two quasars with larger red shifts. OH 471 was observed to have a red shift of 3.40 and OQ 172 a red shift of 3.53. These values correspond to recession velocities of 90% of the speed of light and distances near 10,000,000,000 light-years.

The first determination of a large red shift by radio means also was achieved during the year. Although radio observations led to the discovery of quasars, the determination of their red shifts had always been a

Photomosaic of Mercury transmitted by Mariner 10 in March from a distance of about 210,000 km. (130,000 mi.). Extensive cratering, which is evident in this view, is important in the history of the planet and of this part of the solar system generally.

Solar flares appear as white areas in this photo taken with red light in July at Boulder, Colo. Sunspot activity was unusually heavy during 1974.

task for optical spectroscopy, using the many spectral lines occurring in the optical and ultraviolet regions. Now, however, the 21-cm. hydrogen line has been detected in absorption in 3C 286 at a red shift of 0.69. This is 81% of the emission-line red shift of 3C 286, indicating that the radio line arises in an intervening galaxy.

A significant discovery during the year was that of a giant 180° arc of neutral hydrogen gas stretching across the southern sky. The feature was named the Magellanic Stream because of its clear association with the Large and Small Magellanic Clouds, where it is most intense; it also has a long tail stretching to the south galactic pole and beyond, and there is evidence for a bridge to the galactic plane. If it is at the distance of the Magellanic Clouds, the mass of hydrogen in the Magellanic Stream is 1,000,000,000 times that of the sun. How did such a stream originate? One possibility is that it was pulled out of the Small Magellanic Cloud and our galaxy by gravitational forces during a close approach between the two some 500 million years ago. There is convincing evidence for such gravitationally produced tails in a number of other pairs of galaxies. In the present case, however, there are difficulties caused by the presence of the Large Magellanic Cloud and the observed smoothness of the motions between the two Clouds. It may well be that the Magellanic Stream is simply leftover material from the original intergalactic medium out of which the Clouds collapsed at their formation.

Jupiter, Venus, and Mercury. The year was an exciting one in planetary research with the Pioneer 10 flyby of Jupiter on Dec. 3, 1973, the close approach of Pioneer 11 a year later, and the Mariner 10 encounters with Venus on Feb. 5, 1974, and with Mercury on March 29, 1974. Pioneer 10 passed within 130,000 km. of Jupiter's cloud tops, while Pioneer 11 passed within 44,000 km. of Jupiter as it

looped around the planet and continued toward a rendezvous with Saturn. Mariner 10 investigated Venus and Mercury at heights of 5,800 and 700 km., respectively.

Jupiter is the largest planet in the solar system, containing two-thirds of all the planetary material and having a radius of 71,600 km. In addition to transmitting some excellent pictures of Jupiter, Pioneer 10 made many important discoveries about the planet's physical properties. The magnetic field of the planet was found to be much more intense than previously thought, having 400 million times the stored energy of the earth's field and extending outward to 100 planetary radii. The field is inclined about 10° to the rotation axis and is also offset by 8,000 km. from the centre of the planet. A flat, disk-shaped system of high-energy electrons, protons, and helium nuclei was also encountered.

Jupiter was confirmed to be emitting 2.5 times as much energy as it receives from the sun, implying an internal source of heat; Pioneer 10 found that the cloud-top temperature remains the same even on the side away from the sun. The temperature at the core is thought to be 30,000° K, and the planet seems to be composed almost entirely of liquid. The Great Red Spot is believed to be the vortex of a gigantic "storm," which typifies the convective currents seething throughout the planet's atmosphere.

Pioneer 11 gave astronomers their first good view of Jupiter's polar regions. On the approach to the planet the instruments aboard the probe detected what appeared to be a polar icecap on Callisto, the second largest of Jupiter's moons.

Venus, with a radius of 6,050 km., is very similar to the earth in size. Alone of the inner planets of our solar system, its surface is totally obscured, being shrouded in a thick, cloudy atmosphere composed largely of carbon dioxide, CO_2. Mariner 10 transmitted television pictures of the clouds in the visual and the near-ultraviolet regions of the spectrum, which showed that they swirl around the planet in a retrograde zonal motion with speeds of almost 100 m. per sec. At the point nearest the sun, however, these streams are disturbed by large-scale convection that persists in spite of the zonal motion.

Mercury, of only 2,420 km. radius, is the closest planet to the sun. Mariner 10 transmitted excellent pictures of its surface, revealing a heavily cratered terrain like that of Mars and the moon. As on Mars and the moon, the cratering is unevenly distributed, covering about half the surface while smoother plains cover the rest. Mercury displays one unique set of surface features, cliffs of from one to several kilometres in height and hundreds of kilometres in length.

Instruments and Techniques. During the year ground-based observers at dry sites continued to open up new regions of the infrared spectrum. Observations between 28 and 40 microns, made near Tucson, Ariz., involved three planets, four cool stars, and four galactic dust clouds, and revealed an atmospheric transmission of about 10%.

New instrumentation of the 5-m. telescope at the Hale Observatory on Palomar Mountain in California included a near-infrared Fourier spectrometer and a radial-velocity spectrometer. The former is capable of producing high-resolution (to 0.015 cm.$^{-1}$) spectra in the 1–2.5 micron region and was successfully tested on planets and a number of stars. With the introduction of an infrared guider, the spectra of cool objects will be observed in the daytime, thus greatly increasing the usage of the telescope at no cost to other programs. The radial-velocity spectrometer is an improved version of a device that uses the photoelectrically detected variation of light transmitted through a specially prepared diaphragm to indicate the shift of the spectral lines and, therefore, the stellar velocity. The instrument will provide velocities with errors of only 0.1 km. per sec. for tenth-magnitude stars.

New telescopes recently coming into commission included the 100-m. radio dish at Bonn, W.Ger., and the 3.9-m. Anglo-Australian optical telescope which joined the 1.2-m. Science Research Council Schmidt telescope at Siding Spring Observatory, New South Wales, Austr. (D. J. FAULKNER)

See also Earth Sciences; Space Exploration. [131.A.3; 132.B and D; 133.C; 10/32.A.1.f and g]

ENCYCLOPÆDIA BRITANNICA FILMS. *Controversy over the Moon* (1973).

Australia

A federal parliamentary state and a member of the Commonwealth of Nations, Australia occupies the smallest continent and, with the island state of Tasmania, is the sixth largest country in the world. Area: 2,967,900 sq.mi. (7,686,850 sq.km.). Pop. (1974 est.): 13,268,600. Cap.: Canberra (pop., 1971, 141,795). Largest city: Sydney (metro. pop., 1971, 2,725,084). Language: English. Religion (1971): Church of England 31%; Roman Catholic 27%; Methodist 8.6%; Presbyterian 8.1%. Queen, Elizabeth II; governors-general in 1974, Sir Paul Hasluck and, from July 11, Sir John Kerr; prime minister, Gough Whitlam.

Domestic Affairs. Australia faced a major constitutional crisis in 1974. On April 11 both houses of Parliament were dissolved, and a double-dissolution election was faced on May 18. In what was described as one of the most daring gambles in Australian political history, Prime Minister Whitlam created a Senate vacancy by appointing one of his most bitter opponents, Sen. Vincent C. Gair of Queensland, former leader of the Democratic Labor Party (DLP), as ambassador to Ireland. With five seats, the DLP held the balance of power in the Senate. Gair's departure decreased the DLP's chances of retaining the balance in the elections for half the Senate seats, scheduled for May 18, while giving Whitlam's Australian Labor Party (ALP) a chance to win a majority.

Hoping to capitalize on the government's embarrassment when the Gair affair became known, the leader of the opposition Liberal-Country Party, Sen. Billy Snedden, threw down the gauntlet and instructed the LCP senators to vote against three appropriation bills giving the government A$170 million to carry on until the start of the financial year. DLP leader Sen. Frank McManus, believing that Gair's diplomatic assignment was an attempt by Whitlam to gain control of the Senate by stealth, sided with the opposition in its threat to defeat the money bills. Such an action by the Senate was unprecedented and aroused considerable criticism. The Senate deferred consideration of the money bills, but Whitlam treated this as a failure to provide supply and responded by asking the governor-general to dissolve both houses.

During the election campaign Snedden concentrated on the issue of inflation. He branded inflation as La-

bor's greatest failure and pushed it squarely to the forefront as the central issue of the campaign, pledging that the Liberal Party would release the nation from the "mire of crippling price rises, savagely rising taxation and unbearable interest rates." The Liberal-Country coalition had a clear and carefully developed plan comprising a tax cut of A$600 million that would "increase take-home pay without pushing up costs and prices"; a reduction in the rate of growth of government spending; a national conference of unions, employers, and state governments to establish a framework for voluntary restraint of wage and price increases; immediate meeting with the state premiers to remove waste between levels of government; and a pledge to transform the inflationary budget deficit of 1973–74 into a domestic surplus.

Whitlam faced a hostile rural electorate. The government's decision to ban a subsidy of A$60 million on superphosphate was especially unpopular, and Whitlam was heckled and abused by militant farmers in March in Victoria and in Western Australia over this issue. The ALP tried to ban a Liberal Party television advertisement authorized by the premier of New South Wales, Sir Robert Askin. The offending advertisement featured an Estonian migrant woman explaining why she was not going to vote Labor in the election. "Today I can see Labor is disguised socialism, but for me it is disguised Communism." The result of the election was a victory for Whitlam. Although the ALP failed to gain control of the Senate, it had the satisfaction of seeing the old splinter party, the DLP, entirely swept out of the chamber. The ALP had a majority of five in the new House of Representatives. As he had foreseen, Whitlam had the numbers to pass through a joint sitting of both houses of Parliament the bills that had been the occasion of the election, including a series of bills on national health, electoral redistribution, extra Senate seats for the Australian Capital Territory and the Northern Territory, and mineral exploration and industrial development, introduced before the dissolution. In the new government James F. Cairns (*see* BIOGRAPHY) replaced Lance H. Barnard as deputy prime minister. In December the Queensland state elections recorded a surprising 16% swing away from the ALP.

On Christmas Day, Cyclone Tracy struck the city of Darwin on Australia's northern coast. The immediate death toll was set at 44, but many more were injured or missing; some 90% of the buildings were destroyed, and at least 25,000 of the city's 32,000 people were without shelter. Relief was difficult because of Darwin's remote location, across the continent from the centres of population and accessible by only one road. Civilian and military aircraft began shuttle flights, carrying supplies in and evacuating refugees, while ships of the Australian Navy, dispatched with further supplies, arrived about a week later. Prime Minister Whitlam, who cut short a European trip because of the disaster, pledged that the city would be rebuilt.

On July 11 Sir John Kerr (*see* BIOGRAPHY) succeeded Sir Paul Hasluck as governor-general.

Foreign Affairs. On April 4 Lance Barnard, then deputy prime minister as well as minister for defense, and Donald R. Willesee, foreign affairs minister, met with Albert Maori Kiki (*see* BIOGRAPHY), Papua New Guinea's minister for defense, foreign relations, and trade. Although the Australian government believed that decisions on Papua New Guinea's defense forces rested with that country's government (Papua New

93

Australia

Guinea had been granted internal self-government formally on Dec. 1, 1973), Barnard discussed the continuance of Australian support in the fields of finance, personnel equipment, and training after full independence. (*See* DEPENDENT STATES; PAPUA NEW GUINEA.)

On February 8, following the United States-British announcement about the development of U.S. naval facilities at Diego Garcia in the Indian Ocean, Willesee stated that the building up of facilities by any great power in the Indian Ocean or the introduction of additional naval forces did not contribute to the achievement of Australia's long-term objective, namely, that the Indian Ocean should be an area free from great power rivalry. Attorney General Lionel Murphy added that Australia would in no way encourage or favour the further growth of Soviet military and naval power in the Indian Ocean. On March 22–23 Australian representatives in Washington and Moscow urged the U.S. and the U.S.S.R. to agree to exercise mutual restraint so that a further escalation of rivalry would be avoided in the Indian Ocean.

In 1974 Whitlam was determined to ensure that Australia was accepted as a good neighbour and a cooperative and helpful member of the Asian and Pacific region. Whitlam toured Southeast Asia during January 28–February 13, visiting Malaysia, Thailand, Laos, Burma, Singapore, and the Philippines. Whitlam's first objective was to emphasize to the leaders of Southeast Asia the continuing and undiminished importance that the Labor government attached to its relations with Southeast Asian nations. The foreign minister continued to extend Australia's dialogue with North Korea (diplomatic relations were formally established on July 31), in pursuance of the policy of having normal diplomatic relations with all countries regardless of ideological considerations. Australia also recognized the annexation of the Baltic states of Latvia, Estonia, and Lithuania by the U.S.S.R.

There was a meeting in Canberra during April of the secretaries-general of the Association of Southeast Asian Nations (ASEAN) and Australian government officials. Foreign Minister Willesee informed the secretaries-general that the Australian government would make available a sum of A\$5 million for ASEAN economic projects suitable for cooperation between ASEAN and Australia. Australia offered its training facilities to help ASEAN countries improve techniques for the handling and storage of grains and transportation of livestock and perishable foodstuffs, and proposed to help overcome protein deficiency in the region by soybean processing.

The U.S. ambassador to Australia was the victim of a prolonged verbal attack by Labor Sen. William W. C. Brown of Victoria. Brown described Ambassador Marshall Green as a "hatchet man" and asked, unsuccessfully, for his recall. He also called Green the "principal contractor who subcontracts out to the CIA" and alleged that he had interfered with the internal democratic processes of Australia by addressing groups of businessmen and urging them to support the LCP in the May elections.

Economic and Social Affairs. The reelected Labor government faced inflation and increased unemployment as its major problems. In July unemployment jumped by 18.7%. The labour minister, Clyde R. Cameron, admitted that the sharp fall in the demand for labour and the big rise in unemployment to 1.59% of the work force were in marked contrast to normal movement in July. The government came under strong pressure to avoid anti-inflation measures that might aggravate unemployment. Average weekly earnings in Australia rose by A\$16 to A\$113 in the March 1974 quarter. The 17% rise in earnings over the 12-month period was the highest recorded. Over the year 1973–74 Treasurer Frank Crean calculated that prices in Australia had risen by 13.6%. This was the largest increase since the early 1950s and five times the average annual increase during the 1960s. The Labor government took a number of steps to reduce inflation, including a reduction of excessive liquidity, the lowering of tariffs to make imports cheaper, and the establishment of a Prices Justification Tribunal.

Two former Liberal prime ministers called for action to beat inflation. Sir Robert Menzies said that if there was one thing that could bring the country down, it was "unbridled greed" on the part of some sections

continued on page 96

Prince Charles rides "Mr. Eh" in the yard of the Barrule Outstation during a visit to southern Queensland in October.

WIDE WORLD

STRIKES IN AN AFFLUENT SOCIETY

By Philip Bentley

Since the end of World War II, Western industrialized society may be described as "the affluent society," a phrase popularized by the famous Harvard economist John Kenneth Galbraith. In the late 1950s—with real incomes advancing rapidly, relatively little unemployment, and rising aspirations in most sectors of society—it was thought that the old battle lines between capital and labour would become blurred and previously embittered working classes would become a part of the middle class and acquire their more conservative values. These developments, it was suggested, would lead to attitudes of consensus and a withering away of the strike.

In hindsight, this diagnosis of the course of Western society appears to have been misplaced. In the late 1960s and early 1970s a number of countries—Australia, Belgium, Canada, West Germany, Italy, The Netherlands, New Zealand, Sweden, the U.K., and the U.S.—experienced an increase in strike activity. In Australia and the U.K. this increase has continued unabated, but whatever the recent experience there seems to be a general feeling that Western societies are experiencing the effects of having a more educated and inquiring work force, one in which people are less willing to accept things at face value, are less tolerant of things that they believe to be wrong, and a work force that has seen the benefits that can be exacted through collective action. In almost every Western society there is growing interest in the area of worker participation, either through the Scandinavian model of replacing assembly lines by semiautonomous groups of workers, or the West German model of representation on supervisory and management boards. (*See* INDUSTRIAL RELATIONS: *Special Report.*)

Factors Influencing Strike Activity. In the postwar period in Australia the proportion of women in the work force has increased, the proportion of white-collar workers has increased, and installment (hire purchase) payments have increased as a proportion of disposable income. The same is generally true in other Western societies. Each of these changes would have been expected to reduce the propensity to strike, but the recent upsurge in Australian strike activity is notable for the fact that it has not been confined to the male, blue-collar area. Nurses in hospitals, female assembly-line workers, male and female schoolteachers, and shop assistants of both sexes recently have taken part in their first strike. There clearly has been a marked change in attitude toward the use of the strike weapon.

Vast increases in the installment purchase of consumer durables have not had an impact on the frequency of strikes, though the need to keep up the payments probably has reduced the length of strikes. Strikers with good credit ratings have been able to defer repayments, and in some cases trade union credit schemes have eased the financial pressures on workers. More important, however, has been the increase in the number of families

Philip Bentley is a research fellow in social sciences and a research associate of the Institute of Labour Studies at the Flinders University of South Australia. He is the author of a number of articles on industrial conflict, trade unions, and incomes policies.

receiving more than one income. Such families are more capable of withstanding the financial strains that have always arisen during a strike. Much of this increased protection from the hardships of striking would not have been possible if the Australian economy had not operated at a relatively full-employment level. This has had effects of its own because more hours are worked and there is a greater chance of friction occurring, the bargaining power of unions is increased, and higher incomes and the possibility of overtime work increase the ability of workers to afford more strikes.

Other factors that may have played a minor role in encouraging workers to more readily use the strike weapon are the increased technological interdependence of economies, the use of progressive rates of income tax, and the spread of multinational corporations. Australian oil-tanker drivers, for example, have demonstrated the widespread need for oil by their strikes, workers in electric power stations nearly caused unemployment in other industries dependent on electric power, and a strike by bank clerks stressed the need of the business community for the processing of checks. In addition, rising incomes have produced larger groups of people who are taxed at higher rates, and rates that can increase very rapidly with small changes in income. Research indicates that this effect has been important in changing middle-class attitudes toward the use of the strike weapon.

The Role of Inflation and Education. All Western countries have expended considerable energies in grappling with their endemic inflation problem. Though there is considerable controversy over the causes of inflation, its effects on industrial behaviour are clear. Inflation has caused feelings of anxiety about the purchasing power of wage agreements; it has aroused resentment because some groups have experienced larger increases in income than others; and it has given rise to heated debate over the distribution of income and wealth. Governments have been compelled for political reasons to combat inflation by the use of wage and price policies. Because of market forces and unequal controls, these policies usually have not been successful, and they have given rise to new disputes about inequitable treatment. Not surprisingly, strikes have been prominent in this scenario of uncertainty, anxiety, and unfairness.

It is too easy to look at industrial relations in isolation from the rest of the society, however. During the late 1960s a number of institutions in affluent societies came under challenge from a more questioning, less tradition-bound, and more restive society. Marked changes were taking place within the family unit because of the changing attitudes of women and children. Educational institutions were confronted with students demanding to participate in decision-making. Churches were finding members and clergy less willing to accept previously unquestioned tenets of faith. And in many urban areas in the world, local action groups were formed to resist or alter governmental or commercial decisions about the quality of life in local communities. All these changes result from improved mass communications and a greater preparedness of people to question authority structures. In the case of the Vietnam war protests in the U.S., the stimulus for the protest movement largely came from the young, in the universities. The demonstrations were seen on television screens in the living rooms of a substantial number of households. Though the initial impact of these protests was one of reaction, the eventual impact was a demonstration of the efficacy of collective action.

The industrial relations arena has been unable to immunize itself from these clamours for change. The details of the experience have varied considerably, but industrial relations in affluent societies is in a state of turbulence. Though it would be wrong to generalize about the future role of strike activity in different countries, it seems safe to suggest that one of the most crucial influences in the immediate future will be the ability of Western society to combat the pressures of rising inflation and unemployment. If governments are unsuccessful, then political instability may become a force to be reckoned with.

continued from page 94

of the community. "We don't need economists' theories," said Menzies, "but a great mood of unselfishness." J. R. Gorton suggested that the Commonwealth Parliament should be given power over prices and wages. He said that, once prices and wages could be fixed, there ought to be a bipartisan approach to inflation, with states, the Commonwealth, employers, and employees all conferring on a way to combat Australia's most serious national problem.

On August 7 the Labor government abandoned its heavy restrictions on the entry of foreign capital into Australia by slashing the Variable Deposit Requirement from 25 to 5%; this clamp on foreign capital inflow had been imposed three weeks after the Labor government took office in December 1972 (and was raised to 33⅓% from October 1973 to June 1974). Treasurer Crean said that the 25% requirement increased the cost of overseas borrowing by one-third. Figures released in August 1974 showed that the government clamp on foreign investment reduced the net capital inflow in 1973–74 to the smallest gain since 1952–53. This state of affairs led to the dramatic decision, on Sept. 24, 1974, to devalue the Australian dollar by 12%.

In September Crean introduced what he called a budget of social progress, proposing a 34% increase in expenditure on a wide range of social services and reductions in personal income tax, particularly for lower-paid workers, together with the abolition of television and radio licenses. As against these measures, he proposed a new capital gains tax, a 10% property surcharge, the cessation of tax concessions to mining (excluding gold-mining) companies, and a reduction of income tax deductible against education. He made it clear that, as well as containing inflation, the government must carry out Labor's program to make Australia a fairer society and that it would not countenance mass unemployment as a means of combating inflation. In November, Whitlam announced a series of measures designed to stimulate the economy and reduce unemployment, including lower taxes for most wage-earners and a reduction in company taxation. In addition, the Prices Justification Tribunal would be asked to take the need for an adequate return on industrial investment into account in its recommendations on prices.

The Labor government tried to iron out difficulties in the trading relationships with Southeast Asian coun-

tries. In 1973–74 Australia had a favourable trade balance of A$225 million with these countries. This situation, if neglected, was likely to generate friction, so Whitlam made a point of explaining to Southeast Asian leaders the 25% tariff cut made by the government in July 1973 and the greatly expanded scheme of tariff preferences for less developed countries, which came into force on Jan. 1, 1974. A special service was established in the Department of Overseas Trade to help less developed countries in market research and commercial contracts. In September Australia formally withdrew from the sterling area system, upon the decline of its sterling holdings. Early in December Crean and Cairns exchanged their respective portfolios of the treasury and overseas trade.

The minister for aboriginal affairs, Sen. James Cavanagh, said on February 25 that the implementation of the Labor government's aboriginal affairs policy had been a financial disaster. The auditor-general, Duncan Craik, asked the Department of Aboriginal Affairs to explain expenditure running into hundreds of thousands of dollars. Craik came to the conclusion that from the outset the department had failed to organize itself so as to control the expenditure of large amounts of public money. The department, burdened with new initiatives and with an inadequate and inexperienced staff, had failed to take early and resolute action to ensure proper financial controls.

In December the government announced new, restrictive regulations concerning immigration, representing a significant change both in Labor policy and in Australia's long-established practice of encouraging immigration. Citizens from other Commonwealth countries would be required, for the first time, to obtain visas before entering the country, and first priority among applications for immigration would be given to those with relatives in Australia and to persons with needed skills. Overseas advertising for settlers was ended, and efforts to deport persons residing in Australia without valid work permits were intensified.

On April 8 the government announced that "Advance Australia Fair" would be the new Australian national anthem, replacing "God Save the Queen." As a compromise "God Save the Queen" would still be used to honour the queen, and on occasions when it was necessary to emphasize Australia's links with Britain. (A. R. G. GRIFFITHS)

[977.B.2]

AUSTRALIA

Education. (1972) Primary, pupils 1,820,534, teachers 69,496; secondary, pupils 1,020,417, teachers 60,935; higher, students 108,263, teaching staff 10,484 (excluding teacher training at third level, students 26,598).

Finance. Monetary unit: Australian dollar, with (after devaluation of Sept. 24, 1974) a free rate of A$0.76 to U.S. $1 (A$1.77 = £1 sterling). Gold, SDRs, and foreign exchange, reserve bank: (May 1974) U.S. $5,408,000,000; (May 1973) U.S. $4,396,000,000. Budget (1972–73 actual): revenue A$9,449,000,000; expenditure A$10,223,000,000. Gross national product: (1972–73) A$40,570,000,000; (1971–72) A$35,-810,000,000. Money supply: (March 1974) A$7,-830,000,000; (March 1973) A$7,038,000,000. Cost of living (1970 = 100): (Jan.–March 1974) 133; (Jan.–March 1973) 117.

Foreign Trade. (1973) Imports A$5,382,-300,000; exports A$6,729,500,000. Import sources: U.S. 22%; Japan 18%; U.K. 16%; West Germany 7%. Export destinations: Japan 32%; U.S. 12%; U.K. 8%; New Zealand 6%. Main exports (1972–73): wool 17%; meat 14%;

iron ore 7%; transport equipment 5%; nonferrous metals 5%; coal 5%.

Transport and Communications. Roads (1971) 884,148 km. (including 192,700 km. paved roads). Motor vehicles in use (1972): passenger 4,273,900; commercial (including buses) 1,024,000. Railways: (government; 1971) 40,269 km.; freight traffic (1972–73) 26,680,-000,000 net ton-km. Air traffic (1972): 11,308,-000,000 passenger-km.; freight 253.1 million net ton-km. Shipping (1973): merchant vessels 100 gross tons and over 373; gross tonnage 1,160,205. Shipping traffic (1973): goods loaded 147,258,000 metric tons, unloaded 26,764,000 metric tons. Telephones (Dec. 1972) 4.4 million. Radio licenses (Dec. 1973) 2,852,000. Television licenses (Dec. 1973) 3,030,000.

Agriculture. Production (in 000; metric tons; 1973; 1972 in parentheses): wheat 11,500 (6,-551); barley 2,132 (1,780); oats 1,361 (752); sorghum 942 (1,228); corn 188 (214); rice 316 (248); potatoes 752 (822); sugar, raw value 2,823 (2,816); apples (1972) 389, (1971) 442;

oranges (1972) 346, (1971) 296; wine (1972) 276, (1971) 251; wool, greasy 737 (875); milk 7,135 (7,130); butter 185 (196); beef and veal 1,434 (1,164); mutton and lamb 708 (956). Livestock (in 000; March 1973): sheep 140,109; cattle 29,130; pigs 3,257; horses c. 450; chickens (1972) c. 23,300.

Industry. Fuel and power (in 000; metric tons; 1973): coal 60,576; lignite 24,677; crude oil 19,136; natural gas (cu.m.) 4,099,000; manufactured gas (cu.m.; 1971–72) 5,484,000; electricity (kw-hr.) 67,067,000. Production (in 000; metric tons; 1973): iron ore (65% metal content) 83,568; bauxite 17,814; pig iron 7,659; crude steel 7,683; zinc 296; aluminum 207; copper 147; lead 191; tin 6.9; nickel concentrates (metal content; 1972) 36; sulfuric acid 2,383; cement 5,247; cotton yarn 30; wool yarn 25; gold (troy oz.; 1972) 755; silver (troy oz.; 1972) 22,506; passenger cars (including assembly; units) 378; commercial vehicles (including assembly; units) 85. Dwelling units completed (1973) 152,000.

Austria

A republic of central Europe, Austria is bounded by West Germany, Czechoslovakia, Hungary, Yugoslavia, Italy, Switzerland, and Liechtenstein. Area: 32,375 sq.mi. (83,850 sq.km.). Pop. (1974): 7,478,600. Cap. and largest city: Vienna (pop., 1971, 1,614,841). Language: German. Religion (1971): Roman Catholic 88%. Presidents in 1974, Franz Jonas to April 23 and, from July 8, Rudolf Kirchschläger; chancellor, Bruno Kreisky.

The death of President Jonas (see OBITUARIES) on April 23, 1974, necessitated a presidential election, which was held on June 23. The candidate of the Socialist Party of Austria (SPÖ), Foreign Minister Rudolf Kirchschläger (see BIOGRAPHY), defeated the Austrian People's Party (ÖVP) candidate, Alois Lugger, the mayor of Innsbruck. The new president, a lawyer and career diplomat, received a total of 2,392,151 votes (51.7%). He was sworn in before the National Assembly on July 8, together with two new Cabinet members, Erich Bielka as foreign minister and Günter Haiden as secretary of state for agriculture and forestry. In regional elections held in Vienna, Upper Austria, Salzburg, and Lower Austria between October 1973 and June 1974, the ÖVP gained nine seats and the Austrian Freedom Party lost two seats. The position of the SPÖ remained unchanged.

As a nonpermanent member of the UN Security Council, Austria was particularly concerned in all UN peacekeeping operations, especially in the Middle East where it agreed to increase its contingent to a total of 599. During 1974 eight Austrians lost their lives in UN service: five on the Golan Heights on the Syrian-Israeli border and three in Cyprus. In March Chancellor Kreisky led a delegation of the Socialist International to Egypt, Syria, Israel, and Jordan. The visit provided an opportunity to improve relations between Austria and Israel, which had been seriously affected by the 1973 closing of the Schönau camp for Soviet Jews in transit to Israel.

In July the Austrian government approved the establishment of yet another international organization in Vienna, the European Research and Development Centre for Social Welfare. Work on the UN City project continued according to plan, despite fierce criticism of both the government and the Vienna city authorities. The opposition demanded that substantial cuts be made in the program to reduce the extremely high construction costs. The Vienna city authorities also came under criticism during the year as the result of an investment scandal in which a building society run by the city authorities sustained losses amounting to millions of schillings.

Implementation of the government's social reform program continued. Further steps were taken in the reorganization of Austrian penal and family law; new measures gave workers a greater share in decision-making at work; a civilian alternative to military service was introduced; and further progress was made with the reform and democratization of the educational system. New regulations were introduced in relation to trade, land development, and environmental control. State development aid was more efficiently organized and coordinated, and an income tax reform

was introduced that reduced the burden on middle-income taxpayers.

In August the deaths of two members of the federal Army as a result of overstrenuous training methods led to a major controversy. In the course of the debate, the opposition called into question the whole basis and efficacy of the Austrian military system. Another controversy concerned the reorganization of the state broadcasting service (ÖRF). The opposition maintained that the government's plans threatened the political independence of the news service. A motion of no confidence was brought before Parliament, and court actions were instituted in an effort to have the new law declared unconstitutional.

The relaxation of the abortion laws continued to arouse strong opposition. In mid-1974 a movement known as Action Life emerged, dedicated to bringing about a repeal of the new law by means of public protests and demonstrations. Meanwhile, the government introduced measures designed to avoid unwanted pregnancies through efficient use of contraceptive techniques, while at the same time providing financial and social incentives to promote population growth.

AUSTRIA

Education. (1972–73) Primary, pupils 978,692, teachers 48,267; secondary, pupils 160,500, teachers 7,737; vocational, pupils 261,845, teachers 4,190; teacher training (including higher), students 13,330, teachers 1,564; higher (including 17 institutions), students 64,806, teaching staff 5,924.

Finance. Monetary unit: schilling, with (Sept. 16, 1974) a free rate of 18.90 schillings to U.S. $1 (43.70 schillings = £1 sterling). Gold, SDRs, and foreign exchange, central bank: (June 1974) U.S. $2,558,000,000; (June 1973) U.S. $2,948,000,000. Budget (1973 est.): revenue 132,558,000,000 schillings; expenditure 148,664,000,000 schillings. Gross national product: (1973) 546.3 billion schillings; (1972) 474.7 billion schillings. Money supply: (May 1974) 105.4 billion schillings; (May 1973) 99.4 billion schillings. Cost of living (1970 = 100): (May 1974) 130; (May 1973) 118.

Foreign Trade. (1973) Imports 137,848,000,000 schillings; exports 102,046,000,000 schillings. Import sources: EEC 65% (West Germany 42%, Italy 7%, U.K. 5%); Switzerland 7%. Export destinations: EEC 49% (West Germany 22%, Italy 11%, U.K. 8%); Switzerland 11%. Main exports: machinery 21%; iron and steel 10%; textile yarns and fabrics 8%; timber 7%; chemicals 7%; paper and board 6%. Tourism (1972): visitors 10,252,000; gross receipts U.S. $1,667,000,000.

Transport and Communications. Roads (1972) 96,500 km. (including 585 km. expressways). Motor vehicles in use (1972): passenger 1,460,000; commercial 138,000. Railways (1972): state 5,883 km., private 636 km.; traffic (state only) 6,768,000,000 passenger-km., freight (1973) 10,269,000,000 net ton-km. Air traffic (1973): 579.2 million passenger-km.; freight 7,749,000 net ton-km. Navigable inland waterways in regular use (1972) 358 km. Telephones (Dec. 1972) 1,694,000. Radio licenses (Dec. 1972) 2,154,000. Television licenses (Dec. 1972) 1,695,000.

Agriculture. Production (in 000; metric tons; 1973; 1972 in parentheses): wheat 917 (863); barley 1,011 (977); rye 430 (402); oats 281 (255); corn 850 (712); potatoes 2,167 (2,341); sugar, raw value 337 (359); apples (1972) 156, (1971) 243; wine (1972) 260, (1971) 181; meat c. 424 (433); timber (cu.m.; 1972) 12,500, (1971) 12,400. Livestock (in 000; Dec. 1972): cattle 2,514; sheep 119; pigs 3,256; chickens 12,231.

Industry. Fuel and power (in 000; metric tons; 1973): lignite 3,600; crude oil 2,579; natural gas (cu.m.) 2,270,000; electricity (kw-hr.) 31,329,000 (59% hydroelectric in 1972); manufactured gas (Vienna only; cu.m.; 1972) 628,000. Production (in 000; metric tons; 1973): iron ore (30% metal content) 4,208; pig iron 3,006; crude steel 4,529; magnesite (1972) 1,429; aluminum 178; copper 23; lead 10; zinc 17; cement 6,260; paper (1972) 1,193; fertilizers (nutrient content; 1972–73) nitrogenous 230, phosphate 139; cotton yarn 21; woven cotton fabric 16; rayon, etc., filaments and fibres (1972) 96.

At the height of the oil crisis in November 1973, the social partnership of unions, employers, and farmers united to organize more efficient means of conserving fuel supplies, industrial raw materials, agricultural products, and medical supplies. Measures included the introduction of a "motorless day" (discontinued in July) and speed limits on the roads.

Apart from these difficulties, the economy developed satisfactorily, with a rise in gross national product higher than that of any other European industrial nation and an inflation rate of less than 10%. A further 10% reduction on January 1 brought tariffs between Austria and the EEC to 60% of the original levels. There was a marked expansion in exports, while the floating of the schilling in May brought an upward revaluation of 3% against the West German mark, designed to promote stability and reduce the effect of "imported inflation." However, tourist traffic fell by some 20%. (ELFRIEDE DIRNBACHER)

[972.B.2.a]

Progressive Liberal Party (PLP) government among working-class voters was somewhat eroded by inflation and high unemployment. Abaco, a dollar-earning Out Island with a roughly equal population of whites and blacks totaling 6,500, continued to agitate for home rule. Some U.S. investors, under the umbrella of "Friends of Abaco," supported such a move, whereby Abaco might become a new tax haven.

The comparative tourist statistics for 1973 showed a small rise of 0.54% over 1972 (1,520,007 as against 1,511,858), with some decrease in 1974 as against 1973 but with tourism from Western Europe expected to continue to rise from the total of 41,925 in 1972. The national food bill for 1973 was approximately B$70 million, of which only 15% was produced domestically. Food and transport were the major contributors to the rising cost of living in early 1974. Some neglect of social services was reported.

(SHEILA PATTERSON)

[974.B.2.d]

Bahamas, The

A member of the Commonwealth of Nations, The Bahamas comprise an archipelago of about 700 islands in the North Atlantic Ocean just southeast of the United States. Area: 5,382 sq.mi. (13,939 sq.km.). Pop. (1973 est.): 189,000. Cap. and largest city: Nassau (urban area pop., 1970, 101,503). Language: English (official). Religion (1970): Baptist 28.8%; Anglican 22.7%; Roman Catholic 22.5%; Methodist 7.3%; Saints of God and Church of God 6%; others and no religion 12.7%. Queen, Elizabeth II; governor-general in 1974, Sir Milo B. Butler; prime minister, Lynden O. Pindling.

The Bahamas' first year of independence ended with reports of a revival of outside and expatriate confidence in the political and investment spheres. The strict immigration controls were abated, and essential skilled foreign personnel gained admittance more smoothly. On the other hand, moves were reported in June to round up and repatriate or deport members of the 40,000-strong community of illegal immigrants or exiles from Haiti. The property market remained quiet, but industrial development was reported in Freeport. The adverse image created earlier by the presence of a number of questionable banking institutions among the more than 300 banks functioning in The Bahamas was dispelled by the closing down of all but one or two. The popularity of Lynden Pindling's

Bahrain

An independent monarchy (emirate), Bahrain consists of a group of islands in the Persian Gulf, lying between the Qatar Peninsula and Saudi Arabia. Total area: 256 sq.mi. (662 sq.km.). Pop. (1974 est.): 239,200. Cap.: Manama (pop., 1974 est., 98,300). Language: Arabic (official), Persian. Religion (1971): Muslim 95.7%; Christian 3%; others 1.3%. Emir in 1974, Isa ibn Sulman al-Khalifah.

In 1974 Bahrain's vital and expanding role as a commercial and communications centre for the Persian Gulf was underlined in various ways. Work began on the construction of a $250 million dry dock financed by eight Arab oil states and designed to handle, initially, 350,000-ton tankers. The expansion of Bahrain Airport to take jumbo jets was started, and multiple work shifts were introduced at Manama Port to handle the rapidly increasing trade there. Oil revenues were double the estimates for 1974 owing to price rises of crude, and the budget showed an 18 million dinar surplus despite heavy increases in expenditures. The government successfully negotiated a 60% share in the output of the Bahrain Petroleum Co. (BAPCO), in which Standard Oil of California and Texaco each owned 20% shares.

Various steps taken to improve living conditions included subsidies, increased family allowances, and cheap housing. In June the economy was severely

BAHAMAS, THE
Education. (1970–71) Primary, pupils 30,880, teachers 707; secondary, pupils 19,650, teachers 548; vocational, pupils 427, teachers 61; teacher training, students 500, teachers 32; higher (1969–70), students 252, teaching staff 40.
Finance and Trade. Monetary unit: Bahamian dollar, with (Sept. 16, 1974) a free rate of B$1 to U.S. $1 (B$2.32 = £1 sterling). Budget (1973 est.): revenue B$114 million; expenditure B$104 million. Foreign trade (1973): imports B$378,870,000 (47% from U.S., 14% from U.K., 6% from Italy); exports B$418,-390,000 (91% to U.S.). Main exports (1972): petroleum products 78%; pharmaceuticals 9%; cement 5%. Tourism (1972): visitors 1,443,400; gross receipts U.S. $286 million.
Transport and Communications. Shipping (1973): merchant vessels 100 gross tons and over 143; gross tonnage 179,494. Telephones (Dec. 1972) 49,000. Radio receivers (Dec. 1972) 84,000. Television receivers (Dec. 1964) c. 4,500.

BAHRAIN
Education. (1973–74) Primary, pupils 41,546, teachers (1971–72) 1,611; secondary, pupils 15,973, teachers (1971–72) 657; vocational, pupils 769, teachers 92; higher, students 612, teaching staff 69.
Finance and Trade. Monetary unit: Bahrain dinar, with (Sept. 16, 1974) a free rate of 0.40 dinar to U.S. $1 (0.91 dinar = £1 sterling). Budget (1974–75 est.) balanced at 53 million dinars. Foreign trade (1973): imports 127,819,000 dinars; exports (excluding oil) 32,012,000 dinars. Import sources: U.K. 19%; U.S. 14%; Japan 12%; Australia 10%; China 6%. Export destinations: Saudi Arabia 52%; Dubai 8%; Iran 6%; Qatar 5%. Main exports: crude oil and petroleum products.
Industry. Production (in 000; metric tons; 1972): crude oil 3,508; petroleum products 11,544.

Automobile Industry:
see Industrial
Production and
Technology;
Transportation

Automobile Racing:
see Motor Sports

Aviation:
see Defense;
Transportation

threatened by strikes at the ALBA aluminum complex, which led to police intervention and arrests, including one member of the ruling Khalifah family described as an instigator. The management of the complex threatened a complete shutdown.

In October Bahrain announced that the U.S. could keep its naval base on Bahrain Island, though a notice for its closing had previously been delivered. The U.S. in June appointed Joseph W. Twinam its first resident ambassador to Bahrain.   (PETER MANSFIELD)

[978.B.4.b]

Bangladesh

An independent republic and member of the Commonwealth of Nations, Bangladesh is bordered by India on the west, north, and east, by Burma in the southeast, and by the Bay of Bengal in the south. Area: 55,126 sq.mi. (142,776 sq.km.). Pop. (1974): 71,316,517. Cap. and largest city: Dacca (pop., 1974, 1,310,976). Language: Bengali. Religion: Muslim 80%, with Hindu, Christian, and Buddhist minorities. President in 1974, Muhammadullah; prime minister, Sheikh Mujibur Rahman.

Domestic Affairs. The devastating floods of July–August 1974, two and a half years after the liberation war of 1971, dealt a crippling blow to the country's reconstruction and development efforts. Floods, drought, or typhoons had alternately ravaged Bangladesh many times in the past, but the inundation of 1974 was the worst in more than two decades. Some 32,000 sq.mi., or more than half the area of the country, were submerged, almost all the standing crops were destroyed, and the threat of famine began to loom as the hard-pressed government sought international assistance to meet the crisis. The official death toll in the month-long floods was placed at 1,500, while nearly one-third of the population was directly affected. Experts estimated that the country would need $320 million worth of food and flood relief and half that much again to enable the various industries to resume operations.

The problem of law and order became worse during the year. A total of 15,000 persons had been killed and another 2,000 were missing in various parts of Bangladesh in raids by terrorist elements since the liberation. Political rivalry and personal vendettas were behind most of the killings. Officials admitted that the government's failure to absorb the former freedom fighters into the armed forces or give them gainful employment and education had led to a worsening of the situation.

The most serious incident occurred in April 1974 when a gang of masked gunmen sprayed machine-gun bullets into a group of students on the Dacca University campus, killing seven of them. Press reports attributed the tragedy to political rivalry between the student and youth wings of the ruling Awami League. Sheikh Mujib's repeated warnings that he would take drastic steps to deal with the terrorists brought no response and on December 28, as lawlessness continued, a state of emergency was declared empowering him to institute measures he considered necessary to restore law and order and to deal with the country's worsening economy.

The sheikh made some attempts to streamline his Cabinet and to eliminate corrupt and inefficient administrators. He dropped nine ministers from the Cabinet in July, redistributing their portfolios and himself taking charge of the vital jute affairs ministry. He had earlier relinquished the post of Awami League president to devote more time to government affairs. A newly established National Economic Council liberalized terms for both domestic and foreign investment. Parliament also enacted a law providing for death sentences for smuggling, hoarding, and black-marketeering.

Muhammadullah, who was made acting president on the resignation of Abu Sayeed Choudhury in December 1973, was officially elected president in January. Bangladesh's first census was taken during February–March. In June a provisional report gave the total

Transport by rowboat in flooded Dacca.

CAMERAPIX/KEYSTONE

Balance of Payments:
see Exchange and Payments, International

Ballet:
see Dance

population as 71,316,517, an increase of 40.2% since the East Pakistan census of 1961.

Foreign Affairs. The Dacca government's foreign policy paid dividends as Pakistan, which had withheld recognition for more than two years, finally granted it on Feb. 22, 1974. Sheikh Mujib made a triumphant entry into the Islamic summit conference held in Lahore, Pak., the same month and forged closer relations with several Arab heads of state. The tripartite agreement signed with Pakistan and India in New Delhi in April brought to a close the vexing problems of repatriation of Pakistani prisoners of war, Bengalis stranded in Pakistan, and Biharis in Bangladesh who wanted to go to Pakistan. Under the agreement Bangladesh also gave up its plans to try 195 Pakistani prisoners for war crimes.

Pakistani Prime Minister Z. A. Bhutto's hopes for a reconciliation with former East Pakistan were dashed in June, when his official visit to Dacca ended in a fiasco. The sheikh and Bhutto could not solve the vital issues of division of assets and the number of Pakistani nationals to be repatriated from Bangladesh to Pakistan. Nonetheless, the Pakistani recognition had removed the last remaining obstacle to the republic's admission to the UN, which accepted Bangladesh unanimously in September. China was the only major world power that had not yet recognized Bangladesh, but officials in Dacca believed recognition would soon be established.

Relations with the Soviet Union and India became closer. Sheikh Mujib spent nearly a month in Moscow early in the year undergoing treatment for chronic bronchitis. In May he made an official visit to New Delhi and signed a joint declaration and a border demarcation agreement with Prime Minister Indira Gandhi. India pledged to cooperate in checking smuggling. It also agreed to extend credits totaling Rs. 380 million ($50.6 million) for setting up four projects— a cement plant, a fertilizer plant, and a sponge iron plant in Bangladesh and a clinker plant in Meghalaya, east India, to supply clinker to Bangladesh.

The Economy. Economic activity in Bangladesh, already sluggish, faced new challenges as Sheikh Mujib's regime attempted to deal with rising oil prices, worldwide inflation, and such internal problems as corruption, mismanagement, hoarding, and smuggling. Industrial output for 1973–74 was about 20% higher than in 1972–73 but 10% below the target set by the government. The jute industry, which earned 80% of the country's foreign exchange, remained disorganized. Official statistics showed that only 2.7 million bales of raw jute could leave the country during 1973–74, compared with the target of 3.5 million bales. Production had fallen to 6 million bales from the 1969–70 peak of 7.2 million bales. According to economic experts, smuggling across the border to India had accounted for at least 1 million bales. All essential commodities were in short supply, and the prices of rice, kerosene, and cloth rose by three to four times in one year. The taka, officially at par with the Indian rupee, was bringing twice as much in the black market. An International Monetary Fund suggestion to devalue the currency was rejected by the government for political reasons.

Despite generous help in foreign aid—about 7,340,-000,000 taka from the West and Japan since independence—Bangladesh could make little headway economically. By the end of June 1974, foreign exchange reserves had hit a new low of about $80 million, far less than estimated needs for essential imports in July–December. Rice output during 1973–74 was put at 11.8 million tons, compared with the 12,580,000-ton target. After the floods it was stated that Bangladesh would need to import at least 2.8 million tons of rice to prevent starvation in the coming months.

In June Finance Minister Tajuddin Ahmed submitted to Parliament a 1974–75 budget showing revenues and expenditure balanced at 4.7 billion taka. A separate development budget envisaged expenditure of 5,250,000,000 taka, including 3,940,000,000 taka to be covered by foreign loans and grants.

(GOVINDAN UNNY)

[976.A.3.b]

BANGLADESH
Education. (1972–73) Primary, pupils c. 6 million, teachers 124,146; secondary, pupils c. 1.7 million, teachers c. 63,000; vocational and primary teacher training, students 11,300, teachers 887; higher and third-level teacher training, students 45,014, teaching staff 3,073.
Finance. Monetary unit: taka, with a free rate (Sept. 16, 1974) of 7.80 taka to U.S. $1 (18 taka = £1 sterling). Foreign exchange (March 1974 est.): U.S. $95 million. Budget (1973–74 est.): revenue 4,113,000,000 taka; expenditure 2,953,000,000 taka (development budget 5,253,000,000 taka). Cost of living (Dacca; 1970 = 100): (Feb. 1974) 255; (Feb. 1973) 184.
Foreign Trade. (1972) Imports 1,027,700,000 taka; exports 2,273,186,000 taka. Export destinations (jute only; 1970–71): U.K. 14%; Belgium-Luxembourg 8%; West Germany 5%; France 5%. Main exports: jute products c. 36%; jute c. 24%; tea 13%.
Transport and Communications. Roads (1972) c. 24,000 km. (including c. 4,000 km. with improved surface). Motor vehicles in use (1972): passenger 66,700; commercial (including buses) 23,300. Railways: (1971) 2,858 km.; traffic (1970–71) 2,095,000,-000 passenger-km., freight 1,022,000,000 net ton-km. Navigable waterways (1972) c. 8,000 km. Shipping (1973): merchant vessels 100 gross tons and over 90; gross tonnage 60,601. Shipping traffic (1972): goods loaded 275,000 metric tons, unloaded 2,141,000 metric tons. Telephones (Dec. 1972) 48,000. Radio licenses (March 1969) 531,000.
Agriculture. Production (in 000; metric tons; 1973; 1972 in parentheses): rice c. 19,050 (c. 14,387); dry beans c. 60 (c. 55); potatoes c. 800 (753); onions c. 180 (160); jute c. 972 (c. 1,170); tea c. 27 (23); tobacco c. 39 (35); fish catch (1970) 247, (1969) 277. Livestock (in 000; 1972–73): horses c. 45; cattle c. 26,000; buffaloes c. 700; sheep c. 700; goats c. 11,900; chickens c. 28,500.
Industry. Production (in 000; metric tons; 1971–72): cement 23; nitrogenous fertilizers (plant nutrient content; 1972–73) 98; jute fabrics (1969–70) 589; cotton yarn 21; paper (1969–70) 79.

Barbados

The parliamentary state of Barbados is a member of the Commonwealth of Nations and occupies the most easterly island in the southern Caribbean Sea. Area: 166 sq.mi. (430 sq.km.). Pop. (1973 est.): 241,500, 91% Negro; 4% white; 4% mixed. Cap. and largest city: Bridgetown (pop., 1970, 8,868). Language: English. Religion: Anglican 53%; Methodist 9%; Roman Catholic 4%; Moravian 2%; others 32%. Queen, Elizabeth II; governor-general in 1974, Sir Winston Scott; prime minister, Errol Walton Barrow.

Early in March 1974 the government put before the House of Assembly the 1973–77 National Development Plan. Among its goals were the creation of 11,300 new jobs mainly in manufacturing and 4,000 in construction, and tourist growth requiring an addi-

Banking:
see Money and Banking

Baptists:
see Religion

BARBADOS
Education. (1972–73) Primary, pupils 43,246, teachers 970; secondary, pupils 24,640, teachers 1,020; vocational (1971–72), pupils 1,121, teachers (1969–70) 64: higher, students 1,099, teaching staff 75.
Finance and Trade. Monetary unit: Barbados dollar, with (Sept. 16, 1974) a free rate of Bar$2.07 to U.S. $1 (official rate of Bar$4.80 = £1 sterling). Budget (1973–74 est.): revenue Bar$120.7 million; expenditure Bar$146.9 million. Foreign trade (1973): imports U.S. $168,550,000; exports U.S. $53,540,000. Import sources: U.K. 25%; U.S. 21%; Canada 11%; Trinidad and Tobago 8%. Export destinations: U.K. 34%; U.S. 17%; Windward Islands 9%; Trinidad and Tobago 8%; Canada 6%. Main exports (1972): sugar 32%; clothing 6%; rum 5%. Tourism (1972): visitors 210,000; gross receipts c. U.S. $60 million.
Agriculture. Sugar production, raw value (in 000; metric tons; 1973) c. 119, (1972) c. 113.

tional 2,000 jobs and 1,800 hotel beds. If these goals were reached, unemployment would be reduced from 11% in 1974 to 8% by 1977. A labour force of 110,000 was expected by 1977. The forecast expenditure on capital projects during the development period was Bar$175.6 million, external institutions providing much of the development funds.

Barbados was hit by rising import costs, inflation, economic slowdown, and increased unemployment. In June the all-items index of retail prices stood at 254.3, compared with 182.4 in June 1973 (October 1965 = 100). The 1974 sugar crop was expected to yield just under 109,000 tons, a small decrease from the 1973 crop, but large world price increases augmented revenue by about £4 million.

In the summer Errol Barrow's Democratic Labour Party (DLP) government put forward proposals for constitutional changes, vesting additional power in the executive. They concerned the attorney general's powers, judicial and public service appointments, citizenship restrictions, and parliamentary disqualifications, and they aroused protest from the official Barbados Labour Party opposition and other bodies. Nevertheless, the House of Assembly, with its DLP majority, passed the controversial amendments on August 29. (SHEILA PATTERSON)

Baseball

The Oakland A's, continuing to thrive on a combination of mutinous tendencies and brutally efficient skills, won the World Series of baseball for the third successive time in 1974. Prospering despite clubhouse fights, legal infringements, and assorted other inner turmoils, the A's cut down the Los Angeles Dodgers, 4 games to 1, to make a shambles of the first all-California Series on record. Four of the five games in the post-season classic were determined by scores of 3–2.

It was a year in which three of baseball's mountainous individual barriers, two statistical and one sociological, fell by the wayside. Hank Aaron (see BIOGRAPHY) of the Atlanta Braves shattered Babe Ruth's home run record, probably the most prestigious mark in sports. Lou Brock (see BIOGRAPHY) of the St. Louis Cardinals broke Maury Wills's stolen base record. Frank Robinson was named baseball's first black manager by the Cleveland Indians.

Aaron entered the season-opening three-game series at Cincinnati with 713 home runs, only one behind Ruth's lifetime total. In deference to Atlanta's home fans, the Braves originally announced that Aaron might be withheld from the lineup in Cincinnati in an effort to save his historic 714th and 715th homers for Atlanta Stadium. But baseball Commissioner Bowie Kuhn ordered the Atlanta management to start Aaron in at least two of the three games in Cincinnati. So it was that Aaron, in his first swing in the first inning of the first game of the new season, smashed his 714th off the Reds' Jack Billingham to tie the record. It was Aaron's lone hit of the game. He sat out the second game and had no hits in the third. That brought Aaron and the Braves back to Atlanta for their nationally televised home opener. The date was April 8 when Aaron batted against left-hander Al Downing of the Los Angeles Dodgers with a count of one ball and no strikes. On the next pitch the 40-year-old right-handed slugger rifled his 715th home run over the left-centrefield fence, some 400 ft. distant, to end his dramatic chase of Babe Ruth's ghost. Aaron ended the season with 733 home runs.

Brock stole 118 bases in 1974, wiping out Wills's mark of 104 set in 1962. Wills had broken another of baseball's sacred records, the 96 stolen bases for one season of Ty Cobb, a standard once deemed unbeatable. Brock's 105th steal came against Philadelphia at Busch Stadium in St. Louis on September 10 and he concluded the year with a lifetime total of 753, surpassing Max Carey's modern National League record of 738. Cobb continued to hold the major league high of 892.

Frank Robinson was appointed to the Cleveland managerial job on October 3, replacing Ken Aspromonte. Robinson, a 19-year veteran in the majors, was the only man ever to win Most Valuable Player honours in both the American and National leagues.

Al Kaline of the Detroit Tigers collected his 3,000th hit in a game at Baltimore on September 24. He was the 12th man to reach that total and the first in the American League since Eddie Collins in 1925.

California Angels fireballer Nolan Ryan pitched his third career no-hitter on September 28, striking

Final Major League Standings, 1974

American League
East Division

Club	W.	L.	Pct.	G.B.	Balt.	N.Y.	Bos.	Clev.	Mil.	Det.	Cal.	Chi.	K.C.	Minn.	Oak.	Tex.
Baltimore	91	71	.562	—		11	10	12	8	14	7	5	8	6	6	4
New York	89	73	.549	2	7	—	7	11	9	7	9	8	8	7	8	8
Boston	84	78	.519	7	8	11	—	9	10	11	4	8	4	6	8	4
Cleveland	77	85	.475	14	6	7	9	—	10	9	9	4	8	6	5	4
Milwaukee	76	86	.469	15	10	9	8	8	—	9	9	4	1	6	5	7
Detroit	72	90	.444	19	4	11	7	9	9	—	7	5	7	3	5	5

West Division

Club	W.	L.	Pct.	G.B.	Oak.	Tex.	Minn.	Chi.	K.C.	Cal.	Balt.	Bos.	Clev.	Det.	Mil.	N.Y.
Oakland	90	72	.556	—		8	13	11	10	12	6	4	7	7	7	5
Texas	84	76	.525	5	10	—	9	7	10	9	8	7	8*	7	5	4
Minnesota	82	80	.506	8	5	9	—	11	10	10	6	6	6	9	6	4
Chicago	80	80	.500	9	7	9	7	—	11	8	7	4	8	7	8	4
Kansas City	80	82	.494	8	8	8	8	7	—	10	4	8	4	5	11	4
California	68	94	.420	22	6	9	10	8	10	—	5	8	3	5	3	3

*—Includes forfeit awarded in game of June 4.
Ties—Chicago 3; California, Minnesota, Texas.

National League
East Division

Club	W.	L.	Pct.	G.B.	Pitt.	St.L.	Phil.	Mon.	N.Y.	Chi.	Atl.	Cin.	Hou.	L.A.	S.D.	S.F.
Pittsburgh	88	74	.543	—		7	8	9	11	9	8	4	7	8	9	8
St. Louis	86	75	.534	1½	11	—	9	9	12	13	3	6	4	6	7	6
Philadelphia	80	82	.494	8	10	9	—	7	11	10	4	4	6	5	8	6
Montreal	79	82	.491	8½	9	8	11	—	9	13	3	6	6	4	6	6
New York	71	91	.438	17	7	6	7	9	—	10	4	3	6	7	6	6
Chicago	66	96	.407	22	9	5	8	5	8	—	8	5	4	2	6	6

West Division

Club	W.	L.	Pct.	G.B.	L.A.	Cin.	Atl.	Hou.	S.F.	S.D.	Chi.	Mon.	N.Y.	Phil.	Pitt.	St.L.
Los Angeles	102	60	.630	—		12	10	13	12	16	10	8	5	6	4	6
Cincinnati	98	64	.605	4	6	—	11	14	11	12	7	6	9	8	6	6
Atlanta	88	74	.543	14	8	7	—	6	8	17	4	9	8	8	4	9
Houston	81	81	.500	21	5	4	12	—	10	11	8	6	6	6	5	8
San Francisco	72	90	.444	30	6	7	10	8	—	7	6	8	6	4	4	6
San Diego	60	102	.370	42	2	6	1	7	11	—	6	6	7	3	5	

Tie—Atlanta, Cincinnati.
Source: *The Sporting News.*

Sal Bando of the Oakland A's tags Bill Buckner, Dodger outfielder, on a close play at third base in the fifth game of the World Series. Oakland went on to win the game and the championship, defeating Los Angeles four games to one.

out 15 and walking 8 in a 4–0 conquest of the Minnesota Twins. Sandy Koufax of the Dodgers holds the record for no-hitters with four. Ryan's feat came three weeks after four Rockwell International scientists had clocked his fastball at a record 100.8 mph in a game at Anaheim, Calif. The previous fastest unofficial clocking was the 98.6 mph attributed to Bob Feller in 1946.

Two other no-hitters were recorded in 1974. Steve Busby of the Kansas City Royals stopped Milwaukee, 2–0, thus becoming the first pitcher to post a no-hitter in each of his first two seasons in the majors. Cleveland's Dick Bosman handcuffed Oakland, 4–0, missing a perfect game as the result of his own throwing error.

Bob Gibson of the St. Louis Cardinals recorded his 3,000th strikeout on July 17. Only Walter Johnson, with 3,508, previously had reached that milestone. Ironically, Gibson's feat came on the same day that former Cardinal pitching great Dizzy Dean died.

Relief star Mike Marshall (*see* BIOGRAPHY) of the

Hank Aaron hits his 715th home run, surpassing Babe Ruth's lifetime total.

Dodgers pitched in a record 106 games, including 13 straight, another record. Cleveland pitcher Gaylord Perry won 15 games in a row, one short of the American League record.

The National League turned down a request by financially troubled C. Arnholt Smith to sell the San Diego Padres to Washington, D.C., interests. Ray Kroc (*see* BIOGRAPHY), the McDonald's hamburger king, then bought the Padres for a reported $10.1 million and kept the team in San Diego.

The Hall of Fame at Cooperstown, N.Y., added six members. Present for induction ceremonies were Mickey Mantle and Whitey Ford of the New York Yankees, umpire Jocko Conlan, and James ("Cool Papa") Bell, the Ty Cobb of the Negro leagues. Sam Thompson and "Sunny Jim" Bottomley were honoured posthumously.

Major Leagues. Three of the four divisional races in the major leagues were not settled until the last days of the season. In the National League the Pittsburgh Pirates won the East Division laurels on the final night of the regular season, beating the Chicago Cubs, 5–4, in ten innings to oust St. Louis by $1\frac{1}{2}$ games. Los Angeles clinched the West Division title on the next-to-last night of the season. Cincinnati finished second, four games out. In the American League, the Baltimore Orioles beat the New York Yankees by two games in the East Division in another race that went down to the next-to-last night. Oakland won more easily, taking the West Division by five games over the surprising Texas Rangers.

In the American League play-offs Oakland won the three-out-of-five series, 3 games to 1. Los Angeles topped Pittsburgh, 3 games to 1, for the National League pennant.

The World Series opened at Dodger Stadium in Los Angeles, and the A's beat the Dodgers, 3–2. Jim ("Catfish") Hunter, the ace Oakland starter, was summoned in relief this time to record the final out after Jim Wynn's two-out solo home run and a subsequent single had put the tying run on first. Hunter, who had started and won the American League play-off clincher three days earlier, relieved Rollie Fingers, the winning pitcher. Fingers had replaced starter Ken Holtzman in the fifth inning to put down a Los Angeles threat. Reggie Jackson homered off losing pitcher Andy Messersmith in the second inning. The A's made it 2–0 in the fifth inning on Holtzman's double, a wild pitch, and Bert Campaneris' squeeze bunt. Holtzman was batting in a game for the first time all season because the American League's designated hitter rule could not be used in the Series. An error led to the first Los Angeles run in the bottom of the fifth, but Fingers came on with two on and one out to pitch $4\frac{1}{3}$ effective innings of relief. Third baseman Ron Cey's wild throw enabled the A's to score their decisive third run in the eighth.

Los Angeles evened the Series in the second game by the same 3–2 score. Mike Marshall came on in relief for the Dodgers after a hit batsman and Jackson's double had imperiled winning pitcher Don Sutton's 3–0 lead. Joe Rudi singled for two runs, but Marshall then proceeded to pick off Herb Washington, pinch-running for Rudi at first. Washington, a former Olympic Games sprint champion, had been signed by the A's earlier in the year solely as a pinch runner. Joe Ferguson's two-run homer off loser Vida Blue in the sixth provided the Dodger victory margin. Steve Yeager had singled home the first Los Angeles run in the second.

The Series switched to Oakland Coliseum for the third game, and the habit-forming trend of 3–2 final scores continued. Oakland won by that familiar margin to pull in front, 2 games to 1. Hunter and Fingers pitched for the winners again, combining to hold the Dodgers to seven hits. Hunter, the winner, started and spread five hits over 7⅓ innings, departing when Bill Buckner homered to pare Oakland's lead to 3–1. Fingers finished up, yielding a homer to Willie Crawford in the ninth but escaping later as second baseman Dick Green of the A's initiated a double play for the third time in the game. An error by catcher Ferguson, his first of two, gave Oakland one run and set up another during a two-run third inning off loser Al Downing. Campaneris' single sent home the other A's run in the fourth.

Holtzman was the star of the fourth game, his bat and arm triggering Oakland to a 5–2 triumph and a commanding Series margin of 3 games to 1. He homered off the loser, Messersmith, for the game's first run in the third inning and checked the Dodgers on six hits before giving way to Fingers in the eighth. Los Angeles grabbed a 2–1 lead in the fourth on Bill Russell's two-run triple, but a four-run A's sixth, highlighted by Jim Holt's pinch two-run single, settled the issue. A spectacular stop by Green at second base started a double play to kill off the final Dodger threat in the ninth.

Oakland won its third world title, 4 games to 1, by staving off Los Angeles by that customary 3–2 score in the fifth game. A seventh-inning home run by Rudi off reliever Marshall snapped a 2–2 tie. The blast came after the game had been held up temporarily to clear off debris thrown by unruly fans at Oakland Coliseum. Fingers, who pitched in relief in all four A's wins, came on in the eighth and mopped up Los Angeles quickly; he was voted Most Valuable Player of the Series.

Rod Carew of the Minnesota Twins captured his fourth career American League batting title and third straight by hitting .364. Dick Allen of the Chicago White Sox topped the home run list with 32, and Jeff Burroughs of the Texas Rangers led the league in runs batted in with 118. Ralph Garr of the Atlanta Braves won the National League batting championship with a .353 average. Philadelphia's Mike Schmidt grabbed home run honours with 36, and Johnny Bench of Cincinnati led in runs batted in with 129.

The National League whipped the American League in the All-Star game for the 11th time in the last 12 outings. The score was 7–2 at Three Rivers Stadium in Pittsburgh. Steve Garvey of the Dodgers was voted Most Valuable Player for his two hits and fine defensive play. The winning pitcher was Ken Brett of the Pittsburgh Pirates, the loser Luis Tiant of the Boston Red Sox. The Nationals led the series, 26–18, with one tie.

Most valuable player awards went to Steve Garvey in the National League and Jeff Burroughs in the American. Cy Young awards for outstanding pitching were won by Mike Marshall in the National League and Catfish Hunter in the American. Mike Hargrove of the Texas Rangers was named American League rookie of the year, and Bake McBride of the St. Louis Cardinals won the award in the National League. Manager of the year in the National League was Walter Alston of the Dodgers and in the American, Billy Martin of the Texas Rangers.

Hunter in December became the most highly paid baseball player in history when he signed a five-year contract with the New York Yankees estimated at $3,750,000. He had been declared a free agent by an arbitrator, who ruled that Oakland owner Charles Finley reneged on part of Hunter's 1974 contract.

Amateur. The University of Southern California won its tenth national championship and fifth straight by beating Miami of Florida, 7–3, in the finale of the NCAA College World Series at Omaha, Neb. The winning pitcher on the strength of a five-inning relief job was George Milke, his third tournament win. Milke was voted the Most Outstanding Player award.

The New Jersey Division on Civil Rights in April ordered Little League teams in the state to allow girls to play alongside boys. Faced by suits to end sex discrimination in other states, the board of directors of Little League Baseball, Inc., announced in June that they would permit girls to play on the teams. Kao Hsiung of Taiwan won the Little League World Series, 12–1, over Red Bluff, Calif., in August. It was the fourth consecutive year that a Taiwan team had taken the title. In November it was announced that in the future only continental U.S. teams would be allowed to participate. (JACK BRICKHOUSE)

Japanese. The Lotte Orions of Sendai won the World Series of Japan, 4 games to 2, over the Chunichi Dragons of Nagoya. The Dragons had taken the pennant of the Central League for the first time in 20 years, while the Orions captured the pennant in the rival Pacific League by defeating the Hankyu Braves of Nishinomiya, 3–0, in a best-of-five play-off series.

After making a good start, the Dragons once fell to the bottom, but by mid-July they closely followed the front-running Hanshin Tigers of Osaka. In August they overtook and passed the Tigers after winning six straight games.

Attracting the most attention during the season was whether the Yomiuri Giants of Tokyo could win the Central League title for the tenth straight year. However, the Giants failed, chiefly because of the high average age of their players and an overall poor pitching performance. Especially cited as an unfavourable element was the marked decline of Shigeo Nagashima, nicknamed "Mr. Giants," who had been a dominant player for the past 17 years. Nagashima later announced his retirement.

In the Central League, Sadaharu Oh of the Giants hammered 49 home runs, hit .332, and batted in 107 runs, winning the triple crown for the second straight season. He was also named as the league's Most Valuable Player.

In the Pacific League, Clarence Jones of the Kintetsu Buffaloes of Osaka, who had 38 home runs, became the first foreign player from the West to win a title since the present two-league system came into being in 1950. Isao Harimoto of the Nippon Ham Fighters of Tokyo was crowned as the league's leading hitter with a .340 average. Tokuji Nagaike of the Braves had the most runs batted in with 96. Tomehiro Kaneda of the Orions was the league's leading pitcher with a 16–7 record, and also won the Most Valuable Player award for his contribution to bringing his team to victory. (RYUSAKU HASEGAWA)

[452.B.4.h.iii]

Basketball

United States. *Professional.* The Boston Celtics lived up to their illustrious heritage in 1974 by winning the championship of the National Basketball

UPI COMPIX

Cornell Warner of the Milwaukee Bucks evades the Celtics' John Havlicek in the sixth game of the NBA championship finals.

Association (NBA). The title was a record 12th for the Celtics but their first since 1969. Fittingly, one of the two players left from that last championship team, John Havlicek, led the way to victory. Havlicek, a veteran of 12 seasons, shifted from forward to guard and back again without missing an important shot or a vital defensive assignment as Boston toppled Buffalo, defending champion New York, and Milwaukee.

The success of the Celtics' fast-break style flew in the face of the slower and, so some critics said, duller pace at which many successful NBA teams had played since Bill Russell retired as Boston's centre in 1969. While Havlicek knew the running game best, each of his fellow Celtics got a chance to demonstrate that the tradition had been placed in reliable hands.

Boston won the league's Atlantic Division by 6½ games and went into the play-offs against the Buffalo Braves, who, led by 6-ft. 9-in. centre Bob McAdoo, suddenly ceased to resemble the mere third-place team they were. Stepping to the foul line in the sixth game, Jo Jo White sank two free throws, giving Boston a 106–104 win and the series, four games to two.

The New York Knickerbockers were the defending NBA champions and they were fresh from vanquishing their perennial play-off opponents, the Capital Bullets, but they were no match for Boston. The Celtics went into high gear against New York, with Havlicek, centre Dave Cowens, and forward Paul Silas providing the impetus, and the best-of-seven series ended in five games.

Impressive as had been Boston's first two series, its opponent in the finals, the Milwaukee Bucks, did even better by losing just one play-off game in nine. Generating most of Milwaukee's power was 7-ft. 2-in. Kareem Abdul Jabbar, the game's most dominant player on offense and defense. Except for the lone quarterfinal game lost to the Los Angeles Lakers, Jabbar brought victory to the Bucks almost at will. After he scored 38 points and grabbed 24 rebounds to conclude a four-game sweep of Chicago, the Bulls' coach, Dick Motta, wondered publicly if his team could beat Jabbar playing by himself.

It often did seem as though Jabbar was on the court alone when Milwaukee met Boston in the finals. Havlicek, Silas, and Don Nelson, the three forwards employed most frequently by Celtic coach Tommy Heinsohn, devastated their opposition, while Don

Chaney, a long-armed, 6-ft. 5-in. guard, harassed Milwaukee's aging Oscar Robertson unmercifully. But still the Bucks traded victories with Boston up to the seventh and deciding game. The reason, quite simply, was Jabbar, who scored 35, 36, 26, 34, 37, 34, and 26 points in the series and who led a defense that kept the explosive Celtics under 100 points five times.

One of the two games in which Boston broke 100 was a double-overtime 102–101 loss that Jabbar won by sinking a long hook shot with three seconds remaining. Experts placed the battle among the most memorable ever seen in the play-offs, but the Celtics forgot about it in time for the deciding game. Cowens, their aggressive, muscular, 6-ft. 9-in. centre, neutralized Jabbar with long shots good for 28 points, and Havlicek and the other Celtics continued their usual feverish pitch. The result was a 102–87 victory and a return to NBA glory for Boston.

When individual honours were handed out at the season's end, Jabbar, who averaged 27 points and 14.5 rebounds a game, was named the NBA's most valuable player for the third time in his five-year career. He also found himself at centre on the league's all-star team, surrounded by Havlicek of Boston and Rick Barry of Golden State at forward and Walt Frazier of New York and Gail Goodrich of Los Angeles at guard.

Youth found its place among the veterans when it came to statistics. Buffalo's McAdoo became, at age 22, the youngest player ever to win an NBA scoring title. He averaged 30.6 points a game and also topped the league with a .547 field goal percentage, the first leading scorer to do that since Wilt Chamberlain in 1966. Ernie DiGregorio, a 6-ft. guard from Buffalo who was voted rookie of the year, led in assists (8.2 a game) and free throw percentage (.902). The premier rebounder in the NBA was Elvin Hayes of the Capital Bullets, with an 18.1 average. Watching the action were 6,885,289 customers, approximately 51,000 more than paid to get into games in 1973.

The NBA assumed a different look after the season. New Orleans was awarded a franchise, later nicknamed the Jazz. It was stocked by a player draft that produced veteran centre Walt Bellamy of Atlanta and guard Dean Meminger of New York, as well as by a trade that provided Atlanta's controversial, high-scoring Pete Maravich.

Age and injuries forced long-time NBA stars Oscar Robertson of Milwaukee, Jerry West of Los Angeles, and Willis Reed and Jerry Lucas of New York into retirement after the 1973–74 season. A third Knickerbocker standout, Dave DeBusschere, gave up playing to become the general manager of the New York Nets of the American Basketball Association (ABA).

Change came to the ABA as well in 1974. The domination of the league by the Indiana Pacers was ended, and the youthful Nets defeated the Utah Stars four games to one to capture the championship. New York's first-year coach, Kevin Loughery, molded the Nets around forward Julius Erving, whose 27.3 points a game made him the ABA's top scorer and most valuable player. Erving was named to the league's all-star team with Kentucky centre Artis Gilmore, who averaged a season high of 18.3 rebounds a game, forward George McGinnis of Indiana, and guards Jimmy Jones of Utah and Mack Calvin of Carolina. The ABA's rookie of the year was Erving's fellow forward on the Nets, Larry Kenon.

Attendance in the league held steady at 2.6 million. One franchise, the Carolina Cougars, ran into trouble because of a lack of fans and an abundance of administrative problems, and it wound up being moved to St. Louis, an abandoned NBA stronghold, and renamed the Spirits.

Moses Malone, the draft choice who created the biggest sensation in the ABA, did not play college basketball in 1974 because he was still attending Petersburg (Va.) High School. The subject of an intense recruiting war among the nation's leading basketball schools, the 6-ft. 11-in. Malone had signed a letter of intent to play at the University of Maryland and was preparing to register for classes when he finally agreed to a $1 million, five-year contract with the Utah Stars. In doing so, he became one of the few players to move directly from high school ball to the professional level.

As Malone was coming onto the scene, another big man, 7-ft. 2-in. Wilt Chamberlain, announced that he was retiring from his $600,000-a-year job as coach of the San Diego Conquistadors. Chamberlain had ended his record-setting playing career in the NBA in 1973 with Los Angeles. A lawsuit over his services as a player prevented him from performing for the Conquistadors.

Collegiate. The new face under the championship crown of the National Collegiate Athletic Association (NCAA) in 1974 belonged to North Carolina State. With an attack built around David Thompson, the Wolfpack smashed any doubts about its right to such stature by defeating powerful UCLA on the way to the title. But because of the record seven consecutive championships the Bruins had won before their fall, 1974 would undoubtedly be remembered chiefly as the year UCLA lost.

UCLA charged into the season as rich in talent as ever. The same Bruins who had set an NCAA record with 75 wins in a row—6-ft. 11-in. Bill Walton and sharpshooting Keith Wilkes, to name but two—tacked on 13 more triumphs, including an 84–66 victory over North Carolina State, before they ran into Notre Dame. The Irish came from 11 points behind with three minutes to go and won 71–70 on a jump shot by guard Dwight Clay with 29 seconds left. Ironically, the last loss the Bruins had suffered had been on the same South Bend, Ind., court in 1971.

Little more than a month later, the Bruins were upset again, this time in back-to-back games by Oregon State and Oregon. It was the first such embarrassment for UCLA since 1966, but the experience slowed them only momentarily in their quest for the Pac Eight Conference championship, the first step toward another NCAA tournament.

On the other side of the country, North Carolina State was trying to prove it was as good as had been indicated by its 27–0 record in 1973, when it was barred from postseason play for recruiting violations. Although the Wolfpack still had its leader, the 6-ft. 4-in. Thompson, who leaped as high as his foot-

Another two points for Purdue, en route to an 87–81 triumph over Utah in the NIT championship final.

taller teammate, Tommy Burleson, success came slowly at first. Victories were by close margins, and the season's lone loss, to UCLA, marked the low point. The Wolfpack needed to muster all the strength it could to go undefeated through the Atlantic Coast Conference, which placed three teams among the nation's ten best, North Carolina State, Maryland, and North Carolina.

The hardest thing North Carolina State had to do in winning the NCAA's Eastern Regionals was to play 30 minutes against Pittsburgh without Thompson. After leading the Wolfpack past Providence 92–78, Thompson went up to block a shot early in the Pittsburgh game and came crashing down on his head. He escaped with a 15-stitch gash, but all he could do for the rest of the day was watch Burleson, who scored 26 points, and Towe pull the rest of the team together to win 100–72.

No one was safe in the Mideast Regionals. Notre Dame, buoyed by its victory over UCLA and led by such outstanding performers as 6-ft. 9-in. John Shumate and freshman forward Adrian Dantley, was upset by Michigan 77–68. Then Marquette, which had defeated Vanderbilt 69–61, surprised Michigan 72–70 with gritty play by rebounder Maurice Lucas and shooter Bo Ellis.

More surprises cropped up in the Midwest Regionals, and for a time it appeared that Oral Roberts University, in only its third season of NCAA play, was going to spring most of them. First Oral Roberts eliminated Louisville, and then the shooting of guard Sam McCants put it seven points ahead of Kansas with only three minutes to go. But the Jayhawks injected some haste into their usually deliberate style and, with Roger Morningstar and Rick Suttle showing the way, were rewarded with a 93–90 victory in overtime.

As expected, UCLA won the Western Regionals, but not without putting in some overtime of its own against Dayton. Mike Sylvester threw in 36 points from every conceivable angle for the Flyers as they took the Bruins into three overtimes before running out of steam 111–100. Everything was back to normal

Major College Champions, 1974	
League	Team and location
Eastern (Ivy)	Pennsylvania (Philadelphia)
Atlantic Coast	North Carolina State (Raleigh)
Southeastern	Vanderbilt (Nashville, Tenn.)
Southern	Furman (Greenville, S.C.)
Ohio Valley	Austin Peay (Clarksville, Tenn.)
Big Ten	Indiana (Bloomington) and Michigan (Ann Arbor)
Mid-American	Ohio (Athens)
Big Eight	Kansas (Lawrence)
Missouri Valley	Louisville (Ky.)
Southwest	Texas (Austin)
AAWU (Pacific Eight)	UCLA (Los Angeles, Calif.)
Western Athletic	New Mexico (Albuquerque)

for UCLA against San Francisco, with Wilkes and Walton leading an 83–60 runaway.

The real NCAA championship game was in the semifinals when UCLA and North Carolina State played for the second time. The Wolfpack had revenge working for it. Thompson had to show that he was better than Wilkes, who had outdone him earlier, and Burleson and Towe had to prove that the maturity they had gained during the season was no illusion. When North Carolina State was trailing by 11 points at the outset of the second half, its three stars began doing what they set out to and did not stop until they had done away with UCLA 80–77.

The Wolfpack's final game, against Marquette, conqueror of Kansas 64–51, was more of a formality than anything else. The Warriors could do little to avert defeat 76–64, and the championship belonged to North Carolina State.

Victory paid off in a host of individual honours for the Wolfpack. Wire services, sports publications, and assorted athletic associations named Norm Sloan coach of the year and Thompson player of the year.

The *Sporting News* selected Thompson to its All-American team, putting him at forward with Marvin Barnes of Providence. The team's centre was Walton of UCLA and the guards were Tom Henderson of Hawaii and Dennis DuVal of Syracuse.

The final statistics of the college basketball season found only one first-team All-American among the leaders, Barnes, who grabbed 18.7 rebounds a game. Pacing the scorers with a 33.4 average was sophomore forward Larry Fogle of Canisius. From the foul line, the best shot was Rickey Medlock of Arkansas, who made 87 of 95 free-throw attempts. The most accurate shooter from the field was Al Fleming of Arizona, who connected on 136 of 204 attempts for a .667 percentage that tied the NCAA record held by UCLA's Lew Alcindor (now Kareem Abdul Jabbar) and Abilene Christian's Kent Martens.

Alcindor's record career field-goal percentage of .639 was topped by his replacement at centre at UCLA, Walton, who made 65% of his shots in three years. Oddly, Walton never won a season field-goal percentage championship.

Morgan State, featuring 6-ft. 11-in. centre Marvin Webster, beat Southwest Missouri 67–52 to become the first team in 17 years to win the NCAA college division championship in its first try. Unheralded West Georgia College upset Alcorn State of Mississippi 97–79 to become the champion of the National Association of Intercollegiate Athletics.

(JOHN SCHULIAN)

World Amateur. At its meeting on July 10, 1974, at San Juan, P.R., the Central Bureau of the International Amateur Basketball Federation admitted into membership China's Basketball Federation. Basketball in China was hampered by lack of contact with the rest of the world, but it was expected that regular exchanges would take place, and the English Basket Ball Association was invited to send its men's team to China in July 1975. Women's basketball was scheduled to be included in the Olympic Games for the first time in 1976.

In the world championships, held in Puerto Rico in July, the U.S.S.R. added the world championship title to its controversial 1972 Olympic gold medal. It was not easily achieved. In the final round Yugoslavia beat the Soviets 82–79 but lost to the U.S. 91–88, and the U.S.S.R. chalked up a victory against the U.S. 105–94. This left the three teams with equal points,

and the final placings had to be decided by goal average, which resulted in Yugoslavia's being second and the U.S. third. Cuba, Spain, and Brazil occupied the next three positions.

In the 1974 edition of the European Cup, Real Madrid (Spain) was back on the throne, beating Ignis Varese (Italy) 84–83 in a memorable final at Nantes, France. In the 17 years of the cup competition, Soviet clubs had won eight times, Spanish five, and Italian four. In the Cup Winners' Cup, Crvena Zvezda Belgrade (Yugos.) defeated Spartak Brno (Czech.) 86–75. In the Korac Cup, Birra Forst Cantu (Italy) secured a trophy for Italy by beating KK Partizan Belgrade (Yugos.).

In the Women's Cup, once more, predictably, Daugava Riga (U.S.S.R.) defeated Clermont Ferrand (France). The scores were 96–67 in the Soviet Union and 69–53 in France. In recent years Clermont Ferrand had been the only club capable of giving the magnificent Latvian team a reasonable game. Daugava won this cup for the 11th time in a row. The U.S.S.R. also took the honours in the Women's Cup Winners' Cup final: Spartak Leningrad (U.S.S.R.) snatched the trophy from GEAS Sesto San Giovanni (Italy), the fine performance in Italy when GEAS beat Spartak 65–57 not being sufficient to overcome the ten-point deficit when Spartak won in Leningrad 68–58.

In 1974 a new cup appeared, the European Cup for National Teams. Played on an experimental basis, it proved such a success that it was decided to continue it in 1975. Six teams competed. The final team standings were Italy, Yugoslavia, Greece, Turkey, France, and West Germany.

Seoul, South Korea, was the site of the fifth Asian Basketball Championships for women. In the final round South Korea and Japan played outstandingly, and the result was a close and exciting game with South Korea finishing strongly 76–70 to take the championship.   (K. K. MITCHELL)

[452.B.4.h.iv]

Behavioural Sciences

Behavioural science research during 1974 was strongly influenced by changing mores. The annual psychological and sociological association meetings, prodded by the women's liberation movement, gave high priority to sex role stereotyping. The controversy over the use of IQ and other tests that result in the labeling of children and adolescents continued to receive attention, but much of the hysteria evidenced in earlier years was absent. Behavioural scientists were more worried about job opportunities, research funding, and inflation.

Psychology and Law. New laws affecting research on human subjects and the use of behaviour modification techniques in prisons and mental hospitals were certain to influence the work of behavioural scientists. However, some scientists turned the tables by involving themselves in legal proceedings. They helped defense lawyers in a number of notable conspiracy trials of militant leaders, including the American Indians tried in connection with the 1973 occupation of Wounded Knee, S.D. Their work centred mainly on the jury selection or *voir dire* procedure and involved such sophisticated techniques as the construction of computer profiles of the "ideal" (from a defense standpoint) juror.

This type of advocate psychology was criticized by some social scientists who expressed concern that it could prevent fair trials. A wealthy defendant, for instance, would have an advantage over the prosecution unless both sides could avail themselves of the same techniques. Social scientists, of course, did not invent the jury-selection procedure, in which each side is allowed a given number of peremptory challenges that can be used to excuse prospective jurors without stating a reason. Lawyers for both defense and prosecution have long used homespun psychology in their efforts to obtain a jury that will favour their side.

A social psychologist and a legal scholar, of the University of Chicago, examined how peremptory challenges work under actual trial conditions. With the cooperation of three federal judges, they were able to study ten cases, each of which had one real jury and two experimental ones: an "English" jury, chosen at random from the jury pool, and another made up of individuals challenged by either the defense or the prosecution. The two mock juries received the same treatment as the real one.

In the ten cases, the real jury voted guilty five times and not guilty five times. The challenged jury voted guilty eight times. The English jury found the defendant guilty every time. The judges, asked what their verdicts would have been, voted guilty in nine of the cases. Post-trial analysis showed that both defense and prosecution had used their challenges effectively in eliminating jurors likely to vote against them. When asked why prospective jurors were challenged, both defense and prosecution mentioned race most often, followed by demeanour, occupation, residence, sex, and age. On the basis of how jurors actually voted, challenges based on race were most likely to be correct (80% of the time) and those based on sex were least likely to be correct (44%).

Sex Stereotyping. Several studies indicated that sex-role stereotyping begins in the delivery room and continues from then on. Questioning of 30 sets of parents within 24 hours of the birth of their first child by asking them to describe their baby, rating the child on 18 adjective scales (firm/soft, big/little, relaxed/nervous, and so on), yielded interesting results. Although hospital records showed no significant differences between the 15 male and 15 female children, the parents of daughters saw their children as softer, finer-featured, smaller, and more inattentive than did the parents of boys.

In another study, 11 mothers were observed while in a nursery playing with a six-month-old boy. Five saw the child dressed in blue pants and were told his name was Adam. The other six saw him in a pink dress and were told his name was Beth. Three toys were available for play: a fish, a train, and a doll. Though all the mothers agreed that there were no sex differences in the way six-month-old children should play and were not aware that they treated Beth/Adam differently, the mothers who thought they were playing with a girl handed the baby a doll more often while those who thought he was a boy tended to give him the train. There was no difference in the handling of the sex-neutral fish.

At the University of Wyoming 40 male and 67 female college students were asked to rate, on an approval/disapproval scale, ten sentences describing young children engaged in activities usually considered more appropriate for the opposite sex: a boy playing with dolls; a girl playing baseball. All the students were more disapproving of "inappropriate"

behaviour by boys than by girls, while male students expressed greater disapproval of such behaviour by both boys and girls than did the female students.

The fact that adults accept tomboy behaviour more freely than sissy behaviour helped to explain the results of a psychological study at Bowling Green (O.) State University. When women students in a class on the psychology of women were asked to write autobiographical accounts, 78% reported having been tomboys. Thinking this might be a specialized group, the researchers questioned young girls at a summer camp and found that 63% considered themselves tomboys and 60% said they had been tomboys when they were younger. In a random group of adult women at a shopping mall, 51% reported they had been tomboys when they were girls. These findings led the investigators to speculate that "tomboyism is not so much abnormal as it is typical."

Nonverbal Communication. Several Harvard psychologists developed a Profile of Nonverbal Sensitivity Test (PONS, for short). The subject is shown a series of scenes in which a woman is either seen, heard, or both for just two seconds. After each scene, the subject says which of two possible situations he has just witnessed; e.g., "expressing jealous anger" or "talking about one's divorce." Females, as early as the third grade, scored consistently higher than males in interpreting nonverbal clues, though men in occupations requiring artistic or expressive behaviour—for example, actors, artists, and clinical psychologists—tended to score high.

Child Development. It was learned that the rhythm of a heartbeat and the rhythm of human speech strongly affect newborn babies. Observing that mothers at New York Hospital consistently held infants on the left side, researchers exposed a group of newborn babies day and night to the sound of a recorded heartbeat; it was found that the babies cried less and gained more weight than a control group. Interestingly, mothers who had been separated from their children for 24 hours or more after birth did not show this tendency. It appears that a mother's tendency to hold the baby near her heartbeat also fulfills her baby's need—a need that might have been imprinted before birth.

Sound films of infant-adult interactions at Boston University Medical Center were compared for sound and movement, frame by frame. It was found that

Electric shock therapy is used on a convicted child molester in an effort to achieve behaviour modification.

infant movements of mouth, body, and limbs tended to change direction and speed at natural breaking points in the adult's speech. It was concluded that day-old children already react to the particular speech patterns of their culture, long before they start to use them in actual speech.

Good Samaritans. In an effort to find those personality traits associated with helping behaviour, 40 students at Princeton Theological Seminary were first tested for three types of religiosity, summarized briefly as religion as means, religion as end, and religion as quest. The students were then given a passage to read (in one case a discussion of possible future jobs for seminary students; in the other the biblical parable of the Good Samaritan). Finally, they were asked to go to another building to record a short talk on the subject of the passage. Each was told either that he was late for his appointment, that the assistant with the recorder was ready for him, or that he had plenty of time. On the way to the next building, the subject passed a supposed victim, slumped in a doorway with head down and eyes closed, coughing or moaning intermittently.

Sixteen men offered some type of aid; 24 did not. Neither the passage read nor the subject's type of religiosity seemed to predict how he would react. The one significant factor was how hurried he was. In the low hurry condition, 63% helped; medium hurry, 45% helped; high hurry, only 10% helped. It was concluded that "the frequently cited explanation that ethics becomes a luxury as the speed of our daily lives increases" is at least an accurate description.

(PATRICE DAILY HORN)

[441.A.3.a; 432.C.2.4.c; 523.A.2.a.i; 553.F.3.a; 10/51.B.6]

ENCYCLOPÆDIA BRITANNICA FILMS. *The House of Man, Part II—Our Crowded Environment* (1969); *View from the People Wall: A Statement About Problem Solving and Abstract Methods* (1973).

Belgium

A constitutional monarchy on the North Sea coast of Europe, Belgium is bordered by The Netherlands, West Germany, Luxembourg, and France. Area: 11,782 sq.mi. (30,514 sq.km.). Pop. (1973 est.): 9,756,600. Cap. and largest urban area: Brussels (pop., 1973 est., commune 153,400, urban agglomeration 1,063,300). Language: Dutch, French, and German. Religion: predominantly Roman Catholic. King, Baudouin I; prime ministers in 1974, Edmond Leburton until January 19 and, from April 25, Léo Tindemans.

The tripartite coalition government, comprising Socialists, Social Christians, and Liberals under the leadership of Edmond Leburton, resigned on Jan. 19, 1974, after the withdrawal of Iran from the joint oil refinery project in the Liège area, which was to have been run by the Iranian-Belgian Refining and Marketing Company (IBRAMCO). The Liberals and Social Christians had strong doubts about the potential profit-making capacity of the state-run enterprise, the Liberals stressing that private industry had not defaulted, while the Socialists continued to uphold their long-standing demand for state intervention in the crucial energy sector. As a result, arguments within the government dragged on beyond the time limit set by the Iranians, who promptly announced their withdrawal from the project. The Socialists regarded the issue as a test case for their beliefs on the subject of state intervention and many considered the matter a good issue on which to fight a general election.

For the second time in six months a bomb explodes in front of the Iberia Air Lines office in downtown Brussels.

In the first instance, however, King Baudouin asked the leader of the Flemish wing of the Social Christians, Deputy Prime Minister Léo Tindemans (*see* BIOGRAPHY), to try to form a government. Only when this attempt failed, due to Tindemans' inability to obtain sufficient support from the Walloon wing of his party, was Parliament dissolved and a general election called for March 10. The results were: Social Christians 72 seats; Socialists 58; Liberals 30; Walloon and Brussels federalists (Rassemblement Wallon and Front Démocratique Francophone) 25; Flemish federalists (Volksunie) 22; Communists 4.

Since the Socialists had rejected the tripartite formula, prime minister-designate Tindemans commenced negotiations on the basis of a coalition between Social Christians and Socialists. However, serious disagreements on the crucial and long-standing issue of regional devolution, as well as on the subjects of abortion law reform, state intervention in industry, and educational problems, led him to abandon the attempt and turn to the Liberals. The latter urged him to invite the federalist parties to join in a broad coalition that would command the two-thirds majority required to pass legislation on the controversial matter of devolution of powers to French-speaking Wallonia, Dutch-speaking Flanders, and the bilingual Brussels district.

On April 19–20 a conference of leaders of all parties, excluding the Socialists and Communists, took place at Steenokkerzeel Castle near Brussels. A number of differences between Flemings and Walloons were ironed out in a marathon 23-hour session, but it proved impossible to reach any mutually acceptable agreement on the limits of the Brussels region. However, the conference did pave the way for a minority government of Social Christians and Liberals headed by Tindemans, with the tacit support of the federalist parties who were expected to join in at a later stage.

The new government, which was sworn in on April 25, consisted initially of 13 Social Christian ministers and 6 Liberals, with 3 Social Christian and 3 Liberal secretaries of state. Of the federalists, only the Rassemblement Wallon eventually joined the government, with one minister and three secretaries of state. The Volksunie and the Front Démocratique Francophone remained at loggerheads over the limits of the Brussels region. Finally, just before the summer recess, Parliament approved provisional legislation on the devolution issue which did not require the special majority. The bill, which provided for the setting up by October 1 of three ministerial councils, one for each of the regions, was passed by a total of 108 votes in favour, with 78 against and 13 abstentions.

On taking office, the new government was immediately faced with a crisis in the energy sector. The outgoing government had consistently refused to grant higher prices for oil products, and on March 12 distribution had come to a halt. Four days later an interim increase was agreed to, but the oil companies regarded this as inadequate and on April 4 all refineries ceased production and strategic stocks had to be used until production was resumed on April 23. Finally, on September 24, IBRAMCO was dissolved.

Problems also arose in the educational sector when the schools reopened and teachers refused to supervise children outside normal school hours. Moreover, news that Belgium would issue school registration certificates to foreigners illegally residing in the country led to an influx of immigrants from other states. Inflation became a major concern for the new government. In the first nine months of 1974 the consumer price index climbed more than 11%. The 1975 budget called for increased company and motor vehicle taxes. Farmers' dissatisfaction with EEC agricultural policies and the rising cost of oil products and foodstuffs led to a series of demonstrations in September.

In the sphere of foreign affairs, on February 11 the government concluded an agreement with Zairian Pres. Mobutu Sese Seko providing for BFr. 4 billion compensation for the giant mining company Union Minière and for Belgian aid in the construction of a new copper refinery in Zaire.   (JAN R. ENGELS)

[972.A.7]

Bhutan

A monarchy situated in the eastern Himalayas, Bhutan is bounded by China, India, and Sikkim. Area: 18,000 sq.mi. (47,000 sq.km.). Pop. (1973 est.): 1,129,000. Official cap.: Thimphu (pop., approximately 10,000). Administrative cap.: Paro (population unavailable). Language: Dzongkha (official). Religion: approximately 75% Buddhist, 25% Hindu. Druk gyalpo (king) in 1974, Jigme Singye Wangchuk.

Eighteen-year-old King Jigme Singye Wangchuk was officially crowned in Thimphu on June 2, 1974. The week-long ceremony was attended by the presidents of India and Bangladesh, by diplomatic representatives of the five permanent members of the UN Security Council, including China, as well as those of other countries, and by royalty from Sikkim and Nepal. Before the coronation, Bhutanese officials announced that Tibetan refugees had plotted to assassinate the king and that 30 persons, including Deputy Home Minister Phuntsho Dhondup and the police commandant, had been arrested. Gyalo Thendhup, a brother of the Dalai Lama in exile in India, was said to be their ringleader. Speaking after the coronation, the king praised India for its economic aid to Bhutan and expressed satisfaction at the working of the Indo-Bhutan treaty of 1949, but declared that Bhutan's aim was greater self-reliance.

Indian aid continued to be the major factor in Bhutan's development. In March an agreement was signed under which India was to finance a Rs. 830 million hydroelectric project; surplus power was to go to India. In September the UN Children's Fund (UNICEF) agreed to provide $600,000 in 1974–75 to improve health services for children and expectant mothers. Bhutan's first currency notes were released in Thimphu in April. Called ngultrums, they were at par with the Indian rupee, which would remain legal tender.   (GOVINDAN UNNY)

King Jigme Singye Wangchuk on his throne following his installation in Thimphu.

BELGIUM
Education. (1968–69) Primary, pupils 1,008,444, teachers (1967–68) 47,902; secondary, pupils 309,137, teachers (1967–68) 40,074; vocational, pupils 518,-709, teachers (1966–67) 47,956; teacher training, students 19,282, teachers (1967–68) 6,089; higher (4 universities; 1970–71), students 75,106, teaching staff (1967–68) 5,489.
Finance. Monetary unit: Belgian franc, with (Sept. 16, 1974) a free rate of BFr. 39.51 to U.S. $1 (BFr. 91.40 = £1 sterling). Gold, SDRs, and foreign exchange, central bank: (June 1974) U.S. $4,070,000,-000; (June 1973) U.S. $4,449,000,000. Budget (1973 actual): revenue BFr. 427,089,000,000; expenditure BFr. 512,725,000,000. Gross national product: (1972) BFr. 1,583,000,000,000; (1971) BFr. 1,419,000,000,-000. Money supply: (Feb. 1974) BFr. 562.6 billion; (Feb. 1973) BFr. 520.8 billion. Cost of living (1970 = 100): (June 1974) 132; (June 1973) 117.
Foreign Trade. (Belgium-Luxembourg economic union; 1973) Imports BFr 851.1 billion; exports BFr. 868.7 billion. Import sources: EEC 71% (West Germany 25%, France 19%, The Netherlands 16%, U.K. 7%); U.S. 6%. Export destinations: EEC 73% (West Germany 24%, France 21%, The Netherlands 18%, Italy 5%, U.K. 5%); U.S. 6%. Main exports: iron and steel 16%; machinery 10%; chemicals 10%; textile yarns and fabrics 8%; motor vehicles 10%; nonferrous metals 6%. Tourism (1972): visitors 6,952,-700; gross receipts (Belgium-Luxembourg) U.S. $435 million.
Transport and Communications. Roads (1972) 92,666 km. (including 898 km. expressways). Motor vehicles in use (1972): passenger 2,247,000; commercial 220,000. Railways: (1972) 4,081 km.; traffic (1973) 8,092,000,000 passenger-km., freight 8,164,-000,000 net ton-km. Air traffic (1973): 3,644,000,000 passenger-km.; freight 247,608,000 net ton-km. Navigable inland waterways in regular use (1971) 1,536 km. Shipping (1973): merchant vessels 100 gross tons and over 236; gross tonnage 1,161,609. Shipping traffic (1973): goods loaded 36,917,000 metric tons, unloaded 60,762,000 metric tons. Telephones (Dec. 1972) 2,324,000. Radio licenses (Dec. 1972) 3,560,000. Television licenses (Dec. 1972) 2,289,000.
Agriculture. Production (in 000; metric tons; 1973; 1972 in parentheses): wheat c. 900 (924); barley 660 (653); oats 240 (249); rye 63 (76); potatoes c. 1,400 (1,337); apples (1972) c. 238, (1971) 272; sugar, raw value c. 778 (c. 685); pork c. 545 (511); beef and veal c. 260 (258); milk (1972) c. 3,680, (1971) 3,604; fish catch (1972) 59, (1971) 60. Livestock (in 000; May 1973): cattle c. 2,865; pigs c. 4,412; sheep 69; horses c. 60; chickens (1972) c. 43,500.
Industry. Fuel and power (in 000; 1973): coal (metric tons) 8,873; manufactured gas (cu.m.; 1972) 3,165,000; electricity (kw-hr.) 41,071,000. Production (in 000; metric tons; 1973): pig iron 12,655; crude steel 15,526; copper 372; lead 113; zinc 282; tin 4.5; sulfuric acid 2,594; cement 7,042; cotton yarn 65; cotton fabrics 72; wool yarn 84; woolen fabrics 37; rayon and acetate yarn and fibres 32.

BHUTAN
Education. (1969) Primary, pupils 10,150, teachers (1968) 275; secondary (1968), pupils 2,559, teachers 141; vocational, pupils 197, teachers 19; teacher training, students 53, teachers 6.
Finance and Trade. Monetary unit: ngultrum, at par with the Indian rupee, with (Sept. 16, 1974) a free rate of Rs. 8.20 to U.S. $1 (official rate of Rs. 18.97 = £1 sterling). Budget (1971–72): revenue Rs. 27.5 million; expenditure Rs. 69.1 million. Third five-year development plan (1971–76) total expenditure (est.) Rs. 350 million (including c. Rs. 330 million from India). About 95% of external trade is with India. Main exports (1963–64): timber Rs. 1,250,000; coal Rs. 220,000.

Biography 1974

The following is a selected list of men and women who influenced events in 1974.

AARON, HENRY

On April 8, 1974, Hank Aaron picked out a 1 and 0 fastball thrown by Los Angeles Dodger left-hander Al Downing and drove it over Atlanta Stadium's left-centre field fence, just to the right of the 385-ft. marker. That home run, the 715th of his career, broke Babe Ruth's lifetime record, which had stood for almost 40 years and which many believed would never be exceeded. Shortly after the season ended, Aaron was traded by the Braves to the Milwaukee Brewers of the American League. He hit 398 of his 733 home runs before the National League Braves moved from Milwaukee to Atlanta after the 1965 season and had expressed a desire to return.

Aaron began the season with 713 home runs, and it was all but inevitable that he would break Ruth's record. Detractors took up their refrain of the season before, namely that the modern baseball is livelier than in Ruth's day and that Aaron had played in more games than Ruth. Aaron's defenders countered that he had to contend with the slider, a breaking pitch not introduced until after Ruth retired, and a high percentage of night games. Aaron smiled politely through the turmoil, which included a large measure of hate mail, much of it of a racial nature.

Born on Feb. 5, 1934, in Mobile, Ala., Aaron played with the Indianapolis Clowns of the Negro American League until June 1952, when the Boston Braves paid $10,000 for his contract and signed him for $350 a month. In 1954, after a stint in the minors, he joined the Braves, who by then had moved to Milwaukee. Aaron suffered a broken ankle in September, but came back the next season to hit .314 with 27 home runs and 106 RBIs. He won the National League batting championship with a .328 average in 1956 and was named the league's most valuable player in 1957. His last contract with the Braves called for $200,000 a year.

The 1974 season began with pressure on Aaron from within baseball as well as from without. The Braves had planned to hold him out of a three-game series in Cincinnati so he would have a chance to break Ruth's record in Atlanta. However, baseball Commissioner Bowie Kuhn ordered Aaron to play opening day in Cincinnati, and Henry tied Ruth's record with his first swing of the season. Kuhn also ordered that he play in the third game, but he failed to get a hit. The feat was thus saved for a cool, overcast day in Atlanta. Aaron told the cheering crowd, "I just thank God it's all over."

(J. TIMOTHY WEIGEL)

ADAMS, RICHARD GEORGE

Continuing in the British animal-fantasy tradition of A. A. Milne, Lewis Carroll, Kenneth Grahame, and J. R. R. Tolkien, Richard Adams produced a saga of wild rabbits that became one of the most popular novels of 1974. *Watership Down*, published in England in 1972 and in the U.S. in 1974, is a fable of survival: a group of rabbits, forced to flee their warren by human housing developers and guided by a gentle and persuasive leader, roam the English countryside in search of a new home, encountering and overcoming various dangers along the way. In addition to the anthropomorphic, but not sentimentalized, rabbit personalities he created, Adams invented a complete rabbit culture, including a language, folklore, and culture hero.

The novel developed out of stories Adams told to his two young daughters. When he decided, at the urging of one daughter, to write the stories down, he studied R. M. Lockley's *The Private Life of the Rabbit* (1964), which provided much of the plausible detail of rabbit life that contributed to the book's success. The novel thus began as a children's book, although its appeal to adults as well made it a best-seller. Adams maintained that he did not intend to create an allegory of the human condition or a political parable (although the book was so interpreted by some readers) but "to write a cliffhanging story, to pay tribute to the beauty of this part of the English countryside—and to provide a study of leadership."

In 1973 the book won the Carnegie Medal and the Guardian Award for children's fiction. The critical acclaim the book received in England was not entirely echoed in the U.S.—one New York reviewer found Adams' creatures to be male chauvinist rabbits—but that did not seriously affect the book's popular appeal. The novel was also purchased for a full-length animated movie.

The author, who was in his mid-50s, was born and brought up in Berkshire, Eng., near the Watership Down area that he described in his book. He studied history at Worcester College, Oxford, and served in the Royal Army Service Corps during World War II. After the war he entered government service and was assistant secretary (head of the air pollution department) of the Department of the Environment when *Watership Down* was published. Adams retired from his government position in 1974 to devote full time to writing. He had already completed his second novel, *Shardik*, about an empire led by a bear-god.

(JOAN NATALIE REIBSTEIN)

ADLER, MORTIMER JEROME

In the rather staid publishing world of scholarly books and reference works, the month of February 1974 must be regarded as a benchmark of some significance. The new 15th edition of the *Encyclopædia Britannica* burst upon the scene amidst a torrent of publicity releases, reviews, and national advertising. Startlingly new in concept, design, and content, this total revision of the venerable *Britannica* occasioned no little surprise—even the name had been altered. The new *Britannica 3,* so designated because of its tripartite format, represented years of planning and preparation under the guiding genius of Mortimer Adler, *Britannica's* man for all seasons.

Adler has been variously described as a philosopher, educator, editor, and businessman, and it is fair to say that his career reflects and encompasses each of these diverse callings. As an honours student under John Erskine at Columbia University in the 1920s, Adler became impressed with the value of readings and discussions based on great books—the best-sellers of the ages, as it were. When he later joined Robert Hutchins in the halcyon years of educational ferment at the University of Chicago, the two men did much to promote the concept that study of great books could provide the core of a liberal education. They attempted to make such an education available to all adults through publication of the 54-volume *Great Books of the Western World* in 1952. The *Syntopicon* of this set is a two-volume index of great ideas devised by Adler. It has served as the seminal source for a host of additional works, including *The Great Ideas Today* (1961–).

Many of his books were written or edited at the Institute for Philosophical Research, which Adler directed from 1952. Most notable are *The Conditions of Philosophy* (1965), *The Difference of Man and the Difference It Makes* (1967), *The Time of Our Lives* (1970), and the widely acclaimed 20-volume compilation of Americana entitled *Annals of America* (1968). The latter set, produced for *Britannica,* includes a two-volume *Conspectus* treating great issues in American history, also devised by Adler.

A man of boundless energy characterized by tireless ferocity in pursuit of an idea, Adler at 72 was still to be found everywhere, seemingly doing everything at once. He would address a luncheon at the Harvard Club, return to his Institute to confer on manuscript progress, stride to *Britannica* headquarters to meet with and inspire the sales force, appear on a television talk show, lecture at the University of Chicago, jet to Aspen or Santa Barbara to hold seminars, and on and on. Little wonder that this man was chosen to direct the massive undertaking of planning the new *Britannica*—and that he accepted the challenge. By reason of his breadth of knowledge, perseverance in the face of adversity, and good common sense, Adler welded the editors of the several parts of the circle of knowledge to common purpose so that in 1974, at last, the final obstacles were overcome and the great work completed. The classification of knowledge is apart from the actual creation of knowledge and, in this sense, can be considered an artifice, or nonscholarly enterprise. But in the absence of classification there can be no order and, in the final analysis, no rational scheme for compiling an encyclopædia. The production of a new *Britannica* is no little thing; rather, it is the event of a lifetime and the capstone of a career. Mortimer Adler had good reason to be proud of his efforts in 1974.

(LAWRENCE K. LUSTIG)

AHMED, FAKHRUDDIN ALI

India's fifth president and the second Muslim to hold the office, Fakhruddin Ali Ahmed succeeded V. V. Giri on Aug. 24, 1974. A Congress Party veteran of more than 40 years' standing, he had been a member of the party's central parliamentary board from 1964. In the political crisis of 1969, in which the Congress Party split into two distinct parliamentary factions, he had stood firmly by Prime Minister Indira Gandhi.

Born in Delhi on May 13, 1905, the son of an army doctor from Assam, Ahmed attended St. Catherine's College, Cambridge, graduating in 1927, and was called to the bar by the Inner Temple the following year. Back in India, he threw in his lot with Gandhi and Nehru and opposed the sectarian politics of the Muslim League. Elected to the Assam legislature in 1935, he became the province's minister of finance and revenue in 1938. He was responsible for some radical taxation measures and was the first in India to impose a levy on agricultural income.

The outbreak of World War II led to a confrontation between the Congress Party and the British power, and Ahmed spent most of the war years in prison. Released in April 1945, he lost to a Muslim League candidate in the election of that year. A year later he was appointed advocate general of Assam, a post he held for six years. After a term in the national Parliament, he returned to Assam politics and was a minister from 1957 until 1966, when Mrs. Gandhi included him in her first Cabinet. At the national level he held a variety of portfolios. As minister of industrial development, he piloted the antimonopolies bill through Parliament.

Unflamboyant and soft-spoken, Ahmed on occasion had disarmed Parliament by his quiet humour. When a member charged that he had married a woman many years his junior, he replied: "The honourable member is correct. I did indeed marry an 18-year-old girl, but that was 20 years ago!" Begum Abida and he were married in 1945; they had two sons and a daughter. The new president's pastimes were Urdu poetry, classical Indian music, and tennis. He was president of the All-India Lawn Tennis Association.　　(H. Y. SHARADA PRASAD)

ALMIRANTE, GIORGIO

Political secretary of the neofascist Italian Social Movement-National Right (MSI-DN) party, Giorgio Almirante gained attention during 1974 following the proceedings of an inquiry by Milan judge Luigi Bianchi D'Espinosa that aimed at prosecuting Almirante for reconstitution of the Fascist Party, barred by Italian law. In May 1973, during a debate in the Chamber of Deputies concerned with obtaining permission to proceed legally against a member of Parliament, Almirante had voted in favour of allowing such permission in the hope that a new inquiry would disprove the conclusions reached by Judge D'Espinosa. The authorization was granted by 485 votes to 59, and the papers in his case were therefore transmitted for competence to Rome judge Carmelo Spagnuolo. On Jan. 24, 1974, Almirante was interrogated for two hours, and inquiries continued throughout the year.

Almirante's name also became front-page news a few days after the August 4 bomb explosion on the "Italicus" train, which killed 12 people. He claimed that he had been warned of it and had informed the proper authorities. His gesture was regarded as an attempt to establish a moral alibi since extreme right-wing terrorists were held to be responsible for the planting of the bomb.

Born at Salsomaggiore on July 27, 1914, Almirante embraced Fascism and the Mussolini cult as a student, becoming a member of a group that aimed at keeping peace and order—Fascist-style—at his university. A journalist at 18, with *Il Tevere,* the newspaper edited by Fascist theoretician Telesio Interlandi, he later became assistant editor before joining as a volunteer for the war in Abyssinia. Returning to Italy, he worked as a teacher and then again as a journalist. After July 25, 1943 (when the Fascist government was overthrown), he joined the Army, became a prisoner of the Germans, and later joined the Italian Social Republic. When it fell, he disappeared for 18 months, during which time he worked at odd jobs until he was able to return to teaching. He was elected to the Italian Parliament in 1948 and advanced within the MSI until he became its secretary-general following the death of former leader Arturo Michelini in 1969. After shedding some of his extreme

Giorgio Almirante

KEYSTONE

views, he brought together the MSI and the Monarchist Party to form the right-wing MSI-DN coalition of which he became leader.

AMIN, IDI DADA OUMEE

A burly, extroverted soldier who became president of Uganda in January 1971 after a military coup against Pres. Milton Obote, Idi Amin survived army mutinies and assassination attempts in 1974 by acting swiftly. He gained a reputation as an increasingly dangerous and difficult man to cross. He accused two neighbour states, Tanzania and Zambia, of planning to attack Uganda. When the International Commission of Jurists published a harsh indictment of the conduct of affairs in Uganda, Amin countered by establishing his own commission to inquire into the disappearance of prominent citizens and their unexplained deaths, including those of a former chief justice and the lately dismissed foreign minister. He separated from his three wives, of whom one was subsequently arrested and charged with smuggling while another died under circumstances about which conflicting reports were published. On November 28 he suddenly dismissed Elizabeth Bagaya (formerly Princess Elizabeth of Toro), foreign minister since February 19, for alleged misconduct in Paris and had her placed under brief house arrest. A revealing French documentary film of Amin's personal rule,

G. WURTZ—FRANCE MATCH / CAMERA 5

by the Swiss director Barbet Schroeder, was widely distributed in 1974.

Born about 1925 in the village of Koboko and a devout Muslim from the small Kakwa tribe, Amin was largely self-taught, having joined the British colonial army as a young man. He saw service in the Burma campaign in World War II with the King's African Rifles, an East African regiment. Subsequently, he fought against the Mau Mau rebellion in Kenya. Under the colonial regime he rose to the highest noncommissioned rank and became an officer only a year before Uganda achieved its independence in 1962. Four years later he was made army commander. Most at ease with the rank and file of the Army, Amin was for ten years heavyweight boxing champion of Uganda and an enthusiastic rugby football player. He was closely involved with Obote in dealing with previous attempts at coups and assassinations in Uganda. But the two men became increasingly estranged after 1969, when Obote decided on changes in the army structure. These disagreements turned into hostility, and Amin was on the point of being dismissed when he staged his successful coup.
　　(COLIN LEGUM)

ARAFAT, YASIR

Wearing the familiar checkered kaffiyeh, dark sunglasses, and an unmistakable air

of triumph, Yasir Arafat, chairman of the Palestine Liberation Organization (PLO), appeared before the UN General Assembly on Nov. 13, 1974. His arrival in New York triggered one of the most massive security operations ever undertaken in that city because Arafat personified the "enemy" to its large Jewish population. His speech did little to dispel such antagonism, for Arafat proclaimed as his goal the organization of a new secular Palestinian state, one which would include Muslims, Christians, and Jews. Opponents were quick to equate this aim with elimination of the state of Israel as presently constituted—an Arab dream since 1948.

Arafat's appearance represented the culmination of a long struggle among several Arab factions. At issue had been the question of who would speak for the displaced Palestinians of the Gaza Strip, the West Bank of the Jordan River, and those still farther removed from their original homeland. When the West Bank fell into Israeli hands following the Six-Day War of June 1967, King Hussein of Jordan asserted his fundamental sovereignty over the territory and was thus acknowledged as the refugees' principal spokesman. The discontent produced by Israel's victory in that war, however, led to seizure of control of the PLO by Arafat's preexisting guerrilla group, Al Fatah (an acronym in reverse for Palestine Liberation Movement). He became chairman of the PLO in 1969 and this organization was named the sole legitimate representative of all the Palestinian people at an Arab summit meeting held in Rabat, Morocco, in October 1974. This stunning political defeat for King Hussein also dashed hopes for an early settlement of the Middle East situation.

Arafat was born in Ramallah (or possibly Jenin), north of Jerusalem, in 1929. He received a civil engineering degree from Cairo University and during the 1956 Suez conflict served as a lieutenant in the Egyptian Army. He subsequently joined the firm of Emile Bustani, which operated in Beirut and the Persian Gulf area generally, and did not become seriously concerned with Palestinian politics until the early 1960s.

However one might view Arafat's role in Middle East affairs, his ascent to the UN podium must be considered remarkable for a man who but a few years earlier lived in caves in the desert, hiding from agents of both Israel and King Hussein. Some observers thought it likely that he would ultimately emerge as the head of a government-in-exile, but others, aware of the volatility of events in the region, suggested that his influence might wane as rapidly as it had arisen.　　(LAWRENCE K. LUSTIG)

ARIAS NAVARRO, CARLOS

The terrorist bomb that blew Premier Luis Carrero Blanco and his car over a church wall on Dec. 20, 1973, cleared the way for Carlos Arias Navarro to become, on December 29, the unexpected first civilian premier of post-Civil War Spain, a personal choice of Franco over three candidates put forward by the Council of the Realm. Less a politician than a personal servant of General Franco, Arias Navarro was characterized chiefly by a capacity for ruthlessness. Though recently described as courteous, approachable, and willing to listen, he retained an unyielding nature. His unpredicted 11 changes in the 19-man Cabinet demonstrated his independence.

While staunchly supporting the maintenance of law and order, Arias Navarro accepted that expediency required the introduction of a modest degree of political liberalization in Spain. His cautious moves in that direction met with fierce hostility from the right wing of the regime. In defending his policy he showed tenacity, individuality, and resourcefulness, which delineated him more clearly in the public eye.

Arias Navarro was born on Dec. 11, 1908, in Madrid, where he went to the university and became a doctor of law. In 1929 he entered the technical services of the Ministry of Justice and six years later was appointed a state prosecutor. At the outbreak of the Civil War in 1936, Arias Navarro swiftly transferred his allegiance from the republic to General Franco. He was captured and imprisoned in Málaga by the Republicans, and then freed on the arrival of Franco's forces. He was made a military prosecutor and gained recognition for his harshness.

Between 1944 and 1957 he held various civil governorships and was then appointed director general of security. The eight years during which he occupied this position were noted for the vindictiveness displayed toward opponents of the regime. As mayor of Madrid, during 1965–73, he appeared in a more favourable light, achieving advances in the fields of education and transport, and even making some headway in tackling the city's acute environmental problems. In June 1973 he was named minister of the interior in Adm. Carrero Blanco's Cabinet.

(JOAN PEARCE)

BARZANI, MULLA MUSTAFA AL-

In March 1974 Mulla Mustafa al-Barzani was once again leading an insurrection against the Iraqi government to secure autonomy for the Kurds of northeastern Iraq. Born in about 1902 as a member of the leading Kurdish Barzani clan, Mulla Mustafa was the younger brother of Sheikh Ahmed, a religious eccentric who led the Kurdish national struggle from World War I until the late 1930s when he retired from politics. Mulla Mustafa then took over the leadership and headed the Kurdish Democratic Party (KDP), formed in 1945. In 1946 he

Mulla Mustafa al-Barzani

C. SIMONPIETRI—SYGMA

commanded the army of the short-lived autonomous Kurdish Mahabad Republic, established with Soviet support in a strip of Iranian territory on the Iraqi and Turkish borders. When Soviet troops were withdrawn from Iran, the Mahabad Republic collapsed and the territory was reoccupied by Iran. Mulla Mustafa and the other Barzanis escaped over the Soviet frontier.

Mulla Mustafa remained in the Soviet Union until allowed to return to Iraq by Abd al-Karim Kassem's regime after the overthrow of the Iraqi monarchy in 1958. He lived in Baghdad, which he was not allowed to leave, until 1960, when he escaped to the Kurdish areas and organized a new revolt against the Baghdad regime. His efforts were a major factor in the overthrow of Kassem in February 1963, but after a short respite the war was resumed against Kassem's Baath Party successors. Another lull followed the downfall of the Baathists in November 1963, but an agreement with Iraq in 1966 was abortive and tension, with frequent clashes, continued until a new 15-point agreement with the new Baathist government in March 1970 appeared to give Barzani and the KDP their main objectives. It was their insistence that Iraq had failed to implement this agreement in good faith—and, especially, had not included the oil-rich Kirkuk area in the autonomous Kurdish region—that led to the renewed fighting in 1974.

A generally taciturn man of commanding presence and proved qualities as a guerrilla leader, Mulla Mustafa was opposed in 1974 by a minority group of younger Kurds, including one of his own sons, who regarded him as too conservative and tribalistic and deplored his connections with the Iranian government. But most Iraqi Kurds were expected to rally to his support in any internal struggle. At the end of November 1974 rumours that he had died in an Iranian hospital were denied. (PETER MANSFIELD)

BECKENBAUER, FRANZ

Known throughout West German soccer circles as "Kaiser Franz," Franz Beckenbauer realized a double ambition in 1974 when he led his country to the world championship and his club, Bayern Munich, to European Cup success over Atletico Madrid of Spain. His World Cup medal was achieved on the third attempt, for he had played in the 1966 finals in England, where West Germany lost the final to the host country, and in Mexico in 1970, where the West Germans finished third, losing in the semifinals to Italy.

Born in Munich on Sept. 11, 1945, Beckenbauer joined his local club, Bayern, after leaving school and started as a centre back. He was soon drafted onto the senior team, operating in various positions, including midfield, striker, and sweeper.

During his long tenure on a regular first team, Beckenbauer helped his club to four national league titles, the European Cup-Winners' Cup (1967), and four national cup victories as well as the 1974 European Cup. He also helped West Germany win the European championship in 1972 and participated in the 1966 and 1970 World Cup appearances. Over this period Beckenbauer was voted European Footballer of the Year in 1973, and with 72 international appearances for his country surpassed the record previously held by Uwe Seeler.

Off the soccer field Beckenbauer had interests in insurance and would have gone into that business had he not taken up football for a living. Although in his most recent seasons he played as a centre back, he never lost his thirst for attack, and his long-range dipping shots caught many a goalkeeper unaware. His talent was recognized in 1974

with an award by the West German government following the World Cup success.

(TREVOR WILLIAMSON)

BENN, ANTHONY NEIL WEDGWOOD

In Britain in 1974 the English language acquired a new word: Bennery. It was used to encapsulate the Labour government's program for extending state ownership and intervention in industry, and it was associated with the name of Tony Benn, appointed secretary of state for industry in the Wilson government in March and confirmed in that post after the October election.

In practice, "Bennery" might be taken to imply a commitment to nationalization and state intervention, plus worker participation in management, or outright worker control that went further than the government's declared program but reflected Benn's own ideological commitments. It was reported that the official White Paper on British industry was a much watered-down version of Benn's original draft.

Because of his highly contentious views, Benn became anathema to the Confederation of British Industry and to the City of London, but a favourite of the Labour left wing. At the November party conference he headed the poll in the election of constituency members of the executive, suggesting that the hostile publicity he had attracted had not harmed his political standing, at least within the party. In December came a spectacular application of "Bennery" to Britain's ailing automotive giant, British Leyland, with the partial revelation of plans for state intervention to secure its survival.

Born in London on April 3, 1925, the son of the first Lord Stansgate, Benn was educated at Westminster School and, after World War II service as a pilot, at Oxford. Elected a Labour MP in 1950, he had to relinquish his seat on succeeding to the peerage in 1960. Subsequent legislation allowing peers to renounce their titles enabled him to return to the House of Commons in 1963. Later he discarded other outward signs of his family background, eliminating references to his education in his *Who's Who* entry and dropping Wedgwood from his name. Minister of technology from 1966 to 1970, he was a leader of the anti-EEC group in the Labour Party and insisted that the question of British membership be settled by a referendum. (HARFORD THOMAS)

BLATTY, WILLIAM PETER

The *enfant diable* of screenwriters in 1974 was William Peter Blatty, a Jesuit-educated former publicist. Author of *The Exorcist,* which sold nine million copies, he converted the novel into a film that raised many eyebrows, swelled other people's gorges, and turned more than one stomach.

Based on a documented case, the story involves the demonic possession of a young girl (played by Linda Blair, 13). Inexplicably, her normally pleasant personality and her surroundings begin to change: her room turns cold; her bed tosses her like an infernal trampoline; she desecrates a chapel, has evil prescience, speaks in tongues. Convinced that the child is possessed, her mother (Ellen Burstyn) turns to Georgetown University (Blatty's alma mater) for help. A young priest (Jason Miller) and a venerable Jesuit archaeologist (Max von Sydow) begin an exorcism while the girl levitates, masturbates with a crucifix, and twists her head 360° while screaming obscenities. Both priests die in the ordeal, but the girl becomes her old self again.

Released the day after Christmas 1973, the film grossed $2 million in the first month as people flocked to it like crippled pilgrims to Lourdes. But not all of them could stay. Some fled, others fainted or vomited. The movie's popularity was linked to other occult fads such as astrology and witchcraft, and theologians, critics, and social observers joined in a debate over its significance. *New York Times* critic Vincent Canby sneered that it treated diabolism with the kind of slickness "movie makers once lavished on the stories of saints." *Newsday* argued that it "creates the experience of evil and sustains it for two hours." A Catholic writer called it "an exceedingly well-made bad picture." The Academy of Motion Picture Arts and Sciences agreed. Though nominated for ten Oscars, it won only two—for the sound track and the screenplay adaptation.

The scenarist and producer of the film, Blatty was born Jan. 7, 1928, in New York City. While at Georgetown he read of the suspected real-life possession of a suburban boy. He took a doctorate at American University, served as a psychological warfare officer with the Air Force, and held several public relations jobs while trying his hand at screenplays. His screen credits included *A Shot in the Dark* and *John Goldfarb, Please Come Home.*　　(PHILIP KOPPER)

BOERMA, ADDEKE HENDRIK

When Addeke Boerma became director general of the UN Food and Agriculture Organization (FAO) in 1968, the Green Revolution in the less developed countries gave promise of making them self-sufficient in food and dispelling the Malthusian spectre forever. Indeed, one of the chief problems that he stressed at a 1970 World Food Conference in The Hague was that of employing labourers who would not be needed on the land as modern farming methods took over.

By 1974 a combination of economic dislocations and weather anomalies had changed the picture drastically. World grain reserves were at a 20-year low. Even in affluent countries, food was being priced out of reach of the poor, and the first UN World Food Conference in November faced (though it did not solve) the reality of widespread famine and malnutrition.

The most immediate problem coming to rest on Boerma's desk in 1974 was as old as his term of office, though the six-year drought in Africa's Sahel region had not come to public attention until 1973. In January he estimated that 500,000 tons of grain and 60,000 tons of high-protein foods were needed if widespread starvation and malnutrition were to be avoided. In March the Carnegie Endowment for International Peace issued a study charging that the U.S. government and various international agencies had contributed to the deaths of 100,000 people in Africa because they were slow to prepare relief programs. The FAO chief denied this, saying that he had seen no evidence that governmental bodies were at fault. At the same time, Boerma tried to direct the world's attention to a longer term aspect of the food problem. He sent a telegram to the governments of 38 countries pointing out that the world production of fertilizer was in danger of declining because of the increase in energy costs.

Boerma is an international civil servant who avoids the publicity so often courted by other men of his station. An agricultural engineer from The Netherlands, he has been with the FAO for more than 25 years. He was born April 3, 1912, and graduated from the State Agricultural University in Wageningen. In 1938 he entered government service in The Netherlands as an officer in charge of preparing for food distribution in case of war. After World War II he became involved in the preparatory planning for an international food organization, and in 1948 was appointed regional representative of the FAO for Europe. He became director general in 1968.　　(FRANCIS S. PIERCE)

BOUMÉDIENNE, HOUARI

A puritan soldier who had already led Algeria along an austere but determined road toward self-sufficiency and industrialization, Pres. Houari Boumédienne emerged in 1974 as a champion among the third world states against what he saw as the economic domination of developed and industrialized nations.

Boumédienne had given an indication of the trend toward "economic liberation" when he chaired the fourth conference of nonaligned nations at Algiers in September 1973. That conference had readily followed Algeria's lead, and Boumédienne carried his leading role further by calling for a special session of the UN General Assembly to consider the third world's problems. The assembly responded to his call, and Boumédienne made the keynote speech at the special session on raw materials and economic development held in New York in April 1974. He urged the less developed countries to nationalize their resources and the industrialized nations to collaborate with, rather than confront, the third world in their economic dealings.

Born Muhammad Boukharouba (Houari was a nickname and Boumédienne a pseudonym) on Aug. 23, 1927, the son of a small farmer, he had a mainly religious education at the Islamic Institute in Constantine, Alg., and at al-Azhar University in Cairo, Egypt. In December 1954, a month after the outbreak of the war against France, he switched from religious to military studies in Egypt and then took further training in Morocco. In 1955 he joined a guerrilla unit in western Algeria and three years later was in charge of all operations in the western sector. In 1960 he was put in charge of the National Liberation Army force with headquarters in Tunisia.

After independence was achieved, the 30,-000 troops under Boumédienne's command were the decisive factor in the struggle for power, and he led them into Algiers in September 1962 in support of Ahmed Ben Bella. He was rewarded with the Defense Ministry and set about transforming a guerrilla army into a modern fighting force. But he was soon disillusioned with Ben Bella's

Houari Boumédienne

ABBAS—GAMMA

left-leaning coterie, and while vice-president he seized power in June 1965. After taking over the presidency he eschewed the speechmaking, promises, and political philosophizing of his predecessor in the belief that his people wanted bread, schools, and economic progress.　　(PETER KILNER)

BOUTEFLIKA, ABDEL-AZIZ

The United Nations' choice of Abdel-Aziz Bouteflika, foreign minister of Algeria, to be president of its 29th General Assembly was yet another indicator of the growing determination of the third world to use its voice more effectively. It indicated also the special role that Algeria had come to play as a spokesman for the "have-nots." Bouteflika, only 37 at the time of his election in September 1974, already had more than a decade of ministerial experience in international affairs. In 1963 he had become the world's youngest foreign minister.

Bouteflika came to the General Assembly presidency with a reputation as a tough negotiator; as an accomplished diplomat despite a lack of formal education; and as one whose earlier anti-Western stance had gradually softened during the years he guided his country's foreign policy toward an impartial pragmatism. His youthful appearance belied an iron determination to make full use of his year as president in the service of the new nations, which formed a majority among the UN's members. His ability to express this majority will, at the expense of older UN conventions, was displayed particularly during the special debate on Palestine in November. At home, Bouteflika had long been identified with and overshadowed by Pres. Houari Boumédienne (*q.v.*), for almost 20 years his close associate, but he was far from merely speaking with his master's voice.

Born at Tlemcen, in western Algeria, on March 2, 1937, Bouteflika was the son of a small-time merchant who settled at Oujda, just across the Moroccan border. He was studying at Oujda when the Algerian revolution broke out in 1954 and soon afterward joined the guerrillas, being attached to the sector commanded by Boumédienne. He followed Boumédienne to Tunisia when the National Liberation Army's external headquarters were established there. With Algeria's independence in 1962, Bouteflika was elected member for Tlemcen in the National Assembly and was given the portfolio of youth and sport by Ahmed Ben Bella, the country's first president. A year later Ben Bella moved him to foreign affairs, but strained relations developed between the two; it was Ben Bella's threat to dismiss Bouteflika that finally led Boumédienne to oust Ben Bella and seize power himself.　　(PETER KILNER)

BROCK, LOU

The 1974 baseball season was one of glorious achievement and bitter disappointment for Lou Brock. The man destined perhaps to become the most proficient base stealer in baseball history set a major-league stolen base record (118) for the St. Louis Cardinals. He also, at the age of 35, batted .306 and scored 106 runs. But he did not win the National League's most valuable player award. That honour went instead to Los Angeles Dodger infielder Steve Garvey, and only a mighty effort in self-control kept Brock from spilling his bitterness on the public.

Brock was in Chicago the day the award-winner was announced and had already scheduled a press conference in anticipation of his victory. However, after Garvey was named, Brock called off the conference and granted no interviews. In no mood to answer questions, he was willing to pose one of his own: What did he have to do to win the award that he had not done already?

Indeed, Brock's accomplishments in 1974 were awesome. His total of 118 base thefts shattered the old mark of 104, set by Maury Wills. Brock broke the record on September 10 in St. Louis when he stole numbers 104 and 105 against the Philadelphia Phillies. He finished the 1974 campaign with a career total of 753 stolen bases, a new National League record. The only man still ahead of him was Ty Cobb, and his all-time record of 892 seemed within Brock's reach.

Brock was born on June 18, 1939, in El Dorado, Ark., one of nine children. He was awarded a $30,000 bonus with the Chicago Cubs in 1961 and hit a home run on the first pitch thrown to him in his professional career, at St. Cloud, Minn., in the Northern League. He played two seasons in Chicago and then was shipped to St. Louis in a trade that turned into a true "steal" for the Cardinals. Six players were involved in that deal of June 1964, and by 1974 Brock was the only one still playing baseball.

Brock led the Cardinals to a pennant during that 1964 season and was also a prime mover in the flags won by St. Louis in 1967 and 1968. In 1968 he also led the National League in doubles, triples, and stolen bases, a feat not accomplished since Honus Wagner garnered the honour in 1908. The only man to steal seven bases in a single World Series, Brock did this twice, in 1967 and 1968. His 14 steals overall in World Series play tied him with Eddie Collins. Brock would like to increase his marks before retirement but claimed that he was not aiming at Ty Cobb's lifetime total.   (J. TIMOTHY WEIGEL)

BUTHELEZI, GATSHA MANGOSUTHU

Considered to be one of the ablest and most dynamic black leaders in South Africa, Chief Gatsha Buthelezi, while cooperating with the government in his capacity of chief executive councillor of KwaZulu (formerly Zululand), remained openly critical of South Africa's policy of separate development and ultimate independence for the Bantu homelands, or Bantustans.

A descendant of the royal line of the warrior Zulu nation through his mother, Buthelezi was born Aug. 27, 1928, at Mahlabatini, where his father was chief of the Shenge tribe. Brought up in the royal kraal at Nongoma, the KwaZulu capital, he received a degree in history and native administration from Fort Hare University College, South Africa's main higher educational institution for Africans only. At the age of 25 he was elected acting chief of his tribe, and in 1958 full chieftain.

Traditionally the Buthelezi family provided the chief councillors, or "prime ministers," to the Zulu rulers. For 16 years Buthelezi was chief councillor to Paramount Chief Cyprian; he became chief executive councillor for the KwaZulu homeland in 1972 when, after years of opposition to the apartheid Bantustan concept—led by Buthelezi himself—the four million-strong Zulu people accepted Bantustan status. He made no secret of the fact that he cooperated in the existing system because it gave him a platform for expressing his views and opportunities for influencing events and obtaining

as much benefit for his people as possible. He dismissed the idea that KwaZulu, fragmented as it was, could become genuinely independent and he saw no future in the government's consolidation proposals.

Ideologically, Buthelezi was a disciple of Chief Albert Lutuli (1898–1967), former head of the African National Congress (banned in 1960) and 1960 Nobel Peace Prize winner. His basic philosophy was one of equal rights for all South Africans, preferably in some form of federation. He was a prolific writer and a widely traveled speaker whose voice commanded respect both in and outside South Africa. A devoted member of the Anglican Church, in 1963 he was one of the three diocesan delegates from Zululand to the World Anglican Congress in Toronto.   (LOUIS HOTZ)

CABRAL, LUIS

When the Republic of Guinea-Bissau became independent of Portuguese colonial rule on Sept. 10, 1974, its first president was Luis Cabral, the 45-year-old half brother of Amilcar Cabral, the noted revolutionary who led the African Party for the Independence of Guinea and Cape Verde (PAIGC) until his assassination in January 1973.

Luis Cabral was born at Bafatá, Portuguese Guinea, in 1929, of mixed European and African parents who came originally from the Cape Verde Islands. He did not follow his brother to the university in Lisbon but began his working life as a clerk in Bissau, the capital of Portuguese Guinea. He became an active labour leader in the late 1950s, took part in the founding of PAIGC in 1956, and was the main organizer of the longshoremen's strike at Pidgiguiti in August 1959. The strike resulted in the shooting of 230 African workers (50 of whom died) by Portuguese police. As a result Cabral went into exile in neighbouring Guinea, where in 1964 he became an executive member of the PAIGC, mainly concerned with party organization.

In 1965 Cabral was sent by PAIGC to Cuba, where he successfully enlisted support from its prime minister, Fidel Castro. In 1972 PAIGC prepared to proclaim the Republic of Guinea-Bissau, and the Cabral brothers busied themselves in organizing regional councils and elections for those areas that had been freed from Portuguese control. After Amilcar Cabral's death Aristide Pereira headed PAIGC, and he and Luis Cabral continued the struggle until talks with the Portuguese were begun in May. A Marxist like his late brother, Cabral nevertheless proved himself to be both tolerant and pragmatic in his negotiations with Portugal for his country's independence.
      (COLIN LEGUM)

CAIRNS, JAMES FORD

When James F. Cairns displaced Lance Barnard as deputy prime minister of Australia, the conservative triumvirate (Prime Minister Gough Whitlam, Treasurer Frank Crean, and Barnard) that had led the country in the first Whitlam ministry was shattered. Cairns' promotion came after the Australian Labor Party faced and won its second election in two years.

In 1970 Cairns had been virtually written off as a possible Labor minister because of his leadership of the antiwar Vietnam moratorium movement. But the parliamentary party elected him deputy in July 1974, and almost immediately speculation began as to whether he was running the country. It seemed as though the prime minister had been kicked upstairs to titular head of the government while Cairns, who was also, and still is, minister of trade, had been left with the day-to-day management of the economy.

Cairns indeed tried to break away from the Treasury formula for combating inflation. According to the Treasury, businesses were to be forced to stop paying higher wages and charging higher prices through Treasury-induced losses, and workers were to be made to give up wage claims by manipulation of the unemployment level. In the Chifley Memorial Lecture at Melbourne University in August, Cairns said: "What is needed is not just a way to control inflation but a way to reform society so that it may avoid inflation. We need to stop treating society as if it were just an economy . . . and remember that it is a community."

Cairns was born at Carlton, Victoria, in 1914. He was a Victorian police officer (1935–44) and enlisted in the 2nd Australian Imperial Force in January 1945, serving with the Army Educational Corps in Australia and Morotai. Before he entered Parliament he was a senior lecturer in economic history at Melbourne University. He was elected to the House of Representatives for Yarra in 1955 and for Lalor in 1969, and when Labor took power in December 1972 he became minister for overseas trade and secondary industry.   (A. R. G. GRIFFITHS)

CALDWELL, SARAH

The first lady of opera in America in 1974 did not sing a note. Sarah Caldwell was a stage director and operatic conductor, at once the driving force and personification of the Opera Company of Boston. Paul Hume, the Washington Post's music critic, believed "she is a special treasure in the world of opera, one of the geniuses of our time." She was all the more a phenomenon for belonging to a select fraternity dominated by men.

Miss Caldwell was born in Maryville, Mo., in 1929. A music and mathematics prodigy, she graduated from high school at 14, studied psychology at the University of Arkansas, and went on to the New England Conservatory of Music. She became the protégée of impresario Boris Goldovsky and for 11 years was his assistant at the New England Opera Company.

In 1957 she founded the Boston Opera Group, which became the Opera Company of Boston in 1965. The city had razed its old opera house, but she put it back on the operatic map with an astonishing series of spectaculars performed in derelict movie theatres and college gyms. Her reputation for joining musical perfection with stagecraft unknown elsewhere in opera earned her national attention and brought many of the world's greatest voices to Boston.

Among other American premieres, she presented Luigi Nono's Intolleranza (after fighting the State Department for his visitor's visa), Schoenberg's monumental Moses und Aron, Schuller's The Fisherman and His Wife, Bartok's The Miraculous Mandarin, and Stravinsky's Rake's Progress. When she staged The Bartered Bride, the sad-faced circus clown Emmett Kelly played a role. In a production of Don Quichotte her knight-errant actually spun around on the windmill because the script called for it. In Berlioz' Les Troyens she included a 900-lb. Trojan horse and sacked the city with "fire, smoke, tumbling temples and crumbling statues" in a five-hour extravaganza.

In 1974 her masterpiece was a rare full-length presentation of Prokofiev's War and Peace that brought audiences to their feet at Washington's new Wolf Trap Park amphitheatre. Generally unconcerned with her appearance, she dresses shabbily except during performances and has been known to roll up in a carpet to sleep in a theatre aisle after a marathon rehearsal.   (PHILIP KOPPER)

CALLAGHAN, (LEONARD) JAMES

In March 1974, James Callaghan was appointed foreign secretary in Britain's new Labour government. With the single exception of Prime Minister Harold Wilson, no one in the Cabinet had had longer experience in office. First elected to Parliament in 1945, he became a junior minister in Clement Attlee's government in 1947. Then, in the Wilson governments of 1964 to 1970, he held key Cabinet posts as chancellor of the Exchequer and home secretary (in the latter he found himself responsible for handling the outbreak of civil strife in Northern Ireland). From 1957 he had a place on the Labour Party's executive, and as party chairman in 1973–74 he took a leading role in the preparation and presentation of the Labour program at the two general elections of 1974.

In moving to the Foreign Office, he took charge of one of the most crucial issues raised by Labour's return to power: Britain's relationship with the European Economic Community. Labour had promised that the terms of Britain's entry to the EEC, accepted in 1972 by Edward Heath's Conservative government, would be renegotiated and that the decision on whether or not to stay in would be put to the country by a referendum. With Labour deeply divided on this question, Callaghan's undoctrinaire middle of the road position and his equable, pragmatic temperament were natural advantages.

At the beginning of negotiations with the European foreign ministers in April, Callaghan said he was looking for "successful renegotiation from which the right terms for continued membership will emerge." Apart from the EEC negotiations, Callaghan was anxious to improve relations between Europe and the U.S. In these highly charged areas, his bluff, no-nonsense style seemed to be paying off. When war broke out in Cyprus between Turks and Greeks, Callaghan was the principal peacemaker in talks at Geneva. By dogged persistence, he was instrumental in bringing about first a cease-fire and then an interim settlement.

Born on March 27, 1912, in Portsmouth, Callaghan was educated at local schools, and in the ten years before World War II he worked first as a tax official in the Inland Revenue, then as trade-union officer of the Inland Revenue Staff Federation. On election to Parliament in 1945, he was quickly spotted and brought on by Hugh Dalton, then chancellor of the Exchequer.

(HARFORD THOMAS)

CÂMARA PESSOA, DOM HELDER

The award in February 1974 of a "People's Peace Prize" to Dom Helder Câmara, archbishop of Olinda and Recife in Brazil, did more than recognize Câmara's "fight for peace, freedom, justice, and human dignity against oppression and exploitation"; it also underlined widespread dissent over the award of the previous year's Nobel Peace Prize (for which Câmara had been a nominee) jointly to U.S. Secretary of State Henry Kissinger and North Vietnam's Le Duc Tho. The "alternative" peace prize resulted from a campaign in Norway and other countries that collected 1,510,000 kroner for the purpose. At a ceremony in Oslo on February 10 it was presented to Archbishop Câmara, who stated that the money would be used to train poor agricultural workers in northeastern Brazil. Earlier in February he was nominated by six members of the Norwegian Storting (parliament) for the 1974 Nobel Peace Prize.

Dom Helder first began to attract international attention at the Second Vatican Council in Rome (1962–65). He belonged to a group of bishops who wanted the church to be poor, both in reality and in appearance. In Brazil he had been an advocate of radical reform. The plans of the military government for opening up the northeastern region seemed to him like the substitution of foreign-dominated capitalism for feudalism. He denounced the use of torture. One of his closest associates, Father Antônio Henrique Neto, was murdered in mysterious circumstances in 1969. Yet the revolution he preached was one of charity and justice. He was accused of being naive and also, more damagingly, of being a Communist. A self-styled spokesman of "those who have no voice," he made lecture tours around the world. From time to time the government placed restrictions on his movements or on reporting them. At one stage, the Vatican appeared to have backed up the government, only to relent later.

Dom Helder was born in Fortaleza in February 1909 and ordained priest in 1931. In the 1950s he was secretary of Catholic Action and then auxiliary bishop of Rio de Janeiro. His first conflicts with the authorities came when he launched "Operation Hope" to rehouse shantytown dwellers. He was appointed archbishop of Olinda and Recife in April 1964.

(PETER HEBBLETHWAITE)

CEAUSESCU, NICOLAE

A Communist leader who enjoyed considerable popularity in his country, Nicolae Ceausescu had accumulated great power by 1974, when he was made president of the Socialist Republic of Romania on March 28. He had already been named general secretary of the Romanian Communist Party (RCP) on March 22, 1965, and chairman of the State Council on Dec. 9, 1969. The presidency was proposed by the Central Committee of the RCP and endorsed by the Grand National Assembly. As president, Ceausescu was chief of state and supreme commander of the armed forces, but also continued to chair the State Council.

Born a peasant's son on Jan. 26, 1918, at Scornicesti, Olt district, Ceausescu joined the illegal Union of Communist Youth at the age of 15. During the German occupation of Romania he played an active part in the struggle against the occupying Nazis and their Romanian accomplice, Gen. Ion Antonescu. After King Michael's coup d'etat of Aug. 23, 1944, when the Communist Party became legal after 20 years of underground militancy, Ceausescu was elected to its Central Committee. He joined the party's secretariat in 1954, when Gheorghe Gheorghiu-Dej ceased to be first secretary and was succeeded by Gheorghe Apostol. The following year Gheorghiu-Dej reassumed control of the party as first secretary of the Central Committee, and Ceausescu was elected to the Politburo.

After Gheorghiu-Dej's death the ninth congress changed the party's name from Romanian Workers' to Romanian Communist Party, and the country's name from People's Republic to Socialist Republic. At the same time, Ceausescu's role was given the wider title of general secretary of the RCP. In the *Draft Program of the Romanian Communist Party* (a booklet of 178 pages), adopted by the Central Committee on Sept. 14, 1974, Ceausescu averred that in the 1920s the activity of the party had been difficult because "it took an incorrect stand on the national question" (referring to Bessarabia, won from the U.S.S.R. in 1918 and lost in 1940) and because some leaders of the party, "sent by the Comintern," were ignorant of the "country's realities." Ceausescu, indeed, had the self-confidence to inspire the 11th party congress in November to make an unpar-

Luis Cabral

Dom Helder Câmara Pessoa

Lou Brock

alleled statement of independence from Soviet political domination, to the effect that the activities of Communist parties could no longer be centrally controlled.

(K. M. SMOGORZEWSKI)

CHIRAC, JACQUES RENÉ

From the outset of his career Jacques Chirac, nominated to head France's new government by Pres. Valéry Giscard d'Estaing (*q.v.*) on May 27, 1974, at the early age of 41, had stood out as the very model of the *jeunes loups* ("young wolves") of French political life. In 1962, only three years after graduating from the École Nationale d'Administration—the nursery of France's top civil servants—he had become head of the personal staff of Georges Pompidou (then premier), who referred to his protégé as "my bulldozer." Although more of a "Pompidolian" than a Gaullist, he had been an approved

A.G.I.P. / PICTORIAL PARADE

member of de Gaulle's entourage, being related by marriage to the general's sole companion at the time of the June 1940 *Appel*.

As state secretary at the Ministry of Economy and Finance (1968–71) he had worked closely with Giscard d'Estaing, who then headed the ministry. No doubt the new president, not himself a member of the Gaullist Union des Démocrates pour la République (UDR), saw in the essentially pragmatic Chirac the qualities needed to reconcile the "Giscardian" and "non-Giscardian" factions of the parliamentary majority. As premier, indeed, Chirac quickly set about persuading the Gaullists that, despite the social reforms promised by President Giscard, the basic tenets of Gaullism, such as national and European independence, would be retained. By an astute move he secured his election as secretary-general of the UDR in the face of potential opposition from the party "barons" and soon afterward consolidated his hold over the majority by easily defeating an opposition motion of censure.

Jacques Chirac was born in Paris on Nov. 29, 1932, the son of a company director. He was educated at the Carnot and Louis-le-Grand lycées in Paris, graduated from the Institut d'Études Politiques, and attended Harvard University's Summer School before entering the École Nationale d'Administration in 1957. Elected a deputy in 1967, he was made a junior minister the same year and a senior minister in charge of relations with Parliament in 1971. He first attracted international attention as minister of agri-

culture (1972–74), when he castigated U.S., West German, and European Commission agricultural policies that conflicted with French interests. As minister of the interior from March 1974 he was entrusted by President Pompidou with preparations for the presidential election, then scheduled for 1976 but brought forward by Pompidou's death.

(PIERRE VIANSSON-PONTÉ)

CLERIDES, GLAFKOS JOHN

A prominent Greek Cypriot lawyer and deputy president of the republic of Cyprus after August 1960, Glafkos Clerides became interim president on July 23, 1974, after Nikos Sampson, the nine-day "president" installed by Greece's military government, was whisked away to Greece. Clerides soon removed the government established by Sampson and brought in a new team of liberals and moderates, thus creating a climate of confidence, which, he hoped, would enable him to pursue reconciliation with the Turkish community. Konstantinos Karamanlis (*q.v.*), the new Greek prime minister, expressed his confidence in Clerides and agreed with him that no peaceful settlement of the Cyprus problem was possible on the basis of partition of the island in two federated parts, with an exchange of populations. Both men also agreed that the president, Archbishop Makarios (*q.v.*), should not return immediately, and Clerides continued to serve as interim president until Makarios reentered Cyprus on December 7.

Clerides was born in Nicosia, Cyprus, on April 24, 1919, the son of the attorney general with the governor's executive council when the British ruled Cyprus. He studied law at King's College, London University, and later at Gray's Inn. His law studies were interrupted by World War II, during which he served in the Royal Air Force. Taken prisoner when his Wellington bomber was hit over Germany, Clerides escaped from captivity three separate times. After the war he returned to Cyprus and joined his father's law firm in Nicosia.

As did every Greek Cypriot, he sympathized with the *enosis* movement for union with Greece. During the revolt that started in 1955 he defended many political prisoners in court. In 1960, after the first elections to the House of Representatives of the republic of Cyprus, he was elected speaker and ex-officio deputy president of the republic. The ablest of President Makarios' advisers, he stood aloof from the intrigues that led to the breakdown of the 1960 constitution as well as from the widespread fighting between the Greek and Turkish communities that started in December 1963. Attempts at mediation by the U.S. and the UN, as well as by Greek and Turkish governments, failed. During the summer of 1968 direct talks began between Clerides and Rauf Denktash (*q.v.*), president of the Turkish Cypriot Communal Chamber, and these continued after the Turkish occupation of 1974. They were, however, interrupted by Makarios' return.

(K. M. SMOGORZEWSKI)

COGGAN, (FREDERICK) DONALD

Donald Coggan's appointment as archbishop of Canterbury had seemed unlikely until the untimely death in October 1972 of Ian Ramsey, bishop of Durham, who was the expected successor to the present archbishop, Arthur Michael Ramsey. Thereafter, the field appeared wide open. Because of the seniority of his see, the archbishop of Canterbury has a primacy of honour—although not of jurisdiction—in the worldwide Anglican Communion, and it had even been suggested that the next archbishop might come from outside England. Pressure had also

built up for ecclesiastical appointments to be decided by the Church of England itself rather than by the secular government. Ramsey's resignation was announced in March 1974, to take effect on November 15. In July the church's General Synod voted in favour of controlling its own appointments, but Coggan's nomination had already been announced on May 14.

A noted biblical scholar and member of the team that produced the New English Bible, Coggan, until his consecration as bishop of Bradford (1956), had pursued an almost exclusively academic career. A small-ish, quiet man in spectacles, loathing ostentation, he had become an efficient and discreet administrator. His theology was orthodox to the point of conservatism and firmly Bible-based. An "evangelical" churchman who had voted for the abortive scheme of union with the Methodists, he nevertheless transcended church party distractions. As archbishop of York (from 1961), he drew Roman Catholics as well as Free Churchmen into his "Call to the North" evangelism program. Because he was 65 and Anglican bishops now retire at around 70, he could, for that and other reasons, be labeled a "caretaker" archbishop (though it might be remembered that Pope John XXIII was initially cast in that role).

Born on Oct. 9, 1909, in Highgate, London, Coggan was educated at Merchant Taylors' School and the University of Cambridge. After holding a lectureship in Semitic languages at the University of Manchester (1931–34) and a working-class London curacy (1934–37), he was appointed professor of New Testament at Wycliffe College, Toronto (1937–44), returning to England to become principal (1944–56) of the London College of Divinity. (STEPHANIE MULLINS)

CONNORS, JIMMY and EVERT, CHRIS

It was a starry night in July and the band played "The Girl That I Marry" as Jimmy Connors and Chris Evert led off the traditional first dance at the Wimbledon Ball. The darlings of the centre court had already aroused more public interest than any sports romance in history. When they then became the first engaged couple to win both the men's and women's singles titles at Wimbledon, the most prestigious tournament in tennis, public imagination ran wild.

The 21-year-old Connors said he had dreamed of winning at Wimbledon since he was six, and the 19-year-old Miss Evert said she had been afraid to dream of winning because she was so young. The tennis world dreamed of the scheduled November wedding of the two young superstars.

But as in all dreams, everyone had to awaken. The November 8 wedding date came and went without a ceremony. Chris said she still had the 1½-carat diamond that had been mined especially for her in South Africa, and Jimmy still had his gold and elephant-hair bracelet. The wedding was said to be "just postponed" because of the unyielding demands of their tennis schedules, but many thought that the postponement might prove to be permanent.

Even if romance seemed a temporary loser, the Connors-Evert team did little but win on the tennis courts during the 1974 season. Connors established himself as one of the greatest male players in the game with his smashing wins over Ken Rosewall in the finals of both Wimbledon and the U.S. Open. The native of Belleville, Ill., and former UCLA student put on an awesome display of power as he smashed Rosewall 6–1, 6–0, 6–1 in the U.S. Open at Forest Hills, N.Y.

The victory was the climax of a typically mercurial year for the controversial Connors.

He won three of the "Big Four" tournaments (Australian, Wimbledon, and the U.S. Open), but was barred from the fourth, the French Open. He sued the Association of Tennis Professionals for $10 million, alleging that they illegally excluded him from the French event.

Miss Evert also enjoyed a big year, winning in the Australian, Wimbledon, French, and Italian tournaments. But Evonne Goolagong upset her at Forest Hills, thus breaking her amazing 10-tournament, 56-match winning streak.

The pony-tailed prodigy, born Dec. 21, 1954, in Fort Lauderdale, Fla., first burst into America's imagination in 1971, when at 16 she became the youngest semifinalist ever at Forest Hills. Her father, Jim Evert, was a national indoor tennis champion, and her sister and two brothers are also outstanding players.   (J. TIMOTHY WEIGEL)

CRUYFF, JOHAN

Star of the 1974 World Cup finals in West Germany, Johan Cruyff led the Dutch soccer team in the decisive game against the host nation in Munich on July 7. But there this brilliant young athlete, born in Amsterdam in 1947, just missed attaining every football player's ambition of a winner's medal.

Cruyff started his career at 16 as a junior with the local club, Ajax—its stadium was just around the corner from his birthplace—and was given number 14. He retained it throughout his career in The Netherlands, where he became known simply as "No. 14." Cruyff helped his club to seven national titles, four national cup triumphs, three successive European Cup victories, and an Inter-Continental Cup success; he himself won several other cups for The Netherlands. He was also voted Europe's top football player in 1971 and 1973. However, even his brilliance could not help The Netherlands gain the World Cup finals in Mexico in 1970. His footwork—delicate as Delft china—control, and shrewd football brain continually showed up in Ajax's achievements, yet through it all he remained cool and modest.

After his tremendous success with the Amsterdam club in 1973 came a new chapter in his life and a new nickname, "El Salvador." Barcelona, wallowing in the relegation zone of the Spanish League, paid $2,250,000 for the Dutch superstar, who thus rejoined his old coach Rinus Michels. Cruyff immediately gave the lie to the old axiom

that one man does not make a team. His arrival started a winning streak for Barcelona, which eventually won the league championship.

While millions thrilled to the marvelous football skills of this young athlete through television, his business interests, which made him a rich man, were guided by his father-in-law, Cor Corster. These activities included making a film in Dutch and Spanish entitled *No. 14,* and a variety of appearances in advertisements. Yet Cruyff remained quiet and unassuming despite the fame engendered by his ability on the soccer field to pass with computer accuracy, create openings for others, and round off efforts with a bazooka-like shot. Even more important, he was a good team captain.   (TREVOR WILLIAMSON)

DAVIDSON, GARY

Described by the *New York Times* as the "greatest organizer of professional sports leagues America has produced," Gary Davidson received his first major setback on Oct. 29, 1974, when he resigned as commissioner of one of his creations, the World Football League (WFL), after an emergency meeting with league owners. For Davidson, who remained on the WFL's executive committee, it was an uncharacteristic defeat in a remarkable career that began in 1967 when he was the prime mover in the organization of the American Basketball Association. In 1972 he guided the formation of the World Hockey Association (WHA).

Conventional wisdom had it that there was a major league structure in each of these sports, and assumed, therefore, that whoever wanted to play (as athlete or investor) had to go where the action already was. Davidson changed that, leading *Business Week* to observe in January that he "is riding the crest of one of the most glamorous tax shelters to be found." He expanded professional sports by creating new leagues, opening up new investment and competitive opportunities for backers and players, and cutting more cities in on the pie. In the process he made considerable money by creating and selling franchises.

"There are a lot of people around with plenty of money who want to get involved in sports," he said. "There are also more capable athletes than the older leagues could ever absorb, and more cities with stadiums or arenas than are being used. My job is to bring these things together, line up financing,

block out how things should work, get it all organized."

Davidson's role in forming the leagues was to sketch the idea, line up backers and interested cities, incorporate the organization, and then, as in the case of the WHA, sell franchises for $25,000 apiece. Three years later franchises were reselling for $2.5 million, even though the teams were losing money. At the end of 1974 the future of the WFL appeared more doubtful. Two of the franchises folded during the season, and financial problems forced several others to move to different cities.

Davidson was born in Missoula, Mont., Aug. 13, 1934. He gained undergraduate and law degrees at UCLA and set up legal practice in southern California. A weekend athlete himself, he became interested in the franchising business through an amateur basketball league.   (PHILIP KOPPER)

DENKTASH, RAUF

Turkish Cypriot political leader and vice-president of the republic of Cyprus from February 1973, Rauf Denktash declared after the Turkish invasion of the island that Greek Cypriots must realize that the door to *enosis,* or union with Greece, was closed forever. On Aug. 15, 1974, when the Turkish Army completed its occupation of the northern part of Cyprus, Denktash spoke of partition under a federal system as a possible settlement of the Cyprus issue.

Denktash was born on Jan. 27, 1924, at Ktima, near Paphos, the youngest child of a judge. Having completed his elementary and secondary schooling in Cyprus in 1941, he worked as interpreter, court clerk, and teacher until 1943, when he went to England to study law at Lincoln's Inn (1944–47). On returning to Cyprus, he practiced law and in 1948 was appointed a member of the Consultative Assembly set up by the British colonial government to consider the application of self-government to Cyprus. In 1949 he was appointed junior crown counsel to the attorney general's office, four years later was crown counsel, and in 1956 became solicitor general. He resigned as solicitor general in 1957 after being elected chairman of the Federation of Turkish Associations.

Early in 1959 Denktash advised the Turkish government as to the guarantees required by the Turkish Cypriot community before acceptance of the so-called Zürich compromise on the conditions of Cypriot independence. He led the Turkish Cypriot delegation at the Athens conference dealing with the military side of the treaty that established the republic, and was the principal Turkish Cypriot member of the committee that drafted the new nation's constitution. In 1960 he was elected president of the Turkish Communal Chamber.

In 1964 Denktash led the Turkish Cypriot delegation at the London conference and attended the UN Security Council. On his return from New York he was prohibited from entering Cyprus by Archbishop Makarios and resided in Turkey until October 1967, when he secretly landed on the island but was captured and detained by the Greek Cypriot police for 13 days. Public pressure secured his release, but he was sent back to Turkey. Denktash was allowed to return to Cyprus on April 13, 1968, when he immediately resumed his duties as president of the Turkish Communal Chamber. When the intercommunal talks began in June 1968, he became the Turkish community's spokesman.
    (K. M. SMOGORZEWSKI)

Johan Cruyff

Jimmy Connors and Chris Evert

DEWHURST, COLLEEN

When the "Today" show interviewer remarked that the lady was "discovered" every few years, Colleen Dewhurst smiled in rueful agreement. A professional actress of the first magnitude for nearly 30 years, she was rediscovered again in 1974 when she won her second Antoinette Perry (Tony) Award for portraying Josie Hogan in Eugene O'Neill's *A Moon for the Misbegotten* with Jason Robards, Jr.

The problem was that Dewhurst was a character actress with a broad range and an abiding interest in the classics. While a Bardot is discovered once and stays on top as long as people want to watch the same sex symbol, Dewhurst was a differently earthy woman in every part. Seeing her play a new role was to discover a new character. Also, though she had won every major stage and television acting prize, she rarely appeared in films.

Born in Montreal in 1926, she left Downer College for Young Ladies (now part of St. Lawrence University) to go to New York. She studied acting while working as a Carnegie Hall usher and as an instructor in a reducing gym. Joseph Papp tended her career before he became famous as the producer of Shakespeare in New York's Central Park. She appeared as Tamora in *Titus Andronicus*, Kate in *Taming of the Shrew*, Gertrude in *Hamlet*. She was featured in *Camille* and Wycherley's *The Country Wife*. Other credits included starring roles in *Antony and Cleopatra*, Cocteau's *The Eagle Has Two Heads*, Albee's *The Ballad of the Sad Cafe* and *Who's Afraid of Virginia Woolf?*, Brecht's *The Good Woman of Setzuan*, and Sartre's *No Exit*.

She was an old hand at O'Neill, and this was the third time she had played Josie under José Quintero's direction. "I love the O'Neill women," she said. "They move from the groin rather than the brain. To play O'Neill . . . you can't sit and play little moments of sadness or sweetness."

Time's critic wrote of her performance, "No woman has been big enough for the part before. Not only physically [she is 5 ft. 8 in.] but in generosity of heart, mind and spirit." Clive Barnes wrote that "she spoke O'Neill as if it were being spoken for the first time."

Offstage she lived with her two sons in a 200-year-old farmhouse in Westchester, N.Y., commuting distance from Broadway. She met their father, actor George C. Scott, onstage at the Circle in the Square theatre in New York when they appeared together in *Children of Darkness*. They were married and divorced twice.   (PHILIP KOPPER)

DUGDALE, BRIDGET ROSE

After pleading "proudly and incorruptibly guilty," Rose Dugdale, daughter of wealthy landowning parents, was sentenced in Dublin on June 25, 1974, to nine years' penal servitude for receiving paintings (valued at £8 million [$19.2 million]) stolen from the Irish country home of Sir Alfred Beit. The armed robbery, in which she almost certainly took part, was the culmination of a career of increasingly vocal and criminal activity directed against the English "establishment," in furtherance of which she had identified herself and worked with unofficial Irish Republican Army (IRA) groups. Superficially, Rose Dugdale could be considered an English Patricia Hearst (*q.v.*), a child of riches and privilege turned revolutionary. But whereas chance apparently precipitated Patricia's "conversion," Rose seemingly had been mo-

tivated by a need to act out a conflict with her father, the roots of which must lie deep in her earlier life.

Daughter of an ex-army officer turned Lloyd's underwriter, Rose Dugdale, born in March 1941 near Axminster in Devon, was educated at private schools, "came out" as a debutante, and then read philosophy, politics, and economics at St. Anne's College, Oxford (1959–62). There she learned the theories that were to provide rationalization for her later activities; but for a while longer her career remained "respectable" (work in the Ministry of Overseas Development and a lectureship at Bedford College, London University, where she received her doctorate). She was already helping the underprivileged in north London when her meeting in 1972 with Walter Heaton precipitated her development into a full-fledged revolutionary. Heaton, an ex-soldier, shop steward, and ex-convict, left his wife and daughters to live with Rose and share her work; they also made trips to Northern Ireland, on which, the police suspected, they smuggled arms to the IRA. Rose gave large sums to Heaton's wife and to the needy; a consequent shortage of funds, together with an increasingly bitter and almost obscene animosity against her father, probably motivated the burglary of her parents' Devon home (June 1973), for which Heaton was imprisoned. Rose received only a suspended sentence, and on its expiry apparently moved to Belfast. There she began to act with unofficial groups of the Provisional IRA and in January 1974 was allegedly involved in the attempted aerial bombing of Strabane police station. The Beit robbery, in April, was naively conceived and ineptly conducted, almost certainly independent of IRA authorization.   (STEPHANIE MULLINS)

ECEVIT, BULENT

When Bulent Ecevit became prime minister of Turkey on Jan. 25, 1974, at the head of a coalition of his Republican People's Party (RPP) and the Islamic National Salvation Party (NSP), the long-standing feud between secular progressives and religious conservatives in Turkish political life appeared to have ended. A humanist and social democrat in home affairs, whose first action as prime minister was to secure an amnesty for all political prisoners, Ecevit surprised many in the West when he authorized Turkey's military intervention in Cyprus on July 20 following the Greek-led coup there. The success of the operation greatly enhanced his reputation, and he became a force to be reckoned with in Turkey. Consequently, he felt strong enough to dispense with his NSP partners and on September 18 he resigned, in the expectation of then being able to form an alternative coalition. This he was unable to do, and a prolonged governmental crisis ensued. (*See* TURKEY.)

Like many Turkish reformers in the last century, Ecevit was a Western-trained intellectual. Born in 1925, he went to the prestigious American Robert College in Istanbul. He developed a taste for literature, and after a spell as a junior embassy official in London, returned to Turkey to become a writer and journalist. This led him into politics, and he gravitated toward the RPP, which his father had represented in Parliament. He was elected to Parliament in 1957 and two years later he joined the party council. He gradually emerged as leader of the left-of-centre group, whose policy the party adopted but which the electorate rejected in 1965. As minister of labour (1961–65) he legalized strikes for the first time in Turkish history. In 1966 he became RPP secretary-general under Ismet Inonu's leadership, but the hold that he established over

Bulent Ecevit

the party seemed destroyed after March 12, 1971, when, against Ecevit's advice, Inonu backed the national coalition imposed on Parliament by the military commanders. Ecevit fought back, defeated Inonu, and became leader of the party on May 14, 1972. His criticism of military intervention in politics alienated many of the party's traditional supporters but was rewarded in the Oct. 14, 1973, election, in which the RPP won the major share of the popular poll and a plurality in Parliament. (ANDREW MANGO)

ETEKI MBOUMOUA, WILLIAM AURELIEN

The new key figure in the Organization of African Unity (OAU), William Eteki Mboumoua was elected on June 16, 1974, at Muqdisho, Somalia, to succeed Nzo Ekangaki, a fellow countryman from the Cameroon Republic, as the administrative secretary-general of the OAU.

William Eteki (by which name he was best known) was an experienced administrator and politician. Born on Oct. 20, 1933, in Akwa, Douala, he was given a scholarship at the age of 14 to study in France. He qualified as an administrator in the École Nationale de la France d'Outre Mer, the school for overseas administration, in 1956 and went on to take a law degree before returning home in 1959. He was employed by the French colonial administration as a prefect, or district officer, in the Samaga-Maritime division, a notoriously rebellious area, and won a reputation as a sympathetic administrator. A year after Cameroon achieved its independence in 1960, he was made minister of national education, youth, sports, art, and culture. In 1971 he was appointed as a special technical adviser to the president. He also served for a year in 1970 as president of the UNESCO assembly in Paris, and subsequently wrote two books, *Un Certain Humanisme* (1970) and *Democratiser la culture* (1974).

Eteki was described as an elegant and soft-spoken diplomat. In his new job, which had proved to be intractably difficult for his immediate predecessor, he was required to be both diplomatic and firm, two qualities which he seemed to have acquired from his political experience during which he successfully made the transition from colonial official to Cabinet minister in a newly independent state.   (COLIN LEGUM)

EVERT, CHRIS: see CONNORS, JIMMY.

Michael Foot

FELKER, CLAY

As the editor and founder of *New York* magazine and the president of its parent company, Clay Felker became involved in a controversy surrounding the 1974 corporate merger of the magazine with the *Village Voice,* a New York City newspaper. When the merger was announced in June, writers and editors of the *Village Voice,* as well as some *New York* staff members, expressed concern about the editorial independence of their publication and asked for a guarantee that the current editor and publisher would retain control over editorial matters. Felker refused to relinquish absolute authority, but maintained that, notwithstanding his plans for expanding the *Village Voice,* the two publications would keep their independent identities, staffs, and facilities. By midyear, however, the *Village Voice* editor had resigned.

At the time of the merger, the *Village Voice,* founded in 1955, was a tabloid with a circulation of 150,000. It represented a generally radical, counterestablishment perspective in politics and entertainment. *New York* magazine, on the other hand, founded by Felker in 1967, was a weekly with a circulation of 355,000 and was directed toward relatively affluent and liberal New Yorkers.

Felker was born in St. Louis, Mo., on Oct. 2, 1928. He received his B.A. in 1951 from Duke University, where he served as editor of the *Duke Chronicle.* As a correspondent for *Life* magazine from 1951 to 1957, he worked in New York City and Washington, D.C. He was features editor for *Esquire* magazine from 1957 to 1962 and editor of the Sunday magazine of the *New York Herald Tribune* and its successor, the *New York World Journal Tribune,* from 1963 to 1967. This Sunday magazine became the basis for Felker's *New York* magazine, which appeared as an independent publication in 1968. After a weak start, *New York* —with such writers as critics John Simon (theatre) and Judith Crist (movies), contributing editors Gael Green and Gloria Steinem, and "new journalists" Tom Wolfe and Jimmy Breslin—established itself firmly in the publishing business.

(JOAN NATALIE REIBSTEIN)

FOOT, MICHAEL

After a lifetime in British politics, Michael Foot got his first job in government at the age of 60 when in March 1974 he was brought into the Cabinet of Harold Wilson in the key position of secretary for employment. His first task was to help bring an end to the miners' strike and the three-day workweek. He was then committed to the repeal of the Industrial Relations Act of 1971, which had been enacted by the outgoing Conservative government in the face of bitter trade union hostility. He had to oversee the dismantling of wage controls and their replacement (at a time of unprecedented inflation) by a form of voluntary wage restraint embodied in the so-called social contract between the Labour government and the unions.

Foot was chosen for this formidable assignment as an ardent Socialist whose position had been plainly on the left wing of the party since he first entered Parliament in 1945. Beginning in 1960 he represented Ebbw Vale, a Welsh mining constituency.

Born July 23, 1913, in Plymouth, Eng., Foot did not come of working-class background himself. He was one of a notable family of Liberals, his father being a Liberal MP for more than 20 years, while his brother Sir Dingle Foot started his political career as a Liberal; another brother, Lord Caradon, was U.K. representative at the UN (1964–70). At Oxford University Michael seemed to be following in the family footsteps, becoming president of the Oxford Union and of the university Liberal Club. But a meeting with the family of Sir Stafford Cripps (chancellor of the Exchequer in the Labour government of 1947–50) led him to join the Labour Party in 1935.

Foot made his name in politics as an outstanding parliamentary debater from the back benches, as a writer (his biography of Aneurin Bevan was a classic of contemporary political history), as a journalist (for some years on the staff of the London *Evening Standard*), and as a television celebrity. He won a reputation as an outspoken rebel of the left and was one of those most adamantly opposed to Britain's entry into the EEC.

(HARFORD THOMAS)

FORD, GERALD RUDOLPH

Gerald Ford, a man of the Congress who had always seemed likely to remain there, became the 38th president of the United States on Aug. 9, 1974. Confirmed as vice-president only eight months earlier, he spent much of the intervening time crisscrossing

Gerald Rudolph Ford

the country, expressing faith in Pres. Richard Nixon (*q.v.*), who had nominated Ford for the office. By late July, however, the Watergate scandal could no longer be brushed aside, and Nixon resigned rather than face impeachment. Ford walked with him to the helicopter in which he would begin his journey into retirement, and two hours later took the oath of office.

His first words to the nation were a message of healing: "My fellow Americans, our long national nightmare is over." Promising "openness and candor," he made himself available to the press and congressional leaders. With his wife and four outspoken children, he seemed unintimidated by the high office—the needed antidote for the secretiveness and suspicion of Nixon's last days.

The end of the honeymoon came a month after Ford took office, when he granted a full pardon to Nixon "for all offenses against the United States" that he may have committed while in office. Ford's opinion poll ratings plummeted. To counter the widespread outcry, Ford voluntarily appeared before a House subcommittee on October 17 to explain his reasoning—the first time a sitting U.S. president had formally testified before a committee of Congress.

With Watergate relegated to the courts, the country's economic ills emerged as a first priority. Ford convened an "economic summit meeting" to suggest ways of coping with inflation and the energy crisis, but it produced little more than evidence that economists tend not to agree. Confirmation of his choice for vice-president, Nelson Rockefeller (*q.v.*), was delayed by a long congressional investigation. There were personal troubles, too—in September Mrs. Ford underwent surgery for breast cancer.

With the November congressional elections approaching, Ford undertook a vigorous campaign tour—which did not, however, prevent an overwhelming Democratic victory. Though Henry Kissinger (*q.v.*), retained as secretary of state, continued to dominate foreign policy, Ford traveled to Japan, South Korea, and the Soviet Union in late November; at Vladivostok he signed a preliminary agreement with Soviet party leader Leonid I. Brezhnev on limitation of strategic missiles. As the year drew to a close, and recession replaced inflation as the major economic woe, there were indications that Ford planned to drop his stalemated anti-inflation program in favour of measures to stimulate the economy.

Ford was born July 14, 1913, in Omaha, Neb. He graduated from the University of Michigan and received a law degree from Yale. After service in the Navy during World War II, he was elected to the House of Representatives from Michigan. He was chosen Republican minority leader of the House in 1965 and held that position until October 1973, when he was nominated to replace former vice-president Spiro Agnew.

(STANLEY WILLS CLOUD)

FUJINO, CHUJIRO

At 73, Chujiro Fujino, chairman of Mitsubishi Shoji and vice-president of the Tokyo Chamber of Commerce, was given the top chair in the "Mitsubishi Group," Japan's most powerful business empire. On Nov. 1, 1974, Fujino was chosen chairman of the Kinyokai, the real nucleus of power in the Mitsubishi Group. As chairman of Mitsubishi Shoji, he ran the massive trading firm that is well known in other countries as the Mitsubishi Corp. The entire Mitsubishi

Group, however, constituted scores of companies, of which Mitsubishi Shoji was just one. Some 26 top executives from Mitsubishi Shoji, the Mitsubishi Bank, Mitsubishi Heavy Industries, Mitsubishi Estates, Nippon Yusen Kaisha (NYK), and Tokyo Marine Fire Insurance held regular meetings in a huge boardroom on the 15th floor of the Mitsubishi Building in the Marunouchi district of Tokyo, where they exchanged information and discussed the management strategy of the Mitsubishi syndicate. This meeting was called "Kinyokai," or the Friday Conference, since it was held on the second Friday of every month.

This conglomeration of companies grew up in the control of the Iwasaki family, but the family lost its proprietorship as a result of the Decentralization Law, by which the U.S. occupation of Japan after World War II outlawed the *zaibatsu*, or financial combines. Quite obviously, however, Mitsubishi has risen again to the position of dominance it had held before the war, thanks to the booming Japanese economy. The strength of the Mitsubishi Group in 1974 was illustrated by the fact that its annual sales were equal to 10% of Japan's total GNP.

Fujino was an appropriate choice to head such a combine. A 40-year career in foreign trade and a reputation as one of the best informed Japanese in world economic matters give him unique qualifications to steer his company through trying times. After graduating from the economics department of Tokyo Imperial University, which subsequently became Tokyo University, he joined Mitsubishi Shoji. During his early career, he lived at various places in North America and had an opportunity to observe closely the Depression of the 1930s. During World War II, he managed Mitsubishi's branch in Talien, China.　　(MASAKI MATSUBARA)

GAIRY, ERIC

The tiny (133-sq.mi.) West Indies island of Grenada became an independent nation Feb. 7, 1974, thus ending 324 years of colonial rule, first by France and then by Great Britain. Full independence had been approved Dec. 11, 1973, by the British House of Commons. But the change in status was at best a mixed blessing for the 105,000 people who lived on the island. The transition was marked by violence, crippling strikes, and political controversy, at the centre of which was the prime minister, Eric Gairy.

As Grenada moved toward independence, Gairy's opponents—including left-wing intellectuals, wealthy landowners, businessmen, and religious leaders—had mounted a major campaign to drive him from office. They considered Gairy a ruthless dictator and feared that he would extend his one-man control over the country after independence was granted. Late in 1973, Gairy's opponents organized a series of demonstrations and strikes, causing political and economic chaos. Despite harsh countermeasures taken by Gairy and his secret police, the strikes continued through independence day. Businesses closed and hundreds of Grenadians fled the island. Tourism dropped off markedly. By the end of the year, however, the situation had quieted.

Born on Feb. 18, 1922, in Grenada and privately educated, Gairy was a schoolteacher in the late 1930s. He was employed in 1940 at Dutch oil refineries in Aruba, where he became involved in the labour union movement. When he returned to Grenada in 1951, he continued to work as a

union organizer, concentrating his efforts on small plantations on the island. As a result, the wages paid to farm workers soon doubled—a fact, according to Gairy, that underlies the continuing hostility many plantation owners feel toward him.

Gairy's career as a government official began in 1951, when he was first elected to the Legislative Council. In 1956 he became minister of trade and production and in 1961 chief minister and minister of finance. After 1953 Gairy's United Labour Party won every election but one. Gairy became Grenada's premier in 1962, a position he held until independence, when his title was changed to prime minister.

(STANLEY WILLS CLOUD)

GEISEL, ERNESTO

On March 15, 1974, Gen. Ernesto Geisel took office as Brazil's fourth successive military president in ten years. An austere, colourless man who shunned unnecessary public appearances, Geisel was almost completely unknown to most Brazilians when the rigidly censored national press announced his candidacy in 1973. Geisel was the choice of incumbent Pres. Emílio Médici and the ruling military junta, and his ratification by the generals' ARENA Party-controlled electoral college was a foregone conclusion. Formerly director of Petrobrás, Brazil's powerful state-owned petroleum monopoly, he was a political conservative whose commitment to the status quo ensured his adherence to the junta's goals of rapid economic development and controlled social change.

Some who had followed Geisel's career hoped for a degree of liberalization of the generally repressive military regime during his five-year term of office. In 1966, he successfully opposed the dissolution of Congress by the generals. While campaigning for president on the slogan of "development and security," he stressed continuing economic growth rather than combating political subversion. By the year's end, however, Geisel's government had not proved significantly different from the other military dictatorships that preceded it.

The fifth and youngest child of a poor schoolteacher who immigrated from Stuttgart, Ger., Geisel was born Aug. 3, 1908, in Rio Grande do Sul, the southernmost Brazilian state. When his sister Amalia won the state lottery, his family used the money to send Ernesto and his older brother Orlando, now minister of the Army, to military college. Before reaching the rank of general at age 53, Geisel held a number of important Army and civil service positions including secretary of finance and public works in the state of Paraiba, superintendent of a government oil refinery, and as a member of the National Petroleum Council. He neither drinks nor smokes, is fluent in five languages, and plays chess for relaxation.

(DONNA ZIMMERMAN)

GIELGUD, SIR (ARTHUR) JOHN

Hailed by many critics as Britain's foremost Shakespearean actor, Sir John Gielgud in 1974 celebrated his 70th birthday and the 53rd anniversary of his professional debut by appearing as Prospero in Peter Hall's production of *The Tempest* for the National Theatre Company at London's Old Vic Theatre. Later in the year he played Shakespeare in Edward Bond's semibiographical drama of the poet's last days, *Bingo*, at the Royal Court Theatre. The latter performance, praised as much for its psychological insight as for Gielgud's unique talent for making theatrical bricks out of a dramatist's straw, came as a fitting climax to the dis-

DOUGLAS H JEFFERY

Sir John Gielgud

tinguished career, by no means exhausted, of an actor, director, and producer renowned on both sides of the Atlantic.

Born in London on April 14, 1904, Gielgud was descended on his mother's side from the famous Terry family, Ellen Terry being his great-aunt. Destined for the theatre from early childhood, he studied privately and at the Royal Academy of Dramatic Art (as it was to become) before entering the profession as a bit player, understudy, and stage manager. Following his professional debut as the Herald in *Henry V* in 1921, he soon made his mark as a leading juvenile actor in both classical and modern drama. A period of apprenticeship with the Oxford Repertory Company, and another with Theodore Komisarjevsky's London-based troupe, led him to the Old Vic in 1929, the year after his New York debut.

Shakespearean roles definitively interpreted by Gielgud included Hamlet, Romeo, Richard II, Angelo, Lear, Cassius, Leontes, and Prospero. Equally memorable in the modern repertoire were his John Worthing in Oscar Wilde's *The Importance of Being Earnest* and Gayev in Chekhov's *The Cherry Orchard*. On both sides of the Atlantic he won critical acclaim and awards as Harry in David Storey's *Home*. Gielgud also became a major screen character actor, appearing in such films as *The Barretts of Wimpole Street, The Charge of the Light Brigade,* and, most recently, *11 Harrowhouse* and *Murder on the Orient Express.* He was knighted in 1953 and holds honorary degrees from Oxford and St. Andrews universities. His autobiography is set forth in three volumes: *Early Stages* (1938); *Stage Directions* (1963); and *Distinguished Company* (1972).　　(OSSIA TRILLING)

GIROUD, FRANÇOISE

Appointed secretary of state for women's affairs on July 16, 1974, Françoise Giroud, at the age of 57, moved directly from journalism into politics to take up a post in the French government specially created for her by Pres. Valéry Giscard d'Estaing (*q.v.*). Previously she had been editor in chief of the news magazine *L'Express,* the first woman editor of a major French weekly outside the specialist field of fashion and "women's interests." A self-made woman of strong convictions, she was well suited to take on the task of bettering the life of French women, having brilliantly bettered her own through strength of character, intelligence, and appetite for work.

Born in Geneva, Switz., on Sept. 21, 1916, daughter of the director of the Ottoman Telegraph Agency, Françoise Gourdji went to school in Paris. At 16 she began work as a salesgirl in a Left-Bank bookshop. There she was noticed by the film producer Marc Allégret, who engaged her as a typist and assistant script girl. After becoming script girl, she worked on Allégret's production of Marcel Pagnol's *Fanny* (1932) and with Jean Renoir on *La Grande Illusion* (1936). She then became assistant director and also wrote scripts and lyrics. During World War II she joined the Resistance and was afterward decorated for the part she played. Turning to journalism after the war, she served her apprenticeship on the leading French women's magazine *Elle,* under Hélène Lazareff. In 1953 she joined with Jean-Jacques Servan-Schreiber in founding *L'Express,* a French version of the *Time* magazine format. She became in 1971 editor in chief of *L'Express,* having been named a member of the board of the publishing company Express-Union in 1970.

Although not politically committed, Mme. Giroud had called on her readers to vote for François Mitterrand, the candidate of the Socialist-Communist alliance, in the 1974 presidential election. Her appointment as a junior minister reflected President Giscard d'Estaing's need to give his administration a more liberal image in view of his declared intention to transform French society. Mme. Giroud was far from being a militant women's liberationist. A woman, she held, had the "right . . . not to become an *ersatz* for man." Furthermore, she said, "I reject the term of equality between men and women, when it claims to ignore biology."

(PIERRE VIANSSON-PONTÉ)

GISCARD D'ESTAING, VALÉRY

As a boy of 12 Valéry Giscard d'Estaing informed his schoolmates that one day he would be president of France. That early prediction came true in May 1974 when, still only 48, he succeeded Georges Pompidou (*see* FRANCE; OBITUARIES) as the Fifth Republic's third president.

Leader of the Independent Republicans—moderate allies of the Gaullists—Giscard had promised electors social and political reform and an "open, modern style of government." At his May 27 inauguration he threw off the chains of protocol and tradition and entered on his seven-year term of office visibly relaxed and with an elegant ease of manner.

Valéry Giscard d'Estaing

A.G.I.P./BLACK STAR

But although the new presidential style and image were initially popular, and liberalization measures such as reduction of the voting age to 18, cessation of wiretapping, and reform of abortion and divorce legislation found favour, Giscard's reforming zeal made little impact against current economic realities. With inflation and unemployment mounting, he was criticized for lack of firm guidance, and by the end of November, following a period of widespread strikes, opinion polls showed his popularity at a low ebb. Criticism extended to his mode of life and of working, the influential newspaper *Le Monde* pointing out that the president's family had not moved into the Elysée Palace as was customary, and that his own whereabouts were sometimes unknown.

A number of summit meetings brought consolation. Prime Minister Pierre Trudeau of Canada's visit in October closed the rift caused by de Gaulle's "long live free Quebec" speech of 1967. Soviet leader Leonid I. Brezhnev's visit early in December emphasized the continuing importance to the Soviet Union of its French connection. The meeting in Paris, at Giscard's invitation, of the EEC heads of government seemed to increase the likelihood of Britain remaining a member. Finally, Giscard's meeting with U.S. Pres. Gerald Ford in Martinique (December 14–16) marked a new French attitude of cooperation with the U.S., in particular over energy problems.

Born in Koblenz, Ger., on Feb. 2, 1926, Giscard came from a patrician background, his family owning land at Estaing in the Auvergne. After a brilliant academic career he became an inspector of finances in 1954 and was elected *député* for Puy-de-Dôme in 1956. Secretary of state at the Ministry of Finance from 1959, he was minister of finance during 1962–66 and 1969–74.

(PIERRE VIANSSON-PONTÉ)

GONÇALVES, VASCO DOS SANTOS

After the resignation of Pres. António de Spínola on Sept. 30, 1974, power in Portugal seemed to be divided between Gen. Francisco da Costa Gomes, the country's new president and military chief of staff, and Col. (later Brig. Gen.) Vasco dos Santos Gonçalves, premier from July 12 and also a career officer. Gonçalves was regarded as the principal architect of the April 25 coup that overthrew the government of Marcello Caetano, but he was unknown to the country at large. After he had formed his new Cabinet, Gonçalves and the more conservative Spínola disagreed on almost all important policy issues. Where Spínola saw anarchy, Gonçalves saw a healthy popular vigilance. But with Costa Gomes, Gonçalves had much more agreement on policy and therefore was in a far better position to clarify the situation with his analytical, political mind. Reportedly the first choice of the Armed Forces Movement (AFM) as the man to design and implement its program, he saw his task as doing so without provoking economic dislocation and a consequent right-wing backlash.

Gonçalves was born in Lisbon on May 3, 1921, son of an international football player of the celebrated Benfica team. He became a career army officer and specialized in engineering, becoming a captain in 1954, major in 1963, and lieutenant colonel in 1967. His various commissions were technical and connected with his specialty, for he was a brilliant engineer. He served in Goa during 1955–56, as well as in Mozambique and Angola; during his time in Africa he served with General Costa Gomes, and the two became friends. Together they participated in the April coup and in formulating

the program of the AFM. During the first provisional government after the coup, Gonçalves worked as chairman of the movement and served with the directorate of the engineering branch of the Army, until called to the premiership.

(MICHAEL WOOLLER)

GREENE, JOE

When the Pittsburgh Steelers won the championship of U.S. professional football by defeating the Minnesota Vikings 16–6 in the Super Bowl on Jan. 12, 1975, they established the remarkable record of holding Minnesota to a gain of only 17 yd. rushing. The Viking running attack was completely thwarted by one of the greatest defensive lines in the history of professional football, a foursome consisting of Dwight White, Ernie Holmes, L. C. Greenwood, and "Mean" Joe Greene (a nickname he disclaimed). For 6-ft. 4-in., 275-lb. tackle Greene, the game was a high point in an outstanding career that had already gained him national awards for his defensive play.

Greene was born Sept. 24, 1946, in Temple, Tex. During his senior year at North Texas State he was the unanimous choice as the top college defensive lineman in the nation. After the season he played in the Senior Bowl and was voted the outstanding lineman for the South.

In the 1969 professional draft of football players Pittsburgh chose Greene in the first round. He was named defensive rookie of the year by the Associated Press, and in 1971 and each year thereafter was elected to the National Football League all-star team. The Associated Press named him the NFL's most valuable defensive player in 1972. During one game that year he sacked the opposing quarterback five times in one of the finest defensive performances ever witnessed in the NFL.

Greene clearly helped lead Pittsburgh from its position as perennial doormat to a divisional championship in 1972. The Steelers reached the American Conference finals in that year before losing to Miami. In 1973 they gained the conference play-offs but lost in the semifinal game to Oakland. But Greene and his fellow front linemen gained revenge in 1974, holding the Raiders to 29 yd. rushing in a 24–13 victory that qualified the Steelers for the Super Bowl.

(DAVID R. CALHOUN)

GUILLAUME, GÜNTER

The arrest on April 24, 1974, of Günter Guillaume on suspicion of being an East German spy led to the resignation less than two weeks later of the West German chancellor, Willy Brandt. In mid-December the federal public prosecutor's office announced that Guillaume would be tried for treason and espionage early in 1975.

In 1972 Guillaume was appointed as a liaison officer between the chancellor's office and the Social Democratic Party (SPD). In this capacity he was in almost daily contact with the chancellor and had access to secret information. When he was arrested, he confessed to being an officer of the East German National People's Army and an official of the East German State Security.

Born on Feb. 1, 1927, in Berlin, Guillaume joined the Nazi Party in 1944 when he was 17. After World War II he worked for a state publishing company in East Berlin. He came to the West in 1956, ostensibly as a refugee, and joined the SPD in 1957. Enthusiastic and efficient, he quickly rose to a position of influence in the party in Frankfurt, and was eventually appointed a senior party functionary in that city (1964–68). He joined the staff of the Chancellery in 1970.

Former colleagues described him as a right-winger who was in favour of throwing young dissidents out of the party. Guillaume fell under suspicion of being a spy in the summer of 1973, and Brandt was told about this. But on the advice of the security authorities Brandt continued to employ Guillaume. It was later established that for many years Guillaume had been collecting intelligence material and sending it to his East German masters.

At a parliamentary commission of inquiry into the Guillaume affair (which cleared Brandt of any direct blame), Brandt said that although he accepted political responsibility for any negligence that had occurred, he had been kept in complete ignorance of how the security services were handling the situation. Until immediately before Guillaume's arrest he had not been told that their suspicions had been confirmed.

(NORMAN CROSSLAND)

HAILE SELASSIE

Emperor of Ethiopia and Lion of Judah, diminutive but imposing, Haile Selassie lost his throne on Sept. 12, 1974, when a provisional military government was established. His long rule had lasted since 1916, when, at the age of 24, as the then Lij Tafari, he became regent; after the death of Empress Zauditu he was crowned emperor in 1930. For the next 44 years, except for an interregnum during the Italian occupation (1935–41), he exercised his imperial power with considerable skill, toughness, and, recently, with tolerance and moderation. His outstanding achievement was to unify his empire and to begin the process of modernizing Ethiopia's ancient feudal society. He also succeeded in capturing a leadership position in the modern Pan-Africanist movement, making his capital, Addis Ababa, the seat of the Organization of African Unity. His proud defiance of Benito Mussolini's military occupation of Ethiopia was memorably symbolized by his lonely but dignified appeal to the League of Nations in 1936 for world support; this he failed to get until the Allies went to war against the fascist dictators in 1939, liberating Ethiopia in 1941.

Haile Selassie was born near Harer on July 23, 1892, a nobleman of royal blood but not close to the throne. Although he introduced a number of modern reforms, he was most proud of the written constitution he conferred on his subjects at his silver jubilee in 1955. But his rule suffered from two major defects: with an old man's doggedness he clung stubbornly to his imperial supremacy, refusing to surrender any of the effective powers of his questionably used patronage system; and he refused to submit to pressures to allow for a smooth transition of his imperial crown to his son, Crown Prince Asfa Wossen. It was only after the beginning of the military coup in February 1974 that he finally agreed to proposals to convert the role of the emperor into that of a constitutional monarch. But the young army officers, who had increasingly made themselves the political masters of Ethiopia, suspected that he was only playing for time to manipulate the situation. Unable to use the emperor to legitimize its radical reforms, the Military Council eventually decided to dethrone him. The emperor was accused of corruption and trickery, and then detained.

(COLIN LEGUM)

HALSTON

Quiet, classic, comfortable—these words described the women's clothing designed by Halston, twice winner of the Coty "Winnie" Award, the fashion world's highest honour. Shrewd, energetic, successful—these words described Roy Halston Frowick, who started his own salon in 1968 and in October 1973 sold out to a conglomerate for $10 million in stock.

Born in Des Moines, Ia., in April 1932, Halston made his first hat in 1945 as a gift for his mother. High school friends remembered how beautifully he dressed and how rich girls would drive him around in their convertibles. As a student at the Art Institute of Chicago, he supported himself by making window displays for the Carson Pirie Scott department store and, in his spare hours, created hats in his apartment. When these were displayed at Chicago's Ambassador Hotel, they won such acclaim that he opened a millinery salon.

Halston moved to New York City in 1958 to work for designer Lilly Daché, left a year later for Bergdorf Goodman, and soon became head of Bergdorf's custom millinery department. When Jacqueline Kennedy asked him for hats to wear during her husband's 1960 presidential campaign, Halston designed the beige felt pillbox that became a nationwide fad. His other customers included Perle Mesta, Mrs. William Paley, and Mrs. Henry Ford. He won a Coty Special Award in 1962 for millinery and four years later began to design complete ensembles.

With capital supplied by a wealthy Texas socialite, Halston entered business on his own in 1968. He established a custom millinery and clothing salon on New York City's Upper East Side and also designed ready-to-wear fashions. His first solo collection, in 1969, won a second Coty Special Award. Halston emphasized casual, comfortable wear with long flowing lines. He brought back the cardigan sweater of the '50s, used clinging jersey fabrics in dresses, and became the first designer to work successfully with man-made suede. In October 1973, with his sales approaching $28 million, he sold out to the Norton Simon conglomerate. Freed to devote most of his time to designing new products for what was now a subsidiary, he continued to work as vigorously as ever. Going against the trend toward longer, looser clothes, he shocked the audience at his fall showing by introducing the "skimp"—the miniskirt revisited.

(VICTOR M. CASSIDY)

HARTONO, RUDY

In March 1974, for a record-breaking seventh consecutive time, Rudy Hartono of Indonesia won the men's singles title at the All-England Badminton Championships at Wembley, Eng., generally accepted as the unofficial world championships. Hartono won his first All-England title in his first attempt in 1968, and in accomplishing this emulated the feat of such distinguished predecessors as Conny Jepsen (Denmark and later Sweden) in 1947, David G. Freeman (U.S.) in 1949, and Tan Joe Hok (Indonesia) in 1959.

Hartono was 18 years old when he won his first All-England title, the youngest man ever to do so. He has also won major national championships in many other parts of the world. An aggressive player, he tries to win his points as rapidly as possible, hits very hard when given the slightest opportunity, and does not rely on defense, which is the strategy employed by many leading singles players. His shots are noted for their accuracy and for deceptiveness that remorselessly works his opponent out of position.

Hartono was born in Surabaja, East Java, Aug. 18, 1949, and was educated at Trisakti University, Jakarta, where he majored in economics. He also studied medicine, civil aviation, and acting. Raised in a family that strongly emphasized physical fitness, he has a sister, Utami Dewi, who is also a national champion in badminton.

In Indonesia Hartono is considered a national hero and frequently makes front-page headlines for his achievements in badminton. Despite the fact that one of his gifts was a house, most of the time he lives in simple quarters along with Indonesia's other badminton stars at Jakarta's vast Senayan Sports complex. His national fame and international mastery of the game have been a powerful stimulant to Indonesian youth.

(JACK H. VAN PRAAG)

HAYNIE, SANDRA

Almost every prize in women's golf had been won by Sandra Haynie as 1974 drew to a close. Only topping the yearly money list and taking the Colgate-Dinah Shore tournament escaped her. The 5-ft. 5-in. 120-lb. Texan was the second highest money-winner of all time in women's professional golf, behind only Kathy Whitworth. Beginning in 1962 Miss Haynie won 34 major tournaments, and in 1974 she took two out of the "big three" by winning the U.S. Women's Open and the Ladies Professional Golf Association (LPGA), both in July.

Still, the nagging query "Sandra who?" seemed to follow her as she played along the women's circuit. Most observers agreed that her public recognition had not kept pace with her success on the golf courses. Other performers such as Kathy Whitworth, Jane Blalock, JoAnne Carner, and Carol Mann seemed to enjoy higher public profiles and more lucrative endorsement contracts to supplement their golf earnings. But the soft-spoken Texan never protested her obscurity.

Miss Haynie finished the 1974 campaign with approximate earnings of $75,000, third behind Mrs. Carner and Miss Blalock. This was a considerable improvement over her 1973 earnings of $47,000. In fact, steady improvement and remarkable consistency have marked her 17 years of competition.

Miss Haynie was born in Fort Worth, Tex., on June 4, 1943. She began her golf career at the age of 11 when Warren Cantrell, a teaching professional at the Lubbock Country Club, told her father she had the "gait of a born golfer." Three years later, she won the Texas Amateur championship at the age of 14 and the following year took the Trans-Mississippi, her first national title. Always an intense worker, Sandra blistered her hands by swinging a club for three hours the first time she got hold of one. As of 1974 she had not stopped swinging and insisted that practice was the major reason for her improvement.

(J. TIMOTHY WEIGEL)

HEALEY, DENIS WINSTON

Within nine months of being appointed the U.K. chancellor of the Exchequer in March 1974, Denis Healey had introduced three budgets—an indicator of the pace at which the economic crisis in Britain was developing in 1974. His reputation in the Labour Party as one of its most powerful intellects had been built up first as a specialist in foreign affairs and then as defense minister for the six years of the 1964–70 government of Harold Wilson. While the party was in opposition during the government of Edward Heath, Healey turned to financial and economic affairs as "shadow" chancellor.

Born in Mottingham, Kent, on Aug. 30, 1917, Healey was educated at Balliol College, Oxford. Although he had been an MP since 1952 and before that had worked in

Haile Selassie

MERMAID III · Kenichi Horie

the Labour Party's secretariat in the international department, he had moved up through the party hierarchy somewhat more slowly than some of his contemporaries, becoming a member of the party executive only in 1970. His tough, hardheaded view of what needed to be done to revive economic activity in the U.K. by helping companies to improve their profits and their capacity to invest caused some Labour MPs to regard his November 1974 budget as too soft on industry. This mood was reflected later in the month at the party conference elections, when Healey only narrowly held his place on the executive.

But in 1974 Healey was not exclusively preoccupied with Britain's economic problems. He took a leading role in the international meetings of finance ministers called to devise ways of dealing with the problem of handling the vast surplus of "petrodollars," initiating a plan of his own for recycling the earnings of the oil producers. Healey also warned his fellow finance ministers of the danger of a world slump on the scale of the 1930s, and urged them not to take defensive measures nation by nation that would create a worldwide recession. He suggested that a watershed in world history had been reached, and that a new period was beginning when economic growth would encounter material restraints.

(HARFORD THOMAS)

HEARST, PATRICIA
At 19, Patricia Hearst, granddaughter of one of the country's most powerful publishers, the late William Randolph Hearst, was to all appearances an easygoing California girl living quietly with her boyfriend in a Berkeley apartment. By her 20th birthday, she was the central figure in one of the most bizarre blends of street crime and political protest the nation had ever seen.

On the night of Feb. 5, 1974, two women and two men, later identified as members of a small, loosely organized group of former convicts and self-styled radicals called the Symbionese Liberation Army, kidnapped Patty Hearst from her flat, beat her fiancé, and fled in a hail of bullets to ward off pursuers. As ransom, the SLA demanded food for the poor, and Patty's wealthy father, publisher Randolph A. Hearst, then spent $2 million for food that was given away in poor sections of San Francisco. On April 3 a tape recording was received on which Patty declared that she had chosen to "stay and fight" on the side of her captors for the "freedom of oppressed people." She assailed her father as a "corporate liar" and called the food giveaways a "sham."

During the April 15 robbery of a San Francisco bank, hidden cameras photo-graphed Miss Hearst training an automatic rifle on bank employees. But they also showed other SLA members apparently covering her, and her family insisted she had been coerced or brainwashed. Meanwhile, the intensive police and FBI search went on, and on May 17, 400 law officers laid siege to a small, shabby stucco house in Los Angeles. In 70 minutes more than 1,000 rounds of ammunition were expended, and the house eventually burned to the ground. Six bodies were recovered from the debris and coroners identified them as known SLA members; Patty Hearst was not among them.

In a later tape she claimed she had been in love with one of the victims. Thought to be in the company of the last remnants of the SLA, she was sought unsuccessfully on a federal fugitive warrant for her part in the bank robbery. An aging gangster, Mickey Cohen, claimed to have known something of her whereabouts, and she was variously reported in Cleveland, Texas, and Canada. The FBI refused comment, and the mystery of Patty Hearst continued.

(JOHN F. STACKS)

HORIE, KENICHI
In Japanese fashion, Kenichi Horie usually masked his emotions, but he could not hold back the tears when, on May 4, 1974, he nosed his three-ton sloop "Mermaid III" into Osaka harbour. He had fulfilled a lifelong dream, circumnavigating the earth alone nonstop. The 30,000-mi. voyage took 276 days, breaking the record of 292 days set in 1971 by Britain's Chay Blyth.

Blue water was in the 35-year-old Horie's blood. In 1962, at the age of 24, he became the first man to sail the Pacific alone without a halt. The 5,000-mi. Osaka-to-San Francisco crossing took him 93 days aboard the tiny 19-ft. "Mermaid." After acquiring a wife, Nobuko, and opening a small restaurant, Horie began planning his round-the-world adventure. With the money he earned and contributions from sailing enthusiasts, he quietly began building "Mermaid II." He set out on Nov. 12, 1972, hoping to girdle the earth in 290 days or less. But 70 mi. SSW of Osaka one of the masts snapped in a storm, and he suffered the humiliation of being towed back to his home port.

Undaunted, he went to work on "Mermaid III." On Aug. 1, 1973, he set sail from Osaka again, heading westward into the Indian Ocean from the Pacific in September and October, then rounding the Cape of Good Hope to enter the South Atlantic at the beginning of November. Early in January 1974 he bucked high winds and towering seas to force a passage through the narrow strait named after Sir Francis Drake at Cape Horn, South America's southernmost tip.

Turning northward, he made Hawaii in mid-March. The rest was plain sailing.

Though he became an authentic Japanese hero through his exploits, Horie retained his modesty. Born Sept. 8, 1938, the oldest son of an auto parts dealer in Osaka, he became interested in sailing while a freshman at Kansai University's First High School, where he joined the yacht club. He concealed his plan to sail the Pacific, departing without a passport and arriving in the U.S. without a visa. Both governments indulgently forgave him. (JOHN P. RODERICK)

ISHIHARA, SHINTARO
One of Japan's best-known politicians and most widely read novelists, Shintaro Ishihara shocked many Japanese in June 1974 when he said his country might have had a better working democracy if Emperor Hirohito had been tried and executed after World War II. Ishihara wrote in the monthly *Jiyu* that the U.S. decision not to try the emperor left unanswered the question of his responsibility for the war. Had he been executed after testifying to his role, Ishihara said, Japan would have been able to digest democracy more slowly and would have understood it better.

Late in 1973 Ishihara helped form the Seirankai or "Blue Storm Society," a group of 31 ultraconservative members of the Diet belonging to the ruling Liberal-Democratic Party. Anti-Communist and pro-Taiwan, Seirankai led an unsuccessful fight to prevent Prime Minister Kakuei Tanaka from concluding an aviation agreement with China. Commercial service between Japan and China began Sept. 29, 1974, but the Nationalist government on Taiwan retaliated by canceling the Tokyo–Taipei route.

The reactionary nature of Seirankai—it resorted to violence in the Diet and had signed its founding document in blood—turned more moderate Japanese against it. By year's end it had lost ten of its members, but Ishihara remained a prominent and controversial figure. He refused his party's bid to run for governor of Tokyo in 1975 and threatened to create a new party to foster his ideas.

Startling his compatriots was a specialty of the 42-year-old Ishihara. Born Sept. 30, 1932, in Kobe, he began the process in 1956, while still a student at Hitotsubashi University, with his first novel, *Taiyo-no-Kisetsu* ("Season in the Sun"). It portrayed his contemporaries as amoral and selfishly individualistic. More novels, plays, and movies followed depicting the youthful Japanese "Sun Tribe," as they soon were called. Ishihara's younger brother, Yujiro, became a movie star in film versions of the books. When Shintaro turned to politics in 1968 he won a landslide election to the House of Councillors (upper house) of the Diet, then moved to the ruling House of Representatives in 1971. Though he was the nation's top vote getter, he remained nonconformist. (JOHN P. RODERICK)

JAWORSKI, LEON
As the federal government's second special Watergate prosecutor, Leon Jaworski presided over the crucial phase of an investigation that toppled a U.S. president and brought men who had once been among the most powerful in the government to the bar of justice. The assignment was a difficult and sensitive one, and when Jaworski returned to private life on Oct. 25, 1974, there was general agreement that he had car-

ried it out with care and responsibility, even though much work remained to be done.

Jaworski, a Texas attorney, was appointed to the special prosecutor's job by Pres. Richard Nixon to replace the first special prosecutor, Archibald Cox, whom Nixon ordered fired on Oct. 20, 1973. Cox had gone beyond his franchise, Nixon felt, in demanding White House tape recordings as evidence and in carrying his investigation into areas of alleged wrongdoing not directly related to Watergate. Congress, however, had insisted on independence for Cox, and provided even more safeguards for Jaworski. Still, when Jaworski's nomination was announced, it received a mixed reaction —his integrity was never in doubt but his record as a Nixon supporter in 1972 led some observers to predict that he would be less aggressive than Cox.

To be sure, even after Jaworski stepped down, there were those who thought he had been too flexible in his plea bargaining with defendants and that he should at least have attempted to indict Nixon, either before or after the president's resignation. But these criticisms notwithstanding, Jaworski was widely praised for his work. He pursued investigations into the Watergate affair begun by Cox: the break-in of Daniel Ellsberg's psychiatrist's office by the White House "plumbers," election "dirty tricks," the misuse of campaign funds, and other matters. The evidence he presented to a federal grand jury led to the indictment, on charges related to the Watergate cover-up, of seven important figures in both the Nixon administration and the Committee for the Re-election of the President.

The evidence also persuaded the grand jury to name Nixon as an unindicted coconspirator in the cover-up. Furthermore, Jaworski and his staff were able to obtain a number of guilty pleas and convictions in 1974, including the conviction of John Ehrlichman, Nixon's former domestic affairs adviser, in connection with the Ellsberg burglary. Perhaps most important, Jaworski successfully challenged Nixon's attempt to withhold from the special prosecutor subpoenaed tapes and documents of 64 presidential conversations. On July 24 the U.S. Supreme Court sustained Jaworski's arguments in an 8–0 opinion.

Leon Jaworski

PICTORIAL PARADE

Jaworski was born Sept. 19, 1905, in Waco, Tex., the son of a Protestant minister who had migrated from Poland. He attended Baylor University in Waco and received a law degree there in 1925. Later he joined a leading Houston, Tex., law firm and became a senior partner in 1951. He served as president of the American Bar Association (1971–72). When he resigned as special prosecutor, he was replaced by his assistant, Henry S. Ruth, Jr.

(STANLEY WILLS CLOUD)

KARAMANLIS, KONSTANTINOS

After 11 years of self-imposed exile in Paris, Konstantinos Karamanlis, who had held power in Greece for a record near-eight successive years (1955–63), returned to Athens on July 24, 1974, and was sworn in as prime minister. He demanded and obtained the subordination of the armed forces to civilian authority, and averted a catastrophic war with Turkey over Cyprus without loss of prestige. He had been recalled by Pres. Phaidon Gizikis, who had dismissed the government of the military junta after the disaster of its attempted coup against Cyprus on July 15 and its miscalculation about Turkey's reaction.

Karamanlis was born in 1907 at the village of Proti, near Serrai, in Greek Macedonia (then still a Turkish province), the eldest of the seven children of a schoolteacher. After graduating from the law school of the University of Athens in 1932, he practiced law in Athens. Launched into politics by the Populist Party, he was elected to Parliament in 1935 for Serrai. In 1950 he joined the Greek Rally of Field Marshal Alexandros Papagos, which at the Nov. 16, 1952, elections obtained 239 out of 300 seats. He entered the Papagos government as minister of public works and earned popularity by his energetic road construction program. When Papagos died in October 1955, King Paul chose the young and successful administrator as prime minister.

Karamanlis formed not only his government but also his own party, the National Radical Union (ERE), and at the Feb. 19, 1956, elections obtained 161 seats. He improved Greece's relations with Yugoslavia, but those with Turkey, and especially with Great Britain, remained strained owing to the Cyprus issue. In order to restore friendly relations with the NATO powers, Karamanlis decided to disentangle the awkward Cyprus problem by the establishment of an independent republic on the island. On Feb. 5–11, 1959, he met Adnan Menderes, the prime minister of Turkey, in Zürich, Switz., and reached a compromise endorsed eight days later by the British prime minister, Harold Macmillan. On Oct. 29, 1961, Karamanlis won his third election with 176 seats, but on June 11, 1963, he resigned following King Paul's rejection of his advice that the king's state visit to London should be postponed.   (K. M. SMOGORZEWSKI)

KARDELJ, EDVARD

A close colleague of Tito since the days of the 1941–45 partisan war, Edvard Kardelj emerged in 1974 as the 82-year-old Yugoslav president's chosen successor. Kardelj, the leading theoretician of his country's "road to socialism," was entrusted with the task of preparing the new constitution, which was adopted in February. A long and complex document, it embodied most of Kardelj's thinking on workers' self-management as the basis of Yugoslavia's political, economic, and social system.

Throughout the year the mass media strove to present Kardelj—a rather dry, schoolmasterly man without much sense of

humour or charisma—in a more attractive light. Perhaps more important, Kardelj took an increasing share in running the country's foreign policy, which had always been Tito's jealously guarded preserve. The most important of several foreign missions that he undertook in 1974 was his visit to Moscow at the beginning of September to discuss the degree of Soviet involvement in a conspiracy uncovered in Montenegro in April.

Tito had had several heirs apparent, all of whom had fallen into disgrace. The best known were Milovan Djilas, who fell out with Tito because of his insistence on more rapid liberalization in 1954, and Aleksandr Rankovic, who was dismissed in 1966 for plotting against Tito and preparing a conservative regime to follow his disappearance. Because of his lack of strong support, either in his native republic of Slovenia or with other groups in Yugoslavia, Kardelj remained essentially a lonely figure, respected but not loved and therefore vulnerable to coups from left and right.

A member of Yugoslavia's collective state presidency and of the Presidium of the League of Communists, Kardelj was born in Ljubljana on Jan. 27, 1910, into a working-class family. Having joined the party's youth organization at 16, he spent two years in prison in Yugoslavia and from 1934 to 1936 lived in Moscow. In 1939 he published a study of the national question in Slovenia, the first of a long series of theoretical works. He was closely involved in the development of the whole Yugoslav politico-social system after 1945.   (K. F. CVIIC)

KARPOV, ANATOLY

The official challenger to Bobby Fischer for the 1975 world chess championship, Anatoly Karpov was certainly the best prospect for winning the title that the Soviet Union had produced since the advent of Mikhail Tal and Boris Spassky. His recent career had been an almost uninterrupted series of successes, and it was only against Viktor Korchnoi, whom he eventually beat by the odd game in the final of the 1974 candidates' matches, that he experienced any real difficulty.

Born May 23, 1951, at Zlatoust in the southern Urals, Karpov learned chess at the age of four and at nine was rated a first-category player—the equivalent of a first-class amateur in the U.S. or the U.K. At 15 he won an international tournament, contended by many adult masters, and later he won the 1967–68 junior international tournament at Groningen, Neth., an event subsequently recognized as the European junior championship.

In 1969 he became world junior champion and in 1970 the world's youngest grand master. The following year he was fourth in the 39th Soviet championship at Leningrad and equal first with Leonid Stein at the Alekhine Memorial Tournament in Moscow. He was equal first (with Korchnoi) at the 1971–72 Hastings (Eng.) Congress Premier Tournament and at San Antonio, Tex., in 1972 (with Tigran Petrosian of the U.S.S.R. and Lajos Portisch of Hungary). In the 1973 Leningrad Interzonal Tournament he again tied for first with Korchnoi. He beat Lev Polugayevsky and Spassky easily enough in the quarter- and semifinals of the 1974 candidates' matches.

A student at the Leningrad State University, Karpov was modest, unassuming, of deceptively small stature and almost frail-looking, but endowed with remarkable powers of endurance. His style of play was that of the complete grand master, without any noticeable weaknesses except, perhaps, that he much preferred attack to defense and was occasionally liable to wilt under the pressure of a fierce onslaught. However, should the match for the world title with Fischer take place, there was no doubt that he would make a thoroughly worthy adversary. His first press statement was on the subject of curtsying. He wished it to be known that the ladies' curtsy to the governor-general ought to be replaced by shaking hands. He favoured the shaking of hands as a reciprocal gesture of greeting and respect but added that a slight bow to the governor-general and his wife by both men and women at the time of shaking hands would not be inappropriate.

Since the governor-general's main function was to open sessions of Parliament, give the royal assent to acts of Parliament, and act as the queen's viceroy and chief of state, Kerr made no controversial statements and took no part in domestic politics. Arriving at the vice-regal residence via a distinguished but esoteric law career—unlike most of his predecessors, who had been involved in spectacular political or military pursuits—he had an air of aloof mystery which the nature of his office did little to dispel.

KERR, SIR JOHN ROBERT
Sworn in as governor-general and commander in chief of the defense forces of Australia at Parliament House on July 11, 1974, during a ten-minute ceremony in the Senate, Sir John Kerr, chief justice of the Supreme Court of New South Wales, took over the office from Sir Paul Hasluck. From the first Sir John adopted a note of informality. His first press statement was on the subject of curtsying. He wished it to be known that the ladies' curtsy to the governor-general ought to be replaced by shaking hands. He favoured the shaking of hands as a reciprocal gesture of greeting and respect but added that a slight bow to the governor-general and his wife by both men and women at the time of shaking hands would not be inappropriate.

Kerr was born in Sydney, Austr., on Sept. 24, 1914. Admitted to the New South Wales bar in 1938, he served with the 2nd Australian Imperial Force (1942–46). He became a queen's counsel in 1953; a judge of the Commonwealth industrial court in 1966; a Supreme Court judge of the Australian Capital Territory in 1966, and of the Northern Territory in 1970. He played an important part in Australian industrial relations as deputy president of the Trade Practices Tribunal (1966) and as a member of the Courts of Marine Inquiry (1967–72). His administrative ability was recognized by his appointment as chairman of the committees on the review of administrative decisions (1968) and on reviewing the pay of the armed forces (1970).   (A. R. G. GRIFFITHS)

KIRCHSCHLÄGER, RUDOLF
The nomination of Rudolf Kirchschläger by the Austrian Socialist Party (SPÖ) as its candidate for the presidency in succession to Franz Jonas (*see* OBITUARIES) caused general surprise. Previously, the SPÖ's candidates had always been highly placed in the party hierarchy, whereas Kirchschläger, a lawyer and diplomat who had been foreign minister since 1970, was not. However, his candidacy was successful, and he won 51.7% of the votes cast in the election of June 23, 1974. On July 8 he was sworn in as president of Austria.

Kirchschläger was born on March 20, 1915, in the Upper Austrian village of Obermühl. His youth was marked by poverty and deprivation. Orphaned at the age of 11, he had to earn money for his studies, but these were interrupted when he was drafted for military service during World War II, in the course of which he was twice seriously wounded. After the war he entered the justice department of the civil service, working first in Horn in Lower Austria and then in Vienna as a district judge. In 1954 he joined the foreign service. At that time the State Treaty granting Austria full sovereignty was under preparation. As legal ad-

viser, Kirchschläger took part in 1955 in negotiations with the great powers and collaborated in drafting the constitutional law of perpetual Austrian neutrality.

Subsequently, he was active in various branches of the Ministry for Foreign Affairs, as leader of delegations to numerous international conferences, as chief secretary to foreign ministers Lujo Tončić-Sorinj and Bruno Kreisky, and as ambassador in Prague. Meanwhile, he also taught international law and collaborated in the writing of a number of legal publications. When in 1970 Kreisky became chancellor, he appointed Kirchschläger foreign minister. In this capacity he defined the goal of Austrian foreign policy as the maintenance and strengthening of the republic's independence; Kirchschläger viewed Austria's neutrality as fundamental both to the preservation of its independence and as a stabilizing element in the maintenance of international peace.   (ELFRIEDE DIRNBACHER)

KISSINGER, HENRY ALFRED
Through more than five years, first as assistant for national security affairs to U.S. Pres. Richard Nixon and then also as secretary of state, Henry Kissinger had demonstrated that he was a statesman of extraordinary energy and ability. He became very nearly indispensable to Nixon and then, in the late summer of 1974 when Nixon resigned as a result of the Watergate scandals, Kissinger demonstrated that he was also a political man of unusual skill.

From the beginning of the Nixon presidency, foreign affairs were the president's chief preoccupation, and Kissinger was the president's chief instrument in formulating and executing U.S. foreign policy. When Nixon began his struggle to avoid impeachment, it was his administration's success abroad that was used as the main argument against his being ousted. Kissinger's role then became double-edged. He began the year telling the public that Nixon, rather than himself, was still in charge of the nation's foreign policy despite the growing impeachment threat. Yet the denial was not believed; Kissinger had helped Nixon to his administration's successes, but his very excellence diminished the president's own claim on indispensability.

Kissinger continued his world travels throughout the year, and appeared indefatigable in the many long negotiations he attended. His marathon, 32-day flying-shuttle diplomacy between Israel and Syria produced on May 31 the first signed accord between those two hostile states since the

Henry Alfred Kissinger

DENNIS BRACK—BLACK STAR

armistice ending the 1948 war for Israeli independence. Kissinger also paved the way for Nixon's summit meeting with Soviet leaders in Moscow in June, and continued on that trip and on a subsequent journey in October to negotiate toward a further limitation on strategic nuclear weapons. He organized Pres. Gerald Ford's first meeting as president with Soviet Communist Party general secretary Leonid I. Brezhnev in Vladivostok.

As the pressure of Watergate on Nixon increased, Kissinger himself came under greater scrutiny for his role in the early Nixon years in establishing wiretaps on some newsmen and on his own National Security Council employees. In June an FBI memorandum was published which identified Kissinger as the initiator of the taps. He had denied such a role and repeated that denial.

During the year Kissinger became concerned with the continued functioning of U.S. diplomacy in the face of the eroding stature of the Nixon government. That problem was finally solved in early August when Nixon left office, a course counseled and guided by Kissinger.

Kissinger was born in Fürth, in what is now West Germany, on May 27, 1923. He became a U.S. citizen after fleeing Nazi Germany with his family in 1938. Before his appointment in 1968 as Nixon's assistant he was a professor of government at Harvard University. In 1974 he married Nancy Maginnes, an aide to former New York governor Nelson Rockefeller.

(JOHN F. STACKS)

KNIEVEL, EVEL
The year's most dramatic failure was Evel Knievel, a petty thief turned motorcycle exhibitionist who tried to vault Idaho's Snake River Canyon and ended up at its bottom.

The attempt, on Sept. 8, 1974, was also the year's nonevent, a publicity man's outlandish dream that somehow mesmerized a nation still rocky from its summer-long constitutional crisis. Knievel flashed a $6 million check, purportedly his advance fee from admission and closed circuit TV receipts. Promoters promised a $1 million party, which turned out to be a free round of beer in a drive-in. They claimed 200,000 people were coming to tiny Twin Falls to watch the stuntman soar across the canyon. And a few motorcycle gangs did appear, along with some spaced-out young people and others looking for kindred spirits. The news media showed up in force. Two newsmen were beaten, one by Knievel personally, and a couple of girls were willingly stripped and then mauled.

Then, after a week of raucous idleness, Knievel climbed into his steam-powered Sky-Cycle for "the jump." Before the vehicle had cleared the launch ramp the landing parachute popped out—deployed prematurely either by a malfunction or by Knievel's own nervous thumb—and the vehicle drifted down to the water's edge. Rescue helicopters reported that he was not hurt. And the party was over.

Robert Craig Knievel was born in Butte, Mont., Oct. 17, 1938. By his own admission he started stealing hubcaps as a teenager, and he later supported himself as a con man, card shark, and sneak thief. A semipro athlete, hunting guide and sports promotor for a while, he became a motorcycle dealer, then took to stunt riding—taking off from wooden ramps and sailing over lines of

Evel Knievel

parked cars or snarls of rattlesnakes. On New Year's Day 1968 he gained some national attention trying the same trick in Las Vegas. He managed to clear the fountains at Caesar's Palace hotel but botched the landing. He boasted that this and other accidents had broken every major bone in his body except his neck. Still, he was deemed a contemporary phenomenon, featured in *The New Yorker* and *Business Week,* which reported on the successful commercial exploitation of his notoriety. There had even been a movie about the man who called himself "the last gladiator in the New Rome."

(PHILIP KOPPER)

KROC, RAY

"Over 15 Billion Served." The familiar sign had to be changed every four months in 1974 as McDonald's restaurants sold a billion more hamburgers at 2,300 locations in the U.S., Canada, Europe, and Japan. Total

sales in 1974 exceeded $1 billion, making McDonald's a bigger supplier of food than the U.S. Army.

Twenty years earlier there had been only one McDonald's, and Raymond A. Kroc was an obscure, moderately prosperous businessman. Born Oct. 5, 1902, in Chicago, Kroc worked at a series of occupations, including ambulance driver in World War I, jazz pianist in Chicago nightclubs, and Florida land salesman, before becoming exclusive distributor of the Prince Castle Multimixer, a gadget that stirred six milkshakes at once. In 1954 one restaurant purchased eight multimixers. Startled, Kroc traveled to San Bernardino, Calif., to find out what sort of operation could sell so many meals. He saw a prosperous fast-food restaurant that served hamburgers, french fries, and milkshakes only. It was owned by two brothers, Maurice and Richard McDonald. Hoping to sell more multimixers, Kroc approached the McDonalds with a scheme to franchise their idea. He began franchising in 1955 and soon went into it full time. Capital was not easy to find in the early '60s, but Kroc persevered and by 1965 he owned the business outright. The rest was history.

With Harry Sonneborn, an early business associate since retired, Kroc devised a franchising system whereby the parent company bought a site, constructed a restaurant, then leased the operation for a percentage of sales. A franchise holder, who paid roughly $150,000 to enter the business and could expect to net about $50,000 per year, had to learn his trade at the company's Hamburger University in Elk Grove Village, Ill. A McDonald's hamburger, for example, consisted of precisely 1.6 oz. of beef with no more than 19% fat; it was placed on a 3½-in. bun and had to be thrown away if not sold within ten minutes.

Early in 1974 Ray Kroc bought the San Diego (Calif.) Padres, a baseball team wretched in both performance and attendance. Early in the season, he chastised the entire team over the stadium's public address system—later apologizing for this understandable display of emotion. The team finished last, as usual, but Ray Kroc, of all people, knew the value of perseverance.

(VICTOR M. CASSIDY)

KUROISHI, TSUNE

Tsune Kuroishi believed that women could scale any mountain on earth. She spoke from lofty experience. On May 4, 1974, she led an 11-member, all-Japanese women's climbing team that conquered 26,760-ft. Mt. Manaslu in the Himalayas. Three women, Mieko Mori, Masako Uchida, and Naoko Nakaseko, made it to the top and claimed a record for women climbers. The feat was marred by the death the day before of Teiko Suzuki on a smaller peak.

Kuroishi, a veteran of 24 years of mountaineering, directed the team from camp no. 1 at 17,160 ft. Two of the women, Uchida and Nakaseko, reached the summit without oxygen masks, which they discarded as too heavy. Originally, the team had planned to go up the menacing and hitherto unclimbed east ridge, but on April 1 the women gave up that attempt and turned to the traditional glacier course. A Japanese men's team had first climbed Manaslu—the world's seventh highest mountain—in 1956. The previous record for women climbers was claimed by Setsuko Watanabe of Tokyo, who reached the 26,240-ft.-high South Col of Mt. Everest in 1971.

Preparations for the expedition were difficult, Kuroishi said, because the Jungfrau Alpine Club had little money and fundraising was slow. The assault had been planned for five years and cost more than

$100,000. In choosing Manaslu they tackled a killer mountain. It was regarded as one of the deadliest of the Himalayan peaks, its hanging glacier a mass of shifting snow and ice reached by clambering over the steep rocky face below. Avalanches killed 15 members of a South Korean team in 1972.

Kuroishi took over the team's direction after its leader, Kyoko Sato, was stricken with a kidney ailment and had to be returned to Japan. Born in Yamagata, Aug. 5, 1925, she started climbing in 1950 after graduating from Tokyo Women's Medical College. Over the years she scaled most of the prominent Japanese mountains, climbed in the Peruvian Andes, and had done some trekking in Nepal. A doctor of internal medicine, she regarded mountaineering as a hobby, like golf. Neighbourhood doctors took care of her patients when she was away on long climbs. Married to an economist turned drugstore owner, she has no children—and thinks men are superior mountain climbers. (JOHN P. RODERICK)

LAUGERUD GARCÍA, KJELL EUGENIO

A 44-year-old army general, Kjell Laugerud García was elected president of Guatemala on March 3, 1974, over two other soldier-candidates in a contest that was basically like a division of opinion on a military promotion board. He won because he was the handpicked successor to the outgoing president, Carlos Manuel Arana Osorio, also an army officer, and because there was little real difference in the slightly right-of-centre positions of the three candidates. When army backers of the two losing candidates from the Demócrata Cristiano and Revolucionario parties chose not to challenge the election, Laugerud was inaugurated for a four-year term on July 1.

Laugerud was born Jan. 24, 1930, in Guatemala City, the son of a Norwegian immigrant father and a native-born Guatemalan mother. He rose to eminence by way of the Politécnica, Guatemala's military academy, where he graduated in 1949 and eventually became superintendent in 1965. He later served as military attaché in the U.S. and was defense minister of Guatemala until resigning in 1973 to run against Gen. José Efrain Ríos Montt of the Partido Demócrata Cristiano and Col. Ernesto Píaz Novales of the Partido Revolucionario.

Laugerud was the candidate of the combined Movimiento de Liberación Nacional (MLN) and the Partido Institucional Democrático (PID), a mildly rightist coalition that had successfully elected Arana four years earlier. Laugerud declared himself unalterably opposed to the return of Cuba to full membership in the Organization of American States. And, as all Guatemalan politicians must, he asserted Guatemala's claim to sovereignty over the British colony of Belize.

Laugerud faced serious economic problems in Guatemala, which suffered considerably from the higher prices it had to pay for imported oil. With Marxist guerrilla movements remaining a potential threat to the nation's stability, Laugerud was expected to remain a firm friend of the U.S.

(JEREMIAH A. O'LEARY)

LECANUET, JEAN ADRIEN FRANÇOIS

Appointed minister of justice in the new French government formed after the May 1974 election of Valéry Giscard d'Estaing (*q.v.*) as president of the republic, Jean Lecanuet became a leading member of the regime he had once effectively opposed. In 1965 he had himself been a candidate for the presidency; then youthful-looking at

45, with a brilliant smile, he made television appearances during the presidential election campaign that charmed 15% of the voters (against an expected 2–3%) into casting their votes for him, and so forced the founder and leader of the Fifth Republic, Gen. Charles de Gaulle, to a second ballot. For the Gaullists this was a kind of lese majesty, and consequently during the remainder of de Gaulle's presidency and the ensuing five years of Georges Pompidou's, Lecanuet was confined to a posture of ineffectual opposition.

Following Pompidou's death, the scene changed. Lecanuet, whose Democratic Centre Party had in 1972 joined with the Radical Party of Jean-Jacques Servan-Schreiber to establish the Reform Movement, rallied to Giscard, bringing to the latter the votes of a large portion of the former Christian Democrats who formed the rank and file of the Democratic Centre. The Reform Movement lost its cohesion and, eventually, its formal existence, after Servan-Schreiber, who became minister of reforms in the new government, was dismissed for criticizing French nuclear policy; but Lecanuet's Democratic Centre Party remained an indispensable ally of President Giscard's Independent Republicans in developing policies of social change and liberalization.

Lecanuet was born on March 4, 1920, in Rouen. Active in the Resistance during World War II, he was arrested once by the Germans but escaped. After the war he helped form the (Roman Catholic) People's Republican Movement (MRP), of which he became president in 1963 and which in 1966 merged into the Democratic Centre. Lecanuet became a deputy in 1951 and served in Edgar Faure's government of 1955. As mayor of Rouen and president of the Regional Council he established a solid personal power base in Normandy.

(PIERRE VIANSSON-PONTÉ)

LÉGER, JULES

On Jan. 14, 1974, Jules Léger became Canada's 21st governor-general. As such, he was the representative of Queen Elizabeth II in Canada, charged with the duties of summoning and dissolving Parliament, giving the royal assent to parliamentary bills, and reading the speech from the throne at the opening of each session of Parliament. He was unable to perform that duty when the 30th Parliament opened on September 30, however. He was convalescing from a stroke suffered on June 8, and the speech was read by Chief Justice Bora Laskin. The chief justice had been sworn in on July 2 as administrator of Canada, a post filled only when the governor-general has died or is absent or incapacitated.

Jules Léger

CANADIAN PRESS

Léger was the second governor-general of French Canadian origin. A brother, Paul Émile Cardinal Léger, had been archbishop of Montreal but gave up that post to work among lepers in Africa. Jules Léger was born in St. Anicet, Que., on April 4, 1913, and was educated in Canada and France. After receiving his B.A. from Valleyfield College in Quebec (1933), he studied law at the University of Montreal (1933–36) and the Sorbonne in Paris.

A quiet, reflective man, a scholar, art collector, and man of letters, Léger has been called "one of the most brilliant minds in the public service." After joining the Canadian government as third secretary in the Department of External Affairs in 1940, he saw service in Chile, Mexico, England, Italy, France, Belgium, and Luxembourg. He was adviser to the Canadian delegation to the UN General Assembly in Paris (1948–49) and ambassador to NATO (1958–62). Within Canada, he had served as undersecretary of state for external affairs (1954–58) and undersecretary of state for arts, cultural support, bilingualism, education, and citizenship (1968–73). In August 1973 he was made a Companion of the Order of Canada.

In Léger's view, the office of governor-general symbolized the stability of Canadian national life and the permanence of Canadian institutions. He valued both Canadian cultures and had regard for all aspects of Canadian life.   (DIANE LOIS WAY)

LÓPEZ MICHELSEN, ALFONSO

On Aug. 7, 1974, after an overwhelming electoral victory as standard-bearer of the Liberal Party, Alfonso López Michelsen was inaugurated president of Colombia. It was the first time in 16 years that Colombia had departed from the Frente Nacional arrangement, in which, by agreement, the Liberals and Conservatives alternated in the presidency—a system adopted to end the political violence between the two factions.

López, a lawyer who was considered a leftist radical in his youth, was the son of the reformer Alfonso López Pumarejo, one of the greatest presidents Colombia had had in this century. In the April 21, 1974, national election, López ran up a margin of more than a million votes above his nearest rival, Álvaro Gómez Hurtado of the Conservative Party. María Eugenia Rojas de Moreno Díaz, leader of the populist National Popular Alliance and daughter of the former dictator Gen. Gustavo Rojas Pinilla, ran a poor third.

Once an open radical who advocated relations with Cuba when that was far from popular in the rest of Latin America, López made his peace with the orthodox Liberals in 1967 and became a state governor and then foreign minister from 1967 to 1970. By the time he became president, Colombia was in the forefront of the political battle to restore Cuba to full membership in the Organization of American States.

Born in Bogotá on June 30, 1913, López was educated at the Lycée Pascal in Paris, the University of Chile, and at the Georgetown University School of Foreign Service in Washington, D.C. He taught administrative law at Bogotá National University and became immersed in politics at an early age. In 1962 he was defeated in his first bid for his country's presidency but was elected a senator, opposing the Liberal-Conservative coalition.

Even though the Frente Nacional arrangement ended formally with López' election, the system of parity between the Liberals and Conservatives was to continue for four more years in regard to the appointments

of governors, mayors, and Cabinet ministers. Then Colombia was scheduled to return to freewheeling partisan politics amid hopes that there would be no repetition of the Liberal-versus-Conservative violence that took some 200,000 lives from 1948 until 1957 when the Frente Nacional was first established.   (JEREMIAH A. O'LEARY)

McGIBBON, PAULINE MILLS

On April 10, 1974, Pauline McGibbon was installed as the 22nd lieutenant governor of Ontario, the first woman to hold a viceregal post in Canada. As a lover of the theatre, she had an appreciation for the ceremony of her office, which included a horse-drawn carriage to ride to the opening of the legislature where, as representative of Queen Elizabeth II in Ontario, she would read the speech from the throne.

She did not intend to appear in a uniform, but had she decided to wear one, she would have had ample medals for it. An officer of the Order of Canada and a Dame of the Order of St. Lazarus of Jerusalem, she had received the Canadian Drama Award for outstanding service to theatre (1957), the Canadian Centennial Medal (1967), and Toronto's Civic Award of Merit (1967).

Coming from "a generation of women who didn't take up professional careers," Mrs. McGibbon went into volunteer work. Without children, she had no chance of election to the school board, so she made a career of service to education and the arts, working through a seemingly limitless list of organizations and offices: national president of the Imperial Order of the Daughters of the Empire (1963–65), first president of the national Children's Film Library, chairman of the board of the National Theatre School of Canada (1956–68), vice-president of the Canadian Conference on the Arts, director of the Canadian Association for the Mentally Retarded. In 1971 she became the first woman chancellor of the University of Toronto; she had received her B.A. from the university's Victoria College in 1933.

Her first speaking engagement as lieutenant governor was in Sarnia, Ont., where she was born Pauline Emily Mills on Oct. 10, 1910. She had been married since 1935 to another Sarnia native, Donald W. McGibbon, the treasurer of Imperial Oil Ltd. Mrs. McGibbon believed her appointment could not have happened ten years earlier, before the women's movement had changed community attitudes. Viewing her post as principally one of public relations, she looked forward to touring the province and encouraging those who were trying to improve the quality of life. (DIANE LOIS WAY)

MACHEL, SAMORA MOISES

When the Portuguese revolution in April 1974 heralded the imminent end of Portugal's long era of colonialism in Africa, Samora Machel became the foremost contender for the post of first president of Mozambique, which by agreement with the new Portuguese government was to achieve full independence the following year. As military commander of the Front for the Liberation of Mozambique (Frelimo), established in 1962 under the leadership of Eduardo Mondlane, Machel became a member of the triumvirate formed following Mondlane's assassination in 1969. In 1970 he was elected Frelimo's president.

Machel was born in Gaza, southern Mozambique, in October 1933. When his eldest brother was killed in an accident in the

South African mines (for which $25 compensation was paid), his parents could not afford to keep him at school, but he managed to pay his own way through primary school by working in the Protestant mission school's fields. He then trained as a male nurse and studied after hours in a secondary school for adults. He met Mondlane in 1961, at a time when the anti-Portuguese struggle had just begun in Angola. The following year he crossed into Tanzania to join Frelimo's guerrilla forces. Returning to the Mozambique bush after military training in Algeria, he quickly distinguished himself as a military leader and in 1968 was given command of the guerrilla forces.

Machel's appearance was gentle rather than military. He was by nature a conciliator, but could be a man of iron when the occasion demanded. The greatest influence on his thinking had been Pres. Julius Nyerere of Tanzania, who preached an essentially African approach to socialism. Although a committed Pan-Africanist, Machel was expected to be pragmatic in his relations with South Africa. He behaved with warm friendship and tolerance toward the Portuguese in response to their change of policies. When on Sept. 20, 1974, a provisional Mozambican administration was installed, Machel emphasized that Frelimo had never "fought against the Portuguese people or against the white race." (COLIN LEGUM)

MAKARIOS III

Archbishop of the Greek Orthodox Church of Cyprus, ethnarch (national leader) of the Greek population of the island from Oct. 18, 1950, and president of the republic of Cyprus from Dec. 13, 1959, Makarios narrowly escaped assassination on July 15, 1974, when the Greek Cypriot National Guard, officered by mainland Greeks, attempted a coup to achieve *enosis*, or union, with Greece. Planned in Athens by the military junta, the coup was sparked by a letter of July 2 from Makarios to Gen. Phaidon Gizikis,

Makarios III

the Greek president, asserting that more than once Makarios had sensed the risk of assassination from Athens. On March 8, 1970, in fact, he had escaped unhurt after shots had downed his helicopter. Later, two more attempts were made to kill Makarios, as a traitor to *enosis*.

In his letter Makarios asked Gizikis to recall the Greek officers of the National Guard. In the morning of July 15, the guard's tanks and artillery attacked Makarios' residence in Nicosia. At 10 A.M. his death was announced over the radio, and at 2:55 P.M. Nikos Sampson was sworn in as president. But Makarios had succeeded in fleeing to Paphos, from which he was eventually flown to Malta and London. In October he pleaded his cause at the United Nations in New York City, and then went to Athens at the end of November. On December 7 he was given a rapturous welcome by Greek Cypriots when he returned to Nicosia.

Makarios (Mihail Khristodolou Mouskos) was born at Ano Panayia, near Paphos, Cyprus, on Aug. 13, 1913. He attended the University of Athens, and in 1946 was ordained a priest. He later studied sociology and theology at Boston (Mass.) University. In 1948 he was elected bishop of Kition in Cyprus. Engaging in politics, he organized a national movement in Cyprus for *enosis* but later considered full independence to be a preferable alternative. In 1956 he was deported by the British to the Seychelles because he was alleged to be involved in the terrorist campaign to achieve independence. Released from exile in 1957, he returned to Cyprus in March 1959 after the signing of the London agreement on Cyprus. In December he was elected president, taking office in August 1960 when Cyprus attained full independence. (K. M. SMOGORZEWSKI)

MAORI KIKI, ALBERT

A key figure in Papua New Guinea's march toward independence, Albert Maori Kiki faced added responsibilities in 1974. Following the death of Paulus Arek, he was given the trade portfolio in Papua New Guinea's administration. As he was already minister for defense and foreign minister, he had substantial duties. His major task was to consult with Australia over defense policy in the period immediately following the territory's independence (set back from the target date of December 1 until some time in 1975). In the diplomatic field he directed the establishment of Papua New Guinean consulates or high commissions in Sydney, Canberra, Suva (Fiji), Jakarta (Indonesia), Wellington (N.Z.), Tokyo, and at the United Nations. He took no part in the controversial public discussions on the post-independence constitution.

At his April 4 meeting with the Australian deputy prime minister, L. H. Barnard, Maori Kiki emphasized that the ultimate decisions on Papua New Guinea's defense capabilities and the structure of its defense forces must rest with the Papua New Guinea government. He was willing to discuss continued Australian support after independence in the fields of finance and personnel and equipment, and he also looked forward to the continuance of cooperation in other ways, such as the joint training and exercising of Australian and Papua New Guinean defense forces.

Maori Kiki was born in Orokolo village, Gulf District, in 1931. He was educated at a mission school at Sogeri, and at a medical school in Fiji. He worked as a patrol and welfare officer, was founder of Papua New Guinea's first labour union and president of the Port Moresby Council of Trade Unions, and served as a member of the National Education Board. He left a promising career in the Public Service to found the Pangu Pati (the independence party). Maori Kiki organized the Pangu Pati's election campaign in 1968, and helped to devise the slogan and platform "One name, one country, one people." He was himself unsuccessful in the election, narrowly losing the seat of Kikori, but subsequently under his guidance the emerging nation developed sound lines of foreign policy and defense.
(A. R. G. GRIFFITHS)

MARSH, JEAN

Part Edwardian comedy of manners, part superior soap opera, the London Weekend Television series "Upstairs, Downstairs" became the hit of U.S. public television in

1974. Set in one of the great houses of pre-World War I London, the series' self-contained episodes counterpointed the lives of the upper-class Bellamy family and of the servants below stairs—Hudson the butler, Mrs. Bridges the cook, and Rose the head housemaid, the last a role that had made Jean Marsh a star.

Marsh had been partly responsible for starting the series in the first place. She and fellow actress Eileen Atkins conceived the idea when they discovered they both had parents who had been in domestic service and decided that, instead of the walk-on parts usually assigned to them, the servants should be given equal time with the masters. Atkins was to have played Sarah, the rebellious maid featured in the early episodes. Other commitments prevented it, but Marsh went on to make Rose a vital part of the series, slightly enigmatic, suggesting a private personality that was never made fully explicit.

The series was an immediate success in Britain. Thirteen of the first 26 episodes appeared on U.S. public television early in 1974 (with Alastair Cooke summarizing the missing sections), and by popular demand another 13 were shown in the winter of 1974–75. In Britain, meanwhile, the story had been carried into the Great War, and a final series had been filmed but had not yet been shown.

Jean Marsh was born in London in the mid-1930s. Paralyzed by shock during the blitz, she was enrolled by her parents in a dancing class in the hope that it would help her recover. This was her first contact with the stage, and by 16 she was playing leading roles in repertory and bit parts in movies. In the late 1950s she appeared on Broadway in *Much Ado About Nothing* with Sir John Gielgud, and subsequently her credits ranged from a robot girl in the TV series "Twilight Zone" to a neurotic secretary in Alfred Hitchcock's movie *Frenzy*. But it was "Upstairs, Downstairs" that brought her public acclaim. In 1972 she was voted Britain's best female television personality, and in 1974 she received the Variety Club of Great Britain award as ITV (Independent Television) personality of the year.

(DAPHNE DAUME)

MARSHALL, MIKE

Many of his Los Angeles Dodger teammates considered Mike Marshall an intellectual snob—a physical education major masquerading as a member of the cognoscenti. But those same teammates did appreciate Marshall's strong right arm, which made them richer while making Marshall the premier relief pitcher in baseball.

Marshall helped propel Los Angeles to its first National League pennant in eight years in 1974 as he appeared in a record-setting 106 games. That broke the mark of 92 he had set in 1973 while still with the Montreal Expos. Marshall also registered a won-lost record of 15–12 and saved 21 games for the Dodgers in their drive to the pennant.

The reward for his achievement was the National League's coveted Cy Young Award for most outstanding pitcher. Marshall became the first relief pitcher ever to win that lofty prize. In fact, the only other reliever to win a major award from the Baseball Writers Association of America was Jim Konstanty, then with the Philadelphia Phillies, who was the National League's most valuable player in 1950.

After receiving the Cy Young Award, Marshall said he was strongly considering retirement. He expected to receive a doctorate in physiological psychology from Michigan State University, and maintained that he might rather teach than play baseball. But Dodger officials who paid Marshall $87,000 for the 1974 campaign, fully expected him to report for duty in the spring.

Born on Jan. 15, 1943, in Adrian, Mich., Marshall bounced around the minor leagues for eight years and finally broke into the majors with a 3–10 record for the Seattle Pilots in their solitary season in the American League in 1969. From there, he moved to the Detroit Tigers and then to the Houston Astros, who used him for four games before shipping him to Montreal.

Marshall did not get rolling until the 1971 season, when his assortment of sliders, screwballs, and fastballs, plus his remarkable stamina, made him a star. He saved 23 games that year and then in 1972 won 14, lost 8, and carved an incredible earned run average of 1.78. The following year, he appeared in 179 innings and thus became the first relief pitcher to qualify for the earned run title. He finished fourth in that category with a 2.66 mark and was traded the following winter to Los Angeles for outfielder Willie Davis.

(J. TIMOTHY WEIGEL)

MILLER, ARNOLD

If it had not been for a particularly bestial murder, Arnold Miller in 1974 would still have been subsisting in the wretched coal-mining town of Ohley, W.Va., while his adversary resided in Washington, D.C., riding in a Cadillac and drawing an executive salary. But Miller's story really began more than a decade earlier, when John L. Lewis retired after 30 years as head of the United Mine Workers.

Arnold Miller

Lewis' handpicked successor as president of the 207,000-member union was W. A. ("Tony") Boyle. By the late 1960s Boyle faced a strong insurgent movement, led by Joseph A. ("Jock") Yablonski, and in 1969 Yablonski challenged Boyle for the union presidency. He lost, after a violence-marred campaign. On Dec. 31, 1969, three hoodlums hired by Boyle with $20,000 in embezzled union funds entered Yablonski's home and shot him, his wife, and daughter.

On the day of Yablonski's funeral, a group of his supporters met to plan their strategy. Joseph L. Rauh, Jr., a liberal labour lawyer, would work through the courts while Mike Trbovich, a miner, led a new insurgent movement, later named Miners for Democracy. Arnold Miller, though not a founder, joined at once. Born in 1922, Miller had dropped out of school in the ninth grade to work in the pits. Severely wounded at a Normandy beach in World War II, he later returned to the mines and eventually became head of the Black Lung Association. He was himself a victim of black lung disease, which results from constant exposure to coal dust.

A series of court cases exposed corruption in the union, and in 1972 a U.S. district court declared the 1969 election invalid— the new one was to be monitored by 1,000 Department of Labor poll watchers to ensure an honest count. To everyone's surprise, the Miners for Democracy nominated Miller rather than Trbovich, though Miller had done considerable quiet politicking beforehand. He campaigned on a platform of pensions, greater mine safety, and opposition to corruption, traveling from mine to mine with an armed bodyguard. When the votes were counted, he had 70,373 to Boyle's 56,334. Yablonski's killers were caught rather easily, and from them the trail led upward until Boyle was found guilty on three counts of first-degree murder. In 1974 Arnold Miller, taking advantage of the new leverage the energy crisis had given to coal, led the miners through a 24-day strike to a new contract that would raise their total compensation 54% over three years. He had sold the union's Cadillacs.

(VICTOR M. CASSIDY)

NAMATH, JOSEPH WILLIAM

Dec. 8, 1974, was a windy, rainswept Sunday in New York, and the playing field for the last home game of the season in Shea Stadium was a sea of mud. Only 32,805 loyal fans assembled in the inclement weather to watch a relatively undistinguished New York Jets team take on the much stronger Buffalo

Bills, who had already gained a play-off spot in the American Football Conference. With the Jets trailing 10–6 and only four minutes left in the game, Jet quarterback Joe Namath faded back and threw a 36-yd. touchdown pass to Jerome Barkum in the end zone, thereby beating the Bills and continuing the football heroics his fans had come to expect.

It was the fifth straight victory for the Jets, and the following week they beat Baltimore to even their season's won-lost mark at 7–7 after a disastrous beginning. Namath was voted the most valuable player on the squad, and the passing statistics for 1974 attest to the correlation between his efforts and the Jets' success. During the first eight games Namath completed about 50% of his passes and had 17 intercepted. During the Jets' subsequent six-game winning streak, however, his completions increased to 58% and his interceptions numbered only five.

Thus, the season was concluded in style. Indeed, style was virtually synonymous with the name of this premier quarterback of professional football, whom many consider the best passer the game has seen. The legend began prior to the 1969 Super Bowl when Namath boasted that his New York Jets, of the then fledgling American Football League, would handily beat the mighty Baltimore Colts, champions of the old, established National Football League. The prediction seemed ludicrous, and the Colts were favoured to win by three touchdowns. But Namath completed 19 of 28 passes that day and led the Jets to an astonishing 16–7 win that will long be remembered in football annals.

Unmarried at 31, Namath has become widely known as one fond of the good life off the field. He was often seen in the company of beautiful girls, and his image as a playboy has been enhanced by two notable television commercials, one involving shaving cream—and girls—and the other showing him clad in panty hose. He also appeared in motion pictures and was at one time part owner of a New York nightclub.

Namath played out his option with the Jets in 1974 and the Shea Stadium legions may not see his like again. Some thought that the former University of Alabama All-American from Beaver Falls, Pa., would retire from the game because of his oft-injured legs, but others held that "Broadway Joe" would throw again, perhaps for some other club, if the price was right.

(LAWRENCE K. LUSTIG)

NEVELSON, LOUISE

Her earliest memory is of a candy shop, its glass jars set together on tiers of shelves, light streaming through to make a rainbow of colour. Perhaps Louise Nevelson has carried this impression into her art; today, she is best known for sculptural walls produced during the 1950s and 1960s. She coloured found objects and odd bits of lumber, glued them into open-faced wooden boxes similarly painted, and then stacked these on top of each other to make free-standing walls. Several such large works, carefully positioned and lighted in a gallery, formed an environment or tableau.

Nevelson saw the candy shop in 1903. She was four then, traveling from her birthplace in Kiev, Russia, to join her father, Isaac Berliawsky, who had emigrated somewhat earlier to Maine where he owned a lumberyard and worked as a building con-

Jack Nicholson

tractor. Nevelson spent her youth in Maine and at age nine fiercely declared that she would someday sculpt rather than paint since she considered colour a crutch. Instead of going directly to art school, however, she married Charles Nevelson, a businessman, in 1920 and went with him to live in New York City. There she studied all the arts—voice, painting, dance—and chafed at her social duties as an upper middle class matron. After years of indecision, she abandoned husband and child and went to Europe.

After studying in Europe, Nevelson returned to New York and worked for a time as assistant to the Mexican muralist Diego Rivera. She exhibited for the first time in various group shows during 1933 and 1934; her blocky sculptures, usually clay, showed strong Cubist influence. In 1943 she exhibited her first environment, a group called "The Circus—the Clown is the Center of the World." This show, though well-received, brought no sales.

After some years of infrequent exhibitions, Nevelson in 1958 began her work on sculptural walls. This occurred when a friend sent her a carton of liquor for Christmas. After removing the bottles, she suddenly saw the cardboard box and its square compartments as a sculpture in itself. She then fashioned wood reliefs by placing various objects in boxes—everything being painted black. About this time, she began to win genuine recognition. In 1959, New York's Museum of Modern Art showed a group of her columns, boxes, free-standing objects and walls, all painted white to everyone's surprise, rather than the black used previously. New York's Whitney Museum of American Art presented the first major Nevelson retrospective in 1967.

In the late 1960s and early 1970s Nevelson began to experiment with metal and plexiglass, producing large sculptures quite different from her works in wood. Geometric elements replaced found objects; she arrested the viewer by bolting plexiglass together instead of gluing it invisibly as other artists did. By 1974 she was working with

wood again and was also taking up aluminum. (VICTOR M. CASSIDY)

NICHOLAS, CINDY

Sixteen-year-old Cindy Nicholas did not intend to begin her swim of Lake Ontario that morning in August 1974. She and her party had driven from Toronto to Youngstown, N.Y., merely to examine lake conditions. But both the weather and water were ideal, and her swimming coach decided she should not wait.

Hasty preparations were made. The U.S. Coast Guard was asked to accompany the party's 14-ft. outboard motorboat to Canadian waters, but the request was refused because of bureaucratic red tape. However, four young Americans who lived nearby agreed to go part way in a 33-ft. motorized sailboat. So, after a quick snack on board the sailboat, Cindy dove into the water at 2:32 A.M., Aug. 16, 1974, and was on her way to becoming the second person to swim Lake Ontario. With her were her father, coach Al Waites, pacer Bruce Waites, and a Toronto reporter.

Cindy set a pace of 72 strokes a minute, slowing occasionally to 68. At 6:25 A.M. the American boat turned back, leaving the party alone, since none of the expected Canadian boats had appeared. Currents and drift add several miles to the 32-mi. distance between Youngstown and Toronto, but Cindy did not realize the extent of this and at one point thought she was almost done when there were actually 12 mi. left. Undaunted, she later confided that she "could have gone another 20 if necessary." Cindy reached the shore at Toronto at 5:45 P.M. and was greeted by a flotilla of pleasure craft and several city dignitaries. According to her stopwatch, the 40-mi. swim had taken 15 hours and 10 minutes.

Cynthia Maria Nicholas was born in Toronto on Aug. 20, 1957. Introduced to the water at the age of two by her father, a school vice-principal, she began competitive swimming when she was five. She had read articles about Marilyn Bell, who as a 16-year-old became the first person to swim Lake Ontario in 1954, and she had a great desire to prove that today's teenagers can do as well as the last generation. The good weather even enabled her to take six hours off Marilyn's record.

That ambition accomplished, for the moment Cindy was concentrating on her grade 12 schoolwork. She hoped to become either a research chemist or a teacher. But someday, she admitted, she might attempt to swim the Juan de Fuca Strait between Vancouver Island and Washington state.

(DIANE LOIS WAY)

NICHOLSON, JACK

"The people who never saw my [early] movies are better off in life than I am," said the star of *Cry-Baby Killer,* which was widely unseen in 1958. In 1974, however, Jack Nicholson took whatever roles he wanted for almost any price he named. He had worked, trained, and hustled his way to the top of the film trade as an actor's actor with an immense popular following. Almost uniquely, he was a star without a stock screen image. As a British critic wrote, "He is one of the few major screen actors around who, like Olivier, can change his physical identity from part to part."

Born in Neptune, N.J., on April 22, 1937, Nicholson started acting in high school because "all the chicks that I liked were doing plays." Ranked among the top 2% of all college entrance candidates, he avoided college by going to Los Angeles where his sister was working as a showgirl. He landed a job as a $30-a-week mail clerk at MGM and signed up for Jeff Corey's acting class with two other neophytes, James Coburn and Sally Kellerman. He found acting work where he could—with Boris Karloff once and on television's "Divorce Court" countless times as a habitual co-respondent.

In 1969 he was the production chief and budget overseer for Dennis Hopper and Peter Fonda, who had begun making an unconventional motorcycle epic. When Rip Torn threw over the key supporting role of a drunken, small-town, Dixie lawyer, Nicholson stepped in. He stole the show, made *Easy Rider* a memorable film, and won the New York Film Critics' Award. He went on to appear as the misanthropic pianist turned oil rigger in *Five Easy Pieces,* the emotional brute in Mike Nichols' *Carnal Knowledge,* the soulful, salty, madcap sailor in *The Last Detail,* the inscrutable opportunistic detective in Roman Polanski's *Chinatown.*

He seemed to prove a seminal point in

Louise Nevelson

AL MOZELL—THE PACE GALLERY/COURTESY, ART NEWS

Chinatown in 1974. As an actor, Nicholson could be all things to all people—an anti-hero to film cultists, a who-done-what hero to mystery lovers, a romantic match for Faye Dunaway fans, a near nemesis for villainous tycoon John Huston, a brilliantly adaptable talent for the demanding Polanski, the critics' darling, and the best thing for a theatre's income since popcorn.

(PHILIP KOPPER)

NIXON, RICHARD MILHOUS

In 1974 Richard Nixon became the first president of the United States to resign his office. He did so on August 8, faced with the virtual certainty that he would be impeached and convicted by Congress for his part in the Watergate scandals. Nixon's resignation was submitted two years and 52 days after burglars employed by his Committee for the Re-election of the President were arrested in the Democratic Party's national headquarters at the Watergate complex in Washington.

Nixon's political and legal defenses had been crumbling gradually since the break-in. In 1974 they collapsed. Seven of his close associates and advisers were indicted by a federal grand jury in March on Watergate-related criminal charges. The same grand jury named Nixon himself as an unindicted co-conspirator. On July 24, the U.S. Supreme Court ruled 8–0 that Nixon could not withhold from Watergate Special Prosecutor Leon Jaworski (*q.v.*) 64 subpoenaed White House tape recordings. Then, on August 5, Nixon revealed that one of the subpoenaed tapes showed that he had participated in the Watergate cover-up as early as June 23, 1972.

Nixon's admission effectively eliminated whatever chance he had of remaining in office until 1976. Watergate had dominated his entire second term, and never more so than in 1974 when it severely limited the administration's ability to deal with a wide range of serious domestic and international problems.

After his resignation, Nixon sought seclusion at his San Clemente, Calif., estate. But he could not escape the repercussions of Watergate. On September 8, his successor, Gerald Ford (*q.v.*), issued a controversial "full, free and absolute pardon" for any crimes Nixon may have committed as president. Nixon's physicians, meanwhile, insisted that he could not testify at the trial of his former associates because of a blood clot in his left leg, for which he was hospitalized in late September and operated on in late October. Nixon went into shock following surgery, and for a time there was serious concern for his life. Later, a panel of three court-appointed physicians examined Nixon and recommended that he not be forced to testify at the Watergate defendants' trial in 1974. Judge John Sirica concurred and ordered the trial to continue.

Nixon was born Jan. 9, 1913, in Yorba Linda, Calif. He attended Whittier College and received a law degree from Duke University Law School. Following duty in the U.S. Navy during World War II, he served in the U.S. House of Representatives and later the U.S. Senate before he was elected vice-president in 1952. He ran unsuccessfully as the Republican candidate for president in 1960, but tried again in 1968 and narrowly defeated Hubert Humphrey. Nixon was reelected by a landslide margin over George McGovern in 1972. His administration's most notable achievements were in international relations, achievements symbolized by his tour of the Middle East in June and his Moscow summit meeting with Soviet leaders in July.

(STANLEY WILLS CLOUD)

ODUBER QUIRÓS, DANIEL

A protégé of his Central American country's national hero, José "Pepe" Figueres, Daniel Oduber Quirós was elected president of Costa Rica on Feb. 3, 1974, for a four-year term. His victory as candidate of the Partido de Liberación Nacional marked the first time one party had won consecutive elections in modern Costa Rican history.

Oduber was inaugurated on May 8. It soon became apparent that the well-read middle class intellectual and lawyer was off on a new and independent political and economic tack in contrast to his earlier position. Once, like Figueres, an ardent foe of Prime Minister Fidel Castro of Cuba and a close economic and political ally of the U.S., Oduber and his government took the lead in the fight within the Organization of American States to lift the economic sanctions against Cuba. He also presided over a government that was in the forefront of the movement by banana-producing nations to form a cartel to raise the cash value of that fruit crop. (*See* Panama.)

Oduber was foreign minister of Costa Rica in 1963 when his country was one of the most outspoken enemies of the Cuban dictatorship and favoured a show of force in order to remove the Soviet troops on the island. But, like much of Latin America, Costa Rica had swung around to the position of wanting the return of Cuba to the hemispheric family.

Oduber was born in San José on Aug. 25, 1921. He worked his way through college and law school in San José and then opened a law firm there. Later he studied at McGill University in Montreal and at the Sorbonne in Paris.

Oduber first became active in politics at the age of 19. In 1956 he became secretary-general of the Partido de Liberación Nacional and two years later was elected to Congress. He made an unsuccessful bid for the presidency in 1961 and served as foreign minister from 1962 to 1966.

Oduber was narrowly defeated in 1966 as his party's candidate for the presidency and resigned as president of the legislative assembly to run again in 1974. In this at-

tempt he won over seven other candidates, gaining 43% of the vote.

(JEREMIAH A. O'LEARY)

ONODA, HIROO

Controversy over possibly latent Japanese militarism revived in 1974 with the formal surrender in the Philippines of Imperial Army 2nd Lieut. Hiroo Onoda, 52, after he had received a direct order from his former commanding officer. For more than 29 years, Onoda had obeyed his last order, to gather intelligence and conduct guerrilla operations even if the Japanese Army had surrendered. Lubang islanders claimed that armed Japanese on these missions had killed 30 and wounded perhaps 100. Philippine officials, however, blamed many casualties on Filipino bandits.

Deemed the second "last soldier" of World War II (the first "last soldier" of Japan, Shoichi Yokoi, surrendered in the jungles of Guam in 1972), Onoda had preserved his rifle, ammunition, hand grenades, and sword along with a helmet and uniform. Onoda evaded intensive air and ground searches of tiny Lubang Island (74 sq.mi.). He ignored pamphlets reprinting Emperor Hirohito's surrender and pleas by megaphone from his two brothers who accompanied private Japanese search parties.

The English-speaking Onoda listened to the world over a transistor radio. But he told the 24-year-old Japanese adventurer Norio Suzuki, who lured him from hiding in February 1974, that as a Japanese officer he could not surrender without a cancellation of his orders. Former Maj. Yoshimi Taniguchi, now 63 and a bookstore owner, flew to the island and read to his wartime subordinate the surrender order issued in September 1945.

Military protocol culminated in Manila where Pres. Ferdinand Marcos, a guerrilla fighter against the Japanese during the war, accepted Onoda's proffered sword, returned it, praised his devotion to duty, and par-

DAVID BURNETT—GAMMA

Richard Milhous Nixon

doned him. The dissenting view was summarized by a Manila columnist: "Onoda is a perfect example of the fanatical soldier peculiar to Japanese militarism." Many Japanese echoed this view. Admiration was general for the qualities of courage, loyalty, and self-sacrifice—traditional expressions of the "Japanese spirit." But the *Asahi Shimbun* in a typical editorial commented: "Onoda is an alarm bell tolling a warning to all Japanese against taking the road of the recent past."

Perhaps confirmation that, by objective consensus, Japan today essentially is pacifist came from Onoda himself. Gradually he came to tell friends, "Perhaps it was all useless, but what else could I do as a soldier?" In October he flew to Brazil where his brother operates a flower farm near São Paulo. Offered 120 ha. of land to farm, Onoda decided to start his new life in Brazil. His circumstances were somewhat overshadowed at the end of the year when still another "last soldier" was captured on the remote Indonesian island of Morotai. Like Yokoi and Onoda, Teruo Nakamura was motivated to hold out in the jungles by fear of capture and an unfailing fidelity to orders.

(ROLAND GOULD)

PANOV, VALERY AND GALINA

He wanted to practice his art and to worship God. She refused to abandon her husband. For these unspeakable crimes, Valery and Galina Ragozina Panov suffered two years of constant persecution until an international campaign secured their release from the Soviet Union. Ironically, Panov had replaced Rudolf Nureyev in many principal roles at Leningrad's Kirov Ballet after Nureyev defected to the West in 1961. The Kirov had provided the West with a remarkable stream of dance artists, beginning with George Balanchine in 1924 and continuing with Nureyev, Natalia Makarova, and, most recently, Mikhail Baryshnikov.

Panov's troubles began in 1959 when the dancer, then 20, was on tour in San Francisco. The secret police who accompany all traveling Soviet groups noticed that he was friendly with Americans. A police spy told Panov he must return home because one of his parents had died—a brutal lie concocted to get him back to the U.S.S.R.—and he was not allowed to dance outside the Soviet Union again. The authorities later accused him of talking to Zionists, though at the time Panov, a Jew, did not know what Zionists were.

Despite official suspicions, Panov rose steadily in the Kirov, while his wife, Galina Ragozina (b. 1949), danced with the company as a soloist. Though fully in agreement with the Kirov's classical approach to ballet, Panov, like many of his predecessors, felt artistically shackled there, so in March 1972 he applied for a visa to emigrate to Israel.

The Panovs summed up the next 27 months as "daily sadism." Valery lost his job and his union membership and was convicted of "hooliganism." The secret police cut off the couple's telephone and mail and, worst of all, confined them to a small apartment where they had no room to practice. Galina was demoted from soloist to the corps de ballet and resigned. In their campaign of harassment, the police even accused her of selling pornography.

Meanwhile, a coalition of admirers in the U.S. and Great Britain campaigned for the Panovs' release. Led by Lord Olivier and British Actors Equity, the group approached Soviet officials, picketed touring Soviet groups, and forced cancellation of a U.S. tour by the Kirov. In June 1974 the Soviets abruptly expelled the Panovs, possibly because they feared the uproar threatened détente with the West. Several months of practice in Tel Aviv returned the couple to proper condition, and they made a stage appearance in November. Valery hoped to form a National Ballet of Israel, which had no classical company. "We shall try to dance everywhere," he said, "but . . . always come back to Israel."

(VICTOR M. CASSIDY)

PARK CHUNG HEE

In a flagrant show of dictatorial paranoia, South Korea's Pres. Park Chung Hee decreed in 1974 a total of four emergency measures, one of which made antigovernment criticism punishable by from 15 years' imprisonment to death. Reacting to a growing movement to revise the constitution, which effectively gave him unlimited powers, Park used "the fluctuations of the international economy" and the threat of renewed attack by North Korea as excuses for ruthlessly stamping out political opposition. By August 1974 more than 280 enemies of Park had been arrested—a number had been tried and sentenced to death or life imprisonment. Park's increasing intolerance to criticism included barring foreign journalists who published anything uncomplimentary to his regime. The foreign press was, in fact, prohibited from criticizing its own censorship.

Park was unknown outside of the Army when he engineered the military coup that brought him to power on May 16, 1961. Although he muzzled the press and dissolved the legislature, he was believed to be a genuine reformer dedicated to eradicating corruption. Elected to his first presidential term in 1963, he swore "never to permit the resurgence of dictatorship under any guise or pretext." In 1969 he changed the constitution in order to obtain a third term, later promising to retire in 1975. Then in 1972 Park forced through a new constitution making him president for life.

Born Sept. 30, 1917, near Taegu in southern Son Son Province during the period in which Japan controlled Korea, Park was graduated from Taegu Normal School at the top of his class in 1937 and taught primary school for three years. He served as a second lieutenant in the Japanese Army during World War II and in 1947 was commissioned a captain in the Korean Constabulary. A year later Park was sentenced to death for taking part in a Communist revolt led by Korean officers. Pleading that he had been misled by anti-Japanese nationalism, he was pardoned and returned to full rank after supplying a list of persons involved in Communist activities. After that his military career advanced steadily, and he served as an officer in the Korean War. Always an efficient but puritanical martinet, he refused to take up golf and learned little English while attending the U.S. Army Artillery School at Ft. Sill, Okla., as a brigadier general in 1953. He later prided himself on being one of the few Korean officers without an American nickname.

In August 1974, as Park gave a commemorative speech on the 29th anniversary of Korean liberation from Japanese rule, his second wife, Yook Young Soo, was struck by a bullet during an assassination attempt on Park. Presumably unaware of the seriousness of the wound, he resumed his speech as she was rushed to the hospital, where she died eight hours later.

(DONNA ZIMMERMAN)

PÉREZ, CARLOS ANDRÉS

Barely two months after taking office on March 12, 1974, Pres. Carlos Andrés Pérez of Venezuela requested and received from Congress one year of "emergency economic powers" to reconstruct the economy. Though it was one of the world's major oil producers, Venezuela had a 17% unemployment rate and a highly unequal distribution of wealth. By the end of June the Pérez government had issued 211 economic decrees.

U.S. steel companies learned that their iron-ore concessions would immediately revert to the state. In August, Pérez surprised U.S. oil companies by the speed, if not the content, of a draft bill for their impending nationalization. Still, foreign oilmen might be around for some time. At the current production rate, existing oil reserves could last only 11 years, and Venezuela lacked the

Valery and Galina Panov

technology to develop the crude oil pool of the Orinoco basin. Partly to ensure access to this technology, Pérez planned to invest some of the $11 billion in 1974 oil revenues outside the country.

Pérez was born Oct. 27, 1922, in Rubio, Tachira. A political activist at 16 for the Acción Democrática party, he won his first parliamentary campaign at 22. After Marcos Pérez Jiménez came to power in 1952, he was imprisoned, then exiled. Returning after Pérez Jiménez was overthrown in 1958, he became minister of the interior in Pres. Romulo Betancourt's government. During the '60s he was responsible for the harsh suppression of leftist guerrillas and left office with a tough-cop reputation that he found difficult to overcome.

Employing a U.S. consulting firm to help plot his 1973 presidential campaign, Pérez walked all over the country to create the image of a vigorous reformer. One of 12 candidates in the December 9 election, he received almost 49% of the vote. As president of one of the last remaining democracies in Latin America, he believed Venezuela's success or failure would have a critical effect on other nations: "We are compelled to demonstrate by our example that democracy . . . provides the necessary energy to confront the faces of capitalism."

(DONNA ZIMMERMAN)

PERÓN, MARÍA ESTELA MARTÍNEZ DE

The first woman chief of state in the Western Hemisphere, María Estela Martínez de Perón inherited the presidency of Argentina July 1, 1974, on the death of her 78-year-old husband, Juan Domingo Perón. Isabelita, as she prefers to be known, also inherited economic and political problems that Perón himself, had he lived, probably could not have resolved. In addition to widespread unemployment, severe shortages, and a 30% annual rate of inflation, the nation was torn by chaos within Isabelita's own Justicialista Party, containing both left- and right-wing extremists. More than 100 political assassinations were carried out in 1974; kidnapping and terrorism were so frequent that U.S. and foreign firms virtually stopped all capital investment in Argentina. On November 6, after the assassination of the federal police chief and his wife and a former union official, Mrs. Perón placed the country under a state of siege.

Born to a middle-class family Feb. 4, 1932, in impoverished La Rioja Province, María Estela Martínez was the sixth and youngest child of a bank official who died in 1938. Her formal education having ended in the sixth grade, she studied music and dance and left home in her early 20s to tour Central America with a folk dance troupe called "Joe and His Ballets." While playing the Happyland nightclub in Panama City in 1956, she met the exiled Perón, who had been overthrown in a military coup the previous year. Isabelita became his secretary and companion, following him finally to Spain where they married in 1961. For 17 years she remained in the background, typing manuscripts of his books, answering his correspondence, and watching over his health.

During Perón's triumphant return from exile in June 1973, Isabelita took an increasingly visible role despite the jeering scorn of Argentines who regarded her as cold and ruthless and resented her obvious efforts to emulate Eva Duarte, Perón's immensely popular second wife. Perón outraged both supporters and foes in August 1973 when he announced that Isabelita would be his vice-presidential running mate.

As vice-president Isabelita assumed a strong role, making state visits to China,

María Estela Martínez de Perón

Spain, and Italy. Still, it was generally believed that in the event of Perón's death she would ensure an orderly succession of power by modestly stepping down to allow a strong male figure to become president in new general elections. In 1974, however, she showed no signs of resigning, and no strong male emerged to replace her.

(DONNA ZIMMERMAN)

PONIATOWSKI, MICHEL CASIMIR

"France of the *châteaux* and government by princes" was the mischievous and cutting phrase used by Michel Jobert, former minister of foreign affairs under Georges Pompidou, to describe the new regime of Valéry Giscard d'Estaing (*q.v.*). The remark was clearly directed against Prince Michel Poniatowski, a descendant of the Polish royal family and the power behind the Fifth Republic of Giscard.

An enigmatic man, deceptively stolid in appearance, this close and faithful friend of the youthful chief of state seemed less a zealous aide than a mentor, almost a father figure. Content to take third place in the government, as minister of state and of the interior, he nevertheless readily gave advice—if not instructions—to the premier, Jacques Chirac (*q.v.*), whose post would certainly have been his for the asking.

Grand strategist of the Independent Republicans (Giscardian partners of the Gaullist parliamentary majority), Poniatowski in a speech to the Anglo-American press in Paris on October 22 stated that the government of Giscard d'Estaing would be a long-lasting one. He spoke of "our desire to liberalize French life," and in reference to recent tensions between the Socialist and Communist parties called the latter "totalitarian and fascist in tendency." The Communist paper *L'Humanité* responded with a tart reference to the "minister of police" and to attempts to conceal the "brutally reactionary" nature of the Giscard regime.

Michel Poniatowski, who was born in Paris on May 16, 1922, numbered a marshal of France, an Austrian field marshal, and a king of Poland among his forebears. After graduating in law at Cambridge University, he attended the École Nationale d'Administration for a year and in 1948 joined the Ministry of Finance. After spells at the Ministry of Finance and as financial attaché at the French embassy in Washington (1956), he served briefly in 1958 as economic

and financial counselor at the French embassy in Morocco. From 1959 onward he was closely associated with Giscard d'Estaing at the Ministry of Finance. Elected Independent Republican deputy for the Val-d'Oise in 1967, he was the party's secretary-general during 1967–70.

(PIERRE VIANSSON-PONTÉ)

RABIN, YITZHAK

When Yitzhak Rabin became prime minister of Israel at the head of a Labour-dominated coalition government on June 3, 1974, he shouldered a mantle perhaps weightier than that of any of his predecessors. The shock of the October 1973 war had brought a sobered people back to the realization that they were only 3 million facing 80 million Arabs enjoying vast resources. For many Israelis General Rabin was a welcome change from Prime Minister Golda Meir's "kitchen Cabinet." The man who had presided over Israel's lightning victory in the 1967 Six-Day War and who, as ambassador to the U.S. (1968–73), had raised Israeli-U.S. relations to a new peak, was sufficiently removed from the Meir government's failures to be untainted in the public mind.

Following the first-ever visit of an incumbent U.S. president to Israel in June, Rabin accepted Richard Nixon's return invitation, renewed by Pres. Gerald Ford, and set out for a five-day state visit to Washington, D.C., on September 10. In reply to President Ford's acknowledgment of Israel's spirit of concession, Rabin stressed "Only a strong Israel, which has the capacity . . . to defend herself successfully . . . has a chance of winning peace." In his message for the Jewish New Year, 5735, Rabin declared that Israel would "probe every possible avenue that might lead to the end of the conflict. . . . But Israel will not surrender its vital security in return for palliative arrangements that go by the name of a settlement." While recognizing the need for territorial concessions in

Yitzhak Rabin

return for an Egyptian declaration of non-belligerent status, he utterly rejected, following the Arab leaders' promotion of the Palestine Liberation Organization (PLO) at their Rabat, Morocco, summit meeting, the possibility of negotiations with the PLO ("a body that . . . resorts to violence and terror") on the formation of a Palestinian state between Jordan and Israel.

Born in Jerusalem on March 1, 1922, Rabin took part in the Allied invasion of Syria in 1941 and in 1948 was prominent in the battle for Jerusalem. In 1953 he graduated from the British Staff College and in January 1964 became Israel's seventh chief of staff. On retirement from the Army four years later he was appointed ambassador to the U.S. In the December 1973 election Rabin gained a Knesset seat representing the Labour alignment. Golda Meir made him her minister of labour, and following her resignation in April 1974 he became Labour candidate for the prime ministership.

(R. J. M. DENNERSTEIN)

REDFORD, ROBERT

Robert Redford continued to walk to the beat of his own drummer in 1974. One of Hollywood's established superstars, he avoided offscreen publicity, stayed happily married to his wife of 16 years, kept living in the Utah mountain house he had built with his own hands, and kept on making celebrated movies. He also spent $450,000 for the film rights to a book far too controversial for most filmmakers—*All the President's Men,* the account by *Washington Post* reporters Bob Woodward and Carl Bernstein of how they helped break the story of the Watergate scandals.

Meanwhile, Redford starred in *The Great Gatsby,* an adaptation of F. Scott Fitzgerald's classic novel. Expectations for the film were high because of the original material, the lavish $6 million production, and the cast of talented young actors. But Redford saw an advance screening and—wisely, as it turned out—bucked protocol and boycotted the premieres.

"The golden loner," as *Newsweek* called him, was born in Santa Monica, Calif., Aug. 18, 1937. He won a baseball scholarship to

Robert Redford

the University of Colorado, but soon dropped out, worked in California oil fields, and went to Europe where he painted and eked out a living in Florence and Paris. In New York City he worked as a mail clerk, lived in a slum, and entered art school at Pratt Institute before switching to the American Academy of Dramatic Arts. After appearing in *Tall Story,* he landed the lead role in Neil Simon's Broadway comedy *Barefoot in the Park.* He then appeared in several forgettable movies before taking his Mormon wife and children to Spain.

Redford returned a year later to star in the film version of *Barefoot in the Park.* He then began to concentrate on films with a common thread: the involvement of a questing individual in a particularly American context, past or present. These films included the fabulously successful *Butch Cassidy and the Sundance Kid* with Paul Newman, about an engaging pair of ill-starred outlaws, *Tell Them Willie Boy Is Here, Jeremiah Johnson, The Way We Were,* with Barbra Streisand, and *The Sting,* a gangster adventure that reunited him with Newman and swept the 1974 Academy Awards. After *Downhill Racer,* perhaps the best skiing movie ever made, he met an Olympic champion. "We agreed that it's much more important, and much more fun, trying to get up the mountain than it is once you're there." (PHILIP KOPPER)

RICHLER, MORDECAI

With *The Apprenticeship of Duddy Kravitz* showing signs of becoming the Canadian film industry's first big commercial success in the United States, the author of both the screenplay and the 1959 novel of the same title, Mordecai Richler, long a successful novelist and journalist, was becoming known to an even wider public. The film deals with themes familiar in Richler's writings—the lives of poor Jews in modern Canada and the search of a rootless individual for success in some form—in the comic mode that marks his style. The Duddy of the title is a hustler, a poor boy on the make using means that are often less than savoury, in the Jewish ghetto of Montreal in the late 1940s.

Although his characterizations have earned Richler the accusation of anti-Semitism in some quarters, Richler himself does not see his characters as unsympathetic. Born Jan. 27, 1931, in Montreal, he was raised in the Orthodox Jewish tradition in the ghetto that he writes about, although he lived in England and France during most of his adult life.

The son of a junkyard operator, Richler received his early education in a Jewish religious school and later attended Sir George Williams University. He dropped out of school in 1951 because he wanted to write. After his first novel, *The Acrobats,* was published in 1954, he left Canada, which he found provincial and suffocating, for London, and did not return to his native land permanently until nearly 20 years later. Yet Richler feels himself thoroughly Canadian, and much of his work deals with Canadians, resident or expatriate. In Canada, his special area is the old Jewish ghetto of Montreal: "I do feel forever rooted in Montreal's St. Urbain Street. That was my time, my place, and I have elected myself to get it right."

Richler was writer in residence at Sir George Williams University in 1968–69 and was named visiting professor at Carleton University, Ottawa, in 1972. He received the Canadian Governor-General's Award for Literature in 1969 and 1972. *Son of a Smaller Hero* (1955), *A Choice of Enemies* (1957), *The Incomparable Atuk* (1963), *Cocksure* (1968), and *St. Urbain's Horseman* (1971) are his novels. His short stories, essays, and

reports have been collected in *Hunting Tigers Under Glass* (1968), *The Street* (1969), *Shovelling Trouble* (1973), and *Notes on an Endangered Species and Others* (1974).

(JOAN NATALIE REIBSTEIN)

ROCKEFELLER, NELSON ALDRICH

On Dec. 19, 1974, Nelson Rockefeller, former governor of New York, long-time public servant and politician, and member of one of the world's richest families, was sworn in as vice-president of the United States. He

was the second to be chosen under the terms of the 25th Amendment to the U.S. Constitution, which provides that when the office is vacant a new vice-president shall be nominated by the president and confirmed by Congress. The first was Gerald Ford (*q.v.*), who was nominated by Pres. Richard Nixon when Spiro Agnew resigned in 1973 and then succeeded to the presidency upon Nixon's resignation in August 1974. Thus, for the first time in the country's history, neither the president nor the vice-president had been elected by the people.

Rockefeller was confirmed only after prolonged and grueling hearings in Congress, mostly centring around the question of whether a man of such great wealth could possibly avoid conflicts of interest. Could he take any actions in office that would not affect his vast holdings (net worth $62.6 million) or those of his family? Did lavish gifts he had made to friends and associates represent attempts to buy political support? (Rockefeller denied any improprieties but promised to stop the practice.) Also at issue was a derogatory biography of Arthur J. Goldberg, Rockefeller's opponent in one gubernatorial election, that had been financed with family money. While the hearings were going on, Rockefeller's wife, Margaretta ("Happy"), underwent two operations for breast cancer. In the end, he was confirmed fairly easily—by 90–7 in the Senate and 287–128 in the House.

Rockefeller had held major appointments in the Roosevelt and Eisenhower administrations. He defeated Democrat W. Averell Harriman in the 1958 New York gubernatorial election and was reelected in 1962, 1966, and 1970. In December 1973 he resigned to head the Commission on Critical Choices for Americans, considered a poten-

Peter Wallace Rodino

tial vehicle for a presidential bid. Rockefeller had unsuccessfully sought the Republican presidential nomination in 1960, 1964, and 1968. The 1976 election appeared to be his last chance, but after Ford's accession the nomination seemed certain to go to Ford if he wanted it.

Rockefeller was born July 8, 1908, at Bar Harbor, Me. He was graduated from Dartmouth College, Hanover, N.H., and had a brief business career before entering public life.   (STANLEY WILLS CLOUD)

RODINO, PETER WALLACE

When the constitutional machinery for impeaching a U.S. president clanked to life for the first time in a century, leaders of the U.S. House of Representatives were concerned to find that an obscure 64-year-old Democrat from Newark, N.J., was in charge of a critical part of that mechanism. The leaders' first instinct was to attempt to bypass Peter W. Rodino's House Judiciary Committee by establishing a select committee to consider the impeachment charges against Pres. Richard M. Nixon (q.v.). Rodino, a 25-year veteran of the House whose best-known accomplishment had been making Columbus Day a national holiday, resisted that move.

With no apparent relish, Rodino began preparing himself for the ordeal by reading on the question of impeachment. He set about the problem of staffing the impeachment inquiry, and while other congressmen fumed that he was moving too slowly, Rodino scoured law schools and conferred with bar association leaders in search of a committee counsel. He finally chose John Doar, a Republican. Rodino was well aware that whatever the outcome of the impeachment proceedings, they had to be conducted on an apparently nonpartisan basis. That Doar was a Republican made little difference, however, because soon he and Chairman Rodino were accused by Nixon and his supporters of conducting a Democratic vendetta against the president. It quickly became clear that those in the president's camp were eager to discredit beforehand any negative result the committee might produce.

On the other hand, Rodino's patience and painstaking fairness upset some anti-Nixon members of his own committee. The hearing process, which went on for 11 weeks and produced some 7,200 pages of evidence and testimony, included, when Rodino gave his consent, all six of the defense witnesses that presidential lawyer James St. Clair (q.v.) had requested. In mid-June many liberals on the Judiciary Committee and even some members of the House Democratic leadership feared Rodino had waited too long, and that the momentum for impeachment had waned. Rodino did manage to placate members on both sides of the question, and finally, at 7:05 P.M. on July 27, the committee produced, by a bipartisan vote of 27–11, a

bill calling for the impeachment of Richard Nixon. Within days, however, new evidence that had been withheld from the committee was made public, and even the 11 members supporting the president joined the cry for his impeachment.

Rodino was born in Newark on June 7, 1909, and received his law degree from the University of Newark (Rutgers) in 1937. He served in Europe during World War II with the U.S. Army, then returned to practice law, and in 1948 was elected to Congress. Rodino at one time aspired to be a poet and wrote an unpublished novel about his youth in a tough Italian section of his hometown. The pace of the impeachment inquiry and the unending string of 18-hour days put Rodino in Bethesda Naval Hospital briefly in February, when he feared a heart attack. He was pronounced exhausted and sent home. "If I had it to do over," Rodino joked afterward, "maybe I'd have worked harder to be a poet." But by the fall, Rodino was back in the thick of a political struggle when his committee began hearings on the nomination of Nelson Rockefeller (q.v.) as vice-president. On December 12 the committee recommended Rockefeller's confirmation by a vote of 26–12.   (JOHN F. STACKS)

RODNINA, IRINA

The first ice pair skater to win six world championships, Irina Rodnina achieved the feat in consecutive seasons with two partners. This completed a decade of Soviet dominance in an event first instituted in 1908. The four straight successes of Oleg and Ludmila Protopopov (1965–68) heralded an era when Soviet pairs were supreme, despite the curious fact that a world or European title had yet to be gained by a Soviet solo figure skater.

The classical elegance and technical proficiency of the Protopopov pair was a national breakthrough that inspired their compatriots. With a faster, more robust style, Rodnina joined Aleksey Ulanov in four world victories (1969–72), also winning the Olympic gold medal at Sapporo, Jap., in their final season together. When the partnership broke up, Rodnina showed who had been the real master. With Aleksandr Zaitsev, a then relatively unknown skater, she won her fifth world crown in 1973, incredibly skating half the performance without music. After they had skated half of their five-minute program, their record stopped. They elected to continue without accompaniment and provided a display containing some of the greatest pair movements ever seen, including a memorably brilliant double twist lift. With precisely matched jumps and spins, they put superiority beyond question in a scintillating performance of near-perfect cohesion. The referee afterward offered them the chance to skate again but they agreed to be marked. All nine judges awarded 5.9 for technical merit and seven gave the same mark for

artistic impression. It was an occurrence without precedent.

When they decisively retained the title, in Munich, W.Ger., in March 1974, the Moscow couple were not quite so impressive but nevertheless quite good. In an event where the male is expected to take charge, it was clear that his stocky partner was much the better skater and the guiding force. Born in Moscow on Sept. 12, 1949, Irina Rodnina began to skate at the age of six. She and her two partners were trained by Stanislav Zhuk, whose knowledge of technique and psychological handling was a key factor in molding the most outstanding woman pair skater since championships began.   (HOWARD BASS)

ROWLING, WALLACE EDWARD

When Prime Minister Norman E. Kirk (see OBITUARIES) died on Aug. 31, 1974, New Zealand's parliamentary Labour Party elected "Bill" Rowling to succeed him. As minister of finance in Kirk's Cabinet, faced with inflation and difficulties with foreign trade, Rowling had had a big job on his hands. But then the party caucus looked past a number of senior ministers to entrust him with a still bigger job, to try to replace the seemingly irreplaceable.

Rowling acknowledged that he was no Norman Kirk. At 46—the youngest man ever voted to the post—he was as physically and vocally unimpressive as Kirk was commanding, differing markedly in manner from his more homespun predecessor. But the requirement of the moment was not so much charisma as it was a grasp of economics to prevent the nation from sliding into a depression.

Rowling's approach to his new job was not so unassuming as to cause him to forego the foreign affairs portfolio, which had become a tradition with New Zealand prime ministers, but in the prevailing economic crisis he confined his first journeyings to islands in the South Pacific. He soon showed he would involve the Cabinet team more than did Kirk, streamline procedures, and surround himself more comfortably with top bureaucratic advisers. He knew he would succeed or fail by one test, the battle to retrieve the economy, and in 1974 he was feeling his way through the first rounds of that endeavour.

Born in the small apple orchard centre of Motueka at the top of the South Island on Nov. 15, 1927, Rowling was educated at Nelson College, took a master's degree, and was a schoolteacher before he entered politics. Beginning in 1962 he represented Buller, one of New Zealand's most rural and colourful electorates, and he became party president eight years later. When the third Labour government came to power in November 1972, Rowling was appointed finance minister over the head of the party spokesman on finance, Robert James Tizard. After Rowling was named prime minister, Tizard took over the finance portfolio and also became deputy prime minister.   (JOHN A. KELLEHER)

ST. CLAIR, JAMES DRAPER

Many U.S. presidents have had counsel to advise them on the legal technicalities of their job. But in 1974, Richard Nixon (q.v.) needed a criminal lawyer to help him deal with the many charges leveled at him as a result of the Watergate investigation. Nixon chose James Draper St. Clair for the job. A skilled and sophisticated man with a reputation as a courtroom wizard, St. Clair accepted a federal salary of $42,500 a year and devoted a prodigious amount of time and energy to Nixon's cause. But the weight of the evidence was too great, and in the end Nixon was forced to resign the presidency.

St. Clair spoke for Nixon in a variety of forums. He participated in the House Judiciary Committee's impeachment hearings and argued before the U.S. Supreme Court that Nixon was justified in refusing to yield tapes and documents of 64 presidential conversations that had been subpoenaed by Special Watergate Prosecutor Leon Jaworski (q.v.). St. Clair based his arguments on the largely untested and ill-defined doctrine of "executive privilege," by which presidents from time to time have attempted to maintain the confidentiality of their official records and memorandums. But Jaworski, insisting that the tapes were necessary as evidence in criminal cases he was preparing, took the matter to court. In July, despite an impressive presentation by St. Clair, the Supreme Court ruled 8–0 against Nixon.

Surprisingly, St. Clair said he had conducted the case up to that point without having informed himself about the evidence on the subpoenaed tapes. Following the Supreme Court's ruling, however, he did review transcripts that Nixon had recently ordered prepared. In the process, St. Clair came across the transcripts of the June 23, 1972, meeting between Nixon and his former White House chief of staff, H. R. Haldeman. The transcripts showed that Nixon already knew much of the Watergate story only six days after the break-in at Democratic Party headquarters in the Watergate complex and had taken steps to prevent others—including FBI investigators—from learning the facts. Repeated public statements by both Nixon and St. Clair were thus flatly contradicted by the transcripts, and St. Clair had little choice but to insist that the president release them immediately. The president did so on August 5, and the overwhelmingly negative public and congressional reaction forced his resignation just three days later.

St. Clair was born April 14, 1920, in Akron, O. He graduated from the University of Illinois and received his law degree from Harvard. Joining the Boston firm of Hale & Dorr, he gained a reputation as an outstanding trial lawyer. In 1954 he was chief assistant to his senior partner, Joseph N. Welch, when Welch defended the U.S. Army before Wisconsin Sen. Joseph R. McCarthy's special investigations subcommittee. St. Clair returned to his firm shortly after Nixon's resignation.   (STANLEY WILLS CLOUD)

SANYA DHARMASAKTI

As Thailand struggled to evolve a viable democratic system after four decades of military dictatorship, two men emerged as central characters with a decisive hold on events. King Bhumibol played his role quietly from the sidelines as befitted a titular monarch. Sanya Dharmasakti tried to remove himself to the sidelines as well, but he was forced by public demand to remain at centre stage as a somewhat reluctant prime minister.

It was Sanya's utterly noncontroversial background as judge, educationist, and Buddhist activist that had made him appear the ideal prime minister when a sudden wave of violence swept the previous military government out of power in October 1973. When fresh violence, strikes, and political dissensions rocked the country in 1974, Sanya was criticized as a weak leader. He resigned in

apparent frustration in May, but at that point all sections of opinion clamoured for his return. The country seemed to feel that no other universally acceptable public figure was available. The king reappointed Sanya prime minister on May 27.

Born in Bangkok on April 5, 1907, Sanya studied at the Assumption College in Bangkok and then at the Bangkok Law School, becoming a Thai barrister at law. Later he went to England on a scholarship and was called to the bar by the Middle Temple. Beginning his career as a judge in the Ministry of Justice, he rose to become chief judge of the Supreme Court of Thailand. He retired at the age of 60 but continued to serve the king as privy councillor. Subsequently, he was appointed rector of Thammasat University, Bangkok, where he lectured in law for several years.

Sanya's abiding interest was Buddhism. Many prominent men in Thailand share this interest, but he seemed more deeply involved than most others. He was at one time vice-president of the World Fellowship of Buddhists, as well as of the Buddhist Association of Thailand. When he resigned as prime minister he announced a desire to enter a Buddhist monastery.   (T. J. S. GEORGE)

SAVALAS, TELLY

The meanest, toughest—and most popular—cop on television in 1974 was "Kojak," with a weekly audience of 35 million viewers. Telly Savalas, the man who portrayed him, won the Emmy Award as the year's best TV dramatic actor.

The series' success was due only in part to Savalas' acting. It depended on a special blend of heroics and rock-bottom realities, in the show as a whole and in the central character of the New York City detective lieutenant. While Kojak himself rode the whitest of horses, his corral was seamy and his boots were soiled. The worst guys lost and the best won, but gray characters on either side of the moral fence thrived and bled. "Kojak" emerged as a series from a made-for-TV film based on the real-life case of a man wrongfully imprisoned for murder.

Savalas himself was a romantic realist who could give vent to outrage. "I don't know when in history we've been any lower. In our stupidity we have put the focus on the outhouses of the world." Bald as a brick, as warm looking as Tierra del Fuego, and glowering like a shaved buffalo, he nonetheless had a certain appeal. Though his credits included such nonendearing roles as Al Capone, Pontius Pilate, and a "swinish, shaven-headed weirdo" in the film *The Dirty Dozen,* he was once voted the third sexiest man on the screen. He quoted his mother (who named her sons Aristotle, Socrates, Demosthenes, and Praxiteles) as telling him, "Telly, you've been beautiful for a thousand years. Go look at the Parthenon and see your face."

Aristotle Savalas was born in Garden City, N.Y., to a prosperous Greek family that was ruined in the Depression. After World War II army service, he graduated from Columbia University with honours in psychology, wrote for the Voice of America, was an executive director of the U.S. Information Service, and then moved to ABC as director of news and special events. He came to acting accidentally when he auditioned for a part no one seemed able to fill. "The second show I did on TV I was the lead . . . you ask yourself 'What kind of boat ride is this?' I remembered my father's words: 'From Roosevelt to me, my son, it's all a racket.'"

          (PHILIP KOPPER)

SCANLON, HUGH PARR

After six years as head of Britain's Amalgamated Union of Engineering Workers

(AUEW), Hugh Scanlon had won a reputation as the left-wing militant ogre of the British labour movement, both in the Trades Union Congress (TUC) and in the Labour Party. When in 1974 the government of Harold Wilson tried to bring wage increases under voluntary control through a "social contract," Scanlon's intransigence seemed likely to present a major obstacle.

Scanlon's opposition to any form of incomes policy had become a characteristic and consistent stance. He had led left-wing resistance in 1968–69 to the Labour government's policy for regulating industrial relations (set out in its White Paper, "In Place of Strife"), and his attitude hardened when Edward Heath's Conservative government passed its Industrial Relations Act in 1971. Scanlon and his union rejected the authority of the National Industrial Relations Court established by the act and in 1972 incurred a £50,000 fine for contempt, which they refused to pay. The issue was only settled by the repeal of the Industrial Relations Act when Labour took office in 1974.

Born in Australia on Oct. 26, 1913, Scanlon moved to England with his parents as a boy and spent most of his working life in and around Manchester. Beginning work at 14 with the electrical engineering firm of Metropolitan Vickers, he became a shop steward at 22 and his union's Manchester divisional organizer at 35. As a young man he educated himself at night school, studying economics and industrial psychology and becoming a convinced Marxist. For some years he was a member of the Communist Party but left it in 1955. Elected to the Amalgamated Engineering Union (later renamed AUEW) executive committee in 1963, he was elected the union's president for life in 1968, succeeding Lord Carron, who had retired in 1967.   (HARFORD THOMAS)

SCHEEL, WALTER

Fourth president of West Germany from July 1, 1974, succeeding Gustav Heinemann, who retired, Walter Scheel was elected on May 15 on the first ballot, having won an absolute majority of the votes in the electoral college (composed of all the members of the Federal Parliament and an equal number of representatives of the Länder, or states). Scheel, a Rhinelander and essentially a jolly man—his recording of a folk song reached the top of the West German hit parade—had been West Germany's vice-chancellor and foreign minister since 1969.

A politician of wide experience, Scheel was elected to the Bundestag as a member of the small Free Democratic Party (FDP) in 1953. In 1961, when the Free Democrats were in coalition with the Christian Democrats, he became minister for economic cooperation, responsible for development aid to the less developed countries. He headed this department until 1966 when the FDP left the coalition, a move that led to the downfall of the government of Christian Democrat Chancellor Ludwig Erhard. In his capacity as chairman (since 1968) of the FDP, Scheel joined forces with the Social Democrats under Willy Brandt in 1969. This, more than anything else, brought about the end of Christian Democratic government in Germany after 20 years.

Born on July 8, 1919, in Solingen, Scheel served in World War II in the Air Force as a night fighter pilot. From 1945 to 1953 he was an executive in the steel industry and then, as an independent industrial adviser, set up his own firm. As foreign minister, he became one of the most popular politicians in West Germany and enabled his party to retain its own identity in the coalition government. He was regarded at EEC headquarters in Brussels as a shrewd diplomat, adept at restoring harmony after disputes among the EEC partners.

(NORMAN CROSSLAND)

SCHMIDT, HELMUT H. W.

Elected federal chancellor of West Germany by the Bundestag on May 16, 1974, to succeed Willy Brandt who had resigned over the Günter Guillaume (q.v.) spy affair, Helmut Schmidt had long been regarded as the nation's "crown prince." In many respects he was the opposite of his predecessor: whereas Brandt was an idealist and a dreamer, Schmidt was a pragmatist with his feet firmly on the ground.

Before his election to the chancellorship, Schmidt had made it clear that West Germany would not risk its economic stability and the prosperity of its people by making heavy financial sacrifices to bolster a European Community that was incapable of action. His statement of policy to the Bundestag on May 17 reemphasized this theme. He stressed the importance of maintaining economic stability and painted a gloomy picture of the state of the EEC. His friendship with the French president, Valéry Giscard d'Estaing (q.v.), resulted in the strengthening of cooperation between Paris and Bonn and led to comments about a French-West German axis. During October 28–31 Schmidt visited Moscow to discuss long-term cooperation with the Soviet leadership, and on December 5–6 he visited Washington, D.C., for talks with Pres. Gerald Ford (q.v.) on the economic crisis. He also visited London on November 30 to address a special Labour Party conference on the merits of Britain's remaining in the EEC and was applauded for his urbane, witty, and persuasive speech.

Schmidt was born on Dec. 23, 1918, in Hamburg, the son of a grammar school teacher. He passed his university entrance examinations but was called up in World War II to serve with an armoured division on the eastern front and later took part in the Ardennes offensive. He joined the Social Democratic Party (SPD) immediately after the war, studied economics in Hamburg, and then worked from 1949 to 1953 in the department of economics and transport in the city administration. He was elected to the Bundestag in 1953. In 1961 he gave up his seat and returned to Hamburg as senator (minister) for internal affairs but was back in the Bundestag four years later. He served as defense minister from 1969 to 1972, minister of economics and finance from July 1972 to December 1972, and then as minister of finance until his election to the chancellorship.

(NORMAN CROSSLAND)

Helmut Schmidt

KEYSTONE

SIMON, WILLIAM EDWARD

Largely because of the instability generated by the Watergate scandal, the administration of U.S. Pres. Richard Nixon in its waning months became something of a merry-go-round for its Cabinet and sub-Cabinet officers. Many men rode a few turns and departed; others changed horses quickly and stayed. William E. Simon, a 47-year-old bond salesman and multimillionaire, joined the Nixon team in January 1973 as deputy secretary of the treasury. By the end of that year, he was named director of the Federal Energy Office, the agency created to cope with the nation's mounting difficulties with fossil fuels. By April 1974 Simon had succeeded his original boss, George Shultz, who had himself held three Cabinet-level posts in five years, as secretary of the treasury.

Simon earned his Cabinet job by quickly building a reputation in Washington as a ferocious taskmaster who demanded dedication and long hours of his deputies, but who matched and often exceeded their output with his own. He also was capable of quick decision-making in enormously complicated policy areas. As "energy czar," Simon succeeded in managing the nation's response to the Arab oil boycott and in the process distinguished himself from his more careful colleagues with his often tart tongue.

In July Simon toured the Middle East to discuss financial investments, trade, and oil policy with leaders of four nations. A conference with Egyptian Pres. Anwar as-Sadat yielded permission for four U.S. banks to open offices in Egypt, the first foreign institutions to enter that country in 17 years. As a Cabinet officer, Simon served under difficult circumstances. His power, both as energy office director and as treasury secretary, was in constant dispute by other powerful Nixon advisers, such as Office of Management and Budget Director Roy Ash. Simon and Ash clashed in February over the length and severity of the energy problem. Ash called it "manageable, one-time, and short-term"; Simon, faced with leading an energy conservation program, believed otherwise and told Ash to "keep his cotton-pickin' hands off energy policy." When Gerald Ford became president in August, Simon continued as treasury secretary, sharing economic policymaking functions with other presidential advisers.

Simon was born on Nov. 27, 1927, in Paterson, N.J. The scion of a family that had owned a successful silk-dyeing business, which failed in the Depression, Simon received a degree from Lafayette College, Easton, Pa., in 1951. He began amassing his fortune (now in a blind trust) while a senior partner with Salomon Brothers, a New York investment banking firm. (JOHN F. STACKS)

SOARES, MÁRIO

After two periods of exile imposed by the prerevolutionary regime in Portugal, Mário Soares, leader of the Portuguese Socialist Party (PSP), returned to Lisbon from Paris after the April 1974 coup to become foreign minister in the first provisional government headed by Adélino da Palma Carlos. Soares retained his post when Carlos was succeeded by Col. Vasco dos Santos Gonçalves (q.v.) and when Gen. António de Spínola (q.v.) was succeeded as president by Gen. Francisco da Costa Gomes.

One of Soares' first tasks on taking office was to visit major European capitals to explain the new government's policy. In London on May 2 he stated that the greatest dangers facing Portugal were economic disintegration, which could result in a countercoup, and the threat of a unilateral declaration of independence in the overseas states.

Soon afterward he became intensively involved in negotiations for the independence of the African territories, meeting first in London, then in Algiers, Dar es Salaam, Tanzania, and Lusaka, Zambia. These negotiations led to the independence of Guinea-Bissau on September 10 and agreement that Mozambique should become independent in June 1975.

Born Dec. 7, 1924, in Lisbon, Soares graduated in law from the university there. He was a founder member of the United Democratic Movement and a member of its central executive (1946–48). After several key appointments in the opposition to the Salazar government, he became a member of the commission supporting the election of Gen. Humberto Delgado to the presidency in 1958. He was then arrested and later exiled to São Tomé. In October 1968, soon after Marcello Caetano took over from the stricken Salazar, Soares was allowed to return to Lisbon. In 1970 he undertook a lecture tour in Europe and the U.S. during which he made speeches critical of the Caetano government. On his return, to attend the funeral of his father, he was given the choice of leaving Portugal within eight hours or being put under arrest without bail. Soares chose exile. In 1973, at the PSP convention in Bonne, France, he was elected secretary-general of the party.

(MICHAEL WOOLLER)

SOLZHENITSYN, ALEKSANDR ISAEVICH

On Feb. 13, 1974, the Soviet Union through its ambassador asked if the West German government would receive the noted Soviet author Aleksandr Solzhenitsyn. That same afternoon he arrived in Bonn by plane from Moscow. The Soviet government had learned in December 1973 that Solzhenitsyn had given permission for his new work, *The Gulag Archipelago*, a description of the Soviet labour camp system, to be published in the West. On January 2 a violent propaganda campaign against the writer opened in the Soviet press, radio, and television, branding him a traitor. He refused summonses on February 8 and February 11 to appear at the state prosecutor's office, and on February 12 he was arrested and threatened. But the government had already decided to expel him and deprive him of citizenship.

After a few days in Bonn and Zürich, Solzhenitsyn traveled to Denmark and Norway. He then settled in Zürich, where his wife Natalya Dimitrievna, her mother, his stepson, and his own three sons rejoined him later. On December 10 in Stockholm he received his Nobel Prize for Literature for 1970 (he had not left the U.S.S.R. to receive it in that year).

Solzhenitsyn was born on Dec. 11, 1918, at Kislovodsk, Russia, in the Caucasus. His father, a Cossack squire, died before his birth. In 1924 his mother moved to Rostov-on-Don. He studied mathematics and physics at Rostov University, graduating in 1941. Solzhenitsyn joined the Army in October of the same year and served as an artillery lieutenant. He was twice decorated for bravery and early in 1945 was promoted to captain. Soon afterward he was arrested for criticizing Stalin in letters and was sentenced to eight years' hard labour. On his release in 1953 he was sent into "perpetual exile." After Stalin's death, he was freed in 1956 and "rehabilitated" a year later.

In 1962 Solzhenitsyn's first novel, *One Day in the Life of Ivan Denisovich*, was published, an explosive literary debut made possible because Premier Nikita Khrushchev himself authorized it. After Khrushchev's fall in 1964 only one short story by Solzhenitsyn appeared in print in the Soviet Union. After *Cancer Ward* (1968) and *The First Circle* (1968) appeared in the West, he was expelled in 1969 from the Union of Soviet Writers.　　　　　(K. M. SMOGORZEWSKI)

SOMARE, MICHAEL THOMAS

In 1974 Michael Somare, chief minister of Papua New Guinea, was often forced to chop and change as he steered his country toward the complete independence it was expected to achieve the following year. For example, he had to review his policy of decreasing the number of expatriate staff in the Papua New Guinea public service. Under a government plan announced in 1972, each department was supposed to cut employment of expatriates by 15% annually. But by 1974 the rate was reaching 30%, and the loss of experienced staff was threatening to damage Papua New Guinea's social and economic programs. "We would rather employ people from overseas for as long as is necessary," Somare said, "than have these programs fail because of a shortage of manpower."

Somare made a strong effort to prevent Papua New Guinea from being denuded of its indigenous art by banning the export of artifacts made before 1952. This had a deleterious effect on the economy of the Sepik villages and the Maprik area, where many artisans had become so expert in aging their carvings that they could not convince the authorities they were of recent manufacture. He also set in train an investigation into the Burns Philp Group (one of the largest and most highly diversified companies in Papua New Guinea), observing that there had been "the smell of a rat" about some of the company's dealings.

Somare faced a major reverse following his disagreement with the justice minister, John Kaputin. After a dispute over a planning committee's report on the new Papua New Guinea constitution, Somare asked Kaputin to resign. Kaputin refused, was stripped of his portfolio, but managed to depict the sacking as an affront to the Tolai people of his electorate. When public meetings demanded Kaputin's reinstatement, Somare was forced to back down. This led some Australian newspapers to doubt Somare's capacity to lead Papua New Guinea in its days of independence.

Michael Somare was born on April 9, 1936, in Rabaul. He first came to national prominence in 1968 when he was elected to the House of Assembly for the East Sepik Regional Electorate. A former schoolteacher and journalist, he became parliamentary leader of the Pangu Pati, and as chief minister accomplished the difficult task of holding the territory's coalition government together.
　　　　　(A. R. G. GRIFFITHS)

SOUPHANOUVONG, PRINCE

Every time peace had been established in recent years in Laos, it had been on the basis of a coalition between the rightists in the government and the Pathet Lao Communists, and 1974 was no exception. The Pathet Lao leader Prince Souphanouvong left his hideout in April and journeyed to the capital city of Vientiane for the first time in 11 years. In public life the "Red Prince" had usually lived in the shadow of his older half brother, Prince Souvanna Phouma, the premier. But his quiet determination and ideo-

logical convictions combined to give him considerable influence. Within days of his arrival in the Laotian capital he established himself and the Pathet Lao wing of the new coalition as "more equal" than their non-Communist partners.

Souphanouvong was born in 1912. His father, Prince Boun Khong, was a collateral member of the royal family, but because his mother was a commoner he was denied the privileges other princes enjoyed. Aided by one of his four half brothers, Souphanouvong went to France to study engineering. After completing his studies he spent a year working on the docks at Le Havre, where he got to know French Communists. On returning home he took employment in the French colonial administration and was posted to the central coast of South Vietnam. There his career took a political turn. His Marxist father-in-law introduced him to political contacts who finally took him to Ho Chi Minh, already an oracle of Indochinese revolution. Under Ho's tutelage, Souphanouvong quickly evolved as an ideologically charged underground leader.

At the end of World War II Souphanouvong became active in the resistance against France. The Pathet Lao was founded in 1950. For the best part of the next two decades his guerrillas fought government forces under the leadership of Souvanna Phouma. But the personal relationship between the two princes always remained warm. In 1962 Souphanouvong joined the coalition government as vice-premier, but the government collapsed in a year and he found himself in jail. He escaped and set up a fortress in a complex of caves in the province of Sam Neua. On his return to Vientiane in 1974 he stayed out of the Cabinet, preferring to be chief of the powerful Joint National Political Council.　　　　(T. J. S. GEORGE)

SPÍNOLA, ANTÓNIO SEBASTIÃO RIBEIRO DE

A monocled cavalryman who wished to save his country, Gen. António de Spínola during his brief term as president of Portugal, from May 15 to Sept. 30, 1974, saw democracy return to that country and colonialism disappear from Portuguese Africa. The publication in February of his book *Portugal e o Futuro* ("Portugal and the Future"), which boldly sketched out a nonmilitary policy of gradual change in Portuguese Africa, was an awakening call.

Born April 11, 1910, at Estremoz and entering the cavalry at the age of 20, Spínola became a career army officer. He began his

António de Spínola

SVEN SIMON/KATHERINE YOUNG

tour in Africa in Angola in 1961, being promoted to brigadier general in 1966 and serving as governor and commander in chief of the armed forces in Portuguese Guinea, 1968–73. During his term there he pledged himself to promote the integration of the black community into political life. In 1973 Spínola returned to Portugal, where he was proclaimed a national hero and named deputy chief of staff of the armed forces. After unrest had led to the detention of young officers in March 1974, Marcello Caetano's government called on senior officers to swear an oath of loyalty publicly. Gen. Francisco da Costa Gomes, the commander in chief, and General Spínola failed to attend the ceremony and were dismissed from their posts, although retaining their ranks.

After Caetano was overthrown in the April 25 coup by the Armed Forces Movement, in which he played no direct role, Spínola sought to become more than a figurehead president but lost his political battles from the beginning. The attempt to create a balance between the centre and the left did not work, and Spínola was forced to accept Col. Vasco dos Santos Gonçalves (*q.v.*) as premier. Gonçalves and the more conservative Spínola fought on almost all important issues. Overtaken by the demands of the left, General Spínola made his famous appeal to the "silent majority," and woke the fear that he was appealing over the heads of the Armed Forces Movement for enough personal power to be able to obtain the presidency at the promised elections. On September 30 Spínola resigned, warning that Portugal was being taken over by leftists and faced anarchy, crisis, and chaos, and retired into private life.　　　　(MICHAEL WOOLLER)

STIRLING, (ARCHIBALD) DAVID

Founder and leader during World War II of the British Special Air Services (SAS), which mounted raids behind German lines in North Africa, Col. David Stirling found himself the focus of political attention in Britain during the summer of 1974. Newspapers disclosed that he was masterminding a secret organization called GB 75, "a nonmilitary force of patriotic volunteers" whose purpose was to counter strikes that might immobilize power stations, factories, and other important installations. His organization was reported to be ready to take over the running of essential services in an emergency.

Stirling already had experience in some newly independent countries of providing specialized security expertise for the protection of heads of state. This was done by means of an organization called Watchguard, formed in 1967 but later dissolved. He complained that his political position had been misrepresented in reports of his activities, saying that he was nonpolitical and that he had "no truck with the extreme right wing and neo-fascists." While living in Rhodesia and Kenya after the war he had formed the Capricorn Africa Society, which had a program for interracial understanding. "I abominate class and colour barriers," he said.

Stirling's preoccupation with industrial unrest in the U.K., particularly after the miners' strike early in 1974, was representative of the mood of a significant section of Conservative opinion, but his plans for dealing with it did not seem to be fully worked out. "The left wing rumbled us before we were ready," he complained. He was critical of a parallel organization called Unison (later renamed Civil Assistance), directed by Gen. Sir Walter Walker (formerly commander in chief, Allied Forces Northern Europe), because, he said, it was "apparently highly militaristic and very right wing."

Stirling was born Nov. 15, 1915. He attended Ampleforth College and, briefly, Cambridge University. When he returned to Britain from Africa in 1959, he set up a business in London called Television International Enterprises Ltd.   (HARFORD THOMAS)

TENG HSIAO-PING

The perennial question in China "After Mao, who?" was overtaken in 1974 by a new one: "After Chou, who?" For it was Premier Chou En-lai who dominated the headlines during the year with news of heart attacks and prolonged hospitalization. The premier's failing health in turn pushed into the limelight one of the most controversial of China's leaders, Teng Hsiao-ping.

This was a curious turn of history. In 1966 Teng, then secretary-general of the Communist Party and therefore one of the most powerful men in Peking, had been unceremoniously stripped of all powers and humiliated. At the height of the Cultural Revolution, he was accused of supporting the "bourgeois reactionary line" against Mao. Red Guards called him a "demon" and a "freak." For six years Teng was never seen in public. Then, suddenly, on April 12, 1973, he appeared at a banquet in Peking and was subsequently named a deputy premier.

Born in Szechuan Province in 1904, Teng joined a high-school program that qualified him for higher education in France. There he met Chou and joined the Chinese Communist Party when he was 20. Two years later he returned home via the Soviet Union. Starting out as an underground organizer in Shanghai, Teng established himself as a political commissar in Red Army units and took part in the fabled Communist Long March of 1934–35. After the Communist triumph in 1949 he occupied various administrative-financial positions. He went to Moscow more than once for major negotiations and won Chou's approval as a skilled negotiator. In 1954 he became secretary of the party, and from December 1963 until April 1965 was acting premier.

Teng's return to power in 1973 was generally attributed to his being one of Chou's men. Indeed, it was believed that Chou brought him out of oblivion precisely for the purpose of establishing him as his successor. There was no indication, however, that the power struggle in Peking had resolved itself. While the Chou En-lai moderates might accept Teng, the Shanghai radicals were said to be against him.   (T. J. S. GEORGE)

TINDEMANS, LÉO

The choice of Léo Tindemans as Belgium's prime minister-designate was no surprise once results of the March 10, 1974, general election were known; his party, the Flemish Social Christians (CVP), had waged its campaign under the banner "With Tindemans, it will be different." Just how different was soon to become apparent. Not only did he refuse to enter into protracted negotiations with the Socialists, the second largest party, but he was also the first politician of one of the three traditional parties (Social Christians, Socialists, and Liberals) to call on the federalist language parties to help form a government. (In the end, only one of these parties, the Rassemblement Wallon, was represented in the new government.)

Tindemans was born at Zwijndrecht, Antwerp Province, on April 16, 1922. Bright, studious, and determined, after taking a master's degree in economics he began his career in journalism but soon joined the Social Christian political study centre. He quickly became a familiar figure among the political leaders of his party, of which he became national secretary in 1958. Three years later he succeeded in Parliament one of

the great Flemish pre-World War II Roman Catholic leaders, Frans Van Cauwelaert (on whom he later wrote a thesis for his master's degree in political and social science). Tindemans' appointment as secretary-general of the European Union of Christian Democrats gave scope for his strong interest in foreign affairs, and in that capacity he was able to establish close contact with such prominent European politicians as Konrad Adenauer, Mariano Rumor, Jean Lecanuet, and Alain Poher. In 1968 Tindemans accepted Prime Minister Gaston Eyskens' invitation to join his government as minister of community relations, and teamed up with his Walloon counterpart, Freddy Terwagne, to form an efficient working partnership. As minister of agriculture in the short-lived second Eyskens government he showed great firmness and integrity in deciding, in the face of powerful lobbying, that Belgium should comply at once with international treaties banning the popular and long-established practice of trapping migrating birds. In the tripartite government of Edmond Leburton early in 1973 Tindemans was the undisputed Social Christian leader. He was made deputy prime minister, in charge of the budget and institutional reforms.   (JAN R. ENGELS)

TRUDEAU, MARGARET and PIERRE ELLIOTT

After the October 1972 election, Canadian Prime Minister Pierre Elliott Trudeau was left with only a shadow of his former political dominance of the country. From his earlier position as a kind of matinee idol and national hero, he was reduced to running Canada with a minority government dependent upon the coalition support of the socialist New Democratic Party (NDP).

For a year and a half Trudeau's Liberal Party faced no less than 20 no-confidence votes in Parliament, turning back each one narrowly until, on May 8, the NDP deserted on a vote on Trudeau's budget, defeating the prime minister's party and precipitating a national election. The 54-year-old leader had learned from his 1972 defeat and turned away from his usually lofty and contemplative political lectures. During the seven-week campaign, Trudeau crisscrossed the country at least once a week, campaigning hard and welcoming the assistance of party professionals whom he had largely ignored in 1972.

Trudeau also changed his mind about involving his beautiful young wife in political affairs. Shortly after his 1971 marriage to Margaret Sinclair, the daughter of a former Cabinet minister, Trudeau said he did not like the idea of mixing his family up in politics—"the whole idea is repugnant to me." But in the early summer campaign, Margaret traveled with her husband and took campaign trips on her own. She was well received and her assistance was credited with helping the campaign enormously. It plainly did not help her, however. In September, 25-year-old Margaret was hospitalized for treatment of what she termed "severe emotional stress." In October, in a remarkably candid interview on national television, she talked about her hospitalization. The pressures of being a political wife, she said, were "a total catastrophe in terms of my identity. I'm pretty much an outfront, straightforward chick, and I get a bit confused by expectations. It's certainly not the glamorous exciting life people think it is."

But for her husband the 1974 election was anything but catastrophic. Despite growing inflation and unemployment and a Conservative campaign that harped on those problems, Trudeau and the Liberal Party swept to a surprisingly clear majority in the July 8 election. They increased their seats

in Parliament from 109 to 141, giving Trudeau a four-year mandate to run Canada. Among his first efforts was a trip to France where he and French Pres. Valéry Giscard d'Estaing (q.v.) accomplished a formal reconciliation of differences between the two nations that had smoldered since the days of Charles de Gaulle's public and disruptive support of the French separatist movement in Quebec. The rapprochement was part of Trudeau's effort to steer a middle course in the face of deepening and spreading feelings of nationalism and a decided resentment of the U.S. He had previously strengthened Canadian ties with Pacific nations, then with the Soviet Union and China, and the trip to France was the first round in improving diplomatic and trade relations with Western Europe and the EEC. These improved relationships, Trudeau hoped, would lessen Canadian dependence on the U.S.

Trudeau was born in Montreal on Oct. 18, 1919. He received his law degree from the University of Montreal, his master's from Harvard, and attended L'École des Sciences Politiques in Paris and the London School of Economics. Trudeau sought and won his first elective office, a seat in the House of Commons, in 1965. Three years later he was elected leader of the Liberal Party, and succeeded Lester B. Pearson as prime minister on April 20, 1968.

Margaret Sinclair Trudeau was born on Sept. 10, 1948, in Vancouver, B.C. She attended Simon Fraser University in Vancouver. The Trudeaus, married on March 4, 1971, have two sons, both born on Christmas Day—Justin in 1971 and Sacha in 1973.   (JOHN F. STACKS)

WALTERS, BARBARA

Just before the alarm goes off she pulls herself out of bed; she hates to hear it ring. It is 4:45 A.M., and after a hasty, highly idiosyncratic breakfast (e.g., brownies or cheese and crackers) she rides to the studio. By seven Barbara Walters, co-host and commentator of the "Today" show, is ready to begin the day for millions of U.S. television viewers.

"Today" is an early morning program of news, weather, feature presentations, and interviews that was seen over 218 stations in 1974. It was the most successful show of its kind, making over $10 million in profits each

Barbara Walters

SAHM DOHERTY—CAMERA 5

year for the NBC television network. Walters received nearly $400,000 as salary.

Things were not always so. Born Sept. 25, 1931, in Boston, Mass., the child of a vaudeville and nightclub impresario, Walters had a solitary and unsettled childhood. While in college she hoped to teach, but after getting a job at a New York TV station she decided to become a journalist. Later came a stint at CBS, where she wrote material for such stars as Jack Parr and Dick Van Dyke. CBS fired her—for economy reasons—and in 1961 she began with "Today," where she prepared programming of interest to women and did occasional news features. In those days, the female on the program was called the "Today Girl." Her job was to look pretty, engage in small talk, and occasionally deliver a bit of fashion news, but solid journalism went to the man. In 1964, when the latest in a long line of "Today Girls" resigned, Walters got the job on a temporary basis. Soon she began to expand the dimensions of her role by delivering hard news. Grudgingly the network gave her leeway, and before long she was demonstrating a remarkable talent for getting famous people to appear on "Today" for penetrating, often sensational, interviews.

Possibly on the theory that only a woman could compete with a woman, CBS hired Washington newspaperwoman Sally Quinn for its own early morning show, but Quinn lacked the Walters magic and the experiment was short-lived. Just how far Walters had come from the "Today Girl" image was plain when NBC began searching for a new male co-host after the death of Frank McGee in April. Most members of the news staff were mentioned at one time or another before Jim Hartz was finally chosen, and the chief criterion by which they were judged was how well they would work with Barbara Walters.

(VICTOR M. CASSIDY)

WILLIAMS, SHIRLEY VIVIEN TERESA BRITTAIN

In Britain's new Labour government formed in March 1974, the sensitive post—at a time of rapid inflation—of secretary of state for prices and consumer protection went to Shirley Williams. With a seat in the Cabinet at the age of 43, Mrs. Williams was looked on as one of the few women in British politics with a chance of becoming prime minister. She had obtained a junior ministerial post in the previous Labour government in 1966, and was quickly promoted to minister of state, first for education and science and then at the Home Office. With this experience behind her, she moved up to a place in the Labour shadow cabinet while the party was in opposition from 1970 to 1974, taking responsibility for consumer affairs in 1973. She gained a reputation for being tough and decisive in an area exposed to many pressures.

Shirley Williams was born July 27, 1930. Her father, Sir George Catlin, and her mother, the writer Vera Brittain, were both prominent in left-wing politics in the 1930s, and as a child Shirley knew many of the Labour Party leaders of that time. At Oxford University after World War II she was the first woman chairman of the Oxford University Labour Club. It was natural that she should seek a career in politics, but she had to fight three elections unsuccessfully before being elected as a member of Parliament for Hitchin in 1964. Meanwhile, she was general secretary (1960–64) of the Fabian Society, the leading organization for socialist intellectual activity and research.

On one issue differences within the Labour Party seemed to threaten Mrs. Williams' political future. She had long been an absolutely committed supporter of British membership in the European Economic Community. On this she declined to be silenced, and during the campaign for the October elections she antagonized the anti-EEC group in the Labour Party by saying at a press conference that if a Labour government advised against staying in the EEC she would resign from the Cabinet.

(HARFORD THOMAS)

WILLIAMSON, DAVID

Already an established dramatist in his native Australia, in 1974 David Williamson added considerably to his international reputation. In September his comedy *What If You Died Tomorrow?* opened in London's West End with the full cast of the original production, first staged at the Sydney Opera House in October 1973. It was his fifth full-length play, and his second to reach the London stage.

Williamson made his debut as a dramatist with a one-act play in 1967. His first full-length play, *The Coming of Stork* (1970), was subsequently filmed as *Stork*. Of two plays staged in 1971, *Don's Party,* having the return to power of the Australian Labor Party as its background, and *The Removalists,* a "study of violence in Australian society," the second won the George Devine Award for the best play of the year to be performed in London. This was the first time the award had been given to a writer from outside the United Kingdom. *Don's Party* was acquired for production in London in February 1975 and was to be directed by Michael Blakemore at the Royal Court Theatre.

Jugglers Three (1972) received the Melbourne critics' Erik Award for the year's best Australian play. Williamson's most recent play, *The Departure* (1974), commissioned by the South Australian Theatre Company, was to receive its world premiere in 1975. Just as *The Removalists* was, in the author's words, an attack "not on the police force but on authoritarianism," so all Williamson's plays looked at some aspect or other of man's selfishness or brutality or both. In *What If You Died Tomorrow?,* a sharp and funny comedy about a young novelist's sudden success, he examined the selfishness of individual members of a family, their friends and associates, and described with telling realism the hurt they are able to inflict on one another.

Born in Melbourne, Victoria, in 1942, the son of a bank official, Williamson went to Bairnsdale School in northeast Victoria and graduated in mechanical engineering at Monash University. He lectured in thermodynamics and psychology at Swinburne Technical College, Melbourne, until 1972, when he left teaching for full-time writing.

(OSSIA TRILLING)

WILSON, ERICA

Nowhere was the burgeoning interest in handcrafts in the U.S. more evident than in the art needlework department of any large store. Where cross-stitch dresser scarves and needlepoint cabbage roses had once reigned supreme, aspiring needlewomen (and men) could now choose from a riot of kits and materials, reproducing the best of the past or applying traditional techniques to modern designs. Much of the credit belonged to Erica Wilson, an Englishwoman, a graduate of London's Royal School of Needlework, and head of a thriving business.

Born and raised in England, Erica Wilson became interested in needlework as a child. At the Royal School of Needlework she

COURTESY, ERICA WILSON NEEDLE WORKS

Erica Wilson

studied crewel, a form of embroidery with yarn dating back to the 16th century, Elizabethan black work, church embroidery, and other forms of needlecraft, and later became an instructor. Soon after going to the U.S. in the early 1950s, she began to teach at Cooper Union Museum in New York City and helped to found the Millbrook Needlework Guild of New York. In 1958 her husband, Vladimir Kagan, encouraged her to enlarge her mimeographed instructions for crewel into a correspondence course, which by 1974 had enrolled more than 10,000 students.

Her first book, *Crewel Embroidery* (1962), became a standard work in the field; an abridged version, *The Craft of Crewel Embroidery,* was published in 1971. *Fun with Crewel Embroidery* (1965) was an introduction for children, and *Erica Wilson's Embroidery Book* (1973) was a comprehensive introduction to needlecraft. Her television series, a 26-week program entitled "Erica" that began on public television in 1971, was the first to teach needlework. The projects shown on the series were collected in a forthcoming book, *Needleplay.*

Now in her mid-40s, Miss Wilson ran several needlework shops, designed exclusive mail-order kits for the Erica Wilson Creative Needlework Society as well as kits for nationwide distribution, lectured, taught, and conducted seminars. Among the items she designed were cushions for Gracie Mansion, the New York mayor's residence, kneeling cushions for the National Cathedral in Washington, D.C., and for St. Mark's Episcopal Church in New Canaan, Conn., and work for the Jared Coffin House in Nantucket, Mass. (JOAN NATALIE REIBSTEIN)

WILSON, (JAMES) HAROLD

Twice during 1974, and for the fourth time in ten years, Harold Wilson led Britain's Labour Party to victory in a general election. After the election of February 28 he took over as prime minister with a minority of seats in the House of Commons. Though Labour was the largest party, its position was so insecure that Wilson called another election in October, to win again by a bare overall majority. But this election gave Labour in effect a working majority because an ill-assorted collection of splinter groups and independent MPs would have to coalesce with the Conservatives to threaten the Labour government.

Wilson became leader of the Labour Party after a split in its ranks, following the death of Hugh Gaitskell (1963). His dexterity in balancing rival groups was in the historical tradition of the Labour Party, but it earned him a reputation for deviousness, although it could also be seen as political professionalism based on experience unmatched by anyone else in British political life; he had been a member of Clement Attlee's government formed in 1945, and had won a place in the Cabinet at the age of 31.

Born March 11, 1916, in Huddersfield, Wilson went to school in Yorkshire and Cheshire and won a scholarship to Oxford University. During World War II he entered the civil service and swiftly rose to a senior position in the Ministry of Fuel and Power. He was elected a member of Parliament in 1945 and took his place in the first postwar government. His resignation from the Attlee government in 1951 on the issue of imposing National Health Service charges established his position on the left of the party, although once he had become party leader he moved toward the centre.

Wilson was not identified with any doctrinaire commitment: indeed, on the key issue of British membership in the EEC he started negotiations for British entry while he was prime minister in the late 1960s, but then turned against the terms of entry accepted by the Heath government. Later, he met the objections of the Labour anti-EEC group by promising that a Labour government would renegotiate the terms and submit the decision to a referendum.

(HARFORD THOMAS)

WISEMAN, CLARENCE

In 1974 Clarence Wiseman took command of the world's largest private army. It had 2.5 million members in more than 80 nations and 17,000 meeting places—often situated in seamy areas of big cities—where recruitment proceeded daily. He frequently talked to his commander in chief but had never seen Him. The movement's symbol was a red shield.

Wiseman was the tenth general of the Salvation Army. He was elected on May 13, 1974, by that organization's High Council and assumed command in July. A Canadian, he was only the second non-Briton to head the international, nonpolitical, religious and charitable movement. Born in 1908 to an Army couple, he joined in 1927 at Guelph, Ont., and played in a Salvation Army band. Assignments in his native country followed his graduation from Officer Training School. Then, in 1939, he became a chaplain with the Canadian Army in Britain and eventually directed all Salvation Army work with Canadian forces in Europe, the Middle East, and India. While a young officer, he began one of the first religious programs on radio.

After World War II, Wiseman returned to Canada, directed the Army in Newfoundland for eight years, then served successively as field secretary and chief secretary for the entire country. In 1960 he became territorial commander in East Africa, where he established a home known as Joytown for crippled children. Two years later, the Army called Wiseman to England where he was principal of the training college. Known as an indefatigable worker, he also represented the Army at meetings of the World Council of Churches and in 1966 conducted a highly successful missionary campaign in Finland. In 1967 he returned to Canada as territorial commander, assuming responsibility for 1,400 officers and several thousand employees. He was then married to Janet Kelly, an Army captain.

Wiseman believed the Salvation Army must remain flexible, but he planned no radical changes. He emphatically declared, for example, that the familiar officer's uniform should be retained. He also continued to en-courage indigenous leadership in the less developed countries and to emphasize youth work. Always the missionary, he hoped to see "an army of young people, marching through the world, telling other young people about Jesus."   (VICTOR M. CASSIDY)

WITTEVEEN, HENDRIKUS JOHANNES

A Dutch economics professor and financial administrator moved onto the world stage in 1974 with a plan to recycle the tide of oil dollars pouring into the Middle East from the industrial countries. The financial crisis caused by the sudden raising of prices by the oil-producing countries had brought predictions of disaster from many experts. They feared that the oil-importing countries would be led to correct their international payments balances by cutting their trade with each other, producing a worldwide deflation resembling that of the 1930s.

H. Johannes Witteveen, the academician who manages the International Monetary Fund (IMF), came forward in January with a plan that brought temporary hope to the hearts of some financiers. In a speech to the Economic Club of Detroit on May 6, he explained his idea that one way to help the oil-importing countries meet the high prices would be to have the producing countries lend them back their money.

Witteveen proposed to have the oil-producing nations "lend" to the IMF from their surplus oil revenues to help establish an "oil facility" that would make currency loans to oil-importing countries. The idea was to help ensure that "the surplus funds of the oil countries will find their way to where they are most needed."

Subsequently, the oil facility was established after the oil-producing countries had been approached for subscriptions. They signed agreements to lend over $3 billion to the facility.

For many years a professor of economics in Rotterdam, Witteveen was also a Liberal Party member of the Dutch legislature's First Chamber and an adviser to the Anglo-Dutch Unilever company. He twice served as the nation's finance minister, in 1963–65 and 1967–71, and in 1973 became managing director of the IMF.

Born in Zeist on June 12, 1921, Witteveen grew up in Rotterdam. (His father, a municipal architect, was involved in the rebuilding of Rotterdam after its destruction in World War II.) He was widely known in The Netherlands as an ardent member of the Sufi religious sect, a movement that tries to combine Christianity with the Oriental outlook in religion.   (FRANCIS S. PIERCE)

WONDER, STEVIE

Astride the pop music world like a colossus, Stevie Wonder in 1974 alone won four major Grammy Awards, the Nobel Prizes of the recording industry. A professional for half his life, he had sold more than 40 million records by the time he was 24. More important, his influence was unmatched among contemporary musicians, from former Beatle Paul McCartney to soul queen Roberta Flack to orchestrator Henry Mancini. Moreover, he was born black and blind in Saginaw, Mich., May 13, 1950.

Sources agreed he was christened Steveland but differed as to whether his surname was Hardaway or Morris. As a child in Detroit's ghetto, Stevie became known as a musical prodigy. He played bongos, danced on front porches for neighbours, and wore out toy drums until a Lions Club gave him a real set for Christmas. He played toy harmonicas until they broke and learned keyboard performing on a hand-me-down piano.

When Stevie was nine, a friend's older brother, who sang with the Miracles, arranged an audition for the boy with Motown, the already thriving black record company. Stevie took to hanging around the studio, making a pest of himself but also impressing everyone with his native talent. By the age of 12 he had written two concertos and recorded for Motown his first hit, "Fingertips." He attended the Michigan School for the Blind, which arranged for a tutor and a special curriculum so that he could go on tour with other Motown performers. By then his reputation as a tiny miracle had given rise to "Little Stevie Wonder," a *nom de disque* that stuck until he was six feet tall and the "little" was dropped.

By the time he reached his majority Wonder had such credits as "Fingertips Part 2," "Signed, Sealed, Delivered," "Uptight," "For Once in My Life," "My Cherie Amour," "I Was Made to Love Her," and other songs, many recorded by such leading performers as Barbra Streisand and Frank Sinatra. He eventually gained enough influence to do the unspeakable: demand that Motown renegotiate his contract and give him total musical freedom. It was as if Pinto had demanded—and gotten—absolute marketing and racing freedom from the Ford Motor Co.   (PHILIP KOPPER)

(ABOVE) DAVID GAHR; (RIGHT) WIDE WORLD

Clarence Wiseman

Stevie Wonder

Bolivia

A landlocked republic in central South America, Bolivia is bordered by Brazil, Paraguay, Argentina, Chile, and Peru. Area: 424,165 sq.mi. (1,098,581 sq.km.). Pop. (1973 est.): 5,331,000, of whom more than 50% were Indian. Language: Spanish (official). Religion (1971 est.): Roman Catholic 94.5%. Judicial cap.: Sucre (pop., 1972 est., 52,100). Administrative cap. and largest city: La Paz (pop., 1972 est., 574,200). President in 1974, Col. Hugo Banzer Suárez.

In February 1974, after the Cochabamba peasant uprising (see below), most of the leaders of Bolivia's Falange Socialista Boliviana (FSB) and Movimiento Nacionalista Revolucionario (MNR), the base of President Banzer's political support, left the loose federation of the Frente Popular Nacionalista (FPN), which consisted of the above parties and the armed forces. The president then appointed an almost wholly military Cabinet. Before dawn on June 5 a group of young army officers attempted a coup, but government forces quickly reestablished control. In July a new Cabinet was appointed. The abortive plot was seen to have involved senior members of the armed forces, and the possibility of continued military cohesion in support of the president seemed increasingly doubtful. The conspirators' demands were allowed to be published after the coup had failed, and they included the resignation of the president, the establishment of a military government without the involvement of the political parties, and the calling of elections without an official candidate. President Banzer announced that elections would take place in October 1975 and that power would be handed to an elected government. To accomplish this, the Consejo Nacional de Reformas Estructurales and the Consejo Político Nacionalista would be set up. On November 10, however, after an abortive revolt at Santa Cruz (see below), he said that a military government of reconstruction would take over until 1980.

The president's position was one of perpetual crisis, threatened by the powerful agro-industrial interests of the southwest, which had brought him to power, and by the various military factions whose rivalries kept him there. Inflation, running at 35% in 1973,

largely wiped out the benefits to the economy of high export prices, while four major across-the-board pay increases since the middle of 1973 served to keep demand for staples and food imports high. The cotton, rice, and sugar producers flatly refused to be taxed, and so there was a permanent shortage in government revenues. Even President Banzer's hold over the peasants of the Cochabamba region could not be taken for granted after the Army was called out there in January to quell an uprising in protest against economic measures raising food prices; approximately 100 peasants were killed in the conflict. On November 7 another revolt, at Santa Cruz, was quelled by Banzer himself with paratroops.

The external economic picture, however, proved brighter with record exports of $268.3 million—though with record imports of $255.5 million—in 1973. The government was successful in attracting major foreign loans from both private and international sources. The Inter-American Development Bank loaned $35 million for road improvement between Cochabamba and Oruro and $46.5 million for a project to expand oil-refining capacity.

On May 22 the presidents of Bolivia and Brazil signed an agreement for industrial cooperation in return for sales of Bolivian natural gas to Brazil. A pipeline was to be built between the two countries to deliver 240 million cu.ft. of gas a day to São Paulo in Brazil. Brazil would provide financial support to construct a development zone in the Santa Cruz area at an estimated cost of $600 million. By August the government had signed 11 exploration and development contracts with foreign oil companies. During

Army troops disperse peasants in Cochabamba during the uprising in January.

UPI COMPIX

1973 crude oil exports reached 11.9 million bbl., an increase of 9% over the year before, while natural gas exports to Argentina increased by 71% to 1,719,000,-000 cu.m. Argentina and Bolivia were to cooperate in building a pesticide factory at Oruro with financial assistance from the Corporación Andina de Fomento, which was also to grant lines of credit of $1 million to Bolivia to help expand the metalworking industry and increase Bolivian participation in and exports to the Andean Group. (MICHAEL WOOLLER)

[974.D.3]

Botswana

A landlocked republic of southern Africa and a member of the Commonwealth of Nations, Botswana is bounded by South Africa, South West Africa, and Rhodesia. Area: 222,000 sq.mi. (576,000 sq.km.). Pop. (1973 est.): 646,000, almost 99% African. Capital: Gaborone (pop., 1971, 18,799). Largest city: Francistown (pop., 1971, 21,083). Language: English (official) and Tswana. Religion: Christian 60%; animist. President in 1974, Sir Seretse Khama.

In the general elections held on October 26, Pres. Sir Seretse Khama's Botswana Democratic Party was returned to power for another five years, winning 27 of the National Assembly's 32 seats. Botswana's internal and external problems intensified after the January 1974 uprising in Lesotho. Refugees from Lesotho crossed its borders and guerrillas passed through Botswana on the way to fighting South African troops in South West Africa (Namibia). Botswana found it difficult to decide whether those seeking its sanctuary were genuine political refugees or criminals who should be extradited.

Botswana is bound by economic ties to South Africa, which supplies 80% of its imports and accepts much farm and mine labour from it. In February, Quet Masire, Botswana's vice-president and minister of finance, visited 12 countries to explain the problems faced by his nation in the light of the oil embargo on South Africa. Because South Africa refines and transports oil for Botswana, cuts in the oil supply would mean a reduction in the output of the Botswana mining industry, a reduction in tourism, and the expenditure of considerable money to improve alternative road transportation via Zambia.

In April leaders of Botswana, Lesotho, and

BOTSWANA
Education. (1973) Primary, pupils 95,511, teachers 2,698; secondary, pupils 6,152, teachers 311; vocational, pupils 1,521, teachers 123; teacher training (including higher), students 392, teachers 46; higher (at University of Botswana, Lesotho, and Swaziland), students 132, teaching staff 23.
Finance and Trade. Monetary unit: South African rand, with (Sept. 16, 1974) a free rate of R 0.70 to U.S. $1 (R 1.62 = £1 sterling). Budget (1973–74 est.): revenue R 36,850,000; expenditure R 36,820,-000. Foreign trade (1972–73): imports R 86.9 million (65% from South Africa in 1966); exports R 41 million (18% to South Africa in 1966). Main exports: mineral products 44%; meat and products 42%.
Agriculture. Production (in 000; metric tons; 1972; 1971 in parentheses): sorghum 74 (73); corn 12 (18); millet 7 (3); peanuts c. 6 (6). Livestock (in 000; 1972): cattle 1,800; sheep 402; goats 1,035.
Industry. Production (in 000; 1972): diamonds (metric carats) 2,446; manganese ore (metric tons) 0.3; electricity (kw-hr.) 32,000.

Swaziland met to form a joint commission to cooperate in matters of common interest and to pool resources. During the year diamond mining increased in production and value, but schemes to develop Okavango River waters, though economically advantageous, were held up by political considerations.

(MOLLY MORTIMER)

[978.E.8.b.ii]

Bowling and Lawn Bowls

Tenpin Bowling. *World.* A market review indicated that in 1974 there were in the world more than 40 million men, women, and children who engaged in bowling. Of those more than 10 million competed in leagues and, through their national federations, were members of the Fédération Internationale des Quilleurs (FIQ), whose membership grew from 48 to 53 affiliates through the addition of Thailand, Netherlands Antilles, Bolivia, Channel Islands, and Guam.

In April seven countries competed in the third FIQ Asian championships in Tokyo. The winners were: *men:* teams of five, Japan, 5,854; teams of three, Thailand, 3,466; doubles, Singapore, 2,398; singles, Tien Tsai, Taiwan, 1,199; masters, Katsuyuki Saito, Japan, 3,140; all-events, S. Y. Loh, Singapore, 4,684; *women:* teams of four, Philippines, 4,411; teams of three, Thailand, 3,384; doubles, Philippines, 2,340; singles, S. Pinibal, Thailand, 1,160; masters, J. Baker, Australia, 2,305; all-events, R. Kompeerasut, Thailand, 4,502.

Also in April teams from ten European countries competed in the second FIQ European Youth Championships in The Netherlands. The idea of the tournament was to promote bowling as a sport for young people. The winners were: teams of five, Great Britain, 5,305; doubles, Sweden, 2,148. Each of the above consisted of six games, and an additional six-game singles brought the total number of games to 18; the 18 games decided the individual championship, which went to C. McCarthy, Great Britain, 3,274.

In addition to these competitions, there were other international events. The Bowling World Cup, the most important annual singles tournament, held its 1973 finals in Singapore. The national eliminations had been bowled in almost 50 different countries, and the men and women winners of those tournaments were flown to Singapore for the finals. In the men's competition Great Britain's Bernie Caterer defeated Canada's Glen Watson in a three-game final match with the smallest possible difference, 643 to 642. In the ladies' division, as in 1972, Mexico and Thailand were again represented in the final match, in which Pimolrat Srivises of Thailand defeated Luisa Delgado of Mexico, 569 to 495. The annual Tournament of the Americas, bowled for the 12th time in July in Miami, Fla., under the sponsorship, as always, of the city of Miami, enjoyed a record entry of 22 countries. Winners of the most important events were: *men:* doubles, U.S., 3,591; singles (15 games), Alfonso Rodriquez, Mexico, 2,902; all-events (36 games), Robert Hart, U.S., 7,216; *women:* doubles, U.S., 3,316; singles (15 games), Mary Lou Graham, U.S., 2,979; all-events (36 games), Graham, U.S., 6,903.

(YRJÖ SARAHETE)

United States. Earl Anthony, of Tacoma, Wash., a left-handed bowler competing on the Professional Bowlers Association (PBA) tournament circuit at a time when few other left-handers were successful, was

Larry Laub winning the U.S. Open Bowling Tournament for his third championship of 1974.

a likely candidate for 1974 Bowler of the Year honours as the year neared completion. The 36-year-old Anthony, winner of seven PBA meets in four previous years as a professional, scored a 216–213 victory over Johnny Petraglia, New York, N.Y., in the final of the $125,000 Firestone Tournament of Champions in Akron, O., to win the PBA's richest prize, $25,000. Anthony then captured the PBA national championship in Downey, Calif., and added PBA titles in San Jose and Fresno, Calif. Named in January 1974 as 1973 Bowler of the Year was Don McCune.

The Masters Tournament, a match play event that pays off more in prestige than money, was won by Paul Colwell, a PBA member from Tucson, Ariz., who defeated all seven of his opponents in four-game duels and averaged a record 234.17 while doing so. Colwell received $5,620. The Masters is conducted annually by the American Bowling Congress (ABC) on the same lanes used for the ABC tournament that is open to all members. Colwell defeated Steve Neff, Sarasota, Fla., 967–905, in the title match.

In the ABC meet, staged over a 79-day period in Indianapolis, Ind., Jim Godman established a Classic Division (for professionals) all-events record by totaling 2,184 for nine games. The Lorain, O., bowler became the first ABC contestant to roll 700 or better in each of three events, shooting 731 in the team event, 749 in doubles, and 704 in singles. Godman helped the Ebonite club, of Hopkinsville, Ky., composed of a quintet of traveling professionals, win the Classic Division team title with a score that was just one pin higher than that of the Munsingwear No. 3 team from Minneapolis, Minn. The score was 3,117 to 3,116. Bob Perry, Paterson, N.J., and Tye Critchlow, Claremont, Calif., won the Classic doubles with 1,359, and the singles championship went to Ed Ditolla, Hackensack, N.J., who shot 747.

In the ABC Regular Division the winners were: team, Olympia Beer, Omaha, Neb., 3,186; doubles, Chuck Sunseri and Bob Hart, Detroit, Mich., 1,419; singles, Gene Krause, Cleveland, O., 773.

The 55th annual Women's International Bowling Congress (WIBC) national tournament was held in Houston, Tex., and the outstanding performer was the 1973 Woman Bowler of the Year, Judy Cook Soutar, of Kansas City, Mo. Mrs. Soutar captured the Open Division all-events title with a nine-game series of 1,944, including a 624 for Kalicak Construction, from Kansas City, the winner of the Open team title

with 2,973. Carol Miller, Waukesha, Wis., and Janie Leszczynski, Milwaukee, Wis., totaled 1,313 for the doubles crown in the Open Division, and Shirley Garms, Chicago, Ill., topped the singles with 702.

Duckpins. The Marchone Italian Deli group, from Wheaton, Md., won the men's team title in the National Duckpin Tournament, held at Long Meadow Bowl, Hagerstown, Md. Other men's winners were: doubles, Bob Burchard and Bob Devine, Providence, R.I., 925; singles, Smith Greene, Providence, R.I., 489; all-events, Basil Boone, Annapolis, Md., 1,337. Women's Division: team, Scallops, Popes Creek, Md., 1,899; doubles, Nancy Gawor and Jean Stewart, Baltimore, Md., 844; singles, Lori Cabral, Providence, R.I., 432; all-events, Phyllis Rapson, Manchester, Conn., 1,239. Mixed Division: team, Romer's Rollers, Richmond, Va, 1,872; doubles, Anita Rothman and Bill Mueller, Baltimore, Md., 862.   (JOHN J. ARCHIBALD)

Lawn Bowls. The British Commonwealth Games at Woolaston, N.Z., and the second Women's International Championships held at the Victoria Club, Wellington, N.Z., were the major events in lawn bowls in 1974. At the former, David Bryant set a record by winning the singles for the third time in succession; this accomplishment, added to his world championship victory in 1966, stamped him as perhaps the greatest player to date in the history of lawn bowls. Yet Woolanga showed that Australia had a potential gold medalist in Clive White, one of the two men to beat Bryant, as he did again later in the year when Bryant traveled to Newcastle, New South Wales, for the International Masters. Willie Wood of Scotland, winner of the South African mini-Olympic singles in 1973, was Bryant's other conqueror. White finished second and Wood third in the singles. In the pairs Jack Christie and Alex McIntosh won the gold medal for Scotland. John Evans and Peter Line (Eng.) were second, and Phil Skoglund and Bob McDonald (N.Z.) finished third. New Zealand deservedly captured the fours title through the sound teamwork of Kerry Clark, Ray Baldwin, John Somerville, and Gordon Jolly. Australia placed second and Scotland third.

The Women's Championships were dominated by the New Zealanders, with Elsie Wilkie as their outstanding player. She took the singles without losing a match, while Mavis Steele (Eng.) came in second with six wins out of seven matches. Australia won the pairs and New Zealand the triples and fours.

During the year forthcoming complications about amateur-professional definitions could clearly be discerned. South Africa was finally given the go-ahead by the International Bowling Board (IBB) for the 1976 World Bowling Championships, and in England an enterprising travel agency hit upon the idea of promoting a tournament with two package tours to Johannesburg and pocket money to spend as prizes. The tournament would be for officials connected with the 34 counties that made up the English Bowling Association (EBA). These officials were likely to prove vital in gathering together members of the 1,000-strong party that the English intended to send in support of their team. South Africa challenged the provision of pocket money, but the EBA had already forbidden the agency to hand over cash. Yet, even without pocket money, the value of the prizes far exceeded traditional ideas of amateurism. Newspaper articles and books also raised awkward questions, and by the year's end it was clear that open bowls would come into being during the next decade.   (C. M. JONES)
[452.B.4.h.vi]

Boxing

Muhammad Ali (U.S.) staked his claim to join the all-time greats in boxing by regaining the world heavyweight championship, knocking out George Foreman (U.S.) in eight rounds at Kinshasa, Zaire, on Oct. 30, 1974. It was the first world title fight staged in Zaire. Ali at the age of 32 became only the second heavyweight in history to recapture the world title, a feat previously achieved by Floyd Patterson (U.S.) at the age of 25. Ali had first won the world championship in 1964. He never lost the championship in the ring but was stripped of the title when he refused to join the U.S. Army. He remained inactive throughout 1968 and 1969 before announcing his retirement in 1970. He decided to come back later that year and regained the title ten years after he had first won it. Foreman, who earlier in the year had stopped Ken Norton in two rounds in Caracas, Venezuela, was the first world champion never to have fought for the title in the U.S., having won it in Jamaica and defended it in Japan, Venezuela, and Zaire. Ali had taken part in only one other fight earlier in the year, outpointing Joe Frazier (U.S.), a former champion, in New York City.

The world light heavyweight championship changed hands after six years. Bob Foster (U.S.), veteran champion, was held to a draw by Jorge Ahumada (Arg.) at Albuquerque, N.M., and then declined to defend the title against John Conteh (Eng.). Both the World Boxing Council (WBC) and the World Boxing Association (WBA) declared the title vacant. The WBC recognized Conteh as the new champion when he outpointed Ahumada in London. Victor Galindez (Arg.) was recognized by the WBA when he stopped Len Hutchins (U.S.) in 12 rounds in Buenos Aires, Arg., in December.

Carlos Monzón (Arg.) continued to be recognized as world middleweight champion by the WBA after stopping the world welterweight champion, José Nápoles (Mex.), in six rounds in Paris and Tony Mundine (Austr.) in seven in Buenos Aires. But the WBC withdrew recognition and accepted Rodrigo Valdes (Colombia) as champion after he knocked out Benny Briscoe (U.S.) in seven rounds at Monte Carlo. The world junior middleweight championship was won by Oscar Alvarado (U.S.), who stopped Koichi Wajima (Jap.) in 15 rounds in Tokyo. Alvarado then retained his crown by defeating Ryu Sorimachi (Jap.) in seven. José Nápoles retained the world

George Foreman drives a left to the ribs of Muhammad Ali in their title bout at Kinshasa, Zaire. Ali knocked out Foreman in the eighth round, thus becoming only the second fighter in history to regain the heavyweight championship.

welterweight title he had won five years earlier, stopping Hedgemon Lewis (U.S.) in nine rounds in Mexico City. Antonio Cervantes (Colombia) retained the WBA junior welterweight championship, beating Chang Kil Lee (South Korea) in six rounds, Victor Ortiz (P.R.) in two, and Yasuaki Kadoto (Jap.) in eight. The WBC, however, recognized Perico Fernandez (Spain) as champion after he outpointed Lion Furuyama (Jap.) in Rome. This followed the relinquishing of the title by Bruno Arcari (Italy).

Roberto Durán (Panama) retained the WBA lightweight championship, stopping Esteban de Jesus (P.R.) in 11 rounds. Gattu ("Guts") Ishimatsu (Jap.) carried on as WBC champion, stopping Rodolfo González (U.S.) in eight rounds and drawing with Arturo Pineda (Mex.), both fights taking place in Tokyo. Kuniaki Shibata (Jap.) won the WBC junior lightweight crown from Riccardo Arredondo (Mex.) in Tokyo. The WBA version was retained by Ben Villaflor (Phil.), who drew with Apollo Yoshio (Jap.) and stopped Harugi Uehara (Jap.). New WBC and WBA featherweight champions were crowned. Bobby Chacon (U.S.) received WBC recognition by stopping Alfredo Marcano (Venezuela) in nine rounds for the vacant crown. Ruben Olivares (Mex.) became WBA champion in another contest for the vacant

Division	World	Europe	Commonwealth	Britain
	Boxing Champions			
	As of Dec. 31, 1974			
Heavyweight	Muhammad Ali, U.S.	Joe Bugner, Eng.	Danny McAlinden, N. Ire.	Danny McAlinden, N. Ire.
Light heavyweight	John Conteh, Eng.*	vacant	John Conteh, Eng.	vacant
	Victor Galindez, Arg.†			
Middleweight	Rodrigo Valdes, Col.*	Kevin Finnegan, Eng.	Tony Mundine, Austr.	vacant
	Carlos Monzón, Arg.†			
Junior middleweight	Oscar Alvarado, U.S.	José Durán, Spain	Charkey Ramon, Austr.	Maurice Hope, Eng.
Welterweight	José Nápoles, Mex.	John Stracey, Eng.	Clyde Gray, Can.	John Stracey, Eng.
Junior welterweight	Perico Fernandez, Spain*	vacant	Hector Thompson, Austr.	Joey Singleton, Eng.
	Antonio Cervantes, Col.†			
Lightweight	Gattu Ishimatsu, Jap.*	Ken Buchanan, Scot.	Percy Hayles, Jam.	vacant
	Roberto Durán, Pan.†			
Junior lightweight	Kuniaki Shibata, Jap.*	Sven-Erik Paulsen, Nor.	...	...
	Ben Villaflor, Phil.†			
Featherweight	Bobby Chacon, U.S.*	Gitano Jiminez, Spain	David "Poison" Kotey, Ghana	Evan Armstrong, Scot.
	Alexis Arguello, Nic.†			
Bantamweight	Rodolfo Martinez, Mex.*	Bob Allotey, Spain	Paul Ferreri, Austr.	Dave Needham, Eng.
	Soo Hwan-Hong, S. Korea†			
Flyweight	Shoji Oguma, Jap.*	Franco Udella, Italy	Jim West, Austr.	John McCluskey, Scot.
	Susumu Hanagata, Jap.†			

*World Boxing Council champion.
†World Boxing Association champion.

The new WBC lightweight champion, Gattu ("Guts") Ishimatsu, sends Rodolfo González (U.S.) to the canvas for the third and last time in their Tokyo title bout.

title by defeating Zensuke Utagawa (Jap.) in seven. Later, Olivares lost the WBA title when stopped in 12 rounds by Alexis Arguello (Nicaragua). Rafael Herrera (Mex.) retained the WBC bantamweight championship by knocking out Romero Anaya (Mex.) in six rounds but then lost the title to Rodolfo Martinez (Mex.), who stopped him in four rounds. Soo Hwan Hong (South Korea) took the WBA crown on points from Arnold Taylor (S.Af.). Chartchai Chionoi (Thailand) defended the WBA flyweight title, outpointing Fritz Chervet (Switz.), but he then lost the crown to Susumu Hanagata (Jap.) in six rounds. Betulio Gonzáles (Venezuela) retained the WBC version by knocking out Franco Udella (Italy) in ten rounds but then lost it when outpointed by Shoji Oguma (Jap.).

In Europe Joe Bugner (Eng.) continued to dominate the heavyweights, stopping Mario Baruzzi (Italy) in nine rounds in Copenhagen. John Conteh held the light heavyweight crown with victories over Tom Bogs (Den.) and Chris Finnegan (Eng.), but relinquished the title after becoming WBC world champion. Domenico Adinolfi (Italy) won the crown in December by knocking out Karl Heinz Klein (W.Ger.).

Kevin Finnegan (Eng.) won the middleweight title with a victory on points over Jean-Claude Bouttier (France). José Durán (Spain) became the new junior middleweight champion with a points win against Jacques Kechichian (France). A new welterweight champion was crowned when John Stracey (Eng.) defeated Roger Menetrey (France) in eight rounds. The junior welterweight championship went to Perico Fernandez (Spain), who stopped Antonio Ortiz (Spain) in 12 rounds. Fernandez relinquished this title after becoming WBC world champion.

Ken Buchanan (Scot.) won the lightweight crown from Antonio Puddu (Italy) with a sixth-round knockout, while Sven-Erik Paulsen (Nor.) took the junior lightweight title from Lothar Abend (W.Ger.). Gitano Jiminez (Spain) retained the featherweight championship defeating Daniel Vermandere (France) and Elio Cotena (Italy). The bantamweight championship became vacant when Johnny Clark (Eng.) retired because of eye trouble; Bob Allotey (Spain) became the new champion, outpointing Guy Caudron (France). Franco Udella was crowned the new flyweight champion, knocking out Pedro Molledo (Spain) in five rounds of a contest for the vacant title.

(FRANK BUTLER)

[452.B.4.h.vii]

Brazil

A federal republic in eastern and central South America, Brazil is bounded by the Atlantic Ocean and all the countries of South America except Ecuador and Chile. Area: 3,286,488 sq.mi. (8,511,965 sq.km.). Pop. (1974 est.): 104,641,500. Principal cities (pop., 1970): Brasília (cap.) 271,570; Rio de Janeiro 4,251,918; São Paulo 5,924,612. Language: Portuguese. Religion: Roman Catholic 93%. Presidents in 1974, Gen. Emílio Garrastazú Médici and, from March 15, Gen. Ernesto Geisel.

Political Affairs. On March 15 Gen. Ernesto Geisel (*see* BIOGRAPHY) and Gen. Adalberto Pereira dos Santos were sworn in at Brasília as the republic's president and vice-president, respectively, for the five-year period ending on March 15, 1979. Afterward, Geisel made a brief speech in which he emphasized that his administration would endeavour to continue the general policies of the 1964 revolution, which were summarized as "development" and "security."

Geisel had been publicly declared by President Médici in mid-1973 to be the administration's candidate for the presidency in the elections of 1974. This selection was later endorsed by the government's political party (National Renewal Alliance, known as ARENA). In September 1973 the opposition party, Brazilian Democratic Movement (MDB), nominated its own candidates: Ulysses Guimarães and Barbosa Lima Sobrinho for president and vice-president, respectively. In the political campaign that followed, General Geisel, after resigning his position as president of Petrobras (the government-owned oil monopoly), limited himself to the study of plans for his future administration. The MDB candidates carried on throughout the country what was called a symbolic "countercampaign," protesting against the indirect system of presidential elections, calling for the immediate amnesty of all political dissenters, the abolition of censorship, the reinstatement of habeas corpus, and other traditional democratic tenets.

As expected, on Jan. 15, 1974, Geisel and Pereira dos Santos were duly elected by the electoral college gathered at the Chamber of Deputies in Brasília for that purpose, as provided by the 1967 constitution and the implementing law of August 1973. They received 400 votes out of a total of 497. The MDB candidates had 76 votes, and a number of opposition party delegates abstained from voting.

At his first Cabinet meeting President Geisel again emphasized that the basic aim of his government would be to assure the country's economic development and security. He added that he would welcome the participation of responsible elites and of the general public but that he would not tolerate "turbulent or errant minorities" that might upset the nation's normal life. He further declared that he anticipated a general rise in prices because of higher prices to be paid for imported oil. To reduce the nation's dependence on imported oil, Geisel announced that he planned greater development of the country's hydroelectric potential, preparation for Brazil's entrance into the nuclear energy age, and better use of the existing coal and shale-oil deposits. He added that he intended to promote the redistribution of wealth, the strengthening of the capital market, and the eradication of illiteracy.

The tenth anniversary of the revolution was commemorated on March 31. The ten-year ban on political activities of 106 leaders (known as *cassados* or "the annulled ones") of the regime overthrown in 1964 was lifted a few days later (April 10). The list included three former presidents (Juscelino Kubitschek, Jânio Quadros, and João Goulart), several former government ministers, congressmen, and military officers. Many of these people had left the country; they could now return and resume political activity although the administration warned that the ban could be reimposed if there was sufficient cause for it.

Elections for Congress (all 310 members of the Chamber of Deputies and 22 of the 66 senators) took place Nov. 15, 1974. The result was a surprising victory for the MDB. The opposition captured 20 Senate seats and, by winning more than a third of the seats in the Chamber, it obtained the right to form investigative committees and summon government officials to testify. Effective power, however, remained with the executive.

For some time, the relations of the government with the country's Roman Catholic Church leaders had been strained. Priests and nuns accused of subversive activities were arrested. A Catholic-owned radio station in São Paulo was taken off the air, allegedly for technical violations. At the beginning of President Geisel's administration, church leaders had indicated their desire to end the feud. Geisel showed consideration toward the church by consulting certain Catholic leaders before choosing his Cabinet. His inauguration was attended by church leaders. When Agnelo Cardinal Rossi, prefect of the Vatican's Congregation for Evangelization, visited Brazil in July, he was cordially received by the president. After that, relations between the government and the church were believed to have improved considerably.

The Economy. Brazil's economy was hard hit by the oil crisis of 1973–74. For some time the country had been importing as much as 75–80% of its annual oil consumption. After the Arab oil embargo the price of imported oil rose from $3.38 (September 1973) to $11.73 (February 1974) per barrel, an increase of almost 350%. To illustrate the effect of the increase, Brazil paid $327 million in 1971 for its imported oil; it was estimated that it paid about $3 billion in 1974. Although there was no gasoline rationing, the price of gasoline went up 10% in November 1973 and another 6–10% in January 1974.

To minimize the effects of the rise in oil prices, the government sought to enter into long-term purchasing contracts with the Arab oil-producing states and barter deals were negotiated with some. In May it was announced that Brazil had arranged for the sale of armoured vehicles built in Brazil, equipped with guns supplied by France, in exchange for oil from Qatar. The total value of this transaction was estimated at $100 million.

Increased prospecting for oil was undertaken by Petrobras, which became seriously interested in the use of shale oil. It was claimed that Brazil had the second-largest deposits of shale oil in the world.

BRAZIL

Education. (1971) Primary, pupils 13,623,388, teachers 510,285; secondary, pupils 3,464,088, teachers 228,143; vocational, pupils 797,487, teachers 68,846; teacher training (including higher), students 495,762, teachers 39,223; higher (including 44 official universities; 1972), students 493,171, teaching staff 58,278.

Finance. Monetary unit: cruzeiro, with a free rate (Sept. 16, 1974) of 7 cruzeiros to U.S. $1 (16.20 cruzeiros = £1 sterling). Gold, SDRs, and foreign exchange, official: (March 1974) U.S. $6,397,000,000; (March 1973) U.S. $5,879,000,000. Budget (1973 est.) balanced at 43,834,000,000 cruzeiros. Gross national product: (1972) 296,566,000,000 cruzeiros; (1971) 231,546,000,000 cruzeiros. Money supply: (March 1974) 97,357,000,000 cruzeiros; (March 1973) 63,175,000,000 cruzeiros. Cost of living (São Paulo; 1970 = 100): (May 1974) 198; (May 1973) 125.

Foreign Trade. Imports (1972) 28,060,000,000 cruzeiros; exports 23,580,000,000 cruzeiros. Import sources: U.S. 28%; West Germany 14%; Japan 8%; U.K. 5%; Argentina 5%. Export destinations: U.S. 23%; West Germany 8%; The Netherlands 8%; Italy 7%. Main exports: coffee 25%; iron ore 6%; cotton 5%.

Transport and Communications. Roads (1972) 1,260,331 km. (including 59,372 km. main roads). Motor vehicles in use (1971): passenger 2,786,700; commercial (including buses) 687,200. Railways (1972): 31,190 km.; traffic 11,489,000,000 passenger-km., freight 18,080,000,000 net ton-km. Air traffic (1973): 7,340,000,000 passenger-km.; freight 329,450,000 net ton-km. Shipping (1973): merchant vessels 100 gross tons and over 469; gross tonnage 2,103,319. Shipping traffic (1973): goods loaded 64,054,000 metric tons, unloaded 38,487,000 metric tons. Telephones (Dec. 1972) 2,190,000. Radio receivers (Dec. 1972) 6 million. Television receivers (Dec. 1972) 6.6 million.

Agriculture. Production (in 000; metric tons; 1973; 1972 in parentheses): corn *c.* 15,338 (*c.* 14,892); rice *c.* 8,200 (*c.* 7,309); cassava (1972) *c.* 31,000, (1971) 30,258; potatoes *c.* 1,750 (*c.* 1,720); sweet potatoes (1972) *c.* 2,200, (1971) *c.* 2,210; wheat 1,800 (680); coffee *c.* 1,026 (*c.* 1,475); cocoa *c.* 200 (*c.* 185); bananas (1972) *c.* 7,000, (1971) *c.* 6,806; oranges (1972) *c.* 3,200, (1971) *c.* 3,150; cotton, lint 640 (673); sisal (1972) *c.* 210, (1971) *c.* 210; tobacco *c.* 233 (*c.* 250); peanuts *c.* 650 (*c.* 920); sugar, raw value *c.* 7,156 (*c.* 6,350); dry beans *c.* 2,683 (*c.* 2,439); soybeans *c.* 4,900 (*c.* 3,666); beef and veal *c.* 2,195 (*c.* 2,041); pork *c.* 800 (*c.* 772); rubber *c.* 24 (*c.* 26); timber (cu.m.; 1972) 163,800, (1971) 164,600; fish catch (1971) 581, (1970) 517. Livestock (in 000; Dec. 1972): cattle *c.* 100,500; horses *c.* 9,100; pigs *c.* 68,464; sheep *c.* 24,900; goats (1971) 14,500; chickens (1971) *c.* 300,000.

Industry. Fuel and power (in 000; metric tons; 1973): crude oil 8,284; coal 2,317; natural gas (cu.m.) 1,180,000; electricity (kw-hr.; 1972) 53,767,000 (85% hydroelectric in 1971). Production (in 000; metric tons; 1973): pig iron 5,515; crude steel 7,151; iron ore (metal content; 1972) 28,628; bauxite (1972) 324; manganese ore (metal content; 1971) 1,150; gold (troy oz.; 1972) 166; cement 13,342; asbestos (1968) 345; wood pulp (1972) 1,000; paper (1972) 1,540; passenger cars (including assembly; units) 492; commercial vehicles (including assembly; units) 251.

Jacomea Ecreu, one of two chiefs of the Bororos, an Indian tribe whose survival is threatened by development schemes in the Amazon rain forest.

MARVINE HOWE—THE NEW YORK TIMES

Petrobras also resorted to an increase in the sugarcane alcohol percentage added to the gasoline it sold to the public. An agreement was announced in August between Petrobras and the U.S.S.R. for the purchase of approximately 500,000 tons of crude oil by the end of 1974.

The oil crisis represented a severe setback to the remarkable economic growth of Brazil, which since 1968 had been estimated at an average annual rate of better than 9% according to a published report of the World Bank Group in the Americas. To accomplish this, the government intervened in the economic activities of the country in order to harmonize the interests of the public with private national and foreign interests. Under this system, commonly known as the "Brazilian model," certain economic activities, especially agricultural and industrial production, were promoted jointly by the state and private concerns. A "gradualist system" of combating inflation was adopted under which prices, salaries, and interest rates were controlled.

Brazil's agricultural production did increase immensely, stimulated by greater opportunities in foreign markets. This was especially true in regard to sugar and soybeans. The nation sold large quantities of sugar to the Soviet Union, China, and the U.S. Diplomatic relations with China were reestablished on Aug. 15, 1974, with the expectation that trade between the two countries would increase.

In April 1973 Brazil and Paraguay signed an agreement to construct a large hydroelectric plant at Itaipu, 25 mi. upriver from Iguaçu Falls. In May 1974 Brazil agreed to cooperate in the economic development of southeastern Bolivia. Brazil was to buy natural gas from Bolivia, and a gas pipeline between the two nations was to be constructed.

In September Finance Minister Mário Henrique Simonsen declared before the Economic and Finance Committee of the Chamber of Deputies that inflation would probably reach a rate of 32% by the end of the year. An unfavourable balance of payments was forecast, but this was expected to be offset by incoming foreign capital and loans.   (RAUL D'ECA)

[974.G]

Bulgaria

A people's republic of Europe, Bulgaria is situated on the eastern Balkan Peninsula along the Black Sea, bordered by Romania, Yugoslavia, Greece, and Turkey. Area: 42,823 sq.mi. (110,912 sq.km.). Pop. (1974 est.): 8,642,600. Cap. and largest city: Sofia (pop., 1972 est., 926,300). Language: chiefly Bulgarian. First secretary of the Bulgarian Communist Party in 1974 and chairman of the Council of State, Todor Zhivkov; chairman of the Council of Ministers (premier), Stanko Todorov.

The outstanding event of 1974 was the celebration on September 9 of the 30th anniversary of the socialist revolution in Bulgaria. Many prominent personalities of the socialist bloc, headed by Pres. Nikolay V. Podgorny of the U.S.S.R., were present in Sofia for the occasion, though not a single Communist party leader attended. Chairman Zhivkov proclaimed that without the "fraternal friendship" of the Soviet Union and the cooperation of other socialist countries, Bulgaria's considerable economic achievements would have been impossible. Pledging that the Bulgarian Communist Party would continue to follow "the line

of Marxism-Leninism and proletarian internationalism," he said rather significantly that Bulgaria was making "constant efforts to improve relations with neighbouring Yugoslavia" and added, "We want to expand ties with Albania, too." Podgorny, the chief speaker among the fraternal delegates, congratulated the Bulgarian party for its "implacable struggles against the enemies of the working class."

The transformation of Bulgaria from an agrarian country into an industrial one had indeed been remarkable. Prior to World War II the ratio between industry and agriculture was 25:75; in 1974 it stood at 81:19 in favour of industry. National income in 1972 exceeded 11 billion leva, or seven times as much as in 1939, and in 1973 it increased by another 8.7%. Some three-quarters of the national income was set aside for consumption, either directly or through social welfare funds, while the rest was invested in the national economy. Industry accounted for 51% of national income. Total industrial production had expanded more than 43 times since 1945.

Major changes in the Bulgarian party leadership took place in July. After a dramatic plenary meeting of the Central Committee on July 3, it was announced that 43-year-old Ivan Abadjiev, elected candidate member of the Politburo and appointed secretary of the Central Committee of the 1971 party congress, had been dismissed from both bodies. It had been generally assumed that Abedjiev was Zhivkov's probable successor. Two other candidate members of the Politburo were also removed: Venelin Kotsev, a deputy premier, and Kostadin Gyaurov, member of the Council of State and chairman of the Trade Unions Central Council. Two secretaries of the Central Committee, Grisha Filipov and Aleksandr Lilov, became full members of the Politburo, and four new candidate members were elected: Gen. Dobri Djurov, minister of defense, Peter Mladenov, minister of foreign affairs, and the party provincial secretaries of Plovdiv and Varna.

There was also a purge in the state administration: Khristo Panayotov, minister of chemical industry, was replaced by Georgi Pankov; Misho Mishev was appointed chairman of the Trade Unions Central Council while Kyril Tsarev, previously governor of the Bulgarian National Bank, succeeded him as minister of labour; and Vesselin Nikiforov, till then chairman of the State Planning Commission, became governor of the National Bank. These changes, as well as many other replacements of party and state functionaries, suggested that, after a sudden visit to Moscow in May, Zhivkov felt strong enough to rout a faction within the party.

Diplomatic relations were established with West Germany in December 1973 and with Portugal in June 1974.   (K. M. SMOGORZEWSKI)

[972.B.3.d]

Burma

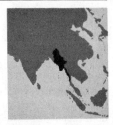

A republic of Southeast Asia, Burma is bordered by Bangladesh, India, China, Laos, and Thailand. Area: 261,789 sq. mi. (678,030 sq.km.). Pop. (1974 est.): 29.5 million. Cap. and largest city: Rangoon (metro. pop., 1971 est., 1,844,000). Language: Burmese. Religion (1970): Buddhist 85%. Chairman of the State Council in 1974, U Ne Win; prime ministers, Ne Win until March 2 and, from March 4, U Sein Win.

In the long-awaited general election held in January–February 1974, candidates of U Ne Win's Burma Socialist Program Party (BSPP) won 99% of the seats in the 451-member unicameral People's Assembly, the few remaining seats going to government-backed independents. The election, provided for in the new constitution approved in a 1973 referendum, was the first since Ne Win seized power in 1962.

Ne Win and his military colleagues continued to hold undisputed sway over the state, now renamed the Socialist Republic of the Union of Burma. At its first session on March 2, the Assembly elected a 28-member State Council which in turn chose Ne Win as the first president. The election of the State Council was widely publicized since the constitution designated it as the supreme authority of the state. Ne Win also made the formal gesture of transferring state authority to the Assembly, as he had promised during the drafting of the constitution in 1973. However, his choice of General San Yu, a long-time companion and former vice-chairman, to be secretary-general of the State Council was criticized. An 18-member Council of Ministers, chosen two days later by the State Council, was headed by U Sein Win as prime minister.

There was awareness that the union's future stability would depend largely on how the new team attacked the economic morass in which Burma now found itself. In May and June what began as riots against the inadequate government rice rations soon

BURMA
Education. (1971–72) Primary, pupils 3,198,670, teachers 71,136; secondary, pupils 813,144, teachers 25,461; vocational, pupils 6,307, teachers 576; teacher training (including higher), students 4,269, teachers 307; higher, students 52,661, teaching staff 3,700.
Finance and Banking. Monetary unit: kyat, with (Sept. 16, 1974) a free rate of 4.86 kyats to U.S. $1 (11.25 kyats = £1 sterling). Gold, SDRs, and foreign exchange, official: (March 1974) U.S. $125 million; (March 1973) U.S. $53.9 million. Budget (1972–73 est.): revenue 8,734,000,000 kyats; expenditure 9,702,-000,000 kyats.
Foreign Trade. (1973) Imports 471.5 million kyats; exports 532.2 million kyats. Import sources (1972): Japan 27%; China 10%; West Germany 9%; India 7%; U.K. 7%; U.S. 5%. Export destinations (1972): Sri Lanka 14%; Japan 12%; U.K. 9%; Singapore 9%; West Germany 5%; Mauritius 5%. Main exports: teak 37%; rice 14%; oilcakes 8%.
Transport and Communications. Roads (1972) c. 25,000 km. (including c. 13,700 km. all-weather). Motor vehicles in use (1972): passenger 31,000; commercial (including buses) 33,400. Railways: (1971) 3,098 km.; traffic (1973) 2,593,000,000 passenger-km., freight 708 million net ton-km. Air traffic (1972): 162 million passenger-km.; freight 2.3 million net ton-km. Shipping (1973): merchant vessels 100 gross tons and over 40; gross tonnage 54,977. Telephones (Dec. 1972) 28,000. Radio licenses (Dec. 1972) 600,000.
Agriculture. Production (in 000; metric tons; 1973; 1972 in parentheses): rice c. 8,580 (7,559); sesame seed c. 115 (c. 115); peanuts (1972) c. 520, (1971) 502; dry beans c. 150 (c. 145); onions c. 110 (106); sugar, raw value c. 100 (c. 98); cotton, lint (1972) c. 17, (1971) 14; jute c. 99 (c. 90); tobacco c. 52 (52); rubber c. 10 (c. 10); timber (cu.m.; 1972) 16,-200, (1971) 15,900. Livestock (in 000; March 1973): cattle c. 7,350; buffalo (1972) c. 1,620; pigs c. 1,700; goats (1972) c. 600; sheep c. 190.
Industry. Production (in 000; metric tons; 1973): crude oil 914; electricity (excluding most industrial production; kw-hr.) 634,000; cement 193; lead concentrates (metal content; 1971) 9.1; zinc concentrates (metal content; 1971) 2.9; tin concentrates (metal content; 1972) 0.6; tungsten concentrates (oxide content; 1971) 0.5.

turned into widespread student and worker demonstrations and strikes in factories. At least 22 people were killed before the Army and police restored order. Ne Win promised that rations would be increased and that rice exports, the major foreign exchange earner, would be stopped if necessary. The government also announced plans to import 30,000 tons of wheat and flour, 2,000 tons of sugar, and 30,000 tons of powdered soap. The rice procurement and distribution policy was only partly successful, since farmers, despite a 40% increase in the procurement price, withheld deliveries.

Burma lifted its isolationist curtain a bit during 1974 by deciding to compensate previous owners of nationalized properties and to invite foreign consortiums to explore for offshore oil and mineral resources. In June the Myanma Oil Corporation, the state oil enterprise of Burma, signed agreements with the Arakan Oil Development Co. of Japan, with a three-nation Western European consortium, and with a U.S. consortium, which included Esso, for offshore drilling for oil near the Arakan coast. The agreements were on a 70–30 profit-sharing basis in Burma's favour.

Presenting the 1974–75 budget to the Assembly, Deputy Prime Minister and Minister for Planning and Finance U Lwin warned that an all-out effort was needed to rescue the economy. He proposed to limit imports to essential items, to reorganize unprofitable state enterprises, and to curtail government spending severely. The budget estimates showed a deficit of 582 million kyats; expenditure was placed at 11,797,-000,000 kyats and revenues, including foreign loans and grants, at 11,215,000,000 kyats. U Lwin also submitted the draft second four-year plan envisaging a total investment of 5,910,000,000 kyats and an annual increase in the net national output of 4.5%.

On December 5 students at Rangoon seized the body of U Thant (*see* OBITUARIES), former secretary-general of the UN who had died in New York November 25, and later buried it, in defiance of the government, at a site of their own choosing. The body was subsequently recovered by government troops.

In March the Assembly enacted legislation offering amnesty to insurgents, and some gave themselves up before the deadline of June 16. Nevertheless, the hard core of the Burmese Communist Party insurgents and the Shan and Karen rebels continued to menace security in the countryside. (GOVINDAN UNNY)

[976.B.1]

Burundi

A republic of eastern Africa, Burundi is bordered by Zaire, Rwanda, and Tanzania. Area: 10,747 sq.mi. (27,834 sq.km.). Pop. (1973 est.): 3.6 million, mainly Hutu, Tutsi, and Twa. Cap. and largest city: Bujumbura (pop., 1970 est., 110,000). Language: Kirundi and French. Religion (1964): Roman Catholic 51%; Protestant 4%; animist 45%. President in 1974, Michel Micombero.

Through massive suppression of the Hutu (85% of the population), President Micombero during the year maintained control of the government by the Tutsi ethnic minority. A study of the situation by the Minority Rights Group, London, estimated that 100,000 Hutu (over 3% of the population) had been killed in the tribal warfare, which began in 1972. The leadership elite of the Hutu was believed to have been wiped out. The republic's first constitution was promulgated on July 11; widest power continued to be vested in the president, who remained head of the only legal political party as well as supreme commander of the armed forces.

The government improved Burundi's relations with neighbouring Rwanda and Zaire at a June summit meeting. By May the compensation due to Tanzania for the 1973 border clashes between the two countries had been paid in full, though the problem of Hutu refugees in Tanzania remained. Landlocked Burundi depended on Tanzanian outlets for about 80% of its exports, and a World Bank loan of TShs. 2.5 billion to finance a joint rail link for Burundi

nickel exports was initiated during the year. A National Trade Office was established by presidential order to oversee trade agreements such as the January economic and technical agreement with Romania, to carry out government commercial policy, and, by so controlling imports, to ensure the supply of commodities for state administration of the economy. In May Burundi was reported to have signed a trade agreement with the U.S.S.R.

Much of the 1974 budget expenditure of BurFr. 2,820,000,000 was for national security, while revenue at BurFr. 2,531,000,000, mainly from taxation and customs duty, showed the country's continued dependence on foreign aid, largely Belgian. Britain provided £5,000 for fishing development, while the International Development Association granted $5 million for road development under the 1974–78 maintenance and development plan. (MOLLY MORTIMER)

Cambodia

A republic of Southeast Asia, Cambodia (officially known as the Khmer Republic) is the southwest part of the Indochinese Peninsula. Area: 69,898 sq.mi. (181,035 sq.km.). Pop. (1973 est.): 7,190,000, including (1962 est.) Khmer 93%; Vietnamese 4%; Chinese 3%. Cap.: Phnom Penh (pop., 1971 est., 479,300). Language: Khmer (official) and French. Religion: Buddhist. President in 1974, Gen. Lon Nol; premier, Long Boret.

On March 18, 1974, Pres. Lon Nol celebrated the fourth anniversary of the overthrow of Prince Norodom Sihanouk; it was also, essentially, the fourth anniversary of the Cambodian war. Although U.S. bombing was halted in 1973, the war continued unabated, largely because of vastly increased supplies of U.S. armaments. Fighting followed the pattern set earlier: government troops, reduced to a defensive strategy,

BURUNDI
Education. (1970–71) Primary, pupils 182,664, teachers 4,982; secondary, pupils 3,969, teachers 397; vocational, pupils 1,115, teachers 173; teacher training, students 3,085, teachers 284; higher, students 470, teaching staff 67.
Finance. Monetary unit: Burundi franc, with (Sept. 16, 1974) an official rate of BurFr. 78.80 to U.S. $1 (free rate of BurFr. 181.97 = £1 sterling). Gold, SDRs, and foreign exchange, central bank: (June 1974) U.S. $19.3 million; (June 1973) U.S. $19,680,-000. Budget (1973 actual): revenue BurFr 2,806,000,-000; expenditure BurFr. 2,746,400,000.
Foreign Trade. (1973) Imports BurFr. 2,495,000,-000; exports BurFr. 2,380,000,000. Import sources: Belgium-Luxembourg 24%; France 12%; West Germany 9%; Kenya 5%. Export destinations: U.S. 55%; Italy 11%; West Germany 10%; U.K. 9%; Spain 5%. Main export coffee 86%.
Agriculture. Production (in 000; metric tons; 1972; 1971 in parentheses): corn *c.* 250 (247); cassava *c.* 1,580 (*c.* 1,580); sweet potatoes *c.* 1,100 (*c.* 1,060); millet *c.* 25 (22); sorghum *c.* 55 (53); dry beans *c.* 170 (*c.* 150); dry peas *c.* 36 (*c.* 36); coffee (1973) *c.* 23, (1972) 19; cotton, lint *c.* 3 (*c.* 3).

CAMBODIA
Education. (1972–73) Primary, pupils 471,493, teachers 20,150; secondary, pupils 98,358, teachers (1969–70) 5,292; vocational, pupils (1969–70) 5,789, teachers (1967–68) 464; teacher training, students 580, teachers 96; higher (including 5 universities), students 7,527, teaching staff 1,101.
Finance. Monetary unit: riel, with (Sept. 16, 1974) a free rate of 420 riels to U.S. $1 (970 riels = £1 sterling). Budget (1973 est.): revenue 24,658,000,000 riels; expenditure 34 billion riels.
Foreign Trade. (1971) Imports 4,346,000,000 riels; exports 825 million riels. Import sources: U.S. 40%; Singapore 13%; Japan 13%; Hong Kong 6%. Export destinations: Hong Kong 17%; France 15%; Japan 14%; Singapore 12%; Senegal 9%; Dahomey 7%. Main exports (1970): rice 42%; rubber 16%; corn 5%; beans 5%.
Transport and Communications. Roads (1972) *c.* 11,000 km. Motor vehicles in use (1972): passenger 27,200; commercial (including buses) 11,100. Railways: (including sections not in operation; 1972) *c.* 650 km.; traffic (1973) 54,070,000 passenger-km., freight 9,780,000 net ton-km. Air traffic (1972): 34 million passenger-km.; freight 700,000 net ton-km. Inland waterway (Mekong River; 1972) *c.* 1,400 km. Telephones (Dec. 1972) 9,000. Radio receivers (Dec. 1972) 1.1 million. Television receivers (Dec. 1969) 50,000.
Agriculture. Production (in 000; metric tons; 1973; 1972 in parentheses): rice 953 (2,138); corn (1972) 62, (1971) 122; rubber *c.* 20 (15); bananas (1972) *c.* 135, (1971) 134; dry beans *c.* 25 (22); jute *c.* 5 (5). Livestock (in 000; Dec. 1972): cattle *c.* 2,300; buffalo *c.* 700; pigs *c.* 1,150.

Business Review:
see Economy, World
Butter:
see Agriculture and
Food Supplies

attempted to preserve enclaves of control, while insurgents struck deep into the capital city but were unable or unwilling to seize it.

The heaviest attack on Phnom Penh took place in late January. From the north a rebel Communist force of about 7,500 troops drove to within three miles of the Pochentong airport and then suddenly stopped, while from the south rockets and artillery pounded the city, its suburbs, and a refugee camp for four days, killing 85 persons. The Communists captured Oudong, a provincial capital 24 mi. NW of Phnom Penh, in March. Informed estimates of the cost of war were grim: approximately 300 Cambodians killed or wounded every day, some 200,000 refugees since the bombing stopped—taking the total to 3 million, or nearly half the population of the country—more than 200,000 children orphaned, and 50,000 war widows registered with the government.

The war raged against a background of rising popular unrest in Phnom Penh and confusion in government ranks. Students and teachers led antigovernment demonstrations, which rose to a tragic climax in midyear. Campus unrest had become militant by late 1973, and teachers went on strike on December 20 demanding that salaries be trebled. A month later four students aged between 14 and 18 were found hanged inside their jail cells. Their deaths were attributed to suicide by the government, but to torture by others. Public schools were closed, though sporadic protest demonstrations continued. In the last week of May the arrest of 61 students and a teacher on charges of subversive activities provoked renewed anger, and moves were made to form a coalition of schoolteachers, university students, and Buddhist monks.

On June 4 hundreds of students marched in procession to protest against the arrest of students and teachers, stormed the Ministry of Education, and forced Minister Keo Sangkim and his aide Thach Chea to accompany them (some reports said the officials were abducted). Moving to the Lycée 18 March, the students held the officials in a classroom and refused to free them until the arrested teachers and students were released. Police surrounded the school, and ultimatums, taunts, and stone-throwing followed; in the subsequent struggle both Keo Sangkim and Thach Chea were killed.

The police claimed that students had stabbed and shot the minister and his aide, but a newsman at the scene was quoted as saying that the officials were shot by military policemen when the students used them as human shields, and two other witnesses said that nonstudent infiltrators had fired the fatal shots. According to the police, 2 students were killed, 8 wounded, and 48 arrested. A curfew was imposed on Phnom Penh. On September 2 it was announced that a military tribunal had sentenced two high school students to death and ten others to long prison terms for the killing of the officials. Earlier, the prosecutor had told the tribunal that a 30-year-old engineer leading a commando unit of seven was responsible.

Deep disquiet followed the tragedy of Lycée 18 March, and the governing coalition itself disintegrated. Lon Nol reacted by resorting to his familiar technique in times of crisis—the announcement of a new Cabinet. In April he had established a new apex body called the High Executive Council, consisting of himself, Premier Long Boret, Maj. Gen. Sosthène Fernandez, the army chief of staff, and former strongman Lieut. Gen. Sirik Matak, but after the killing of the education minister six Cabinet members re-

Government forces in action against the Khmer Rouge insurgents near Kruos in May.

signed. In the new Cabinet Lon Nol retained Long Boret as premier but kept the opposition Republican Party out of office. It was generally seen as another round in what had come to be known as Cambodia's "musical chairs."

In early July Lon Nol proposed peace talks with the insurgents "without prerequisites or conditions." The offer came after two weeks of talks between government leaders and U.S. Ambassador John Gunther Dean, but there had been no contact with what Lon Nol called "the other Cambodian side." Earlier, the U.S. defense secretary had said in Washington, D.C., that the Nixon administration would accept a Laotian-style coalition government (including Communists) in Cambodia. Within hours of the Lon Nol offer, Sihanouk said in Peking that there could be no negotiations with the "traitors." Sihanouk's position offered no hope of a compromise, although Lon Nol had retreated from his 1973 stand that North Vietnamese troops must withdraw from Cambodia before negotiations could start. It was suggested that Lon Nol's annual peace offers were timed to coincide with the U.S. congressional debate on aid to Cambodia and the UN debate on who should have Cambodia's seat in the world body.

For the second successive year, an attempt led by China and some third world nations to allot Cambodia's UN seat to the Sihanouk government failed by a narrow margin. The vote, which took place in the early morning hours of November 28, was 56 for, 54 against, and 24 abstentions. The voting pattern was unusual in that the Asian, African, and Arab nations failed to vote as a bloc. However, the results of the UN vote were expected to have no more than a psychological effect, leaving the politico-military situation in Cambodia unchanged. As if to emphasize the determination of the Royal Government of National Union of Cambodia (GRUNK) to fight on, the leader of the Communist guerrilla movement, Khieu Samphan, visited fraternal countries in May and June. The tour, which ended with visits to the Communist areas of Laos and South Vietnam, helped to establish Khieu Samphan, officially vice-premier and commander in chief of GRUNK, as the central political figure while Sihanouk remained the titular head of state.

In four years of fighting the state of the Cambodian

economy had become so hopeless that no one seemed interested in examining it any longer. Phnom Penh's cost of living soared at an annual rate of 300%. The riel was devalued on May 1 from 375 to 418 to the U.S. dollar. Two army battalions demonstrated outside the presidential palace claiming they had not been paid in four months. The sole prop maintaining the economy and the government was U.S. aid, reported to be running at nearly $2 million a day, although the actual flow was considered to be much higher. (T. J. S. GEORGE)

[976.B.4.f]

Cameroon

A republic of west equatorial Africa on the Gulf of Guinea, Cameroon borders on Nigeria, Chad, the Central African Republic, the Congo, Gabon, and Equatorial Guinea. Area: 179,558 sq.mi. (465,054 sq.km.). Pop. (1973 est.): 6,090,000. Cap.: Yaoundé (pop., 1972 est., 190,000). Largest city: Douala (pop., 1972 est., 252,000). Language: English and French (official), Bantu, Sudanic. Religion: mainly animist, with Christian and Muslim minorities. President in 1974, Ahmadou Ahidjo.

Despite the intransigent nationalism evinced in President Ahidjo's attitudes, particularly in the sphere of his country's relations with its former French rulers, he remained unable to overcome the opposition of certain sectors of the country's elites. In February a fierce controversy developed between Ahidjo's government and the Cameroonian National Union of Students as a result of disturbances at the University of Yaoundé. The students alleged that three of their number had been killed and that an additional 60 had been injured in the disturbances. The authorities, however, continued to deny the allegations.

The Cameroon government continued its policy of

a major reorganization of its relations and agreements with France, and in February a series of new accords between the two countries was finally signed in Paris after five months of laborious negotiations. In all, about ten new agreements were signed. However, neither the French nor the Cameroonians gave any indication as to the content of the agreements either at the time of signing or later in the year when President Ahidjo had talks with French Pres. Valéry Giscard d'Estaing.

In August, a few days after the expiration of the normal one-year period of notice required for Cameroon's withdrawal from the Common African and Mauritian Organization (OCAM) to become final, action was taken making Cameroon an official member of the Central and East African organization set up at the instigation and under the de facto leadership of Zaire. Meanwhile, OCAM transferred its headquarters from Yaoundé, the Cameroonian capital, to the Central African Republic's capital of Bangui.

(PHILIPPE DECRAENE)

Canada

Canada is a federal parliamentary state and member of the Commonwealth of Nations covering North America north of conterminous United States and east of Alaska. Area: 3,851,809 sq.mi. (9,976,139 sq.km.). Pop. (1974 est.): 22,479,000, including (1971) British 44.6%; French 28.7%; other European 23%; Indian and Eskimo 1.4%. Cap.: Ottawa (metro. pop., 1973 est., 619,000). Largest city: Montreal (metro. pop., 1973 est., 2,775,000). Language (mother tongue, 1971): English 60.1%; French 26.9%; others 13%. Religion (1971): Roman Catholic 46.2%; Protestant 42.1%. Queen, Elizabeth II; governors-general in 1974, D. Roland Michener and, from January 14, Jules Léger; prime minister, Pierre Elliott Trudeau.

At a time when unstable governments seemed to be the rule in Western countries, Canada in 1974 replaced a minority government with one holding a solid electoral majority. The federal general election of July 8 saw the administration of Pierre Elliott Trudeau (*see* BIOGRAPHY) win a substantial vote of confidence from the Canadian people. Trudeau's victory also represented a break with the recent Canadian past. Since 1957, when a period of political instability set in following the defeat of the long-established Liberal government, Canada had elected minority administrations in five out of seven national elections.

Parliamentary strengths before the July election were Liberals 109, Progressive Conservatives 106, New Democratic Party (socialist) 31, and Social Credit 15. (The 264-seat House of Commons also included one independent [the speaker] and there were two vacant seats.) The Social Credit members tended to vote with the Conservatives, so that the life of the Trudeau government depended on holding the support of the 31 New Democratic Party (NDP) members. This the government had managed to do, surviving 16 confidence votes during the first session of the 29th Parliament. In the second session it won four more votes of confidence. But the NDP was becoming increasingly restless; although it had gained some desired legislation, it was fearful of losing its identity to the electorate through close collaboration with the

CANADA

Education. (1973–74) Primary, pupils 3,779,-900, teachers (1970–71) 166,700; secondary, pupils 1,885,100, teachers (1970–71) 101,800; vocational (1970–71), pupils 322,000; higher (including 68 university institutions), students 543,250, teaching staff 45,700.

Finance. Monetary unit: Canadian dollar, with a free rate (Sept. 16, 1974) of Can$0.99 to U.S. $1 (Can$2.28 = £1 sterling). Gold, SDRs, and foreign exchange, official: (June 1974) U.S. $5,780,000,000; (June 1973) U.S. $5,682,000,-000. Budget (1972–73 est.): revenue Can$16,-602,000,000; expenditure Can$16,116,000,000. Gross national product: (1973) Can$118,680,-000,000; (1972) Can$103,410,000,000. Money supply: (April 1974) Can$25.1 billion; (April 1973) Can$21,980,000,000. Cost of living (1970 = 100): (June 1974) 128; (May 1972) 134.

Foreign Trade. (1973) Imports Can$24,937,-000,000; exports Can$26,216,000,000. Import sources: U.S. 68%; EEC 10%. Export destinations: U.S. 65%; EEC 12% (U.K. 6%); Japan 7%. Main exports: motor vehicles 19%; metal ores 8%; timber 8%; crude oil and natural gas 7%; nonferrous metals 7%; newsprint 5%;

wheat 5%. Tourism (1972): visitors 37,148,000; gross receipts U.S. $1,344,000,000.

Transport and Communications. Roads (1971) 831,682 km. (including 2,765 km. expressways). Motor vehicles in use (1972): passenger 7,407,300; commercial (including buses) 2,059,200. Railways: (1971) 71,057 km.; traffic (1973) 2,688,000,000 passenger-km., freight 183,-186,000,000 net ton-km. Air traffic (1972): 18,-022,000,000 passenger-km.; freight 508 million net ton-km. Shipping (1973): merchant vessels 100 gross tons and over 1,235; gross tonnage 2,422,802. Shipping traffic (includes Great Lakes and St. Lawrence traffic; 1972): goods loaded 98,980,000 metric tons, unloaded 62,024,000 metric tons. Telephones (Dec. 1972) 10,979,000. Radio receivers (Dec. 1972) 17,932,000. Television receivers (Dec. 1971) 7,610,000.

Agriculture. Production (in 000; metric tons; 1973; 1972 in parentheses): wheat 17,112 (14,-514); barley 10,333 (11,287); oats 5,041 (4,-630); rye 363 (344); corn 2,767 (2,528); potatoes 2,133 (2,001); tomatoes c. 390 (343); rapeseed 1,207 (1,300); linseed 493 (447); soybeans 397 (375); tobacco c. 124 (85); beef and veal c. 897 (898); pork c. 635 (632); timber

(cu.m.; 1971) 119,700, (1970) 121,500; fish catch (1972) 1,169, (1971) 1,290. Livestock (in 000; Dec. 1972): cattle 12,734; sheep 605; horses 342; pigs 7,303; poultry c. 91,000.

Industry. Labour force: (May 1974) 9,676,-000; (May 1973) 9,335,000. Unemployment: (May 1974) 5.4%; (May 1973) 5.3%. Index of industrial production (1970 = 100): (1973) 122; (1972) 113. Fuel and power (in 000; metric tons; 1973): coal 17,700; lignite 3,717; crude oil 88,310; natural gas (cu.m.) 98,906,000; electricity (kw-hr.) 262,272,000 (75% hydroelectric and 3% nuclear in 1972). Metal and mineral production (in 000; metric tons; 1973): iron ore (shipments; 55% metal content) 48,198; crude steel 13,385; copper ore (metal content) 815; nickel ore (metal content; 1972) 233; zinc ore (metal content) 1,351; lead ore (metal content) 388; aluminum (1972) 907; uranium ore (metal content; 1972) 3.8; asbestos (1972) 1,535; gold (troy oz.) 1,925; silver (troy oz.) 48,156. Other production (in 000; metric tons; 1973): wood pulp 18,171; newsprint 8,135; sulfuric acid 2,-951; synthetic rubber 229; passenger cars (units) 1,228; commercial vehicles (units) 348. Dwelling units completed (1973) 246,580.

Liberals and unhappy at the government's failure to tax corporation profits more heavily and to reduce business exemptions.

The critical test came on May 6, when Finance Minister John Turner unveiled his budget. He rejected the temporary wage and price controls demanded by the Conservatives to fight inflation, a strategy that he termed unworkable. A more important consideration was whether his taxation measures would appeal to the NDP. Although Turner imposed stiffer taxes on mining and petroleum companies, he rejected most of the NDP's other requirements. NDP leader David Lewis' call for an excess-profits tax gained only a limited response in the revision of company taxation outlined in the Turner budget.

Opposition parties were quick to express their strong dislike of the proposed budget. On May 8 an NDP amendment moving a lack of confidence in the government came to the vote. The Conservatives joined

the 31 NDP members in support of the amendment, outvoting 108 Liberals and 15 Social Credit members. When the results of the vote, 137–123 (with one Liberal member absent because of illness), were announced the chamber erupted in confusion as members tossed papers in the air in their excitement at the outcome. The dramatic scene marked only the third time in Canadian parliamentary history that a government had fallen through losing a vote of confidence and the first time that a government had failed to win support for its budget in the House of Commons. According to the Canadian constitution, a government is obliged to resign or seek a fresh mandate when it loses the confidence of a majority of the House of Commons on a vital subject. Prime Minister Trudeau asked Governor-General Jules Léger to dissolve Parliament and a general election was called for July 8.

The long campaign that followed was less exciting

Campaign '74 on the Trudeau Express, in Rimouski, Que.

CANADA'S NATIVE INDIAN PEOPLES

By Verna J. Kirkness

Our struggle will be over when we have in our own way found our place amongst the many peoples of the earth. And when that time comes, we will be a people identifiable and independent and proud.

The words are those of David Courchene, past president of the Manitoba Indian Brotherhood. They summarize the aspirations of Canada's native peoples, who in the 1970s are striving toward self-realization after a century of subservience and dependency.

Although archaeological discoveries have shown that Indians occupied what is now Canada for many thousands of years prior to the arrival of the Europeans, little is known about these native peoples before European contact. In the last 500 years, significant social, cultural, educational, religious, economic, and political changes have occurred among all peoples in Canada. Gradually, Canadians have come to share similar life-styles, including modes of dress, accommodations, entertainment, and adaptation to technological advancement. But this process of change, basically European-oriented, has had many adverse effects upon the native Indian peoples.

The Treaties and the Indian Act. Before the coming of the white man, Indians lived as members of independent tribes. Each tribe controlled the religious, social, cultural, medical, economic, and political activities of its people. All this changed with the white man's arrival. White immigration, commercialization of the fur trade, and the emphasis on agriculture encroached on the Indian way of life. The result was a straining of relationships between the Indians and the white men as well as among the Indian tribes themselves.

In this situation, the land to which the native peoples had aboriginal title became a central issue. Beginning in the mid-19th century, the government attempted to solve the problem by initiating "treaties" with the Indians. These treaties were designed to forestall quarrels between the Indians and whites over land, to facilitate the spread of white settlements, to maintain traditional military alliances with the Indians, and, most importantly, to extinguish legally the Indians' aboriginal land titles. In return for the Indians' surrender of their interests in the land, the crown undertook to set aside reserves, areas for their exclusive use. The crown also undertook to pay annuities of $3 to $5 per person and to provide schools and other services. Only a few treaties were made before confederation in 1867. The post-confederation treaties number 11 in all, with the first major one, Treaty Number 1, having been signed in Manitoba on Aug. 3, 1871. The terms of all the treaties are similar.

The treaties brought about a split among the native peoples. The federal government recognized as Indian only those members of Indian bands who signed treaties. Those who opted not to sign were given an outright payment for their land rights, after which they were regarded as having the status of ordinary Canadian citizens. Their descendants today are called Métis and are, in the main, people of mixed Indian and white blood. However, a large number of Métis still identify with the Indians in language, values, and customs.

Verna J. Kirkness is a consultant on Indian education in Canada with a long-standing concern about the needs of native peoples. Her published works include Indians Without Tipis *(1973).*

Other legal distinctions were made among the native peoples. For example, the Indian Act of 1876 provided that Indians in the Maritimes, Quebec, the Yukon Territory, and most of British Columbia were to be regarded as "legal" Indians. Their descendants are "registered" Indians with a status similar to that of the treaty Indians, even though their ancestors neither signed treaties nor received outright payment for their land.

Until 1960 neither treaty nor registered Indians had the right to vote in federal elections. At any time, a treaty or registered Indian may choose to become enfranchised, but in so doing he forgoes his rights as a legal Indian. He receives an outright payment and is accorded the status of an ordinary Canadian citizen. A legal Indian woman automatically loses her status upon marriage to a person not of legal Indian status. However, an Indian man's spouse automatically gains the status of a legal Indian even if she has no Indian blood at all.

By law, therefore, Canada's Indians can be described as a diverse group, though culturally they are very similar. Most of this legal diversity stems from the provisions of the Indian Act, which codified the status, reserves, rights and privileges, and the general overall government of Indian people. This is the basic law governing Indians, although Indians as individuals are subject to federal, provincial, and municipal laws as well.

To administer the Indian Act, the federal government established a department, presently known as the Department of Indian Affairs and Northern Development. Over the years it has developed into a large bureaucracy with a staff of about 7,000, located at the headquarters office in Ottawa, at regional offices in the various provinces, and on or near Indian reserves.

The department serves a population of over 250,000 legal Indians. The number of Indians without legal status cannot be counted accurately, but they are believed to exceed the legal Indian population. It is estimated that the native peoples are increasing at a rate of 2.8% per year, compared with 1.5% for the Canadian population as a whole.

The Indian Becomes Visible. Approximately 100 years have passed since the signing of the treaties and the passage of the Indian Act, and the colonial type of government they imposed on the native peoples has taken its toll. For almost a century, the Indians of Canada remained passive under government restraints —a period that today's Indians remember as a tragic time. The reserve system restricted the traditional mobility of the Indians and caused an arbitrary split among the native peoples. When the land could no longer support a viable hunting, trapping, and fishing economy, no alternatives were provided or even explored. The once proud and self-sufficient Indian became dependent on a protectivist and paternalistic state. As a result, he developed attitudes of submission and servitude toward government that have had lasting effects.

In the late 1950s this began to change. Indians throughout Canada began to show concern for the conditions under which they found themselves. Some startling facts were brought to light: a disproportionately high percentage of Indians lived on welfare; almost 50% of Indian families earned less than $1,000 a year; the infant mortality rate for Indians was twice the national average; life expectancy of Indians was 34 years, compared with the national average of 62 years; Indian housing was far below standard; 90–97% of Indian children failed to complete high school. By the latter half of the 1960s, Indian organizations dedicated to improving these conditions were emerging as strong, active forces all across the country.

In 1969 the government issued a White Paper defining a "new Indian policy," and Indian organizations throughout Canada rallied together and reacted vehemently to it. The thrust of the policy was to remove legal distinctions between Indians and the general Canadian population. Services that had been the responsibility of the federal government were to be provided by the provincial governments, and their transfer would be negotiated between the federal government and the provinces. This was recognized as an abrogation of the treaties, under which the federal government was bound to recognize the special status of the Indians. The provinces are not bound by any means to honour these agreements. The policy was viewed by Indians as a scheme to divest them of their aboriginal, residual, and statutory rights. Even before the announcement of the new policy, a movement had been under way among the Indian people to break the cycle of paternalism and engage in constructive efforts toward self-sufficiency. The new policy prompted a greater determination to move toward this goal—a determination shared by Indians in all parts of the country. Stronger bonds developed among Indians, and joint-action projects for identifying goals and objectives were in process. By organizing provincially and nationally, the Indians were establishing forceful and creative political units. Needs were being articulated that reflected their desire to be responsible for their own destiny.

Toward a New Self-sufficiency. Within the last decade, significant gains have been achieved in the political, economic, educational, cultural, and social spheres. As late as five years ago, Indian chiefs and their band councils exercised only token authority; the real power to set policy and make decisions was vested in government civil servants. There are still many bothersome government restrictions, but today each reserve is administered, in the main, by the chief, his council, and a small staff. In the field of economic development, many local services once provided by non-Indians are being taken over by the Indian people. These include small businesses such as stores, service stations, and coffee shops. There is a movement toward tourist-area development. Cooperatives are being established on the reserves, and corporations are being formed to deal in industry and commerce on a larger scale.

The Indian people are taking the position that they, and not the Department of Indian Affairs and Northern Development, must control Indian education. Over 100 years of education under the government system has proved ineffective, as witnessed by the fact that over 90% of Indian students drop out before the 12th grade. Indians blame this on the failure of the system to provide a meaningful educational program.

Indians are presently attempting to identify the means whereby they will control education. It is anticipated that greater involvement by native people will lead to a more meaningful education for Indian children. It will be an education rooted in Indian philosophy, relevant to the environment, and in keeping with today's needs. All these aspects are outlined in "Indian Control of Indian Education," a policy paper prepared by Indians representing various organizations in Canada.

As the Indian people struggle toward more direct control of their own affairs, one of the main obstacles they have encountered is the very system that was established to serve them. It is difficult to alter or reduce a bureaucratic structure, and the Indian Act itself has restrictive and discriminatory sections. The Indian approach to these shortcomings is to work for revision of the act rather than for its abolition. Whatever its faults, the Indian Act is legislation that was meant to protect and guarantee Indian treaty and aboriginal rights.

The Métis are often overlooked in writings on the native peoples, although a large majority of them identify with an Indian way of life. They are generally regarded as Canadian citizens with no special status, and governments have been slow to recognize them as an identifiable group. Yet they face many of the same problems as the Indians, and their plight is sometimes said to be even worse. Their struggle is for economic, cultural, educational, and even social survival.

In the last decade they, too, have founded their own organizations. Like the Indians, they desire greater autonomy, the means to become self-sufficient, and improved education for their children. But though the Indians and Métis have similar problems and are striving for similar solutions, cooperation between them is inhibited by the fact that they must deal with different levels of government—the Indians with the federal government and the Métis, because of their status as ordinary Canadian citizens, with the provinces. Nevertheless, wherever possible both groups of native peoples are working together for their common good.

For Canada's native peoples, these are years of intense activity, bringing new insights into the past, a better understanding of the present, and new hope for tomorrow. The long tradition of dependency, the dominance of European culture and its adverse effects, can be counteracted only by restoration of the pride, equality, freedom, and involvement that are the Indians' birthright; by psychological renewal, social rebirth, and cultural renaissance. Given the opportunity, Indians believe they can effect positive changes that will provide them, once again, with the feeling of true citizenship.

Women of the Hare tribe work at handcrafts in Fort Franklin, Mackenzie District, Northwest Territories.

"Then it's agreed, under the new government restrained-spending policy we switch to the giant jumbo economy dispenser . . . the one with the shorter handle."

continued from page 153

than the last days of the 29th Parliament. Conservative leader Robert L. Stanfield continuously attacked the Trudeau government for its failure to curb inflation and manage the economy. At every opportunity he put forward the Conservative program: a 90-day period of controls on wages and prices, followed by more flexible measures as needed. He also promised that a Conservative administration would reduce government spending.

Most Liberal Cabinet ministers spent the weeks that followed dissolution cultivating their own constituencies, leaving Trudeau the task of bringing the Liberal message to the mass of Canadian voters. Trudeau attacked the Conservative program of controls as unrealistic in a country dependent on imports of many foodstuffs and manufactured goods. Inflation was not an issue, he claimed, but a worldwide problem from which Canada could not isolate itself. In spite of a sharp rise in consumer prices, wages and salaries had risen even more rapidly. Trudeau had no dramatic solutions to the problem of inflation nor did he attempt to gloss over the seriousness of the Western world's economic difficulties. Throughout the campaign the Liberals unveiled new policies. A special effort would be made to assist Western farmers through ending inequities in freight rates and improving rail transportation for grain shipments. The concern about the threat to Canada's economic independence would be met by a plan to require a 50% Canadian interest in future resource ventures in forestry, mining, energy, fisheries, and pipeline construction.

NDP leader Lewis attempted to repeat his successful 1972 election strategy by claiming that private corporations, especially in the resource field, gained unjustified exemptions under federal taxation policy. His argument that high prices and unreasonable corporate profits were a prime cause of inflation failed, however, to have the impact that it had in 1972.

Election day dawned clear and hot across Canada. Commentators had been predicting another minority government as the outcome, although they were divided as to whether it would be of a Liberal or Conservative stamp. The first results came from the Atlantic provinces and showed, surprisingly, a Liberal tide in Conservative leader Stanfield's own region. The

tide continued strongly through the traditional Liberal stronghold of Quebec and rolled through the large and electorally decisive province of Ontario, where Liberal gains were recorded in both city and rural areas. Overall the Liberals gained 32 seats, to emerge with a clear parliamentary majority of 141 seats in the 264-member House of Commons. They increased their popular vote in eight of the ten provinces, winning 42.4% of the vote, compared with 38% in the 1972 election. Their most significant advances came in Ontario, where their representation rose from 36 to 55, and in British Columbia, where they won 8 seats compared with the 4 they had held before the polling. All but one of the 28 ministers of the Trudeau Cabinet were reelected. The exception was Jack Davis, minister of the environment and fisheries, defeated by 4,000 votes in his British Columbia riding of Capilano, north of Vancouver. Davis, in fact, was the only Liberal running for reelection in 1974 who failed to be returned by his constituency.

For the Conservatives the election was a bitter setback. In 1972 they had come close to forming the largest party group in the House of Commons. (After the 1972 election they had 107 members to the Liberals' 109.) In 1974 they dropped to 95 seats, losing 15 seats in the metropolitan Toronto area and in southwestern Ontario. They could take comfort from the fact that nationally their share of the popular vote remained at 34.8% and that in Quebec, where they faced the hardest task, they increased their popular vote by almost 4%. For Stanfield, defeated in three successive general elections by Trudeau and the Liberals, the 1974 campaign was his last as party leader. The NDP was the real loser in the 1974 election. Its share of the popular vote fell from 17.2 to 15.1% and, more drastically, its parliamentary representation was cut from 31 to 16 members. In Ontario the NDP lost three seats; in British Columbia it lost nine. Party leader David Lewis was defeated in his own Toronto riding of York South and announced his retirement from public life. The Social Credit Party retained most of its seats in Quebec but made no impact on the rest of Canada. Party leader Réal Caouette campaigned quietly in Quebec, managing to hold 11 of the party's 15 seats, although Social Credit's total share of the popular vote dropped from 7.4 to 4.9%.

Trudeau rearranged his Cabinet on August 8 after evaluating the election results. Mitchell Sharp, minister for external affairs since the formation of the administration in 1968, moved to the post of president of the Privy Council, with responsibility for steering legislation through Parliament. He was succeeded in the external affairs portfolio by the previous government House leader, Allan MacEachen, a popular and effective member of the Pearson and Trudeau Cabinets. Eight ministers were transferred to different departments, but major portfolios such as defense, justice, and finance were left undisturbed. Six ministers were dropped from the Cabinet. One of these, Paul Martin, a member of Parliament since 1935 and on several occasions a candidate for the Liberal leadership, left the post of Liberal leader in the Senate to become high commissioner to Britain.

Domestic Affairs. The first session of Canada's 29th Parliament began on Jan. 4, 1973, and lasted until Feb. 26, 1974. The last few months of the session saw a number of important pieces of legislation passed, four of which were given royal assent on Jan. 14, 1974. One of these measures had been the centre of public discussion for years. It dealt with the controversial subject of election campaign expenses. The bill provided that donations of more than $100 to an electoral campaign be publicly disclosed and that there must be an accounting of commercial services provided by a backer. Another bill was the subject of a disagreement between the House of Commons and the appointed upper house, the Senate. It regulated the use of wiretapping by police departments and outlawed electronic surveillance by individuals or private organizations. The House of Commons had inserted a clause in the Protection of Privacy bill that the attorney general must inform the subject of a wiretap within 90 days of the removal of the device that he had been under surveillance. The Senate deleted this clause the first time it passed the bill, but eventually accepted it without change. Parliament also passed the Energy Supplies Emergency Act, setting up a five-member board to proceed with plans for dealing with emergencies in oil deliveries, and an export tax on petroleum, first collected in October 1973 as an excise tax, was given statutory authority in the Oil Export Tax Act.

The second session of the 29th Parliament convened on February 27. The speech from the throne was read by Canada's new governor-general, Jules Léger (*see* BIOGRAPHY), who had been sworn into office on January 14. The speech presented no startling initiatives but outlined an economic and social program designed to assist the minority Trudeau government in a hostile House of Commons. The session lasted until May 8 when the Trudeau government was defeated over its budget proposals. Its legislative accomplishments were meagre; 27 bills remained at various stages in the legislative process. Among the measures were amendments to the Canada Pension Plan, a bill to establish a national petroleum corporation, and the Canadian Football Act, which would have prevented the U.S. World Football League from expanding into Canada. According to Canadian law they could not be carried over to a new Parliament, but would have to be reintroduced. The Liberal government promised to revive these measures when it had a chance to meet Parliament following the election.

This opportunity occurred when the first session of the 30th Parliament opened in Ottawa on September 30. The speech from the throne, read by Chief Justice Bora Laskin acting for Léger, who had suffered a stroke in June, mentioned as subjects of impending legislation a number of the items considered in the previous Parliament. In addition the government promised to improve intercity transportation services, to reform Parliament's rules, to redistribute seats, to require a majority of directors of federally incorporated firms to be Canadians, and to promote more processing of natural resources within Canada. There was also a new budget to be introduced, with tax changes that had been outlined in the May budget. The most pressing business before the 30th Parliament in its early weeks, however, was the settlement of a six-week strike of grain handlers on the British Columbia coast. Parliament imposed a settlement based on a conciliation report that had been accepted by the union but turned down by the grain elevator companies.

Three provincial general elections were held in 1974. All resulted in the return of a sitting government while two, held in Nova Scotia and Prince Edward Island in April, presaged the federal Liberal victory in July. The Nova Scotia election of April 2 saw the Liberal government win 31 seats in comparison with the 23 they had secured at the polls four years before. The

Progressive Conservatives dropped 6 seats to win only 12, while the NDP captured the remaining 3 seats in the 46-member house. Canada's smallest province, Prince Edward Island, went to the polls on April 29 and gave a comfortable majority to the eight-year-old Liberal administration. In New Brunswick, which voted November 18, Richard Hatfield's Conservative government was returned to power, winning one more seat than when it was first elected in 1970. The Conservatives won 33 seats and the Liberals 15, although each party captured about 47% of the vote.

In July the Quebec National Assembly passed the Official Language Act making French the only official language of the province. Two English-speaking Liberals broke from the party to vote against the bill, which passed 92–10.

Foreign Affairs. The supply and price of oil dominated relations between Canada and the U.S. in 1974. Canada survived the world oil shortage in the winter of 1973–74 without restricting consumption. Oil supplies for eastern Canada, dependent on foreign oil, were augmented by domestic oil from Alberta and Saskatchewan. In January the government announced that the Interprovincial Pipe Line, running from the Canadian Prairies to Ontario and the U.S. Midwest, would be extended from Sarnia, Ont., to Montreal to serve the eastern market.

Canada's new petroleum policy to give domestic oil requirements first priority in the development of domestic supplies contained implications for its oil exports to the U.S. The decision in September 1973 to impose a tax on oil exports to the U.S. was sharply criticized in the U.S. Senate early in 1974. As world oil prices continued to rise, the Canadian tax was raised in stages to $6.40 a barrel after February 1. At the time of this increase Canada's Energy Minister Donald Macdonald met with William Simon, U.S. energy administrator, to explain the new tax. Macdonald argued that it was unfair to claim that the tax had been imposed to extract more money from the U.S. in its critical oil shortage. In reality the price charged for Canadian oil in the U.S. had been about half the cost that Canadian consumers dependent on offshore imports had to pay and below the price U.S. consumers were paying to other suppliers. The tax, based on the world price for imported non-Canadian oil at Chicago, meant that additional profits resulting from inflated world oil prices would go to the Canadian government, not to the oil companies. A large part of the revenues would be used to offset the high price Canada paid for imported oil for its eastern market.

At the Washington, D.C., energy conference in February, Mitchell Sharp, minister for external affairs, stated that Canada had little additional oil that it could share with the rest of the world in a crisis. The year 1974, in fact, saw a reduction of exports to the U.S. compared with the peak levels reached in 1973. January export figures were down about 12% from a year before, and 1974 oil shipments to the U.S. averaged about 900,000 bbl. a day. On November 22 the Canadian government announced that it planned to cut this back to 800,000 bbl. as of Jan. 1, 1975, with a further reduction the following July, if Alberta and Saskatchewan agreed, and a total phaseout by 1982. The proposal was one of the principal subjects of discussion at the meeting between U.S. Pres. Gerald Ford and Trudeau in Washington in December.

Further changes in Canadian oil policies relating to the U.S. followed a meeting of Prime Minister Trudeau and the provincial premiers on March 27. At that time it was announced that the price of domestic crude oil would be set at $6.50 a barrel across Canada, transportation charges additional. A revised export tax of $5.20 a barrel would come into existence on June 1, to be adjusted with changes in the long-term world price. Although the Organization of Petroleum Exporting Countries (OPEC) increased prices in October, the Canadian export price remained at the June level. In November, in fact, the tax on exports of heavy crude oil was reduced, reflecting the world glut in oil products in the latter months of 1974.

Canada served as an active peacekeeper in 1974. About 1,100 Canadian troops provided logistic support in the Suez Canal area for the UN force set up after the 1973 Arab-Israeli war. Following the Israeli-Syrian disengagement at the end of May, between 100 and 150 men were dispatched from this force for observation duties in the Golan Heights. When fighting erupted in Cyprus, Canada announced that it would double its UN peacekeeping contingent there, but the human costs of peacekeeping were brought home: three Canadians were killed on Cyprus; nine died in the crash of a transport plane brought down by Syrian antiaircraft guns while on a UN flight from Beirut, Lebanon, to Damascus, Syria, three died when their vehicle collided with an Egyptian Army truck, and a thirteenth also died in the Middle East. On June 15 Canada withdrew its small delegation to the International Control Commission for Laos.

A major NATO meeting was held in Ottawa June 18–19, the occasion of the 25th anniversary of the formation of the collective defense system. The meeting produced the Declaration on Atlantic Relations, which affirmed that in spite of détente, the alliance provided "the indispensable basis" for the security of its 15 member states. Although the declaration was formally signed in Brussels, it seemed fitting that it was worked out in the country that symbolized the link between North America and Western Europe.

Protest demonstration in Laval, Que., against the enforced use of English by French-speaking students.

LEN SIDAWAY—CANADIAN PRESS

Prime Minister Trudeau emphasized Canada's concerns with Europe during the course of a visit to France and Belgium in October. Meetings with French Pres. Valéry Giscard d'Estaing were particularly important, for they marked an end to the diplomatic iciness that had existed between Canada and France since the late Charles de Gaulle's encouragement of Quebec separatism during his visit to Canada in 1967. After the meeting it was announced that efforts to expand trade between the two countries would be undertaken and that study groups would be set up to examine cooperation in the development of Canadian energy supplies. In Brussels Trudeau met with EEC and NATO leaders to promote a most-favoured-nation trade agreement between Canada and the EEC. This would place Canada's exports to the EEC, its second-largest market, on a more assured basis, but the EEC remained cool to what would constitute a precedent-making agreement between the trading bloc and a major industrialized nation.

Relations with India suffered a relapse when India exploded an underground nuclear device on May 18. Canada's displeasure arose from the fact that it had helped India build two nuclear power plants for nonmilitary purposes and had trained Indian scientists in nuclear technology. The Cabinet decided that it would immediately suspend shipments of nuclear equipment to India and terminate exchanges in the technical field. Food shipments and agricultural assistance would be continued, however.

The Economy. As in most industrialized countries, the Canadian economy experienced a condition of weakness in 1974. Export volumes declined; there was a slowdown in the growth of consumer spending and a slump in real terms in business capital investment. Real growth in the gross national product was expected to be only 5.5%, providing a total of about $137.6 billion for the year. With the Canadian economy tied closely to that of the U.S., the economic slump there created difficulties for Canada. The housing slowdown in the U.S., for instance, meant a seriously reduced demand for Canadian lumber. Exports from Canada to all countries for the first nine months of 1974 totaled $23,172,300,000, a gain of 28% over the same period in 1973. Imports, at $22,661,400,000 for the same period, showed a larger growth, leading to a deteriorating trade balance.

No significant reduction in unemployment occurred in 1974. The labour force continued to grow but September figures showed unemployment standing at 5.8% (seasonally adjusted). The consumer price index rose by 10.9% in the first nine months, below the average for the 24 major industrialized countries but the highest increase in Canada since the Korean War, leaving Canada to deal with the difficult combination of rapidly rising prices and little real economic growth.

Finance Minister Turner's rejected May budget had forecast revenues of $23,950,000,000 for the 1974–75 fiscal year, with expenditures of $24.4 billion—a deficit of $450 million, smaller than in 1973. A second budget was introduced November 18. Turner proposed new measures to deal with inflation and the declining economy. Revenues for the fiscal year 1974–75 were now calculated at $25.1 billion and expenditures at $24,850,000,000, leaving a budget surplus of $250 million. (D. M. L. FARR)

[973.B]

ENCYCLOPÆDIA BRITANNICA FILMS. *The Legend of the Magic Knives* (1970); *The Canadians: Their Cities* (1974); *The Canadians: Their Land* (1974).

Central African Republic

The landlocked Central African Republic is bounded by Chad, the Sudan, Congo, Zaire, and Cameroon. Area: 240,378 sq.mi. (622,577 sq.km.). Pop. (1973 est.): 1,716,000. Cap. and largest city: Bangui (pop., 1968, 298,579). Language: French (official); local dialects. Religion: Protestant, about 40%; animist and Catholic, about 30% each. President and premier in 1974, Jean-Bédel Bokassa.

During a private visit to France in September 1974 President Bokassa announced after a meeting with French Pres. Valéry Giscard d'Estaing that the French chief of state would be paying an official visit—the first by a French president in office since the establishment of the African nation in 1960—to the Central African Republic in the near future. President Bokassa did not give any indication of the expected date or duration of the visit, however.

During the year, however, relations between the Central African Republic and its former colonial rulers were far from ideal. A long series of "pinpricks" had characterized the Central African authorities' attitude to France as well as to other European countries with interests in the republic. These included the arrest and expulsion of various French nationals accused of antigovernment sympathies or activities, the banning of the sale of French newspapers throughout the country, and the introduction of nationalization measures hampering the activities of foreign press agencies as well as foreign companies engaged in the petroleum and forestry industries. Moreover, the French consulate general in Bangui was summarily closed and the exploitation of uranium deposits in the region of Bakouma, which was to have been undertaken by a joint French and Central African company but which had never properly been started, was brought to a standstill.

In home affairs, the only event of significance was a major Cabinet reshuffle in June. In August the capital of the Central African Republic was the scene of a conference of heads of state of member countries of the Common African and Mauritian Organization (OCAM). Indeed, OCAM had been saved from collapse by the personal efforts of President Bokassa, and this was doubtless an important factor in the unanimous decision of the organization's leaders to transfer its headquarters to Bangui from the capital of Cameroon, the latter country having withdrawn from OCAM the previous year. (PHILIPPE DECRAENE)

[978.E.7.a.ii]

Chad

A landlocked republic of central Africa, Chad is bounded by Libya, the Sudan, the Central African Republic, Cameroon, Nigeria, and Niger. Area: 495,750 sq.mi. (1,284,000 sq.km.). Pop. (1973 est.): 3,869,000, including Saras, other Africans, and Arabs. Cap. and largest city: N'Djamena (until Nov. 28, 1973, known by its former French name, Fort-Lamy; pop., 1973 est., 193,000). Language: French (official). Religion (1964): Muslim 41%; animist 30%; Christian 29%. President and premier in 1974, N'Garta (formerly François) Tombalbaye.

The main features of Chadian foreign policy in 1974 were increasing tension in relations with France and a rapprochement with the Arab states. President Tombalbaye was particularly irked at the French government's refusal to hand over political opponents of his regime with French nationality who had sought refuge in France. He was especially worried about the activities of the former Chadian ambassador to West Germany, Toura N'Gaba, and of members of the Mouvement Démocratique de rénovation tchadienne (MDRT), whose leader, Outel Bono, had been assassinated under mysterious circumstances in Paris the previous August.

In January the then French secretary-general for African affairs, Jacques Foccart, toured capitals of the states of the Sahel affected by drought (see AGRICULTURE AND FOOD SUPPLIES: *Special Report*) but had to avoid Chad due to President Tombalbaye's persistent accusations that he was plotting against the regime. However, relations eased after a meeting of the joint Franco-Chadian commission in the Chadian capital in February. France agreed to provide substantial assistance to those areas affected by drought. U.S. food aid was halted by the Chadian government in late October after a *New York Times* article accused persons close to leadership of corruption and inefficiency.

In March Col. Muammar al-Qaddafi of Libya, who had previously supported the rebel Chad National Liberation Front (Frolinat), paid an official visit to

---

CENTRAL AFRICAN REPUBLIC
Education. (1970–71) Primary, pupils 176,300, teachers 2,784; secondary, pupils 9,691, teachers 293; vocational, pupils 1,363, teachers 130; teacher training, students 225, teachers 34; higher, students 88, teaching staff 6.
Finance. Monetary unit: CFA franc, with (Sept. 16, 1974) a parity of CFA Fr. 50 to the French franc and a free rate of CFA Fr. 240.50 to U.S. $1 (CFA Fr. 556.50 = £1 sterling). Budget (1972 rev. est.) balanced at CFA Fr. 13.8 billion.
Foreign Trade. (1971) Imports CFA Fr. 9,053,-000,000; exports CFA Fr. 8,939,000,000. Import sources: France 62%; West Germany 6%; U.S. 6%; Italy 5%. Export destinations: France 56%; Belgium 12%; Israel 9%. Main exports: diamonds 34%; coffee 24%; cotton 23%.
Agriculture. Production (in 000; metric tons; 1972; 1971 in parentheses): cassava c. 1,100 (c. 1,100); millet and sorghum c. 50 (c. 50); sweet potatoes c. 49 (c. 49); peanuts c. 85 (c. 85); bananas c. 170 (c. 170); coffee c. 11 (c. 11); cotton, lint c. 17 (c. 18). Livestock (in 000; 1972–73): cattle c. 450; pigs c. 59; sheep c. 68; goats c. 535; chickens c. 1,150.
Industry. Production (1972): diamonds 524,000 metric carats; cotton fabrics 11 million m.; electricity 47.3 million kw-hr.

CHAD
Education. (1971–72) Primary, pupils 183,840, teachers (public only) 2,587; secondary, pupils 10,079, teachers (1969–70) 313; vocational, pupils 609, teachers (1970–71) 70; teacher training (1970–71), students 423, teachers (1969–70) 33.
Finance. Monetary unit: CFA franc, with (Sept. 16, 1974) a parity of CFA Fr. 50 to the French franc and a free rate of CFA Fr. 240.50 to U.S. $1 (CFA Fr. 556.50 = £1 sterling). Budget (1973 est.) balanced at CFA Fr. 17,018,000,000. Cost of living (N'Djamena; 1970 = 100; Dec. 1971) 155.
Foreign Trade. (1972) Imports CFA Fr. 15,476,-000,000; exports CFA Fr. 9,028,000,000. Import sources: France 48%; Nigeria 11%. Export destinations: France c. 20%; Zaire c. 7%; West Germany c. 6%. Main export cotton 67%.

Chad, indicating a marked rapprochement between the two countries. In September an agreement between Chad and Saudi Arabia provided for the financing by Saudi Arabia of the construction, in the Chadian capital, of the largest mosque in black Africa.

Information on the activities of Frolinat was increasingly difficult to obtain, but the rebels were clearly not unduly deterred by the Libyan change of attitude. When a group of Europeans, including a West German physician, was kidnapped in April, West German officials succeeded in obtaining the release of the doctor by direct negotiations with the rebels. President Tombalbaye indicated his displeasure by breaking off diplomatic relations with West Germany.

(PHILIPPE DECRAENE)

Chemistry

Physical and Inorganic. *Measurement of Gaseous Radical Concentrations by Laser Magnetic Resonance Spectroscopy.* Scientists at the U.S. National Bureau of Standards, Boulder, Colo., developed a technique for measuring the concentration of hydroxyl (OH) radicals at levels as low as 2×10^8 molecules per cc, a factor of about 10^4 lower than previously possible. This technique, laser magnetic resonance, is similar to such other magnetic resonance measurement methods as electron spin resonance (electron paramagnetic resonance) and nuclear magnetic resonance. The molecule or molecular species being detected absorbs radiation corresponding to a transition between rotational energy levels. In paramagnetic species, such as radicals, the rotational energy levels split into a specific number of sublevels in the presence of a magnetic field, and the differences in energy between these sublevels depend upon the intensity of the applied field. It is possible to take a species whose rotational levels are separated by an energy difference similar to the energy of light from a laser source and "tune" the molecule to have rotational energy transitions that correspond exactly to the laser radiation. When the molecule is tuned, its absorption of laser light becomes an extremely sensitive and quantitative detector of that particular species.

This method was used to obtain rate constants for several hydroxyl radical reactions, and these values

compared favourably with those derived by conventional methods. Other species being investigated by the new technique included CH, CHO, and HO_2.

Rare Earth Antiknock Compounds. Efforts were intensified to find a replacement for tetraethyl lead (TEL) as an antiknock agent in gasoline. Apart from its possible long-term effect as a health hazard, TEL had to be removed from gasoline if automobiles were to be fitted with catalytic afterburners and converters to meet more stringent exhaust emission standards. The alternative to finding a suitable substitute for TEL was to increase the aromatic content of gasoline, but this led to further undesirable exhaust emissions.

Workers at the U.S. Air Force Aerospace Research Laboratories at Wright-Patterson Air Force Base, Ohio, discovered that rare-earth metals and their compounds had better antiknock properties than TEL in some applications. The best results were obtained with cerium compounds, in particular cerium(2,2,6,6-tetramethyl-3,5-heptadionate)$_4$, also referred to as $Ce(thd)_4$. Tests with a supercharged engine that simulated an aircraft during takeoff showed that $Ce(thd)_4$ had better antiknock characteristics than TEL, whereas in a conventional automobile engine $Ce(thd)_4$ exhibited significant antiknock properties but was not as good as TEL.

Phosphazene High Polymers. Significant advances were made in research on a new group of inorganic polymers, the polyorganophosphazenes. These materials aroused considerable technological interest and were thought to have potential applications in excess of the only other significant group of synthetic inorganic polymers, the silicones.

Phosphazenes (also termed phosphonitriles) are cyclic or linear molecules containing alternate phosphorus and nitrogen atoms in the skeleton with two substituents on each phosphorus atom. The cyclic trimeric and tetrameric chlorophosphazenes had long been known from the reaction of ammonium chloride and phosphorus pentachloride. These molecules could be converted by heating to a transparent elastomeric polymer known as "inorganic rubber." Crosslinked polydichlorophosphazene would be useful except that it reacts slowly with atmospheric moisture to yield phosphoric acid, ammonia, and hydrochloric acid.

H. R. Allcock and his research group at Pennsylvania State University devised methods of synthesizing linear polyphosphazenes in which nonhydrolyzable organic substituent groups replaced the chlorine atoms. To bring about the substitution reaction it was first necessary to synthesize a polydichlorophosphazene that was free from crosslinks. Such a polymer was isolated by polymerization of hexachlorocyclotriphosphazene under rigorously controlled conditions. Solutions of the noncrosslinked polymer reacted rapidly and quantitatively with sodium alkoxides or aryloxides or with primary or secondary amines.

The organo-substituted polymers prepared in this way were stable elastomers of thermoplastics that were extremely resistant to hydrolysis. Poly[bis(trifluoroethoxy)phosphazene], $[NP(OCH_2CF_3)_2]_n$, an example of this type of polymer, formed strong, translucent, flexible films that superficially resembled polyethylene. Unlike many organic polymers, it retained its flexible properties over a temperature range of $-66°$ to $+242°$ C. In addition, the polymer was more water-repellent than Teflon and was highly crystalline, so that it could be converted by stretching to yield strong fibres.

(J. A. KERR)

[121.A.12; 122.A.6.e; 122.D.2.f]

Glenn T. Seaborg (left) and Albert Ghiorso announce the successful synthesis of element 106 at the American Chemical Society meeting in New Jersey.

WIDE WORLD

Organic. The development of synthetic forms of two substances that have great therapeutic value, insulin and the prostaglandins, was a major goal of organic chemists during the year.

Synthetic Insulin. The protein hormone insulin was first obtained in crude form from the pancreas in 1922 and its vital role in regulating the metabolism of carbohydrates was then demonstrated. Since that time insulin, obtained from the pancreases of cattle, sheep, and hogs, has provided the most effective means of controlling the chronic disease diabetes mellitus. The continual increase (about 5% per year) in the incidence of diabetes is raising the demand for insulin so much that it is likely that the quantities needed will eventually exceed those available from slaughtered animals. Serious attention is therefore being given to the development of an inexpensive method of producing insulin synthetically.

Before a chemist can undertake the synthesis of any organic compound, he must know its molecular structure. Elucidation of the structure of insulin, announced in 1955, was one of the major feats of 20th-century organic chemistry. Like all proteins, insulin is made up of amino acids, about 20 different nitrogen-containing organic compounds that can be combined into long chains in living cells. The insulin molecule contains two of these chains linked into loops by chemical bonds between the sulfur atoms present in cysteine, one of the kinds of amino acid units in the chains. Knowledge of the structure furnished the target for laboratory preparative procedures, but the synthesis of insulin posed two problems far beyond the techniques known to organic chemists in 1955: assembly, in the proper order, of the chains of 21 and 30 amino acids; and combination of the two chains in the way peculiar to the natural hormone.

By the mid-1960s the techniques needed for building up the chains had been developed. Attempts to unite the two chains into the final loops, however, were almost fruitless, because there was no way to ensure the proper pairings of the cysteine sulfur atoms. Apparently, the pancreatic cells exert this control by some mechanism that the chemists had not been able to simulate. These initial efforts, though inefficient, did produce the first traces of artificial insulin.

The insight that the chemists needed was provided by the discovery, reported in 1967, that in the pancreas the two chains of the insulin molecule do not form independently. Instead, they are the end segments of a longer single chain, proinsulin **1,** which folds up to bring the pairs of cysteine units into proximity. After the loops close, the middle section of the chain of amino acids is detached. The chemists' exploitation of this finding has been the use of a simple compound—instead of the natural chain of amino acids—to hold the chains together while the loops close. It has recently been shown experimentally that insulin can be formed by this method, in a much less wasteful way than was the case in the earlier syntheses of the hormone. The promise of this scheme is great enough to lead workers in the field to believe that commercial production of synthetic insulin could become a reality during the next 15 years.

Prostaglandins. The prostaglandins are a class of organic compounds that have attracted increasing attention in recent years. The intense physiological activity of the prostaglandins was first recognized upon the observation, made in 1930, that fresh semen could either contract or relax uterine muscle. The first of these compounds was obtained from extracts

BASED UPON CHEMICAL & ENGINEERING NEWS, APRIL 29, 1974, P. 19, AFTER DIETRICH BRANDENBURG AND A. WOLLMER

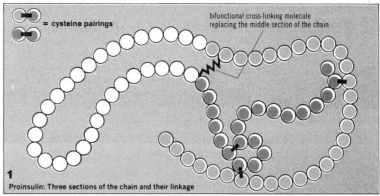

= cysteine pairings

bifunctional cross-linking molecule replacing the middle section of the chain

1 Proinsulin: Three sections of the chain and their linkage

of the vesicular glands of sheep, but about 15 of them have since been identified in various mammalian tissues and fluids and in species of Caribbean corals as well. For many years the quantities obtainable were too small to permit extensive clinical or chemical investigation, but by the mid-1960s the detailed chemical structure of several prostaglandins had been determined, and procedures for their synthetic preparation had been developed. The resulting availability of both the naturally occurring compounds and closely similar ones stimulated broadened studies of their possible therapeutic usefulness. By 1974 two prostaglandins **2** (those denoted E_2 and $F_{2\alpha}$) were being offered by pharmaceutical manufacturers, and several others were undergoing clinical evaluation.

Preparation of these compounds posed a formidable challenge to chemists who were trying to duplicate them in the laboratory. It was necessary to devise methods that would ensure the proper spatial arrangement of the different molecular groups attached to a ring of five carbon atoms while at the same time restricting the experimental conditions so that labile portions of the compounds are not disrupted.

The prostaglandins are used for inducing childbirth labour or for terminating pregnancy during the second trimester. They are being investigated in several other applications, including control of hypertension,

The three polypeptide chains of proinsulin and their linkage.

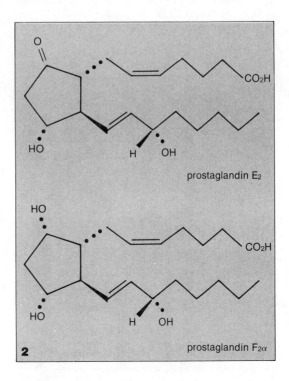

prostaglandin E_2

prostaglandin $F_{2\alpha}$

2

gastric ulcers, and asthmatic attacks. A foreseeable role for chemists will be the preparation of analogous substances that will exert sustained physiological action and in which a chosen one of the diverse effects will be enhanced while others are suppressed; for example, such a drug might regulate the secretion of gastric acids but have no appreciable influence upon blood pressure. (JOHN V. KILLHEFFER)

[122.E.1.n.; 123.H; 321.C.4.b; 424.G.7]

Chess

Though he did manifest some interest in chess matters during 1973 and 1974, the world champion, Bobby Fischer (U.S.), still refrained from playing chess and it became doubtful whether he would defend his title when the time came in 1975. During the World Chess Federation Congress at Nice, France, in June a telegram was received from Fischer resigning his International Chess Federation world championship title. The World Chess Federation asked him to reconsider but received no answer. Nevertheless, the candidates' matches went forward, with Anatoly Karpov (U.S.S.R.; see BIOGRAPHY) emerging as the official challenger.

In August 1973 the 11th Rubinstein Memorial Tournament at Polanica Zdroj, Pol., ended in a tie for first place between M. Dvoretsky (U.S.S.R.) and W. Schmidt (Pol.). The U.S. National Championship, held at El Paso, Tex., in September, also ended in a tie, between John Grefe and Lubomir Kavalek. At Leipzig, E.Ger., in October, an international tournament ended in a tie between V. Hort (Czech.) and A. Lutikov (U.S.S.R.). Bent Larsen (Den.) won first prize in a strongly contested tournament at Manila. The Marlboro International Classic, also in the Philippines, was won by Kavalek.

Valentina Kozlovskaya (U.S.S.R.) won the ladies' interzonal at Minorca, Spain, thus qualifying for the candidates' stage of the world championship. There was a tie for the remaining two qualifying places among four Soviet players: N. Alexandria, N. Konopleva, I. Levitina, and M. Shul. Alexandria and Levitina were successful in the play-off at Kislovodsk,

U.S.S.R., some months later. First prize at the strong international tournament in Madrid went to Karpov. A match tournament at Tbilisi, U.S.S.R., between the U.S.S.R. and Yugoslavia was won by the former, 31–15. A training match in Solingen, W.Ger., was won by V. Korchnoi (U.S.S.R.) against R. Hubner (W.Ger.), $4\frac{1}{2}$–$3\frac{1}{2}$, in December. Jan Timman (Neth.) was first in the Guardian Royal Exchange Tournament in London. The ladies' European Championship at Vrnacka Banja, Yugos., was won by Alla Kushnir (U.S.S.R.). R. Kholmov (U.S.S.R.) and M. Tal (U.S.S.R.) tied for first at the international tournament at Dubna, U.S.S.R.

The Hastings, Eng., international tournament ended in January 1974 in a four-way tie between G. Kuzmin (U.S.S.R.), L. Szabo (Hung.), Tal, and Timman. The European Junior Championship at Groningen, Neth., was won by S. Makarychev (U.S.S.R.). William Hartston became British champion after a play-off against Michael Basman. In the quarterfinals of the candidates' matches to decide who should challenge Fischer, Korchnoi beat H. Mecking (Braz.) at Augusta, Ga.; Boris Spassky (U.S.S.R.) beat Robert Byrne (U.S.) at San Juan, P.R.; T. Petrosian

Anatoly Karpov waits for Boris Spassky to move during their chess match in Leningrad.
The 23-year-old grand master went on to defeat Spassky, a former world champion.

СПАССКИЙ КАРПОВ

WIDE WORLD

Ruy Lopez (by transposition), Steinitz Defense Deferred (played in an international tournament at Halle, E.Ger., 1974)

White M. Tal	Black R. Knaak	White M. Tal	Black R. Knaak
1 P—K4	Kt—QB3	13 P—KR3	B—R4 (d)
2 Kt—KB3	Kt—B5	14 Kt—B5	O—O—O
3 B—Kt5	P—QR3	15 B—Kt5	Kt—Kt1 (e)
4 B—R4	P—Q3	16 B×B	Kt×B
5 O—O	B—Q2	17 Q—Kt5	Kt×Kt (f)
6 P—Q4	Kt—B3	18 P×Kt	P—KKt3
7 B×Kt (a)	B×B	19 P—KKt4	Q—B3
8 R—K1	B—K2 (b)	20 P—B6 (g)	P—Q4
9 Kt—B3	P×P	21 R—K7	P—R3
10 Kt×P	B—Q2	22 Q—K5	P—Q5 (h)
11 Q—B3	B—Kt5 (c)	23 Kt—K2	R—Q4
12 Q—Kt3	B—Q2	24 Kt×P (i)	resigns

(a) More usual here is 7 R—K1. (b) And not 8 . . ., Kt×P; 9 P—Q5, winning a piece; while after 8 . . ., B×P; 9 Kt—B3, White has the advantage. (c) Again more usual was 11 . . ., O—O; 12 B—B4, R—K1 with about equal chances. (d) If he retreats the bishop to the centre by 13 . . ., B—K3 then 14 P—K5, P×P; 15 Kt×B, P×Kt; 16 Q×KP, with considerable advantage to White. (e) After 15 . . ., B—Kt3; 16 Kt×B ch, Q×Kt; 17 Kt—Q5, Q—K3; 18 B×Kt, P×B; 19 Q—QB3, White wins a pawn with the better game. (f) Tal afterward thought that Black could have put up a more tenacious resistance by sacrificing a pawn by 17 . . ., Kt—B3; 18 Q×B, P—KKt3; 19 Kt×P ch, K—Kt1 when White intended playing 21 P—QR3. (g) 20 P×B, P×P would be much too dangerous for White; but now he threatens 21 Kt—Q5. (h) Setting the ingenious trap 23 Kt—K4, R—Q4; 24 R×P ch, K—Kt1! (i) Decisive; if now 24 . . ., R×Q; 25 Kt×Q, wins, as does 24 . . ., Q—B5; 25 R×P ch, Q×R; 26 Q×R.

Petroff Defense (sixth game of the final match in the World Championship Candidates' series in Moscow, 1974)

White A. Karpov	Black V. Korchnoi	White A. Karpov	Black V. Korchnoi
1 P—K4	P—K4	17 Kt×B	B×Pch
2 Kt—KB3	Kt—KB3	18 R×B	Kt×R
3 Kt×P	P—Q3	19 K×Kt	Q—Q3
4 Kt—B3	Kt×P	20 Kt—Kt5 (g)	R—KB1
5 P—Q4	P—Q4	21 Q—R3	Q—Q1 (h)
6 B—Q3	B—K2	22 B—B4	P—KR3
7 O—O	Kt—QB3	23 Kt—B3	R—K1
8 R—K1	B—KKt5	24 B—Q3	R—K5
9 P—B3 (a)	P—B4	25 P—KKt3 (i)	R—B3
10 Q—Kt3	O—O	26 Q—B5	P—Kt4
11 QKt—Q2 (b)	K—R1 (c)	27 Kt×P (j)	P×Kt
12 P—KR3	B—R4 (d)	28 B×KtP	R(K5)—K3
13 Q×KtP	R—B3	29 R—K1	Q—KKt1
14 Q—Kt3	R—Kt3	30 P—KR4 (k)	R—Kt3
15 B—K2	B—R5	31 R×R	and black
16 R—B1 (e)	B×Kt (f)		lost on time (l)

(a) White does not win a pawn by 9 B×Kt, P×B; 10 R×P, on account of 10 . . ., B×Kt; 11 Q×B, Q×P; 12 Q—Q3, Kt—K3 with equality. (b) Not wishing to endure the attack Black would have after 11 Q×P, Q—Q3; followed by R—Kt1. (c) Safer was 11 . . ., Kt×Kt; 12 Kt×Kt, R—Kt1. (d) Again he should have protected his pawn by 12 . . ., B×Kt; 13 Kt×B, R—QK1. (e) And not 16 Kt×B, Q×Kt; 17 Kt×Kt, Q×Kt; 18 P—B3, B×P when Black wins. (f) To 16 . . ., Q—K2, White intended replying 17 Q—Q1, threatening Kt—K5. (g) A move that both threatens (Kt—B7ch) and defends (the KKt3 point). (h) Exchange of queens would help White to get down to a won ending. (i) Acceptance of the offered exchange would be too risky; e.g., 25 B×R, BP×B; 26 Kt—K5, R—B3. (j) Very strong and not really a sacrifice. (k) Better than 30 B×R ch, R×B; when Black threatens 25 P—B5. (l) In any case he loses another pawn and the game might go 31 . . ., R×R; 32 B—Kt5, Kt—Q1; 33 Q×BP.

(U.S.S.R.) beat L. Portisch (Hung.) at Palma de Majorca, Spain; and Karpov beat L. Polugayevsky (U.S.S.R.) in Moscow. In the semifinals Karpov beat Spassky in Leningrad, and Korchnoi beat Petrosian in Odessa. In the final match, held in Moscow September 16–November 22, a long and exciting struggle ended in a narrow victory for Karpov by 3 wins, 2 losses, and 19 draws. The U.S. National Open at Las Vegas, Nev., was won by A. Bisguier (U.S.). Ulf Andersson (Swed.) won the international tournament at Camaguey, Cuba. The Clare Benedict International Team Tournament at Minorca, Spain, was won by England.

The 21st Olympiad took place at Nice in June, and the U.S.S.R. had little difficulty in retaining the World Team Championship. The U.S.S.R. was first in the World Students Team Championship tournament at Thornaby, Eng., in July. In the World "Cadet" (under 16) Championship at Pont-Sainte-Maxence, France, first place went to A. J. Mestel (Eng.). The first prize at the second World Open Tournament in New York was won by Larsen, and Kavalek and Polugayevsky tied for first place at Solingen. The 23rd U.S. championship at Chicago, Ill., was won by Walter Browne. The World Junior Championship at Manila was won by Tony Miles (Eng.). There was a tie for first place in the U.S. open championship at New York between V. Hort (Czech.) and P. Benko (U.S.). (HARRY GOLOMBEK)

[452.C.3.c.ii]

Chile

A republic extending along the southern Pacific coast of South America, Chile has an area of 292,258 sq.mi. (756,-945 sq.km.), not including its Antarctic claim. It is bounded by Argentina, Bolivia, and Peru. Pop. (1974 est.): 10,494,400. Cap. and largest city: Santiago (metro. pop., 1973 est., 3,435,900). Language: Spanish. Religion: predominantly Roman Catholic. President of the four-man military junta and, from June 27, 1974, supreme chief (chief of state), Gen. Augusto Pinochet Ugarte.

During 1974 it became apparent that the military leadership of Chile had no intention of handing control of the nation back to the electorate in the near future. According to General Pinochet, the military would retain control for as many years as it deemed necessary to restore stability and domestic tranquillity. Congress had been abolished following the military uprising that overthrew the elected Marxist regime of Pres. Salvador Allende in 1973, thus ending the democratic form of government that had prevailed in Chile for 46 years. The ban against political parties and activities remained in effect, and the traditional non-Marxist parties, such as the Christian Democrats, Radicals, and National (conservative) Party, were functionally out of business.

The military and a group of law professors were preparing a new constitution, although too little was known about it even for speculation. There were indications that Chile's military leaders might be planning some variation of the system evolved by the Brazilian military, which had abolished the traditional parties and replaced them by a government party and a non-military opposition. Meanwhile, the Chilean officers

COURTESY, UNITED NATIONS

Food production continued on this cooperative farm near Santiago despite political changes in Chile during the year.

brooked no opposition. Censorship and the nighttime curfew continued, although the curfew hours had been eased and foreign correspondents were permitted to move about freely. Some of the 7,000 known or suspected Marxists and Allende sympathizers seized after the coup, among them former defense minister Orlando Letelier, were released and sent into exile.

Information that emerged in the U.S. in connection with investigations into the Watergate affair threw some light on U.S. activities in Chile prior to the coup. It appeared that the Central Intelligence Agency, with the approval of Henry Kissinger, then the president's national security adviser, had carried out an $8 million clandestine campaign against Allende by making payments to opposition politicians, newspapers, and radio stations. There was no evidence that the CIA or Kissinger, who later became secretary of state, had any role in the revolution itself. Information made available through the U.S. Congress indicated that the CIA role was to try to make it impossible for Allende's Marxist experiment to succeed. It was also claimed that, at U.S. instigation, Chile had received little or no financial assistance from international organizations prior to the coup.

The rate of inflation in Chile had not improved markedly since the Allende period, when it had reached a level in excess of 300%. However, the military leaders hastened to make their peace with foreign investors, notably the copper companies expropriated by Allende. The nationalization of the companies was irreversible, but the government settled the claims of Cerro Corp. and Anaconda Co. and talks with Kennecott Copper Corp. continued. A new foreign investment law, decreed during the summer, was designed to lure foreign investors even at the expense of relations with other Latin-American countries, most notably those in the Andean Group. By guaranteeing remittance of profits and ensuring that the rules of investment would remain stable, Chile hoped to attract the kind of investment needed to make the national economy viable. These moves significantly improved Chile's credit, which had evaporated in the last months of the Allende regime. The country's attractiveness to foreign investors was further enhanced when the government began to return private companies, taken over by the previous regime, to their owners. The ultimate aim of the military appeared to be the creation of a corporate state, somewhat like

Child Welfare:
see Education; Social
  and Welfare
  Services

Mussolini's Italy, dedicated to capitalism and strongly opposed to Marxism in any form.

On the anniversary of the coup, General Pinochet declared in a speech that the state of internal war had been reduced to a state of siege, but the military still appeared to consider itself at war with Marxism. A decree published on June 26 had given Pinochet sole executive power and he was sworn in as president the following day. Legislative powers were assigned to the commanders of the three branches of the armed forces and to the national police, while Pinochet retained his position as army commander. On July 10 he carried out a Cabinet reshuffle in which eight ministers were replaced and two new portfolios were created. However, the new Cabinet was still overwhelmingly military, with only 3 civilians as opposed to 14 officers. As 1974 drew to a close, the Chileans were making vigorous efforts to acquire planes and tanks from the U.S. and other sources, allegedly because of a suspicion that Peru might attempt to recover territories lost to Chile nearly 100 years earlier in the War of the Pacific.   (JEREMIAH A. O'LEARY)

[974.E]

CHILE
Education. (1971) Primary, pupils 2,200,160, teachers (public only; 1969) 35,588; secondary, pupils 238,651, teachers (1969) 11,900; vocational, pupils 127,448, teachers (1969) 8,600; teacher training (1969), students 5,745, teachers 580; higher (including 8 universities), students (1970) 78,430, teaching staff (1965) 8,835.
Finance. Monetary unit: escudo, with (Sept. 16, 1974) a multiple exchange rate system including a rate for converting copper exports of 860 escudos to U.S. $1 (1,990 escudos = £1 sterling), a "bank" rate of 990 escudos to U.S. $1 (2,290 escudos = £1 sterling), and a "broker's" rate of 1,050 escudos to U.S. $1 (2,552 escudos = £1 sterling). Budget (1973 est.): revenue 167,568,000,000 escudos; expenditure 301,038,000,000 escudos. Gross national product: (1971) 119,069,000,000 escudos; (1970) 90,799,000,000 escudos. Money supply: (Feb. 1973) 65,822,000,000 escudos; (Feb. 1972) 23,401,000,000 escudos. Cost of living (Santiago; 1970 = 100): (March 1974) 3,402; (March 1973) 899.
Foreign Trade. Imports (1972) U.S. $941.1 million; exports (1973) U.S. $1,230,500. Import sources: U.S. 17%; Argentina 15%; West Germany 9%; U.K. 6%. Export destinations (1972): Japan 17%; West Germany 14%; U.K. 11%; U.S. 10%; The Netherlands 8%; Italy 7%; Argentina 6%. Main exports: copper (1970) 77%; iron ore (1972) 5%.
Transport and Communications: Roads (1972) 63,656 km. Motor vehicles in use (1971): passenger 193,009; commercial 135,667. Railways: (1972) 10,820 km. (including 8,218 km. state railways); traffic (principal railways only; 1971) 2,481,000,000 passenger-km., freight 2,718,000,000 net ton-km. Air traffic (1973): 1,111,200,000 passenger-km.; freight 55,570,000 net ton-km. Shipping (1973): merchant vessels 100 gross tons and over 138; gross tonnage 383,886. Telephones (Dec. 1972) 415,000. Radio receivers (Dec. 1972) 1.5 million. Television receivers (Dec. 1972) 500,000.
Agriculture. Production (in 000; metric tons; 1973; 1972 in parentheses): wheat 747 (1,195); barley 107 (139); oats 109 (111); corn 294 (283); potatoes 624 (733); rapeseed 40 (78); dry beans 65 (83); onions c. 63 (c. 65); sugar, raw value 112 (153); apples (1972) c. 98, (1971) c. 93; wine c. 500 (670); beef and veal c. 100 (118); wool (1972) c. 12, (1971) c. 10; timber (cu.m.; 1971) 8,200, (1970) 7,600; fish catch (1971) 1,487, (1970) 1,181. Livestock (in 000; 1972–73): cattle c. 3,155; sheep c. 6,900; pigs c. 1,203; horses c. 420.
Industry. Production (in 000; metric tons; 1972): crude oil 1,613; coal 1,332; natural gas (cu.m.) 4,080,000; electricity (kw-hr.) 8,934,000 (58% hydroelectric); iron ore (63% metal content; 1973) 9,706; pig iron (1973) 457; crude steel (ingots; 1973) 508; copper ore (metal content) 723; nitrate of soda (1970) 516; manganese ore (metal content) 6.7; sulfur (1971) 106; iodine 2.1; molybdenum concentrates (metal content) 5.9; gold (troy oz.) 95; silver (troy oz.) 2,860; woven cotton fabrics (m.) 85,000; fish meal 116.

China

The most populous country in the world and the third largest in area, China is bounded by the U.S.S.R., Mongolia, North Korea, North Vietnam, Laos, Burma, India, Bhutan, Sikkim, Nepal, Pakistan, and Afghanistan. From 1949 the country has been divided into the People's Republic of China (Communist) on the mainland and on Hainan and other islands, and the Republic of China (Nationalist) on Taiwan. (*See* TAIWAN.) Area: 3,691,500 sq.mi. (9,561,000 sq.km.), including Tibet but excluding Taiwan. Pop. of the People's Republic (1974 official est.): nearly 800 million. Cap.: Peking (metro. pop., 1970 est., 7,570,000). Largest city: Shanghai (metro. pop., 1970 est., 10,820,000). Language: Chinese (varieties of the Mandarin dialect predominate). Chairman of the Communist Party in 1974, Mao Tse-tung; premier, Chou En-lai.

Early in 1974, China returned to more militant attitudes by heightening the anti-Confucius and anti-Lin Piao campaigns initiated by Chairman Mao, who advocated perpetual revolution and periodic upheaval as necessary measures to guard against bourgeois tendencies. Therefore, these campaigns were designed to advance the struggle against any possible restoration of capitalism, to consolidate "the dictatorship of the proletariat," and thus to arrive at a new ideological consensus in conformity with "The Thought of Mao." The campaigns followed three years of relative internal calm and actively pragmatic diplomacy that had identified Chinese interests with the third world of nonaligned nations and had sought to improve relations with the West in order to blunt the Soviet threat.

The nationwide ideological movement to criticize Lin Piao and Confucius, characteristic of the ideological debate of the 1965–69 Cultural Revolution, carried a particular undertone of hostility to the established authority of Chou En-lai, China's premier since 1949. The increasing intensity of these ideological campaigns and the pressing problem of succession were accentuated by the aging of Chairman Mao and the illness of Premier Chou, who was forced to retreat from his full foreign and domestic responsibilities. The result was an internal power struggle, shattered political stability and unity, a sense of uncertainty at home and abroad, and decreased support for liberation movements in Africa, Asia, and Latin America.

Internal Politics. The movement against the legacy of the ancient sage Confucius and the late Defense Minister Lin Piao, the "closest comrade-in-arms" and once heir apparent of Chairman Mao, had its roots in the past two congresses of the Communist Party. The ninth congress, held in April 1969, officially concluded the Cultural Revolution, which had been directed against traditional and bureaucratic ideas, internal and external revisionism of Communist doctrine, and specific political opponents of Chairman Mao. It disposed of "capitalist roaders," including the head of state Liu Shao-ch'i; proclaimed Mao and Lin Piao as the supreme leaders; elected a Central Committee with a larger military representation; and laid down the guidelines for the reconstruction of the Communist Party in Mao's image. However, the increased power of the military in the political structures intensified the conflict with the civilian leadership and led to the downfall of Lin. Over a year after his demise in 1971 Peking confirmed Lin's abortive coup to seize power and his death in a plane crash while trying to flee toward the Soviet Union.

The tenth congress, in August 1973, held in unprecedented secrecy, formally disposed of the Lin affair, ratified the reconstituted leadership bodies, and deemphasized the cult of Mao so as to revitalize the party's institutional authority. The congress unanimously reelected Chairman Mao and elected five vice-chairmen in the following order: Premier Chou En-lai; Wang Hung-wen, a former worker in Shanghai; K'ang Sheng, a member of the previous Politburo and the Cultural Revolution Group; Yeh Ch'ien-ying, acting defense minister and a close associate of Premier Chou; and Li Teh-sheng, then head of the Army General Political Department and military commander in the capital region. Although he was not officially designated as Mao's successor, Chou's ascendancy to the position next to Mao was confirmed. The rise of Wang Hung-wen, only in his 30s, suggested Mao's design in the new succession and a delicate balance of power among the radicals, moderates, and the non-Lin Piao military in the new ruling coalition.

By virtue of his second place in the hierarchy and with the State Council as his power base, Premier Chou became a dominant figure in the new ruling coalition of moderates, or pragmatists, and radicals, or idealists. The two groups differed in their fundamental approach to the art of government, and the struggle between the "Red" and the "Expert" persisted. Just before the convocation of the tenth congress a movement was initiated under the slogan "Going Against the Tide," opposing the decisions of the moderate central administration. Evidently, Chou's policy of détente with the U.S., which brought about greatly increased contacts with Western ideas and travelers, had created tensions with the radical leaders. Soon after the conclusion of the congress, a campaign was launched to criticize Confucius and exalt the Ch'in emperor Shih Huang Ti, the first monarch to smash feudalism and unify the Chinese empire in 221 B.C. Ruling the country by force instead of adhering to the teachings of Confucius, the emperor had burned the Four Books of Confucius and massacred Confucian scholars. He was regarded by Mao's ideological movement as a model of political behaviour.

Meanwhile, the central leadership succeeded with considerable finesse in December 1973 in reorganizing the military high command by reshuffling 8 of the 11 regional military commands in order to bring the military establishments in the provinces more closely under civilian control from the capital. The transfer of Vice-Chairman Li Teh-sheng, commander of the Peking region, to the Shenyang region in Manchuria and his replacement by Commander Chen Hsi-lien, known as Premier Chou's close associate, were considered significant developments. Shortly afterward, Teng Hsiao-ping (see BIOGRAPHY), who had been the second-ranking target of criticism during the Cultural Revolution, reappeared as a Politburo member. Teng was the former superior of many army men now holding important posts, and his reemergence strengthened the position of the moderates.

Although the initial anti-Confucius movement was obliquely aimed at Premier Chou, he endorsed and defused it by directing the attack onto Lin Piao and his followers and by placing the movement under the supervision of the Communist Party. Early in February, the name of the campaign was changed to "criti-

An urban Chinese girl working on a state farm near Harbin. This is one aspect of the government's continuing effort to have everyone engage in farm labour for certain periods of time.

cize Lin-Confucius movement," and the *People's Daily* declared it a nationwide mass movement against feudalism, capitalism, and revisionism. The radicals were instructed that the campaigns must be carried out under the leadership of the party, and that they should not be used to attack personal enemies or political foes as in the early part of the Cultural Revolution.

With the organization of youth, workers', and women's associations to join the campaign of criticizing Lin Piao and Confucius, the movement was intensified. The mass rallies and criticism sessions subsequently organized throughout the country proved to be the largest mobilization since the Cultural Revolution. Large posters airing grievances and criticizing leaders proliferated. Premier Chou began to take a more militant posture in his remarks on foreign relations. Although the movement indicated no basic change of diplomatic and trade policies, there was a shift in Peking's attitude toward greater opposition to Western music and other cultural influences.

In April a reconciliation between the moderates and radical leaders appeared likely when the government dispatched a delegation headed by Deputy Premier Teng Hsiao-ping to attend the special session of the UN General Assembly. Except for Chairman Mao all the Politburo members, including Chou and Chiang Ch'ing, came to the airport to bid Teng farewell and to welcome him back. Speaking to the General Assembly, Teng explained that the campaign to criticize Lin Piao and Confucius was aimed at ensuring that "socialist China will never change her colour."

In the meantime, Premier Chou began to withdraw from some frontline political and diplomatic duties. He was absent for the first time from a state banquet, in honour of Pakistani Prime Minister Zulfikar Ali Bhutto. After May, Deputy Premier Teng acted in Chou's place at important official functions. However, it was not clear then whether Chou's initial withdrawal from an active role was voluntary or under pressure. In July it was officially made known that Chou had been hospitalized because of a heart ailment. Early in September when a U.S. congressional delegation headed by Sen. J. William Fulbright (Dem., Ark.)

was in Peking, Chou was unable to receive them because of his illness.

On September 30, the eve of the 25th anniversary of the People's Republic, Chou made his first major appearance in public in two months and gave a reception for all high officials, including foreign dignitaries. In his speech Chou declared that "We will continue to criticize Lin Piao and Confucius, persist in continuing the revolution under the dictatorship of the proletariat, [and] adhere to the principle of independence and self-reliance." However, the Lin Piao crisis and the ideological dispute continued to cause divisions within the Communist Party, government, and Army, and long delayed the convocation of the fourth National People's Congress first announced by Chou in August 1973.

Economic Development. China claimed in 1974 that it had achieved self-sufficiency in food supplies, although it continued to import wheat, corn, soybeans, and cotton. U.S. agricultural exports to China for 1973 amounted to $700 million. Statistics on grain production were not available, but China called the 1973 grain output a record harvest of about 250 million metric tons. The 1974 production was expected to be higher than that of 1973.

Much of the nation's most recent industrial development was directed to serving the needs of agriculture by producing farm machinery, fertilizers, and pesticides. Another major part of China's recent economic development program was to improve its transportation system. Jet transports, helicopters, trucks, oil-drilling rigs, and steel and chemical plants were purchased from Japan and the West.

In the world energy crisis, China played a role as an important oil supplier to Japan, Thailand, the Philippines, and Hong Kong. According to Premier Chou, China's oil production reached a record of 50 million metric tons in 1973 (roughly 350 million bbl.), compared with 30 million tons for the previous year. Beginning in November 1973 U.S. companies sold to China about $10 million of oil equipment. There were preliminary talks about joint exploitation of China's potentially large onshore and offshore oil reserves.

Foreign Relations. Foreign policy in 1974 continued to follow the line expounded by Premier Chou and endorsed by Chairman Mao at the tenth party congress. It consisted of the following major elements: opposition to the domination of the U.S. and the Soviet Union in world affairs; détente with the U.S. and friendship for Japan and Western Europe as a counterweight against the threat of Soviet aggression against China; and solidarity with the third world against both the "socialist imperialism" of the U.S.S.R. and the "capitalist imperialism" of the U.S. and Western Europe.

Concerning the international situation in 1974, Premier Chou repeatedly declared that U.S.-Soviet contention for dominance was the cause of world tensions. This theme was reiterated in greater detail at the UN General Assembly by Chinese delegates Teng Hsiao-ping and Chiao Kuan-hua. Teng said that the two superpowers were the largest exploiters and oppressors, while Chiao (who replaced Chi Peng-fei as foreign minister in November) hailed the Arab countries' use of oil as a political weapon.

In China's view of the world balance of power, Western Europe and Japan had become important components. After Japan, China had become the European Community's second largest trading partner in Asia. Peking's courtship of Western Europe was most pronounced in its invitation to U.K. Conservative Prime Minister Edward Heath to visit China and another invitation to his Labour Party successor. In May, Heath visited Peking and was greeted by ceremonies equivalent to those for a head of government. To strengthen Sino-French ties, Teng Hsiao-ping made a special trip to Paris to hold talks with French Premier Pierre Messmer. Peking also concluded a contract with an industrial complex in West Germany to build steel mills in China and to train a large number of Chinese engineers.

A new full-scale trade agreement between China and Japan was signed in Peking on January 5, granting the most-favoured-nation treatment in commercial relations between the two Asian powers and providing an exchange of journalists. Following the conclusion of an aviation pact in April, direct regular air services between Tokyo and Peking were inaugurated in September, and fishery and shipping agreements were under negotiation. After the completion of those agreements a new peace treaty of friendship was scheduled to be negotiated.

During the year a dozen heads of state or government and several other high state officials visited China to seek closer political and economic ties with Peking. In chronological order, the heads of government paying state visits included: Pres. Houari Boumédienne of Algeria; Pres. Julius Nyerere of Tanzania; Pres. Kenneth Kaunda of Zambia; Pres. Léopold Sédar Senghor of Senegal; Prime Minister Zulfikar Ali Bhutto of Pakistan; Archbishop Makarios, president of Cyprus; Prime Minister Tun Abdul Razak of Malaysia; Gen. Yakubu Gowon of Nigeria; Gen. Gnassingbe Eyadema, president of Togo; Pres. Moktar Ould Daddah of Mauritania; Pres. Omar Bongo of Gabon; and Prime Minister Poul Hartling of Denmark. Some of them were paying their second or third visits to Peking, but they were

A new tower under construction at the Shanghai oil refinery. The installation processes about four million tons of crude oil per year.

CAMERA PRESS / PHOTO TRENDS

all granted audience by Chairman Mao. In previous years, Mao had only received heads of state but in 1974 he received Japan's foreign minister, the former prime minister of the U.K., and Mme Imelda Marcos, wife of the Philippine president. However, he did not meet with U.S. Secretary of State Henry Kissinger during the latter's trip to Peking in November.

In attempts at regional diplomacy, China began to show goodwill to countries in Southeast Asia, where more than 15 million Chinese resided, by advising the overseas Chinese to be loyal to their country of adoption. In the negotiations for establishing diplomatic relations with Malaysia, Peking declared that it gave no material support to the insurgencies in Malaysia, which became the first member of the Association of Southeast Asian Nations to recognize the Peking regime as the sole legal government of China. In negotiations to establish diplomatic relations with Indonesia, Thailand, and the Philippines, Premier Chou assured them that China would neither support nor encourage rebellions in their countries.

Sino-Soviet Relations. During the year Sino-Soviet relations showed no improvement as the two nations continued their territorial and ideological disputes and rivalry for leadership in the Communist world. The Soviet press accused the Peking leadership of anti-Soviet policy and anti-Communism, while the Chinese media called Moscow the worst imperialist power and accused it of attempts at subversion within China. The Soviet move to call a world Communist congress to ostracize China from the orthodox Communist movement failed to win the support of some national Communist parties.

In Peking's view the ideological quarrel between the two powers would not stand in the way of restoring good relations if Moscow would agree on the demarcation of the long boundary between the two and would pull back the huge number of Soviet troops from the Chinese frontier. The U.S.S.R. was unable to meet Peking's terms, and so the border issues remained unresolved after four years of prolonged negotiations. Early in the year the complex border issues were aggravated and overshadowed by two incidents involving spy charges and countercharges. On January 19 Peking expelled five Soviet nationals, including two diplomats, their families, and an interpreter, on charges of espionage activities. The Chinese asserted that they had been caught a few days earlier in a Peking suburb while delivering espionage material and documents to their agent, Li Hung-shu, who had been trained by Soviet military intelligence. The Soviet Union denied the charges and, in apparent retaliation, arrested and expelled from Moscow two days later a young Chinese diplomat accused of spying. The Chinese indignantly rebutted the charge.

Another spying incident occurred on March 14 when a Soviet military helicopter with a three-man crew strayed over the Sinkiang border and landed on Chinese territory. In a protest note of March 23, the Chinese charged that the helicopter had been on a spying mission. Moscow rejected the charges and demanded the return of the craft and crew. On the eve of U.S. Pres. Richard Nixon's visit to Moscow and in a gesture of Soviet conciliation, Leonid F. Ilyichev, the chief Soviet negotiator, returned to Peking on June 25 to resume border negotiations after nearly a year, but he left for Moscow two months later. In November, on the occasion of the Soviet celebration of the Bolshevik Revolution, China somewhat abruptly indicated that it was interested in a non-

CHINA
Education. Primary (1959–60), pupils 90 million, teachers (1964) c. 2.6 million; secondary (1958–59), pupils 8,520,000; vocational (1958–59), pupils 850,-000; teacher training, students (1958–59) 620,000; higher (1962–63), students 820,000.

Finance. Monetary unit: yuan, with (Sept. 16, 1974) an official exchange rate of 1.96 yuan to U.S. $1 (4.63 yuan = £1 sterling). Gold reserves (1972 est.) U.S. $2,250,000,000. Budget (1960 est.; latest published) balanced at 70,020,000,000 yuan. Gross national product (1971 est.) U.S. $129 billion.

Foreign Trade. (1973) Imports c. U.S. $4,670,-000,000; exports c. U.S. $4,120,000,000. Import sources (1972): Japan c. 24%; Canada c. 10%; West Germany c. 6%. Export destinations (1972): Hong Kong c. 23%; Japan c. 16%; Singapore c. 6%. Main exports: industrial and mining products (textiles and clothing, crude oil, metal ores; etc.) 65%; fruit and vegetables; rice; hides and skins.

Transport and Communications. Roads (1970) c. 800,000 km. (including c. 300,000 km. all-weather). Motor vehicles in use (1971): passenger c. 1,030,000; commercial (including buses) c. 780,000. Railways: (1972) c. 35,000 km.; traffic (1959) 45,670,000,000 passenger-km., freight (1971) 301,000,000,000 net ton-km. Air traffic (1960): 63,882,000 passenger-km.; freight 1,967,000 net ton-km. Inland waterways (including Yangtze River; 1972) c. 160,000 km. Shipping (1973): merchant vessels 100 gross tons and over 323; gross tonnage 1,478,992. Telephones (1951) 255,000. Radio receivers (Dec. 1970) c. 12 million. Television receivers (Dec. 1969) c. 300,000.

Agriculture. Production (in 000; metric tons; 1973; 1972 in parentheses): rice c. 107,000 (c. 102,000); corn c. 29,700 (c. 28,500); wheat c. 35,000 (c. 34,-500); barley c. 19,500 (c. 18,500); millet and sorghum c. 23,000 (c. 22,000); potatoes c. 32,400 (c. 32,000); dry peas c. 3,472 (c. 3,450); soybeans c. 11,-700 (c. 11,500); peanuts c. 2,600 (c. 2,500); rapeseed c. 1,150 (c. 1,150); sugar, raw value c. 3,500 (c. 3,-500); pears c. 1,000 (c. 975); tobacco c. 856 (c. 853); tea c. 205 (c. 203); cotton, lint c. 1,690 (c. 1,409); jute c. 520 (c. 510); beef and buffalo meat c. 1,966 (c. 1,957); pork c. 9,398 (c. 9,183); timber (cu.m.; 1971) 174,000, (1970) 171,000; fish catch (1972) c. 6,920, (1971) c. 6,880. Livestock (in 000; 1972–73): horses c. 7,000; asses c. 11,650; cattle c. 63,-250; buffalo c. 29,700; sheep c. 72,000; pigs c. 235,-000; goats c. 58,500.

Industry. Fuel and power (in 000; metric tons; 1973): coal (including lignite) c. 450,000; coke (1971) 18,000; crude oil c. 50,000; electricity (kw-hr.; 1960) c. 58,500,000. Production (in 000; metric tons; 1972): iron ore (metal content) c. 25,300; pig iron c. 28,000; crude steel (1973) c. 25,000; lead c. 100; copper c. 100; zinc c. 100; aluminum c. 140; tungsten concentrates (oxide content) c. 8.8; cement (1971) c. 12,000; salt (1971) c. 15,000; sulfuric acid (1966) c. 2,500; fertilizers (nutrient content; 1972–73) nitrogenous c. 2,245, phosphate c. 1,031; cotton yarn (1969) c. 1,450; cotton fabrics (1971) c. 9,000; man-made fibres c. 65; paper c. 4,550.

aggression pact with the U.S.S.R., but the Soviets reportedly found the proposal "unacceptable."

Sino-U.S. Relations. Following Secretary of State Kissinger's visit to China in February 1973 and as a step toward full diplomatic relations, liaison offices, each headed by a chief liaison officer, were established in April 1973 in Peking and Washington, D.C. However, internal Chinese politics, President Nixon's resignation, and the firm U.S. commitments to the Nationalist Chinese government on Taiwan delayed normalization of relations between the two countries.

China was irritated over the quick appointment of so senior a U.S. diplomat as Leonard Unger to the ambassadorship in Taiwan. Peking's representative in Washington protested the appointment as contrary to the 1972 Shanghai communiqué issued by President Nixon and Premier Chou. However, Teng Hsiao-ping assured Washington of Peking's cautious but determined policy of accommodation.

Early in June, Secretary of State Kissinger stated to private U.S. organizations advocating early recognition of Peking that "the normalization of relations and essential element of our foreign policy. . . ." After his return from a week's visit in Peking early in July, Sen. Henry M. Jackson (Dem., Wash.) proposed that the U.S. raise its diplomatic liaison office in Peking to the level of an embassy and at the same time reduce its embassy in Taipei to a liaison office.

Hours after Gerald Ford had taken the oath as president on August 9, Secretary of State Kissinger assured Huang Chen that there would be no change in U.S. policy concerning China. In the meantime, a personal letter from Premier Chou to President Ford was believed to reflect Peking's desire to establish good relations with the new U.S. administration. On September 4 President Ford named George Bush, the Republican Party national chairman, to be the U.S. envoy to China, succeeding David K. E. Bruce. At the invitation of the Chinese People's Institute of Foreign Affairs, a bipartisan congressional delegation of seven members headed by Senator Fulbright made a two-week tour of China early in September.

Immediately after the Ford-Brezhnev summit meeting in Vladivostok on November 22–23, Secretary of State Kissinger made his seventh visit to Peking (November 25–29) to confer with Chinese leaders. He held talks with Vice-Premier Teng and with Foreign Minister Chaio, with whom he had drafted the Shanghai communiqué. Although he did not meet with Chairman Mao, he did visit Premier Chou in the hospital. At the end of his visit a short communiqué was issued reaffirming the two countries' "unchanged commitment to the principle of the Shanghai communiqué" and announcing that President Ford would visit China in 1975.

(HUNG-TI CHU)

See also **Taiwan.**
[975.A]

Cities and Urban Affairs

The Energy Crisis. The decision of oil-producing countries at the end of 1973 to restrict production and place an embargo on the delivery of supplies to the U.S. and The Netherlands forced an awareness of the importance of energy upon the world. It might well prove to have been the spark that set in motion a reversal of the way cities had developed over the past three decades.

The enormous rise in private ownership of the automobile, perhaps more than any other phenomenon, had profoundly affected cities and towns. Daily commuting had become, for many, a normal way of life. The increased volume of cars in turn led to demands for more and enlarged road surfaces, and the hearts of many cities were disfigured by four-lane, multistory highways, cutting neighbourhoods in two, destroying city landscapes, and ultimately attracting ever more traffic. The ease and convenience of private transportation led to declining demand for public transport, which virtually disappeared in many cities, causing further hardship to the aged, the physically handicapped, and the poor.

As the more affluent moved beyond the old city boundaries, the built-up area spread into the surrounding countryside, using up land needed for other purposes, such as green space and leisure activities, and greatly extending travel distances. Suburbanization also widened the social cleavage between those who could leave the increasingly congested, deteriorating, and dangerous cities and those who, for

reasons of age, race, or income, had to remain behind.

The many advantages of the private motorcar had long blinded owners and city officials alike to the disadvantages, for the city, of its unlimited use. Despite bumper-to-bumper lines of traffic, limited parking space, and rush hour congestion, it was not until people became aware of the danger to their own health from polluted air and of the need to maintain the ecological balance that measures were taken to control the use of automobiles in cities. These included closing narrow shopping streets in the old cities of Europe to motor traffic, construction of pedestrian malls in new and reconstructed city centres in all parts of the world, bans on parking, planting trees to absorb automotive exhaust fumes, and halting further major highway construction. Yet it was difficult for people to imagine a life in which the motorcar did not play a central role.

The day came, however, when world events made this a reality for people in several European countries. Several governments introduced the carless Sunday; this was accepted as a temporary necessity, but by the time it was abolished, many city residents regretted its passing. There had been a rare opportunity to experience life in a city without motorcars. Public transport came into its own. Families took afternoon walks or went bicycling. The many attractions of the city came to be more appreciated.

Although carless Sundays and gasoline rationing had vanished by the end of 1974, the need for cautious use of energy, immediately and in the future, remained. The fact that the world's energy supplies were limited gained increasing acceptance, although there was less general agreement on the management of these resources. Nevertheless, for cities and towns, certain guideposts stood out clearly: alternative means of transportation must be developed and promoted; cities must be less dispersed; environmental protection must be continued.

Efforts to find alternative transport modes centred on the improvement of conventional systems and the development of new ones. Technological advances included the propulsion system, using the electric motor, which had environmental advantages; vehicle support systems—air cushion and magnetic support; lighter structures and miniaturization, applied to conventional systems such as buses; and automatic guidance systems, which involved replacing drivers with automatic control systems and conductors and inspectors with automatic ticket stamping facilities. Developments that could narrow the gap between public and private transport included the dual-mode bus, which used guideways but could be driven like any other vehicle on ordinary roads, and the various "dial-a-ride" systems that would allow passengers to summon public transport to collect them from and deliver them to named destinations. (*See* TRANSPORTATION.)

In Europe the bicycle came back into vogue. The Netherlands and Denmark had long been countries of cyclists and, more recently, of motorcycle riders. In The Netherlands, where 76% of the population owned bicycles, special bicycle paths were a feature of city traffic circulation patterns. Often special traffic lights at intersections gave cyclists a five-second advantage over motor traffic. The bicycle was rated so convenient that not even difficult weather conditions restricted its widespread use. Bicycles were becoming increasingly popular in Great Britain. One New Town, Stevenage, took the lead in catering to the cyclist—and the pedestrian—by setting up two separate circulation networks, one for automobiles and one for cycles and pedestrians. About 23 mi. of bicycle paths and some 90 underpasses were provided. Bicycle paths carried two-way traffic and often ran alongside main roads, from which they were separated by grass verges. Västerås in Sweden closed its centre to all but cyclists, pedestrians, buses, and delivery vehicles. Special bicycle routes were provided in other areas of the city.

Bicycles were less widely used in the U.S., although there were at least 80 million bicycles and more cycles were sold than automobiles. In university towns a large percentage of young residents were bicycle owners and riders. The bicycle had many advantages in cities that made proper provision for it; it was quiet, nonpolluting, healthy, efficient, and inexpensive. Sixteen bicycles could be parked in the space required by one car, and the cost per square metre of a cycle path was about one-sixth that of an expressway. A four-metre cycle path had five times the carrying capacity of an eight-metre motor road. There were disadvantages to bicycle transportation in cities, however, mainly because insufficient provision was made to separate cycles from motor traffic. Bicyclists in the U.S. were known to travel the shortest route, whether or not this coincided with the bicycle paths, and cities were not able to enforce the use of cycle routes because bicycles were not recognized as a means of transportation and therefore were not included in the motor code. In The Netherlands, by contrast, cyclists who did not use the pathways, where they existed, or who did not abide by the general traffic code could be cited for a traffic violation.

New Plans for Cities. Even before the energy crisis, many experiments to provide alternative means of transportation were under way, but similar efforts to optimize energy use through alternative plans for the development of cities and towns had yet to be made. An analysis of the consequences for energy use of wide-scale suburbanization in the New York region, by the Regional Plan Association and Resources for the Future, showed that energy used per resident rose as density declined and that use of residential electricity per dollar of income was three times as high in the suburban counties of the New York region as in the denser areas. Low densities proved expensive in terms of residential energy use and of the development of commercial, industrial, and public facilities. Higher densities led to more efficient energy use for public transport as well as for the provision of clean water, sewage disposal, and the recovery of solid waste resources.

Research organizations made several suggestions, aimed at both governments and private individuals, for incorporating energy conservation into the design of residential areas. Construction of free-standing shopping centres, strip highway commerce, isolated office and educational campuses, and other land uses that characterized urban sprawl should be restricted. Homes should be built on small lots, with imaginative landscaping used to provide a feeling of privacy. Private and public developers should plan a better relationship between various space uses, such as housing, shops, work places, and cultural and recreational facilities. For many years zoning patterns had separated different land uses to such an extent that accessibility in terms of time and distance had been greatly limited. With better grouping of land uses, access could be improved, individual time and energy saved, and the attractions of city living enhanced.

Land as well as energy was in short supply and would need to be well managed in the future. Multiple residences and the terraced townhouse type of home would have to become the choice of more and more city dwellers. Many criticisms of such dwellings— lack of privacy, noise, pollution, inconvenient layouts, lack of modern equipment, difficult access to the out-of-doors, uninteresting outlook, and a general lack of space—were valid, but these disadvantages were not inherent. Technology could overcome such defects, provided building research was given priority in government budgets and the funds needed to incorporate new techniques into modern constructions were made available.

Aerial view of Expo 74 grounds at Spokane, Wash.

BLACK STAR

Economic development
is changing the face
of Paris, as indicated
by this view near
the Eiffel Tower.

More choice in housing types would also be needed. People's knowledge and experience of housing was often limited to traditional types, and it was not necessarily true that they would reject new kinds of homes, neighbourhood patterns, and overall city designs if they knew of them. Increased choice and changed attitudes could encourage citizens to match their housing with stages in the life cycle. The newly married couple, the family with growing children, the older person in ill health—all required dwellings suited to their particular needs. The more limited the choice, the less the opportunity for such matchings, and the less efficient the use of total housing facilities and space resources.

If, as a result of the energy crisis, city renovation efforts could be intensified, new life would come to deteriorating downtown centres. Preservation of what was usable or of historic value, limited renewal where deterioration had reached the point of no return, and widespread renovation, when possible, needed encouraging. City centres containing only offices and commercial buildings were dead during nonworking hours. If these areas were to be utilized fully, housing, shops, and traffic-free areas where people could walk unhindered, sit and rest, refresh themselves at outdoor cafes, or enjoy open-air entertainment would all be required.

Environmental Protection. There was some danger that the need to conserve energy resources might lead city officials and city dwellers to call for relaxation of some of the strict environmental measures that had recently been adopted. It would be unfortunate if the gains so painfully made were to be given up for reasons of inconvenience and because of unwillingness to modify a current way of life. In the U.S. the deadline for the installation of emission controls in new cars was postponed for one year. The controls, supposed to eliminate 90% of the polluting emissions, would reduce the efficiency of the automobile and require the use of more gasoline. Demands for heavier cars, larger engine sizes, and, particularly in warm climates, air conditioning all placed new burdens on energy supplies.

Setbacks in controlling the pollution caused by heating were also to be expected. One reason for the sharp drop in air pollution in London, resulting in the disappearance of the famous London fog, had been the ban on the burning of soft coal for home use. If in Great Britain—as elsewhere—domestic coal could be substituted for costly imported fuel oils, the resulting savings and the reduction in international pressures might be so convincing that governments would find it difficult to resist. Should it come to a choice between insufficient heating and the use of a fuel with a higher pollution content, the outcome would not be difficult to predict. The same arguments would also hold true for industrial fuel, particularly in a world where economic growth was a major national priority. Difficult choices would face cities in the months ahead as the full implications of decreased oil supplies and increased costs became evident.

Local Government Reform. The precarious balance between the ever increasing responsibilities of local governments, especially in the field of public and personal social services, and their limited resources continued to lead to more or less drastic structural reforms in many countries. Most such reforms started from the viewpoint that "bigger local government is better local government." The efficiency principle meant that services must cover substantial numbers of actual and potential clients and users if the costs to the community—i.e., the local, regional, and national economies and the taxpayer— were to be kept within reasonable limits. The usual pattern of reform involved the amalgamation of units too small to be viable and/or the transfer of competences and tasks to units covering larger numbers of citizens.

In few countries did local government reorganization assume such ambitious and controversial dimensions as in Great Britain. Following the publication of a royal commission report (1969) and a White Paper (1971), the latter refuting some crucial recommendations of the former, the Local Government Act 1972 was passed, marking the end of a structure dating back to 1888 and 1894. The White Paper had stated that the areas of many existing authorities no longer reflected the pattern of life and work in modern society. There were too many authorities, and many of them were too small to support the services citizens had come to expect.

The Local Government Act, which introduced what some called "the quiet revolution" and others termed a "cataclysmic change and near-chaos," came into force in stages. In October 1973, 26 new district councils were created in Northern Ireland; on April 1, 1974, England and Wales saw their 1,424 local government areas reduced to 456; and by April 1975 the 432 local government units in Scotland would have been replaced by 65 new district councils. The 1974 reorganization in England did not include London, where governmental reform had been carried through separately in the mid-1960s.

Coincident with the local government reorganization, the National Health Service was restructured and new Area Health Authorities were charged with personal health services. Regional water authorities were also created. Both changes inevitably affected local government competence.

Characteristic of the reorganization was the adoption of a two-tier system, with the new county as the first tier, covering the wider areas necessary for effective management of certain services. The district or borough, which formed the second tier, somewhat nearer to the local community, was created by the merging of former units too small for adequate performance. In the interest of local democracy, citizen involvement, and community life, especially in rural areas, the parish was retained as the smallest unit of local government. In larger urban areas, new nonstatutory bodies might come to perform the same functions for neighbourhoods and small communities within cities that the parishes provided in rural areas.

In the most densely populated parts of the country, six urban counties were temporarily designated metropolitan counties. They consisted of a number of districts or boroughs, each one large enough in population and resources and sufficiently compact in size to be responsible for education, personal social services, and certain other local functions that in other areas belonged to the competence of the new counties. The county boroughs, local governments of big towns with excellent records in providing public services, were not retained because they could not be fitted to the new pattern without perpetuating a separation between town and country that the drafters of the Local Government Act deemed undesirable.

The new counties, as envisaged by law, were in no sense a continuation of the former county authorities. Rather, they were entirely new authorities intended to bind together—in most cases for the first time— all the urban and rural areas within their boundaries. Where possible, existing county boundaries were retained in order to maximize existing loyalties and minimize administrative problems. Nevertheless, the transitional period was crucial. Within a few months, new councillors had to create a management structure, appoint councillors and chief executives to responsible posts, provide accommodations and equipment, and still maintain existing services without interruption. In the words of some experts, reorganization plunged all those employed in local government into a sea of uncertainties. The challenge stimulated many, but for others it brought unhappiness and frustration. Some of the new authorities had populations of almost two million, more than the total population of either Panama or Northern Ireland.

One aim of the reorganization was to promote vigorous local democracy. Thus the parish was retained to counterbalance the trend toward the larger units required by effective services management. The White Paper of 1971 had stated its determination "to return power to those people who should exercise decisions locally, and to ensure that local government is given every opportunity to take that initiative and responsibility effectively, speedily, and with vigour." Local government spokesmen were not so sure about the outcome, and whether the end result would be a new local government structure that was as perplexing to the electorate as the old remained to be seen. Many people found the new structure confusing where no confusion had existed before. A British local government journal remarked that local government would undoubtedly "look very untidy for some time" and that the problem of contact with the public would have to be resolved. A local government information office was certainly needed.

Mention should be made, however, of various initiatives in Britain that were not directly related to the reorganization but that offered encouraging prospects for the future relations of local government with citizens. In February 1974, for example, the first planning advice centre was set up in the London borough of Lambeth. Very shortly it was handling up to 200 citizens' inquiries each week on such matters as clearance and conservation areas, historic buildings, and town centre renewal plans. This initiative met with general approval, and the impression of the staff was that the average citizen had a much greater understanding of planning problems than was sometimes assumed. The Lambeth initiative was followed by Leeds, where a planning advice centre was established in April, and by Winchester, where the centre was a joint venture of the Department of the Environment, the Winchester District Council, and the Hampshire County Council.

The prevailing mood was perhaps best reflected in the words of a local government magazine: "It would be fair to say that a large number of people in local government have never been in favour of reorganization. But there was widespread resignation to the fact that change was inevitable—and that it would be imperfect whichever government carried it out." Without doubt, reorganization would require the skill and dedication of many thousands of newly elected representatives on county and district councils, and of their newly appointed chief executives and other officers, for years to come.

In Great Britain, London government had been reformed first, followed by local government in the rest of the country. Denmark's reorganization followed the reverse sequence. On April 1, 1974, the 37 members of the Metropolitan Council, embracing Copenhagen, Frederiksberg, and the counties of Copenhagen, Frederiksborg, and Roskilde, took office under the new Metropolitan Council Act of 1973. This area had not been included in the Local Government Act which came into force in 1970. The 1973 act reduced the number of first-tier units from 1,300 to 277 and of second-tier units from 25 to 14, redistributed competences and powers between the various levels of local government, and took into consideration the possibility of further decentralization in the future.

The members of the Copenhagen Metropolitan Council were appointed by the five municipalities and counties within the area from among their council members, in accordance with the principle of political and geographic proportional representation. Competences of the Metropolitan Council included physical

		World's 25 Most Populous Urban Areas*			
		City proper		Metropolitan area	
Rank	City and country	Most recent population	Year	Most recent population	Year
1	Tokyo, Japan	8,708,311	1974 estimate	23,457,133	1970 census
2	New York City, U.S.	7,716,600	1973 estimate	16,179,100	1973 estimate
3	Osaka, Japan	2,826,796	1974 estimate	15,389,971	1970 census
4	London, U.K.	7,281,080	1973 estimate	12,704,300	1973 estimate
5	Shanghai, China	...	...	10,820,000†	1970 census
6	Mexico City, Mexico	7,768,033	1973 estimate	10,223,102	1973 estimate
7	Paris, France	2,425,000	1974 estimate	10,022,000	1974 estimate
8	Ruhr, West Germany‡	—	—	9,813,000	1970 estimate
9	Buenos Aires, Argentina	2,976,000	1973 estimate	8,352,900	1970 census
10	São Paulo, Brazil	5,924,612	1970 census	8,139,705	1970 census
11	Peking, China	...	...	7,570,000†	1970 estimate
12	Moscow, U.S.S.R.	7,255,000	1973 estimate	7,410,000	1973 estimate
13	Rio de Janeiro, Brazil	4,251,918	1970 census	7,092,627	1970 census
14	Chicago, U.S.	3,380,634	1973 estimate	7,048,500	1973 estimate
15	Calcutta, India	3,148,746	1971 census	7,031,382	1971 census
16	Los Angeles, U.S.	2,814,806	1973 estimate	6,944,800	1973 estimate
17	Nagoya, Japan	2,077,031	1974 estimate	6,633,958	1970 census
18	Bombay, India	...	...	5,970,575†	1971 census
19	Cairo, Egypt	5,517,000	1973 estimate	5,925,400	1970 estimate
20	Seoul, South Korea	...	...	5,525,262†	1970 census
21	Manila, Philippines	1,473,557	1974 estimate	5,369,892	1974 estimate
22	Jakarta, Indonesia	...	...	4,915,265†	1973 estimate
23	Detroit, U.S.	1,514,063	1970 census	4,446,800	1973 estimate
24	Tientsin, China	...	...	4,280,000†	1970 estimate
25	Wu-han, China	3,000,000	1970 estimate	4,250,000†	1970 estimate

*Ranked by population of metropolitan area.
†Municipality or other civil division within which a city proper may not be distinguished.
‡A so-called industrial conurbation, within which a single central city is not distinguished.

Prefabricated housing is used in development of Churchill, Man. The Canadian government is spending large sums to improve this Arctic seaport on the shore of Hudson Bay.

planning powers at the regional level, the setting of land use and town development priorities, and the location of major roads and water supply and sewerage systems. The council also set time schedules for implementation of the various phases of the plans, which were binding on the municipal and county councils. Experience had taught that such powers were essential if metropolitan council decisions were to be effective.

A Metropolitan Fund was created to allocate revenue funds to various projects—which would be determined by the council annually on the basis of applications from the municipalities and counties in the metropolitan area—for such purposes as land purchase, town development and renewal, water supply plants, and regional parks. The funds would be provided as either grants or loans, with or without interest. The Metropolitan Council also had responsibility for public transport. A Metropolitan Traffic Council would coordinate the location and construction of traffic lines, schedules of services, and fares, and recommend a scheme for unified operation of all public transportation. A new Metropolitan Bus Company would take over all publicly owned or dominated bus companies. Part of the boards of these new bodies were appointed by the Metropolitan Council. On environmental matters, the Metropolitan Council was given functions similar to those of a regional body, especially with regard to planning the main sewerage system and to water pollution technology. Other powers might be given to the council in due time. The reorganization was generally considered as a first step, with revisions tentatively projected for 1976–77.

In contrast to the bold reorganizations carried through in Great Britain and Denmark, change in French local government was cautious. The reorganization set in motion by a 1971 law concerning the amalgamation and redivision of the local communes gradually developed in the course of 1974. Although the approach tended toward the prudent, the 38,000 local communes were to be reduced by 1,000. Ten years earlier few people in France would have expected any such move. Thus, a needed reform was accepted, though with resignation rather than enthusiasm. The cases of amalgamation dealt with by the Conseil d'État seemed to wake little protest or, if protests did arise, they appeared to be growing less virulent.

Again, it was the cost of public and social services that provided the impetus toward larger units, especially in the rural areas where declining populations and small communities could no longer afford to provide essential facilities. The 1971 law required the prefectural assemblies to study the local communes within their area and classify them as: (1) communes that could function on their own; (2) communes that should share resources in order to guarantee good administration and proper development; and (3) communes that should be amalgamated with others. Proposals for amalgamation were submitted by the prefect to the municipal councils concerned, but if a municipality rejected the amalgamation, it did not take place.

The municipalities were left with a choice between simple amalgamation and a merger involving the creation of one or more associated communes. The rigours of amalgamation were further mitigated by the possibility of a local referendum, but, significantly, demands for referenda were infrequent. The law was less cautious concerning the urban municipalities, districts, and communal syndicates. Their very existence was not at stake, and only part of their powers would be affected. Since the adoption of a special law in 1970, new agglomerations could be created in urban areas. This was done on the advice of the prefectural assembly, the municipal councils, and, sometimes, the metropolitan authority concerned. The new agglomerations could take either of two forms: the "communal planning syndicate," representing the metropolitan authority until the agglomeration reached a size that would justify the creation of a new municipality; or the "urban combination" (*ensemble urbain*), chosen by the municipal councils concerned and, again, to be superseded by a new municipality when the population grew large enough. New agglomerations were mainly in the Paris Region, with two exceptions, Vaudreuil in Normandy and Sabolas near Lyons.

Innovation of Local Administrations. These country-wide reorganizations represented one attempt to relieve the financial burdens and improve the effectiveness of local governments. Another such attempt, often combined with the first, was the introduction of innovation and the modernization of the way in which local administrations functioned. Two efforts in updating administrative practices were topics of much discussion in 1974, namely the "corporate approach" to local administration and the fuller exploitation by local governments of advanced technology.

The Corporate Approach. The local government reorganization in Great Britain was accompanied by suggestions concerning the form of internal organization and management most appropriate for the new local authorities. Emphasis was on the desirability of the "corporate approach," the major purpose of which would be to integrate operations and to enable the various local committees and administrative departments to make use of local resources. It was suggested that local government could be made more flexible so that it could better adapt policies and actions to the requirements of a changing society. The main features of the corporate approach were systematic contacts and the sharing of information and resources between the various departments and committees; a major role for a management team of chief officers and the chief executive, rather than for the chief executive alone, and a predominant role for a policy and resources committee.

The principle behind this approach was that few, if any, major decisions could be made that did not have some effect on others' areas of responsibility. Corporate management provided a means whereby a local authority could plan, review, and adjust its activities as a whole in relation to changing needs and problems. Although many new authorities adopted the corporate approach, it was of necessity an evolutionary process. Nor was corporate management topical only in England. In September 1974, a seminar on the subject was arranged in The Netherlands for Dutch municipal officials.

Given the crucial function of communication in the corporate approach, a basic requirement for its effectiveness was the development of a policy for distributing common data among the various local administrations. Computer systems provided the appropriate means. This, in turn, led to an examination of the research and development efforts of local governments in their quest for equipment that would help improve the quality of services.

Technological Innovation and Local Government. An important contribution to discussions on the use of advanced technology for local government was made when the International Institute for the Management of Technology (IIMT) and the International Union of Local Authorities (IULA) organized, in May 1974, an expert meeting on Research and Development for Local Government at Milan, Italy. The participants, who represented European research and development organizations and local government associations from Europe, the U.S., and other parts of the world, agreed that urban local government the world over faced severe problems resulting from urbanization; natural population growth or decline; rising standards of living; and the social and environmental effects of private sector activities.

Typically, expenditures by local governments in industrialized countries were growing more rapidly than gross national product. The quality of the services provided by local governments, which largely determined the quality of life in urban areas, appeared to be the only variable in a situation where limited resources had to be stretched to cover widening gaps between demand and supply. Research and development were the means of upgrading the quality of services, and they should be used to foster exploitation by local governments of technological advances made in the private sector and in such public sectors as health care, education, aerospace programs, and defense. It was important, therefore, that direct links be established between local governments and the sources of innovation in these sectors. For this purpose, IIMT and IULA invited representatives of research and development organizations and local governments to discuss the feasibility of closer and more systematic cooperation. Of first importance was an understanding of the various concepts involved.

Innovation implied that local governments be involved from the beginning of the process to the end. It required that local governments be able to state their needs to research and development organizations and be willing and able to take the development risk. In a few cases, local governments had their own research facilities. In the majority of cases, however, innovations were solicited from private sector suppliers to match more or less accurate specifications. Such innovations were generally sectorial and marginal, primarily because the climate in local government was not very innovative. Change implied risk, and risks were not easily taken. In addition, funds for experimental projects were either limited or not available.

Technological transfer was an attempt to exploit an innovation for a purpose it was not initially designed to serve. Once the usefulness of an innovation in one area had been demonstrated, the transfer process was one of adapting it to new applications, in this case the urban environment. The process had recently received considerable attention as attempts were made to distribute the benefits of research and development in defense and aerospace over more mundane areas of governmental concern. In the U.S. there were concerted efforts in which local and regional governments participated, including the creation of Public Technology Inc. (PTI), a nonprofit organization sponsored by federal, state, and local agencies.

Technology diffusion was the process whereby innovation moved from one urban environment to another. This process had a number of channels such as conferences, exhibitions, visits, publications, and twin-city arrangements. One very strong argument for technology diffusion was that it began with demonstrated public acceptance, a crucial issue in local government innovation. Indications were that this process was the vehicle for most local government innovations. It required, however, that at least one local authority take the initial risk.

The situation with regard to local government innovations differed from country to country. Some countries considered local government innovation of primary importance and had already institutionalized efforts to improve operations, *e.g.,* the Local Government Operations Research Unit (LGORU) in Great Britain. A project was under way in West Germany to determine a federal strategy with regard to local government innovations. In Cologne a research project was nearing completion on the development of an automatic data processing (ADP)-based information system as an aid in planning and decision making in a large municipal administration. Cologne had participated in the project with the Siemens enterprise and the scientific institution DATUM e.V., with the federal government providing financial support. The most important factor in achieving progress would be a broadening of the circle of users who put tech-

173

Cities and Urban Affairs

Demonstrators occupy Centre Point, the 32-story office building in London's West End which has been vacant since its construction in 1963. Approximately 300 persons fought police efforts to remove them before the building finally was cleared.

LONDON DAILY EXPRESS/PICTORIAL PARADE

nological innovations into practical use. Numerous departments and individuals had been writing and speaking about information systems, but too few institutions were willing to accept the risks of active engagement in the field. In the long run, only an increase of users would shape ADP into a tool that could be put to good use for planning and decision-making purposes.

Experts agreed that there was an obvious need to develop a systematic approach to harnessing science and technology for the benefit of local communities. A key element in this development would be the creation of mechanisms to define the needs of local government and to channel them to the appropriate organizations. Much could be gained and unnecessary duplication could be avoided by active international cooperation. The experts meeting in Milan invited IIMT and IULA to study the possibilities of creating international machinery for the application of science and technology to local and regional problems, including both hard and software and intermediate technology. Such an organization would not itself undertake research and development but would act as a broker between the users and their associations on the one hand and research and development institutes on the other. (IULA)

See also Architecture; Crime and Law Enforcement; Environment; Historic Preservation; Housing; Law.

[525.B; 542.A.1.c; 737]

ENCYCLOPÆDIA BRITANNICA FILMS. *The House of Man, Part II—Our Crowded Environment* (1969); *The South: Roots of the Urban Crisis* (1969); *The Industrial City* (1970); *The Rise of the American City* (1970); *What Is a Community?* (1970); *Our Changing Cities: Can They Be Saved?* (1972); *The Image of the City* (1973).

Colombia

A republic in northwestern South America, Colombia is bordered by Panama, Venezuela, Brazil, Peru, and Ecuador and has coasts on both the Caribbean Sea and the Pacific Ocean. Area: 439,737 sq.mi. (1,138,914 sq.km.). Pop. (1974 est.): 23,952,100. Cap. and largest city: Bogotá (pop., 1974 est., 2,975,200). Language: Spanish. Religion: Roman Catholic (91%). Presidents in 1974, Misael Pastrana Borrero and, after August 7, Alfonso López Michelsen.

Political activity in early 1974 culminated in the presidential and congressional elections on April 21. The elections were the first to be held since 1958 in which the result had not been largely predetermined by the Frente Nacional arrangement, whereby the two major parties had agreed to alternate in the presidency and to maintain parity in the Congress during a period of 16 years. The outcome was a convincing victory for the Liberal Party candidate, Alfonso López Michelsen (*see* BIOGRAPHY), who received 56% of the votes cast and led his nearest rival, the Conservative Álvaro Gómez Hurtado, by more than a million votes. At the same time, the Liberal Party gained 67 out of 113 seats in the Senate and 113 out of 199 in the Chamber of Deputies. Parity between the two major parties was to continue in the Cabinet for another four years; in fact, several of those appointed to Cabinet posts by President López Michelsen were considered to be technocrats rather than politicians.

Guerrilla groups were active early in 1974. The Communist Colombian Revolutionary Armed Forces (FARC) was operating in Bogotá in January; and the National Liberation Army (ELN) lost a leader-priest in a clash with troops in Antioquía Department in

February, his death reportedly leaving only one surviving ELN leader.

The rapid growth of the economy in 1973, when the gross domestic product rose by 7.5%, was maintained in 1974. There was a marked expansion of both production and capacity in industry, particularly in construction, which grew at an annual rate of about 20%. Unemployment fell below 7%, as compared with an average of 12% in the late 1960s. The performance of the external sector remained satisfactory. The overall balance of payments was in surplus, and though for the year up to August 24 there was a deficit on the current account of $42.2 million, this was due to a slight decline in income from coffee exports, an increase in the cost of imported crude oil, an exceptionally large import bill for food products, notably wheat, in July, and the habitual deficit on services. Earnings from exports of manufactured goods and products continued to increase rapidly, amounting to $182 million in the first half of 1974, as compared with $82.2 million in the same period of 1973; the outstanding sectors in this respect were textiles, machinery, and chemicals and pharmaceuticals.

The most serious problem besetting the economy was inflation; the rate reached 25% in 1973, and was expected to rise to at least 30% for 1974. In the early months of 1974 the government introduced a series of measures aimed at stemming inflation: the monthly import quota was raised from $100 million to $120 million, both to absorb excess liquidity and to ensure

COLOMBIA

Education. (1971–72) Primary, pupils 3,282,387, teachers 93,980; secondary, pupils 688,746, teachers 21,511; vocational, pupils 7,769, teachers 405; teacher training, students 95,967, teachers 3,558; higher (including 16 state universities), students 109,639, teaching staff 5,304.

Finance. Monetary unit: peso, with (Sept. 16, 1974) a free rate of 23.47 pesos to U.S. $1 (54.30 pesos = £1 sterling). Gold, SDRs, and foreign exchange, central bank: (June 1974) U.S. $490 million; (June 1973) U.S. $463 million. Budget (1974): revenue 24,984,-000,000 pesos; expenditure 26,361,000,000 pesos. Gross national product: (1972) 180,520,000,000 pesos; (1971) 150,080,000,000 pesos. Money supply: (Dec. 1973) 41,647,000,000 pesos; (Dec. 1972) 31,854,000,-000 pesos. Cost of living (Bogotá; 1970 = 100): (April 1974) 188; (May 1972) 238.

Foreign Trade. (1972) Imports 18,413,000,000 pesos; exports 18,553,000,000 pesos. Import sources: U.S. 39%; West Germany 10%; Japan 8%; U.K. 6%; Spain 5%. Export destinations: U.S. 34%; West Germany 14%; Spain 6%. Main export coffee 41%.

Transport and Communications. Roads (1971) 45,873 km. (including 20,017 km. main roads). Motor vehicles in use (1971): passenger 268,200; commercial (including buses) 86,900. Railways: (1972) 3,424 km.; traffic (1973) 427 million passenger-km., freight 1,332,000,000 net ton-km. Air traffic (1973): 2,284,-000,000 passenger-km.; freight 90.5 million net ton-km. Shipping (1973): merchant vessels 100 gross tons and over 54; gross tonnage 223,881. Telephones (Dec. 1972) 1,010,000. Radio receivers (Dec. 1972) 2,255,-000. Television receivers (Dec. 1972) c. 1.2 million.

Agriculture. Production (in 000; metric tons; 1973; 1972 in parentheses): corn c. 1,000 (955); rice c. 1,100 (996); barley c. 115 (110); potatoes c. 1,176 (1,147); cassava (1972) 1,600, (1971) 1,395; sorghum c. 300 (230); soybeans c. 132 (c. 122); coffee c. 516 (c. 432); bananas (1972) 828, (1971) 804; cane sugar, raw value c. 840 (c. 824); palm oil c. 42 (37); cotton, lint c. 150 (145); tobacco c. 49 (36). Livestock (in 000; Dec. 1972): cattle c. 23,000; sheep c. 2,111; pigs c. 1,542; goats (1971) 660; horses (1971) 859; chickens (1971) 33,515.

Industry. Production (in 000; metric tons; 1973): crude oil 9,493; natural gas (cu.m.; 1971) 1,563,000; coal (1972) c. 2,800; electricity (kw-hr.; 1972) c. 10,300,000 (74% hydroelectric in 1969); crude steel 263; gold (troy oz.; 1972) 188; salt (1972) 1,023; cement 3,220.

adequate supplies of raw materials and machinery for industry and agriculture; the bank rate was raised from 14 to 16%; the banks' rediscount facilities with the Banco de la República were reduced; price controls were reinforced; the Instituto de Mercadeo Agropecuario was empowered to create a permanent stockpile of basic foodstuffs; government expenditure was cut back; and exports of some products, mostly foods, were prohibited.

Within a week of taking office on August 7, President López Michelsen took action to revise the mechanisms and application of monetary policy, with a view toward controlling the money supply. To facilitate the introduction of further economic measures, and after consultations between the government, labour unions, and industry, the president declared a 45-day state of economic emergency on September 17. This was the first declaration of an economic emergency since such an eventuality was provided for in the 1968 constitution. It empowered the government to conduct economic policy by decree, without seeking the approval of Congress, though the latter could subsequently reverse the measures.   (JOAN PEARCE)

[974.C.2]

Commercial and Trade Policies

The unprecedented boom in production and investment that had characterized the first half of 1973 came to an abrupt end in 1974, giving way to accelerated inflation and the possibility of a serious and protracted recession. While the boom in commodity prices and in international trade extended into the second and third quarters of 1974, definite signs of softening in the prices of certain commodities in the third quarter gave rise to apprehensions of a possible decline in trade and a deterioration of the improved terms of trade of the less developed countries. Uncertainties about the future development of prices in general and about availabilities of energy resources and foodstuffs further aggravated the already ominous economic outlook for 1975.

The reaction of the international economic community took several forms. In the area of commercial policies, industrial countries recognized that the sharp decline in their payments balances required joint international action and restraints on mutually conflicting policies designed to improve individual competitive positions. They declared their intention to refrain, at least for one year, from imposing any further restrictions on imports or other current account transactions and from artificially stimulating visible and current invisible exports.

Those less developed countries that participated in the commodity price boom were able to offset higher prices for their imports of manufactured goods, but the poorer (and more populous) less developed countries faced even larger foreign exchange deficits than in previous years. Prospects for these countries were particularly critical.

The principal unanswered question at the end of 1974 was whether industrial countries would be able to achieve sufficient coordination of their individual policies to cope with oil-induced balance of payments deficits, or whether each would resort to stringent deflationary measures, stepped-up export performance, and possibly import restraints.

Against this background, both the industrial and the less developed countries felt the need to take stock of the world economic situation and to develop, to the extent possible at this stage, joint action programs of an international character. The UN and its organs and agencies, notably the UN Conference on Trade and Development (UNCTAD), the International Monetary Fund (IMF), and the World Bank, were called upon to play a major role. Other international organizations such as the General Agreement on Tariffs and Trade (GATT) and the Organization for Economic Cooperation and Development (OECD) also made important contributions.

The General Assembly Special Session. The special session of the UN General Assembly, called on the initiative of Algeria in April 1974, focused on the special problems of the less developed countries, especially the low-income countries that are not oil producers and that depend heavily on imports of energy, food and fertilizer, and manufactured products. In a Declaration on the Establishment of a New International Economic Order, it restated, with considerable urgency, several of the major action programs championed by UNCTAD and other UN bodies over the preceding decade.

While it did not break new ground, the special session recognized that immediate help was needed by those populous, low-income countries that would be most severely affected by the high costs of their vital imports. It therefore issued an urgent appeal to the industrial countries and "other potential contributors" to make emergency financial contributions to a UN-operated fund, established to meet the substantial costs of a major rescue operation. As the year drew to a close, the success of the operation was still in the balance.

UNCTAD. Although somewhat overshadowed by the special session, UNCTAD continued to pursue its established program, including its ad hoc intensive intergovernmental consultations on commodities and the development and expansion of the less developed countries' trade in manufactured products. Consultations were held on a wide variety of commodities, but no concrete proposals for action resulted. A similar lack of success had attended the UN Sugar Conference in October 1973, convened by UNCTAD for the purpose of negotiating a new International Sugar Agreement to take the place of the one that expired at the end of 1973. The only agreement that could be reached was to keep the Sugar Organization alive. As with other commodity agreements, the Sugar Agreement fell victim, at least for the moment, to international commodity price movements and to profound changes in supply-demand relations in world trade.

The UNCTAD Trade and Development Board, meeting in August–September 1974, further emphasized the interdependence of reforms in the international trade and monetary systems and stressed the difficulties encountered by the non-oil-producing less developed countries in coping with the rising prices of their imports. The board encouraged an early start to multilateral trade negotiations as one avenue whereby less developed countries might be able to improve, or at least protect, their access to the markets of the industrial countries.

OECD. The OECD, at its ministerial-level meeting in Paris in May, appealed to industrial countries to coordinate their anti-inflation policies and warned of the dire consequences of a nationalistic approach to growing deficits. OECD countries were enjoined to "avoid policies that would transfer unemployment problems from one country to another." The ministers agreed that it would be mutually destructive to insist on unilateral policies aiming at increased export performance to recoup the foreign exchange needed for oil imports. They therefore agreed on a one-year standstill on the application of new restrictions on trade and current invisible transactions and on any new artificial stimulation of exports. Many if not all of the OECD countries were likely to face serious external financial difficulties. The ministers therefore agreed to cooperate fully to facilitate the necessary and appropriate financing arrangements and reaffirmed their support for an early start of multilateral trade negotiations within the framework of GATT.

There was concern about the acute economic problems that certain less developed countries with low per capita income were certain to experience as a result of expected economic dislocations. Members of the Development Assistance Committee would provide these countries with relief assistance over the next 18 months on a case-by-case basis, in the form of special aid for essential imports and debt relief. Shipments of fertilizers to less developed countries with urgent needs would at least be maintained, and fertilizer production in less developed countries would be encouraged.

GATT. Almost 50 governments reached agreement on a new Arrangement Regarding International Trade in Textiles under GATT auspices in late December 1973. The arrangement, which would run for four years, entered into force on Jan. 1, 1974. In addition to a standstill on further unilateral and bilateral restraints on textile imports, and to a gradual phasing out of existing bilateral restraints, it provided for a major improvement for the position of exporting countries through more balanced and equitable criteria for import restraints than had pertained under the older Long-Term Textile Arrangement. It was hoped that the new arrangement would secure a substantial increase in less developed countries' foreign exchange earnings from textile exports and yield for them a larger share of the world textile market.

The most striking innovation was the establishment of a Textile Surveillance Body, consisting of nine members, with important responsibilities for the implementation of the arrangement. The new arrangement also had broader coverage than the old one, since it included all manufactured textile products of cotton, wool, and man-made fibres and their blends except for artificial and synthetic staple fibre.

Long-standing negotiations instituted under art. xxiv:6 by a number of GATT countries, notably the U.S., with the European Economic Community (EEC) with a view to obtaining compensatory concessions for the damage caused by the enlargement of the Community were mostly concluded by mid-1974. They were not entirely satisfactory to the U.S. and Australia, which reserved their rights to seek compensation for their loss of grain exports. Nevertheless, several U.S. spokesmen welcomed the agreement as a significant breakthrough in U.S.-EEC economic relations.

The multilateral trade negotiations launched at Tokyo in September 1973 under GATT auspices marked time awaiting final passage of the U.S. trade reform bill. In the meantime, technical consultations and discussions moved forward in three meetings of the Trade Negotiations Committee (TNC), established in Tokyo with the mandate to prepare the negotiations and procedures in detail. TNC membership

had risen to 90 by late October. Roughly a quarter of the prospective participants were not contracting parties to GATT and three-quarters qualified as less developed countries. Since the committee and its technical subgroups worked on the basis of working hypotheses rather than firm guidelines, their conclusions and recommendations remained tentative and provisional until the negotiating authorities of the major trading countries were more clearly defined.

U.S. Trade Reform Act. U.S. participation in the round of multilateral trade negotiations scheduled to begin in February 1975 was assured when Congress approved a compromise trade reform bill on Dec. 20, 1974. The bill had passed the House of Representatives by a margin of two to one in December 1973. Hearings in the Senate Finance Committee were completed in October 1974, when a compromise solution was finally found for the controversial section linking the grant of export credits and most-favoured-nation treatment for nonmarket countries to their emigration policies. Once this was settled the long-stalled bill was passed by the Senate, with House and Senate conferees reporting resolved differences between House and Senate versions on December 19.

Though the publicity concerning the bill focused on the link between Soviet emigration policy and U.S. trade concessions, the bill also gave the president broad authority to enter into trade agreements—an authority that had terminated in 1967 with the expiration of the 1962 Trade Expansion Act. The provisions of the 1974 act were indicative of new thinking in commercial policy matters. Negotiating powers granted to the president included the authority to sharply raise or reduce U.S. tariffs; the authority to reduce, eliminate, or harmonize nontariff barriers; and the power to retaliate against unreasonable foreign restrictions on U.S. trade by imposing duties or other restraints on an offending country's exports to the U.S. The president was also empowered to reduce or suspend import duties in order to combat rising prices in the U.S. Other provisions emphasized increased trade rather than foreign aid to help less developed nations, by allowing goods to enter the U.S. duty-free.

EEC. The EEC stated the basic principles of its general approach to the multilateral trade negotiations in a document published in June 1973. In a second, informal statement, published in October 1974, the Community outlined some of its basic concepts in greater detail and in light of recent developments.

On reduction of tariffs in the industrial sector, the EEC proposed "differential reductions" of current duty levels; this would entail a greater reduction of very high duties and lesser reductions in duties that were already low. The objective would be to reduce duties in such a way that the maximum would be no more than 20%. On nontariff barriers, the EEC restated the position that it is important to set priorities for their removal or reduction and hinted that differentiated treatment of less developed countries might be acceptable.

The EEC position concerning negotiations on the agricultural sector was that they should be conducted in accordance with special rules, separate and distinct from those applicable to the general negotiations. This contrasted with the U.S. position, which would apply the general rules, agreed to for the negotiations as a whole, to agricultural negotiations, at least in principle. The subject of safeguards against market disruption would form a major part of the forthcoming negotiations. The EEC called for the replacement of current GATT provisions on safeguards with an international surveillance system.

The EEC believed that liberalization of trade could no longer be the sole aim of multilateral negotiations, and that trade agreements concluded within the framework of these negotiations must recognize possible shortages of agricultural supplies. It therefore called for an "organization of world markets" through surveillance machinery, stabilization systems, storage provisions, and international agreements. Whether or not customs duties for certain agricultural products should also be reduced remained an open question.

The EEC subscribed to the Tokyo Declaration, which stipulated that less developed countries are not under obligation to give reciprocity to industrial countries and that special measures on behalf of the least developed are desirable.

Two basic conventions governing relations between former dependent countries and members of the EEC, the Yaoundé and the Arusha conventions, would expire in early 1975. For some time negotiations had been in progress looking toward a new convention that would govern relations between the EEC and its current 19 associates, principally former French and Belgian dependent areas; the African, Caribbean, and Pacific "associables"; independent Commonwealth countries; and certain others such as Ethiopia.

These negotiations were given new impetus by a ministerial conference, held in Jamaica in July 1974. Under the previous conventions, the eligible countries were granted duty-free access to the EEC markets, in return for which they granted Community exports duty- and quota-free access to their markets unless their development needs warranted otherwise. In the negotiations, the associates and associables pursued four main objectives: free and unlimited access to EEC markets for all their exports; elimination of tariff reciprocity; more generous origin rules than those granted in the Yaoundé Convention; and measures to stabilize export earnings. The ministers agreed on the broad outlines of a stabilization fund for export earnings and accepted the proposal that less developed countries should be under no obligation to reciprocate the trade concessions. Negotiations on a series of other issues continued.

International Action on Trade and Payments. The IMF Committee of Twenty, at its final meeting in June 1974, agreed on a program of immediate action to cope with the rapidly changing monetary situation and the serious deterioration of the reserve positions of both developed and less developed countries. The program provided for pledges by countries "on a voluntary basis not to introduce or intensify trade or other current account measures for balance of payments purposes without a finding by the Fund that there is . . . justification."

This and other recommendations were adopted by the IMF and World Bank meetings in September 1974. While the monetary institutions could not reach any concrete decisions on monetary reform, they established a special financial facility within the Fund to deal with the problem of "recycling borrowed petrodollars." This facility in the IMF and others in the World Bank were to deal with the expected major shift in the world's monetary reserves over the next decade from industrialized to oil-producing countries and redirect their flow toward the most needy areas. The meeting also established a high-level committee that would give its special attention to the needs of

the less developed countries. Its terms of reference called for a focus "on all aspects of the broad question of the transfer of real resources to developing countries." (C. CHUNG-TSE SHIH)

See also Agriculture and Food Supplies; Commodity Trade; Development, Economic and Social; Trade, International.

[534.F.2–3; 544.A.3.e]

Commodity Trade

Prices and Terms of Trade. The upsurge in world commodity prices, which began in late 1972, continued unabated through 1973 and until April 1974. After that, with a few exceptions such as petroleum, gold, and steel, prices of most commodities showed definite signs of weakness in the face of slumping demand and rising inventories. In the United States, the spot market price index of 22 basic commodities compiled by the U.S. Department of Labor at the end of 1974 stood at 207.9 (1967 = 100), down nearly 17% from its all-time high of 249.9 in late July and barely above a year earlier. Most of the weakness occurred in the industrial segment (13 commodities) of the index, which was down to 179.2 (1967 = 100), off 25.6% from its peak of 240.9 in early April 1974. Following a different pattern, largely reflecting various shortages, the foodstuffs segment (9 commodities) of the index remained relatively strong, standing at 257.5. This was down 11.2% from the record 290 (1967 = 100) reached in mid-November but was nearly 30% higher than it had been a year earlier.

Another leading commodity indicator, the *London Economist* index—which includes 28 raw commodities traded in world free markets for which there are daily spot or nearby futures quotations for specified grades and quantities—peaked in late April and early May; it had risen about 175% in the preceding three years. During the last eight months of 1974, the index fell about 10%. During the same period, the *Economist*'s indicator of world industrial commodity prices declined some 40%. But after some weakness, world food prices, as measured by the *Economist* index, were at the end of 1974 about 30% higher than a year earlier. The downturn in commodity prices generally was gaining momentum and was expected to continue in 1975.

Prices of some of the major commodities traded in world markets seemed likely to dip below their cost of production. Spot copper wirebars at London, which sold at a record $1.524 per pound in early April 1974, were selling at about 56 cents per pound late in the year. Copper at the latter price and natural rubber at 30 cents per pound and less were close to being produced at a marginal loss from the less efficient mines and plantations. With both commodities being prime sources of employment and foreign exchange for the less developed countries, production cuts would be made with extreme reluctance and difficulty.

Many cuts in production of basic commodities, both real and threatened, presumably would be financed with money from oil-rich nations, such as Venezuela, which agreed to finance coffee stockpiles of several Central American countries. However, those oil producers that invest funds in surplus commodities during a world recession may face storage problems. Also, they probably will earn little or no interest on their money and will have relatively poor prospects of benefiting by capital gains. In addition, unwanted surpluses cause prices to weaken rather than strengthen.

Commodities, Primary: *see* Commodity Trade

Slaughter of more than 500 calves by members of the National Farmers Organization, near Curtiss, Wis. The move was designed as a protest against rising feed costs and sagging beef prices.

Virtually all of the drop in commodity prices was restricted to those traded in the free markets of New York, Chicago, London, and large centres. In contrast, prices of industrial raw materials such as aluminum, cement, paper, nickel, and steel continued to rise. The prices of those commodities were fixed by producers' costs and not by supply and demand factors in free markets.

While devastating to many producing nations, the collapse of free-market commodity prices helped the balance of payments of major importing nations. Great Britain, for example, expected to pay considerably less for imported copper and cocoa beans in 1975 than in 1974. However, some manufacturers who accumulated late stocks of copper and other metals were suffering heavy inventory losses.

Any decline in commodity earnings of the less developed countries, already burdened with an oil debt estimated at $22 billion a year, would intensify their hardship position. On the other hand, the boom of the preceding three years improved the terms on which commodity-exporting countries trade with the industrial world. Basic commodities, including oil, exported by those countries in early 1974 accounted for about 48% of world trade at that time, against only 38% in 1970. Recession in the developed countries would be extremely hard on the less developed nations. Their export earnings would decline sharply, limiting their ability to import vital industrial materials, while their oil bills would continue to rise.

Commodity Futures Trading. Reflecting the deepening recession and unprecedented price volatility of some commodities, the rate of growth in commodity futures trading tailed off sharply in 1974. Although volume set a record for the sixth consecutive year, activity in some commodities fell sharply, with the increase in volume the smallest in three years. Before 1974 the lack of trading confidence had been in the stock market, and people were switching their money into commodities. In 1974, however, the entire economy deteriorated and people lacked trust in everything. During 1974, about 27.7 million contracts were traded on the 11 major U.S. exchanges that had futures markets in commodities, according to the Association of Commodity Exchange Firms Inc., a trade group. This trading was up about 4.6% from 1973, but was well below the jump of nearly 45% in 1973 over 1972.

Normally, price volatility is prized by speculators in commodities because it increases the potential profits that can be made by trading on rapid price swings. But in 1974 some markets were too hectic for many speculators. During a 75-day trading period in the summer, cattle futures moved up or down the daily limit (the amount a commodity's price is allowed to rise or fall in a single trading session) 72 times. Too often, this meant that a trader was "locked in" to a certain position. When a market makes a "limit move," trading often slows or even stops. If the market goes up the limit, potential sellers, as might be expected, tend to hold on to their contracts and sell them the next day when prices conceivably will resume their upturn. In this situation, a "short," someone who has sold a contract he does not own and has to buy to cover his position, might have to wait until the next day to do so because of a lack of sellers. When a market falls the limit, buyers tend to disappear because they expect even lower prices the next day. In this situation, offers to sell at the limit do not find any takers.

Margins, the amount of money a trader must put up to buy a futures contract, were increased for some contracts in 1974 to discourage undue speculation. It is obvious that when contracts are higher for a period of time, a given amount of capital can support a smaller number of trading units than previously. The withdrawal of speculators from the market tends to create a vicious circle. Fewer buyers and sellers are present to cushion price moves, which become more pronounced and thereby discourage more speculators.

Among major commodities, 1974 futures trading in pork bellies and shell eggs was down substantially, while activity in sugar, coffee, cotton, live cattle, orange juice, and broilers also declined. Spectacular exceptions to the downturn in trading were provided by corn and wheat. Compared with a year earlier, the 4.7 million corn contracts traded on the Chicago Board of Trade during 1974 represented a rise of about 10%, while wheat trading of nearly 2.4 million contracts was almost double. Activity in the corn and wheat markets was encouraged by weather damage to crops and heavy export demand. Total trading on the Chicago Board of Trade, which accounted for more than 50% of all U.S. futures trading in commodities in 1974, was up 10% for the year. Increased use of the Board of Trade by commercial interests, such as grain exporters and processors, partly offset its decreased use by speculators.

Meanwhile, two former champion items on the Chicago Mercantile Exchange, the nation's second largest with about 17% of futures trading in commodities in 1974, were in a severe slump. Through November, shell-egg trading dropped 43% from a year earlier, to 335,200 contracts, and activity in frozen pork bellies fell 39%, to 661,400 contracts. Total trading on the Chicago Mercantile Exchange, excluding volume on the international money market during 1974, declined 18% from a year earlier.

U.S. Pres. Gerald Ford on Oct. 23, 1974, signed into law a bill reforming commodity trading in the United States. Beginning April 21, 1975, a Commodity Futures Trading Commission was to oversee all U.S. futures markets. Futures trading in gold, which began Dec. 31, 1974, was also covered but futures trading in foreign currencies among banks was not. The new commission, which would replace the Commodity Exchange Authority in the U.S. Department of Agriculture, was to be an independent agency with five commissioners appointed to five-year terms by the president.

Commodity Policies, National Policies. Pres. Carlos Andrés Pérez of Venezuela, on Dec. 7, 1974, announced that, effective Jan. 1, 1975, the government of Venezuela would nationalize the iron-ore mining industry operated by subsidiaries of two U.S. companies, Bethlehem Steel and U.S. Steel. This takeover was expected to serve as a model for the nationalization of the more important oil industry sometime in 1975. President Pérez said that compensation to the two U.S. companies would not exceed the net book value of the iron-mining holdings, but gave no specific figure. Payment was to be made over ten years in government bonds at 7% interest.

Until late 1974, U.S. citizens were able to buy and sell gold only for industrial and numismatic purposes. Therefore, it was a historic occasion on August 14, when President Ford signed Senate Bill 2565, which contained a clause making it legal for U.S. citizens generally to buy, sell, and hold gold for the first

time in more than 40 years. The effective date of the gold-ownership clause was Dec. 31, 1974. Once trading began on December 31, most Americans showed little interest in gold. Bankers and brokerage houses generally reported disappointing demand for bullion, most of the activity being on commodity futures exchanges. After going as high as $190.50 per ounce, the January 1975 contract on the New York Commodity Exchange fell to $182.50. Gold offerings from U.S. Treasury stocks severely depressed the market. At the first Treasury offering of 2 million ounces (from a total stockpile of 276 million ounces) on Jan. 6, 1975, bid prices ranged from $188 per ounce down to $135.

President Ford on November 18 set the U.S. sugar import quota at 7 million short tons, raw value, per calendar year, effective Jan. 1, 1975. This quota, which was to be applied on a global first-come first-served basis, replaced country quotas under the U.S. Sugar Act, which was allowed to expire Dec. 31, 1974. With foreign prices of sugar often as high or higher than U.S. prices, the Sugar Act in 1974 proved ineffective in guaranteeing sufficient supplies of sugar for the U.S. market.

The government of Australia on Aug. 27, 1974, announced that it would guarantee funds up to A$200 million in order to allow the Australian Wool Corporation (AWC) to operate a minimum floor price equivalent to 250 Australian cents per kilogram (clean basis) for 21-micron (average 64s) wool throughout the 1974–75 season. This action was taken to avoid a collapse in the wool market and to provide both growers and users with confidence in the future. The AWC would still continue a flexible reserve price above 250 cents per kilo. The government guarantee was conditional upon the growers agreeing to contribute a 5% levy on the proceeds of all sales.

Legislation to expand the power of the AWC was introduced into the Australian Parliament on November 19. The corporation was to be allowed greater freedom in its trading policies and was to receive specific statutory authority to operate the floor price scheme and to manage the supply of wool offered for sale. On November 20, legislation was introduced to appropriate an additional A$200 million to finance

continued purchases of wool by the AWC under its floor price scheme and provide advances to growers whose wool is withheld from sale.

International Policies. On Dec. 13, 1974, oil ministers of the 13-nation Organization of Petroleum Exporting Countries (OPEC) boosted their average selling price of oil by 38 cents per 42-gal. barrel to $10.12. This action brought OPEC into line with three of its Persian Gulf members, Saudi Arabia, Qatar, and the United Arab Emirates, which had adopted the higher price unilaterally a month earlier.

In addition to increasing the rates, OPEC also announced a new pricing system for oil to replace the posted price—an artificial figure used for assessing taxes and royalties. Under the new system, the oil producers charged the companies a single "market price," on top of which the oil companies would add 11 cents for production costs and 50 cents for profit. Thus, the new price was $10.73 a barrel, versus the previous $10.35.

Hoping to shore up declining prices of copper, members (Chile, Peru, Zambia, and Zaire) of the Intergovernmental Council of Copper Exporting Countries (CIPEC) on Nov. 19, 1974, announced that they would cut back exports of copper by 10%, effective Dec. 1, 1974. (*See* Special Report.)

After meeting for two weeks in London, the executive board of the International Coffee Organization (ICO) on Sept. 20, 1974, agreed to extend the present International Coffee Agreement (ICA) for another year, until Sept. 30, 1976. Also, the board postponed the date for completing the negotiations for a new agreement from Sept. 30, 1974, to May 31, 1975. Meanwhile, the 1974–75 coffee harvest, including a bumper crop in Brazil, was expected to be the largest since 1965–66. As a result, prices dropped and there was renewed interest in putting "teeth" back into the ICA. Soon after the close of the ICO meetings, 18 of the world's coffee producers, accounting for more than 80% of world coffee exports, agreed to withhold about 16 million bags (132.3 lb. each) of coffee during the 1974–75 season.

Despite the inclusion of most of the world's major

continued on page 182

ARE CARTELS INEVITABLE?

By Andrew W. Staines

Producers of primary commodities, eager to emulate the success of the Organization of Petroleum Exporting Countries (OPEC) and to fix the prices of the products that they export, made various attempts in 1974 to form "quasi-cartels." Ideological differences and past enmities were set aside in the drive to achieve the largest possible returns, although some countries were drawn reluctantly into the militant new producer groupings by their urgent need to offset the increased cost of oil imports.

Moves to improve returns on resources by higher price structures, increased royalties, and greater participation in operating companies met with only limited success. Phosphate rock and bauxite proved notable exceptions, the producing countries having acted before the onset of the economic depression, which by midyear had overtaken many industrialized countries. The dramatic price increases planned by producers of iron ore, natural rubber, copper, and tungsten for the second half of the year were effectively muted by slack demand and ailing economies in the consuming countries.

Phosphate Rock. Producers of phosphate rock, a major constituent of fertilizers and detergents, succeeded in raising prices from around $15 a ton to $65–$75 a ton within nine months, with Morocco, Senegal, Algeria, Togo, and Tunisia acting in concert. Oceanic producers and Spain followed suit, and U.S. producers raised prices to levels only slightly below those set by the North African militants. In Togo, where production of phosphate rock exceeded two million tons a year, Pres. Gnassingbe Eyadema fully nationalized the major Compagnie Togolaise des Mines du Bénin only a few weeks after raising Togo's stake in the operation from 35 to 51%. Senegal acquired a larger stake in its Western-operated mining companies and established a premium price of around $76 a ton for its high-purity rock.

The price increases were well-timed, with world demand for fertilizers running well ahead of supply. However, phosphate nutrients remain in the soil longer than most other fertilizer materials, and if annual application should prove to be unnecessary, demand from Europe and the U.S. would fall. Predictably, price increases had the greatest effect in India, the Far East, and other areas dependent almost entirely on imports. As prices of two major phosphate-based fertilizers, diammonium phosphate and triple superphosphate, doubled and then trebled, less developed countries were unable to afford them.

There was evidence that the moves on phosphate rock were the brainchild of one man, Muhammad Karim Lamrani, former prime minister of Morocco and head of Morocco's Office Chérifien des Phosphates. Lamrani, aiming to establish a Moroccan fertilizer industry to rank with the powerful U.S. and European companies, took heavy aid from the U.S.S.R. for the construction of plants that would come into operation in the mid-1970s. In consequence, European phosphoric acid operators, lacking any real control over raw material supplies, canceled expansion and considered leaving an industry that would soon be heavily dominated by North Africa.

Andrew W. Staines is an industrial journalist specializing in oil, chemicals, and natural resources. He is deputy editor of European Chemical News.

Phosphate rock also became involved in Morocco's dispute with Spain over the Spanish Sahara. At Bu Craa, Spanish Sahara, production was expected to reach three million tons a year. Phosphate from the mines carried by conveyor system to the port of El Aaiún for shipment became the target of local guerrillas, encouraged at arm's length by Morocco, and Spanish troops had to be stationed at strategic points along the route. The purchase of large quantities of Moroccan phosphate rock for home consumption allowed Spain to obtain premium export prices for high-purity rock from Spanish Sahara. In July, however, Morocco cut Spain to 25% of its previous offtake of Moroccan rock in an attempt to drive the Spanish Saharan material off world markets and back into Spain.

Phosphate rock-producing countries completed the year firmly established in world fertilizer markets. Several countries emulated Morocco's plant construction program, with large complexes being built or planned in Jordan, Syria, and Brazil. Much of the financing for such projects was obtained from the increased phosphate rock prices and the actions of a cartel ranking second only to the OPEC in terms of success.

Bauxite. Representatives of the major producers of bauxite—the main raw material for aluminum—met in Belgrade, Yugos., in January 1974 to set up "an association to safeguard and further their interests"; as a result, the International Bauxite Association (IBA), consisting of the seven major producers—Australia, Guinea, Guyana, Jamaica, Sierra Leone, Surinam, and Yugoslavia—was formed in March. Jamaican Prime Minister Michael Manley described the move as "a response to the . . . disproportionate power of the multinational corporation."

There was general agreement among IBA members for improving returns from bauxite, but the structure of the bauxite business precluded the formation of a cartel proper, because bauxite was not a freely traded international commodity with a determinable free market price, and six aluminum companies with 76% of non-Communist aluminum production were virtually the sole buyers. Because Australia, the world's biggest bauxite producer but with close ties with Kaiser Aluminum & Chemical Corp. and Aluminum Co. of America, acted against the formation of a true cartel, and with several smaller bauxite-producing countries highly dependent on bauxite revenues, the association ruled out an OPEC-style production cut to boost prices.

The Caribbean countries had different ideas on realizing the full potential of their resources. Rather than equity participation in the companies it supplied (as, for example, Guinea wanted), Guyana preferred further nationalization, while Jamaica, opting for greatly increased royalty payments from the mining companies, approved a sixfold increase in bauxite royalties to be levied against U.S. and Canadian companies, and imposed additional taxes. The moves would raise Jamaica's bauxite revenues from some $25 million to around $200 million annually.

The Dominican Republic, a relatively small producer, pressed for an increase in bauxite royalties from $2.73 a ton to $5 a ton, but it was doubtful whether the republic could sustain such a move in the light of the new slowdown in aluminum market demand. In July, Guyana, the world's fifth-largest producer, announced nationalization of its bauxite industry. Control of 51% of the Reynolds Metals Co. bauxite mines in Guyana was sought, and a levy linked to profits was introduced.

Bauxite producers also made plans to integrate deeper into aluminum production and, in June, Jamaica, Guyana, and Trinidad and Tobago announced a joint venture, a $500 million aluminum smelter, to handle 200,000 tons a year and be based at Point Lisas in Trinidad. The smelter would enter production in 1977, with Jamaica and Guyana providing the bauxite and Trinidad supplying oil to power the operation.

Copper. Throughout the early part of 1974 it was feared that the long-established Intergovernmental Council of Copper Exporting Countries (CIPEC) would combine to establish a minimum floor price. However, copper presented a classic case of plans thwarted by the world economic downturn.

At a meeting in Lusaka, Zambia, in June, CIPEC's four members (Chile, Peru, Zaire, and Zambia), accounting for around 60% of international copper trade, were "unable to agree on any action" to implement a proposed floor price. Chile had publicly advocated a minimum floor price believed to be around £800 a ton, and the three other members had supported the plan in principle, but the problem was that no decision would be binding on the many smaller copper exporting countries outside the organization. An agreement to cut copper exports by 10% was reached by the four CIPEC members at a subsequent meeting, held in Paris in November, and Chile announced plans to close one of its major mines for six months. With demand low, however, the move seemed unlikely to have any dramatic effect.

Mercury. In 1974 seven of the world's major mercury producers (Spain, Italy, Mexico, Turkey, Yugoslavia, Algeria, and Canada) took first steps toward forming a cartel as a means of improving returns from a declining market. Mercury's main use—the chemical production of chlorine—had steadily decreased as the outcry grew against the environmental pollution caused by the process. In Japan mercury pollution from chlorine plants was held directly responsible for the notorious Minamata disease, and chemical companies had to scrap mercury process chlorine plants and replace them with the pollution-free diaphragm process. The mercury process had also fallen from favour in Europe and the U.S. Mercury producers decided to go for higher returns while there was still time, and late in 1973 they agreed on a general price policy and on the formation of the Mercury Producer Countries Organization. In May 1974 they decided on a 25% increase in the price of mercury and established a minimum floor price of $350 a flask. For most of mercury's specialized applications, however, flask prices were not the critical factor in production, and despite continuing falls in demand, producers might be expected to risk asking for further price increases. The major producers had always exercised a high degree of control over world prices, and the cartel action formalized this control.

Natural Rubber. Trade in natural rubber had been conducted on an international commodity basis with prices dictated by speculative buying by industrialized user countries, rather than by demand. When the effects of the 1974 oil crisis pushed up prices for rival oil-based synthetic rubbers (some 67% of overall world rubber consumption) by nearly 250%, natural rubber prices rose in tandem. Authoritative estimates suggested that natural rubber could win back much of the market share lost to synthetic rubber over the previous decade, particularly if synthetic rubber production continued to be restricted by limitations in supplies of oil-based chemical feedstocks.

Thus encouraged, the newer and smaller producers of natural rubber—Sri Lanka, Liberia, Nigeria, and South America—called for group producer action to press home what appeared to be a heaven-sent economic advantage. But a full-scale producer cartel in natural rubber did not materialize, and as slack demand and easing availability of chemical feedstocks stabilized synthetic rubber prices, natural rubber prices reverted to a position slightly below those for rival synthetic materials. Malaysia did attempt a minor degree of cartel-type action when it cut production by 15%, an attempt to inject some strength into prices. The move was not particularly successful. Rubber demand went from bad to worse and the improvement in prices was barely noticeable.

Evidently, cartel action to improve returns from natural rubber was unlikely to succeed until demand improved. Installed world plant capacity for synthetic rubber remained adequate to meet demands. Malaysia and Indonesia, together producing over two-thirds of world natural rubber supplies, planned to diversify into the manufacture of rubber products as a means of adding value to their material, and their reluctance to join an all-out rubber cartel proved a decisive factor in limiting its success.

Iron Ore. Major exporters of iron ore met in Geneva in July. Behind the meeting lay a 15-year history of price erosion largely caused by the combined buying strength of the world's major steel companies. Producing countries had had to contend with increased costs of labour, materials, and mine-handling equipment—much of it supplied by the very countries to whom lower-priced ore was being shipped—and a degree of producer militancy at the Geneva meeting was therefore inevitable. Brazil, India, Venezuela, and Mauritania were anxious to create an "iron ore OPEC" to prevent further deterioration of their fortunes. The problems of establishing a successful iron ore cartel were, however, immense. World iron ore reserves were not confined to a politically sensitive area, as was oil in the Middle East, nor were ore supplies likely to dry up. Australia, Canada, and Sweden, three of the world's major iron ore exporters, were reluctant to join a major cartel, although each sent observers to producer meetings and all would welcome higher prices. The more militant producers could be expected to band together when demand from the highly cyclical steel industry proved sufficiently strong to offer some chance of success.

Other Sectors. During the course of the year, producers of chrome ore, tungsten, manganese ore, and tin held meetings to discuss prices and market conditions. Where potential power lay in the hands of very few producers, cartel action was a distinct possibility, and with the groundwork done, much would depend on the revival of industrialized economies. Fears of a cartel in tin proved groundless because of the existence of the International Tin Agreement, embracing over 20 consumer members and 7 major producer members. But even in this relatively conservative sector unrest could be found, and Malaysia, producer of nearly 40% of the world's tin, issued advertisements in the world press headed "A cartel? Not with tin."

Consumer Countries' Response. The moves toward cartels on materials other than oil were slowly recognized in the industrialized world. Initial statements and reactions, particularly in the U.S., were designed to shock the large, complacent user companies into recognition of a potentially huge problem. In one hard-hitting speech, the U.S. Bureau of Mines chief said that "a U.S. minerals crisis" was "only a short distance down the road." Subsequent U.S. action took the form of increased diplomatic activity in sensitive raw materials-producing areas and attempts to halt the depletion of strategic stockpiles.

The EEC, dependent on outside supplies for between 70 and 100% of its various primary product needs, set up a working party in February to examine the effects of possible disruptions in supplies of raw materials. In July its report concluded that the EEC faced little risk of immediate raw material shortages but identified a number of "sensitive" products that could prove difficult and recommended that efforts be made to tie these products into international agreements with producing countries. Concern was expressed about underinvestment in mining and prospecting, but the report was optimistic that the EEC could resist producer action on most raw materials and added that the value of the Community's non-oil raw material imports was only 4% of their value as industrial products.

Japan, almost completely dependent on outside sources for major raw materials, moved to expand already strong ties with Australia, a source of abundant natural resources. Major Japanese companies expanded outside investment through joint ventures with resource-rich countries in the Middle East and South America, and efforts were made to improve trade with China.

Conclusion. The depressed state of the industrialized economies in 1974 served to act against the formation of successful raw material cartels. But OPEC action had shown that effective cartel moves must be taken when demand booms, and incentives for such action increased. Economic and technological factors served to limit possibilities, by encouraging both substitution between materials and materials recovery. Moreover, in many producer countries the need to maintain local labour levels would make cuts in production a questionable approach. As the year advanced the immediate threat to the industrialized countries of widespread raw material cartel action appeared to recede, although the new mood of the less developed world and diminishing resources indicated that the story was by no means ended.

Changes in International Prices of Selected Major Commodities

Commodity, unit, country of origin, and market	Wholesale price in U.S. dollars				
	1966	1971	1972	1973	July 1974
Aluminum (100 lb.) Canada	24.50	28.40	26.80	27.20	34.50
Beef (100 lb.) U.S. (N.Y.)	35.44	42.51	49.76	63.67	52.86
Butter (100 lb.) New Zealand (London)	36.35	46.43	54.92	44.19	50.66
Cocoa (100 lb.) Ghana (N.Y.)	24.43	26.77	32.26	63.96	106.93
Coffee (100 lb.) Brazil (N.Y.)	40.79	45.17	50.74	66.53	69.95
Copper (100 lb.) U.K. (London)	69.22	49.02	48.56	80.88	86.96
Copra (100 lb.) Philippines (Manila)	6.48	6.29	4.68	12.62	26.51
Cotton (100 lb.) Egypt (Liverpool)	49.96	61.72	65.29	74.15	163.78
Hides (100 lb.) U.S. (Chicago)	17.90	14.50	29.60	34.30	25.80
Jute (short ton) Bangladesh (N.Y.)	384.00	346.00	356.00	366.00	390.00
Lead (100 lb.) U.S. (N.Y.)	15.00	13.90	15.40	16.40	24.50
Newsprint (short ton) U.S. (N.Y.)	136.20	157.00	163.20	170.40	207.10
Peanuts (100 lb.) Nigeria (London)	8.47	11.39	11.52	17.76	33.49
Petroleum (bbl.) Venezuela (La Cruz)	2.80	2.80	3.21	4.40	11.22
Rice (100 lb.) U.S. (New Orleans)	8.30	8.70	9.80	18.00	25.00
Rubber (100 lb.) Malaysia (Singapore)	21.36	15.06	15.05	33.73	30.50
Sugar (100 lb.) Caribbean (N.Y. for exp.)	1.92	4.52	7.52	9.65	25.23
Tea (100 lb.) Sri Lanka-India (N.Y.)	48.30	48.70	50.70	48.30	63.80
Tin (100 lb.) Malaysia (Penang)	159.40	154.70	166.70	208.10	383.10
Tobacco (100 lb.) U.S.	64.50	73.23	80.03	83.83	87.67
Wheat (bu.) Canada (Fort William)	1.91	1.75	1.93	4.00	5.26
Wool (100 lb.) U.S. (Boston)	62.20	35.10	48.80	85.00	62.00
Zinc (100 lb.) U.K. (London)	12.75	13.98	17.13	38.50	49.61

Source: International Monetary Fund, *International Financial Statistics*.

continued from page 179

producers, most experts believed that the agreement would have little effect on world coffee prices in the foreseeable future. Coffee supplies were large, and many producing countries might be forced to sell stocks to earn needed foreign exchange.

The Cocoa Council, the governing body of the International Cocoa Agreement, approved in September 1974 an increase of 6.50 cents per pound in the pact's price range and reduced annual export quotas by 87,900 metric tons. The new price range under the agreement was 29.50 cents to 38.50 cents per pound, compared with 23 cents to 32 cents previously. Basic annual export quotas under the agreement were cut from 1,467,300 metric tons to 1,379,400 metric tons.

Reflecting consumer resistance to high prices, spot cocoa beans, which sold in the New York market at a record high of $1.305 per pound on May 3, 1974, slumped to about 80 cents by the year's end. Even so, prices were more than double the upper end of the agreement's price range.

The seventh session of the UN Food and Agriculture Organization's subgroup of tea exporters was held in Rome in June 1974. Global export quotas for black tea, covering India, Sri Lanka, and 13 smaller producers, were revised to 658,000 metric tons for the 1974–75 marketing year (April 1–March 31), representing a cut of 23,000 from the quota set at the sixth session in July 1973. Also, a global quota of 682,000 tons was set for the 1975–76 marketing year.

(NORMAN R. URQUHART)

See also Agriculture and Food Supplies; Commercial and Trade Policies; Development, Economic and Social; Exchange and Payments, International; Food Processing; Mining and Quarrying; Trade, International.

[533.A.2]

Commonwealth of Nations

For the Commonwealth 1974 was a year of consolidation after the "spirit of Ottawa" meeting of 1973 and of preparation for the Kingston, Jamaica, heads of government meeting in 1975. It was a year of "nuts and bolts," of regular technical and functional cooperation rather than of political action, although it began with the independence of Grenada (February 7), continued with the Cyprus crisis from July onward, and ended with Papua New Guinea on the verge of independence and Malta's becoming a republic.

Common Market:
see Commercial and Trade Policies; European Unity

Pacific. The year was typified by the tenth Commonwealth Games, a New Zealand triumph of quiet efficiency, and was epitomized by Norman Kirk, whose untimely death deprived New Zealand and the Commonwealth of a wise prime minister (*see* OBITUARIES) with a great concern for "third world" peoples in the Pacific. Kirk was a chief supporter of the South Pacific Forum, and one of his last acts was to put forward the creation of a South Pacific Council. Meeting in the Cook Islands on March 20, the fifth forum welcomed Papua New Guinea as an internally self-governing member; endorsed the work of the economic bureau and of Tonga, Fiji, and Western Samoa in relation to the EEC; and discussed the immigration policies of Australia and New Zealand.

Australia was concerned during the year with the rising claims of its own aboriginal population. Although Prime Minister Gough Whitlam doubled national expenditure on the welfare of aboriginals and set up bodies to voice their wishes and to examine land claims, their leaders remained dubious about the status of their mineral rights, and some of their growing population demanded full self-determination and control of resources.

Canada and the Caribbean. Pierre Trudeau's Canadian government, returned with a large majority in July, showed itself in Land Rights Year 1974 ready to face the claims of Canada's one million Indians as well as the challenge of an Amerindian Conference for the whole continent. (*See* CANADA: *Special Report.*) The Caricom (Caribbean Common Market) heads of government meeting at St. Lucia in August recommended Shidath Ramphal from the Caribbean to replace Canadian-born Arnold Smith as next Commonwealth secretary-general. Many of the Caribbean inhabitants of African descent were becoming increasingly interested in strengthening ties with West Africa.

Africa. Under Nigerian leadership, Commonwealth Africa showed unity of purpose in negotiations with the EEC, but little political constructiveness. The disintegration of the East African Community (set up in 1967) was hastened by the bad relations among Tanzania, Uganda, and Kenya. Tanzania's 20% increase in charges for the use of its ports led to difficulties for Zambia, which still kept its Rhodesian border closed. In December, Zambia was host to discussions between Rhodesian Prime Minister Ian Smith and black nationalist leaders.

Asia and Cyprus. Commonwealth Southeast Asia speeded up its effort to strengthen regionalism. The Malayan elections returned Tun Abdul Razak's national front multiracial party with a massive majority, while the "global city" of Singapore mended its fences with Indonesia by an exchange of visits between Prime Minister Lee Kuan Yew and President Suharto; both promised added support to ASEAN (Association of Southeast Asian Nations) for regional defense.

Although the Commonwealth took no direct part in the Cyprus crisis, the fact that two non-Commonwealth countries were fighting over a member of the Commonwealth affected all members, especially Britain, which still held sovereign bases there. Some observers believed that a referendum in the island on its Commonwealth connection might show a preference for keeping its membership in that organization rather than for its partition between Greek and Turkish communities. The Royal Air Force base at Akrotiri demonstrated the dependence of NATO forces on maintaining bases in Cyprus. (*See* DEFENSE: *Special Report.*)

Economic Affairs. Commonwealth economic relations were dominated by the uncertainty of Britain's future with the EEC and the crisis concerning world oil prices. Ironically, as the British attitude, with Commonwealth interests in mind, grew more cautious toward the EEC, the 44 associated and associable African, Caribbean, and Pacific states pressed for quicker agreement on EEC trade and industrial cooperation to replace the Yaoundé conventions, which were to expire in February 1975. (*See* Commercial and Trade Policies.) Although protocol 22 of the Treaty of Accession of the EEC, offering Commonwealth association, applied only to Africa, the Caribbean, and the Pacific, the new EEC agreement with India was viewed optimistically as a sign of extension of EEC cooperation to Asia.

The Commonwealth primary producing countries, with the example of the Arab oil producers before them, became increasingly aware of their own power to demand higher prices and guarantees for their products, as world prices soared, an instance being the formation by Australia, Jamaica, Guyana, Sierra Leone, and three non-Commonwealth countries of the International Bauxite Association. (*See* Commodity Trade: *Special Report.*) Jamaica, Guyana, and Barbados in January ceased exporting sugar to the U.K. and did not resume until March after the U.K. agreed on an increase in the price it paid to £83 per ton. World sugar prices continued to rise, and in September the U.K. paid Guyana £140 a ton (it obtained more than £300 per ton on the U.S. market); a struggle then took place in the EEC over Britain's negotiation for a five-year sugar contract with Australia, an old Commonwealth supplier.

The Commonwealth Development Corporation had a record year in 1973 with new commitments at £48,260,000, over 50 of them in Africa, and an increased total commitment of £243.5 million in 233 projects. The disbursement of £25.1 million brought investment to £180.7 million. Gross trading income reached a record figure of £16.3 million with an operating surplus of nearly £14 million. Although the majority of projects were agricultural, projects were also begun in the industrial, housing, and power sectors. More nationals of less developed countries were trained in new skills, and in particular a new agricultural management centre in Swaziland was fully utilized by Commonwealth students. The effect on production in other Commonwealth countries of encouraging development of a commodity in a particular Commonwealth nation, such as that of tea in Kenya to the detriment of tea planting in Sri Lanka, was considered at a Commonwealth tea symposium in London in December 1974. The symposium was convened because Commonwealth countries supplied four-fifths of world trade in black tea and the 1969 price and quota agreements needed revision.

The 23rd meeting of Colombo Plan ministers took place in Wellington, N.Z., from Nov. 27 to Dec. 6, 1973, and admitted Papua New Guinea as a full member. Commonwealth aid shifted toward the encouragement of mutual and self-help, with Canada leading the way. British assistance to less developed countries, nearly 90% of them in the Commonwealth, totaled £249.8 million net in 1972 (a £100 million increase over 1970 figures) and £262.5 million in 1973. Together with an estimated flow of £344 million from private sources, the 1972 amount totaled £593.8 million, or 0.96% of the U.K.'s gross national product. Asia, with India as largest single recipient, received nearly 50% of the total official bilateral aid dispensed, with Africa following at 33%, largely on behalf of Kenya. More than 11,000 technical personnel (including some 1,700 volunteers), nearly half of them in education, served overseas. At the same time, nearly 83,000 overseas, mainly Commonwealth, students and trainees were taking courses in the U.K.

Commonwealth trade figures were difficult to evaluate: for instance, an increase of £50 million in trade between the U.K. and Nigeria was almost entirely due to 1973 inflated prices for oil, tin, and cocoa, with still higher figures expected for 1974. The year 1974 saw above all a steady increase in regular functional cooperation within the Commonwealth: the expansion (with a 1974 budget of £3 million) of the Commonwealth Fund for Technical Co-operation as a multilateral channel of expertise exchange to quicken the advancement of less affluent areas. New ground was broken in legal, medical, youth, and planning developments under the aegis of the Commonwealth Foundation (£2,250,000 disbursed, 1966–73). Commonwealth meetings during the year ranged from the tenth Commonwealth Games mentioned above to the 20th Commonwealth Parliamentary Association conference at

UPI COMPIX

Finance ministers
from 34 countries
of the Commonwealth
assemble in Ottawa
to consider the world's
economy and matters
of joint concern.

Colombo, Sri Lanka, the sixth Educational Conference in Kingston, Jamaica, the fourth Medical Conference in Nairobi, Kenya, and the Press Union in Hong Kong.

(MOLLY MORTIMER)

See also articles on the individual countries and political units.

[542.A.1.a; 972.A.1.a]

Communist Movement

In contrast to the dramatic shifts in political leadership, scandals, conflicts, inflation, and shortages that beset so many non-Communist nations in 1974, the Communist states on the whole presented a picture of political and economic stability. Instability in the West, coupled with the fact that Communism and the Soviet Union no longer appeared as threatening as they once had, helped open new opportunities for the Communist parties in several countries to participate in government.

However, a number of problems continued to confront the Communists. There were contradictions connected with the effort to combine a policy of détente with one of intensified ideological struggle against bourgeois ideas. Along with economic advantages, the new ties with the capitalist countries brought unwelcome outside influences and inflationary pressures. The crackdown on dissent in the Communist states tended to retard détente and also to damage the image of Communists in the West who were pursuing a popular front policy. Furthermore, the very stability of the Communist governments appeared in several cases to be the result of political stalemate and contributed to a virtual gerontocracy in some countries.

Alvaro Cunhal, secretary-general of Portugal's Communist Party, receives a warm reception in Lisbon.

JACQUES HAILLOT—L'EXPRESS

Problems of Soviet Policy. General Secretary Leonid I. Brezhnev continued to strengthen his image as the most authoritative figure in the Soviet party's collective leadership, but there were indications of opposition in the Politburo to some of his policies. The Soviet military in particular seemed skeptical of the advantages to be derived from Brezhnev's détente policy, and their opposition could account for the failure to reach any major agreement on strategic arms limitation when U.S. Pres. Richard Nixon visited the U.S.S.R. in June. The "momentum of détente" appeared to have resumed with the strategic arms agreement reached by Brezhnev and Nixon's successor, Gerald Ford, at Vladivostok in November. Nevertheless, the growing criticism of certain aspects of détente in the West aroused concern. Further, besides Nixon, two other major partners in this policy disappeared during the year: French Pres. Georges Pompidou, who died in April, and West German Chancellor Willy Brandt, who resigned in May.

Brezhnev's détente policy had consistently been accompanied by an internal ideological crackdown, but the decision to expel rather than imprison Nobel Prize-winning author Aleksandr Solzhenitsyn (*see* BIOGRAPHY) in February demonstrated that at least some Soviet leaders were sensitive to Western opinion. A similar ambivalence could be seen in the expulsion of dissident leader Pavel Litvinov; the granting of exit permits to a number of prominent Jewish dissidents, as well as to certain non-Jews; the release of dissident Gen. Pyotr Grigorenko from a mental asylum; and the decision to allow an exhibition of unofficial art in Moscow after the disruption of an earlier exhibit caused an uproar in the West. To gain the benefits of U.S. trade and calm Western critics of détente, the Soviet leaders reluctantly and unofficially agreed in October to allow at least 60,000 Jews and members of other minority groups to leave the country annually. However, the renewed emphasis on the need to improve ideological work seemed to indicate that pressures for a harder line were still strong.

Sino-Soviet relations showed no improvement. The two Communist powers continued to polemicize against one another. Several Soviet diplomats were arrested and expelled from China as spies in January, and a Chinese diplomat was later expelled from Moscow on similar charges. A Soviet helicopter, which the Chinese said was on a spy mission, was captured in China's Sinkiang Province and its crew imprisoned in March. New disputes over the Amur-Ussuri border developed, and an attempt at negotiations during the summer quickly broke down.

Beginning late in 1973, Soviet spokesmen and leaders of various closely associated Communist parties urged the convocation of a new World Communist Conference to discuss changes in world conditions since the last such conference in 1969, to promote greater unity within the movement, and, if possible, to excommunicate the Chinese Communists. However, considerable opposition to the expulsion of China was evident both at the conference of Western European Communist parties in Brussels in January and at the Consultative Meeting of European Communist Parties in Warsaw in October.

Eastern and Western Europe. Soviet leaders devoted a large amount of time and energy to maintaining personal contacts and coordinating policies with their Eastern European allies during 1974. In April Brezhnev and Premier Aleksey N. Kosygin went to Warsaw to attend the first meeting of the Warsaw

Pact's Political Consultative Committee in more than two years. Brezhnev and his associates used anniversary celebrations in various countries as occasions to visit their allies and to emphasize the unity of the Communist camp. The leaders of most of the European Communist states also visited the Soviet Union, but for the first time since 1971 there was no formal meeting of Eastern bloc party heads in the Crimea.

Romania continued to demonstrate the peculiar combination of almost Stalinist conservatism at home and independence in its dealings with the Soviet Union that had characterized its behaviour for a decade. Nicolae Ceausescu (*see* BIOGRAPHY) further consolidated his personal position as supreme leader of the party and state in March when he had the constitution altered to allow him to assume the new title of president. At the same time, several officials, including the old and independently prestigious Premier Ion Maurer, were replaced by men more personally loyal to him. In foreign policy Ceausescu tried to assume a position only slightly closer to the Soviet camp than that of the nonaligned Yugoslavs. Although in the last few years Romania had been somewhat more cooperative with its Warsaw Pact neighbours, it was rumoured to have taken a negative attitude toward granting Soviet troops the right of passage to Bulgaria where Warsaw Pact exercises were held.

As usual, Bulgaria distinguished itself by its ultra pro-Soviet stance. The February session of the Bulgarian party's Central Committee was devoted to the need to improve ideological work, and the subsequent campaign for vigilance was accompanied by a well-publicized trial of a Jewish former Bulgarian UN official as a Western spy. The East German Communists remained a troublesome ally for those Soviet leaders interested in improving relations with the West. It was an East German spy, Günter Guillaume (*see* BIOGRAPHY), who caused Willy Brandt's resignation, and an East German effort to deny West German government officials access to West Berlin set off a sort of mini-crisis in late July.

The efforts of the Czechoslovak and Polish Communists to win popular support on the basis of increased economic well-being appeared to have succeeded in 1974. The crackdown on "ideological subversion" within Czechoslovakia continued, but the regime seemed to be stable as the Czechoslovaks enjoyed, along with the East Germans, the highest standard of living in Eastern Europe. Similarly, in Poland, higher wages, better housing, and more abundant consumer goods appeared to have mollified the volatile workers whose riots upset the regime in 1970. Party leader Edward Gierek was the first Communist leader to visit the U.S. to meet President Ford. In Hungary, on the other hand, growing demands from spokesmen of the working class placed severe pressures on liberal Communist Party leader Janos Kadar. In March, Rezso Nyers and Gyorgy Aczel, the leading party advocates of the New Economic Mechanism and of cultural tolerance, respectively, were removed from the party Secretariat.

Nonaligned Yugoslavia drew closer to the Soviet Union as aging President Tito attempted to combat problems of national divisiveness and runaway inflation. Internally, the drive to promote party and national unity was expressed in the continued purge of party officials associated with the earlier decentralization policy. The revival of Yugoslavia's old dispute with Italy over Trieste and annoyance with U.S. policy in the Mediterranean and Middle East also

Janos Kadar (left), first secretary of the Hungarian Communist Party, drives to the Kremlin with General Secretary Leonid I. Brezhnev. The two leaders met in Moscow to discuss possible agricultural barter arrangements.

contributed to the pro-Soviet attitude. Old fears of Soviet intentions reemerged in September with the discovery and trial of 32 members of a "Cominformist plot," but after an initial outburst of rumours concerning a direct Soviet involvement, the whole issue was played down.

In Western Europe the Communist movement experienced substantial—and in some cases unexpected—gains. The Western European Communists who gathered in Brussels in January agreed on the need for Communists to forge broad alliances with all democratic and progressive forces. As the economic and political instability in Italy worsened, the Italian Communist Party indicated that, if it were given a place in the government, it would be willing to work within the framework of the Common Market and NATO. In France the candidate of the Communist-Socialist alliance, Socialist Party leader François Mitterrand, won 49.3% of the vote in the final round of the presidential election in May. In Britain the Communists won a position on the General Council of the Trades Union Congress.

The major breakthroughs of the year came with the collapse of the dictatorships in Portugal and Greece. In late April the previously outlawed Portuguese Communist Party was given a place in the military junta's provisional government, and the strength of the Communists was evident in the events leading to the removal of Pres. António de Spínola in October. In Greece in September the Communists were allowed to operate legally for the first time in 27 years. Encouraged by these events and by the illness of Francisco Franco during the summer, the still outlawed Spanish party vigorously reiterated its willingness to work within a broad political coalition.

Communism in Asia. In October, when the Chinese Communists celebrated 25 years in power, it was clear that age was finally taking its toll among the leaders. Premier Chou En-lai was ill and hospitalized for much of the year, and many of his duties in foreign relations were taken on by a slightly younger deputy premier, Teng Hsiao-ping (*see* BIOGRAPHY). Mao Tse-tung, though still able to meet certain foreign dignitaries in private, was apparently too frail to attend public ceremonies. In these circumstances, the mini-Cultural Revolution that developed during the first half of 1974 around the mass campaign to criticize Confucius and former Defense Minister Lin

Piao had all the earmarks of a struggle for succession. However, the campaign subsided in the autumn, and a renewed emphasis on unity seemed to be connected with the growing conviction that the Soviet "social imperialists" did not actually intend to launch a direct attack on China.

The Chinese leadership showed particular concern about the growth of Soviet influence in South and Southeast Asia. Shortly after Thailand's foreign minister issued a statement in January calling on the Soviet Union to take a larger role in settling the problems of Southeast Asia, Chou En-lai urged Thailand's visiting defense minister to beware of the Soviet drive for hegemony in the area and informed him that China had ceased supporting insurgents in Thailand, Laos, and elsewhere. In discussions leading to the establishment of relations with Malaysia in May, Chinese leaders similarly indicated that China considered the Communist insurgency there to be a purely internal matter. More surprising, while assuring Pakistan of continued Chinese support, Chinese leaders indicated that they hoped to normalize relations with all countries of the subcontinent. Subsequent events, however, including India's explosion of an atomic device, led to a resumption of Chinese polemics against the Soviet Union's main Asian ally.

Although the North Vietnamese tried to maintain good relations with both of the Communist giants, they were clearly antagonized by the Chinese seizure of the Paracel Islands from South Vietnamese government forces in January. China was the only Communist government that did not send a representative to the third congress of the North Vietnamese trade union federation. In April, as evidence was increasing that relations between the indigenous Khmer Rouge and North Vietnamese forces in Cambodia were deteriorating, Peking chose to greet the visiting commander of the Khmer Rouge forces, Khieu Samphan, in a manner befitting a head of state. Meanwhile, Laos enjoyed relative calm as the Laotian Communists, the Pathet Lao, gained increasing influence within the neutral coalition government. The North Korean Communist regime of Kim Il Sung also tried to maintain a neutral stance in the Sino-Soviet dispute. Its success could be seen in the fact that no Communist state had yet responded to South Korea's attempt to "open the doors" to relations with all nations.

Communism in the Americas. For the Cuban Communists the events of 1974 were gratifying. Although Cuba's image had become considerably less revolutionary in recent years, it was not until Brezhnev's delayed visit to Cuba in late January that Cuban leader Fidel Castro explicitly endorsed all aspects of his détente policy. In the months that followed, one Latin-American country after another reestablished diplomatic and economic relations with Cuba, and even the U.S. government appeared compelled to move in the same direction.

Elsewhere in Latin America the picture was bleak for the Communists. The military regimes in Chile, Brazil, Bolivia, Uruguay, Paraguay, and Guatemala ruthlessly suppressed them. The Soviet press was particularly vitriolic concerning the fact that the Chinese did not break relations with Chile following the 1973 coup, though it could not object when China established relations with Brazil in August since relations between the U.S.S.R. and the Brazilian regime had improved considerably. Where the pro-Moscow Communist parties were legal they made slight headway in their efforts to form broad democratic coalitions.

The Peruvian Communists lent their support to the military government's takeover of the press, and the Argentine Communists, legalized by the Peronist government, backed the government's efforts to suppress terrorism. (DAVID L. WILLIAMS)

See also Soviet Bloc Economies; and articles on various countries.
[541.E.3.d.ii]

Computers

One of the most exciting and significant new developments in computer technology in many years was the microprocessor, which went into quantity production at several semiconductor manufacturing companies during 1974. A microprocessor is a single large-scale integrated circuit with much of the capability of the central processing unit of a much larger computer; it is limited by its speed and by a generally restricted instruction set, but it is much smaller and cheaper than conventional equipment.

The major significance of the microprocessor lies in its impact on conventional engineering design. When transistors and integrated circuits first became available in large quantities and at low costs, they often replaced electromechanical relays and switches in control systems; however, they continued to be permanently wired together and, therefore, difficult to alter when mistakes were discovered or improved designs were worked out. In microprocessors, much of this permanent wiring is replaced with sequences of instructions in a program similar to that of a large computer. To change or correct a design, only the program needs to be changed; the wiring is untouched. Changing the program may require the physical replacement of a read-only memory, a relatively simple operation, or only the reloading of a read-write memory, an electrical operation that can take place literally quicker than a wink.

Applications benefiting from microprocessors included automatic weighing and batching machines, highway traffic lights, monitoring for air pollution, mobile terminals in police cars (giving the patrolman direct access to data files in police headquarters), point-of-sale terminals (the new electronic machines that were replacing cash registers in many department stores), and automatic cash dispensers in banks.

Automobile manufacturers began to show strong interest in microprocessors. In their search for cost-effective ways to implement various automotive functions, the manufacturers found microprocessors an attractive component. They could be used, for example, in the engine controls now required to maintain stringent air-pollution and fuel-economy standards, including spark timing, emission control, and automatic transmission control.

Microprocessors also began to appear widely in such applications as laboratory instruments. Among these was a data-acquisition system that could scan and record 20 to 1,000 measurements at 20 per second and perform statistical operations on the accumulated readings. The measurements could indicate voltage, current, temperature, or special functions.

Most microprocessors were built with metal-oxide-semiconductor (MOS) technology and could perform arithmetic and logic functions on 4, 8, or perhaps 12 bits at once; this could increase to 16 bits when several processors were used together. Intel Corp., which had started the commercial microprocessor

Communications:
see
Telecommunications;
Television and Radio

business in earnest with relatively slow four-bit and eight-bit MOS units in 1972, prepared to introduce an improved four-bit device, and also came up with two much faster microprocessors: an eight-bit MOS device about ten times as fast as its earlier one, and a two-bit unit made with the intrinsically faster bipolar process. The bipolar microprocessor was combinable in two-bit increments to achieve a level of computing that permitted relatively long words.

In Japan, Tokyo Shibaura Electric Co. (Toshiba) revealed details of a 12-bit MOS microprocessor, an unusually large device with many powerful features yet measuring only 5.5 by 5.9 mm. European producers were also at work in microprocessor development, the front runner appearing to be Siemens AG, in West Germany.

Technology. Medium-scale and large-scale integrated (LSI) circuits made possible in several new computers the inclusion within the main processor frame of controllers for communication lines, magnetic disk storage units, and other peripherals. This was the latest development in a trend away from separate cabinets for such controllers, a trend that accelerated as LSI technology advanced.

Semiconductor memories continued to make inroads as a major form of data storage for computers, although they had not yet displaced ferrite-core memories, the standard technology since the early 1950s. In 1974 the cost of semiconductor memory systems first became competitive with ferrite-core systems as 4,096-bit integrated circuits—four times the previously most widely used capacity—became generally available and appeared in numerous new machines, especially minicomputers. However, the advent of these circuits presented new problems. For example, they were difficult to test. A thorough test often involved checking for possible interactions between all pairs of cells. In such a circuit there are 16 million possible pairs of 4,000 things, and testing them all, even at submicrosecond cycle times, took so much time that users searched for new ways to carry out rigorous tests.

After several years of development, the first working, fully populated magnetic-bubble memory was produced at Bell Telephone Laboratories, Inc. It had a capacity of about 500,000 bits on two substrates that together fit in the palm of a man's hand. They could move data at 700,000 bits per second; a full read-write cycle was accomplished in 5.1 microseconds, and average access time was 2.7 milliseconds. Magnetic domains in a thin film of garnet can be made to move around within the film under control of an external magnetic field that is guided by metal patterns deposited on the film.

Business. The antitrust case of the U.S. Department of Justice against International Business Machines Corp. (IBM) moved slowly during 1974. Judge David N. Edelstein demanded that the case be scheduled to go to trial in October, but short additional delays were encountered. Finally, in December, a new trial date of Feb. 18, 1975, was set and agreed to by both sides.

Late in 1973 four of IBM's competitors—Control Data Corp., Honeywell, Inc., Sperry Rand Corp., and National Cash Register Co. (which later changed its name to NCR Corp.)—had presented a joint statement of their views on how the case should be prosecuted. Although these and other competitors of IBM found that IBM's lopsided share of the market—about 65%—made life difficult for them, and although the Justice Department had cited as one of its objectives the breakup of IBM into several smaller companies, the four competitors opposed such a dismemberment because each of the successor companies would itself be very large and, in totality, would present at least as difficult a competitive situation as did IBM alone.

Meanwhile, the IBM-Telex antitrust case moved through the appeal process. Telex Corp., a manufacturer of peripheral equipment compatible with IBM computers, had sued IBM, charging monopolistic practices. IBM countersued, charging theft of trade secrets. Both parties won their suits in September 1973; Telex was awarded $352.5 million, later reduced to $259.5 million, while IBM was awarded $21.9 million. Both parties appealed, the appeals were consolidated, and a decision of the U.S. Court of Appeals in Denver, Colo., was awaited.

In a venture that presaged head-to-head competition between the largest computer company and the largest common carrier, IBM bought a large share of a subsidiary of Communications Satellite Corp. (Comsat). The purchase, subject to approval by the Federal

GENERAL AUTOMATION, INC.

The trend toward microprocessors continued in the computer industry. The MOS unit at right now equals the performance of an earlier minicomputer packaged on six printed-circuit boards at left.

Communications Commission, aroused strong opposition among several communications companies, among them American Telephone and Telegraph Co., which believed that it violated antitrust laws.

Unidata, the European computer-manufacturing combine, announced its first computer in January and was expected to follow with another later in the year. Called the Unidata 7720, the machine was actually a modification of a computer previously under development at Philips' Gloeilampenfabrieken, the Dutch participant in the Unidata venture.

Unidata seemed to be doing well but still faced enormous difficulties before it could be sure of success. If a fourth company—Britain's International Computers Ltd.—could be brought into the combine alongside Philips, Siemens AG (West German), and Compagnie Internationale pour l'Informatique (French), it would be stronger, but that possibility seemed remote. Meanwhile, Siemens acquired another West German company, Telefunken Computer, as a subsidiary from Nixdorf Computer AG, and was expected to merge it into Unidata. Late in 1974, a proposal was made to combine Honeywell-Bull with CII, thus strengthening the latter, giving Honeywell Information Systems Inc., the U.S. parent of Honeywell-Bull, access to new European markets through Unidata, and providing a U.S. market for Unidata.

Minicomputers enjoyed a healthy sales boom in Japan, where sales in fiscal 1973 were 50–60% higher than those of the year before. The boom was part of an 18% increase for all types of computers, in a market that most observers expected would grow another 20% in 1974.

Two of Japan's three groups of computer manufacturers announced new computers. Nippon Electric Co. and Tokyo Shibaura Electric Co. brought out machines competitive with the smaller models of IBM's System 370, while Mitsubishi and Oki announced a large scientific and control computer. Both new computers had been developed with government subsidies that had been offered to maintain Japanese competitiveness while liberalizing the nation's importing and licensing restrictions. This liberalization was the result of pressure by the U.S. to admit U.S. computers and technology to Japan.

Applications. A minicomputer was applied to the reduction of traffic congestion on the San Francisco–Oakland Bay Bridge in California. It sensed traffic volume at the centre of the bridge and controlled traffic signals at the bridge approaches to admit cars onto the bridge at intervals designed to keep all the cars moving as steadily as possible.

An upgraded computer system for the San Francisco Bay Area Rapid Transit system, the first fully automatic subway in the U.S., was prepared during the summer of 1974 by rewriting the control programs. After nearly two years of limited operation, first on the east side of the bay and later in San Francisco itself, trains finally began to operate through the transbay tube, joining both sides of the bay in a single rapid-transit system.

The U.S. National Weather Service installed the beginnings of what would eventually be a giant network of computers intended to streamline the forwarding of forecast information from station to station across the country. It was designed to reduce the amount of time spent by weathermen ripping copy from teletypewriters and thumbing through hundreds of daily charts and maps. The full system was scheduled to be installed by 1981.

Products. Three and a half years after taking over the computer manufacturing business of General Electric Co. and adding the GE machines to its own line, Honeywell Information Systems Inc. introduced a new line, the Series 60. It completed the consolidation of the two product lines. All models in the series used semiconductor memories, and a few large models used high-speed buffer memories in front of the relatively slow main memory to boost system performance—a technique that previously only IBM had used extensively but that shortly afterward also appeared in new computers from several other companies.

Two computer models called the Naked Mini LSI 1 and 2 were brought out by Computer Automation, Inc. This company had long specialized in minicomputers sold for use as part of larger industrial systems. Offering these without such essentials as power supply and control panel, intending the customer to provide them in his larger system, the company dubbed its line the "Naked Mini." Both new models, compatible with their predecessors, made extensive use of large-scale integrated circuits to provide full minicomputer capability on one 16 in. by 17 in. printed-circuit board. The Naked Mini LSI 1 used MOS integrated circuits; the Naked Mini LSI 2 achieved faster performance at a small increase in physical size by using bipolar integrated circuits. (WALLACE B. RILEY)

[735.D; 10/23.A.6–7]

ENCYCLOPÆDIA BRITANNICA FILMS. *What Is a Computer?* (1971); *A Computer Glossary* (1973).

Scientists at Bell Laboratories listen to synthetic speech produced by new computer techniques requiring only one-fiftieth the amount of digital data previously needed.

COURTESY, BELL TELEPHONE LABORATORIES

Congo

A people's republic of equatorial Africa, the Congo is bounded by Gabon, Cameroon, the Central African Republic, Zaire, Angola, and the Atlantic Ocean. Area: 132,047 sq.mi. (342,000 sq.km.). Pop. (1974 prelim.): 1,300,100, mainly Bantu. Cap. and largest city: Brazzaville (pop., 1974 prelim., 310,500). Language: French (official) and Bantu dialects. Religion: mainly animist, with a Christian minority. President in 1974, Maj. Marien Ngouabi; premier, Henri Lopez.

On Jan. 1, 1974, the government at Brazzaville signed new cooperation agreements with France. The agreements set up a permanent joint commission and permitted citizens from either country to travel to the other's territories. They also provided for cultural exchanges, scientific and technical cooperation, and agreements on taxes, merchant marine, higher education, fishing, and military technology. During the same month, the National Assembly voted to proceed with the nationalization of eight petroleum-product distributing companies operating in the Congo. Cultural and trade agreements with Senegal were signed on the occasion of Pres. Léopold Senghor's visit to the Congo, February 23–26.

As a consequence of the terms of the amnesty announced in October 1973, some exiled former opposition leaders returned to the country, notably Prosper Gandixion, minister under Abbé Fulbert Youlou (president 1960–63), and Gilbert Pongault, Christian labour-union leader. But this was not enough to stifle discontent. In January the government suspended the General Union of Congolese Students and High School Pupils, and security forces moved into the capital's educational institutions on several occasions.

Changes in military organization were made in October. President Ngouabi issued decrees setting up two new defense bodies, both headed by himself: a defense committee functioning as a military high command, and a supreme defense and security council. At the same time an assistant to the president for defense and security matters and a chief of staff for the Army were appointed.

At the international level, the Congolese government was apparently intensifying its efforts to establish relationships with the states of Central and East Africa and also sought to play a part in the settlement of the future of Angola, particularly in support of the leaders of the Popular Movement for the Liberation of Angola (MPLA). But it also gave some support to the establishment of Cabinda as a state, separate from Angola. According to a report of the Organization of African Unity (OAU) the Congo was among the 9 of the OAU's 42 member states not severely affected by the oil crisis. Agreements were signed with Tanzania in September on economic and cultural cooperation.

(PHILIPPE DECRAENE)

[978.E.7.iii]

CONGO
Education. (1972–73) Primary, pupils 277,386, teachers 4,373; secondary, pupils 49,984, teachers 948; vocational, pupils 4,228, teachers 331; teacher training, students 671, teachers 23; higher, students 2,098, teaching staff 194.
Finance. Monetary unit: CFA franc, with (Sept. 16, 1974) a parity of CFA Fr. 50 to the French franc and a free rate of CFA Fr. 240.50 to U.S. $1 (CFA Fr. 556.50 = £1 sterling). Budget (1973 est.) balanced at CFA Fr. 27,475,000,000.
Foreign Trade. (1972) Imports CFA Fr. 22,608,-000,000; exports CFA Fr. 13,212,000,000. Import sources: France 62%; West Germany 5%; U.S. 5%. Export destinations: France 29%; West Germany 9%; other European 23%. Main exports (1971): timber 56%; fertilizers 14%; sugar 11%; diamonds 7%.
Transport and Communications. Roads (1971) c. 11,000 km. (including 310 km. with improved surface). Motor vehicles in use (1971): passenger c. 7,500; commercial c. 5,500. Railways: (1972) 795 km.; traffic (1973) 171 million passenger-km., freight 517 million net ton-km. Air traffic (including apportionment of Air Afrique; 1972) 87 million passenger-km.; freight 8.7 million net ton-km. Telephones (Dec. 1972) 11,000. Radio receivers (Dec. 1972) 70,000. Television receivers (Dec. 1972) 2,500.
Agriculture. Production (in 000; metric tons; 1972; 1971 in parentheses): cassava c. 460 (c. 460); peanuts c. 20 (c. 20); sugar, raw value c. 40 (c. 70); coffee c. 2 (1.9); palm kernels c. 2.5 (c. 2.6); palm oil c. 6 (c. 6). Livestock (in 000; 1972–73): cattle c. 30; sheep c. 33; goats c. 45; pigs c. 15.

Consumerism

Soaring inflation and the steep rise in consumer prices in 1974 served in most countries to reemphasize the need for measures to protect and inform the consumer, for whom it had become more important than ever to get the best value for his diminishing resources. This fresh emphasis on the role of consumerism had a dual influence on its development in 1974. It accelerated the growth of the organized consumer movement, and it encouraged many consumer organizations to increase their pressure on governments to implement measures to help the consumer.

In the United States the automobile manufacturers, suffering their worst sales year in more than a decade, blamed their difficulties in part on government action. They claimed that the antipollution equipment the federal government had required to be installed in each car had contributed substantially to a price increase and, therefore, to the subsequent consumer resistance to the new models.

In its biennial report issued at the end of the year, the International Organization of Consumers Unions (IOCU) revealed that its membership had grown faster in 1974 than in any previous year since its founding in 1960. IOCU, which by December comprised nearly 100 member organizations in approximately 50 countries, also reported a higher than average rate of increase in the memberships of its affiliated organizations and in the readership of consumer magazines.

The fastest and most dramatic growth in the consumer field in 1974 occurred once again in the less developed countries, where inflation hit hardest. In those nations it aggravated the deprivation experienced by poorer sections of the population. Consumer organizations in those areas worked primarily to alleviate suffering and to ensure that the effects of inflation were not exaggerated by hoarding and speculation on the part of big firms or by uninformed buying on the part of consumers.

The rising level of interest in consumerism within the less developed countries was evidenced at the IOCU Seminar for Asia and the Pacific, held in Singapore in February. Almost 100 representatives of some 20 countries within the region met for the first time to discuss collaboration on consumer programs. As a result of this meeting, an IOCU regional office was established in Singapore in June.

Consumer Protection. A national consumer protection organization was formed in the U.S. in June. Consisting of state, county, and city consumer affairs officials from throughout the country, it planned to press for federal and state consumer legislation, to exchange information on consumer problems, and to provide a competing voice to that of business. In 1969 there were no governmental consumer administrators in the U.S., but by 1974 their numbers had grown to more than 200.

The U.S. Consumer Product Safety Commission (CPSC) in June issued guidelines concerning protection from faulty television sets and aluminum wiring in homes. Consumers had testified before the commission that the defective TV sets could cause fires and electric shocks, several of which had been fatal, and that homes equipped with aluminum wiring could suddenly burst into flames without warning. The commission announced that it planned to write mandatory

Congregational Churches: see Religion

Conservation: see Environment

Construction Industry: see Engineering Projects; Housing; Industrial Production and Technology

safety standards for television sets and would investigate aluminum wiring to determine whether it posed an unreasonable risk of injury.

Condominiums were a major focus of consumer concern in the U.S. during the year. These living units, in which the buyer owns his apartment and holds joint ownership with the other residents in the "common areas," had become increasingly popular during the 1970s. However, consumer provisions in the state laws governing condominium sales were generally either primitive or nonexistent. Consumers complained increasingly of shoddy construction, unfair and unannounced increases in the monthly maintenance fees for keeping up the common areas, and prolonged control over the condominium's facilities by the builder.

The federal government's response to the complaints about condominiums was summed up by James Lynn, secretary of housing and urban development: "This is certainly an area where, if the evidence continues to develop that there are substantial problems, action will have to be taken." Lynn added that he favoured a disclosure law that would inform the consumer about what he was and was not getting rather than a regulatory statute that would establish specific standards.

A sharp rise in consumer complaints about automobile repairs was reported at a meeting of consumer affairs officials in Washington, D.C., in June. The most commonly reported complaints dealt with shoddy or unperformed work, followed by those concerning warranty coverage, parts defects, overcharging, slowness of delivery, and fraudulent practices. Most of the officials agreed that emission control mechanisms posed a new and formidable challenge to repairmen and that the problem was likely to get worse.

The CPSC in August warned consumers that approximately 200,000 household "trouble lights" or "mechanic's lights" sold during the previous 12 months could cause a serious or fatal electric shock. The commission recommended to consumers that they cease using the light immediately and that they take extreme care not to touch any metal parts when disconnecting it from the electrical outlet. The lights, which bore no brand name, label, or other distinguishing mark, had been sold nationally by such stores as Woolco, Zayre, Korvettes, and Food Fair.

Bicycles were the subject of action by the CPSC during the year. In July the commission published mandatory safety regulations that were to apply to all bicycles sold in interstate commerce after Jan. 1, 1975. The required safety features included: reflectors on the front, back, sides, and pedals to make bicycles visible at night; protective edges on metal fenders and coverings for protruding bolts; locking devices to secure wheel hubs to frame, seat, handlebar, and stem clamps; chain guards for bicycles with pedals that cannot be reversed; brakes capable of stopping the bicycle within 15 ft. when ridden by a person weighing more than 150 lb. at a test speed based on the gear ratio; and instructions for the vehicle's maintenance.

A research group inspired by the work of consumer advocate Ralph Nader surveyed nine hearing-aid dealers in New York City and found that seven of them recommended aids for investigators with normal hearing who posed as customers. The dealers denied the accusation, but Nader said that the study supported the findings of similar surveys conducted in Minnesota, Michigan, Iowa, Vermont, Maryland, and Massachusetts.

Many consumer officials feared that rising unemployment and inflation would lead to an upsurge in consumer fraud, and they warned the public to beware of confidence men. Of particular concern, because it was comparatively unfamiliar to most consumers, was the buying and selling of gold bullion, which became legal in the U.S. on Dec. 31, 1974, for the first time in more than 40 years. The public was advised to beware of fraud in the assaying of gold, the verification of its weight and pureness. Because there were no federal or uniform state standards governing assayers, consumers were told to take particular care in finding one who was qualified.

In addition, the Assay Division of the U.S. Mint recommended that consumers find out which method of verification the assayer planned to use. According to the Mint only two methods were reliable: fire assay, which subjects the gold to heat and lead, and spectrographic assay, which employs a special instrument to produce a spark that indicates by means of its colours the metals that are present.

Consumer Education. The theme of the IOCU February seminar, "Community Education for Consumer Protection," demonstrated another of the effects of inflation—the realization of the need for more consumer education. Particularly in the less developed countries, where most families spent 80% or more of their incomes on food, it was vital that consumers should be taught how they could best spend what resources they had; for example, they should buy food that had the highest possible nutritional value for the money available. Similarly, the UN World Population Conference at Bucharest, Rom., in August aligned itself with the consumer movement in stressing that birth control education should form just one part of a comprehensive education in the basics of life, such as health, hygiene, nutrition, and housing. The objective was to give the consumer in the less developed countries a sound basis of knowledge as a protection against malnutrition and exploitation.

In the industrialized countries too, programs for consumer education, particularly in schools, had the support of both governments and consumer associations. In Norway, for example, consumer education became a compulsory part of the syllabus of the comprehensive schools. In the U.K. the Consumers' Association launched a scheme to provide a central bank of information on consumer education, to be available to all countries.

Consumer Credit. Several new laws dealing with consumer credit were included in an omnibus bill passed by Congress and signed by U.S. Pres. Gerald Ford in October. Under the Equal Opportunity Act, sex discrimination was banned in the granting of credit. Previously, some stores and credit card companies had denied credit to applicants solely because they were women. This act was to go into effect on Oct. 28, 1975. Also to become effective on that date was the Fair Credit Billing Act. It included provisions that required a creditor to take action within 90 days on a computer error in a consumer's credit account, if informed of it, and also prohibited credit card companies from preventing stores that accepted their cards from offering discounts to cash customers. In an amendment to the Truth in Lending Act, a consumer buying a home must be given the closing costs at the time the creditor makes the loan commitment and not at the actual closing time, as had been required previously.

In advance of the Fair Credit Billing Act, the American Express Co. in April had agreed to allow merchants that used its credit card to offer discounts to customers who paid cash. Consumers Union then dropped an antitrust suit against the company, calling the agreement a "tremendous victory" for consumers. The Union estimated that cash-paying customers might expect price cuts of 3–6% per item.

Four former investigators for the Retail Credit Co., the nation's largest credit investigation firm, testified before a U.S. Senate subcommittee in February that they had been forced to falsify credit reports in order to keep their jobs. All four told of being compelled to produce adverse information on a certain percentage of applicants for insurance, usually ranging from 6 to 10%, in order to demonstrate that Retail Credit was more thorough than other firms. As one of the former investigators put it, "The one who can get more adverse information can net more contracts." Retail Credit denied the allegations.

International Organizations. For consumers in the less developed countries, the difficulty of making ends meet in 1974 was aggravated by the continuing growth of the multinational companies. The president of IOCU explained how these companies acted in a way that was detrimental to consumer interests. From the consumer standpoint, he said, marked concentrations of economic power and severe imperfec-

tions of competition were always danger signals, for they meant price increases. In June, a study group recommended that a watchdog commission be set up to keep the subject under constant review, and also urged governments to set limits on the permissible public activities of these companies.

Protection of the consumer against action of large companies was also considered at the World Food Conference in Rome in November, when IOCU drew attention to companies that were adding to inflation in the less developed countries by "playing the commodity market as they had once played the Stock Market." Against this and other evils IOCU put forward a plan calling for greater supervision of commodity exchanges by national and international agencies and better cooperation among governments to control speculation; for international arrangements to make prices less volatile; and for the development of a code of ethics in the international food trade. Finally, IOCU demanded the discouragement—or even banning—of sale or excessive promotion of high-cost and nutritionally undesirable food products in poor countries.

The tenth session of the FAO-WHO Codex Alimentarius Commission, meeting in Rome in July with the participation of IOCU representatives, had already considered the possibility of formulating a code of ethics for the international food trade. Their other plans to help the less developed countries included setting up national Codex committees to take account of the differing needs of particular areas. Meanwhile, for the industrialized countries, it was stated that many members of the commission had accepted Recommended Codex Standards or parts of them. For example, the EEC had acted on the Sugar Standards and had drawn up an action program that included most of the commodities covered by the recommended standards.

The Council of Europe was active on both the consumer education and the consumer protection fronts.

Trouble light is called a "death trap" by the U.S. Consumer Product Safety Commission because of the possibility of fatal electric shock for its user.

WIDE WORLD

Housewives protest
the soaring price of sugar
at St. Clair Shores, Mich.

Working Party No. 2, on Education and Information, met twice in Strasbourg, France, while the Council's Committee of Experts on the Liability of Producers sought to place on the producer the responsibility for damage or injuries caused by defective products. Strasbourg was also the site for a round table on consumer education, organized by the European Centre for Social and Economic Progress, which drew up resolutions on consumer education in schools, the increased responsibility of the press in consumer matters, and the role of national and international organizations in consumer education.

The consumer voice was also heard more clearly in the EEC in 1974. Britain provided two, and Denmark one, of the independent consumer members on the Economic and Social Committee, a body that must be consulted on all EEC legislation. From the outside, the Bureau Européen des Unions de Consommateurs (BEUC) exerted its influence on the Common Market Commission. (BEUC is a federation of consumer organizations from the nine European Community countries, and its job is to try to ensure that consumers are heard when anything that concerns them is being decided.)

In June the EEC published a greatly extended program on behalf of the consumer. Three main areas of Community action were proposed: protection against unsafe and defective goods and unfair trading practices; redress for the consumer and help in asserting his rights; and better labeling, comparative testing, and more consumer information. During the year the EEC also advanced proposals for consumer protection that concentrated on health and safety standards, labeling, misleading advertisements, and supply of unsolicited goods.

Legislation. Much legislation was initiated during the year to counteract the effects of inflation, but the bulk of the consumer legislation was enacted to protect the individual in those areas, such as pollution of the environment, where his essential weakness adversely affected his interests at the hands of state or industry. At the international level, the Scandinavian countries joined together to set up a Working Group for Research and Protection of the Environment, and arranged to cooperate on environmental problems. At the national level, many laws were passed to prevent pollution. Norway in particular was active in this field and gave greater powers to local authorities to deal with pollution of the rivers and the coastal waters. (*See* ENVIRONMENT.)

A number of countries also increased the scale of

direct government participation in consumer protection, through the introduction or expansion of official consumer agencies. In the U.K., for example, the Labour government created a new Department of Prices and Consumer Protection, with a secretary of state and a minister.

In the U.S. the House of Representatives approved a bill establishing a national consumer protection agency that would represent consumers in proceedings before a wide range of federal agencies. However, after four unsuccessful efforts to end a filibuster on the bill, the Senate tabled it.

Pressure for tightening controls on advertising came from many countries. In May a new Code of Advertising Practice was launched in the U.K., strengthening the old regulations and bringing in new ones dealing with sales promotion practices. The U.S. made compulsory the substantiation of claims (for example, the efficacy of patent cold remedies must be proved), and corrective advertising for a fixed period was also made law.

Many nations were concerned with better and more informative labeling, both of clothing and of foodstuffs. West Germany and Sweden also prepared bills to give the purchaser certain rights if goods were either unsatisfactory or not delivered on time, rights that could not be invalidated by exclusion clauses in the small print on the packaging. The most important legislation in this area was the Prices Act in the U.K. Under its terms the display of average and comparative prices of goods of the same quality was made compulsory.

Important acts were passed on consumer credit in Australia and in the U.K. The Consumer Credit Act (U.K.) brought the consumer full disclosure of the terms offered, including the cost of credit in cash and percentage per year. The Australian bill improved borrower protection in credit transactions involving small and medium-sized sums. Also in the field of credit, several countries were concerned about the accuracy of, and access to, the information stored on individuals by credit information banks. Legislation in the U.K. insisted that access to such information be given to those on whom information was held, and a similar bill was introduced in Sweden.

To help the consumer both with the everyday problems of life and with more specialized problems of price and credit information, many countries either set up or proposed the establishment of consumer information and advice centres. West Germany's Consumer Council recommended displays of comparative prices and the establishment of a price information system independent of producers and advertisers. Ireland worked on improving consumer information and on enabling consumers to lodge price complaints at regional information centres. Australia passed the Consumer Protection Act, which set up tribunals for consumers' actions; it also outlawed pyramid selling, and extended the powers of the director of consumer affairs.

A high proportion of consumer-oriented activities in 1974 had the aim of helping the consumer make ends meet. In recognition of the special urgency of this objective, IOCU announced at the year's end that the next World Consumer Congress, to be held in Sydney, Austr., in March 1975, would have "The Cost of Living" as its main theme.

(JOHN CALASCIONE; DAVID R. CALHOUN)

See also Advertising.
[532.B.3; 534.K]

Contract Bridge

The bridge world was temporarily split in 1974 by a proposal to introduce the use of "screens" in top-level international bridge. In an ideal bridge-playing world every player would make his every bid and play at an even tone and tempo, but since bridge players are not automatons this had to be recognized as an unattainable ideal. The fact also had to be recognized that occasionally a player may have to give more than usual thought to a particular bid and that inferences may be drawn from the fact. Players are required not to allow themselves to be influenced by their partners' speed of action, but with all the best intentions in the world situations frequently arise where one or the other side is embarrassed by a "slow" bid or pass.

The president of the World Bridge Federation, Julius L. Rosenblum of New Orleans, sought to limit the embarrassment by the use of "screens" in the 1973 world championships. A screen is placed diagonally across the table at the beginning of the bidding so that each player can see only one opponent and cannot see his partner. Players make their bids with the aid of a silent bidding device, and a scorer announces the bids, two by two, at regular intervals so that no player is able to know whether a delay has been occasioned by his own partner's deliberation. At the end of the bidding the screen is removed. The proposal was favourably received in the United States, and successful experiments were carried out at na-

tional championships. Europe on the whole reacted unfavourably and considered the proposal one that would bring the game into disrepute. The Italians, who were to host the 1974 Bermuda Bowl contest, the world championship, in Venice, categorically refused to have screens used for the first time on their territory. The championship was played without screens, but a firm decision was taken to use them at the 1975 Bermuda Bowl contest which was to be staged in Bermuda in late January.

Italy retained the world championship in 1974, though with a performance that fell short of the team's high standards. In the final, against North America, Italy led by 70 points after 56 boards (hands) of the 96-board match. After board 74 the margin had been reduced to only five points, and a packed theatre saw the closest finish in many years. Italy finally drew away at the end to win by a score of 195–166. In the semifinal round Italy beat Indonesia, and North America defeated Brazil; France and New Zealand had been eliminated earlier in the round robin tournament. Brazil won the play-off for third place. The round robin, in which the same hands were played in all three matches, produced the most dramatic hand of the championship (*see* box).

The winning Italian team contained only three of the original Blue Team, in the persons of Pietro Forquet, Benito Garozzo, and Giorgio Belladonna. It seemed likely that the team that would defend the 1975 championship would do so without Forquet, whose retirement was imminent. The loss of Forquet was expected to make the Italian team much more vulnerable. Garozzo and Belladonna, who were established as the world's top pair (though Bobby Wolff and Robert Hamman of the U.S. won the Paris Olympiad), turned professional and headed a team that played in the name of the Lancia automobile. The Lancia team cars consequently became a familiar sight at European tournaments. The European bridge championship was won by France from Italy, while the women's event was won by Italy from France.

Preeminent in women's bridge was the British pair, Mrs. Rixi Markus and Mrs. Fritzi Gordon. They were runaway victors in the women's Pairs Olympiad. In three of the four Olympiads they had appeared as a pair, finishing first, second, and first, and on the fourth occasion, when they each took on a new partner, they were, respectively, fourth and fifth. The U.S. was no less outstanding in the Mixed Team Championship, winning the first four places. In first place were Bobby and Peggy Lipsitz, Mrs. Jo Morse, Steve Parker, and Steve Robinson, all from Washington, D.C.

(HAROLD FRANKLIN)

[452.C.3.a.i]

```
                NORTH
              ♠ A Q J 4 2
              ♥ J 8
              ♦ 3
              ♣ K 8 7 6 3
WEST                        EAST
♠ 6                         ♠ 10 9 8 3
♥ A K 6 5 4 3 2             ♥ Q 10 9 7
♦ A J 9                     ♦ K Q 7 4 2
♣ J 9                       ♣ None
                SOUTH
              ♠ K 7 5
              ♥ None
              ♦ 10 8 6 5
              ♣ A Q 10 5 4 2
```

Dealer, North. North-South game.

North	East	South	West
Belladonna	F. Manoppo	Garozzo	S. Manoppo
1 ♣	2 ♦	3 ♣	3 ♥
4 ♣	4 ♥	4 no trumps	5 ♦
Pass	Pass	5 ♠	Pass
6 ♣	6 ♥	6 ♠	Pass
Pass	Pass		

East led the seven of hearts, and declarer took one heart ruff, five trump tricks, and six clubs for a score of plus 1,660. A diamond lead and a club return, not an easy defense to find, would have given the Indonesians plus 200. In the event this would still have been a losing board, for in the other room the Indonesian North-South pair showed less accurate judgment when they doubled six hearts. After a club lead declarer had no difficulty in taking all 13 tricks for a score of plus 1,310 and a swing on the board of 1,970. Michel Lebel and Christian Mari, for France against Brazil, played in six spades doubled. A more inspired East, Gabriel Chagas of Brazil, led the queen of diamonds. His partner got the message and overtook with the ace to return a club and defeat the contract. But all this was to no avail, since at the other table the French were allowed to play in a contract of five hearts for a winning board. Bobby Goldman for North America against New Zealand found the same excellent lead against six spades and the same cooperative defense from his partner, Mark Blumenthal. And again to no avail, since in the replay the New Zealanders were permitted to play in six hearts doubled.

Cooperatives

Cooperative movements in a number of countries underwent change in 1974. In West Germany it was decided to convert the central organization into a holding company and to establish independent organizations for trade, production, and service. In the U.K. the second regional plan for reducing the 247 individual consumer societies to 26 regional societies was approved by the congress of the Cooperative Union.

In Finland the progressive consumer movement reached agreement on structural reform involving the establishment of larger economic units. The national assemblies of the Norwegian and Swedish consumer movements approved new programs to promote consumer interests. In Austria consumer cooperatives opened more large-scale sales units. The Swiss Coop Group abolished dividend stamps and introduced other incentives to attract new members.

The annual congress of Nordisk Andelsförbund, the joint buying and project organization of the Nordic consumer cooperatives, decided to establish a holding company to enlarge the field of joint cooperative production and to promote joint marketing schemes. In June the International Cooperative Trading Organization Ltd., owned by cooperative societies in Southeast Asia, was registered in Singapore to engage in and encourage trade between cooperative organizations all over the world. The Indian Farmers Fertilizer Cooperative, assisted by cooperatives in the U.S. and government agencies in the U.S., the U.K., and The Netherlands, started production of high-analysis fertilizers.

Nineteen major U.S. farm supply cooperatives formed an international trading company to undertake a broad-based search for sources of energy. The organization, known as the International Energy Cooperative Inc., intended to negotiate directly with major oil-producing countries for supplies needed by cooperatives to meet rural energy needs.

The third International Conference on Cooperative Thrift and Credit, organized by cooperative and mutual savings banking organizations, was held in London in June.

The International Labour Organization (ILO) conference on cooperative education and population, held in Nairobi, Kenya, in May, concluded that cooperatives could play an important role in advancing family welfare with particular regard to population issues. The joint committee for the promotion of aid to cooperatives (Copac), on which the International Cooperative Alliance (ICA), the ILO, the UN Food and Agriculture Organization, and the UN Social Development Division were represented, held a symposium in Hungary in September on the promotion of cooperatives in less developed countries.

The International Co-operative Alliance. In October the ICA Central Committee met in Vienna. The main theme was "Collaboration Between Cooperatives," and some of the problems involved in collaboration between producer and consumer cooperatives were discussed. The constitution of the ICA Women's Committee was approved. Following the political changes in Greece, the Panhellenic Confederation of Unions of Agricultural Cooperatives was readmitted to the ICA after a lapse of seven years.

The ICA Workers' Productive Committee, with the assistance of its Polish member organization, established a Centre for the Promotion of Industrial Cooperatives in Warsaw. The International Cooperative Housing Committee set up a working group to study the financing of cooperative and nonprofit housing. The Organization for Cooperative Consumer Policy held its first General Assembly in Vienna in October. INTER-COOP, the committee representing wholesale and retail interests, considerably increased collaboration among cooperatives in the food sector and registered progress in the nonfood sector.

Educational activities of the ICA Regional Office for Southeast Asia included a conference in Jakarta, Indon., in June that brought together the principals of national cooperative training institutions in the area to discuss the possibilities of mutual support and the introduction of new educational technology.

Copper:
see Mining and Quarrying

Corn:
see Agriculture and Food Supplies

Cosmetics:
see Fashion and Dress

Membership and Trade. At the end of 1974, the number of cooperative federations in membership with the ICA totaled 165 in 65 countries. The latest available statistics showed an increase in the number of societies from 624,900 in 1971 to 655,223 in 1972, while membership within these societies rose from 305 million to 327 million. The largest membership was reported from India (65.2 million), followed by the U.S.S.R. (62 million) and the U.S. (49 million). Of the total membership, the greatest proportion was in consumer societies (39.47%), followed by credit societies (30.14%), agricultural societies (18.78%), miscellaneous societies (6.66%), building and housing societies (2.84%), workers' productive and artisanal societies (1.46%), and fisheries societies (0.65%).

Agreements to promote trade relations were signed between the Central Cooperative Union of Bulgaria and the Central Union of Agricultural Cooperatives of Japan and between the Union of Polish Consumer Cooperatives and the consumer cooperatives of the Lega Nazionale delle Cooperative, Italy. The national organization of consumer cooperatives of the U.S.S.R., Centrosoyus, agreed to expand trade with consumer cooperatives in India.   (LOTTE KENT)
[534.E; 534.H.5]

Costa Rica

A Central American republic, Costa Rica lies between Nicaragua and Panama and has coastlines on the Caribbean Sea and the Pacific Ocean. Area: 19,652 sq.mi. (50,898 sq.km.). Pop. (1973 prelim.): 1,845,731, including white and mestizo 97.6%. Cap. and largest city: San José (pop., 1973 prelim., 215,023). Language: Spanish. Religion: predominantly Roman Catholic. Presidents in 1974, José Figueres Ferrer and, after May 8, Daniel Oduber Quirós.

The presidential election held on Feb. 3, 1974, was won by Daniel Oduber Quirós (*see* BIOGRAPHY), who polled 43% of the votes cast; the result ended the 25-year-old pattern of the two main political groups alternating in the presidency. However, the president's party, the Partido de Liberación Nacional, lost its overall majority in the Legislative Assembly; of the 57 seats, it had 27, while the Partido de Unificación Nacional had 16, the Partido Nacional Independiente 6, and five smaller parties occupied the remaining 8. At his inauguration on May 8, President Oduber outlined the government's economic policy for the next four years. The country's mineral resources were to be actively developed and basic industries expanded. To stimulate the modernization and diversification of agriculture, Costa Rica hoped to join with other Central American countries in seeking markets for agricultural exports outside the region.

The emphasis on greater cooperation with fellow members of the Central American Common Market (CACM) derived partly from the reduction of Costa Rica's trade deficit with the rest of the CACM, which fell to $5.2 million in the first half of 1974, as compared with $8.2 million and $20.1 million in the same periods of 1973 and 1972, respectively. The additional cost of oil imports by Costa Rica in 1974, estimated at $20 million, other pressures on the balance of payments, and, more particularly, the deteriorating fiscal situation led to the introduction on April 25 of a comprehensive exchange reform, accompanied by measures designed to control external indebtedness and to tax exports. The two-tier exchange system was unified at the previous free-market rate, representing an effective depreciation of the colón amounting to 23% against the U.S. dollar and 36% against gold, and all existing exchange restrictions were removed, though some were later reintroduced.

Agricultural products continued to account for the majority of export earnings. The attempt to find new markets met with some success: in the first quarter of the 1973–74 season, the Soviet Union bought more Costa Rican coffee than any other country except the U.S.; in 1974 Venezuela imported 25,000 beef cattle, a fast-growing sector; and Israel showed interest in buying both meat and sugar. Friction arose over foreign investment in the banana industry when the Standard Fruit & Steamship Co. opposed the tax of $1 a crate imposed by Costa Rica and other members of the Union of Banana Exporting Countries that was formed in March. Costa Rica obtained noticeable publicity for the exporting countries' case when the matter was raised before the United Nations and the Organization of American States. Subsequently, the government lowered the tax to 25 cents, and Standard Fruit announced that it would continue to operate in Costa Rica.

Students and workers protested against price increases in February; and in March there were protests against modification of the extradition law to permit financier Robert Vesco, a friend of President Figueres, to remain in Costa Rica, where he had invested $25 million, and avoid extradition to the U.S.

(JOAN PEARCE)

[974.B.2.e]

Cricket

The English cricket team was the only one to have a full international season in 1973–74. They toured the West Indies and drew a five-match series, and later at home beat India and drew with Pakistan in three-match rubbers. Australia met New Zealand twice, home and away, in three-match rubbers. They won 2–0 at home and drew 1–1 away, one match in each rubber being drawn.

The controversial but, from the playing point of view, successful reign of R. Illingworth as captain of England ended when Pakistan won an overwhelming victory at the end of 1973. After much speculation M. H. Denness, captain of Kent but relatively untried in international cricket, was appointed to lead England in the West Indies.

West Indies v. England. The rubber began disastrously for England, which comprehensively lost the first test by 7 wickets, despite 174 by D. L. Amiss and 93 by G. Boycott, and only saved the second because of a quite remarkable 262 not out by Amiss that ensured a draw. The batting of A. W. Greig, A. P. E. Knott, and K. W. R. Fletcher saved the third test after L. G. Rowe had made 302 for West Indies, and the fourth was a rain-spoiled draw. England in a last-ditch effort won the fifth test to draw the series after superb batting by Boycott and match-winning bowling by Greig, who had changed his style from fast-medium to slow-medium off-cutters and took 13 wickets. England's faster bowlers, G. G. Arnold, R. G. D. Willis, and C. M. Old, made little impact on the tour, and the slow men, D. L. Underwood and P. I. Pocock, did most of the work in support of Greig. West Indies was, on paper, the stronger team, but apart from Rowe, A. I. Kallicharran, and R. C. Fredericks, its experienced batsmen, especially R. B. Kanhai, C. H. Lloyd, and G. S. Sobers, had a poor season. The West Indians had no genuine fast bowler but instead relied on fast-medium B. D. Julien, K. D. Boyce, and V. A. Holder; offspinner L. R. Gibbs was the chief slow bowler, aided by the versatile Sobers, who used both his fast-medium and slow styles.

West Indies under Kanhai won the first test at Port of Spain, Trinidad, by 7 wickets: England 131 and 392 (Amiss 174, Boycott 93, Gibbs 6 for 108); West Indies 392 (Kallicharran 158, Julien 86 not out, Pocock 5 for 110) and 132 for 3 (Fredericks 65 not out). The second test at Kingston, Jamaica, was drawn: England 353 (Boycott 68, Denness 67) and 432 for 9 (Amiss 262 not out); West Indies 583 for 9 declared (Rowe 120, Fredericks 94, Kallicharran 93, Julien 66, Sobers 57). The third test at Bridgetown, Barbados, was drawn: England 395 (Greig 148, Knott 87, Julien 5 for 57) and 277 for 7 (Fletcher 129 not out, Knott 67); West Indies 596 for 8 declared (Rowe 302, Kallicharran 119, D. L. Murray 53 not out, Greig 6 for 164). The fourth test at Georgetown, Guyana, was drawn: England 448 (Greig 121, Amiss 118; Knott 61); West Indies 198 for 4 (Fredericks 98). England won the final test at Port of Spain by 26 runs: England 267 (Boycott 99) and 263 (Boycott 112); West Indies 305 (Rowe 123, Lloyd 52, Greig 8 for 86) and 199 (Greig 5 for 70).

Australia v. New Zealand. In Australasia, Australia under I. M. Chappell easily won at home against a New Zealand team at half-strength, but in New Zealand the home side achieved its greatest triumph

Cotton:
see Agriculture and Food Supplies; Industrial Production and Technology
Council for Mutual Economic Assistance:
see Soviet Bloc Economies
Council of Europe:
see European Unity
Credit and Debt:
see Exchange and Payments, International; Government Finance; Money and Banking

Sadiq Mohammad hooks
for four as David Lloyd
ducks during play
on the first day
of the England-Pakistan
match at Lord's
in London.

by beating for the first time a full-strength Australia in the second test after the first had been drawn. Australia revenged this defeat by winning the third test to draw the series. In Australia, New Zealand under B. E. Congdon was easily beaten in the first test, but was desperately unlucky not to win the second after leading by 150 in the first innings and adding another 305 in the second; at this time, rain rescued Australia from an impossible position. However, the Australians reasserted their superiority by winning the third test by an innings and 57 runs. In New Zealand, the first test was remarkable for the deeds of the Chappell brothers. Greg Chappell made the highest aggregate by any individual in a test, 380 for once out. Ian Chappell also made two centuries in the same match to establish another record, brothers scoring two centuries each in the same match. Congdon and B. R. Hastings also made centuries in this high-scoring match, and G. M. Turner made a century in each innings of the second test, which New Zealand won by 5 wickets after Congdon had bravely sent Australia in to bat. Two more centuries in the third test, by K. D. Walters and I. R. Redpath both not out, ensured a comfortable victory for Australia.

In Australia, the home side won the first test at Melbourne by an innings and 25 runs: Australia 462 for 8 declared (K. R. Stackpole 122, Walters 79, Greg Chappell 60, Ian Chappell 54); New Zealand 237 (K. J. Wadsworth 80) and 200. The second test at Sydney was drawn: New Zealand 312 (J. M. Parker 108, Wadsworth 54) and 305 for 9 declared (J. F. M. Morrison 117, Hastings 83); Australia 162 and 30 for 2. Australia won the third test at Adelaide by an innings and 57 runs: Australia 477 (R. W. Marsh 132, Walters 94, K. J. O'Keeffe 85, D. R. O'Sullivan 5 for 148); New Zealand 218 and 202 (Congdon 71 not out, G. Dymock 5 for 58).

In New Zealand, the first test at Wellington was drawn: Australia 511 for 6 declared (Greg Chappell 247 not out, Ian Chappell 145) and 460 for 8 (Greg Chappell 133, Ian Chappell 121, Redpath 93); New Zealand 484 (Congdon 132, Hastings 101). New Zealand won the second test at Christchurch by 5 wickets: Australia 223 (Redpath 71) and 259 (Wal-

ters 65, Redpath 58, I. C. Davis 50); New Zealand 255 (Turner 101) and 230 for 5 (Turner 110 not out). Australia won the third test at Auckland by 297 runs: Australia 221 (Walters 104 not out) and 346 (Redpath 159 not out); New Zealand 112 (G. J. Gilmour 5 for 64) and 158 (Turner 72).

England v. India. England, again under Denness, proved far too strong for India, led by A. L. Wadekar. India made a fight of the first test but surrendered in the other two, in each case by an innings, to lose the series 3–0. England then rubbed in its superiority by winning the two one-day internationals by 4 and 6 wickets. India had no fast-medium bowler of any class, and its spin bowlers, B. S. Chandrasekhar, B. S. Bedi, and E. A. S. Prasanna, so deadly in their own country, were countered and finally put to flight by England's attacking batsmen. India's own batting collapsed against the seam bowling of Arnold, Old, and M. Hendrick. England's batsmen scored seven centuries, India's only one.

England won the first test at Old Trafford, Manchester, by 113 runs: England 328 for 9 declared (Fletcher 123 not out, Amiss 56, Greig 53) and 213 for 3 declared (J. H. Edrich 100 not out); India 246 (S. M. Gavaskar 101, S. Abid Ali 71) and 182 (Gavaskar 58, G. R. Viswanath 50). England won the second test at Lord's, London, by an innings and 285 runs: England 629 (Amiss 188, Denness 118, Greig 106, Edrich 96, Bedi 6 for 226); India 302 (F. M. Engineer 86, Viswanath 52) and 42 (Old 5 for 21). England won the third test at Edgbaston, Birmingham, by an innings and 78 runs. India 165 (Engineer 64 not out) and 216 (S. S. Naik 77); England 459 for 2 declared (D. Lloyd 214 not out, Denness 100, Amiss 79, Fletcher 51 not out).

England v. Pakistan. Pakistan under Intikhab Alam provided much tougher opposition for England than had India. All three matches were drawn, with rain ruining close finishes in the first two tests. In the first test, England needed 44 to win with 4 wickets standing, but rain prevented any play on the fifth day. In the second test Pakistan suffered a cruel stroke of luck when water seeped under the covers and transformed a good batting pitch into one ideal for Underwood, who took 13 wickets in the match. But justice was done when additional rain helped Pakistan to save the game. In the decisive third test on a slow easy pitch, Pakistan made 600 and England 545, which proved that the batting of both sides was too strong for the bowling. The fast-medium bowling of Asif Masood and Sarfraz Nawaz was an admirable counter to England's seam bowlers, who confined the strong Pakistan batting to only one major individual score, 240 by Zaheer Abbas, while for England Amiss and Fletcher made centuries in the same match. Pakistan then won the two one-day internationals decisively, by 7 and 8 wickets.

The first draw took place at Headingley, Leeds, where Pakistan made 285 (Majid Khan 75, Sarfraz 53) and 179; England 183 and 238 for 6 (Edrich 70, Fletcher 67 not out). The second draw took place at Lord's where Pakistan made 130 for 9 declared (Underwood 5 for 20) and 226 (Mushtaq Mohammad 76, Wasim Raja 53, Underwood 8 for 51); England 270 (Knott 83) and 27 for no wicket. The third draw took place at the Oval, London, where Pakistan made 600 for 7 declared (Zaheer Abbas 240, Majid Khan 98, Mushtaq Mohammad 76) and 94 for 4; England 545 (Amiss 183, Fletcher 122, Old 65, Intikhab Alam 5 for 116).

County Cricket. Worcestershire dethroned the reigning champion, Hampshire, in a dramatic finish in which bad weather played a crucial part. Hampshire, which had led in the standings for most of the season, was prevented by four consecutive days' rain from clinching its position, while Worcestershire, which had chased them hard throughout the season, was able to score the points necessary for the lead on the one day on which cricket was possible in a drier part of the country. Worcestershire, with six test players, mostly from overseas, was a fine all-round side, as was Hampshire, for whom A. M. E. Roberts from Antigua was the fastest bowler in England and took 119 wickets. B. A. Richards and G. G. Greenidge were as talented a pair of opening batsmen as were Turner and R. Headley for Worcestershire. Northamptonshire retained third place, and Leicestershire finished fourth. Winners of the one-day competitions were Surrey, which beat Leicestershire by 27 runs in the Benson and Hedges final; Kent, which beat Lancashire by 4 wickets to win the Gillette Cup; and Leicestershire, which won the John Player League by two points from Somerset.

Chief run getters in the championship were R. T. Virgin (Northamptonshire) with 1,936 and J. A. Jameson (Warwickshire) with 1,932. C. H. Lloyd (Lancashire) headed the first-class averages with 1,458 runs, and Roberts took 119 wickets, 25 more than his nearest rival, V. A. Holder (Worcestershire).

National Cricket. In Australia, Victoria won the Sheffield Shield; in South Africa, Natal won the Currie Cup; in New Zealand, Wellington won the Plunket Shield; and in West Indies, Barbados won the Shell Shield. Mysore, renamed Karnataka, won the Ranji Trophy in India, thus breaking Bombay's 15-year sequence of victories, and North Zone won the Duleep Trophy. In Pakistan, Railways won both the Patron's Trophy and the Qaid-i-Azam Trophy. (REX ALSTON)

[452.B.4.h.ix]

Crime and Law Enforcement

Trends in Crime. Unprecedented levels of criminal violence were experienced internationally in 1974. Assassinations and bombings by terrorists wrought death and destruction in numerous countries. During one September week alone: In South Vietnam a man in soldier's uniform burst into the cockpit of an Air Vietnam jet and demanded to be taken to Hanoi. When the pilot refused, the hijacker exploded hand grenades, demolishing the aircraft and killing everyone on board. In Northern Ireland, Irish Republican Army (IRA) gunmen executed two of the province's most respected judges—one of them in front of his young daughter. In Argentina, where terrorists killed an average of one person daily, guerrillas kidnapped two rich grain dealers, leaving behind the bodies of another businessman and a chauffeur.

Violence and Terrorism. The kidnapping of executives for ransom in Argentina was reported to be that country's most lucrative crime. While worldwide publicity focused mainly on such spectacular abductions as that which brought the People's Revolutionary Army, a Marxist guerrilla group, a record $14.2 million ransom for the general manager of Exxon Corp.'s Argentine subsidiary, relatively few of those kidnapped were foreigners. Of the more than 500 people seized in 1974 for ransoms totaling more than $50 million, only 29 were not Argentine citizens. Argen-

tine police noted the slaying of 30 kidnappers in thwarted attempts and the solving of 11 abductions in the 12-month period ending August 1973.

Dismal records for solving kidnapping cases were not limited to Argentine law enforcement officers. In the U.S., the Federal Bureau of Investigation (FBI) admitted being baffled by the sensational kidnapping in February of Patricia Hearst (*see* BIOGRAPHY), daughter of newspaper owner Randolph A. Hearst, by members of the Symbionese Liberation Army (SLA). Although a number of leading SLA members were killed in a bloody shootout in May in Los Angeles, the whereabouts of Patricia Hearst remained a mystery. Meanwhile, FBI Director Clarence M. Kelley predicted that Latin-American-style kidnappings of members of the business community and their families would increase dramatically in the U.S. On February 20 J. Reginald Murphy, editorial page editor of the *Atlanta* (Ga.) *Constitution,* was abducted. Telephone calls identified the kidnapper as a colonel of the "American Revolutionary Army." Two days later Murphy was released unharmed when the *Atlanta Constitution* paid $700,000 in ransom. FBI agents and local police closed in on a suburban Atlanta home a few hours after Murphy's release, arresting the kidnapper and his wife and recovering almost all of the ransom money.

In the U.K. the annual report of Sir John Hill, chief inspector of constabulary, released in July, revealed that violent crime and sexual offenses in the preceding year surpassed records in England and Wales. In March a gunman fired several shots into a limousine carrying Princess Anne and her husband, Capt. Mark Phillips, in an apparent kidnapping attempt. A bodyguard and the chauffeur were wounded but Princess Anne and her husband were unharmed. After the attack, the gunman dashed into St. James Park where he was apprehended. Officials said that a letter addressed to the queen demanding ransom had been found; the man was found to be mentally deranged.

In Ireland an armed gang burst into the mansion of Sir Alfred Beit near Dublin on April 26 and stole 19 paintings, including works by Velázquez, Goya, and Vermeer, valued at $19.2 million. A ransom note offered to restore five paintings in exchange for the transfer to jails in Northern Ireland of two sisters and two men, all members of the IRA, who were in Brixton Prison, London, serving life sentences for bombings. The note also demanded the equivalent of $1.2 million for the return of the remaining 14 paintings. On May 4 all 19 paintings were recovered undamaged by Irish police in a cottage outside Glandore. Bridget Rose Dugdale (*see* BIOGRAPHY), a British partisan of the IRA cause, was subsequently convicted of receiving the paintings.

The Italian government began a shakedown of its security forces in 1974 in the wake of a series of political bombings and kidnappings, most of which remained unsolved. A new antiterrorist centre was set up in an attempt to coordinate the overlapping investigations into these crimes by the country's three major law enforcement groups, the Carabinieri, the Public Security Police, and the Finance Guard. Italian officials reported that the crime rate throughout the country had increased 16% during 1973. On Jan. 16, 1974, Italian police arrested three men on charges of having kidnapped J. Paul Getty III, grandson of billionaire J. Paul Getty. Young Getty was released on Dec. 15, 1973, after having been held captive for five months. The arrested men were charged with kidnapping, criminal association, and having caused serious personal injury. Police attributed the kidnapping to the underworld in the southern province of Calabria.

In France Paris officials reported a sharp increase in crime in the city's subway system, the Metro. Police figures revealed that at least 1,000 attacks occurred on the Metro in 1973, a 40% increase over 1972. The subway workers' union asserted that the number of offenses was probably ten times that shown by official figures, since only about one in ten people who were attacked reported the incident. In August 1974 a Metro official said that at least 20 handbags were stolen every day at one station near the Place Pigalle. On one occasion at the Boulevard St. Michel Station, in the heart of the Latin Quarter, a group of 40 youths boarded a train and terrorized the passengers, whom they roughed up before stealing wallets and handbags.

In West Germany the city of Frankfurt am Main reported the highest crime rate of any major German city in 1974. Demands for added police protection were met by the addition of some 300 officers to the force of 2,200 uniformed officers and 500 detectives. Blame for much of the crime increase was placed on the influx of foreign workers into West German cities.

Police in Brazil reported that during the first three months of 1974 there were 342 killings with intent in Rio de Janeiro, as compared with 741 for the whole of 1973. Rio's leading daily, *Jornal do Brasil,* opened a campaign against crime in the city. The newspaper gave Rio the dubious title of "the third most violent city in the world"—after Chicago and New York City.

Reports from China indicated that street crime in Peking and some other cities had increased to the point where neighbourhoods were being patrolled day and night by militia units. These patrols were backed by a poster campaign urging public support for the fight against "hooliganism." Offenses ranged from petty theft to murder, and some residents hesitated before walking the streets alone at night. The biggest threat to public order reputedly came from the estimated 50,000 young drifters who had made their way back to the cities illegally from enforced resettlement in the countryside under a program initiated by Chairman Mao Tse-tung during the Cultural Revolution of 1966–69.

Tokyo, the world's most populous city with some nine million people, was probably also the least crime-troubled big city anywhere in the world. In 1973 Tokyo had 196 murders while New York City, with

a population of only eight million, had 1,680. During the same year, New York, with a 31,000-man police force, had 72,750 reported robberies, Tokyo had 361; New York had 3,735 reported rapes, Tokyo had 426. While cities across the U.S. and Europe had experienced spiraling rates of crime over the past decade, Tokyo's overall crime rate did not increase and, in the category of major crimes, the rate actually dropped despite steady population growth.

A prime cause of escalating crime rates in most nations, and particularly property crimes, was said to be soaring inflation. In the U.S., which in 1973 had experienced only a slight increase in the rate of crime, the statistics for the first six months of 1974 revealed a renewed surge in criminal activity, apparently related to the nation's deteriorating economic situation. Crimes against property, such as burglary, larceny, and car theft, rose 17% between January and June, while violent crimes such as murder increased by only 6%. Shoplifting increased from $5.2 billion in losses in 1973 to an estimated $5.8 billion in 1974, according to the U.S. Department of Commerce. Retail stock losses, including both shoplifting and employee theft, grew from a stable 1.97% of sales in 1972 and 1973 to 2.07% in 1974. The passing of bad checks also increased sharply during the first six months of 1974.

Law enforcement officials, while acknowledging the effect of economic conditions upon the crime rate, were careful to point out that this was only one of several factors affecting the state of crime. During the depression of the 1930s, crime rates in many U.S. cities remained relatively low, although unemployment and other economic hardships were widespread.

A disturbing trend for those Americans who had fled the crime-ridden inner city areas during the 1960s for the safety of suburbia was the rising level of crime in both suburban and rural districts. The raw statistics for 1973 showed crime was up 6% nationally, 10% in rural U.S., and 9% in suburbia. In the first six months of 1974, crime was up 16% nationally, 19% in rural U.S., and 21% in suburbia. In 1973 many larger cities showed either little growth in crime or, in some cases, a decline. Explanations for this trend included the fact that there were simply more Americans living in the suburbs than in the city centres. There was also greater social diversity in suburban areas, as well as more opportunity for committing crime. Criminals displayed greater mobility generally in the offenses they committed, traveling by car along freeways from major city areas into the suburbs and rural districts to commit their crimes.

Tense scene at Schiphol airport near Amsterdam. Three Japanese terrorists held 11 hostages at the French embassy in The Hague, including Ambassador Jacques Senard. They demanded release of a Japanese prisoner, who was flown from Paris to Schiphol aboard this plane. The outcome, in the words of Dutch authorities, was most fortunate because release of the hostages was safely accomplished.

KEYSTONE

In San Francisco, on the night of Jan. 28, 1974, black gunmen cruising in cars killed four white persons at random and wounded another. The shootings were similar in nature to a series of killings that had started on Nov. 25, 1973. By April 16, 12 persons had been slain. The murders became known as the Zebra killings because of the radio channel used by special police investigators—"Z" for zebra. In connection with these crimes four Black Muslims were indicted by a state grand jury in San Francisco on May 16 and charged with murdering three white persons and conspiring to kill whites at random. In the testimony of an informer, it was asserted that members of a black militant group called Death Angels took pictures of each other murdering whites in order to win promotions within the organization. The informer charged that the mission of Death Angels was to kill white people, with special credit for mutilation, and testified that he had been taken along on ten murder missions by Death Angels.

Mrs. Martin Luther King, Sr., the 71-year-old mother of the slain civil rights leader, was fatally wounded on June 30 when a young black man went on a shooting spree while she was playing the organ in Atlanta's Ebenezer Baptist Church. Also killed in the fusillade of shots was a church deacon. Police identified the assailant as Marcus Wayne Chenault of Dayton, O. Investigators stated that there was no evidence of any conspiracy in the shootings, which occurred just a little over six years after Martin Luther King, Jr., was assassinated in Memphis, Tenn. Chenault told police that he had received orders from his god to come to Atlanta and kill the Rev. Martin Luther King, Sr. He shot Mrs. King because she was nearest to him and the other persons because they were worshiping a false idol. On September 12 a superior court jury in Atlanta convicted Chenault of the murders of Mrs. Martin Luther King, Sr., and the deacon, Edward Boykin.

Violent crimes committed by youth gangs in New York City were on the increase according to state legislative investigators, who reported increasing violence by 315 gangs with 8,061 verified members and an overall alleged total of 19,503 members in the four boroughs of Bronx, Manhattan, Brooklyn, and Queens. In 1973 city police made 2,223 arrests of youthful gang members for major crimes, an increase of 30% over 1972. An average of 37 gang incidents and 62 arrests occurred every week during the year, and instead of the switchblade knives and zip guns that were formerly common, police now recovered large quantities of automatic rifles, pistols, grenades, and even army bazookas and mortars.

Use of Firearms. In the U.S., "Saturday night specials" (guns made domestically from imported parts) continued to show up again and again in street crimes involving violence. There were estimated to be over 30 million of these handguns, in addition to 100 million rifles and shotguns, owned privately by U.S. citizens. Given this massive armoury, and the abject failure of past attempts to curb the possession of firearms, many proponents of gun control were looking with keen interest at a new approach adopted by police in Baltimore, Md., for removing guns from citizens. Under this approach, police offered a bounty for each gun turned in to the authorities. In less than one month, 12,000 firearms were collected and more than $600,000 paid in bounties. This cache of weapons was estimated to represent, at most, a scant 10% of the firearms in Baltimore, a city of one million

people, and the evidence of a reduction in crimes involving guns was inconclusive. Critics of the program labeled it a costly gimmick, and the U.S. Justice Department estimated privately that it would cost $1.5 billion to buy back handguns alone nationwide.

The danger of accidental shootings was emphasized by a research study in Cleveland, O., which indicated that a gun purchased to protect a family against an intruder was six times more likely to be used to kill a family member or friend. The study revealed that the death rate from accidents involving guns in the Cleveland area had increased fivefold for urban populations and had doubled for suburban populations during a 14-year time span. Deaths from firearms increased more than those from any other type of accident in the Cleveland region.

The FBI reported that firearms, mostly handguns, were responsible for the deaths of 120 of the 127 law enforcement officers killed in 1973 due to felonious criminal action in the U.S. More officers were killed attempting arrests than in any other circumstances. Intervention in family disputes was also a hazardous police activity, 30 officers being slain responding to "disturbance calls" of this type. Many police forces continued to provide special training for their officers in handling family crisis interventions in an attempt to reduce the rate of fatalities and injuries of both law enforcement officers and the disputants. More realistic training was also given police in the use of their firearms in emergency situations. One new and widely used training technique was to show police motion-picture films depicting simulated high-risk situations. Officers in the classroom were asked to fire guns, loaded with blanks, at the screen at the point in the film at which they believed such intervention was justified. Discussions followed concerning details of the event portrayed and the appropriateness of the police response.

Despite the continuing and growing levels of terrorist activities sparked by the conflict in Northern Ireland, British police continued to remain predominantly unarmed. For example, only 10% of the metropolitan police force in London was authorized to bear firearms, and they were issued during 1973 on an average of fewer than six occasions a day. Guns were actually fired in just two incidents. Instead of using added weaponry to deal with an outbreak of U.S.-style muggings that occurred in London at the rate of four cases a day, Scotland Yard dispatched special squads into the area plagued by these street robberies. In a three-month period the muggings were reported to have declined by almost one-third, although police tactics aroused some resentment among minority group members who accused the antimugging squads of harassment.

Nonviolent Crime. In New York City federal narcotics officials disclosed that they had seized 170 lb. of heroin, worth $112 million, which had been concealed in a shipment of simulated antique furniture from France. Agents traced the heroin to a Queens warehouse where it was confiscated on August 9. Four French citizens and an Argentine were arrested. The head of the Justice Department's Drug Enforcement Administration, John R. Bartels, Jr., noted that this was the first seizure since the Turkish government announced its intention of allowing farmers to resume growing poppies for opium. Turkey was identified as the source of supply for the so-called French connection smuggling route through Marseilles into New York. (*See* DRUG ABUSE.)

Marcus Wayne Chenault of Dayton, O., is led from the courthouse following his conviction for the murder of Mrs. Martin Luther King, Sr., and Edward Boykin. They were both slain in Ebenezer Baptist Church in Atlanta, Ga., in June.

Empty frames are mute witness to the theft of 19 masterpieces from Sir Alfred Beit's collection in his home in Blessington, Ire., in April 1974.

Carmine Tramunti, described as boss of the organized crime family in New York City formerly headed by the late Thomas Lucchese, was sentenced on May 7 to 15 years' imprisonment for narcotics conspiracy. Tramunti was the alleged banker for the conspiracy. Joseph DiNapoli, another defendant in the trial in which 15 persons were convicted on March 13, was sentenced to 20 years. DiNapoli had been arrested with a suitcase containing almost $1 million in cash, allegedly from the narcotics operation. Vincent Aloi, reputedly the acting head of an organized crime family in New York, was sentenced in a federal district court in New York on February 5 to nine years' imprisonment in a stock fraud case. The sentence was ordered to be served consecutively with a seven-year sentence for perjury imposed in 1973 by a New York state court. The federal conviction involved a fraudulent $300,000 stock offering for a car-leasing company known as the At Your Service Leasing Corp.

Nineteen persons were indicted in a federal district court in Brooklyn on March 5, charged with the theft of over 7,000 blank airline tickets, resulting in a loss to carriers of more than $2 million. Although ticket thefts had plagued airlines for years, security officials stated that this crime had increased sharply since 1970. Gangsters with organized crime connections were involved with the theft of large numbers of tickets, and organized groups systematically stole tickets from travel agents, airline offices, and printers' shipments. The tickets were validated through the use of stolen or counterfeit travel agency or airline validation plates and were used by customers to fly to various places throughout the world. One of the persons arrested in connection with this racket was a promoter of flights for gamblers to Las Vegas, Nev. It was revealed in May that Pan American World Airways had secretly paid thousands of dollars to an organized crime ring to buy back approximately 2,000 blank flight tickets that had been stolen. Some of the tickets had been stolen from travel agencies but most were taken from shipments of tickets from a printing plant to airline offices. Pan Am's decision brought criticism from some security specialists at other airlines, who contended that the purchase could encourage additional thefts. Some of the individuals involved in the Pan Am thefts were among the persons indicted on March 5.

Law Enforcement and Criminology. Adoption of new and advanced technology to combat crime was reported in 1974 by many of the world's law enforcement agencies. In Washington, D.C., controversy raged on Capitol Hill when plans were announced by some U.S. companies to exhibit sophisticated law enforcement equipment at the Krimtekhnika-74 exhibition to be held in Moscow in August. Following congressional criticisms pointing out that the logical buyer of such equipment was the KGB (the Soviet secret police), the administration agreed to examine the possibility of imposing export controls on the sale of such crime-detecting machines as voice identifiers and lie detectors. Under current law, only technology that could harm the national security of the U.S. required export permits.

Wealthy Americans began turning to detective and security agencies for protection and advice. The two major U.S. private investigation companies, Pinkerton and Burns, reported swelling business both nationally and internationally for protective services. Although the private security business relieved some of the pressure on the world's hard-pressed police forces, the rash of terrorist activities produced new problems for law enforcement authorities. As extremist groups began increasingly to operate across continents and national borders, bomb disposal and antiterrorist experts sought closer liaison with one another.

In the U.S. the National Bomb Data Center, established in 1972, accumulated data and disseminated know-how on bomb technology to the nation's police forces. In 1974 most U.S. cities reported they possessed a full or part-time bomb squad. The largest of these forces, that of the New York City Police Department, dealing annually with some 5,000–8,000 bomb threats and approximately 600 suspicious packages, was confronted at year's end with a spate of bombings of major Manhattan banks. The bombings were believed to be the work of a terrorist group seeking independence for Puerto Rico. The group promised more bombings if their demands, which included the release of a number of "political prisoners" held in federal jails, were not met.

In the U.K. police received the benefits of new technology, including expanded use of computers and helicopters. Saturation policing was another technique adopted by Scotland Yard to fight street crime. A 200-man mobile reserve, used to saturate areas imperiled by crime, effected 21% more arrests in 1973 than in the previous year. A further fruitful source of arrest assistance was the police television program broadcast for ten minutes each Friday night by the independent television channel in London. The program reconstructed unsolved crimes using a variety of visual aids and appealed for public help. In 1973, 323 separate appeals led directly to 137 arrests.

In Japan a government White Paper attributed the country's unique success in crime fighting to the efficiency of the police and to strict controls on weapons and drugs. Japanese police, among other things, continued to be organized on a neighbourhood basis. In Tokyo, for instance, police booths, or *kobans*, were located every few blocks throughout the city, and were manned by 1 to 12 men who patrolled their neighbourhoods constantly. Every *koban* policeman had responsibility, on the average, for about 150 households, each of which he was required to visit twice a year. Apart from the efficiency of their police, Japan was well known for ruthless enforcement of antidrug laws and for equally relentless bans on guns and swords. The outcome was few reported crimes by addicts desperate for a fix, and the use of a karate chop rather than a blast from a "Saturday night special" in robberies.

The deluge of criminal violence around the world sparked renewed attention in many countries to the controversial issue of capital punishment. In the U.S. law enforcement authorities urged the reintroduction of the death penalty as a deterrent for crimes of terror. Support for the proponents of capital punishment was found in public opinion polls and in statements by such dignitaries as the nation's chief law officer, Attorney General William Saxbe. By late 1974, 29 states in the U.S. had restored the death penalty following the 5–4 ruling by the U.S. Supreme Court in 1972 invalidating almost all existing capital punishment laws. In U.S. prisons 147 men awaited the executioner pending the outcome of fresh legal challenges to the constitutionality of the death penalty. Bombings by the IRA in England, in which a number of persons were killed, led to a campaign to reinstate the death penalty, but Parliament rejected the proposal.

Countries continuing to use the death penalty for various types of violent crimes included Saudi Arabia, Iran, Iraq, Turkey, and South Africa. Unlike other Muslim countries, which in the main had adopted Western legal codes, Saudi Arabia continued to follow Koranic tradition in legislative and judicial proceedings. Habitual thieves, for instance, were still liable to have their hands cut off as punishment. In murder cases, Saudis continued to follow the traditional principle of vengeance. A victim's family was given the option of receiving compensation, having the state execute the offender, or doing it themselves. Executions, and occasional floggings, were performed in public after Friday noon prayers.

Preliminary results of a federally funded survey of crime victimization throughout the U.S. added further fuel to the furor about the overall rate of crime. The survey findings from a National Crime Panel (NCP) of the Law Enforcement Assistance Administration (LEAA) showed that unreported crime was twice as high as reported crime in eight cities initially studied. The NCP material showed that nearly half of the victims of assault, robbery, burglary, and larceny of $50 and above did not report the incidents to police. The nonreporting rate of larceny below $50 was 80%. The most common reason cited was that the victim felt police could not do anything about the incident, or felt the incident was not important enough to report.

The key findings of another major U.S. research study, directly challenging the fundamental premise of police organizations around the world that regular patrol by uniformed officers deters crime and reassures the public, also received widespread attention. The patrol experiment study, financed by a large grant from the Police Foundation, a Washington-based offspring of the Ford Foundation, involved 148,000 persons living in a 32-sq.mi. area in Kansas City, Mo. Fifteen patrol sectors, or beats, were divided into three groupings with similar patterns of reported crime, income levels, and population characteristics. The area covered included shopping centres, apartment houses, and single family houses. On a random basis, the matched sectors were given one of three levels of patrol. In each of the five sectors in the first group there was no regular uniformed patrol and police cars entered only when citizens made specific requests for service. In the five sectors of the second group a single patrol car roamed the streets, as had been the practice

for many years. In the five sectors of the third group two to three times the normal number of cars provided highly intensive patrol. Surveys of citizens and businesses both before and at the end of the experiment found that the varying levels of patrol had no significant effect on burglaries, auto thefts, larcenies involving auto accessories, robberies, or vandalism, all traditionally considered to be deterrable through preventive patrol. It was also found that citizen fear of overall crime was not affected by the experimental additions, and that, generally, the attitudes of businessmen and other residents toward crime and police services did not change as a result of intensive patrolling.

According to the best estimates, local governments in the U.S. diverted at least one-third of their annual expenditure for police protection to maintaining and operating uniformed patrol forces. It remained to be seen what the effect of the Kansas City experiment would be upon these expenditures.

A further important topic of criminology research in the U.S. was the victim of crime. Particular attention was devoted to the crime of rape—a crime in which the attitudes and behaviour of criminal justice personnel were believed to have a profound effect upon the victim and upon the outcome of enforcement and prosecution efforts. The FBI termed rape the fastest growing violent crime in the nation, and law enforcement officials stated that about 80% of attacks went unreported because of the victims' shame, fear of reprisals, or concern that a court proceeding would bring further embarrassment.

To counter some of these reporting difficulties and to improve the criminal justice system's handling of the crime of forcible rape, late in 1974 the LEAA funded a major national study of the crime of rape by the Battelle Law and Justice Study Center in Seattle, Wash. Meanwhile, several states across the country passed laws designed to protect rape victims and help prosecute offenders. Among other measures being taken was the establishment of 24-hour rape crisis hotlines from which victims could anonymously seek advice.

Criminal Justice. The hardship produced by jury service was a point of citizen dissatisfaction with the criminal justice system in the U.S. The matter was highlighted when a number of the members of the Watergate cover-up grand jury lost their jobs when the inquiry ended following two years of investigation. In another Watergate-related trial lasting ten weeks, that of former U.S. attorney general John Mitchell and ex-Nixon Cabinet member Maurice Stans, two jurors lost their jobs at the completion of their jury service. The result of these juror job losses was an attempt to secure federal legislation protecting those citizens who served on juries from subsequently being terminated in their employment.

The effect of Watergate was felt not only in the field of jury service but throughout the U.S. system of criminal justice. The pardoning of former president Richard Nixon by his successor, Gerald Ford, together with the involvement in criminal activities of many in the Nixon administration who had professed such strong support for the concept of law and order and "equal justice," produced substantial public cynicism about the working of the system at large, although the long-term effects of this cynicism remained to be measured.

A further product of Watergate was an increasing emphasis upon the prosecution of "white collar" or economic crimes in the United States. In the past such crimes, involving a wide variety of business and allied frauds, were viewed with substantial tolerance by a criminal justice system whose major efforts were directed toward violent or traditional and less complex offenses against the person and property. Even when successfully prosecuted and convicted, white collar criminals frequently received lenient sentences from the courts. Seeking to change this situation, an LEAA-funded action research program assisted 15 prosecutors' offices around the U.S. to establish special economic crime prosecution units. In their first year of operation, these units achieved striking successes in the prosecution of numerous frauds upon consumers.

(DUNCAN CHAPPELL; VIRGIL W. PETERSON)

International Criminal Police Organization. Interpol's affiliate membership rose to 120 countries in 1974. The 43rd General Assembly was held in Cannes, France, September 19–25. Among the subjects covered in the reports submitted were international illicit drug traffic, international currency counterfeiting, import and export of small firearms and international exchange of information involving firearms, ammunition, and explosives purchased by private individuals abroad, and international police cooperation.

A second Asian Regional Conference was also held in Cannes in September. A symposium organized by the Interpol General Secretariat for heads of police colleges was held in Saint-Cloud, France, in November 1973 and was attended by 80 participants from 43 countries. Another symposium, on international fraud, was held in Paris in September 1974.

Activity by the National Central Bureaus (NCBs) during the course of the year involved the exchange of 246,319 items of information and led to 1,991 arrests. Between June 1973 and June 1974 the General Secretariat examined 25,679 cases resulting in 1,481 arrests; 10,160 items of information were supplied to NCBs, and 571 persons were the subject of international notices.

See also Drug Abuse; Law; Prisons and Penology; and Race Relations.

[522.C.6; 543.A.5; 552.C and F; 737.B; 10/36.C.5.a]

ENCYCLOPÆDIA BRITANNICA FILMS. *Our Community Services* (1969).

Cuba

The socialist republic of Cuba occupies the largest island in the Greater Antilles of the West Indies. Area: 42,827 sq.mi. (110,922 sq.km.), including several thousand small islands and cays. Pop. (1973 est.): 8,915,800, including (1953) white 72.8%; mestizo 14.5%; Negro 12.4%. Cap. and largest city: Havana (pop., 1970, 942,348). Language: Spanish. Religion: predominantly Roman Catholic. President in 1974, Osvaldo Dorticós Torrado; prime minister, Fidel Castro.

Cuba enjoyed political stability and made some economic progress in 1974. Prime Minister Castro puzzled observers by making few public appearances during the year, but his leadership remained unchallenged. Progress was made toward establishing municipal assemblies throughout the country as part of the official policy to create institutions permitting civilians some decision-making voice. The preliminary selection of candidates for assemblies in the province of Matanzas was completed in June, and the assemblies met for the first time on July 12.

In April the U.S. government lifted its ban on the sale of motor vehicles to Cuba by U.S.-owned companies; subsidiaries of General Motors, Ford, and Chrysler in Argentina concluded transactions valued at $75 million in April and June. It was reported in August that the U.S. was considering lifting the trade embargo, which had been in force since the early 1960s, the sales to Cuba by the automobile companies in Argentina being the first signs of the possibility of such a move. The U.S. secretary of state, Henry Kissinger, had reportedly requested the Mexican foreign minister to discuss Cuban relations with the U.S. and Latin America with Prime Minister Castro during his visit to Havana, and Castro had then stated that Cuban representatives would attend the Latin-American foreign ministers' meeting in 1975 "in a constructive spirit." In August U.S. Pres. Gerald Ford hinted at a press conference that his administration was studying a renewal of ties; many commentators considered that an announcement would be made after the U.S. congressional elections in November. On April 23 the U.S. Senate Foreign Relations Committee had unanimously approved a resolution calling for an end to the embargo and a resumption of U.S.-Cuban commercial and diplomatic relations, but this resolution was not binding on the president. Late in September Sen. Jacob Javits (Rep., N.Y.) and Sen. Claiborne Pell (Dem., R.I.) visited Cuba and met with Castro. They expressed the belief that Castro desired improved relations with the U.S., even though the prime minister during their visit had denounced U.S. "imperialist policies" in a major speech.

Cuba enjoyed considerable success in strengthening ties with other Latin-American countries. At a meeting of the 24 Latin-American and Caribbean foreign

CUBA

Education. (1972–73) Primary, pupils 1,852,714, teachers 68,699; secondary, pupils 222,481, teachers 17,724; vocational, pupils 41,940, teachers 4,652; teacher training, students 25,910, teachers 2,268; higher (at 4 universities), students 43,261, teaching staff (1970–71) 4,129.

Finance. Monetary unit: peso, with (Sept. 16, 1974) an official rate of 0.80 peso to U.S. $1 (free rate of 1.92 pesos = £1 sterling). Budget (1966; latest published) balanced at 2,718,000,000 pesos.

Foreign Trade. (1972) Imports 1,189,000,000 pesos; exports 739 million pesos. Import sources (1970): U.S.S.R. 53%; U.K. 5%; France 5%. Export destinations (1970): U.S.S.R. 51%; Japan 10%; Czechoslovakia 5%; East Germany 5%. Main exports (1970): raw sugar 68%; nonferrous metal ores 16%; refined sugar 7%.

Transport and Communications. Roads (1972) 13,343 km. (including 1,144 km. of the Central Highway). Motor vehicles in use (1971): passenger *c.* 72,000; commercial (including buses) *c.* 32,000. Railways: (1972) 14,494 km. (including 9,441 km. plantation); traffic (1971) 987 million passenger-km., freight 1,598,000,000 net ton-km. Air traffic (1972): 550 million passenger-km.; freight 12.6 million net ton-km. Shipping (1973): merchant vessels 100 gross tons and over 271; gross tonnage 416,305. Telephones (Dec. 1972) 278,000. Radio receivers (Dec. 1972) 1.5 million. Television receivers (Dec. 1968) *c.* 575,000.

Agriculture. Production (in 000; metric tons; 1973; 1972 in parentheses): rice *c.* 370 (*c.* 350); corn *c.* 120 (*c.* 120); cassava *c.* 220 (*c.* 220); sweet potatoes (1972) *c.* 260, (1971) *c.* 260; tomatoes *c.* 50 (*c.* 50); sugar, raw value *c.* 5,400 (*c.* 4,388); coffee *c.* 30 (*c.* 29); oranges (1972) *c.* 130, (1971) *c.* 130; tobacco *c.* 32 (*c.* 46); jute *c.* 7 (*c.* 7). Livestock (in 000; 1972–73): cattle *c.* 7,400; pigs *c.* 1,450; sheep *c.* 308; goats *c.* 83.

Industry. Production (in 000; metric tons; 1972): crude oil 117; petroleum products (1971) 4,310; electricity (kw-hr.; 1971) 5,208,000; copper ore (metal content) 3; chrome ore (oxide content; 1967) 11; manganese ore (metal content; 1968) 28; nickel ore (metal content) 37.

Crops:
see Agriculture and Food Supplies

"First, let me explain our conditional amnesty program. . ."

In a speech on May 1 the secretary-general of the central labour organization emphasized the need to link wages more closely to productivity and announced that workers who exceeded their production targets would receive cash bonuses. Castro announced in May that private farmers' cooperatives would be given scope to increase their activities.

The government was concerned during the year about the political apathy of young people and their failure to take advantage of the opportunities offered them for higher education. The minister of armed forces, Raúl Castro, in a speech early in May to the Communist Youth Union (UJC), stated that the proportion of young Communists in relation to the mass of adolescents was far too low and that the number of young people between the ages of 13 and 16 who studied had not increased significantly since 1972; he expressed the hope that young people would not be unduly influenced by "decadent ideas of the past" and "the influence of consumer societies." The speech coincided with a campaign in the press and mass media against the high levels of consumption.

(ROBIN CHAPMAN)

[974.C.2.c]

Cycling

British amateur cyclists won four of the seven championships contested at the Commonwealth Games in January 1974 at Christchurch, N.Z. Ian Hallam of the U.K. won two gold medals, one silver, and one bronze. The expected challenge from New Zealand riders did not materialize, but the Australians rode strongly to take the other three titles. Caribbean trackmen did well, Xavier Mirander of Jamaica being the final challenger to star Australian sprinter John Nicholson.

Meanwhile, European professional road riders prepared for their own long season. The first real test was the eight-day Paris–Nice contest in March, which was of special interest owing to the presence of a Polish national team, the first meeting in a major race

ministers in Washington, D.C., on April 17 and 18, it was decided to poll member nations as to whether to invite Cuba to send a representative to the next meeting, to be held in Buenos Aires, Arg., in March 1975, as a first step toward discussions of the country's return to the Organization of American States. The poll revealed that a majority opposed Cuba's readmission to the OAS. At the request of Costa Rica, Colombia, and Venezuela, a special meeting of the OAS foreign ministers was held in Quito, Ecuador, in November to consider the question of lifting political and economic sanctions against Cuba. After five days of intensive negotiations, the vote fell two short of the required two-thirds majority.

In December 1973 a Mexican trade mission visited Cuba, returning with orders valued at about $8.8 million; the Mexican foreign minister, Emilio Rabasa, visited Havana in March, and the formation of a Cuban-Mexican shipping line was announced early in May. A Peruvian commercial mission visited Cuba in May, and it was announced during the same month that Cuba was to purchase from a Peruvian concern five tuna boats valued at over $8 million. There was also a notable expansion in trade with Argentina; in February agreements were signed providing for Argentine exports worth $500 million.

Relations with the Soviet Union continued to be close. The general secretary of the Communist Party of the Soviet Union, Leonid I. Brezhnev, visited Havana late in January. Under the terms of an agreement signed in Moscow in February, Cuban-Soviet trade in 1974 was to amount to $1.8 billion, an increase of 18% over the figure for 1973; efforts were to be made to speed up the flow of trade through improvements to ports and air terminals; and the U.S.S.R. undertook to meet Cuba's requirements for petroleum and its by-products, and to increase shipments of machinery and equipment to modernize the sugar industry.

There were indications of improvement in the economy, with substantial increases in overall agricultural and industrial output during the first nine months of the year as compared with the same period of 1973.

Group of cyclists pass through Béthune, France, during the 61st Tour de France, won by E. Merckx of Belgium.

A.F.P./PICTORIAL PARADE

Currency:
see Money and Banking

Cybernetics:
see Computers

1974 Winners		
Event	Winner	Country
WORLD AMATEUR CHAMPIONS—TRACK		
Men		
Sprint	A. Tkac	Czechoslovakia
Tandem sprint	V. Vackar, M. Vymazal	Czechoslovakia
Individual pursuit	H. Lutz	West Germany
1,000-m. time trial	E. Rapp	U.S.S.R.
Team pursuit	West Germany	
50-km. motor-paced	J. Breur	West Germany
Women		
Sprint	T. Piltsikova	U.S.S.R.
Pursuit	T. Garkushina	U.S.S.R.
WORLD PROFESSIONAL CHAMPIONS—TRACK		
Sprint	P. Pedersen	Denmark
Individual pursuit	R. Schuiten	The Netherlands
100-km. motor-paced	C. Stam	The Netherlands
WORLD AMATEUR CHAMPIONS—ROAD		
Men		
100-km. team time trial	Sweden	
Individual road race	J. Kowlaski	Poland
Women		
Individual road race	G. Gambillon	France
WORLD PROFESSIONAL CHAMPIONS—ROAD		
Individual road race	E. Merckx	Belgium
NATIONAL ROAD-RACE CHAMPIONS		
(professional unless otherwise stated)		
Belgium	R. Swerts	
France	G. Talbourdet	
Italy	E. Paolini	
Luxembourg	R. Gilson	
Netherlands, The	C. Priem	
Portugal	F. Mendes	
Spain	V. Lopez-Carril	
Switzerland	R. Salm	
West Germany	G. Haritz	
U.K., professional	K. Lambert	
amateur	W. Nickson	
women	B. Burton	
MAJOR PROFESSIONAL ROAD-RACE WINNERS		
Het Volk	J. Bruyère	Belgium
Tour of Flanders	C. Bal	The Netherlands
Gent-Wevelgem	B. Hoban	U.K.
Milan-San Remo	F. Gimondi	Italy
Paris-Roubaix	R. de Vlaeminck	Belgium
Amstel Gold Race	G. Knetemann	The Netherlands
Flèche Wallonne	F. Verbeeck	Belgium
Liège-Bastogne-Liège	R. de Witte	Belgium
Grand Prix of Frankfurt	W. Godefroot	Belgium
Bordeaux-Paris	R. Delepine	France
	H. van Springel	Belgium
Paris-Tours	F. Moser	Italy
Paris-Brussels	M. de Meyer	Belgium
Grand Prix des Nations	D. Wells	U.K.
time trial		
Tour of Lombardy	R. de Vlaeminck	Belgium
Tour de France	E. Merckx	Belgium
Tour of Italy	E. Merckx	Belgium
Tour of Spain	J.-M. Fuente	Spain
Tour of Switzerland	E. Merckx	Belgium
Tour of Belgium	R. Swerts	Belgium
Paris-Nice	J. Zoetemelk	The Netherlands
Dauphiné-Libéré	A. Sainty	France
Four Days of Dunkirk	W. Godefroot	Belgium
Midi-Libre	J.-P. Danguillaume	France
Tour of Luxembourg	F. Maertens	Belgium
Tour of Sardinia	R. Van Linden	Belgium

to win the tours of Spain and Italy as well. In fact, he finished only fourth in Spain and was a nonstarter in the other two. Merckx refused tempting cash offers to ride the Tour of Spain, his first long race being the 21-day Tour of Italy in late May and June. Although winning this, his fifth victory, by only 12 seconds from the new Italian star Giambattista Baronchelli, he rode economically with an eye on races still to come and in the next event "soft-pedaled" to take the shorter Tour of Switzerland from Gösta Pettersson (Swed.). Then, winning eight of the daily stages, Merckx scored his fifth overall Tour de France win in six years, eight minutes ahead of French veteran Raymond Poulidor. On June 29 riders and officials crossed the Channel from Brittany for the second stage at Plymouth, the first Tour de France visit to Britain. Merckx capped a great second half to 1974 by winning the world road championship at Montreal in August, the runner-up again being Poulidor.

Riders from Poland and The Netherlands were prominent in many major amateur road events. World champion Szurkowski did not enter the 1,150-mi. Warsaw–Berlin–Prague (the "Peace Race"), which he had won three times, compatriot Stanislav Szozda scoring in his absence. Szurkowski arrived in Britain a clear favourite for the 14-day Tour of Britain but succumbed by seven seconds to Roy Schuiten (Neth.), already winner of his own national tour. Schuiten's high class was confirmed when he turned professional and won the 5,000-m. track pursuit world championship in Montreal.

Canada's organization of the world series for the first time since 1899 was praised, and the racing was excellent. A surprise was the elimination of Daniel Morelon (France), six times winner of the amateur sprint title. There was like disappointment for the 1973 women's champion, Sheila Young (U.S.), but another American girl, Sue Novara, rode well to reach the final, finishing runner-up to Tamara Piltsikova of the U.S.S.R., whose riders again dominated the track events.

As at the opening of the season the closing phase was enlivened by an "open" stage race, a team of Belgian professionals accepting an invitation to ride the previously all-amateur Tour of Poland. It was expected that the Poles would avenge their Paris–Nice defeat in March, but the visitors were soon on top and André Delcroix was the overall winner of the ten-day race.   (J. B. WADLEY)

[452.B.4.h.x.]

of Eastern European amateurs and leading Western European professionals. The test was inconclusive. With no hard training the Poles rode well for four days—world amateur champion Ryszard Szurkowski matched Eddy Merckx in strength and speed—but were dominated by the better-trained professionals in the last hilly stages. Surprisingly, Merckx lost the race on the final mountain test and finished third to Joop Zoetemelk (Neth.), whose fine start to the season was marred by a serious accident in May.

In recent years a Merckx setback was usually followed by a brilliant series of victories. This pattern, however, was not repeated in 1974. The Belgian was usually among the leaders but lacked zip, and the list of early-season classic winners did not include his name. The most spectacular victory of these races was by the reigning world champion, Felice Gimondi (Italy), in the 180-mi. Milan–San Remo. Later in the season Merckx's Tour de France clash with Luís Ocana, winner of the 1973 event in which Merckx did not take part, was awaited with interest. The Spaniard, however, was too ambitious. Instead of concentrating, as in 1973, on the French marathon, Ocana planned

Cyprus

An island republic and a member of the Commonwealth of Nations, Cyprus is in the eastern Mediterranean. Area: 3,572 sq.mi. (9,251 sq.km.). Pop. (1973 est.): 632,000, including Greeks 79%; Turks 18%. Cap. and largest city: Nicosia (pop., 1973, 116,000). Language: Greek and Turkish. Religion: Greek Orthodox 79%; Muslim 18%. Presidents in 1974, Archbishop Makarios III; Nikos Sampson (named president following the July 15 coup), July 15 to July 23; and Glafkos Clerides (acting president), July 23 to December 7.

In July 1974 Cyprus became the focal point of international attention when a coup engineered by the Greek-officered National Guard ousted Archbishop

Makarios (*see* BIOGRAPHY) from the presidency and subsequent intervention by the Turkish Army brought about the fall of the military regime in Greece and caused a crisis within NATO. (*See* DEFENSE: *Special Report.*)

Talks between representatives of the Greek and Turkish communities in Cyprus, which had been reactivated in June 1972, had continued through the winter of 1973–74. They were limited to a discussion of the scope of Turkish Cypriot local autonomy within an "independent, sovereign, and unitary state of Cyprus." The Greek Cypriot side was willing to grant the Turks autonomy in communal affairs and representation in the central government. The Turkish side sought to limit governmental supervision and administrative control over their local government bodies.

The Cyprus government believed that satisfaction of the Turks' demands would lead to the creation of a state within a state and subsequently to union of the Turkish Cypriot lands with Turkey (because, it was thought, the Turkish Cypriots would have no basis for economic survival as an independent unit). The intransigence of the Turkish Cypriots was mainly due to their fear that a union of the whole island with Greece might eventually be effected unless they had powerful institutions of their own at central and local government levels. The deadlock compelled the UN Security Council to extend the mandate of the UN peace force on the island until December 1974.

Although *enosis* (union with Greece) remained, in Archbishop Makarios' words, "the national aspiration of the Greek Cypriots," the government was opposed to any solution of the Cyprus problem that would involve partition. The principal Greek Cypriot opponents of Makarios, the members of EOKA B, doubted his sympathy for *enosis*. They made an attempt on the archbishop's life on Oct. 7, 1973, and murdered two of his supporters early in January 1974. Makarios believed a policy that would satisfy these nationalists would only promote partition. He was unable to exercise the fullest power of the state against them because numerous mainland Greek officers in the National Guard supported EOKA B. The guard indeed posed a constant threat, and the president was obliged to maintain a paramilitary Presidential Guard and a Police Tactical Reserve.

Gen. Georgios Grivas, the leader of EOKA B, died on January 27 (*see* OBITUARIES). The president granted amnesty to Grivas' followers, but antigovernment manifestations during and subsequent to Grivas' funeral compelled him late in April to declare EOKA B an illegal organization. At the beginning of April the intercommunal talks were suspended because of a demand by the new Turkish prime minister, Bulent Ecevit, for a federation of the Greek and Turkish communities in Cyprus. Immediately, UN Undersecretary-General Roberto Guyer visited Ankara, Athens, and Nicosia to discuss the suspension. Thanks to this UN initiative, the Greek and Turkish Cypriot interlocutors, Glafkos Clerides and Rauf Denktash (*see* BIOGRAPHY), resumed the talks on June 11.

In June relations between the president and the National Guard worsened, especially when he took measures to weaken this body by reducing the period of military service for Greek Cypriots. Early in July Makarios was driven to protest to the Greek government about interference in the internal affairs of Cyprus by the guard's Greek officers, and he insisted that 650 of them be withdrawn by July 20. He explained that he was provoked into taking this action

The age-old horrors of war are revealed by a bulldozer near Famagusta, Cyprus. Greek Cypriots allegedly massacred 57 Turkish villagers and buried them in a mass grave. One of the survivors mourns at right.

by the refusal of the National Guard to dismiss from its training school some 50 cadets who had been kept there contrary to the wishes of his government.

Some members of the Greek government had long opposed Makarios because he enjoyed the support of the powerful Cyprus Communist Party and had good relations with the Soviet Union and with other Communist and socialist states. The Cyprus government understood that its position was now dangerous but appeared to believe the president's large following in Cyprus and the possibility of Turkish intervention would prevent an openly illegal course of action. When the National Guard carried out a coup on July 15, the president was surprised and barely escaped with his life. (He left Cyprus the following day.)

The organizers of the coup gave the title of president to Nikos Sampson, an old EOKA terrorist. This extraordinary action was to have fateful consequences. On July 16, while the National Guard was overcoming the last armed resistance of Makarios' supporters, the Turkish Army was put on the alert. The next day Denktash, as leader of the Turkish Cypriot community, demanded the return of Makarios. On July 20 a Turkish force landed at Kyrenia with the professed aim of overturning Sampson's government. Numerous Greek Cypriots rallied to the support of the National Guard, but the rebels obtained no assistance from the Greek government and were driven back by the Turks. On July 23 the Greek president dismissed his Cabinet and called on the exiled politician Konstantinos Karamanlis (*see* BIOGRAPHY) to form a new government. On the same day, Sampson was relieved of his post by the National Guard; Clerides, president of the Cyprus House of Representatives, was made interim president; and a cease-fire was proclaimed.

On July 30 the three guarantors of the Cyprus constitution, Great Britain, Greece, and Turkey, agreed at Geneva on safeguards to ensure the cease-fire. Nonetheless, a real cease-fire did not come into effect until August 9. On August 8 the foreign ministers of the guarantor powers met again at Geneva, but their talks broke down on August 14 because the Turkish government required an agreement that would satisfy, once and for all, the aspirations of the Turkish Cypriot community. On August 14 the Turkish Army made a new advance, one purpose of which was to

Education. (Greek schools; 1972–73) Primary, pupils 64,186, teachers 2,280; secondary, pupils 43,871, teachers 2,031; vocational, pupils 4,198, teachers 296; teacher training, students 267, teachers 17; higher, students 654, teaching staff 74. (Turkish schools; 1972–73) Primary, pupils 16,014; secondary, pupils 7,190; vocational, pupils 753; teacher training, students 13.

Finance. Monetary unit: pound, with (Sept. 16, 1974) a free rate of C£0.37 to U.S. $1 (C£0.86 = £1 sterling). Gold, SDRs, and foreign exchange, monetary authorities: (May 1974) U.S. $260.6 million; (May 1973) U.S. $337.2 million. Budget (1973 est.): revenue C£49,590,000; expenditure C£43,940,000.

Foreign Trade. (1973) Imports C£157,850,000; exports C£63,130,000. Import sources: U.K. 25%; West Germany 9%; Italy 8%; U.S. 7%; France 7%; Greece 6%. Export destinations: U.K. 42%; West Germany 7%. Main exports: citrus fruit 26%; potatoes 14%; copper 11%; wine 7%.

Transport and Communications. Roads (1971) 8,319 km. Motor vehicles in use (1972): passenger 75,595; commercial 16,317. Air traffic (1973): 371 million passenger-km.; freight 2,932,000 net ton-km. Shipping (1973): merchant vessels 100 gross tons and over 589; gross tonnage 2,935,775. Telephones (Dec. 1972) 54,000. Radio licenses (Dec. 1972) 171,000. Television licenses (Dec. 1972) 66,000.

Agriculture. Production (in 000; metric tons; 1973; 1972 in parentheses): barley c. 10 (81); wheat (1972) 83, (1971) 97; grapes c. 185 (c. 185); potatoes (1972) 175, (1971) 178; oranges (1972) c. 130, (1971) 169; grapefruit (1972) c. 55, (1971) 57; olives 8 (c. 16). Livestock (in 000; 1972–73): sheep 480; cattle c. 34; pigs 125; goats 380.

Industry. Production (in 000; metric tons; 1972): sulfur 285; asbestos 27; copper ore (exports; metal content) 16; chromium ore (oxide content) 14; cement (1973) 456; electricity (kw-hr.; 1973) 829,000.

The Presidential Palace of Archbishop Makarios after his overthrow by Greek elements supporting enosis, or union with Greece. The Turkish invasion of Cyprus swiftly followed.

protect the scattered Turkish Cypriot communities from irregular supporters of the National Guard. When international pressure brought about a cease-fire on August 16, the Turks controlled the northern third of Cyprus.

By this time some 250,000 Greek Cypriots had become refugees. On August 22 the Soviet government issued a statement that an international conference should be called to discuss the Cyprus problem, and this was favourably received by the Greek government. The Turkish government, on the other hand, required a resumption of the Geneva talks. Preliminary discussions between Denktash and Clerides began early in September. Their negotiations—interrupted for several days after the discovery of the corpses of over 80 Turkish Cypriots at Maratha—led (September 11) to an agreement about an exchange of prisoners of war, and by September 28, 1,900 prisoners had been exchanged. However, there was no settlement of the refugee problem. About one-third of the island's population was living in the open or in tents—the autumn rains were approaching, and the economy of Cyprus was in ruins. Makarios returned to Nicosia December 7 to an emotional and enthusiastic reception, but his presence seemed unlikely to provide any impetus toward solution of the island's problems. The Turks indicated that they recognized him only as leader "of the Greek community."

Cyprus had faced economic difficulties even before the coup and the Turkish invasion. The year 1972 had been a poor one for agriculture, but in 1973 the island had suffered its worst drought in many years, cereal output having decreased to 10,000 tons. The government was obliged to spend £16 million on imports of wheat and barley, causing a balance of payments deficit of £5 million. The output of milk, vegetables, tobacco, and olives also declined. To counter the effects of the drought, the government accepted a 30-year

loan of DM. 2.5 million from West Germany in February 1974. On January 30 the World Bank had agreed to grant Cyprus a long-term loan of £14 million for a water development project.

The worldwide energy and economic crises created additional financial difficulties. The retail price index rose 7.8% in 1973. On Jan. 7, 1974, the government, employers, and trade unions agreed on a prices and incomes policy. At the end of February the Council of Ministers fixed the wholesale and retail prices of sugar, rice, and iron, froze the prices of 21 other items until further notice, and took measures to prevent hoarding. Inflation abroad posed a threat to the tourist trade, so early in February the government also froze the prices of all-inclusive vacations in the island for foreigners until October. Many tourists were trapped for a short time after the coup.

The situation in Cyprus was so uncertain that there was little hope the refugees might soon return to their homes. It was reported that numerous cattle had died and that crops and much capital equipment had been destroyed or damaged. On September 6 the foreign minister declared that the Cyprus economy had suffered losses in the region of £350 million since July 15, and that the Turkish forces occupied territories which had hitherto produced 70% of the country's wealth. Reports that the Turks envisaged a solution to the Cyprus problem that would legalize a de facto transfer of population gave rise to fears among the Greek Cypriot refugees that their temporary privations might become permanent. (L. J. D. COLLINS)
[978.A.4]

Czechoslovakia

A federal socialist republic of central Europe, Czechoslovakia lies between Poland, the U.S.S.R., Hungary, Austria, and East and West Germany. Area: 49,374 sq.mi. (127,877 sq.km.). Pop. (1974 est.): 14,686,255, including (1970 est.) Czech 65%; Slovak 29%. Cap. and largest city: Prague (pop., 1973 est., 1,091,449). Language: Czech and Slovak (official). General secretary of the Communist Party of Czechoslovakia in 1974, Gustav Husak; president, Ludvik Svoboda; federal premier, Lubomir StroEqual.

Czechoslovakia edged closer toward normal relations with the West in 1974. The ratification of the Czechoslovak-West German treaty on the normalization of relations by the West German Bundestag on July 8 and by the Czechoslovak Federal Assembly on July 15 (the treaty had been signed in Prague on Dec. 11, 1973) paved the way for a visit to West Germany by the Czechoslovak foreign minister, Bohuslav Chnoupek, July 18–20. Relations with Austria deteriorated in February after the publication in Austria of disclosures about alleged Soviet and Czechoslovak plans against Austria and Yugoslavia in 1968 made by Gen. Jan Sejna, a former senior Warsaw Pact commander living in the U.S. Prague Radio called the publication of the Sejna article in an Austrian news magazine and an interview with Sejna on Austrian television an attempt by "antidétente circles" to sabotage East-West talks in Geneva and Vienna. A number of frontier incidents soured relations still further. But by June these relations were improving, and on June 25 the Czechoslovak Federal Assembly passed a bill ceding to Austria a small strip of territory at the confluence of the Danube and Morava rivers where Austria, Slovakia, and the Czech province of Moravia meet.

An agreement settling mutual financial claims between the U.S. and Czechoslovakia was reached in Prague on July 6. Czechoslovak spokesmen expressed the hope that the agreement would pave the way for more trade with the U.S. The main point at issue had been the U.S. decision to freeze Czechoslovak gold held by the U.S. until Czechoslovakia had paid compensation for U.S. property nationalized in Czechoslovakia after 1948. Party leader Gustav Husak visited Finland on September 16–19. During his visit, an agreement on the gradual removal of mutual trade barriers was signed.

Relations with the Vatican took a turn for the worse as a result of the sudden death on April 7 of Stepan Cardinal Trochta, archbishop of Litomerice in Slovakia. The cardinal had died of a heart attack after a long interview with a government official on the same day, and Catholic circles in the West claimed that the official had abused and threatened the cardinal. The Czechoslovak government denied these charges.

In December 1973 two additional deputy premiers were appointed: Rudolf Rohlicek, formerly finance minister, and Vlastimil Ehrenberger; Leopold Ler became finance minister, and other changes in the

This pastoral area in Moravia was witness to a record wheat harvest during 1974.

federal Cabinet were made. Hopes of a greater tolerance toward political opponents remained unfulfilled. At the time of the funeral of Josef Smrkovsky (*see* OBITUARIES), one of the most popular leaders during the 1968 reform period, who died of cancer in January, police prevented the attendance of a number of Smrkovsky's friends. In a letter of condolence addressed to Smrkovsky's widow, Alexander Dubcek, party leader in 1968–69, complained that he, Dubcek, and his wife were "dishonoured and undefended" under the present system of "personal power and bureaucratic control" in Czechoslovakia. Dubcek's letter was ignored in the Czechoslovak press but was published in an Italian Communist weekly in March. On the fifth anniversary (April 17) of Dubcek's replacement by Husak in 1969, *Rude Pravo* and other party organs restated the party's line and sharply attacked "right-wing revisionists" such as Dubcek who had brought Czechoslovakia into "mortal peril" in 1968. Pavel Kohout, a prominent dissident writer, told West German correspondents in Prague on February 6 that the literary atmosphere there bore comparison with that in the Soviet Union under Stalin. But two well-known critics of the regime, journalist Jiri Hockmann and writer Ota Filip, were allowed to leave for the West in the summer. In London on March 27 Amnesty International issued a condemnation of deteriorating prison conditions in Czechoslovakia for political prisoners. A law that came into force on July 1 gave the security forces extended powers, to be used circumspectly, to "override civil rights and liberties if the social system, the socialist state, public order or the security of persons or property require it."

In contrast with the rather depressed political scene, the economic one looked a good deal brighter in 1974. Industrial output increased by 6.2% in the first half of the year as compared with the same period in 1973. About 90% of the increase was reported to have been achieved by higher productivity. The ten million-ton grain harvest was a record, and other economic indicators were also positive. The number of live births was 18.8 per 1,000 persons in 1973, as compared with 14.9 in 1968. There was also a corresponding drop in the number of abortions. But Czechoslovakia continued to suffer from an acute labour shortage.

The volume of foreign trade increased by 12.6% in 1973. Imports from the West increased by 24%. In

CZECHOSLOVAKIA

Education. (1973–74) Primary, pupils 1,890,081, teachers 96,781; secondary, pupils 119,563, teachers 7,829; vocational and teacher training, pupils 560,572, teachers 26,900; higher (including 6 main universities), students 108,646, teaching staff 16,697.

Finance. Monetary unit: koruna, with (Sept. 16, 1974) a free exchange rate of 5.90 koruny to U.S. $1 (13.65 koruny = £1 sterling) and a tourist rate of 12.46 koruny to U.S. $1 (23.80 koruny = £1 sterling). Budget (1972 est.): revenue 223.5 billion koruny; expenditure 216,570,000,000 koruny.

Foreign Trade. (1972) Imports 30,912,000,000 koruny; exports 35,588,000,000 koruny. Import sources: U.S.S.R. 33%; East Germany 13%; Poland 8%; West Germany 6%; Hungary 6%. Export destinations: U.S.S.R. 34%; East Germany 11%; Poland 9%; Hungary 5%; West Germany 5%. Main exports: machinery 37%; iron and steel 9%; motor vehicles 9%; chemicals 5%.

Transport and Communications. Roads (1972) 143,886 km. (including 23 km. expressways). Motor vehicles in use (1972): passenger 1,009,075; commercial 216,797. Railways (1972): 13,299 km. (including 2,631 km. electrified); traffic 16,154,000,000 passenger-km., freight (1973) 64,941,000,000 net ton-km. Air traffic (1973): 1,138,400,000 passenger-km.; freight 17,964,000 net ton-km. Navigable inland waterways (1972) 483 km. Shipping (1973): merchant vessels 100 gross tons and over 11; gross tonnage 86,510. Telephones (Dec. 1972) 2,233,000. Radio licenses (Dec. 1972) 3,808,000. Television licenses (Dec. 1972) 3,305,000.

Agriculture. Production (in 000; metric tons; 1973; 1972 in parentheses): wheat c. 4,300 (4,017); barley c. 2,980 (2,651); oats c. 670 (726); rye c. 570 (634); corn c. 690 (642); potatoes c. 4,600 (5,058); sugar, raw value c. 743 (c. 753); beef and veal c. 370 (377); pork c. 684 (681). Livestock (in 000; Jan. 1973): cattle 4,466; pigs 6,093; sheep 889; poultry 39,170.

Industry. Index of industrial production (1970 = 100): (1973) 130; (1972) 131. Fuel and power (in 000; metric tons; 1973): coal 27,776; brown coal 81,828; crude oil 170; electricity (kw-hr.) 53,420,000. Production (in 000; metric tons; 1973): iron ore (30% metal content) 1,672; pig iron c. 8,600; steel 13,149; cement 8,381; sulfuric acid 1,214; fertilizers (nutrient content; 1972–73) nitrogenous 410, phosphate 334; cotton yarn 123; cotton fabrics (m.) 582,000; woolen fabrics (m.) 56,000; rayon and acetate yarn and fibres 72; nylon, etc., yarn and fibres 45; passenger cars (units) 164; commercial vehicles (units) 59. Dwelling units completed (1973) 166,000.

the first six months of 1974 imports from the West went up by 55%, while exports increased by 35.5% in comparison with those of the first half of 1973. Czechoslovakia was affected by international inflation, and about 6 billion koruny (crowns) were earmarked in 1974 to cover increased prices of raw materials and fuels imported from abroad, especially from the non-Communist countries. The first 6.7-km. (4.2-mi.) section of the new Prague underground railway was opened to traffic in May; the whole 93-km. (58-mi.) network was to be completed by the year 2000.

(K. F. CVIIC)

[972.B.2.c]

Dahomey

A republic of West Africa, Dahomey is located north of the Gulf of Guinea and is bounded by Togo, Upper Volta, Niger, and Nigeria. Area: 43,475 sq.mi. (112,-600 sq.km.). Pop. (1973 est.): 2,993,000, mainly Dahomean and allied tribes. Cap.: Porto-Novo (pop., 1971 est., 90,000). Largest city: Cotonou (pop., 1971 est., 152,000). Language: French and local dialects. Religion: animist, with Christian and Muslim minorities. President in 1974, Lieut. Col. Mathieu Kerekou.

The most significant features of the general policy adopted during 1974 by President Kerekou's military regime in Dahomey, which had seized power in October 1972, were continued efforts toward the redefinition of the country's relations with its former French rulers in the light of the new situation, and the adoption of a more pacific attitude toward those who had participated in the previous regime. The three members of the former Presidential Council—former president Hubert Maga, former president Justin Ahomadegbe, and Sourou Migan Apithy, whose turn as president would have come in 1974 but for the seizure of power by Kerekou—continued to be kept under house arrest, but in January and March a number of those who had served as ministers in the previous administration were set free.

In December President Kerekou, in a move apparently aimed at strengthening his regime, announced the establishment of "Defense of the Revolution Committees" in all Dahomean businesses. The committees were charged with the responsibility of

DAHOMEY

Education. (1971–72) Primary, pupils 186,000, teachers (1968–69) 3,594; secondary, pupils 27,000, teachers (1970–71) 505; vocational, pupils 2,000, teachers (1968–69) 102; teacher training, students 2,553; higher, students 600, teaching staff 52.

Finance. Monetary unit: CFA franc, with (Sept. 16, 1974) a parity of CFA Fr. 50 to the French franc and a free rate of CFA Fr. 240.50 to U.S. $1 (CFA Fr. 556.50 = £1 sterling). Budget (1974 est.): receipts CFA Fr. 12,485,000,000; expenditure CFA Fr. 13,-572,000,000.

Foreign Trade. (1971) Imports CFA Fr. 21.2 billion; exports CFA Fr. 11,650,000,000. Import sources: France 38%; West Germany 6%; The Netherlands 6%; U.S. 6%; Japan 5%; U.K. 5%. Export destinations: France 42%; West Germany 13%; Japan 9%; The Netherlands 6%; U.K. 5%; Nigeria 5%. Main exports: palm products 34%; cocoa 24%; cotton 19%.

Agriculture. Production (in 000; metric tons; 1973; 1972 in parentheses): sorghum c. 30 (c. 40); corn (1972) c. 170, (1971) 175; cassava (1972) c. 750, (1971) c. 740; sweet potatoes c. 39 (c. 39); dry beans c. 25 (c. 25); peanuts c. 55 (c. 70); palm kernels c. 60 (c. 55); palm oil c. 45 (c. 42); coffee (1972) c. 2, (1971) 2.5; cotton, lint c. 20 (c. 17). Livestock (in 000; 1972): cattle c. 690; sheep c. 670; goats c. 650; pigs c. 400.

Dairy Products:
see Agriculture and
Food Supplies

Dams:
see Engineering
Projects

disclosing and denouncing "all acts of sabotage." Kerekou criticized various sectors of the population for "mocking" the revolutionary regime.

In September discussions that promised to be both laborious and time-consuming were opened in Paris. Their goal was a new series of cooperation agreements between the French and Dahomean governments. At home, however, relations with the French community in Dahomey, which had deteriorated sharply after the seizure of power by Kerekou's regime, continued to be less than cordial. Indeed, on receiving the pledges of representatives of the Cotonou Chamber of Commerce in January, President Kerekou made no secret of his attitude to that French-dominated organization when he openly described it as a "disreputable institution." (PHILIPPE DECRAENE)

Dance

A major U.S. event in the 1974 dance year was the opening in April of the Harkness Theater in New York City. The building itself, a former movie-vaudeville house and later a television studio, was purchased for more than $1 million and totally renovated especially for dance at a cost of $5 million by dance benefactress Rebekah Harkness, founder-director of the Harkness Ballet, an international troupe, which opened the new theatre with a brief repertory season. The elaborate renovations included proscenium murals that featured nude dancing bodies and a heroic representation of the patroness herself in flowing draperies, and simulated gold fixtures for the rest rooms. Dance figures from all over the U.S. and many from abroad were flown in for opening night as Harkness guests.

Tremendous increases in operating costs caused some established dance institutions to collapse in 1974. After 42 years of daily performances, the oldest resident ballet company in New York City, the Radio City Music Hall Ballet Company, was disbanded, leaving the Rockettes as the Music Hall's only permanent dance troupe. Since the opening of the Music Hall in 1932, many famous dancers had performed there as guest stars, and several teenage girls destined to become ballerinas (Nora Kaye and Melissa Hayden among them) started out in that corps de ballet. Another major departure from the dance scene was the National Ballet of Washington, D.C. Founded in 1963, at the time of its demise it was well established as a successful touring troupe and a regular seasonal performing unit at Washington's Kennedy Center. Also undermined by financial problems was the San Francisco Ballet, one of the oldest dance troupes in the country. Funds to meet a huge deficit and assure production and performing futures were needed if the historic company was to survive.

Grants from the Rockefeller Foundation and the Shubert Foundation and assistance in the form of theatre space brought a new company, the Eliot Feld Ballet, into existence. The company opened May 30 at the New York Shakespeare Festival's Newman Theater. Two new works, both on Jewish themes, *Sephardic Song* and *The Tzaddik*, were presented during the repertory season.

The Dance Theatre of Harlem, the first all-black classical ballet company, made its Broadway debut in the spring following several seasons of touring. Repertory included the traditional *Le Corsaire* pas de deux, George Balanchine's *Concerto Barocco* and

Agon, other works in classical idiom, and ballets with Afro-jazz roots. Among new works offered by the group were Geoffrey Holder's *Dougla* (an adaptation of earlier Holder dances of the same name), Talley Beatty's *Caravanserai,* and Milko Sparemblek's *Ancient Voices of Children.*

The City Center Joffrey Ballet, directed by Robert Joffrey, included among its new works Gerald Arpino's *The Relativity of Icarus* (Gerhard Samuel), Jonathan Watts's *Evening Dialogues* (Robert Schumann), and new productions of Leonide Massine's *Pulcinella* (Stravinsky-Picasso), Sir Frederick Ashton's *Monotones* (Erik Satie), and Jerome Robbins' *New York Export, Op. Jazz* (Robert Prince) with decor by Ben Shahn.

Sharing a long-range, multimillion-dollar Ford Foundation grant with the New York City Opera, the New York City Ballet, with Balanchine and Lincoln Kirstein as its directors, presented several new works at its home theatre in Lincoln Center and one—*Coppélia*—in its summer home at Saratoga Springs, N.Y. *Coppélia* (Délibes) was staged by Alexandra Danilova and Balanchine after Marius Petipa, based on the Saint-Léon Paris original with some newly choreographed sections. Patricia McBride and Helgi Tomasson headed the cast. Other new pieces included Robbins' *Dybbuk* (Leonard Bernstein), based on a Yiddish drama about possession and exorcism; Balanchine's *Variations pour une porte et un soupir;* Robbins' *Four Bagatelles* (Beethoven); and Jacques d'Amboise's *Saltarelli* (Vivaldi).

The American Ballet Theatre opened its season at Lincoln Center with Alvin Ailey's *The River,* dedicated to the memory of its composer, Duke Ellington (*see* OBITUARIES). Other productions included the U.S. premiere of John Neumeier's *Le Baiser de la Fée* (Stravinsky); *Divertissements from Napoli,* extracts from the August Bournonville Danish ballet; and Lar Lubovitch's *Three Essays* (Charles Ives). The company also introduced to New York audiences the Kirov Ballet's Mikhail Baryshnikov who had defected while dancing with a touring unit of the Bolshoi Ballet in Canada. The Soviet star danced *Giselle, La Bayadère,* and the *Don Quixote* grand pas de deux with an earlier Kirov defector, Natalia Makarova. Ballerina Gelsey Kirkland left the New York City Ballet to join the American Ballet Theatre in the fall to dance with Baryshnikov at his request.

Among ballet companies visiting the U.S. were Britain's Royal Ballet in a repertory that featured the U.S. premiere of Kenneth MacMillan's full-length *Manon.* The National Ballet of Canada featured Neumeier's *Don Juan,* with Rudolf Nureyev as guest star in the title role, and Bournonville's *La Sylphide,* also with Nureyev. "Stars of the Bolshoi Ballet" featured the celebrated Soviet ballerina Maya Plisetskaya in a repertory of divertissements and extracts. The U.S. debut of both the Royal Swedish Ballet and the Norwegian National Ballet brought some traditional ballets as well as works that were wholly new to American audiences.

The Pennsylvania Ballet was named a resident company of the Brooklyn Academy of Music and produced new pieces, among them Robert Rodham's *American Rhapsody* (George Gershwin) and John Butler's *Black Angel* (George Crumb). The Boston Ballet, the Cincinnati (Ohio) Ballet, Ballet West, and a number of other non-New York-based professional ballet companies were active in their communities and on extensive regional tours, and the more than

200 nonprofessional ballet companies worked toward major appearances in ballet festivals from coast to coast.

In modern dance, the José Limón Dance Company, which continued to function after the death of its founder, was reconstituted with Ruth Currier, once a principal dancer with the group, as director. The company was not only to perform the works of Limón and the late Doris Humphrey and supervise productions of Limón dances by other companies, both ballet and modern, but also would commission new choreographies. The troupe was engaged as resident unit at the Young Men's and Young Women's Hebrew Association in New York City, which celebrated its 100th anniversary in 1974.

The Alvin Ailey City Center Dance Theater added several new works and revivals to its repertory, among them Janet Collins' new *Canticle of the Elements* (Bach and Villa-Lobos) and John Jones's *Nocturnes.* Other modern dance and avant-garde dance events employing close to 50 dancers and/or groups were those involving Paul Taylor, who created a new full-length work, *American Genesis,* and engaged Nureyev for guest appearances in his *Aureole;* Merce Cunningham, who produced "Events" programs combining new, old, and adapted creations of his own; the Nikolais Dance Theatre (on Broadway) in the premieres of *Cross-Fade* and *Scrolls* as well as older Alwin Nikolais works; the Murray Louis Dance Company (on Broadway) in premieres of *Porcelain Dialogues* and *Scheherazade;* and many others.

Ethnic dance groups and solo artists included Slask (Poland), the Moiseyev Dance Company (U.S.S.R.), Ritha Devi and Bhaskar (India), and representatives

Laura Brown and Paul Russell of the Dance Theatre of Harlem, the first black classical ballet company, opened on Broadway in April to highly favourable notices.

MARTHA SWOPE

of Sri Lanka, Senegal, Hungary, Ecuador, Jamaica, Haiti, Guyana, Spain, Japan, and Korea.

Special events included the formation of the Dance Critics Association, composed of more than 100 North American dance critics, with William Littler of the *Toronto Star* elected as first president. Fernando Bujones won a gold medal at the International Ballet Competition in Varna, Bulg. (the first time a U.S. dancer had won a gold medal in the ten-year history of this competition). The 23rd annual Capezio Dance Award was earned by Robert Joffrey, and the annual Dance Magazine Awards were won by Gerald Arpino, Antony Tudor, and Maurice Béjart. Summer dance highlights centred upon the famed Jacob's Pillow Dance Festival at Lee, Mass., the American Dance Festival at Connecticut College, New London, and the open-air New York Dance Festival in Central Park.

(WALTER TERRY)

The 1973–74 dance season in Britain saw an enormous amount of creative activity with all the companies strengthening their repertories. This was rather less apparent with the Royal Ballet's Covent Garden company, which concentrated more on consolidating its repertory of works suited to an established opera house situation. The main creation was Kenneth MacMillan's *Manon*. MacMillan also revived his *Seven Deadly Sins* (Kurt Weill), originally created for Western Theatre Ballet at the 1961 Edinburgh Festival, and Jerome Robbins revived his *In the Night* (Chopin).

More adventurous was the smaller touring Royal Ballet New Group with new creations from Hans van Manen, *Septet Extra* (Saint-Saëns); David Drew, *Sword of Alsace* (Raff); Ronald Hynd, *Charlotte Brontë* (Douglas Young); and Ashley Killar, *The Entertainers* (Pergolesi). Also revived were John Cranko's *Card Game* (Stravinsky) and Michel Fokine's *Les Sylphides* (Chopin). As well as continual provincial touring, the company gave regular seasons at Sadler's Wells Theatre.

Ballet Rambert also made Sadler's Wells its principal London theatre. To celebrate this, Louis Falco came from the U.S. to create *Tutti-Frutti* (Burt Alcantara). Christopher Bruce created *Duets* (Brian Hodgson) and Norman Morrice, *Isolde* (John Lewis).

In addition, the company's work continued in non-proscenium theatres. For a spring season at the Round House, there were further new works from Bruce, *Weekend* (Hodgson), and from Morrice, *Spindrift* (Lewis). The autumn of 1974 brought the resignation of Morrice, who as artistic director of Ballet Rambert over eight years had been largely responsible for the company's transformation. His co-director, John Chesworth, took over.

The principal touring by a large company to Britain's provincial cities and overseas was again undertaken by London Festival Ballet. Regular London seasons were also given. The repertory of full-length classics gained Ben Stevenson's *Cinderella* (Prokofiev). Revivals included Hynd's *The Fairy's Kiss* (Stravinsky), previously created for Munich; Béjart's *Rose Variations* (Tchaikovsky and Kevin Nutty percussion); and Massine's *Parade* (Satie)—the first time a British company had given this historic piece originally created for Diaghilev in 1917. The major creation was Barry Moreland's *Prodigal Son* in ragtime style (Scott Joplin, Grant Hossack, and others).

For Britain's first regional company, the Scottish Ballet (formerly Scottish Theatre Ballet), it was a year of great development. Director Peter Darrell extended his former second act of *The Nutcracker* (Tchaikovsky) into a full-length work. The repertory of full-length works was enlarged with Bournonville's *La Sylphide* (Lövenskjöld), revived by the Danish ballet master Hans Brenaa. The revival of these classics made it possible for the company to undertake its first overseas tour, across Australia, with Margot Fonteyn as guest ballerina. The other regional company, Northern Dance Theatre based in Manchester, enlarged its repertory with Charles Czarny's *Brandenburg Three* (Bach), Jonathan Thorpe's *Part Exchange* (no music) and *A Woman's Love* (Schumann), and Simon Mottram's *Tchaikovsky Suite* (Tchaikovsky) and *In Concert* (Shostakovich).

Two more regional companies opened up in 1974, though the Irish Ballet, based in Cork, strictly speaking belonged to Europe rather than Britain. The first creations included Joan Denise Moriarty's *Overture* (Tchaikovsky) and Peter Darrell's *Asparas* (Massenet). The first dance company for Wales, Welsh

Antoinette Sibley and Anthony Dowell of the Royal Ballet as they appeared in a sterling performance of "Manon" in London.

ANTHONY CRICKMAY

Rudolf Nureyev and Merle Park performed Stravinsky's "Apollon Musagète" at Versailles in June.

Dance Theatre, was started in the autumn of 1974 in Cardiff and planned to give seasons in the several university theatres in Wales as well as providing a demonstration group for smaller towns and villages.

In a year when London saw more visiting companies than ever before, there were seasons by the Bolshoi, the Royal Danish Ballet, Ballet Théâtre Contemporain, Ballet of the 20th Century, the Australian Ballet, the Dutch National Ballet, and the Netherlands Dance Theatre. From the U.S. came the Louis Falco Dance Company and the Dance Theatre of Harlem.

One of the most important developments in Europe had been the phoenix-like reemergence of the Paris Opéra as a company that not only upheld its great classical traditions but was also moving with contemporary trends in dance. The repertory of classics always associated with the company, such as *Giselle* and *La Sylphide,* had been enlarged with the addition of Pierre Lacotte's *Coppélia.* Other revivals included Léo Staats's *Soir de Fête* (Délibes) and Clustine's *Suite de Dance* (Chopin). Following the practice started in the previous year of devoting an entire evening to a single composer, the company mounted one of Stravinsky works only—Balanchine's *Agon, Orpheus, Apollo,* and *Capriccio* and Robbins' *Scherzo Fantastique.* This practice had also become the policy of the French company Ballet Théâtre Contemporain, now firmly established in Angers. Its Stravinsky program included John Butler's *Kill What I Love,* Lar Lubovitch's *Sans Titre,* Dirk Sanders' *Pasdansés,* and François Adret's danced and sung version of the opera *Le Rossignol.*

Changes of directors brought new life to some of the principal West German ballet companies. John Neumeier, formerly artistic director of the Frankfurt Opera Company, took up the same position with the Hamburg State Opera Ballet. He took with him his new production of *Romeo and Juliet* (Prokofiev); his first major creation for Hamburg was *Meyerbeer/Schumann.* Neumeier was replaced in Frankfurt by

Alfonso Cata, formerly of the Geneva Ballet, who mounted an intimate version of *Sleeping Beauty* (Tchaikovsky) for only 30 dancers. The director to take over the Stuttgart Ballet, as successor to the late John Cranko, was Glen Tetley. The appointment was made after Tetley had created *Voluntaries* (Poulenc).

In The Netherlands, the Dutch National Ballet started to emerge as an important European company. In addition to the full-length classics there were many creations. The director, Rudi van Dantzig, created *Ramifications* (Ligeti/Purcell) and *Orpheus* (Stravinsky); from Hans van Manen came *Adiago Hammerklavier* (Beethoven), *Daphnis and Chloë* (Ravel), and *Rite of Spring* (Stravinsky). The Netherlands Dance Theatre enlarged its repertory with works from Louis Falco and Jennifer Muller.

In Belgium, the Ballet of the 20th Century increased its repertory of works by Béjart with *Golestan* (Iranian traditional) and *Stimmung* (Stockhausen). For the Royal Danish Ballet in Copenhagen it was more a year of revivals with Taylor's *Aureole,* Limón's *The Moor's Pavane,* and Balanchine's *Orpheus,* principally for Nureyev who danced all three as he had at the Paris Opéra. Eske Holm created a new version of *The Firebird* (Stravinsky), and Flemming Flindt an important ballet in the opera *Die Fledermaus* (Strauss). (PETER WILLIAMS)

See also Music; Theatre.
[625]

Defense

The most significant military event of 1974 was the Soviet Union's achievement of strategic superiority vis-à-vis the U.S. When coupled with continuing technical advances making it possible for the two superpowers to engage in controlled, limited, strategic nuclear exchanges, the Soviet drive for strategic supremacy suggested that the leadership expected this military advantage to be exploitable for political ends. No other explanation seemed possible for the massive Soviet investments in strategic forces far in excess of those needed to deter any nuclear threat from the U.S. or China. The U.S., therefore, felt compelled to reenter, however reluctantly, the strategic arms race, which it had sought to contain by the strategic arms limitation talks agreements of May 1972, known collectively as SALT I. The two superpowers were thus engaged in a qualitative and quantitative arms race of unprecedented complexity and expense, while the effects of the preliminary SALT II agreement signed at Vladivostok in November remained, as yet, a largely unknown quantity.

The main elements in the strategic forces of the U.S. and the U.S.S.R. were land-based intercontinental ballistic missiles (ICBMs), submarine-launched ballistic missiles (SLBMs) carried in nuclear-powered ballistic missile submarines (SSBNs), and manned strategic bombers. ICBMs in emplacements known as silos, hardened to withstand overpressures of up to 300 lb. per sq.in. (psi), had formed the perfect system for mutual deterrence; since it took at least four attacking ICBMs to destroy one in its silo, a disarming counterforce first strike was a technical impossibility. This relative invulnerability to surprise attack had been eroded, however, by the development of multiple independently targeted reentry vehicles (MIRVs), which were much more accurate than single warheads and represented a more efficient division of the

Controversial B-1 bomber rolls out at Palmdale, Calif., October 26. Soaring production costs and strategic considerations led a number of congressional critics to question the necessity for this U.S. Air Force program.

ICBM's payload into several smaller warheads. Instead of a single one-megaton warhead, a typical U.S. MIRV for the Minuteman III ICBM carried three warheads of 200 kilotons each. At the same time, the accuracy of ICBMs had been improved, and the U.S. was even developing multiple reaimable reentry vehicles (MARVs), in which the individual warheads could make last-minute adjustments in their course.

When such cumulative improvements were combined with the very large carrying capacity or throw weight of Soviet ICBMs, the result was a significant Soviet capability for a first strike aimed at knocking out the U.S. Minuteman force. Under SALT I, the U.S.S.R. was allowed a maximum of 313 heavy ICBMs of the SS-9 type. A force of 300 SS-9s, with a probable circular error of 25 nautical miles, a reliability of 0.8, and a payload of six two-megaton MIRVs could destroy about 94% of the U.S. force of 1,000 Minuteman ICBMs in hardened silos. Conversely, although the U.S. had tried to avoid acquiring the capability for attacking Soviet missile silos, the current Minuteman MIRV program, when completed, would give the U.S. the ability to destroy some 80% of a Soviet force of 1,500 ICBMs.

Given this increased vulnerability of ICBMs, the superpowers had two alternatives: they could take partial countermeasures to protect their ICBM forces by greater hardening, improved communications facilities, reprogramming capabilities that would enable ICBMs to be retargeted quickly, and the development of mobile ICBMs, or they could scrap them. The U.S. had considered proposing a complete ban on ICBMs at the Conference of the Committee on Disarmament, but rejected the idea as placing too much reliance on the SLBM and the manned bomber. In any case, the U.S.S.R.'s commitment to the ICBM as its preferred means of acquiring strategic superiority made Soviet agreement to such a proposal unlikely. Instead, both the U.S. and the U.S.S.R. were modernizing their ICBM forces while developing doctrines for their use in limited strategic nuclear exchanges that would be confined to strikes at military targets.

In many ways, "strategic arms race" was an inadequate description of the complex relationship between the strategic force programs of the U.S. and the U.S.S.R. The U.S. had unilaterally held its strategic forces to 1,054 ICBMs, 41 SSBNs, and about 300–500 manned bombers and was engaged in relatively limited modernization, including MIRV, while the U.S.S.R. had engaged in a massive expansion of its strategic forces that stressed quantitative programs.

By mid-1974 the Soviets had 1,575 ICBMs, of which 1,018 were SS-11s, first deployed in 1966 and comparable to the U.S. Minuteman, with a range of 6,500 mi. and armed with a one- or two-megaton warhead or three multiple reentry vehicles (MRVs) in the kiloton range. The much larger SS-9, of which 288 were deployed, had a range of 7,500 mi. and carried a warhead of 20–25 megatons or three 4–5-megaton MRVs. There were also 209 of the older SS-7s and SS-8s, with a range of 6,900 mi. and a five-megaton warhead, plus 60 SS-13s with a 5,000-mi. range and a one-megaton warhead. In addition, the Soviets had 12 ordinary ICBM silos and 25 heavy silos under construction, which would give them 1,587 ICBMs out of the ceiling of 1,618 allowed under SALT. Four new ICBMs were being developed: the SS-X-18 liquid-fueled missile similar to the SS-9; the SS-X-17 and the SS-X-19, two liquid-fueled missiles intended to replace the SS-11 but with a throw weight three to five times greater; and the SS-X-16, a solid-fueled ICBM similar to the SS-13. Once these were deployed, the Soviet throw weight would increase from the current 6 million–7 million lb. to 10 million–12 million lb., against 1 million–2 million lb. for the U.S., and the U.S.S.R. would be able to deliver 7,000 separately targeted warheads in the megaton range, compared with the U.S. ability to deliver 2,000 similar warheads.

The Soviets had 33 Y-class SSBNs, each carrying 16 SS-N-6 SLBMs with a range of 1,750 mi., and 9 D-class SSBNs, each carrying 12 SS-N-8 SLBMs with a range of 4,800 mi.; both missiles had warheads in the megaton range. There were also 8 H-class SSBNs, each carrying 3 SS-N-5 SLBMs with a range of 750 mi., plus 20 diesel submarines carrying short-range SLBMs that were essentially obsolete and were not counted as strategic missiles under SALT I. Thus the Soviet Union had increased its SLBM force to 720

Approximate Strengths of Regular Armed Forces of the World

Country	Military personnel in 000s Army	Navy	Air force	Warships Aircraft carriers (CV)/ cruisers (CA/CL)	Submarines*	Destroyers/ frigates	Total major surface combat vessels	Jet aircraft Bombers†	Fighters	Tanks‡	Defense expenditure as % of GNP
I. NATO											
Belgium	65.0	4.2	20.0	—	—	—	—	80 FB	36	482	2.0
Canada	33.0	14.0	36.0	—	4	24	24	96 FB	66	332	1.8
Denmark	21.5	6.0	9.5	—	6	6	6	60 FB	40	200	1.9
France§	331.5	69.0	102.0	2 CV, 2 CA	19, 3 FBMS	45	49	236 FB, 36 SB	120	910	3.1
Germany, West	340.0	39.0	111.0	—	13	23	23	476 FB	60	3,560	2.9
Greece	121.0	18.0	22.0	—	7	13	13	120 FB	54	860	3.4
Italy	306.5	44.5	70.0	3 CA	9	20	34	135 FB	90	1,300	2.9
Luxembourg	0.5	—	—	—	—	—	—	—	—	—	1.0
Netherlands, The	75.0	19.0	20.0	1 CA	6	16	17	108 FB	36	885	3.3
Norway	18.0	8.0	8.9	—	15	5	5	70 FB	16	116	3.3
Portugal	180.0	19.5	18.5	—	4	8	8	30 FB	30	100	4.7
Turkey	365.0	40.0	48.0	—	15	14	14	162 FB	58	1,800	3.7
United Kingdom‖	178.3	86.1	98.2	3 CV, 2 CA	22, 8 N, 4 FBMS	67	72	150 B, 210 FB	135	900	4.9
United States‖	997.5	551.0	645.0	15 CV, 5 CA, 4 CL	12, 61 N, 41 FBMS	95	177	1,400 FB, 503 SB	1,240	...	6.2
II. WARSAW PACT											
Bulgaria	120.0	10.0	22.0	—	2	—	—	72 FB	148	2,000	2.5
Czechoslovakia	155.0	—	45.0	—	—	—	—	168 FB	252	3,400	3.8
Germany, East	100.0	17.0	28.0	—	—	2	2	40 FB	294	2,000	5.3
Hungary	90.0	0.5	13.0	—	—	—	—	36 FB	72	1,500	2.5
Poland	220.0	25.0	58.0	—	4	4	4	30 B, 200 FB	432	3,400	3.7
Romania	141.0	9.0	21.0	—	—	—	—	80 FB	200	1,700	1.7
U.S.S.R.	1,800.0	475.0	900.0	1 CV, 33 CA	140, 30 N, 42 FBMS, 8 N/BMSS, 20 BMSS, 40 N/CMS, 25 CMS	76	110	700 B, 3,000 FB, 100 SB	4,000	33,600	5.4
III. OTHER EUROPEAN											
Albania	30.0	3.0	5.0	—	4	—	—	—	72	85	...
Austria	33.0	—	4.3	—	—	—	—	38 FB	—	320	0.9
Finland	30.3	2.5	3.0	—	—	3	3	—	47	...	1.5
Ireland	11.3	0.4	0.6	—	—	—	—	—	3	—	1.3
Spain‖	208.0	43.0	33.0	1 CV, 1 CA	6	20	22	145 FB	—	550	1.9
Sweden	57.6	14.8	13.7	—	20	12	12	150 FB	360	...	3.1
Switzerland	33.5	—	9.0	—	—	—	—	240 FB	30	620	1.7
Yugoslavia	190.0	20.0	20.0	—	5	1	1	125 FB	110	2,150	4.5
IV. MIDDLE EAST AND MEDITERRANEAN; SUB-SAHARAN AFRICA; LATIN AMERICA¶											
Algeria	55.0	3.5	4.5	—	—	—	—	115 FB, 30 B	35	400	4.5
Egypt	280.0	15.0	28.0	—	12	5	5	238 FB, 30 B	210	2,000	32.8
Iran	175.0	13.0	50.0	—	—	7	7	196 FB	—	1,160	9.3
Iraq	100.0	2.0	10.5	—	—	—	—	80 FB, 8 B	130	1,300	9.4
Israel♀	12.5/375.0	4.5/5.0	16.0/20.0	—	2	—	—	408 FB, 10 B	42	1,900	47.8
Jordan	70.0	—	4.6	—	—	—	—	32 FB	18	490	15.3
Lebanon	14.0	—	1.0	—	—	—	—	8 FB	10	60	...
Libya	25.0	2.0	5.0	—	—	1	1	20 FB	32	271	2.8
Morocco	50.0	2.0	4.0	—	—	1	1	24 FB	24	120	3.5
Saudi Arabia	36.0	1.5	5.5	—	—	—	—	55 FB	35	55	21.8
Sudan	40.0	0.6	3.0	—	—	—	—	17 FB	24	130	5.9
Syria	125.0	2.5	10.0	—	—	—	—	90 FB	200	1,600	14.9
Ethiopia	40.9	1.4	2.2	—	—	—	—	12 FB, 4 B	8	50	2.8
Nigeria	200.0	5.0	5.0	—	—	1	1	21 FB, 3 B	—	—	2.0
S. Africa	34.5	4.5	8.5	—	3	8	8	95 FB, 18 B	56	120	2.5
Zaire	49.0	—	0.8	—	—	—	—	—	15	—	2.0
Argentina	85.0	36.0	17.0	1 CV, 3 CA	6	11	15	75 FB, 11 B	12	120	1.3
Brazil	130.0	43.0	35.0	1 CV, 1 CA	7	21	23	—	16	190	2.1
Chile	32.0	18.0	10.0	3 CA	2	7	10	—	32	76	2.7
Colombia	50.0	7.2	6.0	—	2	5	5	—	18	—	1.0
Cuba	90.0	6.5	20.0	—	—	3	3	15 FB	190	600	6.2
Mexico	65.0	11.0	6.0	—	—	11	11	12 FB	—	—	0.7
Peru	39.0	8.0	7.0	3 CL	4	7	10	15 B	30	260	2.9
V. FAR EAST AND OCEANIA¶											
Australia	31.2	16.1	21.5	1 CV	4	9	10	66 FB, 8 B	—	143	3.3
Bangladesh	17.0	0.5	1.0	—	—	—	—	—	18	—	...
Burma	145.0	7.0	7.0	—	6	1	1	—	—	—	2.9
Cambodia	200.0	11.0	9.5	—	—	—	—	—	—	—	...
China‖δ	2,500.0	230.0	220.0	—	47	17	17	500 FB, 400 B	3,100	1,500	3.1
India	826.0	30.0	100.0	1 CV, 2 CL	6	24	27	257 FB, 60 B	400	1,700	3.2
Indonesia	200.0	40.0	30.0	—	5	9	9	17 FB, 32 B	27	520	0.8
Japan	154.0	38.1	40.9	—	14	43	43	120 FB	250	520	0.8
Korea, North	410.0	17.0	40.0	—	4	—	—	328 FB, 70 B	200	900	24.9
Korea, South‖	580.0	20.0	25.0	—	—	6	6	200 FB	—	1,000	3.8
Laos	60.0	—	2.3	—	—	—	—	—	—	—	11.0
Malaysia	56.1	4.8	5.3	—	—	2	2	16 FB	—	—	4.3
New Zealand	5.5	2.9	4.3	—	—	4	4	24 FB	—	—	1.7
Pakistan	365.0	10.0	17.0	—	3	6	6	245 FB, 10 B	21	950	5.5
Philippines	35.0	11.0	9.0	—	—	1	1	16 FB	20	—	1.3
Taiwan‖	375.0	36.0	80.0	—	—	18	18	90 FB	98	800	7.2
Thailand‖	130.0	23.5	42.0	—	—	7	7	11 FB	—	—	3.6
Vietnam, North	570.0	3.0	10.0	—	—	—	—	100 FB, 8 B	90	900	21.5
Vietnam, South‖	465.0	40.0	60.0	—	—	9	9	132 FB	—	600	21.4

Note: Data exclude paramilitary, security, and irregular forces. Naval data exclude vessels of less than 100 tons standard displacement. Figures are for July 1974.
*Nuclear hunter-killers (N); fleet ballistic missile submarines (FBMS); (nuclear/) ballistic missile submarines, short-range (BMSS, N/BMSS); (nuclear/) long-range cruise missile submarines (CMS, N/CMS).
†Medium and heavy bombers (B), fighter-bombers (FB), and strategic bombers (SB).
‡Medium and heavy tanks (31 tons and over).
§French forces were withdrawn from NATO in 1966, but France remains a member of NATO.
‖Includes Marine Corps.
¶Sections IV and V list only those states with significant military forces.
♀Second figure is fully mobilized strength.
δApproximate.
Sources: International Institute for Strategic Studies, 18 Adam Street, London, *The Military Balance 1974-1975, Strategic Survey 1973.*

(92 more than a year earlier) in 70 SSBNs and would reach the SALT I ceiling of 62 modern SSBNs by 1977, when the SLBM total would be 744 as against the SALT I ceiling of 950. The U.S.S.R. also maintained a small strategic bomber force composed of 100 Tu-95s and 40 Mya-4s. In addition, the new Backfire bomber was expected to enter service with a range and refueling capability that would enable it to function as a strategic bomber.

In reply, the U.S. was trying to modernize its existing forces while developing new systems for later deployment. Its ICBM forces comprised 21 Minuteman Is and 450 Minuteman IIs, both with a range of 8,000 mi. and carrying warheads in the one–two-megaton range, or three smaller MRVs, plus 529 Minuteman IIIs, each with three 200-kiloton MIRVs. There were also 54 Titan II liquid-fueled missiles with warheads in the five–ten-megaton range. The current MIRV program called for deployment of 550 Minuteman IIIs by 1975. All Minuteman silos were to be hardened to withstand more than 300 psi, and a new command data buffer system that allowed rapid retargeting was to be installed. Other projects that would be started if the U.S.S.R. did not display restraint included improvements in the accuracy of Minuteman III, deployment of MARV, and, ultimately, the development of a new, large-payload ICBM capable of being launched from existing silos.

The U.S. had devoted more attention to its SLBM force, which consisted of 22 submarines carrying 352 Poseidon SLBMs with a range of 2,880 mi. and 10–14 50-kiloton MIRV warheads, and 19 submarines carrying 160 Polaris SLBMs with a range of 2,880 mi. and three 200-kiloton MRVs. The program for converting 11 Polaris submarines to carry Poseidon was scheduled for completion by mid-1977. This would leave the U.S. within the SALT I ceilings. Thereafter the surviving Polaris submarines would be replaced by the new Trident submarine, carrying 24 Trident I missiles with a range of 4,600 mi. and MIRV/MARV warheads. The Trident I SLBM could also be deployed in SSBNs that were carrying the Poseidon. The U.S. strategic bomber force had been reduced to 277 B-52s and 66 FB-111As, all fitted with the new short-range attack missile (SRAM). Any decision on replacing the B-52s with B-1 supersonic bombers was unlikely before 1976.

DISARMAMENT

Against this background, efforts to restrain the development and deployment of new weapons continued to be made, though whether they could abate the intensive superpower competition in strategic and conventional weapons remained to be seen. On November 24 U.S. Pres. Gerald Ford and Soviet General Secretary Leonid Brezhnev signed a preliminary agreement placing overall limits on the number of strategic delivery vehicles and MIRVs that could be deployed by each superpower. Although the details remained to be worked out, the published information suggested that within the agreed limits there was still considerable room for qualitative and quantitative improvement. Earlier, in July, Brezhnev and then U.S. Pres. Richard Nixon concluded a comprehensive test ban treaty— but with a threshold of permitted explosions sufficient to allow continued testing of small nuclear weapons—and formalized the de facto limitation of antiballistic missile (ABM) deployment to one site each. Meanwhile, India detonated its first nuclear device, nominally described as a peaceful nuclear ex-

plosive, and the countries of the third world continued to insist that they had a right to conduct their own conventional arms races.

The preliminary SALT II agreement was announced with almost no advance publicity at a summit meeting held in Okeanskaya (a resort area in Vladivostok) on the Soviet Pacific coast. According to the joint statement issued on November 24, the new agreement, the exact terms of which were to be negotiated at SALT II in Geneva beginning in January 1975, would incorporate the relevant provisions of the Interim Agreement Limiting Offensive Missiles (SALT I), which was due to expire in October 1977, and would cover the period from October 1977 to Dec. 31, 1985.

Information released following President Ford's return to the U.S. indicated that the aggregate limit on strategic delivery vehicles (including ICBMs, SLBMs, and strategic bombers) was to be set at about 2,400 for each power. Each bomber would count as a single launcher. Within this aggregate, about 1,300 ICBMs and SLBMs apiece could be equipped with MIRV—a limit that the U.S. was not expected to reach until Trident was deployed in the mid-1980s. U.S. Secretary of State Henry Kissinger, who described the agreement as a "breakthrough," told a press briefing that no current U.S. military programs would be affected.

Earlier, during his visit to Moscow in March to prepare for the June–July summit meeting between Nixon and Brezhnev, Kissinger had sought unsuccessfully to bring about a "conceptual breakthrough" in SALT II that would halt MIRV programs where they were, limit testing of MIRVs, and limit the throw weight of total strategic forces, including those not covered by SALT I. The Soviets rejected this even in principle, and the summit produced only the largely symbolic test ban and ABM agreements.

A comprehensive test ban treaty had long been regarded as the most important single qualitative restraint on superpower acquisition of potentially destabilizing capabilities. To launch a disarming counterforce first strike, the attacker would first need to have very high confidence in the reliability of his MIRV, and this could only come from an extensive testing program. The 1963 partial test ban treaty allowed underground detonations, which could be used for this purpose, but a comprehensive ban would prevent the testing of MIRVs, as well as of ABM warheads and the new generation of miniature nuclear weapons (mininukes) being developed by the U.S. The treaty signed in Moscow in July allowed underground nuclear explosions up to 150 kilotons, sufficient to test most MIRV warhead designs and to develop mininukes, and even this very limited ban would not come into force until March 31, 1976.

The July 1974 agreement to hold ABM deployment at one site apiece was of minor importance, since neither the U.S. nor the U.S.S.R. was anxious to deploy more of its existing ABM systems when new ones were becoming available. The U.S. Safeguard ABM defense for the Minuteman force at Grand Forks, N.D., would become operational in mid-1975. The U.S.S.R. was holding its ABM system defending Moscow to 64 Galosh long-range interceptors, with a new interceptor being tested.

Prospects for containing nuclear proliferation declined in 1974. The nonproliferation treaty of 1968 had attempted to persuade states with nuclear weapons not to disseminate them or the technology for their manufacture, while the nonnuclear states agreed not to seek nuclear weapons or the capability for making them. Of the nuclear powers, the U.S., the U.K., and the U.S.S.R. signed while France and China did not. Of the nonnuclear powers with a significant capability for manufacturing nuclear weapons, India, Argentina, Brazil, and South Africa had refused to sign while Japan had signed but had not ratified.

All the nonnuclear states had insisted on their rights to develop nuclear energy for peaceful purposes, chiefly the generation of electricity, and to use "peaceful nuclear explosives" for releasing oil and natural gas and for large-scale excavations; hence India's claim that its first nuclear device, detonated at Rajasthan on May 18, 1974, was a peaceful nuclear explosive. Unfortunately, the nuclear technology needed for peaceful purposes was also suitable for rapid conversion to military uses.

The pessimistic view was that India's lead would be followed by other states, the most likely being, in order of probability, Israel, Japan, Egypt, Argentina and Brazil, and South Africa. The optimistic view was that proliferation would remain relatively slow, relatively manageable, and limited. Although the future rate of proliferation would probably fall somewhere between the two estimates, it was clear that the overall prospects for effective arms control were much less bright.

After 50 years, the U.S. Senate finally ratified the 1925 Geneva Protocol against chemical warfare, although the administration retained reservations concerning certain uses of herbicides and tear gas. The Senate also ratified a 1972 treaty outlawing the production and stockpiling of biological weapons.

NATO

The negotiations on mutual and balanced force reductions (MBFR) in Europe, which had opened in Vienna on Oct. 30, 1973, symbolized the problems facing NATO. Geographic and political considerations—the U.S.S.R. was much closer to Central Europe than the U.S. and faced none of the political difficulties that might inhibit a U.S. defense of Europe in a conventional war—introduced asymmetries into the NATO-Warsaw Pact balance in Europe that favoured the WP. To lessen these asymmetries, NATO was seeking a reduction of the WP's superiority in the means for surprise attack, chiefly tanks. In contrast, the WP was seeking equal percentage reductions in the two forces, a process of mutual force reductions (MFR) rather than MBFR.

The initial proposals by the two sides reflected their different objectives. The Soviets suggested a three-stage reduction proportionate to the size of the WP and NATO forces. In Stage I (1975) there would be an equal manpower reduction of 20,000 from each of the two sides; in Stage II (1976) the reduction would be 5% on either side; and in Stage III (1977), a further 10%. The Stage I reductions would include nuclear and air force units, as well as ground forces, and all reductions would be symmetrical, the withdrawal of a given WP unit being matched by the withdrawal of a NATO unit comparable in size and type. Foreign units that were withdrawn would take their equipment with them while indigenous units would be disbanded. Subsequently, the Soviet and other WP delegations insisted that the first phase must cover all 11 direct participants (the U.S.S.R., Czechoslovakia, East Germany, and Poland for the WP; the U.S., Canada, Belgium, The Netherlands, Luxembourg, the U.K., and West Germany for NATO), though this stand was later abandoned in favour of initial reductions by the two superpowers. The Soviets also advocated—both at the Vienna talks and in SALT II—a reduction in the U.S. forward based systems for delivering tactical nuclear weapons which, to the Western Europeans, symbolized the U.S. nuclear guarantee.

The U.S. proposal suggested a two-phase reduction. In Phase I the U.S. would withdraw 20,000 men from unspecified units while the Soviets would withdraw 68,000 men, all from specified tank units. In Phase II, to be negotiated after Phase I had been agreed, both sides would come down to a common ceiling of 700,-000-man ground forces. There was little sign of progress in the negotiations after the initial proposals were introduced. The only possibility for an agreement appeared to be a political decision by the U.S. to accept a token cutback by the superpowers of 20,000–30,000 men each, with symbolic allied reductions, the whole package symbolizing détente. President Ford was reported to be opposed to such a concession, as were West Germany, France (which was boycotting the negotiations), and the U.K. Meanwhile, the difficulty of maintaining NATO forces at their current level in an age of superpower détente was emphasized by the Dutch decision, temporarily postponed under NATO pressure, to cut 20,000 men from The Netherlands' 113,000-man armed forces.

That the military balance favoured the WP rather than NATO was still disputed by the U.S. Quantitatively the WP was certainly superior. The NATO figures used in the MBFR negotiations set WP ground combat forces at 925,000, as against 770,000 for NATO, and main battle tanks at 15,500 for the WP, compared with NATO's 6,000. Of these forces, 199,-000 were U.S. ground units, out of a total for U.S. forces in Western Europe (including air and naval units) of 310,000, compared with Soviet ground forces of 470,000 on the Central Front. The latest U.S. studies suggested that NATO's qualitative superiority would enable the alliance to conduct a successful conventional defense for up to 90 days, but this conclusion was rejected by the Western European NATO members.

On the broader political front, relations between Washington and its Western European allies eased somewhat after the strains caused by the 1973 Arab-Israeli war and the resulting oil crisis, an improvement reflected in the Declaration on Atlantic Relations, signed June 19 at Ottawa, in which the allies promised to consult together more fully on matters of common interest. How far they would live up to this obligation remained open to question. President Nixon's resig-

continued on page 218

"All God's chillun got N-power."

OLIPHANT, THE DENVER POST 1974 © THE LOS ANGELES TIMES SYNDICATE

CYPRUS AND THE GREAT POWER BALANCE

By Robert J. Ranger

The Turkish invasion of Cyprus in July–August 1974 demonstrated the truth of the dictum that war is an extension of diplomacy by other means. In ten days of fighting, Turkey achieved the security of the Turkish Cypriots—a minority of 116,000 in a population of 632,000—for which it had unsuccessfully negotiated with Greece for ten years. Conversely, Greece, by attempting a coup in Cyprus that it lacked the military strength to support, lost the gains of the past decade and set off a chain of events that brought down the military junta that had ruled since 1967.

This limited fighting between two of its members imposed great strains on the NATO alliance, but these were not as serious as they first appeared, since the so-called southern flank of NATO would only be threatened in the unlikely event of a direct Soviet military thrust. Nevertheless, the military balance in the southern Mediterranean had certainly swung in favour of the Warsaw Pact. The real losers seemed likely to be the U.S., which was attempting to maintain bases in Greece and Turkey in the face of local opposition, and the U.K., which maintained two Sovereign Base Areas in Cyprus of extreme importance to NATO.

The Military Action. Under the Zürich-London agreements of 1959, Cyprus had been established as a state whose independence was guaranteed by the U.K., the former colonial power, and Greece and Turkey as representatives of the two main national groups on the island. Fighting between the Greek and Turkish Cypriots in 1964 had led to the establishment of the UN Peacekeeping Force in Cyprus (UNFICYP) to supervise the cease-fire between the two groups.

By 1974 the Cypriot president, Archbishop Makarios, faced opposition on two fronts: the Greek military regime was continuing its pressure aimed at *enosis*, the union of Cyprus with Greece, while the Cypriot Communist Party had polled about 30% of the votes in recent elections. On July 15 Greece moved to head off this growing Communist influence by instigating a coup in Cyprus, headed by Greek officers of the Cypriot National Guard whom Makarios had been trying to remove. (*See* CYPRUS.) Turkey responded by placing its armed forces on alert, and on July 20 a Turkish force, estimated at 6,000 troops and 40 tanks, was landed from an invasion force of 5 destroyers/destroyer escorts, 20 medium landing craft, and 5 small landing craft, operating under a Turkish air umbrella.

These forces met negligible opposition. A temporary cease-fire was declared on August 9 but, after Turkey had brought in reinforcements raising its forces to some 40,000 men with about 400 tanks, artillery, and air support, fighting was renewed on August 14. By the time the cease-fire announced on August 16 actually took effect, Turkey had advanced to a line from Lefka to Nicosia to Famagusta and thus effectively controlled the northern 40% of the island. It seemed likely that Turkey would be

Robert J. Ranger is assistant professor of political science at St. Francis Xavier University, Antigonish, Nova Scotia, and a long-time contributor to the Britannica Book of the Year.

able to legitimatize its military gains through diplomatic negotiations, since there was no countervailing military force.

The relatively easy Turkish conquest of northern Cyprus was made possible by Turkey's military superiority as compared with Greece and the geographic position of Cyprus, which is much closer to Turkey.

A rough comparison of forces indicates Turkey's overwhelming quantitative superiority: an army of 365,000 men to Greece's 121,000; 1,800 medium tanks to Greece's 860; reserves of 750,000 to Greece's 230,000. In air power, the Turkish Air Force of 48,000 men and 290 combat aircraft was marginally superior to Greece's 22,700 men and 220 combat aircraft. The 40,000-man Turkish Navy, though small, was adequate to ferry troops and tanks from Turkey to Cyprus and considerably overbalanced the Greek Navy of 17,500 men. Turkey was also better provided with air transport.

Qualitative factors were also important. Once Turkey decided to intervene in Cyprus, it could be sure of the local air and sea supremacy needed to land and supply enough troops to overwhelm the few Greek Cypriot forces. Greece could counter only by threatening a limited attack against Turkish positions on its border, but such threats would have lacked military or political credibility. In addition, the prolonged involvement of the Greek military in politics had made political, rather than military, qualities important in gaining and holding promotion. Thus Greece was reported to have experienced considerable difficulties, including the absence of equipment apparently sold on the black market, when it attempted a limited mobilization.

The NATO Connection. Under these circumstances, the Greeks' only hope of halting Turkey's military offensive in Cyprus lay in mobilizing NATO's other members, especially the U.S., against Turkey. But it was by no means clear that Greece could do this, or that such pressure as other NATO countries might bring to bear would suffice to turn Turkey back from what it saw as a legitimate use of force in defense of its vital national interests and honour.

The U.S. and its secretary of state, Henry Kissinger, were in a particularly delicate position. U.S. military and financial aid had enabled the Greek military junta to survive for seven years. Furthermore, it was widely believed that the U.S. Central Intelligence Agency (CIA) had had advance notice of the July 15 coup attempt and had condoned—if not encouraged—it because it appeared to be anti-Communist. Turkey was therefore disinclined to listen to Kissinger's appeals to stop the fighting in Cyprus. At the same time, Kissinger was caught in a wave of Greek anti-Americanism, directed at his failure to halt Turkey and at U.S. support of the junta that had just been replaced by a civilian government under Konstantinos Karamanlis.

Kissinger threatened to withhold U.S. financial and military aid if a conflict broke out between Greece and Turkey, but the pressure he could put on Turkey was limited by its greater military importance to the U.S. and NATO. Turkish facilities at the alliance's disposal included U.S. naval bases at Istanbul, Izmir, and Iskenderun and a NATO airbase at Adana. In addition—and probably crucially—the U.S. depended on radar and electronics warfare facilities in Turkey to track Soviet intercontinental ballistic missiles on the test range in the southern U.S.S.R. These facilities alone were vital to the U.S. Greece, on the other hand, was of relatively less importance. The basing facilities for the U.S. 6th Fleet at Piraeus were not yet fully developed and were a source of domestic criticism in the U.S. The only other naval facility was at Suda Bay, in Crete, where there was also a NATO airbase at Iraklion.

The most important NATO facilities in the area were the British Sovereign Base Areas at Akrotiri and Dhekelia in Cyprus, established under the Zürich-London agreements. These provided bases for maritime reconnaissance over the eastern Aegean, as well as the Syrian, Lebanese, Israeli, and Egyptian coasts, thus enabling the U.K. to monitor the activities of the Soviet Mediterranean squadron. There were also highly important facilities

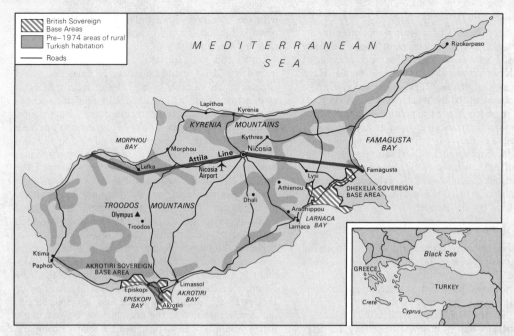

MEDITERRANEAN SEA

Rizokarpaso

Lapithos
Kyrenia
KYRENIA MOUNTAINS
MORPHOU BAY
Kythrea
FAMAGUSTA BAY
Morphou
Attila Line
Nicosia
Lefka
Nicosia Airport
Famagusta
Lysi
Athienou
DHEKELIA SOVEREIGN BASE AREA
Dhali
TROODOS MOUNTAINS
Aradhippou
Olympus ▲
LARNACA BAY
Troodos
Larnaca
Ktima
Paphos
AKROTIRI SOVEREIGN BASE AREA
Limassol
Episkopi
AKROTIRI BAY
EPISKOPI BAY
Akrotiri

Black Sea
GREECE
TURKEY
Crete
Cyprus

Map of Cyprus showing the Attila Line, a demarcation zone between Turkish forces to the north and Greek Cypriot forces to the south.

for electronics warfare against the U.S.S.R. and for nuclear strikes against the U.S.S.R. in time of war, as well as large stockpiles of equipment for use in a limited war in the Middle East. The conflict in Cyprus was thus of more than purely local significance, since it exposed the relative strategic vulnerability of NATO's southern flank to Soviet pressure.

The Other Side. The military balance in the area certainly favoured the Soviet Union. In the southern U.S.S.R. there were 21 mechanized infantry and 2 tank divisions—each with about 10,000 men—with approximately 6,000 medium tanks, although these forces were not combat ready. Perhaps more important were seven airborne divisions, with a total of about 70,000 men, and a sizable air transport force. The local Soviet air force, with about 1,000 aircraft plus naval air force units on the Black Sea coast, could probably gain and hold local air superiority. The Soviet Black Sea Fleet, which provided the base from which the Mediterranean squadron was drawn, comprised 20 submarines and 60 major surface combat vessels, usually including one of the two Moskva-class antisubmarine warfare (ASW) helicopter cruisers, Kara- and Kresta-class ASW cruisers, and various classes of destroyers, many equipped with surface-to-air and surface-to-surface missiles. This naval force also had about half the total force of some 17,000 naval infantry, the Soviet equivalent of the U.S. Marines, organized in brigades and equipped with standard infantry weapons.

Besides these Soviet forces, there were those of its Warsaw Pact allies. Bulgaria, bordering on Turkey, was a loyal ally of the U.S.S.R. and fielded substantial forces, including an army of 120,000 men composed of eight motorized rifle divisions and five well-equipped tank brigades. The 22,000-man Air Force had 267 combat aircraft, including 72 MiG-17 fighter-bombers and 148 interceptors. The Navy was limited to coastal defense. Romania, between the U.S.S.R. and Bulgaria, was the only Warsaw Pact country not occupied by Soviet forces and had shown considerable independence in its foreign policy. In the last resort, however, it would be forced to side with the U.S.S.R., certainly if the Soviets moved against NATO's southern flank. This would add Romania's army of 141,000 men, composed of two tank and eight motorized rifle divisions, two mountain brigades, and one airborne regiment, and its air force with 21,000 men and 290 combat aircraft.

Of the other two Balkan powers, Yugoslavia did not belong to the Warsaw Pact and, unlike the Pact members, did not have a bilateral treaty of friendship and mutual assistance with the U.S.S.R. Yugoslavia's forces were intended to delay a Soviet invasion as long as possible, creating an opportunity for Western

intervention and making the costs and risks involved greater than any gains the Soviets might hope to achieve. Yugoslavia spent 4.5% of its gross national product on defense. It had an army of 190,000 with some 2,150 medium tanks, an air force of 20,000 with 275 combat aircraft, among them 110 MiG-21 fighters, and a 20,000-man navy. The Territorial Defense Force (reserves) was being increased from one million to three million, suggesting that Yugoslavia feared Soviet military action in the Balkans or eastern Mediterranean in the near future. These Yugoslav forces could not, therefore, be said to threaten Greece, despite the long Yugoslav-Greek border. Yugoslavia's other southern neighbour, Albania, was a political anomaly, with a neo-Stalinist government allied to China and opposed to both Yugoslavia and Greece. Albania's military forces were negligible.

The Larger Balance. This preponderance of Warsaw Pact forces in the eastern Mediterranean explained NATO's perennial fear for its southern flank, represented by Greece and Turkey, and its reaction when their hostility to one another nearly led them into war over Cyprus. They were sandwiched between the Soviet Union—anxious to control the Dardanelles and thus its access to the Mediterranean from the Black Sea—to the north and the U.S.S.R.'s Arab allies, notably Syria, to the south.

Yet, paradoxically, the vulnerability of Greece and Turkey to direct Soviet military pressure enabled them to feel free to use force against each other in Cyprus. Because they were vulnerable militarily they were not vulnerable politically. Since any concessions to the U.S.S.R. would inevitably lead to more demands, they could not afford to make the first concession. In the end any Soviet threat of military action against either Greece or Turkey or both would certainly be met by a NATO counterthreat, ultimately resting on U.S. willingness to use the tactical nuclear weapons it had stationed in those countries for their defense. Thus the Soviets could exploit their military superiority against Greece and Turkey only in the context of a general European conflict in which their fate would be essentially irrelevant.

An uneasy truce could be expected to prevail in the eastern Mediterranean area between Greece and Cyprus. UNFICYP with its 4,400 men would continue to police whatever boundary line was drawn between the Turkish and Greek Cypriot areas, but it would lack the power to punish any violations of the ceasefire or to prevent a renewal of fighting by Greek Cypriot guerrillas against the Turkish invaders. In a broader sense, Turkey's controlled use of military force for clearly defined political ends served as a reminder that force remained the most effective instrument of diplomacy, even in a nuclear age. The lesson would not be lost in either the Arab nations or Israel.

continued from page 215

nation deprived NATO of a strong supporter in the White House, although his successor seemed equally well disposed to the alliance. The appointment of President Nixon's top aide, Gen. Alexander M. Haig, Jr., as the new supreme Allied commander, Europe (Saceur), was resented by Washington's NATO partners, who regarded him as a political general whose highest combat command had been as a colonel. His appointment was delayed until December 15 in case he should be implicated in the Watergate scandals. The lack of unity within NATO was epitomized by the July-August clash between Greece and Turkey in Cyprus, which nearly led to a war between two NATO members. (*See* Special Report.)

UNITED STATES

The new U.S. strategic targeting doctrine announced by Secretary of Defense James Schlesinger in 1974 represented the most significant change in U.S. defense policy since the withdrawal from South Vietnam. There was much opposition to Schlesinger's argument that the U.S. must be prepared to fight a limited strategic war if this was necessary to deter aggression, but the new doctrine reflected a growing questioning of the strategic policy adopted under Robert S. McNamara (secretary of defense, 1961–68) and continued by Melvin R. Laird (1969–73).

The two key concepts of the McNamara strategy were mutual assured destruction (MAD) and damage limitation. The basic objective of U.S. strategic forces was to deter a deliberate nuclear attack on the U.S. or its allies by maintaining the ability to inflict an unacceptable degree of damage on any aggressor or combination of aggressors, even after absorbing the most effective surprise first strike they could launch. Unacceptable damage was defined, for the U.S., as the ability to destroy 20–25% of the Soviet population and 50% of the U.S.S.R.'s industrial capability. Conversely, a Soviet capability for inflicting a similar level of damage on the U.S., even after a U.S. first strike on the U.S.S.R., would, in this view, deter a U.S. attack. The superpowers would thus be in a position to inflict assured destruction on each other.

As long as the ICBM and SLBM remained ineffective counterforce weapons—that is, as long as it took more than one attacking missile to knock out an ICBM in its silo—the marginal utility of procuring strategic forces beyond those needed for MAD was very low, since they would only represent an overkill capability. Additional forces would therefore be needed only for limiting damage to the U.S. population and industrial capacity should deterrence fail. Under MAD the cities of each superpower existed as mutual hostages for each other's good behaviour.

The U.S. had assumed that the U.S.S.R. would accept the MAD-plus-damage-limitation formula for determining the level of its strategic forces, enabling the superpowers to freeze these forces quantitatively via the SALT I agreement and qualitatively through a subsequent SALT II agreement. However, these assumptions were being invalidated by changes in strategic technology and doctrine that raised the possibility of the Soviet Union using its strategic superiority to exert political pressure on the U.S. Both superpowers were now acquiring a combination of accuracy, throw weight, and variable warhead size that would enable each of them to threaten a significant counterforce strike against the other. With collateral damage to civilian targets lowered to an "acceptable" level and

with the necessary command and control facilities in place, a limited strategic nuclear war would be possible by the late 1970s.

Under these circumstances, the level of forces required for MAD would no longer be fixed but would depend on the relative capabilities of each side for a counterforce first strike that could reduce its opponent's forces below those required for MAD. Additional strategic forces would be necessary for both sides if they were to preserve their MAD capabilities, and these additional forces in turn could function in a counterforce role. As a result of these changes, the static notion of MAD had to be replaced by a more flexible strategic doctrine. Furthermore, the political prudence and morality of maintaining a strategy based on holding populations and cities as hostages seemed questionable when alternatives were available.

Hence the new Schlesinger doctrine, announced on January 10 and expanded in his annual defense statement to Congress on March 4. Schlesinger's two new criteria for determining the size and capabilities of U.S. strategic forces were sizing and selective targeting. Sizing meant that the adequacy of U.S. strategic forces would now be determined by relative comparisons with those of the U.S.S.R., taking into account Soviet capabilities for a counterforce first strike. This suggested that the U.S. would insist on meaningful symmetry, offsetting any Soviet attempt to acquire significant qualitative or quantitative advantages. Selective targeting involved the separate but related idea that the U.S. president should have selective options for retaliation in the event of a limited Soviet move against the U.S., rather than being confined to noncredible threats against Soviet cities. Underlying both concepts was the belief that criteria for deterrence had to be reassessed in an era of counterforce capabilities and an apparent Soviet belief that such capabilities would produce political gains. This was especially true for the U.S., which had to protect both itself and its allies in Western Europe and elsewhere.

The U.S. continued to reduce its conventional strength. Manpower was lowered by 78,900 to 2,174,-000, and defense expenditure, at $85.8 billion or 6.2% of GNP, was at its lowest level in real terms since before the Korean War. The last draftees in the armed forces were discharged in November. The Army, which was experiencing difficulty recruiting enough volunteers, had 782,000 men, manning three armoured, one armoured cavalry, four mechanized infantry, three infantry, one airmobile, and one airborne division, plus three armoured cavalry regiments, one brigade in Berlin, and two special mission brigades in Alaska and Panama. Most of these forces were oriented for the defense of Western Europe, and two armoured and two mechanized infantry divisions, one mechanized infantry brigade, and two armoured cavalry regiments, totaling 190,000 men, were stationed there with the 7th Army. In the U.S. one armoured and two mechanized divisions assigned to reinforce the 7th Army had most of their equipment stockpiled in Western Europe. The Strategic Reserve comprised one armoured cavalry, one infantry, one airmobile, and one airborne division, plus one infantry brigade. Other forces overseas included one infantry division of 26,-000 men in South Korea, maintained despite attempts by the U.S. to persuade the South Koreans that this force could be reduced, and one infantry division, less one brigade, in Hawaii. New equipment included the Lance short-range surface-to-surface missile (SSM), replacing the Honest John and Sergeant in the 20 SSM battalions. A new main battle tank, the SM-1, was being developed.

The Marine Corps also constituted a strategic reserve force, maintained at a constant strength of three 18,000-man divisions, with 428 medium tanks, each with integral air support from three air wings totaling 550 aircraft. Two divisions/air wings were in the U.S. and one was in the Pacific. The Navy continued to be centred around its aircraft carrier striking forces. These included one nuclear-powered carrier, the USS "Enterprise" (a second was ready for commissioning), eight large Forrestal/Kitty Hawk- and three Midway-class carriers with 80–90 aircraft each, and three smaller Hancock-class carriers with 70–80 aircraft. Construction started on a fourth nuclear-powered aircraft carrier, 30 destroyers, 5 nuclear-powered frigates, and 27 nuclear-powered attack submarines to add to the 61 in service.

U.S.S.R.

The Soviet Union continued to expand its conventional, as well as its strategic, forces. Manpower was raised by 100,000 to 3,525,000. Defense expenditure was estimated at approximately $96 billion out of a GNP calculated in 1971 at $547 billion, making defense spending 5.4% of GNP, compared with 5.7% in the preceding year. These calculations involved considerable margin for error, however, and it was likely that the U.S.S.R. was continuing to spend substantially more of its GNP on defense than the U.S.

The nominal strength of the Soviet Army rose by three mechanized divisions to 110 mechanized, 50 tank, and 7 airborne divisions. These were at three degrees of combat readiness: category 1, between three-quarters and full-strength, with complete equipment; category 2, between half and three-quarters strength, with complete fighting vehicles; and category 3, essentially a reserve, with one-third strength and older fighting vehicles. The category 1 divisions were concentrated in Central and Eastern Europe, where the U.S.S.R. maintained 20 divisions (10 tank) in East Germany, 2 tank divisions in Poland, 4 divisions (2 tank) in Hungary, and 5 divisions (2 tank) in Czechoslovakia. The tank force totaled 9,025 medium tanks, with the T-62 replacing the T-54/55. There were a further 63 divisions (about 22 tank) in the European U.S.S.R., a few at category 1 and the rest divided between categories 2 and 3. The other area of military concentration was the Sino-Soviet border, where 45 divisions (about 8 tank) were maintained, including 2 in Mongolia. Soviet forces were deployed outside the Warsaw Pact area in Afghanistan (150 personnel); Algeria (600); Cuba (1,000); Egypt (500); Iraq (600); North Vietnam (1,000); Somalia (1,000); Syria (2,000–3,000), and Yemen (Aden) (200).

All Soviet forces continued to be built around the concept of rapid armoured advances of up to 100 km. per day, on the model of the offensives against Germany in World War II. The Soviets stressed the use of tactical nuclear weapons to prepare the openings for such advances, and nuclear-capable SSMs were organic to their formations. These included the Frog 1–7 (10–45-mi. range); the Scud A (50-mi.), the Scud B (185-mi.), and the Scaleboard (500-mi.), all with warheads in the kiloton range.

The Air Force was divided into the Air Defense Forces and the tactical and the long-range air forces. The Air Defense Forces comprised 500,000 personnel with 2,650 interceptors, including 650 obsolete MiG-17s and MiG-19s; 750 Su-9s; and 1,250 Yak-28P

A record speed of 80 knots (92 mph) was attained by this U.S. Navy Surface Effect Ship during trials near Panama City, Fla., in April.

Firebars, Tu-28P Fiddlers, and Su-11 and Su-15 Flagon-As. The advanced MiG-25 Foxbat had been brought into service. Some 9,800 surface-to-air missiles (SAMs), deployed at about 1,650 sites, included about 4,500 SA-2 Guidelines with Fan Song radar and a slant range (launcher to target) of about 25 mi., effective between 1,000 and 80,000 ft.; the SA-3 Goa low-level SAM with a slant range of 15 mi.; the SA-4 Ganef mobile, air-portable, long-range SAM; the SA-5 Griffon, with a slant range of 50 mi. and a limited anti-missile capability; and the SA-6 Gainful, used successfully in the 1973 Arab-Israeli war, with a slant range of 17 mi. About 75% of the long-range air force was based in the European U.S.S.R. and most of the remainder in the Far East.

About half the tactical air force was oriented against Western Europe and a quarter against China. It had 400,000 personnel and about 5,350 combat aircraft, including a tactical force of 800 obsolete MiG-17s, 500 Su-7 fighter-bombers, 300 MiG-23 interceptors, and more than 1,350 MiG-21 interceptors. The Air Transport Force had about 1,706 aircraft, including 870 Il-14s, An-8s, and An-24s, 800 An-12 and Il-18 medium transports, and 30 of the An-22 heavy transports used to supply the Arabs in the 1973 war. There were also 2,500 helicopters.

With personnel of 475,000, 221 major surface combat ships, and 70 nuclear and 245 diesel submarines, the Soviet Navy enjoyed virtual parity with the U.S. except in aircraft carriers. The first Soviet aircraft carrier, a 40,000-ton Kuril-class vessel with about 25 vertical/short takeoff and landing (V/STOL) aircraft and 36 helicopters, was entering service and a sister ship was building. The naval air force had 75,000 personnel and 715 combat aircraft, including 280 Tu-16 Badgers with Kipper and Kelt air-to-surface missiles (ASMs), 55 Tu-22s, 20 Il-28s, 50 Tu-95 Bears, and 150 Tu-16 Badgers used for strike and reconnaissance duties. These units were shore-based near the northwest and Black Sea coasts. Like the other services, the

Combat readiness training continues for troops of the U.S. Army's 2nd Division, stationed in South Korea. The men of this unit constitute the last U.S. force in the country, more than 20 years after the large-scale hostilities of the Korean War.

large surface fleet was designed and organized to fight a war in which individual units would be committed to combat until destroyed and then replaced by new units. This produced a preference for large numbers of comparatively small units, able to deliver more intensive fire over a short time than their U.S. opposite numbers, which were designed to fight a longer war in which damaged units would be pulled out, repaired, and fed back. This explained the provision for three separate missile systems in the three Kara-class cruisers.

UNITED KINGDOM

The major issue in U.K. defense policy was the commitment by the Labour government of Prime Minister Harold Wilson (confirmed in office by the October 10 general election) to reduce defense spending. At $8,721,000,000, the 1974 defense budget was a relatively high 4.9% of GNP, compared with 2 to 3.5% for most other Western European governments.

The government's proposals, announced to the House of Commons on December 3 by Defense Secretary Roy Mason, would save an estimated £290 million in the next year and more than £4,700 million over the next ten years. As outlined by Mason, the major reductions would be made in the Navy and the Royal Air Force. Within ten years, the armed services would lose some 35,000 men and women, half of whom would come from the RAF. The remnants of Britain's commitments east of Suez would be largely eliminated with the calling back of most of the men serving in Singapore under the five-power defense arrangement between Britain, Australia, New Zealand, Malaysia, and Singapore and some of the contingent in Hong Kong. Removal of the small forces on Mauritius and on Gan in the Maldives was considered to be largely symbolic, as was the decision to end the agreement with South Africa for use of the Simonstown naval base. No reductions were to be made in the British Army of the Rhine (BAOR) stationed in West Germany under NATO. Significant cuts were to be made in the forces on Cyprus, however, suggesting some pullback from the eastern Mediterranean. Mason proposed a reduction in the number of naval support ships on the ground that there would be less need for the Navy to move around the Cape. Some 30,000 civilian jobs would be abolished.

U.K. overseas deployments in 1974 included one infantry battalion group in Singapore, one Gurkha battalion in Brunei, 9,300 troops in Hong Kong, one infantry battalion in Gibraltar, and one infantry battalion and one armed reconnaissance squadron with the UN peacekeeping force in Cyprus, plus a similar force (temporarily increased as a result of the Turkish invasion in July 1974) to garrison the Sovereign Base Areas there. The Royal Navy, with 78,100 personnel and 74 major surface combat vessels, was the largest in Western Europe. It included a significant amphibious landing capability, with air cover provided by one aircraft carrier with 14 Buccaneer light bombers. These forces were expensive and of limited military value, although they were politically useful to the U.K. as a rapid reinforcement of NATO forces on the northern flank, especially Norway. The strategic forces comprised four SSBNs, each with 16 Polaris A-3 missiles. Although Labour had always attacked the concept of an independent deterrent in theory, they had maintained it in practice. An underground test of a new U.K. thermonuclear MRV was carried out in U.S. testing grounds in June.

The all-volunteer Army of 178,300 included 55,500 in the BAOR. The maintenance of forces in Northern Ireland was proving increasingly difficult as opinion in the U.K. appeared to be moving in favour of withdrawal. (See UNITED KINGDOM.) There were signs that the armed forces could become involved in politics; two prominent ex-officers, Col. David Stirling (see BIOGRAPHY) and Gen. Sir Walter Walker, were reported to be forming so-called private armies directed against strikers, though both said their planned organizations were strictly nonmilitary.

FRANCE

The election of Valéry Giscard d'Estaing as president of France meant the continuation of modified Gaullism in defense and foreign policy. The clearest manifestation of this policy was the French nuclear striking force, the *force de frappe*, which had cost over $12 billion between 1960 and 1971. Further tests of atomic (fission) triggers for the force's thermonuclear (fusion) warheads were held at Mururoa Atoll in the Pacific, despite protests from Australia and New Zealand, but these tests were said to be the last France would conduct in the atmosphere. The French announced that they would deploy MRVs as a prelude to MIRVs, if these could be developed.

The nuclear forces included two squadrons of nine SSBS S-2 intermediate-range ballistic missiles (IRBMs) each in silos in the Plateau d'Albion, with a third squadron under construction and three SSBNs. A fourth SSBN was scheduled to become operational in 1976, one more was under construction, and a sixth would probably be built so that two could be on patrol at all times. There were also 36 Mirage IV-A strategic bombers, with 18 more in reserve. The new Pluton tactical missile was in service, and some Mirage III strike aircraft could also deliver tactical nuclear weapons. The weakest point in the *force de frappe* was its reliance on fission warheads with yields limited to the kiloton range.

The main roles of the Air Force were protection of the *force de frappe* and tactical air support. The Air Defense Command had 9,000 personnel manning the automatic Strida II air defense system and 45 Mirage III-C interceptors, 30 Mirage F-1 interceptors (with a third squadron forming), and 45 Super Mystère B-2 interceptors. The Tactical Air Force had 13,500 personnel and included 120 Mirage III-Es, 30 Mirage Vs, 56 F100-Ds, and 30 Jaguar fighter-bombers, plus 45

Mirage III reconnaissance aircraft. The 30 Vautour light bombers were being withdrawn as obsolete.

The strength of the Army and Navy remained approximately constant. The 331,500-man Army (including 216,000 conscripts) was divided into the *force de manoeuvre*, with two mechanized divisions in West Germany and three in France, and the Strategic Reserve (*force d'intervention*). There were some 12,000 troops stationed outside Western Europe and 52,000 troops in France for territorial defense. The Navy had 69,000 personnel (16,500 conscripts) and 49 major surface combat vessels, including two aircraft carriers with 40 aircraft each, equipped with Exocet SSMs, Masurca and Tartar SAMs, and Malafon ASW missiles. The Naval Air Force comprised 13,000 personnel and 181 combat aircraft.

WEST GERMANY

The West German defense budget fell slightly as a percentage of GNP, to 2.9%, but at $10,764,000,000 it still provided the largest force on the NATO Central Front. Furthermore, the relative size of that force would increase in the event of MBFR/MFR. The Army of 340,000 men, including 190,000 conscripts, manned 13 armoured brigades of 4,000–5,000 men each and 12 armoured infantry, 3 motorized infantry, 2 mountain, and 3 airborne brigades, organized in 3 corps and 12 divisions. Equipment included 2,200 of the newer Leopard medium tanks, 1,360 M-48A2 Patton medium tanks, over 7,000 armoured personnel carriers; and over 1,000 tank destroyers, including 316 with SS-11 antitank guided weapons. Missiles included 1,000 Redeye SAMs, Cobra, Milan, and TOW antitank guided weapons, and 71 Honest John and 19 Sergeant SSMs. These forces were supported by the Territorial Army with a peacetime strength of 35,000 (including 5,000 conscripts) and a mobilization strength of 218,700.

The 111,000-man Air Force (39,000 conscripts) had 408 combat aircraft. Replacement of the F-104G Starfighter by the F-4F Phantom continued, but there were still 104 fighter-ground attack and 72 fighter F-104Gs in service. Other aircraft included 60 reconnaissance RF4-Es and 168 G-91R 3 fighter-ground attack planes.

The Navy, with 39,000 personnel (11,000 conscripts), remained geared to coastal operations in the Baltic. Eleven coastal submarines were ordered to reinforce the existing 13. Surface vessels included 11 destroyers, 3 with the Tartar SAM; 6 fast frigates; 5 ASW frigates; 11 fast combat support ships; and 40 fast patrol boats, 14 of which were armed with the Exocet SSM. The Naval Air Arm had 148 combat aircraft, including 128 F-104Gs and RF-104G fighter-bomber/reconnaissance planes.

THE MIDDLE EAST

The cease-fire agreements of Oct. 22–25, 1973, which ended the so-called Yom Kippur war between Israel and the Arab states of Egypt, Syria, Jordan, and Iraq, were followed by separate disengagement agreements between Israel and, successively, Egypt and Syria. These agreements established buffer zones between the combatants policed by UN forces, but the zones were too small to offer serious obstacles to a renewal of hostilities. The real deterrent was the U.S. interest in preserving the cease-fire and converting it into a lasting peace. However, Secretary Kissinger faced what appeared to be insuperable obstacles in his efforts to bring this about.

The Arabs felt that use of the oil weapon could put such pressure on the U.S. that it, in turn, would force Israel to agree to what the Arabs regarded as acceptable peace terms. It was by no means clear that these terms would include survival of the Israeli state, of which the U.S. was the implicit guarantor, or that any compromise was possible between the respective sets of peace terms that the Arab and Israeli leaders could sell to their internal critics. Thus, by increasing the Arabs' expectations of long-run victory, the oil weapon had lessened the short-run chances of peace. Although Egypt's Pres. Anwar as-Sadat had accepted Kissinger's efforts toward a peaceful settlement, Pres. Hafez al-Assad of Syria remained opposed to any concessions to Israel. It seemed likely, therefore, that the next conflict would be concentrated on the Israeli-Syrian front.

There were ample reserves of men and matériel for a future war, since the Soviet and U.S. resupply operations had continued on only a slightly reduced scale after the cease-fire. Quantitatively, both sides were as well equipped as they had been in October 1973, and qualitatively their positions had improved. The most serious combat losses had been in skilled personnel, but even these were unlikely to inhibit a resumption of fighting. The arms shipments by the superpowers meant that defense budgets in the Middle East underestimated military investment, but even these figures reinforced the impression that the Middle Eastern countries were engaged in the most dangerous arms race in the world.

Thus Syria spent $460 million, or 14.7% of GNP, on defense. The Army totaled 120,000 men, and equipment included 100 T-34 and 1,000 T-54/55 medium tanks, as well as 500 of the new T-62s. For the first time the U.S.S.R. had supplied Frog 7 and Scud SSMs. With a range of 185 mi., the larger Scud was potentially able to strike at Israeli cities, but it was under Soviet control. The Air Force had about 300 combat aircraft, including 60 MiG-17 day fighter/ground attack planes, 30 Su-7 fighter-bombers, 200 MiG-21 interceptors, and an unknown number of MiG-23 interceptors supplied for the first time. The air defense network comprised 24 batteries with SA-6 SAMs for use against low-level attacks.

The Egyptian defense budget of $3,177,000,000 (32.8% of GNP) provided Egypt with the largest single Arab army—280,000 men, or 20,000 more than in October 1973. Armoured forces included 2,000 JS-31 T-10 heavy tanks and T-54/55 and T-62 medium tanks, plus 2,000 armoured personnel carriers. The U.S.S.R. had supplied about 24 Scud SSMs; it retained control over them but not over the shorter-range Frog 7 and Samlet SSMs or the SAM air defense network, which included 80 SA-2s, 65 SA-3s, some SA-6 launchers, missile radars, and 37-, 57-, 85-, and 100-mm. antiaircraft guns. The Air Force had 200 MiG-21 interceptors with the Atoll air-to-air missile (AAM), linked to the air defense system, 25 Tu-16 medium bombers, 5 Il-28 fighter-bombers, 38 Mirage fighter-bombers (transferred from Libya, despite Libyan promises to the French suppliers), and 100 Su-7 and 100 MiG-17 fighter-bombers. The Navy included 12 submarines and 5 destroyers.

To counter these large Arab forces, Israel spent $3,688,000,000 (47.8% of GNP) on defense, a dramatic rise from the 20.9% of GNP spent in 1972 but one that reflected the expenses of the 1973 war. Israel retained its two-tier system, with a first-line force of regulars and conscripts providing a screen for the mobilization, within 72 hours, of the second-line forces. This Israeli dependence on securing enough time to mobilize had nearly proved fatal in 1973 and led to pressure in late 1974 for a preemptive Israeli strike against the Arabs, probably aimed at destroying Syria as a military force for the rest of the decade.

Israeli forces included an army of 15,000 regulars, 110,000 conscripts, and about 128,000 reserves, divided into ten armoured, nine mechanized, nine infantry, and five parachute brigades. Of these, seven brigades were normally at full strength, five at half to full strength, and the rest at cadre strength. Equipment included 1,900 medium tanks, among them modified World War II Shermans with 75- and 105-mm. guns, Centurions, M-48s, and M-60s, plus captured T1-67s, T-54/55s, T-62s, and PT-76 light tanks, and 3,500 armoured fighting vehicles. The 280-mi.-range Jericho SSM was in production, raising the possibility of an SSM exchange between Israel and the Arabs, aimed at each other's cities, in any future conflict. The Air Force had 15,000 regular and 1,000 conscript personnel and reserves of 4,000. The 466 combat aircraft, now almost wholly U.S.-supplied, included 150 Phantom F-4E fighter-bomber/interceptors and 180 A-4E/H Skyhawk fighter-bombers, with more of both types on order. Of the older French aircraft, 25 Mirage III-B/C fighter-bomber/interceptors were still in service and 10 Vautour light bombers and 30 Ouragan fighter-bombers were in storage. There were ten SAM batteries equipped with the Hawk. The Navy was small.

Additional Arab forces that could intervene in the event of war included Jordan's Army of 70,000 men, equipped with 590 medium tanks, and its Air Force of 4,600 men with 32 Hunter fighter-bombers, 18 F-104A interceptors, and 36 F-5E fighter-bombers on order from the U.S. The Iraqi Army of 100,000 men had 1,300 medium tanks, and its Air Force of 10,500 had 60 Su-7 and 20 Hunter fighter-bombers and 30 MiG-17 and 100 MiG-21 interceptors, but most of Iraq's forces were deployed against Iran.

With U.S. and U.K. support, Iran was emerging as the dominant power in the Persian Gulf. Militarily and economically, Iran was potentially on a par with the industrialized countries of Western Europe, and its armed forces, when trained, would put it in the front rank of medium powers. The 175,000-man Army had 300 Chieftain tanks, the largest and most powerful tank in service in the world, and 480 more on order—a force comparable to that of the British Army of the Rhine. Aircraft for the 50,000-man Air Force included 32 F-4P and 64 F-4E Phantoms and 100 F-5A fighter-bombers, with 80 F-14 Tomcats and 70 F-4Es and 141 F-5Es on order. The Navy was able to control the Persian Gulf and could land a battalion of troops anywhere in the Gulf in 45 minutes.

SOUTHEAST ASIA

Although U.S. forces were no longer directly involved in combat in Southeast Asia, the war continued, with North Vietnam and the Communist forces in Cambodia opposing South Vietnam and the Cambodian government. Casualties in Vietnam were estimated at about the same level as in 1973, including 42,000 Communists and 14,000 South Vietnamese.

North Vietnam had apparently decided to wage a political struggle for control of South Vietnam, with the combat-ready field units of the North Vietnamese People's Army (PAVN) stationed outside the North putting military pressure on South Vietnam and Cam-

bodia. Communist strength in Vietnam was estimated at 140,000 combat and 50,000 administrative PAVN troops and 30,000 regulars and 30,000 guerrillas of the People's Liberation Armed Forces (PLAF), giving a total Communist force of 250,000, with 600 tanks, 50 armoured personnel carriers, and 500 artillery pieces. This compared with 230,000 combat and 235,-000 administrative personnel of the Army of the Republic of Vietnam (ARVN) and paramilitary forces comprising 325,000 Regional Forces, 200,000 Popular Forces, and 1.4 million in the People's Self-Defense Force (militia), armed with 450 tanks, 1,000 armoured personnel carriers, and 1,500 artillery pieces.

Since the cease-fire of Jan. 27, 1973, the PAVN and PLAF forces in South Vietnam had risen by about 40,000, and supplies were believed sufficient for a three–ten month campaign. To balance this, the U.S. had supplied South Vietnam with large quantities of advanced military equipment, including 600 M-48 medium and 1,000 M-41 light tanks, 1,000 M-113 armoured personnel carriers, 72 F-5A jet fighters, with 36. in storage and 68 F-5Es on order, 220 A-37 fighter-bombers, and 56 gunships. This made it unlikely that the North could defeat the South in a single military campaign, and the war seemed likely to drag on. The long-term prospect was for a Northern victory, probably a Pyrrhic one.

In Cambodia the Communists controlled 70% of the country and 50% of the population but failed to take the capital of Phnom Penh, despite intensive fighting. The Communist forces, including 50,000 Khmer Rouge and 10,000 North Vietnamese, were equipped with Soviet and Chinese small arms and light artillery, including captured U.S. 105-mm. howitzers. The government forces comprised a 200,000-man army with U.S. armoured personnel carriers and howitzers and an air force of 9,500 with 48 T-28 ground-attack aircraft, 13 AU-24 counterinsurgency aircraft, and 6 AC-47 gunships. The 150,000-man paramilitary forces were of doubtful utility.

The Laotian peace agreements of Feb. 21, 1973, had led to an uneasy truce, with the Communist Pathet Lao holding three-quarters of the country while the government controlled most of the population. Pathet Lao strength was estimated at 35,000, plus 60,000 North Vietnamese and 17,000 Thai irregulars, while the government had an army of 62,800. In 1974 a coalition government was formed, with Premier Souvanna Phouma heading a Cabinet that included neutralists and Pathet Lao representatives. (*See* LAOS.)

In Thailand, as yet untouched by war, the U.S. 7th Air Force retained its bases and some 40,000 personnel. The Thai armed forces were substantial, including an army of 130,000 men equipped with U.S.-supplied armoured personnel carriers and 105- and 155-mm. howitzers and an air force of 42,000 with 11 F-5A fighters and 92 counterinsurgency aircraft.

INDIA AND PAKISTAN

India's detonation of a nuclear device on May 18 confirmed long-held suspicions that India intended to become the world's sixth nuclear power. The real significance of the Indian bomb was political: it was expected to give India the status of a regional Asian great power, analogous to that enjoyed by China. In India's eyes, China's nuclear weapons program was the crucial factor that compelled the U.S. and the U.S.S.R. to respect its interests and aspirations. Although China's nuclear capability had appeared threatening in the aftermath of the 1962 Sino-Indian border war, the Chinese had not subsequently indulged in nuclear diplomacy against India. The Indians did not, therefore, need nuclear weapons as a deterrent against China, except in the unlikely contingency of a Chinese attempt at nuclear blackmail.

Thus the most paradoxical effect of the Indian bomb was how little it changed India's defense needs and costs. Despite the development of a nuclear option, India's defense budget had been held at $2,443,000, or 3.1% of GNP. The costs of developing a limited delivery system would be relatively modest, especially since it would include adaptation of a program nominally aimed at peaceful research into missile launch vehicles. If India followed the Chinese pattern of nuclear development, the initial fission bomb would provide a suitable trigger for a fusion bomb, which could be produced over the next ten years. Whether India would do so was open to question, however. Since the Indian bomb was essentially a prestige weapon, it did not need to be a credible deterrent against China and would not threaten the U.S. or the U.S.S.R. for many years.

India's real strategic need was for an army and air force that could contain Pakistan, China, and the Naga and Mizo (Lushai) border guerrillas while maintaining internal order. Among Asian forces, the Army of 826,000 men was second only to China's; it was also well equipped, with 1,000 T-54/55 and Vijayanta medium tanks, armoured personnel carriers, and over 3,000 25-pounder guns, plus SS-11 and Entac antitank guided weapons and Tigercat SAMs. The 100,000-man Air Force was equipped with 60 Canberra light bombers, 77 Su-7BKLs, and 50 HF-24 Marut 1A fighter-bombers, all capable of delivering tactical nuclear weapons over a 1,000-mi. radius, as well as 130 Hunter F-56 fighter-bombers, 220 MiG-21 PFM interceptors, and 180 Gnat F-1 interceptors. The Navy's 1 aircraft carrier, 2 cruisers, and 22 frigates gave India control over its immediate coastline, including Sri Lanka.

Compared with these Indian forces, Pakistan's were barely adequate to ensure its own defense, though they consumed $575 million or 5.5% of GNP. This provided an army of 365,000 men, including 25,000 Azad Kashmir troops, with 900 medium tanks, about 900 25-pounder guns, and Cobra antitank guided weapons. The 17,000-man Air Force had 10 B-57B Combine light bombers, 21 Mirage III-EP interceptors, 28 Mirage Vs, 75 F-86s, and 140 MiG-19-F6 fighter-bombers. The Navy had only three French Daphne-class submarines, four destroyers, and two frigates.

FAR EAST

In contrast to the balance of deterrence between the U.S., its Western European allies, and the U.S.S.R., where the use of force for political objectives was a very real threat, the balance of military forces in the Far East provided a standoff between the Communist powers of China and North Korea on the one hand and Japan, Taiwan, and South Korea on the other. China remained the dominant military power without being the dominant political power.

As a nuclear power, China was preoccupied with deterring a possible Soviet attack. The slow but steady buildup of its nuclear force continued. The nuclear test, of about one megaton, held in June 1974 was the 16th since tests started a decade earlier. Nuclear production facilities had been expanded so the existing stockpile of 200–300 weapons could be increased rap-

The RAF's most recent weapons system, the Jaguar, was unveiled at Lossiemouth, Scot., in June when the first squadron became operational.

idly. A multistage ICBM with a range of 3,500-mi., able to reach Moscow and most parts of Asia, was ready for operational deployment, and a longer-range ICBM able to reach major targets in the U.S. was being deployed. About 20–30 IRBMs and 50 medium-range ballistic missiles were deployed operationally in at least four locations, all under the control of the 2nd Artillery, the missile arm of the People's Liberation Army (PLA). These missiles were all liquid fueled, but solid fueled versions were expected to become available in the near future.

The PLA remained a defensive force, lacking the facilities, equipment, and logistic support for protracted large-scale military operations outside China, although weapons and logistic capability were being improved. There were 2.5 million personnel in the Army, manning 7 armoured, 6 airborne, 4 cavalry, 119 infantry, and 20 artillery divisions, plus 41 railway and construction engineer divisions. The Air Force of 220,000 had about 3,800 combat aircraft, including 50 Tu-16 and some Tu-14 medium bombers, 200 Il-28 and 100 Tu-2 light bombers, and about 1,700 MiG-17, 1,300 MiG-19, 50 MiG-21, and 400 Chinese-designed and built F-9 fighters. The air defense system provided a limited defense of key urban and industrial areas, and military installations.

In December 1973 there was a major reshuffle of military commanders in 8 of the country's 11 military regions, including Peking, intended to reduce the political power of regional military leaders who had assumed administrative and political functions after the Communist Party had been weakened by the Cultural Revolution. There was still no defense minister to replace Lin Piao, who had died after an apparent attempt to take over the government in 1971, and no chief of staff for the PLA. Estimates of China's defense expenditure varied from $4 billion to $12 billion out of a GNP estimated at $105 billion–$140 billion.

In contrast, Japan's $3,835,000,000 defense budget represented only 0.8% of its GNP of $439,400,000,-000. Its forces were intended to provide a limited conventional defense against a Chinese attack that was improbable and in any case was deterred by U.S. nuclear and conventional forces. Army personnel totaled 154,000, organized in one mechanized and 12 infantry divisions of 7,000–9,000 men each, equipped with 500 Type 61 medium tanks, 430 Type 60 armoured personnel carriers, and 140 Hawk SAMs. The Air Force of 40,900 had 385 combat aircraft, including 120 F-86F Sabres and 130 F-104J, 40 F-4E, and 80 F-86F interceptors, plus 5 SAM groups equipped with the Nike-J. The 38,100-man Navy included 27 destroyers with helicopters and ASROC ASW missiles, 14 general purpose destroyers, 11 ASW and 5 general purpose destroyer escorts and frigates, and 14 submarines. The Naval Air Arm had 110 combat aircraft.

Taiwan was similarly equipped to defend itself against China without being able to use its forces outside the country although, at $774 million, the Taiwanese defense budget was 9.4% of GNP. This provided an army of 340,000, 60,000 of whom were deployed on the island of Quemoy off the Chinese coast and 20,000 on the neighbouring island of Matsu. The Air Force had 80,000 men and 206 combat aircraft, including 90 F-100A/D fighter-bombers, 35 F-5A/B and 63 F-104G interceptors, and 8 RF-104Gs. The 36,000-man Navy was designed for coastal defense. The marine force included 35,000 men.

In Korea the Northern and Southern forces were relatively balanced. The North had a 410,000-man army with 900 T-34, T-54/55, and T-59 medium tanks and an air force of 40,000 men with 590 aircraft, including 300 MiG-15 and MiG-17 fighter-bombers and 70 MiG-19 and 130 MiG-21 interceptors. Against this, the South had an army of 560,000 with 1,000 M-4, M-47, M-48, and M-60 medium tanks and an air force of 25,000 men and 210 combat aircraft, including 30 F-4D, 100 F-86F, and 70 F-5A fighter-bombers.

AFRICA SOUTH OF THE SAHARA

The strategic picture in southern Africa was dramatically altered by the military coup of April 25, 1974, in Portugal. The military government that came to power reversed the previous government's policy of retaining Portugal's African colonies by force in favour of immediate negotiations with the guerrilla movements in these colonies, looking toward an end to the fighting and independence. The consequences for Rhodesia appeared grave. South Africa seemed likely to survive, though its long-run chances were lessened.

Before the coup, Portugal had been spending some 4.7% of its GNP on a defense budget of $523 million, representing about 45% of all government spending in a poor country that was also trying to develop economically. This provided an army of 179,000, with conscripts serving for two years, an air force of 18,-500 with a three-year period of service, and a navy of 19,500 with a four-year period of service. About 25 infantry and 4 parachute battalions, plus supporting units, served in Africa, and these, together with locally enlisted forces, gave Portugal a total of 27,-000 troops in Portuguese Guinea, 50,000 in Mozambique, and 57,000 in Angola.

The key group in the coup was the Captain's Movement, later the Armed Forces Movement (AFM), composed of junior officers who had served three or four tours of duty in Africa and were aware of the costs of the war for ordinary soldiers. They were convinced that the guerrillas could not be defeated and equally certain that the government of Premier Marcello Caetano would never negotiate a political settlement and would blame the Army for any military defeat. The African wars had thus brought the Portuguese Army into politics, while the conscription system had made the younger officers aware of the gen-

eral dissatisfaction with the existing government. Their symbolic leader was Gen. António de Spínola, deputy chief of the general staff and former military governor of Portuguese Guinea, whose book *Portugal and the Future* had argued that the guerrilla wars in Africa could not be won militarily and that political solutions must be found. After the April 25 coup, General Spínola headed a Junta of National Salvation, based on the AFM. He later resigned as a result of pressure from the left.

In August the new Portuguese government announced that it would withdraw from Portuguese Guinea and Mozambique and intended to withdraw from Angola, though this would be more difficult. In Portuguese Guinea (Guinea-Bissau) there were only 3,000 whites in a population of some 510,000. On August 26 the African Party for the Independence of Guinea and Cape Verde (PAIGC) was recognized as the government of Guinea-Bissau and the colony became independent on September 10; the Cape Verde Islands were to become independent in 1975. In military terms, the changeover in Guinea-Bissau was not important. The territory had no strategic significance and no valuable raw materials.

Mozambique was strategically significant, since it bordered on white-dominated Rhodesia and South Africa and contained the Cabora Bassa Dam, scheduled for completion in 1975, which would be a major source of electrical power for South Africa. The population of Mozambique included about 220,000 whites, 60,000 Asians, and over 8 million blacks. The Front for the Liberation of Mozambique (Frelimo) had emerged as the leader of the guerrilla groups, which had become increasingly active in Tete District where the Cabora Bassa Dam was being built. Frelimo was recognized by Portugal as the government of Mozambique and independence was to be granted in 1975. Subsequently, an attempted coup by the whites to forestall independence failed when it was unable to gain any support from the Army.

The future of Angola was less clear. It had a far larger white population, some 500,000, as compared with 250,000 of mixed race and over 5 million blacks. Angola was also the most valuable of Portugal's African territories economically, with sizable mineral deposits and a favourable balance of payments. The guerrillas had not been able to expand much beyond the frontier regions and were divided among themselves, the largest groups being the Popular Movement for the Liberation of Angola and the National Front for the Liberation of Angola. However, the new Portuguese government, under pressure from the younger, more radical officers of the AFM, seemed likely to insist on an end to Portuguese occupation.

These developments left Rhodesia and South Africa even more dependent on their military forces. The Rhodesian Army of 3,500 regulars, 10,000 Territorial Forces, and 8,000 British South African Police seemed insufficient to enable the white population of 273,000 to contain a black population of 5.8 million indefinitely. South Africa remained the dominant military power in Africa, with an army of 34,500, some of whom were operating against African guerrillas in the Caprivi Strip in Namibia (South West Africa). Elsewhere in Africa, the dominance of the military in politics continued. In Ethiopia, Emperor Haile Selassie was deposed by his army. (*See* ETHIOPIA.)

(ROBERT J. RANGER)

See also Space Exploration.
[535.B.5.e.ii; 544.B.5–6; 736]

Demography

Birth Statistics. Provisional statistics indicated that both the number of live births and the birthrate in the U.S. continued to decline in 1973 and the first eight months of 1974, although the rate of decline slowed markedly. The number of births and the birthrate per 1,000 population fell 4% from 1972 to 1973, compared with a 10% decrease between 1971 and 1972, and the decrease for the first eight months of 1974 was only 1% below 1973. These figures, plus the leveling off of the seasonally adjusted fertility rate since late 1973, suggested that the birth and fertility rate declines in process since about 1960 had stopped, at least for the time being.

The crude birthrate and the fertility rate (births per 1,000 women aged 15–44 years) were 15 and 69.3, respectively, in 1973, compared with 15.6 and 73.4 in 1972. For the first eight months of 1974 the birthrate, 14.7, and the fertility rate, 67.1, were slightly below the rates for the corresponding period in 1973. This slowing of the decline in total births and the crude birthrate was at least partly explained by a continuing increase in the number of women of childbearing age.

The rate of natural population increase (excess of births over deaths per 1,000 population) continued its decline, falling from 6.2 in 1972 to 5.6 in 1973. However, it rose slightly in the first eight months of 1974 because the number of deaths decreased more than the number of births. The recent rate of natural increase had been less than half the rate of about 16 per 1,000 population observed in the mid-1950s.

The latest U.S. birth data by colour, age of mother, and other characteristics were for 1971. The rate for the white population, 16.2, continued to be much lower than for all other groups, 24.7. The fertility rate for white women in 1971, 77.5, was only 71% of the rate for women of all other races, 109.5. A total of 5.6% of white births were illegitimate in 1971, compared with 37.3% of nonwhite births. The number of white illegitimate births declined 7% from 1970 to 1971, while the number for nonwhites increased over 6%.

Birthrates and numbers of births declined between 1970 and 1971 for women of all ages. The largest decline, about 15%, was for women 40 years and over, and the smallest, 5%, for women 15–19 years of age. Rates for all birth-order groups fell in 1971, from 4 to 8% for first, second, and third births and from 11 to 17% for fourth and higher-order births. Recent data collected by the U.S. Bureau of the Census in its current Population Survey indicated that this trend toward fewer births per mother was likely to continue. According to the results of a June 1974 survey, married women 18 to 39 years old expected to have an average of 2.55 children, compared with an expected 3.12 children in 1967. There was strong evidence that the two-child family was regarded as the preferred size by an increasing majority of women.

Table I. Life Expectancy at Birth, in Years, for Selected Countries

Country	Period	Male	Female
Africa			
Burundi	1965	35.0	38.5
Egypt	1960	51.6	53.8
Liberia	1970	50.8	57.4
Malagasy Republic	1966	37.5	38.3
Nigeria	1965–66	37.2	36.7
Upper Volta	1960–61	32.1	31.1
Asia			
Cambodia	1958–59	44.2	43.3
Hong Kong	1971	67.4	75.0
India	1966–70	48.2	46.0
Israel	1971	70.1	73.4
Japan	1972	70.5	75.9
Korea, South	1970	63.0	67.0
Pakistan	1962	53.7	48.8
Taiwan	1971	66.1	71.7
Thailand	1964–67	53.9	58.6
Europe			
Albania	1965–66	64.9	67.0
Austria	1971	66.6	73.7
Belgium	1959–63	67.7	73.5
Bulgaria	1965–67	68.8	72.7
Czechoslovakia	1969	66.2	73.2
Denmark	1969–70	70.8	75.7
Finland	1961–65	65.4	72.6
France	1970	68.6	76.1
Germany, East	1967–68	69.2	74.4
Germany, West	1966–68	67.6	73.6
Greece	1960–62	67.5	70.7
Hungary	1970	66.3	72.1
Iceland	1966–70	70.7	76.3
Ireland	1965–67	68.6	72.9
Italy	1964–67	67.9	73.4
Netherlands, The	1971	71.0	76.7
Norway	1971–72	71.2	77.4
Poland	1965–66	66.9	72.8
Portugal	1970	65.3	71.0
Romania	1968	65.5	69.8
Spain	1970	69.7	75.0
Sweden	1967–71	71.9	76.8
Switzerland	1960–70	69.2	75.0
United Kingdom	1969–71	68.6	74.9
Yugoslavia	1968–70	64.8	69.2
North America			
Barbados	1959–61	62.7	67.4
Canada	1965–67	68.8	75.2
Costa Rica	1962–64	61.9	64.8
Guatemala	1963–65	48.3	49.7
Mexico	1965–70	61.0	63.7
Panama	1960–61	57.6	60.9
Puerto Rico	1969–71	69.0	71.9
United States	1971	67.4	74.9
Oceania			
Australia	1960–62	67.9	74.2
New Zealand	1965–67	68.7	74.8
South America			
Argentina	1965–70	64.1	70.2
Brazil	1975*	58.8	63.1
Chile	1969–70	60.5	66.0
Peru	1960–65	52.6	55.5
Surinam	1963	62.5	66.7
Uruguay	1963–64	65.5	71.6
Venezuela	1970–75*	62.9	66.7
U.S.S.R.	1968–69	65.0	74.0

*Projection.
Source: United Nations, *Demographic Yearbook* (1972); official country sources.

Table II. Birth Rates and Death Rates per 1,000 Population and Infant Mortality per 1,000 Live Births in Selected Countries, 1973*

Country	Birth-rate	Death rate	Infant mortality	Country	Birth-rate	Death rate	Infant mortality
Africa				Portugal§	20.3	10.5	41.4
Egypt†	34.8	13.1	103.3	Romania	18.8	9.2	40.0
Kenya†	17.2	3.8	55.0	Spain	19.2	8.5	15.1
Mauritius§	25.2	7.9	65.1	Sweden	13.5	10.5	9.6
Tunisia	37.3§	7.5§	76.3†	Switzerland	13.6	8.9	12.8
Asia				United Kingdom	13.9	12.0	17.5§
Cyprus	19.1	9.1	33.3	Yugoslavia	18.0	8.7	43.3
Hong Kong	19.8	5.1	16.8	**North America**			
Israel	27.2	7.1	22.8	Bahamas, The	30.4	8.4	45.4
Japan	19.4	6.6	11.7§	Barbados§	22.1	8.5	30.9
Kuwait	45.5	5.2	44.1	Canada	15.7	7.4	16.8
Lebanon	24.5	4.3	13.6‖	Costa Rica§	31.2	5.9	54.4
Philippines§	24.8	7.3	67.9	Cuba§	28.3	5.5	34.4†
Singapore	22.1	5.5	20.4	El Salvador§	40.7	8.6	52.5†
Thailand§	32.8	6.9	22.5	Guatemala	43.4	15.4	79.1
Europe				Jamaica	31.3	7.2	26.2
Austria	12.9	12.3	23.7	Mexico§	44.7	9.1	60.9
Belgium	13.3	12.1	17.0	Panama	34.0	6.0§	33.7§
Bulgaria	16.3	9.4	25.9	Puerto Rico§	24.1	6.7	27.1
Czechoslovakia	18.8	11.5	21.2	United States	15.0	9.4	17.6
Denmark	14.3	10.1	13.5†	**Oceania**			
Finland	12.2	9.3	10.1	American Samoa	31.0	4.4	20.2
France	16.4	10.7	12.9	Australia	18.9	8.5	16.7§
Germany, East	10.6	13.7	17.7§	Fiji§	27.8	5.0	26.1
Germany, West	10.2	11.8	20.4§	Guam§	35.1	4.5	15.3
Greece§	15.5	8.6	27.8	New Caledonia†	35.9	9.6	41.1
Hungary	15.0	11.8	33.5	New Zealand	20.5	8.5	16.2
Iceland	20.7	7.1	11.6§	Western Samoa	32.1	4.2	40.7§
Ireland	22.5	11.0	17.8	**South America**			
Italy	16.0	9.9	25.7	Ecuador†	38.7	10.2	78.5
Luxembourg	10.9	12.0	15.5	Paraguay†	32.3	5.8	38.6
Malta	17.1	9.3	24.0	Uruguay§	20.9	9.8†	40.4†
Netherlands, The	14.5	8.2	11.6	Venezuela§	36.8	6.6	49.7†
Norway	15.5	10.1	12.8†	U.S.S.R.§	17.7	8.7	26.3
Poland	17.9	8.3	26.1				

*Registered births and deaths only.
†1971.
‡1970.
§1972.
‖1960.

Sources: United Nations, *Population and Vital Statistics Report*; various national demographic publications.

In other countries where birth registration was considered to be 90% or more complete, UN reports indicated that the birthrate declined in 28 countries between 1972 and 1973 and increased in only 4. In the early months of 1974, 21 reporting countries showed lower rates than for the corresponding periods in 1973, 6 reported increases, and 1, no change. Thus the pattern of a falling birthrate observed for the U.S. also held for most other reporting countries. The most recent UN estimates for countries with incomplete registration showed that birthrates around the world ranged from about 11 per 1,000 population to over 50.

The birthrate was now the most dynamic factor affecting rates of population increase in all parts of the world. The rate of natural increase ranged from well below 10 in the U.S. and most European countries to over 30 in many countries of Africa, South America, and Asia. The recent rates for some of the largest countries were Egypt 21.7; Nigeria 24.7; the U.S. 6.2; China 17.8; India 26.1; Japan 12.7; Pakistan 32.5; and the U.S.S.R. 9.5.

Death Statistics. The provisional crude death rate in the U.S. in 1973 was 9.4 per 1,000 population, unchanged from 1972. However, the rate for the first eight months of 1974, at 9.2, was substantially lower than the rate of 9.5 for the corresponding period in 1973. Although the crude rate did not change, certain age-sex-colour-specific rates reached new lows for the U.S. in 1973: for white males 35–44, 45–54, 55–64, and 65–74 years of age; for all other males aged 65–74; for white females aged 65–74; and for all other females aged 15–24, 25–34, 45–54, and 55–64.

The most recent available age-adjusted U.S. death rates were for 1971. Although the rates for all sex-race groups had declined in the past few years, they continued to show substantial differences. The rate for males was 9.1 and for females, 5.3; for white persons the rate was 6.7 and for all others, 10. By major causes of death the rates were much higher for males than for females, except for diabetes, and much lower for whites than for all other races except for arteriosclerosis, suicide, and bronchitis, emphysema, and asthma.

The ranking of the ten leading causes of death in the U.S. in 1973 is shown below. The only change from 1972 involved cirrhosis of the liver and certain causes of mortality in early infancy, which reversed rank orders. The rate for cirrhosis of the liver was the highest ever recorded in the U.S. The rate for diabetes declined significantly from 18.8 per 100,000 population in 1972 to 17.4 in 1973. For the first seven months of 1974, the rates for accidents, influenza and pneumonia, and bronchitis, emphysema, and asthma fell significantly.

Cause of death	Estimated rate per 100,000 population
All causes	942.1
Diseases of the heart	359.5
Malignant neoplasms (cancer)	168.4
Cerebrovascular diseases	102.3
Accidents	54.8
Influenza and pneumonia	29.1
Diabetes mellitus	17.4
Cirrhosis of the liver	16.0
Arteriosclerosis	15.9
Certain causes of mortality in early infancy	14.8
Bronchitis, emphysema, and asthma	14.4

As in the U.S., the crude death rates in European countries, Canada, Australia, and New Zealand had fluctuated within very narrow limits for a decade or longer. The few countries in other parts of the world that had reasonably complete statistics had generally shown a trend toward lower rates, reflecting improvements in health services and standards of living. Among countries that had at least 90% complete registration, 13 reported higher rates in 1973 than in 1972, 11 reported lower rates, and 8 reported no change. For the early part of 1974, 5 countries reported increases and 22 reported lower rates compared with the corresponding months of 1973.

Infant and Maternal Mortality. The provisional infant mortality rate for the U.S. continued its long downward trend, falling from 18.5 deaths under one year per 1,000 live births in 1972 to 17.6 in 1973. Rates for both whites and nonwhites were the lowest ever recorded for the U.S., 15.2 for white infants and 28.8 for nonwhite infants. Both the neonatal rate (infants under 28 days) and the post-neonatal rate (28 days to 11 months) fell, the former from 13.7 to 12.9, the latter from 4.8 to 4.7. Improvement continued in the first eight months of 1974 as the total infant mortality rate fell from 17.7 in 1973 to 16.7.

Among countries with 90% or more complete registration, the infant mortality rate in 1972 ranged from 11 to 12 for Finland, Iceland, Japan, The Netherlands, Norway, and Sweden to 25 to 40 for Bulgaria, Austria, Greece, Hungary, Poland, Portugal, and Yugoslavia. The U.S. rate of 18.5 in 1972 was higher than the rates for Canada, Japan, Australia, New Zealand, and many European countries. The rates for most countries in Africa, Asia, and South America were estimated to range from 75 to over 200, but reliable figures were not available.

The provisional maternal mortality rate for the U.S. in 1973 was 15 deaths per 100,000 live births, the lowest ever recorded for the country and substantially below the rate of 24 for 1972. The most recent figures available by race, for 1971, indicated that the rate for mothers of all races other than white was about $3\frac{1}{2}$ times higher than the rate for white mothers.

Expectation of Life. The estimated expectation of life at birth in the U.S. in 1973 was 71.3 years, the longest ever attained for the entire population. In the preceding ten years about one year had been added to life expectancy, which is the average number of years that an infant could be expected to live if the age-specific death rates observed during the year of its birth were to continue unchanged throughout its lifetime. In 1972, the latest year for which detailed statistics were available, the life expectancy of a white male baby was 68.3 years; of a white female, 75.9 years; of a nonwhite male, 61.5 years; and of a nonwhite female, 69.9 years. Between 1971 and 1972 life expectancy increased for all these groups except white males.

Throughout the world life expectancy in recent years had ranged from less than 40 years in some less developed nations to 70 to 77 years in the most highly developed countries. Generally, in the advanced countries, female life expectancy was five to six years longer than for males. In the less technically advanced countries the female advantage was usually two to three years; in a few countries the expectation for females was less than for males. (*See* Table I.)

Marriage and Divorce. The provisional number of marriages in the U.S. in 1973 was only slightly larger than in 1972. The crude marriage rate (marriages per 1,000 total population) remained the same as in 1972, 10.9. In the first eight months of 1974 there was a 2.9% drop in the number of marriages and a 3.6% fall in the rate, compared with 1973. The more refined marriage rates based on the populations of unmarried women 15 years and over and 15 to 44 years, rather than total population, had been falling since 1969. Thus at least a temporary halt in the rise of the marriage rate was evident, despite the continuing increase in the number of persons entering the marriageable ages.

Statistics available for 1971 showed that the highest rate of marriage occurred in the age period 20–24 years. This was true for both first marriages and remarriages. The rates of remarriage of previously divorced women and men were much higher than for those previously widowed. For example, among previously divorced men and women aged 25–44, the remarriage rates were 338.4 and 176.1, respectively. For previously widowed men and women in this age group, the corresponding rates were 201.3 and 70.4.

Among countries where reporting was at least 90% complete, the marriage rate rose from 1972 to 1973 in 10 countries ånd fell in 17, with no change in one country. Thirteen countries showed higher rates for the early months of 1974 and 12 reported lower rates, as compared with the corresponding months of 1973. Marriage and divorce statistics were available for even fewer countries than other vital statistics, and were also less complete. Marriage rates were also affected by the frequency of common-law marriages, which were not included in official statistics, and by differences in the age composition of the populations.

Both the number and rate of divorces and annulments in the U.S. continued to increase, a trend that began about 1958. After reaching a peak of 4.3 divorces per 1,000 in 1946, the crude rate had declined to 2.1 in 1958. In 1973 it rose to 4.4, 10% above the rate for 1972 and the highest rate in U.S. history. Data for the first eight months of 1974 indicated that the increase continued, from 4.3 in 1973 to 4.5.

Latest detailed divorce statistics for the U.S. indicated that the median duration of marriages terminated by divorce or annulment in 1971 was 6.7 years. Median duration of marriages ended by divorce had declined steadily since 1963, when it was 7.5 years. The average number of minor children affected was 1.2 per divorce in 1971, representing a slight decline from the 1.3 average that prevailed during most of the 1960s.

Among countries reporting divorces with some reliability, the U.S. consistently had the highest rate. Next highest in 1972 was the U.S.S.R. with 2.6. Hungary, Czechoslovakia, East Germany, and Sweden also had higher than average divorce rates. Divorce was not recognized, was infrequent, or was not reported in most countries of Africa, Asia, and Latin America. The general trend of the divorce rate in most reporting countries had been upward for a decade.

(ROBERT D. GROVE)

See also Populations and Areas.
[338.F.5.b; 525.A; 10/36.C.5.d]

Denmark

A constitutional monarchy of north central Europe lying between the North and Baltic seas, Denmark includes the Jutland Peninsula and 100 inhabited islands in the Kattegat and Skagerrak straits. Area (excluding Faeroe Islands and Greenland): 16,629 sq.mi. (43,070 sq.km.). Pop. (1973 est.): 5,007,500. Cap. and largest city: Copen-

JAN PEHRSSON—NORDISK PRESSEFOTO/PICTORIAL PARADE

hagen (pop., 1973 est., 767,967). Language: Danish. Religion: predominantly Lutheran. Queen, Margrethe II; prime minister in 1974, Poul Hartling.

The chronic political and economic instability that had plagued Denmark for years continued to be a problem in 1974. During the summer a marked rise in the level of unemployment became apparent, with repercussions on the atmosphere in the business community. Inflationary price rises, which had been a feature of Danish economic life for a decade, were widely blamed on the country's system of automatic wage adjustments based on the consumer price index. Moreover, for several years Denmark had held the European record for high levels of interest as well as taxation. Almost 50% of the country's gross national product was being swallowed by the enormous public sector, and ordinary mortgage bonds bore an effective interest rate of up to 18% per year.

In spite of all this, Danish exports had increased steadily from year to year. However, imports had risen even more rapidly, and invisible earnings were insufficient to prevent an ever growing deficit. The balance of payments position continued to deteriorate, and the accumulated foreign debt had reached a total of almost 30 billion kroner.

Moreover, Denmark was almost entirely dependent on imports to meet its energy requirements, the Danish sector of the North Sea oil fields providing no more than about 1.5% of the country's needs. It was estimated that developments in the world energy situation would lead to a rise in Denmark's "normal" balance of payments deficit from about 3 billion kroner to almost 8 billion kroner in 1974.

Lis Helbo, 22 years old and pregnant, is also a sergeant in the modern Danish Army. Given permission by the authorities to wear civilian clothing, she continued to perform her military duties, as in this inspection of troops near Copenhagen.

DENMARK

Education. (1972–73) Primary, pupils 395,289, teachers 47,729; secondary, pupils 386,246, teachers 52,272; vocational, pupils 70,064, teachers 4,485; teacher training, pupils 19,839, teachers 1,513; higher (including 4 main universities), students 93,175, teaching staff 5,503.

Finance. Monetary unit: Danish krone, with (Sept. 16, 1974) a free rate of 6.24 kroner to U.S. $1 (14.43 kroner = £1 sterling). Gold, SDRs, and foreign exchange, central bank: (June 1974) U.S. $716 million; (June 1973) U.S. $1,054,800,000. Budget (1973–74 est.): revenue 53.5 billion kroner; expenditure 49,-470,000 kroner. Gross national product: (1972) 145,390,000,000 kroner; (1971) 127,870,000,000 kroner. Money supply: (Feb. 1974) 39.1 billion kroner; (Feb. 1973) 37,390,000,000 kroner. Cost of living (1970 = 100): (April 1974) 137; (April 1973) 120.

Foreign Trade. (1973) Imports 46,243,000,000 kroner; exports 37,548,000,000 kroner. Import sources: EEC 46% (West Germany 20%, U.K. 11%, The Netherlands 5%); Sweden 16%; U.S. 6%; Norway 5%. Export destinations: EEC 45% (U.K. 19%, West Germany 13%, Italy 5%); Sweden 14%; U.S. 7%; Norway 7%. Main exports: machinery 20%; meat and meat products 18%; chemicals 6%; ships and boats 5%; dairy products 5%.

Transport and Communications. Roads (1972) 64,300 km. (including 270 km. expressways). Motor vehicles in use (1972): passenger 1,228,900; commercial 173,300. Railways: state (1972) 1,999 km.; private (1970) 538 km.; traffic (1971–72) 3,723,000,000 passenger-km., freight 1,907,000,000 net ton-km. Air traffic (including Danish part of international operations of Scandinavian Airlines System; 1972): 1,918,-000,000 passenger-km.; freight 86.4 million net ton-km. Shipping (1973): merchant vessels 100 gross tons and over 1,362; gross tonnage 4,106,525. Shipping traffic (1972): goods loaded 8,320,000 metric tons, unloaded 32,360,000 metric tons. Telephones (including Faeroe Islands and Greenland; Dec. 1972) 1,918,000. Radio licenses (Dec. 1972) 1,636,000. Television licenses (Dec. 1972) 1,411,000.

Agriculture. Production (in 000; metric tons; 1973; 1972 in parentheses): wheat 520 (592); barley 5,450 (5,572); oats 460 (637); rye 140 (155); potatoes c. 709 (709); sugar, raw value c. 396 (341); apples (1972) c. 125, (1971) 115; butter (1972) 136, (1971) 124; cheese (1972) 131, (1971) 120; pork c. 745 (765); beef and veal c. 156 (171); fish catch (1972) 1,443, (1971) 1,401. Livestock (in 000; July 1973): cattle c. 2,750; pigs 8,294; sheep c. 57; horses (1972) 48; chickens (1972) c. 16,000.

Industry. Production (in 000; metric tons; 1973): cement 2,890; pig iron (1972) 204; crude steel 449; fertilizers (nutrient content; 1972–73) nitrogenous 77, phosphate 97; manufactured gas (cu.m.) 370,000; electricity (net; kw-hr.; 1972) 19,368,000. Merchant vessels launched (100 gross tons and over; 1973) 921,-000 gross tons.

Dissatisfaction continued to be expressed in many quarters with the increasing consumption of resources by the public sector and the concomitant rise in taxation. Despite signs of a marked increase in unemployment, it was widely felt that public expenditure would have to be curtailed, even at the price of a diminution in public services.

Political instability was no new phenomenon for Denmark, but the general election of December 1973 had produced a more precarious situation than usual. The previous Social Democratic minority government, supported by the Socialist People's Party, had given way to a Liberal government under Prime Minister Hartling that had only 22 seats in the 179-member Folketing (parliament). Another interesting feature was the growing popularity of the Progress Party founded by Copenhagen tax lawyer Mogens Glistrup, whose trial on charges of tax evasion began in October. Based on the abolition of income tax, a simplified legislature, and drastic cuts in the public sector, the Progress Party was second only to the Social Democrats in terms of parliamentary seats.

Nevertheless, a considerable amount of new legis-

lation was brought in by the new government. A proposal to limit the automatic wage system by giving wage earners tax-free compensation instead failed to gain the necessary support, but after laborious negotiations a "cost-limiting subsidy" was introduced that allowed employers to partially neutralize some of the price increases that would otherwise have resulted. Opinions on the effectiveness of the scheme differed. Prices continued to rise, but many claimed increases would have been even greater without the new system.

A form of compulsory saving was introduced whereby taxpayers with incomes above a certain amount were obliged to deposit a stated sum in a bank or savings bank for a set period of years. In May a number of increases in indirect taxation were introduced, to the accompaniment of widespread protests and strikes. Building activity was cut back, and a stringent credit policy was applied. Further proposals aimed at a considerable reduction in direct income taxes, with the prerequisite of substantial economies in the public sector.

A special parliamentary session called in September to deal with the new proposals proved highly dramatic. The government survived no less than four no-confidence motions proposed by different party groupings. Although the proposals ultimately passed, with a government resting on only 22 seats and 10 parties represented in the Folketing nothing in the session was ever a foregone conclusion. In December, Hartling called for an election in January 1975 on the issue of his economic policy.

It was small comfort that many of Denmark's troubles—increasing balance of payments deficit, inflation, rising unemployment, and a general atmosphere of instability and disenchantment with Parliament and politicians—were shared by other Western states. Denmark's dependence on imports for energy and raw materials, together with one of the highest per capita foreign trade totals in the world, made its problems exceptionally difficult to solve and constituted a source of constant worry to politicians and ordinary citizens alike.   (STENER AARSDAL)

[972.A.6.a]

Dependent States

The major event in the dependent territories in 1974 was the dissolution of Portugal's colonial empire following the coup in Lisbon on April 25. The independence of Portuguese Guinea was recognized on September 10 (see GUINEA-BISSAU); Mozambique was promised independence in 1975; Angola was negotiating the terms of its independence; and similar steps were being taken with regard to Portugal's smaller possessions. Elsewhere, the majority of the world's dependent territories were fostering independence movements.

Grenada became the first of the six states associated with the U.K. to achieve independence (February 7), so encouraging the possible creation of five more nonviable ministates for Commonwealth and UN membership. Very few dependent territories were self-sufficient, but they did not regard that as an obstacle to at least nominal independence.

Africa. *French Africa.* On June 19 the premier of the Territory of the Afars and Issas, Ali Aref Bourhan, and the French secretary of state for overseas départements and territories, Olivier Stern, signed

Dentistry:
see Health and Disease

an accord. Under its terms more internal control passed to the territory, French technicians would be sent to the country, and new aid would be forthcoming. Aref, in an interview, countered Somalia's claims to the territory by saying that the Somalis represented no more than 25% of its population and that the majority of people wished the French to stay for some time. Aref also said that when the French left the territory would seek the protection of the Organization of African Unity (OAU). The OAU, however, urged the French president to grant independence to the "Somali Coast."

Portuguese Africa. In Angola guerrilla activity was not particularly pronounced, but in Mozambique recriminations concerning the alleged Wiriyamu massacre led to charges by both the Portuguese and their opponents of acts of cruelty in various parts of the territory. The forces of the Mozambique Liberation Front (Frelimo) carried their campaign farther to the south, the railway line between Beira and Malawi territory being a favourite target. In February, Gen. António de Spínola (*see* BIOGRAPHY), who had been for five years governor of Portuguese Guinea, published a book claiming that a military solution was unattainable and that a political approach was essential. For these opinions he was dismissed as deputy chief of the general staff in March, but six weeks later a coup by army officers in Lisbon overthrew Marcello Caetano's government and Spínola was called upon to lead the military junta that replaced it.

Within the new government there was a difference of opinion about the future of the African territories. Spínola favoured self-determination by stages with a referendum in each territory to determine who should form the new government and with the hope that Portugal would retain a federal relationship with the former dependencies. Others, however, advocated immediate troop withdrawal and complete independence. Frelimo proposed to continue military operations and to reject a federal solution, and the white settlers in Mozambique announced their determination to remain in the country and oppose any handing over of power to a militant resistance movement. However, Frelimo aggression began to undermine their resolve, more particularly after the South African government announced on May 20 the cessation of military cooperation with Mozambique. Talks early in June between Mário Soares (*see* BIOGRAPHY), the new Portuguese foreign minister, and Samora Machel (*see* BIOGRAPHY), representing Frelimo, were adjourned for a month when Machel rejected the idea of a referendum. In July Frelimo started new operations in the province of Zambézia, and labour strikes took place.

In Angola the white settlers at first responded more optimistically to news of the Lisbon coup, partly because the independence movement in that territory was less united than in Mozambique and partly because they believed that their role in that much wealthier territory would be secure, even after independence. The Popular Movement for the Liberation of Angola (MPLA) remained active, however, and in June its leader, Agostinho Neto, denied that he had agreed to a cease-fire. But two weeks later he announced that the MPLA had ceased its military operations and would take part in political discussions; nevertheless, in mid-July fierce fighting broke out in Luanda between whites and blacks and many were killed. Portugal ordered that the government of Angola should be taken over by a local military council

charged with restoring order, and a number of people were expelled from the country or imprisoned.

African leaders in both Angola and Mozambique watched the negotiations between the Portuguese government and independence leaders in Guinea-Bissau in May and June. The talks resulted in Portugal's acknowledgment in August of the republic's independence, which was formally proclaimed on September 10 (*see* GUINEA-BISSAU); the Cape Verde Islands, associated with the Guinea-Bissau independence movement, remained in Portuguese hands with a promise of independence in 1975, a policy also established in regard to São Tomé and Príncipe. Almost simultaneously, the Portuguese government announced its program for the independence of Angola. A cease-fire was demanded before formal negotiations could begin, after which a provisional government representing all the liberation movements as well as the chief African ethnic groups and the white settlers would be set up. The provisional government would formulate an electoral law guaranteeing freedom of expression on the basis of one-man one-vote and propose a scheme for the relationship between the new state and Portugal; it would then hold an election for a constituent assembly before the end of a two-year period and the assembly would draft a constitution in preparation for new elections. The National Front for the Liberation of Angola, led by Holden Roberto, expressed its reservations, and the difficulty of reconciling conflicting opinions in Angola became apparent.

It was in Mozambique, however, that the situation seemed most explosive. In the middle of August rioting Africans destroyed homes and shops along the northern coast and Europeans and Asians fled to take refuge in the town of Nampula. Mário Soares, however, opened discussions with Frelimo leaders in Dar es Salaam, Tanzania, on August 16 and, in spite of a delay in plans to establish a temporary ruling junta in Mozambique, agreement was reportedly reached on a date in June 1975 for the country's independence. This postponement was acceptable to Frelimo because it was anxious to prepare the way for its assumption of power as securely as possible; meanwhile, its leaders were willing to head a provisional government to be set up in September. These developments produced a hostile response from some white settlers, who early in September seized Mozambique's main radio station and broadcast an appeal for independence without Frelimo. Portuguese troops broke up the rebellion within a few days. By agreement reached in Lusaka, Zambia, on September 7, transferring power to Frelimo, independence was agreed for June 25, 1975; in the meantime, a new Mozambique government took office on September 20. It consisted of six Frelimo ministers and three Portuguese. The premier was Joaquim Chissano, welcomed by many Portuguese who regarded him as one of the more moderate Frelimo leaders.

South Africa. South Africa stepped up its multinational developments in South West Africa (Namibia), the status of which as Republic of South Africa territory was contested by the UN. The republic had set up in 1973 a nominated South West African Advisory Council, which at a meeting in September 1974 endorsed the establishment of a constitutional conference of representatives of all racial groups (including European), chosen by the groups themselves, to decide whether South West Africa should be a single self-governing territory or a federation of several. In October the South African government reintroduced the

Training of militiamen in Angola includes defense against simulated attacks on villages, as in the Cuando-Cubango district shown here.

An ambush of Portuguese troops in Mozambique produces classic response: disperse—take cover—radio headquarters for assistance.

idea of partition to allow the Ovambo, the largest ethnic group, to unite in an independent state with their fellow people in Angola while the rest of the territory would retain its connection with the republic. But the South West African People's Organization (SWAPO), the dominant black political group, rejected partition and demanded complete independence.

Spanish Africa. The demand for independence continued to be voiced in Spanish Sahara, where the only brake on open conflict seemed to be the rival claims of neighbouring Morocco, Algeria, and Mauritania. In Morocco King Hassan II's government made urgent and threatening demands for the territory for political and economic reasons. Morocco feared that a referendum in the territory under UN auspices, agreed to by Spain, could result in complete independence. This would place beyond Morocco's influence the phosphate seam at Bou Craa, said to be the world's largest, which with production raised to 20 million tons a year was competing with the phosphate exports vital to Morocco's economy. Spain faced a dilemma: to grant independence, with or without a referendum, would anger Morocco, but to hand over the territory to Morocco would displease Algeria and Mauritania and also the European consortium working the phosphates. Eventually it was arranged that a referendum under UN supervision would be held in early 1975.

Caribbean. The Caribbean Common Market (Caricom), established by Barbados, Guyana, Jamaica, and Trinidad and Tobago on Aug. 1, 1973, moved nearer to regional integration in 1974, with the less developed territories (Belize, Dominica, Grenada, Montserrat, St. Kitts-Nevis-Anguilla, St. Lucia, and St. Vincent) signing the treaty of accession between April and July. Premier Robert L. Bradshaw of St. Kitts-Nevis-Anguilla signed on behalf of the breakaway island of Anguilla. The conference adopted the principle of dual nationality, permitting nationals of member states to travel on a common travel document. Cooperation was also agreed upon with the Central American Common Market and the Andean Common Market. Haiti and Surinam applied to join Caricom, and diplomatic relations were established between Caricom countries and Cuba.

In the five British "associated states" (Grenada,

the sixth, having become independent on February 7; *see* GRENADA) earnings for sugar, bananas, and other produce rose, but not sufficiently to offset the steep rise in the cost of living. The island territories of Leewards and Windwards were particularly affected by uncertainty over the debt-ridden Leeward Islands Air Transport (LIAT), purchased in 1973 by the Court Line, a British package-vacation firm that collapsed in August 1974. In St. Vincent the independent one-man majority government of James F. Mitchell fell in September following the resignation of Ebenezer T. Joshua and his wife, Ivy. Joshua, the deputy premier and minister of finance, accused Mitchell of bringing St. Vincent to the "edge of bankruptcy."

In May elections, Premier John Compton of St. Lucia and his United Workers' Party were returned to power with a three-seat majority, fewer than expected. Seven out of the 17 seats at stake went to the opposition St. Lucia Labour Party. Black power elements in Dominica were increasingly active, holding antiwhite and antitourist demonstrations. After attacks on tourists, including one murder, Deputy Premier Patrick John announced that the government would stamp out antiwhite racism. The island's newest hotel closed down because of a slump in tourist trade. Edward O. LeBlanc, premier since 1962, resigned in July, and John became leader of the Labour Party and premier.

In Bermuda tourism increased, and there was no flight of international business from this select and impeccably run tax haven. The Cayman Islands, another offshore tax haven, experienced a tourist boom, but were less fortunate in the financial field, with the collapse in September of the International Bank of Grand Cayman, the Sterling Bank and Trust, and others. Grand Cayman Island achieved unwanted recognition when two suspects in the theft of $4.3 million from the vault of an armoured car service company in Chicago were arrested there; authorities believed that much of the money had been deposited in the secret, numbered accounts used by Grand Cayman banks. Early in 1974 the Turks and Caicos Islands petitioned Britain to end association status, replacing it with some form of association with Canada. In Belize (British Honduras) elections held in late October, with independence as a major issue, were overshadowed by Guatemala's threat to invade in support of its "inalienable and sovereign rights" there. An opposition front of conservatives captured 5 of the 18 seats, denting the hold of George Price's labour union-based People's United Party.

In the French Caribbean, Martinique experienced a general strike in February, after localized conflicts including a three-month strike by the staff of the newspaper *France-Antilles.* Violent clashes followed between police and demonstrating plantation workers, resulting in two deaths. Police reinforcements were sent in from Guadeloupe and French Guiana. On his arrival at Fort-de-France on December 14 to meet with U.S. Pres. Gerald Ford, French Pres. Valéry Giscard d'Estaing was welcomed by a large crowd, although he gave up a visit to the town hall because of left-wing demonstrations.

At a three-day conference in The Hague, Neth., in May, the prime ministers of The Netherlands, Surinam, and the Netherlands Antilles decided to dissolve the 20-year-old statute under which the Dutch colonies in the Caribbean were given autonomy except in defense and foreign affairs. Surinam was to gain complete independence at the end of 1975, while the principles of the statute were to continue to apply to the Antilles for at least five years. In the Surinam elections of late 1973 the prime minister's Progressive National Party and a four-party opposition front favouring independence won 22 out of 39 seats.

Indian Ocean. *French Dependencies.* A referendum held in the Comoro Islands on Dec. 22, 1974, under the government of Pres. Ahmed Abdullah, resulted in an overwhelming vote (almost 95% of a poll exceeding 90%) in favour of independence from France. On the island of Mayotte, however, where a separatist movement favoured self-determination within the French orbit and apart from the other Comoros, 64% of those voting opposed independence. President Abdullah subsequently visited Paris for discussions with the French government.

British Dependencies. African pressure was also stepped up against the Seychelles. The Organization of African Unity openly supported the opposition to James Mancham's party, which after achieving phased independence in 1975 wished to remain within the Commonwealth, join the OAU, and associate with the EEC. Despite third world protests that the Indian Ocean should be a peace zone, work went ahead to expand Anglo-U.S. naval and air facilities on the island of Diego Garcia.

Pacific. *British Pacific Territories.* In July two Arab-financed merchant banks were established in Hong Kong. Both sought to invest throughout Southeast Asia and farther east. Immigrants continued to flow into Hong Kong from China; new housing estates on islands in the New Territories were planned to cope with the rising tide, estimated at 6 million, but resources were taxed fully. In the British Gilbert and Ellice Islands colony the Ellice Islands voted by referendum in October to become a separate colony. The Solomon Islands Protectorate, under its new constitution looking toward independence in the 1980s, elected its first chief minister in August.

Portuguese Pacific Territories. The governor of Portuguese Timor, Col. Fernando Aldeia, announced at the beginning of June that a referendum would be held in 1975 to determine the status of the territory. Three political groups with divergent aims, one wishing to keep the Portuguese presence, another demanding complete independence, and a third seeking integration with Indonesian Timor, were already active. In Macau, a new acting military commander, Gen. Francisco Ribelo Gonçalves, was appointed in June; some of the 500 Portuguese troops stationed there had already become restless and had denounced their senior officers.

French Pacific Territories. Social unrest continued in New Caledonia, and demands for self-government were re-echoed, though perhaps less stridently than before. In March 1974 agreement was reached between Le Nickel and the Pétroles d'Aquitaine companies for joint exploitation of New Caledonian mineral resources. During Bastille Day celebrations on July 14 several hundred young Melanesians clashed with security forces at Nouméa, and 42 demonstrators were arrested. On September 24, the anniversary of French annexation, there were further disturbances; the three independence parties—the Union Calédonienne, the Union Multiraciale, and the Mouvement Populaire Calédonien—did not appear to have initiated them but nevertheless supported their instigators. In October the labour unions called a four-day strike, resulting in partial satisfaction of their demands.

Australian and New Zealand External Territories. Having attained self-government on Dec. 1, 1973,

Papua New Guinea, under Chief Minister Michael T. Somare (*see* BIOGRAPHY), looked forward to achieving full independence in 1975, after a constitution had been drawn up by the House of Assembly. Meanwhile, a land nationalization measure was to return foreign-owned land to the government. Somare sought complete indigenization of the country and its economy and avoidance of a multiracial society. Australia agreed to continue providing economic and military aid after independence. (*See* PAPUA NEW GUINEA.)

U.S. Territories. United independence seemed as far off as ever for the U.S. Trust Territory of the Pacific Islands (American Micronesia), though 42 delegates were elected for the 1975 constitutional conference aimed at independence in 1980. But the Marshall Islands kept their political options open, while the Marianas moved toward separate agreement with the U.S. to give them Puerto Rican-type status and a closer relationship with Guam, the major U.S. base in the Western Pacific.

Indian Associated State (Sikkim). The decision of India, effective from Sept. 4, 1974, to change the status of the kingdom of Sikkim from an Indian protectorate to an Indian associated state was a logical sequence to earlier events. As arranged for by the Tripartite Agreement of 1973 among the chogyal (king), the Indian representative, and leaders of Sikkim's three major political factions, Sikkim held its first general election on April 15–16, 1974. It gave 31 (out of 32) seats in the Sikkim Assembly to the pro-Indian Sikkim Congress and only 1 to the chogyal-supported Sikkim National Party. Under a new democratic constitution approved on June 20 and signed reluctantly by the chogyal on July 4, the chogyal became a constitutional head of state acting on the advice of the Indian chief executive, who officially headed the administration. The National Congress formed the first five-man Council of Ministers, headed by Chief Minister Kazi Lendup Dorji; the council comprised two Lepchas, two Nepalis, and one Bhutia. The Assembly also quickly passed a unanimous resolution seeking Sikkimese participation in India's political and economic institutions, the move that led to India's decision to change Sikkim's status. India maintained its economic support, undertaking to finance the Rs. 200 million fourth five-year plan.

(PHILIPPE DECRAENE; KENNETH INGHAM; MOLLY MORTIMER; SHEILA PATTERSON; GOVINDAN UNNY)

See also African Affairs; Commonwealth of Nations; South Africa; United Nations.

Leader of the Sikkim Congress Party and winner of the 1974 elections, Kazi Lendup Dorji headed the new government.

KEYSTONE

Development, Economic and Social

The usual demarcation between developed and less developed countries is the level of output and income per capita, the former being between approximately $50 and $500 per capita in the less developed countries and between $1,000 and $5,000 in the developed countries. Behind these statistics are stark contrasts in economic and social conditions, including modes of production, nutrition, health, education, employment, housing, and life expectancy. In recent years it has become increasingly difficult to separate trends in the less developed countries from trends in the entire world economy. The poor countries remain a specialized field of inquiry, but neither their existing economic conditions nor their social and political re-

Table I. Selected Economic Indicators for Less Developed and Industrialized Countries by Income Group

Average annual real growth and shares in GNP (%)

Income group	Total GDP	Agricultural production	Manufacturing production	Population	GDP per capita	Gross investment	Shares in GNP Gross investment	Shares in GNP Gross national saving
Less developed countries*								
1966–70	5.8	3.1	7.8	2.5	3.3	7.0	19.3	16.9
1971	5.5	3.5	7.8	2.3	3.1	6.3	20.1	17.9
1972	5.4	—0.9	10.1	2.5	2.8	7.8	20.6	18.1
1973†	7.3	6.1	...	2.4	4.8	...	...	...
Oil exporters‡								
1966–70	7.0	1.9	7.8	2.5	4.4	10.1	20.8	21.6
1971	6.7	0.9	10.9	3.0	3.5	14.5	23.4	26.2
1972	7.5	2.0	9.0	2.8	4.9	14.7	24.6	25.9
1973†	10.4	3.2	10.5	3.0	7.2	...	...	...
Higher-income countries§								
1966–70	6.1	3.1	8.3	2.4	3.6	7.0	20.9	18.6
1971	6.6	5.5	7.9	2.4	4.1	6.0	20.9	18.2
1972	7.5	1.5	11.2	2.4	5.0	10.5	21.5	18.3
1973†	7.1	3.9	10.8	2.4	4.5	...	...	...
Middle-income countries‖								
1966–70	5.7	2.5	9.6	2.7	2.9	9.5	19.2	14.2
1971	6.6	6.5	10.1	2.5	4.1	2.4	19.1	13.9
1972	4.8	1.8	8.9	2.5	2.3	—3.8	18.1	13.5
1973†	7.7	4.7	...	2.6	5.0	...	...	...
Lower-income countries¶								
1966–70	4.4	3.9	3.4	2.4	1.9	2.7	14.7	12.0
1971	1.4	1.2	3.3	2.5	—1.1	3.1	16.5	14.0
1972	—0.7	—5.2	6.5	2.6	—3.2	1.9	16.6	14.6
1973†	5.1	9.5	...	2.3	2.9	...	...	...
Industrialized countries♀								
1966–70	4.6	2.1	5.4	1.0	3.6	5.4	22.2	22.7
1971	3.3	4.8	1.3	0.9	2.4	1.4	22.4	22.9
1972	5.2	1.1	6.6	0.9	4.2	6.5	22.3	22.7
1973†	6.2	1.0	9.6	0.9	5.3	...	...	...

*Includes 86 countries identified in footnote * of Table III.
†Preliminary.
‡Oil exporters: Algeria, Ecuador, Gabon, Indonesia, Iran, Iraq, Nigeria, Venezuela.
§Higher-income countries: Argentina, Botswana, Brazil, Chile, Colombia, Costa Rica, Cyprus, Dominican Republic, Fiji, Greece, Guatemala, Guyana, Israel, Jamaica, Malaysia, Malta, Mexico, Nicaragua, Panama, Peru, Singapore, Spain, Taiwan, Trinidad and Tobago, Tunisia, Uruguay, Yugoslavia, Zambia.
‖Middle-income countries: Bolivia, Cameroon, Congo, Egypt, El Salvador, Ghana, Honduras, Ivory Coast, Jordan, South Korea, Liberia, Mauritius, Morocco, Paraguay, Philippines, Senegal, Swaziland, Syria, Thailand, Turkey, South Vietnam.
¶Lower-income countries: Afghanistan, Bangladesh, Burma, Burundi, Central African Republic, Chad, Dahomey, Ethiopia, The Gambia, India, Kenya, Lesotho, Malagasy Republic, Malawi, Mali, Mauritania, Niger, Pakistan, Rwanda, Sierra Leone, Somalia, Sri Lanka, Sudan, Tanzania, Togo, Uganda, Upper Volta, Yemen (Aden), Zaire, plus East African Community.
♀Includes 22 countries identified in footnote † of Table II.
Source: World Bank.

actions can be comprehended fully outside the context of a global economy and society.

Inflation and Commodity Prices. The events of 1973–74 bore dramatic testimony to this situation. At least three interrelated factors on the world scene were of major significance for development: inflation; the tremendous increase in the price of petroleum products; and the general boom in the price of most other primary commodities. Inflation affected the less developed countries in several important ways: it imposed disproportionate penalties on the poor; it eroded the value of official development assistance; and the lowered growth rates in the developed nations resulted in reduced demand for the less developed countries' exports. The tremendous increase in petroleum prices fell most severely on the poorest countries, which did not have the flexibility to adjust or the margin to reduce consumption. The boom in most other primary commodities benefited some less developed countries, but it substantially reduced the terms of trade (the relationship between the prices of exports and imports) for those countries that could not offset the higher prices of oil, fertilizer, food, and minerals by raising the prices of their own exports.

Available figures showed that the rate of domestic inflation increased sharply during 1973 in both the more developed and less developed primary producing countries. However, the approximately 25% rise in consumer prices in the less developed countries between 1972 and 1973 was far exceeded by the increase of nearly 40% that occurred over the year ending with the first quarter of 1974. The average prices of internationally traded goods rose at an annual rate of 10%

in 1968–73 and by 14% in 1974, compared with less than 1% per year in the decade prior to 1960. Although inflation reduced the debt service burden of the less developed countries, this was more than offset by the deterioration in the terms of trade. It also meant a decrease in the real value of concessionary aid, from 0.34% of the gross national product (GNP) of Organization for Economic Cooperation and Development (OECD) countries in 1972 to 0.30% in 1973.

Petroleum was a special problem. In the 12 months from October 1973, the price of petroleum rose 400% relative to the export prices of manufactured goods, resulting in a global imbalance of payments of unprecedented size. There were two important consequences for less developed countries. First, the cost of their current volume of imported oil rose by some $10 billion, equal to 15% of their total import bill and to 40% of the entire net inflow of external capital in 1973. As a result, some countries were forced to curtail their development programs. Second, if the current situation remained unchanged, the oil-exporting countries taken together would have a continuing balance of payments surplus of some $30 billion–$60 billion per year (in 1974 prices), about three-quarters of which was with developed countries. This placed a strain on the developed nations' economies and on international financial markets, making it more difficult for less developed countries to expand export earnings and finance balance of payments deficits.

In theory, the effect of increased petroleum prices on the balance of payments of less developed countries could be diminished somewhat by reducing energy consumption or through development of domestic sources of energy. However, the one billion people in countries with per capita incomes below $200 consumed only about 1% as much energy per capita as citizens of the U.S. Any significant further reduction could only depress industrial and agricultural production, with the resultant lowering of living standards that were already at the poverty level. Some countries —India, Pakistan, Brazil, and Turkey, for example— possessed potential alternative energy sources in the form of hydropower, geothermal power, coal, lignite, or nuclear fuel. But development of these sources would require time and large capital investments that would draw money away from other much needed development projects.

Prices of commodities exported by less developed countries had increased rapidly after mid-1972 as a result of exceptionally rapid growth in almost all industrialized nations and the failure of the wheat and rice crops in some areas in 1972 and 1973. In 1973 prices of primary commodity exports reached the peak levels of the Korean War period. However, this mainly benefited the richer primary producers, and in any case the situation was not expected to last. Growth prospects in the industrialized countries were much less promising than in the 1960s and early 1970s. The GNP of the OECD countries appeared to be growing at only 1.3% in 1974, compared with rates of 5 and 6% in previous years, and as lower growth rates were translated into reduced demand, prices of primary commodities (possibly excepting oil and some minerals) would lose their buoyancy. Once again, the poorest countries suffered the most. The OECD countries accounted for 75% of the total exports of the oil-importing less developed nations. It was estimated that, by the end of the decade, these very poor countries would probably suffer a decline of over 20% in their terms of trade.

These heavy burdens on the balance of payments of less developed countries reduced the amount of savings available to finance investment. At the same time, the amount of capital required by less developed countries to achieve even modest rates of growth had increased tremendously. Additional capital flows would be required to make up the difference, but the outlook for such increases was not optimistic. Market borrowings had provided funds for less developed countries with high credit standing, but this source was not open to the lower income countries. Of $8.8 billion raised by the less developed countries in 1973, $3.3 billion went to just three countries, Mexico, Brazil, and Peru, and an additional $2.1 billion went to the oil- and mineral-exporting countries.

Lower income countries depended mainly on concessionary flows, principally official development assistance. The 62% increase in the money value of such assistance between 1970 and 1974 barely maintained the real value at the 1970 level. However, the members of the Organization of Petroleum Exporting Countries (OPEC) were beginning to use some of their huge foreign exchange surpluses to help meet the less developed countries' capital requirements. In drawing on these surpluses, the less developed countries faced considerable competition from industrialized nations wishing to finance their own balance of payments deficits, but some OPEC countries were already providing more aid in relation to their GNP than the OECD nations. Moreover, the OPEC countries had taken a number of steps that might lead to even larger increases in the flow of their development aid. These included agreements by Iran and Iraq to supply India with specified quantities of oil on deferred payment terms, creation of the Saudi Arabian Development Fund, and expansion of the Kuwait and Abu Dhabi development funds.

Regional Comparisons. The effects of the recent and rapid changes in commodity prices, high rates of inflation, and the economic uncertainties within developed countries had repercussions throughout the less developed world, but they were mitigated or augmented by special factors in different areas. By and large, the most seriously affected countries were those of southern Asia and Africa.

East Africa. Most East African countries depended on a narrow group of commodity exports; all were net importers of petroleum and petroleum products and imported nearly all their capital goods. Drought had severely affected parts of the area in

Table II. Selected Foreign Trade Indicators

In U.S. $000,000

	1965	1966	1967	1968	1969	1970	1971	1972	1973*
Exports									
World	184,139	201,370	211,892	236,342	269,668	308,806	344,463	385,527	547,771
Developed market economies†	125,853	138,681	146,200	164,647	189,648	218,903	244,883	269,594	395,205
Centrally planned economies‡	19,950	21,148	23,054	25,162	27,780	30,893	33,717	39,910	54,500
Less developed market economies§	38,336	41,541	42,538	46,533	52,240	59,010	65,863	76,023	98,066
Major oil exporters‖	10,720	11,432	12,035	13,433	14,490	16,284	20,901	24,502	33,591
Higher-income countries‖	16,291	18,283	18,838	20,478	24,084	27,549	29,293	33,977	41,940
Middle-income countries‖	6,326	6,424	6,572	7,207	7,909	8,899	9,419	11,358	15,828
Lower-income countries‖	4,999	5,402	5,093	5,415	5,757	6,278	6,250	6,186	6,707
Imports									
World	190,879	208,792	219,210	243,818	277,187	318,233	353,921	411,501	558,048
Developed market economies†	128,540	141,393	149,539	168,039	193,166	222,577	247,706	290,351	400,318
Centrally planned economies‡	19,657	20,615	22,025	23,927	26,372	30,179	32,722	40,286	55,500
Less developed market economies§	42,682	46,784	47,649	51,852	57,649	65,477	73,493	80,864	102,230
Major oil exporters‖	6,134	6,166	6,604	7,480	8,428	9,395	10,925	13,354	19,976
Higher-income countries‖	21,383	23,780	24,602	27,077	30,984	36,452	41,145	45,673	57,360
Middle-income countries‖	8,037	9,392	9,413	10,318	11,250	12,363	13,640	15,215	18,183
Lower-income countries‖	7,128	7,446	7,030	6,977	6,987	7,267	7,783	6,622	6,711
Export quantum indices (1963=100)									
All commodities	118	127	134	151	167	183	194	213	244
Developed	120	130	137	155	173	189	202	200	250
Less developed	113	118	124	136	147	160	168	186	226

*Preliminary.
†Developed market economies: Australia, Austria, Belgium, Canada, Denmark, Finland, France, West Germany, Iceland, Ireland, Italy, Japan, Luxembourg, The Netherlands, New Zealand, Norway, Portugal, South Africa, Sweden, Switzerland, United Kingdom, United States.
‡Centrally planned economies: Albania, Bulgaria, Czechoslovakia, East Germany, Hungary, Poland, Romania, U.S.S.R., Yugoslavia.
§Less developed market economies: Those countries listed in footnote * of Table III and the following: Africa—Guinea and Libya; East Asia—Cambodia, Laos, and Papua New Guinea; Middle East—Kuwait, Lebanon, Saudi Arabia, and Yemen (San'a'); South Asia—Nepal; Western Hemisphere—Barbados and Haiti.
‖Definition same as notes ‡, §, ‖, and ¶ of Table I.
Source: United Nations.

Table III. External Public Debt Outstanding of 86 Less Developed Countries* by Region and Income Group

In U.S. $000,000

		By region						By income group		
Year	Total	Africa	East Asia†	Middle East‡	South Asia	Southern Europe§	Western Hemisphere	Oil exporters‖	Higher-income countries‖	Middle-income countries‖	Lower-income countries‖
1965	38,067	7,686	3,968	2,357	9,115	4,033	10,907	5,927	14,587	6,444	11,109
1966	43,376	8,528	4,447	2,990	10,865	4,284	12,262	6,459	16,157	7,637	13,123
1967	50,343	9,192	5,302	3,917	11,697	5,114	15,120	7,326	20,139	8,681	14,197
1968	56,883	10,124	6,373	4,723	13,097	5,676	16,890	8,449	22,661	9,835	15,939
1969	63,468	11,035	7,833	5,488	14,093	6,418	18,601	10,010	25,006	11,233	17,220
1970	72,878	12,798	9,302	7,504	15,336	7,087	20,851	12,084	29,009	12,614	19,172
1971	85,143	14,632	11,361	9,243	16,942	8,548	24,418	14,990	34,466	14,543	21,144
1972	99,376	16,248	13,824	11,036	18,384	10,309	29,576	17,667	41,933	16,708	23,068

Note: Detail may not add to total given because of rounding.
*Includes the following countries: Africa—Algeria, Botswana, Burundi, Cameroon, Central African Republic, Chad, Congo, Dahomey, Egypt, Ethiopia, Gabon, The Gambia, Ghana, Ivory Coast, Kenya, Lesotho, Liberia, Malagasy Republic, Malawi, Mali, Mauritania, Mauritius, Morocco, Niger, Nigeria, Rwanda, Senegal, Sierra Leone, Somalia, Sudan, Swaziland, Tanzania, Togo, Tunisia, Uganda, Upper Volta, Zaire, Zambia, plus East African Community; East Asia—Fiji, Indonesia, South Korea, Malaysia, Philippines, Singapore, Taiwan, Thailand, South Vietnam; Middle East—Iran, Iraq, Israel, Jordan, Syria, Yemen (Aden); South Asia—Afghanistan, Bangladesh, Burma, India, Pakistan, Sri Lanka; Southern Europe—Cyprus, Greece, Malta, Spain, Turkey, Yugoslavia; Western Hemisphere—Argentina, Bolivia, Brazil, Chile, Colombia, Costa Rica, Dominican Republic, Ecuador, El Salvador, Guatemala, Guyana, Honduras, Jamaica, Mexico, Nicaragua, Panama, Paraguay, Peru, Trinidad and Tobago, Uruguay, Venezuela.
†Does not include publicly guaranteed private debt of the Philippines, estimated at U.S. $396,000,000 in 1972.
‡Does not include the undisbursed portion of the debt of Israel for the years 1965-70.
§Does not include the nonguaranteed debt of the "social sector" of Yugoslavia contracted after March 31, 1966.
‖Definition same as notes ‡, §, ‖, and ¶ of Table I.
Source: World Bank.

1973–74, most notably the northern provinces of Ethiopia.

East African exports of mineral products, sugar, cotton, and wool benefited from the shift in commodity prices. Rising oil prices tended to offset the favourable effects of this boom, but the low level of industrialization kept the demand for petroleum products relatively low. Taken as a whole, the countries of East Africa made some economic progress.

West Africa. Development in West Africa was impeded by drought and inflation. The coastal countries benefited from commodity price increases, particularly Nigeria, Gabon, and Congo, which export petroleum. However, the long drought in the Sahel had disastrous consequences for the economies of Chad, Mali, Mauritania, Niger, Senegal, Upper Volta, and Dahomey. (*See* AGRICULTURE AND FOOD SUPPLIES: *Special Report.*) Agriculture, which directly supported 70% of the area's population, had actually declined. For the region as a whole, economic growth had barely kept pace with population growth, and income disparities within and between countries had widened.

Europe, the Middle East, and North Africa. The resources, economic structures, and levels of development of countries in this region varied widely, and they had been affected very differently by the petroleum situation. At one end of the range were major petroleum exporters such as Algeria, Iran, Iraq, Kuwait, Libya, Oman, Qatar, Saudi Arabia, and the United Arab Emirates, whose earnings had risen from $15 billion in 1972 to $26 billion in 1973 and were expected to reach about $90 billion in 1974. The problem of absorptive capacity assumed a high priority for these countries. They recognized the need to develop modern economic systems and had also become a source of funds for other countries. The oil revenues of Syria and Tunisia had increased considerably but were still small in relation to their development needs.

Egypt and Romania exported about as much petroleum as they imported. The other less developed countries in the region—Afghanistan, Cyprus, Finland, Greece, Iceland, Ireland, Israel, Jordan, Lebanon, Morocco, Spain, Turkey, Yemen (San'a'), Yemen (Aden), and Yugoslavia—were net importers of oil and their import bills were rising significantly.

Asia. Though there was tremendous diversity among the less developed countries in this region, from the economic point of view they could be considered in three groups: those possessing abundant natural and mineral resources; those making economic progress despite the lack of such resources; and those that remained depressed.

For the first two groups, the past few years had been marked by significant increases in GNP. The Philippines, Thailand, Indonesia, and Malaysia had all experienced rapidly growing demand for their primary exports and favourable changes in their terms of trade. Expansion had been most rapid in Taiwan, South Korea, and Singapore. South Korea had a highly successful development strategy combining the advantages of an ample labour force with modern technology oriented to producing competitively for world markets. Singapore, with a very small population, had exploited its geographic position between the Indian and Pacific oceans and its excellent harbour. In both countries foreign capital had been welcomed to help implement national development strategies.

South Asia presented a strong contrast to these buoyant trends. World demand for the traditional exports of Bangladesh, India, and Sri Lanka—tea and jute—had been depressed for more than a decade, and the problem was aggravated by the worldwide inflation which increased import bills for energy, food, and capital goods. Despite severe flood damage in 1973, Pakistan's GNP rose about 6% in real terms because of favourable world markets for its main products—cotton, cotton goods, and rice—and the devaluation of the Pakistan rupee in early 1972. India's agricultural production had recovered from the 1972 drought, but depleted food stocks, inadequate foreign exchange, inflation, and lowered real investment combined to make 1974 a very difficult year. Few of India's major exports obtained higher prices. However, some areas, notably the northern states of Punjab and Haryana, continued to make economic progress.

Higher petroleum prices greatly influenced the short-term economic outlook throughout Asia. Only Indonesia stood to gain much financially from increased prices for its oil exports. Malaysia was a small net importer of oil, though its exports would exceed its imports in dollar value. For Sri Lanka, costlier petroleum, fertilizer, and food had been offset to some degree by higher prices for coconut products and rubber.

International Initiatives. The International Development Strategy for the UN's Second Development Decade (1971–80) "has not yet taken hold with anything like the force needed," according to a working paper prepared by the Committee on Review and Appraisal and revised by the UN Economic and Social Council (Ecosoc) during its 55th session in Geneva. Preliminary evidence suggested that the average annual rate of growth of gross domestic product (GDP) of the less developed countries in 1970 and 1971 did not quite reach the annual average of 5.5% experienced during the First Development Decade (1961–70) and was considerably smaller than in the closing years of the 1960s. The average rate of growth of per

Table IV. Flow of Financial Resources from DAC Countries* to Less Developed Countries and Multilateral Institutions

In U.S. $000,000

	1965	1966	1967	1968	1969	1970	1971	1972	1973†
Net disbursements									
Total, official and private‡	10.32	10.39	11.44	13.51	13.78	14.93	17.25	18.82	22.80
Total official	6.20	6.43	7.06	7.05	7.19	7.98	9.03	10.25	11.93
Official development assistance§	5.90	5.98	6.54	6.31	6.62	6.83	7.76	8.67	9.42
Grants‖	3.71	3.70	3.58	3.34	3.25	3.32	3.63	4.37	4.48
Multilateral contributions	0.35	0.34	0.74	0.68	1.05	1.12	1.34	1.90	2.25
Bilateral loans	1.83	1.95	2.23	2.28	2.32	2.38	2.79	2.40	2.68
Other official flows¶	0.30	0.45	0.52	0.74	0.57	1.15	1.27	1.58	2.52
Total private	4.12	3.96	4.38	6.46	6.59	6.95	8.22	8.58	10.87
Direct investment	2.47	2.18	2.11	3.15	2.92	3.56	3.87	4.41	5.87
Bilateral portfolio investment	0.66	0.48	0.80	0.95	1.20	0.73	0.76	2.07	3.17
Multilateral portfolio investment	0.25	0.18	0.47	0.77	0.42	0.47	0.77	0.67	0.26
Private export credits	0.75	1.12	1.01	1.60	2.05	2.19	2.81	1.43	1.58
Volume indicators (net disbursements)									
Total flow as share of GNP (%)‡	0.77	0.71	0.73	0.79	0.74	0.73	0.76	0.73	0.73
Official development assistance as share of GNP (%)	0.44	0.41	0.42	0.37	0.36	0.34	0.35	0.34	0.30
Private and other official flows as share of GNP (%)‡	0.33	0.30	0.31	0.42	0.38	0.39	0.41	0.39	0.43

Note: Details may not add to total given because of rounding. All data at current prices and exchange rates.
*Australia, Austria, Belgium, Canada, Denmark, France, West Germany, Italy, Japan, The Netherlands, New Zealand (which joined DAC in 1973), Norway, Portugal, Sweden, Switzerland, United Kingdom, and United States.
†Preliminary.
‡Excluding grants by private voluntary agencies. From all DAC countries, these totaled an estimated $858 million in 1970, $913 million in 1971, $1,033,000,000 in 1972, and $1,348,000,000 in 1973. In each year, these figures represented about 0.04% of GNP.
§Official Development Assistance (ODA) is defined as all flows to less developed countries and multilateral institutions provided by official agencies, including state and local governments, or by their executive agencies which meet the following tests:
(a) They are administered with the promotion of the economic development and welfare of less developed countries as their main objective.
(b) Their financial terms are intended to be concessional in character.
‖ Including "grant-like" flows denominated in recipients' currencies.
¶"Other Official Flows" include, in particular:
(a) Official bilateral transactions which are not concessional or which, even though they have concessional elements, are primarily export facilitating in purpose.
(b) The net acquisition by governments and central monetary institutions of securities issued by multilateral development banks at market terms. Rediscounting of trade instruments by central monetary authorities is not included.
Source: OECD.

capita GDP was not much above 2.5% and in many countries was considerably lower. In 1972 food production in the less developed countries actually declined.

The International Development Strategy stated that the growth of per capita GDP of the less developed countries as a whole during the Decade "should be about 3.5% in order at least to make a modest beginning towards narrowing the gap in living standards between developed and developing countries." Among the goals of the Strategy was an average annual growth rate in GDP of at least 6%.

Redistribution of income had made insufficient progress and unemployment loomed large, but the working paper noted some improvement in spreading the benefits of economic growth through education, health facilities, and low-cost housing. However, malnutrition remained widespread. The policies and action of the developed countries continued to have considerable influence on the economies of less developed countries. Most developed countries had not introduced any major policy changes in support of the Strategy. As ameliorative measures, the working paper urged developed countries to be receptive to international commodity agreements and to implement a generalized scheme of preference for imports of manufactured and semimanufactured goods from less developed countries.

The subject of multinational corporations was examined by an international Group of Eminent Persons established by Ecosoc. Meeting in September and November 1973 and March 1974, the group considered the effect of multinational corporations on world development and international relations and heard the views of government officials, labour unions, special interest groups, and multinational corporation executives and officials. It also considered a voluminous report, "Multinational Corporations in World Development," prepared by the UN Department of Economic and Social Affairs.

The report proposed the establishment of new supranational machinery to lay down universally accepted principles for multinational corporations. The ability of multinational corporations to tap worldwide resources, develop new technology, and provide needed productive and managerial ability could be used in the service of mankind, the report stated, but action was needed to give substance to the concept of "corporate social responsibility." Although only one-third of the direct investment by multinational corporations was in the less developed countries, their relative significance was much greater there than in developed market economies. Among the less developed countries the Western Hemisphere had attracted an estimated 18% of total worldwide foreign investment; Africa accounted for 6%, Asia for 5%, and the Middle East for 3%.

At the 57th session of Ecosoc in Geneva, UN Secretary-General Kurt Waldheim stated that the reemergence of scarcities constituted "the most visible symptom in the malfunctioning of the world economy today." This was especially true as regards the production and availability of food, where a combination of natural factors and growing demand had created an alarming situation. During 1972–73 world wheat and rice production declined by a little more than 4% while corn (maize) and other coarse grains fell more than 3%, and by the early summer of 1974 world grain reserves were at a new low. Early in 1974 it was thought that the 1973–74 world grain crop would be

the largest in history, but poor weather in several important growing areas appeared to have frustrated these expectations. Meanwhile, the world fish catch was declining both absolutely and in per capita terms.

Many factors had affected the food situation. The great increase in demand had resulted not only from population growth but also from changed eating habits —in many cases brought about by improved living standards. The Green Revolution, which had held such promise of increasing agricultural yields in the less

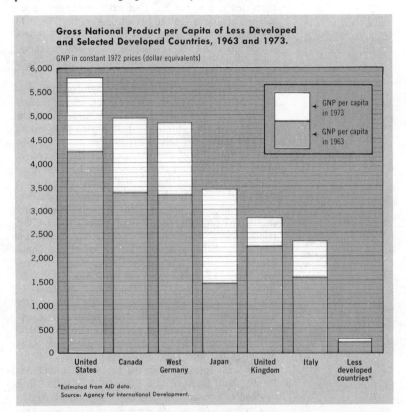

Gross National Product per Capita of Less Developed and Selected Developed Countries, 1963 and 1973.

GNP in constant 1972 prices (dollar equivalents)

GNP per capita in 1973

GNP per capita in 1963

*Estimated from AID data.
Source: Agency for International Development.

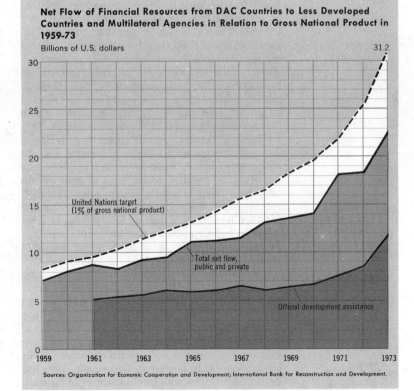

Net Flow of Financial Resources from DAC Countries to Less Developed Countries and Multilateral Agencies in Relation to Gross National Product in 1959-73

Billions of U.S. dollars

31.2

United Nations target (1% of gross national product)

Total net flow, public and private

Official development assistance

Sources: Organization for Economic Cooperation and Development; International Bank for Reconstruction and Development.

developed countries, was highly dependent on fertilizer and pesticides, both of which were affected by the petroleum situation. As a result, the less developed countries faced the possibility of increases in their food import bills comparable to those in their outlays for oil. In 1973 food-grain imports into non-oil-exporting countries had risen to an estimated $7 billion, compared with $2.8 billion in 1972, and a further rise to $8 billion–$9 billion was anticipated in 1974. Over the past two decades the position of the less developed countries as a whole had changed from approximate self-sufficiency in food to one of dependency. In 1973 the negative trade balance in food grains of the less developed countries (excluding trade among themselves) contributed $3.5 billion to improving the trade balances of developed areas.

Conflicts of interest between developed and less developed countries and, in some cases, among the less developed countries themselves, were apparent at the three major UN conferences held during the year to consider aspects of this situation. The third Conference on the Law of the Sea, in Caracas, Venezuela, aimed at creating an international legal regime governing all aspects of marine affairs, including fishing rights and the development of submerged mineral resources, but it adjourned without having made any substantive progress. (*See* LAW: *Special Report.*) The relationship of development to population control created sharp divisions among the less developed countries at the World Population Conference in Bucharest, Rom. (*See* POPULATIONS AND AREAS: *Special Report.*) The World Food Conference in Rome in November approved establishment of a new UN agency to supervise world food aid and endorsed several other long-term measures but accomplished little in the way of immediate assistance programs. (*See* AGRICULTURE AND FOOD SUPPLIES.)

The sixth special session of the UN General Assembly, held in April and May 1974, was the first devoted to economic matters. A Program of Action was adopted to provide emergency relief measures for the less developed countries most seriously affected by the economic crisis. As a first step, an emergency operation was set up with the aim of maintaining "unimpaired essential imports for the duration of the coming 12 months." Raúl Prebisch, former secretary-general of the UN Conference on Trade and Development (UNCTAD), was appointed to take charge of this operation. As part of the program, a special fund to provide relief and development assistance was to begin operations by Jan. 1, 1975, at the latest. In a report to a 36-nation special committee overseeing this assistance program, Prebisch declared that $3 billion to $4 billion would be needed to save those less developed countries on the brink of economic disaster as a result of soaring import costs. The EEC indicated that it would contribute one-sixth of the proposed fund, up to a limit of $500 million, if other industrial and oil-producing countries would bear their fair share. In October it was announced that $150 million of this would be released unconditionally.

International Development Assistance. In his address delivered at the annual meeting of the International Bank for Reconstruction and Development and the International Monetary Fund (IMF), Sept. 30, 1974, Robert McNamara, president of the World Bank, set forth his institution's program for the year. Primary emphasis was to be placed on increasing the productivity of the poorest 40% of people in the less developed countries, with special attention to the small

farmers and landless workers who migrate to larger towns and cities for offseason employment. The aim of the program was to increase productivity so that by 1985 output would be growing by 5% per year, double the rate of the 1960s. McNamara envisaged expanding the total lending of the World Bank to $36 billion for the fiscal years 1975–79, compared with $16 billion in 1970–74. This represented an increase of 125% in money terms, but it would provide an increase of only 40% in real terms because of inflation.

In accordance with a decision of the IMF executive board on June 13, 1974, a temporary supplementary facility was set up by the IMF to help members in balance of payments difficulties as a result of increases in the cost of petroleum and petroleum products. On August 22 the Fund announced that agreements had been completed with seven lenders to provide the equivalent of just over 2.8 billion SDRs (special drawing rights; somewhat over $3 billion).

Expenditures of the UN Development Program (UNDP) neared the $600 million mark in 1973, including $269 million from its own resources and over $325 million provided by the less developed countries themselves. Of these outlays, 30.9% were made in Africa, 23.6% in Asia, 21.7% in Latin America, and 21.7% in Europe, the Mediterranean area, and the Middle East. The remainder went into worldwide and interregional projects. Some 28.4% of the program was devoted to agriculture, 15.5% to trade, transport, and communication, 14% to industry, 10.1% to economic and social planning, 8.2% to education, 7.7% to health and social services, 6.7% to science and technology, 4.9% to natural resource development, and 4.5% to other related sectors.

An Asian Development Fund was set up as the facility for the concessional lending operations of the Asian Development Bank. It would be the sole vehicle for the bank's soft loans and was designed to be of particular benefit to smaller countries.

Economic Trends. The real rate of growth of less developed countries as a whole was 7.3% in 1973, compared with 5.4% in 1972 and 5.5 in 1971. The lowest rate was 4.7% in Africa, representing a slight decline from 1972. The Middle East and East Asia had by far the highest rates: 10% and 11.1%, respectively. Although South Asia's rate of 5.4% was one of the lowest, it was a marked improvement over the negative growth rate of 1972.

The overall real growth rate for agricultural production in the less developed countries was 6.1% in 1973, compared with −0.9% in 1972. However, there were striking disparities between geographic areas. The real rate of growth was −1.7% in Africa in 1973, −0.6% in southern Europe, −0.5% in the Middle East (7.1% in 1972), 9.1% in East Asia (1.4%), 11.3% in South Asia (−6.3%), and 4.6% in the Western Hemisphere (1.2%).

Figures indicating the growth rate of manufacturing in less developed countries as a whole and in some of the individual regions in 1973 were not yet available. Those that were showed a marked increase for East Asia (16.5% in 1973, compared with 12.9% in 1971 and 1972) and a considerable drop in South Asia (2.4% from 6.6%). In 1972 marked increases occurred in Africa (12.3% in 1972, compared with 8.6% in 1971) and in southern Europe (13% compared with 6.7%). In the Middle East the growth rate of manufacturing fell from 14.4% in 1971 to 12.2% in 1972. Southeast Asia and the Western Hemisphere both showed gains.

Diamonds:
see Mining and
Quarrying

Considering the less developed countries by income group, there were significant increases in the rates of growth of total GDP for 1973 in the oil-exporting countries (from 7.5 to 10.4%), the middle income countries (from 4.8 to 7.7%), and the lower income countries (from −0.7 to 5.1%). The improvement in the oil-producing countries was almost entirely due to petroleum. In the higher income countries agricultural production rose in 1973 but manufacturing declined, while in the middle and lower income countries the improvement was in the agricultural sector.

In the lower income countries, the rate of growth of GDP per capita rose from −3.2% in 1972 to 2.9% in 1973. However, this was still much lower than that for any other group and contrasted markedly with the 7.2% rate in 1973 of the oil-exporting countries. The higher income countries showed a decline, from 5 to 4.5%. (*See* Table I.) Among regions, sharp increases occurred in East Asia and South Asia—in East Asia the rate rose from −4 to 3.2%. Africa was the one area in which the growth rate of GDP per capita declined to any extent in 1973, falling from 2.9% in 1972 to 2%.

The annual growth rate of world external trade more than doubled between 1972 (18.8%) and 1973 (38.1%), and the rise was even larger for less developed market economies than for the developed market economies. The export quantum index (1963 = 100) was 244 for all commodities in 1973, compared with 213 in 1972; the index for less developed countries was 226. Reflecting worldwide inflation, the value of exports grew much more rapidly than the trade quantum index, resulting in an improvement in the less developed countries' trade balance of over $4 billion. According to an UNCTAD report, however, the trade deficit of less developed countries other than the major oil exporters in 1974 was expected to deteriorate by $5 billion–$9 billion compared with 1972, with a prospect of further deterioration of $13 billion–$23 billion in 1975. (*See* Table II.)

Gross investment and savings did not change appreciably between 1971 and 1972 for the less developed world as a whole. (Figures for 1973 were not yet available.) Gross investment amounted to 20.6% of GNP in 1972 and gross national savings to 18.1%. The lowest rates were in South Asia and the highest in southern Europe and the Middle East. Gross investment for all less developed countries in 1972 was about 2% below that for industrialized countries, while gross savings showed a larger differential of 4.6%. The oil-exporting countries had higher gross investment (24.6%) and savings (25.9%) than any other group of countries, including the industrialized nations. (*See* Table I.)

The total outstanding external debt of less developed countries had been increasing rapidly, from $38 billion in 1965 to $99 billion in 1972. It was estimated that by the end of 1974 it would exceed $120 billion and that debt service would amount to more than $10 billion. (*See* Table III.)

Official disbursements from members of the Development Assistance Committee (DAC) of the OECD to less developed countries and multilateral institutions in 1973 totaled $11,930,000,000, compared with $10,250,000,000 in 1972. Total private disbursements were $8,580,000,000 in 1972 and $10,870,000,000 in 1973. Total flow as a share of GNP remained at 0.73%; official development assistance declined from 0.34 to 0.30%, but private and other official flows rose slightly from 0.39 to 0.43%. Multilateral aid increased from $1.9 billion to $2,250,000,000 but was still only a small fraction of the total flow of financial resources from DAC countries to less developed countries. (*See* Table IV.)　　　　　(IRVING S. FRIEDMAN)

See also Agriculture and Food Supplies; Commercial and Trade Policies; Commodity Trade; Energy; Exchange and Payments, International; Industrial Production and Technology; Investment, International; Trade, International.
[537.A.5]

Disasters

The loss of life and property in disasters during 1974 included the following.

AVIATION

Jan. 1 Near Turin, Italy. An Italian twin-engine Fokker F-28 jetliner, on a flight from Cagliari, Sardinia, to Geneva, crashed in bad weather while approaching Turin airport for a stopover; only 4 of the 42 persons aboard were rescued from the flaming wreckage.

Jan. 6 Johnstown, Pa. A Beechcraft 99 twin-engine commuter turboprop struck a bank of runway lights at the Johnstown-Cambria (Pa.) County Airport, flipped over, and broke almost in half; 11 died and 6 were critically injured.

Jan. 26 Izmir, Turk. A Fokker F-28, taking off from Izmir's military airport on a domestic flight to Istanbul, crashed and burst into flames; 65 of the 73 aboard died.

Jan. 30 Pago Pago, American Samoa. A Pan American Boeing 707, arriving from Auckland, N.Z., crashed during heavy rains about one mile short of the Pago Pago airport runway; with its wings severed and fuselage torn apart, the plane burst into flames, killing 96 of the 101 persons aboard.

March 3 Near Paris. In the worst air disaster to date, a Turkish Airlines DC-10 jumbo jet, shortly after taking off from Paris' Orly Airport, crashed into a pine forest 26 mi. NE of the city; 346 bodies were recovered over a wide area that was strewn with wreckage and personal belongings; the disaster was apparently caused by a defective rear cargo door that suddenly burst open.

March 8 Hanoi, North Vietnam. A Soviet-made North Vietnamese airplane crashed as it attempted to land at Hanoi's military airport; 13 Algerian journalists and 3 radio reporters were killed.

March 14 Bishop, Calif. A chartered twin-engine Convair, taking a television crew from location in Bishop back to Burbank, Calif., crashed into a mountain ridge shortly after takeoff; 31 cast and film crew members and 5 members of the plane's crew were killed.

March 15 Teheran, Iran. A chartered Danish airliner, returning vacationers to Copenhagen after a tour of the Far East, burst into flames as it taxied into position for a takeoff from Teheran airport; of the almost 100 persons aboard, at least 16 died and many were hospitalized.

April 4 Francistown, Botswana. A DC-4, transporting gold miners home to Malawi after work in South Africa, caught fire shortly after takeoff and crashed as it attempted to return to the Francistown airport; 77 lost their lives but 7, thrown clear by the crash, survived.

April 11 SW of Hilo, Hawaii. A twin-engine Beechcraft, flying tourists from Hilo to the island of Maui, crashed into a mountain 31 mi. from the Hilo airport; a rescue team recovered all 11 bodies.

Wreckage from the worst air disaster in history lies in a forest near Paris. On March 3 a Turkish Airlines DC-10 crashed, killing 346.

AGIP/PICTORIAL PARADE

Smoke rises from the ruins of the Nypro chemical plant at Flixborough, Eng., destroyed in an explosion and fire on June 1 that killed 28 and caused extensive damage to nearby buildings.

April 22 Bali. A Pan American Boeing 707, carrying an international group of passengers from Hong Kong to Sydney, Austr., by way of Bali, crashed into a precipitous mountain as it began its approach to the international airport at Denpasar; rescue teams eventually recovered all 107 bodies.

April 27 Leningrad. A four-engine turboprop Ilyushin-18, departing on an Aeroflot flight to Krasnodar, crashed shortly after leaving the runway at Leningrad airport; 118 persons reportedly died in the flaming wreckage.

May 2 Andes Mountains, Ecuador. A twin-engine DC-3 owned by the local Ecuadorean airline, Atesa, crashed in the Andes Mountains east of Quito, while on a flight from Pastaza to Ambato; 22 persons were killed.

May 26 Celebes, Indon. An Indonesian Air Force aircraft crashed into a mountain killing all 10 crew members.

June 8 Colombia. A Colombian airliner crashed and burned at night in a jungle area near the Venezuelan border; all 43 persons on board were killed.

June 28 Battambang, Cambodia. A Cambodia Air Commercial plane, piloted by a Taiwanese crew, crashed on takeoff; 20 of the 25 persons aboard were reported killed.

Aug. 12 Near Linoghin, Upper Volta. An Air Mali Ilyushin turboprop, on a flight from Jidda, Saudi Arabia, to Bamako, Mali, crashed during a violent storm as the Soviet pilot apparently attempted an emergency landing when his plane ran out of fuel; though 13 survived, at least 47 others perished.

Aug. 14 Margarita Island, Venez. A four-engine turboprop of the government-owned Aeropostal airline was driven into a hill by hurricane-strength winds while on a flight from Caracas; the 49 casualties included two "stowaway" teenage girls who were allowed to board by a stewardess friend; only one person survived the crash.

Aug. 18 Near Kisangani, Zaire. A C-130 Zaire Air Force transport crashed with the loss of all 31 aboard.

Sept. 7 Near Telukbetung, Indon. An Indonesian Airways Fokker F-27, on a flight from Jakarta, was driven off course by a thunderstorm as it neared Telukbetung airport, crashed into an abandoned house, and burned; 28 persons were reported killed, 7 hospitalized, and 3 missing.

Sept. 8 Ionian Sea. A TWA Boeing 707, on a flight from Tel Aviv to New York City by way of Athens and Rome, crashed into the sea after flying westward across Greece; all 88 persons aboard died on impact or drowned.

Sept. 11 Charlotte, N.C. An Eastern Airlines DC-9, flying to Charlotte from Charleston, S.C., burst into flames and disintegrated when it crashed into a wooded area more than two miles from the Charlotte runway; 72 of the 82 persons aboard were killed.

Sept. 18 Ponta Pora, Braz. A Brazilian Air Force transport exploded and crashed shortly after taking off from Ponta Pora; 2 generals and an army base commander were among the 23 officers killed; one survived.

Oct. 30 Near Melville Island, N.W.T. A four-engine Lockheed Electra, operated by Panarctic Oils Ltd., crashed into Byam Channel while on a routine flight from Edmonton; only 2 of the 34 persons aboard survived when the plane hit the ice-covered channel.

Nov. 20 Nairobi, Kenya. A West German Lufthansa airliner, probably impaired by malfunctioning wing flaps, plunged into a muddy field and burned moments after taking off from the Nairobi airport; of the 157 persons involved in the first fatal crash of a Boeing 747, 59 died, 23 were hospitalized, and 75 escaped without serious injury.

Dec. 1 Upperville, Va. A TWA Boeing 727, battling heavy rains, crashed into a wooded slope near a secret U.S. government installation while approaching Dulles International Airport, Washington, D.C., on a flight from Columbus, O.; all 92 persons aboard the jetliner were killed.

Dec. 4 Central Sri Lanka. A chartered Dutch DC-8 jetliner, carrying 182 Indonesian Muslim pilgrims to Mecca, Saudi Arabia, crashed into a hillside 70 mi. SE of Colombo, while approaching Bandaranaike International Airport; all 182 pilgrims and 9 crew members were killed.

Dec. 22 Near Maturín, Venez. An Avensa Airlines DC-9, on a domestic flight to Caracas, exploded and crashed shortly after taking off from Maturín airport; 77 persons died.

Dec. 28 Near Tikal, Guatemala. A chartered Lockheed Lodestar airliner, carrying a group of U.S. tourists back to Guatemala City after a visit to Mayan ruins in the north, crashed in flames shortly after taking off from the Tikal airport; all 21 passengers were killed along with the 3 Guatemalan crew members.

FIRES AND EXPLOSIONS

Jan. 23 Heusden, Belg. A night fire, possibly started by illicit smoking and fueled by wooden partitions and bedding, swept through Sacred Heart College dormitory; 23 teenage boys were asphyxiated or burned to death.

Feb. 1 São Paulo, Braz. A fire, started by an electrical short circuit in an air conditioner, engulfed the upper 14 stories of a newly constructed 25-story bank building, trapping hundreds of workers as the flames fed on combustible interior-finish materials; due to inadequate escape facilities, at least 227 persons lost their lives.

March 11 Dublin, Ire. In the worst private home fire in Dublin in almost 30 years, a news vendor, his pregnant wife, and 10 of their 13 children were burned to death.

June 1 Flixborough, Humberside County, Eng. A violent explosion completely destroyed the recently completed Nypro chemical plant located about 180 mi. N of London; 28 persons died, some perhaps victims of the raging fire or of toxic fumes that required evacuation of neighbouring areas.

June 17 Lahore, Pak. A building was completely gutted by a fire that took at least 40 lives; six entire families reportedly perished.

June 30 Port Chester, N.Y. Heavy smoke and flames from a cellar fire next door poured into a crowded two-level discotheque on the New York-Connecticut border, trapping scores of dancers who struggled blindly for the exits after the lights failed; of the 24 persons who died, some were apparently trampled to death in the panic.

Aug. 1 Alcalá de Henares, Spain. A raging prison fire claimed the lives of the warden and 13 inmates.

Sept. 5 Southern Nigeria. Fire swept through a riverboat in southern Nigeria; 67 persons were killed and more than 180 were injured.

Oct. 16 Sumatra, Indon. The Swedish tanker "Palma" caught fire and burned in a Sumatra harbour; the captain and 12 crewmen were missing and believed dead.

Oct. 17 Seoul, South Korea. Fire erupted on the fifth floor of the ten-story New Namsan Hotel in downtown Seoul; 15 persons died and more than 20 others were injured.

Oct. 31 Near Allahabad, India. Two coaches of the Upper India Express exploded and burned with the loss of 52 lives; about 60 were injured.

Nov. 3 Seoul, South Korea. A seven-story hotel and entertainment centre known as Daewang Corner was badly ravaged by a fire; of the 88 persons who lost their lives, 72 died in the Time Club discotheque.

Nov. 9 Tokyo Bay, Jap. The Liberian freighter "Pacific Ares" collided with the 43,700-ton Japanese tanker "Yuyo Maru," which was carrying butane, propane, and naphtha; 21 persons died and 12 others were missing as a result of violent explosions and raging fires that destroyed both vessels.

Dec. 15 Nottingham, Eng. An early morning fire accompanied by heavy smoke swept through a city-owned nursing home; 18 of the 49 residents died, most from asphyxiation.

MARINE

Jan. 5 Central Philippines. The ferry "Tagbilaran" sank in high seas and strong winds shortly after midnight; 37 bodies were recovered but another 45 of the 217 persons aboard were reported missing.

Jan. 17 English Channel near Guernsey. The 2,000-ton Cypriot timber freighter "Prosperity" was wrecked on a reef by a 100-mph gale; 16 bodies were recovered and 2 other crewmen were presumed drowned.

Jan. 18 near Pilottown, La. The U.S. tanker "Key Trader" collided with the Norwegian ore freighter "Baune" in the mouth of the Mississippi River; exploding oil and gasoline caused the deaths of 5 persons; 8 were reported injured and 11 missing.

Feb. 8 Arctic Ocean. The ultramodern 1,106-ton British trawler "Gaul" apparently foundered and sank in stormy seas and freezing temperatures north of Norway; after an extensive but futile eight-day air and sea search all 36 crew members were presumed dead.

Feb. 22 Off Chungmu, South Korea. A South Korean Navy tug, returning from a training cruise with 311 recruits and a crew of 5, sank in Chungmu Harbour; 15 were known to have died, but 144 others were missing.

Late March Mato Grosso, Braz. Two navy ships collided while rescuing flood victims in Mato Grosso, a state in the west region of Brazil; 13 persons died in the accident, which increased the flood death toll to 38.

April 3 Piauí, Braz. A barge carrying 80 persons was reported to have gone down in the Paranaíba River; at least 30 persons lost their lives.

April 12 Off Cape Hino, Jap. The 999-ton South Korean freighter "Kaiei Ho" collided with the 21,467-ton American container ship "President Pierce"; 18 of the 26 Korean seamen were missing after their ship split in two.

April 12 Off Cape Shinono, Jap. In a pre-dawn accident, the 284-ton fishing boat "Shohei Maru" collided with the 11,144-ton freighter "Ocean Sovereign"; 14 of the 17 Japanese tuna fishermen were missing and presumed drowned.

April 23 SE of Rangoon, Burma. A fishing schooner was reported sunk some 155 mi. from Rangoon with a loss of about 100 lives.

May 1 Bay of Bengal. A motor launch capsized in waters off Bangladesh, killing 250 persons.

Late August Off southwest coast, South Korea. Six fishing boats, battered by severe gales and heavy rains, were presumed to have capsized with the loss of 71 lives.

Mid-September Black Sea. A Kashin-class Soviet destroyer, armed with guided missiles, exploded and sank with the loss of its entire crew, according to unofficial sources; the death toll was conservatively estimated at 225—and may have exceeded 300—making it one of the worst peacetime naval disasters in modern history.

September Bay of Bengal. A ferryboat capsized in the Bay of Bengal, drowning about 160 persons.

Sept. 28 Hong Kong. The Panamanian freighter "Sun Shang" sank after being caught in a typhoon 400 mi. E of Hong Kong, killing 31 of 34 crewmen aboard.

Late October Near Fiji. A burned-out Korean fishing boat, minus lifeboats and crew, was discovered on Nov. 1; all 22 aboard were presumed to have drowned.

Nov. 20 Near Sundarbans, Bangladesh. A ferryboat capsized about 90 mi. from Dacca with the loss of at least 85 lives.

Nov. 28 Bay of Bengal. A cyclone that struck Bangladesh was believed to have claimed the lives of 79 fishermen who were still missing after a sea and air search.

MINING AND TUNNELING

March 10 Near Soko Banja, Yugos. Methane gas exploded in a coal pit in eastern Yugoslavia taking the lives of 12 miners; 3 other workers were missing and presumed dead.

May 11(?) Near Erzurum, Turk. A coal mine explosion in eastern Turkey took the lives of at least 10 miners.

Dec. 27 Liévin, France. An explosion and fire of uncertain origin took the lives of 42 miners working 2,300 ft. below the surface in the state-owned Liévin coalfields.

MISCELLANEOUS

May 26 Central Kuwait. Three floors of an office building suddenly collapsed during construction; 14 workers were reportedly killed despite frantic efforts to rescue those trapped alive beneath the wreckage.

Early June India. In the worst smallpox epidemic of the century, centred mainly in the state of Bihar but extending in a lesser degree to other far-flung areas of the country, an estimated 20,000 persons were reported to have died in Bihar alone.

October Bahia State, Braz. Several hundred cases of bubonic plague were reported in Bahia State; some 40 deaths were confirmed with others expected to follow.

October São Paulo, Braz. A prolonged epidemic of meningitis was reportedly abating after it had caused at least 1,500 deaths.

Dec. 5 Teheran, Iran. The concrete-slab roof above the main lobby of the newly enlarged airport terminal at Teheran collapsed after a heavy snowfall; 17 deaths were confirmed but the fatality list was expected to grow.

Dec. 31 Mecca, Saudi Arabia. During a religious pilgrimage to Mecca, 28 Nigerian Muslims contracted cholera and died.

NATURAL

Mid-January Australia. Floodwaters in eastern Australia claimed 17 lives and left homeless an estimated 1,000 persons; in New South Wales and Queensland tens of thousands of sheep and cattle were killed.

Mid-January Situbondo, Indon. Heavy rains and tidal waves in East Java destroyed homes, washed out bridges, and ruined rice crops; 19 died and some 2,000 were made homeless.

Jan. 21(?) Tatra Mountains, Czechoslovakia. Three avalanches, brought on by a sudden temperature rise, brought death to 12 Czechoslovak ski students, their instructor, and a mountaineer.

Late January Eastern Australia. Prolonged storms caused record flooding over vast areas of the eastern half of Australia; Queensland, the most devastated region, reported at least 15 deaths and damage to crops, cattle, and homes well in excess of $100 million.

February NW Argentina. Torrential rains inundated half of Santiago del Estero Province, virtually destroying the entire cotton harvest; similar destruction occurred in ten other provinces; at least 100 persons were killed and more than 100,000 were forced to evacuate their homes.

Feb. 10 Natal, S.Af. Rivers, swollen by an intense rainfall, overflowed their banks in northern Natal and swept away huts and shacks during the night; more than 50 persons were believed dead, many of them children.

Late March Tubarão, Braz. After months of drought, torrential rains poured into the Tubarão River, which reportedly rose 36 ft. within hours, overflowed its banks, and virtually destroyed the city; reports estimated that between 1,000 and 1,500 persons died and that 60,000 of the city's 70,000 people were made homeless.

Early April Grande Kabylie, Alg. Several days of torrential coastal rains caused severe flooding; at least 50 persons were reported killed and 30 injured.

April 3 United States. A series of tornadoes, nearly 100 of which struck during an eight-hour period, caused more than $1 billion in damage as they wreaked havoc in 11 U.S. Southern and Middle Western states and in Canada; early reports showed 72 confirmed deaths in Alabama, 71 in Kentucky, 58 in Tennessee, 52 in Indiana, 34 in Ohio, 16 in Georgia, 5 in North Carolina, 3 in Michigan, 2 in Illinois, and 1 each in Virginia and West Virginia; 8 deaths in Windsor, Ont., raised the death toll to 323.

April 16 Okuura, Jap. A storm-triggered landslide buried about 80 homes in mud in an area of old mine tunnels about 190 mi. N of Tokyo; 8 bodies were recovered but 9 other persons were missing and believed killed.

Yugoslav soldiers help extricate passengers from a train wreck in Zagreb, Yugos., on August 30. The accident killed 124.

A man leaps to his death from a burning 25-story bank building in São Paulo, Braz., on February 1. The fire took 227 lives.

April 25 Central Andes, Peru. Heavy rains and earth tremors caused parts of three mountains to shear loose in gigantic landslides that virtually obliterated several villages; in all, more than 1,000 may have been killed, an estimated 200 in Mayunmarca, 150 in Huacoto, and 100 each in Perseverancia and Ropas.

Early May NE Brazil. Heavy rains caused landslides that reportedly brought death to 91 persons; all told, floods claimed about 200 victims, mostly in the state of Ceará.

May 9 Izu-hanto, Jap. A powerful earthquake, striking 90 mi. SW of Tokyo, damaged or destroyed hundreds of homes and killed more than 30 persons.

June 8 Oklahoma. A series of night tornadoes swept through Oklahoma killing an estimated 14 persons and injuring hundreds; 6 others were killed in Kansas and 4 in Arkansas.

June 17 Near Acapulco, Mex. Torrential rains carried by Hurricane Dolores devastated a poverty area on the outskirts of Acapulco; at least 13 persons were killed and 35 injured; the fate of 16 others was unknown.

June 28 Quebradablanca, Colombia. A huge avalanche of rocks and mud thundered onto 800 yd. of twisting highway engulfing 6 crowded buses and more than 20 other vehicles, some of which were hurled into a ravine; officials estimated the death toll to be in excess of 200 and the injured to number about 100.

July 6–7 Japan. A typhoon that dumped as much as 12 in. of rain on some areas of western and southern Japan killed 33 persons; some 50 others were injured and 15 were reported missing.

July 11 Japan. Prolonged rains in various parts of the country brought death to at least 108 persons and caused damage estimated at nearly $400 million.

Mid-August Bangladesh and northeastern India. Two Himalayan rivers, at flood stage for several weeks, were reported to have caused at least 800 deaths in Bangladesh and 100 deaths in seven states of northeastern India; an additional 1,500 deaths in Bangladesh were caused by a cholera outbreak brought on by the flooding.

Mid-August Luzon, Phil. Week-long monsoon rains, which flooded vast expanses of 13 of the 24 provinces of the island of Luzon, killed at least 94 persons; more than one million refugees of the disaster required emergency relief.

Aug. 15 West Bengal State, India. A cyclone killed at least 20 persons and injured about 100 others before moving on to Jamshedpur, where 800 families had to be evacuated.

Aug. 20 Along the Irrawaddy River, Burma. Widespread flooding, brought on by monsoon rains, inundated nearly 2,000 villages and took the lives of at least 12 persons; about 500,000 persons were left homeless and stranded when roads and railway lines were washed away.

Sept. 20 Honduras. Hurricane Fifi, battering the northern coast of Honduras with 130-mph winds and torrential rains, brought death to an estimated 5,000 persons and caused extensive damage to crops, buildings, roads, bridges, and communications facilities; relief teams flew in food, clothing, and medical supplies to assist the injured and the tens of thousands made homeless by the disaster.

Sept. 29 Medellín, Colombia. A landslide that crashed into a slum settlement on the outskirts of the city took the lives of an estimated 90 persons.

Oct. 3 Peru. A violent earthquake, measuring 7.8 on the Richter scale, caused extensive damage in Lima and in the coastal cities of Cañete, Pisco, and Ica; early reports indicated that the quake killed more than 73 persons, injured some 2,000, and badly damaged or destroyed thousands of homes.

Oct. 3 Chorillos, Peru. An earthquake that demolished numerous buildings killed 44 persons and injured hundreds.

Oct. 23 São Tomé. A landslide that rumbled through a ravine killed at least 30 persons.

Nov. 19 Silopi, Turk. Floodwaters from a small river swollen by heavy rains trapped members of a nomadic tribe camping nearby; 33 persons lost their lives.

Nov. 29 Off Cox's Bazar, Bangladesh. A 12-ft. tidal wave swept over offshore islands in the southeastern Bay of Bengal in the wake of a cyclone that left thousands of people homeless in Bangladesh on November 28; 20 people were killed by the tidal wave.

Dec. 20 Neskaupstadhur, Iceland. An avalanche of snow and ice roared down on the fishing town of Neskaupstadhur; 12 bodies were recovered from the debris.

Dec. 25 Darwin, Austr. Cyclone Tracy ripped through the port city of Darwin, in what was described as Australia's worst natural catastrophe. Ninety percent of the city was destroyed and the death toll was reported to be more than 50.

Dec. 28 Northern Pakistan. A violent earthquake destroyed at least nine villages situated at the base of the Karakoram Range; rescue teams placed the death toll at about 5,200 and the number of injured at 15,000.

RAILROAD

Jan. 7 Zeytinlik, Turk. Two passenger trains collided at a station in southern Turkey, killing at least 25 persons and injuring some 50 others.

March 27 Near Lourenço Marques, Mozambique. A Mozambique freight train, loaded with petroleum products, collided with a Rhodesian passenger train about 31 mi. N of the Mozambique capital; of the estimated 60 persons who died, most were burned to death in a raging fire; about 50 others were hospitalized in serious condition.

May 29 Rio de Janeiro, Braz. Two suburban freight trains passing each other created a powerful slipstream that tore loose the grip of habitual hitchhikers clinging to the sides of the cars; 16 were killed and many others injured.

June 17 Banha, Egypt. A crowded train bound for Alexandria collided with a truck at the Banha crossing, about 30 mi. from Cairo; 18 persons died and more than 98 others were injured.

Aug. 30 Zagreb, Yugos. An eight-car passenger train derailed when the engineer, probably dozing with fatigue, failed to slow the train down as it swept into Zagreb station and hit a curve; 124 persons were reported killed and about 100 others injured.

Dec. 20 Near Bamako, Mali. A speeding passenger train jumped the tracks as it rounded a curve before entering Bamako station; 20 persons were killed and 180 injured.

TRAFFIC

Jan. 19 Karachi, Pak. When a gasoline tanker truck collided with a bus, leaking fuel set fire to nearby buildings; at least 24 persons were killed and 40 injured.

Jan. 28 Peru. A bus that plunged into a river in the Andes was swirled 400 yd. downstream; at least 35 persons died.

Jan. 29 Colombia. A bus toppled over a precipice and into the Ovejas River, killing 17 persons and badly injuring 10.

Feb. 11 Banphot Phisai, Thailand. Two buses collided about 165 mi. N of Bangkok; 25 persons were reported killed and 50 injured.

March 14 (?) Nigeria. A truck, moving along the road between Kontagora and Zura, went off the road and plunged into a river; 23 persons were killed and 14 injured.

April 12 Near Acapulco, Mex. A double-level truck, swerving to avoid a horse, went off the road and into a 21-ft. gully; 14 passengers, returning home from Good Friday services, lost their lives; more than 100 others suffered injuries.

May 20 Eastern Tabasco State, Mex. A bus filled with vacationers crashed into the Carizales River, killing 36 persons.

May 21 Ganges River, India. A crowded bus, being driven onto a tug that served as a river ferry, slid off the boat and into the Ganges; at least 50 persons were believed drowned.

July 25 Near Mexico City. Two bus crashes, both near Mexico City, took the lives of 24 persons and injured 71.

July 28 Belém, Braz. A bus collided with a truck 250 mi. S of Belém, killing 69 persons and injuring 10.

Aug. 11 Near Bolu, Turk. A collision between two buses traveling along the Ankara–Istanbul highway took the lives of 21 persons and injured 41.

Sept. 9 Lusaka, Zambia. A bus accident caused the death of 26 persons, including one member of Parliament.

Dec. 20 Sterkstroom, S.Af. A truck overturned near Sterkstroom, killing 33 African railway workers and injuring 26 seriously.

Dec. 27 Nova Iguaçu, Braz. An interurban train passing a suburban railroad crossing north of Rio de Janeiro crashed into a bus; 18 persons died and 18 others were injured.

Dominican Republic

Covering the eastern two-thirds of the Caribbean island of Hispaniola, the Dominican Republic is separated from Haiti, which occupies the western third, by a rugged mountain range. Area: 18,658 sq.mi. (48,323 sq.km.). Pop. (1973 est.): 4,431,700, including (1960) mulatto 73%; white 16%; Negro 11%. Cap. and largest city: Santo Domingo (pop., 1973 est., 817,303). Language: Spanish. Religion (1971 est.): Roman Catholic 92%. President in 1974, Joaquín Balaguer.

The national presidential elections clearly dominated political events in 1974. The principal opposition to the incumbent Reformist Party was the Coalition of Santiago, headed by presidential candidate and rancher Silvestre Guzmán. It was formed from a combination of parties, including the left-wing Dominican Revolutionary Party (PRD), the nationalist Social Christian Revolutionary Party (PRSC), and the right-wing Quisqueyan Democratic Party (PQD). The coalition abstained from the presidential race two days before the May 16 elections, alleging lack of constitutional guarantees for a free election. Joaquín Balaguer was reelected for a third term, defeating the

DOMINICAN REPUBLIC

Education. (1971–72) Primary, pupils 820,215, teachers 14,752; secondary, pupils 122,565, teachers 2,131; vocational, pupils 6,923, teachers 409; teacher training, students 621, teachers 51; higher (1970–71), students 19,336, teaching staff 1,038.

Finance. Monetary unit: peso, at parity with the U.S. dollar, with a free rate (Sept. 16, 1974) of 2.31 pesos to £1 sterling. Gold, SDRs, and foreign exchange, central bank: (June 1974) U.S. $122.1 million; (June 1973) U.S. $40.7 million. Budget (1974 est.) balanced at 383.4 million pesos. Gross national product: (1971) 1,604,200,000 pesos; (1970) 1,446,300,000 pesos. Money supply: (Feb. 1974) 257.3 million pesos; (Feb. 1973) 218.3 million pesos. Cost of living (Santo Domingo; 1970 = 100): (May 1974) 143; (May 1973) 122.

Foreign Trade. (1973) Imports 485.9 million pesos; exports 442.1 million pesos. Import sources: U.S. 59%; Japan 9%; West Germany 7%. Export destination U.S. 65%. Main exports: sugar 45%; coffee 10%; tobacco 7%; cocoa 5%.

Transport and Communications. Roads (1970) c. 6,250 km. Motor vehicles in use (1972): passenger 50,700; commercial (including buses) 24,200. Railways (1972) c. 1,700 km. (mainly for sugar estates). Telephones (Jan. 1973) 66,000. Radio receivers (Dec. 1972) 170,000. Television receivers (Dec. 1972) 150,000.

Agriculture. Production (in 000; metric tons; 1973; 1972 in parentheses): rice c. 183 (c. 191); corn (1972) 50, (1971) c. 47; sweet potatoes (1972) c. 95, (1971) c. 91; cassava (1972) c. 195, (1971) c. 184; dry beans c. 32 (c. 30); tomatoes c. 60 (c. 60); peanuts c. 67 (c. 83); sugar, raw value c. 1,270 (c. 1,200); oranges c. 63 (c. 62); bananas (1972) c. 290, (1971) c. 286; cocoa 28 (44); coffee c. 45 (c. 43); tobacco c. 35 (c. 28). Livestock (in 000; June 1973): cattle c. 1,500; sheep c. 87; pigs (1972) c. 400; horses c. 170; chickens c. 7,500.

Industry. Production (in 000; metric tons; 1972): bauxite 1,087; cement 678; electricity (kw-hr.) 1,201,000.

small Popular Democratic Party (PDP). A wave of unrest accompanied the elections as neighbourhoods within several cities went on 24-hour strikes.

In response to the opposition protests against his continuing in office, President Balaguer on August 16 presented four amendments to the constitution. Among them, he proposed that a person not succeed himself as president for more than two consecutive terms in office. The right to freedom of speech was returned to several opposition leaders, among them José Peña Gomez, the PRD secretary-general.

In late September, members of the leftist 12th of January Freedom Movement, led by Radames Méndez Vargas, kidnapped seven persons and held them hostage in the Venezuelan consulate in Santo Domingo. Among the hostages held for ransom were the Venezuelan consul and vice-consul, the director of the local U.S. Information Service office, a Spanish priest, and four Dominicans. The ransom demanded by the kidnappers included freedom for 36 political prisoners, $1 million, and safe exit from the country. All the demands were refused but the last one; the kidnappers released their hostages unharmed, and in early October were allowed to leave for Panama.

The Dominican Republic served as host country for the 12th Central American and Caribbean Olympic Games, held in Santo Domingo city from February 27 to March 13, 1974. Approximately 3,000 athletes representing 23 countries competed in 16 sports events. The Games subsequently stimulated participation in sports throughout the republic. Volleyball increased in popularity, and basketball began to share baseball's role as a spectator sport. The rivalry between Naco and San Lazaro, with the latter team winning the national basketball championship, was instrumental in increasing that sport's popularity.

The government's large-scale building and restoration programs continued throughout 1974. In Santo Domingo city, two new developments were completed: Independence Square, housing public office buildings, and the Cultural Centre, composed of several large museums and halls for the performing arts. The restoration of colonial sites continued, as public and private investments helped Dominicans rediscover and preserve the nation's history. In the rural areas, top priority on the construction list was being given to the extension of irrigation works and the building of farm-to-market roads.

The republic continued economic diversification in 1974, as illustrated by the inauguration of a free port and industrial park in Santiago city. Tourism was another important investment area. Development focused on beach-front properties along the north coast near Puerto Plata, to the northeast on Samana Peninsula, and to the south at Boca Chica, a popular resort located a half hour's drive from the capital city.

(GUSTAVO ARTHUR ANTONINI)

[974.B.2.b]

Drug Abuse

The claim that marijuana (*Cannabis sativa*) is harmless (often advanced by those who would like to see it legalized) was questioned further in 1974. In March William Paton of the University of Oxford reported that evidence of the drug's toxicity was accumulating rapidly, but that study of possible long-term effects on habitual users was difficult because little was known about how the body deals with tetrahydrocannabinol (THC), the chief active ingredient. It was known that the drug accumulates in fat. From 20 to 30 breakdown products of THC had been identified, but scientists had yet to discover if and how any of these chemicals interfere with other tissues. The drug had been shown to produce birth defects in three species of animals.

A team of researchers at Columbia University reported experiments suggesting that smoking marijuana may lower resistance to certain viral and fungal infections, and perhaps to cancer. The workers found that THC reduces the activity of certain white blood cells (lymphocytes) concerned with the immune response, the mechanism whereby the body attempts to destroy "foreign" cells. The activity of lymphocytes from 50 regular marijuana smokers was about half the normal level. Earlier, Australian workers had found that tobacco smokers appear to suffer similar damage.

Research at the Reproductive Biology Research Foundation, St. Louis, Mo., suggested that the use of *Cannabis* produces a significant reduction in the level of the male sex hormone, testosterone, circulating in the blood of heterosexual men. The subjects were 20 young men who had used marijuana at least four times a week for at least six months. The reduction of the hormone in the blood was proportional to the quantity of *Cannabis* taken, and in men who had been smoking ten or more marijuana cigarettes a week, the testosterone level had fallen by 60%. However, only two of the smokers admitted any falling off in their capacity for sex. The Missouri workers pointed out that THC can pass the placental barrier from the blood of a pregnant woman to her fetus, and since a proper level of testosterone in the tissues of the developing male child is necessary for the formation

Drama:
see Motion Pictures; Theatre

Dress:
see Fashion and Dress; Furs

UPI COMPIX

Customs official examines part of the almost 19 tons of marijuana confiscated from smugglers at Nogales, Arizona, on September 20. Believed to be the largest single seizure of the drug in the U.S., it had a street value estimated at $10.9 million.

of the male sex organs, they suggested that a marijuana-using mother might run the risk of producing a sexually malformed infant.

Despite the accumulation of experimental evidence, there was still no firm clinical evidence that marijuana users are, in fact, more liable to any particular ills of the flesh than the rest of the community. This fact provided little excuse for complacency, however, in view (for example) of the very long time it took to recognize any connection between tobacco smoking and disease. Moreover, since marijuana was illegal, most users would not admit their habit, thus obscuring any pattern of disease that might exist.

A study of 60 patients admitted to a poisoning treatment centre at Edinburgh Royal Infirmary as a result of a "bad trip" on the hallucinogen LSD established several interesting points. None of the patients died. The only treatment needed was sedation. Only one out of six was thought to be in need of psychiatric help. There were three times as many men patients as women. Most of the admissions occurred during the weekend. The patients' average age was 20, and well over half were younger. The great majority were "working class," two out of five were unemployed, and almost the same proportion had been convicted of some offense. These facts suggested that LSD might be somewhat less dangerous than was generally supposed. More importantly, they implied that "mind bending" drugs were not primarily the playthings of a privileged generation searching for "kicks" but were, instead, a means of temporary escape from reality for young people for whom the world was a cheerless and inhospitable place.

In the area of opiate abuse, research continued to centre on the development of antagonists. Reports from current studies of the long acting, methadone-

like drug LAAM indicated that it would be at least as safe and efficacious as methadone as a replacement therapy for heroin addiction. Research on the antagonist Naltrexone continued and studies of its short-term efficacy and safety were being made. The U.S. government initiated three studies to determine the efficacy of propoxyphene napsulate in the treatment of chronic heroin addiction, particularly as a detoxification agent.

International Supplies and Traffic. The latest available figures furnished by countries reporting to the International Narcotics Control Board (INCB) indicated that production of opium in these countries reached a peak of 1,550 tons in 1972 (1,388 tons in 1971). The increase was almost entirely attributable to production of 374 tons by Iran, which produced opium exclusively for the maintenance treatment of its own addicts and where production was controlled by the authorities in accordance with the demand. The opium harvest in India was the highest since World War II, 991 tons, compared with 883 tons in 1971. Production in the U.S.S.R. declined for the second successive year, falling from a peak of 226 tons in 1970 to 114 tons in 1972. In its last year of production before the abortive ban, Turkey produced 66 tons, continuing the decline of the previous 20 years. Some 170 tons of morphine were produced from opium, poppy straw, and concentrate of poppy straw, 3% less than in 1971. As in previous years, the bulk of the morphine (88.4%) was converted into codeine.

Peru produced 10,022 tons of coca leaf in 1972, virtually the same as in 1971. Only 5% of the Peruvian production was used for medical purposes; 18 tons went for the manufacture of cocaine and 522 tons were exported to the U.S. for the manufacture of aromatic products not containing alkaloids and for the extraction of cocaine. Bolivia, the other country producing coca leaf, did not furnish information to the board in 1972.

In 1974 Turkey repealed the ban on the growing of opium poppies instituted following a bilateral agreement with the U.S. in 1972. Turkish farmers, for whom poppy growing was an established culture, had been vociferous in their opposition, and the U.S. pledge of $35.7 million was considered insufficient. The Turkish government did plan to collect the whole poppy pod, rather than the opium gum, in an effort to decrease the amount of gum purchased illegally.

U.S. hopes for salubrious results from the Turkish agreement had diminished long before, however. For a short period there were indications of a decreased supply of heroin, especially on the East Coast, and evidences that other drugs, including cocaine, were supplanting it. But before long Mexican brown heroin began to surface across the U.S., and heroin from the Golden Triangle of Southeast Asia followed the Vietnam veterans home.

Mexico became the number one priority country in U.S. international narcotics-control efforts. The Mexican opium crop and heroin laboratories were the current source of "a very large percent" of heroin available in the U.S., and a large proportion of marijuana entering the U.S. was produced in Mexico. U.S.-Mexican cooperative measures included the use of helicopters to locate and eradicate illegal crops of opium poppies and marijuana in Mexico's otherwise inaccessible western mountains. Other countries where the U.S. was active were Colombia, the major transit point for illegal shipments of cocaine entering the U.S. market, and Jamaica, a transit point for smuggled cocaine and opium, and second only to Mexico as a supplier of marijuana. The emergence of a domestic drug problem in France in 1970 resulted in increased cooperation between France and the U.S. in shutting down laboratories located in the Marseilles area. U.S. international control efforts in Southeast Asia centred in Thailand, the major transit area for opium grown in Burma.

Through the initiative of the UN Commission on Narcotic Drugs, groups of states in the Middle and Far East had been brought together to encourage the coordination of activities to counter drug abuse and illicit trafficking. These initiatives were financed by the UN Fund for Drug Abuse Control, which also funded other national and international control projects ranging from systems of crop substitution to the establishment of a Central Training Unit for enforcement officers. In 1974 the Fund financed a World Health Organization study aimed at clarifying components of the international drug problem.

Management of the Problem. Ignorance continued to be the principal obstacle to intelligent and effective management of the drug problem. Little was known of the factors encouraging drug abuse, its true extent, or how it affected either the individual or society as a whole. Only a tiny proportion of drug users came under medical care or into conflict with the law. This fact alone suggested that illicit drugs do not produce evident abnormalities in most users.

The curiously ambivalent attitude of authority toward illegal drugs was illustrated when a proposal by a voluntary London organization named Release, for setting up an analysis service to which drug users could submit possibly false or adulterated substances without risk of prosecution, gained immediate respectable support. In the U.S. it appeared that the population was developing a tolerance of drug dependency. Where only a few years earlier public concern over marijuana smoking was all-pervasive, in 1974 marijuana use could be termed ubiquitous within most age groups in all regions of the country. Even in relation to heroin addiction, people were expressing concern not so much over the drug's effect on the user as over the incidence of drug-related crime.

In the high-flying rhetoric of 1971–73, the U.S. president had proclaimed that "we have turned the corner of heroin abuse," but in October 1974 the director of the Special Action Office for Drug Abuse Prevention (SAODAP) testified before a congressional committee that "we are still far from winning the 'war against drugs.'" Generally speaking, state and federal approaches to the drug problem continued to be more political than social; more punitive than permissive; and were typified by pragmatism, in the absence of a guiding set of principles. The federal effort was fragmented with the Drug Enforcement Administration (DEA) in the Department of Justice, the Department of State, the National Institute on Drug Abuse (NIDA), and SAODAP each assuming responsibilities for limited segments of the problem.

Some trends were apparent. Testifying at a congressional hearing, federal narcotics officials stated that heroin use had increased during the year in Chicago, Los Angeles, San Francisco, San Diego, Calif., and parts of the Southwest and had spread into smaller cities. Requests for treatment in federally supported programs appeared to coincide geographically with changes in patterns of heroin use. In 1974 the number of persons in treatment in California had risen from 16,000 to 23,500. In Illinois (identified by

DEA as a major distribution point for Mexican brown heroin) the number of persons in treatment had tripled in a year and a half. Use of heroin along the Texas-Mexico border had spread north to Austin. New York City reported a sharp increase in the number of heroin detoxifications performed in the Manhattan House of Detention (the Tombs) and the Brooklyn House of Detention.

Litigation in the courts challenging the right of the U.S. military establishment to mandate urinalysis as a means of detecting use of drugs appeared to have resulted in increased narcotics use within the armed forces. Since 1971 urinalysis data had been collected regularly for all U.S. military services, and beginning in September 1973 there were indications of a decrease in both the percent and the number of personnel identified as drug positive. In July 1974 the Department of Defense suspended all tests while awaiting a decision as to whether mandatory urinalysis was to be legally classed as an invasion of privacy or as a permissible health measure. After the order went into effect, data reported by SAODAP indicated increased drug use within the military. Simultaneously, the number of personnel in treatment dropped from over 20,000 to about 17,000.

As of 1974, the federal government was providing support for approximately 2,000 drug treatment programs across the U.S., some 700 of which provided methadone maintenance while the remainder provided drug-free therapies. In October 1974 approximately 75,000 clients were receiving treatment in these programs, and the number was rising. Meanwhile, the controversy over treatment continued. Those favouring the substitution of the narcotic methadone for heroin, followed by maintenance of the patient on methadone, claimed it was the most effective method of dealing with heroin addiction, while those who opposed it said the procedure merely traded one addiction for another. Additionally, it had proved impossible to prevent diversion of methadone to illicit use.

Controversy was not limited to methadone maintenance. Drug-free therapies of various types continued to operate, but no acceptable method of evaluating them had been designed. The training branch of the National Institute on Drug Abuse, attempting to evaluate the state of the art of training drug abuse personnel, could agree only on the need for primary prevention of drug use and early intervention with young people who had just begun to experiment. The

Opium poppy is harvested in Turkey. After a two-year ban, Turkey in 1974 resumed cultivation of the poppy, formerly the primary source of about 80% of the heroin that reached the U.S.

need for a preventive approach was heightened by the fact that approximately 30% of those treated in federally funded programs had abused drugs other than opiates. The patterns of polydrug use were diverse, and such persons were extremely difficult to treat.

Those who favoured prevention programs contended that some of these drug experimenters—especially young people—would respond to activities in which "highs" could be developed that were more interesting and exciting than those obtained from drugs. That the new U.S. administration of Pres. Gerald Ford favoured a preventive approach was indicated in November, when the Alcohol and Drug Abuse Education Act Amendments of 1974 were adopted and signed into law. Under the statute, Congress appropriated $90 million to "encourage the development of new and improved curricula on . . . drug abuse."

It was worth noting, however, that drunkenness and alcoholism were increasing in many countries, including Britain, France, the U.S.S.R., and the U.S. In 1973 convictions for drunkenness in England and Wales were 10% higher than in the previous year, and this was the largest annual rise since 1962. More people were smoking than ever before, with U.S. consumption reaching a record 583,000,000,000 cigarettes in 1973, while in Britain sales more than recovered from the temporary slump that followed a Royal College of Physicians report on smoking and health in 1971. These trends made it clear that the continuing widespread use of illicit drugs was only one facet of an almost universal appetite for some kind of chemical crutch for the mind.

(DONALD W. GOULD; CHRISTOPHER JOHN TRAIN;
STANLEY F. YOLLES)

[522.C.9]

ENCYCLOPÆDIA BRITANNICA FILMS. *The Drug Problem: What Do You Think?* (1973).

Earth Sciences

Continental drift, climatic change, circulation of the ocean currents, seafloor spreading, and earthquake prediction were among the many subjects under study by earth scientists in 1974.

GEOLOGY

The Apollo program and two unmanned Soviet landings provided scientists with information on lunar rocks from eight sites. Only a small fraction of the approximately 800 lb. of rock brought back had been thoroughly examined by the end of 1974, but the work continued. Although the sites provided only a limited sampling, the results were generally uniform and suggested that the geology of the moon is simpler than that of the earth.

The passage and reflection of waves generated by moonquakes has shown that the moon's crust is about 65 km. (40 mi.) thick, and the material thrown out of large craters reveals that the crust is chiefly composed of anorthosite, a relatively rare, feldspar-rich rock. All the anorthosite on the moon, like that on the earth, was formed during the early part of its history. Apparently at that time the outer part melted and differentiated into crust and mantle and then froze again. The mantle is believed to consist of denser rocks rich in iron and magnesium.

The nature of the moon from 1,000 km. (620 mi.) below the surface to its centre 1,738 km. deep re-

mained less certain, and the information about it was of two kinds. During the year measurement of the moon made by the use of laser beams from the earth and reflectors placed on the moon reduced the accepted value of the moon's moment of inertia from about 0.4 to 0.395. This means that the mass of the moon is more strongly concentrated toward its centre than was previously believed to be the case. Consequently, it is possible for the moon to have an iron core up to 500 km. in radius or one that is a mixture of iron and sulfur up to 700 km. in radius. The other evidence is the magnetization of many of the moon's rocks, indicating that they have been in a magnetic field. If the moon's core had once been liquid, it could have generated a magnetic field by a dynamo action. This field has now vanished, so many scientists believe that the core is now solid. Others believe that the magnetic field was an external one and this hypothesis permits a wider choice for the nature of the moon's core.

The regularities apparent in the solar system suggest that it all formed at the same time. Various lines of evidence, but chiefly the maximum age of meteorites, indicate that this happened about 4,600,-000,000 years ago. During the year a rock from the moon was dated and found to be of about that age. During the formation process the energy of impacts probably led to melting, differentiation, and rapid resolidification. Over a short period of time about 4,000,-000,000 years ago, about a dozen large bodies struck the moon, forming large craters on a crust already rigid enough for them to persist. The debris from the craters was thrown for long distances, and it has been proposed that the successive falls of material have remained as identifiable layers over much of the lunar surface.

From about 3,200,000,000 to 3,800,000,000 years ago partial melting in the moon's interior generated basalt lavas that welled up and filled most of the large craters to form the dark circular maria in evidence today. The added load of lava produces noticeable increases in gravity over the maria. Since then the only disturbances have been the impacts of smaller meteorites, which have churned up the surface rocks.

Following the successful study of Mars by television cameras in 1973, the Mariner 10 mission to Mercury obtained excellent pictures of a quarter of the planet's surface in March 1974. The structure of the surface is extremely similar to that of the moon, with a multitude of craters of various sizes, but one set of features seems to be unique. Scarps estimated at up to 3 km. in height and 500 km. in length are widely distributed. These could be explained if Mercury had once melted and differentiated into a silicate crust and a large, dense, iron-rich core. Because the surface looks like the moon's, which is known to be silicate rock, and because the average density of Mercury, 5.4 g./cc, is much higher than that of silicates (about 3), this is plausible. The scarps could have been formed by compression of the crust at the time when the molten iron core cooled and shrank.

Chilling a Lava Flow. The results of one of mankind's successful efforts to combat a natural disaster were assessed in 1974. During the first six months of 1973 the volcano Eldfell on Heimaey Island off the southwest coast of Iceland was in eruption. Starting suddenly, it poured out millions of cubic yards of viscous liquid lava and more millions of cubic yards of volcanic ash and tephra (dust and fragments formed when molten, red-hot lava is blown high into the air to cool and solidify before falling back to the ground).

Earthquakes:
see Disasters;
Earth Sciences

Early in the eruption it was seen that if the red-hot lava continued to flow into the harbour it would become choked and the fishing industry ruined. Therefore, seawater was pumped onto the leading edge of the lava flow, causing it to freeze and form a wall that diverted the flows. Eventually, 47 large pumps on barges were deployed and the effort to divert the flows was successful. The lava added a square mile to the area of the island, which was only five times that size. The ash, which threatened to bury the town, was cleared with bulldozers and used to extend the island's airport and to provide level ground upon which to rebuild.

Artificial Satellites. The Earth Resources Technology Satellite (ERTS-1), launched in 1972, scans the greater part of the earth every 18 days on a variety of spectral bands of visible and infrared light. The results are telemetered to earth and reproduced as excellent pictures with high resolution, which are used for such purposes as mapping and studies of crops, forests, snow cover, pollution of both air and water, and several features of geologic interest.

For geologists ERTS-1 traced faults marked by linear features up to several hundred miles long. Many of these had not been detected on the ground. Some were shown to be active, by the offsets noted along them or by alignment of shallow earthquakes along them. The intersections of pairs of faults provide guides to prospecting for oil or metals, particularly mercury, copper, tin, and tungsten. ERTS pictures were also used to map the spread of waters during the 1973 Mississippi River flood.

Continental Drift. Now widely accepted, continental drift is held to be caused by relative motion between the huge crustal plates that make up the surface of the earth. A frequent question is whether this motion can be measured. The answer is that where the boundary between plates is on land, as along the San Andreas Fault in California, repeated surveys suffice to measure that these motions never exceed a very few inches a year. Unfortunately, most boundaries lie beneath the oceans and few methods of surveying can measure the changes in width of oceans with the precision of an inch a year. Attempts were being made by using laser beams reflected from the moon and long-range interferometry of distant quasars. In 1974 a report claimed success in measuring the drift between Europe and North America by a method involving the 45 astronomical observatories that measure time on those continents.

Few quantities can be as accurately measured as time, and modern atomic clocks have errors of less than one part in 1,000,000,000. These records can be compared with time as measured by the rate of rotation of the earth relative to the stars. Comparisons show that one day may be more than one-thousandth of a second shorter or longer than the next and also reveal seasonal variations. Most of these discrepancies are believed to be due to the effect of weather upon the distribution of snow, ice, and seawater, but there are residual long-term differences. These show that over the past ten years North America has been losing time relative to Europe by a very small amount, which can only be interpreted as due to the widening of the Atlantic Ocean so that the fixed stars cross the meridian later. The rate of separation of a few inches in a year is similar but rather greater than that derived from indirect arguments. (J. TUZO WILSON)

[133.C.1.a; 133.E.4 and 5; 212.D.4; 213.A; 232.B.2; 241.F.2; 738.C.4]

Largest turtle ever found, eight feet long and six feet wide, this fossil was pieced together by Arnold Lewis and Gabrielle Dundon of Harvard University. A freshwater member of the family Pelomedusidae, found in 1972 in northern Venezuela, it lived six million years ago.

METEOROLOGY

Droughts, floods, and killing frosts in many regions during 1974 seriously curtailed or completely wiped out growing crops and reduced the food supply for people everywhere. Weather and climate as the major uncontrolled variables in agricultural production were thus pushed further into the arena of world politics and human welfare.

In most parts of the world in 1974 applied meteorology maintained slow development and extension of facilities and services, particularly in the automation of field operations and services (AFOS). The advances in weather data gathering during recent decades, such as automatic weather-observing stations, earth-orbiting satellites, and radar, had become daily routine operations. The globe-covering system of weather reporting and forecasting functioned with remarkable continuity under the umbrella of cooperation provided by the World Meteorological Organization (WMO), comprising approximately 140 member states and territories.

Research and Development. In the WMO *Bulletin* for July the fluctuations of climate were reviewed and charts with data reaching back to ancient eras were published. The possible long-term influences of men's activities on climate were considered. The latter aspect, especially in application to individual cities and industrial complexes, was the subject of many research studies and technical papers. In one of these studies the "heat dome" produced by artificial warming of buildings, ground, and air over St. Louis, Mo., and environs was graphically summarized and described. Changes in patterns of precipitation and temperature downwind from urban centres were described in many other articles. Observations and conclusions showed such great variation in different cases that relatively few general principles could be found that would apply to all cities and manufacturing centres; rather, every locality had to be surveyed to reveal individual environmental features.

Another important research contribution toward the understanding of climate was undertaken by the U.S. National Center for Atmospheric Research (NCAR). The conclusions of this study supported views of many climatologists that the slightly higher temperatures over the earth as a whole during most of the first half of the 20th century, with their crest during 1945–49, had been replaced in recent years by a trend that might take the averages back to the cooler decades of 1850–

Table I. Selected Weather Headlines, 1974

Date	Place	Kind of weather	Casualties, damage, or nature
Jan. 15–25	North Atlantic Ocean	Unusually severe storms	Heavy seas damaged shipping, high jet stream delayed aircraft
Feb. 13–20	North Pacific Ocean	Severe storms	Fishing vessels sunk in heavy seas; 29 men lost
April 3–4	Canada; midwestern U.S.	Ninety-one tornadoes in 24 hr.	Worst outbreak of tornadoes in 49 years; over 300 persons killed
April 3	Xenia, Ohio	Destructive tornado	Total destruction in path 3 mi. long; deaths 30–35
May 28–30	Bangladesh	Cyclone ("hurricane")	Gale winds caused storm surge from Indian Ocean. Many drownings
June	Southwestern and midwestern U.S.	Tornadoes	Intensified jet stream high over southwestern U.S. induced record number of tornadoes
July 23–30	Argentina and Chile	Severe gales and snowstorms	Winter storms over southern tip of South America prolonged; isolated most places
August	Sahara and west-central Africa	7-yr. drought ends with flooding rains	Famine-stricken desert peoples relieved, in part, by storms
Sept. 18–20	Honduras, Central America	Hurricane Fifi; flood rains, bad mud slides	An estimated 5,000 deaths from torrential rains, record floods; mud slides buried towns
Sept. 21	West coasts of Central America	Typhoon Orlene, extension of Fifi	Hurricane crossed Central America, renamed Orlene; reduced intensity
Oct. 12 and 17	Philippines and Hong Kong	Typhoons strike Philippines and east coast of China	Typhoons Bess and Carmen made thousands homeless; many drownings
Dec. 25	Northern coast of Australia	Cyclone Tracy	About 90% of city of Darwin destroyed

Table II. Maximum Recorded Snowfall in Selected Cities of Canada and U.S.

Place	Snowfall within 24-hr. period (in.)	Snowfall during one-month period (in.)	Snowfall during an entire season (in.)	Maximum accumulation on ground (in.)
Boston	19½	41	89	23
Chicago	20	43	77	28
Denver	23	57	118	33
Detroit	25	38	78	26
Montreal	18	63	174	40
New York City	26	31	63	26
Ottawa	16	43	183	46
Pittsburgh	20	36	79	23
Quebec	22	82	200	52
St. Louis	20	29	68	20
Toronto	19	46	124	28
Washington, D.C.	25	35	54	34

1900. A significant view not yet proven was that the weather is more variable during cool years, resulting in greater extremes of hot and cold, worse droughts, and more flood-producing storms. Although the statistics were fragmentary, it was noted that 1973, which brought an all-time record number of tornadoes in the U.S., supported the NCAR supposition.

Scientists have long assumed that if they collected sufficient data based on a worldwide sampling of the atmosphere, these comprehensive observations could be analyzed and the physical and chemical processes that explain weather and climate could be understood. Logically, this would open the way to accurate and long-range predictions. Because of the endless interactions and interrelations in both space and time of the many "parcels" of the atmosphere, thousands of research programs have looked for more observations in regions where data have always been sparse or entirely lacking, the polar areas and the uninhabited equatorial zone. These two contrasting areas—the hot, humid intertropical zones and the frigid Arctic and Antarctic—are the main sources of energy that drive the "heat engine" that constitutes the mechanism of the earth's general atmospheric circulation. Accordingly, the decade of the 1970s could be characterized in meteorology as the period when the meteorological organizations of the world launched their maximum efforts to gather comprehensive observations of the atmosphere over polar and equatorial regions. With programs coordinated through the WMO and its technical commissions, the Polar Experiment (Polex) and the GARP Atlantic Tropical Experiment (GATE) held prospects for obtaining enough data for improved analysis and modeling of the general circulation.

Polex and GATE were basically subprograms of GARP, the Global Atmospheric Research Program, which had been inaugurated in the late 1960s to achieve the complete coverage in observations required for forecasting weather and climate throughout the world. In fact, a primary goal of GARP was to discover the degree to which weather can be predicted with scientific justification long into the future or whether there are random, indeterminate factors that inherently limit the time range to a few days. This problem was still unresolved in 1974, and prospects for solution seemed years away.

In a conference and workshop on climatology held in Asheville, N.C., in October the subject of energy and the atmosphere was viewed from another aspect. Solar radiation, rainfall, wind power, and other components of climate were examined as sources of energy to supplement the earth's diminished oil resources.

In Europe much of the research reported during the year treated the subjects that have been the main themes of meteorological studies in recent decades. These included three-dimensional models of the general circulation, convective phenomena in the air, cloud physics, and precipitation mechanisms. France, Great Britain, The Netherlands, Norway, Sweden, and the Soviet Union continued among the leaders in reporting results of research.

Air turbulence is caused by various agents, among them convection, waves produced on the boundaries of air currents with different velocities, and mountainous barriers. Knowledge of these conditions is important in order to avoid certain hazards to aircraft and to identify some of the factors responsible for the genesis of local storms. About 1970 several investigations had brought to light the causative factors of severe air turbulence at high altitudes in clear air, primarily those identified with transitory wave motions on the boundaries between different layers of wind movement. This knowledge led to the development of techniques for locating and predicting cases of extreme turbulence so that by 1974 pilots were usually able to avoid hazardous places. However, much remained to be discovered and explained as regards turbulence in the atmosphere. To pursue solutions to these problems, the WMO cosponsored with the American Meteorological Society a symposium on atmospheric diffusion, air pollution, and turbulence, in Santa Barbara, Calif., in September. The results of more than 90 research papers presented in this symposium contributed significantly to knowledge about these subjects.

Weather Modification and Observation. Progress on weather modification during 1974 was discouragingly slow, and the matter of success or failure remained highly controversial, as it had been since the beginning of Project Cirrus in the late 1940s. For three decades a preponderance of reports about field experimentation in artificial methods for increasing the amount of rainfall and other desired weather elements had been optimistic. However, heated controversy about these achievements arose between some experimenters and many respected scientists. A review by budget investigators published in *Science* magazine in October found that very little real progress had been made in recent years in the methods and techniques of weather modification; questions of success or failure in the innumerable thousands of rainmaking attempts made every year were still mostly unresolved. The status summaries of past years remained valid: essentially, there are certain special and limited

View of earth from SMS-1 weather satellite on May 28 shows Western Hemisphere with west coast of Africa at far right. Cloud motions are used to infer wind speed and direction.

cases in which the quantity of rainfall or snowfall can be increased or decreased, but the outcome of individual cases is uncertain and most certainly the conditions of a widespread and prolonged drought cannot be overcome by any practical artificial means so far discovered.

Weather modification also deals with methods for dispelling fog over airports, for suppressing hail, and for preventing frost. Worthwhile success was attained in these areas in certain limited cases.

The most spectacular breakthrough in meteorological techniques ever to be achieved was the adoption of space satellite techniques for worldwide views of cloud systems, temperature and wind profiles, and other atmospheric conditions. Further advances made in 1974 permitted daily, sometimes almost continuous, watches for cyclones developing at sea and for other features vital for warnings of storms and other weather disturbances.   (FRANCIS W. REICHELDERFER)

[224.A.3.e; 224.B; 224.D]

OCEANOGRAPHY

Potential and actual worldwide shortages of food, raw materials, and energy during 1974 highlighted interest in the oceans, not only as possible direct sources of these essentials but also as a perhaps major influence in establishing the global climatic regimes upon which agricultural and marine biological sources of food and raw materials are crucially dependent. Direct exploitation of such marine resources appears most feasible in the relatively shallow water of the continental shelves. However, precisely because of the proximity of these regions to national coastlines, the political problems inherent in guaranteeing equitable distribution of such marine resources have grown acute as the technology for their recovery advanced and as the need for them increased.

Reconciliation of these international needs with claims of national sovereignty was the general subject of the third United Nations Conference on the Law of the Sea, an international meeting of more than 5,000 delegates from 137 countries lasting over two months during the summer of 1974 in Caracas, Venezuela. The discussion articulated the many conflicting points of view that must be reconciled in the writing of an international treaty regulating exploitation of the resources of the sea and of the seabed. Elements of any final

agreement that could be visualized on the basis of the discussions included a relatively narrow (perhaps 12-mi. wide) territorial sea, with a considerably wider (typically to 200 mi.) adjoining zone of economic priority in the development of water and seafloor resources. But the details of any such agreement remained to be specified, and it was clear that much further work would be required before a widely subscribed international treaty became a reality. (*See* LAW: *Special Report*.)

Against this challenging background of resource shortage and political uncertainty, studies of ocean circulation were aimed at understanding not only how the oceans store and distribute dissolved and suspended substances but also how they absorb, transmit, and release heat, thus potentially exerting a profound influence on the global climate. Studies of the ocean bottom continued to deal with the worldwide structure of the seafloor but added an emphasis on detailed knowledge of conditions at one spreading centre.

The second phase of the Geosecs (Geochemical Ocean Sections) chemical study of ocean circulation ended on June 10, 1974, when the research vessel "Melville," operated by the Scripps Institution of Oceanography, La Jolla, Calif., put into port after a 35,000-mi., ten-month expedition that took it from Antarctica to the Bering Sea. This cruise was the Pacific sequel to the first phase of Geosecs, a nine-month Atlantic cruise in 1973 by the research vessel "Knorr," operated by the Woods Hole (Mass.) Oceanographic Institution. Both cruises were planned to follow the presumed trajectories of deep western ocean currents, hypothesized to supply the deep and bottom waters of these two major ocean basins.

In addition to the traditional oceanographic measurements of temperature, salinity, and oxygen (made, however, in far more detail than had previously been routine), Geosecs concentrated upon measurements of dissolved constituents such as radioisotopes, both natural and man-made, and of constituents present as suspended particulate matter in the sea. Radioisotopes, with their intrinsic decay rates, serve as self-dating tracers, indicating the age as well as the origin of different water parcels. The distribution of particulate matter, which ranges in composition from remains of organisms to meteoric dust, is of interest because the pattern of occurrence of many elements in the deep sea is strongly influenced by the dissolution of particles falling from surface layers.

Geosecs results generally confirmed the previously held notion that the Atlantic and the Pacific differ greatly in their deep circulations. The Pacific Geosecs cruise provided new observations and understanding of the Pacific Benthic Front, a gently sloping deep discontinuity in water properties (temperature, salinity, nutrients) believed to mark the boundary between the waters of the central Pacific and the underlying deep water of immediate Antarctic origin. The front deepens from New Zealand across the Equator and was detected as far north as Hawaii.

The results of Geosecs would, when completely analyzed, shed light on the overall ability of the oceans to accept and store materials over many years and to distribute them slowly throughout the major ocean basins. But this ability is the end result of many processes operating over shorter times and lengths. During 1974, a great deal of attention was devoted to the study of such processes on the basis of data collected by the MODE (Mid-Ocean Dynamics Experiment), especially during an intensive field program in 1973. Emphasis in MODE was on the careful description of oceanic eddies that are roughly 100–200 km. (60–120 mi.) across and require weeks or months to complete a rotation, and upon exploring their role in establishing basin-wide patterns of ocean flow and transport. Carrying out the fieldwork required using many new techniques of measurement, and much of the analysis of the data in 1974 was devoted to comparisons of different measurements for purposes of validating measurement techniques.

While the data were undergoing analysis, computer models of ocean circulation were constructed in which eddies similar to those observed during MODE appear spontaneously as the computed flow patterns evolve. The interaction between the eddies and the basin-sized components of the flow is intense in these calculations, and it was being systematically explored in further computations. Many more oceanic observations would be needed to establish which of the many theoretically possible eddy configurations actually characterize the real oceans. Plans for future eddy observations included a cooperative program of fieldwork, POLYMODE, between the U.S. and U.S.S.R. The ultimate insight sought in this work is essential to the formulation of a predictive model of the oceans for global forecasts of climate and pollution spread.

While Geosecs and MODE studied the dynamics of the ocean itself, other projects aimed at the interaction between the atmosphere and the ocean. Of these, Norpax and GATE were climatologically oriented in a broad sense, while CUEA was primarily oriented toward one particular aspect of the overall air-sea interaction, coastal upwelling.

Norpax (North Pacific Experiment) is an attempt to understand the observed apparent correlation between shifts in the pattern of sea surface temperature in the Pacific and Northern Hemisphere climatic fluctuations. During the winter of 1974, Norpax experimenters carried out the first of a series of projected studies aimed ultimately at understanding how ocean surface temperature anomalies form and thus providing the information needed to design a system for long-term monitoring of ocean surface

conditions as part of a climatological forecast plan. The winter's fieldwork included airborne and ship-borne measurements of near-surface ocean and atmosphere thermal structures over a North Pacific region roughly 200 km. (120 mi.) in diameter centred on "Flip," a "ship" of uniquely stable spar-like design from which direct measurements of air-sea fluxes and of ocean currents were made. Drogues and radar-tracked drifters were also employed to further delineate the flow field. The results of this work enabled proper interpretation of the significance of individual measurements made at widely separated locations, as would be the case in any imaginable ocean-wide monitoring effort. Plans for 1975 centred on basin-wide sections of near-surface thermal structures taken repeatedly from regularly scheduled ships and aircraft.

Coherence between climate and ocean temperature has been documented in equatorial as well as middle latitudes, and it has been suggested that the oceans exert their causative effect upon climate primarily in the tropics rather than in middle latitudes. During the summer of 1974, GATE (Global Atmospheric Research Program, Atlantic Tropical Experiment) held a multinational three-month program of fieldwork ending in September and involving ships, aircraft, and moored buoys concentrated in the near-equatorial Atlantic in an effort to understand the tropical interaction of the ocean and the atmosphere. Discussion of the results awaited reduction of the data.

Coastal upwelling is a process occurring most conspicuously along the western coasts of continents, especially of the Americas and of Africa. In these regions, surface winds blowing toward the Equator plus the rotation of the earth work together to force surface water seaward and hence to bring up in its place (upwell) cold and nutrient-rich water from depths of several hundred metres. Approximately 50% of the world's fish catch is taken from such areas. CUEA (Coastal Upwelling Ecosystem Analysis) studied both the physical and biological aspects of upwelling, attempting to develop predictive skill at forecasting its onset and duration as well as the sequence of concentrations of living organisms leading ultimately to rich fish harvests. Previous fieldwork by CUEA was concentrated on the west coast of the United States. In 1974, upwelling in the area of Cape Blanc off the west African coast was studied during an international experiment scheduled from February through March. The data, still under analysis, appeared to contain several upwelling events and could yield new insight into the initiation of upwelling.

Study of the ocean floor was continued by DSDP (the Deep Sea Drilling Project) aboard the specially outfitted drilling ship "Glomar Challenger." The past five years of deep ocean drilling by DSDP generally confirmed the idea of seafloor spreading, according to which the ocean's crust spreads laterally from mid-ocean rises or ridges at speeds of several centimetres per year and moves toward trenches and zones of convergence, where it plunges beneath the surface. Drilling in the South Atlantic in 1974 discovered a seaward extension of the Falkland Plateau, 750 mi. (1,200 km.) E of the Falkland Islands, and thus provided a final element in the reconstruction of the relative positions of South America and Africa about 150 million years ago, when they were adjacent.

A portion of the Mid-Atlantic Ridge, some 220 mi. (360 km.) SW of the Azores, was studied in unprecedented detail during repeated dives by the U.S.

Mechanical claw operated from the U.S. deep-diving craft "Alvin" gathers a sample of lava forced up through the floor of a rift valley in the Mid-Atlantic Ridge.

submersible "Alvin" and the French undersea vehicles "Archimède" and "Cyana" to depths of about 9,000 ft. (almost 3,000 m.). The dives were part of Project FAMOUS (French-American Mid-Ocean Undersea Study) and were carried out during the summer of 1974. The Mid-Atlantic Ridge is believed to mark the source of the seafloor underlying the Atlantic Ocean. During Project FAMOUS, this spreading region was studied visually and by sample gathering in a way previously possible only on land. Numerous formations indicating frequent extrusion of lava were observed with evidence of modern activity confined to a very narrow zone on either side of the centreline of the ridge's rift valley.　　(MYRL C. HENDERSHOTT)

[223.A; 223.C; 231.D]

SEISMOLOGY

The year 1974 was marked in the U.S. by an increase in official recognition of the earthquake problem. Based on a new law passed by the California legislature requiring communities to amend their general plans to include four new elements—safety, seismic safety, noise, and scenic highways—the Los Angeles Regional Planning Commission issued recommendations for safety to be used as a guide to city planners throughout the county. An advisory panel was set up to investigate seismic risk. More stringent restrictive ordinances concerning known fault areas and specifying construction techniques were adopted. Land uses in fault zones were limited to parks, golf courses, archery ranges, parking lots, and others requiring minimal construction. As an example, the San Fernando Veteran's Hospital, which was demolished with a loss of 47 lives during the earthquake of Feb. 9, 1971, had been replaced by a memorial park.

In another action the California State Division of Safety of Dams had required a seismic study of four Santa Clara Valley Water District dams. While these dams were all built prior to World War II, they were built to the most rigid specifications and had shown no structural weakness; nevertheless, they were to undergo sophisticated testing, including core drillings, as the first step in a program that would eventually test all earthfill dams in earthquake-prone areas throughout the state.

A similar concern was noted in many other areas of the world. Soviet scientists completed a seismic risk map of the Balkans in a study, under UN auspices, aimed at the planning of earthquake-resistant buildings. The Ottawa regional council considered the earthquake hazards attendant upon the Hazeldan Fault, which transects an area of high population density in the vicinity of the Canadian capital.

Methods of attaining greater protection from earthquake hazards were developed in several aspects of construction. Nuclear power plants have always had to meet rigorous seismic safety standards. To help with this problem a vibration simulator capable of reproducing the complex motions generated by earthquakes was developed. While most other simulators can produce only one type of wave, usually a unidirectional sinusoidal wave, the new machine was capable of moving a 64-ft. mounting platform as much as 12 in. horizontally and 9 in. vertically. Three hydraulic actuators, two vertical and one horizontal, generate the desired waveshapes. Prerecorded signals from a tape deck or minicomputer are furnished to the servoelectronic units which drive the actuators. Any waveform can be simulated, including those formed by the combination of various frequencies

and random directions. The facility, located near Los Angeles, began operations in May. It tested a reactor core, which after being subjected to an equivalent of 200 earthquakes the size of the 1906 San Francisco earthquake, emerged with no damage to its graphite absorption blocks.

The theory of dilatation, with its series of precursor phenomena that result in an earthquake, continued to gain acceptance among seismologists. This theory postulates an expansion and subsequent weakening of the material in the earthquake's central region. One of the measures of this sequence is a gradual decrease in the speed of compressional seismic waves (P waves). James Whitcomb and his colleagues at the California Institute of Technology had noted a drop in the velocity of P waves passing through a region east of Riverside, Calif. This change continued for a period of 13 months, after which the velocities returned to normal. Based on this information, the investigators had predicted an earthquake of magnitude 5.5 would occur within three months. A shock did occur within the specified time at the designated location except that its magnitude was only 4.1 The difference in magnitude was attributed to strike-slip faulting at the source rather than the thrust faulting on which the prediction had been based.

Two methods of earthquake prediction were developed and tested in the U.S.S.R. Soviet scientists developed a generator to predict the time, place, and magnitude of impending shocks. Through 1974, the earth's crust had been probed to a depth of 30–40 km. (18–25 mi.) in field tests of a portable generator of this type. In Tashkent, a large city in an area of high seismic activity, geologist Abamubdi Sultankhodzhaer predicted successfully at least four minor shocks between 40 and 60 hours prior to their occurrence by noting the abrupt change in the chemical composition of groundwater at a depth of 2,450 m. (about 8,000 ft.). He was confident that he would be able to detect an incipient shock of major size in time to evacuate the city.

Interest in earthquake prediction in China increased in recent years. Three groups, the Geophysical Institute, the Geological Institute, and the Institute of Engineering Mechanics, were engaged in extensive programs for the study of premonitory phenomena such as ground tilts, variations in gravity, and variations in crustal strain.

More general aspects of prediction included the correlation of the Chandler wobble with periods of high seismicity. The rotation of the earth varies periodically, and as it slows, the amplitude of this wobble of the earth's axis increases. These two conditions were in effect during the last two eras of major earthquake activity, 1896–1911 and 1932–1942, and because a similar period is approaching, Don Anderson of the California Institute of Technology expected increased seismic activity in the near future.

(RUTLAGE J. BRAZEE)

[213.B]

See also Antarctica; Disasters; Energy; Industrial Production and Technology; Law; Life Sciences; Mining and Quarrying; Physics; Space Exploration; Speleology.

ENCYCLOPÆDIA BRITANNICA FILMS. *Reflections on Time* (1969); *Heartbeat of a Volcano* (1970); *How Level Is Sea Level?* (1970); *A Time for Rain* (1973); *A Time for Sun* (1973); *Earthquakes: Lesson of a Disaster* (1973); *Fog* (1973); *Geyser Valley* (1973); *Glacier on the Move* (1973); *The Atmosphere in Motion* (1973); *The Ways of Water* (1973); *Volcanoes: Exploring the Restless Earth* (1973); *Monuments to Erosion* (1974); *Storms: The Restless Atmosphere* (1974); *The San Andreas Fault* (1974).

Tiltmeter installation at Pacaya volcano in Guatemala monitors seismic disturbances. Measurements are transmitted from the site via satellite.

Eastern Orthodox Churches: *see* Religion

Ecology: *see* Environment; Life Sciences

Economics

Simultaneous inflation and recession posed a dilemma for economists in 1974. The conventional wisdom since John Maynard Keynes's *General Theory of Employment, Interest and Money* of 1935 has attributed inflation to an excess of effective demand and recession to a deficiency of effective demand. Thus, the remedy for inflation is to decrease effective demand and the remedy for recession is to increase it. The coexistence of inflation and recession suggested that fiscal and monetary policies, the traditional weapons for controlling effective demand, were insufficient to curb inflation. Apart from excess demand, inflation may arise from a wage-price spiral or a shortage of specific commodities, so that fiscal and monetary restraint is not always an appropriate remedy.

Economists have viewed unemployment (recession) as a more serious problem than inflation because the former results in a loss of real income and wealth to society as a whole, whereas inflation leads primarily to their redistribution. Although the fear that inflation as such can destroy a nation is misleading, inflation may result in gross inequities through an arbitrary redistribution of income and wealth. G. L. Bach of Stanford, examining this issue (*Challenge,* July-August, 1974, pp. 48–55), found that money wages in the U.S. did not lag behind the cost of living in the post-World War II period except during the inflation of 1973–74.

Debtors gain and creditors lose from inflation except to the extent that the inflation is anticipated and allowed for in loan contracts. After allowing for these anticipations, Bach concluded that from one-half to two-thirds of $1 billion was transferred from creditors to debtors in the U.S. between 1946 and 1971. Among households, Bach found that the chief gainers from unanticipated inflation were the middle and upper-middle income groups and that the chief losers were the very poor and the very rich. The very poor are not debtors because they are unable to borrow, and the very rich do not need to.

Indexation is a plan by which contracts extending over time are expressed in terms of money of constant purchasing power. Escalator clauses in wage contracts are an example. If all economic transactions were indexed, everyone would remain in the same relative position irrespective of the inflation rate. Milton Friedman of the University of Chicago recommended that indexation be legislated for all government trans-

"Keep flapping, everyone— it's all under control!"

actions, including income taxes and bonds (*Essays on Inflation and Indexation*, 1974, p. 26); for the rest of the economy, it should be voluntary but given encouragement. Friedman's proposal would prevent the government from taking automatically, as taxes, an increasing share of individual incomes, which is what happens under inflation in the absence of some protective device. Interest on government bonds would be guaranteed in real terms, and the repaid principal would have the same purchasing power as the money used to purchase the bonds initially. Friedman did not claim that indexation would eliminate inflation, but he believed it would make inflation more tolerable.

Confronted with the inadequacies of economic theory and policy, economists reexamined the received theory and its policy implications. Sir John Hicks, Oxford's Nobel laureate, wrote *The Crisis in Keynesian Economics* (1974) in which he attempted to reconstruct Keynesian theory. Wassily Leontief, another Nobel laureate, recommended an economic planning board for the U.S. (*Challenge,* July-August, 1974, pp. 35–40). Leontief's planning board would provide an information system of detailed and systematic data designed to improve the operation of the market. It would, for example, anticipate shortages before they occurred. He defended the profit motive but expressed the view that it should be controlled within a planning framework in order to move the economy toward social goals. The information system would include a primary concern with microeconomics, in contrast to the existing Council of Economic Advisers, which operates primarily with economic aggregates.

In his presidential address to the American Economic Association, Kenneth J. Arrow, another Nobel laureate, examined some of the strengths and weaknesses of neoclassical economic theory (*American Economic Review,* March 1974, pp. 1–10). One line of his thinking ran as follows: Private optimizing under capitalism depends on the existence of markets. Optimizing takes place among present alternatives and also between present markets and future alternatives for which very few markets exist. The nonexistence of future markets leaves the optimizer at the mercy of his own expectations and, since expectations based on uncertain future events are highly unstable, market failures frequently result. Arrow illustrated this point with reference to durable capital assets, the demand for which depends on the expected prices and sales of products to be produced by the capital assets sometime in the future. Uncertainty about these future prices and sales may result in a failure of the market for capital goods, which in turn creates further uncertainties. A logical inference from Arrow's analysis is that indicative planning as an information system can reduce uncertainties and improve the performance of market capitalism.

Robert M. Solow of MIT, in the Ely lecture on "The Economics of Resources and the Resources of Economics" (*American Economic Review,* May 1974, pp. 1–14), explored the economic theory of exhaustible resources such as petroleum. One of the weakest links in neoclassical economics has been the pricing of exhaustible resources in a manner consistent with their optimal rate of exploitation. Solow suggested that indicative planning can play a constructive role by providing improved information and coordination in the utilization of scarce natural resources.

The Mideast oil crisis posed some interesting problems. Historically, international cartels in raw materials have not succeeded in maintaining artificially

OLIPHANT, THE DENVER POST © 1974 LOS ANGELES TIMES SYNDICATE

high prices for long. Internal conflicts among members of the cartel are one force tending toward its breakup. Further, to the extent that the cartel does hold together, it provides incentives for new production to enter the market. In the case of petroleum, the very high price of crude oil fixed by the Organization of Petroleum Exporting Countries created incentives for an intense search for new sources of petroleum and for oil substitutes. Based on this analysis, many economists predicted that the price of crude oil would fall in the future. (DUDLEY DILLARD)

See also Nobel Prizes.
[531; 10/36.D]

Economy, World

All major industrial economies during 1974 experienced a deepening slippage into recession amid virulent inflationary pressures. The downturn was not a mere aftereffect of the shock caused by the energy crisis; it was not a mere rolling adjustment similar to cyclical slowdowns earlier in the past quarter century; it was a new economic condition aptly described by such words as "inflationary recession," "stagflation," or even "slumpflation"—words coined to recognize not just that inflation coexisted with recession, stagnation, or slump, but that inflation brought about such conditions.

A Brutal Change. The change in economic trends throughout the industrial world was brutal. The violent boom of 1972 and 1973, which occurred simultaneously throughout the industrial world, was followed in 1974 by an equally simultaneous downturn that, at the year's end, pointed toward a still weaker economic picture in 1975. The boom had been unsustainable because demand had been allowed to build to a point that exceeded the limits of available capacity; the turnaround, which had begun slowly in

mid-1973, gathered momentum during 1974. It was spurred by the oil crisis, the effects—after a time lag —of restrictive policies enforced by governments to hold down the pace of inflation, and the gradual weakening of demand as "real" after-tax incomes declined because of price inflation and heavier taxation.

For industrial countries as a whole, the "real" output of goods and services—the so-called "real" gross national product (GNP) after correction for price increases—stagnated in 1974 (*see* Tables I and II). The GNP actually declined in the U.S., the U.K., and Japan; the drop in Japan, the biggest industrial country outside the U.S., followed the nonstop expansion of the previous 25 years. France showed an increase, but with growing difficulty; Italy also had an increase for the year, but activity there fell abruptly during the second half. The Canadian economy, which had unused resources, continued to grow, as did most of the smaller continental European countries.

In the U.S., whose GNP was nearly one-third of gross world product (excluding the Soviet Union, China, and their satellite countries), the decline from 1973 was 2.2%—the greatest decline in a single year since 1946. During the last three months of 1974, GNP was, at a seasonally adjusted annual rate, 9.1% below its peak in the last quarter of 1973.

In all industrial countries, declines in GNP spread through all sectors of the economy; but unlike the earlier cyclical downturns, which usually originated in the subsidence of capital investment booms, the drop in 1974 was decidedly influenced by the pronounced weakness of consumer buying. West Germany was a notable exception. The crucial factor that weakened consumer buying was inflation. Consumers held back their buying as income gains lagged behind price increases, as in the U.S. and Japan, or failed to increase as much as in earlier years, as generally was the case in Europe. The sharp decline in bond and stock prices was also a factor; many

Table I. Growth of Real Gross National Product

Country	Annual percent changes 1960-72	1973	1974
France	5.8	6.0	4.8
Italy	5.5	6.0	4.8
Canada	5.0	6.8	4.5
West Germany	4.9	5.3	1.0
United Kingdom	3.1	5.3	—0.5
United States	4.1	5.9	—1.8
Japan	11.0	10.2	—3.3
Seven major countries	5.5	6.5	—0.3
Spain	7.3	7.9	5.5
Austria	5.1	5.5	5.0
Belgium	4.9	6.1	4.5
Norway	5.0	3.7	4.0
Finland	5.4	6.0	3.3
Sweden	4.2	1.5	3.0
Ireland	4.0	6.8	2.5
Netherlands, The	5.2	4.2	2.5
Australia	4.8	5.6	2.3
All industrial countries Of which:	5.4	6.3	0.3
Europe	5.1	5.4	2.8

Source: Adapted from OECD, *Economic Outlook* (December 1974).

Table II. Price Trends in Industrial Countries*

Country	Annual percent increases 1960-72	1973	1974
West Germany	3.8	5.8	6.5
France	4.5	7.3	10.0
United States	2.8	5.6	10.0
Canada	3.1	7.6	13.0
Italy	4.5	10.5	15.3
United Kingdom	4.5	7.3	11.0
Japan	4.8	12.0	26.0
Major countries	3.6	7.2	12.5

*As measured by deflators of gross national product.
Source: Adapted from OECD, *Economic Outlook* (December 1974).

Table III. Industrial Countries Ranked by Price-Cost Performance

Item	Percent change in 1974*	1973	1972
Consumer prices			
West Germany	7.5	7.0	5.6
Canada	10.0	6.1	3.5
United States	11.5	5.5	2.6
France	13.8	7.1	6.2
United Kingdom	14.8	8.6	6.7
Italy	19.3	10.8	5.7
Japan	25.0	11.7	4.9
Hourly earnings in manufacturing			
West Germany	11.0	10.7	8.7
United States	11.0	6.8	6.7
Canada	13.0	8.5	7.3
United Kingdom	16.0	12.6	12.8
France	19.0	12.4	11.3
Italy	23.0	24.3	10.4
Japan	27.0	23.6	15.6
Wage costs per unit of output in manufacturing (expressed in national currencies)			
United States	8.3	2.6	1.0
Canada	8.8	4.2	3.0
West Germany	9.3	4.9	3.6
France	14.2	5.4	3.9
United Kingdom	14.5	5.5	9.8
Japan	18.4	3.9	5.7
Italy	...	12.0	5.3
Wage costs per unit of output in manufacturing (expressed in U.S. dollars)			
France	7.1	19.6	14.0
United States	8.3	2.6	1.0
United Kingdom	8.3	3.3	12.9
Canada	11.5	3.2	5.0
Japan	12.4	16.6	21.5
West Germany	20.1	26.1	13.3
Italy	...	12.2	11.7

*For consumer prices and hourly earnings in manufacturing, 1974 as estimated by the OECD; for wage costs per unit of output, 1974 to date compared with the same period of 1973.
Source: Adapted from OECD, *Economic Outlook* (December 1974).

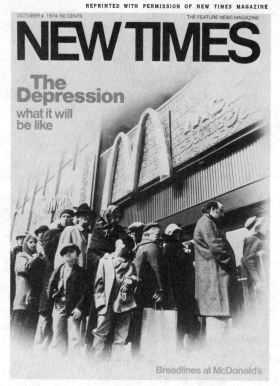

OCTOBER 4, 1974/60 CENTS　　THE FEATURE NEWS MAGAZINE

NEW TIMES

The Depression
what it will be like

Breadlines at McDonald's

Sardonic view of deteriorating U.S. economy by "New Times" magazine shows a breadline forming at a McDonald's Restaurant.

people hesitated to make purchases as the value of their fixed assets fell disastrously. Penny-pinching became a necessity. The rise in food prices, partly because of bad crops, was a critical factor because expenditure on food is stable in volume.

The confidence of the consumers was battered not only by rising unemployment and economic uncertainty but also by the absence of strong national leadership in the U.S. and other major countries. Much of the buying weakness was concentrated in the areas of home construction, which was also depressed by very high interest rates, and automobiles, which had already been hit earlier in the year by fears of a gasoline shortage.

Business spending on plant and equipment, which was a strong component of demand in 1973 in all countries except West Germany, held more or less steady in 1974. It softened in some industries but strengthened in others, principally in energy and in basic materials. But prospects for an increase in business spending were eroded by the falling off in utilization of capacity, by the rise in interest rates and more difficult access to credit, by the inadequate level of profits, and by the deteriorating financial position of enterprises. The key element was the decline in profitability, which weakened the incentive for adding to basic industrial capacity and brought about a decline in corporate liquidity. Business spending on inventories, meanwhile, dropped appreciably—a turnaround reflecting the sensitivity of inventory accumulation to tight credit conditions and high short-term interest rates. To some extent, the performance of inventories reflected involuntary buildups, such as stocks of unsold automobiles. In countries where demand for exports is a strong component of GNP—West Germany, Japan, and the small European nations—an appreciable measure of stimulation came from the buying of manufactured goods by such countries as France, Italy, and the U.K. as well as by oil-producing nations and other primary producers.

Industrial production also turned downward but

less than did GNP. (*See* Chart 1.) It was supported by exceptionally strong demand for exports and by involuntary additions to stocks. Important differences developed in the various industrial sectors; for example, there were strains in steel and chemicals, but there was considerable slack in automobiles and textiles. In the U.S., where industrial production peaked in November 1973, the decline through December 1974 was 7.2%.

Reflecting the weakening trend in output, average hours worked declined, part-time work appeared, and unemployment rose, especially in West Germany and the U.S. In the U.S., 7.1% of the labour force, or 6.5 million workers, were unemployed in December 1974, the highest level in 13 years. The rate for married men, regarded as a good general indicator of both tightness in the labour market and family hardship caused by unemployment, stood at 3.7%, up from 2.2% a year earlier. Total employment of workers on nonfarm payrolls stopped rising and actually dropped by over one million in November and December to 82 million. In Japan, despite the drop in GNP, the unemployment rate rose little. In continental Europe, the picture was complicated by the movements of several million migrant workers; restrictions on their recruitment were introduced in West Germany in 1973, and in France and some other countries in 1974.

Virulent Inflation. Despite stagnation or actual declines in GNP, price inflation continued (*see* Chart 2 and Tables II and III; the latter shows at a glance where countries stood relative to one another). Money depreciated at rates of 8–12%, even in countries that had had a relatively good record in earlier years (*see* Table IV). West Germany was the main exception to the disastrous decline in the buying power of paper money. In the U.S., the rate of depreciation of the dollar during January–November 1974 was 9.9%, up from 5.8% in 1973, which itself was up from 3.2% in 1972. At the 1974 rate of depreciation, the dollar would lose half of its buying power in only seven years; this process would take ten years if the dollar depreciated at the 7% annual rate that was hoped for in late 1975.

Inflation in the industrial world had changed in nature. In 1973, a surge in prices of base metals and other raw materials resulting from worldwide excess demand played a large part in the inflationary process; but, beginning in the second quarter of 1974, prices of most non-oil commodities declined spectacularly. The rise in food prices remained a critical factor in 1974, together with the oil price explosion. In the U.S. petroleum products accounted for 15–20% of the increase in major price indexes in 1974. This was about the same as the figure attributable to food and food products.

Although governments tried to prevent the rise in commodity prices from leading to large increases in wages, they failed. In the U.S., real wage incomes declined in 1973 and early 1974 but began to catch up rapidly later in the year. A veritable avalanche of wage claims descended on the industrial world as wage gains were left behind price increases and as inflationary expectations became rigidly entrenched. Wage claims were more moderate in West Germany than in other countries; relative to productivity prospects, they were high in the U.S., Canada, France, and Japan and were especially high in Italy and the U.K. To protect wages (and also pensions, including Social Security benefits), new labour contracts as well as other private and government arrangements made increasing use of automatic cost-of-living escalator clauses linked to cost-of-living indexes. Such linkage (technically called indexation) quickly translates higher prices into higher wages.

The wage eruption occurred at a time when productivity gains slowed down, as they generally do in periods of sluggish economic growth; West Germany was again a major exception. In the U.S. productivity declined. As a result, unit labour costs rose rapidly (*see* Table III) and strong pressures thus developed on final product prices except when the price rise had brought about large profit increases that could be shaved—as the recession halted the acceleration in final goods prices—to mitigate the pressure of costs on prices.

In view of the differences in rates of domestic inflation and productivity from country to country, the rise in wage costs per unit of output varied greatly (*see* Table III, bottom). Unit wage costs, together with effective exchange rates, which were less volatile

in 1974 than in 1973, changed the competitive positions of the principal countries. At the same time, the decline in the value of the dollar magnified the effect of foreign inflations on the U.S. price level as higher prices for foreign currencies raised the dollar prices of imported goods.

Inflation Demoted. The inflationary process that had penetrated the industrial economies as never before during peacetime was not controllable through any single drastic, powerful policy. In fact, official measures to dampen inflation had little success. It is true that after mid-1974 the inflationary bulge receded somewhat, but the same forces that caused

Table IV. Depreciation of Money

Country	Indexes of value of money (1963=100) 1968	1973	Annual rates of depreciation (percent) '63-'73*	'72-'73	'73-'74†
Industrial countries					
West Germany	87	70	3.6	6.5	6.7
Netherlands, The	80	57	5.6	7.3	8.3
Norway	81	58	5.3	7.0	8.3
Luxembourg	87	69	3.6	5.7	8.4
Sweden	81	61	4.9	6.4	8.5
Austria	84	65	4.2	7.0	8.8
Switzerland	84	64	4.4	8.0	9.2
New Zealand	82	58	5.4	7.6	9.5
Canada	86	68	3.8	7.1	9.6
South Africa	86	64	4.3	8.7	9.8
United States	88	69	3.7	5.8	9.9
Belgium	84	66	4.0	6.5	10.7
France	86	64	4.4	6.8	11.7
Australia	86	66	4.1	8.6	12.9
Denmark	76	56	5.7	8.5	13.0
United Kingdom	83	58	5.3	8.4	13.3
Spain	70	49	6.8	10.2	13.3
Ireland	80	52	6.3	10.2	13.7
Italy	84	64	4.4	9.7	14.0
Finland	72	54	5.9	10.5	14.7
Turkey	74	42	8.3	14.2	15.5
Japan	78	56	5.7	10.5	19.7
Portugal	80	49	6.9	11.4	20.8
Iceland	59	30	11.4	18.2	21.9
Greece	90	69	3.8	13.4	23.7
Less developed countries					
Venezuela	93	80	2.2	3.8	6.9
Iraq	94	75	2.8	4.7	6.9
Honduras	89	76	2.7	4.3	11.7
Guatemala	98	82	2.0	12.6	11.9
Iran	92	72	3.2	8.9	12.8
Peru	54	39	9.1	8.7	14.2
Morocco	94	80	2.2	3.9	15.7
Argentina	32	8	22.7	37.6	16.2
Pakistan	78	58	6.9	17.1	16.2
Yugoslavia	48	25	13.0	16.5	16.8
Colombia	60	33	10.5	18.6	18.0
South Korea	52	31	11.1	3.1	18.4
Thailand	88	72	3.2	10.5	19.4
Ecuador	83	56	5.6	11.3	19.4
Paraguay	90	69	3.7	11.3	20.4
Brazil	14	6	24.5	13.4	20.5
Singapore	93	71	3.5	20.8	20.6
India	63	46	7.4	14.4	21.6
Jamaica	86	54	5.9	16.6	22.3
Israel	79	48	7.1	16.6	26.7
Mexico	87	64	4.3	14.2	27.3
Philippines	79	48	7.1	6.6	29.9
Indonesia	22	11	19.7	23.7	30.5
Uruguay	6	1	90.0	49.2	41.7
Chile	29	2	33.4	77.9	86.8

Note: Depreciation of money is measured by rates of decline in the domestic purchasing power of national currencies (as computed from reciprocals of official cost-of-living or consumer price indexes), not by rates of price inflation. For example, a rate of inflation of 100% is equivalent to a 50% rate of depreciation of money.
*Compounded annually.
†Based on average monthly data available for 1974 compared with corresponding period of 1973.

CHART 1.

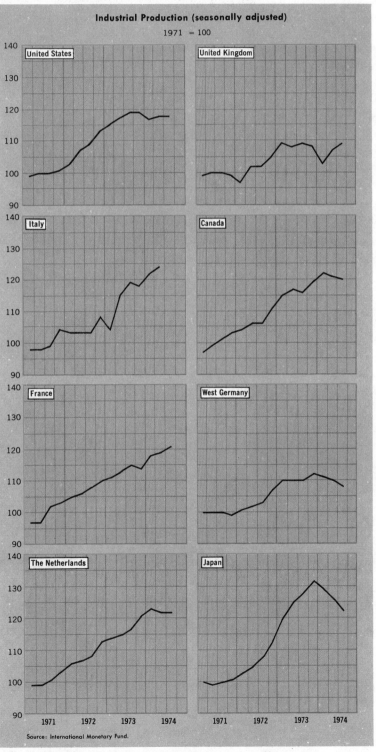

Industrial Production (seasonally adjusted)
1971 = 100

United States • United Kingdom • Italy • Canada • France • West Germany • The Netherlands • Japan

Source: International Monetary Fund.

CHART 2.

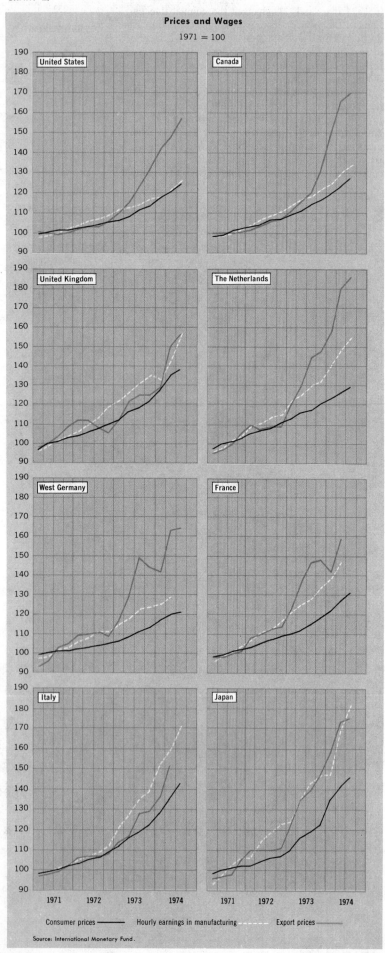

Prices and Wages
1971 = 100

Consumer prices ———   Hourly earnings in manufacturing - - - -   Export prices ———

Source: International Monetary Fund.

prices to rise so sharply also produced the weakening of consumption and investment and, therefore, led to some easing in the pressure on resources and on commodity markets.

Even before mid-1974, monetary and fiscal policies had involved a combination of one foot on the accelerator and one foot on the brake. Monetary policy was restrictive but—despite soaring interest rates, which were the consequence not only of the credit squeeze but also of the depreciation of money—was not rigid, as evidenced by the rapid monetary growth. Short of risking a severe liquidity crisis and a sharp downturn in the economy, the monetary authorities had little choice but to allow rising costs and prices to be financed. This fact of life—together with large government budgetary deficits, huge flows of funds between currencies, and other factors—reflected the limited effect that monetary policy could exert on inflationary forces of the kind and intensity that plagued the major nations in 1974.

This monetary posture evolved in late 1974 into actions aimed at keeping the rate of monetary expansion low enough to hold down the rise in prices but high enough to bolster economic activity somewhat. West Germany's central bank was the first to release the brake, with the stated objective of stimulating investment. The U.S. Federal Reserve System, which made it known during the period of restraint that "in no event will a credit crunch occur," visibly eased monetary policy toward the year's end. The Bank of England, which energetically shored up the domestic financial structure, had the hardest job; it was faced with the awkward combination of a low pressure of internal demand, a large balance of payments deficit, and high cost inflation.

As a matter of stabilization policy, a number of countries sought to curb the growth of government spending, but without much success. In the U.S., Pres. Gerald Ford proposed in October a fiscal package framed to provide a small overall tax increase together with selected tax reductions and selected increases in outlays, but without any net budget stimulus; by not moving toward a more stimulative stance, the president's program differed strikingly from the postures that had been adopted at similar stages of previous business cycles. As the recession gathered force at the end of 1974, however, this package was quietly shelved. The new strategy was to be decidedly expansionary.

Direct controls on prices, wages, and dividends had a checkered history in 1974. In the U.S., the controls, imposed in 1971 and run through four phases, were lifted in April 1974. In the U.K., mandatory controls set up in 1973 were replaced by a voluntary arrangement on incomes, the "social contract." A new package of prices and incomes policies was introduced in New Zealand. In many countries, established price-wage policies were severely tested but no longer had to contend with excess demand. West Germany and Japan had no direct price-wage policy.

In the U.S. and the U.K., proposals were repeatedly advanced during the year to revive controls over wages and prices so that the government could release additional demand and thus raise the number of jobs and the level of output without fear of further price-cost increases. Some of the credit for the moderate 6–7% annual rise in hourly earnings in the U.S. during 1971–73 was given to the wage guidelines and the way in which the control authorities helped bring those guidelines to bear on wage negotiations. The difficulty was that they could not be maintained for long because of the grievances, complications, inequalities, and lack of fairness they entailed. But while acknowledging that earlier efforts failed, economists also came to realize that market power could be abused to everybody's detriment. As the recession began to bite in late 1974, political leaders—apprehensive lest the social tensions that might arise as a consequence of increased unemployment (even if tempered by government help to the unemployed) would be more insidious than the actual tensions arising from inflation—shifted toward open stimulative action. This was done by means of fiscal measures aimed at a moderate growth of demand—moderate, that is, by the standards of the past decade.

Cassandra on LDCs. Among the less developed countries (LDCs), the "haves"—the oil-exporting nations—not only gained reserves and built up investments in the industrial world but also found themselves on a high-flying magic carpet, able to disregard financial constraints in their efforts to industrialize, diversify, and develop their economies. Euphoria was, however, mixed with apprehension. For countries with educational systems and technical skills that also called for improvement, the difficulty in developing ways to spend money efficiently was enormous. Inflation was strong (Table IV) and the additional strains of running a faster-paced economy were unmistakable. Doors were open to foreign enterprises and technicians eager to take advantage of the massive opportunities opened by a boom that would, they hoped, continue for years. Oil-producing countries pledged $3 billion to a special "facility" in the International Monetary Fund to help particularly hard-pressed countries cope with oil-price increases. The oil producers also purchased bonds issued by the World Bank and regional development banks, and extended direct assistance within the Asian and Middle Eastern regions, especially Egypt. As elsewhere in the world, much money went into purchases of arms.

Another group of LDCs that also did well in 1974 were the producers of such important commodities as copper, zinc, cotton, wool, and rubber, and the already relatively wealthy manufacturers such as Brazil, Malaysia, Argentina, the Philippines, and Colombia. But as 1974 ended the prices of many commodities were well below the peaks established during the first half of the year. Several Latin-American countries borrowed in the international market to finance their payments deficits. With regard to oil, Colombia, Ecuador, and Mexico were self-sufficient, and Argentina and Brazil produced a large part of what they consumed. Asian and African countries that did not produce oil were compelled to cut oil imports.

Inspired by the example of oil producers, the countries producing metals and other primary commodities came to believe that their "scarce" materials could be treated with the same magic as oil. (*See* COMMODITY TRADE: *Special Report.*) In April, the LDCs proclaimed a "charter for a new economic order" at the United Nations. Thereafter, as the industrial world found itself in recession, sharp declines in commodity prices brought disillusionment. All LDCs are heavy debtors and benefited from the worldwide inflation in that the burden of their debt service was reduced in relation to the value of their exports. At the same time, however, the prices of industrial goods imported from North America, Europe, and Japan continued to rise even after those of primary commodities had begun to drop; as a result, the terms of

trade of the LDCs deteriorated, a deterioration that offset the advantage of the relatively lighter debt service.

The poorest LDCs, countries in Asia and Africa that represented one billion people and accounted for half of the population of all LDCs, had a hard year. Famine struck parts of India and Bangladesh. Floods and a lack of fertilizers—not to mention the population explosion, the oil-price upheaval, and global inflation—also posed a critical threat to these nations, but their hungry people were often fed only on "a diet of words," as Lord Boyd Orr, first director general of the Food and Agriculture Organization, once said.

Official development assistance, severely eroded by inflation because the donor countries did not increase aid to offset the rise in prices, declined in 1974. It proved difficult to mobilize assistance in an environment in which real incomes of the donors declined and in which all industrial countries suffered from unemployment and uncertain growth prospects. It was often said that the oil-producing nations ought to pick up more of the general development burden; however, their liquidity was only one year old and was based on the sale of a nonrenewable resource.

The Communist World. Inflation, unemployment, and the decline in output in the West were chronicled in the Communist world as yet another phase of "the crisis of capitalism." As Lenin once observed, nothing is more likely to sound the death knell of the capitalist method of ordering society than the collapse of the monetary system around which the entire edifice revolves. Official propaganda bragged about monetary stability in the Communist world, as attested by the retail price indexes. But, in sober reality, the Communist world did not lick inflation entirely: it merely repressed it. Official price indexes took no account of prices in the relatively free markets where peasants sold the produce from their private plots; they ignored price increases disguised whenever higher priced "new" or "improved" products are marketed; and they failed to reflect frequent shortages of goods in unevenly supplied markets. High rates of savings in societies eager to consume more were yet another sign of repressed inflation.

D.P.A./PICTORIAL PARADE

Victims of the energy crisis, unsold new BMW cars sit in January in a company parking lot in Munich, W.Ger.

Though too much money chased too few goods, it nevertheless appeared that inflation in Communist countries (except Yugoslavia, which is outside the Eastern European grouping) was less pervasive than in the West. This apparent monetary stability, together with further concessions by the leadership to people clamouring for more consumer goods, made it easier for governments to conduct economic affairs. There were continuing problems, however, as confirmed at the year's end by the Soviet government's announcement of "incomplete fulfillment" of the current five-year plan, with growth put at 5% in 1974, against the 6.5% called for in the plan. The unsatisfactory performance was attributed to poor management, inefficiency, and lagging productivity.

Against this background, and also because of harvest shortages, the Soviet Union sought trade and credits in the capitalist world. A long-term agreement between the U.S. and the U.S.S.R. to facilitate economic, industrial, and technical cooperation was signed in Moscow in June but subsequent developments were less promising. In October, after the U.S. adopted a "voluntary system of cooperation in the regulation of grain exports" in the light of unfavourable crop forecasts, grain exports to the U.S.S.R. until at least the summer of 1975 were to be reduced to only about two-thirds of what had been arranged. In December, the Trade Reform Act authorized President Ford to grant the Soviet Union most-favoured-nation status for 18 months only, with subsequent annual presidential extensions contingent upon the whole context of détente including the treatment of Soviet Jews. Congress also limited Export-Import Bank credits to finance Soviet purchases to $300 million over a four-year period.

China also officially reported retail price stability. The country experienced what was described by observers as probably the worst trade and economic difficulties since it recovered from the Cultural Revolution. Workers and young people wanted more political participation and better living conditions than a vast developing country could afford to give them. Like the Soviet Union, China sought to import capital goods and know-how on a deferred-payment basis, a move away from the credo of self-sufficiency in trade.

Requiem for a Troubled Year. The deficiencies of Eastern Europe's economic performance did not prevent the Communist and socialist parties in Western Europe and Japan from claiming that a centrally controlled economy would cure inflation and unemployment. In the U.S., the thought of direct government intervention in the economy gained advocates even in quarters that did not regard recession with inflation as proof of the structural vulnerability of contemporary capitalism. The view that the Western world's political and economic systems would gain over the Communist ones because they were politically freer and economically more efficient thus appeared less convincing to many people as inflation became a sign of economic inefficiency and recession seemingly called for government intervention. These postures were accompanied by agitation to cut defense expenditures without awaiting matching reductions from the Communist side.

Living standards of people in the industrial world as well as in the less developed, non-oil countries were threatened at the very time that high expectations continued to be generated. Evidently, the drain from the stream of consumption spending into oil-producing countries was becoming a new fact of economic life. Much more critical, however, were the shortages of food and industrial materials and the distinct limitations on the capacity of economies to achieve rates of growth comparable to those of the past decade. Some bottlenecks were physical whereas others stemmed from the shortage of capital. The latter was severely aggravated by the reduction in liquidity of enterprises in an environment of inflation, which cut profits in real terms, and by inadequate long-term capital formation, itself a consequence of the decline in thrift and sobriety. The practical inhibitions of liberal democracy made it difficult for governments to abandon the full employment goal, or to deal successfully with inflation.

In the face of this tumult and turbulence, leadership was required to demonstrate that there was nothing irreversible in the economic decline. Such leadership must possess stability at home and mutual cohesion on the international plane that would enable governments to rise to the occasion.

(MIROSLAV A. KRIZ)

See also Economics; Employment, Wages, and Hours; Exchange and Payments, International; Income, National; Industrial Production and Technology; Industrial Relations; Prices; Profits; Savings and Investment; Stock Exchanges; Taxation; Trade, International.

[531.B–E; 532.B; 536.A, C–D; 537]

Ecuador

A republic on the west coast of South America, Ecuador is bounded by Colombia, Peru, and the Pacific Ocean. Area: 109,484 sq.mi. (283,561 sq. km.), including the Galápagos Islands (3,075 sq.mi.). Pop. (1974): 6,480,801. Cap.: Quito (pop., 1974, 597,133). Largest city: Guayaquil (pop., 1974, 814,064). Language: Spanish, but Indians speak Quechuan and Jivaroan. Religion: mainly Roman Catholic. President in 1974, Brig. Gen. Guillermo Rodríguez Lara.

While the gains that Ecuador had experienced since it began exporting oil in 1972 were undeniable, the government had failed to deal with the accompanying social pressures. These had come to the fore with the gradual realization that, despite admirable plans, the government had been unable or unwilling to channel the massive oil revenues into productive uses. This resulted in growing inequality in favour of the coastal traders and businessmen—not to mention the government and the armed forces—and against the vast mass of the rural population. The latter suffered great hardship because of shortages of essential foodstuffs and high prices caused by stagnating agricultural production. In 1973 the cost of living index rose by 20.5%, compared with 6.9% in 1972, and even the conservatives were showing some alarm at the rapidly widening gap between rich and poor.

In an attempt to improve matters, the government finally enacted its agrarian reform program late in 1973. However, no limit was set on the size of landholdings and the only criterion for expropriation was the degree of efficiency with which the land was farmed. Thus, its principal aim was increased productivity rather than any real redistribution of wealth. Moreover, the large landowners retaliated by refusing to invest in the land because of alleged insecurity, an attitude interpreted by the government as a deliberate challenge to the reform program. The result-

ECUADOR

Education. (1970–71) Primary, pupils 1,024,413, teachers 27,099; secondary, pupils 195,154, teachers 11,160; vocational, pupils 22,597, teachers 3,487; teacher training (1969–70), students 18,163, teachers 1,052; higher (including 7 universities), students 42,-394, teaching staff (1969–70) 2,454.

Finance. Monetary unit: sucre, with (Sept. 16, 1974) an official rate of 25 sucres to U.S. $1 (57.55 sucres = £1 sterling). Gold, SDRs, and foreign exchange, central bank: (June 1974) U.S. $437.6 million; (June 1973) U.S. $177.1 million. Budget (1974 est.) balanced at 11.2 billion sucres. Gross national product: (1972) 50,860,000,000 sucres; (1971) 42,240,000,-000 sucres. Money supply: (March 1974) 9,949,000,-000 sucres; (May 1973) 7,758,000,000 sucres. Cost of living (Quito; 1970 = 100): (April 1974) 164; (April 1973) 127.

Foreign Trade. Imports (1973) U.S. $516.6 million; exports (1972) U.S. $335.8 million. Import sources (1972): U.S. 38%; Japan 12%; West Germany 11%; U.K. 6%; Colombia 5%. Export destinations: U.S. 35%; Japan 15%; West Germany 8%; Trinidad and Tobago 5%. Main exports: bananas 36%; coffee 14%; cocoa 8%; sugar 6%; fish products 6%.

Transport and Communications. Roads (1972) 18,345 km. (including 1,392 km. of Pan-American Highway). Motor vehicles in use (1971): passenger 30,100; commercial (including buses) 44,300. Railways (1971): 1,070 km.; traffic 62 million passenger-km.; freight 55 million net ton-km. Air traffic (1972): 218 million passenger-km.; freight 4.5 million net ton-km. Telephones (Dec. 1972) 120,000. Radio receivers (Dec. 1971) 1.7 million. Television receivers (Dec. 1971) 280,000.

Agriculture. Production (in 000; metric tons; 1973; 1972 in parentheses): barley c. 85 (c. 90); corn (1972) c. 240, (1971) 261; potatoes c. 500 (c. 473); rice (1972) 110, (1971) 150; cassava (1972) c. 415, (1971) c. 413; dry beans c. 30 (26); bananas (1972) c. 3,100, (1971) c. 2,500; coffee c. 54 (c. 66); cocoa c. 71 (c. 65); oranges (1972) c. 187, (1971) c. 186; sugar, raw value c. 293 (275); cotton, lint (1972) c. 8, (1971) c. 6. Livestock (in 000; 1972–73): cattle c. 2,580; sheep c. 2,010; pigs c. 1,410; horses c. 260; chickens (1971–72) c. 5,500.

Industry. Production (in 000; metric tons; 1972): petroleum products 1,260; crude oil (1973) 10,706; electricity (kw-hr.) 1,117,000; cement 482; gold (troy oz; 1970) 8.5; silver (troy oz.) c. 70.

ing ineffectiveness of the program led to growing tension in the countryside and to a clash between farmers and police in Chimborazo province, with the farmers receiving considerable support from the local clergy. The government's attempts to counter the unrest by pointing to impressive figures demonstrating the country's expanding economy were of little avail in the absence of any convincing evidence that this wealth was being redirected toward the needy inhabitants of the interior.

Ecuador's external economic position had indeed shown a dramatic improvement as a result of its oil exports. The nation's trade deficit of $40 million in 1971 was transformed into a surplus of $199 million by 1973, the first full year of exports. With the trans-Andean pipeline working at full capacity after October 1973, foreign exchange earnings from petroleum alone covered the entire import bill. However, during 1974 the government took steps to extend the life of proved reserves (20–25 years) by establishing maximum production levels. Meanwhile, the construction of a state refinery meant that by 1976 export earnings would receive a boost from the sale of refined as well as of crude petroleum.

The government's decision to finance the construction of the refinery with its own funds provoked some criticism, as many believed that priority should be given to projects less attractive to foreign investors. It was hoped that the massive oil revenues would solve the country's budgetary problems and, in addi-

tion to facilitating the import of raw materials and capital goods required for industrial development, would meet the need for long overdue improvements in public works. However, such improvements would tend to increase incomes without increasing production, thus enhancing the inflationary spiral.

Following the revision of the oil companies' contracts, government revenue from oil was expected to reach approximately $1 billion in 1974. Furthermore, on the advice of the Organization of Petroleum Exporting Countries (OPEC), in which Ecuador had been accorded full membership in November 1973, negotiations were being speeded up to acquire large shares in the operation of the oil companies.

The crucial importance of oil both economically and politically was demonstrated later in the year by the dismissal of the strongly nationalist minister of power and natural resources, Capt. Gustavo Jarrín Ampudia, who had long been a critic of "excessive profits" by the oil companies and a militant voice in OPEC. The dismissal followed his denunciation of U.S. Pres. Gerald Ford's alleged "imperialist threats" against the oil-producing countries. The Ecuadorian president hastened to express a more conciliatory attitude toward the U.S.　　　(ANNE PARSONS)

[974.D.1]

Education

The United Nations World Population Conference, held in Bucharest, Rom., in August 1974, afforded a stark reminder to the world's educators of the growing magnitude of the task that faced them. As Kurt Waldheim, secretary-general of the UN, put it, each year 127 million children are born and 95 million come of school age—and these totals were likely to rise steeply in the years ahead. Judging from figures produced for the conference by the UN, the increased annual rates of enrollment in the 1960s had not been maintained into the 1970s. It was estimated that at current rates of population growth and school enrollment the number of children who would not go to school would increase by about 17 million every year.

World enrollment figures are difficult to judge, particularly for China, North Korea, and North Vietnam, though one estimate put the 1974 total for the three nations at somewhat over 150 million for the age-range 5 to 24. Adding this figure to the UN estimate for the rest of the world from age 5 to 24 gives a total of approximately 650 million. It was estimated that in the less developed countries the size of the school population aged 5 to 14 would rise to 914 million by 1985, a 42% increase over 1970. In the developed countries, the estimate was for a rise of about 11% to 215 million.

Expenditure on education, therefore, continued to expand in 1974, though in most countries attempts were made to contain the rate of increase. This was especially true in the developed countries, where secondary and higher education in particular had markedly expanded during the 1960s.

Progress in the less developed countries was uneven, though there was evidence of renewed advance in China and, perhaps most dramatically, in the nations of the oil-rich Middle East. Outstanding among the latter was Saudi Arabia; King Faisal's regime sharply reinforced its commitment to education in 1974. The Saudis anticipated that their oil resources would not last indefinitely, perhaps 30 years at the

Ecumenical Movements *see* Religion

most. A conscious decision was therefore taken by the Saudi government to provide the nation with resources of educated manpower similar to those in the countries of the West. At all events, Saudi expenditure on education in 1974 was approximately 13% of the national budget and was expected to increase to 25% in 1980. The 1974 illiteracy rate of 70% would, it was expected, be reduced to 20% by 1994, and by 1979 about 95% of the 6–11-year-old age group should be at school.

Unfortunately, the same reason that allowed the Saudis and others in the Middle East to look forward to a period of euphoric advance, namely the increased cost of oil, had the opposite effect in most other countries. The result there was an attempt to reduce public expenditure and, with it, spending on education.

In the United States, a nation mired down psychologically and politically in the Watergate situation, and also beset by inflation and an energy crisis, little special attention was devoted to education. Educators functioned with large but stabilized enrollments and budgets, financial crises, and generally relaxed students and citizens.

Elementary school enrollments dropped 2.2% in 1974, the third consecutive year of a decline that was likely to continue. The 1974 elementary enrollment was 31.5 million contrasted to 34 million in 1970. Total private and public enrollments in 1974 at all levels dropped from 60.1 million in 1973 to 59.4 million in 1974. Approximately three million teachers, supervisors, and administrators staffed the nation's schools. Of the total U.S. population, 29% were involved as students and staff personnel in educational activities. Education in 1974 cost $108 billion, or 8% of the gross national product. Costs escalated $11 billion over 1973 even though enrollments dropped.

Speaking at a presidentially convened conference on the economics of health, education, and welfare, James A. Harris, president of the 1.5 million-member National Education Association, called for 15% annual pay hikes to keep up with inflation. Other delegates warned that social welfare programs should not suffer fiscal cutbacks, even though the gross national product was suffering its largest drop in 14 years.

Polls taken throughout the U.S. showed negative feelings about major institutions, traditional values, and the presidency. A University of Michigan survey found the military on top in public respect, followed by universities. The public schools were approximately in the middle, while the federal government branches were at the bottom. Christopher Arterton (Massachusetts Institute of Technology) reported that grades 3-4-5 students were totally negative about the presidency, a startling reversal of almost complete admiration reported in previous years. A poll by Daniel Yankelovich of noncollege persons aged 16–25 showed a significant decline from 1969 to 1974 in belief in country, God, family, political institutions, and hard-work payoffs. Tensions related to the war in Vietnam continued to fade away on college campuses; demonstrations became only harrowing memories to administrators.

Holders of the top posts in the federal educational hierarchy changed with their customary frequency. Virginia Y. Trotter became assistant secretary for education in the Department of Health, Education, and Welfare and Terrell H. Bell became the fifth U.S. commissioner of education in the past seven years. The drying up of federal educational funds pointed to declining influence for federal education officials, a decline intensified by the frequent leadership changes, slowness of the federal establishment in adapting to conditions, and the complexity of exercising leadership in a large bureaucracy. The main focus of action was increasingly moving to the states.

Although implementation of educational opportunities guidelines for women was delayed for many months, their release by the Department of Health, Education, and Welfare eventually should have great influence on coeducational classes, athletics, hiring, and other educational practices. Carrying out the spirit of the 1964 Civil Rights Act, Rutgers University provided reparations of $375,000 to 210 female and minority group male employees.

Other federal legislation in 1974 protected the rights and privacy of students and parents in relation to files and records. Students were granted rights to previously confidential records, while others, including parents of college students, found records closed to them.

Nursery and Primary Education. There had been expectations that by 1974 most of the developed countries would begin to redress the imbalance of investment between primary and higher education. Unfortunately, and largely for economic reasons, those expectations were not adequately fulfilled. In Australia, for example, the reelected Labor Party prime minister, Gough Whitlam, promised an ambitious preschool education program to cost A$130 million the first year, but by the fall of 1974 this had been scrapped. There were also cutbacks in Great Britain, where local education authorities found that they did not have the resources to provide new nursery schools or even to fulfill the plan to replace the primary schools built before 1900.

Proposals were introduced by the French government in September to establish free nursery education from the age of 2 to 6. It was already the case in France that almost all 5-year-olds were in school, 75% of 3–4-year-olds, and 25% of 2–3-year-olds. The classes were, however, large, at least half being over 40. The proposals were that for the 2–4-year-olds there should be a ratio of one "education helper" to ten children. The helpers were to be provided with special training. But in France—as in Britain whenever similar proposals had been made—there was strong criticism from the teachers' unions that the

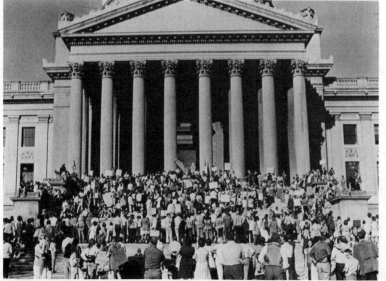

Demonstrators gather at the West Virginia Capitol on October 28 to protest the use of "dirty" and "godless" textbooks in the Kanawha County public schools.

UPI COMPIX

World Education

Most recent official data

Country	1st level (primary) Students (full-time)	1st level Teachers (full-time)	1st level Total schools	General 2nd level (secondary) Students (full-time)	General 2nd level Teachers (full-time)	General 2nd level Total schools	Vocational 2nd level Students (full-time)	Vocational 2nd level Teachers (full-time)	Vocational 2nd level Total schools	3rd level (higher) Students (full-time)	3rd level Teachers (full-time)	3rd level Total schools	Literacy % of population	Literacy Over age
Afghanistan	620,576	16,022	3,226	160,895	7,317	716	9,331	868	33	11,695	1,498	22	8.0	15
Albania	555,300	18,944	1,374	32,867	7,157	46	50,072	1,205	85	25,500	926	5	71.0	9
Algeria	2,244,844	51,461	7,139	278,843	9,892	422	64,550	3,933	259	26,522	...	15	67.0	9
Angola	494,800	11,668	5,070	50,825	2,613	162	16,047	1,207	99	2,435	273	1	30.0	...
Argentina	3,508,406	189,456	20,648	422,652	59,521	1,720	703,063	88,962	2,695	423,824	38,964	788	92.9	10
Australia	1,820,534	69,496	8,237	1,020,417	60,935	2,262	...	...	...	134,861	10,984*	117	...	...
Austria	978,692	48,267	5,659	160,500	7,737	293	266,847	4,190*	1,005	73,134	6,148	35	98.0	15
Bangladesh	6,000,000	124,146	30,446	1,700,000	63,000	5,983	11,300	887	86	45,014	3,073	68	22.7	15
Bolivia	748,506	27,046	8,887	86,365	4,116	383	8,114	1,060	80	37,692	3,026	16	39.8	15
Botswana	95,511	2,698	308	6,152	311	14	1,866	158	28	179	44	1	10.6	15
Brazil	13,623,388	510,285	153,142	3,464,088	228,143	9,323	1,098,038	108,069	6,318	688,382	58,278	1,930	65.9	15
Brunei	30,652	1,478	134	12,127	720	25	532	60	4	—	—	—	64.0	15
Bulgaria	1,025,921	49,775	3,739	109,173	6,891	304	293,226	18,252	571	115,113	8,736	51	91.4	8
Burma	3,198,670	71,136	18,299	813,144	25,461	1,748	8,735	756	35	54,502	3,827	20	68.3	8
Cambodia	471,493	20,150	1,483	98,358	2,410†	88	580	...	96	7,797	1,107	31	74.0	15
Cameroon	754,101	14,703	3,450	65,360	2,719	191	21,547	961	134	3,559	322	11	68.3	8
Canada	3,779,900	269,200‡	16,000‡	1,885,100	‡	‡	...	...	...	543,250	45,700	272	95.4	14
Chile	1,980,906	35,500†	7,302	178,887	7,374†	461	92,014	6,574	276	52,937	...	8	83.6	14
China	90,000,000	...	...	8,520,000	...	...	1,470,000	...	...	820,000	...	...	40.0	...
Colombia	3,282,387	93,980	31,901	688,746	21,511	2,457	103,745	3,963	358	109,639	5,304	45	78.5	15
Congo	277,386	4,373	940	49,984	948	67	4,899	354	31	2,098	194	2	30.0	...
Costa Rica	356,171	12,109	2,530	78,224	...	121	7,679	462	19	17,366	1,275	5	84.7	15
Cuba	1,852,714	68,699	15,474	222,481	17,724	498	67,850	6,920	163	43,261	...	4	...	...
Czechoslovakia	1,890,081	96,781	10,247	119,563	7,829	339	560,572	26,900	1,548	108,646	16,697	44	98.5	15
Denmark	395,289	47,729	2,341	386,276	52,272	...	70,064	4,485	165	113,014	7,016	108	100.0	10
Dominican Republic	820,215	14,752	4,916	122,565	2,131	933	7,544	460	8	19,336	1,038	...	67.2	15
Ecuador	1,024,413	27,099	7,472	195,154	11,160	720	22,597	3,487	...	42,394	2,454	10	69.6	10
Egypt	3,873,297	99,351	8,415	1,268,060	44,197	1,705	289,812	14,300	261	241,690	5,378	106	26.3	14
El Salvador	509,985	13,919	2,787	60,870	3,531§	300	27,437	§	114	9,615	751	9	49.0	...
Fiji	130,440	4,015	635	21,079	862	87	1,703	152	25	981	110	1	72.2	15
Finland	380,865	19,273	4,236	408,464	23,402	1,099	110,016	6,466	745	63,303	7,223	26	100.0	15
France	7,309,000	184,326†	61,500	3,774,228	251,243	8,273	615,425	...	3,762	886,000	31,039	36	100.0	7
Germany, East	2,608,074	151,989‡	5,042	51,609	‡	288	431,963	14,692	1,035	145,717	17,015	54	100.0	15
Germany, West	6,888,669	221,065	24,811	2,217,079	112,890	4,691	2,212,472	44,080	6,081	528,474	38,165	3,361	100.0	10
Greece	907,446	29,336	9,513	422,022	12,958	871	117,006	...	1,166	76,198	3,483	5	85.8	10
Guatemala	585,015	16,451	5,902	86,215	5,934	493	15,810	1,380	...	21,715	1,314	5	37.9	15
Honduras	415,851	11,354	4,245	33,392	2,516	110	7,089	2,689	13	9,204	533	4	47.3	10
Hong Kong	704,536	21,470	1,135	282,195	10,307§	297	18,901	§	38	15,834	1,826	16	82.0	10
Hungary	1,032,786	64,605	4,978	212,734	13,689	295	110,176	7,209	245	60,408	11,155	43	98.0	15
India	78,000,000	1,602,515	404,418	8,600,000§	538,684§	124,360	§	§	§	2,540,000	119,000	3,721	33.3	15
Indonesia	13,201,730	414,799	65,950	1,394,593	58,947	6,446	696,519	34,057	3,733	241,800	13,430†	390	58.1	10
Iran	2,788,000	91,606	18,396	1,134,000	28,244	2,600	66,000	2,682	...	84,000	2,900	6,474	22.8	15
Iraq	1,908,839	58,445	6,817	388,624	14,519	1,093	23,415	1,375	70	49,123	12,108	46	16.3	15
Ireland	538,318	16,844	3,972	226,821	8,882	867	4,025	224	80	28,614	1,404	55	100.0	15
Israel	537,516	27,035	1,856	74,833	5,133	349	72,591	5,229	356	81,243	954	47	91.2‖	14‖
Italy	4,968,900	245,900	35,080	1,190,656	245,628	8,868	1,894,831	249,031	6,639	802,603	44,622	77	91.6	7
Ivory Coast	556,689	12,216	2,377	83,456	2,804†	115	3,284¶	130¶	12¶	4,699	...	2	20.0	...
Japan	9,816,536	392,793	24,592	7,153,337	445,388	14,070	1,561,580	...	1,413	1,926,108	102,396	977	99.9	15
Jordan	352,696	9,408	1,143	121,579	5,706	836	4,349	268	10	8,186	416	16	43.8	15
Kenya	1,779,938	53,812	6,698	179,280	7,344	973	12,850	849	26	2,883	756	1	43.0	15
Korea, South	5,618,768	107,436	6,315	2,460,152	62,318	2,548	451,032	13,996	476	257,610	12,847	185	88.5	13
Kuwait	94,087	5,033	162	88,922	7,283	176	3,034	488	9	3,339	152	5	61.0	10
Laos	273,357	7,320	2,125	14,633	613	37	5,977	413	27	625	106	3	34.3	15
Lebanon	497,723	32,901‡	2,319	167,578	‡	1,241	7,836†	...	159	50,803	2,313	13	88.0	...
Lesotho	187,459	3,951	1,087	12,559	551	56	553	86	9	446	61	1	56.5	15
Liberia	120,245	3,384	889	15,494	918	195	1,308	919	...	1,109	164	3	23.6	5
Libya	467,204	18,840	1,869	67,161	5,093	299	14,365	4,364	106	8,220	414	11	27.0	6
Luxembourg	35,525	1,667	516	9,889	727†	17	7,473	657†	38	357	91	2	100.0	15
Malawi	537,301	9,204	2,028	13,779	677	59	1,792	142	19	1,097	153	1	16.5	15
Malaysia	1,834,390	57,378	6,355	790,358	28,575	1,193	22,466	1,084	85	28,002	2,081	21	60.8	10
Mali	229,879	6,614	873	3,507	290	10	4,937	424	24	731	151	4	20.0	15
Mauritius	154,830	5,270	235	55,893	1,870	126	1,210	93	10	1,263	65	2	61.6	12
Mexico	9,127,226	182,454	46,010	1,008,205	71,057	4,530	419,251	30,540	1,107	247,637	17,103	374	76.2	9
Morocco	1,337,931	37,585	1,609	361,725	23,701	...	2,567¶	120¶	...	20,055	620	...	11.2	15
Mozambique	496,381	6,607	4,095	17,831	1,150	96	2,754	292	25	1,145	213	9	...	...
Nepal	478,743	11,490	7,260	257,245	3,334	1,041	365¶	19¶	...	25,000	1,070	49	11.5	0
Netherlands, The	1,539,676	56,745	9,173	662,145	41,738	1,502	448,735	40,600♀	2,050	83,212	7,500♀	336	100.0	15
New Zealand	521,871	19,831	2,562	202,876	11,223	394	2,231	...	19	35,268	3,006	31	100.0	15
Nicaragua	314,425	8,154	2,115	54,139	1,587	185	6,945	429	44	11,618	694	6	57.6	15
Nigeria	4,391,197	130,355	14,536	399,732	16,720	1,209	53,857	3,085	214	22,927	2,341	18	25.0	15
Norway	375,004	19,109	3,395	268,197	17,799	312	57,215	5,405	598	56,664	5,491	106	100.0	15
Pakistan	4,200,000	95,000	44,637	1,270,000	61,000§	5,893	3,000	§	193	55,000	1,500	421	16.3	5
Panama	319,124	10,578	2,116	74,484	3,440	77	37,116	1,960	149	21,616	705	2	79.4	15
Papua New Guinea	227,699	7,381	1,658	24,335	1,079	71	7,951	602	91	3,088	...	12	32.7	10
Paraguay	459,393	15,871	2,709	66,746	6,829	652	848	66	2	11,194	1,388δ	4	79.7	15
Peru	2,562,695	64,004	20,034	547,316	21,863	1,451	145,207	7,408	414	124,700	13,900	124	61.1	15
Philippines	6,764,501	247,439	42,833	1,723,365	59,473	3,955	112,654	2,414□	683	688,259	27,625	674	83.4	10
Poland	4,841,300	206,700	...	608,800	23,800	...	1,856,285	78,442	...	361,100	38,188	...	95.7	15
Portugal	988,559	30,444	16,586	328,354	19,552	1,623	161,220	10,845	488	51,510	3,111	62	66.5	15
Puerto Rico	471,716	17,565	1,717	311,453	11,999	474	22,449	769	80	78,009	4,246	8	88.1	15
Rhodesia	836,541	21,417	3,732	65,341	3,420	199	6,802	375	35	2,125	303	6	28.6	16
Romania	2,720,199	135,089	14,899	349,980	16,107	532	521,646	24,772	1,078	143,985	14,488	187	100.0	8
Rwanda	397,752	7,777	2,003	7,488	1,487	177	3,047	736	85	735	86	4	23.0	15
Saudi Arabia	530,181	22,705	2,530	106,045	6,117	573	15,192	1,191	80	18,585	1,450	43	10.0	...
Senegal	283,276	6,294	...	59,236	2,198	89	7,408	920	124	7,773	...	...	6.0	14
Singapore	345,284	12,112	408	173,109	7,767	124	5,789	848	13	13,487	858	4	74.7	10
Soviet Union	49,324,000‡	2,360,000‡	...	‡	‡	...	4,437,000	183,000	...	4,630,000	201,000	...	99.7	...
Spain	5,261,920	176,242	133,828	1,274,097	60,925	3,053	421,029	25,195	1,137	267,628	18,268	241	90.1	15
Sri Lanka	2,117,706	...	6,970	480,264	98,925‡	1,673	12,936	895	39	12,074	1,329	5	78.1	10
Sudan	1,031,390	30,328	4,089	199,613	7,874	944	9,804	1,114	41	18,888	732	22	20.0	9–45
Sweden	690,497	40,000	4,000	574,649§	61,000§	800§	§	§	§	102,000	7,000	40	100.0	15
Syria	924,969	25,132	5,261	315,803	10,651	813	2,424	201	41	40,537	1,192	20	100.0	15
Taiwan	2,431,440	61,517	2,349	1,140,260	45,094	788	232,574	8,876	171	263,551	12,678	99	82.7	15
Tanzania	937,609	19,786	4,705	34,303	2,199	114	6,017	472	...	2,060	308	1	...	...
Thailand	6,228,469	192,318	30,933	666,755	28,064	1,705	178,866	12,044	278	63,940	8,348	26	82.3	10
Togo	257,877	4,403	983	24,521	778	72	2,712	228	16	1,369	93	1	10.5	...
Tunisia	922,861	19,421	220	163,353	6,931	154	8,207¶	600¶	...	9,413	304	13	32.2	10
Turkey	5,268,811	159,599	40,383	1,263,802	33,619	2,933	186,225	11,688	563	180,689	10,703	81	54.7	6
Uganda	786,899	24,032	2,937	53,887	2,341	159	6,242	501	31	4,018	470	2	31.0	15
United Kingdom	6,228,702	248,107	28,451	4,061,002	242,436	6,481	330,629	63,787	826	389,659	50,788	283	100.0	15
United States	35,100,000	1,260,000	78,392	15,510,000	1,076,000	57,342	7,278,523	235,658	...	8,370,000	607,000	27,342	99.0	14
Uruguay	366,756	13,436	2,430	138,422	8,154	233	44,203	3,251	97	18,650	2,201	1	90.3	15
Venezuela	1,918,655	54,387	10,591	564,167	15,665	1,018	17,429	1,199	...	99,745	9,105	35	77.1	10
Vietnam, South	2,718,036	49,194	7,978	711,240	23,305	886	35,794	1,031	60	56,608	1,221	14	80.0	...
Yugoslavia	2,856,491	123,860	13,761	193,275	9,508	443	509,261	9,679	631	328,536	19,197	272	80.3	10
Zaire	3,088,011	69,999	4,756	185,370	2,516	646	67,864	3,232	557	12,363	1,386	32	15.0	15
Zambia	777,873	16,491	2,628	60,051	2,779	110	4,057	164¶	18	1,934	214	2	34.3	5

*Excludes teacher training. †Public schools only. ‡Data for primary include secondary. §General includes teacher training and vocational. ‖Jewish population only.
¶Teacher training only. ♀Estimate. δExcludes private 3rd level teacher training. □Private schools only.

UPI COMPIX

Girl consults a textbook to find the answer to a question "asked" her by "Leachim," a computerized robot. Said to have a memory capable of storing thousands of historical and mathematical facts, the robot was designed by New York doctoral student Michael Freeman.

education provided by the "helpers" would be much less than adequate.

The primary education of the growing numbers of immigrant children in Western European countries caused more and more concern. In England, where it was estimated there were 450,000 immigrant children under the age of 14, the position was exacerbated by the fact that they were not only concentrated in some of the larger towns but were almost all coloured and, like immigrants elsewhere in Europe, had problems of language. The West Indians had the advantage of knowing English, but it was frequently of a Creole type. The language problems of Indian and Pakistani children, the other major group, were more severe, but it was found that the parental attitudes to education of these children were very positive and Asian children on the whole did better in school than West Indians.

In West Germany there was similar evidence of anxiety about the educational standard of immigrant children, notably in Bavaria where a report of the minister of education described them as half-educated, both in their native language and in German. In France, where there were estimated to be 800,000 immigrant children of school age in 1974, again mainly living around large towns such as Paris, some progress in concluding agreements to recruit and pay teachers from the native countries of the immigrants was made in the case of Italy, Portugal, Algeria, Tunisia, Spain, and Yugoslavia.

Following the April 25 coup in Lisbon, the new Portuguese regime put great emphasis on the expansion of education. Indeed, one of the priorities declared by the new minister of education, Vitorino Magalhães Godinho, was the setting up of nursery schools for children under seven, the age when primary education began in Portugal. On a more modest scale, another Portuguese-speaking country, Brazil, showed progress in 1974 with the almost intractable problem of illiteracy. It was announced by the minister of education that in 1975 an attempt would be made to extend "Mobral," the Brazilian adult literacy drive, to 9–14-year-olds in the schools. Experiments had already shown that the use of "Mobral" could cause student dropout rates, approximately 70% in

Brazil's elementary schools, to be reduced to 3%. The 1975 experiment was intended to apply to some five million children. It seemed, however, that success was closely related to a school lunch program that went hand-in-hand with the scheme.

Elementary and Secondary Education. The $25.2 billion bill amending the Elementary and Secondary Education Act cleared the U.S. Congress halfway through the year and received the president's signature. Under the amendments, which were to extend through fiscal 1978, programs for the handicapped rose from $47.5 million to $500 million annually. The act forbade court-ordered busing past a student's second-nearest school unless constitutional rights of minority-group children were being violated. The legislation authorized an Advisory Council on Women's Education Programs and directed that a comprehensive review of sex discrimination in education be undertaken. It also contained provisions for career education, education about the metric system, community schools, and gifted children.

Bilingual, multicultural education also was encouraged in the 1974 amendments. Dual-language instruction was expected to promote learning as well as dignity and self-respect for minority-group Americans for whom English was the second tongue. The act's provisions included high priority for training of bilingual teachers, research and demonstration, and monies for state bilingual programs. The U.S. Supreme Court early in 1974 ruled that positive action must be taken to alleviate the learning problems of poor Chinese students in San Francisco who do not speak English. The ruling was likely to affect other non-English-speaking groups, who commonly have high dropout rates, lower standardized-test scores, and below-average college entry rates.

Desegregation action was largely completed in the South and moved to the North and West. Boston received the major attention as federal court-ordered busing moved students out of traditional ethnic enclaves. Violence marked the change. (*See* RACE RELATIONS.) The 1964 U.S. Civil Rights Act changed the number of black students attending school with white students in the South from 2 to 90%. Assistant Attorney General J. Stanley Pottinger claimed that the North lagged in applying the act.

Violence erupted in West Virginia during September and October as parents protested against new textbooks that were being introduced into the Kanawha County public schools. Led by a small group of Fundamentalist ministers, the protesters focused their attack on a grade 7–12 language-arts series, which they described as "anti-Christ," "dirty," and "godless." Demonstrators outside the schools were often joined by striking coal miners, and many parents staged a boycott and kept their children home. In October two schools were bombed and one damaged in a rural area east of Charleston. In an effort to deal with the situation the Kanawha County school board withdrew the disputed books from the schools and subjected them to a 30-day review by an 18-member citizens' committee. On October 8 the committee voted 11–6 to return the books to the schools, but the antibook group continued its protest.

The Education Commission of the States advocated an amendment to the U.S. Constitution that would make education a fundamental right. Equality of educational opportunity could not be denied or abridged on the basis of the student's economic status or any other factor.

Finances emerged as the top state education topic. Efforts were made to maintain fiscal stability. The immense increase in the price of oil escalated fuel costs, and galloping inflation created financial crises in public schools and colleges. For private institutions with limited means of increasing income, the outlook was especially gloomy.

A California state superior court judge ruled that the state must find alternatives to district-by-district financing of public schools by property taxes. The ruling was the first major one following the U.S. Supreme Court's 1973 decision that Texas school inequities had to be ended by statewide action.

Parents in New Hampshire were given a controversial choice between public and private schools. The Department of Health, Education, and Welfare authorized $3 million in funds for the experiment. Under the voucher system used in the experiment, parents were given certificates that could be cashed to cover costs of educating their children. The nation's only previous experience with such a system had been in Alum Rock, Calif., where only public school options were available to parents.

Oregon became the first state to put a teacher-dominated Teacher Standards and Practices Commission into full effect. The commission determined policies on teacher licensing, revocation and other disciplinary action, and accreditation of teacher-education programs.

Albert Shanker attained another step in his climb to power within the education and union establishment, toppling David Selden from the presidency of the 425,000-member American Federation of Teachers (AFT). The AFT and the National Education Association forged alliances with the national union of federal, state, and local government workers. NEA and AFT merger talks became snagged early in the year, and the groups exchanged charges on why the negotiations broke down.

The Representative Assembly of the National Education Association acted to oppose performance contracting, revenue sharing, voucher plans, tax credits, and evaluations by private, profit-making groups. The NEA Representative Assembly approved $50,000 to develop Watergate-antidote curriculum materials. They were to be about fair play, participatory democracy, ethics, and theoretical concepts of democracy.

The most arresting, if not the most significant, educational event of 1974 in Europe was the publication of a report by a commission studying Sweden's school structure, chaired by a well-known educationist, Jonas Orring, the director general of the National Board of Education in Sweden. During the 1960s Sweden had established itself as the European country with the most advanced educational ideas. SIA, the Swedish abbreviation for the report, was an attempt to bring to the nine-year comprehensive schools (ages 7–16) a curricular content that would link school more closely with life. The central concept was that of an integrated school day, the purpose of which was "to make the nine-year compulsory school a living educational and social centre." The report envisaged schools being open from six in the morning until late in the evening. The obligatory part of the school day would average about six hours for the younger children and seven hours for the older ones and would be used not only for formal lessons but also for a wide range of activities. Thus, the aim of the SIA proposal was "a community-orientated, open institution playing a central role in the life of our

growing generation"; the traditional school, nursery classes, and leisure centres would be rolled into one. There was a good deal of emphasis, too, on parents. Indeed, the commission even proposed giving them a statutory right to spend a day with their children at school every three years.

To some extent the motivation behind SIA was economic, incorporating what in Britain, for example, was known as "dual use" of school buildings. It might also economize on teaching staff. Needless to say it did not get an altogether warm reception from the teachers' unions in Sweden. At the same time the commission reported that SIA had been tried out experimentally in 25 communities throughout the country and was found to work well.

In Britain the Schools Council for the Curriculum continued to produce curriculum proposals for various subjects, though the emphasis in its work turned toward disseminating previous findings rather than opening up new fields of research. As in other countries, the British were beginning to find that it was one thing to propose curricular innovations and improvements and quite another to get teachers to apply them. There was a good deal more stress on teacher training and in-service training, though the economic climate restricted this development.

In France discussion was almost obsessively concerned with the reform of secondary education. This was begun by Joseph Fontanet in 1973, but after the death of Pres. Georges Pompidou he was replaced as minister of education by René Haby in April 1974, with the result that discussions began all over again. Unfortunately, Haby had less success than Fontanet in gaining support for his reforms from the teachers' unions and other interests.

One among Haby's ideas was a change in the form of the baccalaureat, a peculiarly sensitive area in French education because it is the examination that provides automatic entry to a university. The minister's proposals were to spread the baccalaureat over two years and then to follow it with a final year, or *terminale,* devoted to pre-university specialization.

It was a proposal bound to give rise to suspicion because it implied that the route to a university education might too readily be closed. In continental Europe the notion that there should be open access

Pres. Richard M. Nixon presents a plaque to the 1974 Teacher of the Year, Vivian Tom, at the White House. Miss Tom is a teacher of social studies at Lincoln High School, Yonkers, N.Y. The Teacher of the Year awards are sponsored by the Encyclopædia Britannica Companies, the Council of Chief State School Officers, and the "Ladies' Home Journal," which featured an article on the 1974 winner and five finalists in the May issue.

UPI COMPIX

to a university for those who had successfully completed the final secondary school examination was strongly established. Yet it was clear that the opposite principle, the careful selection of university entrants, was inevitable in view of the need to contain the high cost of university education.

The principal bone of contention over secondary education, however, was the same as in most other European countries outside Scandinavia; namely, that secondary education was not sufficiently comprehensive. In Britain, and more particularly in West Germany, the issue was further complicated because of its political overtones. In West Germany the Social Democrats were committed to comprehensive schools and the Christian Democrats inclined to resist them. Thus in 1974, Bavaria, dominated by the Christian Democrats, had no more than 3 comprehensive schools, whereas Social Democrat-controlled Hesse had as many as 64. Hesse announced that it planned to go entirely comprehensive by 1985, but received a setback in June 1974 when the Darmstadt administrative court upheld a petition by parents against the conversion of a grammar (academic college preparatory) school into an integrated comprehensive, arguing that Hesse's school administration law merely permitted "experiments with comprehensive schools."

In Britain, a similar though more muted division appeared in 1974 between the Conservatives and the Labour Party. In the campaign preceding the October 1974 general election, the Conservatives argued strongly that grammar schools should be allowed to coexist with comprehensives. The Labour Party, however, won the election and immediately reaffirmed its policy to introduce comprehensive schools throughout the country. However, despite the fact that the Labour Party had been in office from 1964 to 1970, less than half the secondary school population was in comprehensive schools and two out of every five comprehensives in England had to coexist with grammar schools, thus preventing them from being truly comprehensive. Even so, England, and more especially Wales and Scotland, moved much further along the path toward comprehensive education than West Germany, where in 1974 there were only 105 genuine comprehensives, compared with some 2,000 gymnasiums, or grammar schools, and 25,000 other secondary schools.

In the Scandinavian countries, however, comprehensive schools became more firmly established in 1974. In Norway in June a law was passed establishing the nine-year school (ages 7–16) with an additional 16-plus stage involving a year of common studies followed by some measure of specialization. This was much the same development that had already taken place in Sweden. Denmark also arrived at a similar pattern, as set out in the Højby Report published in June 1973. This provided for the age group 16–19 having the choice of three types of education—vocational, technical, and college preparatory—but financial constraints led to its being delayed in 1974.

One unanticipated consequence of comprehensive education, together with the extension of secondary schooling to the age of 16 and over, was the growing demand in 1974 that there should be some monitoring of standards. The demand was linked especially with concern about the decline of discipline, notably in Britain when the school-leaving age was raised in 1973–74 and large numbers of reluctant 16-year-olds had to be contained in the schools. Politically, pressure came mostly from the Conservative side. In Swe-

den a parliamentary commission was established to inquire into "goals and evaluation in secondary schools," the aim being to establish certain standards for all pupils leaving school. In England and Wales, an Assessment of Performance Unit was established by the Department of Education.

Not surprisingly, the biggest change of orientation in secondary education took place in Portugal following the collapse of the regime of Premier Marcello Caetano in April 1974. There followed an immediate and thorough revision of teaching programs, particularly in such sensitive areas as history, politics, philosophy, and Portuguese literature. There was much more teacher consultation, and teachers were allowed freedom to select their own texts instead of having to rely on prescribed work by the ministry. Needless to say, finance placed a severe restraint on expansion, particularly as some attempt had to be made to increase teachers' salaries; the salaries of secondary-school teachers under the Caetano regime had been as low as £750 ($1,800) a year.

But complaints about the rigidity of the curriculum and examinations were not restricted to countries like Portugal. In June 1974 in New Zealand it was announced that teachers were to have more influence in decisions on the secondary-school curriculum, and in the state of Victoria in Australia the Secondary School Teachers' Association threatened to refuse to teach matriculation classes (classes for the pre-university entrance examinations) in 1975. They argued that the examination dominated the curriculum and gave unfair advantage to middle-class children.

Higher Education. The beginning of a collision course between the demand for the expansion of higher education, following the expansion of secondary education, and the need for economic constraint became evident in 1974. The predictions of the European Cultural Foundation (ECF), under the chairmanship of Henri Janne of Brussels, envisaged continued expansion. The minimal forecast made by the ECF group was that 15% of the population aged 20–24 would be enrolled in universities in 1980 in Western Europe and 30% in the year 2000, while the maximal forecast was for 20 and 40% for those two years, respectively. In cost terms this would mean that West Germany, for example, would have to give over 2.5% of its national income to the universities in 1980 and 4.1% in the year 2000. Given the maximal ECF forecast, this latter figure could rise as high as 19%.

At the same time, almost all countries were decelerating the expansion of higher education. The exceptions were, as might be expected, many of the oil-rich countries and, more surprisingly, Australia. In Saudi Arabia plans were announced for the massive expansion of the University of Riyadh, the technological university devoted to petroleum technology and mineralogy in Dhahran, and the Abdul Aziz University in Jidda. Despite the insistence that men and women had to be educated separately, provision was made for women students to be included in the expansion. Already, by 1974, there were 900 women at the university in Jidda out of a total of 4,200 students. Yet no male lecturer was allowed to appear in front of the women, except via closed circuit television. In Australia, where university funding had fallen behind in recent years, the federal government took over complete responsibility for universities from the states and the budget was increased by approximately 50%. The number of universities was also scheduled to be increased from 15 to 18 in 1975.

In Western Europe, however, retrenchment was the order of the day. In France there was a cut in university building of 19% between 1973 and 1975. The possibility of introducing a two-semester year to make better use of university buildings was also discussed. In the U.K. almost every university announced cutbacks in expenditure except for the Open University, which the Labour government announced would be allowed to accept up to 20,000 students (6,000 more than the previous year) in January 1975. The Open University had been planned as a means of teaching older home-based students who wished to take a university degree in a minimum period of four years by part-time study using correspondence courses, television and radio programs, and short summer-school courses. The teaching methods and course content of the Open University were the subject of widespread interest in 1974 in a number of countries outside Britain.

Decisions were taken in several European countries to reduce the output of teachers and to reinforce the quality of their training. In England and Wales it was decided that a teaching force of 510,000 previously planned for 1980 would need to be cut back by about 20,000 to 30,000 because of the unanticipated drop in the birthrate. In France it was announced that, whereas there were 22,500 new teaching posts in 1974, there would be only 10,000 in 1975. In West Germany the University of Essen claimed that by 1981 there would be a surplus of 160,000 teachers, though this was, needless to say, not accepted by the teachers' organizations.

In addition to restricting the output of teachers, the government in England and Wales also planned to stiffen the pre-entry qualification for teaching so that it would be equivalent to university entry and in the long term to make teaching into an all-graduate profession. Similar moves were planned in Poland, where it was announced that the teachers' institutes providing three-year courses would become part of the universities. The Polish government also stated that all male teachers under 40 and women teachers under 35 would have to undertake a part-time university course (and having completed it would get a 25% increase in salary). In the Soviet Union the periodic assessment of teachers was to begin in 1975. Assessment for all teachers, except chief administrators, would take place every five years.

In Eastern Europe there was evidence of greater cooperation, though not without tensions, among the various members of the Council for Mutual Economic Assistance (Comecon). A "qualitative new stage" that would integrate the economic forecasting of the Comecon members up to 1985–90 was planned to begin in 1976. This, it was said, would inevitably involve closer integration of higher education. Late in 1973 the *Higher Education Quarterly* of the Eastern European countries began to be published in Warsaw.

At the other end of the Communist world, in China, it seemed that higher education was still emerging from the trauma of the Cultural Revolution. The insistence that students in institutions of higher education must combine academic work with productive labour was if anything reinforced. It was reported that unless applicants for university places had spent five years working in field or factory they were unlikely to be accepted. Moreover, application had to be via a Revolutionary Committee, whether that of a commune, a factory, or the People's Liberation Army. Thus low academic qualifications would not

necessarily be a deterrent, but presumably the very high staff-student ratios (less than one in three in some universities) would help to make good these disadvantages.

The divisions between East and West in higher education were sharply manifest at the conference of European rectors and vice-chancellors (CRE) held in Bologna, Italy, in September. This standing conference emerged in the early 1950s and by 1974 had grown to represent 25 nations. At the November 1973 UNESCO meeting of European ministers of education, however, a resolution had been passed calling for a new body to be established to promote European understanding at university level. This appeared to undermine the CRE, and following the Bologna conference a working party was established to try to work out an accommodation. One of the sticking points was that the CRE members were unwilling to be part of an organization that was subject to governmental influence.

Access to college remained unequal for students in the U.S. Low-income families, minority groups, people from large cities and rural areas, and women were the major groups with less access, according to the National Commission on the Financing of Postsecondary Education after months of study. Persons living in small metropolitan areas had the best access to college, and Orientals, with 58%, had the highest percentage of persons with some college education, topping the 53% of whites who had some college. The 1974 convention of the American Federation of Teachers advocated complete and open access to

Children attend public school in the jungle in newly independent Guinea-Bissau.

higher education, coupled with counseling and other actions to assure student success.

Although large numbers of teacher trainees could not get teaching jobs during the year, a Gallup Poll in 1974 revealed that about 25% of college students planned to enter teaching. (The 25% figure equaled three-fourths of the current teaching force.) The National Education Association claimed that there would be no teacher surplus if class sizes were lowered to an adequate level, if kindergarten and special education classes were increased, and if other efforts to raise standards were made.

Federally guaranteed student-loan defaults by post-secondary students reached new highs, particularly at profit-making training schools. Students dropped classes and decreased commitments to repay loans. In eight years, approximately 168,000 defaults had been reported. The defaults reflected student and parent inability to meet increasing costs as well as a growing respectability for dropping out of post-secondary education and entering nonprofessional job fields.

Tenure, traditionally almost a guaranteed position for life in return for professional services, was shaken on campus. Inflation-hit budgets and declining (or stabilizing) student populations combined to reduce the need for some senior, tenured staff. Harder hit were junior professors and new graduates seeking positions, particularly at regional universities and state colleges. A few private colleges cut their staffs by as much as 40%.

The Ford Foundation considered cancellation of its philanthropic program, much of which was devoted to education. It decided instead to curtail programs and continue studies on how to survive. Cuts of 50% in programs were discussed. The foundation's assets dropped from $3 billion to $2 billion in 1974, while inflation decreased the value of available moneys. Other foundations faced similar financial problems.

International Cooperation. The European Community, although ostensibly strengthened by the addition of the U.K., Ireland, and Denmark, made little progress on the educational side. There was almost no movement toward the mutual recognition of each country's academic degrees, though a determined effort was made to get mutual recognition of medical qualifications. At the June meeting of the Community ministers of education in Luxembourg, however, an education committee was established, though it was restricted chiefly to preparing better statistics, improving contact between institutions of higher education, and collating information about the education of immigrant children.

The biennial exhibition of educational materials, Didacta, took place in June at Brussels. This is a well-established and important marketplace for the sale of materials and equipment for schools and colleges, and this, the 12th Didacta, attracted exhibitors and buyers from places as widely dispersed as China, Thailand, Iceland, and South Africa. West German exhibitors were in the majority with 205; the British came next with 158 exhibitors; the French had 100, and, surprisingly, the U.S. was represented by as many as 61 companies.

(TUDOR DAVID; JOEL L. BURDIN)

See also Health and Disease; Libraries; Motion Pictures; Museums.

[562; 563]

ENCYCLOPÆDIA BRITANNICA FILMS. *Learning with Today's Media* (1974).

Eggs:
see Agriculture and Food Supplies

Egypt

A republic of northeast Africa, Egypt is bounded by Israel, Sudan, Libya, the Mediterranean Sea, and the Red Sea. Area: 386,900 sq.mi. (1,002,-000 sq.km.). Pop. (1973 est.): 35,619,000. Cap. and largest city: Cairo (pop., 1973 est., 5,517,000). Language: Arabic. Religion: Muslim 93%; Christian 7%. President in 1974, Anwar as-Sadat; prime ministers, Anwar as-Sadat and, from September 25, Abdul Aziz Hegazy.

In 1974 Egypt pursued its efforts for a resumption of Middle East peace talks that would lead to an Israeli withdrawal from Egyptian territory, but with limited success. Internally, there were moves toward the liberalization of the economy and political life. Friendly relations with the United States were maintained, but at year's end earlier indications of a rapprochement with the Soviet Union were in doubt.

Relations with Israel and the Palestinians. Egypt and Israel continued their talks in Geneva on military disengagement during the first week of January, but it required the intervention of U.S. Secretary of State Henry Kissinger (*see* BIOGRAPHY), who shuttled between Aswan and Jerusalem from January 11 to 17, to achieve an agreement. By the terms of this accord, which was approved by both sides on January 18, reduced Egyptian forces were stationed in a strip six miles wide along the east bank of the Suez Canal. Israel withdrew from its last positions on the canal on March 4.

The disengagement made it possible to begin work on clearing bombs and mines from the canal bed and banks and on removing sunken ships. The U.S., British, and French navies helped the Egyptians with the work, but hopes that the canal could be reopened to international shipping during 1974 were not fulfilled; May 1, 1975, became the date forecast for reopening. Work also began on rebuilding the shattered and semi-deserted canal towns of Suez, Ismailiyah, and Port Said. President Sadat visited the east bank of the canal in June and announced a target of restoring the canal towns to normal life by the end of the year. The former inhabitants began flocking back, and by July 10 it was reported that 235,000 had already returned. After the clearance of Port Said at the beginning of the summer, the harbour was brought into use to relieve congestion in Alexandria.

Realizing that the greatest obstacle to a resumption of the Geneva talks was the question of Palestinian representation at Geneva, Sadat tried persistently to achieve a compromise between King Hussein of Jordan and the Palestine Liberation Organization (PLO). After a visit by King Hussein to Egypt on July 16–18, President Sadat announced his agreement that the PLO should represent all Palestinians except those living in Jordan. This was unacceptable to the PLO, and, after a meeting with the Syrians and the PLO in Cairo in September, Egypt apparently reversed its position by agreeing that the PLO should represent all Palestinians. However, Sadat continued to work for a compromise and played a major role in the one that was achieved at the Arab summit meeting in October. (*See* MIDDLE EASTERN AFFAIRS.)

Kissinger's next visit to Cairo early in October yielded little result, and the prospects of a resumption

EGYPT

Education. (1971–72) Primary, pupils 3,873,297, teachers 99,351; secondary, pupils 1,240,192, teachers 42,025; vocational, pupils 289,812, teachers 14,300; teacher training, students 27,247, teachers 2,172; higher (including 6 universities), students 241,690, teaching staff 5,378.

Finance. Monetary unit: Egyptian pound, with (Sept. 16, 1974) an official rate of E£0.39 to U.S. $1 (E£0.94 = £1 sterling) and a tourist rate of E£0.62 to U.S. $1 (E£1.43 = £1 sterling). Gold, SDRs, and foreign exchange, central bank: (May 1974) U.S. $436 million; (May 1973) U.S. $206 million. Budget (1971–72 est.): revenue E£1,922 million; expenditure E£2,001 million. Gross national product: (1970–71) E£3,078 million; (1969–70) E£2,927 million. Money supply: (April 1974) E£1,311 million; (April 1973) E£1,030.5 million. Cost of living (1970 = 100): (Dec. 1973) 114; (Dec. 1972) 107.

Foreign Trade. (1973) Imports E£357.5 million; exports E£444.2 million. Import sources (1972): U.S.S.R. 13%; Australia 9%; U.S. 9%; France 7%; West Germany 7%. Export destinations (1972): U.S.S.R. 26%; U.K. 5%; West Germany 5%. Main exports: cotton 43%; crude oil 11%; cotton yarn 10%; rice 6%.

Transport and Communications. Roads (1970) c. 50,000 km. (including 22,100 km. with improved surface). Motor vehicles in use (1972): passenger 151,700; commercial (including buses) 39,200. Railways: (1973) 5,006 km.; traffic (1971–72) 7,306,000,000 passenger-km., freight 2,976,000,000 net ton-km. Air traffic (1972): 1,095,000,000 passenger-km.; freight 17.8 million net ton-km. Shipping (1973): merchant vessels 100 gross tons and over 137; gross tonnage 268,747. Telephones (Jan. 1969) c. 365,000. Radio licenses (Dec. 1972) 5 million. Television licenses (Dec. 1971) 584,000.

Agriculture. Production (in 000; metric tons; 1973; 1972 in parentheses): corn c. 2,400 (2,421); wheat c. 1,840 (1,618); barley c. 110 (109); millet and sorghum c. 850 (831); rice c. 2,680 (2,507); potatoes c. 500 (596); sugar, raw value c. 680 (c. 653); tomatoes c. 1,650 (1,668); onions c. 470 (519); dry broad beans (1972) 361, (1971) 256; dates (1972) 350, (1971) 340; oranges (1972) c. 750, (1971) 707; tangerines and mandarin oranges (1972) c. 90, (1971) 101; lemons (1972) c. 75, (1971) 74; grapes (1972) c. 128, (1971) 122; cotton, lint c. 523 (514); cheese (1972) c. 181, (1971) c. 180; beef and buffalo meat c. 226 (218). Livestock (in 000; 1972–73): cattle c. 2,138; buffaloes (1971–72) c. 2200; sheep 2,140; goats (1971–72) c. 1,350; asses (1971–72) c. 1,400; camels c. 125; chickens (1971–72) c. 25,150.

Industry. Production (in 000; metric tons; 1973): cement 3,626; iron ore (50% metal content) 603; crude oil 8,367; petroleum products (1971) 4,860; fertilizers (nutrient content) nitrogenous 152, phosphate 115; salt (1971) 385; sulfuric acid 115; cotton yarn 180; cotton fabrics (m.) c. 570,000; electricity (kw-hr.; 1972) 8,030,000.

of the Geneva talks receded. Sadat continually emphasized, however, that he would not consider a separate peace with Israel and that Egypt was as much concerned with the recovery of other occupied Arab territories as of Sinai. The possibility of a further partial agreement between Egypt and Israel in which Israel might withdraw in Sinai in return for free navigation rights in the Suez Canal and an Egyptian declaration of nonbelligerency was widely discussed in diplomatic circles. However, Israel was reported to be refusing to give up the Sinai oil fields, while Egypt maintained that it would refuse to reopen the Suez Canal while the Israelis remained on the shore of the Gulf of Suez.

Relations with the Superpowers. President Sadat's wooing of the United States and his exceptional friendliness with Kissinger led to the full resumption of Cairo-Washington diplomatic relations on February 28 after seven years. On April 24 Pres. Richard Nixon asked the U.S. Congress for $250 million in aid for Egypt, and he received a great popular welcome when he visited Egypt on June 12–14 at the start of his Middle East tour. Nixon promised aid to strengthen the economy and provide Egypt with a U.S. nuclear reactor. The U.S. encouraged Egypt's moves toward the liberalization and opening-up of the economy to foreign capital.

Although the U.S. secretary of defense said that his country might consider military aid for Egypt, such a move seemed doubtful, and Egypt remained dependent on the U.S.S.R. for arms. France was a possible alternative source of supply after it raised its arms embargo on the Middle East belligerent states in August, but France strongly denied it was selling 50 Mirage F-1 aircraft to Egypt (although some Mirages sold to Saudi Arabia, Kuwait, and Abu Dhabi were expected to reach Egypt with French knowledge). Egypt's greatest need was for modern fighters to replace the 150 lost in the October 1973 war. After the cease-fire the U.S.S.R. had supplied Egypt with some tanks and MiG-21s, but Soviet arms supplies slowed down when the extent of Egypt's commitment to the U.S. became clear.

The Egyptian foreign minister, Ismail Fahmy, visited Moscow in January and gave an account of Egypt's disengagement agreement with Israel, but Soviet-Egyptian relations subsequently deteriorated. There was little improvement even after Soviet Foreign Minister Andrey A. Gromyko's Cairo visit in March, and throughout the spring and summer President Sadat was openly critical of the Soviet Union, which, he said, had consistently failed to give Egypt equal support to that provided by the U.S. for Israel. The Soviet press replied with criticisms of Egypt's move to the right. However, between June 27 and July 2 Sadat paid successful visits to Romania and Bulgaria, and by September there were clear signs of a rapprochement. After the Egyptian foreign minister visited Moscow in October it was announced that Soviet leader Leonid I. Brezhnev would visit Egypt in January 1975. However, during a further visit to Moscow by Fahmy and the Egyptian defense minister in December, the cancellation of Brezhnev's visit was announced, supposedly because of disagreement over military aid.

Relations with the Arab States. During 1974 Egypt had fair success in cultivating its relations with the Arab states and maintaining Arab solidarity. In January President Sadat visited 11 Arab states in five days. Relations with Jordan were delicate because of the PLO issue. Close ties with Syria were maintained despite Syrian doubts about Egypt's pro-U.S. moves, but Egypt was most successful in strengthening its relations with Saudi Arabia and Algeria, at opposite ends of the Arab political spectrum. Saudi King Faisal visited Egypt from July 30 to August 7 and pledged $300 million in aid. Oil-rich Kuwait and Abu Dhabi also agreed to increase their support. Iraq was still critical of Egyptian policy, but in August agreed on joint economic ventures worth $1 billion. Pres. Gaafar Nimeiry of Sudan visited Cairo in February and agreed with President Sadat on measures for "political and economic integration."

Despite a sudden reconciliation visit to Cairo by Libyan Pres. Muammar al-Qaddafi in February, Egyptian-Libyan relations worsened, especially after Egypt accused Libya of involvement in an armed attack on the Military Technical Academy in Cairo in April, in which 11 were killed, and later, in August, after Libyan Mirage jets were discovered on Egyptian territory. President Sadat criticized President Qaddafi in strong terms, and some of the 200,000 Egyptians employed in Libya returned home.

HMS "Wilton" (foreground) and salvage craft take part in clearing the Suez Canal of unexploded weapons. The Anglo-U.S.-French-Egyptian operation began April 11.

Domestic Affairs. The year 1974 was marked by *al-infitah,* or the opening-up of the economy, the lifting of censorship in February on the Egyptian and foreign press, and an open debate on the rights and wrongs of the era of Pres. Gamal abd an-Nasser. There was much discussion of "de-nasserization." In January and October a number of prisoners charged with political offenses under the Nasser regime were released. On February 1, Ali Amin, exiled under Nasser, replaced Muhammad Heikal as editor of the influential newspaper *al-Ahram.* However, there was some counterreaction by Nasserist and left-wing intellectuals, and in May one of them, Ahmad Baheddin, replaced Amin, who moved to the less influential *Akhbar al-Yaum.* There were indications that President Sadat felt that "de-nasserization" had gone too far, and he made clear that his aim was to remedy the defects of the Nasser era but maintain its achievements. On April 24 Sadat formed a new Cabinet with himself as prime minister but with Finance Minister Abdul Aziz Hegazy, a strong advocate of economic liberalization, promoted to first deputy prime minister. On May 15 Sadat's "October program" for political, economic, and social reforms was endorsed by 99.95% of a popular vote. On September 25 Sadat, in a long-expected move, relinquished the post of prime minister to Abdul Aziz Hegazy, who formed a 37-man government with key ministers unchanged.

Left-wing students were openly critical of Egypt's new friendship with the U.S. There was also some right-wing opposition, allegedly supported by Libya, represented by the attack on the Cairo Military Technical Academy. Discontent with shortages of some basic commodities was expressed, and in October industrial workers at Helwan went on strike. Heavy defense expenditure and the annual population increase of 800,000 continued to apply heavy pressure on the balance of payments. A government spokesman estimated Egypt's debts at $1.5 billion, mainly on account of defense. In June the People's Assembly passed a law giving foreign investors liberal tax relief and freeing them from many controls, including the requirement of 51% Egyptian participation in companies. Liberalization measures, combined with the financial backing of the oil states, helped to create a new climate for investment in Egypt. However, by the end of 1974 some disappointment was being expressed at the delayed fulfillment of promises of aid, and foreign investors were complaining of continuing obstacles from Egyptian bureaucracy.   (PETER MANSFIELD)

[978.B.3.e]

Eire:
see Ireland

Electrical Industries:
see Energy; Industrial Production and Technology

Electronics:
see Computers

El Salvador

A republic on the Pacific coast of Central America and the smallest country on the isthmus, El Salvador is bounded on the west by Guatemala and on the north and east by Honduras. Area: 8,098 sq.mi. (21,975 sq.km.). Pop. (1974 est.): 3,926,500. Cap. and largest city: San Salvador (pop., 1974 est., 416,900). Language: Spanish. Religion: Roman Catholic. President in 1974, Col. Arturo Armando Molina.

The effects of the 1969 war between El Salvador and Honduras continued to be reflected in 1974 in the Salvadorean economy. The border between the two countries remained closed to each other's trade to the especial detriment of El Salvador, the most densely populated, industrialized, and trade-dependent of the Central American republics. Efforts in 1974 to restore trade between the two nations were unsuccessful. As the economic situation worsened in El Salvador, where the unemployment rate was at least 20%, the under-employment rate twice that, and inflation running at an annual rate of 60%, the government increasingly found itself pressured by opposition parties to resolve differences with Honduras.

The economic news was especially dispiriting for El Salvador in 1974 as a result of a substantial drop in the price of the nation's key commodity, coffee, which accounted for more than one-third of the nation's foreign exchange earnings. The 1973–74 crop year was considered the greatest setback ever between one year and another.

In the wake of the 1969 war the government had promised to undertake agrarian reform programs. But

EL SALVADOR
Education. (1970) Primary, pupils 509,985, teachers 13,919; secondary, pupils 60,870; vocational, pupils 27,437; secondary and vocational, teachers 3,531; higher, students 9,615, teaching staff 751.
Finance. Monetary unit: colón, with (Sept. 16, 1974) a par value of 2.50 colones to U.S. $1 (free rate of 5.79 colones = £1 sterling). Gold, SDRs, and foreign exchange, central bank: (June 1974) U.S. $63.4 million; (June 1973) U.S. $106.9 million. Budget (1974) balanced at 557.9 million colones. Gross national product: (1972) 2,862,000,000 colones; (1971) 2,673,000,000 colones. Money supply: (June 1974) 533.3 million colones; (June 1973) 393.4 million colones. Cost of living (1970 = 100): (March 1974) 119; (March 1973) 105.
Foreign Trade. (1973) Imports 943.1 million colones; exports 880 million colones. Import sources (1972): U.S. 28%; Guatemala 17%; Japan 11%; West Germany 8%; Nicaragua 5%; Costa Rica 5%. Export destinations: West Germany 23%; Guatemala 20%; U.S. 16%; Japan 14%; Costa Rica 8%; Nicaragua 6%. Main exports: coffee 45%; cotton 10%.
Transport and Communications. Roads (1971) 10,733 km. (including 625 km. of Pan-American Highway). Motor vehicles in use (1972): passenger 37,900; commercial (including buses) 21,900. Railways (1972) 720 km. Telephones (Dec. 1972) 43,000. Radio receivers (Dec. 1971) 350,000. Television receivers (Dec. 1971) 125,000.
Agriculture. Production (in 000; metric tons; 1973; 1972 in parentheses): corn c. 400 (237); sorghum c. 161 (146); rice c. 55 (c. 55); dry beans c. 37 (27); coffee 134 (129); sugar, raw value c. 187 (c. 187); cotton, lint 69 (68); jute 5 (5). Livestock (in 000; 1972–73): cattle c. 1,100; pigs c. 420; horses c. 65; poultry (1971–72) c. 8,100.
Industry. Production (in 000; metric tons; 1972): cement 218; petroleum products 467; cotton yarn (1971) 5; electricity (kw-hr.) 820,000.

none was attempted until a token gesture was made at the beginning of 1974 by President Molina in an effort to avoid serious unrest. Molina issued a decree to alleviate rural poverty by promising a minimum rural wage of 2.75 colones ($1.10) per day and a minimum daily food ration of corn (700 grams) and beans (110 grams) plus salt. These proposals were flatly refused by the ruling landowners, and Molina abandoned his agrarian reform efforts. That precipitated, in February, the resignation of Agriculture Minister Roberto Llach Hill and his deputy, Antonio Cabrales Caceras, after only four months in office. They were replaced by Mauricio Eladio Castillo and Col. Roberto Escobar García.

In spite of these problems, and pressures from opponents, the ruling National Conciliation Party (PCN) won congressional and mayoral elections on March 10, retaining its position as the governing party. Election results gave 32 of the 52 legislative seats to the PCN, 14 to the National Opposition Union (UNO), 4 to the Salvadorean People's Party (PPS), and 2 to the United Independent Democratic Front (FUDI). A majority of the 261 mayoral posts at stake were won by PCN candidates, but a UNO member, José Antonio Morales Ehrlich, was elected mayor of San Salvador.   (ALLEN D. BUSHONG)

[974.B.1.c]

Employment, Wages, and Hours

The economic boom of 1973 was brought to an abrupt halt in 1974 by the oil crisis, which had the dual effect of causing both recession and accelerated inflation: because consumers spent more on petroleum they had correspondingly less to spend on other goods, and expenditure by the oil-producing countries did not fill the gap. Meanwhile, higher energy costs were working their way through all economies, raising prices generally. The recession was likely to worsen because, although the richer countries could borrow to finance their increased oil bills, the poorer countries could not, and so the third world was resorting to cuts in imports other than oil. Exports from industrial countries were therefore likely to fall, aggravating the recession.

The world economy was also suffering a crisis in food production. During the 1950s and 1960s agricultural output in most countries managed to keep up with population growth, largely through the application of fertilizers in the context of advancing agricultural technology. But in the late 1960s more countries began to import food to cope with the growing pressures of population. Then, in 1973–74, the price of fertilizers rose sharply owing to increasing shortages, the rise in oil prices, and the fact that Morocco, the world's most important supplier of phosphates, trebled the price of phosphate at the end of 1973 to protect its economy from the effects of higher oil prices. As the prices of inputs to agricultural production rise, food prices, too, must rise if farming is to continue profitable, and this rise in prices will be brought about by a reduction of food supply as farmers cut their losses. This can have catastrophic effects, particularly for the poorer sections of the community.

The problems emerging from the 1973–74 crisis were ones with which the world economy was likely to become increasingly familiar as world population pressed against the limits of natural resources. The fundamental importance of population growth as the basic factor of economic history cannot be over-stressed. In 1970 UN population estimates put the world's population at 3.6 billion, and this was projected to rise to 6.5 billion by the year 2000—most of the increase being concentrated in the less developed regions where population was expected to double from 2.5 billion to 5 billion. Population in the more developed regions was projected to rise from 1.1 billion to only 1.5 billion.

In the less developed regions the fast growth of population meant that school-age children formed a higher proportion of the population than in developed regions. Correspondingly, the focus of social policy in less developed regions was on education but, once the young were educated, the provision of sufficient productive jobs became a major economic and social problem. Education and employment were closely associated with the food crisis, and many third world countries were adapting school curricula to the needs of a progressive agriculture, so that productive employment in farming could ease both the food and the unemployment crises.

One of the more important demographic changes in the developed regions was the growing proportion of older persons in the population. The problems of elderly retired persons consequently required greater attention, in particular, providing adequate retirement pensions in the face of accelerating inflation. After the price inflation caused by the Korean War ended, prices rose by only about 3% a year during the 1950s and 1960s. In the 1970s, however, this stability disappeared as shortages appeared, fundamentally caused by continued rapid population growth, but aggravated by the economic boom. Even before the oil crisis, prices were rising at a rate three or four times faster than their historic average.

Employment and Unemployment. Beginning late in 1972 and continuing into 1973 the world economy experienced a sharp boom in economic activity, and unemployment in most countries fell during 1973.

Table I. Employment, Unemployment, and Population

Changes for 1972 over 1971 (%)

Country	Employment Nonagri-cultural	Employment Manu-facturing	Numbers unem-ployed	Popula-tion
Third world				
Chile	...	10.1	−30.1	1.6
El Salvador	6.1	7.1	...	1.9
India	3.8	...	28.8	2.1
Korea, South	0.5	18.6	4.8	1.8
Malawi	12.0	6.4	...	2.6
Philippines	...	−3.3	...	3.0
Puerto Rico	4.4	4.5	6.7	3.2
Sierra Leone	−9.5	11.3	−15.3	1.5
Singapore	11.4	22.6	−4.2	1.9
Zambia	1.8	−0.4	23.5	2.8
Average	3.8	8.5	2.0	2.2
Industrial market				
Australia	1.3	−1.7	43.7	1.6
Austria	2.4	2.1	−5.6	0.4
Belgium	...	...	22.4	0.4
Canada	3.7	1.7	1.8	1.2
France	0.1	0.7	13.4	0.9
Germany, West	−0.3	−1.1	33.0	0.6
Italy	−0.2	−0.9	14.4	0.8
Japan	1.3	−0.3	14.1	1.3
Netherlands, The	...	−5.1	74.0	1.1
Sweden	0.5	−0.7	5.9	0.2
United Kingdom	0	−3.4	10.8	0.3
United States	3.3	2.2	−3.1	0.9
Average	1.2	−0.6	18.7	0.8
Centrally planned				
Hungary	0.4	−0.7	...	0.3
Poland	4.7	4.0	...	0.8
Romania	...	5.5	...	0.9
Yugoslavia	4.5	5.4	8.6	1.0
Average	3.2	3.6	...	0.8

Source: United Nations, *Monthly Bulletin of Statistics* (August 1974).

However, this fall was sharply reversed by the oil crisis, and by mid-1974 most industrial market economies were experiencing rises in unemployment. Employment in manufacturing in the third world and in centrally planned economies continued to expand at a rapid rate.

Third World Economies. Some economies showed rapid increases in manufacturing employment in 1972 (Table I). In South Korea and Singapore employment rose rapidly as exports rose by 57 and 40%, respectively. In Chile the last full year of the Allende government saw a continued fall in unemployment and a further rise in manufacturing employment as internal demand rose. In Zambia there was a downturn of economic activity in 1972 following restrictive fiscal measures, and employment fell in all sectors of the economy, including the public sector and especially in construction, while unemployment rose (Table II). This trend was reversed as copper mining expanded during the 1973 boom.

In India the growth of recorded unemployment was rapid in 1972 and 1973 as agricultural production continued to do poorly. Food prices rose by 7.7% in 1972 and by 21.2% in 1973, while prices generally rose by 17.3% in 1973. The trade unions responded to the higher prices with demands for large wage increases, and in the first half of 1974 there were several large strikes in support of their claims. In July 1974 the Indian government imposed an effective freeze on wages and salaries, at the same time cutting back the amounts payable to workers in compensation for rises in the cost of living.

Industrial Market Economies. The simultaneous expansion of economic activity that affected most industrial economies in 1973 was seen in the general and substantial declines in unemployment for that year, when unemployment fell by 8.9% on average (Table III). The boom in economic activity that began in 1972 was strongly synchronized by 1973, and labour markets throughout the industrial world became tight. It was this unprecedentedly synchronized expansion that placed severe strains of rapidly rising demand upon world commodity markets in 1973, leading to shortages of such things as paper, fertilizers, and oil. Additionally there was considerable speculative buying of stocks, and prices for many commodities rose to record levels, accelerating the rate of worldwide inflation. Some of these price rises benefited third world primary producers, providing a temporary upsurge in their reserves of foreign exchange. This boom was brought to an abrupt end by the oil crisis, and the suddenness of the change can be seen by comparing the changes of unemployment in 1973 with those in the second quarter of 1974, when unemployment rose by 5.2% on average (Table III).

In the U.S., unemployment rose by 7.8% in the second quarter of 1974, having fallen by 11.1% in 1973. This slowdown was caused partly by shortages of capacity on the side of production, but also by reduced demand due to tighter fiscal and monetary policies. The rate of growth of manufacturing employment fell from 4.7% in 1973 to 0.8% in the second quarter of 1974.

In Japan the bottom of the slump was reached in 1972, when unemployment rose by 14.1%. The government then adopted an expansionary budget supplemented by additional public expenditures. By mid-1973 nearly all the slack in the economy had been absorbed both by rising domestic demand and by increased exports, so that unemployment fell by

9.8%. However, the growing tightness of the Japanese labour market was indicated by the relatively slow growth of manufacturing employment of 1.3%. In response to the oil crisis, the government cut domestic demand, causing exports to rise sharply, and the Japanese economy was not experiencing the rising unemployment typical of other industrial economies.

In Australia the turning point of the cycle also came in mid-1972 and by 1973 unemployment had fallen by 19.2%. This boom resulted partly from expansionary fiscal policies of the 1972–73 budget together with increased social security benefits, so that in 1973 private consumption expenditure rose by 6% in volume. Added to this was an export boom of a magnitude not enjoyed since the Korean War. Expansion was hampered by increasing shortages of labour, slightly mitigated by the increased participation of women in the labour force, but considerably worsened by an upsurge of strikes in support of wage demands.

Early in 1973 the West German government reacted to the signs of accelerating inflation. In May a comprehensive anti-inflationary program was introduced including a tax on investment, suspension of depreciation allowances, extensions of income tax surcharge to middle-income groups, reduction of public spending, and a tighter monetary policy. This quickly led to a moderation of both investment and consumption expenditures, and consequently unemployment rose by 14.2% in 1973, against the international trend. By the second quarter of 1974 unemployment had more than doubled the 1973 level. The reduction of imports and expansion of exports associated with this early cutback in demand while other countries were still expanding put the West German balance of payments and the whole economy in a better position to withstand the impact of the oil crisis, and in December 1973 the government adopted a cautious policy of expansion so that unemployment was unlikely to rise much further. In Norway the strong and continued fall in unemployment may have been due less to movements in the economy than to the fact that, with the lowering of the retirement age in 1973 from 70 to 67, about 1% of the labour force retired.

The growth of industrial output in the U.K. was rapid toward the end of 1972 and in the first half of 1973, due mainly to a boom in consumer spending aimed at "beating" the introduction of value-added tax (VAT) in April 1973. Activity in the building industry also expanded considerably. Consequently, unemployment fell sharply from its high level of 1972, but there was no expansion of manufacturing employment as most of the extra output was provided by greatly increased labour productivity. As consumer expenditure slowed in the second half of 1973, private investment (especially in North Sea oil exploration) and exports continued to provide momentum to the economy, despite the three-day workweek imposed in response to the coal miners' strike and the need to conserve supplies of energy. Then, as investment and the export boom both dwindled, the economy went into a recession and unemployment was expected to rise sharply in 1975.

Centrally Planned Economies. The growth of manufacturing production and employment continued in most centrally planned economies owing to an increase in exports and better agricultural harvests, which boosted internal demand (Table IV). In the U.S.S.R. the grain crop recovered from the low harvest of 1972 and most other crops also did better. At the end of 1973 the government announced plans for a rationalization of the use of agricultural labour in the country's 33,000 collective farms and 15,000 state farms. This was to be effected through crop specialization, with food processing and other light industries making better use of farm labour during the slack season. In 1970 the labour force of the U.S.S.R. totaled 117 million, of whom 17.2 million were engaged on collective farms, 11.4 million were employed as wage earners in agriculture, while 300,-000 worked as farmers outside the cooperative and state sectors. With one-quarter of the total labour force engaged in agriculture, increased efficiency in the utilization of farm labour could be an important source of economic growth. (By contrast, in 1972 the total labour force of the U.S. numbered 89 million, of whom only 3.7 million, or 4%, were engaged in agriculture.) The U.S.S.R. planned to spend more than a quarter of total investment in the material and technical base of agriculture. In industry high rates of labour turnover continued to be a severe problem: one recent estimate was that 20 million–30 million workers changed jobs every year, losing about one billion working days in the process.

Industrial growth in Poland during 1973 was rapid and manufacturing employment expanded, drawing on unemployed workers as well as agricultural labour. Unemployment fell from 75,000 in the first half of 1972 to 46,000 in the first half of 1973, and the out-migration from the agricultural sector, which employed about 39% of the economically active population, was causing shortages of farm labour with agricultural production becoming increasingly dependent on older workers. Much of the industrial growth arose from higher labour productivity, and real wages rose substantially in line with the new policy of rewarding workers for their increased efficiency and relating wages to enterprise profits. The worsening shortage of labour in Poland was shown by the fact that about 40% of persons of retirement age were still working, mostly in agriculture, boosting the total labour force by 9%.

Yugoslavia's stabilization measures of a freeze on service sector wages during the first half of 1973 and a 10% cut in the wages of employees in unprofitable enterprises slowed the rate of growth of incomes in 1973 and real wages fell. Yugoslavia initiated a "social contract" for wage increases that specified guidelines for the division of enterprise income between wages and surplus, the basic goal being to increase, or at least maintain, the proportion of earnings retained for investment in the expansion of the enterprise.

Wages. *Industrial Market Economies.* The rate of inflation continued to accelerate in 1973 and 1974 and containing the rise in prices and money wages was a central concern in all countries. The average rate of growth of prices in the Organization for Economic Cooperation and Development (OECD) countries rose from 8.6% in 1973 to 12.5% in 1974, while the rate of growth of money wages rose from 13.7 to 16.7% (Table V). The rate of growth of real wages did not accelerate, and some countries experienced declines in real wages.

The introduction of statutory wage and price controls in the U.S. in August 1971 seemed to have had some success in controlling the rate of inflation during 1972, a year of rapid economic expansion. Although this was a controversial area, most econometric studies indicated that, if past relationships had held, prices and wages would have risen faster than they did in 1972, and the difference between actual price and wage changes and those expected in a period of expansion could be ascribed to the effects of administrative controls. The success of price controls may have helped to moderate wage settlements indirectly, supplementing direct restrictions on wage increases. However, price controls were relaxed at the beginning of 1973 and price inflation during that year accelerated markedly, largely due to the effect of rises in food prices following the large Soviet purchases of wheat in 1972. Following this came the impact of oil prices, and the rate of inflation, now more than 10% a year, became the government's major worry.

In Japan growing shortages of labour led to an un-

Casualties of the energy crisis, laid-off workers in Detroit, most of them from the Chrysler Corp., line up on February 4 to apply for unemployment benefits.

UPI COMPIX

usual rise in wage costs per unit of output, with wages rising in excess of productivity causing domestic inflation on top of considerable imported inflation. Thus in 1973 wages rose by 23.6% and by the second quarter of 1974 wages were 30.3% higher than a year previously. Given this pressure of costs the annual rate of price inflation almost doubled from 11.7 to 22.7%.

In Australia the rate of price inflation moderated during 1972 but the rate of wage increase remained high, causing pressures of increased unit labour costs which led to a sharply accelerated rate of price inflation in 1973 and 1974. On top of this domestically generated inflation, import prices began to rise, and the rate of wage increase rose still further as trade unions aggressively stepped up their demands. In December 1973 the government was defeated on a referendum proposing that it have direct power over wages and prices.

West Germany's relatively low rate of price inflation, due largely to policies of demand management, combined with a slight acceleration in the rate of wage increases resulting from aggressive trade union action, gave German workers a high rate of increase of real wages in 1974. In France 1973 saw a rapid rise of the legal minimum wage—from October 1972 to October 1973 the minimum wage rose by 23.7%, compared with an increase of 13.1% for all wages. No general wage increases were negotiated in Norway during 1973 and wages rose in line with prices through indexation, with the government attempting to reduce the effect of indexation through food subsidies and postponements of price increases in the public sector. In Austria the tight labour market led to an acceleration in the rate of wage

Table II. Unemployment: Third World

Changes over previous years (%)

Country	1972	1973
Burma	20.2	13.6
Chile	−30.1	...
Cyprus	−11.6	31.3
Ghana	69.6	−15.7
Greece	−21.5	−11.8
Guatemala	−6.1	...
Guyana	−23.8	...
India	28.8	30.1
Korea, South	4.8	...
Malaysia, West	2.3	−3.7
Malta	28.8	−3.5
Mauritius	12.4	...
Nigeria	6.3	...
Puerto Rico	6.7	0.9
Sierra Leone	−15.3	−17.5
Singapore	−4.2	−1.4
Sri Lanka	4.8	4.1
Surinam	−10.4	...
Trinidad	0	...
Zambia	23.5	−26.2
Average	6.4	0

Source: United Nations, *Monthly Bulletin of Statistics* (September 1974).

Table III. Employment in Manufacturing and Total Unemployment: Industrial Market Economies

Changes over previous years (%)

Country	Employment 1973	Employment 1974*	Unemployment 1973	Unemployment 1974*
Canada	5.0	4.2	−7.5	−0.4
United States	4.7	0.8	−11.1	7.8
Japan	1.3	0.3	−9.8	−7.6
Australia	1.9	3.3†	−19.2	−2.7
Austria	2.0	0.1†	−18.0	3.1
Belgium	−3.2	...	5.7	7.0
Denmark	4.0	2.2†	−33.3	43.6
Finland	1.0	5.8†	−10.5	−26.5†
France	1.8	1.1	3.7	14.2
Germany, West	0.6	−0.8†	14.2	117.9
Ireland	3.0	3.5†	−8.3	2.1
Italy	1.8	6.2	−4.0	−34.1
Netherlands, The	...	...	1.9	15.3
Norway	0.8	2.3	−13.3	−30.5
Sweden	1.9	6.2	−4.2	−16.1
United Kingdom	−0.1	−0.6†	−28.5	−9.2
Average	1.8	2.5	−8.9	5.2

*Second quarter 1974 over second quarter 1973.
†First quarter 1974 over first quarter 1973.
Source: Organization for Economic Cooperation and Development, *Main Economic Indicators* (September 1974).

Table IV. Output, Employment, Wages, and Prices: Centrally Planned Economies

Change in 1973 over 1972 (%)

Country	Manufacturing production	Manufacturing employment	Average earnings	Consumer prices
Bulgaria	10.9*	1.9	6.8	...
Czechoslovakia	6.8	1.2	3.5	0.3
Hungary	6.5	1.2	10.8	3.6
Poland	11.6	2.8	5.4	0.5
U.S.S.R.	7.8	1.7†	...	...
Yugoslavia	6.3	3.2	17.7	21.4

*Industrial sector.
†Estimated by applying productivity growth of 6% to output growth.
Sources: United Nations, *Monthly Bulletin of Statistics* (September 1974); Economist Intelligence Unit, *Quarterly Economic Reviews* of individual countries.

Table V. Money and Real Wages in Manufacturing and Consumer Prices: Industrial Market Economies

Changes over previous years (%)

Country	Money wages 1973	Money wages 1974*	Real wages 1973	Real wages 1974*	Prices 1973	Prices 1974*
Canada	8.5	11.9	1.0	1.1	7.4	10.7
United States	7.1	7.5	1.4	−2.9	5.6	10.7
Japan	23.6	30.3	10.7	6.2	11.7	22.7
Australia	12.2	14.1†	2.2	0.4†	9.8	13.6†
Austria	10.9	16.0	2.6	5.6	8.1	9.9
Belgium	15.7	14.2†	7.8	5.4†	7.3	8.4†
Denmark	18.6	27.0†	9.0	11.2†	8.8	14.2†
Finland	16.8	20.9†	4.8	3.6†	11.4	16.7†
France	12.4	17.8	4.9	3.7	7.1	13.6
Germany, West	10.1	12.7	2.7	5.2	7.2	7.1
Ireland	19.5	18.6†	6.8	4.6†	11.9	13.4†
Italy	24.3	27.9†	12.2	12.5†	10.8	13.7†
Netherlands, The	12.7	18.6	4.5	9.0	7.8	8.8
Norway	10.7	11.7†	3.5	3.0†	7.0	8.4†
Sweden	8.0	12.2	1.8	−1.3	6.1	13.7
Switzerland	9.2	10.2†	0.4	−0.2†	8.8	10.4†
United Kingdom	12.5	12.4	2.8	−3.2	9.4	16.1
Average	13.7	16.7	4.7	3.8	8.6	12.5

*Second quarter 1974 over second quarter 1973.
†First quarter 1974 over first quarter 1973.
Source: Organization for Economic Cooperation and Development, *Main Economic Indicators* (September 1974).

Table VI. Money and Real Wages in Manufacturing and Consumer Prices: Third World

Changes over previous year (%)

Country	Money wages 1972	Money wages 1973	Real wages 1972	Real wages 1973	Prices 1972	Prices 1973
Barbados	...	...	...	...	11.8	16.9
Chile	62.6	...	−8.5	...	77.8	352.8
El Salvador	3.1	4.0	1.4	−2.3	1.7	6.5
Greece	9.2	16.4	4.6	0.9	4.4	15.4
Guatemala	2.3	...	1.8	...	0.5	14.4
Korea, South	15.9	11.1	3.8	7.7	11.7	3.2
Malawi	10.3	−7.5	6.2	−12.0	3.8	5.1
Puerto Rico	7.0	6.5	3.7	−0.7	3.2	7.3
Sri Lanka	17.2	...	10.3	...	6.3	9.6
Venezuela	7.1	−0.1	4.0	−4.3	3.0	4.4
Average*	9.0	5.1	4.5	−1.8	5.2	9.2

*Excluding Chile.
Source: United Nations, *Monthly Bulletin of Statistics* (September 1974).

Table VII. Weekly Hours of Work in Manufacturing

Country	1972	1973	Absolute change
Industrial countries			
Australia	38.7	38.8	0.1
Austria	36.4	36.0	−0.4
Canada	40.0	39.6	−0.4
Finland	38.2	...	...
France*	44.1	43.7	−0.4
Germany, West	42.7	42.8	0.1
Ireland	42.3	42.2	−0.1
Japan	42.3	42.0	−0.3
Netherlands, The	43.8	43.3	−0.5
Norway	34.4	34.0	−0.4
Switzerland	44.3	44.2	−0.1
United Kingdom	43.6	44.1	0.5
United States	40.6	40.7	0.1
Czechoslovakia	43.7	43.6	−0.1
Average	41.1	41.2	−0.1
Third world			
El Salvador	46.4	47.0	0.6
Greece	44.6	43.4	−1.2
Guatemala	46.5	...	...
Korea, South	51.6	...	...
Puerto Rico	37.1	37.4	0.3
Average	45.2	42.6	−0.1

*All activities.
Sources: United Nations, *Monthly Bulletin of Statistics* (September 1974); Organization for Economic Cooperation and Development, *Main Economic Indicators* (September 1974).

increases partly because of shorter, more frequently renegotiated contracts. In The Netherlands anti-inflationary policies and direct price controls successfully contained the rate of inflation in 1973.

In the U.K. the prices and incomes policy of 1973 successfully contained the rate of growth of money wages, but the rate of price inflation rose from 7.1% in 1972 to 9.4% in 1973. By the second quarter of 1974 prices were rising at an annual rate of 16.1% and accelerating, causing a decline in real wages that put severe strains upon the "social contract"—the Labour government's understanding with the trade unions that the former would refrain from a direct incomes policy if the latter moderated their wage demands. From the second quarter of 1974 the rate of increase of money wages accelerated sharply. This was partly due to "threshold agreements," which permitted additions to wages of £0.40 per week for every 1 percentage point rise of the cost-of-living index above its level of October 1973. By May 1974, when the first of these threshold payments came into force, such agreements covered about three-quarters of the labour force, and successive thresholds had added £4.40 to weekly earnings by the time the scheme came to its scheduled end in November 1974.

Third World Economies. The less developed countries were badly affected by the world economic crisis. Annual rates of price inflation accelerated from an average of 5.2% in 1972 to 9.2% in 1973, and the trend was continuing (Table VI). During 1973 some third world economies were cushioned from the effects of international inflation by rising commodity prices, but after the onset of recession these prices began to fall and third world reserves of foreign exchange were dwindling rapidly. Faced with steep increases in the oil and food import bills, these countries were resorting, perforce, to direct cuts of imports other than oil and food. This meant that exports from industrial countries to the third world would decline sharply, intensifying the world recession. Further excess purchasing power of employees in the third world, which could no longer be spent on imports, posed serious problems for domestic economics.

Hours. On average, hours of work changed little during 1973 (Table VII). This was against the long-term trend toward a shorter working week and there were counteracting forces seeking to lengthen the working week as tight labour markets encouraged a more intensive use of labour. As pressure in labour markets slackened in 1974 with the rise in unemployment, weekly hours of work fell in several industrial countries: from the peaks reached in 1973 weekly hours had declined by mid-1974 in the following countries by the following amounts: U.S. 4.2 hours; Canada 3.5 hours; Japan 4.3 hours; West Germany 2.8 hours; U.K. 1.5 hours; and France 1.1 hours. (D. A. S. JACKSON)

See also Economy, World; Income, National; Industrial Production and Technology; Industrial Relations; Prices.
[534.C.1]

ENCYCLOPÆDIA BRITANNICA FILMS. *The Industrial Worker* (1969); *The Rise of Big Business* (1970).

Energy

In the field of energy 1974 made its mark in history through the actions of the Organization of Petroleum Exporting Countries (OPEC) and the Arab members of that body, the Organization of Arab Petroleum Ex-porting Countries (OAPEC). In reaction to the war between Israel and the Arab states in the fall of 1973, OAPEC instituted an embargo on oil shipments to certain countries whose foreign policies did not meet with their approval. The embargo originally applied to The Netherlands and to the United States, its possessions, and certain Western Hemisphere refineries supplying it. In December it was extended to Portugal, South Africa, and Rhodesia. Moreover, because of production cutbacks in the Arab nations a general world shortage of oil developed.

The reaction in Europe and Japan was one of near panic, as governments strove to reduce oil consumption in the face of a loss of supply the duration of which could only be guessed. Several countries imposed gasoline rationing (some rationed heating oil as well); others banned Sunday driving, lowered speed limits, or ordered service stations closed on weekends. Electricity consumption was also reduced in order to conserve the heavy fuel oil used for power generation.

The U.S. prepared for gasoline rationing by printing coupons, but the embargo ended before it became necessary. Allocation programs for fuel oil were, however, set up under a new agency, the Federal Energy Office (later established by Congress as a permanent agency, the Federal Energy Administration). Other measures included the establishment of a federal highway speed limit of 55 mph, year-round daylight savings time throughout the country, and a program to encourage the conservation of energy. Thermostats were turned down; lighting, both indoor and outdoor, was reduced; and the public was urged to cut back on the use of electricity and oil products as much as possible. A program was also established to reconvert oil-burning power plants that had previously been converted from coal, but this ran into problems of coal supply and a conflict with air pollution regulations.

The effect of the embargo on heating oil supplies was minimized by the fortuitous occurrence of an unusually warm winter. The effect on gasoline supply, however, was severe, even in the absence of rationing. During February and March it became increasingly common (especially in the Northeast) to see long lines of cars at the few service stations that were open at any one time. Waits of several hours in line were the rule and, once at the pump, the unfortunate motorist was limited to only a few gallons or a few dollars' worth by the station attendants. In an effort to ease the situation several states adopted "alternate day" programs in which motorists could get gasoline only on odd- or even-numbered days of the month, according to whether their license plate numbers were odd or even.

For the U.S. the embargo was lifted on March 18 (although Libya and Syria did not join in the move until later in the year), but for The Netherlands it continued until July 10 and for Portugal, Rhodesia, and South Africa it remained in effect throughout the year. The economic effects of the embargo in the countries that were its victims were on the whole minor. Some unemployment and lost production resulted, but in general the burden was one of inconvenience.

The same could not be said, however, for the actions of OPEC with respect to the price of oil. OPEC's successful imposition of the embargo demonstrated its economic power and led, in January, to the tripling of the posted price of oil in the OPEC countries. Throughout the year other actions, such as increased royalties or taxes and changes in the formulas by which they were computed, further raised the cost of OPEC oil by a few percentage points. Anticipating the reaction of oil demand to the higher prices, the OPEC countries announced that their production would henceforth be controlled to maintain the new price levels, and during the year production cutbacks were in fact instituted. A further small increase was decided on at the December meeting of OPEC in Vienna, but the oil producers promised that prices would remain stable for the next nine months.

These actions stunned the oil-importing countries of the world, which included all the industrialized nations except the Soviet Union. Oil is the largest single item in international trade, and never before in history had the price of a basic raw material risen by so much so fast. For some of the oil-producing countries the additional annual income during 1974 was itself larger than the country's gross national product in 1973. For Europe, with its heavy dependence on imported oil, the new prices posed serious balance of payments problems. The U.S., dependent on imports for about one-third of its total supply, was more fortunate but still felt the shock. The effect was most serious in those less developed nations that did not produce oil and already had serious economic problems. Those countries desperately tried to reduce oil consumption so as to conserve foreign exchange.

In Europe oil consumption fell in response to the new price levels. There was also some cutback in the U.S. in the use of oil products, especially gasoline; but the chief U.S. response to the twin shocks of the embargo and the price increases was the adoption of a new energy policy, "Project Independence." Announced by Pres. Richard Nixon in November 1973, the policy established the goal of complete self-sufficiency in energy for the U.S. by 1980, to be accomplished through reliance on domestic energy resources (coal, oil shale, and nuclear fuels) together with accelerated development of the petroleum resources of the outer continental shelf.

The high level of oil prices was a powerful stimulus to the search for new sources of oil throughout the world. Although the effects of this stimulus would not be known for several years, important new discoveries were made in several parts of the world as the result of already ongoing search activities. Additional large oil discoveries continued to be made in the North Sea and in Indonesia (both onshore and offshore). A surprise was the discovery of a large oil field in the Aegean Sea, 10 mi. off the coast of northeastern Greece. Significant new discoveries were also made in the Canadian Arctic. (Exploration activities in that area included the successful demonstration of the practicability of drilling on the floating ice sheet, 8 mi. offshore from Melville Island.)

In the U.S. a new world depth record of 31,441 ft. was set by a well drilled in western Oklahoma. The well unexpectedly encountered molten sulfur at a temperature of 450° F, which flooded into the well and solidified, "freezing" the drill string in the hole. Construction of the trans-Alaska pipeline, long delayed by opposition on environmental grounds, began in April. Carrying oil from the Prudhoe Bay field on Alaska's northern coast 800 mi. to the port of Valdez on the southeastern coast, the pipeline was expected to make its first deliveries in 1977.

Natural gas discoveries included the first large find in the Beaufort Sea, offshore from Canada's Mackenzie River delta, and the announcement of what

appeared to be the world's largest gas field. Actually discovered in 1973, the field is in the Kangan region of southeastern Iran.

Coal prices moved up sharply during the year in response to the pressure on coal supplies from consumers seeking to cope with the oil embargo and with the high oil prices. For the first time in memory U.S. electric utilities and steel companies began importing coal and coke from such sources as Canada, Europe, and South Africa. The coal industry, having suffered a declining demand for many years in the face of competition from alternative fuels and nuclear power, was in no position to meet the sudden upsurge in demand. The short-term supply difficulties were intensified by a strike by U.S. coal miners in November which lasted more than three weeks. Among other developments in coal were, in January, the first commercial production of methane in the U.S. directly from coal seams and, in April, the signing of a Soviet-Japanese agreement for the development of the rich coal resources of the Yakut S.S.R. for use in the Japanese steel industry.

The development of unconventional energy resources in the U.S. moved forward on two fronts with the institution of federal leasing programs. In January the first lease sale under these programs was held for oil shale lands in Colorado. This was followed by lease sales later in the year for tracts in Wyoming and Utah. Also in January the government held the first lease sale of geothermal lands, in California. In October prospects for early commercial development of oil shale received a setback, however, with the announcement that construction of the first commercial plant, scheduled to have begun in early 1975, had been indefinitely postponed because of economic and national energy policy uncertainties.

Plagued by higher prices for its fuels, historically high interest rates, and a decline in the rate of growth of sales because of energy conservation, the electric utility industry in the U.S. experienced severe financing difficulties. The industry deluged the state regulatory commissions with requests for rate increases, which were vigorously contested by both industrial and individual consumers. Although the number and size of rate increases granted during the year set a record, the rate relief was not sufficient to forestall a wave of postponements and cancellations of construction projects for new generating capacity, both fossil and nuclear. These difficulties did not, however, have any effect on the industry's ability to meet current system loads.

In a speech to a joint session of Congress in October, Pres. Gerald Ford outlined his program for dealing with the nation's energy problems. He announced the establishment of a Cabinet-level National Energy Board, chaired by Secretary of the Interior Rogers Morton, whose first assignment was to reduce oil imports by one million barrels per day by the end of 1975. The president also established 1980 as the target date for eliminating all oil-fired generating plants and called for legislative action on the deregulation of natural gas supplies and "responsible use" of the naval petroleum reserves. By year's end it was apparent that the voluntary energy conservation measures called for by the president were not having the desired effect, and some form of mandatory program was expected early in the new year.

(BRUCE C. NETSCHERT)

ENCYCLOPÆDIA BRITANNICA FILMS. *Energy: A Matter of Choices* (1973).

COAL

With shortages of oil causing an energy crisis late in 1973, it became clear that coal would play a more important role as a source of power over the next decade. In recent years coal had been increasingly neglected, but because many power stations were equipped to burn either coal or oil, increased coal consumption might provide an easy solution to the problems of oil shortages and higher costs. Where mines had been shut down because they had been unprofitable, coal mining could not be easily expanded, but planned contraction was substantially slowed down in 1974. Where expansion was possible, it would take some years for investment to yield results.

World hard coal production in 1973 amounted to an estimated 2,241,976,000 metric tons, an increase of 23 million tons over 1972. The trends of previous years continued, with increases in production in the U.S.S.R., China, Poland, and Australia; U.S. output showed a slight decline.

In Western Europe production remained at the same level as in 1972, stemming the previous downward trend. Eastern European production (including the U.S.S.R.) increased 1.9%. China, with an output estimated at 410 million metric tons, an increase of 10 million tons, remained the world's third largest producer, and was reported to be expanding output, not only to supply home needs but also for export.

U.S.S.R. In 1973, 668 million metric tons of raw coal were produced from about 800 underground mines and 68 open pits; this was an increase of almost 2% over 1972. Total production consisted of 434.5 million metric tons of bituminous coal, 77.5 million tons of anthracite, and 158 million tons of lignite. Open-pit operations expanded steadily, accounting for nearly 30% of total production. New facilities commissioned had an annual capacity of 34 million tons of ungraded coal and lignite.

Japanese importers expressed interest in Siberian coal, and there was a proposal to construct power stations at pitheads in Siberia in order to distribute electricity over an extensive area. The Donets Basin maintained record production in 1973 with 219,408,000 tons.

United States. In 1973 coal demand exceeded supply, mainly because of increased requirements by public utilities and coke plants; however, production fell short of the 1972 total. Some 591 million short tons of bituminous coal and lignite were produced, 46.6% from strip-mining operations. The decline from 1972 of 4.4 million tons was attributed to work stoppages, absenteeism, and mine closings. Underground productivity had declined from 15.61 tons per man-day in 1969 to 11.20 in 1973.

Anthracite production again declined with a 5.1% drop to 6.7 million short tons. Exports fell by 3.1 million tons, although shipments to Japan increased by 6% to 19,190,000 short tons and Japan regained the position of primary importer of U.S. coal. By mid-1974 exports were running well above the level of 1973. In 1973 the number of men working daily in the underground mines increased by 6.8% over the average for 1972, to 110,900. U.S. coal production by the year 2000 was forecast at 1,500,000,000 short tons a year. Blessed with abundant reserves, the U.S. industry seemed in a position to reach this target provided adequate financial incentives could be found.

European Economic Community. Total hard coal production in 1973 for the enlarged Community—which included the U.K. after January—amounted to 263.5 million metric tons, a decrease of 116 million tons from the equivalent figure for 1972. Increases in oil costs led governments to review energy policies and resulted in measures, announced in 1974, to stabilize, or in certain cases increase, production levels, which had been steadily falling for the previous decade.

Belgium produced 8.8 million metric tons, a reduction of 15.8% from 1972. France showed a decrease of 4,080,000 metric tons for a total of 25,680,000 metric tons, and in Italy the underground mines were closed during the year, although lignite production regained the 1971 level of 1.3 million metric tons. The two remaining mines in The Netherlands produced 1,718,000 metric tons, though the planned closing of those mines during 1974, in the light of the country's dependence on imported oil, was under review.

In West Germany demand exceeded supply, yet hard coal production fell by 5% to 97.3 million tons. However, lignite production increased by 7.2 million tons to 117.6 million tons, and lignite supplied 25% of the country's electricity needs.

In the U.K. the four-week miners' strike in February 1974 and the preceding 13-week overtime ban resulted in an output loss of 20 million long tons. The National Coal Board (NCB) ended the financial year with a deficit, after interest repayments, of £130.7 million. Deep-mined output was 97.1 million long tons during 1973–74, with an additional 8.9 million tons from surface operations and about 500,000 tons produced by licensed deep mines and open pits.

During 1974 plans were announced to expand deep-mined production to about 130 million tons. Part of this would be achieved by developing the recently discovered Selby coal field in Yorkshire. Open-pit operations were to be increased to 15 million tons a year, and despite labour troubles the future of the industry looked much brighter.

Poland. Hard coal production rose to a record 156.6 million metric tons, an increase of 3.9% over 1972. The future for the industry was good, marked by increased domestic demand and expanding exports. In 1974 the combined output of coal and lignite was expected to exceed 200 million tons.

Since the late 1950s Poland had invested heavily in developing new collieries and had expanded and reconstructed existing mines. Consequently, annual output doubled during that period.

India. Although hard coal production in 1973 increased by 3,250,000 metric tons to 78 million metric tons, it was greatly restricted by power shortages, labour troubles, and transportation bottlenecks. Planned output for the final fiscal year of the fifth five-year plan (1978–79), an ambitious 135 million metric tons, included 34 million tons for metallurgical purposes.

Japan. Japan's coal imports during 1973 attained a record high of 56,854,460 metric tons, an increase of 15.4% over the 1972 total. Australia remained Japan's principal supplier of coal, providing 24.9 million metric tons, an increase of 4.4 million tons over 1972. In the first four months of 1974, the U.S. supplied more coal to Japan than did Australia, and levels were 8% above those for the same period of 1973.

Japan's indigenous production fell by 5.7 million metric tons to 22,414,000 metric tons, and again it remained cheaper to import. But, with the nation badly hit by the oil crisis, it was proposed to stimulate home production by means of government subsidy.

South America. Coal production in 1973 was 8.1 million metric tons, an increase of 685,000 tons over 1972. Colombia, the largest producer, had 3.3 million metric tons. Brazil produced 2.6 million and Chile 1,350,000 metric tons. In Colombia plans were announced in 1973 to develop the high-quality bituminous reserves of the El Cerrejon deposit. Initial annual production was forecast at 5 million tons.

Africa. Of an estimated total of 67.4 million metric tons in 1973, 62.4 million were produced by South Africa and 3 million by Rhodesia. South Africa's bituminous coal production, at 60,940,000 metric tons, showed a gain of 3.8 million metric tons while anthracite production again dropped, to 1,410,000 tons in 1973. Though exports only amounted to 1,940,000 tons, there were excellent future prospects of a worldwide export trade.

Australia. Production of bituminous coal continued to rise in 1973 to just over 60 million metric tons, compared with 59.6 million in 1972. Approximately two-thirds of the production was from New South Wales, most of the balance coming from recently developed collieries in the Bowen basin region of Queensland. Lignite production increased to 24.1 million metric tons in 1973.

Canada. Production in 1973 reached a record 22.5 million short tons, an increase of 1,840,000 tons over 1972, and was expected to rise to 25 million tons in 1974. Exports were again a record, at 12 million short tons, with exports to Japan representing 97.4% of the total. British Columbia showed a gain of 19% to 7.8 million short tons. Lignite production in Saskatchewan increased 23% to 4,028,280 short tons. Imports of coal from the U.S. were down slightly, to 17.5 million short tons.

(R. J. FOWELL)

ELECTRICITY

In the wake of the energy crisis, the use of indigenous rather than imported power-generating resources was encouraged. A switch to coal provided an easy answer, but could only be applied where coal mining could be expanded or the rate of its contraction slowed down. When the proper technology could be developed, virtually inexhaustible amounts of primary energy might

Vertical axis windmill, designed to convert wind power into electricity, is under study at NASA's Langley Research Center in Hampton, Va.

Installed Capacity and Production of Electric Power in Selected Countries, Dec. 31, 1972				
	Hydroelectric power		Total electric power	
	Operating plants			
Political division	Installed capacity (000 kw.)	Production (000,000 kw.-hr.)	Installed capacity (000 kw.)	Production (000,000 kw.-hr.)
World	...	...	...	5,646,700
Afghanistan	190*	...	207*	439
Algeria†	262*	360	613*	2,270
Angola	227	680	346	838
Argentina	915	1,502	7,611	25,319
Australia†	4,221	11,746	16,215	61,020
Austria	5,691	17,238	8,308	29,388
Belgium‡§	503	581	8,024	37,461
Bolivia	171‖	...	252*	872
Brazil	10,974	...	13,489	53,767
Bulgaria	895	2,095	4,659	22,271
Burma¶	103	397	256	600
Cambodia†	10	—	55	165.6*
Cameroon	193*	1,080	221*	1,133
Canada‡§	32,500	178,169	49,944	237,627
Chad♀	—	...	38	51.3
Chile	1,068	5,226	2,782	8,934
Colombia	...	...	2,700¶	10,300
Costa Rica	243	1,105	320	1,266
Cuba†	44	...	873	4,212
Czechoslovakia	1,593	2,810	11,898	51,402
Denmark	9	24	5,282	19,368
Ecuador	105	445	357	1,117
Egypt†‡	2,448	5,135	3,847	7,371
El Salvador†	108	429	180	780
Ethiopia	91.4¶	...	...	585*
Finland	2,320	10,211	5,924	22,302
France‡§	15,459	48,417	41,494	163,412
Gabon†	...	4.7	36.8	133.6
Germany, E.‡§	680	1,224	14,182	72,828
Germany, W.‡§	4,839	13,689	57,617	274,769
Ghana	900	...	976	...
Greece†	1,040	2,670	2,857	12,033
Guatemala*†	96	...	174	830
Honduras†	70	303	131	333
Hong Kong♀	—	...	1,838	6,193
Hungary	20*	108	2,932*	16,323
Iceland†δ▢	364	1,703	454	1,768
India*‡§	6,615	28,031	16,889	66,385
Indonesia†	312	1,425†	684	2,368†
Iran†	800	...	1,977	6,862
Ireland*	219*	6,746	1,678*	6,923
Israel♀	—	...	1,450	8,478
Italy‡§δ▢	15,554	42,820	37,044	134,930
Jamaica†	18	130	315	1,106
Japan‡§δ▢	20,734	88,023	85,296	428,577
Kenya†	71	320*	186	556*
Korea, South†	341	1,368	3,872	11,839
Lebanon†	246*	807	483*	1,545
Liberia†	34	241	82.9	330
Libya♀	—	—	168	...
Luxembourg†	932	936	1,138	2,107
Malagasy Rep.†	...	142	...	213
Malaysia	...	1,154	1,024.3	4,309
Mauritius	26.0	68	68.7	164
Mexicoδ	3,321	15,392	8,502	34,457
Morocco†	300¶	1,573	439¶	...
Mozambique*†	114	...	264	671
Netherlands‡§♀	—	...	12,392	49,551
New Zealand†δ▢	3,271	14,109	4,093	17,253
Nicaragua†	100	287†	217	516¶
Nigeria†	320	1,447*	753	1,912*
Norway	14,075	67,630	14,225	67,793
Pakistan¶	586	2,524	1,850	6,773
Panama*	15.2	84†	171.6	919†
Paraguay	...	...	156	273
Peru*	989	4,283	1,797	5,949
Philippines†	593	2,536	1,770	7,941
Poland	821	1,935	16,125	76,475
Portugal	1,690	7,115	2,498	8,350
Rhodesia	705	5,292	1,192	6,091
Romania	2,100	7,343	9,357	43,439
Singapore♀	—	—	727	3,144†
South Africa	160	814	12,600	59,081
Spain‡§	11,057*	36,520	19,073*	68,910
Sri Lanka	195	856	281	995
Sweden‡§	11,261	53,772	17,850	71,682
Switzerland‡§	9,700	...	11,320	31,300
Syria	...	...	354	1,223
Tanzania†	...	...	131.4	469
Thailand†	475	2,048*	1,302	5,083*
Tunisia†	29	53	277	869
Turkey	877	3,209	2,742	11,242
Uganda†	150	796	154	800
U.S.S.R.‡§	34,846	122,899	186,239	857,435
U.K.‡§	2,158	4,305	75,446	263,681
U.S.‡§δ▢	57,244	276,123	418,457	1,853,390
Uruguay†	236	1,470*	503	2,289*
Venezuela†	908*	6,020	2,753*	14,656
Vietnam, South	...	...	838	1,483
Yugoslavia	4,624	17,982	8,545	33,231
Zaire	15.0*†	3,348	31.4*†	3,842
Zambia*	425	3,076	655	3,297

*1971. †Public sector only. ‡Includes nuclear (in 000 kw.): Belgium 11; Canada 2,126; France 2,709; East Germany 70; West Germany 2,307; India 580; Italy 670; Japan 1,836; The Netherlands 55; Spain 1,073; Sweden 477; Switzerland 1,006; U.S.S.R. 2,621; U.K. 5,614; U.S. 15,301. ‖1969. ¶1970. ♀Thermal only. §Includes nuclear (in 000,000 kw-hr.): Belgium ...; Canada 6,739; France 13,800; East Germany 385; West Germany 9,137; India ...; Italy 3,626; Japan 9,480; The Netherlands 326; Spain ...; Sweden 1,465; Switzerland ...; U.S.S.R. ...; U.K. 29,378; U.S. 54,031. δIncludes geothermal (in 000 kw.): Iceland 2; Italy 391; Japan 31; Mexico 3; New Zealand 192; U.S. 322. ▢Includes geothermal (in 000,000 kw-hr.): Iceland 22; Italy 2,582; Japan 248; New Zealand 1,175; U.S. 1,453.
Source: United Nations. (FRANK H. SKELDING)

School in suburban Minneapolis, Minn., is heated by solar energy. A water-glycol solution circulating through the collector panels is heated by the sun to 130°–150° F and is then used to heat air for the school building.

be produced from solar, geothermal, wind, and tidal power, but in 1974 none of these could supply the output needed to feed electric grids without vast, costly, and usually unacceptable installations.

Consequently, there was little choice but to fall back on nuclear power, which raised problems in use but appeared to have advantages that outweighed the disadvantages. Distribution of uranium, although sparse, was better than that of most fossil fuels. Also, its energy-weight ratio was high, and when supplies were assured and breeder reactors perfected, consumption would be so low that fuel costs would be only a small proportion of the total cost of electricity.

Worldwide research favoured the sodium-cooled fast-breeder reactor fed by mixed uranium and plutonium oxides. Prototypes were built in the U.S.S.R., whose 150-Mw. BN350 came into service in July 1973; in France, where Phénix reached its full 250-Mw. capacity in March 1974; and in the U.K., where the 250-Mw. Dounreay went critical in March. Work on fast breeders continued in the U.S.S.R., West Germany, the U.S., and Japan. France, Italy, and West Germany agreed to build a 1,200-Mw. breeder, derived from the Phénix prototype, at Creys-Malville, France. Construction was to begin in 1975.

Nuclear Electric Power. In 1973 output from the world's nuclear power stations totaled 188,000,000,000 kw.-hr., or 3% of the global total from all forms of generation. Of this, 62,000,000,000 kw.-hr. were produced by pressurized water reactors (PWRs), 60,000,000,000 kw.-hr. by boiling water reactors (BWRs), 44,000,000,000 kw.-hr. by gas-graphite reactors, 17,000,000,000 kw.-hr. by heavy water reactors, and the balance by various other types. Approximately 776,000,000,000 kw.-hr. had been generated by nuclear power stations up to January 1974, by which time 409 nuclear reactors with a total generating capacity of 276,000 Mw. were in service, under construction, or on order.

On Jan. 1, 1974, the U.S. had 42 reactors in service, 56 in various stages of construction, and 101 on order. Total capacity was 204,473 Mw. Nuclear power had become highly competitive both in the U.S. and in France, where, by the end of the year, generating costs were half those of the oil-burning stations.

The U.K.'s first nuclear power program, begun in 1956 and completed in 1971, had been followed in 1965 by a second, to build five advanced gas-cooled reactors (AGRs). Work on these had been delayed by technical difficulties, but they were due to go into service by 1976. For the U.K.'s future program the authorities had vacillated between ordinary water, heavy water, and high-temperature reactors, but in July, despite representations by the Central Electricity Generating Board (CEGB) in favour of a U.S.-designed light water reactor (LWR), the government selected a British design, the steam generating heavy water reactor (SGHWR). It was similar to the Canadian Candu reactor, but burned slightly enriched, rather than natural, uranium. The program was a modest one, with small power stations of 600 to 650 Mw., but after 1980 the U.K. could look forward to ample oil supplies from the North Sea.

France, with little coal and virtually no oil, was particularly hard hit by the energy crisis, and the government set about major expansion of the country's nuclear installations. These, in January 1974, consisted of 10 reactors with a total capacity of 2,888 Mw. An additional 20 reactors, mostly PWRs but including two BWRs, with a total capacity of 17,725 Mw., were under construction or planned for completion by 1980.

In West Germany the Biblis A 1,200-Mw. PWR station came into service in July, bringing the number of reactors in use to 11. Nine more reactors under construction would increase total capacity to 12,488 Mw. The long-delayed fourth nuclear program involved construction of 13 reactors with a total capacity of 15,542 Mw.

Italy's three nuclear power stations had a total capacity of 592 Mw. A fourth, consisting of an 840-Mw. BWR, was under construction, and two additional reactors were on order. Sweden had two 450-Mw. nuclear power stations in use, with nine more under construction or on order for completion by 1981. A national commission of inquiry reported in August in favour of nuclear power, provided that installations were sited at least 20 km. (12½ mi.) from large urban centres.

In Canada the seven nuclear power stations in operation had a total capacity of 2,534 Mw. The largest, the Ontario Hydro Commission's Pickering plant, comprised four natural uranium reactors moderated and cooled by heavy water under pressure (PHWRs). Additional reactors under construction or on order included the 2,980-Mw. Bence power station, to be equipped with four 745-Mw. PHWRs.

The world's hundredth nuclear power station came into service at Atucha in Argentina in January 1974. Later in the year Argentina ordered a Canadian 600-Mw.-capacity PHWR, to be built at Río Tercero in Córdoba Province.

By January 1974 the U.S.S.R. had 18 reactors in service, totaling 3,931 Mw., and another 15 under construction or on order. A graphite-moderated, ordinary water-cooled reactor, capacity 1,000 Mw., had come into operation in December 1973.

Thermoelectricity. In those countries that had sizable reserves, coal returned to favour. In the U.S., a number of public utilities ordered coal-burning groups with a capacity of 400–500 Mw. each. In Canada, the Ontario Hydro Commission signed a contract with the U.S. Steel Corp. for the joint working of a coalfield in Pennsylvania to supply the Nanticoke power station with an annual 3 million tons.

In the U.K. strikes during the winter of 1973–74 resulted in severe restrictions on

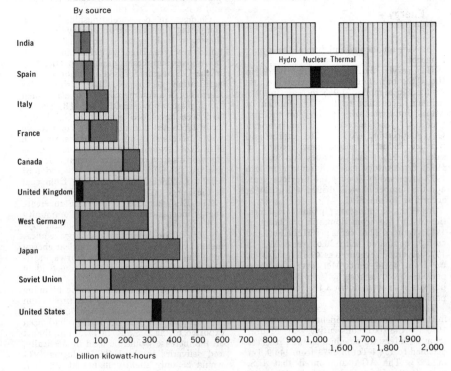

Electrical Power Production of Selected Countries, 1973

By source

Hydro Nuclear Thermal

India
Spain
Italy
France
Canada
United Kingdom
West Germany
Japan
Soviet Union
United States

0 100 200 300 400 500 600 700 800 900 1,000   1,600 1,700 1,800 1,900 2,000

billion kilowatt-hours

Sources: United Nations, *Monthly Bulletin of Statistics; World Energy Supplies, 1968-1971.*

Reactor at the nuclear power station in Biblis, W.Ger., is filled with uranium rods. The station, one of the world's largest, began producing electricity in July.

consumption. Late in 1973 the first two groups, of 660 Mw. each, at the Drax power station in Yorkshire were linked to the grid. In May 1974 the CEGB ordered three 660-Mw. turbogenerators, for the Littlebrook D power station in Kent; these were to utilize fuel oil. Construction began late in 1973 on the Peterhead power station in Scotland; its two 660-Mw. groups would burn either fuel oil or gas.

West Germany planned a giant power station that would use 23 million metric tons of coal from the Ruhr mines and produce 50,000,000,000 kw-hr. and 15,000,000,000 cu.m. of gas a year. In the U.S.S.R., the Syr-Darya power station in Uzbekistan became operational late in 1973. When completed, it would have a total capacity of 4,400 Mw. and consume 7,000,000,000 cu.m. of natural gas each year.

Hydroelectricity. In Canada work began in September 1973 on fitting out the James Bay installation on the La Grande River, total capacity 4,400 Mw., in 16 groups. Three additional power stations were to have capacities of 1,500 Mw., 1,500 Mw., and 920 Mw. A project for a tidal power installation on the Bay of Fundy, between Nova Scotia and New Brunswick, judged uneconomic in 1968, was reexamined.

In Brazil the government decided to build two hydroelectric plants, one on the Tocantins River at Tucuruí, and the other on its tributary, the Araguaia. The potential of the river basin was estimated at 18,000 Mw. The national power concern, Electrobras, ordered a feasibility study on the hydroelectric potential of the Amazon basin, hitherto neglected because of its distance from the centres of consumption. However, with the harnessing of Itaipu (Sete Quedas), capacity 12,000 Mw., on the Paraná, Electrobras had already faced the problem of transporting electricity a considerable distance to the São Paulo region.

In the U.S. the last of six reversible turbo-pump groups at the pumped storage station at Ludington, Mich., came into operation

late in 1973, bringing total capacity of the station to 1,872 Mw. The installation supplied peak-hour power to the Detroit and Michigan grids.   (LUCIEN CHALMEY)

GAS

In the U.S. 1974 may have proved to be a benchmark year in a trend of lessened growth for the natural gas industry that was anticipated to continue for the rest of the decade. There remained a greater demand for natural gas than there was an increase in reserves, but the difference was smaller than expected because of a slowdown in industrial growth. Yet, the price of gas was expected to continue upward.

Based on the industrial pace the U.S. had become accustomed to before the slowdown, the U.S. Federal Power Commission (FPC) estimated that by 1980 production would fall short of demand by 3–4 Tcf (trillion cu.ft.). By 1990 total supply was expected to range between 14 and 44 Tcf. One-half of the gas produced in U.S. history had been produced since 1960, and it represented more than what was left underground in the contiguous 48 states.

The U.S. government continued to work for the deregulation of price on all new natural gas, for conservation in its use, and for more research and development funds. Many linked the supply shortage to speculative anticipation of higher prices.

Generally agreed upon means of solving the situation included improvement of offshore leasing policy; extension of controls to the intrastate market, where gas prices had been higher than in the regulated interstate market; greater competition; more effective regulation; and independent government reserve estimates. The FPC strove for curtailment of nonessential uses, improvement in maintenance, added insulation for buildings, elimination of ornamental uses, and reduction of thermostat settings.

The FPC proposed regulations to require all companies to report proved domestic gas reserves. It said that industry surveys failed to provide an adequate picture of the supply situation.

Gas served 31.2% of energy needs in the U.S., but shortages and curtailed use resulted in a modest 1.9% increase in 1973 demand, according to the U.S. Bureau of Mines. Industrial sales declined for the first time in 35 years, according to the American Gas Association (AGA). The utility and pipeline industry posted new records in sales (up 12%) and revenues (up 9%) in 1973. Exploratory gas well footage in late 1973 increased 44% over the previous year, and the number of wells drilled was up 24%, according to the FPC.

At 33 major interstate pipeline companies, the cost of gas from domestic producers in 1973 averaged 22.62 cents per Mcf (thousand cu.ft.), compared with 20.69 cents/Mcf in 1972. Average revenue was 49.37 cents/Mcf, up from 45.14 cents/Mcf over the same period. Revenues rose 5.4% to $8.3 billion, but gas sales were down 3.1% for the companies.

The FPC reported that gas reserves committed to interstate pipelines declined in 1973 for the sixth consecutive year. Figures from 63 interstate pipelines showed reserves declined to 134.4 Tcf in 1973 from 146.9 Tcf in 1972. The AGA announced that U.S. proved reserves dropped 6% in 1973, the fifth decline in six years. It estimated proved reserves (including Alaska) in 1974 at 250 Tcf, the lowest level since 1957.

The FPC set a single uniform national base rate of 42 cents per Mcf on sales begun after 1972. It also provided for fixed annual escalations of 1 cent/Mcf and a gathering allowance for certain producing areas of 1–2½ cents/Mcf. Additional provisions for offshore gas and special relief in unusual circumstances as well as biennial review were also established.   (JOSEPH J. ACCARDO)

At the fourth International Conference on Liquefied Natural Gas (LNG), held in Algeria in June 1974, Pres. Houari Boumédienne said that Algeria's investment in developing its gas reserves would total about $10 billion over the next seven years and would double by the end of the century. For such investments Algeria would require fair financial returns that would take into account both development needs and the depletion of reserves.

Algeria continued to expand its LNG export business and early in 1974 delivered its first shipment to Spain under an 18-year contract signed two years previously with Sonatrach, the Algerian state agency. Moving gas from producer to buyer involved vast sums in shipping and pipeline contracts, and Algeria secured loans from the World Bank totaling $70 million for the new LNG terminal at Bethioua. Sonatrach signed a 20-year contract to ship 159 Bcf (billion cu.ft.) a year in Spanish-built tankers to Spain's Empresa Nacional del Gas. The LNG would be regasified in Spain at Bilbao and Valencia, and a pipeline built from Valencia to Madrid. With an Algeria–Italy pipeline already a possibility, Spain also considered the construction of a pipeline to link it with Algeria.

During the year Iran unilaterally doubled the price of the 100 million cu.ft. of gas a day sold to the U.S.S.R. Iran was reported as seeing more of a future in chemicals than in energy and planned a major chemicals investment program. A pact between Iran and France involved $5 billion: France would build plants in Iran and a natural gas pipeline to Europe, and both nations planned

joint construction of a gas liquefaction plant and a fleet of LNG tankers.

Changes in price relationships between competing fuels caused secondary fuel producers to look again at previously uneconomic reserves. High oil prices and uncertainty over supplies of naphtha, particularly in the U.S., again focused attention on coal gasification techniques. The British Gas Corp. began a commercial test of a modified Lurgi plant at Westfield, Scot. The process had been developed by British Gas in the early 1960s but had not proved competitive with processes using other feedstocks. In Fife, Scot., several thousand families became the world's first consumers of synthetic natural gas (SNG) made by the methanation of lean gas, which itself was made from coal in the Lurgi gasifiers at Westfield.

The EEC launched a program to create energy independence within the Community and advocated that natural gas should supply 30% of the Community's energy requirements by the year 2000, with nuclear energy supplying 50%. During 1974 Norway ratified the sale of gas from the Frigg field in the North Sea to British Gas.

Afghanistan was reported to be planning a 100% increase in natural gas production over the next two years. Some 96.5 Bcf of the nation's 100 Bcf production had been exported to the U.S.S.R. in 1973, but almost all the increase would be used domestically, and deliveries to the U.S.S.R. during 1974 would be only slightly higher at 105 Bcf. Egypt planned to use the output from the Nile delta's Abu Madi gas field in chemical complexes in the Cairo area. Production from the field, believed likely to have a life of 30 years, was expected to reach 290 million cu.ft. daily.

A Dutch partnership was formed to bring Dutch North Sea gas ashore. A 110-mi. pipeline under construction was designed to bring an estimated 3.5 Tcf to Uithuizen, where a treatment plant with two output lines would be built. N. V. Nederlandse Gasunie completed a 20-year contract to buy all the gas from the Noordwinning Group's K 13 block in the Dutch sector of the North Sea. Deliveries were to begin in late 1975 at an average rate of nearly 42 Bcf a year.

The U.S.S.R. sought more than $1 billion in Japanese loans to develop Siberian natural resources, including the Yakutsk gas field, which was estimated to have reserves of 459 Tcf. Another Soviet discovery in the Caspian Sea was said to have been tested at a total of 35 million cu.ft. a day from three wells at 16,000 ft. The Soviet Union also reported the opening of its Orenburg gas field in southern Russia, where reserves were estimated at 85 Tcf.

Gas discoveries reported during the year included offshore fields capable of producing a total of 21 million cu.ft. a day in the Gulf of Martaban, off Burma; and a gas and oil strike 70 mi. NW of Jakarta in the Java Sea. Test flows on the gas indicated between 7 million and 9 million cu.ft. a day. Phillips Petroleum Co. announced a gas discovery offshore of West Irian, Indonesia. The well was tested to 135 million cu.ft. a day. A group headed by Continental Oil Co. of Indonesia opened a new discovery area in Indonesian waters northeast of Singapore. Cumulative flow rates for gas from six zones in the South China Sea produced 24 million cu.ft. per day.

The Soviet Union continued to find gas in the far north. A 35 million-cu.ft.-a-day well on Cape Kharasavei was the fifth natural gas field discovered during the year in Western Siberia's Tyumen Province, all five being found on the Yamal Peninsula. In Japan, after discovering gas 25 mi. off the east coast of Honshu Island in November

1973, an Exxon Corp. subsidiary and Japan's Teikoku Oil Co. tested another well in the area at 26 million cu.ft. a day.

Significant reserves of natural gas were found off the southern coast of Ireland by Marathon, a U.S. company. The field, in the area known as the Celtic Sea, had reserves of 1 Tcf. There were no plans, however, to develop natural gas for household use in Ireland. Following the success of an oil find in Dorset, British Gas drilled for oil and gas on the Isle of Wight. Since signing the Frigg contract, the corporation had been reassured by indications that large amounts of gas, much of it associated with oil, existed in the northern North Sea. Gas found in the Shell-Esso Brent field was at least equal to the reserves in the Norwegian sector of the Frigg field and could provide 6 Bcf of gas per day by the end of the 1970s.

British Gas predicted that the gas industry's 23% share of Britain's total useful heat output could reach 33 to 40% by the early 1980s, and that the present 35 to 40% share of the domestic market could rise to about 50%. The program of conversion from town to natural gas in Britain, scheduled to be 90% complete by the end of March 1975, would take in nearly 12 million out of a total of almost 13.5 million customers.

(DAVID R. BUTLER)

PETROLEUM

In 1974 nobody was in any doubt of the international repercussions of the oil crisis or the dominant role of petroleum in national economies. The economic balance had tilted decisively to the oil-producing countries. They asserted their collective strength to obtain large price increases for crude oil; they controlled production; and they used oil embargoes as a means to achieve political ends. In consequence, the year saw an extensive reappraisal of oil within the context of total energy requirements, and a review of the implications and the effects of surplus oil revenue funds on existing world financial institutions.

The Arab-Israeli war of October 1973 had been followed by a selective withdrawal of oil supplies. In November even more stringent cuts were announced, and while some were never fully implemented, they were not entirely rescinded until July 1974. The interruption of supplies induced certain governments, notably France, Japan, and the U.K., to anticipate oil shortages by negotiating bilateral deals, and pressured certain purchasers to take up options at excessive prices, $17.34 per barrel being paid for nonembargoed Iranian crude. Considerable confusion ensued in the oil markets. The situation was aggravated by the unprecedented decision taken by the Organization of Petroleum Exporting Countries (OPEC) in October 1973 to raise prices from 70 to 100%. This was followed by further stiff increases in December even though such increases were in direct breach of the Teheran and Geneva agreements. In less than two months, the posted price of Arabian light 34° rose from $2.591 to $11.651 per barrel. It soon became apparent that the previous pricing system and structure were no longer operative, and that henceforth pricing and production were to be the sole prerogative of the producing countries.

A timetable had been drawn up in 1972 for countries to achieve 51% participation in the companies operating concessions on their territory by 1981. In January 1974 the Kuwait Oil Co. acceded to a government request for 60% participation. Qatar and Abu Dhabi followed suit. Saudi Arabia, after initially claiming 60% of Aramco, the world's largest producing company, was negotiating a 100% takeover at year's end.

Libya, which had demanded an immediate 51% shareholding, had already nationalized three U.S. companies for noncompliance. Nigeria negotiated 35% in 1973, and Iran, by an agreement dated June 1973, received additional payments for its crude oil.

Reactions of consuming governments to reduced supplies and increased costs varied, but there were attempts at rationing, speed limits, and nondriving days. In the U.S. Pres. Richard Nixon launched "Project Independence" to make the country self-sufficient in energy. The trans-Alaska pipeline was authorized in the same month. In Europe the EEC sought to establish a common energy policy, but the complexity of the economic problems and political indecision impeded real cooperation. In February 1974 the U.S. government called a meeting of 12 governments in Washington to discuss joint action, but France refused to be associated with the issued policy statement.

Later in the year more rational approaches emerged, and as the effect of oil price increases on inflationary pressures came to be understood, efforts were made to reconcile the interests of producing and consuming countries in maintaining a stable world economy. Saudi Arabia, with U.S. support, led in proposing a reduction in oil prices which was partially successful in that it slowed the rate of increase, and at the OPEC conference in June posted prices were frozen for three months, although royalties were increased by 2%. In Vienna, in September, there were further price adjustments, apparently aimed at reducing the profits of the oil companies, and in December, in Vienna, it was agreed that prices would be stabilized, at a slightly higher level, for nine months. In several speeches during September, President Ford took the oil-producing countries to task, and a search was launched for a formula that would be acceptable to all parties, would preserve oil revenues from inflation-produced reductions, and would ensure security of supplies. In Paris, on November 15, 16 oil-consuming nations formed the International Energy Agency, established within the framework of the Organization for Economic Cooperation and Development, with the aim of pooling energy resources in an emergency. In a speech in November, U.S. Secretary of State Henry Kissinger proposed that the industrialized oil-consuming nations create an international fund to rescue the economy of any nation threatened with financial ruin by selective Arab investments.

Accompanying efforts to stabilize prices came initiatives from the International Monetary Fund (IMF) to set up an oil facility to recycle the surplus oil funds. UN Secretary-General Kurt Waldheim also tackled the problem. A report issued in September predicted that because of the increased prices of oil and other exports, 32 nations with a population totaling 900 million people faced a disastrous situation with projected deficits for 1974 that would amount to $2.3 billion or more.

The French government considered oil rationing, and in the U.K. a government-sponsored committee produced a report on energy conservation that called for better standards of insulation and smaller cars. In Detroit, Mich., in September, the ninth World Energy Conference pressed for a more rapid advance toward nuclear energy and a relaxation of environmental standards. In July 1974 the Labour government in the U.K. proposed nationalizing the oil beneath the North Sea. In June a UN-sponsored Conference on the Law of the Sea examined the implications of offshore drilling. (*See* Law: *Special Report*.)

The growth of production in the first half of 1974 was 3% more than in the corresponding period of 1973. Middle East production rose 4.8%, far less than the 19% increase of the previous year. In the context of 1974 emerging Chinese production, said in January to be equivalent to 1 million bbl. a day, assumed a new significance.

Reserves. At the beginning of 1974 total world proved and probable oil reserves were 634,700,000,000 bbl., compared with 672,700,000,000 bbl. for the previous year. The Western Hemisphere share was 82,700,000,000 bbl., 12.8% of the total. The Middle East continued to account for the largest share of world reserves, 349,700,000,000 bbl., 55.4% of the world total. U.S. reserves, at 6.2%, remained much the same as in the preceding year, while those of the U.S.S.R., Eastern Europe, and China increased to 103,000,000,000 bbl., or 16.3%.

Production. During 1973 world crude oil production increased by 8.7% to 57,710,000 bbl. a day, compared with a 5.4% increase in 1972. The Middle East again dominated production with an increased share of 36.8% for a total of 21,070,000 bbl. a day. Saudi Arabia increased production by 27.8% to 12.9% of the total, 7,345,000 bbl. a day. Iran followed with an increase of 16.4%, giving it a 10.3% share of the total with 5,895,000 bbl. a day. Iraq and Abu Dhabi registered large increases of 34.7 and 23.8%, respectively. Kuwait, however, reduced production by 18%, and Libya's output fell by 2.9%. U.S. production at 10,925,000 bbl. a

day was approximately the same percentage share of the total at 18.3%, but was down 2.7% from 1972. Venezuelan production, 3,445,000 bbl., an increase of 4.2%, accounted for 6.3% of the total share. Indonesia with 22.2% and Nigeria with 12.6% both recorded increases, as did West Africa and Southeast Asia.

Consumption. World petroleum consumption in 1973 was 56,425,000 bbl. a day, an increase of 7.3% over 1972. Japanese demand at 5,425,000 bbl. a day, an increase of 14% over the previous year, was 10% of total world consumption. The U.S. remained the largest single consuming nation at 16,815,000 bbl. a day, an increase of 5% that maintained its share of the world total at just below 30%. Western European consumption was 15,155,000 bbl. a day, an increase of 8.2%, with West Germany at 3,070,000 bbl., France 2,555,000 bbl., the U.K. 2,285,000 bbl., and Italy 2,100,000 bbl. a day as the chief consumers. Spain registered the greatest increase over 1972, with 20%, and France followed with 10.2%. The U.S.S.R., Eastern Europe, and China, with a consumption of 8,775,000 bbl. a day, 15.7% of the total, showed an increase of 10.2%.

The pattern of imports changed little in 1973. The Middle East continued to supply most of the consumption of Japan and Western Europe, and increased its supplies to the U.S. to 820,000 bbl. a day, compared with 475,000 bbl. a day in 1972.

Products. In the U.S. gasolines continued to dominate demand, followed by middle distillates and fuel oil; increases over the previous year were 4.1, 4.6, and 9.4%, respectively. The Benelux countries continued to show large increases for gasolines, Belgium and Luxembourg 11.8% and The Netherlands 18.1%. The last-named showed a 10.4% decline in fuel oil demand as natural gas replaced it. In Japan fuel oil at 2,330 bbl. a day accounted for 50% of demand.

Refining. World refining capacity in 1973 was 64,510,000 bbl. a day, an increase of 7.7% over 1972. The capacity of the Western Hemisphere was 23,090,000 bbl. per day, 35.8% of the total and an increase of 5.6%. Western Europe, with 18,615,000 bbl. a day, had 28.8% of the total and an increase of 7.8%. Capacity in the U.S. declined to 22.1% of the world total, although, at 14,250,000 bbl. a day, it was 4.5% higher than in 1972. Mexico at 24% and Spain, 20.2%, registered large increases. Japan, with an increase of 10.5%, had a 7.5% share of the total at 4,870,000 bbl. a day. Southeast Asia registered an increase at 15.8%, accounting for nearly 4% of the total share.

Petrochemicals. Measures to reduce the lead content ratio in gasoline resulted in more aromatics being added to maintain octane numbers and antiknock values, but as aromatics were also vital for the petrochemical industry the pressure on the availability of supplies and the increasing cost of chemical feedstock caused problems. Naphtha costs quadrupled in 1974. In the U.S. petrochemical demand in 1973 was 4,200,000,000 gal. of ethane, 3,200,000,000 gal. of propane, and 1,600,000,000 gal. of butanes, most of it consumed in the production of oil fuels. Total U.S. production of ethylene was 21,700,000,000 lb. Further large investments were scheduled for the Middle East, particularly in Iran. (R. W. FERRIER)

See also Engineering Projects; Environment; Industrial Production and Technology; Mining and Quarrying; Transportation.
[214.C.4; 721; 724.B.2; 724.C.1-2; 737.A.5]

Section of the production platform for British Petroleum's Forties oil field in the North Sea is towed through the Cromarty Firth to the site.

BRITISH PETROLEUM CO. LTD.

Engineering Projects

Bridges. *Suspension and Cable-Stayed.* In 1974 Nanhae Island was linked to Hadong on the South Korean mainland by a 2,165-ft.-long suspension bridge with a main span of 1,325 ft., the largest structure of its type in the Far East outside Japan. For spans of that length, however, cable-stayed bridges often proved more economical than suspension bridges because they did not require the construction of expensive anchorages. Thus in France work was nearing completion on a cable-stayed bridge across the Loire estuary, between Saint-Nazaire and Saint-Brévin. With a centre span of 1,325 ft. flanked by two spans of 518 ft., it would outclass the 1,148-ft. Duisburg–Neuenkamp (W.Ger.) bridge. Two 223-ft.-high steel pylons in the form of an inverted V were capped by a short vertical element to hold the cables, which fanned out on two oblique planes to reach their anchorages on the lateral surfaces of the box girder forming the deck. On either side of this main metal structure were access viaducts of prestressed concrete girders, comprising, respectively, 22 and 30 166-ft. spans.

Under construction during the year were the Deggenau bridge near Deggendorf on the Danube in West Germany, consisting of two cable-stayed metal spans of 476 ft. and 951 ft.; the Kiev bridge in the U.S.S.R., due for completion in 1975, with a main span of 984 ft.; and the Suehiro bridge over the port of Tokushima on Shikoku Island, Japan, with three cable-stayed spans (361 ft.; 820 ft.; 361 ft.).

Metal Girder Bridges. The 9.4-mi. bridge across the Bay of Guanabara in Brazil, between Rio de Janeiro and Niterói, was opened to traffic. It comprised a metal structure consisting of an 85-ft.-wide orthotropic plate on twin box girders that crossed the navigable channel in three spans (656 ft.; 984 ft.; 656 ft.) and flanking viaducts of prestressed concrete built by successive corbeling of prefabricated voussoirs.

The Avonmouth bridge over the River Avon in England consisted of three main spans (370 ft.; 570 ft.; 370 ft.) extended by 17 approach spans varying in length from 100 to 240 ft. Twin box girders 20 ft. wide and varying in height from 10 to 25 ft. carried a 132-ft.-wide orthotropic plate.

Other Metal Bridges. The 600-ft.-long metal arch bridge across the port of Milwaukee, Wis., opened early in 1974. Its metal deck, sited midway across the bow, provided a width of 112 ft. for traffic and clearance of 120 ft. above the navigable channel. In Japan the Nanko cantilever bridge across the Bay of Osaka neared completion. With its 1,683-ft. main span, between two spans of 776 ft. each, it would be the third longest of its type in the world, after Quebec's old railway bridge (1,800 ft.) and the Forth bridge in Scotland (1,710 ft.). The 614-ft.-long central section, weighing 5,000 metric tons, was winched into place 170 ft. above water level in only three and a half hours, despite a wind reaching 32 mph.

Concrete Cable-Stayed Bridges. Concrete structures were being built to increasingly daring designs, easily bearing comparison with the most spectacular metal bridges. In France work began during the year on the Meules bridge over the Seine River, downstream from Rouen. Its main structure of prestressed concrete was to comprise three cable-stayed spans, of which the 1,050-ft. centre span would beat the world record set by the 940-ft. centre span of the Wadi Kuf bridge in Libya. The deck, formed of 9.8-ft.-long voussoirs 12.5 ft. high in section, was being launched out from the piers by successive corbeling. Approach viaducts, also being built by corbeling, would bring the total length to 4,265 ft. (0.8 mi.).

In Argentina the Chaco–Corrientes bridge over the Paraná River, opened to traffic in late 1973, consisted of three main cable-stayed spans (537 ft.; 804 ft.; 537 ft.).

Concrete Girder Bridges. For traditional structures, successive corbeling remained the method of construction by which the most spectacular results were achieved. In the U.S. mobile rigs were used to build the Pine Valley Creek, Calif., bridge, completed in 1974, with a 450-ft. main span. The deck comprised two box girders, each of uniform 19-ft. depth, supporting a 42-ft. roadway. A space was left between the girders to allow for later widening of the roadways, by insertion of a central girder, should traffic conditions demand it.

The same construction method was used for the Felsenau viaduct crossing the Aare River near Bern, Switz., at a height of 200 ft. in four spans (309 ft.; 2 of 472 ft.; 309 ft.). The single box girder, varying in depth between 26.2 and 9.8 ft., carried an 86-ft.-wide deck.

The main innovation in the construction of concrete bridges lay in the use of lightweight aggregates. Widespread adoption of these materials had been hampered by both high costs and inadequate understanding of their mechanical properties. Dutch engineers appeared to have established a lead in this field, and three identical structures spanning the Meuse–Waal canal near Nijmegen, Neth., were brought into service. Each of these was built by successive corbeling and consisted of three spans (156 ft.; 368 ft.; 156 ft.), only the centre spans being constructed in lightweight concrete. It was clear that the material would come into its own in the construction of wide spans, where the dead load factor was most restricting, and it was to be used in the planned viaduct over the West Scheldt in Zeeland, Neth., which would have eight 525-ft. spans.

(ROBERT CHAUSSIN)

Buildings. In 1974 the future of housing for low- and middle-income people in the United States was bleak. Construction, property, and financing costs had risen to such high levels as to put the prices of unsubsidized houses out of the reach of these income

Kanmon bridge, at 1,068 m. the longest span in the Orient, connects the Japanese islands of Honshu and Kyushu.

groups. Inflation had wiped out the cost benefits of construction technology and long-term mortgage financing. These conditions also placed greater constraints on the development of subsidized housing. In 1974 monthly rentals of $100 per room were reported as required to cover investment cost, as compared with $30 in 1968.

Despite these conditions it was possible to see in 1974 the results of subsidized housing projects of substantial scale. These were projects that had come to fruition or were nearing completion as the result of years of planning and the participation of builders, developers, architects, government officials, citizens' groups, and individuals.

The New York architectural firm of Davis, Brody and Associates was one that in 1974 could show a substantial contribution to subsidized housing in New York City's boroughs of Manhattan and the Bronx. This firm, which was organized in 1953, had worked with builder-developers and others in New York for more than two decades to bring better housing design into housing projects. Two of the firm's projects—Waterside, which was completed in 1974, and Harlem River Housing, which was nearing completion at the year's end—illustrated the nature of the firm's contributions. Waterside was built on a site that was originally a part of the East River. Rather than being constructed on land or on a fill, it was built on 2,000 concrete pilings that went down 80 ft. or more through the water to the bedrock underneath.

The Harlem River project was located across the river from the Bronx on the east side of the Harlem River. Its development involved a major effort to attach it to the community, which was separated from it by the expressway. In 1974 a new bridge was being constructed over the traffic to supplement the existing bridge and to provide ready access to a parking structure that was a part of the development. Not only did the Harlem River project provide housing that incorporated pleasant architectural features, it also took advantage of an elaborate recreational complex that existed just north of it.

In *Architecture Plus* it was reported that the buildings of the Berlin Free University were completed in 1974 and that they represented or embodied the most radical architectural departure of the 1960s. According to the report, the architecture included a type of building never considered to be architecture before. Such a building embodied the concept that its physical parts should be built so that they could be modified or changed over time to better accommodate the needs of the users. The architectural design, made in 1963 by the Paris firm of Georges Candilis, Alexy Josic, and Shadrach Woods, consisted of a network of circulation paths with four parallel major paths stretching the length of the 30-ac. site and joining the two groups of existing buildings. Spaces for activity were to be built as they were required. The purpose of the design was to accommodate change and growth over a period of time. It was difficult to assess fully the merits of the architectural design or its flexibility features. The flexibility in the building elements might prove to be useful, yet at the same time might prove expensive and unwieldy. Nevertheless, it was significant that a new idea was emerging in the design of buildings—one that recognized the possible need for change during the ongoing construction process or at any later period.

The World Trade Building in New York City was one that provoked much discussion among engineers

A new bridge across the Elbe River at Hamburg, W.Ger., expected to be used by more than 30,000 vehicles per day, was opened in the fall.

and architects in 1974. It embodied the engineering features of load-bearing walls as opposed to cage construction. Reporting in *Architecture Plus*, Henry Wright, the director of research in the School of Architecture at New York's City College, expressed the view that there were fundamental reasons why the load-bearing wall might bring about a new era of tall building design. He pointed out that the cage frame type of building had been dictated by engineering requirements, noting that for 88 years skyscraper architects had been dealing with one problem, to provide socially acceptable exteriors for post-and-beam bays of 20–25 sq.ft. multiplied in three dimensions. Wright believed that the load-bearing wall design of the World Trade Center would open up an entirely new approach to the exterior design of tall buildings.

(CARTER C. OSTERBIND)

Dams. *Europe.* In Spain the Guadalhorce–Guadalteba rock-fill dam (height 272 ft., volume 4,185,600 cu.yd.) was completed in 1974. Also finished was the Arenos rock-fill dam on the Mijares River (height 344 ft., crest length 1,427 ft., volume 2,563,680 cu.yd. filler, 1,438,800 cu.yd. clay; storage 105,680 ac.-ft.). It had an inclined watertight core, separated from the rock fill by means of two filter layers, and protected upstream with a filter and a rock-fill layer in contact with the reservoir.

The Piastra concrete gravity dam on the Gesso River and the Passante solid gravity dam on the Passante River were under construction in Italy. In Greece construction continued on the Kardamakis earth and rock-fill dam on the Aliakmon River. It was designed to supply three Francis turbines of 360 Mw. installed capacity.

In the Soviet Union the Zeyskaya buttress dam on the Zeya River, a tributary of the Amur River, was completed. The Serebryansk earth and rock-fill dam on the Voronya River and the Sayano-Shushenskaya dam in Siberia, which would be the world's biggest power plant, with a capacity of 6,400 Mw., were under construction.

Asia. The Tarbela earth and rock-fill dam on the

Construction continues on the Ust-Ilim hydroelectric power station on the Angara River in the Soviet Union.

V. CHERNOV—CAMERA PRESS PHOTO TRENDS

Indus River in Pakistan, the world's largest of its kind, neared completion, although a setback occurred in August when the tunnel gates—the biggest ever made in the history of dam construction—were damaged. Tarbela, when complete, would have a total capacity of 2,100 Mw., but it was built primarily for irrigation. Cost of the project was estimated to exceed $800 million.

In India the Idikki thin (tapering to 25 ft. at its crest from 75 ft. at its base), double-curvature, parabolic arch dam on the Periyar River was completed. It was the first of its kind to be built in that country. The Idikki hydroelectric system included two other dams under construction: the Kulamavu masonry dam and the Cheruthoni concrete gravity dam. The three-dam system would impound 1.7 million ac-ft. of water to feed a high-head (2,200 ft.) underground power station housing six 130-Mw. units.

To supply the ever increasing demand for water, approximately 60 dams over 130 ft. high were under construction in Japan. A number of high dams were built for pumped-storage hydroelectric power, specifically to meet peak demand. Dams completed during the year included the Oto concrete gravity dam on the Niyodo River (height 328 ft., crest length 1,080 ft., volume 956,000 cu.yd., storage 53,500 ac-ft.); the Kajigawa concrete gravity dam on the Kaji River

(height 351 ft., crest length 876 ft., volume 554,600 cu.yd., storage 18,293 ac-ft.); the Sameura concrete gravity dam on the Yoshino River (height 348 ft., crest length 1,378 ft., volume 1,570,000 cu.yd., storage 256,910 ac-ft.); and the Nikappu rock-fill dam on the Nikappu River (height 338 ft., crest length 1,070 ft., volume 4,002,480 cu.yd., storage 117,886 ac-ft.). The Kusaki concrete gravity dam on the Watarase River and the Managawa arch dam on the Mana River neared completion.

North and South America. In the U.S. the Pueblo massive-head, concrete buttress and earth-fill dam on the Arkansas River in Colorado (height 190 ft.; crest length: right embankment 4,875 ft., left 3,575 ft.; buttress 1,750 ft.; earth-fill 11 million cu.yd.; concrete 500,000 cu.yd.; storage 357,000 ac-ft.) was completed in 1974. To make winter work possible, the forms had been insulated with a foam-spray coating and rubber mats hung on the concrete. Construction continued on the Raccoon Mountains rock-fill dam on the Tennessee River to provide the upper reservoir in a pumped-storage scheme; on the Crystal double-curvature arch dam on the Gunnison River in Colorado; on the New Melones rock-fill dam on the Stanislaus River in California; and on the Back Creek rock-fill dam on the Little Back Creek in Missouri.

In Brazil the Passo Real earth and rock-fill dam on

Major World Dams Under Construction in 1974*

Name of dam	River	Country	Type†	Height (ft.)	Length of crest (ft.)	Volume content (000 cu.yd.)	Gross capacity of reservoir (000 ac-ft.)
Auburn	American (N. Fork)	U.S.	A	685	4,150	6,000	2,300
Balimela	Sileru	India	E	230	15,200	29,600	3,100
Beas	Beas-Indus	India	E	435	6,400	45,800	6,600
Bilandi Tank	Bilandi	India	EG	105	2,320	26,907	51
Cabora Bassa	Zambezi	Mozambique	A	561	994	667	51,900
Chirkeyskaya	Sulak	U.S.S.R.	A	764	1,109	1,602	2,252
Chivor	Bata	Colombia	ER	778	1,089	14,400	661
Cochiti	Rio Grande	U.S.	E	251	28,200	46,640	513
Dartmouth	Mitta Mitta	Australia	ER	591	2,198	20,000	3,000
Fierze	Drin	Albania	E	518	1,312	916	2,124
Finstertal	Finstertal-bach	Austria	ER	518	2,034	5,742	49
Hasan Ugurlu	Yesilirmak	Turkey	ER	574	1,427	11,827	874
Ilha Solteira	Paraná	Brazil	EG	291	20,300	35,741	17,172
Inguri	Inguri	U.S.S.R.	A	892	2,513	4,967	891
Itaipu	Paraná	Brazil-Paraguay	EG	558	26,717	36,624	23,511
Itumbiara	Paranaiba	Brazil	ER	348	21,983	44,426	13,804
Kara Kaya	Euphrates	Turkey	A	591	1,293	1,779	7,767
Keban	Euphrates	Turkey	RG	679	3,598	19,600	25,110
Kölnbrein	Malta	Austria	A	650	1,969	2,093	162
Kolyma	Kolyma	U.S.S.R.	R	427	2,461	16,415	12,000
Las Portas	Camba	Spain	G	498	1,587	977	609
Marimbondo	Grande	Brazil	EG	295	12,297	24,328	5,184
Melones, New‡	Stanislaus	U.S.	ER	625	1,600	15,970	2,400
Mratinje	Piva	Yugoslavia	A	722	879	971	713
Nagarjuna Sagar	Krishna	India	EG	407	15,257	73,575	9,165
Nurek	Vakhsh	U.S.S.R.	E	1,040	2,390	75,864	8,424
Oosterschelde	Vense Gat Oosterschelde	Netherlands, The	E	148	29,529	91,560	2,351
Oymapinar	Manavgat	Turkey	A	607	1,181	739	243
Patia	Patia	Colombia	R	755	1,540	26,000	11,200
São Sinão	Paranaiba	Brazil	EG	394	11,848	31,435	10,134
Sayano-Shushenskaya	Yenisei	U.S.S.R.	A	794	3,504	11,916	25,353
Sterkfontein	Nuwe Jaanspruit	South Africa	E	292	10,007	20,274	2,156
Tachien	Tachia	Taiwan	A	591	951	562	188
Takase	Takase	Japan	EG	577	1,115	13,996	62
Tarbela	Indus	Pakistan	ER	486	9,000	186,000	11,100
Toktogul	Naryn	U.S.S.R.	A	705	1,476	3,787	15,800
Ukai	Tapi	India	EG	226	16,165	33,375	6,900
Ust-Ilim	Angara	U.S.S.R.	EG	344	11,695	11,382	48,100
Warm Springs	Dry Creek	U.S.	E	318	2,999	30,385	245
Yacyreta-Apipe	Paraná	Argentina-Paraguay	EG	125	16,405	37,493	14,079
MAJOR WORLD DAMS COMPLETED IN 1973 AND 1974*							
Carters Lake	Coosawattec	U.S.	E	450	2,050	14,300	475
Dworshak	Clearwater, (N. Fork)	U.S.	G	717	3,287	6,500	3,453
El Chocón	Limay	Argentina	ER	243	7,448	15,892	17,000
Emosson	Barberine	Switzerland	A	590	1,818	1,400	182
Gokcekaya	Sakarya	Turkey	A	525	1,542	850	737
Idikki	Periyar	India	A	555	1,201	609	1,618
Kanev	Dnepr	U.S.S.R.	E	82	52,950	49,520	2,125
Krasnoyarsk	Yenisei	U.S.S.R.	G	407	3,493	5,685	59,425
Libby	Kootenai	U.S.	G	446	2,240	4,200	5,850
Mica	Columbia	Canada	R	800	2,600	42,000	20,000
Reza, Shah Kabir	Karun	Iran	A	656	1,247	1,570	2,351
Zeyskaya	Zeya	U.S.S.R.	G	369	2,343	3,139	55,452

*Having a height exceeding 492 ft. (150 m.); or having a total volume content exceeding 20 million cu.yd. (15 million cu.m.); or forming a reservoir exceeding 12 million ac-ft. capacity (14,800 x 10⁶ cu.m.).
†Type of dam: E=earth; R=rock-fill; A=arch; G=gravity.
‡Replacement of existing dam.

(T.W. MERMEL)

the Jacuì River (height 184 ft., crest length 2,000 ft., volume 3,270,000 cu.yd., storage 2,967 ac-ft.) was completed. The plant included two earth-fill embankments, each 11,000 ft. long, and a concrete spillway. Dams under construction included: the São Simão dam on the Paranaiba River, southwest of Minas Gerais state; the Foz do Areia dam on the Iguaçu River; the Itumbiara earth and rock-fill dam on the Paranaiba River; and the Itaipu solid gravity dam on the Paraná River, between Brazil and Paraguay.

In Argentina the El Chocón earth and rock-fill dam on the Limay River, with impervious clay core inclined downstream, had been completed in 1973. Two earth and rock-fill dams, Futaleufú and Los Reyunos, were under construction. The Agua del Toro double-curvature arch dam on the Diamante River, the first of its type in the country, neared completion.

Africa. In Morocco the Bou-Regreg earth and rock-fill dam on the Oued Bou-Regreg, with central impervious core (height 328 ft., crest length 1,115 ft., volume 3,924,000 cu.yd., storage 463,415 ac-ft.), was completed in 1974. The Idriss 1 hollow gravity dam on the Oued Inaouene (height 236 ft., crest length 1,466 ft., volume 588,600 cu.yd., storage 1,032,520 ac-ft.) had been completed in 1973. The Le Roux arch dam on the Orange River, 75 mi. downstream from the Hendrik Verwoerd dam, which was to have the highest concrete arch in South Africa, was under construction. (ALDO MARCELLO)

Roads. In the planning of road systems, two concepts gained increasing recognition in 1974. First, the pioneer road thrust into a developing area or region gained new importance. Second, the idea gained credence that the development of any road system and, in fact, of the whole transport system of a region had to be planned to keep pace with the overall development plans for that area.

Brazil could best illustrate the use of the pioneer road concept. As part of the National Integration Program of 1970, a decision had been made to invest in an undeveloped region, the vast area north of the Amazon. The Brazilian government already had experience with the pioneer road as an agent for development, having constructed the Belém–Brasília Highway, part of the Trans-Brazilian Highway linking the river port of Belém on the Amazon estuary to Aceguá on the border with Uruguay. When the southern part of the road was almost complete, the government decided to build another great highway from the Atlantic coast. The new road passed through densely populated regions in the northeast, intercepted the Belém–Brasília Highway, penetrated deep into tropical forests, and then ran through fertile valleys to connect with roads to Peru and Bolivia.

The opening of continental road networks in Africa, South America, and Asia caused greatly increased world expenditure on road building. World expenditure in the 1950s was probably about $6 billion a year, but by 1974 it had risen to more than $50 billion a year. The dramatic increases in the prices of oil products during 1974 seemed likely to affect future road-building trends. Road-building programs in Europe and North America were expected to continue but at a slower rate. In the less developed countries, however, transport was an essential key to primary production. In Mexico, for example, some 12 million of the population of 53 million were not linked to the rest of the nation by roads passable in all weathers. The government aimed to increase the national network of roads from 43,500 to 93,000 mi. by 1976.

The Asian Highway Network, which already linked 15 countries from west to east, was connected to the European Highway Network at the Iran-Turkey border and to the Middle East Highway Network at the Iran-Iraq border. The Asian Highway Network, 40,000 mi. long overall, was two-lane paved for 48% of its length and one-lane paved for an additional 27%. Another 11% was surfaced with gravel or stone. In poor weather an additional 4% was passable by car and 3% by jeep, but 7% of the network was still not passable at all.

Construction of the last link of the Pan-American Highway, the Darien Highway in Panama, was delayed by an outbreak of foot-and-mouth disease in Colombia. The 9-mi.-long Cañitas-Bayano River project neared completion, and work commenced on the Cañazas–Canglon section.

In Morocco the 97-mi.-long Chemaia–Agadir road opened, and the time of the trip from Casablanca to Agadir was thereby cut by an hour. The 70-mi. Guidam–Romji and Madaoua section of the Niamey–Zinder road opened in Niger. In northern Thailand a new 60-mi.-long road was built through difficult mountainous country between Sri Satchanalai and Phrae, and a 40-mi. length of new construction on the Rong Kwang–Song–Nagao Highway opened. The 1,060-mi. Baja California Peninsular Highway opened in the U.S.

France planned to build 335 mi. of expressway by 1978, bringing the national network up to 3,750 mi. The expressway between Paris and Orléans and the Les Pennes–Mirabeau–Martiques expressway opened. Italy opened many short sections of expressway.

Nearly 57 mi. of new expressway opened in the U.K., bringing the total in use to 990 mi. An additional 197 mi. were under construction, and 574 mi. were in the planning stage. With 27 mi. of expressway in Wales, and 90 mi. in Scotland, the expressway network in Great Britain totaled 1,107 mi. The long-term objective of the British road program was a 3,500-mi. network of strategic trunk roads to connect all major centres of population and industry with each other and with the ports. (R. S. MILLARD)

Tunnels. An event of major significance for international cooperation on tunneling matters took place in Oslo, Nor., in April 1974, when representatives from 15 nations agreed to form an International Tunneling Association. A committee was formed with a

Tunneling shield of a new design, used in the construction of the Fleet Line extension to London's Underground (subway).

SCOTT-SHIPSIDES LTD.

Road tunnel
at Shakespeare, Eng.,
near Dover, is part
of the system that
provides access
to the starting
point of construction
on the Channel Tunnel.

permanent secretariat at Bron in France, and it was hoped to hold the first meeting of the new association in West Germany in 1975.

On both sides of the English Channel the second stage of preparatory works for the Channel Tunnel proceeded during the year, although financial difficulties were being encountered. On the English side access tunnels were driven to the grade of the future central service tunnel prior to the installation of a full-face tunneling machine. On the French side a similar operation was taking place, using a U.S. tunneling machine. An additional practical development in tunnel technology in the U.K. was to be continued on a sewer tunnel at Warrington, Lancashire, where a Bentonite shield was to be used following its successful trials on the new Fleet Line subway in London.

Work began on the Furka Railway project in Switzerland, where hydraulically powered drilling equipment was to be used for the entire 20 km. of tunnel required for the project. Advantages claimed for this system, apart from the greatly improved working conditions at the face, included a high rate of penetration—up to 1,600 mm. per minute in hard granite. Work continued on the St. Gotthard Tunnel, which, when completed, would be the longest road tunnel in the world. It was in 1974 the largest construction project in Switzerland. Also in Switzerland, two of the world's largest drill jumbos were in use on the twin-bore, 9-km.-long Seelisberg tunnel, which, when completed, would form part of the N2 highway linking Switzerland and Italy.

In Austria, which planned to construct approximately 200 km. of new road tunnels in the next 25 years, work began on the world's second longest road tunnel, comprising 12.5-km.-long twin bores through the Arlberg Massif. Work continued on the construction of the Munich, W.Ger., rapid transit system, where two U.S. full-face tunneling machines were successfully driving through difficult wet ground conditions.

The Dutch maintained their lead in the construction of immersed tube tunnels by building four of them in 1974. In Amsterdam work continued on the underground section of the city's first subway line. This was proving to be one of the most difficult underground railways to be constructed anywhere in the world. Two methods of construction were being used: the first involved sinking precast concrete caissons into the subsoil using water jetting; the second was a wall and in situ roofing system using Bentonite slurry walls or contiguous bored piling. Work was expected to be completed in 1977.

Considerable engineering problems were being overcome in Italy during the driving of two tunnels on a section of the Genoa–Savona expressway on the outskirts of Genoa. To avoid subsidence on one section, a rock-splitting tool operated by compressed air was in use, eliminating the use of explosives. Elsewhere on those works extensive use was being made of Shotcrete to provide support in bad ground. Construction of the rapid transit subway system in central Oslo involved technically interesting methods of using explosives in urban areas.

In Hong Kong there was considerable tunneling activity. Work proceeded on the construction of three trial tunnels to prove construction methods prior to the letting of a contract for a 53-km. subway system. In Japan excavation began for the main and service tunnels for the 54-km. Seikan crossing, the longest railway tunnel in the world, to be completed by 1979.

The San Fernando tunnel in California was completed slightly more than three years after the June 1971 explosion in the tunnel that had cost 17 lives. In New York City, 22 km. of hard-rock tunnel were being driven as part of one of the largest municipal water supply contracts ever let in the Western Hemisphere. Depth of the tunnel varied from 100 to 250 m., with diameters ranging from 6 to 8 m. The Manhattan subway extension called for considerable engineering ingenuity. Almost every conceivable ground condition was being encountered, and both hard-rock tunneling and cut-and-cover methods were being used.

(DAVID A. HARRIES)

[733; 734.A]

ENCYCLOPÆDIA BRITANNICA FILMS. *The Mississippi System: Waterway of Commerce* (1970).

Environment

Throughout 1974 the world's media were absorbed with reports of economic and political crises, and environmental issues appeared to assume a minor role. Two major UN conferences, which debated the law of the sea and world population (*see* LAW: *Special Report;* POPULATIONS AND AREAS: *Special Report*), received little press coverage. A third conference, held under the auspices of the Food and Agriculture Organization (FAO) of the UN in Rome in November, discussed the world food situation, an issue of more immediate relevance to the ordinary citizen.

A major factor in the high rates of inflation experienced in all industrial countries was the sharp rise in the price of oil and other commodities, combined with a continued shortage of food. Except for a few weeks very early in the year when the Arab oil-producing countries withheld supplies to countries they regarded as friendly to Israel, oil was not in short supply; indeed, there were problems of storage as surpluses accumulated all over the world. Nevertheless, prices remained high, imposing a severe strain on the economy of consumers, and many actions taken to alleviate the situation had environmental implications.

NATIONAL DEVELOPMENTS AND POLICIES

The U.S. Energy Crisis. Fearing the economic repercussions of the energy problem, the U.S. convened a conference of oil-consuming nations in Washington in February. A communiqué issued on February 13 called for conservation of supplies, a system for allocating supplies in times of shortage, and economic measures to safeguard the less developed countries. The participants agreed "to accelerate wherever practicable their own national programs of new energy sources and technology which will help the over-all worldwide supply and demand situation." The industrial nations agreed to make the maintenance and improvement of the natural environment an "important goal of their activity" while exploiting energy resources, but environmentalists were not convinced that this would be given a high priority. The U.S. had declared its determination to achieve self-sufficiency in energy, and to this end environmentalists believed their objections would be neglected.

In November 1973 Congress removed the last legal obstacle to construction of the trans-Alaska pipeline, which would carry oil from Prudhoe Bay on the North Slope to the port of Valdez in the south, and work began during 1974. However, the change in the world energy situation made the Alaskan reserves even more valuable and encouraged the companies to accelerate the rate at which they were to be exploited. On March 21 the Alaskan Arctic Gas Pipeline Co. and Canadian Arctic Gas Pipeline Ltd. filed the first applications for construction of a gas pipeline, to run southeast from northern Alaska to the Mackenzie delta, then south through Alberta to Montana, with the possibility of further extensions west into Washington state and east through the Dakotas toward Chicago.

On May 19 an article in the *Anchorage* (Alaska) *Daily News* stated that the gas from Alaska would be used to power coal gasification plants under development in Montana, Wyoming, North Dakota, and New Mexico, where large coal seams were available for strip-mining. Although the Sierra Club's prolonged campaign against the first pipeline had at least ensured important safeguards for the tundra through which it passed, the new pipelines would cause major ecological disturbance in Alaska or the Northern Plains states, or both. Fears were also expressed that the availability of energy and the rising world prices for minerals would lead to the strip-mining of parts of Alaska for uranium, nickel, mercury, lead, and tungsten. Beneath the land reserved for oil exploitation in Alaska there were believed to be some 130,000,000,000 metric tons of coal. (*See* ARCTIC REGIONS.)

As the year went on, U.S. environmentalists found themselves fighting a series of rearguard actions. An emergency energy bill that would have permitted significant relaxations in the control of air pollution was divided into two separate acts, but the Energy Supply and Environmental Coordination Act of 1974 was passed by the House of Representatives before a joint House-Senate conference committee agreed to its amendment. On May 30 the conference committee agreed to reduce the number of power plants that the previous legislation would have permitted to convert from oil to coal, standards for emissions from automobiles were delayed for one year, and there were other relaxations in environmental standards for transport. The Clean Air Act was extended for a year, but pollution controls were eased. On August 16 the Sierra Club's *National News Report* stated that Pres. Gerald Ford had recommended that "the country's environmental concerns take second place to its energy needs."

Energy Conservation and Transport. Although the need to accelerate the production of primary sources of energy caused increased environmental problems, it was paralleled, and to some extent balanced, by the need to conserve energy. Environmentalists had long held that a direct relationship exists between energy use and environmental deterioration. In Britain the Transport 2000 group continued to press for an increase in rail transport. In June an independent transport commission called for an integrated transport system, and the main political parties began to recognize the need to improve public transport services, all of which were losing money and finding it difficult to recruit sufficient staff to maintain services.

In the U.S. most motorists returned to their cars after the winter gas shortage eased, although public transport systems, overall, reported a small but consistent increase in riders. There was some evidence that cars were being driven less, but it appeared that the high cost of gas rather than conservation was the motivating factor. President Ford urged further voluntary reductions in car use as part of his anti-inflation program. Large, low-mileage cars, almost un-

salable during the shortage, made something of a comeback, but smaller models continued to hold a large share of a shrinking market. All three major car makers reported sharply reduced profits.

As of July 1, high-volume gas stations in the U.S. were required to sell the lead-free gasoline needed for use with the catalytic converters that were standard on 1975 models. For the moment, at least, the catalytic converter was Detroit's answer to the pollution problem. One study, however, claimed that though it lowered the emission of certain pollutants, it increased others, chiefly sulfur dioxide, that might cause even more serious problems in the long run. Interest in the low-polluting rotary engine waned because of its alleged high gas consumption.

The controversial plan to build a third London airport at Maplin was abandoned during the year. British politicians showed renewed interest in the proposed Channel Tunnel, although its cost increased almost daily. The Labour government reaffirmed its original intention of proceeding with the Concorde supersonic airliner project, but among the alternative transport systems being considered, the cargo-carrying airship, capable of conveying a load of over 400 tons for up to 1,000 mi., was the subject of intensive research. It was calculated that a fleet of five airships and their ground facilities, costing about £60 million, could move the whole of the traffic flow projected for the Channel Tunnel by 1980. In West Germany work continued on a new design for sailing ships that might compete successfully with steam- and nuclear-powered vessels for certain cargoes. Inland, there was renewed interest in rivers and canals. (*See* TRANSPORTATION.)

Alternative Energy Sources. There was a markedly increased interest in economy measures that could be effected by householders. The U.K. Department of the Environment announced on January 25 that it intended to double insulation standards for new housing. To draw attention to the economies that were possible, Friends of the Earth, a voluntary environmental pressure group, insulated 50 old people's dwellings free of charge. Several local authorities encouraged experimental installations utilizing solar energy for domestic water and space heating.

Sir Kingsley Dunham, director of the Institute of Geological Sciences in London, appealed for funds to sink experimental geothermal boreholes at several British sites. Geothermal energy, derived from the heat of the earth's mantle where this approaches the surface in the form of "hot rock" or from subterranean reservoirs of superheated steam, was being exploited in Italy, as it had been since the early 1900s, and experimental drillings were being made in the U.S.

Environmentalists tended to welcome the use of such "free" energy, which would help conserve fossil fuel stocks and, they believed, would be less damaging to the environment than conventional alternatives. This view was challenged during the year, however. Geothermal energy, which reaches the surface as superheated steam, may carry highly noxious substances, especially hydrogen sulfide, in solution. Even hydrogen, favoured by some experts as the most practicable alternative to petroleum as a fuel for transport, was shown by experiments conducted at the Monsanto laboratories in the U.S. to produce considerable quantities of hydrogen peroxide when it is burned. Hydrogen peroxide is a reactive substance that can initiate processes leading to the production of substances that damage living tissue. It seemed likely that vehicles powered by hydrogen would require emission control equipment at least as expensive as that required by oil-burning engines.

Nuclear Power. The main controversy in the energy field, however, centred on nuclear power. Environmentalists in the U.S. and Europe urged caution as all the leading industrial nations began to accelerate their nuclear reactor programs. At times views became polarized, with proponents of the programs arguing that no danger existed and their opponents holding that under no circumstances could nuclear power be safe. The U.S. Atomic Energy Commission, after a two-year study, concluded that the risk of mass destruction resulting from reactor failure was about the same as the risk from falling meteors, but critics challenged the AEC's statistical analysis and cited its alleged bias toward the nuclear industry. The U.K. secretary of state for energy, Eric Varley, announced on July 10 that Britain's program would be based on the British steam generating heavy water reactor (SGHWR) rather than the U.S. light water reactor (LWR). Apart from the obvious encouragement to British industry, the decision reflected growing concern, often voiced by environmentalists, over the safety of the LWR.

In his statement, Varley referred to the environmental implications of the storage and disposal of radioactive wastes: "We shall keep a close watch over the environmental implications of . . . radioactive wastes. The Royal Commission on Environmental Pollution is examining these and related issues." The environmentalists were not completely satisfied. In their view, the problem of waste disposal had not been solved and probably could not be solved. In the longer term, the development of the fast-breeder reactor, which produces its own fuel in the form of plutonium as a by-product of its own process, presented additional problems. Plutonium is one of the most poisonous substances known, and its very existence has environmental and public health implications.

Early in July, the British Committee for Environmental Conservation, the Royal Society of Arts, and the Institute of Fuel issued a report stating that "it is difficult to believe that there will not be a serious accident somewhere in the world [in a nuclear plant] before A.D. 2000, particularly as the care of these installations passes to less skilled and dedicated men." These three organizations, representing among them a wide range of environmental, scientific, and industrial interests, were reflecting the views of such groups as the Conservation Society and Friends of the Earth, as well as those of the distinguished Swedish physicist Hannes Alfvén, president of Pugwash, the international scientists' peace movement. In the same week, Alfvén told an audience at the University of Birmingham that the problem of avoiding a world "filled with radioactive poison and nuclear bombs" dwarfed all other international issues.

The Ozone Shield. A new environmental threat appeared during the year, this time from aerosol sprays. For several years there had been warnings about the dangers implicit in any reduction in the belt of ozone that surrounds the planet. Ozone absorbs incoming ultraviolet radiation, and a diminution in the shield might have serious effects on living organisms at the surface. In June 1974 a report in *Nature* described the most authoritative measurements made so far of actual ozone levels, by the Australian Commonwealth Scientific and Industrial Research Organisation. They showed that there was a continuous downward trend in ozone concentrations below the 30-km.

level from 1965 to 1973, whereas above 30 km. the concentration appeared to be increasing. Though previous measurements had shown a regular rise and fall in concentrations that could be related to the solar cycle, the new trend was continuous and cut across the solar cycle.

In 1972 and 1973 the threat was believed to come mainly from rockets, high-flying aircraft, and industrial pollutants, but a paper published in *Science* (September 27) suggested that the main cause might be the propellants used in aerosols. The chemicals most commonly used (chlorofluoromethanes) are relatively inert and rise into the stratosphere where they are broken down by ultraviolet light, releasing chlorine atoms which react with atmospheric ozone. Warning of this danger came from F. S. Rowland, of the University of California at Irvine, in an address given in September at the annual meeting of the American Chemical Society in Atlantic City, N.J.

Natural Resources. Although earlier environmentalist warnings of the impending exhaustion of global oil reserves were not borne out in the energy crisis of 1973–74, prices of other commodities did reflect scarcity and therefore higher extraction costs. In his Graham Clark Lecture to the Council of Engineering Institutions in London on January 8, Sir Kingsley Dunham warned that silver, lead, mercury, and zinc might be exhausted within 20 years. Other metals, such as copper, molybdenum, iron, possibly nickel, tin, tungsten, and gold, could be extracted in quantities adequate to meet projected demands, but only if the supply of energy was sufficient to permit the mining of progressively lower grades of ores. Their extraction, as well as the extraction and refining of aluminum, "will create environmental disturbance on a scale hitherto not seen, or will demand oceanic equipment."

The implications of commodity price rises, combined with the world shortage of food, led a team of British environmentalists to consider the feasibility of increasing home food production. Their first discussion paper, *Losing Ground,* published in July by Earth Resources Research Ltd., suggested that Britain should aim to grow more of its own food, but that it could gain no real advantage if it planned to do so by increasing the use of agricultural chemicals, machinery, and feedstuffs, all of which Britain imported. The entire question was complicated by the fact that intensive, high-yield agriculture involved the use of fertilizers and pesticides that were often environmentally suspect. In the U.S. the Environmental Protection Agency banned the manufacture of two widely used pesticides, aldrin and dieldrin, because of their alleged carcinogenic properties.

Inevitably, conflicts arose over land use. A meeting of pulp and paper experts arranged by the FAO in Rome in May warned of an impending world shortage of paper, implying a need to increase the world's afforested areas. Vigorous campaigning by U.S. environmentalists helped to secure the inclusion of environmental safeguards in a bill regulating stripmining, but President Ford vetoed the legislation.

INTERNATIONAL COOPERATION

Although the third UN Conference on the Law of the Sea adjourned without reaching general agreement on any major issue, some progress was made during the year in protecting the marine environment. The FAO convened a meeting of countries bordering the Mediterranean. The areas with the most severe pollution problems were identified as the stretch from the Ebro River in Spain to the Arno in Italy, the northern part of the Adriatic, and the coastal waters of Lebanon and Israel. The principal cause of pollution was said to be the release of untreated sewage and industrial effluents, including mercury and pesticides. A general convention was proposed, covering specific matters such as the regulation of dumping, cooperation in pollution emergencies, discharge of oil from ships, land-based pollution, and pollution related to seabed exploitation.

On March 22 the Soviet Union and six other states bordering the Baltic signed a convention to protect the Baltic Sea from all forms of pollution. A five-year Anglo-Soviet environmental protection agreement, signed in London on May 21, covered joint action in combating air and water pollution, use of water resources, environmental monitoring, and the protection and management of ecological systems. On June 11 ten countries (Denmark, France, Iceland, Luxembourg, The Netherlands, Norway, Spain, Sweden, the U.K., and West Germany) signed a convention for the Prevention of Marine Pollution from Land-Based Sources. In the view of the U.K. Department of the Environment, this "Paris Convention," together with the Oslo Convention signed in February 1972 and conventions of the Inter-Governmental Maritime Consultative Organization, provided "a comprehensive framework for the control of pollution in the North Sea and the North-East Atlantic." In Britain the Dumping at Sea Act 1974 received royal assent on June 27.

On January 23 the Organization for Economic Co-operation and Development (OECD) published the findings of its study of transfrontier air pollution, in which ten member countries were participating. It found that pollutants are carried at altitudes of up to 2,000 m. for distances of several thousand kilometres, and it estimated that, if current policies remained unchanged, emissions of sulfur and nitrogen oxides would nearly double by 1980. The main areas of emissions were the United Kingdom, the Ruhr (W.Ger.), and parts of The Netherlands, Belgium, and France, as well as East Germany and parts of Czechoslovakia and Poland outside the OECD area. Significant rises in pollution levels were revealed in regions remote from pollution sources, such as northern Norway and the Faroe Islands. The OECD study was to continue until 1975.

In Nairobi, Kenya, the UN Environment Program (UNEP), created by the General Assembly following the 1972 Stockholm Conference on the Human Environment, reported on its progress in establishing the Earthwatch global monitoring system; in providing a training and information referral system and training and technical assistance on environmental matters for experts and institutions; in halting the spread of deserts and aridity; in protecting the marine environment; in the conservation of genetic resources; in "nonhazardous" pest control; in environmentally sound technologies for human settlements; and in the creation of a registry for potentially toxic chemicals being produced by factories. June 5, the second anniversary of the opening of the Stockholm conference, was again designated World Environment Day, but the occasion received little publicity.

Cooperation between the U.S. and the U.S.S.R. on environmental programs received further support at a July meeting between Pres. Richard Nixon and Soviet party leader Leonid I. Brezhnev. In the words of their final communiqué, they "agreed to designate in the territories of their respective countries certain natural areas as biosphere reserves for protecting valuable plant and animal genetic strains and ecosystems, and for conducting scientific research needed for more effective actions concerned with global environmental protection."

The year's second main UN conference, on world population, was held August 19–30 in Bucharest, Rom. It exposed once again the wide gulf between the developed countries, which urged population control, and the less developed countries, which regarded it as a subtle form of genocide. An innocuous Plan of Action was adopted, but there was little genuine agreement on what many environmentalists believed to be the main issue facing the world.

The Club of Rome, whose 1972 publication *The Limits to Growth* had predicted imminent catastrophe, took a slightly more optimistic stand. *Mankind at the Turning Point,* published during 1974, employed more sophisticated computer analyses than those used in *Limits,* and it treated the world by regions rather than as a monolithic whole. Urgent action was still seen as necessary, and shortages and overpopulation might still lead to disaster, but the authors at least held out the possibility that man could act to save himself. Even the blanket proscription of growth was modified; thus some industrialization in less developed regions was seen as desirable, though it should be balanced by less industrialization in more advanced countries. (MICHAEL ALLABY)

IAN STEWART—THE NEW YORK TIMES

Observers identify species among a flock of migratory birds near Kooragang Island in New South Wales, Austr. Plans by the Australian government to set aside part of the island for industrial development threaten the existence of these and the thousands of other birds that migrate there each year.

Man is stricken by "acid mist" in Chicago, caused by the leakage of silicon tetrachloride from a chemical storage tank on April 26.

THE NATURAL ENVIRONMENT

Although the energy supply crisis eased as the year advanced, forward-looking countries took stock of their real assets in terms of environmental values. Howard Brabyn, editor of the UNESCO magazine *Nature and Resources,* maintained that protected areas, representative of widespread ecosystems, were needed as standards for judging the effects of human use or modification elsewhere. Biosphere reserves should include completely untouched natural ecosystems, man-modified systems maintained by long-established land use practice, and even ravaged areas that showed potential for restoration.

The U.S. Earth Resources Technology Satellite (ERTS) continued to scan the whole earth every 18 days from a height of 550 mi. and to transmit electronic images back to its base. When suitably programmed, it could detect, measure, and interpret many of the large-scale dynamic disaster processes that are constantly occurring on the earth's surface. It could detect smoke from volcanic eruptions or from large-scale industrial centres and monitor ice conditions in Arctic regions, sandbanks in coastal waters, types of forest cover, the pattern of lands used for cultivation, or even the extent of land afflicted by exceptional drought. Its information was immediately available to scientists of all nations, but so far response, in the form of remedial measures by the national authorities concerned, had been slow.

Land Conservation. Addressing the tenth Commonwealth Forestry Conference at Oxford, Eng., in September, a distinguished ecologist, Sir Frank Fraser Darling, stressed the need for conserving the world's tropical forests as vital resources for timber supply, water control, and biological studies. Clearances made by small native populations of slash-and-burn cultivators, he said, did little harm and could even aid forest regeneration, but technology and vastly increasing overall human population made possible severe attacks on the forest. Replacement of indigenous forests by plantations of quick-growing conifers, such as Caribbean pines, was not an adequate recompense for the loss of age-old systems of plant and animal life, based on the local complex of rock, soil, and water regime.

A measure of the areas at risk was provided by the FAO, which estimated that 4,000,000,000 ha., or about one-third of the world's land surface, is wooded. Between 5 million and 10 million ha. were irretrievably destroyed each year. In the Far East there were 24 million "shifting cultivators" who felled 8 million ha. annually, though much of this was allowed to regenerate. The great danger was that accelerated destruction might outstrip replacement. Paul Richards, a leading U.S. tropical silviculturist, forecast the disappearance of true tropical forests within 30 years.

In the U.S. the Advisory Panel on Timber and the Environment, sponsored by the American Forestry Association, made a 20-point recommendation to the president, asking him to give timber resources their proper place in the national economy. Comprehensive conservation programs should include expansion of recreation and wilderness areas, protection of water supplies and fragile soils subject to erosion, protection of wildlife, including rare and endangered species of plants, animals, and birds, controlled timber harvesting commensurate with the forest's productive capacity, and improved utilization of wood fibre in all its forms. A Forestry Incentives program, announced in January, allocated $10 million for use in tree planting and timber stand improvement. Meanwhile, a controversy arose over the government-backed campaign that for 31 years had used the symbol of Smokey Bear to urge the public to help prevent forest fires. Some ecologists claimed the danger had been overstressed, to the point where much time and money had been spent extinguishing the naturally occurring fires that were actually a necessary part of the forest ecology. (*See* FORESTRY.)

Famine continued in the African belt of semidesert south of the Sahara. Suggestions for long-term solutions included control of nomadic grazing, planned pasture management, and encouragement of arable farming using high-yielding strains of grain, though none of these measures could be applied easily among the area's nomadic inhabitants. (*See* AGRICULTURE AND FOOD SUPPLIES: *Special Report.*)

Investigations by a team of Oxford and Cambridge University scientists into the history of the Thar, or Great Indian Desert, showed that desert conditions should not be regarded as stable over long periods of time. A. S. Goudie reported the discovery, in Gujarat, eastern Punjab, and Rajasthan, of an extensive series of "fossil sand dunes." Excavations revealed buried soils beneath these, with pottery surviving as evidence of human occupation on relatively well-watered land in prehistoric times. In modern times the dunes had become stabilized under a heavy vegetation of grass and acacia trees. Increased rainfall, now around 28 in. instead of the 10 in. considered critical for dune formation, was believed responsible for this amelioration, although changing agricultural and pastoral practices probably also played a significant part.

A problem in land conservation was reported from the Northern Jarrah forests of Western Australia, where a light tree cover of *Eucalyptus* invited clearance for productive pastures. The underlying saprolite rock was very saline, and removal of the forest, which had its own self-contained soil-water system, led to an influx of salty waters that in turn checked the growth of useful grasses. Similar problems were anticipated as strip mining for bauxite ores extended through the state forests, where mineral leases had been granted on an ill-advisedly lavish scale. Though mining leases provided for restoration of surface soil and vegetation, this might present major technical problems over such potentially saline lands.

In Ireland and Finland rising world fuel prices gave impetus to the harvesting of peat as an industrial fuel. The world reserve of this remarkable surface fuel, which consists of plant remains that have failed to decay because of prevailing sodden conditions, was estimated at 200,000,000,000 tons, fully dried. Allowing for differences in calorific value, this was equivalent to 100,000,000,000 tons of oil, or all the world's known proven oil reserves. The Irish State Peat Board, which was already exploiting 130,000 ac. of bogs by highly mechanized methods, decided to extend production by another 40,000 ac. to meet, overall, nearly one-third of the national energy requirement. Land conservation was written into the program. A substantial bottom layer of peat was left for mixing with the mineral soil below, which was drained to provide extensive areas of permanent pasture.

Water Conservation. Floods on several continents demonstrated man's failure to come to terms with the varying incidence of rainfall. In January exceptionally heavy rainstorms struck eastern Australia, with Brisbane recording 25 in. of rain within 72 hours. Freak high tides, associated with Cyclone Wanda, checked normal outflow of rivers to the sea, and vast areas were flooded, rendering thousands of people homeless. In the adjoining state of New South Wales over a million cattle and sheep were drowned, and losses were estimated at U.S. $240 million. Following days of nonstop rain, vast areas of central Australia, normally an arid desert, became a great inland sea.

In January there was also serious flooding in Kufra, a region in southeast Libya that is normally desert, and in March severe flooding over seven Brazilian states caused widespread loss of life. In August exceptionally heavy monsoon rains along the Himalayan ranges resulted in exceptional flooding in Pakistan, India, and Bangladesh. In the west the Indus burst its banks near Nawabshah, Pak., and overwhelmed great expanses of low-lying ground that were normally protected by extensive embankments linked to irrigation schemes. In the east the tributaries of the Ganges were estimated to have flooded half of the land surface of Bangladesh. Similar overflows struck Burma, where the Irrawaddy broke its banks, and Thailand and the Philippine Islands were also affected by floods.

In East Africa concern was expressed over the risk to water supplies inherent in the large-scale application of chemical fertilizers and pesticides to land that drained toward inland lakes. A critical area lay around Lake Victoria, a large but shallow body whose shores are shared by Uganda, Kenya, and Tanzania. Rising world prices made it profitable for peasant farmers to buy expensive imported chemicals to raise crop yields. Residues inevitably went downstream to the lake, where they threatened the valuable fishing industry. The persistent insecticide DDT, which had been used to protect the cotton crop, was being superseded by less toxic compounds such as endosulfan, which could be applied through ultra-low-volume sprayers needing minimal water supplies.

Pollution of Lake Superior by iron-ore wastes led to what Russell E. Train, head of the U.S. Environmental Protection Agency, called a "classic confrontation" between economic and environmental interests. After three years of effort by the federal government had failed to stop the Reserve Mining Co. from discharging waste from its Silver Bay, Minn., plant into the lake, suit was brought against the company by the

Justice Department, the states of Minnesota, Michigan, and Wisconsin, and five environmental groups. Some 67,000 tons of ground taconite rock were discharged into the lake daily. Residues had been found in the Duluth water supply, and the plaintiffs claimed they contained elements similar to those causing cancer among asbestos workers. A U.S. district judge ordered an immediate end to the dumping; and the plant closed for two days before the order was stayed. In June a federal appeals panel ruled that evidence of an immediate health hazard was insufficient to justify closing the plant, one of the area's chief employers. The ruling virtually assured that Reserve could continue dumping in the lake during the estimated three and a half to five years needed to convert to disposal on land.

As part of the UN Man and the Biosphere (MAB) program, a symposium held in Delhi, India, highlighted the problems raised by waterweeds in tropical water conservation. By ensuring constant supplies of clear water, often enriched by the residues of fertilizers, irrigation schemes provide ideal habitats for rapidly growing vegetation. The most serious pest, the water hyacinth *Eichhornia crassipes*, originated in South America but had since spread to most tropical countries. This and similar weeds check the desired slow flow of irrigation water, compete with semi-aquatic crops such as rice for nutrients, and interfere with navigation, fishing, and bathing. The symposium considered many means of combating these persistent, quick-growing weeds, including chemical herbicides, mechanical clearance, and biological enemies such as insects and fungi. The most effective measures appeared to be the planned, but temporary, drying-out of irrigation canals and the encouragement of weed-eating species of fish.

A serious water management problem arose in the Palm Coast development in northern Florida, where the International Telephone and Telegraph Corp. was sponsoring a program of marshland reclamation involving 92,000 ac. of swamps. The intention was to drain the area intensively by open canals, which would also serve for landscaping, fishing, and boating. The project was opposed by the Florida state authorities, who valued the marshland as a wilderness region and feared pollution of coastal recreation and fishing waters.

The increasing prosperity of the oil-rich but arid states of the Persian Gulf led to unusual developments in irrigation. At Abu Dhabi, for example, a U.S. team led by James Riley of the University of Arizona set up an Arid Lands Research Centre. One successful project used fresh water, obtained by the desalination of seawater and enriched with chemicals, in large greenhouses. To maintain humidity and lower temperatures, which often reached 100° F outside, the air circulating in the greenhouses was sucked in through curtains of waste water from the desalination plant. Growth in this controlled environment was so rapid that the resulting fresh vegetables and fruit could be marketed at prices competitive with imports.

A reduction of rainfall in northern Europe made the planning of future freshwater supplies a matter of critical importance. The British Water Resources Board published its long-term strategy in January. In the U.S. the Environmental Protection Agency ordered a nationwide study of drinking water after traces of organic chemicals identified as possibly carcinogenic were found in the New Orleans, La., water supply.   (HERBERT L. EDLIN)

Fish in an electrode chamber is subjected to various pollutants that cause it to "cough," a normal gill-clearing process to remove debris that has settled on the gills. A polygraph indicates the rate of the coughing. Such fish might be used as "watchdogs" to monitor the pollution levels of lakes and streams.

Wildlife. Anxiety over the continued existence of birds of prey and efforts to assure their survival continued. In the U.S. 300 eagles, mostly golden eagles, were said to be electrocuted yearly by power transmission lines. In Maine the only bald eagle nest contained a single addled egg, but two fertile eggs were transferred from Minnesota and the young raised. In southern France the Hawk Trust reported that helicopter training flights prevented the nesting of golden, short-tailed, and bonelli eagles in gorges. In Great Britain the osprey restoration project of the Royal Society for the Protection of Birds was again successful, with ten pairs raising 21 young.

Increased efforts were made to bring the traffic in captive wild birds under control. On May 4 customs officials at London Airport intercepted an illegal consignment from Thailand of five black-winged kites (*Elanus caeruleus*) and five shikra hawks (*Astur bandius*). One kite and two shikras died but the others were returned to Thailand and released. In August the International Council for Bird Preservation, at its world conference in Canberra, Austr., drew attention to the "massive and widespread abuses to wild birds and their populations" from the traffic in captured birds. All governments—especially those of Thailand, Singapore, and Great Britain (on behalf of Hong Kong)—were urged to take prompt and effective measures to reduce this traffic, and to ratify the Washington Convention on International Trade in Endangered Species of Wild Fauna and Flora. By October, 47 nations had signed the convention, but only the U.S., Nigeria, Switzerland, Togo, and Tunisia had ratified it.

In Queensland, Austr., the brindled rat-tail wallaby (*Onychogalea fraenata*), long thought to be extinct, was rediscovered. Five species of fish new to science were reported when a mobile barge oil rig was brought to the surface off the northwest coast of Australia. On May 16 the Bia national park, formerly part of the Bia South forest reserve, was established in Ghana to protect the olive, red, and black and white colobus monkeys, chimpanzee, giant forest hog, Red River hog, elephant, and a wealth of birds.

Lake Nakuru national park in Kenya was enlarged from 15,000 to over 50,000 ac. With the assistance of a donation of more than $400,000 from the World Wildlife Fund, the Kenya national parks administration had bought large tracts around the lake inhabited by defassa waterbuck, Bohor and Chanler's reedbuck, leopard, black rhinoceros, black and white colobus monkeys, and rock hyrax. The West German government provided funds for a sewage farm so that un-treated sewage from Nakuru town would not foul the lake water. In May 300 young Kenyans, organized by the International Student Movement, removed the town rubbish dump from the lake neighbourhood.

In May the Wildlife Conservation Organization of Ethiopia arranged to move as many Swayne's hartebeest (*Alcelaphus buselaphus swaynei*) as possible from Sankalle in the central plains, when they were endangered by pastoralists and mechanized farming, to Awash national park and to Nechisar, where a national park was proposed. Ninety hartebeest were moved to Awash and 120 to Nechisar. The operation was completed with only seven casualties.

An increase to 200 of the walia ibex (*Capra ibex walie*) in Ethiopia's Semien national park was reported, chiefly as a result of better control of poaching. From Arabia came reports that the Arabian oryx (*Oryx leucoryx*) had become so reduced by hunting that its survival as a wild animal was unlikely, although its survival in captivity seemed assured. In an article in *Oryx*, the journal of the Fauna Preservation Society (FPS), D. F. Owen warned that all spectacular butterflies were in danger from collectors and the butterfly trade, and that even in Great Britain 20 of the 56 resident species were threatened. The breakup of a British ring of traffickers in rare birds' eggs led to the arrest of Charles G. Sibley, a respected professor of ornithology at Yale University, who claimed that he had purchased the illegally gathered eggs for research purposes.

Scant help for the world's dwindling whale stocks could be found in the decisions of the 26th session of the International Whaling Commission, held in London in June. For the first time, geographic considerations and the size of whales killed were taken into account in fixing annual quotas—formerly numbers had been the sole criterion—but the ten-year moratorium on commercial whaling, considered urgently necessary at the 1972 Stockholm conference, was again rejected.

In September the International Union for Conservation of Nature (IUCN) called for drastic measures against elephant poaching and illegal traffic in ivory, which together threatened the survival of the African elephant. The imposition of minimal penalties, the subornation of those charged with enforcing controls, and the high price of ivory were blamed. With the aid of a grant from the FPS, IUCN had sent Paul Leyhausen, chairman of the cat group of its Survival Service Commission, to the small island of Iriomote in the Ryukyus, Japan, to investigate the situation of the newly discovered Iriomote cat. Leyhausen found urgent need for protection of the cat and also reported a dwarf pig, either a new species or a new subspecies of the wild boar (*Sus scrofa*). Subsequently half of Iriomote was declared a national park.

(C. L. BOYLE)

See also Agriculture and Food Supplies; Cities and Urban Affairs; Energy; Fisheries; Life Sciences.

[355.D; 534.C.2.a; 724.A]

ENCYCLOPÆDIA BRITANNICA FILMS. *The House of Man, Part II—Our Crowded Environment* (1969); *Problems of Conservation—Forest and Range* (1969); *Problems of Conservation—Minerals* (1969); *Problems of Conservation—Water* (1969); *The Garbage Explosion* (1970); *Problems of Conservation—Our Natural Resources* (1970); *Problems of Conservation—Soil* (1970); *Problems of Conservation—Wildlife* (1970); *A Field Becomes a Town* (1970); *The Aging of Lakes* (1971); *Turn off Pollution* (1971); *Poison Plants* (1972); *The Great Lakes* (1972); *The Environment: Everything Around Us* (1972); *Buffalo: An Ecological Success Story* (1972); *Controversy over Industrial Pollution: A Case Study* (1972); *The Ways of Water* (1973); *Noise: Polluting the Environment* (1973).

Epidemics:
see Health and Disease

Episcopal Church:
see Religion

Equatorial Guinea

The African republic of Equatorial Guinea consists of Río Muni, which is bordered by Cameroon on the north, Gabon on the east and south, and the Atlantic Ocean on the west; and the offshore islands of Macías Nguema Biyogo (until 1973 called Fernando Po) and Paglu (formerly Annobón). Area: 10,830 sq.mi. (28,050 sq.km.). Pop. (1974 est.): 303,000. Cap. and largest city: Malabo (formerly Santa Isabel), on Macías Nguema Biyogo (pop., 1970 est., 19,341). Language: Spanish. President in 1974, Francisco Macías Nguema.

Sovereignty over Mbanie Island in the Bay of Corisco had been disputed since 1972 by Equatorial Guinea and neighbouring Gabon, and in 1974 Gabon took the step of decreeing that it would only permit vessels flying the Gabonese flag to approach the island. An additional dispute concerning the border between Equatorial Guinea and Gabon was settled in July when President Nguema and Pres. Omar Bongo of Gabon visited the area and Nguema accepted the existing boundary as legitimate; it was presumed that the Mbanie question had also been resolved.

Reports circulated in Madrid in December by Equatorial Guinean exiles listed more than 300 opponents of the regime believed executed since independence in 1968. They alleged wholesale political and religious persecution and economic mismanagement under conditions of absolute dictatorship.

[978.E.7.b]

EQUATORIAL GUINEA
Education. (1970–71) Primary, pupils 49,500, teachers 635; secondary, pupils 5,200; vocational, pupils 720; teacher training, students 210; secondary, vocational, and teacher training, teachers 175.
Finance and Trade. Monetary unit: ekpwele, at par with the Spanish peseta, with (Sept. 17, 1974) a free rate of 57.54 ekpwele to U.S. $1 (133.12 ekpwele = £1 sterling). Budget (1969–70 est.): revenue 712.5 million ekpwele; expenditure 1,139,000,000 ekpwele. Foreign trade (1966): imports 1,278,000,000 ekpwele (58% from Spain in 1965); exports 1,817,000,000 ekpwele (97% to Spain in 1965). Main exports (1965): cocoa 44%; coffee 21%; timber 19%. Trade with Spain (1973): imports 863,316,000 ekpwele; exports 761,966,000 ekpwele.
Agriculture. Production (in 000; metric tons; 1973; 1972 in parentheses): sweet potatoes c. 28 (c. 28); bananas c. 12 (c. 12); cocoa c. 13 (15); coffee c. 6 (c. 7); palm kernels c. 2.1 (c. 2.1); palm oil c. 4.2 (c. 4.1). Livestock (in 000; 1972): sheep c. 30; cattle c. 3; pigs c. 6; goats c. 7; chickens c. 79.

Ethiopia

A kingdom of northeastern Africa, Ethiopia is bordered by Somalia, Afars and Issas, Kenya, the Sudan, and the Red Sea. Area: 471,800 sq.mi. (1,221,900 sq.km.). Pop. (1974 est.): 27,800,800. Cap. and largest city: Addis Ababa (pop., 1974 est., 1,046,300). Language: Amharic (official) and English. Religion: Ethiopian Orthodox (Coptic) and Muslim, with various animist minorities. Chiefs of state: Emperor Haile Selassie I

and, from Sept. 12, 1974, Crown Prince Asfa Wossen (nominated king); prime ministers in 1974, Aklilu Habte-wold until February 27, Endalkachew Makonnen until July 22, and Michael Imru until September 12; chairmen of the Provisional Military Administrative Council, Lieut. Gen. Aman Michael Andom from September 12 to November 23 and, from November 28, Brig. Gen. Teferi Benti.

In 1974 the revolt against the long-established feudal order in the empire of Ethiopia finally amassed sufficient force and popular backing to initiate a process of fundamental change. The movement began in mid-February when strikes and demonstrations by students, taxi drivers, and trade union organizations paralyzed life in the capital. The civilian demonstrators were joined by the armed forces in Addis Ababa, Asmara, and Harar, who were motivated by a number of considerations including the demand for increases in pay. Habte-wold's Cabinet resigned on February 27, and Endalkachew Makonnen formed a new Cabinet. After a series of events, including minor Cabinet changes and widespread action against corrupt officials throughout the country, the movement culminated on September 12 (the first working day of the Ethiopian New Year) with a proclamation ending the imperial rule and with the deposition and imprisonment of Emperor Haile Selassie I (*see* BIOGRAPHY). The throne was offered by the Provisional Military Administrative Council to Haile Selassie's named heir, 57-year-old Crown Prince Asfa Wossen, who was recuperating in Geneva from a serious stroke. According to the Military Council, the king would act as chief of state but would have no constitutional powers.

These changes were accompanied by measures against the old ruling group of aristocratic families and palace appointees. The Cabinet of former prime minister Habte-wold had already been arrested and his successor, Endalkachew, was arrested in July, together with several of his colleagues. On August 16

Demonstrators in Addis Ababa urged removal of Prime Minister Endalkachew Makonnen in March. Other demands, including freedom of the press and land for the poor, combined to bring about the eventual overthrow of Emperor Haile Selassie's regime in Ethiopia.

the Crown Council was abolished along with the Chilot (the emperor's final court of appeal) and the emperor's Private Cabinet. The Haile Selassie Foundation and the Haile Selassie Prize Trust were placed under the Ministry of Finance. Officials connected with such organizations and other prominent personalities from the old regime were incarcerated and awaited trial by a military tribunal on charges of corruption and maladministration. The emperor was detained with the expectation that he would be tried for alleged crimes against the people.

Parliament was suspended from September 12, together with the 1955 revised constitution (a new constitution, prepared by a committee formed under Endalkachew's government, was rejected by the Military Council). A civilian Technical Advisory Council, composed of 50 representatives from the various ministries, from the 14 provinces, and from such active organized groups as the teachers and trade unions, began work in October to propose a new constitution to the Dirgue (Amharic for "committee" and the commonly used name for the Military Council). The council itself was composed of 120 representatives of the armed forces and the police, under a chairman, Lieut. Gen. Aman Michael Andom (*see* OBITUARIES). General Aman as chairman of the council was effectual head of state, and replaced Michael Imru, who

served briefly as prime minister after Endalkachew's removal.

The Dirgue declared its intention to "return to barracks" when conditions were ready for civilian government. In the meantime, although it issued broad policy statements under the slogan of *Ethiopia Tikdem* ("Ethiopia First"), specific courses of action in key areas such as land reform were not defined. Guerrilla activities by the secessionist Eritrean Liberation Front late in the year posed a threat to the Dirgue's hold on national unity.

On November 23, Aman, who was generally considered a moderate, was abruptly removed from office. The following day Radio Ethiopia announced that he had been killed, and there were reports that he had died while resisting arrest. At the same time, 60 aristocrats and former officials, including Habte-wold and Endalkachew, were summarily executed (*see* OBITUARIES). On November 30 the government announced that the former emperor had signed papers authorizing the transfer of his fortune to the newly established Ethiopian Drought Relief and Rehabilitation Commission. It was unclear, however, whether the transaction could be consummated, since much of the money was in Swiss banks which, under Swiss law, cannot honour transfers of assets made under duress. Brig. Gen. Teferi Benti, who was said to have had no role in the executions, was elected chairman of the Military Council on November 28.

In the meantime, serious famine conditions continued in the provinces of Wallo and Tigre and there were indications that similar problems now had to be faced in virtually all provinces except Arusi. The Drought Relief and Rehabilitation Commission estimated in October that possibly 2.6 million people were affected.

[978.E.5.a]

ETHIOPIA

Education. (1970–71) Primary, pupils 655,427, teachers (1969–70) 11,964; secondary, pupils 135,300, teachers (1969–70) 3,971; vocational, pupils 6,200, teachers (1969–70) 508; teacher training, students 2,800, teachers (1969–70) 131; higher, students 4,543, teaching staff (1969–70) 503.

Finance. Monetary unit: Ethiopian dollar, with (Sept. 16, 1974) a par value of Eth$2.07 to U.S. $1 (free rate of Eth$4.79 = £1 sterling). Gold, SDRs, and foreign exchange, central bank: (June 1974) U.S. $235.7 million; (June 1973) U.S. $155.3 million. Budget (1973–74 est.): revenue Eth$832 million; expenditure Eth$857 million. Gross national product: (1971) Eth$4,702,000,000; (1970) Eth$4,470,000,000. Money supply: (May 1974) Eth$665.1 million; (May 1973) Eth$486.6 million. Cost of living (Addis Ababa; 1970 = 100): (May 1974) 113; (May 1973) 105.

Foreign Trade. (1973) Imports Eth$448.2 million; exports Eth$501.2 million. Import sources (1972): Italy 16%; Japan 15%; West Germany 11%; U.K. 9%; U.S. 9%; Iran 6%. Export destinations (1972): U.S. 35%; Italy 8%; West Germany 7%; Japan 6%; Saudi Arabia 6%; Afars and Issas 6%. Main exports: coffee 38%; pulses 16%; hides and skins 13%; oilseeds 10%.

Transport and Communications. Roads (1972) *c.* 23,400 km. (including 8,170 km. main roads). Motor vehicles in use (1972): passenger 31,933; commercial 7,410. Railways (1971): 1,088 km.; traffic (including traffic of Afars and Issas portion of Djibouti–Addis Ababa line) 80 million passenger-km., freight 243 million net ton-km. Air traffic (1972): 430.6 million passenger-km.; freight 15.3 million net ton-km. Telephones (Dec. 1972) 54,000. Radio receivers (Dec. 1972) 170,000. Television receivers (Dec. 1972) *c.* 21,000.

Agriculture. Production (in 000; metric tons; 1973; 1972 in parentheses): barley *c.* 1,500 (1,601); wheat *c.* 850 (923); corn *c.* 1,000 (1,004); millet *c.* 150 (158); sorghum *c.* 1,100 (1,138); sweet potatoes (1972) *c.* 256, (1971) *c.* 256; potatoes *c.* 169 (*c.* 166); linseed *c.* 66 (*c.* 66); sesame *c.* 100 (*c.* 105); sugar, raw value *c.* 145 (127); chick-peas *c.* 196 (*c.* 194); dry peas *c.* 133 (*c.* 132); dry broad beans *c.* 145 (*c.* 143); lentils *c.* 110 (*c.* 110); dry beans *c.* 78 (*c.* 76); coffee *c.* 180 (*c.* 175). Livestock (in 000; 1972): cattle *c.* 26,450; sheep *c.* 12,950; goats *c.* 11,370; horses *c.* 1,430; mules *c.* 1,460; asses *c.* 3,930; camels *c.* 994; poultry *c.* 50,000.

Industry. Production (in 000; metric tons; 1970–71): cement 183; petroleum products (1972) 367; cotton yarn 9.6; cotton fabrics (sq.m.) 79,000; electricity (kw-hr.) 585,000.

European Economic Community: *see* Commercial and Trade Policies; European Unity

European Unity

Toward the close of 1974, barely two years after Denmark, Ireland, and the U.K. had entered the European Economic Community (EEC) full of hope and expectation, a disillusioned Community was wondering whether it would survive as a "growing union of Western Europe," as U.S. Pres. John F. Kennedy had called it in 1962. The total disruption of the orderly monetary system designed at Bretton Woods, N.H., in 1944 had been followed in late 1973 by the oil-producing countries' decisions tripling the price of crude oil. The price of most other raw materials also rose rapidly. For the Community, the strain was almost too great. The balances of payments of the member countries, with the exception of West Germany and The Netherlands, moved into massive deficit, with Britain and Italy in the worst position. Unable to reach a common position on energy, the Nine went their divergent ways and quarreled bitterly with the U.S. in the process. The Nine were scarcely more united in their attitudes toward Israel and the Arab states in the wake of the October 1973 war.

Against this background, the new Labour government in Britain, fresh from its victory in the general election of February 1974, declared its intention of "renegotiating" the terms of British entry set out in the Treaty of Accession, which had been solemnly signed by Britain two years earlier and duly ratified. The British people, according to Labour, would be given "the final say—through the ballot box" on acceptance or rejection of EEC membership terms. As the year passed, however, the British government's attitude seemed to undergo a substantial change. By year's end it was clear that "renegotiation" meant little more than the normal process of continuing negotiation within the Community institutions.

Throughout most of the year, the Community made little progress toward the goals set at the Paris summit meeting of October 1972. The European Commission prepared its reports largely on time, but there was virtually no real progress on economic and monetary union, industrial policy, research and technology, the environment, the reorganization of Community institutions and decision-making processes, democratization and participation, and world trade negotiations under the General Agreement on Tariffs and Trade (GATT). Only in the negotiations with the 44 African, Caribbean, and Pacific (ACP) countries was there a significant advance.

Under these circumstances, the summit meeting held in Paris on December 9–10 was surprisingly harmonious. Progress was made in a number of areas, although serious economic and energy issues remained to be resolved. The Regional Development Fund to assist deprived rural regions and areas of contracting industry, regarded as vital by the British, Irish, and Italians, was set up with an allocation of 1.3 billion units of account (roughly $1.6 billion) over three years. In a move toward closer cooperation, it was agreed that the heads of government of the Nine would meet three times a year as the European Council rather than at an annual summit. Other decisions looked toward strengthening of the Community institutions, creation of a uniform Community passport, and harmonization of social security benefits in the member countries.

Britain's "Renegotiation." The Labour government's claim to renegotiation was first set forth by Britain's new foreign secretary, James Callaghan, to the Community's Council of Ministers on April 1, 1974. Its tone made an immediate bad impression on Britain's partners. Callaghan said his government would prefer a successful renegotiation rather than British withdrawal, but he then proceeded to attack the "dangerously overambitious" plans for economic and monetary union and European union by 1980. He also assailed the common agricultural policy (CAP), partly on the assumption that cheap food was still available somewhere for Britain. Finally, he claimed a "fair deal" on Britain's contribution to the Community budget on the ground that Britain would be paying more than its proper share.

In a second major statement on June 4, Callaghan modified his tone considerably. He limited the fields to be covered by renegotiation to four: the Community budget, CAP, improvements in trade and aid arrangements for the Commonwealth and less developed countries, and regional and industrial policies. Above all, he made it clear that Britain was not insisting on immediate renegotiation of the Treaty of Accession but was seeking changes in matters that could be handled initially by the Council of Ministers, though the budget issue would require special consideration. Callaghan estimated that Britain would be providing 24% of the Community's "own resources" by 1980, while its share in the Community's gross domestic product (GDP) would be only 14%.

At the December Paris summit, Prime Minister Harold Wilson reiterated that Britain was seeking revision of the budgetary formula rather than treaty renegotiation. While the communiqué emphasized that the "own resources" formula was basic to the Community (a point insisted on by France), the Commission was asked to formulate a "corrective mechanism" that would apply to members in economic difficulties.

Energy. The Community's failure to react effectively to the collapse of Western Europe's world position, following the united action of the Arab petroleum-exporting countries to raise oil prices and to cut back supplies to the West, had been exemplified in the Community's statement of Nov. 6, 1973, on energy. This was widely interpreted as a gesture of appeasement to the Arab governments. The statement published after the Copenhagen summit of December 14–15 confirmed the common position on energy and set out concrete measures to be taken. These included the drawing up of an energy balance sheet by the Commission and of proposals to resolve the energy crisis; concerted measures to limit energy consumption; a program on alternative sources of energy; negotiations on comprehensive arrangements with oil-producing countries; and the establishment of an energy committee.

The quarrel with the U.S. resulted from the refusal of the Nine, under French pressure, to consult with the U.S. over its projects for long-term cooperation with the Arab states. In March 1974, with relations seemingly at the breaking point, U.S. Pres. Richard M. Nixon threatened cuts in the number of U.S. troops in Europe. This produced the desired effect. The Nine agreed to consult with the U.S. collectively through the member country currently in the chair in the Council of Ministers. The U.S. tried to achieve an international energy program with 12 other oil-importing countries, including Canada, Japan, Norway and the Community countries, through the Energy Coordinating Group, while France attempted to marshal the Community separately. On July 31 the Arab League countries and the Nine took their first step toward economic cooperation by setting up joint machinery, including a European-Arab commission, which held its first meeting in November.

On November 15, in Paris, 16 oil-importing nations formed the International Energy Agency to replace the Energy Coordinating Group. The IEA, set up within the framework of the Organization for Economic Cooperation and Development, included all the members of the Coordinating Group except Norway, plus Austria, Spain, Sweden, Switzerland, and Turkey. Once again, France refused to join. Energy was a major subject of discussion at the Paris summit, but no concrete agreements were reached. On December 17 the EEC energy ministers, meeting at Brussels, agreed on joint objectives for energy use by 1985 and adopted a program of energy-saving measures.

Economic and Monetary Union. Economic and monetary union made no progress during the year. The worldwide inflation had an uneven effect on the member countries, thus widening the stability gap that had opened up in 1973 between the new "D-mark zone"—five Community countries (West Germany, The Netherlands, Belgium, Luxembourg, and Denmark) and two nonmember countries (Norway and Sweden) whose currencies were floating jointly—and the "free floaters" (Britain, Italy, and France). Consumer prices were rising by 15–20% in Britain and Italy, by only 7% in West Germany, and by less than 10% in The Netherlands. A second major divergence, which appeared in 1974, was in growth rates. Growth of GDP had been remarkably even throughout the

Community in 1973, generally within a range of 5–6%. In 1974 Britain's GDP actually declined, by about 1%, while GDP grew slowly (about 2%) in West Germany and Denmark and rapidly (4–5%) in France, Italy, Belgium, and Luxembourg.

Finally, the balance of payments problems of the Community became acute. The deficit of the Nine on current account was likely to amount to $16 billion–$20 billion in 1974, against a surplus of $1 billion in 1973. Within this total, the performances of the member countries were widely divergent. Italy and Britain were expected to have deficits of $10 billion, while West Germany was expected to record another huge surplus and the Dutch position appeared to be even better than its average performance over the previous ten years. The halt in the rise of most raw material prices by the summer, and a decision by the Community's finance ministers on October 21 to raise loans up to a total of $3 billion from oil-producing countries to help member states in balance of payment difficulties, provided two rays of light, albeit somewhat dim ones.

Industrial and Regional Policy. In December 1973 the Community had adopted a timetable for attaining the industrial policy targets set out in the Commission's memorandum of the preceding May. Fiscal barriers to mergers were to be removed gradually during 1974 and 1975, and two further directives on company law were to be produced; minimum standards would be set for a number of foodstuffs

This determined contingent of tractors rolled through Düsseldorf in November as German farmers protested the effect of Common Market policy on prices.

before 1978; and common policies would be adopted during 1974 for the aerospace, shipbuilding, and paper industries. However, the arrival in power of the Labour government halted any progress in the adoption of new common policies in 1974.

Agriculture. It was ironic that agreement among the Nine to examine the revision of CAP should come at a time (Oct. 2, 1974) when CAP was playing a major part in ensuring stability of food prices within the Community in the face of massively increased world price levels. Nevertheless, Community farm-product prices had to be raised twice during the year. The first increase, authorized on March 23, averaged $8\frac{3}{4}$%, while the second was a 5% across-the-board increase in support prices, accompanied by a 5% increase in the premiums for delaying slaughter of beef cattle and an extension of the ban on beef imports introduced in July.

The Commission was to submit a "stocktaking" of CAP, with recommendations, to the Council in February 1975. The British and West Germans both hoped to cut the cost of the policy, which was estimated at 3.8 billion units of account ($4.6 billion) for 1974, or 76% of the Community's total operating budget. Nevertheless, the total reversal of the earlier situation, in which Community farm-product prices had been well above world levels, had already transformed the operation of CAP. By October 1974 export subsidies had been suspended by the Community on most farm products. Far from restricting imports, the Community had by then imposed very tight export restrictions on cereals, rice, and sugar and was imposing levies on the limited amounts of cereals and sugar allowed to be exported and on exports of oils and oilseeds. More discerning observers, mindful that a shortfall of 1 or 2% in supplies could send prices shooting upward, were also taking a much more favourable attitude toward stocks—the so-called mountains of beef, butter, and some other commodities. In October Britain accepted an offer by the Community to make up its sugar shortage at the very favourable Community price of about £130 a ton (involving some element of subsidy), compared with the (November 8) world price level of £530.

Restrictive Practices and Monopolies. The Commission continued its action against restrictive practices and monopolies in 1974, and its decisions were upheld by the Community's Court of Justice in Luxembourg in two key cases. In one of them, the court found that a U.S. firm, Commercial Solvents Corp., was abusing a monopoly position by withholding supplies of an essential ingredient of a drug from one of its competitors in Italy. For the first time, the Commission used its powers to impose daily penalties on the company as long as it continued the practice. In the other judgment, the court upheld a Commission decision that HAG, a company producing decaffeinated coffee, was abusing trademark rights by preventing the import of its legitimately licensed products from one Community country to another in order to divide up the market. Alleged monopoly abuses by General Motors and BMW automobile companies, major oil companies, IBM, and Radio Luxembourg were investigated during the year.

Living and Working Conditions. On Jan. 21, 1974, the Council of Ministers adopted a three-stage social action program for 1974–76. The first set of seven projects was presented soon afterward, and on June 10 the Council adopted three of them, covering Social Fund aid for migrant and disabled workers,

WIDE WORLD

other help for disabled workers, and the setting up of a Community industrial safety committee. The other projects included a directive on equal pay for men and women, achievement of a 40-hour week and four weeks' annual paid vacation by 1976, the setting up of a European foundation for improvement of the environment and living and working conditions, and a directive on legislation covering collective dismissals of workers.

Relations with Other Countries. In one of their most positive achievements of the year, the Nine, on July 28 in Kingston, Jamaica, reached a broad outline agreement on trade and aid with the 44 ACP countries. The arrangement was to come into force on Feb. 1, 1975. The ACP countries obtained a significant concession from the Nine when the latter agreed that a financial guarantee on the ACP countries' earnings from their exports to the Nine could cover goods other than eight named primary products. The Community also undertook to ease its rules of origin for ACP goods and to reduce as far as possible barriers to ACP exports arising from CAP. The Nine confirmed that they no longer sought reciprocal concessions for their exports to the ACP countries. Still to be decided were the terms of development aid from the Community as well as a long-term agreement on sugar.

The Commission proposed, for 1975, a series of improvements in the Community's generalized system of preferences, available to all less developed countries. These included extension of the list of processed agricultural products covered by the system and increases in the margins of preference for most processed agricultural products. The Community offered to contribute $500 million to a $3 billion UN fund to aid the less developed countries most seriously affected by the rise in the cost of oil, provided the remainder was pledged by other countries (one half by the oil-producing countries themselves). In October the Nine agreed to release $150 million of this sum unconditionally as an outright grant.

The delay in passage of the U.S. trade bill until late in the year meant that the GATT negotiations on worldwide reduction of trade barriers were unable to get under way in 1974. On October 30 the Commission sent new proposals for a negotiating mandate to the Nine, replacing the somewhat vague proposals agreed on in June 1973. (*See* COMMERCIAL AND TRADE POLICIES.) Following the demise of the military regime in Greece, preliminary steps were taken toward full reactivation of that country's association agreement with the Community.

Council of Europe. With the enlargement of the Community to nine members and the extension of its purview to new fields of policy, the question of the Council of Europe's usefulness became acute. In March 1974 the Council published a report announcing that it would concentrate its efforts on eight specific areas: human rights (in which it had played a notable role), education, youth programs, migrant workers, public health, environment, local authorities, and the administration of justice. A new secretary-general, Georg Kahn-Ackermann, a Social Democrat member of the West German Bundestag, took office with the announced intention of making the Council cost-effective. (DEREK PRAG)

See also Defense; Exchange and Payments, International; Taxation; Trade, International; and articles on the various countries.

[534.F.3.b.iv; 971.D.7]

Exchange and Payments, International

The rise of oil prices, together with the aftermath of the inflationary boom of 1973 and the subsequent slippage into recession (*see* ECONOMY, WORLD), created severe turbulence in international payments during 1974. The oil crisis began in mid-October 1973, after a new outbreak of war in the Middle East, with the decision of Arab oil-producing countries to curtail production of crude oil, place an embargo on oil exports to the U.S. and The Netherlands, and raise the price of oil. The non-Arab members of the Organization of Petroleum Exporting Countries (OPEC, which included Algeria, Ecuador, Indonesia, Iran, Iraq, Kuwait, Libya, Nigeria, Qatar, Saudi Arabia, the United Arab Emirates, and Venezuela) subsequently also raised their prices.

At first, the prospective supply shortages appeared to be the greatest threat to the industrial world; but the embargo on the U.S. was lifted in March 1974, and by April the output of Saudi Arabia, the world's largest producer, had returned to the September 1973 level. Thus, the critical problem was not quantity but price. Before the price increase in October 1973, the average payment to producing countries for a barrel of oil was less than $2; by late 1974, it exceeded $10.

Petrodollars. The quintupling of the oil price had a brutal impact on the balances of payments of industrial nations, for a change of only ten cents per barrel translated itself into an increase in the import bill of nearly $1 billion. The U.S. alone spent about $27.5 billion on oil imports in 1974, up from $8.8 billion for substantially the same volume of oil in 1973. In the aggregate, payments to OPEC countries by oil-importing nations, which had amounted to $15 billion in 1972 and $22 billion in 1973, reached $90

Table I. External Surplus and Investment of Oil-Exporting Countries, January–November 1974

Item	$000,000,000	Percent
Eurocurrency deposits	18.0	39
Investments in the U.S.	10.5	23
Investments in the U.K.	7.5	16
Investments in and loans to other industrial countries*	5.0	11
Loans to international financial institutions	3.0	7
Aid to less developed countries	2.0	4
Total investable surplus	46.0	100
Memorandum item: Increase in published official reserves of oil-exporting countries†	24.1	

*Does not include private loans, purchases of real estate and corporate securities, and other investments in Europe and Japan.
†January–October 1974.
Sources: U.S. Treasury Dept. and International Monetary Fund.

Table II. Current Accounts of Industrial Countries

	($000,000,000) Total current balances			1974 balance	
Country	1972	1973	1974	Increase in net oil imports(−)	Adjusted current balance*
Germany, West	1.0	4.5	9.0	−6.3	15.3
United States	−8.4	0.5	−3.3	−14.8	11.5
Japan	6.6	−0.1	−4.8	−12.0	7.2
Netherlands, The	1.1	1.8	1.5	−0.5	2.0
Belgium	1.4	1.4	0.3	−1.2	1.5
France	0.3	−0.7	−7.5	−6.3	−1.2
Canada	−0.6	−0.4	−1.5	0.3	−1.8
Italy	2.0	−2.4	−8.3	−5.0	−3.3
United Kingdom	0.2	−3.1	−9.0	−5.2	−3.8
All others	0.9	0.9	−13.8	−7.5	−6.0
Total	4.5	2.5	−37.5	−59.0	21.5

*Current account balance excluding increases in net expenditures on oil in 1974.
Source: Adapted from OECD, *Economic Outlook* (Dec. 1974).

Evangelical Churches:
see Religion

CHART 1.

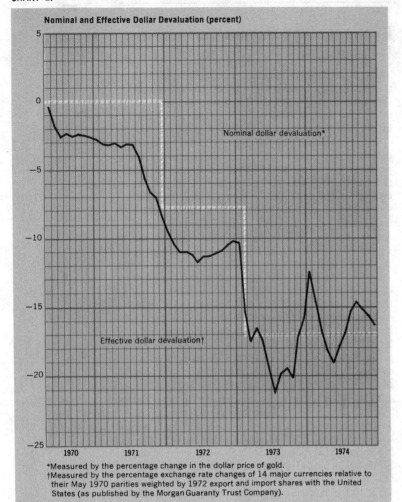

Nominal and Effective Dollar Devaluation (percent)

Nominal dollar devaluation*

Effective dollar devaluation†

*Measured by the percentage change in the dollar price of gold.
†Measured by the percentage exchange rate changes of 14 major currencies relative to their May 1970 parities weighted by 1972 export and import shares with the United States (as published by the Morgan Guaranty Trust Company).

and, outside Europe, the Philippines, Mexico, and Brazil also borrowed heavily.

Some OPEC countries—Indonesia, Iran, Nigeria, and Venezuela, in particular—increased their imports considerably during 1974; the economies of these nations had large absorptive capacity. Other oil-exporting countries, having small populations and undiversified economies, would be unable for years to spend on imports more than a fraction of their oil earnings and income from investments abroad. On the other hand, oil-importing countries, which could reduce oil imports only gradually by conservation and creation of substitutes, would have deficits that they, as a group, would have to cover by the use of reserves and borrowed funds.

By mid-1974 it came to be realized that private markets could not continue much longer to take the risks of accepting large amounts of petrodollars, which were for the most part repayable at short notice, and of lending them out for a number of years to countries that were already heavily in debt. The U.K. and the continental European Economic Community (Common Market) countries other than West Germany favoured an International Monetary Fund (IMF) "facility" of up to $30 billion to soak up OPEC dollars and lend them out to oil-importing countries. The U.S. proposed a "common loan and guarantee facility" to redistribute up to $25 billion in two years—a "financial safety net" linked to the OECD (Organization for Economic Cooperation and Development), an organization composed exclusively of industrial countries. As 1974 drew to an end there was increasing recognition that "recycling" petrofunds meant merely the piling of debt on top of debt. It could not be a substitute for the adjustment of unsustainable imbalances.

Oil and Non-oil Deficits. The overlay of oil deficits was superimposed on trade imbalances that stemmed from factors other than oil, such factors as differences in the degree and the pervasiveness of inflation and their consequences for costs, productivity, and economic efficiency. Only West Germany had a large surplus on current account; Belgium and The Netherlands had small surpluses. Other large European industrial countries and Japan had deficits on trade and services (see Table II). These deficits were matched by borrowings abroad, mainly in the U.S. and Eurodollar markets. In January the U.S. lifted all restrictions on lending abroad, which opened up the U.S. to foreign borrowers for the first time since 1963.

West Germany's current surplus was bigger than in 1973. Most of the surplus was achieved through sales to other European countries, especially Italy, France, and the U.K. In effect, West Germany's trade surplus exceeded its oil deficit. In the U.S., a trade deficit of $3 billion was recorded in 1974—a sharp reversal from the $1.4 billion surplus in 1973. But the 1974 deficit was fairly small when it is recognized that the cost of oil imports was almost $17 billion larger than the year before. The non-oil trade balance thus improved sufficiently to cover most of the increase in the cost of oil imports. The non-oil surplus was helped by higher export prices; much of it was earned in trade with Western Europe.

The entire current account of the U.S. showed a substantial deficit in 1974, in part because of the increase in payments to foreigners on their investments. The so-called basic balance, which includes long-term capital transactions, was heavily in deficit. Canada, despite a foreign trade performance that ended

billion in 1974. In addition, payments to OPEC countries for other exported goods and for services, including income from investments abroad, amounted to $5 billion. But imports of OPEC countries, although rising rapidly in percentage terms, fell far short of their increased oil revenues. As a result, these nations had a surplus of approximately $60 billion for 1974. These "petrodollars," which could not be spent, were invested for the most part in the major industrial countries.

The investment of OPEC surpluses could be identified only roughly (see Table I). Most of the funds were placed in the U.S., British, and Eurocurrency markets. In the Eurocurrency market they were almost entirely in Eurodollars (U.S. dollars held in banks outside the U.S., including foreign branches of U.S. banks). Large acquisitions by Arab interests of businesses in the U.S. and Europe were regarded with misgivings, and in defense industries were not approved by governments.

Most of the petrodollars invested in the U.S. market originated in Venezuela, Indonesia, and African oil-exporting countries. Middle East funds were placed principally in the Eurodollar market. Funds from Kuwait, the United Arab Emirates, and Nigeria, which had traditional ties to London, were also invested in sterling, as was a part of Saudi Arabia's moneys.

The largest Eurodollar borrower was the U.K., replacing Italy, which had that unenviable ranking in 1973; France was the second largest borrower. Spain in surplus, had a current-account deficit. However, it was easily covered by capital inflows.

A number of nations, such as the U.K., France, and Italy, ran deficits not only with oil-exporting countries but also with other oil-importing countries. There was a growing realization that they should try to secure a better balance of payments on non-oil trade without attempting to improve their overall balances by deflating domestic demand, depreciating exchange rates, or imposing restrictions on imports. Governments thus pledged themselves to avoid beggar-my-neighbour policies. The difficulty was that as the relatively easy initial stage of the new oil situation came to an end, the full effect of inflated oil prices on the payments balances, on domestic economic policies, and on trade policies among these oil-importing nations would be felt only in 1975.

Generalized Floating. The strains created by the abrupt increase in oil prices and the wide swings in the balances of payments did not lead during 1974 to particularly large fluctuations in exchange rates among the main currencies. Indeed, the changes were much smaller than in 1973 when, beginning in March, the major currencies entered the condition of generalized uncoordinated floating.

In this perspective, movements in the effective exchange rate of the dollar relative to other major currencies (see Chart 1) were significant. From mid-March to early July 1973, the dollar fell sharply; from early July 1973 to late January 1974, it strengthened appreciably—at first, because of a recovery in the U.S. balance of payments and, beginning in October 1973, because of the general feeling that the U.S. was in a better position than Europe and Japan to withstand both the domestic and balance of payments effects of the rise in oil prices.

In late January 1974, however, the opinion developed that the rise in the dollar exchange rate had been overdone and that the U.S., too, was exposed to the adverse effects of the new oil situation; the removal in January of controls on U.S. capital outflows was also a factor. In late May, the dollar rate fell to a point at which it was only 2½% of where it had stood when the floating began in February 1973. Thereafter, from June through September, the dollar strengthened, principally because of the rise in U.S. interest rates; but, beginning in October, as U.S. interest rates trended downward and Arab governments were reportedly diversifying their foreign exchange holdings, the dollar again sagged. At the end of December, it stood only 0.5% below its level of February 1973; it had climbed above that level by as much as 2% in early September.

The fluctuations of several leading currencies in terms of the dollar were also affected by conditions in each of the countries concerned (see Chart 2 and Table III). The French franc was "temporarily" floated in January 1974; in March the French and the Italian dual exchange rate systems, established in 1971 and early 1973, respectively, were abolished and commercial rates became applicable for all transactions. The Spanish peseta was floated in January; the Austrian schilling was upvalued de facto in May; the South African rand was floated in June; the Australian and New Zealand dollars were devalued in September by 12 and 9%, respectively; the Israeli pound was devalued by 43% in November; and the Hong Kong dollar was floated in November. The currencies of the oil-producing countries remained stable in terms of the dollar and, therefore, depreciated

against the stronger continental European currencies.

The generalized float had evident benefits. It relieved pressures in foreign exchange markets and, above all, relieved central banks—especially those that had to absorb large speculative fund inflows—of the obligation to expand domestic money supplies by purchasing foreign exchange at rates declared in advance to the markets. "In other words," as the Bank for International Settlements—which ought to know—commented in its 1974 annual report, "the authorities did not present the same sitting target for attack as they did formerly. Of course, those inflows were not simply a consequence of exchange rates being fixed. They were due rather to the maintenance of unrealistic exchange rates in situations of major disequilibrium."

The drawbacks of floating rates became visible even more forcefully in 1974 than in 1973. First, the wide and erratic movements that had little to do with the behaviour of basic purchasing power relationships among currencies made dealings in foreign currencies both tempting and risky. The market became a speculative playground. Speculation offered opportunity for profits, which accrued to private operators as well as to central banks. Widely publicized losses were, however, incurred by banks and others in the U.S., Switzerland, West Germany, Britain, Italy, and Belgium. Furthermore, floating rates became a factor in the acceleration of inflation. For those currencies that floated downward, the decline in their value on the foreign exchange markets forced up the costs of imports.

But the large swings in exchange rates also gave an impulse to inflation in that they contributed to distrust in money. Finally, floating was, more often than not, "dirty": some countries with payments deficits were unwilling to accept the depreciation of their currencies that market forces would have brought about. To prevent this from happening, Italy, the U.K., and Japan intervened in the markets with billions of dollars that they borrowed rather than owned. It was also feared that governments might use intervention to make exports cheaper.

To counter exchange-rate manipulation, governments agreed, through the IMF, on a code of good conduct for floating currencies. These guidelines are reviewed below. And to help prevent crises that would damage the fragile confidence in the international banking system, the central banks of key countries in September worked out safeguards "for the provision of temporary liquidity" to commercial banks, "if and when necessary." The commitment for central banks to act as lenders of last resort in Eurocurrency markets was deliberately worded very vaguely, for

Currency	Parity on May 5, 1971 In dollars per unit	Appreciation or depreciation (−) against the U.S. dollar (%)		Cumulative change	Market rate on Dec. 31, 1974 In dollars per unit
		May 5, 1971 to Dec. 31, 1973	Dec. 31, 1973 to Dec. 31, 1974	May 5, 1971 to Dec. 31, 1974	
Swiss franc	.2287	34.5	28.3	72.5	.3945
Austrian schilling	.0385	30.8	18.3	54.7	.0595
German mark	.2732	35.3	12.2	51.9	.4149
Dutch guilder	.2762	28.1	13.1	44.8	.4000
Norwegian krone	.1399	24.6	10.9	38.3	.1935
Danish krone	.1333	19.2	12.0	33.5	.1780
Swedish krona	.1933	12.9	12.7	27.3	.2460
French franc	.1800	18.2	6.1	25.4	.2257
Japanese yen	.0028	28.4	−6.8	19.7	.0033
Belgian franc	.0200	21.0	−5.9	13.9	.0228
British pound	2.4000	−3.2	1.1	−2.1	2.3490
Italian lira	.0016	2.8	−6.7	−4.1	.0015

Table III. How the Currencies Fared: 1971–74

the authorities were anxious to avoid giving the impression that they would automatically bail out any bank that found itself in trouble.

The regime of floating that was to assure freedom for market participants resulted in controls. These included the policing of exchange markets; steps to repulse unwanted dollars (as in West Germany and Switzerland in November, reversing an earlier liberalization of fund inflows); and import restrictions (as in Italy and Denmark in May). There were also limitations, prohibitions, or taxes on exports (as in the U.S. on grain exports, with exports to the Soviet Union reduced to only two-thirds of what had been arranged). Barter of product for product, which thrives during times of inflation, slump, and uncertainty, came to be practiced increasingly even among the countries outside the sphere of influence of the Soviet Union.

Monetary Reserves. The first fact of international life with regard to monetary reserves in 1974 was the visible reluctance of deficit countries to reduce their holdings of gold. Governments were reluctant to sell gold because of the wide disparity between the official price of $42.22 an ounce and the price in the international market, which during the year ranged from $116.50 to $197.50 per ounce. In June the U.S. and other major countries agreed that gold reserves could be used as collateral, at market-related prices, for international loans. Italy, which had a large proportion of its reserves in gold, borrowed $2 billion from West Germany in September, with gold supplied as collateral valued at $120 per ounce (80% of the average market price during July–August).

Other governments, most prominently those of the U.K. and France, preferred to retain monetary reserves as a support for borrowing and, as already noted, borrowed substantial amounts of dollars. Such loans boosted the reserves of those nations, but reserves ceased to provide an accurate reflection of the pressures on the currency. In fact, movements in the reserves of deficit countries were surprisingly small.

It had been, more often than not, taken for granted that exchange-rate floating would reduce the extent to which governments would want to retain reserves for intervention in the exchange market. But, despite widespread floating, governments continued to value their reserves. There were several reasons for this. First, the authorities were determined to manage the float rather than to allow it to occur without intervention. Second, even under the regime of floating, governments wanted to display reserves to help pre-

serve confidence in them in the U.S. and Eurodollar markets, thereby enabling them to borrow large sums of money. Last, but perhaps not least, governments may have wanted to leave open the option of returning, when circumstances permitted, to fixed (but, of course, adjustable) exchange rates. Such a move would require respectable reserves appropriate for the circumstance. Smaller countries that pegged their currencies to a major floating currency wanted reserves to deal with greater uncertainties all around.

Another fact of international monetary life in 1974 was the buildup of monetary reserves by oil-exporting countries. The nine principal OPEC countries increased their reserves, as reported to the IMF, by $25 billion during the 12 months ended September 1974 to $38 billion. Saudi Arabia alone added during the period $7.5 billion to its reported reserves; these stood at $11.5 billion in September, the fourth largest in the world (after West Germany, the U.S., and Japan).

Massive foreign currency borrowings by deficit countries and massive additions to reserves by the surplus countries exporting oil, together with sizable additions to reserves by a number of non-oil, commodity-producing countries, brought about an extraordinary rise in the world total of monetary reserves: $210 billion in September 1974, compared with $188 billion a year earlier (*see* Chart 3). In 1974, for the fifth year in succession, global monetary reserves—measured in terms of U.S. dollars but with gold still valued at the $42.22 per ounce official price—thus expanded in ways that had very little to do with the growth in the volume of world trade. The principal cause lay in worldwide inflation and the oil price increase, with the foreign exchange component, principally dollars, the largest factor in the growth. Also significant was the increase in U.S. liquid liabilities to foreign governments and central banks and to international monetary institutions. Apart from this increase in official international liquidity, there was a sharp rise in private international liquidity (holdings of liquid assets that can be realized readily to settle international debts; domestic liquidity consists of assets to settle domestic debts).

The Deadlock on Gold. Confronted with huge balance of payments deficits, the governments of countries that rebuilt their gold stocks after World War II (*see* Table IV) sought to make the most of the international reserve asset they possessed in relatively large quantities. At first, they had envisaged gold settlements among the Common Market countries at market-related prices; but, in the wake of the oil crisis, they began to realize that gold could not be left unused worldwide. It was not that the oil-consuming countries would want to barter gold against oil; rather, it was that they would be much less worried about using dollars, whether owned or borrowed, when they had gold reserves carrying a higher valuation behind them.

In April the Common Market finance ministers reached a sufficient degree of agreement about utilizing gold stocks as instruments of international settlements to approach the U.S. government, but they had no success. Meanwhile, the Italian crisis broke out, and in mid-June the U.S. and other financial powers accepted the political necessity of allowing the hard-pressed Italian government to pledge monetary gold, of which Italy was one of the main holders, as backing for foreign loans at market-related prices. This arrangement, as already noted, led to the $2 billion

Table IV. Monetary Gold Stocks

Country	September 1949 $000,000,000	September 1949 % of total	September 1974 $000,000,000	September 1974 % of total
United States	24.7	70.9	11.7	23.4
Germany, West	—	—	5.0	10.0
France	0.5	1.5	4.3	8.5
Switzerland	1.5	4.3	3.5	7.0
Italy	0.3	0.7	3.5	7.0
Netherlands, The	0.2	0.5	2.3	4.6
Belgium	0.7	2.1	1.8	3.6
United Kingdom	1.4*	4.1	0.9	1.8
Japan	—	—	0.9	1.8
All countries	33.4	95.7	43.1	86.5
International institutions†	1.5	4.3	6.7	13.5
Total	34.9	100.0	49.9	100.0

Note: Valued at $35 per fine ounce in September 1949 and at $42.22 per ounce in September 1974.
*Includes a small amount of U.S. and Canadian dollars held in the exchange equalization account.
†IMF, Bank for International Settlements, etc.

West German credit to Italy in September. In December at a meeting in Martinique, U.S. Pres. Gerald Ford and French Pres. Valéry Giscard d'Estaing agreed that "as one specific measure to strengthen the existing financial framework . . . it would be appropriate for any government which wished to do so to adopt current market prices as the basis of valuation for its gold holding." Subsequently, France announced that, beginning in January 1975, it would value its gold stock at market-related prices.

At the same time, the IMF was studying "the arrangements for gold." The matter was of real urgency because governments sought, under the periodic five-year review, a substantial increase in IMF quotas; however, if quota increases were authorized, 25% of the increased subscriptions would have to be paid in gold. Governments did not want to use gold for this purpose, and the IMF charter was to be amended in 1975 to permit payment in hard currencies or SDRs.

The U.S. Treasury's position remained that gold should be deinstitutionalized as an international monetary instrument. This had already taken place in U.S. domestic monetary arrangements, with the last vestige eliminated in 1968 when gold ceased to be used as partial backing for Federal Reserve notes. In the view of U.S. Secretary of the Treasury William E. Simon—as stated on December 3 in announcing a sale of gold out of the Treasury's stock in early January 1975, after Americans had, on Dec. 31, 1974, recovered the right to own gold in any form they chose—a wide range of international agreement had already been reached on gold: "One important part of that agreement is that the international monetary role of gold should be reduced and that we should move toward the situation internationally in which gold is accorded a legal status no different from that of other commodities."

On December 5, Federal Reserve Board Chairman Arthur F. Burns, while reluctantly supporting the Treasury's sale of a small amount of gold, pointedly disagreed with Simon on the ground that "it would hardly be desirable to dispose of any sizable part of our reserve assets," especially because "the precise role of gold in the international monetary system is yet to be determined." Gold, at $11.7 billion, represented in October the bulk of U.S. liquid international assets, which totaled $15.9 billion; the difference consisted almost entirely of IMF positions and SDRs.

At the end of 1974, world gold matters, which are political in the final analysis, were thus in full evolution. Governments seemed to accept the thought that, in the future, inflows of gold into the official monetary reserves could not be relied upon to provide the bulk of new liquidity; liquidity was to be "managed" through SDRs, which would become "the principal reserve asset." Gold was to be divested of its traditional function as the common denominator of currencies and the yardstick of monetary values; the SDR was to do the job. In brief, no government sought to return to the gold standard.

Under the law of Aug. 14, 1974, and beginning on Dec. 31, 1974, the right of private gold bullion ownership was restored after 41 years of prohibition. A year earlier, in December 1973, it may be recalled, the U.S. Department of the Treasury reinterpreted its gold regulations to permit the purchase of any gold coins originally minted prior to 1960, including re-strikes of those coins in subsequent years. During 1974, Americans bought these so-called bullion coins,

CHART 2.

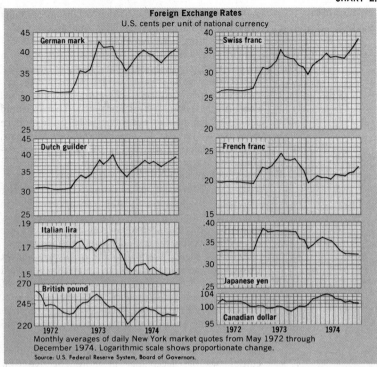

Foreign Exchange Rates
U.S. cents per unit of national currency

Monthly averages of daily New York market quotes from May 1972 through December 1974. Logarithmic scale shows proportionate change.
Source: U.S. Federal Reserve System, Board of Governors.

CHART 3.

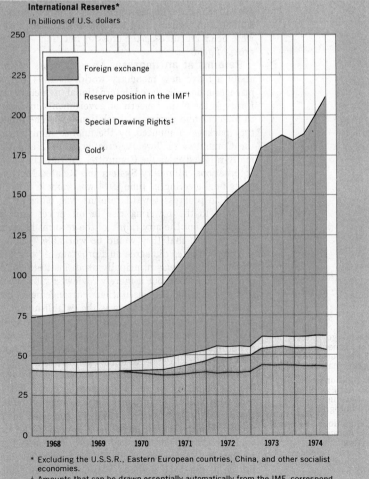

International Reserves*
In billions of U.S. dollars

- Foreign exchange
- Reserve position in the IMF†
- Special Drawing Rights‡
- Gold§

* Excluding the U.S.S.R., Eastern European countries, China, and other socialist economies.

† Amounts that can be drawn essentially automatically from the IMF, corresponding to members' gold subscriptions *plus* amounts of their currencies sold by the Fund to other members (net) *plus* outstanding lendings to the Fund.

‡ Special Drawing Rights are unconditional international reserve assets created by the IMF; they are allocated to participating members in proportion to their IMF quotas.

§ Valued at $35 an ounce from 1966 to September 1971; at $38 from December 1971 to December 1972; and at $42.22 thereafter.

Source: International Monetary Fund.

mainly of Mexican and Austrian origin, in amounts estimated at 3.5 million–4 million ounces.

The Treasury and the Federal Reserve were opposed to the restoration of private gold ownership in bullion form on a fixed date; but, in early December, the Treasury made it known that it would not recommend congressional reconsideration of that fixed date. At the same time, it announced that it would sell 2 million ounces out of its 276 million-ounce stockpile on January 6. The Federal Reserve Board chairman endorsed the Treasury's sale, without enthusiasm, as a means of limiting the risks of transition to private ownership. The Treasury reassured Congress that "later sales" of gold would be for "smaller amounts." By selling gold, the Treasury sought to reduce the import demand for the metal, since output in the U.S. was much smaller than the country's use of gold in jewelry, the arts, dentistry, and industry.

Political, social, economic, and monetary unrest throughout the world in 1974 led to a strong demand for gold as a hedge against inflation or as a means of protection against a decline in the exchange value of a country's currency. But while seeking protection by purchasing gold individually, people were by no means ready to recognize that the way to get out of the world's seemingly intractable monetary difficulties was the acceptance of more effective constraints on the use that governments make of their ability to print money. Having been taught for decades to blame the depression of the 1930s on the gold standard, Americans had not yet realized that they were being crucified on the cross of inflation—not the cross of gold.

Reforms at an Impasse. After 12 years of talk about a brave new monetary world, in 1974 the oil price eruption displaced international monetary reforms as the main concern of governments in regard to financial and commercial relationships. The monetary package announced by the finance ministers of the Committee of Twenty, created in 1972 and formally referred to as the Committee on Reform of the International Monetary System and Related Matters, at its final meeting in June 1974 was modest. The inability to progress toward reforms was officially attributed to the towering rise in oil prices and its aftermath; but the airy fabric of the reforms held out little promise that they would be workable.

The committee did agree on a program of "immediate action" that was principally of an institutional or procedural nature, but it merely reviewed substantive matters. Among the institutional arrangements accepted by the governments was the establishment of an interim committee of the IMF Board of Governors that, after amendment of the charter, would become a permanent council with "the necessary decision-making powers to supervise management and adaptation of the monetary system, to oversee the continuing operation of the adjustment process and to deal with sudden disturbances which might threaten the system." The interim committee consisted of 27 finance ministers and central bank governors, an unwieldy body to deal efficiently with delicate monetary matters in a suspicious world. A joint ministerial committee of the IMF and the World Bank was established to "study" the transfer of real resources to less developed countries and to recommend measures in that regard.

Another institutional innovation, which became effective on July 1, was the adoption, "for an interim period," of a method of valuation of the SDR based on a basket of 16 currencies; the change was of an operational nature and, pending an amendment to the charter, the SDR remained defined in gold at $35 an ounce. Its attribute as the principal unit of account did not, however, make the SDR the principal reserve asset. Only a new supply of SDRs sufficient to meet the demand for reserves would make it the principal reserve asset; there was in 1974 no prospect of an SDR issue on that scale. Among procedural innovations were arrangements for consultation and surveillance of the adjustment process and guidelines for the management of floating rates.

Disagreements remained on substantive matters, above all on the very nature of the reformed exchange-rate regime, to be based on "stable but adjustable par values," with floating rates "recognized as providing a useful technique in particular situations." From this lack of uniformity of view about the relative importance of stability of exchange rates and their adjustability stemmed three additional disagreements. The first was concerned with the method of establishing the need for exchange rate adjustments. The U.S. advocated an "objective indicator" in the guise of disproportionate gains or losses of monetary reserves, and most other countries advocated discretionary adjustment. The second disagreement revolved around convertibility of the dollar into primary reserve assets of gold and SDRs, with the U.S. taking the view that if the surplus countries were happy to hold dollars, such an option would introduce flexibility into the system. The third disagreement was about the management of global liquidity; this issue included the phasing out of gold, the severance of the present link of SDRs with gold, and a substantial relaxation of the present rules and safeguards governing SDRs.

Thus, as 1974 ended it appeared that the reconstruction of an organized international monetary system would start modestly—and experimentally—from exchange rate postures, practices, and policies that might prove mutually compatible under the guidelines agreed upon by governments, in a general way, during the year. But action must necessarily begin at home: a sustainable international monetary order requires reasonable domestic monetary discipline in each of the monetarily important countries.

(MIROSLAV A. KRIZ)

See also Commercial and Trade Policies; Commodity Trade; Economy, World; Investment, International; Money and Banking; Prices; Trade, International. [536.B]

Fashion and Dress

Though blue denim was still the favourite of the junior crowds browsing and buying along London's King's Road and Fulham Road, as well as on the sidewalks and café terraces of Paris' Saint Germain des Prés, 1974 turned out to be a year of transition from pants to skirts and away from the long-lived unisex silhouette.

To the blue denim panoply, which already included jeans, jackets, bags, and shoes, was added the ankle-length blue denim skirt, buttoned and flared, wrapped, or gently gored to the hem, but always very flat over the hips. The other ankle-length favourite was in printed cotton with a small all-over floral design and one or two deep hem frills, more reminiscent of an old-time petticoat than a skirt. It was worn with a plain T shirt, with a more elaborate blouse with

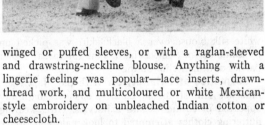

winged or puffed sleeves, or with a raglan-sleeved and drawstring-neckline blouse. Anything with a lingerie feeling was popular—lace inserts, drawn-thread work, and multicoloured or white Mexican-style embroidery on unbleached Indian cotton or cheesecloth.

The feminine and romantic impression was emphasized by the ubiquitous crocheted wool shawl, dipping in back like a poncho, in very open stitch and deeply fringed, and by the flower-trimmed hat. But it was contradicted by the clumsy clogs that still retained the juniors' favour and by the popular shoulder bag so weighted down with contents that it was closer to a plumber's kit than to a girl's handbag. Laura Ashley's prim Victorian look, with the petticoat-skirt and blouse outfit or the square-necked, shoulder-strapped, long pinafore, was as popular in Paris as in London. In a warmer version of lightweight plaid flannel, it advanced well into the fall.

For adults it was a soft and fluttering spring. The newest and smartest street look comprised a fluted mid-calf skirt and matching jacket with lifted shoulder line, short puffed sleeves, a waist seam, and a biased peplum, all in a small-patterned floral design. Boots were worn to start the season, as if to fight off the possible aging effect of the new length, but when this was well accepted they were replaced by high-heeled ankle- or T-strapped shoes and, during the summer, by open-toed, strapped sandals. Later in the season the street look changed to a scoop-necked T shirt with a flower-printed skirt, softly gathered instead of bias-cut. The T shirt was worn either over the skirt with a narrow belt or tucked into it under a pulled-in waist. The most popular flower prints were in small crowded patterns.

The classical tailored shirt was replaced by soft, fluid blouses. The wide, elbow-length sleeves were in keeping with the new, easy, wide-at-the-top silhouette, which carried through into the fall. The look originated with the collections of two leading ready-to-wear designers in Paris, Karl Lagerfeld's for Chlöe and Kenzo's for Jap.

With *The Great Gatsby, The Sting,* and *Stavisky* on the screen, there was certain to be an influence on fashion. It was called Revival in the U.S., Nostalgia in Great Britain, and Retro in France, but all were on the same wavelength. It influenced the leading ready-to-wear designers in Paris, and the urge to discover quality materials, embroidery, drawn-thread work, and hand-sewn clothes drew crowds of young Parisiennes to the famous Flea Market in search of anything that could be called antiuniform. Pure silk crepe de chine in period prints was the most sought after material in town. Many designers turned to reference books of the 1920s and '30s for colours and designs and had them specially reproduced.

Paris haute couture—and particularly Yves Saint Laurent, who always had a weakness for the '30s—made a big effort to bring back the suit in the spring. Saint Laurent's suit was in hairline flannel, with tailored lapels and a carnation at the buttonhole, accompanied by rows of pearls over a softly tied blouse and worn by a model with a curly, shoulder-length hairdo. But women still bypassed the suit, preferring the long cable-knit jacket to accompany their printed silk skirts. It looked less formal.

Another silhouette straight from the late 1920s appeared in the form of a loose overblouse topping skinny-hipped skirts, once again in the favourite fabric of the season, plain or printed crepe de chine. Skirts had a low biased flare or, occasionally, knife pleating, always covering the knees if they did not descend to mid-calf. One of the advantages of the Retro fashion was that no length was compulsory; the most flattering was the best.

The summer evening look also indicated that skirts were gaining favour over pants. The exceptions were some very full and soft pajama outfits in plain or printed crepe. Separate evening skirts, no longer floor length but to the ankles, were worn with tops that featured plunging necklines, front and back, and transparent effects created by circular band inserts of Irish lace. White on unbleached cotton crepe was very popular. Soft and fluttering evening dresses—also

The man of leisure, international style, dressed by Braemar.

ankle length because full length was considered far too matronly—appeared in all the materials and colours of the 1930s: crepe de chine, crepe georgette, and chiffon in shades of shell pink, peach, coral, salmon, old rose, and jade green. The look was completed by gold or silver sandals.

On the beaches, and particularly at St. Tropez where the gendarmes took a severe attitude toward total nudity, the "string" with mini triangles attached was adopted for sunbathing (though it was considered precarious for diving and swimming). Runners-up were gathered and draped tops, worn with high-cut briefs that revealed most of the hip or with boxer shorts. The one-piece bathing suit, if more scarce, was the newest; its draped top and cut-out back were reminiscent of the 1950s. For a cover-up on the beach, the year's choice was the terry-cloth sweat shirt, plain or striped, over the new wide-legged shorts or with bermudas. The latter were often seen with a matching white cotton-jersey blouson. The all-white look, however, was more for the well-turned-out crowd at Deauville. There a belted blouse top, Russian style, was one of the favourite accompaniments for well-tailored matching pants.

Clothes gained in volume as autumn set in. After-hugging their shawls in the wind and facing pouring rain under the shelter of their new flared raincoats, girls made their first autumn buy in the form of a wool cape. This could be in speckled tweed, reflecting autumn shades of rust and copper, in natural camel hair or cashmere, or in flannel or plain loden that could be khaki or one of the murky autumn fashion colours—olive green, smoky blue, or eggplant. But whatever the choice of material, capes had to be super-wide, swinging, and unlined to avoid bulk and weight. To look right, autumn clothes had to be animated.

Coats followed the direction of capes. With deep armholes, capelets, and pelerines, they were frequently in the Inverness style. Underneath could be worn a suit, a knitted jacket with separate flared or gathered soft skirt, or the newly recreated chemise dress. A heavy knit bonnet that hugged the head, a slanted beret tipping the right eyebrow, or a funny little brimmed hat were all acceptable headgear, but the newest was the jersey turban, wrapped and clinging to the head in the style of Paul Poiret.

The look was incomplete without the indispensable high-heeled boots, crushed instead of zipped this season. The newest and most expensive Paris-made ones were in black patent leather. Also part of the autumn fashion story were long, flowing, knitted scarves in wool, worn trailing to hem, wound around the neck and twisted by twos, or attached to the collar and then matched to the knit jacket, cardigan, or sweater.

Flared culottes, always flat on the hips, occasionally took the place of skirts, but they looked best on tall girls. Sometimes they were tucked into the boots. Plain flannel or discreetly flecked tweed was the best choice for this type of garment, which the French named "knickers." They were shown in the subdued colours of the season—brick, rust, gray, and black.

For many reasons the untiring efforts of fashion designers to reinstate the dress had been met by the obstinate refusal of pace-setters who preferred the multilayered look, but in the fall the dress finally reentered the scene. With volume at the height of fashion, it looked very different. Sometimes like a coat, more often like an overdress or a smock, cut with deep kimono armholes and hardly any seams, it

could be worn with a sweater or blouse underneath. The effect was very easy and effortless, with lots of swing. Pulling in the waist with a belt balanced volume at the top for those who had small measurements.

The right choice of accessories and bangles turned this new dress shape into a multioccasion garment. Loden, camel hair, and corduroy were among the favourite daytime materials, while the late-day choices were printed wool challis and printed silk crepe de chine, again mostly in florals. In the softer versions shoulder yokes, back and front, were used to introduce gathers, but a circular yoke and dropped shoulder seams were more usual. The Yves Saint Laurent version was seamed and gathered below a high bustline and at mid-thigh level and had long sleeves that puffed over the wristband.

In tune with the free-flowing capes, particularly in black, was the Russian look, which swept through the Italian collections in Rome. Galitzine and Lancetti showed many variations of the Cossack blouse with gathered neckline, worn over boyar pants tucked into boots. Yves Saint Laurent had introduced the Russian Cossack overblouse the year before; it was far more subdued and accidental in his winter collection, but it looked pretty in white silk broché worn with a braided black velvet suit. In the fall, the idea of the white silk blouse over a black skirt was picked up by a number of Saint Laurent fans for casual dinner parties and nightclub outings.

Cosmetics and Hairstyles. With the "Jazz Age" influence still strong in clothes, offshoots naturally appeared in cosmetics and hairstyles. Girls wearing fluttering clothes attempted to look pale and pretty in an effort to resemble Daisy in *The Great Gatsby*. Lustrous eyes were the first objective and sparkling, vivid lips the second. Luminous eye shadows enforced the accent on the eyes, and the return of black for lashes heightened the desired deep passionate gaze.

To dramatize the look, Helena Rubinstein proposed drawing a fine line of Automatic Eyeliner "Black" on the upper lid and thickening the lashes with Long Lash Mascara "Black." Elizabeth Arden's suggestion for fall was "Rhapsody in Plumberry" with a "Plumberry" crayon line traced along "Yellow Gold" eyeshadow. New browns and blacks came from Estée Lauder. Among many others who voted for smoky eyes, Charles of the Ritz favoured "Smoky Blue," "Pearly Pewter," and "Cobblestone Grey." For Revlon it was "Misty Grey" shadow and for Helena Rubinstein, "Black Pearl" and "Mauve Pearl."

Lips sparkled with "Blazing Red" from Estée Lauder or with "Emperor Red" from Elizabeth Arden. Some girls preferred the softer hues of chestnut brandy and copper red, in keeping with their clothes, and chose Helena Rubinstein's "Tender Moka" and "Tender Frost." Nail polish matched lipstick with blazing reds or the more subdued dark brandy and copper shades.

In the spring, complexions, light and transparent, still had a touch of amber with a bronzed beige overtone, but in the fall the "pale and pretty" mood demanded a porcelain skin with a touch of rouge on the cheeks. Cheek rouge was taken up by the young in a quite emphatic manner. Estée Lauder launched a soft film compact rouge, "New Geranium," and a new Tender Blusher, "Misty Red," that one could even dab on forehead and chin tip. The porcelain complexion was highlighted by Elizabeth Arden with "Cocoa Rose" blush.

Long, straight, gypsy-style hair was replaced by bobs and waves in the fall, and even by some shingles straight out of the 1920s and '30s. Heads needed to become smaller to balance the new overpowering clothes, and square cuts, curly waved bangs, and even frizzed hair with an all-over permanent served the purpose. The aim was to free the nape of the neck. Flowered fragrances completed the Gatsby era revival, with Caron's "Fleurs de Rocaille" and Guerlain's "Jicky" among the most popular.

(THELMA SWEETINBURGH)

Men's Fashions. The elegant, classically styled two-piece suit remained the foundation of male fashion in most countries in 1974, although it appeared to be losing some ground in the U.S. Emphasis tended to be on the fabrics rather than the fashions. Suitings included new pure woolens and worsteds, new blends of one or more natural fibres, blends of natural and man-made fibres, and mohairs, in which there was a resurgence of interest. Woven fabrics were firmly entrenched for suits; knitted fabrics still presented no serious challenge.

The IMBEX trade show, in London in February, provided further evidence of the trend to "country" colours, the rich, autumnal shades of brown and green. The International Men's Fashion Week at Cologne, W.Ger., in August confirmed these colours and also the continuing trend to more comfortable clothing for leisure wear. The new cottons predominated for summer and vacation styles.

Variations of safari and blouson-style jackets were shown in cotton, linen, or lightweight Donegal tweed with either matching or contrasting slacks. The "put together" suit of patterned jacket with plain trousers —or vice-versa—gained in popularity. Some had waistcoats (vests).

More double-breasted styles began to emerge, and the blazer, mostly in the double-breasted style, regained some of its former popularity. Nevertheless, the single-breasted suit, either three- or two-buttoned, still headed the list in all categories of suits. Lapels on jackets were narrower. Gatsby-look styles enjoyed only a short lease on life.

Sales of shirts rose in most countries, with coloured shirts far outstripping the plain whites. The slim-fit style was more popular with the younger age groups. The fashionable ties were 4 to $4\frac{1}{2}$ in. wide, in bright colours and sharper patterns. The bigger bow tie, in velvet for evening dress wear and in silk, cotton, or man-made materials for day wear, gained in popularity. The trend in topcoats and raincoats was to shorter lengths. As in suits, the main emphasis was on the fabrics. (STANLEY H. COSTIN)

See also **Furs.**

[451.B.2.b; 451.B.2.d.i; 629.C.1.a]

ENCYCLOPÆDIA BRITANNICA FILMS. *Culture and Costumes: The Great Clothes Put-On* (1974).

Fiji

An independent parliamentary state and member of the Commonwealth of Nations, Fiji is an island group in the South Pacific Ocean, about 2,000 mi. E of Australia and 3,200 mi. S of Hawaii. Area: 7,055 sq.mi. (18,274 sq.km.), with two major islands, Viti Levu (4,011 sq.mi.) and Vanua Levu (2,137 sq.mi.), and several hundred

FIJI
Education. (1973) Primary, pupils 130,440, teachers 4,015; secondary, pupils 21,079, teachers 862; vocational, pupils 1,277, teachers 117; teacher training, students 426, teachers 35; higher (University of the South Pacific), students 981, teaching staff 110.
Finance and Trade. Monetary unit: Fiji dollar, with (Sept. 16, 1974) an official rate of F$0.80 to U.S. $1 (free rate of F$1.85 = £1 sterling). Budget (1972 actual): revenue F$56.8 million; expenditure F$64 million. Foreign trade (1973): imports F$232 million; exports F$105 million. Import sources: Australia 30%; Japan 16%; U.K. 14%; New Zealand 13%; U.S. 5%. Export destinations: U.K. 28%; U.S. 23%; Australia 11%; New Zealand 6%; Canada 5%. Main exports (1972): sugar 67%; gold 8%; coconut products 5%. Tourism (1971): visitors 152,000; gross receipts U.S. $38 million.
Transport and Communications. Roads (1972) 2,316 km. (including 2,004 km. all-weather). Motor vehicles in use (1972): passenger 16,300; commercial (including buses) 6,300. Railways (1972) *c.* 7,000 km. (for sugar estates). Shipping (1973): merchant vessels 100 gross tons and over 25; gross tonnage 7,151. Ships entered (1972) vessels totaling 2,431,000 net registered tons; goods loaded (1972) 479,000 metric tons, unloaded 719,000 metric tons. Telephones (Dec. 1972) 22,000. Radio licenses (Dec. 1972) 53,000.
Agriculture. Production (in 000; metric tons; 1973; 1972 in parentheses): sugar, raw value *c.* 380 (303); sweet potatoes *c.* 16 (*c.* 16); cassava (1972) *c.* 88, (1971) *c.* 87; copra *c.* 29 (29); bananas (exports) *c.* 3 (3). Livestock (in 000; Sept. 1973): cattle *c.* 130; pigs *c.* 29; goats *c.* 30; horses *c.* 29.
Industry. Production (in 000; 1972): cement (metric tons) 90; gold (troy oz.) 76; electricity (kw-hr.) 191,000.

smaller islands. Pop. (1974 est.): 553,700. Cap. and largest city: Suva (pop., 1973 est., 65,530). Language: English, Fijian, and Hindi. Religion: Christian and Hindu. Queen, Elizabeth II; governor-general in 1974, Sir George Cakobau; prime minister, Ratu Sir Kamisese Mara.

On Oct. 10, 1974, Fiji celebrated the centenary of its cession to Britain and the fourth anniversary of independence. Prince Charles attended the ceremonies.

Cyclone Lottie caused widespread damage and claimed almost 100 lives in December 1973. The island had not yet fully recovered from the effects of Hurricane Bebe in 1972.

Concern over the failure to formulate a new International Sugar Agreement was dispelled by the rise in sugar prices, and record prices were received for copra. However, export receipts and invisible earnings could not match escalating import costs, the consequence of the fuel crisis and spiraling freight rates. In August controls over the outward capital flow were tightened. In January the Fijian dollar had been linked to the U.S. dollar to minimize the effects of currency fluctuations.

Unpopular wage and price controls provoked industrial action and a short strike by 3,000 civil servants. The new Fijian National Party gained some increased support as a result of the dissatisfaction with economic conditions. The party demanded paramountcy for indigenous Fijian interests and questioned multiracialist policies. (BARRIE KEITH MACDONALD)

[977.A.3]

Finland

The republic of Finland is bordered on the north by Norway, on the west by Sweden and the Gulf of Bothnia, on the south by the Gulf of Finland, and on the east by the U.S.S.R. Area: 130,129 sq.mi. (337,032 sq.km.). Pop. (1973 est.): 4,665,300. Cap. and largest city: Helsinki (pop., 1973 est., 505,719). Language: Finnish, Swedish. Religion (1970): Lutheran 92.5%. President in 1974, Urho Kaleva Kekkonen; prime minister, Kalevi Sorsa.

The world energy crisis dominated trade developments in Finland during 1974. Massive price increases, especially for Soviet oil (which comprised 65% of Finnish supplies), seriously threatened the economic stability of the country.

In an effort to maintain its neutral position with regard to European trade, in 1973 Finland had participated in the establishment of a joint commission with the Eastern European trading organization Comecon, and had ratified an agreement on free trade in industrial goods with the EEC. However, as a result of the increased oil bill, the Soviet Union became the country's leading trading partner, supplying 20% of total Finnish imports by value, compared with only 10% until 1973. To overcome the effect of the increased cost of fuel, Finland signed a number of long-term trade agreements with the Soviet Union and concluded several large deals, including a 1.5 billion markkaa contract to build a copper smelting plant in Soviet Siberia. In April the Ministry of Foreign Trade in Helsinki announced that Finnish-Soviet trade would regain equilibrium by 1978.

Throughout the year Finland continued to negotiate with Eastern European states on the progressive aboli-

tion of tariffs and other trade barriers in an effort to bring them into line with its terms of trade with the Soviet Union and Western Europe. Agreements were reached with Hungary, Czechoslovakia, and Bulgaria during 1974, while negotiations continued with Poland and Romania.

On March 19 Sorsa's four-party coalition government reached a significant wage and price agreement with the trade unions and industry, designed to limit wage increases to 10% over a two-year period. With a 20% inflation rate forecast for 1974, the government in June announced a massive program to improve the short-term balance of trade, including a 300 million markkaa export surcharge on the paper industry.

The 35-nation Conference on Security and Cooperation in Europe remained the dominant foreign policy issue, although, because of limited progress at the second phase in Geneva, the third phase, which Finland hoped would open in Helsinki in July, was postponed. Meanwhile, on March 22, another major conference in Helsinki produced the world's first international agreement on the protection of the marine environment: a seven-nation convention on the protection of the Baltic Sea from pollution.

Relations with the two German states were further consolidated. On May 27 Foreign Minister Ahti Karjalainen made the first official post-World War II visit to East Berlin by a Finnish Cabinet minister, and on September 18 he paid a similar visit to Bonn. Negotiations with both German states on the settlement of outstanding legal and financial questions continued throughout the year.

The Finnish government took an active role in the international movement against the military regime in Chile. An international inquiry commission into the crimes of the Chilean junta met in Helsinki in March, and on September 11 a solidarity meeting for the people of Chile was held in the Finnish Parliament. In the UN, Finland departed from its principle of bloc voting with the Scandinavian states to support rejection of South Africa's credentials. Diplomatic ties with Pretoria remained intact, however.

A new party, the Constitutional Party, made its appearance in the Finnish Parliament at the end of 1973. Occupying 2 seats out of the total of 200, it brought the number of parliamentary parties to ten. The constitution came under lively attack during 1974, and a government committee was set up to study its revision. The key question was the status of the president, the powerful central figure in Finnish politics. There were calls for subjecting the presidency to Parliament, but President Kekkonen authoritatively blocked all proposals for reform.

A complete politicization of the national broadcasting service took place on May 23 when the politically appointed administrative board decided that all editorial staff should be selected on the basis of their political views in direct proportion to party strengths in Parliament. (COLIN NARBOROUGH)

[972.A.6.d.i]

FINLAND

Education. (1972–73) Primary, pupils 380,865, teachers (full-time) 19,273; secondary, pupils 408,464, teachers 23,402; vocational, pupils 108,330, teachers 6,284; teacher training, students 1,686, teachers 182; higher (including 11 universities), students 61,746, teaching staff 6,759.

Finance. Monetary unit: markka, with (Sept. 16, 1974) a free rate of 3.80 markkaa to U.S. $1 (8.78 markkaa = £1 sterling). Gold, SDRs, and foreign exchange, central bank: (June 1974) U.S. $672.3 million; (June 1973) U.S. $505.7 million. Budget (1974 est.) balanced at 17,127,000,000 markkaa. Gross national product: (1972) 54,710,000,000 markkaa; (1971) 47,180,000,000 markkaa. Money supply: (Dec. 1973) 6,111,000,000 markkaa; (Dec. 1972) 4,960,-000,000 markkaa. Cost of living (1970 = 100): (June 1974) 146; (June 1973) 126.

Foreign Trade. (1973) Imports 16,548,000,000 markkaa; exports 14,609,000,000 markkaa. Import sources: Sweden 18%; West Germany 17%; U.S.S.R. 12%; U.K. 10%; U.S. 5%. Export destinations: U.K. 19%; Sweden 15%; U.S.S.R. 12%; West Germany 10%. Main exports: paper 28%; timber 16%; wood pulp 8%; machinery 7%; ships 6%; clothing 6%; plywood 5%.

Transport and Communications. Roads (1973) 73,210 km. (including 161 km. expressways). Motor vehicles in use (1973): passenger 894,104; commercial 119,898. Railways (1972): 5,954 km.; traffic 2,594,-000,000 passenger-km., freight (1973) 7,011,000,000 net ton-km. Air traffic (1973): 1,061,600,000 passenger-km.; freight 32,385,000 net ton-km. Navigable inland waterways (1972) 6,674 km. Shipping (1973): merchant vessels 100 gross tons and over 390; gross tonnage 1,545,626. Telephones (Dec. 1972) 1,412,000. Radio licenses (Dec. 1972) 1,896,000. Television licenses (Dec. 1972) 1,183,000.

Agriculture. Production (in 000; metric tons; 1973; 1972 in parentheses): wheat 462 (462); barley 992 (1,140); oats 1,169 (1,245); rye 124 (119); potatoes c. 716 (716); sugar, raw value c. 85 (91); butter c. 84 (84); timber (cu.m.; 1971) 43,000, (1970) 45,100; fish catch (1972) 67, (1971) 70. Livestock (in 000; June 1973): cattle c. 1,884; sheep 145; pigs 1,139; horses 48; chickens 8,109.

Industry. Production (in 000; metric tons; 1973): iron ore (66% metal content) 751; pig iron 1,412; crude steel 1,385; copper (1972) 38; cement 2,125; sulfuric acid 935; petroleum products (1972) 8,640; plywood (cu.m.; 1972) 675; cellulose (1972) 3,990; wood pulp (1971) mechanical 2,008, chemical 4,238; newsprint 1,680; other paper and board (1972) 3,568; electricity (kw-hr.) 28,930,000; manufactured gas (cu.m.) 40,160.

Fisheries

The third UN Conference on the Law of the Sea, at Caracas, Venezuela, was the central event in developments affecting the world's fishing industry during 1974. (*See* LAW: *Special Report.*) With few exceptions, nations aimed at a 200-mi. "exclusive economic zone" and a 12-mi. exclusive fishing zone.

No firm decision was reached, but the mood of the conference encouraged the U.S., Canada, Iceland, and Norway to announce their intentions of establishing a 200-mi. zone. But while the trawlers of Massachusetts welcomed the promise of reduced competition on their home ground, the tuna fishermen of California and owners of the 9,000 shrimp boats of the Mexican Gulf foresaw problems, as did the salmon fishermen of Alaska and Washington. How could a coastal state accept responsibility for tuna ranging far into the Pacific Ocean? If salmon belonged to the state in whose rivers they spawned, what conservation could that state exercise over them outside the 200-mi. zone?

One school of thought held that a "species approach" and an international controlling body could best protect stocks of these fish. International tuna commissions already existed, but U.S. tuna boats had another problem. For years they had fished illegally inside the unilaterally declared 200-mi. limits of states such as Ecuador and Peru, backed by the U.S. government, which paid their fines if caught (over $1 million in 1973). Once the 200-mi. limit became the accepted norm, those fishing grounds would really be closed. There were also clashes of interest in Britain, Norway, and elsewhere. Scottish fishermen feared a government trade-off of west coast herring for Norwegian cod; Norwegian small-boat cod fishermen feared the incursion of British deep-sea trawlers. In Britain the big fishing companies, foreseeing restrictions on their distant-water fleets, began to invest in smaller coastal vessels in the profitable 70–80-ft. class.

In late 1973 fish prices were high, demand was good, and shipyards' order books were bulging, but the fuel crisis, which tripled the cost of fuel, substantially raised operating costs. In Spain, 14,000 small-boat fishermen demanded, and got, a government subsidy, but most fishermen were left to recoup costs as best they could. The fuel crisis also had other repercussions. With spending power cut, fish prices went down, not up, and large stocks of fish bought when prices were high were still choking the cold stores in Europe and the U.S. months later.

The world catch in 1974 seemed unlikely to break records. The Peruvian anchoveta catch showed no signs of complete recovery, and catches of whitefish were not encouraging. Fishing trials continued on the deep-sea grenadier off northwest Ireland, blue whiting in the North Sea, and capelin off Newfoundland. Even the long-neglected silver smelt came under consideration. The failure of Peruvian anchoveta in 1972–73 had raised the international price of fish meal to a level that made "trash" fish more attractive.

Another factor was the newly introduced "fleshbone separator," a device developed in the U.S. to separate chicken flesh from bone. It also worked with fish, and could be used to salvage the last 5% of meat from fish skeletons after filleting or to remove the flesh from fish too small to be filleted economically or unmarketable in whole form. Since the resulting product could be processed into fish cakes, fish sticks, or even blocks of 100% fish meat, fishing no longer had to be a matter of seeking only salable fish. (H. S. NOEL)

See also Environment.
[731.D.2.a]

WIDE WORLD

Nets are spread at a fish-breeding farm in Anhwei Province, China. This hatchery raised 7.5 billion frying fish between 1967 and 1973.

Food Processing

Environmental pollution, food additives and contaminants, the effect of processing on the nutritive value of foodstuffs, control of the microbiological safety of foods, and carcinogenic hazards inherent in certain traditional processes received much attention both nationally and internationally in 1974. There were no major legislative changes except for a trend toward greater restriction of chemical additives. The U.S. Food and Drug Administration (FDA) proceeded with its review of the GRAS (Generally Recognized as Safe) list and issued many reviews on the toxicology, teratology, and mutagenicity of numerous additives. The Codex Alimentarius Commission issued a list of food additives that had been evaluated for safety in use. A market research report indicated that the annual value of food additives used in Britain was approximately £40 million, the most important being thickening agents, emulsifiers, and acidulants. The U.S. and Britain instituted a review of the safety of plastic food containers following reports of a cancer hazard associated with vinyl chloride monomer. There was renewed interest in natural plant pigments as alternatives to synthetics in both the U.S. and Britain. The FDA deferred reconsideration of cyclamates pending further investigations but no further restrictions were applied to saccharin. A new sweetener known commercially as Aspartame ran into trouble immediately after approval by the FDA. The possible formation of carcinogens from nitrates and nitrites in cured meats caused much international activity and the imposition of certain restrictions in the U.S., Britain, and some other countries. Investigations were extended to nitrate contamination of certain foodstuffs and drinking water resulting from the excessive use of nitrogenous fertilizers.

An International Commission on Food Safety and Supply was formed and authorized to "examine and report on the societal benefits and risks that accrue from the application of science, technology, and law to the food supply." The EEC formed a Scientific Committee for Food to consider the protection of human life and health with particular regard to the composition of foods, use of additives, and the presence of contaminants; it recommended that sweets and sugar-rich products be restricted in schools. An Australian nutritionist reviewed the responsibilities of the food industry and advocated a reduction in sophisticated foods and more emphasis on those containing nutrients in their natural proportions. The need for nutrient labeling was not accepted in Britain but a research unit began the routine monitoring and nutritional evaluation of convenience foods used in school meals.

Technology. The U.S. Department of Agriculture (USDA) developed a novel method of preparing aroma concentrates from spices by extraction with liquid carbon dioxide whereby the aromatic substances can be obtained in highly concentrated form after evaporation of the carbon dioxide at a low temperature, which avoids heat damage and loss of aroma volatiles. Interest in the development of many types of new foods from novel proteins stimulated work in many countries on meat aroma and the development of improved flavourings for meat substitutes. Improved flavour retention was achieved by a U.S. process for slush evaporation which removes water by a combination of evaporation and sublimation from the partly frozen product. This process was claimed to be superior to freeze-drying. Another U.S. process giving good aroma retention combined spray-drying with continuous through-flow bed drying of products such as milk, coffee, juices, vegetable extracts, and flavourings. A novel and compact spiral freezing tunnel was developed by an Italian company utilizing a fluorocarbon refrigerant. The plant handled up to 1,000 lb. per hour of vegetables, fruit, fish, meatburgers, precooked meals, or ice cream. An improved flame sterilizer suitable for canned milk, cream, custards, rice puddings, and seafoods was developed in Australia and had means for recording the temperature of individual cans and economizing cooling water. A U.S. innovation was a self-refrigerating can for beverages. The can has an inner capsule containing refrigerant under pressure that when released reduces the temperature of the contents to 40° F in about 90 seconds.

Retortable pouches, developed independently in Japan and Britain, were exhaustively tested as alternatives to cans and made possible the introduction of a new line of convenience meals that could be prepared for eating within five minutes by heating in boiling water. The packaging of beer and carbonated soft drinks in plastic pouches made great strides and a new £5 million pouch manufacturing plant was planned in the U.K. In the U.S. a group was commissioned to investigate plastic alternatives to metal cans and reported favourably on the utility and advantages of flexible packaging for heat-processed foods. An ingenious U.S. innovation was a special container for the microwave reheating of frozen meals whereby meat and vegetables could be warmed to 140° F while ice cream placed in the same tray remained frozen; a hospital reported a saving of two cents per meal in labour costs. A pneumatic conveyor for vegetables that used air for cooling instead of water was developed in the U.S. This saved water, reduced capital costs, and minimized loss of solids through leaching. Increased demand for lettuce induced workers at the USDA to develop a mechanical harvester with a novel X-ray lettuce-head selector to provide standard-sized lettuce heads at lower cost. Australian scientists developed an efficient machine for the mechanical harvesting and drying of sultanas.

Products. U.S. scientists found that certain bacteria that help preserve cultured dairy products could be used to prolong the shelf life of meat products without impairing acceptability. Canada Agriculture investigated the suitability of various protein emulsifiers for pulverized meats and the possibility of replacing some of the meat protein with plant or poultry protein. A U.S. company developed a process for producing steaks tailored to satisfy market requirements in respect to taste, chewability, and appearance by taking frozen flaked meat and melting it in special molds under hydraulic pressure at a low temperature. A British dairy group commissioned a £4 million cheddar cheese factory, one of the world's largest, to produce 80 tons of cheese daily using the latest automatic equipment. Another U.K. dairy group introduced aseptic single-portion equipment for the filling and capping of plastic pots with milk and cream at 600 per minute. In The Netherlands a dairy installed an automated 200,000-gal. milk reception facility that required only one man to operate. A Norwegian group undertook a $17.5 million turnkey project in Poland for the erection of one of Europe's largest dairies.

Floods:
see Disasters;
Engineering
Projects

Folk Music:
see Music

The Australian government allocated A$20 million for the reconstruction of its dairy industry.

British agriculturalists investigated the long-term storage of corn (maize) and wheat in Kenya. It was found that strategic reserves could be maintained in good condition for 24 months in hermetically sealed silos of simple construction because any infesting insects quickly died. The utilization of cassava for starch and fermented products production including food protein was studied. A modern factory for the manufacture of ten tons of gari daily was erected by a British company in Nigeria. Canada funded a project for the establishment in Colombia of a specialized information centre covering all aspects of cassava technology. In Brazil a simple and inexpensive process was developed for the nutritional enrichment of tortillas with soy protein. A soybean-processing plant with a rated annual capacity of 150,000 tons was commissioned in Yugoslavia and a plant was installed in Canada for the annual production of 5,000 tons of rapeseed protein concentrate. A mushroom factory with a roof spanning 22 ac. was erected in Malaysia for $6 million.

Fisheries. The UN Food and Agriculture Organization (FAO) reported that aquaculture was contributing about six million metric tons of fish valued at $2.5 billion and that it was making a significant contribution to human nutrition in Asia and the Far East. It provided employment for close to one million people in these areas. A U.S. company developed a controlled-environment silo system that was claimed to increase fish cultivation by 500 times over natural pond production. The survival of fingerling trout and salmon had increased from less than 1% to more than 70% with improved feed conversion. Progress was made in British shellfish cultivation, and feed utilization of oyster spat was improved 20% by feeding three or four times daily instead of continuously. Successful experiments were made with rope frameworks to encourage the settlement of scallop spat. Frozen whole krill, now plentiful due to the depletion of whales, found a ready market in Japan following the first successful trawl. Krill paste was produced in the U.S.S.R. by squeezing out the liquid content and heating it to coagulate the protein. The South African government constructed a large trout hatchery in the eastern Transvaal with a capacity of 15 million ova a year. Mexican scientists developed a bland product from species of fish normally discarded and used it successfully as a protein supplement in tortillas and tacos.

Irradiation. South African and Arab scientists independently demonstrated that irradiation successfully extends the shelf life of perishable subtropical fruits and would make possible their export when permitted. Workers at the International Project in the Field of Food Irradiation, Karlsruhe, W.Ger., raised the problem of introducing irradiated foods despite the apparent benefits, arguing that their potential had not been adequately realized except among those responsible for their development and that this, combined with the unproven economic advantages, the unknown consumer reactions, and the availability of alternative conventional methods, was the main reason for slow progress. In The Netherlands recommendations were made for the establishment of an international centre for the promotion of food irradiation technology to help bridge the gap between research and commercial exploitation. Researchers in Thailand showed that losses of onions from rotting

This delectable group of sweets and desserts emerged from research on a new artificial chocolate flavour for confectioneries.

and sprouting could be greatly reduced by irradiation and that salmonella could be eliminated from frozen and dried egg.

New Foods. The development of new protein-rich products from bacteria, yeasts, fungi, and algae continued unabated but their use as human food made little progress because of the application of increasingly severe safety criteria. A UN study recommended that products derived from yeasts grown on carbohydrate substrates and methyl and ethyl alcohols were preferable for human use, and processes developed in Switzerland and the U.S. for growing yeast on methanol attracted worldwide interest. A U.S. company built a plant to produce initially ten million pounds of food yeast annually from methanol manufactured from petroleum. Petroprotein production in France was handicapped by technical problems and incurred losses exceeding Fr. 17 million. Interest was reactivated in the preparation of edible protein from the juices of lucerne, alfalfa, and other green vegetation, and an establishment was set up in Britain for its promotion and to support feeding trials. A bland protein concentrate from alfalfa was developed in the U.S. A Japanese company made plans to produce 3,000 tons of leaf protein annually under Hungarian license.

The extraction of protein from cheese whey by ultrafiltration and its use in the manufacture of baby foods, protein-enriched beverages, and as a protein supplement made good progress, and production began in Sweden, Denmark, Britain, France, and the U.S. British scientists developed meat substitutes by spinning protein from slaughterhouse blood plasma.

The FAO surveyed the future of textured vegetable proteins from soybean, rapeseed, sunflower seed, wheat, oats, cottonseed, and other vegetable sources as meat extenders and replacers. A Japanese company developed meat substitutes from wheat gluten. Textured substitutes from defatted soy flour and soy protein concentrates were increasingly used internationally as meat extenders for institutional feeding in view of shortages and the high price of natural meat. Good consumer acceptance in the U.S. was accorded to a ground beef/soy protein preparation, and convenience foods containing meat substitutes were introduced into school lunch programs. An investigation on the acceptability of meat substitutes in the school meals service was commenced in Britain.

Soft margarines enriched with polyunsaturated fat accounted for two-thirds of the spreads used in the U.S., and similar preparations gained ground in Europe. This stimulated the commercial development of polyunsaturated butter utilizing Australian technology, while New Zealand scientists developed both soft and hard butter for different climates by fractionation of milk fat. Progress in the separation of the major components of foodstuffs, namely proteins, fats, and carbohydrates, and their subsequent recombination made possible the introduction of many new foods tailored for convenience, novelty, and economy. Such "commerciogenic" foods were criticized by some U.S. nutritionists on the grounds that they tend to impair the nutritional status of those in greatest need by diverting limited resources from the purchase of staple foodstuffs to those with high acceptability and convenience. Approximately 500 such new foods were introduced into the U.K. market, but a statistical survey showed that of 6,000 such products introduced during the previous 14 years only half attained national distribution and most disappeared within five years.

The U.S.S.R. developed the world's first automatic installation for the manufacture of simulated caviar at the rate of 50 kg. per hour. Made from milk protein and gelatin, it was claimed to be highly nutritious and as acceptable as the natural product. A Canadian inventor made synthetic currants and other soft fruits from fluid compositions encapsulated with calcium alginate or pectate gels. New snack foods having a honeycomb structure were developed in Switzerland. U.S. Army scientists developed a new class of compressed foods that regain their normal textural properties when rehydrated; these included fruit bars, potato salad, coleslaw, chocolate pudding, chicken and rice, barbequed pork, chicken a la king, chili with beans, scrambled eggs, and apple pie filling. Other U.S. introductions included refrigerated peach slices which largely replaced dried peaches, a convenience food consisting of ground beef and rice wrapped in cabbage leaves, and pasta supplemented with nonfat dry milk.

(H. B. HAWLEY)

See also Agriculture and Food Supplies; Commodity Trade; Fisheries; Prices.
[451.B.1.c.ii; 731.E–H]

ENCYCLOPÆDIA BRITANNICA FILMS. *Milk: From Farm to You* (1972).

Football

Association Football (Soccer).
The unhappy saga of violence on and off the field continued in association football during the 1973–74 season and the 1974 World Cup finals. Although permits for fans and trenches, moats, barricades, and other constraining impedimenta were employed, the problem was only reduced, not eradicated, and no simple solution was found.

Table I. Association Football Major Tournaments

Event	Winner	Country
World Cup	West Germany	
European Super Cup	Ajax, Amsterdam	The Netherlands
European Champions' Cup	Bayern Munich	West Germany
European Cup-Winners' Cup	FC Magdeburg	East Germany
UEFA Cup	Feyenoord	The Netherlands
South American Champions' Cup	Independiente	Argentina
UEFA Youth Cup	Bulgaria	
Inter-Continental Cup	Independiente	Argentina

Food Supplies:
see Agriculture and Food Supplies

World Cup. West Germany's 2–1 victory over The Netherlands in the final of the World Cup in Munich on July 7, 1974, was the climax of the year. The Germans had battled their way through to their second victory in this premier competition in soccer from among 16 nations that had reached the final round in the tournament. The others, along with The Netherlands, were Argentina, Australia, Brazil, Bulgaria, Chile, East Germany, Haiti, Italy, Poland, Scotland, Sweden, Uruguay, Yugoslavia, and Zaire. The final was a fine spectacle; it opened in dramatic fashion when The Netherlands made 15 passes from the kickoff without a German player's touching the ball and was awarded a penalty by Referee Jack Taylor (Eng.) because Johan Cruyff (*see* BIOGRAPHY), the Dutch captain and star of the tournament, was brought down in the penalty area by Uli Hoeness. Johan Neeskens calmly thundered the ball past West German goalkeeper Sepp Maier. But the Dutch failed to consolidate the advantage. They allowed the home side, led by Franz Beckenbauer (*see* BIOGRAPHY), veteran of the 1966 final in England, to regroup and swing back to gain a measure of control and, ultimately, command of the game.

Helmut Schoen, the West German manager, revealed afterward that the team had decided the best way to beat The Netherlands was to put a man onto Cruyff to shut him out of the game. This difficult job was entrusted to Berti Vogts, and he carried it out almost to perfection. The Dutch captain was never a real force after those opening minutes. In fact, within 25 minutes the West Germans had tied the score, again by means of a penalty goal. This time Dutch defender Win Jansen tripped Bernd Hoelzenbein as he was on the point of shooting. Paul Breitner equaled the earlier Neeskens blow with similar studied calm. Jan Jongbloed, the Dutch goalkeeper, was more successful with an effort by Vogts and a shrewd free kick by Beckenbauer. But he had no chance with what was to prove the winning goal two minutes before the interval. A West German attack developed on the right with Rainer Bonhof making a brave run down the flank and crossing the ball. The speedy Gerd Müller was so quick to size up the situation that he was ahead of the ball and had to turn back and swivel before lashing it into the far corner of the net, despite the desperate efforts of Arie Haan. The Dutch had earlier chances to score, but Johnny Rep, when slipped the ball by Cruyff, unaccountably missed and Ruud Krol forced Beckenbauer to head the ball gratefully over his own bar for a corner, just before Müller struck.

In the second half The Netherlands was committed to offense and set up many dangerous situations, but the final finishing touch to their countless attacks was missing and they became frustrated. At the same time, the subduing of Cruyff by Vogts enabled Beckenbauer to play a more positive role as the game progressed. Thus, West Germany won the world soccer championship for the second time, and it was the fourth time in the ten finals that the host country had triumphed.

A day earlier in the same stadium Poland, which won the Olympic title there in 1972, beat Brazil, one of the precontest favourites, in the third-place play-off with a single goal by Grzegorz Lato about 15 minutes from the end of an entertaining game that saw Rivelino, the Brazilian captain, parade some of his superb ball skill. The Poles were reinforced by the return of Andrzei Szarmach, their star striker.

European Cup. For the first time since the trophy's inception in 1956, the premier club title in Europe went to West Germany when Bayern Munich crushed Atletico Madrid 4–0 in a replayed final in Brussels on May 17. The men from Munich were completely in command in the Heysel Stadium, though 48 hours earlier they had not tied the score in the first game until the last few seconds of extra time, when George Schwarzenbeck dashed through from deep defense to drive home the equalizer from about 20 yd. out; before that Atletico appeared to be sailing into the record books on the strength of a goal by Suarez Luís from a free kick just outside the penalty area after 116 minutes of play. In the replay, the first in the history of the competition at the final stage, Hoeness and Müller, responding to the changed tactics of coach Udo Lattek that put the emphasis on attack, each scored twice. Hoeness drove in the first from a pass by Schwarzenbeck after 29 minutes; shortly after the break Müller added two more, and Hoeness a fourth goal 9 minutes from the end.

European Cup-Winners' Cup. FC Magdeburg became the first team from East Germany to win the trophy by convincingly toppling AC Milan of Italy 2–0 in the final at the Feyenoord Stadium, Rotterdam, Neth., on May 8. The East Germans played some thrilling attacking soccer, and their speedy young side, averaging just over 23 years, proved too elusive for the famed but aging Milan defense. The first goal came two minutes from the end of the first half when Martin Hoffman set off on a brilliant run from the

Gerd Müller (left) scored the second and winning goal as West Germany defeated The Netherlands 2–1 in the World Cup soccer final in Munich.

halfway line and then swung over a low cross, causing Enrico Lanzi to turn the ball into his own net despite a valiant attempt by goalkeeper Pierluigi Pizzabella to save. The East Germans, who had earlier won their own domestic league competition, continued to carry the battle to their opponents after the interval and were rewarded with a second goal, again from the resourceful Hoffman.

UEFA Cup. Feyenoord, the first Dutch club to win the European Cup in 1970, emulated that feat in the UEFA Cup by defeating Tottenham Hotspur, Eng., in a two-legged final in May 1974. In the second leg, at Rotterdam on May 29, fans of the English club rioted, fighting with Dutch supporters and clashing with police. UEFA fined Feyenoord £3,500 for failing to keep proper crowd control, and the Tottenham Hotspurs were banned from staging their next two home UEFA matches within 300 km. of their home ground at White Hart Lane, London. The damage, estimated at £10,000, was split between the two clubs.

In the first leg at Tottenham on May 21 the Hotspurs scored twice, both times by Welsh international centre back Mike England; the Dutch were equal to them and answered first through W. van Hanegem and then Theo de Jong to tie the score at 2–2. The return match in Rotterdam found Feyenoord in top form, skillfully using possession play to keep Tottenham's defense at full stretch and its attackers frustrated. Feyenoord won 2–0, scoring being done by Wim Rijsbergen and Peter Ressel. Thus, the Dutch team ended the British monopoly of this trophy and its predecessor, the Inter-Cities Fairs' Cup, a domination that had begun in 1968.

British Isles Championship. A 2–0 victory over England at Hampden Park, Glasgow, on May 18 enabled Scotland to share the British Isles title with their victims and was a timely fillip for Scottish morale before setting off for the World Cup. Ironically, Scotland's goals came from deflections by two English defenders of shots by Joe Jordan (Leeds United) and Ken Dalglish (Celtic). That the Scots deserved their success was undeniable, because the England defense could never contain the fiery Scottish raiders until Joe Mercer, England caretaker-manager, substituted Dave Watson (Sunderland) for Leeds' Norman Hunter in the second half. The same day, at Wrexham,

Table II. Association Football National Champions		
Nation	Cup and league winners	
Austria	Cup	Austria WAC
	League	Voest Linz
Belgium	Cup	Waregem
	League	Anderlecht
Bulgaria	Cup	Levski Spartak
	League	Levski Spartak
Czechoslovakia	Cup	Slovan Bratislava
	League	Slovan Bratislava
Denmark	Cup	Vannaese
	League	Randers Freja
England	Cup	Liverpool
	League	Leeds United
Finland	Cup	Reipas Lahti
	League	Kuopi Palloseura
France	Cup	Saint-Étienne
	League	Saint-Étienne
Germany, East	Cup	Carl Zeiss Jena
	League	FC Magdeburg
Germany, West	Cup	Eintracht Frankfurt
	League	Bayern Munich
Greece	Cup	PAOK Salonika
	League	Olympiakos Piraeus
Hungary	Cup	Ferencvaros
	League	Ujpest Dozsa
Iceland	Cup	Valur
	League	Akranes
Ireland	Cup	Finn Harps
	League	Cork Celtic
Italy	Cup	Bologna
	League	Lazio
Luxembourg	Cup	Jeunesse d'Esch
	League	Jeunesse d'Esch
Netherlands, The	Cup	PSV Eindhoven
	League	Feyenoord
Northern Ireland	Cup	Ards
	League	Coleraine
Norway	Cup	Strømgodset
	League	Viking Stavanger
Poland	Cup	Ruch Chorzow
	League	Ruch Chorzow
Portugal	Cup	Sporting Lisbon
	League	Sporting Lisbon
Romania	Cup	Jiul Petroseni
	League	Universitatea Craiova
Scotland	Cup	Celtic
	League	Celtic
Spain	Cup	Real Madrid
	League	Barcelona
Sweden	Cup	Malmö
	League	Åtvidaberg
Switzerland	Cup	FC Sion
	League	FC Zurich
Turkey	Cup	Fenerbahce
	League	Fenerbahce
U.S.S.R.	Cup	Ararat Erevan
	League	Ararat Erevan
Wales	Cup	Cardiff
Yugoslavia	Cup	Hajduk Split
	League	Hajduk Split

Wales ended its four-year goal famine in this tournament when, midway through the opening half, David Smallman of the home club lobbed the ball over goalkeeper Pat Jennings (Tottenham Hotspur) to defeat Northern Ireland. On the opening day of the 1974 tournament, England had beaten Wales at Ninian Park, Cardiff, 2–0. Stan Bowles (Queen's Park Rangers) and Kevin Keegan (Liverpool) scored. Meanwhile, in Glasgow, Northern Ireland beat Scotland by a single goal, scored by Tommy Cassidy (Newcastle United), and owed its victory in large part to the goalkeeping of Jennings. Scotland introduced Jordan in this game in place of Denis Law (Manchester City), and he kept the no. 9 shirt during the World Cup.

Scotland beat an injury-hit Wales 2–0, both goals coming in the first half from Dalglish and on a penalty kick by fullback Sandy Jardine (Glasgow Rangers). England struggled to beat Northern Ireland at Wembley Stadium, London, by a single goal, scored by Keith Weller (Leicester City), following the substitution of his club colleague Frank Worthington for Bowles.　　　　　　　　　　(TREVOR WILLIAMSON)

Rugby. *Rugby Union.* The 1973–74 period was a time of much international touring, the main event being the 22-match tour of South Africa by the Lions of the British Isles in May, June, and July 1974. The Lions became the first international touring team on a major tour to win a test series in South Africa since 1896. Captained by Bill McBride and coached by Syd Millar, both of the Ballymena club in Northern Ireland, the Lions won all but one of their test series games against South Africa's Springboks, the fourth, which was drawn 13–13 at Johannesburg. The Lions won the first three tests decisively, by 12–3 at Cape Town, 28–9 at Pretoria, and 26–9 at Port Elizabeth. The main strength of the British team was in the forwards, who outscrummaged the Springboks in the set scrums and outpaced them in the loose. By these means the Lions were able to apply pressure on their opponents, especially on the halfbacks, with the result that handling mistakes and errors of judgment were induced from which the Lions scored tries or kicked penalty goals. In one of their lesser matches the Lions set a record score by beating South-West Districts 97–0 at Mossel Bay. This was the highest score achieved by any Lions team, and the highest recorded in a first-class match in South Africa. Alan Old, the England standoff half, scored 37 points in this game, a record for a player from overseas on tour in South Africa.

The period between September and December 1973 was a time of international activity in the British Isles and Europe. The chief tourists, Australia, played nine matches in England, Wales, and Italy. They were short of powerful forwards and were beaten 24–0 by Wales at Cardiff and 20–3 by England at Twickenham. They then defeated Italy 59–21 at L'Aquila. Their final record was: played 9, won 3, lost 5, drawn 1; points: for 144, against 152.

In the same period both Japan and Argentina made their first visits to the British Isles. The Japanese played 11 matches, winning 2 and losing 9. Their main disadvantage was the relatively small physical stature of their forwards. In their chief matches they were beaten 62–14 by Wales at Cardiff, 30–18 by France at Bordeaux, and 19–10 by England Under-23 at Twickenham. Argentina played eight games in Ireland and Scotland, winning two, drawing two, and losing four. In their two major matches they were beaten 21–8 by Ireland in Dublin and 12–11 by Scotland at

Murrayfield. Their tour was marred by late and dangerous tackling, especially in their first game, against the Munster provincial side at Limerick, which the referee brought to a halt several minutes early.

For the first time the ten matches of the home international championship were squeezed into five nominated Saturdays with two weeks between each instead of being played during January–March. This new system created problems, but interest in the outcome of the championship was maintained until the last Saturday. At that time Ireland became champion for the first time since 1951. The Irish owed their success mainly to the strength and experience of their forwards and to the all-around excellence of Mike Gibson in the centre. They took some time to assert themselves, being beaten 9–6 by France in Paris in their first match, thanks to a last-minute penalty goal kicked for France by Jean-Louis Berot, and then being held to a 9–9 draw by Wales in Dublin. This was a match they could have won if their goal-kicking had been more accurate. In their third match the Irish acquired a commanding lead of 26–9 over England at Twickenham before eventually winning 26–21. This was the highest number of points Ireland had ever scored in a match against England. They followed this victory by beating Scotland 9–6 in Dublin and then had to sit back and wait for the results of the last Saturday's two matches—in which they were not directly involved—when Scotland beat France 19–6 at Murrayfield and England beat Wales 16–12 at Twickenham.

These outcomes meant that Ireland finished first with five championship points; Wales, Scotland, and France each had four points and England trailed with three. Wales for once could not find a really powerful pack of forwards, and though they started their campaign by beating Scotland 6–0 at Cardiff, their draw with Ireland and their defeat by England, together with another draw, 16–16 with France at Cardiff, left them below Ireland in the final standings. Scotland had five excellent tight forwards, but they lacked loose forwards and an established pair of halfbacks. A late penalty goal by Andy Irvine enabled them to snatch a victory, 16–14, over England at Murrayfield, and their win over France lent a happy ending to their season, but their other games brought nothing but frustration.

France had a vigorous set of forwards but as a whole played without the flair usually associated with French teams. England had a season of missed opportunities in which their goal-kickers and their midfield backs generally failed to draw profit from the sterling work of their forward line. They did, however, hold France to a 12–12 draw in Paris, and their 16–12 defeat of Wales was their first victory over the Welsh since 1963 and their first over them at Twickenham since 1960. Phil Bennett, Wales's standoff half, created a new individual record of 36 points for Wales in a season, beating the mark set by Barry John in 1972.

During the Southern Hemisphere season of 1974, the International Board held its annual meeting in Sydney for the first time in order to mark 100 years of rugby in Australia. Australia also played host to the All Blacks, who won their three-match test series 2–0 with the other game drawn, the scores being 11–6, 16–16, and 16–6. The All Blacks' final record in Australia was: played 12, won 11, drawn 1.

Rugby League. The main event of the season was the long tour of Australia and New Zealand made by Great Britain in June, July, and August 1974. Opening in Australia, Great Britain lost the first test 12–6 in Brisbane, drew level by winning the second 16–11 in Sydney, but then were beaten 22–18 in the third and last, also in Sydney. In this third match G. F. Langlands of Australia scored 13 points and so became the first player ever to score more than 100 points in tests between those two countries. Great Britain won a test match series in New Zealand 2–1: 8–13 in Auckland, 17–8 in Christchurch, and 20–0 in Auckland.

(DAVID FROST)

[452.B.4.h.xxiv]

U.S. Football. The Pittsburgh Steelers were crowned champions of professional football for the first time in their 42-year history when they defeated the Minnesota Vikings 16–6 in the National Football League's Super Bowl on Jan. 12, 1975, in New Orleans. The top-ranked college teams, according to two different polls, were Oklahoma and Southern California.

College. Oklahoma would have been the undisputed number one college football team of 1974 except for one problem: the Sooners were on probation for violating the recruiting regulations of the National Collegiate Athletic Association (NCAA). As a result, Oklahoma was banned from national television appearances and postseason bowl games.

Taking different positions on the issue were the Associated Press and United Press International, conductors of the country's most prominent football polls. UPI, which reflected the sentiments of 35 college coaches, refused to so much as mention Oklahoma in its weekly ratings and selected the once-beaten University of Southern California as its top team. The AP, relying on the opinions of 63 sportswriters, kept Oklahoma in its ratings all season, a stance that was justified—at least on athletic grounds—when the Sooners emerged as the only unbeaten, untied team in major college football.

In their 11 victories, the Sooners, who compiled a 29-game winning streak, intimidated their opponents both offensively and defensively. The offense was easier to see, as when All-American running back Joe Washington, who gained 1,321 yd., led the way to a 63–0 romp over Kansas State and a 72–3 slaughter of Utah State. But the Oklahoma defense, anchored by All-American linebacker Rod Shoate, was there when it had to be. It received its sternest test against Nebraska, when it had to keep the Cornhuskers from increasing a 14–7 third-quarter lead while Sooner quarterback Steve Davis plotted the way to a 28–14 come-from-behind win.

The logical bowl game opponent for Oklahoma would have been Alabama, which had an 11–0 record in regular-season play. By defeating Notre Dame in the Orange Bowl, Alabama conceivably could have been ranked first in both polls. But the Fighting Irish, playing their last game for coach Ara Parseghian, who was resigning, spoiled that dream 13–11.

Southern California used that upset and one of its own making on New Year's Day to achieve first place in the UPI rankings and second in the AP poll. The Trojans got off to a disappointing start by losing their first game to Arkansas, but then regrouped their forces and were undefeated the rest of the year. They reached what many observers believed was their peak by spotting Notre Dame 24 points and coming back to win 55–24 on the strength of four touchdown runs by All-American Anthony Davis. But the Trojans had to be better on New Year's Day against Ohio State in the Rose Bowl, and they were. With barely two min-

utes left in the game, quarterback Pat Haden threw a touchdown pass and a two-point conversion pass to give the Trojans an 18–17 victory.

Ohio State's Archie Griffin had run for more than 100 yd. in 22 consecutive games, an NCAA record, before Southern California held him to 76 yd. in the Rose Bowl. He was a major factor in the considerable success of the Buckeyes. They raced through eight wins before being upset by Michigan State 16–13. Then they came back to beat undefeated Michigan 12–10 on four field goals by Tom Klaban. The Big Ten Conference's athletic directors voted to send Ohio State to the Rose Bowl for the third straight year. This prompted Michigan coach Bo Schembechler, whose team had the same regular-season record (10–1) as the Buckeyes, to protest the conference's rule that its teams can play in no other bowl.

In the final AP poll Michigan finished third, one place ahead of Ohio State. Alabama was fifth, Notre Dame sixth, Penn State seventh, Auburn eighth, Nebraska ninth, and Miami of Ohio, which had only a tie marring its 11-game schedule, tenth.

Yale, which featured star running back Rudy Green and a stingy defense, had a legitimate chance to win the Lambert Trophy as the best team in the East until it came up against Harvard and its All-American receiver, Pat McInally, in their traditional meeting. Milt Holt, the Crimson's quarterback, ran for a five-yard touchdown in the waning moments of the game to upset Yale 21–16 and give the Lambert Trophy to Penn State. In the country's other major traditional game, Bob Jackson scored two touchdowns to lead Navy to a 19–0 win over Army. Central Michigan crushed Delaware 54–14 in the Camellia Bowl and was crowned champion of the NCAA's Division II, for smaller schools.

Griffin of Ohio State, whose 1,620 yd. gained led all major college players, became only the fifth junior to win the Heisman Trophy, symbolic of the top individual effort. The Outland Trophy, awarded annually to the outstanding lineman, went to Maryland defensive tackle Randy White.

Franco Harris of the Pittsburgh Steelers set a new Super Bowl rushing record, gaining 158 yd. in 34 carries against the Minnesota Vikings.

"Mean" Joe Greene pursues Minnesota Viking quarterback Fran Tarkenton in the Super Bowl. The game was won by Pittsburgh 16–6, largely as a consequence of an outstanding defensive performance by Greene and his teammates.

Confrontation of NFL players on the picket line was common during the 1974 preseason. Most veteran players supported the strike but rookies, who had yet to win places on their teams, generally played in preliminary contests in an effort to prove their worth.

Despite Griffin's superior yardage total, Louie Giammona of Utah State averaged 153.4 yd. for ten games to lead in that category. Giammona also led the NCAA's special category of all-purpose running by averaging 198.4 yd. a game rushing, pass receiving, and returning punts and kickoffs.

Temple University quarterback Steve Joachim led major college players in total offense with 222.7 yd. per game passing and running. The leading passer in the country, Steve Bartkowski of California, connected 182 times in 325 attempts, but his .560 completion average was well behind that of North Carolina's Chris Kupec, whose .694 (104 of 150) established an NCAA record. Dwight McDonald of San Diego State averaged 7.8 pass receptions a game to lead the nation, and Wisconsin running back Bill Marek paced scorers with 12.7 points per game.

As would befit a team as explosive as Oklahoma, the Sooners led the nation in total offense (507.7 yd. a game), rushing offense (438.8 yd.), and points per game (43). The toughest team in the country to score against was Michigan, which surrendered a scant 6.8 points per game.

After completing its 77th season, Vermont became the first state university to drop intercollegiate football. The school gave the burgeoning cost of the sport as its main reason, and economy-conscious officials at other institutions indicated that they might follow Vermont's example.

The need to save money was pointed up when total attendance at college games dropped for the first time in 20 years, putting an added burden on school athletic treasuries. Suggested was a return to one-platoon football, which allows only limited substitution and would therefore mean fewer scholarships.

Professional. The Pittsburgh Steelers defeated the Minnesota Vikings in the Super Bowl at the end of a season during which the National Football League's most significant battles were taking place off the field. A players' strike, soaring expenses, declining fan interest, and a court ruling that the player-reserve system was illegal all contributed to the gloom.

Preseason practice and exhibition games were hindered severely by the walkout in July and August, with the annual College All-Star game in Chicago, which was canceled, the most prominent casualty. The first formal strike in NFL history was resolved only superficially when the players elected to return to blocking and tackling without a new contract.

One of the contract issues for which the NFL Play-

ers Association was campaigning was ruled on favourably later in the year by U.S. District Court Judge William T. Sweigert. Acting on a suit brought by former quarterback Joe Kapp, who had been forbidden to play for the New England Patriots unless he signed a standard contract, Judge Sweigert determined that the reserve system violated antitrust laws. This meant that a player who has fulfilled the option clause of his contract becomes a free agent and can sign with any other team in the league, without that team having to compensate the one he left. Further legal wrangling should prevent the effect of the Kapp decision from being felt for several seasons.

The year ended with the NFL awaiting another federal court decision that could prove even more unsettling. The case hinged on a claim by the Internal Revenue Service that team managements should not be able to place a monetary value on players and use their depreciation to build a tax shelter.

In 1974 attendance dropped below ten million, and many more than a million other fans purchased tickets in advance for games and then failed to show up for them. Explanations for the shrinking crowds revolved mainly around the tight economy, which made $10 and $12 tickets a luxury, and the abundance of free football on television. But there was also a 9% decline in TV ratings for the league's games.

Despite these troubling developments, there were some happy people in the NFL. The happiest of all may have been in Pittsburgh, where the Steelers had played for 42 years before making it to a championship game. This is not to say, however, that the Steelers were spared rough moments during the season. Their offense was sporadic much of the time, and the team was split over whom it wanted as a starting quarterback—Terry Bradshaw, a white native of Louisiana, or Joe Gilliam, who won the job at the start of the year and was acclaimed nationally because he was a black man succeeding at a position no member of his race had ever held in the NFL.

By the time Pittsburgh won the American Conference's Central Division, Bradshaw was playing ahead of Gilliam. He proved that he belonged there when he directed the Steelers to a 32–14 victory over Buffalo, the first of their final two obstacles on the road to the Super Bowl. In addition to completing 12 of 19 passes for 203 yd. and one touchdown, Bradshaw directed his offense masterfully, catching Buffalo asleep with surprise plays and silencing the critics who had questioned his football intelligence quotient.

The Pittsburgh defense shackled Buffalo's O. J. Simpson, who ran for 1,125 yd. during the regular season and finished third behind league-leading rusher Otis Armstrong of Denver. But it was against the Steelers' second obstacle, the Oakland Raiders, that the defense reached its zenith.

A fierce line, led by tackle Joe Greene (*see* BIOGRAPHY) and end L. C. Greenwood, held the Raiders as a team to only 29 yd. on the ground. Linebackers Andy Russell and Jack Lambert helped apply the pressure that led to the interception of three Oakland passes. The rest of the time, Rocky Bleier and Franco Harris were running for 98 and 111 yd., respectively, as Pittsburgh's offense put across the points for a 24–13 win and the American Conference title.

The satisfaction felt by the Steelers' 73-year-old owner, Art Rooney, who founded the team in 1933, must have been as great as the disappointment of the Raiders. Although they had made the play-offs six

Table III
NFL Final Standings and Play-offs, 1974

AMERICAN CONFERENCE
Eastern Division

	W	L	T
Miami	11	3	0
*Buffalo	9	5	0
New England	7	7	0
New York Jets	7	7	0
Baltimore	2	12	0

Central Division

	W	L	T
Pittsburgh	10	3	1
Cincinnati	7	7	0
Houston	7	7	0
Cleveland	4	10	0

Western Division

	W	L	T
Oakland	12	2	0
Denver	7	6	1
San Diego	5	9	0
Kansas City	5	9	0

NATIONAL CONFERENCE
Eastern Division

	W	L	T
St. Louis	10	4	0
*Washington	10	4	0
Dallas	8	6	0
Philadelphia	7	7	0
New York Giants	2	12	0

Central Division

	W	L	T
Minnesota	10	4	0
Detroit	7	7	0
Green Bay	6	8	0
Chicago	4	10	0

Western Division

	W	L	T
Los Angeles	10	4	0
San Francisco	6	8	0
New Orleans	5	9	0
Atlanta	3	11	0

*Fourth qualifier for play-offs.

Play-offs
American semifinals
Oakland 28, Miami 26
Pittsburgh 32, Buffalo 14

National semifinals
Minnesota 30, St. Louis 14
Los Angeles 19, Washington 10

American finals
Pittsburgh 24, Oakland 13

National finals
Minnesota 14, Los Angeles 10

Super Bowl
Pittsburgh 16, Minnesota 6

times in the last seven seasons, the Raiders had not been to the Super Bowl since the 1967 season, when they unsuccessfully represented the old American Football League. In 1974 they had the best regular-season record in pro football (12–2), and they reached the conference finals by defeating the Miami Dolphins 28–26 in a game that could only be described as a classic.

The Dolphins, the defending Super Bowl champions, appeared to have won the game with about two minutes left when rookie Benny Malone tightroped his way for 23 yd. down the sideline to put Miami ahead 26–21. But Oakland quarterback Ken Stabler, who had already thrown for three touchdowns in the game, coolly directed the Raiders down the field and, with 26 seconds remaining, passed to the diving Clarence Davis for a fourth score and victory.

The style with which the Minnesota Vikings marched to the Super Bowl was neither as heartening—they were back for the second year in a row—nor as dramatic as Pittsburgh's. Minnesota, which won its division handily with a 10–4 record, took care of its first play-off opponent, the St. Louis Cardinals, 30–14. The game was tied 7–7 when the Vikings broke it open with 16 points in five minutes during the third quarter. Fred Cox kicked a 37-yd. field goal, cornerback Nate Wright returned a recovered fumble 20 yd. for a touchdown, and quarterback Fran Tarkenton threw his second scoring pass of the day to John Gilliam to kill the St. Louis hopes.

The Los Angeles Rams, who won their first play-off game over the Washington Redskins 19–10, gave Minnesota more of a struggle, but in the end their mistakes did them in. Los Angeles lost three fumbles, had two passes intercepted, and was pressured into a variety of penalties, bobbles, and other mistakes by Minnesota's Carl Eller, Jim Marshall, and Alan Page, aging defenders once revered as the "Purple People Eaters." Their work was enough to make a Tarkenton touchdown pass to Jim Lash and a 1-yd. scoring plunge by Dave Osborne stand up for the 14–10 win that clinched the National Conference title.

Defense dominated the Super Bowl as Pittsburgh outlasted Minnesota 16–6 on a wet and slippery field in New Orleans. The Steelers' redoubtable line held the Vikings to 17 yd. rushing and frequently batted down Fran Tarkenton's passes just as they left his hand. Pittsburgh fullback Franco Harris set a Super Bowl rushing record with 158 yd. in 34 carries. The Steeler scores came on a safety (the only score in the first half), a 9-yd. run by Harris, and a 4-yd. pass by Terry Bradshaw to Larry Brown. Minnesota tallied when Terry Brown recovered a blocked punt in the Pittsburgh end zone.

The World Football League had enough trouble in its first year of business to fill any ten NFL seasons. Early in the season it was disclosed that some of the WFL's 12 teams were inflating their attendance figures. By the end of the season there were only ten teams left, Detroit and Jacksonville having gone out of business, and two of those ten had to move to survive, New York to Charlotte and Houston to Shreveport. The U.S. Internal Revenue Service filed liens against the holdings of Birmingham, Jacksonville, and Portland. According to conservative estimates, the WFL was $10 million in debt.

Part of that debt was salaries owed to players on seven teams, including the two in the league's championship game, the Birmingham Americans and the Florida Blazers. Players from both teams threatened to boycott the first World Bowl, which Birmingham won 22–21.

The league's owners eventually ousted WFL founder Gary Davidson (*see* BIOGRAPHY) as president and replaced him with Chris Hemmeter, one of the operators of the Hawaii franchise. The plan at the year's end seemed to be to tread water until the arrival of the 60-odd NFL players who had signed with WFL teams. But Oakland's Stabler was trying to find a legal way out of his contract with Birmingham, and others seemed sure to follow suit.

Canadian Football. Defense proved to be the salvation of the Montreal Alouettes as they surprised the favoured Edmonton Eskimos 20–7 in the Grey Cup game, the Canadian Football League's version of the Super Bowl. Living up to their regular-season reputation, the Alouette defenders repeatedly left their offense in scoring position and Edmonton's far back in its own territory on a waterlogged neutral field in Vancouver.

Perhaps the most telling blow of the game was delivered by end Junior Ah You and tackle Glen Weir on the shoulder of the Eskimos' star quarterback, Tom Wilkinson, shortly after he threw a first-quarter touchdown pass. Wilkinson went reeling to the sidelines, and Edmonton proceeded to flounder to its second Grey Cup defeat in two years.

Montreal got its first score on a five-yard touchdown run by halfback Larry Sherrer, but thereafter everything revolved around kicker Don Sweet. Sweet's four field goals broke a 33-year-old Grey Cup record and established a margin Edmonton could never overcome. (JOHN SCHULIAN)

[452.B.4.h.xiii]

Forestry

According to the Food and Agriculture Organization (FAO) of the United Nations, 1973 was the most favourable year for all sectors of the forest products market in some time, and early reports indicated that the trend continued in 1974. After a period of several years with rising costs but static prices, production in 1973 reached peak levels and prices rose sharply resulting in better profits.

Preliminary estimates published by the FAO indicated that world roundwood production rose 4% between 1972 and 1973, an appreciably higher rate of increase than in previous years. Growth in the production of roundwood resulted in sharp increases in trade, with substantial price increases also reported worldwide. The volume in trade of coniferous roundwood increased by 16% and its value by 84%. Volume in trade of non-coniferous (mainly tropical hardwood) logs increased by 20% and its value by 98%.

World production of sawn softwood rose 3% between 1972 and 1973, to 345 million cu.m. This increase occurred mainly in Western Europe, with production in the U.S. down slightly from the 1972 level. The National Forest Products Association reported total sawn wood (including softwood and hardwood) in the U.S. for 1973 at 89,420,400 cu.m. This was down slightly from the 1972 total of 90,279,440 cu.m. Estimated U.S. production of sawn wood for the first quarter of 1974 indicated a 5.3% drop from the corresponding period of 1973, a decrease attributed to the slump in housing construction.

Pulpwood production increased by 4% in 1973 to 114.7 million tons but this was not sufficient to meet the demand from the papermaking industry. Difficulties in obtaining pulp and paper supplies were experienced worldwide, with the result that pulp prices increased 50% between July 1973 and July 1974. Pulp and paper mills were operating at full capacity in sharp contrast to earlier years, and a supply-demand imbalance was expected to remain until new investments were made to increase capacity. The industry estimates that it takes at least three years to bring new mills into production.

A new ruling that would affect world trade was put into effect by the U.S. Department of Agriculture (USDA) in March 1974. The ruling bans log exports from national forest lands west of the 100th meridian. It also stipulates that timber from western national forests will no longer be sold to replace timber cut from private lands for export. Japan, which receives 85% of U.S. log exports, was expected to turn to Canada and the U.S.S.R. for its log needs and had already increased imports from the U.S.S.R. in 1973.

A National Academy of Sciences (NAS) committee Report published in March 1974 on "The Effects of Herbicides in South Viet Nam" concluded that serious, long-term damage had been inflicted by the U.S. over a nine-year period in an effort to defoliate Vietnamese forests for military purposes. The extent of damage to the inland forests, which cover about 62% of South Vietnam, depended on the number of times sprayed and the bomb damage; the committee concluded that large-scale rehabilitation of these areas could restore them to productive forestry. Damage to coastal mangrove forests, which cover 2% of South Vietnam, was greater, and it was concluded that "under present conditions of use and natural regrowth, it may take well over 100 years for the mangrove area to be reforested."

The ban on the use of DDT in the U.S. was lifted in February 1974 to allow the U.S. Forest Service to spray about 410,000 ac. in the Blue Mountains of Oregon and Washington to control a particularly severe outbreak of the tussock moth. The moth infestation had spread to nearly 800,000 ac., mainly Douglas fir trees, and had caused varying degrees of damage to the trees ranging from complete death to loss of

A ranger examines a fallen giant in Sequoia National Park, California. Carpenter ants have been found in nearly all such trees, and it is thought that their nesting habit, which tends to hollow out the sequoias, is a contributory cause of the destruction.

less than a quarter of the crown. The net timber loss, minus salvageable timber, was estimated by the U.S. Forest Service at $43 million. DDT, a persistent pesticide, had been banned by the Environmental Protection Agency in December 1972, except in the case of an emergency in which no alternative chemical would be effective. The Forest Service said that the tussock moth outbreak was such an emergency and the EPA "reluctantly" granted approval for its use. Following the spraying, which took place over a period of six weeks in June and July, the area was closely monitored for adverse effects on water and wildlife. Environmentalists claimed that the infestation, which occurs at periodic intervals, would eventually have succumbed to natural controls. The EPA said that the one-time lifting of the ban on DDT was not to be considered a precedent.

Recreational demands on the national forests continued in the U.S. with the result that the Forest Service had to limit public access to one of the most popular mountain areas in the country—Mt. Whitney and adjacent peaks in the Sierra Nevada Range in California. Starting with the summer season of 1974, only 75 persons per day were allowed to climb the 14,494-ft. mountain. Previously as many as 250 persons per day used the mountain trail. The area, in the Inyo National Forest, was set aside as a wilderness area, but the Forest Service said the intense use caused a multitude of problems, not the least of which was loss of wilderness solitude.

An Endangered Species Act was passed by the U.S. Congress and became law in late December 1973, supplanting the previous Endangered Species Conservation Act of 1969. The new law includes plants as well as animals and covers threatened as well as endangered species. Under the law the secretary of the Smithsonian Institution was directed to review the species of plants that are now or may become threatened and to report to Congress recommendations for conserving such species. Nearly 50 species of trees were proposed for review, including the American elm, threatened by disease, and the Monterey cypress, threatened by loss of habitat.

The United States proclaimed March 21, 1974, as World Forestry Day, and it was proposed that the event be made an annual one. The date was selected because it marks the first day of spring in the Northern Hemisphere. World Forestry Day had the endorsement of the European Federation of Agriculture and the FAO.   (IRENE MC MANUS)

See Environment; Industrial Production and Technology.
[724.C.8.a–b; 731.B.3; 732.C.8]

ENCYCLOPÆDIA BRITANNICA FILMS. *The Coniferous Forest Biome* (1969); *Problems of Conservation—Forest and Range* (1969); *Problems of Conservation—Our Natural Resources* (1970).

WIDE WORLD

France

A republic of Western Europe and head of the French Community, France is bounded by the English Channel, Belgium, Luxembourg, West Germany, Switzerland, Italy, the Mediterranean Sea, Monaco, Spain, Andorra, and the Atlantic Ocean. Area: 210,039 sq.mi. (543,998 sq.km.), including Corsica. Pop. (1974 est.): 52,343,000. Cap. and largest city: Paris (pop., 1974 est., 2,425,000). Language: French. Religion: predominantly Roman

FRANCE

Education. (1972–73) Primary, pupils 7,309,-000, teachers (state only; 1970–71) 184,326; secondary, pupils 3,743,000; vocational, pupils 915,000; secondary and vocational, teachers (1969–70) 248,934; teacher training (1969–70), students 31,228, teachers 2,309; higher (including 36 universities), students 886,000, teaching staff (1969–70) 31,039.

Finance. Monetary unit: franc, with (Sept. 16, 1974) a free rate of Fr. 4.81 to U.S. $1 (Fr. 11.13 = £1 sterling). Gold, SDRs, and foreign exchange, official: (June 1974) U.S. $7,707,000,-000; (June 1973) U.S. $10,997,000,000. Budget (1973 actual): revenue Fr. 230,040,000,000; expenditure Fr. 222,710,000,000. Gross national product: (1972) Fr. 1,001,900,000,000; (1971) Fr. 899.6 billion. Money supply: (Dec. 1973) Fr. 332.1 billion; (Dec. 1972) Fr. 302,520,000,000. Cost of living (1970 = 100): (June 1974) 136; (June 1973) 119.

Foreign Trade. (1973) Imports Fr. 167,250,-000,000; exports Fr. 162,460,000,000. Import sources: EEC 55% (West Germany 23%, Belgium-Luxembourg 12%, Italy 9%, The Netherlands 6%, U.K. 5%); U.S. 8%. Export destinations: EEC 55% (West Germany 19%, Italy 12%, Belgium-Luxembourg 11%, U.K. 6%, The Netherlands 5%); Switzerland 5%; U.S. 5%. Main exports: machinery 18%; motor vehicles 11%; chemicals 10%; iron and steel 7%; cereals 6%; textile yarn and fabrics 5%. Tourism: visitors (1971) 14.7 million; gross receipts (1972) U.S. $1,920,000,000.

Transport and Communications. Roads (1973) 793,826 km. (including 2,426 km. expressways). Motor vehicles in use (1973): passenger 14,620,000; commercial 1,980,000. Railways: (1972) 34,710 km.; traffic (1973) 44,547,000,000 passenger-km., freight 73,824,-000,000 net ton-km. Air traffic (1973): 19,492,-000,000 passenger-km.; freight 835,995,000 net ton-km. Navigable inland waterways in regular use (1972) 7,136 km.; freight traffic 14,156,-000,000 ton-km. Shipping (1973): merchant vessels 100 gross tons and over 1,376; gross tonnage 8,288,773. Telephones (Dec. 1972) 10,338,000. Radio licenses (Dec. 1972) 17,034,000. Television licenses (Dec. 1972) 12,279,000.

Agriculture. Production (in 000; metric tons; 1973; 1972 in parentheses): wheat 17,792 (18,-123); rye 327 (331); barley 10,844 (10,426); oats 2,203 (2,464); corn 10,635 (8,190); potatoes 7,449 (7,966); rice 71 (52); rapeseed 661 (722); sunflower seed 91 (73); tomatoes c. 490 (490); onions c. 168 (168); apples 3,239 (2,811); pears 490 (469); flax fibre (1972) 46, (1971) 53; sugar, raw value c. 3,150 (2,981); wine c. 8,000 (5,854); tobacco 51 (48); beef and veal c. 1,360 (1,456); pork c. 1,650 (1,541); milk (1972) c. 30,350, (1971) 28,693; butter (1972) c. 573, (1971) c. 502; cheese (1972) c. 863, (1971) 816; fish catch (1972) 783, (1971) 742. Livestock (in 000; Oct. 1972): cattle 21,902; sheep 10,218; pigs 11,525; horses 480; poultry (1972) c. 190,000.

Industry. Index of production (1970 = 100): (1973) 120; (1972) 112. Fuel and power (in 000; 1973): coal (metric tons) 25,681; electricity (kw.-hr.) 174,080,000; natural gas (cu.m.) 7,539,000; manufactured gas (cu.m.; 1972) 6,071,000. Production (in 000; metric tons; 1973): bauxite 3,104; iron ore (32% metal content) 54,232; pig iron 20,287; crude steel 25,-264; aluminum 590; lead 159; zinc 268; cement 30,717; cotton yarn 272; cotton fabrics 211; wool yarn 151; wool fabrics 66; rayon, etc., filament yarn 49; rayon, etc., staple fibre 86; nylon, etc., filament yarn 112; nylon, etc., staple fibre 155; sulfuric acid 4,383; petroleum products (1972) 108,600; fertilizers (nutrient content; 1972–73) nitrogenous 1,472, phosphate 1,620, potash 1,672; passenger cars (units) 3,202; commercial vehicles (units) 394. Merchant vessels launched (100 gross tons and over; 1973) 1,123,-800 gross tons.

Catholic with Protestant and Jewish minorities. Presidents in 1974, Georges Pompidou until April 2, Alain Poher (interim president), and, from May 27, Valéry Giscard d'Estaing; premiers, Pierre Messmer and, from May 27, Jacques Chirac.

The most momentous events of 1974 were the sudden death of Pres. Georges Pompidou (*see* OBITUARIES) on April 2 and the election of former minister of economy and finance Valéry Giscard d'Estaing (*see* BIOGRAPHY) as his successor after France's most exciting election campaign in many years. The extremely narrow margin by which Giscard d'Estaing defeated the United Left candidate, François Mitterrand, testified to a further increase in the widespread desire for change that had been evident in the legislative elections the previous year, a factor that the new government could not afford to ignore.

Domestic Affairs. During the first three months of 1974 President Pompidou faced the first consequences of the economic and financial crisis brought about by the quadrupling of the price of oil. At an extraordinary meeting of the Council of Ministers held on January 19, it was decided to float the franc for a period of six months. A censure motion proposed by the left in the National Assembly failed by a wide margin.

It was in this context that Foreign Minister Michel Jobert visited Saudi Arabia, Kuwait, and Syria in order to negotiate bilateral agreements with the oil-producing Arab states that would guarantee France a quarter of its total requirements. In the long term, France remained in favour of calling a conference of European and Arab states to seek a general solution to the problem.

In the sphere of industrial relations France's longest strike, that at the Lip watch factory in Besançon which had lasted almost a year, came to a satisfactory conclusion at the end of January. However, the stock exchange and banks in Paris were paralyzed by strikes lasting several weeks and industrial disputes affected various other sectors including the Atlantic dockyards, the major hotels of Paris, and Air France.

In an effort to increase the "cohesion and solidarity" of the government, President Pompidou decided at the end of February to reshuffle the Cabinet, the second of Premier Messmer's term of office. Messmer, who had succeeded Jacques Chaban-Delmas in July 1972, had been confirmed in his position after the legislative elections of 1973. Contrary to general expectations, however, his third Cabinet was not markedly different from the second. The main changes were as follows: Jacques Chirac (Union des Démocrates pour la République, UDR) replaced Raymond Marcellin (Independent Republicans, IR) as minister of the interior, while Marcellin took over Chirac's former position as minister of agriculture; Alain Peyrefitte (UDR) replaced Maurice Druon (nonparliamentary) and Robert Poujade (UDR) as minister of cultural affairs and the environment; Valéry Giscard d'Estaing (IR), who retained the portfolio for economy and finance, became a minister of state.

A few days after the reshuffle Messmer inaugurated the new Charles de Gaulle airport at Roissy to the north of Paris, which would gradually replace Orly as the capital's main airport with an eventual capacity of 8 million–10 million passengers a year.

The interruption of radio and television programs on April 2 for the announcement that Pres. Georges Pompidou had died suddenly just after 9 o'clock in the evening came as a profound shock to the people of France. While it was widely known that the president had been ill, perhaps even gravely ill, for some time, and although he had appeared very tired during his meeting with Soviet party leader Leonid I. Brezhnev at the Black Sea resort of Pitsunda in March, even those closest to him were shocked by his death.

Perhaps the hallmark of Georges Pompidou's presidency and the qualities for which the French would remember him were above all his physical endurance, his courage in adversity, and his personal contribution to the reconstruction of France, following in the wake of his illustrious predecessor, Charles de Gaulle. As requested in his will, Pompidou was buried quietly at the village of Orvilliers, after a mass at the church of St. Louis-en-l'Île in Paris. On April 6, a day of national mourning, a solemn memorial service at the cathedral of Notre Dame was attended by many foreign dignitaries. The previous day, the president of the Senate, Alain Poher, had moved to the Élysée Palace to carry out the duties of interim head of state for the second time in his career.

A bank holiday on August 15 was celebrated in Paris by closing part of the famed Champs-Élysées to traffic. Scores of pedestrians enjoyed a stroll on the usually congested roadway.

The Presidential Election. No less than 12 candidates stood for election in the first round, held on May 5, representing all shades of political opinion. The major figures, however, were the candidate of the Socialist-Communist alliance, Mitterrand, and the two candidates of the ruling majority, Chaban-Delmas (UDR) and Giscard d'Estaing (IR). The result of the first ballot was remarkable less for the easy victory of Mitterrand, which had been expected, than for the very large turnout (over 25 million out of some 30 million voters) and above all for the ease with which Giscard d'Estaing outstripped Chaban-Delmas, providing further clear evidence of the desire for change and the loss of impetus Gaullism had suffered after 16 years in power. Chaban-Delmas was thus eliminated from the second round, which according to law was to be fought out between the two best-placed candidates in the first round in the event neither secured an absolute majority at that stage.

The fortnight's interval between the two ballots saw Mitterrand and Giscard d'Estaing join battle in a fierce contest. Both candidates toured the country promising change and reform, the campaign culminating in a televised encounter between the two. On the eve of the ballot public opinion polls still placed the two candidates neck and neck. Certainly no election in recent years had aroused such interest and excitement, as witnessed by the record turnout of electors (86.17%) on May 19. Out of the 26,367,807 votes cast, Giscard d'Estaing gained the necessary absolute majority with 13,396,203 (50.81%) as against 12,-971,604 (49.19%) for Mitterrand.

The narrow margin of just over 400,000 votes that separated the two candidates meant that if the new president wished to regard himself as "president of all the French" he would have to take into account the views of that half of the French population that had not voted for him. In fact, with more than 49% of the votes cast, the left had achieved its greatest electoral success since 1946.

On May 27 the new president took up his official quarters at the Élysée Palace. Having based his electoral campaign on promises of change and innovation, Giscard d'Estaing lost no time in instituting various innovations in the inauguration procedures. Shunning the usual processional pomp, the new president made the last part of his journey to the palace, from the statue of Clémenceau to the Élysée, on foot. After the ceremony, for which he wore a business suit instead of the customary morning dress, he set out once again on foot along the Champs-Élysées from the Avenue George-V to the Arc de Triomphe, cheered by an enthusiastic crowd.

The president's passion for change went far beyond symbolic changes in the inauguration ceremony, however. Within three days Premier Messmer had been replaced by the 42-year-old Jacques Chirac (UDR; *see* BIOGRAPHY), a new government had been formed, and the inaugural address pronounced in Parliament. The new government was completed on June 8 by the addition of 21 secretaries of state and presented a very different image from the previous administration. The ousting of many of the Gaullist "barons" of the UDR, the largest group within the ruling majority, and the bringing in of a strong contingent of reformers and centrists marked the end of the Gaullist continuity that had been the hallmark of the Fifth Republic. The surprise election of Chirac as secretary-general of the UDR on December 14 was expected to bring about a further dissolution of traditional Gaullism.

The new government was composed as follows: premier, Jacques Chirac (UDR); minister of state and of the interior, Michel Poniatowski (IR; *see* BIOGRAPHY); justice, Jean Lecanuet (Reform Movement, Ref.; *see* BIOGRAPHY); defense, Jacques Soufflet (UDR); reforms, Jean-Jacques Servan-Schreiber (Ref.); foreign affairs, Jean Sauvagnargues (nonparliamentary); economy and finance, Jean-Pierre Fourcade (nonparliamentary); education, René Haby (nonparliamentary); cooperation, Pierre Abelin (Ref.); public works, Robert Galley (UDR); agriculture, Christian Bonnet (IR); quality of life, André Jarrot (UDR); labour, Michel Durafour (Ref.); health, Simone Veil (nonparliamentary); industry, Michel d'Ornano (IR); commerce and small traders, Vincent Ansquer (UDR).

By the evening of June 9, however, Servan-Schreiber had lost his job as minister for reforms. He had expressed opinions, criticizing the government's policy of continuing nuclear tests in the Pacific despite worldwide protest, which were regarded as being contrary to the "essential principles of government solidarity" and he was promptly dismissed. A week later his colleague on the political weekly *L'Express,* editor in chief Françoise Giroud (*see* BIOGRAPHY), was appointed secretary of state for women's affairs.

In his first press conference on July 25, in which he defined himself as a "traditionalist who loves change," and in his broadcast address on August 27 three months after taking office, President Giscard d'Estaing stressed the changes that had taken place since the beginning of his term of office. The three main axes of his policy in the short term were the transformation of society, the battle against inflation, and the political construction of Europe.

In his second press conference, on October 24, traditionally devoted to foreign policy, the president broke with the practice of his predecessors in addressing himself above all to economic problems. On the question of the world energy crisis, Giscard d'Estaing proposed calling a conference early in 1975 to bring together representatives of the major oil-exporting nations, the industrialized consumer countries, and the nonindustrialized importing countries. He envisaged a system that would guarantee supplies for the consumer countries and revenues for the producing countries based on lower price levels than those currently obtaining.

On the Palestinian problem, the president stressed that the problem would have to be dealt with as a whole in an international context and that the "Palestinian fact" would have to be recognized by all sides just as it had been recognized by the UN. Only then could a lasting settlement be achieved. The proposals were hailed as "realistic and progressive" by the Palestine Liberation Organization, but the Israeli government was quick to express its disappointment.

Parliament. The normal session of Parliament that had been interrupted by the presidential elections duly came to an end on June 28, but was prolonged by an extraordinary session of some ten days so that the first steps toward the new administration's "transformation of society" could be undertaken without delay. On June 6 Premier Chirac's declaration of general policy had been favourably received by the National Assembly by 297 votes to 181, giving him the support of all the UDR, IR, and Union Centriste members as well as almost all those of the Reformers.

Social legislation included measures liberalizing the law on contraception and abortion (passed by the National Assembly on November 29 and by the Senate on December 15), together with increases in old age pensions and other social benefits. A bill reducing the age of civil and electoral majority from 21 to 18 was passed by both houses at the end of June.

The government's interim measures for "cooling down" inflation were also passed by the National Assembly, with 291 votes in favour to 182 against. Company tax was raised by 18% and the surtax on high individual incomes from 5 to 15%. The price of oil and other fuel products was raised slightly.

After lengthy debates, the long-mooted legislation for the reform and reorganization of the Office de Radiodiffusion et Télévision Française (ORTF) was passed by the National Assembly and by the Senate at the end of July. While eschewing the idea of turning the national radio and television network over to private enterprise, the legislation nevertheless provided for the breaking down of the massive organization into six separate publicly owned companies and the closing of its centralized headquarters. (*See* TELEVISION AND RADIO.)

On October 21 members of Parliament meeting in congress at Versailles gave the required three-fifths majority vote to a new constitutional measure that would allow a fixed number of parliamentarians (60 deputies or senators) to demand that the Constitutional Council examine any piece of legislation to establish whether it was constitutional.

The budget debates in the autumn took place in an atmosphere clouded by threats of rising unemployment. By the end of September the number of unemployed had risen to about half a million, a record figure for France and an increase of some 30% over the previous year's figures, a fact that could hardly fail to provoke a new wave of social unrest despite the government's efforts to deal with the problem. Two months later the figure had risen further to

689,200. (Worst affected was the automotive industry; state aid of Fr. 1,450,000,000 to the Citroën and Renault concerns was announced in December.)

Industrial and Social Unrest. Industrial agitation continued to be fostered by Georges Séguy and Edmond Maire, leaders of the powerful Confédération Générale du Travail (CGT) and Confédération Française Démocratique du Travail (CFDT), respectively. During the summer, while peasants protested falling prices for agricultural produce coupled with rising production costs, outbreaks of violent protest by detainees in French penal institutions led to the deaths of several wardens and the preparation of government plans for the "humanization" of the prison system. In September the crew of the liner "France" forced its captain to drop anchor just off Le Havre where the ship remained for some time while the crew protested plans to scrap the liner and demanded guarantees regarding future employment of its crew.

In the last four months of the year the government launched its "operation price brake," designed to reduce the effects of inflation and to encourage people to redevelop the skill of "shopping around" for bargains. As part of the campaign, some 200,000 shopkeepers agreed voluntarily to reduce the prices of a set range of goods by 5%, the range of goods involved to vary at three-month intervals.

On September 11 President Giscard d'Estaing took a step unprecedented in recent times and called a Council of Ministers at Lyons. The council approved a bill to give equal social protection to all by Jan. 1, 1978. This was followed on October 14 by the signing of an agreement between employers and labour unions guaranteeing payments equal to a year's real wages to any employee dismissed from his post. This was widely regarded as a momentous occasion in the history of the struggle for social security.

However, this did not prevent the outbreak of a fresh series of strikes in the autumn, the most spectacular being the postal strike that paralyzed French mail services for several weeks. In addition, there were sporadic stoppages in the coal-mining and transport industries and in various public services.

Foreign Affairs. "The construction of Europe is the great aim of our foreign policy," declared Foreign Minister Sauvagnargues to the National Assembly at the beginning of November. Indeed, this was the thrust of French foreign policy under Giscard d'Estaing, despite the fact that the new president was in many ways more favourably disposed toward the Atlantic alliance than his predecessors.

Thus it was that three times in as many months the French president met his West German counterpart, Chancellor Helmut Schmidt (*see* BIOGRAPHY), as the Franco-German team did its best to pull Europe out of the economic rut. Sauvagnargues put forward on behalf of France proposals for a series of measures aimed at reinforcing the cohesion and solidarity of the EEC, and further initiatives in this direction were expected. For the moment, the problem was made more difficult due to the uncertainty surrounding Great Britain's membership in the EEC since the coming to power of Harold Wilson's Labour government and its proposals for renegotiating the terms of Britain's treaty of accession. At his meeting with Wilson in Paris in July Giscard d'Estaing stated that France was not prepared to agree to renegotiations of the type demanded by Britain and the position remained uncertain throughout the rest of the year. A summit meeting of EEC heads of government in

Paris in December led to a verbal confrontation between the two when Wilson accused Giscard d'Estaing of blocking renegotiations and hindering progress, although the final communiqué issued after a meeting of foreign ministers left room for hope that the problems of Britain's relationship with the EEC in general and France in particular might be overcome.

NATO's Ministerial Council opened its session at Ottawa in June and allowed Sauvagnargues and U.S. Secretary of State Henry Kissinger to iron out Franco-U.S. differences. It also paved the way for President Giscard d'Estaing's three-day summit meeting with U.S. Pres. Gerald Ford in December. The meeting took place on the French Carribbean island of Martinique, a major topic of discussion being the world energy crisis. A communiqué issued after the discussions proposed the holding of a preparatory conference of oil-exporting and consuming countries in March 1975, to be followed as soon as possible by a world energy conference. Earlier in December Giscard d'Estaing had received Soviet party leader Leonid I. Brezhnev, continuing the policy of regular talks pursued by his predecessors, and the two had signed an agreement for France to build a Fr. 6 billion aluminum plant in Siberia.

As a result of agreements concluded during the visit to Paris of the shah of Iran and Empress Farah at the end of June and Chirac's visit to Teheran in December, France had become one of Iran's principal trading partners. President Giscard d'Estaing was invited by Algerian Pres. Houari Boumédienne to pay an official visit to Algiers in 1975, the first by a French head of state since Algerian independence.

Canadian Prime Minister Pierre Trudeau's visit to Paris in October was the first by a Canadian prime minister in ten years, as well as the first since de Gaulle's notorious "Long live Free Quebec" speech in Montreal in 1967, and marked a definite step forward in Franco-Canadian economic cooperation.

During the summer the decision was taken to lift the embargo on deliveries of arms to the Middle East imposed by de Gaulle in 1967, and in October Foreign Minister Sauvagnargues took up his predecessor's policy of rapprochement with the Arab states with a visit to the Middle East. The trip was significant above all for his meeting with the leader of the Palestine Liberation Organization, Yasir Arafat, a clear indication of France's own recognition of the "Palestinian fact." In December it was announced that Saudi Arabia had placed a Fr. 4 billion arms order with France.   (JEAN KNECHT)

[972.A.2]

Furs

Despite the economic difficulties confronting the Western world in 1974, fur sales maintained the good pace of the previous two years and may even have shown a modest increase. In the U.S., where inflation and high interest rates dampened general consumer spending, retailers were genuinely surprised by the number of furs purchased in the preseason months of June, July, and August. Similar gains were registered in Western Europe and Japan. Among the major consuming nations, only Italy fell behind, and this was attributed to the heavy import duties and sales taxes imposed by the Italian government.

Pressed for an explanation, analysts suggested that the traditional customer for expensive furs was not seriously hurt by the economic situation and/or that people were inclined to put their depreciating money into luxuries. Another possibility was that the energy crisis and the falling stock market had made travel and investments less attractive, so that money was available for other purchases.

Complete figures were not yet available at year's end, but Jess Chernak, executive secretary of the American Fur Industry, central association for the U.S. trade, estimated that 1974 sales were somewhat above the previous year's total of $440,841,000. His analysis, based on reports from manufacturers and retailers, was that low- and high-priced fur garments had moved well while furs in middle ranges had lagged. This appeared to reflect the economic pressure on the middle classes. The wealthy were largely unaffected, while the consumer at the lower end of the scale saw furs as representing a greater intrinsic value than cloth.

The association's projections indicated that fur sales in the U.S. rose by $30 million or more for the year. Allowing for an average price increase of about 10%, this would mean a slight decrease in the number of units sold. However, the association's statistics did not take into consideration inexpensive jackets and coats made of rabbit and pieced furs imported from Canada and the Far East and sold by large department and specialty stores. It was estimated that these garments accounted for an additional $50 million.

High interest rates and tight money caused major problems for U.S. fur manufacturers. Retailers delayed paying for their merchandise even after they had sold it, since it was considerably cheaper to use the money for operating expenses than to borrow from banks. As a result, manufacturers were forced to borrow at high interest rates to cover their own obligations, thereby cutting down their profits.

With some minor variations, fur skin prices held firm at the previous year's levels. The price of mink skins, still the mainstay of the industry, advanced about 5% on average. Certain longhairs, such as fox and lynx, declined a bit from the record highs of 1973, mainly because Italian skin buyers were less active.

According to the Crop Reporting Board of the U.S. Department of Agriculture, mink pelt production in the U.S. in 1973–74 totaled 3,037,000, or 2% more than in the preceding crop year. This was the first increase in almost a decade, reflecting two years of higher prices. Fifteen states accounted for 95% of U.S. mink production, and five—Wisconsin, Minnesota, Utah, Oregon, and Illinois—produced 63%. Standard dark types represented 35.8% of the total, pastel 35.4%, pearl 10.2%, violet 8.6%, and sapphire 4.5%; the balance included white, gunmetal, lavender, pale brown, and platinum. There were 1,329 ranchers producing mink at the beginning of 1974, compared with 1,380 a year earlier.

U.S. mink prices for the year averaged about $23 for darks and $20 for mutations (all other colours). This was only 5% above 1973 levels, while ranchers' costs had risen at least 10%. Indications at year's end were that 1975 output might rise slightly, since production is planned two years in advance, but that 1976 could see a further decline. For both U.S. and Scandinavian ranchers, much would depend on the prices obtained in the 1975 season. With costs of feed, labour, maintenance, and overhead all rising, it appeared that a 15% price increase would be needed merely to hold the line.

One category in which prices fell substantially during the year was Alaska fur seal, reflecting sharply diminished demand for that item in the U.S. and the falloff in Italian purchases. (SANDY PARKER)

See also Fashion and Dress.
[724.C.8.e; 732.C.4]

Gabon

A republic of western equatorial Africa, Gabon is bounded by Equatorial Guinea, Cameroon, the Congo, and the Atlantic Ocean. Area: 103,347 sq.mi. (267,667 sq. km.). Pop. (1973 est.): 980,000. Cap. and largest city: Libreville (pop., 1970, 105,080). Language: French and Bantu dialects. Religion: traditional tribal beliefs; Christian minority. President in 1974, Omar Bongo.

New agreements with France, reached in Paris on Feb. 12, 1974, featured a rise in the price of raw materials supplied by Gabon to France. Gabon would remain in the franc zone, and a detachment of French troops would continue to be stationed in Gabon. Prices to France were raised again in May. Government participation was introduced and increased in French-owned industries and mines.

On May 22 Gabon announced the termination of its cooperation agreements with Libya, none of which had been implemented by the latter. The Organization of African Unity reported that of its 42 members Gabon was one of the nine unaffected by the oil crisis; it had become in the course of two years a modestly significant producer of crude oil.

After refusal of the World Bank and the European Investment Bank to finance the trans-Gabon railway project, the European Commission on May 22 agreed to provide $7 million from EEC funds; a number of countries, including the U.S., Canada, and South Africa, also joined in. The railway would open up the interior and transport Gabon's raw materials other than

GABON
Education. (1972–73) Primary, pupils 110,472, teachers 2,436; secondary, pupils 11,734, teachers 373; vocational, pupils 2,419, teachers 212; teacher training, students 301, teachers (1970–71) 22; higher, students 533.
Finance. Monetary unit: CFA franc, with (Sept. 16, 1974) a parity of CFA Fr. 50 to the French franc (free rate of CFA Fr. 240.50 = U.S. $1; CFA Fr. 556.50 = £1 sterling). Budget (1973 est.): revenue CFA Fr. 34.3 billion; expenditure CFA Fr. 26.2 billion.
Foreign Trade. (1972) Imports CFA Fr. 35 billion; exports CFA Fr. 50.3 billion. Import sources: France 58%; U.S. 11%; West Germany 10%. Export destinations: France 35%; U.S. 9%; West Germany 7%; Netherlands Antilles 6%. Main exports (1971): crude oil 44%; timber 23%; manganese 19%; plywood 6%.
Transport and Communications. Roads (1973) 6,848 km. Motor vehicles in use (1970): passenger 7,100; commercial 5,800. Railways (1973) 372 km. Construction of a Trans-Gabon railway (332 km.) was begun in 1974. Telephones (Dec. 1972) 18,000. Radio receivers (Dec. 1971) 65,000. Television receivers (Dec. 1971) 1,300.
Agriculture. Production (in 000; metric tons; 1972; 1971 in parentheses): corn *c.* 2 (*c.* 2); coffee *c.* 1 (*c.* 0.9); cocoa *c.* 5 (5); bananas *c.* 10 (*c.* 10); timber (cu.m.; 1972) 3,200, (1971) 3,200. Livestock (in 000; 1972): cattle *c.* 5; pigs *c.* 5; sheep *c.* 55; goats *c.* 60.
Industry. Production (in 000; metric tons; 1972): manganese ore (metal content) 988; crude oil (1973) 7,598; uranium 0.2; petroleum products 903; electricity (kw-hr.) 134,000.

petroleum—iron, manganese, timber, and uranium—more easily to the coast.

President Bongo in October paid an official visit to China, recognized by Gabon in March. (*See also* EQUATORIAL GUINEA.) (R. M. GOODWIN)
[978.E.7.a.iv]

Gambia, The

A small republic and member of the Commonwealth of Nations, The Gambia extends from the Atlantic Ocean along the lower Gambia River in West Africa and is surrounded by Senegal. Area: 4,467 sq.mi. (11,569 sq.km.). Pop. (1973): 494,279, including (1963) Malinke 40.8%; Fulani 13.5%; Wolof 12.9%; Dyola 7%; Soninke 6.8%; non-African 1.9%. Cap. and largest city: Banjul (named Bathurst until April 24, 1973; pop., 1973, 39,476). Language: English (official). Religion: predominantly Muslim. President in 1974, Sir Dauda Jawara.

President Jawara's February 1974 visit to Libya resulted in technical, financial, and cultural agreements, with Libya granting more than $1 million toward radio and educational equipment and the establishment of health centres and a public transport corporation. In June the president's official visit to London produced a £600,000 loan for economic development; the U.K. had already granted £500,000 toward modernizing Yundum airport. In his 1974–75 budget statement, Finance Minister Alhaji Garba-Jahumpa, while warning of future uncertainty, allowed a significant increase in development expenditure as a result of British and World Bank aid. There had also been a record peanut crop (accounting for over 90% of exports) at unprecedented world prices, averaging 747 dalasis per ton (and reaching over 1,000 dalasis) as against 491 dalasis in 1973. The government's acquisition of the local crushing and refining mills marked another step in nationalization.

Britain was The Gambia's chief trade partner, taking 40% of exports and supplying nearly 40% of imports. The Gambia's high 1973 population census figure (showing a growth rate of 4.6% since 1963; UN estimate 2.1%) was questioned as a possible overestimate due to annual migrations of farmers and inclusion of refugees from the drought-stricken Sahel area. The Gambia itself was affected by the Sahelian drought and received UN Food and Agricultural Organization relief. (*See* AGRICULTURE AND FOOD SUPPLIES: *Special Report.*) The problem of rural-urban migration was accentuated, and Banjul, the only large urban centre, experienced population pressure and unemployment. (MOLLY MORTIMER)
[978.E.4.b.ii]

GAMBIA, THE
Education. (1972–73) Primary, pupils 19,421, teachers 677; secondary, pupils 5,373, teachers 247; vocational, pupils 178, teachers 21; teacher training, students 165, teachers 16.
Finance and Trade. Monetary unit: dalasi, with (Sept. 16, 1974) a free rate of 1.73 dalasi to U.S. $1 (par value of 4 dalasis = £1 sterling). Budget (1973–74 est.): revenue 20,658,000 dalasis; expenditure 22,279,000 dalasis. Foreign trade (1973): imports 53,390,000 dalasis; exports 39,950,000 dalasis. Import sources: U.K. 28%; China 12%; Japan 8%; France 5%. Export destinations: France 54%; U.K. 18%; West Germany 8%; Italy 7%. Main exports (1973–74): peanuts 52%; peanut oil 33%; peanut meal and cake 11%.

Hang gliders for skiers appeared in Switzerland during 1974. The demonstrator pictured here has made more than 500 successful flights in Alpine terrain.

New toys for 1974 included models of various business enterprises familiar to the younger set. A particular favourite was this "McDonald's" ® drive-in by Playskool.

Games and Toys

Worldwide shortages of raw materials and plastics during 1974 resulted in a dearth of new and exciting toys, as many companies held back on new products in the belief that it would be difficult enough to supply the required quantities of their existing lines. Nevertheless, the industry did well, supporting the toy makers' belief that a downturn in the economy brings a greater demand for toys. The lack of raw materials and international currency fluctuations caused a number of pricing problems, and inflation kept prices at a very high level. Although the supply situation eased somewhat toward midyear, inevitably prices remained much higher than previously and the year ended disappointingly as the anticipated seasonal upswing in sales failed to reach expectations.

Despite prophecies of recession in the industry the order situation at the major toy fairs at the beginning of the year was extremely healthy. At Brighton and Harrogate, the two big British trade fairs, many customers were ordering two or three times the amount of goods they needed, on the assumption that material shortages would result in manufacturers' operating "quota" systems. The Nürnberg, W.Ger., show, however, was probably more indicative of the general trading situation. Orders there were still substantially above 1973 but nowhere near double.

Buying trends continued on the same lines as during the previous year with dolls, board games, and educational and preschool toys dominating sales. Among the year's doll innovations was the British firm Model Toys' Havoc, a sort of female James Bond character. With several outfits available, designed by Mary Quant, she was equipped to fit a variety of play situations. From the French toy makers Clodrey came a "magic" doll that was the hit of the Salon International du Jouet in Paris. This soft, colourful doll was supplied with a blank face area, allowing a child to draw in any desired features. In the U.S., Creative Playthings offered a doll whose expression changed as its head was tilted.

Dress-up manikins, like Barbie and Sindie, continued to outsell their traditional counterparts. And the popularity of male dress-up dolls, such as Palitoy's Action Man and Louis Marx's new Lone Ranger, was perhaps partly responsible for the growth in the "unisex" toy market, particularly evident in the U.S. Randolph P. Barton, president of Toy Manufacturers of America, said after the American Toy Fair in New York City that more and more toys were being designed for use by both sexes. The latest packaging reflected this, showing boys and girls in play situations with the same toys.

New educational toys included a pushbutton toy based on the television series "Sesame Street" and a U-Drive-It game simulating actual driving conditions. Miniature-car racers could build their own models with Pour 'N Play kits containing molds, pouring compounds, wheels, axles, and paint.

Sales of wheeled toys generally rose sharply throughout the world. Bicycles were especially popular and Raleigh, the world's largest cycle manufacturers, with annual sales running at approximately $130 million, had another record-breaking year. Orders at the beginning of February were 120% above those of the previous year. At the Milan toy show the demand for cycles, roller skates, Go-Karts, and similar items was particularly noticeable.

Television played an increasingly important part in toy marketing plans, with giants such as Dunbee-Combex-Marx and Palitoy spending enormous sums to promote their wares through this medium. In England alone Louis Marx (part of the DCM group) spent about £85,000 on pre-Christmas advertising spots. Television also helped to boost the growth of "character" merchandising, and world markets were flooded with Rupert Bear and other well-known cartoon characters in a variety of different forms. The biggest character merchandising success was Pedigree's Womble soft toys, promoted on television and through comics, records, and "live" appearances on both sides of the Atlantic. The demand rapidly exceeded the company's capacity to produce.

Board games continued to sell well, with old favourites such as Monopoly and Scrabble maintaining their popularity along with the more recent Cluedo, Diplomacy, and others. The most successful newcomer was probably Master Mind, winner of the British Toy Manufacturers Association's Game of the Year award. In a different category, the ancient game of backgammon continued its spectacular comeback.

Inspired by the feats of daredevil Evel Knievel (see BIOGRAPHY) were a Stunt and Crash Car, a Canyon Sky Cycle, and a Stunt Stadium. Playskool brought out a miniature copy of a McDonald's restaurant, equipped with everything from restrooms to the golden arches. Electronic games included Finders Beepers, an electronic hide-and-seek game, and a table tennis game in which an electronic screen showed a ball moving from side to side.

Hong Kong retained its position as the world's largest toy exporter, with sales in 1974 estimated at about $230 million. Increasing competition at the cheaper end of the market came from Taiwan and South Korea, and to combat this Hong Kong started to concentrate on goods of better quality. Among countries that considerably increased their toy exports were Italy (with export sales of about 68 billion lire); Spain (about 3,220,000,000 pesetas); and Israel. Australia had a year of steady growth, and the Australian market was thought to be worth about $230 million at retail value.

In Britain, still a major export force with 1974 sales of about £180 million, more stringent safety regulations were introduced. These included lower limits on the amount of lead and other toxic substances in the paint used on toys; also, for the first time, safety requirements were introduced for electrical toys. (A. A. WHITE)

[452.B.6; 452.C–D]

CRAFTSMEN WITHOUT NUMBER

By Susan Nelson

Man's hands are the ultimate machine. That appeared to be the conclusion of both participants and visitors at the World Crafts Council exhibition, "In Praise of Hands," held in Toronto from June 11 through Sept. 2, 1974. The nearly 1,000 contemporary handcrafts on display, gathered over three years from the council's nearly 80 member nations, ranged from Ecuadorean dough figures to whimsical Czechoslovakian blown-glass sculptures to porcupine quill and leather breastplates made by Sioux Indians. Each object was fashioned as art with a useful function—the most basic definition of crafts—and each was wrought of "natural" materials, namely clay, fibre, glass, metal, or wood.

Earlier in the year, Chicago's Field Museum of Natural History celebrated contemporary African crafts with a seven-month-long show of examples collected throughout Africa. The Field Museum festival, like that of the World Crafts Council, featured related films, appearances and demonstrations by the craftsmen, and music integral to their lives.

Such varied expositions were the latest wave in a craft movement touching the entire world. In the United States, in recent history the most modern, throwaway-minded of cultures, handcrafts were experiencing a renaissance. Professional craftsmen were gaining new and widespread respect. Collectors combed the byways for examples of folk art. Home crafts hobbyists—possibly as many as one of every two Americans over the age of 12—were spending billions of dollars on the supplies needed to make thousands of objects they could buy ready-made but preferred to create with their own hands. Inherent in handcrafts as a genre is a vital spontaneity that allows us to know more about our present and our past, and invites us to try to create our own objects of unique, personal beauty.

Old Arts Rediscovered. Skills that aided settlement of America had emerged as a fresh challenge to modern man, from furniture making and house building to pottery and weaving, the fastest growing of the crafts. The applied (or decorative, or folk) artist, who was helped through the depression of the '30s by Works Progress Administration programs and then abandoned during the post-World War II technical boom, again was viewed with interest by the federal government. But this time he was seen as one of the group of people who could help preserve America's unique cultural heritage.

For crafts are as old as man. Archaeologists have learned that even prehistoric man fashioned objects to make his life more comfortable, his work more expedient, his body more attractive. He applied his imagination and his sense of beauty to his practical needs. Modern man's denial of the value of crafts is understandable. As machines were devised that could produce objects man once made by hand, machine-made goods became "modern" and handmade goods, "backward." But the resurgence of handcrafts is just as understandable.

Such books as Alvin Toffler's *Future Shock* (published in 1970) and Studs Terkel's conversations in *Working* (1974) pointed up what had already become apparent: that American

Susan Nelson is a writer and editor for the Chicago Tribune Magazine. *During the 1974–75 academic year she held a professional journalism fellowship at Stanford University.*

man feels himself to be only an insignificant spoke in the wheel of the technological machine. Many elements enter into this sense of disenchantment: an uncertain economy that makes the purchase of new goods worrisome, the energy crisis, the political confusion of a country that provided Richard Nixon with a landslide victory in 1972 and felt relieved when he resigned two years later. No wonder the average American—or any other citizen of the industrialized West—confronting an increasingly insecure world of rising prices and changing values, questions the meaning of his life and trembles when he finds no reassurance in the assembly-line objects that surround him.

As man fears, he looks for something to steady him. Clearly the boom in handcrafts suggests our longing for a surer past. Antiques, most of them handcrafted, already are big business. So are the movies, plays, fashions, and music of the nostalgia movement. The surprising popularity of such television shows as "The Waltons" and its imitators suggests an even more personal longing for close-knit family life.

But handcrafts are not necessarily an escape from reality. The same family that buys a pocket calculator to simplify its existence may own a loom or a kiln to craft items that will soften or humanize its members' lives. The woman who travels extensively may also sew her own clothes; of the more than 52 million American women of all ages who used sewing machines at home, one-quarter had incomes well above $15,000.

Modern man has the chance to choose both the best of what technology offers and the best of the creative skills developed through humanity's long history. In 1974 classes in crafts were springing up across the United States as community centres and colleges, private workshops, and high school night classes instructed adults in weaving, pottery, sewing, and such decorative arts as macrame, needlework, decoupage, papier tole, and paper quilling. Specialized books and magazines were brisk sellers. Ten times as many colleges and universities granted degrees in craft fields as had been the case as recently as 1960.

Clearly, America was in a golden age of crafts. There was a darker side to this newly reborn appreciation for the handcrafted object, marked by the unique, personal touch of its creator. It was represented by wealthy collectors whose willingness to invest in pre-Columbian or African or classical artifacts encouraged smuggling and theft and threatened to wipe out the cultural inheritance of nations unable to defend themselves. But for the ordinary man or woman the craft movement offered new opportunities for self-fulfillment, for finding a satisfying hobby or even a new way of life.

Crafts for Fun and Profit. In many parts of the world, handcrafts long supposed to be on their way to extinction were flourishing. Interest in perpetuating them had been renewed in the most vulnerable of cultures, those just becoming industrialized, by governments that took to heart Mohandas Gandhi's emphasis on spinning and weaving programs. In ethnic and regional enclaves of more modernized countries, young people were taking pride in the interest collectors and tourists showed in their cultures, and some were learning the crafts of their ancestors as a way to earn their own livings.

Nowhere was this strengthening of traditional crafts more apparent than in the United States, where many of the craft products of ethnic and regional groups were rapidly achieving the rank of status symbols. The demand for works of American Indians and Eskimos was greater than the supply. The silver and turquoise jewelry of the Southwestern Indians commanded especially high prices; in what was almost a parody of the craft movement, a kit appeared on the market that enabled the purchaser to put together an imitation of the much-prized Navajo squash blossom necklace.

In Appalachia, the mountain settlers, who had never stopped creating quilts and furniture and whimsical objects to brighten their lives on drab, impoverished land, were newly recognized as brilliant artisans. Crafts cooperatives, established to ensure that the workers received fair prices for their painstaking efforts and to work with half a dozen or so government agencies in publicizing and encouraging specific regions, now included some 300,000 members. One of the best known, Mountain Artisans of West Virginia, was a project of Sharon Percy Rockefeller, member of two socially and politically prominent families; many of the quilts and other products of its craftswomen were sold through exclusive boutiques and galleries.

Such traditional handcraft areas—and New England and California as well—had become magnets for those who had turned to crafts. In fact, rural areas in all 50 states were attracting crafts people, and even in the largest cities colonies of craftsmen were thriving in out-of-the-way neighbourhoods. Many of these people were highly trained professionals who had dropped out of their competitive fields in order to work with their hands. A lawyer might become a cabinetmaker, a business executive might open a crafts gallery, a schoolteacher might sell her weavings, a journalist might become a potter.

For most adults, of course, responsibilities of job and family prevented such total changes. Thus, perhaps, the popularity of handcrafts to be learned and then practiced at home. No longer the mere do-it-yourself projects of America's post-World War II home-building boom—or quaint busywork that would keep the Devil at bay—today's crafts suggested that modern man, as well as exploring his creative potential, was striving for quality objects that would outlast machine-spewn plastics.

Crafts and Art. Increasingly, crafts were being viewed as art. Purists might argue, but in fact the divorce between the two had come relatively late in history, when machines began to produce the articles of everyday life and the appellation of "art" was confined to the relatively useless. England's Arts and Crafts Movement of the mid- to late 19th century was as much a protest by craftsmen at being excluded from "art" as it was a protest against the dehumanization—including the loss of handwork—stemming from the Industrial Revolution. But the exhibition of medieval tapestries, mounted in 1974 by New York's Metropolitan Museum of Art, showed the heights to which "crafts" could rise. Navajo rugs were recognized as abstract art, and American

A chairmaker plies his craft in accord with age-old practice, pulling each strand taut by strength of hand.

Spinning, carding, and weaving yield in the end both cloth and satisfaction for this young woman.

quilts, hung like oversized paintings in 1971 in New York's Whitney Museum, were rapidly achieving the same rank. Conversely, artists were turning to crafts as mediums, producing, for example, constructions of macrame and crochet work and "paintings" of embroidery or appliqué.

As the line between art and craft diminished, so did the assumption that certain handcrafts were "masculine" and others "feminine." Former defensive lineman Roosevelt Grier with his needlepoint disputed the notion that stitchery is the exclusive realm of women and effeminate men; women's magazines with their "handyman" columns were assuring women that anyone can learn to build a coffee table or a window box. In the schools, boys were beginning to learn the skills formerly subsumed under the heading of home economics as readily as girls were learning such shop crafts as woodworking.

Skeptics might warn that the omnipresence of handcrafts was just one more American fad—and cite as an example the New Jersey physician who prescribed basketmaking for his obese patients to help them forget about nibbling (though the use of crafts as therapy for the mentally and physically handicapped has a long and useful history). More thoughtful observers saw creative crafts as a link in life that modern man had temporarily displaced. Decoupage, macrame, and tie-dying might follow one another as the "in" craft. Stained-glass kits and do-it-yourself Tiffany lamps might come and go. But the basic human need that informs them all will remain.

It is this deeper meaning of handcrafts that concerns Mexican poet and essayist Octavio Paz. In his introduction to the book *In Praise of Hands,* published in conjunction with the Toronto exhibit, he suggests that "between the timeless time of the museum and the speeded-up time of technology, craftsmanship is the heartbeat of human time. A thing that is handmade is a useful object but also one that is beautiful; an object that lasts a long time but also one that slowly ages away and is resigned to so doing; an object that is not unique like the work of art and can be replaced by another object that is similar but not identical. The craftsman's handiwork teaches us to die and hence . . . to live."

Gardening

High prices and fear of food shortages led to an upsurge in home gardening throughout the U.S. in 1974. Families that never before had grown vegetables dug up parts of lawns and flower beds to plant tomatoes, beans, squash, and greens. Community gardens were started in many cities so that persons with little or no land also could grow food for themselves. Pres. Gerald Ford encouraged the trend as an antiinflation measure. A trend that continued into 1974 was the enthusiasm for house plants, at least partly an outgrowth of the ecology movement and the resultant popularity of "natural" materials and motifs in interior decoration. Books on the subject were good sellers, and plant shops, specializing in house plants and accessories, were a common sight in urban centres.

A group of U.S. plant scientists spent nearly a month (August 26–September 23) in China arranging the exchange of information on advancements in crop and forestry research and on improved plants and seeds. The last such exchanges with China had ended 20 years earlier. A delegation of Chinese plant scientists also visited the U.S., bringing with them a gift of more than 200 lots of seeds.

Every year trees, weakened by decay, are blown over in the wind, causing deaths, injuries, and property damage, but there has been no easy way to determine whether a standing tree was sound or not. In 1974, after seven years of studies and tests, a portable electronic meter was developed that permits on-site testing of trees and poles for strength and safety. Named the Shigometer for one of its originators, Alex L. Shigo of the U.S. Department of Agriculture (USDA), it takes advantage of the fact that electrical resistance to a pulsed current is much less in decayed wood than in sound wood. A short series of electrical currents is sent through the wood to determine the soundness of the material.

Cornell University researchers reported major progress in their efforts to find an artificial method of increasing cold hardiness in plants. In a paper presented at the annual meeting of the American Society of Plant Physiologists in June, they reported that when the membrane of the chloroplast, the cellular particle in which photosynthesis takes place, is frozen and thawed at a slow rate, certain proteins break loose from the membrane and biological activity stops. Using a biochemical process worked out at Cornell and elsewhere, they succeeded in bringing these proteins back to the membrane.

The British Glasshouse Crops Research Institute developed a growing technique, useful for both crop and pot plants, in which black polythene film is placed in gulleys dug into the soil; the roots of the plant are introduced into the gulleys and fed by a continually circulating nutrient solution. Yields of tomatoes indicated that this technique could be commercially viable. The Dutch Institute for Horticultural Engineering found that rock wool, used as a growing medium, helped to facilitate mechanical crop handling. In the U.K., the John Innes Institute used tissue culture techniques to extend the range of species in which mature cells of a developed leaf can be made to divide repeatedly to form new plants.

The International Convention of the World Federation of Rose Societies was held in Chicago, September 1–12. It was the third worldwide rose convention ever held and the first under the aegis of the World Federation formed three years earlier in New Zealand. Other notable international conferences held during the year included a five-day congress in Vienna sponsored by the International Federation of Landscape Architects and the International Federation of Park and Recreation Administrations and centred on the need for ecological balance in the environment. Research into microclimates in plastic structures was described at an international meeting on plastics in horticulture, held in England. The International Council of Museums sponsored an international conference in England that included discussion of electronic data-processing methods for classifying plant collections.

Good yellow roses are rare, but one such rose, a pure yellow hybrid tea named Oregold, was a 1975 All-America award winner. Oregold was hybridized by the R. M. Tantau Nursery in West Germany. Other 1975 winners were Arizona, a bronze and copper grandiflora hybridized by Ollie Weeks of Ontario, Calif., and Rose Parade, a light coral-pink floribunda hybridized by Benjamin Williams of Silver Spring, Md.

Six annuals won All-America awards for 1974. A gold medal was awarded to Scarlet Ruffles, a brilliant, deep scarlet hybrid zinnia with fully double blooms on long stems that are ideal for cutting. The Showboat, a dwarf triploid marigold with deep-yellow colouring, was the first flower ever to win an award in All-America Selections, All-Britain Trials, and Fleuroselect (the European flower trials). The other All-America winners were the Peter Pan Orange zinnia, Red Fox celosia, Magic Charms dianthus, and Diablo cosmos.

Improvements in vegetables are much more difficult to breed than in flowers, but two new vegetable varieties were given 1974 All-America awards. One was Table King, a bush acorn squash developed by the University of Connecticut, which received a silver medal for the extra large size of its dark, glossy, green fruits and the compact, bushy habit of the plants. The other was Goldcrop, a flavourful, disease-resistant bush wax bean developed by the USDA in cooperation with Washington State University.

The U.K. Royal National Rose Society awarded the Henry Edland Memorial Medal for the most

The Showboat, an early-flowering hybrid marigold, of deep-yellow colour, was the 1974 All-America, All-Britain, and Fleuroselect winner. Standing 12–15 in. tall, with flowers 2–2½ in. wide, this bushy plant was the first triple winner to be introduced.

COURTESY, FERRY-MORSE SEED COMPANY

fragrant rose to Compassion, an orange-salmon climber raised by R. Harkness & Co. Ltd. Harkness also won the gold medal at the City of Belfast International Rose Trials, with Alexander, and the Golden Thorn, with Southampton. The Golden Rose of The Hague was awarded to Esperanza. The Madrid sweet pea, Showboat marigold, and the *Rudbeckia hirta* Rustic Dwarfs won bronze medals in the 1972 All-Britain Flower Trials. The first two were raised in the U.S. by the Ferry-Morse Seed Co. and the third by Hurst, Gunson, Cooper, Taber.

A new variety of blueberry, called Harrison, was developed by the North Carolina Agricultural Experiment Station. It was described as high yielding and suitable for hand or machine harvesting. Three new chrysanthemum varieties were introduced by the University of Minnesota, Wendy Ann (fawn yellow), Minnruby (dark red), and Lindy (lavender-pink). A new variety of Manchurian crabapple, Midwest, was released by the USDA Soil Conservation Service for use in conservation plantings. The crabapples remain on the trees in winter where they can be harvested by birds and small animals.

After a ten-year trial period, the French Fruit Research Station at Angers released General Leclerc, a midseason pear said to yield earlier and more heavily than Williams. Malling Jet, a new, heavy-yielding black currant, was released by the East Malling Research Station in Britain. The first of several new cultivars being developed for specific purposes, it was easy to pick mechanically and flowered late, thus avoiding spring frosts.

(J. G. SCOTT MARSHALL; TOM STEVENSON)

See also Agriculture and Food Supplies; Life Sciences. [355.C.2–3; 731.B.1]

Geography

A return to emphasis on environmental studies may well have rekindled the eclecticism that characterized geography before 1960. If the majority of research articles in U.S. geographic journals in 1974 did not bear the stamp of environmental studies per se, the incidence of environmental and ecological language and methodology in the published research seemed to indicate such a pervading influence. Although the analytical studies in both physical and cultural geography continued to emphasize theoretical and metho-

dological discourse, college course titles and programs sponsored by geography departments, new collections of readings, and popular geographic writing substantiated the profession's concern with environmental problems.

The National Geographic Society's contributions to understanding and illuminating environmental problems ranged from *Vanishing Wildlife of North America*—a special publication in 1974—to several educational filmstrips and films for television on topics such as the plant kingdom, energy, plant and animal life cycles, ecology, and the solar eclipse. Its journal articles included studies of the wilderness, timber, drought in the Tuareg area of Africa, oil, and communion with nature. Many of the society's biological articles also dealt with ecological topics and a number of important research grants supported studies on endangered species, the historical ecology of early Mexican cultures, the ecology of gorillas, and the impact of coral reef destruction on the islands in the Southwest Pacific.

Perspectives on Environment was released by the Association of American Geographers (AAG) in 1974. This collection of 12 original essays summarized research and various environmental problems, exposed the dimensions of new environmental problems, and demonstrated the distinctive aspects of geographic modes of inquiry that are of particular value in dealing with environmental issues.

The annual meeting of the AAG in Seattle, Wash., in April, offered several sessions on environmental problems, and past president Wilbur Zelinsky's address, although ostensibly peripheral to environmental issues, emphasized the need for intellectual commitment designed to cope with human wants and needs. The AAG also completed a land use project for the Geographic Applications Programs of the United States Geological Survey, including an inventory of the status of land use planning and mapping in each of the 50 states and a determination of the compatibility or incompatibility of their land use classification systems with the Geological Survey's system. Information was also collected on land use data sources, map scales and projections, minimum mapping units, and land use update rates. A pilot study was completed on possible applications of land use data obtained for urban areas of the U.S. from remotely sensed imagery available for and developed by the Geographic Applications Program. The study developed

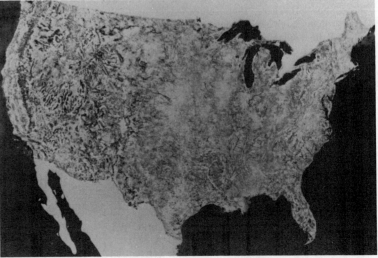

The first photomosaic of the 48 contiguous United States, this map was produced from 595 cloud-free images returned from the first Earth Resources Technology Satellite. The scale is 1:1,000,000.

WIDE WORLD

a cross-sectional spatial model and an urban growth model of land use. Finally, an illustrated manual documented urban and regional land use analysis tasks represented by Geographic Applications Program projects.

The AAG also embarked upon two important projects: developing an environmental education source book for undergraduate colleges, where environmental courses were proliferating, and conducting a national survey of natural environment-based education programs for effectiveness and quality. The association continued its projects on black America and comparative metropolitan analysis, conducted a seminar in Yugoslavia for U.S. graduate students, and began a revision of its high school geography course.

Basic and applied research continued on social problems, especially urban problems, but ranged from studies on modeling spatial entropy and optimal facility locations in one-dimensional spatial markets to prostitution in Nevada and the ecological study of fisheries in Lake Izabal, Guatemala. The important National Geographic Society archaeological programs in east Africa at Olduvai Gorge, Tanzania, and Lake Rudolf, Kenya, continued with exciting prospects for significant reappraisals of the age of man.

The American Geographical Society and the Arctic Institute of North America jointly published the *Icefield Ranges Research Project Scientific Results,* vol. 4, which included the major reports of research carried out between 1966 and 1970 as part of the High Mountain Environmental Project, a program affiliated with the ice field project. Many of the climatologic and meteorologic studies, water and snow studies, geologic and geomorphologic studies, and biologic studies presented in this volume had never been published before.

The time-honoured concerns for integrating human and earth sciences will provide the profession with increased opportunities to contribute to the solution of problems of resource adequacy, environmental quality, less developed nations, destructive exploitation of resources, the demographic crisis, and the revolution of rising expectations. The concern with environmental studies has created demands for biogeographers, landform and soil geographers, and climatologists.

(SALVATORE J. NATOLI)

See also Antarctica; Earth Sciences.

[10/33.B.1]

ENCYCLOPÆDIA BRITANNICA FILMS. *Earth: Man's Home* (1970).

German Democratic Republic

A country of central Europe, Germany was partitioned after World War II into the Federal Republic of Germany (Bundesrepublik Deutschland; West Germany) and the German Democratic Republic (Deutsche Demokratische Republik; East Germany), with a special provisional regime for Berlin. East Germany is bordered by the Baltic Sea, Poland, Czechoslovakia, and West Germany. Area: 41,768 sq.mi. (108,178 sq.km.). Pop. (1973 est.): 16,951,250. Cap. and largest city: East Berlin (pop., 1973 est., 1,088,800). Language: German. Religion (1950): Protestant 81.3%; Roman Catholic 11%. First secretary of the Socialist Unity (Communist)

UPI COMPIX

Party (SED) in 1974, Erich Honecker; chairman of the Council of State, Willi Stoph; president of the Council of Ministers (premier), Horst Sindermann.

The leadership of the Socialist Unity (Communist) Party (SED) had every reason to be in the best of spirits in 1974, the 25th anniversary of the founding of the German Democratic Republic. East Germany had gained worldwide recognition, and its capital, East Berlin, had become an international diplomatic centre. In September diplomatic relations were established with the U.S., the last NATO ally to grant formal recognition to East Germany. The conclusion of negotiations had been delayed by the Americans in protest against East German interference with transit traffic between West Germany and West Berlin in July. (*See* GERMANY, FEDERAL REPUBLIC OF.)

At a celebration of the anniversary on October 10, First Secretary Honecker said that the creation and growth of the state were proof of the wisdom of the teachings of Marx, Engels, and Lenin. As far as the size of countries was concerned, East Germany was 104th in the world table, and in terms of population 36th. But, said Honecker, when it came to industrial production East Germany was in tenth place. In the first year of its foundation the country had had a national income of M. 22 billion—in 1973 it was M. 127 billion. Now East German industry was producing as much in the space of six weeks as it produced during the whole of 1949. The celebration was attended by Soviet Communist Party leader Leonid I. Brezhnev.

At its 13th session, on September 27, the East German People's Chamber approved a law amending the constitution. The legislative period of Parliament was extended from four to five years; the voting age was reduced to 18; and, more important, all reference to the German nation was deleted. The West German government, which accepted the existence of two German states, retaliated with a statement that it continued to adhere to the unity of the German nation. Bonn was confident that "the feeling among Germans of belonging together would not be impaired by this step."

Representatives of the two German states signed an agreement in Bonn on March 14 to set up permanent missions in their respective capitals. They were to perform the functions of embassies, but were not referred to as such because of West Germany's insistence that the relationship was a special one, based

The United States and East Germany end 29 years of cold war history. Formal diplomatic relations commenced September 4, following signing of an agreement to this effect at the State Department in Washington, D.C.

Geology: *see* Earth Sciences

**German
Democratic
Republic**

New buildings
in the Gothic style
have been constructed
in Rostock to blend
with adjacent medieval
structures. The Hanseatic
trade centre has enjoyed
a boom since 1953
when the government
designated Rostock
the country's principal
port.

on the claim that there was still only one German
nation. The West Germans won a number of concessions. The senior official of each mission was to be
called head or chief, and not ambassador as the East
Germans had wished. The special character of the
arrangement was further underlined by the fact that
the East German mission in Bonn would deal through
the federal chancellor's office and not through the Foreign Ministry. An important provision in the agreement was that the West German mission in East Berlin would also represent the interests of West Berlin.
The status of officials in the missions would be governed by the terms of the Vienna Convention of 1961
on diplomatic rights, giving them the same protection
and privileges as diplomats. The head of the West German mission in East Berlin was Günther Gaus, a state
secretary in the chancellor's office. Michael Kohl, also
a state secretary, was appointed head of the East
German mission in Bonn. It was not until June that
the two men handed over their credentials in the respective capitals, an act that set the final seal on the
long process of mutual recognition. The ceremony
would have taken place earlier, but the West German

government postponed the event as a gesture of anger
over the Guillaume spy case. (*See* GERMANY, FEDERAL
REPUBLIC OF.) In Bonn the ceremony was played in
a low key, but in East Berlin it was afforded full military honours.

In July the foreign ministry announced that East
Germany was maintaining diplomatic relations with
109 countries, and that the policy of peaceful coexistence pursued by East Germany toward states with
different social systems was part of the coordinated
foreign policy practiced by the community of socialist
states. Ten-year agreements on economic, industrial,
and technical cooperation were concluded with France,
Italy, Britain, Denmark, Belgium, and The Netherlands, and others were being prepared.

The decision of the East German government to
reduce the sum of money that had to be exchanged
for East German marks by visitors to East Germany
and East Berlin was seen in Bonn as a modest gesture
of goodwill on the eve of the visit of West German
Chancellor Helmut Schmidt to Moscow in October.
On Nov. 5, 1973, the sum to be exchanged for each
day's stay in East Germany had been doubled to M.

GERMAN DEMOCRATIC REPUBLIC

Education. (1972–73) Primary, pupils 2,608,-
074; secondary, pupils 51,609; primary and secondary, teachers 151,989; vocational, pupils 431,-
963, teachers 14,692; teacher training, students
18,579, teachers (1969–70), 20,115; higher (including 7 universities), students 145,717, teaching staff (1969–70) 17,015.

Finance. Monetary unit: Mark of Deutsche
Demokratische Republik, with (Sept. 16, 1974)
an official exchange rate of M. 1.78 to U.S. $1
(nominal rate of M. 6 = £1 sterling). Budget
(1972 est.): revenue M. 86,951,000,000; expenditure M. 85,764,000,000. Net material product (at 1967 prices): (1972) M. 120.1 billion;
(1971) M. 113.6 billion.

Foreign Trade. (1973) Imports M. 27,330,-
000,000; exports M. 26,171,000,000. Import
sources: U.S.S.R. 32%; Czechoslovakia 9%;
West Germany 8%; Poland 8%; Hungary 6%.
Export destinations: U.S.S.R. 36%; Czechoslo-

vakia 10%; Poland 9%; West Germany 6%.
Main exports (1970): machinery 38%; transport
and equipment 11% (ships and boats 5%);
chemicals; lignite; textiles.

Transport and Communications. Roads
(1973) 129,900 km. (45,645 km. main roads,
including 1,495 km. autobahns). Motor vehicles
in use (1972): passenger 1,400,400; commercial
205,800. Railways (1973): 14,317 km. (including
1,383 km. electrified); traffic 20,691,000,000 passenger-km., freight 46,776,000,000 net ton-km.
Air traffic (1972): 1,098,500,000 passenger-km.;
freight 29,229,000 net ton-km. Navigable inland
waterways in regular use (1972) 2,546 km.;
freight traffic 2,304,000,000 ton-km. Shipping
(1973): merchant vessels 100 gross tons and over
432; gross tonnage 1,219,037. Telephones (Dec.
1972) 2,232,000. Radio licenses (Dec. 1972)
6,050,000. Television licenses (Dec. 1972) 4,820,-
000.

Agriculture. Production (in 000; metric tons;
1973; 1972 in parentheses): wheat *c.* 2,800 (2,-
744); rye *c.* 1,670 (1,904); barley *c.* 2,500 (2,-
592); oats *c.* 850 (890); potatoes *c.* 12,140
(12,140); sugar, raw value *c.* 655 (*c.* 642);
onions *c.* 100 (*c.* 100); rapeseed *c.* 205 (234).
Livestock (in 000; Dec. 1973): cattle 5,481;
sheep 1,742; pigs 10,849; goats 78; horses used
in agriculture 82; poultry 45,667.

Industry. Index of production (1970 = 100):
(1973) 120; (1972) 112. Production (in 000;
metric tons; 1973): lignite 246,244; coal 751;
petroleum products (1972) 13,420; manufactured
gas (cu.m.) 4,814,000; electricity (kw-hr.) 77,-
908,000; iron ore (24% metal content) 250; pig
iron 2,202; crude steel 5,892; cement 9,547;
potash (oxide content; 1972) 2,458; sulfuric
acid 1,059; synthetic rubber 133; rayon, etc.,
filaments and fibres (1972) 165; passenger cars
(units) 147; commercial vehicles (units) 31.

20 and for visitors to East Berlin to half that amount. This was taken in the West to be contrary to the spirit of the East-West German treaty, and especially to the agreement under which several million West Germans living near the border were allowed to visit the border areas on the other side. The consequence had been a sharp drop in the number of visitors and particularly of old-age pensioners who could no longer afford the luxury of crossing the border to meet their relatives. Despite representations by Bonn, the East German government had refused to return to the former rates; instead they decided that a visitor to East Germany must exchange M. 13 a day and to East Berlin, half that amount, which led to an immediate increase in the number of visits.

President Tito of Yugoslavia visited East Germany in November for the first time since 1965. He was treated like a revisionist who had come in from the cold, and was awarded East Germany's highest decoration, the Karl Marx Order. (NORMAN CROSSLAND)

[972.A.3.b.iii]

Germany, Federal Republic of

A country of central Europe, Germany was partitioned after World War II into the Federal Republic of Germany (Bundesrepublik Deutschland; West Germany) and the German Democratic Republic (Deutsche Demokratische Republik; East Germany), with a special provisional regime for Berlin. West Germany is bordered by Denmark, The Netherlands, Belgium, Luxembourg, France, Switzerland, Austria, Czechoslovakia, East Germany, and the North Sea. Area: 95,980 sq.mi. (248,587 sq.km.). Pop. (1974 est.): 62,075,300. Provisional cap.: Bonn (pop., 1974 est., 283,260). Largest city: Hamburg (pop., 1974 est., 1,751,620). (West Berlin, which is an enclave within East Germany, had a population of 2,047,950 in 1974.) Language: German. Religion (1970): Protestant 49%; Roman Catholic 44.6%; Jewish 0.05%. Presidents in 1974, Gustav Heinemann and, from July 1, Walter Scheel; chancellors, Willy

Brandt, from May 7 Walter Scheel (caretaker), and, from May 16, Helmut Schmidt.

The resignation of the federal Chancellor Willy Brandt on May 6, 1974, less than two weeks after the arrest of one of his personal aides, Günter Guillaume (see BIOGRAPHY), on suspicion of being an East German spy, overshadowed the year. Walter Scheel acted as chancellor in a caretaker capacity until May 16, when Brandt was succeeded by Helmut Schmidt (see BIOGRAPHY), formerly finance minister. In the face of continued inflation and rising unemployment, the new chancellor placed the emphasis of his policy on promoting economic stability.

Domestic Affairs. The Guillaume case caused a heavy loss of support for the Social Democratic Party (SPD), whose fortunes had been fading for many months, and on May 1 a research institute reported that only 30% of a representative sample of voters most trusted the SPD, as compared with 54% for the opposition Christian Democratic Union and its Bavarian sister party, the Christian Social Union (CDU/CSU). Even so, the announcement of Brandt's resignation came as a great shock. In his letter of resignation, Brandt said he accepted political responsibility for negligence in connection with the spy affair. But it became clear that he had used the case to step down from a post that was becoming an increasing burden to him.

Subsequent events showed that there was little reason why Brandt should have taken the blame for neglect in the Guillaume affair. A report of an independent commission, published in November, accused the security services of neglect and recommended the appointment of a commissioner to coordinate the work of the nation's three security organizations.

In March the SPD suffered heavy losses in the state election of Hamburg and in local elections in Schleswig-Holstein and the Rhineland Palatinate. In Hamburg, a traditional stronghold of Social Democracy, the SPD lost its overall majority in the state Parliament, polling 10.3% fewer votes than at the previous election. The SPD poll also went down in the Lower Saxony state election in June, but by only 3.2%—an improvement that was partly attributed to the change of government in Bonn. However, the trend in favour of the CDU/CSU continued in the state elections in

Germany, Federal Republic of

GERMANY, FEDERAL REPUBLIC OF

Education. (1971–72) Primary (including special), pupils 6,888,669, teachers 221,065; secondary, pupils 2,417,868, teachers 112,890; vocational, pupils 2,212,472, teachers 44,080; teacher training, students 69,211; higher (at 44 universities), students 528,474, teaching staff (1970–71) 38,165.

Finance. Monetary unit: Deutsche Mark, with (Sept. 16, 1974) a free rate of DM. 2.67 to U.S. $1 (free rate of DM. 6.17 = £1 sterling). Gold, SDRs, and foreign exchange, central bank: (June 1974) U.S. $32,673,000,000; (June 1973) U.S. $30,944,000,000. Budget (federal; 1973 actual): revenue DM. 121.1 billion; expenditure DM. 122,480,000,000. Gross national product: (1972) DM. 828.9 billion; (1971) DM. 758.5 billion. Money supply: (May 1974) DM. 130.6 billion; (May 1973) DM. 125.2 billion. Cost of living (1970 = 100): (June 1974) 127; (June 1973) 119.

Foreign Trade. (1973) Imports DM. 144,510,000,000; exports DM. 178,230,000,000. Import sources: EEC 52% (The Netherlands 14%, France 13%, Italy 10%, Belgium-Luxembourg 10%); U.S. 8%. Export destinations: EEC 47% (France 13%, The Netherlands 10%, Italy 8%, Belgium-Luxembourg 8%, U.K. 5%); U.S. 8%; Switzerland 6%; Austria 5%. Main exports: ma-

chinery 31%; motor vehicles 14%; chemicals 12%; iron and steel 7%; textile yarns and fabrics 5%. Tourism (1972): visitors 7,565,000; gross receipts U.S. $1,854,000,000.

Transport and Communications. Roads (1973) 459,452 km. (including 5,481 km. autobahns). Motor vehicles in use (1973): passenger 17,036,000; commercial 1,246,000. Railways: (1972) federal 29,191 km. (including 9,304 km. electrified), other 3,482 km.; traffic (1973) 41,-265,000,000 passenger-km., freight 67,257,000,-000 net ton-km. Air traffic (1973): 11,105,000,-000 passenger-km.; freight 873,678,000 net ton-km. Navigable inland waterways in regular use (1972) 4,393 km.; freight traffic 43,969,000,000 ton-km. Shipping (1973): merchant vessels 100 gross tons and over 2,234; gross tonnage 7,914,-679. Telephones (Dec. 1972) 16,521,000. Radio licenses (Dec. 1972) 20,290,000. Television licenses (Dec. 1972) 18,064,000.

Agriculture. Production (in 000; metric tons; 1973; 1972 in parentheses): wheat 7,134 (6,-608); rye 2,574 (2,914); barley 6,622 (5,997); oats 3,045 (2,887); potatoes 13,675 (15,036); apples 1,748 (1,217); sugar, raw value c. 2,348 (2,214); wine c. 850 (686); milk (1972) 21,318, (1971) 21,165; butter (1972) 494, (1971) 471;

cheese (1972) c. 540, (1971) 522; beef and veal 1,090 (1,169); pork 2,238 (2,314); fish catch (1972) 419, (1971) 508. Livestock (in 000; Dec. 1972): cattle 13,892; pigs 20,028; horses used in agriculture 283; chickens 100,401.

Industry. Index of production (1970 = 100): (1973) 113; (1972) 106. Unemployment: (1973) 1.2%; (1972) 1.1%. Fuel and power (in 000; metric tons; 1973): coal 97,340; lignite 118,657; crude oil 6,637; coke (1972) 34,-449; electricity (kw-hr.) 299,000,000; natural gas (cu.m.; 1972) 17,452,000; manufactured gas (cu.m.) 16,903,000. Production (in 000; metric tons; 1973): iron ore (28% metal content) 5,-069; pig iron 37,091; crude steel 49,521; aluminum 861; copper 406; lead 304; zinc 551; cement 40,864; sulfuric acid 5,067; cotton yarn 216; woven cotton fabrics 187; wool yarn 65; rayon, etc., filament yarn 71; rayon, etc., staple fibres 98; nylon, etc., filament yarn 398; nylon, etc., fibres 412; fertilizers (1972–73) nitrogenous 1,471, phosphate 986, potash 2,498; synthetic rubber 397; plastics and resins 6,407; passenger vehicles (units) 3,643; commercial vehicles (units) 306. Merchant vessels launched (100 gross tons and over; 1973) 1,854,000 gross tons. New dwelling units completed (1973) 714,000.

Hesse and Bavaria in October, and in both states these parties made progress not only in rural areas, but also in big cities and among young voters. To a large extent, the SPD's losses and those of the Free Democratic Party (FDP), its junior partner in the federal coalition, were attributed to inflation and rising unemployment. By the end of October the number of unemployed had risen to over 672,000, a quota of 3%. But inflation—at a rate of about 7% for much of the year—was considerably lower than in other industrial countries. And, at the end of January, a record trade surplus for 1973 of DM. 33 billion had been announced; later a trade surplus of DM. 25.2 billion, almost double the comparable figure for 1973, was recorded for the first six months of 1974.

The change of federal government proceeded smoothly. It was taken for granted as soon as the news of Brandt's resignation was announced that Helmut Schmidt would succeed him. In his statement of policy to the Bundestag on May 17, Schmidt said the slogan of his government would be continuity and concentration, concentration in the sense that priority would be given to those problems that stood the best chance of being solved. The statement dealt mostly with domestic affairs, but contained the assurance that NATO remained the basis of West Germany's security.

In May Walter Scheel (*see* BIOGRAPHY) was elected federal president to succeed Gustav Heinemann, who retired from office effective the end of June. This necessitated a Cabinet reshuffle. Hans-Dietrich Genscher (FDP) took over from Scheel as foreign minister, while Werner Maihofer, formerly minister without portfolio, succeeded Genscher as minister of the interior. Hans Apel, formerly parliamentary state secretary in the Foreign Ministry, took over the vital job of finance minister from Schmidt. The government's stability program was based on big cuts in public expenditure, coupled with a credit squeeze. But, as unemployment rose, credit policy was eased and large sums of money were made available to local authorities for such projects as hospitals, schools, and roads—a boost for the job market. Additional stimulatory measures were announced in December.

A leading member of the Baader-Meinhof group of urban guerrillas, Holger Meins, died in his prison cell

at Wittlich on November 9, after two months on a hunger strike during which he had been fed by force. With other members of the group he was due to stand trial at Stuttgart in the spring of 1975. The charge sheet against the 30 or more members listed a variety of offenses, including murder, manslaughter, bank robbery, and arson. The news of Meins's death caused demonstrations in several cities, and on November 10 the leading West Berlin judge, Günter von Drenkmann, was murdered by men who forced their way into his home.

Foreign Affairs. The year started badly for relations between Western Europe and the U.S., and in March Pres. Richard M. Nixon warned the Western allies of "dire consequences" should they persist in what he described as ganging up against the U.S. The president and U.S. Secretary of State Henry Kissinger, who had felt badly let down by the allies in the October war in the Middle East in 1973, were now annoyed at the EEC plans to open talks with the Arabs that were designed to increase economic cooperation. Scheel, in his capacity during the first half of the year as president of the EEC Ministerial Council, made proposals for improving consultations between the EEC and the U.S. While continuing to seek better relations with the U.S.S.R. and its allies, the Schmidt government placed its main foreign policy emphasis on strengthening ties with the West and promoted integration of the EEC partners: the union of Europe was the central theme of Bonn's foreign policy.

The change of leadership in both West Germany and France brought to power in those respective countries two men who had become friends as finance ministers, Schmidt and Valéry Giscard d'Estaing (*see* BIOGRAPHY). In their new roles they had frequent consultations over and above the terms of the 1963 treaty of friendship between their two countries, and there was even talk of a French-West German axis. During his visit to Bonn in July the French president talked of the parallelism of their respective policies, and the two leaders said that their relationship provided the basis for the revival of efforts to create European union. These developments tended to leave Britain, still arguing whether to stay in the EEC or not, out in the cold, although Schmidt said in November that Britain's departure from the Community would be deeply regretted.

With the ratification of the treaty between West Germany and Czechoslovakia, signed in Prague in December 1973, the foundations of the *Ostpolitik* were finally completed. Under the treaty, West Germany accepted that the Munich Agreement of 1938, by which the Sudetenland was ceded to Nazi Germany, was invalid. In June President Tito of Yugoslavia paid a three-day state visit to West Germany, shortly after the West German government had approved a DM. 700 million loan to Yugoslavia to promote industrial development.

Schmidt and Foreign Minister Genscher, accompanied by a delegation of industrialists, went to Moscow in October, but the talks between the chancellor and Soviet leader Leonid I. Brezhnev made little headway on political issues. The industrial delegation drew up a deal, the third of its kind, under which a West German consortium would supply gas pipes to the U.S.S.R. in return for the delivery of natural gas to West Germany. There was also agreement in principle that West Germany should be fed with nuclear power from reactors to be built by the West Germans at Kaliningrad (formerly Königsberg in East Prussia).

Willy Brandt, former West German chancellor, congratulates Helmut Schmidt (left) who was nominated as his successor. Brandt resigned the post on May 6.

HENRI BUREAU—SYGMA

Walter Scheel accepts the post as fourth president of the Federal Republic of Germany.

West Berlin. In spite of the four-power agreement, signed in 1972, events in 1974 showed that West Berlin could still become a centre of international tension. In July West Germany set up a federal Environment Protection Office in West Berlin. East Germany had said that establishment of a federal agency, with all the attributes of a West German ministry, would violate the four-power agreement which maintained that West Berlin was not part of West Germany. Notes issued by Britain, the U.S., and France said that the office did not violate the agreement and held the U.S.S.R. responsible for maintaining open travel routes to West Berlin. For several days the East Germans carried out spot checks at the border crossing points so as to deter officials of the environment office from using the transit routes. In one case a senior official was refused access. West Germany and its allies stated this was a contravention of the transit agreement between the two German states. Another instance of East German sensitivity over West Berlin occurred in July when East German television and party newspapers attacked President Scheel, in West Berlin for his first official visit, for calling his visit a symbol of the West German presence in West Berlin and for promising to repeat this "offense" by regular visits in future.

The subject of West Berlin played an important role in the talks between Schmidt and Brezhnev at the end of October. Schmidt told Brezhnev that whereas for the U.S.S.R. Berlin was perhaps only a detail of its *Westpolitik,* it was the cardinal point of Bonn's *Ostpolitik.*

The chancellor had good reason to feel uneasy about Brezhnev's policy on Berlin. In a speech during Schmidt's visit Brezhnev had spoken of the need for strict adherence to the four-power Berlin agreement, carefully omitting the second part of the joint statement issued by himself and Brandt in 1973 which referred to "strict adherence and full implementation." After hours of discussion Brezhnev reluctantly concurred that the final statement on the Schmidt visit should contain a reaffirmation of the full reference. Differences as to how these principles should be interpreted remained unresolved, however.

West Berlin could expect to be fed with nuclear power from Kaliningrad, but the Soviets moved only marginally, if at all, on the demand that a series of agreements with West Germany—on scientific and technical cooperation, cultural exchanges, tourism, and cooperation between courts of law—which were awaiting signature, should include West Berlin.

(NORMAN CROSSLAND)

[972.A.3.b.ii]

Ghana

A republic of West Africa and member of the Commonwealth of Nations, Ghana is on the Gulf of Guinea and is bordered by Ivory Coast, Upper Volta, and Togo. Area: 92,100 sq.mi. (238,500 sq.km.). Pop. (1973 est.): 9,190,000. Cap. and largest city: Accra (pop., 1970, 564,200). Language: English (official); local Sudanic dialects. Religion (1960): Christian 43%; Muslim 12%; animist 38%. Chairman of the National Redemption Council in 1974, Col. Ignatius Kutu Acheampong.

After a plot in December 1973 by followers of former Ghanaian leader Kwame Nkrumah to overthrow the National Redemption Council in favour of a supreme revolutionary council, death sentences were passed on the leaders; these were later commuted to life imprisonment. Colonel Acheampong tightened his personal control of the country, adding the finance portfolio and retaining that of defense. The universities were closed during February 11–March 15 because of the activities of "subversive elements," and several Soviet officials were deported for spying.

In his speech on Jan. 13, 1974, the second anniversary of the revolution, Colonel Acheampong, though making no reference to a return to civilian rule, announced the establishment of a civilian National Advisory Council on political affairs. He further announced the "demilitarization of economic life" and the inauguration of a 33-member National Economic Planning Council, to be charged with evolving a system to include every Ghanaian in the nation's self-reliance program. The council also was to launch a second five-year plan to increase agricultural diversification, develop mining of bauxite and other minerals, and encourage light industry for export. At its first meeting on May 9, Colonel Acheampong laid emphasis on the improvement in the economy, though the annual growth rate of 3% barely kept pace with the population increase. Despite large increases in foreign reserves, real growth was not easy to estimate because of the oil crisis and also because the Central Statistics Bureau in Accra had collapsed. The economic situation was helped by the Debt Settlement Agreement of March 13, which rescheduled medium-term debts to Western creditors and resulted in an immediate resumption of aid. It allowed a 10-year grace period for capital repayment, to be followed by an 18-year period for repayment at 2.5% interest.

German Literature: *see* Literature

GHANA

Education. (1970–71) Primary, pupils 1,419,838, teachers 47,957; secondary, pupils 59,669, teachers 3,388; vocational, pupils 23,152, teachers 1,130; teacher training, students 16,478, teachers 1,324; higher (including 3 universities), students 5,426, teaching staff 902.

Finance. Monetary unit: new cedi, with (Sept. 17, 1973) an official rate of 1.15 cedi to U.S. $1 (free rate of 2.66 cedis = £1 sterling). Gold, SDRs, and foreign exchange, official: (June 1974) U.S. $161.2 million; (June 1973) U.S. $174 million. Budget (1972–73 rev. est.): revenue 402 million cedis; expenditure 503 million cedis. Gross national product: (1972) 2,787,000,000 cedis; (1971) 2,449,000,000 cedis. Money supply: (April 1974) 568.3 million cedis; (April 1973) 430.9 million cedis. Cost of living (Accra; 1970 = 100): (Jan. 1974) 145; (Jan. 1973) 127.

Foreign Trade. (1972) Imports 393,330,000 cedis; exports 513,980,000 cedis. Import sources: U.S. 18%; U.K. 16%; West Germany 13%; Japan 6%; France 5%; U.S.S.R. 5%. Export destinations: U.K. 19%; U.S. 13%; West Germany 11%; The Netherlands 9%; U.S.S.R. 8%; Switzerland 7%. Main exports: cocoa 56%; timber 12%.

Transport and Communications. Roads (1972) c. 31,000 km. (including 10,350 km. main roads). Motor vehicles in use (1972): passenger 51,700; commercial (including buses) 37,600. Railways (1971): 953 km; traffic 448 million passenger-km., freight 292 million net ton-km. Air traffic (1973): 150.5 million passenger-km.; freight 2,773,000 net ton-km. Shipping (1973): merchant vessels 100 gross tons and over 73; gross tonnage 165,565. Telephones (Dec. 1972) 51,000. Radio receivers (Dec. 1972) 775,000. Television receivers (Dec. 1972) 21,000.

Agriculture. Production (in 000; metric tons; 1973; 1972 in parentheses): corn c. 350 (389); cassava (1972) c. 2,390, (1971) 2,388; taro (1972) c. 1,100, (1971) c. 1,080; yams (1972) c. 1,100, (1971) 909; millet c. 110 (98); sorghum c. 160 (151); rice (1972) c. 65, (1971) 55; peanuts c. 100 (89); cocoa 396 (420); palm oil c. 60 (c. 60); timber (cu.m.; 1970) 10,200, (1969) 9,200; fish catch (1972) 281, (1971) 220. Livestock (in 000; 1972–73): cattle c. 930; sheep c. 1,400; pigs c. 290; goats (1971–72) c. 1,700.

Industry. Production (in 000; metric tons; 1972): bauxite 340; petroleum products 932; gold (troy oz.) 724; diamonds (metric carats) 2,659; manganese ore (metal content) 244; electricity (kw-hr.; 1971) 2,944,000.

Ghana's foreign trade figures continued to move upward, with a record trade surplus of 198.1 million cedis, though rocketing prices accounted for much of this, particularly in the case of cocoa. Ghana accounted for one-quarter to one-third of world production of this commodity, which contributed 70% of the country's foreign exchange reserves. The 1973–74 crop showed only 343,000 tons as against 410,000 in 1972–73, but prices soared to £900 a ton in July 1973 and £975 by March 1974. Apart from the danger of a price decline, the cocoa industry faced problems of disease, labour dissatisfaction, and large-scale smuggling. Timber, the second-largest export, likewise benefited from world demand and rising prices (138 million cedis in 1973–74, as against 33 million cedis in 1971); but by March 1974 overproduction and the high price of Ghana hardwoods had already led to a large log pileup at Takoradi. Record production of gold, 728,821,331 fine ounces, took place in 1973 while prices rose from $90 a fine ounce in 1973 to a record $170 in 1974.

By mid-1974 the rise in the price of oil and world inflation were affecting Ghana's boom, and the trade surplus fell. In June a government decree unified import and export control with stiff punishment for evasion; similar central coordination was established for home and overseas investment. Though long-term prospects remained fair, the immediate future, both politically and economically, seemed likely to show strain. (MOLLY MORTIMER)

[978.E.4.b.ii]

Golf

Although Johnny Miller commanded the tournament scene with eight victories and official prize money of $353,021, well over $100,000 more than Jack Nicklaus, who was second in the list, Gary Player of South Africa undoubtedly was the world golfer of 1974. Not only did he win the Masters and the British and Australian opens, but he finished among the top eight in the U.S. Open and in the Professional Golfers' Association (PGA) championships. His second round of 59 in winning the Brazilian Open equaled the lowest score ever returned in an important event, and he won or was second in numerous others in America, South Africa, and Europe.

Player's tally of major championships, three British Opens, two Masters, two PGAs, and one U.S. Open, was surpassed only by Nicklaus, Walter Hagen, and Ben Hogan among professionals. No golfer of modern times had had a greater span between his first and most recent victories: from 1959, when Player won the British Open at Muirfield, to his win in that tournament at Royal Lytham and St. Anne's in 1974. His determination to prove himself the greatest of golfers and his remarkable fitness enabled him to rise to the challenge of great occasions, and to withstand the pressures of constant air travel and time changes. By the end of 1974 he had flown upward of four million miles, a total that must be unapproached by any other players of games.

Miller could hardly do wrong on the U.S. circuit. He opened his season with three successive wins and also annexed the two largest prizes, in the World Open at Pinehurst, N.C., and the Westchester (N.Y.) Classic. When he won the Kaiser International, he equaled Arnold Palmer's 1960 total of eight victories,

Lee Elder, first black man to qualify for the Masters, blasts from the rough in the April Tournament of Champions.

UPI COMPIX

the highest since Byron Nelson in 1945. Ironically, though, Miller could not summon this form in the major championships; he was never in contention in any one of the four, and his best finish was tenth in the British. Nevertheless, he established himself as one of the world's finest golfers, with a superb swing and a wonderfully aggressive game.

The foundation of Player's victory in the Masters at Augusta, Ga., was a third round of 66, which brought him within a stroke of Dave Stockton. The final day was dramatic with five men in contention for the title, but all except Player faltered slightly. Nicklaus and Tom Weiskopf missed the green of the short 16th, and Stockton could not hole the necessary putts. Few then noticed the cool, quiet Hale Irwin, who was fourth, but two months later his name was heard around the world as the U.S. Open champion.

Rarely had that championship been played on a course as ruthlessly demanding as Winged Foot, near New York City. The greens, firm and fast, were small targets for anything but finely placed tee shots to narrow fairways. The golf was a severe exercise in control, and it was clear that par for the event would not be broken. Only Player matched it with a 70 on the first day. When he shared the lead after 36 holes with Irwin and, to everyone's delight, Palmer, it seemed he had his foot firmly on the second rung of the Grand Slam. But a disastrous few holes the next day set him back. By then only Palmer of the great names was in contention, but he fell away and Irwin's admirably steady golf and poise under pressure prevailed by two strokes over Forrest Fezler. Irwin's total of 287 was the most over par since 1963. Some thought Winged Foot too tough and that the par should have been 72 and not 70, but the Open produced a worthy winner.

That Irwin was no sudden flash was confirmed later in Britain when he beat Player over 36 holes in the final of the Piccadilly match-play championship. And with better support from Lee Trevino he could have won the World Cup for the U.S. in Venezuela. This was a triumph for the South Africans, Bobby Cole and Dale Hayes, total age 48, the youngest ever to win. Cole played beautifully, hitting enormous distances and returning the lowest individual score of 271, five ahead of Masashi Ozaki of the Japanese team, which was second. The Americans, with Irwin scoring seven strokes lower than Trevino's disappointing 285, were third.

The British Open was a resounding triumph for Player, who led throughout. After 36 holes he was five strokes ahead and, although Peter Oosterhuis and Nicklaus closed on him the next day, the South African swept ahead again and was never really threatened. Oosterhuis finished second; easily the year's outstanding British golfer, he had victories in the French and Italian opens. For the fourth successive season, a record, he led the Order of Merit and in November easily obtained his tournament player's card in the PGA qualifying school in California.

For the first time the 1.68-in.-diameter American-size ball was used in the British Open, and Player's total of 282, two under par, showed that it could be managed even in the considerable winds that at times attacked the course. Its use also indicated that the large ball might eventually supersede the small one, at least in championship competition.

Not since 1969 had Nicklaus failed to win a major title, and Trevino spoiled his last chance when he beat him by a stroke in the PGA championship.

Sandra Palmer sinks a two-foot birdie to win the Burdines Invitation Golf Tournament in a sudden death play-off in Miami, Fla.

Nicklaus, however, did win the first Tournament Players Division championship. Trevino won the World Series of Golf after seven sudden-death holes with Player.

U.S. teams dominated the amateur internationals. In the world championships at La Romana, Dominican Republic, Jerry Pate (the champion), George Burns, Gary Koch, and Curtis Strange won the Eisenhower Trophy, ten strokes ahead of Japan. The U.S. women's team, led by the champion, Cynthia Hill, won by the overwhelming margin of 16 strokes from South Africa and Great Britain and Ireland in the contest for the Espirito Santo Trophy. This was the sixth U.S. victory in the championships. The American women also gained their 14th victory in the 18th Curtis Cup match in San Francisco. The British visitors were only one point down in the two sets of foursomes but lost 9 of the 12 singles.

JoAnne Carner, Jane Blalock, and Sandra Haynie (see BIOGRAPHY) were the most successful women professionals. Mrs. Carner's winnings of $88,400 surpassed the previous record held by Kathy Whitworth. A five-time winner of the U.S. amateur title, Mrs. Carner had won the Open in 1971 and was fulfilling one of the finest talents to appear in the women's game. Miss Haynie won the Open and the Ladies' PGA championships, and Jo Ann Prentice took the year's richest prize of $32,000 in the Colgate-Dinah Shore tournament in Palm Springs, Calif. The Colgate Co. also promoted the first professional tournament for women ever held in Europe, at Sunningdale, Berkshire, Eng., in August. In difficult, unfamiliar conditions, Judy Rankin showed great control in winning by five strokes.   (P. A. WARD-THOMAS)

[452.B.4.h.xiv]

Government Finance

The makers of economic policy faced a double challenge in 1974. Inflation continued apace in the industrialized countries, with prices rising at annual rates of over 10% in most of them. Anti-inflationary policies were made difficult, however, by a downturn in economic activity that went on throughout the year and seemed likely to continue well into 1975. This confronted policymakers with a wholly new problem: the existence of inflation in a period of economic downswing. Strong measures against inflation were almost certain to increase unemployment, whereas efforts to create jobs were likely to make inflation worse. Most governments sought to follow restrictive monetary and fiscal policies—*i.e.*, reducing the quantity of money and credit available, raising taxes, and cutting government expenditures—while at the same time they tried to ease the burden this placed on the lower-income levels. But among professional economists and financial experts there was little agreement on a course of action; their views tended to vary according to whether they thought inflation was a greater long-run problem than unemployment. Some felt that the inflation would soon work itself out, whereas others regarded it as a serious illness against which drastic measures were needed.

United States. "A policy of fiscal responsibility" was the phrase Pres. Richard Nixon used to describe the budget for fiscal 1975, which he sent to Congress early in 1974. The keynote of government policy was to be a continuing fight against inflation. The chief weapons were a tight monetary policy and restraints on government spending. At the same time the administration admitted that it was concerned with growing unemployment and promised that it would not pursue a deflationary policy to the point of bringing on a recession. "If we have to bust the budget to prevent it," said one top official, "we'll bust the budget."

This began a public discussion of national economic policy that continued throughout the year. As in other industrialized countries, the question was what to do about a high rate of inflation at a time of declining economic activity, when an attack on one problem was likely to aggravate the other.

President Nixon had entered office five years before as a fiscal conservative. Ironically, his five previous budgets, together with increases voted by Congress, had raised total outlays by $108 billion, an average of 11% a year. Over the same period the dollar value of gross national product (GNP) had risen by a similar amount, however, so that the size of the federal budget in relation to GNP remained about the same.

The 1975 budget reflected significant changes in the national economy and also in the administration's policies. At the beginning of 1973 the economy had been on an upturn from the recession of 1970 and 1971. The administration had committed itself to holding down spending in fiscal 1974 in an effort to keep the upturn from becoming inflationary. It had undertaken to "impound" nearly $8 billion in funds already appropriated by Congress and it requested reductions in new appropriations. But the effort failed. A number of court decisions cast doubt on the president's power to impound funds already appropriated. Congress refused to reduce new appropriations and went on to vote a major increase in Social Security benefits.

In the 1975 budget the administration seemed to have given up its effort to reduce spending and appeared to be seeking a rapprochement with Congress. The proposed budget for fiscal 1975 (the year from July 1974 to June 1975) set expenditures at $304.4 billion, or nearly 11% above the expected outlays in fiscal 1974. The increase was largely a result of the growth of "uncontrollable" programs in the fields of social security and health. The budget projected a deficit of $9.4 billion, attributed to an anticipated slowdown in economic activity which would lead to reduced tax receipts.

Subsequent months brought a mounting concern with the problem of inflation throughout the country, together with a continuing increase in unemployment. In August President Nixon resigned over the Watergate issue and was succeeded by Gerald Ford. The new president focused on inflation as "public enemy No. 1." He initiated a series of "summit discussions" in Washington among leading economists, representatives of management and labour, and officials of the administration. The discussions produced nothing new for government financial policy. One critic, Herbert Stein, who had been chairman of the Council of Economic Advisers under President Nixon, complained that the economists' discussions tended to support the policy of moderation and compromise of the previous ten years—"a monetary and fiscal policy that is only fitfully restrictive, supplemented from time to time by softer or harder variants of price control."

Publicly, nonetheless, President Ford took up a tough budget-cutting stance. In a nationally televised speech to a joint session of Congress on October 8, he proposed to cut expenditures in fiscal 1975 to $300 billion from a projected outlay of over $305 billion. He also proposed a one-year temporary 5% income tax surcharge on corporations and upper-income persons. The tax would raise an estimated $5 billion to pay for increased unemployment benefits and a standby program of public works.

Ford softened his budget-cutting position on November 26, when he sent a revised budget to Congress. This called for a spending total of $302.2 billion in fiscal 1975, with a projected deficit of $9.2 billion. It assumed that Congress would enact his previous tax proposals, but most observers thought this unlikely. The administration had now been brought to admit that the country was in a recession, and Treasury Secretary William Simon predicted that the decline would continue through the first quarter of 1975 with unemployment climbing to at least 7% of the labour force (a figure that was, in fact, reached in December). By year's end, there were indications that new economic proposals to be presented early in 1975 would include a tax cut and other stimulatory measures.

As compared with other governments, the U.S. government clearly lacked control over some of the basic

Summary of the U.S. Federal Budget

In $000,000,000

			Fiscal year ending June 30	
Item	1973 actual	1974 actual	1975 estimate*	1975 revised estimate†
Budget receipts	232.2	264.8	295.0	293.0
Budget outlays	246.5	268.3	304.4	302.2
Actual surplus or deficit (—)	—14.3	—3.5	—9.4	—9.2

*February 1974.
†November 1974.
Source: Office of Management and Budget.

budgetary decisions. The president's budget message to Congress was only a set of requests that were subject to a vortex of political forces in the House and Senate. Congress itself lacked integrated control over the various appropriations bills that made their way through its standing committees, with consequences that were sometimes surprising. In June, however, Congress took a giant step toward a more efficient way of processing the budget. It passed a bill creating new budget committees in both the House and the Senate to oversee expenditures and revenues as a whole. It also established a budget office to provide itself with the sort of expert knowledge that the executive branch of the government has in the Office of Management and Budget. It changed the starting date of the government's fiscal year from July 1 to October 1 beginning in 1976 and set up a procedure under which either of the two houses could veto impoundments of funds by the president. The president would have to submit his budget message to Congress by February 15 rather than January 20.

Japan. The chief concern of economic policy in Japan in 1974 was inflation. The upward spiral began in 1972 and was exacerbated by the rise in oil prices late in 1973. In presenting the fiscal 1974 budget to the Diet, Minister of Finance Takeo Fukuda said that 1974 would be "a year of trial for Japan." The budget for fiscal 1974 (April 1, 1974–March 31, 1975) called for heavy restraints on government spending. Major public works programs were curtailed, and the scale of projects for government-owned railways and telecommunications was trimmed. On the other hand, expenditures on social security programs were to increase, since these merely redistributed income without generating new demand for goods. This restrictive budget was accompanied by a tight monetary policy. Changes were also made in the tax structure to reduce the burden on wage and salary workers. The personal income tax was reduced, while the corporation income tax and certain excise taxes were increased. The effect of these policies was to reduce domestic demand for goods while stepping up exports—particularly to less developed and Communist countries.

The formula did not succeed in overcoming Japan's inflation, although it did produce a recession with rising unemployment as in other industrialized countries. Particularly hard hit were the electrical, construction, and textile industries. It was expected that the GNP would show little or no real increase in 1974, for the first time since World War II. But as the government set about compiling its budget for fiscal 1975, it continued to regard inflation as the main threat. The new finance minister, Masayoshi Ohira, announced in September that the next budget would be about 20% larger than the 1974 budget in monetary terms. Since the general price level would have increased by perhaps more than 20%, the predominant view among Japanese economists was that this would hold the nation's real economic growth rate to a low level in fiscal 1975.

West Germany. The vicissitudes of oil, inflation, and unemployment fell lightly upon the West German economy. In his budget speech on September 18 Finance Minister Hans Apel boasted to the Bundestag that "we are the country with the lowest rate of price increase, with the fewest days lost in strikes, with the highest currency reserves, with one of the world's best systems of social security, with one of the highest wage levels in the Western world, and at the same time with a high level of employment."

Introducing the draft budget for 1975, Apel said that the government intended to continue past anti-inflationary policies. While the country had by no means escaped inflation, the rate of 7% was low compared with the double-digit inflation in other industrial countries. In contrast to the trade deficits of most other countries, West Germany reported a record trade surplus of DM. 25.2 billion, or nearly 3% of the GNP, for the first six months of 1974.

The finance minister criticized some neighbouring countries for their efforts to get West Germany to cut its trade surplus. They complained, he said, that the German export drive was cutting into their markets abroad. Apel countered that these countries were not losing their markets because of Bonn's stability policy but because of their own inflationary policies, which were running up the prices of their exports. The government's restrictive financial policy—the money supply actually shrank in the second quarter of the year—had admittedly led to growing unemployment, which was most severe in the construction industry. Overall, however, unemployment stood at only about 2.3% of the labour force.

The 1974 budget was expected to be in deficit by $4 to $5 billion. A tax cut due to take effect January 1 would raise the deficit to nearly $6 billion in 1975, but would add more than $5 billion to total purchasing power. It was designed to offset the effects of inflation on persons in the lower- and middle-income brackets and give stimulus to the domestic economy, which had not shared in the prosperity of the export industries. Toward the end of the year, as unemployment continued to mount, the government determined on a more expansionary policy and the budget deficit for 1975 was reestimated at nearly $10 billion.

United Kingdom. The critical state of Britain's economy in 1974 caused much uncertainty among economic policymakers. Like other Western countries, the U.K. was faced with two dangers: runaway inflation on the one hand and rising unemployment on the other. A Labour government took office in March after winning a narrow victory over the Conservatives. A second election in October kept Labour in office by another narrow margin. These economic and political uncertainties were reflected in the three successive budgets introduced in March, July, and November. The first budget was based on estimates that supplies of most goods would be short because of the slowdown in the first part of the year, when industry was put on a three-day workweek in response to the oil crisis. The chancellor of the Exchequer, concerned at the danger of inflation, brought in a budget intended to restrain demand. It increased taxes on various consumer goods, including tobacco, gasoline, and beverages; raised income taxes on higher-income groups; and increased the tax burden on corporations. At the same time the budget sought to hold down the cost of living so as not to trigger off a round of wage increases. Toward this end it increased subsidies to food and housing and raised social insurance benefits. The benefits to consumers were somewhat offset by big price increases for nationalized industries (30% in electricity, 25% in steel, 15% for rail freight, and up to 20% in telecommunications). Companies in the private sector, however, were given little opportunity to raise their prices under the tight system of price controls.

In July the government announced a new budget, this one intended to stimulate the economy rather than to deflate it. The major danger now was seen as unemployment rather than inflation. The new budget canceled out much of the effect of the previous one. It was designed to stimulate demand and to lighten the tax burden on corporations so as to encourage business expansion. It reduced sales and excise taxes by about as much as the March budget had increased them. Large employers of labour in regions of high unemployment were given special tax relief.

Still a third budget was announced in mid-November, a month after the new election had kept the Labour government in power. This budget was largely neutral as between deflating demand on the one hand and stimulating it on the other. What it did was to shift resources from the personal consumption of the public to business. Chancellor of the Exchequer Denis Healey (*see* BIOGRAPHY) told Parliament that he hoped to increase the annual rate of economic growth by 2% between the second half of 1974 and the first half of 1975. One effect of the budget was to increase the cost of living slightly. The subsidies for the nationalized industries, amounting to $2.4 billion a year, were to be eliminated gradually. In addition, there would be increases in local tax rates. Business firms were given some relief from strict price controls. The hoped-for cut in the corporation tax was not forthcoming, but companies were required to pay less tax on inventory profits. The government hoped that the trade unions would adhere to the so-called social contract and forbear pressing for higher wages. (*See* INDUSTRIAL RELATIONS.)

France. The government of Pres. Valéry Giscard d'Estaing, which took office in May, addressed itself to a chronic inflation that seemed to be growing worse. In the first quarter of 1974 the general price level had risen at an annual rate of well over 10%. In June the government announced a series of anti-inflationary measures that differed from previous ones in being directed at business expansion. Earlier measures had sought to reduce demand without discouraging business investment, in line with the policy of fostering a high rate of economic growth. To that end efforts had been made to slow down the growth of the money supply and to control bank credit while making funds available for long-term capital expansion.

The measures introduced in June included an 18% increase in corporation taxes, tighter credit controls, and lower tax write-offs on investments. Personal income taxes were also raised at the highest levels. The new taxes were expected to bring increased revenues of Fr. 8 billion. An additional Fr. 1 billion was to be found by trimming government expenditures for the year (on items other than public works).

Canada. Inflation became a major political issue in 1974, with the consumer price index in June standing 11.4% above the level of a year earlier. In May the Liberal government of Prime Minister Pierre Trudeau fell when his parliamentary opposition passed a motion of no confidence in the government's budget policies. The proposed budget for the fiscal year ending March 31, 1975, had rejected wage and price controls and certain fiscal measures demanded by the opposition parties. It had proposed a reduction of personal income taxes together with a 10% surtax on corporation income, higher excise taxes, a removal of the 12% sales tax on clothing, and abolition of taxes on machinery, bicycles, and buses. The left-of-centre New Democrats joined with the right-of-centre Progressive Conservatives to bring down the government—the first time that a Canadian government had fallen in a vote on its budget. In national elections held in July, Trudeau's party won a large majority

in Parliament and he formed a new government. The new budget, presented in November, repeated the main proposals of the May budget but reduced the federal tax burden on the oil and mining industries while increasing the cut in personal income taxes. The aim was to deal with inflation and slower economic growth through tax cuts, restricted government expenditure, and by giving stimulus to private capital investment. (FRANCIS S. PIERCE)

See also Economics; Economy, World; Exchange and Payments, International; Taxation.

[534.G; 535.B.1 and 4; 543.B]

Greece

A republic of Europe, Greece occupies the southern part of the Balkan Peninsula. Area: 50,944 sq.mi. (131,944 sq.km.), of which the mainland accounts for 41,227 sq.mi. Pop. (1972 est.): 8,889,000. Cap. and largest city: Athens (pop., 1971, 867,000). Language: Greek. Religion: Orthodox. Presidents in 1974, Phaidon Gizikis and, from December 18 (ad interim), Michael Stassinopoulos; prime ministers, Adamantios Androutsopoulos and, from July 24, Konstantinos Karamanlis.

For Greece 1974 was a momentous year, culminating in the restoration of democracy, the first fully free elections since 1964, and popular rejection of the former monarchy.

The New Junta. The downfall on Nov. 25, 1973, of Georgios Papadopoulos, toppled by military police chief Brig. Gen. Demetrios Ioannidis and his new junta, generated a curious climate of euphoria among the people of Greece. During this spell of optimism Ioannidis pieced together a government under Adamantios Androutsopoulos, who had served Papadopoulos as minister of finance and of interior. Androutsopoulos' first public statement dispelled hope of political evolution, however. Nonconformist newspapers were shut down and, though censorship was officially lifted, editors received daily orders from a military police major. Promises that hundreds arrested after the revolt at the National Technical University of Athens would be freed were belied by fresh arrests, and the notorious concentration camp on Yiaros Island was reopened.

Konstantinos Karamanlis takes the oath of office as prime minister of Greece, replacing the military regime. Gen. Phaidon Gizikis (centre) remained president temporarily.

The regime tried to gain credit in February 1974 by emphasizing the discovery of "significant deposits of oil and natural gas" off the island of Thasos in the northern Aegean Sea. Then it was found that, also in February, the Turkish government had already granted oil exploration concessions in the eastern Aegean, west of the Greek islands that hug the Anatolian coast. An acid exchange of diplomatic notes followed, in which both sides invoked the 1958 Geneva convention on the continental shelf. A NATO Aegean naval exercise was suspended on March 31, and there was an exchange of angry speeches and articles.

U.S. and NATO interventions eased the tension. The Greek and Turkish foreign ministers met in Ottawa (June 20) and agreed to have formal discussions on the Aegean issue, but five days later, when the prime ministers of Greece and Turkey met in Brussels for this purpose, Androutsopoulos rejected such negotiation. If the Aegean dispute diverted popular attention from domestic problems, it also made the regime realize the extent of its political isolation from the international community—other than countries willing to help in its rearmament plans, such as the U.S. and France.

Even relations with the U.S. declined; negotiations for an extension of the U.S. Navy's use of the Athens area as a home port for one of its two aircraft carriers in the Mediterranean and for use of Akrotiri, Crete, as an air base broke down in January because the Greeks demanded, in return, the total renovation of their air force's arsenal. Relations with Britain deteriorated when the Labour government canceled (March 14) a scheduled naval visit.

While the arrest of such opponents of the regime as liberal leader Georgios Mavros (March 16) and even of critics became a daily occurrence, the regime also acted against officials of the deposed Papadopoulos regime. Ex-minister Ioannis Agathanghelou was banished to Yiaros for subversive conversation and, in June, ex-Col. Michael Balopoulos of the 1967 junta was convicted before a military tribunal, together with 39 of Papadopoulos' Ministry of Trade officials and meat importers accused of bribery and fraud. However, domestic events were overshadowed by the mounting tension between Greece and Turkey, mainly over Aegean rights. Greek orders for armaments from the U.S. and France, the breakdown of the Brussels talks, and rumours that Turkey was hiring a U.S. seismographic ship for preliminary oil exploration in the Aegean touched off another spell of sabre rattling late in June.

At this point the Cyprus problem flared up again after a period of quiescence during negotiations between the Greek Cypriot and the Turkish Cypriot representatives. Archbishop Makarios (*see* BIOGRAPHY), the president of Cyprus, sent a letter (July 2) to the Greek president, Gen. Phaidon Gizikis, asking that the 650 Greek Army officers and NCOs on loan to the Greek Cypriot National Guard be recalled because of evidence that they were planning a coup to seize the island for Greece. He asked verbally that half these officers be withdrawn by July 20. On July 15 the National Guard, led by the Greek officers and supported by the Greek Army contingent stationed in Cyprus, under orders from Ioannidis, staged a coup with the aim of seizing power and killing Makarios, whom the Athens junta had always regarded as a traitor to the cause of *enosis* (union of Cyprus with Greece). Makarios escaped, and the coup leaders, unable to find a more respectable substitute for him,

named a journalist, politician, and gunman, Nikos Sampson, as president.

Initially, Ioannidis and the junta did not believe the Turkish threat to invade Cyprus. A few hours before the Turkish landing of July 20, Ioannidis claimed that the Turks were "bluffing, once again." After the landing he attempted to intimidate Turkey by ordering a 12-hour general mobilization that threw Greece economically and militarily out of gear. The next day Ioannidis and the junta ordered the chiefs of staff to attack the Turkish invasion forces and also to start shelling across the Evros River (the Greek-Turkish border). The chiefs balked, declaring they were equipped to defend, not to attack. Nonetheless, a flight of ten antiquated transport planes with crack troops did make the 600-mi. dash and landed with heavy losses at Nicosia airport, just before it ceased being operational. (*See* DEFENSE: *Special Report.*)

Democracy Restored. On July 22 the Greek chiefs of staff asked President Gizikis to summon political leaders for consultations. The leaders were summoned the next day and were told by Gizikis and the chiefs that the armed forces had decided to surrender power to them in order to save the nation. It was decided to invite Konstantinos Karamanlis (*see* BIOGRAPHY)

Athens rejoices: July 23, 1974.

CAMERA PRESS/PICTORIAL PARADE

to become prime minister, and the man who had been prime minister of Greece from 1955 to 1963, and then quit politics in disgust, returned from Paris to a hero's welcome. Sworn in at 4 A.M. on July 24, Karamanlis within 48 hours set up a Cabinet with Mavros as deputy prime minister and foreign minister. Political prisoners were freed and the military police stripped of political powers. Mavros flew to Geneva for marathon talks on Cyprus with his British and Turkish counterparts; the result was an uneasy cease-fire in Cyprus, but the fears of war were dispelled.

The 1952 constitution abolished by the dictatorship was reinstated, except that the future of the monarchy was to be determined by plebiscite. The government and local government were purged. Within three months Ioannidis had been placed on retirement, his henchmen had been suspended, torturers were facing trial, and army units had been moved from Athens. By October 9 martial law had been lifted in all except a few border areas; ex-dictator Papadopoulos and four of his associates had been banished to Kea Island; and judicial inquiries were in progress against over 100 junta functionaries on charges of high treason and moral instigation to mass murder. The breakdown of the Geneva talks on Cyprus in mid-August and the Turkish occupation of 40% of the island prompted a declaration that Greece would withdraw its forces from NATO.

The new government next set out to prepare the country for elections, the first in ten years. Karamanlis himself founded the New Democracy Party. Mavros was elected leader of the liberal Centre Union, which was joined by the New Political Forces, a group that included intellectuals who had resisted the dictatorship. Andreas Papandreou, son of the late prime minister Georgios Papandreou, returned from exile and set up the Pan-Hellenic Socialist Movement

(Pasok), which preached nationalization of private enterprise and a nonaligned foreign policy. On September 23 Karamanlis lifted the 27-year-long ban on the Greek Communist Party (KKE), whose two warring factions set up a United Left with the extreme United Democratic Left (EDA). Principal issues during an exceptionally orderly campaign were retribution for the junta and its henchmen and guarantees against military coups in the future.

When the Greeks went to the polls on November 17 they gave Karamanlis the massive majority he had asked to empower him to put through constitutional reforms. His New Democracy won 220 seats, Mavros' Centre Union-New Forces 60, Pasok 12, and the United Left 8. Of the 4,912,356 valid votes cast, New Democracy received 2,670,804 or 54.37%; the Centre Union-New Forces, 1,002,908 or 20.42%; the Pan-Hellenic Socialist Movement, 666,806 or 13.58%; and the United Left, 464,331 or 9.45%.

In a referendum held December 8, restoration of the monarchy was emphatically rejected, the electorate voting about 2 to 1 for a republican form of government. On December 18, three days after Gizikis had resigned, Michael Stassinopoulos became interim president. A draft of a new constitution was made public December 23. (MARIO MODIANO)

[972.B.3.d]

Grenada

A parliamentary state within the Commonwealth of Nations, Grenada, with its dependency, the southern Grenadines, is the southernmost of the Windward Islands of the Caribbean Sea, 100 mi. N of Trinidad. Area: 133 sq.mi. (344 sq.km.). Pop. (1973 est.): 105,000, Negro 53%, mixed 42%, white 1%, and other 4%. Cap.: Saint George's (pop., 1969 est., 8,644). Language: English. Religion: Christian. Queen, Elizabeth II; governor until Jan. 14, 1974, Dame Hilda Louisa Bynoe; governor-general, from February 7, Leo de Gale (acting governor January 24–February 6); prime minister, Eric Gairy.

Grenada became an independent state and the 34th member of the Commonwealth of Nations on Feb. 7, 1974, in an atmosphere of extreme political unrest. The ceremony was boycotted by the prime ministers of the independent Commonwealth Caribbean states, and Prince Richard of Gloucester did not attend as the queen's representative for security reasons.

The opposition to independence was, to a large extent, opposition to control by Prime Minister Eric

GREECE
Education. (1970–71) Primary, pupils 907,446, teachers 29,336; secondary, pupils 422,022, teachers 12,958; vocational, pupils 117,006; higher (including 5 universities), students 76,198, teaching staff 3,483.
Finance. Monetary unit: drachma, with (Sept. 16, 1974) a par value of 30 drachmas to U.S. $1 (free rate of 69.27 drachmas = £1 sterling). Gold, SDRs, and foreign exchange, central bank: (June 1974) U.S. $916.2 million; (June 1973) U.S. $1,061,700,000. Budget (1974 est.): revenue 92.5 billion drachmas; expenditure 99 billion drachmas. Gross national product: (1973) 488.8 billion drachmas; (1972) 376.8 billion drachmas. Money supply: (April 1972) 87,020,-000,000 drachmas; (April 1973) 76,360,000,000 drachmas. Cost of living (1970 = 100): (June 1974) 159; (June 1973) 122.
Foreign Trade. (1973) Imports 102,747,000,000 drachmas; exports 42,812,-000,000 drachmas. Import sources: EEC 50% (West Germany 20%, Italy 9%, France 8%, U.K. 6%); U.S. 8%; Japan 7%. Export destinations: EEC 55% (West Germany 22%, Italy 9%, U.K. 7%, The Netherlands 7%, France 7%); U.S. 6%. Main exports: petroleum products 14%; textile yarns and fabrics 9%; iron and steel 8%; dried fruit 6%; cotton 6%; chemicals 5%; fresh fruit 5%. Tourism (1972): visitors 2,436,400; gross receipts U.S. $393 million.
Transport and Communications. Roads (1972) 35,512 km. (including 11 km. expressways). Motor vehicles in use (1972): passenger 301,900; commercial 130,200. Railways: (1972) 2,572 km.; traffic (1973) 1,615,000,000 passenger-km., freight 798 million net ton-km. Air traffic (1973): 3,729,000,000 passenger-km.; freight 57,759,000 net ton-km. Shipping (1973): merchant vessels 100 gross tons and over 2,536; gross tonnage 19,295,143. Telephones (Dec. 1972) 1,438,-000. Radio receivers (Dec. 1971) 1 million. Television receivers (Dec. 1972) 520,000.
Agriculture. Production (in 000; metric tons; 1973; 1972 in parentheses): wheat 1,738 (1,919); barley 856 (867); oats 102 (107); corn 656 (579); potatoes c. 715 (683); rice c. 82 (74); tomatoes c. 1,165 (c. 1,100); apples (1972) c. 240, (1971) 239; oranges (1972) c. 430, (1971) 362; lemons (1972) c. 140, (1971) 125; sugar, raw value c. 168 (126); olives c. 970 (c. 1,090); olive oil 225 (c. 255); wine c. 550 (489); raisins (1972) c. 140, (1971) c. 150; currants and sultanas (1972) 141, (1971) 161; figs (1972) c. 150, (1971) c. 150; tobacco 78 (85); cotton, lint c. 127 (136). Livestock (in 000; Dec. 1972): sheep c. 7,620; cattle c. 993; goats (1971) 4,185; pigs c. 380; horses (1971) 216; asses (1971) 345; chickens c. 25,500.
Industry. Production (in 000; metric tons; 1973): lignite 13,118; electricity (excluding most industrial production; kw-hr.) 13,544,000; petroleum products (1972) 6,200; bauxite 2,739; magnesite (1972) 917; cement 6,449; sulfuric acid 903; fertilizers (1972–73) nitrogenous c. 220, phosphate c. 150; cotton yarn 52. Merchant vessels launched (100 gross tons and over; 1973) 151,000 gross tons.

GRENADA
Education. (1970–71) Primary, pupils 30,355, teachers 800; secondary, pupils 3,039, teachers 129; vocational, pupils 985, teachers 20; teacher training, students 57, teachers 12.
Finance and Trade. Monetary unit: East Caribbean dollar, with (Sept. 16, 1974) a free rate of ECar$2.07 to U.S. $1 (official rate of ECar$4.80 = £1 sterling). Budget (1973 est.): revenue ECar$20,428,000; expenditure ECar$20,329,000. Foreign trade (1970): imports ECar$44,080,000; exports (main only; accounting for 94% of total in 1969) ECar$10,497,000. Import sources (1968): U.K. 33%; U.S. 10%; Canada 10%; The Netherlands 5%. Export destinations: U.K. 40%; U.S. 10%. Main exports: cocoa c. 37%; nutmegs c. 28%; bananas c. 22%; mace 6%. Tourism (1972): visitors 132,000; gross expenditure ECar$24,-380,000.

Gairy (*see* BIOGRAPHY). His support had traditionally come from the rural areas. More recently, however, he recruited a strong-arm squad of police aides known as the Mongoose Squad, some of whom were criminals, allegedly for protection against Communist subversion. By late 1973 he was opposed by the Committee of *22*, a group ranging from business and professional men and urban white-collar workers to the young radical intellectuals of the New Jewel Movement (Joint Endeavour for Welfare, Education, and Liberation). On Jan. 1, 1974, the Committee of *22*, as a protest against police brutality, called a general strike. The government countered this with legislation making it illegal for business premises to close down during normal trading hours. In the weeks before independence there were daily anti-Gairy demonstrations and marches; a continued general strike; a business shutdown; a cutoff of fuel, electricity, and telephone service; shortages of food; looting; violence; the killing of labour union leader Rupert Bishop, father of New Jewel's coordinating secretary, Maurice Bishop; and the collapse of the tourist business. Labour unions in Trinidad refused to handle cargoes consigned to Grenada as a gesture of solidarity with striking Grenadian workers. Efforts by Caribbean labour unions, church groups, and others to mediate proved in vain, as did appeals to the British government to defer independence. Instead, Britain gave Grenada an independence present of £100,000.

A new wave of arrests occurred after independence day, and the strikers went back to work on February 23. Many Grenadians fled the island. The economy, based on tourism, cocoa, nutmeg, and bananas, was reported to be in a perilous condition, with up to 90% of normal revenue lost. By May some normality had returned to the island, but the economy remained precarious. Grenada joined the Caribbean Common Market (Caricom), and there were plans to turn the island into a tax haven. On September 17 the UN General Assembly elected Grenada as a member state of the United Nations. (SHEILA PATTERSON)

Guatemala

A republic of Central America, Guatemala is bounded by Mexico, Belize, Honduras, El Salvador, the Caribbean Sea, and the Pacific Ocean. Area: 42,042 sq.mi. (108,889 sq. km.). Pop. (1973): 5,211,930. Cap. and largest city: Guatemala City (pop., 1973, 717,320). Language: Spanish, with some Indian dialects. Religion: predominantly Roman Catholic. Presidents in 1974, Carlos Manuel Arana Osorio and, from July 1, Kjell Eugenio Laugerud García.

Following the presidential elections held on March 3, Gen. Kjell Laugerud García (*see* BIOGRAPHY), the candidate of the ruling coalition of the Partido Institucional Democrático and the Movimiento de Liberación Nacional, was declared the winner. A coalition headed by the Partido Demócrata Cristiano, whose candidate, Gen. Efraín Ríos Montt, was widely believed to have polled the most votes, voiced a strong protest, and opposition members of Congress boycotted the session in which the result was confirmed. President Laugerud took office on July 1 for four years; the weakness of his mandate was reflected in his choice of ministers, most of whom had either

served in or been closely associated with the previous administration.

In his inaugural speech President Laugerud referred to the need for social reform, including income redistribution and greater equality of opportunity. His first major policy step, however, was the announcement on August 13 of an action plan to deal with inflation. This problem, which had been intensifying since 1973, was attributed to a shortage of staple foods, an excess of monetary liquidity arising from high prices received for commodity exports, and the

Kjell Laugerud García, new president of Guatemala, addresses an audience of Indians in March.

GUATEMALA

Education. (1973) Primary, pupils 585,015, teachers 16,451; secondary, pupils 86,215, teachers 5,934; vocational (1970), pupils 15,810, teachers (1969) 1,380; teacher training (1970), students 7,980, teaching staff (1969) 1,008; higher (including 4 universities), students 21,715, teaching staff (1970) 1,314.

Finance. Monetary unit: quetzal, at par with the U.S. dollar (free rate, at Sept. 16, 1974, of 2.31 quetzales to £1 sterling). Gold, SDRs, and foreign exchange, central bank: (June 1974) U.S. $221.9 million; (June 1973) U.S. $203.7 million. Budget (1974 est.) balanced at 355.6 million quetzales. Gross domestic product: (1972) 2,164,000,000 quetzales; (1971) 1,985,000,000 quetzales. Money supply: (Feb. 1974) 302.6 million quetzales; (Feb. 1973) 232 million quetzales. Cost of living (Guatemala City; 1970 = 100): (May 1974) 125; (May 1973) 116.

Foreign Trade. (1973) Imports 431 million quetzales; exports 436.2 million quetzales. Import sources (1972): U.S. 32%; El Salvador 14%; West Germany 9%; Japan 9%; Venezuela 5%. Export destinations (1972): U.S. 29%; El Salvador 14%; West Germany 10%; Costa Rica 8%; Japan 8%; Nicaragua 5%. Main exports: coffee 34%; cotton 11%; sugar 6%.

Transport and Communications. Roads (1972) 13,449 km. (including 824 km. of Pan-American Highway). Motor vehicles in use (1972): passenger 46,000; commercial (including buses) 30,000. Railways: (1972) 822 km.; freight traffic (1970) 106 million net ton-km. Air traffic (1973): 47.6 million passenger-km.; freight 3,690,000 net ton-km. Telephones (Dec. 1972) 54,000. Radio receivers (Dec. 1968) 559,000. Television receivers (Dec. 1972) 85,000.

Agriculture. Production (in 000; metric tons; 1973; 1972 in parentheses): corn *c.* 783 (*c.* 666); cane sugar, raw value *c.* 211 (192); sorghum *c.* 51 (*c.* 48); tomatoes *c.* 79 (*c.* 74); dry beans *c.* 66 (65); coffee *c.* 132 (*c.* 135); bananas (1972) *c.* 550, (1971) *c.* 495; cotton, lint 93 (81). Livestock (in 000; March 1973): cattle *c.* 1,800; sheep *c.* 650; pigs 983; chickens (1972) *c.* 9,900.

Industry. Production (in 000; metric tons; 1971): cement 235; petroleum products (1972) 871; lead ore (metal content) 1; zinc ore (metal content; 1971) 0.5; electricity (kw-hr.) 830,000.

high cost of some imports, particularly petroleum. The official figure for the increase in the cost of living over the first eight months of the year was 17%, and unofficial sources estimated that the inflation rate for the year as a whole would be 30%. The countermeasures adopted included restrictions on exports of foodstuffs and other raw materials, government financing for imports of staple foods and fertilizers, price controls for some basic commodities, price subsidies for petroleum products used in industry, and an indefinite freeze on rents. In addition, salary increases were granted.

The inflationary situation caused the economy to grow more slowly than in 1973, at a real rate of less than 5%. There was a decline in activity in the construction industry because of sharp rises in the cost of building materials. Hotel construction expanded, however, reflecting the rapid growth of the tourist trade. Unofficial figures for the number of tourists in the first quarter of 1974 were higher than for the whole of 1973, and it was believed that income from tourism in 1974 might exceed $200 million.

Production was adversely affected by two natural disasters. In mid-September Hurricane Fifi struck the northern part of the country, destroying banana plantations and staple crops. Two weeks later, volcanic eruptions began to occur in the southwest, the richest agricultural region of Guatemala, causing widespread damage to cotton and coffee plantations and to grain crops. These setbacks, coupled with the decline in world prices for some of Guatemala's more important exports, notably coffee, cotton, and meat, seriously harmed the agricultural sector, still the mainstay of the economy, and the minister of finance predicted that 1975 would be a difficult year. In contrast, the longer-term outlook became more encouraging, with the discovery in June of an oil well at Rubelsanto capable of producing 3,000 bbl. of petroleum a day, or some 15% of the nation's current needs.

(JOAN PEARCE)

[974.B.1.a]

GUINEA

Education. (1970–71) Primary, pupils 191,287, teachers 5,304; secondary, pupils 59,918, teachers 2,360; vocational, pupils 2,013, teachers 150; teacher training, students 1,478, teachers 275; higher (1968–69), students 942, teachers (1965–66) 95.

Finance. Monetary unit: sily, with an official rate (Sept. 16, 1974) of 20.46 silys to U.S. $1 (free nominal rate of 47.30 silys = £1 sterling). Budget (1972–73 est.) balanced at 4.5 billion silys.

Foreign Trade. (1972) Imports *c.* 1.8 billion silys; exports *c.* 1.2 billion silys. Import sources: France *c.* 31%; U.S. *c.* 13%; Belgium-Luxembourg *c.* 12%; U.S.S.R. *c.* 12%; Italy *c.* 5%; West Germany *c.* 5%. Export destinations: Spain *c.* 16%; Norway *c.* 15%; West Germany *c.* 14%; Cameroon *c.* 10%; Switzerland *c.* 5%; Yugoslavia 5%. Main exports (1970): aluminum and bauxite 65%; coffee 11%; palm products 6%.

come Guinea-Bissau officially on September 10, and President Touré received the credentials of Guinea-Bissau's first ambassador as early as February 12; on May 12 Guinea's envoy presented his credentials to Guinea-Bissau's president, Luis Cabral.

At a meeting in Conakry, Feb. 28–March 8, 1974, the International Bauxite Association was formally established by the seven leading bauxite-producing countries. (*See* COMMODITY TRADE: *Special Report.*)

The economy was helped by an African Development Fund loan to improve Conakry's water supply and by the announced prospecting for offshore oil by a U.S. company with the Guinean government's participation. A new dam was being built at Koukoutamba to bring electric power to southeastern Guinea, and a Canadian firm agreed to build a trans-Guinea railway at a cost of $555 million.

Following the deposition of Emperor Haile Selassie of Ethiopia in September, Guinea was one of the few African countries to make official representations for the preservation of the former monarch's life.

(R. M. GOODWIN)

[978.E.4.b.ii]

Guinea

A republic on the west coast of Africa, Guinea is bounded by Guinea-Bissau, Senegal, Mali, Ivory Coast, Liberia, and Sierra Leone. Area: 94,926 sq.mi. (245,856 sq.km.). Pop. (1973 UN est.): 4,208,000; however, a census held on Dec. 30, 1972, reported 5,143,284 persons, of whom 1.5 million were living abroad. Cap. and largest city: Conakry (pop., 1972, 525,671). Language: French (official). Religion: mostly Muslim. President in 1974, Sékou Touré; premier, Louis Lansana Beavogui.

In presidential and general elections held on December 27, Pres. Sékou Touré was returned unopposed for a third seven-year term, securing 100% of the 2,432,129 votes cast. Electors also approved the choice by the Central Committee of the Democratic Party of Guinea (the single, governing party) of 150 deputies, as against 75 in the previous assembly.

In Guinea's quarrel with Senegal and the Ivory Coast over the alleged harbouring of dissident Guinean exiles, President Touré was persuaded in February by Nigeria's Gen. Yakubu Gowon, as chairman of the Organization of African Unity (OAU), to withdraw the matter from the UN and settle it amicably within the OAU. Guinea had strongly supported the African nationalists in Portuguese Guinea, to be-

Guinea-Bissau

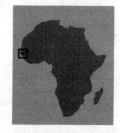

An independent African republic, Guinea-Bissau has an Atlantic coastline on the west and borders Senegal on the north and Guinea on the east and south. Area: 13,948 sq.mi. (36,125 sq.km.). Pop. (1973 est.): 510,000. Cap.: Madina do Boé (pop. a few hundred). Largest city: the former colonial capital, Bissau (metro. area pop., 1970, 71,169). President in 1974: Luis Cabral.

Guinea-Bissau officially became independent on Sept. 10, 1974, by agreement with Portugal and became a member of the UN on September 17. Luis Cabral (*see* BIOGRAPHY), half brother of Amilcar Cabral, founder of the African Party for the Independence of Guinea and Cape Verde (PAIGC) who had been killed in 1973, became the first president.

The PAIGC claimed to have set up the independent republic of Guinea-Bissau in September 1973. Despite Portugal's insistence that this assertion was fictitious, African guerrillas controlled most of the country. More and more African and other nonaligned countries gave their support, and in November the republic was admitted as the 42nd member of the Organization of African Unity. The PAIGC was encouraged by

A meeting of the PAIGC in April. The banner honours former party leader Amilcar Cabral, whose brother, Luis, became first president of Guinea-Bissau.

this, as well as by Sweden's gift of $3.6 million in September and the offer of a further $770,000 from Nigeria in November. The republic was granted an observer seat at the UN in March 1974. The coup in Portugal in April brought in as president Gen. António de Spínola (*see* BIOGRAPHY), formerly governor of Portuguese Guinea, who was known to oppose the continuance of military colonial rule. Mário Soares (*see* BIOGRAPHY), now Portugal's foreign minister, initiated discussions with Aristides Pereira, secretary-general of the PAIGC, in Dakar, Senegal, in May, and further talks were held in London and Algiers in May and June. The success of the talks was threatened first by the question of the Cape Verde Islands, regarded by the PAIGC as an integral part of an independent republic. The Portuguese were reluctant to surrender their hold, however, and the inhabitants (many of Portuguese descent) had no strong links with the mainland. The second problem arose from the PAIGC's insistence that Portugal recognize the state of Guinea-Bissau before negotiations began.

The talks in London and Algiers ended in deadlock, but after secret negotiations, supervised by Spínola himself and encouraged by Pres. Léopold Senghor of Senegal, Portugal announced, in August, its willingness to recognize the PAIGC as the governing body within the republic and to sponsor Guinea-Bissau's application for UN membership. In addition, Portugal would continue to supply doctors, teachers, and other essential personnel, while the Portuguese Army was to begin withdrawal before the end of the month. The future of the Cape Verde Islands was left in abeyance (in December it was announced that they would become independent in 1975). PAIGC intended to retain the economy's agricultural basis, but the new government hoped that Portugal would give financial aid to promote development.   (KENNETH INGHAM)

·[978.E.4.b.ii]

Guyana

A republic and member of the Commonwealth of Nations, Guyana is situated between Venezuela, Brazil, and Surinam on the Atlantic Ocean. Area: 83,000 sq.mi. (215,000 sq.km.). Pop. (1973 est.): 758,000, including (1970) East Indian 51%; African 30.7%; mixed 11.4%; Amerindian 4.4%. Cap. and largest city: Georgetown (pop., 1970, 63,184). Language: English (official). Religion: Protestant, Hindu, Roman Catholic. President in 1974, Arthur Chung; prime minister, Forbes Burnham.

Cheddi Jagan, former prime minister and leader of the majority Indian community, continued his boycott of Parliament in 1974. Publication of his daily newspaper, the *Mirror*, was made irregular by harassment; Jagan's house and party headquarters were raided in July, and Jagan himself was later fined for illegally possessing a pistol. The editors of other nongovernmental newspapers were forced out of their jobs, and in October Prime Minister Burnham introduced a ban on "subversive" literature. Earlier Burnham had quashed the appointment to the University of Guyana's chair of history of black militant Walter Rodney, a Guyanan expelled from Jamaica in 1968 who had taught in Tanzania for the previous six years. The Guyana Trades Union Conference supported the protest against Burnham's action by the university staff, and a rally led by the African Society for Cultural Relations with Independent Africa (ASCRIA) condemned the ban. ASCRIA had earlier agreed with the Indian Political Revolutionary Associates (IPRA) to work jointly for the dignity and equality of those of African and Indian descent in

GUYANA

Education. (1970–71) Primary, pupils 130,484, teachers 4,485; secondary, pupils 62,093, teachers 2,262; vocational, pupils 3,060, teachers 72; teacher training, students 656, teachers 61; higher, students 1,182, teaching staff (1968–69) 110.

Finance. Monetary unit: Guyanan dollar, with (Sept. 16, 1974) a free rate of Guy$2.26 to U.S. $1 (official rate of Guy$5.21 = £1 sterling). Gold, SDRs, and foreign exchange: (May 1974) U.S. $13,170,000; (May 1973) U.S. $25.1 million. Budget (1974 est.): revenue Guy$364.2 million; expenditure Guy$395.2 million.

Foreign Trade. (1973) Imports Guy$372.5 million; exports Guy$293 million. Import sources: U.K. 25%; U.S. 24%; Trinidad and Tobago 18%; Canada 5%. Export destinations: U.K. 29%; U.S. 21%; U.S.S.R. 6%; Trinidad and Tobago 6%; Jamaica 6%; Canada 5%. Main exports: bauxite 48%; sugar 31%; alumina 9%; rice 9%; fish 5%.

Agriculture. Production (in 000; metric tons; 1973; 1972 in parentheses): rice *c.* 170 (147); sugar, raw value *c.* 295 (*c.* 320); cassava (1972) *c.* 14, (1971) *c.* 14; oranges (1972) *c.* 11, (1971) 10; copra *c.* 7 (*c.* 7). Livestock (in 000; 1972–73): cattle *c.* 254; sheep *c.* 96; goats *c.* 35; pigs *c.* 82.

Industry. Production (in 000; 1973): bauxite (metric tons) 3,560; diamonds (metric carats; 1972) 47; electricity (kw-hr.) 362,000.

Guyana, but the Mahatma Gandhi Association's general secretary expressed the view (rejected by the government and the Muslim community) that integration had failed and the division of Guyana into two provinces should be considered.

At the end of the year, the government, which had become a founding member of the International Bauxite Association in March, agreed on $14.5 million compensation to Reynolds for the takeover of its bauxite-mining operations, scheduled for early 1975. Also in December, the government assumed control of all foreign trade. Guyana was hard hit by the energy crisis, but extra earnings from bauxite and sugar were expected to help. The cost of living was kept down by food subsidies of about Guy$31 million in 1974.   (SHEILA PATTERSON)

[974.B.2.d]

Haiti

The Republic of Haiti occupies the western one-third of the Caribbean island of Hispaniola, which it shares with the Dominican Republic. Area: 10,714 sq.mi. (27,750 sq.km.). Pop. (1974 est.): 4,513,600, of whom 95% are Negro. Cap. and largest city: Port-au-Prince (pop., 1971, 458,680). Language: French (official) and Creole. Religion: Roman Catholic; Voodooism practiced in rural areas. President in 1974, Jean-Claude Duvalier.

A feature in Haiti's power balance in 1974 was the consolidation of President Duvalier's support in the Cabinet and among the armed forces. After a reshuffle on March 19, the Cabinet reflected a compromise, with some old-guard Duvalierists remaining, together with "technocrats" chosen by the president.

An economic recovery had brought about an annual growth rate in the gross national product of about 5% in the three years 1971–73. Exports of assembled products in 1973, competitive because of a minimum wage for workers of $1.30 per day, reached a total of more than $32 million, and projections for 1974 and 1975 suggested similar rates of growth. The importance of this sector was being emphasized by the government, which reported that only retail commerce employed more Haitians in the Port-au-Prince area. Tourism also showed considerable growth, with receipts in 1974 almost 50% over those of 1973, and hotel construction was expanding. Remittances from Haitians living abroad increased to about $20 million a year, with many "economic exiles" becoming eager to invest in Haiti's growth.

But the boom occurred exclusively in the capital and involved only a tiny proportion of the urban population. New jobs were created in the baseball and

Fishing boats in the harbour at St. Marc.

GRAPHIC HOUSE/EB INC.

brassiere factories, in hotels, and on numerous building sites, but the increased economic activity was taking place entirely in the services and export industries and did not result in expanded output for the home market. The boom thus resulted in a sharp rise in inflation so that even the 25,000 or so holders of new jobs found their wages eaten away by the increased cost of living and were little better off than before. But for the 75% of Haiti's inhabitants who lived outside the cash economy in remote overcrowded valleys or on badly eroded mountain slopes, conditions had deteriorated since 1971. With the population growing at 2.1% annually and agricultural production stagnant or shrinking, it was usual for things to get worse in the countryside. The bureaucracy was badly paid and consequently corrupt and inefficient, and was thus unable to absorb large amounts of aid. Haiti was desperately short of technicians, professionals, and skilled workers, a problem aggravated by the "brain drain" to the U.S.; an estimated 90% of the physicians left the country within two years of graduating.

A fundamental problem was the lack of an adequate road structure. If agricultural production was to be stimulated, only farmers within walking distance of the urban centres would be able to profit. The government could not therefore be faulted for giving priority to the improvement of the country's roads, and it obtained a World Bank loan for $10 million to improve the Port-au-Prince to Cap-Haïtien highway and a $22.5 million Inter-American Development Bank loan to modernize the road west to Les Cayes. Once this work was completed, in perhaps five years, work could start on interior access roads.

Haiti was one of the most densely populated countries in the Western Hemisphere, but it also had the highest rate of infant mortality, the main killer being umbilical tetanus. Yet, if a campaign were launched to reduce it, the real birthrate would jump and population pressures would rise.   (MICHAEL WOOLLER)

[974.B.2.a]

Health and Disease

General Overview. Although there has been no slackening in the advance of medical technology, 1974 saw the continuation of a general trend toward the idea that effective health care demands a good deal more than is provided by the orthodox "scientific" doctor. In particular, there has been a growing reaction to the assumption that powerful remedies offered by the pharmaceutical industry provide the cure for all remediable ills. In May a conference called by the U.S. National Institute of Mental Health to discuss the many problems arising out of the escalating use of antianxiety drugs was told that in the U.S. the use of preparations like Valium is increasing at the rate of seven million prescriptions a year.

In the less developed nations shortages of trained doctors, nurses, and other health workers have led to an increasing acceptance of China's "barefoot doctor" policy, involving the use of people with a minimal training in elementary health care to satisfy the simpler needs for medical aid. During the year several reports appeared describing pilot experiments in the use of such workers in, among other places, Guatemala, Tanzania, and Iran. They encountered some resistance among people conditioned to the idea that an almost magical wisdom, of a kind only vouchsafed to "proper doctors," is necessary for the effective management of human ills, but it seems inevitable that this method of meeting a high proportion of the demand for primary medical care will spread rapidly, if only because it is the one way in which the greater part of the world can be given any kind of medical care at all.

The problem is not confined to less developed areas. In New York there is a scheme for entrusting the dispensing of contraceptives and contraceptive advice to anyone who can survive a fairly rigorous three-month training course. In Britain contraceptive pills can only be dispensed with a doctor's prescription, but there was growing pressure to allow nurses and other health workers to provide this invaluable agent, referring the applicant to a doctor when some special health problem seems to make this course advisable. There has also been much talk in the developed nations about schemes for having nurses or trained paramedics deal with all manner of illnesses and health needs in the first instance, leaving the doctors to see only those patients whose condition requires their specialized skills and knowledge, or patients who, for their own peace of mind, specifically ask to see a doctor.

In the U.S., however, both the government and organized medicine now have agreed that the shortage of physicians decried a few years ago does not really exist. The problem, they say, is that doctors are not evenly distributed where the patients need them, particularly in rural areas and the urban ghetto. Federal health planners have pointed out the tendency of specialists to clump together in urban areas, already rich in medical resources. In late September the Senate overwhelmingly approved legislation to induce medical and dental schools to designate 25% of their students for future service in shortage regions. At the same time the Senate voted down a proposal to require the periodic relicensure of physicians and dentists. At present, licensure is a state-controlled matter and only two states, New Mexico and Oregon, reexamine physicians for medical competence. A number

Harbours:
see Transportation

Harness Racing:
see Horse Racing

Hay:
see Agriculture and Food Supplies

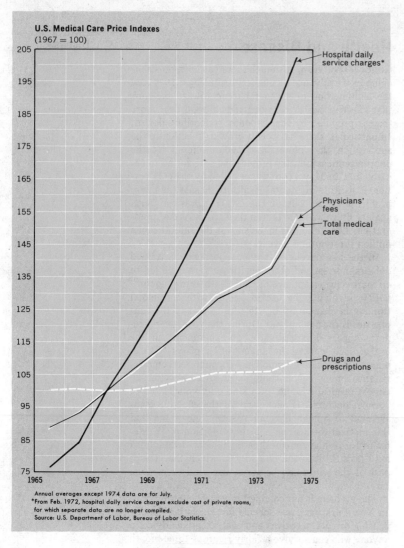

U.S. Medical Care Price Indexes
(1967 = 100)

- Hospital daily service charges*
- Physicians' fees
- Total medical care
- Drugs and prescriptions

Annual averages except 1974 data are for July.
*From Feb. 1972, hospital daily service charges exclude cost of private rooms, for which separate data are no longer compiled.
Source: U.S. Department of Labor, Bureau of Labor Statistics.

considered essential for just maintaining the quality of medical care, let alone developing and improving the service. The discontent of ancillary medical staff such as nurses, radiographers, physiotherapists, and laboratory technicians, all of whom had been notoriously ill-paid since the service began, came to a head in the summer with a series of strikes by radiographers, nurses in mental hospitals, and hospital domestic workers. The domestic workers made the existence of a small number of private beds in NHS hospitals the overt reason for their revolt and in some places refused to serve the private wings. Attempting to restore peace, Barbara Castle, secretary of state for social services, assured the strikers that the Labour government would expedite its already stated policy of abolishing private practices in NHS hospitals, but she managed to give the impression that she had agreed to abolish private beds under pressure from the hospital domestics. This enraged a number of hospital doctors, who promptly threatened to quit the NHS and set up their own private health scheme if denied the right to private practice. Eventually the nurses were awarded a 30% pay increase. Other ancillary workers were given less with promises of more to come, and some of the cuts in health service spending were restored. By autumn an uneasy but clearly transient peace had been restored within the service.

Not all medical debate existed on a political or economic level. As U.S.-China détente grew firmer, more medical experts traveled to see the wonders of acupuncture at first hand. An Ohio State University specialist reported that electrically stimulated needles did produce pain relief in some of his patients. But several famous patients, including Alabama's Gov. George Wallace, were disappointed by results of their therapy. After an inspection visit of medical facilities in China, a University of Washington anesthesiologist pointed to the core of the problem. Too little research has been done to explain how, or even if, acupuncture works. A cooperative U.S.-Chinese study might do more than solve the acupuncture controversy—it might tell us the nature of pain, something of a puzzle to clinicians and patients alike.

Another major mystery that yielded somewhat to recent medical investigation concerned what goes on in the womb. A National Foundation-March of Dimes study estimated that over 38% of the more than 5,160,000 conceptions that occurred in the U.S. during 1973 ended with the death of the fetus. Induced abortions terminated nearly a third of these pregnancies, but some 1,340,000 fetal deaths were unplanned. The causes for most of these so-called spontaneous abortions were unknown, but scientists do know that many were caused by flaws in the genetic structure of the unborn child. The first case of successful correction of one of these errors in the womb was recorded at Tufts-New England Medical Center in Boston. By making careful taps of the amniotic fluid that surrounded a young woman's fetus, clinicians determined that an enzymatic defect was present. (Another child born to the woman had died from the condition, methylmalonic acidemia.) During the last two months of her pregnancy the woman received massive doses of the vitamin B_{12}. The vitamin injections resulted in the uneventful birth of a healthy girl.

Another significant cause of perinatal death is undetected venereal disease. Two years of federal campaigning to detect and combat syphilis and gonorrhea might be paying off. The first half of 1974 showed a

continued on page 345

of other states were considering such measures, however, and the American Academy of Family Practice instituted mandatory recertification for its members. A number of other specialty societies have instituted voluntary programs in which members can reevaluate their skills.

Early in 1976 Professional Standards Review Organizations (PSROs) were to become operational throughout the U.S. and were intended to monitor the standards of medical practice in all cases where medical care is paid for by taxes from a federal source. This would include care of patients under Medicare and Medicaid, and presumably any national health insurance plan that might emerge from Congress. Only two basic national health insurance plans had survived several years of congressional compromise and maneuver. One would be financed almost entirely through the Social Security system and was favoured by social reformers and the more liberal Democrats, principally Sen. Edward Kennedy (Dem., Mass.). It was given less of a chance for final passage than a more conservative plan, backed by most congressional Republicans, medical leaders, and economists, which would depend heavily on private insurance firms and only partly on Social Security.

In the U.K. the people most dissatisfied with the National Health Service (NHS) during the year were those employed in it. Complaints centred around poor pay and a cutback in the funds available for new buildings, equipment, additional staff, and other items

DEFINITIONS OF ILL HEALTH

By Barbara Starfield

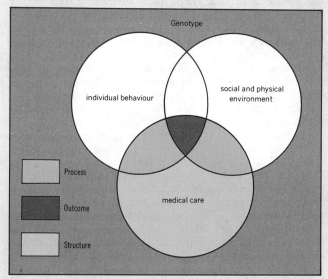

Determinants of Health Status

The preamble to the constitution of the World Health Organization, chartered in 1948, defines health as "a state of complete physical, mental, and social well-being and not merely the absence of disease or infirmity." This definition represented the aspirations of a world that had just experienced the holocaust of 1940–45, with its attendant threat of nuclear annihilation, and conveys all the idealism and hope of people striving to achieve harmony with nature. Realistically, the expressed goal is unachievable, for conflict between man and the environment will always be present and provide a necessary stimulus for progress. The definition serves, however, as a constant reminder that there is a chasm between the current state of affairs and the ideal state of affairs, which society should aim at narrowing, but the definition is silent on issues concerning whether and how much we must sacrifice in present health for future health, and whether there are trade-offs between the health of individuals and the health of populations. Such considerations are indeed important, for the measures chosen as indicators will implicitly or explicitly favour one choice over the other.

Decisions to label problems as "illnesses" are largely social and cultural; therefore, concepts of "normal" health may be expected to change. Normality is perceived in many ways and is perhaps most commonly posed as a dichotomy: someone either is or is not healthy. Alternatively, normality can be described in statistical terms as the modal, or most common, state; or, it can be defined in a social sense according to values, by comparison with what "ought to be." Although it may never be possible to agree on the standards to which we might aspire, it should be possible to arrive at a consensus regarding the direction in which society should move, and in what way the progress should be measured.

A framework for viewing the primary determinants of health can be seen in the accompanying figure. The potential for health is determined by the genotype, the inherited genetic material that determines how individuals respond to the range of possible stimuli. Although the ability to manipulate and change an individual's genotype is theoretically possible, this is still far in the future. Altering the frequency of inherited disease by influencing reproductive behaviour of individuals with genetic defects is a more likely possibility, but moral and ethical considerations are powerful deterrents.

The other determinants are relatively easily observed and manipulated. Of these, by far the most important is the social and physical environment. The history of medicine and public health provides vivid demonstration of the primacy of social and physical conditions as determinants of health and disease, and how health and disease change as the environment is altered. Improvements in health derive largely from forces external to the individual. Even within the last century, the decline in mortality and morbidity can be attributed more to efforts to improve

Barbara Starfield is associate professor of health care and pediatrics at the Johns Hopkins University and consultant to the U.S. Department of Health, Education, and Welfare. She has published numerous professional papers on childhood illness and general health care.

living conditions than to specific medical interventions. Traditional medical care—the second determinant—influences health primarily by modifying the manifestations of illness; unfortunately, it has yet to contribute dramatically to the prevention of illness. The third determinant, individual behaviour, is of great importance for health is clearly influenced by the nature and extent of participation of individuals in health, illness, and sick-role activities. Most health-related activities are carried out apart from any contact with organized health care; behaviour such as food choices, smoking, or decisions to wear seat belts significantly influences health, but is at most only tangential to the relationships of individuals with health practitioners.

The formal health care system is represented by that portion of the framework that involves the system of medical practice and its overlap with the behaviour of individuals, known as the "structure" and "process" of health care. "Structure" involves the nature of health facilities and personnel, and "process" involves the interaction between patients and providers, which includes the extent of use of health services, the nature of problem recognition, diagnosis, management activities by professionals, and the patient's understanding of and compliance with the professional's recommendations. Although "structure" and "process" have been used as measures of the adequacy of the health of a population, they are, at best, only proxy measures of health. Health is the result of a complex interaction of the social and physical environment, the health care system, and the behaviour of individuals on the genotype, and changes in health status can rarely be attributed to isolated changes in any one of the determinants. People, both individually and collectively, are interested more in the outcome of efforts to assure good health than in the efforts themselves. Although there is considerable emphasis on measuring the activities that influence health, attention is rapidly shifting to the outcome itself.

Historical Views of Health. Until the Renaissance, disease was an individual phenomenon, generally attributed to poor living habits or the sinfulness of the person unfortunate enough to develop an illness. As scientific knowledge grew and society developed, there was increasing conflict between those who viewed disease as derangements within individuals and those who viewed it as manifestations of derangements in society. The invention of the compound microscope in the 16th century, the revelations about the anatomy and function of the bodily systems, and the discovery of microbial organisms and their role in disease causation resulted in increasingly narrow concepts of disease. Sickness could now be viewed not only as a characteristic of the individual but as localized to subunits of the individual, a philosophy that was reflected in a system of taxonomy that fragmented illness into diseases, signs, and symptoms of anatomic, physiologic, or microbiologic nature. For those who subscribed to this approach, disease would be conquered by attacking the pathologic process within the body with specific agents—the antecedent of the modern armamentarium of medicines.

Others saw the cause of illness in social conditions, a viewpoint that originated in the Industrial Revolution when epidemics appeared in factories and tenements consequent to industrialization and urbanization. The development of industry, moreover, removed the responsibility for maintaining health from the individual to society, for the majority of people depended for their livelihood on the labour market, over which they had no control. With the growth of the factory (and the city along with it) health conditions rapidly deteriorated. Close, crowded quarters provided conditions in which disease flourished and spread. There was little interest in sanitary arrangements since expenditures for such facilities were not considered remunerative.

By the 19th century, when available knowledge and organization of resources made it possible to systematically attack the roots of disease, the opposing forces crystallized. Biologically oriented scientists, relying on the germ theory, insisted on treatment of the individual. The hygienists, in contrast, maintained that more would be gained by controlling the environment, particularly with sanitary measures. Although the bioscientific movement has been credited with vastly improved mortality rates for the major contagious illnesses, it was undoubtedly the efforts of the hygienists who, by attacking the milieu in which germs flourished rather than their effects on individuals, were responsible for the marked improvement in death rates.

At a time when disease was considered a phenomenon localized within the individual, the concept of statistics had no meaning. As illness began to take on social aspects, church records of baptisms, burials, and marriages became useful for planning in the secular realm. Toward the end of the 17th century efforts were made to justify investments in transporting sick people outside the city and caring for them to increase their probability of survival and hence ability to work, but disease continued to reduce the productivity of the work force. Whereas deaths could be and were counted, calculations of the impact of deaths on a population depended on an accurate census of the population. In the mid-18th century in Sweden, a system of population registers was established, making it possible for Per Wargentin to calculate mortality tables by age and sex. His data were the first to show that the death rate of males exceeds that for females. By the early 1800s many countries had adopted regular censuses and it was observed that not only was the working population more severely attacked by outbreaks of illness than other segments of the community but the outbreaks were creating an economic loss that adversely affected all segments of the population.

The publication in England in 1885 of William Farr's *Vital Statistics* marked the beginning of broad-based population health statistics dealing with mortality, and in 1902 the U.S. Congress established the Permanent Census Office and the annual federal collection of mortality statistics. By this time it was generally accepted that the physical strength of a nation is among the chief determinants of national prosperity. British experience with conscription for the Boer War and World War I showed that many young men examined for military service were physically unfit, prompting the government to initiate a wave of studies of infant mortality and its causes as a measure to "conserve" this national manpower resource.

It is important to recognize a pattern here that has characterized not only maternal and child health work but community health as a whole. Advances are determined far more by social, economic, and political needs than by humanitarian concerns. In 1919 the U.S. Public Health Service was faced with the care of thousands of disabled World War I veterans. As a result, many states passed laws to reorganize their health departments and many communities retained the organizations that had been established to aid the war effort. Special programs such as

malaria and VD control became permanent activities in a number of state health departments.

In the late 1930s there was a renewal of activity. The depression had resulted in the destitution of a large portion of the work force, and there was a growing realization that U.S. entry into the war would be inevitable. The National Health Survey of 1936–37, initiated under these circumstances, essentially ushered in the era of modern public health. Programs created in the 1940s to deal with the needs of the war period were directed not only at servicemen, but also their wives and children, providing a wealth of information on the distribution of illness in the country.

Following World War II, statistics showed that chronic diseases were increasing and communicable diseases were waning as causes of death. This shift produced problems in classifying and interpreting the statistics on cause of death. The primary cause of death was easily determined when that cause was acute, but in chronic illness the multiplicity of pathological conditions made the cause more difficult to specify. The growing dissatisfaction with mortality statistics was accompanied by a parallel demand for data on prevalence of illness, and in 1956 the U.S. Congress authorized the annual collection of statistics on illness and disability as they existed in the population, whether or not care had been sought or death had resulted.

Characteristics of Health Statistics. Health statistics had their origin as indicators of social conditions and their development followed developments in the level of understanding of disease. When little was known of specific disease processes, death served as the main indicator of poor health. Recognition of specific syndromes enabled the development of a classification of diseases. More recently, technology has provided the means to identify problems at a highly disaggregated level. It is now possible to identify an illness even before it is symptomatic in the affected individual and to detect its predisposing states before it becomes an identifiable "disease." It has become increasingly evident that the definition of illness depends upon the perspective of the definer. Patients define illness as impairment that conforms with what society accepts as being "sick." Modern medicine defines illness as that which is organic and measurable; that is, that which is biomedically explainable. Clearly, any widely acceptable indicator of health must incorporate both of these aspects.

Effective medical therapy became available only within the 20th century, and it is only within the last several decades that improvements in health could be attributed to specific medical interventions. It was perhaps understandable, therefore, that these interventions themselves become measures of "health." Moreover, concerns about the particularly poor health of various segments of the population, particularly among the indigent and the nonwhite, focused attention on inequities in the availability of health services in different groups. Thus, *Medical Care for Americans* (1929), which arose out of an intensive study by the Committee on the Costs of Medical Care, is devoted almost entirely to documenting the lack of equality in number and type of services available to the poor of the U.S. Subsequent efforts were devoted to providing financial aid (considerably short of comprehensive health insurance) and limited direct services to needy groups. Although the tendency to measure health status by means of counts of professional manpower or services (number of physicians per population, number of hospital beds, number of hospitalizations, number of physician visits) still lingers, attention has shifted to measures that demonstrate the effects of the services. Advances in techniques of measurement have facilitated this shift. Refinement of social survey tools has enabled the obtaining of reliable and valid information from individuals in their homes; relatively skillful interview techniques can provide data on the extent of disability and symptoms, and technologic advance has made possible the recognition of signs of morbid or premorbid conditions. Development of techniques to sample populations and statistical procedures that evolved out of a need for methods of interpreting the large amounts of data that were being collected encouraged the development of more complex measures of health status.

How "Health" Is Measured. Modern health indicators reflect a variety of interacting forces. The needs of society for productive capacity, the ability of technology to provide tools of measurement, the effectiveness of the health care system in influencing health and disease, and consumer demands for equitable distribution of efficacious services all have an impact in determining which indicators will be chosen to reflect health status, and the way in which they are interpreted.

There are three major types of indicators currently used as measures of health status: those associated with the health of persons and populations; those related to the physical and social environment; and those concerned with the provision and use of health services.

Those indicators dealing with individual or population health can be further categorized as dealing with mortality, morbidity, disability, or with other modes of adaptation to stress.

Trends in morbidity and differentials in mortality among population groups remain very useful as indicators of shifts in the cause of disease. For example, observation of rising mortality from chronic respiratory disease has focused attention on the important and increasing role of smoking and environmental pollution as etiologic agents. Mortality data are widely available and relatively well reported, making possible comparisons among groups within a country and among countries. However, many illnesses that cause great discomfort and disability are not lethal and, therefore, do not contribute to mortality, making mortality statistics an incomplete indicator of a population's health. Moreover, serious inconsistencies in the recording of causes of death or death certificates hamper accurate interpretation of reasons for death, particularly when comparisons are made between one time period and another.

Morbidity data, while more representative of the ills with which people suffer, has its own limitations. Counts of diseases are notoriously incomplete and unreliable. Except for contagious diseases that are a threat to the community, there is no legal requirement that illnesses be reported. Furthermore, not all individuals with illnesses seek medical care and of those who do, not all undergo uniform diagnostic procedures. Many individuals with definitive illnesses, therefore, are unrepresented in morbidity statistics. In the U.S. existing morbidity statistics are derived primarily from hospitals that tabulate diagnoses on discharge or death. Although hospitals have not been required to routinely provide data on diagnoses, many local surveys and the hospital discharge data collected have provided information on the frequency, distribution, and care of illnesses requiring institutionalization, but such data are clearly unrepresentative of the entire spectrum of disease in the population.

Most medical care in the U.S. is provided in individual offices rather than in hospitals or organized health centres, and most practitioners compile no statistics on the illnesses that they diagnose and treat. Within the last few years, the National Center for Health Statistics has developed a procedure whereby office practices are provided with uniform reporting forms that are completed on a sampling basis. This procedure, known as the National Ambulatory Care Survey, is beginning to provide information regarding the nature of complaints that patients bring to physicians and their relationship to the diagnoses made by the physicians; it also will elucidate patterns of medical care throughout the U.S.

The National Center for Health Statistics instituted a Health Examination Survey in 1959 to obtain information on diseases that remain undiagnosed, unrecognized, or unreported. On a sample basis, noninstitutionalized individuals were asked to report to a specially equipped centre to provide a complete medical history and undergo a physical examination and selected laboratory tests. The results of this survey indicated a significant amount of unrecognized illness in the population—there were, for

example, twice as many unknown as known diabetics. Although the techniques of examining a sample of individuals are sufficiently well developed to make such a survey a useful tool, limitation on the ability to examine for certain conditions—even those as common as cancer and stroke—makes such efforts useful only for certain illnesses.

If mortality and morbidity data are useful in reflecting causes of death and serious illness in the population, what information is available regarding less serious, but often very frequent, illnesses? Disability measures are an approach to determining the impact of illnesses of all severities and durations as they influence the social participation of members of the population.

During the 19th century, the primary cause of absenteeism among workers was occupational injuries. This was not because the workers were unusually "healthy," but rather because workers who were relatively plentiful and unskilled and therefore easily replaced were either at their machines or out of a job. As an increasingly skilled labour force became organized and workers began to win sick benefits, the trend shifted. By World War I industry employed an ever growing number of highly skilled workers who were well paid and worked efficiently; for such workers, the consequence of the loss of working days resulted in failure to achieve projected outputs and caused greater economic losses.

Depression in the 1930s drew further attention to the connection between economics and medical care. Labour, which previously had opposed compulsory social insurance schemes operated by the government on the grounds that this would lead to control of the union movement, shifted in 1934 to advocacy of health insurance as workers became far more concerned with economic loss resulting from illness.

Partly as a result of these developments, in 1934–35 the U.S. Public Health Service conducted a National Health Survey, which showed that the frequency of illness was disproportionately higher among the poor and unemployed than among the employed. Another survey, conducted by the Cost of Living Division of the Department of Labor, further substantiated the fact that the amount and quality of medical care received were correlated with the family's income. Because different types of questions were employed in the various surveys, it was not possible to compare one set of findings against another or derive accurate data on trends in disability. The 1959 survey standardized the collection of information on disability, making comparisons between successive periods possible.

Despite the standardization of instruments of measurement, interpretation of trends regarding disability is fraught with difficulty. As society increases its social welfare benefits, particularly its provisions for sickness insurance, the prevalence of reported disability due to illness increases. From the early 1930s to the present, reported disability rates have almost doubled. Moreover, prior to the institution of social welfare, many disabled individuals were discharged from the working force so that their disabling conditions, while present, were not associated with inability to carry on "regular activities." Other limitations of disability data derive from their nonspecificity: any given degree of disability can be a manifestation of a variety of illness conditions. Measures of disability, therefore, are useful primarily for indicating the impact of illness on productivity rather than as direct measures of the "health" of an individual or populations. They do, however, have utility as indicators of how well health services succeed in minimizing the limitations on activity imposed by noncurable diseases.

In contrast to the measures that reflect health status itself, the other two types of indicators are at best only indirectly related to health status and, therefore, merit only brief mention. Indicators related to the physical and social environment that are commonly accepted as useful correlates of the health of a community include levels of education, level of unemployment, proportion of the population receiving welfare benefits, Selective Service rejections, ambient levels of radioactivity or pollution, and adequacy of sewage disposal facilities. Many of these factors are known to be causes of ill health; others are characteristics of individuals or communities that are generally highly related to levels of health. In neither case are they direct measures of health status. Their increasing use as proxy indicators testifies to the tendency to make the health professions responsible for a wide range of derangements, despite the evidence that much of the cause and management of illness lies outside the realm of traditional medical care.

Just as the onus for the effects on health of the social and physical environment has fallen on the health professions, so also has there been a tendency to assume that provision of health care assures improved health. As a result, measures of access to and use of resources have been widely used as criteria of health status, even though other factors are far more important as determiners of health. Indicators that are employed include such statistics as doctor visits per year, hospitalizations per year, visits to a dentist per year, and availability of regular sources of care. Such information is regularly obtained by national health surveys in household interviews and was employed in the arguments that led to the health legislation of the 1960s and in the testimony currently under way regarding national health insurance and the reorganization of health services. The relative ease with which the information is obtained undoubtedly explains the frequency with which it is used as evidence of health needs. It is important to recognize, however, that the need for health services depends upon the assumption that traditional health services are a critical determinant of the health status of individuals or populations and evidence for this is at best tenuous.

The Population's "Health." Selected information on mortality, morbidity, and disability sets the stage for a discussion of new developments that hold promise for the future. Average life expectancy in the U.S. increased dramatically in this century until the last decade when the increase leveled off. Examination of death rates within specific age groupings indicates that the increase in life expectancy can be attributed to decreased death rates in infants, young children, and the very elderly, and very little to changes in death rates at ages 5 through 75. Most of the major causes of death, however, have changed radically since 1900. Although there is evidence that deaths attributed to diseases of the heart may be decreasing, this remains the most commonly designated cause of death in the population as a whole. Trends in infant mortality are of interest because they are a major determinant of the expected length of life of a population, and because of their worldwide acceptance as the most sensitive indicator of the level of living in a country.

A number of studies undertaken have shown a general lack of correlation between the conditions that bring people to physicians and those that appear with the greatest frequency as causes of hospitalization or death. In contrast, there is a comparatively good relation between ranking of causes of visits to physicians and causes of limitation of activity. Such differences in the distribution of complaints and problems brought to physicians and the distribution of diagnoses listed as causes of hospitalization or death highlight the importance of using multiple types of information—mortality, morbidity, and disability—for planning or evaluation. Each may serve a different purpose in the need to rationally organize institutions and manpower resources, educate health professions, and carry out research to illuminate the causes and natural history of illnesses.

New Directions for Indicators of Health. "The history of public health," said Sir Geoffrey Vickers, "might well be written as a record of successive redefinings of the unacceptable." That which was once unfathomable is now potential, and will tomorrow be possible. So it is with man's aspiration for health, and therefore with measures used to assess it. The range of health, rather than a single continuum, is better conceptualized as a spectrum made up of many components that are social, biological, and psychological. Health statistics merely define points along the various continua. The type of health statistics that proves most

meaningful or most useful depends on the purpose for which it is intended. If an indicator is to be used primarily for planning in the health sector, its characteristics are likely to be different than if it is intended primarily for evaluation purposes. For planning purposes, it is often sufficient to choose a measure that is not a health indicator at all, but a social indicator generally correlated with levels of health. For assessment of the effectiveness of specific interventions, however, it is necessary to employ indicators that are more directly related to the achievement that is intended. Technological advances are facilitating the procurement and assimilation of information on health care and health status. It is now possible, with the help of computers, to link information from one source with that from another, making it possible to learn how diseases are distributed in the population, what influences their manifestation and course, and how medical therapy can interrupt or deflect this course.

Scientific and social changes in the last half of the 20th century are focusing increasing attention on the nature of current health indicators and will continue to influence the direction of development of new ones. Whereas it has been customary to view disease as having a primary cause, it is now certain that the important causes of ill health are multifactorial, and include genetic predisposition, environmental influences, patient behaviour, and medical intervention. Realization of the vast social impact of disease will bring about the training and deployment of a wider variety of types of health professionals. This development alone will call for widening the scope of health indicators. As each type of professional is likely to have his own type of goal, broader measures of effectiveness will be required.

Trends in life expectancy indicate that with the presently available tools for intervening in the processes of aging and biologic degeneration man may be approaching the asymptote for the upper limits of age. Recognition of the inability to significantly prolong life carried with it the realization that heightened attention must be devoted to improving the quality of that life. Thus, health statistics that reflect the increasing importance of chronic conditions, the coexistence of several conditions within an individual, the impact of new conditions without known cause or cure, the influence of a multiplicity of interacting environmental and personal characteristics, and the ability of individuals to adapt to and cope with illness are necessary. The ability to carry out normal functions in comfort, the achievement of inherent potential, and the ability to overcome adversity will soon come to be important components of health statistics.

It will no longer be sufficient to judge health by one measure or one type of measure. More useful will be a profile that incorporates the variety of aspects of health: longevity, activity, comfort, satisfaction, disease, achievement, resilience. Each of these aspects would first be evaluated separately and then viewed together to give a "picture" of health. Longevity, judged at any point in time, has at one extreme death and at the other extreme a prognosis for life expectancy that is average for that individual's age. Activity can be judged to fit anywhere along a continuum from one extreme which signifies complete disability to the other at which there is maximal function. Similarly, the scope of comfort extends from uncomfortable to comfortable, and satisfaction with health from satisfied to dissatisfied. It will always be important to incorporate physiologic measurements into a profile of health. As we recognize the importance of the quality of life as a reflection of health, it will become important to measure the extent to which individuals are attaining the potential given to them by their inheritance and training. Efforts are now being addressed to developing and refining measures for assessing some of these different aspects of health, particularly those related to the various levels of function, disability, and the assessment of severity and prognosis of specific disease states. At the same time as these attempts to assess the effects of adversity are becoming operational, attention is beginning to focus on our ability to anticipate threats to health and to develop the means to cope with them more adequately.

continued from page 340

decline in primary and secondary syphilis and a leveling off of the decade-old rise in gonorrhea, according to the U.S. Public Health Service. Although the summer months elicited an increase in both types of infection, public health officials were hopeful that the year would show an overall decline.

Research continued into the manifold effects and potential uses of prostaglandins—the remarkable natural body substances that influence the activity of all cells and organs, which were isolated and named by the Swedish physiologist and Nobel Prize-winner Ulf von Euler some 40 years ago, and then almost forgotten until a recent revival of interest led to the realization that they play a central role in many bodily functions. Particular attention has been paid to the effect of certain prostaglandins on the uterus, and trials continued in the use of prostaglandins for inducing labour and also as apparently efficient and safe agents for producing an abortion without surgical interference or any dangerous side effects, even after the 12th week of pregnancy. (*See* CHEMISTRY: *Organic*.)

In 1971 researchers at the Royal College of Surgeons in London had shown that aspirin probably prevents the manufacture of prostaglandins in the body, suggesting the possibility that aspirin might influence some of the events of pregnancy and childbirth. The results of a study of the records of women who had babies at the New York Hospital-Cornell Medical Center, New York City, showed that women who had taken over ten aspirin tablets a day had their pregnancies prolonged beyond the normal span by more than a week on average, and that many had been more than two weeks overdue. The duration of their labour was almost twice as long as usual, and they lost, on average, 50% more blood than other women.

Although the relationship between aspirin and prostaglandins shows that the action of aspirin on the body is probably far more complex than had been suspected, the drug was still accepted as a relatively safe household remedy. During the year the highly dangerous nature of another popular pain killer—phenacetin (acetophenetidin)—was tardily acknowledged in Britain. Phenacetin can cause death by producing permanent kidney damage. From mid-1974 a government order restricted the sale of preparations containing the drug to pharmacists and from the beginning of 1975 the drug would be obtainable only on prescription. Other countries have been ahead of Britain in controlling the over-the-counter sale of potentially dangerous medicines (preparations containing more than small quantities of phenacetin and paracetamol have been supplied by prescription only in Belgium since 1972, for example), and the new British regulations were only part of a general trend toward tighter controls over all kinds of medicines.

In the U.S. the American National Red Cross and 24 other medical groups were attempting to set up an all-volunteer blood donor system to replace the significant amounts of purchased serum and plasma. The rationale of their effort was that some of the purchased blood was infected by the hepatitis virus, which in turn was carried by repeat donors who sold their blood to pay for their sometimes unhealthy ways of living. Another type of living tissue bank, this for bone marrow, was becoming increasingly frequent. Scores of patients who had developed aplastic anemia, certain types of leukemia, and immune disorders were surviving after marrow transplants. Usually the donor was a close relative, but an international registry of donors was being formed. A National Institutes of Health team already had recorded the tissue types (an analog of blood types) of more than 9,000 persons who would form the core of the bank. The objections of some religious sects to blood transfusions were being overcome by perfection of the technique of autotransfusion. Hundreds of U.S. hospitals had the equipment to collect blood as it was lost, filter and process it, then return it to the body after corrective measures had been taken. Autotransfusion eliminates the hazards of cross matching, allows surgery on those with rare blood types, and reduces transfusion costs.

Arguments about the role of diet in coronary heart disease (CHD) continued. The report of a three-year study by the Department of Health and Social Security in Britain stated that diets containing a high proportion of polyunsaturated fats (nonanimal fats of the type present in margarine) afford no protection against heart attacks. The report did, however, recommend a reduction in the total fat content of the diet, the study having found that the risk of death from CHD correlates well with fat intake. The report also recommended weight reduction, caution in the large-scale introduction of water-softening programs (studies have shown that CHD is commoner in soft-water areas), and reduced sugar consumption. While not accepting as proved the theory that sucrose (ordinary household sugar) is a direct cause of the arterial damage leading to heart attacks, the experts held that eating less sugar was well worthwhile "if only to diminish the risk of obesity and its possible sequelae." (See *The Heart Attack Epidemic,* below.)

The belief that an intensive care unit, equipped with elaborate machinery and staffed by eager experts, is the best possible place for any patient during the days immediately following a heart attack has been questioned. Harold Mather, a cardiologist working in Bristol, Eng., reported the results of a survey carried out in his area with the help of local family doctors. He found that men over the age of 60 who had suffered a heart attack, but had not developed shock or heart failure, were twice as likely to survive if left at home instead of being moved to a hospital and subjected to intensive care. Mather listed the relatively few and simple resources needed by the family doctor for adequate care of coronary patients in their own homes, and held that the lack of monitoring equipment and apparatus necessary for correcting grossly

A surgical stapler is prepared for use in the course of an operation. The device currently is used in more than 5,000 operations per week and the stapling technique is taught in more than 50% of the medical institutions in the U.S.

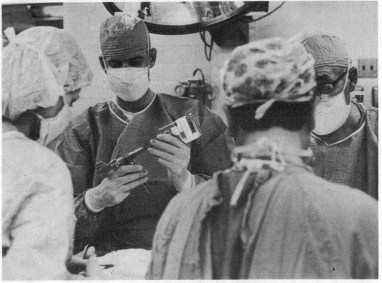

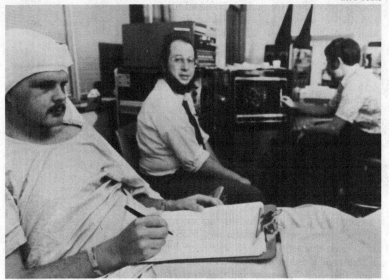

The blind can "see" again by means of electronic stimulation of the brain. This sightless Vietnam veteran draws a transmitted image in experiments at the University of Western Ontario.

abnormal contractions of the heart muscle by means of an electric shock was more than compensated for by the benefits of familiar, quiet surroundings, the absence of seriously ill patients in neighbouring beds, and avoidance of the rigours of an anxiety-ridden ambulance journey in the immediate aftermath of a frightening happening. The perils of the ambulance ride were also underlined in a report from Belfast, N.Ire., which showed that one-third of all patients with a heart attack suffered a dangerous increase in pulse rate as a result of the handling involved in getting them to a hospital. The Belfast report recommended the use of a particular drug to prevent this rise in heart rate, but it seems likely that opinion may be moving away from the ideal of immediate vigorous and intensive treatment for all heart attack victims in favour of a more conservative approach, stressing the value of keeping the physical and emotional strain on the patient to a minimum except in the case of those patients in whom acute and life-threatening complications demand rapid and active intervention.

Heart transplants—the surgical "miracle" of the late 1960s—were still being performed by scattered teams worldwide, but most medical scientists returned to their workbenches to develop artificial heart machines or study the tissue rejection reaction that destroyed many of the transplants. Approximately one heart transplant a month was being performed at Stanford University by a team headed by a codeveloper of the surgical technique, Norman Shumway. Twenty-four of the first 73 patients with heart transplants at Palo Alto were alive in the summer of 1974, most at least a year after surgery, while only 13 of the other 164 heart recipients in operations done elsewhere since 1967 were surviving at that time. As with bone marrow transplants, long-term heart transplant survival seems predicated on matching donor and recipient tissues by sophisticated and expensive immunologic techniques.

The atomic-powered heart pacemaker had been used in the U.S. for more than a year by 15 pioneer recipients. They were part of some 200 persons in the U.S. selected as the first group to wear the plutonium-powered devices for regulating heartbeat. About 600 other heart patients worldwide also had had the atomic pacemaker implanted, and no significant problems had thus far developed. A number of conventional pacemaker recipients whose devices were dis-

rupted by microwave emissions were not so lucky. No fatalities had occurred, but warning signs were posted near microwave ovens, such as those used to warm "fast foods" in public snack bars.

Environmental hazards were identified in a number of previously unsuspected industrial situations. In late summer, several employees of a Massachusetts semiconductor plant evidenced apparent symptoms of carbon monoxide poisoning. An inadequate ventilation system was determined as the culprit. A surprising finding was that workers who smoked had been most seriously affected and tests confirmed that the blood levels of smokers contained at least 5% higher CO levels even without exposure to the plant environment.

The appearance in Kentucky of clusters of cases of a relatively rare liver cancer caused industrial physicians to indict a material used in making plastic products. Chronic exposure to vinyl chloride, a monomer used in synthesizing polyvinyl chloride, was pinpointed as a probable cause by the federal Occupational Safety and Health Administration (OSHA). A subsequent investigation of the harmful properties of over 400 other potentially toxic substances resulted in a general tightening of industrial safety regulations.

Breast cancer was discovered in the wives of U.S. Pres. Gerald Ford and Vice-Pres.-designate Nelson Rockefeller. The operations performed on Mrs. Betty Ford and Mrs. Margaretta "Happy" Rockefeller were essentially the same: radical mastectomy. (Mrs. Rockefeller also subsequently underwent a simple mastectomy.) The procedure sparked anew the surgical controversy as to whether or not these extensive operations improve cancer survival. The American Cancer Society reported that earlier and more frequent diagnoses were being made by women conducting the much-publicized monthly self-examination. This factor, as well as advancing techniques in post-surgical therapy, somewhat clouds the question about the effectiveness of the radical procedure. However, a survey of physicians by a national medical magazine showed that, if the physician's own wife or daughter discovered breast cancer, the overwhelming majority would recommend the radical procedure. Meanwhile, a study was being formed to evaluate the effect of less disfiguring, simpler procedures.

A promising step toward the development of an artificial liver was reported by workers at London's King's College Hospital. Twenty-two patients who were deeply unconscious and close to death as a result of acute liver failure and who had not responded to other therapy were treated by passing their blood through cylinders containing activated charcoal. The charcoal absorbed several of the substances in the blood that accumulate when the liver fails, producing brain damage and coma. These include the amino acids phenylalanine, tyrosine, and the methionine acids. Eleven of the patients treated recovered consciousness and ten left the hospital cured. This recovery rate of almost 50% compares well with an average survival figure of only 10% among patients suffering acute liver failure treated by other means, and presages the early evolution of a "liver machine" that may prove as valuable a lifesaver as the now well-proven artificial kidney.

A similar technique may lead to the production of simpler and cheaper artificial kidneys. T. M. S. Chang of McGill University, Montreal, described a "microcapsule artificial kidney," only 8 cm. high and 10 cm. in diameter, in which blood from the patient flows through a bed of specially coated fine granules of activated charcoal. No pump is required. Although the miniature artificial kidney prevents the dangerous accumulation of metabolites, it does not cope with the removal from the body of excess water, but, as a leading article in the British journal *Lancet* remarked, the system "may be the basis of tomorrow's artificial kidney for chronic renal failure patients."

In the U.S. influenza and pneumonia deaths stayed mostly below the epidemic threshold in 1973–74, although the Middle Atlantic states suffered a brief severe attack of influenza type A in the early spring at the end of the "flu season." Overall, Americans were not as troubled by "the bug" as in previous winters, but a previously rare influenza complication known as Reye's syndrome did appear, resulting in the deaths of close to half of the over 300 victims, primarily children. The disease, a degeneration of brain and blood, seemed to occur primarily in specific geographic areas of the Midwest. Previously, this unexplained complication of viral infection had been even more infrequent than rheumatic fever.

No available flu vaccine ever has been entirely effective because each individual victim of influenza actually has been infected by a "new" virus and each human transmission changes the structure of influenza's cell walls. About 2,000 New York City area schoolchildren received a "hybrid" vaccine in the fall of 1974, developed by investigators at the Mount Sinai School of Medicine. It was hoped that this potpourri of the minor components of several past flu strains would be more effective in blocking replication of neuraminidase, the key protein of such viruses.

Several vaccines that have proved effective against such diseases as polio, diphtheria, and red (rubeola) and German (rubella) measles have been ignored by parents in recent years. The result was a potential "epidemic pool" of five million unprotected children, many approaching school age. A nationwide inoculation campaign was launched by a conglomerate of medical groups, led by the American Academy of Pediatrics and the U.S. Public Health Service, to update preschool immunization programs. The alternative, public health specialists feared, would be a recurrence of the crippling epidemics familiar as recently as the late 1960s.

A new vaccine against nature's family of viruses is directed against the principal type of cerebrospinal meningitis. Licensed by the U.S. Food and Drug Administration (FDA) after extensive proof that it protected Army recruits against group C meningococcus, the vaccine would be used where civilian epidemics threaten, as they do in some cities each summer.

Not fatal but still discomforting, the "common cold" remains unconquered. Canadian and U.S. investigators gave cautious endorsement to the preventive role of vitamin C, and a number of controlled clinical trials of the controversial cold-preventive, advocated by Nobel laureate Linus Pauling, indeed indicated some protective effect. Prolonged ingestion of "megavitamin" doses was still discouraged, however, as potentially harmful. A daily glass of orange juice, or a cold tablet supplemented by the vitamin, is harmless and perhaps helpful.

Two new antiviral drugs, tested principally in other nations by U.S. pharmaceutical firms, showed promise for treatment of a broad spectrum of infections, from serious forms of the familiar "cold sore" (herpes simplex) and hepatitis to mild influenza. Systemic adenine arabinoside (ara-A) and ribavarin created much excitement among U.S. pharmacologists be-

cause of their potential as new weapons for a variety of serious ills, but until further clinical studies were completed, U.S. physicians could apply them only to life-threatening situations. Hepatitis infects over 40,-000 Americans annually and a vaccine would be the ideal way to combat this serious liver disease. Until recently scientists could not find the virus that apparently causes it, but investigators at several universities have now definitely established the "Dane particle" as a virus associated with serum hepatitis. They are now trying to grow the virus, first sighted by British scientists in 1970, in sufficient quantities to help manufacture a vaccine.

The epidemic of cholera that claimed more than 20 lives and disrupted the tourist trade in Italy in 1973 was repeated in Portugal during the summer of 1974. By the end of September over 2,000 cases had been reported, and the disease had spread to the island of Madeira. However, just as happened in Italy, the Portuguese authorities, afraid of losing tourist trade, never conceded that a breakdown in public health control had taken place, and at the height of the epidemic insisted that the situation was "under control." The responsible germ was the same El Tor type of *Vibrio cholerae* that had caused outbreaks in the Middle East, North Africa, and southern Europe during recent years, and that had begun spreading to neighbouring countries from Indonesia in 1961. In view of the short-lived and incomplete protection provided by cholera vaccine, and the poor standards of hygiene and sanitary engineering in many Mediterranean countries, it seemed likely that cholera would remain endemic in Europe for some time to come.

By the beginning of 1974 smallpox was endemic in only four countries—Bangladesh, India, Pakistan, and Ethiopia. In 1967, when the World Health Organization (WHO) intensified its campaign for the total eradication of smallpox, it was endemic in 30 countries, including most of Africa, Brazil, and Indonesia. This rapid and dramatic reduction in the number of communities harbouring the infection seemed to indicate that WHO's target of getting rid of all permanent pockets of the disease could be reached quite soon. And despite the recent epidemics in India and Bangladesh, Halfdan Mahler, WHO's new director general, confidently predicted in May that "next year the world will have seen its last case of smallpox."

Malaria was another disease that WHO hoped to eradicate by a worldwide program of attacks upon the mosquito, which spreads the infection to man, and a mass drug treatment of human victims and carriers of the malarial parasites. Launched in 1964, the program had achieved remarkable results to the extent that over 1,300,000,000 of the more than 1,800,000,-000 people originally living in malarial areas were now free of the disease, but a report published in May outlined the difficulties of ridding the world of malaria altogether. These include the emergence of mosquito strains resistant to available insecticides and drug-resistant strains of malarial parasites. Moreover, the cost of insecticides had escalated to the extent that the communities where the disease was still endemic simply could not afford to sustain effective antimalarial campaigns. The WHO experts now recognize that the final disappearance of malaria must depend upon improvements in living standards, health services, and the physical environment—changes far more profound than anything this one specialized agency of the UN has either the resources or authority to accomplish. This was just one example of the increasingly apparent truth that statesmen and politicians have at least as much influence upon and responsibility for the health of mankind as medical scientists and technicians.

(DONALD W. GOULD; BYRON THORPE SCOTT)

[423; 424; 10/35]

MENTAL HEALTH OVERVIEW

Consideration of significant developments in the field of mental health leads to a definition of the parameters of the concept. Definitions of mental health often do no more than state that mental health is the absence of mental disease. Matthew Dumont, community psychiatrist, defines mental health as freedom. Marie Jahoda in *Current Concepts of Positive Mental Health* (1958) found six overriding principles of mental health in psychiatric parlance—environmental mastery, attitudes toward the self, self-actualization, integration, autonomy, and perception of reality. The complexity of the problem is shown in the preface to Dumont's *Absurd Healer* written by Leonard Duhl:

> It seems to me as though many years have passed since I was an intern in Brooklyn and was called to see a patient in a fifth floor slum tenement. After climbing the stairs with the ambulance attendant and two policemen who were there to protect me, I entered a room which appeared to be no more than 12 feet square. In it were a dozen people joined by giant rats circling under the sink and cockroaches on the walls and ceiling. Under the single bulb which lit the room were people preparing food, children playing, couples performing sexual acts, people coughing, smoking—all huddled together in poverty and despair. In the far corner of the room was a woman lying in a pool of blood, having just delivered a baby and the afterbirth. Spontaneously, without a thought, I turned to the ambulance driver—perhaps to cover my own anxiety—and asked, "Which one is the patient?"

"Which one is the patient?" The answer to the question clearly resides in the diversity of programs that come under the rubric of mental health. First, consider the psychiatric patient who has been hospitalized and the nature of the treatment programs offered in the hospital. The trend throughout the U.S. has been to significantly decrease the number of patients who are in residence. Second, hospitalized patients are spending much less time within the hospital than in past years. California moved very rapidly toward the elimination of all state hospitals for the mentally ill except for patients convicted of felonies and considered potentially dangerous to society. Illinois reduced its state hospital population

from 38,137 in 1964 to 7,590 in 1974. New York emptied its state hospitals in much the same fashion. Communities were not receptive to an influx of state hospital patients returning to the community, and many sought legislation to keep the "undesirables" out. (*See* Special Report.)

The increasing emphasis on the use of short-term hospital care was intimately tied to the nature of the patient's insurance program. Only a very limited number of patients can afford long-term care. Therefore, the hospital has become a relatively transient place for psychiatric patients. In many hospitals group and milieu therapy replaced individual treatment. In group therapy, problems of patients were discussed within the group and treated by group therapists. Milieu therapy involved treatment in which there is adaptation to the environment of the unit that seeks to create a beneficial emotional climate. The nature of treatment continued to be predominantly one in which drugs were used so that acute symptoms would recede. The end result was that many patients had better controls enabling them to leave the hospital. Economics carry the message "get out of the hospital before the insurance program lapses," and mental health programs in the U.S. were inexorably woven to the political system of city, state, and federal government.

The continued growth of behaviour modification therapeutic programs was evident in 1974. Instead of treating the origin of the symptoms, the symptoms themselves became the primary object of attention. In the U.S. one area of behaviour modification was the subject of criticism because civil rights were seen as violated. A token economy was one in which, as patients learned to respond in behaviour defined as more appropriate, they received tokens. The tokens enabled the patient to buy snacks, to gain certain privileges that were given in exchange for tokens earned. However, members of the legal profession took the position that tokens did not meet minimum-wage standards and therefore the patients were placed in a state of peonage. If this argument held up in court, there seemed little question that significant changes would have to be made in the token economy. Again a picture emerged in which therapeutics were governed by social, political, or legal

continued on page 352

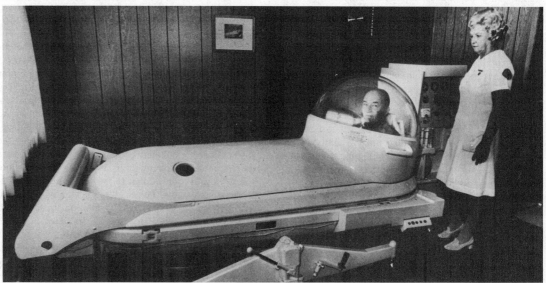

A patient is subjected to hyperbaric oxygenation (the introduction of oxygen to the bloodstream under high pressure) in this apparatus at the Miami Heart Institute. The process may cure memory loss and senility in some cases.

WIDE WORLD

INSTITUTIONAL CARE AND MENTAL ILLNESS

By William G. Smith

Since the mid-1950s there has been a gradual movement of mentally ill patients in the United States from large remote state hospitals to a wide array of local facilities. Sharp controversy surrounds this trend, and many professionals actually view hospitalization as harmful by its very nature. They argue that long confinement robs a person of his social skills and retards recovery. In addition, civil libertarians have become increasingly concerned about involuntary hospitalization. Laws have become more stringent so that commitment procedures are often limited to situations in which a mentally ill person is considered dangerous, and then only after careful and complex legal review.

On the other hand, concern has been raised in many communities that patients are released from institutions prematurely and without adequate supervision, medical care, or financial support. They are often unable to manage their own affairs, neglect their health, and fall prey to unscrupulous individuals who take advantage of them. Many people continue to be frightened by the unconventional behaviour of disturbed persons. Some professionals feel these seriously disabled persons would be managed more humanely in an institutional setting, even if no specific treatment is available to remedy their basic illness. They believe that the emphasis on legal procedures actually perpetuates the stigma associated with mental illness by treating its victims as quasi-criminals.

It appears that this controversy has arisen precisely because of the differences between mental illness and most other diseases. Mental illness strikes at an individual's ability to make rational judgments in the conduct of his life. Normally, when a person experiences a physical disease, he is aware that he is ill and seeks appropriate help. Often this is not the case with mentally ill persons who do not recognize their disturbance and its effect upon their ability to function—hence the need for involuntary institutional care with its attendant problems.

The Roles of Institutions. The quality of care available to persons with serious mental illness is not uniform. Wide variations in resources and staffing exist across the country, and this makes broad generalizations difficult. However, it is possible to describe in principle the roles of various types of institutions in the delivery of mental health care.

In the wide range of services required for comprehensive professional care of the mentally ill, hospitals and institutions continue to fulfill important functions. Institutions provide a protected and orderly environment conducive to helping patients reorganize their psychological equilibrium; intensive and specialized services directed toward rehabilitation; a protective milieu for the patient when suicide is a threat or the patient is unable to care for himself; and protection of society when a patient's judgment and control are so disorganized that he presents a physical danger to others.

William G. Smith is professor of psychiatry at the Rockford School of Medicine, University of Illinois. The focus of his principal works has been the seriously disturbed patient and the community health care concept.

Considerable overlap exists among institutions serving these functions. Frequently, persons suffering from mental illness are first hospitalized in special psychiatric units in general hospitals. Patients receive thorough physical and psychiatric evaluations and are treated with some combination of psychotherapy, medication, activity therapy, and, when appropriate, electroshock treatments. Generally these units are small and a great deal of interaction takes place between staff and patients. Most admissions to such units are voluntary, and the typical length of stay is between two and three weeks.

A patient requiring further treatment may be sent to a specialized hospital operated privately or by a county or state or, depending on the availability of a general hospital psychiatric unit, the patient's economic resources, and the choice of the patient or his family, he may be admitted to such an institution directly. Eligible patients may enter federal facilities, such as those of the Veterans Administration. Longer-term hospitals utilize a variety of treatment modalities similar to those employed in acute short-term hospitals, but with special emphasis on techniques to rehabilitate a patient's social and vocational function. These hospitals tend to be large, though the better run facilities are divided into treatment units of about 30 patients. The length of hospitalization in specialized facilities may vary from a few weeks to many years, but for the most part ranges from several months to a year.

About one-third of admissions for mental illness are involuntary; *i.e.*, the patient is committed for treatment without his consent. Most state codes require that an involuntary patient be examined by a licensed physician and that the physician certify the patient as mentally ill and, as a result of his illness, dangerous to himself or others. These certifications are reviewed by a court, which has final authority concerning the commitment. In many states a periodic reexamination and court review are required, and the patient has the right of appeal.

Even after adequate and intensive treatment, some patients continue to have residual symptoms. Most of these patients can be supported in the open community with the aid of medication, counseling, and a variety of social services including financial assistance, help in locating proper housing, vocational training, and job placement. Coordination of these services, which are often scattered among diverse agencies, remains an important challenge to mental health professionals.

Between 10 and 15% of hospitalized mental patients need some form of extended institutional care following their hospital stay. Halfway houses were developed as transitional facilities where patients could readjust to life in the community. Typically 10 to 20 patients reside in a halfway house, which is staffed by experienced mental health workers. Using the house as a home base, patients gradually assume more and more responsibility until they are capable of fully independent living. Another type of transitional care, partial hospitalization, has gained some popularity, especially in urban areas. This may involve either day or night care. Some chronic patients can be maintained at home provided they have structured and constructive activities during the day. Other patients may work during the day and return to the hospital for therapy in the evening.

A smaller group of patients requires semipermanent placement in special facilities. Geriatric patients can often be managed in nursing homes or group homes for the aged after their illness has been stabilized. A patient with physical infirmities may be cared for in a licensed nursing home. Physically healthy patients who are unable to live independently or with their families are often placed in sheltered-care facilities. In addition to general living services, these facilities provide active recreational programs and many are affiliated with sheltered workshops. Almost all patients in extended-care facilities require continuing state economic support.

In recent years the lodge has emerged as another option. A lodge consists of a "family" of 6–12 patients who live and work together as a unit, assisted by a mental health worker who acts

Patients in the Rhode Island Institute of Mental Health.

as business manager and counselor. Together, the patients operate a business venture, such as a small retail store or a janitorial service. While many chronic patients cannot meet the work standards in regular industrial jobs, as a group they can often provide their basic economic needs. At the same time, the lodge gives them more personal freedom and a greater sense of self-esteem than would be possible in a long-term hospital. The lodge approach also saves tax dollars. This concept must still be viewed as experimental, but it appears promising.

At present, on any given day, a community is likely to have about 30 persons per 100,000 population in acute psychiatric inpatient facilities, another 30 to 50 per 100,000 in long-term hospitals, and twice this many in extended-care facilities.

Origins of the State Hospital. To understand the contemporary situation, it is necessary to review briefly the history of institutional care for the mentally ill in the U.S.

In early colonial times society treated the dangerous mentally ill person harshly and the harmless one with indifference. Agitated persons were imprisoned as common criminals; others were simply run out of town. The most humane treatment available was to board disturbed persons with families where they were either locked in strong rooms or employed as domestics. When the population began to grow in the 18th century, almshouses and workhouses came into use as the principal means of harbouring the indigent mentally ill. Conditions were poor but not much worse than the treatment afforded any dependent or impoverished person at the time.

In 1751 the Pennsylvania Hospital in Philadelphia became the first medical institution in the U.S. to admit mental patients with the intent of trying to effect a recovery. In practice this noble ideal fell far short of its goal. According to Thomas G. Morton, "Their scalps were shaved and blistered; they were bled to the

point of fainting; purged until the alimentary canal failed to yield anything but mucus, and in the intervals, chained by the waist or ankle to the cell wall." Such treatment may seem deliberately cruel, but it was endorsed by most physicians of the time, including Benjamin Rush, the father of American psychiatry. He believed that agitation was caused by an inflammation of the brain due to engorgement with blood—hence the bloodletting. He also believed patients had to fear their doctor if he were to influence them. Rush did gradually introduce a number of reforms. He recommended kindly treatment of patients, regular occupational therapy, and emotional catharsis through having patients write out their feelings and experiences. He insisted that hospital attendants be carefully selected and that hospitals for the mentally ill be clean and have adequate heat and ventilation.

During the first quarter of the 19th century, "moral treatment" was introduced in the U.S. through the Society of Friends at its hospital near Philadelphia. The tenets of moral treatment had been developed by the Tukes, a Quaker family who had founded a small retreat for the mentally ill in York, Eng. Patients were to be treated with kindness and respect in tranquil country settings in the hope that this respite would be conducive to their recovery. Mechanical restraint and physical punishment were minimized. By 1825 nine states had an institution for the mentally ill and Virginia had two, all applying the moral treatment approach. However, most of the mentally ill continued to be confined in jails and in overcrowded almshouses.

Toward the middle of the 19th century, several factors led to a massive expansion of state-supported mental hospitals. In a popular book recounting his travels in the U.S., a retired English naval officer named Basil Hall decried the condition of inmates in poorhouses and praised the treatment patients received at the Hartford Retreat, where a remarkably high cure rate of 90% was reported. His account gave impetus to "the cult of curability" and a surge of hospital construction. It appeared from the statistics presented that patients who were hospitalized early in the course of their illness had an extraordinarily good outlook for recovery and that hospitalization in itself led to cure. Prominent psychiatrists of the day endorsed this concept, and legislators became convinced that building hospitals would lead to quick cures and obviate the need to support mental patients throughout their lives. At about the same time, Dorothea Lynde Dix, a retired schoolteacher, became intensely interested in improving the lot of the mentally ill. With evangelical fervour, she campaigned for state hospitals in nearly every state east of the Rockies. In almost every instance, she succeeded in getting a state hospital established or existing institutions expanded.

Unfortunately, the claims of cure were exaggerated. In 1887 Pliny Earle wrote *The Curability of Insanity,* based on careful research of hospital records. He pointed out that simple discharge from a mental institution was taken to mean the patient was cured, and that duplications on lists of recovered patients falsely inflated the recovery rate. For instance, within a single year one woman was discharged as "cured" six times from Bloomingdale Hospital in New York and seven times from the Worcester hospital in Massachusetts. As a result of these findings, the pendulum swung from undue optimism toward undue pessimism.

In retrospect, the facts did not support either attitude. State hospitals were clearly an advance over the neglect of the mentally ill that had prevailed. Hospitalization itself, however, became viewed as the main therapeutic tool. Certainly a benign atmosphere was more conducive to recovery than outright neglect, but this progressive step was not accompanied by genuine scientific understanding of mental illness. A mental hospital did not differ basically from an almshouse, except that it had a new label, was sometimes better run, and housed only mentally ill persons. To have expected that this in itself would result in cure now appears naive, but the confusion between humane care and scientific cure ultimately led to disillusionment. Gradually, state hospitals became custodial institutions where many patients remained for life.

These patients at the Throgg's Neck Community Health Center, N.Y., engage in creative therapeutic pastimes as part of their treatment.

In 1866 an acrimonious debate erupted at the annual meeting of the Association of Medical Superintendents of Asylums for the Insane (later the American Psychiatric Association). New York had established the Willard Hospital for the incurably insane. Those opposing such segregation argued that all mentally ill persons should be entitled to active treatment, and that no one could accurately predict who was incurable. The association rejected the plan for separate institutions, but in practice the development of the cottage system in state hospitals meant that acute patients and long-term patients were treated in separate buildings. It now appears that both viewpoints had some validity. Chronic patients do require different approaches to their care, but to segregate them and label them as hopeless often leads to their neglect and diminishes the chances of maximizing their full potential. No completely satisfactory solution to this problem has emerged to date.

Another heated debate that arose toward the close of the 19th century also contains lessons for today, viz., whether patients should be cared for in small, local (county) institutions or large state hospitals. In the end, most states opted for the state hospital plan, though Iowa and Wisconsin held to the county system. The facts indicate that both systems can work, but neither eliminated the vexing problem of caring for the nonresponsive patient and neither proved more economical than the other.

Meanwhile, government hospitals continued to grow in size. In 1851 Thomas Kirkbride had recommended a maximum hospital capacity of 250 patients, but by the 1950s some hospitals housed more than 10,000. Most institutions were overcrowded, understaffed, and underfunded. Once committed, patients tended to remain hospitalized for many years. Daily hospital routine was monotonous. Due to these conditions and the remoteness of state hospitals, many patients lost contact with normal ways of living, thus adding a secondary disability of desocialization to their crippling mental illness.

The Community-Based Approach. By 1925 several progressive innovations had been introduced as psychiatry became an established medical speciality. Advances had been made in the classification of mental illnesses and the use of psychotherapy. Better trained staff, especially nurses and social workers, became active in the field. Receiving hospitals and outpatient clinics began to appear in metropolitan areas, at first in connection with medical schools. The receiving hospitals provided observation and evaluation of newly admitted patients and short-term care of acute problems. Outpatient clinics and private psychiatrists focused on less severe emotional disturbances and provided aftercare for previously hospitalized patients.

A further stimulus toward outpatient care came during World War II, when it was discovered that severe battle stress neuroses responded best to intensive front-line crisis intervention. Then, in 1957, the major tranquilizers were introduced on a massive scale. Serious symptoms and much bizarre behaviour came under control, and patients who had spent many years in state hospitals could be discharged. The introduction of effective antidepressants in the early 1960s reinforced the trend.

All these factors, added to the deteriorating conditions in state hospitals, gave impetus to the community mental health movement. The goals of this movement were to improve society's acceptance of those afflicted with major mental illness, to minimize the deleterious effects of long-term hospitalization, to enable the mentally ill to live more normal lives in the open community, and to improve the quality of care. There was the further hope that if patients received vigorous, early treatment close to home, chronic mental illness would be averted. Some professionals viewed any hospitalization as unnecessary or even harmful. Public campaigns sometimes labeled involuntary or prolonged hospital care as imprisonment. Under the stimulus of the Community Mental Health Centers Act of 1963, local centres sprouted throughout the country. Hospitals rapidly discharged patients back to their communities as every effort was bent toward reducing hospital populations.

By 1974, after nearly 15 years, substantial progress had been made in achieving the goals of the community mental health movement. The number of inpatients in state and local government hospitals, which peaked at 558,000 in 1958, had fallen to 248,000 in 1973, despite the growth of the population as a whole. With increased funding, community facilities had expanded and the level of humanitarian care available for the mentally ill had been raised. Staff to patient ratios had improved markedly. The mentally ill were more accepted by the public.

There was also a more sober side to the picture. A regional mental health authority sent half of all 1967 admissions from a nine-county area in northern Illinois to a new centre operated according to the tenets of the community mental health orientation, while the other half were sent to traditional state hospitals. Both groups were matched and followed for three full years. None of the evidence indicated that the community-oriented thrust was superior in decreasing social disability due to serious mental illness, and costs proved to be higher. It was noted, however, that this first study bore a heavy load of unfavourable cases. Only 26% were coming into the hospital for the first time. The balance had previously spent an average of 320 days in a mental hospital.

A second investigation centred exclusively on patients experiencing their first admission had a more positive outcome.

Results indicated increased effectiveness for a crisis-intervention strategy as compared with traditional hospital care. The regional centre group showed fewer days of institutionalization and somewhat better social functioning. Even though these patients received three times as many outpatient services, the overall cost per capita was lower by over $1,300. Centre patients and their families were more frequently pleased with the services received. Nevertheless, a similar small proportion in both groups completely failed to make a community adjustment.

Recently a great deal of attention has focused on the dilemma of the nonresponsive patient. Under public pressure generated when many former patients were found to be living in poverty and squalor, California backed away from a plan to close its state hospitals, though a reduction in their number and size certainly seemed justified. Both the American Psychiatric Association and the American Hospital Association issued policy statements underlining the continuing need for adequate long-term care for those "comparatively few mentally ill or disabled individuals who cannot be maintained in the community." In spite of vigorous efforts to rehabilitate patients for community living, 10 to 15% still required some form of institutional care and 2 to 5% remained too disturbed for discharge from the hospital. It was clear that the new organization of mental health services had not eliminated the most difficult patients. While genuine progress in the humane care of the mentally ill had been made, this should not be confused with a scientific advance in treatment.

Public facilities for the care of the mentally ill came into being and continue to exist precisely because of the chronicity associated with serious disturbance. No sure technology has been found that will prevent chronicity in some patients. While psychiatry must persist in its search for a breakthrough, means still have to be provided to care for long-term patients. Crisis intervention centres, short- and long-term hospitals, partial hospitalization, and community extended-care facilities are all needed if society is to ensure quality care for the full spectrum of its human casualties. With such a mix of facilities, careful clinical judgment can be exercised in designing an appropriate plan for each individual patient, and the demoralization that has historically followed the pursuit of unproven professional enthusiasms will be avoided.

continued from page 348

considerations. This development was on the rise. Sen. Sam Ervin (Dem., N.C.) commented, "There is a real question whether the government should be involved at all in programs that potentially pose substantial threats to our basic freedoms." Further, "The subcommittee found that the federal government, through a number of departments and agencies, is going ahead with behavior-modification projects, including psychosurgery, without a review structure fully adequate to protect the constitutional rights of the subjects."

About one-third of all severely mentally retarded babies are mongoloids. In the U.K. in April an official report on the working of the Abortion Act advocated prenatal diagnosis, whereby women carrying mongoloid fetuses could have their pregnancies terminated. The diagnosis would involve amniocentesis, in which a needle is inserted through the belly wall into the cavity of the womb, and a sample of the amniotic fluid that surrounds the fetus is withdrawn. Laboratory culture of the sample will reveal whether the abnormal extra chromosome, evident in the cells of those afflicted with mongolism (Down's syndrome), is present. The report recommended that pregnant women over the age of 40 should be encouraged to undergo amniocentesis, since the risk of a mongoloid baby being born rises sharply with the age of the mother and is in excess of 1 in 40 at the age of 45 or over. The report also noted recent research suggesting that the existence of spina bifida could be detected by the presence of an abnormal level of a particular protein in the amniotic fluid. The inclusion of such observations in a document concerned with the law on abortion underlined the increasing emphasis being placed upon prenatal diagnosis, followed by termination of pregnancy when appropriate, as a powerful means for reducing the large number of mentally handicapped children born each year.

Some controversy arose in Britain during the year over the use of drugs for the treatment of criminals convicted of sexual offenses. The experimental use of such agents had been going on for more than a decade, but while countries such as Denmark, West Germany, and the U.S. employed irreversible procedures such as surgical castration and brain surgery to modify the behaviour of sexual offenders and violent criminals, the U.K. had had little experience in this field. A drug called cyproterone acetate, which neutralizes the activity of the male sex hormone, testosterone, and which thus, among other things, dampens or abolishes the sex drive in men, was approved for release by the Committee on Safety of Medicines in the U.K. in January 1974, and the manufacturers, Schering Chemicals, announced its general availability to British doctors in June. This produced the renewal of an argument that flared up a few months earlier when it became generally known that a number of "volunteer" prisoners convicted of serious sexual offenses had been given another drug, Benperidol, designed to reduce their sexual drive. The dispute reflected doubts concerning the ability of a prisoner to exercise a truly free choice when offered any "treatment" by authority and, even more importantly, revealed a mounting disquiet about the use of drugs and other medical and psychological techniques to alter the attitudes or the behaviour of citizens who fail to conform to official ideas of normality.

The concern for the British prisoners, who appeared to have willingly accepted treatment that might protect them from further conflicts with the law, was nourished by continuing reports from the U.S.S.R. of the committal of prominent dissidents to mental asylums. This apparently blatant abuse of psychiatry by the Soviets in the interests of the civil power greatly embarrassed the organizers of a symposium held under the auspices of the World Psychiatrists' Association that took place in Soviet Armenia in October 1973 and produced formal protests from several national psychiatric organizations during 1974.

In July at a meeting on circumpolar health held at Yellowknife, N.W.T., several speakers reported the disastrous effects upon the mental health of Eskimos (from Alaska to Greenland) of increasing contact with white civilization to which they had been subjected since World War II. There had been an escalating incidence of mental illness, homicide, and suicide, often associated with heavy drinking.

By contrast, Britain had the lowest suicide rate for a decade in 1973, despite a lack of any reduction in the general level of mental illness. Reporting this fact, and noting that U.K. suicide figures showed a marked and steady decline after 1963, whereas the rate in comparable countries had been static or rising, a British psychiatrist, Richard Fox, suggested that the Samaritans deserved much of the credit. This voluntary organization maintained a nationwide network of 150 centres, staffed 24 hours a day by counselors ready to talk on the telephone to anyone seeking sympathy, encouragement, and advice during a crisis of anxiety or despair. But while the British suicide death rate fell by one-third, there was a large increase in attempted suicides, so that the total of "unsuccessful" suicidal acts showed a substantial increase. This supported the supposition that a great majority of those who survived an apparent suicide attempt had no wish to die but were making a dramatic bid for desperately wanted attention and concern.   (ALAN K. ROSENWALD; DONALD W. GOULD)

DENTISTRY OVERVIEW

During 1974 dental scientists intensified their efforts to unravel the many puzzling aspects of the causes of periodontal, or gum, disease. The ultimate goal was a method to chemotherapeutically control this disorder, which is the greatest cause of tooth loss among adults. Recent research has found that the tissue inflammation of periodontal disease appears to be linked to immune reactions that occur when people become sensitized to products of particular bacteria. These suspect organisms are clustered closely against the gums for long intervals in a film of dental plaque, the sticky, colourless substance that collects at the base of teeth. It was found that immune reactions were either caused by sensitized gum tissue cells or by a family of serum proteins, scientifically labeled as complement, which circulate in the bloodstream or form on cell surfaces.

One mark of progress was the discovery that prostaglandin E (PGE) occurs at high levels in inflamed human gum tissues and that, during tissue culture experiments, PGE can cause bone to disappear or resorb. Animal experiments have also supported the concept of the bone damaging action of certain serum proteins through the addition of radioactive calcium. The immunologic concept of periodontal disease was further upheld in a study by the National Institute of Dental Research (NIDR) which indicated that patients whose immune systems have been suppressed to retain kidney transplants have a lower incidence of gum disease than those individuals with intact immune mechanism. These findings imply that drugs given to kidney transplant patients to prevent immune responses affect their oral tissues in the same manner. For patients with advanced periodontal disease and subsequent bone loss, a new bone grafting technique has been tested successfully in cases where the advanced stage of the disease has created deep pockets in the soft tissue as well as bone loss around the teeth. Bone tissue is removed from an unaffected area of the mouth, usually the bony ridge near the back teeth, by a small high-speed rotating bur. A suction hose then transmits the bone particles to the defective area. Host acceptance usually is not a problem because the transplanted bone comes from the patient himself.

As spiraling inflation continued to plague the U.S. economy, American Dental Association (ADA) officials noted that even after the lifting of wage-price controls dental costs increased at a slower pace than other consumer services, particularly physicians' fees and hospital charges. A national health insurance plan remained a high priority in Congress and dental leaders continued their insistence that if any such program is adopted at least dental care for chil-

dren must be incorporated, plus the option for a phased- in program of emergency dental care for older individuals. As the prospects for some form of governmental overview of health care services grew more imminent—for instance, the passage of the Professional Standards Review Organizations (PSROs) law —dental leaders pledged the profession's cooperation as long as dental services were being reviewed under the provisions of the PSROs law. They indicated that they would seek amendments of sections of the law that present potential danger to the profession and its patients and seek repeal of the law if it permits unwarranted interference with appropriate judgments made by professional health care providers or if it adversely affects peer review mechanisms already developed by the dental profession throughout the country.

Expansion of fluoridation scored a major triumph when Los Angeles adopted the measure in September. The decision affected three million residents of the city. Nationally, there were now more than 100 million Americans who resided in areas with fluoridated community water systems. An Armed Forces Institute of Pathology dental scientist reported that there may be more to fluoride action in preventing cavities than the strengthening of tooth enamel crystals. Experiments conducted on extracted wisdom teeth indicated that fluorides may intercept acid production in bacterial plaque that forms on teeth. Plaque is chiefly implicated in the development of tooth decay and gum disease and the significance of these findings, if the results can be duplicated, lies in the fact that plaque control at the clinical level may be made more effective by intensified fluoride chemotherapy applied to the teeth of adults as well as children.

Because sucrose, or table sugar, has long been implicated in the development of tooth decay, scientists have been exploring whether sucrose substitutes might be less harmful to oral health. Studies at the University of Alabama on human subjects and animals, however, have shown contradictory results on whether substitutes for sucrose would cause dental decay. While one team of investigators reported that xylitol, a sucrose substitute, seems to have no ability to encourage decay in humans, another group found just the opposite result in substituting xylitol in the diet of rats. The first group of researchers tested fructose, or fruit sugar, and sucrose and found that both can be considered equal in contributing to incipient or early tooth decay in humans. They ranked the four other sugars in descending order of impact on dental decay as follows: melibiose (from molasses); raffinose (from sugar beets and cottonseed oil); sorbitol (from the sorbus tree); and xylitol (wood sugar). However, the sorbitol results were disputed by the other research team in their experiments with rats in which no decrease in the decay rate was detected.

Progress in the search for vaccines against tooth decay was reported by several scientists but any momentous breakthrough to permit practical application in everyday dental practice appeared to lie in the distant future. One encouraging note was sounded by Fred G. Emmings of the School of Dentistry, State University of New York at Buffalo, who related that experimental vaccines can help prevent organisms suspected of causing tooth decay from colonizing as dental plaque on monkeys' teeth. The animals received injections of *Streptococcus mutans* bacteria into the salivary glands, which stimulated production of salivary antibodies against the decay-causing bacteria and dramatically reduced the amount of *Strepto-*

COURTESY, DR. HENRY J.
SKERMAN, BOSTON UNIVERSITY

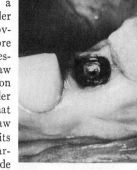

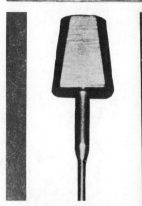

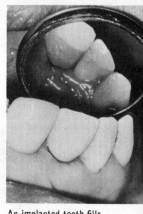

An implanted tooth fills the gap. From the top, a vitreous-carbon plug is implanted in the gum to firmly hold a steel post (middle pictures), which is then capped (bottom) to provide a perfect match.

coccus mutans in dental plaque. Although this achievement is encouraging, much work remains to be done before a vaccine can be tested in man. In a similar vein William Bowen of the NIDR National Caries Program observed that even though the dental enamel affected by the disease is not in direct contact with the immunological system of the body, a vaccine against dental decay may be feasible by having the antibody enter the mouth through the salivary glands and through the gum tissues. The antibody as shown in Emmings' experiments could then combine with microorganisms and prevent them from colonizing the tooth surface.   (LOU JOSEPH)

[422.E.1.a.ii; 10/35.C.1]

THE HEART ATTACK EPIDEMIC

Atherosclerosis is a specific type of arteriosclerosis, or hardening of the arteries—by far the most important type in terms of human sickness and death. It is a disease process and not an aspect of normal aging. Its hallmark is the deposition of cholesterol and other fatty substances in the walls of arteries. At first these deposits involve only the innermost layer of the artery wall, but as the disease progresses —and as the arterial cells respond with a tissue reaction to the harmful effects of the excess fats—the entire wall is involved. It becomes thick and inelastic, and the channel for flow of arterial blood is progressively narrowed.

Severe atherosclerosis with its complications—*e.g.*, clot formation (thrombosis)—is the underlying disease process in most cases of heart attack, angina pectoris, and other forms of coronary heart disease (CHD). It is also responsible for a high proportion of strokes (cerebrovascular disease) and arterial disease of the trunk and lower extremities. But atherosclerotic coronary disease is by far the most prevalent cause of serious illness, disability, and death, not only for elderly persons but also for persons in the prime of life.

Hollis Haines of Biloxi, Miss., is believed to be the youngest pacemaker recipient on record. Born with a congenital heart defect, the infant had the device implanted when he was 18 hours old.

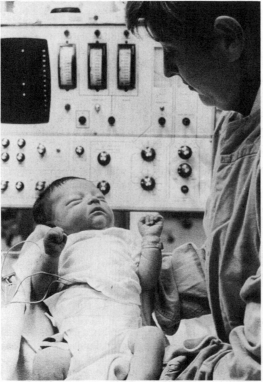

UPI COMPIX

The World Health Organization (WHO) has determined that an epidemic of premature atherosclerotic coronary heart disease (*e.g.*, before age 65) is currently raging, especially in the industrialized countries. At present in the U.S. about 175,000—one in four—of the 700,000 annual CHD deaths occur prior to age 65. Coronary heart disease in young adulthood and middle age has a marked predilection for men. The ratio of heart attacks in U.S. men compared with women is 10 to 1 or higher prior to age 50; 3 to 1 prior to age 65. This is a major factor accounting for the shorter life expectancy of men compared with women—and for the important social problem of widespread premature widowhood. A high proportion of the coronary deaths occur suddenly—instantaneously or in less than an hour. About a quarter of all first heart attacks manifest themselves as sudden death. This marked tendency of heart attack to kill suddenly accounts for the fact that about 70% of coronary deaths occur outside the hospital. For every fatal case of heart attack, one to two nonfatal cases occur. In the U.S. coronary heart disease is the number one cause of disability for workers—men and women, white and black. The estimated economic costs to the nation are correspondingly high and, of course, no dollar estimates can be put on the toll of physical and psychological human suffering.

Study of the history of epidemic diseases compels a basic generalization most relevant for the CHD problem: Epidemic disease occurs only in those populations experiencing a confluence of multiple causes essential for the massive onslaught of sickness. Epidemic disease never has a single cause, not even when there is a clear-cut single necessary cause for the given disease. Thus, the tuberculosis organism is indeed the necessary cause for TB but by itself is not sufficient cause for the development of the disease in epidemic proportions. Undoubtedly TB bacteria have been abroad among human populations for centuries and millennia. It was not until the 19th century that TB became epidemic as the great white plague and major health problem of the era. The etiological prerequisites for epidemic TB were the social circumstances generated by the Industrial Revolution—rapid chaotic expansion of towns into cities, with inadequate housing, mass overcrowding, poor sanitation, inadequate public health and medical care, etc. These were the multiple socioeconomic and sociocultural factors—the confluence of several causes, together with the bacterium—producing epidemic TB.

In the course of the 20th century, coronary heart disease has replaced TB as the great epidemic disease of the era in the industrialized countries. CHD is the epidemic disease of mature, advanced industrial society, as TB was the epidemic disease of that society in its childhood and adolescence. Extensive evidence is available indicating that a confluence of sociocultural circumstances is responsible for the emergence of CHD as the 20th century epidemic disease of developed countries. One key circumstance is that the mass of the population in affluent countries has for the first time in history been able to enjoy a "rich" diet high in animal products (meats and dairy foods), and not been restricted to inexpensive starchy foods (bread, potatoes, pasta, oatmeal, cornmeal, etc.). This modern diet—excessive in calories in relation to energy expenditure, high in total fat, saturated fat, cholesterol, sugar, and salt—leads to high prevalence rates of hypercholesterolemia (high levels of blood cholesterol) in the adult population. Sustained hypercholesterolemia—due particularly to the high intake of saturated fat, cholesterol, and calories—markedly increases risk of premature severe atherosclerotic disease and its clinical sequelae. This diet also contributes significantly to current high prevalence rates of obesity and, as one important consequence, of high blood pressure—another important coronary risk factor.

A second aspect contributing to the CHD epidemic has been the development of mass consumption of cigarettes since World War I. There is no longer any doubt that cigarette smoking is a major factor adding substantially to risk of CHD, at least among the populations of the advanced countries, with the nutritional-metabolic prerequisites for the development of atherosclerosis.

A third circumstance is the emergence of sedentary living and poor cardiopulmonary fitness—a result of increasing use of nonhuman energy in large-scale production, the motorcar, television, etc. Aside from any other negative effects, this change certainly contributes to chronic caloric imbalance and frequent obesity, *e.g.*, prevalence rates of 20 and 50% among teenagers and middle-aged adults, respectively, in the U.S., with all the consequences. Although the evidence is not entirely airtight and consistent, there is good reason to believe that lack of exercise—habitual inactivity at work and leisure—is another important aspect of the modern mode of life increasing susceptibility to premature CHD. Data are also available indicating that the stresses, tensions, and conflicts of modern life in highly urbanized society—the pace, turmoil, mobility, and change and their effects on personality and behaviour—along with the "rich" diet, cigarette smoking, and sedentary living, seem to be playing an important role in the causation of the CHD epidemic in the developed countries.

That the epidemic of premature coronary heart disease is a consequence of sociocultural factors, of the evolution of life-style in the 20th century, is further buttressed by data comparing the U.S. with other countries. Chart 1 presents such data for 21 developed areas. These statistics are recent mortality rates per 100,000 population per year for men aged 45–54, compiled by the U.S. Public Health Service. The CHD mortality rates for middle-aged men differ substantially and significantly among these countries and these differences are paralleled generally by corresponding differences in rates for all causes of death. Several of the European countries with CHD and total mortality rates lower than those for the U.S. are the countries whence the ancestors of tens of millions of Americans migrated. Undoubtedly the gene pool of the populations of these countries is essentially similar to that of the U.S. The differences in coronary disease mortality cannot be attributed, therefore, to differences in population genetics—they must be consequences of differences in mode of life.

The International Cooperative Study on Epidemiology of Cardiovascular Disease yielded data on the role of dietary fat and blood cholesterol, along with evidence on the contributory influence of hypertension and cigarette smoking, in accounting for international differences in rates of occurrence of premature CHD. A ten-year study of 18 population samples in seven countries—Finland, Greece, Italy, Japan, The Netherlands, the U.S., and Yugoslavia—dealt with observations on approximately 12,000 men, originally of age 40 to 59. Marked differences in the rates of occurrence of coronary heart disease were recorded among

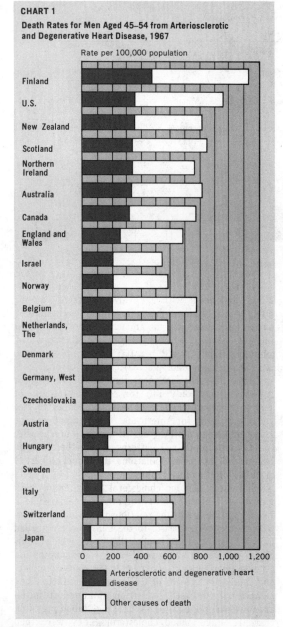

CHART 1

Death Rates for Men Aged 45–54 from Arteriosclerotic and Degenerative Heart Disease, 1967

Rate per 100,000 population

Finland
U.S.
New Zealand
Scotland
Northern Ireland
Australia
Canada
England and Wales
Israel
Norway
Belgium
Netherlands, The
Denmark
Germany, West
Czechoslovakia
Austria
Hungary
Sweden
Italy
Switzerland
Japan

0   200   400   600   800   1,000   1,200

■ Arteriosclerotic and degenerative heart disease

□ Other causes of death

the population samples from the seven countries. The highest five-year incidence rates were recorded for men from eastern Finland and the U.S.—over 120 and 80 per 1,000 population, respectively. In contrast, five-year incidence rates were about 20 or less per 1,000 for men in the Greek islands of Corfu and Crete, Dalmatia, Yugos., and Japan. Amount and type of fat habitually eaten—especially saturated fat, and inevitably cholesterol—varied markedly among the population samples studied. In Kyushu, Jap., total fat constituted 9% of calories, saturated fat 3%. In several of the European communities (*e.g.*, Corfu and Crete; Velika Krsna and Dalmatia, Yugos.; Montegiorgio and Crevalcore, Italy) saturated fat intake was also low (7–10% of calories). Polyunsaturated fat intake was never high (3–7%). In contrast, analyses of the diets ingested by the men under study in Finland, The Netherlands, and the U.S. revealed high saturated fat intakes, in the range of 17–22% of calories (total fat 35–40%). Men from eastern Finland exhibited the highest levels of saturated fat ingestion—22% of total calories.

It has also been shown that the pattern of rise in

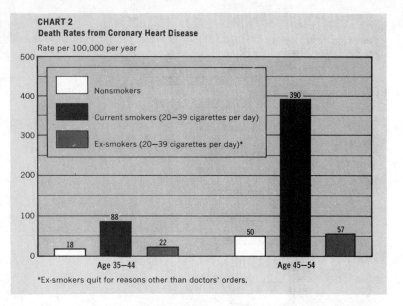

CHART 2
Death Rates from Coronary Heart Disease

Rate per 100,000 per year

Nonsmokers

Current smokers (20–39 cigarettes per day)

Ex-smokers (20–39 cigarettes per day)*

Age 35–44: 18, 88, 22

Age 45–54: 50, 390, 57

*Ex-smokers quit for reasons other than doctors' orders.

blood cholesterol with age varies markedly among different populations, depending upon habitual diet, particularly saturated fat and cholesterol intake. At birth, levels are very similar throughout the world, averaging about 80 mg. per 100 ml., as measured on umbilical cord blood. Thereafter they diverge conspicuously. By the late teens they are about 180 for Americans, but only 140 for southern Italians or Japanese. Blood cholesterol levels continue to rise steadily with age for Americans, plateauing at average levels of 220 or more by age 35 or 40, whereas with the different nutritional patterns among the southern Italian and Japanese populations, they level off earlier at much lower average values.

Differences in blood cholesterol levels among individuals in a given country or area make possible a further evaluation of the relationship of blood cholesterol to coronary disease. In the U.S. in the so-called national cooperative Pooling Project, which combined results from several long-term population studies, thousands of men aged 30–59 were examined, and those free of signs of CHD were identified. They were classified based on various findings at initial examination (done in the 1950s); e.g., blood pressure, cigarette usage, blood cholesterol. They were then followed long-term, to evaluate the relationship between their risk factor findings and subsequent rates of heart attack. The attack rate was more than doubled for men with baseline blood cholesterol levels of 250–274 or 275–299 (mg. per 100 ml.), more than trebled for those 300 and above, compared with those with good low normal readings under 200. The amassed data further indicated that there is a steady increment in premature CHD as blood level of cholesterol rises. As cholesterol concentration increases, risk increases. The relationship is continuous. This is true at all ages, at least from young adulthood through middle age. There is no evidence of a critical level that divides "normal" subgroups (i.e., subgroups "immune" to premature coronary disease) from CHD-prone "abnormal" subgroups. This conclusion is of the utmost practical importance with regard to measures for prevention. The greater the risk, the greater the need for prophylaxis—but no single "screening level" exists to separate those in need of prophylaxis from those not in need of prophylaxis.

A practical consequence for both diagnosis and treatment of hypercholesterolemia and other risk fac-

tors is the importance of evaluating the entire immediate family. For example, children inherit both their parents' genes and living habits. The latter are amenable to environmental influence. Identification of susceptibility in a parent must, therefore, immediately call attention to his or her children and to parental siblings; the converse is equally true. Hence, prevention, especially early prevention, should be an intrinsic part of family medicine. The basic aim is, by changing family living habits, to control heritable risk factors and thus mute or negate genetic predisposition to premature coronary heart disease.

International data demonstrate a high-order and significant correlation between average per capita consumption of cigarettes and coronary heart disease mortality rates for both middle-aged male and female populations of the developed countries. In regard to differences in cigarette smoking habit among individuals and their relationship to risk of atherosclerotic disease, extensive data from several studies in the U.S. and the U.K. demonstrate a clear-cut, significant relationship.

The largest study of cigarette smoking—under the aegis of the American Cancer Society—involved one million men and women originally aged 40–84. It has furnished follow-up data showing that for each sex and age group coronary heart disease mortality increased with intensity of cigarette smoking. The younger the age group, the higher the relative risk associated with cigarette smoking. The youngest men smoking two or more packs of cigarettes a day were at highest relative risk. Excess risk remained high for cigarette smokers throughout middle age. In addition, autopsy studies have shown that atherosclerosis of the aorta and/or the coronary arteries was more severe at autopsy in persons who had been habitual cigarette smokers, compared with those who had never smoked.

Elevated blood pressure is another major risk factor for atherosclerotic disease, in this instance for both premature coronary and cerebrovascular disease. The autopsy data of the International Atherosclerosis Project demonstrated a significant relationship between hypertension and the severity of atherosclerosis. Data from the International Cooperative Study on the Epidemiology of Cardiovascular Disease indicate that differences among the populations of the seven countries in five-year CHD incidence rates were attributable, at least in part, to differences in the prevalence of hypertension among the samples of middle-aged men.

The data from epidemiologic studies now permit clear definition of the quantitative impact on coronary incidence and mortality—and on mortality from all causes—of the major treatable risk factors (hypercholesterolemia, hypertension, and cigarette smoking), not only singly, but most importantly in combination. Analysis of data from the Pooling Project illustrates this. The analysis was a simple and crude one in that only a single measurement at entry examination was utilized to characterize each man. Moreover, his status with respect to the specified risk factors was designated either high or not high, utilizing the specified cutting points. Obviously, as already emphasized, a serum cholesterol level of 240 is by no means an optimal level in terms of risk, and similarly with respect to diastolic blood pressure of 88. Nevertheless, for purposes of this analysis, such values were designated not high. Presence of only one risk factor—as compared to none—was associated with a more

Major Food Groups in the U.S. Diet and Percentage Calories, Total Fat, and Cholesterol Derived from Each

Food group	Calories	Total fat	Cholesterol
Meat, fish, poultry	22	38	35
Fats and oils	12	29	6
Dairy products	13	15	16
Commercial baked goods	6	4	8
Eggs	2	4	35
All other food groups	45	11	—

than 100% increase in probability of a major coronary event over the next decade, and an increase in risk of almost 100% for the fatal end points, including total mortality. When combinations of these major risk factors—any two or all three—were present, susceptibility to overt CHD and fatal disease was substantially higher, attaining levels four or five times greater than for the group with none of the risk factors.

The reasons for the coronary epidemic are clear as are the key elements of a strategy for controlling the epidemic. It is reasonable to infer that by improvement in life-styles, beginning in infancy and childhood when primary habits are formed, upcoming generations can be influenced so that a much lower percentage of adults are in the very high risk group. It is also important to identify high risk persons as early as possible by a variety of means, including screening programs and the work of family physicians. And, having identified cases, to give attention to encouraging family life-styles to eliminate or blunt the impact of risk factors—through improvements of diet to lower blood cholesterol, encouragement of cessation of cigarette smoking, encouragement of reduction of weight to lower elevated blood pressure, and introduction early of pharmacologic therapy for hypertension when appropriate.

Data from the Chicago Heart Association Detection Project in Industry demonstrate that a sizable proportion of the general population of young and middle-aged adults are hypertensive. But a majority of these people are unaware of their condition. Moreover, only about a half of those giving a history of hypertension are being treated, and for those being treated, only about half are being treated vigorously enough and are adhering well enough to prescription to have their blood pressure normalized. Of the estimated 24 million hypertensives in the U.S., about three million are receiving treatment adequate enough to normalize blood pressure.

Reports from the U.S. Veterans Administration cooperative study on antihypertensive treatment indicated that there is little or no doubt regarding efficacy of sustained effective treatment for high blood pressure. This is not only true for persons with severe hypertension (diastolic pressures averaging 115 mm. of mercury and greater), but also true for persons with so-called "moderate" hypertension (diastolic pressures averaging less than 115). Over the years of this study, the untreated group had a rate of morbid events of all types of almost 60%. In contrast, the treated group—with blood pressure markedly lowered by modern antihypertensive drugs in combination—had a rate of only 20%. Therapy was about 70% effective. Side and toxic effects were of limited frequency and severity, so that the benefit to risk ratio with this judicious treatment was excellent.

Ability of physicians to influence risk is not confined to such pharmacologic modalities of treatment as drugs for hypertension. One of the key areas is

cigarette smoking. Undoubtedly a high percentage of cigarette smokers can be prevailed upon to quit. This is illustrated by the findings of the Chicago Heart Association large-scale surveys in industry. Even for the younger group, aged 25–44, 35% of the men who had ever smoked listed themselves as ex-users of cigarettes, as did 27% of the women. The quit rate was even higher for the older age group (45% for men, 30% for women). Chart 2 includes data from a 1958 study of hundreds of thousands of veterans, illustrating that it pays to quit, even in late middle age, after decades of heavy cigarette smoking, and the evidence is that habits are changing, especially among middle-aged men.

Similarly, with changes in eating habit, it is entirely possible to accomplish and sustain a reduction in blood cholesterol. The table illustrates the key food groups in U.S. diets, in terms of dietary saturated fat, cholesterol, and calories. The key foods high in saturated fats and/or cholesterol—the fat from dairy products, meats, egg yolks, and commercial baked goods—need to be deemphasized, while the positive nutritional value of low-fat dairy products, lean meats, fish and poultry, egg whites without yolks, and the use of unsaturated oils and margarines needs to be emphasized. There is a great deal for Americans to learn from the life-styles of people in places where average blood cholesterol levels and heart attack mortality rates are substantially lower. Some of the finest cooking in the world, *e.g.*, from the Mediterranean basin and from the Far East, is considerably lower in saturated fat, cholesterol, and calories than the usual U.S. diet, and the populations from these areas of the globe have much lower average blood cholesterol levels and lower coronary death rates.

At least three long-term studies—in Chicago, Los Angeles, and New York City—have yielded encouraging data on the possibility of preventing heart attacks in this way. Extensive evidence exists as to the possibility of turning the flank of the coronary epidemic—first and foremost by developing better approaches to life-style, from infancy on, for whole families and for whole communities, especially with regard to eating, smoking, and exercise habits.

(JEREMIAH STAMLER)

[422.A.1 & 2]

Radiographs are examined for evidence of successful application of urokinase in treating heart attack victims. Urokinase, made from human male urine, was used experimentally in 1974 to evaluate the condition of a patient's coronary vessel after a heart attack.

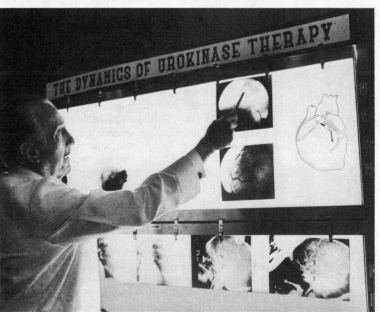

JACK MULCAHY—CHICAGO TRIBUNE

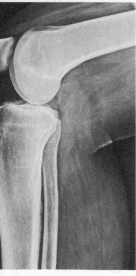

Conventional (top)
and electron radiograph
of a patient's knee
shows the greatly enhanced
image provided by this
new diagnostic technique.

RADIOGRAPHY
The Detection and Diagnosis of Disease.
Before 1900 doctors were dependent on surgery to examine internal structures of patients. Aside from directly accessible body cavities, only the patient's history and an external examination provided other clues as to the nature and cause of patient symptoms. The discovery of X rays in 1895 offered the first means for direct examination of internal structures. So powerful was this new method that X-ray studies were performed extensively in many countries within a year of their discovery, beginning a new era of medical practice.

There are two basic types of X-ray examination. The first, radiography, provides a still picture of the patient's anatomic structures. The second includes fluoroscopy and several of its more modern modifications; these are multiple sequential images that show bodily functions as they occur; for example, gastrointestinal and circulatory studies use sequential images. However, only radiography can yield full resolution of fine structural details with permanent records for later reference. Radiography is therefore used not only alone, but also almost always in combination with other X-ray studies.

In addition to X-ray examinations, modern medical diagnosis benefits from sophisticated laboratory and nuclear medicine studies, as well as from two other new techniques. Nuclear medicine employs radioactive isotopes attached to biologically active chemicals. When introduced into the patient's body, these tagged chemicals as measured from their radioactive signals are used to evaluate body function, physiologic status, and even morphologic details. Recently the method has been extended to tests that permit accurate measurement of unbelievably tiny amounts of specific antibodies, and has in general greatly extended frontiers of both laboratory and X-ray studies.

Ultrasonic medicine is a more recent addition that uses sound waves of 0.5 to 25 MHz. These sounds are ultrasonic, or of too high frequency to be heard, and are used to map body structures as well as to measure blood flow, motion, and many other functions. The method works primarily as a result of sound reflections from tissue and cell interfaces; these include lung-muscle, fluid-tumour, fetus-amniotic fluid, and plasma-blood cell boundaries. Both pictorial and movement data result.

The other new diagnostic technique is thermography, which photographically portrays the surface temperatures of the body, based on self-emanating infrared radiation. This method of skin-heat-emission mapping is chiefly useful in detecting breast abnormalities and a number of circulatory problems.

All of the above methods aid the physician to ascertain bodily function and to pinpoint specific pathology. X-ray examinations remain essential, however, and diagnostic radiology is an important aspect of the diagnostic effort. Of the two basic types of X-ray examinations, radiography is performed most frequently because it yields a maximum of useful information quickly and efficiently.

Conventional Radiography.
X rays are produced by allowing high-energy electrons to strike a small metallic area of an X-ray tube. Part of the electrons' energy appears as X rays that diverge in all directions. Some of these rays are allowed to strike the area of interest on the patient; all others are excluded by appropriate shielding means. The intensity of the impinging X rays is modified to varying degrees by bone and tissue in traversing the patient. As a result the intensity across the emerging beam varies in a way reflecting the patient's anatomy and hence any pathology reflected in disturbed morphology. In this way an "X-ray image" results with the desired diagnostic information.

Because X rays are invisible to the eye, the X-ray image must be converted to visible form to be useful. Special photographic films are used for this purpose, in two basic ways. The first involves direct film darkening by the X rays, producing an extremely sharp, nongranular image. Unfortunately X rays readily penetrate film emulsions without much interaction, necessitating considerable patient irradiation for usable film darkness. As a result this method is restricted to radiography of the teeth, breast, and body extremities, for which higher X-ray dose levels are more medically acceptable than for most other parts of the body.

For virtually all other radiographic studies, special "intensifier" fluorescent screens are used in conjunction with double-coated, light-sensitive film; this reduces required patient dosage to levels 20–80 times lower than those for film alone. In practice two such screens generally sandwich the film; the fluorescent light they release during X-ray irradiation exposes the adjacent film emulsions, accounting for well over 97% of the final film darkening and achieving great reduction in required X-ray exposure. Screen-film combinations produce images less distinct than films exposed directly, but this is usually an acceptable penalty for the substantial patient dose reduction. New screens designed for use with special films give promise of even greater dose reduction. An immediate benefit is in certain applications where they can permit the reduction of required X-ray machine and tube output capacity, with significant reduction in initial capital outlay and operating costs—ultimately benefiting the patient. The table describes the procedure followed in conventional radiography: preparation, exposure, development, fixing, and viewing.

Important limitations exist for screen film or "conventional" radiography; these have led to a search for alternative methods. As indicated above, light spread from intensifying screens inevitably reduces detail resolution, even when great care is taken to assure intimate screen-film contact. Another problem is the altered density versus exposure response characteristics of useful combinations. This can result in excessively black and white areas on the final film, so that it is difficult to see anatomic sites of differing X-ray absorption; often extra studies are required to examine an extensive body area. For example, soft tissues near bony structures appear dark if one exposes properly for the bone; lung fields are seen well only with underexposure of spine and diaphragm areas. Recently an important economic factor has entered the picture. Silver bromide is the sensitive chemical in photographic film and silver is becoming a scarce, expensive metal, so X-ray film costs have risen and will likely rise at an increasing rate.

Work has been carried out for several years to produce electrostatic images, similar to those produced by most copying machines. Such images are made using pigmented plastic powder called "toner," of the order of five microns down to well below one micron diameter. Such toner can be attracted to charged areas on a film, rendering an electric image visible, just as is done in the familiar copier units.

The earliest work was the xeroradiography process, in which X rays discharge a selenium plate roughly in

Steps in Radiography		
Item	Conventional radiography	Electron radiography
Preparation	Double-emulsion film, dark-loaded between intensifying screens	Blank plastic film discharged, inserted into chamber, and gas pressure and high voltage started
Exposure	X rays from patient produce latent chemical image	X rays from patient produce latent electric charge image
Development	Latent image made visible by chemical means, as silver crystals	Latent image made visible by electric attraction of pigmented powder, not silver
Fixing	Chemical means—excess silver bromide removal, emulsion hardened	Physical means—solvent or other bonding of pigment to self and plastic sheet
Viewing	As transparency on bright viewbox	As transparency on bright viewbox

proportion to the X-ray exposure; the plate is used to produce a transfer image on paper, then reprocessed and reused several times. The method unfortunately is at present an order of magnitude slower than conventional radiography, and has some other disadvantages that have limited its use for most radiographic applications. Another method utilizes a gas-discharge chamber to deposit electric charges on a sheet of plastic; the resulting electrostatic image is then developed by a toner method. Early work has suffered from both very low sensitivity and limitation to very small image areas of about 4 × 4 in. as against 14 × 17 in.

Electron Radiography. A team of U.S. scientists accomplished a breakthrough in electrostatic imaging of X-ray irradiation in late 1971 using a discharge chamber system of novel design. Use of optimal electrical field arrangement and xenon gas at high pressure (combined with other designs) produced a system that yields full-size radiographs of good quality employing patient dose levels comparable to those of medium-speed screen-film technique. The final image is produced on conventional X-ray film base (a sheet of transparent plastic without photographic emulsion) and is studied on a bright viewbox in the usual manner. Thus, the dream of an X-ray detection system without silver halide is now close to fulfillment.

The exposure of an electron radiograph image is similar to that of any other imaging system; existing X-ray machines and tubes can be used without change to produce electron radiographs (*see* table). High-pressure xenon gas is combined with a high-voltage field to yield great sensitivity with good detail resolution, especially when development is optimal. Fixing is by means of solvent or heat fusion of the plastic particles to each other and to the sheet of plastic base, or by some alternative method.

Recent work has been directed to evaluating the potential of the new system, employing a model provided and continually updated by the investors. Briefly stated, the objective is to confirm the sensitivity (acceptable patient exposure) and imaging capability of the system, and to give some estimate of its practical potential. Exposure levels and imaging ability are not independent variables in this connection. Ideally, one would hope for both better images and reduced patient exposure, but image improvement must be stressed so long as patient dose is not excessive. The primary objective is to show more diagnostic information and to display it in a manner making diagnosis more certain. An incidental benefit could be to reduce the number of needed examinations without compromising diagnostic accuracy. The approach has been and continues to be two-pronged.

First, relevant physical parameters are measured: patient exposure as well as image properties, such as edge sharpness and enhancement and graininess, which affect detail visualization. Second, final clinical verification must be done. This involves exposing electron and conventional radiographs of the same parts of the same patients in direct sequence. The resulting radiograph pairs can then be evaluated for information content, using techniques ranging from simple subjective comparison of appearance to sophisticated information-yield studies (performed on statistically controlled sets for many different anatomic areas containing marginally detectable pathology).

A major two-year effort is in progress to delineate the exact areas of promise of the new system and to objectively evaluate its potential and limitations. However, extensive measurements and visual comparisons by many consultant radiologists on a national level have indicated great potential for the basic system. The test model for the system has produced diagnostically acceptable radiographs using exposure factors identical to those used in conventional radiography. Thus, the first basic requirement is met—acceptable patient exposure—since it is very likely the more advanced model will require even less exposure than the present unit.

Of equal or greater importance are the electron radiograph system image qualities. Image "latitude" has been found to be much greater than in screen-film systems, and a wide range of anatomic densities are demonstrated on a single radiograph with useful density. Thus, soft tissues near bone, lung fields and spine and heart shadow in chest studies, and the full human pelvis are demonstrated with more uniform density than in conventional radiographs. Provided that desired diagnostic details are shown adequately, this can result in two benefits. First, a single electron radiograph can help detect pathology that would not usually be observed with a conventional radiograph where the abnormality might be either subliminally displayed or completely invisible (in whiter areas of the film). Second, increased latitude makes exposure technique less critically dependent on patient variables, so fewer repeat examinations are required. The image latitude is combined with an ability to "enhance" edges of many desired details. The result is that contrast of some types of details is retained or even increased despite the increased

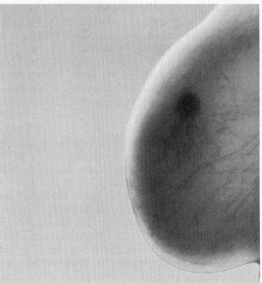

A mammogram, or X-ray photograph, can clearly reveal early malignancy before it becomes palpable. This view of a female right breast discloses such a malignancy in the dark area in the upper part of the breast.

ALBERT EINSTEIN MEDICAL CENTER / AMERICAN CANCER SOCIETY

image latitude. Combined with an inherently sharper image (unlike screen-film images, which are produced indirectly, electron radiographs are produced directly in a single step), edge enhancement can emphasize details of diagnostic importance.

The electron radiograph system is quite versatile in that it is possible to vary edge effects and image latitude over a wide range while still retaining adequate detail resolution. This versatility may make possible optimizing images for various types of studies, such as of the chest, abdomen, and bony structures, to highlight desired information. Potential benefits promised in the final design units are fourfold: (1) detection of some pathology now often seen only in retrospect, by highlighting of essential details; (2) at least moderate reduction in patient exposure, with fewer repeat exposures; (3) reduction in materials cost, due to elimination of silver bromide and chemical processing; and (4) all of the above without basic modification of existing X-ray generators. (LEONARD STANTON; LUTHER WELDON BRADY)

[10/35.B.1.a]

THE COSTS OF U.S. MEDICAL EDUCATION

Early in 1974 the Institute of Medicine of the National Academy of Sciences submitted a report on the "Costs of Education in the Health Professions" to the U.S. Congress and the Department of Health, Education, and Welfare. This was the report of an 18-month study carried out under the provisions of the Comprehensive Health Manpower Act of 1971. Because it was increasingly involved in the financing of educating health professionals, Congress sought guidance on a series of critical issues: The cost of educating physicians, dentists, and other health professionals during their undergraduate years; the factors responsible for the wide range in costs among different schools; and the criteria that should be used to determine the amount of federal support for the education of health professionals.

Between the beginning and the end of the study, marked shifts were made in the basic assumptions held about the trends in health manpower by the Congress, the administration, professional groups, and the public. When the study was authorized in 1971, the predominant view was that the U.S. faced a severe shortage of physicians (usually estimated at 50,000, or the equivalent of the total number of graduates for five years). Conservatives, as well as liberals, believed that the federal government should increase the scale of its financial support for the health system as a whole, including funding for medical education.

By early 1974 the mood had shifted. The concern about a physician shortage had been replaced by a growing conviction that the nation might soon have surpluses of doctors as a result of the substantial increases in the annual output of U.S. medical schools, reinforced by large inflows of foreign medical graduates. In 1972 the number of new foreign medical graduates, 12,000, exceeded the total number of U.S. medical school graduates. The steep rise in total annual federal expenditures for health in the period 1965–73 —from $5 billion to $33 billion—led many in the Congress and the administration to reconsider their earlier premise that the government should increase financial support of the health industry, including medical schools. The administration concluded that it should cut back radically its support for medical education in the face of a prospective oversupply and the large

number of qualified applicants, and indicated a strong preference to shift support from institutions to students, from grants to loans.

In order to understand the critical dimensions involved in such questions as who pays, who benefits, and who should determine policy with respect to medical education, the following background facts must be considered. In 1972–73 there were 112 medical schools in operation in the U.S., 19 more than in 1965; of this total, 64 were public and 48 were under private control. In 1965 the number of medical school graduates was 7,400; it was anticipated that the number of graduates in 1976 would be 12,200, an increase of approximately two-thirds. Most of the gain reflected increased enrollment in existing schools; less than 1,000 would be graduated from new schools.

The federal government became an important source of financial assistance to medical schools when it undertook the large-scale financing of biomedical research in the early post-World War II years. In 1965 it offered its first specific support for health education aimed at increasing enrollments and assisting low-income students. Medicare and Medicaid led to a substantial infusion of new funds via reimbursement for the care of patients in the teaching hospitals of medical schools. Legislation in 1968 went further to permit the federal government to assist medical schools in financial distress. This support was broadened by legislation in 1970 that enabled the federal government to assist new medical schools. In 1971, in the Comprehensive Health Manpower Training Act, Congress provided an array of manpower-focused assistance to medical schools, including capitation grants, increased loans and scholarships, and incentive grants for physicians to locate in underserved areas.

In 1971–72 only 7 medical schools were free-standing, 34 were under university auspices, and the largest group, 52, were organized as health sciences centres of universities, which means that they were linked with one or more health professional schools in the fields of dentistry, pharmacy, veterinary medicine, nursing, etc. Thus, in 1972, medical schools were involved in the education and training of 43,000 undergraduate medical students, 32,000 house staff, 18,-000 graduate students, and 17,000 undergraduates in other disciplines. In addition, these schools engaged in almost $1 billion annually of biomedical research and provided about $7 billion of patient care, approximately 20% of the nation's total hospital bill.

The modern U.S. medical school at a large university therefore is a multipurpose institution that provides a wide range of educational services, is heavily focused on biomedical research, and is directly involved through its teaching hospital or hospitals in the provision of inpatient and outpatient services that run the gamut from emergency room care to tertiary levels of care for patients who travel hundreds or thousands of miles to seek help from the professional staff. It is not possible to discuss the financing of medical education from the vantage of individual or social costs and benefits without acknowledging the fact that the education of a physician is only a small part of the multiple and complex functions performed by medical schools.

The fact that all medical schools are engaged in more than a single product—a physician—makes it difficult but not impossible to estimate the costs of educating a physician and to determine the resources available to cover these costs. The determination of costs and income under conditions of joint supply depends, however, on the accounting traditions and involves many judgments about the best way to allocate resources used and revenues received in the production and sale of joint products.

The Institute of Medicine's study was based on a sample of schools whose faculties were asked to allocate their time among three principal activities—teaching, research, and patient care. It found that the educational costs per medical student in 1972–73 totaled $12,650, of which $7,650 represented instruction, $3,250 research, and $1,750 patient care. The range among medical schools was substantial: from a low of $6,900 to a high of $18,650—a difference of about 270%.

The $12,650 average cost per medical student represented total educational costs and included all resources used, without reference to compensating revenues from research and patient care, part of which may be available to cover educational costs. From the viewpoint of public policy, a key consideration was how much of total educational costs were unfunded. In the study the concept of net educational costs was developed to focus on this critical element. Net educational cost was derived by subtracting income from research and patient care that was available for educational purposes from total educational costs. Available income from research amounted to $2,100 and from patient care, $1,300. The average net educational cost was therefore between $9,000 and $10,000. The range was reduced at both the upper and lower levels but remained wide: from slightly over $14,000 to slightly over $5,000.

A few important generalizations on available revenues can be ventured from the study. In neither public nor private schools was tuition a significant source of revenue; it accounted for no more than 11% of total income in any school and, more typically, it accounted for less than 5%. State appropriations are the most important source of revenue in publicly supported schools, providing approximately two-fifths of their total income. State appropriations are also relatively important (about 15%) in the revenues of some private schools.

The most striking finding about income was the significant role that research and patient care revenues represent of the total incomes of both public and private medical schools. Among the former, these two sources accounted for almost half of all income; in all but one of the latter, these sources provided considerably more than 50% of all income.

Although the foregoing data have been presented to sketch the financial parameters of the medical educational system in the early 1970s, it is relatively easy to move from these broad considerations to a consideration of costs and benefits to the individual student. In 1972 the average tuition of a student who attended a publicly controlled medical school was just under $800 while the comparable figure for students attending private institutions was $2,500. Since net educational costs averaged between $5,000 and $14,000, it at once becomes clear that the subsidy that a typical student receives over a four-year period is substantial—between $20,000 and $30,000.

The growing disquietude about medical subsidies, which are overwhelmingly derived from tax dollars and not from endowment and gifts, stems not only from the size, substantial as it is, but even more from the low tuition charged by public institutions and the high earning potential of physicians after graduation. The issue cannot be dismissed; it raises a host of com-

Approximately 300 doctors in Copenhagen, half of them Danish, take the special examination to qualify for a U.S. license to practice medicine.

plex problems that should be delineated and evaluated. A number of reform proposals have been advanced. The federal government should make loans available to students instead of making grants to medical schools as it now does. Moreover, it should tie the availability of loan funds to medical schools' raising their tuition to a respectable level; i.e., to around $2,000 or $3,000 instead of the $800 or so that is now paid by state residents who attend public institutions. The federal government should broaden its present programs of forgiveness if graduates agree to serve in designated doctor-short areas. Another approach might be to establish a special surtax on the earnings of physicians and recapture the whole or part of the training subsidy they earlier received.

While it might appear desirable for the federal government to exert leverage on the states to raise their tuition in medical schools, more careful deliberation suggests that it might be improper for Congress to stipulate how a state should support its institutions, whether through taxes or tuition, or in what combination. The use of federal leverage is questionable, especially in an era of new federalism, in light of the long history of difficult federal-state relations.

A related and, in fact, an antecedent question was why the federal government should single out health professional schools for direct subsidy, when this practice was not followed for any other segment of higher education. The answer that proved convincing to the steering committee of the Institute of Medicine study was that, for its health care, the U.S. relies on a mixed pattern of private and public institutions, limited in number, which are not distributed according to a logical pattern but whose facilities represent and should be treated as a national resource. It would be exceedingly costly for the federal government to turn its back on the financial viability of medical schools since it finances almost one-third of the total costs of all health services.

A related question bears on the desirability and feasibility of the federal government's shifting from institutional support based on capitation to a large-scale student loan program. The objections are not trivial: if most students had to borrow enough money to cover their full tuition plus their living expenses, before long the loan program would cost billions of dollars which at prevailing or even somewhat lower rates of interest would represent a significant carrying cost to the federal government. Also, the more expensive schools would be under pressure to lower their tuitions in the face of a probable loss of the better qualified students who would seek admission where costs are considerably lower. It is hard to see how the steeply rising number of women students—up from 6% in the early 1960s to 20% in 1974—could be maintained. Efforts to increase the number of low-income and minority students would also be undermined by higher tuition.

Against the backdrop of these policy considerations, it can be better understood why the steering committee favoured a more conservative approach, including the continuation of the present system of capitation at a rate between 25 and 40% of net educational costs, which suggests a federal contribution of around $3,000 per medical student per year, to provide a stable source of financial support to medical schools (as well as to other health professional schools), with no stipulation that this support be linked to changes in enrollment or to the length of the course. The steering committee also recognized the need for a mechanism in both the administrative and legislative branches of the federal government to coordinate the flow of funds into medical schools from other than the capitation route; that is, via monies for research and patient care. At present, different committees of the Congress act on these matters, and each is concerned that the funds it authorizes and appropriates are used only for the functions indicated, but no federal agency has an overview of the costs and revenues. This explains why the Congress in 1973 authorized a second study of the costs of graduate medical education to help it obtain a more comprehensive view.

Who pays for medical education? In descending order of importance: the federal government, state governments, patients and prospective patients via insurance, philanthropy, and students (or their parents). Who benefits? The nation as a whole, the overwhelming majority of the people who use the medical care system or who know that it is available to them in case of need, and the physician who derives satisfaction, status, and a good income from his work. The question of to whom the physician should be responsible raises a host of questions that transcend the issue of the financing of medical education. In 1973–74 the total expenditures for the health services industry in the U.S. would probably top $105 billion. The total expenditures of all medical schools in 1972–73, according to the Institute of Medicine's study, amounted to approximately $2 billion, of which about $400 million or 0.4% of the total national outlay for all health services was spent for undergraduate medical education.

Many critical issues face the American people as they seek to improve access to, availability of, and the quality of health services. And almost all of these issues involve the medical profession directly or indirectly. Finding answers, even partial answers, to these problems will not be easy, but it is an issue that both physicians and the public must undertake for their mutual benefit.   (ELI GINZBERG)

See also Demography; Drug Abuse; Life Sciences; Social and Welfare Services.

[425.A]

ENCYCLOPÆDIA BRITANNICA FILMS. *Ears and Hearing* (1969); *Muscle: Chemistry of Contraction* (1969); *Muscle: Dynamics of Contraction* (1969); *Radioisotopes: Tools of Discovery* (1969); *Respiration in Man* (1969); *The Nerve Impulse* (1971); *Health (Eye Care Fantasy)* (1972); *Health: Toothache of the Clown* (1972); *Work of the Kidneys* (2nd ed., 1973); *Regulating Body Temperature* (2nd ed., 1973); *Venereal Disease: The Hidden Epidemic* (1973); *Alcohol Problem: What Do You Think?* (1973); *Tobacco Problem: What Do You Think?* (1973); *Intern: A Long Year* (1973); *Exercise and Physical Fitness* (1973).

Historic Preservation

The convention on the protection of the world's cultural and natural heritage, adopted by the General Conference of UNESCO in 1972, was ratified first by the U.S. in December 1973, then by Egypt, Bulgaria, Sudan, Algeria, the Dominican Republic, and Australia; a number of other states were expected to act shortly. At its spring 1974 session, the Executive Board of UNESCO approved a preliminary study on the feasibility of an international instrument for the preservation of historic quarters and cities. It also recommended the preparation of a report and draft instrument, to be submitted to the General Conference at its 19th session in 1976.

Buildings in Telc, Czech., have been restored in detail.

Progress continued on two major international schemes. In Egypt the cofferdam around the island of Philae, site of a group of ancient temples, was completed, and pumping began to lower the water level preparatory to moving the temples to the island of Agilkia, which was being prepared to resemble ancient Philae. Contributions toward the project included some $1,270,000 from the U.S.S.R., $1 million from the U.S., and $10,000 from Japan. Installation of equipment for dismounting the northern face of the Buddhist monument at Borobudur, Indon., was well under way. After studying reports on alternatives, the International Executive Committee recommended adoption of a modified plan to protect the monument from seismic movements. The most important change was to maintain in place those sides of the monument that had not been seriously affected by soil movements and showed promise of continued stability. This would also help keep costs closer to the original estimates. In March 1974 the site was visited by Queen Elizabeth II, and it was announced that the U.K. would contribute almost $150,000 to the project. The U.S. committee reported that it had raised over $1 million, and new contributions and pledges were received from Burma, Ghana, Malaysia, Singapore, Spain, and Thailand.

Plans for safeguarding Venice were hampered by economic and political problems in Italy. An aqueduct was completed that would permit closing the artesian wells that had contributed to the subsidence of the island, and a second aqueduct was authorized, with construction scheduled to begin in the spring of 1975. Plans for a modern sewerage system awaited the release of funds by the government. Regulations on atmospheric pollution had been adopted, but regulations to control the expansion of industry and govern new construction in the outer zone of the city were in abeyance. Many feared that these would not be sufficiently stringent. There was also dissatisfaction with the solution proposed for dealing with high water. It was thought that the only dependable solution—which was also the most costly—was to construct gates to close the major shipping channels leading into the lagoon.

In Pakistan a special authority had been set up to safeguard the Bronze Age site of Mohenjo-daro. Work had begun on two experimental tube wells, and it was expected that detailed cost estimates could be made by early 1975. An intensive fund-raising campaign would then be launched.

The Cuzco-Puno area of Peru provided an example of a restoration program forming part of an overall plan to improve the economy and promote tourism, while at the same time improving the living standards of a largely underprivileged group of inhabitants. With the aid of funds from the UN Development Program, experts were sent by UNESCO to study and work on the restoration of Inca and Spanish colonial monuments in the area. This involved problems of town planning in Cuzco, as well as the need to stabilize the Inca site of Machu Picchu. Cost of the government's overall program for hotel construction, improvement of communications, training, and restoration was estimated at approximately $72 million. The Inter-American Development Bank had agreed to contribute some $29.3 million in loans. It was hoped that the loan and investments could be amortized from future tourist revenues.

European Architectural Heritage Year 1975, launched by the Council of Europe in 1974 under the

The J. P. Morgan mansion in New York City lost its city landmark status in June.

chairmanship of Duncan Sandys, made rapid progress, with many Eastern European states either participating or developing parallel programs. In the U.K. the Civic Trust offered special Heritage Year awards for practical conservation schemes, and similar projects were under way in other countries. The campaign, which was designed to interest national and local authorities in conservation projects, was to reach its climax in Amsterdam in October 1975 (the 700th anniversary of the city's founding) with an exhibition showing the achievements of participating states. Findings accumulated during the campaign were expected to serve as guidelines for future work.

Another project going beyond national boundaries was a series of programs on conservation projects, planned by the Japan Broadcasting Corporation in consultation with UNESCO. The series would demonstrate the similarity of problems in different countries and encourage action on conservation. Foreign-language versions were planned for distribution outside Japan.

National programs were also evolving rapidly. In the U.S. more funds were being made available for conservation, and the "homesteading" scheme, whereby citizens could gain title to dilapidated houses by repairing them and living in them for a minimum period, was gaining in popularity. However, the number of historic buildings being destroyed was still alarming. Many municipal planning regulations, particularly those encouraging high vertical densities, actually encouraged such destruction. With the approach of the bicentennial of the Declaration of Independence in 1976, many towns showed increased interest in the preservation of buildings embodying earlier traditions and architectural styles. In Vermont plans were made to maintain railroad tracks, coaches, and steam locomotives that would otherwise have been scrapped and to use them for special tours.

In the U.K. several new projects took account of changes in industrial practice, notably those involving conversion and preservation of docksides and quays that were inadequate for modern shipping. Old warehouses along the Albert Dock in Liverpool were being converted to provide modern facilities for students at the city's large polytechnic. The cost of the project was below that of new construction. In Hull, an important fishing port, the Princess Dock had been bought by the city council with grant aid from the Department of the Environment, and plans were under way to convert it into a marina with an adjacent maritime museum. The Glasgow city authorities promoted a study of the River Clyde and a competition for ideas to develop over 200 ac. of land and water within the city. Winning entries featured parks, convention facilities, and marinas as well as housing.

On several occasions, France's Pres. Valéry Giscard d'Estaing used his power of veto in favour of conservation. He vetoed a plan approved by the Paris municipal authorities for an expressway along the city's historic Left Bank directly opposite the Île de la Cité and the cathedral of Notre Dame. He also vetoed development plans for the historic Cité Fleurie in the 19th arrondissement, where tenants had resisted attempts to demolish the historic artists' studios built with materials salvaged from the 1878 Paris Exhibition. With the preservation of the Cité assured, a campaign was launched to raise funds to purchase the land from the developers.

The French president's most important conservation decision, however, related to the area once occupied by the historic pavilions of Les Halles, the old central food market. Plans approved by his predecessor, Pres. Georges Pompidou, for a major international trade centre with convention hall and underground shopping centre were vetoed as inappropriate to the surroundings, which included the historic church of St. Eustache. The only surface construction in the original plan to escape the veto was a new building for a museum of modern art. For the rest of the site, President Giscard requested that a design for a park be submitted by October.

In October the French secretary of state for culture announced plans for preserving 19th- and 20th-century architectural features in 100 towns. The Luxembourg government decided to adopt the recommendations of UNESCO experts to safeguard the historic abbey and gardens of Echternach from being divided by the major highway leading into the city from West Germany. A costly tunnel underneath the gardens would not only ease the flow of traffic but also permit the realization of another of the experts' suggestions—the closing of the historic city to motor traffic.

In Senegal UNESCO recommendations for tourist development of the island of Gorée included restoration of the historic fortress guarding the entrance to the port of Dakar and its old slave barracks. The recommendations also provided for a limited scheme to ensure that beach facilities remained for Dakar's expanding population. Another project concerned the restoration of the island of St.-Louis, which had de-

clined in importance with the expansion of Dakar. It was suggested that the interesting old brick houses with their wrought iron balconies be restored and adapted to modern standards.   (HIROSHI DAIFUKU)

See also Architecture; Museums.

[612.C.2.d]

Hockey

Ice Hockey. *North American.* An outstanding event of 1974 in professional ice hockey was a series matching an all-star team from the World Hockey Association (WHA) with a team from the Soviet Union. The Soviets won the rancorous eight-game tournament with four wins, one loss, and three ties. The first four games were played in the Canadian cities of Quebec, Toronto, Winnipeg, and Vancouver, and the last four in Moscow. About 2,700 fans followed the WHA squad on its trip to Moscow. In the fall of 1972 a National Hockey League (NHL) all-star team narrowly beat the Soviets in a similar series with four wins, three losses, and one tie.

Competition for talent between the WHA and NHL sent scouts from both leagues scurrying to Europe for players. Soviet players were not permitted to go to another country, but the North Americans raided the national teams of Sweden, Finland, and Czechoslovakia. The Toronto Maple Leafs of the NHL recruited Borje Salming, one of Sweden's leading defensemen. In his rookie NHL season, Salming ranked among the four or five best rear guards. The Toronto Toros of the WHA encouraged two impressive players, Vaclav Nedomansky and Richard Farda, to defect from the Czechoslovak national team, and the Winnipeg Jets of the WHA began the 1974–75 season with four Swedes and two Finns in their lineup.

The Philadelphia Flyers won the Stanley Cup to become the first so-called expansion team to capture

Table I. NHL Final Standings, 1973/74

	Won	Lost	Tied	Goals	Goals against	Pts.
EAST DIVISION						
Boston Bruins	52	17	9	349	221	113
Montreal Canadiens	45	24	9	293	240	99
New York Rangers	40	24	14	300	251	94
Toronto Maple Leafs	35	27	16	274	230	86
Buffalo Sabres	32	34	12	242	250	76
Detroit Red Wings	29	39	10	255	319	68
Vancouver Canucks	24	43	11	224	296	59
New York Islanders	19	41	18	182	247	56
WEST DIVISION						
Philadelphia Flyers	50	16	12	273	164	112
Chicago Black Hawks	41	14	23	272	164	105
Los Angeles Kings	33	33	12	233	231	78
Atlanta Flames	30	34	14	214	238	74
Pittsburgh Penguins	28	41	9	242	273	65
St. Louis Blues	26	40	12	206	248	64
Minnesota North Stars	23	38	17	235	275	63
California Seals	13	55	10	195	342	36

Table II. WHA Final Standings, 1973/74

	Won	Lost	Tied	Goals	Goals against	Pts.
EAST DIVISION						
New England Whalers	43	31	4	291	260	90
Toronto Toros	41	33	4	304	272	86
Cleveland Crusaders	37	32	9	266	264	83
Chicago Cougars	38	35	5	271	273	81
Quebec Nordiques	38	36	4	306	280	80
New Jersey Knights	32	42	4	268	313	68
WEST DIVISION						
Houston Aeros	48	25	5	318	219	101
Minnesota Fighting Saints	44	32	2	332	275	90
Edmonton Oilers	38	37	3	268	269	79
Winnipeg Jets	34	39	5	264	296	73
Vancouver Blazers	27	50	1	278	345	55
Los Angeles Sharks	25	53	0	239	339	50

Table III. World Amateur Ice Hockey Championships

GROUP A	Won	Lost	Tied	Goals	Goals against	Pts.
U.S.S.R.	9	1	0	64	18	18
Czechoslovakia	7	3	0	57	19	14
Sweden	5	4	1	38	34	11
Finland	4	4	2	34	39	10
Poland	1	7	2	22	64	4
East Germany	1	8	1	21	71	3

Philadelphia goalie blocks Boston shot in Stanley Cup action.

the major team prize in the NHL. The Flyers, led by combative Bobby Clarke at centre and stingy Bernie Parent in the goal, beat the Boston Bruins four games to two in the final round. Philadelphia had been added to the NHL in 1967.

The Kansas City Scouts and the Washington Capitals joined the NHL in 1974, increasing the league's membership to 18 and causing a radical rearrangement of the divisions. The former East and West alignment was broken up into four divisions: the Lester Patrick, the Conn Smythe, the James Norris, and the Charles F. Adams.

Massive realignment also occurred in the WHA. The addition of the Indianapolis Racers and Phoenix Roadrunners boosted league membership from 12 teams to 14. The WHA regrouped in three divisions, the Eastern, Western, and Canadian. WHA franchises continued to fold in one community and resurface elsewhere. The New Jersey Knights abandoned Cherry Hill, N.J., to become the San Diego Mariners, and the Los Angeles Sharks left California to be re-incarnated in Detroit as the Michigan Stags.

The Houston Aeros won the Avco Cup, representative of the WHA championship, defeating the Chicago Cougars in the final series four games to none. Gordie Howe, a distinguished right wing for 25 years in the NHL, was a Houston star at the age of 46. Howe came out of retirement to play with his two sons, 19-year-old Mark and 20-year-old Marty.

The Hershey Bears defeated the Providence Reds four games to one in the championship series in the American League. In their last season in the Western League, the Phoenix Roadrunners beat the Portland Buckaroos four games to one for the title in that conference. The Dallas Black Hawks made the 4–1 margin unanimous at the minor league professional level, defeating the Oklahoma City Blazers by that result in the Central Pro final.   (R. H. BEDDOES)

European and International. Ice hockey at amateur and professional levels in Europe was stimulated in the 1973–74 season by the formation and example of the London Lions, a strong professional club based at Wembley, Eng., financed by the owners of the Detroit Red Wings, and staffed by highly rated Canadian, U.S., and Swedish players. Their 71 matches in nine countries—they won 53, lost 12, and tied 6—inspired the International Ice Hockey Federation (IIHF) to create a European League, to start in 1974–75, with the expectation that the continent's leading clubs would enter and amateurs be permitted to compete with professionals.

The 41st world amateur championships were contested by 22 nations during March and April. The six leading teams competed for the title in Group A at Helsinki, Fin., each playing the other twice. After an unimpressive start the U.S.S.R. retained the title, its 11th victory in 12 years. Its early 7–2 defeat by Czechoslovakia (runner-up) looked decisive, but the Soviet players recovered well in their other matches and all hinged on the second encounter between these arch-rivals; in this, although Jiri Holik opened the scoring for the Czechoslovakians, the tide soon flowed relentlessly the other way and the Soviets won 3–1. Sweden (third) and Finland (fourth) each had a match result reversed for fielding a player who failed to pass a drug test; one of these reversed results kept Poland above the bottom team, East Germany, which was relegated to Group B. The three outstanding players of the tournament were Vladislav Tretyak, Soviet goalkeeper, Lars-Erik Sjöberg, Swedish defenseman, and Vaclav Nedomansky, veteran Czechoslovakian forward.

The U.S., leader of the eight teams in Group B, at Ljubljana, Yugos., moved up to Group A after winning all its seven games. The order after the U.S. was Yugoslavia, West Germany, Japan, The Netherlands, Romania, Norway, and Austria, the last two being relegated to Group C. Switzerland and Italy gained promotion to Group B by finishing first and second, respectively, in Group C, played at Grenoble, France. Bulgaria finished third, followed by Hungary, France, China, Australia, and North Korea. Canada, winner of the world title most times, stayed out for a fifth successive year and seemed likely to remain on the sidelines until the championship should be declared open to professionals.

Djurgården of Sweden won the international club competition for the Ahearne Cup. Moscow Dynamo was runner-up.   (HOWARD BASS)

Field Hockey. In 1974 The Netherlands added the first women's World Cup to the men's World Cup, which it had won the previous September; Spain won the men's European Cup, defeating both The Netherlands and West Germany; Frankfurt 1880 took the European Club Cup for the fourth year in succession; Pakistan defeated India in the final of the Asian Games, winning the replay (2–0) that followed a 1–1 draw. Although the two world titles were held in Europe, the victory of Pakistan in a seven-nation international tournament at Christchurch, N.Z., from a field that included the world champions was a sign that the Asians, former world leaders, were still a force to be reckoned with.

The women's World Cup, the first world championship for women, was held in France at Mandelieu under the auspices of the International Hockey Federation (FIH). Because of absentee countries the field was not fully representative, but competition was

U.S. shot on goal in world ice hockey play. The Americans beat Austria 6–0 in this match to score their fifth straight victory.

keen among the ten competing nations, the semifinals and final all being decided by scores of 1–0. In the final, The Netherlands did not score its goal against Argentina until very near the end of extra time. The small number of contestants in the tournament was a reminder of the rift between the FIH, the international controlling authority of men's hockey, and the International Federation of Women's Hockey Associations, to which 36 national associations and women's sections of national associations were affiliated. The rift centred on the organization of international women's hockey tournaments.

The FIH celebrated its 50th anniversary with a match between representative European and Asian teams in Brussels. The weather was unfriendly, the field very wet, and the result a 0–0 tie.

Spain's victory in the European Cup in Madrid ranked as that nation's best performance ever in international competition, though it had been runner-up to Pakistan in the first World Cup tournament at Barcelona in 1971. This time, in Madrid, the Spaniards defeated The Netherlands, the world champions, 1–0 in the semifinals and West Germany, the Olympic champions, by the same score in the final.

In the series between the four home countries, Wales had the best record of the four, defeating England, Ireland, and Scotland in the same season for the first time. England defeated Ireland but lost to Scotland and Wales. The championship of the four, however, remained incomplete because the game between Ireland and Scotland was canceled. The England women's team had a mixed season, losing to New Zealand and The Netherlands, beating Scotland and Wales, and drawing with Ireland and the U.S.

A branch of hockey achieving widespread growth and popularity was the indoor game, pioneered by West Germany and since practiced increasingly in most European countries. The first European Indoor Championship took place in 1974 with the following result: (1) West Germany; (2) The Netherlands; (3) Switzerland; (4) Belgium; (5) Scotland; (6) Austria.

After years of patient preparation, the International Hockey Rules Board (men) and the Women's International Hockey Rules Board finally agreed on a common code of rules to come into force at the start of the 1974–75 season.   (R. L. HOLLANDS)

Hogs:
see Agriculture and Food Supplies
Holland:
see Netherlands, The

[452.B.4.h.xvi]

Honduras

A republic of Central America, Honduras is bounded by Nicaragua, El Salvador, Guatemala, the Caribbean Sea, and the Pacific Ocean. Area: 43,277 sq.mi. (112,088 sq.km.). Pop. (1974 est.): 2,653,857, including 90% mestizo. Cap. and largest city: Tegucigalpa (pop., 1974, 303,879). Language: Spanish; some Indian dialects. Religion: Roman Catholic. President in 1974, Gen. Oswaldo López Arellano.

Honduras' most devastating natural calamity in the 20th century occurred Sept. 19 and 20, 1974, when Hurricane Fifi struck the north coast, killing at least 5,000 persons, damaging or destroying 182 communities through flooding and landslides, and leaving more than 150,000 homeless and many on the verge of starvation. The valleys drained by the Aguán, León, and Ulúa rivers were hardest hit. One town, Choloma, lost 2,800 inhabitants when they were buried by an avalanche of debris that left the community under 12 ft. of mud. Disaster aid was rapidly forthcoming from the International Red Cross and through private efforts in the Americas and Europe, but poor roads, inadequate organization, and fuel shortages in Honduras slowed the assistance efforts.

Damage to the economy was severe. Some 60% of the banana crop, the nation's leading source of export

HONDURAS

Education. (1972) Primary, pupils 412,050, teachers 11,354; secondary (1970), pupils 28,949; vocational (1970), pupils 7,089; teacher training (1970), students 3,801; secondary, vocational, and teacher training, teachers (1968) 2,689; higher (1973), students 9,204, teaching staff 533.

Finance. Monetary unit: lempira, with (Sept. 16, 1974) a par value of 2 lempiras to U.S. $1 (free rate of 4.63 lempiras = £1 sterling). Gold, SDRs, and foreign exchange, central bank: (June 1974) U.S. $34,-030,000; (June 1973) U.S. $44,860,000. Budget (1974 est.) balanced at 329 million lempiras. Gross national product: (1972) 1,576,000,000 lempiras; (1971) 1,467,000,000 lempiras. Money supply: (May 1974) 240,910,000 lempiras; (May 1973) 218.5 million lempiras. Cost of living (Tegucigalpa; 1970 = 100): (June 1974) 128; (June 1973) 114.

Foreign Trade. (1973) Imports 524.6 million lempiras; exports 473.5 million lempiras. Import sources (1972): U.S. 45%; Venezuela 8%; Japan 8%; Guatemala 5%. Export destinations (1972): U.S. 51%; West Germany 14%; Canada 9%. Main exports: bananas 34%; coffee 20%; timber 17%.

Transport and Communications. Roads (1972) c. 5,700 km. (including 153 km. of Pan-American Highway). Motor vehicles in use (1971): passenger 13,800; commercial (including buses) 16,900. Railways (1972) 1,059 km. (mainly for banana plantations). Air traffic (1972): 174.5 million passenger-km.; freight 3.2 million net ton-km. Shipping (1973): merchant vessels 100 gross tons and over 57; gross tonnage 67,274. Telephones (Jan. 1973) 16,000. Radio receivers (Dec. 1972) 150,000. Television receivers (Dec. 1971) 25,000.

Agriculture. Production (in 000; metric tons; 1973; 1972 in parentheses): corn c. 360 (c. 290); coffee c. 42 (c. 47); sorghum c. 42 (c. 40); sugar, raw value c. 90 (96); dry beans c. 58 (c. 32); bananas (1972) c. 1,366, (1971) c. 1,500; oranges (1972) c. 52, (1971) c. 50; cotton, lint (1972) c. 5, (1971) c. 2; beef and veal c. 43 (c. 41); timber (cu.m.; 1972) 4,-400, (1971) 4,300. Livestock (in 000; 1972–73): cattle c. 1,628; pigs c. 740; chickens (1971–72) c. 7,300.

Industry. Production (in 000; metric tons; 1972): petroleum products 599; silver 0.11; gold (troy oz.; 1970) 2.5; lead ore (metal content; 1971) 16; zinc ore (metal content; 1971) 20.8; electricity (excluding most industrial production; kw-hr.) 333,000.

Devastating effect
of September's hurricane
in Central America
included inland scenes
such as this in Honduras.
The buildings of this
town were either destroyed
or buried in mud
by the floodwaters.

revenue, and 40% of the cattle were lost. More than half of the rice and corn, both staple items in the Honduran diet, also were destroyed. The effect of Fifi on the economy would be felt into 1975, when exports were expected to decline by at least 23% and imports to rise by 10%.

The blow fell on an already troubled economy that had never completely recovered from the effects of the war with El Salvador in 1969. That dispute remained unresolved, despite continuing efforts to restore diplomatic relations and reopen the border shared by the two nations. Until Honduras and El Salvador resolved their differences, the strength of the Central American Common Market, from which Honduras withdrew in 1971, remained diluted.

In January President López announced a 15-year national development plan calling for cooperative agricultural communities to replace very large and very small landholdings, government support for collective bargaining, a minimum wage scale, gradual nationalization of the nation's forest resources (the most extensive in Central America), and an end to lucrative mining concessions to foreign companies. Investment in new industries, with carefully controlled government incentives, was an additional feature.

The national development plan was highly popular among peasants and industrial workers. Landowners and some businesses had an opposite reaction, and there was even a threat on President López' life. The agrarian reform segment of the plan, though drastic by Central American standards, was mild. There was no proposal to expropriate holdings above a certain size; only idle or badly farmed land would be appropriated and redistributed, and the owners would be compensated with 20- to 30-year bonds.

As the third largest exporter of bananas in the Western Hemisphere (after Ecuador and Costa Rica), Honduras joined a new union of banana-exporting nations. In March the union decided to impose an export tax of up to $1 per 40-lb. crate on the producing companies. The companies retaliated, and though Honduras imposed only a 50 cent crate charge on April 25, the Standard Fruit and Steamship Co. halted exports, cut production, and destroyed crates of bananas. In May the company did resume exports, but at one-third of normal output and with the exports going to new markets where the tax did not apply. (*See* PANAMA.)   (ALLEN D. BUSHONG)
[974.B.1.b]

Horse Racing

Thoroughbred Racing. *United States.* The exploits of Ruffian, Foolish Pleasure, Forego, and Chris Evert highlighted the U.S. Thoroughbred racing season in 1974. Ruffian, a two-year-old filly, and Foolish Pleasure, a two-year-old colt, were undefeated. Forego, a four-year-old gelding, competed in 13 consecutive stakes and won eight of them. Chris Evert dominated the three-year-old filly division.

Locust Hill Farm's Ruffian, larger than 16 hands and daughter of `Reviewer-Shenanigans, by Native Dancer, generated tremendous excitement with her sheer speed. She won by 15 lengths in her debut at Belmont Park late in May, equaling the 5½-furlong track record of 1 min. 3 sec. The Kentucky-bred filly won the Fashion Stakes in identical time and then swept to victory in three other stakes—the Astoria, Sorority, and Spinaway—before a hairline fracture of a phalanx bone in the right hind ankle sidelined her early in October after she had earned $134,073.

Only one more race, the Selima Stakes at Laurel, had been under consideration for Ruffian, although many horsemen had been prodding trainer Frank Y. Whiteley, Jr., to start her against colts. Whiteley responded that he might do so in 1975.

Ruffian won her five races by an average margin of more than nine lengths and usually without being unduly urged. In the Spinaway, her final start, she ran the fastest six furlongs (1 min. 8⅗ sec.) ever recorded by a two-year-old at Saratoga.

Honduras, British:
see Dependent States

Hong Kong:
see Dependent States

John L. Greer's Foolish Pleasure (What A Pleasure–Fool-Me-Not, by Tom Fool) launched his career with a victory at Hialeah early in April. He then won six consecutive stakes, including the season-ending one-mile Champagne at Belmont Park in which his winning margin was six lengths. Foolish Pleasure also annexed the Dover, Tremont, Sapling, Hopeful, and Cowdin stakes while competing at six race tracks. Completely dominating his division, he was at his best at the end of his campaign. A Florida-bred colt, Foolish Pleasure amassed earnings of $284,595.

Lazy F Ranch's Forego, which in time might be ranked with or above such predecessor geldings as Exterminator, Armed, and Kelso, was as versatile as he was huge. Carrying high weights all season, he won at distances varying from seven furlongs to two miles. Even in defeat he was not disgraced. The Kentucky-bred son of Forli–Lady Golconda, by Hasty Road, outranked only by Secretariat during his three-year season in 1973, started 1974 by defeating persistent rival True Knight three consecutive times in Florida, in the Donn, Gulfstream Park, and Widener handicaps. Forego was then sent north by trainer Sherrill Ward and competed solely on New York tracks the remainder of the year.

Forego won his first start in New York, the seven-furlong Carter Handicap, and he was first in the Brooklyn Handicap at $1\frac{1}{8}$ mi. three races later. He suffered three defeats and then finished the season by winning the $1\frac{1}{2}$-mi. Woodward, the seven-furlong Vosburgh, and the 2-mi. Jockey Club Gold Cup to account for 1974 earnings of $545,086.

Carl Rosen's Chris Evert (Swoon's Son–Miss Carmie, by T. V. Lark) won four races while starting only seven times, all in stakes, but her average earning per start was more than $75,000. The major reason for the high average was her victory over Miss Musket in a $350,000 winner-take-all match race at Hollywood Park in July. Chris Evert, a slight underdog, took the lead at the break and then gradually pulled away to a 50-length decision over her floundering rival, negotiating the $1\frac{1}{4}$ mi. in 2 min. 2 sec.

Chris Evert earlier had won the Triple Crown for her division, taking one half of the split Acorn Stakes, and the Mother Goose and Coaching Club American Oaks. She was defeated narrowly by Quaze Quilt in the Alabama at Saratoga early in August, and a week later she completed her season by racing against colts in the Travers and finishing a respectable third to Holding Pattern and Little Current.

Ruffian, Foolish Pleasure, Forego, and Chris Evert were crowned champions in their respective divisions in the coordinated poll conducted by the *Daily Racing Form*, National Turf Writers Association, and the Thoroughbred Racing Association. Forego won the ultimate honour as horse of the year and also was named the best sprinter.

Other award winners were: Darby Dan Farm's homebred Kentucky colt Little Current in the three-year-old colt or gelding division; H. T. Mangurian, Jr.'s Florida-bred Desert Vixen, older filly or mare; N. B. Hunt's homebred Kentucky filly, the four-year-old Dahlia, grass horse; and Mrs. F. A. Clark's eight-year-old Chilean-bred Gran Kan, steeplechaser or hurdler.

Laffit Pincay, Jr., was voted champion jockey for the second consecutive year, while other honours were won by apprentice jockey Chris McCarron, trainer Sherrill Ward, and owner Dan Lasater, whose horses earned the most money for the second consecutive season. The 19-year-old McCarron, who had never ridden in a horse race until January 29, rode 547 winners in 1974, a new one-year record.

There were several contenders in the three-year-old division, and Little Current gained the title chiefly through seven-length triumphs in the Preakness and Belmont Stakes. Cannonade scored in the Kentucky Derby, a trouble-racked race that drew a record 23 starters. Other prominent three-year-olds were Agitate, Holding Pattern, and Stonewalk. Little Current was retired late in summer after suffering a leg injury.

Desert Vixen, champion three-year-old filly of 1973, was slow to reach her best form. Her most important victories came in the Beldame and Matchmaker. Making her first start on turf, she lost narrowly to Admetus in the Washington (D.C.) International after setting the pace.

Dahlia, a 3–5 favourite, finished third in the International after winning two other turf classics, the Man o' War and the Canadian International Championship Stakes. These were Dahlia's only races in the U.S. after winning three of seven starts in the U.K. and France. (JOSEPH C. AGRELLA)

Canada. In a 1974 racing season replete with outstanding performances, some of the brightest stars emerged from the two-year-old division. J.-L. Levesque's homebred L'Enjoleur, a son of champions Buckpasser and Fanfreluche, won six stakes in Canada and the prestigious Laurel Futurity in the U.S. to establish himself as one of the best juvenile runners in Canadian history. At sprint distances, however, W. P. Gilbride's Greek Answer was almost invincible. The colt's blazing speed carried him to victory in three Canadian stakes and in the rich Arlington-Washington Futurity at Chicago. Stafford Farm's Royal Selari won two stakes in a brief but impressive spring campaign that marked him as a top prospect for the Canadian three-year-old classics in 1975. In Western Canada, Elmbrook Stable's Western Dangler established all-time Alberta records for two-year-olds, winning five consecutive stakes.

Outstanding among a fine crop of two-year-old fillies was Jim Dandy Stable's Ruthie's Run, by Outing Class. Slow to develop, she recorded four straight victories in the month of September, three of them in major stakes events.

For the second consecutive year, the classic Queen's

Miguel Rivera boots home Little Current to win the Belmont Stakes by seven lengths.

UPI COMPIX

Plate for three-year-olds was won by a Stafford Farm colour-bearer. Amber Herod splashed through a sloppy track to victory in the 115th edition of the Plate, which carried a record purse of $148,525. Amber Herod won three stakes over the season but had several strong rivals for divisional honours. A. Minshall's western-bred Rushton's Corsair finished third in the Queen's Plate but won the next leg of the Canadian Triple Crown, the Prince of Wales Stakes at Fort Erie, and also captured top money in the rich Manitoba Derby at Winnipeg's Assiniboia Downs. The final Triple Crown event, the Breeders' Stakes at Woodbine, went to Gardiner Farm's Haymaker's Jig, a late-blooming son of Bolero. Jack Diamond's homebred Battling Craig compiled an outstanding stakes-winning record in western Canada and the United States, but in the British Columbia Derby at his home track, Vancouver's Exhibition Park, he was upset by an Eastern invader, Kinghaven Farm's Norland. Norland also won the Quebec Derby. Other contenders for the national three-year-old championship included G. C. Hendrie's Native Aid, the Queen's Plate runner-up and winner of two other stakes, and the TV Stable's Canadian Derby winner, Progressive Hope.

In the latter part of the season, T. A. Morton's Lost Majorette rose to prominence among three-year-old fillies with two major stakes victories and also defeated many of the top three-year-old males. Earlier, D. Banks's Trudie Tudor, a Canadian champion at two in 1973, won four stakes events for fillies, including the prestigious Canadian Oaks at Woodbine.

In the handicap division, Gardiner Farm had two leading performers, U.S.-bred Carney's Point, winner of two major turf events, and homebred Henry Tudor, winner of four stakes prizes in Canada and another in the U.S. Sam-Son Farm's U.S.-bred Selari Spirit used front-running tactics to capture four added-money distance events, and veteran homebred Fabe Count was a multiple stakes winner again for the Parkview Stable.

The $125,000 added Canadian International Championship, a triumphant finale to the great Secretariat's career in 1973, was a showcase for champions again in 1974. The smashing winner of the one-mile-and-five-furlong turf event at Woodbine was Nelson Bunker Hunt's magnificent four-year-old filly Dahlia. In adding the Championship to her record of major victories on both sides of the Atlantic, Dahlia defeated Windfields Farm's Snow Knight, 1974 winner of the historic English Derby at Epsom, and other leading turf performers from France, West Germany, Chile, the United States, and Canada.

(ERIC A. ASTROM)

Europe and Australia. The undisputed hero of the 1973–74 National Hunt racing season in Britain was N. Le Mare's nine-year-old gelding, Red Rum. Trained by D. McCain and ridden by Brian Fletcher, he won the Grand National Steeplechase for the second year in succession, carrying the maximum weight of 168 lb.—23 lb. more than he carried in 1973—and beating L'Escargot by seven lengths. Three weeks later he won the Scottish Grand National from Proud Tarquin and became the only horse to win both races in the same season. At Cheltenham the Champion Hurdle was won by Lanzarote from Comedy of Errors; Pendil, the favourite, was brought down in the Gold Cup Steeplechase, which was won by the Irish horse Captain Christy from the previous year's winner, The Dikler. The Hennessy Gold Cup Steeplechase at New-

Captain Christy clears the last fence to win the Cheltenham Gold Cup.

bury was won by Red Candle by a length from Red Rum, and the Whitbread Gold Cup Steeplechase by The Dikler. Proud Tarquin finished first in the Whitbread, but an objection against him for hampering The Dikler was sustained. R. Barry was National Hunt champion jockey. At the end of 1974 a scandal broke in France over the fixing of a 1973 hurdle race at Auteuil, carrying the large *tiercé* betting pool, by a number of jockeys in the race who, it was alleged, had been bribed or intimidated by a racing mafia. Some arrests were made.

On the flat in 1974, as in 1973, the fillies were distinctly better than the colts. Daniel Wildenstein's Allez France and Nelson Bunker Hunt's Dahlia, both four-year-olds trained and principally raced in France, were outstanding, the former superior to any other horse in Europe. Trained by Argentine-born Angel Penna and ridden by Y. Saint-Martin, Allez France won Europe's richest race, the Prix de l'Arc de Triomphe at Longchamp, from Comtesse de Loir; her other 1974 victories included the Prix Ganay, from Tennyson, and the Prix d'Harcourt. In three seasons Allez France won more than $1 million in stakes, a European record. Trained by M. Zilber, Dahlia, though always defeated by Allez France, was her nearest rival. She won the Grand Prix de Saint-Cloud from On My Way and, ridden by L. Piggott, won the King George VI and Queen Elizabeth Stakes at Ascot from Highclere (becoming the first horse to win the race twice since its inception in 1951). Dahlia also won the Benson and Hedges Gold Cup at York, and later went to the U.S., where she won the Man o' War Stakes, and to Canada, where she won the Canadian International Championship Stakes in record time. Her season's earnings of $1,206,705 surpassed those of Allez France.

In England, Queen Elizabeth II's filly Highclere, trained by W. Hern and ridden by J. Mercer, won the One Thousand Guineas from Polygamy and later traveled to France to win the Prix de Diane (Oaks). Polygamy won the Oaks from Furioso, a race in which Dibidale's saddle unfortunately slipped under her just as she was making her challenge. Dibidale went on to win the Irish Oaks easily; then, after winning the Yorkshire Oaks, she jarred herself while training for the Arc de Triomphe and had to be retired. The French colt Nonoalco won the Two Thousand Guineas in style; Snow Knight, trained by P. Nelson and ridden by B. Taylor, won a disappointing Derby (from Imperial Prince) and nothing else of importance. Bustino won the St. Leger for Lady Beaverbrook. Surprise of the classic season was the failure of Irish trainer Vincent O'Brien's Apalachee and Cellini, who had both been brilliant as two-year-olds. Giacometti also disappointed his trainer, H. Price, but was nevertheless second in the Two Thousand Guineas, third in the Derby, second in the St. Leger, and won the Champion Stakes.

The French equivalents of the Two Thousand and One Thousand Guineas were won by Moulines from Mississipian and by Dumka from Hippodamia, respectively; the French Derby went to the outsider Caracolero, who beat the favourite, Marcel Boussac's Dankaro, winner of the Prix Lupin and the Prix Greffulhe; and the Prix Royal Oak (St. Leger) was won by Busiris. Récupéré won the Prix du Cadran, the French equivalent of the Ascot Gold Cup, from Lassalle, the previous year's winner. Sagaro won the Grand Prix de Paris from Bustino, and the Prix Vermeille went to Paulista, from Comtesse de Loir. The Irish Two Thousand and One Thousand Guineas were won by Furry Glen from Pitcairn and Gaily (trained by Hern) from Northern Gem; English Prince won the Irish Derby from Imperial Prince, and Mistigri the Irish St. Leger from Richard Grenville. Wohlgemuth won the Italian Derby, but the French colt Ribecourt won the Gran Premio d'Italia from Wohlgemuth. Marduk won the German Derby and St. Leger.

The duke of Norfolk's three-year-old Ragstone won the Ascot Gold Cup from Proverb and Lassalle (the 1973 winner), but Proverb went on to win the Goodwood Cup and the Doncaster Cup. Buoy won the Yorkshire Cup, the Coronation Cup, from Dahlia, at Epsom, and the Princess of Wales's Stakes at Newmarket and was then sent to Australia. Boldboy won the Lockinge Stakes, Coup de Feu the Eclipse Stakes, and Ace of Aces the Sussex Stakes. Among the sprinters, Blue Cashmere beat Rapid River and Saritamer in a fine race for the Nunthorpe Stakes. Saritamer won the Cork and Orrery Stakes at Royal Ascot, the Newmarket July Cup, and Ascot's Diadem Stakes.

Leading two-year-old colts in England were Grundy (Champagne Stakes); R. Tikkoo's Irish colt Steel Heart (Gimcrack Stakes, Middle Park Stakes, and Dewhurst Stakes), whose Irish trainer, D. Weld, was making a name for himself; Red Cross; and Auction Ring. Among the fillies Cry of Truth (Lowther Stakes and Cheveley Park Stakes) was the best, and Highest Trump and Roussalka ran well. In France the Prix Morny and the Prix Robert Papin were won by Broadway Dancer and Sky Commander, respectively; the Grand Criterium was won by Dandy Lute.

P. Eddery was champion jockey in England. Women jockeys competed for the first time against male amateurs, with success. The trainers P. Walwyn (96 races won and £206,783 in stakes) and Hern (53 races won in England and £201,850 in stakes, with four classics in England, France, and Ireland) had their best seasons. Not unexpectedly, bloodstock sales at Newmarket slumped badly from the levels of previous years.

In Australia the six-year-old New Zealand horse Battle Heights won the 2-mi. Sydney Cup from Grand Scale and Dayana. The Melbourne Cup was won by Think Big from Leilani and Captain Peri.

(R. M. GOODWIN)

Harness Racing. In a year of worldwide feminine liberation two superior females, the five-year-old trotting mare Delmonica Hanover and three-year-old pacing filly Handle With Care, humbled male opposition and scored the major triumphs of North American harness racing in 1974.

Delmonica Hanover, owned by W. Arnold Hanger and Delvin Miller and trained by Miller, defeated Europe's best trotting horses with a spectacular stretch rush in the grueling 2,600-m. Prix d'Amérique at Vincennes in Paris in late January. She then returned to win the $200,000 Roosevelt International at $1\frac{1}{4}$ mi. for the second straight year at Roosevelt Raceway in New York in July, was sold at auction for a record $300,000 in mid-November, and capped her most successful season by receiving harness horse of the year honours from the U.S. Trotting Association and the U.S. Harness Writers' Association. Delmonica Hanover ended the year with lifetime earnings of $709,799, making her the richest harness horse currently racing.

Though it is not unusual for a mare to hold supremacy among trotters, females almost never are dominant in pacing, and for a three-year-old filly to defeat the best older male pacers in the sport is a racing rarity. Handle With Care, which had won 17 races against fillies without defeat as a two-year-old, stretched that unbeaten skein to 24 before losing to arch-rival Joanna's Time but then resumed winning ways and concluded her season by winning the $59,165 Western Pace at Hollywood Park in California in world record time. Her mile in 1 min. 54$\frac{4}{5}$ sec. was the fastest ever by a filly or mare, and only one-fifth of a second slower than the world race record set by Albatross when that champion was a four-year-old. Handle With Care also paced the third fastest mile in history by a Standardbred, a 1 min. 54$\frac{2}{5}$ sec. at Lexington, Ky., in a time trial in October. She finished the season with 19 victories in 24 starts and seasonal earnings of $226,274.

Handle With Care was trained and driven in most of her races by 51-year-old Bill Haughton, the world's leading money-winning harness race driver, but Haughton's 20-year-old son, Peter, was in the sulky when the filly established her world mark in California. Young Haughton also won the $113,350 American Pacing Classic at Hollywood Park with Keystone Smartie for his third $100,000 race, a feat never before accomplished by a driver of his age. Earlier in the season, he had won the $150,000 Prix d'Été at Blue Bonnets Raceway in Montreal with the three-year-old pacer Armbro Omaha and later won the $117,095 Colonial Trot at Liberty Bell Park in Philadelphia with the three-year-old colt Keystone Gabriel.

While young Haughton was winning that trio of $100,000 events, his father was driving the winners of five others, an unprecedented accomplishment for one driver and for a stable. The elder Haughton drove Christopher T. to victory in the $160,150 Hambletonian, harness racing's premier event for three-year-old trotters, and also won the $104,350 Adios, $132,630 Little Brown Jug, $151,043 Messenger, and $100,000 Shapiro, all with Armbro Omaha. Owned by J. Elgin Armstrong, Armbro Omaha was voted three-year-old pacer of the year and was the richest Standardbred money-winner of 1974 with $336,644 in earnings.

Although Christopher T. won the Hambletonian, giving Bill Haughton his first victory in that classic, the colt did not emerge as the three-year-old trotting champion. That honour went to Dream of Glory, a colt that had not been nominated for most of the important stakes races in the three-year-old division. Without him, wide-open competition flourished. Surge Hanover won the $112,380 Dexter Cup at Roosevelt Raceway; Buckeye Count the $63,665 Vernon Downs Gold Cup; Golden Sovereign the $34,018 Review Futurity in Springfield, Ill.; Anvil the $51,855 Horseman Futurity in Indianapolis; Spitfire Hanover the $125,822 Yonkers Trot; and Waymaker the $100,000 Kentucky Futurity (Nevele Diamond and Dancing Party also won miles in that four-heat battle). When Dream of Glory raced he usually won, and his victories included the $31,716 Old Oaken Bucket at Delaware, O., and the $50,000 Leland Stanford and $51,700 Pacific Trot at Hollywood Park.

The two-year-old pacing division produced four champions of exceptional class, two colts and two fillies. The colts, the two fastest in the history of the sport, were Alert Bret and Nero. Nero was unbeaten in his first 11 races and had defeated Alert Bret three times before their meeting in the $53,790 International Stallion Stake at Lexington, Ky., in October. The race produced the fastest mile in history by a two-year-old, 1 min. $55\frac{4}{5}$ sec., with Alert Bret outbattling Nero in a memorable final quarter-mile stretch duel. The standout pacing fillies were Silk Stockings and Tarport Hap. Tarport Hap won more races (20 of 26) and more money ($150,051, a record for a two-year-old pacing filly) than Silk Stockings, but the latter had a faster time for the mile, 1 min. $58\frac{2}{5}$ sec. to 1 min. $58\frac{4}{5}$ sec. for Tarport Hap.

Bonefish was voted best two-year-old trotting colt of the year, with Meadow Bright earning that honour among fillies after Edith Lobell, dominant late in the season, broke a bone and was forced into retirement. Exclusive Way and San Juan had shown the best form among the trotting fillies earlier in the year.

Colonial Charm, a four-year-old trotting mare from Castleton Farm, set a new world record of 1 min. $56\frac{1}{5}$ sec. at Lexington, Ky., fastest trotting mile ever by a filly or mare, and Savoir won the $108,000 American Trotting Classic in California to push his career bankroll to $688,806, best among older trotting horses.

Pacer of the year was Armbro Nesbit, which won 16 races (11 of them 1-mi. victories in two minutes or faster) and $312,279 for owner Duncan MacDonald and trainer-driver Joe O'Brien. The horse was retired to stallion duty at Hanover Shoe Farm at the end of the season. Sir Dalrae won two of the three $50,000 legs of Harness Tracks of America's United States Pacing Championship, while the two richest races for older pacers, the $96,563 Roosevelt Realization and $101,598 American National Maturity, both were won by Otaro Hanover, guided by 34-year-old driver Hervé Filion.

Filion was the leading money-winning driver for the fifth straight year and leading race-winning driver for the seventh straight year, establishing an all-time record of more than $3 million in purses won by his mounts in 1974 and becoming only the second harness driver in history, after Hans Frömming of West Germany, to drive more than 5,000 career victories. Filion also broke his own previous world record for wins in a single season with 631.

Despite a faltering national and world economy, the market for trotters and pacers remained strong.

The sport's two major auction sales, in Harrisburg, Pa., and Lexington, Ky., produced record grosses of $7,857,400 and $6,350,900, respectively.

(STANLEY F. BERGSTEIN)

In New Zealand in 1974 Maurice Holmes in his final season as a reinsman won the drivers' championship for the 17th time in his 49 years in competition. The New Zealand Cup and the Auckland Cup were won by Arapaho; the Dominion Trotting Handicap went to Philemon; and Koarakau took the New Zealand Derby. Find of the year was the two-year-old pacer Noodlum, which scored 11 consecutive wins and was being hailed as the equal of the legendary Cardigan Bay. In Australia the Inter-Dominion Championships final, marred by a string of accidents, was won by the top-class pacer Hondo Grattan for the second year in succession. Brilliant two-year-old John Oliver won the Breeders' Plate, Youthful Stakes, and Sapling Stakes at Harold Park, Sydney, but was defeated in the final of the Challenge Stakes by Abercorn Kid. Top money winner Welcome Advice broke the Queensland record with a 1-min. $58\frac{2}{5}$-sec. time trial at Albion Park and retired to stud. Champion four-year-old Paleface Adios won the Futurity Stakes, Lord Mayor's Cup, and Four-Year-Old Championship in Sydney, earning more than $100,000. Monara took his earnings past $100,000 in winning the Hunter Cup in Melbourne, where Maori's Wonder won the Trotters' Derby.

Star event of the year in Europe was the World Driving Championship, in which drivers from Australia, New Zealand, Canada, the U.S., and most European countries drove in a series of 20 races in various countries. Joe Marsh, Jr., from the U.S. captured eight races to win the championship, with Kevin Brooke from Australia second. Marsh was the first U.S. driver to win the title. In Italy the Premio Nazionale for three-year-olds, raced in Milan, went to Andraz, which set a European record of 2 min. 5 sec. for 2,100 m.; the Premio Duomo in Florence for aged trotters was won by Top Hanover. Medoc easily won the $30,000 Derby for four-year-olds in Trieste. The Premio della Fiera in Milan went to Timothy T. In France, the Prix d'Amérique of 1974 drew 18 starters in the richest harness race ever ($250,000) and was won in the last stride by Roosevelt International winner Delmonica Hanover. At Vincennes the Prix René Pallière for aged trotters was won by the champion French "saddle" trotter Bellino II,

A long shot at 50–1 odds, Snow Knight shows his heels to the pack in winning the Epsom Derby. Originally purchased for less than £6,000 ($14,400), Snow Knight is now worth £1 million ($2.4 million) at stud.

beating harness horses of the calibre of Timothy T., Castar, and Axius. The Prix de Paris was taken by Italian-owned Timothy T.

The Finnish "Great Mastership" for aged trotters went to the Swedish-bred Damokles. Soviet-bred Titan won the final of the Finnish Trotting Championship. The Trotting Derby at Helsinki was won by the Swedish-bred filly Butch Girl. Grain won the Swedish Derby, for four-year-olds; the International Elite Trot was won by U.S.-bred Timothy T. to bring his season's earnings past $140,000. In Norway, the Grand Prix for international horses over three heats saw Pimpernel II declared the winner. In Denmark, the Petit Prix was won by the U.S. import Chaco S., while O'Man defeated the Danish Championship winner Osman Bobo in winning "The Grand." The Scandinavian Championship, raced in Copenhagen, was won by Air France (Sweden). The Moscow Hippodrome in 1974 was the scene of a series of match races between teams from Moscow and Helsinki. Races were won by Mynttorg (Fin.), Pavlin (U.S.S.R.), the U.S. trotter Uncle Sam, and the Soviet-bred Othello. The championship was awarded to Othello.   (NOEL SIMPSON)

[452.B.4.h.xvii]

Housing

The housing situation in many Western countries in 1974 was a matter of grave social and political concern, as the effects of the energy crisis and continuing world inflation made themselves felt in housing markets. However, it was not true, as was sometimes said, that the difficulties in the field of housing, such as rising costs of dwellings and materials, serious declines in housing production, bankruptcies in the building industries, shortages of mortgage finance, and increasing homelessness, were entirely the results of inflation and economic insecurity. Rather, the economic situation exacerbated an inbuilt tendency toward imbalance and instability in many housing markets. In 1973 the cost of houses already was rapidly escalating with a consequent rise in real homelessness in a number of industrialized countries, well before world inflation reached its 1974 levels.

In general, the countries that suffered most from the "housing crisis" were those with a poorly developed public sector to their housing programs; countries with significant public sectors were able to stabilize housing production and the costs to consumers by increased government intervention. The housing problems of the poorer and less developed countries remained unchanged. They involved, fundamentally, stretching scarce resources in an attempt to make some inroads on tremendous housing shortages; providing a minimum standard of accommodation for at least a section of the population; and coping with the continuing and ever increasing flight from rural areas to the cities and the consequent unplanned and seemingly unstoppable growth of urban shantytowns that defied even the most basic concepts of public health.

Construction Performance. Table II records the achievements of 30 countries in housing construction during 1972–74. It should be noted that because of differences in definition and methods of statistical compilation, international comparisons serve at best only as a guide.

The table shows average monthly construction performance in the first part of 1974, the same period in 1973, and for the whole of 1973 and 1972. The most meaningful comparison for the 1974 data is with that for the same period in 1973 rather than the whole of that year because there frequently are seasonal variations during a year in monthly performances. On this basis, more countries suffered a decrease in housing construction in 1974 as compared with the same period in 1973 than improved their performance (17 decreased and 13 increased).

Some of the reductions in housing construction were very large. Turkey's housing output in the first part of 1974 was 52% lower than in early 1973; for Czechoslovakia the reduction was 51%; for Japan 34%; and for the U.S. 32%. Of the countries that managed to increase housing output in the first part of 1974, Ireland achieved the largest increase (57%), followed by Yugoslavia (40%) and South Korea (26%).

Relative achievements as between different countries are better shown by figures in Table I. Marriage figures in themselves do not provide precise measures of housing need or demand, but they do give some indication of the potential rate of new household formation and, therefore, the demand for separate dwellings. The ratio of housing construction to marriage rate thus gives a rough indication of the extent to which potential demand is being met.

The Housing Crisis. As a consequence of the general economic conditions, some U.S. experts were predicting the worst housing crisis since the 1930s depression. It was a situation repeated, although perhaps not in such an extreme form, in many other countries. There were several aspects to the crisis and its manifestations varied as between countries, but certain features were common. Inflation affected housing directly in a number of countries, as evidenced by soaring house prices, repair and maintenance costs, and costs of building materials.

In the U.S. the median price of a new house rose to $35,500 in June 1974, double the figure in 1963 and 34% higher than five years earlier. Prices rose comparably in a number of European countries, notably France and Italy, and in Australia house prices in the first quarter of 1974 were up 5% over the last quarter of 1973. In marked contrast, after the steep rises in 1972 and 1973, prices in the U.K. leveled off and in some areas fell significantly in 1974. During the course of the year, however, this downward trend ceased and prices began to creep up again.

Allied to the steep increases in the costs of houses

"It was rather naive of me to think that was the cost of the house."

ULUSCHAK—EDMONTON JOURNAL, CANADA/ROTHCO

Horticulture:
see Gardening

Hospitals:
see Health and Disease

Table I. Average Monthly Housing Construction in Early 1974 per 1,000 Marriages			
Country	Monthly construction per 1,000 marriages	Country	Monthly construction per 1,000 marriages
Australia	1,265	New Zealand	1,373
Canada	1,218	Norway	1,327
Czechoslovakia	588	Panama*	448
Finland*	2,325	Poland†	445
France*	1,871	Portugal*	456
Germany, East	841	Puerto Rico†	633
Germany, West	742	Spain	612
Ireland	1,534	Sweden	2,375
Israel†	1,358	Switzerland	710
Italy	285	U.K.†	605
Japan	1,144	U.S.	680
Netherlands, The	1,262	Yugoslavia	170

*Construction figures for final quarter of 1973.
†1972 marriage rates.
Source: United Nations, *Monthly Digest of Statistics.*

themselves were sharp rises in repair and maintenance costs (up by 41% since 1969 in the U.S.); in the cost of building materials (up 11% over the past year in the U.S. and 27% in the U.K.); and in the costs of servicing loans for home purchase, with mortgage interest rates creeping into double figures in a number of European countries (U.K., France, Italy) and fast approaching that level in the U.S. and Australia.

An aspect of the housing crisis common to many countries was—ironically—in large measure the result of government policies to stem inflation. These policies caused a tightening of money supplies, which reduced the flow of funds to home builders and to potential purchasers. Italy, France, the U.K., the U.S., and Australia, among many other countries, experienced a considerable reduction in the flow of funds into lending institutions and as a result far fewer homes were sold during the year. As a consequence of this, and of lack of funds, private builders retrenched, and very large reductions in construction of private homes occurred during the first nine months of 1974 in some countries. Thus, in Australia, orders for private homes were down by 25% compared with early 1973; in France, completions of private homes declined by 20%; in Italy only very expensive homes and second homes were selling in any volume; in the U.S. housing starts were running at an annual rate of 1,335,000 in July 1974, more than 800,000 below the figure for July 1973; and in the U.K. contracts for private housing in the period May–July 1974 showed a 55% drop over the corresponding period in 1973. It was interesting to note that in both the U.S. and the U.K. construction was down but mortgage rates were up, and many homes were standing unsold; this was accompanied in the U.K. by significant declines in the cost of housing but in the U.S. by continually rising prices.

Some consequences of the crisis were already apparent, but others would only show themselves in years to come. Many young couples and low-income families found themselves priced out of the housing market and were having to settle for rental apartments, as in the U.S., or to move to less expensive areas, which in France produced fears that Paris might become the preserve of the rich and in England left London short of schoolteachers. Longer term effects would result from the depressed state of the building industry in many countries, with profits down and bankruptcies on the increase in the U.S. and the U.K., and from the virtual cessation of speculative private building. Without government intervention this situation could lead to very considerably increased housing shortages in 1975 and 1976.

Government Intervention. A feature of the disturbances produced in housing markets by the year's economic conditions was that the countries worst affected were those with a poorly developed public housing program. Had there not been a large government injection of funds into the public sector in the U.K., the record on overall housing construction would have been far worse. As it was, while the private sector suffered a reduction of more than 50%, the expansion of the public sector almost made up for it; in consequence, total housing completions were only down by approximately 5% during the first part of the year.

Recognition of the growing importance of government intervention, either directly into the private housing market or by a more vigorous public housing policy, led in the U.S. to the introduction of legislation to give more financial assistance to home buyers and to inject more aid into public housing. The latter move was a reversal of the trend during the Nixon administration. In France it was argued that a more vigorous intervention by the state Habitations à Loyer Modéré (HLM) organization could help to preserve the social heterogeneity of Paris by preventing the exodus of the poorer people.

Even countries unaffected by the economic crisis, such as the oil-producing nations of Bahrain, Saudi Arabia, and Kuwait, took steps in 1974 to produce plans for government-instigated and administered housing programs. Most Eastern European countries, by continuing their policy of providing housing as a

New York building is constructed from top to bottom. The two central pillars, housing stairwells and elevators, were erected first, and ground-assembled single floors were then raised in turn and fastened in place.

KEYSTONE

Table II. Housing Construction in Early 1974, Compared with 1973 and 1972

Country	Monthly* average (early 1974)	Monthly* average (early 1973)	Monthly average (1973)	Monthly average (1972)	New or total†	Type of measure
Australia	11,907	11,686	12,637	12,124	Total	Buildings completed
Canada	19,993	18,107	20,548	19,352	New	Buildings completed
Czechoslovakia	6,927	14,201	13,844	9,543	New	Buildings completed
Denmark	4,023	4,542	4,631	4,167	New	Buildings completed
Finland	6,773‡	5,876§	5,131	4,175	Total	Buildings completed
France	62,584‡	59,784§	55,835	53,094	Total	Building permits issued
Germany, East	9,639	9,100	10,486	9,752	Total	Buildings completed
Germany, West	24,527	27,452	59,519	55,053	Total	Buildings completed
Ireland	2,905	1,856	2,001	1,736	Total	Buildings completed
Israel	3,420	4,690	4,256	3,946	Total	Buildings completed
Italy	9,898	9,913	15,108	20,014	Total	Buildings completed
Japan	103,296	156,323	150,632	150,632	Total	Buildings started
Korea, South	9,455	7,483	8,046	5,314	Total	Building permits issued
Kuwait	358	533	451	419	New	Building permits issued
Morocco	1,431	1,695	1,654	1,430	New	Building permits issued
Netherlands, The	11,305	12,307	12,951	12,689	New	Buildings completed
New Zealand	3,013	2,879	3,330	2,500	New	Building permits issued
Norway	3,065	3,632	3,730	3,634	New	Buildings completed
Panama	240‡	302§	344	291	New	Building permits issued
Poland	11,500	11,900	13,900	12,600	Total	Buildings completed
Portugal	3,223‡	2,897§	2,623	2,384	Total	Buildings completed
Puerto Rico	1,818	2,165	2,262	2,089	New	Building permits issued
South Africa	1,173	1,099	1,114	1,119	New	Private buildings completed
Spain	13,685	12,469	14,777	15,868	Total	Buildings completed with state aid only
Sweden	7,572	8,253	8,123	8,670	New	Buildings completed
Switzerland	2,361	2,273	2,573	2,315	New	Buildings completed
Turkey	7,777	16,135	16,243	13,827	Total	Building permits issued
U.K.	24,265	25,581	25,372	27,475	New	Buildings completed
U.S.	129,900	191,037	171,500	198,200	New	Buildings started
Yugoslavia	2,611	1,861	3,397	3,390	Total	Buildings completed

*Wherever possible, figures for early 1974 and 1973 relate to the same time period.
†New=new dwellings only. Total=new dwellings plus conversions, extensions, etc.
‡Figures relate to final quarter of 1973.
§Figures relate to final quarter of 1972.
Source: United Nations, *Monthly Digest of Statistics*.

social commodity, managed to keep rents down to a level between 4 and 8% of average household income.

Housing and Development. The crisis of housing in the Western world in 1974 still paled into insignificance beside the chronic need for even the basic essentials of shelter that persisted in many less developed countries. Mass exodus from rural areas continued unabated, and squatter settlements around the large cities continued to spread. One interesting and hopeful development during the year, however, was the extension in a number of countries of a policy to capitalize on the ingenuity and effort of squatter settlers. This was achieved by providing the necessary conditions for a more stable and healthy environment and the means, under government supervision, for settlers to construct their own homes with more functional materials. Indications were that by adopting such policies, rather than complex and expensive housing programs, the production of new homes of a tolerable standard would increase rapidly.

(JOHN EDWARDS)

See also Architecture; Cities and Urban Affairs; Economy, World; Industrial Production and Technology; Money and Banking.

[451.B.3.a–d; 525.B.3.b]

ENCYCLOPÆDIA BRITANNICA FILMS. *Equality Under Law— The California Fair Housing Cases* (1969); *The House of Man, Part II—Our Crowded Environment* (1969); *The Image of the City* (1973).

Hungary

A people's republic of central Europe, Hungary is bordered by Czechoslovakia, the U.S.S.R., Romania, Yugoslavia, and Austria. Area: 35,920 sq.mi. (93,032 sq.km.). Pop. (1974 est.): 10,449,000, including (1970) Hungarian 95.8%; German 2.1%. Cap. and largest city: Budapest (pop., 1974 est., 2,042,900). Language (1970): Magyar 95.8%. Religion (1956): Roman Catholic 67%; Protestant 27.3%; Orthodox

HUNGARY

Education. (1973–74) Primary, pupils 1,032,786, teachers 64,605; secondary and vocational, pupils 212,734, teachers 13,689; higher (including 18 universities), students 60,408, teaching staff 11,155.

Finance. Monetary unit: forint, with (Sept. 16, 1974) an official exchange rate of 9.39 forints to U.S. $1 (21.70 forints = £1 sterling) and a tourist rate of 24.87 forints to U.S. $1 (56.09 forints = £1 sterling). Budget (1973 est.): revenue 229.5 billion forints; expenditure 232.2 billion forints. National income (net material product): (1973) 354 billion forints; (1972) 319.4 billion forints.

Foreign Trade. (1973) Imports 37,299,000,000 forints; exports 42,039,000,000 forints. Import sources: U.S.S.R. 34%; East Germany 9%; West Germany 9%; Czechoslovakia 8%; Poland 5%. Export destinations: U.S.S.R. 33%; East Germany 11%; Czechoslovakia 9%; Italy 6%; West Germany 6%; Poland 6%. Main exports (1972): machinery 21%; transport equipment 12%; chemicals 8%; fruit and vegetables 6%; livestock 5%; iron and steel 5%; meat 5%; clothing 5%.

Transport and Communications. Roads (1973) 109,649 km. (including 158 km. expressways). Motor vehicles in use (1973): passenger 407,551; commercial 98,304. Railways: (1972) 8,603 km.; traffic (1973) 13,888,000,000 passenger-km., freight 20,686,000,000 net ton-km. Air traffic (1972): 326 million passenger-km.; freight 5.9 million net ton-km. Telephones (Dec. 1972) 924,000. Radio licenses (Dec. 1972) 2,542,000. Television licenses (Dec. 1972) 2,085,000.

Agriculture. Production (in 000; metric tons; 1973; 1972 in parentheses): corn c. 6,000 (5,554); wheat 4,500 (4,095); rye 176 (173); barley 876 (807); oats 70 (64); rice c. 65 (61); potatoes c. 1,400 (1,349); sugar, raw value c. 372 (c. 326); tomatoes c. 400 (367); onions c. 178 (171); rapeseed c. 75 (52); sunflower seed c. 145 (134); dry peas c. 85 (84); apples (1972) c. 600, (1971) 621; wine c. 600 (503); tobacco c. 17 (17); beef and veal (1972) c. 175, (1971) 183; pork (1972) c. 480, (1971) 416. Livestock (in 000; March 1973): cattle 1,965; pigs 6,990; sheep 2,259; horses 189; chickens (1972) 61,216.

Industry. Index of production (1970 = 100): (1973) 120; (1972) 112. Production (in 000; metric tons; 1973): coal 3,411; lignite 23,371; crude oil 1,990; natural gas (cu.m.) 4,814,000; electricity (kw.-hr.) 17,635,000; iron ore (25% metal content) 681; pig iron 2,110; crude steel 3,332; bauxite 2,600; aluminum 68; cement 3,405; petroleum products (1972) 7,167; sulfuric acid 648; fertilizers (1972–73): nitrogenous 374, phosphate 181; cotton yarn 57; wool yarn 13; commercial vehicles (units) 11.

2.5%; Jewish 1.5%. First secretary of the Hungarian Socialist Workers' (Communist) Party in 1974, Janos Kadar; president of the Presidential Council (chief of state), Pal Losonczi; president of the Council of Ministers (premier), Jeno Fock.

A reshuffle in both the party leadership and the government, initiated by the Central Committee of the Hungarian Socialist Workers' Party on March 20–21, 1974, forecast changes in the functioning of the New Economic Mechanism, the only economic system within the Comecon group allowing some freedom of decision to state enterprise managers and a range of fair market prices. Rezso Nyers, principal architect of NEM, was removed from the post of party secretary and relegated to virtual obscurity as director of the Economics Institute of the Academy of Sciences; he was succeeded by Karoly Nemeth, a member of the Politburo and head of the Budapest party organization. Gyorgy Aczel, another party secretary and a supporter of Nyers, who had been in charge of Hungary's relatively liberal cultural policy for seven years, was made deputy premier, and his job in the secretariat was given to Imre Gyori, a member of the Central Committee. There were now four hard-liners in the six-member secretariat surrounding Kadar. Lajos Feher, one of the five deputy premiers and also a supporter of Nyers, was retired and succeeded by Janos Borbandi, a member of the

Central Committee. However, Nyers, Aczel, and Feher remained in the 13-member Politburo.

Speaking on March 28 at Nyiregyhaza, Kadar himself commented on this "regrouping of cadres": they were unavoidable, since the new party congress would assemble the following spring and preparations for a congress always raised cadre problems, but work for the party's good was the criterion. Alluding to foreign relations, Kadar went on: "Hungarian foreign policy cannot be ambiguous. We must speak the same language in Budapest, in New York, and in Moscow. We stand by the U.S.S.R."

Kadar also referred to Hungarian-Vatican relations, to the talks conducted between Hungary and the Vatican for several years, and to the Vatican's decision concerning the archbishopric of Esztergom. "I think," said Kadar, "that those who suppose that Pope Paul VI deprived Mindszenty of the archbishopric of Esztergom on pressure from us overestimate our influence and underestimate the Vatican." Jozsef Cardinal Mindszenty had agreed in September 1971 to leave his 15-year refuge in the U.S. embassy in Budapest, where he had fled during the 1956 revolution, and to go abroad, but he had refused to resign as archbishop of Esztergom and primate of Hungary because the Hungarian government declined to clear him of the false charges for which he had been sentenced to life imprisonment in 1949. However, both the Holy See and the Hungarian Bishops' Conference wished to restore church administration in Hungary to normality. Therefore, on Jan. 30, 1974, Pope Paul VI wrote to Cardinal Mindszenty, who was residing in Vienna, to inform him of the measures he had decided to adopt. On February 5 Vatican Radio announced that the primatial see of Esztergom had been declared vacant and that Msgr. Laszlo Lekai, apostolic administrator of the diocese of Veszprem, had been appointed apostolic administrator of the archdiocese of Esztergom.

A party and government delegation from Hungary, led by Kadar, paid an official visit to the U.S.S.R. September 25–30. Kadar also visited Prague in April and met Leonid I. Brezhnev, general secretary of the Communist Party of the U.S.S.R., in the Crimea at the beginning of August. In April President Tito of Yugoslavia visited Budapest. Premier Fock paid a visit to East Berlin in February, and Piotr Jaroszewicz, the Polish premier, arrived in Budapest in August.

In October the internationally known writer Gyorgy Konrad, the sociologist Ivan Szelenyi, and the poet Tamas Szentjoby were arrested and charged with subversive activity. The arrests caused a wave of foreign protests and on October 28 the three were released and offered the chance to emigrate.

(K. M. SMOGORZEWSKI)

[972.B.2.b]

Iceland

Iceland is an island republic in the North Atlantic Ocean, near the Arctic Circle. Area: 39,769 sq.mi. (103,000 sq.km.). Pop. (1973 est.): 213,499. Cap. and largest city: Reykjavik (pop., 1973 est., 84,333). Language: Icelandic. Religion: 98% Lutheran. President in 1974, Kristjan Eldjarn; prime ministers, Olafur Johannesson and, from August 28, Geir Hallgrimsson.

Early in 1974 the three-year-old coalition of leftist parties under Prime Minister Johannesson began to show signs of discord, mainly over economic issues. On May 9 Parliament was dissolved, fully one year before its four-year term ran out, and a new election was called for June 30. The election produced gains for the Independence Party, which received 42.7% of the vote and 25 out of 60 seats in the legislature. On August 28 a new coalition government was formed

Iceland lies astride the Mid-Atlantic Ridge and is thus subject to volcanism as well as sea-floor spreading processes. The rift shown here, northeast of Reykjavik, is proof of this activity. Laser measuring devices have indicated a widening of one to two inches during the last few years.

THEODORE L. SULLIVAN—THE NEW YORK TIMES

Hurricanes:
see Disasters;
    Earth Sciences

Hydroelectric Power:
see Energy;
    Engineering Projects

Ice Hockey:
see Hockey

under the premiership of Independence Party leader Geir Hallgrimsson.

Negotiations begun in 1973 to revise Iceland's 1951 defense pact with the U.S. and move U.S. troops out of Iceland were formally terminated in October. The new regime decided that the U.S.-operated NATO base at Keflavik would remain open.

The "cod war" with Great Britain ended in November 1973, but no settlement was reached with West Germany over fishing rights within the claimed fishing zone of 50 mi. In July 1974 Iceland rejected a judgment by the International Court of Justice that favoured the U.K. and West Germany. (*See* Law.) Skirmishes between Icelandic coast guard boats and West German trawlers continued on a reduced scale. In September and October Iceland stepped up its efforts to pressure German vessels out of the 50-mi. zone while at the same time renewing active negotiations with Bonn. West Germany barred Icelandic fishing vessels from its ports in November.

Although 1973 was a prosperous year for the Icelandic economy (national income in real terms increasing by some 9.5% despite the loss of productive capacity due to the volcanic eruption at Heimaey), matters took a turn for the worse in 1974. Export prices, mainly for fish meal and oil, declined from their high 1973 level whereas import prices rose. The balance of payments, therefore, became unfavourable and real national income leveled off. Meanwhile, the forces of world inflation combined with heavy cost increases at home produced an inflation rate exceeding 36%. The króna was twice devalued (initially by 4% and then by 17%).

Construction of a 150-Mw. power station at Sigalda in the southwest continued in 1974 and was scheduled for completion in 1976. A portion of the electricity produced by the station would be used by a ferrosilicon plant to be constructed in 1975 and jointly owned by the Icelandic government and Union Carbide Corp. of the U.S.   (BJÖRN MATTHÍASSON)
[972.A.6.d.ii]

ICELAND
Education. (1971–72) Primary, pupils 27,727, teachers 1,153; secondary, pupils 18,753, teachers 974; vocational, pupils 13,897, teachers 259; teacher training, students 701, teachers 39; higher (at Reykjavik University), students 2,000, teaching staff 123.
Finance. Monetary unit: króna, with (Sept. 16, 1974) a free rate of 119 krónur to U.S. $1 (free rate of 274 krónur = £1 sterling). Gold, SDRs, and foreign exchange, central bank: (June 1974) U.S. $64.7 million; (June 1973) U.S. $86.3 million. Budget (1973 est.): revenue 21,970,000,000 krónur; expenditure 21,457,000,000 krónur. Gross national product: (1972) 66,270,000,000 krónur; (1971) 53,210,000,000 krónur. Money supply: (June 1974) 12,563,000,000 krónur; (June 1973) 9,548,000,000 krónur. Cost of living (Reykjavik; 1970 = 100): (May 1974) 199; (May 1973) 138.
Foreign Trade. (1973) Imports 31,859,000,000 krónur; exports 26,039,000,000 krónur. Import sources: U.K. 11%; West Germany 11%; Norway 10%; Denmark 9%; Sweden 8%; U.S. 7%; The Netherlands 7%; U.S.S.R. 6%. Export destinations: U.S. 27%; West Germany 12%; U.K. 11%; Denmark 8%; Switzerland 5%; Portugal 5%. Main exports: fish 56%; aluminum 17%; fish meal 14%.
Transport and Communications. Roads (1973) 11,137 km. Motor vehicles in use (1972): passenger 50,595; commercial 5,857. There are no railways. Air traffic (1973): 1,982,000,000 passenger-km.; freight 30,058,000 net ton-km. Shipping (1973): merchant vessels 100 gross tons and over 325; gross tonnage 142,777. Telephones (Dec. 1972) 78,000. Radio licenses (Dec. 1972) 65,000. Television licenses (Dec. 1972) 46,000.
Agriculture. Production (in 000; metric tons; 1972; 1971 in parentheses): potatoes c. 11 (11); hay (1971) c. 410, (1970) 289; milk c. 125 (122); mutton and lamb c. 12 (11); fish catch 726 (685). Livestock (in 000; Dec. 1972): cattle 65; sheep 829; horses 39; poultry 200.
Industry. Production (in 000): electricity (public supply only; kw-hr.; 1973) 2,278,000; aluminum (metric tons; 1971) 41.

Ice Skating

The growing appeal of ice skating was reflected in 1974 by an increase of television coverage. Another trend, the growing demand for municipally owned rinks, was prompted by a realization that overall operating costs could be much reduced by putting a swimming pool and an ice rink in adjacent buildings and designing a common power plant for the two. Prominent among several new rinks in warm-climate countries was South Africa's first truly international-sized rink, opened on July 4 in Johannesburg. The popularity of ice dancing was recognized by the conferring of Olympic status on this branch of ice skating, to take effect from 1976. Technical progress was demonstrated by Gordon McKellen of the U.S. during training, when he became the first person to achieve a triple axel jump, requiring three and a half midair rotations.

New singles champions emerged when 22 nations were represented by 128 skaters in the world ice figure and dance championships in Munich, W.Ger., on March 5–9. Jan Hoffmann of Dresden, E.Ger., took the undefended men's title with three great triple leaps—Lutz, Salchow, and toe loop—but really owed his victory to a vital lead in the figures. The U.S.S.R.'s Sergei Volkov narrowly finished second ahead of Toller Cranston of Canada, who was by far the best free skater, producing two triple Salchows in a superbly original performance and receiving two well-deserved sixes for artistic presentation.

Nine judges voted 6–3 to award the vacant women's crown to Christine Errath, a stocky East German from Berlin. Thanks to her earlier advantage in the figures, she was able to thwart a last-ditch stand by Dorothy Hamill, the U.S. runner-up, who outpointed the new champion in the free skating and scored a six for artistic presentation. Dianne de Leeuw, the U.S.-domiciled Dutch skater, finished third.

In the pairs competition mockery was made of the once-revered six mark—meant to denote perfection—when one judge gave it for technical merit to Aleksandr Zaitsev and Irina Rodnina (*see* BIOGRAPHY) of the U.S.S.R.; the Moscow couple decisively retained the title but made three blatant errors. It was Miss Rodnina's sixth successive pairs title, a record; she had been partnered the first four times by Aleksey Ulanov, the latter on this occasion a worthy runner-up with his wife, Ludmila Smirnova. Third were Wolf Östereich and Romy Kermer of East Germany.

Perhaps inspired by the news of the forthcoming Olympic status of their event, Aleksandr Gorshkov and Ludmila Pakhomova gained a record fifth successive ice dance victory. Skating with admirable cohesion and slick changes of tempo, the Soviet couple reached new heights in the best performance of their careers, scoring seven sixes for artistic presentation and another for technical merit. Only Glyn Watts and Hilary Green, the British runners-up, seemed to be in a comparable class, comfortably ahead of the third-place Genadi Karponosov and Natalya Linicuk of the U.S.S.R.

Irina Rodnina
and Aleksandr Zaitsev
perform in Munich where
the Moscow couple
captured the world
figure skating title
for pairs. It marked
Miss Rodnina's sixth
successive victory
in the event.

Sten Stensen of Norway took the overall title in the men's world ice speed championship at Inzell, W.Ger., on February 9–10. He won both the long-distance events, 5,000 m. and 10,000 m. Harm Kuipers of The Netherlands and Göran Claesson of Sweden were second and third overall, but neither won an individual event. Hans van Helden, another Dutchman, took the 1,500 m., and Masaki Suzuki of Japan won the 500-m. sprint. Many brows were raised by the performance of Colin Coates of Australia, whose fourth place in the 10,000 m. was a remarkable feat for a skater from a country with no speed rink.

In the women's world speed championship at Heerenveen, Neth., on February 23–24, Atje Keulen-Deelstra of The Netherlands won the overall title for a third successive year and equaled the record total of four victories attained nine years previously by Inga Voronina of the U.S.S.R. Mrs. Keulen-Deelstra was first in three of the four events. Sheila Young of the U.S. won the 500 m., but Tatjana Averina and Nina Statkevich, both of the U.S.S.R., took second and third overall places. Separate world sprint titles for men and women were won by Per Bjørang of Norway and Leah Poulos of the U.S. at Innsbruck, Aus., on February 16–17.

Two women's world records were improved in April, both by Miss Averina at Medeo, U.S.S.R. She set a new time of 1 min. 26.4 sec. for the 1,000 m. (a distance to be added to the next Olympic men's schedule) and lowered the 1,500-m. mark to 2 min. 14 sec.

(HOWARD BASS)

[452.B.4.g]

Income, National

The world economy in 1973 continued its rapid growth of output in real terms (that is, after allowing for price changes), following the rapid expansion of

1972. The rate of growth in both years was well above the trend of the decade 1960–70. For the countries of the Organization for Economic Cooperation and Development (OECD) and the other developed nations, with the exception of Malta and South Africa, the rate of growth was about 5.8% in 1972 and 6.2% in 1973. However, in 1974, under the impact of the international payments crisis created by oil price rises and the adoption of deflationary policies by governments concerned primarily with inflation, the OECD countries barely grew at all, the overall rate being only 0.25%. The OECD also forecast continued slow growth with only 0.5% increase in 1975.

The record of growth of gross domestic product (GDP) in recent years is given in Table I for individual countries. The figure for the most recent years should be regarded as provisional. The 1974 figures are taken from OECD *Economic Outlook* for December 1974 and are based on the latest available evidence. Similar estimates by the European Commission published in the autumn of 1974 in *The Economic Situation in the Community* suggested a GDP growth rate of 2.7% in 1974 for the enlarged Common Market, following growth of 5.6% in 1973 and 3.7% in 1972; this compares with OECD estimates of 2.5% growth in 1974, 5.5% in 1973, and 4% in 1972 for the nine EEC countries.

The world recession of 1974 was most marked in the major economies of Japan, the United States, and the United Kingdom, where output fell in real terms. West Germany's growth was cut back to about 1%. However, Canada, France, and Italy were each able to grow by between 4 and 5%, and some of the middle ranking countries (in terms of total output) were also able to expand to some extent. The EEC report referred to above had similar estimates for Common Market countries, and included an estimate of 4.5% growth for Luxembourg in 1974. OECD figures on a calendar year basis suggest about 2.2% growth in

Australia and 3.8% growth in New Zealand in 1974, following growth rates of 5.6 and 5.3%, respectively, in 1973. These figures thus differ from those in Table I, which are for financial years.

For the less developed countries as a whole the general picture in 1973 was of continued growth. The Inter-American Development Bank in its report *Economic and Social Progress in Latin America* estimated that the Latin American countries grew by 6.8% in 1973, 6.7% in 1972, and 6.2% in 1971 following an average growth rate of 5.5% in the years 1961–70. However, the effect of the recession in the industrial countries and of higher import bills for oil and for other products, including manufactured goods, was likely to have created severe economic difficulties for a number of less developed countries in 1974.

Among the individual less developed countries, Brazil, Ecuador, South Korea, and the Philippines achieved growth rates of 10% or more in 1973. The higher prices that it charged for its oil in 1973 created a growth rate of 33% in Iran. The growth rate fell to 2% or below in Ethiopia, Morocco, Tunisia, Zambia, Uruguay, Syria, and Burma.

Table II shows for more than 90 countries the latest available figures for gross domestic product and national income, converted from national currencies to U.S. dollars, on both a total and a per capita basis. The concept of GDP is designed to measure the value of domestic production; it is the sum of all domestic current expenditures by consumers and public authorities, investment expenditures, *plus* exports of goods and services, *less* imports of goods and services.

The concept of national income is related to GDP. GDP *plus* the net factor income from abroad (payments such as interest and dividends arising in one country and paid to residents of another country) is called gross national product (GNP). National income is GNP *minus* an allowance for the depreciation of the country's stock of fixed capital during the year. Defined in these ways, GDP, GNP, and national income are said to be measured in terms of market prices. The table includes all countries that had a national income of $1 billion or more in 1970.

The national figures are converted to U.S. dollars at current exchange rates. Two important qualifications must be made about this procedure. First, the use of current exchange rates determined for foreign trade and payments purposes may not adequately reflect differences in the purchasing power of the various national currencies. For most countries the exchange rates used are the "trade conversion factors" published by the IMF in *International Financial*

Table I. Growth of Real Gross Domestic Products, 1960–74

Country	Annual % change 1960-70	1971	% change from preceding year 1972	1973	1974*	Country	Annual % change 1960-70	1971	% change from preceding year 1972	1973	1974*
Industrial countries						Tanzania♀	5.5¶	3.9	5.3	...	...
Austria	4.7	5.6	7.2	5.6	5	Tunisia	4.9	9.1	17.9	1.3	...
Belgium	5.0	3.4	5.2	5.7	4½	Uganda	4.6¶	2.4	...	...	...
Canada	5.2	5.6	5.7	6.8	4½	Zambia	6.1	−13.4	5.0	0.7	...
Denmark	4.8	3.7	4.5	3.5	1½	**Caribbean and Latin America**					
France	5.8	5.3	5.3	6.0	4¾	Argentina	4.2	3.9	3.8	5.5	...
Germany, West	4.9	2.9	3.3	5.3	1	Bolivia	5.5	3.8	5.1	6.0	...
Italy	5.6	1.6	3.1	6.4	4¾	Brazil	6.0	11.3	10.4	11.4	...
Japan	11.1	6.8	8.9	10.2	−3¼	Chile	4.4	7.7	1.4	...	...
Luxembourg	3.4	1.7	4.6	7.4	...	Colombia	5.2	5.5	6.7	7.3	...
Netherlands, The	5.4	4.4	4.2	4.2	2½	Costa Rica	4.9¶	5.0	...	...	...
Norway	5.0	5.5	4.5	3.7	4	Dominican Republic	5.2	9.9	12.5	...	...
Sweden	4.5	0.1	2.5	1.5	3	Ecuador	5.0	2.1	8.4	13.3	...
Switzerland	4.3	3.8	5.7	3.5	1½	El Salvador	5.6	...	...	...	...
United Kingdom	2.7	2.3	3.1	5.3	−½	Guatemala	5.5	5.6	7.3	7.5	...
United States	4.2	3.1	6.0	5.9	−1¾	Haiti	1.0	6.4	3.7	...	...
Other developed areas						Honduras	4.8	5.1	4.0	...	...
Australia†	5.2	2.9	4.5	5.5	...	Jamaica	4.9	1.7	−0.2	...	...
Finland	5.2	2.3	7.2	7.0	3¼	Mexico	7.0	3.4	7.3	7.6	...
Greece	7.8	7.0	10.0	9.5	...	Nicaragua	7.2	5.8	4.0	2.4	...
Iceland	4.1	10.1	6.5	5.5	...	Panama	8.0¶	8.8	6.3	6.5	...
Ireland	4.2	3.5	3.3	6.8	2½	Paraguay	4.5	4.6	5.3	7.2	...
Malta	4.9	2.5	5.8	...	...	Peru	5.2	5.9	5.8	5.3	...
New Zealand‡	3.9	3.0	5.2	5.0	...	Puerto Rico‡	7.4	5.6	5.4	...	...
Portugal	6.3	5.8	8.7	7.0	...	Uruguay	1.6	−1.0	−1.5	1.0	...
South Africa§	6.0	4.1	3.6	4.1	...	Venezuela	5.5	2.2	4.5	6.0	...
Spain	7.5	4.3	7.8	7.9	5½	**Asia, Middle East**					
Turkey	5.5	9.5	6.7	4.6	...	Cyprus	6.3	12.2	5.0	...	...
Centrally planned economies‖						Iran‡	6.6	12.2	13.8	33.0	...
Albania	8.3	...	...	...	...	Israel	8.7	9.8	9.9	3.5	...
Bulgaria	7.7	6.9	7.0	7.2	...	Saudi Arabia†	10.0	15.4	...	...	...
Czechoslovakia	4.3	4.7	5.5	5.2	...	Syria	7.9	10.1	9.7	−0.1	...
Germany, East	4.4	4.5	5.7	5.5	...	**Asia, East and Southeast, and Oceania**					
Hungary	5.5	6.6	5.1	7.4	...	Bangladesh†	...	...	−2.6¶	...	...
Mongolia	3.3	3.9	...	...	...	Burmaδ	2.9¶	4.1	2.4	1.1	...
Poland	6.1	8.1	10.2	11.6	...	Fiji	7.0¶	6.9	7.5	6.2	...
Romania	8.4	12.9	10.2	10.8	...	Hong Kong	8.1¶	1.8	8.0	8.6	...
U.S.S.R.	7.1	5.5	4.0	6.3	...	India‡	3.7	2.0	1.0	3.0	...
Yugoslavia	6.7	8.9	4.4	5.0	...	Indonesia	3.6	5.9	...	...	...
Less developed areas						Korea, South	8.7	9.8	7.3	16.9	...
Africa						Malaysia	6.3	8.9	7.1	9.7	...
Egypt†	3.5¶	3.9	...	...	...	Nepal†	1.6¶	−0.1	2.0	2.0	...
Ethiopia	4.0	4.5	4.4	2.0	...	Pakistan†□	5.1	0.0	5.3	...	...
Ghana	2.7	7.9	...	...	...	Philippines	5.1	7.9	5.2	10.0	...
Kenya	6.5¶	7.3	5.2	6.0	...	Sri Lanka	5.5¶	1.4	2.5	...	...
Libya	24.0¶	−7.8	...	...	...	Thailand	8.0	5.8	3.1	8.3	...
Malawi	6.5¶	14.2	10.5	7.7	...	Vietnam, South	3.2	3.7	0.9	3.7	...
Morocco	3.9	5.0	4.8	1.5	...						
Rhodesia	5.6¶	10.5	7.2	...	...						

*OECD estimates, based on incomplete data.
†Financial year beginning July 1 (ending July 15 for Nepal).
‡Financial year beginning April 1 (March 21 for Iran).
§Includes Namibia.
‖Growth of material product. See text for discussion of comparability with other figures.
¶Burma, Libya, Paraguay, Saudi Arabia, 1962–70; Uganda, 1963–70; Egypt, Kenya, Malawi, Tanzania, 1964–70; Fiji, Rhodesia, 1965–70; Costa Rica, Hong Kong, Nepal, 1966–70; Bangladesh, 1969/70 to 1972/3 (annual rate).
♀Former Tanganyika only.
δFinancial year ending September 30.
□Excludes Bangladesh from 1969.
Sources: Publications of the UN, OECD, and IMF, various national sources.

Statistics. They are averages of the effective exchange rates for international trading. The general effect of using such exchange rates is probably to make the recorded gaps in levels of national income and GDP between the less developed and the industrial countries somewhat greater than they would be if the data were available to make more refined calculations. The second qualification is that the figures in national currencies are themselves estimated in a variety of ways, and there are differences in the systems of national accounting used among various countries. Although the per capita figures given have been rounded to the nearest $10 to avoid a spurious appearance of accuracy, it is still unwise to place much reliance on small differences between countries. The net effect of the devaluations and currency floats of recent years was to reduce the size of GDP and national income for the U.S. and U.K. in relation to most other countries. On these calculations the U.S. economy was approximately three times the size of Japan's economy and between seven and eight times larger than that of the United Kingdom.

Comparisons between Eastern European and other countries are difficult because the former exclude from national income accounts certain "unproductive services," such as public administration and personal and professional services. If such items were included, the growth rates in those countries would probably be somewhat lower than those recorded in Table I. Growth in Czechoslovakia and East Germany in 1973

Table III. Estimates of Gross National Product for Centrally Planned Economies, 1971 (with comparative figures)

Country	Total (U.S. $000,000,000)	Per capita (U.S. $)
Centrally planned economies		
Germany, East	37	2,190
Czechoslovakia	31	2,120
U.S.S.R.	343	1,400
Poland	44	1,350
Hungary	12	1,200
Bulgaria	7.0	820
Romania	15	740
Yugoslavia	15	730
Cuba	4.4	510
Albania	1.1	480
Mongolia	0.5	380
Korea, North	4.4	310
China	126	160
Vietnam, North	2.2	100
Selected free-market economies		
United States	1,068	5,160
France	172	3,360
Germany, West	197	3,210
United Kingdom	136	2,430
Japan	223	2,130
Italy	101	1,860
Argentina	29	1,230
Dominican Republic	1.8	430
Korea, South	9.2	290
Vietnam, South	4.3	230
India	61	110

Source: International Bank for Reconstruction and Development, *World Bank Atlas.*

was similar to that in 1972, while the other countries increased their growth rates.

Interest is often expressed in comparisons of levels of national product between free-market and centrally

Table II. Total and Per Capita Gross Domestic Product and National Income

Country	Year	Gross domestic product U.S. $000,000	Gross domestic product U.S. $ per capita	National income U.S. $000,000	National income U.S.$ per capita	Country	Year	Gross domestic product U.S. $000,000	Gross domestic product U.S. $ per capita	National income U.S. $000,000	National income U.S.$ per capita
Industrialized countries						*Caribbean and Latin America*					
Austria	1973	27.9	3,710	24.9	3,310	Argentina	1971	29.7	1,260	27.6	1,170
Belgium	1973	45.6	4,670	40.9	4,190	Bolivia	1972	1.2	220	1.1	210
Canada	1973	119.8	5,410	105.1	4,750	Brazil	1972	50.8	510	47.8	480
Denmark	1973	27.5	5,460	25.1	4,980	Chile	1972	12.3	1,220	11.2	1,110
France	1973	254.9	4,890	226.9	4,350	Colombia	1972	8.4	370	7.6	340
Germany, West	1973	348.3	5,620	309.5	5,000	Costa Rica	1972	1.2	630	1.1	580
Italy	1973	137.8	2,510	125.9	2,290	Dominican Republic	1971	1.6	390	1.5	360
Japan	1973	413.3	3,810	360.4	3,330	Ecuador	1973	2.6	390	2.4	350
Luxembourg	1973	1.8	5,220	1.5	4,340	El Salvador	1973	1.3	350	1.2	330
Netherlands, The	1973	59.3	4,410	54.8	4,080	Guatemala	1973	2.6	470	2.4	440
Norway	1973	19.0	4,790	16.1	4,070	Haiti	1972	0.6	110	0.6	110
Sweden	1973	49.9	6,140	45.2	5,560	Honduras	1972	0.8	300	0.7	270
Switzerland	1973	40.5	6,290	36.9	5,730	Jamaica	1972	1.6	830	1.4	720
United Kingdom	1973	172.3	3,080	157.6	2,820	Mexico	1973	49.7	920	47.5	880
United States	1973	1,274.1	6,060	1,184.1	5,630	Nicaragua	1973	1.1	550	1.0	510
Other developed areas						Panama	1973	1.5	930	1.3	820
Australia*	1972/73	52.5	4,020	47.7	3,650	Paraguay	1973	1.0	370	0.9	350
Finland	1973	16.8	3,610	15.1	3,230	Peru	1972	7.5	520	6.6	460
Greece	1973	16.0	1,790	15.5	1,730	Puerto Rico*	1972/73	6.4	2,220	5.9	2,040
Iceland	1972	0.8	3,650	0.7	3,140	Uruguay	1973	1.4	470	1.3	450
Ireland	1973	6.5	2,150	6.1	2,010	Venezuela	1973	17.8	1,570	14.7	1,300
Malta	1973	0.3	990	0.3	1,010	*Asia, Middle East*					
New Zealand†	1972/73	8.7	2,990	8.0	2,750	Cyprus	1972	0.8	1,160	0.7	1,060
Portugal	1972	8.6	1,000	8.1	950	Iran†	1972/73	17.6	570	15.3	500
South Africa‡	1973	26.9	1,100	26.0	1,070	Iraq	1971	4.2	430	3.3	340
Spain	1973	60.3	1,730	55.8	1,600	Israel	1972	7.0	2,280	6.2	2,010
Turkey	1973	20.0	530	19.6	520	Jordan	1973	0.8	310	0.8	330
Less developed areas						Kuwait†	1971/72	4.0	4,950	3.1	3,810
Africa						Lebanon	1970	1.5	530	1.5	520
Algeria	1973	7.1	450	6.4	410	Saudi Arabia	1971	6.3	790	4.6	580
Angola	1970	1.7§	300§	...	...	Syria	1971	2.4	290	2.3	280
Cameroon	1970	1.1	190	1.0	170	*Asia, East and Southeast, and Oceania*					
Egypt*	1971/72	7.7	220	7.5	220	Afghanistan	1970	...	...	1.4	80
Ethiopia‖	1971/72	2.0	80	2.0	80	Bangladesh*	1972/73	5.6	80	...	...
Ghana	1972	2.2	240	2.0	220	Burma♀	1972/73	2.3	80	2.0	70
Ivory Coast	1972	1.9	420	1.7	370	Fiji	1973	0.4	680	0.4	650
Kenya	1973	2.3	180	2.2	180	Hong Kong	1973	5.9	1,410	...	...
Libya	1972	4.9	2,340	3.8	1,850	India†	1970/71	53.1	100	50.0	90
Malawi	1973	0.5	110	0.5	100	Indonesia	1972	10.9	90	9.9	80
Morocco	1973	4.4	270	...	...	Korea, South	1973	12.5	380	11.4	350
Mozambique	1970	1.9§	240§	...	...	Malaysia	1973	5.7	510	...	...
Nigeria†	1970/71	3.9	70	...	...	Nepal‖	1972/73	1.1	90	...	...
Rhodesia	1971	1.7	310	1.6	280	Pakistan*δ	1972/73	5.9	90	5.6	90
Sudan*	1971/72	2.2	130	2.0	120	Philippines	1972	8.8	220	7.7	200
Tanzania¶	1972	1.4	100	1.5	110	Singapore	1973	3.9	1,770	3.8	1,720
Tunisia	1973	2.5	460	2.4	430	Sri Lanka	1971	2.2	180	2.1	160
Uganda	1971	1.5	140	1.4	140	Taiwan	1973	8.9	580	8.3	540
Zaire	1972	2.8	120	2.3	100	Thailand	1973	9.2	230	8.5	210
Zambia	1972	1.7	390	1.5	340	Vietnam, South	1973	3.1	160	...	...

*Year beginning July 1.   †Year beginning April 1 (March 21 for Iran).   ‡Includes Namibia.   §Gross national product: the figures for GDP are unlikely to be noticeably different.   ‖Year ending July 7 for Ethiopia; ending July 15 for Nepal.   ¶Former Tanganyika only.   ♀Year ending September 30.   δExcludes Bangladesh.
Sources: Publications of UN, OECD, IMF, and World Bank; various national sources.

planned economies. One international source provided estimates for 1971 of gross national product (GNP) per capita for both groups of countries. The qualifications expressed about the estimates in Table II apply with even stronger force to the estimates shown in Table III. The estimates of total GNP were obtained by multiplying the GNP per capita figures by the population figures given in the same source. They suggest that total output in the U.S.S.R. was less than one third of U.S. output and that East Germany had a per capita output similar to that of the United Kingdom.   (M. F. FULLER)

See also Economy, World.
[534.D.3.a]

India

A federal republic of southern Asia and a member of the Commonwealth of Nations, India is situated on a peninsula extending into the Indian Ocean with the Arabian Sea to the west and the Bay of Bengal to the east. It is bounded (east to west) by Burma, Bangladesh, China, Bhutan, Sikkim, Nepal, and Pakistan; Sri Lanka lies just off its southern tip in the Indian Ocean. Area: 1,266,602 sq.mi. (3,280,483 sq.km.), including the Pakistani-controlled section of Jammu and Kashmir. Pop. (1974 est.): 586,056,000; Indo-Aryans and Dravidians are dominant, with Mongoloid, Negroid, and Australoid admixtures. Cap.: New Delhi (pop., 1971, 301,801). Largest cities: Calcutta (metro. pop., 1971, 7,031,382) and Greater Bombay (metro. pop., 1971, 5,970,575). Language: Hindi and English (official). Religion (1971): Hindu 82.7%; Muslim 11.2%; Christian 2.6%; Sikh 1.9%; Buddhist 0.7%; others 0.9%. Presidents in 1974, Varahagiri Venkata Giri and, from August 24, Fakhruddin Ali Ahmed; prime minister, Mrs. Indira Gandhi.

In 1974 India accomplished its first nuclear explosion, but it was also a year of mounting economic hardship, political tension, and Jaya Prakash Narayan's agitation in Bihar.

Domestic Affairs. Elections were held in February to legislative assemblies in four states, Uttar Pradesh, Orissa, Nagaland, and Manipur, and a union territory, Pondicherry. The ruling Congress Party just managed to secure an absolute majority in Uttar Pradesh and formed a government under the chief ministership of H. N. Bahuguna. In Orissa the Congress formed a minority government with Mrs. Nandini Satpathy as chief minister. In Nagaland the United Democratic Front obtained a majority, and a Cabinet headed by T. Vizol took office. In Manipur a non-Congress coalition under the leadership of Mohammed Alimuddin assumed office. In Pondicherry the Anna Dravida Munnetra Kazhagam (DMK) and the Communist Party formed a coalition; it resigned three weeks later, and president's rule was reimposed on the territory.

Early in January, students in Gujarat went on strike demanding lower food prices in hostels. The action quickly escalated into an antigovernment movement. Legislators were subjected to *gherao* (physical surrounding, a form of political pressure that had become increasingly common in India), and their resignation from the State Assembly was demanded. On February 9 the chief minister, Chimanbhai Patel, resigned, and the state was placed under president's rule. A month later the Assembly was dis-

solved. Chimanbhai Patel was expelled from the Congress Party and formed his own party.

Gujarat quickly returned to normal, but student trouble then flared up in Bihar. Jaya Prakash Narayan, veteran leader of the Sarvodaya movement (a branch of the movement begun by Mohandas Gandhi), took charge of the agitation. He advocated the overhaul of the country's parliamentary system in order to eliminate the power of money in elections as his larger aim and the removal of the Abdul Ghafoor ministry and dissolution of the state legislature as his immediate objective. He formed citizens' committees and preached boycott of the legislature, government offices, and colleges, and nonpayment of revenue. Most opposition parties (with the marked exception of the Communist Party of India) backed the movement, but only about 40 of the 318 legislators of the state resigned during the first six months of the movement. There were repeated clashes between crowds and authority, and charges and countercharges of preplanned mob violence and police vindictiveness. A meeting between Mrs. Gandhi and Narayan on November 1 was unproductive. Three days later Narayan was injured in a demonstration in Patna.

Another challenge to the government was a strike on the national railway system in May. Officials claimed that only 8% of the 1.7 million railway workers were involved, but before it collapsed after 20 days the strike imposed additional strain on the economy. To the opposition, the strike was an opportunity to accuse the government of being antilabour. The sessions of Parliament were acrimonious throughout most of the year, and charges of corruption were leveled against the government as a whole and also against individual ministers. But two motions of no confidence were defeated, the first on May 10 by voice vote and the second on July 25 by 294 votes to 61.

Seven opposition parties, led by the Swatantra Party, the Bharatiya Kranti Dal, and the Samyukta Socialist Party, formed a new party, the Bharatiya Lok Dal, under the chairmanship of Charan Singh from Uttar Pradesh. Some of the opposition parties had made a determined bid to challenge the Congress Party at the time of the presidential election by fielding a candidate, Tridib Kumar Chaudhuri, to oppose the official nominee, Fakhruddin Ali Ahmed. However, Ahmed (*see* BIOGRAPHY) won by a large margin, securing 765,587 votes of the electoral college against Chaudhuri's 189,196. Ahmed took over from V. V. Giri on August 24. B. D. Jatti was elected vice-president to succeed G. S. Pathak. Earlier, the government had sought the Supreme Court's opinion as to whether the validity of the electoral college as the body that elects the president was affected by the dissolution of the Gujarat Assembly. The court, in a judgment on June 5, held that the election of a new president must be held before the expiration of the term of the incumbent president even if a state assembly or assemblies had been dissolved, as in the case of Gujarat.

Mrs. Gandhi's supremacy in party and government remained unchallenged. In January she inducted K. Brahmananda Reddy and K. D. Malaviya into the central Cabinet. In October, to fill the place vacated by Ahmed and to redeploy ministerial talent to meet the economic crisis, she made far-reaching changes in the Council of Ministers. All three members of the inner Cabinet were moved: Jagjivan Ram from defense to agriculture, Swaran Singh from external affairs to defense, and Y. B. Chavan from finance to external affairs. C. Subramaniam was assigned finance; K.

Brahmananda Reddy home affairs; and U. S. Dikshit was named minister without portfolio. The president of the Congress Party, S. D. Sharma, was also given the Cabinet berth for communications, and the petroleum and chemicals minister, D. K. Barooah, resigned from the Cabinet to head the party.

An amendment of the constitution was undertaken to provide representation to Sikkim, as an associate state, in both houses of Parliament. (*See* DEPENDENT STATES.) Two other constitutional amendment bills were passed. The 33rd Amendment Act was intended to prevent resignation from a legislature under duress, and was a reaction to the agitations in Gujarat and Bihar. The 34th Amendment Act was designed to protect land tenure legislation in several states.

An event criticized vehemently abroad but popular within the country was an underground nuclear explosion carried out on May 18 by scientists of India's Atomic Energy Commission in the Rajasthan desert. The commission's chairman, H. N. Sethna, said that it was a wholly contained explosion in the range of 10–15 kilotons and took place at a depth of 100 m. (330 ft.) using an implosion device. The official announcement declared that the experiment was "a part of the research in peaceful uses of nuclear explosives," particularly for mining and earth moving, and that India had no intention of producing nuclear weapons. Canada, which had assisted India in the construction of nuclear reactors, responded with particular sharpness to this development. India maintained that all the plutonium used in the explosion had been produced within the country by Indian scientists and that the expenditure on nuclear explosion research amounted to less than 0.1% of the national budget.

An internal development that aroused great interest was the endeavour to reach an understanding with Sheikh Mohammad Abdullah, the Kashmir leader who had been removed from that state's chief ministership in 1953. Negotiations were still in progress at the year's end. Following a judgment by the Supreme Court on an election petition, an ordinance was issued on October 19 to clarify that under the Representation of the People Act election expenses incurred by a political party would not be deemed as an expenditure incurred by a candidate. Opposition leaders assailed the ordinance.

The Economy. The monsoon of 1974 proved erratic. Rains were 20 to 59% below normal over large parts of Gujarat, Rajasthan, Orissa, West Bengal, southern Bihar, Haryana, and Punjab. Kerala and northern Bihar were subjected to severe floods. Consequently, a shortage of seven million tons in the summer crop of food grains was feared. The possibility of importing large quantities of grain was also restricted owing to high world prices. In the climate of scarcity many growers held onto their stocks, and there was also a considerable amount of clandestine trading. In Orissa and West Bengal low stocks of grain and lack of purchasing power led to famine conditions in rural areas.

The government adopted a series of measures to curb money supply, curtail expenditure, and raise more revenue. The annual budget of the union government, presented on February 28, imposed new levies of Rs. 1,860,000,000 to take the revenue earnings for 1974–75 to an estimated Rs. 56,410,000,000 as against an expenditure of Rs. 54,080,000,000. With capital receipts of Rs. 30,990,000,000 and capital expenditures of Rs. 34,570,000,000, an overall deficit of Rs. 1,250,000,000 was expected, as compared with a

India was crippled in May as two million rail workers went on strike.

MORGAN CHUA—FAR EASTERN ECONOMIC REVIEW

"Let them eat plutonium!"

deficit of Rs. 6.5 billion in 1973–74. On July 31 an additional dose of taxation was announced to collect Rs. 1,360,000,000 in the remaining months of the financial year. Railway and postal rates were also increased.

Although higher allowances were given to workers to compensate for the rise in the cost of living, ordinances were issued in July by which half the subsequent increases were to be placed in a special deposit, thus immobilizing them temporarily. Orders were passed imposing curbs on the use of cement and steel for construction. The bank rate was increased to 9%, and curbs were enforced on dividend distribution and on credits in order to check speculative trading in food and inventory building. In spite of these measures, the general price index on August 31 was 30.6% higher than in August 1973.

Foreign Affairs. The foreign ministers of Bangladesh, India, and Pakistan met in New Delhi in April and signed a tripartite agreement by which Bangladesh announced its decision to drop, as an act of clemency, the trial of 195 Pakistani prisoners for war crimes. Pakistan in turn expressed deep regret for any crimes

that might have been committed. India arranged to return the 195 prisoners by the end of the month, thus completing the repatriation of all prisoners of war captured in the war of 1971. Pakistan undertook to speed the return to Pakistan of the non-Bengalis from Bangladesh.

After the Indian nuclear explosion in May, Pakistan refused to attend a meeting with Indian representatives scheduled for June, but talks were eventually held in September at which accord was reached on resumption of telecommunications and travel between the two countries. An agreement to resume trade relations, interrupted since the 1965 war over Kashmir, was signed November 30. Earlier, after a visit by Bangladesh's prime minister, Sheikh Mujibur Rahman, India and Bangladesh exchanged some territorial enclaves and announced their decision to find a solution to the problem of the sharing of the waters of the Ganges River. Another major foreign policy decision during the year was the recognition of Sri Lanka's title to Kachchativu Island, thus ending an old dispute. Mrs. Gandhi and the shah of Iran exchanged visits and formulated a program for sizable

INDIA

Education. (1971–72) Primary, pupils 78 million, teachers (1970–71) 1,602,515; secondary and vocational, pupils 8.4 million, teachers (1970–71) 523,341; teacher training (1968–69), students 207,289, teachers 15,343; higher (including 86 universities), students 2,540,000, teaching staff (1970–71) 119,000.

Finance. Monetary unit: rupee, with (Sept. 16, 1974) a free rate of Rs. 8.20 to U.S. $1 (Rs. 18.97 = £1 sterling). Gold, SDRs, and foreign exchange, official: (March 1974) U.S. $1,324,-000,000; (May 1973) U.S. $1,219,000,000. Budget (1972–73 actual): revenue Rs. 44,770,000,-000; expenditure Rs. 50,010,000,000. Gross national product: (1970–71) Rs. 397.7 billion; (1969–70) Rs. 330,019,000,000. Money supply: (April 1974) Rs. 112,640,000,000; (April 1973) Rs. 95,540,000,000. Cost of living (1970 = 100): (April 1974) 152; (April 1973) 120.

Foreign Trade. (1973–74) Imports Rs. 29,-209,000,000; exports Rs. 24,832,000,000. Import sources: U.S. 17%; Iran 9%; U.S.S.R. 9%;

West Germany 7%. Export destinations: Japan 14%; U.S. 14%; U.S.S.R. 11%; U.K. 10%. Main exports: cotton fabrics 9%; jute manufactures 9%; animal feedstuffs 7%; leather 7%; tea 6%; iron ore 5%.

Transport and Communications. Roads (1972) 1,021,819 km. (including 28,819 km. main highways). Motor vehicles in use (1972): passenger 646,463; commercial 346,020. Railways: (1972) 60,041 km.; traffic (1971–72) 125,469,000,000 passenger-km., freight 133,311,-000,000 net ton-km. Air traffic (1972): 4,557,-000,000 passenger-km.; freight 151.4 million net ton-km. Shipping (1973): merchant vessels 100 gross tons and over 430; gross tonnage 2,886,595. Telephones (Dec. 1972) 1,396,000. Radio licenses (Dec. 1972) 12,772,000. Television licenses (Dec. 1971) 49,000.

Agriculture. Production (in 000; metric tons; 1973; 1972 in parentheses): wheat 24,923 (26,-410); rice c. 67,500 (57,950); barley 2,327 (2,577); corn c. 6,500 (6,206); millet c. 10,000

(7,183); sorghum c. 8,300 (6,443); potatoes c. 5,079 (4,834); cassava (1972) 5,939, (1971) 5,130; tea c. 465 (454); chick-peas 4,469 (5,081); bananas (1972) c. 3,100, (1971) c. 3,300; sugar, raw value c. 4,300 (3,383); tobacco 364 (419); rapeseed 1,853 (1,433); linseed 439 (530); peanuts c. 6,000 (3,924); cotton, lint c. 1,160 (1,164); jute c. 1,224 (876). Livestock (in 000; Oct. 1972): cattle c. 176,900; sheep c. 43,300; pigs c. 4,780; buffalo c. 55,000; goats c. 69,000; poultry c. 118,000.

Industry. Production (in 000; metric tons; 1973): coal 77,077; lignite 3,304; iron ore (61% metal content) 34,426; pig iron 7,517; crude steel 6,870; electricity (excluding most industrial production; kw-hr.) 63,079,000; aluminum 152; cement 15,006; cotton yarn 998; woven cotton fabrics (m.; 1972) 8,024,000; petroleum products (1971) 17,884; sulfuric acid 1,313; caustic soda 419; gold (troy oz.; 1972) 106; manganese ore (metal content; 1972) 612.

expansion of Indo-Iranian economic cooperation. Successful talks were held with Burma, Sri Lanka, and Indonesia on the demarcation of the continental shelf.

A solution was found to the problem of the rupee funds accumulated by the United States through aid loans. Under an arrangement worked out in December 1973 and formally signed on Feb. 18, 1974, after endorsement by the U.S. Congress, Rs. 16,640,000,000 were to be regarded as granted to India toward development and social welfare while Rs. 8,621,000,000 were to be kept interest-free by the U.S. embassy in the public account of the government of India. The U.S. secretary of state, Henry Kissinger, visited New Delhi at the end of October in an effort to place Indo-U.S. relations on a new basis of maturity.

(H. Y. SHARADA PRASAD)

See also Bangladesh; Pakistan.
[976.A.2]

Indonesia

A republic of Southeast Asia, Indonesia consists of the major islands of Sumatra, Java, Kalimantan (Indonesian Borneo), Celebes, and Irian Jaya (West New Guinea) and approximately 3,000 smaller islands and islets. Area: 782,663 sq.mi. (2,027,087 sq.km.). Pop. (1973 est.): 124,602,000. Cap. and largest city: Jakarta (pop., 1973 est., 4,915,300). Language: Bahasa Indonesian (official); Javanese; Sundanese; Madurese. Religion: mainly Muslim; some Christian, Buddhist, and Hindu. President and prime minister in 1974, General Suharto.

Domestic Affairs. During 1974 the lengthy political honeymoon between the Suharto administration and the country's students and intellectuals collapsed in widespread rioting in the capital. For the first time under Suharto, who had assumed the reins of government following the abortive 1965 Communist coup, Indonesia appeared to lose confidence and direction, and entered a period of political uncertainty. By the close of the year, however, the stability and tranquillity that had been the trademarks of the Suharto government were restored.

Three days of rioting, known as the January 15 incident, began when students massed around the presidential palace while Suharto conferred with Japanese Prime Minister Kakuei Tanaka, a state guest then completing a tour of Southeast Asia to ease rising tensions between Japan and its regional trading partners. The students were soon joined by unemployed youths, squatters, and criminal gangs, and all roamed through Jakarta's business quarter, smashing automobiles, looting shops, and ransacking office buildings. The targets were primarily Chinese-owned stores and buildings that housed the branch offices of large Japanese firms. The Western community was ignored.

In essence, the rioting was a reaction to Suharto's daring economic strategy. In a bid to make up for the years "lost" under the rabble-rousing, inefficient, expansionist Sukarno regime, the president had taken painful economic steps. He enlarged Indonesia's dependence on foreign aid and foreign technology with heavy emphasis on attracting private and foreign investment, notably that of the aggressive and efficient Japanese and local Chinese businessmen who had traditionally dominated the Indonesian economy. Neither Chinese nor Japanese are especially popular in Indonesia, the former because of their disproportionate leverage over Indonesia's retail and wholesale markets and the latter because of a generally overbearing manner that reminded many Indonesians of the ruthless Japanese occupation of their homeland during World War II.

The economy responded vigorously, but as the living conditions of some impoverished Indonesians rose arithmetically, the abyss between rich and poor widened geometrically. A newly prosperous Indonesian class emerged which lived extravagantly and ostentatiously. The press, students, and intellectuals became increasingly vocal against the spread of "corruption," a code word not only for graft but for the abuse of power by elite groups.

Aware of the discontent, Suharto initiated a dialogue with his critics. When the rioting broke out in January, Suharto believed that the students had broken a pledge not to take their case to the streets. In the aftermath, a curfew was imposed, 11 persons were killed and scores injured, the publishing permits of several crusading newspapers were canceled, and 820 persons were arrested (778 were released within two weeks). Forty-two prominent student leaders and intellectuals, including members of Parliament, were charged with undermining the government. During the summer the first of their cases went to trial. The trials, which were open to the public, the press, and foreign observers, were expected to continue into 1975.

In some respects the rioting had a useful effect. For example, Suharto issued new regulations prohibiting army officers and/or their wives from acquiring controlling shares in commercial firms; authorized

---

INDONESIA

Education. (1970) Primary, pupils 13,395,000, teachers 347,500; secondary, pupils 1,260,900, teachers 87,810; vocational, pupils 544,830, teachers 48,780; teacher training, students 124,-900, teachers 9,645; higher, students 236,892, teaching staff (1967) 21,309.

Finance. Monetary unit: rupiah, with (Sept. 16, 1974) an official rate of 415 rupiah to U.S. $1 (free rate of 960 rupiah = £1 sterling). Gold, SDRs, and foreign exchange, central bank: (June 1974) U.S. $1,364,000,000; (June 1973) U.S. $774 million. Budget (1974–75) balanced at 1,577,000,000,000 rupiah. Gross national product: (1972) 4,407,000,000,000 rupiah; (1971) 3,726,-000,000,000 rupiah. Money supply: (Sept. 1973) 639,710,000,000 rupiah; (Sept. 1972) 424,350,-000,000 rupiah. Cost of living (Jakarta; 1970 = 100): (June 1974) 204; (June 1973) 142.

Foreign Trade. (1973) Imports U.S. $2,541,-800,000; exports U.S. $3,061,500,000. Import sources (1972): Japan 36%; U.S. 15%; West Germany 8%; Singapore 6%. Export destinations (1972): Japan 48%; U.S. 15%; Singapore 11%; The Netherlands 5%. Main exports: petroleum and products 49%; timber 18%; rubber 13%.

Transport and Communications. Roads (1972) 84,891 km. Motor vehicles in use (1972): passenger 277,210; commercial 131,175. Railways (1972): 8,596 km.; traffic 3,302,000,000 passenger-km., freight 1,042,000,000 net ton-km. Air traffic (1972): 1,253,800,000 passenger-km.; freight 22,452,000 net ton-km. Shipping (1973): merchant vessels 100 gross tons and over 573; gross tonnage 668,964. Telephones (Dec. 1972) 240,000. Radio receivers (Dec. 1970) 13,796,000. Television receivers (Dec. 1971) 95,000.

Agriculture. Production (in 000; metric tons; 1973; 1972 in parentheses): rice c. 20,321 (18,-031); corn c. 2,500 (2,269); cassava (1972) 10,099, (1971) 10,042; sweet potatoes (1972) 1,944, (1971) 2,154; sugar, raw value c. 950 (889); tea c. 67 (64); copra c. 800 (c. 820); soybeans c. 480 (515); palm oil c. 300 (269); peanuts c. 467 (455); coffee c. 198 (189); tobacco c. 76 (c. 75); rubber c. 797 (760); fish catch (1972) 1,268, (1971) 1,244. Livestock (in 000; Dec. 1972): cattle c. 6,250; pigs c. 4,300; sheep c. 3,000; horses c. 670; buffalo c. 2,900; goats c. 7,600; chickens c. 67,500.

Industry. Production (in 000; metric tons; 1973): crude oil 67,120; petroleum products (1972) 14,374; coal (1972) 179; tin concentrates (metal content) 22; bauxite (1972) 1,278; electricity (kw-hr.; 1971) 2,368,000.

a crackdown on graft; raised the salaries of civil servants as much as 400%; and revised the country's second five-year plan to put greater emphasis on a more evenhanded distribution of wealth.

The Economy. The surfacing of political stresses notwithstanding, Indonesia's economy continued its brisk upward movement. This was all the more remarkable given rising economic disequilibrium in the world at large. A major factor in Indonesia's continued success was oil.

The principal oil producer in the Far East, Indonesia during its first five-year plan (1969–74) increased its oil production by a spectacular 53.2% to reach a total of 1.5 million bbl. per day. Under the second five-year plan (1974–79), the nation hoped to double its production. After the Arab oil embargo during the winter of 1973–74 and the subsequent quadrupling of oil prices, Indonesia earned about $3.8 billion in foreign exchange from oil sales alone. In a politically astute move, however, Jakarta conspicuously pegged the price of its oil lower than Arab prices in a maneuver to win friends among less developed Afro-Asian countries and to maintain an atmosphere of accommodation among developed nations, the principal sources of the capital investment needed for Indonesia's expanding economy.

Foreign Affairs. On the surface, foreign affairs appeared quiescent. But in reality, 1974 was profoundly disturbing to the country's leadership, underscoring the thesis, accepted by both Suharto's supporters and critics at home, that Indonesia cannot afford the luxury of domestic political turmoil. For a country without a steel mill, with little hope of developing a nuclear

capability in the near future, with an almost non-existent navy and air force, the year was a period of deepening uneasiness about the ability of Indonesia to maintain its future independence and integrity.

After the Communist Party's collapse in Indonesia in 1965, China reasserted a claim to sovereignty over islands in the South China Sea that were internationally recognized as Indonesian territory. In the spring of 1974 China launched an air-naval military action to establish its sovereignty over islets in the area claimed by South Vietnam. Without fanfare, Jakarta reacted to the Sino-Vietnamese military encounter by officially claiming that its territorial boundary in the South China Sea extended to the Natuna Islands. During the summer, Indonesia announced the discovery of offshore oil deposits in the Natunas.

A completely unanticipated problem developed when the dictatorship of Marcello Caetano in Portugal was overthrown in April and the new Lisbon government announced plans to give Portuguese overseas territories the right of self-determination. These territories included Portuguese Timor (the eastern half of the island of Timor; the western half is Indonesian). Jakarta announced that it would respect the decision of the 600,000 people of Portuguese Timor, who were scheduled to vote on their future in 1975. But there was a feeling among observers that Indonesia might absorb this last Portuguese possession in Southeast Asia rather than face the prospect of a tiny, independent Timor with a substantial Chinese minority that might inject an element of instability into the area.   (ARNOLD C. BRACKMAN)

[976.C.1]

Riots erupted in Jakarta in January, the focus of antagonism being Prime Minister Tanaka of Japan who was visiting Indonesia at the time.

Industrial Production and Technology

In 1974 the fight against inflation caused many countries to adopt restrictive monetary or fiscal policies. Depressed demand, rapid inflation, and the temporary uncertainties over energy supplies generated a fairly widespread confidence crisis which, coupled with high interest rates and the reduced profitability and liquidity of the corporate sector, significantly lowered investment activity. Thus the boom year of 1973 was followed by a slack 1974, and although industrial activity might have recovered somewhat by the end of the year, 1974 was expected to show hardly any increase in manufacturing as compared with 1973.

In 1973 world industrial activity had exceeded the high rate of growth of 1972, with manufacturing production 10% higher than in the previous year, when the advance was 7%. The 18% rate of increase of those two years together was probably the fastest since World War II. All the industrialized countries had participated in the exceptionally fast rise, and the less industrialized nations had also raised their manufacturing output at almost the same rate, although progress among them was not quite so uniform.

Most of the growth in 1973 took place during the first half of the year; there was little advance after midyear, and in the last months industrial activity was disturbed by the cutback of oil supplies from the Arab oil-producing nations. Energy problems remained the characteristic feature of 1974. In the beginning months the reduction of supplies continued and added to the other difficulties that were starting to mount: rising inflation, unprecedentedly high commodity prices, and weakening demand. Total industrial output of the developed countries fell in the first half of 1974, chiefly as a result of declining activity in the United States, in Japan, and, because of the coal miners' strike, in the United Kingdom. Almost everywhere else stagnation followed the 1973 boom. Although the normal rate of oil deliveries was restored by midyear, tripled oil prices deflated activity everywhere and created enormous balance of payments problems for many countries. (*See* ENERGY.)

Various industries had fared differently in the 1973 boom. Within an overall 10% increase in manufacturing output, the heavy industries grew at 12%, twice the rate of the light industries. Output of the industries producing basic metals and metal products increased the fastest, 13%, followed by the chemical industries with 11%, the timber and furniture industries with 9%, and nonmetallic minerals with 8%. Food, beverages, tobacco, textiles, paper, and printing made somewhat less progress with 5–6%, and lagging behind them came the clothing-footwear group, with 3%. Interestingly, in most industries growth rates in the industrial and the less industrialized countries were comparable; however, clothing and footwear output rose by 11% in the less developed countries in 1973 and by only 2% in the industrial countries.

Although industrial activity in developed non-Communist nations grew at only a marginal rate in the second half of 1973, it did grow. In the first half of 1974, however, it fell. In many countries the initial deceleration resulted primarily from shortages of capacity, but, under the impact of general fuel stringency and tightening monetary policies, the deceleration turned into an actual decline in a number of countries, to be followed by a fractional recovery later in the year. Output for the first six months of 1974 was lower than for the second half of 1973 in the U.S., Japan, and the U.K., and in most other countries the growth of manufacturing activity was limited. An actual physical shortage of energy was most acute in the U.S., where crude oil imports were down by about 20% in the first quarter of 1974, and in the U.K., where the prolonged strike of the coal miners caused severe coal and power shortages.

The rate of growth of industrial activity throughout the world remained dependent on the U.S., whose industry accounted for more than 40% of the world total, excluding the U.S.S.R., China, and Eastern Europe. U.S. production stopped growing in the autumn of 1973, but, even so, had achieved an increase of almost 10% over 1972. The decline, which was most pronounced in residential building, quickly spread to consumer spending, already squeezed by rising prices. The automobile industry bore the brunt of the effects of the energy shortage and the high gasoline prices, and the fall in motor vehicle production in the first half of 1974 accounted for nearly all of the reduction in consumer spending. The decline continued throughout the year.

In Canada the spectacular rate of advance of 1973 slowed down toward the end of that year although the Canadian economy was less affected by the oil crisis. Some growth continued into 1974, though at a slower rate. Demand was strong in both years, with marked increases in consumption and business investment.

In Japan manufacturing output had risen by a record 18% in 1973, and high demand pressures from all sectors had led to serious capacity bottlenecks by the autumn. Fiscal measures to restrict demand had no time to show any major effect because the oil cutbacks sparked off a marked recession. Of all the industrial countries, Japan relied the most heavily on oil as a primary source of energy, and under the impact of the oil shortage, soon supported by weakening demand both at home and abroad, industrial production fell by some

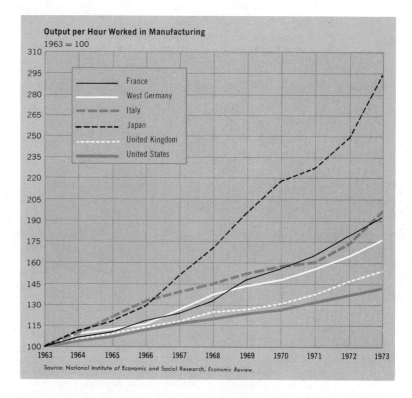

Output per Hour Worked in Manufacturing
1963 = 100

France
West Germany
Italy
Japan
United Kingdom
United States

Source: National Institute of Economic and Social Research, *Economic Review.*

Source: UN Monthly Bulletin of Statistics.

Table I. Index Numbers of World Production, Employment, and Productivity in Manufacturing Industries
1963=100

Area	Relative importance 1963	Relative importance 1973	Production 1971	Production 1972	Production 1973	Employment 1971	Employment 1972	Employment 1973	Productivity* 1971	Productivity* 1972	Productivity* 1973
World†	1,000	1,000	154	165	182	...	...	...	...	...	...
Industrial countries	876	862	152	163	179	...	...	...	...	...	...
Less industrialized countries	124	138	171	186	203	...	...	...	...	...	...
North America‡	480	440	140	152	167	...	...	...	...	...	...
Canada	28	29	157	168	182	115	117	123	137	144	148
United States	452	411	139	150	165	109	111	117	128	135	141
Latin America§	49	57	179	194	211	...	...	...	...	...	...
Mexico	8	10	196	212	225	...	...	...	...	...	...
Asia‖	88	132	219	236	273	...	...	...	...	...	...
India	16	13	139	148	150	...	...	...	...	...	...
Japan	55	99	258	277	327	121	121	125	213	229	262
Pakistan	3	3	164	169	196	...	...	...	...	...	...
Europe¶	350	333	153	160	173	...	...	...	...	...	...
Austria	7	7	164	179	187	104	106	108	158	169	173
Belgium	11	10	148	158	169	107	...	NA	138	...	...
Denmark	6	6	153	166	174	105	104	108	146	160	...
Finland	4	4	166	186	195	119	121	...	139	154	...
France	51	54	162	177	194	101	101	103	160	175	188
Germany, West	89	86	159	165	177	105	104	104	151	159	170
Greece	2	3	204	231	269	125	130	138	163	178	195
Ireland	1	1	159	167	184	115	116	119	138	144	155
Italy	36	33	150	156	170	108	107	109	139	146	156
Netherlands, The	12	13	172	181	193	99	94	...	174	193	...
Norway	4	3	148	151	158	...	...	...	...	...	...
Portugal	2	2	176	205	218	...	...	...	...	...	...
Spain	12	19	218	255	297	127	132	...	172	193	...
Sweden	14	13	153	157	167	96	95	97	159	165	172
Switzerland	10	8	146	150	157	94	91	90	155	165	174
United Kingdom	73	56	126	129	140	97	93	94	130	139	149
Yugoslavia	13	15	191	206	219	125	132	136	153	156	161
Rest of the world⊘	33	38	...	...	...	...	...	...	...	...	...
Australia	14	12	143	143	158	120	118	120	119	121	132
South Africa	5	5	162	167	182	160	164	...	101	102	...
Centrally planned economiesδ	...	...	193	209	228	...	...	...	...	...	...

*This is 100 times the production index divided by the employment index, giving a rough indication of changes in output per person employed.
†Excluding Albania, Bulgaria, China, Czechoslovakia, East Germany, Hungary, Mongolia, North Korea, North Vietnam, Poland, Romania, and the U.S.S.R.
‡Canada and the United States.
§South and Central America (including Mexico) and the Caribbean islands.
‖Asian Middle East and East and Southeast Asia, including Japan.
¶Excluding Albania, Bulgaria, Czechoslovakia, East Germany, Hungary, Poland, Romania, and the U.S.S.R.
⊘Africa, the Middle East, and Oceania.
δThese are not included in the above world total and consist of Albania, Bulgaria, Czechoslovakia, East Germany, Hungary, Poland, Romania, and the U.S.S.R.
Sources: UN Monthly Bulletin of Statistics; U.K. National Institute of Economic and Social Research, Economic Review.

Table II. Manufacturing Production in the U.S.S.R. and Eastern Europe
1963=100

Country	1971	1972	1973*
Bulgaria†	237	257	285
Czechoslovakia	184	210	209
Germany, East	163	173	184
Hungary	163	173	184
Poland	195	216	241
Romania	258	287	...
U.S.S.R.	192	205	221

*Provisional.
†General (all industries).
Source: UN Monthly Bulletin of Statistics.

5% between the autumn of 1973 and the spring of 1974. In the late autumn of 1974 there were signs of some modest recovery, and after the lifting of restrictions on industrial oil consumption in August industry seemed likely to be edging out of recession.

Manufacturing in the United Kingdom had advanced at the rate of 9% in 1973, but that level had been achieved in the first quarter of the year and after that there had been no further progress. The chief sources of demand were private consumption and exports, while investment grew at only a moderate rate. The refusal by the coal miners to work overtime, which began in November, combined with the oil cutbacks to produce a more severe energy shortage in the U.K. than elsewhere, and there was further deterioration when a full-scale strike stopped coal production entirely early in 1974. To protect power station coal stocks, the government forced a three-day workweek on industry, with the exception of the food industry and newspaper printing, which lasted into March. Yet manufacturing activity in the first quarter of 1974 was only 5% lower than it had been earlier. Full recovery, however, was slow, and total output for 1974 was likely to fall somewhat below that of 1973.

Manufacturing in France, which had grown approximately 10% in 1973, was relatively well maintained in 1974. In contrast to other countries, further growth was limited by capacity, in both physical and human terms. Shortage of labour became increasingly acute in almost all branches of industry, and in the summer of 1974, for the first time in more than 25 years, the number of unfilled vacancies in French industry exceeded the number of people looking for work.

Output of manufacturing industry in West Germany, by far the most important in Europe, grew by more than 7% in 1973. Order books remained full, and further growth appeared to be restricted only by limitations of capacity. The setback that followed in the first half of 1974 was not general. The West German automobile industry was severely hit by the oil crisis, and the building and construction industries and their suppliers also suffered a slump. But other industries, notably those producing steel and other intermediate materials, continued to work to the limits of their capacity until the early autumn of 1974. By then, there were signs of recovery in the domestic market. Exports of West German manufactures had continued at their previous high level without any interruption.

Despite a considerable number of industrial disputes, manufacturing in Italy rose by 9% in 1973, following years of slow growth and underinvestment. Although a major setback was avoided in 1974, the prospects for further growth were slight because of political and labour troubles, reduced industrial confidence, and the reliance on exports to markets where demand in 1974 was slack.

Advance was variable in 1973 in other European countries. Manufacturing output rose by 16% in Spain and Greece and by 10% in Ireland. There was medium growth, 6–7%, in Belgium, The Netherlands, Sweden, Yugoslavia, and Portugal; while in Austria, Denmark, Finland, Norway, and Switzerland the growth rate was 4–5%. In several countries where the manufacturing industries were already highly developed, limitations of capacity prevented faster progress. These countries also felt the effects of the generally weaker economic activity of the major industrial countries, but most succeeded in avoiding a decline in production, although growth rates slowed.

Elsewhere, there were wide differences in 1973. Most marked was the slow growth of manufacturing in India, at 1½%, in strong contrast to that of Pakistan, at 16%. In both Australia and South Africa the increase amounted to about 10%.

Among the centrally planned economies, output in Czechoslovakia stagnated after two years of spectacular growth. Poland and Bulgaria had the fastest growth rates of Eastern Europe; both exceeded 10% in 1973. In East Germany and in Hungary, by contrast, manufacturing output rose by only 6%. Industry in the U.S.S.R. increased by 8%.

High growth rates favoured productivity advance. Output per hour worked in manufacturing rose fastest in Japan and Italy, with more than 10%, followed by France and West Germany with 7–8%. The advance in the U.K., at 5½%, and in the U.S., at 3½%, was slower, and generally the growth of productivity slowed considerably in 1974. (G. F. RAY)

AEROSPACE

Despite the gloomy outlook of the new year, the world's aerospace industry generally showed healthy growth in 1974, thanks largely to defense sales. The 6% growth in U.S. turnover forecast by market analysts in the fall of 1973 seemed to have been achieved, and the Society of British Aerospace Companies forecast that the 1974 value of exports would be the highest ever. Inflation and other financial troubles, however, hit a number of companies. Lockheed ran into difficulties, and a complicated refinancing operation with the U.S. firm of Textron was begun. Aérospatiale of France, one of the major European aerospace firms, had a bad deficit in 1973 and requested emergency government aid. Worst hit were the airlines. (*See* TRANSPORTATION.)

The Anglo-French Concorde continued to be the spearhead commercial aviation project. Efforts centred on completing the trials needed to certify the supersonic transport for airline service in 1976. Following a crucial meeting of the two governments, with Britain seemingly wanting to cancel the project and British Airways claiming that compulsory operation of Concorde could badly affect its financial results, continuing finance for 16 aircraft was agreed.

In March a combined Lockheed and Rolls-Royce team demonstrated a TriStar in Moscow. The long-range version of this wide-body transport was launched in September, when Saudi Arabian Airlines announced that its four TriStars would be fitted with the uprated Rolls-Royce RB. 211-524 engines. This was a significant event for the British company, demonstrating that it once again could compete with the big fan engines from the U.S. Plans were also made to fit the engine to the recently ordered Boeing 747s of British Airways.

The first major accident involving a wide-body airliner killed 346 people and destroyed a McDonnell Douglas DC-10 in March. The 747 suffered its first fatal crash in November when 59 were killed shortly after takeoff from Nairobi, Kenya. Overall, fatality rates for the big planes had been low during their four years of operation, but under pressure from the U.S. Federal Aviation Administration design modifications were to be embodied in the DC-10 beginning in 1975. The smallest of the wide-body transports, the twin-engined Airbus A-300B, built by a consortium of European firms, entered service between Paris and London during the summer. Despite U.S. skepticism about these big "twins," there were about 40 orders for the U.S.-powered aircraft by the year's end.

Boeing's 727 continued as the most successful jet airliner of all time, and in 1973 the company sold 86. Its success depressed the market for any new aircraft in its class, and the Seattle, Wash., firm's own plan for a family of transports to replace the 707 and 727 was shelved indefinitely. At the lower end of the scale, the British Hawker Siddeley HS.146 feederliner, launched in July 1973, ran into financial difficulties as a result of inflation; with government help, the project would be maintained at design stage.

Two successes were announced at the Farnborough International Air Show: Short's SD3-30, a derivative of the well-known Skyvan, made its first sale, to a New York operator, and Fairey-Britten-Norman announced the sale of 100 Islanders to the Philippines.

In October the British government confirmed that it was to nationalize the aircraft industry. The two largest airframe manufacturers, British Aircraft Corp. (BAC) and Hawker Siddeley, would merge into a new British National Aerospace Corp., but the rest of the industry, such as the lesser airframe companies, the aero engine business, and the manufacturers of electronics equipment, were excluded from the plans.

One of the most notable military aviation events of the year was the first flight of the European Multi-Role Combat Aircraft (MRCA) in September. Though the plane was long-delayed owing to difficulties with the engines, Britain, West Germany, and Italy all publicly affirmed their resolve to bring the new fighter into service as rapidly as possible.

The Anglo-French Jaguar fighter-bomber, which entered service with the RAF and the French Air Force earlier in the year, broke into the export market with £80 million worth of sales to Oman and Kuwait. The Hawk trainer, replacing the RAF's two-seater Gnat, made its first flight just before the Farnborough show opened. The new B-1 intercontinental bomber, built by Rockwell International Corp. and intended to replace the U.S. Air Force's B-52, made its first test flight in December.

In September a bitter battle broke out between France and the U.S. about the supply of a replacement fighter for the Starfighters of The Netherlands, Belgium, Norway, and Denmark. France had offered a version of the new Dassault Mirage F.1 with a Snecma M.53 engine. The U.S., in a drive to reduce balance of payments problems, made a high-powered sales pitch for its products and backed it with the decision to put the winner of its lightweight fighter competition—between Northrop's YF-17, which, as the Cobra, had been on offer to The Netherlands for several years as a combined U.S.-European work package, and General Dynamics' YF-16—into U.S. Air Force service. The decision by the European nations was to be made early in 1975. Switzerland chose another Northrop design, the F-5E version of its Freedom Fighter, to maintain the air-superiority role in its air force.

The U.S. again dominated the space scene. The third, and final, manned Skylab flight came to a successful conclusion early in the year, and only a few weeks later man's first close-up view of the planet Mercury was transmitted over television from NASA's Mariner 10 spacecraft as it sped past the planet at a range of 700 km. By means of superb guidance and navigation, the spacecraft was brought into the vicinity of Mercury for another flyby in September. Two unmanned satellites, the Earth Resources Technology Satellite (ERTS-1) and the Applications Technology Satellite (ATS 6), showed impressively how space technology could help man. The ERTS-1 continued to return a stream of pictures and data showing new details about the earth. The ATS 6 was used for a number of significant experiments, such as the transmission of medical data and the setting up of a pilot education service to the scattered villages of India and Alaska. The satellite could broadcast directly to small, cheap aerials and receiving equipment costing only a few hundred dollars per set.   (MICHAEL WILSON)
[732.B.1]

AUTOMOBILES

The number and diversity of obstacles to the growth and prosperity of the automobile industry during 1974 had an aggregate effect little short of catastrophic. Although the scarcity (and unprecedented rise in price) of petroleum and all its derivatives was by far the most serious of those obstacles, causing sharp declines in sales and production, other inflationary pressures continued to push up manufacturing costs. In many countries, fiscal restrictions upon compensatory increases in selling price reduced profit margins and cash flows to such an extent that the funds essential to the continuance of research, development, and retooling became dangerously reduced. In the long term, threats to the resources available for meeting the many engineering projects necessitated by the energy crisis, by environmental pressures, and by tougher safety standards were probably the most serious consequence. An inevitable short-term effect was that comparatively few new models were introduced.

A comparison between car production figures for the first six months of 1974 with those of the same period in 1973 showed that the United States suffered a decline of nearly 30%. For West Germany and Japan the drop in production was approximately 20%, while for the U.K. it was about 10% and for Canada less than 7%. In France and

Two new Japanese planes designed for corporate use are the Mitsubishi MU-21 (foreground) and MU-2M.

KEYSTONE

Italy the level of car production did not decline seriously until the latter part of the year.

The pattern of commercial vehicle production differed considerably from that of passenger cars during the first half of the year and generally presented a less disturbing picture. As in earlier years (*see* Table III), European countries and Japan exported a very much higher proportion of their vehicle production (both passenger cars and commercials) than did the U.S.

The worldwide drop in sales during 1974 was accompanied by changes in the size and price of cars preferred by customers. In an industry geared to production on a very large scale it was physically impossible to alter the "mix" of a diversity of models at short notice; furthermore, the fluidity of an unprecedented marketing situation involved the danger that, while production facilities were being revamped, there might well be another shift in demand. No one could confidently predict the eventual effects of the shortage and high cost of gasoline, the frequent and substantial increases in car prices, and the statutory limitations on speeds that were applied, by many governments, as a device to reduce fuel consumption.

During the early part of the year, marketing uncertainties were most acutely felt in the United States, where the sharp drop in total sales was unevenly distributed across the spectrum of car sizes and prices; in general, big cars and "intermediates" suffered heavily, but the decline in demand also affected "compacts" and subcompact models. Unexpectedly, the market penetration achieved by imported cars (which were mostly small in size) likewise decreased, though only slightly. Later in the year, the large cars began to stage a comeback, and the intermediate and compact models regained some ground. But the steep increases in price that accompanied the introduction of the 1975 models in the fall again caused reduced demand and led to widespread layoffs and many plant closures.

In order to meet the U.S. federal standards for 1975 (which required reductions of 50% in the emission of hydrocarbons and 46% in the case of carbon monoxide, from the already low levels required in 1974), most of the U.S. cars introduced in the fall were fitted with catalytic converters. These devices facilitated the conversion of the unwanted pollutants into water and carbon dioxide. The successful development of these converters, housed in stainless steel in order to last for the 50,000 mi. demanded by statute, was a technological achievement of great importance but one that necessarily added substantially to the price of the vehicle. Another consequence was that it became imperative for cars so equipped to operate on unleaded gasoline (lead having a damaging effect upon the catalyst).

General Motors was the most powerful proponent of the catalytic converter, insisting that this new method for controlling pollutants made it possible to back off from some of the distortions to engine specifications previously needed to meet emission standards (which had adversely affected drivability and, especially, fuel economy). Other compensations for the cost of reducing pollutants included the longer life and reliability of the ignition systems (including spark plugs), which had to be achieved in order to safeguard the converter from the effects of misfiring. American Motors de-

cided to use the catalytic converter made by GM for nearly all its 1975 models. Ford and Chrysler adopted a catalytic converter of different internal design for most of their 1975 models, but adopted a more cautious approach than GM, continuing to offer options with engines modified to meet federal requirements without the aid of a converter and therefore able to use either leaded or unleaded fuel.

In general, the lineup of 1975 models reflected the new importance of operating costs, especially in terms of mileage per gallon, but, paradoxically, new high-performance options were also introduced. Chevrolet added a Monza coupe to the Vega range (with optional V-8 engine), and GM also launched a Pontiac Astre, an Oldsmobile Starfire, and a Buick Skyhawk, all based on the Vega chassis but with a revived and updated version of a former V-6 engine. Ford managed to find room for a V-8 engine option, with automatic transmission, in the Mustang II and offered a West German-built V-6 engine as a Pinto option. However, the most important of the Ford announcements concerned two new and luxuriously equipped cars in the somewhat larger "compact" category (overall length no more than 200 in.): a Ford Granada and a Lincoln Mercury Monarch, expressly designed to give the refinement and quietness normally found only in much larger models. Chrysler announced a new Cordoba coupe and offered an "overdrive-4" manual transmission on the Dodge Dart and Plymouth Valiant. American Motors adopted the (British) Laycock automatic overdrive for the six-cylinder Gremlin and Hornet.

In the troubled field of safety legislation the mandatory interlocking of seat belts with engine electrics and the projected airbag program were thrown out by a vote of 339 to 49 in the U.S. House of Representatives in August. Interlock systems had proved unpopular (and easily bypassed), while the controversial airbag, despite its attractions, would have been a costly innovation of uncertain reliability.

Of all the European Community countries, West Germany suffered the greatest decline in car production. Floating exchange rates strengthened West German currency to the extent that the price of the products became prohibitive to many export customers. The converse effect helped the U.K. and Italy to remain competitive in important

export markets, but their advantage was progressively undermined by a combination of unprecedented inflation and industrial unrest. British Leyland, hampered by inadequate resources to finance essential plant and product development, was promised £50 million in government aid toward year's end, with the prospect of undefined state participation in management. The liquidation of Aston Martin Ltd., maker of luxury high-performance cars, was announced at the end of December.

Early in the year the British motor industry also suffered from the imposition of a three-day workweek, a government measure taken to conserve coal stocks during a national strike by miners. Nevertheless, Britain's total motor vehicle exports (including components) were 13% higher during the first eight months of 1974 than in the same period in 1973 while its motor imports dropped to a small extent.

The pattern of demand for cars of varying size and price did not swing in Europe to the extremes experienced in the U.S.; very small and "smallish" cars, which traditionally held the largest share of the European markets, gained some extra penetration. The losers were mainly in the "medium" class, approximately the size of an American subcompact.

Increased interest was shown in diesel engine options, for which Mercedes-Benz and Peugeot were traditionally the main sources. The former company announced a five-cylinder version of its 220 D four-cylinder model, thereby stepping up engine size and performance by 25%, and Peugeot offered a diesel option in its small "204" front-drive model to supplement the existing 404 and 504 diesels.

Volkswagen announced a new, small front-drive three-door coupe, named the Scirocco, at the Geneva motor show in March, followed later by the Golf (Rabbit in the U.S.) sedan and the Audi 50. There was speculation about all three as probable successors to the Beetle, the 18 millionth of which came off the assembly line in October. Volvo launched a new 240 series of cars in September, notable for an advanced V-6 engine in which aluminum alloy die castings were largely used. This was the first product of the new engine plant at Douvrin (near Paris), which was a cooperative venture undertaken by Volvo, Peugeot, and Renault. The same basic engine was used

**Table III. Production and Exports of Motor Vehicles
by the Principal Producing Countries**
In 000 units

	1971		1972		1973	
Country	Passenger cars	Commercial vehicles	Passenger cars	Commercial vehicles	Passenger cars	Commercial vehicles
Production						
United States	8,583.7	2,088.0	8,828.2	2,482.5	9,667.2	3,014.3
Germany, West	3,696.8	285.9	3,521.5	294.5	3,649.9	299.2
France	2,694.0	316.3	2,992.9	335.3	3,202.4	393.8
United Kingdom	1,741.9	456.2	1,921.3	408.0	1,747.3	416.7
Japan	3,717.9	2,092.9	4,022.3	2,272.1	4,470.6	2,612.2
Italy	1,701.1	116.0	1,732.4	107.4	1,823.3	134.7
Canada	1,096.1	276.0	1,154.5	319.9	1,227.4	347.4
Australia	391.2	78.9	366.6	81.2	376.3	86.6
Sweden	287.4	29.7	317.9	33.0	341.5	36.8
U.S.S.R.	518.0	612.0	730.0	649.0	917.0	685.0
Other countries	1,604.9	559.1	1,857.7	490.6	2,080.9	724.5
World total	26,033.0	6,911.0	27,445.3	7,473.5	29,503.8	8,751.2
Exports						
Germany, West	2,155.9	163.2	2,097.6	167.0	2,203.6	182.4
United Kingdom	721.1	194.7	627.5	139.9	598.8	163.1
France	1,148.6	65.4	1,240.0	69.7	1,340.0	75.2
Italy	640.2	40.3	659.1	40.6	656.3	49.1
United States	386.6	99.1	410.2	119.9	509.2	150.8
Sweden	212.5	23.4	195.2	23.7	183.2	25.9
Japan	1,299.4	479.7	1,407.3	547.5	1,450.9	616.7
Canada	822.3	390.7	979.4	372.7	892.3	315.9

Source: British Society of Motor Manufacturers and Traders, *The Motor Industry of Great Britain.*

in new 504 coupe models introduced by Peugeot. This tripartite consortium was said to be unaffected by the surprise announcement, in the fall, that a merger was being planned between Peugeot and Citroen. Citroen's financial plight proved so serious that government support of around $300 million had to be provided to permit completion of the deal.

Despite economic difficulties, Citroen's entirely new front-drive CX sedan was one of very few outstanding exhibits at the Paris motor show in October. Renault, after weathering a difficult year exceptionally well, had little to attract attention. Opel introduced a new turbocharged version of its Manta Berlinetta coupe.

A dearth of new models also detracted from the London automobile show, held in October. The revamped Ford Capri II hatchback coupe and Granada Ghia coupe, a Vanden Plas deluxe version of the Austin Allegro, and a 2300 S edition of the Vauxhall Victor sedan set a trend seemingly at odds with economic austerities. In the sports car class the new Lotus Elite combined an advanced technical specification with attractive styling. Chrysler, although strongly represented in London and Paris, made few changes to its European products for the 1975 model year.

The biennial commercial vehicle show, held in London in September, was notable for the introduction of an entirely new range of heavy Bedford trucks by Vauxhall (a GM subsidiary), backed by an investment of £50 million for engineering development and productive equipment. Bedford had not previously competed in the heavyweight class.

An unprecedented decline in the domestic sales of automobiles in Japan, accentuated by restrictive fiscal measures, completely swamped a creditable export performance, although the situation improved somewhat later in the year. The hard-pressed motor vehicle industry also faced stiffer emission standards for cars and the extension of emission controls to diesel trucks and buses. Japanese cars retained their dominance among imports into Australia.

A report published by the Industries Assistance Commission of the Australian government in August suggested that the market for motor vehicles in Australia was not big enough to support local manufacture by more than the three best-established companies, GM-Holden, Ford, and Chrysler. This intensified the troubled situation of British Leyland in that country and precipitated its decision to dispose of a large manufacturing plant at Zetland. In November Australia took steps to curb car imports and encourage domestic manufacture of components.　　(MAURICE PLATT) [732.B.2]

BUILDING AND CONSTRUCTION

The total expenditure for new construction in the United States at midyear 1974 was at an annual rate of $138 billion; however, it was estimated that construction during the last half of the year would drop considerably below that level and that for the entire year total outlays would fall far below the record total of $135.4 billion reached in 1973. One major sustaining force in construction during the first half of the year was the high level of spending for public construction. On a seasonally adjusted basis, these expenditures in July 1974 were at an annual rate of $39.6 billion, compared with total outlays of $32.5 billion in 1973. Expenditures for private construction during the first half of 1974 were below those for the comparable period of 1973, and it

Some 12 million bricks are stockpiled in London because of the housing decline.

appeared that during the last half of the year these outlays would drop to much lower levels.

All types of private construction were being influenced adversely by inflation and the shortage of mortgage funds. These influences were especially noticeable in residential construction. In 1972, in the United States, a record number of 2,378,500 housing units had been started. In the following year the starts had dropped to 2,057,500; by the third quarter of 1974 it appeared that housing starts for the entire year would be less than 1.4 million units. Housing starts in August 1974 were down almost 50% from August 1973.

While inflation had pushed the prices of houses up and the downturn in the economy had undoubtedly affected the number of buyers, the main contributor to the sharp decline in housing starts in 1974 was the acute shortage of mortgage funds. Mortgage funds available in 1974 were sufficient to finance only about 60% of the number of new homes that had been financed in 1972.

One of the most disturbing features of the collapse of the mortgage market was that it occurred despite the U.S. government's major effort to direct credit into that sector of the economy. Starting in 1968 the government had authorized the Federal National Mortgage Association to buy conventional mortgages from lending institutions, had authorized the Government National Mortgage Association to support the market in government-backed mortgages, and had created the Federal Home Loan Mortgage Corp. to buy mortgages held by the savings and loan associations. On Dec. 31, 1968, these federal agencies held 5.3% of the home mortgages in the United States, but by June 30, 1974, they held 9.9%. This was a gain of 87% in the share of mortgages held. During this same period the share held by savings and loan associations gained only 11% (from 43.9 to 49.1%), while the share of mutual savings banks declined 21% (from 13.9 to 11%) and that of life insurance companies 53% (from 11.5 to 5.4%).

Builders were confronted during the first half of 1974 with a continued upward movement in construction costs. In July 1974 the United States Department of Commerce Composite Construction Cash Index stood

at 171 (1967 = 100). In 1973 the index was 152, having moved from 144 in January to 158 in December.

In Canada residential construction was being held back by mortgage rates of 12% or more. Inflation and a general economic downturn were evident in Western Europe during 1974. In the U.K. the output of the construction industry grew slightly more than 2% in 1973 but was on a declining trend throughout that year. In 1974 the industry was in a serious recession. The starts of private houses were expected to be about 150,000, compared with 215,000 in 1973. In most countries of Western Europe construction was curtailed or the industry was in recession as a result of the unfavourable economic developments in 1974. In Japan inflation was having a strongly adverse effect and was imposing severe constraints on construction.　　(CARTER C. OSTERBIND) [733.A]

CHEMICALS

All the vital signs for the first three quarters of 1974 pointed to a chemical industry that was in excellent physical health. But some indications of sluggishness began appearing in the early part of the fourth quarter. And the industry was facing a number of gnawing problems that to some degree were taking the glow off the shining statistical profile.

The U.S. Department of Commerce reported that shipments of chemicals and allied products in 1973 amounted to $67,034,000,-000, 16.7% higher than 1972's $57,437,000,-000. During the first six months of 1974, they shot up to $40,142,000,000, 18.6% higher than the $33,861,000,000 recorded during the same period of 1973. Chemical production, according to the Federal Reserve Board's index of quantity output, went from 139.6 (1967 = 100) in 1972 to 150.2 in 1973 and increased during the first seven months of 1974 to 156 (preliminary, seasonally adjusted) in July.

After an extended period on a near plateau, chemical prices started to move up in 1973 and then increased sharply during the first half of 1974. The U.S. Department of Labor's index of wholesale prices for chemicals and allied products averaged 110 (1967 = 100) in 1973, up from 104.2 in 1972. It then increased during each of the first seven months of 1974, reaching 148.4 in July.

Chemical exports soared during the first half of 1974 and were helping in some measure to offset the huge trade deficits being run up by the U.S. because of its increased imports of expensive crude oil. U.S. Department of Commerce figures showed that U.S. chemical exports rose 39% in 1973, from $4,132,800,000 in 1972 to $5,748,500,000. They rose 63.9% in the first half of 1974, from $2,593,800,000 for the first half of 1973 to $4,252,100,000. Chemical imports, meanwhile, climbed only 21% in 1973, from $2,-014,600,000 in 1972 to $2,436,700,000. They reached $1,664,000,000 in the first half of 1974, a 35.8% increase over the $1,225,000,-000 imported during the first half of 1973. As a result, the balance of chemical trade for the U.S. rose 56.3% in 1973 from $2,118,-200,000 in 1972 to $3,311,800,000. It came to $2,588,100,000 for the first half of 1974, 89.1% higher than the $1,368,800,000 for the first six months of 1973.

With demand strong and profits healthy, chemical companies were planning ambitious expansion programs. The McGraw-Hill annual survey of capital expenditures in May 1974 reported manufacturers of chemicals and allied products in the U.S. spent $3,450,-000,000 for new plant and equipment in 1972 and $4,460,000,000 in 1973. They were planning a 36.1% increase in 1974 to $6,070,-000,000. The company's August 1974 survey of capital spending by U.S. companies overseas showed chemical companies planned to boost expenditures outside the U.S. to $2,-465,000,000 in 1974, 68% more than in 1973, and to raise that to $3,205,000,000 in 1975 and to $3,686,000,000 in 1976.

The expansion plans, although impressive by any measure, were distorted by inflation. A Union Carbide study during the first half of 1974 found that plant and construction costs, which had increased 4.7% per year from 1958 through 1973, were 16% higher in 1974 than in 1973. By the end of the third quarter, the costs seemed to be escalating at an even faster rate. Most chemical companies were sticking to their dollar commitments but were cutting back on some expansion projects.

Cost and availability of feedstocks and energy were among the worrisome problems facing the chemical industry. Spot disruptions were experienced during the winter of 1973–74, but the industry managed to survive without serious cutbacks. Coping with shortages of a broad range of materials became a way of life for those in the industry during the period, but the cause was usually a lack of capacity rather than an actual scarcity of raw materials or energy. Chemical companies were learning to design and operate plants to utilize energy more efficiently and were striving for maximum flexibility in their ability to use different forms of energy.

A number of chemical products drew the fire of environmental and other groups during 1974. One of the most notable was vinyl chloride monomer (VCM), which was linked to workers who had contracted angiosarcoma, a rare form of liver cancer. Most of the cases had occurred in plants making polyvinyl chloride (PVC) from VCM. (See *Plastics,* below.)

The chemical industries in other industrialized countries were experiencing, in varying degrees, the same prospects and problems as the U.S. industry. In West Germany, chemical sales rose about 15% in 1973 to an estimated $23.9 billion. Chemical exports were up 21% to $9,520,000,000, while chemical imports increased 16% to about $5.1 billion. Sales during the first quarter of 1974 were 22.8% ahead of the corresponding period of 1973, and chemical exports rose 44.3%. The industry, however, was affected by high costs for raw materials, and the increase in sales and export volumes in part reflected inflationary factors.

Japan's chemical industry weathered the Arab oil embargo and energy problems of 1973–74 far better than had been expected. Chemical sales for 1973 increased 14% to approximately $14.8 billion, and chemical companies boosted both sales and profits for fiscal year 1973 (which ended March 31, 1974). One advantage was the relatively large inventories of the manufacturers. Synthetic fibre makers, though faced with high raw materials costs and price controls on their products, showed profit increases for 1974, in one case of 283%. The country's Ministry of International Trade and Industry said that synthetic fibre production in fiscal 1973 rose 15.9% to 1,390,000,000 met-

ric tons. Demand, however, rose 40.1% to 1,420,000,000 metric tons. Worrying fibre makers and other chemical companies in Japan were the 30% wage increase negotiated by the major labour unions in the spring of 1974, electricity costs that were expected to nearly double, and continued rising costs of raw materials.

The United Kingdom's chemical industry rode out the economic upheavals in that country better than most other industries. Preliminary estimates placed chemical sales for 1973 at over $13 billion, an 11% rise over 1972. And while total manufacturing output declined by 4.7%, British chemical sales gained 4% during the first quarter of 1974. The industry continued to make a contribution to trade. Chemical exports were up only 32% in 1973, while imports rose 36%. Still, with chemical exports of $2.9 billion and imports of $2 billion, net exports amounted to $900 million. Chemical exports were rising faster in 1974. For the first seven months, according to the U.K.'s Chemical Industries Association, they rose more than 66% to $2.8 billion. The association placed new investment in chemicals at $550 million in 1973 and was expecting an expenditure of $989 million in 1974.   (DONALD P. BURKE)
[732.D.1]

ELECTRICAL

A high rate of monetary inflation in all industrialized countries in 1974, shortages and wide price fluctuations in raw materials, and government measures to arrest inflation all combined to distort the results presented in most of the annual reports of companies in the electrical industry. New accounting systems to allow for the effects of inflation and revision of financial legislation were the objectives of intensive industry lobbying of governments.

In May, as the energy crisis and the quadrupling of oil prices caused countries to turn to electricity generation using coal and nuclear energy, Westinghouse Electric Corp. Chairman Donald C. Burnham envisaged increased opportunities for the electrical industry. But, plagued by high interest rates and dwindling credit resources, U.S. utilities delayed the construction of many nuclear power reactors and even abandoned plans for others. In October, the U.S. Atomic Energy Commission reported that the 102,000 Mw. of nuclear capacity planned for 1980 had dropped to 85,000 Mw. The role of government finance in the expansion of nuclear power would clearly be large, and much would depend on the willingness of the oil producers to invest on a long-term basis in capital markets.

In Britain the Department of Industry's survey of investment intentions in September showed that electrical manufacturers' capital expenditure would rise by 5% between 1973 and 1974. Only a year previously the forecast for the same period had been 15%. Also in September, Westinghouse Electric sought to renegotiate long-term contracts with utilities for generators, transformers, and circuit breakers. Price increases of 6–8% were being asked. At the same time, the management of Brown Boveri's West German group indicated that it was not too optimistic about the future performance of the company because of delays in contracts for power station equipment.

The General Electric Co. in Britain increased sales in 1973 by more than 10% but said that the proceeds in real terms had gone to the government through increased taxation and that neither the employees nor the stockholders had benefited from the improved productivity and profits. In West Germany sales by Siemens in 1973 rose only

2%, but an improvement, mainly from exports, was predicted for 1974. Business in West Germany was tending to stagnate, the company said. Net earnings were 2.8% of sales, but the board aimed to raise this to 5% "in closer alignment with our international competitors." British Insulated Callenders Cables' net earnings in 1973 were 7% of sales, but finance charges were 50% higher, due partly to higher copper costs.

In Sweden, Allmänna Svenska Elektriska Aktiebolaget (ASEA) reported net earnings in 1973 of 6% of sales and said that it planned to concentrate on technical improvements to plant control systems in order to reduce electrical power consumption. The company also announced that it would try to balance material and production costs against energy savings.

Three principles of energy conservation, which would lead to different research and development goals than those based on commercial criteria, were enunciated by Chauncey Starr of the U.S. Electric Power Research Institute. First, built-in obsolescence of products should be eliminated; second, materials requiring considerable energy for their production should be used in such a way that they could be reused for further applications; and third, industrial processes should be integrated to minimize waste in reheating, and process plants should be located close to their market areas.

A new electric motor, one-third the size and weight of previous designs, was developed for use in domestic appliances by Philips in The Netherlands. Ceramic ferrite permanent magnets were used in place of copper field windings. Other examples of designs based on material conservation principles were under development in industrial laboratories around the world.

Product design changes were also being brought about in the countries of the European Economic Community following publication of the EEC Commission's Low Voltage Directive. The object of this directive was the removal of trade barriers by ensuring standardization of safety regulations for all electrical equipment designed for operation at voltages below 1,000 v. New safety standards were being adopted in all nine member countries, and approval schemes by recognized testing houses were being set up for domestic appliances and portable tools.

Although European proposals for a new design of plug and socket to connect domestic appliances and portable tools to the electricity supply were likely to lead to the publication shortly of an international standard, the design would in practice be confined to Europe. Domestic wiring installations in the U.S. were usually designed for 125 v., and it seemed unlikely that a changeover to 230–240 v. would be made in the foreseeable future. The "Europlug" would be rated at 16 amp. 250 v. and would be unfused.

In regard to public electricity supply networks, the major product development in recent years had been metal-clad switchgear using sulfurhexafluoride gas for insulation and arc interruption during switching operations. From the time this equipment was first seriously considered in the late 1950s, commercial development was rapid, particularly in France and West Germany. Many utilities were adopting the design in Europe and the U.S., and those manufacturers able to offer such equipment could look forward to increasing commercial success in world markets.   (T. C. J. COGLE)
[732.C.6; 10/37.B.5.d]

GLASS

Shortages, rising costs, and inflation assailed the glass industries in 1974, at least in the developed countries. In three significant areas—soda ash, fuel oil, and wages—there were fluctuations that significantly affected productive capacity and costs. (Soda ash, with sand and limestone, is one of the basic raw materials for glass manufacture.)

The year began with an upsurge in demand for glass products in most Western countries. Suppliers of raw materials were able to cope with the resultant pressure except for soda ash manufacturers, who operate a capital-intensive catalytic process as opposed to the basically extractive processes of the sand and limestone producers. In the U.S. major producers had to close down two plants when the Environmental Protection Agency maintained that effluent was polluting rivers with sodium nitrate. In the U.K. the three-day week and, later, some labour problems caused shortages. In Europe supply lagged behind demand.

More serious was the rapid rise in the cost of fuel oil, which, with natural gas, is one of the two principal means of obtaining the energy to melt glass. This caused glass manufacturers to examine their processes more closely to see whether a more effective use of energy might be made. Finally, the rate of inflation affected wage rates. There were no major strikes, but the glass industries had to concede wage payments at a rate consistent with rises in the cost of living.

Glass-container manufacturers continued to be subjected to pressures from governments and environmental agencies. In Norway there was a move toward banning non-returnable containers, and many container makers showed interest in setting up systems for returning used containers for remelting. Energy conservation could create demand in the flat-glass industries, due to demand for double glazing, and in the glass-fibre sectors, for insulation. In the latter field, Saint-Gobain-Pont-à-Mousson of France announced a new process that could help in both energy conservation and the secondary use of waste glass.

Czechoslovakian glass technologists announced a breakthrough in the speed of manufacturing sheet glass by the Fourcault process by electrical boosting. To what extent this might affect the traditional methods of manufacturing flat glass in the face of the spread of the float process was a matter of interest to all manufacturers in this field. One area of dispute was Scandinavia, where the U.K. patent holders of float glass, Pilkington Brothers Ltd., were interested in setting up a plant and invited sheet-glass manufacturers to join the project. Other investment plans totaling £150 million were deferred by Pilkington in October pending "changes in taxation and price control."

In Poland, where investment had been low for several years, 18 new glass and ceramic plants were to be completed over two years. The only two producers of container glass in Belgium, Verlica-Momignies and Bouteilleries Belges Réunies, were discussing closer cooperation to create a unit large enough to meet foreign competition.

From the safety point of view, some countries favoured toughened glass for car windscreens (windshields), while others preferred laminated glass. The U.K. company Triplex announced a development that appeared to combine the best of both processes in a laminated shield that shattered into blunt particles, as in toughened glass, rather than large splinters. (CYRIL WEEDEN)

[724.C.5.a; 733.A.4.a.vii]

IRON AND STEEL

For a considerable time the fortunes of the world steel industry had followed a well-established pattern. Demand, and consequently prices and profitability, fluctuated with the cycles to which the steel industry is particularly subject, yielding, for various reasons, a generally insufficient financial return over the cycle. In contrast, a number of significant new developments of an economic character took place in 1974: some were already emerging early in 1973, while others were unheralded.

The first such feature was the energy crisis, which began near the end of 1973. The initial impact was severe in physical terms and created great uncertainty and loss of confidence, particularly in the steel industries of those countries whose economies were most dependent on oil imports, most notably Japan. Later, as the initial crisis passed, the chief effects were seen to be in the sharp boost given to inflationary trends generally and especially to the cost of all imported energy sources.

A second major development was that the general inflation that was a feature of 1973 became more marked. The energy crisis stimulated substantial increases in domestic, and even more in imported, coking coal prices; iron ore prices rose significantly; scrap became acutely short and expensive in many areas, a development exacerbated by the decision of the U.S. authorities in mid-1973 to restrict scrap exports; and labour costs rose by varying extents but everywhere substantially.

The third feature of the year was the steel shortage in many major producing areas. This was not, as had most commonly been the case in the past, a consequence of boom demand outrunning existing capacity. Rather, physical shortages of raw materials, and in some cases labour and technical problems, held steel production significantly below the levels that the industry should have been capable of producing from its installed capacity. Thus, steel output was likely to rise worldwide from its 1973 level of 695 million metric tons to about 710 million metric tons in 1974, whereas it seemed certain that considerably more steel, perhaps over 720 million metric tons, could have been absorbed if available. Similarly, although there was clear evidence that the current steel cycle was now over the peak, and the rate of demand growth could be expected to decline in 1975, continuing supply problems were likely to maintain the industry in a stronger position in the world market than had been experienced at a similar stage in past cycles.

A fourth important development was the tentative indication of a wider general understanding that continuing inadequacy of profit in steel would result in serious long-term shortages through insufficient investment, and consequently in high prices on the world market. The result, therefore, might be that the current cyclical improvement in steel profits would be maintained to a greater extent than had been the case for some time.

In many respects, the steel situation in the U.S. typified the world steel picture in 1974. Economic activity declined somewhat from the exceptional levels attained in 1973; this was the case especially in the consumer goods and housing sectors. On the other hand, the investment sector continued strong, and although overall estimated steel consumption was expected to decline by about 4% from 1973, the tight world market and consequent high prices attracted increased U.S. exports and tended to reduce imports. The voluntary restraint agreements first undertaken by the Japanese and EEC producers in 1969 and renewed for three years in 1972 remained theoretically in force. They had no effective impact, however, because world steel market and international

currency considerations continued to render the U.S. relatively unattractive to imports. It appeared virtually certain that the agreements would not be renewed beyond the expiration date of January 1975. At the same time, the U.S. steel industry experienced certain production limitations during the year, largely for technical reasons, so that steel shortages continued in the domestic market. A three-week coal strike late in the year caused temporary production cutbacks at some steel mills.

Substantial price increases following the relaxation of price controls in the spring created a more favourable profit climate for most U.S. steel companies, and investment, which had been languishing for three years and required an increase if serious shortages were to be avoided later in the decade, turned sharply upward. Expenditure in 1974 was estimated to be about 45% higher than in 1973 (including inflation).

By the standards of the Japanese steel industry, 1974 was a difficult year. The oil crisis made a great impact initially, and restrictive national economic policies cumulatively resulted in a decline of approximately 6% in domestic steel consumption during the year. The strong world steel market made possible a substantial increase in exports, especially to less developed countries, but the industry experienced difficulties with supplies of necessary raw materials. Overall, it was probable that steel production would do no more than equal the 1973 level (119 million metric tons) and might even fall slightly below this. Some revival of domestic demand in 1975 was likely to result in a resumption of growth in steel output at a moderate rate.

The experience of the European Community steel industries varied substantially from one country to another. Domestic consumption in the original six member states rose modestly (by about 2%), but within this group Italian demand grew quite strongly while that in West Germany fell slightly. In the latter part of the year new orders declined significantly. But exports were strong, and raw material shortages and labour difficulties tended to restrict production; therefore, the market remained fairly tight and prices were held at generally profitable levels, despite substantial cost increases. Steel output in the six countries was likely to rise by about 10% over the year.

The U.K. position differed in important respects. A coal strike during the early part of the year, followed by continuing coking coal and scrap shortages, technical problems at the factories, and to some extent industrial disputes in the steel industry, restricted output. Production was likely to be about 23 million metric tons in 1974 against 26.6 million metric tons in 1973. On the other hand, domestic consumption fell only slightly, the balance being supplied from producers' stocks, sharp reduction of exports (which were restricted by license early in the year), and substantially increased imports. The U.K. was likely, most unusually, to be a net importer of steel in 1974. Certain products were in short supply for much of the year, and producers were therefore able to raise prices and to operate profitably.

The Soviet countries made an unusually strong impact on the world steel market in 1974. Although their production continued to increase by about 3% annually, consumption developed at a faster rate than usual so that imports from the West expanded

Table IV. World Production of Pig Iron and Blast Furnace Ferroalloys
In 000 metric tons

Country	1969	1970	1971	1972	1973
World	406,720	425,930	422,550	446,940	495,430
U.S.	86,620	83,300	74,110	81,110	91,611
U.S.S.R.	81,640	85,930	89,250	92,300	94,900
Japan*	58,150	68,050	72,740	74,060	90,000
Germany, West	33,760	33,630	29,990	32,000	36,830
France	18,210	19,220	18,340	19,000	20,290
United Kingdom	16,650	17,670	15,420	15,320	16,850
China†	15,500	16,500	19,000	21,000	23,000
Belgium	11,310	10,960	10,530	11,900	12,660
Italy	7,800	8,350	8,550	9,440	10,030
India	7,390	6,990	6,940	7,020	7,340
Czechoslovakia	7,010	7,550	7,960	8,360	8,530
Canada*	6,740	8,220	7,830	8,490	9,540
Poland	6,730	6,980	7,190	7,420	8,140
Australia*	5,810	5,960	6,240	6,000	7,660
Luxembourg	4,870	4,810	4,580	4,670	5,130
South Africa	3,990	3,950	4,040	4,430	4,330
Brazil*	3,720	4,200	4,690	5,290	5,470
Romania	3,490	4,210	4,380	4,890	5,710
Netherlands, The	3,460	3,590	3,760	4,290	4,710
Spain*	3,330	4,160	4,850	5,930	6,290
Austria*	2,820	2,960	2,850	2,850	3,000
Sweden	2,500	2,610	2,580	2,360	2,570
Germany, East	2,100	1,990	2,030	2,150	2,200
Hungary	1,750	1,830	1,980	2,060	2,110
Mexico*	1,700	1,650	1,680	1,890	2,800
Yugoslavia*	1,200	1,280	1,510	1,820	1,960
Bulgaria	1,100	1,200	1,340	1,510	1,610

*Pig iron only.
†Estimated.
Source: British Steel Corporation.

Table V. World Production of Crude Steel
In 000 metric tons

Country	1969	1970	1971	1972	1973	1974 Year to date	No. of months	Percent change 1974/73
World	574,000	595,000	581,000	629,000	694,300	...	...	...
U.S.*	128,150	119,310	109,270	120,750	136,460	100,040	9	− 1.7
U.S.S.R.	110,310	115,880	120,640	126,000	131,000	67,300	6	+ 3.5
Japan	82,170	93,320	88,560	96,900	119,320	88,460	9	+ 0.5
Germany, West	45,320	45,040	40,310	43,700	49,520	39,980	9	+ 8.7
U.K.	26,850	28,320	24,180	25,320	26,650	16,760	9	−16.3
France	22,510	23,770	22,860	24,050	25,260	19,940	9	+ 7.8
Italy	16,430	17,280	17,450	19,810	21,000	17,720	9	+17.5
China†	16,000	18,500	21,000	23,000	25,000	...	...	...
Belgium	21,830	12,610	12,440	14,530	15,530	12,420	9	+ 8.6
Poland	11,250	11,750	12,690	13,480	14,060	7,210	6	+ 2.9
Czechoslovakia	10,800	11,480	12,090	12,730	13,160	6,830	6	+ 3.2
Canada	9,350	11,200	11,040	11,860	13,390	10,050	9	− 0.1
Australia	7,030	6,840	6,750	6,750	7,680	5,580	9	− 0.4
India	6,560	6,280	6,100	6,860	6,970	5,040	9	− 4.1
Spain	5,980	7,390	8,020	9,530	10,510	8,460	9	+ 4.7
Romania	5,540	6,520	6,800	7,400	8,160	...	...	...
Luxembourg	5,520	5,460	5,240	5,460	5,920	4,860	9	+ 9.9
Sweden	5,320	5,500	5,270	5,260	5,660	4,390	9	+ 5.2
Brazil	4,920	5,390	6,000	6,570	7,150	5,720	9	+ 9.2
Germany, East	4,820	5,050	5,350	5,750	5,890	3,020	6	+ 2.8
Netherlands, The	4,720	5,030	5,080	5,570	5,620	4,310	9	+ 1.5
South Africa	4,620	4,760	4,880	5,340	5,630	4,220	9	− 0.4
Austria	3,930	4,080	3,960	4,070	4,240	3,530	9	+10.5
Mexico	3,470	3,880	3,820	4,360	4,700	3,810	9	+10.1
Hungary	3,030	3,110	3,110	3,270	3,330	1,710	6	+ 3.3
Yugoslavia	2,220	2,230	2,450	2,590	2,680	1,640	7	+ 3.1
Argentina	1,690	1,820	1,910	2,110	2,150	1,750	9	+10.0
Bulgaria	1,510	1,800	1,950	2,120	2,250	940	5	+ 3.1

*Excludes production of independent foundries.
†Estimated.
Source: International Iron and Steel Institute; British Steel Corporation.

greatly, making a significant contribution to the strength of the world steel market during the year. (TREVOR MACDONALD)
[724.C.3.g; 732.C.2]

MACHINERY AND MACHINE TOOLS

The threat of a continuing energy crisis and other pessimistic economic forecasts did not seriously affect the machinery and machine tool industry in 1974. In the U.S., machine tool orders in March reached record levels, which surpassed all bookings for a single month since the National Machine Tool Builders' Association started keeping combined totals of metal-cutting and metal-forming machine tools in 1956.

The industry reported that many of the new orders were from automobile producers, which were tooling up for production of small engines. Demand for machine tools also came from farm machinery producers, off-the-road equipment manufacturers, and producers of electrical generating equipment and other energy-related industries, such as mass transportation equipment producers and companies making equipment to produce oil.

The trend that was established in early 1974 continued into the second and third quarters, and the shipment of machines by the industry in the first nine months was up 35% over the comparable period in 1973. Orders for the industry did not rise as much, but were ahead of the totals for the first nine months of 1973 by 14%.

In September, at the International Machine Tool Show in Chicago, manufacturers of machine tools expressed optimism. Many companies reported that they were enjoying one of their best years. The money shortage was their greatest concern and appeared to be the major factor that would influence orders in the fourth quarter of the year. Cancellations of orders in the industry were at a normal level and not rising.

The machinery requirements of the Soviet Union's Kama River truck complex provided a major market for U.S. exports. One leading U.S. manufacturer announced the completion of a $20 million machinery line for this project, with many additional millions in equipment being supplied by other U.S. manufacturers.

Some manufacturers of machine tools faced severe problems in finding skilled machinists and other skilled workers. Shortages of materials and component parts also limited production in many plants.

Japanese production of machine tools rose approximately 40% in 1974, and manufacturers were anticipating a record output for the year. However, they were also feeling the effect of tight money in their world markets. No longer did they have an advantage on the price of their equipment.

The advent of the industrial robot in the 1960s and its continued use into the 1970s was an important factor in machinery production throughout the world. In 1970 there were approximately 200 of these robots in the U.S. There had been an accelerated increase in their use since that time, and industry spokesmen indicated that the Occupational Safety and Health Act (OSHA) of 1970 provided a significant stimulus to the use of the robots. These machines can perform jobs in areas that are unsafe for man. In many applications it is more economical to buy a robot than to change a whole operation to meet OSHA standards. As of 1974, robots were being used with a high degree of success in forging, welding, stamp pressing, machine-tool operation, die casting, injection and compression molding, investment casting, spray coat applications, and material transfer. In Japan about 1,500 industrial robots were in use and there were more than 50 manufacturers of the robots.

Recent developments in ultrasonic machining proved to offer the advantages of longer tool life, faster and smoother cutting, and minimum shelling and chipping. Ultrasonics was more widely used in assembling than in machining and was finding increased uses in testing, cleaning, and measuring.

By the end of 1974 there were ominous signs of doom for many industries throughout the world, but most machinery and machine tool manufacturers believed that unless catastrophic economic problems occurred in 1975 that year should also be a good one. Shortages in agricultural, mining, oil-production, and earth-moving equipment were expected to continue into 1975, promising to benefit not only the makers of such equipment but also the producers of machine tools. The automobile industry was the hardest hit of the consumers of machine tools and had the gloomiest outlook going into 1975. (ORLAND B. KILLIN)

[722.B–C; 732.C.7]

NUCLEAR INDUSTRY

The Arab oil embargo brought home the fact that oil supplies were not infinite and that the world's dependence on cheap oil was at an end. The embargo placed a tremendous strain on the economic and technical resources of the developed countries during 1974, and electricity utilities were particularly hard hit. Having found it difficult to raise funds for investment projects for some time, they were now in desperate need of finance for nuclear projects.

In the U.S., the crunch came in the latter half of 1974. Approximately 42,000 Mw. of new nuclear-electric capacity were on order at the end of 1973 and the rate of ordering continued into 1974, but it then fell off. By October, orders for over 100,000 Mw. of generating capacity, over half of it nuclear, had been delayed or canceled. This was the result partly of talk of a decline in consumption, an energy resource conservation program, and increased coal utilization.

Some nuclear projects, such as those of the Detroit Edison Co., were stopped in midstream due to lack of funds. Experts were afraid, however, that declines in consumption and energy conservation measures might not produce as much decrease in demand as expected, and that the utilities might therefore find themselves unable to meet their legally imposed obligations to supply power. By October there were already signs that the rate of increase of consumer demand for electric power had again reached its previous level of 7% per year.

France made the biggest new commitment to nuclear power in 1974, Électricité de France ordering 13 reactors in February and announcing that an additional 6 reactors would be ordered each year for the rest of the decade. Creusot-Loire Framatome, building pressurized water reactors (PWRs) under license from Westinghouse, was to build 12 of the units, while the 13th was to be the first boiling water reactor (BWR) built by the Compagnie Générale d'Électricité Alsthom Group under a General Electric Co. license.

In Britain, despite considerable pressure in favour of U.S.-designed Westinghouse PWRs and the Canadian Candu system, the government decided to base its nuclear program on the British-designed steam generating heavy water reactor (SGHWR) system. Only 4,000 Mw. of capacity was scheduled to be built over the next three years.

As the political situation within the U.S. stabilized, the government completed plans for dismembering the all-powerful Atomic Energy Commission (AEC), which had been under attack for favouring industry at public expense. Research functions were to be handed to the newly created Energy Research and Development Administration (ERDA), and a Nuclear Regulatory Commission was to take responsibility for regulatory activities. The long-awaited Rasmussen report was published during the year. It concluded that the worst possible consequences of a severe nuclear accident were far less serious than the antinuclear lobby, led by Ralph Nader, had forecast.

Several smaller industrial and less developed countries planned to extend their nuclear capacity, including Sweden, Belgium, The Netherlands, Egypt, and Iran. France was to supply Iran with five 1,000-Mw. reactors, and Israel was reported to be making similar arrangements. The UN's International Atomic Energy Agency estimated that the less developed nations could absorb approximately 60,000 Mw. of nuclear capacity, but that reactors would have to be smaller than 500 Mw. Technological development of such systems was, however, held back by the general economic situation.

India, having long wanted nuclear explosives for use in canal digging, for underground gasification, and for other peaceful purposes, created a political storm by exploding its first nuclear device. Almost at once, Canada, the U.S., the U.S.S.R., and the U.K. suspended nuclear aid to India, whose actions resulted in a resurgence of worldwide fears of the wider availability of nuclear weapons and thereby lent force to the arguments of the antinuclear lobbies.

During 1974, attention focused on the nuclear fuel cycle and on the supply situation for uranium. The price of uranium ore doubled during the year, from $10 to $20 per pound, but did not generate the needed investment in exploration. Canada and Australia limited both exports of, and exploration for, the ore in the hopes of recouping greater financial returns later, and both planned to establish processing industries in anticipation of exporting the completed fuel rather than the cheaper ore. In the U.S., a government-backed attempt to interest private industry in uranium enrichment failed, but Canada, Australia, and Japan started discussions on enrichment with the U.S. France, through Eurodif, was already committed to building a large enrichment plant. Urenco-Centec began to accept enrichment services contracts, but its members, the U.K., The Netherlands, and West Germany, resolved to take more independent control of their own shares of the project, thereby illustrating the continuing difficulties of maintaining international cooperation on nuclear matters once projects reached the commercial stage. The fuel reprocessing industry suffered a considerable setback when a General Electric Co. plant for that purpose, due to begin operating during the year, was judged unworkable; full-scale modifications or dismantling the plant were advised.

Nuclear propulsion of ships attracted increasing interest during the year, and there were several projects under development. In Japan, however, local fishermen stopped the prototype NS "Mutsu" from leaving port, and when the ship finally reached the sea and started its reactor, neutron radiation was discovered, causing extreme embarrassment and many problems for the authorities.

Development of new uses of radiation and sophisticated instrumentation continued to expand, and new applications for radionuclides (isotopes of elements that are unstable and undergo radioactive decay) were found in environmental monitoring, research into human metabolism, and treatment of cardiovascular disease and cancer. Several countries ordered irradiation units for sterilization and for food preservation, and Switzerland planned to use a unit for sewage treatment. Computer imaging techniques based on radioactive tracers made further strides. (RICHARD W. KOVAN)
[721.B.9]

PAINTS AND VARNISHES

The foreboding that had afflicted the paint and varnish industry at the outset of 1973 gave way in 1974 to alarm that in some cases approached panic. Since many of its raw materials are derived from petroleum, the industry had soon felt the effects of oil shortages and of steeply higher costs. These were only partly recouped by price increases, which were estimated at some 15% for the European paint industry as a whole.

The industry also suffered from other shortages. Failures of oilseed crops led to reduced availability and higher prices of natural drying oils. High demand for titanium dioxide, the main white pigment, coincided with reduced output due to pollution restrictions and insufficient capacity. It was generally agreed that prices had to rise to encourage adequate investment in new plant to meet anticipated demand later in the decade.

Despite the difficulties, paint output in 1973 showed a healthy increase throughout Europe, ranging from a 13% gain in Switzerland to about 4% in France and The Netherlands. U.K. production expanded by 12.6% in tonnage and some 17% in value, compared with a growth of only 5% in GNP, but the introduction of the value-added tax was thought to have distorted the picture. Thus, decorative paint sales were up 10–12% by volume, against 5–7% for industrial coatings. U.K. paint exports rose to a record £23.8 million, compared with record imports of £7.5 million.

In other areas the paint industry also reflected movements in GNP and general industrial activity. Thus production in the U.S. showed only moderate gains in volume and value. In Australia the second half of 1973 was a boom period, and statistics for the whole year were expected to exceed the 5.9% growth noted in the first half.

Emulsions continued to gain popularity among household and do-it-yourself users. Factors contributing to this growth were convenience and an acceptable finish. Published statistics also showed sharp increases in sales of thinners and bituminous coatings.

Leading experts believed that waterborne paints were establishing a dominant position for the future. In the U.S., for example, the total output of industrial finishes rose 23% between 1970 and 1972, from 399 million to 485 million gal., while production of waterborne coatings grew from 34 million to 73 million gal., or over 110%, in the same period. Estimates for 1975 indicated that solvent-based stoving finishes would be 23% below 1973, while waterborne materials were

expected to be some 120% above current levels.

During 1973 high-quality waterborne coatings had become available for application by all the widely used industrial methods, including spraying, dipping, flow coating, and electrodeposition. Only in specialized areas such as primer-surfacers were solvent-based materials still supreme.

(LIONEL BILEFIELD)
[732.D.7]

PAPER AND PULP

World production of paper and paperboard again rose sharply in 1973. Output totaled some 155 million metric tons, or 7.6% more than in 1972, and would have been still higher except for prolonged strikes in North America. The volume increase was the largest ever recorded and also exceeded the long-term average growth rate, which had been running at about 5% per year. This reflected rapid economic expansion in all of the chief paper-using regions, especially North America, Europe, and Japan.

The situation contrasted sharply with the earlier part of the decade. Throughout 1970, 1971, and part of 1972, there was a sizable excess of world capacity for manufacturing many pulp and paper products. As a consequence, the industry in the leading producing nations suffered severe declines in production

Semispherical balls are used to trap odours from this Japanese industrial waste pond.

WIDE WORLD

and earnings, and incentive to invest in new mills and new paper machines was greatly reduced.

So rapid was the turnaround, beginning in mid-1972, that shortages of some products, especially chemical wood pulp, developed in world markets and continued throughout 1973 and most of 1974. Toward the end of 1974, however, as the economies of many industrial countries slowed—some to recession pace—it appeared likely that supply and demand in paper and paperboard would achieve a reasonable balance, at least for a time.

Meanwhile, expansion plans in the paper industry were being accelerated somewhat, in response to improved earnings and the generally favourable long-term outlook. Nevertheless, rapidly rising capital costs, high interest rates, and some uncertainty about the shorter-term outlook were causing many companies to follow fairly conservative investment policies.

In the U.S., the world's largest producer, it was estimated that manufacturing capacity for paper and paperboard would increase by an average of 2.7% annually during the three years 1973–76, compared with an average of 4% annually in the preceding 20-year period. Similarly, in Canada, the second largest producer, a 3.2% growth rate was forecast for 1973–76, compared with an actual 3.8% annually during the previous 20 years.

World production of paper and paperboard in 1973 was divided approximately as follows: North America 69 million metric tons (66 million in 1972); Europe 52 million (48 million); Asia 27 million (24 million); Latin America 4.7 million (4.2 million); and Africa 1.2 million (1 million). World trade in pulp, paper, and paperboard amounted to over 40 million tons during the year. The largest exporter was Canada, with more than one-third of the total.

Many countries were largely self-sufficient in production of paper and paperboard but required substantial imports of wood pulp. Thus the world pulp shortages that arose in 1973 and 1974 were of serious concern, especially in regions with steadily rising cellulose fibre deficits, such as the EEC and Japan. This kindled greater interest than ever before in obtaining more pulp from recycled paper and paperboard, and also in investing in pulp mills in such forest-rich regions as North America and Latin America. Particularly striking was the interest shown in Brazil by many multinational pulp and paper companies. Several large new pulp mills were under construction there, and it was expected that Brazil would become one of the world's leading pulp exporters over the next decade.

World pulp and paper prices rose considerably in 1973 and 1974 after a decade of relative stability. Return on investment, which in Canada, for example, declined to some 2% in 1971, had risen to far healthier levels by late 1974. However, in the face of rapid inflation, it seemed unlikely that there would be a return to the overexpansion that had occurred periodically in the past.

(GORDON MINNES)

[732.D.3]

PHARMACEUTICALS

The energy situation and concurrently developing shortages of a few selected raw materials created some concern among pro-

ducers of pharmaceuticals during 1974. For example, there were shortages of cortisone, some steroids (key ingredients in oral contraceptives), petroleum jelly, and even opium—giving Turkey its justification for resuming cultivation of the opium poppy. More significant were shortages of petroleum-based raw materials and packaging components, ranging from alcohol to packaging films and plastic bottles. Petroleum feedstocks are also used to make aspirin, sulfa drugs, antihistamines, and vitamins, and the rising price of oil accounted in part for 5–10% increases in the prices of these drugs by midyear.

On the whole, however, these problems did not seriously affect a robust industry that had experienced a 10–12% growth in sales for several years. According to the Pharmaceutical Manufacturers Association, worldwide sales of prescription drugs exceeded $9 billion in 1973, 11% more than in the preceding year. Though 1973 figures were not yet available, in 1972 the prescription drug industry employed 257,000 persons, 144,000 of whom were in the U.S.

More than one-quarter of total sales consisted of products for the central nervous system, including tranquilizers, amphetamines, and barbiturates. Antiinfectives, of which antibiotics constituted the major portion, and those drugs used to combat neoplasms and endocrine disorders constituted the next two largest product categories.

Downward price pressures were brought to bear against pharmaceutical producers in several countries. The governments of Britain and West Germany exercised legal measures to drive down the prices of Librium and Valium, two tranquilizers produced by Hoffmann-La Roche, Inc., of Switzerland. In the U.S. more subtle pressures resulted from the expiration of patents on important antibiotics and tranquilizers; much publicized Senate hearings on drug pricing, promotion, and testing procedures and policies; and a rise in so-called third party prescription payment plans, especially those administered by unions, community and regional health plans, and Medicare. There were also efforts at the state level to permit prescription drug price advertising and to force the designation of drugs in prescriptions by generic name. Nevertheless, drug industry profits continued to be relatively high.

Research and development expenditures among drug companies probably exceeded $800 million in 1973, 11% above the previous year. The figure is somewhat deceptive, however. Compared with R and D expenditures in the 1950s, it would hint at the possibility of a flood of new drugs in the next decade. In reality, a large part of it went for the vastly increased cost of assembling the therapeutic data now being required for every new drug—and, to a lesser degree, for checking out adverse reactions to drugs already on the market. Also, new drugs were becoming more difficult to discover, since most of the "easy" therapeutic categories had been heavily investigated during the preceding 20 years. (DONALD A. DAVIS)
[732.D.4]

PLASTICS

Worldwide, the plastics industry began 1974 in bad shape. This was readily understandable in view of its almost total dependence on petrochemical (i.e., oil-derived) raw materials. These were in short supply to varying degrees even before the Middle East war of October 1973, due to the combined effects of low investment in additional refinery capacity and an unexpectedly rapid increase in demand. There was also a tendency to give priority to gasoline (petrol) and other

fuel uses for crude oil rather than to chemicals, although petrochemicals account for only 5–7% of oil.

When the Middle East oil producers restricted output, placed a complete embargo on exports to certain markets, and began massively increasing prices for crude, world plastics markets—with those for the rest of the chemical industry—were reduced to near chaos. With restricted petrochemicals output and hoarding by speculators, acute scarcities developed and prices rocketed. In the case of styrene, admittedly the worst example, the regular price in Europe rose by around 500% in some 18 months, up to the spring of 1974. Prices asked on the black market increased as much as tenfold.

In most areas demand for plastics materials by processors continued at a high level throughout the first half of the year, but the supply position progressively stabilized, and the black market generally collapsed during the summer. In the second half of 1974 a more general downturn of business became apparent, with processors reducing inventories. This had the effect of somewhat alleviating the feedstock problem for the time being, although many materials such as nylon remained in short supply.

Assuming no further complications in crude oil supply, the prospects were that the level of economic activity in most industrialized countries would recover by the end of 1975 or early 1976. This, together with natural growth in plastics demand, seemed likely to result in the reemergence of an acute material supply problem, since not enough additional petrochemicals capacity would be completed by then. A stable balance between supply and demand was unlikely much before the end of 1977.

With the increase in crude oil prices, costs of plastics naturally followed suit. This gave rise to much speculation about the future competitiveness of plastics as against other basic materials, such as metals, wood, and paper. A study carried out in the U.K. by Imperial Chemical Industries Ltd. revealed that a 300% increase in crude oil prices resulted, for instance, in rises of 200% for ethylene and 100% for polyethylene molding materials, but only 30% for polyethylene bags and 40% for extruded pipe. These figures were typical for the large-tonnage commodity thermoplastics. The ICI report concluded that price increases for articles made from these plastics were of the same order as those for articles made from competing materials; that to make articles from plastics required, in general, less energy than to make them from traditional materials, even allowing for the oil used for feedstock; and that the long-term growth prospects for such thermoplastics, especially polypropylene, were if anything improved by the increases in oil prices.

In all these areas, greater attention was being paid to improved flame-retardant properties to meet higher standards imposed by regulatory bodies. Research into these problems was tending to concentrate on the development of new polymer systems rather than on the traditional approach through additives. Other work concerned improved plastics-forming methods, with renewed interest in rotational molding and structural foams. Higher prices meant more attention to recycling, filled materials, and better process control.

An acute environmental problem arose in 1974 as a result of allegations that contact with vinyl chloride monomer could cause a rare form of liver cancer. (See HEALTH AND DISEASE.) With the U.S. taking the lead, extremely severe limitations on the permissible atmospheric concentration of vinyl chloride in manufacturing locations were issued. Although the evidence related only to the monomer, a cloud was also cast on polyvinyl chloride (PVC), causing tremors throughout the whole of the huge industry concerned with the manufacture and use of this, the largest-tonnage plastic of all. This was particularly true since a considerable proportion of PVC applications involved contact with food, beverages, or potable water, and there was a suggestion that unreacted monomer might be present in some cases as a residue. Whatever the outcome, it was certain that increasingly stringent standards would be required of food-grade plastics, involving exhaustive and expensive testing.

Final estimates for world plastics production in 1973 by *European Plastics News* put the total at 43.3 million metric tons (Western Europe 16.5 million tons; Eastern Europe 5.1 million tons; U.S. 13.2 million tons; Japan 6.5 million tons; remainder of the world 2 million tons). Industry performance in 1974 was unusually difficult to predict before the appearance of firm statistics, but some expansion did take place. U.S. plastics production in the first half of the year rose by about 4% compared with the same period in 1973.　　(ROBIN C. PENFOLD)
[732.D.5]

PRINTING

Severe paper shortages continued to harass the printing and publishing industries in 1974, and there were further heavy increases in the prices of all types of paper. Careful preplanning and cost control became meaningless as publishers and print buyers faced ever rising costs and wages and severe increases in postal and freight charges.

Web offset lost its supremacy. Mass circulation magazine and mail order producers looked afresh at gravure, with its ability to give high-fidelity colour reproduction on cheap, lightweight papers, and at letterpress rotary printing. Gravure still suffered from the mystique of being difficult to master, but in The Netherlands a large-scale reproduction operation trained out-of-work coal miners to become skilled craftsmen. In West Germany, compact electronic cylinder engraving machines were introduced by Dr.-Ing. Rudolf Hell. Graphicart and Daetwyler of Switzerland and West Germany's Langbein-Pfannhauser, THM, Walter of Munich, and Saueressig produced sophisticated, fully automatic, cylinder processing systems.

In letterpress, photopolymer plates became commonplace in newspaper and book production. Letterflex of the U.S. began manufacture in Britain and recorded many new users worldwide, including the Asahi Shimbun newspapers of Japan, home of its main plate competitors, APR and Napp. DuPont introduced a photopolymer plate for flexographic printing and, in West Germany, BASF Nyloprint announced a similar development.

The move to electronic colour scanners became a tide, with the Japanese printing industry an enthusiastic convert. Crosfield Electronics and Sun Graphic Systems in the U.S. sold Magnascan 460 scanners to the Far East in batches of 20. With Spain's printing industry expected to become a major European growth sector, Hauser y Menet in Madrid installed three Magnascan units alongside two existing Chromagraph-Hell scanners. In response to a long-standing need of the printing industry, new black-and-white electronic scanning systems were announced by Crosfield in Britain and Hell in West Germany; the latter made a special-purpose scanner for black-and-white, and the British company offered attachments that extended the range of applications of

Arnold Grunwald of the Argonne National Laboratory, Argonne, Ill., demonstrates a portable machine of his invention that can translate data on a magnetic tape into Braille. A blind person would "read" by touching an endless plastic belt on which the Braille is stamped.

its colour scanners. Linoscan was first with simultaneous scanning of several colours.

In France, Logabax introduced a direct-screening four-colour photographic colour separation system, bringing scanner-like automation to this method of reproduction. A more modest system was introduced by Vannier. In West Germany, Klimsch offered complete automation by electronics on large reproduction cameras.

In Paris, at the International Paper Printing and Graphic Arts Industries Exhibition (TPG), the major European printing show, König & Bauer achieved the coup of the year in sheet-fed printing with the introduction of Rapida III. Using a novel sheet-laying drum system, the offset two-colour machine could print 15,000-plus sheets per hour. Four-colour versions were promised. Solna Offset of Sweden offered the Model 164 machine for single-button control, relieving the operator of the need to handle several sequential operations in press control—an advantage wherever skilled labour was scarce.

In Scotland, Wm. Collins & Sons, producers of over 70 million books a year, laid claim to the title of the world's largest book-production unit and installed a second Roland 800 and an American Cameron book printing press that could print and deliver complete books in a single operation. By mid-1974, 14 such presses had sold worldwide. Swedish printers set new records in low manning for printing machines. At *Sala Allehanda*, only two men controlled a six-unit Solna web offset press.

Transfer printing became big business. Strachan & Henshaw in Britain, anticipating demand for several hundred presses a year, designed extra-wide presses, and Cobden Chadwick, also of Britain, Windmöller & Hölscher of West Germany, and several U.S. companies followed suit. The Far East became a major market for transfer printing on substrata, for transfer to textiles and other materials.

Phototypesetting consolidated gains of previous years. Linotron 303 was launched as a lower priced system of cathode-ray-tube (CRT) photosetting. The Monotype Corp. broke with its own tradition by introducing the 400/8 phototypesetter, operated from 8-level tape instead of the 31-channel Monotype spool. From the U.S., Photon reported a growing number of European installations of the APS-4 CRT system. At the Scottish *Daily Record*, phototypesetting and

web offset combined to produce the world's largest web offset daily.

Electronic editing systems, once considered an expensive gimmick, were adopted by newspapers, particularly in the U.S., where the world's first all-electronic newsroom was installed at Davenport, Ia. The two major U.S. news agencies, AP and UPI, placed multimillion-dollar orders for CRT editing and correction systems. The *Nieuwe Rotterdamse Courant* in The Netherlands and the *Baltimore* (Md.) *Sun* became the first large newspapers with completely electronic text and advertising handling. The use of the Krantz computer editing system was pioneered by *WAZ* of West Germany.

Gannett Newspapers in the U.S. was pioneering laser engraving of printing plates directly from film or pasteup. By using a combination of the Pagitron system of Optronics Inc. with the Laserplate of Lasergraphics Inc., both U.S. companies, the photographic stages in typesetting, reproduction, and platemaking could be completely bypassed. The combination made it possible to electronically scan pictures (in black and white), electronically generate letter images, and assemble both according to a layout sketch on a display screen. Once the page imposition was displayed, a pushbutton activated the laser beam, which engraved printing plates or exposed coatings on the plates.
(W. PINCUS JASPERT)

[735.E.3-4]

RUBBER

Shortages of materials plagued the rubber industry during 1974. In addition to petrochemical-based materials, many other chemicals, fillers, and miscellaneous materials used in rubber manufacture were scarce, although some so-called shortages were later found to be the result of maldistribution. The need to find substitutes resulted in some innovations in rubber compound formulation. Prices of raw materials based on petroleum reflected increases in the price of crude oil. Prices of other materials also rose drastically as a result of higher labour costs and price increases reflecting the supply and demand situation.

The oil crisis affected the rubber industry in other ways. The marked increase in sales of small cars could have some effect on rubber consumption, since they use smaller tires that require considerably less rubber. This was further compounded by the trend toward fewer miles of driving.

Table VI. Natural Rubber Production
In 000 metric tons

Country	1971	1972	1973*
Malaysia	1,319	1,325	1,566
Indonesia	819	819	886
Thailand	316	337	382
Sri Lanka	141	140	155
India	99	109	123
Liberia	74	83	84
Nigeria†	62	54	68†
Zaire	40†	40†	40†
Brazil	24	26	23
Others†	184	180	166
Total†	3,078	3,113	3,493

*Preliminary.
†Estimate, or includes estimate.

Table VII. Synthetic Rubber Production
In 000 metric tons

Country	1971	1972	1973*
United States	2,277	2,455	2,627
Japan	780	819	967
France	323	368	458
United Kingdom	277	307	353
Germany, West	306	300	350
Netherlands, The	191	186	263
Canada	197	195	230
Italy†	160	200	230
Germany, East	129	133	134
Brazil	78	95	125
Poland	66	78	94
Romania	71	73	85†
Spain	45	60†	75†
Belgium†	60	60	65
Czechoslovakia	52	52	50†
Argentina†	38	44	47
Mexico†	45	40	45
Australia	43	42	43
South Africa	30	30	28
Others†‡	915	988	1,026
Total†‡	6,083	6,525	7,295

*Preliminary.
†Estimate, or includes estimate.
‡Includes estimated production for the Soviet Union (about 980,000 tons in 1973) and China (about 25,000 tons in 1973).
Source: The Secretariat of the International Rubber Study Group, *Rubber Statistical Bulletin.*

Disposal of scrap tires was a major environmental problem. Workers in Australia and the U.S. reported that ground tire scrap is an excellent mulch and soil conditioner. Jones and Laughlin Steel Corp. found that whole scrap tires thrown into their basic oxygen high carbon steel furnaces act as a defoamer. The Oil Shale Corp. of Golden, Colo., was collaborating with Goodyear Tire on a 25-ton-per-day pilot plant for recovering oil from scrap tires. Reports from the Firestone Tire and Rubber Co. indicated that other valuable chemicals such as antioxidants and tackifying resins were being obtained from depolymerized scrap rubber.

Natural rubber was one of the few raw materials used in rubber manufacture that did not reflect a marked price change. On Oct. 1, 1973, it was 34 cents per pound and on Oct. 1, 1974, it was 32 cents, although it reached 55 cents in February at the height of the shortage of petroleum-based synthetic rubber feedstocks. Consumption of natural rubber had essentially equaled production for several years.

World production of natural rubber in 1974 was estimated at 3,650,000 metric tons, up 200,000 tons from 1973. The Management Committee of the International Rubber Study Group (IRSG), meeting in London in June, estimated natural rubber supplies at 3.7 million metric tons in 1974; synthetic rubber supplies at 7,350,000 metric tons; and world consumption at some 3,480,000 metric tons of natural rubber and 7.2 million metric tons of synthetic rubber.

The U.S. remained the largest single buyer of natural rubber, using 696,435 metric tons in 1973. World consumption of natural rubber latex (dry basis) in 1973 was estimated at 297,500 metric tons. Statistics on world consumption of synthetic latices were incomplete, but the U.S. alone consumed 130,441 tons (dry basis) of the SBR type. Total consumption of both natural and synthetic rubbers worldwide was estimated at 10,525,000 metric tons. Production of reclaimed rubber increased somewhat from 280,000 metric tons to 295,293 metric tons.

A Dunlop tire expert described the tire of 1984 as pneumatic with a height to width ratio of 40%, reinforced by high modulus textile, steel, or other fibres only in the belt with no carcass fabric or beads, made of rubber by an injection or transfer molding technique, and with run-flat capability. However, it seemed probable that such a tire could be in use considerably sooner. In 1974 Goodrich announced development of a conventional radial tire with the ability to seal punctures up to one-quarter inch by use of a special sponge rubber innerliner. Metzeler announced the production of a nonstudded winter tire that incorporated silica treated with silane in place of carbon black—one of many attempts to circumvent legislation outlawing studded tires. The new tire was said to be essentially equal to studded tires in winter traction, but it did not damage highways as many claimed studs do.

One-third of the new cars manufactured in the first half of 1973 were equipped with radial tires. It was estimated that approximately 80% of the 1975 General Motors cars were equipped with radial tires conforming to GM specifications and bearing a GM specification number, though they were made by various manufacturers. Other carmakers were expected to adopt this system.

One of the developments helping to offset the styrene shortage was the use of (poly)-butadienes with polymerization conditions altered to increase the vinyl content of the (poly)butadiene and make it perform more like styrene-butadiene (SBR) rubber. The use of chemicals such as the silanes to promote adhesion of rubbers to pigment particles or fibres was increasing.

The U.S. Supreme Court ruled the General Tire and Rubber Co. patent on oil-extended SBR invalid. Most manufacturers of OESBR could cease paying royalties and some funds would undoubtedly have to be returned. A second development, of less importance, was the withdrawal of Firestone from the development and manufacture of racing tires for Indianapolis type races.   (J. R. BEATTY)
[732.D.6]

SHIPBUILDING

Until mid-1974 the flow of orders into the world's shipyards was sustained at only a little below the rate recorded toward the end of 1973, and by the end of July ordered tonnage since January 1 totaled 134 million gross registered tons (grt). For the same period in 1973 the figure was 105,316,423 grt. This was remarkable in view of the reduced output of oil from the Arab-controlled fields and the huge rise in fuel costs, which combined to lower both the dry cargo and tanker freight markets.

Nearly all shipyards had orders stretching well into 1977, and in some cases—Japan, for example—into 1978. Japan continued to hold first place with a record order book of more than 62 million grt, although rises in labour and material costs might eliminate the profit on many contracts. Well behind Japan lay Sweden with over 11 million grt on order, followed by the West German yards, which achieved a remarkable 7.7 million grt, and Spain, which almost matched the West German figure. Largely because the bulk of the new orders represented giant tankers of over 250,000 tons deadweight (dw.), the U.K. order book stood at a modest 7.5 million grt.

Several major shipyards, including some

Giant gantry crane used in Swedish shipyards to lift extremely heavy ship sections into place during construction.

COURTESY, KOCKUMS

in Japan, abandoned fixed price contracts, and yards with a heavy investment in building docks for 700,000-tonners were becoming anxious as orders for vessels over 400,000 tons became harder to obtain. The possibility of the Suez Canal reopening in 1975, plus the slowing down in the rate of increase in world oil consumption, caused owners to pause in their rush to order very large and ultralarge crude carriers, and in many cases orders were modified or changed. Despite their high cost (currently about $16 million for a 25,000-tonner), the products carriers were becoming popular, and the average size on order rose from 25,000 to 50,000 tons dw. Demand for these vessels might be expected to increase as more refineries were built by the Arab oil-producing countries.

In September a Spanish consulting and engineering company, Sener, started work on a new shipyard designed for the production of liquefied natural gas (LNG) and liquefied petroleum gas carriers of up to 130,000-cu.m. capacity. The shipyard, known as Crinavias, would produce approximately four vessels a year, each valued at about $104 million. The new Setenave shipyard in Portugal, part of the Lisnave group, was in production on a site only 30 mi. S of Lisnave's own giant repair yard at Lisbon. Malta was chosen by China as the site of a new building dock for 400,000-tonners.

After years in the doldrums, the larger private U.S. shipyards enjoyed an unprecedented peacetime boom. Orders for 55 vessels were placed with U.S. yards, and 16 ships were converted to modern container vessels. The energy crisis and the U.S. Project Independence would ensure a steady flow of orders for offshore drilling rigs and tankers, but a critical shortage of skilled manpower was a problem.

French shipyards remained among the major builders of LNG carriers, but they were also moving into the 500,000-ton tanker class. After a surge of large tanker building, Dutch shipyards concentrated on smaller vessels of all types, particularly supply vessels for oil rigs. Shipyards that had specialized in dredging vessels for several years were now producing drillships and pipe-laying barges.

All Scandinavian and Finnish yards were fully occupied. Kockums of Sweden added a second gantry crane that could lift 1,500-ton steel sections, and the Uddevalla yard was being expanded to build 485,000-tonners. Early in 1974 U.K. yards had orders (excluding naval work) worth over £1,300 million and work in hand was running at over 7 million tons gross. The U.K. industry was in its best position for many years, but was being threatened with outright nationalization by the Labour government.

(W. D. EWART)

[734.E.7]

TEXTILE INDUSTRY

For textile industries around the world, 1974 was far from being a happy year. Protracted labour disputes in much of British industry had an adverse effect on the textile raw materials situation, causing production and distribution problems in home and overseas markets. Unprecedented increases in the prices of oil products were added to political and economic uncertainties. Escalating prices for finished products quickly led to falling demand, reflected in reduced sales of yarns and cloths. By the end of the year, some British spinning and weaving plants were working short-time. With a similar situation in most textile-producing countries, the immediate future was uncertain.

Despite these difficulties, there were no-

table advances in machinery and accessory development. In Britain research centred on spin-texturing man-made filament yarns and on crimping properties of bicomponent fibres. A Yorkshire firm's new industrial fabric rapier looms were said to eliminate weft waste completely. A ten-spindle, 2,000-rpm, fully automatic machine converted yarns into skeins of various sizes, and a new yarn breakage detector operated equally well on slow or fast moving yarns of coarse or fine denier.

West German firms produced a shuttleless double-plush loom with double-lift jacquard, new designs for dye centres, an improved dye cone for synthetic yarns, an open-end spinning machine for man-made fibres in medium staple lengths, and an electronically controlled, single-bed, large-diameter circular knitting machine to produce imitation fur and other plush-type fabrics.

One Swiss firm brought out a new open-width machine for tensionless washing-off treatment of woven and printed cottons and synthetics. Another produced a new open-width washing machine to handle cloths up to two metres wide. A high-speed multicolour needle loom for narrow fabrics utilized full-width or sectional warps, or individual bobbins. A multihead automatic embroidery machine incorporated a device allowing infinite length of stitch.

A French company's new colour coordinator could create over 100,000 variations in tone. A U.S. specialized contract carpet yarn program offered considerable scope and flexibility in carpet yarns. A Dutch firm's extension to a rotary screen printing machine would print transfer paper.

Experts from ten countries attended a symposium in Budapest, Hung., on modern sizing materials, sizing technology and equipment, and problems of desizing. European flax fibre research organizations met in Paris. The European Disposables Association became the European Disposables and Non-Wovens Association.   (ALFRED DAWBER)

Natural Fibres. *Cotton.* Although world production in the 1973–74 season declined marginally, from 60 million to 59.6 million bales, an increase in opening stocks raised the total volume of global supplies to 81.7 million bales, the highest in eight years. During the season cotton prices rose to unprecedented heights. At the peak in January 1974, the average quotation was nearly three times the low point in September 1972.

To some extent the higher prices reflected rising consumption as well as near-record levels of international trade. Consumption had increased steadily for a decade, and in 1973–74 it rose by more than 1.5 million bales over the previous season. Most of the gains were in Asia, notably Taiwan and Korea, but stock rebuilding also occurred because of sharp increases in output in the two previous seasons.

A fall of 3.5% in world planted acreage was almost offset by record yields averaging 355 lb. per ac. Notable increases in productivity were achieved in the Communist countries, Central America, Syria, and the Sudan. Serious floods in growing areas in the U.S. depleted the crop despite near-record yields, while significant gains were made in the Soviet Union and China as a result of improved harvesting methods.

World stocks at the beginning of the 1973–74 season showed the first significant increase since 1968–69, when former heavy surpluses had been liquidated. The initial carry-over was equivalent to about 4.5 months' consumption, compared with the very low level a year earlier when stocks were sufficient to meet only about 4.2 months' requirements.

The Liverpool index of average values

began the 1973–74 season at nearly 70 cents a pound. Sharp advances were posted in subsequent months, with a new peak of $91\frac{1}{2}$ cents registered in mid-January. Subsequent movements were invariably downward; 70 cents was quoted in April, 60 cents at the end of August, and $53\frac{1}{2}$ cents in mid-October.

Little if any increase in output was forecast for 1974–75, as the predicted expansion in planted acreage failed to materialize because of unfavourable weather conditions. Growers were discouraged by the decline in prices and higher production costs. Harvesting was also affected by shortages of important agricultural chemicals.

Continuation of the high rate of consumption growth seemed unlikely as most countries reported economic stagnation, surging inflation, and financial difficulties. In the less developed areas of Asia, South America, and Africa, the rising trend in aggregate cotton consumption was expected to persist but at a considerably reduced rate.

(ARTHUR TATTERSALL)

Silk. The future of the world's silk trade continued to appear uncertain in 1974. In early 1973 China had raised its raw silk prices by some 80% in two steps, and buying had virtually ceased. This situation continued until August 1973, when the Chinese lowered prices by 10%. This arbitrary move had the result of snuffing all confidence, and the first reaction of Western manufacturers was to switch to other fibres.

In earlier years the defection of Western consumers might not have influenced the market unduly, since Japan had been anxious to lay hands on any available silk to satisfy the booming domestic market. But credit measures in Japan were proving effective, and by October 1973 there were indications of resistance in the demand for kimonos. This was followed by the shock of Arab oil prices, and by the turn of the year both cocoon farmers and reelers viewed the future anxiously.

In January 1974 Japanese reelers put up a large sum of money to take surplus silk off the market, and in February a voluntary ten-day shutdown of all filatures was implemented, despite protests by the government. A ban on raw silk imports was called for, but was opposed by the government as being contrary to the policy of trade liberalization and likely to provoke retaliation.

Meanwhile, with the cocoon crop drawing nearer, the farmers maintained unremitting pressure on the government both to raise the authority of the semi-official Raw Silk Corporation for the purchase of silk from 30,000 to 60,000 bales and to limit imports. However, it was not until July 1974, when stocks had risen to 56,000 bales, that the government acted. It was then announced that as from August 1 the Raw Silk Corporation would be granted exclusivity for raw silk imports for a period of ten months, while its authority to purchase on the home market would be increased to 50,000 bales.

Meanwhile, the Chinese reduced prices by 17% in November 1973 and then held firm until June 1974, when they announced a further 19% reduction. It was thought that this latter drop had been planned for March, but that the Chinese were persuaded by Japanese farmers to hold their hand until cocoon prices had been fixed in Japan. In the fall of 1974 silk stocks were high, demand was dwindling, and the next move was awaited with some trepidation.

(PETER W. GADDUM)

Wool. Booming wool prices in 1972–73 had reached a peak in March 1973. Merino prices then fell sharply, but a relatively high and indecisive price trend was maintained until the closing months of the year. Continued demand from wool-consuming countries clearly played a vital part in preventing a price slump. Another important factor was the more general boom in all commodity prices, culminating in the extreme rise in the price of oil and associated products, which meant that synthetic fibres became substantially more expensive.

The price for 64s (21-micron) merino wool quoted by the Australian Wool Corporation (AWC) at the beginning of 1974 was 390 cents (Australian) per kilogram (clean basis), compared with the 1973 peak of 590 cents. By July 1974 the AWC was buying more than half the offering to maintain its promised floor price level, based on 300 cents for this quality. The subsequent reluctance to buy wool stemmed partly from the price selected in Australia as a "floor," but primarily from a developing recession in the main consuming countries, particularly Japan, whose demand for wool in 1972–73 had appeared almost insatiable. By mid-1974 the picture was one of high stocks of semi-manufactures and fully manufactured textiles in the consuming countries, financial pressures making stock reduction the policy at every stage of manufacture and distribution, and general forecasts of a serious world trade recession.

Wool-growing countries were thus faced with urgent marketing decisions. The AWC had barely enough money to maintain its floor price for a matter of weeks after the scheduled opening of the 1974–75 selling season in August, assuming that substantial support would be required. The opening was postponed. Eventually government financial support was promised, but only at a floor price of 250 cents per kilogram for 21-micron wool (clean basis) as a basis for the clip.

After purchasing 56% of the offering in the first eight weeks of selling, the AWC held total stocks of 635,000 bales costing about A$135 million. The intention to maintain the floor with government aid throughout the season was reaffirmed at this stage. South Africa and New Zealand followed similar marketing policies with less publicity.

The year, therefore, saw a decisive move toward controlled marketing, with government financial backing either promised or probable in an emergency. Inadequate demand from consuming countries was still putting these policies under severe test toward year's end. For woolgrowers there was slight consolation in signs of a small shift in demand back to virgin wool, primarily at the expense of man-made fibres. However, with demand for all textile fibres low and recession looming, 1974 ended on a gloomy and anxious note.

(H. M. F. MALLETT)

Man-Made Fibres. In 1974 man-made fibre producers were confronted with the most serious recession since World War II, as shortages and high prices at the beginning of the year gave way to excess capacity and considerable pressure on prices. Faced with greatly increased raw material costs arising from the oil crisis, fibre producers cut back output in preference to price cutting. By year's end it was estimated that throughout Western Europe producers were running at only about 55% of capacity. Despite this, new factories were planned in most devel-

oped countries, although building programs in some less developed countries were slowed.

It was expected that polyester and polyamide (nylon) would emerge as the more expensive fibres, since they were based on somewhat more complex chemicals and produced by more involved processes than the acrylics and polypropylene. Polypropylene already showed signs of gaining ground and was even being used by some carpet manufacturers as a direct replacement for wool.

Acrylics were severely affected by the recession, but the situation was unlikely to continue indefinitely since this class of fibre is inherently cheaper than the polyesters. In polyester fibres there was a clear trend toward the use of textured filament yarns in both warp and weft for a wide range of woven fabrics. A hindrance to the wider use of this type of product had been the glitter that prevented it from being widely accepted for menswear. Now fibre producers were marketing octalobal and pentalobal cross-section fibres that, when woven, could hardly be distinguished in appearance from worsted-spun yarns.

Texturizing is mainly performed by false twisting yarns, and it appeared that friction twisting had taken this process to its final economic limits. There was a renewed interest in air-texturizing filament synthetic yarns to produce bulky yarns of minimum weight. It was a fairly simple, high-speed process capable of producing a variety of effects.

The development in Britain of epitropic fibre as a solution to the problem of static generation was a major technological step. Epitropic fibre is defined as a fibre whose surface contains partially or wholly embedded particles that modify one or more of the fibre's properties. Initial development was based on using carbon particles to make fibres electrically conductive so that, when they were incorporated in all-synthetic materials, static charges would be effectively grounded. (PETER LENNOX-KERR)

[732.C.1; 732.D.9]

TOBACCO

Output of tobacco products in 1973 was estimated to have increased by about 6%, which compared well with the average increase of recent years. But because of the development of techniques designed to economize on leaf tobacco usage, the rate of leaf utilization was not matching the product growth rate, particularly when that of cigarettes was measured by units rather than by weight. In Western Europe, for example, it was estimated that while in recent years the number of cigarettes manufactured had risen by 3.8% annually, leaf utilization only increased by 1.7% a year. Early indications were that product output in 1974 would remain buoyant, with leaf consumption probably showing an overall increase of 3–4% at annual rates.

The most serious threat to the long-term future of tobacco growing continued to be the accelerating pace of the development of synthetic tobacco. With New Smoking Materials Ltd., a subsidiary of the Imperial Group and Imperial Chemical Industries, investing £13 million in a British plant that would have an annual capacity of 20 million–30 million lb. of its synthetic, NSM, and the Celanese Corp. in the U.S. building a plant in Maryland with an initial capacity of 9 million lb. of Cytrel, it seemed that these manufacturers at least were confident of having developed a practical and safer alternative to tobacco leaf. Consumer tests of both products were conducted in 1974, but it seemed unlikely that the general sale of cigarettes containing these cellulose-based products would begin before early 1976. De-

mand for leaf tobacco would inevitably be affected should the synthetics find widespread acceptance; in the U.S. tests, a preference for products containing 70% tobacco and 30% synthetic was observed.

World production of leaf tobacco in 1973 was estimated to have increased by 3% to 10.5 billion lb., equaling the 1967 record crop. The increase owed more to better weather than to any increase in the area harvested, which only expanded by 1%. Provided no threat from the weather developed, early indications were that this growth rate would be improved in 1974 with an additional increase of about 5%. Such an increase would help considerably to ease the tight supply situation that had developed over recent years for flue-cured, Burley, and oriental leaf. In 1973 world tobacco stocks dropped to probably the lowest level for a generation—though the improved leaf production in 1973–74 should arrest this decline—and for this reason, as well as because of worldwide inflationary pressures, the cost of tobacco continued to increase.

Increases in both domestic consumption and exports led to a record 644 billion cigarettes being produced in the U.S. in 1973, 7½% more than in 1972 and the highest rate of increase for many years. The proportion of filter-tipped cigarettes continued to rise, reaching 83.7% of the total. Most of the increase came from the extra-long 100-mm. cigarettes.

In spite of continuing antismoking campaigns and advertising restrictions, the number of cigarettes sold in the U.S. in 1973 rose 4½% to a record 591 billion. This upward trend continued in 1974 with production up 5% to 647 billion pieces in 1973–74 (July–June) and consumption up by 4% to 600 billion pieces.

In the U.K. the publication of the government's first tar and nicotine tables in 1973 appeared to have no significant impact; cigarette sales rose by nearly 7 billion pieces to 137.4 billion. Sales of filter cigarettes accounted for 83% of total sales.

During intergovernmental consultations in Rome in mid-1974—part of a series on various primary commodities held by the Food and Agriculture Organization (FAO) and the UN Conference on Trade and Development (UNCTAD)—methods of increasing the tobacco export earnings of the less developed countries were discussed. Consideration was given to liberalization of tobacco trade by reducing customs duties, taxes, and other nontariff barriers; the adoption of appropriate pricing policies; and improvement of the ability of the less developed countries to produce high-quality tobacco. Delegates from the less developed countries supported FAO suggestions for the supply of technical and financial aid to improve tobacco cultivation, leaf quality, and extension services, and to establish suitable curing, processing, and marketing facilities. They also supported the UNCTAD views on the desirability of changes in the tariff structures of developed countries, the reduction of tariffs, and the removal of export and production subsidies in the EEC and other developed tobacco-producing countries. The general view reported from the consultations was that, despite certain national problems, the situation of the world tobacco economy was reasonably satisfactory. (VIVIAN RAVEN)

[731.B.4.e]

See also Advertising; Agriculture and Food Supplies; Alcoholic Beverages; Cooperatives; Economy, World; Employment, Wages, and Hours; Energy; Food Processing; Forestry; Games and Toys; Housing; Industrial Relations; Marketing and Merchandising; Metallurgy; Mining and Quarrying; Prices; Television and Radio; Trade, International.

Industrial Relations

The intensity of the involvement of employees in labour unions and the degree of concern with which unions are regarded by employers and governments depends on the intensity of economic and political crises and the manner in which they impinge on various interests. The year 1974 was a time of such crises. The energy crisis created repercussions that affected price levels and the balance of payments and had direct and immediate effects upon the lives of ordinary people. Rising prices and shortages of commodities gave rise to intensified collective action in Western industrialized countries. In less developed countries these factors added to the already highly unstable positions of governments, many of which were military ones where the reactions to crises occurred more in the form of intensified government control or oppression than of heightened collective action.

Industrialized Countries. Labour relations in the U.S. were destined to be intense in 1974, for the energy crisis and mounting inflation occurred in a context of uncertainty over government policy concerning wage and price controls, fears about a recession, and intense collective bargaining activity as a large number of contracts came up for renewal. Major agreements were to be negotiated in steel, canning, aluminum, construction, communications, electrical machinery, aerospace, longshoring, railroads, and coal mining. Bargaining began lightly and increased during the year. The United Mine Workers (UMW) prepared for contract renewal at its 46th convention in Pittsburgh, Pa., under the leadership of its president, Arnold Miller (*see* BIOGRAPHY). In a major break with past practices, the union decided that settlements should be approved by a majority of the members concerned. On February 24, after a bitter 21-month strike, the Farah Manufacturing Co., which largely produces blue jeans, announced it would recognize the Amalgamated Clothing Workers of America as bargaining agent for its 8,000 employees. The union had conducted an international boycott that caused Farah to close four plants late in 1973. In a ballot of 7,703 members, 62% voted in favour of union recognition.

The number of man-days lost through strikes in the U.S. increased from 1,142,000 in February to 6,267,000 in May, while the number of strikes rose from 350 to 740. The construction industry was particularly affected by strikes. Some major agreements, however, were concluded without strikes. The steel industry's 14-year-old nationwide strike-free record was maintained when a contract was agreed 3½ months before expiry date in August. United Air Lines and the International Association of Machinists reached agreement about ten hours before strike deadline. No agreement, however, was reached in the coal mining industry before the expiry of the UMW wage contract, and early in November more than 100,000 miners came out on strike. Fears of a fuel crisis were renewed as coal stocks became depleted, particularly in the steel industry. A three-year contract drawn up by bargaining agents for the UMW and the coal industry was ratified by the miners in early December.

In general the U.S. trade union movement had not extended its influence significantly in recent years. The size of the U.S. work force had increased at a faster rate than trade union membership. The percentage of union members in the total labour force fell from

24.2 in 1958 to 21.8 in 1972. Similarly, the percentage of union members among employees in nonagricultural establishments fell from 33.2 to 26.7 in the same period. Within the labour force the manufacturing sector showed a declining union membership while women and white-collar workers accounted for a steadily increasing proportion of all organized labour. In 1972 women accounted for 24.9% of all union members while white-collar workers accounted for 22.6%.

The situation in Britain at the end of 1973 contained the ingredients for industrial problems in 1974. British coal miners had submitted a wage claim that was supported with an overtime ban. This coincided with the oil crisis and precipitated the government's declaration of a state of emergency and the imposition of a three-day workweek, from Dec. 31, 1973, to conserve fuel. Electrical power workers banned standby duties and caused voltage reductions in order to obtain the implementation of an already signed agreement. The Industrial Relations Act continued to be ignored by most unions in most matters.

In a climate of mounting tension the executive of the National Union of Mineworkers (NUM) decided in January to poll its members on the issue of striking to support their wage claim. The result showed that 81% of the miners were in favour of strike action. In South Wales the strike majority was 93%. A national miners' strike was called from February 10, whereupon Prime Minister Edward Heath called a general election on the issue of "who governs Britain." The strike itself was uneventful but it continued through the election campaign and was central to it. The Conservative Party was defeated in the February 28 election and, on March 4, Labour Party leader Harold Wilson became prime minister and appointed Michael Foot as minister of employment. Foot negotiated a strike settlement under which the miners received substantial pay increases.

The new Labour government repealed the Industrial Relations Act in July but was compelled to retain certain antiunion clauses because of pressure from the Liberal Party and the House of Lords. Industrial disputes broke out in the National Health Service as hospital nurses took industrial action, and in May the government set up an independent inquiry into nurses' pay. Nonetheless, strikes, overtime bans, and marches by nurses continued, with dissatisfaction spreading to radiographers and other hospital technicians. In some hospitals, workers refused to service private patients in a move to eliminate private beds in public hospitals. The inquiry into nurses' pay reported in September and recommended substantial pay increases which the nurses' organizations accepted.

At its annual meeting in September the British Trades Union Congress (TUC) agreed to a "social contract" with the government that imposed obligations on both government and unions. The government was expected to pursue a policy of redistributing incomes, improving low pay and social security, and generally raising real wages. The unions were asked to restrict wage demands to those needed to keep pace with cost of living changes, to allow 12-month intervals between agreements, to give priority to agreements that had a beneficial effect upon productivity, to eliminate discrimination, and to negotiate raises in the basic minimum rates within the respective industries to reach the TUC-recommended level of £30 per week. The government agreed to maintain voluntary collective bargaining. The social contract played an important part in the Labour Party's second general election campaign of the year in October, for it was Labour's alternative to the legislative control of unions and statutory incomes policies.

The reality of the social contract, insofar as unions were concerned, lay in their separate interpretations of it within their particular contexts. Workers in the Ford Motor Co., Rolls-Royce, in road haulage, and in road passenger transport in Scotland, in particular, were guided by their own immediate needs rather than the guidelines of the contract and secured wage rises beyond cost of living changes. The crucial union, again, was the NUM. In July negotiations began between the NUM and the National Coal Board over a productivity scheme. After many arguments, the issue was voted on in November, with the miners rejecting the productivity scheme by more than 61%.

Labour union events in Japan have become ritualistic. Each year begins with the tail end of the campaign of the previous year and the planning of the "spring wage offensive." The offensive begins in April and carries on into the summer, when there is a lull before the penalties are meted out for illegal strikes. Hundreds of workers in the public services are fined for taking part in industrial action; only the intensity of the struggles and the achievements of the unions vary. These differences are largely determined by economic conditions. In preparation for the 1974 wages campaign, the joint Spring Labour Offensive Committee, set up by the labour unions Sohyo and Churitsuroren, formulated wage demands for an increase of 21.5%. The offensive began with a mass rally in Tokyo on February 25. The first wave of action was experienced on March 1 when railway workers walked out and paralyzed the National Railways. On March 26 about 2,440,000 workers, mainly in transport, participated in a "quasi-general strike." The third wave occurred in April when a nationwide transportation strike was called. In their struggles the unions demanded not simply wage increases but protection against inflation, the right to strike for public service workers, and relief for the underprivileged. These wider demands evoked a widespread response. The strike of April 9–13 was the largest in the history of the spring wage offensive and included postal and communications workers and teachers. The unions succeeded in obtaining an average increase of about 30%, which just barely compensated for the inflationary cost of living increases. Wage increases in the coal industry amounted to 55.4% and the government set in motion the steps to give public employees the right to strike.

The labour relations situation on the continent of Europe confirmed that there was a pattern in the industrialized countries of intensive struggles during 1974. West Germany, which had been increasingly exposed to strike action after 1969, had a rising level of unemployment and difficulties with its 2.5 million immigrant workers. Early in 1974 the German government considered paying a departure bonus to migrant workers to alleviate the unemployment situation. The large I.G. Metall trade union made a demand late in 1973 for a 15% wage increase and stated that it was not prepared to accept less. Negotiations were deadlocked in January and thousands of metalworkers engaged in warning strikes. In February the Public Service and Transport Union started a three-phase industrial action program after 79% of its members had voted for strike action. This was the first action of its kind by the union. At the same time 89.8% of the

unionized railway workers voted for a strike in a ballot in which 93.6% of the union members participated. Municipal bus, streetcar, and urban railway services were idle on February 11. Some airports were affected and in most areas the refuse disposal services came to a halt. Selective strikes of postal workers began. Five large unions had mandates for strikes for pay increases, involving about two million workers. The strikes escalated until February 13 when agreements were reached for an 11% wage increase, after an original offer of 7.5%. I.G. Metall rejected the 11% offer and in March 52,000 workers in Bremen and Bremerhaven went on strike. On March 28 the strike was called off as the workers agreed to a 12% wage increase.

Industrial action continued in France, involving a wide range of industries. In November 1973 there was a widespread strike of produce retailers against "iniquitous and arbitrary" price controls and, for the first time in its history, all the dock operations in the port of Marseilles were stopped by a strike over pay and conditions. In Lorraine the coal mines were closed because of a strike by surface workers and 10,000 miners were sent on an enforced holiday for six days in January 1974. When they were not paid for this holiday, 90% of the miners went on strike themselves. There were big antigovernment demonstrations by state-sector employees on March 14. Bank clerks were on strike at that time and at one Crédit Lyonnais bank the police forced an entry in order to evict 50 bank clerks who were occupying it. In October French postal workers struck, not for higher pay but for measures to improve postal service. The strike went on throughout November and coincided with a spate of strikes in other industries, particularly in the public sector. A general strike against the government's anti-inflation austerity program was called by the Confédération Générale du Travail (CGT) and the Confédération Française Démocratique du Travail (CFDT) in November. Railway workers, gas and electricity workers, and Paris garbage collectors had deep grievances against the government's policy.

The phenomenon of calling general strikes against government policy as a matter of tactics was also common to Italy. The intention was not to topple governments or to impose extreme economic sanctions but largely to indicate warning signs. When the three main trade union organizations were planning a concerted general strike in February they expressly stated that it was not their aim to bring down the government but to stimulate it. On February 7 more than one million Italian workers staged strikes of between one and eight hours' duration to protest against inflation and to press for social reforms. In some areas such as Milan the strikes were general. Later in the month 13 million workers engaged in a brief general strike. In Rome and its environs most activity stopped for the day. In the rest of the country work was suspended for four hours. Even doctors conducted a 48-hour strike in July in protest against government health reform proposals. The doctors wanted new hospitals and better services.

The collapse of the military dictatorship in Portugal allowed free trade unionism to emerge there. In May, 8,300 shipyard workers struck for higher pay. The shipyard, however, was not completely closed because the workers agreed to work two hours a day for the sake of the economy. Unofficial strikes occurred at textile plants, and at the end of May strikers in Lisbon left the city without bread and buses. Nearly all the

35,000 post office workers in Portugal struck for higher wages in June and refused a government appeal to carry on work during negotiations. Telephone and telex services were not affected and essential services for hospitals, fire stations, and the like were maintained. Workers on the daily paper *Journal do Comercio* went on strike in September for the dismissal of its director, who was considered to have worked too closely with the ousted Caetano regime.

Spain continued to be a centre of trade union oppression. The pattern of earlier years was maintained. Despite the fact that strikes were illegal, Spain had had the most numerous, the longest, and the largest strikes of any country in Europe. In the last week of January 1974 strikes, demonstrations, lockouts, and dismissals spread to various parts of Spain. On January 28 strong police reinforcements forced about 6,000 workers out of the Spanish subsidiary of the International Telephone and Telegraph Co. (ITT) after a series of stoppages about pay. About 1,300 workers occupied a plant in Pamplona that was a subsidiary of the British Leyland automotive firm. The police removed them from the works and they were locked out. When the workers met to discuss their pay claim in Pamplona cathedral, with the permission of church authorities, armed police drove them out, contrary to the Concordat between Spain and the Vatican which specifies that police must not carry out any official act inside a church without the permission of the hierarchy "except in a case of urgent necessity." Many workers were arrested. Representatives of the powerful illegal Workers Commission forecast widespread strikes at a secret press conference in southern Spain in June. The forecast was confirmed when 13,660 workers at the Fasa-Renault car factory in Valladolid were locked out after repeated strikes over wages and working conditions.

Less Developed Countries. Although less developed nations were affected by inflation in much the same way as industrialized ones, this was not a dominant factor in labour relations in those countries. Less developed countries in the Middle East that produce oil did not have, in the main, trade union movements that could exercise pressure on employers. In any event, their wage-earning forces were small. The main issue for wage earners there was the absence of political freedom to take industrial action. Elsewhere the prime issue was also about political freedom because an increasingly large number of countries were subject to military or quasi-military rule. These countries possessed small segments of wage-earning activity in predominantly peasant economies in which the pressures to take protective collective action were present. Most of them possessed organized trade union movements, a legacy of colonialism in many cases, but the unions were usually subjected to strict legislative control or simply contained by the forces of governments.

South Africa was a case where, despite the absence of the formal freedom to organize and strike, black workers nonetheless asserted their collective power, and with some degree of success. In October 1973 the South African minister of labour announced that the government would not give way to the demands of black workers for the recognition of their trade unions, nor would it abolish job reservation. He believed that black workers had the opportunity—through the Bantu Labour Relations Regulations Amendment Act—to negotiate with employers, and to recognize unions would be to create unnecessary duplication. This belief was not confirmed by black

workers; early in 1974 there were strikes by more than 10,000 textile workers at eight factories in Durban. Police were called in and arrested 250 of the strikers. The unrecognized, newly formed, National Union of Textile Workers blamed the dispute on the fact that black Africans had no voice in the determination of wages. Each of the arrested workers was given a fine of R 5 ($7.50) or a sentence of ten days' imprisonment. The strikers returned to work on January 23 after having been promised immediate pay increases. Migrant gold mine workers in the Orange Free State struck in June; violence occurred during the dispute, and four men died. The South African Trade Union Council called for an inquiry into a mine where 30 miners had died in disputes beginning in January. In June the Chamber of Mines announced a 66% increase in the starting wage for African miners.

India was the scene of a bitter and violent strike during the summer. The unions organizing 1.7 million railway workers demanded pay parity with other public sector employees and an annual bonus equal to a month's wages. The unions called for a national rail strike on May 8 and the government attempted to preempt it by arresting more than 300 senior trade union officials. Before the strike started more than 700 officials had been arrested on the ground that the strike notices were illegal under the emergency regulations issued during the 1971 war with Pakistan. Many Indian cities were paralyzed by protest strikes organized by the Communist and Socialist parties in conjunction with the trade unions. By the day of the strike more than 3,600 arrests had been made and the government threatened strikers with penalties ranging from loss of leave and retirement benefits to outright dismissal and imprisonment. There were contradictory reports of the incidence of strike action but in Delhi, Calcutta, and Bombay millions of commuters were without rail transport. Paramilitary units and regular and territorial soldiers were used to dispel picketing strikers, to patrol and guard installations, and to protect strikebreakers. By the end of the first

continued on page 405

Government scientists stage a protest march from the British Museum to Downing Street, where they petitioned Prime Minister Harold Wilson for higher pay.

THE GUARDIAN, LONDON & MANCHESTER

THE QUALITY OF WORKING LIFE

By Richard E. Walton

In 1972 a highly publicized strike occurred at the General Motors assembly plant at Lordstown, Ohio. Many observers viewed this incident as a forerunner of a rash of spontaneous and angry refusals to work initiated by younger workers fed up with meaningless jobs and authoritarian managers. As it happened, wholesale plant unrest has not materialized. Nevertheless, interest in long-term reform in workplaces has continued to grow, and the sense of urgency has remained high in the Western industrialized countries.

During 1974 observers gave a great deal of attention to issues having to do with the quality of working life. And instead of dwelling on symptoms of alienation (the "blue collar blues" and the "white collar woes"), as writers had done in earlier years, they were giving more measured treatment to underlying causes and proposed solutions.

Beginning with the Industrial Revolution, managers sought to increase productivity by rationalizing the production processes. Progressively, jobs were fragmented and deskilled, planning and implementing were separated, management controls were substituted for craft pride and self-discipline, and automation was substituted for human judgment. These approaches eventually produce worker disaffection, and as a result they may no longer serve the goal of productivity or they may do so only at a high human cost. Companies in a variety of industries in many countries have found that they can create a more satisfied, committed, and capable work force and can obtain equal or better quality and quantity of output by restructuring work along different lines: by combining jobs to create whole tasks; by assigning these tasks to teams with responsibilities for inspection, maintenance, planning, scheduling, and work assignment; by cross-training workers for broader flexibility; by adopting more participative management patterns; and by designing pay schemes to reward individual learning and group productivity.

Several attitudes are promoting this reversal of long-established trends. One is rising expectations on the part of employees. Another is greater public consciousness about the quality of work life. Most important of all is a growing belief among managers that work restructuring often leads to improvements not only in the quality of work life but also in productivity.

The Issues. In the United States and other Western industrialized countries, workers are measuring the quality of work life by criteria such as the following:

Adequate and fair compensation. Does pay received meet socially determined standards of sufficiency and the recipient's subjective standard? Does pay received for certain work bear an appropriate relationship to pay received for other work?

Safe and healthy environment. That employees should not be exposed to physical conditions or work arrangements that are unduly hazardous or unhealthy is widely accepted. In the future,

---

Richard E. Walton is Edsel Bryant Ford Professor at the Harvard Graduate School of Business Administration. His published works in the field of industrial relations include A Behavioral Theory of Labor Negotiations (*1965; with R. B. McKersie) and* Interpersonal Peacemaking (*1969*). *Support for the research on which that report is based was provided by the Ford Foundation.*

when health will be less the issue than comfort, even more stringent standards may be imposed. These may include minimizing odours, noise, or visual annoyances.

Constitutionalism. What rights does the worker have and how can he or she protect these rights? The labour unions have sought to protect employees from arbitrary or capricious actions by employers, and in a few unions U.S. workers now enjoy some of these same rights vis-à-vis the union structure itself. In unorganized employment, there are wide variations in the extent to which the organizational culture respects the worker's personal privacy, tolerates dissent, adheres to high standards of equity in distributing rewards, and provides for due process in work-related matters.

Development of human capacities. To what degree does the job enable the worker to use and develop his skills and knowledge? To what extent does it involve the worker, foster self-esteem, provide a challenge?

Advancement. Three questions are involved here: the extent to which an employee's assignments contribute to expansion of capabilities rather than obsolescence; whether newly acquired knowledge and skills can be used in future work assignments; and whether opportunities for advancement are provided in terms that peers and family members will recognize.

Human relations. The employee's personal identity and self-esteem are influenced by such attributes in the climate of the workplace as freedom from prejudice, a sense of community, interpersonal openness, and the absence of stratification in the organization.

The total life space. The role of work should not overbalance a person's life. Ideally the work should create involvement without the imposition of schedules, career demands, and travel requirements that take more than a limited portion of the person's leisure and family time, and it should provide advancement and promotion without requiring repeated geographic moves that disrupt family and community life.

Social relevance. Organizations acting in a socially irresponsible manner may cause employees to depreciate the value of their work and careers. For example, does the worker perceive the organization to be socially responsible in its products, waste disposal, marketing techniques, employment practices, and participation in political campaigns?

The first three of these issues—compensation, safety, and rights—relate to traditionally recognized aspirations of workingmen and have been the subject of legislation and collective bargaining. By 1974 the last two issues—total life space and social relevance—were growing in importance, but could still be thought of as mainly in the future. So the work-restructuring efforts discussed below relate primarily to the opportunity to use and develop one's capacities, the opportunity to advance in a career, and the existence of constructive human relations in the workplace.

One of the reasons why employee expectations have increased with regard to these three issues is that the educational level has risen. Another is that levels of income and security have also risen from decade to decade, so that pay and security are taken more for granted than they used to be. Still another factor is the decreased emphasis given by churches, schools, and families to obedience to authority. Instead, they have promoted individual initiative, self-responsibility and self-control, the relativity of values, and other social patterns that make subordination in a traditional organizational structure increasingly difficult to accept for each successive wave of entrants into the work force.

Work in America, the report of a special task force to the U.S. secretary of health, education, and welfare in 1973, lists a variety of adverse consequences of modern-day organization of work. In the workplace, symptoms of the growing gap between employee expectations and the reality of existing jobs include employee indifference to quality, turnover and absenteeism, work disruptions, and even sabotage to plant and equipment. Work was found to be related to mental and physical health, family stability, educational attainment, and national economic well-being.

As HEW Secretary Elliot Richardson expected when he released the report, it stirred controversy. Some observers assert that dissatisfaction is not a serious problem, arguing either that the proportion of dissatisfied workers is not large or that dissatisfaction with work is a normal state of affairs. Moreover, among many workers, trade-union officials, and managers there is an assumption that the content of jobs and the way work is organized cannot really be changed. They believe that although work may be a "central life interest" for some people, it is not for others. Presumably those others lack an intrinsic interest in the work itself. If the pay and fringe benefits are good and employment is reasonably secure, the jobs can be narrow, repetitive, and devoid of any intellectual or manual challenge.

Those who urge the restructuring of work reply that one cannot be expected to evaluate a state of affairs one has never experienced. Many workers who do not, in advance, express a desire for more autonomy, more responsibility for making decisions, and an opportunity to learn new skills nevertheless state firmly, after they have participated in work restructured to provide autonomy, responsibility, and growth, that they do not want to go back to the earlier way.

Pioneering the Restructuring of Work. Awareness of rising expectations and the potential costs and risks of not meeting them has led to innovations in the restructuring of work in different countries. These experiments are occurring in a large number of leading industrial firms. In the U.S. they include General Foods, Procter & Gamble, General Motors, TRW, Cummins Engine, Scott Paper, and General Electric, and in Europe, Volvo, Saab-Scania, Shell U.K., Philips, Olivetti, and Fiat.

Two recent examples of work restructuring that have received a great deal of publicity are the Volvo assembly plants in Sweden and a General Foods plant at Topeka, Kan. Volvo is significant because the conventional automobile assembly line is viewed as particularly alienating in character. The experiment at Topeka is significant because it is so comprehensive in the aspects of work that have been restructured and so radical in the degree to which workers participate in managerial functions.

Volvo. Faced with a very high rate of labour turnover in 1969, Volvo initiated a program of work restructuring that has affected a large proportion of the workers in its existing plants and has led to the design of a new kind of automobile plant.

Along the assembly lines of the existing plants in Lundby and Torslanda, the jobs of many workers were enlarged, allowing longer work cycles and hence more control over pace, as well as reducing the repetitive tedium. In some groups jobs were rotated once or several times daily, depending on the nature of the

work and the workers' preferences. In many parts of the plants, production teams of three to ten persons with common tasks were created and given responsibility within the requirements set by management. Each team allocated tasks among its members, ensured quality, and elected its own leadership. Finally, consultative groups were formed to permit supervisors and production engineers to meet monthly with representatives chosen by workers to discuss common problems. The program had the joint sponsorship of union and management. Moreover, with few exceptions, the new arrangements were applied to a particular work situation only when the workers directly involved decided they wanted the changes.

Volvo claims positive results, including more employee satisfaction, less labour turnover, less absenteeism, improved quality, and fewer final adjustments. The sizes of crews and their output, however, have not varied, because they are fixed by agreement with the union. Modifications in the assembly line have added costs such as duplicate tools, space for extra inventory, and training, but the company says the benefits outweigh these costs.

Encouraged by these results, Volvo designed a truly revolutionary plant at Kalmar, which began production in the spring of 1974. Assembly work at Kalmar is performed by 25 groups, each typically composed of about 15 workers. A group has responsibility for a complete component of the car, such as the electrical system, instrumentation, or wheels and brakes. Employees can develop professional pride as they acquire expertise in an entire subsystem of the automobile. The members of the team can influence the working procedures, the internal distribution of jobs, and variation in the rate of work. The team is responsible for supplies of materials and plays an active part in quality inspection. With team members accepting greater responsibility, the foreman can devote more time to long-range planning and coordination between areas.

The building has been designed to create a small workshop atmosphere. Each group has at its disposal a floor area screened from the view of the other teams, and each has a separate place for relaxation. Instead of moving on a conveyor line, car bodies are transported on battery-driven trolleys, carefully designed to reduce physical strain on the part of the workers. The screened work areas, the trolleys, sound-absorbent ceilings, and silenced power tools all contribute to an exceptionally quiet plant, with a noise level generally at 65 decibels or less. A computer system with scanner displays in each team area provides teams with information pertinent to their work. All this required a rather high investment, and it remains to be seen whether the results will justify the additional expense.

In 1974 Volvo decided to build an auto assembly plant in the U.S. with similarly advanced forms of job design and work

The traditional and the experimental: assembly line production (left) and Volvo's team approach at the Kalmar plant in Sweden (above).

organization. The firm is committed to working with trade unions in the innovative programs, and Leonard Woodcock, president of the United Auto Workers, indicated a willingness to cooperate. Such a collaborative venture by the UAW and Volvo could significantly affect the attitudes of U.S. employers and unions generally toward the new ideas.

General Foods. The pet food plant opened by General Foods at Topeka in 1970 was designed to provide a high quality of work life, enlist unusual human involvement, and result in high productivity. By 1974 these results had indeed been achieved to an impressive degree. The author was involved in the original design as a consultant and has continued to monitor developments. Employees praise the variety, dignity, and influence that they enjoy, the team spirit, open communication, and mastery of new skills with commensurate pay. Managers report favourably on the capacities and sense of responsibility that the workers have developed. The plant has been manned with 35% fewer employees than if the work had been organized along traditional lines. Even more important, economic benefits include improved yields, less waste, avoidance of shutdowns, and lower absenteeism and turnover.

Some observers argue that this plant is a special case because it is a small facility set in a rural area, or because the workers were selected from a large number of applicants and thus are unusually well motivated. These criticisms make a valid point, namely, that such conditions as the size of the plant, its location, and the nature of the work force can affect the success or failure of work restructuring. But many other experiments, such as that at Volvo, have been effective in larger plants, in urban plants, and without the benefit of selective hiring.

The effectiveness of the Topeka plant results from a number of features. Self-managing work teams assume collective responsibility for large segments of the production process. The teams are composed of from 7 to 14 members, large enough to embrace a set of interrelated tasks and small enough to allow effective face-to-face meetings for decision making and coordination. Activities typically performed by separate units—maintenance, quality control, custodianship, industrial engineering, and personnel—were built into the operating team's responsibilities. For example, team members screen job applicants for replacements on their own team.

An attempt was made to design every set of tasks to include functions requiring higher human abilities and responsibilities, such as planning, diagnosing mechanical problems, and liaison work. The aim was to make all sets of tasks equally challenging, although each set would comprise unique skill demands. Consistent with this aim was a single job classification for all operators, with pay increases geared to the mastery of an increasing number of jobs. Employees were encouraged to teach each other, and they had no reason not to because there were no limits on how many team members could qualify for higher pay brackets.

In lieu of the "foreman," a "team leader" position was created with the responsibility of facilitating team development and decision making. After several years, the self-management capacities of teams were so well developed that these "team leader" positions became unnecessary and were being eliminated. Operators were provided information and decision guidelines that enabled them to make production decisions ordinarily made by higher levels of supervision.

As for plant rules, management refrained from specifying any in advance. Rather, such rules evolved over time from collective experience. The technology and architecture were designed to facilitate rather than discourage the congregating of team members during working hours. Status symbols of the sort that characterize traditional work organizations were minimized. For example, a single entrance leads into both the office and the plant.

Diffusion of the Innovations. As in the case of Volvo, General Foods managers were encouraged with the results of their pilot project and adopted a policy of promoting work restructuring throughout the firm's many plants in the U.S. and abroad. In

the mid-1970s diffusion within General Foods was proceeding somewhat more slowly than within Volvo, however, and the same contrast existed between the U.S. and Sweden in general.

It is instructive to analyze the factors that have promoted diffusion in Sweden. First, there is a powerful commitment of Swedish society to democracy, to relative equality, to the development of human potential through education, and to collaboration and peaceful resolution of conflict. These commitments are also evident in other countries, but in Sweden they are exceptionally strong.

Further, the Swedish work force is well educated, relatively prosperous, and enjoys a relatively high level of economic security. A third factor has been the initiative shown by Swedish management, especially its willingness to import work-restructuring ideas from Norway's Industrial Democracy Projects in the 1960s. Several sharp incentives existed for management to innovate in this area. Sweden has had a scarcity of labour and high rates of turnover. Swedish industry emphasizes quality, precision, and the kinds of products and production systems that benefit especially from a flexible and quality-conscious work force. Government sickness benefits, which ensure that a worker who is absent from work suffers no loss in real income, tend to increase absenteeism.

Swedish union officials have supported work restructuring more than their counterparts in other countries. Very high percentages of blue-collar and white-collar workers belong to unions, and the union institution is very secure. Strong central control gives the union leaders confidence in dealing with job-satisfaction issues and enables them to create, or strongly encourage, nationwide changes. Moreover, their close association with the government gives them a national view and therefore an appreciation of the importance of Swedish productivity. At the same time, an unusually effective federation of employers exists to bargain nationally with trade unions, and it has undertaken to formulate and implement policies on work restructuring. Finally, these strong national institutions of unions and employers are elaborately linked with academic and other independent institutions capable of providing research, training, and counsel.

Other countries do not have institutional mechanisms quite equal to those that fostered work restructuring in Sweden. Still, a review of developments in other countries shows that many programs for improving the quality of work are being sponsored by national and state governments, among them the National Quality of Work Council sponsored by the U.S. Productivity Commission; the Ohio Quality of Work Project sponsored by the Governor's Business and Employment Council; and the Unit for the Quality of Work Life sponsored by the South Australia Department of Labour and Industry.

In 1974 an International Council on the Quality of Working Life was established in Geneva to serve a network of quality-of-work centres in nine countries of North America, Europe, and Asia and to catalyze the creation of new centres in other countries. The council, which had its origins in a conference on the subject sponsored by the Ford Foundation a few years earlier, is a private organization, and expects to receive support from foundations and government agencies in the countries of participants. It will promote the development and dissemination of a body of systematic knowledge that can be used in the training of social scientists, engineers, accountants, trade unionists, lawyers, and administrators who will work on issues relating to the quality of work life.

Thus, the quality of work movement, stimulated in part by visible symptoms of disaffection in the workplace and supported by changing social values, has led to a number of instructive innovations in the way work is structured in particular firms. It has also produced some private networks and public commissions whose purpose is to promote further experimentation and the diffusion of effective innovations. The timetable for actually effecting major reform, however, must be measured in decades rather than years.

continued from page 401

week it was claimed that more than 15,000 railway workers had been arrested. The rail workers action committee called off the strike unilaterally after 20 days, claiming that more than 50,000 workers had been arrested, more than 10,000 dismissed, and nearly 30,000 evicted from their homes.

Trade unions were involved in the troubles in Ethiopia in 1974. Violence and deaths occurred during strikes by teachers and taxicab drivers for higher pay in February. Following the military uprising at the end of February, the Confederation of Ethiopian Labour Unions, representing about 85,000 workers, called a nationwide strike for an improved minimum wage and 15 other demands. Altogether, about 120,000 workers struck for four days and achieved most of their demands.   (V. L. ALLEN)

See also Employment, Wages, and Hours; Race Relations.
[521.B.3; 534.C.1.g; 552.D.3 and F.3; 554.D.4]
ENCYCLOPÆDIA BRITANNICA FILMS. *The Industrial Worker* (1969); *The Rise of Big Business* (1970); *The Progressive Era* (1971).

Insurance

Good news of continuing high growth rates of 8% or more in private insurance in 1974 was offset by bad news of record-breaking disasters in many areas. The highest death toll ever registered in a single aviation loss occurred in March, when a Turkish Airlines DC-10 aircraft crashed in France with the loss of 346 lives. The more than $40 million loss would fall mainly on British insurers, although it would be spread widely by reinsurance. In June 1974 an estimated $100 million loss was suffered in the explosion of a factory producing caprolactam, used in the manufacture of nylon, in Flixborough, Eng. The effects of an April series of tornadoes in the U.S. were devastating for many insurers, with losses exceeding $430 million. Generally, the underwriting profitability of several recent years turned to underwriting losses in most types of property and liability insurance.

Sagging securities markets also caused concern. Investment returns, including realized capital gains and losses, were high, but the sharp decreases in stock market values caused portfolio values and policyholders' surpluses to shrink by billions of dollars. Property-liability insurers faced rising property damage and injury costs due to inflation.

Life Insurance. Growth and results were generally more favourable for life insurance than for other sectors. Canada continued to have the highest ratio of life insurance in force to national income; more than 11 million Canadians owned life insurance at the beginning of 1974, with a total of more than $170 billion in force. In the U.S. some 145 million policyholders owned life insurance valued at almost $2 trillion. More than half was ordinary life insurance, purchased individually, while group life insurance, mostly written through employers, exceeded 40% of the total.

U.S. life insurance company assets at mid-1974 totaled $258 billion, 5% above a year earlier; a little less than one-third of these assets were invested in mortgages, about 40% in bonds, 8% in policy loans, and the remainder in real estate and other uses. During the same period, policy loans had risen 14%. Purchases continued at a near-record level of more than $250 billion. New individual ordinary life contracts averaged approximately $14,000 in value. Women

were buying more life insurance; they accounted for 25% of new contracts and 14% of the total purchased.

Annual premium receipts of U.S. life insurance companies exceeded $50 billion for the first time in 1974. More than half was for life insurance, more than one-third for health insurance, and 15% for annuities. Of the more than $20 billion paid in benefits, about $9 billion was for death benefits and the remainder for "living benefits" including dividends, surrender or matured values, and annuity or disability payments.

Probably the most significant development of 1974 for the U.S. life insurance industry was the enactment of the Employee Retirement Income Security Act. Under this law, an employee's benefits must be fully vested within 15 years, and a governmental Pension Benefit Guaranty Corporation would guarantee payment of these benefits, within certain limits. Retirement plans for self-employed individuals were broadened to permit a maximum tax-deductible annual contribution of 15% of earned income up to $7,500, and individuals not covered by retirement plans could set up their own plans and deduct 15% of salary up to $1,500.

In the U.K. life insurance premiums rose by almost 9% in 1973 to nearly £2,500 million; invested funds totaled more than £18,000 million and investment income, £1,300 million. U.K. insurers owned 30% of all British quoted equity stocks, and the proportion was expected to rise to 50% in the next ten years. One company, Nation Life, went into liquidation in July 1974 mainly as a result of difficulties stemming from newly introduced property and income bonds sold as life insurance contracts.

Property and Liability Insurance. U.S. premium volume approached $45 billion in 1974, but a reversal of the underwriting gains recorded during the previous three years appeared inevitable. Midyear reports showed $500 million in underwriting losses, the worst six-month results ever recorded. With the sharp drop in the securities market and the effects of inflation, it appeared that the $20 billion policyholder surplus would be decreased by several billion dollars by year's end.

About two dozen states had adopted automobile no-fault laws by late 1974, but many were of the limited type that did not severely restrict tort liability lawsuits. The Federal Crime Insurance Program, inaugurated three years earlier and written by the Federal Insurance Administration in 13 states, made little progress. The FAIR (Fair Access to Insurance Requirements) plans for property coverage in urban areas, operating in almost 30 states, were experiencing increasing trouble. Underwriting losses exceeded $40 million in 1973 and the number of premiums written was declining. In contrast, the federal flood insurance program, backed by reinsurance through the Department of Housing and Urban Development, gained momentum as total property values insured rose beyond $7.5 billion.

Mounting problems in medical malpractice liability insurance were accentuated by rapidly rising losses and costs and severe restriction in market availability. A phenomenal growth in products liability claims was noted, allegedly because of the broadened requirements of the new Consumer Product Safety Act and because attorneys were shifting their attention from automobile liability to product liability cases. Among the newest developments in U.S. insurance was a trend toward group legal expense insurance as an employee fringe benefit.

WIDE WORLD

The foundation slab is all that remains of a house in Xenia, Ohio, in the wake of the disastrous tornado that struck April 3.

Information Science and Technology:
see Computers

Member companies of the British Insurance Association showed a profit on their worldwide nonlife underwriting in 1973 for the third successive year. The profit was £19 million, and premium income rose by 16.4%. However, a reversal of these trends was indicated by early 1974 figures. British companies drew 38% of their general premium income from the U.K., 24% from the U.S., and 38% from the rest of the world, where their underwriting loss in Canada and Australia was particularly unprofitable. In Australia losses arose because worker's compensation legislation increased the cost of outstanding claims.

U.K. fire damage, insured and uninsured, rose 65% in 1973 to a record £179 million. The figure fell in the first quarter of 1974 but reached new heights in the second quarter. A rise of 7% in crime losses under household and "all risks" policies was counterbalanced by a fall in claims under money policies and insurances on commercial and industrial premises. The profitability of marine, aviation, and transport insurance in recent years had attracted many newcomers to the market. Lloyd's underwriters numbered a record 7,000 in 1974.

Some progress was made toward establishing a common market in insurance within the EEC. Directives coordinating supervisory legislation and permitting nonlife insurers in one Community country to set up business in any other were adopted in 1973. In May 1974 checks at the frontiers of EEC countries on third-party motor insurance were abolished for motorists of member countries and some others.

Although U.K. insurance companies earned an underwriting profit (2.7%) on automobile insurance in 1973 for the first time in five years, profitable results for 1974 appeared doubtful. The average cost of a claim rose by 16%, partly because of increasing repair costs and partly because of higher awards of damages for bodily injury. On the other hand, claim frequency was held in check by higher fuel costs and the speed limits imposed temporarily during the fuel crisis in the winter of 1973–74. Rising interest rates increased investment income, a short-term benefit of inflation. One large U.K. company, against the trend, reduced automobile insurance premiums by 5% in July 1974.

New Zealand set up a scheme to compensate wage earners and housewives for all kinds of road, work, and other accidents. The common law liability for such injuries was abolished, and the scope of private liability insurers was severely restricted. The scheme was financed mainly by levies on employers and self-employed persons and on the owners or users of automobiles.　(DAVID L. BICKELHAUPT)

See also Cooperatives; Disasters; Industrial Production and Technology; Social and Welfare Services.
[534.J.]

Investment, International

Major changes in the rate of inflow and outflow of funds to the main industrial countries took place during 1973 and 1974. Among the important features of this period were changes in administrative controls over the movement of funds. During the first half of 1973, faced with the weakening of the dollar, some European countries extended their controls on the inflow of funds. Later in 1973 and in 1974, with the recovery of the dollar and the adverse movement of trade balances following oil price rises, these controls were dismantled. Unfortunately, this freedom was short-lived, for, with worsening trade balances, certain countries began to impose restrictions on the outflow of funds in 1974.

United States. The main development in U.S. international investment in 1973–74 was the removal in January 1974 of the restraints imposed in 1963–68 on the outflow of capital. These included the interest equalization tax on U.S. portfolio investment, the restrictions on the transfer of funds abroad for foreign direct investment by U.S. firms, and guidelines for voluntary restraint by U.S. financial institutions. This relaxation of restrictions had little effect on capital flows during the first half of 1974, but a longer term effect was expected.

Direct investment abroad by U.S. firms in 1973 increased by $1.3 billion above its 1972 level, with an increase of $1.8 billion in the flow of capital to Western Europe, divided equally between the U.K. and the rest of the EEC (see Tables I and II). On the other hand, U.S. investment in Japan fell from $230 million to $36 million. A marked change took place in the industrial composition of the investment, with manufacturing dominating in 1973 whereas petroleum

Table I. U.S. Investment Abroad

In $000,000

Item	1969	1970	1971	1972	1973	1974*
Direct investment						
New funds	3,271	4,410	4,943	3,517	4,872	4,356
Reinvested profits	2,604	2,948	3,157	4,521	...	...
Total	5,875	7,358	8,100	8,038	...	...
Portfolio investment	1,494	942	966	654	807	2,006
Total	7,369	8,300	9,066	8,692	...	...

*First half year, seasonally adjusted; at annual rate.
Source: U.S. Department of Commerce, Survey of Current Business.

Table II. U.S. International Investment and Earnings, by Region, 1973

In $000,000

Area	Investment* Direct*	Portfolio	Total	Earnings* Direct*	Portfolio	Total
Canada	540	569	1,109	1,126	1,164	2,290
Latin America	673	107	780	1,622	822	2,444
EEC	2,601	83	2,684	2,035	541	2,576
Other Western Europe	338	33	371	435	178	613
Japan	36	−256	−220	222	375	597
Other countries	641	377	1,018	3,790	531	4,321
International organizations and unallocated	43	−106	−63	185	130	315
	4,872	807	5,679	9,415	3,741	13,156

*Excluding reinvested profits.
Source: U.S. Department of Commerce, Survey of Current Business.

Table III. U.S. Investment Earnings

In $000,000

Item	1969	1970	1971	1972	1973	1974*
Direct investment						
Repatriated profits	5,074	5,330	6,385	6,925	9,415	18,136
Reinvested profits†	2,470	2,788	3,004	4,382	...	...
Total	7,544	8,118	9,389	11,307	...	...
Portfolio investment						
Total income	2,267	2,597	2,556	2,697	3,741	5,650
Total earnings	9,811	10,715	11,945	14,004	...	...

*First half year, seasonally adjusted; at annual rate.
†Excluding interest but before deducting foreign withholding taxes.
Source: U.S. Department of Commerce, Survey of Current Business.

Table IV. Foreign Investment in the U.S.

In $000,000

Inflow of funds	1969	1970	1971	1972	1973	1974*
Direct investment	832	1,030	−115	383	2,537	3,500†
Portfolio investment	3,130	2,190	2,289	4,507	4,061	2,168
Total	3,962	3,220	2,174	4,890	6,598	6,168
Total earnings‡	3,686	4,032	2,965	3,209	4,858	10,942

*First half year, seasonally adjusted; at annual rate.
†Including one special transaction of approximately $2.1 billion.
‡Excluding undistributed profits.
Source: U.S. Department of Commerce, Survey of Current Business.

had been most important in the previous two years. During the first half of 1974 there was a sharp reduction in the outflow of capital in the petroleum industry, but increases in all other industries reflected the eased restrictions.

U.S. portfolio investment in 1973 was at a level similar to that of previous years. Purchases of foreign bonds were about $1 billion in 1973 (as in 1972), but U.S. investors reduced their holdings of foreign stocks by $200 million (compared with $400 million in 1972). Substantial selling of Western European stocks in 1972 gave way to purchases of $130 million in 1973, and the reverse happened with Japanese stocks, U.S. investors selling nearly $200 million in 1973. In the first half of 1974 there was a marked increase in outflow, with purchases of foreign bonds amounting to $1.1 billion, more than during all of 1973. The bulk of this increase was attributable to new issues by Canada. Net sales of foreign stocks continued at a rate similar to that of 1973.

Earnings on U.S. foreign direct investments recorded a marked increase in 1973 (see Table III), with petroleum investments accounting for 60% of the total gain. Investments in Latin America brought an increase in earnings of $700 million, while earnings from Asia and Africa rose from $2.2 billion to 3.3 billion. There was a marked increase in portfolio investment earnings, reflecting higher interest rates and the depreciation of the dollar; gains were evenly spread between regions. In the first half of 1974, U.S. direct investment earnings were running at a rate almost double that of 1973. Earnings by U.S. petroleum companies benefiting from oil price rises accounted for almost two-thirds of the total earnings.

The total inflow of foreign investment funds into the U.S. increased sharply in 1973 to $6.6 billion, exceeding the outflow of $5.7 billion (it should be noted that both figures exclude reinvested profits, which would add more to U.S. than to foreign investment). Investment by the U.K. and by other EEC countries each increased by $500 million, and there was a $300 million increase in Japanese investment. Also included was a $500 million payment by an oil-producing country for participation in a U.S. oil company. For the first half of 1974 the data in Table IV are complicated by a special transaction involving a U.S. oil company; apart from this, the inflow took place at a rate lower than in 1973. The sharp increase in foreign portfolio investment in the U.S. was largely due to increased purchases of U.S. stocks by European investors, and the fall in 1974 reflected selling of the stocks by those same investors.

United Kingdom. The rate of British investment in other countries in 1973 was much the same as in the previous year, but within this unchanging total figure were some marked changes in particular cate-gories. Direct investment rose sharply, and there was also a considerable increase in the oil and miscellaneous category; however, a marked decline took place in portfolio investment. In 1974 direct investment continued at the same level, but disinvestment was recorded in the other two categories and the total outflow fell sharply. The main influence appeared to be the tightening in March 1974 of regulations governing direct and portfolio investment abroad by British residents. In particular, investment in sterling area countries and in EEC nations could no longer be financed from the official exchange market but had to be financed with funds obtained in the investment dollar market or by borrowing abroad.

British direct investment abroad increased rapidly in 1973 to reach a level almost double that of 1971 (see Tables V and VI). Much of this increase was due to a reinvestment of profits abroad, but the outflow of new funds also recorded a large increase because of a number of large acquisitions of foreign companies by U.K. firms. Portfolio investment had reached very high levels in 1972, largely financed by foreign currency borrowing. This was not repeated in 1973. Early in that year British investors began to reduce their holdings of foreign securities, influenced partly by unfavourable investment conditions in U.S. stock markets. This disinvestment continued at a similar rate into 1974.

Foreign investment in the U.K. increased considerably in 1973 (see Table VII). There was a small decline in foreign currency issues by U.K. companies, but foreign purchases of U.K. company securities returned to its 1971 level of about £100 million. This demand was not maintained in 1974.

Table VI. U.K. Direct Investment and Earnings: by Region*
In £000,000

Area	Investment				Earnings			
	1970	1971	1972	1973	1970	1971	1972	1973
North America	185	156	161	...	144	159	214	...
Latin America	13	22	35	...	32	29	44	...
EEC	78	263	222	...	101	104	149	...
Other Western Europe	38	16	56	...	35	33	46	...
Others	2	31	30	...	27	32	37	...
Total nonsterling area	316	488	504	961	341	357	490	763
Total sterling area	230	187	227	384	369	360	425	657
Total	546	675	731	1,345	710	717	915	1,420

*Excluding oil companies.
Source: U.K. Balance of Payments.

Table V. U.K. Investment Abroad
In £000,000

Item	1965	1970	1971	1972	1973	1974*
Direct investment†						
New funds	141	225	346	264	490	...
Reinvested profits	167	321	329	467	855	...
Total	308	546	675	731	1,345	1,400
Portfolio investment‡	−94	112	38	605	−229	−220
Oil and miscellaneous§	154	144	153	72	266	−270
Total	368	802	866	1,408	1,382	910

*Estimate based on first half of year.
†Excluding oil.
‡Net disinvestment in 1965, 1973, and 1974.
§Net disinvestment in 1974.
Sources: U.K. Balance of Payments; Economic Trends.

Table VII. Foreign Investment in the U.K.
In £000,000

Item	1965	1970	1971	1972	1973	1974*
Direct investment†						
New funds	79	175	263	79	260	...
Reinvested profits	118	179	182	284	312	...
Total	197	354	445	363	572	560
Portfolio investment	−26	83	188	155	229	80
Oil and miscellaneous	67	303	392	235	639	870
Total investment	238	740	1,025	753	1,440	1,510
Total earnings	557	889	970	1,176	1,457	1,720

*Estimate based on first half of year.
†Excluding oil.
Sources: U.K. Balance of Payments; Economic Trends.

Table VIII. U.K. Investment Earnings
In £000,000

Item	1965	1970	1971	1972	1973	1974*
Direct investment†						
Repatriated profits	233	389	388	448	565	...
Reinvested profits	167	321	329	467	855	...
Total	400	710	717	915	1,420	1,366
Portfolio investment	158	171	166	162	189	232
Oil and miscellaneous	434	533	612	612	943	1,360
Total	992	1,414	1,495	1,689	2,552	2,958

*First half of year, seasonally adjusted; at annual rate.
†Excluding oil.
Sources: U.K. Balance of Payments; Economic Trends.

There was a very large increase in U.K. investment earnings in 1973, a rise that continued in 1974 (see Table VIII). This reflected increased profits from stock appreciation, higher interest rates, and increased oil revenue. Foreign earnings in the U.K. also increased in 1973 and 1974, but the U.K. surplus on this account widened.

Other Industrial Countries. Statistics of international investment by, and in, other industrial countries in 1972 and 1973 are given in Table IX.

Belgium. The level of Belgian international investment fell slightly in 1973 from the high level of the previous year. Direct investment increased slightly, but there was a lower level of Belgian purchases of foreign bonds and securities. In 1974 there was a sharp decline in both direct and portfolio investment. Foreign direct investment in Belgium increased sharply in 1973; there was much investment by U.S., West German, and Dutch firms in oil refining, textiles, metal manufacturing, and services. Foreign portfolio investment in Belgium in 1973 also rose, and in 1974 there was another rise in foreign direct investment.

France. Whereas 1972 had been a year in which there was a small net inflow of capital into France, in 1973 a modest outflow took place. French investment, both direct and portfolio, increased, but the main feature was a sharp reduction in 1973 in foreign purchases of French securities.

West Germany. There had been a large net inflow of capital into West Germany in 1972, much of this being purchases of West German bonds and securities by foreign investors. Regulations had been introduced in mid-1972 requiring mandatory authorization for the acquisition of West German bonds by foreign investors. These regulations were extended in February 1973 to cover the acquisition of all West German securities by nonresidents. As a result the inflow of funds was sharply reduced though not completely halted. Toward the end of 1973 the strengthening of the dollar further reduced the desire of foreign investors for West German assets. West German residents again reduced their holdings of foreign bonds and securities in 1973 although not to the same extent as in 1972. There were no marked changes in West German direct investment abroad or in foreign direct investment in West Germany, both of which were, as in 1972, about DM. 5

billion. For the year as a whole in 1973 there was a net inflow of capital of DM. 3.3 billion, much below the DM. 15.2 billion inflow of the previous year. In February 1974 some of the restrictions on capital inflows were reduced; mandatory authorization was no longer required for borrowing abroad by residents or for purchases of domestic securities by nonresidents, except for bearer bonds or bonds payable to order.

Italy. The rate of outflow of capital from Italy increased sharply in the first half of 1973, and various measures were adopted to curb the outflow of portfolio investment in view of the adverse effect on the balance of payments. Italian direct investment abroad increased slightly in 1973, although the outflow of funds to North Sea oil prospecting was sharply reduced as this activity was increasingly financed by overseas borrowing. Foreign direct investment in Italy was at the same level as in 1972 and was concentrated in engineering, chemicals, oil, and property development. The inflow of foreign portfolio investment consisted almost exclusively of listed Italian shares and retained its predominantly speculative nature.

Japan. The large increase in Japanese international investment in 1972 continued in 1973, Japan emerging during the year as a major exporter of long-term private capital. In addition to the easing of restrictions in 1969, this sharp increase could be attributed to three factors: the growing domestic labour shortage and rapid rise in wage rates in recent years; the anxiety to secure supplies of industrial raw materials to meet growing domestic demand; and the increasing difficulty in expanding industrial facilities in Japan because of environmental pollution and land shortages. The trend toward increasing the proportion of investment in Western industrialized countries continued in 1973 and 1974.

In 1973, as in the previous year, there was also a marked increase in Japanese purchases of foreign bonds and securities, partly in response to policy measures designed to encourage the outflow of capital to offset the earlier large trade surplus. As a result, the total outflow of capital from Japan exceeded 1 trillion yen in 1973, almost double the outflow of 1972 and approximately five times the rate of 1971.

Foreign investment in Japan had been kept at a minimum up to 1967, when the Japanese government first relaxed its restrictions. The final relaxation in May 1973 permitted 100% foreign ownership. With the removal of regulations came a steady increase in the inflow of foreign capital, with U.S. corporations accounting for 60% of the total. This steady rise was halted temporarily in 1973 due to some selling of assets. Foreign portfolio investment in Japan, which had been at a high level in 1971 and much of 1972, swung sharply into disinvestment in 1973.

The Netherlands. Dutch international investment in 1973 was at a slightly higher rate than in 1972. Direct investment remained the same, but portfolio investment increased by about 15%. Dutch investors increased their purchases of foreign shares and bonds. Foreign direct investment in The Netherlands increased by about 20% in 1973. In 1972 there had been considerable purchasing by foreign investors of Dutch shares, amounting to over 700 billion guilders. This, however, changed in 1973 to net selling of Dutch shares, mostly by British and U.S. investors. Restrictions had been introduced in September 1971 on foreign purchases of quoted guilder bonds from residents. This had the desired effect of reducing the capital inflow; purchases fell to a modest level in 1972, and

Table IX. Other OECD Countries' International Investment 1972–73

In billions of national currency unit

| Country | 1972 | | | 1973 | | |
	Direct	Portfolio	Total	Direct	Portfolio	Total
Belgium						
Outflow	7.6	37.1	44.7	8.0	33.0	41.0
Inflow	16.6	8.0	24.6	27.0	9.0	36.0
Net	−9.0	29.1	20.1	−19.0	24.0	5.0
France						
Outflow	...	...	7.6	...	...	...
Inflow	...	...	8.1	...	...	...
Net	...	...	−0.5	...	...	1.4
West Germany						
Outflow	5.0	−4.0	1.0	4.6	−0.4	4.2
Inflow	5.5	10.7	16.2	5.0	2.5	7.5
Net	−0.5	−14.7	−15.2	−0.4	−2.9	−3.3
Italy						
Outflow	125.0	411.0	536.0	149.0	418.0	567.0
Inflow	364.0	30.0	394.0	366.0	−225.0	141.0
Net	−239.0	381.0	142.0	−217.0	643.0	426.0
Japan						
Outflow	221.0	364.0	585.0	552.0	518.0	1,070.0
Inflow	52.0	181.0	233.0	−12.0	−229.0	−241.0
Net	169.0	183.0	352.0	564.0	747.0	1,311.0
The Netherlands						
Outflow	2.1	2.2	4.3	2.1	2.5	4.6
Inflow	1.9	0.9	2.8	2.3	−0.2	2.1
Net	0.2	1.3	1.5	−0.2	2.7	2.5

Sources: Annual Reports of International Monetary Fund, Bank for International Settlements, and national banks.

became net sales in 1973. These regulations were revoked in February 1974. (A. G. ARMSTRONG)

See also Development, Economic and Social; Exchange and Payments, International; Trade, International. [536.B]

Iran

A constitutional monarchy of western Asia, Iran is bounded by the U.S.S.R., Afghanistan, Pakistan, Iraq, and Turkey and the Caspian Sea, the Arabian Sea, and the Persian Gulf. Area: 636,000 sq.mi. (1,648,000 sq.km.). Pop. (1974 est.): 32,794,000. Cap. and largest city: Teheran (pop., 1972 est., 3,858,000). Language: Farsi Persian. Religion (1966): Muslim 96%; Christian, Jewish, and Zoroastrian minorities. Shah-in-shah, Mohammad Reza Pahlavi Aryamehr; prime minister in 1974, Emir Abbas Hoveida.

The general rise in the world price of crude oil greatly strengthened the financial resources of Iran during 1974. The Iranian government did not approve of the use of oil supplies as a political weapon against the policies of Western countries on the Palestine question; government policy was to strike advantageous bargains with its Western customers in order to promote Iran's own economic development. Thus, during the early months of 1974 bargains were struck with France (a $3 billion framework agreement made during the shah's visit to Paris in June), Great Britain, and West Germany (where Iran also bought a 25% stake in the Krupp steel-making subsidiary) for numerous economic projects—nuclear power stations, petrochemical plants, additional oil refineries, natural gas utilization, and other enterprises—as well as for increased imports of the commodities that Iran needed, such as synthetic rubber, man-made fibres, newsprint, and special steels. In the case of Britain, additional supplies of 5 million tons of crude oil at the price of $7 a barrel obtained for Iran various imports likely to amount to £110 million during 1974 and early 1975, while arrangements were also made to increase Iran's sterling holdings in London. In June Iran agreed to loans to Egypt totaling $1 billion and in July offered Britain a credit of $1.2 billion. Apart from special arrangements to assist Turkey and Pakistan (Iran's partners in the Regional Cooperation for Development, or RCD), commercial agreements were concluded with India and Bangladesh.

Iran's financial strength, with an expected balance of payments surplus of $10 billion at the end of the fiscal year in March 1975, enabled the New Iran Party under Prime Minister Hoveida to progress with its program of economic development and social reform. Plans for rural reconstruction through cooperatives went ahead and the network of good roads was extended. Work continued on the international highway linking Turkey, Iran, and Pakistan, which would not only promote the further growth of through traffic but would facilitate the expansion of the tourist industry in all three countries. Iran was now the wealthiest of the RCD partners and was imparting fresh impetus to existing arrangements for cooperation in the fields of commerce, industry, technology, and finance. Iran's increasing revenues and accelerated rate of economic growth called for improved administrative machinery, and in April 1974 there was a major reorganization

IRAN
Education. (1971–72) Primary, pupils 2,788,000, teachers (1970–71) 91,606; secondary, pupils 1,134,-000, teachers (1970–71) 28,244; vocational (1970–71), pupils 30,579, teachers 2,181; teacher training (1970–71), students 13,288, teachers 461; higher (including 8 universities), students 84,000, teaching staff 2,900.
Finance. Monetary unit: rial, with (Sept. 16, 1974) an official rate of 68.17 rials to U.S. $1 (free rate of 155 rials = £1 sterling). Gold, SDRs, and foreign exchange, central bank: (June 1974) U.S. $5,381,000,-000; (June 1973) U.S. $1,140,000,000. Budget (1971–72 actual): revenue 256.5 billion rials; expenditure 302.8 billion rials. Gross domestic product: (1972–73) 1,287,800,000,000 rials; (1971–72) 1,062,300,000,000 rials. Money supply: (April 1974) 244,950,000,000 rials; (April 1973) 230,290,000,000 rials. Cost of living (1970 = 100): (June 1974) 141; (June 1973) 120.
Foreign Trade. (1973) Imports 238 billion rials; exports 480,220,000,000 rials. Import sources: West Germany 19%; Japan 14%; U.S. 14%; U.K. 10%; U.S.S.R. 5%; France 5%. Export destinations: Japan 32%; West Germany 11%; U.K. 10%; Italy 8%; The Netherlands 7%; U.S. 6%; France 5%. Main export crude oil 91%.
Transport and Communications. Roads (1972) 43,442 km. Motor vehicles in use (1972): passenger 354,800; commercial (including buses) 101,300. Railways (1972): 4,560 km.; traffic 1,955,000,000 passenger-km., freight 3,693,000,000 net ton-km. Air traffic (1972): 859 million passenger-km.; freight 12.5 million net ton-km. Shipping (1973): merchant vessels 100 gross tons and over 93; gross tonnage 192,386. Telephones (Jan. 1973) 447,000. Radio receivers (Dec. 1972) 7 million. Television receivers (Dec. 1972) 1 million.
Agriculture. Production (in 000; metric tons; 1973; 1972 in parentheses): wheat c. 4,775 (4,500); barley c. 1,200 (1,009); rice 1,500 (1,200); sugar, raw value c. 643 (c. 657); onions c. 260 (258); tomatoes c. 143 (c. 140); dates (1972) c. 300, (1971) c. 280; grapes (1972) c. 650, (1971) 648; raisins c. 60 (c. 60); sunflower seed c. 43 (c. 43); tea c. 22 (22); tobacco c. 24 (24); cotton, lint c. 201 (c. 207). Livestock (in 000; Oct. 1972): cattle c. 5,640; sheep c. 37,000; goats (1971) c. 14,700; horses c. 380; asses c. 2,020; chickens c. 31,500.
Industry. Production (in 000; metric tons; 1973): crude oil 269,296; petroleum products (1972) c. 25,-250; natural gas (cu.m.) 19,707,000; cement (1972) 3,600; coal (1972–73) 1,000; lead concentrates (metal content; 1972–73) 33; chrome ore (oxide content; 1972–73) 86; electricity (excluding most industrial production; kw-hr.) 8,719,000.

of Hoveida's Cabinet. The ministries of finance and of the economy were combined, and separate portfolios were created for industry and mines, commerce, and oil affairs.

In the international field Iran's armed forces, equipped with sophisticated weaponry purchased from Western countries, now enabled it both to protect its own interests and to exercise a powerful stabilizing influence throughout western Asia. Opposition at home, some of it externally inspired, was less formidable than before; nevertheless, in January, 12 persons were brought to trial on charges of terrorist activities, including plotting to assassinate the shah and kidnap the empress; 7 were executed and others received terms of imprisonment. Iran did not take sides in the Arab-Israeli dispute, and in Cyprus it gave guarded support to the Turkish government. Its only serious conflict of interest was with Iraq, not only in the Persian Gulf area but also on the frontier between the two countries, where some serious clashes took place during 1974 until a cease-fire was signed in May. Iran's friendship with the United Arab Emirates and its support for the sultan of Oman against rebel forces supported by Yemen (Aden) continued.

Resentment against Iraq continued because of the Iraqi government's support of Soviet-Afghan schemes to encourage secessionist elements in the Pakistani

In 1974 the Iraqi economy, after 15 years of relative stagnation, showed signs of rapid expansion as a result of a massive increase in oil revenues. At the same time, the country's stability was severely threatened by renewed fighting with Kurdish nationalists, which endangered the principal northern oil fields.

At the end of the eighth Regional Congress of the Baath Party held in Baghdad in January, President Hassan al-Bakr was reelected secretary-general of the party, and the country's strong man, Saddam Takriti, was named deputy secretary-general. The Baathist regime broadened its base by appointing three members of the Iraqi Communist Party Central Committee to the National and Progressive National Front. The Kurdish Democratic Party (KDP), led by Mullah Mustafa al-Barzani (*see* BIOGRAPHY), refused to join the front and rejected as inadequate and insincere the terms of the new Kurdish autonomy law announced on March 11, in accordance with the 15-point Iraq-Kurdish cease-fire agreement of 1970. The chief point of dispute was whether Kirkuk and the surrounding oil-producing areas should be part of the region of Kurdish autonomy. The five Kurdish members of the government resigned and were replaced by anti-Barzanist Kurds. The government allowed 15 days grace for the KDP to change its mind, and when the KDP still rejected the terms the government unilaterally decreed the autonomy law and offered a 30-day amnesty, later extended, to all Kurdish officials who had joined the Barzanists. Fierce fighting broke out in which the Kurdish Pesh Merga forces, estimated

The shah and shabanou of Iran (centre) at a dinner given them by French Pres. Valéry Giscard d'Estaing (right) and Mme Giscard d'Estaing (left) at Versailles Palace.

provinces of North-West Frontier and Baluchistan. The movements for the creation of an independent Pakhtunistan and a "Greater Baluchistan" were opposed by Iran not only because they would weaken its ally Pakistan but because there was a considerable Baluchi population within Iran's own borders. Moreover, the establishment of a land corridor between Afghanistan and the Arabian Sea, composed of states that would be too weak to stand alone, held the risk of bringing Soviet influence uncomfortably close to the Persian Gulf, which the shah had described as "Iran's jugular vein." (L. F. RUSHBROOK WILLIAMS)

See also Afghanistan.
[978.C.1]

Iraq

A republic of southwestern Asia, Iraq is bounded by Turkey, Iran, Kuwait, Saudi Arabia, Jordan, Syria, and the Persian Gulf. Area: 168,928 sq.mi. (437,522 sq.km.). Pop. (1974 est.): 10,413,000, including Arabs, Kurds, Turks, Assyrians, Iranians, and others. Cap. and largest city: Baghdad (pop., 1970 est., 2,183,-760). Language: Arabic. Religion: mainly Muslim, some Christian. President in 1974, Gen. Ahmad Hassan al-Bakr.

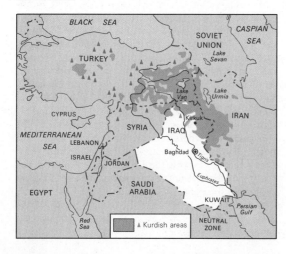

Kurdish areas

IRAQ
Education. (1973–74) Primary, pupils 1,908,839, teachers 58,445; secondary, pupils 388,624, teachers 14,519; vocational, students 16,010, teachers 1,255; teacher training (1971–72), students 7,405, teachers 120; higher (including 6 universities; 1971–72), students 49,123, teaching staff 12,108.

Finance. Monetary unit: Iraqi dinar, with (Sept. 16, 1974) an official rate of 0.296 dinar to U.S. $1 (free rate of 0.682 dinar to £1 sterling). Gold, SDRs, and foreign exchange, central bank: (June 1974) U.S. $2,845,300,000; (June 1973) U.S. $1,199,200,000. Budget (1972–73 est.): revenue 391,510,000 dinars; expenditure 352,170,000 dinars (excluding development expenditure of 130.5 million dinars). Gross national product: (1971) 1,268,700,000 dinars; (1970) 1,108,-000,000 dinars. Money supply: (April 1974) 351.8 million dinars; (April 1973) 274.3 million dinars. Cost of living (Baghdad; 1970 = 100): (June 1974) 121; (June 1973) 110.

Foreign Trade. (1973) Imports 270.3 million dinars; exports 689.6 million dinars. Import sources (1972): U.K. 10%; U.S.S.R. 7%; Czechoslovakia 7%; France 6%; Italy 5%; West Germany 5%. Export destinations (1972): France *c.* 20%; Italy *c.* 18%; Brazil *c.* 7%; Greece *c.* 5%; U.K. *c.* 5%. Main export crude oil 95%.

Transport and Communications. Roads (1973) 10,824 km. Motor vehicles in use (1973): passenger 77,317; commercial 34,336. Railways: (1972) 2,203 km.; traffic (1972–73) 538 million passenger-km., freight 1,465,000,000 net ton-km. Air traffic (1973): 268 million passenger-km.; freight 2.7 million net ton-km. Shipping (1973): merchant vessels 100 gross tons and over 46; gross tonnage 228,274. Telephones (Jan. 1973) 121,000. Radio receivers (Dec. 1971) 1,072,000. Television receivers (Dec. 1972) 520,000.

Agriculture. Production (in 000; metric tons; 1973; 1972 in parentheses): wheat 957 (2,625); barley *c.* 400 (980); rice *c.* 240 (268); tomatoes *c.* 300 (368); onions *c.* 85 (78); dates *c.* 300 (*c.* 300); lemons (1972) *c.* 24, (1971) *c.* 23; sesame *c.* 13 (12); linseed *c.* 6 (4); tobacco *c.* 15 (*c.* 10); cotton, lint (1972) 16, (1971) 14. Livestock (in 000; 1972–73): sheep *c.* 16,218; goats *c.* 2,600; cattle *c.* 2,030; buffaloes *c.* 290; camels *c.* 300; horses *c.* 130; asses *c.* 600.

Industry. Production (in 000; metric tons; 1971): cement 1,856; crude oil (1972) 71,125; petroleum products (1970) 3,496; electricity (excluding most industrial production; kw-hr.) 2,261,000.

at 45,000 regulars with some 50,000 militia, gained control of much of the Kurdish mountain area including the 450-mi. border with Turkey. Hundreds of Kurds, including many professional men, went from the south to join the rebels. The Iraqi Air Force bombed Kurdish villages, and most of the 100,000-strong Iraqi Army was thrown into the battle. In July and August the Iraqi forces were reported to have recaptured some strategic roads and towns, but the Kurds claimed to have inflicted at least 4,000 casualties and shot down 44 Iraqi Air Force planes. Kurdish forces blew up oil pipelines and during the summer were reported within shelling distance of the Kirkuk oil fields.

The Iraqi belief that the Kurds were receiving arms and support from Iran did not help to improve the already sensitive relations between Iraq and Iran. After severe border clashes in February and March about 100 mi. E of Baghdad, the two sides agreed on a cease-fire and the reference of the dispute to a UN investigator. A decision to hold direct negotiations was formally welcomed by the UN on May 28, although Iran was reportedly unhappy because Iraq had not been named as the aggressor. The talks, held August 12–30, reportedly ended with "mutual understanding," but small-scale clashes still continued and in September Iraq claimed that Iran was massing troops on the border.

Despite continued Iraqi criticisms of both Egypt and Syria for their conduct of the October 1973 war against Israel and their willingness to reach disengagement agreements with Israel through U.S. mediation, relations with both countries improved during 1974. In August Iraq and Egypt agreed on a variety of joint economic ventures worth $1 billion. Iraq also offered 50 million dinars (about $170 million) in aid to Syria. In August Iraq reached joint agreements with both Syria and Turkey on sharing the waters of the Euphrates River. The 1974 river flow was exceptionally low and caused severe shortages of drinking water.

During 1974 Iraqi oil production was more than 2 million bbl. a day, an increase of 43% over 1972, and it was planned to increase this to 3.5 million bbl. per day by 1975. The main focus of oil development was being moved from the north to the Basra region in the south. It was reported during the year that 38 foreign oil companies had made 20 bids for oil exploration concessions but that all had been turned down. Total oil revenues for 1974 were estimated at more than $5 billion. The budget for 1974 was 2,933,000,000 dinars, a 50% increase over 1973.

On April 10 Iraq and the U.K. restored diplomatic relations. They had been broken off by Iraq at the end of November 1971 when Iraq blamed Britain for Iran's takeover of three small islands in the Persian Gulf.　　　　　　　　　　　　(PETER MANSFIELD)

[978.B.3.c]

Ireland

Separated from Great Britain by the North Channel, the Irish Sea, and St. George's Channel, the Republic of Ireland shares its island with Northern Ireland to the northeast. Area: 27,136 sq.mi. (70,283 sq.km.), or 83% of the island. Pop. (1973 est.): 3,029,000. Cap. and largest city: Dublin (pop., 1971, 567,866). Language

(1971): non-Irish, mostly English (72%), and Irish (28%). Religion: predominantly Roman Catholic (95%). Presidents in 1974, Erskine Childers until November 17 and, from December 19, Carroll O'Daly; prime minister, Liam Cosgrave.

Though beset by many economic problems during its second year in office, the republic's coalition government was mainly concerned in 1974 with the Northern Ireland situation and the collapse of power-sharing there. After having contributed substantially to the working out of the Sunningdale agreement at the end of 1973, and having given its wholehearted support to the Executive coalition led by former prime minister Brian Faulkner, the republic's government was faced in January 1974 with a High Court action brought by a former Fianna Fail Cabinet minister, Kevin Boland, challenging the constitutionality of the signing of the agreement. This put an immediate strain on relations between Faulkner and Cosgrave and led to a "summit" between them on January 16, aimed at clarifying differences of interpretation. An enlarged meeting between the two leaders, each accompanied by seven ministers, took place near Belfast on February 1. Through March, April, and May, Cosgrave attempted to assure Northern opinion that the Council of Ireland, which formed part of the Sunningdale agreement, was not an "attempt by stealth" to unite Ireland. This view was reinforced by British Prime Minister Harold Wilson's statement

Pesh Merga rebel soldiers train to fight a guerrilla war for Kurdish independence from Iraq.

IRELAND
Education. (1972–73) Primary, pupils 538,318, teachers 16,844; secondary, pupils 226,821, teachers 8,882; vocational, pupils 4,025, teachers 224; higher, students 28,614, teaching staff 1,404.

Finance. Monetary unit: Irish pound, at par with the pound sterling, with a free rate (Sept. 16, 1974) of U.S. $2.31 = £1. Gold, SDRs, and foreign exchange, official: (June 1974) U.S. $916 million; (June 1973) U.S. $988 million. Budget (1973–74 est.): revenue £755.4 million; expenditure £794.7 million. Gross national product: (1972) £2,232 million; (1971) £1,899 million. Money supply: (April 1974) £559.6 million; (April 1973) £470.4 million. Cost of living (1970 = 100): (May 1974) 151; (May 1973) 130.

Foreign Trade. (1973) Imports £1,115 million; exports £870,509,000. Import sources: U.K. 51%; West Germany 8%; U.S. 7%; France 5%. Export destinations: U.K. 55%; U.S. 10%; West Germany 6%; France 5%. Main exports: meat 15%; livestock 10% (cattle 7%); textiles and clothing 11%; dairy products 9%; machinery 7%; chemicals 7%. Tourism (1971): visitors 1,692,000; gross receipts U.S. $185 million.

Transport and Communications. Roads (1971) 87,762 km. Motor vehicles in use (1973): passenger 476,721; commercial 49,040. Railways (1972): 2,189 km.; traffic 844 million passenger-km., freight (1973) 517.2 million net ton-km. Air traffic (1973): 1,757,-000,000 passenger-km.; freight 88.5 million net ton-km. Shipping (1973): merchant vessels 100 gross tons and over 97; gross tonnage 229,349. Telephones (Dec. 1972) 341,000. Radio licenses (Dec. 1971) 615,000. Television licenses (Dec. 1972) 520,000.

Agriculture. Production (in 000; metric tons; 1973; 1972 in parentheses): potatoes c. 1,320 (c. 1,230); wheat 215 (260); oats 155 (180); barley 900 (935); sugar, raw value c. 190 (c. 171); milk (1972) c. 3,750, (1971) 3,633; butter (1972) c. 76, (1971) c. 75; cheese (1972) c. 31, (1971) c. 30; beef and veal (1972) c. 325, (1971) c. 338; pork (1972) c. 165, (1971) 154; fish catch (1972) 92, (1971) 74. Livestock (in 000; June 1973): cattle 6,545; sheep c. 4,277; pigs c. 1,198; horses (1972) c. 115; chickens (1972) c. 11,000.

Industry. Index of production (1970 = 100): (1973) 119; (1972) 108. Production (in 000; metric tons; 1973): coal 62; cement 1,680; petroleum products (1972) 2,618; electricity (excluding most industrial production; kw-hr.) 7,236,000; manufactured gas (cu.m.) 270,000; beer (hl.; 1969–70) 3,751; wool fabrics (sq.m.) 6,200; rayon, etc., fabrics (sq.m.) 7,700.

on April 18 that there was no alternative to Sunningdale and power-sharing in Northern Ireland.

On May 14, however, the Ulster Workers' Council challenged the Executive coalition by calling a general strike, and on May 28 Faulkner resigned and the executive collapsed. The result of this was severe disappointment in the republic, followed by a cool reaction toward North-South cooperation from Cosgrave who, on June 13, in a speech in Dublin, talked of violence in the North "killing the desire for unity in the republic." This was followed by assertions that relations between the government in the South and the politicians representing the minority in the North (members of the Social Democratic and Labour Party) were worsening. At their meeting on August 12, Cosgrave told Wilson that the republic still believed the only solution was through power-sharing. But public statements by government ministers during the summer were low-key and underlined the disappointment felt at the failure of Sunningdale.

The continued successes of the extremists added to this disappointment. On August 18, 19 members of the Provisional wing of the Irish Republican Army (IRA) broke out of the top-security prison at Portlaoise and, despite extensive police searches throughout the country, only one was recaptured. On September 28 a plane was hijacked at Dundalk and used in a bombing raid across the border, though the bomb dropped did not explode. Earlier in the year a helicopter was taken in County Donegal and used in a bombing raid on Strabane. Milk churns packed with explosives were dropped on the Royal Ulster Constabulary barracks in the town, but they landed in a nearby field and no one was injured.

Bank robbers Keith and Kenneth Littlejohn, who claimed to have worked for British intelligence, escaped from Dublin's Mountjoy Prison on March 11; Keith was immediately recaptured. On April 26, pictures valued at £8 million were stolen from the home of Sir Alfred Beit outside Dublin, and a ransom note demanded the movement of four imprisoned IRA guerrillas, including the sisters Marian and Dolours Price, from prison in Britain to Northern Ireland. On May 4 the paintings were recovered, and in June Bridget Rose Dugdale (*see* BIOGRAPHY) was convicted of receiving them and sentenced to nine years' imprisonment. Miss Dugdale was subsequently

convicted of implication in the Strabane aerial bombing. On June 4 the earl and countess of Donoughmore were kidnapped by IRA extremists, but they were released five days later as a result of widespread public indignation.

On June 26, as a result of the continuing activities of extremist groups in the country, Cosgrave announced the formation of a special civilian security force to patrol towns and villages, but he took no further action on the proposal. The worst single act of violence ever known in the republic, and the worst in the whole of Ireland since the troubles began in 1969, occurred in Dublin on Friday, May 17, when three massive bombs exploded at the height of the rush hour in centre city streets. Twenty-three people were killed and 137 injured. The next day the recall of Ireland's contingent of soldiers serving with the UN in Sinai and Cyprus was announced.

The economy suffered from continuing inflation; in the third quarter the consumer price index was 17.9% above the same period in 1973, and unemployment rose steeply. Though exports continued to expand, imports outstripped them by a substantial amount. The tourist season was poor, due in part to the political situation in the North, and the country was expected to have a balance of payments deficit in the neighbourhood of £300 million. Economic uncertainty was aggravated by a taxation White Paper, issued by the government at the beginning of the year, which proposed the introduction of a capital gains tax and wealth tax. In his April budget, the minister for finance, Richie Ryan, introduced a form of income tax for farmers—who had not been subject to it since 1969—and this, coupled with the poor return to small farmers in Ireland from the EEC common agricultural policy, caused considerable controversy. There were further difficulties for farmers in October and November, when British farmers prevented the importation of Irish cattle by force and disrupted the container traffic through Britain to Europe.

An attempt was made by the government to secure passage of legislation legalizing the use of contraceptives. This was made necessary by a Supreme Court decision that made it unconstitutional to deprive a married woman of the means for contraception. Cosgrave decided on a free, conscience vote and then, with another minister and five backbenchers, voted against his own government's bill. The legislation was defeated by 75 votes to 61.

On November 17, President Childers (*see* OBITUARIES) died following a heart attack he suffered while making a speech. By agreement of the three major parties, he was succeeded by Carroll O'Daly (Cearbhall O'Dalaigh), former chief justice and attorney general, who was sworn in as the fifth president of the Irish republic on December 19.

On May 14 President Childers had made a state visit to Belgium, the first to a European country by an Irish chief of state. Earlier in the year Ireland sent its first ambassador to Moscow, Edward Brennan, and Anatoli Stepanovich Kaplin arrived as Soviet ambassador to Dublin. Diplomatic relations were also established for the first time with an Arab state, Libya, and with Japan. The Irish poet Austin Clarke (*see* OBITUARIES) died in March at the age of 77. In October, Sean MacBride became the first Irishman to win the Nobel Peace Prize. (*See* NOBEL PRIZES.)

(BRUCE ARNOLD)

See also United Kingdom.
[972.A.1.b.i]

Bomb wreckage on Talbot Street in Dublin after a terrorist attack on May 17. Three bombs exploded almost simultaneously in various parts of the Irish capital, leaving more than 20 dead and scores injured.

Israel

A republic of the Middle East, Israel is bounded by Lebanon, Syria, Jordan, Egypt, and the Mediterranean Sea. Area (not including territory occupied in the June 1967 war): 7,992 sq.mi. (20,700 sq.km.). Pop. (1974 est.): 3,356,500. Cap.: Jerusalem (pop., 1973 est., 326,400). Largest city: Tel Aviv-Yafo (pop., 1973 est., 367,600). Language: Hebrew and Arabic. Religion: predominantly Jewish. President in 1974, Ephraim Katzir; prime ministers, Mrs. Golda Meir and, from June 3, Yitzhak Rabin.

The last weeks of 1973 and the first six months of 1974 were dominated by the course and the cost of the October 1973 war; the second half of 1974 was shaped largely by the consequences—political, economic, and psychological—of that war. As a result, it was a year during which Israel and Israelis sought to restore the equilibrium that the war's impact, rather than the war itself, had upset. From the cease-fire of Oct. 25, 1973, and the preliminary disengagement negotiations, succeeded by the abortive opening of a Geneva peace conference on December 21 (adjourned December 22), Israel's public opinion and the political world, including a large segment of the armed forces, suffered a largely self-induced psychological shock. The military cost and consequences of the war were exaggerated out of all proportion. A kind of witchhunt was unloosened in the press, among the public, and to a degree even in the government against those who were said to be responsible for the "blunder" of unpreparedness in face of the Arab surprise attack on the Day of Atonement.

The principal target of these attacks was the minister of defense, Moshe Dayan, and, to a lesser degree, the prime minister, Golda Meir. The attack was accompanied by an emotional campaign to win the release of Israeli prisoners of war in Egyptian and Syrian hands, which forced the government to trade over 8,000 Egyptian prisoners for 241 Israelis and make large concessions to Syria in return for fewer than 100 Israelis. Public opinion was similarly emotionally distorted on the question of casualties. At the final official count on June 5, 1974, the number of Israelis killed in the October war was 2,521; there were 7,056 wounded, of whom some 3,500 were considered to be permanently maimed. In order to assuage the public mood and the political discontent, the government appointed a committee of inquiry under Chief Justice Shimon Agranat to consider the causes that led to the initial setbacks for the Israeli forces on Oct. 6, 1973.

The postponed general election was held on December 31, and served only to add to the political disorientation, which appeared to be getting worse rather than better. The Labour Party alignment list remained the largest single party but won no outright majority. On the contrary, it lost a number of seats to the combined right-wing opposition, the Likud, which had been formed by the Herut, Liberal, and Free Centre parties. Mrs. Meir's Labour alignment won 39.9% of the votes and 51 of the 120 seats in the Knesset. Likud won 27.4% of the votes and 39 seats. The National Religious Party lost two seats, thus having only ten in the new Knesset; the Torah Religious Front lost one and

had five members; the New Communists had four, and various left-wing and civil-rights groupings gained a total of four seats. Uri Avneri's much publicized Haolam Hazeh group lost both its seats.

After much political bargaining, Mrs. Meir was unsuccessful in organizing a workable coalition government. On March 10, 1974, largely under pressure of great tension on the Syrian border, she formed a minority government and persuaded Dayan to rejoin it as defense minister, although he had previously refused to do so. The border crisis and the new government were short-lived. The attacks on Dayan increased rather than lessened, and not even the publication on April 2 of a preliminary report by the Agranat committee, which seemed to clear him of direct responsibility, dampened the political attacks on Mrs. Meir's minority administration. On April 10 she announced her resignation.

Meanwhile, Mrs. Meir had had talks in Washington with U.S. Pres. Richard Nixon; U.S. Secretary of State Henry Kissinger came and went; and the talks with the Egyptians continued. On January 18, Gen. David Elazar for Israel and Gen. Muhammad Ghamasy for Egypt signed the disengagement agreement and the accord on "the United States proposal" on the limited deployment of Egyptian and Israeli forces in the forward zone. After a bitter debate, the Knesset approved of the agreement on January 22 by 76 votes to 35, and on February 21 the withdrawal of all Israeli troops from "Africa," the bridgehead on the western bank of the Suez Canal, was completed. The preliminary report of the Agranat committee blamed the chief of staff, General Elazar, for some of the military shortcomings in the October war and recommended that he be replaced. It also criticized the chief of Israel's military intelligence, Eliahu Zeira, and three of his principal assistants for a mistaken doctrine that led them to misread the warnings of the Israeli secret services about Arab preparations for war. Zeira and his assistants were also to be replaced. The committee made a number of important recommendations with regard to the reorganization of the intelligence services. Mrs. Meir accepted the recommendations, and the chief of staff was replaced on April 14 by Maj. Gen. Mordechai Gur, a former paratroop commander. On April 22 the Central Committee of the Labour Party voted on the succession to Mrs. Meir. The 52-year-old former chief of staff and ambassador to the U.S., Yitzhak Rabin (see BIOGRAPHY), won 298 votes against 254 for the runner-up, Shimon Peres, for many years David Ben-Gurion's confidant.

But forming a new government coalition proved to be more difficult than had been expected, and it seemed for a time as if Rabin would have to exchange one set

Antigovernment demonstrators outside the Knesset in Jerusalem stage a mock Purim holiday play; masked players impersonate Israeli Defense Minister Moshe Dayan (second from left) and Prime Minister Golda Meir.

The view
from the shattered
apartment building
in which three Palestinian
terrorists died
after killing 18 persons
and wounding 16 others
in April
in the northern Israeli
town of Kiryat Shmone,
near the Lebanese border.

pound from I£4.20 to U.S. $1 to I£6. This was accompanied by drastic austerity measures, sharp increases in food and fuel prices, and a six months' ban on imports of a range of nonessential consumer goods.

A number of murderous raids by Palestinian groups inflicted grievous casualties on civilians in border towns inhabited largely by immigrants from Arab countries. Mainly women and children were killed in attacks, on Kiryat Shmone (Qiryat Shemona; April 11), Maalot (May 15), Shamir (June 13), Nahariya (June 24), and Beth Shean (Beisan; November 19). In their way, they were a prelude to the appearance in November of Yasir Arafat (*see* BIOGRAPHY), leader of the Palestine Liberation Organization (PLO), at the UN General Assembly. Israel considered Arafat's presence at the UN an affront. The problem became more acute after the General Assembly voted on November 22, without clarifying Israel's position, that the Palestinians should be entitled to return to their land and property. Rabin, with massive national support, reaffirmed that Israel would never negotiate with the PLO, while the PLO proclaimed its continuing war of terror. Israel's growing isolation was further emphasized in November, when the UNESCO General Conference refused to admit Israel

of recriminations for another. This arose from his desire to reshape the face of the government and from the determination of some former members not to serve under him. Dayan would serve only in a Cabinet of national unity. Pinhas Sapir, king maker of Labour-controlled Cabinets since the resignation of Ben-Gurion, moved over to become chairman of the Jewish Agency rather than serve under Rabin. Abba Eban would serve only as foreign minister, a position pre-empted by Rabin's erstwhile commander and colleague, Yigal Allon.

The last act of Mrs. Meir's administration was to request the Knesset on May 30 to ratify the Golan Heights disengagement agreement with Syria. The Knesset approved with a 76 to 36 vote, and then Mrs. Meir's "October government" stepped down. Rabin presented his new government to the Knesset on June 3 and received a vote of confidence of 61–51 with 5 abstentions. The religious parties had refused to join Rabin's government, but the three members of the Civil Rights Movement supported him, and Mrs. Shulamit Aloni, its best-known member, joined the Cabinet. Peres became minister of defense, and Yigal Allon foreign minister.

Immediately important was the need to provide the country with a sense of direction. Rabin and Peres set about restoring the priorities. The defense forces were overhauled and reequipped with the aid of massive financial support and supplies of new equipment from the U.S.; Congress had voted $2.2 billion in emergency aid in December 1973 and President Nixon ordered new weapons to be taken from stocks in the U.S. in order to reequip Israel. By the end of November 1974 Israel's forces were proportionately larger than in October 1973, and qualitatively they were greatly improved in equipment, preparedness, and training. Defense was given priority over all else, and it was reflected in the partial mobilization ordered by the government on November 14 when Israel feared a possible Syrian coup in the Kuneitra (Arabic, Qunaytirah) area.

But as 1974 drew to a close, the economic problems had so outgrown expectation, with a record $3.5 billion balance of payments deficit and inflation running at 40%, that the Cabinet on November 9 ordered a drastic devaluation, reducing the value of the Israel

ISRAEL

Education. (1973–74) Primary, pupils 537,516, teachers 27,035; secondary, pupils 74,833, teachers 5,133; vocational, pupils 72,591, teachers 5,229; higher (including 4 universities), students 81,243, teaching staff (1969–70; universities only) *c.* 4,650.

Finance. Monetary unit: Israeli pound, with (following the devaluation of Nov. 9, 1974) a par value of I£6 to U.S. $1 (free rate of I£14 = £1 sterling). Gold, SDRs, and foreign exchange, central bank: (June 1974) U.S. $1,392,000,000; (June 1973) U.S. $1,387,-400,000. Budget (1973–74 est.): revenue I£13,752 million; expenditure I£15,130 million. Gross national product: (1972) I£28,958 million; (1971) I£23,357 million. Money supply: (June 1973) I£6,196 million; (June 1972) I£5,075 million. Cost of living (1970 = 100): (June 1974) 207; (June 1973) 150.

Foreign Trade. (1973) Imports I£17,809 million (including I£5,481 million military goods); exports I£6,067 million. Import sources: U.S. 19%; West Germany 17%; U.K. 16%; The Netherlands 5%; Italy 5%; Belgium-Luxembourg 5%; France 5%. Export destinations: U.S. 18%; U.K. 10%; West Germany 9%; The Netherlands 7%; Hong Kong 7%; Japan 6%; Switzerland 6%; Belgium-Luxembourg 5%; France 5%. Main exports: diamonds 43%; citrus fruit 11%; chemicals 8%; machinery and transport equipment 7%; clothing 6%; preserved fruit 5%. Tourism (1972): visitors 679,800; gross receipts U.S. $215 million.

Transport and Communications. Roads (1972) *c.* 9,300 km. (including 3,336 main roads). Motor vehicles in use (1972): passenger 201,130; commercial 82,500. Railways: (1972) 789 km.; traffic (1973) 355 million passenger-km., freight 445 million net ton-km. Air traffic (1973): 3,354,000,000 passenger-km.; freight 127.1 million net ton-km. Shipping (1973): merchant vessels 100 gross tons and over 90; gross tonnage 645,391. Telephones (Dec. 1972) 620,000. Radio receivers (Dec. 1972) 680,000. Television licenses (Dec. 1972) 370,000.

Agriculture. Production (in 000; metric tons; 1973; 1972 in parentheses): wheat *c.* 190 (301); barley (1972) 30, (1971) 18; sorghum *c.* 37 (40); potatoes *c.* 145 (143); onions *c.* 51 (50); oranges (1972) 1,179, (1971) 1,106; grapefruit (1972) 334, (1971) 361; lemons (1972) 40, (1971) 46; grapes (1972) *c.* 70, (1971) 67; sugar (1972) 28, (1971) 32; tomatoes *c.* 175 (185); olives *c.* 18 (*c.* 25); bananas (1972) *c.* 60, (1971) 56; cotton, lint *c.* 37 (40); fish catch (1972) 29, (1971) 28. Livestock (in 000; Dec. 1972): cattle 274; sheep 188; goats (1971) 134; chickens (1971) 11,349.

Industry. Index of production (1970 = 100): (1972) 123; (1971) 110. Production (in 000; metric tons; 1973): cement 1,216; petroleum products (1972) 5,770; sulfuric acid 193; electricity (kw-hr.) 8,719,-000; salt (1971) 79; potash (oxide content; 1972–73) 622. New dwelling units completed (1973) 51,000.

to any of its regional groupings and condemned it for allegedly altering and possibly damaging historical features of Jerusalem. Nor were Rabin's difficulties lessened when he finally brought the National Religious Party into the government at the end of October at the cost of losing the support of Mrs. Aloni and the Civil Rights Movement.   (JON KIMCHE)

See also **Middle Eastern Affairs.**
[978.B.3.d.i]
ENCYCLOPÆDIA BRITANNICA FILMS. *Israeli Boy: Life on a Kibbutz* (1973).

Italy

A republic of southern Europe, Italy occupies the Apennine Peninsula, Sicily, Sardinia, and a number of smaller islands. On the north it borders France, Switzerland, Austria, and Yugoslavia. Area: 116,313 sq.mi. (301,245 sq.km.). Pop. (1973 est.): 55,154,400. Cap. and largest city: Rome (pop., 1973 est., 2,833,100). Language: Italian. Religion: predominantly Roman Catholic. President in 1974, Giovanni Leone; premiers, Mariano Rumor until October 3 and, from November 23, Aldo Moro.

The year 1974 was one most Italians would be happy to forget. On the home front a succession of government crises, a series of politically motivated acts of violence, and an outburst of kidnappings were able to overshadow the keenly awaited and controversial referendum on the divorce law. The oil crisis, inflation, and the urgent need to secure oil supplies and foreign loans dictated every aspect of Italian foreign and economic policy.

Domestic Affairs. On February 28 the resignation of the treasury minister, Republican Ugo La Malfa, in open disagreement with the terms of a $1.2 billion loan to Italy, which he had himself negotiated in the U.S., caused the first government crisis of the year. Premier Rumor offered his resignation on March 2, but four days later he was asked by President Leone to form a new government on the same lines as the previous one (a four-party coalition of Christian Democrats, Socialists, Social Democrats, and Repub-

licans). The new Cabinet, which was almost the same as its forerunner, was voted in by the Chamber of Deputies (343 votes to 231) and later by the Senate (183 to 119).

Great controversy was generated by the approval of a bill for the financing of political parties from public funds, amounting to 45 billion lire a year and an extra 15 billion in election years. Later, signatures were collected throughout Italy in an attempt to force a referendum on the matter.

Another referendum had already been taken by the opponents of the 1970 divorce law, who collected more than 1.3 million signatures, and what was to be a decision for the conscience of Italians turned into a fierce political struggle. Two parties, the Christian Democrats and the neofascist Italian Social Movement-National Right (MSI-DN), led by Giorgio Almirante (*see* BIOGRAPHY), campaigned for a vote to repeal the law. All other parties declared themselves in favour of the divorce law, and their position proved to be the winning one when, on May 12, the law was retained by a majority of 59.1% of votes. The regions of Italy where the antidivorce lobby gained a majority, and then only by a small margin, were few, whereas industrial cities such as Turin voted for divorce with a majority nearing 80%.

The Christian Democrats' standing was greatly weakened by their losing campaign, and it came as no surprise when a month later, on June 10, Premier Rumor again offered his resignation. This time President Leone took the unusual step of rejecting the resignation, and after compromise was reached among the coalition partners, Parliament gave its vote of confidence to the Rumor government on June 28. Local elections in Sardinia on June 16 further emphasized the difficulties of the Christian Democrats: their majority decreased from 44.6% (1969) to 38.3%; a net gain was made by both Socialist parties and by the Communists (from 19.7 to 26.8%).

Premier Rumor again resigned on October 3, after the Social Democrats walked out on the coalition. This crisis was not as easy to solve as the previous ones. Former premier and present Christian Democrat secretary Amintore Fanfani was asked on October 14 to form a new government, but after a series of unsuccessful consultations he gave up on October 25.

Pro-divorce demonstrators rally support in Rome prior to the national referendum on repealing Italy's divorce law.

ITALY

Education. (1973–74) Primary, pupils 4,968,-900, teachers 245,628; secondary, pupils 2,517,-341, teachers (1972–73) 249,031; vocational, pupils 1,699,647, teachers (1972–73) 86,342; teacher training, students 195,184, teachers (1972–73) 18,239; higher (1972–73; including 37 universities), students 802,603, teaching staff 44,622.

Finance. Monetary unit: lira, with (Sept. 16, 1974) a free rate of 664 lire to U.S. $1 (1,533 lire = £1 sterling). Gold, SDRs, and foreign exchange, official: (June 1974) U.S. $4,959,000,-000; (June 1973) U.S. $5,609,000,000. Budget (1973 actual): revenue 14,496,000,000,000 lire; expenditure 20,258,000,000,000 lire. Gross national product: (1972) 68,976,000,000,000 lire; (1971) 63,120,000,000,000 lire. Money supply: (Dec. 1973) 54,070,000,000,000 lire; (Dec. 1972) 46,006,000,000,000 lire. Cost of living (1970 = 100): (June 1974) 143; (June 1973) 123.

Foreign Trade. (1973) Imports 16,224,000,-000,000 lire; exports 12,969,000,000,000 lire. Import sources: EEC 49% (West Germany 20%, France 15%, The Netherlands 5%); U.S. 8%. Export destinations: EEC 50% (West Germany 22%, France 14%, U.K. 5%); U.S. 9%; Switzerland 5%. Main exports: machinery 24%; mo-

tor vehicles 9%; chemicals 7%; textiles, yarns, and fabrics 7%; clothing 6%; petroleum products 5%; footwear 5%; iron and steel 5%. Tourism (1972): visitors 10,977,700; gross receipts U.S. $2,178,000,000.

Transport and Communications. Roads (1973) 288,400 km. (including 5,090 km. expressways). Motor vehicles in use (1973): passenger 13.6 million; commercial 1,025,000. Railways: (1971) 20,116 km.; traffic (1972) 35,-394,000,000 passenger-km., freight 17,120,000,-000 net ton-km. Air traffic (1973): 11,124,000,-000 passenger-km.; freight 426,115,000 net ton-km. Shipping (1973): merchant vessels 100 gross tons and over 1,726; gross tonnage 8,867,-205. Telephones (Dec. 1972) 11,345,000. Radio licenses (Dec. 1972) 12,488,000. Television licenses (Dec. 1972) 10,951,000.

Agriculture. Production (in 000; metric tons; 1973; 1972 in parentheses): wheat 8,958 (9,-423); corn 5,052 (4,802); barley 448 (388); oats 425 (461); potatoes c. 2,800 (3,002); rice 970 (751); dry broad beans 284 (348); onions 435 (421); sugar, raw value c. 1,168 (1,257); tomatoes 3,284 (3,068); wine 6,988 (5,919); olives 2,890 (1,870); oranges (1972) 1,554, (1971) 1,462; tangerines and mandarin oranges (1972) 265, (1971) 304; lemons (1972) 726,

(1971) 818; apples (1972) 1,873, (1971) 1,698; pears (1972) 1,526, (1971) 1,705; peaches (1972) 1,319, (1971) 1,249; figs (1972) 177, (1971) 176; tobacco 92 (84); cheese (1972) c. 485, (1971) 478; beef and veal (1972) c. 730, (1971) 754; pork (1972) c. 640, (1971) 612. Livestock (in 000; Jan. 1973): cattle 8,571; sheep 7,805; pigs 7,990; goats 950; horses, mules, and asses 620; poultry c. 110,000.

Industry. Index of production (1970 = 100): (1973) 114; (1972) 104. Unemployment: (1973) 3.5%; (1972) 3.6%. Fuel and power (in 000; metric tons; 1973): lignite 1,302; crude oil 1,040; natural gas (cu.m.) 15,326,000; manufactured gas (cu.m.) 3,161,000; electricity (kw-hr.) c. 144,000,000. Production (in 000; metric tons; 1973): iron ore (50% metal content) 522; pig iron 10,251; crude steel 20,775; aluminum 191; zinc 156; lead 37; cement 36,254; cotton yarn 149; rayon, etc., filament yarn 66; rayon, etc., fibres 98; nylon, etc., filament yarn 150; nylon, etc., fibres 231; fertilizers (nutrient content; 1972–73) nitrogenous 1,045, phosphate 500; sulfuric acid 3,037; petroleum products (1972) 114,046; passenger cars (units) 1,825; commercial vehicles (units) 135. Merchant vessels launched (100 gross tons and over; 1973) 781,-000 gross tons.

The seemingly inexorable advance of lagoon waters surrounding the city forces Venetians to use raised boardwalks to cross St. Mark's Square at high tide.

The choice then fell on Aldo Moro, who was foreign minister in the Rumor Cabinet and a former premier. On November 23 he formed a new two-party government of Christian Democrats and Republicans with the outside support of Socialists and Social Democrats. The Senate voted the government in by 190 to 113, and the Chamber of Deputies by 355 to 226.

Episodes of political violence, mainly attributed to right-wing movements, renewed fears of a coup d'etat. On May 28 a bomb exploded in Brescia during an antifascist rally, killing 6 people and injuring 94. Two days later a fascist military camp was discovered by the national police in the mountains at Racino, near Rieti. In the shooting that followed, a young extremist was killed and two police agents were injured. On June 17 two men were killed in the MSI-DN office in Padua; left-wing extremists were suspected. A bomb was exploded on the "Italicus" express train, between Florence and Bologna, on August 4; 12 people were killed and 48 injured. One police officer was killed on October 15 during an incursion in a hideout of the Red Brigades, a Communist-oriented group disowned by the Communist Party. In November bombs attributed to fascists rocked Savona.

Controversy was caused, in the second half of the year, by the disclosure of activities that had been aimed at achieving right-wing coups in Italy in 1970 and 1974. In the plan for 1974 Premier Rumor was to be kidnapped together with other Cabinet ministers. Secret service activities in the matter were investigated, together with the establishment of a right-wing organization based in Padua and called Rosa dei Venti ("Rose of the Winds"). A number of people were arrested including industrialist Andrea Piaggio and high military officers.

Kidnappings occurred during the year with alarming frequency. Most were carried out for extortion, some for political purposes. Student Piergiorgio Bolis was seized in Bergamo and released after 20 days and a payment of 500 million lire. Industrialist Luigi Rossi di Montalera (of Martini e Rossi vermouth fame) was found and freed by accident after four months' imprisonment and before a ransom had been paid. The greatest speculation, however, was caused by the disappearance of the Genoa judge Mario Sossi on April 18. He was freed by the Red Brigades on May 23 after the Genoa tribunal had agreed to set free eight followers of the left-wing October 22 group.

The promise was not kept. Other kidnappings followed in the autumn. Police inquiries achieved some success: some of the gangs involved in the kidnappings were arrested.

Foreign Affairs. Italian foreign involvement was aimed at securing oil supplies and credit for a shaky economy. At the end of January Foreign Minister Moro went on an oil-finding mission to Abu Dhabi, Kuwait, Iran, and Saudi Arabia, shortly after receiving in Rome the oil ministers of Algeria and Saudi Arabia. In this striving for Arab friendship even the old project of a Muslim mosque in Rome, which had often been postponed under Vatican pressure, was at last given the official go-ahead. After visits to President Leone by Mexican Pres. Luis Echeverría Álvarez (February 8) and by Soviet Foreign Minister Andrey Gromyko (February 19), the oil search was taken up again when Premier Rumor received in Rome, with full honours, Libyan Prime Minister Abdul Salam Jalloud (February 22). On September 26 Leone began an official visit to U.S. Pres. Gerald Ford. Again on the oil trek, Leone paid a very successful visit to the shah of Iran in December.

The Economy. In order to contain the national deficit within 7.4 trillion lire, as estimated at the beginning of 1974, a series of economic plans were suggested. Tax reform came into effect on January 1; later, limits were set on the export of currency, and a special deposit fund was established against all imported goods. The price of gasoline was increased in two stages from 200 to 300 lire a litre. A once-only tax was charged on cars, according to size, and on houses, payable by owners.

The price freeze ended on July 31, and inflation thereafter was almost uncontrolled. At the end of November prices had increased by 26.2% as compared with November 1973. Industrial production had shown encouraging signs at the beginning of the year, but the increase had fallen to 7.4% by November. This was due largely to the crisis in the automobile industry; Fiat was forced to put 71,000 workers on a three-day week after October 7 and to bring forward 1975 holidays, giving workers a three-week holiday between Dec. 20, 1974, and Jan. 13, 1975. On August 31 West German Chancellor Helmut Schmidt and Rumor negotiated a crucial West German loan to Italy of $2 billion.   (FABIO GALVANO)

[972.A.4]

Italian Literature: *see* Literature

Ivory Coast

A republic on the Gulf of Guinea, West Africa, the Ivory Coast is bounded by Liberia, Guinea, Mali, Upper Volta, and Ghana. Area: 123,484 sq.mi. (319,822 sq.km.). Pop. (1973 est.): 4,641,000. Cap. and largest city: Abidjan (pop., early 1970s est., 650,000). Language: French and local dialects. Religion: animist 65%; Muslim 23%; Christian 12%. President and premier in 1974, Félix Houphouët-Boigny.

The main features of Ivory Coast policy in 1974 were the strengthening friendship with France, the rejuvenation and renewal of the governing team, and the continued pursuit of economic expansion.

At the conclusion of a meeting between President Houphouët-Boigny and French Pres. Valéry Giscard d'Estaing in Paris in August, the two heads of state stressed their "complete identity of views." Later in the year the French minister for cooperation, Pierre Abelin, paid an official visit to Abidjan.

In July a major Cabinet reshuffle allowed Laurent Dona-Fologo, the youngest member of the political bureau of the country's sole political party, to become the minister of information. Among the new governing team's first important decisions were major promotions within the armed forces.

In the realm of economic affairs, expansion continued under favourable conditions despite the effects of the world oil crisis on the country's industrial sector. The continued growth of the economy despite soaring oil prices was due in part to the higher prices being obtained for certain agricultural products such as coffee and cocoa, but also resulted from what had proved to be a highly intelligent policy on hydroelectric power development which had been pursued by the government for several years despite the discouraging predictions of some international experts. Under these favourable economic circumstances it was planned to set up a savings bank to encourage Ivoirian savings activities. In October an Ivoirian citizen was appointed governor of the Central Bank of the States of West Africa.

It was reported in the South African press in December that meetings had taken place in September in the Ivory Coast town of Yamoussoukro between the South African prime minister, B. J. Vorster, President Houphouët-Boigny, Pres. Léopold Senghor of Senegal, and representatives of Gabon and Zambia.

(PHILIPPE DECRAENE)

Jamaica

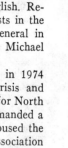

A parliamentary state within the Commonwealth of Nations, Jamaica is an island in the Caribbean Sea about 90 mi. S of Cuba. Area: 4,244 sq.mi. (10,991 sq.km.). Pop. (1974 est.): 1,997,900, predominantly Negro, but including Europeans, Chinese, Indians, and persons of mixed race. Cap. and largest city: Kingston (pop., 1974 est., 169,800). Language: English. Religion: Christian, with Anglicans and Baptists in the majority. Queen, Elizabeth II; governor-general in 1974, Florizel Glasspole; prime minister, Michael Manley.

Jamaica's economic and social problems in 1974 were compounded by the world energy crisis and inflation. Jamaica quadrupled the export tax for North American bauxite mining companies and demanded a share in their operations. Jamaica, which housed the secretariat of the International Bauxite Association (IBA), set up in February–March 1974, later agreed with Trinidad and Guyana to build two aluminum smelting plants. (See COMMODITY TRADE: *Special Report.*) Austerity measures, massive borrowing, and its work program enabled the government to raise currency reserves from Jam$76.1 million early in the year to Jam$190.8 million in August. The cost of living was estimated to have increased by about 30%.

Increasing violence, including the killing of four prominent Jamaicans, led the government to set up a special Gun Court, in which persons arrested on firearms charges would be tried swiftly and, if found guilty, would undergo indefinite detention. Illegal

---

IVORY COAST

Education. (1972–73) Primary, pupils 556,689, teachers 12,216; secondary, pupils 83,456, teachers (1970–71) 1,944; vocational (1970–71), pupils 4,807, teachers 613; teacher training, students 3,284, teachers 130; higher, students 4,699, teaching staff (1970–71) 220.

Finance. Monetary unit: CFA franc, with (Sept. 16, 1974) a parity of CFA Fr. 50 to the French franc (free rate of CFA Fr. 240.50 = U.S. $1; CFA Fr. 556.50 = £1 sterling). Gold, SDRs, and foreign exchange, central bank: (May 1974) U.S. $91.6 million; (May 1973) U.S. $109.5 million. Budget (1974 est.) balanced at CFA Fr. 97.7 billion. Money supply: (May 1974) CFA Fr. 134.8 billion; (May 1973) CFA Fr. 108,640,000,000.

Foreign Trade. (1973) Imports CFA Fr. 157,540,-000,000; exports CFA Fr. 190,880,000,000. Import sources: France 47%; U.S. 11%; West Germany 8%. Export destinations: France 28%; West Germany 15%; Italy 12%; U.S. 11%; Spain 5%. Main exports: timber 29%; coffee 23%; cocoa 15%.

Agriculture. Production (in 000; metric tons; 1973; 1972 in parentheses): corn *c.* 110 (*c.* 108); yams (1972) 1,550, (1971) 1,550; cassava (1972) 570, (1971) 567; rice (1972) 360, (1971) 385; millet *c.* 30 (30); peanuts *c.* 42 (42); coffee *c.* 210 (*c.* 300); cocoa 190 (181); bananas (1972) *c.* 219, (1972) 188; palm kernels *c.* 20 (24); palm oil *c.* 83 (81); cotton, lint *c.* 20 (25); rubber *c.* 14 (14); timber (cu.m.; 1972) 9,800, (1971) 9,400. Livestock (in 000; 1972–73): cattle *c.* 460; pigs *c.* 190; sheep *c.* 920; goats (1971–72) 894; poultry (1971–72) 6,000.

JAMAICA

Education. (1971–72) Primary, pupils 414,919, teachers (1969–70; including preprimary) 7,491; secondary, pupils 75,134, teachers (1969–70) 2,163; vocational, pupils 8,638, teachers (1969–70) 251; teacher training, students 2,104, teachers (1969–70) 144; higher, students 2,751, teaching staff (1969–70) 311.

Finance. Monetary unit: Jamaican dollar, with (Sept. 16, 1974) a par value of Jam$0.91 to U.S. $1 (free rate of Jam$2.11 = £1 sterling). Budget (1973–74 est.): revenue Jam$419 million; expenditure Jam$432 million.

Foreign Trade. (1973) Imports Jam$607,460,000; exports Jam$354,710,000. Import sources (1972): U.S. 37%; U.K. 19%; Canada 7%; Venezuela 5%. Export destinations (1972): U.S. 44%; U.K. 22%; Norway 11%; Canada 5%. Main exports (1972): alumina 40%; bauxite 23%; sugar 12%. Tourism (1972): visitors 407,800; gross receipts U.S. $135 million.

Agriculture. Production (in 000; metric tons; 1973; 1972 in parentheses): sweet potatoes *c.* 22 (*c.* 22); yams (1972) *c.* 120, (1971) 117; cassava *c.* 18 (*c.* 18); sugar, raw value *c.* 341 (*c.* 379); bananas (1972) *c.* 183, (1971) *c.* 185; oranges (1972) *c.* 80, (1971) *c.* 75; grapefruit (1972) *c.* 33, (1971) *c.* 33; lemons (1972) *c.* 10, (1971) *c.* 10; copra *c.* 16 (16). Livestock (in 000; 1972–73): cattle *c.* 270; goats *c.* 126; pigs *c.* 135.

Industry. Production (in 000; metric tons; 1973): bauxite 13,490; cement 404; petroleum products (1972) 1,671; electricity (kw-hr.; 1972) 1,983,000.

arms were connected particularly with the airborne smuggling of cannabis and Jamaican currency (its transfer forbidden in 1972) to the U.S. The U.S. Federal Reserve Bank reported U.S. $39 million was held by Jamaicans and Jamaican concerns in U.S. banks at the end of 1973, as compared with U.S. $19 million two years earlier. Moves toward closer relations with Cuba and a number of African nations continued, and Kingston was the venue for the meeting in July between the ACP (Africa, Caribbean, and Pacific) associated and associable states and the EEC.

(SHEILA PATTERSON)

[974.B.2.d]

Japan

A constitutional monarchy in the northwestern Pacific Ocean, Japan is an archipelago composed of four major islands (Hokkaido, Honshu, Kyushu, and Shikoku), the Ryukyus (including Okinawa), and minor adjacent islands. Area: 145,728 sq.mi. (377,435 sq.km.). Pop. (1974 est.): 109,155,600. Cap. and largest city: Tokyo (pop., 1974 est., 8,708,300). Language: Japanese. Religion: primarily Shinto and Buddhist; Christian 0.5%. Emperor, Hirohito; prime ministers in 1974, Kakuei Tanaka and, from December 9, Takeo Miki.

Domestic Affairs. In 1974 Japan, like other advanced industrial countries, suffered from "stagflation," a severe drop in the growth rate of the economy and steadily soaring consumer prices. In February the Economic Planning Agency (EPA) announced that during 1973 Japan's inflation was the worst among the ten leading industrial countries in the world. In December 1973 wholesale prices had registered an abnormally steep rise of 29%. During the first 20 days of January, Tokyo's consumer price index jumped 4% over that of the same period in December; this resulted in an increase of 20.4% over

the previous January, the highest rate of annual increase in 22 years. The Tokyo index faded to a 3.6% monthly increase in February and by May registered only slight gains. Nonetheless, by that time the consumer price index for Tokyo's 23 wards stood at 149.8 (1970 = 100); Osaka's index was 149.6. By September, Tokyo's index had shot up again by a 1.9% monthly, or 22% annual, inflation rate.

The inflation, of course, had political repercussions. In February the Diet began a special three-day session on price problems. Presidents of the major trading firms, under sharp questioning by members of both majority and opposition parties, admitted to price "irregularities" in the operation of their companies and promised corrective action including the recycling of "excess profits." In May the Tokyo High Public Prosecutor's office indicted the Petroleum Association of Japan, including 12 major petroleum refining companies and 17 of their executives, for alleged collusion in price fixing and curtailment of production. Dependent on imports for a large proportion of its energy, Japan acutely felt the effects of the world oil crisis.

By midyear, some bright spots appeared in the economic picture. A report on trade performance stated that Japan's monthly validated exports in May topped the $5 billion mark for the first time. Major items of export included steel, automobiles, and ships. After foreign exchange reserves registered a low of $11.6 billion at the end of January, they showed an increase of $452 million in May to total $13.2 billion at the end of the month, according to the Finance Ministry.

On June 3 the marathon 185-day (72nd) regular session of the Diet, convened in the midst of the oil crisis, came to a quiet close. The status of the economy and inflation had been the major concerns of the session. Legislative questioning of business leaders had been followed by organized labour's spring drive for higher wages, which called on the Diet to deal with the effects of inflation. Two results were the Land Utilization bill and a special corporate income tax. Both marked a new departure in compromise between the majority and the opposition parties as they moved from confrontation to negotiation of differences. Only the Japan Communists voted against the land bill, which was designed to freeze skyrocketing real estate prices. The other opposition parties threw their weight behind the measure because it began to deemphasize further industrial development.

The Diet also approved several treaties, including the antihijacking pact (known as the Montreal Treaty) and a long-range trade accord with China. Unresolved controversies over educational and electoral reforms were raised by Prime Minister Tanaka, as well as a disputed bill that would have placed the Yasukuni shrine (dedicated to war veterans) under state protection.

At the end of the 72nd Diet session, party representation was as follows: (lower) House of Representatives: Liberal-Democrats (LDP) 279, Japan Socialists (JSP) 118, Japan Communists (JCP) 40, Komeito (KMT) 30, Democratic Socialists (DSP) 20, independents 1, vacancies 3 (total 491); (upper) House of Councillors (number up for election July 7 in parentheses): LDP 135 (71), JSP 59 (25), KMT 23 (13), DSP 11 (6), JCP 11 (4), Niin Club 4 (3), independents 2 (1), vacancies 7 (3) (total 252 [126]).

During 1974 the Japanese public had ample opportunity in national and local elections to express concern over the state of the economy. Results constituted something of a deadlock. On April 7 two leftist

Fearful of radioactive pollution of their fishing waters, protesting Japanese fishermen use their boats to prevent the new nuclear ship "Mutsu" from leaving its home port.

SANKEI SHIMBUN

Education. (1972–73) Primary, pupils 9,816,-536, teachers 392,793; secondary, pupils 7,153,-337; vocational, pupils 1,561,580, secondary and vocational, teachers (1970–71) 478,221; higher (including 38 main state universities), students 1,926,108, teaching staff 102,396.

Finance. Monetary unit: yen, with (Sept. 16, 1974) a free rate of 300 yen to U.S. $1 (free rate of 692 yen = £1 sterling). Gold, SDRs, and foreign exchange, official: (June 1974) U.S. $12,-781,000,000; (June 1973) U.S. $14,532,000,-000. Budget (1973–74 est) revenue 16,440,000,-000,000 yen; expenditure 17,640,000,000,000 yen. Gross national product: (1973) 112,871,-000,000,000 yen; (1972) 90,694,000,000,000 yen. Money supply: (May 1974) 40,994,000,-000,000 yen; (May 1973) 35,776,000,000,000 yen. Cost of living (1970 = 100): (June 1974) 151; (June 1973) 123.

Foreign Trade. (1973) Imports 10,404,400,-000,000 yen; exports 10,023,400,000,000 yen. Import sources: U.S. 24%; Australia 9%; Indonesia 6%; Canada 5%; Iran 5%. Export destinations: U.S. 26%; South Korea 5%. Main exports: machinery 24%; iron and steel 14%; motor vehicles 13%; ships 10%; textile yarns and fabrics 7%; chemicals 6%.

Transport and Communications. Roads (1973) 1,049,710 km. (including 1,403 km. expressways). Motor vehicles in use (1973): passenger 14,473,600; commercial 10,422,400. Railways: (1971) 27,919 km.; traffic (1973) 310,822,000,000 passenger-km., freight 58,882,-000,000 net ton-km. Air traffic (1972): 20,836,-000,000 passenger-km.; freight 641.9 million net ton-km. Shipping (1973): merchant vessels 100 gross tons and over 9,469; gross tonnage 36,785,-094. Telephones (Jan. 1973) 34,021,000. Radio receivers (Dec. 1972) 70,794,000. Television licenses (Dec. 1972) 24,194,000.

Agriculture. Production (in 000; metric tons; 1973; 1972 in parentheses): rice 15,580 (15,-281); wheat 203 (284); barley 216 (325); sweet potatoes (1972) 2,107, (1971) 2,155; potatoes c. 3,200 (3,537); sugar, raw value c. 694 (615); tea c. 97 (95); onions c. 1,100 (c. 1,100); tomatoes c. 800 (c. 792); apples (1972) 1,003, (1971) 1,007; pears (1972) c. 456, (1971) 441; oranges (1972) c. 448, (1971) 337; mandarin oranges and tangerines (1972) c. 3,200, (1971) 2,489; grapes (1972) 269, (1971) 242; tobacco c. 154 (c. 144); pork (1972) 885, (1971) 843; timber (cu.m.; 1971) 46,000, (1971) 49,800; fish catch (1972) 10,248, (1971) 9,949; whale

and sperm oil (1972–73) 20, (1971–72) 60. Livestock (in 000; Feb. 1973): cattle c. 3,485; sheep 19; pigs c. 7,430; goats (1972) 157; horses (1972) 104; chickens (1972) c. 222,300.

Industry. Index of production (1970 = 100): (1973) 130; (1972) 110. Fuel and power (in 000; metric tons; 1973): coal 22,414; crude oil 703; natural gas (cu.m.) 2,890,000; manufactured gas (cu.m.; 1971) 3,387,000; electricity (kw-hr.) 436,377,000. Production (in 000; metric tons; 1973): iron ore (55% metal content) 1,008; pig iron 92,041; crude steel 119,322; petroleum products (1972) 189,495; cement 78,-023; cotton yarn 554; woven cotton fabrics (sq.m.) 2,380,000; rayon, etc., filament yarn 128; rayon, etc., fibres 415; nylon, etc., filament yarn 592; nylon, etc., fibres 716; sulfuric acid 7,115; fertilizers (nutrient content; 1972–73) nitrogenous 2,214, phosphate 729; cameras (units) 5,865; radio receivers (units) 24,485; television receivers (units) 14,416; passenger cars (units) 4,323; commercial vehicles (units) 2,-600; motorcycles (units) 3,763. Merchant vessels launched (100 gross tons and over; 1973) 15,736,000 gross tons. New dwelling units started (1973) 1.9 million.

candidates contested for the governorship of the ancient capital prefecture of Kyoto. The 77-year-old Torazo Ninagawa, governor for the past 24 years and backed by the JCP, won another four years in office but by a slim margin. Local elections held April 21–22, however, resulted in 22 LDP victories out of 23 mayoral contests and the election of LDP candidate Hanji Ogawa to an upper house seat representing Kyoto.

On June 22 some 339 candidates took to the streets in Tokyo and in other strategic cities, campaigning for half the seats at stake in the House of Councillors. All the candidates were pledged to arrest inflation by one means or another. Despite a highly publicized and heavily financed campaign led by Prime Minister Tanaka, the LDP suffered a setback in the elections on July 7, although managing to maintain a bare majority in the upper house. Election results (with total strength in parentheses) were as follows: LDP 62 (126), JSP 28 (62), KMT 14 (24), JCP 13 (20), DSP 5 (10), Niin Club 1 (1), independents 7 (9) (total 130 [252]), with all 7 vacancies filled.

Recession and inflation, coupled with the poor showing of the majority LDP in the July election, threatened the position of Prime Minister Tanaka as both national and party leader. On July 12, Deputy Prime Minister Takeo Miki resigned from the Tanaka Cabinet to protest the style of the LDP's campaign in July and to devote himself to the "modernization of the Liberal-Democratic Party." One week later, Tanaka suffered another blow as his arch-rival within the LDP, Finance Minister Takeo Fukuda, resigned from the Cabinet. Also resigning was Shigeru Hori, who had been director of the Administrative Management Agency. Tanaka named Foreign Minister Masayoshi Ohira to replace Fukuda and Toshio Kimura, who had played a major role in the Japan–U.S. negotiations concerning Okinawa, to succeed Ohira.

On November 26, plagued by the poor economy and also by charges that he had profited illegally by means of his office, Tanaka announced his intention to resign. In the intensive political maneuvering that followed, it soon became clear that the choice of either of the two leading contenders to succeed him, Fukuda or Ohira, would seriously damage party unity. Finally, on December 2, the LDP leadership announced the surprise selection of Miki as a compromise choice. Miki was formally elected leader of the LDP on De-

cember 4 and prime minister by the Diet on December 9. His Cabinet included Kiichi Miyazawa as foreign minister, Ohira as finance minister, and Fukuda as deputy prime minister and head of a new council of economic ministers set up to coordinate economic policy.

Other signs of unrest in Japan included strikes from April 11 to April 13 of some 400,000 public school teachers, directed by the powerful Japan Teachers Union. The stoppages were indirectly in protest against Tanaka's repeated recommendations for the reintroduction of "ethics" into the curriculum and directly against legislation that would lend legal status to head teachers. Since teachers' strikes were banned under civil service laws, on June 1 police arrested 19 union leaders in Tokyo, Saitama, and Hokkaido.

On May 9 a violent earthquake centring on the southern Izu Peninsula, Shizuoka Prefecture, killed 29 persons, injured 77 others, and destroyed 171 houses. The quake's intensity of magnitude on the Richter scale was 6.8. On August 30 the efficiently policed and usually peaceable metropolis of Tokyo was shattered by a bomb explosion near the entrance of the Mitsubishi building in the crowded Marunouchi district. Eight persons were killed and over 300 injured in the blast. Police speculated that the bomb was in protest against the Mitsubishi combine, which was said to account for half the military equipment production in Japan. On October 14 a similar explosion at the Mitsui head office in Nishi-shimbashi, Minato ward, Tokyo, injured 16 persons, 2 seriously.

Foreign Relations. Within a "balanced" foreign policy Japan, according to the Foreign Ministry, attempted to maintain its "close relationship" with the U.S. Foreign Minister Ohira, on his return from the U.S. in late May, stated that current Japan–U.S. relations involved no special problems. He had held talks with Pres. Richard Nixon and former ambassador to Japan Robert S. Ingersoll, who had become assistant secretary in charge of Asian affairs. Nevertheless, in Japan the long-delayed arrival of a new U.S. ambassador was having an adverse effect on Japanese relations. More than six months elapsed after Ingersoll had left Tokyo before the new appointee, James D. Hodgson, a Lockheed Aircraft Co. executive, arrived (July 15).

On August 17, following President Nixon's resigna-

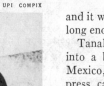

An unhappy Mona Lisa
with shopping basket
joins organized labour's
campaign for higher
wages in an advertising
gimmick inspired
by the exhibition
of Da Vinci's masterpiece
in Tokyo.

tion, Foreign Minister Kimura stated that basic relations between Japan and the U.S. would remain unchanged under the new U.S. administration. Prime Minister Tanaka met Pres. Gerald Ford in Washington on September 21. At that time, Ford announced that he would become the first U.S. president to visit Japan while in office. The visit was later scheduled for November.

Meanwhile, Japan's famous "nuclear allergy" threatened to throw a cloud over the Ford visit. Controversial testimony delivered before a congressional committee in Washington by retired Adm. Gene LaRocque indicated that U.S. warships had regularly entered Japanese ports without unloading their nuclear weapons. The testimony seemed to confirm opposition suspicion that conservative Japanese governments had been duped by, or were in collusion with, the U.S. in circumventing Japan's prohibition of nuclear arms. On October 15, in a statement delivered to Tokyo, the U.S. indirectly denied LaRocque's testimony, described as "given by a private citizen" who "could not in any way represent the views of the U.S. government." Foreign Minister Kimura told the press that the U.S. "has faithfully honoured"—and would continue to honour—its commitments under the Japan–U.S. mutual security treaty. On October 19, Prime Minister Tanaka pledged that Japan would reject a request to introduce nuclear weapons into the country if the U.S. made such a request in accordance with the "prior consultation" arrangement based on the treaty.

Nonetheless, these exchanges left a certain impression of ambiguity in many Japanese minds. On October 21 about 300,000 persons rallied throughout the country to mark International Antiwar Day. Mass rallies called for peace and protested the alleged introduction by U.S. forces of nuclear weapons into Japan. As the time for President Ford's arrival approached, threats of disruption were reminiscent of those that aborted the planned visit by U.S. Pres. Dwight Eisenhower in 1960. Accordingly, the visit, which took place November 18–21, was held under extremely tight security. A joint communiqué issued on November 20 emphasized the "friendly and cooperative relations" between the two countries and their "dedication to the maintenance of world peace," but contained little in the way of substantive decisions. In part this was attributed to the fact that Tanaka's resignation was already widely rumoured,

and it was believed that he would remain in office only long enough to serve as Ford's host.

Tanaka's brief visit to Washington was squeezed into a busy itinerary, which also included visits to Mexico, Brazil, and Canada on what the Japanese press called "energy resources diplomacy." Tanaka conferred with Pres. Luis Echeverría Álvarez in Mexico City, September 12–15; he met Pres. Ernesto Geisel in Brazil, September 16–20; and consulted with Prime Minister Pierre Trudeau in Ottawa, September 23–26. Earlier, in January, he had completed a goodwill tour of the Philippines, Thailand, Malaysia, Singapore, and Indonesia, a trip which to some extent boomeranged. He was greeted by student demonstrations in Bangkok and more serious riots in Jakarta. The experience led Japanese leaders and the public to contemplate Japan's often ugly overseas image of an "economic animal." Late in October, Tanaka toured Australia, New Zealand, and Burma.

Closer to the homeland, relations between Japan and South Korea continued to be strained by misunderstanding and outright animosity. In June, Foreign Minister Ohira stated that his government had "particular concern" over South Korea's handling of the explosive Kim Dae Jung affair. (In August 1973, Kim had been kidnapped in Tokyo and removed to virtual house arrest in South Korea.)

On August 15 the wife of Park Chung Hee died as the result of an assassination attempt directed at Park, during a nationally televised speech marking Korea's liberation from Japan in 1945. Mun Se Kwang, a South Korean national who had previously lived in Japan and was a member of the Chongryun, an organization of pro-North Korean residents in Japan, was subsequently convicted of the killing. Prime Minister Tanaka personally delivered condolences to President Park in Seoul on August 19. However, on September 6 a group of South Korean youths stormed into the Japanese embassy in Seoul, tore down the Japanese flag, ransacked offices, and set fire to an embassy vehicle. The demonstrators demanded the "truth" about the attempted assassination of President Park. The Foreign Ministry in Tokyo instructed Ambassador Torao Ushiroku to file a formal protest. After returning from talks with Park and Prime Minister Kim in Seoul in September, former foreign minister Etsusaburo Shiina stressed the need for Japan and South Korea to continue efforts to develop closer relations. A memorandum pledged that Japan would strictly control any criminal act mounted on its territory that aimed at overthrowing the republic. Mun Se Kwang was executed on December 20.

Turning to contacts with another mainland neighbour, in April Japan and China signed a civil aviation agreement one year and seven months after the two nations had normalized relations. On September 29 flag carriers of both nations initiated scheduled air service between the countries.

During the year, however, the air between China and Japan was not always so calm. In June the Japanese government lodged a strong protest with China over its most recent atmospheric nuclear test. With evenhandedness, Tokyo filed a similarly strong protest against a French nuclear test in the South Pacific. Earlier in May, Japan was shocked by, and strenuously objected to, India's first nuclear test.

These various activities gave rise to two opposing Japanese reactions with regard to ratification of the nuclear nonproliferation treaty—delay and promotion. It had been six years since the pact had been brought into effect and four years since Japan had signed the treaty, but Japan had yet to ratify it. Ratification was opposed for three quite different reasons. First, some Japanese argued that, although the nation maintained a policy not to equip itself with nuclear weapons, Japan had the capacity and even the right to do so for self-defense. Second, others objected to Japan's being subjected to international inspection under the treaty. Third, still others felt that the major purpose of the treaty was maintenance by the U.S. and the Soviet Union of their nuclear supremacy.

In this climate, Japan's intellectuals considered the news of former Prime Minister Eisaku Sato's selection as a 1974 Nobel Peace Prize recipient "dismaying" and "ironic," coming as it did at the time the country was seething over the LaRocque testimony. Certainly, the critics said, the award could not be for signature of the nonproliferation treaty, since Japan had not yet ratified the agreement. Sato himself said he thought the distinction was earned by his efforts toward the reversion of Okinawa to Japanese control, marking the "true end" of World War II.

As to relations with the Soviet Union, on April 1 Foreign Minister Ohira told the Diet that Tokyo was not yet in a position to comment on a Soviet proposal to build a new Siberian railway, a project for which the Soviets were seeking Japanese assistance. Critics had pointed out that no headway was being made toward a peace treaty between Japan and the U.S.S.R. and that the new rail link would constitute a distinct strategic threat to Japan.

On June 3 Japan and the Soviet Union did, however, sign an agreement on the joint development of coking coal in southern Yakutsk. Japan was to provide a $450 million bank-to-bank loan and was to receive 104 million tons of coking coal from 1979 to 1998. During 1974 Tokyo and Moscow had six major development projects under study or in negotiation, involving crude oil in Tyumen, natural gas in Yakutsk, oil and natural gas in Sakhalin, coking coal in southern Yakutsk, forestry development in the Soviet far eastern region, and paper and pulp in Siberia.

(ARDATH W. BURKS)

[975.B.2.e]

Jordan

A constitutional monarchy in southwest Asia, Jordan is bounded by Syria, Iraq, Saudi Arabia, and Israel. Area (including territory occupied by Israel in the June 1967 war): 36,832 sq.mi. (95,394 sq.km.). Pop. (1973 est.): 2,577,000. Cap. and largest city: Amman (pop., 1973 est., 565,000). Language: Arabic. Religion (1961): Muslim 94%; Christian 6%. King, Hussein I; prime minister in 1974, Zaid ar-Rifai.

Jordan's hopes for participation in a Middle East peace conference leading to an early Israeli withdrawal from its territory suffered a severe setback in 1974. It became apparent that, having avoided direct confrontation with Israel during the October 1973 war, Jordan lacked the bargaining power to secure a preliminary disengagement of forces. In a speech on May 1 King Hussein proposed the disengagement of Jordanian and Israeli forces on the West Bank prior to the Geneva peace conference. He also said that if it was the unanimous wish of the Arabs that the Palestine

Liberation Organization (PLO) should be the sole representative of all Palestinians, Jordan would accept this but would abandon its responsibility for the recovery of lost Palestinian territory. At a meeting in Alexandria, Egypt, with Pres. Anwar as-Sadat of Egypt in July, King Hussein reached a compromise recognizing the PLO as the sole legitimate representative of the Palestinians except for those residing in Jordan. Thus Egypt hoped to pave the way for the formation of a joint Palestinian-Jordanian delegation to attend the Geneva talks. However, the PLO strongly rejected this compromise of their claim to represent all Palestinians. In September Egypt reversed its position at a meeting with Syrian and PLO representatives and recognized the PLO as sole legitimate representative of the Palestinians. King Hussein angrily rejected this decision and refused to attend a Cairo meeting with the PLO to discuss the matter although he agreed to attend the Arab summit meeting scheduled to begin October 26 in Rabat, Morocco.

At the summit conference a resolution was passed naming the PLO as the sole legitimate representative of all of the Palestinian people and affirming the right of the Palestinians to establish an independent state in their old homeland. King Hussein signed the resolution and in return secured the right to take part in future negotiations with Israel. Jordan also reportedly was to receive a $300 million annual subsidy from Saudi Arabia.

U.S. Pres. Richard Nixon received a warm welcome in Amman on June 17–18, although Hussein used the occasion to emphasize Jordan's insistence on recovering all its territory from Israel. The U.S. provided about $77.5 million in nonmilitary aid during 1974.

Yasir Arafat, head of the Palestine Liberation Organization, at the Arab summit conference in Rabat, Morocco.

KEYSTONE

During a visit to Washington, D.C., in August, King Hussein had talks with Pres. Gerald Ford and Secretary of Defense James R. Schlesinger on the Middle East and a military assistance program. Jordanians claimed that by 1975 their air force would have more than 100 modern warplanes, including squadrons of U.S. F5-E fighter-bombers. Prime Minister Zaid ar-Rifai visited Washington in September to discuss the possibilities of disengagement. Jordan suffered a diplomatic setback when it was revealed during September that it had made a £7 million deal with South Africa, reported by the British press in August but denied by Jordan, for the sale of Centurion tanks and Tigercat close-range missiles.

Internally, the year was not eventful. In January press censorship was relaxed but was almost immediately reimposed. On February 6 there were reports of a mutiny in army units with demands for pay increases and for the dismissal of the prime minister; army pay was raised, but the king maintained his confidence in the prime minister.   (PETER MANSFIELD)

See also Middle Eastern Affairs.

[978.B.3.d.ii]

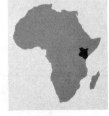

Kenya

A republic and a member of the Commonwealth of Nations, Kenya is bordered on the north by Sudan and Ethiopia, east by Somalia, south by Tanzania, and west by Uganda. Area: 224,961 sq.mi. (582,646 sq.km.), including 5,172 sq.mi. of inland water. Pop. (1974 est.): 12,935,000, including (1969) African 98.1%; Asian 1.5%. Cap. and largest city: Nairobi (pop., 1974 est., 663,000). Language: Swahili (official) and English. Religion (1962): Christian 57.8%; Muslim 3.8%. President in 1974, Jomo Kenyatta.

As soon as President Kenyatta announced in March 1974 that elections would take place later, excitement began to increase in Kenya. In June the president demonstrated that he was intent upon victory by stating that he would crush anyone who attempted to form a rival political party. Former detainees were also prohibited from standing for election unless they had been Kenya African National Union (KANU) members for

Kenya national park employees holding elephant tusks captured from poachers in the Tsavo East Park. The growing sophistication and organization of poachers are generating deep concern throughout Africa for the continent's threatened wildlife.

KENYA
Education. (1973) Primary, pupils 1,779,938, teachers 53,812; secondary, pupils 179,280, teachers 7,344; vocational, pupils 3,420, teachers 213; teacher training, students 9,430, teachers 639; higher (at University of Nairobi), students 2,883.
Finance. Monetary unit: Kenyan shilling, with (Sept. 16, 1974) an official rate of KShs. 7.14 to U.S. $1 (free rate of KShs. 16.56 = £1 sterling). Gold, SDRs, and foreign exchange: (June 1974) U.S. $214.6 million; (June 1973) U.S. $299.5 million. Budget (1973–74 est.): revenue KShs. 3,320,000,000; expenditure KShs. 4,440,000,000. Gross national product: (1972) KShs. 14,026,000,000; (1971) KShs. 12,672,-000,000. Cost of living (Nairobi; 1970 = 100): (Feb. 1974) 131; (Feb. 1973) 113.
Foreign Trade. (1973) Imports KShs. 4,305,000,-000; exports KShs. 3,234,000,000. Import sources: U.K. 23%; Uganda 13%; Japan 12%; Tanzania 10%; West Germany 9%; U.S. 8%; Iran 7%. Export destinations: U.K. 12%; West Germany 8%; The Netherlands 5%; U.S. 5%. Main exports: coffee 22%; tea 11%; petroleum products 8%.
Transport and Communications. Roads (1973) 48,206 km. Motor vehicles in use (1973): passenger 116,984; commercial 18,487. Railways: (1972) 2,070 km. (operated under East African Railways Corp., serving Kenya, mainland Tanzania, and Uganda with a total of 5,860 km.); traffic (total East African; 1966) 4,529,000,000 passenger-km., freight (1972) 3,792,-000,000 net ton-km. Air traffic (East African Airways Corp., including also Tanzania and Uganda; 1973): 798 million passenger-km.; freight 30,240,000 ton-km. Telephones (Dec. 1972) 94,000. Radio receivers (Dec. 1972) 500,000. Television receivers (Dec. 1972) 37,-000.
Agriculture. Production (in 000; metric tons; 1973; 1972 in parentheses): corn *c.* 1,300 (1,660); wheat (1972) *c.* 185, (1971) *c.* 206; millet and sorghum *c.* 330 (*c.* 330); coffee *c.* 62 (*c.* 72); tea *c.* 57 (53); sugar, raw value *c.* 114 (*c.* 100); sisal (1972) *c.* 41, (1972) *c.* 45; cotton, lint *c.* 5 (*c.* 5); fish catch (1972) 30, (1971) 35. Livestock (in 000; May 1973): cattle *c.* 9,500; sheep *c.* 3,172; pigs *c.* 77; goats *c.* 4,000; camels *c.* 320; chickens (1972) *c.* 14,000.
Industry. Production (in 000; metric tons; 1972): salt 50; soda ash 164; cement (1973) 792; petroleum products 2,372; electricity (kw-hr.; 1973) 723,000.

three years, were accepted by KANU, and made a cash deposit accompanied by a declaration of loyalty. Oginga Odinga and nine other former leaders of the rival Kenya People's Union unsuccessfully sought Kenyatta's permission to become candidates. The elections, which were held October 14, resulted in the defeat of more than half the incumbent members of Parliament, including several Cabinet ministers. Among them was Foreign Minister Njoroge Mungai, who was replaced by Munyua Waiyaki in the new Cabinet named by Kenyatta October 31. Kenyatta himself was reelected to his seat without opposition.

There were rumours of corruption in high places, and the chairman of the public accounts committee gave warning of a public scandal concerning members of the government and civil service arising out of malpractices in the distribution of low-interest loans and the allocation of the best land in the former White Highlands. In October an English newspaper accused high-ranking members of the government of corrupt dealings in connection with wresting control of a valuable ruby mine from the two U.S. geologists who had discovered it. There were a number of strikes, and after one by bank workers at the end of July all strikes were banned until further notice.

On March 12 Mwai Kibaki, financial and planning minister, introduced a new five-year development plan costing $4.2 billion. But he warned that his target could not be achieved without economies by the public. Rising oil prices and general inflation would also necessitate adjustments in the program. The government's policy of restricting the price of corn had caused middlemen to conclude that there was no profit in dealing in cornmeal (a basic food), and some wholesalers attempted to trade illegally with Uganda and Somalia. Nor was the atmosphere in the commercial world improved by the president's insistence upon the complete africanization of trade before the end of 1974. On February 24 Kenyatta had ordered that all noncitizen traders who had received quit notices must leave the country as soon as their businesses had been handed over. In July Swahili replaced English as Kenya's official language.

Foreign relations called for careful handling. It was announced in March that the country's armed forces would not take part in the UN cease-fire patrols along the Suez Canal, a peacekeeping operation that might have brought Kenya prestige; possibly, fear of developments in Uganda and along the Somali frontier made the government reluctant to weaken its defenses. Although Kenyatta and Pres. Idi Amin of Uganda had resolved their differences, the former was undoubtedly wary of his neighbour's unpredictable actions and was not unaware of the buildup of Uganda's arms with the assistance of the U.S.S.R. At the same time, the relatively peaceful situation that had existed along the Somali frontier since the end of the Shifta war in 1969 was threatened by a demand from a group calling itself the United Liberation Front of Western Somalia for the transfer of a considerable area of territory from Kenya to Somalia. Relations with Tanzania became strained in December, and cross-border traffic was suspended.   (KENNETH INGHAM)

[978.E.6.b.v]

Korea

A country of eastern Asia, Korea is bounded by China, the Sea of Japan, the Korea Strait, and the Yellow Sea. It is divided into two parts at the 38th parallel.

The hopes of Korean unity, generated by secret talks in 1972 and precariously propped up by a propaganda truce in 1973, disappeared in 1974. The old spectre of an imminent invasion from the North was raised anew by the South as it went through traumatic disturbances climaxing in the assassination of Pres. Park Chung Hee's wife. Formal contacts between the two Koreas did take place, and Red Cross negotiators agreed to open working-level meetings for the resumption of full-scale talks. But the momentum of political events rendered the Red Cross exercise largely meaningless.

Republic of Korea (South Korea). Area: 38,025 sq.mi. (98,484 sq.km.). Pop. (1973 est.): 33,177,000. Cap. and largest city: Seoul (pop., 1970, 5,525,262). Language: Korean. Religion: Buddhist; Confucian; Tonghak (Chondokyo). President in 1974, Gen. Park Chung Hee; prime minister, Kim Chong Pil.

It was a bad year for President Park (see BIOGRAPHY). The unprecedented outburst of mass protests in 1973 had apparently hardened his resolve to fight back. In early December 1973 he reconstituted his Cabinet, retaining Kim Chong Pil as prime minister. What followed was a rigorous clamping down on dissenters. During Christmas week the government issued new press laws that banned reports and editorials critical of the president and his political reforms. Violation of the laws was to be treated as a matter of national security. The press laws were followed by tough new emergency measures in January 1974. One proclamation (January 8) prohibited all opposition to the constitution, which had been introduced in 1972 under martial law, with up to 15 years' imprisonment as punishment. Violators were to be tried by "emergency courts-martial." On April 3, after student demonstrations against the constitution, such demonstrations were made a capital offense.

Trials, most of them secret, began soon after the new decrees were promulgated. By mid-May it was announced that 31 dissidents had been sentenced to 5 to 15 years in prison. Another group of 67, including two Japanese, was to go on trial at the same time on charges of antigovernment activities. Altogether, 253 persons were officially transferred to the jurisdiction of the emergency courts-martial. On July 11 the court found 21 persons guilty of plotting student uprisings. Seven were sentenced to death, eight to life imprisonment, and six others to 20 years. By this time trials had become numerous. Among those before

Khmer Republic:
see **Cambodia**

KOREA: Republic

Education. (1973–74) Primary, pupils 5,618,-768, teachers 107,436; secondary, pupils 2,460,-152, teachers 62,318, vocational, students 451,-032, teachers 13,996; higher (including 27 universities), students 240,069, teaching staff 11,749.

Finance. Monetary unit: won, with a free rate (Sept. 16, 1974) of 400 won to U.S. $1 (923 won = £1 sterling). Gold, SDRs, and foreign exchange, central bank: (June 1974) U.S. $1,020,-600,000; (June 1973) U.S. $886.7 million. Budget (1973 actual): revenue 880,210,000,000 won; expenditure 891,050,000,000 won. Gross national product: (1973) 4,993,600,000,000 won; (1972) 3,860,000,000,000 won. Money supply: (Dec. 1973) 730.2 billion won; (Dec. 1972) 521.5 billion won. Cost of living (1970 = 100): (June 1974) 158; (June 1973) 129.

Foreign Trade. (1973) Imports 1,680,000,-000,000 won; exports 1,280,040,000,000 won. Import sources: Japan 41%; U.S. 28%. Export destinations: Japan 39%; U.S. 31%. Main exports: clothing 23%; textile yarns and fabrics 13%; electrical machinery and equipment 10%; plywood 9%; iron and steel 6%.

Transport and Communications. Roads (1973) 43,580 km. (including 1,013 km. expressways). Motor vehicles in use (1972): passenger 70,200; commercial (including buses) 72,100. Railways: (1972) 5,650 km.; traffic (1973) 10,492,000,000 passenger-km., freight 8,394,000,000 net ton-km. Air traffic (1972): 957 million passenger-km.; freight 59.1 million net ton-km. Shipping (1973): merchant vessels 100 gross tons and over 617; gross tonnage 1,103,925. Telephones (Dec. 1972) 755,000. Radio receivers (Dec. 1971) 4.1 million. Television receivers (Dec. 1972) 956,000.

Agriculture. Production (in 000; metric tons; 1973; 1972 in parentheses): rice 5,730 (5,500); wheat 257 (241); barley 2,110 (1,965); potatoes c. 459 (459); sweet potatoes (1972) 1,877, (1971) 1,901; soybeans c. 257 (224); tomatoes c. 60 (c. 60); onions c. 88 (c. 88); apples (1972) c. 230, (1971) 221; grapes (1972) c. 42, (1971) 34; tobacco c. 96 (c. 94); fish catch (1972) 1,-339, (1971) 1,074. Livestock (in 000; Dec. 1972): cattle c. 1,260; pigs c. 1,450; goats c. 95; chickens c. 24,000.

Industry. Production (in 000; metric tons; 1973): coal 13,572; iron ore (50% metal content) 467; steel 1,157; cement 8,175; tungsten concentrates (oxide content; 1972) 2.5; zinc (1972) 10; kaolin (1971) 124; fluorite (1971) 51; limestone (1971) 11,213; gold (troy oz.; 1972) 17; silver (troy oz.; 1972) 1,672; sulfuric acid 454; petroleum products (1972) 12,-108; electricity (excluding most industrial production; kw-hr.) 14,827,000.

KOREA: Democratic People's Republic

Education. (1970–71) Primary, secondary, and vocational, pupils c. 3 million, teachers c. 100,-000; higher, students 214,000, teaching staff (1966–67) 9,244.

Finance and Trade. Monetary unit: won, with (Sept. 16, 1974) an official exchange rate of 0.96 won to U.S. $1 (free nominal rate of 2.30 won = £1 sterling). Budget (1973 est.) balanced at 8,544,000,000 won. Foreign trade (excluding trade with China; 1972 est.): imports c. U.S. $500 million (57% from U.S.S.R., 20% from Japan); exports c. U.S. $300 million (52% to U.S.S.R., 11% to Japan, 6% to France). Main exports (1964): metals 50%; minerals 12%; farm produce 11%.

Agriculture. Production (in 000; metric tons; 1973; 1972 in parentheses): rice c. 2,800 (c. 2,800); corn c. 1,800 (c. 1,800); barley c. 275 (c. 275); potatoes c. 1,000 (c. 1,000); sweet potatoes (1972) c. 290, (1971) c. 280; millet c. 350 (c. 350); apples (1972) c. 120, (1971) c. 120; fish catch (1964) 770, (1963) 640. Livestock (in 000; Dec. 1972): cattle c. 760; pigs c. 1,450; sheep c. 200; goats c. 175; chickens (1971) c. 15,800.

Industry. Production (in 000; metric tons; 1972): iron ore (metal content) c. 4,350; pig iron c. 2,600; steel c. 2,500; coal (1971) c. 24,300; lead 65; zinc c. 120; magnesite (1971) 1,724; electricity (kw-hr.; 1965) 13,300,000.

UPI COMPIX

In the aftermath of the assassination attempt against President Park, an anti-Japanese demonstrator in South Korea hacks off a finger, a bizarre form of protest employed by 14 others outside the Japanese embassy in Seoul. Their effort to deliver the severed fingers, bundled in a South Korean flag, to the Japanese ambassador was rebuffed by police.

the courts were students, priests, professors, and Yun Po Sun, a former president of South Korea. Those already convicted included South Korea's best-known poet, Kim Chi Ha. Some of the death sentences, including that of Kim, were subsequently commuted to life terms. New sentences ranging from five years to life were announced in August, and a Roman Catholic bishop was tried.

On August 15, Independence Day, at a rare public appearance by Park, a man later identified as Mun Se Kwang, a 22-year-old Korean living in Japan, fired shots at the president. He failed to hit him, but a bullet struck Mrs. Park, who was sitting behind her husband. She died some hours later. The Cabinet resigned as a mark of respect and apology, but Park reappointed all except the home minister and the security chief. Two of the four emergency decrees suppressing political activity were lifted, but Park refused to release those in jail or on trial.

From Tokyo the Japanese police said that they had discovered a handwritten memo indicating that Mun had been planning the assassination for a year. In Seoul officials charged that Mun (executed on December 20) was under North Korea's orders. North Korea emphatically denied the allegation and called it part of the Park regime's "dying struggles." Japan, more than North Korea, seemed to be the target of South Korean wrath. Massive demonstrations against Japan broke out in Seoul, with some men resorting to a traditional style of expressing hatred—cutting off one's little finger in public. (U.S. reports said later that the men who did this were former convicts who had been paid by the government to do so.) South Korea officially threatened diplomatic action against Japan. Although Japanese Prime Minister Kakuei Tanaka personally attended Mrs. Park's funeral, South Korea did not seem to be pacified. Eventually, under reported U.S. urging, the two governments said they had officially ended their conflict over the case.

The government's tough policies alienated significant foreign backing, especially in the U.S. Prominent U.S. personalities publicly urged their government to cut further aid to South Korea. Echoing this sentiment, the foreign aid appropriation bill for fiscal 1975,

passed by the U.S. Congress in December, placed a $145 million ceiling on military assistance to South Korea, to be raised to $165 million if the president reported that the country had made substantial progress in observing human rights. U.S. Pres. Gerald Ford himself reaffirmed U.S. military support for South Korea during his brief visit to Seoul November 22–23. The visit sparked an outbreak of antigovernment demonstrations. Opposition members of the National Assembly staged a three-day sit-in in December.

The possibility of a reduction in U.S. aid cast a shadow across South Korea's economy, once among the healthiest in Asia. Although a 12% growth rate was foreseen, as against the 10% which the government wanted, inflation had become a major problem. The trade deficit was expected to double in 1974, and deterioration of relations with Japan could seriously disrupt the whole structure of the economy. The won was devalued by 20% on December 9.

Democratic People's Republic of Korea (North Korea). Area: 46,800 sq.mi. (121,200 sq.km.). Pop. (1973 est.): 15,090,000. Cap.: Pyongyang (metro. pop., 1970 est., 1.5 million). Language: Korean. Religion: Buddhist; Confucian; Tonghak (Chondokyo). General secretary of the Central Committee of the Workers' Party of Korea, president, and chairman of the Council of Ministers (premier) in 1974, Marshal Kim Il Sung.

What had come to look like "routine progress" for Kim Il Sung's enduring government took on added lustre in 1974 against the background of South Korea's turmoil. Kim began the year by rejecting a South Korean proposal for a nonaggression pact on the plea that it would perpetuate the U.S. presence in the South as well as the division of the country. Instead he reiterated his own call for a peace agreement. While the South's leadership was suffering an erosion of international sympathy, North Korea made some diplomatic headway. It established diplomatic relations with Australia, Guinea-Bissau, and Libya.

The U.S. continued to be singled out for hostile treatment. On May 9, a U.S. spokesman said, North Korea had fired on two U.S. Army helicopters near the demilitarized zone. The UN Command in Panmunjom lodged a protest; the North Korean delegate rejected it. For its part, the Pyongyang government condemned the U.S. when it announced the shifting of a squadron of F-4 Phantom bombers from Thailand to South Korea.

As usual President Kim's attention seemed equally divided between foreign policy and economic planning. A series of meetings early in the year set guidelines for several sectors of the economy. The fifth Central Committee of the Workers' Party of Korea, meeting from February 11 to 13, called for "general mobilization of all efforts" to fulfill ten major production goals to be attained "in the next perspective plan." Exact target achievements continued to be given in the form of percentages, and the usual claim that they had all been fulfilled ahead of time accompanied the percentage figures.

In late February Kim proclaimed a decree reducing the prices of manufactured goods by an average of 30%. He said the successes achieved in industry and agriculture had led to markedly increased production of mass consumption goods. Reports from Pyongyang in May said that during the past year geologic prospectors had found ten promising ore deposits and 300 ore veins in the country. Sizable coal deposits were also claimed to have been found. Meeting in March, the Supreme People's Assembly abolished all taxes in North Korea. These had constituted less than 2% of the government's revenue.   (T. J. S. GEORGE)

[975.C]

Kuwait

An independent emirate, Kuwait is on the northwestern coast of the Persian Gulf between Iraq and Saudi Arabia. Area: 6,880 sq.mi. (17,818 sq.km.). Pop. (1973 est.): 883,000. Cap.: Kuwait (pop., 1973, 93,050). Largest city: Hawalli (pop., 1973, 125,310). Language: Arabic. Religion (1970): Muslim 94.7%; Christian 4.6%. Emir in 1974, Sheikh Sabah as-Salim as-Sabah; prime minister, Crown Prince Sheikh Jabir al-Ahmad al-Jabir as-Sabah.

During 1974 Kuwait used its increased oil revenues to step up its aid and loans to Arab countries and to invest more funds in the West. In March the capital of the Kuwait Fund for Arab Economic Development was increased from 200 million dinars (about $680 million) to 1 billion dinars, giving it a lending potential of $10 billion. Loans to Egypt, Syria, Tunisia, and Yemen (Aden) were approved during the year. The government and the National Assembly also made a grant of $360 million "for the Arab cause," about two-thirds of which went to Syria. In September the Kuwait Investment Office in London caused a stir in financial circles with a successful £107 million bid for the shares of a major London property company. In December the West German government disclosed that Kuwait had purchased a 14% interest in the automobile-manufacturing firm of Daimler-Benz.

On January 29 Kuwait acquired a 60% share in the Kuwait Oil Co. Ratification was delayed until May 14, as many deputies, supported by unions and students' associations, demanded full nationalization; this was effected on December 22, when a 100% takeover of the operating companies, British Petroleum and Gulf Oil, was announced. The 1974–75 budget showed a 73% increase in oil revenues over 1973–74. The government resisted demands for a 50% reduction in oil output to maintain prices and conserve reserves, although production, at about 2.6 million bbl. a day, was below the pre-October 1973 level of

some 3 million bbl. a day. In January the government put up 85 million bbl. of its own oil for auction, but a month later the Kuwaiti press reported that only 18 million bbl. had been sold and this below the posted price of $11.55 per barrel.

Five terrorists representing the Popular Front for the Liberation of Palestine and the Japanese left-wing Red Army occupied the Japanese embassy in Kuwait on February 6, holding hostages and demanding free passage for fellow terrorists trapped in Singapore; their demands were met. (*See* SINGAPORE.)

The cost of living was officially declared to have risen 13% in 1973. In June a 20–25% increase in all government workers' salaries was decreed, but bank workers, who had been offered a 15% rise, struck for a week. In June a Free Democratic Group was formed, mainly of professional men and university lecturers, with a program that included equal employment and property rights for non-Kuwaitis and votes for women. During 1974 Kuwait allocated $1.2 billion to strengthen its armed forces; $312 million went to buy 32 French Mirage aircraft.   (PETER MANSFIELD)

[978.B.4.b]

Laos

A constitutional monarchy of Southeast Asia, Laos is bounded by China, North and South Vietnam, Cambodia, Thailand, and Burma. Area: 91,400 sq.mi. (236,800 sq.km.). Pop. (1973 est.): 3,181,000. Administrative cap. and largest city: Vientiane (pop., 1973, 176,637). Royal cap.: Louangphrabang (Luang Prabang; pop., 1973, 44,200). Language: Lao (official); French and English. Religion: Buddhist; tribal. King, Savang Vatthana; premier in 1974, Prince Souvanna Phouma.

The third attempt in 20 years to establish a neutral Laos got under way in April 1974 with the formation of the long-awaited coalition government. It was not easy. For more than a year after the Laos cease-fire agreement was signed, the Vientiane government and Communist Pathet Lao argued about administrative details. The main bone of contention was the neu-

KUWAIT
Education. (1973–74) Primary, pupils 94,087, teachers 5,033; secondary, pupils 88,922, teachers 7,283; vocational, pupils 2,187, teachers 390; teacher training, students 847, teachers 98; higher (1972–73), students 3,116, teaching staff 152.
Finance. Monetary unit: Kuwaiti dinar, with (Sept. 16, 1974) a par value of 0.296 dinar to U.S. $1 (free rate of 0.677 dinar = £1 sterling). Gold and foreign exchange, official: (June 1974) U.S. $935.3 million; (June 1973) U.S. $544.9 million. Budget (1973–74 est.): revenue 568 million dinars; expenditure 470.1 million dinars. Money supply: (March 1974) 195.9 million dinars; (March 1973) 179.4 million dinars.
Foreign Trade. (1973) Imports 310.6 million dinars; exports 1,129,800,000 dinars. Import sources (1972): Japan 16%; U.S. 13%; U.K. 10%; West Germany 8%; Lebanon 5%; Italy 5%. Export destinations (1972): Japan 17%; U.K. 13%; France 12%; The Netherlands 12%; Italy 9%; Singapore 5%. Main export petroleum 92%.
Industry. Production (in 000; metric tons; 1973): crude oil 138,357; natural gas (cu.m.) 6,580,000; petroleum products (1971) 22,893.

LAOS
Education. (1972–73) Primary, pupils 273,357, teachers 7,320; secondary, pupils 14,633, teachers 613; vocational, pupils 1,946, teachers 186; teacher training, students 4,031, teachers 227; higher, students 625, teaching staff 106.
Finance. Monetary unit: kip, with (Sept. 16, 1974) an official exchange rate of 600 kip to U.S. $1 (nominal free rate of 1,400 kip = £1 sterling). Budget (1973–74 est.): revenue (excluding foreign aid) 12.5 billion kip; expenditure 27.5 billion kip (including defense expenditure of 13 billion kip).
Foreign Trade. (1972) Imports 26,205,000,000 kip; exports 1,753,000,000 kip. Import sources: Thailand 47%; U.S. 16%; Japan 9%; Indonesia 8%. Export destinations: France c. 41%; Thailand c. 30%; Malaysia c. 19%. Main exports: tin 60%; timber 37%.
Transport and Communications. Roads (1972) 7,300 km. (including c. 3,300 km. all-weather). Motor vehicles in use (1972): passenger 12,700; commercial (including buses) 2,200. Air traffic (1972): 21 million passenger-km.; freight 500,000 net ton-km. Telephones (Dec. 1972) 4,000. Radio licenses (Dec. 1971) 51,000.
Agriculture. Production (in 000; metric tons; 1973; 1972 in parentheses): rice c. 750 (700); corn (1972) 36, (1971) 28; coffee c. 3 (c. 3); tobacco c. 4 (c. 4). Livestock (in 000; 1972–73): cattle c. 450; buffalo c. 950; pigs c. 1,200; chickens c. 13,000.
Industry. Production (in 000; 1972): tin concentrates (metric tons) 1.9; electricity (excluding most industrial production; kw-hr.) 64,000.

Labour Unions:
see Industrial Relations

tralization, as stipulated in the cease-fire agreement, of the political and royal capitals, Vientiane and Luang Prabang. Agreement was finally reached on February 6 on the organization of a joint police force and neutral administration for the two towns. Private parleys continued in the two camps about the groups and personalities to be included in the Cabinet and in the National Political Council, the all-important advisory committee that was to set broad policy guidelines. With the lists completed and Pathet Lao anxiety about reliable security arrangements for its leaders assuaged, the coalition was launched.

On April 3 the Pathet Lao leader, Prince Souphanouvong (see BIOGRAPHY), landed at Vientiane airport. He and his party colleagues had left their mountain hideout in Sam Neua three days earlier and had gone to Hanoi first. In an emotional scene at the airport the "Red Prince" embraced his half-brother, Prince Souvanna Phouma, the premier, then drove three miles to his new residence to the cheers of tens of thousands of people massed on both sides of the road. Two days later the Cabinet (consisting of 12 members, 5 of each side and 2 neutrals) and the National Political Council (42 members, 16 of each side and 10 neutrals) were sworn in. Souvanna Phouma remained as premier, while the Pathet Lao leader Phoumi Vongvichit became vice-premier and minister for foreign affairs. The Pathet Lao also received the portfolios of economy and planning, information, public works, and religion. The Vientiane side received a vice-premiership and the portfolios of education, defense, interior, finance, and public health. Two neutrals were appointed ministers of justice and of posts and telegraphs. Prince Souphanouvong became president of the National Political Council with two vice-chairmen drawn from the two sides.

Despite the meticulousness of the balancing act, the Pathet Lao quickly emerged as the dominant partner in both the Cabinet and the council. On May 11, Constitution Day, the National Assembly did not open its session as it should have done. The Pathet Lao members of the Cabinet argued that the old National Assembly (elected while the war was still being fought and mostly right-wing) was not representative of the people. Subsequently, the assembly was dissolved (see below). Constitution Day also served to highlight the brittleness of Vientiane's political temper. The night before, Phoumi Vongvichit telephoned the International Control Commission (ICC) to say that tanks were closing in on his Pathet Lao villa. An ICC military official toured the town and found no tanks. Nevertheless, leaflets appeared the next day accusing the right of plotting a coup. Many took the incident as a genuine case of nerves (Phoumi had been arrested when the first coalition Cabinet collapsed), but others considered it Pathet Lao pressure tactics.

The functioning of the National Political Council also underlined the power of the Pathet Lao. On May 10 Prince Souphanouvong gave a lengthy speech in the council. Two weeks later the council adopted an 18-point program for a "peaceful, independent, neutral, democratic, united, and prosperous Kingdom of Laos." The program closely followed the recommendations of the Pathet Lao leader. A Pathet Lao-supported candidate became the mayor of Vientiane. The Pathet Lao view that no foreign aid money should be used for family planning in Laos prevailed. Sam Neua and the four-fifths of Laos under Communist control remained out of bounds to neutralist and rightist officials from Vientiane.

The rightists in the Cabinet and outside began to grow restive, but their efforts to choose a leader of strength were in vain because no one leader was able to command the loyalty of all of them. In an act of apparent desperation, the rightists staged a demonstration in Vientiane on July 9. They also assembled about 1,000 persons to protest against the continued North Vietnamese military presence in the country. Government police cordoned off the assembly and the crowd dispersed after 12 hours. The government, at a Cabinet meeting, dissolved the National Assembly on July 10. On July 12, Premier Souvanna Phouma suffered a mild heart attack. The two vice-premiers were put in charge of day-to-day affairs during the premier's illness. But Pathet Lao's Phoumi Vongvichit was considered "more equal" than the rightist Leuam Insisiengmay. In early August, Phoumi Vongvichit was named acting premier.

One issue over which some headway was made during 1974 was that of the withdrawal of foreign troops. The agreed deadline for withdrawal was June 4. Two weeks ahead of it the last Thai troops left, ending a decade of direct military involvement in Laos. This was also seen as the end of direct U.S. involvement, for the Thai mercenaries had been maintained by the U.S. Central Intelligence Agency (CIA). The number of U.S. troops in Laos was reduced from 1,100 at the cease-fire to 472 at the withdrawal deadline. North Vietnamese troops reportedly remained in Laos although they had "withdrawn into the scenery." Western sources estimated their strength as between 30,000 and 60,000.

It was too early to say how the Laotian economy, long dependent on U.S. aid, was faring under the new regime. Immediately after the government was formed, the U.S., Britain, France, Japan, and Australia renewed their aid to Laos. This aid, in the form of donations to a foreign exchange operations fund, was customarily administered by agreement between Laos and the five donor countries. Rumours that the kip might be devalued sent the currency on a downward spiral. But the Cabinet decided against devaluation and planned to introduce foreign exchange control, import restrictions, a revised tax structure, and new export regulations.

The Cabinet made it clear that it intended to accept economic aid from Communist and non-Communist countries. But U.S. Sen. Edward Kennedy (Dem., Mass.) expressed concern in June that U.S. aid, going exclusively to the non-Communist side in Laos, might perpetuate the political divisions there. For the fiscal year beginning July 1, the U.S. administration asked for $86.1 million in military aid to Laos. Officials acknowledged that according to plans then current most of the aid would go to the "Royal Laotian" side because the U.S. was continuing existing programs, which were naturally in areas controlled by the former non-Communist government.   (T. J. S. GEORGE)

[976.B.4.e]

Latin-American Affairs

Relations with the U.S. A two-day meeting of the 22 foreign ministers and one representative of the Organization of American States (OAS) was held in Washington, D.C., on April 17–18, 1974, immediately before the OAS general assembly at Atlanta, Ga., to discuss a "new dialogue," worked out at Tlatelolco, Mex., on February 21–23. At the Mexico meeting the

Latin-American delegates considered that they had been successful over two major issues, which were formulated in the Declaration of Tlatelolco: the promise of a maximum effort by the Nixon administration of the U.S. to secure passage of legislation on preferential tariffs in 1974, and the avoidance of any new measures that would restrict access of Latin-American goods to the U.S. market. U.S. Secretary of State Henry Kissinger's visit to Panama, where on February 7 he signed a "declaration of principles" on a new Panama Canal Zone treaty, added weight to the general feeling prevalent at the Mexico conference that the U.S. Department of State would take action on the various issues raised in the Tlatelolco declaration. Subsequently, however, the Watergate debate, the Middle East crisis, and the fostering of the U.S.-Soviet détente frustrated any serious attempt by Kissinger to improve Western Hemisphere relations. Even the Panama initiative was thwarted when 32 U.S. senators on March 29 voted a "declaration of doubt" on the new canal deal. The U.S. standpoint was still that of maintaining "perpetual" sovereign rights over the canal, whereas the Panamanians were intent on winning back control over the area. An additional complication to the negotiations was the U.S. proposal to build a sea-level canal to accommodate larger vessels; the Panamanians were reluctant to accept such a project.

With the resignation of Richard Nixon from the presidency of the United States on August 9, many observers felt that Latin America stood to benefit substantially. These expectations were seriously dampened, however, following the reports of U.S. intrigue and covert activity in Chile that had been aimed at the overthrow of the administration of Salvador Allende. Kissinger's responsibility in these matters seemed likely to lose him credibility in Latin America as a whole, as well as to destroy much of the goodwill he had earned. His delicate position might however be restored by the choice of Nelson Rockefeller to fill the post of vice-president and of William D. Rogers that of assistant secretary of state for inter-American affairs. Both men had long been associated with Latin America, and were known to hold "realistic" views on the U.S. role in the region.

Some progress was made in resolving the Cuban question. It was reported in August that the U.S. was considering lifting the trade embargo in force against Cuba since the early 1960s; the sales to Cuba by subsidiaries in Argentina of General Motors, Ford, and Chrysler in May and July were thought to be the first signs of such a move. Kissinger reportedly requested the Mexican foreign minister to discuss Cuban relations with the U.S. and Latin America with Fidel Castro during his visit to Havana. As a result of these discussions Castro stated that Cuban representatives would attend the Latin-American foreign ministers' conference in 1975 "in a constructive spirit." In August U.S. Pres. Gerald Ford hinted that his administration was studying a renewal of ties with Cuba.

Most Latin-American countries considered the isolation of Cuba as an example of U.S. imperialistic thrust, and the U.S., with the failure of the trade blockade, realized that Cuba was in fact no more than a nuisance in the way of hemisphere development. Pressure on the OAS was brought to bear by Costa Rica and Colombia, which wanted action to come from the OAS by joint approval and not by a series of withdrawals from the blockade concept.

At the request of Colombia, Costa Rica, and Vene-

The Organization of American States convenes in the House of Representatives chamber of the Georgia State Capitol in Atlanta.

zuela the foreign ministers of the OAS met in November at Quito, Ecuador, to consider lifting the Cuban blockade. The final vote was 12 in favour and 3 against with 6 abstentions. Thus, the measure failed by two votes to gain the necessary two-thirds majority, and the sanctions against the Castro regime remained in force. Voting in favour were Costa Rica, Colombia, Venezuela, Honduras, Argentina, El Salvador, Ecuador, Trinidad and Tobago, Mexico, Peru, Panama, and the Dominican Republic. Chile, Paraguay, and Uruguay voted against, and the U.S., Brazil, Bolivia, Guatemala, Haiti, and Nicaragua abstained.

The agreement between the U.S. and Peru on compensation for nationalized U.S. properties was an important step by the Nixon administration toward easing the position of all U.S. companies in Latin America. Under the agreement a total settlement of $150 million was to be made by Peru, $74 million to be paid directly to five companies and $76 million to the U.S. government for distribution to the U.S. companies. The Peruvian government specifically listed only 11 companies with legitimate claims, but a 12th was the International Petroleum Co. (IPC), the Exxon subsidiary that had been nationalized in 1968. Although the expropriated companies had been expecting compensation of more than $200 million, the deal was a diplomatic masterpiece, especially regarding the controversial IPC issue, which had soured relations between the two countries since the takeover by the military regime in 1968.

U.S. relations with Chile continued to improve after the overthrow of Allende. Although Chile had settled compensation claims with Anaconda and the Cerro Corp., a similar agreement with the Kennecott Copper Corp. for the nationalization of its local copper-producing subsidiaries was still pending. Despite the protracted negotiations the "fair" image that Chile had acquired for itself in the international financial community was unlikely to be affected. Another point that would further improve relations with the U.S. and foreign investors in general was the passing of a new Chilean foreign investment statute, which labeled foreign capital as "indispensable" and guaranteed to it the same rights and duties as those granted to local firms. A range of incentives was offered, including total or partial exemption from tariffs on imports of capital goods, guaranteed repatriation of capital, and the right to remit profits abroad. By granting overtly favourable conditions to foreign capital, however, Chile risked alienating some of its Andean Group partners with whom it had agreements for a common investment policy as embodied in Decision No. 24 of the Cartagena Agreement (*see* below). Decision No. 24 specified that foreign firms were to be subject to an annual remittance limit of 14% of registered capital and provided for the gradual transformation of a foreign company into a mixed or national concern.

Inter-American Development Bank. The 15th meeting of the Board of Governors of the IDB was held in Santiago, Chile, on April 1–3. Despite record levels of activity the bank needed new capital to maintain growth, and on terms that would enable it to maintain its ratio of concessionary loans. The major items approved at the meeting were a Venezuelan proposal to establish a special trust fund to be administered by the IDB; a study of the bank's charter to verify whether there were impediments to financing exports to countries outside the region; and the acceptance, in advance, of applications for membership by Guyana and The Bahamas. The discussion of a project for 12 Western European and Pacific nations to join the bank as associate members and provide $500 million in funds was postponed to the meeting of the governors in November. At this meeting 12 European countries and Japan were accepted as associate members, paying total subscriptions of $755 million ($450 million of it in cash) and having two executive directors and 8% of the votes.

In preparation for the October meeting the Board of Governors met in June to study a report from the bank's Executive Board on the possibility of increasing the bank's resources. The report stated that the bank planned to raise the annual level of loans from $884 million in 1973 to $1 billion by the end of 1974, and to exceed this volume from 1975 onward.

International Bank for Reconstruction and Development. The IBRD stated in its 1972–73 annual report that the combined gross national product (GNP) of the Latin-American and Caribbean countries increased by an average annual rate of 5.6% during the 1963–72 decade and that annual growth reached 7% in the last four years of that period. The increase in population, at a rate of 3% a year, was accompanied by a massive exodus from the rural areas, transforming basically rural societies into mainly urban ones in which progress was not shared either by all the countries or by all the social levels. This change in population distribution coincided with the transformation of the economic structure; the share of agriculture both in the GNP and in the labour force declined while the industrial, construction, and transport sectors expanded. Despite the large increase in the population, the income per capita rose substantially, standing in 1972 at $590, whereas the corresponding figure for the less developed countries of the world as a whole reached only $250.

Regional and Subregional Integration. Notwithstanding the weaknesses and failures of the Latin American Free Trade Association (LAFTA) as a viable integration mechanism, some progress was recorded in the expansion of intraregional trade: imports within LAFTA were valued at $2,069,000,000 in 1973, representing an increase of 27% over the figure for 1972. The principal importers in 1973 were Brazil ($589 million), Argentina ($440 million), Chile ($267 million), Peru ($174 million), Mexico ($126 million), and Uruguay ($122 million); the main exporters were Argentina ($747 million), Brazil ($543 million), Mexico ($156 million), Venezuela ($142 million), Chile ($127 million), and Colombia ($123 million). LAFTA exports to, and imports from, the rest of the world totaled $15,915,000,000 and $16,383,000,000, respectively, in 1973, representing increases of 28 and 19% over the 1972 figures. The resulting trade deficit of $468 million compared with one of $1,333,000,000 in 1972.

With regard to the Andean Group (Bolivia, Chile, Colombia, Ecuador, Peru, and Venezuela [joined 1973], with Argentina reported in October to be considering membership), significant progress was made in 1974 to maintain the momentum of integration already achieved. The all-important joint industrial planning mechanism was gradually getting under way, though there was dissension on the implementation of Decision No. 24 on foreign investment. By 1974 Peru and Venezuela were the only countries to have fully introduced Decision No. 24, and new foreign capital was unlikely to be attracted to the subregion until all the rules of the game had been clearly defined. Several industrial programs involving the region still had to be negotiated before the deadline at the end of 1975, when products reserved for sectorial development would automatically revert to the general trade liberalization procedure if they had not already been incorporated into individual programs.

A uniform interpretation of Decision No. 24 was expected to be made more difficult to formulate in view of the very liberal stance taken by Chile toward foreign investment. The Chilean military junta issued its new foreign investment law (Decree-Law No. 600) in July, and it appeared to have little in common with Andean legislation: the new law made no provision for the gradual transformation of a foreign company into a mixed or national concern nor did it establish a maximum limit for the remittance of profits abroad. By making its own legal framework more attractive to foreign investors, Chile allowed its national economic priorities to take precedence over Andean Group considerations. At a meeting in September, Chile's partners agreed that the Chilean statute contravened the spirit of Decision No. 24, but at a further meeting in November it was decided that Decree-Law No. 600 did not violate Decision No. 24. It was unlikely, however, that foreign investors who took advantage of the favourable Chilean foreign investment law would be allowed to benefit from the trade advantages afforded by the Cartagena Agreement to mixed and national companies.

In regard to the Central American Common Market (CACM; Costa Rica, El Salvador, Guatemala, Honduras, and Nicaragua), scant progress was made toward regional economic integration. Despite the significant increase in the absolute value of regional trade, its share of total trade was the same (23%) in 1973 as in 1972. The high-level committee that was studying the restructuring of the CACM presented constructive plans for industrial development and tariff harmonization, but there was doubt as to the extent of the political consensus needed to implement the proposals. The chief obstacle continued to be the unresolved dispute between El Salvador and Honduras stemming from their war in 1969. Both countries faced domestic problems that hampered the granting of concessions. El Salvador was experiencing a high level of unemployment, while the agrarian reform program in Honduras was making little headway. Elsewhere, too, more pressing difficulties drew attention away from the integration process. The reconstruction problems in the aftermath of the Managua earthquake in Nicaragua, and later the severe damage caused by Hurricane Fifi in Honduras further delayed any marked progress toward integration.

(WILLIAM BELTRÁN)

[971.D.8; 974.C-H]

ENCYCLOPÆDIA BRITANNICA FILMS. *Venezuela: Oil Builds a Nation* (1973); *Central America: Finding New Ways* (2nd ed., 1974); *Costa Rica My Country* (2nd ed., 1974).

Law

Court Decisions and Related Developments. Important judicial decisions throughout the world were somewhat overshadowed in 1974 by the "presidential tapes" case handed down by the U.S. Supreme Court, which was an instrumental, if not the critical, turning point in the decision of Richard Nixon to resign from the office of president of the United States. The work of the Supreme Court was also significant in the areas of censorship and free speech and press, as were decisions on these matters from Great Britain, West Germany, Denmark, and Spain. The Supreme Court of Ireland and trial courts in Israel and France also decided cases of major importance and worldwide significance.

United States of America v. *Richard M. Nixon.* On March 1 a grand jury returned an indictment against seven former Nixon administration staff members and campaign officials, charging them with various offenses, including conspiracy to defraud the United States and to obstruct justice. The seven defendants were former attorney general John N. Mitchell; former White House chief of staff H. R. Haldeman; former domestic affairs adviser John D. Ehrlichman; Charles W. Colson, former White House lawyer; Robert C. Mardian, Nixon's 1972 campaign coordinator; Kenneth W. Parkinson, lawyer for the Committee for the Re-election of the President; and Gordon C. Strachan, an assistant to Haldeman. All had responsibilities in their work directly connecting them to President Nixon. In this work certain tape recordings of conversations they had had with President Nixon had been made by him, and he also had certain documents prepared relating to these conversations. The special prosecutor filed an appropriate motion to subpoena these tapes and documents for use in the prosecution of the seven defendants. Nixon, claiming executive privilege, filed a motion to quash the subpoena. District Court Judge John J. Sirica ruled that the president must obey the subpoena and turn over the tapes and documents to him for a private review of their contents. This review, he held, would protect the president from having divulged in court, or otherwise, any materials affecting the national security. Nixon appealed to the United States Supreme Court, arguing two basic propositions: (1) that the dispute between him and the special prosecutor was "nonjusticiable"—that is, a nonreviewable political matter—between him and another member of the executive branch of the government; and (2) that the judicial branch of government lacked authority to review his assertion of executive privilege because of the constitutional doctrine of separation of powers which makes coequal the three branches of government—the executive, the legislative, and the judicial. This second point was buttressed by the argument that, irrespective of the principle of separation of powers, the need for confidentiality of presidential conversations overbalanced any need for testimony in any given criminal trial. On July 24, in a landmark decision, the Supreme Court rejected all these contentions and ordered President Nixon to turn over the tapes and documents as directed by Judge Sirica. Nixon complied with the decision, avoiding a constitutional confrontation of major proportions. Shortly thereafter he resigned his office in the wake of revelations from the tapes and documents that apparently implicated him in the criminal activities charged against the seven defendants.

Although the immediate and dramatic effect of the decision was to cause the resignation of the president of the United States, the importance of *United States* v. *Nixon* as a milestone of constitutional law cannot be exaggerated and may well prove to be the more enduring aspect of the case. Specifically, the court decided two issues that had been hotly debated: (1) that it has the power to review interbranch disputes occurring in the other branches of government; and (2) that neither the doctrine of separation of powers nor the need for confidentiality of high-level communications can sustain an absolute presidential immunity from judicial process. The real importance of the decision, however, lies in the fact that it establishes the proposition that the courts, and only the courts, have the authority to resolve constitutional issues with finality.

This proposition was sharply denied by President Nixon's attorney, James D. St. Clair (*see* BIOGRAPHY), in his presentation of the case to the Supreme Court. He insisted that the court was not the final arbiter of the range and scope of presidential privilege because of separation of powers doctrine, and that it had no business trying to resolve a dispute between the president and the special prosecutor, since both are members of the executive branch of the government. His presence in court, he argued, was not an admission that the court had jurisdiction to resolve these questions. "This matter," he said, "is being submitted to this court for its guidance and judgment with respect to the law. The president, on the other hand, has his obligations under the Constitution."

Special Prosecutor Leon Jaworski (*see* BIOGRAPHY) also approached the case through the same issue. "When boiled down," he argued to the court, "this case really presents one fundamental issue: who is to be the arbiter of what the Constitution says?" To him the answer was clear, that this power reposed with the court. The president cannot be the judge of his own constitutional powers, he contended, because if he is wrong on these matters "there is no one . . . to tell him so." This would leave him "free to pursue his course of erroneous interpretations [and] what then becomes of our constitutional form of government?" The court accepted Jaworski's views and rejected those of St. Clair.

Unasked in the Nixon case was the obverse of Jaworski's question: If the court is wrong on a matter of constitutional interpretation, who is there to tell it so? What limits are there on its freedom to pursue a course of erroneous interpretation? If there is none, what then becomes of the constitutional form of government? The court inferentially answered one of these questions: when there are disputes as to the meaning of the Constitution resort must be made to some umpire, and under the U.S. Constitution the

Latin-American Literature: *see* Literature

Latter-day Saints: *see* Religion

umpire is the U.S. Supreme Court. This answer and the other two unanswered questions will constitute the subject matter of serious debate for years to come.

Censorship. Justice John Harlan once referred to the "intractable obscenity" problem that was plaguing the Supreme Court by requiring it to determine in each case whether allegedly obscene materials could be suppressed or were protected by the First Amendment to the Constitution. The Supreme Court thought it had solved this problem by its decision in *Miller* v. *California* (1973). That case reaffirmed earlier holdings that the test of obscenity involved a consideration of: (1) whether the work depicted or described, in a patently offensive way, sexual conduct specifically defined by the applicable state law; and (2) whether the work taken as a whole lacks serious literary, artistic, political, or scientific value. But *Miller* held that these tests were to be made in terms of whether an average person, applying contemporary community standards, would find that the work, taken as a whole, appeals to prurient interests. By permitting local juries to "apply contemporary community standards" rather than speculate on national standards, the court made it clear that the finding of obscenity would no longer be made on a uniform basis and that what was obscene in a small town might not be found to be obscene in New York City. By being relieved of the obligation to find particular material either obscene or not obscene for all places, the court had hoped that it had solved this "intractable problem." But in 1974 the case of *Jenkins* v. *Georgia* showed that this hope was too optimistic. In that case Jenkins, the manager of a theatre in a small town in Georgia, had been convicted of violating the Georgia obscenity statute for showing the film *Carnal Knowledge.* This film had been critically acclaimed as one of the ten best pictures of 1971 and Ann-Margret, its star, had been nominated for an Academy Award for her performance in the picture. Nevertheless, the jury found the film to be "patently offensive" when tested by community standards. The Supreme Court reversed the conviction, pointing out that the use of contemporary community standards as the basic approach to determining whether or not material is obscene does not give juries the unbridled discretion to find that something is obscene simply because it is offensive to them. Although community standards are the basic framework, it is still necessary to find in the light of them that the particular material depicts or describes, in a patently offensive way, sexual conduct specifically identified as obscene in the applicable state statute, and that the work, taken as a whole, lacks serious artistic, literary, political, or scientific value. Findings on these matters are subject to appellate review. In a concurring opinion, Justice William Brennan observed that it is now clear that the new formulation in *Miller* "does not extricate us from the mire of case-by-case determinations of obscenity."

In *Hamling* v. *United States,* however, the court upheld a conviction of four individuals and two firms for mailing an obscene advertisement. The materials advertised for sale an illustrated version of the 1970 report made by the President's Commission on Obscenity and Pornography and contained a number of explicit photographs that depicted various aspects of sex described in the report. The case was tried in San Diego, Calif., and the defense had offered as evidence the results of a survey of "local standards" of obscenity which showed that the majority of people

in the San Diego area did not regard the advertisement as obscene. The trial court rejected this offer of proof on the ground that the advertisement was being circulated nationally and therefore must be judged by national standards. The Supreme Court appeared to agree with this approach.

Freedom of Speech and Press. In *Gertz* v. *Welch* the Supreme Court clarified its position on defamation actions brought against publishers and broadcasters. In a case decided in 1964, *Times Co.* v. *Sullivan,* the court had held that a public official could not hold a newspaper liable for defamatory remarks unless he could prove that they had been made maliciously. Any other rule, it opined, could lead to intolerable self-censorship, for it would compel a publisher or broadcaster to guarantee the accuracy of his factual assertions. The *Gertz* case in 1974 substantially restricted this broad doctrine by limiting it to public officials and figures. Gertz, a private person without much public standing, was permitted to recover damages for libelous statements made in good faith by a monthly newspaper. In writing the opinion Justice Lewis Powell reaffirmed the holding of *Times Co.* v. *Sullivan* for public officials but pointed out it did not apply to private persons: "The communications media are entitled to act on the assumption that public officials and public figures have voluntarily exposed themselves to increased risk of injury from defamatory falsehoods concerning them. No such assumption is justified with respect to a private individual."

The impact of *Gertz* v. *Welch,* however, was somewhat limited by another decision of the Supreme Court in 1974, namely *Letter Carriers* v. *Austin.* In that case Austin and two other postal employees who had not joined the letter carriers' union were defamed in a newsletter published by the union. Although Austin and the others were not public figures, the court held that the union was not guilty of libel. The court, through Justice Thurgood Marshall, argued that U.S. labour policy was to encourage uninhibited, robust, and wide-open debate in labour disputes and, accordingly, "statements of fact or opinion relevant to a union organizing campaign are protected . . . even if they are defamatory and prove to be erroneous, unless made with knowledge of their falsity."

In *Miami Herald Publishing Co.* v. *Tornillo* the U.S. Supreme Court held unconstitutional the "right-to-reply" statute of the state of Florida. This statute gave political candidates the right to reply, free of cost and with equal space and conspicuousness, to any criticism by a newspaper. The court said that this statute violated freedom of the press.

Important decisions on freedom of speech and press were also handed down in Europe in 1974. In Denmark the editor of a leading newspaper was sentenced to prison for 14 days for invasion of privacy. His crime was the publication of a nude picture of a woman who had been murdered. In West Germany, where the news media had won a significant legislative victory in 1966 when a "press law" was passed giving editors, journalists, and broadcasters the right to refuse to reveal their sources of information, the Federal Constitutional Court declared in 1974 that the "press law" was void to the extent that it gives editors, journalists, and broadcasters a greater privilege to refuse to supply evidence than is provided by the Criminal Procedure Ordinance. The Criminal Procedure Ordinance gives them the privilege to refuse to reveal their sources only in criminal proceedings where the content of the publication may be criminal.

In Spain a military court acquitted a lawyer on a charge of insulting the armed forces. This celebrated case involved a lawyer who had suggested that the police explanation of a shooting incident was "inexact." The House of Lords, Great Britain's highest court, was called upon to construe sec. 134 of the Industrial Relations Act of 1971. This act guarantees the right of "peaceful picketing." The court affirmed this right, but held that it does not include the right of a picket to stop an automobile or to force a person to listen to him.

Several other interesting cases from Europe involved the questions of the movement of people and goods. In a decision that surprised many legal observers, the Supreme Court of Ireland declared unconstitutional a provision of the criminal law which barred the importation of contraceptives. The decision made it clear, however, that the sale of contraceptives still remained illegal. The Supreme Court of Ireland also was involved in an emotional case concerning the conflict in Northern Ireland. The case dealt with an effort by Northern Ireland to extradite two men from the Republic of Ireland for purposes of trying them on charges of possessing explosives and attempted murder. The court held that these charges were political and therefore outside the scope of the Extradition Act.

The British Court of Appeal had occasion in 1974 to reconcile the English Immigration Act of 1971 with a maxim of international law that "the home state of expelled persons is bound to receive them on the home territory." The Immigration Act of 1971 divides immigrants into "patrials" and "nonpatrials." Under this law a nonpatrial requires leave to enter the country. The court held that certain Asian citizens of Uganda who had been expelled by that country were nonpatrials because they had become citizens of Uganda after that country became independent of Great Britain. In writing the opinion, Lord Denning held that the statement "the home state of expelled persons is bound to receive them in the home territory" probably is not a rule of international law. Even if it is, he argued, it is enforceable only between the various states and not by private individuals.

Two judicial developments from Israel and France proved to be interesting and important. A district court of Jerusalem held that the Russian Orthodox Church Outside of Russia is the true owner of some extremely valuable real estate in Israel. The property had been acquired by the Russian Orthodox Church prior to 1917 and taken over by emigré priests after the Russian Revolution. The church in the Soviet Union claimed title to the property, but refused to be joined in the lawsuit. In France a scandal that threatened the Bordeaux wine industry finally found its way to court. Several prominent wine dealers were convicted of adulterating and mislabeling inferior wine to make it appear to be Bordeaux wine. The publicity attending the apprehension and trial of the defendants greatly depreciated the value of Bordeaux wine specifically and injured the French wine industry generally. (WILLIAM D. HAWKLAND)

International Law. The major event in the field of international law during 1974 was the third UN Conference on the Law of the Sea; but the subject was too big and the changes of attitude were too fundamental for the ten-week session to have more than

an educational function, and all decisions were postponed to a continuation of the conference in 1975. The vital importance of a successful outcome, however, was emphasized by a steady progression throughout 1974 of both technological advances and legal developments. (*See* SPECIAL REPORT.)

In such a context the judgment of the International Court of Justice in July holding that Iceland was in breach of its international law obligations in unilaterally extending its fishery limits to 50 mi., while being impeccable as a statement of law, give a Canute-like impression in face of the almost irresistible tide of political pressures. In fact Iceland, refusing to recognize the jurisdiction of the court, ignored the judgment and was preparing an extension to 200 mi. More significantly, Norway was preparing to follow suit, but for slightly different reasons. After suffering for many years from violence on its northern fishing banks between foreign trawlers and native line and drift fishermen, Norway was proposing a general ban on trawl-fishing to extend beyond its current 12-mi. limit within roughly a 50-mi. line. An extension of full fishery jurisdiction to 200 mi. was likely to await the outcome of the law of the sea conference before being implemented.

Violence between different types of fishermen also was reported or feared off Bermuda and in the Irish Sea. But international fishery-sharing agreements were concluded between Poland and other Baltic states, Spain and Morocco, East and West Germany, and the U.K. and Iceland. The North East Arctic Cod Quota Agreement, signed in London in March by the U.K., the U.S.S.R., and Norway, was denounced by the Soviet Union in August because of excessive fishing by other nonparty states. The Faeroes Fishery Agreement, however, between the Faeroes, the U.K., Belgium, Denmark, France, West Germany, Norway, and Poland (signed in December 1973), came into force in January. Other marine wildlife activity included the opening for signature in Oslo in November 1973 of a convention that would prohibit nearly all hunting of polar bears in the Arctic.

The continental shelves continued to attract interest as more areas were opened up for mineral exploration and the technology to develop the rich North Sea oil fields resulted in major engineering advances. Agreements delimiting shelf boundaries were reached between Canada and Denmark and Greenland, France and Spain, and Italy and Spain. Turkey claimed a median line in the Aegean Sea, which was disputed by Greece partly on the basis of the archipelago principle; while Sweden and the U.S.S.R. made little progress because of disagreement over the effect of the island of Gotland. Indeed, the legal rights of

continued on page 434

John W. Dean III (left), former White House counsel to President Nixon, sentenced to one to four years' imprisonment for his part in the Watergate coverup; (below) Maurice H. Stans, left, former U.S. secretary of commerce, and John N. Mitchell, right, former U.S. attorney general, after being acquitted of all charges in connection with a secret cash contribution made to Nixon's reelection campaign.

WIDE WORLD

TYRONE DUKES—THE NEW YORK TIMES

THE LAW
OF THE SEA

By Tony Loftas

Almost imperceptibly, the oceans are becoming one of the major flashpoints in international relations. The powder is the growing interest of all countries, both rich and poor, in marine resources and the use of the oceans. The fuse is the perilous state of the international law of the sea. Efforts to bring lasting order to the oceans, the major part of the earth's surface, have been unsuccessful. The most recent attempt, the third United Nations Conference on the Law of the Sea, held its opening session in Caracas, Venezuela, in 1974, but it failed to agree on any substantive issue other than to continue meeting. This failure could prompt more countries to take unilateral action to protect their maritime interests, thus reducing the prospects for an international regime and increasing the chances of future conflict.

The present crisis in international law reflects changes in the political balance of the world. For centuries the power to shape the law of the sea rested essentially with a few advanced maritime states. Their guiding principle was the freedom of the seas advocated in 1609 by Dutchman Hugo Grotius on behalf of his country, then a major maritime power. Over the years this freedom has suited the merchant and fishery enterprises of the advanced nations as well as, in recent times, their military strategy. Such freedom does not necessarily accord, however, with the aspirations of other, less developed countries.

The birth of many new nation-states since 1960 has strengthened the argument for revision, or even replacement, of laws formulated at two previous law of the sea conferences in 1958 and 1960. These new nations, as well as other less developed countries, are concerned that the last great natural resource on the earth should be denied them by the rich, technologically superior nations. Many less developed countries, for example, have seen their coastal fisheries exploited by itinerant fleets from developed nations, and they have witnessed the advances in marine technology. The demand of these countries, therefore, is for a body of international law that protects each country's coastal resources while guaranteeing it an equitable share in the wealth of the deep sea and open ocean.

The Road to Caracas. Pres. Harry S. Truman's proclamation of 1945 is generally considered the starting point of a new era in the role of seabed resources. This unilateral proclamation laid claim to the resources of the entire American continental shelf, on the ground that it represents nothing more than an extension underwater of the continental land mass. Other countries followed suit. Some of them, lacking any significant area of shelf, claimed expanses of ocean that contained important living resources.

An international commission was asked to study the question, and its findings prepared the way for the 1958 Geneva Convention on the Continental Shelf. This convention recognized the prerogative of the coastal state to exercise sovereign rights over the continental shelf, defined as "the sea-bed and the sub-soil adjacent to the coast but outside the area of the territorial sea, to a depth of 200 metres or, beyond that limit, to where the depth

Tony Loftas is a specialist on marine affairs who has been consultant to the FAO and special adviser to the UN. His publications include Wealth from the Oceans (*1967*) *and* The Last Resource: Man's Exploitation of the Oceans (*1970; revised 1973*).

of the superjacent waters admits of the exploitation of the natural resources of the said areas." These rights were to be independent of "occupation, effective or notional" or "any express proclamation." Nevertheless, the convention approved most acquisitions made in previous unilateral declarations.

Unfortunately, by introducing the ambiguous concept of exploitability, the convention became an open-ended document. According to some interpretations, it removed any restraint on moving into the ocean deeps for minerals and oil. Thus, a clause recognizing that geologic formations do not obey arbitrary limits set by international law became a serious loophole. As advances were made in marine technology, it soon became clear that some countries would be able to exploit resources lying well beyond the continental shelf. With exploitability as the passport to the deep oceans, the wealth of this last resource would pass automatically to a handful of advanced, industrialized countries.

One of the first less developed countries to raise the alarm was Malta. In a rousing speech to the UN General Assembly, the ambassador for Malta brought to the attention of the ocean "have-nots" the threats posed by the great powers' growing domination of the oceans generally and the seabed in particular. Following this initiative, an ad hoc committee was formed to study the uses of the seabed beyond territorial waters. The ad hoc group metamorphosed first into the Sea-Bed Committee and then, after the General Assembly's decision in December 1970 to hold another conference, into the Preparatory Committee for the Law of the Sea Conference.

The Issues. Some countries, notably the advanced maritime nations, would have preferred to restrict the new conference to those issues left unresolved at the two previous conferences, but the General Assembly decreed otherwise. The conference was to be a comprehensive one dealing with seabed resources beyond territorial waters, the breadth of territorial seas, fishing and the conservation of living resources of the high seas, and the preservation of the marine environment. As was clear from the experience of the Sea-Bed Committee, many sources of disagreement lie within these broad headings.

In the past, the advanced military and/or maritime nations favoured the concept of a narrow territorial sea with a further narrow "contiguous zone" in which they could exercise certain rights, such as limited policing and exclusive fishing. Although they sought control of the seabed through the Continental Shelf Convention, the limited jurisdiction over the waters above it accorded with their common interest in the freedom of trade and navigation. On the whole, these countries were openly hostile toward states that attempted to obtain exclusive control over rich fish resources off their coasts.

The battle was more or less decided once the coastal states began to realize the potential resource assets that lay at their doorstep. Increasingly the trend, spearheaded by the Latin-American coastal states, has been toward an exclusive zone, called by various names, extending to a distance of 200 mi. offshore. The remaining issues are restriction of the territorial sea to 12 mi. and preservation of the right of passage through the hundred or so international straits that would then fall completely within national waters. The question of resource control is of less concern, since both developed and less developed countries are among the major beneficiaries of wider marine resource ownership.

In contrast, the distribution of resources is of direct interest to landlocked (no sea) and shelf-locked (little sea) nations. They object to seeing other nations divide the richest parts of the marine real estate. Many coastal states in Africa, for example, are pressing for a 200-mi.-wide exclusive economic zone (EEZ). They have offered the 14 landlocked African countries access to the sea and its living resources, but they have been less magnanimous with the mineral resources of the continental shelf. In such circumstances, landlocked and underprivileged coastal states could benefit more from a reduction in the area of seabed under exclusive national control, thereby adding to the value of the "common heritage" in which they can expect to share.

Living resources pose particularly difficult problems in international law. Their general mobility along coasts or between coastal and oceanic waters calls for a flexibility that contrasts sharply with the "fixed" assets of marine minerals. International fishery commissions exist to manage particular fish populations or areas, but they have not always proved effective. Many coastal states endeavour to reserve offshore fisheries by declaring wide territorial or resource limits. Others try to protect their inshore resources while retaining the right to exploit such wide-ranging fish as tuna and salmon elsewhere.

The less developed countries share a common concern over scientific research by foreign scientists in or close to their coastal waters. They suspect that knowledge gained in the course of scientific research is used to commercial advantage by advanced maritime and industrialized countries. Furthermore, given some evidence of military espionage and the often close association between civilian and military oceanography, some less developed countries feel that their national integrity may be threatened. For their part, marine scientists tend to see the law of the sea as an albatross about their neck, delaying advances in the world's understanding of the oceans.

Certainly the restrictions currently imposed on marine research conflict with the need for environmental data to protect the marine environment. Although some progress has been made in the prevention of marine pollution, the issue is far from resolved. The most serious difficulty is that many of the pollutants that threaten the health of the oceans come from the land. Many countries resent the fact that a legal regime intended to protect ocean space could become an instrument for controlling activities within their sovereign territory.

The Caracas Conference. With so many sensitive issues confronting it, few people believed that the third UN law of the sea conference would be able to resolve them in the first substantive meeting, even though it was to last for ten weeks (June 20 to August 29). Nevertheless, the delegations present, representing over 130 of the 148 countries invited, began with a certain amount of optimism. In the past two or three years, many states had come to realize that political trade-offs would be necessary. The maritime powers, for example, could be outvoted by countries

Some authorities fear that the whale may be destined for extinction if fishing is not limited.

lacking their preoccupation with the traditional freedoms of the sea. Similarly, the aspirations of those less developed countries that stood to gain most from extensive EEZs could be thwarted by landlocked and other disadvantaged states.

In the event, the conference proved a disappointment. Rather than displaying the hoped-for spirit of cooperation, many delegations merely reiterated well-known positions. The conference became something of a muscle-flexing exercise, with delegations apparently preparing for a follow-up meeting where the real negotiating was expected to begin. The next meeting was finally fixed for March 1975 in Geneva, with a final session in Caracas when or if substantial agreement was reached.

During the course of the Caracas meeting, considerable support was given to the proposal for a 12-mi. territorial sea with an EEZ extending to a total distance of 200 mi. from the coastline. Even the maritime powers, such as the U.K., the Soviet Union, and the U.S., moved cautiously toward accepting it. The difficulties arose over the details. The maritime states were anxious to guarantee free movement of their commercial and naval ships

World map of the distribution of oceanic resources in relation to the 200-mi. limit.

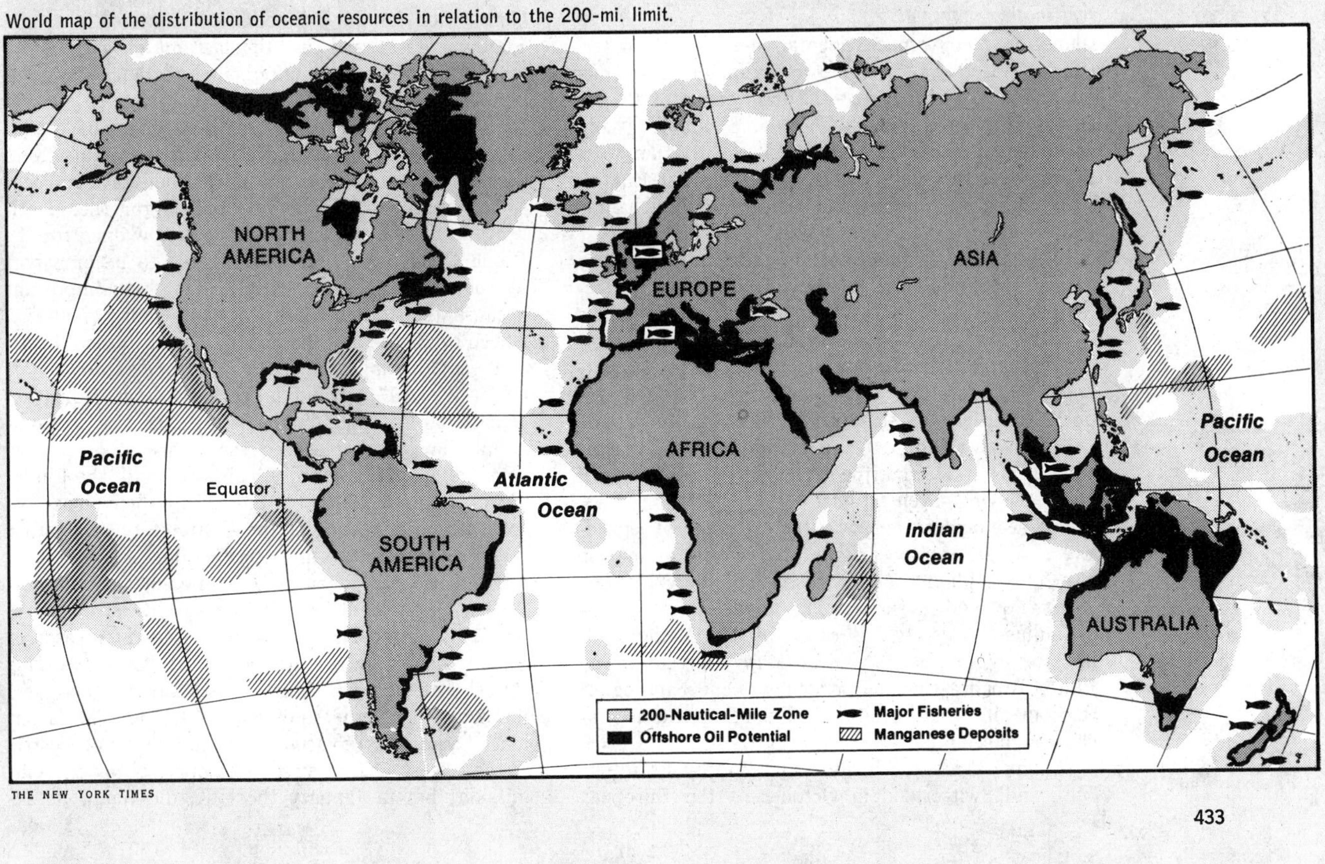

NORTH AMERICA

EUROPE

ASIA

Pacific Ocean

Pacific Ocean

Equator

Atlantic Ocean

AFRICA

Indian Ocean

SOUTH AMERICA

AUSTRALIA

200-Nautical-Mile Zone
Offshore Oil Potential
Major Fisheries
Manganese Deposits

through straits falling within the extended territorial seas. Some countries felt that such movements should be severely restricted, with notification or even authorization required beforehand.

The EEZ fared no better. The maritime states wanted the least restrictive interpretation of this concept. Many coastal states, including Canada, New Zealand, Australia, and most African and Latin-American countries, wanted powers of jurisdiction that would make the EEZ little different from extended territorial waters. Countries consisting of island archipelagoes pressed for extensive areas lying within their compass plus an EEZ. States with islands or island protectorates supported them. The U.K., for example, has several island protectorates that could provide it with access to resources in ocean areas far removed from Western Europe. Most less developed countries opposed the granting of economic zones to dependent island territories, but is it equitable in law to deny such dependencies access to resources that might make them economically viable?

The equity of resource distribution arose in many guises. The richer fishing grounds of the world occur in the vicinity of a comparatively small number of coastal states, not all of which have the capacity to exploit them. The maritime countries objected to the exclusion of their fleets from these areas, although they recognized that the coastal state would need to license foreign vessels operating in its EEZ. In fact, the distribution of both living and nonliving resources is such that equality in law with respect to exclusive exploitation rights can never correspond to equality of opportunity—a point not lost on the land-locked and shelf-locked countries. They saw their salvation in an international marine authority or other form of political compromise guaranteeing them a greater share in marine resources.

As for the establishment of an international ocean authority and a legal regime for the seabed, this seemed no nearer after Caracas even though it was to be a major work of the meeting. In fact, this issue above all others divided the developed and less developed countries. Three basic questions are involved: the area to be governed; the legal nature of the regime and its relationship with coastal states; and, finally, the nature, structure, and function of the authority. Lacking agreement on the first two questions, the dispute eventually centred on whether the authority was to be merely a licensing body or an operating authority empowered to exploit deep-sea minerals, perhaps even marketing them and distributing the income.

The majority of the less developed countries, known as the Group of 77, wanted a strong international seabed authority with extensive powers over the exploitation of resources. The industrialized countries, particularly the U.S., pressed for a much weaker authority that would simply grant licenses to individuals or corporations permitting them to mine the seabed. The Group of 77 found this totally unacceptable, especially since some mineral-exporting members feared that deep-sea nodules mined for copper and cobalt could reduce their own revenues.

The control of the authority was also the subject of sometimes heated debate. Should each nation on its controlling body have a single vote, or should the voting powers be "weighted" in favour of the technologically advanced countries, the only ones with the ability or potential to carry out deep-sea mining? The less developed countries, now a majority in the UN, wanted to be able to control an authority that could enrich or, in the case of some mineral-exporting countries, impoverish them. The industrialized countries, on the other hand, dismissed the prospect of investing heavily in deep-sea technology for the benefit of others.

Beyond Caracas. The results of the conference show that, contrary to popular belief, the great ocean debate has really just begun. One thing is certain: the international law of the sea will never be the same again. In a shrinking world, the beliefs of Hugo Grotius can no longer hold sway.

Many separate issues must be resolved and many different national interests served. Basically, the less developed countries want to maximize their revenues from marine resources. The developed countries fear that "creeping national jurisdiction" over the sea will curtail their freedom to carry out research, military, and most commercial activities. A degree of international control in the waters of coastal states appears inevitable, and the industrialized nations must be prepared for some devolution of power to an international authority. Lack of progress on these points could trigger off a "land" race unparalleled in history.

continued from page 431

islands to their own continental shelves beyond territorial waters had become a major point of dispute, illustrated further by the Irish denial of British claims to the shelf around the North Atlantic island of Rockall and by the French-U.K. arbitration compromis over the shelf boundary in the West English Channel, necessitated by the position of the Channel Islands close to the French coast.

In the area of marine pollution, the emphasis moved to outflow. Following the Paris Convention of December 1973 on Pollution from Rivers and Outfalls in North West Europe, a further convention to limit the discharge of toxic products into rivers and outfalls flowing into the North Sea and the North Atlantic was opened for signature in Paris in June. The Oslo Convention of 1972 against dumping of wastes from ships and aircraft entered into force in April after receiving seven ratifications.

One new development was the extension of legislative activity into the private law aspects of marine law. This applied not only to the Hamburg Conference in April on revision of The Hague Rules on Bills of Lading but also to ratification by The Netherlands in January of the 1965 European Convention on Pirate Broadcasting and its subsequent banning of the four pirate radio stations off the Dutch coast, including the famous Radio Veronica.

Human Rights. With the ratification by France in May and Switzerland in October of the European Convention for the Protection of Human Rights and Fundamental Freedoms, the last major gaps in its application were filled. Of equal importance, all member states of the EEC were now parties to it; and with the *Nold* judgment of the EEC Court of Justice in May, which reiterated that human rights were part of EEC common law and added that international treaties might be referred to for the identification of such rights, the way was now open for the Rome Convention (Human Rights) to become part of the Rome Treaty (EEC). This was important because the Italian Constitutional Court (*Frontini,* December 1973) and the Federal Constitutional Court of West Germany (*Internationale Handelsgesellschaft mbH,* May 1974), while accepting full subordination of national law, including constitutional law, to Community law, both reserved the right to control the compliance of Community legislation with the fundamental rights of citizens protected by their respective constitutions "so long as the Community legal order failed to provide the same protection."

The European Court of Human Rights also was experiencing an increase in its work, with an increased readiness of the EEC Commission to refer cases to it and the emergence of important cases involving states that had not been defendants in the past: Sweden, The Netherlands, and the U.K. The latter, indeed, had now replaced West Germany and Austria as the largest single source of complaints to the Commission; but in January the U.K. did renew its acceptance of the right of individual petition (for a further two-year period).

The UN General Assembly approved on Nov. 30, 1973, a new International Convention on the Suppression and Punishment of the Crime of Apartheid. In January the UN Commission on the Status of Women decided to prepare a draft convention on the elimination of discrimination against women. And a five-week diplomatic conference in Geneva ended in March without reaching agreement on two protocols to strengthen the 1949 Geneva Conventions on the laws of war; a further session was scheduled for 1975.

National developments in freedom of expression included the judgment in January of the Federal Constitutional Court of West Germany holding that the press laws of the constituent Länder were beyond legal authority insofar as they entitled journalists and broadcasters to refuse to reveal their sources when asked to give evidence in criminal cases. (The Länder have legislative powers over the press, the federal government over criminal procedure.) The government immediately followed with a draft bill to give workers in the press and broadcasting an unlimited right to withhold such evidence. In January the Swedish government set up committees to report on the protection of informants' anonymity in cases of police raids on newspaper offices, on provisions of the Criminal Code on crimes against the security of the state, and on the borderline between freedom of the press and criminal law. The move was prompted by the "IB affair," in which the editor of a radical magazine was imprisoned under the official secrets laws for revealing details (mostly culled from public sources) of the operations of the Swedish secret service.

Law and Order. Following the spate of kidnappings of diplomats and others by dissident groups, the UN General Assembly adopted a Convention on Punishment of Crimes against Diplomatic Agents in December 1973. In January the Council of Europe crowned many years of negotiation with the opening for signature of the European Convention on the Non-Applicability of Statutory Limitation to Crimes against Humanity and War Crimes.

International Organizations. Within the EEC area, the agreement setting up the Benelux Court of Justice came into force, the court was formed and its first case referred. The U.K. referred its first case to the EEC Court of Justice under art. 177 (*Van Duyn* v. *Home Office*), and the Court of Appeal in *H. P. Bulmer Ltd.* v. *J. Bollinger S.A.* delivered a long judgment setting out its policy toward Community law. The Republic of Ireland was the first of the new member states to bring (and win) a case directly before the Court of Justice in *Ireland* v. *European Community Council*. No EEC judicial activity emerged from Denmark, however. The free trade agreements between the EEC and the EFTA countries came into force in January, and meetings of the joint councils provided for in the agreements began to take place.

Commercial Law. The 1971 revision of the Universal Copyright Convention came into force in July. New problems in the field of industrial property led to the signature in May of a convention relating to the Distribution of Program-Carrying Signals transmitted by satellite, aimed at regulating the copyright position of broadcasts transmitted via satellite and picked up outside the intended country of reception. Complaints were made against similar unauthorized nonsatellite reception and retransmission of television programs by cable television (CATV) companies,

Bridget Rose Dugdale, English heiress turned Irish Republican revolutionary, was sentenced to nine years in prison for receiving 19 paintings, valued at $19.2 million, after they were stolen from the home of Sir Alfred Beit near Dublin, Ire.

Belgium being particularly singled out since that country is very widely equipped with transmission lines and the originators of programs in the surrounding countries object to losing their Belgian royalties. In Italy the situation became more complex, arising out of the activities of private CATV companies in the north transmitting to their subscribers foreign programs, especially from Switzerland and Austria. The objections were less from those countries than from the Italian government and the state broadcasting company, RAI-TV, which found its monopoly being broken. An attempt to enforce the monopoly by criminal proceedings against Telebiella, a CATV company, led to an appeal to the European Commission of Human Rights under art. 10 (freedom of expression) in May, as well as a reference to the EEC Court of Justice, which gave its ruling in April (*State* v. *Sacchi*), denying in principle any Community objection to RAI's monopoly. In midsummer the Italian government issued a decree closing down the independent CATV companies (by force, if need be); but in July the situation was reversed by a judgment of the Constitutional Court holding that commercial CATV companies with a restricted territorial range were entitled to operate and RAI could only enforce its monopoly against a competing national network.

The EEC Patent Convention, which was intended to supplement the European Patent Agreement signed in Munich in 1973 and to have been agreed to at a conference in Luxembourg in May, was postponed at the request of the U.K. government. However, the EEC Court of Justice, developing its case law under art. 30–36 of the EEC Treaty, held in *Van Zuylen Frères* v. *Hag A.G.* that trademarks owned by different holders in different EEC countries but deriving from a common origin could not be mutually exclusive within the EEC. Courts in The Netherlands had already held that the territorial nature of exhaustion of patent rights had been attenuated by the EEC Treaty.

Trading practices were the subject of a variety of cases and legislation. A UN Conference on Trade and Development working group in Mexico City concluded the drafting of a Charter of Economic Rights and Duties of States, which was then passed to the UN General Assembly. The UN Committee of Experts on Multinational Companies submitted to the secretary-general its report that included 51 guidelines for the treatment of such companies.

The U.K. Fair Trading Act, 1973, which combines in one instrument and under one director general of fair trading the machinery for consumer protection and control of monopolies and restrictive trade practices, came into force in January. The French "Loi Royer" to control the building of hypermarkets in competition with smaller shops was passed in December 1973 and came into force early in the year. The Swedish Credit Ratings Act, passed in December 1973, supplemented the earlier Data Act and closely regulated the supply of credit rating information on privacy protection grounds. Credit as such was the subject of the massive U.K. Consumer Credit Act.

Product liability was becoming increasingly important, and a number of reports were being prepared, by the Council of Europe and others. The thalidomide tragedy resulted in further settlements in favour of the victims. But the issue of liability for the deaths of a number of women from thromboembolisms following consumption of contraceptive pills was being fought by the drug companies in a series of cases being brought in Sweden and proposed in Denmark. In Norway, the first such plaintiff, in *Hudecz v. Schering A.G.,* won damages at first instance but lost on appeal.

(NEVILLE MARCH HUNNINGS)

See also Cities and Urban Affairs; Crime and Law Enforcement; Environment; Race Relations; United Nations; United States.

[552; 553]

ENCYCLOPÆDIA BRITANNICA FILMS. *Equality Under Law —California Fair Housing Cases* (1969); *Free Press vs. Fair Trial by Jury—The Sheppard Case* (1969); *The Schempp Case—Bible Reading in Public Schools* (1969); *United States Supreme Court: Guardian of the Constitution* (2nd ed., 1973).

Lebanon

A republic of the Middle East, Lebanon is bounded by Syria, Israel, and the Mediterranean Sea. Area: 3,950 sq.mi. (10,230 sq.km.). Pop. (1970 est.): 2,126,325, excluding (1972) 191,000 Palestinian and other refugees. Cap. and largest city: Beirut (pop., 1970 est., 475,000). Language: Arabic. Religion: Christian majority with strong Muslim minority. President in 1974, Suleiman Franjieh; prime ministers, Takieddin as-Solh and, after October 31, Rashid as-Solh.

Palestinians raise their flag amid the ruins of their camp in Lebanon following an attack by Israeli planes.

UPI COMPIX

Law Enforcement:
see Crime and Law Enforcement

Lawn Bowls:
see Bowling and Lawn Bowls

Lawn Tennis:
see Tennis

Lead:
see Mining and Quarrying

LEBANON

Education. (1972–73) Primary, pupils 497,723; secondary, pupils 167,578; primary and secondary (1970–71), teachers 32,178; vocational (public only), pupils 4,603, teachers (1969–70) 508; teacher training (public), students 3,233, teachers 218; higher (including 4 universities), students 50,803, teaching staff 2,313.

Finance. Monetary unit: Lebanese pound, with a free rate (Sept. 16, 1974) of L£2.23 to U.S. $1 (L£5.15 = £1 sterling). Gold, SDRs, and foreign exchange, central bank: (June 1974) U.S. $1,068,300,000; (June 1973) U.S. $894.6 million. Budget (1974 est.) balanced at L£1,385 million. Gross national product: (1972) L£6,359 million; (1971) L£5,646 million. Money supply: (May 1974) L£2,648 million; (May 1973) L£2,348 million. Cost of living (Beirut; 1970 = 100): (March 1974) 125; (March 1973) 111.

Foreign Trade. (1972) Imports L£2,619 million; exports L£1,080 million; transit trade L£2,430 million. Import sources: U.S. 13%; West Germany 11%; France 9%; Italy 9%; U.K. 8%; Japan 5%; Iraq 5%. Export destinations: Saudi Arabia 17%; Kuwait 10%; Syria 8%; Libya 7%; U.S. 7%; Iraq 6%. Main exports: fruit and vegetables 13%; machinery 12%; chemicals 8%; aircraft 8%; clothing 5%; textile yarns and fabrics 5%. Tourism (1972): visitors 1,663,700; gross receipts U.S. $204 million.

Transport and Communications. Roads (1971) 7,400 km. Motor vehicles in use (1971): passenger 146,300; commercial 15,600. Railways: (1972) 417 km.; traffic (1973) 2.9 million passenger-km., freight 35 million net ton-km. Air traffic (1973): 1,420,000,-000 passenger-km.; freight 394.9 million net ton-km. Shipping (1973): vessels 100 gross tons and over 81; gross tonnage 119,468. Telephones (Jan. 1973) 227,-000. Radio receivers (Dec. 1971) 605,000. Television receivers (Dec. 1972) 320,000.

Agriculture. Production (in 000; metric tons; 1973; 1972 in parentheses): potatoes *c.* 110 (117); wheat (1972) 39, (1971) 29; sugar, raw value (1972) *c.* 25, (1971) *c.* 27; tomatoes *c.* 70 (73); grapes (1972) *c.* 95, (1971) *c.* 90; olives *c.* 50 (40); figs *c.* 13 (*c.* 13); bananas (1972) *c.* 32, (1971) *c.* 32; oranges (1972) *c.* 200, (1971) *c.* 200; lemons (1972) *c.* 60, (1971) *c.* 60; apples (1972) *c.* 140, (1971) *c.* 160; tobacco (1972) *c.* 8.3, (1971) 8.3. Livestock (in 000; 1972–73): cattle *c.* 86; goats *c.* 300; sheep *c.* 240; chickens *c.* 6,100.

Industry. Production (in 000; metric tons; 1973): cement 1,659; petroleum products (1972) 2,038; electricity (excluding most industrial production; kw-hr.) 1,791,000.

For Lebanon 1974 was a fairly prosperous year in most sectors of the economy, which continued to benefit indirectly from the rising incomes of the Arab oil states. Manufacturing exports were more than double those of 1973 in value. But the government was beset by socio-political problems that reached crisis levels in the autumn.

Despite promises made by the Palestinian guerrillas to cease their raids into Israel from Lebanese territory, Palestinian refugee camps and Lebanese villages in the south of the country suffered throughout the year from retaliatory Israeli air and ground attacks. The heaviest attacks, resulting in several hundred casualties, were on April 12–13, May 16–21, and June 16–21, following the guerrilla operations against Qiryat Shemona, Maalot, and Shamir in Israel. After an Arab attack by sea on Nahariya, Israeli gunboats on July 8 destroyed Lebanese fishing boats in Tyre, Sidon, and Ras a-Shak. In May the government adopted a bill for compulsory military service for 18-year-olds.

The Israeli attacks caused unrest among Lebanon's predominantly Shi'ite Muslim southern population, who protested that the government was failing to protect them. Increasingly, their spokesman and leader was their imam, Mousa Sadr, who exonerated the Palestinians and blamed the regime. At an Arab League Defense Council meeting in Cairo in July, the Palestinian guerrillas asked for sophisticated weapons to repel the Israeli attacks; the Lebanese government feared

Israel would use this as a pretext to occupy southern Lebanon and asked for Arab aid to strengthen its own forces. For the first time Lebanon decided to buy ground-to-air missiles and antiarmour weapons from the Soviet Union, for a reported $2.8 million, and in September Libya offered $44 million in military aid. In September Israeli aircraft over Lebanon met with missile resistance.

The relations between Palestinians and Lebanese remained sensitive, and there were clashes between right-wing Phalangist Party militia and Palestinian guerrilla groups. These conflicts were the main cause of the fall of the Solh government on September 25 after ministers supporting the socialist leader Kamal Jumblatt resigned on the issue of the disarmament of the population. Right-wing groups led by Pierre Gemayel and former president Camille Chamoun insisted their followers should carry arms unless Palestinian guerrillas were disarmed. After a delay, during which Saeb Salam was invited to make an attempt, Rashid as-Solh, a cousin of Takieddin as-Solh, succeeded in forming a Cabinet on October 31.

Inflation and consequent strikes and social unrest were a serious problem, and the government established a Price Control Council in January with limited success. Businessmen and merchants protested strongly against attempts to control profit margins. Concessions through family allowances and reduced taxes narrowly averted a general strike on April 2. After prolonged student unrest in the American University of Beirut, the police stormed the university campus on April 24.   (PETER MANSFIELD)

[978.B.3.a]

Lesotho

A constitutional monarchy of southern Africa and a member of the Commonwealth of Nations, Lesotho is entirely within South Africa. Area: 11,720 sq.mi. (30,355 sq.km.). Pop. (1974 est.): 1,155,700. Cap. and largest city: Maseru (pop., 1972 est., 18,800). Language: English and Sesotho (official). Religion: Roman Catholic 38.7%; Lesotho Evangelical Church 24.3%; Anglican 10.4%; other Christian 8.4%; non-Christian 18.2%. Chief of state in 1974, King Moshoeshoe II; prime minister, Chief Leabua Jonathan.

Fears that a one-party state was developing and the government's threats to arrest parliamentary opposi-

---

LESOTHO

Education. (1972–73) Primary, pupils 187,459, teachers 3,951; secondary, pupils 12,559, teachers 551; vocational, pupils 170, teachers 27; teacher training, students 383, teachers 59; higher (University of Botswana, Lesotho, and Swaziland), students 446, teaching staff 61.

Finance and Trade. Monetary unit: South African rand, with (Sept. 16, 1974) a free rate of R 0.70 to U.S. $1 (R 1.62 = £1 sterling). Budget (1971–72 rev. est.): revenue R 11.1 million; expenditure R 11.6 million. Foreign trade (1972): imports R 43.3 million; exports R 6.2 million. Main exports: cattle 28%; mohair 15%; wool 15%; diamonds 11%; peas and beans 9%; wheat 6%. Most trade is with South Africa.

Agriculture. Production (in 000; metric tons; 1972; 1971 in parentheses): corn 59 (c. 70); wheat 21 (58); sorghum 14 (c. 60); wool c. 2.3 (c. 2.2). Livestock (in 000; Sept. 1972): cattle c. 565; goats c. 910; sheep c. 1,720.

---

tion leaders led to an armed uprising in January; police posts were attacked and many deaths were reported in the ensuing disorders. Ntsu Mokhehle, leader of the Basutoland Congress Party, escaped to Zambia. A government bill adopted in February made it an offense to obtain funds from abroad for acts of terrorism. In June Gerard Ramoreboli, leader of the opposition (which was boycotted by Mokhehle), agreed to the government's plan for a five-year political holiday, provided that the interim National Assembly was made more representative. Chief Jonathan, who had become increasingly anti-South African, partly to pacify internal opposition, met B. J. Vorster, South Africa's prime minister, in April to patch up diplomatic differences.

Lesotho's politico-economic problems were sharpened by the oil crisis. The Arab oil-exporting countries had guaranteed Lesotho a proportion of its oil requirements, but it could only import via South Africa, which was under a total embargo. Following intertribal riots in the Rand gold mines in South Africa, 15,000 Basuto returned jobless to Lesotho at a loss to the country of R 20 million plus R 8 million in deferred pay.   (MOLLY MORTIMER)

[978.E.8.b.ii]

Liberia

A republic on the west coast of Africa, Liberia is bordered by Sierra Leone, Guinea, and Ivory Coast. Area: 43,000 sq.mi. (111,400 sq.km.). Pop. (1974): 1,496,000. Cap. and largest city: Monrovia (pop., 1974, 180,000). Language: English (official) and tribal dialects. Religion: mainly animist. President in 1974, William R. Tolbert, Jr.

President Tolbert declared on January 23 that Liberia's constitution, flag, national anthem, and national slogan—"Love of Liberty Brought Us Here"— must all be changed. In a 3½-hour speech to a joint session of the Senate and House of Representatives in Monrovia, Tolbert said that the existing forms of those symbols no longer appropriately reflected "our national aspirations and concepts." The president recommended that a national commission be formed to study possible constitutional changes. His proposals reflected demands in recent years from Liberian youth that the present national flag be discarded. It had been designed by freed American slaves and was based on the United States flag, but with only one star.

One of Tolbert's proposals, that the constitution be amended to allow for presidential terms of eight years, came in for considerable criticism. Many Liberians believed that an eight-year term was too long. Defending himself, Tolbert argued that two four-year terms would be inadequate because the president would have to spend at least half of his first term running for reelection.

The Movement for Justice in Africa (MOJA), a Liberian organization, asked the government to establish strict origin-labeling requirements for packaged foods. MOJA stated that it believed certain items marked "foreign products" were imports from South Africa. A Liberian executive order prohibited trade with South Africa.

Liberia asked the Soviet Union for technical assistance to improve its fishing industry following a meeting between officials of the Soviet Ministry of Fisheries and Liberia's Ministry of Agriculture. The Soviet delegation agreed to begin research on waters

adjacent to Liberia and to provide fellowships for
Liberians who wished to study the fishing industry in
the Soviet Union.

The U.S. also extended economic aid to Liberia.
Page Communications Engineers, a U.S. firm, signed
a three-year contract for a communications project
financed by an $8 million loan from the U.S. Agency
for International Development. The project called for
the establishment of telecommunications links between Monrovia, Harper, and Tabou in Ivory Coast.

There were intimations of trouble on the agricultural front. The drought conditions afflicting sub-
Saharan Africa began making themselves felt in Liberia in 1974, the foreign ministry announced in late
March.   (RICHARD L. WORSNOP)

[978.E.4.a]

Libraries

At its autumn 1973 meeting, UNESCO's International Advisory Committee on Documentation, Libraries, and Archives had promised general support
for UNISIST, the network of cooperative scientific
information systems launched in 1971. In February
1974, UNISIST outlined its own program for 1975–
80. It was also active in organizing the International
Symposium on Information Systems, held at Varna,
Bulg., in October.

In other actions, the UNESCO committee recommended that more attention be paid to the development of libraries in cultural centres, such as the
maisons de culture in France; approved the development of the Computerized Documentation Centre and
its associated training program at UNESCO headquarters in Paris; approved the foundation of the Information System on Research in Documentation
(ISORID), which by late 1973 had over 80 national
information links; and recommended that during
1975–80 priority be given to library services in less

developed countries, further development of universal
bibliographical control, the study of users' needs, and
the promotion of standards, research, and modern
techniques for disseminating information.

By 1974 the International Centre for Scientific and
Technical Information, Moscow, initiated in 1969 by
Comecon, was producing about 200 publications to
serve a network within Eastern Europe, later to be
linked with UNISIST. The fourth and last of
UNESCO's regional meetings on national planning of
documentation and library services, this time devoted
to the Arabic-speaking countries, was held in Cairo
in February. These regional meetings culminated in
UNESCO's International Conference on Planning of
National Overall Documentation, Library, and
Archives Infrastructures in Paris in September. In
November the International Federation of Library
Associations (IFLA) took up the theme of national
and international planning of libraries at its annual
General Council in Washington, D.C.

With a view toward greater efficiency and economy,
West Germany planned a centralized book selection
service for libraries, to be administered by the
Einkaufszentralstelle (Central Library Supply Centre) in Reutlingen. Similar considerations motivated
the search for a standard classification scheme for
books and documents. In Western countries the
dominant systems were the Dewey Decimal, Universal Decimal, Library of Congress, and Bliss classi-
fications (the Colon Classification was also used in
India), while in the U.S.S.R. and Eastern Europe
librarians had a simpler choice between the Universal
Decimal and the Soviet BBK. In the field of subject
indexing and mechanized information retrieval, work
proceeded in East Germany on the coordination of
German and Russian thesauri and on multilingual coordination under the auspices of UNESCO. A basic
work on classification, *Grundlagen universaler Wis-
sensordnung* by I. Dahlberg, appeared in West Germany.

Twenty-two principles for drafting coordinated
public library laws were set forth in *Public Library
Legislation*, written by F. M. Gardner and published
by UNESCO. In Canada the 1971 governmental recommendations on multiculturalism were taking effect
with the development of the services to immigrants at
the Toronto Public Library and the foundation of a
multicultural language and literature centre at the National Library in Ottawa. The question of payment to
authors whose works were lent by libraries continued
to receive attention in several countries. West Germany was still attempting to devise a fair system of
payment under the law of January 1973.

In the U.S. a radical plan to combine the resources
of four major libraries was announced in March by
the president of the New York Public Library. Under
the plan, the noncirculating division of the New York
Public Library and the libraries of Columbia, Harvard,
and Yale universities would systematically exchange
publications and photocopies of works in their collections. The exchanges would be coordinated by
means of open telephone lines, Teletype machines,
and computer-compiled centralized catalogs. The initial installation was expected to cost between $10
million and $15 million, but it was believed that in the
long run money would be saved through elimination
of duplicate purchases of expensive and/or little used
works. The plan was vigorously attacked by the Association of American Publishers and other groups representing authors and the book trade.

Among university libraries, an audiovisual centre was integrated into the library of Bochum in West Germany, and new buildings were completed at Dortmund and Freiburg im Breisgau. A new library building at the University of Zambia provided open access to subject sections. Other new library buildings included the Bibliothèque universitaire de Poitiers in France, the National Library of the Ivory Coast at Abidjan (designed by Canadian architects with advice from the Direction des Bibliothèques in Paris), and the Fundamental Library of the Social Sciences of the U.S.S.R. Academy of Sciences in Moscow.

Contrasts remained in the training of librarians. In the U.K., for example, the tendency was toward making librarianship a graduate profession, while the firm policy in the U.S.S.R. was to train library technicians for work below management level in the public libraries. Among less developed countries, B.A. and M.A. courses had become available at the universities of Teheran and Tabriz in Iran, and a new library school was started in Jamaica under UNESCO auspices. (ANTHONY THOMPSON)

[441.C.2.d; 613.D.1.a; 735.H]

ENCYCLOPÆDIA BRITANNICA FILMS. *Library of Congress* (1969).

Libya

A socialist republic on the north coast of Africa, Libya is bounded by Egypt, the Sudan, Tunisia, Algeria, Niger, and Chad. Area: 675,000 sq. mi. (1,749,000 sq.km.). Pop. (1973 census): 2,257,037. Cap. and largest city: Tripoli (pop., 1973 census, municipality, 551,477). Language: Arabic. Religion: predominantly Muslim. Leader of the Revolutionary Command Council in 1974, Col. Muammar al-Qaddafi; prime minister, Maj. Abdul Salam Jalloud.

Libya enjoyed a threefold increase in oil revenues in 1974 as a result of the world increase in oil prices following the Arab-Israeli war in October 1973. Estimates indicated that oil earnings rose from $2,210,000,000 in 1973 to $6,701,000,000 for 1974. Libyan policy was not always in line with that of other Arab oil producers, notably Saudi Arabia, the dominant OAPEC (Organization of Arab Petroleum Exporting Countries) member, which showed itself to be in favour of a reduction of crude oil prices once the energy crisis of the winter of 1973–74 had passed and the perilous state of the world monetary situation had been revealed. Colonel Qaddafi, however, remained adamant about the importance of the continued political role of oil in Middle Eastern affairs and in the Palestinian question in particular, and in addition was in favour of further increases in price. His stand on price reflected a reasonable uneasiness about the long-term economic position of Libya, where the oil reserves were small as compared with those of some other OAPEC members. In November, Libya agreed to pay British Petroleum £17.4 million compensation for properties nationalized in 1971.

The first part of the year, until August, was marked by poor relations between Libya and Egypt. Qaddafi accused Pres. Anwar as-Sadat of Egypt of sabotaging the proposed federation of Egypt, Syria, and Libya, and relations reached a very low level in April when Libyan involvement in an attack on the Military Tech-

nical Academy in Cairo was suspected by the Egyptian authorities. Angry exchanges followed, including accusations that a Qaddafi-initiated submarine attack on a Jewish tourist cruise through the Mediterranean on the British liner "Queen Elizabeth II" in 1973 had only been prevented by a countermanding order from Sadat. The latter's revelation in early August of the presence in Egypt of Libyan French-made Mirage jets was also extremely embarrassing to both the Libyan and French governments. Subsequently, more friendly positions were adopted. Meanwhile, early in May, Pres. Gaafar Nimeiry of the Sudan had accused Libya of plotting against his nation.

A proposed union with Tunisia was negotiated and preliminary merger documents signed on January 12, but the project was almost immediately shelved. The move was regarded as an attempt to register a continued commitment to Arab unity while recognizing the estrangement at that time of Libya and an Egypt led by Sadat. At the end of a six-day visit to France in March by Prime Minister Jalloud, a long-term Franco-Libyan cooperative agreement was signed. Under it, in exchange for oil, France would assist Libya in the construction of nuclear power stations and in other industrial energy projects and also in banking and finance. In April it was announced that Colonel Qaddafi would lay aside political and administrative functions and devote himself to "ideological and mass organizational work," and it was expected that more work would therefore devolve upon Jalloud. Jalloud visited Moscow in May, and an agreement on trade and economic, scientific, and

LIBYA

Education. (1972–73) Primary, pupils 467,204, teachers 18,840; secondary, pupils 67,161, teachers 5,093; vocational, pupils 3,375, teachers 415; teacher training, students 10,990, teachers 989; higher, students 8,220, teaching staff 414.

Finance. Monetary unit: Libyan dinar, with (Sept. 16, 1974) a par value of 0.296 dinar to U.S. $1 (free rate of 0.685 dinar = £1 sterling). Gold and foreign exchange, central bank: (June 1974) U.S. $2,989,000,000; (June 1973) U.S. $2,710,000,000. Budget (1971–72 est.) balanced at 632 million dinars (including petroleum revenue of 560 million dinars). Gross national product: (1972) 1,356,000,000 dinars; (1971) 1,298,000,000 dinars. Money supply: (April 1974) 655 million dinars; (April 1973) 425.1 million dinars. Cost of living (Tripoli; 1970 = 100): (Dec. 1973) 108; (Dec. 1972) 96.

Foreign Trade. (1972) Imports 341,450,000 dinars; exports 759.1 million dinars. Import sources: Italy 26%; West Germany 10%; U.K. 9%; France 7%; U.S. 6%; Japan 6%. Export destinations: West Germany 25%; Italy 20%; U.K. 14%; France 9%; U.S. 8%; The Bahamas 5%; The Netherlands 5%. Main export crude oil 99%.

Transport and Communications. Roads (with improved surface; 1972) c. 5,200 km. (including 1,822 km. coast road). Motor vehicles in use (1970): passenger 100,100; commercial (including buses) 45,400. A 149-km. railway line was under construction in 1974. Air traffic (1972): 350 million passenger-km.; freight 4.4 million net ton-km. Ships entered (1970) vessels totaling 4,381,000 net registered tons; goods loaded (1971) 132,753,000 metric tons, unloaded 3,012,000 metric tons. Telephones (Dec. 1971) 42,000. Radio licenses (Dec. 1972) 100,000. Television licenses (Dec. 1972) 2,500.

Agriculture. Production (in 000; metric tons; 1973; 1972 in parentheses): barley c. 70 (116); wheat (1972) 80, (1971) 18; potatoes (1972) 21, (1971) 23; tomatoes (1972) 143, (1971) 131; olives c. 50 (95); dates (1972) 60, (1971) 66. Livestock (in 000; 1972): goats c. 1,100; sheep c. 2,400; cattle 108; camels c. 100; asses c. 80.

Industry. Production (in 000; metric tons): salt (1970) 11; crude oil (1973) 105,222; petroleum products (1972) 435; electricity (Tripolitania; excluding most industrial production; kw-hr.; 1971) 508,000.

technical cooperation was reached with the U.S.S.R.

Preparations were made for increasing the rate of investment of the rising oil revenues in all sectors of the economy. Agricultural self-sufficiency was the goal indicated by the massive capital allocations to irrigation schemes in the remote south in Kufrah, Sarir, and Fezzan. The potential of marginal grazing was being investigated with a view toward improvement through regulated use. The Libyan authorities had begun to follow a policy of seeking contractors and advice from less developed countries as well as from the more usual sources in Western Europe, the U.S., and the Eastern European nations. As a result contracts were awarded to India for rail transportation and to Brazil for a sugar refinery and other industrial plants. (J. A. ALLAN)

[978.D.2.a]

Liechtenstein

A constitutional monarchy between Switzerland and Austria, Liechtenstein is united with Switzerland by a customs and monetary union. Area: 62 sq.mi. (160 sq.km.). Pop. (1974 est.): 23,600. Cap. and largest city: Vaduz (pop., 1973 est., 4,120). Language: German. Religion (1970): Roman Catholic 90.1%. Sovereign prince, Francis Joseph II; chiefs of government in 1974, Alfred Hilbe and, from March 27, Walter Kieber.

In national elections for the Landtag (parliament) on Feb. 1 and 3, 1974, the Progressive Citizens' Party (PCP), known locally as the Blacks, regained the parliamentary majority it had lost to the Fatherland Union (VU; the Reds) in the 1970 elections. Previously the Blacks had held a majority for 42 years. The PCP won eight seats as against seven for the VU. The third party, the Christian Social Party, failed to gain a seat. The three parties were all Catholic, royalist, and conservative, and the principal difference appeared to be active PCP support of a program of cheap and abundant housing. On March 27, after two months of intensive bargaining, the Landtag approved a Cabinet composed of three PCP and two VU members. Alfred Hilbe was replaced as chief of government by Walter Kieber, the nominal head of the PCP.

The exclusion of the Christian Social Party from the Landtag resulted in part from a constitutional amendment approved by the voters in a referendum held prior to the elections. The amendment required a party to draw 8% or more of the total vote nationwide in order to qualify for a seat in the Landtag. Previously, a party could obtain a seat if it received 18% or more of the vote in any one electoral district.

On June 20 the president of the Supreme Court of the principality, Walter Hildebrand, was shot and killed during a session in his court by a Swiss national,

LIECHTENSTEIN
Education. Primary (1972–73), pupils 2,541, teachers 97; secondary, pupils 796, teachers 36; vocational, pupils 919, teachers 43.
Finance and Trade. Monetary unit: Swiss franc, with (Sept. 16, 1974) a free rate of SFr. 3.01 to U.S. $1 (SFr. 6.96 = £1 sterling). Budget (1973 est.): revenue SFr. 78,495,000; expenditure SFr. 78,050,000. Exports (1972) SFr. 421 million. Export destinations: Switzerland 44%; EEC 26%. Main exports: metal manufactures, furniture, pottery. Tourism: visitors (1972) 82,000; gross receipts (1971) c. SFr. 18 million.

Life Insurance:
see Insurance

Reinhold Glatt, who appeared to have been crazed by the judgment rendered against him in a lawsuit. In May the U.S. Securities and Exchange Commission charged that the former directors of the bankrupt Penn Central Railroad had illegally diverted over $4 million to Liechtenstein banks. (ROBERT D. HODGSON)

Life Sciences

It seemed probable that 1974 would be remembered as the year when, under the influence of worldwide food shortages and of UN conferences on the law of the sea, population (see LAW: *Special Report;* POPULATIONS AND AREAS: *Special Report*), and food, the conquest of hunger began to replace that of disease as the dominant aim of biological research. The main requirements were higher food production combined with lower demands for water, fertilizers, and pesticides. The importance of the new techniques available to the plant breeder was shown by the presence of representatives of nearly 50 nations at the third International Congress of Plant Tissue and Cell Culture held at the University of Leicester, Eng., in July. Continued work aimed at increasing the range of nitrogen-fixing crops and at the biological control of pests contributed toward reduced dependence on expensive and potentially polluting chemicals. The anticipated need to reduce the amount of arable land devoted to animal husbandry gave new significance to studies on the ecology of the fauna of the uncultivated regions of the world, including interesting work on the physiology of the African dik-dik and eland, both of which show remarkable capacities for tolerating high temperatures with minimal demands for water.

Acknowledgment of the dominant role of molecular biology in almost every branch of the life sciences was made when the Central Committee of the Communist Party and Council of Ministers of the U.S.S.R. decreed that this was an important research area and charged all ministries (including agriculture) with ensuring the necessary rate of its development. The last traces of the deadening influence of T. D. Lysenko on Soviet science were at last wiped out.

Progress is not without its dangers, and the techniques of genetic engineering that were proving so useful to botanists (e.g., in creating new nitrogen fixers) were realized to hold such potential and unpredictable hazards to human health when applied to the bacterial commensals of the mammalian gut that a number of leading workers in this field took the unprecedented step of appealing through the National Academy of Sciences of the U.S. for a worldwide moratorium on this area of research (see *Genetics,* below). This U.S. initiative also was followed by Britain's Medical Research Council.

An important consequence of the advances in molecular biology was this discipline's unifying influence on disparate fields of biological study. For example, further discoveries of actin and myosin (formerly regarded as characteristic of muscle cells) in a widening range of cell types gave rise to the suggestion that they are involved in all kinds of cell movement—those of whole cells (muscular, amoeboid, embryonic), intracellular movements concerned with cell and nuclear division, and even those movements of cell organelles concerned with secretion of hormones or with the transmission of nerve impulses. More and more processes were traced back to activities of the cell membrane. Its involvement showed much in common between neurotransmission, both in the peripheral nervous system and in the brain, and the antibody-antigen reaction. It might even be significant that the reactions of the surface membrane of the bacterium *Escherichia coli* to complex stimuli revealed a data-processing capacity in some ways analogous to that of the brain. In studies of biological clocks, whose accuracy over a wide range of temperatures shows that they cannot depend on ordinary biochemical reactions, J. Woodland Hastings *et al.* at Harvard University suggested that the basic mechanism involved a feedback loop in the ion-transport mechanism across the cell membrane with temperature constancy maintained by temperature-regulated changes in its lipid composition. Brain studies of diverse kinds, ranging from psychological to pharmacological, physiological, and anatomical, and from a wide variety of animals (from man and other mammals to nematode worms and other invertebrates), continued to be a major field of research and, again thanks to advances in molecular biology, an appreciable closing of the gaps became apparent. (HAROLD SANDON)

BOTANY

Interest in the various pathways of photosynthetic carbon assimilation in higher plants continued in 1974. In three-carbon (C_3) plants atmospheric carbon dioxide is fixed directly into intermediates of the Calvin-Benson cycle, while in four-carbon (C_4) plants additional steps result in the carbon first being fixed into malic acid (malate) before being fed into the Calvin-Benson cycle. In addition, C_4 plants are characterized by the presence of concentric layers of bundle-sheath cells and mesophyll cells associated with the veins of the leaf. Despite good indications that C_4 metabolism has evolved independently many times, no transitional form had been found in nature; even in synthetic hybrids having structural features and enzyme systems of both the C_3 and C_4 parental types, photosynthetic carbon assimilation was in no way intermediate between the types. A report in 1974, however, indicated that one species, *Mollugo verticillata*, not only had some of the anatomical and biochemical features of both C_3 and C_4 plants, but also actively utilized both pathways of carbon fixation. *M. verticillata* may therefore represent a transitional stage in the evolution of C_4 photosynthesis. Of additional interest was the observation that, although low photorespiration rates (characteristic of the highly efficient C_4 plants) were measured in *M. verticillata*, the concentric mesophyll layer, which is one of the anatomical features thought to be necessary for such low rates, was not present.

It was also suggested that guard cells may have specialized pathways of carbon fixation that are different from those found in the mesophyll cells of the leaf. These pathways appeared to be similar to those found in all species of the family Crassulaceae and a number of other desert plants, in which fixation of carbon dioxide into malic acid occurs at night, followed by transfer of carbon into the Calvin-Benson cycle during the day. This fixation method is known as crassulacean acid metabolism (CAM). Evidence was presented that in *Tulipa* and *Commelina*, non-CAM plants, high levels of the enzymes necessary for the dark fixation of carbon dioxide are present in the epidermal cells of the leaf, and probably are localized primarily in the guard cells. It was also shown that epidermal cells (and possibly the guard cells specifically) fix carbon dioxide in light and dark at the same rates, and that the primary products are those

HENRY W. ART, WILLIAMS COLLEGE, MASSACHUSETTS

In the Sunken Forest on New York's Fire Island trees grow profusely and intricately branched, an adaptation to their salt-spray environment.

typical of CAM plants, malate and aspartate. The carbon fixed in this manner is eventually transferred to Calvin-Benson cycle intermediates and into starch, which in the epidermis is present only in the guard cells. High levels of malate were also reported in guard cells of *Vicia faba*, lending support to the hypothesis that such cells have specialized carbon fixation pathways.

The role of inorganic nutrients in the establishment and maintenance of ecosystems continued to receive the attention of plant ecologists. Although much of the nutrient supply in many systems comes from weathering of bedrock, some soils are extremely deficient in plant nutrients. This situation occurs in a forest community on a sand-barrier island off Long Island, N.Y. However, it was demonstrated that salt spray trapped by the forest canopy provides sufficient nutrients to compensate for the poor soils. The trees in this sunken forest are prevented from growing above the level of the protective sand dunes by excess ocean spray and wind. As a result of this, a canopy of large surface area develops that plays a major role in the entrapment of salt-spray nutrients and their transfer, via precipitation, to the forest floor. It was suggested that where high levels of nutrients are available from meteorological sources, rates of succession can be greatly accelerated.

It also was demonstrated in 1974 that the successional plant species are important in maintenance of stability in climax communities, even when such species may be absent from the climax forest. Pin cherry is one species that can become established very rapidly following clearing of northern hardwood forest, and it is maintained for 20–25 years before eventual replacement by the dominant climax species. The pin cherry trees come from seeds that remain viable after being buried for long periods in the soil of the climax forest; germination of such seeds appears to be a response both to aging and to the disturbance of the system resulting from clearing. Once the pin cherry becomes established, nutrients are retained in the ecosystem, thus allowing more rapid reestablishment of the climax community.

For the past few years the possibility of transferring foreign genes into whole plants or into cultured plant cells had received attention. In 1974 a report of results obtained with intact *Arabidopsis* plants indicated that a genetic deficiency in *Arabidopsis* could be corrected by the incorporation of certain bacterial DNA, and that the corrected phenotype could be inherited. Some seeds of a thiamine-requiring strain of *Arabidopsis* will germinate to give plants that can synthesize thiamine if they are immersed in a solution containing high-molecular-weight DNA from bacterial cells capable of catalyzing the reaction that is missing in the deficient strain. The "transformed" plants grow in the absence of thiamine, although at a slower rate than normal plants; more significantly, however, sexually derived offspring of those plants also grow in the absence of externally supplied thiamine. Thus, while there was no information as to the molecular mechanisms involved, clearly the condition responsible for the altered phenotype can survive not only through many mitotic divisions, but also through meiosis. (*See also* GARDENING.)   (PETER L. WEBSTER)

[322.A; 332.B.C; 338.D]

MARINE BIOLOGY

During 1974 results were published of long-term marking and recapture experiments with cod, *Gadus morhua*. Of 18,822 marked fish released off Newfoundland in 1954–55, 26% were recovered in commercial catches up to 1970. Results gave information on intermingling of some Newfoundland Bank stocks and confirmed that other stocks are relatively isolated. Most of the fish remained in the northwestern Atlantic, but some were taken off Greenland, one in the North Sea, and two were recovered as far north as the Barents Sea. Tracking of individual cod in a Scottish sea loch was perfected by a new technique involving a pulsed ultrasonic transmitter inserted into the fish's stomach. Signals received by an array of omnidirectional hydrophones plotted movements over long periods, during which initial high activity was followed by a nocturnal cycle of activity.

Marine pollution studies were becoming more physiological in their approach. The poverty of marine flora off County Durham, Eng., had long been attributed to the direct results of pollution, and the absence of the alga *Himanthalia elongata* was now shown to be due to light reduction by silt. This cuts down light for growth of newly settled zygotes and forms an unsatisfactory substrate for their highly specialized mode of adhesion. Also, estuarine isopod crustaceans at low salinities were shown to be more influenced by heavy-metal pollution than are marine forms in full seawater. This argued against an earlier view that estuarine organisms, which are tolerant of wide changes of salinity and temperature, might also be more tolerant of pollutants than their counterparts in the open ocean.

Adaptation to polluted conditions had already been demonstrated in the polychaete *Nereis,* which in areas of high copper concentration has more copper in the tissues and is more tolerant of the metal in laboratory experiments. New work showed that *Nereis* from zinc polluted areas do not have higher zinc concentrations but are nevertheless zinc tolerant, probably by actively regulating their zinc content. Basic management of the coastal zone would require judgments of expected genetic changes of marine organisms due to the effects of pollutants, as shown by work on changes in gene frequency in the ectoproct *Schizoporella errata* in relation to environmental differences around Cape Cod, Massachusetts.

The deep-sea environment, characterized by high hydrostatic pressure and low temperature, had been considered to be unfavourable for the activities of most microorganisms; microbial decomposition at great depths is 10–100 times slower than at the surface. Japanese work with bacteria collected at a depth of 6,000 m. and cultured in situ with automatically added nutrients suggested that at least some bacteria at that depth are capable of organotrophic activity at the same rate as surface living forms. Off California high rates of population growth were reported for salps; a single swarm of these pelagic tunicates of the species *Thalia democratica* covered 3,500 sq.mi. With an average number of 275 salps per cu.m. to a depth of 70 m., this amounted to 10^{14} animals in the swarm. A considerable amount of energy must be required to support such populations of these filter feeders, which feed nonselectively and have incomplete digestion. Their fecal pellets probably carry significant amounts of carbon out of surface waters. Biochemical work on plankton demonstrated the occurrence of wax-ester metabolism in copepods. This was particularly high in *Calanus finmarchicus* feeding at the surface at night, and wax-esters are important metabolic energy reserves in this species. This kind of metabolism might be an adaptation to life in a partly anaerobic environment and calanoids were known to be abundant at oxygen tensions as low as 0.2 ml. per l. There was additional strong evidence for anaerobic, energy-yielding pathways in other marine invertebrates, particularly mollusks. Physiological work on fish reported on the mechanism of a remarkable "heat-exchanger" in the vascular system of *Tuna,* which permits these fast-swimming fish to retain metabolic heat and raise the body temperature by up to 20° C above ambient sea temperature. Physiological work also began on the coelacanth. After it had been first discovered in 1938, about 70 specimens were caught, mostly in poor condition, but material from a joint British-French-U.S. expedition to the Comoro Islands, between Madagascar and the African continent, permitted study of respiration and muscle proteins in this fish, which occupies a remarkable position in the evolution of vertebrates.

Behavioural studies were directed toward the little-studied settlement of coral planula larvae. Planulae of *Fungia* at settlement show negative phototaxis, which was surprising in view of the importance of light in coral growth, but it is protective in permitting the initial settlement stage to avoid predation. In other behavioural work the adaptive value was demonstrated in associations between hermit crabs and anemones. The hermit crab *Dardanus arrosor* in aquariums at first seeks out the anemone *Calliactis* and places specimens on the shell, but later this behaviour is lost and anemones may be eaten. However, if the octopus *Eledone* is introduced, *Dardanus* quickly reacquires the habit of placing *Calliactis* on its shell. Evidently the anemone affords protection against octopus predation. Other work on *Calliactis tricolor* demonstrated that fed anemones discharge fewer nematocysts than unfed animals when exposed to a food stimulus. Since nematocysts were usually thought to be independent effectors, this work raised the possibility of as yet undiscovered nervous or nonnervous control pathways. A remarkable daily rhythmicity is seen in the synchrony of parental behaviour and egg development of the lobster *Homarus gammarus*. Female lobsters emerge from their burrows and release larvae for a period of one minute after dusk each night for several weeks. It is not possible to stimulate artificial release of larvae before or after the hatching time, thus confirming a circadian rhythm in the embryo.

Experts on marine isopods had for some time been involved in controversy over the age of deep-sea faunas, Soviet workers favouring ancient origins and U.S. workers favouring recent origins. New Soviet work analyzing the distribution of isopods in the world oceans now suggested that the deep-sea isopod families are the youngest and that these families were derived from the Antarctic fauna in the Late Cretaceous Period. (The Cretaceous ended about 65 million years ago.)

(ERNEST NAYLOR)

[345.B]

MOLECULAR BIOLOGY

Biochemistry. The largest gap in the evolutionary sequence of living things is that between the prokaryotes, which do not contain subcellular organelles such as mitochondria, plastids, or nuclei, and the eukaryotes, which do. Prokaryotes encompass the bacteria and the blue-green algae and simpler forms such as mycoplasmas and viruses; the eukaryotes include all of the more complex organisms, both microscopic and macroscopic. Because the transition between these two classes of organisms must have occurred at least 1,000,000,000 years ago and must have involved tiny creatures, it is not likely that fossil records of this momentous transformation exist. Attempts to understand how this bridge was crossed are restricted to the creation of reasonable theories that can be supported by observations of present life but that can probably never be proved definitely.

There are two contrasting theories that deal with the transition from prokaryotes to eukaryotes. One suggests that all intracellular organelles developed gradually by a stepwise process in which cell membranes formed invaginations that ultimately pinched off to form membrane-enclosed vesicles, which then evolved their present complex internal structures and functions. The other theory supposes that mitochondria and plastids were acquired at once as the result of endocellular symbiosis, the invasion of one kind of cell by another to the mutual advantage of both cells. This theory proposes that a hypothetical precursor of the eukaryotes, a protoeukaryote, perhaps capable of anaerobic respiration, engulfed an aerobic prokaryote, giving rise to a stable and successful symbiosis. The prokaryote that had been engulfed achieved a secure living, while the host cell gained by adding the virtuosity of its new partner to its own metabolic repertoire. Gradual mutual adaptations, during the millennia following the original symbiotic event, would complete the conversion of the endosymbiont into mitochondrion or chloroplast. There are examples of endocellular symbiosis in the modern biosphere that serve as models of this original event.

If mitochondria did indeed evolve from an endosymbiotic prokaryote, similarities should exist between mitochondria and bacteria and many such similarities have been invoked in support of the symbiotic theory. They do not provide conclusive support, however, because it is possible that they are retained primitive characteristics. Thus, if there was a gradual transformation from prokaryote to protoeukaryote to eukaryote, the protoeukaryote could retain certain of the characteristics of the prokaryote and then conceivably sequester these primitive characteristics into the developing organelles. In this way mitochondria might seem similar to bacteria without having evolved directly from a prokaryotic endosymbiont.

Comparative studies of enzymes known as superoxide dismutases have recently provided data that may be the strongest support yet obtained for the symbiotic theory and that cannot be dismissed as a retained primitive characteristic. Superoxide dismutases serve to minimize the toxicity of oxygen by catalytically scavenging the superoxide radical (O_2^-), which is a common intermediate in the reduction of oxygen. This activity is needed only by cells that metabolize oxygen because only they run the risk of exposure to O_2^-. Obligate anaerobes are consequently devoid of superoxide dismutase. When oxygen was first introduced to the atmosphere of the earth in substantial amounts as a consequence of photosynthesis by blue-green algae, it necessitated the evolution of superoxide dismutases. Suppose that the protoeukaryotes had diverged, in an evolutionary sense, from the prokaryotes during the anaerobic phase of life's history on this planet. When faced with the common threat posed by oxygen, they could then independently evolve distinct superoxide dismutases, which would thereafter serve as unmistakable labels. Thus in any subsequent symbiosis between prokaryote and protoeukaryote the partners to the symbiosis would each carry its unique superoxide dismutase into the union.

Superoxide dismutases have been isolated from several bacteria, including the common *E. coli,* from the cytosols of numerous eukaryotes, and from chicken liver and human liver mitochondria. The superoxide dismutases from bacteria and mitochondria were found to be strikingly similar, whereas the enzymes from the cytosols of eukaryotes were distinct. Studies of the amino acid sequences of several of these enzymes performed at Duke University, Durham, N.C., have now shown that the mitochondrial and the bacterial superoxide dismutases are closely related to each other in a genetic sense, while being unrelated to the corresponding enzyme from eukaryotic cytosols. Because superoxide dismutases are useful only to oxygen-metabolizing cells they would not have been present in the prokaryotes that preceded the blue-green algae. The bacterial type of superoxide dismutase found in a mitochondrion, therefore, cannot be considered a retained primitive characteristic.

It is simple, therefore, to explain the similarities between the mitochondrial and the bacterial superoxide dismutases on the basis of the symbiotic theory of the origin of mitochondria; at the same time it is very difficult to account for these data without invoking symbiosis or a comparable catastrophic event.

(IRWIN FRIDOVICH)

[10/34.B.3.a]

Biophysics. Cellular repair of genetic material in living organisms is a continual process. Chromosomes are composed of tremendously large DNA molecules that, when stretched out into individual Watson-Crick duplexes, are thousands of times longer than their containing cells. Such gigantic molecules are subject to damage during cell growth and division, and for this reason cells have developed different types of repair systems to maintain genetic constancy. It was surprising to learn in 1974, however, that the repair systems first elucidated in the common intestinal bacterium *E. coli* were also observed in mammalian cells. Ultraviolet light is known to produce at least two kinds of lesions in DNA, strand breaks and dimers (chemically bonded pairs between neighbouring DNA bases termed pyrimidines). There are various means by which a cell can repair these lesions before mutation occurs in the DNA. In one process, known as photorepair or photoreactivation, exposure to light activates an enzyme that opens the chemical bond between the dimers and restores the pyrimidines to their original state. Another method of repair occurs in the dark and in cells containing certain repair enzymes. In this process, known as excision repair, a damaged strand on the DNA duplex is removed and replaced by undamaged DNA replicated from the other strand of the duplex. A third process, recombination repair, operates when both strands of the duplex are damaged in the same region and replaces one or both of them with genetic material from another undamaged duplex that has been replicated in the same cell and, therefore, possesses the identical local gene sequence of the damaged area.

The photorepair process was thought to be absent in placental mammals until 1974, when Betsy M. Sutherland of the University of California at Irvine demonstrated the presence of a photoreactivating DNA-repair enzyme in human leukocytes. The implications of this discovery in the search for the chemistry of skin cancer are tremendous. It is known that skin cancer is initiated by exposure to ultraviolet light, but the apparent lack of a photoreactivating enzyme in placental mammals had heretofore prevented direct evaluation of the role of dimers in skin cancer. Sutherland's discovery may be evidence that skin cancer stems from DNA damage and the lack of the photoreactivating enzyme.

A new and important area of radiation research concerned damage to mammalian cellular DNA produced by near ultraviolet (near-UV) radiation, of wavelengths between the visible and far-UV (300–400 nanometres [nm.]). R. J. Wang, J. D. Stoien, and F. Landa (University of Missouri) found that near-UV kills human, mouse, and Chinese hamster cells in tissue cultures. These results were expected because of many similar earlier results with microorganisms. There have been repeated demonstrations of killing and mutagenesis of bacteria and viruses by near-UV, and even of inactivation of purified DNA. Because of its similarity to UV radiation, near-UV was expected to produce similar lesions, and the usual pyrimidine dimers were indeed found. But near-UV also produced other kinds of lesions, in particular, alkali-labile bonds.

Near-UV, especially the component of 365 nm., has another, much more insidious effect: it inactivates cell repair systems. R. B. Webb and his colleagues at the Argonne National Laboratory, Illinois, showed that exposure of normally resistant bacteria to sublethal doses of near-UV prevented excision repair of UV damage. Even more directly, they also showed that 365 nm. radiation destroys the photoreactivating enzyme from yeast; after irradiation the enzyme could no longer monomerize pyrimidine dimers in native DNA. And very recently, Webb and his co-workers demonstrated that 365 nm. radiation also inactivates enzymes in the recombination-repair system.

Studies of the mechanism of action of near-UV have led to the finding of yet another effect not observed with far-UV, that of the synergistic interactions of radiations of different wavelengths in the inactivation of transforming DNA. M. J. Peak, J. G. Peak, and R. B. Webb (Argonne National Laboratory) found that direct inactivation of genetic material with 365 nm. radiation can be doubled or tripled by the prior or simultaneous administration of low doses of 313 nm. or 334 nm. radiation, respectively, even though these latter radiations alone have no observable effects.

Similar results were obtained for killing of bacteria by exposure to radiation at 334 nm. and 405 nm. This invalidates earlier conclusions based on experiments with single wavelengths alone.

It has been known for some time that sunlight can induce skin tumours in mammals, and the results implicated the causal wavelength as a natural near-UV component. That near-UV is indeed involved was shown by P. D. Forbes (Temple University) who produced tumours in mice by a single exposure to this radiation. His result and those discussed above led to a new evaluation of the role of the near-UV component of sunlight in the induction of skin tumours in man. Since the energy in this region of the spectrum accounts for about 6% of the total radiation received by the earth, there is no doubt that sufficient energy is available so that excessive exposure to sunlight must lead to production of genetic lesions in human cells. In addition, because near-UV inactivates cellular repair systems, epidermal cells become more sensitive to the far-UV component in sunlight.

(H. E. KUBITSCHEK)

[10/34.B.3.b]

Genetics. Genetic studies of somatic cells, made possible by a number of recognizable advances that occurred over the last two decades, continued to dominate reports.

Ernest Chu (University of Michigan) selectively obtained about 60 independent isolates in Chinese hamster cells that cannot utilize the sugar galactose. These isolates retained the ability to take up galactose from the medium, so they were not affected in transport of galactose into the cell. Further characterization had identified one of the lesions as affecting an enzyme involved in galactose utilization called phosphoglucomutase. Revertants to the original parental characteristic were recovered. Through cell-fusion studies of different pairs of isolates, a complementation map was developed. In every test, these isolates behaved as true mutations; that is, as altered forms of the galactose gene on the chromosome.

In a continued study, Frank Ruddle (Yale University) fused human cells and mouse cells with the aid of the Sendai virus. Certain enzymes of each cell type were identified using gel electrophoresis. Hybrid cells that retained different human chromosomes were examined to determine if they also produced the human type enzyme. In this fashion, particular traits were associated with certain chromosomes. The X chromosome was the object of study, since its morphology made it readily identifiable. Among X chromosomes, altered forms were obtained that had translocations or had lost segments of the X chromosome. By use of these altered X chromosomes in man-mouse hybrids and identification of human type enzymes, it was possible to assign positions on the long arm of the chromosome to five distinct traits. This important advance pointed the way for genetic mapping of human traits that should prove to be extremely useful in genetic counseling.

Whole, isolated chromosome transfer was reported by John Minna (National Cancer Institute). Chinese hamster fibroblast cells were arrested in the mitotic cycle by colchicine treatment. The cells were disrupted and the highly condensed individual chromosomes were isolated and fed to mouse L-cells that had a defect in the pyrimidine pathway and would not grow in a medium supplied with aminopterin and xanthine. The donor cells from which the chromosomes were isolated had no such defect. About 5% of the total

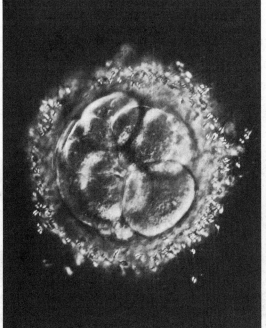

A controversy arose at the July meeting of the British Medical Association when Douglas Bevis of Leeds University claimed that in an experimental program, made by members he refused to identify, human ova had been fertilized in vitro and reimplanted in the women's uterine walls, leading in three cases to normal births. Bevis' announcement of the world's first "test-tube babies" was greeted with skepticism by colleagues familiar with progress in the field. At far left, a human ovum 40 hours after fertilization; left, after 90 hours.

plates made from this cell-chromosome mixture contained clones that grew under these selective conditions. Estimates showed that the formation of these positive clones was about one hundred times more frequent in the presence of the chromosomes than without them. Furthermore, cells from the positive clones contained an enzyme in the pyrimidine pathway identified with that from Chinese hamster cells, even though the cells themselves retained the karyotype and morphology of the mouse L-cells. This indicated that the mouse L-cells had incorporated the Chinese hamster cell chromosome from the medium, an unexpected and most significant finding that would greatly aid the advancement of somatic-cell genetics.

A highly significant discovery was made that was already having far-reaching effects. The work was reported out of the laboratories of Herbert Boyer (University of California, San Francisco) and Stanley Cohen (Stanford University). It involved the use of an enzyme, restriction endonuclease, to cleave DNA molecules in specific ways so that different molecules could be joined together in new combinations. The restriction endonuclease recognized symmetrical sites in DNA base sequences. Certain restriction endonucleases cut the double-stranded DNA molecule symmetrically; that is, between bonds of directly opposite bases. Others, however, cut it asymmetrically or between bonds of bases that are not opposite each other. The asymmetrically cleaving enzyme was used to produce DNA fragments with single-strand ends that matched the single-strand ends of other molecular fragments from different sources. In this manner DNA from one bacterium, a *Staphylococcus* plasmid, was joined to another, a plasmid from *E. coli*. The rejoining of DNA molecules required bringing the single strands into register, a process called annealing, and then forming covalent bonds between the adjacent ends enzymatically. A plasmid is a self-replicating genetic entity, and the cleaved *E. coli* plasmid retained this property when joined to other fragments of DNA. Next the rejoined molecules were introduced in *E. coli* by transformation, a process whereby cells can take up DNA from the medium. Those rare cells that had incorporated a rejoined plasmid were selected

because the *E. coli* plasmid conferred resistance to an antibiotic to that cell. Study of those transformed cells showed that the attached foreign DNA replicated and expressed genetic properties that were new to the cell containing the plasmid. This finding was important because it can be applied to DNA molecules from any source. It was theoretically possible to attach genes from microbes, plants, or higher animals to this plasmid and to have them expressed by *E. coli*, making possible the production of biologically important substances, such as antibiotics and insulin, simply and economically.

A controversy arose over this and other similar experiments. In July, in an unprecedented move, a group of molecular biologists with the backing of the U.S. National Academy of Sciences called for limitations on what they deemed a "potentially harmful" line of genetic-engineering research. The committee of eleven NAS members included four men who were directly involved in DNA recombination research. Their concern stemmed from the possibility that misuse of the bacterium *E. coli*, present in every human intestinal tract and one of molecular biology's favourite tools, might produce a laboratory mutant that was resistant to known antibiotics. The moratorium was aimed at two specific types of experiment: those that involve the introduction into a bacterium of genes that either confer resistance to antibiotics or cause the formation of bacterial toxins, and those that involve the introduction of genes from animal viruses into bacteria.   (JAMES C. COPELAND)

[10/34.B.3.c]

ZOOLOGY

Some interesting findings concerning energy metabolism were reported. C. R. Taylor and co-workers continued their studies dealing with locomotion and compared the energy expenditure of small animals (white mice) and large animals (chimpanzees) while running uphill. They found that the mice used as much additional energy as the chimps per unit weight running up a 15° hill. However, since the mice used about eight times as much energy as the chimps when running on level ground, the relative increase in energy used was much lower for the mice than for the chimps. This results from the fact that the mice have about the same energy cost for lifting one kilogram to a height of one metre as the chimps. Interestingly enough, about 90% of the energy used in running uphill is regained upon running downhill again, because of the acceleration of the limbs by gravity. Field studies were reported by F. L. Carpenter of the hypothermia (decrease in body temperature) during torpor in the Andean hillstar hummingbird (*Oreotrochilus estella*). Birds were found in caves in a state of torpor and their body temperatures determined as a function of the ambient temperature. The torpor occurs more frequently at night and lasts longer in winter, and calculations showed that the increased torpor in winter could not be the result of increased need for energy, because winter birds consumed fewer calories per day than summer birds. It is likely that torpor is a mechanism for conserving energy needed to control body temperature and that it is regulated by an annual rhythm.

R. W. Guimond and V. H. Hutchison studied the relative importance of the various modes of respiration in the hellbender, a large aquatic salamander. Although large lungs are present, they are no more than transparent, poorly vascularized sacs and probably function mainly as hydrostatic structures, in view of the unimportance of aerial respiration. This was found to account for only a small fraction of the external respiration, whereas aquatic respiration accounted for 90% of the oxygen consumption and 97% of carbon dioxide production at all temperatures studied. This in spite of the fact that gills are lacking in this species. It is likely that gas exchange occurs directly through the skin, which is richly vascularized all the way out to the surface, an unusual histological characteristic. Furthermore, the animal is dorsally flattened and skin folds increase the surface area. There is also a behavioural pattern, previously observed but of unknown significance. While underwater, the animals rock or sway, continually breaking the boundary layer between the water and the skin, thus ensuring that the body surface is kept in continuous contact with oxygenated water. This is the largest aquatic vertebrate known that lacks gills and yet uses an almost exclusively aquatic mode of respiration. Another respiratory study has ecological implications. K. L. Smith, Jr., and R. R. Hessler used their newly

developed method for determining the oxygen consumption of individual deep-sea animals. The metabolic activity of two common deep-sea fishes (*Coryphaenoides acrolepis*, a rattail, and the hagfish *Eptatretus deani*) was compared with that of related shallow-water forms. The researchers used their "remote underwater manipulator," a fish trap that permits oxygen consumption measurements, for the study. *C. acrolepis* had an oxygen consumption of only 2.4 ml. per hr. per kg. wet weight, whereas for *Gadus morhua*, a related shallow-water species, the figure was much higher, 55.6. The deep-sea hagfish *E. deani* had a consumption of only 2.2, whereas two shallow-water species, the hagfish *E. stoutii* and the lamprey *Petromyzon marinus*, had figures of 9.4 and 75.5, respectively. The results showed that deep-sea species have much lower metabolic activity than related shallow-water species, and extend earlier results on decreased metabolic activity in the deep sea that may result from a combination of factors; for example, food availability, pressure, and temperature. They hypothesized that deepwater fishes may exist in a quiescent state until food is available, which would be an interesting way of conserving energy in the absence of food.

A variety of studies dealing with behaviour were reported. The evidence that animal grazing produced bare zones (halos) adjacent to chaparral was extended to the marine environment by J. C. Ogden and co-workers, who studied the cause of halos in sea grass surrounding coral reefs in the West Indies. Previous explanations had attributed the halos to physical factors or fish grazing. They found, however, that grazing by the sea urchin *Diadema antillarum* is the cause. The urchins remain active on the reefs during daylight, where they are evidently safe from fish predation. At night they move to the halo areas of the grass, where they feed, and analysis of their stomach contents revealed turtle grass (*Thalassia*) and carbonate sand. The grass shows the characteristic signs of having been bitten off by a sea urchin, not by a fish. Work with homing pigeons by C. Walcott and R. P. Green showed that it is possible to alter the course of homing pigeons by changing the direction of an applied magnetic field. Birds were equipped with a pair of small, battery-powered coils around their heads. If the south magnetic pole was up, they oriented toward home normally under both sun and overcast skies. However, if the polarity was reversed they oriented toward home when the sun was visible, but frequently flew away from home under an overcast, adding to the evidence that bird orientation may be affected by the earth's magnetic field.

A finding of genetic importance was reported by M. S. Calton and T. E. Denton, who studied the chromosomes of the chocolate gourami, *Sphaerichthys osphromenoides*, and found that it has the lowest chromosome number yet reported for fishes. The body cells have 16 chromosomes (diploid number) and the gametes have 8 (haploid number). Other members of the same family, Belontiidae, have diploid numbers of from 42 to 48. The origins of such low chromosome numbers are complex, but the process tends to produce a species that is especially vulnerable to genetic extinction, because loss of one of the remaining chromosomes should cause the loss of vital genes. Indeed, the chocolate gourami is a highly specialized and delicate tropical fish species.

Two studies illustrating the harmful effects that environmental pollution has on animals were reported.

An impression of a 30 million-year-old grasshopper, found in the Ruby River basin in southwestern Montana.

COURTESY, STANDLEY E. LEWIS, ST. CLOUD STATE COLLEGE

D. B. Peakall published data showing that DDE, the major metabolite of DDT, is present in high concentrations in the dried egg membranes of peregrine falcons. These data showed that, at least as early as 1948, DDE was present in peregrine eggs in sufficient concentration to account for the eggshell thinning that started about 1947 in the eggs of predatory birds and helped resolve the controversy surrounding this question. Thus, DDT is probably the major cause of the decline of peregrine falcons in North America and Europe and the termination of their breeding in the eastern United States. Another study suggested that high levels of organochlorine pollutant residues in the mothers of California sea lions are the cause of premature births. R. L. DeLong and co-workers analyzed for residues of DDT and PCBs (polychlorinated biphenyls) in tissues of both premature and normal mothers in 1970 on San Miguel Island. They found significantly higher levels of both DDT and PCB residues in the premature mothers. Premature pups have a variety of defects—*e.g.*, lack of fur, lack of motor coordination, and respiratory problems—and tend to die early. Although the available information does not prove that the organochlorine residues cause the premature births, other information suggests that this may be the case. DDT induces premature birth in rabbits, feeding of PCB compounds causes respiratory failure and death in adult ranch minks, and the presence of organochlorine residues is associated with reproductive failure in ranch minks fed fish from Lake Michigan.   (RONALD R. NOVALES)

[10/34.B.5.1]

Entomology. The U.S. Environmental Protection Agency halted further production of the insecticide dieldrin and its chemical ally aldrin and recommended that their use be phased out. The agency cited evidence that dieldrin produced cancers in mice and rats, and that tests for dieldrin in human autopsies and surgically removed tissues were almost 100% positive and indicated an average body burden almost three times the concentration that had caused cancers in some laboratory rats. The manufacturer countered that there was no evidence that dieldrin had ever caused cancer in humans and the U.S. Department of Agriculture (USDA) defended use of these insecticides, especially in corn and citrus cultivation. In the U.K., the Ministry of Agriculture, Fisheries, and Food banned the use of dieldrin as a seed dressing of winter wheat. Donald Jefferies and colleagues at the Monks Wood Experimental Station reported that sowing of the dieldrin-treated seed caused an almost 70-fold increase in the dieldrin burden of field mice and voles, sufficient to kill most of them, and noted that birds of prey that fed on vermin were then at hazard.

Thomas H. Jukes of the University of California at Berkeley, writing in the journal *Die Naturwissenschaften*, strongly defended the use of DDT, which had been banned in 1972 in the U.S. and was either banned or subject to restricted use in many other countries. He pointed out that DDT had remained unrivaled for economy and effectiveness. It had controlled the insect vectors of a number of tropical diseases and, in controlling the malarial mosquito alone, had saved many millions of lives since 1942. DDT had reduced annual deaths from malaria in Ceylon (Sri Lanka) from nearly three million in 1946 to only 17 in 1963; in 1964, however, its use had been discontinued and deaths from malaria had steadily increased thereafter until in 1968 and 1969 2.5 million people had died of the disease. Jukes claimed that the per-

sistent attacks on use of DDT had been based on untrue or unreliable data. Even in the manufacture of DDT no one had suffered ill effects from prolonged exposure to it, and where serious ecological effects had been attributed to DDT, other insecticides such as dieldrin were often the culprit.

Meanwhile, the world's most grandiose nonchemical insect control program had run into difficulties. The screwworm fly lays its eggs on or near the wounds of cattle, and the maggots develop in the surrounding muscle with devastating effect on the victim. From 1957 the USDA, at enormous cost, had bred hundreds of millions of the flies annually, sterilizing them with gamma radiation and releasing them in order that the sterilized males could mate with wild, fertile females—which then laid infertile eggs. By 1964 the campaign had all but cleared screwworm from the U.S. and, from 1962, the sterilized flies were released in northern Mexico and southern Texas to neutralize the inflow of fertile flies from Mexico. At first the program seemed completely successful, but from 1972 screwworm again built up in the rich cattle-raising districts of the U.S. R. C. Bushland of the USDA, Texas, reported that the laboratory-bred flies were somewhat smaller and lighter in colour than the wild flies and suggested that another wild strain, the females of which distinguished between wild and laboratory bred males and tended to avoid mating with the latter, might have evolved.

Much work continued on the physiology of pheromones—chemicals released by insects that served as sex attractants or in other forms of communication. Earlier research, aimed at trapping or confusing insect pests with synthetic pheromones, had revealed the puzzling fact that a number of species might share the same sex pheromone. What, then, decided who would mate with whom? The answer appeared to lie in the secretion by females of more than one sex pheromone. Yoshio Tamaki and Takashi Yushima of the National Institute of Agricultural Sciences in Tokyo reported that the relative proportions of two pheromones, shared by the cotton leaf worm moth *Spodoptera littoralis* and related species, determined which species was attracted. These scientists also suspected that the females of the one species secreted yet a further substance (or substances) that inhibited the attentions of males of the other. Similarly, L. L. Sower and colleagues of the USDA, Florida, reported that the Indian meal moth *Plodia* and the almond moth *Cadra* shared a sex pheromone but the female *Plodia* secreted an additional, related chemical that inhibited *Cadra* males.

Fundamental studies of the mechanism of insect chemical senses revealed that incoming molecules were initially bound to specific sites on the sensory hairs of insects. S. M. Ferkovitch and colleagues of the USDA, Florida, stated that these sites contained enzymes that broke down the chemical as part of the sensory process; and Osamu Koizumi and colleagues at Kyushu University, Japan, found that the enzymes at the tips of the sugar-tasting hairs of the blowfly were insolubly bound to the cuticle.

Working on other than chemical senses, Philip S. Callahan and Felix Lee, also of the USDA, Florida, offered a new explanation for the fluttering of moths around candles. They found that flying moths emit infrared radiation in rapid pulses owing to the "chopping" effect of the wingbeat, and that the insects appear to have infrared sensing devices on their antennae. Each species has a characteristic emanation,

A member
of the honeycreeper
family, found
on a Hawaiian volcano,
is believed to be the first
new genus and species
of bird discovered
in ten years.

and a flickering candle flame was found to give out a variable pattern of infrared emission that simulates many different species in turn. Callahan and Lee suggested that male moths find night-flying females by these infrared pulses and that this explains why mostly males are attracted to a candle and why some even attempt to mate with the flame.   (PETER W. MILES)

[313.H.5]

Ornithology. In a startling paper P. Ward and A. Zahavi offered a new explanation for social breeding and roosting in birds, namely that these aggregations serve principally as information centres for location of food or of good feeding sites: birds that have fed well the previous day leave the roost in a purposeful manner that is recognized by those that have fed badly and they follow the well-fed birds. The many species for which this was believed to be true included the Eurasian white wagtail, the house sparrow, the cattle egret, and the Quelea finch.

At the 26th Ornithological Congress held at Canberra, Austr., Aug. 12–17, 1973, Janet Kear and R. K. Murton described a new criterion for unraveling the geographic origins of the Australian waterfowl. The breeding responses, species by species, to the same day-length cycle (all birds having been transported to latitude 50° N at Slimbridge, Eng.) helped to show likely affinities between different genera, and whether they had developed these responses in the tropics or in the high latitudes in the Northern or Southern Hemisphere. In Australia waterfowl tend to breed according to the rains; but farther from the Equator day-length is important in determining egg laying, and breeding is predictable.

The Soviet ornithologist Vladimir Galushin showed that raptorial birds that depend on few prey species—especially the rough-legged buzzard, which lives in open tundra habitats, and also species in semidesert and desert belts of Eurasia—undergo local fluctuations that are synchronous with fluctuations in the numbers of their main prey species (e.g., the Norway lemming). He argued that these bird species have evolved, as an important adaptation, the ability to undertake "searching migrations" that enable them to find and settle in areas of adequate food supply, often far removed from the previous breeding area. A new genus and species of honeycreeper (family Drepanididae) was discovered on Haleakala volcano on the island of Maui, Hawaii. It is the size of a house sparrow, but brownish olive above, light buff below, and has a distinctive black face mask. The first checklist for

Yugoslavia was published by S. D. Matvejev and V. F. Vasic, listing 376 species, of which about 256 still bred. Species extinguished in the 20th century include the white pelican, mute swan, crane, great bustard, curlew, snipe, and black-winged stilt. In Dalmatia the Dalmatian pelican had avoided extinction, with 20 pairs known to be in existence.

A study of large herds of nonbreeding whooper swans in Iceland showed that at midsummer when day-length is very long the birds continued feeding all night. Overall, they spent half their time feeding, a quarter resting (regardless of the time of day), and a quarter preening and bathing. In *The Seabirds of Britain and Ireland,* Stanley Cramp, W. R. P. Bourne, and David Saunders reported the results of a huge survey, Operation Seafarer, designed to locate the seabird colonies of the British Isles and assess the numbers of the 24 species concerned. The total population of seabirds was about three million pairs. Contrary to previous estimates, land birds, with some 50 million pairs, far outnumbered seabirds. Some marine birds like the puffin were decreasing. On the other hand, some were more numerous than previously, the fulmar and herring gull being classic examples. Man's part in this spread was not easy to assess, but the availability of garbage, particularly in winter, must have helped the herring gull. The extent to which the fulmar's remarkable spread could be attributed to an increase in fish gutted at sea by more and more trawlers was undecided. Gulls, even the oceanic kittiwake, might well have benefited similarly, and the sharp decline of the great skua in southern Iceland, together with the apparent removal of the birds to Scotland, was believed to have been caused by the decline in trawling in the waters south of Iceland.

In *Born to Sing: an Interpretation and World Survey of Bird Song,* Charles Hartshorne held that birds sing partly to satisfy an aesthetic sense that they themselves have, thus anticipating man in that sense, and argued that this enjoyment supplements rather than conflicts with the territorial and other biological explanations of song. He showed how birdsongs avoid mere regularity unrelieved by deviation and pauses and mere randomness. He also demonstrated the presence in bird music of all the simpler musical devices—e.g., accelerando (wood warbler), ritardando (yellow-billed cuckoo), crescendo (Heuglin's robin-chat of Africa), and diminuendo (grassland yellow finch of the neotropics)—and defined degrees of singing skill in terms of six parameters: loudness, scope, continuity, tone quality, organization, and imitative ability. Out of about 8,600 bird species only 22 rated 46 points or above, out of a maximum of 48. All but two are Oscines. A discography of North American bird-voice phonograph records was published in the journal *Recorded Sound,* listing over 100 disks. About 650 species' voices had been published. An ambitious multi-author work, *Owls of the World,* critically examined the evolution, structure, and ecology of owls.

(JEFFERY BOSWALL)

See also Earth Sciences; Environment; Health and Disease.

[313.J.6]

ENCYCLOPÆDIA BRITANNICA FILMS. *The Ears and Hearing* (2nd ed., 1969); *Muscle: Dynamics of Contraction* (1969); *The Origin of Life—Chemical Evolution* (1969); *Radioisotopes: Tools of Discovery* (1969); *Theories on the Origin of Life* (1969); *The Nerve Impulse* (1971); *Seed Dispersal* (3rd ed., 1971); *Investigating Hibernation* (1972); *A Bird of Prey: The Red Tailed Hawk* (1972); *World of Close-Up* (1972); *How Do They Move?* (1973); *Some Friendly Insects* (1973); *Cactus: Profile of a Plant* (1973); *Nematode* (1973); *The Mayfly: Ecology of an Aquatic Insect* (1973).

Liquors, Alcoholic:
see Alcoholic
Beverages

Literature

The 1974 Nobel Prize for Literature went to two elderly Swedish writers, Eyvind Johnson and Harry Martinson. Each had made a substantial contribution to Swedish literature, Johnson in the 1930s with his "Olof" cycle of autobiographical novels and Martinson as novelist and poet, but they were virtually unknown outside their own culture. (*See* NOBEL PRIZES.)

It was suggested that the Swedish Academy had perhaps not wanted to crowd the centre of the stage should 1970 laureate Aleksandr Solzhenitsyn (*see* BIOGRAPHY) wish to travel belatedly to Stockholm (which he did indeed do in December), and so quietly took the opportunity of honouring two of its own members. Certainly Solzhenitsyn continued to be the focus of much international attention both before and after his expulsion from the Soviet Union, as did the condition of Soviet dissidents as a whole. They were admired more than ever, and, in an abstract sort of way, even envied for their clarity of purpose by writers who felt increasingly impotent in the face of the economic and political storm clouds looming in the West. Addressing "Solzhenitsyn, Bukovsky, Amalrik, Maksimov" and other past and present prisoners of conscience in the U.S.S.R., Eugene Ionesco, in a message to the new magazine *Kontinent* established by émigrés from the European Communist countries, wrote: "Only you and they can still do something for this world of ours. We . . . who have lived in freedom and comfort while you died and were resurrected every minute, only to die again, we have neither your experience nor your authority."

The appearance of *Kontinent* (which would not restrict itself entirely to émigré writers) was an event of some potential significance in view of the quite prodigal export of talent from the U.S.S.R., and at a time when long-established literary magazines, especially in France and the U.S., had been losing money and influence steadily. In London *The New Review* began its career with much goodwill and a series of glossy, lively, and somewhat miscellaneous issues, and a venerable tradition of British literary life ended when John Gross, the new editor of *The Times Literary Supplement* (*TLS*), abolished anonymity for all major reviews. The death occurred in November of critic Cyril Connolly, founder of the influential *Horizon* (1939–50; *see* OBITUARIES).

In Britain, as in most countries, inflation squeezed publishers' profits painfully, causing Penguin Books, for example, to curtail some of the more radical and interesting parts of its program, and making it more difficult for new and experimental work, especially in fiction, to reach its small and important public. There were signs that writers, like other white-collar workers, were feeling the need for collective institutions, as well as agents, to protect their interests. The debate on what a writers' union should be and do continued in West Germany; in Britain argument centred more modestly on how public lending right might bring the greatest good to the greatest number of authors.

It was a year in which the younger media seemed to be feeding on literature, and the novel in particular, with increasing appetite, sometimes paying their way by restoring once popular works to a new readership. Anthony Trollope and Thomas Hardy (and their publishers) were beneficiaries of this transaction in Britain, following immensely popular television adaptations, and F. Scott Fitzgerald began to acquire another generation of readers as a result of a film version of *The Great Gatsby*.

An intriguing mystery of modern literary biography seemed solved when the widow of the enigmatic novelist known as B. Traven (author of *The Treasure of the Sierra Madre;* 1934) declared at a seminar of his work at Tucson, Ariz., that her husband had indeed been also Ret Marut, the German anarchist leader in the Bavarian revolution of 1919. In August the Chinese reported the finding of variant texts, 2,000 years old, of the *Tao-Te Ching* in a tomb near the capital of Hunan Province. The 50th anniversary of the death of Franz Kafka was observed in other parts of the world with more enthusiasm than in Prague, the city of his nightmares. And Vienna mounted a week of lectures and programs to mark the centenary of the birth of its most mordant critic, Karl Kraus, author of *The Last Days of Mankind*.

(W. L. WEBB)

ENGLISH

United Kingdom. "Under pressure of reduced material and psychological circumstances . . . , an unmistakable thinness, corner-of-the-mouth sparsity, sour fastidiousness have developed in the English intellectual, literary tone. The age is less one of anxiety than of envy, hopeful malice." George Steiner, invited to scrutinize "The English Intellectual" in the first issue of the first major literary magazine to be launched in London for years, found the patient's condition to be the same, only worse: still willfully isolating himself from the main modern European traditions of intellectual discourse; struggling petulantly to preserve a native cultural identity, even a linguistic integrity, against "the hammering incursions . . . of the American model"; sourly aware that no talent since D. H. Lawrence had been "at once 'English English' and, beyond cavil, of world rank."

Steiner's recriminations, and even more his rhetoric, were themselves not beyond cavil, but it was hardly a year of high confidence for people preoccupied with the "condition-of-England" question, and the charges of thinness and insularity seemed to stick. Certainly

GODFREY ARGENT—CAMERA PRESS/PICTORIAL PARADE

English novelist Kingsley Amis, whose black comedy of old age, "Ending Up," was published in 1974.

the "leader" of that first issue of Ian Hamilton's glossy, state-aided *The New Review* was insular enough—a straw poll (35 professors of English and 35 writers) on the dimly smoldering question of whether John Gross, the new editor of the *TLS*, should abandon the paper's tradition of anonymous reviewing. Most of them—especially the professors—thought he should, and he did—while restoring anonymity for a considerably expanded Commentary section of high-pop cultural gossip and reportage.

The changes in style and personnel of the still influential cultural magazines were significant ones. They seemed to show that a new, post-"Angry" generation had come through. Children of the Hitler war and the following years of austerity, emancipated pupils of *Scrutiny*-trained teachers (or of F. R. Leavis himself), readers at an impressionable age of Kingsley Amis (*I Like It Here*) and the fine gray lines of Philip Larkin, they carried less, and different, ideological baggage than their contemporaries elsewhere in Europe and on this front at least were not secure against Steiner's charges of insularity. On the other hand, they seemed generally less committed to the doubly islanded traditions of the Oxbridge culture, more in touch with other roots of British life in the regions, and newly resistant to American cultural hegemony (perhaps partly inoculated by outgrown postgraduate infatuation with the power and prestige of American academic criticism, partly by a sense that after Vietnam and Watergate it would be difficult to feel quite the same about the "superior energies" of the American imagination).

Fiction. Of course no new literature sprang into life overnight at the behest of this emergent generation of editors. The map was not greatly altered. "We have an elegant sufficiency of women novelists," wrote Dame Rebecca West in an elegantly sufficient survey of the established best of them for a feature on "Women's Lit" in the new *TLS*. It remained abundantly true: for well-established historical and psychological reasons, women novelists still seemed most at home creatively in times of frustration and deep insecurity. Iris Murdoch produced *The Sacred and Profane Love Machine* (another of her operatically elaborate fictions manipulating this time a psychotherapist and a detective story writer to enact her

Iris Murdoch, whose new novel, "The Sacred and Profane Love Machine," appeared in 1974.

CECIL BEATON—CAMERA PRESS

subtle philosophical speculations on the nature of love, death, and the greedy stratagems of self), and in the stories of *A Scandalous Woman* Edna O'Brien put her "May Queens whose May Days are always rainy" (Rebecca West's neat placing of her generic heroine) through a set of dances gravely gay.

Dame Rebecca added to her list *A Source of Embarrassment,* a subtle comedy by a younger writer, A. L. Barker, about a wife and mother too good for her family to live with, and indeed sentenced to death by cancer, and found it as good as any of the novels by her older sisters. She might also have added *The Bottle Factory Outing* by Beryl Bainbridge (winner of *The Guardian*'s 1974 fiction prize), a novelist whose work does perhaps suggest some characteristics of the sensibility of the generation establishing itself in England. Significantly, her last novel, *The Dressmaker*, was sponsored for the richest British literary prize, the Booker, by Karl Miller (former editor of *The Listener*), who also wrote for *The New York Review of Books* an appreciative retrospective review of her work, noting its close and emotionally intelligent comprehending of the lives of the English working class in their decaying, concrete-patched Victorian cities. Where the earlier work was mostly commemorative of that life in the late 1940s and '50s, as it began to emerge from the isolating narrowness of its traditional poverty, the new novel was of the present, involving two lumpish provincial girls and a coach-load of Italian immigrant workers from a London bottle factory in a bizarrely flirtatious jaunt to a stately home that ends in a kind of comic nightmare. It, too, told much, incidentally, of the other nation of England, but in an entirely individual voice, full of dark wit and formidable vitality: "though there is a kind of pity in the writing," said *The Observer*'s reviewer, "there's a much stronger sense of sheer fixated curiosity."

Novels by two other candidates of the sisterhood, Susan Hill's *In the Springtime of the Year* and Jennifer Johnston's *How Many Miles to Babylon?*, were admired. Miss Hill, already a considerable prize-winner, was the more skillful and assured, but each continued to work that familiar (but yet again fashionable) vein of sensitive and slightly regressive pastoral nostalgia, Jennifer Johnston's nostalgia this time taking her as far back as the world of World War I—which was in fact the world of Susan Hill's previous novel.

If feminine sensibilities generally seemed to handle the novel form more confidently, one male English novelist at least showed no slackening of confidence or vitality: the fecund Anthony Burgess published two novels within the space of three months. *The Clockwork Testament*, subtitled "Enderby's End," wrote off his old poet hero in a blaze of inglorious picaresque adventures in New York and environs where he had been reduced to teaching creative writing to fund the finishing of his epic poem. "That much abused creature of earth and air," wrote Norman Shrapnel, "goes out with spirit, firing from every aperture"—and enabling his creator to settle a score or two in the matter of the filming of *A Clockwork Orange* and its consequences. *Napoleon Symphony*, one of his historical novels, provided a characteristically rich set of variations on Napoleon's life and loves, using Beethoven's "Eroica" for structure rather as Joyce used Homer for *Ulysses*.

Lawrence Durrell's *Monsieur* was Alexandria revisited, with many of the themes of his novel quartet echoed and transposed to Avignon and Venice (lusciously described), dissolving time and space, juggling with sex, theology, and history, and mounting a considerable defense of the Templars and their heresy. Surfeited so sumptuously, most critics complained wistfully of indigestion. No thinness here; but who could afford such prose in these inflationary times? The wordman's book of the year, however, was surely *The Terrors of Dr. Treviles,* which showed Peter Redgrove continuing the attempt of his poems and his previous novel to make a one-man surrealist revival in England. Not strictly one man, however, since this fantastical romance was written with Penelope Shuttle, who also produced a book of poems with him; and the surrealism was of a peculiarly English kind, dreaming densely of Blake and Celtic mythologies. John Fowles, an easier and more fashionable writer, grouped a collection of novellas around his own translation of the 12th-century Celtic romance called *Eliduc,* which was key to the title story, *The Ebony Tower,* an account of a visit to the strange Breton ménage of an old expatriate English painter done with a characteristically teasing shimmer of unresolved sexuality.

There were weeks when death appeared to be the fashionable subject of a rather deadly year. Kingsley Amis, when in form still the best "English English" comic writer of his generation, offered, in *Ending Up,* a geriatric farce about two retired homosexual staff officers in which the crusty fun was occluded by shudders of a *timor mortis* that the author plainly did not have under control. One had to turn to his far from geriatric spiritual great-uncle P. G. Wodehouse and *Aunts Are Not Gentlemen* for reassurance as assured as ever. C. P. Snow added to the fascination with dying the taboo subject of money (*In Their Wisdom*), deploying formidable expertise about expensive surgery, the avoidance of death duties, and other matters of urgent interest to senior citizens of the British upper classes. In *Holiday,* a study of a man cast adrift by the traumas of bereavement and a broken marriage, Stanley Middleton—another traditional realist but with imaginative skills strong and patient enough to keep the form alive—produced scenes from modern provincial life that earned him a salute as the Gissing of our time and a half share of the prestigious Booker Prize. The other half went to Nadine Gordimer for *The Conservationist,* an intricate study of her native South Africa and of its inhabitants.

Among the younger writers were two excellent realists of a similar and unusual kind. Ian Cochrane's *Gone in the Head* (runner-up for *The Guardian*'s fiction prize) and David Cook's *Happy Endings* both achieved not description but a tense enactment of the life of a deprived and damaged British society, Cochrane especially, using the eyes and language of an adolescent boy on a council estate in a raw Ulster town with a quiet skill that, as Robert Nye observed, "gives articulation to an observing of life that does not often find words." Intelligent comedy seems harder for this generation, but David Pownall's *The Raining Tree War* was an almost Marxian romp through the improbable social reality of certain sections of post-colonial Africa, and Tom Sharpe, who conjured dark hilarity from South Africa's nightmares in earlier novels, was almost as funny about the tribal rites of a far from impossible Oxbridge college in *Porterhouse Blue.*

J. G. Ballard and Colin MacInnes speculated in dangerous psychosocial properties, Ballard, in *Concrete Island,* marooning a crashed Jaguar and its driver for 24 chapters in the interstices of a vast motorway junction, and MacInnes projecting the development of a fancy sort of English fascism in *Out of the Garden* (too sentimentally and explicitly for the good of his fiction, though his excellent track record as a short-range social prophet inspired uneasiness). Probably the best historical novel of the year was the ambitious study of St. Joan by the Australian Thomas Keneally, *Blood Red, Sister Rose,* and there were excellent collections of stories by V. S. Pritchett (*The Camberwell Beauty*) and George Mackay Brown (*Hawkfall*). The strenuous half-dozen from Patrick White in *The Cockatoos* mostly suggested that his heavyweight talent needed more room than this form affords.

The year saw the recovery from French of Beckett's early novel *Mercier and Camier* and the *Texts for Nothing,* deeply Irish and refreshingly robust after the bleached bones of the latest prose fragments; also Joyce Cary's unfinished novel *Cock Jarvis,* dangling strangely in the hiatus in reputation that had followed his death; and *Challenge,* Vita Sackville-West's long-suppressed novel about her love affair with Violet Keppel, with its faint echoes of *Orlando.* Three of the wayward fictions of W. B. Yeats's painter brother Jack were reissued, *The Charmed Life* the most rapt and haunting of them; and Macmillan & Co. produced the first volumes of an excellent New Wessex edition of Thomas Hardy.

Biography, History, Letters. There was a modest Romantic Revival: not just a coinciding of the 150th anniversary of Byron's death and attendant publications with new biographies of Shelley and Mary Wollstonecraft and an excellent book on Keats, but a kind of fashionable response to some of these things, reflecting boredom with the modern, skepticism about the superficial rationality of creaking social arrangements, and movement toward feeling (or mindlessness, some would have said). The Romantics apart, neoromanticism reached some sort of climax with the publication of *Conundrum,* in which the writer now called Jan Morris related how she had been struggling to get out of her alter ego, the journalist and traveler, husband and father James Morris, through all his charmed and eventful life; and how eventually he had done the gallant thing and brought her somewhat into being with the help of hormone pills and a Casablanca surgeon's knife. Not least because it had happened to a writer gifted enough to be able to tell it well, it was an extraordinary story, full of incidental insights: for example into the bisexual tone of such English institutions as public schools and smart cavalry regiments. What some critics found improbable was the author's sheer ineffability. "Jan ends by savouring the possibility of 'transcending' both sexes in a manner yet to be devised. Some people are never satisfied," wrote the *TLS* reviewer in a piece headed "Mr. Morris Changes Trains," the last of the *ancien régime*'s notorious puns.

Claire Tomalin's *The Life and Death of Mary Wollstonecraft* gave a clear and thoughtful account of a woman who was thought improperly to play a man's part by her fierce independence of mind and action, and of her loves and milieux, among the radical dissenters of London and the revolutionaries of Paris. *Shelley—The Pursuit,* by the young poet and critic Richard Holmes, told that extraordinary story in great detail in a huge book—"the fullest connected

Lawrence Durrell, whose novel "Monsieur," published in 1974 and set in Avignon and Venice, echoed themes of his earlier "Alexandria Quartet."

account we yet have of Shelley's writing and publishing history," thought Raymond Williams, and particularly good on what another critic, Kathleen Raine, put down as "student politics": giving us a chance to see Shelley much plainer than before. Christopher Ricks's *Keats and Embarrassment,* far from plain, was a highly ingenious argument, with Matthew Arnold and others, about the integrity of Keats's sensuousness, together with a sympathetic account of the letters, of the poet's own physical embarrassments and his exemplariness in coping with them. There was a plurality of books about Byron, that "plural person" as Doris Langley Moore called him in one of the more useful of them, *Lord Byron—Accounts Rendered,* which contributed biographical shading from a study of his bills.

Douglas Day's *Malcolm Lowry* was the first full biography of the author of *Under the Volcano,* a reading persuasive enough to leave a smaller margin of doubt that Lowry mattered. *Malcolm Lowry: His Art and Early Life* was a shorter, personal account by Muriel Bradbrook, the Shakespearean scholar, who came from the same posh suburb of Liverpool as Lowry and was a contemporary at Cambridge. Ian Gregor wrote an excellent study of Hardy's major fiction in *The Great Web,* and Margaret Drabble's *Arnold Bennett* seemed likely to persuade people who were happy to read her to read him.

A. L. Rowse's claim in 1973 to have discovered a palpable and historical "dark lady" was toned down somewhat when he produced his very readable account of the casebook of her "consultant," the astrologer Simon Forman, in *Simon Forman: Sex and Society in Shakespeare's Age.* It did give new and interesting details of "sex and society in Shakespeare's age," as the prithee-come-hither subtitle put it; but as John Buxton wrote, "as so often we come tantalizingly close to Shakespeare without standing in his presence."

It was not a notable year for biography. The Bloomsbury boom mercifully subsided: not much more to take account of than the second volume of the memoirs of Lady Ottoline Morrell, *Ottoline at Garsington,* giving her account of her affair with Bertrand Russell and a rather sad and touching self-portrait. That Sargent among modern biographers, Michael Holroyd, had moved on to Augustus John with a first volume for which Geoffrey Grigson accused him of knowing that John was an inferior painter and yet of carrying on as if he had been important. Kenneth Clark reviewed it more tolerantly, as befitted a man with a highly vulnerable autobiography out in the same season (*Another Part of the Wood,* full of proper names and the highest vulgarization; not innocent of malice nor of a sad self-awareness; but invaluable on the art politics of his time). Sybille Bedford completed her biography of *Aldous Huxley* and Graham Greene refurbished an early unpublished study of the Restoration rake and poet in *Lord Rochester's Monkey,* incidentally claiming Restoration London as an early colony of Greeneland—"sinner with an uneasy conscience . . . a perfect Greene hero," as Martin Dodsworth observed.

Among the less public memoirs, David Thomson's *Woodbrook* was an elegiac and moving meditation on his personal history, as an awkward young man in love with the girl he was tutoring in a shabby Big House in West Cork in the 1930s, and on the rough history of the Anglo-Irish class from which she came: a book that would mark some readers like personal

experience. The finest work by professional historians was to be found in J. C. Beaglehole's masterly *Life of Capt. James Cook,* in John Rosselli's study of the political education of a Liberal imperialist, *Lord William Bentinck,* and in Norman Hampson's *Robespierre,* eccentrically but effectively cast as argument between four friends—a historian, a civil servant, a parson, and a Communist. Arthur Koestler, whose work helped to defrost science, produced a collection of recent essays on American psychiatry, Wittgenstein, intuition, ESP, and other frontier topics in *The Heel of Achilles.*

Geoffrey Moorhouse's account of his west-east camel journey across the "empty quarter" of Africa, *The Fearful Void,* was outstanding among the travel books (another thin category)—a quest into the author's own psychic interior to confront his fear, and a fascinating trip on both levels. Piers Paul Read's *Alive* was an account of the Uruguayan rugby players who survived a plane crash in the Andes by eating companions killed in the landing, well-written but a mite uncritical about the "sacrificial" character of the tragedy.

Finally, the achievement of a glorious work. It was hard to believe that, after a quarter of a century, that great enterprise, Sir Nikolaus Pevsner's Buildings of England, should have come to an end, but with *Staffordshire* and *Oxfordshire* the last two counties were done, and our aesthetical modern Domesday Book was complete. (W. L. WEBB)

Poetry. Following the trend of recent years, 1974 produced an extraordinary number of competent, if not always exciting, first collections; and once again it was the little "shoestring" presses rather than the large publishing organizations that introduced the new poets to a wider public. As in previous years these pamphlet publishers, engaged in a constant struggle with the problems of inflation, continued to exercise an influence upon British poetry far out of proportion to the resources available to them.

One of the most impressive of the new poets was Robin Hamilton, whose *Poems* justifiably won him a Gregory Award during the year. Hamilton's concern with the past and his interest in classical themes and characters as a means of coping with intractable material allowed him not only to project himself imaginatively but also to maintain a stricter control over both diction and emotion. In *High Places* Joan Murray Simpson celebrated the "high places" of spiritual experience and the "blessedness at the heart of things," as well as her love of geographic heights in various parts of Europe. Other first collections were *Ravenswood* by Richard Ryan, *A Fire by the Sea* by Alasdair Clayre, and *Cape Drives* by the young South African Christopher Hope.

Nevertheless, 1974 was more likely to be remembered for a number of very significant books by well-known poets. First, the posthumous poems of W. H. Auden appeared under the title *Thank You, Fog*—an appropriate title as the collection showed Auden's last phase to have been one of relaxed thanksgiving. *The Sleeping Lord and Other Fragments* by David Jones —a combination of legend, history, philosophy, and indictment of modern society—renewed the problems of assessing Jones's achievement, as the title and the author's notes indicated that these "fragments" might eventually form part of a greater work and provide a vital link between his earlier *In Parenthesis* and *The Anathemata.*

Most important of all was the publication of Philip

Larkin's fourth volume, *High Windows,* which some critics welcomed as the "book of a decade." Although Larkin had always firmly rejected the argument that a poet's work should show signs of development over a period, there was indisputable evidence of his own development in this highly praised collection; in it Larkin's earlier defeatism seemed to be countered by a determination to find meaning and purpose in human survival and to celebrate the rituals and customs by which we attempt to limit death's power.

Although in Jon Silkin's *The Principle of Water* such characteristic themes as the 12th-century massacre of the Jews at York were reworked, a group of Shetland poems also demonstrated the poet's ability to capture both the outlook and the life-style of the Shetland islanders, and his long verse play "The People" enabled him to express his sensitivities in a striking new way. Jon Stallworthy's *The Apple Barrel* was a balanced selection from two of his earlier books, though surprisingly enough it included nothing from *Root and Branch* (1969), the best of the three. Stallworthy's latest poems, *Hand in Hand,* exhibited the poet's lyrical powers and his gift for manipulating sensuous imagery against a background of ordinary life, in a sequence describing a love affair.

Anthony Thwaite's *New Confessions* added considerably to the growing reputation of its author. Reminiscent of Geoffrey Hill's *Mercian Hymns* in conception, this collection of poems and prose pieces was based upon St. Augustine, although throughout the volume Thwaite used the commentary on the life and times of the 4th-century bishop of Hippo to contemplate his own experience, at times identifying himself so closely that it became difficult to distinguish between author and subject. *The Sea-Bell and Other Poems* by Susanne Knowles was perhaps the most curious collection in several years, but if the poet's choice of subject tended to be somewhat unconventional—dung beetles, globe artichokes, left-handed whelks, parasites living in the tears of hippopotamuses—her witty attention to detail and her deployment of fascinatingly useless information marked her as an individual poet of remarkable craftsmanship.

Among the collected editions that helped to make 1974 a memorable year were the *Complete Poems* of the late Andrew Young, *Selected Poems, 1946–1968* by R. S. Thomas, *Selected Poems, 1967–1973* by John Pudney, and *In the Trojan Ditch,* which contained the collected poems and selected translations of C. H. Sisson. Other volumes of note were *My Daughters, My Sisters* by Karen Gershon, *The Well-Wishers* by Edward Lucie-Smith, *High Island* by Richard Murphy, *Notebooks of Robinson Crusoe* by Iain Crichton Smith, and *The Faber Book of Irish Verse* edited by John Montague.   (HOWARD SERGEANT)

United States. *Fiction.* It finally became clear in 1974 that the struggle against the extremes of naturalism and symbolism, or raw and rarefied fiction, had been largely won. The novel could now afford a greater confessional power without losing its hold on artistic reality. Thus, trends emergent for a decade began to solidify, as the existential novel of confession and sexual *ressentiment* and the novel as woman both clarified.

The confessional novel did not embody any philosophy; rather, it passionately rendered the growing sense of alienation in the U.S. Its solitary hero found his values in extreme victimization or else gave himself to the void. Never in history had Americans been so driven to expose themselves—in the recent evalua-

tion of values, privacy was one of the big losers. Everywhere in society and the arts people were baring their privates or spilling their guts, from the vogue of confessional poetry to the pervasiveness of pornography, from the New Journalism with its lens turned inward on the reporter himself to the new assertiveness of homosexuals and other increasingly proud minorities.

No writer, not even Mailer or Lowell, contributed more to the confessional climate than Philip Roth. Thanks to *Portnoy's Complaint* a good slice of the year's fiction seemed to come verbatim from the writer's own hours on the couch. In his new book, *My Life as a Man,* which deals with the operatically unhappy marriage of a successful young writer, Roth returned to the quasi-autobiographical mode of *Portnoy* and *Goodbye, Columbus.* Peter Tarnopol, the protagonist-monologist of Roth's new novel, is a cunning sophist and casuist, a narcissist, tireless self-justifier, and wily paranoiac. He is also, of course, Roth recording his life as a man already too recognizable as that of the *mensch manque*—the Jewish boy from New Jersey who was such a nuisance in the public library that he fell into marriage and trouble in his 20s and is now (still) in expensive analysis with Dr. Spielvogel. Standing amid the ruins of his own making, Tarnopol eloquently denounces fate, the world, the universal plot to unman him; yet he manages, in his endless quarrels with himself and the world, somehow to win them all, a triumphant witness to his own dismemberment. At one point, he imagines his wife (a castrating Clytemnestra) suggesting that he call his book "My Martyrdom as a Man." If Mailer's *The Prisoner of Sex* was a self-serving attack on women's lib, *My Life as a Man* was an unpolemical mirror image of its literature, a casebook of male rage and resentment, a contribution to the literature of intersexual victimization.

So, in the face of such despair, whatever its provenance, what's so funny? A good deal, beginning with despair itself and the voice that is its funnel to

JILL KREMENTZ—BANTAM BOOKS

Philip Roth's new novel, "My Life as a Man," continued the confessional mode of erotic anthropology of his "Portnoy's Complaint."

Studs Terkel, whose 1974 best-seller, "Working," was a synthesis of transcribed recordings of some 100 Americans in all walks of life talking about their daily work.

the world—and the tension between the two; the more hysterically the despair insists upon its exalted status as the most wretched the world has ever known, the more the voice, pitched to a scream, an unending *geschrei*, the voice of a depraved saint . . . the more the voice undercuts and nullifies the literary despair it claims as uniquely its own. This, then, baldly basted together, is Roth's very own kind of Jewish intellectual slapstick, worked and reworked from earlier sources and all going back to that primal motherlode of neurosis that has led him through other areas of "erotic anthropology." Like Rousseau's *Confessions* and its modern progeny, *My Life* is reckless in inviting us to view the man rather than the writer; that is part of its appeal. For all its egotism, *My Life* is finally like *Portnoy* a vulnerable and affecting work, which ends with the hero in "sexual quarantine" waiting only "to be weaned from the other sex forever."

Surprising in the light of his ambivalent, even degrading attitudes toward women, Roth's fiction had the most visible influence on the emerging new women writers, who were just getting into the confessional swing when *Portnoy* appeared. They had more barriers to breach, especially in writing about sex, and though a number of women—some very movingly—hewed to the lugubrious line as if they had invented it, some of the recent best like Erica Jong and Sue Kaufman developed a style of exuberant comic recollection enabling them not only to talk about sex but to tell it straight while eluding the trap of ax-grinding and moralizing. Whatever their flaws, Jong's *Fear of Flying* and Lois Gould's *Final Analysis* created a fresh voice that made us want to laugh.

You could almost put them in the same dormitory room if you thought about it—Lois Gould, Erica Jong, and Sue Kaufman—as they let their hair down and raise their consciousness; they had a good deal in common, writing about fashionable young women of talent and worldly experience that they do not know quite how to apply. And all of them managed to make it seem as inanimate and indispensable as their last pair of panty hose. The heroine of *Final Analysis*, Lois Gould's third novel, is another neglected woman shoved to the side of the king-sized bed, who whispers audibly, cries a lot, and weighs under 110 lb. The

confessional "I" who tells this story spends two years and $10,000 discussing her problems with Gould's Spielvogel—Dr. S. Conrad Foxx—her problems mainly being her preference for her own grossly masochistic fantasies to the real thing—she would let her diaphragm "expire with her driver's license."

Fear of Flying was another wayward confessional entertainment by another chafed spirit, Erica Jong. Her heroine, Isadora Zelda, is one of those Marjorie Morningstars who become neurotic Jewish-American princesses or prom queens full of not only their mothers' aspirations but their own fears (flying) and guilts (random sex). The truth's revealed: Freudian psychologists make better lovers than Laingians.

Sue Kaufman's *Falling Bodies*, the fifth novel by the author of *Diary of a Mad Housewife*, was yet another story about the plight of the passive, harassed, neurotic housewife—no feminist tract, but a mocking portrayal of female ineffectuality. All of Kaufman's housewives are pretty much the same and so is their urbanized and unencumbered life—they have yet to pick up any appliance heavier than the Water Pik. Thus Emma Sohier, who has had a bad year, which included her long hospitalization from some fever of unknown origin leaving her unnerved by fugue states involving falling bodies, returns home to a son who burns bedsheets and to a husband whose hypochondriasis has reached unnatural proportions.

Something Happened, Joseph Heller's long-awaited second novel after *Catch-22*, was a major confessional work, a representation of the underachieved contemporary man booby-trapped all the way from his harassment at home to the office where he is making his way up over someone else's body. Perhaps closest to one of Roth's middle-aged self-made victims, full of lapsed hopes and more guilts than any man should have to assume, Bob Slocum, Heller's hero, is seen always on the verge of something ominously imminent—suicide, failure, death—while having experienced a string of little satisfactions, "jobs, love affairs, and fornications." Slocum figures negatively as husband of a wife who now drinks too much even if she has become more amatory in the process, father of a daughter who challenges and undermines him, and nonfather of a son who is retarded and of whom he prefers not to think at all. Obviously there was none of the rogue absurdism or imaginative verve of *Catch-22*, though the work was touted as a masterpiece by critics who panned the first novel; indeed, the work is unrelievedly pessimistic to the degree that Slocum is symptomatic of this age—beleaguered all the way from his bad teeth to his rotten conscience. The novel is a textbook in classical psychoanalysis, taking the hero through a "talking cure" which is essentially an interior dialogue, as private as the confession box. And its tone, like most confessions, is lugubrious and realistic, smothered in angst and high seriousness.

Standing somewhat apart from the confessional trend, a few novels of fantasy (and fewer of paranoid surrealism) achieved prominence. The novel of fantasy is often an intimate of chaos, a strange mutation of comedy; and authors drawn to that form are often geomancers of language, players, and parodists to the bone. Their Nabokovian ironies do not always conceal their desperation, their disgust with reality, or their obsession with death.

The most somber entry was *Long Distance* by Penelope Mortimer, an original, distinguished, puzzling novel inhabited by an unnamed woman in a great white mansion (asylum?) who is doomed to repeat experience until it is remembered—who will be doomed to delete experience that might betray any independence of spirit or show of feeling. She escapes everything but memory; as it was with Sartre's *No Exit,* so here.

William Kotzwinkle's *The Fan Man* was a work of lyric genius, detailing the fantastic light-pawed journeys of that "hippest of the Hip," Horse Badorties, who lives atop, within, and carries around a ziggurat of garbage. Toting his hot-dog umbrella and his Chinese moon-lute, Horse scuttles through the city to have his mystic vision in Van Cortlandt Park. Kotzwinkle makes it all sing, recycling the hum of the humus so that it becomes a new kind of music of the inner-city spheres.

The overblown images from which we all have manufactured our own paranoid visions of the true connections of American society is the subject of Richard Condon's 11th novel, *Winter Kills,* a tour de force depicting an assassination of a president and its ineffectual avenger. The intricacies of its style and construction, especially its masochistic pleasure in cauterizing so many national wounds, spring finally from Condon's feeling of optimism in darkness that only healing satire can truly bring.

A major work of black American fiction was *If Beale Street Could Talk,* James Baldwin's fifth novel, a first-person suspense narrative with a New York street love story into the bargain. The problem: a young black lingers in jail falsely accused of rape while his pregnant lover carries the legal ball and the book. Also notable was Richard Brautigan's *The Hawkline Monster,* a humorous "Gothic Western" by a cracker-barrel surrealist who writes as if he had wandered into a field of ripe cannabis with a pack of Zig Zag papers in his pocket.

Leading the popular field was *Centennial,* another big James Michener novel, more didactic than fictive, sprawling, vast as the Colorado-Wyoming country it describes, loose as the morals of some of its characters, and as interminable as the millions of years of geologic time and human history it encompasses. In more charitable times, *Centennial* would have been hailed as "an epic labour." In the mass-cult market, Peter Benchley's *Jaws* and Gore Vidal's *Myron* rounded out the pop-fiction entries. The first featured a man-eating shark haunting the beaches of Long Island, forcing men to come to piscatorial terms with themselves. The second, another of Vidal's transsexual delicacies, resurrected Myra Breckenridge or rather altered her 25 years later as Myron with a "reconstructed rehnquist between his legs."

Five major short-story collections outwitted the mortality of the genre. Grace Paley's *Enormous Changes at the Last Minute* found a vocation in glorifying the accents of a now vanished and slightly fabulous Second Avenue. Despite Paley's dazzling style, this was a book of losses and failures that added up to one of the most depressing works of fiction in the last decade, hardly a time noted for the prevalence of upbeat writing. Tennessee Williams' *Eight Mortal Ladies Possessed* discovered Williams playing with the word "possessed," implying that his ladies are mad because they hope to own mysteries of the body. They try to dominate others, but find that they, in turn, are slaves to the forces of nature—to mortality itself. Joyce Carol Oates continued her prolificacy with two collections—*The Hungry Ghosts,* seven satiric, allusive comedies on the subject of the foibles

of academia, totally unlike her awesomely serious canon, and *The Goddess,* with her familiar alienated professionals entrapped in suburban garden-variety angst. Finally, Donald Barthelme's *Guilty Pleasures* scored with virtuoso literary legerdemain on themes of popular cultish mythology.

History, Biography, and Belles Lettres. In a year of ouster and crisis, of things steadily becoming shabbier, of shock waves arriving so regularly that many have already forgotten what it felt like to stand on steady ground, the year's historians and social critics were read as much for their quality of truth as for their quality of fantasy—truth being, as Jane Austen once remarked, very excusable in a historian. Possessing greatest power and immediacy, the genre known modishly as New Journalism cut across traditional intellectual disciplines, compounding biography and analysis, anecdote and polemic to reveal the inner stresses of America that permitted both author and reader to create a place for themselves, as persons, in the midst of current complexities.

The big story was broken by Carl Bernstein and Robert ("Bob") Woodward's *All the President's Men,* accomplished by old-fashioned seat-of-the-pants reporting—in other words, lots of intuition and a thick stack of telephone numbers. The real drama, and there was plenty of it, lay in their private-eye tactics. The centrepiece of their own covert operation was an unnamed high government source they called Deep Throat, with whom Woodward arranged secret meetings by positioning the potted palm on his balcony and through codes scribbled in the morning newspaper. Woodward's wee-hours meetings with Deep Throat in an underground parking garage were pure cinema. Then, too, they amassed enough seamy detail to fascinate even the most avid Watergate wallower, breaking Gordian knots of deception that leave the reader giggling with exasperation. As the scandal went public and out of their hands, Bernstein and Woodward seemed as stunned as the rest of us at where their search for the truth had led. Their city editor, Barry Sussman of the *Washington Post,* realized it way back at the beginning—"We've never had a story like this. Just never."

James A. Michener's novel "Centennial," a massive epic of the Colorado-Wyoming country through the ages, was one of 1974's best-sellers.

A number of notable Watergate-related studies also appeared. *The American Condition* by Richard Goodwin, one of the leading apparats in U.S. politics today, focused polemically on the problem of freedom—its abstract, philosophical, political as well as historical dimensions, and its relation to contemporary America. He displayed with great effectiveness the "condition" of America that has produced the very opposite of freedom through the bureaucratic and economic forms it has allowed to develop. The thesis of noted intellectual Michael Novak's *Choosing Our King: Powerful Symbols in Presidential Politics* was that politics is one of America's secular religions; and the president —by embodying the attributes of priest, prophet, and king—its most central and operative symbol.

On the right, William Buckley produced a short, libertarian, antistatist tract called *Four Reforms,* namely: cut welfare for states whose per capita income is above the national average; replace the graduated income tax with a flat 15% tax on personal income; introduce aid to parochial schools; and abolish the Fifth Amendment. More belligerently argued, Ben Wattenberg's *The Real America* was a gloss on almost everything in sight as well as a triple-edged thesis: liberals are unable to govern the country; the U.S. offers more prosperity and social benefits than ever before in its history; and anyone who says it isn't so is a demagogue, an elitist, or a fool.

More traditional history was *The European Discovery of America: The Southern Voyages,* completing brilliant "Whig" historian Adm. Samuel Eliot Morison's monumental study of the Spanish and English explorers who discovered both coasts of the Americas. The author focuses mainly on the voyaging, especially of Columbus, Magellan, and Drake, and how these "robust and persistent mariners" gathered from all the nations of Western Europe set out on voyages that laid foundations for four great empires "with no other motive power than sail and oar." Morison's humaneness was especially revealed in his depiction of Columbus as a spiritually zealous dreamer in search of the Indies, whose strongest epithet was "May God take you."

Other important nonfiction works included Robert Fogel and Stanley Engerman's *Time on the Cross: The Economics of American Negro Slavery,* which promised to generate years of controversy, arguing that Southern slaveholders were shrewd, enterprising capitalists, driven by the profit motive to create a system of bonded labour that was both more efficient and more human than "traditional historians had suspected." Studs Terkel's *Working* printed the spoken words of sustained pain and frustration in a collection of over 100 portraits of people thinking about their work. Most of the portraits are enclosed in human skin, and these people sigh and rage into one's ears. Obviously conceived as an integrated human document, it was probably not conceived to be what it also is: a devastating rebuke to social science research on this topic. Political scientist Thomas Cottle's *Black Children, White Dreams* was a successful humanistic exploration of young people's views of the political process showing that "paying attention" can build the reciprocity of concerns basic to political change. Finally, *The CIA and the Cult of Intelligence,* by Victor Marchetti and John D. Marks, was a commendable, albeit sensational, contribution to the literature of dirty business, making instructive disclosures on CIA structure, its proprietary corporations, and its clandestine services.

The major biography in 1974 was Albert Goldman's controversial *Ladies and Gentlemen—Lenny Bruce!!* Five years in the writing, this biography was well worth the wait—a spectacular achievement, brilliant, depressingly hilarious, and outrageously proper. The oxymoronic character of the book reflected the contradictory elements of Bruce himself, that cruel-kind, villainous-heroic child-man who became the most savage scatological social satirist and stand-up comic of his day, whose attempts to destroy society's sham drove him, finally, to overdose for our sins.

Robert Caro's *The Power Broker: Robert Moses and the Fall of New York* was a remorseless 600,000-word demolition biography of the pharaoh of New York City who created history's largest vista of public works, of parks and beaches, roads and bridges, based entirely around the automobile. Caro's artfully compiled detail ensured that *The Power Broker* would be acclaimed as the definitive monument to Moses, as well as a key study of the web of political figures connected with, and against, Moses' career.

Kissinger, by two noted CBS correspondents, Marvin and Bernard Kalb, was the most detailed study to date of the man whom a 1974 Harris Poll found to be the nation's most admired man. It was also the most detailed analysis yet of U.S. diplomacy in the post cold-war era: worshipful, gravely flawed, and indispensable. Moreover, it contained a "dirty little secret"—that it was Richard Nixon, not Henry Kissinger, who was the main architect and conceptualizer of U.S. foreign policy.

If the Watergate bookshelf became filled during the year, it was also crowded on the island of Lesbos. One imagines Sappho's shade bewildered by the plethora of prophetesses announcing the establishment of the post-male, post-heroic world. Her chief disciple (among many) was Kate Millett, author of *Sexual Politics.* Millett's 545-page autobiography, *Flying,* was a leviathan of self-justification, an unflinching record of her uneasy struggle to practice what she preaches in the trying circumstances of her sudden fame. Celebrating a kind of *exaltatio ad absurdum* of once revolutionary sexual goals, Millett's homosexuality, finally, is a heightening of a deeper sense of inferiority, of not belonging. More entertaining and saner were William O. Douglas' *Go East, Young Man,* a creditable volume one of the autobiography of the longest sitting justice in the history of the Supreme Court (since 1939); and *A Writer's Capital* by Louis Auchincloss—a memoir welcomed by admirers of Auchincloss' fiction, containing at least one memorable portrait, that of Endicott Peabody, his master at Groton.

The high point in belles lettres was the publication of the fifth volume of *The Diary of Anaïs Nin,* a product of considerable genius and breathtaking tenacity. The great diary proceeded, taking on more of the shape of a living machine of words that assaults and defends as much as it reflects and mediates. More and more often, the exquisitely painted masks slipped askew and the diary as artifice—as a stage for self-dramatization rather than as a tool for self-realization —revealed its exasperating limitations. After searching so long (1947–55) with Maxwell Geismar, Malcolm Cowley, James Laughlin, and others for interior and exterior confirmation of her artistic identity, Nin rejected psychedelic and narcotic shortcuts and triumphantly yet tremulously proclaimed "I will not be a tourist in the world of images."

Poetry. If America exists, it was still being discovered this season. Its poets, so disparate in vision and means, continued to survey parcels of the difficult terrain, transforming them to the contours of their own imaginative landscapes.

Galway Kinnell's *The Avenue Bearing the Initial of Christ into the New World* appeared, a collection by one of the most powerful and moving poets of his generation, and containing some of the finest lyric poetry in contemporary American literature. Kinnell's is an elemental poetry of dark woods and snow; of wind, fire, and stars. His subjects are perennial—love illumined and made more precious by the omnipresence of death. The remarkable title of this volume derives from the no less remarkable life-charged poem in which Kinnell, in 1960, celebrated New York City's teeming Avenue C.

The Death Notebooks was Anne Sexton's seventh and last volume of verse, in which the brooding preoccupation with death of one of the country's best and most professional poets came fully to the surface. In these poems, Sexton looks in many places for God, finding him in excremental visions of death and apocalypse while "trying on" her "black necessary trousseau." Two months after this volume appeared, Miss Sexton was a suicide at age 45.

Sphere: The Form of a Motion by A. R. Ammons was a major achievement. This long poem of 155 sections by a former National Book Award winner was punctuated only by colons that thrust the eye forward, deeper into its abstractions, creating its own unfathomable logic—an intergalactic roller coaster into all sorts of hypnotic and rhythmic zones of "perplexing multeity."

American Indian pantheism and the nonegoism of Buddhism underlay Gary Snyder's *Turtle Island*—values Snyder calls "archaic" and "primitive," and which he redefines as the alternative to the bankruptcy of materialistic society. Continuing his efforts to develop America's "ecological conscience," Snyder's observant poems about fishing, Boletus mushrooms, and night herons who "nest in the cypress/ by the San Francisco/ stationary boilers/ with the high smoke stack" strike sharply.

Well-received volumes by younger women were *Cruelty* by Ai, a work of Swinburnean dolorousness: murder, suicide, sexual violence, simple lust, whoredom, and child-beating occur with utmost flatness—the cruelty is everyone's because it is nature's; Jill Hoffman's *Mink Coat,* containing many mature urban lyrics by a sensual woman, well acquainted with her own body, fond of clothing and ornament, and one lyric masterpiece, "Rendezvous," about leaving the husband in bed at night to nurse a child; and Judith Kroll's *In the Temperate Zone,* filled with screams and mutters, the war of the sexes, cowboys and Indians, and persuasive visions of her own death as a blind cancer wobbling like a gyroscope.

(FREDERICK S. PLOTKIN)

Canada. The demands of Canadians for stories based on their own experiences gave rise in 1974 to many outstanding works. Margaret Laurence in *The Diviners* told how Morag Gunn at 47, a stage in her life when she must come to terms with past and future, observes her daughter's struggle toward independence and is haunted by images of her own past struggles and successes. *Crackpot* by Adele Wiseman was a tribute to the indomitable nature of the human spirit. In an environment of ridicule and rejection, fat, whoring Hoda develops into a creature more noble in her suffering than those who sneer at

her. Sinclair Ross's work *Sawbones Memorial* was hailed by critics as a worthy successor to his earlier novels. In it Ross returned to the Prairie town of Upward and recounted the town's reactions at the retirement of the local doctor and the surprises caused by the arrival of his successor. In *Yesterdays* Harold Sonny Ladoo, who died suddenly, told, with a fine sense of the comic and ironic in human relations, of a West Indian trying to finance a Hindu mission to Canada. Matt Cohen's *The Disinherited* dealt with a family struggling against disintegration while the father battles against imminent death. Among other works of new writers were *The Lark in the Clear Air* by Dennis T. Patrick Sears, the tale of an orphaned adolescent who seeks to live with his eccentric, brawling great-uncle, and Ray Smith's *Lord Nelson Tavern,* the starting point of the relationships among a tumultuous troupe of characters.

Alice Munro's *Something I've Been Meaning to Tell You,* a group of short stories, reaffirmed the craftsmanship so evident in her earlier award-winning collection. Other welcome contributors to the growing field of short-story writers were Clark Blaise, whose *Tribal Justice* underlines the myriad problems of widely varied ethnic and religious backgrounds in North America, and novelist Rudy Wiebe, whose first collection of stories, *Where Is that Voice Coming From?,* delineated the isolation, fears, and occasional joys of adult and child in today's complex society.

History and Biography. Barry Broadfoot, a skilled interviewer with a fine sense for detail, recorded the experiences of Canadians during two disruptive historical periods. In *Ten Lost Years: 1929–1939* the anonymous survivors of Canada's worst economic crisis recall the Depression decade with pride, bitterness, and humour. In *Six War Years: 1939–1945* the grim but exuberant memories of Canadians who served on the home front and overseas are recounted.

Using contemporary photographs and personal accounts, Heather Robertson drew an authentic picture of the harsh but rewarding experiences of the homesteaders who settled the Canadian prairies from 1880 to 1914 in *Salt of the Earth.* Robert Craig Brown and Ramsey Cook in *Canada, 1896–1921* added to the Canadian Centenary Series and gave a perceptive synthesis of the dramatic changes in Canadian life during the Borden and Laurier regimes. *Canada Before Confederation* by R. C. Harris and John Warkentin gives the imprint of man on the land in an unusual and often provocative treatment of the historical geography of pre-Confederation Canada. Terry Copp in *The Anatomy of Poverty* reflected the wretched lot of the working poor in Montreal in the period 1897–1929. Abraham Rotstein edited *Getting It Back: A Program for Canadian Independence,* a collection of essays that included suggestions for solutions to the problems of U.S. domination in many areas of Canada's economic and cultural life. Charles Taylor in *Snow Job: Canada, the United States and Viet Nam* revealed Canada as a willing accomplice of the U.S. during every stage of the war in Vietnam in the period 1954–73. Jeremy Manthorpe's *The Power and the Tories* was a witty and penetrating study of Ontario politics from 1943 to the present.

In *Not Bloody Likely, the Shaw Festival, 1963–1973* Brian Doherty, the founding father of the Shaw Festival at Niagara-on-the-Lake, provided a well-documented history of the events that turned a small town into an active international cultural centre. Paul Duval's *High Realism in Canada* presented a crisp and clear view of Canadian painting. The focus was on a small but representative number of artists from the 19th century to the present day who painted in the realist tradition. William Kurelek's *A Prairie Boy's Winter* was more than a nostalgic Canadian story in pictures. Kurelek's primitive technique speaks directly to emotions transcending his Ukrainian immigrant background.

Florence Bird wrote *Anne Francis: An Autobiography,* showing her combination of marriage and her career as journalist, news commentator, and chairman of the Royal Commission on the Status of Women in Canada. Harry J. Boyle's *Memories of a Catholic Boyhood* contained tales of rural Ontario during the Depression. Wilfred Pelletier in *No Foreign Land: The Biography of a Northern American Indian* looked back to his childhood on Manitoulin Island, his attempts at a business career, and his encounters with racism in Toronto.

Poetry and Drama. In 1974 over 200 new volumes of poetry appeared in English Canada with work by new writers predominating. George Bowering presented poems that he wrote after his 30th birthday, *In the Flesh,* demonstrating his sure command of the English language. In *The Collected Poems of A. M. Klein,* compiled and introduced by Miriam Waddington, one is reawakened to the late lawyer-poet's skill in expressing his pride, frustrations, quiet anger, humour, and love. Clear, often brutal images mirror the harsh realities of life in Patrick Lane's *Beware the Months of Fire.* Not a prolific poet, P. K. Page, in *Poems Selected and New,* selected her dominant themes—childhood, nature, and love—with the same concern she accorded each carefully chosen word. In her first volume of verse, *Woman Reading in the Bath,* Annie Szumigalski fulfilled the promise of talent shown in her early work.

Sharon Pollock's dramatic work *Walsh* dealt with the aftermath of the massacre of General Custer and his army at Little Big Horn as it affected Canada. The title character is a Mounted Police officer who attempted to deal fairly with the refugee Sioux Indians and was, in the end, destroyed by the bureaucracy he challenged. Carol Bolt in *Red Emma* wrote a lively and joyous musical play built around the life of Emma Goldman. David French's *Of the Fields, Lately* was a sequel to the highly praised *Leaving Home,* featuring once again the Mercers, a family of Newfoundlanders trying to cope with a faster, more impersonal life in the Toronto of 1960. James Reaney in *Sticks and Stones, Part 1* gave a dramatic account of the Donnelly clan's infamous vendettas.

(H. C. CAMPBELL)

FRENCH

France. *Fiction.* Paul Morand's *Les Écarts amoureux* was a set of three stories whose subjects seemed to have more to do with cruelty than with love, inspired by historical events and executed in a concise, polished style. Jean Mistler's *L'Ami des pauvres,* also a series of three tales, dealt with the inadequacies of contemporary society, one of the tales being inspired by a real-life theft from the Louvre. Marcel Schneider's *Déjà la neige* was a flight into the realm of fantasy in which the author sought to endow fantasy with reality. The work was preceded by a *Discours du fantastique* and, in awarding it the Grand Prix de la Nouvelle, the French Academy also set its seal of approval upon the genre of fantasy. Tenderness merged with atrocity in René Barjavel's *Le Prince blessé,* while Marcel

Brion's *La Fête de la Tour des Âmes* moved subtly from reality to fantasy with a marked strain of black humour. *Les Hommes protégés* by Robert Merle postulated a science fiction fantasy of the U.S. in which the country is ruled by women.

With *Au Plaisir de Dieu,* Jean d'Ormesson almost achieved a masterpiece, embedding into history the story of one century in the life of an aristocratic family gradually disintegrating as its way of life is eroded by modern times. The book showed a remarkable awareness and psychological insight into a milieu of which the author himself was a member. Michel Robida's *Le Déjeuner de Trieste* also dealt with the life and times of a great family, but this time a bourgeois family at the time of World War II. Kléber Haedens' *Adios,* which won the French Academy's Grand Prix du Roman, dealt with a family of petty officials, the story beginning with great verve in Senegal but gradually becoming lost in a web of amorous entanglements.

The historical novel seemed to be undergoing a real renaissance with a number of works evoking the passions and atmosphere of bygone days. Michel Peyramaure's *L'Oeil arraché* was set in Limousin in Merovingian times while Jean-Marie Fonteneau's *Phénix* consisted of a series of stories inspired by such themes as biblical Arabia, Pompeii, and 11th-century Corsica. Andrée Chédid's *Nefertiti et le rêve d'Akhnaton* and Michel Larneuil's *Le Dieu assassiné* both dealt with the same ancient Egyptian figures, while Herbert Le Porrier's *Le Médecin de Cordoue* revived the figure of Moses Maimonides whose science blossomed in Egypt. In *Porporino ou les mystères de Naples* Dominique Fernandez revived 18th-century Naples, dealing particularly with the castrati. The book was awarded the Prix Médicis.

The jury's choice for the coveted Prix Goncourt fell to a work in total reaction to the poetico-pornographic style currently in vogue. Pascal Laîné's *La Dentellière* was an evocation, handled with modesty and restraint, of a love affair between a young country squire and a humble lace-maker who is seduced and abandoned. The whole was written in a concise, polished style worthy of the 19th-century novelists, as was *Le Voyage à l'étranger* by the Swiss-born writer Georges Borgeaud, which dealt with the restrained and platonic passion of a tutor in a noble family for a beautiful visitor. The same reserve characterized Pierre Kyria's two novels, *La Mort blanche* and *Mademoiselle Sarah,* while the Belgian Pierre Mertens' much-discussed *Les bons offices* dealt with a clerical career complicated by romantic attachments. Yves Navarre's *Le Coeur qui cogne* was a savage critique of the bourgeoisie, while two able writers dealt with the subject of lesbianism: Jeanne Galzy in *La Cavalière* and Irène Monesi in *L'Amour et le dédain.*

In *L'Imprécateur* René-Victor Pilhes combined realism and diabolical fantasy in his treatment of the subject of multinational corporations, bringing him both public acclaim and the Prix Fémina. Pierre-Jean Rémy published several works in the course of the year, the most important both in quality and in magnitude being his *Mémoires secrets pour servir à l'histoire de ce siècle,* a strange and captivating work despite the fragmented form of its composition.

Patrick Grainville's *L'Abîme* dealt with a group of old men in a home for the aged, one of whom—lacking neither sexual vigour nor lucidity—dominates the rest. Journalist René Mauriès won the Prix Interallié for *Le Cap de la gitane,* a work inspired by his own reporting and by a serious accident, liberally seasoned with bawdy humour. Jean Roudaut's *Les Prisons* was a novel written in a style close to that of Michel Butor, to whom he devoted a remarkable essay, while *Les Meurtrières* by Frantz-André Burguet, an adept of antiliterature, was inspired by a real-life incident.

Nonfiction. The year brought an unprecedented spate of memoirs and autobiographical journals by eminent people, most of them members of the French Academy. In Jean Guitton's *Écrire comme on se souvient* matters of the mind and spirit took precedence over external events, while Jacques Rivière's posthumous *Carnets,* covering the period of his captivity from 1914 to 1917, showed the same high moral tone in describing the author's experience of the conflict between conjugal love and love for another woman and religious faith. Also in the spirit of a soul in conflict was Julien Green's *Jeunesse,* dealing with the guilty loves of his adolescence, while Henry de Montherlant's *Le Fichier parisien* retained a skeptical, witty, disdainful, and highly polished style. The well-known painter Michel Ciry lamented the vanishing of Western humanism in *Le Buisson ardent* in much the same spirit as J. de Bourbon-Busset's *Complices.* For *Le Temps immobile,* "the work of his life," Claude Mauriac delved into his past to group his thoughts around the feeling and atmosphere of his family, in particular his father. Jacques Chastenet's *Quatre fois vingt ans* fitted the exploits of a soldier, diplomat, writer, and journalist into the wider context of history, bringing in many of the great figures of modern times, while Marguerite Yourcenar's *Souvenirs pieux* was a masterful re-creation of the author's childhood in the very conformist atmosphere, in Liège, of her family and of her marriage. In *La Perpétuité* Maurice Genevoix limited himself to a description, with unfailing humour, of the delicate role of permanent secretary to the French Academy. In *La Boîte à couleurs* André Roussin evoked a carefree childhood in Marseilles, full of humorous incident though to a lesser degree than the author's theatrical works, while in *La Salle des pas perdus* Armand Salacrou progressed beyond a childhood coloured with comical escapades as far as the author's first dramatic successes. Robert Debré, famous physician and father of the former French minister of defense Michel Debré, achieved great success with a detailed account of his brilliant career in *L'Honneur de vivre.* In *Printemps gris* Willy de Spens re-created his childhood among the landed gentry who were wittily castigated in the process, while short-story writer Roger Vrigny looked for the quality of life and the joys of the heart in the period from 1946 to 1963 with *Pourquoi cette joie.* In *Robert Laffont Éditeur* Robert Laffont described the not always easy stages of his career, revealing the underside of the profession with biting humour.

The pretext for André Malraux's *La Tête d'obsidienne,* a sequel to *Antimémoires,* was the work of Picasso, although in fact the book was a superbly written presentation of the author himself and his feelings about universal art as reflected through the painter. *Lazare* was a description of the same author's own journey to the frontiers of death. Julien Gracq's *Lettrines* was a collection of sparkling reflections on art and literature, while in *Répertoire IV* Michel Butor gave free rein to his imagination and astonishing depth of culture to take the reader back to the wellsprings of modern art and literature, from the Flemish school to contemporary painting, from Villon

to Barthes. Claude Roy's *Les Soleils du romantisme* brought together nine of the movement's greatest writers, with a particularly brilliant essay on Victor Hugo. In *Mes contrepoisons* René Étiemble stigmatized contemporary society in a vivid, bold style and with an aggressiveness that was typical of almost all the essayists. In *Le Discours contre la méthode* a new member of the French Academy, Robert Aron, made Descartes indirectly responsible for the triumph of technocracy in modern times, while in *Ce que je crois* Louis Pauwels provided a savage indictment of materialism, reaffirming his faith in the soul and the perfectibility of man. Georges Suffert's *Les Intellectuels en chaise longue* was a cutting, almost Voltairian pamphlet directed against obscurantist, so-called progressive armchair intellectuals; in the same spirit but with even greater virulence Jean Cau denounced egalitarianism as "trash" in *La Grande prostituée.* With less savagery, but with vigour and quiet humour, François de Closets' *Le Bonheur en plus* was an attack on the invasion by technology.

In *L'Irrégulière ou Mon Itinéraire Chanel* Edmonde Charles-Roux produced an astonishing biography of the great couturiere. No one could have written a more accomplished *Frédéric Chopin* than musician and first-rate critic (under the pseudonym of Clarendon) Bernard Gavoty, while Maurice P. Gautier provided a monumental study in *Captain Frederick Marryat.* Despite the closeness of the biographer to his subject, Francis Jeanson's *Sartre dans sa vie* succeeded in remaining objective while providing a large number of revealing details. The Prix des Ambassadeurs went to André Castelot for his masterful *Napoléon III,* while the duc de Castries provided an interesting study in *La Fayette* and Georges Poisson in *Monsieur de Saint-Simon.*

Pierre Chevallier, one of the country's most learned teachers and scholars of freemasonry, published his very full *Histoire de la franc-maçonnerie française,* going back to the original sources of the movement in England. The Bourse Goncourt du Récit Historique, awarded for the first time, went to Georges Bordonove for *Le Naufrage de la Méduse,* a thrilling reconstruction from historical documents of the maritime tragedy immortalized by the painter Théodore Géricault. In a much lighter vein *Notre Patrie gauloise*

Pascal Laîné's novel "La Dentellière" won the 1974 Prix Goncourt, France's most prestigious prize for works of fiction.

A.F.P./PICTORIAL PARADE

was perhaps Gaston Bonheur's best production so far, providing an erudite and humorous account of five centuries of French history from Vercingetorix to Clovis. Alain Decaux finished his learned and entertaining *Histoire des Françaises,* while Pierre Gaxotte, true to his admiration for the monarchy and his contempt for republicanism, nevertheless succeeded in re-editing and completing his *Histoire des Français* without sectarian intrusions.

Poetry. Jean Lebrau's *Singles* conveyed a sense of wonder and a touching experience for the reader, recalling the work of Charles Guérin, a poet who died very young but the centenary of whose birth had just been celebrated with enthusiasm; the latter's *Poèmes choisis* showed brilliance of style while seeming always to spring directly from the heart. Pierre Emmanuel, who had been described as a "dreamer of geneses" on a number of occasions, justified the description with *Sophia,* a vast poem in which he returned to original sources and to the symbol of the eternal wife-mother. In direct opposition to the flowing richness of Emmanuel's verse was the succinct, almost mathematical language, approaching antipoetry, of Eugène Guillevic's *Encoches.* Patrice de La Tour du Pin continued his own spiritual journey with *Psaumes de tous mes temps,* one of the high points of contemporary religious poetry imbued with the rich flowing rhythms of the Psalms. Jean-Claude Renard's *Le Dieu de nuit,* which won the Prix Max Jacob, with its metaphysical and liturgical content provided rather more arduous reading. Robert Mallet's *Quand le miroir s'étonne* expressed the fears and uncertainties of the present century in the style of 16th-century rondeaux, while Pierre Menanteau's *Capitale du souvenir* derived its inspiration from the different quarters of Paris. Maurice Courant's *O toi que le vent glace* was in the polished style of Valéry, while Michel Béguey's *Par des chemins secrets* showed a more vigorous tone and made use of blank verse and elegiac forms. In *Le Florilège poétique* Claude Fourcade illuminated his connection with the 19th-century poet Gérard de Nerval through his own personality while the Belgian Andrée Sodenkamp produced the subtle and spellbinding *La Fête debout.* Pierre Seghers' *La Résistance et ses poètes* scanned the field of French resistance to the World War II German occupation through some of France's greatest poets—Aragon, Éluard, and others of similar stature. Works by two other major poets of the past also appeared: *Collège,* consisting of memoirs in prose by Jean Follain, and *Mystique,* impressions and meditations by Joë Bousquet. The French Academy's Grand Prix de la Poésie went to that master of surrealism, Philippe Soupault. (ANNIE BRIERRE)

Canada. (Quebec). Formerly considered to be marginal literature, by 1974 French-Canadian, or "québécoise," literature occupied a formidable place in the framework of worldwide French literature.

During 1974 the novel developed at a faster rate than poetry, in both quantity and quality. Among new published novels were *Neige noire,* by Hubert Aquin, which pursues and recaptures with spirit the experience of his previous novels; *La Fuite immobile,* by Gilles Archambault, a story about a man between life and death; *Don Quichotte de la Démanche,* by Victor-Lévy Beaulieu, where dream and reality join together more effectively than in other novels with the same theme; *French Kiss,* which revealed the talents of Nicole Brossard; *Moi, mon corps, mon âme,* by Roger Fournier, the story of a young and lonely preg-

nant woman; André Langevin's *Une chaîne dans le parc;* a detective novel entitled *L'Épouvantail,* by André Major, written in a tough style but with sympathetic characters; *Johnny Bungalow,* in which Paul Villeneuve paints a genial picture of life in Quebec; and *L'Enfirouapé,* by Yves Beaulieu, which evokes the atmosphere of events of October 1970.

In poetry, the greats (Gaston Miron, Jacques Brault, Rina Lasnier, and the others) were quiet. On the other hand, younger poets published a number of works but, with the exception of Michel Garneau, author of *Moments,* none of them seemed to take over the genre. Rémi-Paul Forgues's *Poèmes du vent et des ombres,* poems written between 1942 and 1954, was reissued and a publication called *En tous lieux* for French foreign-speaking poets was founded.

In the theatre field, Paris favourably received the production of *Les Belles soeurs* by Michel Tremblay. *Hosanna* from the same writer was staged in New York City. Marcel Dubé wrote a comedy, *Le Testament* or *L'Impromptu de Québec.* The National Theater performed a play by Claude Gauvreau, *La Charge de l'original epormiable.* The Jean Duceppe Company had an immense success with *Charbonneau et le Chef* and Léméac House republished the *Théâtre de Crémazie.* (ROBERT SAINT-AMOUR)

GERMAN

Compared with the previous 12 months, 1974 was a lean year for German literature, and a number of established authors proved disappointing. Heinrich Böll produced his first work since receiving the 1972 Nobel Prize, *Die verlorene Ehre der Katharina Blum,* again a best-seller, which lampooned the reporting methods of the Axel Springer press successfully enough to drive the best-seller lists from Springer's *Welt am Sonntag.* Sloppily written, this minor novel lived purely on its author's indignation. Rolf Hochhuth too managed to please the public and enrage the critics with his comedy *Lysistrate und die NATO;*

Swiss novelist Adolf Muschg, whose "Albissers Grund," published in 1974, satirized attitudes toward foreign workers in Switzerland.

HANNA MUSCHG

more interesting than the play was the long, appended essay on women's emancipation. Peter Handke's *Die Unvernünftigen sterben aus*, a play about capitalists, marked its author's turning to more conventional forms of drama, with recognizable characters in recognizable social situations. Although it read well, the long monologues lacked dramatic tension and it was a failure on the stage. Even the third volume of Uwe Johnson's *Jahrestage* seemed to lack the vigour of the earlier parts, although this could be attributed to the gloom of its subject matter. Covering the period April–June 1968, it included the assassination of Robert Kennedy and increasing tension in Czechoslovakia and, on the more distant time level, the immediate postwar years.

One author to consolidate his reputation was the Swiss Adolf Muschg, whose many-layered novel *Albissers Grund* presented in detective-story form a psychological study of a left-wing teacher, a satire on the relation between the Swiss and their foreign workers, and a variation on the Faust legend. Hubert Fichte's much-discussed *Versuch über die Pubertät* was more private in theme; adolescence appeared to be equated with homosexuality and concrete reminiscences of postwar Hamburg were interspersed with accounts of South American tribal rituals in a novel of undoubted, if at times repulsive, poetic power. Alfred Andersch's novel *Winterspelt* was an impressive montage of the fictitious attempts of a German major to desert with his battalion to the Americans and extracts from historical documents of the closing years of World War II. Minor masterpieces included Jean Améry's *Lefeu*, an "essayistic" novel attacking the contemporary tabula rasa mentality and pleading the cause of the "aesthetics of decay"; also Eva Zeller's *Lampenfieber*, a beautifully presented study of family tensions.

When robbery with violence caused the spectre of anarchist terror to be frequently invoked in the press and on television, crime understandably loomed large in the imagination even of serious authors. Böll's lampoon was about trial by the media. A more carefully reasoned study of the relation between media and violence was Martin Gregor-Dellin's novel *Föhn*: an actual incident, a bank robbery with hostages, generated a study of all the factors involved, not least being the climate—intellectual and meteorological—of the city of Munich. Hans Hellmut Kirst's *Alles hat seinen Preis*, however, with a similar topic and setting, remained on the superficial level of the thriller. More reputable entertainment of this kind was to be found in Hans Herlin's *Freunde*, which, for all its basically melodramatic story, showed some awareness of social and moral problems. More slight, but perhaps more profound, were works by W. E. Richartz and Burkhard Driest. The former's *Noface* was an amusing tale of a man who so lacks identity that the victims of his bank holdups cannot recognize him two minutes later. Driest's *Die Verrohung des Franz Blum* was ostensibly a documentation of life in prison, but in fact an allegory of capitalist society.

An unusual number of eccentricities appeared, usually labeled "roman," a term that appeared now to have little meaning in German. Oddest of these was Michael Vetter's *Handbewegungen*, which consisted, literally, of nothing but carefully executed abstract "doodles." Almost as unexpected, in the context of German literature, was H. J. Stammel's *Die Stunde des Cowboys*, an account in "novel" form of cowboy life in the Texas Panhandle at the end of the 19th century, underpinned—even popular literature was affected by the fashion—with numerous extracts from contemporary documents. Equally eccentric, but in a more traditional way, was Urs Widmer's fantastic *Die Forschungsreise*, a witty parody of adventure stories and at the same time a satire on contemporary overcivilization. Mario Szenessy's *Der Hellseher* seemed to have Uri Geller as godfather, its picaresque hero being gifted with extrasensory perception and psychokinetic powers; unfortunately its excellent beginning, reminiscent of Thomas Mann's *Krull*, was not sustained. Briefer and more consistently entertaining was Renate Rasp's *Chinchilla*; ostensibly a handbook for the prospective prostitute, its insistence throughout on the purely commercial basis of the trade made it clear that the commercial basis of life in general was under attack.

Outstanding in the realm of short prose works was Marie-Luise Kaschnitz's last publication, *Orte*. A collection of brief reminiscences and meditations, it was widely held to represent the pinnacle of its author's career. Dieter Wellershoff published for the first time some short stories, *Doppelt belichtetes Seestück*, a collection that also included poems, radio plays, and *Hysteria*, a scenario for a "multimedia opera." Of more direct social import was Leonie Ossowski's impressive *Mannheimer Erzählungen*, glimpses of the lives of deprived adolescents on probation or in borstals.

Lyric poetry was well represented by collections from Jürgen Becker and Erich Fried. Becker's *Das Ende der Landschaftsmalerei* succeeded in regretting the rape of the countryside in the name of progress without falling into the trap of yearning for the "good old days." His basic skepticism was shared by Fried, whose *Gegengift* was dominated by the concept of "doubt," doubting political commitment but also, in the concluding cycle, doubting language itself. The indefatigable Hermann Kesten, at the age of 74, brought out his first set of poems, *Ich bin der ich bin*.

Memoirs in the literary field included Max Frisch's *Dienstbüchlein*, on his military service 30 years earlier in Switzerland, and Hilde Domin's *Von der Natur nicht vorgesehen*; in the journalistic, Otto Rombach's *Vorwärts, ruckwärts, meine Spur* and Josef Eberle's *Aller Tage Morgen*; in the political, the conservative Gerhard Storz's *Im Lauf der Jahre* and, notably, former West German chancellor Willy Brandt's *Über den Tag hinaus*.

In East Germany important novels appeared by Stefan Heym and Erik Neutsch. The former's *Lassalle* presented the Social Democrat leader in his last year as a subservient opportunist, an interpretation that provoked criticism even in official party ranks. Neutsch's *Auf der Suche nach Gatt* continued a line of works published in both West and East in which the central figure is the subject of investigation rather than analysis; this story of a Communist's failure to keep pace with ideological developments and his later rehabilitation held the attention in spite of the woodenness of the subsidiary characters. Literary Germany lost one of its few remaining links with the 1920s through the death in July of Erich Kastner (*see* Obituaries). (J. H. Reid)

ITALIAN

Does anything ever happen in Italy today worth writing novels about? Or are Italian novelists becoming incapable of responding to what actually goes on in their country? The best-selling novels of 1974 ap-

CASA EDITRICE VALENTINO BOMPIANI

Italian publisher and author Valentino Bompiani published his own memoirs, "Via Privata," in 1974.

peared to be either about manic-depressive characters and their fantasy worlds, or about old memories and past history. Roberto Calasso combined both in *L'impuro folle,* a sort of commentary to the memoirs of Senate President Schreber, the son of a notorious and nefarious 19th-century German educationist and the subject of one of Sigmund Freud's studies. The book was an imaginative attempt to merge fact and fantasy into a sort of poetic metahistory. Another nonnovel was Francesco Leonetti's *Irati e sereni,* a discursive literary metaphor of the emotional and ideological climate in the northern Italian left between 1967 and 1970. Arrigo Benedetti's *Rosso al vento* was set in 1945. Its protagonist, Rinaldo, travels from Rome to Milan through a country ravaged by war and civil strife, awaiting a great conclusive battle that will never be fought. Perhaps Benedetti meant that the final confrontation between reaction and social progress out of which a new Italy might have been born never took place, but he never openly says so. *La morte del fiume* by Guglielmo Petroni was a remembrance of life in the town of Lucca when the protagonist was a young man.

The most ambitious of this crop of memory novels was *La Storia* by Elsa Morante, a slice of Italian history between 1941 and 1947 seen mostly through the eyes of a child, born of a half-Jewish schoolmistress raped by a German soldier. The book was intended to reveal to uncultivated readers, perhaps even to the illiterate proletarians, that history, the cruel machine that first exploits and then crushes them, is "a scandal that has lasted for ten thousand years." It disappointed in many ways, being an undigested mixture of traditional literary rhetoric, stale clichés, novelettish sentimentality, and vernacular vulgarity. Furthermore, the author's babbling toddler with his humanized pets and inadequate mother were weak props to stage convincingly all the drama of recent world history. Only a few good patches here and there recalled how exciting Elsa Morante's writing used to be. Paolo Volponi's *Corporale* displayed a greater stylistic unity, besides many striking pages; and yet it was difficult to gauge its purpose. The fantasy world of Volponi's earlier novels was an effective and powerful way of indirectly portraying a diseased reality: here all contact with reality seemed to

have been lost. Perhaps the answer was found in an aphorism spoken, on the subject of incomprehensible writing, by the archaeologist's daughter in *Umana avventura* by Alberto Bevilacqua: "It is a sign of the highest civilization to be able to face nothingness." Of course, it is very bad criticism to ask questions about characters that are not relevant to the events in the novel, but it may be permissible when the novel is without events: did Bevilacqua's neurotic archaeologist ever do a stroke of work? and how could he financially afford his neurosis? One would like to know. It was a relief to read, after all this, the reminiscences of a hard-working and down-to-earth publisher, Valentino Bompiani, whose *Via privata* ought to become prescribed reading for all reviewers of Italian books. For sheer fantasy one should turn to Italo Calvino's *Il castello dei destini incrociati,* a narrative structure generated by the various possible readings of two square arrangements of tarot cards; and to *Parsifal,* a collection of cruel and macabre stories by Rodolfo Wilcock.

Carlo Cassola's latest novel, *Gisella,* probably did not appeal to Liliana Caruso and Bibi Tomasi who, in their essays *I padri della fallocultura,* sharply criticized him and other prominent Italian writers like Alberto Moravia, Leonardo Sciascia, and Giorgio Bassani for their alleged male chauvinism. To the growing body of serious and intellectually challenging feminist writing Armanda Guiducci contributed an absorbing self-analysis, *La mela e il serpente.* There was not only wit and elegance but a great deal of corrosive truth in Giorgio Manganelli's collected articles on Italian life and customs, *Lunario dell'orfano sannita. A,* by Giovanni Mariotti, was a delicate but emotional treatment of the mother myth, halfway between prose and poetry. Sergio Solmi brought out his collected poems (*Poesie complete*) written between 1924 and 1972, a moving testimonial of sober classicism untainted by fleeting fashion and the passing of time. Most of the words included in Cesare Lanza's *Mercabul,* on the other hand, would be out of date by the end of the decade: the book was a glossary of Italian teenage slang, full of interest for linguists and semanticists.   (GIOVANNI CARSANIGA)

JAPANESE

In Japan 1974 was a remarkable year for its variety and scope in fiction writing. There were two impressive "religious" novels by Shusaku Endo and Kunio Ogawa, a modernistic tour de force by Kobo Abe, two ambitious bouts with contemporary violence by Kenzaburo Ooe and Mitsuharu Inoue, and an analytical evocation of a militaristic boyhood during the Pacific war by Otohiko Kaga.

Shusaku Endo, whose *Chinmoku* (1966) had been translated into English as *Silence* and favourably received by both English and U.S. reviewers, wrote *Shikai no Hotori* ("By the Dead Sea"), which had a contemporary setting in contrast with that of 17th-century feudal Japan in *Silence.* Endo, a sensitive storyteller, deftly juxtaposed the story of a contemporary Japanese visitor to Israel with the episodic evocations of ancient biblical characters. Kunio Ogawa was a Roman Catholic convert, like Endo, but Ogawa's *Aru Seisho* ("A Holy Book") was rather different in tone and technique. This novel was directly concerned with the evocation of the biblical setting and atmosphere, and fabulistic in tone. However, it was deceptively simple, and there was something ambiguous about the whole story.

The first part appears to be a story of naive faith and devotion, but in the second and third parts the story becomes entangled and vague. Religious devotion and political action are intermingled and it is not certain whether the Judas-like character in this novel is really Judas or not.

Kobo Abe, whose important novels have been translated into several foreign languages, including Russian, is an avant-garde type of novelist and his new novel has a strange, surrealistic title, *Hako-Otoko* (*Box Man*). The central character, who remains anonymous throughout the book, decides to hide himself in a box, and continues to live in it. He became a "Box Man" by his own choice. What could it mean, this decision of his? Was he a man of independence or merely a futile escapist? Did Abe intend to suggest any affirmative significance in his preoccupation with closed space, his refusal to belong to any organization or community? In Kenzaburo Ooe's *Kozui wa Waga Tamashii ni oyobi* ("Deluge Rising to My Breast") and Mitsuharu Inoue's *Kokoro Yasashiki Hangyakushatachi* ("Tender Hearted Rebels") the titles were symptomatic. An eschatological mood and forebodings of a "Deluge" permeated Ooe's novel, and the keynote of Inoue's novel was bitter disillusionment and revolt. But both novels were deeply concerned with violence in contemporary society. Otohiko Kaga's *Kaerazaru Natsu* ("Summer of No Return") described the fanatic responses of the young military cadets to the defeat of Japan in 1945.

An impressive contribution by a senior novelist was Kosaku Takaii's *Haijin Nakama* ("A Group of Haiku Poets")—a brilliant masterpiece. Though Takaii was already in his late 70s, this autobiographical novel is vigorous and vivid in its description of local community in the Meiji Period and in the sensitive evocation of his first love affair with a geisha.

(SHOICHI SAEKI)

JEWISH

Hebrew. Hebrew literature in Israel during 1974 continued to demonstrate strength and versatility. The October 1973 war and its aftermath did not stop the presses—all genres of fiction and nonfiction were published, including volumes of topical interest.

Fiction did not produce any "surprises," and the number of volumes published was relatively limited. Nevertheless, M. Shamir's *Yonah me-Hatzer Zara*, an ambitious novel on Jewish life in Israel and abroad, proved of interest, as did A. Oz's selected stories, *Anashim Acherim*, and Y. Kaniuk's *Mot ha-Ir*. In a more realistic vein was the rambling novel by Yonat and Alexander Sando, *Tendu*, while M. Kapeliuk, in *Sippuro shel Jamshee*, portrayed the interplay of attitudes between Israelis and Arabs.

S. H. Bergman's *ha-Filosophia Hadialogit* was a study embracing Kierkegaard and Buber. Trenchant essays by N. Rotenstreich were published in *Zeman u-Mashmout*. Archaeologically instructive was B. Mazar's *Kanaan ve-Ysrael*, a work on Palestine in the so-called Bronze Period. E. Elath in *Shivat Zion ve-Arav* contributed a weighty disquisition on Zionism and Arabism. Autobiographical documents were the volumes by Israeli Prime Minister Yitzhak Rabin (*see* BIOGRAPHY) and Foreign Minister Yigal Allon, both entitled *Bet Avi*. Sh. Lachover's and G. Kressel's bibliography, *Kitvai Zalman Shazar*, of the writings of the late president of Israel, appeared. Volumes of literary criticism were H. Barzel's *Sipporet Ivrit Materialistit* and A. B. Yaffe's *Makbilot ba-Sippur*

Hamoderni, both interpreting mainly Hebrew fiction. B. Y. Michaly's essays *Massa u-Pulmus* were more controversial in tone. A study of the Hebrew works of I. L. Peretz, including a selection of his writings, was Y. Friedlander's *Havaya ve-Chavaya*. E. Schweid dealt with the loneliness and isolation of the contemporary Jew in *ha-Yehudi Haboded veha-Yahadut*.

Poetry as usual dominated the scene, older and younger poets of different schools being represented. Thus A. Shlonsky's *Sefer ha-Sulamot* was the swan song of a leading Hebrew modernist. N. Alterman was another late distinguished poet whose volume *Regayim* was published. Selections by so-called forgotten poets were Y. Lerner's *Shirim* and N. Stern's *Bain Arpilim*. More contemporary in style and method were N. Sach's *Mivhar*, T. Carmi's *Hitnatzlut ha-Mechaber*, M. Wieseltier's *Kach*, and H. Schimmel's *Shirai Malon Zion*. It is noteworthy that T. Carmi and H. Schimmel were American-born. However, in the U.S. itself Hebrew literary activity was almost at a standstill.

(GABRIEL PREIL)

Yiddish. New Yiddish books of poetry and fiction are always numerous and 1974 was no exception. A high point in poetry was the issuance in Tel Aviv of Joseph and Eleanor Mlotek's *Pearls from Yiddish Poetry;* the book was an outgrowth of a poetry page printed in Sunday issues of the New York *Jewish Daily Forward*. The published individual collections of verse included Pinche Berman's *Love*, Eliezer Greenberg's *Memorabilia*, two books by Meir Charatz, *Heaven and Earth* and *In Strange Paradise*, Rachel Kramf's *Clouds Wish to Cry*, and Shifrah Kholodenko's *The Word*. To their previous collections of verse new titles were added by Saul Maltz (*Poems of My Profound Belief*), Abraham Sutzkever (*The Fidlerose*), Malka H. Tuzman (*Under Your Mark*), Freed Weininger (*In the Wide Outside*), Hillel Shargel (*A Window to Heaven*), Isaac Yanosovich (*The Other Side of Wonder*), and Hersh Leib Young (*In the Astral Spheres*). Moshe Brodersohn's *The Last Song* and Roza Nevadovska's *Poems of Mine* were published posthumously. An important event was the publication of the first volume of the *Collected Dramas* by the late poet Aaron Zeitlin.

Notable Yiddish novels included Lily Berger's *Two Storms*, Eliyahu Kaplan's *Incarnations of a Pioneer*, Leibl Kh. Shimoni's *In the Crucible*, published shortly after the author's demise, and Eli Schechtman's tetralogy, *Eve*. In the short-story category belong H. Ayalti's *The Man from De Mille*, Eliezer Cooperman's *From World to World*, Zvi Eisenman's *Between Borders*, Zami Feder's *Closed Fists*, Chaim Goldberg's *Too Much in One Week*, Chaim Grade's *Synagogue and Street*, and B. Shlevin's *Under the Stars of the Negev*.

To the fields of the philosophical essay and literary criticism were added Abraham Golomb's *To the Depths of Jewish Thought*, Noah Griss's *From Light to Darkness*, about the novelist Isaiah Spiegel, Yudel Mark's analytical study *Abraham Sutzkever's Poetic Road*, the *Essays* by Gittel Meisel, and Abraham Yerushalmi's *The Bankruptcy of the Isms*.

Great importance is attached to printing reminiscences or unpublished works by deceased authors, and to the publication of historic or literary documents in general. These categories were enriched by Harry Lang's *Four Generations*, Chaim Ehrenreich's *Remaining Words*, and Isaac Rimon's *Correspondences from Israel (1946–1968)*. Quite substantial was the number of collective volumes devoted to the history of various Jewish communities. Outstanding among them were Leizer Ran's two-volume illustrated *Jerusalem of Lithuania,* by which is meant the city of Vilno, and *The Golden Book of Argentinian Jewry* by Wolf Bressler and Moshe Knapheiss.

(MOSHE STARKMAN)

PORTUGUESE

Portugal. The April revolution marked 1974 as potentially the most significant year in the past half century for Portuguese literature; in the circumstances no literary survey could ignore the work that, without literary pretensions itself, precipitated the fall of the 48-year tyranny—Gen. António de Spínola's *Portugal e o Futuro* (*see* BIOGRAPHY).

The six months prior to the liberation, marked by increasing repression and discouragement, saw little new writing, the most important work by an established poet being the expatriate Jorge de Sena's *Conheço o Sal.* . . . Publication of Herberto Helder's collected poems to date was completed, and Fiama Brandão also published her collected verse, with additions. There was new poetry from Fernando Echevarria (*A Base e o Timbre*), Egito Gonçalves (*Destruição: Dois Pontos*), and Pedro Támen (*Os 42 Sonetos*).

The most interesting work of fiction to appear since the revolution (though written earlier), Mário Cláudio's *Um Verão Assim,* was a palimpsest, in which a summer in the life of a group of young people of the *alta burguesia* at the beach is superimposed on the playing time of a record of Prokofiev, key passages of which are constantly repeated. The discontinuous, fragmentary, "replayable" nature of memory (and, implicitly, of all experience) forms the basis of the work.

The only significant new play, Bernardo Santareno's angry "deposition" *Português, Escritor, 45 Anos de Idade,* would have before April (like most serious contemporary drama) have been consigned, if not to oblivion, at least to silence. The current antiliterary climate might work to the advantage of the theatre, as the genre most easily "taken to the people" and so least open to charges of elitism. A cultural mission, including Santareno, the dramatist L. F. Rebelo, and the fringe theatre company A Comuna, visited Warsaw and Moscow in the fall. Meanwhile, an unexpected and no doubt temporary negative consequence of freedom was not the spate of "socialist realism" some might have feared but a wholesale *trahison des clercs,* lamentably presided over by the veteran Gomes Ferreira, who abjured poetry as a bird that sings sweetest when caged. Although writers who had based their style on censor-proof allusiveness and their themes on protest would now have to do some retooling (and others, given the benefit of the doubt on the assumption they could do better if allowed to, might have their bluff called), such betrayal of the Logos could hardly prosper in a society which for almost 900 years had expressed itself primarily in poetry. (STEPHEN RECKERT)

Brazil. The year 1974 was not one of great effervescence for Brazilian literature. There was the publication of the poetic works of Ledo Ivo, *O Sinal Semafórico,* to commemorate the tenth anniversary of his death. Outstanding among the newcomers were Francisco Alvim, with *Passatempo,* and Geraldo Carneiro, with *Na Busca do Sete-Estrelo.* Stella Leonardos reappeared with two books of poems: *Amanhecência* and *Romançário.* Ariano Suassuna con-

tributed *A Farsa da Boa Preguiça,* following the eminently "northeastern" trend of his works. Novels presented included *As Meninas* by Lygia Fagundes Telles, whose works as storyteller were being republished. Nélida Piñon's *Tebas do Meu Coração* was a thorough and ambitious novel, perhaps influenced by Gabriel García Márquez. Clarice Lispector was present again with *Onde Estiveste De Noite?* and *Via Crucis do Corpo.* Waldomiro Autran Dourado, whose book *O Risco do Bordado* was rather successful in 1971, saw his *Os Sinos da Agonia* published. Although the action described in this book is concentrated in the city of Ouro Prêto during the 18th century, it cannot be classified as a historical novel. From Fausto Cunha came the novel *O Beijo Antes do Sonho* and the essay *Caminhos Reais, Viagens Imaginárias*—a commentary on the novels of Machado de Assis.

Hélgio Trindade produced a serious and objective essay on fascism called *Integralismo, O Fascismo Brasileiro na Década de 30. Quem Matou Vargas* was written with the passionate talent of Carlos Heitor Cony. Edgar Carone presented *A República Nova, 1930–1937. Itinerários* was an interesting arrival, in which Alphonsus de Guimaraens Filho presented the letters he received from Mário de Andrade and Manuel Bandeira. The first two volumes of Pontes de Miranda's *Dez Anos de Pareceres* were published—a collection of juridical opinions planned for ten volumes. Mário da Silva Brito entertained with *Conversa Vai, Conversa Vem.* José Guilherme Merquior produced *Formalismo e Tradição Moderna,* dealing with the problem of the arts in a cultural crisis. Memoirs included *Travessia* by Hermes Lima, *Elos de Uma Corrente* by Laura Rodrigo Otávio, and *Noel Nutels: Memórias e Depoimentos* by Noel Nutels. Part of a writer's diary was published in *A Velha Chama* by Ascendino Leite. Alceu Amoroso Lima contributed two books—*Em Busca da Liberdade* and *Os Direitos do Homem.* (ANTONIO CARLOS VILLAÇA)

RUSSIAN

Soviet Literature. Many works published in 1974 exemplified the tendency of recent years toward broad socio-historical interpretations of life, deep socio-ethical studies of human lives and characters, and broad epic canvases in which the narrative advances on several planes simultaneously. Typical of the numerous novels and novellas centred on events of historical significance were Vasily Smirnov's epic *Discovery of the World,* a chronicle of life in a Russian village on the Upper Volga in the troubled summer of 1917, and P. Proskurin's *Destiny,* ranging over whole decades of the Soviet state's existence.

Among works in a variety of historical genres were A. Shemetov's historical biographical novel *The Breakthrough: The Story of Aleksandr Radischev* and L. Dugin's novellas about Pushkin, *The Lycée,* published in the periodical *Novy Mir.* Many writers turned to the grim, heroic time of World War II, often making use of documentary material, for example B. Polevoi's *Those Four Years: From the Notebook of a War Correspondent.* There was a stirring sense of tradition from father to children in both war and work in V. Roslyakov's novel *The Last War,* E. Nosov's *The Bridge,* and F. Taurin's *No Other Way.*

The effect of scientific and technical progress on the lives of Soviet workers was the theme of novelists such as V. Kozhevnikov, S. Safronov, and Y. Rytkheu. The ethical world of contemporary man was

Aleksandr Solzhenitsyn in exile. In December 1974 the writer traveled to Stockholm to collect his 1970 Nobel Prize for Literature.

treated by V. Shukshin in *Viewpoint: Novella-Fairy Tale* (*see* OBITUARIES).

In portrayals of the life of country folk there was a marked shift from the lyrical narrative of the late 1950s and early 1960s to socio-historical analysis on several levels simultaneously. An example of this was F. Abramov's trilogy *Pryasliny,* a chronicle of the life of a northern Russian village in the difficult war and postwar years. There were interesting reflections on the lives of country people in S. Krutilin's *Broom: Novellas.*

Recent poetry had much to say about the past and present of the Soviet Union, the fraternal commonwealth of the Soviet peoples, and love of one's native countryside. This was reflected in the many translations into Russian from some of the more than 70 languages spoken by various peoples and nationalities of the Soviet Union. Among them were M. Bazhan's *The Spark,* from *Uman Recollections* (1973, translated from Ukrainian); P. Brovka's *We Are Children of One Mother* (1973, from Belorussian); and R. Margiani's *From the Book of Brotherhood* (1973, from Georgian). M. Kanoatov turned to World War II in his *The Voice of Stalingrad* (1973, from Tajik), as did M. Lukonin in his volume *Frontline Verse,* S. Orlov in *Loyalty* (1973), and B. Istru in *Pain of a Shadow* (1973, from Moldavian). The thoughts and feelings of Soviet man trying to interpret the laws of the development of life and understand his role in the creation of the new life were expressed by L. Tatyanichev in *The Honey Season.* (NOVOSTI)

Expatriate Russian Literature. The exiling of Aleksandr I. Solzhenitsyn (*see* BIOGRAPHY) on Feb. 13, 1974, was a significant event in the history of Russian culture, and not just in the chronicles of the current Soviet counterculture. For the Soviet Union, said Andrey Sakharov, the distinguished physicist and the chief leader of political dissent remaining in Moscow, the expulsion was a signal of moral defeat. But for Solzhenitsyn himself it was in every sense a turning point, and speculation centred at once upon the extent to which, uprooted from Russian soil and removed from danger, he would lose his peculiar moral authority, the ready attention of the Western press, and so his political leverage on the Soviet leadership over their handling of internal dissent. So

far as his main tasks as a writer were concerned, his passion for work and the fact that his wife was able to bring out his research material when she joined him in Switzerland meant that he was able to get on with the two parallel projects, Tolstoyan in scale and aspiration, in which he had been reviewing Russia's sufferings in the 20th century. The second volume of *The Gulag Archipelago,* dealing with the actual administration of the prison camps, was published in Paris in the autumn as he was working on the closely interconnected second and third novels in the historical sequence that began with *August 1914.*

The direction and influence of his work as polemicist and pamphleteer on current political events was more problematical, however. In his last years in the Soviet Union he had been spurred on partly by official harassment, but also by a fear that détente amounted to an appeasement which would confirm the Soviet system, indirectly legitimizing its history and emasculating critical Western opinion. This led him to condemn Western liberals who spoke against oppressive right-wing regimes and against Soviet injustices in what he thought was too evenhanded a manner, and to indicate (especially in his *Letter to the Soviet Leaders,* published in Paris shortly after his arrival in Switzerland) a world view that was not only more conservative, nationalist, and pessimistic than that of Western liberals in general but also much to the right of the views of Sakharov, Roy Medvedev, and other Soviet dissidents.

Thus the year made clearer a division in Russia's counterculture remarkably like that which occurred among Russian intellectuals in the mid-19th century, with Solzhenitsyn leading the reborn "Slavophiles" like a latterday Dostoevsky and the more or less revisionist Marxists Medvedev and Sakharov as the chief "Westernizers."

Another symptom of disarray, or alternatively of returning normality in Soviet intellectual life, was the subterranean uproar caused by the appearance of the second book of memoirs, *Hope Abandoned,* by Nadezhda Mandelstam, the formidable widow of one of Russia's great modern poets, Osip Mandelstam. Conformism in official Soviet culture is reinforced by a traditional conservatism that idealizes the artist and makes for a rather hagiographical style in literary history. Mrs. Mandelstam's books, with their naming of names and contemptuous intolerance of the frailty of most of the generation of writers who failed to prevent her husband's disappearance in the camps on the eve of World War II, swept through this cozy atmosphere in a cold and accusing blast. Even an English critic called *Hope Abandoned* a "hair-raisingly unsentimental book," but in Moscow its underground circulation provoked not only verbal recriminations but also a long, outraged letter (sent out for publication abroad by Mrs. Mandelstam herself) from another elderly and respected liberal writer, the novelist V. A. Kaverin, accusing her of self-aggrandizement and "outright abuse . . . or mocking pity" of talented and honourable writers. Critics less intimately involved in the family quarrels, however, were confirmed in their belief that these memoirs were a real addition to Russian literature.

The other internecine quarrel of the year, in which one Russian Nobel Prize winner (Solzhenitsyn) sponsored research designed to show that another (M. A. Sholokhov) was a literary fraud, was set off in the pages of the London *Times Literary Supplement* and proved to be rather a damp squib (although it evoked a long refutation from *Izvestia*), reviving old suspicions but throwing little real light on the problems posed by the great unevenness of *The Quiet Don*, the vast novel on which Sholokhov's reputation uneasily rests.   (W. L. WEBB)

SCANDINAVIAN

Danish. Danish literature was dominated by social preoccupations and memoirs. Tage Skou-Hansen's *Medløberen* (1973) drew a somewhat intricate analogy between a football team and life itself to show how the pressure to conform exerts itself even on the most idealistic. Also an analogy of life was Leif Panduro's *Den ubetænksomme elsker* (1973), a love story about a doctor and a schizophrenic girl. Christian Kampmann's *Visse Hensyn* (1973) was the first part of a trilogy, tracing a family from the 1950s to the present day and indicating the social and political changes that have taken place. Another, bitingly satirical, picture of modern Denmark came from Willy-August Linnemann's *Lovgiveren*. Still with a social purpose but more akin to a thriller was Anders Bodelsen's *Bevisets stilling*. His *Alt hvad du ønsker dig* was superficially a fairy tale about a woman who receives supernatural powers, but essentially a study of human limitations and responsibility. Another fan-

Willy-August Linnemann satirized contemporary Danish society in his novel "Lovgiveren," published in 1974.

GYLDENDALSKE BOGHANDEL NORDISK FORLAG

tastic novel with a message was Henrik Stangerup's *Manden, der ville være skyldig* (1973).

A weightier look at the world and the prospect facing it was to be found in Villy Sørensen's highly intellectual *Uden mal og med* (1973), for which he was awarded the Nordic Council's literature prize. In December 1973 he shared the Danish critics' prize with Aage Dons, whose novel *Nødstedt i natten* won him great acclaim. Sven-Åge Madsen's *Jakkels Vandring* showed different sides of human nature by letting seven different "authors" write their impressions of the same person. Likewise experimental was Henrik Bjelke's *Saturn*, a long, fantastic novel filled with myth and mysticism.

Among the numerous memoirs that appeared in 1974 was Danish Prime Minister Poul Hartling's *Fra 17 år i dansk politik*, while Ole Bjørn Kraft made his contribution in *Frem mod nye tider*. In her *Notater om Karen Blixen* Clara Svendsen told of Karen Blixen as she was in everyday life, while her brother, Thomas Dinesen, wrote of his sister's youth in *Tanne. Min søster Karen Blixen*.

Klaus Rifbjerg made his usual large contribution, including *Sommer,* a collection of short stories ranging from the comic to the brutal and *Du skal ikke være ked af det, Amalia,* which attacked the press.
                                                    (W. GLYN JONES)

Norwegian. Jens Bjørneboe carried his three-volume saga of the white man's atrocities through the ages to a brilliant conclusion with the novel *Stillheten*, in the main devoted to the brutal Spanish destruction of the Aztec and Inca civilizations and to the bestialities of the Vietnam war. A sailing ship doomed to destruction formed the framework of *Haiene*, a tough novel of the sea by the same author. A typical man's world was also the setting for Kåre Holt's outstanding and controversial documentary novel *Kappløpet,* an intense and unflattering report on Roald Amundsen and his race with Capt. R. F. Scott to be the first man at the South Pole. A collection of texts by Cora Sandel, *Barnet som elsket veier,* pointed out what a fastidious master of prose Norway lost at Sandel's death in April 1974 (*see* OBITUARIES). Johan Borgen's *Eksempler* combined psychological analysis of the final stages of the breakup of a marriage with sagacious sidelights on the contemporary human situation in general. A virtuoso mixture of facts and fiction characterized Jens Erik Normann's entertaining thriller *Rakett mot Murmansk.* The conflict between heathen lust for power and the milder Christian morality was at the centre of Vera Henriksen's play *Sverdet,* with St. Olav as the main protagonist.

A plea for the right to free abortion was put forward by Tove Nilsen in the novel *Aldri la dem kle deg forsvarsløst naken,* while ideas of women's liberation in general were discussed in Bjørg Vik's play *To akter for fem kvinner.* Refreshing self-irony seasoned the philosophizing of Stein Mehren's novel *Titanene.* Historical in content but with contemporary overtones was Bergljot Hobæk Haff's novel *Heksen,* centred round a social outsider, a witch living around A.D. 1600. Life in a farming community in southern Norway during the first two decades of the 20th century was depicted by Knut Hauge in the fifth of a series of historical novels, *Spelemannen Siljufløyt.* Wider in scope and covering the first half of the same century was a fascinating collection of autobiographical childhood reminiscences by 17 prominent Norwegians published by Gyldendal Norsk Forlag under the title *Det første halvsekel.*

An amusing literary curiosity was a play by Peter Wessel Zapffe, *Hos doktor Wangel,* peopled by Ibsen characters and published under the pseudonym Ib Henriksen. *Vindharpe* confirmed Hans Børli's central position in Norwegian poetry. Outstanding also were selected poems by André Bjerke, *Med alle mine fugler,* and by Sigmund Skard, *Dikt i utval.*

Two widows provided revealing close-ups of their late husbands, Suzanne Bull in *Ni år. Mitt liv med Olaf Bull,* and Halldis Moren Vesaas in *I Midtbøs bakkar,* covering the first 15 years of her marriage to Tarjei Vesaas. A major event in literary scholarship was the launching of a new history of Norwegian literature in six volumes, *Norges litteraturhistorie,* edited by Edvard Beyer. Johan Riis drew a warm portrait of one of the leading classics in *Alexander L. Kielland. Mannen bak dikteren.*

(TORBJØRN STØVERUD)

Swedish. The death in July 1974 of Pär Lagerkvist (*see* OBITUARIES), winner of the 1951 Nobel Prize for Literature, was followed later in the year by the award of the 1974 prize jointly to two septuagenarian Swedish writers who were internationally less well known: Harry Martinson (whose poems *Tuvor* appeared in 1973) and Eyvind Johnson, whose latest novel, *Några steg mot tystnaden,* was typical in its complex structure and dreams of love. The death occurred also of Olle Hedberg, after the appearance of his novel *Tänk att ha hela livet framför sig....*

Many books dealt with prison life: Kennet Ahl's *Grundbulten,* Inge Ihsgren's *Sociopaten,* and a compilation by 17 prisoners, *Vårdad och fin,* were all based on personal experience behind bars. Journalist Peter Bratt, sentenced for revealing military secrets, wrote *I fängelse* in solitary confinement. The best-seller detective-story team of Maj Sjövall and Per Wahlöö published *Polismördaren,* continuing their critical examination of police and criminals.

Historical imagination was abundant in Artur Lundkvist's study of the painter Goya, *Livsälskare, svart-målare,* a compound of biography, art criticism, and novel. In *Furstarna* Ivar Lo-Johansson published historical short stories dealing with Swedish royalty ("it is only democratic ... after all the commoners I have written about"). Recent history provided the background to Ole Söderström's *Vägen till Nörholm,* whose wartime characters included the Norwegian writer Knut Hamsun, while the main character was a Swedish journalist with personal problems of loyalty and treachery. Sven Delblanc's *Vinteride* was set in 1939–41; a village in neutral Sweden observes the war at a distance, yet has plenty of its own human problems, as the masterly narration makes clear. Per Olov Enquist believed that the spirit of revolt from around 1968 had been replaced by loyalty to the oppressors or political apathy, and in *Berättelser från de inställda upprorens tid* he illustrated this contention in stories set in West Germany and the U.S. Two powerful novels exploring human relationships were Polish-born Rita Tornborg's *Hansson och Goldman* and Per Gunnar Evander's *Måndagarna med Fanny.*

G. Harding and R. Aggestam published an anthology of modern poetry, *Tjugo unga poeter,* Tomas Tranströmer a long poem, *Östersjöar,* Lars Forssell poems entitled *Det möjliga,* and the prolific Lars Norén *Dagliga och nattliga dikter.* Reidar Ekner's *Efter flera tusen rad* was a poem about his eight-year-old daughter as she lay dying of cancer. Astonishingly, this small book spoke of the unspeakable with beauty and hope.   (KARIN PETHERICK)

SPANISH
Spain. The Spanish novel continued defunct in large measure during 1974. There was no new point of departure and no spectacular fireworks. The first of the year yielded an experimentalist first novel, *Cuando 900 mil Mach aprox,* by Mariano Antolín-Rato, and the critics welcomed it as some kind of response to the invasion of the field of Spanish literature by Hispanic-American writers. The year was marked by reappearances of writers who had come to the fore in the late 1950s and had scarcely been heard of since. Two of them, Jesús López Pacheco with his *La hoja de parra* and Luis Goytisolo Gay with *Recuento,* had their books printed in Mexico because of their country's censorship. The third revenant, José Manuel Caballero Bonald, back from the land of lexicography, where he worked on the Spanish Academy's historical dictionary, published an exotic novel appropriately and poetically titled *Agata ojo de gato;* after the author's 13 years of novelistic silence, his book made a great realistic noise: it won the Premio Barral, amid great controversy, and he ended by renouncing this prestigious prize. The noncommercial Premio de la Critica went to Corpus Varga for his novel *Los galgos verdugos;* while the prize for poetry went to Carlos Bousoño for his *Las monedas contra la losa.*

A masterful edition of a most readable classic was that of the *Glosas de sabiduría* by Don Sem Tob, rabbi of Carrión (born *c.* 1300), edited by Agustín García Calvo, whose arrangement of the text was based on a study of the four known manuscripts. For complete reading facility he provided a running paraphrase in modern Spanish (of surprising similarity to the original) clarified so as to make evident that the treatise dealt with the logic of contradiction and moral doubt, and he also furnished a highly useful commentary and introduction.

Another "Jewish" writer of a later date in Spain's racial evolution, from a family of converts who left Spain on the Expulsion, but who was and remained a priest in Italy, provided the theme for a model of lively scholarship, a beautifully proportioned and racy study, *La génesis artística de la lozana andaluza: El realismo literario de Francisco Delicado* by José A. Hernández Ortiz, with a prologue by Juan Goytisolo. Delicado's classic, *Retrato de la lozana andaluza,* was an erotic account of contemporary life and morals mostly among young *pícaros;* Hernández Ortiz did loving justice to his gamy subject.

Still another study of one of the Spanish classics by a writer of Jewish background was devoted to and titled *Fray Luis de León,* that descendant of Jews, Christian monk, translator of the Song of Solomon, and glorious synthesizer of Spanish language, history, and music; the compiler of the book (for it included an anthology of the work of Fray Luis as well as an account of his life and a lyrical appreciation of his work) was Alberto Barasoain, who showed himself possessed of a truly musical ear, something almost totally absent in contemporary Spanish criticism.

A profoundly witty book by the controversial and unique José Bergamín was a collection of varied pieces titled *La importancia del demonio;* its poetic analysis of the "suicidally intense" Spanish gaze, with "eyes that touch" its object but end by seeing nothing, was alone worth its appearance.

One of the more subtle nongenre books of the year was a collection of studies and rare views of 20th-century writers by E. F. Granell under the title of *La leyenda de Lorca y otros escritos.* A telling com-

TOP, KEYSTONE; BOTTOM, LUTFI OZKOK

Swedish authors Eyvind Johnson (top) and Harry Martinson, jointly awarded the 1974 Nobel Prize for Literature.

mentary on the contradictory nature of Spanish censorship was the appearance during the year of no less than three editions of a book long unavailable, the *Guía espiritual* of the heretical Miguel de Molinos, not printed in Spain since 1935, a year before the Civil War. Perhaps the most readily available edition was the one by Claudio Lendínez; another edition was supplied by the poet José Ángel Valente. Camilo José Cela's *Oficio de tinieblas 5,* which appeared at the turn of the year and whose epigraph was Miguel de Unamuno's "Literature is nought but death," was most alive, in a seventh edition by the end of 1974.

An outstanding book of verse was Vicente Aleixandre's *Diálogos del conocimiento.*

(ANTHONY KERRIGAN)

Latin-America. The year 1974 belonged, properly speaking, to the illustrious dead. The deaths of Chile's Pablo Neruda in September 1973, of Miguel Ángel Asturias in June 1974 (both Nobel Prize winners), and the shocking accidental death of the poet and novelist Rosario Castellanos (who was Mexican ambassador to Israel) removed from the literary scene three writers who represented "social" literature at its best. (*See* OBITUARIES.) Neruda, of course, cannot be reduced to any simplistic category. Astonishingly, his posthumous works continued to pour out, almost as if he were writing from his grave. Seven of his books appeared—*La rosa separada, Jardín de invierno, Defectos escogidos, 2000 El corazón amarillo, Libro de las preguntas, Elegía,* and *El mar y las campanas.* At least one critic believed them to be the best poetry Neruda ever wrote. They included the astonishing "Animal de luz," a clear-eyed vision of his own disappearance from the world. In these poems, Neruda faced his own death without self-pity but with a certain caustic wit reminiscent of Picasso. Like Picasso, Neruda kept his amazing creative gifts intact to the end of his life, though the vitalism by which he had always lived proved a tenuous bulwark against death. Both these artists expressed each stage of their lives with verve and candour and met old age with a certain resentment (as well as with resignation) as they sensed the decline of their bodily powers. As he grew older, Neruda tended to look backward more and more, reliving certain privileged moments of experience—his childhood, the East, the Spanish Civil War.

Neruda's widow, Matilde Urrutia, and the Venezuelan novelist Miguel Otero Silva completed the manuscript, with some of Neruda's loose texts, of his memoirs, *Confieso que he vivido.* Unfortunately, they add little to what he told us in his autobiographical poems *Memorial de Isla Negra* (1964).

English translations of Neruda were increased with *Residence on Earth, Extravagaria,* and a selection of poems from *Five Decades,* but as Michael Wood pointed out in the *New York Review of Books* and Donald Walsh in *Hispania,* these works are not valid as legible poetry in the English language and elementary errors make it impossible for those unable to read his works in the original to reach a closeness with the real Neruda.

Miguel Ángel Asturias was never the prolific writer that Neruda was, though he too went through a period of great creativity just before his death and was apparently working on a novel, *Dos veces bastardo.* Like *Viernes de dolores* (1972), it described the Guatemalan middle classes in 1954, on the eve of the overthrow of Arbenz. Rosario Castellanos will be best remembered for her Chiapas novels. She was also an active feminist, a woman of wit and intelligence who would certainly have made a far bigger contribution had she not died tragically at the early age of 48.

The disappearance of these three marked the end of an era of socially conscious literature. All of their works antedated the new novel with its emphasis on the creative participation of the reader. In fact, however, the new novel had itself become repetitive and few really interesting novels appeared in the course of the year. The reason was not the lack of talent but rather the questioning of the genre itself, which has always been associated with a privileged public. More and more of the young talent was looking beyond traditional genres to newer forms or to kinds of art that were not tainted with the original sin of elitism. Symptomatic of this was the interest in popular song, in theatre, and in cinema collectives. Behind this interest, there was still a social concern, but it was being expressed rather differently from the generation of Neruda and Asturias. The concern stemmed, first of all, from a growing realization of the power of the mass media in shaping opinion; hence the spate of articles in literary magazines on comic strips, on popular love stories or television soap operas. Equally symptomatic of this suspicion of cultural elitism was the Cali (Colombia) conference on the novel held by the magazine *La nueva narrativa hispanoamericana.* The organizers' attention to the international scene hurt local Colombian feeling, with the result that Colombian writers, headed by the veteran León de Greiff, signed a protest before the conference opened.

It was not a great year for literary prizes, though Mexico announced its intention to institute an Alfonso Reyes prize with a jury consisting of internationally famous critics. Spain, too, appeared to be planning a "Nobel" prize for the Spanish-speaking world. The annual Casa de las Américas Prize went to Uruguayan Alfredo Gravina, for a collection of short stories, and the Despegues to the Peruvian Marcos Llauria for the novel *En otoño, después de mil años.*

Everything changed in Latin America after the 1973 military coup that overthrew Chilean Pres. Salvador Allende Gossens. It was natural for the Chilean theme to appear in hundreds of books, from poems and compilations of documents such as *El libro negro de la represión en Chile* to novels such as *Salvador Allende* by Enrique Lafourcade. To this genre belongs the newly exiled Chilean Jorge Edwards, who published his diary of experiences in Cuba and in his own country—*Persona non grata.* Published from Edwards' new residence in Spain, the work could not have appeared at a more inopportune time. When the intellectual left found an urgent cause for unity, Edwards (Allende's former representative to Cuba) gave his personal view of the causes of the break between a considerable group of writers on the Latin-American continent and their Cuban friends as a result of the 1971 imprisonment and subsequent self-criticism of the Cuban poet Heberto Padilla.

Of all Chilean exiles the most literarily active was Ariel Dorfman, who published two books of essays and the most interesting experimental novel of the year, *Moros en la costa,* a magnificent tour de force that contained close to 20 novels within the novel. Through its exploration of the limits and possibilities of the genre, *Moros en la costa* was also a testimony of how the Chilean intellectuals answered the challenge of creating a new culture. The central idea of the other two books, *Inocencia y neocolonialismo: ensayos quemados en Chile* and *Superman y sus*

J. M. Caballero Bonald, controversial winner of the Spanish literary prize, the Premio Barral.

amigos del alma, was the denunciation of the values and interests of the U.S. imposed through "pop culture": from comics and TV series to the *Reader's Digest. Superman* contained a second part, by Manuel Jofre, which described how comics used their penetrative force in the construction of socialism in Chile.

Uruguayan novelist Juan Carlos Onetti was the most talked about Latin-American writer, not so much for his excellent short novel *La muerte y la niña* as for the prison term to which he was sentenced by the Uruguayan government. His offense, along with some of his collaborators on the weekly newspaper *Marcha*, was to award a prize to the short story *El guardaespaldas* by Nelson Marra, which attacked police torture and defended the Tupamaro guerrillas.

Fiction. Most of the major writers—among them Juan Rulfo, Gabriel García Márquez, Fernando Alegría, and Carlos Fuentes—were reported to have novels in progress, while comparatively little new talent emerged. The spate of translations in France and the U.S. gave an illusory impression that the boom that characterized the Latin-American novel of the mid-1960s went on unabated. Manuel Puig's *The Buenos Aires Affair* was received with acclaim when it appeared in the U.S. in 1974 and it was speedily followed by Gregory Rabassa's translation of *Paradiso*, a dense novel by the Cuban poet José Lezama Lima. In Latin America itself, the novels that attracted most attention were by writers of the older generation. Ernesto Sábato's *Abaddon, el exterminador*, a novel set in the turbulent year 1972, combined autobiographical elements with Sábato's own private mythology, which readers of his *Sobre héroes y tumbas* will recognize. Alejo Carpentier's novel *El recurso del método* was a major work by this writer and, like several of his previous novels, it has a historical setting—the period just before and during World War I.

Carpentier narrated in the first person the story of a tyrant who belonged to all places and to none. A well-educated dictator who loves French things, the general-president tells how he gained power, overthrew the greedy military, did business, sold his country to foreign interests, and was finally overthrown by an alliance of the people and the students. In spite of his excellent prose, *El recurso del método* (a deliberate echo of Descartes' *Discourse on Method*) sometimes gave the impression that it was written from a European point of view, which sees the Latin-American chaos as a spectacle and not as a tragedy. This objection was not valid in respect to *Yo, el Supremo* by Augusto Roa Bastos, a biography of Doctor Francia, a dictator who ruled Paraguay from 1814 to 1840, literally isolated it from the rest of the world, and in his eagerness to be honest and effective became a despot who made paranoia and terror the nourishment of power. Unwittingly this historical novel became one of the most timely books of 1974.

If the novel flagged, the short story flourished. Jorge Luis Borges was largely responsible for making the story into an art form that was something more than the by-product of the novelist, though he himself had not produced much original work for some time. Several well-known novelists published collections of stories. In *Octaedro,* a collection of eight stories, Julio Cortázar demonstrated the timeliness of the genre and added to his credit two brief masterpieces: "Lugar llamado Kindberg" and "Los pasos en las huellas." Peruvian Alfredo Bryce Echenique, whose outstanding novel *Un mundo para Julius* put him in

Chilean poet Pablo Neruda, 1971 Nobel Prize winner, whose last poems appeared posthumously in 1974.

the front rank of Latin-American writers, brought out a collection of stories, *La felicidad, ja, ja.* A satirist of upper-class life, he portrayed the absurdity of the Lima aristocracy at moments of social change. The lively magazine *Crisis*, published in Buenos Aires, consistently gave over its pages to new talent, publishing anthologies of stories by Peruvian, Argentine, and Uruguayan writers. It presented an impressive selection of 13 young Argentine writers in the February 1974 issue, the best known of whom was Héctor Libertella, recent winner of the Monte Avila prize in Caracas, Venezuela.

In Mexico an outstanding collection of stories was published by José Revueltas. Revueltas, one of the pioneers of the new novel, is an important and neglected writer who recently spent some time in prison, an experience reflected in some of the stories of *Material de los sueños*. A political writer whose politics are not external or rhetorical, Revueltas writes from deeply lived experiences. One of the outstanding stories in *Material de los sueños* was about a common criminal and a political offender, locked together in mutual hatred and in a prison cell. In this and in stories set in the hospital, Revueltas built up an overpowering sense of claustrophobia.

The neglect of Revueltas outside Mexico was symptomatic of the whimsical manner in which Latin-American literature was promoted outside Latin America. Two aspects are particularly overlooked by translators. The first is the strong emphasis on what is called *testimonio* (that is, the direct recording of reality) and the second is the presence of humour. *Redoble para Rancas*, published several years earlier by the Peruvian writer Manuel Scorza, was the prototype of the *testimonio*. Events in Chile and Argentina produced a spate of these works during the year and Scorza himself was at work on a massive series of books, which he called "ballads," based on the struggles of the Indian communes. Humourists, on the other hand, were slow to publish, though the works of writers like Carlos del Parral of Argentina and Augusto Monterroso of Mexico appeared often in magazines and newspapers.

Poetry. Like fiction, poetry was dominated by writers of the older generation, and especially Octavio Paz, whose international reputation was secured by the publication of the majority of his work in Europe and the U.S. A collection of his essays, *Alternating Current,* translated by Helen R. Lane and published in 1973, received an extensive notice in the *New York Review of Books,* and a collection of translations and articles dedicated to his work and first published by *Books Abroad* came out in book form. Edited by Ivar Ivask, *The Perpetual Present* included photographs and an ample bibliography. Paz himself did not publish any original work but brought out a collection of his translations of other poets in *Versiones y diversiones.* An astonishing display of Paz's range of interest, this included versions of poems by Donne and Marvell, by Nerval, by e. e. cummings and William Carlos Williams, by the Portuguese poet Fernando Pessõa, and even versions from Swedish and Chinese. He begged the reader not to look at these poems in an academic light and indeed, as with his criticism, he has a power of incorporating the work of others into his own universe, so that Marvell, for instance, comes out sounding more like Paz than one would have thought possible. A lesser-known contemporary of Paz in Mexico was Efraín Huerta, a truly original poet who published a new collection of about 100 short poems with the title *Los eróticos y otros poemas.* Among younger poets of Mexico, Jaime Reyes, David Huerta, José Joaquin Blanco, and Raul Garduño showed impressive talent though they were as yet published only in periodicals.

Paraguay is not often mentioned in articles on Latin-American literature, but Elvio Romero, Paraguay's best-known poet, continued to be popular and a second edition of his *Antología poética 1947–73* was published by Losada. In Argentina a good deal of poetry was published, notably in the magazine *Crisis,* though it was hard to distinguish any particular trend. An issue dedicated to Peru in April included poems by Antonio Cisneros, Mirko Lauer, Marco Martos, and Enrique Verástegui, though none of these brought out new collections during the year.

The Guatemalan Luis Cardoza y Aragón published *Quinta estación,* which included all of his published poetry. Unfortunately, it was poorly edited, without dates, notes, or bibliography. This was particularly distressing because Cardoza y Aragón was one of the most interesting unknowns in Latin America. A surrealist early in life whose avant-garde *Luna-park* appeared as early as 1923, an art critic and distinguished essayist whose work somehow never attracted much attention, by rights he should have ranked with Carlos Pellicer or Xavier Villaurrutia. Perhaps because he was Guatemalan he never seemed to receive critical notice. This was certainly not the case with Ernesto Cardenal, the Nicaraguan poet whose work was increasingly being translated and published in Europe and North America. During the year his *Homage to the American Indians* appeared in translation, and an edition of his poems in English was scheduled for publication in London. Vallejo, the most difficult of poets to translate, was tackled by David Smith, who published the whole of *Trilce* in translation. J. M. Cohen brought out a translation of *Fuera del juego,* the controversial selection of poems by the Cuban poet Padilla. The English title is *Sent off the Field.*

(JEAN FRANCO; SALVADOR BARROS)

See also Libraries; Philosophy; Theatre.

[621]

A.F.P./PICTORIAL PARADE

The Argentine writer Julio Cortázar, the French translation of whose novel "El libro de Manuel" won France's 1974 Prix Médicis for foreign authors.

ENCYCLOPÆDIA BRITANNICA FILMS. *Bartleby by Herman Melville* (1969); *Dr. Heidegger's Experiment by Nathaniel Hawthorne* (1969); *The Lady, or the Tiger? by Frank Stockton* (1969); *The Lottery by Shirley Jackson* (1969); *Magic Prison* (1969); *My Old Man by Ernest Hemingway* (1969); *James Dickey: Poet* (1970); *The Deserted Village* (1971); *The Lady of Shalott* (1971); *The Prisoner of Chillon* (1971); *Shaw vs. Shakespeare—Part I: The Character of Caesar; Part II: The Tragedy of Julius Caesar; Part III: Caesar and Cleopatra* (1971); *The Greek Myths* (1972); *Walt Whitman: Poet for a New Age* (1972); *Look in the Answer Book* (1972); *The Crocodile by Fyodor Dostoyevsky* (1973); *The Secret Sharer by Joseph Conrad* (1973); *John Keats: His Life and Death* (1973); *John Keats: Poet* (1973).

Luxembourg

A constitutional monarchy, the Benelux country of Luxembourg is bounded on the east by West Germany, on the south by France, and on the west and north by Belgium. Area: 999 sq.mi. (2,586 sq.km.). Pop. (1973 est.): 352,700. Cap. and largest city: Luxembourg (pop., 1973 est., 79,000). Language: French, German, Luxembourgian. Religion: Roman Catholic 97%. Grand duke, Jean; prime ministers in 1974, Pierre Werner and, from June 15, Gaston Thorn.

Prime Minister Werner submitted his resignation on May 27, the day after his ruling Christian Social Party had suffered an unexpected defeat in national elections. Three main factors appeared to have contributed: a desire for change after over five decades of Christian Socialist rule; an increase in parliamentary seats from 56 to 59; and a reduction of the voting age from 21 to 18, which increased the size of the electorate by nearly 7%.

The Christian Social Party's representation fell from 21 seats in the smaller Parliament to 18 in the enlarged one. Of even greater significance, its percentage of the vote dropped from 35.3 to 28%. The CSP coalition partner, the Democratic Party, generally known as the "Liberals," increased its representation from 11 to 14 seats. The opposition Socialists proved

LUXEMBOURG

Education. (1972–73) Primary, pupils 35,525, teachers 1,667; secondary, pupils 9,889, teachers 727; vocational, pupils 7,473, teachers 657; higher, students 357, teaching staff 91.

Finance. Monetary unit: Luxembourg franc, at par with the Belgian franc, with (Sept. 16, 1974) a free rate of LFr. 39.57 to U.S. $1 (LFr. 91.40 = £1 sterling). Budget (1974 est.): revenue LFr. 19,497,000,-000; expenditure LFr. 19,484,000,000. Gross domestic product: (1972) LFr. 59.3 billion; (1971) LFr. 54.8 billion. Cost of living (1970 = 100): (June 1974) 127; (June 1973) 117.

Foreign Trade. See BELGIUM.

Transport and Communications. Roads (1973) 4,465 km. (including 25 km. expressways). Motor vehicles in use (1973): passenger 119,700; commercial 10,010. Railways (1972) 271 km.; traffic 260 million passenger-km., freight (1973) 786 million net ton-km. Air traffic (1972): 113 million passenger-km.; freight 230,000 net ton-km. Telephones (Dec. 1972) 126,000. Radio licenses (Dec. 1971) 160,000. Television licenses (Dec. 1971) 75,000.

Agriculture. Production (in 000; metric tons; 1973; 1972 in parentheses): wheat c. 36 (c. 36); oats c. 37 (37); rye c. 5 (c. 5); barley (1972) c. 54, (1971) 53; potatoes (1972) c. 53, (1971) 65; wine (1972) c. 13, (1971) 12. Livestock (in 000; May 1973): cattle 204; sheep 4; pigs 90; poultry 283.

Industry. Production (in 000; metric tons; 1973): iron ore (30% metal content) 3,782; pig iron 5,093; crude steel 5,925; electricity (kw-hr.) 2,169,000; manufactured gas (cu.m.; 1972) 12,000.

to be the high winners, raising their representation from 12 to 17 seats. Their percentage of the electorate showed a slight decrease, however, and the party chairman, Antoine Wehenkel, was defeated. The Social Democrats and the Communists won five seats apiece.

On June 15, Gaston Thorn, foreign minister in the Werner government, became prime minister in a Liberal-Socialist coalition government. The eight-member Cabinet was equally divided between the two parties.

Inflationary problems faced the new government. From July 1973, the rate of inflation had risen from 6 to 10.1%.   (ROBERT D. HODGSON)

[972.A.7]

Malagasy Republic

The Malagasy Republic occupies the island of Madagascar and minor adjacent islands in the Indian Ocean off the southeast coast of Africa. Area: 226,444 sq.mi. (586,486 sq.km.). Pop. (1973 est.): 7,140,000. Cap. and largest city: Tananarive (pop., 1972 est., 336,530). Language: French and Malagasy. Religion: Christian (approximately 50%) and traditional tribal beliefs. Head of government in 1974, Gen. Gabriel Ramanantsoa.

The process of "malagasization" was further developed in 1974. The French military and naval forces had departed in 1973, and from Aug. 1, 1973, French residents had been obliged to carry identity cards and French visitors to obtain visas like other foreigners. On Jan. 1, 1974, the nation's seven agronomic research institutes were placed under a single Malagasy organization, with Malagasy-financed control. Prior to

MALAGASY REPUBLIC
Education. (1971–72) Primary, pupils 1,004,445, teachers 14,881; secondary, pupils 107,781, teachers 5,181; vocational, pupils 7,194, teachers 594; teacher training, students 2,019, teachers 165; higher, students 7,000; teaching staff 260.
Finance. Monetary unit: Malagasy franc, at par with the CFA franc, with (Sept. 16, 1974) a parity of MalFr. 50 to the French franc (free rates of MalFr. 240.50 = U.S. $1 and MalFr. 556.50 = £1 sterling). Gold, SDRs, and foreign exchange, central bank: (June 1974) U.S. $56.2 million; (June 1973) U.S. $67.2 million. Budget (1973 est.) balanced at MalFr. 89,-080,000,000.
Foreign Trade. (1973) Imports MalFr. 45,060,-000,000; exports MalFr. 44,760,000,000. Import sources (1972): France 55%; West Germany 10%. Export destinations (1972): France 38%; U.S. 20%; Réunion 7%; Japan 5%. Main exports: coffee 30%; vanilla 5%.
Transport and Communications. Roads (1971) 27,019 km. Motor vehicles in use (1971): passenger 52,400; commercial 33,500. Railways: (1972) 884 km.; traffic (1973) 211 million passenger-km., freight 206 million net ton-km. Air traffic (1973): 256 million passenger-km.; freight 10.9 million net ton-km. Shipping (1973): merchant vessels 100 gross tons and over 50; gross tonnage 63,919. Telephones (Dec. 1972) 29,-000. Radio receivers (Dec. 1972) 600,000. Television receivers (Dec. 1972) 6.000.
Agriculture. Production (in 000; metric tons; 1973; 1972 in parentheses): rice c. 1,750 (1,840); corn (1972) c. 121, (1971) 113; cassava (1972) c. 1,310, (1971) 1,213; sweet potatoes (1972) c. 345, (1971) 344; potatoes (1972) c. 126, (1971) 125; dry beans c. 52 (c. 52); bananas (1972) c. 260, (1971) 256; peanuts c. 50 (51); sugar, raw value c. 110 (c. 115); coffee c. 65 (65); tobacco (1972) c. 6, (1971) 5.9; sisal (1972) 21, (1971) 21. Livestock (in 000; Dec. 1972): cattle c. 9,500; sheep c. 500; pigs c. 530; goats c. 820; chickens (1971) c. 11,400.

this, the institutes had been jointly financed by France and the Malagasy Republic. Similarly, the French-directed National Geographic Institute became the Cartographic Institute of Madagascar. The government also took over a controlling share in various public utility companies in the republic.

General Ramanantsoa's rural reorganization (initiated in March 1973) entered its second phase in 1974, and its completion was expected early in 1975; the essence of the scheme was the building up of a widespread economic and social structure based on the self-organization of rural communities, with elected committees; these communities, joined together by mutual interests, would sell their produce directly to a state company and would thereby avoid dealing with middlemen.

The reorganization was attacked by the government's critics as creating a division in the island's life, under which the coastal people would work for the benefit of the plateau-dwelling Merinas. In March lower wages and salaries in the public and private sectors were raised to meet discontent in the face of the steadily rising prices of basic foodstuffs, particularly rice. Later it seemed that the 1974 rice crop might prove to be a record at a forecast 2,160,000 tons. In August a new factory was opened to exploit Madagascar's deposits of marble; it was expected to produce about 78,000 cu.yd. per year, valued at about $470,-000. In October the republic began to take its first population census, to be continued by stages into 1975.

In February Gabriel Ramanjato, editor of the Tananarive newspaper *Bosy Vava*, was sentenced to a year's imprisonment for "defamation" of the Army and police force. The Social Democratic Party of former president Philibert Tsiranana merged in March with the Union Socialiste Malgache to form the Parti Socialiste Malgache under Tsiranana as president and André Resampa as secretary-general.

The republic signed two agreements, for trade and for economic and technical cooperation, with China at Peking in January. Ramanantsoa attended the memorial service for French Pres. Georges Pompidou in Paris in April. The Malagasy Republic joined with other African and Asian nations in denouncing the Anglo-U.S. agreement on the use of the island of Diego Garcia as an Indian Ocean military base.

(R. M. GOODWIN)

[978.E.6.c]

Malawi

A republic and member of the Commonwealth of Nations in east central Africa, Malawi is bounded by Tanzania, Mozambique, and Zambia. Area: 45,747 sq.mi. (118,484 sq.km.). Pop. (1974 est.): 4,916,000. Cap.: Zomba (pop., 1971 est., 20,000). Largest city: Blantyre (pop., 1972, 160,063). Language: English (official) and Nyanja (Chichewa). Religion: predominantly traditional beliefs. President in 1974, Hastings Kamuzu Banda.

Two important development projects were launched in Malawi in the earlier part of 1974. A Canadian loan of $22.4 million enabled plans to be made for the improvement of some 86 mi. of existing railway track and the construction of a further 75 mi. of new track. The plan envisaged the purchase of materials and equipment from Canada, and the whole project, which was to be completed by 1978, would

Machinery and Machine Tools: *see* Industrial Production and Technology
Madagascar: *see* Malagasy Republic
Magazines: *see* Publishing

MALAWI

Education. (1973–74) Primary, pupils 537,301, teachers 9,204; secondary, pupils 13,779, teachers 677; vocational, pupils 480, teachers 42; teacher training, students 1,312, teachers 100; higher (University of Malawi), students 1,097, teaching staff 153.

Finance. Monetary unit: kwacha, with (Sept. 16, 1974) a free rate of 0.85 kwacha to U.S. $1 (1.95 kwacha = £1 sterling). Gold, SDRs, and foreign exchange, official: (May 1974) U.S. $71,630,000; (May 1973) U.S. $42,710,000. Budget (1973–74 est.): revenue 59,440,000 kwachas; expenditure 59,860,000 kwachas.

Foreign Trade. (1973) Imports 113,962,000 kwachas; exports 79,525,000 kwachas. Import sources: U.K. 25%; South Africa 18%; Rhodesia 15%; Japan 6%. Export destinations: U.K. 33%; U.S. 8%; Rhodesia 6%. Main exports: tobacco 38%; tea 17%; peanuts 7%.

Transport and Communications. Roads (1973) 11,814 km. Motor vehicles in use (1973): passenger 10,540; commercial 8,700. Railways: (1972) 592 km.; traffic (1973) 69.8 million passenger-km., freight 290 million net ton-km. Air traffic (1973): 74 million passenger-km.; freight 990,000 net ton-km. Telephones (Dec. 1972) 15,000. Radio receivers (Dec. 1972) 110,000.

Agriculture. Production (in 000; metric tons; 1973; 1972 in parentheses): corn c. 1,000 (c. 1,150); cassava (1972) c. 150, (1971) c. 150; sweet potatoes (1972) c. 49, (1971) c. 46; sorghum c. 35 (c. 35); sugar, raw value c. 38 (c. 38); peanuts (1972) c. 190, (1971) c. 190; tea c. 22 (21); tobacco c. 23 (32); cotton, lint c. 7 (c. 7). Livestock (in 000; 1972–73): cattle c. 565; sheep c. 182; goats (1971–72) c. 640; pigs c. 190; poultry c. 8,500.

Industry. Production (in 000; 1973): electricity (public supply; kw-hr.) 194,000; cement (metric tons) 89.

provide employment for 3,000 persons. The second undertaking was a $13.5 million scheme to raise the cash incomes of 16,300 farmers in the Shire Valley from $11 million to $95 million.

The most important developments on the political front took place outside Malawi. Following the military coup in Portugal in April, the Portuguese government announced on July 23 that it was severing relations with Malawi. The reason given was that Malawi was acting against Portugal's decolonizing policy in Mozambique, more particularly by allowing the former Malawi consul general in Beira, Mozambique, Jorge Jardim, to act against Portugal's interests from Malawi territory. Jardim, a Portuguese and a newspaper proprietor in Mozambique, had certainly urged that the population of Mozambique be allowed to determine its future, but he vigorously denied reports that he had enlisted an army of mercenaries to support his views.

Relations with another friendly power, the U.K., were also in danger of becoming strained when the imprisonment and subsequent expulsion of a British woman for criticizing a speech by President Banda focused attention on the position of British subjects in Malawi. Amnesty International was also concerned about the fate of 26 men sentenced to death in September 1973 in Blantyre; official information about them and about the charges against them was lacking.

Malawi produced a record 53 million lb. of tea in 1973. Tobacco production in that year also rose, to 69 million lb. from 67 million lb. in 1972, but 1974 output was estimated at 64 million lb. because of a bad harvest. External reserves more than doubled from 26.7 million kwachas at the end of 1972 to 56.1 million kwachas at the end of 1973. However, high petroleum prices and the world economic situation in 1974 were posing a threat to Malawi's development.

(KENNETH INGHAM)

[978.E.8.b.iii]

Malaysia

A federation within the Commonwealth of Nations comprising the 11 states of the former Federation of Malaya, Sabah, Sarawak, and the federal territory of Kuala Lumpur, Malaysia is a federal constitutional monarchy situated in Southeast Asia at the southern end of the Malay Peninsula (excluding Singapore) and on the northern part of the island of Borneo. Area: 127,316 sq.mi. (329,747 sq.km.). Pop. (1973 est.): 11,609,000. Cap. and largest city: Kuala Lumpur (pop., 1970, 451,810). Official language: Malay. Religion: Malays are Muslim; Indians mainly Hindu; Chinese mainly Buddhist, Confucian, and Taoist. Supreme head of state in 1974, with the title of *yang di-pertuan agong*, Tuanku Abdul Halim Mu'azzam Shah ibni al-Marhum Sultan Badlishah; prime minister, Tun Abdul Razak.

MALAYSIA

Education. *West Malaysia.* (1974) Primary, pupils 1,554,611, teachers 48,176; secondary, pupils 705,825, teachers 25,361; vocational, pupils 20,649, teachers 901; higher (including 3 universities), students 28,002, teaching staff 2,081. *East Malaysia:* Sabah. (1973) Primary, pupils 121,912, teachers 4,553; secondary, pupils 42,435, teachers 1,593; vocational, pupils 264, teachers 27; teacher training, students 642, teachers 73. *East Malaysia:* Sarawak. (1973) Primary, pupils 157,867, teachers 4,649; secondary, pupils 42,098, teachers 1,621; vocational, pupils 323, teachers 26; teacher training, students 588, teachers 57; higher (1970), students 430.

Finance. Monetary unit: Malaysian dollar, with (Sept. 16, 1974) a free rate of M$2.42 to U.S. $1 (M$5.58 = £1 sterling). Gold, SDRs, and foreign exchange, official: (June 1974) U.S. $1,452,000,000; (June 1973) U.S. $1,239,000,000. Budget (1973 est.): revenue M$3,085,000,000; expenditure M$3,234,000,000. Gross national product: (1972) M$12,904,000,000; (1971) M$12,085,000,000. Money supply: (April 1974) M$3,937,000,000; (April 1973) M$3,001,000,000. Cost of living (West Malaysia; 1970 = 100): (April 1974) 134; (April 1973) 110.

Foreign Trade. (1973) Imports M$5,899,000,000; exports M$7,372,000,000. Import sources: Japan 23%; U.K. 10%; U.S. 9%; Singapore 8%; Australia 7%; China 6%; West Germany 6%. Export destinations: Singapore 23%; Japan 18%; U.S. 11%; U.K. 8%. Main exports: rubber 34%; timber c. 20%; tin 12%; palm oil 6%.

Transport and Communications. Roads (1972) 24,389 km. (including 17,867 km. in West Malaysia). Motor vehicles in use (1972): passenger 340,100; commercial (including buses) 85,800. Railways: (1973) 1,822 km.; traffic (including Singapore; 1972) 755 million passenger-km., freight 1,179,000,000 net ton-km. Air traffic (1973): 868 million passenger-km.; freight 12.2 million net ton-km. Shipping (1973): merchant vessels 100 gross tons and over 117; gross tonnage 226,350. Shipping traffic (1972): goods loaded 16,615,000 metric tons, unloaded 10,086,000 metric tons. Telephones (Jan. 1973) 211,000. Radio licenses (Dec. 1972) 456,000. Television licenses (Dec. 1972) 274,000.

Agriculture. Production (in 000; metric tons; 1973; 1972 in parentheses): rice c. 1,940 (1,908); rubber c. 1,546 (1,325); copra c. 180 (c. 177); palm oil c. 813 (731); tea (West Malaysia; 1972) c. 3.5, (1971) 3.3; bananas (1972) c. 410, (1971) c. 410; pineapples (1972) c. 330, (1971) 332; pepper (Sarawak only; 1972) 26, (1971) 26; timber (cu.m.; 1971) 24,100, (1970) 24,200; fish catch (1972) 359, (1971) 368. Livestock (in 000; 1972–73): cattle c. 357; pigs c. 1,011; goats c. 380; sheep (West Malaysia only) c. 41; buffaloes c. 310; poultry c. 31,000.

Industry. Production (in 000; metric tons; 1973): tin concentrates (metal content) 72; bauxite 1,142; cement (West Malaysia only) 1,279; iron ore (West Malaysia only; 56% metal content) 516; crude oil (Sarawak only) 4,339; petroleum products (Sarawak only; 1972) 2,507; gold (troy oz.; 1972) 48; electricity (kw-hr.) 4,640,000.

The results of the Malaysian general elections held in August 1974 at federal and state level demonstrated the political success of the National Front coalition led by Prime Minister Tun Razak. They marked also a striking test of political stability, given the intercommunal violence that followed the elections of May 1969. In the contest for the federal legislature, the National Front coalition won 135 seats (104 in Malaya, 15 in Sarawak, and 16 in Sabah) out of 154 contested. The only opposition parties to obtain seats in Malaya were the Democratic Action Party with 9 and the Social Justice Party with 1. In Sarawak the Sarawak National Party (SNAP) secured 9 seats for the opposition, while in Sabah 10 prospective Social Justice candidates had been taken into detention 48 hours before nomination day and held until after nominations closed. The National Front secured control of all state assemblies (there were no elections in Sabah). The best opposition performance at the state level was in Sarawak where SNAP obtained 18 seats out of 48 contested. In the new federal Cabinet, Razak continued as prime minister with Hussein bin Dato Onn as his deputy. Significant new recruits included Mahathir Mohamed as minister of education and Mustapha Harun, the chief minister of Sabah, as minister of defense. In April, Tan Siew-sin, leader of the Malaysian Chinese Association (MCA) and federal finance minister, resigned from both offices. He was succeeded in the MCA by Lee San-choon, who became minister of labour and manpower in the new Cabinet.

In February, Prime Minister Razak announced guidelines to restrict foreign acquisition of Malaysian companies through mergers and takeovers, enlarging the share held by indigenous Malaysians by limiting foreign holdings and not by nationalization. In addition, Razak announced in September that it was no longer compatible with Malaysia's national policy to permit foreign domination of the oil industry. For this reason, Petroleum Nasional Berhad, or Petronas, the national petroleum corporation, would seek majority ownership and control of all petroleum projects and participate with the private sector, whether local or foreign, on a joint venture basis.

In March it was announced in Kuching, Sarawak, that since October 1973, 482 Communist insurgents in that state had surrendered to the security forces. This was said to represent 75% of the Communists' total strength there. In June, unknown assassins killed Tan Sri Abdul Rahman bin Hashim, Malaysia's inspector general of police, in Kuala Lumpur.

At the end of May, Razak began a visit to Peking and after talks with Premier Chou En-lai signed an agreement establishing full diplomatic relations between Malaysia and China. It was announced simultaneously in Kuala Lumpur that the Malaysian government was ending all official links with Taiwan. Razak received personal assurances from Chairman Mao Tse-tung that Malaysia's insurgency was considered by China to be an internal problem. In a joint communiqué, China recognized that anyone of Chinese origin who became a Malaysian citizen automatically forfeited Chinese nationality, while residents of Chinese origin who retained Chinese nationality were enjoined to abide by the laws of the government of Malaysia, although their proper rights and interests would be protected by the government of China and respected by the government of Malaysia.

In the third week in June, Kuala Lumpur was the venue for a conference of Islamic foreign ministers

CENTRAL PRESS/PICTORIAL PARADE

The yang di-pertuan agong of Malaysia and his wife, the raja permaisuri agong, guests of honour of Queen Elizabeth II and Prince Philip at Buckingham Palace during a state visit to England.

which, in itself, was a sign of recognition of Malaysia's increasing involvement in Islamic affairs. The occasion was marked by Malaysia's acting in conjunction with Indonesia to shield the Philippines (their fellow member in the Association of Southeast Asian Nations) from undue criticism over its handling of Muslim rebellion on Mindanao. An additional episode of note was the diplomatic exchange between Malaysia and Thailand in which Malaysia reaffirmed its intention not to interfere in Thailand's internal affairs.

Malaysia continued to enjoy a boom economy, even though industrial growth was expected to slow down. The trade balance for 1973 was a favourable M$1,-244,000,000—with high prices for rubber, tin, palm oil, tropical hardwoods, pepper, and oil; export volume increased by 20% and overall export prices by 37%; at the same time import prices rose by 17%. Malaysia's balance of payments showed a surplus of M$576,000,000 in 1973.   (MICHAEL LEIFER)
[976.B.2]

Maldives

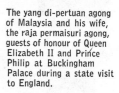

Maldives, a republic in the Indian Ocean consisting of about two thousand small islands, lies southwest of the southern tip of India. Area: 115 sq.mi. (298 sq.km.). Pop. (1974 est.): 131,500. Cap.: Male (pop., 1971, 15,129). Language: Divehi. Religion: Muslim. Sultan, Emir Muhammad Farid Didi; president in 1974, Ibrahim Nasir; prime minister, Ahmed Zaki.

By virtue of its position in the increasingly politicized Indian Ocean, the Maldives had further contacts with the outside world. In March Prime Minister Zaki paid a state visit to India, and in a joint communiqué the two countries supported the concept of the Indian Ocean as a "zone free from Great Power rivalries." India agreed to extend facilities for technical and educational training of Maldivian personnel and to increase economic cooperation. In August, during a visit by Zaki to Sri Lanka, another joint communiqué emphasized "traditional ties of commerce

MALDIVES
Education. (1972–73) Primary, pupils 8,660, teachers 351; secondary, pupils 1,431, teachers 61; vocational (1971), pupils 11, teachers 1.
    Finance and Trade. Monetary unit: Maldivian rupee, with (Sept. 16, 1974) a nominal free rate of MRs. 7.30 to U.S. $1 (MRs. 17 = £1 sterling). Budget (1972) expenditure MRs. 22.6 million. Foreign trade (1971): imports MRs. 20,540,000; exports MRs. 25,520,000. Trade mainly with Sri Lanka. Main exports (metric tons; 1972): fish 5,880; copra 16; shells 14.

MALI
Education. (1970–71) Primary, pupils 229,879, teachers 6,614; secondary, pupils 3,507, teachers 290; vocational, pupils 3,386, teachers 332; teacher training, students 1,551, teachers 92; higher, students 731, teaching staff 151.
    Finance. Monetary unit: Mali franc, with (Sept. 16, 1974) a free rate of MFr. 481 to U.S. $1 (MFr. 1,113 = £1 sterling). Gold, SDRs, and foreign exchange: (Nov. 1973) U.S. $4.2 million; (Nov. 1972) U.S. $4.1 million. Budget (1974 est.) balanced at MFr. 29 billion.
    Foreign Trade. (1972–73) Imports MFr. 40.9 billion; exports MFr. 17,960,000,000. Import sources: France c. 57%; Ivory Coast c. 15%; U.S. 7%; West Germany c. 6%; Belgium-Luxembourg c. 5%. Export destinations: France c. 47%; Upper Volta 11%; Japan c. 8%; West Germany c. 7%; U.K. c. 7%; Ghana c. 6%. Main exports: cotton 39%; peanuts 7%.
    Agriculture. Production (in 000; metric tons; 1973; 1972 in parentheses): millet and sorghum c. 600 (c. 600); rice (1972) c. 150, (1971) c. 170; corn (1972) c. 60, (1971) c. 80; peanuts c. 100 (c. 100); sweet potatoes (1972) c. 71, (1971) c. 71; cassava (1972) c. 160, (1971) c. 160; cotton, lint c. 18 (26); beef and veal (1972) c. 49, (1971) c. 50; mutton and lamb (1972) c. 34, (1971) c. 36. Livestock (in 000; 1972–73): cattle c. 3,700; sheep c. 3,900; horses c. 170; asses c. 460.

and trade" and cooperation in tourism, aviation, and shipping. This was seen as a hopeful sign of normalization after two years of strained relations over trade and commerce. It was agreed that a high-frequency-radio link should be established between Male and Colombo.

In Addu Atoll, Gan Island continued to serve as a Royal Air Force staging post to Singapore and Hong Kong. It was served by 600 RAF personnel, with an additional 50 at Hittadu radio station, and 100 Pakistanis. About 1,000 Maldivians sailed in as day workers from neighbouring islands, for which the RAF provided medical and educational services. The Navy, Army, and Air Force Institutes (NAAFI, supplying goods to service personnel), managed by two Europeans and 37 Singhalese and enjoying an annual turnover of about £1 million, were further licensed to trade with 43 Maldivian vessels. In December the Labour government announced that British personnel on Gan would be withdrawn as part of its program of reducing defense expenditure. (MOLLY MORTIMER)

Mali

A republic of West Africa, Mali is bordered by Algeria, Niger, Upper Volta, Ivory Coast, Guinea, Senegal, and Mauritania. Area: 478,822 sq.mi. (1,240,142 sq.km.). Pop. (1973 est.): 5,376,400. Cap. and largest city: Bamako (pop., 1970 est., 196,800). Language: French (official); Hamito-Semitic and various tribal dialects. Religion: Muslim 65%; animist 30%. Head of military government in 1974, Col. Moussa Traoré.

Drought and famine in the Sahel region continued into 1974 (see AGRICULTURE AND FOOD SUPPLIES: *Special Report*) and ravaged Mali. Tuareg tribes in the region emigrated not only southward but also north into southern Algeria. The Mali administration was accused of not taking the crisis seriously enough. Sidi Coulibaly, minister of production, denied this but admitted that 1,835,000 of the country's population were affected. Improvement in the transportation of emergency food supplies was reported in the second half of the year.

A referendum on a new constitution was held on June 2, with 99% voter approval. Among the constitution's provisions were confirmation of the rule by decree of the Military Committee for National Liberation (which had seized power in November 1968) for an additional period of five years; the president of the republic and head of government would be elected by universal suffrage for a maximum of two five-year terms; persons who had held political office before Nov. 19, 1968, would be excluded from public office. Six years after the coup, former president Modibo Keita, his wife, and 32 other persons were still held under house arrest. Further arrests were made in June in connection with the appearance of a leaflet calling for a negative vote in the referendum.

In May, Mali reached agreement with Mauritania and Senegal on a joint development project for the Senegal River basin. (*See* MAURITANIA.) An agreement to found a joint Libya-Mali bank, to assist development projects in Mali, was signed in Tripoli on September 4. Colonel Traoré announced on September 21 that MFr. 386 billion ($772 million) had been raised for investment in the next five-year development plan, the lion's share going to agriculture, communications, tourism, mining development, and water and energy resources. (R. M. GOODWIN)

[978.E.4.b.ii]

Malta

An island in the Mediterranean Sea, between Sicily and Tunisia, Malta is a republic and a member of the Commonwealth of Nations. Area: 122 sq.mi. (316 sq.km.), including Malta, Gozo, and Comino. Pop. (1973 est.): 298,200. Cap.: Valletta (pop., 1973 est., 14,150). Largest city: Sliema (pop., 1973 est., 20,120). Language: Maltese and English. Religion: mainly Roman Catholic. Queen until Dec. 13, 1974, Elizabeth II; governor-general and, from December 13, president, Sir Anthony Mamo; prime minister, Dom Mintoff.

During 1974 active steps were taken by the government to draw up a new constitution for Malta. Discussions on the proposed amendments were held with the opposition, and government spokesmen reaffirmed that, if no agreement were reached, the constitution would be amended by a simple majority, even where a two-thirds majority in Parliament was required. On December 13, following passage by the House of Representatives of three bills amending the 1964 constitution, Malta was declared a republic. Sir Anthony Mamo, the governor-general, was sworn in as the first president. Malta thus became the 19th republic in the Commonwealth of Nations.

As a result of talks with the U.K., Malta agreed in June to resume repayments of outstanding British Exchequer loans, suspended in 1972. Britain undertook to give Malta £1 million of technical assistance.

Malta.

In July a European Economic Community commission discussed with the government the latter's request for a revision of the 1970 association agreement, intended to include preferential treatment for agricultural products exported to the EEC. Concessions subsequently offered were refused by the Malta government as inadequate.

In November 1973 a national shipping line (Sea Malta) was set up; five months later Air Malta started operating under its own insignia. In April a liability toward the government of M£12.5 million built up by the dry docks over the years was completely written off by the government to enable the dry docks to operate successfully. Work was started on the building of a 300,000-ton tanker dock, super-

vised by Chinese technicians, and a new shipbuilding complex was planned.

In December 1973 the National Bank group found itself in difficulties. The government moved in, constituted the Bank of Valletta with an authorized capital of M£6 million in March, and took up 60% of the equity. The government budgeted for a record expenditure in 1974–75 of M£59 million. By September tourism had registered a 33% increase over the same period in 1973. Texaco Malta Inc. was given the concession, against payment of $10 million, to drill for oil south of Malta.   (ALBERT GANADO)

MALTA
Education. (1972–73) Primary, pupils 37,348, teachers 1,820; secondary, pupils 25,912, teachers 1,592; vocational, pupils 3,886, teachers 191; higher (including Royal University of Malta), students 1,488, teaching staff 346.
Finance. Monetary unit: Maltese pound, with (Sept. 16, 1974) a free rate of M£0.39 to U.S. $1 (M£0.90 = £1 sterling). Gold, SDRs, and foreign exchange, official: (June 1974) U.S. $351.7 million; (June 1973) U.S. $312.9 million. Budget (1973–74 est.) balanced at M£50,733,000.
Foreign Trade. (1973) Imports M£88,098,000; exports M£35,960,000. Import sources: U.K. 28%; Italy 16%; West Germany 9%; France 6%; U.S. 6%; The Netherlands 6%. Export destinations: U.K. 30%; Italy 12%; West Germany 10%; Belgium-Luxembourg 8%; France 5%. Main exports: clothing 37%; textile yarns and fabrics 12%; machinery 9%; rubber products 6%; plumbing fittings 5%. Tourism (1972): 149,900 visitors; gross receipts U.S. $20 million.
Transport and Communications. Roads (1971) 1,239 km. Motor vehicles in use (1972): passenger 47,300; commercial (including buses) 11,400. There are no railways. Air traffic (1973): 181 million passenger-km.; freight 2,560,000 net ton-km. Shipping (1973): merchant vessels 100 gross tons and over 24; gross tonnage 11,022. Ships entered (1972) vessels totaling 1,663,000 net registered tons; goods loaded (1973) 94,000 metric tons, unloaded 941,000 metric tons. Telephones (Dec. 1972) 45,000. Radio licenses (Dec. 1972) 124,000. Television licenses (Dec. 1972) 57,000.

Marketing and Merchandising

The merchandising scene in Europe was dominated by inflation, government anti-inflation measures, and shortages, and the continuing development of large-scale units became of secondary importance. Inflation and recession were dominant factors in marketing and merchandising in North America.

Inflation. In the United States the effects of inflation and recession on retail sales began to be felt in the last third of the year. Earlier, sales advanced steadily to reach their peak of more than $46.5 billion in August. This was a gain of 11% over July and was 11.7% above the corresponding period of 1973. September, October, and November all registered declines, however, with the November total approximately $45.1 billion. This was only 5% above the figure for November 1973 and was more than offset by the 12% rise in consumer prices over the same period. Much of this decline was attributed to the considerable decrease in automobile sales. Retail stores reported their Christmas season was better than expected but unusually late. Many stores featured pre-Christmas sales.

Every country felt the impact of both Middle East oil policies and supply shortages in the world commodity markets. In the U.K., where the increase in the cost of living approached 20% per year, retailing and the food sector bore the brunt of anti-inflation measures. The Labour government imposed a 10% cut in gross profit margins and a three-month interval before price increases could be put into effect. The recession in demand and the inability to pass on genuine and substantial increases in the cost of inputs caused firms to prune expansion plans.

The trust and good will of customers, on which retailers relied, was undermined by the sheer size of price movements in 1974. Of necessity, U.K. retailers turned to improving consumer services, training managers to handle shoppers' grievances more effectively, and introducing the customer into the decision-making process. Fine Fare Ltd., for example, set up a panel of customers on small retainer to be regularly consulted for views, suggestions, and criticisms of the firm's activities. Other stores followed suit, hoping thereby to avoid the experience of U.S. retailers, whose customers had organized picket lines, boycotts, and media attacks on stores following price increases.

The Distributive Industry Training Board (DITB) instituted a system of certificates of merit for retailers with progressive staff training programs. Competition between retailers was such that many were persuaded to take up the scheme and subject themselves to inspection.

For political reasons, food retailers were the government's main target in the U.K., although many of the economic arguments were in their favour. Costs soared in 1974. Profits were never easily made in this highly competitive, stable, slow growing market, and the introduction of subsidies only confused matters. Food retailers asked to be allowed to introduce their own price reductions on certain selected items, while covering themselves on others. Foods having large profit margins, such as fresh meat and dairy products, were favoured at the expense of other foods, and with sales continuing to rise steadily in the nonfood retail sector, the incentives to diversify were clear.

The "own brands" business became a casualty of strained relations between retailers and manufacturers. During the early 1970s retailers sold their own branded foods alongside national brands, often produced by the same manufacturer. Manufacturers' brands were heavily advertised and almost always underpriced by the own brands. However, when in 1974 demand declined in the wake of anti-inflation measures, manufacturers found that their brands were suffering. Consequently, retailers began to find shortages in supplies of own brands as manufacturers concentrated on their named brands, thus hurting those retailers who were heavily dependent on own brands for sales and profits.

The small retailer found price controls and declining demand difficult to bear, but inflation helped to stimulate one development that might in the long run save many independent retailers—voluntary groupings of wholesalers and shopkeepers. By 1974 these embraced a fifth of the retail sector in Britain. Groups gained from economies of scale in ordering, storing, and handling, but retained the traditional advantage of the small unit in providing personal service to the customer.

The price consciousness induced in consumers by inflation produced one growth industry in 1974—freezer supplies. Freezer ownership had soared since 1972, and the increased demand for frozen foods was met initially by new specialist retailers. Established retailers opened specialist freezer offshoots, and by 1974 the Co-op, with 100 such outlets in the U.K., had more than the leading independent, Bejam Bulk Buying Ltd. Sainsbury's announced plans for 40 stores over the next three years, and Tesco's planned 60 over the same period.

A new merchandising idea that could foreshadow developments throughout Europe originated in Sweden, where an automobile supermarket opened in Stockholm. Owned jointly by Volkswagen, Saab, and General Motors, the store held more than 800 new and used cars in a converted multistory garage, with a Swedish motoring organization monitoring and providing detailed reports on every vehicle. Only 12 people were needed to run the business, and prices were well below the average of those elsewhere.

Although business was in recession in 1974 and government controls made life difficult, for some traders expansion was still possible. In the U.K., the mail order industry gained from the reintroduction of hire purchase (installment-plan buying) restrictions in 1974 because its normal repayment periods were too short to fall within the scope of the regulations. However, the future was shadowed by increased postal charges and escalating catalog printing costs and the apparent approach of a situation where sales of one company could increase only at the expense of another.

The trading stamp industry was one of the losers of 1974, being hard hit by the oil shortage when gasoline stations virtually gave up handing out stamps. However, discounting again flourished, and attracted many new entrants, including several established retailers. Woolworth's achieved a new dynamism with the Woolco chain. Great Universal Stores joined the discount business, opening eight specialized stores in its first year. Established retailers had turned to discounting late in the day, but they had the advantage of strong connections with major manufacturers.

Large-Scale Units. Rapid inflation could not halt the opening of large-scale retail units already commissioned. The French-owned Carrefour organization opened two new hypermarkets (retail stores having at least 25,000 sq.ft. of selling area) in the U.K., one in Telford and one in Southampton. Plans drawn up in 1974 were far more cautious. Several applications were rejected, and there were the inevitable appeals and public inquiries. Ministry decisions on proposals

The "Pana Scanner," developed by Matsushita Electric of Japan, a fully automated cash register in which a laser beam is used to read a coded price tag on each item as it is passed over the scanner window. The price tag can also be coded to carry inventory information.

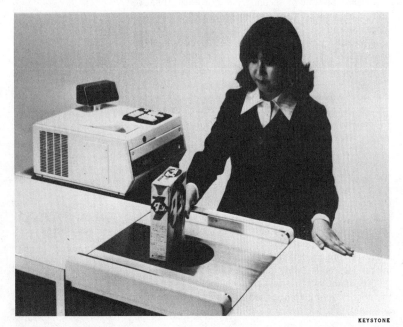

KEYSTONE

for new stores were keenly awaited as guidelines to future government policy.

The 1974 Neilsen Report showed that large units were not as scarce in the U.K. as the publicity about planning applications had suggested, but that such stores tended to be concentrated in the Midlands and in the north of England. Increasing scale characterized the entire retail sector. Sainsbury's new stores that opened in 1974 averaged 17,500 sq.ft.

Hypermarket supporters were not slow to point out that under extreme inflationary conditions any cost reductions made possible by economies of scale would benefit consumers, but their opponents continued to stress the possible destruction of town centres and "green belts" that they might cause. A study made by a firm of chartered surveyors concluded that spending habits of shoppers in Caerphilly, South Wales, after the arrival of Carrefour had been little affected. The store had gained from shoppers drawn from a large surrounding area and, with the effects diffused, there were no omens of catastrophe for smaller retailers.

The experiences of retailers in continental Europe were much the same as those of their U.K. counterparts, but there were differences, particularly in the development of larger units. In Belgium, the takeover of Innovation Bon Marché by G.B. Enterprises created a giant in the distribution sector, approximately four times bigger than its nearest rival. With G.B. Enterprises specializing in out-of-town stores and Innovation Bon Marché in centre-of-town shopping systems, such takeovers appeared to herald a new development—the movement of the hypermarket to the main shopping centre.

The relatively slow growth of hypermarkets in Europe in 1974 was not entirely a natural process; opposition to them was reaching new heights. In West Germany, planning regulations of 1973 were strictly enforced. A new Belgian law forced all shops to close one hour earlier, at 8 P.M., a direct blow to the big stores with their dependence on after-work shopping expeditions. In France, the "Royer law" made it compulsory for every planned superstore to go to a local planning inquiry where vested interests of small retailers would be well represented, effectively checking the superstore development program. Carrefour did announce plans to expand, but in Spain and Brazil rather than within the EEC.

In the U.K., the U.S.-owned Evans Products announced plans for a network of supermarkets selling do-it-yourself products. Also, entry into the EEC, pressures to cut costs, and stagnation of demand boosted the food-brokering concept. New to the U.K., such organizations provided specialist sales forces selling a wide range of noncompeting products to retailers.

A revival in the fortunes of the shopping centre was one consequence of the coming of the hypermarket. In an organized, well-planned shopping community, hypermarkets were an attraction from which other stores benefited, and there was plenty of scope for specialty food and nonfood retailers to operate harmoniously and profitably alongside them. Some proposed out-of-town shopping centres openly canvassed for hypermarkets to join them.

France took up the idea of the large, out-of-town, specifically designed shopping centre. Such centres attracted the interest of traditional department stores and small independent retailers alike. Rosny 2, the fourth Paris centre, opened in 1974. Attractive advanced design and decor, the provision of management services for all the retailers, finance, and no planning problems all added to the centres' attraction, and they seemed the most promising development of an otherwise difficult year.

Merchandising Practices. A new emphasis by U.S. magazine publishers on single-copy sales became evident when it was revealed in September that about 60% of annual retail sales took place in supermarket, drug, and convenience store chains. Those magazines placed on racks at the checkout counters of such stores had sales three to four times greater than magazines located in other display areas.

The U.S. Federal Trade Commission in July charged Sears, Roebuck & Co. with deceptive merchandising of its expensive home appliances. The federal agency accused Sears of employing bait-and-switch tactics: luring customers into a store with promises of low-priced items and then trying to sell them more expensive models. Sears claimed that it was innocent of the charges.

In December the U.S. Department of Agriculture announced that food processors would have until Dec. 31, 1975, to use up existing packaging labels on meat and poultry products. After that time labels using such descriptions as "all" or "pure" or "100 percent" would be banned from packages of meat and poultry that contained more than one ingredient.

(JOHN C. SHOREY)

See also Advertising; Consumerism; Cooperatives; Industrial Production and Technology; Prices.
[534.H.5; 725.D]

Mathematics

The most important unsolved problem in mathematics is generally considered to be the Riemann hypothesis, first studied by the German mathematician G. F. B. Riemann in 1859. It concerns the function $\zeta(s) = 1^{-s} + 2^{-s} + \ldots + n^{-s} + \ldots$. Here, s is a complex number, and it is customary to write $s = \sigma + \sqrt{-1}t$ in which σ and t are real. Initially, one obtains ζ only for $\sigma > 1$, but methods of complex variable theory permit definition of ζ for all s. The question is: for what values of s is $\zeta(s)$ equal to 0? The numbers $s = -2, -4, -6, \ldots$, called the trivial zeros of ζ, are usually excluded from the discussion. (These zeros are called trivial because they are located by a very easy computation; the task of finding the remaining zeros is much harder.) Riemann

SIDNEY HARRIS

thought it likely that σ would have to equal $\frac{1}{2}$ for all other zeros. The question arises in many branches of mathematics and remains unsettled despite extensive study.

About 30 years ago André Weil broadened that inquiry to analogous functions arising in a context (like the clock arithmetic of the "new mathematics") in which adding a suitable number of 1's gives 0. Weil and others achieved significant partial results and in 1974 his Riemann hypothesis was completely proved by the French mathematician Pierre Deligne.

Deligne's success was based in large part on new methods in algebraic geometry developed during the preceding 15 years by Alexandre Grothendieck and his colleagues. Prominent among younger members of this group was David Mumford of Harvard University. His work was honoured in 1974 by one of two awards of the prestigious Fields Prize, the other prize going to Enrico Bombieri of the University of Pisa in Italy for important work in analysis and number theory.

Among other challenging open questions answered in 1974, two concerned groups, perhaps the most basic structure studied in modern mathematics. Groups are abstract objects with a postulated way of combining any two elements so that the familiar laws of algebra are satisfied. If these requirements include the commutative law (meaning that the order in which one takes the elements is irrelevant), the group is called Abelian (honouring the 19th-century Norwegian mathematician Niels Abel). A simple example of an Abelian group is the set Z of all integers (positive, zero, or negative) with addition as the operation.

Sometimes it is possible to decompose an Abelian group G into constituents H and J, H being a subgroup and J the corresponding factor group. (The factor group is formed from G and H by a process resembling the division of one number by another.) One calls G an extension of H by J. Given H and J, there is always a trivial extension formed by naively placing H and J together in a so-called direct sum. One can then take H to be the group Z of integers and inquire what it means for J to have the property that any extension of Z by J must be trivial. It turns out that this occurs if J is a direct sum of copies of Z, such a group being called free. A generation ago the British topologist J. H. C. Whitehead asked whether the requirement being imposed on J would force J to be free. The Israeli mathematician Saharon Shelah gave the answer: on the basis of today's mathematics the question cannot be decided. This was a striking addition to the growing list of propositions that logicians have proved to be undecidable.

In the other group-theoretic question one studies certain groups of matrices, technically called semisimple Lie groups, and wishes to show that all their representations, even the infinite-dimensional ones, conform to a certain standard of behaviour called Type I. For the usual Lie groups over the real numbers this was done many years ago. There is a companion class of Lie groups where p-adic numbers replace real numbers (p-adic numbers differ from real numbers by having a decimal expansion that may run forever to the left instead of to the right). In 1974 the p-adic theorem was proved by I. N. Bernstein of the Soviet Union.

Large-scale computing continued to be used in number theory to achieve results that would have been out of reach in the days of hand computation.

One such result concerned "amicable" numbers. Two numbers are called amicable if each is the sum of all the divisors of the other (1 is counted as a divisor of a number but not the number itself). For example, 220 and 284 are amicable since the divisors of 220 are 1, 2, 4, 5, 10, 11, 20, 22, 44, 55, and 110, adding up to 284, and the divisors of 284 are 1, 2, 4, 71, and 142, adding up to 220. These are the smallest amicable numbers and were known in ancient times. In 1946 a pair of amicable numbers having 25 digits was discovered. This remained the largest known pair until the publication in 1974 of four larger pairs by H. J. J. te Riele of The Netherlands. In the largest of these new pairs each number has 152 digits. It is easy to write these numbers down in a condensed notation. Let $x = 3^4 \cdot 5 \cdot 11 \cdot 5281^{19}$, $y = 2^3 \cdot 3^3 \cdot 5^2 \cdot 1291 \cdot 5281^{19} - 1$, $z = 29 \cdot 89(2 \cdot 1291 \cdot 5281^{19} - 1)$; then the big amicable numbers are xy and xz.   (IRVING KAPLANSKY)

[10/22.B.4.b; 10/22.E.2.a; 10/22.E.2.c.v]

Mauritania

The Islamic Republic of Mauritania is on the Atlantic coast of West Africa, adjoining Spanish Sahara, Algeria, Mali, and Senegal. Area: 398,000 sq.mi. (1,030,700 sq.km.). Pop. (1973 est.): 1,218,000. Cap.: Nouakchott (pop., 1972 est., 55,000). Language: Arabic, French. Religion: Muslim. President in 1974, Moktar Ould Daddah.

The continuing disaster of the Sahel drought and its accompanying famine (*see* AGRICULTURE AND FOOD SUPPLIES: *Special Report*) in 1974 caused most of Mauritania's nomadic population to congregate in the towns of the southwest, where there was a little water and an all-weather road made it possible to transport relief supplies. About 80% of the nomads' livestock perished, and millet and sorghum harvests were poor.

A new political opposition party, the Mauritanian Justice Party, was formed in July. It called for democratic freedom, the liberation of political detainees, and concentration on internal needs.

The Organization for the Development of the Senegal River basin met at Nouakchott in late May and adopted a 40-year development plan (first proposed

Camels being used to draw water in skins from Aroit, one of the few precious wells in the Mauritanian desert.

MAURITANIA

Education. (1972–73) Primary, pupils 38,900, teachers 1,120; secondary, pupils 3,408, teachers 458; vocational, pupils 667, teachers, 156; teacher training, students 237, teachers 33; higher, students 72.

Finance. Monetary unit: ouguiya, with (Sept. 16, 1974) a par value of 1 ouguiya to 5 CFA francs (free rate of 48.10 ouiguiya = U.S. $1; 111.30 ouguiya = £1 sterling). Gold, SDRs, and foreign exchange, central bank: (Jan. 1974) U.S. $44.9 million; (Jan. 1973) U.S. $10.3 million. Budget (1974 est.) balanced at 3,105,000,000 ouguiya.

Foreign Trade. (1972) Imports 3,475,000,000 ouguiya; exports 5,035,000,000 ouguiya. Import sources: France 48%; Japan 8%; U.S. 6%; West Germany 5%. Export destinations: U.K. 25%; Spain 17%; Japan 15%; West Germany 13%; Italy 12%; Belgium-Luxembourg 9%. Main exports: iron ore 73%; fish 10%; copper concentrates 10%.

The rugged and dramatic mountain landscape of Mauritius.

in March 1972) to develop the Senegal River basin on a large scale, including the construction of two dams; finance for the project was to come from, among others, the World Bank, the European Development Fund, and Arab countries. On his return from a ten-day visit to Peking, President Ould Daddah announced that China had agreed to provide Mauritania with a $30 million deepwater harbour and contribute to the building of an east-west highway across the country. Kuwait, Qatar, Abu Dhabi, and Saudi Arabia granted Mauritania $80 million for development of an iron and steelworks, for a fishing port, and for the east-west highway.

As of November 28 the mainly French iron-ore mining company, the Société des Mines de Fer de Mauritanie (Miferma), became nationalized. In 1973 it produced 10.4 million metric tons of iron ore, 1.2 million metric tons more than in 1972; it employed more than 4,000 workers and was the mainstay of the country's economy, accounting for 80% of its exports.

(R. M. GOODWIN)

took over foreign affairs in a Cabinet reshuffle that enlarged the Ministry of Labour, and the three-year ban on 12 trade unions was lifted.

The record 1973 sugar crop of 718,000 tons brought good prices, but the ending of the Commonwealth Sugar Agreement in 1974 led to some uncertainty. On April 17 an agreement was negotiated with the U.S.S.R. for technical aid to increase fisheries output. Development continued in the Mauritius Export Processing Zone, with over 50 light industrial enterprises employing more than 8,000 people and a turnover of $23 million in 1973, while a new industrial estate took shape at Coromandel.

(MOLLY MORTIMER)

Mauritius

The parliamentary state of Mauritius, a member of the Commonwealth of Nations, lies about 500 mi. E of the Malagasy Republic in the Indian Ocean; it includes the island dependencies of Rodrigues, Agalega, and Cargados Carajos. Area: 787.5 sq.mi. (2,040 sq.km.). Pop. (1974 est.): 869,600, including (1972) Indian 50%; Pakistani 16%; Creole (mixed French and African) 31%; others 3%. Cap. and largest city: Port Louis (pop., 1973 est., 136,600). Language: English (official). Religion (1972): Hindu 50%; Christian religions 33%; Muslim 16%. Queen, Elizabeth II; governor-general in 1974, Sir Abdul Rahman Muhammad Osman; prime minister, Sir Seewoosagur Ramgoolam.

In December 1973 the prime minister dismissed four Social Democrats from his coalition government, including his foreign minister, Gaetan Duval, allegedly because of the latter's support of a dialogue with South Africa and a proposal that France should replace its lost Madagascar base with one on Mauritius (France denied the intention). During January 1974 the prime minister suspended four municipal councils, including that of Port Louis, of which Duval was lord mayor, and replaced them with government nominees. In February the prime minister himself

MAURITIUS

Education. (1973) Primary, pupils 150,656, teachers 5,142; secondary, pupils 55,619, teachers 1,859; vocational, pupils 768, teachers 93; teacher training (1972), students 639, teachers (1969) 30; higher, students 1,263, teaching staff 65.

Finance and Trade. Monetary unit: Mauritian rupee, with (Sept. 16, 1974) a free rate of MauRs. 5.77 to U.S. $1 (par value of MauRs. 13.33 = £1 sterling). Gold, SDRs, and foreign exchange, central bank: (June 1974) U.S. $27.4 million; (June 1973) U.S. $65.7 million. Budget (1971–72 est.): revenue MauRs. 294 million; expenditure MauRs. 283 million. Foreign trade (1973): imports MauRs. 922.6 million; exports MauRs. 716.1 million. Import sources: U.K. 22%; South Africa 8%; France 7%; Australia 5%; Iran 5%; Pakistan 5%; West Germany 5%. Export destinations: U.K. 45%; Canada 25%; U.S. 8%. Main export sugar 84%. Tourism: visitors (1973) 68,000; gross receipts (1972) U.S. $10 million.

Agriculture. Production (in 000; metric tons; 1973; 1972 in parentheses): sugar 741 (686); tea c. 5 (5); tobacco (1972) 0.6, (1971) 0.6. Livestock (in 000; April 1972): cattle c. 50; pigs c. 3; sheep c. 3; goats c. 65; chickens c. 410.

Metallurgy

Metallurgy in 1974 continued to be strongly influenced by social and political pressure for pollution control, by reduced energy and fuel consumption, and, in the U.S., by efforts to attain national self-sufficiency for as many resources as possible. High costs together with shortages that ranged from steel scrap to finished metals caused additional problems. Because the problems arose more rapidly than solutions could be found and put into practice, much of the progress made continued to be in the form of laboratory results and construction plans.

Rapid economic changes and future uncertainties hindered construction and financing. Among others, a Japanese steel company stopped work on a major expansion, chiefly because of uncertain petroleum supply. Several proposed plants, especially those that would include new processes, were reported to be awaiting financing.

The potential of hydrometallurgy (treatment of ores by such wet processes as leaching) for solution mining, economical treatment of low-grade ores, and pollution control made it the most rapidly developing branch of metallurgy. The fossil fuel shortage created new interest in uranium, which is extracted almost exclusively by hydrometallurgy. Solvent extraction and the ion-exchange resin processes for selectively removing particular elements from a solution were first used for uranium recovery. In 1974 they were adapted as recovery methods for a number of metals.

Pilot plants for two different hydrometallurgical processes for air-pollution-free copper production neared completion. Doubts were expressed that either would ever be expanded to full-scale production because they required large amounts of electric energy. Although it is difficult to generalize, informed estimates were that hydrometallurgy requires $1\frac{1}{2}$–2 times as much energy for copper production as do pyrometallurgical processes (those involving the application of heat).

Equipment for crushing and grinding ore reflected

the trend to larger units. Crushers with a 66-in. by 84-in. feed opening and a capacity of 3,000 tons per hour of hard rock became available. Many of the new grinding mills were equipped with wrap-around motors, the motor being fastened directly to the mill shell.

A magnetic separation method for weakly magnetic minerals such as hematite was operating on a laboratory scale during the year. If it could be expanded to commercial-scale production, it should lower the cost of beneficiation (preparation for smelting) of the large available deposits of hematite-containing taconite iron ore.

A scrap metal shortage serious enough to affect steel production, especially in the U.K., provided added incentive to recover the metal from all types of waste. Several plants began treating municipal waste by using an air blast to shred and separate the light organic material and then employing a magnet to separate the steel from the other metals and glass; these other materials can be further separated by a variety of processes. A Japanese machine uses nonsharp cutters to chip the insulation off of scrap wire and break the wire into short lengths that can be conveniently remelted. An air blast separates the insulation from the metal. It was found that cooling junk cars to −300° F makes shredding more efficient. Circulating chilled liquefied methane may make such cooling economically practical.

The steel scrap shortage was expected to continue, and the steel producers began considering direct reduced iron as a replacement for scrap. Direct reduction processes use natural gas, or occasionally coal, to produce metallic iron from the iron minerals in the ore or concentrate, but they do not remove any impurities. For ease of handling, the ore is often formed into pellets before reduction.

The chloride process for aluminum production, in which aluminum oxide ores are converted to aluminum chlorides, seemed applicable to extraction of the metal from clay. Both a Soviet and a U.S. process were in the advanced development stage. Obtaining aluminum from clay would make almost every nation independent of foreign sources for ore. Chlorine is also widely used in the final purification step in aluminum production, where it is bubbled through the liquid metal just before casting it into ingots. This source of air pollution can be eliminated with a new process that uses nitrogen gas and a molten salt flux instead of chlorine.

Another pollution problem can be alleviated by using a mechanical substitute for acid pickling to remove oxide scale from metals, eliminating the long-standing problem of how to dispose of the used acid. A Japanese machine uses rapidly rotating brushes made of tightly packed tool steel wires to remove the scale. Shallow surface imperfections can also be removed at the same time.

New developments in superplasticity made these materials, which can undergo extremely large deformation in forming with low power requirements, more applicable. An aluminum-copper alloy that is superplastic at 450° F has properties comparable to other aluminum-copper alloys when below 150°. It was demonstrated that the proper combination of temperature and speed and magnitude of deformation can produce superplasticity in several regular commercial alloys.   (DONALD F. CLIFTON)

See also Industrial Production and Technology; Mining and Quarrying; Physics.
[725.B]

Bales of aluminum beer and soft drink cans enter a shredder in the first step toward recovering the valuable metal. The recycling process yields aluminum at a small fraction of the energy cost of refining ore.

COURTESY, ALCOA

Mexico

A federal republic of Middle America, Mexico is bounded by the U.S., Belize, and Guatemala. Area: 761,605 sq.mi. (1,972,547 sq.km.). Pop. (1973 est.): 54,302,800, including about 55% mestizo and 29% Indian. Cap. and largest city: Mexico City (pop., 1970, city 2,902,970, metro. area 8,589,630). Language: Spanish. Religion: predominantly Roman Catholic. President in 1974, Luis Echeverría Álvarez.

Foreign Relations. President Echeverría paid official visits to West Germany, Austria, Italy, and Yugoslavia in February 1974 and to Costa Rica, Ecuador, Peru, Argentina, Brazil, Venezuela, and Jamaica in July. The goal of the tours was to continue a policy of improving political and economic relations with countries other than the U.S., and to encourage other countries to support the president's proposal for a UN Charter of Economic Rights and Duties of States. The main results of the visits to Latin-American countries were agreements with Brazil for cooperation in technological, scientific, and tourist matters, improvements in sea and air transport systems, and the establishment of a joint committee to meet annually to study ways of strengthening economic relations; with Peru and Ecuador for technical cooperation in the petroleum sector; with Peru for joint action to set up an association of silver-exporting nations; with Venezuela for technical cooperation in the production and supply of petroleum and petrochemicals; and with Argentina for joint action to maintain sugar export prices. On November 26, however, Mexico broke diplomatic relations with Chile. At a meeting on October 21 in Nogales, on the border between Mexico and the U.S., President Echeverría and U.S. Pres. Gerald Ford discussed problems of mutual concern.

Domestic Affairs. The Echeverría administration faced political problems in 1974. An upsurge in terrorist activity caused considerable disquiet. On August 28 the president's father-in-law, José Zuno Hernández, was kidnapped at Guadalajara (Jalisco) and a ransom of $1.6 million and the release of a number of political prisoners were demanded for his life; on May 30, a millionaire labour union leader, Rúben Figueroa, whom some commentators considered to be a possible successor to Echeverría in 1976, was seized in the state of Guerrero. Both men were released early in September without payment of ransom or release of prisoners. There were frequent reports of guerrilla activity in several parts of the country. The government was embarrassed by the assassination in the state of Yucatán in February of Efraín Calderón Lara, who tried to set up an independent labour group outside the jurisdiction of the official trade union organization, the Confederación de Trabajadores Mexicanos (CTM), to which 90% of unionized workers were affiliated. The police chief of the state capital, Mérida, and several of his subordinates were arrested.

The CTM, under its veteran secretary-general, Fidel Velázquez, became increasingly powerful during the year. More and more, the administration relied on it for political support, having alienated a large section of its conservative backing by repeated official statements that reforms would be carried out to bring about a more equitable distribution of income. Velázquez, secretary-general of the CTM since 1941, was confirmed in office for another five-year term beginning in 1975. By August it was apparent that the CTM was the predominant influence in determining the government's economic policies and that its spokesman, the secretary of labour, Porfírio Muñoz Ledo, was the most powerful figure in the Cabinet. In his state of the union message on September 1, the president announced that legislation would be introduced to end discrimination against women.

The Economy. The economic expansion of 1972 and 1973 was maintained during the first eight months of 1974, with production and sales of many industrial items registering substantial increases. President Echeverría announced on September 1 that the rise in gross domestic product for 1974 would be 7%, as compared with 7.3% in 1973. Inflation and the external balance of trade, however, aroused concern.

The national retail price index rose by an estimated 10.4% in the first half of 1974, as compared with 21.4% during the whole of 1973. Contributory causes to the rises of 1973 and 1974 included the increased cost of most imported goods, the growth of internal demand in excess of supply, and sharp upward movements in prices for petroleum products. In August 1973 the government had published a 16-point program to curb inflationary pressures and to permit a

UPI COMPIX

A new 18,000-bbl.-per-day petroleum desulfurization plant built for Petroleos Mexicano at Salamanca symbolizes the vigour of Mexico's growing petroleum industry.

Metals:
see Industrial Production and Technology; Metallurgy; Mining and Quarrying

Meteorology:
see Earth Sciences

Methodists:
see Religion

MEXICO

Education. (1971–72) Primary, pupils 9,127,226, teachers 182,454; secondary, pupils 1,008,205, teachers 71,057; vocational, pupils 359,927, teachers 25,091; teacher training (1969–70), students 59,324, teachers 5,449; higher (including 36 universities; 1970–71), students 247,637, teaching staff 17,103.

Finance. Monetary unit: peso, with (Sept. 16, 1974) a par value of 12.50 pesos to U.S. $1 (free rate of 28.90 pesos = £1 sterling). Gold, SDRs, and foreign exchange, central bank: (April 1974) U.S. $1,432,000,000; (April 1973) U.S. $1,175,000,000. Budget (1974 est.) balanced at 230,960,000,000 pesos. Gross domestic product: (1972) 513.7 billion pesos; (1971) 452.2 billion pesos. Money supply: (Dec. 1973) 83,720,000,000 pesos; (Dec. 1972) 68,250,000,000 pesos. Cost of living (Mexico City; 1970 = 100): (May 1974) 147; (May 1973) 120.

Foreign Trade. (1973) Imports 51,822,000,000 pesos; exports 32,890,000,000 pesos. Import sources (1972): U.S. 60%; West Germany 9%. Export destination U.S. 60%. Main exports (1972): fruit and vegetables 11%; machinery 9%; cotton 8%; sugar 7%; cattle 6%; chemicals 6%; nonferrous metals 5%; coffee 5%; fish 5%. Tourism: visitors (1971) 2,770,000; gross receipts (1972) U.S. $1,787,000,000.

Transport and Communications. Roads (1973) 154,700 km. (including 957 km. expressways). Motor vehicles in use (1973): passenger 1,672,100; commercial 652,000. Railways (1972): 23,272 km.; traffic 4,485,000,000 passenger-km., freight 23,878,000,000 net ton-km. Air traffic (1972): 4,314,000,000 passenger-km.; freight 58 million net ton-km. Shipping (1973): merchant vessels 100 gross tons and over 248; gross tonnage 453,024. Telephones (Dec. 1972) 1,955,000. Radio receivers (Dec. 1972) 15,841,000. Television receivers (Dec. 1972) 3,821,000.

Agriculture. Production (in 000; metric tons; 1973; 1972 in parentheses): corn 9,500 (9,401); wheat 1,980 (1,672); barley c. 300 (294); sorghum c. 2,600 (2,441); rice c. 475 (469); dry beans 800 (809); soybeans c. 510 (344); tomatoes c. 950 (950); bananas (1972) c. 1,250, (1971) 1,219; grapes (1972) c. 225, (1971) 219; oranges (1972) 1,318, (1971) 1,610; lemons (1972) 273, (1971) c. 207; coffee 195 (198); sugar, raw value c. 2,781 (c. 2,526); tobacco 65 (82); sisal (1972) c. 145, (1971) 143; cotton, lint 340 (386); fish catch (1971) 402, (1970) 357. Livestock (in 000; Dec. 1972): cattle 26,548; sheep 5,644; pigs 12,921; horses (1971) 4,423; mules (1971) 2,655; asses (1971) 3,039; chickens (1971) 144,882.

Industry. Production (in 000; metric tons; 1973): cement 9,686; crude oil (1972) 22,163; coal (1972) c. 2,170; natural gas (cu.m.) 19,012; electricity (kw-hr.) 37,068,000; iron ore (metal content) 3,114; pig iron 3,030; steel 4,504; sulfur (1971) 1,243; petroleum products (1972) 24,067; sulfuric acid 1,757; fertilizers (nutrient content; 1972–73) nitrogenous 356, phosphate 220; lead 160; zinc 67; copper, smelter 72; aluminum 39; manganese ore (metal content; 1972) 106; antimony ore (metal content; 1972) 3; gold (troy oz.; 1972) 146; silver (troy oz.; 1972) 37,460; cotton yarn (1972) 131; woven cotton fabrics (1972) 115; wool yarn (1971) 36; rayon, etc., filaments and fibres 37; nylon, etc., filaments and fibres (1972) 87.

reasonable rate of economic expansion. These measures included tighter supervision over government expenditure and the money supply; intensified promotion of new private investment; and a strengthening of official price controls. During the first quarter of 1974 the program appeared to be working well; there was a high level of economic activity and a slight deceleration in the rate of domestic price increases. Nevertheless, it became apparent by June that little progress was being made in restraining inflation, although a reasonable rate of economic expansion continued. The CTM was pressing for an across-the-board pay increase of about 35% and threatened to withhold political support and to take large-scale strike action if this was not granted. It was seeking compensation for the fact that prices of many basic consumer goods had risen by 50–100% since July 1973. Accordingly, late in June 1974, steps were taken to counter inflationary pressures on consumers, including a price freeze until December 31 on 53 basic consumer products and price controls on 100 others; also, the distribution and regulatory activities of the federal agricultural marketing agency were expanded to combat hoarding and speculation.

There was a weakening of the external balance of trade in the first half of 1974. Preliminary official figures established that exports and imports in January–June 1974 were valued at $1,371,000,000 and $2,724,000,000, respectively, representing rises of 50.2 and 50% over the figures for the comparable period of 1973. Official sources considered that if this trend were maintained, there would be a trade deficit of $2,802,000,000 in 1974, as against $1,690,000,000 in 1973. The deterioration in the trade balance was attributed primarily to the higher cost of imports, although the expansion of exports was also constrained by increased domestic demand. A substantial capital inflow in the first half of 1974 was mainly accounted for by new long-term loans contracted by the government; the total foreign debt at the end of June 1974 was estimated at about $10 billion, as compared with $6 billion at the end of 1973.

Two favourable economic developments occurred between January and September. First, the law to promote Mexican and regulate foreign investment, which entered into force on May 8, 1973, appeared to be operating satisfactorily; a considerably larger amount of private direct investment entered Mexico in the first half of 1974 than in the comparable period of 1973. Second, it was officially announced late in July that Mexico had become self-sufficient in the production of crude oil; production from newly discovered wells in the states of Tabasco and Chiapas would shortly permit Mexico to become a net exporter on a considerable scale.   (ROBIN CHAPMAN)

[974.A]

Middle Eastern Affairs

The Arab-Israeli Dispute. The first half of 1974 marked a distinct improvement in the Middle East situation as U.S. mediation helped to secure military disengagement agreements between Israel and both Egypt and Syria. However, the failure to achieve any further progress toward a settlement caused the atmosphere to deteriorate toward the end of the year, and both sides warned of the acute danger of renewed war.

As the year opened, the Egyptian-Israeli disengagement talks that had begun on December 26 at Geneva

Microbiology:
see Life Sciences

were continued, but although UN spokesmen said an important stage had been reached with "a consensus on some principles of disengagement," it was clear that a new impetus was needed for an agreement. This was provided by U.S. Secretary of State Henry Kissinger (see BIOGRAPHY), who arrived in Cairo on January 11 and, after shuttling between that city and Jerusalem, arranged an agreement that was approved by the two sides separately on January 18.

According to the military details of the agreement, which were worked out by the Egyptian and Israeli chiefs of staff, all Egyptian forces east of the Suez Canal were to be deployed west of Line A running about six miles east of, and roughly parallel to, the canal. In this forward zone Egyptian forces were to be thinned out from 70,000 troops and 400 tanks to 7,000 troops and 30 tanks. The area between Line A and Line B, six miles farther to the east, was the zone of disengagement in which a UN Emergency Force was to be situated. Between Line B and Line C, running along the base of the mountains in which the key Gedi (Arabic, Jiddi) and Mitla passes were situated, was the Israeli forward zone, in which its forces were similarly thinned out.

Israeli forces withdrew from their last positions on the Suez Canal on March 4, and work on clearing the canal of bombs and shells began almost immediately. The Egyptian-Israeli disengagement agreement having averted the imminent danger of renewed hostilities on the Sinai front, interest switched to the Golan Heights on the Israeli-Syrian front. The Syrians feared that the Egyptian-Israeli agreement might be at their expense. There were also signs that the Palestine Liberation Organization (PLO) was split over disengagement, which one section of it called a bilateral partial solution that helped Israel and U.S. imperialism. However, the PLO chairman, Yasir Arafat (see BIOGRAPHY), continued in consultation with Egypt, which pressed for PLO participation in renewed Geneva peace talks.

Kissinger pursued his efforts to achieve a Syrian-Israeli disengagement on a new visit to the Middle East in late February. The chief stumbling blocks were the Israeli prisoners of war in Syrian hands and Syria's demand that 17,000 civilians uprooted by the war should be allowed to return. The Soviet government showed its annoyance at having been left out of the Egyptian-Israeli agreement and insisted that it should participate in all future stages of a Middle East settlement. The Soviet foreign minister, Andrey A. Gromyko, visited Damascus in February and March, and again in May, to make this point and express full support for Syria to which Soviet arms were already being supplied in large quantities. Serious Israeli-Syrian clashes occurred in the Golan Heights during March and April, and the military situation deteriorated. The Syrians, however, were prepared to continue indirect negotiations and sent a delegation to Washington on April 9 to discuss disengagement.

With Syrian-Israeli clashes continuing, Kissinger arrived in Algiers on April 29 at the start of a new Middle East mission. His task was made more difficult by Palestinian guerrilla attacks on two northern Israeli towns, Qiryat Shemona (April 12) and Maalot (May 15), which caused many casualties among civilians and hardened the Israeli mood. Both attacks led to heavy Israeli reprisal raids against Palestinian refugee camps in Lebanon. However, Kissinger, after traveling between Middle Eastern capitals throughout the month of May, succeeded, against widespread predictions of failure, in bringing about a Syrian-Israeli disengagement agreement on May 29. This agreement, on similar lines to the one between Egypt and Israel, provided for an Israeli withdrawal to the pre-October 1973 lines minus an additional pocket of territory to include the main Golan town of Kuneitra (Qunaytirah). Both sides agreed to the thinning out of forces in the forward zones. Syria refused Israel's demand that it should promise to control Palestinian guerrilla activity from its territory, and Israel accepted instead a U.S. guarantee of support against guerrilla activity. On June 1 and 6 Syrian and Israeli prisoners were exchanged, and on June 25, after Israeli troops had completed the evacuation of Kuneitra, Syrian civilians were allowed to return. The Syrians, backed by a UN committee that reported in November, accused the Israelis of having razed the city to the ground and refused to repopulate it. The Israelis accused the Syrians of breaking the disengagement by building approach roads and strengthening their defenses in the forward zone. Although the war of attrition ended, the situation remained explosive as Israel began to establish new settlements on the Golan Heights.

The formation of a new Israeli government under Yitzhak Rabin (see BIOGRAPHY) on May 28, without the participation of Moshe Dayan, offered improved hope of a renewal of the Geneva peace talks. The chief obstacle was still the question of the representation of the Palestinians, especially those of the West Bank of Jordan. Egyptian diplomacy was directed both toward securing a Jordanian-Palestinian compromise on this issue and strengthening the hand of those Palestinian elements who favoured participation in the Geneva talks. A meeting in Cairo of the Palestine National Council on June 1–9 adopted a ten-point program for the continuation of the armed struggle, but the question of Palestinian participation in peace talks was barely left open by a decision to meet again "should a fateful decision connected with the future of the Palestinian people arise."

Pres. Richard Nixon's visit to four Arab countries and Israel on June 12–18 symbolized the change in U.S. Middle East policy and the improvement in U.S.-Arab relations. The U.S. restored diplomatic relations with Egypt and Syria. However, it was clear that U.S. aid to the Arabs would stop short of military assistance, and a dangerous Middle East arms buildup continued with the two superpowers supplying opposite sides. President Nixon's visit to Moscow in late June to early July produced no common U.S.-Soviet policy on the Middle East.

On July 18 Jordan and Egypt announced their recognition of the PLO as the legitimate representative of the Palestinians except those living in Jordan. Although this, probably deliberately, failed to say whether Palestinians living in Jordan included those under Israeli occupation on the West Bank, the decision was bitterly attacked by PLO spokesmen and the move failed in its objective of securing a Palestinian-Jordan compromise. In August, Jordan's King Hussein visited the U.S. to put forward his view that Jordanian-Israeli disengagement should precede Geneva peace talks, but this was rejected by Israel and King Hussein's claim to speak for the Palestinians of the West Bank was weakened. Meanwhile, the PLO was making steady progress in its campaign to achieve international recognition. At a meeting in Cairo on September 20–21, Egypt apparently reversed its previous stand by agreeing with Syria and the PLO that the latter should represent all the Palestinians. Jordan's angry response was to freeze all political activity stemming from that decision.

On September 22 the UN General Assembly, overriding strong Israeli objections, included on its agenda for the first time "the Palestine question" as a subject for debate rather than as part of the general question of the Middle East. On October 14, in a historic decision, the assembly invited the PLO to take part in its debate in November on the Palestine question. The voting was 105 in favour, 4 against (including Israel and the U.S.), and 20 abstentions. France and Italy were among Western nations voting in favour. The French foreign minister had the first meeting of any Western statesman with Yasir Arafat, the PLO leader, in Beirut on October 21, and on October 24 the French president said at a press conference that since the Palestinians were now internationally recognized as a people with their own national rights, it was natural that they should aspire to a homeland.

The UN decision had an important effect on the Arab summit meeting held in Rabat, Morocco, on October 26–28. The chief item on the agenda was Palestinian representation at peace talks. Jordan had previously given notice that if other Arab states decided to recognize the PLO as representing the Palestinians of the West Bank it would consider itself released from all responsibility for negotiating an Israeli withdrawal. At Rabat, however, King Hussein came under the combined pressure of all the Arab states to accept the PLO's right to represent the Palestinians in any liberated territory. King Faisal of Saudi Arabia carried special weight with his argument that the Arabs could hardly do less than the UN. Finally, Hussein accepted a resolution which said that any liberated Palestinian territory "should revert to its legitimate Palestinian owners under the leadership of the PLO." It also called for Egypt, Syria, and Jordan to organize their relations in the light of these decisions and established a fighting fund, which was reported to have allocated $1 billion to both Egypt and Syria annually, $300 million to Jordan, and $50 million to the PLO.

The Rabat decision was denounced by the so-called "rejection front," composed of the Popular Front for the Liberation of Palestine (PFLP) of George Habash, the PFLP-General Command, the pro-Iraq Arab Liberation Front, and the Front for the Popular Palestinian Struggle. But although the decision was recognized as enhancing the position of the moderate PLO elements led by Arafat, the U.S. government held the view that it had complicated moves toward a settlement because Israel rejected any possibility of negotiating with the PLO and continued to insist that any

"One thing I've found out about oil . . . it's intoxicating!"

OLIPHANT, THE DENVER POST © 1973 THE LOS ANGELES TIMES SYNDICATE

483

Middle Eastern Affairs

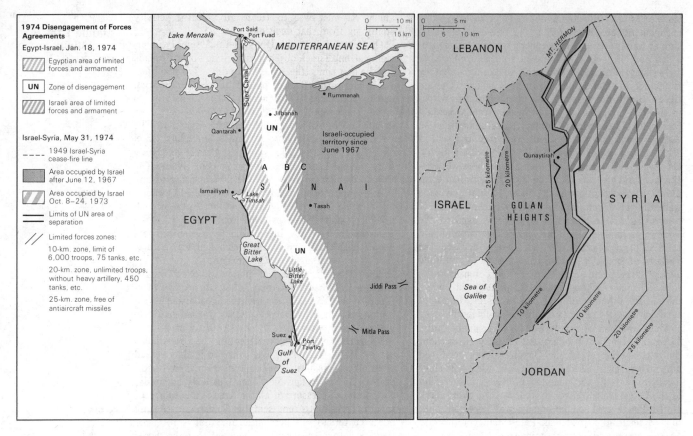

arrangement for the West Bank should be made with King Hussein. The consequence was that Kissinger's next Middle East tour during the first week of November was no more than a sounding-out operation and an attempt to defuse the dangerously tense situation. Israel's line hardened after Rabat, and this allowed the return to the government of the National Religious Party which favoured Israel's retention of the West Bank. Despite Kissinger's assurances, the Israelis were concerned at what they believed might be a change in the U.S. attitude toward the PLO, especially after Pres. Gerald Ford referred to the possibility of Israel-PLO talks at his October 29 press conference. However, when Arafat addressed the UN General Assembly on November 13, there were still no overt indications that the U.S. intended to deal directly with the PLO.

Egyptian diplomacy after the Rabat summit was concentrated on persuading the U.S. to change its attitude toward the PLO and to influence Israel in this direction. However, Kissinger and the Israelis retained the belief that "step-by-step" diplomacy still offered the best prospects and that there were opportunities for a further stage in Egyptian-Israeli disengagement. The difficulty was that while Egypt looked for an additional Israeli military withdrawal in Sinai, Israel was insisting on concessions in return—such as an Egyptian declaration of nonbelligerency, freedom of navigation in the Suez Canal, and an Egyptian withdrawal from the Arab boycott of Israel. Another problem was that Israel was reluctant to give up the Abu Rudeis oil fields on the Gulf of Suez. Although work on clearing the Suez Canal proceeded well enough to make its opening to international shipping technically possible by May 1975, Egyptian Pres. Anwar as-Sadat indicated that he would be unwilling to allow this while the Israelis were still on the shores of the Gulf of Suez.

Inter-Arab Relations. A large measure of the Arab solidarity that was a feature of the October 1973 war and its immediate aftermath was maintained during 1974, as evidenced by the Islamic summit meeting in Lahore, Pak., in February and by the Arab summit in Rabat in October. This spirit of unity was, however, severely tested. The focus was Egypt, which was helped by the new prestige acquired by President Sadat and by its close relations with both Saudi Arabia and Algeria, two key Arab states at opposite ends of the political spectrum. However, Egypt had to deal with Syrian and Palestinian suspicion of its new closer relationship with the U.S. and fears that it was preparing to reach a bilateral settlement with Israel.

For different reasons the odd men out in the Arab world in 1974 were Jordan, Iraq, and Libya. When Jordan found itself isolated over the issue of Palestinian representation, it gave way; King Hussein did not carry out his earlier threat to withdraw from the Arab front, and he set about reorganizing his kingdom to allow for the loss of the West Bank. Iraq maintained its intransigent opposition to a negotiated settlement of the Arab-Israeli dispute and remained highly critical of Syria's and Egypt's acceptance of the cease-fire at the end of the October war. From March onward its Baathist regime was increasingly involved with the uprising of its own Kurdish nationalists. However, its isolation was not total; in August it reached an agreement with Syria over sharing the waters of the Euphrates and with Egypt for joint economic projects worth $2.4 billion.

Libya was unquestionably the most isolated of the Arab states, and during 1974 the Federation of Arab Republics of Egypt, Syria, and Libya virtually ceased to exist. Pres. Muammar al-Qaddafi made a surprise reconciliation visit to Cairo in February and afterward accompanied President Sadat to Saudi Arabia for talks with King Faisal and Pres. Qadi Abdal

Rahman al-Iryani of the Yemen Arab Republic. But Libya soon resumed its bitter criticisms of Egypt, and relations deteriorated sharply after Egypt accused Libya of promoting violent sabotage attempts inside Egypt. In contrast, Egypt moved closer to Sudan. Pres. Gaafar Nimeiry of Sudan paid a friendly visit to Cairo on February 11–12 and agreed on a program of political and economic integration of the two countries. In the new Egyptian government formed on April 25 a minister of Sudanese affairs replaced the former minister of Libyan affairs.

The Joint Arab Defense Council held an emergency meeting in Cairo on July 3–4 at Kuwait's request to discuss support for Lebanon and the Palestinians and made some secret decisions, but nothing positive emerged as Lebanon rejected the help of Arab troops. In May Syria called for an urgent Arab summit to discuss the Arab-Israeli situation. This was fixed for September but in July was postponed to the end of October at Jordan's request. When the summit was held at Rabat, it achieved its main objective of clarifying the Palestinian-Jordanian situation, but the possibilities of bringing about real cooperation between Jordan and the PLO seemed doubtful.

Arab-Foreign Relations. During 1974 there was a marked improvement in Arab-U.S. relations in general, although some Arab states such as Syria remained skeptical that there had been any real change in U.S. policy and others such as Libya and Iraq remained hostile. In March the Arab oil-producing nations decided to lift their embargo on the U.S., with Syria and Libya dissenting. The embargo on The Netherlands was retained until July. In September Arab-U.S. relations were again under a strain as a result of speeches by President Ford and Kissinger that blamed the Arabs for high oil prices and appeared to threaten reprisals if the Arabs were to resume the embargo. During the year the Saudis repeatedly made clear their view that there was a connection between oil supplies and progress toward a satisfactory peace settlement.

There were also signs in the autumn of a thaw in Egyptian-Soviet relations, which was at least partly due to Egypt's need for arms and U.S. promises of large-scale military aid to Israel. However, Sadat made clear on Kissinger's Middle East tour in early November that he still looked to the U.S. as the main factor in helping achieve a Middle East settlement.

Arab-European relations improved during 1974 with France taking the lead in advocating closer ties. In August France announced the lifting of its arms embargo on the Middle East belligerent states, after Egypt had revealed that Libyan Mirages were now in Egypt. This move was welcomed by the Arabs and deplored by Israel. However, reports of immediate Mirage sales to Egypt were denied by France.

On the crucial question of oil pricing, Saudi Arabia was more responsive to the Western desire for cuts than were other oil states such as Algeria, Iraq, or Iran, but it refrained from taking unilateral action. The problem of the rapidly increasing financial reserves of the Middle East oil states, their potential effect on the international monetary system, and the need to recycle the surplus funds was a question of major interest in 1974. Against a background of protests that the Arab states were not doing enough to compensate the less developed nations for rising oil prices, the Arab heads of state decided at Rabat to expand Arab aid to Africa. (PETER MANSFIELD)

See also Energy; articles on the various political units. [978.B]

Migration, International

In 1974 it seemed likely that the energy crisis would have a range of long-term effects on the patterns of world migration. The crisis contributed to the slowing of economic growth and increasing unemployment in industrialized countries, with consequent restrictions on migrant labour and a rise in anti-immigrant sentiment, even though nationals might prefer unemployment (or emigration) to undertaking certain unskilled and disagreeable jobs long performed by migrants.

This was unfavourable to the activities of Patrick Hillery, EEC commissioner for social affairs, who in 1973 undertook to draw up a plan to promote equal living and working conditions for all workers, including migrants and their families, in EEC countries. The EEC Commission's plan was increasingly geared to "long-term" problems, but remained firm on illegal immigration, estimated to provide 10% of the EEC's foreign labour force. Some workers came in with valid permits but stayed illegally after these had expired. Others, arriving illegally and without documents, were especially exposed to abuse. No statistics were available for the numbers of migrants who had gone home as a result of the recession. Italy, as the major labour-exporting member of the EEC, was in a stronger position than other EEC countries to monitor emigration, layoffs, and returns of its nationals.

West Germany, with an estimated 3.5 million migrant workers and their families, mainly from Italy, Turkey, Yugoslavia, and Spain, was the first to introduce definite curbs by suspending nearly all immigration on Nov. 23, 1973. This was linked with a decision

Immigration and Naturalization in the United States

Year ended June 30, 1974

Country or region	Total immigrants admitted	Quota immigrants	Nonquota immigrants Total	Nonquota immigrants Family— U.S. citizens	Aliens naturalized
Africa	6,182	4,242	1,940	1,765	1,591
Asia*	130,662	89,243	41,419	35,019	37,780
China†	18,056	14,376	3,680	3,354	8,692
Hong Kong	4,629	3,991	638	532	...
India	12,779	11,733	1,046	812	1,636
Iran	2,608	1,560	1,048	1,038	562
Iraq	2,281	2,066	215	202	510
Japan	4,860	2,003	2,857	2,394	1,591
Jordan	2,838	2,332	506	470	1,157
Korea, South	28,028	19,659	8,369	5,977	4,451
Lebanon	2,400	1,830	570	529	574
Philippines	32,857	19,281	13,576	12,528	13,573
Thailand	4,956	1,460	3,496	3,156	355
Vietnam, South	3,192	283	2,909	1,870	936
Europe‡	81,212	58,813	22,399	19,797	48,014
Germany, West	6,320	1,614	4,706	4,148	5,785
Greece	10,824	8,617	2,207	2,026	5,551
Italy	15,884	13,235	2,649	2,401	8,898
Poland	4,033	3,083	950	849	3,198
Portugal	11,302	10,247	1,055	957	3,326
Spain	3,390	2,342	1,048	876	940
United Kingdom	10,710	5,854	4,856	4,329	8,554
Yugoslavia	5,817	5,280	537	496	2,479
North America	151,444	105,835	45,609	39,619	36,050
Canada	7,654	3,531	4,123	3,337	4,084
Cuba	18,929	17,583	1,346	357	18,394
Dominican Republic	15,680	11,924	3,756	3,508	1,430
El Salvador	2,278	1,546	732	704	342
Haiti	3,946	3,292	654	621	1,486
Jamaica	12,408	10,442	1,966	1,796	1,533
Mexico	71,586	45,247	26,339	22,952	5,206
Trinidad and Tobago	6,516	5,274	1,242	1,177	699
Oceania	3,052	1,882	1,170	1,018	544
South America	22,307	14,114	8,193	7,624	6,579
Argentina	2,077	1,385	692	597	1,433
Colombia	5,837	3,280	2,557	2,401	1,486
Ecuador	4,795	3,486	1,309	1,260	862
Guyana	3,241	2,637	604	565	420
Total, including others	394,861	274,131	120,730	104,844	131,655

Note: Immigrants listed by country of birth; aliens naturalized by country of former allegiance.
*Includes Turkey. †Taiwan and People's Republic. ‡Includes U.S.S.R.
Source: U.S. Department of Justice, Immigration and Naturalization Service, *1974 Annual Report.*

A Swiss woman votes
in Lugano on an initiative
question, called
for by the National Action
Party, on whether
to reduce the number
of foreign residents
in Switzerland from about
one million to half
that number. The vote
was approximately
60% "no."

to reduce economic growth and combat extra inflation that might result from decreased immigration.

In The Netherlands, where ethnic and racial tensions continued to simmer, particularly in relation to Turks and also Dutch West Indians from Surinam with unrestricted entry, a government memorandum proposed that The Netherlands could not continue to foster its own industrial growth at the expense of less developed countries, and that some of its industries should be aided to move to the third world. The government shortened the list of countries from which foreign workers would be accepted and offered a departure grant to foreign workers returning home after three years.

In France the National Immigration Office (ONI) announced that nearly 350,000 migrants were admitted in 1973, 275,000 of them as workers and the rest as family members. The 132,000 permanent workers admitted included 32,000 Portuguese and 25,000 Moroccans. After outbursts of xenophobia and violence against Algerians, particularly in 1972–73, the Algerian government suspended emigration to France in September 1973 (there were already some 845,000 Algerians in France). In July 1974 André Postel-Vinay, secretary of state for immigrant workers' affairs, resigned because the new government refused to grant more money for the housing needs of France's migrant worker population.

Most Western European receiving countries (Britain, Sweden, The Netherlands, and Belgium excepted) regarded migrant workers as temporary single entities and had no adequate social provisions for them and their families. In Switzerland over 275,000 of the country's 900,000 migrant workers (more than half of them Italian) in 1973 had reached the "establishment permit" phase, and family reunions were increasing. With the highest proportion of migrant workers in Western Europe, Switzerland employed them in the more conservative and xenophobic German-speaking cantons. The hostility toward foreigners expressed in the narrowly lost referendum over the Schwarzenbach initiative of 1970, aiming to reduce the number of foreign residents, came to the fore again with a more extreme initiative. This proposed inter alia to limit naturalizations each year to 4,000 and to reduce the number of foreigners in Switzerland (exclusive of seasonal and border workers) by 1978 from 1.1 million to 500,000 and in any canton (except Geneva) to a maximum of 12% of the Swiss population. At the referendum on October 20, the proposal was more decisively rejected than in 1970, by 1,689,-870 votes to 878,739.

In April, Britain offered an amnesty to illegal Commonwealth or Pakistani immigrants who had entered the country before January 1973. A report by the European Commission on Human Rights published in May condemned the terms of entry into Britain under the 1971 Immigration Act of Asians from Africa holding U.K. passports. In August the act was modified to permit entry of immigrants' husbands and fiancés.

Controls were tightened in 1974 in Canada and the U.S. For the year ended June 30, 1974, the U.S. intake of 395,000 persons was a postwar figure bettered only in 1968 and 1973. Most of the immigrants came from Asia (130,662) and Mexico (71,586), the European intake being 81,212. (*See* Table.) The total intake for the period 1946–74 was 8,051,630. Late in 1974, however, Attorney General William Saxbe spoke of a total of up to 12 million illegal aliens living in the country, and the possibility of opening up new

jobs for U.S. citizens by the extension of the immigration services to locate and remove illegal aliens.

During 1946–73 Canada took in a total of 3,842,963 immigrants, including over one million British, with Italians and West Germans in second and third place. Following a shift in immigration policy to admit "skilled" workers according to a point system, the number of Asians, particularly Chinese, Indians, and Filipinos, increased. In 1974, however, the minister of manpower and immigration, Robert Andras, announced that in view of the "uncertain" employment situation, housing shortages, and strained social services, the point system would be modified so that many immigrants would in future have to have secure jobs waiting for them or be willing to go where their skills were needed, frequently in remote areas. Immigration had nearly doubled from 122,000 in 1972 to an estimated 225,000 in 1974. The curbs would cut the 1975 totals back to 200,000 instead of an expected 250,000.

Australia received 107,401 settlers in 1972–73, down from a peak of 185,099 in 1969–70. About 48,500 of these were British and the great majority still came from European countries despite continuing moves away from the former "white Australia" policy. In October the Australian government announced the temporary suspension for one year of its immigration program (with some exceptions) to ease the unemployment situation. New Zealand had earlier decided to end free entry for British and other Commonwealth passport holders of European origin (except Australians) because of a housing shortage and economic uncertainties.　　　　　　　　　　　(SHEILA PATTERSON)

See also Race Relations; Refugees.
[525.A.1.c]

Mining and Quarrying

Mining company earnings in the first half of 1974 reached record levels, many being 50% higher than for the same period in 1973. Metal and mineral commodity prices also rose to record levels and were the main reason for the high corporate earnings.

The year began with an energy shortage, of both fuels and electricity. In some cases, mining operations had to be curtailed. However, by midyear there was an adequate supply of petroleum, though at higher prices. During the height of the energy shortage, U.S. government officials began to renew warnings that there would be mineral shortages as a result both of growing industrialization throughout the world and of restrictive policies with respect to land use and environmental protection.

Cost inflation during the year was at unprecedented levels. This created disquiet among labour forces, which resulted in some strikes and unusually costly contract settlements when labour contracts fell due.

Industry Developments. In Michigan and Minnesota seven new iron-ore projects were begun, and there were some expansions that were expected to increase pellet capacity by approximately 50%, to a total of about 80 million tons per year by 1978. The first two of these new facilities, the Tilden project and the Empire expansion of Cleveland-Cliffs Mining Co., both in Michigan, came into production in 1974. The seven new facilities were expected to approximately double the capital investment in taconite plants in Michigan and Minnesota.

Natural iron-ore mines were diminishing in numbers

Military Affairs:
see Defense

due to the exhaustion of reserves. The high demand for ore created temporary activity in the extraction of small pockets of ore left in the large pits.

In Arizona, the principal copper-producing state of the U.S., new developments included the commencement of operations at Cities Service's Pinto Valley mine near Miami, which could produce 40,000 tons per day of ore. Magma Copper Co. began development to increase capacity at the underground San Manuel, Ariz., mine from 62,500 to 75,000 tons per day, making it the world's largest underground nonferrous metal mine. Anamax Mining Co. began building an oxide treatment plant at Twin Buttes, Ariz., and studying an expansion of its sulfide plant there. Phelps Dodge's Metcalf mine was to be completed early in 1975 at a cost of nearly $200 million and would add 60,000 tons per year of copper production. The Anaconda Co. announced plans to develop the Carr Fork mine situated east of Tooele, Utah, at an estimated cost of $135 million. This was a noteworthy development, being a new underground operation situated from 2,000 to 5,000 ft. below the surface.

As in previous years, the copper industry continued to make improvements in environmental quality relating to mining and processing operations. In particular, Anaconda's chemical process for converting copper concentrates to electrolytic copper was scheduled to become operational during the year. The process generated no air pollution. At Hidalgo, N.M., the first flash smelter in the U.S. neared completion. This $200 million installation was designed to meet air pollution requirements. At Inspiration, Ariz., the state's first electric furnace copper smelting plant went into operation. This project embraced extensive new facilities designed to meet air pollution statutes.

Because of the energy crisis, the coal industry received great impetus in the development of new mines, in both the eastern and western fields. The U.S. Bureau of Mines reexamined coal resources data and stated that the U.S. reserve figure was 1.6 trillion tons situated less than 3,000 ft. beneath the surface. More than half were in the western states.

Studies of coal gasification and liquefaction continued, but no large-scale commercial plants were under construction. Western Coal Gasification Co. made the most progress with its plan to mine and gasify coal on the Navajo reservation in New Mexico, but this project was delayed pending satisfactory resolution of its environmental impact and Federal Power Commission approval.

The construction of the first commercial oil shale mine and plant was announced in January by Colony Development Operation. In October, the company said that work had to be suspended indefinitely because of inflated costs, environmental problems, and the absence of a national energy policy. The company stated in October that the estimated construction cost had risen 40% in the past six months.

The shortage of zinc smelting capacity in the U.S. showed signs of being alleviated during the year. Because of the pollution it generated and antiquated technology, zinc smelting, which had a capacity of 1.4 million tons per year in the late 1960s, had diminished by 1974 to 600,000 tons per year. American Smelting and Refining Co. approved engineering work for a new smelter at Stephensport, Ky., estimated to cost $160 million and capable of producing 180,000 tons per year of metal. New Jersey Zinc Co. began receiving bids to build a 160,000-tons-per-year smelter at Clarksville, Tenn.

Elsewhere, the trend continued toward local government participation and/or control of enterprises involving minerals. New projects were usually developed on a multinational basis.

Numerous ventures were either in progress or being intensively studied in Africa. In Zaire a consortium led by Charter Consolidated Ltd. was developing a high-grade copper-cobalt deposit on the Tenke Fungurume concessions. Iron ore and, secondarily, bauxite were the targets of activity in Ivory Coast, Guinea, Liberia, and Sierra Leone. In South Africa a wide variety of mineral deposits were under development with gold leading the way.

In South America mining opportunities began to improve in Chile when the Ministry of Economy, Development, and Reconstruction issued Decree-Law No. 600, which clarified regulations and provided guarantees needed to encourage investment. The fact that Chile negotiated a settlement with Anaconda for its expropriated mines and was in the process of doing so with Kennecott Copper Corp. was encouraging. Chile has several important mineral deposits, which, it could be anticipated, would be developed with the help of foreign sources in the near future.

Minero Peru, the government-owned mining development company, was developing the former Anaconda oxide copper deposit, Cerro Verde. Development plans were being augmented to accommodate the large sulfide reserves found underlying the oxide ore. The Cuajone Project of the Southern Peru Copper Co., which was more than 50% finished in 1974, completed its financing during the year. The junta government frankly stated that, although its ultimate goal was complete ownership of mineral resources companies by the people of Peru, agreements now being made with foreign private companies were completely reliable. Meanwhile, Venezuela set the date for nationalization of iron-mining concessions owned by Bethlehem and U.S. Steel for early 1975.

Brazil, viewed by the international community as a favourable place for investment, surged ahead with large new mineral developments in iron ore and bauxite. Amazonia Mineração, S.A., was planning the world's largest iron-ore project, based on an initial production rate of 10 million tons per year. The deposits are in the Amazon River drainage area, previously unknown for iron development, and at 17,800,000,000 tons were the largest known. The project was

The huge and ever growing demand for coal by such energy producers as Wyoming's Jim Bridger power plant, whose conveyor belt (below) carries an endless stream of fuel, threatens to overwhelm social, economic, and ecological considerations in the vast and easily stripped coalfields of the Northern Plains, typified by an already working mine at Gillette, Mont. (bottom).

TOP, WIDE WORLD; BOTTOM, GARY GUISINGER—THE NEW YORK TIMES

owned by U.S. Steel Corp. and the Brazilian government company, Vale do Rio Doce.

In Guyana, the taxes on bauxite were raised drastically, and the Reynolds Metals Co. was on the verge of following the Demerara Bauxite Co. into nationalization. Jamaica's Bauxite Act of 1974 boosted taxes and royalties by more than 700% for six North American firms. In so doing, the country violated long-term contracts. In Surinam and the Dominican Republic, there were also movements for establishing higher levies on bauxite production. The U.S. depended on imports of bauxite, but the increased taxes stimulated interest in domestic low-grade sources.

Canada fell into disrepute among investors because of discriminatory excess profits taxation policies established by some of the provinces, notably British Columbia. That province had experienced a dozen years of a mining boom, but in 1974 exploration work was at a standstill. The Yukon, the Maritime Provinces, and James Bay in the Northwest Territories were achieving good exploration results, but these were relatively small developments. Similarly, Australia was failing to attract new venture capital because of restrictive policies. However, Freeport Minerals' large lateritic nickel-cobalt mine and plant at Greenvale, Queensland, began production during the year.

Technological Developments. Each year brings refinements to machinery and methods that reduce the cost, increase the safety, and improve both underground and open-pit mining operations. For a number of years innovations centred mainly on bigger equipment. By 1974, however, this trend had reached a plateau, and improvements were being made in the mechanics of the equipment.

In open-pit mining the application of rotary drilling was increasing, though a market remained for rotary-percussion drilling and jet piercing. One manufacturer produced an automated drill that could handle 60-ft. pipe for one-pass drilling. The automation of the drilling process was becoming increasingly accepted, and large-capacity hydraulic shovels powered by diesel engines were introduced.

In underground mining much ingenuity was exercised to utilize load-haul-dump units in conjunction with such traditional mining systems as cut-and-fill, undercut-and-fill, shrinkage, caving, and blast-hole stopping. These wheeled, trackless vehicles greatly improved production per man-shift. Swedish manufacturers created many improvements in underground mining equipment and began automating underground rock drills.

International Nickel Co., at Sudbury, Ont., introduced bench drilling and blasting underground to increase productivity. Devices for mechanizing the loading of explosives were introduced. These included vehicles that mixed in transit, and centralized stations from which the blasting agent could be piped to the blast holes by pneumatic force or pumped in slurry.

Much instrumentation was being used for such services as measuring drill holes for depth or obstructions, indicating belt conveyor slip, monitoring mine air continuously for various constituents, and sampling dust. Advances were made in surveying with the introduction of a variety of lightweight measuring devices with direct reading features for determining distance, height differential, and slope.

The UN conference in Venezuela from June through August, which included attempts at establishing international laws to govern mining in the ocean, made no significant progress. (*See* Law: *Special Report*.) However, large-scale experiments in mining nodules from the ocean floor by at least six separate groups were under way.   (JOHN VALENTINE BEALL)

Production. World mineral production increased significantly in 1973, the latest year for which reasonably complete figures were available. Output generally continued high through most of 1974, until recessionary pressures caused production cutbacks in some minerals, such as copper and aluminum, toward the year's end. In at least a few cases, however, producers utilized weakening demand as an opportunity to rebuild their stockpiles, which had been reduced below normal levels. Many mineral producers appeared to be taking a long-term position that viewed the economic weakness of 1974 as a temporary slackening of the inexorable growth in world demand for minerals. Consequently, overall exploration activity remained strong.

Inflation affected mine operations and development in 1974. The cost of all components of production rose drastically during the year. New projects were hard hit because heavy equipment, which has a manufacturing lead time of up to two years, was only being sold with the price to be set at time of delivery. Under such conditions, the final cost of a major new project could be more than double the original estimate. Inflation also affected the price of minerals but not, in many cases, as much as did high demand relative to productive capacity, which resulted in a number of shortages that existed until recession weakened demand late in 1974.

Another factor expected to affect mineral output was the recent move by governments of important mineral-producing countries, particularly the less developed nations, to form cartels in emulation of the Organization of Petroleum Exporting Countries (OPEC). A bauxite group was formed in 1974, and preliminary talks were held involving other commodities, including iron ore, silver, tungsten, and zinc. (*See* COMMODITY TRADE: *Special Report*.)

Of the minerals for which 1973 world production data were available, output of 58 increased an average 7.5% (ranging from 0.2% for magnesite to 54.5% for columbite/tantalite) and output of 19 declined by an average 3.8% (12.6% for monazite to less than 0.1% for industrial diamonds). The U.S. was the largest producer of 32 minerals; the Soviet Union led in 14, and Canada and Japan in 5 each. More than 90% of the world's mineral production (except coal) originated from 1,069 large open-pit and underground mines. These mines were owned by 106 companies and produced 22 minerals. The remaining production came from more than 6,000 known small mines and included the other commercial minerals, ranging from sand and gravel to gemstones and yttrium.

Aluminum. World output of bauxite, the primary ore of aluminum, rose 8.6% to 70.7 million metric tons in 1973. For the second year, Australia (17.8 million tons) led, followed by Jamaica (13.6 million) and Surinam (8.1 million). Aluminum production rose 10.1% to 69.3 million metric tons with no change in rankings: U.S. 4.1 million metric tons, U.S.S.R. 1.4 million, and Japan 1.1 million. The aluminum shortage that developed late in 1972 continued to the last quarter of 1974 and raised the producer price to 39 cents per pound by September 1974, from 29 cents in January.

Antimony. World antimony production in 1973 rose by about 5%, to an estimated total of 71,350 metric tons. The major producers were South Africa (16,000 tons), Bolivia (14,719 tons), China, and the Soviet Union (estimated, respectively, at about 12,000 and 7,000 tons). Output in the U.S. was only about 590 tons, since four months of 1973 production were lost at the Sunshine Mine following a fire in 1972 (the mine normally accounts for 80% of U.S. mine production). Prices in U.S. markets averaged about 48% of the record price levels of 1970.

Asbestos. Despite increasing worldwide attention to the potential health hazards of asbestos, to both mining and industrial processing workers, world production increased by 10.5%, from 3,774,000 metric tons in 1972 to an estimated 4,171,000 tons in 1973. The leading producers were virtually unchanged, except that Canada widened its lead over the Soviet Union slightly (1,791,000 tons and 1,280,000 tons, respectively); most of the remaining production occurred in South Africa (325,000 tons), China (210,000 tons), and Italy (149,000 tons).

Cement. World cement production in 1973 increased about 8.8% over 1972, to 687 million metric tons. The Soviet Union was the world leader with an estimated 109.4 million tons, followed by Japan (78 million tons), the U.S. (74.2 million tons), West Germany (41 million tons), Italy (36 million tons), and France (30.7 million tons). The increase in production reflected strong demand worldwide, although India, Asia's second leading producer, sought to create an export market because utilization of production capacity was only about 61%.

Chromium. World output of chromite rose 7.6% in 1973, to 6.8 million metric tons. The Soviet Union was the leading producer (1.9 million tons), followed by South Africa (1.6 million) and Albania (700,000), which supplanted Turkey in third place. Chromite ore and metal prices rose slowly during 1974. U.S. electrolytic metal went from $1.53 per pound in January to $2.30 at the year's end. Turkish and Rhodesian ore prices also rose.

Cobalt. World mine production of cobalt rose by an estimated 9.6%, to a total of about 25,500 metric tons over the 23,265 tons of 1972. Zaire was the single most important producer (about 55% of the world total) at 14,000 tons; following it were Zambia (2,100 tons), Canada (1,790 tons), Morocco (1,000 tons), and Australia (900 tons). Consumption in the U.S., the leading consumer, rose by about 33%, exceeding the previous high year, 1969, by about 20%. A potentially significant use of cobalt in separating nitrogen and sulfur compounds from shale oil was announced by the U.S. Bureau of Mines.

Copper. In 1973 world output of mine copper increased 7.1%, to 7.2 million metric tons; smelter output rose 6.9%, to 7.1 million tons; and refined increased 3.8%, to 7.3 million tons. The U.S. led in all three categories (mine 1.6 million tons, smelter 1.6 million, refined 1.7 million). Canada (800,000) and Chile (700,000) were second and third in mine output. For both smelted and refined copper, Japan (smelted 800,000, refined 950,000 tons) was second, followed by the U.S.S.R. (smelted 700,000, refined 700,000). Demand for copper remained strong until late in 1974. On the London Metal Exchange, for example, the price of copper reached an all-time high of $1.52 per pound on April 1, 1974, but by late September it had fallen briefly below 60 cents, and it hovered around that level for the rest of the year. Several companies announced reductions of output in the latter part of 1974.

Diamonds. World diamond output fell slightly in 1973; industrial diamonds by less than 0.1%, to 31.2 million carats, and gems by 0.5%, to 12.6 million. Zaire led in the production of industrial stones (11.6 million carats), followed by the U.S.S.R. (7.6 million) and South Africa (4.1 million). South Africa was first in gem production (3.4 million carats), with the U.S.S.R. second (1.9 million) and Angola third (1.6 million). The market in 1974 was weak.

Gold. The decline in world gold production continued in 1973, down 3.7% to 43.1 million troy ounces. There was no change in rank among the largest producers: South Africa 27.5 million troy ounces, U.S.S.R. 7.1 million, and Canada 1.9 million. Beginning April 3, 1974, the price of gold (London final) set several new records, finally reaching $190.50 per troy ounce on November 18. Construction on the Western Hemisphere's largest gold mine, Pueblo Viejo in the Dominican Republic, neared completion, and a number of other new mines, mostly small, were under development in various countries. In August U.S. Pres. Gerald Ford signed a bill permitting U.S. citizens to own gold beginning December 31.

Iron and Steel. During 1973 world output of iron ore rose 10.7%, to 862.9 million metric tons; production of pig iron was up 10.6%, to 504.3 million tons, and raw steel was up 10.6%, to 694.8 million tons. The Soviet Union led in production of both iron ore (215.9 million tons) and pig iron (94.9 million), followed by the U.S. (iron ore 89 million, pig iron 91.6 million). Australia was again third in ore (84.7 million) and Japan in both pig iron (90 million) and steel (119.3 million). Steel was in short supply during 1973, but demand began to decline quite rapidly late in the year.

Lead. World mine output of lead was virtually unchanged as against 1972, with preliminary estimates for the year showing a total production of about 3,430,000 metric tons. The two major producers were the U.S. and the Soviet Union, each producing about 550,000 tons, followed by Australia (400,000 tons), Canada (350,050 tons), and Peru (about 200,000 tons). A strong U.S. market and increased demand elsewhere in the world yielded a significant increase (more than 10%) in world consumption, with the U.S., the leading consumer, increasing its use by almost 14%. Lead prices in the U.S. reached their highest levels since 1952.

Magnesium. World production of magnesium (metal content of ores) was estimated to have increased by only about 1.1% over 1972, to a total (in 1973) of about 233,000 metric tons. The leading producer was the U.S. (111,000 tons), followed by the Soviet Union (52,000 tons), Norway (37,500

tons), and Japan (12,000 tons). World demand exceeded production by about 15%, with most of the deficit being supplied from U.S. strategic stockpiles or current inventories.

Manganese. World mine production of manganese ore rose slightly according to preliminary figures to a total in 1973 of 21.3 million metric tons. The leading producer was thought to be the Soviet Union (7 million tons), followed by South Africa (about 3,450,000 tons), Gabon (2.1 million tons), Brazil (1.8 million tons), and India (1.6 million tons). Much exploration and technological investment was connected with determining the feasibility of exploiting submarine deposits of manganese nodules and associated metals.

Mercury. The decline in world production of mercury continued in 1973, although its magnitude diminished from 6.5 to 0.5% according to preliminary figures. Total production was estimated to amount to 276,200 flasks (of 76 lb. [34.5 kg.] each) in 1973. Spain continued to lead producers with 60,000 flasks, followed by the Soviet Union (52,000 flasks), Italy (32,300 flasks), Mexico (28,000 flasks), and China (an estimated 26,000 flasks). The U.S., until the late 1960s a major producer with almost 30,000 flasks a year, declined to about 2,200 flasks in 1973.

Molybdenum. World mine production rose slightly (less than 3%, according to preliminary figures) in 1973 to a total of 81,650 metric tons. The U.S. continued to be the primary producer, with 48,612 tons (almost 60% of world production), even though domestic production declined by 4.3%; other leading producers were Canada (12,451 tons), the Soviet Union (8,150 tons), and Chile (4,500 tons). Exports from the U.S. were at record high levels in 1973.

Nickel. In 1973 world mine production of nickel increased 4%, to 660,000 metric tons, and smelter production rose by 10.9%, to 670,000 tons, in response to strong demand that continued through most of 1974. The largest mine producers were Canada (241,200 tons), U.S.S.R. (125,000), and New Caledonia (100,000). The leading smelters were Canada (160,000 tons), the Soviet Union (125,000), and Japan (80,000). During 1974 the large new Surigao nickel project went into production in the Philippines. Tight supplies in 1974 helped increase the producer cathode price from $1.62 to $1.85 per pound in May 1974. A later rise to $2.05 per pound in December was expected to fall again because of the lessened demand for stainless steel and, thus, for nickel.

Phosphate. World output of phosphate rock gained 9.2% in 1973, to 98 million metric tons. The U.S. produced 38.2 million, the Soviet Union 21.2 million, and Morocco 16.6 million. The long period of oversupply turned to shortage in 1973–74. In 1974 a number of new phosphate mining projects were announced in various parts of the world (U.S., Australia, Peru), and prices tripled to over $60 per ton.

Platinum Group Metals. During 1973 world production of the platinum metals was estimated to have increased by only about 1%, to a total of about 4,313,000 troy ounces. Virtually all of world production was divided among three countries: the Soviet Union (with an estimated 2,450,000 troy ounces), South Africa (1.5 million ounces), and Canada (288,000 ounces). Imports of refined metals into the U.S., the major consumer, increased markedly, by about 28%, to a total of 2,256,000 ounces; platinum and palladium comprised the bulk of this, both nearly doubling since 1970, while ruthenium increased nearly ninefold. Much of the increased demand in the U.S. could be attributed to the manufacture of catalytic automobile exhaust systems.

Potash. World potash production rose in 1973 by 7.6%, to 21,960,000 tons, in response to strengthening demand. The leading producers were the U.S.S.R. (5.7 million metric tons), Canada (4 million), and West Germany (3 million). Programs for the exploration and development of new mines were well advanced in 1974. Prices strengthened, rising from £19–£23 per ton to £25–£30 in August. The Canadian mines, in Saskatchewan, operated at full capacity in 1974 for the first time since mandatory provincial production and price controls were imposed in 1970. Also in 1974, the provincial government announced new taxes on potash and that it would hold majority ownership in any expansions and full ownership in any new mines to be developed. This brought new activity to the New Mexico potash area, which had been losing markets to the Canadians.

Silver. World mine production of silver rose by 0.9%, according to preliminary figures, to a total in 1973 of 292.8 million troy ounces. Canada was the world leader (48,843,000 ounces), followed by the Soviet Union (thought to be about 41 million ounces), Mexico (38,788,000 ounces), the U.S. (37,233,000 ounces), and Peru (34,257,000 ounces). Handy & Harman estimated world consumption in 1973 to have exceeded mine output by 70%, with the deficit made up from stocks of principal producers and consumers; this increase was estimated to amount to an 18% increase over 1972. Part of the increased consumption could be attributed to consumer and investor uncertainty about paper currencies, especially in the U.S., where the largest increase in any use category was for commemorative and collector silver. The reopening of the Sunshine Mine after a 1972 fire contributed to a substantial recovery of U.S. production.

Sulfur. World production of sulfur in all forms rose 2.7% in 1973, according to preliminary figures, to a total of 26.9 million metric tons. This consisted of approximately 50% elemental recovered sulfur (mostly from natural and industrial gases), 42% native Frasch sulfur (obtained by melting subsurface deposits), and 8% native ores. The leading producer was the U.S., with about 10,182,000 tons from all sources, about 70% Frasch; other major producers were Canada (5,372,000 tons, recovered), Poland (3,545,000 tons, mostly Frasch), and France (1,753,000 tons, recovered). Because domestic U.S. consumption and overseas markets could not absorb the potential production of the U.S. industry, there was a substantial oversupply.

Tin. World mine production of tin declined by more than 5%, from a 1972 total (excluding certain socialist countries) of 195,300 metric tons to 185,300 tons in 1973, and preliminary data for the first half of 1974 indicated a continued decline, with an indicated annual rate of only 181,700 tons for the year. The major producer was Malaysia (72,260 tons), followed by Bolivia (28,570 tons), Indonesia (22,500 tons), Thailand (20,920 tons), and Australia (10,630 tons). Although authoritative data were not available, the production of the Soviet Union was thought to be about 28,000 tons. Producers were generally dissatisfied with the results of 1973 and early 1974 because they did not believe that increased production costs were being returned to them in prices received in world markets. In October 1974 the fourth World Tin Conference was held in Malaysia, bringing together major producers, consumers, and technologists concerned with tin. Producers were told that the future position of tin in world consumption patterns was unlikely to decline and, indeed, in some major uses, such as food canning (especially in the U.S.), might rise by as much as 33% by 1976.

Tungsten. World mine production of tungsten contained in ores rose about 5% during 1973, to a total of about 40,400 metric tons. The two leading producers were thought to be the Soviet Union and China (estimated at about 7,200 and 7,000 tons in 1973, although neither figure was known with certainty); following them were the United States (3,200 tons), Canada (2,628 tons), Thailand (2,500 tons), and Bolivia (2,311 tons). Consumption in the U.S., the major consumer, increased by nearly 10%.

Uranium. Output of uranium oxide in non-Communist countries declined slightly (0.5%) in 1973, to 23,120 metric tons, largely because of a decline in South African production attributable to low prices. The leading producers were the U.S. (12,006 metric tons), Canada (4,354 tons), and South Africa (3,094 tons). Exploration continued strong through 1974, and construction of several new projects was begun. In 1974 uranium prices began to rise. The U.S. spot price for uranium oxide (based on actual sales) was about $7.50 per pound in December 1973. By June 1974 it was $10.50, and at the end of November it had passed $14.50. Prices for future deliveries were even higher; November contracts for 1976 delivery were quoted at $17.15 per pound.

Zinc. World mine production of zinc rose to an estimated total of 5,481,000 metric tons in 1973, showing a slight (1.6%) increase over 1972. Canada continued to be the leading producer (1,231,500 tons), followed by the Soviet Union (650,000 tons), the U.S. (434,000 tons), Peru (404,000 tons), and Mexico (300,000 tons). World smelter production of refined zinc increased slightly (to a total of 5,371,000 tons), although U.S. production declined by a further 15% from 1972 and in 1973 ranked fourth in the world, after Japan (843,000 tons), the Soviet Union (650,000 tons), and Canada (533,000 tons).   (FRANK H. SKELDING)

See also Earth Sciences; Energy; Industrial Production and Technology; Metallurgy.

[724.B.1.a-b; 724.C.3]

ENCYCLOPÆDIA BRITANNICA FILMS. *Problems of Conservation—Minerals* (1969).

Monaco

A sovereign principality on the northern Mediterranean coast, Monaco is bounded on all land sides by the French département of Alpes-Maritimes. Area: 0.73 sq.mi. (1.89 sq.km.). Pop. (1974 est.): 25,000. Language: French. Religion: predominantly Roman Catholic. Prince, Rainier III; minister of state in 1974, André Saint-Mleux.

The social, cultural, and economic life of the principality was dominated during 1974 by the official celebration of the 25th anniversary of the ascension of Prince Rainier to the throne of Monaco. The two-week official celebration, which began on May 8, was highlighted by a solemn mass celebrated by John Cardinal Krol of the U.S. and a garden party to which all Monegasques over the age of 15 were invited. The prince's wife, Princess Grace, unveiled a bronze bust of him in the new Centenary Gardens.

Arguments continued to be raised concerning the development of the principality. Prince Rainier had always sought to promote light industry to supplement

Prince Rainier of Monaco, Princess Grace (seated), and their children (from left), Princess Caroline, Princess Stephanie, and Prince Albert, photographed on the 25th anniversary of Rainier's reign.

such sources of revenue as tourism and postage stamps. During the year, however, Loews Corp. announced the construction of a new luxury hotel, the Loews Monte Carlo, which would occupy six acres of waterfront in the vicinity of the famed casino. Critics claimed that the principality was rapidly becoming another "Coney Island" and that development must cease or be slowed if the elegance, charm, and beauty of old Monaco were to be preserved.

After years of declining tourist income, the principality had reversed the trend by attracting a younger group of visitors than formerly patronized its beaches and cafes. As a result, the Société des Bains de Mer, the parent corporation for the casino, announced a $2.5 million profit. The firm's stock had risen 40% in two years.

The curator of Monaco's Prehistoric Museum announced the discovery of excellent examples of Magdalenian art in two hitherto unexplored caves along the principality's Mediterranean shore. Monaco declared that it accepted, in principle, the General European Patent System, which was to be created by 1976. Monaco did not sign the treaty, but it agreed to adjust its domestic legislation to conform with the new system.   (ROBERT D. HODGSON)

MONACO

Education. (1970–71) Primary, pupils 1,486, teachers 48; secondary, pupils 2,033, teachers 116; vocational, pupils 416, teachers 28.

Finance. Monetary unit: French franc, with (Sept. 16, 1974) a free rate of Fr. 4.81 to U.S. $1 (Fr. 11.13 = £1 sterling). Budget (1973 est.): revenue Fr. 254.9 million; expenditure Fr. 235.4 million.

Foreign Trade. Included with France. Tourism: visitors (1971) 101,900; gross receipts (1966) U.S. $6.1 million.

Money and Banking

Financial and money markets faced serious adjustment problems in 1974, as monetary authorities sought to cope with rampant inflation, large international imbalances, and, increasingly, a weakening of economic activity.

Though its roots went deeper, the dilemma was worsened from the beginning of the year by the steep rise in international crude-oil prices, which intensified cost inflation and caused structural unemployment as energy-related consumer expenditures fell. Concurrently, the oil-exporting countries amassed external current-account surpluses totaling about $50 billion in 1974, which they invested mainly in the Eurocurrency market, in dollar assets in the U.S., and in sterling assets in London. Since the investment of these funds did not match the borrowing needs of the deficit countries, major problems of financial recycling loomed. The many uncertainties put an end for the time being to efforts to work out an international monetary reform based on stable exchange rates.

The monetary explosion that had accompanied the disintegration of the fixed exchange rate system from 1971 to 1973 was followed in 1974 by growing restraint and a slowing down of monetary expansion. Demand pressures moderated, speculative activities were checked, and international raw-material prices fell. But the filtering through of earlier rises in the prices of foodstuffs, raw materials, and oil, together with a renewed wage spiral as labour attempted to restore real earnings, pushed annual rates of consumer price increases as high as 15–25% in some industrial countries. In the absence of effective wage restraint, direct price controls, where applied, led increasingly to market distortions and a squeeze on profits and had to be abandoned or liberalized. Inflationary sentiment became firmly entrenched.

In these circumstances, monetary restraint drove short-term interest rates to record peaks while long-term rates rose progressively. However, in relation to rates of inflation, interest rates frequently were still not high enough to discourage borrowing. With West Germany a notable exception, there was a further strong expansion of bank credit during much of the year. High interest rates had a disproportionately severe effect on housing finance, while sharp falls in bond and stock prices put serious strains on capital-market financing and weakened the asset structures of businesses and some financial institutions.

Central banks tightened their supervisory practices, particularly in relation to the banks' foreign exchange business, and in some cases developed new facilities for assisting banks in difficulties. The lenders themselves became more risk conscious, and risk premiums on all but the highest quality instruments rose. Late in the year money markets tended to ease, though long-term interest rates were slower to respond. Inflation was still viewed as the principal problem, but several countries took action to sustain activity in weak sectors of their economies and began to ease policy generally.

Imbalances between major industrial countries, some exacerbated by the oil-price increase, became extremely large. Italy and the U.K., which already had sizable external problems, not only recorded extremely high rates of inflation—partly a legacy of previous attempts to avoid the external constraint by allowing currencies to depreciate—but also experienced comparatively rapid rates of monetary expansion. On the other hand, West Germany, which enjoyed a favourable external position and a substantially lower rate of inflation, followed quite restrictive monetary policies. The U.S. was in a somewhat similar position. France and Japan gave priority to moderating inflation and reducing their current external deficits.

To finance oil deficits, countries gave official encouragement to borrowing abroad and sought to expand financing facilities within the International Monetary Fund (IMF), the Organization for Economic Cooperation and Development, and the World Bank, while the members of the Organization of Petroleum Exporting Countries (OPEC) established institutions to assist less developed countries. Little progress was made toward reducing dependence on oil. Moreover, the buildup of countries' indebtedness was not matched by increased investment that might help to service it in future years.

Exchange rates continued to fluctuate widely, influenced by divergences in monetary policies, large international capital market operations, and shifting market appraisals of the effect of the oil crisis and inflation on relative currency values. The dollar depreciated by as much as 20% against European currencies between January and May, then recovered

Table I. Rates of Growth of Money plus Quasi-Money

Country	1972 June	Dec.	1973 June	Dec.	March	1974 June	Sept.
United States	9.3	10.8	10.1	8.4	9.0	8.5	8.4
Canada	16.9	14.5	12.1	19.1	20.3	19.4	20.8
Japan	22.8	24.7	24.7	16.8	15.1	13.3	10.9
United Kingdom	23.3	27.6	23.0	28.2	24.6	20.3	15.5
Belgium	16.3	17.5	15.9	13.5	14.6	10.5	9.8*
France	19.2	18.4	14.1	14.9	16.3	16.5	14.0
Germany, West	13.9	17.0	18.3	14.0	10.3	8.3	4.4
Italy	18.5	22.2	20.7	23.3	23.3	23.4	21.4*
Netherlands, The	12.6	11.9	14.9	21.9	21.4	25.9	22.5

*August.

Table II. Selected Interest Rates

Country		1972 June	1973 June	Sept.	Dec.	1974 March	June	Sept.
Belgium	A	4.00	5.50	6.50	7.75	8.75	8.75	8.75
	B¹	2.00	2.96	5.54	7.18	8.96	9.59	9.42
	C	7.07	7.29	7.71	7.79	8.22	8.78	9.26
France	A	5.75	7.50	11.00	11.00	11.00	13.00	13.00
	B¹	3.85	7.46	9.73	11.14	11.88	13.61	13.74*
	C	7.56	8.36	9.00	9.29	10.69	11.45	11.40*
Germany, West	A	3.00	7.00	7.00	7.00	7.00	7.00	7.00
	B²	2.75	7.00	7.00	7.00	7.00	5.63	5.63
	C	7.90	9.90	9.60	9.60	10.40	10.70	10.70
Italy	A	4.00	4.00	6.50	6.50	9.00	9.00	9.00
	B²	5.54	6.00	9.64	8.85	9.64	11.98	15.62
	C	6.42	6.92	6.88	7.06	7.57	9.33	10.26
Netherlands, The	A	4.00	5.00	6.50	8.00	8.00	8.00	8.00
	B²	1.94	3.72	5.87	6.68	6.25	7.31	7.76
	C	7.25	7.75	8.29	8.82	9.95	10.27
Switzerland	A	3.75	4.50	4.50	4.50	5.50	5.50	5.50
	B¹	1.38	1.29	3.00	4.50	2.94	5.25	2.75
	C	5.06	5.36	5.79	6.31	7.09	7.28	7.41
United Kingdom	A	6.00	7.50†	11.50†	13.00†	12.50†	11.75†	11.50†
	B²	5.64	6.96	10.94	12.42	11.98	11.24	10.98
	C	9.32	10.15	11.55	12.50	13.68	14.38	14.95
United States	A	4.50	6.50	7.50	7.50	7.50	8.00	8.00
	B²	3.91	7.19	8.29	7.45	7.96	7.90	8.06
	C	5.59	6.32	6.42	6.35	6.81	7.03	7.30
Canada	A	4.75	6.25	7.25	7.25	8.75	8.75	9.25
	B²	3.58	5.40	6.41	6.38	6.28	8.68	9.03
	C	7.45	7.74	7.72	7.70	8.19	9.46	9.67
Japan	A	4.25	5.50	7.00	9.00	9.00	9.00	9.00
	B¹	4.39	6.30	8.47	10.22	12.23	12.23	12.75
	C	6.45	7.89	8.66	9.35	11.63	10.99	11.28

A=Central bank's discount rate.
B=Money-market rate.
B¹=Day-to-day money.
B²=90-day Treasury bills; in the case of Italy, one-year bills and from September 1973 6-month bills.
C=Long-term government bond yield.
*August.
†Minimum lending rate as of Oct. 13, 1972.

The Tokyo foreign-exchange market suspended trading on January 21 following the floating of the French franc.

much of this loss during the summer before falling to new lows in the autumn. Exchange trading was disrupted for a time in the summer following the announcement of large foreign exchange losses by major banks, but new clearing arrangements in New York and the introduction of tighter controls by several central banks eased the situation. At times, official intervention to smooth sharp fluctuations in rates was substantial.

Eurocurrency and Eurobond Markets. Eurocurrency market activity recorded a strong upsurge in early 1974, as countries dependent on oil imports hastened to cover anticipated external financing needs. Government and public-sector borrowers in France, Italy, and the U.K. obtained commitments for large syndicated loans totaling nearly $10 billion, and officially encouraged borrowings by Japanese commercial banks expanded sharply. Less developed countries continued to make extensive calls on the market. The market was supplied early in the year by substantial U.S. banking outflows, now freed from controls, and thereafter by the growing surpluses of the oil producers.

Borrowers' needs for long maturities and the OPEC investors' preferences for short-term placements were partly reconciled through medium-term variable-rate loans. By summer maturity transformation risks were increasing, however, and the larger banks used by the OPEC countries were becoming reluctant to accept further sizable single deposits. After a number of banks reported foreign exchange losses, some small banks and banks in countries with poor external payments prospects had to pay premiums for refinancing roll-over loans that were above the London interbank rates on which lending contracts had been based. Interbank lending contracted, and the net flows of funds through the Euromarket slowed. Japanese and Italian banks, in particular, reduced their call on the market. Subsequently, as the OPEC countries diversified their placements and final borrowers accepted higher terms and shorter loan maturities, the market showed renewed moderate expansion.

After the termination of U.S. capital-outflow controls at the end of January, Eurodollar interest rates closely followed U.S. money-market rates until the summer. Then the margin increased, with three-month Eurodollar rates reaching a peak of 14% before easing to $10\frac{1}{8}$% at the end of the year. Inflation, exchange-market uncertainties, and a strong preference for liquidity caused traditional Eurobond issues to fall off sharply. With stock prices depressed, the market for convertible issues dried up.

United States. The aim of monetary policy in 1974 was to reduce inflation gradually by keeping the growth of money, on average, significantly below that of nominal gross national product (GNP). After slowing in the fourth quarter of 1973, overall output declined quite sharply in early 1974. Some basic industries were still experiencing demand pressures, however, and consumer prices, increasingly free of controls, were rising rapidly. Following a slight easing around the turn of the year, monetary restraint was resumed, signaled by an increase from $7\frac{1}{2}$ to 8% in Federal Reserve discount rates in April. Federal taxes also had a restrictive effect, and the government's budget deficit in the year ended June 1974 came to only $3.5 billion, down from an estimated $13 billion. A projected rise in the 1974–75 deficit was more than accounted for by the slowdown in the economy.

Bank reserves and the money supply grew moderately during the spring and slowed down sharply in the summer. Business demand for credit remained strong, however, and banks responded by competing aggressively for funds through sales of certificates of deposit. Short-term market rates rose sharply, and banks' prime lending rates went up from their $8\frac{3}{4}$% March low to 12% in July. This process reduced the flow of funds to savings and loan associations and mutual savings banks. Housing activity fell precipitously, despite large compensatory flows from federal agencies to sustain mortgage lending.

New uncertainty was added late in May with the nonpayment of dividends by Consolidated Edison and the announcement of losses in foreign exchange and bond trading by the Franklin National Bank. The latter experienced a run on deposits and was granted substantial Federal Reserve assistance. Thereafter, higher risk premiums appeared in interest rates on all but the highest quality private debt instruments. To further reassure depositors, Federal Deposit Insurance Corporation coverage for individual depositors was doubled to $40,000 per account in October.

By late summer an accelerated rise in wages and unit costs gave a sharp boost to the inflationary spiral, while spreading unemployment and the decline in security values contributed to general retrenchment in demand. Monetary policy was now eased slightly, bringing considerable relief to financial markets. With business as well as mortgage demand for credit now falling, short-term interest rates declined by over two percentage points from their summer peaks, and banks' prime lending rates fell back to around 10% by the end of December. Long-term rates continued to rise until October, but thereafter they too receded.

Incremental reserve requirements against the banks' issues of large certificates of deposit were removed in two stages in the autumn. In November, partly to help meet seasonal liquidity needs, reserve requirements against sight deposits were lowered and requirements against time deposits were restructured to favour those at six months or more. Cost inflation remained a pressing problem, while fixed investment helped to slow the fall in aggregate demand.

Japan. Reflecting the strong economic upswing in 1973, as well as heavy dependence on imported oil, the early months of 1974 saw a sharp increase in the current external deficit and in the rate of inflation. A tight monetary restraint policy was continued throughout the year. Moreover, the expansion of bank lending was kept well below the rate of inflation by strict quantitative limits. By running down their own foreign currency placements with the banks, the authorities for a time strongly encouraged the banks to borrow abroad. This policy was reversed in June, when it became clear that high Eurocurrency indebtedness was obliging Japanese banks to pay an interest rate premium.

After a steep climb in 1973, money-market interest rates edged up further during 1974. Bank credit expansion and the growth of the money supply slowed sharply, while GNP declined faster and over a longer period than at any time since World War II. The external current account improved sharply during the year, thanks partly to favourable international price trends, but domestic prices continued to rise at a fairly rapid rate. The authorities expected some resumption of growth in 1975, although it might be necessary to keep expansion below the economy's potential for some time to come.

Canada. The economy's rapid expansion was interrupted in the summer of 1974, but earlier rises in raw-material prices and accelerating wage increases increased the pace of inflation. The Bank of Canada took steps to restrain the growth of bank reserves and raised the bank rate from $7\frac{1}{4}$ to $9\frac{1}{4}\%$ in three steps between April and July to encourage Canadian interest rates to rise broadly in line with those in the U.S. Bank lending expanded by 20% in the 12 months ended September 1974, though a sharp falloff in mortgage lending approvals became evident after midyear. The broadly defined money supply continued to expand at a high rate, reflecting an upsurge in personal time deposits. With activity now expanding more in line with capacity growth, the authorities believed that further severe monetary restraint would have little effect on inflation. Following declines in interest rates in the U.S., the bank rate was lowered to $8\frac{3}{4}\%$ in November, and steps were taken to ease bank reserve positions.

EEC Countries. The oil crisis further inhibited efforts toward monetary unification. The French franc was floated independently, but West Germany, the Benelux countries, and Denmark continued to manage a joint float against other countries while keeping their own cross rates within margins of $2\frac{1}{4}\%$. The European Monetary Cooperation Fund provided short-term assistance to Italy, converting this into a medium-term loan toward the end of the year. The EEC countries also agreed to set up a fund totaling 2.5 billion units of account in 1975 for recycling oil funds to member countries in deficit.

In the U.K., after a largely unsuccessful attempt to control monetary expansion through interest rates alone, a more effective set of restraints was introduced toward the end of 1973. Apart from a steep increase in interest rates to strengthen sterling and the imposition of installment credit restrictions, banks were required to lodge special blocked deposits with the Bank of England against the growth of interest-bearing liabilities in excess of 8% over the following six months. In early 1974, against the background of a large external deficit and rapidly accelerating inflation, a new crisis was touched off by a miners' strike. A three-day workweek restriction to save coal lasted until March after the election. The new Labour government, announcing fresh credit lines to protect Britain's reserves, increased indirect and direct taxation, particularly on companies, and raised charges for public services. However, the budgetary effect was neutralized by higher pensions and food subsidies. After the miners' strike was settled with a pay award of nearly 30%, the government announced that statutory wage restrictions would be replaced by an undertaking from the unions to keep wage increases broadly in line with the rise in prices.

The rate of increase of the broadly defined money supply decelerated as speculative transactions, which had inflated its growth earlier, slackened. Meanwhile, bank lending and especially personal loans slowed, sales of government stock to the private sector increased, and the external trade deficit, largely financed by public-sector borrowing abroad, drained off corporate liquidity. With stock prices falling drastically, new issue activity came to a standstill. To encourage a lowering of interest rates, the banks' special deposit ratios were reduced from 5% in February to 3% in April and the Bank of England's minimum lending rate was gradually brought down from 13% in January to $11\frac{3}{4}\%$ in May. On the other hand, the reserve

deposit requirement against the growth in the banks' interest-bearing liabilities was extended for six months in July.

Output recovered after the restoration of a full workweek, but by the autumn it was still no higher than a year earlier. However, the annual rate of increase in consumer prices crept up to around 20%. In July new measures were introduced, including a reduction in the value-added tax (VAT), larger regional employment premiums, and a higher limit for permitted dividend increases. Increased public spending to assist the building industry was announced in September. Following a further easing of market interest rates, the Bank of England's minimum lending rate was lowered to $11\frac{1}{2}\%$.

Price controls, together with the mounting cost of wages and inventory financing, squeezed profits and brought corporate liquidity under increasing strain. To avert the threat of a sharp fall in investment and a cutback in output, the government in November announced tax concessions, a relaxation of price controls, and new medium-term credit facilities. But the package added some 2% to consumer price rises and brought the estimated public-sector borrowing requirement in 1974–75 (April–March) to £6,500 million—equivalent to 8% of GNP. Long-term interest rates rose sharply in November.

In West Germany the easing of demand pressures in certain sectors of the economy in late 1973 prompted a selective relaxation of earlier tax and government expenditure restraints, but monetary policy continued to be quite restrictive. Following increases in temporary central-bank credit facilities, the banks' ordinary reserve requirements were lowered in January, and the requirement against the growth of their liabilities vis-à-vis nonresidents was abolished. Later the cash deposit requirement against borrowing abroad by nonbanks was lowered, and controls on long-term capital inflows were liberalized.

With aggregate demand sustained by a substantial trade surplus, the mark recovered strongly from its January low against other European currencies and the dollar. Official intervention to limit the rise was substantial at times, and in May, to forestall an easing of bank liquidity, the banks' utilization of their rediscount lines was restricted. A new situation arose

The Franklin National Bank of New York, the nation's 20th largest bank with assets of $4.5 billion and the largest U.S. bank ever to fail, was quickly taken over by the European-American Bank and Trust Co., owned by a consortium of six major European banks. The Franklin was declared insolvent by the Federal Deposit Insurance Corporation after loans totaling $1.7 billion from the Federal Reserve Bank of New York failed to offset losses.

WIDE WORLD

A silver-refining plant in a suburb of Vancouver, B.C., operates 24 hours a day keeping up with the tide of silverware, coins, and other silver items brought in by private citizens hoping to profit by soaring silver prices.

in late June, however, after the authorities had acted to close a major private bank, the Bankhaus I. D. Herstatt of Cologne. The mark weakened and an element of uneasiness appeared in inter-bank relations.

To ease the situation, the Bundesbank temporarily offered the banks Lombard credit (against securities as collateral) on stock exchange securities at 9% interest and also provided new, selective credit facilities. In September, moreover, the banks' minimum reserve requirements against their domestic liabilities were lowered by 10%, and arrangements were made to refinance unrealizable claims on other banks or sudden deposit withdrawals. Other steps included the introduction of new controls on the banks' open foreign positions and the establishment of a new institution, with Bundesbank participation, to assist basically sound credit institutions threatened with liquidity problems. These measures contributed to some easing of short-term interest rates. The money supply showed very little increase, and long-term interest rates remained fairly stable.

The 12-month increase in consumer prices was kept to under 7%—the best performance among the industrial countries. With unemployment increasing progressively and the economy's external position still strong, monetary policy was eased slightly in October with an across-the-board cut of 8% in the banks' minimum reserve requirements, a lowering of the official discount rate from 7 to $6\frac{1}{2}$%, and an increase in the banks' effective rediscount quotas. Allowing for tax relief for low incomes, the government's budget provided for a DM. 8 billion increase in the deficit in 1975. The release of a modest DM. 1 billion of the very large amount of public sector funds previously frozen at the Bundesbank was announced. In December the official discount rate was cut to 6%.

Economic activity in France continued to accelerate, but the rise in crude-oil prices opened up a large trade deficit and pushed the rise in consumer prices to an annual rate of around 15% by midyear. In January France withdrew from the EEC joint currency float, leaving the franc free to float independently. However, to support the franc and protect official reserves, the government arranged a $1.5 billion medium-term Eurobank loan, negotiated a substantial trade prepayment from Iran, and encouraged public-sector bodies to borrow abroad.

The authorities kept bank credit granting subject to restrictive growth norms throughout the year, though export and energy-saving investment credits were liberalized in stages. A fiscal stabilization package put forward by Pres. Valéry Giscard d'Estaing in June included tax surcharges on corporations and high incomes, budget economies, and the freezing of Fr. 3.5 billion of government funds at the Bank of France. Shortly afterward, the banks' reserve requirements were restructured; those on time deposits were lowered and those on sight deposits were raised. The 33% requirement against the increase in credit granting was abolished, but the penalties for exceeding the credit growth norms were increased. Following a steep rise in interest rates, the official discount rate was raised from 11 to 13% in June.

From summer onward, the banks kept within the 13% ceiling on the 12-month growth of certain credits. Taking exempted credits into account, the rise in total bank lending approached 20%, but the growth of money slowed down. Larger enterprises were encouraged to borrow abroad, but some small enterprises suffered severe liquidity pressures calling for

special credit arrangements. In November the government froze another Fr. 3.5 billion of surplus budgetary revenues at the Bank of France.

Italy's external deficit and inflation reached grave proportions in 1974. Early in the year decisive steps were taken to tighten monetary policy. The Bank of Italy's basic discount and secured lending rates were raised from $6\frac{1}{2}$ to 9%, and the authorities allowed a very steep rise in long- as well as short-term interest rates. In April a ceiling of 15% was placed on the expansion of most categories of direct bank lending during the year ending March 1975, and in May a selective 50% import deposit requirement was imposed, the proceeds of which were to be blocked for six months at the Bank of Italy. This and the external deficit helped to drain liquidity from the economy. Bank credit granting slowed considerably, but the authorities sought to safeguard long-term financing by extending the banks' bond investment requirements and by measures taken in July to facilitate construction financing. A fiscal package including increases in VAT on nonessentials and in tax on higher incomes was adopted in August, but the budget deficit remained enormous and required considerable financing support from the Bank of Italy.

Already heavily indebted abroad, Italian public-sector bodies were able to raise large additional amounts in foreign capital markets only in the early months of the year. Thereafter, Italy had extensive recourse to official credit under EEC arrangements, from the IMF, both under a general standby agreement and under the new oil facility, and from the West German central bank by pledging one-fifth of the country's official gold reserves. Still the lira recorded a further substantial depreciation. In the autumn the monetary aggregates grew more slowly, and the external deficit contracted somewhat.

Economic growth in The Netherlands in 1973 had remained well within capacity limitations, and the oil embargo temporarily caused new demand uncertainties. Hence, monetary policy was kept fairly easy in early 1974. In the struggle against inflation the authorities relied mainly on the earlier exchange appreciation of the guilder, increasingly stringent price controls, and the direct regulation of wages and incomes. To help keep the guilder in the EEC joint float, the authorities eased the banks' terms of access to central-bank credit and adapted money-market conditions by means of dollar swaps with the banks.

Credit to the private sector expanded strongly, and between January and August the broadly defined money supply rose at an annual rate of 30%. From July onward steps were taken to curb the banks' free reserves, and in September their liquidity reserve requirements were raised to $9\frac{1}{2}$%. In general, however, the authorities believed that increased credit demands should be accommodated. With the guilder strong and interest rates falling abroad, the official discount rate was lowered from 8 to 7%.

In Belgium economic activity was bolstered by strong external demand, keeping productive resources under strain until late in 1974. Though still subject to a variety of controls, the rise in consumer prices crept up to around 15%. Continuing its restrictive policy, the National Bank raised its discount rate from 7 to $8\frac{3}{4}$% between November and February and lowered the banks' rediscount coefficients in several stages. In March reserve requirements against time deposits were lowered slightly. The banks remained subject to a government-paper investment obligation, and the 14% year-to-year growth guideline on bank credit was made legally binding. The ceiling arrangements on credit were tightened further at the end of June and, shortly afterward, the government took measures to restrict installment and mortgage credit and imposed a delay on building starts. Under these policies, short-term interest rates rose steeply, bank credit granting slowed, and there was a marked reduction in the rate of monetary expansion. The credit restrictions were prolonged in November, but the authorized year-to-year growth ceiling was raised to 16% and export credits were liberalized.

(JOHN KNEESHAW)

See also Economics; Economy, World; Exchange and Payments, International; Government Finance; Housing; Investment, International; Stock Exchanges.
[534.D.1-2.a-e; 534.K.1-2]

Mongolia

A people's republic of Asia lying between the U.S.S.R. and China, Mongolia occupies the geographic area known as Outer Mongolia. Area: 604,000 sq.mi. (1,565,000 sq.km.). Pop. (1973 est.): 1,359,000. Cap. and largest city: Ulan Bator (pop., 1972 est., 303,000). Language: Khalkha Mongolian. Religion: Lamaistic Buddhism. First secretary of the Mongolian People's Revolutionary (Communist) Party in 1974 and, from June 11, chairman of the Presidium of the Great People's Hural, Yumzhagiyen Tsedenbal; chairmen of the Council of Ministers (premiers), Tsedenbal and, from June 11, Zhambyn Batmunkh.

Mongolian-Chinese relations remained tense throughout 1974, and the 4,673-km. frontier between the two countries bristled with troop concentrations on both sides. In his speech at the anniversary celebrations in Ulan Bator, Soviet party leader Leonid Brezhnev rejected China's protests over the presence of Soviet troops in Mongolia as "totally unacceptable." On November 27 a new Soviet-Mongolian economic cooperation agreement was signed.

On June 11 the Great People's Hural elected 57-

MONGOLIA

Education. (1969–70) Primary, pupils 137,420, teachers 4,362; secondary, pupils 74,344, teachers 3,566; vocational, pupils 8,254; teacher training, pupils 2,239; higher (including University of Ulan Bator), students (1970–71) 6,874, teaching staff (1968–69) 700.

Finance. Monetary unit: tugrik, with (Sept. 16, 1974) an official exchange rate of 3.20 tugriks to U.S. $1 (7.64 tugriks = £1 sterling). Budget (1974 est.): revenue 2,620,000,000 tugriks; expenditure 2,610,000,000 tugriks.

Foreign Trade. (1970) Imports *c.* 430 million tugriks; exports *c.* 310 million tugriks. Import sources: U.S.S.R. *c.* 80%; Czechoslovakia *c.* 5%. Export destinations: U.S.S.R. *c.* 70%; Czechoslovakia 9%. Main exports: agricultural raw materials 58%; raw materials for food 20%; foodstuffs 10%.

Transport and Communications. Roads (1970) *c.* 75,000 km. (including *c.* 8,600 km. main roads). Railways (1972) *c.* 1,400 km. Telephones (Jan. 1973) 26,000. Radio receivers (Dec. 1970) 166,000. Television receivers (Dec. 1973) 34,000.

Agriculture. Production (in 000; metric tons; 1973; 1972 in parentheses): wheat *c.* 300 (*c.* 270); oats *c.* 37 (17); barley *c.* 15 (*c.* 15); potatoes (1972) *c.* 26, (1971) 19. Livestock (in 000; Dec. 1972): cattle *c.* 2,193; sheep 13,717; goats (1971) 4,195; horses (1971) 2,270; camels *c.* 600.

Industry. Production (in 000; metric tons; 1972): coal 106; lignite 2,147; salt 10; cement 141; electricity (kw-hr.) 631,000.

year-old Yumzhagiyen Tsedenbal as chairman of its Presidium. That post had been vacant since May 1972, when Zhamsarangibin Sambuu, its previous incumbent, died. Tsedenbal retained his post of first secretary of the Mongolian People's Revolutionary Party but was succeeded as chairman of the Council of Ministers by Zhambyn Batmunkh, a Politburo member and hitherto a deputy premier. Shortly after his election, Tsedenbal visited Moscow and Budapest. Gen. Batyn Dordzh, minister of defense, visited East Germany in April. In February Mongolia established diplomatic relations with West Germany.

On the occasion of the 50th anniversary of the proclamation of Mongolia's independence in 1924, the Great People's Hural accelerated the chief aims of the national development plan for 1974. During the first half of the year industrial production rose by 9.8% as compared with figures for the same period of 1973. It was expected that the 25 million target for domestic livestock would be reached.

(K. M. SMOGORZEWSKI)

Morocco

A constitutional monarchy of northwestern Africa, on the Atlantic Ocean and the Mediterranean Sea, Morocco is bordered by Algeria and Spanish Sahara. Area: 177,117 sq.mi. (458,730 sq.km.). Pop. (1973 est.): 16,309,000. Cap.: Rabat (pop., 1971, 374,809). Largest city: Casablanca (pop., 1971, 1,506,373). Language: Arabic; Berber. Religion: Muslim. King, Hassan II; prime minister in 1974, Ahmed Osman.

The Spanish Sahara would be "liberated" and reintegrated into Morocco before the end of 1975, King Hassan announced in a speech on July 8, 1974, and this remained the overriding theme of Morocco's policy, both domestic and external, for the rest of the year. Direct talks with Spain on the territory's future were held in Madrid in mid-August. After their failure, King Hassan threatened he would resort to military action if necessary to regain "usurped Moroccan territory." He rejected both a referendum under Spanish supervision to decide on the Sahara's future and the eventual independence of the territory. At the UN General Assembly, the Moroccan delegation moderated the king's more outspoken views and suggested that the Sahara question be referred to the International Court of Justice. In November, 27 people were killed in clashes between Moroccans and Spanish troops in Spanish Sahara. Within Morocco, the government, pursuing its Sahara policy, gave special attention to the development of Tarfaya Province, adjoining the Spanish-administered territory; set up five refugee camps for those said to have fled across the border; and established two new radio stations to beam propaganda on the issue, the one directed to the Sahara itself and the other directed toward metropolitan Spain.

The king's policy on the Sahara provided a point of agreement for the nation's various political groupings. The opposition Istiqlal Party had always pressed for such a policy; the left-wing National Union of Popular Forces saw the new firmer attitude as a step toward national union and, possibly, toward the greater democracy essential, in its view, for the monarchy's survival. Two new parties formed during 1974, the Progressive Socialists and the Progressive Liberals, pledged the king their support on this issue.

In January, 62 people were sentenced to death for

Mormons:
see Religion

MOROCCO

Education. (1973–74) Primary, pupils 1,337,931, teachers 37,585; secondary and vocational, pupils 361,725, teachers 23,701; teacher training (1970–71), students 2,567, teaching staff 120; higher, students 20,055, teaching staff (1970–71) 620.

Finance. Monetary unit: dirham, with (Sept. 16, 1974) a free rate of 4.35 dirhams to U.S. $1 (10.06 dirhams = £1 sterling). Gold, SDRs, and foreign exchange, central bank: (May 1974) U.S. $195 million; (May 1973) U.S. $254 million. Budget (1973 est.): revenue 6,175,000,000 dirhams; expenditure 6,632,-000,000 dirhams. Gross domestic product: (1972) 20,150,000,000 dirhams; (1971) 18,570,000,000 dirhams. Money supply: (April 1974) 8,945,000,000 dirhams; (April 1973) 7,349,000,000 dirhams. Cost of living (Casablanca; 1970 = 100): (Jan. 1974) 126; (Jan. 1973) 110.

Foreign Trade. (1973) Imports 4,684,000,000 dirhams; exports 3,746,000,000 dirhams. Main import sources: France 32%; U.K. 11%; West Germany 8%; Spain 5%; Italy 5%. Main export destinations: France 34%; West Germany 10%; Italy 7%; Spain 5%; U.K. 5%. Main exports: phosphates 21%; citrus fruit 13%; tomatoes 6%; fish 5%. Tourism (1972): visitors 1,062,000; gross receipts U.S. $192 million.

Transport and Communications. Roads (1973) 25,414 (including 14 km. expressways). Motor vehicles in use (1972): passenger 260,411; commercial 84,710. Railways: (1971) 1,756 km.; traffic (1973) 619 million passenger-km., freight 3,319,000,000 net ton-km. Air traffic (1972): 655 million passenger-km.; freight 7.7 million net ton-km. Shipping (1973): merchant vessels 100 gross tons and over 46; gross tonnage 56,125. Telephones (Dec. 1972) 172,000. Radio licenses (Dec. 1972) 1.5 million. Television receivers (Dec. 1972) 225,000.

Agriculture. Production (in 000; metric tons; 1973; 1972 in parentheses): wheat 1,897 (2,161); barley 913 (2,466); corn 221 (368); potatoes c. 226 (226); sugar, raw value c. 265 (245); oranges (1972) c. 695, (1971) 681; mandarin oranges and tangerines (1972) c. 145, (1971) 141; dry broad beans (1972) c. 192, (1971) 243; tomatoes c. 460 (c. 460); wine c. 120 (115); olives c. 330 (c. 250); figs c. 65 (c. 65); dates (1972) c. 92, (1971) c. 90; fish catch (1972) 246, (1971) 227. Livestock (in 000; 1972–73): cattle c. 3,700; sheep c. 16,500; goats (1971–72) c. 8,870; horses c. 420; mules c. 415; asses c. 950; camels c. 235; poultry c. 16,000.

Industry. Production (in 000; metric tons; 1973): coal 565; crude oil 42; cement 1,619; iron ore (55-60% metal content) 374; phosphate rock (1972) 15,105; manganese ore (metal content; 1971) 80; lead concentrates (metal content) 103; zinc concentrates (metal content) 18; petroleum products (1971) 1,344; electricity (kw-hr.; 1972) 2,196,000.

their part in the March 1973 "plot" against the king, and in August seven of these were executed. University, and to some extent secondary school, students continued to stage occasional but large demonstrations to express their concern over the ban on the students' union.

Rabat was the scene of the seventh Arab summit conference in October, which confirmed the Palestine Liberation Organization as the body solely representative of the Palestinian Arabs. Otherwise, Morocco was little involved in Arab affairs in 1974.

The Moroccan economy, still suffering from an imbalance in foreign trade, a fast-growing population, and the need for ever increasing foreign aid, received a boost from the world demand for phosphates. The selling price of Moroccan phosphates, $14 a ton at the end of October 1973, had tripled by the beginning of 1974 and was pushed up to $63 a ton in July. These rises did not inhibit purchasers, and phosphates production was expanded by 20%. From the poorer less developed countries Morocco expressed a willingness to accept payment half in cash and half on long-term credit. In March it was announced that deposits of oil-bearing shale had been discovered in the Middle Atlas Mountains. (PETER KILNER)

[978.D.2.c]

Motion Pictures

The year added to the constant reminders of the advancing age of the motion-picture industry. Among other anniversaries, the Disney organization passed its 50th; and the eternal juveniles of the cinema, Mickey and Donald, Pluto and Goofy, were already distinctly middle-aged. The movies themselves, at 80 years old, were at a critical stage. There was hardly an area of the world where they were not hit by the overwhelming economic factors of a dwindling public and rising costs. Artistically, too, the cinema seemed at a moment of crisis, with signs of an exploration of new directions but also of uncertainty as to where the cinema's new directions would or should lead.

While the gains might be hard to identify, the losses—in terms of the year's obituaries—were undoubted. They included Vittorio de Sica, veteran Italian director and pioneer of "neorealism," at 73; Bud Abbott, of the comic team of Abbott and Costello, at 78; Betty Compson, star of silent films, at 77; Sam Goldwyn, producer since the earliest years of Hollywood, at 91; William Haines, amiable leading man of silent years, at 73; Ranald MacDougall, screenwriter, at 58; Lothar Mendes, veteran international director, at 79; Marcel Pagnol, novelist and filmmaker who romanticized the street life of Marseilles in the *Marius* trilogy, at 79; and Michel Salkind, veteran producer, at 83. (*See also* OBITUARIES.)

English-Speaking Cinema. *United States.* The economics of Hollywood film production continued to depend predominantly upon the occasional outstanding success, such as *The Godfather* or *The Sting,* and upon television production, but there were signs in the U.S. that motion-picture theatre attendance was on the upswing. The show business weekly *Variety* reported that 1974 might ultimately prove to be the best box-office year since 1946. Ironically, most observers credited the attendance rise to the economic recession and the desire to escape, at least temporarily, from the problems of the real world. At the same time, the preoccupations of the Watergate era were reflected in films. One group of movies echoed a skepticism about authority and establishments. David Miller's *Executive Action* (the script was written by Dalton Trumbo, who had learned his skepticism as one of the Hollywood Ten blacklisted at the time of the House Committee on Un-American Activities hearings) dramatized certain speculative theories about the assassination of Pres. John Kennedy and came up with a narrative that seemed at least as valid in dramatic terms as the Warren Commission report. Francis Ford Coppola's *The Conversation,* which won the Grand Prix at the Cannes Film Festival in May, was a hallucinating story about a professional wiretapper, an impressionist study of the morality and the neurosis of eavesdropping. Alan Pakula's *The Parallax View* was again a fictional approach to the theme of public, organized assassination: stylish, intelligent, and with its own speculations about the making of a Lee Harvey Oswald.

The most respected instruments of social order were called in question. Sidney Lumet's *Serpico* dramatized the real-life experiences of a policeman who stood out alone against the corruption he found in the New York City police force, a stand that resulted in exile in Europe as a permanent cripple. Lighter hearted, Aram Avakian's *Cops and Robbers* showed cops *as* robbers—a couple of bored and disillusioned policemen progressing from petty theft to a major Wall Street heist. The stock theme of the suspended policeman who takes the law into his own hands in order to avenge a buddy experienced a new lease on life in the prevailing mood (*e.g.*, Ted Post's *Magnum Force* and John Sturges' *McQ*); alongside these was a new kind of film, a sort of urban Western, which showed the formation of irregular "posses" acting outside the regular forces of law and order to hunt down wrongdoers (*Gordon's War, The Seven-Ups, Law and Disorder*).

Another style that seemed peculiarly characteristic of the period was the film motivated by some catastrophic disaster. *Airport 1975*, depicting the anguish of passengers on a crippled airliner, shrank beside *The Towering Inferno*, concerned with a fire in a vast high-rise building, and above all in comparison with the scope of Mark Robson's *Earthquake*, which (with elaborate special effects) predicted a future Los Angeles earthquake.

Again, it was perhaps natural that nostalgia for a still recent but reassuringly serene past became a significant factor in U.S. entertainment films. *Summer of '42* had its sequel in Paul Bogart's *Class of '44*. *The Way We Were*, a large-scale commercial picture starring Barbra Streisand and Robert Redford (*see* BIOGRAPHY) and based on an Arthur Laurents novel, revisited the 1940s, between the wartime enthusiasm for the U.S.S.R. and the McCarthy era. Daniel Petrie's *Buster and Billie* was a reminiscence of school days in 1948. *Badlands*, a very striking directorial debut by Terence Malick, evoked the world of the "true confessions" magazines of the 1950s, with a simple rustic youth fulfilling his dreams of emulating his movie star idols by becoming a gunman.

Other well-publicized nostalgia films included Roman Polanski's *Chinatown*, set in Los Angeles in the 1930s, which rediscovered some of the patterns of a classical tale and a classical style; and Robert Altman's *Thieves Like Us*, an ironic reexamination of a depression period novel, originally filmed by Nicholas Ray as *They Live By Night*.

Hollywood celebrated its own nostalgia with *That's Entertainment!*, an anthology of scenes from MGM musicals from the 1920s to the 1950s, interspersed with recent shots of the old stars, filmed against the crumbling sets on the MGM lot. The runaway success of this compilation was a sterling tribute to the craft tradition of the former Hollywood and a promise that the film was likely to have successors.

Comedy was sparse; but it tended toward the skeptical and zany, with a preference for the tempting but perilous area of parody. In its burlesque of Western traditions Mel Brooks's *Blazing Saddles* often lacked the engaging idiocy of its title. *Sleeper*, however, in which Woody Allen was a Rip Van Winkle awakening in a terrifying future, was the comedian's most accomplished work as director-star.

Hollywood musicals seemed totally eclipsed: the only example to emerge was Gene Saks's undistinguished transfer of *Mame*. Among the newer formulas bequeathed by recent successes, the most dispiriting were the Mafia cycle that succeeded *The Godfather* and preceded *Godfather II* (for example, Michael Winner's *The Stone Killer* and Richard Fleischer's *The Don Is Dead*), and the post-*Love Story* films preoccupied with sagas of lovely young people in lingering fatal sickness (Joseph Sargent's *Sunshine*).

Two of the best films of the year could not be said to fit into any established formula. *The Sting*, which rapidly took its place among the year's top-grossing films, was a lightweight Runyonesque fable of 1930s gangsterdom, deftly sustained by George Roy Hill. The film played a major role in the rediscovery and rehabilitation of Scott Joplin, the turn-of-the-century piano rag composer, and the music undoubtedly in turn contributed to the international success of the film. *The Last Detail*, starring Jack Nicholson (*see* BIOGRAPHY), showed director Hal Ashby in full mastery of his feeling for odd social and psychological relationships.

The pursuit of literature took young American directors abroad. In Italy, Peter Bogdanovich filmed a *Daisy Miller* of visual splendour but limited by its performances (meanwhile, in France, Claude Chabrol was also filming Henry James, in *De Grey*, while in Britain Tony Scott was shooting *The Author of 'Beltraffio'*). Herman Hesse took Fred Haines to Basel to shoot a psychedelic *Steppenwolf*, and Conrad Rooks to India to film a somewhat too reverential *Siddhartha*.

Among documentary productions, the most notable films—all in one way or another inquisitions into the state of society—were Fred Wiseman's *Juvenile Court* and *Primate*; Jerry Bruck, Jr.'s *I. F. Stone's Weekly*, the portrait of an American individualist and iconoclast; and Peter Davis' *Hearts and Minds*, certainly the best retrospective view of American states of mind in the Vietnam war.

"That's Entertainment!," a celebration of Metro-Goldwyn-Mayer musicals, featured James Stewart (below, right) as one of the present-day narrators and included scenes from "The Wizard of Oz" (below, left with, left to right, Ray Bolger, Jack Haley, Judy Garland, and Bert Lahr) and "Born to Dance" (bottom, with Eleanor Powell).

PHOTOS, COPYRIGHT © 1974, METRO-GOLDWYN-MAYER, INC.

In the annual awards of the U.S. Academy of Motion Picture Arts and Sciences, *The Sting* took the lion's share of the prizes, with awards for best film, best director (George Roy Hill), best original story and screenplay (D. S. Ward), best editing (William Reynolds), best musical scoring (Marvin Hamlisch, based on Scott Joplin piano rags), best art direction (Henry Bumstead, James Payne), and best costumes (Edith Head). The award for best actor went to Jack Lemmon for his performance in *Save the Tiger*; for best actress to Glenda Jackson for *A Touch of Class*; for best supporting actor to John Houseman for *The Paper Chase*; and for best supporting actress to the ten-year-old Tatum O'Neal for *Paper Moon*. The best screenplay based on material from another source was *The Exorcist* by William Peter Blatty (see BIOGRAPHY). The best foreign-language film was François Truffaut's *Day for Night* (*La Nuit Américaine*). A special award was made to Henri Langlois, the founder and for almost 40 years the curator of the French film archive, La Cinémathèque Française, for his services to the cinema.

Britain. While economic prospects continued to look ever more dire, and the correspondence columns of *The Times* were filled with competing ideas for saving the British film industry, the moralists began to move in. A bill introduced by the Conservative government to regulate "Cinematograph and Indecent Displays," which would have seriously threatened the most innocuous cultural activities such as film societies, was lost as a result of the general election that brought a Labour Party administration into office. At the same time, an increasing number of police actions against the exhibitors, distributors, and producers of erotic pornography revealed the growing interest of the Home Office in the cinema.

The talents of British directors, artists, and technicians were much in demand for big-budget international productions. Jack Clayton's *The Great Gatsby*, for instance, though a U.S. production with American stars, was shot in Britain, with Fitzgerald's America re-created on the back lots of Pinewood Studios. The resulting film was visually stunning, but failed through overliteral translation of its original. *Juggernaut*, again a U.S. production, was directed by the Canadian Richard Lester, with a British cast and an unmistakable British look about its effective suspense story of time bombs planted on a big ocean-going liner. Earlier, Lester had directed *The Three Musketeers*, an exceptionally deft and witty interpretation of Dumas. The film was registered as "Panamanian" and shot in various parts of Europe; but again the talents involved were predominantly British.

Other big-budget productions were Ronald Neame's *The Odessa File*, from a Frederick Forsyth novel about the uncovering of a protective society of former Nazi war criminals in 1963 West Germany; and Peter Hunt's *Gold*, which attracted criticism for having been shot on location in South Africa. Despite this, and the naiveté of its melodramatic plot about a group of international tycoons sabotaging a mine, it had a fair commercial success.

Two attractive British productions of the year, going somewhat against the prevailing drift toward increasing violence and sexuality, dealt with children. Anthony Simmons' *The Optimists of Nine Elms*, starring Peter Sellers as an eccentric old street entertainer, was the realization of a project originally designed many years earlier for Buster Keaton. Claude Whatham, attempting quite a different style from his earlier *That'll Be the Day*, filmed the first adaptation of one of Arthur Ransome's children's books, *Swallows and Amazons.*

Otherwise, commercial production in Britain struggled on with stock production-line comedies (*Carry on Girls*), television spin-offs (*Holiday on the Buses*), formula horrors (*Frankenstein and the Monster from Hell*), and softer-than-soft-core comic erotica (*Confessions of a Window Cleaner, Percy's Progress*).

Only in the area of low-budget and independently produced films were there signs of really vigorous activity. The British Film Institute's Production Board showed its first feature films: after Bill Douglas' autobiographical accounts of a deprived Scottish childhood, *My Childhood* and *My Ain Folk*, came Peter K. Smith's *A Private Enterprise*, a sensitive account of life in an Indian community in provincial Britain, which was shown at the London Film Festival; and Kevin Brownlow's *Comrade Jacob*, an adaptation of David Caute's novel relating the tribulations of the Diggers, a commune set up in Cromwell's Britain, with meticulous period detail, rich black-and-white photography, and an individual dramatic sense.

The most distinguished and remarkable independent work, however, was *A Bigger Splash*, made by Jack Hazan and David Mingay. Begun as a simple documentary account of the English painter David Hockney, it ended as a remarkable impressionist view of the artist, his world, and his emotional involvements with a circle of friends and a homosexual lover. Hazan himself photographed the film, and his images succeeded in reflecting and interpreting the visual aspects of Hockney's own imagination.

Canada. There was a continuing official effort during the year to promote Canadian feature films in the world market. A notable success was the award of the Golden Bear at the Berlin Festival to Ted Kotcheff's *The Apprenticeship of Duddy Kravitz*, though it had to be admitted that this novel-like saga of Jewish life and the making of a go-getter owed its festival success largely to the frailty of the competition. Much more interesting and offbeat was André Brassard's realization of some of the characters from the writer Michel Tremblay in *Once Upon a Time in the East*, which filmed the parallel stories of an old woman who wins a fortune in trading stamps and a transvestite beauty contest. Frank Vitale's *Montreal Main* also explored the remoter sides of urban existence.

Australia. The Australian feature cinema seemed to be finding its feet in the international film market, after the success abroad of Bruce Beresford's *The Adventures of Barry McKenzie*. Tim Burstall's *Alvin Purple* aimed at a comparable ribald energy in its comedy about the adventures of a notable sexual gymnast; but Peter Weir's *The Cars That Ate Paris* was an altogether original conception, the reverse of the mock-disparaging Aussie self-congratulation that had characterized the comedies. It was an anarchic horror fantasy about a remote backwoods community living by highway piracy—waylaying and wrecking automobile travelers, looting their goods, and operating on the brains of survivors to turn them into useful, vegetable beings.

Western Europe. *France.* France had always seemed less vulnerable than other cinemas to the effects of economic crisis, and the year found most of France's great names at work and in characteristic form. Claude Chabrol's *Nada* treated the story of a political kidnapping as a gripping thriller. Robert Bresson's *Lancelot du Lac* was a strange and haunt-

ing revisiting of the grail legend, a montage of hypnotic images of armoured men, of the clangour of battle, and of mysterious whispering in the castle shadows. Alain Resnais's *Stavisky* related the career of the celebrated swindler of the 1930s to the larger context of the political life of contemporary Europe. Jacques Tati's *Parade* was a further episode in his comic commentary upon the follies of contemporary urban life. Claude Lelouch's *La Bonne Année* was a characteristically elegant tale of an unsuccessful jewel robbery by two weary old crooks.

At 74, Luis Buñuel continued to prove as fresh and inventive as ever and in *Le Fantôme de la Liberté* (the title taken from Marx) made one of the liveliest French films of the year, a chain of gags which still proclaimed his surrealist and subversive inspirations. Another film of the year which enjoyed, equally, critical and commercial success was Louis Malle's *Lacombe, Lucien,* which showed how easily a young man of ordinary rustic stupidity could drift into wartime collaboration.

Without any critical approval, two films leaped to large box-office success: Édouard Molinaro's *L'Emmerdeur,* a black comedy about an attempted assassination constantly frustrated by the demands for assistance from an incompetent suicide in the next hotel room; and *Emmanuelle,* Just Jaeckin's adaptation of the bestselling novel by Emmanuelle Arsan. The enormous public response to this film seemed in no way affected by the way in which the film reduced the scabrous wit of the book to flaccid erotica.

Switzerland. The resurgence of a young Swiss cinema continued, with German-Swiss artists joining the ranks of the new feature directors—notably Thomas Koerfer, whose *Der Tod des Flohzirkusdirektors* was a Brechtian parable about a man who loses his performing fleas as a result of chemical crop-spraying and, having failed to find compensation, turns his show into a theatre of the plague. Daniel Schmid's *La Paloma* brought a note of flighty eccentricity to the Swiss cinema, with a tale of absurd romantic love treated in a mixture of kitsch and parody-homage both to Hollywood and to the German operetta cinema of the 1930s.

Italy. The Italian cinema was one of the few European industries to survive in a state of reasonable economic prosperity, and the year found most of the old masters (excluding notably Luchino Visconti) working in fairly familiar fields. While Michelangelo Antonioni was at work on an international production, *The Reporter,* shot in West Germany, Spain, and Britain, Federico Fellini created in *Amarcord* a new pageant of provincial life as recalled from his youth in the 1930s.

The latest antique story collection to attract the attention of Pier Paolo Pasolini was *A Thousand and One Nights,* which appeared in his film version sumptuous, sexy, but marked by the director's odd failure to grasp the point of a story. Vittorio de Sica's last film starred Richard Burton and Sophia Loren in a turn-of-the-century tale after Pirandello, *Il Viaggio.* Francesco Rosi reconstructed the life of the celebrated gangster *Lucky Luciano* after his repatriation to Italy in 1946.

Of the newer directors, the brothers Paolo and Vittorio Taviani pursued their interest in 19th-century revolutionary processes, in *Allonsanfan,* a big-budget film with Marcello Mastroianni as a revolutionary of 1816. Liliana Cavani's *The Night Porter* dealt—controversially—with more recent history, in the story of a man and a woman renewing their sadomasochistic concentration camp affair 30 years later.

West Germany. The young West German directors continued to produce a varied program of films within the limits of small budgets. The most prolific remained Rainer Werner Fassbinder, whose *Fear Eats the Soul,* shown at the Cannes Film Festival, told the story of an odd love affair and marriage between a 60-year-old cleaning lady and an immigrant Arab worker half her age. Unsparing but generous, Fassbinder related all the social and psychological difficulties of the unlikely and ultimately doomed match. In an altogether different style, he attempted also an adaptation of Theodor Fontane's novel *Effie Briest*—a film that was stylish, stylized, but ultimately sterile.

Wim Wenders' *Alice in the Cities* was the story, told with an attractive humour and wisdom, of a typical, alienated 1970s hero, who finds himself unexpectedly involved and matured by his association with a small but chirpy girl. Grimmer views emerged in Rudolf Thome's *Made in Germany and U.S.A.,* a garrulous, voyeuristic film about the breakup of a marriage; and in Alexander Kluge's *Part-Time Work of a Domestic Slave,* which examined the role of women through the life of a girl as she progresses from abortionist to illegal labour organizer. An undoubted individualist, Hans-Jürgen Syberberg followed his tableau life of Ludwig II with *Ludwig's Cook,* which looked ironically at the life and character of the monarch through his cook's eyes.

Sweden. Sweden was little represented on the international scene in 1974. The most attractive film, which appeared at both the Vienna and Karlovy Vary festivals, was Bo Widerberg's *Fimpen,* a simple tale about a six-year-old who is not very good at reading or tying his shoes but is such a wizard at soccer that he is recruited to Sweden's international team.

Norway. Mors Hus (Mother's House), which appeared at the Locarno Festival, was a rarity, a chamber work with only three characters observed in the most restricted settings. Per Blom, whose second feature film this was, treated his theme, the possessive, incestuous love of a mother for her son, with discretion and merciless clarity.

Spain. The promised relaxation of censorship did not produce much effect upon the Spanish cinema in 1974. The mainstays of Spanish production were

Scene from Federico Fellini's "Amarcord," a sometimes dreamlike portrayal of life in a small Italian coastal town in the 1930s.

innocuous comedies, horrors, science fiction stories, and "problem" pictures condemning drugs and teen-age sex. Carlos Saura, nevertheless, continued his outspoken commentaries on modern Spanish life and history with *La Prima Angélica,* in which a man returns to the town of his youth and relives in flashbacks the terrors of the 1930s. The film was explicit enough to cause protests and demonstrations on its first showings in Spain. Jaime de Armiñán's *El Amor del Capitán Brando,* the Spanish entry at the Berlin Festival, gave a cruel view of the pressures of provincial life through the story of a 13-year-old's heroic fantasy life.

Eastern Europe. *U.S.S.R.* The Soviet Union, as for some years past, made little impact on the international film scene, despite persistent rumours of the significant work being produced, not in the metropolitan centres of Leningrad and Moscow, but in the studios of the republics. Though *The Ferocious One,* directed by Tolomush Okeyev in the Kazakh Studios —a simplistic fable about the attempt to tame a wolf —did not in itself confirm the rumours, a new film by the director of *Pirosmani,* Georgy Shengelaya, was more encouraging. His *Melodies of the Veriyski Neighbourhood,* a musical of contemporary life in Georgia, had verve and style.

The Red Snowball Tree, directed by Vasily Shukshin, made a deep impression in the Soviet Union— despite heavy cutting at the behest of the censors— by its unsparing picture of a man released after several prison sentences and being dragged helplessly back into the urban underworld. Sadly, Shukshin himself died at the age of 45 in October, while working on a new film (*see* OBITUARIES).

Hungary. Elsewhere in Eastern Europe it was not a year of notable production, and only the Hungarian cinema sustained variety and interest. The master of the contemporary Hungarian cinema, Miklos Jancso, returned from his voluntary exile in Rome to make *My Love, Elektra,* a reinterpretation of the classical story, told in the style of cinema-choreography and lengthy unbroken takes that Jancso, with his cameraman Janos Kende, had made his own.

Istvan Szabo's *25 Fireman's Street* was a brilliant kaleidoscope of the collective dream-memories of the occupants of an apartment house on the eve of demolition—and hence an impressionist recollection of all Hungarian history of the past 60 years. Janos Rozsa's *Dreaming Youth* re-created scenes from the childhood recollections of Bela Balazs, the celebrated Hungarian writer and film aesthetician.

Czechoslovakia. With most of the filmmakers who had created the renascence of the middle 1960s working abroad (the last to go was Jan Nemec, who was forcibly exiled in the fall of 1974), the production of the Czechoslovakian cinema remained rather bland and muted. The best film to be seen abroad during the year was the Czechoslovakian entry at the Karlovy Vary Festival, *People of the Metro,* three stories of workers on the new Prague subway, told with warmth and perception by Jaromil Jires. The gifted animator Karel Zeman made a feature-length animated version of *Sinbad the Sailor.*

Asia. *Japan.* Dominated by strictly commercial production, the Japanese cinema made no impact on the international festivals of 1974, with the exception of Masaki Kobayashi's *Kaseki,* a marathon (3 hours 40 minutes) account of a man dying of cancer who discovers new artistic and sentimental pleasures in the course of a farewell trip to Europe.

India. Promising new directors continued to emerge in India. Shyam Benegal's *Ankur (The Seedling),* shown at the Berlin Film Festival, brought an inventive visual sense to the treatment of social themes. Another film that dealt intelligently and sensitively with the social problems arising from surviving customs of the caste system and marriage arrangements was Awtar Krishna Kaul's *27 Down Bombay-Varanasi Express.* Kaul was drowned only a few weeks before the film's European premiere at the Locarno Festival.

Hong Kong. The cinema of Hong Kong, after many years of prolific production to satisfy a hungry domestic market, suddenly found its products in demand on the international market. Films of the martial arts suddenly became enormously popular with audiences in Europe and America. Despite superficial variations and such novelties as female kung-fu stars (Angela Mao, Nora Miao), the formula of the films was reassuringly consistent.

The major star to emerge from the Hong Kong films was the American-born Chinese Bruce Lee, who died in 1973 but continued to receive an ever-growing posthumous adulation from his audiences. He completed four films—*The Big Boss* and *Fist of Fury,* both made in Hong Kong; *Enter the Dragon,* a U.S.-financed production directed by Robert Clouse; and *Way of the Dragon,* directed by Lee himself with some artlessness but great sensitivity to his own attributes as a star.

Latin America. *Argentina.* The old master of the Argentine cinema, Leopoldo Torre Nilsson, returned strongly to form with *Boquitas Pintadas,* adapted from a novel by the iconoclastic young writer Mañuel Puig. Nilsson and Puig took the formulas of a sentimental romance but reexamined them, in the light of unsparing reality, to expose the spiritual and cultural poverty of a provincial middle class subjugated to social and religious rules and prejudices.

(DAVID ROBINSON)

Nontheatrical Cinema. The development of lightweight equipment, which took the film producer out of the studio into the real world, provided a boost for the documentary film, which was showing new vigour. The documentary was given another assist by the U.S. Federal Communications Commission, which required local television stations to relate more closely to their respective communities. Documentaries made by TV stations were, consequently, expected to increase.

A third stimulant to nontheatrical filmmaking came from the newer medium of videotape recording. Easy-to-operate video recorders were being used more frequently to make routine "films"—tapings of lectures, panel discussions, and straightforward messages. Relieved of the chore of such routine production, filmmakers were able to become more creative in producing other films.

A fourth development related to the nontheatrical film was the surge of films being made by young people. Children as young as fifth graders were making prize-winning animation films. As young people moved through high school and college, a growing number were going into the business for themselves. By late 1974 the number of film production companies in the U.S. exceeded 3,000.

The number of nontheatrical films released in 1973 hit an all-time high mark of 17,230 titles, compared with 15,770 in 1972. In contrast, the amount spent for the 1973 productions dipped 2%, to an estimated $638 million. Business and industry accounted for

Motorboating:
see Motor Sports

Motor Industry:
see Industrial
Production and
Technology

11,530 titles, more than three times as many titles as the 3,470 feature films produced worldwide. Ten percent, or 1,740, of the nontheatrical films were sponsored by federal, state, and local government agencies, the last two showing an increase. One film on safe driving by the California State Highway Department, *License to Kill,* was picked as the top in-plant production of 1974 in two contests.

Venice's Grand Prix was won in 1974 by an industrial film from St. Paul, Minn., *Portrait of a Railroad.* Producer for Burlington Northern Railroad was Francis Thompson of New York. A classroom film, *Space Filling Curves,* by Education Development Center of Newton, Mass., took top prizes in two scientific events at Sydney, Austr., and Padua, Italy.

A sensitive film about two little brothers, one blind and one sighted, was selected for the blue ribbon by the American Film Festival in New York, the premier educational film event in the world.

(THOMAS WALKER HOPE)

See also Photography; Television and Radio.
[623; 735.G.2]

ENCYCLOPÆDIA BRITANNICA FILMS. *Growing* (1969)—a computer-animated film; *Practical Filmmaking* (1972).

Motor Sports

Automobiles. The 1974 season of Formula One Grand Prix motor racing opened in January in Buenos Aires, Arg., over 316.3 km. (53 laps). It looked as if Carlos Reutemann of Argentina would win in a Brabham BT44/1 as he was leading near the end. But his engine developed problems, and it was the veteran Denis Hulme of New Zealand who finished first for Team McLaren, ahead of Austrian Niki Lauda and Gianclaudio ("Clay") Regazzoni of Switzerland in Ferraris. The winning McLaren was an M21/6, which averaged 187.874 kph, but the fastest lap had been made by Regazzoni, at 191.664 kph (1 kph = 0.62 mph).

At the end of January the tour moved to Brazil for the Grand Prix at Interlagos, São Paulo, over 254.7 km. There, Emerson Fittipaldi of Brazil, who had forsaken Lotus, for whom he drove in 1973, to drive for the Texaco-Marlboro McLaren team, returned to form and won at 180.623 kph. He was followed home by Regazzoni in second place with a Ferrari, a combination that again made fastest race lap, at 183.52 kph. Jackie Ickx of Belgium finished third in a Lotus 72 of the John Player team.

Throughout the remainder of the Grand Prix season Fittipaldi showed a clever recognition of the pace required to win the world championship, apparently extending himself fully only when this was called for. In the Grand Prix Premio Presidente Medici, held for the purpose of inaugurating the new autodrome at Brasília, Fittipaldi vanquished Jody Scheckter of South Africa in a Tyrrell and an Iso-Marlborough, at a speed of 174.337 kph for the 219 km.

Before another world championship race was run, there was an interesting interlude on a wet day at Brands Hatch near London, when the Race of Champions for both Formula One and Formula 5000 cars was held. It was won by Ickx in the F1 Lotus 72, while second place went to Lauda in the F1 Ferrari 312B. The next major race was at Kyalami in South Africa at the end of March, where Reutemann won, his Brabham averaging 187.07 kph, to hold off Jean-Pierre Beltoise of France in a BRM P201 and ex-

motorcycle racer Mike Hailwood of the U.K., driving a McLaren M23. The winner made best lap, at a speed of 189.02 kph.

The flat-12-cylinder Ferraris came into their own at Jarama, Spain, where the first two places in the two-hour Spanish Grand Prix went to them. Lauda led Regazzoni home, at 142.396 kph, having set a new lap record of 151.621 kph on his 47th circuit; Fittipaldi finished third. In the Belgian Grand Prix, held over 85 laps of the 3.724-km. autodrome at Nivelles in May, Fittipaldi won, at 182.019 kph, from Lauda's Ferrari and the Tyrrell 007 of Scheckter. Hulme's McLaren lapped fastest, at 188.001 kph. Before the month was over the teams moved to the classic real-road circuit at Monaco, somewhat altered since 1972 and now measuring 2½ km. to the lap. Of the 25 starters Ronnie Peterson of Sweden raised Lotus hopes by doing the quickest lap, on his 72/R8, at 134.252 kph, and going on to victory at 129.540 kph for the 78 laps. Second place was gained by Scheckter for Tyrrell, and the Frenchman Jean-Pierre Jarier, driving a Shadow DN3, was third.

In the Swedish Grand Prix at Anderstorp the Tyrrell 007s made a fine showing, finishing first and second. Scheckter, who averaged 162.723 kph, was the winning driver, followed by his French teammate, Patrick Depailler. James Hunt of Great Britain was third for Lord Hesketh. The frailty of the modern racing car became apparent in this event as evidenced by the number of suspension breakages; 12 cars finished out of 26 starters.

At Zandvoort for the 75-lap, 316.95-km. Dutch Grand Prix in June, the Ferraris were in fighting form, Lauda winning at 184.628 kph from his teammate Regazzoni, with Fittipaldi third. Peterson had the fastest lap. The French Grand Prix was held over 80 laps of the small 3.289-km. Dijon-Premois circuit in early July, Peterson deservedly winning for Lotus. He averaged 192.721 kph for the 263.12 km. of the race, followed in by the two Ferraris of Lauda and Regazzoni. The British Grand Prix, over the undulating 4.26-km. course at Brands Hatch, was marred by mismanagement at the finish. Lauda seemed to have victory in his grasp, when a tire on his Ferrari's right rear wheel deflated. He came in to change it and was unable to get out of the pits road, which was blocked. Scheckter won for Tyrrell, at 186.25 kph, and Lauda's new lap record of 189.31 kph availed him nothing. Fittipaldi was second, Ickx third, and Lauda was afterward permitted to claim fifth instead of ninth place in this so-called John Player Grand Prix.

In August the German Grand Prix over the Nürburgring was as testing as ever of drivers and cars, the

Jackie Ickx of Belgium, driving a John Player Lotus at an average speed of 160.87 kph, wins the Simoniz-"Daily Mail" Race of Champions at Brands Hatch, Eng., in March.

KEYSTONE

latter continuing to suffer alarming breakages. The race was won in fine style by Regazzoni for Ferrari, at 188.825 kph. Scheckter, who made a new lap record for the long and difficult course at 190.689 kph, brought his Tyrrell-Cosworth home second, and third place was filled by Reutemann's Brabham, ahead of Peterson's Lotus. No one headed Reutemann in the Austrian Grand Prix, at the Österreichring. His Brabham BT44 managed 215.81 kph for the 54-lap race. Hulme in the McLaren and Hunt in the Hesketh came in second and third, showing that F1 racing was still wide open and the aging Cosworth-Ford V8 engine by no means past its prime. Regazzoni made a new lap record for the 5.91-km. circuit but was delayed by tire trouble and finished fifth, behind British John Watson's Brabham. Next it was to Monza for the 45th Italian Grand Prix in September. It was hoped locally that the Ferraris would dominate the race, but many thought it would go to Peterson's Lotus. Peterson did win, at a speed of 217.92 kph, although Carlos Pace of Brazil in a Brabham established a new lap record of 220.891 kph. Second place went to Fittipaldi and third to Scheckter.

At the Canadian Grand Prix at the Mosport Park circuit, Fittipaldi drove a good race, to win at 189.13 kph. Behind his McLaren came Regazzoni's Ferrari, Peterson's Lotus, and Hunt's Hesketh, while Lauda made fastest lap in the other Ferrari, at 193.412 kph. There remained only the U.S. Grand Prix at Watkins Glen, N.Y., to decide the much-publicized drivers' championship, and with the result wide open the 1974 season retained its interest to the conclusion. It was, in fact, Reutemann who won, averaging 191.705 kph in the Brabham BT44 to win the $50,000 first prize at the 3.7-mi. road course. Another Brabham driven by Pace was second and Hunt third, but Fittipaldi, by finishing fourth, won the championship. The Ferraris finished the season off form. Regazzoni started the last race of the year equal on points to Fittipaldi, but bad handling dropped him far back to finish in 11th place. The eighth season of Grand Prix competition ended with the Gordon Coppuck-designed M23s of McLaren winning the Constructors' World Championship, the first time McLaren had done so.

The traditional long-distance races for sports-racing cars were continued, with less diverse competition. The Monza four-hour race was won by a BMW 3.5 CSL at 183.817 kph; the Monza 1,000-km. race by an Alfa Romeo 33TT12 at 210.657 kph; the Spa 1,000-km. race by a Matra-Simca 670 at 238.449 kph; the Nürburgring event by a Matra-Simca MS670C at 182.753 kph; the Imola by a Matra-Simca MS670C at 160.9 kph; and the Le Mans 24-hour race by a 3-l. V12 Matra-Simca driven by Henri Pescarolo and Gérard Larrousse, both of France, at 191.940 kph. The Watkins Glen six-hour race was also a Matra-Simca victory, at 174.07 kph. At Brands Hatch the British Airways 1,000-km. race was won by Matra-Simca at 173.021 kph.   (WILLIAM C. BODDY)

The year 1974 was a strange one for U.S. motor sports. Conceived in the depths of the energy crisis and plagued by the spectre of inflation-reduced sponsorships, the programs of the respective sanctioning organizations within and outside the Auto Competition Committee of the U.S. carried forward with more success than might have been expected. There were casualties, among them the 24 Hours of Daytona, the 12 Hours of Sebring, and several Can-Am Challenge Cup events. But the major races drew record or near-record attendance.

Meanwhile, the various groups met the energy crisis with various approaches. The National Association of Stock Car Auto Racing (NASCAR) cut Winston Cup series races 10% in distance; the cut was rescinded for the second half of the season. United States Auto Club (USAC) and the Sports Car Club of America (SCCA) instituted a fuel formula that caused Indianapolis and Formula 5000 competitors to cut speeds in order to make fuel allotments last.

Veterans again dominated the list of champions. Richard Petty drove his STP Dodge to his fifth NASCAR season crown, dueling for the top dollar earnings crown with David Pearson and his Purolator Mercury and Chevrolet-mounted Cale Yarborough. Petty also won the classic Daytona 500 for an unprecedented fifth time. Johnny Rutherford won two legs of the USAC Triple Crown, the Indianapolis 500 and the Pocono Schaeffer 500, plus the Rex Mays 150 in Milwaukee, Wis., but lost the season championship to Bobby Unser.

Rutherford, who won at Indianapolis in his 11th try, led 122 of the 200 laps in what proved to be a safe but uncompetitive race. His victory earned him $245,031 of a record $1,015,686 purse. What competition there was came from pole winner A. J. Foyt (191.632 mph), who led 70 laps before exiting on the 142nd with a broken oil line. Bobby Unser finished second, worth $99,503, and Bill Vukovich third, worth $63,811. The 1973 winner, Gordon Johncock, placed fourth. Rutherford, who averaged 158.589 mph, made eight pit stops—a record for a winning driver as the cars were limited to 285 gal. of methanol fuel. All of the top five cars were powered by turbocharged Offenhausers.

Rutherford also won the Schaeffer 500 and another $62,000, but Unser's fifth place finish there assured him of the best record in the Triple Crown. Unser had won the Ontario, Calif., 500 by an eyelash over his brother Al. He added winning points from Trenton and Phoenix to wrap up the season title early. Meanwhile, Foyt set a new closed-course speed record at the Talladega, Ala., International Motor Speedway in his Indianapolis model car. The 39-year-old driver posted a mark of 217.854 mph.

Although the ending changed occasionally, the leading players in the NASCAR competition remained the same with three men winning 27 of the first 29 events. Petty won ten, including Daytona's 500, the Talladega 500, the Carolina 500, the Capital City 500, the Motor State 400, and the Atlanta Dixie 500. Pearson took the Charlotte World 600, the Daytona Firecracker 400, the Yankee 400, and the Charlotte National 400. Yarborough won ten races in his Carling Beer Chevrolet, including the 25th running of the Southern 500, the Mason-Dixon 500, the Winston Western 500, the Nashville 420, and the Bristol 500. The latter two were protested victories, the Nashville race producing the strange rule that Bobby Allison, who the judges admitted ran one lap more than Yarborough, protested too late because he had not spotted the discrepancy during the contest. Petty and Yarborough finished one-two in the season standings and in money winnings. They and Pearson easily passed $200,000 in season earnings.

Peter Gregg of Jacksonville, Fla., won a reduced SCCA Trans-Am series in an Agor Porsche over the RSR Carrera of Ludwig Heimrath. Another diminished series was the Group 7 car Can-Am—dominated by the UOP Shadows with Belgian Jackie Oliver winning three of the four events.

During the season SCCA and USAC signed an agreement to permit interchange of Formula 5000 single-seater cars and drivers, looking toward a common open wheel series in 1976. The result was that Britisher Brian Redman won the SCCA series with USAC's Mario Andretti second. Andretti continued to have poor luck in Indianapolis cars but showed his versatility by winning the USAC dirt track title.

In USAC stock car racing, Butch Hartman made a late season charge to win his fourth crown. USAC also sanctioned one Bonneville speed record of note as a team of Graham Hill, Luigi Chinetti, Jr., and Milt Minter in a Ferrari GTB4 smashed class marks over a distance of 1,000 km. Bobby Unser also set a record, storming up the 12½-mi. Pikes Peak course in a Dodge kit car in 13 min. 13.16 sec.

Perhaps the most competitive racing during the season came in the International Motor Sports Association series. IMSA had three highly successful series, all backed by sponsors. Elliot-Forbes-Robinson of La Crescenta, Calif., won the VW Gold Cup for Formula Vee single seaters with 7 victories in 13 races. The Camel GT Challenge Series went down to the 11th and final event, at Daytona Speedway, before Peter Gregg won the crown despite an eighth-place finish. Both his challengers, Milt Minter and Michael Keyser, failed to finish. In IMSA's Goodrich Radial Series, there was another race down to the Daytona wire with defending co-champion Nick Craw in a BMW 2002 fighting off George Alderman in the RC Cola Gremlin. Alderman won the Daytona event and the championship.

The U.S. racing world was dealt a serious blow when the Firestone Tire & Rubber Co. announced its complete withdrawal from racing. The company, estimated to have spent in excess of $12 million annually on competition, had been a major source of money for drivers in all facets of the sport.

(ROBERT J. FENDELL)

Motorcycles. In 1974 Phil Read, riding an Italian MV Agusta, again won the 500-cc class of the world championship road-race contest, thereby retaining for the U.K. the most important individual award in motorcycling. In the 350-cc class Giacomo Agostini of Italy, riding for Yamaha after leaving MV Agusta, won his 14th world title. Walter Villa for Aermacchi (both Italy) won the 250-cc class; Kent Andersson of Sweden on a Yamaha, the 125-cc; and Dutchman Hank van Kessel on a Kreidler, the 50-cc. As expected, Klaus Enders (W.Ger.), a BMW driver, won his fifth world sidecar title. Agostini prefaced his world championship rides in Europe with a dazzling display, taking first place in the Daytona meeting in the U.S. Second was Kenny Roberts (U.S.), who later in the year scored the most points in the annual Anglo-U.S. match races held in England at Brands Hatch, Mallory Park, and Oulton Park tracks; the U.K. won the overall competition.

Many of the top riders, such as Agostini and Read, repeated their 1973 boycott of the Tourist Trophy (TT) races in the Isle of Man in June as being too dangerous, and their attitude contributed to the TT's being dropped from the world championship series in 1975. The TT races were in general a Yamaha "benefit," the winners being: open formula, 125 cc, C. Horton (Yamaha), 88.44 mph; 250 cc, C. Williams (Yamaha), 94.16 mph; 350 cc, T. Rutter (Yamaha), 100.44 mph; 500 cc, P. Carpenter (Yamaha), 96.99 mph; 750 cc, C. Mortimer (350 Yamaha), 100.52 mph; 500 cc sidecar, H. Luthringshauser (BMW),

92.27 mph; production race, 1,000 cc, M. Grant (Trident), 99.72 mph; 500 cc, K. Martin (Kawasaki), 93.85 mph; 250 cc, M. Sharpe (Yamaha), 86.94 mph. In September the other Isle of Man road-race event, the Manx Grand Prix for "amateurs," was won by B. Murray (Yamaha) in the 350-cc class at 96.10 mph and the 500-cc at 93.28 mph, and by E. Roberts (Yamaha) in the 250-cc race at 90.35 mph.

In motocross the world championship 500-cc title went to Heikki Mikkola (Fin.), on a Swedish Husqvarna, and the 250-cc to Gennady Moisseev of the U.S.S.R., riding a KTM; the 125-cc FIM Prize, confined to Europe, went to André Malherbe of Belgium, riding a Zündapp. The important team event, the Trophée des Nations, held at Vesouls, France, was headed by Belgium. The Moto Cross des Nations, held in Sweden, was won by the host country, with the U.S., a comparative newcomer to international motocross, second.

In the International Six Days' Trial, held in Italy and marked by accidents and competitors' disagreements, Czechoslovakia won both the Trophy and Vase contests. The classic Scottish Six Days' Trial, a smaller version, for clubs and individuals, was taken by M. Andrews (Yamaha). The chief trials event on the British calendar, the British Experts Trial, was won by M. Wilkinson on a 250-cc Ossa.

In speedway the British team of P. Collins, J. Louis, D. Jessup, and M. Simmons won the World Cup, held at Katowice, Pol. Anders Michanek (Swed.) won the world championship final at Göteborg, Swed., from Ivan Mauger (N.Z.).

The outright world speed record went to Don Vesco (U.S.), with a machine powered by two TZ750 Yamaha engines. He achieved 281.714 mph at Bonneville, Utah. (CYRIL J. AYTON)
[452.B.4.c]

Motorboats. A Miami Beach physician established a motorboat record in 1974 that might stand for many years to come. After two years of painstaking preparation, Robert Magoon piloted a 40-ft. Cigarette hull over the distance from Miami to New York in 22 hr. 41 min. 15 sec. The 42-year-old eye surgeon, winner of five U.S. offshore racing championships, literally assembled the boat piece by piece. With mechanic Gene Lanham, he installed the twin 500-hp MerCruiser stern-drive engines. Navigator for the approximately 1,250-mi. voyage was Bob Connell, a lifelong sailor with experience aboard America's Cup defenders "Constellation" in 1964 and "Intrepid" in 1967. It was his first experience crewing aboard an ocean racing powerboat.

The previous record of 31 hr. 32 min. had been set in 1964 by Charles Johnson in a 41-ft. sport fisherman. No one tried to break the record until Magoon achieved the feat. His average speed for the distance was an incredible 55.40 mph, which meant that he topped 60 mph most of the way.

Meanwhile, unlimited hydroplane racing began its 1974 season with tragedy. George (Skipp) Walther, 27, was fatally injured in a trial run just before the circuit-opening Championship Spark Plug Regatta in Miami. His brother, Dave ("Salt") Walther, had just made a comeback into auto racing after suffering serious injuries at Indianapolis in 1973.

Howie Benns drove "Miss Budweiser" to victory in that first race of the season, and himself was injured in a motorcycle accident late in the year, surrendering his seat to Dean Chenoweth. But it was George Henley in the defending champion boat, the "Pride of

Giacomo Agostini of Italy on his Yamaha wins the Yugoslavian Grand Prix in the 350-cc class.

Carlo Bonomi in his 1,200-hp. "Dry Martini" wins the 1974 Embassy-"Daily Express" International Offshore Powerboat Race with an average speed of 66.9 mph, a new record for the 255-mi. course off the south coast of England.

Pay 'N Pak," who dominated the thunderboat circuit. By late October, in one of the longest unlimited seasons on record, he had won seven of ten races including the prestigious Gold Cup. "Miss Budweiser" won the other three, making it a two-boat contest.

In outboard competition, Gerry Walin was injured while trying to establish a new world straightaway speed record. His Evinrude-powered boat flipped at Lake Havasu, Ariz., while running in excess of 150 mph. The existing record of 136.401 mph, set by Jim Merten with Mercury power in 1973, remained in force.

Italy's Carlo Bonomi won the world offshore powerboat racing championship for the second year in a row, driving "Dry Martini," a Cigarette hull with Kiekhaefer Aeromarine power. Art Norris of Detroit won the U.S. offshore inboard championship, and Juan Fernandez of the Bahamas won the outboard title.

(JIM MARTENHOFF)

[452.B.4.a.ii]

Climbers cross crevasse en route to the top of Lenin Peak in the Pamirs of the U.S.S.R. Eight Soviet women died in a storm on the peak in August.

Mountaineering

In 1974 in the Himalayas there was again much activity and a concentration on routes of considerable technical difficulty. The Nepalese government showed it was determined to see that the rules it laid down for foreign mountaineering expeditions to peaks of

over 20,000 ft. were obeyed, and French and West German parties were penalized for infringing those rules. There was increasing dissatisfaction with the abilities of some of the Sherpa porters available for expeditions, and some talked of forming an elite Sherpa organization. In the Alps an increasing trend was the descent on skis of major snow and ice routes of appreciable difficulty. In the United States the interest in free climbing grew, and many previously artificial routes were climbed free.

In the late summer of 1973 an outstanding new route was a new line on the Eckpfeiler Buttress of Mont Blanc in the Alps. Other new ascents in the Mont Blanc massif were on Mont Blanc du Tacul (three routes), the Aiguille du Midi (northwest couloir), Aiguille des Pélérins (southwest ridge), Aiguille des Deux Aigles (two lines), Petit Dru, Aiguille du Géant, Cardinal, Pointe du Pré de Bar, Aiguille de l'Amône, and Pointe des Améthystes. In the Dauphiné new routes were made on the Rateau and Pic Zsigmondy, and elsewhere in the Alps on the Jägihorn, Tournelon Blanc, Ebnefluh, Monte Rosa (Parrotspitze) and Gross Wiesbachhorn, Piz Badile, and Crozzon di Brenta.

First winter ascents in the Alps in 1973–74 included those of many lines following couloirs, on Mont Blanc du Tacul, Aiguille du Midi, and Aiguille Verte. Several completely new routes were climbed in the winter season, including lines on Mont Blanc du Tacul, the Grandes Jorasses (Pointe Whymper), the Drus, Mont Dolent, the Ruinette, and Mont Blanc de Cheilon.

In the summer of 1974 additional new routes were followed, on the Frêney face and the Eckpfeiler Buttress of Mont Blanc and also on Mont Maudit, Mont Blanc du Tacul, the Aiguilles du Diable, the Aiguille du Midi, Aiguille Verte, Aiguille d'Argentière, and Breithorn. The most noteworthy solo ascents in 1974 were the Cordier route on the Grands Charmoz west face and the traverse of the Aiguilles du Diable.

A new route on the west face of Communism Peak, the highest point of the U.S.S.R., was made by a Polish party in 1973. In the summer of 1974 an international mountaineering camp was organized by the Soviets in the Pamirs, during the course of which British and French parties made new routes on the north face of Lenin Peak (but an independent party of eight Soviet women climbers died in a blizzard there in August), and U.S. climbers made the first ascent of the north face of the 19th Party Congress Peak. In the Hindu Kush new ascents took place on Koh-i-Bandaka in 1973, and on new peaks of Langa Zom in 1974.

After the monsoon in 1973, in the Himalayas the West Germans were successful in the first ascent of Dhaulagiri III and the Japanese in a new route on Kanjiroba. Other Japanese attempts on Kangbachen and Piutha Hiunchuli, a Spanish one on Manaslu, and an Italian one on Annapurna failed, the second and fourth of these each losing several members in avalanche accidents. Successful new ascents before the monsoon in 1974 were the very difficult Changabang (British), Annapurna I (Spaniards, north ridge), Shartse (Austrians), Peak 22270 on Nanda Devi Sanctuary inner rim (Indians), Kanjiroba (south face and east ridge, Japanese), and Lamjung Himal (British). Defeats were Manaslu (by a women's party, one of whom was killed); Jannu, Gangapurna, and Tukuche by Japanese expeditions; and Kangbachen (Polish). British parties failed on

Dhaulagiri IV (with three deaths) and Nampa; Spaniards on Everest; Austrians on Makalu; Americans on Paiju Peak; and Italians on Himalchuli. West Germans were called off Annapurna II because of an irregular ascent of Annapurna IV; and Japanese failed on Annapurna South, Churen Himal, Peak 29, Yalung Kang, the Ogre, and Broad Peak.

In New Zealand during the winter of 1973 the Sheila face of Cook and the south face of Aspiring were climbed, and in summer 1973–74 ascents were made on major faces in the Darran range and other outlying areas. On Ruwenzori, Uganda, new routes were made in 1974 on Baker and the Speke Glacier.

In Greenland there were new ascents in 1973 in Jamesonland and the Angmagssalik areas by British, West German, and Spanish expeditions. In Alaska and the Yukon in 1973 important new climbs were made on Fairweather and Redoubt, and in 1974 on Logan, Dickey, and the Moose's Tooth. A major new ascent in 1974 was the north face of North Twin. Among the major new climbs in the Andes in 1973–74 was Nevado Veronica north face (Poles).   (JOHN NEILL)

[452.B.5.d]

Museums

The museum world reflected society's general concern during the year with acts of political terrorism. Although U.S. museums suffered only one major incident—when Picasso's "Guérnica" was spray-painted at the Museum of Modern Art in New York City—the thefts of significant art works for ransom in Great Britain haunted the security staffs of U.S. museums.

UNESCO and the International Council of Museums (ICOM) were giving particular attention to museum security. After holding a seminar on this subject at Saint-Maximin (France) in May 1973, ICOM set up a special international committee. Meanwhile, UNESCO, in collaboration with the Belgian government, organized in Brussels in November 1973 an international meeting of experts on theft, vandalism, and illicit traffic in works of art. In July 1974 another international meeting held by UNESCO in Paris was devoted to insurance, the high cost of which—due to inflated market values of works of art—was handicapping museums in the protection of their holdings and especially in the organization of temporary or traveling exhibitions and loans.

Financial problems caused by rising costs and, in some cases, reduced income plagued many museums during the year. The situation was especially severe in Italy, where major museums in Milan and Turin were closed for several months.

Even before the financial crises in the U.S. began to affect the museum world, museum workers across the country had begun efforts at unionization. During the year several large museum staffs, such as those of the Art Institute of Chicago and the Brooklyn Museum of Art, moved in that direction. Equally significant was the formation of the Museum Workers Association of New York City, which brought together the personnel from 15 different museums: the natural history, art, craft, and historical museums were represented. The effort was made in order to exchange news and to promote the welfare of the workers and the museums themselves.

The financial problems of the U.S. museum were highlighted at the Pasadena (Calif.) Museum of Modern Art, where the board of directors accepted a complex offer by Norton Simon, an industrialist and well-known art collector. Simon offered to give the museum almost $1 million and to continue to underwrite its debts, in exchange for 75% of its floor space for the display of his own vast collections, valued at hundreds of millions of dollars. "Modern" was then dropped from the museum's title, and several forthcoming exhibitions of recent art were canceled. Critics of the move pointed to Simon's well-known antipathy toward modern art and lamented the loss of a viable showcase for its display.

During 1974, UNESCO and ICOM continued to promote the development of museums. ICOM's tenth General Conference, held in Copenhagen in June, had as its theme "the role of museums in the modern world." UNESCO's General Conference in November adopted a museum program that included seminars on "the adaptation of museums to the needs of the modern world," one of them, for Asian countries, to be held in Tokyo/Kyoto in October 1975, and the other, for African countries, to be organized in 1976. A similar meeting was expected to take place in Latin America in 1977.

Museums held a special relationship to the enactment of national and international measures in favour of the environment. Museums of the environment were appearing or being planned. In November 1974 a remarkable museum—or rather group of museums—was inaugurated at Le Creusot–Montceau-les-Mines in France. It called itself an "eco-museum" and was intended to reveal and stimulate the total life of the community.

Museums in the U.S. were approached from two directions with pleas for resources and action. The Metropolitan Museum of Art, New York City, received $1 million from the Andrew W. Mellon Foundation to establish the Mellon Fund, income from which would be used to encourage the use of museum resources by scholars. The National Endowment for the Arts helped fund the Council on Museums and Education in the Visual Arts; the year-long study undertaken by this group would make available case studies of the educational areas in which museums were operating, and also would further the development of concepts in visual arts education.

Conservation continued to be a prime concern of U.S. museums. Late in 1973 the National Conservation Advisory was founded, and in 1974 new regional laboratories that would be able to handle the problems of the many museums too small to afford their own conservation staffs were being planned. The National Endowment for the Arts continued to distribute federal grants for conservation projects, and the establishment of a National Institute for Conservation was under consideration.

The survey sponsored by the National Endowment for the Arts, *Museums USA*, appeared as the first survey of its kind conducted within the U.S. Based on studies of 1,821 museums in 1971–72, it contained information on which museum officials could base their future planning. For example, it was found that 308 million people had visited those museums in that year; 36% of the museums had cut back facilities, services, and staff since 1966 because of financial pressures; and 37% of the museums charged admission. Total income of the museums in 1971–72 was $513 million, 63% of which came from the private sector. The U.S. museum work force in 1971–72

Motor Vehicles:
see Disasters;
Industrial Production
and Technology;
Motor Sports;
Transportation

Mozambique:
see Dependent States

Municipal Government:
see Cities and Urban
Affairs

Sculpture by Alexander Calder, "Two Discs," stands in front of the Joseph H. Hirshhorn Museum and Sculpture Garden, which opened in Washington, D.C., in October.

relied heavily upon volunteers: 64,200, or 57% of the total of more than 112,000, were nonpaid workers; 30,400 were full-time paid and 18,700, part-time paid. In the area of education the guided tour for children was the most popular activity; only 7% of the museums never offered such tours.

New Facilities. The two newest states of the U.S. were among those announcing new museum building activity. In Hilo, Hawaii, the Lyman House Memorial Museum was to be built; the city of Anchorage, Alaska, raised a $1.2 million bond issue to fund a new wing for the Historical and Fine Arts Museum. The Minneapolis Institute of Arts completed a large $26 million addition to its complex of school, theatre, and museum, the first U.S. buildings by the renowned Japanese architect Kenzo Tange. In Baltimore the $4 million wing at the Walters Art Gallery doubled that museum's exhibition area and would permit it to display more of the 80% of its collection that had been in storage since the museum became public in 1931. The Pennsylvania Academy of Fine Art, in Philadelphia, one of the nation's major collections of early American art, announced a $6 million renovation that would keep its building closed until February 1976.

With the opening of the Neuberger Museum at Purchase, N.Y., the New York State University's museum facility became the largest of any state university system in the U.S. The University of Chicago opened its first major museum facility, the Smart Gallery. In Washington, D.C., the Joseph H. Hirshhorn Museum opened with 4,000 paintings and 2,000 sculptures, housed in a four-story, $16 million cylindrical building; aside from the art works, which comprised the largest single gift ever made by an individual American, Hirshhorn had given $1 million toward the building's construction.

The Römisch-germanisches Museum at Cologne in West Germany was completely reorganized. In France the Chagall Museum at Nice was in a new building. The Ethnographical Museum of Warsaw and a new Art Museum were inaugurated during the year in Poland, while in Spain the Ethnographical Museum of Barcelona opened.

Two museums were still in the planning stage. The Museum of African Art at Dakar (Senegal), which was being designed and organized with the help of experts provided by UNESCO, was to become one of the most important museums in Africa south of the

Sahara. In Afghanistan the old Kabul Museum was to be replaced by an ultramodern institution for which an impressive building was designed by a Danish architect, also provided by UNESCO.

Acquisitions. In the U.S., B. Gerald Cantor donated the world's largest private collection of Rodin sculpture to several museums: 10 works to the Museum of Modern Art in New York City, 29 sculptures to the Los Angeles County Museum of Art, and 88 other works to the Stanford University museum. In New York City, John D. Rockefeller III presented 300 Oriental works to the Asia Society, a museum that he himself had founded in 1956. The well-known photographer Eliot Elisofon bequeathed 600 African sculptures and a 50,000-photo archive on African art to the Museum of African Art in Washington, D.C. The General Services Administration, which had been collecting the works for several years, presented 200 pieces produced for the WPA (Works Progress Administration) and the U.S. Treasury during the depression of the 1930s to the National Collection of Fine Arts of the Smithsonian Institution. The Minneapolis Institute of Art received the Gale Collection of Ukiyo-e art, 100 paintings and 200 prints of the last great flowering of Japanese art.

Two U.S. museums acquired rare old masterworks. The Cleveland Museum of Art obtained a painting, "St. Catherine of Alexandria," by the mysterious 16th-century German artist Matthias Grünewald. The work, from a private German collection, was one of only two Grünewald works in the U.S.; its coming to light especially excited scholars since it is part of a larger altarpiece thought to have been lost at sea in the 17th century. The National Gallery of Art in Washington, D.C., after many years of negotiations with a private source in France, acquired a painting by the 17th-century French artist Georges de la Tour, "The Repentant Magdalene." Only about 40 paintings of this master survive, thus accounting for a purchase price reputed to have been almost $2.5 million. The Los Angeles County Museum of Art acquired "The Holy Family" by Fra Bartolommeo.

In Canada, Henry Moore presented more than 200 of his works to the Art Gallery of Ontario in Toronto. The gift, including 18 bronzes, 41 plaster casts, and numerous graphic works, coincided with the opening of a new building facility by the museum. Also, after four years of negotiation, the National Museum of Man at Ottawa, Ont., acquired the Arthur Speyer, Jr., collection of Canadian Indian artifacts predating 1850. Canada had recently created an Emergency Purchase Fund so that museums could respond quickly to preserve works of art representing the nation's cultural heritage.

Among the outstanding acquisitions of the year in Europe were Edgar Degas's "La Repasseuse," by the Bayerische Staatsgemäldesammlungen in Munich; Amedeo Modigliani's drawing "Tête de profil," given to the French Musée Nationale d'Art Moderne; a Bodhisattva Maitreya Gandara statue, by London's Victoria and Albert Museum; and a 1958 work by the Hungarian painter Victor Vasarely, by the Scottish National Gallery of Modern Art.

The UNESCO General Conference, in November 1974, passed a resolution calling for "the return of cultural property to countries that have been victims of de facto expropriation," including countries occupied in war and those that had been colonized. By the year's end the effect of such claims on present and past museum acquisitions could not yet be foreseen.

There was a growing movement for establishing museum codes of ethics of ensure that the real origin of acquired works of art is known and that the acquisition is legal. Examples in the U.S. of institutions that established acquisition policies involving codes of ethics were the Arizona State Museum, the New York Association of Art Dealers, the American Committee for South Asian Art, the Field Museum of Natural History (Chicago), and the Smithsonian Institution. ICOM began preparing a new international code of ethics. (JOSHUA B. KIND; CONRAD WISE)

See also Art Exhibitions; Art Sales.

[613.D.1.b]

Music

The centenaries of the births of Arnold Schoenberg and Charles Ives occurred in 1974. Both events were celebrated widely throughout the musical world with appropriate revaluations of their work as composers, their influence, and, in Schoenberg's case, his importance as a teacher. To mark the occasion, the University of Southern California established an Arnold Schoenberg Institute and held a centennial celebration from September 12 to 15. At Vienna, in June, the Schoenberg Society held an international congress attended by Schoenberg scholars from all over the world. The society also bought the composer's house in Mödling, Aus., which was to become a museum. At the end of 1973 all Schoenberg's chamber works had been played at concerts in the Queen Elizabeth Hall by the London Sinfonietta conducted by David Atherton. A set of recordings of the chamber works by the same performers was issued during 1974. Schoenberg works were featured in the programs of most major symphony orchestras. His unfinished opera *Moses und Aron* was given a new production by the Hamburg State Opera on March 30, and the same production was taken to the Israel Festival in July.

The Charles Ives Centennial Festival-Conference took place at New York City and New Haven, Conn., October 17–21; it included lectures, symposia, recitals, and concerts. Earlier in the month, a "Mini-Festival Around Charles Ives" was held in New York City. The New York Philharmonic under its conductor, Pierre Boulez, gave, among other works, the Fourth Symphony and *Decoration Day,* and the Chamber Music Society of Lincoln Center, directed by Charles Wadsworth, presented many of the smaller works. The Charles Ives Centennial Festival in Miami, Fla., held later in the year and scheduled to extend into 1975, included nearly all the composer's main works. His orchestral music was also featured in the English Bach Festival at London and Oxford in April, and an exhibition of memorabilia was held at the Queen Elizabeth Hall, London, as part of South Bank Summer Music in August.

The year also marked the centenary of the birth of Gustav Holst, which was quite widely noted in England by performances of his music, several of them directed by his daughter Imogen. Hans Conrad Fischer made an interesting film to mark the 150th anniversary of Anton Bruckner's birth; Bruckner's music was featured in the world's musical capitals, most notably in Vienna, where all his symphonies were included during the summer festival in that city. Even the 125th anniversary of Chopin's death was observed in many recitals of his music in London and elsewhere.

Symphonic Music. The New York Philharmonic, under Boulez, continued its exploration of the less hackneyed paths of music. Its 1973–74 season included performances of Schumann's *Scenes from Goethe's "Faust,"* Mahler's Eighth Symphony, Aaron Copland's *Connotations,* and the premiere of Aribert Reimann's *Cycle for Baritone,* with Dietrich Fischer-Dieskau as soloist. Other New York premieres during the year included Alberto Ginastera's *Serenata* for baritone, cello, and instrumental ensemble, performed by the Chamber Music Society of Lincoln Center; Toru Takemitsu's *Far Away* for piano, by Marie-Françoise Bacquet at the Alice Tully Hall; Luigi Dallapiccola's *Commiato,* by Musica Aeterna; Marvin David Levy's *In Memoriam—W. H. Auden,* by Paul Sperry and the St. Paul Chamber Orchestra; and Ben Johnston's fourth quartet, by the Fine Arts Quartet. Sir Michael Tippett visited the U.S., and conducted his music in various cities during February and March.

The University of Illinois in Urbana presented an American Music Festival from January 30 to February 4. Works included the first performance of George Crumb's *Ancient Voices of Children* and a revival of George F. Bristow's *Rip Van Winkle,* one of the earliest American operas.

The Chicago Symphony Orchestra visited 12 European cities. The Los Angeles Philharmonic Orchestra made a similar tour, taking with them Gerhard Samuel's *Requiem for Survivors,* subtitled "And suddenly it's evening," based on the theme from the Lacrimosa of Mozart's *Requiem.* This new work had been premiered on March 14 in Los Angeles. The Cleveland (O.) Orchestra under its conductor, Lorin Maazel, toured Japan in May. Richard Rodney Bennett's *Concerto for Orchestra* was given its first performance by the Denver (Colo.) Symphony Orchestra on February 25. The 25th season of the Aspen (Colo.) Music Festival, June 28–August 25, had as its theme "Masterpieces of the 20th Century"; it also included a Schoenberg conference. A Charles Ruggles Festival was held at Minneapolis and St. Paul, Minn., between March and June. At Baton Rouge, La., the local symphony orchestra gave the first performance of

Tito Gobbi sings the title role in Verdi's "Falstaff" at London's Royal Opera House in June.

Peter Jona Korn's violin concerto, with Zina Schiff as soloist, on January 16. The Hollywood Bowl Summer Festival, July 9–September 14, included three marathon evenings and a visit from the London Symphony Orchestra under its principal conductor, André Previn.

In London two important premieres of works by Hans Werner Henze were given during the year. On January 4 in the Queen Elizabeth Hall, his *Voices,* 22 songs for mezzo, tenor, and 15 players, was given by Rose Taylor, Paul Sperry, and the London Sinfonietta under the composer's baton. On October 20 his *Tristan* was performed by Colin Davis and the London Symphony. Both had political as well as musical connotations. A new work by Harrison Birtwistle, *Imaginary Landscape,* was given by the BBC Symphony Orchestra, conducted by Boulez, at the Festival Hall on January 16. The Proms in August and September had three premieres: Robin Holloway's *Domination of Black,* a large orchestral work inspired by Schumann; Martin Dalby's viola concerto; and Malcolm Williamson's *Hammarskjöld Portrait,* a setting of the Swedish diplomat's diaries, sung with great fervour by Elisabeth Söderström, who had an *annus mirabilis.* (See *Opera,* below.) The English Bach Festival was distinguished by visits from Maurizio Kagel and Gyorgy Ligeti, who introduced programs of their own music. At South Bank Summer Music, Aribert Reimann's *Tenebrae* was given its first performance by the baritone Barry McDaniel with the composer at the piano. This chamber music festival was notable for some outstanding performances by the Cleveland Quartet, one of the leading young groups of the day, and by Barry Tuckwell's fine horn playing.

Mstislav Rostropovich, having left the Soviet Union for the time being, returned to the Western European concert platform in September. On December 21, at the Maltings, Snape (near Aldeburgh, Eng.), he gave the first performance of Benjamin Britten's third cello suite, written especially for him. In London and elsewhere he appeared as conductor as well as cellist. Antal Dorati was appointed principal conductor of the Royal Philharmonic Orchestra, to take effect from 1975.

With financial stringency the order of the day in Britain, the future of the London orchestras in their existing form again came under review. It was generally agreed that the four main orchestras could not continue their currently exhausting schedules without increased Arts Council grants. The London Symphony continued to prosper under Previn, as did the London Philharmonic under Bernard Haitink, whose Mahler and Bruckner were again notable. The New Philharmonia was feeling its way under its new principal conductor, Riccardo Muti. Its associate conductor, Andrew Davis, was appointed chief conductor of the Toronto Symphony Orchestra. On June 17 and 18 the Berlin Philharmonic Orchestra under Herbert von Karajan made an exciting visit to the Festival Hall to give the four Brahms symphonies.

Outside London, the Hallé Orchestra, which had been in the doldrums for some time, began to prosper under its new principal conductor, James Loughran. Standards were also relatively high in the case of the Scottish National and the Bournemouth Symphony orchestras, the latter under its new principal conductor, Paavo Berglund from Finland. The English Chamber Orchestra again toured successfully under Raymond Leppard and Daniel Barenboim. Of the other chamber orchestras, the Bournemouth Sinfonietta was perhaps the most consistently successful. Leppard was also bringing new life to the BBC Northern Symphony Orchestra. The Leeds Triennial Festival in April revived Peter Racine Fricker's choral work *A Vision of Judgment,* while the Cardiff and Llandaff festivals in the summer featured several new works, mostly by Welsh composers. The City of Birmingham Symphony Orchestra revived Elgar's oratorio *The Apostles,* conducted by Elgar's own apostle, Sir Adrian Boult.

At the Contemporary Arts Festival in La Rochelle, France (previously held in Royan), June 28–July 7, Karlheinz Stockhausen's outlandish new work *Herbstmusik* had its first performance. Barenboim was appointed chief conductor of the Orchestre de Paris in succession to Sir Georg Solti. At the Holland Festival John Tavener's large-scale work *Ultimos Ritos* had its first performance on June 22 at Haarlem; the performance was recorded simultaneously for BBC Television. In Portugal, Iannis Xenakis was featured at the Lisbon Festival in June, and his new work *Cendris* was given there. It called for a large choir and orchestra used experimentally. An International

World's oldest song, dating from the 2nd millennium B.C., is inscribed in cuneiform signs of the Hurrian language (far right) on a tablet unearthed on the coast of Syria. (Right) Richard Crocker, professor of music at the University of California, plays a reproduction of the lyre for which the song was written.

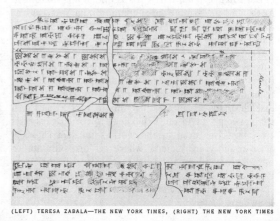

(LEFT) TERESA ZABALA—THE NEW YORK TIMES, (RIGHT) THE NEW YORK TIMES

Congress on New Musical Notation was held at Ghent, Belg., October 22–25.

The year saw the deaths of the composer Darius Milhaud, the conductor Josef Krips, and the violinist David Oistrakh (*see* OBITUARIES). Arthur Rubinstein published the first volume of his autobiography, *My Early Years,* reaching only his 28th year but running to 500 pages. Henri-Louis de la Grange published the first volume of his huge and exhaustive biography of Mahler.

Opera. *United States.* At the Metropolitan the long-drawn-out production of Wagner's *Ring* cycle finally neared completion with *Götterdämmerung* opening on March 8, conducted by Rafael Kubelik, who soon afterward resigned as musical director of the house. His chief assistant, James Levine, was in charge of a new and highly successful production of *I vespri siciliani,* staged by John Dexter, who formed a close association with the Met. The cast included Montserrat Caballé as Elena. Earlier in the season Joan Sutherland appeared in all four soprano roles of *Les Contes d'Hoffmann.* The final new production of the season was a double bill consisting of Bartok's *Bluebeard's Castle* and Puccini's *Gianni Schicchi.* *Death in Venice,* produced by Colin Graham, was the first new production (October 18) of the 1974–75 season, followed by *Jenufa* (November 15) and the original version of *Boris Godunov* with Martti Talvela in the title role (December 16). In November, Anthony A. Bliss, formerly president of the Metropolitan Opera Association, was named executive director of the company, a newly created post that placed him above the general manager, Schuyler G. Chapin. The opening new production at the New York City Opera was *Manon Lescaut* (September 8), followed by *Die Fledermaus* (September 18) and *Un ballo in maschera* (October 29).

At the San Francisco Opera, Leontyne Price sang her first Manon Lescaut in Puccini's opera (September 13). The season also included an outstanding *Parsifal* (September 14), with Kurt Moll as Gurnemanz, and Joan Sutherland in a revival of Massenet's rarely heard *Esclarmonde* (October 23), conducted by Richard Bonynge. At Chicago a special Verdi Congress was held during September. The Chicago Lyric Opera produced *Simon Boccanegra* to run concurrently with the congress, starting on September 20. *Peter Grimes,* a local "first," followed on September 30; *Falstaff* on October 18 with Geraint Evans as producer and singing the title role; *Don Pasquale* on November 2; and *Götterdämmerung,* completing the company's *Ring* cycle, on November 27.

At Houston, Tex., on March 5, Thomas Pasatieri's *The Seagull* had its premiere with Richard Stillwell as Constantin, Frederike von Stade as Nina, and John Reardon as Trigorin. Luchino Visconti's production of *Manon Lescaut* came from Spoleto, Italy, to the Cincinnati (O.) summer season on July 17, and Norman Treigle sang Boris Godunov in a new production of Mussorgsky's opera, in English, on July 24. The summer season at Santa Fe, N.M., included Berg's *Lulu,* conducted by the talented John Mauceri, and Cavalli's *L'Egisto,* with Raymond Leppard in charge of his own edition of the work. The Opera Society of Washington (D.C.) opened its 1974–75 season with *L'incoronazione di Poppea* on October 11; *Die Walküre* followed on December 9, produced by that fine Wotan of the 1950s, George London.

Great Britain. A new *La Bohème* entered the Covent Garden repertory on February 6, staged by John Copley and conducted by Silvio Varviso, with Katia Ricciarelli as a moving Mimi and Placido Domingo an ardent Rodolfo. But the event of the 1973–74 season was the production, the first at the Royal Opera House in the 20th century, of *La clemenza di Tito* on April 22. There were outstanding revivals of *Don Pasquale, Der Rosenkavalier,* and *Jenufa.* The 1974–75 season opened on September 30 with a controversial and exciting production of *Das Rheingold* by Götz Friedrich, conducted at a snail's pace by Colin Davis. *Die Walküre* followed the next evening and *Faust,* produced by John Copley, on November 22. Boris Christoff celebrated his 25th anniversary in the part of Boris Godunov at Covent Garden on November 19.

The Sadler's Wells Opera (which became the English National Opera on August 1) tried its luck with a new opera, Gordon Crosse's *The Story of Vasco,* on March 13 and lost. The company was more successful with new productions of those old favourites *Manon* (January 24) and *Madam Butterfly* (February 28). The 1974–75 season's first new production was *Don Carlos,* disappointing despite the inclusion of some "new" music discovered by musicologist Andrew Porter in the Paris Opéra archives. Henze's *The Bassarids,* in its British premiere (October 10), fared better, although its success as a work was more in doubt. A crippling slowdown by the stage staff closed the house for a time in November.

The Welsh National Opera gave the first performance of Alun Hoddinott's *The Beach of Falesá* (March 26) and Scottish Opera, the premiere of Iain Hamilton's highly dramatic *The Catiline Conspiracy* (March 16). Alexander Goehr's *Arden Must Die* was given its first British performance by the New Opera Company on April 17, and Opera Rara revived Donizetti's *Torquato Tasso* for the Camden Festival (February 27). Thea Musgrave's poetic *The Voice of Ariadne* had its premiere at the Aldeburgh Festival June 11, and for the Holst centenary a double bill of his *Savitri,* with Janet Baker in the title role, and *The Tale of the Wandering Scholar* was given. Alan Bush's Communist-inclined opera *Wat Tyler* had its British premiere at Sadler's Wells Theatre on June 19.

At Glyndebourne, John Cox was responsible for two delightful productions: Richard Strauss's *Intermezzo,* with Söderström outstanding as Christine Storch (alias Pauline Strauss), and *Idomeneo,* both conducted by John Pritchard. At the Edinburgh Festival in August–September, Scottish Opera presented Gluck's *Alceste,* with Julia Varady in the title role, and the Royal Opera of Stockholm gave Götz Friedrich's staging of *Jenufa* with Söderström in the name part—a memorable production and performance. Birgit Nilsson appeared in the company's production of *Elektra.*

Austria. New productions at the Vienna State Opera included *Eugene Onegin* at the end of 1973, Janacek's *Katya Kabanova* (April 19), and *La forza del destino* (September 29). At the Salzburg Easter Festival, Karajan produced and conducted *Die Meistersinger.* At the summer festival he conducted *Die Zauberflöte,* produced by Giorgio Strehler, but the festival's greatest success was *Die Frau ohne Schatten,* conducted by Karl Böhm, who was celebrating his 80th birthday.

Germany. At the Bayreuth (West Germany) Festival (July–August), August Everding produced *Tristan und Isolde,* thrillingly conducted by Carlos Kleiber, with Caterina Ligendza as a beautiful Isolde. Friedrich's production of *Tannhäuser,* in its third year,

Opening night at the new Opera House in Opryland, U.S.A., home of Nashville's Grand Ole Opry.

was another satisfying experience, but the *Ring* badly needed a new staging. At the Munich Festival (July–August), Michael Geliot produced a new *Fidelio;* Fischer-Dieskau was seen in a new production of *Falstaff;* and there was an interesting double bill of Kurt Weill's *Mahagonny Songspiel* and Poulenc's *Les Mamelles de Tirésias,* both produced by Bohumil Herlischka. The regular season included new productions of *La forza del destino,* Henze's *Boulevard Solitude,* and *Die Walküre.* At Hamburg *Moses und Aron* was given on March 30. (*See* above.) The 1974–75 season opened with a production by Herlischka of Mussorgsky's *Khovantchina.* The outstanding new production at Frankfurt was *Katya Kabanova* (January 31). At Cologne Jean-Pierre Ponnelle produced a controversial *Die Entführung aus dem Serail* (June 23), with Lucia Popp a splendid Constanze. At Cassel, James Lockhart was the first British conductor to be in charge of a new staging of the *Ring* in Germany.

Leipzig (East Germany) continued its new look at the *Ring* with Joachim Herz's baroque production of *Die Walküre* on February 20. At the State Opera in East Berlin, Ernst Hermann Mayer's *Reiter der Nacht* was given its premiere in June; it was based on Peter Abrahams' novel *The Path of Thunder.* *Eugene Onegin* (May 4) was the major new production in West Berlin at the Deutsche Oper Berlin.

Italy. At La Scala, Milan, the major new productions were *Salome* (January 28), *La favorita* (January 29) with Fiorenza Cossotto, *Die Walküre* (March 11), and, in April, *Le nozze di Figaro,* conducted by Claudio Abbado, and *Jenufa.* Productions at the Rome Opera included *La Bohème,* Rossellini's *La Reine morte, Pelléas et Mélisande,* and *Don Carlos.* Viviani's *Maria Stuart* had its premiere at the San Carlo in Naples on April 9. Rossini's rarely heard *Matilde de Shabran* was revived at Genoa (March 27), while Spontini's *Fernand Cortez* (January 31) and Donizetti's *Maria di Rohan* (March 14) were revived at Venice.

At the Verona Arena in July there were productions of *Aida, Samson et Dalila,* and *Tosca.* Sherrill Milnes made his Italian debut as Rigoletto at the Macerata Festival on July 14, and Grace Bumbry appeared as Carmen. At the Florence Maggio musicale, the 37th in an illustrious series, Spontini's *Agnes von Hohenstaufen* was revived on May 9, and *La fanciulla del*

West was given (July 5) to mark the 50th anniversary of Puccini's death. Roman Polanski produced *Lulu* at the Spoleto Festival.

France. The new regime at the Paris Opéra continued on its successful way with new productions of Massenet's *Don Quichotte* (January 11); *Cosi fan tutte* (May 17), with Margaret Price as a brilliant Fiordiligi; *Elektra* (May 30), with Birgit Nilsson; *Manon* (July 2), with Ileana Cotrubas; and *Les Contes d'Hoffmann* (October 25). At Strasbourg the Opéra du Rhin gave the first performance of Claude Prey's *Les Liaisons dangereuses* (February 5). The Aix-en-Provence Festival, revived after a year's break, had little success with *La clemenza di Tito* and *Luisa Miller* at the end of July. More enjoyable was a double bill of Pergolesi's *La serva padrona* and Mozart's *Der Schauspieldirektor,* played together! At the Orange Amphitheatre, the mistral disturbed the open-air performance of *Norma* (July 20). On July 23 Christoff sang the title role in a concert performance of Rossini's *Moise.* Leonie Rysanek was magnificent as Salome in Strauss's opera (July 13).

Other Countries. In Belgium, Ernst Poettgen produced an updated *Fidelio* at the Théâtre de la Monnaie in Brussels. At Barcelona, Spain, Matite Salvadori's *Vinatea* was given its first performance (January 19). At the Holland Festival, Gätz Friedrich produced an outrageous version of *Le nozze di Figaro* (June 20), and Agostino Agazzari's *Eumelio* was given its first performance in recent times (June 21). Hans Kox's *Dorian Gray* had its premiere at Amsterdam on March 30. Jan Cikkir's *Coriolanus,* had its premiere during the Prague Spring Festival in May.

Canadian Opera's new productions in Toronto in September were *Bluebeard's Castle, Der fliegende Holländer,* and *L'Heure espagnole.* The Opéra du Québec gave *Madam Butterfly* in Quebec in May and *Falstaff* in Quebec and Montreal in October. Ottawa's Festival Canada at the end of July included new productions of *Le comte Ory* and *Die Entführung aus dem Serail.* Australian Opera gave the first performance of Peter Sculthorpe's long-postponed *Rites of Passage* (September 27).   (ALAN BLYTH)

Jazz. There were several signs during 1974 of the growing tendency, both inside and outside the jazz world, to acknowledge that the music was now old enough to have acquired both a venerable past and a certain cultural respectability, even among the most bigoted. The Soviet Union, which once made the elementary mistake of confusing jazz with the sordid environment from which it had emerged, had so far relented by 1974 as to invite the Canadian piano virtuoso Oscar Peterson to perform a series of concerts in Moscow, Leningrad, and other major cities. Although Peterson's program was only partially fulfilled, through certain inadequacies in Muscovite piano tuning, the tour was a significant indication of the extent to which jazz had outlived its old image.

A different kind of advance, just as important in its own way, was the appearance of the first serious attempt at a day-to-day biography of an important jazz musician, in this case the cornetist-pianist-composer Leon "Bix" Beiderbecke (1903–31). The effort left a great deal to be desired in the literary sense, but the thoroughness of the research and the patent sincerity of the book's intentions suggested that the age of the impressionistic-flapdoodle school of jazz literature might be drawing to a close. Also during the year, the record-buying public benefited from the return of impresario Norman Granz to an active role. Granz had been absent from jazz affairs since the early 1960s. His return, with a new record label, "Pablo," heralded the appearance of new recordings notable for both their catholicity of taste and the bold eclecticism of their performers.

However, all jazz events during the year were dwarfed by the death in May of the most distinguished and sophisticated jazz musician in the history of the music, Edward Kennedy Ellington (see OBITUARIES). Any attempt to summarize Duke Ellington's life is complicated by the fact that he ran several careers and was several different kinds of musician concurrently, although it was as a bandleader that he became world famous. His fortunes, however, were founded on his songwriting achievements. Items like "Solitude," "Mood Indigo," "Sophisticated Lady," and "Satin Doll" place him high in a tradition of which he was never really a part—the Broadway-Tin Pan Alley songwriting world. This prolific melodic gift also manifested itself in literally thousands of brief compositions for his orchestra and, after 1942, in the composition of longer, more formal suites in which the integration between orchestral formality and instrumental improvisation achieved a miraculous balance. "Black, Brown and Beige" and "Such Sweet Thunder" probably rank among the best of his works in this field.

As an instrumentalist Ellington was perhaps the most underrated jazz virtuoso of the last 50 years. His piano style, which was originally formed under the tutelage of the great masters of the "Stride" school of piano playing, James P. Johnson and Willie (The Lion) Smith, developed astonishingly along its own lines, becoming harmonically ornate and intensely romantic in mood. His chief instrument, however, was the orchestra he cherished so dearly and preserved so heroically, for it was through the orchestra that he was able to develop his own compositional fantasies. He was probably the first composer to conceive an original instrumental piece in terms, not of the notes that comprised the piece, but of the individual musicians who were to play it.

Ellington's death overshadowed the death some nine days before of one of his most beloved musicians, the tenor saxophonist Paul Gonsalves (1920–74), who joined the Ellington orchestra in 1950. Gonsalves, a rhapsodic soloist whose stylistic roots could be traced back to the romanticism of Coleman Hawkins, was yet very different from Hawkins and, indeed, from any other saxophonist. A player with an unusually sweet and resilient tone, he also mastered an entirely original harmonic mode of thought that lent his solos a kind of warped symmetry wholly unlike anything else that had been heard in jazz.

Several months after Ellington's death, another occurred that further broke up the texture of the Ellington orchestra. In point of service, the saxophonist-clarinetist Harry Howell Carney (1910–74) was the oldest member of the orchestra, which he had joined in 1926. The first jazz musician to establish the practicability of the baritone saxophone in a jazz context, Carney throughout his long association with Ellington provided an incredibly rich and rock-solid tonal base for all Ellington's saxophone voicings. In later years he tended to play fewer solos, but to the end of his life he continued to perform "Sophisticated Lady" at concerts, a famous parlour trick in which he demonstrated the technique, rare among reed players, of being able to breathe in while holding a sustained note—which meant, naturally, that he could hold it indefinitely. The deaths of Gonsalves and Carney, coming so close to Ellington's own and following the death of Johnny Hodges in 1973, underlined the impracticality of the plan to maintain the Ellington orchestra indefinitely as an effective working group.

(BENNY GREEN)

Popular. Popular music continued to diversify during 1974. A new generation for whom rock was too sophisticated had emerged and demanded its own pop; this was supplied by such artists as Gary Glitter, the Osmonds, and David Cassidy (although Cassidy was trying to change his image). But the musical style derived from earlier years, and there was a general preoccupation with nostalgia. The rock 'n' roll of the 1950s was kept alive both by older stars (Bill Haley) and by young groups re-creating it (Showaddywaddy). Going even further back, there was a revival of classic ragtime, particularly the music of Scott Joplin. British and U.S. sales charts showed a marked difference in taste; in the U.S. musicians such as The Allman Brothers were best-sellers, whereas Britain preferred Slade and Alvin Stardust.

The high standard of rock musicianship resulted in works of symphonic proportions; for example, Yes's "Tales from Topographic Oceans" and "Tubular Bells" and "Hergest Ridge" by the young British musician Mike Oldfield. Yes's former keyboard player, Rick Wakeman, launched his solo career with an entertaining interpretation of Jules Verne's *Journey to the Centre of the Earth*. More avant-garde was the music of Henry Cow and Hatfield & The North.

It was common practice for top musicians to play on one another's albums; for example, Ringo Starr's "Ringo" involved Harry Nilsson, members of The Band, and all four ex-Beatles. The Beatles' publicized reunion failed to materialize as the separate members busied themselves with their own projects. Paul McCartney's band Wings made a million-selling album "Band on the Run."

Theatricalism was less rampant, although some groups (The New York Dolls, Wayne County) still attempted to outrage. Audiences weary of excess were turning to a simpler style; the good pop song was back in favour, neatly performed by such bands as The Eagles and, most notably, Steely Dan. This New York group was led by Donald Fagan (singer/keyboards) and Walter Becker (bass), who had been

Bob Dylan plays his songs in New York City in February, a stop on his first concert tour in eight years.

staff songwriters in a record company and now produced such fine numbers as "Do It Again." British exponents of this style included The Sutherland Brothers & Quiver and the new young group Starry Eyed & Laughing.

Solo artists shared the rock field with groups. David Bowie came out of "retirement" with a new show, two albums, and a television spectacular. New singer/writer Leo Sayer, discovered by 1950s star Adam Faith, toured Britain and the U.S. during the winter of 1973–74 to great acclaim. Adam Faith himself returned to singing with an album, "I Survive." The favourite among female singers was Joni Mitchell.

Group personnel remained more stable than in recent years, but some shifts occurred. Mott the Hoople's original guitarist, Mick Ralphs, joined with Paul Rogers and Simon Kirke (ex-Free) and Boz Burrell to form Bad Company. Swiss musician Patrick Moraz replaced Rick Wakeman in Yes.

There was still a thirst for new talent, and promising acts were heavily promoted. Sparks, an Anglo-American group led by the Mael brothers, won a strong following, and the new English group Cockney Rebel met with spectacular success but split when it was at its height. One of the most individual groups was Gryphon, whose Renaissance-influenced music combined recorders with electric instruments.

The European scene was fronted by The Netherlands' Focus and Golden Earring and the German band Tangerine Dream. Interesting music also came from Finland (Tasavallan Presidentti), France (Magma), and Italy (PFM). From Ireland came Horslips, who combined traditional music with blues. Sweden's Abba won the Eurovision Song Contest with "Waterloo."

Tamla Motown enjoyed another good year, with Stevie Wonder (*see* BIOGRAPHY), Diana Ross, and Marvin Gaye as its outstanding artists. The company issued an "Anthology" series of historic recordings by such stars as Gaye, the Temptations, and The Miracles. "Philly Soul" was very popular, especially in Britain; favourite artists were The Three Degrees and Barry White. The small U.S. record company TK had an international no. 1 hit with George McCrae's "Rock Your Baby." Perhaps the year's biggest success in black music belonged to the four Pointer Sisters from Oakland, Calif.

The British "electric folk" movement thrived, led by Steeleye Span who presented traditional music in a highly entertaining manner. In the U.S. there was a resurgence in country music, rooted in the admittance to Nashville of such artists as John Denver.

Novelty hits included Ray Stevens' "The Streak" and several records by The Wombles, characters from a children's television series that sparked off a craze. The most successful pop musical of the year was *The Rocky Horror Show,* which won the London *Evening Standard*'s award as Best Musical of 1973. Commercial radio came to Britain in the autumn of 1973 and gave exposure to a wide variety of pop. Record sales continued to increase despite the vinyl shortage, but a slump was predicted for the future.

In July 1974 "Mama" Cass Elliot (*see* OBITUARIES) died in London shortly after her season at the Palladium. In August, Bill Chase and three members of his group were killed in a plane crash. Earlier in the year Graham Bond, a founder of the British Rhythm & Blues movement, died after an accident.

The concert business saw artists competing for high attendance figures. Early in 1974 Bob Dylan made a

triumphant tour with The Band; packed audiences heard him sing his old songs in a new way, unsentimental and with no concessions to nostalgia. The "middle" market remained as steady as ever, catering to its large public with pleasant songs and lush orchestral music. This was the province of such singers as Andy Williams and the orchestras led by Bert Kaempfert and Michel Legrand.

With such a wide variety of tastes to satisfy, finding the type of universal heroes that The Beatles had been was virtually impossible—though some artists such as The Carpenters did appeal to more than one market. The pop of the 1960s had matured and was on its way to becoming an art form as separate from popular music as jazz. (HAZEL MORGAN)

Folk Music. Among the many folk festivals, large and small, that took place in all parts of the U.S. in 1974, one of the oldest was the National Folk Festival founded by Sarah Gertrude Knott, which held its 36th annual gathering in Vienna, Va., August 1–4. Probably the most elaborate, the Smithsonian Institution's eighth Annual Festival of American Folklife, took place in Washington, D.C., July 3–14. Folk groups from abroad again participated in the section "Old Ways in the New World." Noteworthy among the summer regional festivals was the 48th Mountain Music Festival of Asheville, N.C., founded by Bascomb Lamar Lunsford. Native American dance teams participated in an Alaskan Native Arts Festival organized in March at the University of Alaska by Thomas Johnston.

Among the many projects in folk music research was a documentary film made by Harold Cook on the Shakers, a small religious sect with a characteristic relation to music. Another film project, to document culture and music in an isolated sector of Montana, was undertaken by Sean Malone. In Canada the 1974 medals of the Canadian Music Council were awarded to three outstanding collectors of folk songs: Helen Creighton, for her work since 1928 in collecting, publishing, and lecturing on the songs and ballads of Nova Scotia; Luc Lacourcière, as a teacher and collector of French-Canadian songs and folklore and especially for his development of the Archives de Folklore at the Université de Laval in Quebec City; and François Brossard, an important folksong collector in French Canada, associated with Lacourcière.

Certain international organizations were paying closer attention to non-European music. Thus, the International Musicological Society (IMS) sent Poul Rovsing Olsen of Denmark on a mission through the Middle East early in 1974, in the course of which he established relations between the IMS and local musicologists. His detailed report on current musicology in these countries was to appear in *Acta Musicologica.* The International Music Council (IMC), affiliated with UNESCO, sponsored its third Rostrum of Asian Music in Alma-Ata, capital of the Kazakh S.S.R., in the fall of 1973.

In February 1974 the IMC sponsored a symposium on traditional and contemporary music of Arabic and North African countries, held in Hammamet, Tunisia. Until recently, interest and research in traditional music outside Europe had been largely the preserve of Europeans and Americans. However, a new trend was emerging, with Asian and African specialists carrying out research in their own music. (BARBARA KRADER)

See also Dance; Motion Pictures; Television and Radio; Theatre.

[624.D-I]

Namibia:
see Dependent States; South Africa

Narcotics:
see Drug Abuse

NATO:
see Defense

Nauru

An island republic in the Pacific Ocean, Nauru lies about 1,200 mi. E of New Guinea. Area: 8.2 sq.mi. (21 sq.km.). Pop. (1973 est.): 7,000. Capital: Yaren. Language: English and Nauruan. Religion: Christian. President in 1973, Hammer de Roburt.

The Nauruan Parliament met in May 1974 to discuss a supplementary finance bill, aimed at raising about A$969,000 to add to the main budget. Bernard Dowiyoyo, member of Parliament, was elected chairman of the Nauruan Workers' Organization after President de Roburt had given sanction to the revival of this body. The NWO focused its attention on inflation; Detonga Deiye, its secretary, pointed out that the prices of basic foodstuffs had doubled over 1973–74, but there had been no review of the basic wage since 1962.

Transport and communications were given high priority in government policy. In May, de Roburt visited Saipan in the Mariana Islands, and subsequently the Nauru Pacific Line was given permission to serve various ports in the area. De Roburt offered to invest A$2 million in the Saipan airport project, to be carried out in the U.S. Trust Territory at a cost of A$6 million, and Nauru subsequently took delivery of a second Fokker F28 jet airliner. Nauru's Local Government Council faced transport difficulties in 1973–74 when the Nauruan vessel "Enna G" was strikebound in Wellington, N.Z. The council took out a writ during December 1973 against three New Zealand seamen's and port workers' unions, claiming A$386,000 damages. Nauru Pacific Line moved into Micronesia with the 6,300-ton chartered ship "Elizabeth Bornhofen," which operated from San Francisco and Honolulu to Majuro and Ponape in the Marshall and Caroline islands. (A. R. G. GRIFFITHS)

[977.A.3]

NAURU
Education. (1973) Primary, pupils 1,506, teachers 87; secondary, pupils 463, teachers 34.
Finance and Trade. Monetary unit: Australian dollar, with (after devaluation on Sept. 24, 1974) a free rate of A$0.76 to U.S. $1 (A$1.77 = £1 sterling). Budget (1971–72): revenue A$7.5 million; expenditure A$7,720,000. Foreign trade (1972 est.): imports A$8.5 million (c. 98% from Australia); exports A$15 million (c. 53% to Australia, c. 39% to New Zealand, c. 8% to Japan).
Industry. Production: phosphate rock (1971–72) 1,906,000 metric tons; electricity (1972) 21 million kw-hr.

Nepal

A constitutional monarchy of Asia, Nepal is in the Himalayas between India and Tibet. Area: 54,362 sq.mi. (140,797 sq.km.). Pop. (1973 est.): 12,020,000. Cap. and largest city: Kathmandu (pop., 1971, 150,402). Language: Nepali (official); also Newari and Bhutia. Religion (1971): Hindu 89.4%; Buddhist 7.5%. King,

NEPAL
Education. (1971–72) Primary, pupils 478,743, teachers 11,490; secondary and vocational, pupils 257,245, teachers 3,334; teacher training, students (1969–70) 365, teachers (1966–67) 19; higher, students 25,000, teaching staff 1,070.
Finance. Monetary unit: Nepalese rupee, with (Sept. 16, 1974) an official rate of NRs. 10.56 to U.S. $1 (free rate of NRs. 24.30 = £1 sterling). Gold, SDRs, and foreign exchange: (March 1974) U.S. $132.3 million; (March 1973) U.S. $106.8 million. Budget (1973–74): revenue NRs. 716 million; expenditure NRs. 506 million (excludes development expenditure of NRs. 1,041,000,000).
Foreign Trade. (1969–70) Imports NRs. 854.7 million (c. 75% from India, c. 10% from Japan); exports NRs. 489.2 million (c. 62% to India, c. 12% to Belgium-Luxembourg, c. 5% to Japan). Main exports: rice 36%; jute 9%; jute products 6%; butter 5%.
Agriculture. Production (in 000; metric tons; 1973; 1972 in parentheses): rice c. 2,550 (c. 2,400); corn c. 800 (785); potatoes c. 293 (293); millet and sorghum c. 130 (c. 120); jute c. 63 (c. 55). Livestock (in 000; 1972–73): cattle c. 6,450; pigs c. 300; sheep c. 2,250; goats c. 2,300.

Birendra Bir Bikram Shah Deva; prime minister in 1974, Nagendra Prasad Rijal.

The maintenance of law and order in Nepal deteriorated during 1974. As the numbers of attacks on police stations in outlying areas rose, arrests of students, politicians, terrorists, and sympathizers with the outlawed Nepali Congress increased. The most serious incident occurred in Biratnagar in March when a grenade exploded about 100 yd. from the Kosi Zonal Review Hall, where the king was making an annual inspection; it killed 2 persons and injured 37 others. In June the government launched intensive operations to recover illegal arms from the Khampa refugees from Tibet, who had settled in the Mustang area. Officials would not confirm that the Khampas, estimated at 8,000, were being subdued to please China; they were known to have made sneak attacks against the Chinese forces in Tibet. The heavily armed Khampas clashed with the Nepalese Army on three occasions with casualties on both sides.

After his official visits to India and China in late 1973, King Birendra claimed that Nepal's relations with both countries were good and that there was no tilt toward either side. But by October strains were visible in relations with India as the Nepalese reacted unfavourably to the Indian Parliament's decision of September 4 to make Sikkim an associate state. India recalled its ambassador for consultations.

Nepal's fifth five-year plan, which envisaged a total expenditure of NRs. 6,570,000,000, had to be revised in 1974 because the rise in oil prices and worldwide inflation made the targets unrealistic. Official estimates put the rate of inflation during 1973–74 at 28.4%. Landlocked Nepal, which depended on India for its oil supplies, sent delegations to Middle Eastern oil-producing countries to purchase its additional oil requirements that India was unable to supply. Foreign aid continued to keep the economy going. A trade and payments agreement was signed with China in May and a trade delegation that visited Peking in April bought more than NRs. 60 million of consumer goods.

In July the minister of state for finance, Bhek Bahadur Thapa, presented the fiscal 1974–75 budget to the National Panchayat. Revenue was estimated at NRs. 1,297,000,000 including foreign aid, and expenditure at NRs. 1,740,890,000. The deficit was to be covered by foreign and internal loans.

(GOVINDAN UNNY)

[976.A.6]

Navies:
see Defense

Netherlands, The

A kingdom of northwest Europe on the North Sea, The Netherlands, a Benelux country, is bounded by Belgium on the south and West Germany on the east. Area: 15,892 sq.mi. (41,160 sq.km.). Pop. (1974 est.): 13,491,000. Cap. and largest city: Amsterdam (pop., 1974 est., 770,800). Seat of government: The Hague (pop., 1974 est., 494,700). Language: Dutch. Religion (1971): Roman Catholic 39.6%; Dutch Reformed 23%; no religion 22.4%; Reformed Churches 7%. Queen, Juliana; prime minister in 1974, Joop den Uyl.

As a consequence of the oil boycott of The Netherlands by the Arab countries, the Dutch government rationed gasoline at the beginning of 1974. The measure was ineffective, however, and was revoked after three weeks (on February 4). The West German and Belgian governments had refused to close their filling stations to Dutch drivers who crossed the frontiers, and the Dutch national organization of filling-station proprietors, who were losing business to foreign pumps, decided to ignore the government's decree and to sell gasoline without restrictions.

On March 3 a British Airways VC-10 plane was seized by two Palestinian terrorists. When it landed at Schiphol Airport, near Amsterdam, the 92 passengers and the crew were forced to disembark. The hijackers set fire to the plane, in reprisal for Britain's having permitted its airports to be used to transport weapons and recruits to Israel during the October 1973 Arab-Israeli war, and then surrendered. The hijackers were tried and were sentenced to five years' imprisonment. They were later released at the request of the Tunisian government in exchange for the 40 passengers and crew of a British Airways VC-10 plane held hostage by Palestinian guerrillas in Tunis.

Elections for the municipal councils (*Gemeenteraden*) took place on May 29. Compared with the March elections for the county councils (*Provinciale Staten*), they showed small gains by the left and right, but the three confessional parties, the Roman Catholic People's Party, the Protestant Antirevolutionary Party, and the Christian Historical Union, still obtained a narrow victory. A main issue in the campaign was the Socialist Party's intention that the executive of mayor and aldermen be chosen by majority vote of the elected council rather than on a representational basis. This was carried out in some large cities. As compared with the corresponding elections in 1970, the elections for the county councils in March resulted in a loss for the three confessional parties.

Early in July the minister of defense, Henk Vredeling, presented a defense plan. Salient proposals were that the defense budget need not rise proportionately with the rise in national income, and that there should be a shift from quantity to quality in weapons and a decrease in numbers of military personnel. The issuance of the plan had been preceded by intensive diplomatic consultations, especially with NATO. An official NATO publication stated that the proposals would seriously affect the treaty organization's defense capability.

From July 29 to August 5 Dutch farmers called attention to a decline in farming income and steeply rising costs by holding traffic-disrupting demonstrations at busy crossroads and by occupying the offices of national agricultural organizations. Activity culminated in a massive demonstration attended by more than 30,000 farmers at a stadium in Utrecht. The government attempted to come to terms with the farmers by acceding to some of their demands, but the farmers remained discontented and turbulent. In response to The Netherlands' request the EEC agreed on an interim 5% rise in the price of some EEC agricultural products. The picture was further darkened by record rains that seriously reduced the potato, onion, and sugar-beet crops in Zeeland.

On September 13, 11 (later reduced to 9) persons, including the French ambassador, Jacques Sénard, were held hostage in the French embassy by three Japanese terrorists. The terrorists, members of the radical (Maoist) Japanese Red Army, demanded the release of Yutaka Furuya, another terrorist then serving a sentence in a Paris prison, his transportation to The Hague, safe-conduct to Schiphol Airport, and an airliner to fly them away. Negotiations with the Japanese were conducted by the Dutch prime minister and the ministers for foreign affairs, justice, and the interior. The French sent Furuya and a Boeing 707 (withdrawing its crew), and transferred responsi-

---

NETHERLANDS, THE

Education. (1972–73) Primary, pupils 1,539,676, teachers 56,745; secondary, pupils 662,145, teachers 41,738; vocational, pupils 438,050, teachers 39,600; teacher training, students 10,685, teachers 1,000; higher (including 10 universities) students 83,212, teaching staff 7,500.

Finance. Monetary unit: guilder, with (Sept. 16, 1974) a free rate of 2.72 guilders to U.S. $1 (6.28 guilders = £1 sterling). Gold, SDRs, and foreign exchange, central bank: (June 1974) U.S. $5,221,000,000; (June 1973) U.S. $5,329,000,000. Budget (1974 est.): revenue 58.2 billion guilders; expenditure 62.8 billion guilders. Gross national product: (1972) 147,480,000,000 guilders; (1971) 129,550,000,000 guilders. Money supply: (April 1974) 37,090,000,000 guilders; (April 1973) 38,780,000,000 guilders. Cost of living (1970 = 100): (June 1974) 136; (June 1973) 125.

Foreign Trade. (1973) Imports 68,623,000,000 guilders; exports 66,918,000,000 guilders. Import sources: EEC 60% (West Germany 27%, Belgium-Luxembourg 16%, France 8%, U.K. 5%); U.S. 9%. Export destinations: EEC 72% (West Germany 33%, Belgium-Luxembourg 14%, France 10%, U.K. 8%, Italy 6%). Main exports: chemicals 16%; petroleum products 13%; textile yarns and fabrics 7%; nonelectri-

cal machinery 6%; meat products 6%; electrical machinery and equipment 6%; iron and steel 6%; transport equipment 5%; fruit and vegetables 5%. Tourism (1972): visitors 2,594,300; gross receipts U.S. $762 million.

Transport and Communications. Roads (1973) 82,488 km. (including 1,367 km. expressways). Motor vehicles in use (1973): passenger 3,230,000; commercial 320,000. Railways: (1972) 2,833 km. (including 1,645 km. electrified); traffic (1973) 8,260,000,000 passenger-km., freight 3,319,000,000 net ton-km. Air traffic (1973): 9,282,000,000 passenger-km.; freight 525.2 million net ton-km. Navigable inland waterways (1972): 4,832 km. (including 1,669 km. for ships of 1,500 tons and over); freight traffic 29,333,000,000 ton-km. Shipping (1973): merchant vessels 100 gross tons and over 1,369; gross tonnage 5,029,443. Ships entered (1972) vessels totaling 142.8 million net registered tons; goods loaded (1973) 88.1 million metric tons, unloaded 261.2 million metric tons. Telephones (Dec. 1972) 4,003,000. Radio licenses (Dec. 1972) 3,776,000. Television receivers (Dec. 1972) 3,353,000.

Agriculture. Production (in 000; metric tons; 1973; 1972 in parentheses): wheat 725 (673); barley 383 (340); rye 105 (151); oats 134

(140); potatoes *c.* 5,400 (5,581); tomatoes *c.* 381 (365); onions *c.* 325 (300); apples (1972) 400, (1971) 520; pears (1972) 100, (1971) 110; sugar, raw value *c.* 807 (*c.* 756); dry peas *c.* 20 (17); rapeseed 41 (45); linseed *c.* 7 (*c.* 7); flax fibre (1972) 12, (1971) 14; milk (1972) 8,860, (1971) 8,392; butter (1972) 163, (1971) 144; cheese (1972) 322, (1971) 307; eggs *c.* 275 (269); beef and veal *c.* 350 (*c.* 345); pork *c.* 780 (*c.* 780); fish catch (1972) 348, (1971) 321. Livestock (in 000; May 1973): cattle 4,675; pigs 6,425; sheep 657; horses used in agriculture *c.* 100; chickens 60,328.

Industry. Index of production (1970 = 100): (1973) 124; (1972) 115. Production (in 000; metric tons; 1973): coal 1,721; crude oil 1,491; natural gas (cu.m.) 70,821,000; manufactured gas (cu.m.) 1,137,000; electricity (kw-hr.) 52,627,000; pig iron 4,706; crude steel 5,624; cement 4,075; petroleum products (1972) 64,779; sulfuric acid 1,545; fertilizers (nutrient content; 1972–73) nitrogenous *c.* 1,205, phosphate *c.* 355; cotton yarn 39; wool yarn 12; rayon, etc., filament yarn 37; nylon, etc., filament yarn and fibres (1972) 113. Merchant vessels launched (100 gross tons and over; 1973) 892,000 gross tons. New dwelling units completed (1973) 155,000.

bility for the affair to the Dutch. In exchange for a ransom of $300,000, safe-conduct to Schiphol, and an unhampered get-away, the Japanese were willing to release the hostages, and on September 17 they were exchanged for a Dutch air crew. Ultimately the plane landed in Damascus, Syria, where the four Japanese surrendered to authorities and returned the ransom to the crew. Later, on October 26, four gun-wielding prisoners, including one of the Palestinians who had set fire to the British Airways VC-10 in March, took 22 hostages in the chapel of Scheveningen Prison near The Hague and demanded, as well as the release of another of the Palestinian hijackers, air transport to freedom. After skillfully conducted negotiations, marine commandos stormed the chapel on October 31, overwhelmed the prisoners, and released unharmed those hostages who had not already been freed.

The confinement of the first group of hostages coincided with the opening of Parliament on September 17, and under the shadow of that dramatic event the opening ceremony was a sober affair. The budget presented by the minister of finance, Willem F. Duisenberg, forecast a deficit. Government expenditures rose by 23% over the previous year, but thanks to higher revenue from natural gas, an increase in taxation was not necessary. In the autumn the minister of economic affairs, Ruud F. M. Lubbers, presented an energy policy directive to Parliament. Its chief proposals were the planned reduction of power; increased government participation in the production, allocation, and use of energy; formation of a strategic reserve of natural gas; and the operation of three new nuclear power stations by 1985. (DICK BOONSTRA)

See also Dependent States.
[972.A.7]

New Zealand

New Zealand, a parliamentary state and member of the Commonwealth of Nations, is in the South Pacific Ocean, separated from southeastern Australia by the Tasman Sea. The  country consists of North and South islands and Stewart, Chatham, and other minor islands. Area: 103,736 sq.mi. (268,675 sq.km.). Pop. (1974 est.): 3,042,800. Cap.: Wellington (pop., 1974 est., 141,800). Largest city: Christchurch (pop., 1974 est., 170,600). Largest urban area: Auckland (pop., 1974 est., 775,460). Language: English (official), Maori. Religion (1971): Church of England 31.3%; Presbyterian 20.4%; Roman Catholic 15.7%. Queen, Elizabeth II; governor-general in 1974, Sir Denis Blundell; prime ministers, Norman E. Kirk and, from September 6, Wallace Edward Rowling.

The death of New Zealand's fourth Labour Party prime minister, Norman Eric Kirk (*see* OBITUARIES), at the age of 51 on Aug. 31, 1974, was received as a national tragedy. The burly, genial, silver-haired enthusiast for a greater sense of unity among the peoples of the Pacific had been in government office for only 21 months, all of it as prime minister, and had given promise of filling a regional vacuum as statesman of the South Pacific when he developed a circulatory ailment after minor surgery in April. He had returned from a six-nation Asian tour earlier in the year and was to have embarked on another tour to Japan and South Korea. Instead, he went through four months

NEW ZEALAND
Education. (1973) Primary, pupils 521,871, teachers 19,831; secondary, pupils 202,876, teachers 11,223; vocational, pupils 2,231, teachers 948; teacher training, students 8,262, teachers 642; higher (at 7 universities), students 27,006, teaching staff 2,415.

Finance. Monetary unit: New Zealand dollar, with (after devaluation on Sept. 24, 1974) a free rate of NZ$0.76 to U.S. $1 (NZ$1.77 = £1 sterling). Gold, SDRs, and foreign exchange, central bank: (May 1974) U.S. $528 million; (May 1973) U.S. $929 million. Budget (1973–74 est.): revenue NZ$2,271,000,000; expenditure NZ$2,605,000,000. Gross national product: (1972–73) NZ$7,056,000,000; (1971–72) NZ$6,261,000,000. Cost of living (1970 = 100): (2nd quarter 1974) 139; (2nd quarter 1973) 126.

Foreign Trade. (1973) Imports NZ$1,591,500,000; exports NZ$1,913,200,000. Import sources: Australia 25%; U.K. 20%; Japan 12%; U.S. 11%. Export destinations: U.K. 24%; U.S. 16%; Japan 14%; Australia 8%. Main exports (1972–73): meat and meat preparations 30%; wool 24%; butter 8%; hides and skins 5%. Tourism: visitors (1969) 148,100; gross receipts (1972) U.S. $62 million.

Transport and Communications. Roads (1973) 92,005 km. (including 116 km. expressways). Motor vehicles in use (1973): passenger 1,064,800; commercial 195,100. Railways: (1973) 4,799 km.; traffic (1972–73) 488 million passenger-km., freight (1973) 3,367,000,000 net ton-km. Air traffic (1973): 3,227,000,000 passenger-km.; freight 85.2 million net ton-km. Shipping (1973): merchant vessels 100 gross tons and over 113; gross tonnage 156,503. Telephones (Dec. 1972) 1,358,000. Radio licenses (Dec. 1971) 713,000. Television licenses (Dec. 1973) 750,000.

Agriculture. Production (in 000; metric tons; 1973; 1972 in parentheses): wheat 420 (427); barley 261 (315); oats 49 (55); corn (1972) 135, (1971) 65; potatoes c. 325 (325); dry peas c. 50 (c. 50); tomatoes c. 61 (c. 60); apples (1972) 161, (1971) 163; milk (1972) 6,289, (1971) 6,135; butter (1972) 249, (1971) 235; cheese (1972) 105, (1971) 108; mutton and lamb (1972) c. 550, (1971) 558; beef and veal (1972) c. 410, (1971) 397; wool 220 (230); timber (cu.m.; 1972–73) 8,800, (1971–72) 8,500; fish catch (1972) 58, (1971) 66. Livestock (in 000; Jan. 1973): cattle 9,088; sheep 56,684; horses c. 80; pigs 507; chickens c. 5,500.

Industry. Fuel and power (in 000; metric tons; 1973): coal 422; lignite 2,046; crude oil (1972) 139; natural gas (cu.m.; 1972) 222,000; manufactured gas (cu.m.) 74,000; electricity (excluding most industrial production; kw-hr.) 17,914,000. Production (in 000; metric tons; 1973): cement 1,058; petroleum products (1971) 2,809; phosphate fertilizers (1972–73) c. 350; wood pulp (1972–73) 601; newsprint (1972–73) 213; other paper (1972–73) 240.

of illness before his death. He was the fifth and youngest New Zealand prime minister to die in office.

Because of the dominance he had come to exert in the Labour Party since he deposed Arnold Nordmeyer as leader in 1965, Kirk had no obvious successor, and it was a fairly open question to whom the party would turn. It decided to bypass Kirk's deputy, Hugh Watt, the only member of the team with previous Cabinet experience, and chose the finance minister, Wallace Edward (Bill) Rowling (*see* BIOGRAPHY), aged 46, a former schoolteacher. As deputy, the parliamentary caucus chose another academic and economics specialist, Robert James Tizard, whom Rowling promptly named finance minister. Watt remained in the Cabinet as minister of works and development. The party was clearly battening down the hatches to ride out the economic storm that was common to most countries that were paying more for imported oil and getting less for their own exports. Foreign-exchange reserves were being drained away as New Zealand obtained less for its meat, dairy products, and wool in overseas markets, fought for continued outlets for cheese after a guarantee worked out during Britain's admission to the EEC would lapse, and battled an inflation that was threatening to surpass 14% for the year.

New Zealand followed Australia with a 9% devaluation at the end of September, and later added 2% to bring it to par with its Commonwealth partner; Australia continued to enjoy a big trade balance at the expense of New Zealand. In April a general pay raise of 9% was granted, along with profit and cost controls that proved ineffective. The budget, at the end of May, limited the size of new homes to conserve building materials, increased pensions, raised loan limits for farmers, and eased depreciation rules for businessmen. A National Development Council set up by the previous government was absorbed into a Cabinet committee. What seemed to be stop-go efforts to cope with costs and the erosion of the balance of payments provided ammunition for the former finance minister, Robert Muldoon, who displaced John Marshall as National Party leader on July 9, in his assaults on the government. In a speech on October 23 Rowling, while making it clear that his government was not prepared to undertake stringent deflationary policies that would generate economic stagnation and unemployment, announced measures to combat inflation. These included a compulsory savings plan for earnings of NZ$60 and more a week, at the rate of 9% of income tax deductions for four months, to be credited against tax paid.

Controversies that distracted New Zealanders from rising costs included abortion, after a police raid on a clinic liberally interpreting the law; the relationship of labour unions to the civil courts and alleged irregularities in the management of some unions; immigration policies, which began to put more emphasis on age and skills and now included British and Irish among those requiring entry permits; reconstruction of the single broadcasting corporation into two corporations for separate TV networks and another corporation for radio; and a hardened attitude toward receiving South African whites-only sports teams, which disqualified not only the sports without merit selection but also the ones that claimed merit selection but were not fully integrated. New Zealand supported Asian countries in their opposition to the enlargement of the Anglo-U.S. Indian Ocean base of Diego Garcia and protested the continued French nuclear testing in the Pacific and China's test.

Violence among nonwhites in urban areas increased during the year. Industrial confrontation lost its edge when the Cabinet was reformed after the death of Kirk; Arthur Faulkner, a former defense minister and big vote-getter in the race for deputy prime minister, was appointed minister of labour. At a time of crisis in petroleum supply it was imperative that New Zealand's lakes should regain their levels for hydroelectric power generation, and one of the wettest winters ever recorded alleviated that difficulty.

New Zealand's most influential visitor was the shah of Iran, on an eastern tour to seek trade relationships with countries other than the major powers.

(JOHN A. KELLEHER)

[977.C]

Nicaragua

The largest country of Central America, Nicaragua is a republic bounded by Honduras, Costa Rica, the Caribbean Sea, and the Pacific Ocean. Area: 50,000 sq.mi. (130,000 sq.km.). Pop. (1973 est.): 2,019,000. Cap. and largest city: Managua (pop., 1971, 398,514). Language: Spanish. Religion: Roman Catholic. Heads of state until Dec. 1, 1974, a triumvirate: Roberto Martínez Lacayo, Alfonso Lovo Cordero, and Ed-

NICARAGUA
Education. (1971) Primary, pupils 314,425, teachers 8,154; secondary, pupils 54,139, teachers 1,578; vocational, pupils 5,613, teachers 336; teacher training, students 1,332, teachers 93; higher (including 2 universities), students 11,618, teaching staff 694.
Finance. Monetary unit: córdoba, with (Sept. 16, 1974) a par value of 7 córdobas to U.S. $1 (free rate of 16.26 córdobas = £1 sterling). Gold, SDRs, and convertible currency, central bank: (May 1974) U.S. $181,270,000; (May 1973) U.S. $134,390,000. Budget (1973 est.) balanced at 878 million córdobas. Gross national product: (1972) 6,648,000,000 córdobas; (1971) 6,138,000,000 córdobas. Money supply: (April 1974) 1,509,100,000 córdobas; (April 1973) 1,133,-400,000 córdobas.
Foreign Trade. (1973) Imports 2,289,000,000 córdobas; exports 1,892,500,000 córdobas. Import sources: U.S. 35%; Costa Rica 9%; Japan 8%; Guatemala 8%; West Germany 7%; Venezuela 7%; El Salvador 5%. Export destinations: U.S. 33%; Japan 18%; Costa Rica 10%; West Germany 7%. Main exports: cotton 23%; coffee 16%; meat 16%; sugar 5%.
Transport and Communications. Roads (1971) 13,147 km. (including 485 km. of Pan-American Highway). Motor vehicles in use (1972): passenger c. 32,-000; commercial (including buses) c. 13,000. Railways: (1972) 348 km.; traffic (1970) 30 million passenger-km., freight 16 million net ton-km. Air traffic (1972): 117 million passenger-km.; freight 1 million net ton-km. Telephones (Jan. 1973) 19,000. Radio receivers (Dec. 1972) 115,000. Television receivers (Dec. 1972) 60,000.
Agriculture. Production (in 000; metric tons; 1973; 1972 in parentheses): corn c. 201 (c. 129); rice (1972) c. 60, (1971) 74; sorghum c. 58 (c. 40); dry beans c. 55 (c. 43); coffee c. 34 (c. 42); sugar, raw value c. 142 (c. 164); cotton, lint c. 105 (c. 104). Livestock (in 000; 1972–73): cattle c. 2,778; pigs c. 660; chickens c. 3,300.
Industry. Production (in 000; metric tons; 1972): petroleum products 456; cement (1971) 99; gold (troy oz.) 82; electricity (kw-hr.; 1971) 649,000.

mundo Paguaga Irías; president after December 1, Anastasio Somoza Debayle.

As expected, the year 1974 ended with the official return of Anastasio Somoza as head of state. Votes cast during the national election on September 1 were not yet tallied when the sole opponent, Edmundo Paguaga Irías of the Conservative Party, conceded defeat. Somoza's eventual margin of victory was about 20–1. The 1950 constitution prohibited the reelection of a president or any of his relatives up to the fourth generation, but in March a new constitution was approved—the country's tenth in 136 years—which provided legitimacy for Somoza's return.

Predictably, strong opposition was displayed against Somoza's perennial candidacy. In June at his own Liberal Party convention, 11 dissident members were summarily expelled from the party. Nine opposition parties were declared illegal because they failed to secure the required signatures of 5% of the electorate, and their leaders lost their political rights. Twenty-seven other prominent Nicaraguans were deprived of political participation after being convicted for defying the constitution by publishing a statement urging Nicaraguans to abstain from voting.

The national election not only returned Somoza to power until May 1, 1981, but also elected 70 members of the lower house, 30 senators, and many minor officials. The winning Liberal Party captured 60% of the seats in the Congress.

Pedro Joaquín Chamorro, Somoza's lifelong enemy, reported in *La Prensa* various charges of government corruption, including a sharp rise in the price of cement, an industry controlled by the Somoza family; an assertion that Somoza and National Assembly Pres. Cornelio Hueck imported automobiles without paying proper import duty; and an accusation that Somoza was involved with Raymond Stansel, Jr., who was charged in the U.S. with illegal drug trafficking.

Censorship was imposed on the news media during April and May, ostensibly to curb inaccurate reports of a strike by hospital and construction workers. Hospital employees asked for a 45% wage increase and settled for a 25% raise; construction workers held their strike in sympathy with the hospital workers.

On December 27 leftist guerrillas seized a group of prominent politicians and business leaders attending a holiday party in Managua. The government acceded to the terrorists' demands and on December 30 released 14 political prisoners, paid the guerrillas a $1 million ransom, and flew the rebels to Cuba, in exchange for the release of the hostages.

Costa Rica and Nicaragua agreed to develop an electric power grid between the two countries, and to build a hydroelectric project in the San Juan River basin. Nicaragua participated in the banana exporters' attempt to raise export taxes. (*See* PANAMA.)

As a result of losses to manufacturing, commerce, and other services caused by the 1972 earthquake, the annual growth rate of the gross national product dropped in 1973 to 2.4%, down 2.6%, and per capita GNP declined from $463 in 1972 to $461 in 1973. Foreign trade grew at a healthy rate with exports increasing 10% in 1973. (GEORGE P. PATTEN)

[974.B.1.d]

Niger

A republic of north central Africa, Niger is bounded by Algeria, Libya, Chad, Nigeria, Dahomey, Upper Volta, and Mali. Area: 489,000 sq.mi. (1,267,000 sq.km.). Pop. (1974 est.): 4,476,000, including (1970 est.) Hausa 53.7%; Zerma and Songhai 23.6%; Fulani 10.6%; Beriberi-Manga 9.1%. Cap. and largest city: Niamey (pop., 1973 est., 121,900). Language: French and Sudanic dialects. Religion: Muslim, animist, Christian. President in 1974 until April 15, Hamani Diori; chief of state from April 17, Lieut. Col. Seyni Kountche.

NIGER

Education. (1970–71) Primary, pupils 88,594, teachers 2,275; secondary, pupils 4,946, teachers 187; vocational, pupils 328, teachers 80; teacher training, students 494, teachers (1969–70) 37.

Finance. Monetary unit: CFA franc, with (Sept. 16, 1974) a parity of CFA Fr. 50 to the French franc (free rate of CFA Fr. 240.50 = U.S. $1; CFA Fr. 556.50 = £1 sterling). Gold, SDRs, and foreign exchange, central bank: (May 1974) U.S. $46.1 million; (May 1973) U.S. $46 million. Budget (1972–73 est.) balanced at CFA Fr. 13,098,000,000.

Foreign Trade. (1973) Imports CFA Fr. 15,281,-000,000; exports CFA Fr. 12,698,000,000. Import sources (1972): France 47%; West Germany 8%; Ivory Coast 8%; U.S. 5%. Export destinations: France 38%; Nigeria 28%; West Germany 7%; Italy 5%. Main exports (1972): peanuts, oil, and cake 47%; uranium 17%; cattle 16%.

Transport and Communications. Roads (1972) 6,998 km. Motor vehicles in use (1972): passenger 11,910; commercial 2,200. There are no railways. Telephones (Dec. 1971) 4,000. Radio receivers (Dec. 1971) 150,000.

Agriculture. Production (in 000; metric tons; 1973; 1972 in parentheses): millet *c.* 480 (*c.* 580); sorghum *c.* 270 (*c.* 270); cassava (1972) *c.* 149, (1971) *c.* 149; rice (1972) 27, (1971) 17; dry beans *c.* 70 (70); peanuts *c.* 100 (*c.* 150); dates (1972) *c.* 6, (1971) *c.* 5. Livestock (in 000; 1972–73): cattle *c.* 3,900; sheep *c.* 2,000; goats (1971–72) *c.* 5,800; camels (1971–72) 350.

The long rule of President Diori's single-party government, uninterrupted since the achievement of independence in 1960, came to an end on April 15, 1974, when Lieut. Col. Seyni Kountche, army chief of staff, carried out a military coup, with little bloodshed, although Diori's wife was killed by a stray shot. On April 17, Kountche declared himself chief of state and head of a supreme military council and a Cabinet of 11 army officers. Diori had been unable to alleviate his people's starvation in the major famine that resulted from the drought in the Sahel (*see* AGRICULTURE AND FOOD SUPPLIES: *Special Report*), and the new regime undertook to devote its energies to combating the Sahel catastrophe above all else. A "superministry" of rural economy, environment, climate, and relief measures was created and placed under Capt. Ali Saib. Three weeks after the coup, Kountche was able to announce that Nigeria was responding with the transport to Niger of 600 tons of relief supplies a day. (The UN World Food Program

As Christian Aid workers look on, cattle in Niger are inoculated against nagana, a bovine form of sleeping sickness.

TOM SHEPPARD— CAMERA PRESS/PHOTO TRENDS

Nickel:
see Mining and Quarrying

announced additional food relief to Niger in April: $2 million of sorghum.)

Although in May Niger ordered the French military detachment stationed at Niamey to be withdrawn, relations between the two countries were not apparently affected. Negotiations concerning an increase in the price of uranium ore supplied to France, which had been opened under President Diori and broken off as unacceptable by the French, were continued. France was concerned about the resource, the extraction of which was operated by French-controlled mines and which was also Niger's only important export and source of national wealth. In May a joint company was founded in Djado by Japanese, West German, and French interests, together with the Niger government, to prospect for uranium in the northeastern part of the country.

Libya and Niger signed a mutual defense treaty on March 22, as well as technical cooperation agreements. As a member of the Chad Basin Committee, Niger cooperated in planning measures to fight the effects of drought, and the country was represented at the meeting of 44 African, Caribbean, and Pacific states in Jamaica to negotiate trade terms with the EEC in July.   (R. M. GOODWIN)

[978.E.4.a.i]

Four convicted armed robbers executed by army firing squad in Lagos for stealing cash and clothing amounting to $400.

Nigeria

A republic and a member of the Commonwealth of Nations, Nigeria is located in Africa on the north coast of the Gulf of Guinea, bounded by Dahomey, Niger, Chad, and Cameroon. Area: 356,669 sq.mi. (923,768 sq.km.). Pop. (1973 census): 79,760,000, including: Hausa 21%; Ibo 18%; Yoruba 18%; Fulani 10%. Cap. and largest city: Lagos (pop., 1973 est., 970,262). Language: English (official). Religion (1963): Muslim 47%; Christian 34%. Head of provisional military government in 1974, Gen. Yakubu Gowon.

Politics in Nigeria in 1974 was influenced strongly by questions of population growth and petroleum production. Provisional 1973 census figures issued in May 1974 gave a total population of 79,760,000, making Nigeria the eighth most populous country in the world and indicating annual growth rates over the preceding ten years ranging from −0.62% in Western State to +7.04% in North-Eastern. Of the 24 million increase since 1963, 21.6 million were counted in the northern states, indicating that these had increased their population by nearly three-quarters in ten years and had 65% of the total population (53% in 1963). The figures sparked off immediate controversy, first because of the bearing of the results upon the promised return to democratic civilian rule by 1976 (it had been intended that the census should provide the basis of a future constitution) and, second, because of their bearing upon revenue allocation. The 1973 census was in fact attacked even more bitterly than that of 1963 and for the same reason: fear in the rest of Nigeria of the political implications of the growing numerical strength of the preponderantly Muslim north. Even allowing for huge migrations into northern Nigeria from the drought-stricken areas of Niger and other countries in the Sahel region, these figures were not acceptable to southern leaders, since under any democratic constitution political control would go to the north. Governors of northern states remained determined that there should be a return to civilian government in 1976.

A second controversy arising from the census figures concerned the allocation of federal revenue, particularly that from oil, which currently favoured the rich producer states as against the poorer northern states. In his Independence Anniversary speech on October 1, General Gowon conceded the impossibility of a return to civilian rule in 1976, because of the dispute over the census and the violent sectional political ambitions that were emerging. Instead, he put forward a program for the 20 billion-naira third National Development Plan, 1975–80, which included measures against corruption, an increase in civilian participation in local administration, the creation of additional new states, the redistribution of oil revenue in favour of the country's poorer states, and the setting up of a constitutional committee. The Army, at a strength of 259,000 the largest in Africa, was allocated more than 30% of current expenditure in the 1974–75 budget.

On his return from China in September, General Gowon charged that there had been plotting against himself and the government. This, together with senior ministerial resignations, indicated that the na-

NIGERIA
Education. (1971–72) Primary, pupils 4,391,197, teachers 130,355; secondary, pupils 399,732, teachers 16,720; vocational, pupils 15,953, teachers 1,178; teacher training, students 37,904, teachers 1,907; higher, students 22,927, teaching staff 2,341.
Finance. Monetary unit: naira, with (Sept. 16, 1974) a free rate of 0.63 naira to U.S. $1 (1.45 naira = £1 sterling). Gold, SDRs, and foreign exchange, official: (June 1974) U.S. $2,106,000,000; (June 1973) U.S. $501 million. Federal budget (1974–75): revenue 2,496,000,000 naira; expenditure 2,634,000,000 naira (including 1,639,000,000 naira capital expenditure). Money supply: (April 1974) 1,233,-200,000 naira; (April 1973) 780 million naira. Cost of living (Lagos; 1970 = 100): (March 1974) 136; (March 1973) 117.
Foreign Trade. (1973) Imports 1,232,900,000 naira; exports 2,209,200,000 naira. Import sources: U.K. 27%; West Germany 15%; U.S. 10%; Japan 9%; France 7%. Export destinations: U.S. 24%; U.K. 19%; The Netherlands 13%; France 13%; Japan 5%. Main exports: crude oil 83%; cocoa 5%.
Transport and Communications. Roads (1971) 88,900 km. Motor vehicles in use (1971): passenger 68,000; commercial (including buses) 44,000. Railways: (1972) 3,520 km.; traffic (1971–72) 961 million passenger-km., freight 1,227,-000,000 net ton-km. Air traffic (1972): 305 million passenger-km.; freight 8.1 million net ton-km. Shipping (1973): merchant vessels 100 gross tons and over 72; gross tonnage 110,015. Telephones (Dec. 1972) 97,000. Radio licenses (Dec. 1972) 1,550,000. Television licenses (Dec. 1972) 75,000.
Agriculture. Production (in 000; metric tons; 1973; 1972 in parentheses): millet c. 2,150 (3,048); sorghum c. 3,000 (3,561); corn c. 600 (1,182); rice (1972) 600, (1971) c. 580; sweet potatoes (1972) c. 204, (1971) c. 204; yams (1972) c. 14,300, (1971) c. 15,365; taro (1972) c. 1,770, (1971) c. 1,650; cassava (1972) c. 9,570, (1971) c. 9,172; tomatoes c. 235 (c. 230); peanuts c. 700 (1,763); palm oil c. 650 (c. 650); cocoa 223 (241); cotton, lint 92 (c. 106); rubber 91 (81). Livestock (in 000; 1971–72): cattle c. 11,400; sheep c. 8,000; goats c. 23,500; pigs c. 880; poultry c. 83,500.
Industry. Production (in 000; metric tons; 1973): crude oil 102,601; natural gas (cu.m.; 1972) 158,000; cement (1972) 1,117; tin 6; petroleum products (1972) 1,946; electricity (kw-hr.; 1972–73) 2,193,000.

tion's stability could be only surface-deep until the question of civilian government was settled.

Nigeria's external relations also were conditioned by its population growth and its oil strength. This was especially true with regard to the creation of the West African Economic Community, the draft treaty of which Nigeria approved despite some points of difficulty with the French-speaking countries of West Africa (secessionist Biafra had enjoyed France's support). Relationships with other African countries depended on whether Nigeria was to be fully aligned with the price-hiking Organization of Petroleum Exporting Countries (OPEC, of which Nigeria was a member) and with the Arab states or would show support for the poorer, sub-Saharan African consumer countries. Nigeria cemented relationships with the U.S.S.R. through General Gowon's state visit to Moscow in May.

Technical assistance from the U.S.S.R. was stepped up, in particular for the establishment of an iron and steel industry, and Soviet oil specialists arrived in Lagos to assist the Nigerian National Oil Corporation. The latter form of help became more significant after the government had made an agreement in 1974 to acquire a 55% share in the five Western companies that had been producing nearly all Nigeria's 2.3 million bbl. a day (it already had a $33\frac{1}{3}$% share in three of them), and to develop its own offshore concessions with Soviet aid. The Nigerian Enterprises Indigenization Decree of April 1, 1974, extended local control of smaller businesses, mainly Lebanese and Asian, with the effect that 22 types of business would pass entirely into African hands and 33 other types would have to have a minimum of 40% indigenous ownership. The danger to foreign investment and lack of local skill permitted exemptions to be granted. The United Africa Co. offered 19 million shares for sale in compliance with the decree, 12 million of them being allocated to state governments.

Despite the huge revenues from petroleum exports, which accounted for about 90% of export earnings, economic performance overall was disappointing and did not approach the 1970–74 plan targets. The economy remained too precariously oil-based, with too great a dependence on imported food.

(MOLLY MORTIMER)

[978.E.4.b.ii]

Nobel Prizes

As always, the 1974 Nobel Prize list contained some surprises, but even the surprises had new twists. The literature laureates were virtually unknown outside their own country, Sweden, whose Swedish Academy chose two of its own members. Stranger still, one peace prize winner was reported to have had the award bought for him through a cleverly concerted campaign.

In Oslo on October 8, former Japanese prime minister Eisaku Sato and Ireland's former foreign minister Sean MacBride, now UN commissioner for South West Africa (Namibia), were named joint recipients of the peace prize. A few days later in Tokyo, two Sato associates revealed that they had conducted a worldwide effort to win the award for him. "We thought it was just about our time to get the prize," said Morinosuke Kajima, a wealthy industrialist who lined up influential domestic support. Former UN ambassador Toshikazu Kase had drummed up foreign

endorsements during a two-month tour as an adviser to the foreign ministry. Meanwhile, a limited English-language edition of Sato's speeches was published, since the Nobel Committee is known to prefer candidates who have written books.

Whatever efforts had promoted MacBride's cause remained secret—even from him. The former chief of staff of the clandestine Irish Republican Army expressed total surprise. He said that a year earlier he had promoted the nomination for the award of Amnesty International, a highly regarded organization without national or doctrinal ties that works for the release of political prisoners throughout the world. He was one of its founders.

The controversy over the literature prize had more in common with the ordinary perils of prize giving. Though Swedish writers Harry Martinson and Eyvind Johnson might be regarded as literary giants in their own country, they were virtually unknown in others. Furthermore, there was enough circumstantial evidence to make the Swedish Academy's motives suspect. Critics charged that either the Academy stooped to national chauvinism, or it chose lesser literary lights to avoid eclipsing the appearance of Aleksandr I. Solzhenitsyn. The Soviet novelist, winner of the 1970 literature prize, was at last scheduled to speak at a Nobel ceremony. Soviet authorities had barred his visit abroad in 1970, but he had since entered exile and, therefore, was free to travel as he pleased.

The prize for economics offered its own conundrum. Gunnar Myrdal and Friedrich von Hayek were named to share the honour, though they had been in opposite economic camps for decades. Myrdal was an architect of Sweden's welfare state, whereas von Hayek was an articulate opponent of socialistic policies.

The awards in the sciences sparked little controversy and even calmed one dissident group. Astronomers, like geophysicists, had long complained that there was no Nobel for their discipline. However, the prize for physics in 1974 was awarded to two British radio astronomers, Sir Martin Ryle and Antony Hewish.

In 1974 each award carried an honorarium worth about $124,000. The prizes were conferred on December 10, the anniversary of Alfred Nobel's death. In-

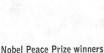

Nobel Peace Prize winners of 1974, Eisaku Sato (left) and Sean MacBride (above).

ventor of dynamite, Nobel bequeathed the bulk of his fortune to establish the awards, which were first given in 1901.

PRIZE FOR PHYSICS

The ancients could do no more than sight stars with the naked eye and measure azimuths with astrolabes. A Dutch optician invented the telescope, and Galileo first focused one on a celestial body in 1609. For more than three centuries astronomers remained shackled to optical instruments, ones that allowed them to observe only those objects that emitted radiation in the narrow visible band of the electromagnetic spectrum. Finally, in the early 1930s, an antenna designed to investigate the causes of radio noise constantly plaguing electronic communications detected a "hiss" of electromagnetic radiation that seemed to emanate from the Milky Way in the region of Sagittarius. In 1937 the first modern parabolic-dish antenna was constructed specifically to gather and focus radio emissions of extraterrestrial origin. Research during World War II into the transmission and detection of highly directed radio waves led to the development of microwave radar and spawned spectacular postwar advances in the technology and application of radio telescopes. Sir Martin Ryle and Antony Hewish were two of the pioneers.

Astronomer Sir Martin Ryle, co-winner of the 1974 Nobel Prize for Physics.

Ryle's outstanding contribution was to invent the technique of aperture synthesis, which might one day enable his successors to define the edge of the universe. Hewish discovered pulsars, the dark remains of once-brilliant stars.

Hewish was born in Berkshire, Eng., May 11, 1924, and took all his degrees at Cambridge University. Following World War II he returned there to work with Ryle at the Cavendish Laboratory. In 1971 he became a professor of radio astronomy at Cambridge. He was also a member of the Royal Society.

Ryle, the son of a physician, was born Sept. 27, 1918. An Oxford University graduate just before World War II, he joined J. A. Ratcliffe's research group at Cambridge, the Telecommunications Research Establishment (now the Royal Radar Establishment) and worked on radar. Following the war he moved to the Cavendish Laboratory and from that time was among the first rank of British scientists. Admitted to the Royal Society in 1952, he was installed in Cambridge's first chair for radio astrophysics in 1959. He was knighted in 1966 and six years later named astronomer royal of Britain.

Ryle became most widely known for his development of aperture synthesis, the technique that allows several small radio telescopes to do the work of an impractically large one. Ryle's theoretical work was also important, and he was a proponent of the "big bang" theory, now widely accepted, which holds that the universe began with a massive explosion of matter.

PRIZE FOR CHEMISTRY

The development of synthetic materials, such as plastics, has, for good or ill, revolutionized modern life. The development of plastics, in turn, depended on the work of Paul J. Flory, who won the 1974 Nobel Prize for Chemistry. He was cited for work "both theoretical and experimental in the physical chemistry of macromolecules."

Specifically, Flory discovered ways of analyzing polymers—macromolecules consisting of chains of smaller molecules—so that it became possible to develop new plastics and other synthetics in a systematic manner. Many of the materials have the interesting ability of increasing the length of their chains; he even discovered the means by which one molecule under growth can stop and pass its growth ability on to another. Recently, he discovered similarities between the elasticity of organic tissues (ligaments, blood vessels, and muscles) and both synthetic and natural plastic materials.

Paul J. Flory, recipient of the 1974 Nobel Prize for Chemistry.

Flory was born June 19, 1910, in Sterling, Ill. He graduated from Manchester College, North Manchester, Ind., and took his doctorate at Ohio State University in 1934. Working with Wallace H. Carothers at the duPont Experimental Station in Wilmington, Del., he helped develop the first nylon and a synthetic rubber, neoprene. Later, he worked for Standard Oil Co. and Goodyear Tire and Rubber Co. Subsequently, he taught at Cornell University and was head of research at the Mellon Institute in Pittsburgh, Pa. In 1961 Flory moved to Stanford, where he was named Jackson Wood professor of chemistry. After his retirement in 1975 he planned to serve as a visiting professor at both the Massachusetts Institute of Technology and the Swiss Federal Institute of Technology in Zürich.

PRIZE FOR PHYSIOLOGY OR MEDICINE

The cell is to living tissue what the atom is to physical matter, a building block so small and fundamental that it was once considered absolutely elementary. But physicists fractured the atom to reveal a family of minuscule components; similarly, specialized biologists probed the living cell to discover its component parts. Three pioneers in this field were Albert Claude, George E. Palade, and Christian de Duve, who shared the 1974 Nobel Prize for Physiology or Medicine. Frequently working in close association, the three were the first to examine intracellular structures and discover their separate functions.

The trio's dean, undeniably, was Albert Claude, director of the Institut Jules Bordet in Brussels. Born in August 1899 and raised in Belgium, he received a medical degree from the University of Liège in 1929. The government awarded him a grant to work abroad and, instead of applying for a job, he proposed a major project to the head of the Rockefeller Institute for Medical Research. His challenge was accepted by what is now known as Rockefeller University, an institution whose researchers have won a total of 15 Nobel Prizes. Having become a U.S. citizen in 1941, Claude performed his most important work at a time when the newly invented electron microscope was being used exclusively by metallurgists and physicists. Given access to the first such instrument in New York City, he demonstrated that it could be adapted to biological studies. He also developed the use of centrifuges to separate cells into their component parts.

In 1945 Claude published the first detailed anatomy of a cell. He discovered mitochondria, which store the cell's energy, and the endoplasmic reticulum, the fibre structure that supports organelles. In 1950 he returned to Belgium and built a cancer research centre at the University of Belgium. In 1946 Claude was discussing his electron microscopy before a New York symposium. After his lecture he was approached by "a polite young man" who asked for an interview. He was George Palade, a Romanian born in Iasi in 1912, who had earned a medical degree at the University of Bucharest in 1940, done research while in the Romanian Army, and then won a two-year visiting professorship to the Rockefeller Institute. Pursuing tangents of Claude's research, he developed improved ways to prepare specimens and advanced centrifuge techniques as well. He discovered ribosomes, the structures that synthesize protein within the cell.

Palade later returned to Romania, but then came back to the U.S. after the Communist takeover and was naturalized in 1952. In 1966 he won the Albert Lasker Basic Research Award and, six years later, left Rockefeller University to direct cell biology studies at Yale University Medical School.

Christian de Duve was born in Thames Ditton, near London, on Oct. 2, 1917. A self-styled "war accident" (his Belgian parents had fled to England to escape World War I), he remained a citizen of Belgium. He graduated from the University of Louvain in 1941 and took a master of science degree in chemistry there five years later. He performed research at the Nobel Institute in Stockholm, and at Washington University in St. Louis, Mo., before returning to the University of Louvain. In 1962 de Duve was lured away to Rockefeller University, where he planned to pursue his research exclusively. But during the transition period, he found he liked working on both sides of the Atlantic. Consequently, he maintained appointments at both universities and built a research organization at each. His particular landmark contribution to cell biology was the discovery of lysosomes, the organelles that ingest a cell's nutrients, breaking down large particles of food for cellular digestion.

PRIZE FOR LITERATURE

Harry Martinson and Eyvind Johnson, the two Swedish authors who shared the literature prize, shared similar characteristics. Both were men of humble origins who were elevated to the fellowship of the Swedish Academy. Both earned reputations as radicals in the 1920s, while, according to a friend, "they would have to be considered rather conservative" today.

The son of a railroad worker, Johnson was born in Svartbjörnsbyn, Swed., July 29, 1900. He began working at a macadam factory at 13, then continued as a timber floater, a candy seller, a box-office attendant, a handyman to an electric fitter, a secretary to a labour union, an engine roughcaster, and a hay-baling presser. In time he became a journalist and studied in Germany and France during the 1920s. Beginning in 1924 he wrote more than 40 novels and collections of short stories. His best-known work that has been translated into English is *Strändernas svall* (*Return to Ithaca: The Odyssey Retold as a Modern Novel*).

Johnson also wrote on political themes. *Drömmar om rosor och eld* ("Dreams of Roses and Fire") involves a 17th-century witchcraft trial in France; the *Krilon* trilogy is a World War II anti-Nazi protest; *Hans nådes tid* ("The Days of His Grace") describes totalitarianism and individualism in Charlemagne's reign.

Martinson was honoured for "writings that catch the dewdrop and reflect the cosmos" in a body of more than 20 volumes of poetry, stories, essays, and full-length fiction. He may be best known for *Aniara,* an epic cycle of poems describing the exodus of 8,000 people from a radiation-ravaged earth. Martinson's other works include *Kap Farväl* (*Cape Farewell*), a seafaring tale, and *Vägen till Klockrike* (*The Road*), a sympathetic examination of tramps and other social outcasts.

Son of a sea captain, Martinson was born in Jämshög May 6, 1904, and spent six years at sea himself. He was elected to the Swedish Academy in 1949.

PRIZE FOR PEACE

"Sean MacBride's efforts for human rights and Eisaku Sato's work for limitation of nuclear weapons and for international conciliation contributed, each in its own way, to securing peace," said the Nobel Committee of the Norwegian Parliament. "Their efforts have come in areas that in our time are central to the work for peace." MacBride's special purview in recent years was the territory of South West Africa. As UN commissioner for that area, he worked for its independence from South Africa, a country whose official policy of total racial segregation (apartheid) made it anathema at the UN.

MacBride was born in Paris on Jan. 26, 1904. His recent activities stand "in sharp contrast with the militancy of his youth." His father was executed by the British in 1916 for taking part in Ireland's Easter Rising of that year. Two years later his mother was imprisoned in London for participating in the Irish struggle for independence. By that time MacBride was an officer in the Irish Republican Army. At 24 he was the IRA's chief of staff and waged civil war against the principle of Ireland's partition. But eventually he accepted the futility of the war and in 1947 entered the Dail (parliament). In 1974 he was supporting a peaceful solution to the problems of Northern Ireland, but he still believed that Ireland should be unified and ruled by the Irish alone.

Prime minister of Japan from 1964 to 1972, longer than any other man since the nation adopted a Cabinet form of government in 1885, Eisaku Sato was cited for curbing the proliferation of nuclear weapons and for improving relations among Pacific nations. His administration was notable for three major achievements: the signing of the nuclear nonproliferation treaty (which, however, Japan never ratified); the negotiated return of Okinawa to Japan by the U.S., which had governed the island since World War II; and the establishment of relations with South Korea.

Born in Tabuse, Jap., March 27, 1901, Sato received his law degree from Tokyo Imperial University in 1924 and worked for the ministry of railways until 1947. In 1948 he became vice-minister for transportation, and later served as chief Cabinet secretary, minister of postal services and telecommunications, minister of construction, and minister of finance.

PRIZE FOR ECONOMICS

Gunnar Myrdal and Friedrich August von Hayek, joint winners of the 1974 Nobel Prize for Economics, were described as "two septuagenarians who still remain active in defending their positions at opposite poles of the monetary policy spectrum." Myrdal, an economic liberal who helped design the Swedish welfare state, somewhat anticipated the monetary theories of John Maynard Keynes and wrote a classic study of the economic problems of U.S. blacks. One of his recent concerns had been the problems of less developed countries. Von Hayek, a Vienna-born University of Chicago professor (emeritus), was an unreconstructed advocate of laissez-faire economics who believed that the more governments try to fight inflation the worse it is likely to become.

Von Hayek's thesis was that governmental control of or intervention in a free market only forestalls such economic ailments as inflation, unemployment, recession, or

Friedrich von Hayek (left) and Gunnar Myrdal (right) shared the 1974 Nobel Prize for Economics.

depression. In 1944 he suggested in *The Road to Serfdom* that mild piecemeal reforms and governmental manipulations inevitably lead to the kind of ultimate domestic disaster that paves the way for totalitarian takeover by a Hitler. Myrdal, on the other hand, adapted Keynes's *General Theory of Employment, Interest and Money,* which holds that a government has a virtual obligation to control business cycles.

Myrdal was born in Gustafs, Swed., Dec. 6, 1898. He studied law and economics at Stockholm University, earning a doctorate there in 1972. He won a Rockefeller fellowship to the U.S. in 1929 and delivered the Godkin lecture at Harvard University in 1938, the year he began directing a study of American Negro problems funded by the Carnegie Corporation. This was published in 1944 as *An American Dilemma,* and it came to be regarded as a classic study of black-white relations. His major focus in 1974 was the economic development of Southeast Asia.

Von Hayek, born May 8, 1899, earned a doctorate from the University of Vienna. In 1931 he took up residence in the U.K. and taught at the London School of Economics until 1950. Then he became professor of social and moral science at the University of Chicago. Reaching retirement age, he took a professorship at the University of Freiburg, W.Ger. (PHILIP KOPPER)

Norway

A constitutional monarchy of northern Europe, Norway is bordered by Sweden, Finland, and the U.S.S.R.; its coastlines are on the Skagerrak, the North Sea, the Norwegian Sea, and the Arctic Ocean. Area: 125,053 sq.mi. (323,886 sq.km.), excluding the Svalbard Archipelago, 23,957 sq.mi., and Jan Mayen Island, 144 sq.mi. Pop. (1973 est.): 3,972,990. Cap. and largest city: Oslo (pop., 1973 est., 468,514). Language: Norwegian. Religion: Lutheran (96.2%). King, Olav V; prime minister in 1974, Trygve Bratteli.

Platform wells in the Ekofisk field in the Norwegian section of the North Sea.

NORWAY

Education. (1972–73) Primary, pupils 375,004, teachers 19,109; secondary, pupils 268,197, teachers 17,799; vocational (1971–72), pupils 57,215, teachers 5,405; teacher training, students 8,795, teachers 784; higher (including 4 universities), students 47,869, teaching staff (1970–71) 5,118.

Finance. Monetary unit: Norwegian krone, with (Sept. 16, 1974) a free rate of 5.57 kroner to U.S. $1 (12.86 kroner = £1 sterling). Gold, SDRs, and foreign exchange, central bank: (June 1974) U.S. $1,546,700,000; (June 1973) U.S. $1,497,900,000. Budget (1974 est.): revenue 34.7 billion kroner; expenditure 41.8 billion kroner. Gross national product: (1972) 95,770,000,000 kroner; (1971) 88,020,000,000 kroner. Money supply: (May 1974) 22,360,000,000 kroner; (May 1973) 20,050,000,000 kroner. Cost of living (1970 = 100): (June 1974) 132; (June 1973) 122.

Foreign Trade. (1973) Imports 36,014,000,000 kroner; exports 27,511,000,000 kroner. Import sources: Sweden 17%; West Germany 14%; U.K. 10%; Japan 8%; Denmark 6%; U.S. 6%; The Netherlands 5%; France 5%. Export destinations: U.K. 18%; Sweden 15%; West Germany 11%; Denmark 8%; Liberia 6%; U.S. 5%. Main exports: ships 20%; machinery 10%; aluminum 8%; fish 7%; chemicals 7%; iron and steel 6%; paper 5%.

Transport and Communications. Roads (1973) 74,796 km. (including 138 km. expressways). Motor vehicles in use (1973): passenger 913,400; commercial 163,000. Railways: (1972) 4,240 km. (including 2,439 km. electrified); traffic (state only; 1973) 1,644,000,000 passenger-km., freight 2,844,000,000 net ton-km. Air traffic (including Norwegian apportionment of international operations of Scandinavian Airlines System; 1973): 2,756,000,000 passenger-km.; freight 96.5 million net ton-km. Shipping (1973): merchant vessels 100 gross tons and over 2,758; gross tonnage 23,621,096. Ships entered (1972) vessels totaling 18,088,000 net registered tons; goods loaded 37,457,000 metric tons, unloaded 20,399,000 metric tons. Telephones (Dec. 1972) 1,262,000. Radio licenses (Dec. 1972) 1,235,000. Television licenses (Dec. 1972) 951,000.

Agriculture. Production (in 000; metric tons; 1973; 1972 in parentheses): barley 530 (522); oats 320 (271); potatoes *c.* 650 (634); apples (1972) *c.* 50, (1971) 51; milk (1972) *c.* 1,780, (1971) 1,738; cheese (1972) 57, (1971) 54; beef and veal (1972) *c.* 56, (1971) 55; pork (1972) *c.* 75, (1971) 69; timber (cu.m.; 1971–72) 8,300, (1970–71) 9,300; fish catch (1972) 3,163, (1971) 3,075. Livestock (in 000; June 1973): cattle *c.* 963; sheep *c.* 1,645; pigs *c.* 721; goats *c.* 77; chickens (1972) *c.* 6,000.

Industry. Fuel and power (in 000; metric tons; 1973): crude oil 1,575; coal (Svalbard mines; Norwegian-operated only) 415; manufactured gas (cu.m.) 28,-400; electricity (kw-hr.) 72,745,000. Production (in 000; metric tons; 1973): iron ore (65% metal content) 3,907; pig iron 1,422; crude steel 963; aluminum 620; zinc 81; copper 26; cement 2,711; petroleum products (1972) 5,793; sulfuric acid 383; fertilizers (nutrient content; 1972–73) nitrogenous 396, phosphate 130; fish meal (1972) 375; wood pulp (1972) mechanical 1,052, chemical 854; newsprint 546; other paper (1971) 830. Merchant vessels launched (100 gross tons and over; 1973) 911,000 gross tons. New dwelling units completed (1973) 44,800.

Norwegian Literature:
see Literature

Nuclear Energy:
see Defense; Energy; Industrial Production and Technology

Numismatics:
see Philately and Numismatics

Nutrition:
see Agriculture and Food Supplies

Nuts:
see Agriculture and Food Supplies

Norwegians continued to enjoy a high level of prosperity during 1974. Demand remained strong for most of Norway's traditional export products, such as metals and paper, and the offshore oil boom created many new jobs in oil service bases and platform-building yards along the western coast. Labour was tight, and wages and prices rose steadily. In the 12 months to mid-September prices had risen by 10.3%. This was, however, a moderate increase as compared with the Organization for Economic Cooperation and Development (OECD) average for the same period. Extensive use of food subsidies, coupled with a tight credit policy, checked inflation.

There was some concern that overhasty exploitation of the offshore petroleum resources could distort Norway's small but well-developed society and economy. In two White Papers published during the spring, the minority Labour government promised to "hasten slowly" in developing offshore oil and gas, by regulating strictly the number of new concessions granted to oil companies and by putting a ceiling on total production, if necessary. The government also announced that the state oil company, Statoil, would be given stakes of 50% or more in future concessions granted south of the 62nd parallel. Moreover, when the waters off Norway's northern coast were eventually opened up for exploration, Statoil would be given the main responsibility for operations in the area.

The allocation of new drilling concessions was postponed several times during 1974. By the end of October it still had not taken place, and by that time it had become clear that only a very few blocks would be distributed, of the 32 for which applications had been invited. The authorities were interested only in exploration on certain blocks along the median line with Britain, in order to locate structures that might straddle the line, as the giant Frigg gas field did. One reason for the delay in issuing new licenses was the discovery of a major new oil and gas field in Norwegian waters, even larger than the giant Ekofisk area. The new field, Statfjord, was believed to have recoverable reserves of at least 2,000,000,000 bbl. of oil and 50,000,000,000 cu.m. of natural gas. Its confirmation almost doubled the proven oil and gas reserves in the Norwegian sector and brought to about 20 the total of hydrocarbon discoveries in the sector—most of them believed to be commercially exploitable. In November negotiations began with the U.S.S.R. on the disputed boundary in the Barents Sea, in an area believed to contain large oil and gas reserves.

Actual output from the one field that was already producing—Ekofisk—was lower than expected during 1974 owing to technical difficulties and exceptionally bad weather. A pipeline to carry oil from the field to Teesside, in the U.K., was completed early in 1974 but was not expected to be put into use until the spring of 1975. Work continued on a pipeline to take natural gas from the field to Emden, W.Ger. By mid-1975 Norway was expected to become Europe's first net exporter of oil.

Work began during the summer on a new petrochemicals complex, at Rafnes in the Telemark district of southeastern Norway. The complex was being built as a joint venture by Statoil, the state-controlled industrial group Norsk Hydro, and Saga Petrokjemi, a private-enterprise group backed by many leading Norwegian industrial, shipping, and financial interests. A shadow was cast over the scheme in October, when Norsk Hydro announced a temporary shutdown of its nearby polyvinyl chloride plant, following reports linking vinyl chloride gas with liver cancer. Hydro had planned a new 300,000-ton-a-year vinyl chloride plant as part of the Rafnes complex, but announced its deferment, in view of concern about health risks, to be studied meanwhile by a medical team. In the same month Borregaard A/S, another Norwegian industrial combine, temporarily withdrew its application to build a vinyl acetate plant in connection with the Rafnes complex because of strong local opposition.

The year saw increased attention devoted to environmental issues. In the autumn the youth organizations of all the country's political parties—from far left to far right—united behind an appeal urging local authorities, organizations, and individuals to fight against the introduction of nuclear power in Norway. Bowing to the trend, the Ministry of Industry told the State Electricity Authority that planning work on nuclear power projects should be taken no further than strictly necessary in order to allow the Storting (parliament) to reach a decision on construction.

The minority Labour government continued to govern without much difficulty, in spite of having only 62 of the 155 seats in the Storting. It sought support for its policies from different groups within the opposition, which was split up among seven parties of varying size.

The budget for 1975 gave substantial tax concessions and was immediately labeled "the Gallup budget" by many of Labour's opponents. They saw it as a bid to regain popularity before the next major political contest—local elections in autumn 1975. Prime Minister Bratteli announced in June that he would not continue in office beyond Labour's 1975 national congress. (FAY GJESTER)

[972.A.6.c]

Obituaries 1974

The following is a selected list of prominent men and women who died during 1974.

ABBOTT, BUD (William A. Abbott), U.S. comedian (b. Atlantic City, N.J., Oct. 2, 1895—d. Woodland Hills, Calif., April 24, 1974), first paired with Lou Costello in 1931 as the straight man of a comedy team that specialized in slapstick routines. They so delighted movie, radio, and television audiences during the 1940s and 1950s that their salaries ranked them among the highest paid entertainers in the country. Their first notable movie success was *Buck Privates* (1941); their last was *Dance with Me, Henry* (1956). The two separated amicably in 1957, two years before Costello's death.

ABRAMS, CREIGHTON WILLIAMS, U.S. Army general (b. Springfield, Mass., Sept. 14, 1914—d. Washington, D.C., Sept. 4, 1974), was a tough, much-decorated officer, whose brilliant military career as a tank commander in World War II was followed by an assignment to Korea and then to Vietnam, where he succeeded Gen. William C. Westmoreland as commander of U.S. forces. In 1972 he was made army chief of staff.

ACHARD, MARCEL, French playwright (b. Sainte-Foy-lès-Lyon, Rhône, France, July 5, 1889—d. Paris, France, Sept. 4, 1974), wrote popular comedies tinged with cynicism. His first success came in 1923 with *Voulez-vous jouer avec Moâ?* and was followed by such other hits as *Jean de la Lune* and *Auprès de ma blonde*. He was elected to the Académie Française in 1959.

ALLAN, ANDREW EDWARD FAIRBAIRN, Canadian dramatist (b. Arbroath, Scot., Aug. 11, 1907—d. Toronto, Ont., Jan. 15, 1974), had a profound influence on the development of Canadian radio drama, for which contribution he received the John Drainie Award in 1969. Allan began his career in 1931 as a radio actor, announcer, writer, and producer in Toronto. Six years later he moved to England to head the radio-shows section of an advertising agency. He rejoined CBC in Vancouver in 1937 to write two weekly radio plays. It was, however, as the director of "Stage" for the CBC radio network in Toronto (1944–56) that his reputation as one of the world's finest radio dramatists was made.

ALSOP, STEWART (Johonnot Oliver), U.S. political columnist (b. Avon, Conn., May 7, 1914—d. Bethesda, Md., May 26, 1974), began his writing career in 1945 as co-author, with his brother Joseph, of a column for the *New York Herald-Tribune*. For 12 years the two commented on national and world affairs in "Matter of Fact," which was syndicated in newspapers all over the country. Background for many of their reports was gathered during extensive travels in Asia and Europe. The pair was twice cited (1950, 1952) by the Overseas Press Club for "best interpretation of foreign news." In 1958 Stewart, on his own, joined *The Saturday Evening Post* as contributing editor for national affairs and from 1962 to 1968 was the *Post*'s Washington, D.C., editor. He then joined *Newsweek* and was as-

Jack Benny

WIDE WORLD

signed the final page of each issue. Alsop often combined political forecasts and an occasional crusade with straightforward reporting.

ANDOM, AMAN MICHAEL, Ethiopian Army officer (b. Eritrea, 1924—d. Nov. 24, 1974), was briefly head of state of Ethiopia after the dethronement of Emperor Haile Selassie. After fighting with partisan forces during the Italian occupation of Ethiopia, he became a regular soldier and served in Korea with the Ethiopian troops attached to the UN. Later he became commandant of the elite military college at Harer and earned the nickname "Desert Lion" for his tough line during a border dispute with Somalia. Andom's demands for political reforms at home, however, so displeased the emperor that he was transferred from the Army to the ineffectual Senate. This forced move so enhanced Andom's reputation with the young army officers who rebeled against the emperor in 1974 that Andom was named chief of staff (with the rank of lieutenant general) and defense minister. When the emperor was deposed in September, Andom became de facto head of state as chairman of the provisional military government. But his liberalism was insufficient to appease the more extreme rebel elements; Andom was forced from office, arrested, and summarily executed.

ARQUETTE, CLIFF(ORD), U.S. entertainer (b. Toledo, O., Dec. 28, 1905—d. Burbank, Calif., Sept. 23, 1974), was at the time of his death one of the most popular guests on the NBC game show "Hollywood Squares." As "Charley Weaver" his humorous attire and zany anecdotes were in sharp contrast to the real Arquette, who was a serious student of U.S. history. The private museum that he opened in Gettysburg, Pa., featured hand-carved Civil War soldiers wearing uniforms painstakingly authenticated through years of research. During his career Arquette appeared on numerous radio and television programs, including "Fibber McGee and Molly" and "Tonight" (later the "Jack Paar Show").

ASTURIAS, MIGUEL ANGEL, Guatemalan novelist, poet, and diplomat (b. Guatemala City, Guatemala, Oct. 19, 1899—d. Madrid, Spain, June 9, 1974), received the Lenin Peace Prize in 1966 and the Nobel Prize for Literature in 1967. Each award, in its own way, acknowledged the power and superb quality of Asturias' writings. Possessed of a rare talent for depicting the wretchedness and desperation of the Guatemalan peasants, he was, in effect, pleading that something be done to uplift his people and restore their hopes. His first major work, *Leyendas de Guatemala* (1930; "Legends of Guatemala"), won critical acclaim for its descriptions of the life and culture of the Mayas before the Spanish conquest. Other important writings include: *El señor presidente* (1946; *The President*), an impassioned denunciation of the Guatemalan dictator Manuel Estrada Cabrera; *Viento fuerte* (1950; *The Cyclone*); *El papa verde* (1954; *The Green Pope*); and *Los ojos de los enterrados* (1960; *The Eyes of the Interred*).

AYUB KHAN, MUHAMMAD, Pakistani politician and field marshal (b. Rihana, Northwest Frontier Province, British India [now in Pakistan], May 14, 1907—d. Islamabad, Pak., April 20, 1974), was president of Pakistan from 1958 to 1969. He attended Aligarh Muslim University in India and the Royal Military College at Sandhurst, Eng., before becoming (1928) an officer in the Indian Army. During World War II he commanded a battalion in Burma. After Pakistan gained independence, Ayub became commander in chief of the Army (1951) and defense minister (1954). Shortly after Pres. Iskander Mirza abrogated the constitution on Oct. 7, 1958, he was exiled to London and Ayub took control under martial law. He introduced a system of local self-governing bodies in 1959, and was subsequently confirmed as president by their representatives. Though efforts were made to restore the economy, stimulate industry, and carry out agrarian reforms, basic problems remained unsolved. Ayub was reelected president in 1965, but student riots in 1968–69 and general disaffection prompted his resignation on March 26, 1969. He then retired to private life.

BATES, HERBERT ERNEST, English author (b. Rushden, Northamptonshire, Eng., May 16, 1905—d. Canterbury, Kent, Eng., Jan. 29, 1974), as "Flying Officer X" gained great popularity with *The Greatest People in the World* (1942)

and *How Sleep the Brave* (1943), stories that conveyed the feeling of wartime flying. His novel *The Darling Buds of May* (1958), introducing the rustic Larkin family, was adapted for film and stage; *The Triple Echo* (1970) became a film and other stories became the basis of the television series "Country Matters."

BEIRNE, JOSEPH ANTHONY, U.S. labour leader (b. Jersey City, N.J., Feb. 16, 1911—d. Washington, D.C., Sept. 2, 1974), became head of the National Federation of Telephone Workers in 1943, then in 1947 reorganized the group as the Communications Workers of America (CWA) with himself as president. He retired in June 1974 after leading three strikes (1947, 1968, 1971) against the Bell Telephone system, but conceded that the effectiveness of strikes had been blunted by automation. As an outspoken member of the AFL-CIO executive council, he sedulously protected the interests of the CWA's half-million members.

BENNY, JACK (Benjamin Kubelsky), U.S. entertainer (b. Chicago, Ill., Feb. 14, 1894—d. Beverly Hills, Calif., Dec. 26, 1974), was a performer whose considerable talent and serious approach to comedy were effectively masked by an appearance of total naturalness. Unlike most comedians, Benny held his audience without such tried and true methods as rapid-fire jokes and outlandish props. His art derived essentially from an uncanny sense of proper timing as he raised an eyebrow, shrugged a shoulder, looked hurt, or stared blankly into space. Year in and year out his cast was allowed to carry the punch lines, with Benny himself the brunt of jokes directed at his miserliness. The mere appearance of his violin (which he could play with commendable finesse) was also enough to set the audience laughing.

Benny joined vaudeville at 18 and made an unspectacular living until he appeared (1932) on Ed Sullivan's radio show. He soon had his own program on NBC radio and by 1948 was such a star that he negotiated a huge contract with CBS. After 23 years he finally went off the air (1955), but had already begun to adapt to the new requirements of television. After irregular scheduling, his program was a weekly feature from 1960 to 1965. Benny never really retired; during his final years he appeared in nightclubs, on television specials, and in benefit performances. His generosity in real life was proverbial.

Marcel Achard

A.F.P./PICTORIAL PARADE

BENTHALL, MICHAEL PICKERSGILL, British stage director (b. London, Eng., Feb. 8, 1919—d. London, Sept. 6, 1974), was director of London's Old Vic Theatre from 1953 to 1961, succeeding Tyrone Guthrie. In 1944 he co-directed *Hamlet* with Guthrie, then directed opera at Covent Garden and Shakespeare productions at both Stratford-on-Avon (including Paul Scofield's *Hamlet*) and the Old Vic (where he staged all 36 plays in the Shakespeare First Folio).

BENTON, HELEN HEMINGWAY, U.S. publisher (b. North Haven, Conn., Sept. 17, 1901—d. Phoenix, Ariz., May 3, 1974), was a woman totally dedicated to excellence in education. Long before the death of her husband, William B. Benton (on March 18, 1973), she shared with him ownership of both Encyclopædia Britannica, Inc., and Encyclopædia Britannica Educational Corp. and was an active member of both boards

EB INC.

of directors. Her influence in helping shape education was perhaps most in evidence during the years it took to plan and write the 15th edition of *Encyclopædia Britannica*. She never questioned the wisdom of investing huge sums of money in a single worthwhile project. Earlier in life she showed a like concern for education when her husband served as vice-president of the University of Chicago and as U.S. ambassador to UNESCO.

BEST, EDNA, British-born actress (b. Hove, Eng., March 3, 1900—d. Geneva, Switz., Sept. 18, 1974), established her reputation in the 1926 production of Margaret Kennedy's *The Constant Nymph*, playing Tessa opposite Noel Coward and later John Gielgud. She made her stage debut in 1917 and her first screen appearance in 1923. During the 1930s she starred in London and New York and was prominent on the U.S. stage and television during the 1940s and 1950s.

BLACKETT, PATRICK MAYNARD STUART BLACKETT, BARON, British experimental physicist (b. London, Eng., Nov. 18, 1897—d. London, July 13, 1974), was awarded the Nobel Prize for Physics in 1948 for his discoveries in cosmic radiation. As a fellow of King's College, Cambridge (1923–33), he worked under Lord Rutherford at the Cavendish Laboratory, where he developed the cloud chamber for the study of the collection of nuclear particles and, in 1933, discovered the positive electron (simultaneously with C. D. Anderson in the U.S.). He was professor of physics, Birkbeck College, University of London (1933–37), and Langworthy professor of physics, University of Manchester (1937–53). During World War II he also served on the Air Defence Committee and then as director of operations research at the Admiralty. At the University of Manchester he created a school of cosmic-ray research and stimulated developments that led to the building of the Jodrell Bank Experimental Station for Radio Astronomy. From 1953 to 1965 he was professor of physics at the Imperial College of Science and Technology, University of London. From 1965 to 1970 he was president of the Royal Society. In 1967 he was awarded the Order of Merit and in 1969 was made a life peer.

BLUNDEN, EDMUND CHARLES, English poet and man of letters (b. London, Eng., Nov. 1, 1896—d. Long Melford, Suffolk, Eng., Jan. 20, 1974), who succeeded Robert Graves as professor of poetry at Oxford University (1966–68), was a Romantic whose late Georgian poetry, filled with grace and intelligence, is represented in *The Poems of Edmund Blunden, 1914–30, Poems, 1930–40,* and succeeding volumes. Blunden wrote biographies of Charles Lamb, Leigh Hunt, and Thomas Hardy, and edited the works of John Clare, William Collins, Christopher Smart, John Keats, Percy Bysshe Shelley, and Wilfred Owen. He was professor of English literature at Tokyo University (1924–27), tutor in English, Merton College, Oxford (1931–43), and cultural liaison officer with the British mission to Japan (1948–50). In 1950 he received the unusual honour of election to the Japanese Academy.

BOHLEN, CHARLES EUSTIS, U.S. diplomat (b. Clayton, N.Y., Aug. 30, 1904—d. Washington, D.C., Jan. 1, 1974), was an acknowledged expert on the Soviet Union. After studying Russian while a member of the U.S. embassy in Paris, he was appointed to the staff of William I. Bullitt, when the U.S. reopened its embassy in Moscow in 1934. His command of Russian and his extensive knowledge of Soviet affairs prompted Pres. Franklin D. Roosevelt to name him as his interpreter (and occasional adviser) at the Teheran and Yalta conferences; he served Pres. Harry S. Truman in the same capacity at Potsdam. He was also an adviser to almost every U.S. secretary of state after World War II and helped devise the Marshall Plan to rebuild Europe and its disrupted economic structure.

Though Bohlen was an outspoken advocate of U.S. military power and had lifelong reservations about Soviet desires for total détente, his willingness to seek limited agreements wherever possible created strong right-wing opposition during hearings that preceded his confirmation as U.S. ambassador to Moscow in 1953. Four years later he was transferred to Manila at the insistence of John Foster Dulles, then secretary of state. Bohlen's last ambassadorial assignment was to Paris from 1962 to 1967.

BOISSIER, PIERRE, Swiss international administrator (b. Geneva, Switz., Dec. 12, 1920—d. Geneva, April 26, 1974), director of the Henri Dunant Institute in Geneva from 1966 and a member of the International Committee of the Red Cross (ICRC) from 1973, was associated with the ICRC from 1948 and carried out critical missions on its behalf in Cyprus, the Middle East, India, Vietnam, and Jordan.

BORGHESE, PRINCE JUNIO VALERIO, Italian nobleman (b. Rome, Italy, June 6, 1906—d. Cadiz, Spain, Aug. 26, 1974), was a militant neo-Fascist leader known as the "black prince." In World War II he commanded the flotilla that carried out a frogman raid on British warships in Alexandria Harbour, Egypt, and later collaborated with the Germans against Italian partisans. Proscribed for a period by a tribunal in Rome in 1949, he launched a subversive neo-Fascist group in 1967.

BOSE, SATYENDRA NATH, Indian theoretical physicist (b. Calcutta, India, Jan. 1, 1894—d. Calcutta, Feb. 4, 1974), was an expert on quantum mechanics, a branch of mathematical physics that deals with the motion of electrons, protons, neutrons, and other subatomic particles. In 1924 Albert Einstein received a copy of "Planck's Law and Hypothesis of Light Quanta," Bose's analysis of particles in connection with photons, or light quanta. Einstein, impressed with the notion that radiation could be considered a form of gas made up of photons, translated the short monograph into German for publication. He also believed that the statistical methods worked out by Bose could be extended to ordinary atoms under an assumption being developed by Louis de Broglie; namely, that material particles have both wave and particulate properties. Though the two scientists never met, they collaborated by mail and gave their names to what is known as Bose-Einstein statistics. Bose graduated from the University of Calcutta and later taught at the universities of Dacca (1921–45) and Calcutta (1916; 1945–56). He was elected a fellow of the Royal Society in 1958.

BRADDOCK, JAMES JOSEPH, U.S. boxing champion (b. New York, N.Y., Dec. 6, 1905—d. North Bergen, N.J., Nov. 29, 1974), came out of

retirement in 1934 to win three successive bouts and a chance to meet Max Baer for the world heavyweight title. On June 13, 1935, Braddock won the crown with a unanimous decision in one of the most stunning upsets in boxing history. On June 22, 1937, no longer in need of government relief to support his family, the former part-time longshoreman defended his title for the first time and was knocked out by Joe Louis.

BRENNAN, WALTER (ANDREW), U.S. actor (b. Lynn, Mass., July 25, 1894—d. Oxnard, Calif., Sept. 21, 1974), won three Academy Awards as best supporting actor during an acting career that lasted half a century and included some 100 films. His prizewinning movie roles were in *Come and Get It* (1936), *Kentucky* (1938), and *The Westerner* (1940). On television he starred in more than 200 episodes of "The Real McCoys."

BROGAN, SIR DENIS WILLIAM, British political scientist (b. Glasgow, Scot., Aug. 11, 1900—d. Cambridge, Eng., Jan. 5, 1974), a professor at Cambridge University from 1939 to 1968, was a leading interpreter of U.S. history and U.S. affairs to the British through such works as *The American Political System* (1933), *U.S.A.: An Outline of the Country, Its People and Institutions* (1941), *An Introduction to American Politics* (1954), and *America in the Modern World* (1960). He also analyzed France and its people in such books as *The Development of Modern France, 1870–1939* (1940) and *The French Nation from Napoleon to Pétain* (1957).

BRONOWSKI, J(ACOB), British science researcher and author (b. Poland, Jan. 18, 1908—d. East Hampton, N.Y., Aug. 22, 1974), produced "The Ascent of Man" (1973), a 13-part BBC television series widely acclaimed for luminously presenting the evolution of civilization and the place of science in human history. He obtained a Ph.D. in mathematics from Cambridge University (1933) before going to the University of Hull as senior lecturer in mathematics (1934–42). His government wartime research included the compilation of statistics on the effects of bombings on industry and economics. Following a visit to Japan in 1945 he wrote a report called "The Effects of the Atomic Bombs at Hiroshima and Nagasaki." After statistical research for the Ministry of Works (1946–50), he directed the Coal Research Establishment at the National Coal Board (1950–59) and was director general of the board's Process Development Department (1959–63), developing smokeless fuels.

From 1964 he was a senior fellow at the Salk Institute for Biological Studies at San Diego, Calif., and was made director of the Council for Biology in Human Affairs in 1970. He broadcast on science and culture, and published *The Poet's Defence* (1939), *William Blake, 1757–1827: A Man Without a Mask* (1944), and *William Blake and the Age of Revolution* (1965). His radio play "The Face of Violence" won the Italia Prize in 1951.

BROOK, CLIVE, British actor (b. London, Eng., June 1, 1887—d. London, Nov. 17, 1974), made his first London stage appearance in 1920. In 1924 he went to Hollywood where his "English" good looks and suave manner earned him a Paramount contract in silent and talking pictures and a succession of leading roles, notably in *Shanghai Express* and *Cavalcade*. He appeared in more than 100 films, made his U.S. stage debut in 1950, and later turned to television.

BROWN, IVOR (JOHN CARNEGIE), Scottish dramatic critic, author, and journalist (b. Penang, Straits Settlements [now Penang, Malaysia], April 25, 1891—d. London, Eng., April 22, 1974), was a foremost London theatre critic for *The Manchester Guardian* (1919–35), the *Saturday Review* (1923–30), and *The Observer* (1929–54); he was also editor of *The Observer* (1942–48). He served as chairman of the British Drama League (1954–65) and was governor of both the Old Vic and the Royal Shakespeare Theatre. Among his writings are *Shakespeare* (1949), *A Word in Your Ear* (1942), *Dickens in His Time* (1963), and *The Way of My World* (1954), an autobiography.

BULMAN, OLIVER MEREDITH BOONE, British paleontologist (b. London, Eng., May 20, 1902—d. London, Feb. 18, 1974), was a leading authority on Lower Paleozoic rocks and fossils and, in particular, on graptolites, extinct colonial marine animals of the Ordovician and Silurian periods. During his lifelong study of graptolites, he was associated with the Imperial College of Science and Technology in London and with Cambridge University. He was elected a fellow of the Royal Society in 1940 and served as president of the Geological Society (1962–64).

BURCKHARDT, CARL JACOB, Swiss diplomat, internationalist, and historian (b. Basel, Switz., Sept. 10, 1891—d. Geneva, Switz., March 3, 1974), was the League of Nations high commissioner in the free city of Danzig from 1937 until World War II broke out in September 1939. As a member of the International Committee of the Red Cross since 1923, and especially as its president (1944–48), he worked for international cooperation. He was ambassador to France from 1945 to 1949 and wrote a noteworthy biography of Cardinal Richelieu.

BUSH, VANNEVAR, U.S. electrical engineer (b. Everett, Mass., March 11, 1890—d. Belmont, Mass., June 28, 1974), developed the differential analyzer, the first electronic analogue computer. In the 1930s, with colleagues from the Massachusetts Institute of Technology, he built an analogue computer capable of analyzing differential equations containing up to 18 independent variables. Among Bush's other accomplishments were a network analyzer that simulated the performance of large electrical networks, and the Rapid Selector, a device using a code and microfilm to facilitate information retrieval.

In 1940 Bush was appointed chairman of the National Defense Research Committee. The following year he became director of the newly established Office of Scientific Research and Development, which coordinated research for the war effort and advised the government on scientific matters. Bush later became chairman of the Joint Research and Development Board (1946–47) and served on the Research and Development Board of the National Military Establishment (1947–48). He was also president of the Carnegie Institution (1939–55).

CAIN, JULIEN, French civil servant (b. Montmorency, France, May 10, 1887—d. Paris, France, Oct. 10, 1974), was general administrator of the Bibliothèque Nationale, France's premier library, from 1930 to 1964, during which time he initiated its reorganization and was largely responsible for the outstanding exhibitions held under its auspices.

CELSING, PETER, Swedish architect (b. Stockholm, Swed., Jan. 29, 1920—d. Stockholm, March 17, 1974), designed the Sergels Torg cultural centre that rose in the heart of Stockholm in the 1960s. The complex also included a new Parliament building. He taught architecture at the Royal Academy Art School, Stockholm (1954–58), and was professor of architecture at the Royal Institute of Technology there (1960–68). His reputation as a sensitive designer of such churches as Harlanda Church, Göteborg, and Gärdet Church, Stockholm, was further enhanced by his happy restorations of old buildings, notably Stockholm's Opera and Royal Theatre.

CHADWICK, SIR JAMES, British experimental physicist (b. Manchester, Eng., Oct. 20, 1891—d. Cambridge, Eng., July 24, 1974), received the Nobel Prize for Physics in 1935 for his discovery of the neutron, which led to the development of atomic energy. He investigated gamma-ray emission from radioactive materials under Ernest Rutherford, at the University of Manchester, then went to Berlin to work with H. Geiger. Interned on the outbreak of World War I, he was able to continue research with aid from German scientists. After the war he followed Rutherford to the Cavendish Laboratory at Cambridge University, where during the 1920s they studied the transmutation of elements under alpha-particle bombardment and investigated the nature of the atomic nucleus. In 1932, as a result of direct experiment, he discovered the neutron, which had been predicted by Rutherford. In 1935 he was appointed Lyon Jones professor of physics at the University of Liverpool, where he had a cyclotron set up and after World War II formed a nuclear physics school. During the war he was engaged in developing the uranium bomb, traveling to the U.S. in 1943 as head of the British team. From 1948 to 1958 he was master of Gonville and Caius College, Cambridge. He was elected to the Royal Society in 1927, knighted in 1945, and in 1970 was made a Companion of Honour.

Erskine Hamilton Childers

CHÊNEBENOIT, ANDRÉ, French journalist (b. Soissons, France, Jan. 5, 1895—d. Feb. 24, 1974), was editor in chief (1944–66) of the influential Paris newspaper Le Monde. A doctor of law, he served in the offices of Raymond Poincaré (premier, 1922–24) and of the president of the Senate before joining the newspaper Le Temps in 1924. From 1928 he was chief subeditor of Le Temps until it ceased publication in November 1942. After the liberation of France he gathered former Temps editors into a new team and, with Hubert Beuve-Méry, brought out Le Monde in December 1944; he remained editor in chief until retirement in 1966.

CHILDERS, ERSKINE HAMILTON, Irish statesman (b. London, Eng., Dec. 11, 1905—d. Dublin, Ire., Nov. 17, 1974), was the fourth president of the Irish Republic and the second Protestant to hold the office. A member of Eamon de Valera's Fianna Fail party, he attained ministerial office in 1944 after a lengthy spell as secretary of the Federation of Irish Manufacturers. Thereafter he held government portfolios for public health, posts and telegraphs, lands, and transport and power before being appointed deputy prime minister in 1969. He supported Prime Minister Jack Lynch's condemnation of the violence in Northern Ireland and his advocacy of a European role for the republic within the EEC. After his election in 1973, Childers was not able to realize his hope of making the presidency a platform for noncontroversial pronouncements and intellectual debate.

CHOTINER, MURRAY M., U.S. lawyer and political tactician (b. Pittsburgh, Pa., Oct. 4, 1909—d. Washington, D.C., Jan. 30, 1974), was a controversial behind-the-scenes political adviser, who greatly influenced the political career of Richard M. Nixon. Chotiner suggested the tactics that won a California congressional seat for Nixon in 1946 and managed Nixon's successful campaign for the U.S. Senate four years later. He also inspired the famous "Checkers speech" that salvaged Nixon's vice-presidential hopes in 1952. As occasional special counsel to the president during the Nixon administration, Chotiner partially formulated then Vice-Pres. Spiro T. Agnew's attacks on "radical liberals."

CLARKE, AUSTIN, Irish poet (b. Dublin, Ire., May 9, 1896—d. Dublin, March 21, 1974), whose Collected Poems (1974) and Collected Plays (1963) reflected the life of Ireland in largely mythological and medieval terms, also wrote three novels (each banned in Ireland on first appearance), memoirs, and criticism. He also helped to organize the Dublin Lyric Theatre Company's seasons of verse plays. In 1932 Clarke was elected a foundation member of the Irish Academy of Letters, served as its president (1952–54), and was awarded the Academy's Gregory Medal in 1968.

COETZEE, BARZILLAI BLAAR, South African politician (b. Hopetown, Cape Province, S.Af., May 14, 1914—d. Cape Town, S.Af., Aug. 29, 1974), was North Rand's outspoken member of

Parliament from 1953, first as member of the United Party and from 1957 of the National Party. He was made deputy minister for Bantu administration in 1966 and joined B. J. Vorster's Cabinet as minister for community development and public works in 1968. He was appointed ambassador to Italy in 1972 but was compelled to retire in 1973 when it became known that he opposed a total ban on black attendance at the Nico Malan Opera House in Cape Town.

COLE, JACK, U.S. choreographer (b. New Brunswick, N.J., April 27, 1914—d. Los Angeles, Calif., Feb. 17, 1974), had, through his work in films, in nightclubs, and on the Broadway stage, a worldwide influence on the development of show dancing. After training at Denishawn School, he danced professionally and later evolved his distinctive style while training others. His last Broadway hit was Man of La Mancha (1965).

CONDON, EDWARD UHLER, U.S. physicist (b. Alamogordo, N.M., March 2, 1902—d. Boulder, Colo., March 26, 1974), was a recognized expert in the fields of quantum mechanics, atomic and molecular spectra, nuclear physics, microwave radio, solid-state physics, and glass manufacturing. He also directed for the U.S. Air Force a widely discussed report on unidentified flying objects. Condon received his Ph.D. in physics (1926) from the University of California at Berkeley. During his diversified career he was associate director of Westinghouse Research Laboratories (1937–45), director of the National Bureau of Standards (1945–51), director of research and development at the Corning Glass Works (1951–54), professor of physics at Washington University in St. Louis (1956–63), and professor of astrophysics at the University of Colorado at Boulder (1963–70). Condon was also science adviser to Encyclopædia Britannica publications.

CONNOLLY, CYRIL VERNON, British critic and writer (b. Coventry, Eng., Sept. 10, 1903—d. London, Eng., Nov. 26, 1974), was an author of considerable wit and brilliance who never quite produced the masterpiece of which he seemed capable. After gaining a reputation for brilliant scholarship at Oxford, he joined The New Statesman and Nation as a book reviewer, and was soon widely read for his witty mastery of parody. In 1939, with Stephen Spender and Peter Watson, he founded the monthly magazine Horizon, which featured among its contributors George Orwell, Evelyn Waugh, Mary McCarthy, T. S. Eliot, W. H. Auden, J. B. Priestley, and André Gide. In 1950 he gave up the magazine to write reviews for The Sunday Times of London. Of his books, the most successful was perhaps The Unquiet Grave, but Connolly's greatest effect on intellectuals was through his numerous critical essays.

CORNELL, KATHARINE, U.S. actress (b. Berlin, Ger., Feb. 16, 1893—d. Vineyard Haven, Mass., June 9, 1974), made stage history as one of America's most accomplished interpreters of romantic and character roles. She brought to each performance a resonant voice and a remarkably expressive face that completely captivated audiences as she made fictional characters believable and often gave them a greater depth of character than was inherent in the script. Cornell began her professional career with the Washington Square Players in New York City in 1916, then played minor parts until she met and married Guthrie McClintic in 1921. During the next 40 years he directed virtually all her performances. Having risen to stardom in 1925 in the role of Iris March in The Green Hat, she formed a new company with her husband in 1931. Two years later, despite the Depression, the "Katharine Cornell Presents" company brought first-rate drama to 77 cities and towns of the U.S. Critics were especially taken with Cornell's performances in Rudolph Besier's The Barretts of Wimpole Street, G. B. Shaw's Candida, and Shakespeare's Romeo and Juliet. For four decades she played countless roles, never at ease with comedy but overwhelming in dramatic parts. She retired in 1961 after the death of her husband.

CRAIG, LYMAN C., U.S. chemist (b. Palmyra, Ia., June 12, 1906—d. Glen Rock, N.J., July

7, 1974), developed the countercurrent technique now widely used to purify drugs and isolate certain chemical compounds. In 1963 he received the Albert Lasker Basic Medical Research Award for this accomplishment.

CROSSMAN, RICHARD HOWARD STAFFORD, British Labour politician and journalist (b. Epping, Eng., Dec. 15, 1907—d. Banbury, Eng., April 5, 1974), was an intellectual whose mental agility sometimes exasperated the steadier-treading members of his party and whose unfettered journalism gave pleasure to many. In 1945 he entered Parliament, representing Coventry East until 1974. Crossman was a leftward backbencher when Hugh Gaitskell made him opposition spokesman on pensions (1956, resigned 1960). Under Harold Wilson's leadership he was minister of housing and local government (1964–66), then an energetic leader of the House of Commons (1966–68), and, lastly, secretary of state for social services. When the government fell in 1970 Crossman became editor of the *New Statesman* (where he had earlier worked), later wrote for *The Times*, and interviewed politicians on the television series "Crosstalk."

DALEY, ARTHUR JOHN, U.S. sportswriter (b. New York, N.Y., July 31, 1904—d. New York, Jan. 3, 1974), was a longtime columnist for the *New York Times* and a great devotee of baseball. He also turned out lively articles on other sports, principally on football, swimming, and track and field. In 1956 Daley won a Pulitzer Prize for "distinguished reporting and commentary." The only other sportswriter ever to win this award was William H. Taylor of the *New York Herald-Tribune* in 1935.

DANIÉLOU, JEAN CARDINAL, French prelate of the Roman Catholic Church (b. Neuilly-sur-Seine, France, May 14, 1905—d. Paris, France, May 20, 1974), was a leader of the Catholic left during his early years, an energetic supporter of ecumenism during the 1960s, and a public defender of the pope during the last years of his life. He entered the Society of Jesus in 1929 after graduating from the Sorbonne and was ordained in 1938. Highly regarded for his intellectual qualities and widely admired for his warmheartedness, he attended the second Vatican Council as an "expert" in theology while concurrently holding the position of dean (1962–69) of the Paris Faculty of Theology. In 1970, the year after he was raised to the cardinalate by Pope Paul VI, he was instrumental in getting 100,000 Frenchmen to sign a letter promising fidelity and obedience to the pope, a direct challenge to the Dutch hierarchy who had denounced obligatory celibacy for the clergy. Among Daniélou's many writings were *Bible et Liturgie* (1951), *Théologie du Judéo-Christianisme* (1958), and *Pourquoi l'Église?* (1972). He was elected to the Académie Française in 1972.

DARVAS, LILI, Hungarian-born actress (b. Budapest, Hung., April 10, 1906—d. New York, N.Y., July 22, 1974), was a celebrated star in Europe when Hitler's troops marched into Austria in 1938. She left Vienna that day and eventually arrived in the U.S. as a refugee. During her long career, which first blossomed under the direction of Max Reinhardt, she played a wide variety of lead roles that ranged from Shakespeare's Juliet to a bedridden old lady in the 1970 Hungarian film *Love*.

DAVES, JESSICA, U.S. fashion editor (b. Cartersville, Ga., Feb. 20, 1898—d New York, N.Y., Sept. 22, 1974), as editor in chief of *Vogue* from 1952 until her retirement in 1963, strove "to educate the public taste" in the realm of women's ready-to-wear fashions. She won several international awards, was a master at editing, and held positions of ever increasing responsibility before reaching the top of her profession.

DAVIES, RODGER PAUL, U.S. diplomat (b. Berkeley, Calif., May 7, 1921—d. Nicosia, Cyprus, Aug. 19, 1974), was deputy assistant secretary of state for Near Eastern and South Asian affairs when appointed to Cyprus, his first ambassadorial assignment. Davies' soft-spoken manner and obvious diplomatic talents marked

him as a logical choice to confront the highly volatile situation then developing in Cyprus. Shortly after Davies arrived in Nicosia, Pres. Makarios was ousted (July 15, 1974). During the hysteria that followed Turkey's invasion of the island, Davies was killed by an assassin's bullet fired into the U.S. embassy from a nearby building.

DAVIS, (DAISIE) ADELLE, U.S. dietitian (b. Lizton, Ind., Feb. 25, 1904—d. Palos Verdes Estates, Calif., May 31, 1974), widely read author and, in recent years, an outspoken guest on television talk shows, gained national fame for her criticism of U.S. eating habits and for her advocacy of organic fruits and vegetables, milk, eggs, liver, fish, vitamin pills, and brewer's yeast. She obtained a B.A. degree (1927) in dietetics at the University of California at Berkeley and later earned a master's degree (1939) in biochemistry at the University of Southern California. Although quite aware of modern research on nutrition, Davis was frequently taken to task for "unscientifically" attributing all manner of diseases to improper diets. Her four books, which together sold more than nine million copies, are: *Let's Cook It Right* (1947), *Let's Have Healthy Children* (1951), *Let's Eat Right to Keep Fit* (1954), and *Let's Get Well* (1965).

DEAN, DIZZY (JAY HANNA DEAN), U.S. baseball player (b. Lucas, Ark., Jan. 16, 1911—d. Reno, Nev., July 17, 1974), became a modern legend as he clowned his way into the hearts of millions while pitching his way into baseball's Hall of Fame. Spotted as a natural athlete on a Texas sandlot, he was signed by the St. Louis Cardinals in 1930. In 1932, already supremely confident of his blazing fast ball, he won 18 games as a 21-year-old rookie. Two years later his 30 wins, coupled with 19 by his younger brother Paul ("Daffy"), paced the rowdy Gashouse Gang to a National League pennant. In the World Series that followed, Detroit won 3 games and St. Louis 4. Each of the Deans got two victories.

Dean's future was abruptly altered when a line drive broke his toe in 1937. By continuing to pitch he hurt his arm, was traded to the Chicago Cubs in 1938, and had to retire in 1941. Later he became a play-by-play sportscaster, his outrageous misuse of the English language proving that you don't have to be a grammarian to win the admiration and affection of those who follow baseball.

DE SICA, VITTORIO, Italian film director (b. Sora, Italy, July 7, 1901—d. Paris, France, Nov. 13, 1974), won worldwide acclaim as director of such neorealist films as *Shoe-shine* (1946), *The Bicycle Thief* (1949), *Miracle in Milan* (1951), and *Umberto D* (1951). He joined an acting company in 1923 and became a star in *Gli uomini, che mascalzoni!* (1932; "Men, What Rascals!"). His first success as a director was *Rose scarlatte* (1939; "Two Dozen Red Roses"). After the great creative upsurge of the postwar period, De Sica continued to act and direct. His *Yesterday, Today and Tomorrow* (1964) won an Academy Award as best foreign-language picture of the year and Sophia Loren was awarded an Oscar for her performance in De Sica's *Two Women* (1961). Another triumph was *The Garden of the Finzi-Contini* (1971), which took the major award at

Vittorio de Sica

KARSH, OTTAWA—CAMERA PRESS/PICTORIAL PARADE

the Berlin Film Festival. De Sica's last film was *The Journey* (1974).

DUNN, ALAN CANTWELL, U.S. social cartoonist, artist, and writer (b. Belmar, N.J., Aug. 11, 1900—d. New York, N.Y., May 20, 1974), had nearly 2,000 cartoons published in *The New Yorker* magazine between 1926 and 1974; he also contributed steadily to *Architectural Record*. The most comprehensive collection of Dunn's works is held by the U.S. Library of Congress.

DUNN, LESLIE CLARENCE, U.S. geneticist (b. Buffalo, N.Y., Nov. 2, 1893—d. North Tarrytown, N.Y., March 19, 1974), gained wide recognition for his studies on heredity, evolution, and race. He rejected the notion of fixed and absolute biological differences between races, attributing perceptible differences between groups of people to evolutionary processes affected by environment. After completing (1920) his doctoral studies in zoology at Harvard University, he spent eight years at the Connecticut Agricultural Experiment Station in Storrs, then settled (1928–62) at Columbia University as professor of zoology. There he founded and directed (1952–58) the Institute for Study of Human Variation, was managing editor of *Genetics* (1936–41), and edited *The American Naturalist* (1950–60). Among the books that bear his name are: *Heredity and Variation* (1932), *Heredity, Race and Society* (1946), *Genetics in the 20th Century* (1951), *Race and Biology* (1951), and *Heredity and Evolution in Human Populations* (1959).

DUTRA, EURICO GASPAR, Brazilian marshal and head of state (b. Cuiabá, Braz., May 18, 1885—d. Rio de Janeiro, Braz., June 11, 1974), restored constitutional democracy while president of Brazil from 1945 to 1951. He became war minister under Getúlio Vargas in 1936, but when Vargas tried to prevent elections in October 1945, Dutra led a successful coup and was elected president in December. His lacklustre administration, however, was repudiated in the 1950 elections and Vargas resumed power.

DUTT, (RAJANI) PALME, British politician (b. Cambridge, Eng., 1896—d. Dec. 20, 1974), was a founder member of the British Communist Party in 1920 and its dominating intellectual. He was dismissed from Balliol College, Oxford, for antiwar Marxist propaganda and was briefly imprisoned, but was permitted to return to the university and complete a double first class in 1918. He worked for the Labour Research Department and in 1920 published his first book, *The Two Internationals;* the following year he began to publish the Marxist *Labour Monthly*. In 1922 he was chairman of a commission to reorganize the British Communist Party, and was a member of the party's executive from 1922 to 1965. Under the leadership of Harry Pollitt, Dutt supplied the brains of British Communism, and was also editor of the party's newspaper, the *Daily Worker*, during 1936–38; he held the party firmly to the Stalinist line at all times, even when Pollitt himself wavered after the Hitler-Stalin pact of August 1939. As the son of a Bengali surgeon (and Swedish mother), he had great influence upon Indian students in England, and thus speeded development of the Indian Communist Party.

ELLINGTON, DUKE (EDWARD KENNEDY ELLINGTON), U.S. musician (b. Washington, D.C., April 29, 1899—d. New York, N.Y., May 24, 1974), was a prolific composer and arranger of jazz whose music enthralled audiences for over half a century in such diverse settings as Westminster Abbey, Carnegie Hall, and the Cotton Club in Harlem, where he first attracted attention. Under his direction many of the most celebrated jazz musicians of America blended sounds in a manner that evoked feelings of classical elegance and sophistication. His compositions, which numbered in the thousands and gave rise to a whole new world of music, included "Mood Indigo" (his first big hit), "Solitude," "Don't Get Around Much Anymore," "Satin Doll," and "East St. Louis Toodle-oo." His longtime theme song, "Take the 'A' Train," was composed by Billy Strayhorn, a close collaborator for many years. Ellington's genius was acknowledged in 1950 by Arturo Toscanini, who commissioned "Harlem" for the NBC Symphony Orchestra. Among Ellington's many memorable performances were "Black, Brown and Beige" (1943), an hour-long suite, and "A Concert of Sacred Music" (1965). Rejecting the unanimous recommendation of its advisory board, the Pulitzer committee withheld a special citation for Ellington in 1965. On hearing the news he remarked: "Fate doesn't want me to be too famous too young." He was 66 years old at the time. His autobiography, *Music Is My Mistress*, was published in 1973.

ELLIOT, CASS(ANDRA) (ELLEN NAOMI COHEN), U.S. pop singer (b. Baltimore, Md., Feb. 19, 1941—d. London, Eng., July 29, 1974), became a big time entertainer singing contralto with the Mamas and the Papas, a folk-rock group formed in 1965. When the group broke up in 1968, Elliot was booked into nightclubs and signed for solo concerts. Her earlier career included some off-Broadway acting.

ELMHIRST, LEONARD KNIGHT, British educationist and agronomist (b. Howden, Yorkshire, Eng., June 6, 1893—d. Beverly Hills, Calif., April 16, 1974), with his wife founded Dartington Hall, an educational trust near Totnes, Devon. The venture developed into a coeducational school with an education program for adults, into a centre for the arts, and into centres for experiments in rural industry and research in agronomy. In India he directed (1921–24) the Institute of Rural Reconstruction at Sriniketan, Bengal, advised the government of Bengal on agriculture (1944–45), and was a member of the Indian Government Committee on Higher Education for Rural Areas (1954–55). He founded the Dartington Cattle Breeding Centre, where he pioneered artificial insemination. He also was president of the International Conference of Agricultural Economists (1929–61) and chairman of the nonpartisan Political and Economic Planning (PEP) organization (1939–53).

EWING, (WILLIAM) MAURICE, U.S. geophysicist (b. Lockney, Tex., May 12, 1906—d. Galveston, Tex., May 4, 1974), opened new avenues of oceanographic research by successfully employing shock-wave techniques to probe marine sediments and ocean floors. His seismic refraction measurements of the Atlantic Ocean basins, the Mid-Atlantic Ridge, and the Mediterranean and Norwegian seas became the basis of later computer analyses. Ewing joined other scientists in suggesting that earthquakes are associated with the central oceanic rifts that encircle the globe, and he theorized that sea-floor spreading is episodic in nature and probably worldwide. During World War II he developed sofar (sound finding and ranging) for the U.S. Navy to provide, through explosion-induced sound waves, a means of underwater communications especially useful as a distress signal. Ewing was educated at Rice Institute, Houston, Tex., and directed the Lamont-Doherty Geological Observatory at Columbia University from 1949 to 1972.

FASSI, MUHAMMAD ALLAL AL-, Moroccan political leader (b. Fez, Morocco, 1906?—d. Bucharest, Rom., May 13, 1974), was prominent from his youth in Morocco's independence movement. His activities in the 1930s to abolish the French and Spanish protectorates led to arrests by the French and eventual exile. In 1956 he returned to head Morocco's right-wing Istiqlal Party. He was King Hassan II's minister of state in charge of Islamic affairs (1961–63) and rector

Duke Ellington

of the Muhammad V University, Rabat, before helping to merge Istiqlal in a united national opposition to the king's new constitution.

FERREIRA DE CASTRO, JOSÉ MARIA, Portuguese writer (b. Salgueiros, Aveiro, Port., May 24, 1898—d. Oporto, Port., June 30, 1974), whose first major novel, *A Selva* (1930; *The Jungle,* 1934), about the Amazon rubber plantations, was translated into 18 languages. He emigrated to Brazil at the age of 12 but returned to Portugal in 1919. His novels and travel books (several of which were translated) included *Terra fria, A Tempestade, A Volta ao mundo, A Lã e a neve,* and *O Instinto supremo* (1968).

FIELDS, DOROTHY, U.S. songwriter (b. Allenhurst, N.J., July 15, 1905—d. New York, N.Y., March 28, 1974), was one of the country's most prolific and successful providers of songs for stage musicals and motion pictures. During her career she collaborated with such renowned composers as Jerome Kern, Sigmund Romberg, Morton Gould, and Oscar Levant, but never quite matched their popular recognition. Of the hundreds of songs that she produced, some of the best known are "I Can't Give You Anything but Love, Baby," "Lovely to Look At" (with Jimmy McHugh), "I'm in the Mood for Love," and "The Way You Look Tonight," which won the 1936 Oscar award. With her brother Herbert she wrote *Annie Get Your Gun* (1946) and *Redhead* (1959), both hits on the Broadway stage.

FOUCHET, CHRISTIAN, French diplomat and politician (b. Saint-Germain-en-Laye, France, Nov. 17, 1911—d. Geneva, Switz., Aug. 11, 1974), was one of Gen. Charles de Gaulle's most trusted counselors and envoys. After the Franco-German armistice of June 1940, he joined de Gaulle in London and in 1944 became the Free French representative to the Polish government at Lublin. He was consul general in Calcutta (1945–47) before returning to France to help organize Gaullist support in the Paris region. He was elected to the National Assembly (1951) and in the Pierre Mendès-France government (1954–55) was minister for Moroccan and Tunisian affairs. He also served as French ambassador to Denmark (1958–62), and was chairman of a European Economic Community commission that drafted plans for a supranational European government that never materialized. In March 1962, as high commissioner, he organized the referendum in Algeria on self-determination and ensured an orderly transfer of power. Later he held Cabinet posts as minister of information (1962), minister of education (1962–67), and minister of the interior (1967–68). After his reelection (1968) to the Assembly, he broke with the Gaullist party (1971) over the policies of Pres. Georges Pompidou. He wrote two books about his association with de Gaulle: *Au Service du Général de Gaulle* (1971) and *Les Lauriers sont Coupés* (1973).

FRASER OF LONSDALE, WILLIAM JOCELYN IAN FRASER, BARON, British soldier and administrator (b. Eastbourne, Sussex, Eng., 1897—d. London, Eng., Dec. 19, 1974), was blinded at the battle of the Somme in 1916, but became a legend for his life of active public service, in particular at St. Dunstan's, a training school for blinded British ex-servicemen, and for the British Legion. Before losing his sight he was the senior cadet officer of the Royal Military College, Sandhurst. He became chairman of the St. Dunstan's council in 1921 and held the post until his death. He also served on the London County Council, 1922–25, entered the House of Commons as a Conservative and sat, with two interruptions, from 1924 to 1958. During 1936–39 and 1941–46 he was a governor of the British Broadcasting Corporation, calling attention to the needs of blind listeners. From 1947 to 1958 he was national president of the British Legion (ex-servicemen's organization) and its advocate in Parliament on pensions and other matters. Fraser was knighted in 1934, was made a Companion of Honour in 1953, and was made a life peer in 1958. He was also a director of numerous companies, including a family business in South Africa. He wrote an autobiography *Whereas I Was Blind* (1942) and *My Story of St. Dunstan's* (1961).

FURSE, (ALICE) MARGARET, British costume designer (b. London, Eng., Feb. 18, 1911—d. London, July 9, 1974), whose convincing period costumes added distinction to many films, studied at the Central School of Art, London, and joined

Motley, a group of young designers of the 1930s. She was nominated six times for an Academy Award, winning the Oscar in 1970 for the costumes used in *Anne of the Thousand Days*. Other notable credits included *The Lion in Winter* (1969), *Scrooge* (1971), and *Mary Queen of Scots* (1972).

FURTSEVA, EKATERINA A(LEKSEYEVNA), Soviet politician (b. Vyshniy Volochek, Kalinin region, Russia, Dec. 7, 1910—d. Moscow, U.S.S.R., Oct. 25, 1974), was minister of culture of the U.S.S.R. from 1960 until her death. She joined the Communist League of Youth at the age of 14 and became a full Communist Party member at 20. In 1937 she entered the Moscow Institute of Fine Chemical Technology, graduating five years later as a chemical engineer. She worked in the Moscow party organization headed by Nikita S. Khrushchev who, appreciating her organizational ability and talent for public speaking, proposed her election in October 1952 to candidate membership of the Central Committee of the CPSU. Her rise was rapid: in February 1956 she was elected a full member of the Central Committee, an alternate member of the Politburo, and its secretary. A year later she became a full member of the Politburo and in May 1960 minister of culture. In October 1961, however, she was dropped from the Politburo. In June 1974 she was not reelected to the Supreme Soviet, which she had joined for the first time in 1954. Rumours attributed her political decline to suspected use of state funds to build a dacha (country house) for her family.

FU TSO-YI, Chinese general (b. Hsiao-yi County, Shansi Province, China, 1895—d. Peking, China, April 19, 1974), made international headlines in January 1949 when, without a battle, he surrendered Peking and 25 divisions of Nationalist troops to attacking Communist forces under Lin Piao. Fu had been Chiang Kai-shek's most reliable commander. He was a graduate of Paoting Military Academy and became a full general in 1935. During the Sino-Japanese War he defended the Suiyuan area and was appointed commander of the 12th War Zone. In 1947 he was assigned to Peking as commander of the newly established North China Communist Suppression Headquarters. After the fall of Peking, Fu announced his support of the Communist cause. He was subsequently given numerous posts in the People's Republic of China but possessed no real power.

FYSH, SIR (WILMOT) HUDSON, Australian airline executive (b. Launceston, Tasmania, Jan. 7, 1895—d. Sydney, New South Wales, Austr., April 6, 1974), co-founded the Queensland and Northern Territory Aerial Services Ltd. (whence Qantas) as a local service in 1920. As Qantas Empire Airways Ltd. it flew the Brisbane-Singapore section of the England-Australia route from 1934. Fysh was a founder-director of Tasman Empire Airways Ltd. (TEAL) in 1940, opening service between Australia and New Zealand. In World War II Qantas flying boats served as Allied transport in the Pacific and in July 1943 reopened the Middle East air route to England, flying the 3,500-mi. Perth–Ceylon stretch. When the Australian government took over Britain's interest in Qantas in 1947, Fysh was named chairman and managing director. He was knighted in 1953.

GAUDIN, A(NTOINE) M(ARC), U.S. mineral engineer (b. Smyrna, Turk., Aug. 8, 1900—d. Boston, Mass., Aug. 23, 1974), was largely responsible for the development of ore-processing techniques that yielded uranium for the earliest atomic bombs. Using ores mined in the Belgian Congo (now Zaire), his team discovered new methods of leaching and ion exchange that were effectively used to extract uranium that was then purified into a metal used in reactors for plutonium production and as a hexafluoride gas for uranium isotope separation. Gaudin also analyzed the principles underlying "flotation," a widely used process for extracting specific metals (*e.g.,* copper) comprising only a small portion of the raw ore. Gaudin taught at Columbia University, his alma mater, before successively joining the faculties of the University of Utah, Montana School of Mines, and the Massachusetts Institute of Technology.

GERARD, RALPH WALDO, U.S. neurophysiologist (b. Harvey, Ill., Oct. 7, 1900—d. Newport Beach, Calif., Feb. 17, 1974), whose studies on the human brain and nervous system contributed significantly to further research on human learning and memory, was among the first to challenge Freudian theories regarding mental disorders. Gerard contended that the probable cause of schizophrenia was abnormal body chemistry, not adverse psychological or cultural environment.

GÉRAUD, CHARLES JOSEPH ANDRÉ ("PERTINAX"), French journalist (b. Saint-Louis-de-Montferrand, Gironde, France, Oct. 18, 1882—d. Ségur-le-Château, Corrèze, France, Dec. 11, 1974), was one of the best known of the international corps of diplomatic commentators that became prominent after the Paris Peace Conference of 1919. He started his career in 1908 as London correspondent of *Echo de Paris*, and became foreign editor in 1917. When that paper ceased publication in 1938, Géraud became editor of *L'Europe Nouvelle*. After World War II he returned to Paris from the U.S. and became a foreign affairs specialist for the newspaper *France-Soir*, retiring in 1960.

GLOUCESTER, HENRY WILLIAM FREDERICK ALBERT, DUKE OF, member of the British royal family (b. Sandringham, Norfolk, Eng., March 31, 1900—d. Barnwell, Northamptonshire, Eng., June 10, 1974), was the third son of King George V and Queen Mary. After an education at Eton College and Cambridge University, Prince Henry entered the Army in 1919. He was created duke of Gloucester in 1928. In 1935 he married Lady Alice Montagu-Douglas-Scott, daughter of the duke of Buccleuch, and by her had two sons, Prince William of Gloucester (b. 1941; killed in a flying accident 1972) and Prince Richard of Gloucester (b. 1944), his heir. The abdication of his brother Edward VIII in 1936 brought the duke's soldiering to an end, his promotion to major general being a royal appointment as the next brother to King George VI. From 1945 to 1947 the duke served as governor-general of Australia. In 1955 he was created a field marshal.

GOLDWYN, SAMUEL (SAMUEL GOLDFISH), U.S. movie producer (b. Warsaw, Pol., Aug. 27, 1882—d. Los Angeles, Calif., Jan. 31, 1974), was one of the great pioneers of the Hollywood movie industry. With Cecil B. DeMille and Jesse L. Lasky he made one of the first feature-length films, *The Squaw Man* (1914), then sold out to a group that founded Paramount. With two brothers, Edgar and Arch Selwyn, he began producing "Goldwyn" pictures, a name he adopted as his own before Goldwyn merged with Metro and Mayer in the early 1920s. As Hollywood's leading independent producer, Goldwyn produced some 70 films, which won 27 Academy Awards in various categories. Among his best known movies were *Wuthering Heights* (1939), *The Best Years of Our Lives* (1946), *Guys and Dolls* (1955), and *Porgy and Bess* (1959). Movie professionals saw in Goldwyn a man whose great talent lay in gathering the finest writers, directors, and movie talent available, whom he then dominated so completely that the final result—always artistic, always in good taste—bore the unmistakable mark of the producer. Public-relations men saw a colourful personality who could be credited with such memorable "Goldwynisms" as "Include me out" and "An oral agreement isn't worth the paper it's written on!" In 1971 Goldwyn was awarded the Medal of Freedom, the nation's highest civilian honour.

GOLENPAUL, DAN, U.S. radio producer, writer, and director (b. New York, N.Y., June 3, 1900—d. New York, Feb. 13, 1974), created the trendsetting "Information Please" quiz program, which proved to be one of NBC's most popular radio shows from 1938 to 1952.

GORDON, JOHN RUTHERFORD, Scottish journalist (b. Dundee, Scot., Dec. 8, 1890—d. London, Eng., Dec. 9, 1974), was editor in chief of the London *Sunday Express* from 1954 until his death. His journalistic proficiency and judgment of the needs and wishes of his readers built up his paper's circulation from 560,000 to 4 million, but he was even better known for his leader page

articles which began during World War II and for his column "Current Affairs," which for many readers was the day's talking point. He was also a director of Beaverbrook Newspapers Ltd. from 1931 to 1969.

GOTTLIEB, ADOLPH, U.S. painter (b. New York, N.Y., March 14, 1903—d. New York, March 4, 1974), was one of the early proponents of Abstract Expressionism, an art form far removed from the social realism that dominated painting during the 1940s. Gottlieb initially developed a pictograph style in which cryptic forms, often derived from mythology and primitive art, were used in rectilinear patterns resembling grids. His abstract landscapes of the 1950s were followed by his second principal style, called "Bursts," in which sunlike, static orb forms float above jagged horizons. Smears, blots, and other characteristic forms of Action painting frequently constitute the lower element.

GRIVAS, GEORGIOS THEODOROS (called DIGHENIS), Greek Army officer (b. Trikomo, Cyprus, May 23, 1898—d. Limassol, Cyprus, Jan. 27, 1974), was the leader of EOKA (Ethniki Organosis Kipriakou Agonos, or National Organization for the Cyprus Struggle), which sought by terrorist means to end British rule in Cyprus and to achieve *enosis*—union with Greece. He took part in the Greek invasion of Turkey (1920–22) and later graduated from the Greek Staff College and the École Supérieure de Guerre in Paris. Following the Italian invasion of Greece (1940–41) he was demobilized (1944) with the rank of lieutenant colonel and under the subsequent German occupation organized a right-wing royalist resistance group in Athens. An unsuccessful candidate in the Greek elections of 1946 and 1950, he returned to Cyprus in 1951 to further Archbishop Makarios' campaign for *enosis*. EOKA's terrorist activities began in 1955, and by 1959 the independence of Cyprus was assured. Grivas then returned to Athens and was promoted general. Creation of the Republic of Cyprus in 1960 was followed by communal strife between Greek and Turkish Cypriots, and in 1964 Grivas returned and was appointed commander of the Greek Cypriot National Guard by President Makarios. However, whereas Grivas was still an ardent advocate of *enosis*, Makarios had rejected it in favour of independence. In 1967 the Greek government recalled Grivas to Athens, but in 1971 he returned secretly to Cyprus to form EOKA B to "prevent a betrayal of *enosis*."

HABTE-WOLD, AKLILU, former Ethiopian prime minister (b. Addis Ababa, Eth., 1908—d. Nov. 24, 1974), was a leading figure in the Ethiopian government for many years and Emperor Haile Selassie's principal adviser on foreign affairs. As prime minister from 1961, he had to contend with growing unrest that culminated in his forced resignation in February 1974. He was later arrested and executed by the forces that overthrew the emperor's rule.

HAHN, KURT MATTHIAS ROBERT MARTIN, German-born educationist (b. Berlin, Ger., June 5, 1886—d. Hermannsburg, W.Ger., Dec. 14, 1974), helped Prince Max of Baden to found (1920) Schloss Salem School, near Lake Constance, then founded (1933) Gordonstoun School in Moray, Scot., after he was expelled from Germany by the Nazis. Pupils from all levels of society, including members of the British royal family, attended Gordonstoun to experience the spartan in-house discipline and the taxing outdoor activities, while following an ordinary academic curriculum. After retiring as headmaster in 1953, Hahn set up about a dozen similar schools in various parts of Europe.

HAILES, PATRICK GEORGE THOMAS BUCHAN-HEPBURN, 1ST BARON, British politician (b. April 2, 1901—d. Nov. 5, 1974), was the urbane chief whip of the Conservative Party from 1948 to 1955. He was private secretary to Winston Churchill, represented the Toxteth (Liverpool) division as MP from 1931 to 1950, and then sat for Beckenham until his elevation to the peerage in 1957. From 1957 until its dissolution in 1962 he was governor-general of the West Indies Federation, and from 1962 to 1973 he was chairman of the Historic Buildings Council for England. He was made a Companion of Honour in 1962.

HATHAWAY, DAME SIBYL MARY, dame of Sark (b. Guernsey, Channel Islands, January

1884—d. Sark, Channel Islands, July 14, 1974), was the 21st feudal governor of the island of Sark, a dependency of the British crown. She largely maintained Sark's feudal character, with some latter-day adjustments. In 1965 she was made a dame of the British Empire.

HEYER, GEORGETTE (MRS. GEORGETTE ROUGIER), British novelist (b. London, Eng., Aug. 16, 1902—d. London, July 5, 1974), wrote popular historical romances, chiefly of the Regency period in England, and some detective stories. Though conventional in plot and character treatment, her novels were well written and well researched, her knowledge of the 1800s and Wellington's armies appearing notably in *An Infamous Army* and *The Spanish Bride*.

HOBLER, ATHERTON WELLS, U.S. advertising executive (b. Chicago, Ill., Sept. 2, 1890—d. Princeton, N.J., Jan. 3, 1974), was founder-chairman of Benton & Bowles, Inc., one of the nation's largest advertising agencies. In 1932 he left Erwin Wasey & Co. to form a corporation with William Benton and Chester Bowles whose agency was already billing $1 million annually. Hobler, whose special interest was radio and television, produced such popular programs as "The Fred Allen Show" and "Show Boat," as well as daytime serials.

HOFFMAN, PAUL GRAY, U.S. business executive and United Nations administrator (b. Western Springs, Ill., April 26, 1891—d. New York, N.Y., Oct. 8, 1974), began his career as an enterprising automobile dealer in Los Angeles with a special talent for organization and an uncommon gift for gentle persuasion. After a series of rapid promotions he was named president, and later chairman, of the Studebaker Corp. When he left industry in 1948 to head the Marshall Plan, he became an international figure as he dispensed $10 billion in less than three years to revive the shattered economies of Europe. Hoffman later served as first president of the Ford Foundation (1951–53), was a member of the U.S. delegation to the UN (1956–57), managing director of the UN Special Fund (1959–66), and head of the UN Development Program (1959–72). He was also a longtime (1937–50) trustee of the University of Chicago and for 31 years a member of the board of directors of Encyclopædia Britannica, Inc. In 1973 he was awarded the Medal of Freedom.

HUNT, H(AROLDSON) L(AFAYETTE), U.S. oil tycoon (b. Ramsey, Ill., Feb. 17, 1889—d. Dallas, Tex., Nov. 29, 1974), was one of the world's richest businessmen at the time of his death. His first successful ventures were the acquisition of profitable oil leases in Arkansas and Louisiana, but it was his shrewd negotiations for oil leases in Rusk County, Tex., that guaranteed his future as a multimillionaire. Following World War I, Hunt Oil Co. explorers found no oil reserves in Pakistan but in Libya brought in one of the largest oil finds on record. Hunt gradually diversified his investments but kept tight control over everything he owned. He was an ardent propagandist for right-wing causes and, except for a luxurious home in Dallas, was content to live

Henry William Frederick Albert, duke of Gloucester

DOROTHY WILDING—CAMERA PRESS/PICTORIAL PARADE

simply, driving an old model car and carrying his lunch in a paper bag.

HUNTLEY, CHET (Chester Robert Huntley), U.S. television newscaster (b. Cardwell, Mont., Dec. 10, 1911—d. Bozeman, Mont., March 20, 1974), became one of America's best-known personalities and most respected reporters as co-anchorman on the weekday news program "Huntley-Brinkley Report." From October 1956 to July 1970 Huntley and David Brinkley, a former Washington, D.C., correspondent, sustained one of television's most consistently popular programs by intermixing humour and human interest with incisive reporting on national and international affairs. After nearly 20 years on the West Coast working alternately for all three major networks, Huntley was called to New York City in 1956 and paired with Brinkley to cover the national political conventions for the National Broadcasting Corp. The chance pairing created such enthusiastic viewer response that NBC assigned them to the nightly news. They subsequently shared every significant award open to television newsmen. After their final broadcast, which concluded as always with "Good night, David—Good night, Chet," Huntley returned to Montana to develop a resort called Big Sky of Montana, Inc., which opened three days after his death.

HUROK, SOL (Solomon Isaievich Hurok), U.S. impresario (b. Pogar [near Kharkov], Russia, April 9, 1888—d. New York, N.Y., March 5, 1974), brought international talent to an appreciative U.S. public for some 60 years. He migrated to the U.S. as a teenager, did odd jobs in Philadelphia, then moved to New York City where he became fully aware of his fascination with the performing arts. While still in his 20s he began arranging performances, always searching for artists who evoked excitement in the audience. One of his greatest discoveries and future stars was Marian Anderson, whom he heard singing in Paris in 1935. Under Hurok's aegis she launched her career with a tour of the U.S. (1935–36). In time Hurok sponsored a vast array of artistic performers and distinguished companies, many of them from his native Russia. Through him many Americans came to appreciate the Bolshoi Ballet, the Royal Ballet, the Old Vic, and such stars as Galina Ulanova, Artur Rubinstein, Isaac Stern, Margot Fonteyn, Anna Pavlova, Andrés Segovia, Maria Callas, Fyodor Chaliapin, and Isadora Duncan. In 1969, when S. Hurok Concerts, Inc. was sold to the Transcontinental Investing Corp., Hurok was given control of TIC for an undetermined period of time. His announced intention was to branch out into motion pictures, television, radio, and rock 'n' roll records (utilizing chain and discount stores for mass distribution) in order to reach the younger generation.

HUSAYNI, HAJ AMIN AL-, Arab leader (b. Jerusalem, 1893—d. Beirut, Lebanon, July 4, 1974), joined the Arab movement in Jerusalem in 1917 to oppose the establishment of a Jewish national home in Palestine. In April 1920 he organized anti-Jewish riots, for which he was sentenced by a British tribunal to ten years' imprisonment. He fled to Transjordan, but returned to Jerusalem under amnesty the following year and was appointed mufti by the high commissioner, Sir Herbert Samuel. He then assumed the title of "grand mufti" and became the leader of the Palestine Arabs. Following the outbreak of World War II, Husayni fled from Lebanon to Iraq, where he played a role in the abortive pro-German coup of Rashid Ali al-Gailani (April–June 1941) and organized a pogrom against the Baghdad Jews. Forced to flee again, he was received in Berlin by Hitler, who authorized him to open the "Arab Bureau." After the collapse of Germany he was given sanctuary in Egypt, where he became the head of the Palestine Arab Higher Committee created by the Arab League. He led an Arab National Guard unit in the Arab-Israeli war that followed Israel's independence (1948). Husayni was instrumental in the assassination in July 1951 of King Abdullah ibn Hussain of Jordan.

ISMAIL, AHMED, Egyptian field marshal (b. Cairo, Egypt, 1917—d. London, Eng., Dec. 25, 1974), was the Egyptian defense minister and commander in chief when he planned the secret attack across the Suez Canal that surprised Israel on Oct. 6, 1973, and opened the October war. Ismail graduated from the Cairo Military Academy in 1938, saw service with the Allies in the Western Desert during World War II, and fought as a brigade commander in the Arab-Israeli war

of 1948. He later trained in Britain, fought the Franco-British-Israeli forces during the Suez operation of 1956, undertook further training in the U.S.S.R., and was a divisional commander in the Six-Day War of 1967. He was made chief of staff in March 1969 but was dismissed by Pres. Gamal Abd-an-Nasser in September, as a scapegoat for successful Israeli raids. Pres. Anwar as-Sadat, however, named him chief of intelligence in September 1970. In October 1972 he accompanied Prime Minister Aziz Sidky on a visit to Moscow and on his return stifled an attempted coup against the president. That same month he replaced the anti-Soviet Gen. Muhammad Sadek as minister of defense and commander in chief and was promoted to full general. His skill as a strategist and his success in reviving the morale of the Egyptian Army became evident in the October 1973 war. Ismail was made a field marshal in November 1973.

JAMIESON, THOMAS, British international refugee administrator (b. Glasgow, Scot., 1911—d. Geneva, Switz., Dec. 18, 1974), served from 1959 to 1972 as director of operations of the United Nations High Commission for Refugees. He involved himself in refugee work at the end of World War II and played a major role in caring for such refugees as those in East Asia, the Near East, Europe, Bangladesh, and Africa.

JOHNSON, EARL J., U.S. journalist (b. Winfield, Kan., April 13, 1900—d. Tucson, Ariz., Jan. 3, 1974), was for 30 years the imperturbable editor of the worldwide news operations of United Press International and of its antecedent, United Press. Johnson helped train some of the best known newsmen and commentators in the country before retiring in 1965 after a 44-year newspaper career.

JOLIVET, ANDRÉ, French composer (b. Paris, France, Aug. 8, 1905—d. Dec. 19, 1974), created his own atonal musical language in the tradition of Arnold Schoenberg and Edgard Varèse, whose pupil he was. While musical director of the Comédie Française (1945–59) he wrote a comic opera, *Dolorès, ou Le Miracle de la femme laide* (1942; Opéra Comique, Paris), and two ballets, *Guignol et Pandore* (1943) and *L'Inconnue* (1950), both produced at the Paris Opéra. From 1966 to 1970 he was professor of composition at the Paris Conservatoire. His interest in primitive ritual and mysticism was reflected in *Mana* (1935; six piano pieces), *Cosmogonie* (1938; orchestral), and *Psyche* (1946; symphonic poem); he also wrote chamber music, symphonies, and pieces for voice and orchestra.

JONAS, FRANZ, Austrian statesman (b. Vienna, Aus., Oct. 4, 1899—d. Vienna, April 23, 1974), president of Austria at the time of his death, was a typesetter, active in the Social Democratic Party, when arrested for high treason in 1935 after attending an illegal revolutionary socialist conference; he was later acquitted. He became local council chairman for his Vienna suburb, Floridsdorf, in 1945, was councillor for food distribution in the Vienna city council in 1948, and took charge of a major housing program in December 1949. He succeeded Theodor Körner as mayor and governor of Vienna in 1951, a position he held for 14 years. He concurrently became a member of the upper chamber of the federal Parliament in 1951 and of the lower chamber in 1953. Jonas strove to improve the social services of Vienna, which he also hoped to develop into an international centre. He was elected federal president of Austria on May 23, 1965, and reelected on April 25, 1971.

KAHN, LOUIS ISADORE, U.S. architect (b. Island of Ösel, Estonia, Russia, Feb. 20, 1901—d. New York, N.Y., March 17, 1974), redefined the form and function of architecture and developed a trend-setting style that immediately set him far apart from such other creative U.S. designers as Frank Lloyd Wright. Kahn's daring innovations first attracted wide attention with the completion (1951) of his first major project, the Yale University Art Gallery, which expressed in brick, glass, and harsh unfinished concrete Kahn's insights into the use of natural light and strong, stark, geometrical forms. More startling still were the bare pipes, uncovered ducts, and open storage spaces, which Kahn viewed as an integral part of his architectural design. His other well-known works include the Kimbell Art Museum in Fort Worth, Tex., the capitol buildings in Dacca, Bangladesh, the Salk Institute in La Jolla, Calif.,

Chet Huntley

and the Richards Medical Research Laboratories at the University of Pennsylvania (where Kahn taught architecture for many years).

KALVEN, HARRY, JR., U.S. law professor (b. Chicago, Ill., Sept. 11, 1914—d. Chicago, Oct. 29, 1974), joined the University of Chicago law school faculty in 1945 and became a highly respected authority on torts, tax laws, and the First Amendment (which guarantees freedom of speech). In 1966 he and Hans Zeisel, a law school colleague, published *The American Jury*. After analyzing surveys covering more than 3,500 jury trials, the authors concluded that U.S. juries have been unquestionably competent and their value indisputable. The two men earlier collaborated on *Delay in the Court* (1959), an account of court congestion. Kalven left a partly finished work on legal theories that underlie the American concept of free speech.

KING, ALBERTA CHRISTINE WILLIAMS, mother of the late civil rights leader Martin Luther King, Jr. (b. Atlanta, Ga., Sept. 13, 1903—d. Atlanta, June 30, 1974), was shot and killed in Atlanta's Ebenezer Baptist Church. Mrs. King, wife of the pastor, died while playing the organ during Sunday morning services. The young black assailant began firing wildly after shouting, "I'm tired of all this. I'm going to take over." A deacon was also killed and one other person wounded. Though Mrs. King chose to remain in the background, those who knew her best believed the support she gave her son and husband made her the most important member of the family.

KIRK, NORMAN ERIC, New Zealand statesman (b. Waimate, Canterbury, N.Z., Jan. 6, 1923—d. Wellington, N.Z., Aug. 31, 1974), was prime minister and minister of foreign affairs from December 1972 until his death. He became an active Labour Party worker in the early 1940s, was mayor of Kaiapoi (1953–57), and entered Parliament as member for Lyttleton in 1957. He was elected vice-president of the New Zealand Labour Party (1963) and president (1964–66), and became (1965) the parliamentary party's youngest leader in history. As Labour prime minister and minister of foreign affairs, Kirk was most effective in foreign policy: with Australian Prime Minister Gough Whitlam, he opposed France's nuclear tests in the Pacific Ocean and took the question to the International Court of Justice at The Hague, Neth.; after Great Britain entered the European Economic Community in January 1973, he made New Zealand a more independent influence in the Pacific and Southeast Asia, while strengthening links with Australia, Canada, and the United States; he banned racially segregated South African sports teams; and he required British immigrants to obtain entry permits from 1974.

KLEIN, ANNE (Anne Klein Rubinstein), U.S. fashion designer (b. Brooklyn, N.Y., Aug. 3, 1922—d. New York, N.Y., March 19, 1974),

Norman E. Kirk

Charles A. Lindbergh

won international acclaim for designing women's clothing that gave casual dress an air of unobtrusive sophistication. Her interests also extended to such accessories as handbags, belts, and jewelry. After establishing (1968) her own manufacturing company, Anne Klein & Co., she marketed her fashions through some 800 outlets in the U.S. She was the only designer to receive the Neiman-Marcus Award for fashion leadership twice (1959, 1969), and was named to the Coty American Fashion Awards Hall of Fame in 1971. At a special fashion show held in Versailles in November 1973, she was one of only ten designers invited to display their creations.

KNOWLAND, WILLIAM FIFE, U.S. newspaper executive and politician (b. Alameda, Calif., June 26, 1908—d. near Monte Rio, Calif., Feb. 23, 1974), was one of modern America's most remarkable politicians. At 25 he was California's youngest assemblyman, at 27 the youngest member of the state Senate, at 32 chairman of the executive committee of the Republican National Committee, and at 37 the youngest member of the U.S. Senate, having been appointed to fill a vacancy by then Gov. Earl Warren. In 1952 Knowland was nominated by both the Democratic and Republican parties for reelection to the Senate and received nearly four million votes, more than any candidate had ever received from a single state for any office. As Republican floor leader from 1953 to 1958, he became known as an ardent foe of Asian Communism. He retired from politics in 1958 after losing the race for governor of California and with it presumed hopes for the presidency. Knowland then became editor and later publisher of the family-owned *Oakland Tribune.*

KNOWLES, THE REV. MICHAEL CLIVE (in religion DAVID), British historian (b. 1896—d. Nov. 21, 1974), was professor of modern history at Cambridge University from 1954 to 1963 and an acclaimed authority on monasticism. He was ordained a Benedictine priest in 1922 but his efforts to institute a stricter form of monastic observance created a conflict that ended only when he was relieved of monastic obligations. In 1944 he took up a fellowship at Peterhouse College, Cambridge, and launched a distinguished academic career. His works include *The American Civil War* (1926), *The Monastic Order in England* (1940), and other books on the history of religion in Europe, to which he brought enormous reserves of classical, medieval, and modern learning. In 1956 he was elected president of the Royal Historical Society. He was also chairman of the British Universities Advisory Committee of *Encyclopædia Britannica.*

KRIPS, JOSEF, Austrian orchestral conductor (b. Vienna, Aus., April 8, 1902—d. Geneva, Switz., Oct. 12, 1974), was best known as an interpreter of the Viennese classics from Mozart to Brückner. He studied at Vienna under Felix Weingartner. Early engagements at Vienna, Dortmund, Ger., and Karlsruhe, Ger. (where he was musical director of the Staatstheater, 1926–33), led to a return to Vienna and the State Opera, with which he was to remain associated, apart from a break from 1938 to 1945. After World War II he helped restart the Salzburg Festival and conducted at Covent Garden before becoming principal conductor of the London Symphony Orchestra (1950–53). Similar appointments followed with the Buffalo (N.Y.) Symphony (1954–

63) and the San Francisco Symphony (1963–70), with frequent returns to Covent Garden and to the London Philharmonic Orchestra.

KROCK, ARTHUR, U.S. journalist (b. Glasgow, Ky., Nov. 16, 1886—d. Washington, D.C., April 12, 1974), was from 1932 to 1953 chief correspondent for the *New York Times* in the nation's capital. He received a Pulitzer Prize in 1935 for general excellence, another in 1938 for an interview with Pres. Franklin D. Roosevelt, and refused the nomination for a third prize in 1950. Instead, he accepted a Pulitzer special commendation for an interview with Pres. Harry S. Truman. In 1955 he received a fourth Pulitzer honour, a special citation for distinguished correspondence. During his more than 60 years as a journalist, Krock became one of the true titans of the U.S. press, writing front page stories and composing his column, "In the Nation," which generally reflected his conservative views of politics and government. He retired in 1966 after serving in the *Times*'s Washington bureau for over 30 years.

KRUGER, OTTO, U.S. actor (b. Toledo, O., Sept. 6, 1885—d. Woodland Hills, Calif., Sept. 6, 1974), was an accomplished Broadway actor long before becoming familiar to movie, radio, and television audiences as an amiable villain. Trained in music from childhood, Kruger became a fine pianist, cellist, and violinist but after graduating from Columbia University resumed an acting career that began at age 15. Major stage hits included *The Royal Family, Private Lives, Counselor-at-Law, The Moon Is Down,* and *Laura.* Of some 100 films in which he appeared, *Saboteur, Magnificent Obsession, Duel in the Sun, High Noon,* and *The Last Command* are among the best remembered.

KUZNETSOV, NIKOLAY GERASIMOVICH, Soviet naval officer (b. Medvedki [now in Archangel Oblast], Russia, 1902—d. Moscow, U.S.S.R., Dec. 8, 1974), was commander in chief of the Soviet Navy during World War II. During the first two years of the Spanish Civil War he served as adviser to the Republican Fleet and from 1937 commanded the Soviet Pacific Fleet. In 1939 he was appointed people's commissar of the navy and consequently commander in chief of Soviet naval forces. When the Navy Commissariat became part of the newly created Ministry of Defense in February 1946, Vice-Admiral Kuznetsov became first deputy minister of defense and navy minister. In 1947 Stalin removed him from his post. A Navy Ministry was restored in 1950 but after Stalin's death it was again absorbed by the Ministry of Defense. Kuznetsov returned to power as first deputy minister of defense and commander in chief of the Navy, but in February 1956 he was dismissed by Nikita Khrushchev.

LAGERKVIST, PÄR FABIAN, Swedish novelist, poet, and dramatist (b. Växjö, Småland, Swed., May 23, 1891—d. Stockholm, Swed., July 11, 1974), was awarded the Nobel Prize for Literature in 1951. After studying at the University of Uppsala, he became interested in socialism, avant-garde art, and literature in Paris. His profoundly disturbed reaction to World War I was reflected in such early works as *Ångest* (1916; "Anguish") and *Kaos* (1919), but his early pessimism was less evident in the 1920s in the tales *Det eviga leendet* (1920; *The Eternal Smile,* 1934), the poems *Den lyckliges väg* (1921; "The Happy

Man's Way") and *Hjärtats sånger* (1926; "Songs of the Heart"), and an autobiographical novel, *Gäst hos verkligheten* (1925; *Guest of Reality,* 1936). By the early 1930s Lagerkvist was preoccupied with Nazism and gave full vent to his thoughts on the power and significance of evil in three principal works: *Bödeln* (1933; *The Hangman,* 1936), a prose work, later dramatized, and two novels, *Dvärgen* (1944; *The Dwarf,* 1945) and *Barabbas* (1950), which was translated into more than 30 languages. Other notable writings included *Den knutna näven* (1934; "The Clenched Fist"), *Mannen utan själ* (1936; *The Man Without a Soul,* 1944), *Seger i mörker* (1939; "Victory over Shadows"), *Ahasverus död* (1960; *The Death of Ahasuerus,* 1962), *Pilgrim på havet* (1962; *Pilgrim at Sea,* 1964), and *Mariamne* (1967; Eng. trans. 1968), published after the death of his wife. He was elected to the Swedish Academy in 1940.

LESCOT, ELIE, Haitian lawyer and politician (b. Saint-Louis du Nord, Haiti, Dec. 9, 1883—d. La Boule, Haiti, Oct. 22, 1974), held various government posts, including that of ambassador to the U.S., before serving as president of Haiti from 1941 to 1946. Though affable of manner, Lescot ruled by martial law and rigorously controlled the press until overthrown by a military coup that was celebrated with wild rejoicing throughout the country.

LESLIE, KENNETH, Canadian poet (b. Pictou, Nova Scotia, Nov. 1, 1892—d. Halifax, Nova Scotia, Oct. 7, 1974), was so attuned to nature that his poems describing rural life in Nova Scotia seemed, and often later were, set to music. In 1938 he received the Governor-General's Medal for a collection of verse entitled *By Stubborn Stars* (1938).

LINDBERGH, CHARLES AUGUSTUS, U.S. pioneer aviator (b. Detroit, Mich., Feb. 4, 1902—d. Kipahulu, Hawaii, Aug. 26, 1974), was an unknown 25-year-old stunt-flyer-turned-airmail-pilot when he left New York City for Paris in his single-engine "Spirit of St. Louis." Late at night on May 21, 1927, after 33½ hours in the air, he completed the first solo nonstop flight across the Atlantic and became an international celebrity. For his daring exploit, the "Lone Eagle" received a $25,000 prize, the Medal of Honor, offers worth millions of dollars, and worldwide acclaim.

Two years later Lindbergh married Anne Morrow. They visited many countries together as Lindbergh plotted new air routes for Transcontinental Air Transport and Pan American Airways. Then, in 1932, their 20-month-old son was kidnapped and murdered. The sensationalism that characterized the subsequent arrest of Bruno R. Hauptmann, his trial, conviction, and execution (April 1936), so disturbed the Lindberghs that they moved to Europe in quest of privacy.

Before World War II broke out in Europe, Lindbergh was twice (1936, 1938) invited to inspect the German Air Force and was decorated by the Nazi government. Convinced that Germany could not be defeated, he gave public speeches (1940–41) warning against American involvement. When he was rebuked by Pres. Franklin D. Roosevelt, Lindbergh resigned his commission (April 1941) in the Air Corps Reserves. Once the U.S. was at war, however, Lindbergh quietly made his way to the Pacific war zone as a civilian employee of United Aircraft Corp. and by war's end had flown 50 combat missions.

In later years Lindbergh was consultant to Pan American Airways and was named a brigadier general (1954) in the Air Force Reserves for longtime service to U.S. government agencies. He wrote several books, receiving a Pulitzer Prize (1954) for *The Spirit of St. Louis,* a recounting of his famous transatlantic flight.

LIPPMANN, WALTER, U.S. journalist (b. New York, N.Y., Sept. 23, 1889—d. New York, Dec. 14, 1974), published millions of words (about 25 books and 4,000 newspaper articles) and became in the process the elder statesman of his profession and one of its most attentively read representatives. For the most part he analyzed domestic and world affairs in the light of political philosophy with little concern for current popular emotions. He was thus more an observer of events than a crusader for special causes. Nonetheless, he publicly opposed such things as the New Deal and the Vietnam war and expressed his preferences for presidential candidates. But it was more typical of him to expose all the facets of a problem and call attention to the dangers of extremes. It was his broad view and perspective that set him apart from most of his contemporaries. Readers sometimes disagreed with what he had to say, but they never dismissed his erudite and carefully reasoned presentations as unworthy of serious consideration.

Lippmann left Harvard University in 1910 after one year of graduate studies. In 1914 he co-founded the *New Republic* and later helped formulate Pres. Woodrow Wilson's Fourteen Points for peace. From 1921 to 1931 he was with the *New York World*, then began writing his "Today and Tomorrow" column for the *New York Herald-Tribune*, later syndicated all over the world. Among the numerous awards that he received were two Pulitzer Prizes (1958, 1962), the Medal of Freedom (1964), and three Overseas Press Club awards (1953, 1955, 1959) for interpreting foreign news.

LITVAK, ANATOLE, Russian-born film director (b. Kiev, Russia, May 21, 1902—d. Paris, France, Dec. 15, 1974), began his career in Germany in 1925, where he worked on G. W. Pabst's *The Joyless Street*, one of Greta Garbo's early films. After directing *Mayerling* in France, he moved to Hollywood to direct such pictures as *Confessions of a Nazi Spy* (1939), *All This and Heaven, Too* (1940), *The Snake Pit* (1948), and *Sorry, Wrong Number* (1948). His film credits, after returning to Europe in 1955, included *Anastasia* (1956), *Goodbye Again* (1961), and *The Night of the Generals* (1967).

LIU SHAO-CH'I, Chinese Communist statesman (b. Ning-hsiang, Hunan Province, 1898—d. reported Peking, October 1974), was chairman (chief of state) of the People's Republic of China from 1959 until his overthrow in 1966 during the Cultural Revolution. The son of a prosperous peasant, he joined the Chinese Communist Party (Kungch'antang or KCT) in 1921 after being sent by the Comintern agent G. N. Voytinsky to Moscow's University for Toilers of the East. He returned to China as a labour organizer and in 1925 was elected vice-chairman of the All-China Federation of Labour. In 1927 he was elected to the KCT Central Committee and in 1934 became a member of the Politburo. During the Communists' Long March to Yenan he worked in areas under Kuomintang (Nationalist) control. In 1939, two years after the Japanese invasion of China, he was appointed head of the Central China Bureau of the KCT. From 1943 he worked in Yenan as deputy chairman of the People's Revolutionary Military Council.

In the central government of the People's Republic of China that was formed in Peking on Oct. 1, 1949, Liu was one of six vice-chairmen serving under Chairman Mao Tse-tung. In 1959 the National People's Congress elected Liu chief of state, succeeding Mao who remained KCT chairman. The Sino-Soviet ideological rift, however, brought into the open a long smoldering rivalry between the two. Liu opposed Mao's collectivist policies and anti-Soviet stance, and Mao viewed Liu as traveling down the "capitalist road." In August 1966, at the 11th plenary session of the Central Committee, Mao launched his Great Proletarian Cultural Revolution. Liu then became the target of a campaign directed against pro-Soviet "revisionists." By December 1966 his public appearances ceased but Peking Radio did not announce until 1968 that he had been deprived of all powers and expelled from the KCT. He spent his last years under house arrest in Peking. In October 1974 the Communist newspaper *Ta Kung Pao* announced that both Liu Shao-ch'i and former defense minister Lin Piao were dead physically as well as politically.

LUNN, SIR ARNOLD, British authority on skiing and author (b. Madras, India, April 18, 1888—d. London, Eng., June 2, 1974), was a devoted Alpinist. He founded the Alpine Ski Club in 1908 and the Kandahar Ski Club in 1924, organized the world's first downhill ski race, at Montana, Switz., in 1911, invented the slalom ski race, at Mürren, Switz., in 1922, and made the first ski ascent of the Eiger mountain in 1924. He was more than once president of the Ski Club of Great Britain, represented Great Britain on the Fédération Internationale de Ski (1928–49), and wrote many books on skiing and the Alps (including guidebooks on Switzerland). The son of a Methodist missionary, he eventually turned to Roman Catholicism (*Now I See*, 1933) and became an energetic Catholic apologist. He was knighted in 1952.

McGEE, FRANK, U.S. newscaster and television host (b. Monroe, La., Sept. 12, 1921—d. New York, N.Y., April 17, 1974), was known to millions of Americans as the affable host of NBC's award-winning morning program "Today." He was a radio and television reporter from 1950 to 1955 in Oklahoma City, where he wrote his own scripts and shot and edited his own film. As news director (1955–57) of an NBC affiliate in Montgomery, Ala., he provided sensitive coverage of racial disturbances that attracted the attention of the network's executives. Transferred to Washington, D.C., in 1957, McGee continued his reports on racial problems and became an expert on the U.S. space program and on politics. He was assigned to New York City two years later and featured on "The Frank McGee Report." When named to the "Today" show in October 1971, McGee was a highly respected journalist who had received among other honours the Peabody Award in 1966 and an Emmy for his coverage of special events.

McGUIGAN, JAMES CHARLES CARDINAL, Canadian prelate of the Roman Catholic Church (b. near Hunter River, P.E.I., Nov. 26, 1894—d. Toronto, Ont., April 8, 1974), became the world's youngest archbishop at age 35 on his appointment to Regina, Sask. He was transferred to Toronto in 1934 and elevated to the cardinalate by Pope Pius XII in 1946—the first English-Canadian to be so honoured. A quiet, happy man with a reputation for excellent administration, McGuigan converted the Archbishop's Palace into a home for children as part of an effort to care for a large postwar influx into Toronto of Catholics. Though he requested to be relieved of his duties in 1961 because of failing health, he carried on with the help of a coadjutor archbishop until his retirement in April 1971.

MAKONNEN, ENDALKACHEW, former Ethiopian prime minister (b. Addis Ababa, Eth., 1926—d. Ethiopia, Nov. 24, 1974), was educated at Oxford, became an expert on foreign affairs, and served as ambassador to London (a post previously held by his father). In 1961 he returned to Addis Ababa as minister of commerce and industry and subsequently became Ethiopia's permanent representative at the UN (1966–69) and minister of communications, telecommunications, and posts (1969–74). In an atmosphere of widespread discontent and charges of inefficiency and corruption, he was called on to form a government in February 1974, following the forced resignation of the previous prime minister, Aklilu Habte-wold. He succeeded in restoring calm, but his moderate policies did not satisfy army extremists. After five months in office, he was forced to resign, was arrested, and executed.

MANNHEIM, HERMANN, German-born British criminologist (b. Berlin, Ger., Oct. 26, 1889—d. London, Eng., Jan. 20, 1974), reader in criminology (1946–55) at London University and honorary director (1956–61) of the Criminological Research Unit at the London School of Economics and Political Science (LSE), established criminology as an academic study in Britain. When he migrated from Germany in 1934 his reputation in legal studies and judicial practice was already well established. His lectures at the LSE were published as *The Dilemma of Penal Reform* (1939) and *War and Crime* (1941); with Sir Alexander Carr-Saunders, director of the LSE, he wrote *Young Offenders* (1942). Mannheim's *Prediction Methods in Relation to Borstal Training* (1955) and *Comparative Criminology* (two vol., 1965) were the products of his lifelong interest in criminology.

MARTIN, FRANK, Swiss composer (b. Geneva, Switz., Sept. 15, 1890—d. Naarden, Neth., Nov. 21, 1974), was best known for his oratorio *Le Vin herbé* (1942; based on the Tristan legend). In Geneva he helped found the Chamber Music Society, where he played both piano and harpsichord, and later he taught at the Jaques-Dalcroze Institute there and at Cologne Conservatory. His early work was influenced by Ravel, Fauré, and Schoenberg. Later compositions include an opera, *Der Sturm* (based on Shakespeare's *The Tempest*), such concertos as the *Petite Symphonie concertante* (1945) for harp, harpsichord, piano, and double string orchestra, and a *Requiem* (1972). From 1946 Martin lived in The Netherlands.

MAUFE, SIR EDWARD, British architect (b. Ilkley, Yorkshire, Eng., Dec. 12, 1883—d. Dec.

12, 1974), received the Royal Gold Medal for Architecture in 1944 and was knighted in 1954. His accomplishments include the Anglican cathedral of Guildford, Surrey; St. Saviour's and St. Bede's, two London churches; new buildings for St. John's and Balliol colleges at Oxford, and the Playhouse Theatre; new structures for Trinity and St. John's colleges at Cambridge, and the Festival Theatre; and numerous renovations.

MENON, (VENGALIL KRISHNAN) KRISHNA, Indian statesman (b. Calicut, Malabar, India, May 3, 1897—d. New Delhi, India, Oct. 5, 1974), who played a controversial role in Indian politics, was his country's first high commissioner (ambassador) in London (1947–52) and its minister of defense (1957–62). Son of a wealthy lawyer, Menon was educated at home by an English tutor and at Madras University, where he became politically minded and an opponent of British rule. In 1924 he left for England where he graduated from the London School of Economics with a master's degree and also became a barrister. He joined the British Labour Party and served as a

WIDE WORLD

councillor of the St. Pancras borough of London (1934–47) while working as a publisher's editor. When India became independent in 1947, Jawaharlal Nehru appointed him high commissioner to the United Kingdom. From 1952 to 1960 he represented India at the UN; during the debates on Suez and Hungary he was highly critical of Western imperialism while condoning Soviet suppression of the Hungarian uprising. Appointed minister of defense by Nehru in 1957, he was forced to resign in November 1962 following China's victory over India in the Assam border dispute. After Nehru's death in 1964 Menon was without friends in the Congress Party, and left it in 1967. Though reelected to the Lok Sabha (lower house) in 1969 as an independent, he failed to regain his former influence.

MESSALI HADJ, AHMAD, Algerian nationalist (b. Tlemcen, Algeria, 1898—d. Paris, France, June 3, 1974), was a leading campaigner for Algerian independence. His activities brought him, from 1929, stretches of imprisonment and exile that ended only with Algeria's achievement of independence in 1962. He spent his last years at Gouvieux, near Chantilly, France.

MEYER, KARL FRIEDRICH, U.S. virologist (b. Basel, Switz., May 19, 1884—d. San Francisco, Calif., April 27, 1974), was responsible for important viral discoveries applicable to public health and veterinary medicine. In South Africa his success in protecting cattle from a deadly tick-borne infection attracted wide attention. He moved to the U.S. in 1910 and successively isolated the virus of eastern and then western equine encephalitis. During his many years

(1915–54) with the Hooper Foundation at the University of California in San Francisco, Meyer solved crucial problems related to typhoid, coccidioidomycosis (valley fever), psittacosis (parrot fever), and leptospirosis (a form of infectious jaundice).

MILHAUD, DARIUS, French composer (b. Aix-en-Provence, France, Sept. 4, 1892—d. Geneva, Switz., June 22, 1974), whose more than 400 works embraced an astonishing diversity of forms, began composing while at the Paris Conservatoire. He accompanied the poet Paul Claudel, appointed French minister to Brazil, to that country in 1916, and acquainted himself with Brazilian folk music (*Saudades do Brasil,* 1920–21). Back in Paris in 1919, he became one of the group of young French composers known as Les Six, under whose stimulus he wrote scintillating scores for ballets, including *Le Boeuf sur le toit* (composed 1919, performed 1920) and *La Création du monde* (1923), as well as his orchestral suite (final version 1919) from Claudel's *Protée* and *Machines Agricoles* (1919), for voice and seven instruments set to a trade catalog. Some of these early works gave cause for scandal with their use of polytonality and strident "unmusical" sounds.

Milhaud's ambitious opera *Christophe Colomb* (1928) triumphed at the Berlin State Opera in 1930 and was followed by incidental music for plays and films, choral, orchestral, and chamber works, works for children, and his first fully orchestrated symphony (1939). During this period he became crippled with rheumatism, and was eventually confined to a wheelchair. At the beginning of World War II he took up a post as professor of composition at Mills College, Oakland, Calif., which he subsequently visited each year. In 1947 he was appointed professor of composition at the Paris Conservatoire, and he continued to compose: Symphony No. 3, liturgical, with chorus (1946); *Service sacrée* (1947); *'adame miroir* (1948, ballet); *David* (1953, opera created at Jerusalem); Symphony No. 12 (1962); *Pacem in terris* (1963, choral symphony on Pope John XXIII's encyclical with special authorization by the Vatican); and *Cantata of Psalms* (1967).

MILTON, ERNEST, U.S.-born British actor (b. San Francisco, Calif., Jan. 10, 1890—d. Northwood, Middlesex, Eng., July 24, 1974), was a sensitive interpreter noted for his fine diction. After acting in the U.S., he joined the Old Vic Company in London in 1918, and in 1926 married the novelist Naomi Royde-Smith. His many outstanding interpretations included the title role in Luigi Pirandello's *Henry IV* (1925, 1929), Pope Paul in Henry de Montherlant's *Malatesta* (1957), and Shakespeare's major tragic roles.

MIRÓ CARDONA, JOSÉ, Cuban politician (b. Cuba, 1902?—d. San Juan, P.R., Aug. 10, 1974), having supported Fidel Castro's rise to power, was named first prime minister (1959) of the new regime and then Cuban ambassador to Spain. Shortly after arriving in the U.S. as Cuban envoy, he defected. When the disastrous Bay of Pigs invasion occurred in 1961, Miró was president of the Cuban Revolutionary Council. At the time of his

Wayne Morse

WIDE WORLD

death he was teaching at the University of Puerto Rico School of Law.

MIRSKY, ALFRED EZRA, U.S. molecular biologist (b. New York, N.Y., Oct. 17, 1900—d. New York, June 19, 1974), made discoveries that provided totally new insights into biological processes. He graduated from Harvard College and Cambridge University (Ph.D. 1926) before joining the Rockefeller Institute for Medical Research in 1927. Mirsky and his colleague Arthur Pollister, working with cells from the liver and thymus of calves, isolated chromatin (a genetic material consisting of DNA, histones, and other proteins) at a stage of cell development in which the DNA and histones are not organized into visible chromosomal structures. Mirsky later discovered that histones play a role in controlling the operation of genes. His research also showed that all human and animal cells have the same amount of DNA with the exception of the sperm and ovum, which receive the second half of their full complement when united through fertilization. Such discoveries helped lay the foundation of molecular biology.

MOJICA, JOSÉ, Mexican tenor (b. Mexico, 1895?—d. Lima, Peru, Sept. 20, 1974), began singing professionally as a teenager, was eventually featured at the Chicago Civic Opera, and starred in numerous films shot in Hollywood, Mexico City, and Buenos Aires. In 1942, at the height of a career that had already lasted three decades, he startled the entertainment world by announcing his retirement. After distributing much of his wealth to the poor, he entered a Franciscan monastery in Arequipa, Peru, and was subsequently ordained a priest. Though Mojica sang publicly from time to time to gather money for religious causes, he returned to movies only once to portray his own life. His autobiography, *I, A Sinner* (1963), sold three million copies in Spanish and was translated into English.

MOLYNEUX, EDWARD HENRY, British fashion designer (b. London, Eng., Sept. 5, 1891—d. Monte Carlo, Monaco, March 22, 1974), was one of the most celebrated dress designers in Paris during the 1920s and '30s. The success of his quietly distinctive clothes was due to a clientele comprising some of the world's most elegant women, among them Princess Marina, the duchess of Kent; Gertrude Lawrence; and Marlene Dietrich.

MOOREHEAD, AGNES ROBERTSON, U.S. actress (b. Clinton, Mass., Dec. 6, 1906—d. Rochester, Minn., April 30, 1974), was a highly versatile performer who graduated from the University of Wisconsin with a master's degree in English and public speaking and from Bradley University with a doctorate in literature. She also attended the American Academy of Dramatic Arts. On radio, television, the stage, and in motion pictures she re-created a wide range of characters and was nominated for five Academy Awards. Her best-known television role was as the witch Endora in "Bewitched." *The Singing Nun,* her final movie, was released in 1966. She last appeared on Broadway in the musical *Gigi.*

MORAES, FRANK ROBERT, Indian journalist (b. Bombay, India, Nov. 12, 1907—d. London, Eng., May 2, 1974), was educated at St. Xavier's College, Bombay, and at Oxford University. He joined the *Times of India,* Bombay, in 1938, serving as war correspondent in Burma and China (1942–45) and as Delhi correspondent. In 1946 he became editor of the *Times of Ceylon* but returned to India in 1948 and became editor of the *Times of India* (1950–57) before going to the *Indian Express,* Delhi, as editor in chief.

MORSE, WAYNE LYMAN, U.S. politician (b. Madison, Wis., Oct. 20, 1900—d. Portland, Ore., July 22, 1974), was for 24 years one of the U.S. Senate's most obstreperous and crusty members. He joined the Senate in 1945 as a Republican from Oregon and in 1952 supported Dwight D. Eisenhower as his party's candidate for president. But when Richard M. Nixon was named as Eisenhower's running mate, Morse switched allegiance and backed Adlai E. Stevenson during the campaign. When Congress reconvened, he announced he was an independent; in 1956 he was reelected as a Democrat. In fiery speeches, replete with "language people can understand," Morse lambasted Democrats and Republicans alike, depending on the issue. He was an early and vocal critic of U.S. military involvement in Vietnam and was one of only two senators to vote against

David Oistrakh

the Gulf of Tonkin resolution in August 1964. Among the causes Morse supported most firmly were civil rights, farm price subsidies, federal aid to education, and the rights of labour unions. At the time of his death, the man who never made a deal was vigorously campaigning to regain the Senate seat he lost in 1968.

MUNCK, EBBE, Danish journalist and diplomat (b. Frederiksberg, Den., Jan. 14, 1905—d. Copenhagen, Den., May 3, 1974), was a newspaper correspondent in Berlin and London before being transferred successively to Spain and Finland to file war reports. While on a later assignment in Sweden (1940–42) he became a member of the Danish Freedom Council and the chief spokesman for the Danish resistance movement. After being named chief liaison officer for the Allies, he effected the escape of the Danish atomic physicist Niels Bohr to Sweden. Later in life Munck held a series of diplomatic posts in Finland and Southeast Asia.

MUNDT, KARL EARL, U.S. politician (b. Humboldt, S.D., June 3, 1900—d. Washington, D.C., Aug. 16, 1974), entered Congress in 1939 as a Republican from South Dakota, then moved into the Senate in 1949. After World War II he gained national prominence as acting chairman of the House Committee on Un-American Activities, which was involved in the Alger Hiss case and in the Joseph McCarthy hearings. He published countless articles and never hesitated to air his strong anti-Communist views, his concern for conservation, and his support for UNESCO, which he helped create. Though incapacitated by a stroke in November 1969, he refused to resign. The Senate finally broke a long-standing precedent in February 1972 when it stripped him of responsibilities that had fallen to him by right of seniority. The following November he ran for reelection but was defeated.

MUNRO, SIR LESLIE KNOX, New Zealand diplomat and politician (b. Auckland, N.Z., Feb. 26, 1901—d. Hamilton, N.Z., Feb. 13, 1974), was president of the UN General Assembly (1957–58). After practicing and teaching law in Auckland, he edited the *New Zealand Herald,* the country's largest daily newspaper (1942–51). He then became (1952–58) New Zealand's ambassador to the U.S. and permanent representative to the UN, serving also on the Trusteeship Council and the Security Council. From 1961 to 1963 he was secretary-general of the International Commission of Jurists. After returning to New Zealand, he sat in Parliament as a member of the National Party from 1963 until retirement in 1972. His book, *United Nations: Hope for a Divided World,* was published in 1960.

O'BRIEN, KATE, Irish author (b. Limerick, Ire., Dec. 3, 1897—d. Canterbury, Eng., Aug. 13, 1974), re-created in her novels and plays Victorian middle-class life in Ireland. Her first works were plays, *Distinguished Villa* (1926) and *The Bridge* (1927). Then came the novels *Without My Cloak* (1931), which won the Hawthornden and the James Tait Black Memorial prizes, *The Ante-Room* (1934), *Mary Lavelle* (1936), *My Ireland* (1962), and *Presentation Parlour* (1963).

ODRÍA, MANUEL ARTURO, Peruvian army general and political leader (b. Tarma, Peru, 1897—d. Lima, Peru, Feb. 18, 1974), became chief of the army staff in 1946 and minister of the interior and chief of police in January 1947. Incensed by the power of the radical Apra party, he led a bloodless coup that ousted Pres. José Luis Bustamante y Rivero in October 1948. Odría assumed the presidency and was confirmed in office by popular election in 1950. His administration, though often ruthlessly intolerant of opposition, carried out some notable social reforms and fostered considerable economic progress. Odría's candidate for the presidency was defeated in 1956, as was Odría himself in 1962.

OISTRAKH, DAVID FYODOROVICH, Soviet violinist (b. Odessa, Russia, Sept. 30, 1908—d. Amsterdam, Neth., Oct. 24, 1974), much admired in the West as the foremost exponent of the Russian school of violin playing, was educated at Odessa's Musical and Dramatic Institute and began touring the Soviet Union as a soloist at the age of 18. In 1930 he won first prize at the Ukrainian Violin Competition in Kharkov and in 1935 received the Wieniawski Prize in Warsaw. His first Western concerts were given in Paris and Brussels in 1937. In 1939 he became professor of violin at the Moscow Conservatory. He reappeared in the West at the Florence Festival in 1951, revisited Paris in 1953, and played for the first time in London a year later. In November 1955 he performed as a soloist at Carnegie Hall, New York City. Oistrakh occasionally appeared with his son and former pupil Igor, also a gifted violinist.

PACKER, SIR (DOUGLAS) FRANK (HEWSON), Australian communications magnate (b. Sydney, New South Wales, Austr., Dec. 3, 1906—d. Sydney, May 1, 1974), was chairman of Australian Consolidated Press and an enthusiastic sportsman who headed the yachting syndicate that unsuccessfully challenged for the America's Cup in 1962 and 1970. His publications included *Women's Weekly*, Australia's largest weekly circulation magazine, *The Bulletin*, a news weekly, and (until they were sold) the *Daily Telegraph*, Sydney's top-circulation morning newspaper, and the *Sunday Telegraph*. Packer set up Australia's first commercial television station and was president of the Australian Newspapers Conference, president of the Australian Newspaper Council, and a director of Reuters.

PAGNOL, MARCEL PAUL, French filmmaker and author (b. Aubagne, Bouches-du-Rhône, France, Feb. 28, 1895—d. Paris, France, April 18, 1974), wrote the play *Les Marchands de gloire* (1925, in collaboration with Paul Nivoix) and *Topaze* (1928, filmed 1932 and 1950). After the arrival of talking pictures he wrote, produced, and sometimes directed films, including the trilogy *Marius* (1931), *Fanny* (1932), and *César* (1936), which inspired the American musical *Fanny*, later adapted to film. Pagnol also wrote novels, three volumes of autobiography, and translated *Hamlet* and some of Shakespeare's other works into French. In 1946 he was elected to the Académie Française.

Juan Domingo Perón

AGIP/PICTORIAL PARADE

PALAZZESCHI, ALDO (ALDO GIURLANI), Italian writer (b. Florence, Italy, Feb. 2, 1885—d. Rome, Italy, Aug. 17, 1974), was best known for his novel *The Materassi Sisters*, a psychological study of the deterioration of two spinsters. For a time he was associated with the Futurist movement, which glorified modern technology and delved into painting, sculpture, and literature of all sorts. Besides novels, he also wrote poetry and short stories and was awarded the Viareggio Prize in 1949.

PARK CHUNG HEE, MADAME (YOOK YOUNG Soo), wife of the president of South Korea (b. Okchon, Korea, Nov. 29, 1925—d. Seoul, South Korea, Aug. 15, 1974), was killed by an assassin's bullet apparently intended for her husband, who was delivering a Liberation Day speech in the National Theatre. A teenaged girl was also killed. Madame Park was active in social work, assisting charities and such organizations as the Red Cross and Girl Scouts. On occasion, she accompanied her husband on diplomatic visits overseas.

PERÓN, JUAN DOMINGO, Argentine chief of state (b. Lobos, Arg., Oct. 8, 1895—d. Buenos Aires, Arg., July 1, 1974), was one of modern Latin America's most remarkable political figures. His rise to power began in 1943 when he and other military officers overthrew Pres. Ramón Castillo. During the next two short-lived regimes, Perón held minor government posts but established a solid political base by initiating desperately needed social reforms to help labourers and the poor. In October 1945 he was suddenly ousted and imprisoned by those who feared his policies and evident ambitions. A huge demonstration, however, was quickly organized in the capital by Eva ("Evita") Duarte and Perón was released. That night, before a crowd of 300,000, he promised the nation over radio that he would build a strong nation if elected president in the upcoming elections. Within a few days he married Eva and in February 1946 won the election.

Perón provided Argentina's "shirtless ones" with low-cost housing, higher wages, and paid vacations. Women for the first time were allowed to vote. Banks and transportation were nationalized, and profits from government controlled exports of meat and other products were used for agricultural and economic development. And Evita Perón (1919–52) became the "little Madonna," whose mere presence among the poor sparked sentiments of religious devotion. However, in carrying out his social programs, Perón was sowing the seeds of deep discontent. He imprisoned opponents, removed judges and teachers, stifled the press, upset the economy with erratic policies, and was unpredictable in foreign affairs. He was easily reelected in 1951, but with inflation rampant, agricultural production down, and foreign reserves depleted, business and industry were nearing revolt. Roman Catholics too became alienated when Perón legalized prostitution and divorce and forbade religious instruction in Catholic schools. In September 1955 he was ousted in a military coup.

For 18 years Perón remained in opulent exile (in Spain from 1960) while a succession of civilian and military governments tried vainly to bring stability to Argentina. In June 1973 a desperate nation welcomed him back amid wild excitement. Perón assumed the presidency on October 12, but quickly discovered that he could not control the left-wing Peronistas or bring order out of chaos. At his death, he left a badly divided country.

PLESCH, ARPAD, Hungarian-born financier and racehorse owner (b. Budapest, Hung., March 25, 1889—d. London, Eng., Dec. 16, 1974), was administrator (1922–33) of the I. G. Farbenindustrie at Frankfurt am Main, Ger., and a successful financier and investment adviser. He was also a racehorse enthusiast, whose mounts won several notable events, including the Epsom Derby (1971), the Prix du Jockey Club, and Prix de l'Arc de Triomphe. Plesch also assembled a collection of rare plants and an outstanding botanical library at his estate at Beaulieu in the south of France and founded the Centre de Recherches Botaniques at Monte Carlo in 1951.

POMPIDOU, GEORGES JEAN RAYMOND, French statesman (b. Montboudif, Cantal, France, July 5, 1911—d. Paris, France, April 2, 1974), was president of the French Republic at the time of his death. The son of schoolteachers, he graduated first in his class from the École Normale Supérieure in Paris before becoming a classics teacher in Marseilles and then at the Lycée Henri-

Georges Pompidou

IV in Paris. In 1935 he married Claude Cahour, who enhanced their official life with her own personal charm.

Gen. Charles de Gaulle chose Pompidou as an aide in 1944, even though he had no Resistance record and no political experience. When de Gaulle resigned in January 1946, Pompidou became deputy director general of tourism (1946–49) and was appointed *maître des requêtes* at the Conseil d'État (the highest administrative court), serving from 1946 to 1954. He then joined the bank of Rothschild Frères, later becoming its director general (1956–62).

When de Gaulle returned to power in June 1958 Pompidou became his *chef de cabinet* and helped draft the constitution of the Fifth Republic. In 1961, while a member of the Constitutional Council, he conducted secret negotiations with the Algerian nationalists that led to the agreement signed at Évian-les-Bains in March 1962. On April 16, still an unknown figure to many Frenchmen and lacking parliamentary experience, he was appointed premier. Although his prestige in the National Assembly rose during the May 1968 student riots in Paris and concomitant industrial unrest, de Gaulle suddenly replaced him with Maurice Couve de Murville after the elections of June 1968. Ten months later, when de Gaulle resigned, Pompidou entered the race for the presidency and was elected on June 15, 1969, receiving more than 58% of the second-round votes.

As president, Pompidou continued in broad outline de Gaulle's foreign policy, maintaining friendship and economic ties with Arab states; he was less successful with West Germany and did not significantly improve relations with the U.S.

When the majority of the Gaullist-dominated ruling coalition was considerably reduced in the March 1973 elections, Pompidou assumed greater independence, overriding his ministers, including his new foreign minister, Michel Jobert.

During his presidency, Pompidou met many world leaders, including Pres. Richard M. Nixon (December 1971, May/June 1973) and the Soviet leader Leonid I. Brezhnev (October 1971, June 1973). Among his most significant travels was a visit to China in September 1973. For almost five years Pompidou provided France with a stable government, strengthened its economy, and made France's political presence felt throughout the world. He supported Great Britain's entry into the European Economic Community, but failed to win wide public support in a national referendum on the enlargement of the EEC. His death was unexpected despite growing evidence of rapidly failing health.

POPE-HENNESSY, JAMES, British biographer and writer (b. Nov. 20, 1916—d. London, Eng., Jan. 25, 1974), won wide acclaim for his official biography (1959) of Queen Mary, consort of George V. His reputation as a biographer was earlier established with works on Monckton Milnes (1950, second part 1952) and Lord Crewe (1955). *West Indian Summer* (1943), *Verandah* (1964), and other colonial studies were inspired by a stay in Trinidad and Tobago (1939) as private secretary to the governor. From 1947 to 1949 Pope-Hennessy was literary editor of *The Spectator*. At the time of his death, he was engaged in research for an authorized biography of Sir Noel Coward.

RAMSAY, THE LADY PATRICIA (VICTORIA PATRICIA HELENA ELIZABETH), granddaughter of

Baldur von Schirach

Queen Victoria (b. Buckingham Palace, London, Eng., March 17, 1886—d. Windlesham, Surrey, Jan. 12, 1974), was the youngest daughter of the duke of Connaught and his duchess, formerly Princess Louise Marguerite of Prussia. Following her marriage in 1919 to Captain (later Admiral Sir Alexander) Ramsay, she relinquished the title of princess and lived a retiring life.

RANSOM, JOHN CROWE, U.S. poet and literary critic (b. Pulaski, Tenn., April 30, 1888—d. Gambier, O., July 3, 1974), was the founder (1939) and for 20 years editor of *The Kenyon Review.* Ransom used the quarterly to propagate his New Criticism, which basically insisted that the text and textual qualities of a literary work were more important than its ideas or social setting. Though Ransom wrote sparingly—often about traditions of the South and the passing of an agricultural economy that he believed enhanced human life—his poems are noteworthy for their gentle eloquence and formal excellence.

RAYMOND, ERNEST, British novelist (b. Argentières, France, Dec. 31, 1888—d. London, Eng., May 14, 1974), wrote the continually reprinted best-seller *Tell England* (1922), later made into a film. The novel was followed by 44 others and a dozen volumes of essays, plays, and autobiography. Raymond's reflective storytelling drew first upon his period of schoolmastering and his service as an Anglican chaplain in World War I (he resigned holy orders in 1923) and then upon middle-class life, mostly in London.

RENOUVIN, PIERRE EUGÈNE GEORGES, French historian (b. Paris, France, Jan. 9, 1893—d. Paris, Dec. 9, 1974), professor of contemporary history at the Sorbonne from 1933, greatly influenced modern historical studies in France. His publications include *Les Origines immédiates de la guerre (28 juin–4 août 1914)* (1925), *La Crise européenne et la grande guerre* (1934), and *Histoire des relations internationales* (1953–58). He was secretary-general of the board that published *Documents diplomatiques français 1871–1914* and was elected to the Académie des Sciences Morales et Politiques in 1946.

RIBEMONT-DESSAIGNES, GEORGES, French poet, dramatist, and painter (b. 1884—d. Saint-Jeannet, Alpes-Maritimes, France, July 9, 1974), was the last poet of Dada, a movement of negation in art and literature precursory to Surrealism. His poems were admired and illustrated by Max Ernst, Joan Miró, and Georges Braque. His plays were edited by Raymond Queneau.

RIDEAL, SIR ERIC KEIGHTLEY, British scientist (b. April 11, 1890—d. London, Eng., Sept. 25, 1974), was a distinguished physical chemist noted for his work in surface chemistry, particularly the study of interfaces, and in polymer chemistry. In 1930 he became Cambridge University's first professor of colloidal physics and in 1946 was appointed director of the Davy-Faraday Research Laboratory and Fullerian professor at the Royal Institution. In 1950 he became professor of physical chemistry at King's College, London, retiring in 1955. He was a fellow of the Royal Society, recipient of the society's Davy Medal, and was knighted in 1951.

RITTER, TEX (Woodward Maurice Ritter), U.S. actor and singer of country and western songs (b. Murvaul, Tex., Jan. 12, 1906—d. Nashville, Tenn., Jan. 2, 1974), was best known for his throaty renditions of "You Are My Sunshine," "Jingle, Jangle, Jingle," and of the theme song from *High Noon* (1952).

ROBERTSON OF OAKRIDGE, BRIAN HUBERT ROBERTSON, 1st Baron, British soldier and administrator (b. Simla, India, July 22, 1896—d. Far Oakridge, Gloucestershire, Eng., April 29, 1974), whose skill and vision helped to bring order and progress to Western Germany immediately after World War II, was appointed deputy military governor of the British Zone of Germany in 1945, commander in chief (promoted to general) and military governor in 1947, and first British high commissioner to the German federal government in 1949; during this period he solved problems posed by economic difficulties and strained relations among the Allies. He returned to army service in 1950 as commander in chief, Middle East Land Forces, but in 1953 was appointed chairman of the British Transport Commission. In 1961 he was created a baron.

ROSAY, FRANÇOISE (Françoise Bandy de Nalèche), French actress (b. Paris, France, April 19, 1891—d. Paris, March 28, 1974), became one of the great ladies of the French cinema; her career lasted some 60 years and included more than 100 films, some of which were American, English, or German. She acted at St. Petersburg (1912–13) and sang as a soprano at the Paris Opéra (1916–18). By the 1930s she was firmly committed to a film career, appearing first in Hollywood in *The Magnificent Lie.* Later pictures included *La Kermesse héroique, Un Carnet de bal, Jenny, Johnny Frenchman,* and *Quartet.* From 1944 to 1947 she was art director of Radio Algiers. Without interrupting her professional career she directed a course in dramatic art in Paris from 1956 to 1967.

ROSEBERY, ALBERT EDWARD HARRY MEYER ARCHIBALD PRIMROSE, 6th Earl of, British nobleman (b. Dalmeny House, South Queensferry, Scot., Jan. 8, 1882—d. Mentmore, near Leighton Buzzard, Eng., May 30, 1974), was a soldier, politician, and all-round sportsman. The elder son of the 5th earl, who was prime minister in 1894–95, he sat as Liberal member of Parliament for Midlothian (1906–10), moved to the Liberal Nationals in the early 1930s, and worked during World War II as regional commissioner (1941–45) and secretary of state (1945) for Scotland. But it was on the turf that Rosebery won popular renown: he was a member of the Jockey Club, was president of the Thoroughbred Breeders' Association, maintained his Mentmore stud, and won five classic races, notably with Blue Peter.

RUBY, HARRY (Harry Rubinstein), U.S. songwriter (b. New York, N.Y., Jan. 27, 1895—d. Woodland Hills, Calif., Feb. 23, 1974), composed numerous popular tunes, especially in collaboration with lyricist Bert Kalmar. Among his best-known songs are "Three Little Words," "Who's Sorry Now," and "I Wanna Be Loved by You." Ruby also wrote Broadway scores and movie scenarios and was an early associate of the Marx brothers, whose comedies he helped produce.

RYAN, CORNELIUS, U.S. author (b. Dublin, Ire., June 5, 1920—d. New York, N.Y., Nov. 23, 1974), was a World War II correspondent whose fascination with the Allied invasion of Normandy sustained ten years of painstaking research that resulted in *The Longest Day* (1959), a best-seller about "the courage of man" that was later made into a movie. Ryan wrote two other highly successful war books, *The Last Battle* (1966) and *A Bridge Too Far* (1974).

RYNDIN, VADIM FEODOROVICH, Soviet stage designer (b. Moscow, Russia, Jan. 2, 1902—d. April 1974), was the creator of stage sets for plays, opera, and ballet and writer of works on stage design. As chief designer at Aleksandr Tairov's Kamerny Theatre, Moscow, he designed productions of L. Pervomaysky's *Unknown Soldiers* (1932), Sophie Treadwell's *Machinal* (1933), and V. Vishnevsky's *An Optimistic Tragedy* (1934). At the Bolshoi Theatre he staged Verdi's *La traviata* and Sergey Prokofiev's *War and Peace.* Ryndin was a member of the Soviet Academy of Arts and was married to Soviet dancer Galina Ulanova.

SAILLANT, LOUIS, French trade unionist (b. Valence, France, Nov. 27, 1910—d. Paris, France, Oct. 28, 1974), was general secretary of the Communist-dominated World Federation of Trade Unions (WFTU) from 1945 to 1969, and although not believed to be a member of the Communist Party, followed Moscow's line. He came to prominence in the clandestine French union movement during World War II, and in 1945, as a result of an agreement between U.S. and Soviet union leaders, was elected first general secretary of the WFTU. A few years later British, U.S., and other trade unionists left the WFTU to protest its pro-Soviet stance. Saillant was awarded the Lenin Peace Prize in 1959, criticized Soviet intervention in Czechoslovakia in 1968, and resigned his WFTU post the following year.

SANTOS, EDUARDO, Colombian politician and journalist (b. Bogotá, Colombia, Aug. 28, 1888—d. Bogotá, March 27, 1974), held numerous government posts before serving as president of Colombia from 1938 to 1942. As owner and publisher of *El Tiempo,* Santos was also one of the best-known journalists in South America. His private library, one of the finest in the country, is a rich repository of materials documenting the life of Simón Bolívar, the man who freed six Latin-American countries from Spanish rule.

SCHIRACH, BALDUR VON, German Nazi leader (b. Berlin, Ger., May 7, 1907—d. Kröv, Rheinland-Pfalz, W.Ger., Aug. 8, 1974), as national director of the Hitler Youth Movement from 1933, personified and propagated the Nazi cult of the blond Aryan. He joined the National Socialist and German Workers' (Nazi) Party in 1927 and the following year, at Hitler's direction, formed the Nazi Students' League. At the outset of World War II he took part in the French campaign, but in 1940 Hitler sent him to Vienna as governor and gauleiter (provincial party boss). In 1946 the Nürnberg war crimes tribunal sentenced him to 20 years' imprisonment for his part in deporting Jews and organizing forced labour. Following his release from Spandau in 1966, he published his memoirs, *Ich Glaubte an Hitler* ("I Believed in Hitler"), in which he stated that it was not until May 1944 that he first heard of the methods used for "the final solution of the Jewish problem."

SEATON, FRED(ERICK) A(NDREW), U.S. businessman and political figure (b. Washington, D.C., Dec. 11, 1909—d. Minneapolis, Minn., Jan. 16, 1974), inherited ownership of a network of Midwest newspapers and radio and television stations, but was best known to the nation as Pres. Dwight D. Eisenhower's secretary of the interior (1956–61), dedicated to acquiring statehood (1959) for Alaska and Hawaii and concerned about conservation, wildlife, and educational programs for American Indians.

SEVERSKY, ALEXANDER PROCOFIEFF DE, U.S. aeronautic engineer (b. Tiflis [Tbilisi], Russia, June 7, 1894—d. New York, N.Y., Aug. 24, 1974), flew more than 50 missions as a czarist aviator after losing a leg in his first combat mission (1915) during World War I. He was in Washington, D.C., in 1918 serving as an assistant naval attaché when his country closed its embassy. Seversky elected to stay in the U.S. During the next half century and more he was an effective advocate of strategic air power, patenting numerous inventions that hastened the arrival of modern aircraft technology. He designed the first fully automatic synchronous bombsight.

SEXTON, ANNE, U.S. poet (b. Newton, Mass., Nov. 9, 1928—d. Weston, Mass., Oct. 4, 1974), whose intensely personal poetry reflected her fascination with death, won the Pulitzer Prize in 1967 for a volume of poems called *Live or Die* (1966). Her first book, *To Bedlam and Part Way Back* (1960), was an intense examination of her mental breakdown and recovery. *All My Pretty Ones* (1962) is also autobiographical. Sexton's talent was widely recognized in the form of special grants, awards, honorary degrees, and teaching positions at Boston University (1970–71) and Colgate University (1971–72). Her last book was entitled *The Death Notebooks* (1974).

SHAZAR, ZALMAN (Shneur Zalman Rubashov), Israeli statesman (b. Mir, Belorussia, Oct. 6, 1889—d. Jerusalem, Israel, Oct. 5, 1974), Israel's third president (1963–73), was a Hebrew scholar and journalist whose political career began in 1906 as secretary of a secret Labour Zionist conference in Minsk, Russia. Later he went to the Academy of Jewish Studies in St. Petersburg and to Germany to study history and philosophy at the universities of Freiburg, Strasburg, and Berlin. He first visited Palestine in 1911, returning there in 1920 as a member of the World Labour Zionist delegation. He settled in Tel Aviv in 1924 and the following year helped to found *Davar*, the daily newspaper published by the Labour Zionist movement, of which he was editor from 1938 to 1948. In 1949 he was appointed minister of education in independent Israel's first government, resigning in 1950 to join the Jewish Agency executive. On May 21, 1963, the Knesset (parliament) elected him president to succeed Yitzhak Ben-Zvi. He was reelected in 1968 and resigned in May 1973.

SHUKSHIN, VASILY, Soviet film director (b. Siberia, U.S.S.R., 1929—d. Moscow, U.S.S.R., Oct. 2, 1974), became a leading figure in modern Soviet cinema after studying at the Moscow Cinema Institute. He appeared as a screen actor and published short stories before his debut as director and scriptwriter of *There Was a Lad* (1964), winner of the Golden Lion of St. Mark at the Venice Festival of Children's Films. Other films were *Your Son and Brother* (1966), *Strange People* (1970), and *The Red Snowball Tree* (1974). In this last film, an unprecedented (although censored) satire on Soviet officialdom, he played the leading role of a former professional criminal. At the time of his death Shukshin was working on an adaptation of Mikhail Sholokhov's *They Fought for the Motherland*.

SIMONDS, GUY GRANVILLE, Canadian general (b. Bury St. Edmunds, Suffolk, Eng., April 23, 1903—d. Toronto, Ont., May 15, 1974), was generally considered Canada's finest tactician and field commander during World War II. He went to Europe in 1939 as a major and in 1941 became the Dominion's youngest general at age 39. After leading the Canadian 1st and 2nd divisions in Africa and Italy, he commanded the II Corps in an assault on Antwerp that opened the port to Allied shipping. After the war he became chief of the general staff and rose to the rank of lieutenant general before retiring in 1955 to enter business.

SINGH, YADAVINDRA, Indian statesman, sportsman, and diplomat (b. Jan. 7, 1913—d. The Hague, Neth., June 17, 1974), succeeded his father as maharaja of Patiala in 1938 and proved to be an enlightened ruler of his state. During World War II he served in the Western Desert, Italy, and Burma. He was the last chancellor of the Chamber of Princes before India's independence (1947) and became rajpramukh of the merged Patiala and East Punjab states (1948–56), a member of the National Defense Council (1962), India's ambassador to Italy (1965–66) and to The Netherlands (from 1971). He captained India at cricket in the 1930s, founded the Asian Games Federation in 1951, was president of the Indian Olympic Association (1936–60), and chairman of the All-India Council of Sports (1960–65).

SIQUEIROS, DAVID ALFARO, Mexican muralist (b. Chihuahua, Mex., Dec. 29, 1896—d. Cuernavaca, Mex., Jan. 6, 1974), whose political activity and social protest gained as much notoriety as his very considerable artistic talent, expressed his Communist beliefs in gigantic, bold, and flamboyant murals. He was jailed several times, most notably in 1960 for inciting student riots. Pardoned after four years, he retired from politics to resume painting with unabated vigour. His best-known murals, depicting historical and revolutionary scenes, are in the gardens of the Hotel de Mexico, on the outside of the National University administration building, inside the National History Museum, and on the exterior and interior walls of the Polyforum, a convention hall in Mexico City. The latter, his largest work, covers 60,000 sq.ft. and is titled "The March of Humanity in Latin America, on the Earth and in the Direction of the Cosmos: Misery and Science." He received the National Art Prize in 1966 and was awarded the Lenin Peace Prize by the Soviet Union in 1967.

SMADJA, HENRY, French journalist (b. Oran, Alg., July 14, 1897—d. Paris, France, July 15, 1974), directed the freewheeling left-wing Paris newspaper *Combat* from 1947 to the time of his death. In 1934 he founded a Tunis newspaper and was elected to the Grand Council of Tunisia

(1934–45). Having bought a printing press in Paris, he became, in 1947, co-director of *Combat*, founded by the writer Albert Camus and others, and sole director from 1950. The circulation of his somewhat erratically directed paper gradually dwindled. After conviction in Tunisia for illicit currency dealing (the prison sentence was quashed on condition of surrender of his Tunisian property) in 1967, Smadja returned to France and moved *Combat*'s office and press to a château outside Paris as an economy measure. However, within two months of his death the paper ceased publication. (*See* PUBLISHING.)

SMRKOVSKY, JOSEF, Czechoslovak Communist leader (b. Velenka, Bohemia, Feb. 26, 1911—d. Prague, Czech., Jan. 15, 1974), was a firm supporter of Alexander Dubcek, who in the spring of 1968 tried to give Czechoslovakia "socialism with a human face." A baker, he joined the Communist Party in 1929. During the German occupation he became a leading figure in the Czech resistance movement. In May 1945, as deputy chairman of the provisional Czech National Council, he opposed the entry of U.S. troops into Prague, thus enabling the "liberation" of the capital the following day by Soviet forces. In February 1948, as commander of the Workers' Militia, he ensured the Communist seizure of power, but subsequently fell into disfavour. Arrested in 1951 and accused of fictitious crimes, he received a death sentence which Klement Gottwald, president of the republic and party boss, hesitated to confirm. Smrkovsky was freed in 1955 and worked as a forester and then as a chairman of a collective farm until his rehabilitation in 1963. In 1966 the 13th party congress elected him to the Central Committee and in January 1967 he became forestry minister. He vigorously supported Dubcek in his struggle against Pres. Antonin Novotny and in March 1968 joined the party's Presidium, being elected president of the National Assembly in April. Immediately after the occupation of Prague by Soviet forces, Dubcek and Smrkovsky were arrested and taken to Moscow. Ludvik Svoboda, then president of the republic, obtained their release and return to Prague, after which they were deposed from office and expelled from the key party bodies.

SOKOLOVA, LYDIA (HILDA MUNNINGS), English ballet dancer (b. Wanstead, Essex, Eng., March 4, 1896—d. Sevenoaks, Kent, Eng., Feb. 5, 1974), became in 1913 the first English dancer to enter Diaghilev's Ballets Russes, where she became a leading ballerina under the choreographers Michel Fokine and, especially, Léonide Massine; she danced in *Petrouchka*, with Vaslav Nijinsky in *Spectre de la Rose*, and in Massine's version of *The Rite of Spring*, among many roles. After Diaghilev's death in 1929 and the dissolution of the company, Sokolova rarely danced again, though she appeared with Leon Woizikowski's company in 1935. Her memoirs, *Dancing for Diaghilev*, were published in 1960.

SPAATZ, CARL ANDREW, U.S. general (b. Boyertown, Pa., June 28, 1891—d. Washington, D.C., July 14, 1974), was a West Point graduate (1914) who very early shared Billy Mitchell's enthusiasm for military air power. In 1947 Spaatz

Ed Sullivan

UPI COMPIX

was named the first Air Force chief of staff when that branch of the military was given equal autonomy with the Army and Navy.

Spaatz went to England in 1940 to evaluate German military might, then took command of the U.S. 8th Air Force in July 1942. He served under Dwight D. Eisenhower in Africa, directed air assaults against Italy, then returned to England with Eisenhower to plan the D-Day invasion of the continent. After V-E Day, Spaatz took over the Pacific Air Force command and though personally opposed to the use of atomic bombs against Japanese cities, carried out Pres. Harry S. Truman's orders to hit Hiroshima and Nagasaki. Spaatz represented the U.S. at the official surrender ceremonies in Germany and Japan.

SPEARS, SIR EDWARD (LOUIS), 1ST BARONET, British soldier and politician (b. Paris, France, Aug. 7, 1886—d. London, Eng., Jan. 27, 1974), was instrumental, as Winston Churchill's representative in France in 1940, in bringing Gen. Charles de Gaulle to England; afterward, with the rank of major general, he headed the British mission to the Free French government-in-exile. After leading a mission to Syria and Lebanon in 1941 Spears served as British minister to the new republics from 1942 to 1944. De Gaulle later accused him of conspiring against France by espousing the Arab cause.

SPOTTSWOOD, BISHOP STEPHEN GILL, U.S. religious and civil rights leader (b. Boston, Mass., July 18, 1897—d. Washington, D.C., Dec. 1, 1974), was ordained in the African Methodist Episcopal Zion Church after graduating (1919) from the Gordon College of Theology in Boston; he then joined the National Association for the Advancement of Colored People (NAACP) and commenced a two-fold career as civil rights activist and pastor of churches in Maine, Connecticut, North Carolina, Indiana, and New York. From 1936 to 1952 he was pastor of the John Wesley National A.M.E. Zion Church in the nation's capital. In 1955 he was elected to the board of directors of the NAACP and in 1961 became board chairman. Though a moderate by nature and a firm believer in economic opportunities for blacks as the most basic requirement for social justice, Spottswood was also capable of righteous anger and personally joined picket lines, organized boycotts, and initiated protests long before such things assumed major proportions during the 1960s.

STRAUSS, LEWIS LICHTENSTEIN, U.S. government official (b. Charleston, W.Va., Jan. 31, 1896—d. Brandy Station, Va., Jan. 21, 1974), became chairman of the U.S. Atomic Energy Commission in 1953 after serving as one of its original members since 1946. After the Soviets exploded their first atomic bomb in 1949, Strauss urged and received approval for the development of a hydrogen bomb. He was supported by Edward Teller and Ernest Lawrence but vigorously opposed by J. Robert Oppenheimer, all three greatly respected physicists. In a highly controversial decision, Strauss joined others in voting to deprive Oppenheimer of his security clearance in 1954. After resigning as chairman of the AEC in 1958, Strauss was nominated secretary of commerce by Pres. Dwight D. Eisenhower. After weeks of hearings and debate, the Senate, perhaps still smarting from previous conflicts with Strauss, rejected the nomination by a vote of 49–46. Earlier in his career, Strauss was a successful Wall Street banker and during World War II attained the rank of rear admiral while serving on several military committees and as assistant to James V. Forrestal, secretary of the navy.

SULLIVAN, EDWARD VINCENT, U.S. impresario and columnist (b. New York, N.Y., Sept. 28, 1901—d. New York, Oct. 13, 1974), was a sports editor, Broadway and Hollywood columnist for the *New York Daily News* (1933–74), and part-time impresario before hosting the "Harvest Moon Ball" on CBS television in 1947. He was thereupon signed as regular host of the CBS variety show "Toast of the Town," which made television history as the "Ed Sullivan Show" by running from 1948 to 1971. Despite a wooden expression and self-conscious mannerisms, Sullivan attained stardom through his

U Thant

shrewd scouting and presentation of entertainers from all over the world. Year after year he provided an endless stream of diverse talent that kept audiences transfixed and ratings at record levels. Among big-name stars who made their first television appearances on Sullivan's show were the Beatles, Elvis Presley, Jack Benny, Liza Minnelli, Dean Martin, Humphrey Bogart, Rudolph Nureyev, Maria Callas, and Jackie Gleason.

SUSANN, JACQUELINE, U.S. author (b. Philadelphia, Pa., Aug. 20, 1921—d. New York, N.Y., Sept. 21, 1974), became a literary phenomenon and a publisher's delight by turning out three successive novels that all reached the top of the best-seller list and then became movies. *Valley of the Dolls* (1966), which became the best-selling novel of all time with 17 million copies, depicted the disintegrating lives of four fading glamour girls and their progressive surrender to drugs and alcohol. *The Love Machine* (1969) detailed the ambitions and love life of a television executive. *Once Is Not Enough* (1973) titillated readers with keyhole glimpses of socially prominent persons and their sexual adventures. Though severely berated by critics for writing books of little literary value, Susann, a former actress and television personality, was undaunted; to her, writing books that were immensely popular (and profitable) was sufficient proof of her writing ability. Her personal favourite was *Every Night Josephine!* (1963), a nonfiction work about herself, her husband of 30 years, and their poodle.

SUTHERLAND, EARL WILBUR, JR., U.S. pharmacologist (b. Burlingame, Kan., Nov. 19, 1915—d. Miami, Fla., March 9, 1974), was awarded the 1971 Nobel Prize for Physiology or Medicine for isolating cyclic AMP, the chemical that enables hormones to perform their function of carrying messages via the bloodstream. In 1956, while serving as director of the department of medicine at Western Reserve University in Cleveland, O., Sutherland discovered cyclic AMP and later demonstrated its vital function as a regulatory substance in the chemistry of living organisms. His breakthrough stimulated a vast range of subsequent research.

Sutherland received his M.D. degree (1942) from Washington University Medical School in St. Louis, Mo., where, after serving in World War II, he worked in the laboratory of Carl Ferdinand Cori, himself a Nobel laureate. Sutherland moved to Vanderbilt University, Nashville, Tenn., in 1963 to devote full time to research. From July 1973 he was on the faculty of the University of Miami Medical School.

TANAKA KOTARO (English name PAUL FRANCIS TANAKA), Japanese jurist (b. Kagoshima, Jap.,—d. Tokyo, Jap., March 1, 1974), as chief justice of the Supreme Court of Japan (1950–60) was responsible for giving Japan's new constitution a definitive interpretation without postwar advice from Western sources. He was the first Japanese Christian to become chief justice and later served (1961–69) as a judge on the International Court of Justice in The Hague,

an elective office conferred by the UN General Assembly. Tanaka, who obtained his law degree from Tokyo Imperial University, visited the U.S. and Europe to broaden his understanding of international law. Among his writings is *Theory of International Law*, for which he received the Asahi Prize in 1935.

THANT, U, Burmese educationist and civil servant (b. Pantanaw, Burma, Jan. 22, 1909—d. New York, N.Y., Nov. 25, 1974), was the third secretary-general (1962–71) of the United Nations. After taking an active role in the Burmese resistance against the Japanese during World War II, he was recruited for government service, became press director (1947), director of broadcasting (1948), and secretary of the Ministry of Information (1949). He was a frequent adviser to Burmese political leaders, including Prime Minister U Nu, and in 1957 began his UN career as Burma's permanent representative. In 1959 he was vice-president of the UN General Assembly. After the death in 1961 of UN Secretary-General Dag Hammarskjöld, Thant was confirmed as secretary-general on Nov. 30, 1962. Among the problems that confronted him during his first term in office were the UN operation in the Congo, the Cuban missile crisis, the India-Pakistan war, and the escalation of the Vietnam war. In 1966 he was reelected unanimously, after earlier indicating his unwillingness to continue in office. In 1967 his decision to withdraw the UN Emergency Force from the border between Israel and Egypt at the Arabs' request was criticized in the West (although legally no other option was open to him). Thant was a man of comprehensive interests but was particularly concerned with the problems of Southeast Asia and with the UN Technical Assistance Program and Development Decade.

TOPPING, DANIEL REID, U.S. sports executive (b. Greenwich, Conn., June 11, 1912—d. Miami Beach, Fla., May 18, 1974), inherited a fortune that enabled him to become co-owner of the New York Yankees, one of the most successful professional baseball teams in history. With Larry MacPhail and Del Webb he acquired the Yankees in 1945 for $2.8 million. Two years later MacPhail sold his interest for $2 million and Topping became president of the Yankee organization. During the next 18 years the Yankees won 15 American League pennants and 10 World Series championships. In 1964 CBS became an 80% shareholder and two years later bought the club outright. Topping opened an advertising agency in 1930 and in 1934 was a leading amateur golfer when he first invested in sports by purchasing an interest in the Brooklyn Dodgers of the National Football League. He later also became part owner of the New York Yankees of the All America Football Conference.

TORRES BODET, JAIME, Mexican educationist (b. Mexico City, Mex., April 17, 1902—d. Mexico City, May 13, 1974), became one of Latin America's most respected intellectuals before serving as director general of UNESCO from 1948 to 1952. After teaching (1924–29) French literature at the University of Mexico, his alma mater, he entered foreign service and was assigned to Mexican embassies in Madrid, Buenos Aires, and Brussels. He then became Mexico's minister of education (1943–46) and foreign minister (1946–48). Throughout his life he was an energetic advocate of well conceived and innovative programs attacking illiteracy, which he viewed as one of the greatest dangers to individual freedom and world peace. His 38 published works include poetry, essays, novels, and memoires (the sixth volume of which was never finished).

UNDÉN, BO ÖSTEN, Swedish statesman (b. Karlstad, Swed., Aug. 25, 1886—d. Stockholm, Swed., Jan. 15, 1974), was one of the chief architects of Sweden's neutrality policy and served twice as foreign minister. From 1917 he taught civil law at the University of Uppsala, of which he was rector (1929–32). A member of the Social Democratic Party, he was elected to the Riksdag and in 1920 became minister of justice in Sweden's first Social Democratic government, under Karl Hjalmar Branting. Adviser on international law to the Swedish Foreign Office from 1917, he became foreign minister (1924–26) in the third Branting government and later under Per Albin Hansson and Tage Erlander (1945–62). He represented Sweden regularly at the general assemblies of the League of Nations in Geneva (1920–39) and also at those of the United Nations in

New York (1946–61). Undén criticized the enlistment of Norway and Denmark into NATO and supported the idea of a Nordic political, economic, and defense community.

VAN BIESBROECK, GEORGE A., U.S. astronomer (b. Ghent, Belg., Jan. 21, 1880—d. Tucson, Ariz., Feb. 23, 1974), whose study of the bending of light from stars provided new evidence confirming Einstein's theory of relativity, was an acknowledged authority on twin stars, asteroids, and comets. For almost 50 years he worked at Yerkes Observatory in Wisconsin, a facility operated by the University of Chicago. He then moved to the University of Arizona where he charted the orbit of Nereid, Neptune's second satellite. During his long career he discovered 11 asteroids and 2 comets.

VANDERBILT, CORNELIUS, JR., U.S. author and journalist (b. New York, N.Y., April 30, 1898—d. Miami Beach, Fla., July 7, 1974), repudiated his inherited social standing by publishing *Farewell to Fifth Avenue* (1935), a personal account of the great and wealthy he had known. Forgoing a life of easy opulence, he turned to journalism, writing newspaper columns and interviewing celebrities. He published tabloids in San Francisco, Miami, and Los Angeles, all financial failures.

VUCHETICH, YEVGENY VIKTOROVICH, Soviet sculptor (b. Dnepropetrovsk, Ukraine, Dec. 28, 1908—d. Moscow, U.S.S.R., April 12, 1974), created the impressive Soviet war memorial in Treptow Park, East Berlin, and the Stalingrad memorial on the Mamai Hill battlefield, which won him a Lenin Prize. He also made the "Let Us Beat Swords into Ploughshares" statue which stands before the UN building in New York City.

WADIYAR, JAYA CHAMARAJENDRA, former maharaja of Mysore (b. Mysore, India, July 18, 1919—d. Mysore, Sept. 23, 1974), was the last in line of a ruling dynasty established in the 14th century. A philosopher, Sanskrit scholar, and student of music and geography, he succeeded his uncle as maharaja of Mysore in 1940 and, in support of the Allied war effort, formed a Mysore squadron of the RAF. After India's independence in 1947 he signed Mysore's accession to the Indian Union and when democratic rule was introduced in 1949, he became first governor. He retained his title of maharaja until 1971 when the princely orders and their privy purses were abolished by the Indian government.

WANG MING (CH'EN SHAO-YU), Soviet-trained Chinese Communist (b. Liu-an County, Anhwei, China, 1905—d. Moscow, U.S.S.R., March 27, 1974), was a prominent revolutionary in the early 1930s who was serving on the Comintern in Moscow when Mao Tse-tung emerged as party leader during the famous Long March (1934–35) to northwest China. On his return to China in 1937, Wang urged Mao to join forces with Chiang Kai-shek against the Japanese. Mao's refusal to follow these Moscow directives initiated a longterm ideological conflict with Wang that culminated in Wang's 1969 denunciation of Mao as an anti-Communist dictator bent only on selfglorification. Though several times elected to the Central Committee of the Chinese Communist

Earl Warren

Party, Wang was progressively removed from positions of influence. In 1954 he was divested of all party authority and retired to Moscow two years later.

WARREN, EARL, U.S. jurist and politician (b. Los Angeles, Calif., March 19, 1891—d. Washington, D.C., July 9, 1974), was chief justice of the United States (1953–69) during an era of precedent-shattering interpretations of U.S. constitutional law. The historic importance of these Supreme Court decisions tended to overshadow Warren's highly successful earlier career as attorney general (1939–43) and governor (1943–53) of California, and his nomination (1948) as Republican vice-presidential candidate.

The first major decision of the Warren court (1954) upset a doctrine that had prevailed since 1896. It unanimously declared that "separate but equal" educational facilities for blacks and whites were "inherently unequal" and therefore unconstitutional. The underlying principle quickly affected all forms of racial discrimination. In 1962 the court held that the Constitution, in accepting the separation of church and state, forbade the recitation of state-composed prayers in public schools.

Regarding criminal law, the court ruled (1961) that illegally obtained evidence, however damaging, could not be used in any U.S. court of law. It later (1966) declared that all arrested persons had a right to counsel before being questioned, that suspects had to be advised of that right, and that free counsel had to be provided to the poor. Moreover, a confession obtained in violation of these rights was inadmissible as evidence. In 1964 the court applied the principle of "one man, one vote" to state legislative districts, thereby necessitating a nationwide realignment of district boundaries. The chief justice remarked with characteristic simplicity that "legislators represent people, not acres or trees." Such decisions dismayed various segments of the population and sparked heated denunciations of the "Warren Revolution." Undeterred, Warren continued to pursue his vision of equal justice and fairness for all, regardless of social status.

In November 1963 Pres. Lyndon B. Johnson tried to reassure a troubled nation by appointing Warren chairman of a commission to investigate the assassination of Pres. John F. Kennedy and the murder of Lee Harvey Oswald, the presumed assassin. The *Warren Report,* published one year later, declared that an exhaustive study failed to uncover any evidence of a group conspiracy.

WATSON, ARTHUR KITTREDGE, U.S. business executive (b. Summit, N.J., April 23, 1919—d. Norwalk, Conn., July 26, 1974), was named vice-president and a director of IBM World Trade Corp. when it was established as a new subsidiary of the IBM Corp. in 1949. During the next 20 years, using the slogan "World Peace Through World Trade," Watson increased IBM's foreign sales 50-fold to $2.5 billion annually. In 1954 he was elected president of IBM World Trade and chairman in 1963. He resigned in 1970 to become U.S. ambassador to France, but two years later returned to IBM as a director and member of the board's executive committee.

WEBB, DEL(BERT) EUGENE, U.S. real estate tycoon and sportsman (b. Fresno, Calif., May 17, 1899—d. Rochester, Minn., July 4, 1974), developed a small carpenter business into the Del E. Webb Corp. worth $100 million. His projects included planned communities for retired persons, business offices, and hotels that extended from Florida to Hawaii. Part of Webb's fortune derived from his co-ownership of the New York Yankees baseball team, which during an 18-year period (1947–64) won 15 American League pennants and 10 World Series championships.

WEBB, JAMES RUFFIN, U.S. screenwriter (b. Denver, Colo., Oct. 4, 1909—d. Hollywood, Calif., Sept. 27, 1974), won an Academy Award for his scenario of *How the West Was Won* (1963) and counted among his other notable screenplay credits such movies as *They Call Me Mr. Tibbs, Trapeze, The Big Country, Vera Cruz,* and *The Hawaiians.* He was founder, president, and chairman of the International Writers Guild, chairman of the Writers Guild of America, founder and president of the Writers Guild Foundation, and board chairman of Actors Equity.

WELLESZ, EGON JOSEPH, Austrian-born musicologist (b. Vienna, Aus., Oct. 21, 1885—d. Oxford, Eng., Nov. 9, 1974), was eminent both as a composer and as a music historian who specialized in Byzantine notation, opera, and early 20th-century music. One of Schoenberg's first pupils, he composed songs, ballets, six operas, symphonies, and string quartets. From 1929 to 1938 he was professor of the history of music at Vienna University. At the time of Hitler's occupation he was invited to Oxford University, where he taught for the remainder of his life. He edited *Monumenta Musicae Byzantinae* and two volumes of the *New Oxford History of Music.* He was created commander, Order of the British Empire, in 1957.

WHEELER, SIR CHARLES (THOMAS), British sculptor (b. Codsall, Staffordshire, Eng., March 14, 1892—d. Mayfield, Sussex, Eng., Aug. 22, 1974), was president of the Royal Academy (1956–66). His works adorn such places as India House, South Africa House, the Bank of England, and the Jellicoe memorial bust and fountain (in collaboration with the architect Sir Edwin Lutyens), all in London; Rhodes House, Oxford; and the RAF memorial, Malta. Sensitive smaller pieces include "The Infant Christ" and "Spring," both in the Tate Gallery, London. Wheeler's presidency of the Royal Academy was marked by the sale of its Leonardo da Vinci Cartoon for £800,000, which restored its finances. His autobiography, *High Relief,* appeared in 1968.

WHEELER, RAYMOND ALBERT, U.S. Army engineer (b. Peoria, Ill., July 31, 1885—d. Washington, D.C., Feb. 8, 1974), graduated from the U.S. Military Academy at West Point in 1911 before working on the Panama Canal. In time he directed engineering projects all over the world, rose to the rank of lieutenant general, received numerous citations, and was chief of the U.S. Army's Corps of Engineers from 1945 to 1949. During World War II he supervised construction of the Ledo Road running between India and China and in 1956 came out of retirement to oversee the clearing of 45 wrecks from the Suez Canal.

WINDGASSEN, WOLFGANG, German operatic tenor (b. Annemasse, France, June 26, 1914—d. Stuttgart, W.Ger., Sept. 8, 1974), was a leading singer and producer at the Württemberg State Theatre, Stuttgart. He made his debut at the Pforzheim Municipal Theatre in 1939 as Alvaro in *La forza del destino.* During 1945–72 he sang regularly at Stuttgart. His Bayreuth debut in 1951 was followed by appearances in major Wagnerian roles that included Parsifal, Siegfried, Lohengrin, Tannhäuser, and Tristan. His New York Metropolitan Opera debut took place in 1957. From 1972 he was director at the Stuttgart Opera.

WOODING, SIR HUGH (OLLIVIERE BERESFORD), Trinidadian judge (b. Trinidad, Jan. 14, 1904—d. St. Augustine, Trinidad, July 26, 1974), was the first chief justice of Trinidad and Tobago (1962–68). He was called to the bar by the Middle Temple, London, in 1928, practiced in the Caribbean, and served as mayor of Port-of-Spain (1943–44). After retiring from the judiciary, he joined the boards of several international companies and became chancellor of the University of the West Indies and chairman of the Trinidad and Tobago Constitution Commission. He was knighted in 1963.

WRIGHT, GEORGE ERNEST, U.S. archaeologist (b. Zanesville, O., Sept. 5, 1909—d. Jaffrey, N.H., Aug. 29, 1974), became an acknowledged expert on Near Eastern archaeology with the publication of *Pottery of Palestine from the Earliest Times to the End of the Early Bronze Age* (1937). He undertook major excavations in Palestine at Shechem (1956–74) and Gezer (1964–65), and in Cyprus at Idalion (1971–74). At Shechem a team under his direction uncovered artifacts dating as far back as 4000 B.C. In 1966 Wright was named head of American Schools of Oriental Research, which represents some 150 scholarly institutions. His name appears on such books as *Shechem: The Biography of a Biblical City* (1965).

ZHUKOV, GEORGY KONSTANTINOVICH, marshal of the Soviet Union (b. Strelkovka, Kaluga Province, Russia, Dec. 2, 1896—d. Moscow, U.S.S.R., June 18, 1974), the son of a peasant, became one of the greatest military commanders in World War II. Conscripted into the Imperial Russian Army in 1915, he was twice decorated for bravery. After the Revolution he joined the Red

Georgy K. Zhukov

Army and became a Communist Party member in 1919. Surviving the 1937 purge of Red Army officers, he was appointed commander of Soviet forces in Mongolia and in August 1939 defeated the invading Japanese Army on the Khalkhin River. He served on Gen. S. K. Timoshenko's staff during the Soviet-Finnish war of 1939–40 and was later appointed commander of the Kiev military district with the rank of army general. In February 1941 he was brought to Moscow as chief of the general staff and deputy commissar of defense. In October 1941 he succeeded Timoshenko as commander of the army group that successfully defended Moscow. A year later he directed the defense of Stalingrad and soon afterward coordinated the operations that in January 1943 resulted in lifting the siege of Leningrad. Created a marshal of the Soviet Union, he planned the great offensives of 1943–44 of the 1st and 2nd Belorussian and 1st and 2nd Ukrainian army groups. In November 1944 he took command of the 1st Belorussian Army Group and pushed on through Warsaw toward Berlin. On the night of May 8–9, 1945, in Berlin-Karlshorst, he was one of the four Allied commanders who accepted the German surrender. He was then appointed Soviet governor and commander in chief in Eastern Germany. In March 1946, however, he was recalled to Moscow where he was made commander of Soviet land forces, and later, through Stalin's jealousy, he was sent to Odessa as military district commander. After Stalin's death, he was appointed first deputy minister of defense, and in 1955 he attended the Warsaw conference where the Warsaw Pact was concluded. In July 1957 Zhukov became the first regular army officer to be named a full member of the Presidium of the Communist Party, but months later N. S. Khrushchev dismissed him from both the ministry and the Presidium for having "violated . . . Leninist principles" by trying to reduce the influence of political commissars among the troops. Following Khrushchev's removal, Zhukov made a formal reappearance at the 1965 VE-Day celebrations in Moscow. In 1966 he was awarded the Order of Lenin. His autobiography was published in 1969.

ZWICKY, FRITZ, Swiss astronomer, physicist, and jet propulsion expert (b. Varna, Bulg., Feb. 14, 1898—d. Pasadena, Calif., Feb. 8, 1974), made valuable contributions to the understanding of supernovas, stars that for a short time are far brighter than normal. He believed that the explosions of supernovas are totally different from those of ordinary novas, occurring only two or three times every 1,000 years in our galaxy. He contended that in supernovas most of the matter of the star is dissipated, leaving little or nothing behind. To confirm his theories, Zwicky studied neighbouring galaxies and between 1937 and 1941, while working at the California Institute of Technology, discovered 18 supernovas; only 12 others had been previously reported. In the early 1930s Zwicky contributed substantially to the physics of solid state, gaseous ionization, and thermodynamics. In 1943 he joined Aerojet Engineering Corp. in Azusa, Calif., where he developed some of the earliest jet engines, including the JATO (jet-assisted takeoff) units used to launch heavy-laden aircraft from short runways.

Oman

An independent sultanate, Oman occupies the southeastern part of the Arabian Peninsula and is bounded by the United Arab Emirates, Saudi Arabia, the Gulf of Oman, and the Arabian Sea. A small part of the country lies to the north of the rest of Oman and is separated from it by the United Arab Emirates. Area: 82,000 sq.mi. (213,380 sq.km.). Pop. (1973 est.): 700,000 to 750,000. Cap.: Muscat (pop., 1973 est., 15,000). Largest city: Matrah (pop., 1973 est., 18,-000). Language: Arabic. Religion: Muslim. Sultan in 1974, Qabus ibn Sa'id.

In 1974 Oman's oil revenues increased substantially, but urgently needed development was held up when funds were diverted to the struggle in the Dhofar region of the southwest against the forces of the Popular Front for the Liberation of Oman and the Arabian Gulf (PFLOAG), supported by Yemen (Aden) and the U.S.S.R. Sultan Qabus' forces claimed progress in the pacification of Dhofar, but clashes continued, especially in the Sarfait area north of Salalah. The presence of some 1,500 artillery-supported Iranian troops fighting alongside the sultan's British-officered Army was denounced by PFLOAG. Sultan Qabus defended their use on the ground that Arab states had refused his requests for aid. At the Arab League foreign ministers' meeting in Tunis on March 25–28 a mediation mission with representatives from Tunisia, Algeria, Kuwait, Egypt, and Syria was formed; in May it visited Oman but not PFLOAG's "liberated areas." PFLOAG later refused to send a delegation to an Arab League meeting in Cairo that was considering Oman. Oman-Kuwait relations suffered because of Kuwait's financial aid to Yemen (Aden).

In July Oman signed an agreement with Petroleum Development (Oman) to increase Oman's participation in the company from 25 to 60% in line with that of other oil-producing states. Annual revenue from Oman's average oil production of 290,000 bbl. a day was estimated at $575 million. A Canadian company reported the discovery of large copper deposits in Lasail Valley in the north.   (PETER MANSFIELD)

[978.B.4.a]

OMAN
Education. (1971–72) Primary, pupils 15,809, teachers 445.
Finance and Trade. Monetary unit: rial Omani, with (Sept. 16, 1974) an official rate of 0.345 rial to U.S. $1 (free rate of 0.08 rial = £1 sterling). Budget (1972 est.): revenue 52 million rials; expenditure *c.* 80 million rials. Foreign trade (1972): imports 51 million rials; exports 50 million rials. Import sources: United Arab Emirates 21%; U.K. 21%; Japan 10%; India 6%; Australia 6%; The Netherlands 5%; China 5%. Export destinations: Japan 32%; France 19%; Denmark 11%; Sweden 9%; Spain 8%; Norway 7%; The Netherlands 6%. Main export crude oil 99%.
Industry. Production: crude oil (1973) 14,620,000 metric tons; electricity (1972) 130 million kw-hr.

Pacifism and Nonviolent Movements

Dramatic developments and some frustration marked 1974 for peace advocates. The resignation under pressure of U.S. Pres. Richard Nixon, the ramifications of the energy crisis, the marked increase in the world price of grains and oil, the sharp debate over unconditional amnesty for war resisters and deserters, tensions in the Middle East, threats of nuclear proliferation and an escalated arms race—these were but a few of the issues to which pacifist and nonviolent movements for social change responded in a year that witnessed striking changes in the sociopolitical landscape.

The *Bulletin of the Atomic Scientists* moved the minute hand of the "Doomsday Clock" on its cover three minutes closer to midnight in the September 1974 issue. The clock, which registered the editors' view of the degree to which the world was endangered by nuclear devastation, was shifted to nine minutes to 12. The *Bulletin* acted in response to the failure of the U.S. and the U.S.S.R. to achieve agreement on significant strategic arms limitations, the development of new generations of nuclear weapons and delivery systems, India's first explosion of a nuclear device, the prospective introduction of nuclear reactors into the Middle East, and the increased threat of nuclear terrorism and sabotage resulting from the proliferation of nuclear energy systems.

Until midsummer much of the energy of the U.S. peace and antiwar movements was focused on the impeachment debate. Whereas most discussion centred on domestic abuses of power, peace leaders also stressed the secret bombing of Cambodia and attacks on civil liberties in general and harrassment of antiwar activists in particular as additional grounds for the formal impeachment and trial of President Nixon. Though considerable minority opinion in the House Judiciary Committee supported these viewpoints, the latter charges were not included in the committee's formal findings, and the issues became clouded after Nixon resigned.

Peace leaders feared that, in the backwash of political disenchantment evident after Watergate, such issues as the need to dismantle the "imperial presidency," to recast campaign financing, and to make governmental representatives truly accountable would be neglected just when their implementation seemed possible. While Congress was beginning to reassert its role in foreign policy, peace advocates pointed to the many steps required to restore true balance between the dominant executive and the legislature. The systematic clandestine involvement of the Central Intelligence Agency in financing acts that "destabilized" the Allende regime in Chile and led to the coup of September 1973 was only one example of congressional oversight in an area where the legislature had formal responsibility.

Peace leaders continued to call attention to U.S. funding of the war in Indochina, where the number of Vietnamese who died during the first 15 months of "peace" was greater than the total of U.S. soldiers killed in ten years of fighting. A united campaign by U.S. peace groups, including the American Friends Service Committee (AFSC), Clergy and Laymen Concerned (CALC), the Fellowship of Reconciliation (FOR), the Indochina Peace Campaign, SANE, the War Resister's League (WRL), the Women's International League for Peace and Freedom (WILPF), and the Coalition to Stop Funding the War, mounted a sustained Tiger Cage Vigil and Fast in Washington, D.C., during the summer. They erected, near the Capitol, a full-scale replica of the "tiger cage" prison cell used in South Vietnam, and combined this display with fasting and lobbying against military appropriations for Vietnam and Cambodia.

In general, protest moved from the streets into legislative offices and corridors. Perhaps the most typical expression of the peace movement's new tactics was the Coalition to Stop Funding the War, composed of over 30 religious, social action, labour, public affairs, and peace organizations. Throughout the year, the coalition lobbied successfully to cut authorizations for military expenditures in Southeast Asia. Most notably, it took partial credit for defeat of a $474 million supplemental military request for South Vietnam in a close House vote, for a Senate vote killing a Pentagon effort to restore $266 million, and for reduction of the military authorization for Indochina to approximately $1 billion, nearly $500 million less than the original administration request. Peace leaders felt they had achieved significant success in cultivating a fragile congressional majority committed to disengagement from Saigon and Phnom Penh.

Peace advocates were far less successful in attacking the overall military budget, however. They failed to block a congressional mandate to pursue research into "counterforce" weapons, though many defense analysts feared these armaments might sharply escalate the arms race. Amendments to stop the B-1 bomber were defeated in both the Senate and House, despite intensive lobbying by such groups as the AFSC, CALC, and SANE, and an effort to slow development of the Trident submarine lost in the House. A budget-reducing amendment sponsored by Rep. Les Aspin (Dem., Wis.), victorious in 1973, lost by 185–209 in 1974. Common Cause, which had played a major role in stopping the bombing of Cambodia in August 1973, focused its congressional efforts on holding the defense budget to the previous year's level, with allowances for inflation.

The Federation of American Scientists (FAS) underlined the seriousness of the failure to achieve even a temporary lid on the strategic arms race when it opposed ratification of the limited Moscow Test Ban Treaty. FAS spokesmen termed the treaty's name a misnomer, since it would not stop underground tests of devices ten times the strength of the bomb that leveled Hiroshima, Jap., and permitted any underground tests as long as they were labeled "peaceful." They urged Congress to reject the treaty and reopen negotiations with the Soviet Union to end all nuclear testing. Further, they proposed that the U.S. urgently seek a phasing out of all land-based missiles in order to promote stability and real disarmament, save defense funds, and reduce the temptation of an adversary to strike first.

While some welcomed Pres. Gerald Ford's limited initiatives toward "earned re-entry" and "clemency" for war resisters and deserters from the military, most movement leaders and organizations pressed for full and unconditional amnesty. War resisters both in the U.S. and in exile denounced the double standard of justice implied by President Ford's full and unconditional pardon of former president Nixon and his cautious, piecemeal, and punitive approach toward draft resisters, deserters, and others jeopardized for offenses committed in relation to the Indochina war.

National peace leaders called for a general, complete, and unconditional amnesty for all those victimized by the continuing U.S. sponsorship of the war. They also urged upgrading of the nearly 560,000 less-than-honourable discharges received by Vietnam-era veterans. The governing board of the National Council of Churches, a federation of over 30 major Protestant and Eastern Orthodox denominations, declared

Brother Roger Schutz (left), founder of the Taizé Community, a village settlement in France dedicated to ecumenism and world peace, receives the German Book Trade Association's prize of peace.

that President Ford's program offered "little more redress than was already available" and pledged to work for "full and genuine amnesty."

The year was marked by further efforts to develop "wholistic" approaches in peace education, combining simple life-styles and movements for peaceful social change. Typical of these efforts was the Life Center of Philadelphia, composed of about 80 adults and children living in a network of 12 houses organized around radical pacifist, communitarian principles. Other groups utilized "macroanalysis" education-action seminar materials, designed to help individuals and groups relate their personal concerns to creative social change. While such efforts were still basically white and middle class in their constituency, some observers felt the combination of simple living and macroanalysis might provide a suggestive challenge to many of the prevailing socioeconomic assumptions in Western industrial society.

In intellectual analysis, two works were crucial to participants in the peace effort. E. F. Schumacher, an English economist, presented his analysis of "economics as if people mattered" in his seminal study *Small Is Beautiful*. He explored an "intermediate technology" that would provide basic needs but would avoid the passion for accelerating growth and production that marked most "developed" economies. His ideas received wide circulation among decentralists, economists, and others attracted by his visions of humane technology, full employment, and broad worker participation in decision making.

Robert L. Heilbroner sharpened his analysis of the "post-industrial age" in his cautionary and provocative *An Inquiry into the Human Prospect*. Focusing on the "civilizational malaise" afflicting both capitalist and socialist systems, he discussed the basic dilemma: the possibility that the quality of life would deteriorate seriously if growth ended and, conversely, the chance that the quality of life would suffer if growth continued. Heilbroner concluded that society exists under a "contingent life sentence" in which, quite possibly, "conclusive change will be forced upon us by external events rather than by conscious choice, by catastrophe rather than by calculation."

Among international and transnational efforts, the Dai Dong movement, founded in 1969 by the International Fellowship of Reconciliation (IFOR), publicized a major statement entitled "Toward a Human Economics." It challenged economists to find a "human economics" and to explore the crisis behind the energy crisis, namely, the plundering of the earth's environment which "drains our finite stock of raw materials and energy."

Peace leaders and groups such as the Committee on New Alternatives in the Middle East struggled to contain the possibility of renewed violence in that region and to work toward a comprehensive resolution of grievances. Many urged increasing attention to the plight of the Palestinian Arabs, suggesting that they be given the chance to live in their own homeland, subject only to the parallel need to assure Israel's existence and safety.

Meeting near Vienna, the 24th Pugwash Conference on Science and World Affairs urged a world meeting of nuclear and militarily powerful nations on disarmament. This was the first unanimous appeal in the 17-year history of the conferences, originally conceived by Albert Einstein, Bertrand Russell, and Cyrus Eaton in the cold war period as a private forum for scientists from both West and East. Representatives from 31 nations attended, although China continued to be unrepresented. Conferees also urged expanded research to examine the hazards associated with nuclear power programs and stressed the need for research into alternative power sources such as solar and geothermal energy.

Sean MacBride, chairman of Amnesty International (AI) and co-winner of the 1974 Nobel Peace Prize, declared that the use of physical and mental torture for political ends was reaching near-epidemic proportions. In its detailed report, the London-based organization stated that at least 64 nations, including democracies as well as police states, were using torture as a systematic weapon of political control. The report accompanied a major conference in Paris in December 1973 initiating AI's worldwide antitorture campaign.

In India the Gandhi Peace Foundation, dedicated to utilizing the ideas of Mohandas Gandhi in social work, education, and in organizing the poor and landless, denounced the Indian government's detonation of a "peaceful" nuclear device. In a widely circulated letter, Radha Krishna, secretary of the foundation, declared the event was "a cruel joke on the people of this country." Asian sensitivities concerning nuclear weapons were underlined in Japan, where extensive protests greeted the discovery of an alleged secret oral agreement that permitted U.S. naval vessels carrying nuclear weapons to enter Japanese ports. The agreement had been kept confidential because of Japanese sensitivity concerning the atomic bombings of Nagasaki and Hiroshima in 1945.

Marking the 11th anniversary of the Diem government's attacks on the An Quang Pagoda and other Buddhist centres, the United Buddhist Church launched a new campaign that placed it in dramatic opposition to the Thieu regime. The church demanded implementation of the 1973 Paris accords and called upon Buddhist members of the armed services to "refuse to take up arms to attack their brothers."

Dom Helder Câmara (*see* BIOGRAPHY), a Roman Catholic prelate known for his work among the Brazilian poor, received $175,000 as part of a "People's Peace Prize" awarded in Oslo, Nor. The IFOR was one of the groups initiating the prize after the 1973 Nobel Peace Prize was awarded to Henry Kissinger and Le Duc Tho for negotiating the Vietnam "peace." SANE's Eleanor Roosevelt Peace Award went to Daniel Ellsberg of the U.S. and dissident Soviet scientist Andrey Sakharov. César Chávez, leader of the United Farm Workers union, received the Martin Luther King, Jr., Nonviolent Peace Prize.

Overall, 1974 was marked by consolidation of efforts, renewed analysis of the relationship between

the U.S. and movements of social change in other countries, and the development of new tactics and strategies to deal with the "postwar war" in Indochina. Some stressed that Vietnam was not an isolated phenomenon, pointing to CIA involvement in Chile and elsewhere.

Many peace advocates, focusing on internal developments within the movement itself, urged continuance of the shift from old forms of mass protest and confrontation. Supporting a "strategy of pervasive struggle," they cultivated peace movement ideas within the black, women's, and men's liberation movements and in enterprises such as food cooperatives, environmental efforts, and communitarian centres. This strategy also demanded a recognition that the opposition was not a monolith and that adversaries had their own internal conflicts and tensions. Further, peace workers attempted to link Watergate, the impeachment process, and the food, energy, and population crises to the building of a world less polarized between haves and have-nots. Attempting to create world community through nonviolent action, they sought not only a moral equivalent of war but a social and political equivalent as well.

(RICHARD O. HATHAWAY)

[524.D.2.b]

Pakistan

A federal republic, Pakistan is bordered on the south by the Arabian Sea, on the west by Afghanistan and Iran, on the north by China, and on the east by India. Area: 307,-374 sq.mi. (796,095 sq.km.), excluding the Pakistani-controlled section of Jammu and Kashmir. Pop. (1973 est.): 66,764,000. Cap.: Islamabad (pop., 1972, 77,000). Largest city: Karachi (metro. area pop., 1972, 3,469,000). Language: Urdu and English. Religion: Muslim 90%, Hindu and Christian minorities. President in 1974, Chaudhri Fazal Elahi; prime minister, Zulfikar Ali Bhutto.

Although 1974 was a difficult year for Pakistan both at home and abroad, there was progress in a number of directions. In the sphere of foreign relations, Pakistan continued to consolidate its links with the world of Islam. The government strongly supported the Arab cause in Palestine, identified itself with the Turkish cause in Cyprus, and played its part in the organization set up by Muslim countries to promote their common interest. Relations with the United States and with China were pursued and improved; those with the Soviet Union became cautiously cordial as Soviet help in the construction of a new steel mill near Karachi materialized.

Pakistan derived both prestige and advantage from the Islamic summit conference held in Lahore on February 22–24. Heads and representatives of 38 Islamic countries attended; included among them were Pres. Anwar as-Sadat of Egypt, King Faisal of Saudi Arabia, Col. Muammar al-Qaddafi of Libya, Pres. Hafez al-Assad of Syria, and Pres. Houari Boumédienne of Algeria. Pakistan promoted a number of projects to strengthen Muslim solidarity by supporting the economic and political development of backward countries with the help of the resources of the wealthy oil-producing states. Pakistan also sought to aid the cause of the Palestine Arabs and to secure

Painting:
see Art Exhibitions;
Art Sales; Museums

Paints and Varnishes:
see Industrial
Production and
Technology

more equitable trading terms for the world's less developed nations.

President Sadat of Egypt and the heads of other Islamic states wished to heal the breach between Pakistan and Bangladesh, and their mediation brought about an arrangement by which Prime Minister Bhutto used the authority conferred on him by the National Assembly in 1973 to recognize Bangladesh on Feb. 22, 1974, while Prime Minister Mujibur Rahman of Bangladesh himself attended the Islamic summit meeting in Lahore. This removed the last obstacle to the full repatriation of the prisoners of war in India by the end of April; by the end of June, the Bengalis in Pakistan and considerable numbers of Biharis in Bangladesh who had opted for Pakistan were also repatriated.

Hopes for the restoration of normal relations between Pakistan and India were temporarily dashed by India's action in exploding a nuclear device on May 18. Pakistan's suspicions were not allayed by India's assertion that it was committed to the peaceful use of atomic energy. The result was that after a meeting in April also attended by Bangladesh talks between Pakistan and India were not resumed until September. By that time Pakistan had secured pledges of support from numerous countries for the idea of declaring South Asia a nuclear-free zone. At the September meeting, Pakistan and India made some progress in restoring travel facilities, postal interchanges, and

Kamal Hossain (left), foreign minister of Bangladesh, Swaran Singh (centre), India's minister for external affairs, and Aziz Ahmed (right), foreign minister of Pakistan, at the conclusion of their repatriation agreement in New Delhi.

overflights, and trade relations were restored in November. A new factor in the establishment of reasonably normal relations between the two countries came into being when India approached the Iranian government for cooperation in a number of economic projects. Since Iran was a friendly neighbour of Pakistan, Indo-Iranian cordiality might well ease relations between New Delhi and Islamabad.

Unfortunately, Kashmir remained a matter of contention between the two countries. Pakistan was concerned that Sheikh Mohammad Abdullah and the Plebiscite Front in Kashmir might be on the point of arranging a definitive agreement with India. Furthermore, the enthusiastic reception accorded to Prime Minister Bhutto when he visited Bangladesh in June was generally regarded as showing friendship for Pakistan and dislike of India's entrenched position in Bangladesh's political and economic life in a manner which embarrassed Sheikh Mujib's government.

The most immediate obstacle to good relations between Pakistan and India was Pakistan's conviction that India was fostering the forces of internal subversion that were aiming to set up new independent states in the North-West Frontier Province (NWFP) and Baluchistan. The links between India and Khan Abdul Ghaffar Khan and his son Khan Abdul Wali Khan were close; their plans to establish an independent Pakhtunistan were favoured by India, and the project had been enlarged to include an independent Baluchistan whose population would also take in Iranian subjects who were Baluchi by race. That explosive project was given new impetus by the support of Afghanistan, whose representatives openly advocated it at the UN on October 7.

Inside Pakistan, the National Awami Party, under Khan Abdul Wali Khan's lead, supported the claims of secessionists in the NWFP and Baluchistan. In its capacity of official opposition, it criticized in the National Assembly the steps that the federal government took to restore order, whereby, the opposition claimed, some 900 people had been killed in air and ground operations. The tribal chiefs in Baluchistan resented the approach of modernism in the form of plans for the improvement of communications and economic development. During 1974 overt resistance began to crumble and, although desultory sniping continued, many "rebels" accepted an amnesty offered by the prime minister. But a hard-core element of resistance to the federal government remained.

PAKISTAN

Education. (1969–70) Primary, pupils *c.* 4.2 million, teachers *c.* 95,000; secondary and vocational, pupils *c.* 1,270,000, teachers *c.* 61,000; teacher training, students *c.* 3,000; higher (at 7 universities; 1972), students *c.* 55,000, teaching staff *c.* 1,500.

Finance. Monetary unit: Pakistan rupee, with (Sept. 16, 1974) a par value of PakRs. 9.90 to U.S. $1 (free rate of PakRs. 22.80 = £1 sterling). Gold, SDRs, and foreign exchange, state bank: (May 1974) U.S. $423 million; (May 1973) U.S. $435 million. Budget (1973–74 est.): revenue PakRs. 9,919,000,000; expenditure PakRs. 8,867,000,000. Gross national product: (1972–73) PakRs. 62,750,000,000; (1971–72) PakRs. 53,370,000,000. Money supply: (June 1974) PakRs. 22,395,000,000; (June 1973) PakRs. 21.1 billion. Cost of living (Karachi; 1970 = 100): (Jan. 1974) 163; (Jan. 1973) 120.

Foreign Trade. (1973) Imports PakRs. 9,788,000,000; exports PakRs. 9,595,000,000. Import sources: U.S. 26%; Japan 9%; West Germany 8%; U.K. 7%; Saudi Arabia 5%. Export destinations: Japan 14%; Hong Kong 13%; Indonesia 9%; U.K. 7%. Main exports (1972): cotton 24%; cotton yarn 16%; cotton fabrics 12%; rice 7%; leather 7%.

Transport and Communications. Roads (1972) 62,800 km. Motor vehicles in use (1972): passenger 74,300; commercial 21,100. Railways: (1972) 8,663 km.; traffic (1971–72) 9,518,000,000 passenger-km., freight 7,721,000,000 net ton-km. Air traffic (1973): 1,484,000,000 passenger-km.; freight 76 million net ton-km. Shipping (1973): merchant vessels 100 gross tons and over 89; gross tonnage 503,429. Telephones (Dec. 1972) 175,000. Radio receivers (Dec. 1971) 1,630,000. Television receivers (Dec. 1972) 129,000.

Agriculture. Production (in 000; metric tons; 1973; 1972 in parentheses): wheat 7,442 (6,890); barley 109 (103); corn *c.* 700 (706); rice *c.* 3,810 (3,487); millet *c.* 350 (304); sorghum *c.* 310 (302); sugar, raw value 479 (399); chick-peas *c.* 520 (516); onions *c.* 260 (253); peanuts *c.* 45 (44); rapeseed *c.* 297 (301); tobacco *c.* 73 (87); cotton, lint 667 (701). Livestock (in 000; 1972–73): cattle *c.* 20,500; buffalo (1971–72) *c.* 12,720; sheep *c.* 17,480; goats (1971–72) *c.* 9,060.

Industry. Production (in 000; metric tons; 1973): cement 2,896; crude oil (1972) 455; coal and lignite (1971–72) 1,251; natural gas (cu.m.; 1972) 3,795,000; electricity (excluding most industrial production; kw-hr.; 1971) 7,449,000; sulfuric acid 39; soda ash (1971–72) 77; nitrogenous fertilizers (nutrient content; 1972–73) *c.* 225; cotton yarn 346; woven cotton fabrics (m.; 1972–73) 636,000.

Pakistan's most effective weapon against internal subversion continued to be the federal government's determination to bring the less developed provinces such as the NWFP and Baluchistan up to the level attained by the Punjab and parts of Sind by means of financial subsidies on a scale never attempted by any previous administration. This was made possible by a remarkable economic revival that brought the foreign trade of Pakistan to a level far exceeding the best figures attained before Bangladesh broke away. Like other countries, Pakistan suffered from the high price of oil; but it received generous economic assistance from Iran ($250 million in 1974, with the promise of $180 million in 1975 and $150 million in 1976), as well as from other countries. Business confidence was restored by the termination of the program of nationalization in January after the banking, shipping, and oil distribution industries had all been incorporated into the public sector.

Disaster struck the northern part of the country in late December when an earthquake destroyed a number of villages at the foot of the Karakoram Mountains, 200 mi. N of Islamabad. Official reports put the death toll well over 5,000, with 15,000 injured, and Prime Minister Bhutto made an urgent appeal for international aid.

(L. F. RUSHBROOK WILLIAMS)

[976.A.3]

Panama

A republic of Central America, bisected by the Canal Zone, Panama is bounded by the Caribbean Sea, Colombia, the Pacific Ocean, and Costa Rica. Area: 29,-209 sq.mi. (75,650 sq.km.). Pop. (1974 est.): 1,618,-100. Cap. and largest city: Panama City (pop., 1974 est., 392,900). Language: Spanish. Religion (1971 est.): Roman Catholic 90%. President in 1974, Demetrio Lakas Bahas.

The resignation of U.S. Pres. Richard M. Nixon led the Panamanian newspaper *Crítica*—tightly controlled by the government—to comment upon a decadent trend in the democratic form of government. On the other hand, the strength of Brig. Gen. Omar Torrijos Herrera's dictatorship in 1974 seemed to be evident in the new apartment houses, schools, higher living standards for the poor, and ubiquitous posters and slogans. These brought him the loyalty of the urban masses, but at the cost of a complaining and dissenting business community. In October 1973 Torrijos required that landlords freeze rents and that banking houses set aside as much as half of their domestic savings to finance low-cost housing. Protests ensued from business and investment interests and opposition also appeared from political groups, probably remnants of former president Arnulfo Arias' supporters.

If these signs of discontent were not menacing, economic problems were insistently pressing upon the Torrijos regime, and commissions were organized to soothe the friction between labour and management, to formulate guidelines for prices and salaries, to implement housing legislation, and to facilitate the import of scarce raw materials. The government, however, could not control import prices, and inflation marched in. Price rises varied from spectacular (in the case of oil and gasoline) to startling (for locally manufactured goods dependent upon imported raw materials). The government expected much from its encouragement of expansion in the sugar, coffee, livestock, and fish industries and continued to support programs of education in the fields of nutrition, health, and vocational capacity, but difficulties remained. Imports were valued at three times exports and Panama's balance of payments deficit climbed rapidly. On the other hand, more Panamanians were finding jobs at higher wages in the Canal Zone, where, for the first time, deficit operations forced a rise in canal tolls.

Torrijos and his associates were willing to tap any foreign sources of help that were available. Late in October 1973 a subsidiary of the First National City Bank of New York had provided a loan with which to refinance the foreign debt. Another loan from the World Bank was granted to finance electrification projects, and funds from the Inter-American Development Bank, intended for the Darien section of the Inter-American Highway, were diverted to other segments of that road.

Early in the year, under the leadership of Torrijos and Pres. José Figueres of Costa Rica, seven Central and South American nations—Guatemala, Honduras, Nicaragua, Costa Rica, Panama, Colombia, and Ecuador—formed the Union of Banana Exporting Countries (UPEB). On March 10 all but Guatemala and

U.S. Secretary of State Henry Kissinger and Panamanian Foreign Minister Juan Antonio Tack sign a declaration of principles on negotiations for a new treaty governing the Canal Zone (right).

Nicaragua announced increases in the export price of bananas ranging from 1–2½ cents per pound, effective April 30. The countries, which accounted for 66% of the world's banana exports, stated that the increase was necessary to offset their soaring petroleum import bills.

One major U.S. fruit company, Standard Fruit and Steamship Corp., threatened to boycott banana shipments from Costa Rica. Also, the head of the Banana Handlers' Council of the International Longshoremen's Association threatened the UPEB heads of state with a boycott of all of their shipments of bananas to the U.S. But these statements, along with later actual reductions by Standard Fruit of imports from Honduras and Costa Rica, only appeared to strengthen the resolve of the UPEB cartel to stand by its decision. The administrative headquarters of UPEB was expected to be established in Panama City.

Another possible source to bolster the Panamanian economy was an increased Canal Zone annuity, but this payment was an inseparable part of the long-standing negotiations between Panama and the U.S. concerning Canal Zone sovereignty. Washington dispatched the experienced diplomat and U.S. ambassador at large Ellsworth Bunker, and for some six weeks in late 1973 and early 1974 he and Foreign Minister Juan Antonio Tack engaged in conversations preparatory to the visit of U.S. Secretary of State Henry Kissinger. Kissinger arrived in Panama City on February 7 to sign the declaration of principles that would serve as a guideline for a new treaty regulating the Canal Zone. It provided for the abrogation of the treaty of 1903 and for the negotiation of a new treaty to endure not in perpetuity but for a fixed term of years. The U.S. was to continue to have the rights to land, water, and air spaces needed to operate and defend the canal but was to surrender certain unused tracts of land in the Canal Zone. Panama was assured a share in administering and defending the canal and in the planning for new or enlarged canal capacity. A more equitable sharing of the monetary benefits of canal operation was included. This new understanding met with immediate and forceful hostility in both houses of the U.S. Congress. The chief point of opposition was the eventual surrender of sovereignty over the Canal Zone to Panama. Without that control, it was contended, defense of the canal would be impossible. A resolution introduced in the Senate calling for continuation of U.S. sovereignty indicated sufficient support to defeat a treaty, but Bunker and Tack continued periodic talks.

In the latter part of August, Panama reversed its policy of isolating Fidel Castro by reestablishing diplomatic relations with Cuba. The move had significance as a spur to the Organization of American States to lift its sanctions and possibly to the U.S. to soften its quarantine of the island republic.

(ALMON R. WRIGHT)

[974.B.1.f]

Papua New Guinea

Papua New Guinea is an internally self-governing state composed of the Australian external territory of Papua and the Australian-administered UN Trust Territory of New Guinea. It is situated in the southwest Pacific and comprises the eastern part of the island of New Guinea, the islands of the Bismarck, Trobriand, Woodlark, Louisiade, and D'Entrecasteaux groups, and parts of the Solomon Islands, including Bougainville. It is separated from Australia by the Torres Strait. Area: 178,260 sq.mi. (461,690 sq.km.). Pop. (1973 est.): 2,563,310. Cap. and largest city: Port Moresby (pop., 1971, 76,500). Language: English (official), Papuan and Melanesian languages, and Pidgin English, the lingua franca. Religion (1966): Roman Catholic 31.2%; Lutheran 27.3%; indigenous 7%. Chief minister in 1974, Michael T. Somare.

After attaining self-governing status on Dec. 1, 1973, the territory of Papua New Guinea entered a transition period at the beginning of 1974 before attempting to achieve full independence from Australia. The inexperienced indigenous government headed by Chief Minister Michael T. Somare (see BIOGRAPHY) seemed to be dealing effectively with the complex problems that faced the undeveloped island nation. According to Minister for Defense and Foreign Affairs Albert Maori Kiki (see BIOGRAPHY), the new administration was giving priority to "bringing the people together." By October, however, hopes to achieve independence were dampened by political strife and long parliamentary arguments over the proposed constitution. The independence day target date of Dec. 1, 1974, was abandoned.

Ever present intertribal tensions continued, and in an attempt to impart a sense of national unity to the 1,000 tribes, which speak more than 600 mutually unintelligible languages, public buildings throughout the territory were plastered with posters reading "Kantri Bilong Yumi," the phonetic spelling of the English "Country belong you me"—meaning "our country" in Pidgin, the English-based common language.

Somare's government attempted to placate the

Palestine:
see Israel; Jordan
Panama Canal Zone:
see Dependent States;
Panama
Paper Industry:
see Forestry; Industrial
Production and
Technology

PANAMA

Education. (1972–73) Primary, pupils 319,124, teachers 10,578; secondary, pupils 74,484, teachers 3,440; vocational, pupils 30,725, teachers 1,701; teacher training, students 6,391, teachers 259; higher, students 21,-616, teaching staff 705.

Finance. Monetary unit: balboa, at par with the U.S. dollar, with a free rate (Sept. 16, 1974) of 2.31 balboas to £1 sterling. Gold, SDRs, and foreign exchange: (Dec. 1973) U.S. $2,188,400,000; (Dec. 1972) U.S. $933.6 million. Budget (1973 est.): revenue 229 million balboas; expenditure 228.2 million balboas. Gross national product: (1972) 1,266,000,000 balboas; (1971) 1,125,700,000 balboas. Money supply (deposits only): (Dec. 1973) 184 million balboas; (Dec. 1972) 164.7 million balboas. Cost of living (Panama City; 1970 = 100): (June 1974) 133; (June 1973) 113.

Foreign Trade. (1973) Imports 488,480,000 balboas; exports 132,660,000 balboas. Net service receipts from Canal Zone (1972) 127.5 million balboas. Main import sources: U.S. 35%; Ecuador 10%; Venezuela 7%; Japan 7%. Main export destinations: U.S. 45%; West Germany 15%; Italy 12%; The Netherlands 7%. Main exports: bananas 48%; petroleum products 18%; shrimps 13%.

Transport and Communications. Roads (1972) 7,016 km. Motor vehicles in use (1971): passenger 50,200; commercial (including buses) 16,200. Railways (1972) 720 km. Shipping (1973): merchant vessels 100 gross tons and over 1,692 (mostly owned by U.S. and other foreign interests); gross tonnage 9,568,-954. Telephones (Dec. 1972) 100,000. Radio receivers (Dec. 1972) 250,000. Television receivers (Dec. 1972) 200,000.

Agriculture. Production (in 000; metric tons; 1973; 1972 in parentheses): rice c. 130 (125); sugar, raw value 81 (80); bananas (1972) c. 920, (1971) c. 940; oranges (1972) c. 84, (1971) 83; coffee 5 (5); cocoa (1972) 0.5, (1971) 0.5. Livestock (in 000; 1972–73): cattle c. 1,350; pigs 188; horses c. 165.

Industry. Production (in 000; metric tons; 1972): petroleum products 3,940; cement (1970) 181; manufactured gas (cu.m.) 16,000; electricity (kw-hr.; 1970) 956,000.

PAPUA NEW GUINEA

Education. (1972) Primary, pupils 227,699, teachers 7,381; secondary, pupils 24,335, teachers 1,079; vocational, pupils 6,015, teachers 389; teacher training, students 1,936, teachers 213; higher (University of Papua New Guinea; 1972), students 1,245, teaching staff 136.

Finance and Trade. Monetary unit: Australian dollar, with (after devaluation on Sept. 24, 1974) a free rate of A$0.76 to U.S. $1 (A$1.77 = £1 sterling). Budget (1972–73) balanced at A$216,166,000 (including A$78,180,000 grant by Australian government). Foreign trade (1971–72): imports A$256,386,-000; exports A$127,181,000. Import sources: Australia 55%; Japan 15%; U.S. 8%. Export destinations: Australia 42%; Japan 17%; West Germany 14%; U.K. 10%; U.S. 8%. Main exports: copper ores 18%; coffee 16%; cocoa 9%; copra 7%; timber 6%; machinery 5%; transport equipment 5%; copra oil 5%.

Transport. Shipping (1973): merchant vessels 100 gross tons and over 56; gross tonnage 27,827.

Agriculture. Production (in 000; metric tons; 1973; 1972 in parentheses): cocoa c. 29 (c. 31); coffee c. 30 (c. 30); copra (1972) 136, (1971) 142; rubber c. 6 (5); timber (cu.m.; 1971–72) 5,500, (1970–71) 5,100. Livestock (in 000; March 1972): cattle 95; pigs 8; chickens 210.

Industry. Production (in 000; troy oz.; 1971): gold 23; silver 17; copper (metric tons; 1971–72) 141.

separatist movements on Bougainville Island (which produces most of the territory's main export, copper) as well as the prosperous agricultural tribes on New Britain Island by offering them what would amount to local autonomy. Other secessionist drives occurred in Papua, one of which was led by the territory's leading feminist and only female member of the 100-seat House of Assembly, Mrs. Josephine Abaijah.

At the end of the year the House of Assembly still faced a number of controversial constitutional questions, and a wider split in the dominant party of the national coalition—Pangu Pati—was envisioned.

Paraguay

A landlocked republic of South America, Paraguay is bounded by Brazil, Argentina, and Bolivia. Area: 157,048 sq.mi. (406,752 sq.km.). Pop. (1974 est.): 2,584,000. Cap. and largest city: Asunción (pop., 1972, 387,676). Language: Spanish (official), though Guaraní is the language of the majority of the people. Religion: Roman Catholic. President in 1974, Gen. Alfredo Stroessner.

President Stroessner's fifth five-year term of office entered its second year in an atmosphere of political stability. Effective opposition was virtually absent, and the president remained firmly in control with the support of the Colorado Party and the armed forces. Rumours of plans to manipulate the constitution so as to make Stroessner president for life had yet to be borne out. However, Stroessner's eldest son, Gustavo, was increasingly brought into the limelight, indicating that potential problems of succession were being kept in mind.

The joint project with Brazil for the 10.7 million-kw. Itaipu hydroelectric plant, embarked on in 1973, had led many people to assume that plans for cooperation with Paraguay's other large neighbour, Argentina, would be shelved. However, in December of that year a similar agreement was reached with Argentina for construction of a 3.3 million-kw. plant at Yacyretá-Apipé, also on the Paraná River. Later both countries agreed to provide funds and assistance for a number of development projects, and it seemed that

Paraguay was successfully playing one against the other. However, some elements criticized the Itaipu agreement on the ground that Paraguay had sold surplus power to Brazil at an unacceptably low price.

On the domestic front, soaring oil and wheat prices led to a massive increase in the cost of living, provoking the country's only legal labour union, the Confederación Paraguaya de Trabajadores, to request a wage increase for the first time in many years. The main source of protest, however, was the traditional alliance of students and clergy on behalf of the peasants. Protests flared briefly at the University of Asunción and were supported in sermons by the archbishop of that city, but calm was restored when about 100 demonstrating students and peasants were rounded up and handed over to military tribunals.

Paraguay continued to benefit from high world prices for its principal exports, notably beef. In 1973 a trade surplus of $5 million was achieved, compared with $3.6 million the previous year. However, while the value of exports rose 47.3%, their volume rose only 4.9%—a disturbing situation in view of the expected leveling-off of meat and other commodity prices. Nevertheless, the achievement of a real gross domestic product growth rate of 7% in 1973 was well above the development plan target of 5.5%. Moreover, while the world energy crisis impaired the external position in the short run, the country's long-term prospects as an energy-producer were considerably enhanced.   (ANNE PARSONS)

[974.F.3]

PARAGUAY

Education. (1973) Primary, pupils 459,393, teachers (including preprimary) 15,871; secondary and vocational, pupils 66,746, teachers 6,829; teacher training (1972), students 1,475, teachers (1968) 1,021; higher, students 9,719, teaching staff 1,231.

Finance. Monetary unit: guaraní, with an official rate (Sept. 16, 1974) of 126 guaraníes to U.S. $1 (free rate of 289 guaraníes = £1 sterling). Gold, SDRs, and foreign exchange, central bank: (June 1974) U.S. $71,260,000; (June 1973) U.S. $43,810,000. Budget (1974 est.): revenue 37,198,000,000 guaraníes; expenditure 37,051,000,000 guaraníes. Gross national product: (1972) 94,950,000,000 guaraníes; (1971) 82,110,000,000 guaraníes. Money supply: (June 1973) 11,907,000,000 guaraníes; (June 1972) 8,318,000,000 guaraníes. Cost of living (Asunción; 1970 = 100): (June 1974) 163; (June 1973) 129.

Foreign Trade. (1973) Imports 15,750,800,000 guaraníes; exports 15,686,300,000 guaraníes. Import sources: Argentina 26%; U.S. 17%; West Germany 11%; U.K. 7%. Export destinations: West Germany 18%; U.S. 13%; Argentina 13%; The Netherlands 8%; U.K. 7%; Belgium-Luxembourg 5%. Main exports: meat 32%; timber 9%; cotton 9%; tobacco 6%; oilseeds 5%.

Transport and Communications. Roads (1970) 11,225 km. Motor vehicles in use (1970): passenger 7,400; commercial (including buses) 10,000. Railways: (1970) 498 km.; traffic (1968) 28 million passenger-km., freight 22 million net ton-km. Navigable inland waterways (including Paraguay-Paraná river system; 1970) c. 3,000 km. Telephones (Dec. 1972) 21,000. Radio receivers (Dec. 1972) 175,000. Television receivers (Dec. 1972) 52,000.

Agriculture. Production (in 000; metric tons; 1973; 1972 in parentheses): corn 300 (209); cassava (1972) c. 1,850, (1971) 1,690; sweet potatoes (1972) c. 142, (1971) 138; soybeans (1972) 128, (1971) 74; peanuts 25 (17); dry beans c. 36 (c. 36); sugar, raw value (1972) c. 66, (1971) c. 61; tomatoes c. 47 (45); oranges (1972) 177, (1971) 197; mandarin oranges and tangerines (1972) 37, (1971) 31; bananas (1972) c. 250, (1971) c. 250; tobacco 24 (18); palm kernels c. 21 (c. 17); cotton, lint 25 (15); beef and veal (1972) c. 115, (1971) c. 111. Livestock (in 000; 1972–73): cattle c. 5,966; sheep c. 335; pigs c. 540; horses c. 710; chickens (1971–72) c. 6,400.

Industry. Production (in 000; metric tons; 1972): cement 75; petroleum products 231; cotton yarn 13; electricity (kw-hr.) 273,000.

Payments and Reserves, International:
see Exchange and Payments, International

Peace Movements:
see Pacifism and Nonviolent Movements

Penology:
see Prisons and Penology

Pentecostal Churches:
see Religion

Peru

A republic on the west coast of South America, Peru is bounded by Ecuador, Colombia, Brazil, Bolivia, Chile, and the Pacific Ocean. Area: 496,-224 sq.mi. (1,285,215 sq.km.). Pop. (1974 est.): 14,370,000, including approximately 52% whites and mestizos and 46% Indians. Cap. and largest city: Lima (metro. area pop., 1972, 3,317,648). Language: Spanish; Indians speak Quechuan or Aymara. Religion: Roman Catholic. President of the military government in 1974, Juan Velasco Alvarado.

The military government of Peru continued to follow a middle road between capitalism and Communism and, politically, survived well during 1974 despite a few setbacks. The policy of nationalization was a key issue. In July, with the publication of the Inca Plan (the original program of the revolution of October 1968), President Velasco emphasized his government's intention ultimately to nationalize air-

PERU

Education. (1970) Primary, pupils 2,562,695, teachers 64,004; secondary, pupils 547,316, teachers 21,-863; vocational, pupils 127,207, teachers 6,333; teacher training, students 18,000, teachers 1,075; higher (including 23 universities), students 124,700, teaching staff 13,900.

Finance. Monetary unit: sol, with a principal official exchange rate (Sept. 16, 1974) of 38.70 soles to U.S. $1 and a free rate of 43.38 soles to U.S. $1 (100.50 soles = £1 sterling). Gold, SDRs, and foreign exchange, central bank: (Jan. 1974) U.S. $477.9 million; (Jan. 1973) U.S. $442.2 million. Budget (1972 actual): revenue 45,112,000,000 soles; expenditure 47,740,000,000 soles. Gross domestic product: (1972) 291.2 billion soles; (1971) 261.2 billion soles. Money supply: (Dec. 1973) 71,590,000,000 soles; (Dec. 1972) 56,220,000,000 soles. Cost of living (Lima and Callao; 1970 = 100): (May 1974) 145; (May 1973) 124.

Foreign Trade. Imports (1972) 30,633,000,000 soles; exports (1973) 40,192,000,000 soles. Import sources: U.S. 30%; West Germany 12%; Japan 8%; Colombia 5%. Export destinations (1972): U.S. 33%; Japan 14%; West Germany 11%; The Netherlands 7%; China 5%. Main exports: copper 27%; fish meal 13%; zinc 9%; sugar 8%; silver 7%; coffee 6%; cotton 6%; iron ore 6%.

Transport and Communications. Roads (1973) 52,102 km. (including 180 km. expressways). Motor vehicles in use (1972): passenger 256,400; commercial 136,100. Railways: (1972) 2,100 km.; traffic (1970) 248 million passenger-km., freight 610 million net ton-km. Air traffic (1972): 355 million passenger-km.; freight 16.1 million net ton-km. Shipping (1973): merchant vessels 100 gross tons and over 663; gross tonnage 448,325. Telephones (Dec. 1972) 269,000. Radio receivers (Dec. 1972) 2 million. Television receivers (Dec. 1972) 410,000.

Agriculture. Production (in 000; metric tons; 1973; 1972 in parentheses): rice 427 (436); corn c. 645 (589); wheat 149 (140); barley c. 165 (170); potatoes 1,888 (1,712); sweet potatoes (1972) 173, (1971) 168; tomatoes 69 (55); onions 177 (162); cassava (1972) 479, (1971) 482; dry beans c. 64 (c. 60); sugar, raw value 923 (922); grapes c. 62 (c. 62); oranges (1972) 236, (1971) 243; lemons (1972) c. 90, (1971) 75; coffee (1972) 72, (1971) 71; cotton, lint c. 65 (86); fish catch (1972) 4,768, (1971) 10,606. Livestock (in 000; 1972–73): cattle c. 4,360; sheep 17,320; pigs c. 2,070; goats (1971–72) 1,946; horses (1971–72) c. 685; poultry (1971–72) 24,363.

Industry. Production (in 000; metric tons; 1972): crude oil 3,194; coal (1971) 92; natural gas (cu.m.) 480,000; cement 1,428; iron ore (metal content) 5,931; pig iron 171; steel 192; lead 86; zinc 66; copper 39; tungsten concentrates (oxide content; 1970) 0.7; gold (troy oz.) 90; silver (troy oz.) c. 40,000; fish meal 900; petroleum products 4,570; electricity (kw-hr.; 1971) 5,949,000.

lines, banks and finance, insurance, and shipping companies, and to assume total control of the mining and petroleum sectors. The campaign against the opposition press had been stepped up, and on July 27 all national daily newspapers were handed over to be run by government-appointed committees, a move that provoked violent right-wing demonstrations in Lima and earlier precipitated the resignation of the minister and commander-in-chief of the Navy, Vice-Adm. Luis Vargas Caballero, and two other high-ranking naval officers and administrators. Earlier in the year several foreign (mainly U.S.) companies were nationalized, including the Cerro de Pasco mining operations; Peru finally agreed to pay $150 million in compensation for U.S.-owned enterprises (see LATIN-AMERICAN AFFAIRS), including the Cerro Corp., W. R. Grace & Co., and various fish meal companies. In April the government approved a law establishing "social ownership" enterprises, with capital to be supplied by the state and full participation by workers in management and profit sharing. Toward the end of the year several small companies were set up under the terms of the new law. The government hoped that this new sector would eventually dominate the economy. Meanwhile, rapid inflation and serious food shortages affected daily life.

Increasing state participation caused confidence in the private sector of the economy to fall, and investment, except by the state, remained at a low level throughout the year. Nevertheless, foreign investors were not discouraged, and large foreign capital inflows were recorded. Substantial amounts were provided by the foreign oil companies, and investment and refinancing loans were granted by other governments, commercial banks, and international financial institutions. Investment capital was provided, in particular, for the Cuajone copper-mine project and for the ambitious Majes irrigation project, in which an international consortium of firms participated. The large capital inflows helped to make the external sector the economy's dominant feature. Although the volume of exports did not increase to any great extent, their value rose because of high world commodity prices, from a record level of $1,119,000,000 in 1973 to over $1.4 billion, with mineral exports accounting for more than $700 million. During the year carefully controlled anchoveta fishing was resumed, with the total catch limited to about four million tons in an effort to allow stocks to return to normal.

Peru's serious foreign debt problem was expected to be of a short-term nature as export earnings from minerals and petroleum would increase substantially by the end of the decade when new copper mines would begin producing (e.g., Cuajone and Cerro Verde, in particular) and large volumes of petroleum would become available. Eighteen foreign oil companies signed contracts for exploration and development of petroleum in the Peruvian Amazon, based on a production split between the government and the companies. Several wells proved successful and prospects were excellent. Peru was currently producing about 60–70% of its total oil requirements but hoped to become a substantial net exporter by the end of the decade. During the year the government arranged about $600 million in financing—principally by Japan and Iran and the banks of a number of other countries—to cover the cost of construction of a 530-mi. trans-Andean pipeline that would carry oil from the Amazon oil fields to the Pacific coast.

Taken as a whole domestic economic growth was

slow, largely as a result of poor performance in agriculture. Steel production increased rapidly, and the government pressed ahead with an expansion program at the Chimbote steelworks and with development of the Nazca integrated steelworks. One of the most successful industries was shipbuilding, and during the year major contracts were won from Cuba, Ecuador, and France. (FRANCES KIRKHAM)

[974.D.2]

Philately and Numismatics

Philately. Aided by the flight from currency, the international stamp market remained extremely buoyant in 1974, with considerably increased turnovers reported by major philatelic auctioneers in Europe and America. Among the most interesting realizations were £24,500 for a block of 12 Lombardy-Venetia 10-centes black (Robson Lowe) and $75,000 for a Japanese stamp of 1871 with an inverted centre (Waverly Trading Co. sale in Tokyo).

Four notable international exhibitions were held. The venues and major award winners were: New Delhi, India—B. Pasti, Italy (Grand Prix d'Honneur), M. A. Bojanowicz, U.K. (Grand Prix International), and D. H. Jatia, India (Grand Prix National); Jerusalem—Louis Abrams, South Africa (Grand Prix International), and Hans G. Sladowsky,

West Germany (Grand Prix National); Basel, Switz. —Luis Cervera, Spain (Grand Prix d'Honneur), Anton Jerger, Austria (Grand Prix International), and Rolf Rothmayr, Switzerland (Grand Prix National); Stockholm—John O. Griffiths, U.K. (Grand Prix d'Honneur), Simone Rubeli, Switzerland (Grand Prix International; the first time a woman collector had achieved this honour), and Julius L. Spencer, U.S. (Grand Prix National).

Other honours included: Lichtenstein Medal of the Collectors Club (New York), Ernest A. Kehr; Royal Philatelic Society Medal (infrequent award), Ewart Gerrish; Philatelic Congress Medal (U.K.), Marjorie M. Humble; Reginald M. Phillips Gold Medal (every fifth year for work in British stamp designing), T. Stuart Rose; and the Gold Medal of the Postal History Society of America to Alan W. Robertson, U.K., for his writings on maritime postal history. New appointments included John O. Griffiths as honorary secretary of the Royal Philatelic Society, London; George Beal as editor of the *Philatelic Magazine,* London; and Hans Hunziker, Switzerland, as president of the International Association of Philatelic Experts.

For the first time since its foundation in 1909, the annual Philatelic Congress of Great Britain was held outside the U.K.—at Enghien-les-Bains, Paris—as part of the 25th anniversary celebrations of the British-based France and Colonies Philatelic Society. The year's new signatories to the Roll of Distinguished Philatelists were Jacques Fromaiget and Raymond Salles, both of France, and Patrick C. Pearson and George South of the U.K. During the year Stanley Gibbons International Ltd. moved into continental Europe by acquiring the Briefmarkenhaus Merkur of Frankfurt am Main, W.Ger., long-established auctioneers and dealers in classic issues. The new Canadian Postal Museum was formally opened in Ottawa in September, and a fund was launched at the Jerusalem international stamp exhibition to found a postal museum in Israel.

The controversy over the practicality of self-adhesive stamps was further stimulated by the issue of a booklet of such stamps by Gibraltar and the experimental issue of a 10-cent self-adhesive Christmas stamp by the U.S. The U.S. Postal Service held three seminars to consider the extension of philatelic facilities through marketing by the Postal Service. Great Britain announced the experimental issue, in January 1975, of its first charity-cum-postage stamps: the Post Office would sell the stamp at $1\frac{1}{2}$ pence above postal value and an independent committee would advise on the distribution of the money among recognized charitable organizations. Two omnibus issues were launched; one, with worldwide support, for the centenary of the Universal Postal Union and the other (largely confined to the British Commonwealth territories) for the centenary of Sir Winston Churchill's birth in 1874. Unlike previous omnibus issues, both included a wide variety of designs by different artists.

The American Philatelic Society published *The Yucatan Affair: The Work of Raoul Ch. de Thuin, Philatelic Counterfeiter,* a record of the forged overprints and postmarks made by de Thuin in Mexico before the APS bought his business and closed it down in 1967. (KENNETH F. CHAPMAN)

Numismatics. The highlight of 1974 was the selection of the three winning designs for use on the U.S. bicentennial quarters, half-dollars, and dollars, and the striking of one each of these coins. The winners

Designs for the new dollar, half-dollar, and quarter coins to be issued in honour of the U.S. bicentennial.

COURTESY, U.S. MINT

COURTESY, THE POST OFFICE, LONDON

A new series of postage stamps issued in Great Britain marked the centenary of the birth (Nov. 30, 1874) of Sir Winston Churchill.

were chosen from among some 1,000 entries by a committee of five artist/sculptors under the supervision of Mary T. Brooks, director of the U.S. Mint.

The entirely new designs would be used on the reverse sides of the quarter, half-dollar, and dollar; no changes would be made on the faces of the coins except that all would bear the double date "1776–1976." Plans were to put the coins into circulation on July 4, 1975, and to produce them in large quantities. Special strikings for collectors would be available, at premium prices, from the Bureau of the Mint through 1975.

One of each coin was struck at the Philadelphia Mint on Aug. 12, 1974, and flown to Bal Harbour, Fla., for exhibition at the annual convention of the American Numismatic Association (ANA). The growing interest in numismatics was indicated by an attendance of over 10,000 at the convention, and by new price records set in the sale of a number of numismatic items. The ANA headquarters in Colorado Springs, Colo., reported that it had accepted nearly 3,700 new members during its last fiscal year.

While U.S. coin collectors had been permitted to hold gold coins as collectors' items, with some restrictions, they as well as the general public looked forward to removal of the federal ban on buying, selling, and ownership of gold as of Jan. 1, 1975. Both the demand for and the prices of rare coins and other numismatic items were rising as a result of inflation, and more and more people were becoming interested in them as investments.

In connection with the 1976 observance of the U.S. bicentennial, the Mint began issuing pewter reproductions of ten of America's earliest medals. The originals were struck in recognition of outstanding commanders and successful Revolutionary War battles. Several new state bicentennial medals were issued during 1974, all produced by private minting firms.

Numerous countries issued new coins during the year, some for regular circulation and others as commemoratives or in observance of events. Among them

were: Austria (125th anniversary of the federal police; Viennese International Garden Exposition), The Bahamas (nine denominations from 1 cent to B$5), Bangladesh, Belize, Canada (centennial of the Winnipeg dollar), Chile, Dominican Republic, Czechoslovakia (composer Bedrich Smetana), East Germany (physicist Johann P. Reis; philosopher Immanuel Kant), Haiti (1973 coins), Iceland (two silver coins for the 1,100th anniversary of settlement), Indonesia, Israel (David Ben-Gurion, 1886–1973), Malawi (tenth year of independence), Norway, Philippines (25th anniversary of its central bank), Poland, Western Samoa, and West Germany.

Canada issued the first 4 coins (dated 1976) of a 28-coin set in observance of the 1976 Olympic Games to be held in Montreal. Private mints issued many commemorative medals, including ones honouring Pablo Casals, Sigmund Freud, composer Charles Ives, Gen. William Tecumseh Sherman, the bicentennial of the arrival of the Shakers in America, and the centennial of the invention of the telephone.

(GLENN B. SMEDLEY)

[452.D.2.b; 725.B.4.g]

Philippines

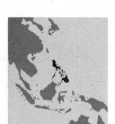

Situated in the western Pacific Ocean off the southeast coast of Asia, the Republic of the Philippines consists of an archipelago of about 7,100 islands. Area: 115,800 sq.mi. (300,000 sq.km.). Pop. (1974 est.): 41,457,170. Capital: Quezon City (pop., 1974 est., 946,390). Largest city: Manila (pop., 1974 est., 1,473,560). Language: Pilipino (based on Tagalog), English, Spanish, and many dialects. Religion (1960): Roman Catholic 84%; Aglipayan 5%; Muslim 5%; Protestant 3%. President in 1974, Ferdinand E. Marcos.

On September 11, to mark his 57th birthday, President Marcos ordered the release of five persons who had been arrested when martial law was declared in September 1972. Each of the five was a political opponent of the president and the most prominent was former senator José W. Diokno, against whom no charges had been filed. His release was described as temporary and it did not absolve him from possible charges of subversion later.

Two other prisoners, a former newspaper publisher and the son of a defeated presidential candidate, went on a hunger strike two months later to protest their two-year imprisonment without trial. The hunger strike lasted ten days until the government announced that it would bring them to trial. No charges against the two had been made, but government spokesmen had accused them of being involved in a conspiracy to assassinate Marcos.

Since the declaration of martial law, the Roman Catholic Church had voiced its concern over the curtailment of basic freedoms in the country. On August 29 Archbishop Jaime Sin of Manila called for a vigil of prayer so that "all of us may live under a regime of truth and justice, peace and freedom." "Martial law and all it connotes . . . is for emergencies only and not for the normal state of things," the archbishop said later. A letter from Secretary of Defense Juan Ponce Enrile to Archbishop Sin, dated November 30, stated that the government was holding 1,792 political prisoners at the time. "No one is without any charges against him, except those the processing of whose charges has taken a little more time than the others."

Petroleum:
see Energy

Pharmaceutical Industry:
see Industrial Production and Technology

More violent opposition to governmental policy was being exerted by the New People's Army, described by Marcos as waging "an armed insurrection and rebellion . . . based on the Marxist-Leninist-Maoist teachings and beliefs." The group, whose activity covered the central and northern provinces of the country, was estimated to comprise 1,800 armed guerrillas, backed by 4,200 propagandists charged with organizing support from the rural population.

Marcos' biggest problem in the south was the continued fighting between the Army and the Moro National Liberation Front. The avowed aim of the Front was complete independence for Muslim-inhabited areas, which included most of the southern portion of the Philippines. A peace plan being considered by the central government was initiated by Islamic groups in other nations. It consisted of creating an autonomous Muslim state within Philippine jurisdiction. A border agreement between the Philippine government and Indonesia led to patrolling of their waters by both countries in order to check the flow of weapons and other contraband into the Philippines. The insurgency in the south had been sustained by a flow of arms and funds believed to have come from Malaysian Sabah.

The economic outlook for the Philippines in 1974 was one of optimism. The gross national product had expanded by close to 10% the previous year and in 1974 increased by an additional 5%. A balance of payments surplus of $64 million was reported for the first nine months of the year. Government revenues for the same period had grown by 46%. As a result of a determined campaign by the Philippine government, foreign investments entering the country during the first half of the year totaled $85 million and accounted for almost 65% of all new investments. Sugar, a major

An elderly resident of the Philippine island of Jolo salvages an oar from the wreckage of the island's capital, ravaged in fighting between government troops and Muslim separatists.

UPI COMPIX

PHILIPPINES

Education. (1971–72) Primary, pupils 6,764,501, teachers 247,439; secondary, pupils 1,723,365, teachers 59,473; vocational, pupils 112,654; higher (including 40 universities), students 688,259, teaching staff 27,625.

Finance. Monetary unit: peso, with (Sept. 16, 1974) an official rate of 6.78 pesos to U.S. $1 (free rate of 15.63 pesos = £1 sterling). Gold, SDRs, and foreign exchange, central bank: (June 1974) U.S. $1,538,000,000; (June 1973) U.S. $845 million. Budget (1973–74 est.): revenue 7,196,000,000 pesos; expenditure 8,606,000,000 pesos. Gross national product: (1972) 57,450,000,000 pesos; (1971) 50,290,000,000 pesos. Money supply: (May 1974) 8,448,000,000 pesos; (May 1973) 6,906,000,000 pesos. Cost of living (Manila; 1970 = 100): (June 1974) 188; (June 1973) 145.

Foreign Trade. (1973) Imports 12,063,000,000 pesos; exports 12,147,000,000 pesos. Import sources: Japan 31%; U.S. 28%; Saudi Arabia 6%; West Germany 5%. Export destinations: U.S. 36%; Japan 36%; The Netherlands 5%. Main exports: coconut products 20%; timber 18%; sugar 17%; copper 16%.

Transport and Communications. Roads (1971) 75,532 km. Motor vehicles in use (1972): passenger 294,300; commercial (including buses) 191,200. Railways (1972): 1,169 km.; traffic 665 million passenger-km., freight (1973) 58 million net ton-km. Air traffic (1972): 1,626,000,000 passenger-km.; freight 41 million net ton-km. Shipping (1973): merchant vessels 100 gross tons and over 404; gross tonnage 947,210. Telephones (Jan. 1973) 391,000. Radio receivers (Dec. 1972) 1.8 million. Television receivers (Dec. 1971) 421,000.

Agriculture. Production (in 000; metric tons; 1973; 1972 in parentheses): rice c. 5,550 (4,415); corn c. 2,200 (1,831); sweet potatoes (1972) c. 680, (1971) 651; cassava (1972) c. 500, (1971) 440; copra c. 1,650 (1,925); sugar, raw value 2,258 (1,859); coffee 52 (52); bananas (1972) c. 1,300, (1971) 1,033; tobacco c. 78 (56); rubber c. 23 (22); manila hemp (1972) c. 68, (1971) 52; pork (1972) c. 334, (1971) c. 301; timber (cu.m.; 1971) 33,300, (1970) 33,700; fish catch (1972) 1,149, (1971) 1,050. Livestock (in 000; March 1973): cattle c. 2,080; buffaloes (1972) 4,711; pigs c. 8,200; goats (1972) 1,083; horses c. 295; chickens (1972) 50,103.

Industry. Production (in 000; metric tons; 1973): coal 39; iron ore (55–60% metal content) 2,235; chrome ore (oxide content; 1972) 124; manganese ore (metal content; 1972) 1.2; copper ore (metal content; 1972) 214; gold (troy oz.; 1972) 607; silver (troy oz.; 1972) 1,800; cement 4,136; petroleum products (1972) 8,363; sulfuric acid 282; electricity (excluding most industrial production; kw-hr.; 1973) 8,718,000.

export commodity, continued to command a high price as the year ended.

On the other hand, inflation raised the Manila consumer price index by 26%. Of the labour force of 14 million, 7% were completely unemployed and approximately 20% were underemployed. A growth rate of 3.1% in the population added half a million new job seekers to the labour market every year. During the year, alternating floods and drought plagued the Filipino farmer. On November 7 President Marcos suspended trading and the export of sugar while assessing damage to the crop caused by six typhoons within the previous five months. Furthermore, the worldwide increase in commodity prices during early 1974, which had provided much of the impetus for the economic boost, proved short-lived.

On November 16 President Marcos took another step toward implementation of land reform by issuing a proclamation limiting all land devoted to the raising of rice and corn to units no more than 17.3 ac. in size; these would ultimately belong to the tenant farmers. The proclamation would permit all of the one million tenant farmers who were working corn and rice fields to take steps toward eventual ownership of the land they tilled. (RAFAEL PARGAS)

[976.C.2]

Philosophy

In 1974 academic philosophy continued its interest in the practical and theoretical problems occasioned by social and political conditions. There was a general interest in the possibility of a philosophy of history that inquires into the prospects for humanity. This concern for the future was exhibited in discussion on the nature of justice, the value of punishment, the justification of civil obedience and disobedience, and moral problems involving sex and race. Philosophy's involvement with history and the human prospect was expressed by Father Theodore M. Hesburgh of Notre Dame University in *The Humane Imperative*. *Philosophy, Morality, and International Affairs*, edited by V. Held and others, included essays on the morality of war, national self-determination, and the relation of social science to foreign policy.

In *Philosophy as Social Expression*, Albert W. Levi treated Plato, Aquinas, Descartes, and G. E. Moore as examples in his argument that philosophical concepts are "*dated* reflections of the time and social contexts in which they originate." *Scientists in Search of Their Conscience*, edited by A. R. Michaelis and H. Harvey, comprised papers from a Brussels international conference on the effect of science on society.

The Philosophy of Karl R. Popper, edited by Paul Schilpp, was added to the Library of Living Philosophers. Papers by Otto Neurath, Rudolf Carnap, Moritz Schlick, and others associated with the development of logical positivism were published in the *Vienna Circle Collection*.

Interest in Arabic philosophy grew in the West in 1974 as demonstrated by the publication of *Al-Kindi's Metaphysics*, a translation edited by Alfred Ivry of the 9th-century Baghdad philosopher's treatise "On First Philosophy." Other examples included *The Life of Ibn Sina* (Avicenna), an autobiography/biography of the 11th-century Persian philosopher edited and translated by William E. Gohlman, and the *Metaphysica of Avicenna*, translated with a critical commentary by Parviz Morewedge.

Among other scholarly publications was Immanuel Kant's *Logic*, translated by R. Hartman and W. Schwarz, the first complete translation to be published in English; *Kant's Political Thought*, by Hans Saner and translated by E. B. Ashton; *Hegel*, by Raymond Plant, a study of Hegel's political thought; and *Galileo: A Philosophical Study*, by Dudley Shapere. *Aristotle*, in two volumes by Anton-Hermann Chroust, concentrated on Aristotle's lost works and on "novel interpretations" of his life. Ludwig Wittgenstein's *Letters to Russell, Keynes, and Moore* was edited with an introduction by G. H. von Wright.

Brand Blanshard's *The Uses of a Liberal Education* was a major contribution to the philosophy of education. *Reason and Compassion*, by R. S. Peters of the University of London, was concerned especially with issues in moral education. *Reason and Teaching*, by Israel Scheffler of Harvard University, concentrated on the nature and meaning of education.

The vitality of existentialism was evidenced by numerous publications. These included Martin Heidegger's *The End of Philosophy*, which was concerned especially with the history of Being; Hazel E. Barnes's *Sartre*; and *Kierkegaard's Thought* by Gregor Malantschuk, edited and translated by H. B. and E. H. Hong.

In his Gifford Lectures, *The Problem of Metaphys-ics*, D. M. MacKinnon was concerned with the impingement of metaphysics upon experience. In *Causality and Determinism*, Georg Henrik von Wright held that the idea of causation derives from the fact that man can affect the course of events.

There was in 1974 no lessening of philosophic interest in art and aesthetic theory. Francis J. Kovach's *Philosophy of Beauty* treated the historical foundations of aesthetics, from Plato to Sartre. In *The Main of Light*, Justus Buchler analyzed the nature of poetry.

The 250th anniversary of the birth of Immanuel Kant was recognized by international congresses at Mainz and the University of Ottawa. Four volumes of the proceedings of the XV World Congress of Philosophy, held in 1973 at Varna, Bulg., were published.

(STERLING M. MCMURRIN)

[10/51; 10/52; 10/53]

ENCYCLOPÆDIA BRITANNICA FILMS. *The Medieval Mind* (1969); *Spirit of the Renaissance* (1971); *The Reformation: Age of Revolt* (1973); *An Essay on War* (1973).

Photography

During 1974 a great many firms produced cameras to take the new subminiature 110 cassette films. A wide range was now available, from the simple, cheap, single-speed type to precision models with automatically controlled electronic shutters. However, no designs had yet been marketed with reflex focusing or interchangeable lenses. An outstanding compact design was shown by Rollei at the 1974 Photokina exhibition in Cologne, W.Ger. Overall size was only $32 \times 44 \times 84$ mm.; it had a 23-mm. $f/2.8$ Tessar lens, and exposure control from 4 sec. at $f/2.8$ to 1/400 sec. at $f/16$ by a silicon photocell. A new 110 camera from Vivitar (a U.S.-Japanese company) had an integral electronic flash unit.

New range-finder 35-mm. cameras included the very compact Rollei 35 S, which was now available with a Sonnar $f/2.8$ five-element lens, and the Konica C35 EF. The latter had a small, retractable, built-in electronic flash that could be programmed for fill-in flash work as well as dim-light photography.

The most interesting camera shown in 1974 was undoubtedly the Rolleiflex SLX, a single-lens reflex cam-

Photographer Minor White with one of 77 works by 69 photographers gathered for his valedictory exhibition at the Massachusetts Institute of Technology.

ARTHUR GRACE—THE NEW YORK TIMES

era taking 6 × 6-cm. pictures. The basic aim of the design was to replace the largest possible number of mechanical functions with electronic controls. Each interchangeable lens contained its own leaf shutter and diaphragm, individually propelled by a newly designed pair of differential electromagnets (described as linear motors), one for the shutter blades and the other for the iris diaphragm. Three silicon cells behind the mirror measured light through the lens and compensated for stray light entering through the viewing screen. Centre-weighted exposure metering was employed for automatic setting of shutter speeds from 30 to 1/500 sec.; there was also manual override. Control was by an integrated circuit chip, approximately one centimetre square, incorporating about 500 different transistor functions. Exposure signals were given by light-emitting diodes alongside the finder screen. Automatic sequence exposures could be made at approximately three frames every two seconds. Another feature was drop-in loading utilizing an inexpensive film holder. The power source was a 9.6-volt nickel-cadmium battery that could be recharged in one hour and provided about 800 exposures (66 rolls).

At first sight, such a radical departure from normal camera design was surprising in the roll-film field. However, initial design was easier in the larger size, and subsequent development could be expected to produce a model for 35-mm. film, which would have 75 times the market potential. Meanwhile, the SLX might well have saved the 120 film size from extinction.

Lenses. A large number of new lenses were introduced during 1974. Most were duplicates, or slightly improved versions, of previously known types, but a few were of especial interest. Vivitar introduced a range of compact solid catadioptric (mirror) lenses, the longest focal length being a 1,200-mm. $f/11$, an 11-element design with an outer diameter of 151 mm. and a total physical length of 172 mm. Fuji revived the idea of variable softness of focus by the deliberate undercorrection of spherical aberration, the basic idea being that, since sharp images were now easily produced, a soft-focus effect was evidence of artistic interpretation and also conferred the old-fashioned look that was currently fashionable. Minolta announced a new 24-mm. $f/2.8$ lens with variable-field curvature. It could be employed to provide greater depth of field

The Rolleiflex SLX, Rollei's fully automated SLR camera featuring electromagnetically driven shutter and diaphragm and motorized film advance.

by suiting the curvature of the image to the main subject shape, which was an interesting departure from the usual assumption that cameras only photograph flat planes. Alternatively, converse action provided selective out-of-focus effects.

Canon stated that it had solved the problems associated with machine production of aspherical surfaces; previously, such lens surfaces had required skilled hand labour. It was estimated that lenses such as 24-mm. $f/1.4$ or 85-mm. $f/1.2$ designs could utilize a single aspherical surface at about half the previous cost.

It was generally accepted that long-focus zoom lenses could now be made with reasonable ease, using computer-derived designs, but that wider angle zooms presented greater difficulty. Nikkor extended the range to produce a 28- to 45-mm. Zoom Nikkor $f/4.5$, thus covering the wide-angle to normal range.

Flash and Lighting. New lamps initiate entire ranges of equipment as manufacturers design apparatus around the lamps. Thorn Electrical Industries Ltd. produced a 10-kw. tungsten-halogen lamp with an average life of 400 hours, about twice that of a conventional type. Several other new tungsten-halogen types appeared, including compact linear designs intended for use with recently introduced motion-picture cameras employing ASA 160 film. There were also several new compact source iodide (CSI) lamps, useful for filming since they could be used in any position, had a short run-up time, provided 50% more light than conventional designs, and permitted the use of lighter-weight housings.

Flashcubes appeared in a smaller size, about one-third the volume of the earlier type. Electronic flash units were introduced in profusion, in both amateur and studio designs. Automatic exposure control was a common feature, and more firms utilized thyristors in series with the capacitors to avoid wasting electricity. Another trend was toward the rapid charging of nickel-cadmium accumulators; this normally necessitated the use of sintered cell construction, which is more durable than the pressed plate method but also more expensive. The trend was toward reduced size and greater versatility but without radical changes.

Films and Processing. Kodacolor II replaced the former Kodacolor X in most parts of the world. Its high definition was essential for the small 110 negatives, but initial production problems were not eliminated until toward the end of 1974. Processing firms tended to delay the purchase of new plant until the future position could be seen more clearly. One difficulty was that the new Kodak processes worked at 100° F (38° C) and demanded very accurate time control. The new Kodachrome colour transparency films became available in the U.S., but it was not possible to introduce them in other countries during 1974. The types were Kodachrome 25 and 64, these figures referring to ASA speeds. An ASA 40 version also was available for motion-picture photography in artificial light.

In 1973 Agfa-Gevaert had introduced an improved colour negative film especially for the 110 size. In the spring of 1974 the same firm introduced an improved reversal film, Agfachrome 64, though supplies during the year were restricted to the U.S. At Photokina a CT 21 film was announced that was twice as fast as the existing CT 18. In general, increased interest was shown in colour photography, and several manufacturers provided kits of chemicals and equipment for home processing. There was general anxiety that the oil crisis would lead to shortages of basic chemicals such as hydroquinone, but in practice the effect was only to raise the price.

Chemicals for black-and-white photography are not normally of great interest, but one introduction in 1974 was outstanding. Aculux, devised by G. Crawley, provided slightly better results than the previous standard D-76, which had been used since 1929, and because it was a concentrated liquid instead of a powder it offered considerable advantages of convenience. The older developer could not be made as a concentrated liquid because the concentration of sodium sulfite (which acted as preservative and gentle silver solvent) was 100 g. per litre in the working solution.

Industry Developments. Worldwide expenditure on photography in 1974 was quoted at about $15 billion, some 20% higher than in the previous year. The 10% devaluation of the dollar, with the simultaneous floating of the yen, essentially canceled out the measures that had been taken to restrict Japanese exports. Hostilities in the Middle East and the ensuing oil crisis resulted in higher prices for raw materials. Other basic photographic costs also rose; the world price of silver nearly doubled during 1973–74, gelatin rose by 85%, raw paper by 35%, and cellulose by 15%. Coupled with higher wages, which particularly affect such labour-intensive industries as camera manufacture, these increases resulted in considerable price inflation.

Japanese production of still cameras during 1973 amounted to 6.8 million units, worth 131 billion yen and representing a 28% increase in volume and a 22% increase in value over the preceding year. The high volume increase was due to the great number of comparatively inexpensive 110 cartridge cameras produced. Of the total production, 43% went to Europe, 38.6% to North America, 10% to Asia, 3.4% to Central and South America, 3.2% to Oceania, and 1.6% to Africa. Importation into Japan totaled some 560,-000 units, representing an increase of 175% over the previous year.

Production in West Germany expanded by 16.1% to over DM. 2.5 billion, while exports rose by 17.8% to more than DM. 1.7 billion. However, profits were severely reduced. Most exports went to the EEC countries, which took 65%; the European Free Trade Area countries accounted for 21% and the U.S. for about 2%. Hardware imports totaled DM. 772.5 million, up 21.8%, but imports of sensitized material rose by only 2.6% to DM. 634.1 million.

In the U.K. expenditure on photography rose to £145 million in 1973, compared with £120 million the previous year. Films accounted for £32 million (£27 million in 1972); processing for £71 million (£56 million); and equipment for £24 million (£37 million). In the U.S. Eastman Kodak sales for 1973 showed a 16% increase to $4,035,520 ($3,477,764 in 1972), and profits rose 18%. Photographic exports from the U.S. exceeded imports by about $500 million.

There was general agreement that the recent rate of expansion in the photographic trade could not be maintained during 1974. The trend toward international cooperation among manufacturers continued and was manifested especially through mergers of West German and Japanese interests. Leitz of Wetzlar, W.Ger., and Minolta of Japan had already formed a connection, and a partnership was set up between Zeiss of West Germany and Yashica of Japan. Late in the year, Yashica was reported to be experiencing severe financial difficulties, attributable partly to poor management and partly to Japan's troubled economy. Rollei, the West German firm manufacturing mainly in Singa-

pore, continued to expand, though additional finance was required from banking organizations. In the search for cheaper labour, the Japanese firms of Canon, Asahi Optical, and Yashica made positive moves toward starting production in Hong Kong and Taiwan; Asahi also began building a factory in São Paulo, Brazil.

Exhibitions and Pictorialism. While the usual major photographic exhibitions, such as those of the Royal Photographic Society, London, were held, nothing of outstanding interest was shown. A transition stage appeared to have been reached between the old-style exhibition, where photographers strove for the approbation of other photographers, and the newer style where pictures were judged by their acceptance in the whole world of visual art. A major accolade to photography was the award of an Arts Council grant to the Photographers' Gallery in London.

An interesting collection of exhibitions was assembled at Cologne for Photokina. The motto "films, photos, multivisions" emphasized that the modern exhibition need not be confined to prints hung on a wall but could also include projected pictures, especially from slides. Some themes were historical, an example being "Movement in Pictures," which showed the state of the art in the last quarter of the 19th century. Two exhibitions from the Kodak Culture Program for Photokina also recalled the past with the "Hill/Adamson Albums" and "Snapshots Yesterday." The former showed photographs taken between 1843

"Advertising Poster," prizewinning entry by Bruce Pinkard in the commercial category of the annual Ilford photographic competition in Great Britain.

BRUCE PINKARD

and 1848; the albums containing the work had lain disregarded in the Royal Academy of Arts in London until plans to auction the pictures attracted public attention. "Snapshots Yesterday" proved that sheer age can enhance the attraction of the most casual photograph. As one critic paraphrased Samuel Johnson, "The marvel is not that they are good pictures, but that they could be taken at all."

"Images d'une France" by André Martin portrayed landscapes in soft pastel shades, sometimes achieving the magic of an Impressionist painting. Use of a very long lens allowed selection of small, characteristic areas of a scene with an absence of definite perspective scale or form. In contrast, "An American Sees Germany" by Ed Holcomb made full use of people in many instances, though again there was predilection for the romantic in scene and setting. Several exhibitions resulted from contests or competitions. "Around the World Cup '74," held jointly by the Deutsche Gesellschaft für Photographie and the German Television Service, attracted 4,399 entries.

Even more international was "One World for All," which supported the World Population Year 1974 proclaimed by the United Nations. The UN, the International Federation of Photographic Art, and the World Assembly of Youth were instrumental in obtaining the photographs. A selection of the 14,000 entries received from 45 countries inspired contemplation of the way of life of different peoples throughout the world.

Noteworthy individual exhibitions were shown by Hans Feurer (Switzerland), who won the 1974 Cultural Prize of the German Photographic Society; by Erwin Fieger (West Germany), known for his books on Mexico and Japan; by Francisco Hidalgo (Spain); by Eikoh Hosoe and Masaaki Nakagawa (both of Japan); by Gunter Sachs (West Germany); and by Tomas Sennett and Sonia L. Sheridan from the U.S. "The Ten Commandments Today," held in conjunction with the Institut für Kulturförderung, featured large placard-like photographs illustrating texts and creating symbols equivalent to the words.

(N. F. MAUDE)

See also Motion Pictures.
[628.D; 735.G.1]

Physics

Nuclear Physics. Although the realm of high-energy nuclear physics is becoming more and more difficult for the average practicing physicist to understand, recent developments in the subject have been quite fascinating. In fact, one nuclear physicist went so far as to say that we are in the midst of "the most exciting time in physics since the second world war."

A major cause of the excitement was the announcement by physicists at two U.S. research facilities that they had detected two new subatomic particles. On November 16 scientists working at the Stanford (Calif.) Linear Accelerator Center and the Brookhaven National Laboratory at Upton, N.Y., revealed that, independently, they had detected a new particle at an energy level of 3.1 GeV (billion electron volts). Named the J particle on the east coast and psi in the west, it had such unexpected properties as a lifetime before decay 1,000 times longer than would have been predicted and a weight $3\frac{1}{2}$ times that of the proton. Many scientists theorized that the new particle might be the long-sought manifestation of the weak force in atomic reactions. One week later the Stanford physicists announced that they had found a second particle, similar to the first, at an energy level of 3.7 GeV.

Results produced by new so-called "colliding beam" experiments, which allow careful studies to be made of electron-positron annihilation as a function of energy, were another cause of the excitement. Theoretical models suggest that the electron, the positron, and other fundamental particles are constituted from even more fundamental particles, quarks or partons. The quark is postulated to be a point particle, and a proton, for example, is made up of three quarks.

If electrons and positrons are made up of point scattering centres, then the scattering during the electron-positron annihilation experiments should exhibit scaling (that is, the scattering cross section should bear a functional relationship to the initial energy involved). The electron-positron experiment can result in the production of a number of hadrons (particles that interact via the strong nuclear interaction), and it is found that the cross section for this interaction is constant with increasing energy and thus seems at variance with the scaling rule. The annihilation experiment can also lead to the production of two muons (particles, in the same category as neutrinos and electrons, that do not participate in strong interactions), and in this case the cross section decreases with increasing energy, as expected. Thus, the overall ratio of cross section of multihadron production to cross section of muon production increases with energy, whereas in scaling theory it remains constant.

The next step for the experimentors is simple: the scaling experiments must be tested at higher energies. Previous experiments may have been conducted at energies too low for scaling to apply. For the theoretician the problem is not so straightforward, and during the year many different explanations were being aired. These ranged from the abandonment of the quark as the fundamental building block of all matter to the approach of Murray Gell-Mann, who first predicted the existence of quarks. He contended that protons, neutrons, and other fundamental particles are made up not simply of quarks but of quarks and "gluons." The gluons can be thought of as binding the quarks together. If Gell-Mann is correct, then current experiments may well have been carried out at too low an energy.

Rare Earth Metals. Research into the physics of the solid state depends for its success on the availability and purity of materials and in particular on pure single crystals. During the year notable progress was made in the purification of the rare earth metals, which initiated a series of new experiments.

The "heavy" rare earth metals, from gadolinium to lutetium in the periodic table, display a wide variety of magnetic structures and therefore have been of great interest to physicists. Only poor material has been available, however, because these elements have an affinity for oxygen, nitrogen, and hydrogen; also, the chemical properties of these elements are almost identical, making chemical separation difficult.

The first research paper on the subject, by R. G. Jordan and D. W. Jones, reported the purification of gadolinium (Gd) with an improvement of a factor of ten over previous techniques. A rod of Gd metal was supported in an ultrahigh vacuum and then heated to 1,100° C. Impurities were either evaporated or driven to the ends of the rod, leaving a pure centre portion. Repetition of this technique produced not only pure material but single crystals as well.

The first test of the new material was the experimental observation of the Fermi surface of Gd. The Fermi surface is the surface in reciprocal space that describes how the electrical conductivity of the metal, due to the conduction electrons, varies with crystallographic direction. The experimental technique requires that the electrons travel large distances in the material without being scattered by defects or impurities. A knowledge of the Fermi surface is vital in understanding the magnetic, electrical, and thermal properties of these materials, and experimental information is necessary to test the current theoretical models. In fact, it seems from the initial data that the theoretical physicists will in some cases have to modify or improve their models.

Work on terbium (Tb) and yttrium (Y) was under way, and successful Fermi surface studies of these materials were made. Samples of Gd, Tb, and Y were being used by various groups in the U.K. to study afresh their physical properties. For example, measurements of specific heat had been bedeviled by anomalous peaks in the range 1°–20° K. In Gd all workers had reported a peak at 3°–4° K. However, measurements by P. Wells, P. C. Lanchester, D. W. Jones, and R. G. Jordan on "pure" Gd found no peak in this range. The anomaly can now be clearly attributed to a Gd_2O_3 impurity present in the previous samples.

Superconductivity. In 1973 it was discovered that a niobium-germanium compound, Nb_3Ge, is the superconductor with the highest known critical temperature (T_c). J. R. Gavaler reported that in a zero applied magnetic field the material, in the form of a sputtered thin film, became superconducting when cooled to 22.3° K. This was supported by workers at Bell Telephone Laboratories, who reported that the T_c for Nb_3Ge is 23.2° K.

This discovery brings much closer the possibility of having superconducting devices that can use liquid hydrogen as refrigerant (the boiling point of hydrogen is 20.3° K). If the Nb_3Ge can be produced in a form suitable for magnetic coils, a breakthrough will be imminent.

Lasers. High-resolution spectroscopy has always been hampered by the problem of Doppler broadening. A monochromatic source of frequency w will have an apparent frequency of $w + w(v/c)$ to an atom moving back along a light beam with velocity v, and an apparent frequency $w - w(v/c)$ to an atom moving with the light beam (c is the velocity of light). Thus, the emitted light from the system will not be monochromatic but will have a Doppler profile characteristic of the temperature of the material under study. This has been overcome in the past by limiting the study to a single-velocity group of atoms, but this technique necessarily reduced the intensity of the emitted light enormously.

During the year three groups of investigators demonstrated that the technique of two-photon absorption can yield high-resolution spectra with no Doppler broadening. Each group studied a particular transition in sodium vapour. The first used a pulsed dye laser pumped with a flash lamp, the second employed a pulsed ultraviolet laser to pump a dye laser of much higher power, whereas the third used a continuous-wave dye laser pumped with an argon laser.

In all experiments the laser light is split into two beams and directed onto the sodium vapour from directions 180° apart. The laser frequency is so chosen that it is exactly half the energy level separation to be

studied; therefore, the simultaneous absorption by an atom of a photon from each beam will cause its transition from the lower to the higher energy. The Doppler shift from one beam is of opposite sign to that of the other beam and is of equal magnitude and thus is eliminated.

The prospect ahead is the full utilization of the single-frequency laser source in spectroscopy. Measurement of energy level separations to an accuracy of 1 in 10^{17} were being discussed, and if this could ever be achieved more accurate length standards would be possible. The technique could also be useful for triggering efficient photochemical reactions with possible applications to uranium and hydrogen isotope separation for reaction use. (S. B. PALMER)

See also Astronomy; Chemistry; Space Exploration. [111.H; 121.A.12; 125.D.8; 128.B.4]

ENCYCLOPÆDIA BRITANNICA FILMS. *Introduction to Lasers* (1973); *Introduction to Holography* (1973).

At the University of California's Livermore Radiation Laboratory, the "2X II" facility is a major tool in the search for ways to harness nuclear fusion as a source of abundant, pollution-free energy.

Poland

A people's republic of Eastern Europe, Poland is bordered by the Baltic Sea, the U.S.S.R., Czechoslovakia, and East Germany. Area: 120,725 sq.mi. (312,677 sq.km.). Pop. (1974 est.): 33,692,000. Cap. and largest city: Warsaw (pop., 1974 est., 1,393,600). Language: Polish. Religion: predominantly Roman Catholic. First secretary of the Polish United Workers' (Communist) Party in 1974, Edward Gierek; chairman of the Council of State, Henryk Jablonski; chairman of the Council of Ministers (premier), Piotr Jaroszewicz.

On July 22, 1974, the Polish People's Republic celebrated its 30th anniversary. The new regime had sought to repair the country's enormous war ravages in the shortest possible time and to transform Poland from an agricultural country into a modern industrial power. Thirty years later this ambitious and difficult task was almost completed. Between 1938 and 1973 yearly per capita income rose in Poland from $200 to $1,300, and in 1973 industrial production was 20 times larger than before World War II and Poland occupied tenth place among the world's industrial powers. Agricultural production in the first postwar years

Pipelines:
see Energy; Transportation

Plastics Industry:
see Industrial Production and Technology

Platinum:
see Mining and Quarrying

Poetry:
see Literature

Polish coal miners, well paid and, in a time of global energy shortage, optimistic about their future.

was low, but by 1970–73 the average yearly harvest of grain, potatoes, and sugar beet was twice as large as that of 1934–38.

Speaking in the Sejm (parliament) on July 21, Edward Gierek attributed these achievements to hard work, correct policy, and cooperation with the Soviet Union and other socialist countries. Replying to Gierek's speech, Leonid I. Brezhnev, general secretary of the Communist Party of the U.S.S.R. and the only prominent foreign guest, congratulated the Poles on their achievement and assured them of Soviet friendship. Gala events began with the opening in Gdansk, on July 18, of the new Northern Port, the largest on the Baltic Sea, which on that day started exporting coal. In 1975 crude oil from the Middle East was to be imported and, accordingly, a refinery was under construction there. In Warsaw the Royal Castle, which was virtually destroyed by the Germans in World War II, was already roofed and the clock in the main tower began working again.

Stefan Olszowski, the foreign minister, paid an official visit to Great Britain on April 8–10. A joint communiqué welcomed the continuing development of mutual economic and commercial relations. Between 1970 and 1973 British exports to Poland rose from £59 million to £111.2 million, while imports from Poland increased from £63 million to £95.1 million. In 1973 Poland overtook the U.S.S.R. for the first time to become Britain's leading market in Eastern Europe. On August 23 a Polish-British cooperation agreement worth £155 million was signed in London with the Massey-Ferguson-Perkins group. In October Britain's Princess Alexandra and her husband, Angus Ogilvy, paid a visit to Krakow and Warsaw. The princess visited the rebuilt Warsaw Royal Castle to present a 14-piece set of antique furniture as a gift from the British people.

Gierek paid an official visit to the United States on October 6–13. After talks with Pres. Gerald Ford and Secretary of State Henry Kissinger, six technical agreements and two political declarations were signed. An official communiqué noted the rapid increase of Polish-U.S. trade. As a result of the freeing of credits by the U.S. Export-Import Bank, Poland's trade turnover with the U.S. grew between 1971 and 1973 from $180 million to $543 million. Among Poland's capitalist partners the U.S. now stood third, after West Germany and Great Britain. It was expected

that in 1974 U.S.-Polish goods turnover would reach a total of $700 million, and $1 billion and $2 billion were forecast for 1976 and 1980 respectively.

Normalization of relations between Poland and West Germany had slowed down somewhat during 1973. In the summer of 1974 Chancellor Helmut Schmidt and Gierek exchanged letters in which they agreed to revive economic talks between Bonn and Warsaw. As a result a ten-year agreement on economic, industrial, and technical cooperation between the two states was signed in Bonn on November 1. Between 1971 and 1973 the trade turnover between Poland and West Germany rose from DM. 1.5 billion to DM. 3 billion.

Michel Poniatowski, French deputy premier and minister of the interior, paid an official visit to Warsaw in September. In a discussion with Deputy Premier Mieczyslaw Jagielski, Poniatowski proposed a barter arrangement under which France would increase imports of Polish coal (2 million tons had been exported to France in 1973) in exchange for French capital equipment. In 1973 French credits to Poland had been increased from Fr. 2,250,000,000 to Fr. 4.5 billion, and now it was agreed to increase them to Fr. 8 billion.

Archbishop Agostino Casaroli, secretary of the Roman Catholic Church's Council for Public Affairs, arrived in Warsaw on February 4 on an official visit. He had talks with Olszowski, Jerzy Kuberski, minister of education, and Aleksander Skarzynski, head of the Office for Religious Affairs. Asked at the end of his five-day visit what was the outcome of his talks with the Polish ministers, Msgr. Casaroli replied that he was "moderately optimistic" but it would be too early to speak about the establishment of diplomatic relations between Poland and the Vatican. Early in July Jozef Czyrek, a deputy foreign minister, visited the Vatican to discuss the matter with Msgr. Casaroli, and it was decided that the Holy See and Poland would initiate "permanent working contacts." At the beginning of October the Polish government appointed Kazimierz Szablewski, an official in the Foreign Ministry, as minister plenipotentiary at the Polish embassy in Rome to maintain "working contacts" with the Vatican. On November 6, after another visit from Czyrek in Rome, the Vatican appointed Msgr. Luigi Poggi as head of its delegation for "working contacts" with Szablewski. In the meantime Kazimierz Kakol

---

POLAND

Education. (1973–74) Primary, pupils 4,778,600, teachers 200,600; secondary, pupils 639,100, teachers 22,800; vocational, pupils 1,922,100, teachers 77,100; teacher training, pupils 24,300, teachers (1970–71) 3,742; higher (including 10 main universities), students 394,300, teaching staff 41,308.

Finance. Monetary unit: zloty, with (Sept. 16, 1974) a basic rate of 20 zlotys to U.S. $1 (46.50 zlotys = £1 sterling) and a tourist rate of 33.20 zlotys to U.S. $1 (75 zlotys = £1 sterling). Budget (1973 est.): revenue 467 billion zlotys; expenditure 466 billion zlotys. National income (net material product): (1973) 1,062,500,000,000 zlotys; (1972) 947.8 billion zlotys.

Foreign Trade. (1973) Imports 26,103,000,000 zlotys; exports 21,355,000,000 zlotys. Import sources: U.S.S.R. 24%; West Germany 12%; East Germany 9%; Czechoslovakia 8%; U.K. 5%. Export destinations: U.S.S.R. 32%; East Germany 10%; Czechoslovakia 8%; West Germany 7%. Main exports (1970): machinery 31%; coal 10%; iron and steel 7%; textiles and clothing 6%; meat and products 6%; ships and boats 5%.

Transport and Communications. Roads (1973) 299,876 km. (including 139 km. express-ways). Motor vehicles in use (1973): passenger 780,874; commercial 324,268. Railways: (1972) 23,558 km. (including 4,359 km. electrified); traffic (1973) 39,647,000,000 passenger-km., freight 116,442,000,000 net ton-km. Air traffic (1973): 1,073,000,000 passenger-km.; freight 11.8 million net ton-km. Shipping (1973): merchant vessels 100 gross tons and over 631; gross tonnage 2,072,531. Telephones (Dec. 1972) 2,087,000. Radio licenses (Dec. 1972) 5,795,000. Television licenses (Dec. 1972) 5.2 million.

Agriculture. Production (in 000; metric tons; 1973; 1972 in parentheses): wheat c. 5,900 (5,147); rye c. 8,300 (8,149); barley c. 3,400 (2,750); oats c. 3,000 (3,212); potatoes c. 45,000 (48,735); sugar, raw value c. 1,740 (1,830); rapeseed c. 570 (430); linseed c. 60 (64); dry peas c. 60 (c. 60); onions c. 326 (326); tomatoes c. 412 (394); apples (1972) c. 560, (1971) 563; pears (1972) c. 150, (1971) 101; tobacco c. 78 (75); flax fibre (1972) c. 55, (1971) 60; butter (1972) c. 215, (1971) 202; cheese (1972) c. 250, (1971) 250; beef and veal (1972) c. 550, (1971) 536; pork (1972) c. 1,350, (1971) 1,313; timber (cu.m.; 1972) 18,700, (1971) 18,300; fish catch (1972) 544, (1971) 518. Livestock (in 000; June 1973): cattle 12,192; horses (1972) 2,422; pigs 19,782; sheep 3,050; chickens (1972) c. 155,000.

Industry. Index of industrial production (1970 = 100): (1973) 133; (1972) 120. Fuel and power (in 000; metric tons; 1973): coal 156,629; brown coal 39,215; coke (1972) 15,874; crude oil (1972) 347; natural gas (cu.m.) 6,026,000; manufactured gas (cu.m.; 1972) 6,942,000; electricity (kw-hr.) 84,287,000. Production (in 000; metric tons; 1973): cement 15,548; iron ore (metal content; 1972) 497; pig iron 8,137; crude steel 14,057; aluminum 62; zinc (1972) 228; copper (1972) 131; lead (1972) 65; petroleum products (1972) 9,182; sulfuric acid 2,914; fertilizers (nutrient content; 1972) nitrogenous 1,147, phosphate 763; cotton yarn 215; wool yarn 89; rayon, etc., filament yarn and fibres 95; nylon, etc., filament yarn and fibres 81; cotton fabrics (m.) 868,000; woolen fabrics (m.) 107,000; rayon and synthetic fabrics (m.; 1972) 108,000; passenger cars (units) 113; commercial vehicles (units) 69. Merchant vessels launched (100 gross tons and over; 1973) 551,000 gross tons. New dwelling units completed (1973) 167,000.

succeeded Skarzynski as head of the Office for Religious Affairs.

On February 16 Stanislaw Wronski was dismissed as minister of culture and art and replaced by Jozef Tejchma, who retained his position of deputy premier. Kazimierz Barcikowski left the party secretariat to succeed Jozef Okuniewski as minister of agriculture. The day before three new secretaries of the Central Committee were elected: Wincenty Krasko, member of the Council of State; Andrzej Werblan, deputy speaker of the Sejm; and Jozef Pinkowski, formerly deputy chairman of the Planning Commission. Further changes followed in June and November, including the replacement of Jan Mitrega by Jan Kulpinski as minister of mining and energy, of Kazimierz Olszewski by Jerzy Olszewski (no relation) as minister of foreign trade, of Stefan Jedrychowski by Henryk Kisiel as minister of finance, and of Wincenty Kawalec by Tadeusz Rudolf as minister of labour, pay, and social service. (K. M. SMOGORZEWSKI)

[972.B.2.d]

Political Science

Politics presented scholars with many challenges in 1974. Two general elections in the United Kingdom, Pres. Georges Pompidou's death and the subsequent presidential elections in France, Chancellor Willy Brandt's replacement in West Germany, and Pres. Juan Perón's death in Argentina would have sufficed to make the year exceptionally eventful. The drama that led to U.S. Pres. Richard Nixon's resignation in August and the international crisis produced by the October 1973 war in the Middle East with the subsequent Arab oil embargo and rise in oil prices could not but attract even more attention.

Such circumstances made it apparent that the debate on the relevance of political science was far from exhausted. The social sciences deal with regularities; it is difficult for them to illuminate single events and individual decisions, which are often the very meat of politics. Rigorous studies of public opinion, attitudes, and bureaucratic behaviour provide indispensable background. They allow political scientists to delineate plausible limits to action and the course of events, but are no substitute for analysis of a far less scientific nature applied to the actions of political leaders.

The complementary nature of the two approaches was very apparent in 1974. Few political scientists of the behavioural persuasion had much to say about the crisis that forced President Nixon out of the White House. The forefront was occupied by constitutional lawyers, long considered somewhat irrelevant to the modern study of politics, and by a small group of so-called psycho-historians. Scientific analysis would undoubtedly contribute much to a deeper explanation of the U.S. political crisis, but its methods were necessarily slow and ill-adapted to singular situations.

In the same way, while in many respects the fourth Arab-Israeli war conformed to the conceptual schemata of international relations theorists, its aftermath was perhaps better analyzed by historians, economists, journalists, and politicians than by the more scientific-minded political scientists.

The wish to combine intellectual rigour and political relevance was apparent in the choice made by the Executive Committee of the International Political Science Association (IPSA) of a general topic for the tenth IPSA Congress, to be organized in Edinburgh,

Scot., in 1976: "Time, Space and Politics." IPSA held a roundtable meeting in Jerusalem in September 1974 on "Problems of National Integration," also a topic of immediate interest in many countries.

At Strasbourg, France, in April, the European Consortium for Political Research (ECPR) held its second round of simultaneous workshops, on a variety of topics. It was apparent that through the efforts of the ECPR, established in 1970, contacts among European political scientists had intensified rapidly, at the very time when the discipline was gaining recognition in countries where indifference or even hostility had greeted previous efforts at establishing it.

In a mail ballot conducted in November 1973, Austin Ranney, of the University of Wisconsin (Madison), was elected president of the American Political Science Association for 1974–75.

Political science journals continued to proliferate. Among recent additions were: *American Politics Quarterly* (Beverly Hills, Calif.); *Black Politician* (Los Angeles, Calif.); *Capitol Studies* (Washington, D.C.); *Études polémologiques* (Paris, France); *European Journal of Political Research* (Amsterdam, Neth.); *International Relations* (Prague, Czech.); *Journal of Contemporary Asia* (Stockholm, Swed.); *Mondes en Développement* (Paris, France); *Ocean Development and International Law Journal* (New York, N.Y.); *Philosophy and Public Affairs* (Princeton, N.J.); *Politeia* (Caracas, Venez.); *Political Science Reviewer* (Hampden-Sydney, Austr.); *Publius* (Philadelphia, Pa.); *Studi parlamentari e di Politica costituzionale* (Rom, Italy); *Theory and Decision* (Dordrecht, Neth.). (SERGE HURTIG)

[541; 542]

ENCYCLOPÆDIA BRITANNICA FILMS. *The Presidency—Search for a Candidate* (1970); *The Progressive Era* (1971); *Where's Your Loyalty?* (1972); *Who Needs Rules?* (1972); *The United States Congress: Of, By and For the People* (2nd ed., 1973); *The United States Supreme Court: Guardian of the Constitution* (2nd ed., 1973); *President of the United States: Too Much Power?* (1973).

Populations and Areas

World population approximated 4,000,000,000 during 1974, representing a gain of about 75 million people. There were no indications of a slowing in the 2% growth rate that would double the number of people on earth in only 35 years unless checked.

Concern over population was being registered throughout the world. The threat of famine in many African and Asian countries, coupled with skyrocketing increases in the prices of food, fuel, and fertilizer, dramatized the need to slow the growth of human numbers. Furthermore, rapid growth seemed to go hand in hand with underdevelopment and poverty.

continued on page 561

Table I. The Ten Largest Nations by Area and Population, 1974

Rank	Area in sq.mi.	Rank	Population
1. U.S.S.R.	8,649,500	1. China	800,000,000
2. Canada	3,851,809	2. India	586,056,000
3. China	3,691,500	3. U.S.S.R.	252,000,000
4. United States	3,615,122	4. United States	211,909,000
5. Brazil	3,286,488	5. Indonesia	127,600,000
6. Australia	2,967,900	6. Japan	109,700,000
7. India	1,266,602	7. Brazil	104,641,500
8. Argentina	1,072,163	8. Nigeria	79,760,000*
9. Sudan	967,500	9. Bangladesh	71,316,500
10. Zaire	905,365	10. Pakistan	69,370,000

*November 1973 census; UN estimate midyear 1973, 59,607,000.

Police:
see Crime and Law Enforcement

WORLD POPULATION YEAR

By Jon Tinker

The United Nations designated 1974 as World Population Year. For the first time, international politicians became fully aware of an issue that could well dominate their thinking for the next half century. To some, the politicizing of the population problem was a matter for rejoicing, because politics is the only means, however imperfect, for solving international issues. To others, politicization was a disaster, for it meant the end of rational and dispassionate discussion. In August delegates from 135 sovereign states came together in Bucharest, Rom., for the first World Population Conference. Their proceedings provided ample evidence to justify both schools of thought.

The Problem. A quick look at the growth of human population makes two points very clear. First, mankind's numbers are increasing rapidly; second, the rate of growth is itself increasing. It took from the dawn of history until 1850 before there were 1 billion (1,000 million) people on earth. The second billion was reached about the time of the 1929 Wall Street crash, and the third billion when John F. Kennedy was elected president of the U.S. in 1960. In 1974 there were about 3.8 billion, and the fourth billion will probably be reached by 1976. For the more distant future, an element of speculation creeps in. If things go on as they are, there will probably be 7 billion by the year 2001 and 13 billion by 2050. If, on the other hand, a staggeringly successful program to persuade people to have fewer children is undertaken within the next decade, there might be 6 billion instead of 7 billion in 2001 and 8 billion instead of 13 billion in 2050. Whether humanity wishes to exercise this option is the question that the World Population Year was meant to ask.

The complexities of human population dynamics are not easy for mathematically sophisticated individuals to grasp, so it is hardly surprising that they are barely comprehended by governments and the general public. For example, an annual net population increase of 3%—the current figure in Ghana, Iran, and Cambodia—sounds comfortably small. Yet if this increase is sustained, the population will double every 24 years.

Perhaps hardest to appreciate is the concept of population momentum, which means that the growth of a predominantly young population is extraordinarily hard to bring to a halt. Clearly, a country where each couple produces two children will eventually have a stable population, for each two parents will leave two children behind them when they die. (In fact, allowing for those who never marry, for childless couples, and for a degree of child mortality, the replacement level of fertility is about 2.1 children per family.) However, a population that suddenly reduces its completed family size to replacement level will not cease to grow at once, because it will still contain a disproportionate number of young people derived from the larger families of previous generations.

A fast-growing population cannot be stabilized until a whole human lifespan after replacement fertility is reached. Japan, for instance, reduced family size down to replacement size in about 1960. But overall Japanese numbers are still growing at an annual rate of about 1%, and are not expected to level off until about the year 2030.

Jon Tinker is a consultant to New Scientist *who has written widely on matters affecting the human and natural environment.*

Taking Sides at Bucharest. As the debates of the World Population Conference quickly showed, there was to be little verbal agreement at Bucharest. One of the countries that fought hard for recognition of the growing crisis was Indonesia, the fifth most populous nation in the world. There, population control already ranks number two in national priorities, second only to economic development. At present, there are about 125 million Indonesians, but by 2001 there could be around 270 million of them. And 70% of Indonesia's population is located on the two islands of Java and Bali, which together are little bigger than Alabama. Most Western and Asian nations were prepared to support the modest action targets of the draft World Population Plan of Action. Such countries as Tunisia, Mexico, Iran, and Jamaica pleaded for urgent action. The delegate from Bangladesh, whose 75 million people are doubling every 25 years, appealed eloquently for the plan. "Our part of the world is sinking under the population explosion. We are short of food, short of educational facilities, short of everything."

The majority, though, dismissed this analysis as "neo-Malthusian." Algeria, Tanzania, and Senegal joined with Argentina and Brazil in the dismemberment of the World Population Plan, a task in which they were aided, for ideological reasons, by the unlikely alliance of China, the U.S.S.R., and the Holy See. China in particular savaged the whole concept of a world population crisis. "It is absurd to suggest that developing countries are poor because of population problems," the Chinese insisted. "The real reasons are colonialism, exploitation, and economic deception."

The draft plan was cut to ribbons. Out went a commitment to give all the world's citizens access to family-planning services by 1985; out went an unqualified invitation to all countries to set birthrate goals and to try and achieve them by 1985. Although well over half the human race lives in countries whose governments are trying to reduce present levels of human fertility, this fact offended the religious or political susceptibilities of many nations and was removed from the conference conclusions. To many observers, the most ludicrous move of all came when China, which operates the largest and most successful program of birth control ever known, demanded the suppression of two UN reports on its population policy and the deletion from the conference documents of all statistics on China's population.

Population and Development. The failure of Bucharest to confront the population crisis was on one level profoundly depressing, and it certainly demonstrated an ominous contempt for the demographic facts of life. The trouble was that relatively few delegations were considering the *world* population crisis, while their estimates of their own national population problems varied enormously. Most of the African states, for example, think themselves underpopulated and are more concerned with reducing their appallingly high death rates than with cutting down on births.

The opposition to the World Population Plan, although frequently expressed in extreme and even nonrational terms, was founded on two points. First, the Afro–Latin-American–Communist bloc argued that the root cause of the third world's problems was underdevelopment and not overpopulation. They clearly suspected that the Western emphasis on population control was a device to turn attention away from what they saw as the rich nations' disproportionate share of the world's money, natural resources, and technology. Second, they considered that a high birthrate and a population explosion were the natural consequence of a low standard of living, and that just as Europe had gone through a demographic transition in which the population rose with industrialization and the birthrate then fell with increasing affluence, so the same pattern would be followed in the rest of the world. Their view may be summed up in the unofficial Bucharest slogan: "Take care of the people, and the population will take care of itself."

The argument between those who hold that overpopulation is caused by poverty and those who say that poverty is caused by overpopulation is, of course, based on a false antithesis. In fact,

(Above) Uncaptioned cartoon by Steve Brodner, first-prize winner
in a competition sponsored by the Population Institute; (right) opening
session of the UN World Population Conference in Bucharest, Rom., August 19.

overpopulation and poverty feed on each other. While some resources (labour power, for instance) increase in proportion to
the population, others (the area of cultivable land, for example)
clearly do not. Given the fact that some resources are inelastic,
the individual's share of the cake is likely to decline as more
people are invited to the party. At the same time, a high birthrate is to some extent caused by poverty and insecurity, especially
in peasant, nonwelfare societies. The more children a couple
have, the more hands there are to work the land and the greater
the number of descendants they will possess to look after them
in their old age.

In this argument, the concept of demographic transition is
crucial. Essentially, this is based on the thesis that the population
explosion in the third world has paralleled that of 19th-century
Europe in its origins and will do so in its disappearance. As a
dogma the idea is no doubt admirable, but as a theory grounded
in historical experience it leaves much to be desired. In England,
for instance, fertility peaked around 1870, over a century after
the Industrial Revolution had started. In France, on the other
hand, fertility began to drop in the 1750s before any significant
industrialization had occurred.

Moreover, even if the demographic patterns of European nations had been similar, the analogy with less developed nations
today would not be encouraging. Most countries in Europe took
nearly a century to double their numbers, and the annual rate
of population growth rarely averaged more than 0.7%. Today,
Asian numbers are growing at an average of 2%, Africa is increasing at 2.4%, and Latin America at 2.9%.

However, the view that "aid" from the rich nations should be
devoted solely to controlling population growth is not held by
any responsible government. Conversely, the laissez-faire argument that it is positively wrong to spend any money on family
planning is advanced only by the most extreme proponents of
uncontrolled demographic expansion. Stripped of the rhetoric,
the dispute is one of balance: how much development, and how
much birth control?

What Was Omitted. One of the major defects of the Bucharest
conference was that many aspects of the population problem were
deliberately ignored. For example, the official speeches and resolutions repeatedly stressed that population was a matter exclusively within the national jurisdiction of each sovereign state,
an attitude that made it difficult to focus attention on the global
aspects of population. This also made it impossible to discuss
demographic aggression. It has, for example, been one of the
conventions of French politics since Napoleonic times that France
must increase its population to counter the growing German
menace from across the Rhine. Again, the vociferously pro-
natalist policies of Brazil have already played a significant part
in stimulating similar attitudes in Peru and Argentina.

Another taboo topic was that of forcing birth control on an
unwilling populace. The city-state of Singapore has come face-
to-face with the population crisis earlier than most. This largely
Chinese nation is confined to a small island, and efforts at limiting population growth have already included methods that stick
unpleasantly in the liberal throat: the refusal of free medical
facilities and schooling after the third child, for instance. There
are also ominous portents for the future. Though the official
birth-control campaign has made great headway among the urban,
educated, Chinese majority, it has been less successful among

the poorer, rural, Malay minority. The Singapore government
is already hinting at more draconian measures, and the potenti-
alities for intercommunal strife are considerable. Nor are these
dangers confined to Singapore; almost every state contains significant minorities that for religious, cultural, or political reasons
might fail to obey a national call for smaller families.

The most humane—some would argue the only humane—
method of reducing the birthrate is contraception. But there are
other means, and they may be used if contraception fails. Abortion as a form of birth control is already accepted in many
countries: Japan and Venezuela, for instance. Unthinkable though
it may seem, infanticide may be next on the list; it was a respected means of birth control for centuries and remains part
of the subculture of the urban European poor. Nor is compulsory
sterilization as inconceivable today as it was a decade ago.

However, there is often a considerable difference between
what national governments feel constrained to say on formal
occasions and what they actually do, as the remarkable contrast
between China's birth-control program at home and its passionate
defense of population explosion abroad showed. Indeed, the
realization of the gravity of the population crisis was more widespread than the official Bucharest resolutions suggest.

An expression of the private feelings of many official delegates
was contained in the "Statement from Bucharest," drafted by
U.S. anthropologist Margaret Mead and signed by the majority of
nongovernmental organizations present.

> The world situation is potentially disastrous. Hundreds of millions
> are suffering from hunger, poverty, persecution, disease and illiteracy.
> The unprecedented rate of population growth, doubling population
> from 3 to 6 billion in a generation, will strain the environment and
> man's social, political and economic institutions to breaking point.
> Action to meet this challenge is imperative. . . . Some countries con-
> sume and waste the earth's resources at a rate that cannot be main-
> tained. Others have densely-settled regions with population growth
> rates of 2 or 3 percent a year that will exert demands on the inter-
> national community which may not be met. The urgency of the global
> crisis must not be ignored nor submerged beneath national ambitions.

Although strictly unofficial, this statement might well be remembered as the Bucharest document most accurately reflecting
the growing anxiety that led to World Population Year.

Table II. World Census Data*

Country	Date of census	Total population	% Male	% Female	% Urban	0 to 14	15 to 29	30 to 44	45 to 59	60 to 74	75 and over	Total	% of total pop.	Agriculture; forestry; fisheries	Mining; mfg.; const.	Service; utilities; finance; govt.
						AGE DISTRIBUTION (%)						ECONOMICALLY ACTIVE				
Afars and Issas	1960–61	81,200	...	...	57.4	...	...	...	...	...	...	...	...	...	...	...
Albania	1960	1,626,315	51.4	48.6	30.9	42.7	...	...	...	...	...	730,762	44.9	...	...	...
Algeria	1966	11,833,126	50.2	49.8	38.8	47.1	22.4	14.9	8.7	5.0	1.8	2,598,100	21.9	50.1	11.7	38.2
American Samoa	1970	27,159	50.4	49.6	28.0	47.4	25.5	14.5	8.8	3.1	0.7	5,385	19.8	2.0	32.9	65.1
Andorra	1971	20,550	...	...	...	...	...	...	...	...	...	...	...	...	...	...
Angola	1970	5,673,046	...	...	14.9	...	...	...	...	...	...	...	...	...	...	...
Antigua	1970	70,000	...	...	...	...	...	...	...	...	...	...	...	...	...	...
Argentina	1970	23,364,431	49.7	50.3	80.4	29.3	24.6	19.9	15.4	8.6	2.2	9,011,450	38.6	14.8	20.6	64.6
Australia	1971	12,755,638	50.3	49.7	...	28.8	24.6	18.3	16.0	9.2	3.1	5,240,428	41.1	7.4	32.5	60.1
Austria	1971	7,456,403	47.0	53.0	51.9	24.4	20.5	18.3	16.5	15.5	4.8	3,097,986	41.5	13.8	40.7	45.5
Bahamas, The	1970	168,812	50.0	50.0	71.4	43.6	24.3	16.8	9.8	4.4	1.1	69,791	41.3	6.9	17.7	75.4
Bahrain	1971	216,078	53.8	46.2	78.1	44.3	25.3	16.9	9.0	3.7	0.8	60,301	27.9	6.6	14.0	79.4
Bangladesh	1974	71,316,517	51.8	48.2	...	...	...	...	...	...	...	...	...	...	...	...
Barbados	1970	235,229	48.0	52.0	3.7	35.9	27.2	12.9	12.8	8.7	2.5	83,669	35.1	21.3	13.8	64.9
Belgium	1970	9,650,944	48.9	51.1	...	23.5	21.0	19.4	17.1	14.4	4.6	3,637,818	37.1	4.5	34.3	61.2
Belize	1970	119,934	50.6	49.4	54.4	49.3	22.5	13.0	8.7	5.0	1.5	...	...	...	...	...
Bermuda	1970	52,976	50.2	49.8	6.9	29.7	25.8	20.5	——24.0——			27,319	52.2	1.6	19.4	79.0
Bhutan	1969	1,034,774	...	...	...	...	...	...	...	...	...	...	...	...	...	...
Bolivia	1950	2,704,165	49.0	51.0	34.9	39.6	27.2	16.6	9.4	5.5	1.7	...	...	...	...	...
Botswana	1971	574,094	45.7	54.3	8.4	46.1	21.7	12.8	9.0	5.0	5.4	51,408	9.0	22.5	20.2	57.3
Brazil	1970	93,139,037	49.7	50.3	55.9	41.7	27.0	——31.3——				29,557,224	31.7	44.3	19.2	36.5
British Solomon Islands	1970	160,998	52.9	47.1	7.0	44.6	25.3	15.9	8.9	4.0	1.3	13,690	8.5	23.2	12.5	64.3
British Virgin Islands	1970	10,298	53.0	47.0	21.9	39.2	29.1	14.7	10.0	5.1	1.9	3,842	37.3	7.8	9.9	82.3
Brunei	1971	136,256	53.4	46.6	63.6	43.4	28.0	15.7	8.1	3.9	0.9	40,012	29.4	11.9	22.1	66.0
Bulgaria	1965	8,227,866	50.0	50.0	46.5	17.8	22.6	23.8	16.5	10.3	9.0	4,267,798	51.9	44.3	26.4	29.3
Cambodia	1962	5,728,771	50.0	50.0	10.3	43.8	24.9	16.8	9.8	4.1	0.6	2,499,735	43.6	80.3	2.8	16.9
Canada	1971	21,568,211	50.0	50.0	76.1	29.6	18.6	25.1	10.6	10.9	5.2	...	...	...	...	...
Canal Zone	1970	44,198	54.9	45.1	5.8	31.8	31.3	19.8	14.1	2.2	0.8	9,776	22.1	1.3	20.3	78.4
Cape Verde Islands	1970	272,071	...	...	19.7	...	...	...	...	...	...	...	...	...	...	...
Cayman Islands	1970	10,249	46.8	53.2	61.1	38.6	——61.4——					...	...	...	...	...
Channel Islands																
Guernsey	1971	53,734	48.2	51.8	30.3	23.1	20.6	17.5	18.3	15.2	5.3	23,813	44.3	23.1	10.4	66.5
Jersey	1971	72,629	48.7	51.3	...	20.5	22.2	19.4	18.0	14.6	5.3	34,641	50.0	18.3	22.5	59.2
Chile	1970	8,884,768	48.8	51.2	75.1	39.0	25.5	16.6	10.4	5.6	2.9	2,624,817	29.5	21.4	17.8	60.8
China	1953	574,205,940	51.8	48.2	13.3	35.9	25.1	18.8	12.9	6.3	1.0	...	...	...	...	...
Colombia	1973	12,962,204	...	...	...	...	...	...	...	...	...	...	...	...	...	...
Comoro Islands	1966	244,905	49.2	50.8	13.9	44.1	23.6	15.7	8.7	4.2	3.8	82,090	33.5	63.9	17.6	18.5
Congo	1974	1,300,120	...	...	39.8	...	...	...	...	...	...	...	...	...	...	...
Cook Islands	1971	21,317	51.2	48.8	0	51.6	22.5	12.5	——14.4——			5,581	26.2	21.9	24.0	54.1
Costa Rica	1973	1,871,780	50.1	49.9	40.6	43.3	27.0	14.2	8.4	4.4	2.7	574,483	30.7	37.5	22.5	40.0
Cuba	1970	8,569,121	51.3	48.7	60.3	27.0	25.0	16.9	12.1	6.8	2.2	2,633,309	30.7	30.0	20.3	49.7
Cyprus	1973	632,000	49.5	50.5	42.1	28.8	27.4	16.9	13.3	——13.5——		...	...	...	...	...
Czechoslovakia	1970	14,344,987	48.7	51.3	55.5	23.1	24.8	18.4	16.7	13.6	3.4	6,982,502	48.7	16.4	48.0	35.6
Denmark	1970	4,937,784	...	...	79.9	23.2	23.8	17.7	17.8	13.4	4.1	...	...	...	...	...
Dominica	1970	70,302	47.4	52.6	46.2	49.1	21.2	11.2	10.0	6.3	2.2	19,617	28.2	39.4	7.9	52.7
Dominican Republic	1970	4,006,405	50.4	49.6	40.0	47.2	24.8	15.2	7.8	3.8	1.2	...	...	...	...	...
Ecuador	1974	6,480,801	50.0	50.0	41.4	...	...	...	...	...	...	...	...	...	...	...
Egypt	1966	30,075,858	50.5	49.5	41.2	...	...	...	...	...	...	8,396,573	27.9	53.2	13.1	33.7
El Salvador	1971	3,541,010	49.6	50.4	39.4	46.2	25.1	15.2	8.2	4.3	1.0	2,376,633	67.1	3.5	3.3	93.2
Equatorial Guinea	1965	254,684	52.5	47.5	...	35.1	——64.9——					...	...	...	...	...
Faeroe Islands	1970	38,612	52.2	47.8	...	31.8	23.0	16.5	16.0	9.4	3.3	...	...	...	...	...
Falkland Islands	1972	1,957	55.2	44.8	44.7	26.7	22.4	——51.9——				926	47.3	48.9	—	51.1
Fiji	1966	476,727	50.9	49.1	33.4	46.7	26.6	14.6	8.2	2.9	1.0	125,809	26.4	55.2	7.0	37.8
Finland	1970	4,598,336	48.3	51.7	50.9	24.3	26.0	18.6	16.6	11.6	2.9	2,118,257	46.1	20.3	34.3	45.4
France	1968	49,654,556	48.7	51.3	70.0	23.7	21.9	19.7	15.9	13.7	5.1	19,961,852	40.2	6.3	15.9	77.8
French Guiana	1967	44,392	54.2	45.8	52.2	35.6	27.4	18.1	12.1	5.5	1.3	17,012	38.3	18.4	28.5	53.1
French Polynesia	1971	117,664	53.1	46.9	19.0	45.5	23.7	16.6	9.0	3.7	1.5	...	...	...	...	...
Gabon	1970	950,009	47.9	52.1	26.9	35.4	19.2	22.2	16.3	6.3	0.6	210,315	22.1	...	...	...
Gambia, The	1973	494,279	50.9	49.1	13.1	41.7	——58.3——					...	...	...	...	...
Germany, East	1971	17,068,318	46.1	53.9	73.8	23.3	19.9	20.1	14.7	16.9	5.1	7,804,100	45.7	12.6	48.8	38.6
Germany, West	1970	60,650,599	47.6	52.4	...	23.2	21.3	19.7	16.6	15.0	4.2	26,493,512	23.5	7.5	48.9	56.4
Ghana	1970	8,559,313	49.6	50.4	28.9	46.9	——53.1——					3,133,047	36.6	57.2	...	...
Gibraltar	1970	26,833	48.1	51.9	91.9	22.9	22.7	21.1	18.7	11.2	3.4	11,748	43.8	—	21.8	78.2
Gilbert and Ellice Is.	1968	53,517	49.3	50.7	14.9	45.5	23.7	14.7	9.7	5.1	1.3	13,121	24.5	65.5	3.8	30.7
Greece	1971	8,768,640	48.8	51.2	53.2	24.9	20.4	21.9	16.5	12.5	3.8	3,283,880	37.5	40.5	24.8	34.7
Greenland	1970	46,531	52.5	47.5	...	43.4	24.8	18.8	8.5	3.9	0.6	...	...	...	...	...
Grenada	1970	96,542	46.2	53.8	...	...	...	...	...	...	...	...	...	...	...	...
Guadeloupe	1967	312,724	51.1	48.9	46.8	43.1	23.9	15.0	10.8	5.5	1.7	89,980	28.8	32.4	25.7	41.9
Guam	1970	84,996	55.7	44.3	25.5	39.7	29.1	19.3	8.9	2.5	0.5	22,112	26.0	0.7	22.8	76.5
Guatemala	1973	5,211,929	50.0	50.0	33.6	45.1	26.7	15.1	8.3	——4.8——		1,547,340	29.7	57.0	13.9	29.1
Guinea	1972	5,143,284	...	...	...	...	...	...	...	...	...	...	...	...	...	...
Guinea-Bissau	1970	487,448	48.7	51.3	11.5	...	...	...	...	...	...	...	...	...	...	...
Guyana	1970	699,848	49.7	50.3	33.3	47.1	25.1	13.4	9.0	4.4	1.0	...	...	...	...	...
Haiti	1971	4,314,628	48.2	51.8	20.4	41.5	25.8	16.5	9.5	5.0	1.7	...	...	...	...	...
Honduras	1974	2,653,857	49.5	50.5	37.5	...	...	...	...	...	...	...	...	...	...	...
Hong Kong	1971	3,948,179	50.7	49.3	...	35.8	24.3	18.1	14.3	6.2	1.3	1,654,907	41.9	2.1	44.5	53.4
Hungary	1970	10,322,099	48.5	51.5	45.2	21.1	23.6	20.5	17.7	13.6	3.5	...	...	...	...	...
Iceland	1970	204,930	50.6	49.4	...	32.3	25.1	16.4	13.7	9.0	3.5	...	...	...	...	...
India	1971	547,949,809	51.8	48.2	19.9	41.9	24.1	17.8	10.2	4.9	1.1	183,605,325	33.5	...	...	...
Indonesia	1971	118,459,845	49.2	50.8	17.5	44.1	24.0	18.6	9.0	3.7	0.6	40,100,070	33.9	61.8	7.5	30.7
Iran	1966	25,788,722	51.8	48.2	38.0	46.1	21.7	17.6	8.0	5.4	1.2	6,190,517	24.0	54.6	21.4	24.0
Iraq	1965	8,047,415	51.0	49.0	44.1	47.9	21.0	15.3	8.7	4.9	2.2	...	...	...	...	...
Ireland	1971	2,978,248	50.2	49.8	52.2	31.3	22.0	15.2	——31.5——			1,119,532	37.6	24.4	27.5	48.1
Isle of Man	1971	56,289	47.0	53.0	55.7	19.9	18.3	14.9	19.0	20.9	7.0	...	...	...	...	...
Israel	1972	3,124,000	53.1	46.9	84.3	...	...	...	...	...	...	1,088,400	34.8	7.5	24.8	67.7
Italy	1971	54,136,547	48.9	51.1	...	24.4	21.2	20.7	17.0	12.8	3.9	18,831,127	34.8	17.2	43.5	39.3
Jamaica	1970	1,813,594	48.8	51.2	41.4	37.5	25.1	15.2	12.4	7.5	2.3	514,639	28.4	...	...	...
Japan	1970	104,665,171	49.3	50.7	72.1	23.7	27.5	22.9	14.4	8.4	3.1	52,409,200	50.1	19.4	16.9	63.7
Jordan	1961	1,706,226	50.9	49.1	43.9	45.4	26.1	13.7	7.9	5.1	1.8	389,978	22.9	35.3	10.8	53.9
Kenya	1969	10,942,705	50.1	49.9	9.9	48.4	25.1	——26.5——				...	...	...	...	...

Table II. World Census Data* *(Continued)*

Country	Date of census	Total population	% Male	% Female	% Urban	AGE DISTRIBUTION (%) 0 to 14	15 to 29	30 to 44	45 to 59	60 to 74	75 and over	ECONOMICALLY ACTIVE Total	% of total pop.	Agriculture; forestry; fisheries	Mining; mfg.; const.	Service; utilities; finance; govt.
Korea, South	1970	31,435,252	48.4	51.6	40.4	42.1	24.9	17.5	10.1	4.5	0.9	10,153,000	32.3	50.8	15.2	34.0
Kuwait	1970	738,663	56.8	43.2	...	43.2	28.8	19.0	6.1	2.2	0.7	233,534	31.6	1.7	16.8	81.5
Lesotho	1966	969,600	48.0	52.0	4.4	37.6	26.2	17.9	11.5	—6.8—		...	...	...	...	...
Liberia	1974	1,496,000	...	...	...	...	...	...	...	...	...	...	...	...	...	...
Libya	1973	2,257,037	53.2	46.8	...	...	...	...	...	...	...	...	...	...	...	...
Liechtenstein	1970	21,350	49.7	50.3	...	27.9			—72.1—			10,251	48.0	6.2	56.6	37.2
Luxembourg	1970	339,812	49.0	51.0	68.4	22.1	20.5	21.4	17.5	14.6	3.9	...	...	...	...	...
Macau	1970	248,636	51.4	48.6	100.0	37.6	28.9	15.0	11.3	5.9	1.1	16,048	6.5	0.4	0.4	99.2
Malawi	1966	4,039,583	47.4	52.6	5.0	43.9	25.2	15.5	9.7	—5.7—		...	...	...	...	...
Malaysia	1970	10,434,034	50.4	49.6	26.7	...	...	...	...	...	...	...	...	...	...	...
Maldives	1972	122,673	52.9	47.1	...	46.0	21.5	19.8	9.0	3.2	0.5	59,040	48.1	6.1	—	93.9
Malta	1967	314,216	47.9	52.1	94.3	29.8	25.9	17.6	13.8	10.2	2.7	94,367	30.0	7.5	24.3	68.2
Martinique	1967	320,030	48.5	51.5	45.8	43.5	22.5	15.2	11.1	5.8	1.9	89,464	27.9	25.4	8.8	65.8
Mauritius	1972	851,334	50.0	50.0	42.9	40.3	28.6	14.5	11.0	4.9	0.7	223,109	26.2	35.0	23.6	41.4
Mexico	1970	48,225,238	49.9	50.1	58.7	46.2	25.6	14.6	8.0	4.4	1.2	12,955,057	26.9	39.4	22.5	38.1
Monaco	1968	23,035	45.2	54.8	100.0	12.9	17.5	18.4	20.9	21.2	9.1	10,093	43.8	0.1	21.5	78.4
Mongolia	1969	1,197,600	49.9	50.1	44.0	...	...	...	...	...	...	...	...	...	...	...
Montserrat	1970	11,458	46.9	53.1	88.9	37.9	20.6	9.8	12.1	10.7	8.9	3,769	32.9	20.4	5.8	73.8
Morocco	1971	15,379,259	50.1	49.9	3.5	46.2	22.4	16.0	8.3	5.3	1.8	3,980,518	26.3	50.6	15.3	34.1
Mozambique	1970	8,233,834	...	...	...	...	...	...	...	...	...	...	...	...	...	...
Nauru	1966	6,055	53.3	46.7	0	40.0	24.7	23.9	9.2	2.1	0.1	2,504	41.4	0.1	31.4	68.5
Nepal	1971	11,555,983	49.7	50.3	13.8	40.5	25.5	18.7	9.7	—5.6—		4,730,376	40.9	96.8	1.1	2.1
Netherlands, The	1971	13,045,785	50.0	50.0	...	27.5	—42.3—		15.6	—14.6—		4,791,610	36.7	...	...	...
Netherland Antilles	1972	223,196	48.8	51.2	...	38.0	26.7	16.7	10.3	6.4	1.9	63,971	28.7	0.9	32.9	66.2
New Caledonia	1969	100,579	52.3	47.7	41.6	34.8	26.6	19.2	12.4	5.4	1.6	39,185	39.0	34.1	18.3	47.6
New Hebrides	1967	77,988	52.1	47.9	12.0	45.6	26.0	15.5	8.5	—4.4—		35,133	45.0	82.5	2.5	15.0
New Zealand	1971	2,862,631	50.0	50.0	81.4	31.8	23.9	16.8	15.1	9.4	3.0	1,118,835	39.1	11.5	34.0	54.5
Nicaragua	1971	1,877,972	48.3	51.7	48.0	...	...	...	...	...	...	564,312	30.0	52.4	15.3	32.3
Niger	1972	4,243,000	49.8	50.2	...	44.5	23.3	17.4	10.1	—4.7—		...	...	...	...	...
Nigeria	1973	79,760,000	...	...	...	...	...	...	...	...	...	...	...	...	...	...
Norway	1970	3,888,305	49.7	50.3	42.6	24.4	22.5	16.0	18.8	13.5	4.8	...	...	...	...	...
Pacific Islands, Trust Territory of the	1973	114,973	...	...	...	...	...	...	...	...	...	...	...	...	...	...
Pakistan	1972	64,892,000	53.0	47.0	...	...	...	...	...	...	...	...	...	...	...	...
Panama	1970	1,428,082	50.7	49.3	47.6	43.4	26.1	15.2	9.6	4.3	1.4	488,668	34.2	...	...	...
Papua New Guinea	1971	2,489,937	52.0	48.0	11.1	45.2	24.5	17.4	9.9	1.4	1.6	521,110	20.9	56.4	4.5	39.1
Paraguay	1972	2,354,071	49.7	50.3	37.4	44.9	25.4	14.5	9.2	4.5	1.5	739,110	31.4	49.5	18.6	31.9
Peru	1972	13,567,939	50.0	50.0	59.6	...	...	...	...	...	...	...	...	...	...	...
Philippines	1970	36,684,486	49.8	50.2	31.8	43.1	27.1	15.4	9.0	4.3	1.1	12,296,583	33.6	51.5	15.6	32.9
Poland	1970	32,642,270	48.6	51.4	52.3	26.4	25.5	20.4	14.6	10.6	2.5	16,943,800	51.9	38.6	34.4	27.0
Portugal	1970	8,545,120	47.4	52.6	...	28.4	21.9	19.0	16.2	11.2	3.3	3,143,940	36.8	31.4	31.5	37.1
Portuguese Timor	1970	609,477	51.9	48.1	...	35.5	25.5	19.9	12.3	5.8	1.0	...	...	...	...	...
Puerto Rico	1970	2,712,033	49.0	51.0	58.1	36.5	26.1	15.9	11.9	7.1	2.5	634,961	23.4	8.1	33.0	58.9
Réunion	1967	416,525	48.8	51.2	42.8	45.7	23.5	15.8	9.7	4.2	1.1	94,334	22.6	29.5	7.3	63.2
Rhodesia	1969	5,099,340	50.3	49.7	16.8	47.2	25.4	15.7	8.4	—3.3—		...	...	...	...	...
Romania	1966	19,103,163	48.9	51.1	38.2	26.3	23.1	23.3	15.3	9.9	2.1	10,362,300	54.2	56.8	19.4	23.8
Rwanda	1970	3,735,585	47.8	52.2	3.2	43.8	24.2	15.2	11.6	—5.2—		...	...	...	...	...
St. Helena	1966	4,649	48.0	52.0	0	39.0	21.2	13.9	13.2	10.0	2.7	1,562	33.6	...	...	...
St. Kitts-Nevis-Anguilla †	1970	44,884	46.9	53.1	31.7	48.4	18.9	9.5	12.1	8.7	2.4	...	...	...	...	...
St. Lucia	1970	101,064	47.5	52.5	54.2	...	...	...	...	...	...	...	...	...	...	...
St. Pierre and Miquelon	1974	5,762	...	...	...	...	...	...	...	...	...	...	...	...	...	...
St. Vincent	1970	89,129	47.4	52.6	...	...	...	...	...	...	...	...	...	...	...	...
São Tomé and Príncipe	1970	73,631	50.3	49.7	11.6	44.2	20.7	18.6	9.8	—6.7—		...	...	...	...	...
Seychelles	1971	52,650	49.8	50.2	26.1	43.4	21.0	15.1	11.2	7.0	2.3	17,868	33.9	28.4	29.7	41.9
Sierra Leone	1963	2,180,355	49.6	50.4	...	36.7	27.2	19.4	9.0	—7.7—		908,147	41.7	75.2	9.8	15.0
Sikkim	1971	204,760	52.8	47.2	...	...	...	...	...	...	...	...	...	...	...	...
Singapore	1970	2,074,507	51.2	49.8	100.0	38.8	28.1	16.9	10.5	4.9	0.8	...	...	...	...	...
South Africa	1970	21,448,169	49.2	50.8	47.9	40.8	26.2	16.7	10.0	5.0	1.3	7,986,220	37.2	28.0	21.3	50.7
South West Africa	1970	746,328	50.8	49.2	24.9	...	...	...	...	...	...	...	...	...	...	...
Spain	1970	33,956,047	48.9	51.1	54.7	27.8	22.0	19.9	16.1	10.8	3.4	11,908,064	35.0	24.8	36.6	38.6
Spanish Sahara	1970	76,425	57.5	42.5	45.3	42.9	27.2	16.3	7.4	4.4	1.8	...	...	...	...	...
Sri Lanka	1971	12,711,143	51.3	48.7	22.4	39.3	27.8	15.9	10.5	5.2	1.3	3,621,988	28.5	50.4	10.0	39.6
Surinam	1971	384,903	50.0	50.0	...	48.0			—52.0—			...	...	...	...	...
Swaziland	1966	374,571	47.7	52.3	7.1	46.7	24.6	14.4	8.5	4.5	1.3	121,063	32.3	19.4	6.9	73.7
Sweden	1970	8,076,903	49.9	50.1	81.4	20.6	22.8	17.4	19.3	14.8	5.1	3,412,668	42.3	8.1	40.3	51.6
Switzerland	1970	6,269,783	49.3	50.7	52.0	23.4	23.7	20.2	16.3	12.5	3.9	3,005,139	47.9	7.6	48.3	44.1
Syria	1970	6,304,685	51.3	48.7	43.5	49.3	22.4	14.3	7.5	4.8	1.7	1,570,776	24.9	47.9	12.7	39.4
Taiwan	1970	14,693,036	52.3	47.7	...	40.5	26.4	17.5	10.9	4.0	0.7	5,062,049	34.5	36.6	19.3	44.1
Tanzania	1967	12,313,469	48.8	51.2	5.5	43.9	24.7	15.4	8.6	4.1	3.3	5,577,567	45.3	91.0	1.7	7.3
Thailand	1970	34,397,374	49.6	50.4	13.4	45.5	24.9	16.1	8.6	—4.9—		16,312,000	47.7	82.1	4.4	13.5
Togo	1970	1,953,778	48.1	51.9	...	...	...	...	...	...	...	...	...	...	...	...
Tonga	1966	77,429	51.5	48.5	...	46.3	25.2	15.6	8.1	3.8	1.0	40,819	52.8	34.0	1.5	64.5
Trinidad and Tobago	1970	931,071	49.4	50.6	...	...	...	...	...	...	...	...	...	...	...	...
Tunisia	1966	4,533,351	51.1	48.9	40.1	46.3	21.4	16.6	10.1	4.4	1.2	1,093,735	24.1	41.0	17.1	41.9
Turkey	1970	35,605,176	50.6	49.4	61.5	41.9	25.0	17.3	8.9	—6.9—		14,533,725	40.8	67.0	11.9	21.1
Turks and Caicos Islands	1970	5,588	47.4	52.6	...	47.1	20.4	12.0	11.1	7.0	2.5	...	...	...	...	...
Uganda	1969	9,548,847	50.5	49.5	7.7	46.2	24.0	15.7	8.3	4.2	1.6	...	...	...	...	...
Union of Soviet Socialist Republics	1970	241,720,134	46.0	54.0	56.3	30.9	19.9	23.5	13.8	—11.8—		115,204,076	47.7	...	...	...
United Kingdom	1971	55,515,602	48.5	51.5	...	24.1	21.0	17.6	18.3	14.3	4.7	25,080,000	45.1	1.7	45.3	53.0
United States	1970	203,211,926	48.7	51.3	73.5	28.6	24.0	17.0	16.3	10.4	3.7	76,553,599	37.7	3.7	32.7	63.7
Uruguay	1963	2,595,510	49.7	50.3	82.1	28.2	22.8	21.6	15.8	9.0	2.6	1,015,500	39.2	17.9	25.8	56.3
Venezuela	1971	10,721,522	50.0	50.0	75.0	35.1	31.7	17.5	10.0	4.4	1.3	3,014,674	28.1	20.3	14.6	65.1
Vietnam, North	1960	15,916,955	48.3	51.7	9.5	44.3			—55.7—			8,119,286	51.0	78.5	6.6	14.9
Virgin Islands (U.S.)	1970	62,468	49.9	50.1	24.4	35.7	28.3	19.4	10.8	4.4	1.4	24,501	39.2	1.2	25.5	73.3
Western Samoa	1971	146,627	51.8	48.2	20.6	50.6	24.3	13.1	7.9	3.3	0.8	37,740	25.7	67.3	—	32.7
Yugoslavia	1971	20,522,972	49.1	50.9	38.6	27.2	24.6	22.7	13.5	9.8	2.2	8,889,846	43.3	43.9	17.7	38.4
Zambia	1969	4,056,995	49.0	51.0	29.6	46.3	24.0	16.6	9.4	3.0	0.7	756,300	18.6	43.7	20.0	36.3

*Any presentation of world census data must necessarily include figures of varying reliability. The tabulation here is of published and unpublished information about the last completed census of population for each country. It excludes estimated data not part of that census, even though no census is more than a body of estimates the quality of which depends on the completeness of the enumeration. Some countries will tabulate only persons actually present whereas others will include persons legally resident, but actually outside the country, on census day. Some will collect age data according to the economic, rather than demographic, interests of the country. No tabulation of economically active population will be identical with any other, although data for developed countries will be more complete and internally consistent; developing countries frequently find it difficult to collect or evaluate information about the workers outside the modern wage-earning sector and the data will, thus, provide little or no information about family and self-employed agricultural and craft workers, although these may be more numerous than the wage-earners.

†Excludes Anguilla, enumerated in 1974 at 6,524 persons.

Table III. Populations and Areas of the Countries of the World, Midyear 1973

Continent and country*	Area† in sq.mi.	Population† in 000	Persons per sq.mi.
AFRICA			
Afars and Issas (Fr.)	8,900	130	14.6
Algeria	896,593	15,772	17.6
Angola (Port.)	481,350	5,715	11.9
Botswana	222,000	646	2.9
Bouvet Island (Nor.)	23	—	—
British Indian Ocean Territory (U.K.)	85	—	—
Burundi	10,747	3,600	335.0
Cameroon	179,558	6,090	33.9
Cape Verde Islands (Port.)	1,557	284	182.4
Central African Republic	240,378	1,716	7.1
Chad	495,750	3,869	7.8
Comoro Islands (Fr.)	863	291	337.2
Congo	132,047	1,280	9.7
Dahomey	43,475	2,993	68.8
Egypt	386,900	35,619	92.1
Equatorial Guinea	10,830	298	27.5
Ethiopia	471,800	26,461	56.1
French Southern and Antarctic Lands (Fr.)‡	2,844	—	—
Gabon	103,347	980	9.5
Gambia, The	4,467	494	110.6
Ghana	92,100	9,190	99.8
Guinea	94,926	4,208	44.3
Guinea-Bissau	13,948	510	31.6
Ivory Coast	123,484	4,641	37.6
Kenya	224,961	12,482	55.5
Lesotho	11,720	1,131	96.5
Liberia	43,000	1,470	39.0
Libya	675,000	2,257	3.3
Malagasy Republic	226,444	7,140	31.5
Malawi	45,747	4,791	104.7
Mali	478,822	5,376	11.2
Mauritania	398,000	1,218	3.1
Mauritius	787	875	1,111.8
Morocco	177,117	16,309	92.1
Mozambique (Port.)	308,642	8,823	28.6
Niger	489,000	4,304	8.8
Nigeria	356,669	71,262	199.8
Réunion (Fr.)	970	473	487.6
Rhodesia	150,873	5,890	3.9
Rwanda	10,169	3,984	391.8
St. Helena (U.K.)	119	6	50.4
São Tomé and Príncipe (Port.)	372	78	209.7
Senegal	78,685	4,137	52.6
Seychelles (U.K.)	107	57	532.7
Sierra Leone	27,925	2,861	102.5
Somalia	246,300	2,965	12.0
South Africa	471,445	23,724	50.3
South West Africa (South Africa; Namibia [UN])	318,261	827	2.6
Spanish Sahara (Sp.)	103,000	99	1.0
Sudan	967,500	12,428	12.8
Swaziland	6,704	479	71.5
Tanzania	364,943	14,372	39.4
Togo	21,925	2,143	97.7
Tunisia	63,379	5,509	86.9
Uganda	91,452	10,810	118.2
Upper Volta	105,869	5,737	54.2
Zaire	905,365	23,563	26.0
Zambia	290,586	4,635	16.0
Total Africa	11,679,800	387,000	33.1
ANTARCTICA			
Australian Antarctic Territory (Austr.)	2,472,000	—	—
British Antarctic Territory (U.K.)§	650,000	—	—
French Southern and Antarctic Lands (Fr.)‖	158,000	—	—
Peter I Island¶	96	—	—
Ross Dependency (N. Z.)	160,000	—	—
Total Antarctica	5,500,000⌀	ẟ	—
ASIA			
Afghanistan	252,000	18,294	72.6
Bahrain	256	229	894.5
Bangladesh	55,126	70,070	1,271.1
Bhutan	18,000	1,129	62.7
Brunei (U.K.-protected state)	2,226	145	65.1
Burma	261,789	29,100	111.2
Cambodia	69,898	7,190	113.2
China	3,691,500	800,000	216.7
Cyprus	3,572	632	176.9
Hong Kong (U.K.)	403	4,160	10,322.6
India	1,266,602	574,216	453.4
Indonesia	782,663	124,602	159.2
Iran	636,000	31,645	49.8
Iraq⌓	168,928	10,413	61.6
Israel	7,992	3,249	406.5
Japan	145,728	107,790	739.7
Jordan	36,832	2,577	70.0
Korea, North	46,800	15,090	322.4
Korea, South	38,025	33,177	872.5
Kuwait	6,880	883	128.3
Laos	91,400	3,181	34.8

Continent and country*	Area† in sq.mi.	Population† in 000	Persons per sq.mi.
ASIA (cont.)			
Lebanon	3,950	3,055	773.4
Macau (Port.)	6	254	42,333.3
Malaysia	127,316	11,609	91.2
Maldives	115	126	1,095.7
Mongolia	604,000	1,359	2.3
Nepal	54,362	12,020	221.1
Neutral Zone (Iraq-Saudi Arabia)	7,000	—	—
Oman	82,000	722	8.8
Pakistan	307,374	66,764	217.2
Philippines	115,800	40,219	347.0
Portuguese Timor (Port.)	5,763	645	111.9
Qatar	4,400	170	38.6
Saudi Arabia⌓	865,000	8,115	9.4
Sikkim (India-protected state)	2,744	206	75.1
Singapore	226	2,185	9,668.1
Sri Lanka	25,332	13,249	523.0
Syria	71,498	6,890	96.4
Taiwan	13,893	15,424	1,110.2
Thailand	198,500	39,787	200.4
Turkey	300,948	38,094	126.6
United Arab Emirates	37,000	320	8.6
Vietnam, North	63,360	22,481	354.8
Vietnam, South	67,293	19,213	285.5
Yemen (Aden)	111,074	1,590	14.3
Yemen (San'a')	77,200	6,217	80.5
Total Asia⌀	17,479,300	2,211,200	126.5
EUROPE			
Albania	11,100	2,315	208.6
Andorra	179	23	129.1
Austria	32,375	7,483	231.1
Belgium	11,782	9,757	828.1
Bulgaria	42,823	8,619	201.2
Channel Islands (U.K.)	75	124	1,653.3
Czechoslovakia	49,374	14,572	295.1
Denmark	16,629	5,008	301.1
Faeroe Islands (Den.)	1,399	42	30.0
Finland	130,129	4,636	35.6
France	210,039	52,200	248.5
Germany, East	41,768	16,980	406.5
Germany, West (inc. W. Berlin)	95,980	61,967	645.6
Gibraltar (U.K.)	2.25	30	1,333.3
Greece	50,944	8,950	175.7
Hungary	35,290	10,416	290.0
Iceland	39,769	213	5.4
Ireland	27,136	3,029	111.6
Isle of Man (U.K.)	221	56	253.4
Italy	116,313	54,888	471.9
Liechtenstein	62	23	371.0
Luxembourg	998	353	353.4
Malta	122	298	2,444.3
Monaco	0.73	25	34,246.7
Netherlands, The	15,892	13,388	842.4
Norway	125,053	3,948	31.6
Poland	120,725	33,277	275.6
Portugal	35,383	8,564	242.0
Romania	91,700	20,828	227.0
San Marino	24	19	791.7
Spain	194,885	34,730	178.2
Svalbard and Jan Mayen (Nor.)	24,197	3	—
Sweden	173,732	8,144	46.9
Switzerland	15,943	6,431	403.4
United Kingdom	94,217	55,933	593.7
Vatican City	0.17	0.7	4,251.0
Yugoslavia	98,766	20,938	212.0
Total Europe⌀	4,056,700	655,000	161.5
NORTH AMERICA			
Antigua	171	74	432.7
Bahamas, The	5,382	189	35.1
Barbados	166	242	1,454.8
Belize (Br. Honduras) (U.K.)	8,866	132	14.9
Bermuda (U.K.)	21	55	2,619.0
British Virgin Islands (U.K.)	59	12	203.4
Canada	3,851,809	22,125	5.7
Canal Zone (U.S.)	362	44	121.5
Cayman Islands (U.K.)	100	12	120.0
Costa Rica	19,652	1,846	93.9
Cuba	42,827	8,916	208.2
Dominica (U.K.)	289	73	252.6
Dominican Republic	18,658	4,432	237.5
El Salvador	8,098	3,864	477.2
Greenland (Den.)	840,000	51	—
Grenada	133	105	789.5
Guadeloupe (Fr.)	687	334	486.2
Guatemala	42,042	5,212	124.0
Haiti	10,714	4,448	415.2
Honduras	43,277	2,608	60.3
Jamaica	4,244	1,968	463.7
Martinique (Fr.)	431	343	795.8
Mexico	761,605	54,303	71.3
Montserrat (U.K.)	40	12	300.0

Continent and country*	Area† in sq.mi.	Population† in 000	Persons per sq.mi.
NORTH AMERICA (cont.)			
Netherlands Antilles (Neth.)	385	234	607.8
Nicaragua	50,000	2,019	40.4
Panama	29,209	1,570	53.8
Puerto Rico (U.S.)	3,421	2,919	853.3
St. Kitts-Nevis-Anguilla (U.K.)	135	65	481.5
St. Lucia (U.K.)	238	107	449.6
St. Pierre and Miquelon (Fr.)	93	6	64.5
St. Vincent (U.K.)	150	91	606.7
Trinidad and Tobago	1,980	1,064	537.4
Turks and Caicos Islands (U.K.)	193	6	31.1
United States	3,615,122	210,396	58.2
Virgin Islands (U.S.)	133	65	488.7
Total North America	9,358,700	329,900	35.3
OCEANIA			
American Samoa (U.S.)	76	29	381.6
Australia	2,967,900	13,132	4.4
British Solomon Islands (U.K.)	10,983	179	16.3
Canton and Enderbury Islands (U.K.-U.S.)	27	—	—
Christmas Island (Austr.)	52	3	57.7
Cocos (Keeling) Islands (Austr.)	6	1	166.7
Cook Islands (N.Z.)	93	20	215.1
French Polynesia (Fr.)	1,261	120	95.2
Gilbert and Ellice Islands (U.K.)	283	63	222.6
Guam (U.S.)	212	94	443.4
Johnston Island (U.S.)	1	1	—
Midway Islands (U.S.)	2	2	—
Nauru	8	7	853.7
New Caledonia (Fr.)	7,366	125	17.0
New Hebrides (Fr.-U.K.)	5,700	90	15.8
New Zealand	103,736	2,975	28.7
Niue (N.Z.)	100	4	40.0
Norfolk Island (Austr.)	14	2	142.9
Pacific Islands, Trust Territory of the (U.S.)	707	115	162.7
Papua New Guinea (Austr.)	178,260	2,563	14.4
Pitcairn Island (U.K.)	2	0.1	—
Tokelau Islands (N.Z.)	4	2	—
Tonga	225	92	408.9
Wake Island (U.S.)	3	2	—
Wallis and Futuna Islands (Fr.)	98	8	77.6
Western Samoa	1,133	151	133.3
Total Oceania	3,285,300	20,300	6.2
SOUTH AMERICA			
Argentina	1,072,163	24,286	22.7
Bolivia	424,165	5,331	12.6
Brazil	3,286,488	101,706	30.9
Chile	292,258	10,229	35.0
Colombia	439,737	23,209	52.8
Ecuador	109,484	6,820	62.3
Falkland Islands (U.K.)	6,150	2	0.3
French Guiana (Fr.)	34,750	52	1.5
Guyana	83,000	758	9.1
Paraguay	157,048	2,415	15.4
Peru	496,224	13,970	28.7
Surinam (Neth.)	70,060	403	5.8
Uruguay	68,536	2,992	43.7
Venezuela	352,144	11,520	32.7
Total South America	6,892,200	203,700	29.6
U.S.S.R.⌀	8,649,500	249,749	28.9
in Asia⌀	6,498,500	62,674	9.6
in Europe⌀	2,151,000	187,075	87.0
World total▲	58,252,000	3,807,200	72.2

Note: Populations given are latest official or UN estimates for midyear 1973. If no estimate for this date was available from either source, an estimate was made where available information permitted, or data for another date were inserted if information was insufficient to make an estimate. A dash (—) in the population column indicates no permanent population; a dash in the density column indicates figure is not meaningful.

*For non-self-governing states, administering power is indicated in parentheses.

†Continent and world totals rounded (independently).

‡Excludes mainland Antarctica portion (Adélie Land); see Antarctica.

§Includes some areas also claimed by Argentina and Chile.

‖Adélie Land only; excludes islands north of 60° south; see Africa.

¶Norwegian claims in mainland Antarctica (Queen Maud Land) are undefined.

⌀Estimated; includes some unclaimed areas.

ẟMay reach a total of 2,000 persons of all nationalities during the summer.

⌓Excludes the Neutral Zone (Iraq-Saudi Arabia), shown separately.

°Asia and Europe continent totals include corresponding portions of U.S.S.R., shown separately at end of table.

▲Area of Antarctica excluded in calculating world density.

continued from page 555

For two decades the wealthier developed nations of North America, Oceania, and Europe had been growing slowly while rates of increase in the poor countries of Africa, Asia, and Latin America continued to rise. Awareness of the problem led to the world's first major population conference, an 11-day series of debates and discussions sponsored by the UN in Bucharest, Rom., in late August. (*See* Special Report.)

In the past few decades world census figures had shown dramatic changes. The U.S., for example, grew rapidly after World War II, but in recent years the American people had begun to limit family size. Officially the population reached 211.9 million in late June 1974, though because of census undercounts the actual figure may have been closer to 217.5 million. However, during the year ended September 1974, the U.S. birthrate had fallen to 14.8 per 1,000, one of the lowest in history. With the death rate stable at 9.2, the annual growth rate was under 0.6%. This meant the U.S. population would take 116 years to double.

In Europe, too, growth had slowed. Europe, including the Soviet Union, was growing at roughly the same rate as the U.S. The most populous country on the continent, the U.S.S.R. (252 million people), was growing at a rate of 0.9%. Similarly, West Germany, the U.K., Italy, and France were all adding less than 1% to their populations each year. Small, isolated Albania recorded the fastest growth rate, 2.5%, the product of a birthrate of 33 and a death rate of 8. Slowest growth was recorded in Austria, where a birthrate of 14 and a death rate of 13 produced a growth rate of 0.1%; at this rate the population would not double for 693 years. East Germany continued to lose population, while West Germany for the first time also showed a loss. Similar patterns were noted in Oceania. Despite a young population and a policy of encouraging immigration, Australia was growing at about 1.7%.

Highest growth was reported in Asia, Latin America, and Africa, all of which had rates of 2.6% or more. This meant they would add another 3,000,000,000 people in little more than a generation. Except in Africa, the high growth rates were due to extremely high birthrates of about 40 and death rates brought down below 20 by improved medical care. In many Muslim countries birthrates of 50 or above were recorded and growth rates surpassed 3% a year.

Asia was home to two of the world's most populous nations: China, with an announced population of about 800 million (estimated unofficially as high as 917 million), and India, with an officially estimated population of 586 million. Though accurate figures were difficult to obtain, both countries were thought to be growing at about 2.5% annually, suggesting an additional 1,500,000,000 people in 25 years. The next largest country, Indonesia, with 127.6 million inhabitants, was increasing by 2.9%. By contrast, Japan was growing by only 1.3%.

The largest African country, Nigeria (79.8 million people announced at the 1973 census but estimated by the UN to be only 59 million in the same year), had a birthrate of 50 and a death rate of 25, resulting in a growth rate of 2.5%. These statistics were typical of many African countries, where births were numerous and deaths among infants were common. As medical care improved, however, growth rates could go higher. In the Arab countries of North Africa they already exceeded 3%.

In Latin America, Brazil and Mexico were growing at 2.8%, fast enough to double in 25 years. In both

countries close to half the population was under the age of 15. The highest growth rate, however, was in El Salvador which, if it maintained its current growth rate of 3.6%, would double its population in 18 years. The slowest growth was in southern South America, where Argentina, Chile, and Uruguay had rates below 2%.

(WARREN W. EISENBERG)

See also Demography.

[525.A]

Members of the Population Action Group gather in Downing Street, London, before delivering a message on population control to the prime minister at his residence.
KEYSTONE

Portugal

A democratic republic of southwestern Europe, Portugal shares the Iberian Peninsula with Spain. Area: 35,383 sq.mi. (91,641 sq.km.), including the Azores (905 sq.mi.) and Madeira (308 sq.mi.). Pop. (1973 est.): 8,564,200. Cap. and largest city: Lisbon (pop., 1973 est., 757,700). Language: Portuguese. Religion: Roman Catholic. Presidents in 1974, Rear Adm. Américo de Deus Rodrigues Tomás, from May 15 Gen. António Sebastião Ribeiro de Spínola, and, from September 30, Gen. Francisco da Costa Gomes; premiers, Marcello José das Neves Alves Caetano, from May 16 Adélino da Palma Carlos, and, from July 13, Brig. Gen. Vasco dos Santos Gonçalves.

The military coup that took place on April 25, 1974, radically changed Portugal internally and in its relationship to the African continent and the world. The coup derived from the work of a group known as the "Captains' Movement," which had been formed in mid-1973 to press for better pay and conditions for junior officers in the armed forces. In early 1974 it became more political, especially after the February publication of Gen. António de Spínola's (*see* BIOGRAPHY) revelatory book *Portugal e o futuro* ("Portugal and the Future"), which stated that the wars in Africa could not be settled by military means but only by a political solution. In early March, after the clandestine circulation by the movement of a document voicing similar aspirations, the government decided to act, seized the movement's leaders, and placed some 200 officers under virtual house arrest until March 12. On March 14 General Costa Gomes and General Spínola were dismissed after they had

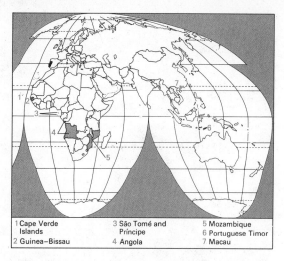

1 Cape Verde Islands	3 São Tomé and Príncipe	5 Mozambique
2 Guinea–Bissau	4 Angola	6 Portuguese Timor
		7 Macau

failed to attend a ceremony to pledge loyalty to Marcello Caetano's government.

On the night of March 15–16 part of an infantry regiment based at Caldas da Rainha (50 mi. N of Lisbon) mutinied. They held their senior officers captive and left for Lisbon but were turned back before reaching Lisbon by police and troops. The ensuing calm was deceptive, however, and early on April 25 a force of about 5,000 men converged on Lisbon. The army insurgents, calling themselves the Armed Forces Movement, overthrew the government, detained Pres. Américo Tomás and Premier Caetano and members of his Cabinet, and installed a "Junta of National Salvation" headed by Spínola. The coup was carried out generally without bloodshed.

General Spínola on April 26 promised a provisional civil government within three weeks; immediate dismissal of Tomás and Caetano and his government; free elections by universal suffrage within a year; freedom of political association and free trade unions; abolition of censorship; disbandment of the secret police in Portugal; immediate amnesty for political

Jubilant Portuguese demonstrate their solidarity with army units taking part in the successful military coup.

KEYSTONE

PORTUGAL

Education. (1972–73) Primary, pupils 970,736, teachers 31,312; secondary, pupils 381,299, teachers 22,057; vocational, pupils 163,284, teachers 10,918; teacher training, students 7,470, teachers 997; higher (including 3 main universities), students 53,999, teaching staff 3,433.

Finance. Monetary unit: escudo, with (Sept. 16, 1974) a free rate of 25.92 escudos to U.S. $1 (59.98 escudos = £1 sterling). Gold, SDRs, and foreign exchange, official: (June 1974) U.S. $2,527,000,000; (June 1973) U.S. $2,599,000,000. Budget (1973 est.): revenue 43,621,000,000 escudos; expenditure 43,597,-000,000 escudos. Gross national product: (1971) 194.9 billion escudos; (1970) 175.5 billion escudos. Money supply: (Dec. 1973) 165.6 billion escudos; (Dec. 1972) 122,290,000,000 escudos. Cost of living (Lisbon; 1970 = 100): (May 1974) 172; (May 1973) 137.

Foreign Trade. (1973) Imports 73,183,000,000 escudos; exports 44,759,000,000 escudos. Import sources: West Germany 14%; U.K. 12%; U.S. 8%; France 7%; Angola 6%; Spain 6%; Italy 5%; Sweden 5%. Export destinations: U.K. 24%; U.S. 10%; West Germany 8%; Angola 7%; Sweden 6%; France 5%; Mozambique 5%. Main exports: textile yarns and fabrics 18%; machinery 11%; clothing 11%; wine 7%; chemicals 7%; cork and manufactures 6%; fruit and vegetables 6%. Tourism (1972): visitors 3,925,300; gross receipts U.S. $391 million.

Transport and Communications. Roads (1972) 43,426 km. (including 66 km. expressways). Motor vehicles in use (1972): passenger 655,700; commercial 34,200. Railways: (1972) 3,563 km.; traffic (1973) 3,226,000,000 passenger-km., freight 860 million net ton-km. Air traffic (1972): 3,419,000,000 passenger-km.; freight 66.7 million net ton-km. Shipping (1973): merchant vessels 100 gross tons and over 438; gross tonnage 1,271,815. Telephones (Dec. 1972) 873,000. Radio licenses (Dec. 1972) 1,449,000. Television licenses (Dec. 1972) 542,000.

Agriculture. Production (in 000; metric tons; 1973; 1972 in parentheses): wheat 489 (612); barley (1972) 55, (1971) 84; oats 76 (85); rye 124 (164); corn 533 (519); rice 180 (164); potatoes 1,049 (1,093); dry beans 49 (51); onions c. 75 (c. 70); tomatoes c. 1,000 (c. 910); figs (1972) c. 200, (1971) c. 180; oranges (1972) c. 121, (1971) 117; apples (1972) 105, (1971) 95; pears (1972) 67, (1971) 41; wine 1,080 (749); olives c. 285 (c. 370); olive oil 40 (54); meat (1972) c. 200, (1971) 201; timber (cu.m.; 1972) 7,000, (1971) 6,400; fish catch (1971) 463, (1970) 498. Livestock (in 000; 1972–73): sheep c. 5,806; cattle (1971–72) c. 1,120; pigs c. 1,500; goats c. 500; asses c. 152; chickens (1972) c. 13,500.

Industry. Fuel and power (in 000; 1973): coal (metric tons) 221; manufactured gas (Lisbon; cu.m.) 131,000; electricity (kw-hr.) 9,658,000. Production (in 000; metric tons; 1973): iron ore (50% metal content) 36; steel 460; sulfuric acid 239; fertilizers (nutrient content; 1972–73) nitrogenous c. 150, phosphate 89; cement 3,123; tin 0.7; manganese ore (metal content; 1972) 2; tungsten concentrates (oxide content; 1972) 1.8; gold (troy oz.; 1972) 14; cotton yarn (1972) 86; woven cotton fabrics (1971) 47; preserved sardines (1971) 40; wood pulp (1972) 481; cork products (1971) 210.

prisoners; and dismissal of the governors-general of the overseas states and all civil governors in metropolitan Portugal and the adjacent islands. The border with Spain was sealed, Lisbon Airport was closed, shipping movements were prohibited, banks and currency offices were closed, and other measures were taken to prevent the flight of capital. The situation was normalized by June. On May 1, declared a public holiday, the inhabitants of Lisbon took part in jubilant celebrations. On May 15 Spínola assumed the presidency, and on the following day a new Cabinet was sworn in comprising mainly centre-left elements, with two members each from the Communist Party and the Democratic Popular Party and three from the Socialist Party, as well as a representative from the Armed Forces Movement and the Portuguese Democratic Movement.

The junta held out the offer of self-determination to Portugal's African overseas territories, and the

Portuguese Socialist leader Mário Soares (see BIOGRAPHY), who had returned from exile on April 28 and was made foreign minister, negotiated at various times throughout the summer with African revolutionary leaders. Spínola himself hoped that a federal solution might be reached and Portuguese and Africans united in some form of partnership, but complete independence was demanded and was granted to Guinea-Bissau; similar self-determination was promised to Mozambique, the Cape Verde Islands, and São Tomé and Príncipe in 1975, and to Angola and Portuguese Timor pending negotiations and arrangements. (See DEPENDENT STATES.)

A governmental crisis arose during July, culminating in the refusal of the Council of State (a 21-member body appointed in May, above the junta and provisional government) to grant the premier, Adélino da Palma Carlos, wider powers; the premier and four other ministers resigned, partly as a result of the postponement of economic and social measures, a controversial decree restraining the promised freedom of press, and the appointment of José Veiga Simão, minister of education under Caetano, as Portugal's representative at the UN. On July 13 Col. (later Brig. Gen.) Vasco dos Santos Gonçalves (see BIOGRAPHY), a "moderate" member of the Armed Forces Movement, became premier, and on July 17 a new Cabinet comprising seven men from the Armed Forces Movement and ten civilians was announced.

Many problems of the Palma Carlos government arose from disagreement between its centre and left-wing members. Although negotiations and legislation dealt with strikes and lockouts, wage increases, and other socioeconomic matters, clear industrial and investment policies and firm economic objectives were needed. Unemployment threatened to become more acute as troops and refugee settlers returned from the African territories. Spínola had begun to feel that rapid progress toward freedom in Portugal and Africa was tending toward anarchy, and his appeal to the "silent majority" to act as a stabilizing influence was feared by the government as an attempt to strengthen presidential authority. So, on September 30, he resigned and was replaced by Gen. Francisco da Costa Gomes, the chief of staff of the armed forces.

Up to the time of Spínola's resignation Portugal's administration had had some success in tackling the country's sizable economic problems. Government planners accepted that the country would have to live temporarily on its reserves—$2,760,000,000 at Dec. 31, 1973, and $2,650,000,000 at June 30, 1974; the reserves remained considerable (half was held in gold) and would offset budget deficits until the reform of the country's economic structure began to take effect. The promised reforms of agriculture and industry would also take time to produce results. With the need to keep the economy buoyant and unemployment at a minimum, the government accepted that inflation would remain high (20–25%).

(MICHAEL WOOLLER)

[972.A.5.b]

Prices

In 1973–74 inflation became a worldwide problem as price increases in many countries reached heights normally associated only with a few Latin-American states. The rapid deterioration was due to a combination of factors. First, in 1973 the level of activity in most industrial countries peaked at more or less the same time, so that shortages of productive capacity and basic materials became widespread. Second, natural disasters and poor climatic conditions in many parts of the world resulted in inadequate supplies of a number of key foodstuffs. Third, sharp increases in prices encouraged large-scale speculative demand for many commodities. Finally, and most dramatic of all, there was a fourfold increase in the price of crude oil over a period of less than one year.

Consumer Prices. The effect of these developments can be judged from Table I. Before 1973 annual price rises in excess of 10% were rare. By 1974 they had become common in industrial countries, while most less developed countries experienced increases of over 20%. The worst rates of inflation among developed market economies were recorded in Japan, Finland, and Italy. Japan suffered greatly from imported inflation because of its heavy dependence on overseas supplies of raw materials and oil; incomes did not become an important factor in the inflationary process until later in the year, following labour negotiations that increased nominal wages by about 30%. Direct price controls introduced in December 1973 for oil products were later extended to cover "essentials." Strong price controls were also in force in Finland, but dependence on imports of raw materials and energy made it very difficult for the country to defend itself against imported inflation. Increases in money wages and farm prices were also blamed for the deterioration. In Italy some of the basic prices, frozen in 1973, were allowed to go up in 1974 to absorb higher costs of imports. There were a number of major strikes in protest against higher prices, as well as the low quality of many public services.

Six other industrial countries experienced price increases of more than 10%. Import prices made a major contribution to the rate of inflation in the U.K. Price controls were in force throughout the year, but income controls were discontinued in the first half of 1974 and replaced by the "social contract" between the new Labour government and the unions. The government was to undertake certain social reforms, repeal the Industrial Relations Act, introduce food subsidies, and raise pensions, in return for which the unions promised to restrain wage demands for a year.

Denmark was another victim of imported inflation. In Australia many of the tariff reductions introduced unilaterally in 1973 were reversed to protect domestic industry and employment as "stagflation" became a major problem. Price controls were relaxed somewhat in France to allow firms to pass on increases in raw materials costs. However, many of the anti-inflationary measures were directed against industry, since excessive demand from this sector was thought to be a major factor in the inflationary process. Imported inflation, chiefly from the U.S., made a major contribution to higher prices in Canada. Sweden was one of the few countries in which economic growth continued. Anti-inflationary policies included subsidies on certain foodstuffs, some price controls, and a reduction of the value-added tax.

Among industrial countries with price increases in the 8–10% range, two, Switzerland and the U.S., had been regarded until recently as examples of price stability. In Switzerland the authorities introduced the familiar mixture of deflationary policies: credit restrictions, cuts in public spending, and increases in direct federal taxes. In the U.S. the new president was opposed to any formal incomes policy and decided to rely on the usual mixture of fiscal and monetary measures. The anti-inflationary package presented in October included a 5% surtax on companies and medium-to-upper income groups, incentives for industrial investment, some additional benefits for the poor and unemployed, and stiffer penalties for violations of the antitrust laws. As the economy slowed, however, stimulation began to assume a higher priority.

In New Zealand the authorities were determined to solve inflation and balance of payments problems while maintaining full employment and economic growth. Appeals were made to all sections of the community to cooperate in restraining increases in wages and prices, restricting imports, and halting increases in land prices. At the same time, new measures were introduced, including a compulsory savings scheme and a form of capital gains tax on land. As the rate of growth slowed down, prevention of unemployment was also given the highest priority in Belgium. Nevertheless, the credit squeeze was tight, and the advance

warning period for price rises was changed from three to six months. The Norwegian economy, on the other hand, was booming. Inflation was kept in check by a tight credit policy, extensive use of food subsidies, and revaluation of the krone in 1973.

As a net exporter of energy, The Netherlands was one of the few countries that benefited from the energy crisis. Nevertheless, tough deflationary measures and price controls were used in an attempt to curb inflation. The government was given special powers to control prices, wages, and dividends without parliamentary consent. Austria's rate of growth was higher and its rate of inflation lower than in most industrial countries. West Germany, however, was the only industrial country where the increase in consumer prices was below 8%. Large balance of payments surpluses led to a sizable revaluation of the mark, minimizing the effect of imported inflation.

Of all the countries listed in Table I, Hungary and Poland recorded the smallest price increases. This was attributable partly to tight central control over the economy and partly to the fact that both countries obtained most of their primary commodities from other Eastern European countries where prices were controlled even more rigidly. The Yugoslav economy was far less "centrally planned" and far more depen-

Table I. Cost of Living—Selected Countries

Country	Index (1970=100) 1972	1973	1974*	Annual % change 1967–71 Average	Annual % changes over preceding year 1972	1973	1974†
Developed market economies							
Japan	111	124	148	6.0	4.7	11.7	24.4
Finland	114	128	144	5.1	7.5	12.3	18.0
U.K.	117	128	143	6.4	7.3	9.4	14.4
Italy	111	123	138	3.4	5.7	10.8	15.0
Denmark	113	123	137	6.0	6.6	8.8	14.2
New Zealand	118	128	137	6.3	7.3	8.5	9.6
Australia	112	123	135	3.9	5.7	9.8	13.4
Netherlands, The	116	125	134	5.9	7.4	7.8	8.9
Switzerland	114	124	133	3.9	6.5	8.8	9.9
France	112	120	132	5.7	5.7	7.1	12.8
Sweden	114	122	131	4.7	6.5	7.0	10.1
Norway	114	122	131	5.7	7.5	7.0	9.2
Austria	111	120	128	3.9	5.7	8.1	8.5
Belgium‡	110	118	127	3.7	5.8	7.3	9.5
Germany, West	111	119	126	3.1	5.7	7.2	7.7
Canada	108	116	125	3.7	4.8	7.4	10.6
U.S.	108	114	123	4.9	3.8	5.6	9.8
Centrally planned economies							
Yugoslavia	135	161	188	9.7	16.4	19.2	19.0
Hungary	105	109	110	1.0	2.9	3.8	1.8
Poland	100	100	105	1.0	0.0	0.0	5.0
Less developed countries							
Chile	214	967	3730	27.1	78.3	351.9	673.8
Cambodia	215	554	1382	21.3	25.7	157.7	296.0
Argentina	214	342	385	17.8	58.5	59.8	17.7
Vietnam, South	148	214	310	25.9	25.4	44.6	66.7
Laos	127	166	224	2.4	25.7	30.7	49.3
Indonesia	111	146	196	32.2	6.7	31.5	46.3
Israel	126	152	196	5.6	12.5	20.6	36.1
Brazil	140	158	188	21.5	16.7	12.8	22.9
Colombia	125	153	181	8.0	14.7	22.4	22.3
Philippines	126	140	177	8.2	9.6	11.1	36.2
Portugal	124	140	168	8.4	10.7	12.9	24.4
Mexico‡	110	128	162	3.4	6.8	16.4	38.5
Jamaica	113	135	162	7.2	5.6	19.5	29.6
Paraguay	115	129	161	1.7	9.5	12.2	27.8
Singapore	104	131	158	0.7	2.0	26.0	30.6
Ecuador	117	132	157	5.9	8.3	12.8	25.6
Korea, South	127	131	156	13.4	11.4	3.1	20.9
Greece	108	124	154	2.3	4.8	14.8	32.8
India	110	128	152	3.1	6.8	16.4	26.7
Jordan	113	124	149	4.6	8.6	9.7	22.1
Ireland	118	132	148	7.3	8.2	11.9	15.6
Spain	117	131	145	5.2	8.3	12.0	15.1
Dominican Republic	112	130	143	2.3	7.7	16.1	15.3
Thailand	106	118	142	1.8	3.9	11.3	23.5
Syria	106	127	140	2.8	1.0	19.8	13.8
Iran	111	122	135	2.6	6.7	9.9	13.4
Puerto Rico	108	116	134	3.4	3.8	7.4	20.7
Cyprus	109	118	134	3.1	4.8	8.2	16.5
South Africa§	113	124	133	3.9	6.6	9.7	9.9
Sri Lanka	109	120	131	5.5	5.8	10.1	13.9
Zambia‡	112	118	127	5.4	5.7	5.4	9.5
Iraq	109	114	124	4.0	4.8	4.6	6.9
Guatemala	100	114	123	1.6	0.0	14.0	9.8
Malta	106	114	120	2.6	3.9	7.5	6.2
Tunisia	108	113	117	3.3	1.9	4.6	2.6
Venezuela	110	117	115	2.6	5.8	6.4	5.5
Ethiopia‡	94	103	111	3.2	−6.9	9.6	9.9

*January–June (average).
†First half 1974 over first half 1973.
‡Excluding rent.
§White population only.
Sources: International Monetary Fund, *International Financial Statistics;* United Nations, *Monthly Bulletin of Statistics;* International Labour Office, *Bulletin of Labour Statistics.*

Table II. Indices of Food Prices in Relation to Cost-of-Living Index

Country (1970=100)	1971	1972	1973	1974*
Developed market economies				
Canada	98	101	107	112
U.S.	99	100	108	111
U.K.	102	103	109	111
Australia	98	96	101	104†
Denmark	100	102	106	104
Japan	100	99	100	103
France	101	102	105	103
New Zealand	99	97	100	101†
Sweden	102	105	104	101
Italy	99	100	101	100†
Austria	99	99	99	98
Germany, West	98	99	99	98
Belgium	98	99	100	98
Finland	98	100	101	98
Norway	100	100	102	98
Switzerland	100	100	97	97
Netherlands, The	97	96	96	94
Centrally planned economies				
Yugoslavia	101	103	105	105†
Poland	102	102	102	104†
Hungary	100	98	99	99
Less developed countries				
Chile	103	125	131	129
Jordan	102	105	113	128
Cambodia	114	116	129	119
Paraguay	103	105	114	115
Laos	99	107	115	115
Ecuador	98	101	108	114‡
Indonesia	98	102	112	114†
Colombia	99	103	110	113‡
Korea, South	105	106	106	108†
Greece	102	102	107	108
South Africa§	99	99	105	106
Venezuela	100	103	106	106
Iraq	101	100	101	105
Cyprus	101	102	103	105‡
Malta	98	99	105	105†
Mexico	99	99	101	104‡
Iran	102	104	102	104‡
Ireland	99	101	106	104‡
Israel	101	98	98	102
Guatemala	98	98	102	102‡
India	98	98	102	102‡
Sri Lanka	99	99	102	102
El Salvador	100	99	100	101†
Peru	100	100	100	101‡
Spain	100	100	101	100†
Argentina	105	108	105	99†
Syria	99	98	100	98†
Ethiopia	99	93	96	97†
Turkey	98	96	99	97‡
Vietnam, South	96	99	101	97
Portugal	97	96	93	95

*January–July (average) except where stated otherwise.
†January–June (average).
‡January–May (average).
§White population only.
Sources: United Nations, *Monthly Bulletin of Statistics;* International Labour Office, *Bulletin of Labour Statistics.*

dent on world markets, but the country might have avoided a good deal of imported inflation if it had not neglected its primary sectors.

The rate of inflation in less developed countries was generally much worse than in the developed economies. In most less developed countries price increases were of the order of 20–40% and one, Chile, was obviously moving into the dangerous sphere of hyperinflation. Sharp price increases coupled with growing balance of payments problems imposed great hardships on many less developed countries. Even Israel, which in many respects was better placed than most, experienced a significant deterioration in the standard of living. In November the Israeli pound was devalued by 43% in an attempt to correct a massive balance of payments deficit. The devaluation was accompanied by a series of drastic measures: food subsidies were halved; wages were no longer to be fully indexed to the cost of living; and imports of many consumer goods, including cars, were banned for six months and were to bear a 15% surcharge after that. The subsequent rise in the prices of a wide range of goods, many of them essentials, led to riots.

Substantially higher prices of essentials, notably food, became a major problem all over the world. This can be seen to some extent in Table II, which shows that there were few countries in which food prices failed to increase even faster than the cost of living in general. (The figures were obtained by dividing the index of food prices by the total index of consumer prices. Consequently, figures over 100 indicate that food prices were rising faster than consumer prices as a whole; and vice versa.) These developments were bound to hit hardest at inhabitants of less developed countries and lower-income groups in industrial coun-

Following a government-ordered rise in the price of pasta, a housewife in Rome restocks her larder. The staple of Italian life had virtually disappeared from grocery shelves before the price hike.

tries, all of whom normally spend a high proportion of their income on food.

Wholesale Prices. The figures in Table III were ominous in the sense that it takes some time before increases in wholesale prices are passed on in higher consumer prices. In 1974 wholesale prices went up by less than 15% in only 6 of the 37 countries included in the table. Toward the end of 1974 there were strong signs that the world economy was both sliding into a serious recession and suffering from an unprecedented and worsening rate of inflation. Perhaps even more depressing was the fact that there was no sign that anybody, anywhere, had a viable solution.

(MILIVOJE PANIĆ)

See also Commodity Trade; Economics; Economy, World; Employment, Wages, and Hours; Exchange and Payments, International; Income, National; Industrial Production and Technology; Investment, International; Marketing and Merchandising; Money and Banking; Stock Exchanges.

[533.B; 534.D.3.b]

Table III. Wholesale Prices for Selected Countries

Country	Index (1970 = 100) 1972	1973	1974*	Annual % change 1967–71 Average	Annual % changes over preceding year 1972	1973	1974†
Developed market economies							
Italy	108	126	167	3.7	4.8	16.7	40.3
Finland	114	134	160	5.7	8.6	17.5	27.0
France‡	107	122	156	4.6	4.9	14.0	33.3
Canada	108	132	155	2.4	6.9	22.2	26.0
Denmark	109	125	149	4.3	4.8	14.7	23.1
Japan	100	116	148	1.3	1.0	16.0	34.5
Sweden	109	121	148	4.0	4.8	11.0	26.5
U.K.§	115	123	143	6.1	5.5	7.0	19.2
New Zealand	120	138	143	6.5	11.1	15.0	7.5
U.S.	108	122	138	3.2	4.8	13.0	16.9
Belgium	103	116	134	2.1	4.0	12.6	18.6
Switzerland	106	117	134	2.3	3.9	10.4	17.5
Norway	108	117	133	3.9	2.8	8.3	17.7
Netherlands, The	105	118	132	2.1	4.0	12.4	15.8
Germany, West	107	114	127	2.6	2.9	6.5	13.4
Austria	109	111	124	3.3	3.8	1.8	14.8
Less developed countries							
Argentina	246	371	399	16.8	75.7	50.8	12.1
Vietnam, South	159	241	375	17.7	33.6	51.6	86.6
Philippines	127	159	237	10.4	9.5	25.2	66.9
Colombia	132	169	216	8.1	17.8	28.0	37.6
Brazil	143	166	202	21.5	19.2	16.1	26.2
Israel	122	145	198	5.4	10.9	18.8	44.5
Greece	110	136	185	2.8	5.8	23.6	51.6
Korea, South	124	132	179	8.4	13.8	6.4	39.8
Yugoslavia‡	128	145	172	6.6	11.3	13.3	24.6
India	118	141	168	2.7	8.2	19.5	27.3
Thailand	108	133	167	−0.5	8.0	23.1	33.6
Syria	105	142	162	3.2	−5.4	35.2	28.4
Mexico	107	124	149	3.7	2.9	15.9	28.4
Portugal	108	120	148	3.7	3.8	11.1	27.6
El Salvador	100	121	148	0.8	5.3	21.0	27.6
Spain	113	124	144	3.1	6.6	9.7	19.0
South Africa	113	128	143	2.8	7.6	13.3	15.3
Iran	113	125	141	3.1	6.6	10.6	17.5
Guatemala	101	116	131	2.9	−1.0	14.8	19.1
Venezuela	107	114	124	2.3	2.9	6.5	11.7
Iraq	102	107	117	3.3	−3.8	4.9	12.5

*January–June (average).
†First half 1974 over first half 1973.
‡Prices of industrial products.
§Prices of finished goods only.
Sources: International Monetary Fund, *International Financial Statistics*; United Nations, *Monthly Bulletin of Statistics*.

Prisons and Penology

Violence and counterviolence marked the year 1974 in prison systems throughout the world. There were jailbreaks, riots, and a major scandal involving brutality and corruption among prison staff. Nineteen prisoners blasted their way out of Ireland's top security prison at Portlaoise with the help of explosives smuggled in with food parcels. Three convicts escaped from a Colorado jail and went on a revenge-inspired rampage against witnesses at their trial, in the course of which they killed a man and a woman, raped two women, and wounded five other persons. Eleven prison officers were arrested on charges of manslaughter, torture, and corruption at the prison at Mannheim, W.Ger., and another 50 were under

Printing: *see* Industrial Production and Technology

The federal minimum security prison at Allenwood, Pa., focus of national attention as the temporary residence of numbers of political figures involved in the Watergate misdeeds.

investigation; among the details that emerged was the story of one prisoner who was found dead in his cell, having choked to death on his own vomit after being savagely beaten and kicked by staff members. Three convicts held 13 hostages captive for ten days in the library of the state prison at Huntsville, Tex., in an attempt to bargain for their freedom; the siege ended with the deaths of two prisoners and two hostages.

Widespread unrest in French prisons during July and August involved more than 40 institutions and resulted in six deaths, some two dozen wounded, and millions of francs worth of damage. At one stage the prisoners themselves attempted to contain the disturbances; at the Santé jail in Paris, prisoners wrote a carefully worded letter urging inmates in all French prisons to be patient and remain calm in view of the reforms that, by then, had been promised by the government. A few days later things turned uglier, however; there were attempts at mass escapes, followed by intervention by riot police and a number of killings. At the same time, prison staff began to express their own discontent over pay and working conditions. This, in turn, temporarily delayed the implementation of some reforms, since the government did not wish to appear to act under duress. Eventually, the atmosphere calmed down and a program to ease the situation was established.

The basic trouble was a shortage of money; only 0.75% of the French national budget was devoted to the prison system and the work of the courts. Grievances included antiquated buildings and lack of suitable work and low earnings for inmates. In addition, many prison rules and regulations—such as those governing visits and other contacts with the outside world—needed revision. Finally, many accused persons were still being held in custody for very long periods before trial. The question of speeding up criminal proceedings and of a much more liberal use of bail arose in France as it had arisen previously in Italy. (In the U.S. bail was used more frequently than in European countries.) As an earnest of the government's intention to introduce the long-overdue reforms quickly, Pres. Valéry Giscard d'Estaing himself visited the Saint Paul and Saint Joseph prisons in Lyons, the most important jail complex in France after those in Paris and Marseilles, and listened to what the inmates had to say.

The question of more liberal use of bail was also examined by a Home Office working party in the U.K.

One of the most important recommendations of their report, *Bail Procedures in Magistrates' Courts,* issued in May, was that the presumption of innocence should extend to the defendant when the question of remand in custody was being considered by the courts: bail should invariably be granted unless the court was completely satisfied that it must be refused. To strengthen this recommendation further, it was suggested that the courts be compelled to state the reasons for refusing bail in writing. Almost parallel with the publication of this report came plans for the establishment of more so-called bail hostels, specifically for the purpose of providing a fixed address for those who had previously been refused bail because they were homeless. Meanwhile, in Belgium, persons who had been "unjustifiably" held without bail had begun to apply for indemnities under the provisions of a 1973 law.

Alternatives to Prison. To an increasing extent, the current use of imprisonment itself was being questioned. For example, in the U.S., in 1973, the federally supported National Advisory Commission on Criminal Justice Standards and Goals had presented the then attorney general, Elliot L. Richardson, with a report proposing, among other reforms, that prison be reserved only for hard-core criminals. A symposium held in Helsinki, Fin., in June 1974 by the International Penal and Penitentiary Foundation discussed the topic "Is There a Future for Imprisonment?" It was attended by leading penal administrators and penologists from many countries, and the broad general conclusion was that, though prison remained necessary (some called it a necessary evil), many countries could considerably reduce their prison population without significant risk to the public.

A few weeks earlier, British Home Secretary Roy Jenkins, in the course of welcoming the report of the Advisory Council on the Penal System, *Young Adult Offenders,* published in May, gave a few approximate international comparisons of prison populations in roughly similar Western European countries. West Germany kept more than 80 of every 100,000 of the total population behind walls; in England and Wales the figure was about 70; while France, Belgium, and the Scandinavian countries ranged from just under 70 to less than 40. However, The Netherlands, as highly industrialized and as densely populated as any of the others, managed to tolerate a prison population of only 22 per 100,000. (The figures for the U.S. were substantially higher than any of these.)

The report included the rather negative results of custodial treatment (65.1% of young men in the 17–21 age group sentenced to borstal training in young offender institutions and as many as 70.1% of those sent to prison in 1968 had been reconvicted after two years) and also the latest findings of research undertaken in both the U.S. and Britain. The two most significant conclusions were that long sentences were no more effective in influencing post-release behaviour than short sentences and, more generally, that there was considerable doubt concerning the effectiveness of imprisonment, as opposed to treatment in the community, in preventing further crime. (*See* Special Report.)

The report proposed a much more sparing use of custodial treatment for shorter periods, and suggested new forms of treatment in the community under the general guidance and supervision of a comparatively large probation service. It quickly aroused interest

continued on page 570

THE PROBLEM OF PRISONS: REFORM OR ABOLITION?

By Jessica Mitford

It is surprising to learn that prison as a place of confinement for the ordinary lawbreaker is less than 200 years old, an institution of purely American origin, conceived by its inventors as a noble humanitarian reform befitting an Age of Enlightenment. There had been prisons and dungeons of sorts for centuries, of course, but these were reserved for persons of quality. Lowlier offenders were detained in prison only while awaiting trial. In colonial America, as in Europe, the standard punishment for the pickpocket, the thief, the highwayman was hanging; for lesser offenders mutilation, the stocks, public brandings and floggings.

Failure of a Reform. Shortly after the American Revolution, a group of high-minded Pennsylvania Quakers set about abolishing these barbarities from the New World. As a result of their efforts, the first penitentiary (their word), the Walnut Street Jail in Philadelphia, was established in 1790. Under Pennsylvania state law, only murder remained a capital offense. The basic feature of the penitentiary was total isolation of the offender from his fellow miscreants. Serving out his sentence in solitude with only the Bible for company, he would in time be brought to penitence for his sins and thus to eternal salvation.

Unfortunately for the Quakers' good intentions, things went wrong from the very beginning. So many convicts went mad or died as a consequence of the solitary regime that by the mid-19th century it was generally abandoned, to be supplanted by the more profitable "congregate hard labour" system. The very corporal punishments the Quakers had sought to replace flourished behind the walls and ever more ingenious tortures to enforce discipline were devised.

That "prisons are a failure" is a cliché dating from the origin of prison, and the failure has given rise to demands for reform. The authors of *Struggle for Justice,* a report prepared by a working party of the American Friends Service Committee, summarize the "reformist prescription" which, they say, is bankrupt:

More judges and more "experts" for the courts, improved educational and therapeutic programs in penal institutions, more and better trained personnel at higher salaries, preventive surveillance of predelinquent children, greater use of probation, careful classification of inmates, preventive detention through indeterminate sentences, small "cottage" institutions, halfway houses, removal of broad classes of criminals (such as juveniles) from criminal to "nonpunitive" processes, the use of lay personnel in treatment—all this paraphernalia of the "new" criminology appears over and over in nineteenth century reformist literature.

Anyone with the fortitude to read that forbidding literature will recognize the formula, and it is repeated in such later documents as a 1931 report of the Wickersham Commission on Law Observance and Enforcement, appointed by Pres. Herbert Hoover in 1929, and "The Challenge of Crime in Free Society," the 1967 report of the President's Commission on Law Enforcement and Administration of Justice. These calls for reform in-

Jessica Mitford is the author of numerous articles and books that have received wide acclaim. She is particularly noted for works of the analytical critique genre, of which The American Way of Death *and* Kind and Usual Punishment *are outstanding examples. The latter work expands upon the theme of this article.*

variably follow in the wake of riots and strikes by prisoners protesting intolerable conditions. Thus the pattern over the past century tends to be circular: an outbreak of prison disturbances —followed by brutal suppression of the insurgents—followed by newspaper clamour for investigation—followed by broad agreement that prisons are horrible, destructive places—followed by a restatement of the penological nostrums of preceding decades.

There have always been those who looked beyond palliative reform proposals to the essential character of prison, found it intrinsically evil, hence have advocated abolishing prisons altogether: George Bernard Shaw, Clarence Darrow, and Federal District Judge James Doyle, to name a few. I share their conviction. But I also agree with the authors of *Struggle for Justice* when they note "the impossibility of achieving more than a superficial reformation of our criminal justice system without a radical change in our values and a drastic restructuring of our social and economic institutions."

The Delusion of Safety. The objectives of prison, as traditionally set forth by penologists, are threefold: protection of the public by locking up the lawbreaker, deterrence, and rehabilitation. (A fourth, punishment, has virtually been dropped from the lexicon, although this is the only objective that prison actually achieves.) Today, few would seriously argue that prison rehabilitates. The proponent of abolition will, however, meet with deeply felt objections on the other counts: "My God, if you let all those killers, rapists, thugs, burglars on the streets, it wouldn't be safe to venture out!" And, "If we had no prisons, the crime rate would soar."

The law-abiding citizen's belief that the prison protects him is, it turns out, illusory. Only a minuscule fraction of lawbreakers are in prison; the vast majority are all around us in the community. The National Commission on the Causes and Prevention of Violence says that for an estimated nine million crimes committed in the United States in a recent year, only $1\frac{1}{2}\%$ of the perpetrators were imprisoned.

What of the categories of crime that send the public temperature soaring the highest—murder, sex offenses, street muggings? Of those murderers who have been caught, prosecuted, and imprisoned, the number who murder again when eventually released (as most of them are) is so negligible that it is not even recorded on the "recidivism" tables so beloved of criminologists. For example, a study by the Philadelphia Bar Association of 215 persons pardoned after serving terms for murder shows that only 7 were later arrested, and of these only one, or 0.5%, for murder. These people have generally acted out some desperate personal frustration, are most likely to repent, least likely to repeat— unless, of course, they are psychotic, in which case they do not belong in prison at all.

Of those convicted of sex offenses (and thereafter forever stigmatized in police records as "sex offenders"), only an estimated 5% have committed crimes of violence. The other 95% are in for activities which, while they may be annoying, do not physically harm anybody, such as voyeurism and indecent exposure, or for types of sexual behaviour arbitrarily labeled "criminal," like statutory rape and homosexuality.

As for street muggers, few are ever caught, since it is in the nature of their crime to strike at night or in unfrequented places. New York is today in the grip of an almost palpable terror of street attacks, muggings, beatings. A white middle-class New Yorker told me: "People are afraid of three main types of criminal: underprivileged blacks and Puerto Ricans, drug addicts, and aberrant psychotics." His views would no doubt be shared by many a ghetto dweller, on whom the burden of such crime falls most heavily. Is prison the solution to any of the problems he enumerated—poverty, drug addiction, insanity? If so, to protect New Yorkers from all who suffer from these disabilities it would be necessary to turn half the city into a prison.

To what extent is fear of prison successful as a deterrent to crime? Obviously those who have been caught and convicted were not deterred, and from the large numbers of repeaters one must infer that the prison experience did not turn them into the paths of righteousness. Criminologists scratch their heads over the deterrent effect of fear of prison on the general populace; most have concluded that respectable people are kept that way mostly from fear of the shame of *any* brush with the law.

As proof that long prison terms do not deter, the California Assembly Committee on Criminal Procedure has cited a number of studies, one of the most striking of which arose out of a 1963 U.S. Supreme Court decision in *Gideon* v. *Wainwright,* in which the court affirmed the right of indigent felony defendants to counsel. As a consequence of the decision, the state of Florida was obliged to discharge, long before the normal release date, 1,252 indigent prisoners who had been tried and convicted of felonies without counsel. The Florida Division of Corrections conducted a study comparing their recidivism rate with an equal number of full-term releases. Result: 28 months after discharge, 25% of the full-term release group had returned to criminal activity, compared with only 13.6% of the early release group.

From these findings the Assembly Committee concluded that "the amount of time served has no measurable effect upon crime among released convicts." It made the further comment that "what is often neglected in official statements is not that prisons fail to rehabilitate but the *active* nature of the destruction that occurs in prison." But it did not explore the next question that logically arises: if prisons were abolished and "time served" reduced to zero, would *this* have any measurable effect on crime?

An Experiment in Abolition. An experiment currently under way in Massachusetts, first of its kind anywhere in the country, may point to some answers. During the '60s the Massachusetts juvenile prisons, housing offenders and abandoned children aged 7 to 17, were notorious for their horrible living conditions, overcrowding, and brutality. In October 1969 the governor appointed a new commissioner of the Department of Youth Services, Jerome G. Miller, whose avowed intention was to abolish all juvenile institutions in the state.

During Miller's first two years in office the population of the juvenile prisons was cut from 1,200–1,500 to 650–750. By the autumn of 1972 the institutional population had been reduced to 80–100. The erstwhile prisoners were released to their own homes or placed in foster homes, prep schools that generally catered to upper- and middle-class youngsters, or residential centres where they were free to come and go. Only those considered "seriously assaultive," about 40 to 50, were housed in the one remaining "secure facility," and these were in the custody of a private ex-convict group. Another 50 to 60 youths deemed "disturbed" were in a special psychiatric facility.

Miller assumes that imprisonment and the threat of imprisonment have no measurable effect on the rate of crime. As of January 1974, his views would seem to have been empirically borne out: preliminary reports showed there was no discernible increase in overall juvenile crime rates as a result of shutting down the prisons—if anything, there had been a slight drop in arrest rates. Moreover, since the closing of the prisons there had been, according to Miller, a "dramatic drop in the amount of violence among those committed to the department." The new programs were not limited to those committed for minor offenses but included offenders in every category, Miller told me. The 80 to 100 kept in secure institutions were youngsters who had committed "really weird, crazy crimes," and even in these cases the goal was to relocate them in the community as soon as possible.

Who Is "Dangerous"? The notion that 75%, or 80%, or 90% of the prison population could be freed tomorrow without danger to the community finds amazingly wide acceptance in prison administration circles. Even the toughest wardens of the roughest prisons will quote some such figure off the record. Should the wardens be taken at their word, and 90% of their captives freed, this would be a giant step in the direction of abolishing prisons.

Yet the very concept of the "dangerous" 10%, and of prison as an appropriate place to confine them, is fraught with peril. Somebody has to decide who is dangerous. The decision rests first of all with the sentencing judge, and there is no consensus among judges as to who is "dangerous." A criminologist told me of a sentencing institute for federal judges in which each judge was given an identical fictional pre-sentence report on a fictional offender. "For the same offense one judge would have given probation; another, twenty years in the penitentiary."

In the current era of prison rebellion, the label "dangerous" is increasingly used by authorities to immure protesters and political militants. Hence the term "political prisoner," originally applied to Vietnam war resisters, civil rights demonstrators, and the like, has been adopted by prison militants convicted of offenses not commonly considered political. They argue that they are victims of class and/or ethnic oppression, that imprisonment is employed to coerce their acquiescence to a status quo of deprivation, indignity, injustice. Is this reasoning valid?

Envision, if you can, a prison system populated primarily by the white and the well-to-do, convicted of crimes that are peculiar to the affluent: price-fixing, purchase and sale of political

Recreation at the federal correctional institution in Fort Worth, Tex., an experimental "coed" prison.

SHELLY KATZ—BLACK STAR

influence, product adulteration, industrial pollution, criminal neglect of industrial safety standards, fraudulent stock manipulation (crimes that, incidentally, cause infinitely more death, injury, and impoverishment than all the "street crimes" put together). That this notion seems like the wildest flight of fancy is already a commentary on the class character of the prison system. It is axiomatic that as long as privileges of class and skin colour prevail in the society, this state of affairs will be reflected in its prisons and will determine who coerces whom.

Most studies of the causes of crime in this decade, whether contained in sociological texts, high-level governmental commission reports, or best-selling books like Ramsey Clark's *Crime in America,* lament the disproportionately high arrest rate for blacks and poor people and assert with wearying monotony that criminality is a product of slums and poverty. Clark invites the reader to mark on his city map the areas where health and education are poorest, where unemployment and poverty are highest, where blacks are concentrated—and he will find these areas also have the highest crime rates.

There is evidence that a high proportion of people in all walks of life have at some time or other committed what are conventionally called "serious crimes." A study of 1,700 New Yorkers weighted toward the upper income brackets, who had never been arrested for anything and who were guaranteed anonymity, revealed that 91% had committed at least one felony or serious misdemeanour. Sixty-four percent of the men and 27% of the women had committed at least one felony for which they could have been sent to the state penitentiary.

If crimes are committed by people of all classes, why the near-universal equation of criminal type and slum dweller? No doubt despair and terrible conditions in the slums give rise to one sort of crime, the only kind available to the very poor: theft, robbery, purse-snatching. The well-to-do commit crimes that are less likely to be detected and punished: embezzlement, sale of fraudulent stock, price-fixing. After all, the bank president is not likely to become a bank robber; nor does the bank robber have the opportunity to embezzle depositors' funds.

Two Roads to Reform. If the criminal justice system, with the penitentiary at the end of it, exists principally as a potent weapon of class control, it becomes imperative to distinguish between two types of reform proposals: those designed to perpetuate and reinforce the system, and those that to one degree or another challenge the whole premise of prison and move in the direction of its abolition.

In the first category are reforms that call for more money for "corrections," more prison employees at higher salaries, more experts, more utilization of the latest scientific know-how in "treatment" of prisoners, building new correctional therapeutic communities to replace the old fortress prisons. These sound attractive to the well-intentioned reformer—and are vehemently opposed by convict organizations, which see them as a mere refurbishing of the facade.

Reform proposals in the second category, most frequently originating with the prisoners themselves, are aimed at reducing the discretionary power of authorities all down the line, at lowering prison populations, and at restoring to prisoners those constitutional rights that will enable them to organize and fight injustice within the system. More than this, they are actions that would restore human dignity to the convict and would remove him from the status of "nonperson" to which he has traditionally been relegated.

If the starting point is that prisons are intrinsically evil and should be abolished, then the first principle of reform should be to have as few people as possible confined and for as short a time as possible. There should be a moratorium on all new prison building. A broad range of offenses should be made noncriminal: prostitution, gambling, adult-consenting sexual acts, all drug use. Cash bail should be abolished, and those now jailed awaiting trial should be released.

Sentences, which for most crimes are longer in the U.S. than in any other Western country, should be greatly reduced in length. Parole, beloved of reformers as a "helping service" and loathed by convicts as an extension of prison servitude, should be abolished and replaced by unsupervised release.

The untrammeled discretion now invested in the authorities via indeterminate sentences should be eliminated. In practice, these set up a penal system within a penal system, the first ostensibly governed by due process, the second totally uninhibited by the vaunted principles of Anglo-Saxon jurisprudence.

The emergent organization of prisoners into something akin to trade unions within the penitentiaries is an entirely new phenomenon, an outgrowth of the prison rebellion of the past decade. For the first time prisoners are attempting to win the right to bargain with their keepers over the conditions of their lives, including prevailing industrial wages for the many jobs they perform. Since a prison regime is absolutist, and hence peculiarly susceptible to the absolute corruptions of power, a ruthless attempt to crush the incipient prison movement is a clear and present danger. Only informed, insistent, massive public support of the prisoners can counter this threat.

When people come upon the celebrated statement of Eugene V. Debs—"While there is a soul in prison I am not free"—they are prone to regard it as an affirmation of extraordinary human compassion. This it is. But it also may be viewed as a profound social insight. And not only because the prison system, inherently unjust and inhumane, is the ultimate expression of injustice and inhumanity in the society at large. Those of us on the outside do not like to think of wardens and guards as our surrogates. Yet they are, and they are intimately locked in a deadly embrace with their human captives behind the prison walls. By extension, we are also there.

A terrible double meaning is thus imparted to the original question of human ethics: Am I my brother's keeper?

A.F.P./PICTORIAL PARADE

Used as a prison since Roman times, the barren Greek island of Yiaros is now deserted. The last 44 prisoners, held for political reasons, were released on July 25.

continued from page 566

in Europe as well as in Canada, Australia, and New Zealand, and there was little doubt that many countries would now seek to deal with the large number of relatively minor offenders (even those with several previous convictions) by means other than imprisonment. Treatment in the community often involved an element of self-help, and it had already been proved that some ex-offenders make good social workers; in helping others to cope with problems they understand from their own experience, they often help themselves.

Among various demonstration projects started in 1974, those based on the crisis intervention theory were especially noteworthy. According to this theory, crises should not be seen as yet another obstacle to frustrated social workers. On the contrary, they provide a special opportunity, since in a crisis situation offenders and their families may be more prepared than normally to reach out toward help or to envisage solutions that they might be reluctant to contemplate at other times. Crisis intervention centres depended on their ability to operate immediately and intensively on a number of different levels, including the provision of accommodation, jobs, and possibly therapy.

Psychiatric Treatment. Prison would have to be retained for dangerous and professional criminals, but there was fresh thinking concerning the area where criminality and mental abnormality overlap. Most modern correctional systems had a psychiatric prison, or at least psychiatric units within particular prisons, and some countries also had special psychiatric hospitals which, though they were not prisons, were nevertheless secure enough to hold the criminally insane. There were many mentally abnormal offenders, however, who could not be dealt with readily and appropriately either in prisons or in ordinary mental hospitals. Among these were a number of helplessly violent offenders whose explosive behaviour could be triggered by almost anything.

There were also passive but highly manipulative and devious prison inmates who managed to make life difficult for others and for themselves; they were criminal but not insane, and exhibited marked character abnormalities that posed endless problems in prison. They were much better dealt with under closed psychiatric hospital conditions, where they could be treated with patience, some form of milieu therapy, and the careful and judicious use of mild mood-controlling drugs. In the U.K. a committee under the chairmanship of Lord Butler proposed in July that 500 such offenders (or one in 70 of the prison population) be removed from prisons and accommodated in small secure psychiatric hospital units, with a high nursing complement and a number of specialists in forensic psychiatry. Eventually these units would become centres of forensic psychiatry.

Prison Regimes. For those in closed prisons, the general tendency in 1974 was to liberalize conditions without loss of security and also to introduce more rewards, such as the possibility of regaining a period of remission lost as a punishment. In the U.K. the bread-and-water diet was abolished in June, and the home secretary decided in July to end the practice of forcibly feeding prisoners who were on hunger strike (given prominence by the hunger strike of the sisters Dolours and Marion Price and other imprisoned members of the Irish Republican Army)—a practice that still existed in many countries, including the U.S.

The purpose of open prisons was increasingly questioned. They served a function in the final stages of long sentences, providing a necessary transition between the sheltered conditions of prison and the demands of outside life. Long-term prisoners, though they might be elated over their impending release, could become very anxious at the thought of facing a world that had probably changed radically since their sentence began. Open prisons also sometimes served as places where experimental regimes could be tried out, as in the "coed" prison at Framingham near Boston, Mass., where men and women worked and had their meals together and went to dances, though they remained separately housed. There was a growing feeling, however, that apart from these situations, prisoners eligible for open prison could be dealt with better—and probably more cheaply—outside prison altogether.

Victims of Crime. Penology was also concerning itself with the victim. Concern for the victim was one of the major factors in public attitudes toward crime, yet neither the law nor society did very much for him. This had not always been so: in Saxon law, one of the primary aims of criminal proceedings was the healing of the breach that the crime had created between people. By contrast, the modern system had largely impersonalized the operation of justice. Victims might sometimes play a part in helping to prove the offense, but otherwise courts concentrated exclusively on the offender.

New Zealand was the first country to introduce (1963) compensation for victims of crimes of violence, and since that time other countries had followed its lead. The ninth Conference of European Ministries of Justice, meeting in Vienna in May 1974, expressed itself as being in favour of more such compensation systems. Meanwhile, penologists pointed out that courts employed no social workers to investigate the plight of victims sympathetically. Proposals were made for a victim casualty service, possibly partly staffed by ex-offenders. In the U.K. voluntary discussion groups composed of victims and offenders enabled offenders to appreciate the consequences of their actions in human terms and victims to correct some preconceptions about offenders.

(HUGH J. KLARE)

See also Crime and Law Enforcement.
[521.C.3.a; 543.A.5.a; 10/36.C.5.b]

Profits

The year 1974 began on a note of optimism. The leading industrial countries had emerged relatively unscathed from the oil embargoes and production cutbacks that were imposed by the Arab countries after the October 1973 Arab-Israeli war. The threat that serious damage might yet result from this action was eliminated when, at the end of 1973, the Arab nations began progressively to increase production and, in March, terminated their embargoes for most nations.

But the optimism was short-lived. Once the acute problem of oil supply receded, other serious issues came to the fore. Attention turned to inflation, which had already surpassed all previous post-World War II records. And there was a growing realization that the unprecedented worldwide boom of 1972–73 was in many countries giving way to recession.

This setting would not appear to provide an auspicious climate for profits. Yet the published data for the current year, which were limited to the United States, Canada, the United Kingdom, West Germany, and Japan, suggested at first glance that corporations had done surprisingly well in the face of adversity. In the U.S. and Canada, pretax profits attained new records in the latest period reported; in the U.K. and Japan, the latest results were second only to the peak level reached in the immediately preceding period; only in West Germany, where data limitations shrouded profits in a veil of ambiguity, was there a hint of significant weakness.

Before proceeding to examine profit developments on a country-by-country basis, it might be well to consider the reasons for this appearance of strength. These reasons relate primarily to the effect of inflation on corporate financial statements. Most obviously, inflation tends to swell all money magnitudes, giving the illusion of growth even though the physical volume of business and the purchasing power of earnings may have declined. But there are also more subtle reasons. By the very nature of their operations, businesses sell in the course of one accounting period merchandise acquired through purchase or production during preceding periods. Their reported profits are largely the difference between the prices they receive currently and the cost of goods being sold, which represents, at least in part, expenses incurred earlier. This introduces no distortions when prices and costs remain stable, but in times of inflation reported profits are magnified by the sale at current inflated prices of goods accumulated when prices were lower. These so-called inventory profits, moreover, enter into total profits and are subject to income tax.

While the national income accounts of several countries endeavoured to identify and to separate inventory profits from operating income, no comparable effort was made to quantify another distorting influence that may be at least as large as the effect of inflation on inventories. This is "under depreciation," or the failure of depreciation based on historical costs to provide for the replacement of plant and equipment during inflation. Businesses use a variety of techniques for spreading the historical cost of their plant and equipment over the estimated service lives of the assets concerned. But, as in the case of inventories, inflation precludes historical cost depreciation from generating the funds needed for asset replacement. If depreciation allowances reflected replacement costs, as would be logical for firms that wish to keep their productive real capital intact, reported profits would have been substantially lower than actually indicated in 1974 statements.

United States. At first glance, corporate profits in the U.S. seemed to defy the downward movement of the national economy. Both before income tax and after, they rose steadily in 1974, reaching the highest levels ever recorded in the third quarter of 1974. At the indicated annual rate of $158.4 billion, pretax profits were 29% higher in that quarter than they were in the same quarter of 1973, and after-tax profits, at $94.9 billion, were 30.2% higher.

As already indicated, however, the glowing appearance of profits reflected more the flush of an inflationary fever than the reality of vibrant health. Inventory profits, rising at an annual rate of $51.7 billion in the third quarter of 1974, were three times as large as in the comparable quarter of 1973 and made up one-third of total pretax profits. Indeed, if inventory profits are deducted from the total, pretax profits fluctuated narrowly about a level of some $106 billion, annual rate, from the second quarter of 1973 through the third quarter of 1974. This meant, of course, that profits actually declined in terms of dollars of constant purchasing power. Yet corporate tax liabilities rose 25% over the same period, illustrating how inflation results in the taxation of capital. And this did not tell the whole story, for the national income statistics made no allowance for underdepreciation.

After-tax profit margins in manufacturing increased steadily, reaching in the second quarter of 1974 the highest level since 1950. But the more analytical measures told a different story. After inventory valuation adjustment, pretax profits fell below 10% of national income in the third quarter of 1973 and continued down to 9.2% in the same quarter of 1974. Thus, they reached the lowest level of the postwar period except for the 1969–70 recession. Moreover, after inventory valuation adjustment and tax, profits had been falling per dollar of gross product originating in nonfinancial corporations since the end of 1972. By the third quarter of 1974, they reached the lowest level ever recorded in the statistics, which date back to 1946.

Canada. The oil crisis was less of a jolt to the Canadian economy than to that of the U.S., for Canada was self-sufficient in energy. Indeed, as an exporter of oil, Canada was a beneficiary of the price increases forced by the cartel of oil-exporting nations (of which Canada was not a member). Thus, Canadian output was better maintained than that of the U.S. in 1974. Nevertheless, real gross national product (GNP) displayed no growth in either the second or third quarter, and many forecasters anticipated that several quarters of decline were in prospect.

Despite the cessation of economic growth, corporate profits surged upward. In the third quarter of 1974 pretax profits attained a new record, one-third higher than in the comparable period of 1973. Although inventory profits rose 50% over the same period, the pretax total, after adjustment for inventory profits, still managed to climb 30%.

Indexes for the manufacturing sector showed that the growth of profits per unit of output exceeded increases in labour income per unit. Thus, from the second quarter of 1973 to the same quarter of 1974, unit profits rose 40% while unit labour costs mounted 9.9%. The concurrent increase in selling prices, which made these simultaneous gains possible, was 20%.

United Kingdom. As in the case of the United States, Britain's profit situation could not be fully understood from a casual reading of the statistics. These showed that total company income reached a new record quarterly rate of £5,450 million at the beginning of 1974, from which they receded only slightly in the second quarter. Indeed, notwithstanding the second-quarter decline, total profits were nearly one-third higher than they were a year earlier. However, operating profits after deducting inventory profits displayed a contrary trend. These had declined since the beginning of 1973, moderately at first and dramatically after the beginning of 1974. During the second quarter of the year, they declined 38% from the year-earlier period. This decline had the extraordinary result of reducing operating profits below inventory profits—so much so, in fact, that they amounted to no more than two-thirds of the latter. Stated differently, inventory profits comprised fully 60% of gross trading profits arising in Britain in the second quarter of 1974. In relation to total domestic income, inventory-adjusted operating income fell in 1974 to the lowest point of the postwar period.

Fortunately for the British companies, rent and nontrading income and income from abroad both increased substantially, thereby cushioning the adverse trend of trading profits on domestic operations. These increased by one-third and two-thirds, respectively, between the second quarters of 1973 and 1974.

The dire straits of British corporations, apparent in the trend of gross trading profits after deducting inventory profits, motivated the British government in its November budget to provide a number of measures to restore liquidity and profitability. Price controls were eased to raise the proportion of labour cost increases that might be passed on to consumers, to permit companies to raise prices for the purpose of financing a portion of new investment expenditures, and to expedite price increases for firms endeavouring to expand investment. Moreover, significant tax relief was provided on inventory gains by allowing companies to deduct from taxable income any increases in the book value of inventories that exceeded 10% of operating profit.

West Germany. The fate of corporate profits in West Germany was difficult to discern, for the data were buried in a catch-all category called entrepreneurial and property income (EPI) that also included the income of professionals and the property income —rent, interest, and dividends—of households. For what they are worth, the data indicated that EPI before tax was slightly lower in the first half of 1974 than in the like period of 1973. The decline in after-tax EPI was more pronounced, reflecting the imposition of a counterinflationary tax surcharge that accounted for approximately DM 1.5 billion of the DM 2.7 billion drop in the net figures. The October *Monthly Report of the Bundesbank* suggested that, since the property income component of EPI "has probably continued to rise sharply," profits must have contracted considerably. Further implying that West Germany's corporate profits were badly squeezed, EPI's share of national income receded to the lowest level of the post-World War II period in the second half of 1973 and then, in the first half of 1974, fell significantly to a still lower proportion.

Additional perspectives on the factors influencing profits were provided by data on productivity, hourly pay rates, unit labour cost, and prices. A comparison of the second quarter of 1974 with the same quarter of 1973 shows that the ratio of price to unit labour cost index, an indicator of profit margins, rose somewhat, from 87 to 90.1%. This suggested that the pressure of wages and salaries was only one element, and perhaps not the dominant one, in a complex of forces impinging on profits—a complex that included the shrinkage of business volume, high interest expense, and increased taxation.

Japan. During the first quarter of 1974, operating profits in current prices reached the highest level in Japan's history. At 4.6 billion yen, seasonally adjusted quarterly rate, they were up more than 40% from the level of one year earlier. In the second quarter, however, they dropped sharply. The peak of net profits occurred one quarter before that of the pretax total. By midyear, after two consecutive quarters of decline, net profits were slightly below 2 billion yen. This represented a drop of nearly one-third from the record level attained at year-end 1973 and the loss of all of the ground gained after the final quarter of 1972. The ratio of operating profits to sales plummeted sharply to 4.5% in the second quarter, reaching the lowest point since the trough of the 1970–71 recession.

Viewed in the perspective of inflation, which carried wholesale prices up almost one-third from second quarter 1973 to second quarter 1974, these profit developments appeared more ominous still. Through the interplay of income taxes, inventory profits, and underdepreciation, such virulent inflation could not have failed to erode the capital base of the business sector. Indeed, the official statistics showed that corporate liquidity, measured by the ratio of cash assets to sales, declined sharply from the beginning of 1973 through mid-1974, even though profits were rising for most of that period.   (GERALD A. POLLACK)

See also Marketing and Merchandising; Stock Exchanges.
[534.C.2.c]

Publishing

The publishing world saw its share of financial problems in the 15 months from October 1973 to December 1974. There were, of course, the difficulties and uncertainties caused by the energy crisis, but publishing throughout the world had to face another crisis just as serious—a shortage in the supply of paper. The United States and Spain had already faced supply difficulties in 1972. Toward the end of 1973 and in early 1974 the shortage became worldwide and led to rising prices, for some qualities by as much as 100%.

The immediate effect of the shortage was an increase in manufacturing costs, and consequently in selling prices, for books, newspapers, and all other printed matter. Obviously, the consumer would not be ready to accept every increase, however much it might be justified. Publishing houses were also affected by increases in the cost of credit, and many firms, especially the smaller and medium-sized ones, were experiencing serious cash flow problems. These were all the more serious in countries where prices were severely controlled, such as France and the United Kingdom.

Newspapers. The crucial problem facing newspapers was one of rising costs: in the U.K., for example, at the beginning of 1974 the cost of taking all the dailies was £1.92 a week; long before the end of the year it had reached £2.95. Despite this massive increase in prices, the year ended with as much uncertainty as it had begun, and in Britain this was demonstrated in the most businesslike terms when the publishing companies produced their annual reports for the financial year April 1973–April 1974.

One of the main problems in this area lay in trying to disentangle publishing interests from the affairs at large of the parent company: two of the most important British newspapers, *The Sunday Times* and the *Daily Mirror,* were part of conglomerates that enfolded not only magazines, local newspaper chains, and book publishing, but anything else from travel (in the case of the Thomson Organization, owners of *The Sunday Times*) to plumbing (Reed International, the *Daily Mirror*'s parent).

Thus, Reed's profit for the six months from April to September 1974 rose from the previous year's £27.6 million to £44.6 million, but virtually all the increase was earned outside Britain. On the publishing front, the rising costs had been met by raising prices, and it was noted that so far there had been no signs of consumer rebellion. But that was before the autumn round of increases and, what was probably more important, before the general economic situation had made a drop in advertising revenue seem inevitable. For a *Financial Times* survey in February had already shown that marketing men planned drastic reductions (of up to 25%) in their annual advertising budgets. In the Thomson report for the same period, April–September 1974, the problems could be seen still more clearly. The profit itself had fallen (from £5.5 million in the same period of 1973) to £1.6 million.

The point was reinforced in the annual report of a smaller company involved almost solely in newspaper publishing. *The Guardian* and *Manchester Evening News* represented together one of the smallest national morning papers and one of the biggest local evening papers. The *Manchester Evening News* supplied the profit to offset *The Guardian*'s loss. The group's figures for 1973–74 showed an increase in trading profit from £1,580,000 to £1,810,000 and a drop of about the same scale in net profit. In October the chairman warned of "substantially lower" profits in the financial year 1974–75.

The situation was not without its ironies: Reed shareholders, for instance, were drawing comfort from the handsome returns of the company's newsprint manufacturing interests—and from the forecast that, with hard economic times making others less likely to invest in the much-needed new plant, prices would continue to rise through 1975.

A further irony lay in the fact that the British press as a whole was well on the way toward a change that some observers had been recommending for years: increasing prices to reduce dependence on advertising. There had been little overall resistance from the readers: total sales of national morning newspapers in the first half of 1974 were 14,882,000, as against 14,866,000 in 1971. In that same period the prices of those papers had risen as much as fourfold. Yet economic conditions erased most of the benefit.

Economies were always being looked for. In June, Vere Harmsworth, chairman of Associated Newspapers, gave warning of the "grave financial crisis" facing the London *Evening News.* He said that success was imperative for the newspaper's future after its September relaunching in a tabloid format. In November its rival, the London *Evening Standard,* stopped publishing its Saturday edition in a drive to

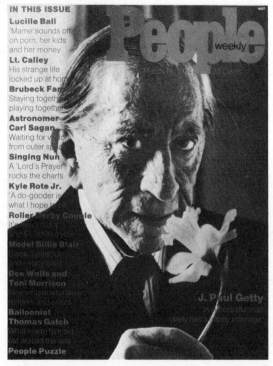

IN THIS ISSUE
Lucille Ball
'Mame' sounds off on porn, her kids and her money
Lt. Calley
His strange life locked up at home
Brubeck Family
Staying together, playing together
Astronomer Carl Sagan
Waiting for word from outer space
Singing Nun
A 'Lord's Prayer' rocks the charts
Kyle Rote Jr.
'A do-gooder is what I hope to be'
Roller Derby Couple
Model Billie Blair
Black, beautiful and nearly bald
Dee Wells and Toni Morrison
Balloonist Thomas Gatch
What made him set out across the sea
People Puzzle

J. Paul Getty

573

Publishing

Capitalizing on the average individual's insatiable curiosity about the affairs of others, "People" was a highly successful 1974 publishing venture.

cut back losses, which reached £130,000 in the first 17 weeks of the financial year alone. The *Evening Standard* was part of the financially troubled Beaverbrook group, which in March had decided to close their Glasgow printing centre and move production of their *Scottish Daily Express* out of Scotland to Manchester, where northern editions of their main title, the *Daily Express,* were printed. This move, which eliminated the jobs of 1,700 journalists and print workers, caused the Labour government to set up a royal commission on the press to examine the factors affecting the maintenance of the independence, diversity, and editorial standards of newspapers and periodicals, and the public's freedom of choice.

Economic problems were worldwide. In one weekend at the end of August, both the French daily newspaper *Combat* and the Dutch daily evening paper *De Tijd* were closed. *Combat*'s death was not perhaps merely a matter of economics. Started as the clandestine voice of the Resistance in World War II, it had Albert Camus as its first editor and Jean-Paul Sartre and André Malraux among its contributors. Recently, however, dwindling circulation had been accompanied by internal dissent, and earlier in 1974 many of the staff had broken away to start a new publication, *Le Quotidien de Paris.* Final closure came after the death of its director, Henry Smadja (*see* OBITUARIES). *Le Quotidien de Paris,* the Catholic *La Croix,* and the Communist *L'Humanité* were all to receive state subsidies in 1975 as "journals of opinion."

The closure of *De Tijd* was of wider interest since it was the first test of The Netherlands' new scheme for government subsidy, a matter of increasing concern in many countries. The Dutch scheme was aimed at preserving a diverse national daily press through reorganization grants to those faced with closing down. In January, *De Tijd,* a quality paper founded 129 years earlier by a Roman Catholic priest, was offered the first such grant. But in August the publishers said they could not meet the second of the two conditions for the grant: that not less than 55,000 copies should be sold and that direct losses should not exceed 3 million guilders.

Elsewhere, the struggle continued, and even in the economic gloom there were some with plans for expansion: *Die Welt,* the Hamburg-based West German daily, announced plans for transferring its central editorial offices to Bonn in 1975 with the aim of becoming the leading national newspaper in a country whose national press was still based on strong regional centres. In May it was announced that *Europa,* the economic monthly published jointly by *Le Monde, La Stampa, The Times* (London), and *Die Welt,* was to be improved and further developed in its second year of publication.

The other main struggle, in 1974 as always, was a basic one for press freedom. In June the new Portuguese military government announced regulations curbing freedom of expression, with penalties including fines of up to about $20,000, 60-day suspension from publication, and indefinite detention. Scarcely a week later the first fine of $4,600 was levied on the Lisbon paper *A Capital,* for a report about two officers who were said to have refused to lead troops against strikers.

In Greece seven years of military rule ended, but many restrictions on public comment and reporting remained. In September there came an attack from Panayotis Lambrias, undersecretary in charge of press affairs in the new government. Lambrias, a journalist for 25 years, charged the Greek daily press with what he called yellow press journalism worse than that of any other country in Europe or North America.

Others continued to suffer more than tongue-lashing. From South America came reports of journalists being shot, imprisoned, put out of work, or censored, almost throughout the continent. In Peru, in July, the six national newspapers were simply expropriated and put under government control. Other regimes acted with little more subtlety. In Rhodesia a three-month ban was imposed on the Roman Catholic weekly *Moto.* The minister of justice, Desmond Lardner-Burke, commented: "For many years this newspaper had taken a line which has been strongly antagonistic against the government and against Europeans generally." (PETER FIDDICK)

For newspapers in the U.S., 1974 was a bittersweet mixture of professional vindication and economic distress. The Watergate affair, which was uncovered by newspaper journalists and pursued with a relentlessness that some readers considered excessive, helped bring about the resignation of Richard Nixon as president of the U.S. That event was seen by many in the profession as an affirmation of the value and legitimacy of investigative reporting, the aggressive, closely researched pursuit of suspected official wrongdoing—a practice that earlier generations of journalists called muckraking. In the wake of Watergate, newspapers across the country began setting up their own investigative reporting units, and a number of those teams came up with consistently worthwhile stories. Pulitzer prizes were awarded to *Washington Star-News* reporter James R. Polk, whose series on the financing of Nixon's 1972 campaign broke the story of the secret $200,000 contribution by Robert L. Vesco, a financier living in Costa Rica; to Long Island's *Newsday,* for an investigative series tracing the route of heroin from Turkish poppy fields to New York streets; and to *New York Daily News* reporter William Sherman, for a series on abuses by physicians in the Medicaid program.

Among the year's more important transactions in the newspaper business were the merger of the Knight and Ridder companies to form the nation's largest newspaper chain, with some 35 papers; the purchase of a controlling interest in the afternoon *Washington Star-News* by Joe L. Allbritton, a Texas banker, for $25 million; and the death of *Chicago Today,* an afternoon daily owned by the Chicago Tribune Co. *Today* had been founded in 1881 as the *Chicago Herald,* and was one of four major dailies left in that city. Immediately upon its closing, the morning *Tribune* became one of a score of "24-hour" newspapers in the U.S. In contrast to most papers, which publish new editions during only part of the day, a "24-hour" newspaper publishes numerous editions throughout the day.

Carl Bernstein and Robert Woodward, the *Washington Post* reporters who first uncovered White House involvement in the Watergate break-in, reaped fame and wealth from that journalistic coup. Their book *All the President's Men,* an account of their work on the story, became a bestseller in 1974, and actor Robert Redford bought movie rights to it.

Watergate and the romance of investigative reporting helped make journalism one of the most popular career goals for young people in 1974. Enrollments in the nation's 213 undergraduate and graduate journalism programs rose by more than 15% over the 48,327 in 1973. That number was nearly four times the journalism enrollment of a decade earlier. However, only about two-thirds of the 11,000 journalism graduates in 1974 had been able to find jobs in the profession by the year's end.

One of the most important events for the newspaper industry in 1974 took place in the U.S. Supreme Court, whose justices unanimously overturned a 1913 Florida "right to reply" law. The statute had been invoked against the *Miami Herald* by Pat Tornillo, a local teachers' association official who had been criticized by the paper in two editorials. The *Herald* refused to print Tornillo's rebuttal, and he claimed a violation of the 1913 law. The court ruled that the statute was unconstitutional because it violated the guarantee of a free press in the First Amendment to the Constitution.

The gross statistics of newspaper growth in 1974 were encouraging. According to *Editor & Publisher International Year Book,* there were 1,451 evening newspapers in the U.S., up from 1,441 a year earlier; evening circulation increased from 36,431,856 to 36,623,140. The number of morning dailies rose to 343 after having dwindled to 337 the year before, and morning circulation rose from 26,078,386 to 26,524,-140. There were 624 Sunday and weekend papers in 1974, up from 603 a year earlier, and their combined circulation rose from 50,000,669 to 51,717,465. Despite signs of a recession, newspaper advertising revenues for the first three quarters of 1974 were at least 6% above the same period in 1973.

Despite those cheering figures, the economic well-being of the newspaper industry was seriously threatened by a crisis involving its most important raw material, paper. The shortage of newsprint that had plagued publishers in 1973 eased somewhat, but the costs of that crucial commodity climbed to unprecedented levels. The price of newsprint rose from $175 a ton in early 1973 to as much as $285 a ton at the end of 1974. The effect of that increase varied from one newspaper to another, but nearly all were adversely affected. The *New York Times,* one of the nation's largest users of newsprint, saw its paper bill jump from $56 million in 1973 to $66 million in 1974. *Times* officials said that they expected the figure to rise to $75 million in 1975.

Publishers responded to the newsprint cost crisis in a number of ways. The American Newspaper Publishers Association reported that nearly half the 1,275 dailies still charging only 10 cents a copy in 1973 raised their newsstand price to 15 cents a copy in 1974. Meanwhile, the *Los Angeles Times,* the *National Observer,* and a number of other papers trimmed their page widths by from one-half inch to about two inches to cut newsprint consumption.

To further reduce costs, newspapers accelerated the installation of automated production equipment in 1974. Some 1,050 of the nation's 1,794 dailies had adopted some form of automated printing, and at least 500 were using one of the most sophisticated newsroom devices, the video display terminal. That miniature television set allows a story to be written, edited, and set into type without the intervention of typewriters, lead pencils, and, in some cases, printing employees.

As might be expected, those innovations were not made without strong opposition from the printers. In New York, Washington, and other cities printers' unions went on strike to protest the introduction of automated equipment that threatened to abolish their jobs. At the *New York Times* and *New York Daily News,* printers agreed to accept automated equipment in return for lifetime job security and substantial monetary incentives to early retirement, a pattern that was expected to be repeated as other papers attempted to automate.   (DONALD MATHER MORRISON)

Magazines. The magazine publishing industry was of course subject to all the same economic pressures as newspapers, and in some cases to legal pressures also. Magazine publishing, however, remained a simpler operation than newspaper publishing, and though a major corporation like the U.K.'s International Publishing Corp. (IPC) found it prudent to postpone two major projects planned for the year, others thought it still worth trying for sections of the market with magazines like *Woman's Choice,* based in Ireland. In spite of the economic storm clouds and talk of declining standards of living toward the end of the year, Britain got yet another hi-fi magazine.

Another British newcomer was slightly less dependent on market forces, somewhat to the chagrin of its small-magazine rivals. With the aid of a £6,000 Arts Council grant, *The New Review* was launched, under the editorship of Ian Hamilton, as a critical literary forum. (*See* LITERATURE.)

Changes took place in another famous literary magazine: poet Sergey Narovchatov became editor of the Soviet magazine *Novy Mir,* an appointment welcomed as restoring a literary figure to the chair. Also in the Soviet Union, the *Chronicle of Current Events,* an underground newsletter prepared by Moscow dissidents, reappeared after its suppression in 1972. Three new issues reached Western correspondents in May.

Designed to publicize European Heritage Year in 1975, *European Heritage* was launched in January 1974. Published in French, German, Italian, and English, the magazine was lavishly illustrated. Only five issues were planned, but it was hoped to continue the magazine after 1975. As always in recent years, sex was the basis for a good part of the profit and of the problems in magazine publishing. In Britain, pub-

lishers found themselves saved by the February general election from the complications that had been expected to follow the government's proposals for an "Indecent Displays" law that would have included magazine covers.   (PETER FIDDICK)

Tennis star Billie Jean King scored another victory in 1974, this time over *Sports Illustrated.* Her *WomenSports,* following the format of its male counterpart, dedicated its editorial pages to all aspects of women in national and international sports. By the end of the year the magazine was doing well, as was another publisher's somewhat more modest effort, *Sportswoman.* There were numerous women's magazines of a more esoteric nature added to the growing list of titles dedicated to proving to women—and to men—that a woman is something more than an extension of a vacuum cleaner handle. Tapping what one editor called "the female unconscious" were such titles as *Elima* (a little literary magazine); *United Sisters* (focusing on general material for liberated women); *Gravida* (a women's collective poetry title); and two scholarly titles devoted to the study of women in society: *Quest* and *Feminist Studies.*

Keeping up with the changes in the image of women, *Ladies' Home Journal* and *McCall's* developed special women's liberation columns. However, the most confusing switch was evident in *Viva,* the female counterpart of *Penthouse.* While still claiming to be the "international magazine for women," it was beginning to look more like a man's magazine, possibly because in 1974 the woman editor was replaced by a man. The publishers of *Modern Bride,* however, stated that their advertisements were still directed to the young woman who has harboured "a lifetime dream of floating down an aisle in a cloud of white lace."

General, mass circulation magazines were supposed to be a thing of the past. But several publishers challenged the "truism" in 1974 with such titles as *People,* the Time Inc. publication that was a polished version of material found in the *National Enquirer,* and *National Star,* a tabloid copy of the aforementioned *National Enquirer.* Another 1974 entry was *Mystique,* a black version of *Cosmopolitan.*

Rolling Stone and *Harper's* began publication of political magazines in 1974. For *Rolling Stone,* the "Washington Bi-Weekly" was a test that appeared as part of the music magazine. *Harper's* effort was *Harper's Weekly,* which, despite the title, did not have a fixed publishing schedule. Purchased by Clay Felker (*see* BIOGRAPHY) of *New York Magazine,* the *Village Voice* at first claimed that there would be no changes. By midyear, however, the editor had resigned, and there were rumbles that other staff members would quit. This was because Felker allegedly hoped to turn the voice of the middle-class radical/bohemian into a more modern challenge to *Rolling Stone.* Among somewhat less sensational changes of ownership in 1974, Fawcett purchased *True* magazine from Peterson, planning to add the well-established men's magazine to its list of such titles as *Hot Rod, Motor Trend,* and *Skin Diver Magazine. American Home,* a $2.6 million loser in 1973, was purchased from Downe Communications by a group of investors who hoped to restore it to its earlier position as a leading general home and garden publication.

Magazines given over to particular audiences grew in popularity in 1974. Among the more typical were *Max,* a general title for men and women over 6 ft. tall; *Yankee Gardener,* an eight-page newsletter for

New England residents; *The Bilingual Review,* a source of bibliographical information on new and older titles in Spanish and English; *Places,* which used literature, including poetry, to stress the more imaginative aspects of the study of geography; *Liberty,* an anarchist tabloid with special emphasis on feminism; and *Fitness Magazine,* one of several new titles for those interested in maintaining good health.

Among the fatalities of the year were *Architectural Forum,* which began publication in 1892; *Intellectual Digest,* a 1969 brainchild of *Psychology Today* founders Nicolas Charney and John Veronis; *Singles,* a one-year venture; *Epicure,* which failed to make a dent in *Gourmet* magazine's monopoly over the epicurean audience; and the English version of the slick, expensive *Réalités.*

More than 100 new alternative-culture magazines were published in 1974. These covered every life-style from gay liberation (*Mouth of the Dragon*) to poetry (*Shocks*) to the media (*Rama*) to ecology and social change (*Connecticut Fireside*). Some indication of the growth of little and alternative-culture magazines could be measured by the development of critical reviews, such as Tom Montag's *Margins.* Along the way there were numerous fatalities, such as the well-known *Lillabulero* and *Antioch Review.*

Despite inflation and talk of recession, the Publishers Information Bureau reported slight increases in advertising revenue in 1974 for most commercial magazines. The same bureau reported that the top magazine advertisers in 1974 spent over $15 million.

Besides the ever present threat of inflation, two basic economic issues plagued magazine publishers during 1974: the rising cost of paper and increased postal rates. While major publishing enterprises, such as Time Inc., were not hit by the rise in paper costs because they owned paper mills, the hikes were particularly hard on magazines with small circulations.

Some relief for the small-circulation magazines came from the U.S. Congress when it delayed planned postal rate increases. In an effort to put the postal service in the black, Congress had approved a 127% rate hike in 1972. It was to be initiated over a five-year period, but in 1974 Congress extended the time of the increase another three years.

The prospects of continued increases in the cost of paper, postage, and labour resulted in the cutting back of their circulations by several large publishers. Reducing the number of copies, coupled with a rise in subscription prices, generally balanced the increased costs in other areas. In mid-1974 *Ladies' Home Journal* was considering a cut of 300,000–500,000 in circulation and an introductory rate boost from $3.97 to $4.97; *Time* and *Newsweek* both raised one-year subscription prices by $2; and *American Home* cut its circulation by 1,150,000 and raised the single copy price by about one-third.

A nightmare for libraries was suggested by the ongoing Williams & Wilkins case. In late 1973 the U.S. Court of Claims held in a 4 to 3 decision that there had been "fair use" made of the copyrighted material of the publisher (Williams & Wilkins) by the National Library of Medicine and the National Institutes of Health. Both governmental institutions were challenged by the publisher for duplicating material from its journals. Although Williams & Wilkins lost the decision, they appealed the case to the Supreme Court. The result of the appeal, particularly in view of congressional inability to handle the matter in a revised copyright law, might prevent libraries from copying and distributing articles from magazines.

National magazine awards, by Columbia University's Graduate School of Journalism, were awarded to: *The New Yorker,* for best fiction and reporting excellence; *Scientific American,* for public service; *Sports Illustrated,* for service to the individual; *Texas Monthly,* for specialized journalism; and *Newsweek,* for visual excellence.   (WILLIAM A. KATZ)

Books. Publishers for the educational market were particularly hard hit by the decline in the birthrate, which had already affected enrollments in the early school grades in the U.S., West Germany, France, and the Scandinavian countries. This meant a decline in pressruns, with a consequent increase in unit costs, as well as a decline in educational research. To offset their economic problems at home, publishers in the educational, scientific, technical, and medical fields in the developed countries turned increasingly toward exporting in 1973–74. New markets opened up with the flow of "oil dollars" into a number of countries, including the Arab countries, Iran, Nigeria, and Indonesia. Some book-importing countries, however, met with increasing difficulties; these included India, Pakistan, and Southeast Asia generally (apart from Indonesia). India planned to build up its own exports to the newly wealthy countries. Stiffer competition could be expected in supplying those markets.

Meanwhile, a protectionist reaction was making itself felt in some countries anxious not to see their national book market taken over by foreign publishers. The Canadians began production for the mass paperback market; in Mexico, publishers asked the government to fix import quotas as of Dec. 1, 1974. In several less developed countries publishers were asking for reproduction rights to allow local editions to be printed.

In Britain publishing, in common with other sections of British industry, met with hard times in 1974. Troubles began with the three-day workweek, which disrupted printers' schedules in ways that were still

Members of the independent house union at Harper & Row, one of the major publishing houses in the U.S., picket during their 17-day strike, the first to hit the book trade in decades.

being felt late in the year. There were also acute shortages of paper and other essential materials. Publishers' cash margins were squeezed between government price control and tax policy on the one hand and the soaring costs of printing, binding, and paper on the other. The high cost of money also fell heavily on an exporting industry that did much of its business on long-term credit, while printers and other suppliers demanded ever more rapid payment.

The industry's problems were reflected in a decline in the total number of titles produced in the first six months of 1974 from 16,276 in the corresponding six months of the previous year to 15,245. In light of the problems faced by the industry, this could be looked upon as a modest decline. It remained to be seen whether the problems would be more sharply reflected in later months. Reports from some publishers suggested that this would be the case. Taken across the whole market, however, demand continued to expand and a high export percentage gave the industry a measure of insulation against adverse national conditions.

The number of titles produced in 1973 had risen by some 2,000 from that in 1972, to 35,254. The industry's strength was particularly noticeable in the export field. From 1969 to 1972 the export proportion fell steadily from a peak in the former year of 47% to below 40% in 1972. In 1973, however, the graph moved upward again to about 42%. Areas of particular strength were children's books, where the number of titles produced increased from 2,178 to 2,710, and general adult books. Although there was much talk about the problems of publishing fiction, the number of titles produced increased substantially, from 3,685 in 1972 to 4,145 in 1973.

Title-by-title analysis showed that the price of books rose by over 8% in the first six months of 1974, giving a total increase of 17.7% in the 12 months up to June. This was considerably below the comparable increase in production costs.

In West Germany in 1973 there were 47,749 titles produced, an increase over the 1972 figure. It seemed likely, however, that 1974 would see something of a decline. Belles lettres still led the field, but the increase of titles in the categories of sciences and humanities showed that these two groups were becoming more important to the German book trade. Paperbacks represented 7.4% of total book production, a decline from the 1971 figure of 8.3%. Translations made up 9.7% of all published titles in 1972–73, 64.8% of them from English-language publications. In 1972–73 the average price for a hardback book was DM. 23.25. In 1971 it had been DM. 18.73. As usual, about 50% of the book imports came from Austria and Switzerland, and those two nations were also the most important purchasing countries for West German books. At the 26th Frankfurt Book Fair, the number of countries participating increased from 60 to 62 and the number of publishers represented rose from 3,844 to 3,903.

In 1973 there were 11,640 titles published in The Netherlands, 4,155 of them reprints. There were 7,474 original Dutch titles, the rest being translations. The price of books remained relatively low, largely because of firm price control by the government. There were important changes in the Dutch book trade, however. Mergers over the preceding years had resulted in 80% of the total Dutch book production being in the hands of five publishing concerns. In 1973 the tendency toward amalgamation was concentrated

World Daily Newspapers and Circulations, 1973–74*

Location	Daily newspapers	Circulation per 1,000 of population	Location	Daily newspapers	Circulation per 1,000 of population
AFRICA			China	392	19
			Cyprus	12	124
Algeria	4	16	Hong Kong	81	...
Angola	4	15	India	821	16
Botswana	2	21	Indonesia	85	7
Cameroon	2	3	Iran	39	24
Central African Republic	1	0.3	Iraq	4	...
Ceuta	1	58	Israel	26	...
Chad	1	0.2	Japan	172	519
Congo	3	...	Jordan	4	24
Dahomey	2	0.7	Korea, North	7	...
Egypt	14	22	Korea, South	42	138
Ethiopia	9	2	Kuwait	6	66
Ghana	4	46	Laos	8	...
Guinea	1	1	Lebanon	52	...
Guinea-Bissau	1	1	Macao	7	...
Ivory Coast	3	10	Malaysia	36	63
Kenya	4	14	Mongolia	2	103
Liberia	1	4	Nepal	30	3
Libya	6	...	Pakistan	98	...
Malagasy Republic	13	15	Philippines	18	21
Mali	3	0.6	Ryukyu Islands	10	284
Mauritius	9	78	Saudi Arabia	5	7
Melilla	1	60	Singapore	10	190
Morocco	11	15	Sri Lanka	25	42
Mozambique	4	5	Syria	5	...
Namibia	3	...	Taiwan	32	64
Niger	1	0.5	Thailand	38	...
Nigeria	17	3	Turkey	433	...
Réunion	2	64	Vietnam, North	7	...
Rhodesia	4	15	Vietnam, South	56	67
Senegal	1	6	Yemen (Aden)	5	18
Seychelles	2	55	Total	2,629	
Sierra Leone	5	17			
Somalia	2	1	**EUROPE**		
South Africa	22	...			
Sudan	22	8	Albania	2	50
Tanzania	4	5	Austria	31	328
Togo	3	6	Belgium	47	...
Tunisia	4	28	Bulgaria	13	206
Uganda	7	7	Czechoslovakia	27	279
Zaire	13	9	Denmark	53	361
Zambia	2	17	Finland	60	...
Total	218		France	105	237
			Germany, East	40	425
			Germany, West	393	319
NORTH AMERICA			Gibraltar	2	214
			Greece	104	77
Bahamas, The	3	162	Hungary	27	221
Barbados	1	113	Iceland	5	449
Belize (British Honduras)	1	32	Ireland	7	233
Bermuda	1	250	Italy	78	133
Canada	114	211	Luxembourg	7	463
Costa Rica	8	93	Malta	6	...
Cuba	10	94	Netherlands, The	93	311
Dominican Republic	7	36	Norway	79	390
El Salvador	12	74	Poland	44	226
Guadeloupe	2	144	Portugal	29	...
Guatemala	8	45	Romania	58	174
Haiti	7	16	Spain	115	98
Honduras	12	42	Sweden	114	534
Jamaica	3	100	Switzerland	98	384
Leeward Islands	3	33	U.S.S.R.	647	347
Martinique	2	137	United Kingdom	109	528
Mexico	208	...	Vatican City (Holy See)	1	...
Netherlands Antilles	5	187	Yugoslavia	25	89
Nicaragua	6	27	Total	2,419	
Panama	7	78			
Puerto Rico	3	89	**OCEANIA**		
Trinidad and Tobago	3	134			
United States	1,774	301	American Samoa	1	97
Virgin Islands	3	343	Australia	58	321
Total	2,203		Cook Islands	1	40
			Fiji Islands	1	35
			French Polynesia	4	91
SOUTH AMERICA			Guam	2	237
			New Caledonia	2	112
Argentina	162	154	New Zealand	40	...
Bolivia	17	37	Niue	1	60
Brazil	261	37	Tonga	2	16
Chile	122	89	Total	112	
Colombia	36	109			
Ecuador	22	45	Grand total	8,375	
French Guiana	1	36			
Guyana	4	54			
Paraguay	11	38			
Peru	56	...			
Surinam	6	57			
Uruguay	54	267			
Venezuela	42	93			
Total	794				
ASIA					
Afghanistan	18	6			
Bangladesh	10	...			
Burma	7	10			
Cambodia	26	22			

*Only newspapers issued four or more times weekly are included. Areas not listed had no known daily newspapers.

Sources: *UN Statistical Yearbook 1973* (1974); *Editor & Publisher International Year Book 1974;* other secondary sources.

(WILLIAM A. HACHTEN)

Apprehension pervaded the editorial room of "Chicago Today" when word was received that the newspaper would cease publication in September.

in the field of distribution. Another conspicuous change was that much more nonfiction than fiction was being produced. In terms of sales, the book clubs retained their importance, having more than one million members.

Swiss book production fell in 1973 by 11%, from 6,849 to 6,065 titles. The general trend of decline was reflected in three of the official languages: German, French, and Italian. Surprisingly, the output in Romansh, the fourth language, spoken by a diminishing number of people in mountainous regions, remained steady. Fiction formed the largest category, but dropped from 1,089 in 1972 to 892. Children's book increased by 99 over the 1972 figure of 279 titles.

Australia managed to produce at least three "firsts" of worldwide significance. The Australian Literature Board, established early in 1973, disbursed A$1.4 million in fellowships to young and established writers and on subsidies to publishers; it largely underwrote some 51 Australian titles.

In April 1974 the prime minister announced the immediate introduction of public lending right (PLR); for each book more than 50 copies of which were in public libraries, the authors would receive an annual fee of A$0.50 and the publishers A$0.12½. The distribution to authors would be handled in cooperation with the Australian Book Publishers Association. Australia thus became the only country in the world to allow publishers their legitimate share of PLR and only the fourth country to introduce PLR at all.

At the end of May, in a case against the University of New South Wales, a Supreme Court judge declared that unsupervised photocopying constituted a breach of copyright. A recently established Copyright Agency would negotiate and handle the administrative and financial consequences of the judgment.

The sales value of Australian books increased from A$18.4 million in 1972 to A$24.5 million in 1973, and export sales moved from A$2 million to A$2.5 million. The number of new books and reprints rose to 3,192 in 1973, compared with 2,139 in 1972. However, inflationary pressures, rising costs, and (in some cases) weak management were the probable reasons why these figures did not, on the whole, produce comparable financial results.

Danish book production decreased slightly in 1972–73. The total number of titles published in 1972 was 6,547; the figure for 1973 was 6,500. Fiction decreased from 1,831 titles in 1972 to 1,656 titles in 1973. Children's books, after an increase of approximately 26% in 1972, again decreased from the 635 titles published in 1972 to 617 in 1973. Paperback production showed another decline.

Trade between the Soviet bloc countries and the West increased substantially during 1974. The Soviet Copyright Agency (VAAP) sent out and received several missions to discuss standard contracts for the purchase or sale of copyright. Countries so contacted included the U.S., Japan, Sweden, Finland, Austria, Portugal, the U.K., France, Denmark, and Switzerland, and some contracts were signed. Several countries, including the U.S. and the U.S.S.R., were considering joint projects for co-editions of children's books and technical works. The U.S.S.R. seemed to be trying to respond to the Western publishers' demands in respect to the photocopying of scientific and technical books and journals; there was a rising Soviet demand for subscriptions to Western journals, and mass pirating in the U.S.S.R. seemed to have stopped.

China and Japan discussed projects for co-edition, following several visits to China by Japanese publishers. The Tokyo Book Development Centre, sponsored by the Japanese government and UNESCO, developed a scheme for co-edition of children's books in a number of Asian countries with the help of Japanese publishers.

The revised 1971 texts of the two international copyright conventions came into force on July 10, 1974, in almost a dozen countries, among them some of the biggest book producers—the U.S., the U.K., France, Spain, and some less developed countries. These revised conventions would govern the future relations between the developed and the less developed countries.

Two major events of 1974, U.S. Pres. Richard Nixon's departure from the White House and Aleksandr Solzhenitsyn's from the U.S.S.R., provided the background for the outstanding bestsellers of the year. Following its initial publication in Paris in December 1973, Solzhenitsyn's *The Gulag Archipelago: 1918–*

1956 was translated into all European languages and became a bestseller in every one. Bernstein and Woodward's *All the President's Men* (Simon & Schuster), having been a great success in the U.S., was translated into numerous languages. McGraw-Hill, in collaboration with several foreign publishers, published two long-lost Leonardo da Vinci notebooks that were rediscovered in Madrid in 1967 and became known as "the Madrid Codices I and II."

As far as the English-speaking countries were concerned, the 1974 Frankfurt Book Fair was a success; but for others the volume of business was disappointing and the atmosphere rather gloomy. The fair's director, Sigfred Taubert, who had done much to make it the book capital of the world, retired in December. He would be followed by Peter Weidhaas.

For publishers, 1974 was also a year of preparation for two events that would make publishing history for years to come. In May 1975 an International Book Fair was to be held at Montreal for the first time; it was planned as an annual event. In May 1976 the International Publishers' Association would hold its 20th congress at Kyoto in Japan, the first meeting of the international publishing community to be held in Asia. (x.)

Inflation, shortages, Watergate, unemployment, labour unrest, overproduction, excess inventories—these stresses common to industry in the U.S. in 1974 were shared by book publishing. As with much of the nation, the problems became severe as the second half of the year began.

Between 1963 and 1973, publication of new books in all categories (fiction, textbooks, general nonfiction, new editions, etc.) rose by just under 50%, with 39,951 new titles and new reprints published in 1973. In the first half of 1974, the rate of publication rose again by a full 4%. Then paper costs escalated, and shortages cut deeply into production; bookstores were unable (or unwilling) to stock titles that were not either "sure winners" or were not going to be heavily backed by advertising and promotion. Also, unsold books were cleared from the shelves and returned by retailers for credit (bookstores are permitted to return books to the publisher for almost full credit within a year after purchase).

Thus, the U.S. publishing industry suddenly found itself in trouble. It would not be clear until mid-1975 how many books were canceled and how many projects merely delayed, although the consensus was that production of new titles and new editions may have been cut by as much as 10% in the second half of the year. Not in doubt, however, were personnel cuts in publishing; in October approximately 200 editorial employees of the Macmillan Co. were abruptly dismissed. To a lesser degree the same sort of action took place during the year in many other houses, while some once-successful publishers terminated activities or were absorbed by other companies. In order to save time and editorial costs, leading publishing houses such as Doubleday announced that they would no longer read unsolicited manuscripts, traditionally the way in which new writers had been discovered. The reward of finding new talent appeared not to be worth the expense at a time when the bookstore life of a serious new novel was estimated to be only six weeks.

For the first time in publishing history, sales of mass market paperbacks ($285.9 million) in 1973 exceeded those of adult hardcover books ($264.8 million). When *The Gulag Archipelago* was published in June 1974 with a two million-copy first printing, 250,000 were hardcover ($12.50) and the remaining 1,750,000 were paperbacks ($1.95).

It was a good year for gossip and confession. Members of the Nixon administration, particularly those involved in what former attorney general John Mitchell called the "White House horrors," were pragmatically dollar-rated by publishers: former president Richard Nixon's memoirs were offered at a floor of $2 million, H. R. Haldeman's at $1 million, and so on down through a list of almost two dozen. Warner Paperback Library acquired all rights to the Nixon book other than hardcover rights, which were reportedly available separately for $750,000. There were several "instant" paperbacks of White House tapes, impeachment hearings, and other events leading to the end of the Nixon presidency, and all sold well.

Rarely had politics and books been so interrelated as in 1974. William Morrow & Co. rejected as "unacceptable" the portrait of Richard Nixon written by his former aide (later a *New York Times* columnist) William Safire. Morrow's total advance was to be $250,000; the company demanded repayment of the first installment of $83,000 and refused to publish the work. The controversy was being resolved in open arbitration in late 1974, with Safire insisting that the changed political atmosphere and not the quality of his manuscript had led to the publisher's unusual about-face.

The year produced some outstanding events in U.S. publishing. The new edition of *Encyclopædia Britannica* was widely hailed, with its publication deemed front-page news by the *New York Times*. *Something Happened*, Joseph Heller's second novel, became an instant bestseller; 12 years had passed since publication of his now-classic *Catch-22*.

Alleged sexual discrimination played a part in the first major strike in U.S. book-publishing history. Bernice Krawczyk led the Association of Harper & Row Employees in an effective 17-day demonstration involving regular and merit raises, participation in a profit-sharing plan, and what nearly 200 striking employees called management's policy of taking "advantage of the lower market value of women." Women comprised 75% of the Harper employee roster, a percentage typical of many large publishing houses.

Some 250 "alternate presses" met in New York in September to discuss the problems and opportunities of small publishers lacking the promotional and distributional force of the established houses. Many of these companies specialized in new life-styles involving natural foods, meditation, the mystic and occult, as well as in the publication of experimental poetry and prose.

In the continuing controversy over censorship and obscenity, Victor L. Marchetti's book on the Central Intelligence Agency, written with John D. Marks, *The C.I.A. and the Cult of Intelligence,* was published despite agency opposition. Passages that had been ordered cut from the book (except for some 200 still-deleted phrases, sentences, or paragraphs) were printed in bold type by the publisher, Alfred A. Knopf, to demonstrate the house's belief that the agency had been oversensitive and more concerned with "image" than with secrecy.

(LEONARD R. HARRIS)

[441.D; 543.A.4.e]

ENCYCLOPÆDIA BRITANNICA FILMS. *Newspaper Story* (2nd ed., 1973).

Qatar

An independent emirate on the west coast of the Persian Gulf, Qatar occupies a desert peninsula east of Bahrain, with Saudi Arabia and the United Arab Emirates bordering on the south. Area: 4,400 sq.mi. (11,400 sq.km.). Pop. (1972 est.): 170,000. Capital: Dohna (pop., 1971 est., 95,000). Language: Arabic. Religion: Muslim. Emir in 1974, Sheikh Khalifah ibn Hamad ath-Thani.

For Qatar 1974 was politically uneventful, as the country benefited from steadily increasing oil revenues. Talks were started with the oil companies on an increase in the government's 25% participation. In February the companies agreed to give Qatar 60%

QATAR

Education. (1972–73) Primary, pupils 19,182, teachers 1,002; secondary, pupils 5,279, teachers 347; vocational, pupils 178, teachers 45; teacher training, students 306, teachers 48.

Finance and Trade. Monetary unit: Qatar riyal, with (Sept. 16, 1974) a par rate of 3.95 riyals to U.S. $1 (free rate of 9.18 riyals = £1 sterling). Budget (1972–73 est.) balanced at 700 million riyals (includes capital expenditure of 300 million riyals). Foreign trade (1972): imports c. 560 million riyals; exports c. 1,450,000,000 riyals. Import sources: U.K. c. 28%; Japan c. 14%; U.S. c. 12%; France c. 8%; West Germany c. 7%; Lebanon c. 6%. Export destinations: U.K. c. 26%; The Netherlands c. 24%; France c. 17%; Italy 10%; West Germany 7%. Main export crude oil c. 100%.

Industry. Crude oil production (1973) 27,466,000 metric tons.

The emir of Qatar (left) is welcomed to an August luncheon meeting at No. 10 Downing Street by British Prime Minister Harold Wilson.

ownership of their operations. Qatar Petroleum Corp. was established in July to handle all state oil interests, and Qatar Gas Co., with 30% Shell International Gas participation, was established in September. An agreement was reached with the oil companies to buy back

60% of the government's share of oil output at an average price of 93% of posted prices for the first six months of 1974.

The government showed concern with the social effects of inflation. Rents were frozen, the price of rice was subsidized, and 102 million riyals were allocated in the budget to social services. Penalties had to be imposed on merchants who were failing to use the metric system, which was officially introduced on Nov. 1, 1973. In May a contract was signed with a Japanese firm to establish an earth satellite communications system in Qatar similar to those in Kuwait and Bahrain. The first U.S. ambassador to Qatar was appointed on May 10, U.S.-Qatar diplomatic relations having previously been handled by the ambassador to Kuwait. Plans were announced for the establishment of a university in Qatar.

(PETER MANSFIELD)

[978.B.4.b]

Race Relations

Resurgent or emergent nationalism lay at the root of most major ethnic and racial unrest and conflict in 1974. This derived for the most part from causes of long standing, but in some cases was linked with extreme revolutionary goals. These were often combined with terrorist or urban guerrilla tactics, as in the case of the Palestine liberation movements; the Irish Republican Army (IRA) nationalists in Northern Ireland (where Catholic and Protestant labels were increasingly fictional); an extreme wing of the Basque separatists in Spain; and EOKA B in Cyprus (whose coup in July, for political union with Greece, sparked off Greek-Turkish communal fighting, the Turkish occupation of 40% of the island, and the displacement of over 200,000 persons, mainly Greek Cypriots, into refugee camps). Some ethnic and racial conflicts were taken up by international power blocs, as in the case of the newly oil-rich Arab and Muslim states and their third world nonaligned supporters. What had been justifiable claims for self-determination or for greater recognition of social and cultural identity escalated into an increasing attack on the fragile framework of international law, order, and civilization, with the acceptance of double standards based on race or political leanings, the arbitrary scapegoating of a few targets—notably Israel, South Africa, and Rhodesia—and the increasing acceptance at international assemblies of indiscriminate political terrorists claiming to be national liberation leaders.

The intellectual confusions engendered by this trend emerged on the one side in the *reductio ad absurdum* of Libyan Pres. Muammar al-Qaddafi's readiness to support both the IRA and their Protestant opponents in Ulster, and on the other in the embarrassed if tacit consent accorded by many Western "liberals" and "leftists" to the worldwide spread of violence and terrorism. Meanwhile, some genuine national movements were still in process, notably in Kurdistan, under the impact of bombings and devastation by the Baathist Iraqi government, helped by Soviet arms and expertise. Some aid was rendered to the Kurds by Iran, which itself had over 1.5 million Kurds.

The balance between white and black in southern Africa tilted against the former with the sudden collapse of the Portuguese colonial presence in Mozambique and Angola. The future of these two territories, with their anxious white minorities and a variety of

ROBERT WALKER—THE NEW YORK TIMES

Puerto Rican citizens of New York City demonstrate at City Hall for more jobs for Puerto Ricans and the appointment of a Puerto Rican to head the city's Community Development Agency.

tribal, religious, and political groupings among the African majorities, particularly in Angola, was by no means straightforward. The Lisbon coup nevertheless left white-dominated South Africa and Rhodesia increasingly vulnerable to black nationalist pressures from within and guerrilla attacks from without along their frontiers with black African states. The majority of these black African states, with their tribal, ethnic, and religious divisions and their arbitrary European-drawn frontiers, were ruled by military regimes. Some had convenient internal scapegoats, such as the Asian minorities in East Africa; but Ugandan Pres. Idi Amin (*see* BIOGRAPHY), having expelled all Asians from Uganda, had to look further, toward the thousand or so British still remaining, or at tribal groups like the Acholi and Lango, which traditionally supported former president Milton Obote. Later, he also moved against some soldiers of the Lugbara tribe. In June the International Commission of Jurists accused President Amin of creating a reign of terror through massive violations of human rights, arbitrary arrests, torture, and murder. From the independent African state of Chad came reports of a "cultural and social revolution" led by Pres. N'Garta Tombalbaye and geared to the revival of national identity. In practice this took the form of a substitution of tribal names for Christian names (many Chadians were Protestants), a forced return to tribal initiation rites and fetishist ceremonies, and the closing down of churches and the killing or torture of ministers who objected. From southern Sudan there were happier reports of a huge relief and resettlement movement for up to a million displaced and refugee non-Muslim southerners, carried out after the 1972 cease-fire had ended the civil strife that had gone on sporadically since 1955.

Religious persecution and ethnic prejudice continued to be highly evident in the U.S.S.R. The hostile Soviet treatment of Jews and of Baptists was better known in the outside world than the continuing discrimination against Roman Catholicism in western Ukraine, Lithuania, and Latvia (where the church was seen as a focus for nationalist opposition) and against Islam (which was depicted as a preserver of "reactionary national customs," although in relations with prestigious Muslim states Soviet tolerance was stressed). Not all racially or ethnically plural societies were involved in tensions and conflicts. Probably a majority were relatively tranquil and therefore unre-

ported as, for instance, Canada, Switzerland, Malaysia, and New Zealand. Even the multiracial societies of the Caribbean were comparatively unscathed by the doctrines of Black Power or interethnic rivalries.

South Africa. The fall of the Portuguese empire and the rise of militant independence movements such as the Front for the Liberation of Mozambique (Frelimo) stimulated "black power" thinking among South Africa's blacks, and reanimated old fears among whites. The government attempted to quell black militancy by widespread arrests, coupled with moves against the press and even against any moderate whites who seemed to support black causes. At the United Nations South Africa made a statement of intent involving an apparent disavowal of racial discrimination and embarked on a diplomatic initiative to resurrect dialogue and cooperation with black Africa, in particular Zambia and Mozambique. Adopting the policy of the contracting *laager*, Prime Minister B. J. Vorster pressured Rhodesia to make a settlement and proposed changes in the direction of self-determination in South West Africa (Namibia).

The South African economy and society continued to rest on the migrant labour system. Only 12% of the African labour force came from outside South Africa, usually for work in the mines, and was truly migrant. Otherwise every second African worker (about 1,305,000 men) in South Africa was a permanent migrant by definition in the land of his birth. The small, soil-eroded, fragmented "homelands" and the "border industries" (only 85,000 jobs created after 12 years) could provide work for only a minority of males over 15, who had to register for work and were subject to government-controlled recruitment. Thereafter such migrants were not allowed to have their wives and children with them, but had to live in bleak hostels and compounds where disorder and crime were rife, while workers who had lost their jobs were compulsorily returned home (92,000 in 1973). All migrant workers worked on annual contracts. Workers born in urban areas or who had lived in them for 15 successive years or who had served one employer for ten years could remain in such areas—but even so only on a temporary basis.

The overcrowded homelands (with a population density of 119 per square mile, as compared with 35 for the rest of the republic) served as labour pools for white industry, with consequent gross distortion of community life (in Vendaland there were 3.6 women

Quakers:
see Religion

Quarrying:
see Mining and Quarrying

to 1 man in the age groups between 20 and 54 years). There were also malnutrition, poverty, alienation, desertion and illegitimacy, and the disruption of family and communal life and tribal sanctions. The homelands' populations were increasingly swelled by impoverished people endorsed out of (banished from) white urban areas or evicted from "black spots" (often ancestral lands) or white-owned farms. Widows and deserted wives migrated to jobs in the towns. The resettlement policy was also leading to the uprooting of stable urban communities and the building of more hostels, it being government policy that all urban African labour should eventually be migrant.

While the lot of millions of "migrants" and "homeland" residents was worsening, that of resident urban black workers, albeit eroded by rises in the cost of living, was slowly improving as economic apartheid and job reservation continued to crumble because of the shortage of white skilled and clerical workers. Most Africans moving into "white" jobs were paid at lower rates than whites; nevertheless, rates for unskilled African labour nearly doubled in 1973, under pressure of employers and trade unions, and unofficial black trade unions were slowly gaining strength (22 unions with a membership of 40,000). Leaders of the African homelands like Chief Gatsha Buthelezi (*see* BIOGRAPHY) of KwaZulu wielded a growing influence among and on behalf of their tribesmen in the cities, demanding not only real black development in the homelands but acceptance of the urban workers as permanent inhabitants with full civil rights. Recognition of the need for some change was increasingly evident, not only among the traditional white liberals but also among some Afrikaner Nationalists and churchmen known as Verligtes ("enlightened ones"). Some forms of petty apartheid, such as segregated elevators and park benches, were being done away with in most major cities, insofar as they came under urban regulations, not state legislation. Prosecutions under the pass laws were still high, but far less than a few years earlier. An impediment to mitigation of policy was the fact that the police and prison services were staffed with personnel used to treating nonwhites as racial inferiors. The prison population was 440,922 in 1972 (474,065 in 1971) for an overall population of nearly 25 million (Africans nearly 18 million), as compared with Britain's 40,000 for a population of 55.5 million. In October there was a particularly grievous case of torture and barbaric assaults on prisoners in a Transvaal jail.

A major problem for Prime Minister Vorster was to make his "voice of reason" seem credible to African leaders like Pres. Kenneth Kaunda of Zambia, while at the same time keeping hold of his more uncompromising Nationalist supporters and leading them to make or accept the changes necessary for survival while assuring them that nothing had changed. This explained the seeming illogicality of his public utterances and actions. While Bantustan leaders and older Africans of influence still appeared to prefer reform to revolution, polarization was far advanced among younger blacks. As for the 2.3 million Cape Coloured people, government policies, depriving them of rights, pushed them to make common cause with the African majority. In July the militantly antiapartheid (Coloured) Labour Party captured the Coloured Persons' Representative Council, which the government then prorogued. Vorster on November 9 rejected the Coloured demands for the restoration of some form of parliamentary representation (the

council had demanded 60 seats in the House of Assembly). He offered only a statutory Consultative Cabinet Council and representation on government bodies, proposals that were rejected by the Labour Party. The main reason for the resistance to direct Coloured parliamentary representation was thought to be that Coloured voters would support the opposition parties and could be strong enough to challenge Nationalist Afrikanerdom's long hold on power. Moreover, the acceptance of a renewed Coloured political presence, even though Coloureds could have no separate homeland, would challenge the principle of separate development.

United Kingdom. In Britain coloured immigration and race relations did not emerge as major issues during the two general elections in February and October, despite the stepped-up intervention of candidates of the anti-immigration, extreme right-wing National Front (in the event, all 54 Nationalist candidates in February and all 90 in October failed to obtain the necessary votes in their constituencies. The number of work vouchers for immigrants was kept at 3,500 but the proportion allocated to East African Asians was increased. In 1973 a total of 10,443 U.K. passport holders (East African Asians) were admitted, as compared with 34,825 for 1972. The number of New Commonwealth immigrants admitted for settlement was 20,424 (as compared with 25,025 in 1972), the great majority being dependent women and children.

After the Labour Party won the February general election, the home secretary, Roy Jenkins, took steps to remedy some anomalies and hardships that had arisen in connection with the entry of certain groups and categories, notably Ugandan Asian refugees; husbands not holding U.K. passports would be admitted to rejoin their wives in Britain who held U.K. passports, and students over the age of 21 would be admitted to rejoin parents with U.K. passports. In August the immigration rules were changed to remove the restriction imposed by James Callaghan in 1969 on the admission of husbands and fiancés of women settled in the U.K. This restored the previous situation whereby the rules were equal for men and women. There were also problems for Pakistani immigrants and their dependents following Pakistan's departure from the Commonwealth and passage of the Pakistan Act of 1973 (under which citizens of Pakistan in Britain became aliens on Sept. 1, 1973, but were allowed to remain and apply for British citizenship under various conditions). These involved the large number of Pakistani dependents still waiting to join their husbands or fathers in Britain (about 43,300), the increasing administrative delays in processing them for entry certificates, and the uncertainty as to whether they would be admitted under the aliens rule or the rule for Commonwealth citizens.

In the employment sphere most New Commonwealth immigrants continued to be concentrated in jobs near the bottom of the occupational scale with few opportunities for training or promotion. In a survey of nearly 300 plants it was found that coloured workers were at a disadvantage in the kind of employment offered and in the difficulty of obtaining it; most employers were not promoting the upgrading of coloured workers; and trade unions did little to induct or welcome coloured workers and sometimes allowed discriminatory practices to develop or even encouraged them. Particular problems relating to immigrant workers included the need to provide additional language training, particularly for Asian workers, and the needs of 4,000 young black people, either latecomers from the West Indies or children of West Indian immigrants. A high incidence of unemployment and homelessness was reported for them, and their numbers were seen as likely to increase as more such young people left schools in certain areas of urban stress, where West Indians were showing much lower educational attainments than nonimmigrant children.

The need for practical measures to promote and monitor programs for equal opportunity in employment was stressed by the interim report on employment of the Parliamentary Select Committee on Race Relations and Immigration. Nevertheless, the select committee considered the request for extra compulsory powers by the Race Relations Board (RRB) unjustified until more energetic endeavours had been made to persuade firms to take voluntary action. During 1973–74 the RRB brought several cases of alleged discrimination to court, one of which concerned entry into workingmen's clubs. This issue led to a controversial decision in the House of Lords in October that a workingmen's club which elected its members and operated a colour bar was not guilty of unlawful discrimination when it refused to provide a coloured associate member (one of about one million associates belonging to 4,000 clubs in the country) with goods and services. The RRB reported a 69% increase in cases of alleged discrimination in the northwest industrial region of Britain during 1973–74.

(SHEILA PATTERSON)

United States. The dramatic political events of 1974 did not result in fundamental alterations in U.S. race relations. The civil rights pattern of the 1970s continued, characterized by minor gains, significant reverses, and blatant resistance. Events in minority politics illustrated this trend, with black Americans continuing to win elected offices. In April the Joint Center for Political Studies in Washington, D.C., reported 2,991 elected black officials in 45 states and the District of Columbia. This figure compared with 2,621 in 1973 and 1,185 in 1969, and it included 108

mayors and over 1,000 city councillors. This growth was national in scope with Michigan (194) and Mississippi (191) boasting the largest totals. The Southern advances in black political development were a direct result of the Voting Rights Act of 1965. Under this act the Justice Department in April blocked enforcement of a 1970 Mississippi state law, labeling it potentially discriminatory against blacks. The proposed statute envisioned one open primary requiring a majority vote to win and would have prevented blacks from winning as independents with a plurality in final elections.

But there were also political setbacks for minorities. In March the Democratic Party announced new rules for selecting delegates to their national convention. The proposed rules would have made challenges difficult for any group that felt cheated in the delegate selection process. The accusing group would have to carry the burden of proof. The situation was ameliorated, however, at the party's midterm convention in Kansas City, Mo., in December, when delegates overwhelmingly approved a compromise that tightened the monitoring of affirmative action and removed the burden of proof. At the second National Black Political Convention, held in Little Rock, Ark., in March, Mayor Richard Hatcher of Gary, Ind., called for "unity without uniformity," but black nationalists rejected this formula, and the National Association for the Advancement of Colored People (NAACP) and the National Urban League refused to attend.

In May the U.S. House of Representatives narrowly defeated (204–197) a Senate-passed bill to permit voters to register by postcard for federal elections. This statute could have significantly increased minority voting, but it was stoutly opposed by most Republicans and Southern Democrats. Later in May the House abolished the Office of Economic Opportunity (OEO) and moved many of its programs to other agencies. In December, however, the Senate voted to extend the life of OEO until Oct. 1, 1975. House-Senate conferees then drafted a compromise bill that

School integration in Boston: motorcycle police (left) escort a school bus carrying black students to South Boston High School as helmeted police line the route; (below) more than 1,000 pro-busing demonstrators rally on Boston Common.

A Hopi woman grazes
her sheep on Arizona
land claimed by both
the Hopi and Navajo
tribes. Charges
of overgrazing
complicate and intensify
the dispute in this arid
region.

was passed by both houses on December 20. Under the bill's provisions OEO was to be abolished immediately and replaced by an independent Community Services Administration. After March 15, 1975, Pres. Gerald R. Ford could propose a reorganization plan transferring poverty programs from the new agency to other federal departments and agencies. A two-thirds vote of Congress would be required to block such a transfer. The bill also would extend the programs that had been embraced in OEO through fiscal 1977 and establish new programs that would help the poor deal with the energy crisis and would provide summer recreational opportunities for disadvantaged children.

Two high-ranking minority officials left government office in 1974. Romana Acosta Banuelos, who as treasurer of the United States was the highest ranking person of Spanish descent in the administration, resigned in February. At the end of the year Barbara Watson was replaced as the head of the State Department's Bureau of Security and Consular Affairs. When appointed in 1968, Mrs. Watson was the first black woman to attain a rank equivalent to an assistant secretary of state.

In June in San Juan, P.R., U.S. District Court Judge Luther Youngdahl threw out as "plainly without merit" a petition that Puerto Ricans on the island be allowed to vote for the U.S. president. All Puerto Ricans are U.S. citizens, but Youngdahl maintained that voting was not an inherent right of citizenship.

Native Americans were more successful in court during 1974. In January the U.S. Supreme Court granted the Oneida Indian Nation the right to sue two upstate New York counties for fair rental value of five million acres which the Oneida claimed were illegally ceded to New York State before 1800. And in Phoenix, Ariz., the Justice Department filed its first suit to protect Indian voting rights. It charged that an Arizona redistricting plan discriminated against voters on the Navajo reservation in Apache County.

The mass media focused on the Wounded Knee trial in St. Paul, Minn. Stemming from the seizure in 1973 of the South Dakota village of Wounded Knee, the trial, which began on January 8, involved ten felony charges against Russell Means and Dennis Banks,

leaders of the militant American Indian Movement (AIM). (On February 8, Means was narrowly defeated, 1,709–1,530, by the incumbent, Richard Wilson, for the presidency of the Oglala Sioux in South Dakota.) The trial itself was stormy and marked by delays. At one point, two defense lawyers were jailed overnight after a courtroom fracas. Finally, in September, Federal Judge Fred Nichol dismissed all charges after strongly criticizing the Justice Department's conduct. The judge accused the chief prosecutor of deceiving the court and the FBI of having "stooped to a new low" in dealing with witnesses and evidence.

Black militants who turned to violence fared less well. Clark Squire, a reputed member of the Black Liberation Army, was found guilty in March of the fatal shooting of a New Jersey state trooper in 1973. Squire was sentenced to life imprisonment. In May four Black Muslims from Philadelphia were convicted of the 1973 murders of seven Hanafi Muslims in their District of Columbia home.

In April, San Francisco Mayor Joseph Alioto, running in the Democratic primary for governor, announced a campaign to catch a so-called Zebra killer. In five months, 18 whites had been shot at random in the back, 12 fatally. Alioto ordered that all young black men who appeared to match the description of the killer be stopped, searched, and questioned. The northern California branch of the American Civil Liberties Union (ACLU) called the order a massive violation of the constitutional rights of every black man in the city. A week later, U.S. District Court Judge Alfonso Zirpoli issued a temporary injunction against the "Zebra" search solely on the basis of a "profile." On May 16 four Black Muslims were indicted for murdering three whites and conspiring to murder others.

More significant was a January Supreme Court ruling. The court held that 17 blacks and two whites were not entitled to seek injunctions against local judges and prosecutors in Cairo, Ill., who allegedly engaged in a pattern of setting more excessive bail and harsher punishments for blacks than whites. The majority agreed that, even if discrimination had been proved, federal court injunctions were improper as they would violate federal and state harmony. Justice William O. Douglas, in angry dissent, described the ruling as doing "violence to the conception of even-handed justice envisioned by the Constitution."

An even more ominous Supreme Court decision involved education. The court decided in July, by a narrow 5–4 count, against allowing a metropolitan remedy for the racial segregation of public schools in Detroit. The four Nixon appointees were joined by Justice Potter Stewart, who concluded that "the remedy . . . was not commensurate with the constitutional violation found." The importance of this decision lay in the fact that central cities were becoming increasingly populated with blacks while the suburbs were largely white. Justice Thurgood Marshall called the decision "a giant step backward."

Other court decisions also deterred education desegregation. The Supreme Court upheld the validity of a Knoxville, Tenn., plan that placed most of the city's black students in just nine schools, each two-thirds or more black. The court also refused to disturb a Memphis, Tenn., plan that retained 25 all-black schools. It also declined to rule on a celebrated case involving the law school of the University of Washington. After being denied admission, Marco DeFunis, Jr., a white applicant, sued on the ground that 36 minority applicants with lower grade averages had been admitted. The court's action invited further legal attacks upon "affirmative action" programs that favour minority applicants.

The judicial branch was joined by the legislative and executive branches in its resistance to school desegregation. In July Congress passed a new federal aid to education bill that contained antibusing measures. It prohibited busing for racial desegregation beyond the school next closest to the pupil's home unless the courts determined that more extensive transportation was necessary to protect constitutional rights, and across district lines unless boundaries were found to have been deliberately drawn to foster segregation. In a March radio address, Pres. Richard Nixon scored "excessive forced busing" for desegregation based on "complicated plans drawn up by far-away officials in Washington." Sen. Claiborne Pell (Dem., R.I.) accused Nixon of "reopening a painful wound." But President Ford, soon after taking office, reiterated the attack. He challenged a U.S. District Court order for school desegregation in Boston as not "the best solution to quality education" even as protest and violence raged in the city.

Boston's desegregation of schools had been ordered in June by Judge W. Arthur Garrity, Jr., after his finding that the city had knowingly segregated both teachers and students through special attendance and grading patterns. The initial step involved only about 6,000 "bused" children out of 94,000. Yet violence, white student boycotts, and mass protest parades characterized the carefully organized resistance to the plan's initiation during the fall. Amid scenes reminiscent of the South of the mid-1960s, most local white political leaders joined the effort to subvert the court order, and in December the Boston School Committee voted to appeal to the U.S. Supreme Court. Less publicized were the successful beginnings of extensive desegregation plans in such cities as Springfield, Mass., Denver, Colo., and Minneapolis, Minn.

The South in 1974 boasted more school desegregation than other regions. While in 1964, 98% of Southern black students were in schools with a 90% or more black enrollment, by 1972 the figure was only

9%. But progress had been much slower in the cities of the North and West where 57% of black students in 1972 were still in schools at least 80% black. Citing these data, the Center for National Policy Review charged in September that federal efforts outside of the South had been characterized by "bureaucratic caution, needless delays, administrative inefficiency, and sloppy investigation." Health, Education, and Welfare Secretary Caspar Weinberger defended his department's actions and asserted that the South had been "much more willing to accept desegregation." As if to underscore the charges, the U.S. Court of Appeals in Washington, D.C., held that HEW could not disburse funds to school systems with racially discriminatory teacher assignments. The decision affected $20 million in grants to five Northern cities.

HEW did determine in January that racial discrimination still existed in the schools of Topeka, Kan., one of the original districts in the historic 1954 Supreme Court decision in *Brown* v. *Board of Education* against de jure public school segregation. HEW ordered Topeka to submit corrective plans. In April, HEW cut off federal funds to Pasadena, Calif., because that city had failed to comply fully with a court-ordered desegregation plan. At the higher education level, the Justice Department sued Louisiana, at HEW's request, to force the desegregation of the state-supported university system.

Attention was also focused during 1974 on the educational problems of other minorities. In February the U.S. Commission on Civil Rights issued a stinging indictment of localities and state governments in California, Arizona, Colorado, New Mexico, and Texas for having consistently failed to provide equal educational opportunities to Chicano children. The commission concluded that the Spanish language and Chicano culture had largely been ignored and "even suppressed." It recommended funding sanctions, mandatory bilingual programs, the recruitment of Chicano teachers, and the prohibition of at-large school board elections so as to allow more Chicano representation.

The Supreme Court in January held that San Francisco was in violation of the 1964 Civil Rights Act if it did not provide bilingual education and English-language instruction for 1,800 Chinese-American pupils who did not speak English. Assistant Attorney General Stanley Pottinger promised that the Justice Department would use this decision to ensure equal educational opportunities for the two million students whose first language was Spanish. Similarly, the New York City Board of Education agreed in federal court in August to provide Spanish-language instruction in basic subjects for those among its approximately 200,000 Spanish-speaking pupils who were unable to make progress in English-language courses.

A report released in August by the U.S. Commission on Civil Rights succinctly listed what was needed to combat housing discrimination more effectively: (1) federal subsidies and state and local zoning reforms to allow black entry into the suburbs; (2) real enforcement of fair housing laws by HEW and the Justice Department; (3) as a condition for receiving housing grants, a requirement that states establish agencies with the power to override local barriers to open housing; (4) financial incentives for families to seek housing integration; and (5) requirements for companies with federal contracts to demonstrate the existence of adequate lower-income housing in suburbs where they were located or planning to locate.

Equally pervasive were minority employment problems, though on this front 1974 witnessed advances. The Justice Department and the Equal Employment Opportunity Commission (EEOC) were particularly active in securing court orders and consent decrees with industry and local governments. The El Paso Natural Gas and Georgia Power companies both agreed in January to pay retrospective wages and benefits and over the next five to seven years to increase their employment percentages of minorities to those of the surrounding population. In March seven major trucking firms agreed to fill from one-third to one-half of all vacancies with minority persons. In April a major job agreement was reached in the federal court of Birmingham, Ala. Nine major steel companies and the United Steelworkers union signed an agreement that included $30.9 million in back pay, one-half of openings in trade and craft positions to be filled by minority persons and women, and easier access to jobs previously reserved for white males. The NAACP quickly sued to have these consent decrees with the steel industry set aside as inadequate.

State police forces were also affected. The Maryland State Police in January settled a suit by banning pre-employment tests that discriminated against women and blacks and by agreeing to hire and assign them on a nondiscriminatory basis. The Mississippi Highway Patrol, with only five black officers among 548, was found in March by the 5th Circuit Court of Appeals to be racially discriminating. And the same court upheld in April a lower court decision that the Alabama Department of Public Safety must alter its hiring policies for the highway patrol until it was one-fourth black.

Income data reported in July by the Census Bureau gave further testimony to these economic difficulties. Though only 8% of white Americans lived below the poverty line in 1973, 31% of all blacks and 40% of black children did so. Both races gained in income amounts in 1973, but the black median family income slipped to 58% that of whites. And while whites gained slightly more in 1973 than the inflation in prices (+2.9%), blacks lost in real income (−0.3%).

The Census Bureau reported in January that by mid-1973 black Americans numbered 23.8 million. This figure represented an increase of 1.2 million since 1970. The bureau also recorded 10,580,000 Americans of Spanish descent, 1.5 million more than were listed in 1970. This number included approximately 6,290,000 Chicanos, 1,550,000 Puerto Ricans, and 733,000 Cubans.

Blacks won numerous honours in 1974. In May television Emmy Awards went to "The Autobiography of Miss Jane Pittman" (a fictional account of an elderly ex-slave) as the best drama special, and to its star, Cicely Tyson, as actress of the year in a special. James Bell, renowned star of the old Negro leagues, was named to baseball's Hall of Fame in February. Lee Elder became the first black golfer to qualify for the Masters Tournament when he won a contest in Pensacola, Fla. Frank Robinson became the first black manager in major league baseball when he was named in October to head the Cleveland Indians. The Rev. C. Shelby Rooks became the first black president of the Chicago Theological Seminary of the United Church of Christ. The Rev. Lawrence Bottoms, a minister in Decatur, Ga., was elected to be the first black moderator of the Southern-based Presbyterian Church in the U.S. In San Antonio, Tex., in July, J. Garfield Owens became the first black

pastor of an all-white congregation of United Methodists. (THOMAS F. PETTIGREW)

See also Cities and Urban Affairs; United States.
[522.B]

ENCYCLOPÆDIA BRITANNICA FILMS. *Heritage in Black* (1969); *The Mexican-American Speaks: Heritage in Bronze* (1972); *The American Indian Speaks* (1973).

Refugees

The Office of the UN High Commissioner for Refugees (UNHCR) completed two major special tasks in mid-1974, one concerning Asians from Uganda of undetermined nationality and the other concerning persons who found themselves stranded minorities after the 1971 hostilities in the South Asian subcontinent. Soon afterward it undertook two more—one in Cyprus and the other in Indochina—while at the same time discharging its traditional responsibilities of international protection and material assistance.

UNHCR succeeded in finding permanent resettlement opportunities for the last of the 4,500 Asians who had been brought to transit camps in Europe under its aegis in November 1972 following their expulsion from Uganda. In all, 20 countries admitted these refugees. Denmark, Canada, Sweden, and Switzerland were particularly helpful in admitting aged and sick. In the autumn of 1974 UNHCR obtained the agreement of the Ugandan authorities to act as a channel for claims for compensation from Asians from Uganda of undetermined nationality, and a special unit was established with UNHCR for this purpose. Close coordination was maintained with the British Claims Board, which had submitted claims on behalf of Asians with U.K. passports.

Another operation carried to a successful conclusion was the massive repatriation begun in 1973 in the South Asian subcontinent, under which Bengalis were moved from Pakistan to Bangladesh and non-Bengalis from Bangladesh to Pakistan. The transcontinental airlift organized for this purpose was concluded on July 1 after 241,300 persons had been repatriated.

On August 20 a new challenge arose when UNHCR was appointed by the UN secretary-general to coordinate UN humanitarian assistance in Cyprus. It was estimated that 226,000 people who had been displaced or uprooted during hostilities there were in need of various types of assistance. (*See* CYPRUS.) Requirements from September 1 until the end of the year were assessed at $22 million. Well before the end of the year, the target had been met by contributions in cash and kind made through UNHCR, the International Committee of the Red Cross, or bilaterally. In September another special program was announced entailing rehabilitation measures for uprooted and displaced persons in Laos and Vietnam. A regional office was established at Vientiane, Laos, in October to administer the various projects, which would require $12 million during 1974–75.

Within its regular program, UNHCR was faced with mounting needs in Latin America related to the change in government in Chile in 1973. By the end of March, 2,600 foreign refugees who had sought asylum in Chile prior to the coup and subsequently wished to leave were resettled, with UNHCR's aid, in 39 countries, and UNHCR's *chargé de mission* in Santiago was withdrawn. However, Chileans had also crossed into Argentina and Peru. They were admitted to Peru in transit on the understanding they would soon be reset-

Radio:
see Television and Radio

Railroads:
see Transportation

Recordings:
see Music

Reformed Churches:
see Religion

Mother and son, empty rice bowl in hand, join thousands of other refugees streaming into Da Nang, South Vietnam. Incessant artillery shelling by the North Vietnamese forced them to flee from their villages.

tled elsewhere, and by the end of October about 700 had left for another country. In Argentina, on the other hand, local settlement was the main solution for the 15,000 Chileans who had arrived there, and this entailed heavy expenditure for UNHCR. Mainly because of the increased requirements in Latin America, the financial target for UNHCR's 1974 regular program was raised in the course of the year from $8.7 million to $11.8 million; fortunately, this amount was covered by supplementary contributions.

The Nansen Medal for outstanding service to the cause of refugees was presented for the first time since 1971 to the Right Rev. Helmut Frenz, bishop of the Evangelical Lutheran Church of Chile. Bishop Frenz had taken the lead in organizing a National Committee for Aid to Refugees, which had assisted thousands of refugees in Chile following the coup, particularly through the creation of "safe havens" where refugees could stay while awaiting resettlement.

Africa continued to be the area with the largest number of refugees of concern to UNHCR. Of the 285,000 refugees assisted by UNHCR in 1973, 90% were on that continent, and in 1974 Africa again accounted for the largest allocation to any region within the regular program. The biggest amount allocated to any single country was $2.9 million to Tanzania for assistance to refugees from Burundi. This was occasioned not by a new influx but by the need to transfer 50,000 persons from the Kigoma area to settlements in the Tabora region.

One long-standing problem in Africa—that of refugees from territories under Portuguese administration —appeared likely to be solved at last with the independence of Guinea-Bissau and the rapid progress toward self-government of Angola and Mozambique. UNHCR maintained close contact with recognized liberation movements with a view toward helping organize the expected mass repatriation of refugees from Senegal, Tanzania, Zaire, and Zambia.

Though migration from Europe generally declined in reaction to economic conditions, refugees were given special consideration. This, together with increased movements to European countries such as Sweden and Switzerland, led to a sharp reduction in the number of refugees awaiting settlement.

The high commissioner, Sadruddin Aga Khan, began a third term of office extending through 1978. On several occasions he was obliged to intervene to prevent the forcible return of refugees to their countries

of origin and other abuses. In June he appealed to the 73 countries that had not yet done so to accede to the 1951 Convention Relating to the Status of Refugees, the main instrument in the field of international protection. (UNHCR)

See also Migration, International.
[525.A.1.c.iii]

Religion

The major themes of 1974 in the world of religion were familiar ones: the struggle to achieve ecumenical agreements and understanding among the various Christian bodies; concern over the decline of "the great absolutes of the Judeo-Christian tradition"; the continuing strength of the so-called conservative churches; the increasing interest in evangelism; the effect of the charismatic movement on all churches; and the problems—especially acute in many "mainline" churches and organizations—brought on by declining contributions and inflation.

After the turbulent activism of the 1960s, U.S. churches, especially, were reexamining their relationship to social and political questions. Yet events throughout the world indicated that religion could achieve no easy divorce from worldly affairs, even if that were considered desirable. In southern Africa and in Latin America, churches were deeply involved on all sides of the issues dividing those regions. In Cyprus, Makarios III, the president and primate of the Cypriot Orthodox Church, was the central figure in a conflict exacerbated by religious differences between ethnic Greeks and Turks. In Israel a Greek Catholic prelate was convicted for smuggling guns to the Arabs. Both Catholic and Protestant churchmen were among those arrested in government crackdowns against dissidents in South Korea and the Philippines. (*See* KOREA; PHILIPPINES.)

In the U.S. churchmen continued to be troubled over the effect of the Watergate affair on moral standards. The tapes of White House conversations, released on April 30, raised shocked questions in some church circles about Pres. Richard Nixon's earthy language and more general questions about the moral climate within his administration, which was denounced by church leaders as "insensitive," "reprehensible," and "cynical." Nixon's subsequent resignation and his pardon by Pres. Gerald Ford for any offenses he might have committed while in office opened up far-reaching considerations of Christian mercy (which Ford had invoked) and its relationship to justice. Two clergymen received wide publicity for their support of President Nixon: John McLaughlin, a Jesuit employed by the White House as a staff speechwriter, and Rabbi Baruch Korff, founder and head of an organization known as Fairness to the Presidency.

The ecumenical movement presented a mixed picture in 1974. Father Charles Angell of the Graymoor Ecumenical Institute noted wryly that "everywhere in official ecumenical circles there is a sinking feeling that the same old tired faces shuffle from conference to conference, producing documents which fall on lifeless ears." Nevertheless, there were some signs of progress, although theological understandings and practical cooperation were more in evidence than moves toward real organizational unity.

A series of dialogue sessions between U.S. Lutherans and Jews removed many historical barriers between the two groups. The dialogue, first begun in 1969, frankly attacked the problem of the anti-Semitism prominent in Martin Luther's writings. Lutheran theologians made it clear they were in no way bound by these writings. The Lutheran-Jewish dialogue was summarized in the book *Speaking of God Today: Jews and Lutherans in Conversation.*

In another historic ecumenical step, Lutheran and Roman Catholic scholars agreed that papal primacy "need not be a barrier to reconciliation" between Lutheran and Roman Catholic churches. A three-year study preceded the declaration by Lutheran scholars that a form of the papacy "renewed and restructured under the Gospel" might be an "appropriate visible expression of the Ministry that serves the unity and ordering of the church." Catholic scholars held that "Catholics continue to emphasize that papal primacy is an institution in accordance with God's will." The overall consensus among the theologians was that there must be promotion of unity among all believers. The Lutheran scholars recommended that "our churches earnestly consider if the time has not come to reaffirm a new attitude toward the papacy 'for the sake of peace and concord in the church.'"

Ecumenical relations between the Roman Catholic

Church in Scotland and the Episcopal (Anglican) Church took a forward step when the two groups stated there was now "extensive" agreement on the Eucharist as sacrament and sacrifice. In another development, England's five major churches (Anglican, Roman Catholic, Baptist, United Reformed, and Methodist) agreed to form a national commission for multilateral discussions about practical reunion. Moves toward uniting three Presbyterian bodies in the U.S. were approved at 1974 meetings. (See *Presbyterian, Reformed, and Congregational,* below.)

In Australia, Presbyterians, Congregationalists, and Methodists agreed to unite June 2, 1976, but a substantial majority of the Presbyterians disapproved of the union and might form a continuing Presbyterian church. In New Zealand, Anglicans voted to try again in 1976 to form a five-church merger (Anglican, Presbyterian, Methodist, Congregational, and the Associated Churches of Christ) after an initial church union proposal was defeated by the Anglican Synod. In Canada there were strong doubts that the Anglican Church would join the proposed merger of the United Church of Canada, the Anglican Church of Canada, and the Christian Church (Disciples of Christ). (See *United Church of Canada,* below.) Prospects of union between the national Church of Scotland (Presbyterian) and the Methodist Church in Scotland appeared hopeful when Kenneth Greet, secretary of the British Methodist Conference, told the Presbyterian General Assembly that necessary legal steps were being taken that would allow one section of British Methodism to unite with another church. (See *Methodists,* below.)

The Consultation on Church Union (COCU), a proposal to unite nine U.S. denominations (African Methodist Episcopal, African Methodist Episcopal Zion, Christian Church [Disciples of Christ], Christian Methodist Episcopal, Episcopal, Presbyterian Church in the U.S., United Church of Christ, United Methodist Church, and United Presbyterian Church in the U.S.A.), seemed to have changed directions during 1974. Early tendencies to develop a monolithic united church gave way to a new pluralism more responsive to the various heritages and traditions of the participating bodies.

Two major U.S. denominations found themselves embroiled in bitter controversy. The question of ordaining women to the Episcopalian priesthood created a furor within that church when 11 women were ordained in July. (See *Anglican Communion,* below.) The Lutheran Church-Missouri Synod found itself torn by dissension as a result of extremely conservative creedal positions taken in 1973. (See *Lutherans,* below.)

A major, two-year ecumenical study of Christian church membership in the U.S. was published by the Glenmary Research Center, a Catholic agency in Washington, D.C. The study, compiled by the Rev. Douglas W. Johnson of the National Council of the Churches of Christ in the U.S.A., the Rev. Paul Picard of the Lutheran Church-Missouri Synod, and the Rev. Bernard Quinn of the Glenmary Center, showed that church membership had grown from 45.8% of the population in 1952, when the last such survey was made, to 49.6% in 1971. (*See* Special Report.)

In other surveys of religious trends, the Center for Policy Research showed that the percentage of the population believing in God had fallen from 77% in 1964 to the current 69%. A Daniel Yankelovich survey of youth values indicated that the number of

Faith-healer John Scudder with a patient.

JEFF LOWENTHAL—NEWSWEEK

youth who consider religion very important had declined markedly—from 38 to 28% for college youth and from 64 to 42% for noncollege youth. A Gallup Poll released early in the year showed that 40% of all U.S. adults attended a church or synagogue during a typical week in 1973; this was approximately the same as in 1971 and 1972 but some nine percentage points below 1958.

Statistical reports from various church sectors showed that declining membership was still cause for concern, although in some cases contributions actually increased. Thus, while Lutheran membership in North America dropped for the fifth successive year, the Lutheran Church in America reported a 6% increase in giving. Sunday School attendance also troubled churchmen. According to the *Toronto Star*, for example, Sunday School attendance in Canada had declined nearly 50% within ten years, and some churches reported even greater losses.

The resignation of J. Brooke Mosley as president of Union Theological Seminary (New York) in June exposed a complex set of problems troubling Union in particular and liberal religious institutions in general. Along with financial problems, the seminary suffered from a decline in enrollment, the passing of some of its theological "stars," and tensions among students, faculty, and administration.

Another dispute arose when five veteran staff members of the National Council of Churches took "early retirement." The new NCC general secretary, Claire Randall, said the retirement was part of a previously approved restructuring plan and that finances were not involved, though there were indications that contributions from member churches had diminished. Adding to the uproar was the fact that the five executives were men and that together they had given more than 100 years service to the council.

Meanwhile, at the conservative end of the spectrum, 2,500 delegates from all parts of the world attended the International Congress on World Evangelization in Lausanne, Switz., in July. The main purpose of the congress was to discuss the task of evangelizing the world. Although primary emphasis was on challenging Christian churches to preach the gospel, consideration also was given to the "liberation of the whole man" and the need to implement the social implications of the gospel. Delegates adopted the Lausanne Covenant, which placed heavy emphasis on a conservative interpretation of the Bible.   (ALFRED P. KLAUSLER)

PROTESTANTS

Anglican Communion. The outstanding event of 1974 was the appointment of a new archbishop of Canterbury. Although the appointment rests only with the English authorities, it is the holder of this office who must personally provide the vital, if tenuous, link between the scattered family of autonomous churches that constitute the worldwide Anglican Communion. The decision, made in May, was that Donald Coggan (*see* BIOGRAPHY), who had been archbishop of York since 1961, should succeed the retiring archbishop, Michael Ramsey, at the end of the year. His appointment was received with general approval, despite the fact that at his age of 65 he could expect a tenure of office of only five years at most. The bishop of Liverpool, the Rt. Rev. Stuart Yarworth Blanch, was appointed to succeed him as archbishop of York.

Despite this change in the leadership, which coincided with other comings and goings in various influential Anglican posts (notably the installation in

Following their disputed ordination, the Rev. Alison Cheek (left), the Rev. Carter Heyward (centre), and the Rev. Jeannette Piccard (right), 3 of 11 controversial new women Episcopal priests, celebrate communion at the Riverside Church, New York City.

June of Bishop John Allin as presiding bishop of the Episcopal Church in the U.S.), the prospect of continuity in Anglican policy was strengthened by the reappointment for a further term of office, until 1979, of the Rt. Rev. John Howe as secretary-general of the Anglican Consultative Council. Bishop Howe affirmed his belief that members of the Anglican Communion, with its "structure of local autonomy and global family consultation," had received a blessing beyond anything they might have devised for themselves. At the same time, he warned that indefinite continuance of liturgical experiment, however excellent in itself, might threaten that essential Anglican unity which, historically, had been based on the general use of substantially identical prayer books.

Statistics published in 1974 indicated a small but significant decline in membership among American Episcopalians which was paralleled by a continuing fall in Anglican numbers in the United Kingdom. In England the historic tie between church and state was weakened by the church's decision, given final approval by the General Synod on Feb. 20, 1974, to order its own worship and doctrine without reference, as hitherto, to Parliament (which duly passed the Worship and Doctrine Measure on December 4) and by its proclaimed desire, expressed by vote of the General Synod on July 5, to appoint its own bishops without reference to the prime minister. Meanwhile, the rate of church buildings closed was up to 100 a year, and declining numbers of clergymen in active service and candidates for ordination gave cause for concern.

In the ecumenical movement for Christian reunion (roundly declared by Bishop Howe to be in a sick and feeble state), Anglicans scored no notable successes. Anglican and Roman Catholic theologians did issue an agreed statement on the nature of the priesthood, which optimistic observers thought might conceivably herald some softening of Rome's hitherto explicit rejection of the validity of Anglican orders. The Anglican Church in Wales pledged itself to pursue a "covenant for union" with other denominations, and the Church of England voted to engage in "talks about talks" with other British churches. But such vague declarations did nothing to remove the impression that, in Bishop Howe's words, "a general pattern of denominational Christianity is with us for a long time to come."

Among particular issues of concern to Anglican authorities were the church remarriage of the divorced and the ordination of women to the priesthood. In England, Canada, and several other Anglican provinces, the groundswell of opinion appeared to favour a change in traditional attitudes on both issues. In the U.S. in July violent controversy flared when three retired bishops and a bishop from Costa Rica "ordained" 11 women deacons to the priesthood in a highly publicized ceremony in North Philadelphia. In voting 128–9 to declare the ordination invalid, the House of Bishops, at an extraordinary meeting held August 14–15, based their decision on the fact that the ceremony had been performed contrary to canon law, which among other things requires approval of the bishop within whose diocese an ordination is held and of the standing committees of the candidates' dioceses. Later, at their regular meeting, the bishops endorsed admission of women to the priesthood in principle. The question had been narrowly defeated at the 1973 General Convention and was expected to be reintroduced at the next convention, in 1976.

(R. L. ROBERTS)

Baptists. The worldwide membership of Baptist churches increased by 2¼% during 1973, bringing the total to 33,492,813 according to statistics of the Baptist World Alliance. For the first time Baptists in Asia outnumbered those in Europe—1,160,000 to 1,150,000; the bulk of Asian members were in India and Burma. In the U.S. the National Council of Churches' annual tabulation of religious affiliations showed a decrease of 5% among congregations of the American Baptist Churches in the U.S.A.; the report was strongly contested by Robert C. Campbell, executive secretary of the ABC, who said figures available from his office indicated a 12% increase over the preceding four years. Membership of the Southern Baptists, the largest Protestant denomination in the U.S., rose 2% to slightly over 12 million.

Jaroy Weber, pastor of the 9,700-member First Baptist Church of Lubbock, Tex., was elected president of the Southern Baptist Convention at the annual meeting in Dallas. The SBC expressed the ambivalence regarding the ordination of women that characterized many church groups. Controversy over abortion continued, with the SBC reaffirming a 1971 resolution approving abortion in cases of "rape, incest, clear evidence of likelihood of damage to the emotional, mental and physical health of the mother." The American Baptist Churches were continuing the evangelistic thrust of the interdenominational Key 73 campaign with the Evangelistic Life Style movement. The Fund of Renewal, a joint effort by the American Baptists and the predominantly black Progressive National Baptists to raise money for the education of minorities, was in the process of being implemented.

Pressure continued to be exerted against Baptists in Communist countries, but there were some encouraging developments. In Poland the report issued in 1974 by Michael Strankiewicz, president of the Polish Baptist Union, recorded 2,400 members in 50 churches, served by 40 ministers and over 130 local preachers. According to Aleksey Bichkov, secretary of the All-Union Council of Evangelical Christians-Baptists of the U.S.S.R., the relationship between church and state in the U.S.S.R. was one "of increas-

ing mutual understanding." Membership had increased by 30,000 since 1969. Early in 1974 David Russell, general secretary of the Baptist Union of Great Britain and Ireland, and C. Ronald Coulding, associate secretary of the Baptist World Alliance, visited Romania, where they discussed the relationship between the state and Baptist churches with the chairman and vice-chairman of the government Department of Cults. In Hungary ten new Baptist churches had been opened since 1972, and there were about 12,000 members in 500 churches. Activities of the Baptist churches in Czechoslovakia had become increasingly difficult, however. The state imposed restrictions on Christian activity, and there was little contact between denominations. The Bulgarian government closed the Baptist church in Russe when its leaders failed to give authorities a "satisfactory" list of members' names.

In Chad the U.S.-based Baptist Mid-Missions Agency was ordered to cease its church-related operations, which the government interpreted as contrary to the nation's cultural revolution. About a hundred churches in south-central Chad were closed, the native-born pastors were imprisoned, and six missionary families and six single missionaries were ordered to leave the country. Only a small medical force remained. The American Baptists were very active in the interdenominational effort to use church investments to affect corporate policies in southern Africa. Some investments in their stock portfolio were sold in protest against unethical and un-Christian policies on the part of the companies involved.

In other developments, a Southern Baptist editor urged fellow Baptists to boycott Texas International Airlines because TIA's magazine carried an article favouring legalized gambling. Some three thousand delegates to the executive board meeting of the predominantly black National Baptist Convention voted unanimously to ask poor people to reject the food demanded as ransom by the kidnappers of Patricia Hearst (*see* BIOGRAPHY). In Britain, Welsh Baptists launched a plan to bring about greater cooperation between all Baptists in that country. In England over £300,000 was raised to increase the capital of the ministers' superannuation fund.

(NORMAN R. DE PUY; RONALD WILLIAM THOMSON)

Christian Church (Disciples of Christ). Members of this congregationally governed, 1.3 million-member body gave more than $11 million to the operating fund of the church for the first time in history. The 3.4% gain was the largest in nine years, though well below the rate of inflation in the U.S. economy.

A Disciples missionary couple working in the Philippines for the council of churches there was arrested, held for two weeks, then ordered to leave the country. Mr. and Mrs. Paul Wilson claimed that they and other church leaders were imprisoned because the church had criticized the government.

W. Barnett Blakemore, dean of Disciples Divinity House at the University of Chicago, was elected president of the World Convention of Churches of Christ (Disciples), a confessional fellowship with origins in the Campbellite movement on the American frontier. The election took place in Mexico City. The quadrennial assembly of the International Christian Women's Fellowship drew more than 4,000 delegates to Lafayette, Ind. Mrs. Anderson B. Barnes of Los Angeles was named president, the first black woman to hold that post.

Roman Catholic and Disciples leaders, ending five years of theological dialogue, called on both bodies to "explore as rapidly as possible" the idea of intercommunion. Kenneth L. Teegarden, general minister and president of the church in the U.S. and Canada, and Mrs. Wilfredo Velez, a Disciples member and vice-president of the National Council of Churches, were part of an ecumenical team that visited the U.S.S.R. to discuss continuing relationships between Soviet and American Christians. (ROBERT L. FRIEDLY)

Christian Science. The Church of Christ, Scientist, continued to strengthen its overseas activities in 1974. Early in the year DeWitt John, who became chairman of the board of directors in June, made an official tour of several Asian countries, and in the fall Otto Bertschi, the first European to become a member of the board of directors, visited Africa.

The International Youth Meeting, held at the Christian Science Center in Boston, July 29–31, had as its theme the verse "Lord, what wilt thou have me to do?" from the Book of Acts. Young Christian Scientists from five continents took part in one of the Voice of America's "Religion Today" programs.

At the annual meeting of the First Church of Christ, Scientist, in Boston (June 3) it was announced that more than 20 new translated publications had been issued by the Christian Science Publishing Society during the year and that Portuguese and Spanish editions of the *Heralds of Christian Science* were being published monthly for the first time. Christian healing was the focal point of a program in the CBS television series "Lamp Unto My Feet."

New officers of the Mother Church named during the year included: president, Georgina Tennant of London; first reader, Clem W. Collins of Boston; and second reader, Jane O. Robbins of Boulder, Colo.

(J. BUROUGHS STOKES)

Churches of Christ. Teaching of the Bible was a major emphasis in 1974. Among the programs for Bible teaching of children were the Thursday school for preschool children, designed to give mothers of the community a free day; Children's Worship; and the Busing Ministry, used in cities to reach poverty-area and minority children.

Mass media evangelistic programs and national and international television and radio ministries were expanded during the year. A mass mailing effort, Pathway Evangelism, was begun by Joe Barnett. A new publication, *Campus Journal*, was founded to serve Christian students at 100 state colleges throughout the U.S. The 21 colleges related to Churches of Christ all reported increased enrollments. In the area of world missions, a new printing facility in Vienna was publishing Bibles and tracts for distribution in 20 countries. Some 650,000 persons were enrolled in the Bible correspondence courses offered by the World Bible School, under the direction of James L. Lovell.

Evangelistic campaigns were carried out in both foreign and domestic mission areas. Hundreds of college young people were used in door-to-door visitation and personal work during summer campaigns, and many became missionary recruits. Despite the financial stress caused by inflation, the number of mission workers was larger than in any previous year. Enrollment in preacher training schools and mission training programs on Christian college campuses also increased, although a number of men were leaving the full-time ministry. (M. NORVEL YOUNG)

Church of Jesus Christ of Latter-day Saints. Spencer W. Kimball, a member of the Council of Twelve since 1943 and its president since 1973, was sustained (confirmed) as president of the church at the semiannual conference in April 1974. He had been chosen by the Council of Twelve to succeed Harold B. Lee, who died Dec. 26, 1973, after 18 months in office. Kimball's counselors in the First Presidency were N. Eldon Tanner and Marion G. Romney. The new president of the Council of Twelve was Ezra Taft Benson.

Shortly after he was sustained as president, Kimball suggested that most anticipated organizational changes had been carried out and that emphasis would now be on the implementation of existing programs. Two important changes occurred subsequently, however. In September the church turned over ownership and operation of its 15 hospitals in Utah, Idaho, and Wyoming to a new nonchurch, nonprofit corporation. The second change was the dissolution in June of the Aaronic Priesthood Mutual Improvement Association. Youth activities for boys 12–17 were consolidated under the Aaronic Priesthood, and girls of corresponding ages became part of an organization called simply Young Women.

Church membership continued to grow relatively rapidly, to approximately 3.5 million at the end of 1974. Stakes (dioceses) and missions at midyear were organized into 270 regions, 72 of them in non-English-language areas. In June the church's first stakes in Scandinavia (Copenhagen) and Northern Ireland (Belfast) were established. The temple at Kensington, Md., was dedicated November 18–21.

In July Richard P. Condie stepped down as conductor of the Mormon Tabernacle Choir, a position he had held for 17 years, and was succeeded by Jay E. Welch. (LEONARD JAMES ARRINGTON)

Jehovah's Witnesses. The international society of Christian evangelizers known as Jehovah's Witnesses enjoyed phenomenal growth during 1974. Their work, organized by 34,576 congregations, was carried on in 207 countries and territories; 297,872 new evangelizers were baptized, bringing the worldwide total to 2,021,432. This was achieved despite opposition to the society's work in Eastern Europe, the Arab countries, Greece, Cuba, Singapore, and some African countries.

During the summer a series of 168 "Divine Purpose" conventions were held in the U.S., Canada, the British Isles, and Western European countries; over 1.6 million persons attended the sessions and heard the public discourse entitled "Human Plans Failing as God's Purpose Succeeds." Two completely new Bible study aids in English were released at these assemblies: *God's "Eternal Purpose" Now Triumphing for Man's Good* and *Is This Life All There Is?* The rapid growth of Jehovah's Witnesses was also highlighted by a new peak attendance of 4,550,457 at the annual celebration of the Lord's Evening Meal.

Eight new rotary presses and new bookbinding equipment were ordered for printing plants in the U.S., West Germany, the Philippines, and Japan. During 1974 the Brooklyn plant alone produced 45,718,920 Bibles and bound books and over 268 million magazines. Circulation of the official journal, *The Watchtower*, reached 8,450,000 copies in 77 languages and that of its companion magazine, *Awake!*, 8.3 million copies in 31 languages. (N. H. KNORR)

Lutherans. The ongoing theological feud in the Lutheran Church-Missouri Synod between conservatives, headed by the president, J. A. O. Preus, and moderates reverberated internationally in 1974. The executive committee of the Lutheran World Federation, meeting at St. Olaf College in Northfield, Minn.,

continued on page 594

THE GEOGRAPHY OF RELIGION IN AMERICA

By Martin E. Marty

United States citizens in 1974 enjoyed a rare opportunity to learn something of the geographical distribution of their faiths. The publication of a statistical study and denominational map (*see* opposite page) revealed that regionalism remained strong in American religion. There were fewer "national" churches than many had suspected, and in almost every part of the country one religious group tended to dominate. On a county-by-county basis, large numbers of churches were indeed represented. In that sense, the U.S. was religiously pluralistic, yet in the majority of counties a single church held the allegiance of over 50% of the churchgoing population; in most of the others, one denomination could summon at least 25%.

The study on which the map is based, *Churches and Church Membership in the United States: 1971,* was prepared by a Lutheran and a Roman Catholic research group and an ecumenical agency, the National Council of the Churches of Christ in the U.S.A. The only similar compilation had been made for 1952.

Users of the map who focused only on religious majorities might think the U.S. is largely made up of five church-joining regions. The most intact is Utah, where Latter-day Saints (Mormons) overwhelm all other faiths. Second is a huge domain of Baptists in the South, where the Southern Baptist Convention has a clear majority in most counties. Stretching from Kansas to Pennsylvania, roughly along the latitude of the Ohio River, is a belt of counties where Methodism tends to have over 25% or, more rarely, over 50% of church members' loyalty. Following the path of Scandinavian and German migrations, there is a northwest-trending arc of Lutheran majorities beginning along a line from Nebraska to Wisconsin and reaching through the Dakotas into Montana. Roman Catholicism, which represents 36% of all U.S. Christian church membership (and 44.5% of the membership in this study, in which not all churches took part), dominates in the Northeast, along the industrial belt of the Great Lakes states, on most of the West Coast, in the Southwest, and in the southern tips of Texas, Louisiana, and Florida.

The publishers of the map urged caution upon their readers. The U.S. Census is not permitted to ask questions about religious affiliation, so the statisticians had to rely on data supplied by the churches. These statistics are only relatively reliable, though they appear to be improving. Further, allowance had to be made for different standards for measuring membership.

More important was the omission of a number of religious groups. Most black churches work with estimates instead of scientific counts, and could not be included. For the most part, they would have added to Baptist or Methodist majorities in southern regions or would have been submerged by Roman Catholic majorities in the cities. Because this was a Christian study, Jews were not represented, but it is believed they dominate in only two

Martin E. Marty is a professor of religion in the Divinity School of the University of Chicago, and an associate editor of The Christian Century. *His published works include* Righteous Empire: The Protestant Experience in America. *He also has served as an adviser on religion for the* Britannica Book of the Year.

or three counties in New York. Their presence, along with that of Eastern Orthodox churches—which do not keep accurate figures or did not cooperate—would not have changed the map in any significant way.

A third complicating feature is the inevitable distortion that occurs because of differing population densities; thus the sparsely settled Southwest gives Roman Catholicism an appearance of strength that it may not have nationally. These limitations aside, the materials did provide a reference point for a reassessment of strengths and weaknesses in the various churches. The 1971 statistics located over 100 million U.S. Christians in 53 communions, probably 80% of all church members.

All five of the regionally strong churches appeared as the result of 19th-century revivalism or later immigrations to the U.S. The religious map shows a startling absence of regional power among the three groups that had a virtual monopoly on religious loyalties in the 17th and 18th centuries. Episcopalians accounted for more than 50% of church membership in only one area in Alaska and one county in Colorado and for 25% or more in only four Great Plains counties. The United Church of Christ, the daughter of colonial Congregationalism, was also visible mainly in the Great Plains area, where Episcopalians and Congregationalists had carried on mission work among American Indians. The Presbyterian, the third of the strong colonial groups, was the only one with a predominance in any county east of the Mississippi, but its showing on a regional basis was as weak as the others. All three groups remain sizable. They form the centre of what is often called the "mainline" group of churches, but almost nowhere do they dominate.

Two of the major religious trends of the late 1960s and early 1970s are not revealed by the map. If a cartographer utilized impressions gained at the religion department of a paperback stand, he would probably expect to find millions of individuals devoted to Zen Buddhism, yoga, and various Hindu or Muslim faiths. These groups tend to attract visible but very small minorities, however. It is not likely that they will alter the appearance of the religious map in the next score of years.

The other major trend has been one in which the mainline churches at best held their own while a number of assertively conservative and evangelistic churches prospered. But despite their growth, these churches—with the exception of the Southern Baptist Convention, a church body that has much internal variety but keeps its evangelistic focus—are not found on the map. For example, the Church of God of Cleveland, Tennessee, grew by 120% between 1952 and 1971, but its original base was small and it has no county majority.

The statistics accompanying the map reveal one other feature of considerable note. There are vastly differing degrees of religious loyalty in various regions. In the westward sweep of the 19th century, the churches were effective in the west north central states (Iowa, Kansas, Minnesota, Missouri, Nebraska, and the Dakotas), none of which has less than 51% of its population on church rolls. But that effectiveness diminished farther west. For a variety of reasons, the Pacific region (Alaska, California, Hawaii, Oregon, and Washington) was least churched. No state there has more than 38% of its population formally enrolled. In New England the Roman Catholic presence pushes the total figure to 60%, but the historic Protestant churches are relatively weak.

Two groups of observers had reason to be surprised by the map and statistics released in 1974. One consisted of people who had predicted dramatic declines in institutional religion. Few in the mainline churches were cheered, but their losses tended to be offset by gains among the aggressive and strict denominations. The other group consisted of those who expected the religious map to show fundamental changes as a result of suburban population shifts and upheavals associated with the second Vatican Council and the social controversies of the '60s. Overall, such change is of a glacial character; it is possible that the mapmakers of the 1990s will not need to reach for too many new colours to tell the story of religious loyalty in the U.S.

Predominant Christian churches by counties of the United States in 1971

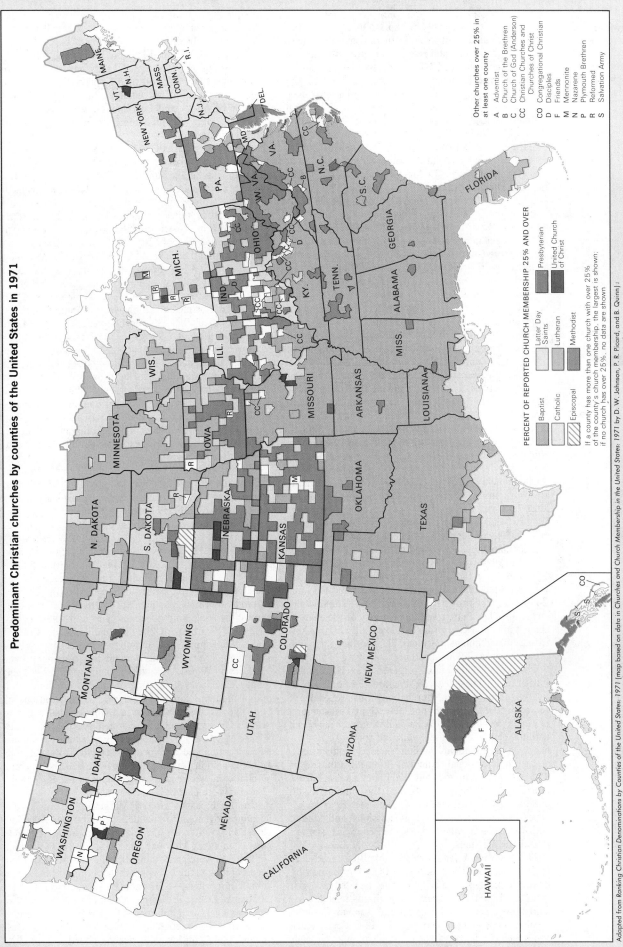

Other churches over 25% in at least one county

A   Adventist
B   Church of the Brethren
C   Church of God (Anderson)
CC Christian Churches and
    Churches of Christ
CO Congregational Christian
D   Disciples
F   Friends
M   Mennonite
N   Nazarene
P   Plymouth Brethren
R   Reformed
S   Salvation Army

PERCENT OF REPORTED CHURCH MEMBERSHIP 25% AND OVER

Baptist
Catholic
Episcopal

Latter Day Saints
Lutheran
Methodist

Presbyterian
United Church of Christ

If a county has more than one church with over 25% of the county's church membership, the largest is shown; if no church has over 25%, no data are shown

Adapted from *Ranking Christian Denominations by Counties of the United States: 1971* (map based on data in *Churches and Church Membership in the United States: 1971* by D. W. Johnson, P. R. Picard, and B. Quinn); map published by Glenmary Research Center, Washington, D.C., 1974; data copyright© 1974 by National Council of the Churches of Christ in the U.S.A.

continued from page 591

was told by its president, Mikko E. Juva of Finland, that "the total body of world Lutheranism is suffering" because "this strong and respected church is torn by a severe internal discord." The executive committee instructed Juva to send "a brotherly letter" to the LCMS expressing the federation's deep concern over the doctrinal dispute that threatened to split the 2.8 million-member denomination, second largest Lutheran body in the U.S.

Earlier, the Lutheran Church in America, at its seventh biennial convention, gave strong support to the moderates in the LCMS. Reaffirming the traditional Lutheran position of fidelity to Holy Scriptures and to the Ecumenical Creeds and the Lutheran Confessions, the LCA statement declared: "We therefore regret all official efforts to legislate adherence to additional documents that serve to fence God's Word and fracture God's people." (Similar resolutions were adopted by the American Lutheran Church at its seventh general convention.) In response, Preus wrote Robert J. Marshall, president of the 3.1 million-member LCA, that "I must categorically reject this judgment on the part of your church body."

The central figure in the controversy, the moderate John H. Tietjen, was suspended late in January as president of Concordia Seminary in St. Louis, Mo., on charges of administrative malfeasance and advocacy of false doctrine. In protest, most of the 600-odd students and a majority of the faculty walked out. A month later they established Seminex or "Seminary in Exile" at St. Louis University's Divinity School, a Roman Catholic institution, and Eden Seminary, affiliated with the United Church of Christ. The Synod's 38 North American district presidents were warned not to place, ordain, or install Seminex graduates without following proper procedures, including interviews and certification by Concordia Seminary. By year's end, however, it appeared that congregations and district presidents were likely to receive most of the Seminex ministerial candidates.

As the 1974–75 academic year began, Concordia at St. Louis, once the largest Lutheran seminary in the U.S., reported 190 students, Seminex claimed 408, and Concordia at Springfield, Ill., had 387. Meanwhile, on October 12, Tietjen was found guilty of the charges against him, and Concordia Seminary's Board of Control dismissed him as president. He also faced possible expulsion as an LCMS pastor.

The Synod's moderates, organized as Evangelical Lutherans in Mission (ELIM), said they did not intend to form another church body but would work for reform within the Synod. The Synod's directors, however, censured ELIM as "substantially a church within a church" because it solicited funds for a seminary, an independent mission society, publications, and an organizational structure. Adopting a budget of $1.5 million at a three-day assembly in Chicago, ELIM indicated that a major portion of the amount would be allocated to Partners in Mission, set up as an independent board for overseas missions and staffed with four persons who had resigned from the Synod's Board for Missions.

The historical-critical method of Bible study, at the core of the LCMS doctrinal dispute, "though by no means the supreme arbiter, must be used as a gift from God in the contemporary discussions among Christians," asserted Lutheran and Roman Catholic theologians who had been engaged in dialogue since 1965. The theologians issued formal findings on their three-year study of papal primacy, in which they said the issue need not be a barrier to reconciliation of the two churches. (*See* Introduction, above.)

The Lutheran World Federation changed leadership when André Appel resigned as its general secretary after nine years and returned to his native France to become president of the Church of the Augsburg Confession of Alsace and Lorraine. He was succeeded by Carl H. Mau, 52, an American with long international experience.

Robert J. Marshall was reelected president of the LCA after a surprisingly strong challenge from Wallace E. Fischer, senior pastor of Holy Trinity Lutheran Church in Lancaster, Pa. The LCA reconsidered use of the title "bishop" but, as in 1972, the nomenclature failed to gain the needed two-thirds majority. The American Lutheran Church authorized experimental use of the title in 1970 but had not taken final action. The ALC elected David W. Preus, cousin of J. A. O. Preus, to his first six-year term as president.

For the fifth successive year, membership in the Lutheran church bodies of North America declined in 1973, to 9,005,213. The five-year loss of 234,061 represented about 2.5% of the all-time high of 9,239,274 recorded in 1968.

Gen. Ernesto Geisel (*see* BIOGRAPHY), the son of Lutheran immigrants, became Brazil's first Protestant president. In France the Lutheran Church of Alsace and Lorraine approved intercommunion with the Roman Catholic Church. In South Africa a five-year ban against Manas Buthelezi, noted Lutheran theologian, was withdrawn without explanation by the government after six months.

Bishop Helmut Frenz, head of the Evangelical Lutheran Church in Chile, was awarded the 1974 Nansen Medal for his "inspiring example" in helping refugees after the 1973 military coup. Meanwhile, conservatives in the church sought the bishop's removal because of his refugee work. (ERIK W. MODEAN)

Methodists. The year 1974 began with a worldwide Vigil of Prayer, starting on the International Date Line at Tonga and encircling the globe. During the 12-hour period of prayer for the mission of Christ's church on earth, participants heard taped messages from the king and queen of Tonga, Bishop Prince Taylor (chairman of the Methodist World Council executive committee), and church leaders from every continent. The vigil was arranged in response to the call of the World Methodist Council meeting in Denver, Colo., in 1971 inviting Methodists to join in an intensified mission to the world. In preparation for positive evangelistic action in 1975, regional planning congresses were held in Europe, North and South America, Africa, India, and Australasia. A World Consultation and Convocation attended by 2,500 people was held in Jerusalem in November 1974, reaching a climax in a commissioning service in the Shepherd's Field at Bethlehem.

In the U.S. the United Methodist Church's continuing movement toward desegregation reached a new level in 1974, with the elimination of all districts based on race. Although the more than 500 districts in the U.S. were predominantly white, because of their geographic nature, 38 had superintendents from ethnic minorities—1 Hispanic, 2 Asian-American, and 35 black. Ethnic leadership also increased at the next highest level, with minority staff persons serving more than 20 of the nation's 70 annual conferences. U.S. membership continued to decline slowly, to 10,192,-

265, but a record $49,407,758 was given for worldwide benevolence and administration. A plan to reduce the number of seminaries from 14 was begun with the merger of two schools in Illinois to become Garrett-Evangelical Theological Seminary in Evanston.

Discussions were held through the year between the official Board of Global Ministries (missions) and an unofficial Evangelical Missions Council, which had accused the board of stressing social-political-economic action to the exclusion of evangelistic concerns. Another evangelical group, known as Good News, expressed opposition to the "doctrinal pluralism" adopted by the denomination's 1972 General Conference. Support of the church for women's rights was expressed, among other ways, in the special assignment of a staff member to work for the ratification of the Equal Rights Amendment to the U.S. Constitution. The Rev. Vivian McFadden became the first United Methodist woman chaplain in the military and the first black woman chaplain in the denomination or in the U.S. Navy.

The bishops of six African nations asked the church's missionary agency to send only missionaries who are "needed and requested by the church in Africa" to fulfill functions determined by those churches. At midyear a total of 794 missionaries from the U.S. were serving in some 50 overseas countries. Rhodesia's Bishop Abel T. Muzorewa was one of six persons honoured by the UN as international champions of human rights. He was unable to attend the presentation because his travel documents had been lifted by the Rhodesian government.

The Methodist Church in South Africa elected its first black president, the Rev. Jotham Charles Mvusi. It agreed to continue membership of the World Council of Churches, despite its disagreement with the World Council's policy of providing grants (though specifically not for military purposes) to guerrilla organizations in southern Africa. It also declared its intention to work toward eventual unity with the Anglican, Presbyterian, and Congregational churches in South Africa and agreed to accept women candidates for the ministry.

The British Conference, meeting at Bristol in June 1974, adopted a *Declaration of the Methodist Church on the Non-Medical Use of Drugs.* The document outlined the facts of the drug situation and then examined the social factors involved and the theological basis for the Christian attitude to drugs, with special reference to alcohol. The report recognized changes in the attitude of many church members toward alcohol and concluded by stressing the importance of individual Christian choice. The conference also adopted a declaration on the use of leisure and a detailed statement opposing euthanasia.

The conversations between the Church of Scotland and the Methodist Church in Scotland continued, with agreement at committee level on doctrinal standards, the structure of the united church, integration of the ministries, qualifications required from candidates for the ministry, and the name for the united church.

(PETER H. BOLT; WINSTON H. TAYLOR)

Pentecostal Churches. Rapid growth continued in the Pentecostal churches in 1974. The American Assemblies of God reported a 6% gain in U.S. membership—from 710,071 to 751,818 in one year; worldwide Assemblies of God membership was placed at 3,938,274; and similar growth was experienced by the 22 other denominations connected with the Pentecostal Fellowship of North America.

The Rev. Sun Myung Moon, South Korean evangelist who is believed by many of his predominantly youthful followers to be the Messiah returned, preaches in Madison Square Garden, New York City, during his U.S. crusade.

Some church officials believed the charismatic renewal movement was an important factor in the growth of Pentecostal churches. Ever larger conferences marked the charismatic movement during the year. Over 4,000 attended the March World Conference on the Holy Spirit in Jerusalem, the largest Christian gathering in Israel since the Middle Ages. Conferences on the Holy Spirit were also held at Princeton Theological Seminary, the Vatican, and in the National Cathedral in Washington, D.C. In June 25,000 Catholic Pentecostals gathered for their annual conference at Notre Dame University. (See *Roman Catholic Church,* below.) There was a growing movement toward détente between charismatic members and officials of the mainline denominations.

Events in the third world were prominently featured during 1974, and the December meeting of the Society for Pentecostal Studies focused on "The Third Force and the Third World." In San Juan a crowd of 50,000, including many Catholics, gathered to protest a decision of the Puerto Rican Supreme Court citing a Pentecostal church as constituting a "public nuisance." Over $60,000 was pledged to Vietnam missions at a convention in the Pentecostal Full Gospel Assembly Church in Seoul, South Korea. In December the Jotabeche Methodist Pentecostal Church in Santiago, Chile (affiliated with the Pentecostal Holiness Church in the U.S.), dedicated a new "cathedral" seating 18,000 persons.

In Great Britain and Ireland, a great Jubilee Rally held on Feb. 14, 1974, packed the Birmingham Town Hall. The annual General Conference, held May 11–18 at Minehead, Somerset, was attended by 5,500 delegates and many registered visitors. A team of "missionary heralds" was formed to evangelize in Malaysia. Home missions had conducted 13 pioneer evangelizing efforts during 1973 and planned six more crusades, while the National Youth Council sponsored two youth rallies, at Manchester and Nottingham. The Publishing House reported a 27% increase in sales, and the official organ *Redemption Tidings* had a circulation of 8,614.   (VINSON SYNAN; AARON LINFORD)

Presbyterian, Reformed, and Congregational. Membership in the World Alliance of Reformed Churches (Presbyterian and Congregational) reached 140 in 1974 with the admission of the Evangelical Church of Bolaang Mongondow (38,000 communicants; the 21st WARC member church in Indonesia), the Waldensian Evangelical Church of the River Plate, with a total communicant membership of 5,000 in Uruguay and Argentina, and the 92,000-strong African Presbyterian Church, the first all-black independent denomination in South Africa and Malawi to join the Alliance.

The 1974 meeting of the executive committee was held in Stony Point, N.Y., in January. This was the first time that the committee's meeting had been closely related to that of the North American Area Council of the WARC, held in the same place a few days earlier. The executive committee unanimously agreed to enter into theological discussions with the Baptist World Alliance. It also decided on a theme ("The Glory of God and the Future of Man") for the next General Council (assembly) of the WARC, scheduled to meet in St. Andrews, Scot., in 1977.

Inflation, coupled with only a slight increase in the churches' contributions, caused concern among WARC executives. Although the anticipated deficit for 1973 was smaller than forecast ($6,000, as against $10,000), 1974 was likely to end with a deficit of $20,000 in a total budget increased from $142,000 to $175,000.

Representatives at the North American Area Council at Stony Point expressed concern over the continuing violation of civil and religious liberty in South Korea. A message conveying this was sent to the two Alliance member churches in Korea, as well as to the Korean National Council of Churches. Later in the year the WARC president, William P. Thompson (U.S.), and General Secretary Edmond Perret (Switzerland) called on Pres. Park Chung Hee to "take constructive steps to unite all citizens under a true, Korean style of democracy." Many Presbyterians were among those sentenced under emergency decrees declared by President Park early in the year.

In 1974 the WARC was given consultative status with the UN Economic and Social Council (Ecosoc). This was done despite opposition from China, which objected to the fact that Taiwan was still represented in the Alliance.

The general assemblies of the highest policy-making bodies of the United Presbyterian Church in the U.S.A. (UPCUSA) and the Presbyterian Church in the U.S. (PCUS) met concurrently in Louisville, Ky., in June 1974; this was the first time they had met in the same city since 1913. The Rev. Robert C. Lamar, a leading advocate of Presbyterian union, was elected moderator of the 186th UPCUSA assembly, and the Rev. Lawrence W. Bottoms, the first black man to be so honoured by his denomination, was elected moderator of the 114th PCUS assembly. Commissioners (delegates) to both assemblies approved proposals aimed at uniting the two bodies, which had been separated since the Civil War, and the Cumberland Presbyterian Church, which had separated from the main body of American Presbyterians in 1810. A *Plan of Union* would be distributed to the churches for comments and recommendations to their 1976 general assemblies.

Merger discussions of the Reformed Presbyterian Church, Evangelical Synod (formed in 1965 by the union of the Reformed Presbyterian Church in North America, General Synod and the Evangelical Presbyterian Church, originally called the Bible Presbyterian Church) and the Orthodox Presbyterian Church moved forward toward final form during the year. The 100th General Assembly of the Presbyterian Church in Canada, held in Kitchener, Ont., in June 1974, placed particular emphasis on restructuring the national administration of the church. The 144th session of the General Assembly of the Cumberland Presbyterian Church, meeting in Bowling Green, Ky., adopted a report calling for a two-year study of Christian unity.

The first black woman minister in UPCUSA, the Rev. Katie Cannon, was ordained by the presbytery of Catawba. The Rev. Florence Dianna Pohlman became the first Presbyterian woman in the U.S. to be endorsed for chaplaincy duty.

In South Africa the six churches involved in union negotiations approved a "Declaration of Intention to Unite." They were the Anglican, Methodist, United Congregational, and three Presbyterian churches, the Presbyterian Church in Southern Africa, the Tsonga Presbyterian Church, and the Bantu Presbyterian Church.

The European Area Committee of the WARC met in Frankfurt am Main, W.Ger., September 13–16. Church representatives continued discussions on the theological basis of human rights (a study project launched by the 1970 world assembly in Nairobi, Kenya) and opened up a new series of discussions on the criteria of theological truth. (See *United Church of Christ*, below.)

(FREDERIK H. KAAN; WILLIAM B. MILLER)

Religious Society of Friends. The year 1974, the 350th anniversary of the birth of George Fox, founder of the Quakers, was marked by continuing emphasis on such traditional Quaker concerns as nonviolence and social change. The award of the 1973 Nobel Peace Prize to Henry Kissinger and Le Duc Tho troubled many Friends, who felt it was not consonant with the original principles governing the award.

The Quaker program at the UN was reviewed at a conference in London in June. It was noted that the Quaker UN team was being recruited from Friends beyond the predominant Anglo-American circle. The European and Near Eastern sections of the Friends World Committee on Consultation met April 11–13 in East Germany, the first time an international Quaker organization had been allowed in Eastern Europe.

Moved by Britain's economic crisis at the beginning of 1974, the society's Social Responsibility Council took on the task of clarifying the Quaker attitude toward change—with emphasis on the traditional testimony on simplicity in living. A report on Friends schools in Britain gave rise to an extended debate. Many British Friends saw the nine schools as privileged establishments.

In the U.S., Intermountain Friends became the newest yearly meeting. Wilburite Friends held the fourth general meeting in their 130-year history in North Carolina, June 21–23, and formed a Northeast Association of Conservative Friends. Louis Schneider became executive secretary of the American Friends Service Committee on June 1; the AFSC continued to serve civilian war victims in Vietnam and provided direct war relief to Israel, Egypt, and Syria.

(DAVID GEORGE FIRTH; J. WILLIAM FROST)

Salvation Army. The High Council of the Salvation Army, meeting in May 1974 at Sunbury-on-Thames, Eng., elected Commissioner Clarence Wiseman (*see* BIOGRAPHY), the territorial commander of Canada, to succeed retiring Gen. Erik Wickberg. Wiseman was the tenth general of the movement and the first Canadian to hold the position. Before retiring on the eve of his 70th birthday, General Wickberg completed a rigorous world tour of Salvation Army centres. He also conducted congresses in Sweden and France, Repentance Day in Germany, and Ascension Day in Switzerland.

In the U.S., 1974 was a Year of Recruitment, following up the Army's involvement in the Key 73 evangelistic program. U.S. membership rose to 361,571, and increased attendance was noted at adult and youth activities. Services to the aging expanded with the dedication in San Francisco of the Army's first federally subsidized high-rise housing complex, built in cooperation with the federal Department of Housing and Urban Development.

Salvationists continued to be active in disaster relief. For several weeks Salvationists served in flooded areas of New South Wales and Queensland in Australia, and relief to the value of A$350,000 was supplied in Brisbane. Relief work was also intensified in Bangladesh, and Salvation Army teams were on duty following a Christmas Day 1973 fire in Hong Kong and the explosion of a chemical factory in Flixborough, Eng. In the U.S., where disaster teams aided thousands of victims of tornados and floods in the Midwest and South, the Salvation Army was officially designated as a recognized disaster agency in new federal disaster legislation passed by Congress.

(ERNEST W. HOLZ; HARRY READ)

Seventh-day Adventists. During 1974 the church celebrated the centennial of its world outreach. On Sept. 15, 1874, the denomination, which had its origin in the U.S., sent John Nevins Andrews from Boston to Europe. Services commemorating his arrival were held in Basel, Switz., Sept. 28–30, 1974. During 1973—the last year for which complete statistics were available—316 new full-time workers and 195 student missionaries were sent to serve overseas. Between 1874 and 1974 church membership had grown from 4,801 to 2,390,124 (including 486,601 in the U.S.), and appropriations for mission work had risen from nothing to a record $76,890,169. Tithes and offerings in 1974 reached a new high of $305 million.

About 2,000 delegates attended three identical eight-day Bible conferences held in the U.S. for Seventh-day Adventist ministers, Bible teachers, and church workers. Their purpose was to examine carefully the church's teachings, making certain that they could be defended on the basis of sound hermeneutical principles. The last such conference was held in 1952.

The denomination's first medical institution, Battle Creek (Mich.) Sanitarium, founded in 1866 by John Harvey Kellogg, again came under church control after 35 years of independence. Members of the church's Loma Linda University surgery team performed the first open-heart operations in South Vietnam.

The first Ellen G. White-SDA Research Center outside the U.S. was opened in early April at the church's Newbold College in England. The centre specialized in early Adventist history, as well as letters, articles, and books written by Ellen G. White (1827–1915), one of the denomination's founders.

(KENNETH H. WOOD)

Unitarians and Universalists. Although acknowledging that individual freedom for inquiry and belief are fundamental to this liberal movement, growing numbers of Unitarian leaders felt that a solution must be found for destructive strains against consensus and community. When freedom and responsibility become separated, erosion and breakdown occur in both the institution and its human constituents.

The Unitarian Universalist Association (U.S. and Canada) claimed 1,008 local congregations in 1974, with 153,750 adult members, 51,655 church school students, and annual expenditures of $22,230,073. The largest number of churches and members were in Massachusetts, New York, and California. Bias against some members of the clergy on grounds of sex and age remained a problem. Of 44 qualified women ministers, only 7 occupied pulpits. The average age of the active clergy was 38.5 years, and their average salary package was $15,300. The number of active ministers had dropped about 4% in the preceding five years, but theological schools reported high enrollment.

The primary denominational instrument for social action and service, the Unitarian Universalist Service Committee, assisted dozens of congregations to launch local projects dealing with problems concerning the courts, police, and prisons. Pilot enterprises in rural Mississippi and urban Boston were exploring innovative uses of video technology to assist community development projects. Additional programs were under way in Peru, Central America, and Haiti.

The 1974 General Assembly of the UUA drew 1,324 delegates and observers to New York City, June 25–30. Preceding the plenary sessions, the official delegates were divided into 100 small groups of eight or nine persons each to discuss the agenda items. In the final resolutions, some passed by small majorities, delegates urged the establishment of an Office of Gay Concerns, support for the United Farm Workers' boycott of nonunion grapes and lettuce, opposition to the restoration of the death penalty, cessation of military aid by all governments to both North and South Vietnam, reform of the courts and penal system, and the right of adults to decide what they should read, hear, and see, free from censorship.

Meadville/Lombard Theological School and the North American Chapter of the International Association for Religious Freedom sponsored an Institute on World Religions, March 14–18, at the University of Chicago. Representatives of various religious cultures led discussions and workshops to consider how religious bodies can acknowledge and celebrate the existence of faiths different from their own.

The Rev. Jacob Davies of Dyfed, Wales, president of the British General Assembly, died on Feb. 11, 1974; this was the first time a president had died in office. At the Annual Meetings in London in April, his place was taken by Mrs. G. J. M. Thomas, also from Wales. During the meetings, delegates and guests from Great Britain and overseas joined in celebrating the 200th anniversary of the founding of the first avowedly Unitarian Church in Great Britain in Essex Street, Strand, London, on the site of the present denominational headquarters. Resolutions carried included one expressing support for Amnesty International's campaign against the use of torture and another asking the government to find means of relieving magistrates of the duty of asking for the religious beliefs of witnesses who choose to affirm rather than take the oath in courts of law.

(JOHN NICHOLLS BOOTH; B. L. GOLLAND)

United Church of Canada. The steady contraction in the church's membership since 1962 had become a matter of serious concern. Baptisms and confirmations had declined to an alarming degree, and attendance generally was down. Some of the falloff could be accounted for by the purging of congregational rolls. This was the case in the largest congregation of the church, where 1,000 names of nonattenders were eliminated. There were other factors, however, which were said to hinder the church's care of its people.

It was suggested that the church had been preoccupied with other continents and countries while political, economic, and social matters in Canada were ignored. The concern among Canada's churches for California grape growers had been strong, but the farm labourers in Canada's Holland Marsh were largely ignored. In addition, some of the programs of the church had not been brought to maturity; for example, union with the Anglican Church of Canada in the near future seemed impossible, although the *Plan of Union* had been overwhelmingly approved by the United Church's General Council. There was little for the United Church to do but be loyal to its own convictions and insights.

Much comment regarding the church's life had come from a group of evangelicals, sometimes referred to as conservatives, who maintained that the United Church was more interested in social action than in promoting the gospel and that it had diluted the faith and mission of the church. There appeared to be some truth in this, although frequently the indictment went too far. One of the most prominent of the evangelicals made it clear that both social action and evangelism are essential to the church's ministry. Evangelism was growing in the United Church; it had the support of some of the best ministers in the church, most of them young.

Women were playing an increasing role in the church. The lay membership of the 1974 General Council consisted of 130 women and 87 men. Three women were chosen as presidents-elect of their conferences, and two women were among the eight nominated for the moderatorship. The number of women candidates for the ministry was rising steadily, and they ranked high in the theological colleges. An increase of both men and women training for the ministry had been evident for some time.

The new moderator of the church, the Rev. Wilbur Howard of Emmanuel United Church, Ottawa, was nominated by three conferences. The Reverend Howard, who is black, had been associate editor of the church's Sunday School publications for 12 years before entering the pastorate.

(ARTHUR GUY REYNOLDS)

United Church of Christ. Brought into being in 1957 by a union of the Congregational Christian Churches and the Evangelical and Reformed Church, both of which had been formed out of previous unions, the United Church of Christ in 1974 had a membership of 1,867,810 in 6,617 congregations. Financial reports for 1973 indicated that though the giving of the members continued to increase (to $196,845,805), the proportion going to mission at the regional and national levels declined. This was due in part to inflation, but there was evidence that local churches were engaging in their own mission work to an increasing extent.

The denomination was not engaged in major efforts to restructure, but it was apparent that decentralization of staff was taking place gradually. For the first time since the denomination came into being, the number of professional staff at the regional or conference level exceeded staff at the national level. A new generation of leaders also had appeared at the conference level. Since 1969 new chief executives had been elected in 27 of the 40 conferences. Among those elected in 1974 was the Rev. W. Sterling Cary, the first black to become conference minister in the denomination, who would serve in the Illinois Conference. He was also the first black to have served as president of the National Council of Churches.

The year saw increased efforts on the part of the UCC to fulfill its commitments to the six predominantly black colleges related to it and to related educational institutions serving minority groups overseas. The 17/76 Fund, a campaign to raise $17 million for these institutions by 1976, had been started among the conferences in late 1972. At the end of 1974, 16 conferences had participated and donations were approaching $5 million. The remaining conferences would participate in 1975.

The new national Office for Church Life and Leadership was approved by the conferences and began operations on July 1. It incorporated functions formerly held by five bodies that had been phased out. Contrary to the practice in other national offices, the staff of the new office was regionalized. It was seen as an experiment in developing new working relationships between conferences and national staff.

For the third year national agencies were engaged in priority programs as authorized by the General Synod of 1971. Prominent among them were Criminal Justice, conducted by the Commission for Racial Justice; Faith Exploration, which combined the techniques of the retreat and the encounter group to enable church members to explore what it means to be Christian; Evangelism; and To Heal a Nation, a program of the Center for Social Action which had dealt with the question of amnesty for Vietnam war resisters, joined other church agencies in aiding minority veterans, and urged complete withdrawal of military aid from Vietnam.

Several of the national agencies that held invested funds continued to offer and support stockholder resolutions calling for fair employment practices in southern Africa and the U.S. by American corporations, representation of minorities and women on boards of directors and in management, and the end of destructive environmental practices. (See *Presbyterian, Reformed, and Congregational,* above.)

(ROBERT V. MOSS)

[827.D; 827.G.3; 827.H; 827.J.3]

ROMAN CATHOLIC CHURCH

Throughout 1974 Pope Paul VI, in the 11th year of his pontificate, laid great stress on the need to prepare for the Holy Year of 1975. In his discourses he dwelt on its twin themes of renewal and reconciliation. Reconciliation, he said repeatedly, involves the church itself and its inner unity, but extends also to other churches, to society as a whole, and to politics and work for peace.

The Synod of Bishops, which met in late September, was subordinate to the Holy Year preparations. The synod's theme was "The Evangelization of the Modern World." One of the principal points at issue was the relation between faith and political commitment. Particularly from Latin America there were demands for a "theology of liberation" interpreting salvation as liberation from injustice and oppression.

Pope Paul VI celebrates
a pontifical Mass
in the Sistine Chapel
at the opening
of the fourth
Synod of Bishops
at the Vatican.

After rejecting, as lacking in substance, three parts of a four-part report to the pope on their month-long discussions, the bishops adopted a hastily drafted general message and a list of major concerns. Among other points, the final text emphasized the need to adapt the faith to local cultures. In his final message to the synod, the pope thanked the bishops for their contributions, but he strongly reasserted his primacy and pointed out that many of the proposals "needed to be placed in proper proportion."

In the speech made on his feast day, Pope Paul had rebuked priests who thought that their mission was primarily social and political, but he conceded that the aim of missionary work was both to preach the gospel and to encourage civil development. This question of priorities was a recurring theme throughout the church during the year.

Initially the Chilean bishops were guarded in their approach to the military junta that took power in 1973, limiting their comments to a call for forgiveness. Later, during Holy Week, Raúl Cardinal Silva Henriquez and Bishop Carlos Camus spent two days sharing the life of the political prisoners, and the experience prompted them to issue a pastoral letter condemning the climate of insecurity and fear brought about by false denunciations and the use of arbitrary arrests and torture. The unity of the Chilean bishops was broken, however, by the bishop of Valparaíso, who postponed the release of the general episcopal statement until he had issued one of his own on reconciliation, as a reply to the Marxists who had "made a principle of class struggle."

The ebb and flow of church-state conflict was evident elsewhere in Latin America. In Argentina a priest was murdered for reasons unknown (though he had belonged to a progressive group called Priests for the Third World), while in Colombia Father Domingo Lain, a Spaniard who had been a strategist with the guerrilla movement, was shot on February 22, almost eight years to the day since the death of the radical priest Camilo Torres in similar circumstances. Less dramatically, the Mexican bishops declared that some form of socialism was needed "to correct the errors and abuses of the system," but they insisted on the importance of private property and thought that

Marxist materialism was incapable of changing the human heart. Early in the year some prominent Catholics were arrested in Brazil, but in July Pres. Ernesto Geisel met Agnelo Cardinal Rossi, formerly bishop of São Paulo and now Vatican official responsible for missions, and the government made a few conciliatory moves. It promised an inquiry into the death of Father Antônio Neto, right-hand man of Archbishop Helder Câmara (*see* BIOGRAPHY), murdered allegedly as a warning to the archbishop. Even so, Brazilian television was not allowed to report Helder Câmara's foreign journeys.

A more substantial example of reconciliation occurred in Zaire, where Pres. Mobutu Sese Seko and Joseph-Albert Cardinal Malula had been in conflict over the scope of the president's "africanization" drive. The president relaxed his ban on meetings of the episcopal conference, gave the cardinal a new residence, and showed other signs of cordiality. No such harmony was to be seen in Rhodesia where the bishops deplored yet again the use of summary arrests, imprisonment without trial, and paid informers. "Rhodesia can only be saved," they said, "by a revolution of love." In Mozambique, shock waves from the military takeover of the Portuguese government in April began to make themselves felt, as the hitherto "rebel" Frelimo guerrilla organization gradually took over the provisional government of the new country during its transition to full independence. This involved some delicate rethinking by bishops, who as recently as January had defended the Caetano regime in Lisbon and offered extenuating explanations for the massacres by Portuguese soldiers at Wiriyamu that had been reported by Catholic missionaries. The Vatican removed the most compromised of them.

In the U.S., too, political movements had their ecclesiastical counterparts. The "revival of ethnicity" was given encouragement by the first Conference of National Ethnic Clergy, whose aim was "to be supportive of one another in rebuilding ethnic communities." They were not challenging the "melting-pot" theory or being anti-American, but simply asserting pluralism. Meanwhile, the Rev. Eugene A. Marino, a 40-year-old black priest, became auxiliary bishop of Washington, D.C., and the country's fourth black bishop. Women were becoming more militant; the National Coalition of American Nuns (NCAN) called for feminine participation in the synod, denounced the presence of a handful of women observers as "tokenism," and pointed out that Jesus sent Mary Magdalene to tell the good news of the Resurrection to the brethren.

In mid-June the Conference on Charismatic Renewal at Notre Dame, Ind., was attended by 25,000 persons, further evidence of the rapid growth of the charismatic movement. The most remarkable feature of the conference was a service of charismatic healing, after which about 50 sick persons registered themselves as cured. A U.S. bishop thought the session "the most emotional and the least theological" he had witnessed at the conference, but Belgium's Leo Cardinal Suenens thought that sensationalism had been successfully avoided. He became the apologist of the charismatic movement, describing it as a "grace for the whole church" and predicting that it would revitalize the sacraments and parish life. In 1975 the Conference of the Charismatic Movement would be held in Rome over Pentecost.

Italy was preoccupied with other worries in 1974. The divorce referendum of May 12–13 proved an unwelcome and unexpected reverse for the hierarchy, which had committed itself to opposing the divorce law as the ruination of the Italian family. Pope Paul said he was "pained and saddened" by the result. Commentators drew the conclusion that Italy had changed radically, that it was rejecting its peasant past, and that it was moving toward pluralism. Over 40 priests who had advocated pluralism were suspended by the hierarchy. The best known was Dom Giovanni Franzoni, formerly abbot of St. Paul's Outside the Walls in Rome, who was expelled from the Benedictine Order.

The Vatican found itself at odds with much of the rest of the world at the UN Conference on World Population held in Bucharest, Rom., in August, where its representative reaffirmed the total ban on artificial contraception. (*See* POPULATIONS AND AREAS: *Special Report*.) On the other hand, concessions were made in dealing with Communist countries. The most notable was the enforced and reluctant resignation of Jozsef Cardinal Mindszenty of Hungary, whose worldwide lecture tours and forthcoming autobiography were causing distress to the Hungarian government. In Poland, despite intense diplomatic efforts by the

Vatican, Stefan Cardinal Wyszynski maintained his mistrustful attitude and was critical of the government's educational proposals which, he said, made education a party matter instead of a national one.

Ecumenism proceeded steadily if unspectacularly. The Anglican-Roman Catholic study on ministry appeared, but it deliberately left in suspense the question of Anglican orders and the controverted question of the papal ministry. This last question was bravely tackled by a Catholic-Lutheran group who reached a surprising measure of consensus on the need for a visible focus for unity that a reformed papacy might provide for all Christians. (*See* Introduction, above.) Elsewhere there were some striking contrasts. While in Strasbourg, France, the Lutherans responded favourably to the archbishop of Strasbourg's openminded position on intercommunion, in England the hierarchy refused to join the British Council of Churches "so as to preserve their right to defend the full teaching of the Catholic Church without reserve."

(PETER HEBBLETHWAITE)

[827.C; 827.G.2; 827.J.2]

EASTERN CHURCHES

The Orthodox Church. The turmoil provoked by the expulsion of the writer A. I. Solzhenitsyn (*see* BIOGRAPHY) from the Soviet Union, the Cyprus crisis, and the political changes in Greece drew attention to several Orthodox personalities involved in these events. In the U.S.S.R. the elderly Metropolitan Serafim, an auxiliary of the patriarch of Moscow, joined Soviet officials in condemning Solzhenitsyn as a traitor. Serafim's statement, however, was countered by Russian prelates in the West who, while remaining under Moscow's ecclesiastical jurisdiction, came to Solzhenitsyn's support. These contradictory assertions clearly diminished the credibility of the Soviet government's attempts to use church officials for propaganda purposes. Solzhenitsyn, who designated himself a faithful Orthodox Christian, had castigated these attempts while he was still in the Soviet Union, although he refrained from direct reference to the subject after his expulsion. Meanwhile, reports from the U.S.S.R. indicated that millions of faithful, including young people, were still crowding the churches. The government, however, repressed any religious activity beyond worship and conventional preaching. In May, Dimitri Dudko, a Moscovite priest, was demoted from his parish position because he had organized regular discussion periods.

Following the resignation of Ieronymos as archbishop of Athens and all Greece, the former metropolitan of Ioannina, Serafim, was elected to succeed him on Jan. 12, 1974. The election was a direct consequence of the coup that had overthrown the Papadopoulos dictatorship in 1973 and replaced it with a new military junta. All bishops who had been consecrated under Ieronymos were excluded from the election under the pretext that Ieronymos had been "uncanonically" elected in 1967. Only 28 diocesan bishops (or metropolitans) took part out of a total of 66, and Serafim, the government candidate, obtained 20 votes. The new archbishop seemed to accommodate himself to the junta's overthrow on July 22, and presided over the swearing in of the new civilian prime minister, Konstantinos Karamanlis. (*See* GREECE.)

Following the overthrow of the Cypriot president, Archbishop Makarios (*see* BIOGRAPHY), the three metropolitans who had been deposed in 1973 after attempting to depose him took up the leadership

The Rev. Joseph O'Rourke, Jesuit priest from New York, baptizes Nathaniel Ryan Morreale, who had been refused baptism by the priests of his parents' own parish in Marlborough, Mass., because of Mrs. Morreale's views favouring abortion.

JOYCE DOPKEEN—THE NEW YORK TIMES

of the church. They had opposed Makarios' involvement in civil government, which they considered incompatible with his ecclesiastical office. Doubt was cast on the future of the Church of Cyprus by the breakdown of the fragile political balance between Greek and Turkish Cypriots, so carefully preserved by Makarios during his presidency. (*See* CYPRUS.)

Observers of the Cypriot crisis feared ominous consequences for the Ecumenical Patriarchate of Constantinople, whose location in Istanbul, in the midst of a hostile Turkish population, became increasingly precarious. The "ecumenical" patriarch had no administrative authority over other Orthodox churches, though he was traditionally respected as the honorary primate among patriarchs. Patriarch Dimitrios I received the newly elected archbishop of Athens and all Greece in July 1974. In ecumenical relations, he adopted a more conservative attitude than his predecessor, Athenagoras I; during a 1973 visit to Istanbul by Jan Cardinal Willebrands, president of the Roman Catholic Secretariat for the Promotion of Christian Unity, he had pointedly insisted on the traditional Orthodox affirmation of equality of all bishops, as opposed to the Roman idea of papal supremacy.

On June 4–8, 1974, a conference of Orthodox theologians from the Middle East, the Soviet Union, Yugoslavia, Bulgaria, Romania, Greece, and America met to discuss "Confessing Christ Today," one of the main themes of the general assembly of the World Council of Churches to be held in Nairobi in 1975. In the U.S. Orthodox theologians joined their Roman Catholic colleagues in "deploring" the trend toward liberalized abortion. The Orthodox Church in America initiated a program for preparing priestly candidates from among Indians, Aleuts, and Eskimos.

Eastern Non-Chalcedonian Churches. The deposition of Haile Selassie (*see* BIOGRAPHY) from the imperial throne of Ethiopia was expected to have long-term consequences, not only for the Ethiopian Church but for all the Non-Chalcedonian churches. The former emperor had always been their fervent supporter and protector, and until recently Ethiopia had been the last surviving medieval theocracy. The Ethiopian Church, which enjoyed numerous privileges and owned vast properties, had not changed its ways of recruiting and educating clergy for centuries. Selassie had taken personal initiatives in favour of some modernization and reforms in education, but the new government was likely to take much more drastic steps in this regard. As yet the church had showed no opposition to the new regime, and the patriarch, Abuna Theophilos, called divine blessings upon the military leaders. (*See* ETHIOPIA.) (JOHN MEYENDORFF)

[827.B; 827.G.1; 827.J.1]

JUDAISM

During the October 1973, or Yom Kippur, war and in the period of uneasy disengagement agreements that followed, Jews throughout the world rose in Israel's support in terms of political action, fund raising, and volunteering. Both within the framework of organized communities, synagogues, and voluntary organizations and as concerned individuals, they tried to swing the attitude of national governments and public opinion in their respective countries toward Israel's cause. Soon, however, enthusiastic manifestations of Jewish solidarity with Israel gave way to deeply felt anxiety, not only about future political and military developments in the Middle East but also about the future of Diaspora Jewry.

The Yom Kippur war, the oil weapon employed so skillfully by the Arab countries, and the subsequent failure of nerve in the Western democracies raised serious questions about the future. Fears were expressed by some Jewish leaders that anti-Semitism had returned in a new guise: as anti-Zionism or anti-Israelism. Two U.S. writers, Benjamin Epstein and Arnold Forster of the Anti-Defamation League of B'nai B'rith, wrote a book called *The New Anti-Semitism* in which they presented the thesis that apathy and indifference to the fate of Israel constitute a covert form of anti-Semitism. In France a spokesman for the Conseil Représentatif des Institutions Juives de France asked his government to check what he described as a wave of anti-Semitism unlike anything seen in France since the end of World War II. The novel aspect of the current wave of anti-Semitism was that it originated not with traditional rightist groups but with leftist organizations linked with the Arabs and enjoying their financial support. Similar groups were also active in Italy, West Germany, and Latin America.

A discussion in the journal *Sh'ma* indicated that the pseudo-messianic aura that surrounded Israel after the June war of 1967 had begun to fade. Many of the Orthodox Jews of Israel persisted in viewing Israel in the messianic perspective, and Rabbi Menachem M. Schneerson, head of the Lubavich Hasidim, joined Israeli rabbis in the claim that Jews dare not give up that which the Lord has given them as an "eternal possession." However, some modern Orthodox Jews and the non-Orthodox in general rejected this dogma and appeared to favour a peace of compromise and reconciliation.

Special concern was felt about the fate of Jews who remained in the Arab countries, particularly those in Syria, which had a Jewish population of some 4,500. Jews were subject to surveillance and some harassment, and the killing of four young Jewish women was reported in March 1974. Jews living in North Africa were leaving rapidly. Before World War II, some 250,000 lived in Morocco alone; now only about 50 Jews remained in Libya, less than 1,000 in Algeria,

Patriarch Pimen, head of the still vigorous and, to a growing number of young Russians, increasingly attractive Russian Orthodox Church, leaves his chambers in Zagorsk, U.S.S.R.

Sally Priesand, the first woman rabbi in the U.S., leads a Hebrew lesson at the Stephen Wise Free Synagogue, New York City, where she is assistant rabbi.

about 8,000 in Tunisia, and some 30,000 in Morocco. Both King Hassan II of Morocco and Pres. Habib Bourguiba of Tunisia repeatedly assured their Jewish subjects of their protection, though in Morocco the opposition daily *L'Opinion* from time to time accused Jews of subversive activities. There were also cases of discrimination, though on the whole little local anti-Jewish feeling was evident among the population, even when reports of the casualties suffered by the Moroccan expeditionary force during the Yom Kippur war became known.

The perennial controversy about "Who is a Jew?" and the ensuing problems centring on the validity of conversions performed by Reform and Conservative rabbis went on unabated. Indeed, it caused a serious political crisis in Israel in May 1974 when the National Religious Party refused to join the coalition government headed by Yitzhak Rabin. (*See* ISRAEL.) A proposal that halakhic conversion (according to Talmudic law) be instituted for all converts to Judaism, but that it be supervised by joint conversion boards in which Orthodox, Reform, and Conservative rabbis would participate, was put forward by a leading U.S. Reform rabbi, Herbert Weiner. The acrimonious controversy over conversions in Israel and the Diaspora could be settled, according to Rabbi Weiner, if Orthodox rabbis agreed to cooperate within such a framework, which would ensure halakhic conversions while enabling the non-Orthodox to instruct converts who had approached them.

The Committee on Jewish Law and Standards of the Conservative movement in the U.S. failed to give official sanction for women to become rabbis and cantors or to serve as witnesses for marriages and in rabbinic courts. However, since some members had voted for the proposals, rabbis might feel free to follow the minority position without fear of punishment by the Rabbinical Assembly. The Reform had accepted women rabbis and cantors some years earlier.

Plans for studying the moral and spiritual aspects of human rights and religious freedom in the Catholic and Jewish religious traditions were agreed on by the International Catholic-Jewish Liaison Committee. The committee, established in 1971, met annually for the purpose of fostering mutual understanding and exchanging information and cooperating in areas of common concern and responsibility.

A new quarterly, *Present Tense,* was launched in the U.S. under the auspices of the American Jewish Committee. It was designed to focus attention on the problems of Jews throughout the world. A University Without Walls, offering a variety of correspondence courses on Judaism and Jewish history, opened under the sponsorship of the American Jewish Committee and the University of Haifa. The response by some 200 enrollees was an indication of the resurgence of interest in higher Jewish learning.

The Synagogue Council of America, an umbrella organization of Orthodox, Conservative, and Reform denominations, reported the establishment of an Institute for Jewish Policy Planning and Research. Headed by Philip Klutznick, former U.S. ambassador to the UN Economic and Social Council, the institute had already published a number of studies of aspects of Jewish life. Another indication of ferment was the formation of the National Jewish Hospitality Committee, with headquarters in Philadelphia. Its purpose was to help mixed and intermarried couples feel at home in the Jewish community.

In 1973, 36,000 Jews from the U.S.S.R. came to Is-

rael, as compared with 31,652 in 1972 and 12,839 in 1971, but there was a serious drop in emigration from the beginning of 1974 due to the precarious political and economic situation in Israel and to various obstacles raised by Soviet authorities. Under the pressure of world public opinion some Soviet Jews were allowed to emigrate, including the distinguished dancer Valery Panov (*see* BIOGRAPHY) and his wife and Silva Zalmanson, who had been imprisoned for her Zionist activities. In October the U.S.S.R. reportedly agreed to permit increased emigration in return for U.S. trade concessions, although later Soviet statements left the matter in some doubt.

(JACOB B. AGUS; PAUL GLIKSON)

[826]

BUDDHISM

The most talked-about figure in the world of Buddhism during 1973–74 was the Dalai Lama, who had been living in India since the abortive Tibetan revolt against China in 1959. In 1973 he had toured ten Western European nations, meeting with the pope, the archbishop of Canterbury, and other leading religious figures and making contacts with institutions that had helped the Tibetan refugees. He was also nominated for the Nobel Peace Prize. During 1973–74 there was widespread speculation that he might visit the Soviet Union and Mongolia and might eventually return to Tibet. There was also an unconfirmed but persistent rumour that the Panchen Lama, the second-ranking Tibetan religio-political leader whom many had believed to be dead, was alive in China and had communicated with the Dalai Lama urging him to return to Tibet. On the other hand, it was reported that China had started the third phase of its communization program, including further destruction of the Tibetan lamaseries.

Two Buddhist states in the Himalayan border area, Sikkim and Bhutan, were taking steps to preserve old Buddhist manuscripts, relics, and images. For example, the Bhutanese government forbade the sale of valuable relics outside the country and retained direct responsibility over the monasteries, providing, among other things, the payment of 25 pais per meal to monks as "curry allowance." The situation in Sikkim might change, however, since real power had passed from its Buddhist king to a chief executive nominated by India. (*See* DEPENDENT STATES.) In another Himalayan border nation, Nepal, the restoration of the Buddha's birthplace, Lumbini, was under way with the support of financial donations from abroad. Even Muslim Pakistan donated Rs. 500,000 to the project.

In India the International Buddhist Dharmaduta Training Centre was established at Sanchi, a Buddhist centre during the reign of King Asoka in the 3rd century B.C. A central organization of Indian Buddhists was being formed with R. D. Bhandate, governor of Bihar, as its president. In Sri Lanka, Jinadasa Samarakkody was elected president of the All-Ceylon Buddhist Congress and O. H. de A. Wijesekera was appointed the editor in chief of the *Encyclopaedia of Buddhism;* both succeeded the late G. P. Malalasekara. Japan's Eiheiji Temple donated a security-glass facade to replace the iron railing enclosing the Sacred Tooth relic at Kandy.

In Thailand a new permanent headquarters of the World Fellowship of Buddhists was built with 3 million baht donated by the Thai government. R. L. Soni, a Burmese lay Buddhist leader, erected a pagoda in the Sagaing Hills of northern Burma in memory of his mentor, the Venerable Lokanatha, an Italian Buddhist monk who had spent 40 years spreading Buddha's gospel in India, Sri Lanka, Thailand, and Burma. A Buddhist research institute was established at the Dongguk University in Seoul, South Korea, where the second international leadership training conference of the World Fellowship of Buddhist Youth was held in 1973. In Japan the Buddhist English Association held its second seminar at Saijoji Zen temple near Odawara. Nikkyo Niwano, president of the influential lay Buddhist organization Rissho Kosei-kai, visited China in April at the invitation of the Buddhist Association of China. According to his report, the Chinese government was helping rebuild Buddhist temples destroyed or damaged by Red Guards during the Cultural Revolution of the late 1960s.

An International Buddhist Congress, held in December 1973 at Neuilly, France, attracted 1,000 delegates from five European nations. A Unitarian-Buddhist group was formed in England. In the U.S., 1974 marked the 75th anniversary of the founding of the Buddhist Churches of America.

(JOSEPH M. KITAGAWA)

[824]

ISLAM

The effects of the October 1973 Israeli-Arab war continued to be felt in 1974, not only in the Middle East but throughout the Muslim world. Announcements from Islamic conferences tended to reflect political and economic situations, and the specific Muslim concern most often expressed related to Israel's control of Jerusalem.

The second conference of Islamic heads of state was held in Lahore, Pak., February 22–24. The conference called for unity to regain territory lost to Israel since 1967, protection of Muslim interests in Jerusalem, and economic cooperation among Arab and other Muslim states. The first Conference of World Muslim Organizations, held in Mecca in April, turned its attention especially to the situation regarding the Qadiani Ahmadi sect in Pakistan, the ongoing disturbances in the southern Philippines, and the Marxist government of Yemen (Aden), as well as concerns relating to Kashmir, Zanzibar, and Albania. In June an Islamic foreign ministers' conference was convened in Kuala Lumpur, Malaysia, where interest centred on the Palestine and Jerusalem questions and, particularly, the Philippine situation.

The communiqué of the Kuala Lumpur conference denounced the Philippine government's actions in the southern Philippines, where disturbances between Muslims and government forces continued. In February Jolo City was reported in ruins with hundreds killed. The Philippine government claimed Malaysia had been aiding the Muslim rebels, who in turn accused the government of attempting genocide. In June riots broke out in Pakistan between Sunni groups and the Qadiani Ahmadis. Some Western observers thought they were the most serious civil disturbances in Pakistan in several years, though the government disagreed. Sunni Muslims regard the Qadiani group, formed in the 19th century in what was then British-controlled India, as heretics.

As the Ethiopian political crisis deepened in the spring, a large Muslim demonstration was held in the capital demanding an end to alleged anti-Muslim discrimination. In August, India selected Fakhruddin Ali Ahmed (see BIOGRAPHY) as president of the country. He was the second Muslim to hold the position.

In the U.S. five Black Muslims went on trial in Washington, D.C., in February on charges of killing seven Hanafi Muslims in a house owned by professional basketball star Kareem Abdul Jabbar. Hanafi leader Hamaas Abdul Khaalis maintained that the murders were in retaliation for letters Jabbar had sent claiming Black Muslim leader Elijah Muhammad taught false Islamic doctrines. Four of the five were convicted in May. In early December 1973, Libya had refused a loan to the Black Muslims, citing Arab disagreement with their all-black philosophy.

In May the government of Morocco stopped work on a motion picture of the life of the Prophet Muhammad, starring Anthony Quinn and directed by the U.S. filmmaker Moustapha Akkad. Filming had begun the previous month, reportedly after sheikhs at al-Azhar University in Cairo had approved the script. Morocco cited religious reasons for its action; Akkad claimed pressure had been brought by other Muslim countries.

Aboud Jumbe, the first vice-president of Tanzania, announced in January that teaching of Islamic principles would be compulsory at all school levels in Zanzibar. He also announced preparation of a new Swahili translation of the Koran. Early in February the National Assembly of Kuwait debated whether Kuwait Airways should serve alcoholic beverages, which are forbidden by Islamic law, on international flights in the Persian Gulf area. Opposing liberal and conservative religious groups appeared to be forming over questions such as this as Muslim countries were drawn more and more into international relationships.

In early April a journalist reported that Yugoslav Communist leaders were complaining that Muslims there still harboured "nationalist" feelings. Israeli Deputy Prime Minister Yigal Allon assisted in laying a cornerstone for a new Islamic seminary in Hebron in July. The institution would receive financial aid from the Israeli government but would be administered under independent Muslim control.

(R. W. SMITH)

[828]

RELIGIONS OF ASIA

A variety of events in Asia during 1973–74 indicated the difficulty of differentiating religious and nonreligious dimensions of life. In sharp contrast to the decade following World War II, when leaders of Asian religions addressed themselves aggressively to social and political problems, it was young people, especially students, who were articulating the concerns of Asian people in the 1970s.

In South Asia religious as well as political tensions were eased by a tripartite agreement reached by India and its two Muslim neighbours, Pakistan and Bangladesh. Internally, however, the discontent of the Indian populace exploded in violent demonstrations and riots. In this situation, several political parties, including some with strong religious bases, such as the Swatantra, attempted to form a single political party, and seven of them eventually merged into the Bharatiya Lok Dal. The ruling Congress Party condemned the activities of such paramilitary groups as the Anand Marg. On January 30, the 26th anniversary of Mohandas Gandhi's murder, his nephew fasted as a protest against violence in Indian society.

Serious discontent was apparent among the youth of Sri Lanka, which had not recovered from the social and economic crisis resulting from the 1971 insurgency. Some 2,400 qualified youths were unable to enter universities because of the shortage of facilities, and many young intellectuals were leaving the country. Sri Lanka signed a pact with India whereby half of the 150,000 stateless Tamil-speaking Hindus of Indian origin residing there would be repatriated as citizens of India, while the other half would remain as full Ceylonese citizens.

Several governments in Southeast Asia were threatened by rebel movements, some of them religiously motivated. Thus, in Burma, Ne Win's regime continued its war against the Karen and Shan insurgents. Meanwhile, former prime minister U Nu resigned from the leadership of the Thailand-based Parliamentary Democratic Party and announced that he hoped to dedicate the rest of his life to the spread of Buddhism. In Thailand Sombat Thamrongthanyawonges, leader of the students whose massive demonstration had helped to topple the military regime of former Prime Minister Thanom Kittikachorn in 1973, was reported to have become a monk to honour the students killed in the disorders.

The bloody Muslim-Catholic conflict in the Philippines continued. The government feared that Muslim nations in the Middle East might deny oil to the Philippines out of sympathy with the Filipino Muslims. In Indonesia the Bahai sect, which had been banned by the late President Sukarno, protested against the government's continued prohibition of its religious activities.

In East Asia, too, religions were deeply involved in political and social dimensions of life. In China, where a mild form of Confucian revival took place in the early 1960s, Confucius came under severe attack from leftists. (*See* CHINA.) In Taiwan Pres. Chiang Kai-shek attacked "totalitarian tyrannies based on materialism and atheism." His government ordered the closing of 17 Christian colleges on the ground that their students were not accredited by the Joint College Entrance Examination.

In the face of growing discontent, Pres. Park Chung Hee of South Korea took strong measures against dissidents. A number of leading Protestant clergymen and Roman Catholic Bishop Daniel Chi Hak Soun received prison terms. (*See* KOREA.) The oil crisis forced the Japanese government to adopt a friendly attitude toward Arab Muslim nations. The Komeito Party, which had suffered a severe setback in the 1972 general election following its break with its parent body, the lay religious group Soka-gakkai, was renewing its relationship with the latter.

Various forms of Asian religions continued to gain adherents in the West. The 16-year-old Maharaj Ji, guru of the Divine Light Mission which claimed large numbers of followers among young people in the U.S., married his 24-year-old American secretary in May.

(JOSEPH M. KITAGAWA)

[823; 825]

WORLD CHURCH MEMBERSHIP

The study of religious statistics is still in its infancy. Some churches keep very exact information on their members but will not release the data to outsiders. Others, and this is particularly true of the ethnic religions and some branches of Christianity with centuries-old ethnic foundations, base their own reports on percentages of population figures. Finally, no census of any kind has as yet been taken in some nations.

Some religions have "adherents," others designate "constituents," and others count "communicants"; only on the mission fields of Christianity, Buddhism, Islam, and Hinduism are precise figures available. A typical instance is Sri Lanka. A reliable government report indicates there are about 6,200 Buddhist temples in the island with about 18,000 priests, and 1,784 Hindu kovils (temples) with about 2,000 officiating kurukkals (priests). The number of adherents in both cases can only be estimated.

Estimated Membership of the Principal Religions of the World*

Religions	North America†	South America	Europe‡	Asia	Africa	Oceania§	World
Total Christian	225,504,750	161,583,500	352,597,100	86,811,000	100,465,100	17,104,000	944,065,450
Roman Catholic	128,884,000	151,600,000	171,748,500	45,122,000	32,039,500	3,188,000	532,582,000
Eastern Orthodox	4,115,000	54,000	65,534,600	1,835,000	17,410,000‖	353,000	89,301,600
Protestant¶	92,505,750	9,929,500	115,314,000	39,854,000	51,015,6009	13,563,000	322,181,850
Jewish	6,346,525	678,700	3,960,700	3,026,150	299,465	75,000	14,386,540
Muslimδ	235,000	191,200	8,730,000	422,208,000	97,678,500	66,000	529,108,700
Zoroastrian□	250	—	—	224,650	475	—	225,375
Shinto○	55,000	90,000	—	62,004,000	—	—	62,149,000
Taoist△	16,000	12,000	—	31,360,700	—	—	31,388,700
Confucian△	96,000	83,000	30,000	205,725,700	500	41,500	205,976,700
Buddhist+	148,000	180,300	220,000	247,951,500	2,000	15,000	248,516,800
Hindu⊕	70,000	502,000	350,000	512,418,000	463,400	629,000	514,432,400
Totals	232,471,525	163,320,700	365,887,800	1,571,729,700	198,909,440	17,930,500	2,550,249,665
Population**	344,950,000	212,139,000	728,724,000	2,255,094,000	384,305,000	21,099,000	3,940,249,000

*Religious statistics are directly affected by war and persecution; for example, recent events in Uganda, Bangladesh, and Cyprus alter the estimates of religious affiliation substantially. There are about 18 million refugees throughout the world who are not as yet integrated into the population statistics and religious estimates of their land of temporary (?) residence.
†Includes Central America and the West Indies.
‡Includes the U.S.S.R., in which the effect of a half century of official Marxist ideology upon religious adherence is evident, although the extent of religious disaffection and disaffiliation is disputed. The same difficulty in estimating religious adherence obtains in other nations with officially Marxist governments, although the degree of persecution varies from country to country and from time to time.
§Includes Australia and New Zealand as well as the islands of the South Pacific.
‖Includes Coptic Christians, numerous in Egypt and Ethiopia.
¶Protestant statistics outside Europe usually include "full members" only, rather than all baptized persons, and are not comparable to the statistics of ethnic religions or of churches counting all adherents.
9Including many sects and cults of recent appearance and rapid growth.
δThe chief base of Islam is still ethnic, although missionary work has lately been undertaken in Europe and America. In countries where Islam is the official state religion, minority religions are frequently persecuted and reliable statistics are scarce. In some, such as Saudi Arabia, no general census has been taken.
□Zoroastrians (Parsees) are found chiefly in Iran and India.
○A Japanese ethnic religion, Shinto has declined markedly since the Japanese emperor gave up the claim to divinity (1947); neither does it transplant readily with Japanese moving out from the homeland, in contrast to Buddhism. Japanese religious statistics are problematical because adherents are frequently related to several different religions simultaneously.
△General population figures for China are highly speculative, although minimal population growth has apparently been achieved. Religious statistics are problematical, with the effect of the Maoist-Marxist revolution not yet measured definitively.
+Buddhism has produced several modern renewal movements, with energetic missions outside the traditional ethnic-Buddhist areas.
⊕Hinduism's strength in India has been enhanced by nationalism but eroded by modern industrialization and contemporary secular ideologies. Modern Hinduism has also developed several modern renewal movements with vigorous missions in Europe and America.
**Source: United Nations, Department of Economic and Social Affairs; data refer to midyear 1974; world total includes adjustment for migration. (FRANKLIN H. LITTELL)

A second major problem for the statistician is the uncertainty of religious reports from areas of persecution. Many millions of the world's refugees are religious as well as cultural, political, and/or economic victims. Their exact religious composition can only be estimated, along with the numbers still left in their lands of origin. The effect of an enforced Marxist ideology in the U.S.S.R. and China, and in allied (Eastern Europe) or occupied (Tibet) areas, can only be estimated. Some official Eastern Orthodox tables still show 100 million Russian Orthodox; a recent government study conceded that there were 30 million "hard core" Christians. Presumably, some place in between is a figure that might be comparable to the statistics of active Christians in Spain, Sweden, or other Western countries.

The data for countries with free churches, where membership is based upon a clear and uninhibited choice, are generally far more reliable than those for areas in which governments have intervened to sponsor or to persecute. That is to say, the statistics of membership of a Zen Buddhist Society in Boston or a Baptist congregation in Burma are "hard" figures; the Buddhist figures for Thailand and the Lutheran figures for Lower Saxony are considerably less dependable, if membership rather than very loose adherence is the issue. Accordingly, though the accompanying table is revised regularly to reflect the latest surveys and informed estimates, the reader is advised to use it with the awareness that mixed styles of reckoning are necessarily involved. (FRANKLIN H. LITTELL)

Rhodesia

Though Rhodesia declared itself a republic on March 2, 1970, it remained a British colony in the eyes of many other nations. It is bounded by Zambia, Mozambique, South Africa, and Botswana. Area: 150,873 sq.mi. (390,759 sq.km.). Pop. (1974 est.): 6.1 million, of whom 95% are African and 5% white. Cap. and largest city: Salisbury (urban area pop., 1973 est., 513,000). Language: English (official) and Bantu. Religion: predominantly traditional tribal beliefs; Christian minority. President in 1974, Clifford W. Dupont; prime minister, Ian D. Smith.

Just before Christmas 1973 terrorists launched a new offensive against Rhodesia. Their main target was the African population rather than the white farmers, and in response the government stepped up its program of building protected villages to house those threatened by the guerrillas. At the same time, the doubling of the number of those drafted for national military service and the formation of a second battalion of the Rhodesian African Rifles, together with the institution of periods of service of up to one month each year for men over the age of 25 with no military commitment, paved the way for a change from defense to attack on the part of the security forces to clear the terrorists from the northeastern districts. The change of regime in Mozambique, after the military coup in Portugal in April, threatened the eastern front, but Rhodesia had been preparing for such an eventuality and the government was confident that it could defend its borders from an attack from that direction. But at the same time, urgent plans were made to open a new railway link with South Africa in case Rhodesia's former outlet to the Indian Ocean through Mozambique should be closed by a hostile government; the vital and only direct link with South Africa, the 90-mi. Rutenga–Beitbridge line, was completed on September 10, far ahead of schedule.

On the home front prospects of rapprochement between the government and the African National Council (ANC) were dismissed early in the year by Edison Sithole, who, speaking for the ANC, said that Prime Minister Smith had shown no willingness to negotiate realistically. The central committee of the ANC flatly rejected the constitutional proposals set out after a year of discussion between Smith and the ANC leader, Bishop Abel Muzorewa, arguing that the proposals, which began with an offer of 22 seats in the Assembly for black members as compared with 50 for whites, would mean that it would take between 40 and 60 years for the blacks to achieve parity with the whites in parliamentary representation. The ANC claimed it could accept nothing less than a constitution in which there was no domination of one race by another. Although this stand seemed like a rebuff for Muzorewa's moderate policy, Sithole maintained that

Zimbabwe guerrillas in camp near the increasingly tense Rhodesian border with Mozambique.

Resources, Natural:
see Environment

Retail Sales:
see Marketing and Merchandising

there was no desire to evict the bishop from his position as leader. Events in Mozambique undoubtedly encouraged the ANC to strengthen its claim for a greater say in the affairs of government, but Smith firmly maintained that only a small minority of the Africans in Rhodesia were in favour of majority rule and that he did not expect it to be introduced during his lifetime.

Support among the white population for Smith's government, already demonstrated by the comfortable victories of the two Rhodesian Front candidates in by-elections in February, was strengthened by the change of government in Mozambique. The resignation, in June, from the Rhodesia Party of its only member of Parliament, Alan Savory, weakened the white opposition to the Smith regime, as did the unsuccessful attempt to form an alliance between the Rhodesia Party and a group of former Rhodesian Front members led by the right-wing William Harper. The strength of support for Smith's government was amply demonstrated on July 30 when in a general election the Rhodesian Front won all 50 of the non-African seats in Parliament (there were 16 African seats).

A radical change in the course of Rhodesian affairs came in December when nationalist leaders Joshua Nkomo of the Zimbabwe African People's Union, Ndabaningi Sithole of the Zimbabwe African National Union, James Chikerema of the Front for the Liberation of Zimbabwe, and Muzorewa, negotiated with Prime Minister Smith at Lusaka, Zambia, by invitation of Pres. Kenneth Kaunda of Zambia. Nkomo and Sithole had been released from government detention for the occasion. At first the talks broke down, but on December 11 Smith, under strong pressure from South African Prime Minister B. J. Vorster to reach an agreement, consented to release all black political detainees and to hold a constitutional con-

ference without preconditions, on the understanding that guerrilla warfare would cease immediately.

The prospects for farmers appeared very much brighter during 1974. Their earnings reached a record level, mainly as a result of the heavy world demand for agricultural produce. Tobacco commanded such high prices that the government was able to hope that it would not need to subsidize growers to ensure that they continued to grow tobacco. Encouraged by the high prices offered for tobacco and the failure of the UN attempt to enforce a trade embargo, Rhodesia's cotton growers sought the government's aid in establishing a cotton research station. The country's mineral production also brought in a record return, which reflected not only a rise in prices but also an increase in output of 14%, and the government was further encouraged when De Beers Consolidated Mines of Johannesburg, S.Af., took another concession to extend its prospecting activities in Rhodesia. Rhodesia's gross national product rose by 6.5% in 1973 and there was a net surplus of R$33 million on the overall balance of payments, but the budget showed a deficit of R$30.7 million in a total of R$349.1 million. Furthermore, the guerrilla war made it necessary to impose a 10% surcharge on income tax.

In one area the outlook seemed more gloomy. Tourist figures showed a sharp decrease in 1974, while immigration figures also declined at a time when more people left the country than in previous years. In spite of the Settler 74 campaign launched at the beginning of the year to encourage immigration, there were grave fears that the demand for skilled labour would not be met from the white community.

(KENNETH INGHAM)

[978.E.8.b.iii]

Romania

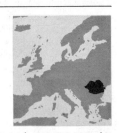

A socialist republic on the Balkan Peninsula in southeastern Europe, Romania is bordered by the U.S.S.R., the Black Sea, Bulgaria, Yugoslavia, and Hungary. Area: 91,700 sq.mi. (237,500 sq.km.). Pop. (1973 est.): 20,828,000, including (1966) Romanian 87.7%; Hungarian 8.5%. Cap. and largest city: Bucharest (pop., 1973 est., 1,528,600). Religion: Romanian Orthodox 70%; Greek Orthodox 10%. General secretary of the Romanian Communist Party, president of the republic (from March 28), and president of the State Council in 1974, Nicolae Ceausescu; chairmen of the Council of Ministers (premiers), Ion Gheorghe Maurer and, after March 26, Manea Manescu.

On Aug. 23, 1974, Romania celebrated the 30th anniversary of what President Ceausescu (*see* BIOGRAPHY) described in his jubilee speech at the Grand National Assembly as "the overthrow of the military-fascist dictatorship and Romania's liberation from Hitler Germany's domination." Summarizing his country's economic transformation since World War II, Ceausescu noted that Romanian industry was now producing some 30 times the previous output. Whereas three decades earlier Romanian steel production amounted to 280,000 tons, in 1974 it exceeded 9 million tons. Electric power generation, meanwhile, had risen from 1,500,000,000 to more than 55,000,000,000 kw-hr. Great progress had also been achieved in agriculture and animal husbandry.

ROMANIA

Education. (1972–73) Primary, pupils 2,720,199, teachers 135,089; secondary, pupils 349,980, teachers 16,107; vocational, pupils 498,071, teachers 23,228; teacher training, students 23,575, teachers 1,544; higher (including 12 universities), students 143,985, teaching staff 14,488.

Finance. Monetary unit: leu, with (Sept. 16, 1974) a commercial rate of 5 lei to U.S. $1 (11.70 lei = £1 sterling) and a tourist rate of 14.38 lei = U.S. $1 (33 lei = £1 sterling). Budget (1973 actual): revenue 175,972,000,000 lei; expenditure 168,091,000,000 lei.

Foreign Trade. (1973) Imports 17,418,000,000 lei; exports 18,576,000,000 lei. Import sources: U.S.S.R. 20%; West Germany 12%; East Germany 6%; Czechoslovakia 6%; France 5%. Export destinations: U.S.S.R. 22%; West Germany 9%; East Germany 7%; Czechoslovakia 6%; Italy 5%; Poland 5%. Main exports: machinery and transport equipment 24%; raw materials 17%; petroleum products 7%; foodstuffs 14%; chemicals 7%.

Transport and Communications. Roads (1972) 76,304 km. (including 96 km. expressways). Motor vehicles in use: passenger (1972) c. 125,000; commercial c. 50,000. Railways (1972): 11,023 km.; traffic 20,184,000,000 passenger-km., freight 53,280,-000,000 net ton-km. Air traffic (1973): 496 million passenger-km.; freight 5,880,000 net ton-km. Inland waterways in regular use (1972) 1,588 km. Shipping (1973): merchant vessels 100 gross tons and over 96; gross tonnage 474,497. Telephones (Dec. 1972) 807,-000. Radio licenses (Dec. 1972) 3,112,000. Television licenses (Dec. 1972) 1,944,000.

Agriculture. Production (in 000; metric tons; 1973; 1972 in parentheses): wheat c. 5,300 (6,041); barley c. 820 (839); oats c. 110 (111); corn c. 9,000 (9,817); potatoes c. 3,600 (3,672); onions c. 270 (283); tomatoes c. 900 (872); sugar, raw value c. 587 (c. 597); sunflower seed c. 875 (850); dry beans c. 90 (90); soybeans c. 230 (186); dry peas c. 100 (91); plums (1972) c. 460, (1971) 459; apples c. 250 (248); wine c. 750 (c. 600); tobacco c. 38 (38); linseed c. 52 (51); hemp fibre (1972) c. 17, (1971) 21; flax fibre (1972) c. 17, (1971) 17. Livestock (in 000; Jan. 1973): cattle 5,677; sheep 14,455; pigs 8,785; horses 631; poultry 64,496.

Industry. Fuel and power (in 000; metric tons; 1972): coal 6,612; lignite 16,547; coke 1,134; crude oil 14,128; natural gas (cu.m.) 26,212; manufactured gas (cu.m.; 1971) 536,000; electricity (kw-hr.) 43,-439,000. Production (in 000; metric tons; 1972): cement 9,212; iron ore (metal content) 842; pig iron (1973) 5,710; crude steel (1973) 8,160; petroleum products (1971) 15,400; sulfuric acid 1,162; fertilizers (nutrient content) nitrogenous 874, phosphate 313; cotton yarn 130; cotton fabrics (sq.m.) 531,000; wool yarn 42; woolen fabrics (sq.m.) 74,000; rayon, etc., filament yarns and fibres 62; nylon, etc., filament yarns and fibres 45; other paper 492; passenger cars (units; 1971) 9,100; commercial vehicles (units) 39,000. New dwelling units completed (1972) 141,000.

No foreign Communist Party leaders attended the Bucharest festivities. The U.S.S.R. was represented by Premier Aleksey Kosygin, who left after a three-day stay without having had any substantial talk with Ceausescu. Moscow's resentment was said to focus on Romanian opposition to a Soviet demand for a new wide-gauge strategic railway line from Odessa to Varna across the Romanian province of Dobruja for the possible transport of troops and equipment from the U.S.S.R. to Bulgaria. On July 8 President Tito of Yugoslavia arrived in Romania on an official visit; his talks with Ceausescu were believed to have included discussion of the proposed railway, a matter of concern to both Bucharest and Belgrade.

At the beginning of July Gheorghe Macovescu, Romanian foreign minister, and Gen. Ion Gheorghe, the chief of the general staff, arrived in Peking. At a banquet for his Romanian guests on July 5, Foreign Minister Chi Peng-fei praised Romania which, "defying brute force, has firmly stood its ground in the face of outside pressure."

On March 28, while retaining his presidency of the State Council and party general secretaryship,

Ceausescu was elected to the newly created presidency of the Socialist Republic of Romania by the Grand National Assembly. Two days earlier, 72-year-old Ion Gheorghe Maurer, chairman of the Council of Ministers since March 1961, had resigned and been succeeded by Manea Manescu.

On November 28 the 11th party congress elected a new Central Committee of 205 members and 156 alternate members. At its first plenary session the Central Committee elected an Executive Political Committee of 23 members and 13 alternate members. On November 29 the Executive Political Committee elected a five-man Standing Committee to "ensure the operative coordination of party and state activity." The congress adopted the 1976–80 five-year plan and also a program mapping out the country's political course to the end of the century. The program rejected the concept of Communist supranationalism: "It is no longer possible to have a centre which coordinates the activities of Communist parties."

Ceausescu continued his foreign travels during the year. He had visited the U.S. in December 1973 to discuss economic cooperation (Romania received a $110 million credit from the World Bank to finance new energy and metallurgical projects). In the new year he visited Libya, Lebanon, Syria, and Iraq in February, Liberia and Argentina in March, Mauretania in April, and Bulgaria in May.

(K. M. SMOGORZEWSKI)

[972.B.3.d]

Rowing

East Germany dominated world rowing in 1974. It was the strongest nation in the men's, women's, and junior world championships, with 15 titles and half a dozen other medals out of a possible 22 events. Two significant features of the 1974 season were the introduction of lightweight classes in the world championships, held at Lucerne, Switz., and the reemergence of the U.S. and Great Britain in eight-oared rowing. Ten nations shared the medals in the men's finals, with East Germany winning six events. Most of the titles were decided by less than a length.

East Germany, the U.S.S.R., and West Germany fought a closely matched contest in coxed fours before East Germany won from the U.S.S.R., with West Germany third. H.-U. Schmied and C. Kreuziger scored the East German triumph in double sculls, and the twins B. and J. Landvoigt gave their country a convincing victory over Romania in coxless pairs. After the favourite, S. Drea (Ire.), had been taken ill, the single sculls title went to W. Honig (E.Ger.). He beat J. Dietz (U.S.), whom Drea had defeated three times earlier in the season. The Russian giant N. Ivanov and his partner V. Eshinov defeated East Germany in coxed pairs, but the situation was reversed in coxless fours when East Germany scored its fifth success. East Germans also became first winners of the new event for quadruple sculls.

The world championship eights proved worthy of the name. New Zealand took an early lead, and until the halfway mark a length covered all six boats. Suddenly West Germany dropped to last place, the U.S. inched past New Zealand, and behind them Great Britain squeezed past East Germany, overtook the U.S.S.R., and then passed New Zealand to finish a quarter of a length behind the U.S. Only 3.02 sec. separated the first five crews at the finish. The U.S.

The Oxford rowing crew sets a record of 17 min. 35 sec. over the 4¼-mi. course and defeats the rival Cambridge crew in their April meeting on the River Thames in London.

in eights and sculls and Australia in coxless fours were winners of the lightweight championships; The Netherlands won silver medals in all three events.

East Germans also dominated the inaugural women's world rowing championships at Lucerne. They won four gold medals, one silver, and one bronze in the six events. The gold medals were gained in the eights, coxed fours, quadruple sculls, and single sculls. The world junior championships were held at Ratzeburg, W.Ger., where East Germany added 5 more titles to the 19 already collected since the championships were officially recognized in 1970. They triumphed in coxed and coxless pairs, coxed and coxless fours, and were first winners of the newly introduced quadruple sculls. West Germans were successful in double sculls and defeated East Germany in the eights. Italy won the single sculls.

At the Henley Royal Regatta, U.S. crews brought their total wins past the 50 mark, and the total of overseas winners at the 135-year-old event reached 170. Soviet crews captured the Grand, Stewards', Silver Goblets, and Double Sculls. Drea retained the Diamond Sculls for Ireland, which also triumphed in the Ladies' Plate. The Thames Cup went to Belgium, and U.S. crews were victors in the Princess Elizabeth Cup (Holy Spirit High School) and the Wyfold Cup (Porcellian Club). Oxford won the 120th university boat race in record time to end Cambridge's six-year run in the series. (KEITH OSBORNE)

[452.B.4.a.ii]

Rwanda

A republic in eastern Africa, and former traditional kingdom whose origins may be traced back to the 15th century, Rwanda is bordered by Zaire, Uganda, Tanzania, and Burundi. Area: 10,169 sq.mi. (26,338 sq.km.). Pop. (1974 est.): 4,062,400, including (1970) Hutu 90%; Tutsi 9%; and Twa 1%. Cap. and largest city: Kigali (pop., 1971 est., 60,000). Language (official): French and Kinyarwanda. Religion (1970): animist 43%; Roman Catholic 46%; Protestant 7%; Muslim 1%. President in 1974, Gen. Juvénal Habyalimana.

President Habyalimana continued his military rule in 1974. He and his government gave high priority to raising the standard of agriculture. Rwanda, one of the poorest, least productive African states, had an annual population increase of 3%. Nonetheless, the government increased expenditure on entertainment. In another action, government employees were forbidden to hold trade licenses. Intertribal relations improved, and one Tutsi was included in the government.

Foreign aid, mainly Belgian and Swiss, was crucial for the economy, there being a substantial imbalance between imports and exports. The International Development Association provided $6.3 million for road projects, and the European Development Fund supplied further aid for tea planting. Coffee remained the chief export, however, with the minerals cassiterite and wolframite following in that order.

During the year the Home de la Vierge des Pauvres, commonly known as Father Fraipont Mission (supported by the Rwandan and Belgian governments and other organizations), became the largest private employer in the country. It produced the cheapest transistor on the African market and made a profit of nearly RwFr. 30,000. A semi-industrial shirt factory at the mission, using local handicapped labour, also captured almost all the local market. The mission's orthopedic workshop produced aids for invalids, and the mission itself had a wholly self-supporting farm.

(MOLLY MORTIMER)

RWANDA

Education. (1973–74) Primary, pupils 397,752, teachers 7,777; secondary, pupils 7,488; vocational, pupils 1,487; teacher training, students 1,560; secondary, vocational, and teacher training (1969–70), teachers 736; higher (1970–71), students 735, teaching staff 86.

Finance. Monetary unit: Rwanda franc, with (Sept. 16, 1974) a par value of RwFr. 92.84 to U.S. $1 (free rate of RwFr. 214.80 = £1 sterling). Gold, SDRs, and foreign exchange, central bank: (June 1974) U.S. $15,020,000; (June 1973) U.S. $15.5 million. Budget (1972 est.) balanced at RwFr. 2,138,000,000.

Foreign Trade. (1973) Imports RwFr. 2,889,900,-000; exports RwFr. 2,794,300,000. Import sources (1972): Belgium-Luxembourg 18%; West Germany 11%; Japan 9%; U.S. 7%; U.K. 6%; France 6%; Iran 6%; Kenya 5%. Export destinations (1972): Kenya 51%; Belgium-Luxembourg 25%; U.S. 8%; U.K. 5%. Main exports: coffee 63%; tin 16%.

Agriculture. Production (in 000; metric tons; 1973; 1972 in parentheses): sorghum c. 154 (145); potatoes 140 (131); sweet potatoes c. 400 (c. 400); cassava c. 350 (c. 350); dry beans c. 135 (131); dry peas c. 56 (55); coffee c. 11 (11); tea c. 3 (2). Livestock (in 000; July 1973): cattle c. 780; sheep c. 234; pigs c. 62.

Sailing

Among the leading events of 1974 was the 25,000-mi. Round the World race, won by Ramon Carlin of Mexico in his Sparkman and Stephens-designed Swan 65 "Sayula II" from the British Royal Naval entry "Adventure," a Nicholson 55 sailed by various crews in relay. The Round Britain race was won by Robin Knox Johnston sailing his huge catamaran "British Oxygen," and once more the America's Cup challenge came to nothing when "Courageous" dominated the series to retain the cup for the U.S.

Early in the year, the Danish sailing maestro, four-time Olympic gold medalist Paul Elvstrøm, proved beyond doubt that his winning days were not behind him. After his disastrous Olympic series in 1972, rivals in the world championship could hardly believe the results when, after three races, Elvstrøm had chalked up three firsts. He collected one more first and a second before the end of the week to beat Olympic Star class gold medalist David Forbes of Australia.

Again, the Southern Ocean Racing Conference (SORC) series was keenly contested and was used as the testing ground for new yachts. If there were any doubts about the improvements made to the one-ton boats, they must have been dispelled by the end of February. The final standings for the SORC series showed only Dick Carter's "Rabbit" preventing a clean sweep for the 27.5-rating yachts—"Robin Too II," "America Jane II," "Country Woman," "Lightnin'," "Magic Twanger," and "Robin." By far the most successful of the large yachts was the Class B 55-ft. "Scaramouche," designed by German Frers, Jr., and owned by Chuck Kirsch.

After the SORC the big yachts sailed north for the season, and the Onion Patch trophy was contested by four teams—U.S., Britain, Canada, and Bermuda. This four-race series ended with the classic Newport-to-Bermuda event. The British team, consisting of "Noryema," "Marionette," and "Oyster," started well and led overall after the first three races, but the U.S. had "Scaramouche," which won the first three races. In the high-scoring Bermuda race, "Scaramouche" won again, and its teammates "Dynamite" and "Robin Too II" took fifth and sixth places to give the U.S. a score of 168 points. Britain and Canada tied for second with 136 points. Overall honours went to "Scaramouche" with yet another Frers design, the Class C "Recluta III" from Argentina, in third place. Second place went to the Sparkman and Stephens-designed "Charisma," a Class B U.S. boat.

The Round the World race had begun in late summer of 1973, and by the New Year the yachts were racing across the dangerous Southern Ocean. The favourite, Eric Tabarly, had already succumbed when his "Pen Duick" lost its mainmast on the first leg to

UPI COMPIX

Cape Town. "Burton Cutter" had sprung a serious leak soon after leaving the Cape, and Chay Blyth's "Great Britain II" did not find its form until the end. So the scene was set for a battle between two fibreglass yachts designed by the two best-known names in yachting, Olin Stephens and Nicholson. The first leg had been won by "Adventure" from "Sayula II"; the second by "Sayula II" with "Adventure" eighth; and the third by "Adventure" with "Sayula II" second. "Adventure" won the final leg with "Sayula II" fourth, but when the times were added up "Sayula II" had won overall by 45 hours.

The Olympic Flying Dutchman class held its world championship in England. World champion Hans Fogh, the Danish-born Canadian sailmaker, was defending his title, and double Olympic gold medalist Rodney Pattisson from the U.K. appeared again suddenly after an 18-month layoff. But it was the East Germans Ilja Wolf and Herbert Huettner who took the honours. Fogh in the heavy weather and Pattisson in the medium had their winning days, but they could not match the two East German crews.

The level-rating "ton" racing series were gradually gathering momentum; the quarter-ton, half-ton, and one-ton had become firmly established, with three-quarter-ton and two-ton gaining increased recognition. The one-ton series held in 1974 off Torquay in the west of England attracted 34 yachts from 13 countries. British-built and owned boats took the first two places, with Jeremy Rogers winning in his Peterson-designed Contessa 35 "Gumboots" from George Stead in his De Ridder-designed "High Tension." The half-ton series, held in France, finished with a stormy race in which only the fittest and most experienced crews survived the full course. West German Eckart Wagner in his Peterson-designed "North Star" won the event with consistent sailing. The quarter-ton series took place in Sweden off Malmö. The Swedes seemed the only ones at home in the sloppy light conditions and had entered boats with big sail areas, heavy displacement, and low wetted surfaces. They took the first two places with prototypes of new production boats.

The American 12-m. "Courageous" leads the Australian challenger "Southern Cross" in the fourth and final America's Cup race off Newport, R.I. The "Courageous" successfully defended the cup with four straight victories.

World Class Boat Champions		
Class	Winner	Country
Soling	P. Elvstrøm	Denmark
Tempest	U. Mares	West Germany
Tornado	R. Jessenig	Austria
Fireball	J. Cassidy	Australia
Hornet	M. Goodwin	U.K.
Laser	P. Commette	U.S.
Flying Dutchman	I. Wolf	East Germany
505	Y. Pajot	France
420	A. Chourgnoz	France
Enterprise	P. Crebbin	U.K.
Solo	F. Imhoff	The Netherlands
Cherub	A. Wilmot	Australia

Once again the centre of publicity in the Round Britain race was on the big boats. As expected, Robin Knox Johnston in his 70-ft. catamaran "British Oxygen," assisted by Gerry Boxall, soon established a lead in this two-man crew event. Co-favourite Alain Colas, in his 70-ft. world-girdling trimaran "Manureva," seemed unable to put the French ahead although he achieved some remarkable averages.

The long-awaited America's Cup challenge and defense took place over the summer months. With both the French and Australians challenging, an elimination series had to be run first. Baron Bich's "France" was soon proved inferior in almost every sailing department and went down four races to nil to Australian Alan Bond's "Southern Cross." While this was going on, the four U.S. yachts, "Courageous," "Intrepid," "Mariner," and "Valiant," were settling down to their final eliminations. "Mariner" and "Valiant" were consistently beaten and the field was left to an absorbing battle between "Courageous," a boat representing the East Coast, and "Intrepid," the California entry. Toward the final days when the selectors would have to make their decision, the older wooden-hulled "Intrepid" appeared to be gaining an edge. Then Ted Hood was put in charge of "Courageous," and this gave it enough of an advantage to win the selection. Thus, the scene was set for the America's Cup challenge between "Southern Cross" and "Courageous." The sharper U.S. crew took the first start and never looked back. The pattern was repeated in increasingly overwhelming style each day, and the Australians realized just what they had missed by not having a keenly contested warm-up series. "Courageous" won the series 4–0.

World sailing speed record attempts were annually held in Britain, but the record in 1974 went to Steve Dashew's D class catamaran "Beowulf" in a timed trial sailed off the U.S. West Coast. Britain's "Crossbow" was said to be preparing a challenge and at the end of 1974 awaited suitable conditions on one of England's largest man-made lakes, Grafham Water.

(ADRIAN JARDINE)

[452.B.4.a.ii]

San Marino

A small republic, San Marino is an enclave in northeastern Italy, 14 mi. SW of Rimini. Area: 24 sq.mi. (61 sq.km.). Pop. (1974 est.): 19,100. Cap. and largest city: San Marino (metro. pop., 1974 est., 4,423). Language: Italian. Religion: Roman Catholic. The country is governed by two *capitani reggenti,* or coregents, appointed every six months by a Grand and General Council. Executive power rests with two secretaries of state: foreign and political affairs and internal affairs. In 1974 the positions were filled, respectively, by Gian Luigi Berti and Giuseppe Lonfernini.

Communists and Socialists made minor gains in general elections held on Sept. 8, 1974. The Commu-

St. Lucia:
see Dependent States

Salvador, El:
see El Salvador

Salvation Army:
see Religion

Samoa:
see Dependent States;
Western Samoa

Sarawak:
see Malaysia

Satellites, Space:
see Space Exploration

SAN MARINO
Education. (1972–73) Primary, pupils 1,683, teachers 99; secondary, pupils 1,115, teachers 83.
  Finance. Monetary unit: Italian lira, with (Sept. 16, 1974) a free rate of 664 lire to U.S. $1 (1,533 lire = £1 sterling); local coins are issued. Budget (1972 est.) balanced at 9,530,000,000 lire. Tourism (1970) 2.3 million visitors.

nists received 3,246 votes, giving them 15 seats in the 60-member Grand and General Council (14 prior to the election), and the Socialists obtained 1,914 votes and 8 seats (7). The Christian Democratic and Social Democratic parties each lost 2 seats, reducing their representation to 25 and 9, respectively. However, with the Socialists, they were able to form a centre-left coalition to rule the republic for the next five years.

This was the first election to be held since passage of a bill in September 1973 allowing women to hold public office and to enter into binding legal and financial commitments. Several women candidates ran for seats on the council, and three, one Christian Democrat and two Communists, were elected.

On Nov. 26, 1973, San Marino established consular relations with East Germany. The republic also ratified the international Convention on Prohibition of the Development, Production, and Stockpiling of Bacteriological (Biological) and Toxic Weapons. In 1974 San Marino applied for membership in UNESCO.

During the energy crisis of late 1973 and early 1974, gasoline stations in the republic were closed on Sundays in an effort to conserve fuel. Sunday driving was not forbidden, since the republic lacked public transportation, but citizens were urged to drive only in emergencies.   (ROBERT D. HODGSON)

Saudi Arabia

A monarchy occupying four-fifths of the Arabian Peninsula, Saudi Arabia has an area of 865,000 sq.mi. (2,240,000 sq.km.). Pop. (1973 est.): 8,115,000. Cap. and largest city: Riyadh (pop., 1965 est., 225,000). Language: Arabic. Religion: Muslim. King and prime minister, Faisal.

Saudi Arabia in 1974 made full use of its growing financial power to exert diplomatic pressure on behalf of the Arabs and Islam and against Zionism and Israel. King Faisal and other Saudi spokesmen persistently warned that unless Israel was made to withdraw from occupied Arab territories the "oil weapon" would again be brought into use. However, Saudi Arabia was generally out of step with other oil producers in the Organization of Petroleum Exporting Countries (OPEC) in advocating a reduction of oil prices to avoid the danger of world recession.

After the Arab oil ministers, except those of Libya and Syria, agreed in Vienna on March 18 to lift the oil embargo on the United States, Saudi oil production was raised to help meet U.S. demand. Output in the summer of 1974 was running about 18% above the level of mid-1973, but was kept by the Saudi government below 8.5 million bbl. a day despite an export capacity of 11.3 million bbl. a day. At the OPEC meeting in Ecuador in June Saudi Arabia refused to raise prices by 4 cents a barrel along with other members, and after the April Vienna meeting it had raised average costs by only 13 cents a barrel, as compared with the 33 cents a barrel decided by other OPEC members. Although Saudi Arabia was still out of line, it was not undercutting the other nations by as much as they had feared. On June 10 it was announced that an agreement in principle had been reached with the Arabian American Oil Co. (Aramco) to raise Saudi participation in the company from 25 to 60%, but at the end of the year it was reported that terms for a 100% takeover had been agreed upon. A U.S. Senate Subcommittee on Multinational Corporations reported that Aramco's net income in 1973 had been $3.2 billion, as compared with $1.7 billion in 1972, and that profits per barrel had risen from $1.25 in 1973 to $4.50 in the early months of 1974. Aramco replied that this grossly overstated the true earnings of its stockholders.

Saudi oil revenues in the 1974–75 budget showed a 346.3% increase over the previous year, and the total national budget of 98,247,000,000 riyals (about $27.7 billion) was 330% above 1973–74. Of the total, 52,-504,000,000 riyals was allocated to development. The government declared that 10% of the budget had been allocated for foreign aid and loans and that this would be future policy. In March Saudi Arabia promised $50 million as a contribution to the World Food Program, making it the second biggest donor after the United States. The budget also included substantial allocations for subsidies for consumer goods and essential services to reduce the cost of living. In September the abolition of customs charges on imports and reduced taxes cut prices further. The price of gasoline was reduced by 40–50% and of electricity by 50–70%. The amount of Saudi surplus funds that could not be absorbed at home was estimated by the oil minister at $17 billion. He said that Saudi Arabia hoped to invest in special U.S. government securities but that Americans need not fear that Saudi Arabia would buy up U.S. industries. In August it was revealed that Saudi Arabia had bought $200 million of debentures in the U.S. Federal National Mortgage Association ("Fannie Mae"). In September it was announced that Saudi Arabia was lending Japan $1 billion.

Part of the trans-Arabian pipeline system near the Ras Tanura oil field in Saudi Arabia. The petroleum flow through such pipes has inundated the desert kingdom with monetary wealth.

SAUDI ARABIA
Education. (1972–73) Primary, pupils 530,181, teachers 22,705; secondary, pupils 106,045, teachers 6,117; vocational, pupils 1,950, teachers 292; teacher training, students 13,242, teachers 899; higher, students 18,-585, teaching staff 1,450.
Finance. Monetary unit: riyal, with (Sept. 16, 1974) a par value of 3.55 riyals to U.S. $1 (free rate of 8.18 riyals = £1 sterling). Gold, SDRs, and foreign exchange, official: (June 1974) U.S. $7,047,000,000; (June 1973) U.S. $3,095,000,000. Budget (1974–75 est.): revenue 98,247,000,000 riyals; expenditure 45,-743,000,000 riyals. Gross domestic product: (1971–72) 28,257,000,000 riyals; (1970–71) 22,921,000,000 riyals. Money supply: (Jan. 1974) 5,272,000,000 riyals; (Jan. 1973) 3,773,000,000 riyals.
Foreign Trade. Imports (1971) 3,667,000,000 riyals; exports (1972) 22,791,000,000 riyals. Import sources: U.S. 17%; Lebanon 13%; Japan 11%; U.K. 9%; West Germany 8%; The Netherlands 5%. Export destinations (1971): Japan 16%; Italy 10%; France 10%; The Netherlands 9%; U.K. 9%. Main exports (1971): crude oil 88%; petroleum products 12%.
Transport and Communications. Roads (1973) 15,680 km. Motor vehicles in use (1973): passenger 54,100; commercial 39,300. Railways (1971): 610 km.; traffic 39 million passenger-km., freight 42 million net ton-km. Air traffic (1972): 777 million passenger-km.; freight 16 million net ton-km. Shipping (1973): merchant vessels 100 gross tons and over 43; gross tonnage 58,530. Telephones (Jan. 1973) 84,000. Radio receivers (Dec. 1971) 87,000. Television receivers (Dec. 1970) 18,000.
Agriculture. Production (in 000; metric tons; 1972; 1971 in parentheses): wheat c. 150 (c. 150); barley c. 36 (c. 35); millet c. 16 (c. 16); sorghum c. 55 (c. 52); dates c. 220 (c. 220). Livestock (in 000; 1971–72): cattle c. 330; sheep c. 3,440; goats c. 2,100; camels c. 570; asses c. 140.
Industry. Production (in 000; metric tons; 1972): cement 910; crude oil (1973) 364,807; natural gas (cu.m.; 1971) 3,000,000; petroleum products 28,977; electricity (excluding most industrial production; kw-hr.) 1,000,000.

U.S. Secretary of State Henry Kissinger visited King Faisal on May 9. When Pres. Richard Nixon went to Jidda on June 14–15 as part of his Middle East tour, his reception, although friendly, was much less effusive than that in Egypt. Earlier in June the Saudi interior minister and second deputy premier, Prince Fahd, widely regarded as the most powerful figure in the country after the king, made a three-day visit to Washington, D.C., and signed a comprehensive agreement for the formation of two joint Saudi-U.S. commissions to plan cooperation in the military and economic fields. In April Saudi Arabia signed a $270 million contract with the U.S. Raytheon Corp. for an advanced Hawk antiaircraft system, which the Saudi defense minister, Prince Sultan, said was "for the protection of the Holy Places." The commander of the National Guard also signed an agreement with the U.S. for $335 million for the development and modernization of the National Guard.

Saudi Arabia maintained good relations with most Arab states except Iraq. On February 2 Pres. Hafez al-Assad of Syria visited King Faisal for "crucial talks," and on February 20 Pres. Anwar as-Sadat of Egypt made an unexpected visit to Jidda with the Libyan leader, Col. Muammar al-Qaddafi, who had in the past been critical of Faisal. In March Prince Sultan visited both Libya and Egypt. Saudi-Egyptian relations remained of prime importance, and on July 30 King Faisal began a nine-day official visit to Egypt, his longest to any Arab country. Afterward it was announced that Saudi Arabia had made Egypt an immediate grant of $300 million. Earlier reports had said a grant of $1 billion and a loan of $500 million had been expected. It was believed that the king had been annoyed by those reports and had restricted his offer. However, it was also reported that Saudi Arabia had made substantial undertakings to help Egypt with the purchase of arms.   (PETER MANSFIELD)

[978.B.4.a]

Savings and Investment

The outstanding and indeed momentous feature characterizing the behaviour of savings and investment in 1974 was the shift of the centre of savings from the industrialized countries of Western Europe, the U.S. and Canada, and Japan to the oil-producing countries of the Middle East, Latin America, and the

Far East. This shift was accompanied by some slowing down in spending on productive assets, dwellings, and business inventories in the advanced countries of the West and the rise in such expenditure in the oil-exporting countries.

The fundamental change in the distribution of savings was the result of a more than fourfold rise in the price of oil after November 1973 and subsequent upward adjustment by way of an increase in participation of oil-exporting countries in the profits of the oil companies. It changed the 1973 balance of payments on current account of 20 industrial countries that are members of the Organization for Economic Cooperation and Development from a surplus of $2,361,000,000 in 1973 to an estimated deficit of $38 billion in 1974. The major industrial countries registering the largest deficits were the U.K., Italy, and France. (*See* Table I.) The oil price increase also contributed to the $8 billion increase in the current account deficit of the less developed countries, from a $13 billion deficit in 1973 to a $21 billion deficit in 1974. The net deficit incurred by the industrial and less developed countries in 1974 relative to the oil-exporting countries reflected the extent to which their total domestic spending, on investment and consumption, was made possible by drawing on the savings generated by the oil-exporting countries; that is to say, by borrowing from them.

While the industrial and less developed countries as a whole had a very large current account deficit relative to the oil-exporting countries, the degree of burden differed between the individual countries. Indeed, one major European country, West Germany, succeeded in having a substantial surplus, estimated at $9 billion. These differences and the fact that financial transactions are carried out mostly in the U.S. dollar, and also to a smaller extent in the pound sterling, was at the heart of the so-called recycling problem. Its essence was how savings—placed in the first instance by the oil-exporting countries in the U.S., and to a smaller extent in the pound sterling and in West Germany, Switzerland, and other Western countries—could be made available to countries with relatively large current account deficits.

Associated with the use of savings of the oil-exporting countries by the industrial and less developed countries was a sharp deceleration in all types of investment expenditures on fixed productive assets, inventories, and dwellings in all the advanced countries, and of course also in savings necessary for them. This rather pronounced deceleration in investment spending can be attributed to deliberate policies pursued by the authorities, aimed at containing strong inflationary pressures by slowing down consumption and reducing imbalances in external payments among the industrialized countries, while also reducing the oil deficit relative to the oil-exporting countries.

Except for Canada and to a much smaller extent France, all major industrial countries experienced an actual decline in spending on all fixed assets, contributing very substantially to deceleration in total economic activity. The continuing buoyancy of total domestic investment spending in Canada and France was due to large outlays by public authorities and/or by industry and commerce on plant and machinery, which functioned to offset deceleration of spending on dwellings.

In the U.S. domestic total outlays on fixed investment and inventories fell in absolute terms as compared with 1973. In the third quarter of 1974 capital

Table I. Current Account of the Balance of Payments of the Major Industrial Countries*

In U.S. $000,000

Country	1972	1973	1974†
U.S.	−9,807	513	−3,250
Canada	−624	−427	−1,500
West Germany	1,040	4,539	9,000
France	290	−677	−7,500
Italy	2,043	−2,418	−8,300
U.K.	186	−3,109	−9,000
Japan	6,624	−136	−4,750
Australia-New Zealand	563	795	−3,200
Other European members of the OECD (Belgium, Luxembourg, Netherlands, Denmark, Ireland, Austria, Finland, Norway, Sweden, Switzerland, Spain)	+2,879	3,281	−9,500
Total	3,194	2,361	−38,000

*With all countries.
†Estimate.
Source: Organization for Economic Cooperation and Development, *Economic Outlook*, no. 15 (July 1974) and no. 16 (December 1974); U. S. Federal Reserve *Bulletin* (August 1974).

Table II. Changes in the Components of Gross Fixed Domestic Investments

In percent

Country	Year	Fixed public investment	Private residential	Private non-residential
U.S.	1972	—	19.3	10.0
	1973	—	−4.1	12.8
	1974	—	−26.0	0.25
Canada	1972	0.7*	9.1	2.5
	1973	4.4*	12.8	11.3
	1974	2.0*	5.25	10.25
West Germany	1972	−6.0*	13.6	0.4
	1973	−3.2*	1.9	1.7
	1974	7.75*	−12.0	−8.0
France	1972	5.5†	8.0	7.6
	1973	4.2†	5.0	8.1
	1974	6.5†	4.25	5.75
Italy	1972	6.3†	1.7	−5.7
	1973	−4.0†	5.4	24.8
	1974	−4.0†	3.0	16.0
U.K.	1972	−5.3†	18.1	5.2
	1973	0.4†	7.6	8.0
	1974	2.0†	−23.5	−4.5
Japan	1972	13.7†	16.4	6.1
	1973	6.1†	17.7	19.2
	1974	−19.0†	−18.0	−7.5

*Exclusive of nationalized industries and public corporations.
†Inclusive of nationalized industries and public corporations.
Source: Organization for Economic Cooperation and Development, *Economic Outlook*, no. 15 (July 1974) no. 16 (December 1974).

Table III. Changes in Gross Domestic or National Product, Fixed Domestic Investment, Stock Building, and Foreign Balance in Main Industrial Countries

In percent

Country	Year	Increase in GDP or GNP	Change in total fixed domestic investment	Change in stock building*	Change in foreign balance*
U.S.†	1972	6.1	12.6	−0.1	−0.3
	1973	5.9	7.9	0.5	1.0
	1974‡	−1.75	−6.25	−0.5	−0.5
Canada†	1972	5.8	3.6	0.4	−1.2
	1973	6.8	10.4	0.5	−1.2
	1974‡	4.5	7.75	1.0	−2.75
West Germany†	1972	3.0	1.9	−0.2	−0.1
	1973	5.3	1.1	0.7	2.0
	1974‡	1.0	−6.75	−1.5	3.75
France§	1972	5.5	7.1	−0.1	−0.1
	1973	6.0	6.5	0.5	−0.1
	1974‡	4.75	5.5	−0.5	0.75
Italy†	1972	3.4	6.3	0.3	0.2
	1973	6.0	9.0	1.2	−1.6
	1974‡	4.75	6.25	−1.25	2.25
U.K.§	1972	3.5	1.7	0.3	−1.8
	1973	5.3	4.8	1.3	−0.5
	1974‡	−4.0	−4.25	−1.25	1.0
Japan†	1972	9.4	10.2	0.5	0.1
	1973	10.2	15.2	1.3	−1.6
	1974‡	−3.25	−12.75	0.5	0.75

*As a percentage of GNP or GDP in the previous year.
†Gross national product at market prices.
‡All 1974 figures are estimates.
§Gross domestic product at market prices.
Source: Organization for Economic Cooperation and Development, *Economic Outlook*, no. 15 (July 1974) and no. 16 (December 1974).

spending experienced its first real decline in four years, causing Commerce Secretary Frederick Dent to urge Congress to boost the investment tax credit for industry. However, while spending on plant and machinery decelerated substantially, spending on housing

Table IV. Savings and Investment in Main Industrial Countries in 1973

Country	House-hold	Non-financial enterprises	Public sector	Financial institutions	Foreign sector	Total
U.S. (in $000,000,000)						
Gross savings	+229.6	+112.6	−8.1	+10.5	−0.1	+344.7
Gross physical investments	−174.1	−160.5	—	−5.0	—	−339.6
Capital transfers and adjustments	+6.0	− 13.8	−5.1	+3.2	+2.2	−7.4
Net financial savings	+61.5	−61.7	−13.1	+8.7	+2.1	−2.3
Financial assets	−130.8	−43.9	−12.2	−217.8	−17.4	−422.1
Financial liabilities	+69.3	+105.5	+25.3	+209.1	+15.3	+424.5
U.K. (in £000,000)						
Gross savings	+5,269	+6,633	+3,031	+824	} +1,269	+15,757
Gross physical investments	−2,982	−7,850	−5,753	−971		−17,556
Capital transfers and adjustments	−320	+347	−35	−51		+1,210
Net financial savings	+1,967	−870	−2,757	−198	+1,269	−589*
Financial assets	−8,139	−2,859	−1,156	−25,033	−13,340	−50,527
Financial liabilities	+6,172	+3,729	+3,913	+25,231	+12,071	+51,116
West Germany (in DM. 000,000,000)						
Gross savings	+77.60	+99.88	+60.78	+11.85	−11.00	+236.38
Gross physical investments	—	−199.84	−31.66	−4.88	—	−236.38
Capital transfers and adjustments	−10.38	+26.89	−15.68	−1.54	+0.71	—
Net financial savings	+67.22	−73.07	+13.44	+5.43	−10.29	—
Financial assets	−70.97	−27.10	−31.23	−126.61	−29.46	−285.37
Financial liabilities	+3.75	+100.17	+17.79	+121.18	+39.75	−285.37
Japan (in 000,000,000 yen)						
Gross savings	+20,264	+14,309	+10,173	—	—	—
Gross physical investments	−12,354	−22,266	−10,851	—	—	—
Capital transfers and adjustments	+2,007	+1,079	−2,395	—	—	—
Net financial savings	+9,917	−6,878	−3,073	—	+ 32	—
Financial assets	−21,131	−29,045	−9,424	−31,479	−993	−92,071
Financial liabilities	+11,213	+35,922	+12,497	+31,479	+961	+92,071

Notes: For gross savings, gross physical investments, and capital transfers and adjustments: + means receipts and − means expenditure; for financial assets: − means spending on assets; for financial liabilities: + means increase in indebtedness. Figures may not add to totals due to rounding.

For the U.S., public sector includes federal, state, and local governments; financial authorities include monetary authorities, sponsored credit agencies, commercial banks, and private nonbank financial institutions; for the U.K., public sector includes central government, local authorities, and public corporations; for West Germany, enterprises includes housing and public sector includes social security funds; for Japan, government includes government financial institutions, administrative activities, local authorities, and non-financial public corporations.

*Excluding residual error.

Sources: Organization for Economic Cooperation and Development, Financial Statistics no. 7D (1974); U.K. Central Statistical Office, Financial Statistics no. 149 (Sept. 1974); U.S. Federal Reserve Bulletin (Sept. 1974).

fell drastically, by nearly 25% in relation to the previous 12 months. The slowing down of spending on productive assets by the corporate sector could be attributed to an absolute decline in savings generated by it, which necessitated a large increase in indebtedness. At the same time, the dramatic fall in spending on dwellings was to a large extent due to the desire of the personal sector to increase its net addition to financial assets by cutting down expenditures on housing. The home-building slump worsened in November when the Commerce Department reported that housing starts were down about 40% from the previous year's level. Spokesmen for the home-building industry contended that government programs to subsidize mortgage rates provided little help because the rates were too high, and the Ford administration was being urged to release funds for low- and moderate-income housing subsidy programs.

In West Germany, where total activity slowed down but did not decline as compared with 1973, the total of spending on fixed investment fell in absolute terms but there was an involuntary rise in inventories. While both private expenditures on dwellings and plant and machinery registered a marked decrease, public sector expenditures rose appreciably. This development reflected the deliberate countercyclical policy pursued by the government, involving a decline in the public sector's savings and a rise in indebtedness. Private industry attempted to reduce its financial deficit by cutting down its outlays on investment, with the personal sector behaving in a similar manner.

In the U.K., where total output, as in the case of the U.S., decreased, spending on fixed assets fell as compared with 1973 in both absolute and relative terms, and outlays on inventories also exerted a depressing influence. Private expenditures on industrial plant and machinery fell and private spending on dwellings decreased very sharply, and there was also a fall in expenditure by public authorities. A deceleration in spending on productive assets by industry was made possible by a substantial increase in the debt of private industry, which exerted a dampening effect on such outlays in the second half of the year. The personal sector tried to maintain its savings by reducing expenditures on dwellings while increasing its capital spending, while the public sector had to raise its indebtedness.

Japan, like the U.S. and the U.K., experienced an absolute fall in total investment spending and total activity. Private spending on plant and machinery fell by about 7.5%, the public sector's outlays on fixed investment fell by about 20%, and there was also a 20% decrease in spending on private housing. The behaviour of individual sectors as regards savings and investment tended to be very similar to that in other industrial countries. Industry increased its indebtedness because, despite the fall in investment outlays, its savings declined, and the personal sector cut down its housing expenditures to maintain its savings. (T. M. RYBCZYNSKI)

See also Money and Banking; Profits; Stock Exchanges. [534.D.2.g.ii]

Senegal

A republic of northwestern Africa, Senegal is bounded by Mauritania, Mali, Guinea, and Guinea-Bissau, and by the Atlantic Ocean. The independent nation of The Gambia forms an enclave within the country. Area: 78,685 sq.mi. (203,793 sq.km.). Pop. (1973 est.): 4,137,200. Cap. and largest city: Dakar (pop., 1973 est., 667,400). Language: French (official); Wolof; Serer; other tribal dialects. Religion: Muslim 90%; Christian 6%. President in 1974, Léopold Sédar Senghor; premier, Abdou Diouf.

To mark the 14th anniversary of Senegal's independence, President Senghor announced on March 20

SENEGAL
SENEGAL
Education. (1973–74) Primary, pupils 283,276, teachers 6,294; secondary, pupils 59,236, teachers 2,198; vocational, pupils 5,482, teachers 465; teacher training, students 1,926, teachers 455; higher (University of Dakar), students 7,773, teaching staff 465.
Finance and Trade. Monetary unit: CFA franc, with (Sept. 16, 1974) a parity of CFA Fr. 50 to the French franc (free rate of CFA Fr. 240.50 = U.S. $1; CFA Fr. 556.50 = £1 sterling). Budget (1973–74 est.) balanced at CFA Fr. 57 billion. Foreign trade (1972): imports CFA Fr. 70,550,000,000; exports CFA Fr. 54,-412,000,000. Import sources: France 49%; West Germany 6%; U.S. 6%. Export destination France 58%. Main exports: peanut oil 37%; phosphates 8%; peanut oil cake 14%; fish and products 5%.

SIERRA LEONE
Education. (1969–70) Primary, pupils 155,697, teachers 5,011; secondary, pupils 29,058, teachers 1,364; vocational, pupils 860, teachers 60; teacher training, students 879, teachers 129; higher, students 1,119, teaching staff 202.
Finance and Trade. Monetary unit: leone, with (Sept. 16, 1974) a free value of 0.87 leone to U.S. $1 (par value of 2 leones = £1 sterling). Budget (1973–74 est.): revenue 65.9 million leones; expenditure 55.8 million leones. Foreign trade (1973): imports 127,930,000 leones; exports 106,570,000 leones. Import sources: U.K. 22%; Japan 9%; U.S. 9%; West Germany 8%; France 8%. Export destinations: U.K. 67%; The Netherlands 6%; U.S. 6%; West Germany 5%; Japan 5%. Main exports: diamonds 61%; iron ore 10%; palm kernels 5%.
Agriculture. Production (in 000; metric tons; 1973; 1972 in parentheses): rice *c.* 470 (*c.* 454); cassava (1972) *c.* 83, (1971) *c.* 83; palm kernels *c.* 50 (*c.* 47); palm oil *c.* 62 (*c.* 62); coffee (1972) *c.* 7.5, (1971) *c.* 6; cocoa 7 (7). Livestock (in 000; 1971–72): cattle *c.* 260; sheep *c.* 60; goats *c.* 160; chickens *c.* 3,050.
Industry. Production (in 000; metric tons; 1972): iron ore (metal content) 1,393; bauxite (1971) 590; petroleum products 304; diamonds (exports; metric carats) 1,647; electricity (kw-hr.; 1971) 208,000.

that all political prisoners would be released. These included former prime minister Mamadou Dia, who had led the attempted coup of December 1962.

New cooperation agreements were signed with France on March 29, 1974, under which the French base at Dakar was transferred to Senegal and token French forces in Senegal were to be reduced in strength. Early in May President Senghor paid official visits to China, India, Bangladesh, and North Korea. He was also a significant mediator at meetings in Dakar between the Portuguese and the African nationalist leaders of Guinea-Bissau. Senegal took part in the meeting in Nouakchott, Mauritania, at the end of May of the Organization for Development of the Senegal River, at which it was agreed to launch the river basin plan. (*See* MAURITANIA.) In the continuing Sahel drought hundreds of thousands of cattle died, and the 1973–74 peanut harvest was cut by a quarter (peanuts are Senegal's principal export). Dakar was a chief point of entry for relief supplies for the Sahel area. (*See* AGRICULTURE AND FOOD SUPPLIES: *Special Report.*)

Production of cottonseed had risen from 268 tons in 1965–66 to 32,600 in 1973–74, and an agreement was reached between Senegal and French interests to set up a joint textile company, with the state holding the majority shares, replacing an older French company which had pioneered cotton growing in Senegal in 1963. In June the nationalization of Senegal's phosphate mines was announced.

A 60% rise in the price of basic foodstuffs permitted by the government in November was only partly relieved by rises, averaging 40%, in basic wages; the government decided to abandon subsidies that favoured the urban population as against rural producers. (R. M. GOODWIN)

[978.E.4.b.ii]

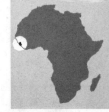

Sierra Leone

A republic within the Commonwealth of Nations, Sierra Leone is a West African nation located between Guinea and Liberia. Area: 27,925 sq.mi. (72,325 sq.km.). Pop. (1973 est.): 2,861,000, including (1963) Mende and Temne tribes 60.7%; other tribes 38.9%; non-African 0.4%. Cap. and largest city: Freetown (pop., 1972 est., 195,800). Language: English (official); tribal dialects. Religion: animist 66%; Muslim 28%; Christian 6%. President in 1974, Siaka Stevens; prime minister, Sorie Ibrahim Koroma.

President Stevens, who had consolidated his one-party state after the 1973 elections, offered government jobs to opposition party members during 1974. Parties other than the governing All People's Congress

Party were obliged, under emergency regulations, to seek permission before meeting.

Neighbourly relationships were developed during the year with The Gambia, Ghana, Nigeria, Guinea, and, especially, with Liberia after the Mano River Declaration of October 1973 providing for economic union with that nation. The African Development Bank approved a $1.5 million loan to finance a direct road link between Freetown and the Liberian capital of Monrovia as a first step.

President Stevens' statement "We've done enough politics and should concentrate on economic progress" was emphasized by the governor of the Bank of Sierra Leone in March as a race to achieve the diversification of agriculture before the diamond boom declined and rising oil costs affected vital foreign aid. The five-year development plan announced during the year emphasized balance between public and private investors and participants; it also stressed the need to end the subsidy for rice imports and make the country self-supporting in rice as it had been before the lure of diamond prospecting began attracting the more enterprising of the agricultural labour force in the mid-1950s.

Diamonds provided over 60% of the nation's revenue in 1973, the value of diamond exports having increased a hundredfold in ten years to reach 31 million leones. Early in the year the government monopoly of diamond exporting ended when five companies were authorized to share in the trade: it was believed that competitive marketing would check the substantial revenue lost through smuggling.

(MOLLY MORTIMER)

[978.E.4.b.ii]

Singapore

Singapore, a republic within the Commonwealth of Nations, occupies a group of islands, the largest of which is Singapore, at the southern extremity of the Malay Peninsula. Area: 226 sq.mi. (586 sq.km.). Pop. (1974 est.): 2,219,100, including 76% Chinese, 15% Malays, and 7% Indians. Language: official languages are English,

Education. (1973) Primary, pupils 345,284, teachers 12,112; secondary, pupils 173,109, teachers 7,767; vocational, pupils 5,429, teachers 746; teacher training, students 360, teachers 102; higher (including 2 universities), students 13,487, teaching staff 1,543.

Finance and Trade. Monetary unit: Singapore dollar, with (Sept. 16, 1974) a free rate of Sing$2.48 to U.S. $1 (Sing$5.74 = £1 sterling). Budget (1974–75 est.): revenue Sing$2,323,000,000; expenditure Sing-$2,299,000,000. Foreign trade (1973): imports Sing-$12,512,600,000; exports Sing$8,907,300,000. Import sources: Japan 18%; Malaysia 16%; U.S. 15%; U.K. 6%; China 5%. Export destinations: Malaysia 18%; U.S. 17%; Japan 8%; U.K. 6%; Hong Kong 5%. Main exports: rubber 18%; machinery 18%; petroleum products 15%. Tourism (1972): visitors 783,-000; gross receipts U.S. $143 million.

Transport and Communications. Roads (1972) 2,070 km. Motor vehicles in use (1972): passenger 169,000; commercial 41,800. Railways (1971) 45 km. (for traffic *see* MALAYSIA). Air traffic (1973): 3,062,-000,000 passenger-km.; freight 74 million net ton-km. Shipping (1973): merchant vessels 100 gross tons and over 387; gross tonnage 2,004,269. Shipping traffic (1973): goods loaded 23,068,000 metric tons, unloaded 39,185,000 metric tons. Telephones (Dec. 1972) 218,-000. Radio licenses (Dec. 1971) 316,000. Television licenses (Dec. 1972) 205,000.

Malay, Mandarin Chinese, and Tamil. Religion: Malays are Muslim; Chinese, mainly Buddhist; Indians, mainly Hindu. President in 1974, Benjamin Henry Sheares; prime minister, Lee Kuan Yew.

In February 1974 four terrorists of the extremist Japanese Red Army and the Popular Front for the Liberation of Palestine tried to blow up the Shell refinery and storage complex on the offshore island of Bukum and, when the attempt failed, hijacked a ferryboat and held its crew as hostages. After a week of negotiations the Japanese government sent an aircraft to pick up the hijackers. In June it was announced that the government had arrested 30 alleged members of the Malayan National Liberation Front, an underground arm of the Malayan Communist Party. At the University of Singapore, a dispute arose in July between student union leaders and the vice-chancellor, Toh Chin-chye, over dress and increases in tuition fees. Students also held an "antirepression week" in which a debate on preventive detention was addressed by Poh Soo-kai, who had been released in 1973 after 11 years in jail.

At the end of August Parliament passed a bill obliging all newspapers published in Singapore to become public companies. The legislation mandated a class of management shares—carrying heavier voting weight than ordinary shares—that could not go to anyone not approved by the minister of culture and that could not be refused to anyone approved by him. Aimed at two major Chinese-language dailies controlled by family groups, the legislation reflected the concern of the Singapore government with the political attitudes of the Chinese-educated community in view of prospective establishment of diplomatic relations with China.

In January Lee Kuan Yew paid his first visit to Manila, and it was noticed that he did not endorse the personal rule of Philippine Pres. Ferdinand E. Marcos. In June the prime minister went to London to discuss the possible withdrawal of British forces stationed in Singapore. President Suharto of Indonesia returned Lee's 1973 visit to Jakarta in August. The two leaders endorsed their common policy of avoiding undue haste in establishing diplomatic relations with China. As a goodwill gesture, Singapore passed on to Indonesia its statistics on trade between the two countries.

Singapore's economy had remained buoyant in 1973, but in 1974 the annual growth rate slowed from 22% to around 7% and there was some increase in unemployment in the face of declining world trade. In 1973 prices had risen by nearly 23%; gross domestic product per capita amounted to Sing$4,065; total trade increased by 36.5%; and there was an overall balance of payments surplus of Sing$256 million.

(MICHAEL LEIFER)

[976.B.2.b]

Skiing

In 1974, the golden jubilee year of the International Ski Federation (FIS), the installation of more plastic practice slopes for preseason training aided the growth of recreational skiing. An ever increasing choice of skis, boots, safety-release devices, and specialized clothing improved the efficiency and appearance of skiers. Better equipment at resorts was a notable feature of the year, especially in North America and in Alpine and Scandinavian areas of Europe. Closer supervision of ski centres meant greater safety control, which reduced the number of accidents proportionate to participants. The year saw the passing of Sir Arnold Lunn (*see* OBITUARIES), the pioneer probably most responsible for the growth of the sport's popularity. In the United States there was rising spectator support for professional freestyle skiing, a form of hazardous acrobatic stunts on skis, including somersaults, with emphasis on spectacular effects.

Alpine Racing. Thirty-five nations were represented by 271 skiers (181 men and 90 women) in the 23rd Alpine World Ski Championships held at St. Moritz, Switz., on February 2–10 and successfully completed despite fog and unseasonably sparse snow. That Austrian skiers won three of the eight gold medals and French and Italian two each was a fair reflection of international strength, but a first-ever gold for the tiny principality of Liechtenstein was as surprising as the relative failure of U.S. racers.

Gustavo Thoeni of Italy, with convincing slalom

WIDE WORLD

Italy's Gustavo Thoeni wins the men's dual slalom at Aspen, Colo., in March.

Christa Zechmeister, a 16-year-old Bavarian girl, wins her second successive international slalom in the Les Gets Grand Prix in January.

Soccer:
see Football

and giant slalom victories, stressed his comparative downhill weakness by not even contesting that event and thus forfeiting a combined rating. Only a great second descent by Hans Hinterseer, the Austrian runner-up, prevented a grand slam in the giant slalom by the Italians, for whom Piero Gros finished third. Some 30,000 spectators lined the fencing on either side of the downhill course to watch David Zwilling and Franz Klammer, both Austrians, take the first two places after Roland Collombin, the Swiss favourite, crashed halfway down; Willi Frommelt, a Liechtenstein racer who trained with the Austrians, prevented a clean sweep by the latter by taking third place. The slalom proved Thoeni's real class when, after finishing eighth in the first run, he made a flawless second descent to narrowly defeat Zwilling, who had seemed a certain winner; a third place for Francisco Fernandez-Ochoa of Spain showed that his victory two years previously had been no flash in the pan. Klammer's consistency in all three events secured him the combined title, ahead of Anderzej Bachleda of Poland and Wolfgang Junginger of West Germany.

The decisive victory of Annemarie Proell-Moser of Austria in the women's downhill was almost a foregone conclusion after her past accomplishments. Her closest rival was Betsy Clifford of Canada, followed by two more Austrians, Wiltrud Drexel and Monika Kaserer. Fabienne Serrat of France won the giant slalom under tricky conditions from Traudl Treichl of West Germany, with another French woman, Jacqueline Rouvier, third. The slalom saw the proud triumph for Liechtenstein of Hanni Wenzel, with Michèle Jacot, the more experienced French racer, runner-up and Lise-Marie Morerod of Switzerland third. Miss Serrat's fourth place clinched the combined title for her, with Miss Wenzel second and Miss Kaserer third.

The eighth World Cup series for the first time appeared to possess greater stature than did the world championships, with growing appreciation that, as compared with success at one meeting, its results reflected consistency of form during 21 events for men and 17 for women from early December 1973 to mid-March 1974 at 22 sites in nine European countries. Gros became the second Italian to win the men's cup, narrowly preventing Thoeni, the runner-up, from scoring a fourth consecutive success; the issue was not resolved until the next to the last event, and the final race determined second place, Hinterseer finishing third. Contrastingly, the outcome of the women's cup was decided halfway through the series, Mrs. Proell-Moser outstripping her rivals for a record fourth successive win. She completed an unprecedented run of 11 consecutive downhill victories (spread over two seasons) to dispel any remaining doubt that she was the greatest woman racer of all time. Second and third, but never any threat, were Miss Kaserer and Miss Wenzel. The Nations' Cup, decided concurrently by combining men's and women's aggregate points, went to Austria.

The fourth Can-Am Ski Trophy series, comprising 18 men's and 17 women's events at 13 North American sites, was won by Gary Aiken of Canada and Leith Lende of the U.S. The third European Cup series winners were Christian Witt-Döring of Austria and Elena Matous from San Marino. Hugo Nindl, an Austrian, was the season's outstanding professional, winning $93,200 as champion of the Benson and Hedges Grand Prix circuit of 14 North American meetings.

Nordic Events. Thirty nations were represented by 324 skiers, including 58 women, in the 30th world Nordic championships at Falun, Swed., held on February 11–24. Overcoming unexpectedly sparse snow conditions, East Germans won five of the seven men's events, and Soviet skiers finished first in all three women's races.

Gerhard Grimmer of East Germany won the grueling 50 km. with nearly two minutes to spare, placed second to Magne Myrmo of Norway in the 15 km., and gained a third medal in East Germany's winning men's relay team. Thomas Magnusson of Sweden won the gold medal for the 30 km. and a third-place bronze in the 50 km. Hans-Georg Aschenbach won both jumping events for East Germany. East Germans also took the first two places in the Nordic combination event, Ulrich Wehling gaining a narrow verdict over Günter Deckert. Galina Kulakova again dominated the women's events, retaining the two individual cross-country titles, 5 km. and 10 km., and gaining a third gold medal as member of the winning U.S.S.R. relay team.

Soviet biathletes were surprisingly overshadowed on their home terrain when Juhani Suutarinen of Finland skied and shot his way to the individual title in the 17th world biathlon championships on March 4 at Minsk. Gheorghe Girnite of Romania and Tor Svendsberget of Norway finished second and third, respectively, but in the relay the Soviets held off a strong Finnish challenge to retain the team title.

(HOWARD BASS)

[452.B.4.h.xxv]

Social and Welfare Services

Social institutions and social security systems underwent changes, modifications, and reforms during 1974 as countries introduced new benefits, improved existing schemes, or put forward important reform proposals for the future orientation of their social security arrangements.

Social Security and Inflation. In several countries improvements were made in the level of social security benefits in an effort to counteract the negative effects of inflation and to prevent the incomes of beneficiaries from falling too far behind those of the working population. In the U.K., for example, the rates of retirement pensions were raised and, for the first time, there were higher increases in long-term benefits (retirement and invalidity [long-term disability] pensions and widows' benefits) than in those for the short term (unemployment and sickness benefits and maternity allowances). Switzerland recorded the largest single increase in its old-age and survivors' pension scheme and aimed to provide the entire population with a statutory pension that would ensure an adequate level of living in retirement. Minimum pensions in Switzerland jumped from SFr. 220 to SFr. 400 per month in 1973, and maximum pensions from SFr. 440 to SFr. 800. Some countries, including the U.S. and Belgium, prompted by rapid rises in both prices and earnings, granted increases over and above those already provided for by automatic adjustment procedures.

In the United States Social Security, welfare, employment assistance, and other social programs were under considerable pressure from inflation and unemployment during the year, and there was concern about how the economy would affect them in the future. Roy Ash, director of the Office of Management and Budget, hinted broadly that the government would not be able to present a balanced budget without reducing future benefits in some social programs. Ash noted that $142 billion, or almost 50% of the federal budget, was earmarked for "entitlement" programs to aid the elderly, poor, handicapped, ill, and veterans. The benefit levels and eligibility requirements of these programs were specified in legislation.

One reason the social services were so greatly affected is that the poor and others who are served by social programs are usually hit first and hardest by economic troubles. A government study found that between August 1971 and December 1973 the cost of living increased about 20% more for the low-income population than for the average wage and salary earner. That trend continued in 1974.

Social Security, which covered 29.1 million Americans, offered a good illustration of how inflation influences social welfare programs. Social Security benefits rose 11% in 1974, the fifth increase since 1969. The main reason for the boosts was to keep pace with the rising cost of living. An escalator clause in the 1972 and 1973 amendments to the Social Security Act provided for annual automatic benefit increases as the cost of living rose.

To meet the cost of the additional benefits, Social Security tax payments also were increased. As of Jan. 1, 1974, the rate was raised to 5.85% for both employee and employer on the first $13,200 of earnings. This meant a maximum annual tax of $772.20 each for an individual and his employer, an increase of $140.40 over 1973 and 4.4 times what was paid in 1965. A self-employed worker paid 7.9% in 1974, or $1,042.80 maximum. As a result of this increase, it was estimated that about half of the wage earners in the U.S. would pay more in Social Security taxes than in regular income taxes.

In 1975 the Social Security tax was to be levied on the first $14,100 of each worker's income. Thus, 19 million workers who earned at least that much would pay $52.65 more than they did in 1974, for a total of $824.85. The self-employed were to pay a maximum of $1,113.90, up $71.10 from 1974. The larger wage base was expected to bring in a total of $1.8 billion additional revenue in 1975.

No boost was slated for the Social Security tax rate until 1978, when it was scheduled to rise to 6.05%; it would then go to 6.30% in 1981, 6.45% in 1986, and 7.45% in 2011. The wage base would rise automatically to reflect higher salary levels and was expected to reach $17,700 by 1978.

Despite these scheduled increases, there was widespread concern that the Social Security system was headed for deficits. Unless corrective changes could be made, officials feared that there would not be enough money collected to pay off the benefits that had been promised. The system was expected to have sufficient revenue until about 1985, but after that it could go into the red if inflation was not curbed. Even if the automatic benefit increases were slowed, Social Security faced serious long-range problems because of the nation's declining birthrate. In future years there would be relatively fewer workers paying taxes to support the growing number of aged and other beneficiaries of the system.

Another area that felt the effect of a sputtering economy and rising unemployment was employment assistance—public job programs and unemployment benefits. In December the U.S. Congress passed a bill appropriating $4.5 billion for an expansion in unemployment compensation and job programs. Approximately $875 million would be distributed to states and communities to provide public service jobs for the unemployed.

In some cases the economic situation was cited by U.S. Pres. Gerald Ford as a reason to curtail rather than accelerate social programs. Ford vetoed a bill to increase education benefits for Vietnam-era veterans because he considered it inflationary. He also proposed significant budget cuts for fiscal 1975 in federal health, welfare, and food stamp programs. These would be accomplished by a variety of means, ranging from the veto to deferring funds previously approved.

The veterans' benefit veto was overridden by votes of 394 to 10 in the House of Representatives and 90 to 1 in the Senate. The measure increased education allowances by 22.7% for 11 million veterans of the war in Vietnam and of the period between the Korean and Vietnam wars. For an unmarried veteran attending college on the GI Bill, this meant a hike in benefits from $220 to $270 a month. Veterans with dependents were to receive slightly larger boosts. The bill also increased on-the-job training funds and vocational aid for disabled veterans, created a new educational loan program, and extended from 36 to 45 months the entitlement period for veterans working on undergraduate degrees.

Governments and social security authorities continued their attempts to establish a closer parallel between changes in earnings and changes in benefit levels. In West Germany, where this concept was called dynamization, there were proposals to extend it from the pension system, where it was already implanted, to unemployment benefits. The French government accepted the principle of guaranteeing a steady progression in the purchasing power of family allowance benefits. Israel adopted automatic adjustment procedures for pensions and joined the long list of countries linking the level of social security benefits to current earnings or prices. In The Netherlands, the government limited increases in social welfare expenditures for 1973–77 to 3% of net national income in an attempt to control the evolution of such expenditure and to fix certain priorities for social security. The level of family allowances, which had been tied to current earnings, was frozen for the first child, and the savings were used to finance additional increases in pension benefits.

Pension Programs. A major piece of social legislation to emerge in the U.S. during 1974 was the first federal law regulating private pension plans. Climaxing a seven-year congressional effort, the measure gave workers some basic protection against the loss of retirement benefits. Companies were not required to establish a pension plan, but the law set standards that must be met if a plan was established. Generally, all employees 25 and over who had worked for at least one year must be enrolled. A firm could choose among three plans for vesting, giving employees part or all of their pension benefits even if they left their job before retirement. Most workers would be fully vested after 15 years.

The new law also set up a Pension Benefit Guaranty Corporation in the U.S. Department of Labor to assure pension payments even if a company goes out of business or goes bankrupt. Stringent rules were established to prevent the misuse of pension fund money.

The railroad retirement fund also got a legislative

Senior citizens demonstrate in Chicago against ageism—the systematic discrimination of American society against the elderly.

overhaul. Spurred by a multibillion dollar deficit in the fund, Congress passed legislation to revamp thoroughly the Railroad Retirement Act of 1937. President Ford vetoed the bill, but Congress overrode the veto. The measure was intended to eliminate a potential $8.5 billion deficit in the railroad retirement fund by authorizing appropriations from general Treasury funds, and to phase out gradually a practice that allowed about 400,000 railroad workers to get both railroad retirement and Social Security benefits.

Welfare. The welfare system, long a target of dissatisfaction in the U.S., remained a major issue in 1974, although there was more talk about it than action. Late in the year Secretary of Health, Education, and Welfare Caspar Weinberger unveiled an "income supplement program." It would guarantee a federal payment for every U.S. family that fell below a certain income level.

The basic cash guarantee from the federal government for a family of four with no other income would be $3,600. If someone in the family went to work, half the earnings would be deducted from the basic benefit until total income reached $7,200. The cash guarantee would replace three established welfare programs: food stamps, Aid to Families with Dependent Children (AFDC), and Supplemental Security Income (SSI).

The demand for change may have been spurred by two studies of welfare programs in the U.S. that were reported during the year. One, prepared by the staff of the Congressional Joint Economic Subcommittee on Fiscal Policy, warned that the nation's present welfare system could encourage family breakup, affect the size of families, and discourage working. It found that a one-child family would gain an average of $1,004 if it were deserted by an unemployed father and that an unemployed childless woman could almost double her cash and food benefits by having a child.

Although major overhaul of the welfare system in the U.S. was postponed, some changes did occur in specific parts of the system during 1974. The idea

of income maintenance was tested in the new SSI program, which went into effect on Jan. 1, 1974, as a replacement for the federal-state assistance for the aged, blind, and disabled.

SSI was the first federal aid program to provide a guaranteed minimum income for any segment of the U.S. population. Recipients were granted enough federal money to bring their incomes to at least $146 a month for individuals and $219 a month for couples. An estimated six million or more persons were eligible in 1974, including some three million not formerly enrolled in the state programs, but early in the program it appeared that large numbers of these were not being reached.

For the first time in 20 years, the number of persons receiving the major welfare assistance, Aid to Families with Dependent Children, declined. After hitting a peak of 11,156,000 parents and children in March 1973, AFDC rolls began dropping and were down to 10,821,000 in May 1974 (the most recent statistics). Welfare officials said that the reduction was the result of a crackdown on carelessness and incompetence in the administration of the program. They noted that increasing unemployment was likely to turn the decline around.

While welfare rolls declined, another form of assistance to the poor, food stamps, increased. Federal spending on stamps and other food assistance rose from less than $1 billion in 1968 to nearly $6 billion in the 1975 fiscal year. An estimated 15 million Americans benefited from the family food distribution programs, and for the first time every county in the nation was participating. In addition, approximately 24 million children took part in the national school lunch program, with more than 9 million receiving a free or reduced-price lunch. Despite these advances, testimony before the Senate Select Committee on Nutrition and Human Needs contended that more than 20 million persons eligible for family food assistance were not receiving it.

European Poverty Program. A comparative poverty profile of the nine EEC member nations was to be one of the first tangible results of the proposed European Poverty Program. The poverty line that would emerge from the profile was not to be arbitrary and determined simply by levels of social security benefits, but would compare the incomes of the poorest with average earnings and the cost of living, and clarify how many people fell below the standards accepted within their own countries. There were suggestions that the U.K., where social security benefits were well below average earnings, would be at the bottom of the scale. Continental members of the EEC had traditionally set their benefits at a high proportion of the average wage.

In the U.K. the Department of Health and Social Security (DHSS) placed emphasis on helping specially defined groups of people—the old, poor families, residents of deprived areas—rather than on an overall attack on basic poverty. That approach was supported by the European Commission, which had already tackled issues of basic poverty elsewhere in its social action programs, but was opposed by virtually everyone else from Britain engaged in the campaign against poverty.

During the summer of 1974 a seminar was held in Brussels to discuss precisely what the European Poverty Program should do. Most of the delegates came prepared to discuss pilot projects that would tackle the social poverty of disadvantaged groups, in line with the British DHSS and the European Commission approaches, but British delegates argued that such projects could only deal with symptoms, and that any "poverty" program worth its name must first attack basic poverty. Until everyone had enough to live on, it would not be possible to define which special groups needed additional help.

The difference of view was not confined to the British group. Countries where basic poverty had been substantially eliminated by tying social security benefits to average earnings—West Germany, Denmark, and The Netherlands—were more concerned with projects that concentrated on the special groups. Those countries where considerable poverty was still known to exist—Italy, Ireland, and Britain—preferred to mount comprehensive welfare rights projects. Projects of both types were included in the final proposals. Money for the poverty program would be channeled through member governments, but in each member state a number of government departments had some responsibility for poverty.

Administrative Changes. Several countries continued their attempts to reorganize social security structures for greater efficiency, to render the administration of social security and welfare provisions more systematic, and to clarify the rights of insured persons under social security systems. The trend was strongest in The Netherlands and in West Germany, where regulations governing the various social security schemes were simplified still further. In West Germany, emphasis was placed on the codification of social security law, and in 1973 a draft version of the major part of the new social security code was presented to the Bundestag.

At one time in 1974, it appeared that the 30-year stalemate over national health insurance in the U.S. might be broken. Both the Nixon administration and leading congressional Democrats were pushing for action and talking of compromise. But a plethora of competing plans (seven major proposals were introduced in Congress) and the impeachment proceedings against Nixon killed hopes for action in 1974.

Some of the major issues included patient cost-sharing; the role of private insurers; administration—should the federal government, states, insurers, or all three run the program; the method of financing; and individual choice—should participation be voluntary or compulsory.

In the less developed countries the situation was often quite different. In most cases, the administration of social security in such countries had been concentrated from the beginning in a centralized national administration, and it was found feasible to introduce sweeping administrative reforms. During 1973 Cameroon, Mexico, Libya, and Togo enacted comprehensive social security codes, grouping under a single legal framework most of the important component parts of their national social security systems.

Two European countries, Denmark and the U.K., made important structural changes. In Denmark, the National Health Security law absorbed approximately 275 existing sickness insurance funds into a national health service that covered the entire population. The scale of cash benefits paid for sickness, maternity, work injury, and family benefits was unified under a single program, with benefits equal to 90% of the loss of income, subject to a maximum.

In the U.K., considerable changes were made during 1974 in the organization of the National Health Service. Local government reorganization for England

Elderly residents of Chinatown in New York City call attention to their need for food, principally hot lunches.

and Wales aimed to unify the various forms of health provision, to improve coordination between health services and local authorities, and to streamline the management of health services. A three-tier organization was established in England, with two-tier groups in Scotland and Wales. Within each of the three the health departments, the DHSS in England, the Scottish Home and Health Department in Scotland, and the Welsh Office in Wales, became responsible for strategic planning, while area authorities became responsible for area planning and operational control of all health services in their regions.

Invalidity Protection. There were important developments in invalidity insurance during 1973–74. Israel and New Zealand both legislated to broaden the scope of invalidity protection. The Israeli scheme covered the entire population, including self-employed, nonemployed, and housewives. Pensions of approximately 20% of the average wage would be paid to those suffering at least 75% disability, and reduced benefits given to those with at least 50% disability. The scheme included vocational rehabilitation and was to be financed by employer contributions and by contributions based on the taxable incomes of self-employed and nonemployed persons.

The New Zealand scheme, by contrast, was primarily an accident insurance plan combining work-related and other accidents within the same program. The new Accident Compensation Act of 1974 entitled all injured earners, self-employed and employees, to 80% of loss of earnings, without having to prove negligence. The scheme also provided for the payment of medical and hospital expenses. Nonearners would be eligible only for medical care benefits, and for lump-sum payments in the event of permanent disability.

In several other countries two separate, but complementary, trends in the provision of invalidity pensions could be noted. Qualifying conditions for invalidity benefits were liberalized, and levels of protection improved. In Finland and Norway it became easier to qualify for an invalidity pension when continued employment would be difficult or impossible. The assessment of invalidity was broadened considerably under earnings-related pension schemes in Finland to take into account the insured person's training, work history, housing conditions, and other factors that might influence his working capacity, and partial invalidity pensions were introduced. The universal pension scheme in Norway was amended to make it possible for persons aged between 64 and 66 whose working capacity had been reduced by at least 50% to be granted an invalidity pension without having to undergo rehabilitation or vocational training.

There were significant improvements in the level of invalidity protection in the Soviet Union, where changes in the methods of calculating benefits resulted in increased payments, and in the U.K., where a special attendance allowance was introduced for people needing care either by day or by night. This was an extension of the allowance that had been paid since 1970 to those who needed constant attention.

Protection for Women. The tendency to eliminate inconsistencies in the treatment of women under social security systems and to improve certain benefits especially relevant to women—maternity benefits, widows' pensions, etc.—continued during 1973–74. In some countries, Ireland for example, important changes were made following the recommendations of special committees charged with examining the economic and social status of women. The Irish Social Welfare Act of 1973 included many provisions affecting the treatment of women, including the creation of a contributory social insurance benefit for deserted wives. This benefit, paid at the same rate as the regular widows' pension, £6.60 a week in 1973, could be claimed by women of more than 40 years of age without dependent children, and by women of any age having at least one dependent child. Also in Ireland a new noncontributory benefit was introduced for unmarried mothers.

West Germany also continued to maintain a special interest in the social security treatment of women. Medical-care costs related to abortion became reimbursable, and a new benefit was introduced to help with the cost of replacing the housewife in case of her illness or hospitalization. Initially, this household assistance benefit was limited to families with at least one child under eight years of age. West Germany, Portugal, and the Soviet Union joined Sweden in providing cash sickness benefits when a mother had to be absent from work to care for a sick child. In West Germany, the benefit was restricted to five days in any one year for each eligible child under eight years of age. In Portugal, the age limit of the child was set at 3 years, and in the U.S.S.R. at 14 years. The Soviet scheme permitted widows, divorced women, and unmarried mothers to claim ten days a year for each child, while other mothers were allowed only seven days a year.

Among the various factors that prompted legislators and administrators in several countries to improve maternity benefits were the greater number of working women, particularly married women, in the labour force, and the policy of certain countries to encourage female employment. Most frequent changes dealt with increases in the rates of cash maternity benefits for insured women. In Libya and in the U.S.S.R. cash maternity benefits were increased to 100% of average earnings, regardless of the length of insured employment. Lump-sum maternity grants were improved in several countries. In Israel a working or self-employed woman adopting a child under ten years of age became eligible for cash maternity benefits at the regular rate.

Protection for Children. In Britain, concern over the "battered baby" issue reached new peaks with the publication of a report on the inquiry into the circumstances in which seven-year-old Maria Colwell had been beaten to death by her stepfather while in the care of a local social services department. The report cited failure in communications between the various agencies concerned with the child as the factor mainly responsible for the lack of protection. A new Children's Bill, published toward the end of 1974 and likely to become law in 1975, contained provisions for a "children's advocate" and for greater protection of all children in adoption, foster-home, and other care situations.

Social and welfare workers, and social services departments, countered the criticism over the Colwell and similar cases with the accusation that the community expected ever increasing standards while resources remained static, or were even cut back. However, based on the economic situation that existed at the end of the year, social and welfare services within the U.K. could only look forward to a leaner 1975.

(DAVID M. MAZIE; ISSA; X.)

See also Education; Health and Disease; Housing; Insurance; Race Relations.

[522.D; 535.B.3.c; 552.D.1]

Somalia

A republic of northeast Africa, the Somali Democratic Republic, or Somalia, is bounded by the Gulf of Aden, the Indian Ocean, Kenya, Ethiopia, and Afars and Issas. Area: 246,300 sq.mi. (638,000 sq.km.). Pop. (1974 est.): 3,085,000, predominantly Hamitic, with Arabic and other admixtures. Cap. and largest city: Muqdisho (pop., 1969 est., 200,000). Language: Somali. Religion: predominantly Muslim. President of the Supreme Revolutionary Council in 1974, Maj. Gen. Muhammad Siyad Barrah.

On Feb. 14, 1974, a special session of the Council of the Arab League admitted Somalia as the league's 20th member. The Somali people, though not Arabs, had throughout their history been part of the Arab world by religion and culture, and this showed itself in their political support for the Arab cause.

The summit conference of the Organization of African Unity was held on June 12–16 at Muqdisho; President Siyad was unanimously elected chairman of the conference. In his opening speech he expressed hope for a solution to the border dispute between Somalia and Ethiopia, but this did not in fact seem any nearer; the dispute was aggravated by incidents along the border and by the propaganda activities of unofficial "liberation" groups. In September a number of people were tried in district courts in the northern region on charges of antirevolutionary conspiracy and of making propaganda against the government. One man was sentenced to death; others to life imprisonment and shorter terms.

The government's efforts in the educational field continued. The mass literacy campaign begun in the towns in 1973 was being carried into rural areas. Universal education to intermediate level was to be made compulsory, and a new National University, with provision for 2,000 students, was to be built with help from the EEC. The Ministry of Planning announced

SOMALIA

Education. (1971–72) Primary, pupils 40,222, teachers 1,133; secondary, pupils 27,263, teachers 1,204; vocational, pupils 730, teachers 87; teacher training, students 351, teachers 17; higher, students 958, teaching staff 51.

Finance. Monetary unit: Somali shilling, with (Sept. 16, 1974) an official rate of 6.30 Somali shillings to U.S. $1 (nominal free rate of 14.50 Somali shillings = £1 sterling). Gold, SDRs, and foreign exchange, central bank: (June 1974) U.S. $33.8 million; (June 1973) U.S. $34.1 million. Budget (1973 est.): revenue 457 million Somali shillings; expenditure 396 million Somali shillings (excludes development expenditure 325 million Somali shillings). Cost of living (Muqdisho; 1970 = 100): (Feb. 1974) 110; (Feb. 1973) 97.

Foreign Trade. (1972) Imports 502.9 million Somali shillings; exports 299.9 million Somali shillings. Import sources: Italy c. 31%; Japan c. 8%; U.S.S.R. c. 7%; U.K. c. 7%; U.S. c. 5%; West Germany c. 5%. Export destinations: Saudi Arabia c. 36%; Italy c. 20%; Kuwait c. 8%. Main exports: livestock 54%; bananas 26%; meat and products 9%; hides and skins 6%.

Transport and Communications. Roads (1971) 17,223 km. Motor vehicles in use (1971): passenger 7,100; commercial (including buses) 4,700. There are no railways. Shipping (1973): merchant vessels 100 gross tons and over 239; gross tonnage 1,612,656. Telephones (Jan. 1971) c. 5,000. Radio receivers (Dec. 1972) 60,000.

Agriculture. Production (in 000; metric tons; 1972; 1971 in parentheses): millet 25 (30); cassava c. 26 (c. 26); sesame c. 6 (c. 6); sugar, raw value 51 (46); bananas c. 150 (c. 150). Livestock (in 000; 1971–72): cattle c. 2,850; sheep c. 3,900; goats c. 5,000; camels c. 3,000.

a new five-year development plan. Aimed at maximum self-sufficiency, its emphasis was to be on agricultural development and communications.

In July Pres. Nikolay V. Podgorny of the Soviet Union paid an official visit to Somalia, and he and President Siyad signed a treaty of cooperation between the two countries.   (VIRGINIA R. LULING)

[978.E.6.b.i]

South Africa

A republic occupying the southern tip of Africa, South Africa is bounded by South West Africa, Botswana, Rhodesia, Mozambique, and Swaziland. Lesotho forms an enclave within South African territory. Area: 471,445 sq.mi. (1,221,037 sq.km.), excluding Walvis Bay, 372 sq.mi. Pop. (1973 est.): 23,724,000, including (1970) Bantu 70.2%; white 17.5%; Coloured 9.4%; Asian 2.9%. Executive cap.: Pretoria (pop., 1971 est., 542,200); judicial cap.: Bloemfontein (pop., 1971 est., 212,503); legislative cap.: Cape Town (pop., 1971 est., 721,350). Largest city: Johannesburg (pop., 1971 est., 1,315,741). Language: Afrikaans and English. Religion: mainly Christian. State president in 1974, Jacobus J. Fouché; prime minister, B. J. Vorster.

Domestic Affairs. With the declared purpose of obtaining a renewed mandate for the government's policies, early parliamentary and provincial elections were held in April 1974. The result was that, with the inclusion of South West Africa (Namibia), the ruling National Party increased its majority in the House of Assembly from 118 to 123, the United Party (the official opposition) lost 6 seats (47 to 41), and the Progressive Party, which had hitherto been represented by one member (Helen Suzman), increased its representation to 7 (counting a by-election victory in June), including its leader, Colin Eglin. In the provincial elections, the National Party retained control of the Transvaal and the Orange Free State (all seats), as well as of the Cape and South West Africa. In Natal the United Party was returned. The Progressives for the first time won seats in the Transvaal and the Cape provincial councils. Neither of the "splinter" parties— the Hertzogite Herstigte Nasionale Party and T. J. A. Gerdener's newly formed Democratic Party—won any parliamentary or provincial seats.

The election was followed by a reshuffling of the Cabinet, and various portfolios were reallocated. Dissension arose in the United Party on matters of leadership and policies between the "Old Guard" and the "Young Turks," or reformists. In the National Party there were differences of opinion between Verligtes ("enlightened ones"), supporting more liberal policies, and Verkramptes ("narrow-minded ones"), who felt the government was departing from traditional Afrikaner-Nationalist racial policies. Organized opposition to a proposed new censorship law to control publications, which abolished appeal to the courts, developed among leading Afrikaans writers and intellectuals. Government warnings of press control led to the formulation by the Newspaper Press Union of a revised press code for voluntary control through a press council empowered to impose penalties for breaches of the code. The code was strenuously opposed by journalists and sections of the press. As a sequel to a commission of inquiry's reports on the activities of certain organizations, the minister of justice prohibited the receipt of funds from foreign sources to assist the cultural and social programs of the National Union of South African Students, which drew most of its financial support from abroad and was declared an "affected organization" under legislation passed in February. Members of the black South African Students Organization and the Black Peoples' Convention were arrested in police action after the staging of a banned mass rally in Durban on September 25 in support of the Frelimo government in Mozambique. The South African Council of Churches in July adopted a resolution urging its members to consider conscientious objections to military service in defense of unjust and discriminatory laws. The resolution aroused controversy in church and political circles. As a result the minister of defense, P. W. Botha, introduced an amendment to the Defense Act which, among other things, made it a severely punishable offense to encourage or incite anyone to refuse to serve under the act. Roman Catholic bishops and other leading churchmen stated that if the legislation were implemented, they might feel themselves bound to break the law as a matter of conscience.

Estimated defense expenditure for the year 1974–75 was R 692 million on revenue account and R 10 million on capital account, as compared with R 472 million in 1973–74. The minister announced that it had been decided to complete an original ten-year defense program in five years. South Africa had become self-supporting in various branches of armament production. Work on a second naval base on Salisbury Island, off Durban, to serve as a subsidiary base to Simonstown, was progressing. At Simonstown itself the building of a new tidal basin, with provision for a protected submarine base, was due to start in 1975. A Defense Planning Council was established to coordinate defense and security activities.

In the light of the worldwide energy situation a pilot plant of the Uranium Enrichment Corporation

Sorghum Grains:
see Agriculture and Food Supplies

A fibreglass minaret tops off the clock tower in the new Oriental Plaza shopping centre in Johannesburg.

of South Africa for the large-scale expansion of uranium enrichment and the production of nuclear fuel was nearing completion at Pelindaba, with West German and other foreign participation. The Atomic Energy Board planned to intensify a fuel development program and the search for more uranium resources. More state funds were provided for the search for oil. Near Pofadder in the northwestern Cape the discovery of extensive deposits of copper, lead, zinc, and related base minerals by U.S. interests was reported. Several new gold mines were planned in the western Transvaal and the Orange Free State. In the Kinross area of the eastern Transvaal the Electricity Supply Commission (Escom) planned a giant thermal power station at an estimated cost of R 600 million, and a hydroelectric project (the Drakensberg scheme) to pipe water across the Drakensberg from the Tugela River in Natal to the Sterkfontein Dam in the Orange Free State was under construction.

The Legislative Assembly of the partially self-governing Transkei decided in March to ask for full independence within five years on condition that land promised to the Transkei under legislation passed by the South African Parliament in 1936 should be so transferred within five years and that such a transfer should not prejudice rights of the Transkei to specific districts originally claimed but not falling within the terms of the 1936 legislation. A recess committee was appointed, with Paramount Chief Kaiser Matanzima, Transkei chief minister, as chairman, to draft constitutional proposals, to consider the financial and diplomatic implications of an independent Transkei, and to establish its boundaries with possible amalgamation with the adjoining Ciskei. In September Prime Minister B. J. Vorster announced government approval of the Transkei's request. Vorster said that the land promised to the Transkei in 1936 would be handed over. The interests of the white and Coloured population in the Transkei (numbering less than 2% of its population of 1,650,000) would be looked after by South Africa. Reacting to the Transkei move, Chief Lucas Mangope, chief minister of the Tswana homeland, said that the minimum for independence would be a more equitable distribution of land and a greater share of South Africa's wealth. In the North Sotho homeland of Lebowa, the report of a special land commission drawn up by the chief minister, Cedric Phatudi, rejected the government's land consolidation

plan and claimed additional land totaling about one-third of the Transvaal. A new departure in the relations between the central government and the Bantustans was a "summit" meeting between Vorster and eight homeland leaders.

To improve productivity and help overcome the shortage of skilled workers, training centres were established. The private sector was encouraged by tax concessions to cooperate in the scheme. An increasing number of Africans were employed, subject to consent by trade unions, in what previously had been whites' jobs. The mining industry planned to train black workers and change its traditional system of recruiting mine labour, with more employment of South African instead of foreign workers. Serious intertribal fighting in the mines, with deaths and many injured, had precipitated the threat of a labour shortage. Wages were raised and the gap between white and black wages narrowed. Pressures from abroad on foreign firms operating in South Africa to improve black workers' wages and working conditions played a part in the process. The government opposed the formation of registered African trade unions as urged by the Trade Union Council of South Africa. (See INDUSTRIAL RELATIONS.)

The political future of the Coloured people continued to be a controversial issue. At its July session in Cape Town the Coloured Persons' Representative Council—partly Coloured-elected, partly government-nominated—rejected by 29 votes to 25 the policy of separate development (apartheid). The defeat of the Federal Party within the council by the Labour opposition led to the council's prorogation. There were outspoken differences of opinion on the issue among Nationalists. The official view, set out by Vorster when he met an all-party deputation of Coloured representatives, headed by the Federal Party leader Tom Schwartz, was that there could be no Coloured representation in the "white" Parliament. The Indian community also aimed at parity with the whites and representation in Parliament, according to H. E. Joosub, chairman of the South African Indian Council (also partly elected, partly nominated). Provisions in the new General Law Amendment bill made it a penal offense to cause or incite hostility between sections of the population. A widely acclaimed clause in the bill repealed repressive century-old master-and-servants

continued on page 626

SOUTH AFRICA

Education. (1970) European: primary, secondary, and vocational, pupils 864,407, teachers 41,603; teacher training, students 12,532, teachers 966; higher, students 53,131, teaching staff 9,889. African (1970) and other non-European: primary, secondary, and vocational, pupils 3,411,924, teachers (1968) 56,242; teacher training, students 11,369, teachers 674; higher, students 5,880, teaching staff 929.

Finance. Monetary unit: rand, with (Sept. 16, 1974) a free rate of R 0.70 to U.S. $1 (R 1.62 = £1 sterling). Gold, SDRs, and foreign exchange, official: (June 1974) U.S. $1,110,000,000; (June 1973) U.S. $1,704,000,000. Budget (1973–74 est.): revenue R 3,163,000,000; expenditure R 3,461,000,000. Gross national product: (1973) R 18,078,000,000; (1972) R 15,103,000,000. Money supply: (May 1974) R 3,568,000,000; (May 1973) R 2,948,000,000. Cost of living (1970 = 100): (May 1974) 134; (May 1973) 122.

Foreign Trade. (1973) Imports R 3,741,200,000; exports (excluding gold) R 2,447,900,000 (outflow of gold U.S. $2,536,000,000). Import sources: U.K. 18%; West Germany 18%; U.S.

15%; Japan 11%. Export destinations: U.K. 29%; Japan 10%; West Germany 8%; U.S. 7%; Belgium-Luxembourg 5%. Main exports: diamonds 15%; wool 8%; iron and steel 8%; copper 6%; metal ores 5%; sugar 5%; cereals 5%.

Transport and Communications. Roads (1973) c. 320,000 km. (including 185,846 km. main roads). Motor vehicles in use (1972): passenger 1,655,000; commercial 513,600. Railways: (1972) 19,909 km.; freight traffic (including Namibia; 1973) 61,184,000,000 net ton-km. Air traffic (1972): 3,545,000,000 passenger-km.; freight 85.2 million net ton-km. Shipping (1973): merchant vessels 100 gross tons and over 252; gross tonnage 490,751. Telephones (Dec. 1972) 1,707,000. Radio receivers (Dec. 1972) 2,350,000.

Agriculture. Production (in 000; metric tons; 1973; 1972 in parentheses): corn 4,300 (9,630); wheat 1,607 (1,746); oats 103 (104); sorghum 270 (556); potatoes c. 700 (c. 650); sugar, raw value c. 1,833 (1,915); peanuts 203 (420); sunflower seed 232 (151); oranges (1972) c. 514, (1971) c. 422; grapefruit (1972) c. 137, (1971)

c. 107; apples (1972) c. 255, (1971) c. 247; wine c. 550 (525); tobacco c. 33 (c. 30); wool c. 49 (58); meat (1972) c. 654, (1971) c. 648; milk (1972) c. 2,850, (1971) c. 2,840; fish catch (1972) 1,123, (1971) 1,165. Livestock (in 000; June 1973): cattle c. 12,480; sheep c. 30,730; pigs c. 1,390; goats c. 5,700; horses c. 420; chickens (on farms and estates) c. 12,600.

Industry. Index of manufacturing production (1970 = 100): (1973) 115; (1972) 105. Fuel and power (in 000; 1973): coal (metric tons) 62,354; manufactured gas (cu.m.; 1972) 1,858,000; electricity (kw-hr.) 64,818,000. Production (in 000; metric tons; 1973): cement 6,866; iron ore (60–65% metal content) 10,952; pig iron 4,885; crude steel 5,631; copper ore (metal content; 1972) 155; asbestos (1972) 321; chrome (oxide content; 1972) 662; antimony concentrates (metal content; 1972) 15; manganese ore (metal content; 1972) 1,362; uranium (1972) 3.1; gold (troy oz.) 27,403; diamonds (metric carats; 1972) 7,395; petroleum products (1971) 10,550; fish meal (including Namibia; 1972) 244.

A WIND
OF CHANGE?

By Helen Suzman

When calling for an early general election in South Africa on April 24, 1974, Prime Minister B. J. Vorster stated that he considered the next few years critical ones for the country, and that for this reason he wanted a stronger mandate to ensure internal and external security and to promote economic progress and political stability within the framework of the government's policy of separate development (apartheid) for the white and nonwhite communities. The voting results returned the Nationalist government with more than a two-thirds majority by the all-white electorate, its seventh successive election victory since 1948. The only unexpected result of the election was the improvement in the fortunes of the small Progressive Party, which advocated a nondiscriminatory multiracial geographic federation. Parliamentary representation of the Progressive Party rose dramatically from one to six (and in a subsequent by-election to seven) at the expense of the official opposition party, the United Party, which advocated a race federation.

The Portuguese Coup. Prime Minister Vorster's prediction of difficult years ahead for South Africa was remarkably well-timed, because the Portuguese coup d'etat, which occurred the day after the election, could have very significant consequences indeed for South Africa. These embrace: national security, landing rights for South African aircraft on Portuguese territory in Angola and on the Cape Verde Islands, use of the important port of Lourenço Marques in Mozambique, the availability of some 100,000 black labourers yearly for the South African gold mines from that territory, and the accessibility of energy for South African industry from Mozambique's vast Cabora Bassa Dam if and when it is completed. A further consequence, which is impossible to measure, is the psychological impact on the indigenous black population of South Africa of the emergence of two or more potentially independent states bordering on South Africa, as a direct result of black militancy.

Mozambique has a small (200,000) white population and a large (8 million) black population, many of whom have openly supported the Mozambique Liberation Front (Frelimo) since the coup. Angola, which has some 300,000 whites and approximately 5.2 million black and mixed, is much more oriented toward a "Brazilian" solution of its race problem, in which a tolerant and easygoing attitude is taken toward racial differences. It is also much richer than Mozambique, having oil wells near Luanda, offshore oil at Cabinda, and mineral and agricultural products. Mozambique is heavily dependent economically on South Africa. According to the latest available figures, South Africa's contribution to Mozambique's gross national product was 42% of the total for 1971. The revenue from black contract mine workers in 1973 amounted to approximately R 50 million. Reliable sources indicate that the deferred wages are paid in gold valued at the official rate. Until now Portugal has benefited from the con-

Helen Suzman has been a member of the South African Parliament since 1953 and was sole representative of the Progressive Party during 1961–74. After the 1974 general election she became the party's parliamentary spokesman on justice and African affairs.

siderable difference in the official and free gold prices to the extent of an estimated R 45 million since 1969. Whether or not a populist black majority government in Mozambique will be able to reconcile its political opposition to South Africa with economic realities remains to be seen.

Bordering on South West Africa (Namibia), Angola has received many blacks as political refugees from that disputed South African territory since the new Portuguese government took over. A sense of urgency has recently crept into the South African government's handling of the Namibian problem. While accepting that Namibia has a separate international status, the government has ignored the resolution passed in 1966 by the UN General Assembly which declared South Africa's mandate over the territory to be terminated. Instead, the government is more and more emphasizing a commitment to "self-determination and independence" for the peoples of Namibia, numbering some 750,-000 (of whom 90,000 are white), who live in 11 "ethnic regions."

Mozambique has a long common border with South Africa. When the territory becomes independent in 1975 and Frelimo-controlled, South Africa's task of defending its borders will become much more demanding. This, significantly enough, is already reflected in an important change in policy, announced as early as June 1974. Blacks are now to be included in South Africa's armed forces, formerly reserved for whites and a few Coloured people, although armed black police have been doing guard duty on the Rhodesian border.

After the Portuguese coup, South Africa's involvement with Rhodesia took on a new dimension. South Africa had been Rhodesia's lifeline since the latter's unilateral declaration of independence in 1965. Now the situation has changed radically. Withdrawal of aid to Rhodesia appears to be a priority demand of black leaders such as Pres. Kenneth Kaunda of Zambia who are anxious for détente in southern Africa. The pragmatic Vorster has seemingly made it clear to Rhodesia that South Africa's interests must be his first concern.

The calls that have been made over the years for the whites of southern Africa to make meaningful changes while they are still in a position of strength take on added significance in the present climate. It has become clearer than ever before that South Africa must move from a situation in which almost all economic and political power and privilege is vested in the white minority to a situation in which people of all races will have equal opportunity to contribute to and benefit from the economic development of the country, and can participate in its decision-making processes. That there is a growing awareness of the need to win the support and loyalty of the indigenous population is evidenced by statements made by Gen. R. C. Hiemstra, former head of the South African Defence Force, who said that no war against guerrillas could ultimately be successful without such support. Anxious leading articles in the pro-government Afrikaans press have reiterated this point of view.

Apartheid and Economics. Economic factors add their impetus for change, because a paradoxical situation exists in South Africa in which economic forces run counter to political aims. Nearly 20 years ago, at the instigation of Hendrik Verwoerd (minister for native affairs from 1950 and prime minister, 1958–66), the Tomlinson Commission produced a blueprint for separate government. Verwoerd was sufficiently intelligent to realize that in the second half of the 20th century the philosophy of racial discrimination was simply not acceptable to the rest of the world. He hoped that a partition plan based on ethnic groups would satisfy internal pressures and external demands for a just solution of the race problem in South Africa. The Tomlinson Commission recommended the rapid development and transformation of the so-called Native Reserves (consisting of 13% of the land area of South Africa) into eight economically viable and potentially independent homelands (Bantustans) for the bulk of the African population. Job opportunities outside of agriculture were to be provided at the rate of 20,000 a year in industrial and 30,000 a year in service occupations, and gradually the majority of the African population living in the so-called white areas was to be attracted back to the homelands. The Tomlinson dream has not, of course, materialized. Nearly two decades have elapsed since the report was presented in Parliament, but less than 25,000 jobs have been created inside the homelands. Moreover, the backup operation of border industries—*i.e.*, white-owned industries encouraged to decentralize on the "white" side of the borders of the homelands—has provided only about 85,000 jobs for homelands inhabitants, at wage rates (as in industries within the homelands) considerably below the minimum statutory rates paid in the other industrial areas in the republic. These facts, when correlated with the inaccuracy of the Tomlinson Commission's population projections—19 million Africans by the year 2000, as against more recent estimates of 35 million–40 million—make nonsense of the homelands solution.

The government insists on a migratory labour system for all Africans seeking employment outside the homelands (except for those born in the urban areas or already there for 15 consecutive years, or who have been employed by one employer for ten years; even these are regarded officially as "temporary sojourners"). Under this policy the men may come to available jobs in the "white" industrial areas as contract workers, leaving their families in the homelands and visiting them for one month annually. This policy has had dire sociological results. It has led to broken families, illegitimacy in town and homelands, and crime and alcoholism among migrants. It runs counter to a major requirement of any modern industrial society, namely, the existence of a stable labour force that can be trained to do skilled and semiskilled work.

Despite official policy, the economic demands of the country have led, and will continue to lead, to considerable modifications in practice. Notwithstanding the absence of free and compulsory education for blacks, long enjoyed by white children, black parents strive to educate their children. Over 80% of African children of school-going age are in school, and although the dropout rate after the first few years is extremely high and less than 1% matriculate, blacks are acquiring skills in increasing numbers. They are performing jobs previously reserved by law and custom for whites. Widespread exemptions from job reservations and modifications of custom have resulted in a slow but sure transformation of the labour market over the last 12 to 15 years. Enlightened self-interest and an acute shortage of white skilled

workers have led even the most reactionary white trade unions to restructure jobs so as to admit black workers. Jobs have been fragmented or "deskilled," and as a result black workers are today performing tasks that traditionally used to be reserved for whites. Moreover, it is obvious that this acquisition of skill by blacks will have to continue at an accelerated pace if the economic growth rate in South Africa is to be maintained. It is estimated that by 1980 South Africa will need 3.7 million skilled workers. At most only 1.7 million could be recruited from the whites, and this would involve the entire economically active white population. The nonwhite population must therefore, of necessity, supply at least two million skilled workers—and the vast majority of these will have to be Africans.

As a result of the need for black workers, there will have to be radical changes in the policy of educating and training Africans. Industry will have to be freed from the many restrictions that handicap the efficient and maximum use of African labour. For example, the remaining statutory and customary job prohibitions must go; the Physical Planning Act, which hinders greater numbers of Africans from being employed in the existing metropolitan areas, must be repealed; and the stringent influx control regulations that prevent rural Africans from entering the cities to seek work (and that result in approximately 160,000 pass prosecutions a year) must be phased out. Most important of all perhaps, if industrial peace is to be preserved, the entire wage structure will have to be revised so as to narrow the wide gap presently existing between low-paid unskilled (black) jobs and high-paid skilled (white) jobs. In 1973, as a result of widespread strikes in Natal involving some 60,000 African workers, the government conceded for the first time, albeit in a very limited form, the right of Africans to strike legally. But the right to join or to form legally recognized trade unions and to enjoy collective bargaining rights, long conceded to white, Coloured, and Asian workers, is still denied to Africans. Yet it is clear to many observers that these rights will have to be granted if industry is not to become a battlefield in the future, for African workers are undoubtedly becoming aware of their economic muscle.

Political Rights. The one field where change is most urgently needed, and where it is least likely to occur, is that of political rights. Under the government's separate development policy, Africans enjoy universal franchise in the homelands, where they may elect legislative assemblies that have limited powers only.

Chief Gatsha Buthelezi appears in full Zulu tribal regalia at the ceremony in which King Goodwill Zwelithini of KwaZulu (one of South Africa's Bantustans) was enthroned.

JAN KOPEC—CAMERA PRESS/PICTORIAL PARADE

The homelands governments are almost entirely dependent financially on monies voted to them by the white Parliament of the republic, and laws passed by them are subject to veto by the white Cabinet. Africans—some eight million of them—who are living in the "white" cities or on the "white" farms exercise an absentee vote for the homelands governments. The four and a half million Africans who live in the urban areas include the migrant workers from the homelands, but many have been in the towns for two or three generations. They are the most sophisticated among their people, and have evolved a way of life very different from the tribal existence. Yet apart from exercising a vote for urban African councils that have no executive power whatever, their only franchise is for the distant homelands governments, which are powerless to effect improvements in their daily lives.

The two million Coloured people have a partially elected and partially nominated Coloured Persons' Representative Council. This body is also entirely dependent for its finances on the white Parliament and is quite impotent to effect any changes in government policies that so radically affect the lives of its constituents. One such policy is reflected in the Group Areas Act, which has already resulted in the forced removal of about 45,000 Coloured families from areas proclaimed for white occupation and ownership and which will eventually lead to the removal of an additional 28,000 families. The same applies to the half-million Asians who have universal franchise for the predominantly nominated Indian Council; 27,000 Asian families have already been moved under Group Areas proclamations, and a further 20,000 families await their fate.

In the homelands the African leaders are using the forums provided for them by the government. Men such as Chief Gatsha Buthelezi (*see* Biography) and Chief Lucas Mangope are demanding more rights and opportunities for their people. All are demanding more land for their poverty-stricken, overpopulated areas, and they protest against the mass removals of their people from "black spots" (pockets of African occupation in areas declared "white") and the ejection of people from the urban areas. (More than one million people have already been "resettled" in the homelands as a result of such removals and of efforts to consolidate the scattered land areas of the homelands.)

South Africa's Isolation. Independence for the homelands, most of the African leaders say, is out of the question until they are economically viable. And independence, of at least one of the homelands, is desperately desired by the Nationalist government as an indication of its sincerity. It hopes thereby to reestablish South Africa's respectability in the outside world. (Negotiations are proceeding with the Transkei homeland for independence within five years.)

Isolation is much abhorred by South Africa, which longs to be reaccepted in the comity of the Western world. The oft-threatened trade boycott is, however, no longer taken very seriously. South Africa fully realizes that its custom is much valued, that its products are much needed, and that United Nations boycott resolutions, for example, are not backed up by enforcement machinery. Nevertheless, the South African government seeks friends in the outside world. It constantly reminds the West that it is an ally against Communism, and of course it deeply resents and suffers from the effects of the sports boycott, which has proved an effective punitive instrument. The government's sports policy has changed considerably over the past few years. More and more concessions have been made to black sportsmen in an unavailing effort to get South Africa readmitted to international sporting events. Recently, an editor of a government-supporting newspaper openly advocated merit selection for South African teams. It remains to be seen if a more liberal policy will be adopted in the entertainment field, as a result of action abroad. The recent resolution by British Equity not to supply the country with television films when television is introduced into South Africa in 1976 could well be a factor in impelling the government to ease up in its rigid separation of the races and to allow "racially mixed" entertainments.

Notwithstanding protestations by South Africa's UN ambassador and by Vorster, the Nationalist government is seemingly determined at all costs to preserve white political supremacy in what it deems "the white republic," claiming that the other races must exercise their political rights in their own areas. That more than half of the African population and the entire Coloured and Asian populations live, work, and will die in the "white republic" is glossed over. The government makes changes only when it has no alternative. "He who fails to read history is doomed to relive it," said George Santayana. It is to be hoped that, before it is too late, South Africa will learn from the history of the rest of Africa that the changes that are demanded today are always greater than those that were rejected yesterday.

Black skilled workers in the Rosslyn automotive factory.

Blacks in training at the Groblersdal counterinsurgency base, an indication of the seriousness with which South Africa views terrorist activity on its borders.

continued from page 622

legislation intended primarily for nonwhite workers.

Demands for the reform of the pass laws and influx control regulations were stimulated by Supreme Court judgments in Natal and Transvaal which ruled as illegal the practice of summarily arresting Africans if they did not have their reference books (passes) on their persons, without giving them time to fetch the document. The government, while appealing against the judgments, undertook to investigate the question.

Foreign Affairs. In September, for the second time in 1974, the General Assembly of the United Nations rejected the credentials of the South African delegation by a 98 to 23 majority, with 14 abstentions, and referred South Africa's position to the Security Council, where a triple veto (U.S., U.K., and France) restored the position. The assembly then took the unprecedented step of suspending South African participation in the current session. For the first time, the South African delegation had included three nonwhite observers.

In South West Africa the governing National Party of South West Africa stated that talks would be held with all other ethnic groups in the territory to decide jointly on its political future. The statement was approved by the South African government and the prime minister's advisory council for South West Africa. The International Monetary Fund deprived South Africa of representation on the board of the Fund and of the World Bank.

In April Pres. Alfredo Stroessner of Paraguay paid a state visit to South Africa and cultural and economic agreements were signed between the two governments. Agreements on nuclear energy, oil, mining, and trade were concluded with Iran. Events in Mozambique brought diplomatic activity by South Africa aimed at détente with black Africa. Vorster and Ian Smith of Rhodesia stated they would not interfere in Mozambique's affairs. Vorster reportedly visited the Ivory Coast in September for talks with several heads of black states. He was influential in securing Smith's agreement to a Rhodesian constitutional conference to be held in 1975. (*See* RHODESIA.)

The Economy. In submitting his post-election budget for 1974–75 in August—a budget largely influenced by the higher price of gold on the world free market—Minister of Finance Nicholas J. Diederichs said that to maintain growth it was necessary to increase productivity, with the help of a skilled labour force. The budget accordingly provided for improved

facilities for the training of workers and the better use of nonwhite labour. With a surplus of R 518 million from the previous year, Diederichs announced cuts in sales duties, lower personal and company taxation, increased social pensions, and incentives to industrialists and exporters. To attract foreign capital the Reserve Bank was empowered to authorize overseas borrowing by the private sector for approved purposes. In June the rand was freed from its fixed parity rate with the U.S. dollar under a policy of independently managed floating. To slow down inflation the bank rate was raised from 7.5 to 8% in August.   (LOUIS HOTZ)

[978.E.8.b.i]

Southeast Asian Affairs

Much of the news of Southeast Asia in 1974—a time of violence and anxiety in the region—was made by the major powers. Those major developments making headlines also contributed to an air of uncertainty. The year began with moves by the superpowers in the Indian Ocean that deeply disturbed Southeast Asian countries. There were reports that the U.S. defense authorities were preparing to establish major air and naval facilities on the British-owned island of Diego Garcia. Other reports during the year confirmed U.S. interest in converting the remote island into a significant military base. The reason officially given was that the Soviet Union was expanding its naval strength in the area.

China was also concerned about Soviet activity in the Indian Ocean. According to an official Peking commentary in March, Soviet activities in the ocean were aimed at building "a great Russian Empire" with bases and seaports in Singapore, Malaysia, Thailand, Indonesia, and Portuguese Timor. The commentary said: "Southeast Asia belongs to the Southeast Asians, not to either of the superpowers." This declaration came within weeks of China's making an excursion of its own into Southeast Asia. A string of archipelagic islands in the South China Sea suddenly became bones of hot contention early in the year. In September 1973 South Vietnam had announced the incorporation of some of the islands and the granting of oil exploration rights to foreign companies. But in a lightning military action on January 19 China took possession of the Paracel Islands, 165 mi. SE of the Chinese island of Hainan, driving away South Vietnamese aircraft and patrol boats. It also laid claims of sovereignty over all the islands in the Spratly group, 400 mi. farther south, and to all the natural resources in the surrounding sea. The Philippines and Taiwan, as well as South Vietnam, claimed islands in the Spratly group.

The Chinese military action brought forth no public pronouncements from Southeast Asian governments except that of South Vietnam. But reports from various capitals showed clearly that it had caused dismay in the region. Moscow's strict hands-off attitude and the stated U.S. position that the Chinese move did not indicate any desire to dominate the region were interpreted as signs that each of the big powers would let the others pursue their interests in the area without interference.

Japan, unexpectedly, contributed another element to Southeast Asian tensions during the year. With Japanese business in a dominant position throughout the region and particularly in Thailand and Indonesia, Prime Minister Kakuei Tanaka decided to embark upon a five-nation tour in January with a view toward removing misunderstandings about Japan among Southeast Asian peoples. Weeks before the tour began, student representatives from different Southeast Asian countries had met and announced their decision to stage a "sensational but constructive" protest against foreign exploitation of Southeast Asia. They mentioned Japan and the U.S. as practitioners of such exploitation. Consequently, Tanaka's tour provided an occasion for massive public demonstrations of resentment and bitterness in many parts of the region. The Philippines, under martial law, was free of incidents. In Singapore also, strict supervision by authorities kept the lid on dissent except for letters written by university student unions protesting against Japanese business practices. Elsewhere, the storm broke. In Malaysia, despite strong control by the government, students organized public demonstrations and burned Tanaka in effigy. In Thailand massive student rallies dogged Tanaka's footsteps from the minute his aircraft landed at the Bangkok airport. Thai student leaders finally met the prime minister at a face-to-face meeting and presented him with various demands. It was in Indonesia that the protests turned to tragedy. Rampaging student mobs brought on Jakarta's first curfew since the Suharto government came to power in 1966. Japanese cars and business establishments were set ablaze, police opened fire on demonstrators, and several were killed.

It appeared that, in part, the Japanese were being used as foils for local people to show their resentment of their own governments' failure to achieve either economic progress or democratic systems. The governments themselves seemed sensitive to their freshly demonstrated lack of popularity; there was a new emphasis on security arrangements in many countries, while Indonesia closed down almost the entire national press and took severe measures against critics of the Tanaka visit.

The one regional development apparently unconnected with the big powers was the internationalization of the Muslim uprising in the Philippines. The Manila government used its full military power to put down the rebellion in its southern provinces but failed. In the process international Muslim solidarity developed over the issue, and relations between the Philippines and Malaysia deteriorated. The extent of it became clear when the fifth Islamic Conference of Foreign Ministers met in Kuala Lumpur on June 21, under Malaysia's stewardship. The Philippine question dominated the conference. In the end the foreign ministers issued what amounted to a condemnation of the Philippine government, calling upon it to "desist from all measures which resulted in the killing of Muslims."

ASEAN. In the light of the dispute between Malaysia and the Philippines, the Association of Southeast Asian Nations appeared somewhat shaky during 1974. But its very attempt to play honest broker between the disputants was cited by some as proof of its usefulness. Its mediation efforts producing no immediate result, ASEAN turned its attention to economic issues with a slightly keener sense of urgency than in the past. This flowed from ASEAN members' appreciation of the seriousness of the world economic crisis. They were also emboldened by their successes in negotiations with the EEC and Japan. When the Japanese government told Japanese synthetic rubber manufacturers to shape their policies after giving due consideration to ASEAN requests on the matter, ASEAN members felt that they did enjoy a measure of bargaining power as a group.

Economic cooperation was the dominant theme when ASEAN foreign ministers met in Jakarta in May for their seventh annual meeting. Inaugurating the meeting, President Suharto said that the present structure whereby ASEAN members exchanged raw materials for manufactured goods no longer provided a satisfactory basis for development. He said that new patterns of relationships were taking shape in Asia and that there was no assurance that outside powers would not interfere in Southeast Asia's internal affairs. In such a situation, he said, the only way ASEAN could remain master of its own political destiny was for each member to improve its political and economic conditions. He called for more efforts for the joint industrial development of the area.

Although there was general satisfaction over the outcome of the meeting, it was understood that the test of solidarity among member countries would come in such sensitive areas as oil sharing. In November 1973 Indonesia had caused all-round dismay by telling Thailand and the Philippines that its considerable oil supplies were already committed to developed countries. Subsequently, Indonesian officials said they were seriously interested in supplying oil to ASEAN neighbours. At the Jakarta meeting the Singapore foreign minister announced that the five ASEAN members would consider cooperating to alleviate one another's shortages.

As if to follow up its resolutions on achieving results, ASEAN decided to give itself a home. The Philippines had asked that the home be in Manila. It later conceded to Jakarta, and the permanent secretariat of the ASEAN was asked to site itself in the Indonesian capital. The meeting also decided to set up procedures to settle disputes among member states and to look into the possibilities of adopting a formal constitution.

The question of the group's enlarging its membership remained as confused as ever. It was no secret that it was quite interested in including the Indochina countries in its fold. However, North Vietnam bluntly refused an invitation to sit in as an observer at the 1974 meeting. South Vietnam, which had attended the 1973 meeting as an observer, was not invited in 1974. Cambodia and Laos sent observers, but Burma did not. Clearly, political affiliations and ideologies were proving decisive in this matter. North Vietnam had bilateral relations with some members of ASEAN, but it denounced Thailand and the Philippines for permitting U.S. bases on their soil. It also attacked ASEAN members for their attitude toward the Provisional Revolutionary Government of South Vietnam. Indonesia, for its part, wanted ASEAN to give fuller support to the beleaguered government of Pres. Lon Nol in Cambodia. The foreign ministers' meeting rejected this proposal but agreed to oppose any UN resolution calling for the recognition of Prince Norodom Sihanouk in place of Lon Nol.

The conflicts within ASEAN over relations with China edged toward resolution following Malaysia's diplomatic recognition of Peking in May. The development marked, in the words of Singapore Prime Minister Lee Kuan Yew, a new phase in Southeast Asia's relations with China. ASEAN reacted warmly to the Malaysian initiative. A spokesman suggested that Malaysia's act was in fact an agreed-upon move and that other members had accepted the principle of following suit.

In South Vietnam the war continued. This North Vietnamese soldier was captured in June, following a hard-fought battle by Saigon's forces to recapture the village of An Dien.

UPI COMPIX

There were some differences of opinion as to how the understanding worked out by Kuala Lumpur and Peking over the Chinese in Malaysia would affect the ethnic problem in other countries. Some 16 million "overseas" Chinese lived in the various Southeast Asian countries, and they had been considered apart from indigenous people in part because of Peking's long tradition of looking upon all Chinese everywhere as its citizens. In later years China had given up this position, but not everybody had felt reassured about Chinese allegiances. Besides, some Chinese residents in Southeast Asian countries had been officially categorized as stateless because they did not hold citizenship papers from any country, for one reason or another. It was generally believed that Peking had agreed not to promote the rights of local Chinese communities or otherwise interfere in ethnic issues in Malaysia. (*See* MALAYSIA.)

ESCAP (ECAFE). The major news of 1974 about the ECAFE (the UN Economic Commission for Asia and the Far East) was that it ceased being ECAFE. During its April meeting in Colombo it decided to rename itself the Economic and Social Commission for Asia and the Pacific. The change signified abandonment of the term Far East, which was deemed to have colonial connotations, as well as a shift in emphasis from the strictly economic to the broader, and it was to be hoped deeper, socioeconomic.

The oil and mineral exploration program launched by ECAFE in 1972 made some headway in 1974 with a pledge of $5 million, of which $1 million was to come from Thailand, Indonesia, Malaysia, Philippines, Cambodia, South Vietnam, and South Korea and $1.5 million from the UN Development Program. Work started on tin and other mineral exploration in the Straits of Malacca and on a survey of the mineral potential of the Malaysian Peninsula.

SEATO. In a published statement the Southeast Asia Treaty Organization's secretary-general, Sunthorn Hongladarom, contended that "China's friendly attitude toward the free world is just an attempt to show the Russians that it has the support of many friends." The statement, which asserted that SEATO was still committed to fighting subversion, was made at a time when the U.S., the main supporter of SEATO, had become a vigorous promoter of friendship with China and when the only two Southeast Asian members of the organization, Thailand and the Philippines, were actively seeking formal diplomatic relations with China. It was clear that, as far as Southeast Asia was concerned, SEATO had already gone into limbo.   (T. J. S. GEORGE)

[976.B]

Soviet Bloc Economies

The year 1974 marked the 25th anniversary of the Council for Mutual Economic Assistance (CMEA or Comecon), created in Moscow by the representatives of the U.S.S.R., Poland, Czechoslovakia, Hungary, Romania, and Bulgaria in January 1949. Albania joined the CMEA the following February but withdrew from it in 1961; East Germany joined in September 1950, Mongolia in June 1962, and Cuba in July 1972. After 1964 an active part in the proceedings of CMEA agencies was played by Yugoslavia, while in May 1973 a cooperation agreement was signed between Comecon and Finland.

Nikolay V. Faddeyev, CMEA secretary-general,

declared on Jan. 6, 1974, that the achievements of the CMEA were remarkable. The member countries, occupying 18% of the world's area and numbering 10% of its population, accounted in 1973 for 33% of its industrial output, compared with 17.8% in 1950. In the Warsaw weekly *Zycie Gospodarcze* (Jan. 13–20, 1974) Faddeyev wrote that the national income of member countries rose almost six times between 1950 and 1973 and industrial production more than eight times. During that period of time the CMEA generation of electric power rose from 135,300,000,000 kw-hr. to 1,216,007,000,000; extraction of crude petroleum from 43.7 million metric tons to 437.9 million; and production of steel from 35.8 million tons to 177.9 million. (*See* Table II.)

Nevertheless, there continued to be a substantial discrepancy between the level of industrial production of the CMEA countries and the volume of their foreign trade. In 1973 the world's exports, amounting to $549.8 billion, included only $52.3 billion (9.5%) for the seven European CMEA countries; their part in the $572.2 billion world's imports reached a total of $53 billion, or 9.2%. (*See* Table III.) Moreover, about two-thirds of the international trade of the CMEA countries was with each other. The U.S.S.R. was the main trade partner of every other CMEA member, though the extent of this predominance varied from country to country. Bulgaria's dependence on Soviet markets was the highest (more than 50% of turnover), and Romania's the lowest (about 25%); for East Germany, Poland, Czechoslovakia, and Hungary the U.S.S.R. took about one-third of their exports and supplied a similar proportion of their imports.

At the 28th plenary jubilee session of the CMEA, held in Sofia, Bulg., on June 18–21, 1974, the official communiqué noted that for the first time since its creation the CMEA had begun to work out a five-year plan (adopted in Bucharest, Rom., in July 1971) of multilateral measures of integration. The heads of government of the seven European member countries signed a general agreement on cooperation in developing the Orenburg gas condensate field and for the construction of a gas pipeline from Orenburg, southern Ural Mountains, to the Soviet-Czechoslovak frontier. As a consequence 15,500,000,000 cu.m. of natural gas would be carried annually via the 1,720-mi. pipeline from the U.S.S.R. to the other participating countries. In addition, an agreement was signed to establish a new international economic complex, Interkhimvolokno, for the speediest possible development of the production of much-needed chemical fibres. Another multinational complex, Intertextilmash, was planned to modernize textile manufacture. The "Friendship" cotton plant being built by Poland and East Germany at Zawiercie, Pol., would be the largest in Europe, producing 12.5 million tons of cotton yarn a year.

Another international economic organization, Interatomenergo, set up within the framework of the CMEA, began to function on June 20, 1974. Its purpose was to coordinate production, deliveries of equipment, and the rendering of technical assistance in the construction of nuclear power plants. The agreement to establish this was also signed by Yugoslavia. General design functions were assumed by the U.S.S.R. Ministry of Power and Electrification, and headquarters were in Moscow.

Natural gas from the Tyumen region in western Siberia reached Moscow in November 1974 through a 1,900-mi. pipeline 4.5 ft. in diameter. The pipeline

Table I. Rates of Industrial Growth in Eastern Europe*

Country	1966–70	1971	1972	1973	1974†
U.S.S.R.	8.5	7.8	6.5	7.3	8.3
East Germany	6.4	5.5	6.3	7.4	7.8
Czechoslovakia	6.3	6.9	6.3	6.3	6.2
Poland	8.3	8.0	10.8	11.0	12.7
Hungary	6.1	5.0	5.6	6.7	...
Romania	11.8	11.5	11.7	14.7	...
Bulgaria	11.2	9.5	8.0	10.6	8.1

*Yearly average percentages.
†First six months.
Source: National statistics.

Table II. Output of Basic Industrial Products in Eastern Europe in 1973

In thousands of metric tons except for natural gas and electric power

Country	Hard coal	Brown coal	Natural gas (million cu.m.)	Crude petroleum	Electric power (million kw-hr.)	Steel	Sulfuric acid	Cement
U.S.S.R.	462,000	204,000	236,000	421,000	915,000	131,000	14,844	109,500
Poland	156,600	38,000	6,000	400	84,300	14,100	2,914	15,500
East Germany	800	246,200	—	—	76,900	5,892	1,058	9,548
Czechoslovakia	27,800	85,000	1,100	...	53,500	13,200	1,209	8,400
Romania	7,200	17,600	29,238	14,287	46,720	8,161	1,311	9,848
Hungary	3,400	23,400	4,813	1,989	17,635	3,332	648	3,405
Bulgaria	400	28,400	—	200	21,952	2,246	561	4,200
Totals	658,200	642,600	277,151	437,876	1,216,007	177,931	22,545	160,401

Table III. Foreign Trade of Eastern Europe

In $000,000

Country	Exports 1960	Exports 1970	Exports 1973	Imports 1960	Imports 1970	Imports 1973
U.S.S.R.	5,564	12,799	21,159	5,628	11,731	20,809
East Germany	2,207	4,577	7,504	2,195	4,843	7,836
Poland	1,326	3,548	6,432	1,495	3,608	7,862
Czechoslovakia	1,929	3,792	5,912	1,816	3,695	5,993
Hungary	874	2,316	4,316	952	2,464	3,767
Romania	717	1,850	3,729	648	1,959	3,496
Bulgaria	572	2,004	3,293	633	1,831	3,251
Totals	13,189	30,886	52,345	13,367	30,131	53,014
Percentages of world trade	10.3%	9.9%	9.5%	9.9%	9.2%	9.2%

Source: National statistics.

started from the Medvezhye fields near the estuary of the Ob River. The gas was to travel to other European countries through the "Northern Light" pipeline, which would serve not only Czechoslovakia but also Austria, East and West Germany, and Italy.

The "Friendship" (Druzhba) oil pipeline, already extended eastward from Almetyevsk in Bashkiria to Samotlor in the Tyumen region, was doubled westward to Mozyr in Belorussia. From there, two branches, also doubled, ran to Poland and East Germany and to Czechoslovakia and Hungary.

Soviet crude petroleum production in 1973 reached 421 million metric tons, of which about 100 million tons were exported. Of these about 43 million metric tons went through the "Friendship" pipeline, 11 million to Plock (Pol.), 17 million to Schwedt (E.Ger.), 10 million to Hrdlo near Bratislava (Czech.), and 5 million to Szazhalombatta (Hung.). Romania's consumption of crude petroleum was covered by its own production (14.3 million metric tons in 1973) and some 3 million imported from the Middle East. Bulgaria received in 1973 approximately 8.5 million metric tons of crude, half of it from the U.S.S.R., by tankers plying between Mirny in the Crimea and Varna, and half from the Middle East. As oil consumption both in the U.S.S.R. and in its European allies had been constantly growing, the Soviet government had in 1966 informed CMEA members that after 1970 it might be unable to cover all their requirements, and advised them to seek additional supplies from the Organization of Petroleum Exporting Countries (OPEC). In consequence a number of deals had been concluded, mainly with Middle Eastern countries. By 1972 about 8.5 million metric tons of crude had been imported, mainly from Iraq and Iran to Bulgaria (4.6 million), East Germany (3.4 million), and Hungary (500,000). In 1973 Poland and Czechoslovakia also began to import oil from the OPEC countries. In that year Poland imported only 570,000 metric tons from these sources, but this figure was expected to rise considerably by mid-1975 when the North Port near Gdansk would be ready to receive tankers and a new refinery would be completed there.

The Soviet leaders and political commentators saw in the high prices of crude oil and oil products an additional cause of economic recession and political crisis in the West. Aleksey N. Kosygin, the Soviet premier, addressing the 25th anniversary CMEA meeting in Sofia, spoke of the capitalist leaders' inability to understand why the socialist countries had no "crisis" of confidence and no clashes of contradictory interests or rivalry.

Until 1973 the CMEA countries ignored the European Economic Community (EEC) and stuck to the principle of bilateral commercial agreements. After the CMEA Sofia session in June 1974 Faddeyev suggested in Brussels that a meeting between him and François-Xavier Ortoli, president of the European Commission, would be useful. In November the EEC secretariat informed the CMEA headquarters in Moscow that the way for a Faddeyev-Ortoli meeting should be prepared by a lower-level discussion on possible cooperation. At the same time, the European Commission wrote to all Eastern European countries that it was ready to negotiate and conclude with them long-term multilateral commercial agreements. Meetings between officials of the CMEA's International Investment Bank and the EEC's European Investment Bank took place in Luxembourg early in December. Following the decision of the UN General Assembly to grant observer status to the CMEA, Faddeyev arrived in New York at the end of November at the invitation of Kurt Waldheim, the UN secretary-general. (K. M. SMOGORZEWSKI)

See also Communist Movement.
[534.F.3.b.vi]

Space Exploration

The year 1974, with the exception of Skylab, was generally a dull one in the history of manned space exploration. Unmanned satellites visited Venus, Mercury, and Jupiter during the year, however, providing a wealth of information not previously obtained. The successful transit of Jupiter by Pioneer 11 also gave promise of data on Saturn's rings when the spacecraft reaches that planet in 1979.

As the age of astronautics advanced, several of its pioneers vanished from the scene, some voluntarily and some otherwise. On March 8, Alan Shepard, America's first man in space, announced his retirement from the U.S. space program. He had made the first U.S. venture into space aboard a Mercury spacecraft on May 5, 1961. He did not orbit the earth as had Yury Gagarin of the Soviet Union. Indeed, Shepard spent only 15 minutes in the weightlessness of a suborbital flight designed to see whether an astronaut could function under such conditions. Subsequently removed from flight status because of an inner ear disorder, Shepard spent six years as chief of the

Jupiter's giant Red Spot and the shadow of Io, one of Jupiter's moons, as photographed by Pioneer 10 from a distance of 2.5 million km. Valuable data on the Jovian composition, atmospheric conditions, and magnetic field were obtained by the unmanned spacecraft.

COURTESY, NASA

The Soviet Soyuz 15 rocket at launch in August. It carried two cosmonauts to the Salyut 3 space laboratory, but an equipment failure prevented a successful docking.

astronaut office at the Lyndon B. Johnson Space Center, selecting his astronaut comrades for missions in the Mercury, Gemini, and Apollo programs. On his own initiative, he undertook treatment of his condition until he was able to pass the flight physical examination, and in 1971 he became the fifth astronaut to walk upon the surface of the moon.

Four days before the announcement that Shepard was retiring, Mikhail K. Tikhonravov died in Moscow. A pioneer in the technological development of rocketry in the Soviet Union from the early 1930s, Tikhonravov had worked with Sergey P. Korolev, the systems engineer who brought the resources of the U.S.S.R. together to produce the Vostok spacecraft and put it into orbit before the U.S. could mount its manned space effort.

In the fall of the year one of the last of the German scientists who had cast their lot with the Americans after World War II decided to retire from his service to the U.S. Kurt H. Debus, who had been director of the John F. Kennedy Space Center, announced his retirement.

Manned Spaceflight. The third and final manned Skylab mission ended on February 8 after a record 84 days in space when U.S. astronauts Gerald Carr, Edward Gibson, and William Pogue landed their Apollo command module in the Pacific. The three had performed scientific experiments in the orbiting Skylab workshop, focusing instruments on the sun and the earth's surface. The Skylab workshop remained in orbit but was deprived of power and life-sustaining atmosphere.

The Soviet Union launched three manned space missions during the year. Soyuz 14 lifted off from the space complex at Tyuratam on July 3, with cosmonauts Pavel R. Popovich, who had previously flown on Vostok 4 in 1962, and Yury P. Artyukhin, who was making his first mission. They docked with the Salyut 3 space station, launched on June 25, and entered it for a 15-day stay aboard the vehicle. During their tour, the pair performed many medical tests, biological experiments, and earth observations. A series of solar flares on July 4–8 caused mission controllers in Kalinin, near Moscow, to consider canceling the mission; however, the cosmonauts were in no danger because of the relatively low altitude of the Salyut.

Several hours before their planned return to the earth, the two cosmonauts began preparing the Salyut for its next occupants. Once the space station was in order, they returned to their Soyuz 14 spacecraft, undocked from the Salyut, and reentered the earth's atmosphere. They landed at a spot approximately 87 mi. SE of Dzhezkazgan, in Kazakhstan, in good physical shape, on July 19.

On August 26, Soyuz 15 was launched from Tyuratam with cosmonauts Lev Demin and Gennady Sarafanov, both space rookies, aboard. However, they failed to achieve a docking with the Salyut because of equipment failure. Soyuz 16, manned by Anatoly V. Filipshenko and Nikolay N. Rukavishnikov, was launched from the Baikonur space centre on December 2. The major purpose of the mission, which lasted six days, was to serve as a rehearsal for the Apollo/Soyuz Test Project (ASTP), the joint Soviet-U.S. manned mission scheduled for July 1975.

Both the U.S. and the Soviet Union continued to work on the ASTP. On April 15 a group of 75 Soviet personnel, including 4 cosmonauts, arrived at the Johnson Space Center for negotiations on the joint space mission. In turn, a 12-man U.S. team journeyed to the Soviet Union on June 23 for a similar mission. They were the first to stay in the newly completed hotel at Zvezdnoy Gorodok (Star City), the Soviet cosmonaut training centre in northeast Moscow. Joint crew training took place at the centre from June 23 until July 15. An additional joint training program took place at the Johnson Center, September 9–30. An agreement was reached that Soviet engineers and flight crew would visit Kennedy Space Center in February 1975, while a reciprocal visit for U.S. personnel to the Soviet launch site at Tyuratam was to be made in May 1975.

In early September the Apollo spacecraft for the mission was shipped to the Kennedy Space Center to begin a series of tests. The U.S. docking mechanism that permits the Apollo to join the Soyuz was checked out in August and was shipped to the U.S.S.R. in October for mating tests with its Soviet counterpart. At Kennedy Space Center, plans were under way to begin preparing the Saturn IB launch vehicle on Jan. 15, 1975.

Unmanned Satellites. A number of significant satellite launchings by various countries took place during the year. The ERTS 1, launched in 1972, provided the most controversial news. On February 21, Sen. Frank Moss (Dem., Utah) announced that photographs taken by the satellite might corroborate the existence of Noah's Ark on Mt. Ararat, in Turkey. He did so at the 12th Conference on Survey, Mapping, and Remote Sensing, held in Salt Lake City.

Moss stated that photographs made by the satellite from an altitude of 550 mi. "show a formation at the lower end of the satellite's resolution capability which appears to be foreign to other materials found on the mountain."

The year 1973 had ended with the launching of Explorer 51, a scientific satellite with the lowest perigee ever experienced by a U.S. craft. The orbit was designed so that the satellite would reach a low point of 98 mi. and a distant point of 2,672 mi. in order to investigate the thermosphere, a little-known region of the earth's upper atmosphere and one previously probed only by a few sounding rockets. By placing the satellite in such an elliptic orbit, scientists reduced considerably the drag of the atmosphere on it in comparison with that which would occur if the orbit were a circle with a radius of 90 mi. Thus, Explorer 51 could dip into the atmosphere, make its measurements, and then race out again. It was equipped with 14 experiments to study the thermosphere, the region in which ultraviolet radiation from the sun and chemical components of the earth's atmosphere interact. Most of the instruments measured the concentration and energy contents of ions, atoms, and molecules. The purpose was to learn more about the processes of energy transfer in the thermosphere, processes that play a major role in the earth's weather.

On April 13 the U.S. launched its first domestic communications satellite, which was owned by the Western Union Corp. Commercial traffic did not begin, however, until July 16. The previous day, Russell W. McFall, president of the company, had initiated the service. Using the original telegraph key of Samuel Morse, borrowed from the Smithsonian Institution for the event, he sent the first message from New York to Los Angeles. It read: "What hath God wrought!"—the same as the first telegraph message sent by wire on May 24, 1844. Five ground stations throughout the U.S. serviced the satellite, which could transmit voice, video, and graphic data.

A new type of weather satellite made its appearance over the U.S. on May 17. Named Synchronous Meteorological Satellite 1 (SMS 1), it was orbited at an altitude of approximately 22,000 mi. over the Atlantic in a position where it could view North and South America as well as western Africa. Its cameras provided 72 hours of constant coverage of the area in two-minute film clips. The satellite was also designed to provide weather data at night and was specifically engineered to seek out hurricanes and conditions that might lead to tornadoes, a mission that it accomplished several times during the year.

On May 30, Applications Technology Satellite 6 (ATS 6) was launched from the Kennedy Space Center and went into synchronous orbit over the Galápagos Islands. It featured a 30-ft.-diameter antenna that deployed after the satellite reached orbit. With the new antenna, the ATS 6 could relay television signals ten times higher in frequency than those of commercial TV channels. Among the tasks set for the satellite were providing educational programs for countries such as India and a communications relay for the forthcoming ASTP mission. The Soviet Union launched its first synchronous communications satellite on July 29, when Molniya 1S was orbited.

A truly multinational space effort took place on October 14 when the Italians launched a British satellite using a U.S. rocket. UK-5, a small scientific satellite, was launched by a Scout from the San Marco facility in Ngwana Bay off the coast of Kenya.

Interplanetary Probes. Mariner 10 was launched on Nov. 3, 1973, for an encounter with a planet never before visited by such a probe from earth. Its target was Mercury, innermost of the sun's natural satellites, which it would visit after first swinging by Venus. On Feb. 5, 1974, Mariner 10 approached within 3,600 mi. of the surface of Venus. Its two cameras photographed the turbulent clouds of the planet's upper atmosphere, and instruments on board probed the dense atmosphere. The gravitational field of the planet swung the probe past it and sped it on toward Mercury.

The 3,400 pictures of Venus taken by Mariner 10 revealed three distinct layers in the planet's atmosphere. The extreme turbulence of the atmosphere showed patterns that scientists said were similar to circulation flows on the earth. Some of the features revealed were jet streams moving at velocities of 220 mph above the Equator, which caused the atmosphere to rotate approximately 50 times faster than does the planet.

Scientific instruments aboard Mariner 10 revealed that Venus has no sensible magnetic field, thereby permitting the solar wind to impinge directly on the planet's atmosphere. They also showed that at an altitude of about 37 mi. above its surface Venus has an atmospheric density similar to that of the earth at an altitude of 40,000 ft. Others showed that oxygen, helium, and carbon dioxide are present in the upper levels of the atmosphere. The planet also appears to be more nearly spherical than the earth.

Mariner 10 flew past Mercury on March 29 and returned photographs of a cratered and pockmarked planet that superficially looked like the moon. But detailed investigation showed features that were unexpected. A large scarp appeared to run for hundreds of miles southward across the planet from its northern hemisphere. Another view showed a huge circular basin approximately 800 mi. in diameter. Crater floors were pocked and "worm-eaten," unlike those on the moon which generally have a central peak.

Most startling were the views of the planet made as the probe approached and left it. On the approach, the surface appeared to vary little and the albedo (fraction of incident light that is reflected) was more or less uniform. In these photographs Mercury resembles the lunar highlands and has no large basins. On the outward bound photographs, there are at least three very large basins and variation in albedo. Also, there are two very prominent large craters with rays, like Tycho on the moon.

After leaving Mercury, the probe suffered a mishap —its tape recorder jammed. However, pictures could still be transmitted at the rate of one every 42 seconds. In May course corrections were made to ensure that the probe would reapproach Mercury at a distance of about 30,000 mi., a height that would be optimum for its long-focal-length lenses. Also, the approach would be from the sunlit side rather than the dark side, as was the case with its first visit.

On September 21, Mariner 10 returned to Mercury and switched on its television cameras to begin taking the first of some 600 pictures. The probe passed over the planet's south pole, taking pictures of features as small as 0.6 mi. In one of these a fresh crater with rays extending from it was clearly visible. Others showed the entire length of the scarp seen in pictures of the first encounter. It has a length of 185 mi., and is about 1 mi. high. Other scarps also were seen. As a result of the random orientation of the scarps, scientists conjectured that they were formed by surface compression.

Pioneer 10, which had been launched on March 2, 1972, reached its target on Dec. 3, 1973, when it approached Jupiter. The probe actually reached the Jovian environment on November 26 when it crossed the bow shock wave formed where the planet's magnetosphere bounds that of interplanetary space. It occurred at a distance of 108 Jupiter radii. Pioneer 10 measurements indicated that the magnetic field strength at the surface of the planet was 4 gauss, a value about eight times greater than that of the earth.

As it approached the planet, Pioneer 10 crossed through the radiation belt surrounding it. The latter was 10,000 times more intense than the earth's similar Van Allen Belts. Infrared sensors aboard the probe indicated that Jupiter emits three times the radiation it receives from the sun. Other sensors measured

Full-scale models of the U.S. Apollo and Soviet Soyuz spacecraft in the linked position they will try to attain during the joint mission in mid-1975.

WIDE WORLD

helium in the atmosphere as well as hydrogen, ammonia, methane, and traces of gases such as acetylene and ethylene. The infrared radiometer data suggested that there was little difference in the temperature of the dark side of the planet and the sunlit side.

Information gained from Pioneer 10 indicates that Jupiter has a very small rocky core surrounded by liquid metallic hydrogen, liquid hydrogen, and gaseous hydrogen. The outer atmosphere, in addition to hydrogen, contains some 17% helium.

Having swung past Jupiter, Pioneer 10 headed for the orbit of Pluto and a trajectory that would take it out of the solar system. Some millions of years from now it may enter the constellation Taurus. If it survives and encounters intelligent life there, its finders may be able to decipher a small plaque on its side. Pictorially, it tells where the craft came from, when the machine began its voyage, and what people on the earth look like.

Pioneer 11 was launched April 5, 1973 and arrived

Major Satellites and Space Probes Launched Oct. 1, 1973–Sept. 30, 1974

Name/country/ launch vehicle/ scientific designation	Launch date, lifetime*	Physical characteristics					Orbital elements			
		Weight in kg.†	Shape	Diameter in m.†	Length or height in m.†	Experiments	Perigee in km.†	Apogee in km.†	Period (min.)	Inclination to Equator (degrees)
Molniya 2G/U.S.S.R./A IIe/ 1973–076A	10/19/73	1,250 (2,756)	Cylinder with conical ends and six panels	1.6 (5.25)	4.2 (13.78)	Communications satellite	503 (313)	39,860 (24,769)	717.9	62.8
Explorer 50/U.S./Delta/ 1973–078A	10/26/73	371 (818)	Sixteen-sided drum	1.35 (4.42)	1.58 (5.17)	Scientific satellite to investigate earth's radiation environment	197.5 (122.7)	228,808 (142,181)	17,286	28.7
Intercosmos 10/U.S.S.R./ B I/1973–082A	10/30/73	1,100 (2,425)	Octagon and octagonal pyramid with eight panels	1.1 (3.61)	2.5 (8.2)	Scientific satellite with experiments provided by East Germany and Czechoslovakia	259 (161)	1,454 (904)	102.1	74
Mariner 10/U.S./Atlas Centaur/1973–085A	11/3/73	503 (1,109)	Octagon with two solar panels	1.38 (4.54)	0.46 (1.5)	Seven scientific instruments, including television camera, to study Mercury	Mercury flyby trajectory			
NOAA 3/U.S./Delta/ 1973–086A	11/6/73	409 (902)	Cube with three rectangular solar panels	1 (3.28)	1.2 (3.94)	Scientific satellite to measure solar proton flux and radiometers to measure temperatures on earth's surface during day and night	1,500 (932)	1,509.2 (937.8)	116.1	102.1
Molniya 1/U.S.S.R./A IIe/ 1973–089A	11/14/73	1,000 (2,205)	Cylinder with conical ends and six panels	1.6 (5.25)	3.4 (11.15)	Communications satellite	566 (352)	39,798 (24,730)	717.9	64.8
Skylab 4/U.S./Saturn 1B/ 1973–090A 2/8/74	11/16/73	30,844 (68,000)	Cylinder with conical end	3.9 (12.8)	10.82 (35.5)	Carried final crew to Skylab space station	148.2 (92.1)	223.3 (138.8)	93.2	50
Molniya 1/U.S.S.R./A IIe/ 1973–097A	11/30/73	1,000 (2,205)	Cylinder with conical ends and six panels	1.6 (5.25)	3.4 (11.15)	Communications satellite	618 (384)	40,830 (25,372)	740	62.9
Explorer 51/U.S./Delta 1973–101A	12/16/73	658 (1,450)	Drum	1.35 (4.42)	1.14 (3.75)	Scientific satellite carrying 14 instruments to study solar ultraviolet radiation and other phenomena	157 (98)	4,300 (2,672)	132.5	68.1
Soyuz 13/U.S.S.R./A II/ 1973–103A 12/26/73	12/18/73	6,600 (14,551)	Sphere and cylinder	3.1 (10.17)	10.7 (35.1)	Test of Soyuz spacecraft	188 (117)	246 (153)	88.9	51.6
Molniya 2H/U.S.S.R./A IIe/ 1973–106A	12/25/73	1,250 (2,756)	Cylinder with cone and six panels	1.6 (5.25)	4.2 (13.78)	Communications satellite	488 (303)	40,809 (25,359)	736.9	62.8
Oreol 2/U.S.S.R./C I/ 1973–107A	12/26/73	550 (1,213)	‡	‡	‡	Joint French-Soviet scientific satellite to study polar lights and upper atmosphere	399 (248)	1,974 (1,227)	109.1	73.9
Skynet 2A/U.K./Delta/ 1974–002A 1/28/74	1/18/74	129 (285)	Cylinder	1.37 (4.5)	0.81 (2.67)	Communications satellite	95 (59)	3,406 (2,116)	121.6	37.6
Tansei 2/Japan/Mu 3c/ 1974–008A	2/16/74	63 (138)	Sphere	0.69 (2.26)		Scientific satellite to test launch vehicle and provide data on upper atmosphere	283 (176)	3,229 (2,007)	121.7	31.2
San Marco 4/Italy/Scout/ 1974–009A	2/18/74	168 (370)	Sphere	0.76 (2.5)		Scientific satellite to measure effects of solar magnetic storms on earth's thermosphere and ionosphere	244 (152)	917 (570)	96.3	2.9
UK-X4/U.K./Scout/ 1974–013A	3/9/74	129 (285)	Cylinder	0.76 (2.5)	0.91 (3)	Telescopically deployed solar cells; first U.K. satellite with three-axis stabilization and attitude control	712 (442)	918 (570)	101.1	97.8
Westar 1/U.S./Delta/ 1974–022A	4/13/74	574 (1,265)	Cylinder	1.83 (6)	1.65 (5.4)	Domestic communications satellite	35,785 (22,237)	35,792 (22,241)	1,436.2	0.0
Molniya 1/U.S.S.R./A II/ 1974–023A	4/20/74	1,000 (2,205)	Cylinder with conical ends and six panels	1.6 (5.25)	3.4 (11.15)	Communications satellite	625 (388)	39,731 (24,689)	717.7	62.9
Meteor 17/U.S.S.R./A II/ 1974–025A	4/24/74	‡	Cylinder with two panels	1.5 (4.92)	5 (16.4)	Meteorological satellite	863 (536)	896 (557)	102.5	81.2
Molniya 2I/U.S.S.R./A IIe/ 1974–026A	4/26/74	1,250 (2,756)	Cylinder with conical ends and six panels	1.6 (5.25)	4.2 (13.78)	Communications satellite	401 (249)	39,955 (24,828)	717.8	62.8
SMS 1/U.S./Delta/ 1974–033A	5/17/74	286 (630)	Cylinder	‡	‡	Meteorological satellite	35,729 (22,202)	35,840 (22,271)	1,436	2
Intercosmos 11/U.S.S.R./C I/ 1974–034A	5/17/74	1,100 (2,425)	Octagon and octagonal pyramid with eight panels	1.1 (3.61)	2.5 (8.21)	Scientific satellite to study upper atmosphere	483 (300)	511 (318)	94.5	50.6
Luna 22/U.S.S.R./D Ie/ 1974–037A	5/29/74	‡	‡	‡	‡	Study lunar surface features and gravitational field	Moon orbit			
ATS 6/U.S./Titan IIIC/ 1974–039A	5/30/74	1,400 3,100	Box with two paddles	0.59 (1.92)	1.47 (4.83)	Educational television and navigational satellite	35,779 (22,233)	35,785 (22,237)	1,435.9	1.7
Hawkeye/U.S./Scout/ 1974–040A	6/3/74	27.22 (60)	Cone and cylinder	0.76 (2.5)	0.76 (2.5)	Scientific satellite to investigate interaction of solar wind with earth's magnetic field near the north polar cap	638 (396)	126,793 (78,789)	3,078.1	89.8
Salyut 3/U.S.S.R./Proton/ 1974–046A	6/25/74	18,960 (41,800)	Cylinder	4 (13.12)	10 (32.81)	Testing changes made to Salyut since 1973	219 (136)	270 (168)	89.1	51.6
Soyuz 14/U.S.S.R./A II/ 1974–051A 7/19/74	7/3/74	6,600 (14,551)	Sphere and cylinder	3.1 (10.17)	10.7 (35.1)	Carried crew to Salyut space station	201 (125)	338 (210)	89.9	51.5
Meteor 18/U.S.S.R./A I/ 1974–052A	7/9/74	‡	Cylinder with two panels	1.5 (4.92)	5 (16.4)	Meteorological satellite	861 (535)	895 (556)	102.5	81.2
Aeros 2/West Germany/ Scout/1974–055A	7/16/74	127 (280)	Cylinder	0.91 (2.99)	0.74 (2.43)	Scientific satellite to investigate physics of upper atmosphere	220 (137)	807 (501)	94.8	97.4
Molniya 2J/U.S.S.R./A IIe/ 1974–056A	7/23/74	1,250 (2,756)	Cylinder with conical ends and six panels	1.6 (5.25)	4.2 (13.78)	Communications satellite	526 (327)	39,840 (24,757)	717.9	63
Molniya 1/U.S.S.R./A IIe/ 1974–060A	7/29/74	1,000 (2,205)	Cylinder with conical ends and six panels	1.6 (5.25)	3.4 (11.15)	Communications satellite	35,787 (22,238)	35,790 (22,240)	1,436.2	0.0
Soyuz 15/U.S.S.R./A II/ 1974–067A 8/28/74	8/26/74	6,600 (14,551)	Sphere and cylinder	3.1 (10.17)	10.7 (34.1)	Carried crew to Salyut space station	188 (117)	210 (130)	88.5	51.6
ANS/The Netherlands/ Scout/1974/070A	8/30/74	135 (298)	Box with two solar panels	0.61 (2)	1.45 (4.75)	Scientific satellite to survey stars that are two to three times hotter than the sun	254 (158)	1,167 (725)	99	98.1

*All dates are in universal time (UT).
†English units in parentheses; weight in pounds, dimensions in feet, apogee and perigee in statute miles.
‡Not available.

(MITCHELL R. SHARPE)

at Jupiter in early December 1974. It came within about 26,600 mi. of the planet's cloud tops, three times closer than Pioneer 10. Although it passed through intense radiation, which caused its electronic systems to mimic radio commands from the earth, Pioneer 11 emerged relatively unscathed from its close flyby. It returned clear images of Jupiter's north polar region and detected a polar icecap on Callisto, the planet's second largest moon.

Pioneer 11 had been retargeted in flight in March 1974 so that it would swing past Jupiter and move on to Saturn, thus becoming the first probe to reach that planet. Arrival was anticipated in September 1979.

Soviet probes also made the news during the period. The Mars 4, 5, 6, and 7 probes launched in July and August 1973 reached the vicinity of Mars in February and March. Mars 4 and 5 arrived on February 10 and 12, respectively. The braking rocket on the former did not function, and Mars 4 continued past the planet. Mars 5, however, entered an orbit about the planet on the latter date. A descent probe from Mars 6 landed on the surface of the planet on March 12, but communications with it were lost just before it landed. A lander from Mars 7, launched from orbit around the planet on March 9, missed Mars by 780 mi.

On May 29, 1974, Luna 22 was launched from Tyuratam for the moon. It entered lunar orbit on June 2. Circling at 132 mi. altitude, it took television photographs of the surface until June 9 when the orbit was changed to an elliptic one of 14 mi. by 146 mi. That orbit was circularized on June 13 to 179 mi. by 108 mi. so that the probe could make studies of the moon's gravitational field. Luna 23 was launched on October 28. Sent to explore the moon's surface and "near-moon space," it entered an orbit ranging from 59 to 65 mi. above the surface on November 2.

Launch Vehicles and Space Shuttle. On Feb. 11, 1974, the Titan IIIE Centaur made its first flight. Launched from the Kennedy Space Center, the flight failed when the Centaur stage did not ignite after the Titan stage burned out and separated. Trouble was traced to the liquid oxygen pump in the Centaur, which failed to operate. There were fears that the malfunction would delay the launching by Titan IIIE Centaurs of an Intelsat communications satellite in November and a Helios solar probe in December. However, corrections were made to the Centaur equipment, and both payloads were launched without delay.

The National Aeronautics and Space Administration announced that about 25 pilots would be needed to fly the space shuttle between 1980 and 1991. Sixteen of the 32 astronauts currently employed were to be used in the early phases of shuttle crew training.

A European project closely tied to the fortunes of the space shuttle was Spacelab. The European Space Research Organization (ESRO) had undertaken to develop the $315 million manned space laboratory that would fit into the cargo bay of the shuttle orbiter. ESRO asked for bids on the laboratory, and a contract was awarded to VFW-Fokker/ERNO in June.

Spacelab as conceived by its designers would permit men to work in a shirt-sleeve environment for a period of one week in orbit. The laboratory would have an enclosed section for experiments not requiring the space environment, and an open section for those that did. It would be accessible through an airlock to scientists dressed in spacesuits.

Although Soviet scientists publicly stated that the U.S.S.R. would develop a space shuttle similar to that of the U.S., such plans might be more fanciful than

factual. The Soviets were still trying to bring to flight status their large, Saturn-class rocket booster, which had been under development and redesign since it blew up on the launching pad at Tyuratam in the summer of 1969. The three-stage, 10 million-lb.-thrust vehicle seemed a step nearer when the Soviets began modifying its static test stand at Tyuratam.

Japan hoped to launch 65 satellites between 1978 and 1987. Launches between 1982 and 1987 would use a hybrid Japanese-U.S. rocket booster, consisting of the U.S. Delta first stage and two Japanese-built upper stages. The first launch of this booster was expected to be in 1975. (MITCHELL R. SHARPE)

See also Astronomy; Defense; Earth Sciences; Industrial Production and Technology; Telecommunications; Television and Radio.

[738.C.2–5]

ENCYCLOPÆDIA BRITANNICA FILMS. *Man Looks at the Moon* (1971); *Space Exploration: A Team Effort* (1972); *Controversy over the Moon* (1973).

Mockup of America's space shuttle, which may be used to transport cargo to and from the earth in 1979.

Spain

A nominal monarchy of southwest Europe, Spain is bounded by Portugal, with which it shares the Iberian Peninsula, and by France. Area: 194,885 sq.mi. (504,-750 sq.km.), including the Balearic and Canary islands. Pop. (1974 est.): 35,225,000, including the Balearics and Canaries. Cap. and largest city: Madrid (pop., 1973 est., 3,409,663). Language: Spanish. Religion: Roman Catholic. Prince of Spain and king-designate, Don Juan Carlos de Borbón y Borbón; chiefs of state in 1974, Gen. Francisco Franco Bahamonde and, from July 19 to September 2, Prince Juan Carlos; premier, Carlos Arias Navarro.

The year 1974 began with the appointment by Arias Navarro (*see* BIOGRAPHY) of a new Cabinet, notable for the virtual exclusion of members of Opus Dei. During the year the premier gained the reputation of being an independent-minded hard-liner who was prepared to allow gradual progress toward greater political freedom provided law and order were not threatened. His first major policy speech, delivered to the Cortes on February 12, included four innovations: a law providing for all mayors and other senior local government officials to be elected rather than appointed; a decree revising the constitution of the Cortes so that a larger proportion of its members would be popularly elected; reform of the state-controlled trade-union organizations to give workers more bargaining power; and a law allowing the right of political association. The speech was interpreted by some as heralding the opening out of political life, and the phrase "the spirit of February 12" was coined.

Hooded men claim responsibility for the death of Spanish Premier Luis Carrero Blanco at a press conference near Bordeaux, France. Photos on the wall are of militant Basques who have died in clashes with the Spanish police.

The government's susceptibility to opposition, direct or implicit, was heightened by the overthrow of Premier Marcello Caetano of Portugal at the end of April. Much attention centred on the chief of the joint chiefs of staff, Gen. Manuel Díez Alegría, who had gained a reputation as a liberal after it was widely rumoured that he had successfully argued against the imposition of martial law following the assassination of Adm. Luis Carrero Blanco in 1973. In June, General Díez Alegría was summarily dismissed, but the prospect of political change acquired fresh immediacy when ill health obliged General Franco temporarily (July 19–September 2) to cede the role of chief of state to Prince Juan Carlos. The interlude produced a crystallization of political groups: on July 30 the Democratic Junta was launched in Paris under the sponsorship of the Spanish Communist Party, and the formation of the Spanish Social Democratic Union (USDE) was announced in Madrid on October 17 by a group of prominent professional figures, the first time a new party had been declared publicly in Spain. On September 13 terrorists exploded a bomb near the national security police headquarters in Madrid, killing 12 persons and wounding 70.

The determination to maintain law and order was displayed in the handling of political activists. Salvador Puig Antich, a member of the left-wing Iberian Liberation Movement, who had been found guilty of killing a policeman when resisting arrest on a charge of bank robbery, was executed by garroting at Barcelona prison on March 2. He was the first political extremist to suffer the death penalty since 1963, and his case prompted numerous appeals for clemency and protests from both within Spain and abroad. Against this background, the bishop of Bilbao, Msgr. Antonio Añoveros, authorized a homily drawing attention to the problem of the rights of the Basques to be read in the churches of his diocese on February 24. The bishop and the vicar-general of the diocese were placed under virtual house arrest, but the Vatican rejected the government's proposal that Msgr. Añoveros be transferred to another diocese and that bishops should submit an advance text of any sermon touching on "temporal" questions. An agreed statement was then issued affirming the right of bishops to comment on such matters and pointing out that the bishop of Bilbao had not advocated separatism. On December 11 a "Day of Basque Unity" combined with a general strike was widely supported throughout the Basque regions.

Internal political uncertainty, together with the coups in Portugal, Cyprus, and Greece, caused a deterioration in Spain's standing in the Mediterranean area. Morocco took this opportunity to initiate a diplomatic campaign (backed by veiled threats of joint Arab action against Spain and a claim by Mauritania) to press demands that Spain give up its colony of Spanish Sahara. The prime ministers of the two countries met in Madrid in mid-August, and on August 21 the Spanish government announced that a referendum on independence would be held in Spanish Sahara in the first half of 1975 under UN auspices.

The regime was unwilling to curb the economic growth that had contributed so much to its political success in recent years, and for much of the year policy concentrated on sustaining a high growth rate at the expense of controlling inflation. Private estimates put the real growth of the gross national product between the first half of 1973 and the same period of 1974 at 6.2%, compared with an increase of 8.5% between the corresponding periods of 1972 and 1973. On the other hand, despite the imposition of a freeze

SPAIN

Education. (1972–73) Primary, pupils 5,261,920, teachers 176,242; secondary, pupils 1,274,097, teachers 60,925; vocational, pupils 385,498, teachers 23,074; teacher training, students 45,531, teachers 2,121; higher (including 27 universities), students 267,628, teaching staff 18,268.

Finance. Monetary unit: peseta, with (Sept. 16, 1974) a free rate of 57.54 pesetas to U.S. $1 (133.12 pesetas = £1 sterling). Gold, SDRs, and convertible currencies, central bank: (June 1974) U.S. $5,976,000,000; (June 1973) U.S. $5,646,000,000. Budget (1973 actual): revenue 499.1 billion pesetas; expenditure 503.7 billion pesetas. Gross national product: (1972) 2,961,000,000,000; (1971) 2,539,000,000,000 pesetas. Money supply: (April 1974) 1,324,900,000,000 pesetas; (April 1973) 1,042,800,000,000 pesetas. Cost of living (1970 = 100): (June 1974) 149; (June 1973) 130.

Foreign Trade. (1973) Imports 557.2 billion pesetas; exports 302.8 billion pesetas. Import sources: EEC 43% (West Germany 14%, France 10%, U.K. 6%, Italy 6%); U.S. 16%; Saudi Arabia 5%. Export destinations: EEC 48% (France 13%, West Germany 12%, U.K. 8%, The Netherlands 6%, Italy 5%); U.S. 14%. Main exports: machinery 10%; fruit 8%; iron and steel 6%; textiles 6%; ships and boats 5%;

footwear 5%; motor vehicles 5%; chemicals 5%. Tourism (1972): visitors 32,506,600; receipts U.S. $2,511,000,000.

Transport and Communications. Roads (1973) 142,136 km. (including 807 km. expressways). Motor vehicles in use (1973): passenger 3,803,700; commercial 887,980. Railways: (1972) 16,345 km. (including 3,771 km. electrified); traffic (1973) 15,650,000,000 passenger-km., freight 11,564,000,000 net ton-km. Air traffic (1973): 9,574,000,000 passenger-km.; freight 193,447,000 net ton-km. Shipping (1973): merchant vessels 100 gross tons and over 2,420; gross tonnage 4,833,048. Telephones (Dec. 1972) 5,713,000. Radio receivers (Dec. 1971) 7,174,000. Television receivers (Dec. 1972) 5,019,000.

Agriculture. Production (in 000; metric tons; 1973; 1972 in parentheses): wheat 3,948 (4,562); barley 4,433 (4,358); oats 429 (440); rye 269 (263); corn 2,019 (1,921); potatoes 5,380 (5,121); rice 378 (329); sorghum 160 (177); dry broad beans (1972) 102, (1971) 128; other dry beans c. 126 (126); chick-peas 109 (82); tomatoes c. 2,300 (2,017); onions 935 (899); apples (1972) 695, (1971) 571; pears (1972) 403, (1971) 401; oranges (1972) 2,027, (1971) 1,771; mandarin oranges and tangerines (1972) 427, (1971) 374; lemons (1972) 165,

(1971) 110; sugar, raw value c. 910 (830); sunflower seed 299 (243); bananas (1972) c. 420, (1971) c. 420; figs (1972) c. 120, (1971) 118; olive oil 564 (491); wine 3,330 (2,645); tobacco 27 (27); cotton, lint 60 (56); meat (1972) 892, (1971) 934; fish catch (1972) 1,617, (1971) c. 1,550. Livestock (in 000; 1972–73): cattle 4,235; pigs 8,048; sheep 17,191; goats 2,368; horses 261; mules 409; asses 327; chickens c. 49,000.

Industry. Index of industrial production (1970 = 100): (1973) 140; (1972) 122. Fuel and power (in 000; metric tons; 1973): coal 9,914; lignite 2,998; crude oil (1972) 143; manufactured gas (cu.m.) 2,507,000; electricity (kw-hr.) 75,765,000. Production (in 000; metric tons; 1973): cement 22,235; iron ore (50% metal content) 6,901; pig iron 6,565; crude steel 10,675; aluminum 168; copper 123; lead 99; zinc 107; sulfur (1971) 1,138; petroleum products (1972) 35,659; sulfuric acid 2,294; fertilizers (nutrient content; 1972) nitrogenous 688, phosphate 631, potash 533; cotton yarn 85; cotton fabrics 78; wool yarn 38; rayon, etc., yarn and fibres 68; nylon, etc., yarn and fibres 133; passenger cars (units) 716; commercial vehicles (units) 107. Merchant vessels launched (100 gross tons and over; 1973) 1,554,000 gross tons.

on wages, prices, and dividends at the end of November 1973, the consumer price index rose faster in the first half of 1974 than in the same period of 1973, and wages increased at about the same rate.

Wage controls were removed in August, largely in response to mounting industrial unrest which had, moreover, spread to regions where labour relations were habitually quiescent. The inflationary situation, combined with higher expenditures on petroleum imports and declining income from tourism and from remittances of Spanish workers abroad, prompted the government to introduce a program of economic austerity in late October. The internal contradictions of this program, which was supposed to maintain full employment, increase production, and stimulate foreign investment while simultaneously stemming inflation and reducing the payments deficit, were sharply criticized by economists and businessmen.

The effect of the program was eclipsed almost immediately by General Franco's dismissal on October 29 of the minister of information and tourism, Pío Cabanillas, who had been responsible for allowing the press a freer hand. On the same day the minister of finance, Antonio Barrera de Irimo, resigned, ostensibly as a gesture of sympathy with his colleague. There followed a wave of resignations among the more progressive members of the regime. On December 20 the Cabinet issued a decree granting Spaniards freedom to form political associations within closely circumscribed limits. It was not expected that currently illegal organizations would be given legal status.

(JOAN PEARCE)

[972.A.5.a]

Speleology

When the connection between the Flint Ridge Cave System and Mammoth Cave in Kentucky was discovered in 1972, the combined length was 144.4 mi. Additional exploration and surveying revealed a total length of 156.9 mi.

In November 1973 cave explorers from Vienna discovered a small but difficult extension in the Mammuthöhle (Dachstein, Aus.). The two new sections included a 150-ft. climb and brought the total length of the system to 16.1 mi.; a large Austrian expedition explored the Lechnerweid Höhle to a total depth of 1,542 ft. and a length of 2.9 mi. A new cave called Anialarra was discovered on the Franco-Spanish border near Pierre Saint-Martin. The entrance was about 6,500 ft. above sea level and the cave approximately 1,345 ft. deep.

Arctomys Pot (British Columbia), discovered in 1912, was reexplored to a depth of 1,719 ft. where it ended in a sump. This made it the deepest cave in both Canada and the U.S. In Venezuela the Sociedad Venezolana de Espeleología explored in February the caves of Los González (320 ft. deep) and Bastimento (460 ft.), without reaching the end in either cave; a subsequent expedition by the Sociedad Venezolana de Ciencias Naturales explored a jungle area at the source of the River Caura, a tributary of the Orinoco, and among large caves explored were the Sima Humboldt (to a depth of 1,050 ft.) and the Sima Eduardo Alfred Martel (to 395 ft.); other expeditions were planned by groups from France, England, Poland, and Romania.

Discoveries made in Lancaster Hole (North Pennines, Eng.) brought the total length of the connected caves in the Easegill System to over 17 mi. If a connection could be established with the associated Pippikin Hole, the overall length would become more than 20 mi. After six years of digging in Mendip Hills, Somerset, Eng., the entrance of Thrupe Lane Swallet was cleared of mud and loose rock to reveal a new cave some 400 ft. deep.

The experienced British cave diver Roger Solari met his death while diving a new sump some two miles inside the cave of Agen Allwedd (South Wales). A Yugoslav diver was drowned in August while attempting to continue downstream from Tkalca jama cave (in the Cerknica drainage system, Slovenia) toward the major rising at Planina. New government regulations were issued in Yugoslavia which made it illegal for foreign speleologists to visit any caves there other than those open to the public, even if they were accompanied by local people.

The bicentennial of J. F. Esper's book *Ausführliche Nachricht von neu entdeckten Zoolithen . . .* fell in 1974. In it he questioned the belief then current that man was more recent than any extinct animal and also put forward some of the earliest reasoned theories of speleogenesis. New books published during 1974 included *The Limestones and Caves of North-West England*, edited by A. C. Waltham, a scientific treatment; *Slovenska Kraška Terminologija* by I. Gams, an international glossary of specialist karst and cave terms; and *American Caves and Caving* by W. R. Halliday, a textbook of exploring and rescue techniques.

(T. R. SHAW)

[232.C.10.c]

A massive stalagmite in New Cave, Carlsbad Caverns National Park, New Mexico. This particular part of the Carlsbad system provides visitors with an experience in cave exploration.

COURTESY, NATIONAL PARK SERVICE

Sporting Record

Rules concerning amateurism in the Olympic Games and equality for women in U.S. college athletic programs were among the major sports stories of 1974. Meeting in Vienna October 21–24, the International Olympic Committee (IOC) approved a revision of its Rule 26. Under the new ruling amateur athletes would be allowed compensation for financial losses incurred during absence from work in order to train. The time limit for training, 60 days, was eliminated. The IOC also permitted an amateur athlete to carry advertising material on his clothing in certain tournaments sanctioned by his national federation (but not in the Olympics) provided that all payment from the advertiser went to the national federation.

At the same meeting the IOC chose Moscow and Lake Placid, N.Y., as the sites for the 1980 Summer and Winter Olympics, respectively.

Earlier in the year the IOC added anabolic steroids, the so-called body-building drugs, to the list of prohibited substances at the Olympic Games. The European Athletic Association announced in November that track and field athletes would be tested for use of the steroids at all major European meets in 1975.

In August the International Amateur Athletic Federation continued its ban against South Africa for all track and field events through 1976, despite that nation's claim that it had made progress toward racial integration in sports. At the same time, the IAAF voted to approve China's participation in the Asian Games, held in September in Teheran, Iran.

In June the U.S. Department of Health, Education, and Welfare (HEW) announced that it intended to enforce fully Title IX of the Education Amendments of 1972, which prohibits discrimination in any university program. For sports, this meant that women were entitled to the same athletic facilities and opportunities as men. The National Collegiate Athletic Association protested to HEW that its enforcement regulations were deficient and showed an "appalling lack" of knowledge about college athletics.

ANGLING

Event	Winner	Country
World casting champion	S. Rajeff	U.S.

ARCHERY

Event	Winner	Country
WORLD FREESTYLE CHAMPIONS		
Individual, men	D. Brothers	U.S.
Individual, women	L. Lessard	Canada
WORLD BAREBOW CHAMPIONS		
Individual, men	L. Berggren	Sweden
Individual, women	E. Schewer	U.S.
EUROPEAN FREESTYLE CHAMPIONS		
Individual, men	T. Persson	Sweden
Individual, women	L. Dapoian	Italy
EUROPEAN BAREBOW CHAMPIONS		
Individual, men	L. Berggren	Sweden
Individual, women	I. Granqvist	Sweden

The West German four-man bobsled crew en route to the 1974 world championship at St. Moritz.

BADMINTON

Event	Winner	Country
WORLD INVITATIONAL TOURNAMENT (Jakarta)		
Men's singles	S. Pri	Denmark
Men's doubles	T. Tjun, J. Wahjudi	Indonesia
Women's singles	M. Beck	U.K.
Women's doubles	R. Masli, S. Minarni	Indonesia
Mixed doubles	C. Hadinata, R. Masli	Indonesia
WORLD INVITATIONAL TOURNAMENT (Glasgow)		
Men's singles	S. Pri	Denmark
Men's doubles	P. Gunalan, D. Soong	Malaysia
Women's singles	H. Yuki	Japan
Women's doubles	M. Aizawa, E. Takenaka	Japan
Mixed doubles	R. McCoig, M. Beck	U.K.
EUROPEAN CHAMPIONS		
Men's singles	S. Jonsson	Sweden
Men's doubles	W. Braun, R. Maiwald	West Germany
Women's singles	G. Gilks	U.K.
Women's doubles	M. Beck, G. Gilks	U.K.
Mixed doubles	D. Talbot, G. Gilks	U.K.
COMMONWEALTH GAMES CHAMPIONS		
Men's singles	P. Gunalan	Malaysia
Men's doubles	E. Stuart, D. Talbot	U.K.
Women's singles	G. Gilks	U.K.
Women's doubles	M. Beck, G. Gilks	U.K.
Mixed doubles	D. Talbot, G. Gilks	U.K.
ALL-ENGLAND (U.K.) OPEN CHAMPIONS		
Men's singles	R. Hartono	Indonesia
Men's doubles	T. Tjun, J. Wahjudi	Indonesia
Women's singles	H. Yuki	Japan
Women's doubles	M. Beck, G. Gilks	U.K.
Mixed doubles	J. Eddy, P. Whetnall	U.K.

BIATHLON

Event	Winner	Country
WORLD CHAMPIONS		
10 km.	J. Suutarinen	Finland
20 km.	J. Suutarinen	Finland
Relay	U.S.S.R.	
10 km., junior	S. Thierfelder	East Germany
15 km., junior	S. Khokhylia	U.S.S.R.
Relay, junior	Finland	

BILLIARDS

Event	Winner	Country
WORLD CHAMPIONS		
Professional	R. Williams	U.K.
Amateur	M. Lafir	Sri Lanka

BOBSLEDDING

Event	Winner	Country
WORLD CHAMPIONS		
Two-man	W. Zimmerer, P. Utzschneider	West Germany
Four-man	M. Schumann, P. Utzschneider, A. Wurzer, W. Zimmerer	West Germany

CANOEING

Event	Winner	Country
WORLD CHAMPIONS—MEN		
Kayak singles	G. Csapo	Hungary
Kayak pairs	Z. Bako, I. Szabo	Hungary
Kayak fours	East Germany	
Canadian singles	V. Yurchenko	U.S.S.R.
Canadian pairs	V. Chessyunas, Y. Lobanov	U.S.S.R.
WORLD CHAMPIONS—WOMEN		
Kayak singles	A. Ohde	East Germany
Kayak pairs	B. Koster, A. Ohde	East Germany

CROSS-COUNTRY

Event	Winner	Country
INTERNATIONAL CHAMPIONS		
Senior, individual	E. de Beck	Belgium
Senior, team	Belgium	
Junior, individual	R. Kimball	U.S.
Junior, team	U.S.	
Women, individual	P. Pigni-Cacchi	Italy
Women, team	England	
NATIONAL CHAMPIONS		
Belgium	Men	E. de Beck
	Women	J. van Santberghe
England	Men	D. Black
	Women	R. Ridley
France	Men	H. Rault
Scotland	Men	J. Brown
	Women	M. O'Boyle
U.S.S.R.	Men, 8 km.	M. Zhelobovskiy
	Men, 12 km.	A. Badrankov
	Women, 2 km.	T. Pangyelova
	Women, 3 km.	L. Demchenko
Wales	Men	J. Jones
	Women	J. Lochhead

CURLING

Event	Winner
WORLD CHAMPIONS	U.S.

EQUESTRIAN SPORTS

Event	Winning rider and horse	Country
WORLD CHAMPIONS		
Dressage, individual	R. Klimke, "Mehmed"	West Germany
Dressage, team	West Germany	
Driving, individual	S. Fuelop	Hungary
Driving, team	U.K.	
Show jumping, individual	H. Steenken, "Simona"	West Germany
Show jumping, women	J. Tissot, "Rocket"	France
Show jumping, team	U.S.	
3-day, individual	B. Davidson, "Irish Cap"	U.S.
3-day, team	U.S.	
EUROPEAN JUNIOR CHAMPIONS		
Show jumping, team	Austria	
3-day, individual	S. Ker, "Peer Gynt"	U.K.
3-day, team	West Germany	

FENCING

Event	Winner	Country
WORLD CHAMPIONS—MEN		
Foil, individual	A. Romankov	U.S.S.R.
Foil, team	U.S.S.R.	
Épée, individual	R. Edling	Sweden
Épée, team	Sweden	
Sabre, individual	M. A. Montano	Italy
Sabre, team	U.S.S.R.	
Nations' Cup	U.S.S.R.	
WORLD CHAMPIONS—WOMEN		
Foil, individual	I. Bobis	Hungary
Foil, team	U.S.S.R.	
WORLD JUNIOR CHAMPIONS—MEN		
Foil, individual	A. Kukie	Romania
Épée, individual	M. Poffet	Switzerland
Sabre, individual	V. Pop	Romania
WORLD JUNIOR CHAMPIONS—WOMEN		
Foil, individual	V. Sidyorova	U.S.S.R.
EUROPEAN CUP—MEN		
Épée, team	BUSC Budapest	Hungary
Sabre, team	CSKA Moscow	U.S.S.R.

Determination was the hallmark of events during the 1974 world curling championship match in Bern, Switz.

GLIDING

Event	Winner	Country
WORLD CHAMPIONS		
Open class	G. Moffat	U.S.
Standard class	H. Reichmann	West Germany

GO-KARTING

Event	Winner	Country
WORLD CHAMPION		
1,000 cc	T. Fullerton	U.K.

GYMNASTICS

Event	Winner	Country
WORLD CHAMPIONS—MEN		
Overall	S. Kasamatsu	Japan
Floor exercises	S. Kasamatsu	Japan
Parallel bars	E. Kenmotsu	Japan
Horizontal bar	E. Gienger	West Germany
Rings	N. Andrianov	U.S.S.R. } (tied)
	D. Grecu	Romania
Pommeled horse	Z. Magyar	Hungary
Long horse vault	S. Kasamatsu	Japan
Team	Japan	
WORLD CHAMPIONS—WOMEN		
Overall	L. Touristcheva	U.S.S.R.
Floor exercises	L. Touristcheva	U.S.S.R.
Asymmetrical bars	A. Zinke	East Germany
Beam	L. Touristcheva	U.S.S.R.
Horse vault	O. Korbut	U.S.S.R.
Team	U.S.S.R.	

HANDBALL

Event	Winner	Country
WORLD CHAMPIONS		
Men	Romania	
Women	Yugoslavia	
European Champions' Cup	VFL Gummersbach	West Germany

HORSESHOE PITCHING

Event	Winner	Country
AAU CHAMPIONS		
Men, singles	C. Daugherty	U.S.
Women, singles	G. Jackson	U.S.

HURLING

Event	Winner
ALL-IRELAND CHAMPIONS	Kilkenny

JUDO

Event	Winner	Country
EUROPEAN CHAMPIONS		
Lightweight	S. Myelnichenko	U.S.S.R.
Welterweight	G. Kruger	East Germany
Middleweight	J. P. Coche	France
Light-heavyweight	G. Zuvela	Yugoslavia
Heavyweight	G. Onashvili	U.S.S.R.
Unlimited weight	S. Novikov	U.S.S.R.
Team	U.S.S.R.	

KARATE

Event	Winner	Country
EUROPEAN CHAMPIONS		
Lightweight	K. Scherer	West Germany
Middleweight	W. Higgins	England
Heavyweight	R. Macfarlane	Scotland
Unlimited weight	J. Kallenbach	The Netherlands

LACROSSE

Event	Winner
WORLD CHAMPION	U.S.

MODERN PENTATHLON

Event	Winner	Country
WORLD CHAMPIONS		
Individual	P. Lednev	U.S.S.R.
Team	U.S.S.R.	
U.K. CHAMPIONS		
Individual	J. Fox	
Team	REME	

ORIENTEERING

Event	Winner	Country
WORLD CHAMPIONS		
Individual, men	B. Frilen	Sweden
Relay, men	Sweden	
Individual, women	M. Norgaard	Denmark
Team, women	Sweden	

POLO

Event	Winner
Coronation Cup	U.S.

RACKETS

Event	Winner	Country
MAJOR TOURNAMENT WINNERS		
U.S. open	W. Surtees	U.S.
U.K. open, singles	H. Angus	U.K.
U.K. open, pairs	G. Atkins, C. Hue Williams	U.K.

REAL TENNIS

Event	Winner	Country
MAJOR TOURNAMENT WINNERS		
U.K. open, singles	H. Angus	U.K.
U.K. open, pairs	N. Cripps, C. Swallow	U.K.
U.K. amateur	H. Angus	U.K.

ROLLER HOCKEY

Event	Winner
WORLD CHAMPION	Portugal

ROLLER SKATING

Event	Winner	Country
WORLD CHAMPIONS		
Mixed pairs	R. Sabo, S. McDonald	U.S.

SKI-BOB

Event	Winner	Country
EUROPEAN CHAMPIONS		
Men	A. Fischbauer	Austria
Women	G. Gebert	Austria

SNOOKER

Event	Winner	Country
WORLD CHAMPIONS		
Professional	R. Reardon	U.K.
Open	J. Spencer	U.K.

Olga Korbut, pixie-like favourite of audiences around the world, performs on the balance beam. The beam championship was captured by L. Tourischeva in 1974, Olga winning the women's horse vault championship.

PICTORIAL PARADE

Mike Hazelwood displays his versatility on water skis during the European championship meet that was won by the U.K. team.

SQUASH RACKETS

Event	Winner	Country
MAJOR TOURNAMENT WINNERS		
World open	G. Hunt	Australia
Australian professional	G. Hunt	Australia
South African open	G. Hunt	Australia
U.K. open	G. Hunt	Australia
U.K. professional	A. Safwat	Egypt
U.K. amateur	Muhammad Khan	Pakistan
U.K. open, women	H. McKay	Australia
European, team	England	
U.S. open	V. Neiderhoffer	U.S.

TABLE TENNIS

Event	Winner	Country
EUROPEAN CHAMPIONS		
Men's singles	M. Orlovski	Czechoslovakia
Men's doubles	I. Jonyer, T. Klampar	Hungary
Women's singles	J. Magos	Hungary
Women's doubles	H. Lotaller, J. Magos	Hungary
Mixed doubles	S. Gomozkov, A. Rudnova	U.S.S.R.
Men's team	Sweden	
Women's team	U.S.S.R.	
ASIAN CHAMPIONS		
Men's singles	N. Hazegawa	Japan
Men's doubles	N. Hazegawa, H. Kono	Japan
Women's singles	K. Edano	Japan
Women's doubles	Chang Li, Cheng Huai-ying	China
Mixed doubles	H. Kono, K. Edano	Japan
Men's team	China	
Women's team	Japan	

TOBOGGANING

Event	Winner	Country
WORLD CHAMPIONS		
Individual, men	J. Fendt	West Germany
Pairs, men	B. Hahn, U. Hahn	East Germany
Individual, women	M. Schumann	East Germany
EUROPEAN CHAMPIONS		
Individual, men	N. Rinn	East Germany
Pairs, men	H. Hildgartner, J. Pleikner	Italy
Individual, women	M. Schumann	East Germany

TRAMPOLINE

Event	Winner	Country
WORLD CHAMPIONS		
Individual, men	R. Tison	France
Pairs, men	J. Cartledge, R. Nealy	U.S.
Individual, women	A. Nicholson	U.S.
Pairs, women	U. Scheile, P. Wenzel	West Germany
EUROPEAN CHAMPIONS		
Individual, men	R. Tison	France
Pairs, men	S. Lobanov, N. Shmelyov	U.S.S.R.
Individual, women	O. Starykova	U.S.S.R.
Pairs, women	N. Korshova, G. Zavzhikova	U.S.S.R.

VOLLEYBALL

Event	Winner	Country
European Champions' Cup	CSKA Moscow	U.S.S.R.

WATER SKIING

Event	Winner	Country
EUROPEAN CHAMPIONS		
Overall, men	P. Seaton	U.K.
Overall, women	W. Staehle	The Netherlands
Team	U.K.	

WEIGHT LIFTING

Event	Winner and Country	Performance
WORLD CHAMPIONS		
Flyweight	M. Nassiri, Iran	232½ kg. (512¼ lb.)
Bantamweight	A. Kirov, Bulgaria	255 kg. (561 lb.)
Featherweight	G. Todorov, Bulgaria	280 kg. (617 lb.)
Lightweight	P. Korol, U.S.S.R.	305 kg. (672 lb.)
Middleweight	N. Kolev, Bulgaria	335 kg. (738 lb.)
Light heavyweight	T. Stoichev, Bulgaria	350 kg. (770 lb.)
Middle heavyweight	D. Rigert, U.S.S.R.	385 kg. (854 lb.)
Heavyweight	V. Ustyuzhin, U.S.S.R.	380 kg. (837½ lb.)
Superheavyweight	V. Alexeyev, U.S.S.R.	425 kg. (935 lb.)
Nations' Cup	Bulgaria	

WRESTLING

Event	Winner	Country
WORLD FREESTYLE CHAMPIONS		
Light flyweight	I. Murselov	Bulgaria
Flyweight	Takada	Japan
Bantamweight	Yumin	U.S.S.R.
Featherweight	Zeveg	Mongolia
Lightweight	N. Nasrulayev	U.S.S.R.
Welterweight	R. Ashuraliev	U.S.S.R.
Middleweight	L. Novoshilov	U.S.S.R.
Light heavyweight	L. Tediashvili	U.S.S.R.
Heavyweight	V. Gulyutkin	U.S.S.R.
Superheavyweight	Ladislav	Romania
EUROPEAN FREESTYLE CHAMPIONS		
Light flyweight	G. Tarzhenakov	U.S.S.R.
Flyweight	O. Nikolov	Bulgaria
Bantamweight	T. Panov	Bulgaria
Featherweight	D. Donchev	Bulgaria
Lightweight	E. Vasilev	Bulgaria
Welterweight	R. Ashuraliev	U.S.S.R.
Middleweight	L. Novoshilov	U.S.S.R.
Light heavyweight	L. Tediashvili	U.S.S.R.
Heavyweight	H. Buettner	East Germany
Superheavyweight	S. Andreyev	U.S.S.R.
EUROPEAN GRECO-ROMAN CHAMPIONS		
Light flyweight	M. Bagandrinov	U.S.S.R.
Flyweight	M. An	U.S.S.R.
Bantamweight	A. Emish	U.S.S.R.
Featherweight	G. Birishkov	U.S.S.R.
Lightweight	O. Paulikenov	Bulgaria
Light middleweight	S. Kurbanov	U.S.S.R.
Middleweight	G. Kostokov	U.S.S.R.
Light heavyweight	G. Malyenkin	U.S.S.R.
Heavyweight	J. Barbuzano	Spain
Superheavyweight	V. Klivodyenko	U.S.S.R.
WORLD NATIONS' CUP—FREESTYLE	U.S.S.R.	

(D. K. R. PHILLIPS)

See also Baseball; Basketball; Bowling and Lawn Bowls; Boxing; Chess; Contract Bridge; Cricket; Cycling; Football; Golf; Hockey; Horse Racing; Ice Skating; Motor Sports; Rowing; Sailing; Skiing; Swimming; Tennis; Track and Field Sports.

[452.B]

Sri Lanka

An Asian republic and member of the Commonwealth of Nations, Sri Lanka (Ceylon) occupies an island off the southeast coast of peninsular India. Area: 25,332 sq.mi. (65,610 sq.km.). Pop. (1973 est.): 13,249,000, including Sinhalese about 72%; Tamil 21%; Moors 7%. Cap. and largest city: Colombo (pop., 1972 est., 607,000). Language: Sinhalese (official), Tamil, English. Religion (1971): Buddhist 67%; Hindu 18%; Christian 7%; Muslim 7%. President in 1974, William Gopallawa; prime minister, Mrs. Sirimavo Bandaranaike.

In his budget speech in November 1973, the finance minister, N. M. Perera, indicated that there had been some improvement in the country's economic situation. He announced cuts in rice distribution and expressed his belief that the crash program initiated by the prime minister in October would result in increased production of rice and of other foods. The economy did benefit considerably from an increase in the price of tea, Sri Lanka's main export, although the huge increase in the world price of oil seriously affected essential fertilizer imports. Efforts were being made to promote tourism, with another large hotel opening in Colombo, and some hopes were aroused by the sinking of an oil well. Nevertheless, the economy was still in a shaky state, with nearly 800,000 persons unemployed in January 1974. Foreign loans were obtained from the International Monetary Fund, Britain (interest free), West Germany, and Sweden.

The main object of the revised constitution of 1972 was to make the National Assembly completely sovereign. The Administration of Justice Act, passed in October 1973, introduced far-reaching changes in the judicial system and procedure. From the political angle, these tended ultimately to prevent the judiciary from determining government actions to be unconstitutional. If unconstitutionality was alleged, the issue would come before a constitutional court, but its decision could be—and was in 1974—overruled by a two-thirds majority of the Assembly. Other legislation of 1973 had weakened the power of the press to criticize the government. Only a few newspapers continued to do so, and they received warnings.

All this further handicapped the opposition. From October 1973, J. R. Jayawardene, leader of the United National Party, had organized a series of rallies, some of a satyagraha (passive resistance) nature, to protest against the government's food and prices policies. In April 1974 as many as 150 rallies were organized for the same day (April 21). Fearing an outbreak of

Stamp Collecting:
see Philately and Numismatics

SRI LANKA

Education. (1973) Primary, pupils 2,117,706; secondary, pupils 480,264; vocational, pupils (state only) 3,648; primary, secondary, and vocational, teachers 98,925; teacher training, students 9,288, teachers 593; higher (1971–72), students 12,074, teaching staff 1,329.

Finance. Monetary unit: Sri Lanka rupee, with (Sept. 16, 1974) a free rate of SLRs. 6.74 to U.S. $1 (SLRs. 15.57 = £1 sterling) and an effective tourist rate of SLRs. 11.13 to U.S. $1 (SLRs. 25.70 = £1 sterling). Gold, SDRs, and foreign exchange, official: (June 1974) U.S. $76 million; (June 1973) U.S. $70 million. Budget (1972–73 est.): revenue SLRs. 3,592,-000,000; expenditure SLRs. 4,913,000,000. Gross national product: (1972) SLRs. 13,374,000,000; (1971) SLRs. 13,151,000,000. Money supply: (March 1974) SLRs. 3,009,000,000; (March 1973) SLRs. 2,394,-000,000. Cost of living (Colombo; 1970 = 100): (June 1974) 133; (June 1973) 119.

Foreign Trade. (1973) Imports SLRs. 2,721,000,-000; exports SLRs. 2,502,000,000. Import sources: U.S. 9%; Japan 9%; France 8%; China 8%; U.K. 7%. Export destinations: U.K. 11%; China 9%; Pakistan 8%; U.S. 7%; Japan 5%. Main exports: tea 50%; rubber 24%.

Transport and Communications. Roads (1973) 22,339 km. Motor vehicles in use (1973): passenger 89,900; commercial 34,400. Railways: (1972) 1,535 km.; traffic (1971–72) 3,101,000,000 passenger-km., freight (1972–73) 319 million net ton-km. Air traffic (1973): 353 million passenger-km.; freight 3,530,000 net ton-km. Telephones (Dec. 1972) 65,000. Radio licenses (Dec. 1972) 505,000.

Agriculture. Production (in 000; metric tons; 1973; 1972 in parentheses): rice *c.* 1,303 (*c.* 1,312); cassava (1972) *c.* 350, (1971) 372; sweet potatoes (1972) *c.* 58, (1971) 57; onions (1972) *c.* 41, (1971) 42; tea *c.* 215 (213); coffee *c.* 10 (10); copra *c.* 250 (*c.* 240); rubber 167 (140). Livestock (in 000; June 1973): cattle *c.* 1,650; buffaloes *c.* 710; sheep *c.* 24; goats *c.* 570; pigs *c.* 112; chickens *c.* 8,000.

Industry. Production (in 000; metric tons; 1972): cement 383; salt 156; graphite (1971) 7.6; petroleum products (1971) 1,516; cotton yarn 4.9; electricity (kw-hr.) 995,000.

violence, Prime Minister Bandaranaike used the government's emergency powers to forbid the rallies and to threaten anyone infringing the prohibition with severe penalties, including confiscation of property. Publication of newspapers supporting the opposition was stopped and a curfew imposed.

During these and earlier debates, the prime minister was accused of nepotism, particularly with regard to her daughter—attacks she indignantly repudiated. Though there was little parliamentary activity, in June an important measure was passed, the Companies (Special Provisions) Act, to come into force in January 1975. The act laid down that any companies working in Sri Lanka must be incorporated there, a provision primarily aimed at ending the considerable and long-standing ownership of tea plantations by British "sterling companies."

In September the annual conference of the Commonwealth Parliamentary Association was held in the Bandaranaike Memorial Hall in Colombo (built and paid for by the government of China). The Tamils of northern Sri Lanka at last obtained their own branch of Sri Lanka University, but the community was still dissatisfied, and talk of federalism and even separation continued. The prime minister took exception to the development of a U.S.-British naval base at Diego Garcia in the Indian Ocean. In conjunction with Indira Gandhi, prime minister of India, she arranged to settle the long-standing problem of the South Indian labourers on Sri Lanka tea estates, some 150,000 of whom were stateless. Half were to be granted Sri Lanka citizenship and the remainder repatriated to India.   (SIDNEY A. PAKEMAN)

[976.A.4]

A former plantation at Kalunadiya has been transformed to a commune by 40 young women. The first crop, being inspected here by a worker, was passion fruit.

WIDE WORLD

Stock Exchanges

The world's major stock markets turned in dismal performances in 1974. With double-digit inflation accompanied by economic recession, record interest rates, and widespread social discontent, 13 of the 15 major industrial stock price indexes outside the North American continent declined between the end of 1973 and the end of 1974 (see Table 1). Reflecting the customarily strong demand for gold during economic and political crises, however, gold shares experienced a bull market in 1974.

The critical factor in worldwide hyperinflation was the fourfold increase in the price of oil instituted by the Organization of Petroleum Exporting Countries (OPEC) following the October 1973 war in the Middle East. The massive shift in real income from oil-consuming nations to OPEC members threatened to disrupt the economic structure of the industrialized world. This fear was heightened when the huge surplus funds of OPEC failed to move rapidly to oil-consuming nations with large deficits. Further aggravating the situation was the inability of deficit countries to apply traditional economic remedies—such as increased government spending—to reflate their economies, because this would add fuel to the inflation fires. The result was that most oil-consuming nations experienced high-level inflation and severe business recession simultaneously.

Soaring interest rates stemmed mainly from three sources. First, an unprecedented demand for money was created by businessmen and speculators. Businessmen were motivated to expand capacity in order to meet shortages and to build inventories. Speculators in the currency and commodity markets, on the other hand, were anticipating higher prices or a breakdown in the world's monetary system. Second, government economic policies to attack stubborn, high-level inflation included a reduction in the supply of money, principally by deceleration in money-supply growth rates. This had the effect of putting further upward pressure on interest rates. Third, the sudden demise of a number of banking organizations in Western Europe tended to heighten investor anxiety over the soundness of the banking system. The result was that investors tended to place their funds in government-guaranteed securities rather than in time or savings deposits in merchant or other lending banks. The diversion of these funds exerted upward pressures on the cost of loans, particularly to less credit-worthy borrowers.

Social discontent also played a role in the bearish trend of stock markets. Public disorders resulted from conflicts between labour and management and threats of nationalization or greater government control over private enterprise. New government leadership in Great Britain, France, Belgium, Italy, West Germany, and Japan also tended to weaken the environment for equity investment due to uncertainties about the future direction of national economic and social policies.

In short, the spectacular rise in petroleum prices in 1974 caused serious economic and political problems in the industrialized world. Moreover, no real solution was apparent for the dilemma of trying to slow inflation while avoiding deep recession and high unemployment. Against this complex background investors chose to be sellers of equities. The investment strategy of avoiding equities was made even more attractive through the relatively high returns of short-term financial instruments, with virtually no risk to capital. As 1974 came to a close equity investors seemed perfectly content to await the resolution of the interlocking problems of high petroleum prices, the drive of international raw material cartels for wealth and power, a highly unstable monetary system, and the possibility of worldwide depression.

United States. The stock market in the United States suffered its worst buffeting in decades during 1974. Prices of most securities and the volume of trading fell sharply on all leading exchanges and in the over-the-counter markets. The Dow Jones industrial average, which reached a high of 892 in March, declined by 35.3% to a low of 577 in December 1974. The prices of many leading stocks fell to the lowest level since the 1950s. As equity values plummeted, institutional investors such as banks, insurance companies, and pension funds were helpless to stop the erosion of the value of their portfolios, and the bond market offered no relief. The combination of double-digit inflation and economic recession simultaneously depressed the prices of both stocks and bonds. The prime rate rose to a record level of 12% in July, reflecting very tight credit. The price of gold hit a record $199 an ounce on the London market on December 30, the day before U.S. citizens were permitted to buy it for the first time since 1933. Margin

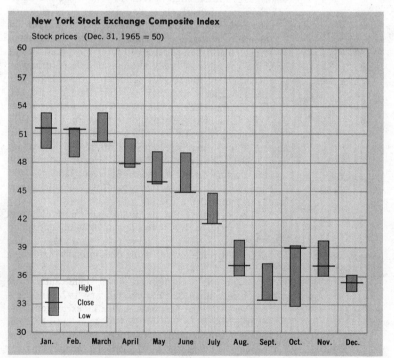

New York Stock Exchange Composite Index

Stock prices (Dec. 31, 1965 = 50)

High
Close
Low

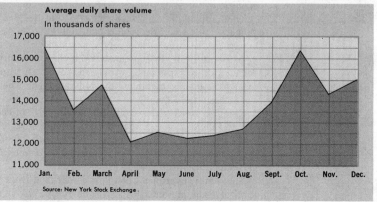

Average daily share volume

In thousands of shares

Source: New York Stock Exchange.

rates on stocks were reduced from 65% to 50% on Jan. 3, 1974, but despite this incentive, margin credit for stock by brokers declined 30% between September 1973 and the corresponding month of 1974. The total value of stocks traded on the New York Stock Exchange fell from $721 billion to $524.5 billion, representing a drop of 27.2%.

Gross national product (GNP) fell more than 2% in real terms in 1974 from $830 billion at an annual rate in the first quarter to under $825 billion in the final quarter. In current dollars GNP rose from $1,358,800,000 in the first quarter to about $1,510,-000,000 in the final quarter. The consumer price index climbed from 139.7% of the 1967 average in January to a high of 154.3% in November, representing a year-to-year increase of 12.1%. The wholesale price index soared from 146.6% in January to 171.9% in November, a gain of 17.3%. Unemployment went from 5% at the beginning of 1974 to 7.1% by year's end, with a strong upward trend. At the end of 1974 there were more than 6.5 million unemployed persons seeking jobs, the highest rate since 1958. From August through November the index of leading economic indicators suffered the sharpest four-month decline since 1949. Automobile sales were off 23% for domestically manufactured cars and 20% for foreign imports. The rate of housing starts sank to an eight-year low in December with residential construction down 40% from the 1973 level. High interest rates and soaring materials costs in early 1974 had a devastating effect on the real estate industry and severely depressed the stocks of mortgage companies, real estate investment trusts, banks, and thrift institutions. Corporate profits hit record levels largely because of inflated prices on accumulated inventories. The worst recession since the 1930s inevitably took its toll in the stock market.

Average prices on the New York Stock Exchange reflected a continuation and acceleration of the 1973 downtrend (see Table II). The 500 stocks in Standard and Poor's composite index fell from 96.11 in January to 68.12 in September before a brief interruption in the decline during October. Between January 1973 and September 1974 the composite index fell from 118.42 to 68.12, a drop of 42.4%.

The 425 stocks in the industrial group slid from 107.18 in January 1974 to a low of 76.54 in September. This represented a nine-month decline of 28.5%. The degree of price erosion from the January 1973 high level was 42.2%.

Public utility stocks were down significantly from the levels of 1973. Between January 1973 and September 1974, the 55 stocks in this index moved from 60.01 to 30.93, a fall of 48.4%. Many utility companies were obliged to postpone major capital improvements because of the adverse money market conditions.

The railroad index, which dipped from 44.37 in January to 31.55 in September, did not suffer as severely as the other leading groups of stocks on a year-to-year basis. In September 1974, the low month for the railroads, the index was 31.55, off 11.1% from the corresponding month of the previous year when the index was 35.49.

Common stock yields continued to climb as prices fell and dividends were maintained. From a level of 2.98% in January 1973, average yields reached 3.98% in January 1974 and 5.55% in August. The 20-month gain was a record high 86.2%.

Long-term government bond prices declined from a level of 60.66 in January to 56.81 in May 1974 (see

Table III). After a short rise in June to 57.11, the average moved within a narrow range during the summer, going to 57.80 in November. At the 1974 low of 54.95 that occurred in August, the average was 6.4% below the corresponding monthly figure of 58.71 during the preceding year. Bond yields rose throughout most of 1974 to levels well above 1973. An average yield of 7.04% was attained in April 1974 and the high for the year occurred in August at a level of 7.33%. By the end of 1974 there was evidence of a declining trend in government bond yields. The Board of Governors of the Federal Reserve System approved reduction in the discount rates at six Federal Reserve banks, including New York, from 8 to 7.75%. The prime rate, which had achieved a high of 12.25% in July 1974, had declined to 10.5% and was still falling in December.

Corporate bond prices fell to 57.6 in August 1974, down from 62.3 in January and well below the level of 66 recorded in January 1973. Yields rose from 7.83% in January to a high of 9.27% in October 1974 (see Table IV). The easing of credit during the late autumn of 1974 resulted in a reversal of the upward trend of corporate bond yields of the highest quality.

The mood of investors was very bearish throughout the year with a widespread feeling that things were going to become worse before they got better. A combination of severe recession, rapid inflation, political uncertainties domestically, an international oil crisis, and international economic problems all tended to discourage investors in the stock market. Major financial institutions withdrew from the equity markets and mutual funds shifted their portfolios from equities to short-term fixed income obligations. The principal positive note in an otherwise gloomy market was the belief that stocks were cheap and the market would tend to anticipate the resumption of economic growth which would result from more aggressive monetary and fiscal policies by the government.

Transactions on the New York Stock Exchange totaled 3,517,742,638 shares in 1974, a drop of 13.2% from the year-earlier level of 4,053,201,306. The average daily volume fell to 13.9 million from 16.1 million shares. The total number of block trades, those of 10,000 shares or more, dropped 21%, to 23,111 from 29,233. Volume was down sharply on the American Stock Exchange with turnover of 482,181,149 shares in 1974, compared with 759,652,005 shares in 1973 and 1,117,971,382 shares in 1972. Between 1972 and 1974 the volume fell by 56.8%. Average daily volume in 1974 was 1,880,000 shares, down from the previous year's figure of 3,020,000. Volume in the over-the-counter market, as reported by the National Association of Securities Dealers, declined from 1,615,816,-300 in 1973 to 1,179,708,948 in 1974, off 27%. The National Stock Exchange members voted to dissolve that exchange in 1975 because of inadequate volume of activity. Bond sales on the New York Stock Exchange dipped 8.4% in 1974, from $4,424,671,800 in 1973 to $4,052,123,400. The decline was sharper on the American Stock Exchange where bond sales were $256,411,000 in 1974 as compared with $457,885,000 in 1973, a loss of 44.1%. The market's performance resulted in fewer new listings and lower prices paid for exchange memberships. Only 47 new issues were listed on the New York Stock Exchange in 1974, less than half the prior year's 97, and 50 were approved for listing on the American Stock Exchange, compared with 59 in 1973. New York Stock Exchange members suffered heavy losses because of declining volume and waning investor interest. Thirty-three big board brokerage firms went out of business and nine merged. An estimated 1,000 fully employed registered representatives quit Wall Street in 1974. On the New York Stock Exchange the value of a seat declined 32% during the year, to $75,000 from 1973's last sale at $110,000. The price of a seat on the American Stock Exchange rose to $70,000, slightly more than double 1973's last sale at $34,000, because of the expectation of a revival of activity resulting from trading in stock options that was scheduled to begin in 1975.

The Securities and Exchange Commission (SEC) determined that the fixed rate system of commissions should be abolished and be replaced by negotiated sales charges. Stock brokers resisted the change with a strong lobbying effort because they felt that this would remove the incentive for exchange membership by removing brokers from supervision by the exchange and drastically reducing the number of buy and sell orders flowing to the trading floor of the exchange. The SEC ordered removal of the fixed commission system to take effect in 1975. In other actions, the SEC urged companies to reflect the market values of securities in their balance sheets and to indicate the effect of higher fuel costs in their annual reports to stockholders. They also proposed regulations requiring corporations to disclose more information in the quarterly financial reports filed with the agency. Companies would be required to provide more information about disputes with their auditors for the purpose of increasing the independence of the auditors from the companies they audit and to increase stockholders' awareness of the auditors' role. The Securities Investor Protection Corporation (SIPC), which insures brokers' accounts up to $50,000 in cash and securities with a $20,000 limit on cash claims, applied for an increase of their limits to $100,000 overall and $40,000 on cash allowances. The SIPC had 4,000 brokerage firm members in 1974.

Canada. The Canadian stock markets suffered a precipitous decline of prices during 1974 despite a relatively strong economy. On the Toronto Stock Exchange the index of industrial stock prices rose from 210 in January to 230 in March, fell to 183 in May, rallied to 200 in June, and dropped to 150 by September. A partial recovery in October and November was followed by a year-end level of 150. The 151 industrials in the average had a high of 228.78 and a low of 150.11 in 1974, a fall of 34.5%. Gold stocks on the Toronto Stock Exchange hit a record high of 622.04 in March 1974 and then fluctuated widely around a sharp downtrend, hitting a low of 284.96 in September, a decline of 54.1%. Base metals and Western oils suffered price declines throughout the year, as did the utility stocks. Yields on long-term Canada bonds were 7.4% in January, slid to 7.2% in February, rose to 8% in April and 9.5% by July before falling back to 8% in November and 7.5% in December. Ninety-day Canadian Treasury bills followed a similar pattern in 1974.

Despite a growth in real GNP of 4.1% by the end of the third quarter of 1974, and pretax profits up 33% above the previous year, unemployment rose to 5.5% and the inflation rate was 11.2%. The newly created Foreign Investment Review Agency entered the market by restricting proposed takeovers to those deemed to be in the national interest. Surveys of executives reflected growing pessimism in Canada about financial conditions. Most felt that the economy would

weaken, unemployment would rise, and it was a bad time for business to expand. By the beginning of September, however, there was a growing belief that the U.S. Federal Reserve Board would soon loosen the financial reins; this improved market sentiment and prices began to creep upward in the securities markets. Short-term fixed income securities sustained slightly declining yields in the last quarter of 1974.

(IRVING PFEFFER)

Western Europe. In 1974 Great Britain suffered its worst bear market since the 1930s. The *Financial Times* index of 30 industrial stocks traded on the London Stock Exchange fell 53% from the end of 1973 to the end of 1974. This equaled the drop in this index from 1929 to 1932. At the 1974 close the index was 70% below its all-time peak set in May 1972 and back to the level of June 1958.

Beginning with the first trading session of 1974 the London Stock Exchange entered a downward phase of major proportions. The government's imposition of a three-day workweek on most of British industry to

643

Stock Exchanges

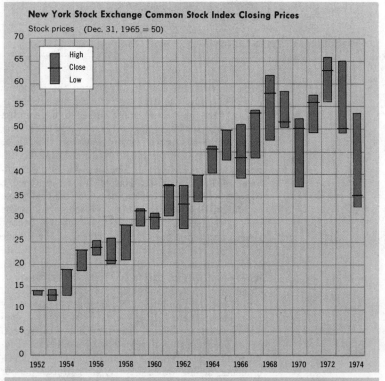

New York Stock Exchange Common Stock Index Closing Prices
Stock prices (Dec. 31, 1965 = 50)

Number of shares sold
In millions of shares

Source: New York Stock Exchange.

conserve fuel and electricity reflected the economic crisis caused by the Arab oil cutbacks that began in 1973. At the same time the nation had to cope with a coal miners' strike, soaring prices, and record interest rates. These events were instrumental in the fall of the Conservative government of Prime Minister Edward Heath on March 4. The new Labour government of Prime Minister Harold Wilson resumed a five-day workweek following the end of the coal strike in March. However, not only were the terms of the coal settlement highly inflationary, but the Labour government's first national budget called for a wide variety of tax increases, including raising the corporate tax rate from 50 to 52%. The new government's narrow majority of only three seats in the House of Commons assured continued political turmoil and divisiveness and dimmed the future outlook for equity investment. The subsequent erosion of equity values was further aggravated by the failure of several brokerage houses. During May and June investor confidence was also impaired by a series of bearish developments, among which were reports of the Labour Party's intention to pursue an aggressive program of nationalization, a new wave of labour disputes, and a terrorist bombing of Parliament. As June came to a close the general economic and political turmoil had carried stock prices 35% below the levels obtaining at the end of 1973.

Stock prices rallied strongly in July, but the recovery was short-lived. Stagnant industrial production and rising unemployment squashed investor hopes for a quick economic recovery. With inflation running at an annual rate of close to 20%, and the lending rate charged by British banks near record levels, an increasing number of business concerns were threatened with bankruptcy. In late October the government announced plans to nationalize the shipbuilding industry and to acquire majority interest in the North Sea oil fields owned by British concerns. Stock prices reached their lowest point in mid-December, but the rebound during the final weeks of 1974 was relatively mild.

The stock market in France also took a beating in

1974—down 33%. The equity index of the Paris Bourse recorded the year's high on January 24, while the low was set on September 26. The January rally was more or less a continuation of the trend started in mid-December 1973 on news of the government's anti-inflationary measures. However, when the annual rate of increase in consumer prices jumped to 11.5% in February from 8.4% in December, widespread public disorders erupted such as had not been seen since the uprisings of May–June 1968. Labour unrest against the rising cost of living produced work stoppages by bank clerks, brokerage-house employees, hotel workers, and a host of trade union members. Moreover, the disruptions did not end with the death of Pres. Georges Pompidou on April 2. The Paris Bourse, for example, was shut due to a strike of exchange clerks from April 3 to May 9. Nor did the May 19 election of former finance minister Valéry Giscard d'Estaing to a seven-year term as president of France seem to generate a renewed sense of national unity. Stock prices dropped almost without interruption from late January until the first week of July.

Following a three-week rally that saw prices regain 8% of their values, the decline resumed. From July 26 to the end of September stock prices dropped 27%. Business failures and bankruptcies increased markedly throughout the summer. In Paris alone 80 failures were reported in July—38% more than in the previous year. The lending rate to the most credit-worthy borrowers reached nearly 16%, while 12% yields were recorded for high-quality industrial bonds.

At the same time, a swelling trade deficit from the quadrupling of oil prices caused the government to ask for national sacrifice. To reduce consumption of petroleum products a flat ceiling on national spending for oil imports was mandated. Selected increases in taxes on corporations and upper-income families were also imposed to control inflation. Nevertheless, as 1974 drew to a close an inflation rate of 17% and strikes among postal workers, garbagemen, and coal miners were tangible evidence that France's economic problems were a long way from being resolved.

In Switzerland the decline in the price index of issues listed on the Zürich Stock Exchange was 37% from the end of 1973 to the end of 1974. After reaching their high in February, equity prices declined on balance until early October. The market made an anemic attempt to rally, but selling pressures built up in December and the year ended with prices at their lowest level. The Swiss stock market was adversely affected during the first half of 1974 by the chaos in foreign exchange markets stemming from the political deadlock in Great Britain, the fall of the Italian government, and the change of political leadership in West Germany. Moreover, the Swiss economy, which in the past had relatively stable price levels, experienced double-digit inflation for the first time on a sustained basis in 1974. Government bond yields, which averaged 5.6% in 1973, cracked the 6% level during the first quarter of 1974 and during September averaged 7.4%. The influence of soaring inflation, coupled with rising yields on fixed-income securities, tended to reduce the incentive for equity investment. As Swiss investors disposed of equities, the proceeds from such sales tended to find their way into the bond market, short-term government securities, or gold bullion to await the outcome of the battle against inflation, resolution of the global oil crisis, and stabilization of the international financial system.

Lower stock prices also prevailed in Denmark. A

downtrend in Danish stock prices developed after reports that revealed the continuing inflationary tendencies prevalent in the economy since the end of 1973. For example, the increase in the consumer price index in 1973 amounted to 10.5%, while the comparable increase for the 12 months ended September 1974 was 15.9%. Government plans to attack the inflationary spiral through changes in the tax laws were greeted by wildcat strikes and mass demonstrations against the economic package. Before the strike actions and demonstrations erupted in May, stock prices had been down 9% from the end of 1973. Following Danish Prime Minister Poul Hartling's inability to gain support for freezing wages and prices in December, national elections were scheduled for Jan. 9, 1975. The year-to-year decline in stock prices amounted to 28%.

After rising 3% in 1973, stock prices in Belgium reversed their bullish pattern in 1974. For the year as a whole, the decline in prices on the Brussels Stock Exchange was 29%. The nation was faced with political divisiveness when Prime Minister Edmond Leburton's coalition government collapsed in January. The crisis was touched off by Iran's decision not to build a major oil refinery in eastern Belgium. Moreover, the March 10 elections were inconclusive, and a new coalition government was not formed until the end of April. In October the new government decided to strengthen price controls and give further tax rebates to lower-income individuals. During the last two months of 1974, stock prices stabilized slightly above the year's lowest levels recorded in mid-September.

The stock markets in Italy and The Netherlands followed similar patterns. However, the average decline in stock prices in Italy was more severe. Equities traded on the Milan Stock Exchange also moved in a much wider range than those on the Amsterdam Stock Exchange. Each exchange recorded its 1974 peak on April 19. At that point stock prices on the Milan Exchange were 35% above the 1973 close, while Amsterdam's index was up 10%. However, by mid-August these gains were wiped out. Prices continued to drop during the remainder of the year, with the Milan Exchange setting its low on December 20 and the Amsterdam Exchange on October 24. The decline in Italy for the year as a whole amounted to 23% while The Netherlands had a 16% decline.

In Sweden equity prices backtracked a mere 8% from the end of 1973 to the end of 1974. Strength in stocks traded on the Stockholm Exchange from the first trading session in January to May 7 (up 33%) reflected rising industrial production and a relatively low inflation rate, due principally to price controls and gasoline rationing. To halt excessive borrowing the Swedish central bank raised its discount rate in April and in August. This rate—which determines the interest rates of commercial banks and other credit institutions—had not changed since the end of 1971. The subsequent drop in equity prices from May 7 to September 20 cut values some 22%. After a rebound had added 11% to values by November 8, the decline resumed. At the year's close, the drop from the November recovery high was 13%.

West Germany's stock market rose 1% from the end of 1973 to the end of 1974. Despite the uncertain political climate caused by the transition of leadership from Willy Brandt to Helmut Schmidt, an increase in labour militancy, and the collapse of Bankhaus I. D. Herstatt in June, stock prices managed to end the first half of 1974 only 1% lower than the 1973 close. Bolstering investor confidence was the favourable position

of the nation's balance of payments. A trade surplus of DM. 8.7 billion was recorded for the first two months of 1974, reportedly the largest ever achieved by any nation during a comparable period. Moreover, the rate of rise in consumer prices in West Germany was the smallest of any European country.

After the initial shock of the Herstatt bankruptcy had passed, stock prices switched direction in July and August. In fact, by mid-August equity values had not only erased the previous decline, but were up 3% since the first of the year. However, the subsequent announcements that three small German banks had to cease operations because of liquidity troubles caused

Table I. Selected Major World Industrial Stock Price Indexes*

Country	1974 range High	Low	Year-end close 1973	1974	Percent change
Australia	536	257	440	298	−32
Austria	2,750	2,508	2,484	2,569†	+ 3
Belgium	132	84	125	89	−29
Denmark	103	70	104	75‡	−28
France	85	48	78	52	−33
Germany, West	609	520	559	564‡	+ 1
Hong Kong	482	153	438	173‡	−61
Italy	154	86	114	88	−23
Japan	4,787	3,355	4,306	3,837	−11
Netherlands, The	141	95	128	107	−16
Singapore	285	147	266	151‡	−43
South Africa	270	154	223	189	−15
Sweden	411	303	333	308	− 8
Switzerland	351	206	326	206	−37
United Kingdom	339	150	344	163	−53

*Index numbers are rounded, and limited to countries for which at least 12 months' data were available on a weekly basis.
†As of Dec. 27, 1974.
‡As of Dec. 30, 1974.
Sources: Barron's, The Economist, Financial Times, and The New York Times.

Table II. U.S. Stock Market Prices and Yields

Month	Railroads (20 stocks) 1974	1973	Industrials (425 stocks) 1974	1973	Public utilities (55 stocks) 1974	1973	Composite (500 stocks) 1974	1973	Yield (200 stocks; %) 1974	1973
January	44.37	42.87	107.18	132.55	48.60	60.01	96.11	118.42	3.98	2.98
February	41.85	40.61	104.13	127.87	48.13	57.52	93.45	114.16	3.99	3.12
March	42.57	39.29	108.98	126.05	47.90	55.94	97.44	112.42	4.11	3.13
April	40.26	35.88	103.66	123.56	44.03	55.34	92.46	110.27	4.29	3.27
May	37.04	36.14	101.77	119.95	39.35	55.43	89.67	107.22	4.42	3.33
June	37.31	34.35	101.62	117.20	37.46	54.37	89.79	104.75	4.51	3.35
July	35.63	35.22	93.54	118.65	35.37	53.31	82.82	105.83	4.99	3.29
August	35.06	33.76	85.51	116.75	34.00	50.14	76.03	103.80	5.55	3.43
September	31.55	35.49	76.54	118.52	30.93	52.31	68.47	105.61	...	3.34
October	33.70	38.24	77.57	123.42	33.80	53.22	69.44	109.84	...	3.37
November	35.95	39.74	80.17	114.64	34.45	48.30	....	102.03	...	3.93
December	....	41.48	....	106.16	....	45.73	....	94.78	...	3.86

Source: U.S. Department of Commerce, Survey of Current Business. Prices are Standard and Poor's monthly averages of daily closing prices with 1941–43=10. Yield figures are Moody's index of 200 stocks.

Table III. U.S. Government Long-Term Bond Prices and Yields
Average price in dollars per $100 bond

Month	Average 1974	1973	Yield (%) 1974	1973	Month	Average 1974	1973	Yield (%) 1974	1973
January	60.66	65.89	6.56	5.94	July	55.97	60.87	7.18	6.53
February	60.83	64.09	6.54	6.14	August	54.95	58.71	7.33	6.81
March	58.70	63.59	6.81	6.20	September	55.13	61.81	7.30	6.42
April	57.01	64.39	7.04	6.11	October	55.69	63.13	7.22	6.26
May	56.81	63.43	7.07	6.22	November	57.80	62.71	6.93	6.31
June	57.11	62.61	7.03	6.32	December		62.37	...	6.35

Source: U.S. Department of Commerce, Survey of Current Business. Average prices are derived from average yields on the basis of an assumed 3% 20-year taxable U.S. Treasury bond. Yields are for U.S. Treasury bonds that are taxable and due or callable in ten years or more.

Table IV. U.S. Corporate Bond Prices and Yields
Average price in dollars per $100 bond

Month	Average 1974	1973	Yield (%) 1974	1973	Month	Average 1974	1973	Yield (%) 1974	1973
January	62.3	66.0	7.83	7.15	July	58.5	63.8	8.72	7.45
February	62.0	65.5	7.85	7.22	August	57.6	61.0	9.00	7.68
March	61.3	65.2	8.01	7.29	September	...	61.2	9.24	7.63
April	60.0	64.9	8.25	7.26	October	...	62.1	9.27	7.60
May	59.7	64.7	8.37	7.29	November	...	62.1	8.89	7.67
June	59.5	64.4	8.47	7.37	December	...	62.9	...	7.68

Source: U.S. Department of Commerce, Survey of Current Business. Average prices are based on Standard and Poor's composite index of A1+ issues. Yields are based on Moody's Aaa domestic corporate bond index.

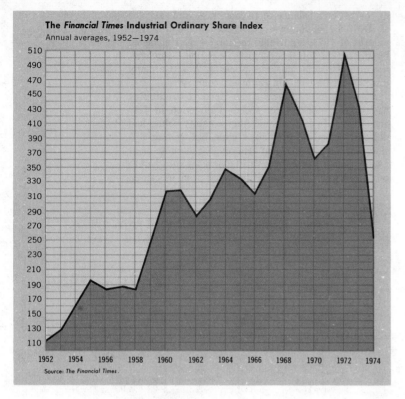

The *Financial Times* Industrial Ordinary Share Index
Annual averages, 1952—1974

Source: The Financial Times.

a major decline in the stock market. Before investor confidence was restored in early October, nearly 10% was chopped off equity values. Although stock prices recovered somewhat, the rally was tempered by government reports that unemployment at the end of October was 3% of the labour force, a total one and a half times the amount a year earlier. Chancellor Schmidt ordered a shift to reflationary policies to boost the domestic economy and reverse the rise in unemployment. The 8% rise in stock prices from the October lows wiped out previous losses and left the market in an uptrend for the year as a whole.

The Austrian stock market was also a star performer in 1974. For the third consecutive year the index of stock prices on the Vienna Stock Exchange ended in plus territory. The rally that got under way in early January accelerated over the next three months. On April 19 stock prices were nearly 11% above the 1973 close. A technical correction over the next five weeks lowered equity values by 3%. Resumption of the rally saw equity prices return to their April peak before profit-takers gained the upper hand. From mid-July until the end of the year the index of stock prices fluctuated within a relatively narrow trading range. At the 1974 close prices were 7% below the July highs and 2% above the January lows. Gross national product in Austria was expected to rise 4.5% in 1974, more than double the 2% growth anticipated for other European countries. The inflation rate was also among the lowest in Europe. On May 16 the government announced that the schilling would be allowed to float independently.

Other Countries. The stock markets in the British crown colony of Hong Kong and in Singapore both experienced severe bear markets in 1974. The Hang Seng index—which measures 33 stocks traded on the Hong Kong Exchange—was the worst performing market indicator outside the North American continent. Its drop of 61% from the end of 1973 to the end of 1974 was substantially greater than the 43% decline in equities traded in Singapore.

The rapid growth of the Asian dollar market in recent years has made Hong Kong and Singapore important international financial centres. Accordingly, neither country was able to insulate itself from worldwide inflation and the liquidity crises in the global money market system caused by spiraling oil prices and the collapse of several international banks. Thus, the equity investment environment in both countries had changed rapidly from one in which the achievement of huge profits in the stock market was not only possible but came to be expected, to one that placed heavy emphasis on the preservation of capital.

In Australia, the stock market declined 32%, on average, in 1974. The drop from the March 4 peak to the low of September 9 was 52%. After only 16 months in office Prime Minister Gough Whitlam was forced into calling elections for May 18, largely due to his program of restricting foreign investment in the mining industry and strong support for other anti-business legislation. Although Whitlam's Labor Party was victorious, his majority in the House and Senate was razor thin. In November Whitlam proposed to attack Australia's high inflation rate with a package of tax cuts for individuals and corporations. Stock prices rallied in the final weeks of 1974 to close 16% above the September bottom.

The trend of the stock market in Japan was also lower. Prices on the Tokyo Stock Exchange fell 10% in 1974, after dropping 17% the year before. The exchange's 225-share index, which during the first half of 1974 had risen 7%, climbed another 4% in the first three weeks of July before bearish sentiment developed. This remarkable performance was achieved despite the fact that the quadrupling of imported petroleum prices threatened massive balance of payments deficits and a sharp curtailment in the nation's standard of living. Oil imports were a higher proportion of total energy requirements in Japan than in any other industrialized country. Reports of raw material shortages touched off a wave of speculative buying, which, in turn, accelerated the rate of inflation. To bring an overheated economy under control the Japanese Diet in March approved a series of measures, including a 10% surcharge on excess corporate profits. Within a matter of months the inflationary psychology began to unwind, many businesses initiated programs of inventory liquidation, and the stock market staged a broad retreat. Selling pressures were so strong during the remainder of the year that only once was the 225-share index able to show two weekly gains in a row. Contributing to bearish sentiment was the resignation of Prime Minister Kakuei Tanaka at the end of November.

Stock prices in South Africa were mixed in 1974. Industrial share prices on the Johannesburg Stock Exchange dipped 15% in 1974, while gold stocks traded on that exchange rose 52%. From January through May the nation's trade deficit was more than double the same period of 1973. Gold sales and a net inflow of foreign capital, however, offset this effect, producing a slight surplus in the overall balance of payments.

Mirroring the price of gold, which moved from about $150 per ounce in late September to nearly $200 in late December, gold stocks were in heavy demand. Nevertheless, the strength in share prices near the end of 1974 was insufficient to move the gold index above the August 16 high.　　　(ROBERT H. TRIGG)

See also Economy, World; Investment, International; Money and Banking; Savings and Investment.

[534.D.2.g]

Sudan

A republic of northeast Africa, the Sudan is bounded by Egypt, the Red Sea, Ethiopia, Kenya, Uganda, Zaire, the Central African Republic, Chad, and Libya. Area: 967,500 sq.mi. (2,505,813 sq.km.). Pop. (1973): 12,427,800, including Arabs in the north and Negroes in the south. Cap. and largest city: Khartoum (pop., 1972 est., 300,000). Language: Arabic; various tribal languages in the south. Religion: Muslim in the north; predominantly animist in the south. President and prime minister in 1974, Maj. Gen. Gaafar Nimeiry.

President Nimeiry, in a speech in April 1974, foresaw a future in which Sudan's role would be that of granary and sugar supplier to the Arab world and beyond. Emphasis on economic development was set toward that objective. Work was in progress on a trunk road system, as well as an oil products pipeline, to link Port Sudan with the capital and the central agricultural region; the Rahad River irrigation project was more than half completed; and contracts were awarded for construction of two new sugar refineries to supplement the two already in operation.

The decline in world cotton prices and severe inflation, running at over 30% annually, made it difficult for the government to sustain bright hopes for the future among a population increasingly disturbed by food shortages, the rising price of sugar (still mainly imported), and the inefficiency of the railways in

Opening of the new Nile bridge at Juba on March 15. Constructed by a specially selected team of Dutch engineers, the span across the White Nile constituted the largest single project within the UN program for the southern Sudan.

transporting supplies. Uncertainty over short-term economic prospects led to a political malaise which the sole permitted party, the Sudan Socialist Union, did not have the vigour to overcome. Elections, under the 1973 constitution, to the 250-member Assembly were held in May. During the year there was a liberalization in political attitudes, at least toward the right. Many political prisoners, including the former leader of the right-wing Umma Party, were released in March, and a general pardon was announced in July, but the Communist Party remained proscribed.

The country's semiautonomous Southern Region started the year with a new government and a new, mainly elected Assembly, which had been inaugurated by President Nimeiry in mid-December 1973. Although eager to go ahead with development plans, the regional government was occupied with resettlement and rehabilitation after the long civil war (ended 1972). The slow pace of progress was the main cause of discontent, and in October a state of emergency was declared after demonstrations at Juba, the regional capital.

President Nimeiry's visit to Pres. Anwar as-Sadat of Egypt in Cairo in February ended a period of tension between the two nations and resulted in agreement on gradual economic integration with Egypt. However, the practical results were few by the year's end. Links with Saudi Arabia proved of greater immediate benefit: that country not only continued its budgetary support with substantial loans but also guaranteed a $200 million Eurodollar loan, assured the Sudan of oil supplies, and financed the construction of an oil refinery at Port Sudan. The Libyan link was the most tenuous one. After fierce verbal exchanges in July, it appeared likely that diplomatic relations would be broken. However, there was hope of an improvement in relations by November, when President Nimeiry made a quick visit to Tripoli.

(PETER KILNER)

[978.E.5.b]

SUDAN

Education. (1973–74) Primary, pupils 1,031,390, teachers 30,328; secondary, pupils 199,613, teachers 7,874; vocational, pupils 4,959, teachers 486; teacher training, students 4,845, teachers 628; higher (including University of Khartoum), students 18,888, teaching staff 732.

Finance. Monetary unit: Sudanese pound, with (Sept. 16, 1974) a free rate of Sud£0.36 to U.S. $1 (Sud£0.83 = £1 sterling). Gold, SDRs, and foreign exchange, official: (June 1974) U.S. $48 million; (June 1973) U.S. $40.8 million. Budget (1974–75 est.): revenue Sud£277 million; expenditure Sud£268 million. Money supply: (May 1974) Sud£187,120,000; (May 1973) Sud£153,210,000. Cost of living (1970 = 100): (March 1974) 147; (March 1973) 117.

Foreign Trade. (1973) Imports Sud£151,840,000; exports Sud£151,170,000. Import sources: U.K. 18%; U.S. 8%; India 7%; Brazil 7%; China 7%; West Germany 7%; U.S.S.R. 6%. Export destinations: India 16%; China 15%; Japan 11%; Italy 11%; West Germany 9%; France 6%; The Netherlands 5%. Main exports: cotton 56%; peanuts 9%; gum arabic 5%.

Transport and Communications. Roads (1972) c. 50,000 km. (mainly tracks, including 335 km. asphalted). Motor vehicles in use (1971): passenger 30,000; commercial (including buses) 18,000. Railways: (1972) 4,756 km.; freight traffic (1971) 2,636,000,000 net ton-km. Air traffic (1972): 158 million passenger-km.; freight 1.9 million net ton-km. Inland navigable waterways (1972) 4,068 km. Telephones (Dec. 1972) 46,000. Radio receivers (Dec. 1972) 1,310,000. Television receivers (Dec. 1972) 70,000.

Agriculture. Production (in 000; metric tons; 1973; 1972 in parentheses): millet c. 370 (353); sorghum c. 1,800 (1,326); sesame 232 (363); dry broad beans c. 13 (c. 13); peanuts 635 (516); sugar, raw value c. 98 (c. 98); dates c. 72 (c. 72); bananas c. 10 (c. 10); cotton, lint c. 199 (c. 244); beef and veal (1972) c. 194, (1971) c. 189; mutton and goat meat (1972) c. 108, (1971) c. 103. Livestock (in 000; 1972–73): cattle c. 15,200; sheep c. 15,400; goats c. 10,200; camels c. 3,300; asses c. 650.

Industry. Production (in 000; metric tons; 1971): salt 55; cement 189; petroleum products 615; electricity (kw-hr.) 259,000.

Swaziland

A landlocked constitutional monarchy of southern Africa, Swaziland is bounded by South Africa and Mozambique. Area: 6,704 sq.mi. (17,364 sq.km.). Pop. (1973 est.): 479,150. Cap. and largest city: Mbabane (pop., 1973 est., 20,755). Language: English and siSwati (official). Religion: Christian 60%; animist 40%. King, Sobhuza II; prime minister in 1974, Prince Makhosini Dlamini.

SWAZILAND
Education. (1973) Primary, pupils 81,694, teachers 2,112; secondary, pupils 12,459, teachers 550; vocational, pupils 483, teachers (1969) 10; teacher training, students 339, teachers (1969) 31; higher, students 395, teaching staff (1969) 15.

Finance and Trade. Monetary unit: lilangeni (plural emalangeni; replaced the South African rand at par from September 1974), with (Sept. 16, 1974) a free rate of 0.70 emalangeni to U.S. $1 (free rate of 1.62 emalangeni to £1 sterling). Budget (1973–74 est.): revenue R 28.1 million; expenditure R 23.9 million. Foreign trade (1972): imports R 53.3 million; exports R 65.5 million. Export destinations (1970): U.K. 25%; Japan 24%; South Africa 21%. Main exports: sugar 29%; wood pulp 17%; asbestos 15%; iron ore 14%; citrus fruit 11%; timber 5%.

Agriculture. Production (in 000; metric tons; 1972; 1971 in parentheses): corn 120 (105); rice 5 (8); sugar, raw value 192 (178); cotton, lint 4 (3). Livestock (in 000; 1972–73): cattle 589; sheep 37; pigs 14; goats 252; poultry 379.

Industry. Production (in 000; metric tons; 1972): coal 143; iron ore (metal content) 1,270; asbestos 34; electricity (kw-hr.) 107,000.

The ban on all political activity continued through 1974 as the royal commission, appointed by King Sobhuza in 1973, had not completed its study on the country's constitutional future. Opposition leader Ambrose Zwane was detained in March for criticizing the government and was threatened with rearrest if he continued his political activities.

Though more prosperous than Botswana and Lesotho, Swaziland shared many of the problems of these landlocked countries. In March and April meetings were held by the three nations to coordinate matters of common interest, in particular problems arising from the oil crisis, monetary policy, and migration (Swaziland had 4,500 nationals, or 1.2% of its labour force, in South Africa, as against Botswana's 4.7% and Lesotho's 20% in 1973). Although remaining in the rand currency zone, Swaziland issued its own currency of emalangeni (singular, lilangeni) and cents, equal to and convertible into rands and backed by the South African Reserve Bank.

In his March budget the finance minister indicated the linkage between the Swazi economy and world inflation. Current high commodity prices indicated good prospects for the nation, particularly in the important sugar industry. Wood pulp exports increased by 5.5% and asbestos by 46%. The value of the cotton crop increased from R 750,000 to R 5 million for the 1974 season, and a textile factory for processing was established in the Nhlangano area after talks with experts from Hong Kong. The tourist industry expanded to a record 92,000 visitors in 1973. Shell Oil Co. was given a concession to develop the extensive coal deposits known to exist in eastern Swaziland. The spectacular increase in government spending was balanced by world prices for Swaziland commodities, but the finance minister pointed out that Swaziland's capacity to absorb loans was limited by lack of skilled personnel to carry out projects rather than by repayment difficulties.   (MOLLY MORTIMER)

[978.E.8.b.ii]

Sweden

A constitutional monarchy of northern Europe lying on the eastern side of the Scandinavian Peninsula, Sweden has common borders with Finland and Norway. Area: 173,732 sq.mi. (449,964 sq.km.). Pop. (1974 est.): 8,160,000. Cap. and largest city: Stock-

holm (pop., 1973 est., 681,300). Language: Swedish, with some Finnish and Lapp in the north. Religion: predominantly Lutheran. King, Carl XVI Gustaf; prime minister in 1974, Olof Palme.

Olof Palme's Social Democratic government—reelected in September 1973 but without a parliamentary majority—was put to an early test in 1974 by the oil crisis. Energy shortages created immediate concern about Sweden's ability to maintain its standard of living, because it was heavily dependent on imported oil, much of it coming from Arab countries. At the end of November 1973 a voluntary campaign was launched to cut oil consumption, and in January 1974 rationing was introduced with the aim of avoiding reductions in industrial production and thus safeguarding employment. Gasoline was rationed for only three weeks, but rationing of heating oil continued until March. Prime Minister Palme told the Parliament (Riksdag) that Sweden was in an exposed position; because of its climate, half of its total energy consumption had to be used to heat homes and places of work, to say nothing of the huge amounts of power required by the steel and forest industries. The situation was further aggravated by Sweden's small refining capacity.

The oil crisis also cast its shadow over the budget for 1974–75, presented in January, which gave priority to labour market security, the working environment, improvements for the handicapped, cultural activities, and energy supply. The revised budget, in May, was more optimistic. It proposed an increase in alcohol excise and a scheme, introduced in the autumn, under which companies making profits of more than 100,000 kronor would set aside a portion of their net profits in a "work environment" fund.

Despite the oil crisis, the Swedish economy performed well during 1974. In June the number of job vacancies exceeded the number of unemployed for the first time in three years. There were indications that this favourable state of affairs would last into 1975, although any deterioration in international trade would cause serious problems for a country so dependent on exports. At the end of January the government introduced a 2.8 billion kronor economic package designed to maintain employment, dampen price increases, and strengthen purchasing power. Similar to the economic measures applied in October 1973, it affected child allowances, old-age pensions, housing construction, energy-saving investments, and the subsidy of basic foods. At the end of February, the government increased the package to 4 billion kronor in a compromise with the Centre and Liberal parties, the main element of which was a decision to lower the 17.6% value-added tax (VAT) by 3% between April 1 and September 15. The bank rate was raised to 6% in April and to 7% in August to counteract a drain on Sweden's currency reserves.

The government had a relatively easy year in Parliament, but there were some hard-fought compromises. The 1973 election had given the Socialist and non-Socialist blocs 175 seats each, leading to fears of deadlock and overmuch use of the Swedish parliamentary practice of drawing lots to decide the issue in the event of a tied vote. There were, in fact, occasions when lots had to be drawn, but in general the government cleverly avoided head-on collisions, and the prospect of a new general election soon receded into the distance. The government did give way over the temporary reduction of VAT and over use of state pension funds to buy shares in private companies.

Education. (1973–74) Primary, pupils 690,497, teachers 40,000; secondary and vocational, pupils 560,971, teachers 60,000; teacher training, students 13,678, teachers 1,000; higher (including 8 universities), students 102,000, teaching staff 7,000.

Finance. Monetary unit: krona, with (Sept. 16, 1974) a free rate of 4.47 kronor to U.S. $1 (10.35 kronor = £1 sterling). Gold, SDRs, and foreign exchange, central bank: (June 1974) U.S. $1,674,000,000; (June 1973) U.S. $2,274,000,-000. Budget (1974–75 est.): revenue 71,489,000,-000 kronor; expenditure 78,595,000,000 kronor. Gross national product: (1972) 198,840,000,000 kronor; (1971) 182,590,000,000 kronor. Money supply: (April 1974) 23,010,000,000 kronor; (April 1973) 19,680,000,000 kronor. Cost of living (1970 = 100): (May 1974) 130; (May 1973) 120.

Foreign Trade. (1973) Imports 46,302,000,-000 kronor; exports 53,019,000,000 kronor. Import sources: West Germany 20%; U.K. 12%; Denmark 8%; Norway 7%; U.S. 7%; Finland 6%; The Netherlands 5%. Export destinations; U.K. 15%; West Germany 10%; Denmark 10%; Norway 9%; Finland 7%; U.S. 6%; France 5%. Main exports: machinery 25%; motor vehicles 10%; paper 9%; iron and steel 8%; wood pulp 8%; timber 7%; ships and boats 6%.

Transport and Communications. Roads (1973) 97,490 km. (including 607 km. expressways; excludes 62,709 km. of subsidized private roads open to the public). Motor vehicles in use (1973): passenger 2,502,600; commercial 147,-980. Railways (1972): 12,114 km. (including 7,520 km. electrified); traffic 4,470,000,000 passenger-km., freight 16,214,000,000 net ton-km. Air traffic (including Swedish apportionment of international operations of Scandinavian Airlines System; 1973): 3,414,000,000 passenger-km.; freight 144,830,000 net ton-km. Shipping (1973): merchant vessels 100 gross tons and over 831; gross tonnage 5,669,340. Telephones (Dec. 1972) 4,680,000. Radio receivers (Dec. 1972) 2,984,-000. Television licenses (Dec. 1972) 2,701,000.

Agriculture. Production (in 000; metric tons; 1973; 1972 in parentheses): wheat 1,255 (1,-150); barley 1,804 (1,883); oats 1,380 (1,630); rye 321 (366); potatoes 997 (1,137); sugar, raw value c. 267 (292); rapeseed 339 (327); apples (1972) 132, (1971) 148; butter (1972) 45, (1971) 43; cheese (1972) 70, (1971) 69; beef and veal (1972) 130, (1971) 146; pork (1972) c. 268, (1971) 248; timber (cu.m.; 1972) 58,-000, (1971) 64,600; fish catch (1972) 225, (1971) 238. Livestock (in 000; June 1973): cattle 1,841; sheep c. 360; pigs 2,264; horses c. 53; chickens (1972) 8,277.

Industry. Index of industrial production (1970 = 100): (1973) 111; (1972) 104. Production (in 000; metric tons; 1973): cement 3,789; electricity (81% hydroelectric in 1972; kw-hr.) 77,279,000; iron ore (60–65% metal content) 34,810; pig iron 2,561; crude steel 5,659; silver (troy oz.; 1972) 4,200; petroleum products (1971) 11,752; sulfuric acid (1971) 769; cotton yarn 8.3; rayon, etc., yarn and fibres 37; wood pulp (1972) mechanical 1,550, chemical 6,764; newsprint 1,075; other paper (1972) 3,-600. Merchant vessels launched (100 gross tons and over; 1973) 2,507,000 gross tons. New dwelling units completed (1973) 97,000.

The government did not mention a reduction in VAT in its January economic package, although this had been forcefully put forward by all the other parties, but after negotiations with the opposition it consented to a 3% drop. The question of the state pension funds revolved around the fourth fund (created in 1973 with a capital of 500 million kronor taken from the three earlier funds), which had the right to purchase an unlimited number of shares in private companies. The Centre and Conservative parties wished to restrict the proportion of shares the fund could purchase to 5% and also proposed that Parliament—not the government—should decide how much extra capital the fund received and that it should be given accounts of the fund's activities. Once again there were drawn-out negotiations, complicated by the trade unions' resolute opposition to the 5% limitation. Finally, the government agreed to the 5% limitation, which would remain until more experience had been gained, and to Parliament's deciding on capital additions and receiving reports.

To finance a proposed reduction of taxes as of January 1975 and the lowering of the retirement age to 65 from 67 in January 1976, the government wanted to increase employers' social charges and raise the payroll tax, but the Liberal Party objected to the latter item. The situation became so serious that the government called unions, employers, and the opposition to a conference at the Haga Manor in Stockholm in May. It was decided that the tax reform would be paid for by an increase in the employers' social charges, but not in the payroll tax, and the retirement age would be lowered as of July 1976 instead of January. The Haga agreement saved the Social Democrats from the threat of a new election and, more significantly, shattered the united front of the non-Socialist opposition.

On February 27 a new constitution, effective Jan. 1, 1975, was adopted for the second time by a new Parliament, as required by law. The constitution reduced the role of the king to that of a figurehead whose formal assent to legislation was no longer required. It would also lower the number of seats in Parliament from 350 to 349, thus avoiding ties and the consequent drawing of lots. In May a new and more liberal abortion law, effective January 1975, was approved. At midyear a state commission proposed the establishment of national gambling casinos to be run by the state. At about the same time the government decided to allow Sweden to become a member of the Energy Coordinating Group on condition that it could withdraw if its neutrality was threatened.

The oil crisis sharpened the continuing debate about nuclear power. The government, conscious that a large body of opinion in Sweden opposed nuclear power and its attendant risks but mindful of Sweden's future energy requirements, was careful not to commit itself. Industry Minister Rune Johansson said that a final decision on Sweden's future energy policy would not be taken until all the facts were known. In November it was revealed that Norway had promised to supply oil to Sweden during the coming decade. During 1974 Parliament approved plans for the construction of a 4.6 billion kronor steelworks in Luleå, northern Sweden, to be in operation by 1980. It would be the largest single industrial investment ever made in Sweden.

The journalists and one of their informants involved in the 1973 "IB affair"—concerning revelations made about Sweden's security service (Information Bureau)—were sentenced in January 1974 to one year's imprisonment. The case led to a lively debate on neutral Sweden's role in espionage activities. The controversy was revived in November when the magazine that had published the original revelations accused the court that rejected the appeal of one of the journalists of being politically motivated. The U.S. and Sweden appointed ambassadors to each other's capitals in March. Diplomatic relations between the two countries had been severed since December 1972 as a result of Swedish disapproval of the U.S. role in Vietnam. (ALAN WILSON)

[972.A.6.b]

A collection of valuable Russian icons is displayed at police headquarters in Stockholm. The relics were smuggled out of the Soviet Union by two employees of the Swedish embassy in Moscow before their discovery and arrest.

UPI COMPIX

Swimming

International regional championships plus a United States-East Germany dual meet in 1974 provided the setting for a record-shattering year in amateur competitive swimming. With the Olympic Games still two years off, the regional championships increased worldwide interest by offering multinational events.

The year's assault on previous records began with the tenth British Commonwealth Games at Christchurch, N.Z., January 25–February 1, when Canada's Wendy Cook, 17, and Australia's 15-year-old Stephen Holland each lowered world marks. The Canadian

Swedish Literature:
see Literature

East Germany's Karla Linke establishes a new world record of 2 min. 34.99 sec. in the women's 200-m. breaststroke competition in Vienna.

high-school student set her record in the 100-m. backstroke, 1 min. 4.78 sec., and the Australian teenager stroked to a record of 8 min. 15.88 sec. for the 800-m. freestyle, on his way to a near-record victory in the 1,500-m. freestyle. Australia won the swimming portion of the 39-nation games with 12 gold and 32 total medals to 9 and 27 for second-place Canada. The Canadians lost seven additional gold medals by a total of 2.35 sec.

In the 13th European Championships on August 18–25 at Vienna, 17 world and 23 European records were set. East Germany continued its ascent to a world ranking just below the U.S., its women winning every event but the 100-m. breaststroke; in that race a world record time of 1 min. 12.55 sec. by West Germany's Christel Justen, 17, prevented an East German sweep. Limited to two entries per race, the East German girls placed one-two in 9 of the 12 individual events, losing only a second place in the 200-m. freestyle and 800-m. freestyle in addition to the breaststroke defeat. Eight of the winning times resulted in world records. The East Germans also triumphed in both relays, winning both the 400-m. freestyle and 400-m. medley, the latter in world record time by almost 10 sec. over their closest rival.

In the men's competition, the 15 titles were shared by five nations. Peter Nocke, 18, of West Germany won both the 100-m. and 200-m. freestyle events and also anchored his country's 400-m. and 800-m. freestyle relays and 400-m. medley relay to victory. Roland Matthes, 24, of East Germany, undefeated in backstroke competition since 1967, easily won the

100-m. and 200-m. backstroke, though not in world record times. East Germany unveiled Frank Pfuetze, a 15-year-old newcomer to international competition, who won the 1,500-m. freestyle in a European record time of 15 min. 54.57 sec. His teammate, Roger Pyttel, 17, won the 100-m. butterfly to give the East German men their fourth gold medal.

Great Britain's David Wilkie, 20, won the 200-m. breaststroke and set a world record of 2 min. 6.32 sec. in winning the 200-m. individual medley. Andras Hargitay, 19, Hungary's 400-m. individual medley world champion, set a world record of 4 min. 28.89 sec. in the event. The Soviet Union was held to two gold medals, Nikolay Pankin, 25, winning the 100-m. breaststroke and Aleksandr Samsonov, 21, the 400-m. freestyle.

In the medal count, East Germany early outdistanced its rivals with 17 gold and a total of 35. West Germany with 6 gold and a total of 12 was a distant runner-up, while the Soviet Union finished third with 2 gold and 13 total.

From August 21 to September 1, Concord, Calif., was the site of outstanding swimming competition. A record attendance of more than 25,000 watched some 1,260 swimmers from the United States, Australia, Canada, and Brazil compete from August 21–25 in the Amateur Athletic Union (AAU) national senior championships. Daily bulletins from the European Championships, being held at the same time, generated intense interest and motivation, resulting in 11 world and 18 U.S. records.

The outstanding performer in the AAU meet was Tim Shaw. The 16-year-old high-school swimmer set world marks in the 200-m., 400-m., and 1,500-m. freestyle. His time of 1 min. 51.66 sec. for the 200-m. freestyle erased Mark Spitz's record of 1 min. 52.78 sec. set at the 1972 Olympics. Shaw's time of 3 min. 56.96 sec. shattered the previous 400-m. record of 3 min. 58.18 sec. by Rick DeMont; Shaw then lowered this to 3 min. 54.69 sec. In the 1,500-m. freestyle, his world record time was 15 min. 31.75 sec. Only one other man, Jon Konrads in 1958, had been able to hold those three world records at the same time.

John Hencken, 20, set a world mark in the 200-m. breaststroke of 2 min. 18.93 sec. Steve Furniss set a world record in the 200-m. individual medley, 2 min. 6.32 sec.

In the women's events, Shirley Babashoff, 17, lowered the 200-m. and 400-m. freestyle world standards to 2 min. 2.94 sec. and 4 min. 15.77 sec., respectively. Australia's Jenny Turrall, 14, lowered her world record in the 1,500-m. freestyle for the fourth time in less than a year as she was timed in 16 min. 33.94 sec. In the same race Jo Ann Harshbarger, 17, was in the lead at 800 m. and was awarded the world record for that length of 8 min. 47.5 sec.

When the East German swimmers arrived at a dual meet at Concord on August 31–September 1, they became the first East German team in any sport to compete in the U.S. The meet attracted more than 12,000 spectators, who saw the U.S. men win every swimming event and the U.S. women win only the 200-m., 400-m., and 800-m. freestyle and the 400-m. freestyle relay. However, the American women captured enough second and third places to give the U.S. a 198–145 victory. Seven world records were broken and three were tied; 16 U.S. records and 4 European marks were also set.

Roland Matthes, East German world recordholder in the backstroke, was defeated for the first time in

World Records Set in 1974			
Event	Name	Country	Time
MEN			
200-m. freestyle	Tim Shaw	U.S.	1 min. 51.66 sec.
400-m. freestyle	Tim Shaw	U.S.	3 min. 56.96 sec.
400-m. freestyle	Tim Shaw	U.S.	3 min. 54.69 sec.
800-m. freestyle	Stephen Holland	Australia	8 min. 15.88 sec.
1,500-m. freestyle	Tim Shaw	U.S.	15 min. 31.75 sec.
100-m. breaststroke	John Hencken	U.S.	1 min. 3.88 sec.
200-m. breaststroke	John Hencken	U.S.	2 min. 18.93 sec.
200-m. breaststroke	John Hencken	U.S.	2 min. 18.21 sec.
200-m. individual medley	David Wilkie	Great Britain	2 min. 6.32 sec.
200-m. individual medley	Steve Furniss	U.S.	2 min. 6.32 sec.
400-m. individual medley	Andras Hargitay	Hungary	4 min. 28.89 sec.
4 x 100-m. freestyle relay	U.S. national team (Andy Coan, Jim Montgomery, Mike Bottom, Tom Hickcox)	U.S.	3 min. 25.17 sec.
WOMEN			
100-m. freestyle	Kornelia Ender	East Germany	57.51 sec.
100-m. freestyle	Kornelia Ender	East Germany	56.96 sec.
200-m. freestyle	Kornelia Ender	East Germany	2 min. 3.22 sec.
200-m. freestyle	Shirley Babashoff	U.S.	2 min. 2.94 sec.
400-m. freestyle	Heather Greenwood	U.S.	4 min. 17.33 sec.
400-m. freestyle	Shirley Babashoff	U.S.	4 min. 15.77 sec.
800-m. freestyle	Jenny Turrall	Australia	8 min. 50.1 sec.*
800-m. freestyle	Jo Harshbarger	U.S.	8 min. 47.5 sec.*
1,500-m. freestyle	Jenny Turrall	Australia	16 min. 48.2 sec.*
1,500-m. freestyle	Jenny Turrall	Australia	16 min. 43.4 sec.*
1,500-m. freestyle	Jenny Turrall	Australia	16 min. 39.28 sec.
1,500-m. freestyle	Jenny Turrall	Australia	16 min. 33.94 sec.
100-m. backstroke	Wendy Cook	Canada	1 min. 4.78 sec.
100-m. backstroke	Ulrike Richter	East Germany	1 min. 4.43 sec.
100-m. backstroke	Ulrike Richter	East Germany	1 min. 4.09 sec.
100-m. backstroke	Ulrike Richter	East Germany	1 min. 3.30 sec.
100-m. backstroke	Ulrike Richter	East Germany	1 min. 3.08 sec.
100-m. backstroke	Ulrike Richter	East Germany	1 min. 2.98 sec.
200-m. backstroke	Ulrike Richter	East Germany	2 min. 18.41 sec.
200-m. backstroke	Ulrike Richter	East Germany	2 min. 17.35 sec.
100-m. breaststroke	Renate Vogel	East Germany	1 min. 12.91 sec.
100-m. breaststroke	Christel Justen	West Germany	1 min. 12.55 sec.
100-m. breaststroke	Renate Vogel	East Germany	1 min. 12.28 sec.
200-m. breaststroke	Anne Katrin Schott	East Germany	2 min. 37.89 sec.
200-m. breaststroke	Karla Linke	East Germany	2 min. 34.99 sec.
100-m. butterfly	Rosemarie Kother	East Germany	1 min. 2.09 sec.
100-m. butterfly	Rosemarie Kother	East Germany	1 min. 1.99 sec.
100-m. butterfly	Rosemarie Kother	East Germany	1 min. 1.88 sec.
200-m. individual medley	Ulrike Tauber	East Germany	2 min. 18.93 sec.
400-m. individual medley	Ulrike Tauber	East Germany	4 min. 52.42 sec.
4 x 100-m. freestyle relay	U.S. national team (Kathy Heddy, Ann Marshall, Kim Peyton, Shirley Babashoff)	U.S.	3 min. 51.99 sec.
4 x 100-m. medley relay	East Germany national team (Ulrike Richter, Renate Vogel, Rosemarie Kother, Kornelia Ender)		4 min. 13.78 sec.

*Watch time, recorded in 1/10 increments.

the backstroke events by John Naber, 18. World records were set by East Germany's Rosemarie Kother, 100-m. butterfly, 1 min. 1.88 sec.; by Ulrike Richter, 100-m. backstroke, 1 min. 2.98 sec.; by Renate Vogel, 100-m. breaststroke, 1 min. 12.28 sec.; and by the U.S. women's 400-m. freestyle relay (Kathy Heddy, Kim Peyton, Ann Marshall, and Shirley Babashoff), 3 min. 51.99 sec. Shirley Babashoff tied her 200-m. freestyle world mark of 2 min. 2.94 sec.

For the United States, world records were set by John Hencken, 100-m. and 200-m. breaststroke, 1 min. 3.88 sec. and 2 min. 18.21 sec., respectively. The quartet of Andy Coan, Mike Bottom, Jim Montgomery, and Tim Hickcox set a record of 3 min. 25.17 sec. for the 400-m. freestyle relay. Steve Furniss tied his world mark of 2 min. 6.32 sec. for the 200-m. individual medley.

Diving. In the European championships at Vienna, August 18–25, Klaus Dibiasi of Italy and Ulrike Knape of Sweden demonstrated that they were the best male and female divers in the world, each winning both the springboard and platform events. The Fern Cup, presented to the country that gains the most points in the combined men's and women's diving events, was won by the U.S.S.R. The Soviets placed second to Sweden in the women's events and second to Italy in the men's but won easily in the combined total with 41 points to runner-up Italy's 35.

In the East German/U.S. dual meet at Concord, the U.S. defeated East Germany 24–20. Janet Ely of the U.S. won the women's platform and Keith Russell, U.S., won the men's 3-m. springboard. East Germany's Christa Koehler won the women's 3-m. springboard and Falk Hoffman, the men's platform.

(ALBERT SCHOENFIELD)

[452.B.4.a.i]

Switzerland

A federal republic in west central Europe consisting of a confederation of 25 cantons, Switzerland is bounded by West Germany, Austria, Liechtenstein, Italy, and France. Area: 15,943 sq.mi. (41,293 sq.km.). Pop. (1973 est.): 6,431,000. Cap.: Bern (pop., 1973 est., 159,100). Largest city: Zürich (pop., 1973 est., 416,100). Language (1970): German 65%; French 18%; Italian 12%; Romansh 1%. Religion (1970): Roman Catholic 49.4%; Protestant 47.7%. President in 1974, Ernst Brugger.

The "total revision" of the federal constitution envisaged a few years earlier was still remote on May 29, 1974, the constitution's 100th anniversary. The preparatory commission published an 860-page report containing the views of many groups. The major problem seemed to be lack of popular interest.

Commercial and cultural contacts with China were increased; an exhibition of Swiss industrial products was held in Peking, and Foreign Minister Pierre Graber visited that city. The exiled Soviet writer Aleksandr Solzhenitsyn asked for and received asylum and settled in Zürich with his family. The violent reaction in Parliament and press to the sanctions voted against Israel in UNESCO in November, and consequent Arab warnings against Switzerland, embarrassed the government in its effort to maintain a neutral position in world affairs.

The separatist movement in the largely French-speaking and Roman Catholic region of the Jura in the canton of Bern continued to attract attention as a test of the ability of the Swiss system to settle minority problems in a constructive way. In June the government of the canton called upon the citizens of the region to vote for or against the establishment of a new, 23rd, canton. A record participation of citizens involved (90%) resulted in a majority in favour (36,802 to 34,057); the northern part of the region was strongly separatist but several districts in the south produced negative majorities. Antiseparatist leaders in the districts wishing to remain in the canton of Bern, therefore, used their right to call for a second plebiscite in their areas, scheduled for March 1975.

The state of the 1974 federal budget was grave. The annually increasing deficit was expected to reach between SFr. 600 million and SFr. 800 million. The deficit was due to a large increase of federal expenditure, especially for social security and welfare, transportation (highway construction) and energy (nuclear power plants), and education. Parliament cut the proposed budget at its pre-Christmas session. How-

SWITZERLAND
Education. (1972–73) Primary, pupils 764,878, teachers (excluding craft teachers; 1961–62) 23,761; secondary, pupils 370,099, teachers (full-time; 1961–62) 6,583; vocational, pupils 142,592; teacher training, students (1970–71) 12,008; higher (including 10 universities; 1971–72), students 44,624, teaching staff 4,318.
Finance. Monetary unit: Swiss franc, with (Sept. 16, 1974) a free rate of SFr. 3.01 to U.S. $1 (SFr. 6.96 = £1 sterling). Gold, SDRs, and foreign exchange, official: (June 1974) U.S. $8,413,000,000; (June 1973) U.S. $8,222,000,000. Budget (1973 actual): revenue SFr. 10,111,000,000; expenditure SFr. 10,786,000,000. Gross national product: (1973) SFr. 131.1 billion; (1972) SFr. 116.1 billion. Money supply: (April 1974) SFr. 53.8 billion; (April 1973) SFr. 53,790,000,000. Cost of living (1970 = 100): (June 1974) 134; (June 1973) 123.
Foreign Trade. (1973) Imports SFr. 36,548,000,000; exports SFr. 29,790,000,000. Import sources: EEC 69% (West Germany 30%, France 14%, Italy 9%, U.K. 6%); U.S. 6%; Austria 5%. Export destinations: EEC 46% (West Germany 14%, France 9%, Italy 8%, U.K. 8%); U.S. 8%; Austria 6%. Main exports: machinery 32% (textile machinery 7%); chemicals 21%; watches and clocks 11%; textile yarns and fabrics 7%. Tourism (1972): visitors 7,131,000; gross receipts U.S. $1,062,000,000.
Transport and Communications. Roads (1973) 60,705 km. (including 557 km. expressways). Motor vehicles in use (1973): passenger 1,656,400; commercial 159,700. Railways: (1971) 5,000 km. (including 4,974 km. electrified); traffic (1973) 8,280,000,000 passenger-km., freight 7,140,000,000 net ton-km. Air traffic (1973): 6,728,000,000 passenger-km.; freight 258,730,000 net ton-km. Shipping (1973): merchant vessels 100 gross tons and over 30; gross tonnage 202,764. Telephones (Dec. 1972) 3,404,000. Radio licenses (Dec. 1972) 1,958,000. Television licenses (Dec. 1972) 1,536,000.
Agriculture. Production (in 000; metric tons; 1973; 1972 in parentheses): wheat c. 390 (400); barley c. 200 (165); oats c. 35 (25); rye c. 48 (55); corn (1972) 100, (1971) 90; potatoes c. 900 (1,000); rapeseed 22 (24); apples (1972) c. 270, (1971) 390; pears (1972) c. 130, (1971) 115; sugar, raw value (1972) 62, (1971) 74; wine (1972) 93, (1971) 82; milk (1972) 3,213, (1971) 3,140; butter (1972) c. 31, (1971) 30; cheese (1972) 96, (1971) 89; beef and veal c. 126 (124); pork c. 230 (218). Livestock (in 000; April 1973): cattle c. 1,909; sheep c. 334; pigs c. 2,129; horses 47; chickens c. 6,610.
Industry. Index of industrial production (1970 = 100): (1973) 110; (1972) 104. Production (in 000; metric tons; 1973): cement 5,420; aluminum (1972) 83; petroleum products (1972) 5,109; rayon, etc., yarn and fibre (1972) 9.1; nylon, etc., yarn and fibre (1972) 73; cigarettes (units; 1972) 32,026,000; watches (units; 1972) 56,955; manufactured gas (gasworks only; cu.m.; 1972) 398,000; electricity (kw-hr.) 37,155,000.

Trapped in the high Alps by early snowfall, hundreds of sheep and lambs are saved only by the efforts of Swiss Army mountain-wise soldiers.

ever, the simultaneous rejection by the people, in a nationwide plebiscite held on December 8, of the proposal to increase revenue from several types of taxes and levies necessitated the subsequent adoption of a stopgap budget.

The federal government's report on defense policy was approved by Parliament in June. After considerable discussion, it was decided to purchase the U.S. Tiger IIF-5E fighter plane rather than the French Mirage 30 or the British Hunter.

The government's economic prognostications early in the year were confirmed later by an Organization for Economic Cooperation and Development report on the Swiss economy. The real increase of domestic demand was expected to decline by about 50% in 1974 as compared with 1973, and the growth of real output was forecast at 2% of the 1973 increase. Because of continued tightness of the labour market, however, this development would not affect the level of employment until 1975. No great problems were expected in the 1974 balance of payments; imports would decrease and exports increase. Moreover, Switzerland would receive a share of the revenue of the oil-producing countries in the form of capital. In November the government limited the influx of foreign capital to prevent the Swiss franc from rising excessively.

Following an exceptionally heated campaign, the people on October 20 rejected, by 1,689,870 votes to 878,739, a "third antiforeign influence initiative" calling for the departure from the country of some 500,000 foreign workers and their families by January 1978. Meanwhile, the government pursued its policy of stabilizing and gradually diminishing the volume of resident foreign workers (596,000 in 1973). (*See* MIGRATION, INTERNATIONAL.)

Recipients of government-financed old-age pensions were given a "13th month" in September, in fulfillment of the eighth revision of the pertinent law. The possible future synchronization of government-operated old-age insurance with the movement of prices (or incomes) remained under discussion.

(MELANIE STAERK)

[972.A.8]

Syria

A republic in southwestern Asia on the Mediterranean Sea, Syria is bordered by Turkey, Iraq, Jordan, Israel, and Lebanon. Area: 71,498 sq.mi. (185,180 sq.km.). Pop. (1973 est.): 6,889,948. Cap. and largest city: Damascus (pop., 1970, 836,668). Language: Arabic (official); also Kurdish, Armenian, Turkish, and Circassian. Religion: predominantly Muslim.

An Israeli soldier looks toward the snowy slopes of Mt. Hermon during a skirmish with Syrian tank and infantry units in April.

SYRIA
Education. (1970–71) Primary, pupils 924,969, teachers 25,132; secondary, pupils 315,803, teachers (1969–70) 10,651; vocational, pupils 10,556, teachers 816; teacher training, students 2,424, teachers 201; higher (including 2 universities), students 40,537, teaching staff 1,192.
Finance. Monetary unit: Syrian pound, with (Sept. 16, 1974) an official exchange rate of S£3.70 to U.S. $1 (nominal rate of S£8.55 = £1 sterling). Gold, SDRs, and foreign exchange, central bank: (March 1974) U.S. $569 million; (March 1973) U.S. $116 million. Budget (1973 est.) balanced at S£3,413 million. Gross domestic product: (1972) S£8,698 million; (1971) S£7,438 million. Money supply: (March 1974) S£4,430 million; (March 1973) S£3,156 million. Cost of living (Damascus; 1970 = 100): (Jan. 1974) 139; (Jan. 1973) 123.
Foreign Trade. (1973) Imports S£2,342 million; exports S£1,341.3 million. Import sources: West Germany 11%; Italy 8%; France 7%; U.S.S.R. 7%; Lebanon 6%; U.K. 5%. Export destinations: U.S.S.R. 15%; Italy 13%; Lebanon 8%; China 8%; Greece 7%; West Germany 5%. Main exports: cotton 38%; crude oil 22%; wool 6%.
Transport and Communications. Roads (1971) 16,710 km. (including 63 km. expressways). Motor vehicles in use (1971): passenger 31,700; commercial 17,500. Railways (1972): 1,148 km.; traffic 107 million passenger-km., freight 154 million net ton-km. Air traffic (1972): 290 million passenger-km.; freight 2.3 million net ton-km. Ships entered (1972) vessels totaling 15,181,000 net registered tons; goods loaded (1973) 34,750,000 metric tons, unloaded 2,212,000 metric tons. Telephones (Dec. 1972) 132,000. Radio receivers (Dec. 1972) 2.5 million. Television receivers (Dec. 1973) 179,000.
Agriculture. Production (in 000; metric tons; 1973; 1972 in parentheses): wheat 593 (1,808); barley 102 (710); lentils (1972) c. 140, (1971) 129; tomatoes c. 300 (c. 443); onions c. 80 (107); grapes (1972) c. 215, (1971) c. 215; figs (1972) c. 50, (1971) c. 50; sugar, raw value (1972) 35, (1971) 30; olives c. 125 (c. 180); tobacco (1972) 13, (1971) 8; cotton, lint c. 140 (c. 163). Livestock (in 000; Dec. 1972): cattle c. 590; sheep 5,166; goats c. 770; horses c. 70; asses c. 230; chickens (1971) c. 3,700.
Industry. Production (in 000; metric tons; 1972): cement 1,004; petroleum products (1971) 2,112; crude oil (1973) 5,521; cotton yarn 28; electricity (kw-hr.) 1,223,000.

President in 1974, Gen. Hafez al-Assad; premier, Mahmoud Ayoubi.

In 1974 Syria took a major step by agreeing to a U.S.-sponsored military disengagement with Israel. However, it constantly emphasized that this was only a preliminary move toward a final settlement and urged the Arab states to be prepared for a new war.

In the winter and spring the danger of a renewed major outbreak between Syria and Israel seemed imminent as Syria conducted a war of attrition against Israel on the Golan Heights. Despite visits to Damascus by U.S. Secretary of State Henry Kissinger on January 20 and February 26, no progress was made toward a disengagement of forces. The main obstacles were the exchange of prisoners, Syria's insistence that 170,000 villagers expelled from their homes should be allowed to return, and Syria's continued demand that the territory captured by Israel in 1967 be returned.

Syria received strong diplomatic support from the U.S.S.R., which was displeased over having been kept out of the Israeli-Egyptian disengagement negotiations. President Assad headed a high-level Syrian delegation to Moscow in April and signed several economic and military agreements. The Soviets supplied Syria with arms, including 180-mm. artillery and T-62 tanks, but reports that the supplies included MiG-23 planes and long-range Scud missiles remained unconfirmed. Syria still recognized, however, that the U.S. remained the key to any Israeli withdrawal and, with strong Egyptian encouragement, continued to negotiate through Washington. In May Kissinger made his supreme effort to achieve an Israeli-Syrian disengagement and, after shuttling as mediator some 20 times between Damascus and Jerusalem, brought about an agreement on May 29. Similar to the January Israeli-Egyptian disengagement, it provided for Israel to withdraw to the pre-1973 boundaries and to relinquish an additional band of territory including the former Golan Heights capital Qunaytirah (Kuneitra). Both sides agreed to the thinning out of forces in the forward zones. On June 6, 382 Syrian prisoners returned from Israel and 56 Israeli prisoners went back to Israel. Each side accused the other of maltreating its prisoners. On June 25 Israeli forces finished evacuating Qunaytirah, in accordance with the agreement, and handed it over to the UN Disengagement Observer Force. The following day Syrian civilians were allowed to return, but the Syrians accused the Israelis of having razed the city to the ground; at the end of the year it remained an empty shell, with the Syrians maintaining that it could not be restored to life unless the agricultural areas surrounding it were returned to Syria.

One consequence of the agreement with Israel was a limited rapprochement with the U.S. Pres. Richard M. Nixon visited Damascus on June 15; the Syrian welcome was friendly but less enthusiastic than in Egypt. Agreement was reached on the full restoration of diplomatic relations, which had been broken off in 1967. Relations were also restored with West Germany on August 7.

Although relations with the West improved during the year, the Soviet Union continued to play a vital role in Syria's affairs. The Soviet foreign minister, Andrey A. Gromyko, visited Damascus on May 5–7 during Kissinger's period of shuttle diplomacy between Syria and Israel, and again on May 28–29. Apart from arms, the U.S.S.R. and other Eastern European states provided substantial economic aid. In August it was announced that the U.S.S.R. would build, in addition to the Euphrates Tabka Dam, which was nearing completion, a large dam on the Nahr el-Kebir near Latakia, which would cost $48 million and irrigate 124,000 ha.

In February the government announced that the economic losses from the October 1973 war against Israel were conservatively estimated at £1 billion with the full cost of repairing power stations, bridges, and other installations still to be assessed; only about one-quarter of the aid promised by the Arab oil states had been forthcoming, but more was hoped for. In February President Assad visited oil-rich Kuwait, Saudi Arabia, and Abu Dhabi. Relations with most Arab states were satisfactory, and there was close alignment with Egypt. On September 20 Syria agreed with Egypt and the Palestine Liberation Organization that the latter would represent all the Palestinians, but Syria subsequently tried to work out a joint policy on Palestinian representation. Anxious to keep Jordan in a common Arab front, Syria continued to press hard for a Jordanian-Palestinian compromise, and President Assad played an important role in the one that was achieved at the Arab summit conference at Rabat, Morocco, in October.

The grain crop was well above average in 1974 although early spring floods in the north prevented it from being as good as had been hoped. The 1974–75 cotton crop was expected to be 10% below that of 1973–74, but 1974 exports were slightly above 1973 with large increases to China and other Communist states. In April the government launched new measures to relax controls on currency and capital exports and to encourage the private sector of the economy. On August 31 a new 31-man Cabinet was formed by Premier Mahmoud Ayoubi. (PETER MANSFIELD)

[978.B.3.b]

Taiwan

Taiwan, which consists of the islands of Formosa and Quemoy and other surrounding islands, is the seat of the Republic of China (Nationalist China). It is situated north of the Philippines, southwest of Japan and Okinawa, and east of Hong Kong. The island of Formosa has an area of 13,815 sq.mi.; including its 77 outlying islands (14 in the Taiwan group and 63 in the Pescadores group), the area of Taiwan totals 13,893 sq.mi. (35,981 sq.km.). Pop. (1974 est.): 15,701,000. Cap. and largest city: Taipei (pop., 1974 est., 1,982,-100). President in 1974, Chiang Kai-shek; president of the Executive Yuan (premier), Chiang Ching-kuo.

The Nationalist regime on Taiwan suffered further diplomatic setbacks in 1974 as Botswana, Brazil, Venezuela, and Malaysia shifted diplomatic recognition from Taipei to the People's Republic of China, but Taiwan's economic growth continued. The growth rate for 1974 was officially estimated at 8.6%, and per capita income rose from U.S. $467 in 1973 to about $500. However, the energy crisis, inflation, and shortages of raw materials affected Taiwan's export-oriented economy and caused some concern.

Chiang Ching-kuo, elder son of 87-year-old President Chiang who became premier in 1972, virtually acted as chief executive and chief spokesman of the government. His economically oriented and populist-style administration appeared to be narrowing the gap between the native Taiwanese majority and the mainland refugee Chinese. The base of the government was broadened; about half the Cabinet posts were held by Taiwanese, and Taiwanese had been appointed to the posts of governor and mayor of Taipei.

Since 1971 the number of countries recognizing the Republic of China as the only legal government of China had fallen from nearly 70 to over 30, most of them (except for the U.S.) smaller nations of Africa, South and Central America, and Asia. On May 31 Malaysia established full diplomatic relations with Peking and, as a result, the Malaysian and Nationalist Chinese consulates general in Taipei and Kuala Lumpur were closed. On the same day, the Nationalist Foreign Ministry issued a statement urging the Malaysian government to protect citizens of the Republic of China in Malaysia from harmful measures that might be taken by the Chinese Communists. About one-third of Malaysia's 11 million people were of Chinese origin, and many had strong ties with Taiwan.

Taiwan's annual trade with Japan, amounting to over U.S. $2 billion, was still greater than Japan's trade with mainland China. In protracted negotiations between Japan and the People's Republic over air and fishery agreements, Peking insisted that the Nationalist-owned China Air Lines be excluded from Japan as a condition for opening direct air service between Tokyo and Peking. Taipei had warned that if Japan submitted to this demand it would stop the lucrative operations by Japan Air Lines and China Air Lines between Japan and Taiwan, but when the agreement was finally signed, on April 27, the then Japanese foreign minister, Masayoshi Ohira, declared that

Pres. Chiang Kai-shek celebrated his 87th birthday in Taipei on October 31.

UPI COMPIX

Japan did not recognize the flag insignia of China Air Lines to be the flag of a nation or the airline itself as representing a state. The Nationalist government, viewing this as a deliberate insult, immediately closed China Air Lines' Tokyo-Taipei routes and forbade Japanese planes to land on or fly over Taiwan.

The Nationalists made determined efforts to strengthen ties with those countries that maintained diplomatic relations with Taiwan and sought to improve relations with other countries through trade and cultural missions. In the spring Vice-Pres. C. K. Yen made a goodwill tour of Costa Rica, El Salvador, Nicaragua, and Honduras, and agreements on trade and technical cooperation were concluded with these countries in addition to agreements with Haiti and Barbados.

The appointment of a well-known diplomat, Leonard Unger, as U.S. ambassador to the Republic of China and Washington's decision to allow the Nationalists to open three new consulates in the U.S. were seen as signs of strengthening U.S.-Taiwan relations. Presenting his credentials to Vice-President Yen on May 25, Unger pledged that the U.S. government would continue to safeguard Taiwan's security. Nevertheless, the U.S. withdrew half its F-4 Phantom jets from Taiwan in July, reducing its forces there to about 4,000. Under the Nixon-Chou communiqué of February 1972, Washington had agreed to withdraw U.S. military forces from Taiwan as soon as tensions ceased in the area, while Peking tacitly pledged not to "liberate" Taiwan by force. (HUNG-TI CHU)

[975.A.6]

TAIWAN

Education. (1973–74) Primary, pupils 2,431,440, teachers 61,517; secondary, pupils 1,140,260, teachers 45,094; vocational, pupils 232,574, teachers 8,876; higher (including 8 universities), students 263,551, teaching staff 12,678.

Finance. Monetary unit: New Taiwan dollar, with (Sept. 16, 1974) a par value of NT$38 to U.S. $1 (free rate of NT$88 = £1 sterling). Gold, SDRs, and foreign exchange, official: (June 1974) U.S. $1,080,000,-000; (June 1973) U.S. $1,241,000,000. Budget (1972–73 est.): revenue NT$65,257,000,000; expenditure NT$62,943,000,000. Gross national product: (1973) NT$356,910,000,000; (1972) NT$292,360,000,000. Money supply: (April 1974) NT$74,880,000,000; (April 1973) NT$60,020,000,000. Cost of living (1970 = 100): (June 1974) 176; (June 1973) 116.

Foreign Trade. (1973) Imports NT$145,077,000,-000; exports NT$167,382,000,000. Import sources: Japan 38%; U.S. 25%; West Germany 5%. Export destinations: U.S. 39%; Japan 19%; Hong Kong 7%; West Germany 5%. Main exports: textiles 28%; electrical machinery and equipment 17%; fruit and vegetables 7%; footwear 5%; plywood 5%.

Transport and Communications. Roads (1972) 15,673 km. Motor vehicles in use (1972): passenger 71,900; commercial 66,500. Railways (1972): 4,400 km.; traffic 7,311,000,000 passenger-km., freight 2,-820,000,000 net ton-km. Air traffic (1970): 954 million passenger-km.; freight 25,175,000 net ton-km. Shipping (1973): merchant vessels 100 gross tons and over 413; gross tonnage 1,467,311. Telephones (July 1973) 437,000. Radio licenses (July 1973) 1,469,000. Television licenses (July 1973) 890,000.

Agriculture. Production (in 000; metric tons; 1972; 1971 in parentheses): rice 2,440 (2,314); sweet potatoes 2,928 (3,391); cassava (1970) 308, (1969) 316; peanuts 94 (98); oranges (1970) c. 156, (1969) 123; tea 26 (27); sugar, raw value (1971) c. 750, (1970) 843; bananas 366 (471); pineapples 334 (359); pork (1972) c. 360, (1971) 354. Livestock (in 000; Dec. 1972): cattle 248; pigs 3,831; goats 178; chickens (1970) 14,269.

Industry. Production (in 000; metric tons; 1972): coal 3,913; crude oil 130; natural gas (cu.m.) 1,264,-000; electricity (kw-hr.) 17,449,000; cement 5,690; crude steel 739; aluminum 32; salt 440; caustic soda 152; petroleum products (1970) 5,030; cotton yarn 91; paper 454.

Tanzania

This republic, an East African member of the Commonwealth of Nations, consists of two parts: Tanganyika, on the Indian Ocean, bordered by Kenya, Uganda, Rwanda, Burundi, Zaire, Zambia, Malawi, and Mozambique; and Zanzibar, just off the coast, including Zanzibar Island, Pemba Island, and small islets. Total area of the united republic: 364,943 sq.mi. (945,198 sq.km.). Total pop. (1973 est.): 14,377,000, including (1966 est.) 98.9% Africans and 0.7% Indo-Pakistani. Cap. and largest city: Dar es Salaam (pop., 1972 est., 396,700) in Tanganyika. Language: English and Swahili. Religion (1967): traditional beliefs 34.6%; Christian 30.6%; Muslim 30.5%. President in 1974, Julius Nyerere.

On July 7, 1974, the Tanganyika African National Union, Tanzania's ruling party, celebrated the 20th anniversary of its founding in 1954 with trade shows, football matches, and other festivities. Seven months earlier, in January, the Zanzibar government celebrated the tenth anniversary of its revolution, which overthrew the sultan's government, by releasing 545

TANZANIA

Education. Tanganyika: (1971) primary, pupils 902,-609, teachers 19,786; secondary, pupils 32,603, teachers 2,199; vocational (1970), pupils 1,546, teachers 145; teacher training, students 4,471, teachers 327; higher (University of Dar es Salaam), students 2,060, teaching staff 308. Zanzibar: (1966) primary, pupils 35,000; secondary, pupils 1,700.

Finance. Monetary unit: Tanzanian shilling, with (Sept. 16, 1974) a par value of TShs. 7.14 to U.S. $1 (free rate of TShs. 16.56 = £1 sterling). Gold, SDRs, and foreign exchange: (June 1974) U.S. $72.5 million; (June 1973) U.S. $133.1 million. Budget (1974–75 est.): revenue TShs. 3,535,000,000; expenditure TShs. 3,661,000,000. Gross domestic product: (1972) TShs. 10,922,000,000; (1971) TShs. 9,732,000,000. Money supply: (June 1974) TShs. 2,964,000,000; (June 1973) TShs. 2,348,000,000. Cost of living (Dar es Salaam; 1970 = 100): (June 1973) 121; (June 1972) 114.

Foreign Trade. (1973) Imports TShs. 3,416,000,-000; exports TShs. 2,581,000,000. Import sources: China 20%; U.K. 14%; Kenya 10%; Japan 8%; West Germany 8%; Iran 7%; Italy 5%. Export destinations: U.K. 10%; Zambia 10%; Indonesia 9%; U.S. 8%; Kenya 6%; West Germany 6%; India 6%; Hong Kong 6%. Main exports: coffee 24%; cotton 17%; cloves 11%; sisal 10%; cashew nuts 7%.

Transport and Communications. Roads (1972) c. 17,500 km. Motor vehicles in use (1972): passenger 34,900; commercial (including buses) 37,600. Railways (1972) 2,560 km. (excluding the new 1,860-km. Tanzam railway linking Dar es Salaam with Zambia; for traffic see KENYA). Air traffic: see KENYA. Shipping traffic (mainland only; 1972): goods loaded 1,257,000 metric tons, unloaded 2,801,000 metric tons. Telephones (Dec. 1972) 44,000. Radio receivers (Dec. 1972) 225,000. Television receivers (Dec. 1969) 4,000.

Agriculture. Production (in 000; metric tons; 1973; 1972 in parentheses): corn c. 650 (984); sweet potatoes (1972) c. 330, (1971) c. 320; millet c. 130 (128); sorghum c. 180 (181); sugar, raw value c. 116 (c. 116); rice c. 180 (185); cassava (1972) c. 6,000, (1971) c. 6,000; dry beans c. 130 (c. 130); coffee c. 48 (52); cotton, lint c. 87 (c. 65); sisal (1972) 157, (1971) 181; timber (cu.m.; 1972) 32,700, (1971) 32,200. Livestock (in 000; 1972–73): cattle c. 13,500; sheep c. 2,700; pigs c. 23; goats c. 4,500; asses c. 160; chickens (1971–72) c. 19,000.

Industry. Production (in 000; metric tons; 1972): cement 237; salt 44; magnesite (exports) 0.5; diamonds (metric carats) 636; petroleum products 771; electricity (excluding most industrial production; kw-hr.) 469,000.

prisoners including three members of the former sultan's Cabinet. Later in the same month the year-long trial for treason of 81 people charged with complicity in the assassination of Sheikh Abeid Karume of Zanzibar came to an end. In all, 54 were found guilty, of whom 34 were sentenced to death. Eighteen of the accused (14 of them sentenced to death in absentia) were being held on the mainland; Nyerere had refused to surrender them for trial in Zanzibar because they would not have been permitted to have defense lawyers and also because under Tanzanian law trials in absentia were invalid.

In March the president paid an official visit to China, as the result of which the Chinese government offered an interest-free loan of about $75 million during the next five years to develop coal and iron ore deposits in southern Tanzania and to link them with the railway system. This offer was followed shortly afterward by a loan of about $400,000 by the government of West Germany to help counter the difficulties arising from increased oil prices and the probability of crop shortages due to poor rainfall. In June, also, Britain resumed economic aid, which had been stopped in 1965 when Tanzania left the Commonwealth and broke off diplomatic relations. The British Ministry of Overseas Development agreed to make available £11 million to assist rural development. The agreement also envisaged the payment of compensation to British farmers whose land might subsequently be nationalized, and one of the first results of this clause was a government proposal to take over British land that was producing mainly coffee and tea in the region of Mt. Kilimanjaro. This caused discontent among uncompensated farmers whose land had been nationalized in October 1973.

Relations with Uganda became tense in July when Pres. Idi Amin (*see* BIOGRAPHY) accused Tanzania and Zambia of planning an invasion of Uganda to restore former president Milton Obote to power. Amin claimed that Tanzanian forces had been assembled on Uganda's southwestern frontier but that the plan had been changed and the force withdrawn. Ugandan troops were moved to the area, however, and the country's armed forces were put on alert after reports that Tanzanian spies had been arrested along the border. Tanzania denied these allegations, and in August Amin canceled his plan for a counterinvasion. A trade dispute with Kenya led to the temporary closing of frontier posts in December.

At the beginning of April the government introduced new price controls, any breach of which rendered traders liable to fines and imprisonment. In September Nyerere made a tour of the Caribbean.

(KENNETH INGHAM)

[978.E.6.b.iii]

Taxation

United States. The major controversy over national tax policy in 1974 developed in the month before the November election, when Pres. Gerald Ford proposed a 5% income tax surcharge for persons with incomes exceeding $15,000. The surcharge was intended to distribute the burden of inflation and of anti-inflation policies more equitably while avoiding increases in the federal budget deficit.

It was apparent from the start that the proposal was not likely to be adopted. The Democratic successes in the congressional elections were thought to

In the U.S., Pres. Gerald Ford proposed a 5% surcharge tax on corporate and upper level incomes to slow inflationary forces.

remove what small chance had previously existed. Objections were made to the imposition of a new tax burden on any group when virtually everyone was suffering from inflation. There was also uncertainty, reflected in the president's October "summit" meetings on inflation and economic policy, regarding appropriate action to be taken when inflation coexisted with recession in certain industries. As unemployment mounted toward year's end, it appeared that the surtax would be dropped entirely and that the administration's economic proposals presented to the new Congress would include a tax cut designed to stimulate the economy.

A second controversy, continuing in a low key throughout the year, centred on a possible increase of 20 cents or more per gallon in the federal excise tax on gasoline. The gasoline excise tax produced about $1 billion for each cent of tax at current consumption levels. The purpose of the tax would have been primarily to conserve energy, and the revenue would have been incidental, though appropriate in an inflation period. Proposals for the tax were coupled with suggestions for offsetting relief, through tax credit or rebates, for low-income individuals. In addition to outcries against a new burden, opponents noted that the tax, insofar as it applied to business uses of gasoline, would increase costs and prices and thus accentuate inflationary pressures. Indications toward the end of the year were that, rather than raising the gasoline tax directly, the administration would propose a tariff on imports of crude oil and an excise tax on oil produced domestically.

Though no major tax legislation was adopted in 1974, the House Ways and Means Committee essentially completed its work on a major revision of the income tax law. The principal issue prompting congressional moves toward tax legislation in 1974 was the large increase in oil company profits in a time of shortages and rising gasoline prices. The most obvious change was the provision that would phase out the oil depletion allowance, which, in effect, reduced the income tax rate on oil production by half. The administration had recommended an excise tax on the "windfall profit" element of the price of new domestic oil, with graduated rates to be applied under a two-tier price system and the tax to be phased out over five years. A credit was to be allowed for reinvested earnings consistent with the national policy of seeking self-sufficiency in energy.

Real estate had been another industry with well-publicized differentially favourable tax treatment. The tentative decisions of the committee would move

Tariffs:
see Commercial and Trade Policies; Trade, International

substantially toward elimination of the artificial use of deductions to reduce ordinary income through partial offsets in subsequent capital gains and of tax-induced purchases and sales of real estate. Continuous ownership, rather than a rapid sequence of owners, might be a useful incidental result.

From the standpoint of many investors, the committee's tentative decision to adopt a sliding scale for capital gains taxation, based on the length of time an asset is held, was a major reform that would reduce both the tax barrier to shifts in investment portfolios and the absorption of part of the nation's capital by taxation. The committee's approach was to exclude an increasing proportion of the capital gain from taxation as the holding period lengthened. The tentative decisions included an extension from six months to a year for qualification as long-term gains, with the effect of this change spread over three years; elimination of the alternative tax at 25% on the first $50,000 of gains; an increase from $1,000 to $3,000 of the amount of capital loss that could be deducted from ordinary income; an increase from $20,000 to $35,000 in the sale price of a principal residence to qualify for exclusion; and elimination of the previous requirement that the seller had to be over 65.

Several tax simplifications were tentatively adopted, including repeal of deductions for payment of state gasoline taxes and medical insurance, sick pay, and the dividend exclusion. Increases were made in the percentage floors for deductibility of medical expenses and drugs, and the child care deduction was modified. As an offset to the loss of some existing deductions, a new "simplification deduction" would be established, equal to $350 plus 2% of adjusted gross income up to a maximum of $650; this would be allowed in addition to the remaining itemized deductions. The low-income allowance and the percentage standard deduction would also be increased, and alimony would be allowed as a deduction in computing adjusted gross income. In a move quite inconsistent with simplification, however, the committee authorized an investment tax credit of 7% on purchases of home garden tools used in the production of home vegetable gardens up to a maximum purchase of $100.

The committee adopted several changes regarding the taxation of foreign source income, the most far-reaching of which was elimination of the per country limitation in computations of the credit for foreign income taxes. The effect would be to permit companies to continue to average out income taxes paid in high-tax and low-tax countries, but to prohibit them from ignoring losses in some foreign countries in calculating total foreign income.

State tax legislation in 1974 showed no pronounced pattern. By mid-September, 14 states had adopted tax reductions amounting to $685 million and 9 states had voted increases of $335 million. The net reductions reflected the continuing expansion of state revenues with a less than corresponding growth of expenditures. Reductions usually took the form of additional deductions or exemptions rather than lower rates, while increases typically involved broadening of tax bases rather than higher rates. Local property tax rates generally continued their inexorable rise, with continuing interest in "circuit-breaker" relief for older homeowners. Substitution of state for local financing of schools proceeded slowly. (DAN THROOP SMITH)

Europe. Several European countries had made major tax changes in recent years, and 1974 was largely a year of consolidation. In the U.K., however, a capital transfer tax was planned, and there were proposals for an annual wealth tax. France instituted three new taxes, and several important measures were announced in West Germany.

Most European countries had large balance of payments deficits, a result of the combined effects of inflation and the oil crisis, and the threat of an international trade recession loomed. Some countries attempted to use fiscal measures to curb energy consumption, and in the U.K. the value-added tax (VAT) was imposed on motor fuels but not on other fuels.

The hoped-for harmonization of the base of VAT within the EEC by January 1975 was acknowledged as impossible by the EEC Commission. Harmonization of the base would be the necessary first step toward a common tax, part of the long-term aim of economic and monetary union.

Denmark. In October 1974 Copenhagen's municipal court began the trial of Mogens Glistrup, member of the Folketing and founder of the antitax Progress Party, the second largest parliamentary party. Glistrup practiced as a lawyer and tax consultant, and the indictment listed some 2,700 charges against him arising out of his tax work. The prosecution claimed that his tax consultancy, which employed 400 people in a fashionable Copenhagen suburb, was for the specific purpose of tax evasion. Glistrup was said to have admitted founding more than 2,000 companies which the prosecution claimed existed only on paper, and to have made large-scale loan transactions to enable clients to gain tax rebates. Glistrup's claim to have kept within the law was supported by several leading jurists.

France. The 1974 budget went some way toward making the income tax more progressive by easing the tax on low-income groups and raising it on high-income groups. It provided for a number of tax concessions, an adjustment for inflation that increased the levels of income subject to each rate of tax, and the insertion of a new starting rate of tax at 5% on individual incomes between Fr. 4,951 and Fr. 5,200. The old system had a starting rate of 10% on incomes between Fr. 3,301 and Fr. 5,750. Corresponding changes were made for other groups.

In December 1973 plans had been announced to help combat inflation by increasing the amount of advance payment required on corporate and individual income tax and by requiring these payments at an earlier date. Planned public expenditure was to be reduced by Fr. 400 million. Further measures were announced in June 1974, including an 18% surcharge on corporation tax and a 5 to 15% surcharge on income tax, the latter to be partly repaid in 1975. Measures were announced to counter tax evasion and two new taxes were introduced: one would tax profits from property deals and the other, a VAT-based *taxe conjoncturelle*, aimed at excess profits resulting from inflation.

In September 1974 an anti-inflation tax on companies, to operate from January 1975, was announced. Nicknamed the "Serisette" after its originator, Jean Serisé, the tax was intended to contain profit margins without damaging investment or increasing unemployment. Some 25,000–30,000 companies with an annual turnover of Fr. 8 million or more were affected. Such companies accounted for more than half of the French gross domestic product. The tax would apply to those companies that exceeded a given margin in the added value between their turnover and their basic outlays, with allowance made for any increase in work force, productive investment, and exports. The tax increased as the permitted margin was exceeded. Half of the revenue would be used to make savings more attractive. The tax would disappear automatically if the retail price index rose by 0.5% or less for three consecutive months.

Italy. With political and economic conditions worsening steadily, the government in July announced a series of measures aimed at bringing in substantial additional revenue. The claim that these would not cause serious unemployment or recession was hard to believe, and several strikes were held in protest.

The proposals, passed in a modified form, would raise the cost of gasoline to 1,200 lire a gallon and public transport costs by an average 30%. Families using more than 58 kw-hr. of electricity each month would pay up to 32% more. Families owning their own homes would pay a once-for all 5,000 lire tax on each room in excess of the number of people in the family; owners of luxury flats with elevators or central heating would pay 50,000 lire for each room; both payments were in addition to the normal property tax. VAT on luxury items was raised from 18 to 30%, and VAT on beef from 6 to 18%. A once-only tax on cars based on horsepower would range from 6,000 lire for the smallest to 200,000 lire for the largest models.

The popular Italian game of tax evasion might be a little more difficult to play if, as announced, the tax office recruited 12,000 more employees. In 1973 the Treasury lost an estimated $420 million from VAT alone—44% of the expected revenue—as a result of evasion. The car tax also seemed to have been widely evaded.

Norway. In October 1974 the government announced substantial tax cuts. These anticipated benefits from North Sea oil, but would produce a deficit for 1975. Income taxes were cut by up to 9%, and people in the middle-income brackets, who had been hard hit by the progressive tax system and rapid increases in prices and wages, gained most. Higher rates, however, were announced for telephone and postal charges, liquor, and public transport.

United Kingdom. In a mini-budget in December 1973, the Conservative government announced a 10% surcharge on the surtax applied to income assessed for the tax year 1972–73. The surcharge did not apply to those who were over 65 as of April 1974. Property companies, which had made some very large profits, would be subjected to a special tax, which was, in fact, put into effect as an interim measure by the new Labour government in March 1974. Certain capital gains arising from the disposal by companies of land and buildings with development value or potential were to be taxed at corporation tax rates: 52% instead of 30%. The first leasing of a nonresidential development would be treated as a disposal for capital gains tax purposes.

The March budget increased the basic rate of income tax from 30 to 33%, inserted a new higher level of tax at 38% on taxable incomes between £4,500 and £5,000, and changed a number of tax allowances. The combined effect of the measures was to exempt 1.5 million people from income tax and to give some relief to lower-income groups at the expense of higher-income groups. Corporation tax was increased to 52%, and accelerated payment was required. VAT was imposed on petrol (gasoline), previously zero-rated, and petrol for the private motorist went up by about 5 pence a gallon. Additional duty of 5 pence per pack

of 20 was imposed on cigarettes, and the tax on spirits and other alcoholic drinks was increased.

The Labour government withdrew tax relief for individuals for private borrowing except for owner-occupied housing. Housing tax relief would be confined to interest on borrowings of less than £25,000. Aggregation of a child's investment income with that of the parents for tax purposes was reintroduced, and stock option and incentive scheme benefits became subject to tax. In July a second budget reduced the rate of VAT from 10 to 8% and increased food subsidies. The regional employment premium, paid to qualifying companies, was doubled to £3 a week to assist company liquidity. Prior to its reelection with a small majority in October, the Labour government had promised to limit the tax relief for house purchase enjoyed by higher-rate taxpayers.

In October the newly elected government found itself in an embarrassing position when it became known that the trust fund to be set up by the Distillers' Company Ltd. to compensate victims of the drug thalidomide would not be tax exempt. Rather than change the law, the government solved the problem by making once-for-all payments to this trust fund, as well as to another trust fund which administered grants for handicapped children, and by promising a full review of the income needs of the disabled.

In November 1974 a complex budget was introduced. Industry was given relief amounting to some £1,600 million, half of which was to come from increased prices allowed by an easing of the Price Code and the rest through deferment of tax on abnormal increases in the value of stocks resulting from inflation. Subsidies to nationalized industries were to be phased out as soon as possible, and substantial increases in post office charges and the prices of steel, electricity, transport, and gas were expected. Additional help for industry was afforded by the provision of £1,000 million at commercial rates for medium-term investment finance. A new tax to apply to deliveries of oil and gas from the continental shelf was announced as a way of taxing oil profits.

VAT on petrol was increased from 8 to 25%. The starting point for the investment income surcharge was reduced from £2,000 to £1,000, or £1,500 for persons over 65. Tax allowances for those over 65 and for blind persons were increased. Pension increases to take effect from April 1975 were announced, with a further review promised for December 1975.

As expected, a capital transfer tax was introduced, designed to prevent estate duty from being drastically reduced through gifts or trusts. The capital transfer tax, which superseded the existing estate duty, applied to all transmissions of wealth, subject to certain exemptions for small amounts and for gifts between husband and wife. The rates were considerably more lenient than the existing estate duty, but the proposals included provisions to remove the tax advantages of trusts and to withdraw the current 45% reduction of duty for farmland and certain business assets, together with the special treatment of woodlands.

A select committee of MPs was to consider proposals for an annual wealth tax, intended to complement the capital transfer tax. At £100,000, the exemption level proposed in a Green Paper (discussion document) was higher than expected, but the proposed coverage included all salable assets, including owner-occupied houses, life insurance policies (at surrender value), business assets and goodwill, and works of art. Tax rates of from 1 to 5% were suggested.

In the U.K., Chancellor of the Exchequer Denis Healey proposes two new levies on the wealthy: a so-called wealth tax and a tax on gifts or capital transfers.

Radical proposals for land were published as a White Paper in September, and the chancellor of the Exchequer announced the introduction of a Land Development Bill with an initial tax rate of 80% to replace the temporary tax on land introduced in March. The bill would give local authorities power to acquire all land needed for private development up to ten years ahead. No significant development would then be allowed except on land owned by, or acquired through, a local authority. Local authorities would be able to buy land at current use value and, in general, would retain the freehold. The community would gain the development value when the land was leased for commercial or industrial purposes. For housing, land would be licensed to builders with provision for house purchasers to buy the freehold.

The terms for Britain's entry into the EEC had allowed the Channel Islands and the Isle of Man to retain their tax advantages. In July 1974, Guernsey, one of the Channel Islands, announced measures to curb profits from speculation in the island's residential property market. A tax of 100% on the "profits," backdated to Oct. 8, 1973, was announced. The measure was not expected to bring in much tax, but it would probably reduce residential property prices.

West Germany. There were sharp differences of opinion between the two parliamentary chambers over tax reforms introduced during 1973–74. The important Land Reform Law made the 1964 assessed values those that would operate for purposes of land tax from January 1974. Transition measures to cushion the resulting tax increases were introduced for the current year. A series of measures in December 1973 largely reversed actions taken in May. The 11% investment tax was removed, and the diminishing balance depreciation system was reintroduced. Tax rebates for private house construction were also reintroduced.

Changes were proposed in the inheritance tax law and in laws affecting property, corporate, and personal income tax. The income tax changes, to take effect from January 1975, would reduce income tax for single persons with incomes up to DM. 40,000 and for married couples with less than twice that amount. Part of the cost would be met by increased tax on higher income groups. The amount at which tax began for single persons would be raised from DM. 1,680 to DM. 3,000 and, after tax allowances, a 22% proportional tax, raised from 19%, would be levied on the next DM. 16,000. The progressive scale would rise to a peak of 56% (old rate 54.6%) on incomes of DM. 130,000. In every case, amounts for a married couple were doubled.   (G. C. HOCKLEY)

See also Economics; Economy, World; Employment, Wages, and Hours; Government Finance; Social and Welfare Services.

[535.B.2; 552.E]

Telecommunications

Mounting awareness of the tremendous significance of technological developments in telecommunications brought about a year in which the developments themselves were eclipsed by the frantic efforts of companies jockeying for position. It appeared that everyone had suddenly become conscious that he who gained the best advantage in 1974 would carry off the glittering telecommunications prizes of the 1980s. Early in the year a marriage of convenience was announced between a French producer of electronic telephone

This 265,000 cu.ft. tethered balloon designed by a subsidiary of Westinghouse provides a stable platform in winds of hurricane force. At altitudes of 10,000 ft. the mini-satellite can provide telecommunications over a 50,000-sq.mi. area.

switching and a British computer manufacturer. After two failures, the British sent their military communications satellite Skynet 2 into orbit. Brazil and Indonesia announced plans for communications satellites. A commanding lead in submarine cables was established by the British subsidiary of a giant U.S. firm, while that same giant nervously watched the activities of another American titan that was beginning to poach perilously close to its own territory. Meanwhile, motivated by a desire merely to be fashionable, British subscribers lent enthusiastic support to an expensive system of establishing telephone connections that promised repercussions of which they could hardly have dreamed.

For the American Telephone and Telegraph Co. (AT&T) the year presented a picture of growing and very real competition. From the Bell System viewpoint, as expressed by Thomas E. Bolger, president of the Chesapeake and Potomac Telephone Co., the threat of the satellite common carriers, the microwave specialized carriers, and others to the telephone company monopoly provided a "serious challenge to the very principles that have enabled our business to offer Americans the best communications system in the world." The increased competition, he noted, has resulted in more reports of equipment trouble and "confusion about who fixes what when trouble occurs."

A major worry of AT&T officials was the Federal Communications Commission (FCC) order issued in April requiring the Bell System's 22 companies to provide interconnections for the specialized carriers. This ended a years-long battle between AT&T and the specialized carriers over the use of customer-owned equipment. The order, which was upheld by the courts, meant that a customer could send his message via a specialized carrier such as MCI Telecommunications Corp., using microwave transmission between ground stations rather than AT&T lines, and then have the transmission hooked into the local Bell System.

The FCC also ruled that state regulatory agencies could take no action in the matter despite suggestions of AT&T and others that the transmissions could be intrastate rather than interstate. The U.S. Court of

Tea:
see Agriculture and
Food Supplies

Appeals finally settled the question when it ruled in September that the FCC was right in issuing its order that the Bell System must furnish the interconnects between its network and the other carriers on a non-discriminatory basis.

The major blow of the year for AT&T took place on November 20 when the U.S. Department of Justice filed a civil antitrust suit against the company and its affiliates. Specifically, the suit asked for divestiture of the entire stock interest that AT&T held in its manufacturing arm, the Western Electric Co., and added that it might also seek divestiture of the stock held in Bell Telephone Laboratories, the company's research division.

The suit charged that the company was illegally monopolizing the telecommunications business by attempts to "prevent, restrict, and eliminate competition from other telecommunications common carriers"; it also charged that through Western Electric the company attempted to prevent, restrict, and eliminate competition from other manufacturers and suppliers. The Justice Department also asked that AT&T either get out of the long distance telephone business or retain the business but give up its interests in some of the 23 local telephone companies that it owned in total or in part.

The reaction from AT&T was predictable and immediate. The day after the Justice Department filed its suit, the chairman of the Bell System, John D. deButts, told a press conference in New York that "I can't understand why Justice would take an action that could lead to dismemberment of the Bell System with the inevitable result that costs would go up and service would suffer . . . it's inevitable because economies of scale that result from our size and our integrated structure would be lost. Western Electric's prices on its products average 70 per cent of the lowest general trade prices for comparable telecommunications products."

DeButts vowed that his company would fight the suit, would not seek a consent decree, and would battle the issue up to the U.S. Supreme Court if necessary. In Washington, most observers saw the legal battle as one that could run as long as ten years and cost up to $70 million for the government to fight.

At the same time that the government was acting against AT&T, a group of nine small telephone equipment manufacturers filed suit in U.S. District Court in Washington, D.C. They asked for $300 million in damages from AT&T, claiming that the company was in violation of the antitrust laws and was trying to drive them out of business. The suit charged that AT&T was duplicating equipment devised by the smaller manufacturers and offering it as its own.

Satellites. The United States entered the satellite communications age on April 16 when Western Union Telegraph Co.'s Westar I was successfully boosted into synchronous orbit, after being launched some three days earlier on April 13. Westar I entered a circular orbit some 22,300 mi. above the earth at longitude 99° W, south of Dallas, Tex., and west of the Galapagos Islands. From there its beam was able to cover all the 50 states and Puerto Rico. The satellite itself was built by Hughes Aircraft Co.

On October 10, Western Union completed the system by launching Westar II. Each of the satellites was capable of relaying eight million words per second and had capacity for voice, video, facsimile, and data transmission. Western Union claimed that its service, which it was leasing to other users, would eventually

result in lower rates to the public and pointed out that at present a leased telephone line on the ground between New York and Los Angeles cost approximately $2,200 per month but the same service via satellite could be had for about $1,000 a month. Initially, the system was to have ground stations at Glenwood, N.J., Chicago, Atlanta, Dallas, and Los Angeles.

The FCC modified an order that would have restricted AT&T from providing private line service via satellite in order to give the smaller and newer companies a first chance at penetrating the field. The new ruling permitted AT&T to launch private line service three years after its satellite was in place.

Challenging the existing common carriers in the U.S., not to mention the Department of Justice, with whom it was involved in an antitrust suit, International Business Machines Corp. (IBM) made a bold move in July to apply its huge technological and financial muscle to building a new kind of telecommunications network in the U.S. In its first acquisition in a decade, IBM surprised both the computer and the communications industries by announcing that it had agreed to take over 55% of CML Satellite Corp. (a consortium of Comsat General Corp., MCI Communications Inc., and Lockheed Aircraft Corp.). Comsat General would have the remaining 45%. The new partners, IBM and Comsat, hoped to submit a plan for a leased-line satellite service to present to the FCC for approval as a specialized satellite carrier. If accepted, the system would be in direct competition with AT&T's land-based services.

Needless to say, the proposed deal soon attracted vociferous opposition from Sperry Rand, Sanders, the Computer Industry Association, all the other domestic satellite carriers, and the U.S. Federal Trade Commission. The opposition culminated in August with an announcement from the EEC Commission that it planned to mount a formal investigation into the European activities of IBM.

Countries Having More Than 100,000 Telephones
Telephones in service, 1973

Country	Number of telephones	Percentage increase over 1963	Telephones per 100 population	Country	Number of telephones	Percentage increase over 1963	Telephones per 100 population
Algeria	211,252	32.5	1.40	Lebanon	227,000	221.1	7.67
Argentina	1,952,109	39.5	8.10	Luxembourg	125,585	85.0	36.40
Australia	4,399,782	74.4	33.95	Malaysia	210,608	91.6	0.25
Austria	1,694,194	110.5	22.72	Mexico	1,957,972	218.9	3.79
Belgium	2,305,218	79.3	23.75	Morocco	175,000	23.8	1.10
Brazil	2,190,000	88.6	2.17	Netherlands, The	4,003,455	112.0	29.91
Bulgaria	581,657	182.2	6.77	New Zealand	1,327,134	56.0	44.61
Canada	10,987,141	73.6	49.98	Norway	1,262,254	56.2	32.00
Chile	419,960	90.4	4.15	Pakistan	175,026	63.1	0.27
China	596,663	396.0	3.90	Panama	107,129	198.0	6.93
Colombia	1,009,791	181.1	4.49	Peru	265,088	125.8	1.81
Cuba*	274,949	26.2	3.16	Philippines	390,595	179.7	1.01
Czechoslovakia	2,232,481	85.0	15.37	Poland	2,087,032	102.5	6.28
Denmark†	1,912,449	60.2	37.93	Portugal	873,339	91.9	9.89
Ecuador	117,961	213.6	1.79	Puerto Rico	380,299	170.9	13.34
Egypt‡	365,000	96.8	1.14	Rhodesia	151,199	64.4	2.62
Finland	1,412,067	107.0	30.47	Romania*	726,554	234.8	3.53
France	10,338,000	107.7	19.91	Singapore	218,430	195.7	10.08
Germany, East	2,232,069	55.5	13.10	South Africa	1,706,794	67.7	7.30
Germany, West	16,521,149	134.4	26.79	Soviet Union	13,198,700	127.6	5.31
Greece	1,437,578	374.7	16.32	Spain‖	5,712,549	172.5	16.45
Hong Kong	795,167	445.7	19.38	Sweden	4,829,047	58.1	59.29
Hungary	923,966	92.7	8.87	Switzerland	3,404,427	81.5	53.95
India	1,479,475	145.5	0.27	Syria	131,760	124.8	2.01
Indonesia	240,210	62.2	0.19	Taiwan	596,663	396.0	3.90
Iran	447,100	188.5	1.49	Thailand*	235,193	372.9	0.61
Iraq	121,500	113.9	1.20	Turkey	728,358	176.1	1.94
Ireland	341,449	85.5	11.33	United Kingdom	17,570,904	97.2	31.39
Israel	619,709	302.5	19.37	United States	131,606,000	62.5	62.75
Italy	11,345,497	143.7	20.76	Uruguay	241,339	35.7	8.11
Japan§	34,021,155	264.4	31.50	Venezuela	470,748	94.9	4.24
Korea, South	748,474	437.2	2.29	Yugoslavia	910,695	200.2	4.38

*1972; increase over 1962. †Including the Faeroe Islands. ‡1969; increase over 1959. §Including the Ryukyu Islands. ‖Including Spanish North Africa.
Sources: American Telephone & Telegraph Co., *The World's Telephones, 1973*; Statistical Office of the United Nations, *Statistical Yearbook 1965*.

After two unsuccessful attempts, including a disastrous failure in January when the U.S. Delta launch vehicle threw the satellite into a wildly eccentric orbit, the first British-built communications satellite, Skynet 2, was launched from the Kennedy Space Center, Florida, in late November. The satellite was intended to carry British defense communications over an area stretching from Britain to Australia, replacing the U.S. Skynet 1 satellites. Meanwhile, the Soviet Union put up its first geostationary satellite. Called Cosmos 637, it was the first of a series of experimental units that were expected to be launched before Soviet engineers put up their first operational telecommunications satellites in 1975–76.

Educational television by satellite was introduced into Brazil in June, using the U.S. National Aeronautics and Space Administration's experimental broadcasting satellite, the ATS-F. Well-developed plans for a national telecommunications satellite awaited the assent of the Brazilian president.

Telephones. Faced with the British Post Office's threat to order £1,000 million worth of TXE4 electronic exchange equipment developed by Standard Telephone and Cable (STC), the British subsidiary of the U.S. firm International Telephone and Telegraph (ITT), Britain's Plessey and the French Compagnie Générale d'Électricité (CGE) announced in March an agreement to develop a new fully electronic digital switching system for the next generation of telephone exchanges. The deal gave Plessey access to the digital switching technology the firm needed to remain in the running as a potential supplier of "System X," the computer-controlled electronic exchange that the Post Office intended to order in the 1980s.

In essence the plan was to link existing French electronic switching gear, the E10, with Plessey's large computer-control system. The result, it was hoped, would be a new type of exchange handling up to 50,000 lines that could be available long before STC had a comparable System X facility to offer the Post Office. The new exchanges, code-named "Felicite," would have unprecedented flexibility of operation and could aptly be named the first hi-fi telephone switching systems. Local exchanges would convert the speech waveform into a train of pulses, and thereafter the entire routing and switching operations would be digital. The advances in microelectronics made it much

more efficient and probably cheaper to transmit signals in this bit-by-bit way and, since the equipment needed only to recognize the presence or absence of pulses to be able to reconstruct the original speech, the quality of transmission would be unaffected by distance.

CGE was also building a 5,000-line demonstration facility in the Soviet Union as a step toward an order for a plant that would produce one million lines per year. A plant producing 100,000 lines per year had already been sold to Poland, a single exchange was to go to Morocco, and a pilot scheme was under way in Mexico. In France itself, however, ITT still had 43% of the market compared with CGE's 32%, and the U.S. company was working on a prototype of a 50,000-line all-electronic exchange designed to meet French specifications.

Within two months of beginning market trials for its new pushbutton dialing telephone late in 1973, the British Post Office received 1,500 requests to install such phones despite a conversion charge of £5 and additional rental charges of £3 per quarter. This took place despite warnings from the Post Office that the new system would not give quicker connections but only quicker dialing. Indeed, the Post Office had to go to some lengths to match the rapid pushbutton dialing speed with the creaking mechanism of its old, Victorian Strowger exchanges, doing so by incorporating a solid-state memory in each pushbutton telephone. The successful development of this memory was expected to lead to a revolution in telephone development over the next few years. For example, if the telephone dial can "remember" the number just dialed, in the event of a connection not being made at the first attempt (a fate that befalls one in three calls in every crowded city), all that the subscriber need do in principle is press a separate button once, and the telephone can re-dial of its own accord.

Several manufacturers brought out designs for a pushbutton telephone that would use a memory to store 32 such numbers. Others took advantage of the solid-state circuitry involved to add a calculator facility to the telephone set. Most far-reaching was work already well under way which would allow letters typed on an ordinary typewriter connected to the telephone line to be transmitted as they are typed to a dialed destination.

Cables. Of the eight submarine cables linking the U.K. with Canada and the U.S., CANTAT 2, the latest to be laid, more than doubled the number of telephone circuits available in all of the previous seven. It was inaugurated on June 21 by a call from Harold Wilson, prime minister of the U.K., to Pierre Trudeau, the Canadian prime minister. With more than 1,800 conversations going into the cable at once, even a modest transmitting power per conversation would quickly burn out the cable, which, although 5,200 km. long, is less than 50 mm. thick. Therefore, transmissions through STC's new cable are made at very low power and amplified every 11 km. by special submarine repeaters that incorporate especially reliable transistors made by a technique invented by the Post Office Corporation research department.

Undersea cables had become so reliable by 1974 that the Italian Post Office ordered from STC a £6 million submarine cable to augment the Rome to Palermo overland trunk route. The new cable was designed to provide up to 5,000 circuits, as many as were available in current telecommunications satellites, and should enter service in 1976.

(DON BYRNE; LAURIE JOHN)

Britain's communications satellite, Skynet 2, under construction in Portsmouth, Eng.

COURTESY, MARCONI SPACE & DEFENSE SYSTEMS, LTD.

International Telecommunication Union. During 1974 membership in the International Telecommunication Union (ITU) increased to 148 with the accession to the International Telecommunication Convention of The Gambia and The Bahamas. The 29th session of the Administrative Council was held at ITU headquarters in Geneva from June 15 to July 5. The council adopted a budget of SFr. 51 million for 1975.

The XIIIth Plenary Assembly of the ITU's International Radio Consultative Committee was held in Geneva from July 15 to July 26. Among the many subjects discussed was the use of satellites for different types of radio services, notably for direct broadcasting and for maritime navigation. (ITU)

[735.I.2-3 and 6]

ENCYCLOPÆDIA BRITANNICA FILMS. *The Information Machine* (1973); *An Introduction to Feedback* (1973).

Television and Radio

Television and radio sets in use throughout the world reached an estimated 1,007,500,000 in 1974. Among the major nations, none lacked some form of radio service. Only South Africa was without some degree of television service, and the government there was considering introducing it in 1975. There were approximately 702.5 million radio sets in use throughout the world, with slightly more than half, or 356.5 million, in the U.S. Television sets throughout the world numbered approximately 305 million, of which about 112 million were in the U.S.

Estimates published in the 1974 *Broadcasting Yearbook* ranked the Soviet Union, with about 30 million television sets, next to the U.S., followed by Japan with 25 million and the United Kingdom with 20 million. Other *Broadcasting* estimates of television sets included West Germany 17 million, France 13 million, Italy 12 million, Canada 7.5 million, and Spain 5.5 million.

There were about 6,435 television stations on the air throughout the world, distributed approximately as follows: 2,100 in the Far East, 2,000 in Western Europe, 947 in the U.S., 910 in Eastern Europe, 175 in South America, more than 80 in Canada, and 35 in Africa. Some 13,850 radio stations were in operation, most of them of the amplitude modulation (AM) variety but with the number of frequency modulation (FM) stations continuing to increase. The U.S. had 7,715, or about 55% of the world's radio stations; of these, 3,296 were FM.

Organization. Broadcasters displayed more ingenuity in arranging satellite relays for international distribution of television programs in 1974 than they did in organizing plans to govern future satellite uses. As the end of 1974 approached, no substantive new effort had been made in the UN to break the stalemate that developed there in 1973 over the form of regulation to be employed when satellite broadcasting from one country directly to home television sets in other countries became feasible, expected within about ten years. In the continuing impasse the U.S. held to its position that the flow of information among countries should not be impeded, while the U.S.S.R., other Soviet bloc countries, and many small nations held that each country must have veto rights over any program importation.

In the absence of UN action, and in the hope of heading off restrictive action, a working committee

A new Thames Television series of seven plays, based on the life of "Jennie, Lady Randolph Churchill," featured Lee Remick in the title role. She is shown here calling to her son Winston (Warren Clarke) in a replica of the tree house Winston Churchill built at Salisbury Hall at the age of 26.

representing several international broadcasting organizations met early in 1974 and developed a draft agreement. While recognizing the sovereign rights of nations, the agreement put its main emphasis on cooperation among broadcasters and opposed creation of a special body to govern international direct telecasting.

The draft was developed by representatives of the European Broadcasting Union, the Asian Broadcasting Union, and two groups representing broadcasters in Spain and Latin America, and U.S. and Canadian networks. They hoped to develop strong international support for the plan and submit it for UN consideration. Reaction was mixed, however. While the Canadian Broadcasting Corporation (CBC) and Canada's CTV television network accepted the draft, two U.S. networks (ABC and CBS) abstained and the third (NBC) approved but only on the condition that it might review its position later. The European Broadcasting Union approved the draft, but the African, Arab States, and Asian broadcasting unions took no position on it. Whether there would be a new effort to achieve greater solidarity among broadcasters was unclear.

Broadcasters were more successful in organizing satellite distribution of international news broadcasts. These hookups had become virtually routine; they were used extensively for round-the-world coverage not only of the year's biggest news story—the resignation of U.S. Pres. Richard Nixon and the inauguration of Pres. Gerald Ford—but also for other news such as Nixon's earlier visits to the Middle East and to Moscow, U.S. Secretary of State Henry Kissinger's Middle Eastern diplomatic missions, and the U.S. House of Representatives Judiciary Committee's impeachment proceedings.

Satellites also enabled U.S. viewers to get a first-hand look at government censorship in action. On July 2, the last day of formal U.S. network coverage of Nixon's summit talks in Moscow, the Soviet Union halted transmissions of TV broadcasts from Moscow by ABC, CBS, and NBC when those networks' newsmen attempted to report on Soviet Jewish dissidence. To U.S. viewers, the correspondents were on-screen one moment and gone the next, the television sets blank and silent. The Central Committee of the Soviet Broadcast Group apologized, blaming the interruptions on satellite technicians and promising that there would be no recurrence, but a day later a CBS news correspondent, Murray Fromson, was balked when he tried to transmit a story dealing with Andrey Sakharov, the dissident Soviet physicist who was then on a hunger strike.

Broadcasters had become capable of arranging sophisticated satellite arrays when needed. An especially complex pattern of relays and retransmissions, involving two satellites and separate routings for audio and video signals, was devised to provide live colour coverage of the world's amateur boxing championships in Havana, Cuba, on August 28–30. It was the first time two satellites—in this case one Soviet and one U.S.—had been used in this way to overcome both distances and technical differences.

In September 1974 the 49th session of the International Radio and Television Organization (OIRT) administrative council was held in Ulan Bator, Mongolia. Chairman of the meetings was S. G. Lapin, president of the State Television and Radio Committee of the Council of Ministers of the U.S.S.R. The session considered the progress of OIRT during 1974, with special reference to various commemorative broadcasts in connection with anniversaries within the Soviet bloc. It urged a greater concentration on the promotion of television news exchanges among Intervision members.

In February 1974 the 24th general assembly of the Union of National Radio and Television Organizations of Africa (URTNA) took place in Benghazi, Libya. The assembly discussed programming and technical progress in African broadcasting and elected Boubacar Kasse, director of Radio Mali, as president of the 11-member administrative council.

There was continued concern about the one-way traffic in TV programs, dominated by the United States, Britain, and continental Western Europe. The problem was analyzed in a report for UNESCO by K. Nordenstreng and Tapio Varis of the University of Tampere, Fin., the first attempt at a detailed picture of world TV trade. It showed that the U.S. imported less than 2% of its program needs, while Britain bought about 12% of foreign material. This compared with Mexico (39%), Australia (57%), and Uruguay (62%).

A number of major communications development programs were proposed. Brazil announced a massive new investment program in telecommunications, which would also improve the basic technical systems for broadcasting. In the Caribbean work began on an 800-mi.-long microwave system linking the chain of islands from Tortola (British Virgin Islands) in the north to Trinidad and Tobago in the south. This would create a basis for an important extension of broadcasting services in the region.

Indonesia decided to include a national communications satellite project in its second five-year development plan (1974–79). The system would provide a broadcasting and telecommunications service to the country's 3,000 islands. Japan announced a space development program that was to include communications satellites. In Europe work progressed on the European communications satellite project.

Europe. There were considerable changes in the structure of broadcasting systems in several countries, reflecting new attitudes to media under social and technological pressures. In France the state broadcasting organization, Office de Radiodiffusion et Télévision Française (ORTF), was to be dissolved and replaced by six public organizations on Jan. 1, 1975. Distribution was to be handled by a public service corporation responsible for the transmitter network. One-half of the board of directors would represent the state, the other half consisting of two political representatives, representatives of the programming companies, and two staff members. Income was to come from license revenue (75%) and advertising (25%). Four national program companies were to be responsible for programming, one for radio and one for each of the three television networks. The state was the only stockholder in these companies, and the governing body of each was to be made up of two state members, one member of Parliament, one representative of the press, one representative of the arts, and one staff member.

The long-awaited reform of the state-owned RAI-ITV network in Italy was delayed by governmental crises. However, in December the Cabinet agreed on a new structure for the network. A 15-man administrative council would exercise control over it, with parliamentary and national committees supervising general broadcasting policy. The two television and three radio channels would have competing independent news services.

Austria adopted a new broadcasting law on July 10, 1974. The independence of Austrian broadcasting was guaranteed by a constitutional law defining broadcasting as not only over-the-air transmission but also wire distribution. Considerations to be taken into account included objectivity and impartiality in reporting, balance in programming, and independence of individuals and institutions.

New legislation in Denmark maintained the state monopoly of Danmarks Radio and assigned it the right to control cable TV distribution. A feature of the law was the setting up of a 16-man radio council to investigate complaints about programs. Dissatisfied listeners could take their cases to a special commission of three members appointed by the government.

Lord Olivier and Joan Plowright in the roles of Shylock and Portia during the ABC television production of "The Merchant of Venice" in March.

UPI COMPIX

In Britain by the end of 1973 almost six million colour television sets had been sold. But the slumping economy affected sales in 1974, and they declined by between 25 and 35%. This particularly affected BBC forecasts of revenue from license fees that would accrue from the more expensive colour licenses. The BBC's financial difficulties led to 10% cuts in television and radio programming at the end of 1974. An increase in the license fee (last raised in 1971) seemed likely in 1975.

The BBC reacted vigorously to Labour Party plans for broadcasting changes that would effectively abolish both the BBC and the Independent Broadcasting Association (IBA), replacing them with a National Broadcasting Commission to collect advertising revenue and allocate funds. The plan suggested that programs be contracted to independent producers and scheduled by two television corporations, each with a national and a regional channel. A Committee of Inquiry into Broadcasting, under the chairmanship of Lord Annan, was to report in 1977.

There was sustained interest in providing for greater participation in broadcasting by the public, including minority groups. A number of programs in which air time was turned over to articulate groups were shown in Britain ("Open Door"), Canada, and West Germany ("Orakel").

Cable television continued to attract attention. In Europe the French government agreed to the setting up of the state-controlled Société Française de Télédistribution to lay down rules and structures for the first French cable TV stations. In The Netherlands a number of cable TV stations continued to produce locally originated programs. The Labour government in Britain decided to allow the four British cable TV stations to continue, but the projects were suffering from lack of funds.

An interesting development in Europe was the referral in May 1974 of the case of the Italian cable TV company Telebiella to the Court of the European Economic Community at Luxembourg. The district court of Como, Italy, sought the EEC court's verdict on whether the Italian firm was within its rights in breaking the monopoly of Radiotelevisione Italiana (RAI) since the Treaty of Rome allowed the free transfer of goods and services inside the EEC. Also, it asked whether broadcasting monopolies such as RAI should be allowed under the antimonopoly laws of the EEC. The court ruled that RAI and the Italian government were not in breach of the treaty and that the state broadcasting monopoly was not inconsistent with the rules on competition.

On June 6 the European Broadcasting Union (EBU) celebrated the 20th anniversary of Eurovision, marking the event with a live gala concert, featuring major international stars, at Cannes, France. Eurovision had begun in 1954 when audiences in eight European countries watched live coverage of the Narcissus Festival from Montreux, Switz.

Eurovision had a growing sound and vision network stretching from the far north of Europe to North Africa. In 1974 the length of the network was 13,080 km. (1 km. = 0.62 mi.). Late in the year, a computer-assisted switching system came into operation to speed up the transmission of programs. The network served approximately 90 million receivers with an audience of 300 million viewers. There were also links with Intervision (the corresponding Eastern European network) and via Intelsat satellites to the networks of many television services outside Europe.

A major broadcasting event for Eurovision in 1974 was coverage of the World Cup soccer finals in West Germany. Months of study, consultations, and negotiations were needed to plan the transmissions. The opening match between Brazil and Yugoslavia on June 13 was transmitted live by 28 television services in Western Europe and 5 in Eastern Europe. It was also relayed by satellite to Australia, Africa, South America, and the Middle East. Thirty-eight matches were transmitted between June 13 and July 7.

Apart from program exchanges, the EBU was also concerned with staff training and exchanges. A major example of this in 1974 was the fourth biennial EBU Workshop for Producers and Directors of Children's Television at Copenhagen, Den. It was attended by representatives of 23 countries, together with delegates from the Arab States Broadcasting Union and Intervision.

The most important radio event of 1974 was the EBU symposium on "Radio in the 1980s," held in Belgrade, Yugos., on November 5–8. The symposium, which was attended by approximately 120 delegates, discussed society in the 1980s; likely technical developments in radio, including home receivers and new recording techniques; the further development of television and its effects on the role of radio; the probable nature of regional, local, and community-operated radio; and whether educational radio had a future. It was agreed that many of the problems raised needed further research and development, and as a result the CBC was designated to host a subsequent conference in 1976.

United States. U.S. homes equipped with colour television sets numbered 48,635,000, or 71% of all TV homes, as of Oct. 1, 1974, a 12-month gain of 5,235,000, or 12%, according to estimates compiled by *Broadcasting.* Except for old movies filmed originally in black and white, virtually all programs broadcast by U.S. networks and stations were transmitted in colour. A study by the American Research Bureau's Arbitron TV service, published in *Broadcasting* in February, estimated that 86% of U.S. TV homes were also equipped to receive signals from ultrahigh-frequency (UHF) stations, 44% had more than one TV set, and 12% were linked to cable television (CATV).

Cable television's progress remained slow in 1974 as some of its principal problems intensified. High interest rates continued to hold down borrowing for construction of new systems, particularly in larger cities. This led operators to put more emphasis on developing old franchises, seeking rate increases for their service, and adding subscribers to existing systems. Earlier visions of "wired cities" and even a "wired nation" thus receded further into the future. CATV won a favourable U.S. Supreme Court decision on its liability under the existing copyright law, but its efforts to obtain favourable treatment in new copyright legislation bogged down with the legislation itself, which seemed destined once again to wait at least another year for final congressional action.

The continuing dispute between the National Cable Television Association (NCTA) and the National Association of Broadcasters over pay cable, CATV's version of pay television, deepened with the approach of a showdown in October: the second oral argument to be held by the Federal Communications Commission (FCC) within a year on possible relaxation of FCC restrictions on the use of movies and sports events—longtime staples of free television—

on pay-cable systems. Scores of participants engaged in the oral argument, with cable interests contending that they should be free to compete for public favour and with broadcasters arguing that the public would be hurt, not served, if cable were permitted to buy up and sell to its subscribers programming that broadcast audiences had been receiving free.

In mid-November the FCC adopted a new policy, which, although many details remained to be filled in, would loosen some restrictions on pay cable's ability to bid for sports and movies but would tighten other restrictions. NCTA officials called it "a cosmetic change in an outrageous rule" and vowed to go to court, if necessary, to obtain a more favourable ruling.

For all its problems, however, or perhaps because of them, the cable industry late in 1974 began gathering its forces for a drive to free itself from most if not all restrictive federal regulation, particularly rules limiting its carriage of broadcast programs and other requirements setting a 1977 deadline for compliance by all CATV systems with strict FCC technical standards. To meet the technical requirements alone, an NCTA official estimated, would require the cable industry to spend more than half as much money ($550 million) on new construction and refurbishing as it had spent since about 1950 in creating and developing the existing CATV system.

U.S. domestic satellite service became a reality in January 1974 when RCA Corp. dedicated its Satcom system, using leased circuits on Telesat Canada's Anik II satellite until the launching of its own satellites in late 1975 and 1976, to link the east and west coasts of the contiguous U.S. and both coasts with Alaska. In mid-1974 Western Union Telegraph Corp. launched the first of its own domestic satellites. On the whole, however, a slowdown in satellite activity had occurred since the FCC adopted its "open skies" policy in December 1972, largely because of a tight money market and high interest rates.

In the experimental area, however, one of the most extensive projects ever undertaken in advanced communications satellite technology was launched in mid-1974. This was a two-year program testing the use of satellites to relay instructional television to teachers and students at multiple reception points in remote areas of the U.S. The project encompassed three educational tests for 1974–75. In one, during the summer of 1974, programming from the University of Kentucky at Lexington was transmitted via satellite to teachers assembled at 16 reception points in 13 states in the eastern Appalachian region. Later, instructional programming was to go by satellite to teachers at the same number of terminals in Alaska. In the most complex test, an $11 million project scheduled to continue throughout the 1974–75 school year, 35 minutes of instructional material per day was being transmitted by satellite to 69 terminals in eight Rocky Mountain states and relayed to some 6,000 junior-high-school students in areas where television was not ordinarily receivable.

ABC and CBS, which with NBC were targets in 1972 of a federal government antitrust suit charging that they improperly controlled prime evening television time, formally countered in 1974 that the suit was politically inspired by the Nixon administration because it did not like the networks' news coverage. The presiding federal judge ruled in May that they should have a chance to prove their charge and ordered the government to identify relevant documents. Subsequently, after President Nixon resigned

and entered an agreement giving him control over access to his tapes and papers, the networks filed for dismissal of the suit on grounds that the government could not comply with the court's order to produce pertinent documents. In mid-November, however, the presiding judge, Robert Kelleher, dismissed the suit "without prejudice." This permitted the government to file, on December 10, a new suit presumably free of the taint of alleged political motivation.

Public broadcasting remained plagued by financial problems in 1974. Operating in fiscal 1974 under a $50 million appropriation, which was $15 million more than it had in 1972 and 1973 but $5 million less than initially authorized, the Corporation for Public Broadcasting had hoped for long-range rather than year-to-year financing. A long-range funding bill was eventually introduced, providing up to $100 million a year for public broadcasting by 1980 on a matching fund basis ($1 for each $2.50 raised by CPB from other sources), but it was still pending at the year's end. Also pending was a subsequent bill under which the Department of Health, Education, and Welfare proposed to allocate $50 million over five years to build new and expand existing public broadcasting facilities.

In September, with the help of a $1,045,000 grant from the Ford Foundation, the Public Broadcasting Service, the distribution arm of public television, launched a major national promotion program. Its aim was to add approximately two million families as "subscribers" to public television by 1977 and thus perhaps increase individual contributions to $60 million a year from the current $20 million.

There was little letup in pressures on broadcasters in 1974. The year's unravelings in the Watergate case and President Nixon's resignation cut off the flow of criticism that members of the Nixon administration had directed at network news coverage over the years, but most of the other problems remained. Broadcasters spent much of the year trying to get relief from challenges to their licenses by local groups, and they came closer to success than in previous years: both the House and the Senate passed bills that contained provisions extending broadcast license terms from three years to five, but the many differences between the two measures could not be reconciled prior to congressional adjournment.

Congressional criticism of violence in television programming continued. Networks were also criticized repeatedly, both by members of Congress and by private critics, for the "maturity" of some of the programs they presented. The FCC's four-year-old proposal to prohibit common ownership of newspapers and television stations in the same market was brought back into the limelight when the Department of Justice petitioned the FCC to deny the license renewal applications of television stations owned by the Pulitzer Publishing Co. in St. Louis, the Newhouse newspaper interests, also in St. Louis, and Cowles Communications Inc. in Des Moines, Ia. Six months later the FCC held oral arguments on its proposed ban, heard 40 witnesses debate the issues, and indicated that a decision would be reached relatively soon.

The FCC did dispose of its three-year-old reappraisal of the fairness doctrine by issuing a report in late June that indicated it would take a restrained rather than expansive approach to ensuring fairness by broadcasters in discussing controversial issues of public importance. In one major provision the commission abandoned, as a fairness doctrine precedent, its historic 1967 ruling that broadcasters who carried commercials for cigarettes must also carry antismoking messages. In the future, the report said, the FCC would apply the fairness doctrine to commercials only if they explicitly raised issues of controversial importance. Another major provision rejected suggestions that the government should give the public a mandated right of access, free or paid, to the broadcast media.

Broadcasters won a major court victory in September, when a U.S. Court of Appeals ruled 2–1 that the FCC had erred in holding that an NBC-TV documentary on pensions, called "Pensions: The Broken Promise," had violated the fairness doctrine. The FCC had held that the broadcast paid too much attention to pension plan failures and not enough to successes and thus failed to achieve the balance required by the fairness doctrine. NBC was joined by other broadcast organizations in arguing that the program was designed as an "exposé-type" examination directed primarily at problems and that the FCC's ruling, if allowed to stand, would "throttle investigative journalism on television."

Programming. Sending news coverage from one country to another by satellite was standard procedure whenever the news warranted in 1974. The public portions of the House Judiciary Committee's impeachment proceedings, President Nixon's resignation address and departure from Washington, and the inauguration of President Ford were among the most widely disseminated broadcasts in television and radio history.

In entertainment programming, comedies, Westerns, and mysteries produced in the U.S. remained prime attractions in many countries. "Gunsmoke," "Bonanza," "Bewitched," "Perry Mason," and "The Carol Burnett Show" were among the most widely sold, each in scores of countries. Foreign sales by U.S. TV film distributors were expected to exceed $100 million in 1974 but would fall short of the record $135 million for 1973. The 1973 figure was about $35 million more than originally expected, with the increase credited largely to an exceptional sales drive by a single company, United Artists Television.

United States. The FCC's prime-time access rule continued to create problems for television programmers in 1974. Recognizing that the rule had not created the new sources of programming that it was originally expected to, the FCC in late 1973 and early 1974 eased some of its restrictions. But in June 1974 a federal appeals court in New York, acting on an appeal filed by a group of independent producers, ordered the FCC to defer the changes for at least a year. This had the effect of requiring ABC, CBS, and NBC to drop one hour of extra Sunday-night programming that each had already scheduled for the 1974–75 season, plus a half hour to an hour per network on various other nights. Consequently, network affiliates found it necessary to develop or acquire additional programming for these suddenly vacated network periods, which they did in most cases by scheduling syndicated game shows, contests, nature shows, or in some cases local public affairs.

Though some FCC members were inclined to scrap the rule, in mid-November a 5–2 majority decided to keep the rule's basic format but to make other changes. It instructed the commission staff to draft a new decision, to be effective Sept. 1, 1975, barring affiliates from carrying more than three hours of network programming per night but providing for a number of exceptions. These would let the networks exceed the

three-hour quota with additional programming of specific types, such as children's shows, public affairs presentations, and documentaries.

The network season that opened in September 1974 was again dominated by situation comedies and action-adventure series, with 12 new entries in each category spread among the three networks. From an audience ratings standpoint, reaction to the new lineup was the most negative in recent years. Less than three weeks after the season opened, executives of all three networks were openly discussing imminent changes; within a month, the first cancellation notices had gone out: ABC was dropping "Kodiak" and "The Texas Wheelers" for replacements yet to be selected; CBS would replace "Sons and Daughters" with a summer hit, "Tony Orlando and Dawn"; and NBC planned to substitute another summer series, "The Mac Davis Show," for "Sierra." Still other changes, to be effective in December and January, were being devised as the season progressed. Among the generally highly rated new shows of the 1974–75 season were "Chico and the Man," "Little House on the Prairie," "Rockford Files," and "Police Woman," all on NBC, and "Rhoda" on CBS.

The networks continued to try to deal with contemporary problems and themes in both regular programming and specials. Rape, homosexuality, prostitution, drug abuse, and legal reform were among the issues being seriously treated and, as usual when sensitive or controversial issues are involved, some viewers thought television was going too far. Most of their criticism, however, seemed directed at what they considered overemphasis on sex and the use of language once taboo on television. Network executives insisted in response that programming was only reflecting contemporary standards, not setting or leading them, and that attempts to deal with today's life in yesterday's terms would alienate rather than attract

Cicely Tyson stars in the title role of a moving CBS production, "The Autobiography of Miss Jane Pittman."

COURTESY, CBS TELEVISION NETWORK

The highly successful "Mary Tyler Moore Show" gave rise to another popular situation comedy in 1974—"Rhoda." Valerie Harper stars as Rhoda Morgenstern, around whom the story is based.

audiences. In any event, they said, programs on sensitive or "adult" subjects were scheduled at hours when audiences would consist primarily of adults and, in addition, were accompanied by "disclaimers" pointing up the nature of the material to follow.

In its 26th annual Emmy Awards, the National Academy of Television Arts and Sciences voted "The Autobiography of Miss Jane Pittman," the story of a black woman from childhood in slavery to the beginnings of the current civil rights movement, as the outstanding TV special of the 1973–74 season. A British series carried on public television, "Upstairs, Downstairs," was chosen as the outstanding dramatic series; "M*A*S*H," the outstanding comedy; "The Carol Burnett Show," the outstanding variety show; and "Marlo Thomas and Friends in Free To Be . . . You and Me," the outstanding children's special.

Sports remained among the biggest and highest priced attractions in 1974. *Broadcasting* estimated that television and radio networks and stations paid $43,245,000, or $860,000 more than the year before, for broadcast rights to major league baseball games, and $80,292,457 for professional and college football games. The football figure represented an increase of more than $10 million from *Broadcasting*'s estimate for 1973, with about $1,350,000 of the increment attributable to payments to the newly formed World Football League.

NFL radio rights costs declined about 10%, to an estimated $2,577,500, because of audience losses suffered under the new law, passed in 1973 as a three-year experiment, which required NFL clubs to permit local telecasting of their home games if sold out at the gate 72 hours before game time. Although this antiblackout law severely hurt radio, the FCC said in a report to Congress that its TV effect was essentially to improve local ratings in some areas. As further evidence of the appeal of sports on television, ABC acquired rights to—and said it had already sold to sponsors at a profit—television coverage of the 1976 Winter Olympic Games for an estimated $15 million and of the 1976 Summer Olympics for $25 million.

The House Judiciary Committee's public impeach-

ment proceedings and President Nixon's subsequent resignation and the swearing-in of President Ford were carried in full by television and radio. *Broadcasting* estimated that 70 million viewers saw some or all of the impeachment proceedings, which were spread over six days and in most cases encompassed prime evening viewing hours. The cost to the three commercial TV networks, which covered the deliberations on a rotational basis, was estimated by *Broadcasting* at about $3.4 million. Entertainment programming competing with impeachment coverage consistently attracted bigger audiences, usually by two or three to one. However, the dignity of the TV coverage was widely commended and credited with contributing to subsequent proposals that congressional sessions generally be opened to broadcast coverage.

When President Nixon announced his resignation on August 8, his prime-time address was carried by all three commercial TV networks live, as were his departure from Washington the next morning and, some three hours later, the inauguration of President Ford. The Nielsen company estimated that 46.9 million homes, representing a TV rating of 70.9, watched some part of those three events on the three commercial networks (not estimated were viewers on public broadcasting and on non-network commercial stations that carried the events). Other sources estimated that 40 million persons listened to Nixon's resignation speech on radio.

Local television stations also expanded their coverage of news in 1974. A special study by *Broadcasting*, published in August, showed that stations were devoting more air time to news, investing more money and manpower in its coverage, and, as highly portable cameras became more readily available, were increasing both the range and the depth of local reporting. The FCC estimated that the country's 686 commercial TV stations devoted, on average, 22.5% of their broadcast time to news, public affairs, and other nonentertainment and non-sports programming.

In radio, a trend back toward the dramatic or comedy series that were the medium's mainstays in its years of greatest popularity became apparent in 1974. Several networks introduced new mystery, science, and other radio series, with considerable success. Some of the classics of earlier years, including "The Shadow," "The Green Hornet," and the "Fibber McGee and Molly" comedy series, were being carried on more than 300 radio stations. Jack Benny, one of the most popular performers on radio and, later, television, died during the year (*see* OBITUARIES).

The Public Broadcasting Service schedule for 1974–75 included a 13-part BBC series on the history of science, called "The Ascent of Man"; another new science entry, "Solar Energy"; the Children's Television Workshop's health series for general audiences, "Feeling Good"; an examination of contemporary life in the U.S., "American Chronicles"; and specialized series on subjects as diverse as yoga, crime prevention, wildlife conservation, jazz, sports, and cooking. In addition, the "Black Journal" and "Black Perspective on the News" series were to be joined by several bilingual series, including "Villa Allegre," "Acción Chicano," and the "Carrascolendas" children's programs. In 1973–74 PBS carried 1,052 new program hours and 640 hours of reruns.

Europe. Films, old and very old, provided a staple of entertainment on many television networks. Because of the decline in the motion picture industry, television networks found that the formerly plentiful supply of unscreened feature films was rapidly dwindling. In Britain the Independent Broadcasting Association (IBA) reported that contemporary themes of sex and violence in the cinema made many films unsuitable for showing on television. Even the Western, standby of many program planners, had, in its quest for realism, introduced degrees of violence which, in the IBA's opinion, were "inappropriate for viewing in the home." The BBC announced that it was prepared to help finance films for the cinema on condition that they would be available (and suitable) for showing on television at a later date.

Radio drama received a boost from a nine-nation collaborative project aimed at attracting top writers to radio through the offer of larger fees. The scheme was proposed by the BBC, and members included Ireland, West Germany, the Scandinavian countries, and the U.S., each member paying its normal author's fee into a central fund. Writers already commissioned for radio in this way included Sir Terence Rattigan, Marguérite Duras, and Tom Stoppard.

In Britain, although networks were criticized for overreliance on old-established programs ("This Is Your Life," "Coronation Street," "Dixon of Dock Green"), home-produced programs continued to find export outlets. A popular British import to the U.S. was London Weekend's "Upstairs, Downstairs," brainchild of actresses Jean Marsh (*see* BIOGRAPHY) and Eileen Atkins. Set in an Edwardian household in London, the series followed the fortunes of the upper-class Bellamy family (the "upstairs" of the title) and their domestic servants ("downstairs"). It was marked by a high level of authenticity in its treatment of social behaviour and attitudes, as well as by consistently solid performances by its cast. The series was also screened in Yugoslavia and Scandinavia.

Period pieces seemed as popular as ever with British audiences. BBC 2's serialization "The Pallisers," based on the novels of Anthony Trollope about the Palliser family, proved almost as successful as the now-legendary "Forsyte Saga." Also well received was "Jennie, Lady Randolph Churchill," a series about the life of Jennie Jerome, mother of Sir Winston Churchill, in which the title role was played by Lee Remick.

Devoted audiences followed the feudings in BBC 1's "The Brothers," a series about a family-owned road haulage business; and one of the year's largest regular followings watched Googie Withers as an immaculate and ever sympathetic prison governor in "Within These Walls"—a series about life in a women's prison. Praised by the critics were Granada's drama series "Sam" by John Finch and Colin Welland's BBC 1 play "Kisses at Fifty."

Another award-winning program was "The World at War," a 26-part Thames Television documentary by Jeremy Isaacs about World War II. The series was named outstanding documentary of 1973 by the Broadcasting Press Guild and was widely sold abroad. Episodes were bought by Eastern European countries, whose film archives were among those that provided historical material for the series.

A "World in Action" screening in which children were offered to the public for adoption caused some controversy. The technique of using television to bring together homeless children and possible adoptive parents had been tried first in the U.S., and the British program brought more than 6,000 responses. Broadcasters, politicians, and the public agreed that the February election was "overkilled" by the radio and television media; consequently, the coverage of the October election was more restrained.

However, in France, the presidential contest between Valéry Giscard d'Estaing and François Mitterrand was a spark of life in an otherwise dormant ORTF scene. A World War II series, "L'Orchestre Rouge" (the code name for the wartime Communist spy network in Europe), aroused criticism from former Resistance fighters. Made in collaboration with Bavarian and Italian television and filmed in West Germany, the series was anti-Communist and anti-Semitic, showing the Gestapo as heroic leaders of the struggle against Communism. The French Resistance leaders, depicted as either cowards or criminals in the series, were allotted viewing time to state their objections. The ORTF presentation "Josse," based on novels by Marcel Aymé about life between the wars, won the Prix Italia.

There were 28 competing broadcasting organizations in the 1974 Montreux Golden Rose contest. A predictably large proportion of the entries were musicals of varying quality, but there were a few bright spots of comic invention. After an initial tie with ATV's "Barbra Streisand Show," the winner, by vote of the president, was the Spanish entry, an elegant, humorous study of the Don Juan legend. This took a satirical look at what myth means to Spanish manhood and (by implication) the Spanish establishment by showing a succession of hopeful would-be Don Juans failing disastrously at a casting session.

Australia. The controversial points system (introduced in August 1973) did little to improve the standard of Australian programs. Initial requirements that both radio and television stations include a specific content of Australian-produced material (with points allotted to programs of a certain type and quality) were easily met within existing programming. Although the top ten shows were locally produced, the overall implication seemed to be that an Australian program, no matter how poor, was rated better than more sophisticated overseas material.

Other moves resulted in the identification of repeat programs in TV guides; the phasing out of cigarette advertising; amendments to the Broadcasting and Television Act to clarify the functions of the Australian Broadcasting Control Board and to allow for variable periods of license renewal; a sharp decline in the number of reported cases of breaches of advertising standards; and the provision for station promotions to be included in permitted hourly advertising

Zero Mostel portrays "nice" and "grouchy" for "The Sesame Street Book of Opposites" and for "Sesame Street" programs.

periods to eliminate advertising "clutter." Australian content in children's programs was raised from four to six hours a month.

Radio was also subject to the quota system. Previously, music performed by Australians had to account for not less than 10% of music broadcasting time, in addition to the requirement that 5% of music broadcast be composed by Australians. This quota was to be increased to 30% within three years. Restrictions on foreign language broadcasting (previously 2.5% of broadcasting time) were removed. This was aimed at encouraging commercial stations to promote foreign-language broadcasts. Between 30 and 50 medium-frequency radio stations were designated to provide programs for minority audiences, public access programs, and educational broadcasting.

Japan. More than 88% of Japanese owned TV sets, and about 95% of all TV programs were in colour. This led to a diversification of viewer preference and some program changes. In particular, progress was made in improving television news coverage. The time-lag problem of overseas news coverage was resolved by full use of communications satellites.

Programming became increasingly keyed to regional tastes, as well as those of various social and economic groups. Through its many regional headquarters, the Japanese state network, NHK, which broadcast nationwide, tried to upgrade programs dealing with regional topics and problems. Commercial stations in major cities introduced afternoon programs, popular with housewives, which featured consumer information as well as entertainment. Another feature of these programs, which generally bore the name of the presenter, was that they encouraged audience participation; viewers aired their opinions on social problems and sought advice on such intimate matters as marriage and sex.

In children's programs, youngsters avidly followed science fiction stories generally called *henshin* (literally "metamorphosis"). Similar fare offered in cartoon form was also popular. Animation also played a vital role in educational programs for toddlers and schoolchildren in the lower grades. NHK's "A Picture Book of Songs," in which geometrical shapes were moved about to the sound of music, was a notable example. NHK also dramatized a widely read classic, "Satomi Hakkenden," as a puppet show that skillfully incorporated those parts of the classic appealing to modern audiences. Japanese children were captivated by the subtle music of the *futosao,* an ancient stringed instrument used in Bunraku puppet plays.

In October 1973 the ninth Japan Prize contest, an international competition for radio and TV educational programs sponsored by NHK, was held in Tokyo, with 54 countries and 86 organizations participating. The top award went to Britain's Open University entry "English Consort Music," for radio, and to "Practice—Emergency Test," West German ZDF's (second network) entry, for television.

(RUFUS W. CRATER; LYNDA GRAY; TERENCE HUGHES; SOL TAISHOFF; ICHIRO TSUJIMOTO; MICHAEL TYPE; BRIAN WILLIAMS)

Amateur Radio. When Hurricane Fifi struck Honduras on Sept. 19, 1974, it left one-third of the country devastated, thousands dead, and many more thousands homeless and in dire need of rescue, food, clothing, shelter, and medical attention. Communications within the country and with the outside world were, of course, totally disrupted.

In this situation, amateur radio operators were quick to respond with their emergency communications services. Within hours Honduran amateurs had established contact and were operating through amateur emergency nets in the U.S. During the weekend of September 21–22, more than 200 amateurs were involved in long hours of message-handling for governments, disaster relief agencies, and medical rescue facilities.

The latest in the series of amateur radio satellites called OSCAR (for Orbiting Satellite Carrying Amateur Radio) was successfully placed in orbit on November 15 from NASA's Western Test Range in Lompoc, Calif. Designated OSCAR 7, the new satellite was declared operational on orbit number 17 and was afterward used by hundreds of amateurs for two-way communications. (MORGAN W. GODWIN)

See also Advertising; Motion Pictures; Music; Space Exploration; Telecommunications.

[613.D.4.b; 735.I.4–5]

ENCYCLOPÆDIA BRITANNICA FILMS. *TV News: Behind the Scenes* (1973).

Tennis

Effective control of the game by the traditional governing body, the International Lawn Tennis Federation (ILTF), continued to be a problem in 1974. Accord was reached with the Association of Tennis Professionals (ATP), to which most leading men players belonged and with which there had been serious dispute in 1973, but the formation in the United States of World Team Tennis complicated the administration of the game. Harmony between the ILTF and ATP was reached in September 1974 with the formation of a Men's International Professional Tennis Council with joint representation. The council was authorized to regulate all men's tournaments offering prize money in excess of $17,500.

World Team Tennis (WTT), a purely commercial organization, began active operations in May. It comprised 16 teams on an intercity league basis with its administration based on the pattern of other professional sports in the U.S. such as baseball and football. The various franchise holders in WTT gave lucrative contracts to leading players of both sexes. Conflicts soon arose between this new form of tennis and the traditional tournaments. The WTT playing schedule had a gap specifically to give its players time to compete in the Wimbledon championships and in any case finished before the start of the U.S. Open championships at Forest Hills, N.Y., at the end of August, but the Italian and French Open championships as well as many lesser events were held to be gravely threatened by the absence of many leading players. After controversy among member nations, the ILTF eventually sanctioned WTT operations, though with conditions that some member nations claimed were not fulfilled. The upshot was that the Italian and French federations banned WTT-contracted players from their respective open championships. Specifically, they refused the entries of two leading professionals, Jim Connors of the U.S. (*see* BIOGRAPHY) and Evonne Goolagong of Australia, causing the two to take legal action.

The new form of tennis promoted by WTT diverged widely from tradition. In its eventual format each intercity match (all were staged indoors) comprised a set each of men's singles, women's singles, men's doubles, women's doubles, and mixed doubles. Each set consisted of no more than 13 games. Deuce and advantage were abolished in the point scoring of games. Substitutes were allowed even in the middle of a set. Spectators were encouraged to be as noisy as possible. The first season was avowedly experimental, expensive for the promoters, and not obviously successful. WTT's estimate of the financial "break-even" point was an average attendance of 4,000 at each match. Toward the end of July WTT published a figure of 2,381 as the average achieved.

A tie-breaking scoring system was officially incorporated into the rules of tennis at the annual general meeting of the ILTF in Amsterdam in July. The diverse experimental systems previously allowed ceased to have legal sanction in 1975 with the adoption of the 12-point method used at Wimbledon and elsewhere. In this system the tie-breaking game was won by the player winning the best out of 12 points and being at least two points in front. The use of the tie-breaking game remained permissive, not mandatory, and the timing of its application was discretionary.

Commercial sponsorship and big prize money continued for some leading events, though the Wimbledon tournament notably maintained its resistance to sponsorship, as did the Davis Cup competition. Vast sums were won by the most successful players, men and women. Total prize money in the U.S. Open championships exceeded $270,000 and, round for round, the women earned the same as the men.

Men's Competition. *Singles.* The Australian championship, played in Melbourne and incorporating the Victorian State championship, was won by Connors, the outstanding player of the year. The defending champion, John Newcombe, lost to a fellow Australian, Ross Case, in the quarterfinals, and Connors' final victory was over another Australian, Phil Dent, by 7–6, 6–4, 4–6, 6–3.

Connors did not participate in the circuit promoted by World Championship Tennis (WCT). A well-established feature of the game, this was divided into three groups of 28 players each who competed in 8 tournaments, 24 in all, at various sites throughout the world. The eight most successful players qualified for a final tournament in Dallas, Tex., in May. They were Newcombe, fellow Australian Rod Laver, Stan Smith and Arthur Ashe of the U.S., Tom Okker of The Netherlands, Jan Kodes of Czechoslovakia, Ilie Nastase of Romania, and Björn Borg of Sweden. In the final Newcombe beat Borg 4–6, 6–3, 6–3, 6–2. Borg, who was 18 on June 6, 1974, had unusually precocious success, notably on hard courts. He won both the Italian and French Open championships, triumphing in the Italian final in Rome against the 1973 champion, Nastase, by 6–3, 6–4, 6–2 when he was still only 17 years old. Two weeks later, having become 18 during the tournament, he beat Manuel Orantes of Spain 2–6, 6–7, 6–0, 6–1, 6–1 in Paris in the final of the French meeting.

The Wimbledon tournament was dominated by the bold and aggressive game of the left-handed Connors, double-fisted on the backhand. In the final he easily beat Ken Rosewall of Australia 6–1, 6–1, 6–4. The second-place finish of Rosewall, 39 years old on Nov. 2, 1973, was the most surprising aspect of the event. He beat the number one seed, Newcombe, in the quarterfinals and the 1972 champion, Smith, in the semifinals, winning the latter match after being within a point of losing. Rosewall's first Wimbledon singles final was 1954. In the year he first competed there, 1952, his final opponent of 1974 was not born. Con-

nors maintained compelling form to take the U.S. Open title at Forest Hills in September. At that tournament Rosewall again surprised by reaching the final, again beating Newcombe in the course of doing so. In the last match Connors overwhelmed Rosewall 6–1, 6–0, 6–1, the most one-sided final on record.

Doubles. No pair in 1974 was dominant to the exclusion of all rivals. An attempt was made to increase interest in this form of the game by the promotion of a WCT final doubles tournament in Montreal and by the Commercial Union Grand Prix, which covered a wide range of tournaments throughout the world, awarding points for doubles as well as singles. The WCT event was won by South Africans Bob Hewitt and Frew McMillan. The Wimbledon title was taken for the fifth time by Newcombe and his fellow Australian Tony Roche. There was consistency of performance by the American pair of Smith and Bob Lutz, runners-up for the French and Wimbledon titles and winners of the U.S. Open.

Davis Cup. The domination of Davis Cup competition by either the U.S. or Australia, unbroken since 1938, ended. The U.S. lost in its first contest, against Colombia early in the year, when a below-strength American side of Harold Solomon, Erik Van Dillen, and Charles Pasarell was defeated 4–1 in Bogotá. In May the defending champion, Australia, was beaten 3–2 by India in Calcutta in the final of the Eastern Zone. Vijay Amritraj took part in all three Indian victories. The Australian team consisted of Bob Giltinan, John Alexander, and Colin Dibley, not its optimum strength. The outcome of the contest was undecided until the fifth match, and the total number of games played in all five was 327, the highest in the history of the competition. South Africa won the American Zone, and Italy and the U.S.S.R. were winners of the two European zones. The U.S.S.R. met India in the first of the interzone contests at Poona. India won 3–1 on the performance of Amritraj and his elder brother Anand. In Johannesburg, South Africa beat Italy 4–1.

The competition ended in anticlimax. The final between South Africa and India resulted in a forfeit victory for the South Africans when India announced its inability, for political reasons, to compete against them. With such a finish the reputation of the Davis Cup suffered more than at any time since its inauguration in 1900.

LONDON DAILY MAIL / PICTORIAL PARADE

Chris Evert in action against Lesley Hunt at Wimbledon. She went on to take the women's singles title rather handily.

Women's Competition. *Singles.* In the absence of Margaret Court of Australia, who gave birth to her second child during the year, the outstanding player was Chris Evert of the U.S. (*see* BIOGRAPHY), born Dec. 21, 1954. She won the Italian, French, and Wimbledon titles, events in which she had finished second in 1973. Miss Goolagong won the Australian title for the first time after three previous years as finalist, beating Miss Evert in the final 7–6, 4–6, 6–0. Miss Evert defeated Martina Navratilova of Czechoslovakia 6–3, 6–3 in the final to win in Rome. In Paris she won the final against Olga Morozova of the Soviet Union 6–1, 6–2 and met the same opponent in the final at Wimbledon, where she triumphed 6–0, 6–4.

Billie Jean King, an outstanding performer at Wimbledon for many years, defended all three titles (singles, doubles, and mixed doubles) with success only in the mixed doubles with the Australian Owen Davidson. This brought her total of Wimbledon championships to 18, one short of the record 19 taken by another Californian, Elizabeth Ryan, from 1914 to 1934. Mrs. King compensated for her Wimbledon losses by taking the U.S. Open at Forest Hills, defeating Miss Goolagong in the final 3–6, 6–3, 7–5.

Doubles. There were three notably successful partnerships. Miss Goolagong paired with Peggy Michel of the U.S. to win the Australian title, and the two, unseeded, later won at Wimbledon. Miss Evert was successful with Mrs. Morozova in both the Italian and French tournaments. Mrs. King played with fellow American Rosemary Casals to win the U.S. Open.

Federation Cup. Held in May in Naples, Italy, the Federation Cup tournament attracted 27 nations. Australia won for the seventh time. The United States, represented by Julie Heldman, Jeanne Evert, and Sharon Walsh, beat Poland, France, and West Germany to reach the final. Australia, represented by Miss Goolagong, Diane Fromholtz, and Janet Young, beat Japan, Italy, and Great Britain and then defeated the U.S. 2–1. (LANCE TINGAY)

[452.B.4.h.xxvii]

Thailand

A constitutional monarchy of Southeast Asia, Thailand is bordered by Burma, Laos, Cambodia, and Malaysia. Area: 198,500 sq.mi. (514,000 sq.km.). Pop. (1973 est.): 39,787,000. Cap. and largest city: Bangkok-Thon Buri (pop., 1970, 2,495,312). Language: Thai. Religion (1964): Buddhist 93.7%; Muslim 3.9%. King, Bhumibol Adulyadej; prime minister in 1974, Sanya Dharmasakti.

Strikes, rallies, violent demonstrations, and political crises marked 1974, Thailand's first year of democracy. At the end of it all a new constitution gave the chastened nation some hope of consolidation.

Soon after Sanya Dharmasakti's (*see* BIOGRAPHY) civilian government took office in October 1973, groups of people began taking advantage of their newfound democratic rights. Long-exploited workers broke out in spontaneous mass action for higher wages and better conditions. Two waves of strikes swept across the spectrum of industry, netting labour a legal minimum wage of $1.25 a day as against 60 cents a year earlier. General labour unrest continued, but even as the strikes started, the government began work to complete a constitution by the stipulated deadline of April.

The students, who had been the heroes of the

"October Revolution" that brought down the military government, were also restive, and anti-Japanese and anti-U.S. feelings ran high. Vocational students, the most active in the 1973 uprising, mobbed a police station at the beginning of January; one of them was killed. Days later another group of young people burned several buses in protest against an increase in fares. Resuming their offensive two weeks later, vocational students occupied the Education Ministry and threatened "drastic" action unless the authorities met their demands for academic rights and privileges.

Prime Minister Sanya was becoming visibly dissatisfied with the growing uncertainties in the country. In the National Assembly some of his early proposals ran into opposition, forcing him to drop hints of resignation. When the deputy education minister decided to leave the Cabinet over a departmental dispute, the premier had had enough. On May 21 he resigned. A military alert was immediately declared throughout the country. Several days of political crisis followed. Fears that the discredited previous military leaders might attempt a comeback gained wide currency. All sections of opinion appealed to Sanya to withdraw his resignation, and on May 27 the king named him prime minister again. A new Cabinet with fewer military men was announced a few days later.

In July the worst rioting of the year broke out in Bangkok's Chinese district, Plabplachai. Street fighting and police firing continued for three days with an estimated 25 persons killed and more than 100 injured. Meanwhile, the student force was dissipating. Differences developed among the leaders, and rival groups sprouted. The public seemed to grow rather bored with student politics as a whole. Assembly politics was a different matter. In August Sanya faced another crisis—and issued another resignation threat—when he refused to comply with an Assembly bill confiscating the assets of three exiled leaders of the previous government on the ground that it was unconstitutional. Eventually he agreed to confiscate "ill-gotten assets" of the deposed men, but only after giving them a chance to contest the action.

It was October, a full year after the new government had come to power and six months after the original deadline, when a constitution was approved by the Assembly. Elections under the new charter were scheduled for Feb. 1, 1975. But there was considerable speculation that generals and former deputies linked to the previous government might gain the most from a general election. The king's own public criticism of parts of the constitution struck many as a discouraging augury. Late in December former prime minister Thanom Kittikachorn was arrested after he had entered the country secretly, allegedly to visit his sick father. The government at first decided to prosecute him but then reversed itself and had him flown to Singapore.

The unsettled domestic situation left Thailand's foreign relations in a state of flux during the year. Considerable strain in relations with the U.S. developed in January with the disclosure that the Central Intelligence Agency (CIA) was actively involved in Thailand's affairs. A CIA operative in insurgent northeast Thailand sent Prime Minister Sanya a false cease-fire offer purporting to be from a Communist leader. There were reports that the U.S. had contingency plans to use air bases in Thailand in the continuing war in Cambodia. In mid-May the U.S. Air Force began a slow pullout from Thailand. Half of the 50 B-52s stationed in the country and 175 other

Textiles:
see Industrial Production and Technology

THAILAND

Education. (1972–73) Primary, pupils 6,228,469, teachers 192,318; secondary, pupils 666,755, teachers 28,064; vocational, pupils 129,025, teachers 8,277; teacher training, students 49,841, teachers 3,767; higher (including 7 universities), students 63,940, teaching staff 8,448.

Finance. Monetary unit: baht, with (Sept. 16, 1974) a par value of 20 baht to U.S. $1 (free rate of 46.95 baht = £1 sterling). Gold, SDRs, and foreign exchange, official: (June 1974) U.S. $1,790,000,000; (June 1973) U.S. $1,242,000,000. Budget (1973–74 est.): revenue 26,520,000,000 baht; expenditure 34,482,000,-000 baht. Gross national product: (1972) 159,840,-000,000 baht; (1971) 145,370,000,000 baht. Money supply: (Dec. 1973) 29,820,000,000 baht; (Dec. 1972) 24,680,000,000 baht. Cost of living (Bangkok; 1970 = 100): (May 1974) 149; (May 1973) 116.

Foreign Trade. (1973) Imports 41,841,000,000 baht; exports 32,277,000,000 baht. Import sources (1972): Japan 37%; U.S. 16%; West Germany 7%; U.K. 5%. Export destinations: Japan 21%; U.S. 13%; Singapore 9%; The Netherlands 8%; Hong Kong 7%. Main exports: rubber 14%; rice 11%; corn 9%; tapioca 8%; tin 6%. Tourism (1972): visitors 820,-800; gross receipts U.S. $131 million.

Transport and Communications. Roads (main; 1972) 17,686 km. Motor vehicles in use (1972): passenger 282,600; commercial 158,900. Railways: (1970) 3,765 km.; traffic (1971) 4,260,000,000 passenger-km., freight 2,381,000,000 net ton-km. Air traffic (1973): 1,751,000,000 passenger-km.; freight 31,760,000 net ton-km. Shipping (1973): merchant vessels 100 gross tons and over 78; gross tonnage 182,-043. Telephones (Dec. 1972) 235,000. Radio receivers (Dec. 1972) 3 million. Television receivers (Dec. 1971) 241,000.

Agriculture. Production (in 000; metric tons; 1973; 1972 in parentheses): rice c. 14,200 (11,669); corn c. 2,500 (1,315); peanuts c. 230 (227); sweet potatoes (1972) c. 270, (1971) c. 260; sorghum c. 130 (81); dry beans c. 211 (c. 195); soybeans c. 58 (c. 56); cassava (1972) 3,687, (1971) c. 3,010; sugar, raw value 761 (709); bananas c. 1,200 (c. 1,200); tobacco c. 45 (c. 49); rubber 360 (337); cotton, lint c. 25 (c. 25); jute c. 10 (c. 10); kenaf c. 487 (c. 390); timber (cu.m.; 1971) 19,000, (1970) 18,600; fish catch (1972) 1,679, (1971) 1,587. Livestock (in 000; 1972–73): cattle 4,751; buffaloes (1971–72) c. 5,800; pigs 4,573; chickens (1971–72) c. 37,000; ducks (1971–72) c. 13,500.

Industry. Production (in 000; metric tons; 1972): tin concentrates (metal content) 22; tungsten concentrates (oxide content) 3.3; lead concentrates (metal content) 1.6; manganese ore (metal content) 6.6; cement (1973) 3,735; petroleum products 6,963; electricity (kw-hr.; 1971) 5,225,000.

aircraft were to go by the year's end, leaving 350 U.S. military aircraft.

Thai contacts with China continued with Air Chief Marshal Dawee Chullasapya, then defense minister, visiting Peking in February. A 14-year-old ban on trade with China was lifted in January. There was talk of establishing "a semigovernmental" relationship between the two countries by the year's end.

The economy remained relatively healthy despite a 15% increase in prices. Financial authorities estimated that inflation induced by the world economic turmoil was the worst since World War II. The outlook for the immediate future was described as bleak.

(T. J. S. GEORGE)

[976.B.3]

Theatre

U.S. and Canada. In the U.S. theatre, the symbolic event of the year was FACT, the First American Congress of Theater, a four-day meeting of theatre people from all parts of the nation, held in June at Princeton, N.J., and organized under the leadership of the Broadway producer Alexander Cohen. The Broadway theatre, traditionally indifferent to subsidized, noncommercial professional theatre, was calling for unity

and asking for help. As Bernard Jacobs, a co-director of the Shubert Organization, which controls more Broadway theatres than any other agency, told the delegates, "Very few people make money in the Broadway theatre anymore. That kind of theatre has ceased to exist, and it will never return." Even if Jacobs was exaggerating, it was a historic statement for a Shubert executive to make.

Walter Kerr wrote in the *New York Times* that if Broadway could not survive as a significant centre of theatrical production, it could still function as a centre for the exhibition of productions from elsewhere. And, indeed, most of the significant work to be seen on Broadway in 1974 did come from elsewhere, either from subsidized, noncommercial U.S. theatres or from Great Britain.

The dramatic success of the 1973–74 Broadway season was *A Moon for the Misbegotten* by Eugene O'Neill. This late play of O'Neill's had been professionally produced in New York twice previously; this time, in a production that originated at the Academy Theatre outside Chicago, it connected fully with both press and public. José Quintero directed a cast that included Jason Robards, Colleen Dewhurst (*see* BIOGRAPHY), and Ed Flanders; Quintero, Dewhurst, and Flanders all won Tony awards.

The musical success of the season was *Candide,* a revival of a Broadway failure of 1956, based on the satire by Voltaire with a score by Leonard Bernstein. It opened Dec. 20, 1973, at the Chelsea Theater Center in the Brooklyn Academy of Music, with a new book by Hugh Wheeler and an inventive, environmental staging by Harold Prince that had the actors dashing among several small stages through the midst of the audience. In March it was moved to the Broadway Theater, which was especially remodeled for the occasion; it won the New York Drama Critics' Circle Award as best musical of the season.

Another success from Brooklyn was *Scapino,* adapted and directed by Frank Dunlop. This free version of Molière's *Les Fourberies de Scapin* was first produced by the Young Vic in London and was brought to the Brooklyn Academy of Music as part of the Academy's British Theatre Season. From there it was transferred first to the Circle in the Square–Joseph E. Levine Theatre, a noncommercial theatre located on Broadway, and then to a regular Broadway theatre. It featured a virtuosic low-comedy performance by Jim Dale.

A number of other Broadway offerings came from Great Britain by various routes. Arriving late in 1973, *Good Evening* was a revue by Peter Cook and Dudley Moore, with Cook and Moore comprising the entire cast; it was received as a sterling example of British hilarity. *Find Your Way Home,* by the British playwright John Hopkins, was not in general well received, but a young U.S. actor named Michael Moriarty became a star as a result of his performance. *Jumpers* by Tom Stoppard, a meditation on modern life in the form of a farcical comedy, came to Broadway in a production mounted by the Kennedy Center in Washington, D.C., directed by Peter Wood, with Brian Bedford in the leading role.

The fall season of 1974 on Broadway was dominated by British imports. The most prominent dramatic success was *Equus* by Peter Shaffer, a play about a boy who is passionately and dangerously drawn to horses. First staged at the British National Theatre, it was presented in New York with two British actors heading the cast, Peter Firth as the boy

Helena Brodin and Jan-Olof Strandberg star in Ingmar Bergman's production of "To Damascus," by August Strindberg, at the Royal Dramatic Theatre, Stockholm.

and Anthony Hopkins as his troubled psychiatrist. The Circle in the Square-Joseph E. Levine Theatre opened its 1974–75 season with *The National Health* by Peter Nichols, a comedy about mortality set in a hospital ward, also first presented by the British National Theatre but shown in New York in a production from the Long Wharf Theatre in New Haven, Conn. The comedy success of the new season was a British farce with serious overtones, *Absurd Person Singular* by Alan Ayckbourn.

Yet another British import was *Flowers*, a mime adaptation of Jean Genet's novel, *Our Lady of the Flowers*, created by Lindsay Kemp, who also played the leading role. The Royal Shakespeare Company sent its productions of two 19th-century plays: *London Assurance* by Dion Boucicault and *Sherlock Holmes* by Arthur Conan Doyle and William Gillette. *Saturday, Sunday, Monday* by Eduardo De Filippo and an all-male production of Shakespeare's *As You Like It* were both restagings, by the original directors but with new casts, of productions originally given at the British National Theatre.

Not everything on Broadway in 1974 was British. *The Freedom of the City*, by the Irish playwright Brian Friel, dealt with the troubles in Northern Ireland and came to New York in a production mounted by the Goodman Theatre Center in Chicago. *Bad Habits*, a pair of sourly witty one-act comedies by Terrence McNally, was transferred to Broadway from off-Broadway (having originated off-off-Broadway). From South Africa (via London and New Haven) came *Sizwe Bansi Is Dead* and *The Island*, two plays by Athol Fugard, John Kani, and Winston Ntshona, performed in repertory by Kani and Ntshona. A revival of *Cat on a Hot Tin Roof* by Tennessee Williams, with Elizabeth Ashley, came from the American Shakespeare Theatre in Stratford, Conn. *Hosanna*, by the French-Canadian Michel Tremblay, was first presented in Montreal and came to Broadway in an English-language production originally mounted by the Tarragon Theatre in Toronto.

Meanwhile, Broadway produced pitifully little on its own. *The Good Doctor*, adapted by Neil Simon from various plays and sketches of Chekhov, opened in November 1973 and was less successful than most of Simon's work. *Ulysses in Nighttown*, an adaptation from James Joyce's novel starring Zero Mostel as Leopold Bloom, was less successful on Broadway than

it had been off-Broadway 16 years previously. There was a comedy about the stresses of New York life (not a new topic) called *Thieves*, by Herb Gardner. *The Magic Show*, starring a young Canadian magician, Doug Henning, was a surprise success.

Broadway also produced a number of nostalgia-laden musicals: *Lorelei*, a reworked version of *Gentlemen Prefer Blondes*, once again starring Carol Channing; *Over Here!*, set during World War II and featuring the two remaining Andrews sisters; a revival of *Gypsy* starring Angela Lansbury; *Mack and Mabel*, about the early days of Hollywood, with Robert Preston and Bernadette Peters; and a revival of *Good News* with Alice Faye and John Payne.

Off-Broadway was in worse shape than Broadway as a centre for commercial productions. A successful production of *Moonchildren*, Michael Weller's sensitive play about a group of brilliant, unhappy young Americans, arrived in November 1973 and ran until the following fall. *Bad Habits* by Terrence McNally was first staged off-off-Broadway and *Why Hanna's Skirt Won't Stay Down* became an off-Broadway production after having been an off-off-Broadway perennial for several years.

During the season, two old-fashioned realistic plays transferred to off-Broadway from one off-off-Broadway theatre, the Circle Repertory. One was a melodrama, *When You Comin' Back, Red Ryder?* by Mark Medoff, and the other a romantic two-character play called *The Sea Horse* by "James Irwin," a pseudonym for Edward Moore, who played the leading role. (Medoff eventually replaced Kevin Conway in the leading role of his play.) These two new writers were the most promising to emerge during this sparse season. In the fall of 1974 another play by Medoff, *The Wager*, was produced off-Broadway after an off-off-Broadway tryout.

It is important not to judge the U.S. noncommercial theatres merely on the basis of the productions that they send to Broadway; their first responsibility is to work in their own communities for their own audiences. Thus, the Dallas Theater Center continued to produce new plays about its own region, including *Jack Ruby: All-American Boy* by John Logan and the *Bradleyville Trilogy*, three plays about West Texas by Preston Jones. In addition to its regular season of classical plays, the Tyrone Guthrie Theater in Minneapolis, Minn., commissioned an original musical presentation, *The Portable Pioneer and Prairie Show* by David Chambers and Mel Marvin, based on Middle Western history.

The Trinity Square Repertory Company moved into its new headquarters in downtown Providence, R.I., late in 1973, and celebrated with a season that included new plays by Stuart Vaughan (*Ghost Dance* —about Sitting Bull), Israel Horovitz (*Alfred the Great*), and Oliver Hailey (*For the Use of the Hall*). The company also produced *Aimee,* a musical about Aimee Semple McPherson, with book and lyrics by William Goyen and music by Worth Gardner. The Yale Repertory Theatre in New Haven successfully produced the Kurt Weill-Bertolt Brecht opera *The Rise and Fall of the City of Mahagonny* and also presented new plays by Sam Shepard (*Geography of a Horse Dreamer*), Adrienne Kennedy (*An Evening with Dead Essex*), and Isaac Bashevis Singer (*Shlemiel the First*), plus Albert Camus's adaptation of Dostoyevsky's *The Possessed,* staged by the Polish film director Andrzej Wajda.

The Arena Stage in Washington, D.C., presented *The Madness of God,* a new play about Russian Jewry by Elie Wiesel. Several British plays made their first American appearances at regional noncommercial theatres. Two plays by David Storey had their U.S. premieres in Washington, D.C.: *In Celebration* was given by the Arena Stage, and *The Farm* by the Folger Theatre Group. *The Sea* by Edward Bond was first produced at the Goodman Theatre Center in Chicago.

For Joseph Papp, the producer of the New York Shakespeare Festival and the most prominent figure in the U.S. noncommercial theatre, it was a relatively poor season. Papp's first production at the Vivian Beaumont Theater in Lincoln Center, *Boom Boom Room* by David Rabe, provoked furious controversy. *What the Wine-Sellers Buy* by Ron Milner, a play about a young man's maturation set in a black ghetto, was presented both at the Beaumont and in the touring Mobile Theater. Papp's only unqualified success was *Short Eyes,* a prison drama written by an ex-convict, Miguel Piñero, and performed, under the direction of Marvin Felix Camillo, by "The Family," a group consisting mostly of ex-convicts. *Short Eyes* was introduced to New York at the Theater of Riverside Church and transferred by Papp first to his Public Theater downtown and then to the Beaumont.

Two widely contrasting avant-garde theatre groups, both based in New York, emerged into prominence during 1974. The Ridiculous Theatrical Company, directed by Charles Ludlam, devoted itself to grotesque transvestite comedy. The La Mama Repertory Company, directed by Andrei Serban, presented a trilogy of Greek tragedies, *Medea, The Trojan Women,* and *Electra,* with music by Elizabeth Swados; the plays were performed in ancient Greek.

In Canada the Shaw Festival mounted a hugely successful production of *Charley's Aunt,* starring Paxton Whitehead, and sent it on tour; the Stratford Festival, in Jean Gascon's last season as artistic director, produced *The Imaginary Invalid* as a vehicle for William Hutt and sent it on a tour of Australia. But the important theatrical news in Canada in 1974 was made by Canadian playwrights. The most prominent among them was Michel Tremblay, whose play *Hosanna,* about a transvestite who is forced to recognize his manhood, was described by the author as a political allegory about the nationhood of Quebec. The English-language production of *Hosanna,* staged by Bill Glassco at the Tarragon Theatre, made a

greater impact in Toronto than it did a few months later in New York. A new play by David Freeman, *Battering Ram,* was produced at the Tarragon and in Vancouver, B.C. The Toronto Free Theatre presented *Red Emma,* a play by Carol Bolt about the anarchist Emma Goldman. James Reaney continued to work on a trilogy entitled *The Donnellys. Sticks and Stones: The Donnellys, Part I,* produced in 1973, was scheduled to be followed (at the Tarragon) by *The St. Nicholas Hotel: The Donnellys, Part II.* George Ryga's new play *Paracelsus* was published in *The Canadian Theatre Review,* a new journal whose very existence was a significant indication of the development of Canadian theatre.   (JULIUS NOVICK)

Great Britain and Ireland. The year began badly, with power restrictions and industrial disputes affecting the theatre particularly severely, and ended even more menacingly as soaring inflation threatened the future of all the arts. The case of the Royal Shakespeare Company was typical: the previous year's deficit could not be met by new grant funds as the expected inflationary rise of 7% turned out to be nearer 20% and a six-figure deficit had to be faced. Moreover, despite the government's offer to counter its effects by increased funding to the Arts Council of Great Britain, the imposition of the value-added tax had brought many theatres to the verge of bankruptcy. The opening of the National Theatre's new three-auditorium complex on the South Bank was postponed yet again, partly due to building delays. While this meant a short-term saving, it left Peter Hall with the problem of what to do with the new works he had bought and the actors he had engaged for them. A bill brought in by the new Labour government ensured finance for completion of the new buildings, though not for future operating costs.

The outlook for the regional and private theatres was equally bleak, though the government promised help for the Arts Council to meet the demand for supplementary grants. Meanwhile, the London theatre continued to be at the mercy of property developers,

Rex Harrison plays the title role in Luigi Pirandello's "Henry IV" at Her Majesty's Theatre in London.

DONALD COOPER

and a campaign to protect historic theatre buildings was strongly supported by leaders of the acting profession. As a result, the Shaftesbury Theatre was saved, but the future of the Criterion in Piccadilly Circus remained in doubt.

The Royal Shakespeare Company's policy of offering new works and classics continued unabated, even if this meant courting occasional unpopularity. David Mercer's symbolic drama of a 20th-century apocalypse, *Duck Song,* and Peter Barnes's scabrous pseudohistorical parody of power politics, *The Bewitched,* failed to stay the course at the company's main London home, the Aldwych; but Tom Stoppard's mock-biographical skit on literature and politics, *Travesties,* hilariously staged by Peter Wood, tipped the scales in the other direction, together with David Jones's realistic production of Gorky's *Summerfolk,* Frank Dunlop's spoof of the traditional thriller *Sherlock Holmes,* and Ronald Eyre's mockingly expressionistic treatment of the English premiere of Frank Wedekind's *The Marquis of Keith.* Transfers from Stratford were *Richard II,* John Barton's rewritten version of Marlowe's *Dr. Faustus,* and *Cymbeline.* A transfer from the company's new Stratford studio theatre, The Other Place, to its third workshop season at London's The Place was Buzz Goodbody's truncated *Lear* for schools with Tony Church as the king. Also at The Place, plays by Strindberg, Victor Lanoux, and Snoo Wilson inaugurated the centenary celebrations of the Stratford Shakespeare Festival.

A similar pattern was set by the National Theatre at the Old Vic, where Peter Hall's reign as manager began with his quasi-operatic production of *The Tempest,* featuring John Gielgud (*see* BIOGRAPHY) as Prospero and spectacular sets by John Bury. A sympathetically acted revival of J. B. Priestley's *Eden End* with Joan Plowright failed to presage a return to favour of the 80-year-old writer; a long-drawn-out domestic drama by John Hopkins, *Next of Kin,* staged by Harold Pinter, and a heavy-handed futuristic comedy by Peter Nichols entitled *The Freeway* fared less well than Jonathan Miller's productions of *Measure for Measure* with the company's mobile troupe and of Beaumarchais' *The Marriage of Figaro.* Wedekind's *Spring Awakening* and A. E. Ellis' *Grand Manoeuvres,* a first play by a novelist about the notorious Dreyfus affair, proved more stimulating.

The Young Vic, under Frank Dunlop, celebrated a spectacular year, with successes both on tour and in the U.S., by severing formal connections with the parent National Theatre Company. Particularly popular was the first performance in two centuries of Henry Fielding's *Tom Thumb.*

The classics were exceptionally well served by two companies of no fixed theatrical abode. The Prospect Theatre, fresh from foreign triumphs, staged a modern-dress *Pericles* and a cycle of three of Shakespeare's chronicle dramas, and the Actors' Company, after a splendid New York season, presented a first-rate repertoire ranging from Shakespeare to Chekhov.

The success of Wedekind at the Old Vic and the Aldwych was accompanied by a wave of German classics and moderns new to London, from Schiller's *The Highwayman* (said to be the first English version of *Die Raüber* in Britain) at the Round House and Carl Sternheim's *Schippel* and *The Snob* at the Open Space to several contemporary plays by Rainer Werner Fassbinder and Franz Xaver Kroetz in other small fringe theatres. Many of these productions were aided by grants from the Goethe Institute. Other pioneering works on the fringe were David Rudkin's semiautobiographical *Ashes* at the Open Space and E. A. Whitehead's *The Sea Anchor* at the Theatre Upstairs (the Royal Court's studio theatre).

At the Royal Court, following three protest dramas by South African playwright Athol Fugard and his black collaborators, Oscar Lewenstein's last season as manager was notable for the West Indian Mustapha Matura's sad comedy *Play Mas,* David Storey's study of a failed art master, *Life Class* (which, like Matura's and two of the Fugard plays, was transferred to the West End), and *Bingo,* Edward Bond's tragedy of the artist in society with John Gielgud as Will Shakespeare and Arthur Lowe as Ben Jonson.

The Greenwich Theatre presented two cycles. The first, subtitled "Family Romances," comprised *Ghosts, The Seagull,* and *Hamlet,* all staged by Jonathan Miller in the same abstract setting and with identical casts. The second, "Norman Conquests," comprised three plays by Alan Ayckbourn about the sexual adventures of his lower middle-class hero Norman, later a great success in the West End. Finally, John Osborne's production of his own *The Entertainer* launched the theatre's Osborne season, with Max Wall in the role created by Sir Laurence Olivier in 1957. The direction of Joan Littlewood's Theatre Workshop, struggling to carry on behind a forest of high-rise buildings, passed to Ken Hill, author of most of the season's entertainments. At the Mermaid the year's best-seller was *Cole,* a biographical revue based on the life and music of Cole Porter.

Among foreign imports, U.S. playwright Sam Shepard received acclaim for several dramas of modern violence, which were receiving their first performance in London. The second play by Australian David Williamson (*see* BIOGRAPHY) to be seen in London, *What If You Died Tomorrow?,* was performed in the West End by its original Australian company. The Round House saw the return of the Paris-based Grand Magic Circus with Jerome Savary's joyous pseudohistorical extravaganza *From Moses to Mao.* Direct U.S. imports were limited to the erotic revue *Let My People Come;* of several American plays to reach the West End the best were *A Streetcar Named Desire* starring Claire Bloom and *The Gingerbread Lady* with Elaine Stritch. *Pygmalion* with Diana Rigg and Alec McCowen achieved a record run in the West

Colleen Dewhurst cradles Jason Robards in a scene from Eugene O'Neill's "A Moon for the Misbegotten" at the Morosco Theatre in New York City.

R. BRAATEN—AUTHENTICATED NEWS INTERNATIONAL

End, outclassing even Pirandello's *Henry IV* with Rex Harrison as its mad hero and *The Waltz of the Toreadors* with Trever Howard as Jean Anouilh's sex-mad General St. Pé. Other West End successes included *Chez Nous* with Albert Finney, *Snap* with Maggie Smith, *A Ghost on Tiptoe* with Robert Morley, *The Dame of Sark* with Celia Johnson, *Birds of Paradise* with Moira Lister, the musicals *Billy* (Michael Crawford) and *Hans Christian Andersen* (Tommy Steele), *The Good Companions* with Judi Dench, *Cinderella* with Twiggy, and the sad story of the Beatles by the Liverpudlian writer Willy Russell with the original Liverpool cast.

In Ireland the Dublin Theatre Festival's new productions broke all records. They included Edna O'Brien's *The Gathering* at the Abbey Theatre, in which bitter hidden conflicts break out during a celebration; Hugh Leonard's Irish comedy of human foibles, *Summer,* and Kevin O'Morrisson's *The Morgan Yard,* both at the Olympia and both first seen in the U.S.; and Ray McAnally's production of *The Gingerbread Lady* at the Eblana and George Furth's *Twigs* at the Gate, both with Anna Monahan. Desmond Cave's portrayal of the title role in Brecht's *The Resistible Rise of Arturo Ui,* directed by Tomas MacAnna at the Abbey, was among the year's finest performances. Two memorable firsts in bomb-scarred Belfast were Michael Poynor's production of Brecht's *Schweik in World War II* and John Boyd's *Guests,* the drama of a returning ghost.

France. Two new ministers of culture since the previous year, novelist Maurice Druon and one-time head of the Paris Autumn Festival Michel Guy, both attracted criticism, the former for decrying leftist tendencies among artists and the latter for wholesale firings and arbitrary appointments. Guy's dismissal of law professor and creator of the Nancy Festival Jack Lang from the management of the Palais de Chaillot complex found some support, however. Lang's successor, André-Louis Perinetti, inherited the reshaped large auditorium and some of Lang's repertoire. This began with Romanian guest director Lucian Pintilie's version of *Princess Turandot* with a cast of dwarfs and ended after Lang's departure with *Atlantis,* a Freudian exploration of a child's view of the world devised and staged by Petrika Ionesco and Radu Buruzescu. The Autumn Festival, planned by Guy before his promotion, included Peter Brook's challenging new-look version of *Timon of Athens,* performed in a gutted boulevard theatre by members of his International Theatre Workshop with a leavening of French actors; Jerome Savary's melodramatic frolic *Goodbye Mr. Freud;* a lugubriously misconceived adaptation of Wedekind's *Spring Awakening;* and Robert Wilson's mischievously named slow-motion "opera" *A Letter from Queen Victoria.*

Besides losing one of its oldest members, Robert Hirsch, to the commercial stage, and its most gifted young apprentice, Isabelle Adjani, to the films after her singular successes in *Ondine* and *The House of Bernarda Alba,* the Comédie Française had to move temporarily to the Marigny to allow the Salle Richelieu to be modernized for its tercentenary in 1980. Robert Hossein made his directing debut with *The House of Bernarda Alba* at the Odéon and with *Hernani* at the Marigny, where Jacques Charon directed and starred in Jean Poiret's revue of the company's 300 years entitled *L'Impromptu de Marigny.*

At the Théâtre de la Ville, Jean Mercure's production of Arthur Miller's *The Creation of the World and Other Business* was sandwiched between Jean-Michel Ribes's skit on Homeric Greece, *A Cup of Tea for the Odyssey,* and a superb production of Brecht's *Petit Bourgeois Wedding.* At the Théâtre de l'Est Parisien, Guy Rétoré, with stunning revivals of *The Good Woman of Setzuan* and *The Tempest* behind him and despite an immensely popular co-production with the Avignon Festival of a musical version of the Alfred Jarry plays called *The Ubs,* was one of the unexplained victims of Michel Guy's new broom. At the Théâtre d'Orsay, Jean-Louis Barrault staged his adaptation of Nietzsche's *Thus Spake Zarathustra* on the large stage, with the world premiere of Slawomir Mrozek's *The Exiles* on the small stage.

Roger Planchon's Théâtre National Populaire featured his drama on the theme of superstition, *The Black Pig,* as well as Michal Vinaver's *Overboard* from Lyons and Tankred Dorst's *Toller.* Other plays by German authors seen in France were Wedekind's *Death and the Devil* and Peter Handke's *The Ride Across Lake Constance.* Dario Fo gave his celebrated one-man show in French, and *The Cloud in Love,* based on the writings of the Turkish poet Nazim Hikmet, found favour both at home and abroad. A controversial world premiere was *The Exile,* Henry Montherlant's first drama set in World War I and proscribed by the author during his lifetime.

Switzerland, Germany, Austria, Belgium, The Netherlands. At the Zürich Schauspielhaus, Manfred Wekwerth paid a return visit to stage a *Richard III* previously tried out in East Berlin and based on the idea that the villainous usurper was a partly comic figure. The same theatre saw the European premiere of Arthur Miller's *The Creation of the World and Other Business* staged by Leopold Lindtberg, a new version of Brecht's *Mother Courage and Her Children, The Three Sisters* staged by Polish guest director Jerzy Jarocki, and Friedrich Dürrenmatt's unorthodox treatment of Gotthold Lessing's *Emilia Galotti.* At the Neumarkt, the world premiere of Handke's anticapitalist allegory, *The Unreasonable Die Out,* was directed by Horst Zankl. In Basel Hans Hollmann made theatrical history by staging, in two parts and on two consecutive nights in the foyers of the uncompleted new City Theatre, the monumental and previously unperformed 55-year-old epic drama *The Last Days of Mankind* by the Austrian satirist Karl Kraus.

In West Germany, Peter Zadek's Bochum Theatre made national headlines with controversial open-stage versions of *The Seagull* and *King Lear,* the latter performed in a movie house with the youthful Ulrich Wildgruber in the title role and Hannelore Hoger as the Fool. Other notable productions were the world premiere of Georg Büchner's translation of Victor Hugo's *Lucretia Borgia;* a documentary about the Baader-Meinhof terrorist gang staged by British guest director Pip Simmons; and a stage version of Heinrich Mann's novel *Professor Unrath* with Hoger in the role of Rosa Fröhlich, immortalized by Marlene Dietrich in the film version (*The Blue Angel*). Among many new productions of British plays in Germany, Luc Bondy's showy version of *The Sea* at the Munich Residenz Theatre won a well-deserved invitation to Berlin. New plays by German writers included Yaak Karsunke's *Germinal,* staged by the Frankfurt TAT Theatre's new manager, Rainer Werner Fassbinder; Wolfgang Deichsel's sociocritical horror-drama *Terror Cell* on the same stage; the first play by the Frankfurt City Theatre's literary manager,

While Robert Shaw (foreground) contemplates, his wife, Zoe Caldwell, turns her anger toward her former lover, Hector Elizondo, in the New York Shakespeare Festival production of August Strindberg's "The Dance of Death."

Horst Laube, a critique of 20th-century Germany entitled *The Marathon Piano Player* and directed with aplomb by Bondy; Rolf Hochhuth's anti-NATO satire *Lysistrata*, staged simultaneously in Essen and Vienna; *Ghosts*, Wolfgang Bauer's drama of mindless egotism, at the Munich Kammerspiele, where two East Berliners, Benno Besson and Adolf Drese, also made their debuts as guest directors; and in Stuttgart Hartmut Lange's parable drama *Staschek, or the Life of Ovid* and Gerlin Reinshagen's study of the experience of death, *Heaven and Earth*. The world premieres of works by Vaclav Havel and Pavel Kohout, banned in their native Czechoslovakia, ranked in importance with the Dutchman Lodewijk de Boer's TV parody *The Family*, spread over four nights in Düsseldorf, and Ramón de Valle-Inclán's trilogy *Comédias Bárbaras*, staged in a single evening by the Argentine Augusto Fernandez in Frankfurt.

In West Berlin a poor start at the Volksbühne was redeemed by Kurt Hübner's striking work in Peter Shaffer's *Equus*. New plays on the Schiller's three stages included: Hartmut Lange's anti-Stalinist *The Murder of Ajax;* the East Berlin writer Heiner Müller's farcical passion play about the cleansing of the Augean stables, *Herakles 5;* Thomas Bernhard's *Hunting Party;* Kroetz's *Maria Magdalena;* and a horror-comic double bill by Harald Mueller, comprising *Silent Night* and *Jetsam*. Hans Lietzau surpassed himself with his staging of Simon Gray's *Butley* and Chekhov's *Ivanov*, both starring Martin Benrath. The Tribüne gave the world premiere of a play by French writer Armand Gatti, while the Schaubühne am Halleschen Ufer offered the first showing in the West of Müller's drama of postwar East Germany, *The Blackleg;* Gorky's *Summerfolk;* and, on two consecutive nights in an exhibition hall fitted out for the purpose, Peter Stein's and Klaus-Michael Grüber's daunting two-part *Antiquity Project*.

The East Berlin Volksbühne's outstanding novelty was *Spectacle II:* a dozen plays and sketches, old and new, three of them by Müller, acted out in various parts of the theatre. Maik Hamburger provided a new translation for Friedo Solter's youthful *The Tempest* at the Deutsches Theater, while the Berliner Ensemble offered *Spring Awakening*, with Brecht's granddaughter in the cast, the Brecht-Marlowe *Ed-*ward II staged by her parents, and a third variant of *The Mother* with Felicitas Ritsch, imposingly directed by Ruth Berghaus.

Gerhard Klingenberg's penultimate season as head of the Vienna Burgtheater featured guest productions of a Carlo Goldoni comedy by Italy's Georgio Strehler, Bernhard's *Hunting Party* by Germany's Claus Peymann, Schiller's *Maria Stuart* by Poland's Erwin Axer, and Pinkas Braun's of his own translation of Edward Albee's *Seascape*. Klingenberg's revival of Arthur Schnitzler's *Anatol* incorporated for the first time the posthumous, previously unperformed sketch, *Das Süsse Mädl*. The same author's *Professor Bernhardi* and *Wild and Free* were directed by Hans Jaray at the Josefstadt Theater and by Gustav Manker at the Volkstheater. Bernhard's *Force of Habit,* about a circus troupe, was staged by Dieter Dorn at the Salzburg Festival.

The stunning revival of Arnold Wesker's *The Kitchen* by British guest director William Gaskill at the Belgian National Theatre in Brussels vied in popularity with the world premiere at the rival Théâtre du Rideau of Paul Willems' whimsical *The Mirrors of Ostende*. Czechoslovakia's Jan Grossman directed a Gogol comedy at Amsterdam's Municipal Theatre, which also offered two new works by the self-exiled Belgian writer Hugo Claus. Meanwhile, Lodewijk de Boer came up with a sequel to his four-part *The Family* entitled *The Family in Heaven*.

Italy. At the Milan Piccolo, Georgio Strehler's poetic approach to Chekhov's *The Cherry Orchard*, set in an all-white tented setting by Luciano Damiani, received great acclaim, while Dario Fo, still at loggerheads with authority, put on a provocative new farce about the evils of a supermarket, *Nobody Pays, Nobody Pays*, at his outlying theatre. The St. Vincent Best Actor Award went to Tino Buazzelli in Edmo Fenoglio's production of Italo Svevo's satire on old age and youth, *Regeneration*. After the previous year's scandal, Harold Pinter's *The Homecoming* had the author's full approval when Mauro Bolognini directed it at the Rome Teatro Valle; at the same theatre, Giorgio De Lullo's evocative staging of Pirandello's *To Find Oneself* established Rossella Falk as Italy's first solo actress-manager. At the Quirino, De Lullo's production of Molière's *The Imaginary Invalid* marked Romolo Valli's debut as actor-manager of a new company. Under Franco Enriquez' management at the Teatro di Roma, Shakespeare's *Taming of the Shrew* with Valeria Moriconi and Glauco Mauri and Oedön von Horvath's *Kasimir und Karoline* staged under canvas were the main draws.

Eastern Europe. At the Moscow Art Theatre the outstanding new play was Mikhail Roshchin's *The Old New Year*, staged by Oleg Yefremov, while revivals of Aleksey Tolstoy's *Tsar Fyodor Ioannovich* and Aleksandr Ostrovsky's *The Thunderstorm* were the choices for the Maly Theatre's 150th anniversary. At the Sovremennik's new premises the chief attractions were Galina Volchyok's production of Mikhail Shatrov's *Tomorrow's Weather* and Leningrad guest director Georgy Tovstonogov's of Sergey Mikhalkov's *Balalaikin and Co.,* adapted from the sociocritical novel by Mikhail Saltykov. Two novelties at the Taganka were Yuri Liubimov's setting of a collage of Pushkin's writings, *Comrade, Believe . . . ,* and *Wooden Horses,* an epic tragedy of village life based on two stories by Fyodor Abramov. For the Satire Theatre's 50th anniversary Valentin Pluchek staged a festive new production of Vladimir Mayakovsky's

The Bedbug, while at the Gogol a curiosity was a drama by Vadim Nekrassov and Tomas Koleshnichenko about the drug scene in the U.S. using tapes of the score of *Jesus Christ Superstar.*

At Warsaw's National Theatre, Adam Hanuszkewicz scandalized orthodox views with his iconoclastic revivals of the classics by introducing motorcycles in Juliusz Slowacki's fairy-tale *Balladyna* and an apple tree in full bloom in the spring but bearing real fruit in the fall in *A Month in the Country.* Jerzy Jarocki's production of Witold Gombrowicz's *The Wedding* at the Dramatic and Erwin Axer's of Mrozek's *Happy Event* at the Contemporary marked the rehabilitation of two writers proscribed for many years. Bruno Jasenski's antibourgeois satire *The Mannequin's Ball* played at the Ateneum, while at the Studio Jozef Szajna staged his parabolic version of *Dante,* based on the *Divine Comedy,* after its world premiere at the Florence Festival. At the Stary Theatre in Krakow, Andrzej Wajda and Konrad Swinarski staged superb revivals of Stanislaw Wyspianski's *November Night* and *Deliverance.* The best news from Prague, where the iron censorship reigned supreme, was the return of the dissident director Otomar Krejca to work on Chekhov's *Platonov* at the outlying S. K. Neumann Theatre. In Belgrade the two hits of the season were Slobodanka Aleksic's folkloric production of *Prometheus Bound* and Branko Plesa's staging of Alexander Sukhovo-Kobylin's *Tarelkin's Death.* In Bulgaria Tania Massalitinova (daughter of the Muscovite actor who created Claudius in Gordon Craig's historic *Hamlet*) appeared in a monodrama about Edith Piaf.

In Bucharest, Rom., Dinu Cernescu scored successes with a production of *Hamlet* and Marin Sorescu's *Mother.* In Budapest, Hung., Istvan Orkeny's latest absurdist allegory about seven unrelated persons all somehow linked was entitled *Kith and Kin.* Moscow designer David Borovski returned to the Comedy Theatre for Istvan Horvai's two-level production of *The Cherry Orchard.* Miklos Szinetar forsook television to put on the Arthur Miller adaptation of *An Enemy of the People* at the National's small stage, while film directors Gyula Hernadi and Miklos Jancso staged their *Red Psalm* at the 25th Theatre, where the Hungarian epic drama of *The Tragedy of Man* reappeared in a controversial format as *M-A-D-A-C-H.*

Scandinavia. Besides Per Sjöstrand's spectacular staging of Bond's *The Sea* at the Royal Dramatic in Stockholm and Alf Sjöberg's of Brecht's *Galileo,* the most talked of production was Ingmar Bergman's eye-catching version of parts 1 and 2 of Strindberg's *To Damascus.* At the City Theatre a children's play by Ionesco, Arnold Wesker's drama about a Jewish capitalist, *The Wedding Feast,* and Lars Forssell's new translation of Part 1 of *Peer Gynt* with Bengt Ernryd's music were world premiered. At the Copenhagen Royal Theatre Kaspar Rostrup made a promising directing debut with Strindberg's *Erik XIV,* while in Oslo Liv Ullmann played Nora in a New Norwegian version of Ibsen's *A Doll's House.* Highlights of the Helsinki season were Pierre Lefèvre's staging of a modern version of Molière's *The Misanthrope* by Tony Harrison at the Swedish National and Heinrich Schnitzler's production of his father's *The Lonely Road* at the Finnish National. (OSSIA TRILLING)

See also Dance; Literature; Music.

ENCYCLOPÆDIA BRITANNICA FILMS. *Shaw vs. Shakespeare Part I: The Character of Caesar, Part II: The Tragedy of Julius Caesar, Part III: Caesar and Cleopatra* (1970); *Medieval Theater: The Play of Abraham and Isaac* (1974).

Togo

A West African republic, Togo is bordered by Ghana, Upper Volta, and Dahomey. Area: 21,925 sq.mi. (56,785 sq.km.). Pop. (1974 est.): 2,197,900. Cap. and largest city: Lomé (pop., 1974 est., 214,200). Language: French (official). Religion: animist; Muslim and Christian minorities. President in 1974, Gen. Gnassingbe Eyadema.

Addressing a crowd of 30,000 people at Lomé on Feb. 2, 1974, President Eyadema announced that the government would take complete control of the important French Compagnie Togolaise des Mines du Bénin, which was working the phosphate mines at Kpémé. (*See* COMMODITY TRADE: *Special Report.*) He held the company's management responsible for the airplane accident in which he nearly lost his life on January 24 and in which four people died. On May 8 he made it known that he had given up his Christian name of Étienne and would use only his African second name of Gnassingbe.

President Eyadema paid a five-day visit to Peking early in September, during which economic and technical cooperation between China and Togo was arranged. On October 27, on his return from a visit to Nigeria, the president announced that the Economic Community of West African States, proposed by Nigeria and Togo in 1972, would be established in May 1975 at Lagos, Nig.; he also said that Nigeria would deliver crude oil to Togo in exchange for phosphates. Togo concluded an agreement with France in October for aid valued at CFA Fr. 337 million for water distribution and cotton growing. During President Eyadema's visit to Paris on November 4–8 the establishment of a Togolese air force and the building of an oil refinery and cement and fertilizer plants were discussed. (R. M. GOODWIN)

[978.E.4.b.ii]

TOGO

Education. (1971–72) Primary, pupils 257,877, teachers 4,403; secondary, pupils 24,521, teachers 778; vocational, pupils 2,506, teachers 214; teacher training (1970–71), students 153, teachers 16; higher, students 1,369, teaching staff 93.

Finance. Monetary unit: CFA franc, with (Sept. 16, 1974) a parity of CFA Fr. 50 to the French franc (free rate of CFA Fr. 240.50 = U.S. $1; CFA Fr. 556.50 = £1 sterling). Budget (1973 est.) balanced at CFA Fr. 13,434,000,000.

Foreign Trade. (1973) Imports CFA Fr. 21,398,000,000; exports CFA Fr. 12,648,000,000. Import sources: France 38%; West Germany 10%; U.K. 7%: The Netherlands 7%. Export destinations: The Netherlands 36%; France 31%; West Germany 12%; Belgium-Luxembourg 5%. Main exports: phosphates 52%; coffee 15%; cocoa 15%.

Tonga

An independent monarchy and member of the Commonwealth of Nations, Tonga is an island group in the Pacific Ocean east of Fiji. Area: 225 sq.mi. (583 sq.km.). Pop. (1973 est.): 92,000. Cap.: Nukualofa (pop., 1972 est., 20,000). Language: English and Tongan. Religion: Christian. King, Taufa'ahau Tupou IV; prime minister in 1974, Prince Tu'ipelehake.

During 1974 Tonga increased its contacts with Japan. After a visit to Japan by King Taufa'ahau Tupou IV in November 1973, proposals for several

TONGA

Education. (1971) Primary, pupils 16,416, teachers
(1970) 658; secondary, pupils 10,164, teachers (1970)
417; vocational, pupils 199; teacher training, students
92, teachers (1970) 11.

Finance and Trade. Monetary unit: pa'anga (dollar), with a free rate (Sept. 16, 1974) of 0.67 pa'anga
to U.S. $1 (1.56 pa'anga = £1 sterling). Budget
(1972–73 est.): revenue 4,238,000 pa'angas; expenditure 4,077,000 pa'angas. Foreign trade (1973): imports 7,997,000 pa'angas; exports 3,245,000 pa'angas.
Import sources: New Zealand 37%; Australia 31%;
Fiji 20%; U.K. 5%. Export destinations: The Netherlands 26%; Australia 23%; New Zealand 21%; Norway 11%; U.K. 6%; Denmark 5%; West Germany
5%. Main exports: copra 67%; desiccated coconut
10%; bananas 9%; watermelons 5%.

joint ventures—including hotels, telecommunications, and an airline—were announced. In 1974, however, the airline scheme was dropped in favour of
cooperation with Air Nauru. After an investigation
by the South Pacific Bureau of Cooperation, Tonga
joined with other Pacific nations in moves to establish
a regional shipping line.

Economically, Tonga had a difficult year despite
record prices for some agricultural products. There
was a small balance of payments credit in 1972–73
but in 1973–74, largely because of the fuel crisis and
imported inflation, there was a deficit of 4,750,000
pa'angas. With the opening of a new sealed airstrip
and increased visits from cruise ships, tourism receipts
rose slightly to reach 1.5 million pa'angas. One-third
of all imports were for food items, a reflection of rapid
population growth, increased urbanization on Tonga-
tapu, and a decline in subsistence agriculture. Frequently, the employment expectations of those migrating to Nukualofa, the capital, could not be met.
Some were able to migrate to New Zealand for short-
term employment, but in 1974 some 2,000 Tongans
who had overstayed their visitors' permits there were
instructed to leave.　　　(BARRIE KEITH MACDONALD)

[977.A.3]

Tourism

Higher oil prices, worldwide inflation, and expectations
of lower economic growth in North America and
Europe combined to moderate the expansion of international tourism in 1974. In contrast to other sectors
of the economy, however, the overall effect of these
economic setbacks on international tourism remained
marginal. While some destinations reported a falloff
in international visitors of 2–7%, many others reported continued gains.

Rapidly rising costs affected the profitability of
such tourism-related businesses as carriers, operators,
and hoteliers, and many of them faced loss situations
that were out of proportion to the modest contraction
of the total market. With their real incomes static or
declining, consumers altered but did not cancel travel
plans. The main beneficiaries of the new situation
were domestic travel and international movements to
neighbouring countries. The main casualties were organized travel and, later in the year, air charter vacations. Business travel remained the staple of the
world's scheduled airlines.

International tourism had made a good start in 1973,
but suffered a minor setback in April when dollar air
fares rose in the wake of the second U.S. dollar devaluation in February. Throughout the summer, Euro-

pean countries reported that U.S. arrivals were down
2–10%, although travel by European residents continued to increase. The cutbacks in oil exports by the
Arab exporting countries in the autumn, and the subsequent higher prices for gasoline and aviation fuel,
hit the industry very hard in the last quarter of 1973.
Year-end figures published by the International Union
of Official Travel Organizations (IUOTO), based on
projections of results for the earlier months of the
year, suggested a continuation of 1972 trends in the
early part of 1973, with arrivals increasing at an annual rate of 7–9%, followed by a slackening in growth
to an annual rate of 5–6%. On this basis, international tourist arrivals, which stood at 198 million in
1972, rose to about 210 million in 1973.

Tourism in 1974 began in very low key, but confidence returned as the effect of fuel costs on prices
became clearer. Operators who had made drastic cutbacks in hotel bookings in response to pessimistic
predictions frequently found themselves unable to satisfy last-minute demand. The international tourist
responded to higher prices in several ways. First,
there was an attempt to stay within the confines of
the previous year's travel budget by substituting lower-
cost air charter travel for scheduled air carriers. Then,
as the effects of higher air transport costs filtered
through to charter lines in the form of fuel surcharges,
there was a drop in bookings of "inclusive tour" arrangements involving considerable air travel. (Long-
distance, intercontinental travel was an exception.)

Finally, fears of economic recession and shorter
workweeks in European industry led to the postponement of travel plans from January–February, the
traditional booking season, to the late spring. This did
not affect the ultimate number of travelers, but it had
serious repercussions on the activities of tour operators, whose slender profit margins could ill withstand
the dual effect of booking uncertainty and a serious
shortage of liquidity, occasioned by the delay in receiving deposits. Public confidence in the financial
standing of operators was dealt a blow by the failure
of Court Line, Britain's second largest tour operator,
and it was apparent that many tourists were choosing
to vacation in their own countries.

There was general agreement that the age of the
low-cost package tour was over. It was predicted that
1975 prices would be 30–50% higher than those of
1973. At the same time, the role that international
tourism earnings could play in offsetting massive oil-
account balance of payments deficits was recognized,
and governments were being urged to turn from promoting tourism to managing tourism. Operators hoped
that governments would abstain from adopting restrictive economic measures toward tourism, such as
the imposition of exchange controls. It was recognized,
however, that measures favouring the industry would
be limited to those that did not conflict with anti-
inflation policies.

International Travel. The publication of final 1973
figures by the major tourist-receiving countries underlined the slower growth trend of that year. Overnight stays by tourists in West Germany and Switzerland declined to 19.9 million (−1%) and 33.4 million
(−2%), respectively. Exchange rates were thought to
have contributed to this drop. Austria (78.3 million)
and Italy (73.3 million) experienced zero growth. An
upward trend continued in Greece and Spain, but the
rate of increase was less than in 1972: there were 16
million overnights in Greece (+14%) and 69.7 million in Spain (+4%). The hotel sector in France

Tornadoes:
see Disasters;
Earth Sciences

recorded 43.8 million overnights for a 3% increase, while in Belgium there was a 6% increase to 7.4 million. Despite an 11% drop in U.S. visitors, the U.K. was still able to register a 6% rise. In Ireland, where U.S. arrivals rose 11%, a 10% increase in total foreign overnights was reported.

Outside Europe, Japan reported 784,700 visitors, an increase of 8%. Kenya, on the other hand, experienced a 10% drop in arrivals from the 420,100 of 1972. Among Caribbean destinations, Jamaica reported a 3% rise in visitors to 418,300. Probably the most impressive increase of 1973 was recorded by the U.S. A substantial promotional effort by the U.S. Travel Service (USTS), lower transatlantic air fares, and the lower value of the dollar heralded a 24% increase in overseas arrivals to 3,554,000. Of this total, 78% were pleasure travelers and 1,623,000, or 46%, came from European countries.

The U.S. also had the highest foreign exchange earnings from international tourism in 1973. Valid comparisons with 1972 are not possible because of exchange rate depreciations, but dollar earnings from tourism in 1973 can be ranked as follows: U.S. $3,250,-000,000; Spain $3,216,000,000; France $2,390,000,-000; Italy $2,373,000,000; Austria $2,190,000,000; West Germany $2,183,000,000; the U.K. $1,672,000,-Q00; Canada $1,446,000,000; Switzerland $1,369,000,-000; and The Netherlands $963,000,000. These ten countries accounted for three-quarters of total world tourist receipts, estimated at $29 billion in 1973, a dollar increase of more than 20% over 1972.

West Germany consolidated its position as the world's largest spender on international travel in 1973. Expenditures by West German tourists totaled $6,504,000,000 in 1973, exceeding those of U.S. tourists by a fifth. The second and third largest travel spenders were the U.S. ($5,371,000,000) and France ($2,155,000,000). France's position as a major travel spender was all the more remarkable in view of the enormous and varied domestic tourism infrastructure of that country. Other major spenders in 1973 were: Canada ($1,742,000,000); the U.K. ($1,665,000,000); Italy ($1,459,000,000); and Japan ($1,251,000,000; a 62% dollar increase over 1972).

The further slowdown in the growth of international tourism in 1974 was apparent from figures published by national tourist offices relative to the early months of the year, although the resurgence of demand in the summer months would probably produce an improvement in year-end figures. Early trends in arrivals were: Denmark −4%; India −2%; Italy −11%; and Portugal −1%. Declines in foreign tourist overnights were noted in West Germany (−6%), Switzerland (−7%), and Yugoslavia (−3%). In Spain the number of arrivals recorded at frontiers in the first six months of 1974 was 10.9 million, 4.7% below the comparable figure for 1973. U.S. citizen departures to Europe were down 14% in the same period, while in the early months of the year Canada experienced a 5% drop in frontier arrivals (mainly automobile arrivals from the U.S.). The U.S. itself registered a 2% drop in arrivals.

The overall picture was not as gloomy as some had foreseen, however. With the exception of reduced travel to the eastern Mediterranean area occasioned by the disorders in Cyprus, the third quarter of 1974 was reportedly satisfactory for most European countries. Newer destinations such as Tunisia benefited from a diversion of traffic at the time of the Cyprus disturbances and the transfer of power from military

to civil authorities in Greece. A number of countries reported an upward trend in the early months of 1974, including The Bahamas, Hong Kong, Kenya, and Turkey. The continuing political tension in Northern Ireland appeared to have been fully discounted as Ireland reported frontier arrivals unchanged in the first six months of the year. In Israel, however, the legacy of the October 1973 war was still apparent in early 1974; arrivals to April 1974 were 8% lower than in the previous year.

An IUOTO survey of 250 major tour operators in Europe, North America, and Japan indicated that 57% of operators experienced a drop in sales in the first four months of 1974, 14% a leveling off, and 29% an increase. All noted the trend to later bookings. Among destinations, 70% reported lower bookings to Spain but increased bookings for travel to neighbouring countries and for domestic tourism (especially in France). Sales of trips to Mexico were high in the case of North American operators. Japanese agents reported increased bookings for all destinations except round-the-world trips. From 60 to 65% of the sample reported more reservations for air travel by scheduled flights and fewer reservations for charter services. Some 59% of operators reported increased bookings for rail travel.

The two U.S. dollar devaluations of December 1971 and February 1973, whatever their other economic repercussions, did much to improve the position of the U.S. as the world's number-one earner of travel receipts. In 1973 the gap between money spent by U.S. tourists abroad and money spent by foreign tourists in the U.S. narrowed by $100 million. The Japanese led in overseas arrivals to the U.S. in 1973; Japanese tourists numbered 640,000, a 45% increase over 1972. Tourists from the U.K. rose 25% to 485,-000; from West Germany, 40% to 334,000; and from France, 23% to 200,000. South American arrivals increased by 15% to 358,000, while the large number of arrivals from Mexico and Canada rose 12 and 13%, respectively. A breakdown of the $3,250,000,000 spent in the U.S. by foreign tourists in 1973 showed Canada in first place with $1,046,000,000, followed by Mexico with $694 million. Japanese tourists spent $334 million, or $520 per arrival.

Soviet liner "Maksim Gorky" enters New York Harbor, its base for Caribbean cruises in the summer of 1974.

In contrast, U.S. travel outlays overseas rose only 8% in 1973, compared with 23% the previous year. Western European countries suffered most from this cutback. The number of U.S. tourists visiting the U.K. dropped 11%, and Italy, Switzerland, Austria, and France all reported declines. A drop of 18% was reported in U.S. travel to Israel. Only Spain, Portugal, and Ireland registered substantial gains. Canada and Mexico appeared to have taken up the slack. Spending in Canada rose 8% to $1,122,000,000, while in Mexico it rose 11% to $1,152,000,000 (exceeding outlays in Canada for the first time). Expenditure in Caribbean and South American destinations also rose. Spending in Japan remained at 1972 levels.

Developments in Tourism. Cruising continued to enjoy popularity in 1973–74. In Mediterranean countries such as Malta and Morocco, cruise arrivals accounted for 15–25% of the total visitor movement. In 1973, 750,000 U.S. residents took cruises, a 14% increase over the previous year. Even so, cruise ship operations were not immune to spiraling costs. The largest cruise ship in the world, the SS "France," was retired prematurely in the face of a continuing need for a government subsidy; public feeling in France ran high, and the crew occupied the vessel in protest.

Recognition of the interrelationship between tourism and environmental considerations came from many quarters. On France's famed Côte d'Azur, the need to safeguard the environment as a means of securing the future of tourism was underlined by the activities of CIPALM (Cellule d'intervention contre la pollution dans les Alpes Maritimes). At dawn each day during the holiday season, a fleet of specially equipped vessels, directed by spotter aircraft, scoured the sea for unsightly oil slicks and detritus.

The U.K. package tour industry was shaken by the Court Line collapse. Operating under the brand names of Horizon and Clarksons, Court was Britain's second-largest tour operator when, following an earlier suspension of stock dealing, it entered liquidation on Aug. 15, 1974. Some 50,000 tourists were temporarily stranded overseas as a direct result, and another 100,000 faced the loss of over $12 million held by Court in booking deposits. In the event, a bonding scheme arranged two years earlier between the Tour Operators Study Group and the U.K. Civil Aviation Authority financed a rescue airlift for the stranded travelers, while protracted negotiations between the travel industry and the trade secretary held out hope for clients' deposits. Among the factors cited for the collapse were Court's relative inexperience; slender profit margins and an assumption that high load factors and occupancy rates would continue indefinitely; a liquidity crisis created by late receipt of deposits; and general uncertainty about 1974 travel plans.

Although supplementary means of accommodation continued to expand faster than traditional hotels, the lack of medium priced hotel accommodations was creating a serious disequilibrium on the supply side of the market. The problem was particularly acute in gateway cities such as Frankfurt, Paris, and London, where the newer luxury-class hotels were badly hit by declining occupancy rates. The phenomenon led to an observable polarization of the tourist influx in big cities. Student tourists, with sleeping bags and camp gear, slept rough or alighted in pensions and hostels, while wealthy tourists stayed in expensive (but well-known) city hotels.

Almost four years after the statutes of the World Tourism Organization (WTO) were signed, at the

Toys:
see Games and Toys

Extraordinary General Assembly of IUOTO in Mexico City in 1970, the Swiss government received the 51st ratification and the WTO began its juridical life on Nov. 1, 1974. The purpose of the new intergovernmental organization was to raise tourism to the level of a full governmental responsibility.

(PETER SHACKLEFORD)

See also Transportation.
[732.F.1]

Track and Field Sports

International Competition. Many track and field experts were disappointed with the premier event of the 1974 season, the European championships, held at the Stadio Olimpico at Rome in September. Though world records fell in the women's competition, many of the men's events failed to live up to expectations because of the humidity, injuries to key men, and the threat of drug tests. Valery Borzov proved himself to be still the best sprinter in Europe in the 100-m. final, surviving the closing rush of 200-m. winner-to-be Pietro Mennea (Italy) to retain his title for the third successive time in 10.27 sec. The hero of the men's events for many was the unheralded Luciano Susanj of Yugoslavia, who won the 800-m. final in 1 min. 44.07 sec. from Steve Ovett (U.K.) and Markku Taskinen (Fin.).

Brendan Foster (U.K.) took the 5,000-m. final in 13 min. 17.2 sec. from Manfred Kuschmann (E.Ger.) and Lasse Viren (Fin.) and enhanced his reputation with an unbeaten season. Ian Thompson (U.K.) won the marathon, more than $1\frac{1}{2}$ min. ahead of runner-up Eckhard Lesse (E.Ger.), his 2-hr. 13-min. 18.8-sec. victory being his fourth win in as many starts. Kuschmann won the 10,000 m. in 28 min. 25.8 sec. from Tony Simmons (U.K.).

Karl Honz (W.Ger.) proved to be Europe's best over 400 m., downing defender Dave Jenkins (U.K.) with a 45.04-sec. victory in Rome, though the top 400-m. man of 1974 was Alberto Juantorena of Cuba, with a string of successes crowned by a 44.7-sec. clocking. Silvio Leonard (Cuba) pulled off a surprise by outleaning Steve Williams' (U.S.) in a 10.1-sec. 100-m. race. Leonard later improved to 10 sec. and also bettered Jamaican Commonwealth champion Don Quarrie over 200 m. (20.2 sec.). Making a big impact over 1,500 m. and 3,000 m. was John Walker (N.Z.), who climaxed his European tour with timings of 3 min. 33.4 sec. and 7 min. 40.6 sec.

The Commonwealth Games at Christchurch, N.Z., were a vindication of the fearless front-running tactics of Tanzania's 1,500-m. runner Filbert Bayi. He overcame John Walker, Ben Jipcho (Kenya), Rod Dixon (N.Z.), and Graeme Crouch (Austr.) by setting off at a fierce pace: his 3 min. 32.2 sec. lowered U.S. Jim Ryun's world record by 0.9 sec. Jipcho collected both the 3,000-m. steeplechase (8 min. 20.8 sec.) and 5,000-m. titles (13 min. 14.4 sec.; after a titanic tussle with Brendan Foster) as a grand finale to his amateur track career. Kenyan John Kipkurgat won the 800 m. in 1 min. 43.9 sec. from his countryman Mike Boit. The 10,000 m. was won by outsider Dick Tayler (N.Z.) from Dave Black (U.K.) in 27 min. 46.4 sec.

Dave Bedford (U.K.) emerged from a winter of injury to win the Amateur Athletic Association's 10,000 m. in July for his fifth successive title, but he was injured soon afterward. The high hurdler of Europe was once again Guy Drut of France. He won the

Dwight Stones of the U.S., world record holder in the high jump, wins the event at the Coca-Cola Invitational Athletic Meeting in London with a leap of 7 ft. 2¾ in.

110-m. hurdle (13.4 sec.) in Rome, and though he lost to Charles Foster and Thomas Hill, both of the U.S., his 13.2 sec. ranked top in the world. Alan Pascoe (U.K.) won the Commonwealth 400-m. hurdles crown in 48.83 sec. and then the European title in 48.82 sec. During the year Jim Bolding (U.S.) ran 11 of his 27 clockings at 49 sec. or better, headed by 48.1 sec. Swedish ace Anders Garderud cut his steeplechase best to 8 min. 14.2 sec. (European record), but Bronislaw Malinowski (Pol.) just beat him in 8 min. 15 sec. in Rome.

Though Dwight Stones (U.S.) retained his world leadership in the high jump, Jesper Toerring (Den.) surprised in Rome, at 2.25 m. (7 ft. 4½ in.), to defeat Kestutis Sapka (U.S.S.R.). Pole vaulter Tadeusz Slusarski (Pol.) gained the world's top ranking with 5.42 m. (17 ft. 9¼ in.), but Vladimir Kishkum (U.S.S.R.) won the European title at 5.35 m. (17 ft. 6½ in.). The best 1974 competitor in the long jump, Valery Podluzhny (U.S.S.R.), won the European title easily with 8.12 m. (26 ft. 7¾ in.) and later jumped 8.17 m. (26 ft. 9¾ in.). Max Klauss (E.Ger.) led the European rankings with 8.18 m. (26 ft. 10 in.). After some great early-season action from Geoff Capes (U.K.), principally a 21.37 m. (70 ft. 1½ in.) effort and a defeat of the feared East German Hartmut Briesenick, the Rome shotput final was a curiously subdued affair. Briesenick's 20.5 m. won it as the others just never got going. Alex Baryshnikov (U.S.S.R.) had set a European record of 21.7 m. (71 ft. 2½ in.) with his discus-turn style but could do no better than fourth in Rome as Ralf Reichenbach (W.Ger.) and Capes collected the other medals. Ricky Bruch (Swed.) led the world in the discus with 68.16 m. (223 ft. 7 in.), but Penti Kahma (Fin.) won the European championship with 63.62 m. Aleksey Spiridonov (U.S.S.R.) twirled 74.20 m. (243 ft. 5 in.) in winning the European hammer throw title from Jochen Sachse (E.Ger.) and later set a world record with 76.66 m. (251 ft. 6 in.) in Munich. Hannu Siitonen (Fin.) won the javelin final in Rome with 89.58 m. (293 ft. 10½ in.).

A decathlon duel was fought out for the European title, before Ryszard Skowronek (Pol.) won with 8,207 pt.; Yves Le Roy (France; 8,146 pt.) and Guido Kratschmer (W.Ger.; 8,132 pt.) finished second and third. Undisputed world leader was Bruce Jenner (U.S.) with a spotless win-loss record and a top score of 8,308. Le Roy improved late in the season to 8,229.

Top female athlete of 1974, Polish sprinter Irena Szewinska, clocked 10.9 sec. (11.13 sec. electrical) for 100 m., 22 sec. (22.51 sec. electrical) for 200 m., and lowered the 400-m. world record by 1.1 sec. to 49.9 sec. In Rome, Riita Salin (Fin.) recorded 50.14 sec. in her 400-m. European victory. Szewinska, meanwhile, defeated Olympic champion Renate Stecher (E.Ger.) in both the 100 m. and 200 m. The Pole ended a memorable meeting by anchoring her 4 x 400 m. relay team with a sensational 48.5-sec. leg. Lilyana Tomova (Bulg.) won the European 800-m. title from Gunhild Hoffmeister (E.Ger.) in 1 min. 58.1 sec. Hoffmeister triumphed by a wide margin in the European 1,500-m. final, over Tomova, in 4 min. 2.3 sec., the second fastest in history. In the 3,000 m. at Rome, the first major championship event at that distance for women, Nina Holmen (Fin.) outsprinted Ludmila Bragina (U.S.S.R.) and Joyce Smith (U.K.) to win in 8 min. 55.2 sec. Annelie Ehrhardt (E.Ger.) remained unbeaten in the 100-m. hurdles, capturing the European title in 12.66 sec. from her teammate, Annerose Fiedler. Her 12.4-sec. hand-timing mark was a world record.

High jumper Rosie Witschas (E.Ger.) won in Rome and raised the world record to 1.95 m. (6 ft. 4¾ in.). In the long jump East Germany's Angela Schmalfeld and Marianne Voelzke shared the year's best mark at 6.77 m. (22 ft. 2½ in.), but in Rome Ilona Bruzsenyak (Hung.) won with 6.65 m. Though Helena Fibingerova (Czech.) topped the world with a late-season record of 21.57 m. (70 ft. 9¼ in.)—the first 70-ft. women's shot put in history—the European title was claimed by Nadyezhda Chizhova (U.S.S.R.), who won with a 20.78-m. mark after a duel with Marianne Adam (E.Ger.). Ruth Fuchs (E.Ger.), rated one of the greatest women athletes of all time, won the European javelin championship with a world record throw of 67.22 m. (220 ft. 6 in.). In the discus, Faina Melnik (U.S.S.R.) still reigned as queen. Her opening throw of 69.00 m. sufficed to keep her in front in Rome, and to cap the year she broke her world record with a 69.90 m. (229 ft. 4 in.) heave. This marked the first occasion in which a women's world record was superior to the equivalent men's mark, though women throw the 1-kg. discus as against the 2-kg. for men. The European pentathlon title was won by Nadyezhda Tkachenko (U.S.S.R.), who scored 4,776 pt. to better Burglinde Pollak (E.Ger.) by exactly 100. Olympic champion Mary Peters retired after winning the Commonwealth title with 4,455 pt. (JAMES COOTE)

United States Competition. Rick Wohlhuter set the pace as runners dominated U.S. track and field activities throughout the year. The University of Chicago Track Club middle distance runner set two world and one U.S. record while winning all his races from 800 m. to one mile. As a result, he was named World Track and Field Athlete of the year by the international selection board of *Track & Field News.*

Wohlhuter's first big race came at Eugene, Ore., on June 8 when he sped through 880 yd. in 1 min. 44.1 sec. This bettered his own world record by 0.5 sec., and while no time was taken at the slightly shorter 800-m. mark, the 880-yd. time became the new U.S. record at the metric distance. Two weeks later, in Los Angeles, Wohlhuter lowered his 800-m. mark to 1 min. 43.9 sec., and he repeated the time at Stockholm.

Turning to 1,000 m., a distance seldom run in the U.S. but a standard fixture in Europe, Wohlhuter captured his second world record. He ran the distance in 2 min. 13.9 sec. at Oslo on July 30 to become the second American ever to hold the 1,000-m. record and the first in 21 years. Moving up to the mile, Wohlhuter defeated several international leaders in European competition, recording a best time of 3 min. 54.4 sec.

Three other U.S. runners set world records, two of which emerged from a particularly competitive sprinting campaign. The first 100-yd. dash to be run in 9.0 sec. was achieved by veteran Ivory Crockett of the Philadelphia Pioneer Club at Knoxville, Tenn., on May 11. Six men had shared the former record of 9.1 sec., first established in 1963. Crockett was later beaten in the Amateur Athletic Union (AAU) national championships by the last man to run an official 9.1 sec. record. The winner was Steve Williams of San Diego State, and his 9.9 sec. for 100 m. equaled the world mark set by six others. The fifth world record by U.S. runners came from Jim Bolding, who capped a long, successful season in the U.S. and Europe by running the 440-yd. intermediate hurdles in 48.7 sec.

Table I. World 1974 Outdoor Records—Men

Event	Competitor, country, date	Performance
100 yd.	Ivory Crockett, U.S., May 11	9.0 sec.
100 m.	Steve Williams, U.S., June 21	9.9 sec.
880 yd.	Rick Wohlhuter, U.S., June 8	1 min. 44.1 sec.
1,000 m.	Rick Wohlhuter, U.S., July 30	2 min. 13.9 sec.
1,500 m.	Filbert Bayi, Tanzania, February 2	3 min. 32.2 sec.
3,000 m.	Brendan Foster, U.K., August 3	7 min. 35.2 sec.
440-yd. hurdles	Jim Bolding, U.S., July 24	48.7 sec.
20,000-m. walk	Bernd Kannenberg, West Germany, May 25	1 hr. 24 min. 45 sec.
2-hr. walk	Peter Frenkel, East Germany, April 14	26,930 m.
	Bernd Kannenberg, West Germany, May 11	27,153 m.
30,000-m. walk	Peter Frenkel, East Germany, April 14	2 hr. 14 min. 21.2 sec.
	Bernd Kannenberg, West Germany, May 11	2 hr. 12 min. 58 sec.
20-mi. walk	Gerhard Weidner, West Germany, May 25	2 hr. 30 min. 38.6 sec.
Hammer throw	Reinhard Theimer, East Germany, July 4	251 ft. 4 in.
	Aleksey Spiridonov, U.S.S.R., September 11	251 ft. 6 in.

Table II. World 1974 Outdoor Records—Women

Event	Competitor, country, date	Performance
60 m.	Andrea Lynch, U.K., June 22	7.2 sec.*
200 m.	Irena Szewinska, Poland, June 13	22.0 sec.†
400 m.	Irena Szewinska, Poland, June 22	49.9 sec.†
	Riita Salin, Finland, September 4	50.14 sec.‡
440 yd.	Debra Sapenter, U.S., June 29	52.2 sec.‡
400-m. relay	East Germany, August 24	42.6 sec.*
	East Germany, September 8	42.51 sec.‡
3,000 m.	Ludmila Bragina, U.S.S.R., July 6	8 min. 52.8 sec.
100-m. hurdles	Annelie Ehrhardt, East Germany, September 7	12.4 sec.†
High jump	Rosemarie Witschas, East Germany, September 8	6 ft. 4¾ in.
Shot put	Helena Fibingerova, Czechoslovakia, September 21	70 ft. 9¼ in.
Discus	Faina Melnik, U.S.S.R., May 27	229 ft. 4 in.
Javelin	Ruth Fuchs, East Germany, September 3	220 ft. 6 in.

*Ties record.
†Hand timing.
‡Electrical timing.

at Turin, Italy, on July 24. Bolding also claimed a U.S. record in the 400-m. hurdles with 48.1 sec.

By far the busiest record breaker on the American scene was Steve Prefontaine of the Oregon Track Club. He set no world marks but claimed an unparalleled total of nine national records in eight events. Indoors, Prefontaine claimed the 2-mi. mark with 8 min. 22.2 sec. at Portland, Ore., on January 26; he soon lowered this to 8 min. 20.4 sec. at San Diego on February 17. In the latter race he was timed in 7 min. 50 sec. for 3,000 m., another U.S. record.

Outdoors, the record-breaking campaign started early. On April 27, at Eugene, Prefontaine earned two records in one race, clocking 26 min. 51.8 sec. for 6 mi. and 27 min. 43.6 sec. for 10,000 m. Once again at Eugene, on June 6, he ran 3 mi. in 12 min. 51.4 sec. Moving to Europe, he ran 5,000 m. in 13 min. 22.2 sec. at Helsinki on June 26, 3,000 m. in 7 min. 42.6 sec. at Milan on July 2, and 2 mi. in 8 min. 18.4 sec. at Stockholm on July 18. In one season Prefontaine took for himself all six U.S. records at the distances from 3,000 m. to 10,000 m.

Two additional national records fell, again to runners. Doug Brown of the University of Tennessee reduced the 3,000-m. steeplechase standard to 8 min. 23.2 sec., and Manhattan College ran the 4-mi. relay in 16 min. 14.4 sec.

In team competition, Tennessee dethroned UCLA in a tight National Collegiate Athletic Association (NCAA) battle, winning 60 to 56 at Austin, Tex. The NCAA Division II championship was shared by Eastern Illinois and Norfolk State, and Ashland won the

Annelie Ehrhardt of East Germany (left) clears the last barrier to win the 100-m. hurdles in the European championships at Rome. Valeria Stefanescu of Romania (centre) placed fourth and Grazyna Rabsztyn of Poland eighth.

WIDE WORLD

Division III meet. The AAU title went to the Beverly Hills Striders at Los Angeles.

Durham, N.C., was the site of the annual U.S. *v.* U.S.S.R. contest. The U.S. won the men's competition 117–102 but lost the women's meet 90–67 and so was beaten in the combined scoring, 192–184. The two countries also met indoors, with the U.S.S.R. winning 89–72, at Moscow on March 2. At home, the Beverly Hills Striders won the AAU indoor tournament at New York on February 22, and the NCAA indoor meet, at Detroit on March 9, was won by the University of Texas at El Paso.

The major record breaker indoors was George Woods of the Pacific Coast Club. He raised the amateur shot put mark first to 69 ft. 10¾ in., then to 70 ft. 4½ in., and finally reached 72 ft. 2¾ in. at Inglewood, Calif., on February 8. This was the longest put ever, indoors or out, amateur or professional.

Tony Waldrop of North Carolina lowered the world indoor mile standard to 3 min. 55.0 sec. at San Diego on February 17, and in the same race received credit for a U.S. indoor record of 3 min. 39.8 sec. for 1,500 m. The 60-yd. high-hurdle record of 6.8 sec. was matched three times by Rod Milburn of the Baton Rouge Track Club, while Dwight Stones of the Pacific Coast Club high jumped 7 ft. 4¼ in., a U.S. indoor best for amateurs.

Turning professional midway through the indoor season, Milburn established a world record of 6.7 sec. for the hurdles. Another member of the International Track Association (ITA) professional touring group, Steve Smith, twice pole vaulted to an indoor record, first 18 ft. 1 in. and then 18 ft. 1¾ in.

In events held less often there were a number of bests-on-record: among the amateurs, Stan Vinson, 62.6 sec. for 500 m.; Steve Williams (San Diego State) and Barry Miller, 10.7 sec. for 100 m.; Williams, 34.1 sec. for 300 m.; University of Chicago Track Club, 7 min. 20.8 sec. for the 2-mi. relay; Marshall Dill, 29.3 sec. for 300 yd.; Indiana, 16 min. 44.8 sec. for the 4-mi. relay; Tom Hill, 7.3 sec. for the 60-m. hurdles; and Cliff Outlin, 6.4 sec. for 60 m. For the professionals, Paul Gibson set a record of 8.7 sec. for the 70-m. hurdles, and John Carlos ran 70 m. in 7.3 sec.

Neil Cusack of Ireland and East Tennessee State University won the Boston Marathon, April 15, in 2 hr. 13 min. 39 sec., the third best time for the event. In cross country, Steve Prefontaine of Oregon won his third NCAA title and led his school to victory. Frank Shorter took the AAU cross country title for the fourth straight year, and his Florida Track Club was an easy team winner.

Among the women, it was also the runners who provided most of the records with Mary Decker and Francie Larrieu heading the list. Larrieu set three U.S. records outdoors: 4 min. 10.3 sec. for 1,500 m., 4 min. 33.1 sec. for 1 mi., and 9 min. 3.2 sec. for 3,000 m. Indoors, she claimed four world marks: 4 min. 12.2 sec. for 1,500 m., 4 min. 34.6 sec. for 1 mi., 9 min. 2.4 sec. for 3,000 m., and 9 min. 39.4 sec. for 2 mi. Indoors, Decker twice lowered the 880-yd. standard to 2 min. 2.3 sec. and ran 800 m. in 2 min. 1.8 sec. and 1,000 yd. in 2 min. 26.7 sec.

The lone outdoor world mark was set when Debra Sapenter equaled the 440-yd. record of 52.2 sec. U.S. records were established by Martha Watson, 21 ft. 7½ in. in the long jump; Maren Seidler, 56 ft. 7 in. in the shot put; Joni Huntley, 6 ft. ¾ in. in the high jump; and Jane Frederick, 4,391 pt. in the pentathlon.

World indoor records were set by Patty Johnson, 13.2 sec. for the 110-m. hurdles; Kathy Lawson, 10.7 sec. for 100 yd.; and Martha Watson and Theresa Montgomery, 7.1 sec. for 60 m. U.S. indoor records included Seidler, 56 ft. 11 in. for the shot put; Huntley, 6 ft. ½ in. for the high jump; Robin Campbell, 1 min. 19.3 sec. for 600 yd.; and the Atoms Track Club, 3 min. 47.5 sec. for the mile relay.

Among the ITA professionals, the sprints, the only women's events on the program, were dominated by Wyomia Tyus, twice Olympic 100-m. champion.

(BERT NELSON)

[452.B.4.b]

Trade, International

The biggest single influence on the level and pattern of world trade in 1974 was, without doubt, the quadrupling of the price of oil at the end of 1973. Many industrial countries attempted to alleviate the effect of the price increase on their balance of payments by reducing the overall level of domestic demand, thus cutting back on their imports. The effect on world trade was immediate, and the growth in the volume of trade in 1974 was expected to be no more than 3%, well below the 15% increase recorded in 1973 and also below the average growth rate in the previous decade of 9%.

The total value of world trade in 1973 had increased by some 37% above its level in 1972. The interacting elements of general inflation, oil price increases, and soaring primary commodity prices strongly influenced the average prices of imports and exports, which rose by over 20%. The volume of trade, however, rose by 15%. This was the highest increase recorded for many years and was due to the rapid expansion of economic activity in all industrial countries. The large price increases for primary commodities enabled the less developed countries also to record large increases in their demand for goods in world markets. During 1973, however, there was a slowing down in the growth of economic activity as some countries ran into balance of payments difficulties and cut back their demand. This resulted in a slowing down in the growth of world trade even before the worldwide increases in oil prices. In the first three quarters of 1973 the volume of world trade had been about 16% above its level a year earlier but in the fourth quarter this dropped to 10%. An additional factor in this slowing down involved supply limitations for certain primary products, including those stemming from droughts and other natural forces.

The movements in the prices of goods in world trade in 1973 were such that the balance of trade of industrial countries, as a group, deteriorated while that of the primary producers improved. The movement in the terms of trade (*i.e.,* the price of exports relative to the price of imports) of the main groups of countries is shown in Table II. The decade from 1960 to 1970 was a period in which there had been a small but definite shift in the terms of trade in favour of industrial countries to the disadvantage of the less developed economies. The increase in oil prices in 1971 had first disturbed this pattern, and the changes were very marked in 1973 with the terms of trade of industrial countries deteriorating by 2.5%. The biggest single improvement was recorded by the oil-exporting countries, but the less developed primary producers also benefited from a 6% increase in their terms of trade. Although the prices of most primary products increased, there were some exceptions; this prevented a larger increase in terms of trade, which was also held back by the rising prices of foodstuffs imported by many less developed economies.

In 1974 the terms of trade shifted against all groups of countries except the oil producers. Those industrial countries with heavy dependence on imported oil and whose exports consisted predominantly of manufactured goods suffered particularly badly. Also badly hit were less developed economies whose exports products either were not sharing in the general upsurge of commodity prices or were among those most severely hit by the slump in prices later in the year. By mid-1974 the terms of trade of industrial countries had fallen 11% below the 1973 level with a consequent marked deterioration in their balance of trade, although they gained some relief from the falling prices of imported primary products.

Estimates made by the International Monetary Fund (IMF) on the balance of trade positions of the main groups suggested that the effect of higher oil prices was likely to increase the overall deficit of industrial countries by some $53 billion in 1974, of other developed areas by $6 billion, and of the non-oil-producing less developed economies by $7 billion. At the same time the major oil producers (i.e., Algeria, Indonesia, Iran, Iraq, Kuwait, Libya, Nigeria, Saudi Arabia, and Venezuela) shared in a similar massive increase in their surpluses.

The rate of growth of both the value and volume of trade of the main groups of countries is shown in Table I. The differential movements in exports and imports resulted in a worsening of the trading position of industrial countries and reduced deficits for primary producing economies.

Primary Producing Countries. The improved trading performance of primary producing countries in 1973 owed a great deal to the rapid increase in world prices for nearly all raw materials and foodstuffs. An upsurge in demand in all industrial countries, together with buying of commodities by speculators, pulled up prices at rates unprecedented since 1951. The index measuring the average export price of primary products (excluding oil) had risen by over 70% between the beginning of 1973 and spring 1974. The index was then slightly more than twice its value in spring 1972, before the upsurge in prices began.

Between the first half of 1973 and the corresponding period in 1974 the market prices of copper, lead, zinc, sugar, and tin had more than doubled, and increases of more than 50% were recorded for cocoa, cotton, and rubber. Although substantial increases in prices were recorded for most products there were exceptions, including tea, jute, bananas, and bauxite, and the fortunes of individual countries were closely linked with the price movements of their predominant export product. In the middle of 1974 many prices turned downward with reduced demand from industrial countries; in addition, much of the speculative demand came to an end.

One of the main features of primary producers' trade balances in 1973 was the difference in the fortunes of particular areas. (See Table III.) The overall balance of the more developed countries deteriorated while the surpluses of the oil exporters increased and the combined deficit of the less developed non-oil exporters was reduced.

The larger deficit of the more developed areas in 1973 was due to the Western European countries, where Spain, Yugoslavia, and Greece all recorded larger deficits. Australia and New Zealand both benefited from higher wool prices, which enabled them to increase both their imports and their trade surpluses. In both countries the value of wool exports in 1973 was more than double the 1971 value.

The major oil-exporting countries further increased their already large surpluses and in 1973, before the full effect of the new level of oil prices had been felt, their trading exports were almost double their imports. The even larger surpluses they built up during 1974 reflected their inability to consume goods as rapidly as they could earn revenue from oil.

Among the other less developed countries fortunes varied, depending on price movements of their main exports. Overall, this large group of countries recorded a sharp reduction in its trading deficit. In Latin America there was only a modest improvement. Venezuela and Colombia improved their trading position as a result of exports of oil and coffee, respectively. Brazilian exports benefited from higher coffee prices but imports also rose rapidly. In the Middle East Israel was the only country among the oil exporters not to improve its trading position in 1973. Despite greatly increased exports of diamonds, its import bill,

Table I. World Trade

Percent change from previous year
(Value in U.S. dollars)

Area		1970	1971	1972	1973	1974*
Imports						
World	value	14.5	11.5	17.0	37.0	...
	volume	9.0	5.5	9.0	13.5	...
Industrial countries	value	15.0	11.5	19.5	37.0	46.5
	volume	9.0	6.0	11.5	11.5	3.5
Other developed areas†	value	19.0	10.0	9.5	41.0	61.0
	volume	13.0	3.5	1.0	17.0	...
Less developed areas	value	12.0	14.0	11.0	32.5	...
	volume	8.0	7.0	3.0	11.0	...
Oil exporters	value	10.5	18.0	20.5	42.0	...
	volume	6.5	12.0	12.0	20.0	...
Others	value	12.5	13.0	9.5	30.5	...
	volume	8.5	6.5	1.5	9.5	...
Exports						
World	value	15.0	12.0	18.5	37.5	...
	volume	9.5	6.0	10.0	15.0	...
Industrial countries	value	15.5	12.0	18.0	35.0	37.5
	volume	9.5	6.5	9.5	13.5	9.5
Other developed areas†	value	12.5	9.5	24.5	45.0	27.5
	volume	8.0	5.5	11.0	16.0	3.5
Less developed areas	value	12.0	13.0	18.5	42.0	...
	volume	8.0	6.0	10.0	9.0	...
Oil exporters	value	13.5	32.0	18.5	56.5	...
	volume	11.0	8.0	7.0	12.5	...
Others	value	11.5	4.5	18.5	36.5	...
	volume	6.5	5.5	9.5	7.0	...

*First six months compared with first six months of 1973.
†Australia, New Zealand, South Africa, and the less industrialized nations of Western Europe.
Sources: International Monetary Fund, Annual Report; United Nations, Monthly Bulletin of Statistics.

Table II. Terms of Trade

Percent changes

Area	Average 1960–70	1970	Change from previous year 1971	1972	1973
Industrial countries	0.50	0.50	−0.50	0	−2.50
Other developed countries	0.50	−1.50	−2.25	4.25	4.25
Less developed countries	−0.50	−1.50	2.00	1.25	10.00
Oil exporters	−2.00	−2.00	17.00	2.75	17.25
Others	0.50	−1.00	−6.50	0.50	6.00

Source: International Monetary Fund, Annual Report 1974.

Table III. Primary Producing Countries' Foreign Trade

In $000,000,000

Area	1972 Exports	Imports*	Balance of trade	1973 Exports	Imports*	Balance of trade
More developed areas†	24.8	32.3	−7.5	34.8	45.8	−11.0
Less developed areas	74.0	71.3	2.7	102.0	94.4	7.6
Major oil exporters	26.3	12.5	13.8	35.7	19.0	16.7
Others	47.7	58.8	−11.1	66.3	75.4	−9.1
Total	98.8	103.6	−4.8	136.8	140.2	−3.4

*Imports, in most cases, include freight and insurance charges.
†Australia, New Zealand, South Africa, and the less industrialized countries of Western Europe.
Source: International Monetary Fund, International Financial Statistics.

even excluding military items, increased by nearly 50%; military items further increased the deficit. India and Sri Lanka were two countries that did not benefit greatly from price changes. Indian exports of jute and tea fell in 1973, and although Sri Lanka gained some compensation from exports of rubber, both countries' trading balances worsened. Malaysia benefited from rising rubber exports and increased its surplus. The features of the improvement in the overall trading balance of African countries were the increased surpluses in Nigeria and Zambia, due largely to oil and copper.

Industrial Countries. The trading positions of the main industrial countries varied considerably in 1973, but all were severely hit by the increase in oil prices in 1974, with the notable exception of West Germany, whose balance of trade increased substantially in both years. (*See* Table IV.) In 1973 the overall balance of the main industrial nations worsened although, like West Germany's, the U.S. trade balance improved. There were marked increases in the Italian and British deficits and a sharp reduction in the Japanese surplus.

The trade balance of the EEC moved into a modest deficit in 1973. The sharp acceleration in imports was fairly evenly spread over all countries, while in the case of exports West Germany and The Netherlands experienced particularly large gains. EEC sales to Japan expanded by over 70% while intra-area sales increased by 35%. The value of EEC sales to North America increased by 20%, which, when allowance

is made for the increase in price, represented a lower volume than in 1972. In previous years one of the most rapidly growing elements of world trade had been trade between industrial countries. However, in 1973, with rising commodity prices, demand in the less developed economies expanded rapidly and their imports from the industrial countries increased by 42% while trade between the latter rose by 35%.

The worsening terms of trade of the industrialized countries in 1973 is noted in Table II. With the increase in oil prices there was a very sharp deterioration in early 1974, and in the first half of 1974 the average terms of trade of the industrial countries were some 11–12% worse than one year earlier. This deterioration was 20% or more in the case of France, Italy, Japan, and the U.K., although it was under 10% for West Germany and The Netherlands. These divergent movements, which reflected varying dependence on imported oil and different exchange movements, explained the different trading performances in 1974, although only in West Germany did the trading balance improve. The overall deficit of the Organization for Economic Cooperation and Development (OECD) countries in 1974 was expected to be close to $50 billion.

In the U.S. an improvement in the balance of trade in 1973 brought with it the long-awaited recovery in the overall balance of payments. With exports increasing by 44% in value and imports by only 25%, a sizable deficit in 1972 was turned into a modest surplus in 1973—an improvement of $6 billion. The

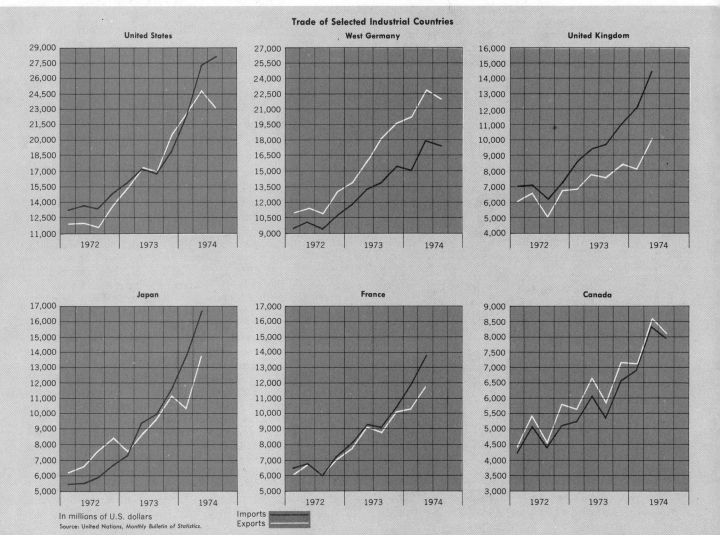

Trade of Selected Industrial Countries

In millions of U.S. dollars
Source: United Nations, *Monthly Bulletin of Statistics.*

Imports
Exports

Darris Moeller inspects his Soviet-built tractor on his farm near Picayune, Miss.

large growth in exports was due to three main factors: (1) the coincident booms in most markets for U.S. industrial goods, where U.S. firms held onto their share after a number of years of declining shares; (2) the cumulative effect of the dollar where the effective exchange rate against major currencies was 10% lower than in 1972; and (3) poor harvests abroad and the failure of the catch of Peruvian anchovies (a major competitor with U.S. soybean exports), which contributed to a 90% increase in the value of agricultural exports. The growth in U.S. imports, which was only 5% in volume terms, was checked by the devaluation of the dollar, although oil imports increased by 75% in value. The U.S. was fortunate among industrial countries in also being an exporter of agricultural products; rising world commodity prices meant that the U.S. terms of trade worsened by only 1.5% in 1973 despite the devaluation of the dollar. Analysis of the regional pattern of U.S. trade showed that the improvement in the trading balance was most marked with Japan and the six original EEC countries. In 1974 the growth in the

volume of U.S. imports and exports continued, although at a lower rate, but a 12% deterioration in the terms of trade (largely due to oil prices) resulted in the reappearance of a sizable deficit.

In West Germany the surplus on the balance of trade, which was already large in 1972, continued to increase throughout 1973 despite an average 12% upward revaluation of the mark. In 1974 there was a further increase in the trading surplus, and West Germany was one of the few countries in the world, apart from the oil exporters, to record an improved trading position. In 1973, despite rising gross domestic product (GDP), there was a relatively modest growth in the volume of West German imports, much less than had been associated with increases in GDP of a similar magnitude in the past. This was partly due to a shift in the structure of German demand away from import-intensive categories such as consumers' expenditure.

The main reasons for the increase in the West German surplus in 1973 and 1974 was the impressive growth in exports, which increased in value by 46% in 1973 and by 27% in 1974. The increase in volume was 18% and was achieved despite the fact that, as a result of the revaluation of the mark, foreign customers were paying, on average, 14% more for West German goods. One reason for this success was the coincident boom in most of West Germany's market areas for exports, but over and above this the country's share in most of these markets increased. Total world exports of manufactured goods increased sharply to over 22% in 1973. (*See* Table V.) A high proportion of these exports was machinery and consumer durables, which are not very sensitive to price changes provided quality and delivery are guaranteed. Further, even where price was an important selling point, the effect of the currency revaluation was offset by both the tendency to higher rates of inflation in competing countries and expectations of further appreciation of the mark. In the first half of 1974 this situation continued very much unchanged. The volume of imports was 1–2% lower than a year earlier while export volume had increased by some 20%. The result was that, despite an adverse movement in the terms of trade, there was a further increase in the surplus on the balance of trade.

In Japan, on the other hand, there was a marked worsening in the trade balance in 1973. After a record surplus in 1972, the rapid expansion of imports relative to exports in 1973 caused a sharp swing into deficit. The appreciation of the yen compared with other currencies to a level about 10% higher in 1973 than in 1972 encouraged the increase in imports, as did the liberalization of tariffs. In addition there was a high level of demand at home, and in some cases there were supply problems. A large part of Japanese imports were of food, raw materials, and fuel, all of which rose rapidly in price; the average price of Japanese imports increased by one-third in 1973 and the value of imports by over 60%. There was a fall in exports of textiles and textile products and other products of price-sensitive light industries. Iron and steel exports increased, but exports of machinery were sluggish and supply problems held back chemical exports. With a 23% worsening in the terms of trade in the first half of 1974, the deficit increased sharply.

The U.K. trade deficit, which was already large in 1972, increased further in 1973 and widened drastically in 1974 under the impact of higher oil prices. As a result of the rapid growth of the economy in

Table IV. Trade of the Main Industrial Countries
In $000,000,000

Country	1973 Exports	1973 Imports	1973 Balance of trade	1974* Exports	1974* Imports	1974* Balance of trade
U.S.	70.22	68.67	1.55	94.78	99.67	−4.89
Canada	25.21	23.31	1.90	31.25	30.45	0.80
EEC	209.73	213.63	−3.90	261.32	278.92	−17.60
France	35.57	36.99	−1.42	46.52	53.41	−6.89
Germany, West	67.47	54.50	12.97	85.90	66.00	19.90
Italy	22.22	27.80	−5.58	26.99	39.29	−12.30
U.K.	30.55	38.92	−8.37	36.56	53.33	−16.77
Japan	36.97	38.32	−1.35	48.11	61.42	−13.31
Total	342.13	343.93	−1.80	435.46	470.46	−35.00

*First half of year, seasonally adjusted, at annual rate.
Source: United Nations, *Monthly Bulletin of Statistics.*

Table V. World Exports of Manufactured Goods
Percent of total value

Year	Total value*	United States	United Kingdom	West Germany	France	Italy	Japan	Others†
1960	52.4	21.6	16.5	19.3	9.6	5.1	6.9	21.0
1965	83.2	20.3	13.9	19.1	8.8	6.7	9.4	21.8
1970	154.4	18.5	10.8	19.8	8.7	7.2	11.7	23.3
1971	174.8	17.0	10.9	20.0	8.8	7.2	13.0	23.1
1972	205.2	16.1	10.0	20.2	9.3	7.6	13.2	23.5
1973	273.2	16.1	9.4	22.1	9.6	6.8	12.8	23.3
1974‡	347.2	16.3	8.6	22.5	9.0	6.4	13.9	23.4

*In $000,000,000, excluding special category exports (mostly arms).
†Belgium, Luxembourg, Canada, The Netherlands, Sweden, and Switzerland.
‡First half of year, seasonally adjusted, at annual rate.
Source: National Institute of Economic and Social Research, London.

1973, bringing with it high demand and supply problems, the volume of imports increased by 14% and of exports by 12%. Since there was a 12% deterioration in the terms of trade, the value increase for imports of 41% greatly exceeded that for exports of 25%; about four-fifths of the increase in the deficit could be attributed to the worsening of the terms of trade. British exports to Western Europe recorded above average growth. The leading sector in the growth of imports was machinery, with a 51% increase. In 1974 the slowdown in the economy reduced the growth in the volume of imports to about 5% in the first half of the year compared with one year earlier. However, with import prices 56% higher, the import bill rose very sharply. Exports were benefiting relatively little from the depreciation of the pound sterling, and the volume growth was a disappointing 7%. (A. G. ARMSTRONG)

See also Commercial and Trade Policies; Commodity Trade; Exchange and Payments, International.

[534.F]

ENCYCLOPÆDIA BRITANNICA FILMS. *Rotterdam—Europort, Gateway to Europe* (1971).

Transportation

The oil crisis dominated transport during 1974, and private transport came under attack both from environmentalists and from the very consumers of the personal mobility it provided. Worldwide, automobile production declined by some 12%. The retail price of gasoline did not rise as fast as crude oil prices because of its high tax element. While crude prices rose 300% within a year, pump prices were 78% higher than in 1970 in Europe and 165% higher in the U.S. When the Arab producers' cutbacks were eased and oil became plentiful again in the spring, previous patterns of consumption were not resumed. Car sales continued at a lower level and many manufacturers predicted a bad year in 1975.

The slump in confidence was not caused solely by the higher price of oil. Fuel accounted for only one-third of the cost of maintaining a car driven 20,000 mi. a year. Other motoring costs also rose rapidly, and car manufacturers appeared to be running short of

techniques to keep cost increases below the level of inflation. The slowdown in world economies made people seek ways to cut spending, and the oil crisis had a large psychological effect on car users. The high cost of antipollution and safety measures proved an additional burden. Most 1975-model cars in the U.S. were required to have exhaust catalysts, and Detroit claimed that this increased the price by several hundred dollars per car.

There was no large-scale switch to public transport. Fast intercity rail services continued to attract more passengers, and many cities found that the decline in the use of bus services was slowing. But the slow speeds of public transport, the long waits for connections, and the sheer rigidity of the routes meant that many journeys were scrapped and people stayed home. In London, at any given income level, car owners traveled more than twice as much as those who did not own cars.

Governments and local authorities continued to promote public transport. Communist bloc countries showed a strong interest in subways. In England, Tyneside started building a light rapid-transit system. Hong Kong went ahead with a subway, and Mexico City planned to extend its system. Financing difficulties meant that many schemes were deferred, however, and buses and even minibuses were considered as low-cost alternatives.

Car and truck interests tried to counterattack, pointing out that road transport accounted for only one-fifth to one-quarter of most countries' oil consumption, the U.S. being a major exception. But road transport was the one major use that could not switch to other fuels, at least with existing technology. Britain placed its hopes largely in North Sea oil, a light crude from which a high percentage of motor fuel could be refined.

Several new means of fuel saving were actively promoted: drag deflectors, improved fans, fuel additives, and carburetor devices. Many fell short of the predicted results, particularly over a long working life or when installed in mass production. British Leyland claimed that fuel economy could improve 50% within a few years, and Detroit worked on such alternatives to the existing internal-combustion engine as the Stirling engine, which would run on peanut oil, the gas

Circular terminal building of the new Charles de Gaulle Airport near Paris dwarfs a Concorde airliner.

THE TIMES, LONDON/PICTORIAL PARADE

Trade Policies:
see Commercial and Trade Policies

Trade Unions:
see Industrial Relations

Traffic Accidents:
see Disasters

CitiCar, manufactured
in the U.S.
by Sebring-Vanguard Inc.,
features a strong
but lightweight plastic
body and an electric
engine that has a range
of up to 50 mi.
and is capable
of cruising speeds of up
to 28 mph.

turbine, stratified charge, and increased application of diesel fuel to cars. Thermal efficiency of the conventional engine was only about 10%. The U.S. postponed introducing new severe antipollution rules, allowing car makers to concentrate on fuel saving. The exhaust catalysts on 1975 cars permitted engineers to tune for fuel economy rather than emissions.

Asia and the Soviet Union remained the two areas of the world where more passengers traveled by public transport than by car. In the U.S. only 1% of travel was by rail and 6% by bus. Railways moved two-thirds of world freight traffic, but in Europe road and rail ran neck and neck. Among Western European countries, France had the highest percentage of freight moving by rail, but 1973 figures showed road haulage was closing the gap. Freight had taken a secondary place in rail investment plans, and increases in passenger-train speeds made it more difficult to schedule slower moving freight trains. Many European rail lines had reached full capacity. Relief lines were proposed, often with the intention that the new line would be purely for fast passenger trains, leaving the old tracks for slower movements.

The effect of the energy crisis was not confined to land transport. Higher fuel prices were a major cause of massive increases in air fares, adversely affecting tourism and causing financial difficulties for some airlines. The realization that oil production might remain fairly static for the rest of the decade threatened the shipping industry's plans for investment in tankers. The prospect of a huge surplus of tankers was only partly ameliorated by higher bunker prices, which made it attractive to slow-steam, thus increasing the number of ships required to deliver the same amount of oil in the same amount of time. The best hope for tanker owners was that contracts with shipyards might be canceled, and the first signs of this appeared in the fall. (RICHARD CASEMENT)

AVIATION

The rising price of jet fuel pushed operating costs sharply upward in 1974, and the fare increases that were introduced were inadequate, and too late, to balance the situation. In addition, it was feared that higher fares themselves would adversely affect traffic. The International Air Transport Association (IATA) estimated that during the first seven months of the year more than $700 million of additional expenditure on fuel was not covered by fare increases.

Passenger traffic growth for 1974 was much lower than for 1973, and some routes showed an actual decline. The London airports reported a 2.5% drop in both aircraft movements and numbers of passengers in the first half of the year as compared with the first half of 1973, and the airports at Zürich, Switz., and Frankfurt, W.Ger., reported only modest growth for the same period. In the U.S. the number of revenue passenger-miles flown by the trunk carriers and Pan American in the first half of 1974 was 5% less than in the comparable period of 1973. IATA's estimates suggested that summer traffic on the North Atlantic routes was 10 to 15% below that of the previous summer.

World air traffic in 1973, relatively little affected by the oil crisis that broke at the end of the year, held up well. International Civil Aviation Organization (ICAO) figures for 1973 scheduled traffic, excluding the Soviet Union and China, showed (comparison with 1972 in parentheses): passengers carried 394 million (+ 7.1%); passenger-kilometres 514,000,000,000 (+ 10.8%); available seat-kilometres 940,000 (+ 9.8%); passenger load factor 54.7% (+ 0.5%); cargo metric ton-kilometres 15,490,000,000 (+ 17.2%); total available ton-kilometres 130,210,-000,000 (+ 10.5%); weight load factor 49.2% (+ 0.5%). Load factors quoted improved again, reflecting the airlines' efforts to fill the additional capacity created by their new wide-body jets. More than 60% of scheduled passenger traffic on the North Atlantic, however, was carried at less than the full fare.

According to IATA, during 1973 capacity continued to outstrip demand on North Atlantic, mid-Atlantic, and certain intra-American routes, but in most areas capacity was far better utilized as carriers were forced by fuel shortages to exercise closer control and governments adopted "new and encouraging" positions regarding rationalization of capacity. The authorization by the U.S. Civil Aeronautics Board (CAB) of inter-airline agreements on capacity was a radical departure from the earlier U.S. policy of maintaining free competition. U.S. scheduled airlines totaled 161,957,307,-000 revenue passenger-mi. (+ 6.3%) at a load factor of 52.1% (− 0.9%). Cargo accounted for 6,035,200,-000 short ton-mi. (+ 9.8%). U.S. domestic trunk airlines totaled 115,352,180,000 revenue passenger-mi. (+ 7.7%), and local service carriers, 9,829,603,000 revenue passenger-mi. (+ 10.5%). Canadian airlines' scheduled passenger traffic in 1973 amounted to 13,-484,454,000 passenger-mi. (+ 18.2%); cargo ton-miles totaled 391,534,000 (+ 8.2%).

The Association of European Airlines (AEA) claimed that intra-European passenger traffic carried by members rose 9% in the year ended June 1974, with capacity up by 6%. Similar figures—10 and 6%, respectively—were given for intercontinental scheduled passenger traffic. AEA members' freight traffic rose 10% within Europe and 18% on intercontinental routes.

Returns by IATA members showed faster-than-average growth in certain areas in 1973. In the Europe-Far East-Oceania market, scheduled passenger traffic rose 37.2%; within the Far East and Oceania the figure was 20.5%. Corresponding cargo figures were 34.5% and 16.7%, respectively. The smaller mid-Atlantic market showed 23.6% passenger traffic growth. At the other end of the scale were the North and Mid-Pacific (+ 1.7%), North-to-Central America (+ 2.3%), and the important North Atlantic routes (+ 7.1%).

Of a total of 14 million passengers on North Atlantic routes in 1973, IATA members claimed to have carried 10,029,000 on scheduled services and 1,671,000 on nonscheduled services. The non-IATA charter airlines, including the U.S. supplemental airlines, carried some 2 million passengers, with a further 300,000 carried by non-IATA scheduled airlines.

During the year ICAO issued its second report on nonscheduled traffic, on which few statistics had been available previously. The report showed that in 1972 (the year covered) nonscheduled passenger traffic, excluding the Soviet Union and China, totaled 98,138,-300,000 passenger-km., 27.5% of which was on inclusive-tour flights. Nonscheduled operators carried 53.7% of the total and the scheduled airlines the remainder. All-cargo services accounted for 2,520,200,-000 revenue metric ton-km., with 48% carried by nonscheduled operators. ICAO estimated that a further 15 operators who did not report accounted for an additional 3,300,000,000 passenger-km.

Statistics released by the CAB showed that in fiscal

World Transportation

Country	Railways Route length in 000 km.	Railways Traffic Passenger in 000,000 pass.-km.	Railways Traffic Freight in 000,000 net ton-km.	Motor transport Road length in 000 km.	Vehicles in use Passenger in 000	Vehicles in use Commercial in 000	Merchant shipping Ships of 100 tons and over Number of vessels	Gross reg. tons in 000	Air traffic Total km. flown in 000,000	Passenger in 000,000 pass.-km.	Freight in 000,000 net ton-km.
EUROPE											
Austria	5.9*	6,768*	10,269*	96.5	1,460.0	138.0	61	96	11	579	7.7
Belgium	4.1	8,092	8,164	92.7	2,247.0	220.0	236	1,162	48	3,644	247.6
Bulgaria	4.2	7,071	16,635	35.7	c.160.0†	c.38.0†	159	757	8	336	6.1
Cyprus	—	—	—	8.3†	75.6	16.3	589	2,936	4	371	2.9
Czechoslovakia	13.3	16,154	64,941	143.9	1,009.1	216.8	11	87	23	1,138	18.0
Denmark	2.0*	3,723*	1,907*	64.3	1,228.9	173.3	1,362	4,107	35‡	1,918‡	86.4‡
Finland	6.0	2,594	7,011	73.2	894.1	119.9	390	1,546	24	1,062	32.4
France	34.7	44,547	73,824	793.8	14,620.0	1,980.0	1,376	8,289	228	19,492	836.0
Germany, East (excluding Berlin)	14.3	20,691	46,776	129.9	1,400.4	205.8	432	1,219	...	1,098	29.2
Germany, West (excluding Berlin)	32.7	41,265	67,257	459.5	17,036.0§	1,246.0§	2,234	7,915	158	11,105	873.7
Greece	2.6	1,615	798	35.5	301.9	130.2	2,536	19,295	38	3,729	57.8
Hungary	8.6	13,888	20,686	109.6	407.6	98.3	21	54	9	326	5.9
Ireland	2.2	844	517	87.8†	476.7	49.0	97	229	20	1,757	88.5
Italy	20.1†	35,394	17,120	288.4	13,600.0	1,025.0	1,726	8,867	156	11,124	426.1
Netherlands, The	2.8	8,260	3,319	82.5	3,230.0	320.0	1,369	5,029	97	9,282	525.2
Norway	4.2	1,644*	2,844*	74.8	913.4	163.0	2,758	23,621	47‡	2,756‡	96.5‡
Poland	23.6	39,647	116,442	299.9	780.9	324.3	631	2,073	18	1,073	11.8
Portugal	3.6	3,226	860	43.4	655.7	34.2	438	1,272	49	3,419	66.7
Romania	11.0	20,184	53,280	76.3	c.125.0	c.50.0	96	474	10	496	5.9
Spain	16.3	15,650	11,564	142.1	3,803.7	888.0	2,420	4,833	116	9,574	193.4
Sweden	12.1	4,470	16,214	97.5	2,502.6	148.0	831	5,669	57‡	3,414‡	144.8‡
Switzerland	5.0†	8,280	7,140	60.7	1,656.4	159.7	30	203	79	6,728	258.7
U.S.S.R.	257.1†	285,792	2,958,000	1,358.9†	c.1,810.0	c.5,100.0	7,123	17,397	...	95,286	2,100.0
United Kingdom	18.6‖	33,902‖	23,012‖	362.5	13,100.0	1,686.2	3,628	30,160	348	26,188	906.8
Yugoslavia	10.4	10,441	20,361	96.2	999.5	248.3	382	1,667	22	1,258	8.6
ASIA											
Bangladesh	2.9†	2,095†	1,022†	c.24.0	66.7	23.3	90	61	...	...	...
Burma	3.1†	2,593	708	c.25.0	31.0	33.4	40	55	6	162	2.3
Cambodia (Khmer Republic)	0.6	54	10	c.11.0	27.2	11.1	3	2	1	34	0.7
China	c.35.0	45,670†	301,000†	c.800.0†	c.1,030.0†	c.780.0†	323	1,479	...	64†	2.0†
India	60.0	125,469	133,311	1,021.8	646.5	346.0	430	2,887	67	4,557	151.4
Indonesia	8.6	3,302	1,042	84.9	277.2	131.2	573	669	32	1,254	22.5
Iran	4.6	1,955	3,693	43.4	354.8	101.3	93	192	13	859	12.5
Iraq	2.2	538	1,465	10.8	77.3	34.3	46	228	6	268	2.7
Israel	0.8	355	445	c.9.3	201.1	82.5	90	645	32	3,354	127.1
Japan	27.9†	310,822	58,882	1,049.7	14,473.6	10,422.4	9,469	36,785	245	20,836	641.9
Korea, South	5.6	10,492	8,394	43.6	70.2	72.1	617	1,104	23	957	59.1
Malaysia	1.8	755¶	1,179¶	24.4	340.1	85.8	117	226	17♀	868	12.2
Pakistan	8.7	9,518	7,721	62.8	74.3	21.1	89	503	20	1,484	76.0
Philippines	1.2	665	58	73.5†	294.3	191.2	404	947	37	1,626	41.0
Syria	1.1	107	154	16.7†	31.7†	17.5†	8	2	6	290	2.3
Taiwan	4.4	7,311	2,820	15.7	71.9	66.5	413	1,467	18†	954†	25.2†
Thailand	3.8†	4,260†	2,381†	17.7	282.6	158.9	78	182	20	1,751	31.8
Turkey	8.1	5,337	6,641	59.3	234.6	159.3	353	757	17	1,649	11.6
Vietnam, South	0.7	170	1	20.9†	58.4†	29.2†	46	38	9	390	4.1
AFRICA											
Algeria	4.0†	1,016	1,533	78.4	165.0	90.8	56	163	14	699	4.9
Central African Republic	...	...	...	c.19.3	5.4†	4.0†	...	...	2δ	82δ	8.5δ
Chad	...	...	...	30.7	4.5†	6.0†	...	...	2δ	94δ	9.4δ
Congo	0.8	171	517	c.11.0†	7.5†	5.5†	5	1	2δ	87δ	8.7δ
Dahomey	0.6	84†	94†	c.7.6	12.8†	7.7†	4	—	1δ	78δ	8.5δ
Egypt	5.0	7,306	2,976	c.50.0†	151.7	39.2	137	269	18	1,095	17.8
Gabon	0.4	...	...	6.8	7.1†	5.8†	9	12	3δ	102δ	8.6δ
Ghana	1.0†	448	292	c.31.0	51.7	37.6	73	166	4	150	2.8
Ivory Coast	0.6	520	344	c.24.8	90.5	57.4	39	89	2δ	84δ	8.6δ
Kenya	2.1	4,529†□	3,792†□	48.2	117.0	18.5	22	22	7°	316°	9.7°
Malawi	0.6	70	290	11.8	10.5	8.7	...	...	2	74	1.0
Mali	0.6	80†	148†	c.13.0	4.5†	5.7†	...	...	2	68	2.3
Morocco	1.8†	619	3,319	25.4	260.4	84.7	46	56	10	655	7.7
Nigeria	3.5	961	1,227	88.9†	68.0†	44.0†	72	110	7	305	8.1
Rhodesia	3.2	...	6,802▲	78.0†	127.0†	56.0†	...	...	6	202	0.9
Senegal	1.0	322†	188†	15.4†	42.7	23.8	43	17	2δ	87δ	8.5δ
South Africa	19.9	...	61,184†	c.320.0	1,655.0	513.6	252	491	47	3,545	85.2
Tanzania	2.6	4,529†□	3,792†□	c.17.5	34.9	37.6	14	28	5°	242°	7.6°
Uganda	1.2	4,529†□	3,792†□	25.7	25.7	13.6	1	6	6°	302°	9.9°
Zaire	5.2	751†	2,482†	c.145.0	81.4	54.3	9	39	13	524	19.8
Zambia	1.3	...	...	35.0	64.0	40.0	1	6	7	340	16.4
NORTH AND CENTRAL AMERICA											
Canada	71.1†	2,688	183,186	831.7†	7,407.3	2,059.2	1,235	2,423	231	18,022	508.0
Costa Rica	0.8†	c.57†	c.13†	c.17.6	47.5	30.1	14	9	6	256	8.3
Cuba	14.5	987†	1,598†	13.3	c.72.0	c.32.0	271	416	9	550	12.6
El Salvador	0.7	...	...	10.7†	37.9	21.9	3	—	...	...	...
Guatemala	0.8	...	106†	13.4	46.0	30.0	6	8	3	48	3.7
Honduras	1.1	174	3	c.5.7	13.8†	16.9†	57	67	6	174	3.3
Mexico	23.3	4,485	23,878	154.7	1,672.1	652.0	248	453	72	4,314	58.0
Nicaragua	0.3	30†	16†	13.1†	c.32.0	c.13.0	11	22	3	117	1.0
Panama	0.7	...	...	7.0	50.2†	16.2†	1,692	9,569	...	...	...
United States	334.8	15,080	1,233,760	6,178.7	101,237.0	23,201.0	4,063	14,912	3,823	260,639	8,826.0
SOUTH AMERICA											
Argentina	39.5†	12,183	12,284	283.8	1,680.0†	788.0†	351	1,453	55	2,963	87.3
Bolivia	3.5†	270†	440†	25.6†	c.19.2†	c.28.8†	...	...	4	177	2.9
Brazil	31.2	11,489	18,080	1,260.3	2,786.7†	687.2†	469	2,103	122	7,340	329.4
Chile	10.8	2,481†	2,718†	63.7	193.0	135.7†	138	384	23	1,111	55.6
Colombia	3.4	427	1,332	45.9†	268.2†	86.9†	54	224	54	2,284	90.5
Ecuador	1.1†	62†	55†	18.3	30.1†	44.3†	23	76	10	218	4.5
Paraguay	0.5†	28†	22†	11.2†	7.4†	10.1†	26	22	...	...	...
Peru	2.1	248†	610†	52.1	256.4	136.1	663	448	8	355	16.1
Uruguay	3.0	...	...	49.6	220.0	80.0	38	143	1	27	0.1
Venezuela	0.5†	36†	13†	44.3	778.6†	256.1†	137	479	33	1,740	77.1
OCEANIA											
Australia	40.3*†	...	26,680*	884.1†	4,273.9	1,024.0	373	1,160	181	11,308	253.1
New Zealand	4.8	488	3,367	92.0	1,064.8	195.1	113	157	41	3,227	85.2

Note: Data are for 1972 or 1973 unless otherwise indicated.
(—) Indicates nil or negligible; (...) indicates not known; (c.) indicates provisional or estimated.
*State system only.
†Data given are the most recent available.
‡Including apportionment of traffic of Scandinavian Airlines System.
§Including West Berlin.
‖Excluding Northern Ireland.

¶Including Singapore.
♀Apportionment of traffic of Malaysia-Singapore Airlines Ltd.
δIncluding apportionment of traffic of Air Afrique.
□Total for Kenya, Tanzania, and Uganda (East African Railways Corp.).
°Including apportionment of traffic of East African Airways Corp. and Caspair Ltd.
▲Including traffic for Botswana.
+Including Namibia (South West Africa).

Sources: UN, *Statistical Yearbook 1973, Monthly Bulletin of Statistics, Annual Bulletin of Transport Statistics for Europe 1972*; Lloyd's Register of Shipping, *Statistical Tables 1973*; International Road Federation, *World Road Statistics 1974; Jahrbuch des Eisenbahnwesens 1973.*

(M. C. MacDONALD)

1973 the U.S. commuter airlines carried 5,508,000 passengers, an increase of 11%. They also carried 42,960 tons of cargo, a 52% increase, and 75,206 tons of mail, up 30%.

The sharp increase in fuel prices was first experienced late in 1973. By mid-1974 prices had doubled and in some cases trebled. CAB records showed that the cost for U.S. trunk and local-service carriers in domestic operations rose from 12.342 cents per U.S. gallon in July 1973 to 23.557 cents in August 1974, 100.6% higher than the average of 11.745 cents for the year ended June 1973. Increases for international operations were even greater. For Pacific and transatlantic operations fuel cost almost trebled, from 12.780 and 13.770 cents per U.S. gallon in July 1973 to 35.546 and 37.365 cents in August 1974.

The rate of increase was greatest in the period between December 1973 and January 1974, which witnessed a 21% jump for U.S. domestic operations. Later the rate tailed off, declining to 1.4% between July and August. Some international fuel prices fell in May and June, but observers' suggestions that a peak had been reached were premature. Fuel prices paid by IATA member airlines were slightly higher than those quoted for U.S. carriers. The association anticipated an average 42 cents a gallon by September 1974, with further rises in 1975–76. IATA noted that the bonded fuel price in the U.S. rose as high as 78 cents a gallon for a time, and in mid-1974 figures of 65.9 cents were recorded in Casablanca, Morocco, and 88.4 cents in New Delhi, India.

Because of the high prices, the airlines' fuel bills, which had remained at a steady 12% of total operating costs for some years, had risen to 25–28% of total operating costs by July 1974. Reviewing the economic picture, IATA estimated that members would suffer an operating loss equivalent to 3.2% of operating revenue in 1974, compared with a 2.3% operating profit in 1973. ICAO estimated the equivalent 1973 figure for all scheduled airlines, excluding the Soviet Union and China, at 3.1% of operating revenue of $26,128,000,-000, or $820 million. Net profit was unofficially estimated at 1% of operating revenue.

All the major U.S. carriers except Pan American and TWA made a profit in the first half of the year. Since the U.S. contribution formed a substantial part of the IATA total, it could be inferred that non-U.S. airlines sustained sizable losses during 1974. According to the CAB, in the 12 months to June 1974 U.S. trunk airlines—international and domestic—made operating

profits of $659 million (+ 31%) and had a net income of $277 million (+ 62.9%) on operating revenue of $12,031,000,000 (+ 16.9%), with an increase of almost 4% in traffic and virtually static capacity (up less than 0.5%). Percentage change figures were slightly distorted by changes in reporting procedures.

In the first half of 1974, both American Airlines and Eastern Airlines turned a first-half loss in 1973 into profit. Eastern had entered 1974 expecting to lose more than $100 million, but following the half-year result it estimated that it would break even for the year, or better. The most profitable airline in the first half year was Delta, followed by United and Northwest. International operations were unprofitable, partly due to the high cost of foreign and bonded fuel. Pan American, as a predominantly international carrier, was hit badly, losing $32,396,000 in the first half year (but improving later to $28 million in the first eight months).

In contrast with the trunks, the supplementals—the U.S. nonscheduled operators—slid into an operating loss of $12.3 million in the 12 months ended March 1974, following a small profit in the preceding period. Operating revenue totaled $397.5 million (+ 13.3%), and operating expenses rose 17.6%. Revenue from military traffic was down 26%, whereas revenue from civil traffic rose 32% to 76% of the total. The National Air Carrier Association (NACA), representing the supplementals, campaigned for liberalization of regulations governing charter services and an end to "below-cost" promotional fares on scheduled services. Illegal fare discounting and rebating seemed particularly prevalent on North Atlantic routes.

The Air Transport Association (ATA), representing the U.S. scheduled airlines, reported that the average scheduled passenger revenue yield in 1973 was 6.34 cents per mile, only 4.1% higher than it had been ten years earlier. Both ATA and IATA reported adverse economic factors other than the price of fuel, specifically employee costs and sharp rises in landing fees and navigation service charges. ATA claimed that employee costs rose from $9,730 per employee in 1967 to $16,464 in 1973. Landing fees rose from 20 cents to 45 cents per 1,000-lb. aircraft weight over the same period.

In September 1974 representatives of the airlines met in San Diego, Calif., to discuss the establishment of a "floor" to charter rates, and the British Civil Aviation Authority (CAA) announced the establishment of minimum rates to become effective in April 1975. The "wholesale" rates would be equivalent to between 2.9 and 3.6 U.S. cents per mile, depending on the season. A tentative agreement envisaged rates about 70% higher than those of 1973 and about 35% higher than current rates. Several nonscheduled airlines refused to accept this, however, and the meeting broke up in indecision. Other governments were expected to follow the lead of the U.K., and the establishment of a charter floor became an integral part of the U.S. administration's policy for ending the financial squeeze on U.S. airlines.

Meeting in Montreal in late September, IATA decided to admit charter carriers to membership for the first time. The vote was unanimous, and charter members operating from the Western Hemisphere across the Atlantic to Europe would be admitted to traffic conferences convened to establish fares. Two major U.S. supplementals immediately claimed that there would be no advantage in joining IATA.

The two chief U.S. international airlines, Pan Amer-

Britain's first battery-powered bus, demonstrated in London, has a range of 40 mi. and a top speed of 40 mph.

DAILY TELEGRAPH, LONDON

ican and TWA, gave cause for concern during 1974. Pan Am's financial difficulties were aggravated by the fuel situation. A plan, announced in March, for a revenue pool and route consolidation on the North Atlantic won initial CAB support but ran into opposition from the U.S. Justice Department and was later withdrawn. Revenue pools, although quite common in Europe and elsewhere, had not so far been permitted under U.S. law.

In April both airlines appealed for government subsidies, and in August Pan Am applied to the CAB for a subsidy of $10,175,000 a month. Toward the end of April the CAB had authorized the two carriers to discuss route sharing in the hope of achieving significant savings. The plea for subsidy, which was not supported by the U.S. Department of Transportation, ultimately failed, but in May the transportation secretary stated that the department would take steps to see that neither airline went bankrupt. In October the airlines announced agreement on the allocation of routes and applied for CAB authorization; however, a provision giving TWA Pan Am's right to serve the Los Angeles–Hawaii route was strongly criticized by other airlines and was deleted from a revised plan submitted to the CAB in late December. At midyear Pan Am forecast an operating loss for 1974 of $123.1 million. Late in the year Congress passed a bill designed to help Pan Am and TWA compete with subsidized foreign airlines. Among its provisions was a directive to federal officials to negotiate reductions in high landing fees and other charges and to take retaliatory steps if negotiations failed. ATA had complained of high charges levied abroad.

Two major airports opened during the year: the new Dallas-Fort Worth (Tex.) Airport in January and the third major Paris airport, known originally as Roissy-en-France and renamed Charles de Gaulle, in March. Tokyo's new Narita Airport, although ready for service, was prevented from opening by environmental protest groups. In July the British government reversed an earlier decision and canceled plans for a third London airport at Maplin, on the Essex coast.

It had been hoped that final airline accident figures for 1974 would show a continuation of improving trends, but the year's record was marred by the two worst commercial air crashes to date. On March 3 a Turkish Airlines DC-10 crashed shortly after taking off from Paris, killing 346 persons. First reports attributed the catastrophe to depressurization through a lower-deck cargo door. There had been an earlier, similar, but nonfatal incident involving a DC-10, and controversy arose over whether the U.S. Federal Aviation Administration (FAA) should have introduced mandatory, rather than recommended, modifications for DC-10 doors. On December 4 a chartered Dutch DC-8 carrying Muslim pilgrims to Mecca crashed in bad weather in the mountains of Sri Lanka, killing 191. On November 20 the first fatal crash of a 747 since that plane entered service occurred in Nairobi, Kenya. Fifty-nine persons died when the West German Lufthansa plane crashed and burned after takeoff, probably as a result of malfunctioning wing flaps. (*See* DISASTERS.)

Preliminary ICAO figures for the world's scheduled airlines (excluding the Soviet Union and China) showed 30 fatal accidents for 1973, with 824 passengers killed (42 accidents and 1,210 passengers killed in 1972). The number of passenger fatalities per 100 million passenger-mi. in 1973 was 0.26, the lowest figure in a decade. The rate of fatal accidents per 100

million aircraft-miles was 0.46. In the U.S. the National Transportation Safety Board reported 42 accidents to aircraft operated by certificated route carriers and supplemental airlines. Nine fatal accidents resulted in the deaths of 200 passengers, 26 crew, and one other person. The rate of fatal accidents per 100 million aircraft-miles was 0.3.

In September air services between Japan and China were established, two years after diplomatic relations between the two countries had been resumed. The bilateral agreement that enabled the service to start had led to the suspension of services between Japan and Taiwan, and informal exchanges aimed at restoring that link took place in September. China's first commercial service to Western Europe, a weekly round trip to Paris, began in October.

In August Qantas abandoned its Mexico–London service; the Australian airline had dropped its U.S.–U.K. service in 1973 and no longer operated around the world. In October British Caledonian Airways announced a major cutback because of the economic situation and talked of suspending transatlantic scheduled services. Laker Airways, whose "Skytrain" no-reservation, low-cost transatlantic service had been approved by the British authorities, grew restive at prolonged delays in obtaining a U.S. decision and announced that it had instituted legal action in the U.S.

As airlines looked forward to a bleak 1975, freight appeared to offer some salvation. West Germany's Lufthansa, original operator of the all-cargo 747, prepared to increase North Atlantic freight capacity, and there were reports that the airline earned more from cargo than from passenger traffic.   (DAVID WOOLLEY)

URBAN MASS TRANSIT

The biggest transport problems occurred in cities. In some cities traffic jams had reduced the speed of movement to no better than horses could have achieved, although the horse-drawn era had been similarly accompanied by traffic jams, pollution, and noise. In London neutral was the gear most commonly used. Cities also had the biggest environmental problems, and in developed countries up to 80% of the population might live in urban areas. Modest schemes for bus lanes and pedestrian-only streets gained ground in 1974, but no government was yet willing to introduce major curbs on car use.

Most urban agglomerations turned first to building railways, either under or over the ground. In Eastern Europe the first four miles of Prague's underground opened in May. Warsaw announced it would have a subway by 1980, and there was talk of subways in Belgrade, Bucharest, and Sofia. Seoul, South Korea, and São Paulo, Braz., opened their first subways, and the tunnel under San Francisco Bay, the last segment of the automated Bay Area Rapid Transit (BART) system, finally entered service. But subways had drawbacks—particularly cost, which ran above $50 million per mile. It was estimated that the price of a subway system for one city could pay for the doubling of the less developed world's bus fleet.

In The Netherlands, Amsterdam's Metro, due to open in 1977, was attacked as a "Dutch Concorde." Costs had risen from 450 million guilders in 1970 to 1.5 billion guilders for an 11-mi. track, only two miles of which were underground. Environmentalists who had at first supported the project now opposed it on the ground that historic buildings would be destroyed. In London estimates for the first three miles of the new Fleet Line rose to £57 million, and there were doubts whether the rest of the line would be built.

In the U.S. voters in the November elections decided several proposed bond issues to support mass transit. In New York, where an earlier, more ambitious proposal by Gov. Nelson A. Rockefeller had been voted down, a $250 million issue was approved. A much larger bond issue for Michigan was defeated. In Los Angeles voters rejected a one-cent sales tax that would have raised $8 billion for mass transit over the next 12–15 years. It would have been spent on increasing the bus fleet by 50%, with special bus lanes on freeways, on 145 mi. of fixed guideway system, and on a railway to the new airport to be built on the other side of the mountains.

One drawback to urban railways was that unless a whole city could be crisscrossed with them, at enormous expense, they would only serve a small part of the city's travel needs, because most places would be far from a railway station. The growth of car ownership and increased affluence had encouraged cities to develop in a suburban sprawl, which did not generate the density of traffic railways require. The proposed Los Angeles rail lines aimed to encourage a greater density of population. In Japan a whole series of dormitory towns, with integrated transport systems, was planned for the Greater Tokyo metropolitan area.

In November 1974 U.S. Pres. Gerald Ford signed a six-year, $11.8 billion urban mass transit bill providing $7.8 billion to continue existing programs of capital grants to mass transit systems and nearly $4 billion that, for the first time, could be used either for capital expenditures or for operating expenses. Thus, money for mass transit was available, but authorities increasingly looked to cheaper proposals than railways. The Institute for Defense Analyses reported to the U.S. Department of Transportation at the end of 1973 that, for the urban commuter market, rail and express buses were about equal in terms of total journey time, assuming adequate roads for buses existed. The cost of providing bus services was much lower—total trip costs were about half and bus systems used less fuel.

A town bus with only 12% of the seats occupied used ten times as much fuel to move a given number of passengers as a full diesel train, but a bus with all its seats filled used little more fuel than the train, and if the bus was freed from wasting fuel in traffic jams it used less. One bus lane into New York City carried 25,000 passengers in the peak hour, more than most commuter rail lines. But building a bus lane could also be prohibitively expensive, unless it was to be heavily used, and it was difficult to put a bus lane underground.

All public transport systems were vulnerable to inflation in 1974. For both buses and trains, between two-thirds and four-fifths of the costs were labour costs, and on many systems even the cost of wages was not covered by revenue from passengers. Governments and local authorities came under increasing pressure to subsidize operating costs. In November the Labour-controlled Greater London Council finally broke its election pledge to keep fares down and approved a 36% fare increase, but even a rise of this order was not nearly enough to make the system viable without subsidy. An increase of 100 to 200% would be needed to make the network self-supporting.

During the height of the oil shortage, car pooling became popular in the U.S., and some local authorities and employers tried various incentives to encourage

them further. The main drawback was that everyone in the same pool had to arrive at, and leave, the place of work at precisely the same time. In some less developed countries, privately run minibuses and shared taxis were common. The taxi drivers worked long hours and charged fares not much higher than the buses. In Hong Kong minibuses were so successful that proposals were made to restrict them on the ground that they contributed to traffic congestion.

In Amsterdam membership in the White Car Cooperative Society reached 1,500. Members had access to two-seater cars that could be picked up from and left at any station on the system; mileage was worked out by computer, and charges were debited to members' bank accounts. Similar "town spider" systems were considered for other cities. Most members of such cooperatives would probably be city centre dwellers, although others might want to leave their cars at the edge of town, ride public transport to the town centre, and use the town spider to move around the city during the day.

Perlach, W.Ger., a new town under construction near Munich, planned a fully automatic "cabinentaxi" system. Small vehicles, carrying two or three passengers plus luggage, would go nonstop to the riders' destination, and vehicles should always be available from any station. The cars would use elevated tracks, separated from road traffic, with separate stopping tracks at stations.

Several attempts were made to encourage people to make at least part-time use of public transport. In Honolulu bus fares were cut substantially, and there were plans to eliminate them altogether. An experiment with free transportation in Rome had failed to cut automobile use, but the changed fuel situation might well produce a different result. Seattle, Wash., inaugurated a "Magic Carpet Service." The free system covered 105 blocks and connected with downtown districts containing city and county offices, the financial and shopping centres, and the city's historic area. In six weeks of operation bus usage rose 56%.

"Dial-a-ride" systems came to several cities. In El Cajon, Calif., riders could go anywhere within the city for a single 50-cent coupon. In the fall London inaugurated "Dial-a-Bus," with 15-seater minibuses operating in an area of poor public transport but high telephone coverage. Passengers called a central controller to be picked up and to tell the driver where to let them off.

There were several proposals to build fully automated, computer-controlled guideways, with from 4 to 40 seats, which would be free of wage inflation and would provide a service between that of the private car and conventional public transport. Toronto designed a system using magnetic suspension, but even that suffered soaring costs, technical doubts, and environmental criticism. An experiment in Morgantown, W.Va., failed on cost grounds, and France scrapped plans for an urban hovertrain.

INTERCITY RAILWAYS

Investment for main intercity railway lines proceeded at a rapid pace in 1974. In March France approved a new high-speed route between Paris and Lyons; the French believed that they had overcome the technical problems of traveling at speeds up to 185 mph. Spain, long a laggard in railway investment, announced electrification plans designed to double traffic by 1980. West Germany planned to build four new lines by 1985 and hoped to increase freight movement by

100% and passenger traffic by 50%. Initially, 125-mph trains were planned, but eventually these should run at 185 mph. In Japan, as an extension of the Shinkansen line from Okayama to Hakata neared completion, the seven-hour, 700-mi.-long trip from Tokyo to Makata became a reality.

In Britain investment in rolling stock for both the High Speed Train, capable of 125 mph, and the Advanced Passenger Train, capable of 155 mph, was approved. In the U.S. Amtrak, the quasi-governmental organization that had taken over passenger services from many existing railways in 1971, opened two new routes. It reported that passengers had increased from 15 million to 18 million but costs had risen faster than revenue. In the Soviet Union 100,000 workers were assigned to build the new Trans-Siberian railway. The existing railway ran perilously near the Chinese border, and the new line would run much farther north. The Chinese-financed and built rail link between Tanzania and Zambia, the Tanzam railway, was nearing completion two years ahead of schedule.

Despite good prospects for intercity passenger travel, with a 1% increase in passengers recorded for every 1% increase in speed, railways continued to suffer grave financial problems. This was partly because so much of the rail network was underutilized. In West Germany one-ninth of the network carried three-quarters of the passenger traffic. Overstaffing and delays in getting fare increases contributed to the problems.

Britain's Railway Act 1974, providing a new system of financial support, received the royal assent on July 31. Total expenditure provided in the bill was estimated at £3.500 million. The £1.500 million for passenger subsidies was supposed to last five years, but officials believed it might run out before that. Rather than blanket subsidies, British Rail wanted the government to subsidize infrastructure costs and then leave the railways with strict commercial targets, but this was said to contravene EEC rules. The support program was criticized because freight was largely neglected and because the passenger services that were to attract the most investment were largely used by businessmen. In the U.S. Pres. Richard Nixon signed a bill early in the year providing a mechanism whereby seven bankrupt railroads in the northeastern part of the country, including the giant Penn Central, could be reorganized into a new tax-supported railroad. A federal court found the law unconstitutional in part, but it was upheld by the Supreme Court late in the year. On December 20 a $30 million grant to the Penn Central under terms of the act was approved by a U.S. district court.

In West Germany losses were predicted at DM. 3 billion for 1974, despite large-scale subsidies. The Bundesbahn banned further hiring and announced plans to close 600 of its 1,000 parcel depots. The investment program was pruned in expectation of a slowdown in the economic growth rate.

Despite emphasis on the energy efficiency of trains, there were signs that the railways might find the environmental issue boomeranging. The planned Channel Tunnel between Britain and France was attacked by people living along the route of the rail link that would be needed between London and the coast. (The rail link was abandoned in November on grounds of cost; this, together with the escalating cost of the tunnel itself and the difficulty of financing it, raised the possibility that the project might be shelved again.)

Research on a substitute for the steel wheel on steel

Section of the Central Asia-Centre Transcontinental Gas Line, the longest natural-gas pipeline in the Soviet Union, is under construction in the Kara-Kum Desert of the southwestern U.S.S.R. When completed, the line will stretch almost 2,000 mi., from Turkmen S.S.R. to Eastern Europe.

rail continued in the U.S., Europe, and Japan. Magnetic suspension was increasingly favoured over the hovercraft principle. In July France scrapped the Aerotrain project, on cost grounds, and in August the British government approved dismantling of the hovertrain test track near Cambridge. The decision to use conventional steel on steel trains for the Paris–Lyons line was a blow to the new technology.

FREIGHT MOVEMENTS

There were signs in the first half of the year that the railways might come back into their own for transporting freight. The West German railways, for example, recorded a healthy increase in traffic, though more time would be needed to determine whether this would be sustained. The European Commission suggested that increased oil prices were unlikely to make more than a marginal difference in the respective shares of road and rail. This conclusion also emerged from a Dutch study. Fuel, as a percentage of total costs for long-distance truck journeys, increased to 14.5%, but this was overshadowed by increased wage costs to which railways were more vulnerable. The use of rail was encouraged by the sheer shortage of diesel fuel for trucks at the beginning of the year and by speed restrictions, which reduced the capacity of truck fleets.

Road haulers came under increasing environmental pressure. In The Netherlands, where short distances, flat landscapes, and modern roads had encouraged the use of trucks, the secretary of state for transport suggested that limits on truck licenses in congested areas would discourage industry from expanding in regions that were already heavily polluted. Planned liberalization of the truck licensing system in France remained in abeyance because of the energy crisis. In Britain increasing numbers of towns put strict controls on the movement of heavier trucks. The government unveiled proposals for compulsory truck routes, which road freight interests criticized sharply because longer journeys would be involved. Everywhere research budgets on freight movements were increased.

Haulage interests were compelled to reduce the

nuisance they caused. The diesel fuel shortage early in the year provided an excuse for cutting out unnecessary trips, for example by restricting deliveries to customers to one a week. Many firms continued the practice even when fuel again became plentiful. Computers were used to schedule routes for trucks, with emphasis on reducing low utilization of capacity. On average, only half of a truck's capacity was used since many trucks made return trips empty. Yet a West German experiment to provide a centralized service for finding return loads failed because of lack of interest from haulers. France had regional bourses to find return loads, but they had many drawbacks; the Institut de Récherche des Transports planned to computerize the booking system.

Despite mixed results from existing transshipment depots, interest continued in reducing the need for heavy trucks to enter city centres. London examined the possibility of setting up a series of small transshipment centres, but a French study showed that the cost of transshipment and warehousing was many times the cost of congestion caused by trucks. Warehousing was high on the priority list of transport companies' investment plans since goods in a hauler's warehouse were more likely to be shipped in his trucks.

A more scientific approach to distribution was needed if the environmental and economic efficiency of haulage was to be improved. A survey by the Whitehead Consulting Group in January showed that only 30% of the British firms responding could identify total distribution costs, only 22% had a distribution man on the board, and only 11% used systematic standards for scheduling.

Many transport customers made insufficient distinction between really urgent goods that had to go by road and those that could afford to go more slowly by rail. French and West German railways considered changing from very long freight trains, which needed long waits to build up a full load and much coupling and uncoupling during journeys, to smaller trains, especially company trains for one customer, with cars built to handle specific goods. British Rail, which had used the company train approach for several years, had cut traction hours per 1,000 tons of traffic by over one-third and increased net ton-miles per traction-hour by two-thirds since 1967. However, Europe had more private sidings and made greater use of carload

Driverless cars stop at a station during test runs in Japan. Designed to be run on an overhead railway circuit, each computer-operated car can accommodate 30 passengers.

KEYSTONE

traffic. In 1974 the British government announced financial help for building private sidings, and British Rail announced a new, modernized carload service to operate between city centres.   (RICHARD CASEMENT)

SHIPPING AND PORTS

After peaking in October 1973, the world dry cargo and tanker markets moved downward, with the tanker market leading the way. By mid-1974 the total world tanker fleet reached 234,179,758 tons deadweight (dw.). The influx of new vessels in the first six months totaled 19 million tons dw. and, if current shipyard deliveries were maintained, a further 25 million tons dw. would be added. It was expected that at the end of the year available capacity would exceed demand by approximately 20 million tons.

The tonnage imbalance was brought about by a reduction in world demand for oil, resulting from high prices and uncertainty over future actions of the exporting countries. Consumption of oil, which until 1973 had been rising at an annual rate of 8% worldwide, was reduced to almost nil growth, and in some areas it was cut by nearly 10%. Tanker owners managed to keep surplus capacity to a minimum by reducing speed and keeping vessels at sea longer. Furthermore, the price of bunker fuel had quadrupled in the course of a year, and a 25% reduction in the speed of a very large crude carrier saved at least 50% of bunker consumption and allowed a larger cargo to be loaded.

Very few owners resorted to laying up vessels, and scrapping was restricted largely to the older, smaller tankers that had become uneconomic to operate. Another helpful factor was the presence in the tanker fleet of nearly 370 combined carriers, totaling 39,464,-000 tons dw. These vessels, some in the 200,000-ton class, could carry oil or other bulk cargoes such as grain or coal. Only 60% of the combined carrier fleet was involved in oil transport by mid-1974, and the future for this type of vessel was fairly good. The demand for moving coal from Australia to Europe and Japan and from the U.S. to Japan encouraged owners to build more combined carriers. One of the most interesting projects was planned by Japanese interests wishing to transport crude oil from the Persian Gulf to Brazil and steel slabs from Brazil to Japan.

A matter of concern for tanker operators was the effect of reopening the Suez Canal, expected to take place in late 1975. If the canal was reopened to allow the transit of vessels drawing 38 ft. of water, it was estimated that within two years a 46-ft. draft would be available, increasing to 70 ft. by 1982. Currently, the bends in the canal could only accommodate vessels of up to 900 ft. in length and, unless the waterway was widened, more passing points would be needed to achieve the required throughput of ships. No indication was given as to the level of canal charges or how they might be assessed. However, it was generally expected that dues would be competitive with the alternative route via the Cape of Good Hope. One tanker authority suggested that opening of the canal would reduce the demand for oil-carrying capacity by only 5%. Assuming an initial 38-ft. draft, it was estimated that approximately 2,000 of the existing fleet of tankers (with a total deadweight of 50 million tons) would be able to transit the waterway. However, nearly all these vessels were of less than 50,000 tons dw., most were between 15 and 20 years old, and many were heavily committed for coastwise and regular trading.

Interest in products carriers continued to grow, and during the first half of 1974 orders were placed for 81 vessels totaling 2.4 million tons dw. Some owners took the view that reopening of the Suez Canal and the siting of new refineries in oil-producing countries, when seen against the background of the age structure of the existing fleet capable of carrying products, served to justify the ordering of products carriers of up to 66,000 tons.

There was an increase in the rate of orders placed for liquefied natural gas (LNG) carriers; 46 were on order with an aggregate capacity of 5,210,700 cu.m. Orders for a further 20 vessels with 125,000-cu.m. capacity each, required by a Norwegian-Iranian consortium, had yet to be placed.

Dry-cargo movements in the early part of 1974 were far less affected by the oil situation. Most of the reduction in world cargo movements was the result of a downturn in world economic activity, particularly in the U.S., Japan, West Germany, and the U.K. For the first few months of the year the growth of trade remained sluggish, but by July a slight recovery became apparent, and it was forecast that the volume of trade would be about 4% higher than in 1973. The total deadweight of dry-cargo capacity available by the end of 1974 was estimated at 106.3 million tons, an increase of 20% over 1973, so that, as in the case of tankers, there would be a surplus of dry-cargo tonnage by the end of 1974. In most sections of the dry-cargo market there was optimism regarding longer-term developments in the grain, coal, and iron-ore trades. Imports into the Arab states raised a demand for more dry-cargo tonnage to Persian Gulf ports, which were being enlarged to handle the increased flow of cargo.

Two events of 1974 would have a long-term effect on world shipping. The first was the proposed Code of Conduct for Liner Conferences, produced at the April meeting of the UN Conference on Trade and Development (UNCTAD). The code aimed at giving less developed countries a greater share in the shipping trade. Each less developed country would be allowed to carry 40% of bilateral trade, with the other partner carrying 40% and "outsider" or third flags, the remaining 20%. Although the proposed code was carried by 72 votes to 7 with 5 abstentions, the countries voting against were maritime nations representing most of the world's cargo tonnage. Member states of the EEC and the Scandinavian countries opposed the code, believing that it would destroy the economics of shipping operations and force up the cost of sea transport.

The second event was the Law of the Sea Conference at Caracas, Venezuela, in August. One of the conference's objectives was agreement on territorial limits and the right of coastal states to develop the oil, gas, and minerals under the seabed off their coasts. The meeting served principally as a platform for ideas and policies. The next meeting, to convene in Vienna in 1975, might see a more conclusive series of debates. (*See* LAW: *Special Report.*)

Port development made good progress during the year in terms of new container facilities and tanker terminals. At Fosse near Marseilles, France, 350,000-ton tankers would be able to discharge in 1975, and the new outer harbour at Dunkirk would soon be able to accept vessels drawing up to 70 ft. At Bilbao, Spain, 500,000-tonners would be able to unload in 1975. A new large terminal for 300,000-tonners (ultimately to be increased to 500,000) was under construction at Brofjorden, near Lysekil, Swed. Container-handling facilities increased at all major ports, particularly in the U.S. and at Singapore and Hong Kong.

In 1973 some maritime nations had appeared to be taking a renewed interest in marine nuclear applications, and during 1974 orders for nuclear-powered tankers were placed in the U.S. and France. Following the success of the experimental West German nuclear cargo ship "Otto Hahn," a West German shipyard started work on a third-generation, 2,000-ton container-carrying ship powered by an 80,000-hp nuclear plant utilizing steam turbines and twin screws. The Japanese nuclear ship "Mutsu" was dogged by misfortune, however. Following a nuclear leak on its delayed trial voyage, it was barred from its home port by fishermen fearing contamination.   (W. D. EWART)

Soviet hydrofoil approaches London's Tower Bridge during its first trip on the River Thames. Commuter service on the river was to be provided by such boats.

PIPELINES

Underwater pipelaying technology was stretched to its limits in 1974 by stormy seas off the east coast of Scotland. Pipelaying experts worked in atrocious conditions, but although they could master the depths of the North Sea, they could not fully master the weather. For the oil industry, their success was crucial. There would be little point in exploring for oil offshore if discoveries could not be commercially exploited because it was technologically impossible to lay pipes to the nearest landfall.

During the year, British Petroleum completed the pipeline linking the Forties oil field to the land terminal at Cruden Bay near Aberdeen. Phillips finished work on the pipeline from the Ekofisk oil field, in Norwegian waters, to a terminal in northeast England, on Teesside. Both projects were behind schedule.

A start was made on three new North Sea projects. Occidental began work on a 32-in. pipeline to carry oil from the Piper and Claymore fields to the Orkneys. Phillips commenced a second pipeline from Ekofisk which would carry natural gas 274 mi. to Emden, W.Ger. Work also began on dual pipelines to take gas from the Frigg field, east of the Shetlands, to a terminal at St. Fergus, Aberdeenshire.

Most important, perhaps, was the decision of 17 oil companies with shares in discoveries northeast of the Shetlands to build, at a cost of £200 million, a single pipeline that could move a million barrels of oil a day —half the U.K.'s current daily consumption—to the islands. The Brent, Dunlin, Hutton, and Thistle oil fields would pipe production to a giant platform in a fifth field, Cormorant; from there, it would be piped 96 mi. through a 36-in. line to a terminal at Sullom Voe in the Shetlands. It made sound economic sense to build one, rather than several lines, and the companies were undoubtedly influenced by the British government's intention to introduce the same "common carrier" rights for offshore pipelines that existed for onshore lines. Any new oil field on the route of an existing pipeline would have the right to link up with that line, provided spare capacity existed. BP and Burmah planned a single line from their Ninian discovery to Sullom Voe, and both Union Oil of California and Total Oil Marine seemed likely to link their nearby fields to the same line.

Elsewhere, ENI, the Italian state energy company, achieved a major technical breakthrough by laying 15 km. of 10-in. pipe in water over 1,000 ft. deep between Sicily and the Italian mainland. ENI undertook to lay six more parallel pipes—part of an ambitious scheme to import 117,000,000,000 cu.m. of Algerian gas to Italy under a 25-year contract—and planned a 1,500-km. trunk line up the Tyrrhenian Sea coast to La Spezia. Italy's gas supply position was further strengthened by the completion of gas import lines from the U.S.S.R. and The Netherlands. A line that could carry 6,000,000,000 cu.m. of gas from the U.S.S.R. via Czechoslovakia to Cremona became fully operational.

Iran planned two new pipelines to move surplus natural gas into Europe. A second trunk line would be built to the Soviet border. The Soviet Union would use 13,000,000,000 cu.m. of gas a year in the southern provinces and make a similar amount available to West Germany. A 1,900-km. pipeline through Iran and Turkey would move some 40,000,000,000 cu.m. of gas a year to the Turkish port of Iskenderun.

The completion, during the summer, of a service road along the route of the trans-Alaska pipeline would enable work to start on the 789-mi., 48-in.-diameter pipeline to transport oil from the North Slope reservoirs to the ice-free port of Valdez for shipment to the U.S. west coast. A parallel 42-in. gas pipeline, planned by El Paso Natural Gas, would move gas found in association with the North Slope oil to Point Gravina, where it would be liquefied and shipped to California. The scheme rivaled the Gas Arctic pipeline to take Alaskan gas into Canada and then to the U.S., together with gas from the Mackenzie River area. (*See* ARCTIC REGIONS.) (ROGER VIELVOYE)

See also Cities and Urban Affairs; Engineering Projects; Industrial Production and Technology.

[725.C.3; 734; 737.A.3]

ENCYCLOPÆDIA BRITANNICA FILMS. *The Mississippi System: Waterway of Commerce* (1970); *The Great Lakes—North America's Inland Seas* (1971); *Rotterdam—Europort, Gateway to Europe* (1971); *Airplane Trip* (4th ed., 1972); *All the Wonderful Things that Fly* (1974).

Trinidad and Tobago

A parliamentary state and a member of the Commonwealth of Nations, Trinidad and Tobago consists of two islands off the coast of Venezuela, north of the Orinoco River delta. Area: 1,980 sq.mi. (5,128 sq.km.). Pop. (1973 est.): 1,064,000, including (1970) Negro 42.8%; East Indian 40.1%; mixed 14.2%. Cap. and largest city: Port-of-Spain (pop., 1972 est., 65,400). Language: English (official); Hindi, French, Spanish. Religion (1960): Christian 66%; Hindu 23%; Muslim 6%. Queen, Elizabeth II; governor-general in 1974, Sir Ellis Clarke; prime minister, Eric Williams.

TRINIDAD AND TOBAGO

Education. (1969–70) Primary (state only), pupils 227,181, teachers 6,380; secondary (state only), pupils 28,457, teachers 1,343; vocational (state only), pupils 3,396; teacher training, students 707, teachers 83; higher, students 2,218, teaching staff 348.

Finance and Trade. Monetary unit: Trinidad and Tobago dollar, with (Sept. 16, 1974) a free rate of TT$2.08 to U.S. $1 (par value of TT$4.80 = £1 sterling). Budget (1972 actual): revenue TT$529 million; expenditure TT$568 million. Foreign trade (1973): imports TT$1,532,700,000; exports TT$1,301,300,000. Import sources: Saudi Arabia 24%; U.S. 16%; U.K. 11%; Venezuela 5%. Export destinations: U.S. 55%; Sweden 7%; ship and aircraft bunker stores 7%; U.K. 5%. Main exports: petroleum and products 79%.

Transport and Communications. Roads (classified; 1971) 4,230 km. Motor vehicles in use (1972): passenger 78,400; commercial (including buses) 20,000. There are no railways in operation. Air traffic (1973): 616 million passenger-km.; freight 13,220,000 net ton-km. Ships entered (1971) vessels totaling 26,296,000 net registered tons; goods loaded 19,280,000 metric tons, unloaded 16,169,000 metric tons. Telephones (Dec. 1972) 66,000. Radio receivers (Dec. 1971) 296,000. Television licenses (Dec. 1972) 82,000.

Agriculture. Production (in 000; metric tons; 1972; 1971 in parentheses): rice *c.* 10 (*c.* 10); sweet potatoes *c.* 20 (20); oranges *c.* 11 (11); grapefruit *c.* 18 (18); sugar, raw value 232 (221); copra 13 (13). Livestock (in 000; 1971–72): cattle *c.* 67; pigs *c.* 55; goats *c.* 38; poultry *c.* 5,550.

Industry. Production (in 000; metric tons; 1972): crude oil 7,246; natural gas (cu.m.) 1,618,000; petroleum products 19,679; cement (1973) 262; nitrogenous fertilizers (nutrient content) *c.* 114; electricity (kw-hr.) 1,308,000.

Trinidad's economy, through offshore oil and natural gas, benefited from the energy crisis of 1973–74. But there remained inadequate education, unemployment, and industrial unrest (especially in the sugarcane industry early in 1974), complicated by interunion struggles and a continuing political malaise under the virtual one-party government of Eric Williams and the People's National Movement.

The Constitution Commission appointed in June 1971 under Sir Hugh Wooding (*see* OBITUARIES) issued its report in January 1974. It recommended a republican form of government; reduction of the voting age to 18; ballot boxes to replace voting machines at elections; and abolition of the Senate and adoption of a single-chamber Parliament. Under the recommended mixed electoral system, 36 members of Parliament (called the National Assembly) would be elected by simple majority and the remaining 36 would be nominated from party lists by way of proportional representation. In October Prime Minister Williams announced that the proposals would be decided on in Parliament, countering moves for immediate elections or the convening of a constituent assembly to design a new constitution.

The government took over the entire assets of Shell Trinidad Ltd. for TT$93.6 million. Trinidad brought together aluminum producers Jamaica and Guyana to build two aluminum smelters, the first in Trinidad, the second in Guyana. Most of the initial expenditure was to be borne by Trinidad, which would also supply the natural gas for energy requirements. Trinidad also urged that a new fund set up by the Caribbean Development Bank should assist the eight less developed members of the Caribbean Common Market (Caricom) and emphasized that Trinidad's surplus funds must be used to further the interest of the Caribbean Community.　　　　　(SHEILA PATTERSON)

[974.B.2.d]

Tunisia

A republic of North Africa lying on the Mediterranean Sea, Tunisia is bounded by Algeria and Libya. Area: 63,379 sq.mi. (164,150 sq.km.). Pop. (1973 est.): 5,509,000. Cap. and largest city: Tunis (pop., 1966, 468,997). Language: Arabic (official). Religion: Muslim; Jewish and Christian minorities. President in 1974, Habib Bourguiba; prime minister, Hedi Nouira.

After two days of talks on the Tunisian island of Djerba, President Bourguiba and Pres. Muammar al-Qaddafi of Libya announced on Jan. 12, 1974, that their two countries would be united in a single state. However, the referendum on this merger that was to have been held on January 18 was postponed, and Muhammad Masmoudi, the Tunisian foreign minister and an architect of the merger, was dismissed on January 14 and replaced by Habib Chatti, head of the presidential secretariat. In spite of a second meeting between Qaddafi and Bourguiba in Geneva, the merger was at last shelved indefinitely in a speech by Bourguiba on March 2.

During 1974 the Tunisian government moved toward the right. At the University of Tunis unrest among the students led to trials and prison sentences for left-wing activists. Forty students sentenced in April were pardoned by the president in July to mark

the 16th anniversary of the republic, but at the trial of alleged left-wing plotters in August, 175 men and women, mostly students and university teachers, were sentenced and 27 were acquitted. Another 31 persons accused of belonging to illegal organizations were on trial in the latter half of December.

In the presidential and general elections of November 3, Bourguiba was reelected unopposed for a fourth term of office, and the ruling Destour Socialist Party (PSD) won all 112 seats unopposed in the new enlarged National Assembly; the government in office continued unchanged. At the ninth congress of the

Security guards on patrol around Dutch airliner at Tunis airport in November. The plane had carried two Palestinians released from jail in The Netherlands on the demand of four Palestinians, who had hijacked a British airliner (top, left).

TUNISIA
Education. Primary (1970–71), pupils 922,861, teachers 19,421; secondary (1969–70), pupils 163,-353; vocational (1968–69), pupils 50,587; secondary and vocational (1969–70), teachers 6,931; teacher training (1968–69), students 8,207, teachers 600; higher (at University of Tunis), students (1969–70) 9,413, teaching staff (1968–69) 304.
Finance. Monetary unit: Tunisian dinar, with (Sept. 16, 1974) a par value of 0.435 dinar to U.S. $1 (free rate of 1 dinar = £1 sterling). Gold, SDRs, and foreign exchange, central bank: (June 1974) U.S. $366.8 million; (June 1973) U.S. $267 million. Budget (1973 est.) balanced at 208 million dinars. Gross national product: (1971) 741.6 million dinars; (1970) 648.7 million dinars. Money supply: (March 1974) 336,080,000 dinars; (March 1973) 289,150,000 dinars. Cost of living (Tunis; 1970 = 100): (May 1974) 115; (May 1973) 115.
Foreign Trade. (1973) Imports 265,970,000 dinars; exports 168,640,000 dinars. Import sources: France 37%; U.S. 9%; West Germany 9%; Italy 8%. Export destinations: France 28%; Italy 16%; U.S. 15%; West Germany 7%; Libya 5%. Main exports: crude oil 31%; olive oil 15%; phosphates 14%; fruit and vegetables 7%; wine 5%. Tourism (1972): visitors 780,400; gross receipts U.S. $147 million.
Transport and Communications. Roads (1973) 18,774 km. Motor vehicles in use (1973): passenger 90,200; commercial 50,200. Railways: (1972) 2,305 km.; traffic (1973) 527 million passenger-km., freight 1,391,900,000 net ton-km. Air traffic (1973): 529 million passenger-km.; freight 4,430,000 net ton-km. Telephones (Dec. 1972) 96,000. Radio licenses (Dec. 1972) 400,000. Television licenses (Dec. 1972) 80,000.
Agriculture. Production (in 000; metric tons; 1973; 1972 in parentheses): wheat 690 (914); barley 210 (236); potatoes (1972) 105, (1971) 80; tomatoes c. 180 (180); wine c. 100 (c. 100); dates (1972) c. 51, (1971) 39; figs (1972) c. 20, (1971) 15; olives 700 (350); oranges (1972) c. 80, (1971) 77; lemons (1972) c. 15, (1971) c. 12. Livestock (in 000; 1972–73): sheep c. 3,200; cattle c. 680; goats c. 450; camels c. 300; poultry (1971–72) 11,060.
Industry. Production (in 000; metric tons; 1973): crude oil 3,878; natural gas (cu.m.) 113,000; cement 528; iron ore (55% metal content) 808; phosphate rock (1972) 3,387; lead 26; petroleum products (1972) 1,043; sulfuric acid 430; electricity (excluding most industrial production; kw-hr.) 963,000.

Trucking Industry:
see Transportation

Trust Territories:
see Dependent States

Tungsten:
see Mining and
Quarrying

PSD at Monastir, September 12–15, Bourguiba had been elected president of the party for life; the congress also wished the constitution to be amended to allow him to be president of the country for life.

During the year Tunisia and Libya cooperated in the fields of agriculture and transport coordination. A $7.8 million trade agreement with Egypt was reached in March. France and Belgium made loans for engineering equipment, telecommunications (second undersea cable to France), rural development, health, and agriculture. For the fourth consecutive year Tunisia's balance of payments showed a surplus in 1973, enabling the country to repay all loans and to clear the deficit in its balance of trade.   (R. M. GOODWIN)

[978.D.2.b]

Turkey

A republic of southeastern Europe and Asia Minor, Turkey is bounded by the Aegean Sea, the Black Sea, the U.S.S.R., Iran, Iraq, Syria, the Mediterranean Sea, Greece, and Bulgaria. Area: 300,948 sq.mi. (779,452 sq.km.), including 9,150 sq.mi. in Europe. Pop. (1974 est.): 39,066,000. Cap.: Ankara (pop., 1970, 1,467,300). Largest city: Istanbul (pop., 1970, 2,203,340). Language: Turkish, Kurdish, Arabic. Religion: predominantly Muslim. President in 1974, Fahri Koruturk; prime ministers, Naim Talu, from January 25 Bulent Ecevit, and from November 17 Sadi Irmak.

In 1974 chronic government instability was combined with bold government action, above all in the Cyprus dispute but also over the amnesty of political prisoners. The political crisis, which had dragged on since the inconclusive general elections of Oct. 14, 1973, was finally resolved on Jan. 25, 1974, when Bulent Ecevit (*see* BIOGRAPHY), leader of the left-of-centre Republican People's Party (RPP), the largest party in the Assembly, formed a coalition with Necmettin Erbakan's right-wing, traditionalist National Salvation Party (NSP). On February 7 the 450-member National Assembly endorsed the new government's program by 235 votes to 136.

Turkish Navy landing craft with army personnel on board steams toward Cyprus in July. Turkey invaded the island on July 20.

TURKEY

Education. (1972–73) Primary, pupils 5,268,811, teachers 159,599; secondary, pupils 1,263,802, teachers 33,619; vocational, pupils 139,862, teachers 9,003; teacher training, students 46,363, teachers 1,685; higher (including 9 universities), students 180,689, teaching staff 10,703.

Finance. Monetary unit: Turkish lira, with (Sept. 16, 1974) a par value of 14 liras to U.S. $1 (free rate of 32.30 liras = £1 sterling). Gold, SDRs, and foreign exchange, central bank: (June 1974) U.S. $2,124,000,000; (June 1973) U.S. $1,793,000,000. Budget (1972–73 actual): revenue 46,730,000,000 liras; expenditure 51,470,000,000 liras. Gross national product: (1973) 294,890,000,000 liras; (1972) 237,760,000,000 liras. Money supply: (Dec. 1973) 37,390,000,000 liras; (Dec. 1972) 28,330,000,000 liras. Cost of living (Ankara; 1970 = 100): (May 1974) 179; (May 1973) 150.

Foreign Trade. (1973) Imports 29,777,000,000 liras; exports 18,038,000,000 liras. Import sources: West Germany 19%; U.K. 10%; U.S. 9%; Italy 8%; France 6%; U.S.S.R. 6%; Switzerland 6%; The Netherlands 5%. Export destinations: West Germany 15%; U.S. 10%; Switzerland 9%; Italy 9%; Lebanon 8%; U.K. 8%; France 6%. Main exports: cotton 23%; tobacco 10%; hazelnuts 9%. Tourism: visitors (1971) 494,000; gross receipts (1972) U.S. $104 million.

Transport and Communications. Roads (1973) 59,279 km. Motor vehicles in use (1973): passenger 234,600; commercial 159,300. Railways (1972): 8,132 km.; traffic 5,337,000,000 passenger-km., freight 6,641,000,000 net ton-km. Air traffic (1973): 1,649,000,000 passenger-km.; freight 11.6 million net ton-km. Shipping (1973): merchant vessels 100 gross tons and over 353; gross tonnage 756,807. Telephones (Dec. 1972) 728,000. Radio licenses (Dec. 1972) 3,941,000. Television receivers (Dec. 1972) 133,000.

Agriculture. Production (in 000; metric tons; 1973; 1972 in parentheses): wheat 10,082 (12,275); barley 2,900 (3,725); corn 1,040 (1,030); rye 700 (755); oats 376 (396); rice (1972) 203, (1971) 280; potatoes 2,150 (2,200); tomatoes 2,100 (2,000); onions 600 (575); sugar, raw value *c.* 815 (*c.* 811); sunflower seed 540 (560); lentils (1972) 110, (1971) 101; chick-peas 156 (183); dry beans 147 (159); oranges (1972) 573, (1971) 545; lemons (1972) 149, (1971) 142; apples (1972) 850, (1971) 780; pears (1972) 200, (1971) 175; peaches (1972) 120, (1971) 84; plums (1972) 120, (1971) 111; grapes (1972) 3,396, (1971) 3,853; raisins (1972) *c.* 315, (1971) *c.* 315; figs (1972) 220, (1971) 195; olives 487 (1,019); tea 22 (47); tobacco 164 (173); cotton, lint 520 (544). Livestock (in 000; Dec. 1972): cattle 13,045; sheep 38,806; horses (1971) 1,027; asses (1971) 1,760; buffaloes (1971) 1,026; goats (1971) 18,863; chickens (1971) *c.* 32,800.

Industry. Fuel and power (in 000; metric tons; 1973): crude oil 3,602; coal (1972) 4,641; lignite (1972) 5,336; electricity (kw-hr.) 12,289,000. Production (in 000; metric tons; 1973): cement 8,936; iron ore (metal content; 1972) 1,143; pig iron 896; crude steel 1,163; sulfur (1971) 27; petroleum products (1972) 10,219; sulfuric acid (1972) 28; fertilizers (nutrient content; 1972–73) nitrogenous *c.* 145, phosphate *c.* 134; manganese ore (metal content; 1971) 5; chrome ore (oxide content; 1971) 352; cotton yarn (factory only; 1970) 185; wool yarn (1971) 26; nylon, etc., filament yarns and fibres (1972) 31.

The government promised a general amnesty extending to ideological crimes, and guarantees for the freedom of thought, expression, and the press. When the amnesty bill came before the Assembly on May 15, some members of the NSP secured the exclusion of political prisoners from the amnesty. On May 18, Ecevit declared that he wished to resign, but he was dissuaded by his party colleagues. On July 3 the Constitutional Court reversed the Assembly's amnesty decision.

In foreign affairs Ecevit's government continued a dispute with Greece over continental shelf rights in the Aegean. In February Greece protested against the granting by Turkey of oil exploration licenses in the disputed area. Turkey replied, proposing negotiations. When Ecevit met the Greek prime minister, Adamantios Androutsopoulos, in Brussels on June 25–26, the Turkish proposal for a permanent commission to discuss all matters arising between the two countries was rejected.

President Makarios (*see* BIOGRAPHY) of Cyprus was overthrown by a military coup on July 15. On July 17, Ecevit and his advisers arrived in London asking that Britain and Turkey intervene jointly in Cyprus in order to give effect to their guarantee of the Cyprus constitution. Two days of talks failed to establish agreement, and at dawn on Saturday, July 20, Turkey began landing troops by sea and air in Cyprus. (*See* CYPRUS; DEFENSE: *Special Report.*) The Turkish government accepted the UN Security Council's resolution for a cease-fire as of July 22, and Ecevit welcomed the collapse of the Greek junta and the appointment of Konstantinos Karamanlis (*see* BIOGRAPHY) as prime minister on July 24. At the first round of talks in Geneva between Great Britain, Turkey, and Greece as guarantors of Cyprus' constitution, beginning on July 24, an agreement for a military standstill was reached on July 30 with a renewal of the cease-fire. At the second round, beginning on August 8, Turkey sought a solution that would give long-term political security and physical protection to the endangered Turkish Cypriot minority. Negotiations broke down after the Turks had rejected a proposed 48-hour recess on August 14. The same day Turkish forces resumed hostilities, till a further cease-fire was established on August 16. In October the U.S. Congress passed legislation cutting off U.S. aid to Turkey as of December 10 unless "substantial progress" was made toward settlement of the Cyprus problem. At the urging of the administration a provision delaying the cutoff until February 5 was included in the foreign aid bill passed in December.

Having won considerable popularity at home as a result of the Cyprus operation, Ecevit dissolved his partnership with the NSP, the resignation of the government being accepted on September 18. Ecevit then failed to form a coalition with other partners. Suleyman Demirel, leader of the Justice Party (JP), was equally unsuccessful, and Ecevit was again asked to try, on October 10. Ecevit, unable to obtain Demirel's cooperation, resigned on November 7, when student rioting at Ankara made U.S. Secretary of State Henry Kissinger cancel a meeting with him there. On November 12 Sadi Irmak, an independent senator, was invited by President Koruturk to form a government to serve until elections could be held. Irmak assumed office on November 17. He resigned November 29 after losing a vote of confidence, but stayed on in a caretaker capacity until a new government could be formed.   (ANDREW MANGO)

See also Cyprus.
[978.A.1–3]

Uganda

A republic and a member of the Commonwealth of Nations, Uganda is bounded by Sudan, Zaire, Rwanda, Tanzania, and Kenya. Area: 91,-452 sq.mi. (236,860 sq.km.), including 15,235 sq.mi. of inland water. Pop. (1974 est.): 11,171,900, virtually all of whom are African. Cap. and largest city: Kampala (pop., 1969, 330,700). Language: English (official), Bantu, Nilotic, Nilo-

Hamitic, and Sudanic. Religion: Christian, Muslim, traditional beliefs. President in 1974, Gen. Idi Amin.

In March 1974 the body of Lieut. Col. Michael Ondoga, dismissed from the post of foreign minister on February 19, was found in the Nile. The news triggered an attempted military coup led by Brig. Charles Arube, a former acting chief of staff. He was supported by soldiers from the Lugbara tribe, who were disaffected as a result of the dismissal of a number of officers from that tribe. President Amin (*see* BIOGRAPHY) acted promptly, and the uprising was crushed. Many dissidents were killed, Arube among them.

Amin was very conscious of the opposition to his government and late in February warned that if another former foreign minister, Wanume Kibedi, and two other former ministers who had fled the country were to speak ill of Uganda in countries friendly to Uganda they would be beaten. Despite this warning Kibedi in June broke the silence he had maintained in order to protect friends and relatives in Uganda and accused Amin of responsibility for the murder of the former chief justice, Benedicto Kiwanuka. Kibedi added that the number of people killed since Amin's seizure of power was almost certainly in excess of the estimated 80,000–90,000. Amin countered by telling a commission of inquiry, which he had appointed to investigate the disappearance of Ugandan citizens, that many reported missing were living abroad and working against his government in collaboration with the former president, Milton Obote. Early in June, however, the International Commission of Jurists accused Amin's government of maintaining a reign of terror in Uganda. Amin responded by threatening to close down the office of the British High Commission in Uganda and to expel all Britons working in the country unless what he claimed to be unfounded allegations against Uganda stopped immediately; at the beginning of November he ordered an immediate reduction of the British High Commission staff from 50 to 5 persons. The British government reacted by ordering a swift corresponding reduction of Uganda High Commission staff in London.

In June Amin urged committed African countries to attack Rhodesia. This followed an earlier call to abandon guerrilla tactics in southern Africa and instead to launch a military attack under African leadership. Amin had offered seven battalions of troops as Uganda's contribution to any such force that might be raised. A month later, in July, he accused Tanzania and Zambia of plotting to invade Uganda and of

Shailesh Mehta raises his hand in a mathematics class at a school in Pennsylvania. He is one of 1,700 Asian refugees from Uganda admitted to the U.S.

UNITED NATIONS HIGH COMMISSIONER FOR REFUGEES

Tunnels:
see Engineering Projects

UGANDA

Education. (1972–73) Primary, pupils 786,899, teachers 24,032; secondary, pupils 53,887, teachers 2,341; vocational, pupils 1,521, teachers 159; teacher training, students 4,721, teachers 342; higher (at Makerere University), students 3,571, teaching staff 425.

Finance and Trade. Monetary unit: Uganda shilling, with (Sept. 16, 1974) a par value of UShs. 7.14 to U.S. $1 (free rate of UShs. 16.57 = £1 sterling). Budget (1973–74 est.) balanced at UShs. 1,241,000,-000. Foreign trade (1973): imports UShs. 1,138,-000,000; exports UShs. 2,290,000,000. Import sources: Kenya 39%; U.K. 17%; West Germany 8%; Japan 5%. Export destinations: U.K. 20%; U.S. 19%; West Germany 7%; Japan 6%; Yugoslavia 5%. Main exports (excluding trade with Kenya and Tanzania): coffee 67%; cotton 15%; copper 5%; tea 5%.

Transport and Communications. Roads (1972) 25,714 km. Motor vehicles in use (1972): passenger 25,700; commercial 13,600. Railways (1972) 1,230 km. (for traffic *see* KENYA). Air traffic: *see* KENYA. Telephones (Dec. 1972) 34,000. Radio receivers (Dec. 1972) 275,000. Television receivers (Dec. 1972) 15,000.

Agriculture. Production (in 000; metric tons; 1973; 1972 in parentheses): millet *c.* 630 (*c.* 630); sorghum *c.* 332 (*c.* 332); sweet potatoes *c.* 713 (*c.* 713); cassava *c.* 2,200 (*c.* 2,200); peanuts *c.* 170 (*c.* 180); dry beans *c.* 270 (*c.* 270); coffee *c.* 171 (*c.* 200); tea *c.* 22 (*c.* 24); sugar, raw value *c.* 108 (117); cotton, lint *c.* 77 (*c.* 75); timber (cu.m.; 1972) 14,700, (1971) 14,300; fish catch (1972) 170, (1971) 137. Livestock (in 000; Dec. 1972): cattle *c.* 4,800; sheep *c.* 750; goats (1971) *c.* 1,970; pigs *c.* 70; chickens (1971) *c.* 10,500.

Industry. Production (in 000; metric tons; 1972): cement 166; copper, smelter 14; tungsten concentrates (oxide content) 0.15; salt (1971) 3; phosphate rock 23; electricity (excluding most industrial production; kw-hr.; 1973) 798,000.

massing troops on Uganda's southwestern border. In retaliation, Ugandan forces were moved to the border, but early in August the president canceled his plan for a counterinvasion of Tanzania.

In this fluctuating political situation, which was scarcely helped by the president's impetuous offers of intervention in various trouble spots around the world, the country's economy remained unsteady. High prices for cotton and coffee exports brought in a welcome flow of foreign currency, and the continuing fall in imports, due to strict controls and to the wariness of overseas traders, improved the country's balance of payments. Nevertheless, the availability of foreign exchange was severely limited and shortages of many commodities such as salt and sugar remained acute. A heavy deficit in government spending in 1973–74 was reported, and the prospects of early payment of compensation for nationalized British businesses seemed slight.　　　　　　　　　　(KENNETH INGHAM)

See also Race Relations; Refugees.

[978.E.6.B.iv]

Unemployment:
see Employment, Wages, and Hours; Social and Welfare Services

Union of Soviet Socialist Republics

The Union of Soviet Socialist Republics is a federal state covering parts of eastern Europe and northern and central Asia. Area: 8,600,340 sq.mi. (22,274,900 sq.km.). Pop. (1973 est.): 249,749,000, including (1970) Russians 53%; Ukrainians 17%; Belorussians 4%; Uzbeks 4%; Tatars 2%. Cap. and largest city: Moscow (pop., 1973 est., 7,255,000). Language: officially Russian, but many others are spoken. Religion: about 40 religions are represented in the U.S.S.R., the major ones being Christian denomina-

tions. General secretary of the Communist Party of the Soviet Union in 1974, Leonid Ilich Brezhnev; chairman of the Presidium of the Supreme Soviet (president), Nikolay V. Podgorny; chairman of the Council of Ministers (premier), Aleksey N. Kosygin.

Domestic Affairs. By 1974 Leonid I. Brezhnev had been at the head of Soviet affairs longer than any of his predecessors, with the exception, of course, of Joseph Stalin, and his dominating position as general secretary of the Communist Party of the Soviet Union appeared unchallenged. Western press rumours about impending changes in the composition of the Politburo were shown to be unfounded when the entire Politburo was confirmed in office by the party's Central Committee in July. Rumours emerged again in late December, however, when it was announced in Moscow that Brezhnev had indefinitely postponed a visit to Egypt, Syria, and Iraq, which had been scheduled to begin in mid-January 1975. At first no explanation was given and the cancellation was regarded as a setback in the Kremlin's efforts to enhance its position in the Middle East. On December 31, diplomatic sources in Cairo reported that illness, not a rift in relations, had caused Brezhnev to postpone his trip to the Middle East and that high Egyptian officials visiting the U.S.S.R. had been received by Brezhnev in a sanatorium outside Moscow.

Despite the evidence of political stability, the undercurrents of discontent continued to cause concern to the authorities. The policy of decapitating the movement of dissent, first introduced in 1972, seemed to have been stepped up; some of its leading spokesmen were either driven into exile or allowed to emigrate. But in some respects the present regime improved on practices of the past. The most famous dissenter, the novelist Aleksandr Solzhenitsyn (*see* BIOGRAPHY), was expelled from the U.S.S.R. and deprived of his Soviet citizenship in February 1974; his family was allowed to join him and they ultimately settled in Switzerland. The expulsion seemed a shrewd move on the part of Soviet authorities—by having the comforts of a Swiss exile thrust upon him, Solzhenitsyn became of less interest to the news media in the West and his influence inside the U.S.S.R. was expected to decline. In March the dissident writer Vladimir Maksimov was allowed to leave, and shortly afterward Pavel Litvinov, a grandson of the former commissar for foreign affairs, who had protested in public against the Soviet invasion of Czechoslovakia in 1968, was granted an exit visa. Solzhenitsyn's friend and defender, the famous cellist Mstislav Rostropovich, and his wife, soprano Galina Vishnevskaya, were granted exit visas to live abroad for two years. In June one of the most notorious cases of detaining political dissidents in insane asylums seemed to have been terminated by the release of former Maj. Gen. Pyotr Grigorenko, who had been incarcerated for five years mainly because of his support for the Crimean Tatars.

On June 28 the dissident Soviet physicist Andrey D. Sakharov began a hunger strike in support of an amnesty for political prisoners who were being detained in Soviet jails. On July 2–3 attempts by U.S. television networks to broadcast interviews with Sakharov and other Soviet dissidents were cut off by the Soviet television station in Moscow. The controversy occurred after Moscow had agreed to allow transmission of any and all news related to the summit meeting of Brezhnev and U.S. Pres. Richard Nixon, which was taking place at that time. A number of outgoing newscasts were blocked in transmission from Moscow as were attempts by U.S. commentators to explain on camera what happened. Soviet television officials claimed that the censored telecasts had no relation to the visit of President Nixon to their country.

The issue of Jewish emigration from the U.S.S.R. had perhaps broader international implications. The Soviet Union's desire for extended economic contacts with the U.S. had to contend with widespread criticism of the treatment of Soviet Jews wishing to emigrate to Israel. Opposition in the U.S. Senate to granting the U.S.S.R. most-favoured-nation trading status, led by Sen. Henry Jackson (Dem., Wash.), was reported to have led to an informal agreement under which restrictions would be eased. The Soviet government later claimed its position had been misinterpreted, and the bill, passed in December, contained some limitations on the granting of most-favoured-nation treatment. The Soviet leaders were obviously taking some note of world public opinion on the issue. Thus, in June, the most publicized case of frustrated Jewish emigration—that of the Jewish ballet dancer Valery Panov (*see* BIOGRAPHY) and his gentile wife, Galina—was resolved when the Panovs were granted permission to leave for Israel; this move coincided with a visit to London by Moscow's Bolshoi Ballet. Yet on the whole, fewer Jews left the U.S.S.R. in 1974 than in 1973: the Intergovernmental Committee for European Migration in Geneva announced in December that the total for 1974 was about 21,000, compared with almost 35,000 in the previous year.

The Soviet authorities have been troubled by the resurgence of clandestinely produced literature and informational material, known as *samizdat*. In particular, the reappearance of the *Chronicle of Current Events* was reported, despite a widely publicized four-year sentence for disseminating underground literature passed on Viktor Khaustov in March. Some nonconformist painters and sculptors also gave expression to their views. In September they organized a nonauthorized exhibition of their works in Moscow, only to have some of their exhibits bulldozed into the ground and some of their pictures ruined. Water-spraying trucks were used to drench onlookers. Two

weeks later, however, municipal authorities gave permission for an exhibition in a park on the outskirts of Moscow, and a crowd estimated at about 10,000 viewed the pictures. It was reported to be the first public display of art works not presubmitted to the state for approval in approximately 50 years. Following the death in October of the long-time minister of culture Ekaterina Furtseva, and her replacement by Pyotr Demichev, cultural policy was expected to undergo some change. In December Demichev was removed from the post he held as national party secretary for cultural and ideological matters but retained his position as a candidate, or nonvoting, member of the ruling Politburo, thus keeping the realm of cultural affairs under the watch of the Central Committee. His removal as party secretary was anticipated as party and government positions are not normally held by the same person in the Soviet political system.

There was relaxation of the severe laws controlling the movement of Soviet citizens inside their own country. In August the internal passport regulations were changed in an attempt to reduce the irritation and inconvenience suffered by the public: internal passports would be of unlimited validity and persons changing their domicile would have to register with the militia within three days rather than 24 hours, as was previously the case. Further changes in the system came in December when it was announced that all citizens from the age of 16 would be issued new internal passports, in what was described as a simplification of travel and residence procedures within the U.S.S.R. The announcement also implied that rural people would be among those receiving the new passports, which were to be issued from 1976 to 1981. Previously, residents of collective and state farms had not been issued internal passports, which all urban dwellers must carry, largely to prevent their migration to jobs in the cities.

The Economy. The most serious economic issue that the world inherited from 1973 was the energy crisis. In this context, Soviet authorities claimed that they had no problem: in September it was announced that oil production in 1974 would amount to 451.7 million tons—an increase of 29.1 million tons over 1973, most of which would be supplied by the new Tyumen fields in Siberia. Natural gas production in

Simas Kudirka, a Lithuanian seaman, inspects his new surroundings in Locust, N.J., after being allowed to emigrate from the Soviet Union on November 5. Kudirka had tried to defect to the U.S. from a Soviet ship in 1970 and had afterward been imprisoned in the U.S.S.R.

U.S.S.R.

Education. (1972–73) Primary and secondary, pupils 49,324,000, teachers (1970–71) 2,360,900; vocational and teacher training, pupils 4,437,000, teachers (1970–71) 183,000; higher (including 116 universities), students 4,630,000, teaching staff (1965–66) 201,000.

Finance. Monetary unit: ruble, with (Sept. 16, 1974) an official exchange rate of 0.78 ruble to U.S. $1 (free rate of 1.78 ruble = £1 sterling). Budget (1973 actual): revenue 181.8 billion rubles; expenditure 181.6 billion rubles.

Foreign Trade. (1973) Imports 15,541,000,000 rubles; exports 15,802,000,000 rubles. Import sources: Sino-Soviet area 59% (East Germany 14%, Poland 10%, Czechoslovakia 9%, Bulgaria 9%, Hungary 7%); U.S. 7%; France 5%. Export destinations: Sino-Soviet area 58% (East Germany 12%, Poland 9%, Czechoslovakia 9%, Bulgaria 8%, Hungary 6%). Main exports: machinery 22%; crude oil 9%; iron and steel 8%; timber 5%.

Transport and Communications. Roads (1969) 1,358,900 km. (including 567,300 km. surfaced roads in 1972). Motor vehicles in use: passenger (1972) *c.* 1,810,000; commercial *c.* 5.1 million. Railways: (1971) 257,100 km. (including 135,400 km. public and 121,700 industrial); traffic (1972) 285,792,000,000 passenger-km., freight (1973) 2,958,000,000,000 net ton-km. Air traffic (1972): 95,900,000,000 passenger-km.; freight 2,200,000,000 net ton-km. Navigable inland waterways (1972) 146,100 km.; traffic 180,300,000,000 ton-km. Shipping (1973): merchant vessels 100 gross tons and over 7,123; gross tonnage 17,396,900. Telephones (Dec. 1972) 13,198,000. Radio licenses (Dec. 1972) 100 million. Television licenses (Dec. 1972) 40 million.

Agriculture. Production (in 000; metric tons; 1973; 1972 in parentheses): wheat 109,700 (85,950); barley *c.* 52,000 (36,810); oats *c.* 20,000 (14,081); rye *c.* 12,000 (9,630); corn 13,400 (9,830); rice 1,770 (1,647); millet *c.* 3,000 (2,123); potatoes *c.* 94,000 (78,329); sugar, raw value *c.* 9,030 (*c.* 8,315); tomatoes *c.* 2,945 (*c.* 2,850); sunflower seed 7,340 (5,048); linseed *c.* 500 (*c.* 413); dry peas *c.* 5,900 (*c.* 4,700); soybeans *c.* 500 (258); wine 3,100 (2,940); tea *c.* 74 (71); tobacco *c.* 310 (*c.* 300); cotton, lint *c.* 2,535 (2,418); flax fibres 445 (485); wool 257 (252); eggs 2,800 (2,643); meat (1972) *c.* 12,206, (1971) 11,715; milk (1972) 82,600, (1971) 82,600; butter (1972) 1,081, (1971) 1,122; cheese (1972) *c.* 550, (1971) *c.* 530; timber (cu.m.; 1971) 384,900, (1970) 385,100; fish catch (1972)

7,757, (1971) 7,337. Livestock (in 000; Jan. 1973): cattle 104,006; pigs 66,590; sheep 139,086; goats (1972) 5,417; horses (1972) 7,320; chickens (1972) 649,000.

Industry. Index of production (1970 = 100): (1973) 123; (1972) 115. Fuel and power (in 000; metric tons; 1973): coal and lignite 667,000; crude oil 427,250; natural gas (cu.m.) 236,500,000; manufactured gas (cu.m.; 1972) 34,345,000; electricity (kw-hr.) 901,100,000. Production (in 000; metric tons; 1973): cement 109,400; iron ore (60% metal content) 216,100; pig iron 96,100; steel 132,900; aluminum (1972) *c.* 1,250; copper (1972) *c.* 1,225; lead (1972) *c.* 460; zinc (1972) *c.* 650; manganese ore (metal content; 1972) 2,682; tungsten concentrates (oxide content; 1972) 9.1; magnesite (1971) *c.* 1,450; gold (troy oz.) *c.* 6,500; silver (troy oz.) 40,000; sulfuric acid 14,784; caustic soda 2,020; plastics and resins 2,300; fertilizers (nutrient content; 1972) nitrogenous 6,551, phosphate 2,929, potash 5,433; newsprint (1972) 1,212; other paper (1972) 6,212; cotton fabrics (sq.m.) 6,581,000; woolen fabrics (sq.m.) 703,000; rayon and synthetic fabrics (sq.m.) 1,345,000; passenger cars (units) 917; commercial vehicles (units) 685. New dwelling units completed (1972) 2,233,000.

1974 would total 257,000,000,000 cu.m., 21,000,000,-000 cu.m. more than in 1973; in 10–15 years the Tyumen deposits would be the main source of this energy supply. In October a 2,000-mi. pipeline connecting the huge Medvezhnye natural gas field in the Tyumen region with Moscow became operative. With an annual capacity of 14,500,000,000 cu.m., the linkup would double the gas supply available to the capital. The line traversed developed areas of the Urals and the central part of the country, and gas could be tapped by consumers along the route. The construction of new petrochemical installations in the Tobolsk and Tomsk areas of Siberia was also initiated in 1974. In November, however, a discreet campaign to encourage people to save fuel was initiated and the official Communist Party newspaper, *Pravda,* warned that "every kilogram of fuel must be treated carefully." Natural gas was of special significance as it represented one of the Soviet Union's major bargaining counters in its commercial dealings with Western countries and in fact figured prominently in some 1974 trade agreements. The case for moderating domestic consumption was a strong one. The exploitation of new oil fields seemed restricted by the failure of Soviet industry to provide enough basic equipment, as was reflected in the official plan implementation reports for 1974. Large quantities of oil and gas were lost by seepage from poor-quality pipelines, and the U.S.S.R. obtained special credits from West Germany for the purchase of nearly a million tons of large-diameter steel pipe.

The need for extending economic ties with the West and broadening access to Western technology played an important role in the U.S.S.R.'s diplomatic activities throughout 1974. An agreement with West Germany concluded in October offered Soviet natural gas; credits to cover the supply of automation equipment from Rheinstahl AG for the new Kama motorworks and for the delivery of 9,000 heavy trucks in 1975–76 were also negotiated. The newly established American-Soviet Commercial and Economic Commission met in Washington in February and in Moscow in October. U.S. Treasury Secretary William Simon visited Moscow to take part in the deliberations and, in a speech at a dinner to mark the

occasion, Brezhnev stressed that the volume of U.S.-Soviet trade in 1974 would amount to $1 billion, compared with only $200 million in 1971. An agreement concluded with Japan in September dealt with the financing of three joint projects in Siberia: the production of coking coal, the extraction of natural gas, and the processing of timber. Trade talks held in London in May produced a ten-year agreement with the U.K. on economic, scientific, technical, and industrial cooperation—computers and scientific instruments being specified as areas of special interest. This followed shortly after an agreement for a £20 million loan by a consortium of British banks for the construction of a plant to produce high-stretch polyethylenes. One of the results of a summit meeting between Brezhnev and French Pres. Valéry Giscard d'Estaing at Rambouillet, France, at the beginning of December was an agreement under which the French would cooperate in the development of a vast aluminum plant in Siberia in exchange for Soviet supplies of natural gas, which by 1980 would account for one-eighth of French consumption.

The development and security of Siberia were of paramount importance, and perhaps the most significant economic development in 1974 was the decision to start the building of a 2,000-mi. railway line from Ust Kut on the Lena River to Komsomolsk on the Amur. This Amur–Baikal railway would cross virgin territory rich in copper and iron ore, asbestos, and coking coal. Some 140 bridges would be built and four tunnels (one of them 10 mi. long) would be constructed. The published plans stressed that the environment of the taiga would be fully safeguarded. The new railway was also of strategic importance, as the present Trans-Siberian runs for thousands of miles along the Chinese border, while the line of the new Amur–Baikal is separated from it by hundreds of miles of very difficult terrain.

The results reported on the Soviet economy in 1974 were impressive. Industrial output in the first ten months of the year increased by 8.4% over the same period in 1973. The Soviet press made much of this success, which exceeded the plan target by approximately 2%, and pointed comparisons were made with the allegedly critically stagnant condition of the

A. STUZHIN—TASS/SOVFOTO

Restoration
of the Spasskaya Tower
of the Kremlin wall
takes place behind a new
granite platform
for spectators at Red
Square in Moscow.

capitalist economies. Generally, labour productivity was up and production costs were down. The production of computers increased by 27%. Official statements, however, reported serious shortfalls in the production of chemicals and in the manufacture of oil industry equipment, harvester combines, and heavy tractors. The total grain harvest in 1974 fell only slightly below the 1973 peak and was described as the second highest on record.

Foreign Policy. The major preoccupation of Soviet diplomacy was the maintenance of international stability, without which a reasonable development of economic relations with the West would be impossible. In the Soviet view, the stability of the international balance depends largely on the mutual understanding of the superpowers, and the pace and content of détente can be determined primarily by them. In this sense, the special relationship between Moscow and Washington represented the level of aspiration of the Soviet leadership in terms of international power politics. At the ideological level this could create problems, but at the moment security, stability, and economic advantage appeared to rank very high on the list of Moscow's priorities. This did not mean that the Soviet Union was prepared to abandon its ideological position, or that it was prepared to forgo any possible gains. In areas such as the Middle East, it tried to tilt the balance in its favour whenever opportunities presented themselves, although this was done with great care in order to prevent any escalation of the successive Middle East crises to a state where a direct confrontation of the superpowers could not be avoided.

There were several reasons why the Soviet Union sought an understanding with the U.S. Basically, the two superpowers share the major responsibility for the prevention of nuclear war. The cost of nuclear arms technology has driven both countries to negotiate about the limitation of strategic nuclear weapons. Soviet policy toward the U.S. was naturally influenced by the opening up of relations between Washington and Peking, and the situation was further complicated by the current fluidity in the international system as the bipolar confrontation of two homogeneous alliance systems gave way to a more flexible continuity of negotiation.

Soviet relations with the U.S. centred largely on nuclear matters. In August 1973 it had been reported that the U.S.S.R. had achieved a major advance in the technology of multiple independently targeted reentry vehicles. President Nixon's negotiating position was relatively weak in view of his domestic difficulties, and when he visited Moscow in June 1974 he obtained little more than an agreement on Soviet-U.S. cooperation on artificial heart research and housing. Nevertheless, in his speech at the dinner given in the Kremlin in Nixon's honour on June 27, Brezhnev described the achievement of "stable peace between the U.S.S.R. and the U.S." as "the chief task in the development of Soviet-American relations. . . . For everything useful that we can achieve in this direction, future generations will remember us with kind words." Throughout the Watergate affair, Soviet comment was reserved and cautious, and the reaction to Nixon's departure from the White House was simply to state that U.S. foreign policy was the result of objective circumstances inherent in the present condition of the international system and therefore not to be identified with any single politician. However, at the end of November, when the new president, Gerald

Ford, met Brezhnev for the first time in Vladivostok, they reached a tentative understanding to limit the numbers of all offensive strategic nuclear weapons and delivery vehicles until 1985. The formal agreement was subject to further negotiations on technical matters and would not be signed before the summer of 1975, when Brezhnev was due to visit the U.S. It seemed clear that the Soviet Union did not want to engage in an unlimited nuclear arms race. Efforts were being made to reduce defense expenditure, and although the defense estimates quoted in Soviet budgets do not include defense spending concealed under other headings, they do at least indicate the image the party is trying to project. Thus, the budget for 1974 set defense spending at 9.1% of all budget expenditure, as compared with 9.9% in 1973, and a further reduction was forecast for 1975. The economic motives behind the Soviet Union's readiness to accept an ill-defined ceiling on offensive nuclear missiles could therefore be genuine. On the other hand, the Soviets might be trying to achieve total superiority over the U.S. deterrent, and they might be using arms limitation agreements merely as a method of gaining time for further technological development—this at least was the view of some U.S. critics of the Vladivostok negotiations. It was more likely that the Soviet leaders believed that their deterrent capabilities still lagged behind those of the U.S. and, if that was the case, then the Vladivostok meeting was an essential move in the process of détente.

In September Soviet Foreign Minister Andrey A. Gromyko told the UN General Assembly that "international developments are dominated by détente." During Gromyko's visit to the U.S. he went to Washington, D.C., to meet with President Ford. In September, also, Gromyko went to Bonn, and in October Helmut Schmidt paid his first visit to Moscow as chancellor of West Germany. Brezhnev's meeting with Giscard d'Estaing in December at Rambouillet led to an important agreement on economic and technical cooperation, and Brezhnev obtained evidence of the new French president's support for his predecessors' policies of détente and cooperation.

The crises in the Middle East and the eastern Mediterranean were, on the whole, treated with cautious moderation, although the Soviet Union continued its diplomatic support of the Arab cause. Exchanges at high level took place during the year, including visits by Syrian Pres. Hafez al-Assad to Moscow, Soviet Defense Minister Andrey Grechko to Iraq, and Soviet Foreign Minister Gromyko to Syria and Egypt. Yasir Arafat, the leader of the Palestine Liberation Organization, was officially welcomed in Moscow in July. In August, in an important speech delivered in Kishinev, the capital of Soviet Moldavia, Brezhnev came out in strong support of the Palestinians' right to a national home: "It is essential finally to carry out the decisions of the United Nations and ensure the liberation of the lands seized by Israel, the satisfaction of the just interests of the Arab people of Palestine and its right to a national home."

There was little change in relations with other Communist countries. Relations with Romania remained cool. Soviet Premier Aleksey N. Kosygin attended the August 22 observance of the 30th anniversary of Communist rule in Romania but spurned invitations to extend his visit and hold more substantive talks with Romanian leader Nicolae Ceausescu. In October a consultative meeting to prepare a conference of European Communist parties was held in Warsaw.

UPI COMPIX

Truck sprays water at fleeing crowd
as Soviet police break up
an unauthorized outdoor exhibit
of abstract art in Moscow
on September 15.

Relations with China remained in a state of plaintive hostility, expressed principally in frequent commentaries in the Soviet press. Thus, for example, at the height of the Cyprus crisis, for which *Pravda* blamed the "despicable activities of NATO," China was accused of supporting the NATO position. In its September issue the ideological journal of the Soviet Communist Party, *Agitator,* took issue with the Maoists in Peking, attacking them for "deformation of the socialist economic basis" by placing too much emphasis on agriculture and indulging in "xenophobia and spy mania." In November, according to reports from Communist sources, Soviet and Chinese troops engaged in a number of clashes on the Mongolian-Chinese frontier, resulting in about 30 men killed or wounded. Brezhnev visited the Mongolian capital, Ulan Bator, during the same month and in a speech there flatly rejected Chinese proposals for easing the situation on the border. Talks on the situation had been deadlocked for a long time and China experts believed that Soviet leaders sought to maintain the tension because of the unstable political situation in Peking. But none of this was new, and a fundamental reappraisal of Sino-Soviet relations might have to wait for structural and personal changes in Peking.

The Ideological Dilemma. While the controversy with China was carried on principally in ideological terms, the dialogue with the Western world in general and the U.S. in particular was conducted at the accepted level of diplomatic intercourse. Inevitably, this created ideological contradictions for the Soviet Communist Party—if, as it is claimed, socialism is far superior as an economic system to capitalism, why should the Soviet Union seek to extend its economic cooperation with the West? What is the ultimate aim of détente, which according to Gromyko "dominates" the development of international relations, as long as the party ideologues maintain: "Considering peaceful coexistence as a special form of class struggle between the countries of socialism and capitalism, the party stresses that it cannot lead to the peaceful coexistence of Communist and bourgeois ideologies"?

Western proposals, put forward at the Conference on Security and Cooperation in Europe for establishing the free exchange of ideas between East and West have been rejected as "a convenient cloak for subtle anti-Soviet propaganda." An important and obviously authoritative article published in *Pravda* on April 2, 1974, under the heading "Socialism and creative freedom," makes this point, emphasizing that therefore "there can be no talk of any 'ideological coexistence' or even 'ideological armistice.' " After giving many examples illustrating the pernicious effect of bourgeois and capitalist values upon true artistic freedom and realism, the paper dismisses the attention paid in the West to a few "dissenting" writers in the Soviet Union as being due to their "raving anti-Sovietism." Somewhat illogically, *Pravda* also claims that "the hypocritical farce conducted under the slogan of 'intellectual freedom' is actually a fierce and determined attempt to block the dissemination of socialism."

The Soviet pursuit of technical cooperation with the West can be related to an important article by Nikolay Inozemtsev, the director of the Institute of World Economics and International Relations, which appeared in *Pravda* on Aug. 20, 1974. The author argues on established lines that the pressures of the energy crisis and of inflation have brought about an intensification of the internal contradictions inherent in the capitalist system; the condition of the West is therefore described as "unstable and tense." In these circumstances, the class war must inevitably grow more acute, leading to a "sharpened political struggle engendering deep social and political crises in a number of countries." The fall of authoritarian regimes in Portugal and Greece was interpreted as a portent of things to come.

If this was in fact the Soviet blueprint for the future, it was difficult to foresee a long and healthy life for the policy of détente. Yet on the other hand it was arguable that the Soviet Union's prospects for economic advance, which must condition the degree of stability and consensus enjoyed by the system, depend on the further development of economic ties with the industrialized West. To ascribe a single monolithic view to the Soviet leadership would almost certainly be far too simple. There were probably differences of opinion about what was likely to happen; the future of détente depended largely upon the resolution of these differences.   (OTTO PICK)

[972.B.1]

ENCYCLOPÆDIA BRITANNICA FILMS. *The Soviet Union: Epic Land* (1971); *The Soviet Union: A Student's Life* (1972); *The Soviet Union: Faces of Today* (1972).

Unions:
see Industrial Relations

Unitarians:
see Religion

Sheikh Zaid (left), president of the U.A.E., met with King Faisal of Saudi Arabia at the Arab summit conference in Rabat, Morocco, which acknowledged Yasir Arafat as spokesman for the Palestinian refugees.

United Arab Emirates

Consisting of seven emirates, the United Arab Emirates is located on the eastern Arabian Peninsula. Area: 37,000 sq.mi. (96,000 sq.km.). Pop. (1974 est.): 430,000, of whom (1968) 68% were Arab, 15% Iranian, and 15% Indian and Pakistani. Cap.: Abu Dhabi town (pop., 1973 est., 60,000). Language: Arabic. Religion: Muslim. President in 1974, Sheikh Zaid ibn Sultan an-Nahayan; prime minister, Sheikh Maktum ibn Rashid al-Maktum.

In 1974 exceptional boom conditions caused by the growing oil revenues of the United Arab Emirates continued. Oil output in Abu Dhabi, main producer of the seven emirates, was running at about 20% above 1973, but in the summer it was announced that Abu Dhabi was holding back further increases to maintain prices. On September 3 agreement was reached after prolonged negotiations to increase Abu Dhabi's share in the Abu Dhabi Petroleum Co. and Abu Dhabi Marine Areas from 25 to 60% (in line with previous agreements reached between Kuwait, Qatar, Saudi Arabia, and the oil companies), retroactive to Jan. 1, 1974. Agreement was also reached for the companies to buy back part of Abu Dhabi's share of crude oil at 93% of posted prices. Sheikh Zaid visited Saudi Arabia on August 19–21 and signed an agreement with King Faisal on the form of reciprocal diplomatic relations and border demarcation, set-

UNITED ARAB EMIRATES
Education. Primary and secondary, pupils (1973–74) 50,000, teachers (Abu Dhabi only; 1968–69) 223.
Finance. Monetary unit: dirham, with (Sept. 16, 1974) a par value of 3.95 dirhams to U.S. $1 (free rate of 9.13 dirhams = £1 sterling). Budget (1973 est.) revenue *c.* 500 million dirhams.
Foreign Trade. (1973 est.) Imports *c.* 3 billion dirhams; exports *c.* 6 billion dirhams. Import sources: Japan *c.* 23%; U.K. *c.* 17%; U.S. *c.* 17%; France *c.* 15%. Export destinations: Japan *c.* 33%; France *c.* 21%; West Germany *c.* 15%; U.K. *c.* 10%; The Netherlands *c.* 5%. Main export crude oil *c.* 100%.
Industry. Crude oil production (1972) 58,140,000 metric tons.

tling in principle outstanding differences over disputed oil-rich areas including the Buraimi Oasis. A joint technical committee was established to fix the borders.

Abu Dhabi in 1974 pledged substantial funds to other Arab states—notably Egypt and Syria—and capital held by the Abu Dhabi Fund for Arab Economic Development was quadrupled to $480 million. Abu Dhabi also loaned $76 million to the World Bank and pledged $400 million in aid to less developed countries. In Dubai, the other main emirate, commercial expansion continued. Contracts were signed for the doubling in size of Port Rashid and the building of a $48 million cement plant. In September a UAE oil tanker company was founded.   (PETER MANSFIELD)
[978.B.4.b]

United Kingdom

A constitutional monarchy in northwestern Europe and member of the Commonwealth of Nations, the United Kingdom comprises the island of Great Britain (England, Scotland, and Wales) and Northern Ireland, together with many small islands. Area: 94,217 sq.mi. (244,021 sq.km.), including 1,191 sq.mi. of inland water but excluding the crown dependencies of the Channel Islands and Isle of Man. Pop. (1973 est.): 55,957,000. Cap. and largest city: London (Greater London pop., 1973 est., 7,281,080). Language: English; some Welsh and Gaelic also are used. Religion: mainly Protestant. Queen, Elizabeth II; prime ministers in 1974, Edward Heath and, from March 4, Harold Wilson.

Two general elections, a change of government, and three budgets were landmarks in a continuing industrial, economic, and political crisis that convulsed the United Kingdom during 1974. A state of emergency had been declared on Nov. 13, 1973, when an energy crisis was threatened by industrial disputes in electric power and coal mining coming on top of cutbacks in oil supplies from the Middle East. In December the situation was further aggravated by a ban on overtime by railwaymen. Precarious energy supplies led to the decision to limit electricity supplies to industry to three days a week. The full effects of the three-day workweek began to be felt early in January 1974. The Conservative government headed by Edward Heath was determined to uphold the limits on wage increases set in Stage Three of its counterinflationary program. But the miners would not give way and the National Union of Mineworkers (NUM), which had been operating a ban on overtime working, decided on February 5 to call an all-out strike, which had the backing of an 81% vote in a miners' ballot.

Elections. Two days later Heath dissolved Parliament and called for a general election, in the minimum time allowable, on February 28. Though he had a small but workable majority in Parliament, he and his Cabinet felt they must have the support of the country in their confrontation with the unions on statutory limits on wage increases. Heath pinned his election campaign to the appeal for a firm mandate and a strong government to fight inflation against the pressures of militant trade unionists. The Conservative manifesto put it bluntly: "the choice is between moderation and extremism." Labour, led by Harold Wilson (*see* BIOGRAPHY), however, fought on a comprehensive program of measures drawn up by the party during 1973, including renegotiation of the terms of

United Church of Canada:
see Religion
United Church of Christ:
see Religion

Prime Minister Harold Wilson waves to the crowd outside 10 Downing St. following the Labour Party victory in the October elections.

British membership in the EEC, with a decision on whether to withdraw or stay in to be made by referendum; a wide-ranging program of social reform to help low-income groups; extension of public ownership of industry under the aegis of a new National Enterprise Board; and the repeal of the Conservatives' Industrial Relations Act, passed in 1971, which set up a system for the regulation of trade unions, together with a return to a voluntary incomes policy. The Liberals, with only 11 MPs in the outgoing Parliament, put forward a scheme for holding back inflation by taxing companies and their employees who forced up either prices or earnings above an agreed annual rate; a minimum wage; a tax credit scheme to help the less privileged; and improvement of industrial relations. But the main weight of the Liberal thrust was against the two-party system itself which they blamed for sterile politics and a self-defeating alternation of conflicting short-term policies.

As the February campaign developed, the opinion polls showed an initial lead for the Conservatives dwindling, and a startling advance (put by some polls at around 25%) by the Liberals. When the results were declared they produced deadlock. In the old Parliament Conservatives had a majority of 16 over all parties. Labour was now the largest single party,

but with a majority of only 5 over the Conservatives which could at any moment be overturned by the 37 members of other small parties. The Liberals suffered the usual fate of third parties under the simple majority system of voting: they trebled their vote (compared with the 1970 election) from two million (7.4%) to six million (19.3%) but the number of Liberal MPs increased by only 3, to 14. Labour, with a handful more seats, had rather fewer votes than Conservatives: Labour 11,654,726 (37.2%); Conservatives, 11,963,207 (38.2%).

The results were so inconclusive that Heath did not immediately resign, though Wilson at once announced that Labour was prepared to form a government. The Liberal leader, Jeremy Thorpe, met Heath on March 2 and 3 to discuss the situation, but on March 4 the Liberal MPs and peers rejected a proposal for a Conservative-Liberal coalition made by Heath, though they called for "a government of national unity." Thereupon Heath resigned and Wilson was called on to form a government.

Wilson's Cabinet—which was to remain unchanged after still another general election in October—was: Edward Short (leader of the House of Commons), Lord Shepherd (leader of the House of Lords), James Callaghan (secretary of state for foreign affairs; *see* BIOGRAPHY), Elwyn Jones (lord chancellor), Roy Jenkins (home secretary), Denis Healey (chancellor of the Exchequer; *see* BIOGRAPHY), Michael Foot (employment; *see* BIOGRAPHY), Eric Varley (energy), Frederick Peart (agriculture), Barbara Castle (social services), Anthony Wedgwood Benn (industry; *see* BIOGRAPHY), Anthony Crosland (environment), William Ross (Scotland), Harold Lever (Duchy of Lancaster, with responsibilities for economic policy), Peter Shore (trade), Shirley Williams (prices and consumer protection; *see* BIOGRAPHY), Roy Mason (defense), Merlyn Rees (Northern Ireland), John Morris (Wales), and Reginald Prentice (education and science).

Though the Wilson government was extremely insecure in the House of Commons, it carried on through the spring and summer, submitting to an occasional defeat, but also bringing in some of its more controversial legislation, including the repeal of the Industrial Relations Act and the abolition of the Pay

---

UNITED KINGDOM

Education. (1972–73) Primary, pupils 6,228,702, teachers 248,107; secondary, pupils 4,061,002, teachers 242,436; vocational, pupils 348,766, teachers 63,547; teacher training, students 1,863, teachers 240; higher (including 42 universities), students 389,659, teaching staff 50,788.

Finance. Monetary unit: pound sterling, with (Sept. 16, 1974) a free rate of £0.43 to U.S. $1 (U.S. $2.31 = £1 sterling). Gold, SDRs, and foreign exchange, official: (June 1974) U.S. $6,570,000,000; (June 1973) U.S. $6,873,000,000. Budget (1974–75 est.): revenue £23,188 million; expenditure £22,203 million. Gross national product: (1973) £71,270 million; (1972) £62,470 million. Money supply: (March 1974) £12,774 million; (March 1973) £12,333 million. Cost of living (1970 = 100): (June 1974) 149; (June 1973) 128.

Foreign Trade. (1973) Imports £15,854.1 million; exports £12,455 million. Import sources: EEC 33% (West Germany 8%, France 6%, The Netherlands 6%); U.S. 10%; Sweden 5%; Canada 5%. Export destinations: EEC 32% (West Germany 6%, France 5%, Ireland 5%, Belgium-Luxembourg 5%, The Netherlands 5%); U.S. 12%. Main exports: machinery 26%; chemicals 10%; motor vehicles 9%; precious

stones 7%; textile yarns and fabrics 5%. Tourism (1972): visitors 7,255,000; gross receipts U.S. $1,380,000,000.

Transport and Communications. Roads (1972) 362,539 km. (including 1,761 km. expressways). Motor vehicles in use (1972): passenger 13,100,030; commercial 1,686,200. Railways (excluding Northern Ireland; 1972): 18,567 km.; traffic 33,902,000,000 passenger-km., freight (1973) 23,012,000,000 net ton-km. Air traffic (1973): 26,188,000,000 passenger-km.; freight 906,793,000 net ton-km. Shipping (1973): merchant vessels 100 gross tons and over 3,628; gross tonnage 30,159,543. Ships entered (1970) vessels totaling 137,888,000 net registered tons; goods loaded (1972) 50,697,000 metric tons, unloaded 206,013,000 metric tons. Telephones (Dec. 1972) 17,572,000. Radio receivers (Dec. 1972) c. 37.5 million. Television licenses (Dec. 1973) 17,293,000.

Agriculture. Production (in 000; metric tons; 1973; 1972 in parentheses): wheat 5,007 (4,780); barley 8,993 (9,244); oats 1,087 (1,250); potatoes c. 6,300 (6,527); sugar, raw value c. 1,184 (c. 965); apples (1972) 381, (1971) 529; pears (1972) 53, (1971) 72; dry peas c. 74 (73); dry broad beans (1972) 166,

(1971) 134; tomatoes c. 120 (111); onions c. 205 (196); eggs 821 (875); milk c. 14,500 (c. 14,200); butter 96 (95); cheese 182 (184); beef and veal 879 (917); mutton and lamb 234 (219); pork 934 (932); wool 32 (31); fish catch (1972) 1,081, (1971) 1,107. Livestock (in 000; June 1973): cattle 14,498; sheep 28,089; pigs 8,905; poultry 144,079.

Industry. Index of production (1970 = 100): (1973) 110; (1972) 102. Fuel and power (in 000; metric tons; 1973): coal 132,025; crude oil 366; natural gas (cu.m.) 27,151,000; manufactured gas (cu.m.) 10,790,000; electricity (kw-hr.) 281,600,000. Production (in 000; metric tons; 1973): cement 19,990; iron ore (28% metal content) 7,130; pig iron 16,868; crude steel 26,649; petroleum products (1972) 104,554; sulfuric acid 3,996; fertilizers (nutrient content; 1972–73) nitrogenous 816, phosphate 467; cotton fabrics (m.) 452,000; woolen fabrics (sq.m.) 192,000; rayon and acetate fabrics (m.) 504,000; passenger cars (units) 1,747; commercial vehicles (units) 416. Merchant vessels launched (100 gross tons and over; 1973) 1,010,000 gross tons. New dwelling units completed (1973) 304,000.

Board, which were its major pledges to the trade unions. It settled the coal strike immediately by making an exception to the Stage Three counterinflationary provisions and allowing wage increases that would add about £100 million to the National Coal Board's (NCB) wage bill, compared with the offer costing about £44 million made under the previous government. The state of emergency was ended on March 11, and a five-day workweek was resumed on March 9. The price of coal for industry was raised by 48% from the Yorkshire and Midlands coalfields, and by an average of 28% from other coalfields, on April 1. The government undertook to write off an NCB deficit of £150 million.

It was clear that another election must be expected soon, and Wilson decided to go to the polls again on October 10 (seeking, as Heath did, an emphatic mandate). Both the Conservatives and the Liberals were focusing attention on the need for a coalition government, and the Liberals' annual party assembly gave the Liberal Party a free hand to decide on what terms it would join in a coalition. The Conservatives in their manifesto promised to consult and confer with other parties after the election: "the nation's crisis should transcend party differences." Labour rejected the idea of a coalition, arguing that the country needed a government with clear-cut policies: "If we believe, as we must, in our own independent political philosophies, there is no meeting point between us and those with quite different philosophies." At the heart of Labour's manifesto was a "social contract" between a Labour government and the trade unions.

The social contract reached with the Trades Union Congress (TUC) during the summer was for voluntary restraint on wage increases to replace statutory control, which came to an end in July. It became a central issue, its critics objecting that in practice it would not be found to be binding on wage settlements. In the version approved by the TUC general council on June 26, the social contract said that the objective in present inflationary circumstances was to maintain (rather than to increase) real incomes. Though this point attracted little attention at the time, toward the end of the year it began to look as though it might be taken to sanction wage increases to cover the expected rate of inflation for the coming 12 months—which would tend to perpetuate any supposed future annual rate of inflation—and this led to some sharp criticism of the effectiveness of the concept of the social contract as a way of damping down wage inflation. While the TUC as a body subscribed to the social contract, the atttitude of some member unions was equivocal, notably that of the Amalgamated Union of Engineering Workers led by Hugh Scanlon (see BIOGRAPHY) and, at the end of the year, of the NUM, whose left-wing elements were pressing the union's executive to endorse a claim for a £30 a week wage increase.

The election of October 10 did not produce a clear majority for Labour, although it increased the Labour lead sufficiently to make it likely that the Wilson government would last for some years. Compared with February there was a 2.1% swing in total votes from Conservative to Labour, which left Labour with a majority of 43 seats over the Conservatives, but with a majority of only 3 over all the parties. The growth of the Liberals, with about 5,350,000 votes and 13 MPs, and of nationalist parties collecting almost 2 million votes with 24 MPs (11 Scottish, 10 Ulster, 3 Welsh), appeared to be a trend away from the two

County boundaries in the U.K. before and after April 1, 1974, the effective redistricting date.

main parties, with neither Labour nor Conservatives taking as much as 40% of the poll either in February or in October.

After losing two general elections, Edward Heath's leadership was widely questioned within the Conservative Party. However, he indicated that he would not resign but would submit to reelection for the leadership. The issue was not immediately pressed, partly because there was no obvious successor.

The Economy. Inflation had been building up rapidly during 1973, fed by world commodity prices and an excessive increase in the money supply at home, and approached crisis proportions after the quadrupling of oil prices by the oil-exporting countries and the industrial disruption caused by the three-day workweek. On December 17 the Conservative chancellor of the Exchequer, Anthony Barber, introduced measures cutting public expenditure by £1,200 million. New and severe taxes were to be imposed on profits from land and property deals to discourage speculation. Credit was cut back by reimposing consumer credit controls and by restrictions on bank lending. A 10% surcharge was put on higher incomes. This "minibudget" was a foretaste of three more to come in 1974.

Labour's chancellor of the Exchequer, Denis Healey, brought in his first budget on March 26. By now the government had to weigh the opposing risks of continuing inflation and possible recession with consequent unemployment. Though Healey said his budget was "broadly neutral on demand," he increased taxation by £1,400 million and planned to reduce the government's borrowing by £1,500 million. Income tax rates were increased by 3 percentage points, and on taxable income over £20,000 the rate reached 83%.

About £500 million additional was to be provided for food subsidies. Healey proposed to finance the balance of payments deficit, already building up to huge proportions largely owing to the oil bill, by overseas borrowing rather than by cutting imports through massive deflation.

Healey promised another budget for the autumn but found that he had to bring in an interim budget in July. Automatic threshold increases in wages linked to the retail price index were already tending to add to wage inflation. Therefore, in a package of measures announced on July 22 he sought to hold back price increases by reducing the value-added tax (VAT) from 10 to 8%, by relief for domestic ratepayers, by increasing rent rebates and allowances, and by additional food subsidies. To help raise money on the market for investment, the dividend control was relaxed to permit increased distribution by up to $12\frac{1}{2}\%$ to shareholders.

By the time Healey brought in his autumn budget on November 12 the financial difficulties of many industrial companies had become critical. He chose to divert about £1,500 million to industry by changes in price controls and by easing the burden of corporation tax on that part of profits arising from inflation in the value of stock. The Confederation of British Industry had asked for help amounting to £3,000 million, but some of Labour's left-wing MPs thought Healey's relatively modest rescue operation was too generous. VAT was raised by 25% on gasoline and a capital transfer tax, or gift tax, was introduced to replace estate duty.

Less than a month after the November budget the government had to come to the rescue of British Leyland, Britain's largest automobile manufacturer, employing 165,000 workers. With sales of around £1,500 million a year, British Leyland saw a 1973 profit of £51 million wiped out in 1974 by the three-day workweek, chronic industrial stoppages, and inflated costs. (*See* INDUSTRIAL PRODUCTION AND TECHNOLOGY.) Earlier in the year the government had come to the rescue of Ferranti (a major supplier of electronic defense equipment), Rolls-Royce (to support production of the RB.211 aero engine), and Court Line (a mix of shipbuilding and package holidays which nevertheless collapsed—to public outcry because it had

been understood that the tourist side of the company was to receive government support).

In the financial world the secondary banks that had mushroomed during the easy credit spree of 1972 and 1973 were in dire trouble when the property market collapsed in 1974. Several market favourites went into liquidation despite a massive rescue operation (primarily to protect depositors) mounted by the Bank of England and the clearing banks. Even the big clearing banks were hit by the steep fall in property and stock market values, and some suffered large losses in foreign currency exchange transactions. It was a traumatic year for the stock market, which saw the *Financial Times* industrial ordinary shares index drop from 500 in January 1973 (it came close to 550 in mid-1972) to around 320 in January 1974, slipping below 200 in August (for the first time since 1958), and to 150 by mid-December. This was a more drastic decline than in the slump of the 1930s. The main causes were low profitability of business and high interest rates, with the Bank of England's minimum lending rate easing only a little from $12\frac{1}{2}$ to $11\frac{1}{2}\%$.

High interest rates were a cause of difficulty in the housing market. The demand for mortgage loans was inflated by the rapidly rising cost of houses in the previous two or three years, but building society funds were hit by competitive interest rates at a time when strong government pressure was put on building societies not to increase the rate of mortgage interest. In April the government made available a loan of £100 million to building societies with provision for another £400 million. Owing to lack of cash flow, many houses were left uncompleted by building firms. The March budget included plans to enable local authorities to purchase unsold houses. The borrowing power of the Housing Corporation, set up in 1964 to encourage voluntary housing associations to build or renovate houses or flats, was raised to £400 million. The Labour government in its first week in office in March froze rents to the end of the year.

Farm economics were dislocated by the worldwide inflation in commodity prices. The high cost of imported feedgrains threatened a collapse in beef-cattle raising when farmers started to sell young animals at knockdown prices because they could not afford to feed them.

The year produced a batch of unprecedented economic statistics. The U.K. deficit on visible trade (exports and imports) was running at over £400 million a month for most of the year, most of it being due to oil. The import bill had risen by about two-thirds since the corresponding months of 1973, while the value of exports had gone up by only one-third— a trend accentuated by the declining exchange value of sterling, with a devaluation of just over 20% against the average of main trading currencies since November 1971. The U.K. terms of trade—the ratio between import and export prices—had worsened by a quarter since 1970, which meant that the U.K. should be exporting correspondingly more to pay for the same amount of imports. In fact, the volume of both imports and exports had risen by about one-quarter since 1970. The U.K. continued to have a flagging production record, with the production index in September up only 9% from 1970. In the same month earnings were up 89% from 1970, with the annual rate of wage increases standing at 21%. Wage inflation was forecast to rise to 23% in 1975 with retail prices almost exactly keeping pace. Though the prices of materials and fuels were leveling out during the year (most

William of Orange, who defeated the Catholics in 1690, is depicted with drawn sword on a building wall in Belfast, N.Ire. Ulstermen's awareness of their past history is at least partly responsible for the presence of barbed wire in the streets today.

JONATHAN HARSCH—CAMERA PRESS/PHOTO TRENDS

at rather more than double the 1970 level), the price of manufactured goods was still increasing in the later months of the year by about 25% over a year earlier. In some sectors, particularly motor vehicles, consumer resistance set in with a consequent threat of unemployment. However, unemployment rose less than expected, to 607,700 in November (2.7%).

The economic situation caused the cancellation or curtailment of a number of high-spending projects. Plans for a third London airport, with a site designated near the mouth of the Thames at Maplin after ten years of bitter controversy, were abandoned on the grounds that existing airports could now cope until the 1990s and that noise nuisance would be reduced by quieter aircraft. The cost of the Maplin project was put at £650 million. The projected high-speed railway link from London to the Channel Tunnel was abandoned and with French agreement preliminary work on the tunnel itself was halted. Cost of the rail link, estimated in 1973 to be £130 million, had escalated to £330 million. Hawker Siddeley called off the development of its HS.146 short-haul 100-seater airliner because it became clear that the necessary financial backing by the government would not be available. The future of the Concorde supersonic airliner was in doubt when in the March budget Healey said no allowance had been made for expenditure beyond the existing program. The sums committed by Britain and France then stood at £1,070 million, with £130 million remaining to be spent by the U.K. At this time Tony Benn, the industry minister, reported that production models of Concorde would necessarily be built at a loss. Development of the Concorde to extend its range and reduce its engine noise would cost the two countries an estimated £220 million. The policy as defined by Healey in his March budget was, "we must avoid spending large sums of money and skilled manpower on projects which use high technology and are unlikely to bring an economic return."

Hopes that Britain would escape from its energy crisis and balance of payments difficulties by the development of North Sea oil were strengthened by the prospect of larger quantities of oil than forecast earlier, but were postponed by delays in development of production platforms and pipelines to bring the oil ashore. While by mid-1974 it seemed likely that production would be running at 100 million tons or more by 1980, the forecast of 25 million tons in 1975 had been cut back to 5 million tons in 1976 (a delay costing the balance of payments £750 million). But with ten proven oil fields in the British sector of the North Sea and the prospect of more discoveries, it seemed probable that Britain would be self-sufficient in oil by the 1980s. To speed up production the government decided in August to take a number of coastal sites in Scotland into public ownership for the construction of oil production platforms, at the rate of about nine a year and at a cost of about £60 million each. In a White Paper published on July 11 the government set out its proposals for taxing the profits of North Sea oil and for establishing a majority state participation in development by the oil companies through a British National Oil Corporation.

On December 9 Energy Minister Varley announced in the House of Commons measures to conserve energy: speed reductions for motorists, with most of the cost of forthcoming oil price rises to be borne by the private motorist, and restrictions on heating levels in most buildings other than living accommodations and hospitals to a maximum of 68° F (20° C). Varley

Bombing of public houses in Birmingham, Eng., in November, reportedly the work of the IRA, caused 19 deaths and 120 injuries.

said that the restrictions were no more than an interim measure.

Domestic Affairs. On March 20 Princess Anne and her husband, Capt. Mark Phillips, escaped a kidnapping attempt. A man, subsequently found to be mentally deranged, blocked the car in which they were traveling with his own, in the Mall near Buckingham Palace, and then fired shots, wounding the couple's chauffeur, their personal detective, and a policeman and a passerby before he was seized.

In April Prime Minister Wilson was questioned on land deals made by Anthony Field, brother of his personal secretary, Marcia Williams (later Lady Falkender), and the forging of his signature on a letter. The forgery was traced to a property dealer, Ronald Milhench, who was convicted, and no impropriety was found on the part of any person attached to the prime minister. At the end of April, Edward Short, leader of the Commons, was questioned about a check for £250 he had received, innocently, from T. Dan Smith, public relations officer and former leader of the Newcastle upon Tyne council. Such inquiries were raised against the background of a local government corruption case (bribery and influence) of exceptional magnitude, involving as principals an architect, John Poulson, and W. G. Pottinger, a senior Scottish civil servant, who were sentenced earlier, and T. Dan Smith and a local government officer, Andrew Cunningham, who both received severe prison sentences. The case led to the prime minister's setting up a royal commission to inquire into "the furtherance of private gain as against public duty." The House of Commons voted on May 22 that members of Parliament must register the names of outside organizations from which they received payments.

Defense. The defense budget was cut three times in 12 months. In December 1973 Conservative Chancellor Barber announced cuts of £178 million, and Healey in his budget in March made another £50 million cut. A searching review of defense commitments followed, and on December 3 Defence Minister Mason announced a long-term program that would save an estimated £4,700 million in ten years and would reduce the proportion of the gross national product (GNP) spent on defense from 5½ to 4½%. The cuts involved withdrawal from most overseas bases in Southeast Asia and the Indian Ocean and some in the Mediterranean, manpower cuts of 35,000 servicemen and 30,000 civilians, and some reductions of equipment. (*See* DEFENSE.)

Foreign Policy. The Wilson government was elected with a pledge to renegotiate the terms of British membership in the EEC. Foreign Minister Callaghan stated the British position (published as a White Paper) at a meeting of the European Council of Ministers on April 1. He said, "I stress that I do not hope for a negotiation about withdrawal. I would prefer successful negotiation from which the right terms for continued membership will emerge." This was the position emphasized on a number of occasions by Prime Minister Wilson. The main points for renegotiation concerned the common agricultural policy (seen to be unfair to the U.K. as a major food importer), the Community budget (likely to impose an unreasonably large share on the U.K.), trade with the British Commonwealth and less developed countries (thought to be unduly restrictive), European union (thought to be unrealistic), the authority of the Community (thought to be unduly restrictive on national policies), and external relations (Callaghan stressed the U.K.'s wish to maintain an effective Atlantic alliance with the U.S.). Negotiations continued throughout the year, with the Labour Party's pledge to put the terms to the test of a referendum repeated at the October election. (*See* EUROPEAN UNITY.) The Labour position sometimes seemed ambiguous because a number of Cabinet ministers were committed opponents of the European idea.

To keep a closer watch on the effect of Community legislation, Parliament set up committees of the Commons and the Lords called Select Committees on European Community Secondary Legislation.

Northern Ireland. Strife between the Roman Catholic and Protestant communities in Northern Ireland became even more murderous after the breakdown of the power-sharing formula for intercommunal government devised by a conference of British, Irish, and Northern Ireland political leaders at Sunningdale, Eng., in December 1973. The power-sharing Executive coalition headed by Brian Faulkner was brought down by the hostility of extreme Protestant·opinion which culminated in May 1974 in a general strike by Protestant trade unionists led by an Ulster Workers Council. The strike was condemned by U.K. Prime Minister Wilson as "a deliberate and calculated attempt to use every undemocratic and unparliamentary means for the purpose of bringing down the whole constitution of Northern Ireland so as to set up there a sectarian and undemocratic state." Faced with this challenge, the British government resumed direct rule from Westminster. Later in the year the situation degenerated into a vendetta feud with an exchange of random assassinations of individual Catholics and Protestants. By the end of November there had been 90 such murders during the year, and 300 since 1969. There was a decline in the number of bombings in Northern Ireland in 1974, but this form of terrorism broke out in Britain, causing 40 deaths in five incidents: 12 died when a bomb wrecked a coach traveling on the M62 motorway; one died and many tourists were seriously. injured by a bomb placed in the White Tower in the Tower of London; bombs planted in public houses killed 5 in Guildford, 2 in Woolwich, and 20 in Birmingham. The Birmingham bombings on November 21 led the British government to hurry through Parliament the Prevention of Terrorism Act giving police new powers of arrest, detention, and expulsion, ban-

ning the Irish Republican Army (IRA), and forbidding the wearing of such traditional IRA emblems as the black beret. They led also to a debate in the House of Commons on December 11 on bringing back the death penalty for terrorist murders, but the motion was defeated by 369 votes to 217. The IRA suspended its activities over the Christmas period.

(HARFORD THOMAS)

See also Ireland.
[972.A.1.a]

United Nations

In presenting his annual report on the work of the UN, Secretary-General Kurt Waldheim identified the organization's two most significant problems as the Middle East crisis and the mounting complexities and dangers of the world's economic situation. He also stressed Cyprus and southern Africa.

Middle East. In the aftermath of the 1973 Arab-Israeli war, the UN found itself deeply involved in Middle Eastern problems. From Jan. 25 to March 4, 1974, the 7,000-man UN Emergency Force (UNEF) supervised the disengagement of Egyptian and Israeli troops and took up positions in the buffer zone between them, according to arrangements worked out largely by U.S. Secretary of State Henry Kissinger. On June 5, after the parties reached agreement in Geneva, a new UN Disengagement Observer Force (UNDOF), comprising about 1,250 Austrian and Peruvian officers and men with logistical support from Canada and Poland, took up positions between Syria and Israel. In late November Waldheim visited the Middle East and secured the agreement of the allegedly reluctant Syrians to renew UNDOF until May 31, 1975.

Syria complained to the UN about the behaviour of Israeli troops before they pulled back in June, and Lebanon and Israel exchanged charges and countercharges throughout the year. On October 14 the General Assembly, which began its 29th session September 17, decided to invite representatives of the Palestine Liberation Organization (PLO) to participate in a debate on the Palestine question. The PLO thus became the first nongovernmental organization in UN history to address a plenary (as opposed to a committee) session of the assembly. Opening the debate on November 13, Yasir Arafat (*see* BIOGRAPHY), the head of the PLO, called for the establishment in Palestine of "one democratic state where Christian, Jew, and Muslim can live in justice, equality and fraternity." Such a state presumably would require the dismantling of Israel, and Israeli spokesmen replied by saying that they, unlike the UN, would never deal with PLO "murderers, assassins, and cut-throats."

The assembly, at the request of its president, Abdel-Aziz Bouteflika (*see* BIOGRAPHY) of Algeria, voted on November 14 to limit states to one major speech, thus restricting Israel, after its initial extended remarks, to brief replies to speeches by 20 Arab delegates. On November 22 the assembly acknowledged the "inalienable rights" of Palestinian refugees "to return to their homes and properties," affirmed their right to self-determination, national independence, and sovereignty "inside Palestine," and, in a second resolution, granted observer status to the PLO, now regarded as "a principal party" in establishing a durable Middle Eastern peace.

Another long-standing Middle East dispute flared up

Member States of the United Nations
Dec. 31, 1974

Afghanistan	Ecuador*	Kuwait	Saudi Arabia*
Albania	Egypt*	Laos	Senegal
Algeria	El Salvador*	Lebanon*	Sierra Leone
Argentina*	Equatorial Guinea	Lesotho	Singapore
Australia*	Ethiopia*	Liberia*	Somalia
Austria	Fiji	Libya	South Africa*
Bahamas, The	Finland	Luxembourg*	Spain
Bahrain	France*	Malagasy Rep.	Sri Lanka
Bangladesh	Gabon	Malawi	(formerly
Barbados	Gambia, The	Malaysia	Ceylon)
Belgium*	German Democratic	Maldives	Sudan
Belorussia*	Republic	Mali	Swaziland
Bhutan	Germany, Federal	Malta	Sweden
Bolivia*	Republic of	Mauritania	Syria*
Botswana	Ghana	Mauritius	Tanzania
Brazil*	Greece*	Mexico*	Thailand
Bulgaria	Grenada	Mongolia	Togo
Burma	Guatemala*	Morocco	Trinidad and
Burundi	Guinea	Nepal	Tobago
Cambodia	Guinea-Bissau	Netherlands,	Tunisia
(Khmer Rep.)	Guyana	The*	Turkey*
Cameroon	Haiti*	New Zealand*	Uganda
Canada*	Honduras*	Nicaragua*	Ukraine*
Central African	Hungary	Niger	U.S.S.R.*
Rep.	Iceland	Nigeria	United Arab
Chad	India*	Norway*	Emirates
Chile*	Indonesia	Oman	United Kingdom*
China*	Iran*	Pakistan	United States*
Colombia*	Iraq*	Panama*	Upper Volta
Congo	Ireland	Paraguay*	Uruguay*
Costa Rica*	Israel	Peru*	Venezuela*
Cuba*	Italy	Philippines*	Yemen (Aden)
Cyprus	Ivory Coast	Poland*	Yemen (San'a')
Czechoslovakia*	Jamaica	Portugal	Yugoslavia*
Dahomey	Japan	Qatar	Zaire
Denmark*	Jordan	Romania	Zambia
Dominican Rep.*	Kenya	Rwanda	

*Signatories to original Charter.

when armed clashes occurred at the Iran-Iraq border in February. Iraq brought the matter to the Security Council, which decided by consensus (February 28) to ask the secretary-general to investigate. In May Waldheim's special representative, Ambassador Luis Weckmann-Muñoz of Mexico, reported that both governments had reaffirmed a cease-fire agreement and consented to abide by the findings of a new joint border delimitation commission.

Cyprus. On July 16 Permanent Representative Zenon Rossides of Cyprus told the Security Council that a coup, led by Greek officers training and commanding the Cypriot National Guard, had deposed the Cypriot president, Archbishop Makarios. The same charges were made before the council by Makarios on July 19. Waldheim said the UN Peacekeeping Force in Cyprus (UNFICYP) was doing all it could to keep the Turkish Cypriot community calm and called for restraint, but Turkey intervened militarily on July 20. The Security Council then asked all states to stop fighting and to withdraw all military personnel not sanctioned by international agreement. The U.K., as a guarantor of the 1960 treaty on the independence of Cyprus, requested Greece and Turkey to open peace negotiations in London on July 21.

On July 30 Britain, Greece (under a new civilian government since July 23), and Turkey issued a declaration in Geneva, also demanding an immediate military standstill on the island. The declaration envisaged new duties for UNFICYP as part of an effort to consolidate the cease-fire. Waldheim asked for troop reinforcements, and Britain, Denmark, Finland, and Sweden sent 1,400 men to join the 2,300 already there.

The Geneva talks subsequently broke down, however, and Turkey launched new attacks. The Security Council issued repeated cease-fire demands (August 14-16) and urged new political negotiations (August 16). After visiting Cyprus, Greece, and Turkey from August 25-27, Waldheim told the council that all parties wanted a negotiated settlement and that UNFICYP needed a new mandate. The plight of 226,-000 persons left homeless by the fighting received

attention from the UN High Commissioner for Refugees. (*See* REFUGEES.)

On September 5 the UN held a memorial service outside its Meditation Room in tribute to 37 members of UN peacekeeping forces killed in Cyprus and the Middle East since the start of the year. The fatalities included 13 Canadians, 8 Austrians, 5 Danes, 4 Finns, 3 Peruvians, 2 from Britain, and 1 each from Indonesia and Panama. Three more Canadians in UNEF died Christmas Eve, when their vehicle collided with an Egyptian Army truck.

World Economic Situation. Food, fuel, and population problems dominated the economic and social side of UN work in 1974. In mid-May the Economic and Social Council (Ecosoc) asked states to redouble their aid for the people of sub-Saharan Africa, which was suffering from extended drought. The Food and Agriculture Organization (FAO) and the UN Sahelian Office had been coordinating international aid programs. (*See* AGRICULTURE AND FOOD SUPPLIES: *Special Report.*)

At the suggestion of Algerian Pres. Houari Boumédienne, the General Assembly met in special session, April 9–May 2, to consider problems of raw materials and development. Waldheim characterized the session as "recognition of the necessity to redress the disparities that afflict our world and the contrasts between affluence and poverty." The assembly adopted, without a vote, a Declaration on the Establishment of a New International Economic Order and a Program of Action to carry it out. The declaration enunciated 20 principles, including sovereign equality of states, embracing full authority over and the right to nationalize natural resources; full compensation for "colonialist exploitation"; the need to spur progress in less developed (especially the poorest) countries; the desirability of regulating transnational companies in the interests of host states; a fair balance between the prices of less developed countries' exports and imports; unconditional aid for less developed countries from the international community; and preferential treatment in transferring financial resources and technology to less developed countries. A 34-article charter of economic rights and privileges incorporating many of the declaration's provisions was adopted by the 29th assembly December 12.

UN delegates applauded Yasir Arafat, head of the PLO, as the General Assembly took up the Palestine question in November.

T. CHEN—UNITED NATIONS/KEYSTONE

On May 8, following up the action program, Waldheim appealed to 44 industrialized and oil-producing states to provide emergency help to poor countries affected by sharp increases in the prices of essential imports. He also opened a special account at UN headquarters for cash contributions for emergency assistance to affected states. A second appeal was issued December 29, but prospects of funding the emergency program were dimmed by U.S. and West German decisions not to participate. On December 7 the U.S. representative, John Scali, warned that the stream of resolutions being adopted over U.S. objections was eroding U.S. support for the UN.

Three major UN-sponsored conferences dealing with aspects of the world economic situation were held during the year. While the conference on the law of the sea, at Caracas, Venezuela, attempted to deal with all aspects of maritime law, fishing rights and the exploitation of other ocean resources figured prominently in the discussions. (*See* LAW: *Special Report.*) Representatives of more than 130 states attending the first UN World Population Conference in Bucharest, Rom., adopted a Plan of Action aimed at coordinating population and development trends. (*See* POPULATIONS AND AREAS: *Special Report.*)

The World Food Conference met in Rome in November against a background of unprecedented world food shortages. In his opening remarks, Secretary Kissinger asked oil-producing nations to supplement an increased U.S. contribution of food for stricken less developed countries and recommended that the conference establish new machinery to fight famine. The conference responded by dealing with long-range problems. Delegates asked the General Assembly to create a World Food Council to work through Ecosoc to coordinate a global war against hunger (the 29th assembly adopted this recommendation); called for a ten-million-ton-a-year food aid program; envisaged an international grain reserve; approved an "early warning system" for pooling information on supply and demand; conceived an agricultural development fund, supported by the oil producers; and endorsed agricultural improvement programs. (*See* AGRICULTURE AND FOOD SUPPLIES.)

Africa. Changes in Portugal in 1974 brought the UN close to objectives that had eluded it for years. The secretary-general visited Lisbon in August and received pledges from the new Portuguese government that it would cooperate fully with UN efforts to decolonize Africa. Guinea-Bissau was admitted to the UN on September 17 (together with Bangladesh and Grenada, raising UN membership to 138). When the Portuguese president, Francisco da Costa Gomes, addressed the assembly on October 17, he confirmed Portugal's intentions to speed decolonization in the Cape Verde Islands, to negotiate with the Mozambique Liberation Front and Angolan liberation movements, and to consider sanctions against Rhodesia.

In October, as in previous years, the assembly rejected the credentials of South Africa's delegation and, in a new move, asked the Security Council to review South Africa's relations with the UN because of its "constant violation" of the principles of the UN Charter and the 1948 Universal Declaration of Human Rights. On October 30 an African draft resolution recommending that the assembly expel South Africa was vetoed by France, the U.K., and the U.S. on the grounds that it would create a dangerous precedent and reduce the pressure of world opinion just when it seemed to be moving South Africa toward more liberal

policies. On November 12 the assembly voted to suspend South Africa for the rest of the session. South Africa recalled its UN ambassador and withheld its financial contribution. (RICHARD N. SWIFT)

See also Development, Economic and Social; Environment.

[552.B.2]

United States

The United States of America is a federal republic composed of 50 states, 49 of which are in North America and one of which consists of the Hawaiian Islands. Area: 3,615,122 sq.mi. (9,363,123 sq.km.), including 78,267 sq.mi. of inland water but excluding the 60,306 sq.mi. of the Great Lakes that lie within U.S. boundaries. Pop. (1974 est.): 211,909,000, including (1970) white 87.3%; Negro 11.1%. Language: English. Religion (early 1970s est.): Protestant 72 million; Roman Catholic 48 million; Jewish 5.9 million; Orthodox 3,850,000. Cap.: Washington, D.C. (pop., 1973 est., 734,000). Largest city: New York (pop., 1973 est., 7,716,600). Presidents in 1974, Richard Milhous Nixon and, from August 9, Gerald Rudolph Ford.

"My fellow Americans, our long national nightmare is over," said Gerald Ford (*see* BIOGRAPHY) in a nationally televised address after taking the oath of office as 38th president of the United States on Aug. 9, 1974. Ford was referring to the two-year-long ordeal of Watergate, the series of political scandals that crippled and finally destroyed the administration of Richard Nixon (*see* BIOGRAPHY). With Nixon's resignation from and Ford's accession to the presidency, it did indeed seem as if the country would be able to cast Watergate aside and begin to grapple with pressing economic problems.

But it was not to be. Ford's honeymoon period with Congress and the public lasted only until September 8, when he granted Nixon a full pardon for all federal crimes he "committed or may have committed or taken part in" during his term in office. Announcement of the pardon unleashed a torrent of criticism, and White House press secretary J. F. terHorst resigned in protest. Confidence in Ford was further eroded by the president's seeming inability to combat inflation, which he described as "public enemy No. 1." At the year's end, inflation and unemployment were both rising and a long recession seemed in prospect.

Nixon's Downfall. As 1974 began, Richard Nixon remained firm in his oft-proclaimed resolve to remain in office until the expiration of his term in January 1977. He used his state of the union message to Congress on January 30 to reiterate that he would not quit—but wished that the Watergate investigators would. "One year of Watergate is enough," the president said. "As you know, I have provided to the special prosecutor voluntarily a great deal of material. I believe that I have provided all the material that he needs to conclude his investigations."

But the special prosecutor, Leon Jaworski (*see* BIOGRAPHY), refused to back down. Rebutting the president's claim, Jaworski said that the White House had not turned over to him all the tapes and documents he had requested. Furthermore, the special prosecutor's office told the U.S. District Court in Washington, D.C., that it had found no evidence to indicate that former White House counsel John W. Dean III had lied in his testimony linking Nixon to the Watergate cover-up.

Trouble was also brewing for Nixon on another front. With only four members voting "nay," the U.S. House of Representatives on February 6 formally granted its Judiciary Committee power to investigate the conduct of the president with a view to determining whether grounds existed for his impeachment. "Whatever the result, we are going to be just and honorable and worthy of the public trust," pledged Judiciary Committee Chairman Peter W. Rodino, Jr. (Dem., N.J.; see BIOGRAPHY).

More bad news for the White House followed soon afterward. Seven former Nixon aides—John Mitchell, H. R. ("Bob") Haldeman, John Ehrlichman, Charles Colson, Robert Mardian, Kenneth Parkinson, and Gordon Strachan—were indicted March 1 by a federal grand jury in Washington for conspiring to hinder investigation of the incident that had triggered the whole Watergate affair, the June 17, 1972, break-in at Democratic Party headquarters in Washington's Watergate complex. In an unrelated development, the staff of the congressional Joint Committee on Internal Revenue Taxation reported on April 3 that Nixon owed $476,431, including interest, in federal taxes for 1969–72. The White House promptly announced that the Internal Revenue Service had reached substantially the same conclusion, and that Nixon would pay the full amount.

After months of such damaging disclosures, the White House was heartened by the acquittal on April 28 of Mitchell and Maurice Stans. Mitchell and Stans, who had held high positions in Nixon's 1972 reelection campaign organization, had been charged with 15 counts of conspiracy, perjury, and obstruction of justice in connection with their handling of a secret $200,000 cash contribution from fugitive financier Robert L. Vesco. Their acquittal by a U.S. District Court jury in New York was viewed by the White House as partial vindication of its protestations of noninvolvement in Watergate.

One day after Mitchell and Stans were acquitted, Nixon went on nationwide television to announce that he was turning over to the House Judiciary Committee edited transcripts of 46 tapes of discussions between himself and his advisers concerning Watergate. The yielding of the transcripts was in response to a committee subpoena on April 11 for 42 tapes of conversations. Although the committee accepted the transcripts, which were made public in a 1,308-page volume on April 30, it voted to inform Nixon that he had not complied with the subpoena. The committee continued to insist on delivery of the tapes themselves.

The edited White House transcripts were widely reprinted and analyzed in newspapers and magazines, and soon appeared in paperback book form. For the most part, reaction in Congress and among the public was highly unfavourable. Many readers expressed dismay at the disjointed and occasionally vindictive tone of the conversations between Nixon and his top aides. And the numerous excisions marked as "unintelligible" or "expletive deleted" aroused curiosity as to the nature of the missing words.

While the White House gave the appearance of cooperating with the Judiciary Committee, it remained firm in its refusal to turn over tapes and documents of 64 presidential conversations sought by Special Prosecutor Jaworski. U.S. District Court Judge John J. Sirica, acting at Jaworski's request, on April 18 ordered a subpoena issued on the White House for the requested material. When Nixon refused to comply with the subpoena, Jaworski petitioned the U.S. Supreme Court to hear the case, and it agreed to do so.

The oral arguments in the tapes case, heard by the court on July 8, turned chiefly on the doctrine of executive privilege. Nixon's lawyer, James St. Clair (see BIOGRAPHY), argued, in essence, that the president alone could determine the limits of executive privilege and decide which records would be surrendered in a criminal inquiry. Jaworski retorted that constitutional government would be in "serious jeopardy if the president—any president—is to say that the Constitution means what he says it does, and that

Pres. Richard M. Nixon bade farewell to all White House personnel in a speech on August 9, just prior to his departure for San Clemente, Calif. Gerald Ford was sworn in as his replacement two hours later before the same assemblage.

United States Senate

(Membership at the opening session of the 94th Congress in January 1975)

State	Name	Party*	Current term expires
Alabama	Sparkman, John J.	(D)	1979
	Allen, James B.	(D)	1981
Alaska	Stevens, Ted	(R)	1979
	Gravel, Mike	(D)	1981
Arizona	Fannin, Paul J.	(R)	1977
	Goldwater, Barry M.	(R)	1981
Arkansas	McClellan, John L.	(D)	1979
	Bumpers, Dale	(D)	1981
California	Cranston, Alan	(D)	1981
	Tunney, John V.	(D)	1977
Colorado	Haskell, Floyd K.	(D)	1979
	Hart, Gary W.	(D)	1981
Connecticut	Ribicoff, Abraham A.	(D)	1981
	Weicker, Lowell P., Jr.	(R)	1977
Delaware	Roth, William V., Jr.	(R)	1977
	Biden, Joseph R., Jr.	(D)	1979
Florida	Chiles, Lawton M.	(D)	1977
	Stone, Richard	(D)	1981
Georgia	Talmadge, Herman E.	(D)	1981
	Nunn, Sam	(D)	1979
Hawaii	Fong, Hiram L.	(R)	1977
	Inouye, Daniel K.	(D)	1981
Idaho	Church, Frank	(D)	1981
	McClure, James A.	(R)	1979
Illinois	Percy, Charles H.	(R)	1979
	Stevenson, Adlai E., III	(D)	1981
Indiana	Hartke, Vance	(D)	1977
	Bayh, Birch	(D)	1981
Iowa	Clark, Richard	(D)	1979
	Culver, John C.	(D)	1981
Kansas	Pearson, James B.	(R)	1979
	Dole, Robert J.	(R)	1981
Kentucky	Huddleston, Walter	(D)	1979
	Ford, Wendell H.	(D)	1981
Louisiana	Long, Russell B.	(D)	1981
	Johnston, J. Bennett, Jr.	(D)	1979
Maine	Muskie, Edmund S.	(D)	1977
	Hathaway, William D.	(D)	1979
Maryland	Mathias, Charles McC., Jr.	(R)	1981
	Beall, J. Glenn, Jr.	(R)	1977
Massachusetts	Kennedy, Edward M.	(D)	1977
	Brooke, Edward W.	(R)	1979
Michigan	Hart, Philip A.	(D)	1977
	Griffin, Robert P.	(R)	1979
Minnesota	Mondale, Walter F.	(D)	1979
	Humphrey, Hubert H.	(D)	1977
Mississippi	Eastland, James O.	(D)	1979
	Stennis, John C.	(D)	1977
Missouri	Symington, Stuart	(D)	1977
	Eagleton, Thomas F.	(D)	1981
Montana	Mansfield, Mike	(D)	1977
	Metcalf, Lee	(D)	1979
Nebraska	Hruska, Roman L.	(R)	1977
	Curtis, Carl T.	(R)	1979
Nevada	Cannon, Howard W.	(D)	1977
	Laxalt, Paul	(R)	1981
New Hampshire	McIntyre, Thomas J.	(D)	1979
	Vacancy†		
New Jersey	Case, Clifford P.	(R)	1979
	Williams, Harrison A., Jr.	(D)	1977
New Mexico	Montoya, Joseph M.	(D)	1977
	Domenici, Pete V.	(R)	1979
New York	Javits, Jacob K.	(R)	1981
	Buckley, James L.	(C-R)	1977
North Carolina	Helms, Jesse	(R)	1979
	Morgan, Robert B.	(D)	1981
North Dakota	Young, Milton R.	(R)	1981
	Burdick, Quentin N.	(D)	1977
Ohio	Taft, Robert, Jr.	(R)	1977
	Glenn, John H., Jr.	(D)	1981
Oklahoma	Bellmon, Henry L.	(R)	1981
	Bartlett, Dewey F.	(R)	1979
Oregon	Hatfield, Mark O.	(R)	1979
	Packwood, Robert W.	(R)	1981
Pennsylvania	Scott, Hugh	(R)	1977
	Schweiker, Richard S.	(R)	1981
Rhode Island	Pastore, John O.	(D)	1977
	Pell, Claiborne	(D)	1979
South Carolina	Thurmond, Strom	(R)	1979
	Hollings, Ernest F.	(D)	1981
South Dakota	McGovern, George	(D)	1981
	Abourezk, James G.	(D)	1979
Tennessee	Baker, Howard H., Jr.	(R)	1979
	Brock, William E., III	(R)	1977
Texas	Tower, John G.	(R)	1979
	Bentsen, Lloyd M.	(D)	1977
Utah	Moss, Frank E.	(D)	1977
	Garn, Jake	(R)	1981
Vermont	Stafford, Robert T.	(R)	1977
	Leahy, Patrick J.	(D)	1981
Virginia	Byrd, Harry F., Jr.	(I)	1977
	Scott, William L.	(R)	1979
Washington	Magnuson, Warren G.	(D)	1981
	Jackson, Henry M.	(D)	1977
West Virginia	Randolph, Jennings	(D)	1979
	Byrd, Robert C.	(D)	1977
Wisconsin	Proxmire, William	(D)	1977
	Nelson, Gaylord	(D)	1981
Wyoming	McGee, Gale W.	(D)	1977
	Hansen, Clifford P.	(R)	1979

*(D) Democratic, (R) Republican, (C-R) Conservative-Republican, (I) Independent.
†Election of Louis C. Wyman (R) challenged by John A. Durkin (D).

there is no one, not even the Supreme Court, to tell him otherwise." In an 8–0 decision handed down on July 24, the Supreme Court ruled that Nixon must provide "forthwith" the material sought by Jaworski. (*See* Law.) After a delay of several hours, St. Clair announced that the president would comply with the court's decision "in all respects."

The Supreme Court's decision was made public the same day that the House Judiciary Committee began nationally televised hearings on whether to recommend that the House of Representatives vote to impeach Nixon, a step that would lead to the president's trial by the Senate and possible removal from office. By the end of general debate on July 25, it was clear that the committee would recommend impeachment by a large bipartisan margin. After some behind-the-scenes redrafting, the committee approved three articles of impeachment, charging Nixon with obstruction of justice in connection with the Watergate scandal, abuse of presidential powers, and attempting to impede the impeachment process by defying committee subpoenas for evidence. The committee rejected two other proposed articles, one charging that Nixon had usurped the powers of Congress by concealing from Congress the secret bombing of Cambodia on and after March 17, 1969, and the other concerning income tax fraud and the unlawful use of government funds on his properties in California and Florida.

Events moved rapidly after the Judiciary Committee recessed on July 30. Although the White House continued to express confidence that Nixon would survive any impeachment vote, support for the president appeared to be eroding steadily in both houses of Congress. Then, on August 5, came the final bombshell. Apparently at the insistence of St. Clair, who had been unaware of their contents, Nixon made public transcripts of three of the taped conversations covered by the Supreme Court decision. They consisted of conversations he had had on June 23, 1972, with Haldeman, who was then chief of White House staff. Informed that the FBI's probe of the Watergate break-in was pointing to officials in his reelection campaign, Nixon instructed Haldeman to tell the FBI, "Don't go any further into this case, period!" While Nixon's earlier statements on the Watergate case attributed his concern over the FBI's investigations to national security problems and possible conflicts with the Central Intelligence Agency (CIA), the June 23 transcripts clearly indicated that political considerations had played a major role.

Release of the transcripts swept away virtually all remaining support for Nixon in Congress. Each of the ten Republican members of the House Judiciary Committee who had voted against all five articles of impeachment announced that he would vote for impeachment on the House floor. Numerous members of Congress urged the president to resign and thus spare the country the ordeal of impeachment and a Senate trial, the outcome of which was no longer in doubt. (*See* Special Report.)

For almost three days, Nixon wavered. Finally, on August 8, he went on nationwide television to announce that he would resign as president the following day. "In the past few days," he said, ". . . it has become evident to me that I no longer have a strong enough political base in the Congress to justify continuing" the struggle to remain in office. Nixon's last address as president was delivered to his Cabinet members and other aides in the East Room of the White House on the morning of August 9. "Always remember," he told the group, "others may hate you, but those who hate you don't win unless you hate them—and then you destroy yourself." Nixon and members of his family then boarded a helicopter on the south lawn of the White House and flew to his home in San Clemente, Calif. Vice-President Ford took the oath of office shortly thereafter.

Transition to Ford. Most Americans greeted Ford's accession to the presidency with a mixture of relief and euphoria. His informal "inaugural address" was

well received, particularly the passage in which he said: "In all my public and private acts as your president, I expect to follow my instincts of openness and candor with full confidence that honesty is always the best policy in the end." In the ensuing days and weeks, Ford was glowingly portrayed as the "great healer," a forthright, plain-spoken man ideally suited to the task of binding up the nation's Watergate wounds. Ford's nomination on August 20 of Nelson Rockefeller (see BIOGRAPHY) to serve as vice-president was widely

United States House of Representatives

(Membership at the opening session of the 94th Congress in January 1975)

State, district, name, party

Ala.—1. Edwards, Jack (R)
2. Dickinson, W. L. (R)
3. Nichols, William (D)
4. Bevill, Tom (D)
5. Jones, Robert E., Jr. (D)
6. Buchanan, John H., Jr. (R)
7. Flowers, W. W. (D)
Alaska—Young, Don (R)
Ariz.—1. Rhodes, John J. (R)
2. Udall, Morris K. (D)
3. Steiger, Sam (R)
4. Conlan, J. B. (R)
Ark.—1. Alexander, Bill (D)
2. Mills, Wilbur D. (D)
3. Hammerschmidt, J. P. (R)
4. Thornton, Ray (D)
Calif.—1. Johnson, Harold T. (D)
2. Clausen, Don H. (R)
3. Moss, John E. (D)
4. Leggett, Robert L. (D)
5. Burton, John L. (D)
6. Burton, Phillip (D)
7. Miller, George, III (D)
8. Dellums, Ronald V. (D)
9. Stark, Fortney H. (D)
10. Edwards, Don (D)
11. Ryan, Leo J. (D)
12. McCloskey, Paul N., Jr. (R)
13. Mineta, Norman Y. (D)
14. McFall, John J. (D)
15. Sisk, B. F. (D)
16. Talcott, Burt L. (R)
17. Krebs, John (D)
18. Ketchum, William M. (R)
19. Lagomarsino, Robert J. (R)
20. Goldwater, Barry M., Jr. (R)
21. Corman, James C. (D)
22. Moorhead, Carlos J. (R)
23. Rees, Thomas M. (D)
24. Waxman, Henry A. (D)
25. Roybal, Edward R. (D)
26. Rousselot, John H. (R)
27. Bell, Alphonzo (R)
28. Burke, Yvonne B. (D)
29. Hawkins, Augustus F. (D)
30. Danielson, George E. (D)
31. Wilson, Charles H. (D)
32. Anderson, Glenn M. (D)
33. Clawson, Del (R)
34. Hannaford, Mark W. (D)
35. Lloyd, Jim (D)
36. Brown, George E., Jr. (D)
37. Pettis, Jerry L. (R)
38. Patterson, Jerry M. (D)
39. Wiggins, Charles E. (R)
40. Hinshaw, Andrew J. (R)
41. Wilson, Bob (R)
42. Van Deerlin, Lionel (D)
43. Burgener, Clair W. (R)
Colo.—1. Schroeder, Patricia (D)
2. Wirth, Timothy E. (D)
3. Evans, Frank (D)
4. Johnson, J. P. (R)
5. Armstrong, W. L. (R)
Conn.—1. Cotter, William R. (D)
2. Dodd, Christopher J. (D)
3. Giaimo, Robert N. (D)
4. McKinney, Stewart B. (R)
5. Sarasin, Ronald A. (R)
6. Moffett, Anthony J. (D)
Del.—duPont, Pierre S., IV (R)
Fla.—1. Sikes, Robert L. F. (D)
2. Fuqua, Don (D)
3. Bennett, Charles E. (D)
4. Chappell, William, Jr. (D)
5. Kelly, Richard (R)
6. Young, C. William (R)
7. Gibbons, Sam (D)
8. Haley, James A. (D)
9. Frey, Louis, Jr. (R)
10. Bafalis, L. A. (R)
11. Rogers, Paul G. (D)
12. Burke, J. Herbert (R)
13. Lehman, William (D)
14. Pepper, Claude (D)
15. Fascell, Dante B. (D)
Ga.—1. Ginn, R. B. (D)

2. Mathis, Dawson (D)
3. Brinkley, Jack (D)
4. Levitas, Elliott H. (D)
5. Young, Andrew (D)
6. Flynt, J. J., Jr. (D)
7. McDonald, Lawrence P. (D)
8. Stuckey, W. S., Jr. (D)
9. Landrum, Phil M. (D)
10. Stephens, Robert G., Jr. (D)
Hawaii—1. Matsunaga, Spark M. (D)
2. Mink, Patsy (D)
Ida.—1. Symms, S. D. (R)
2. Hansen, George V. (R)
Ill.—1. Metcalfe, Ralph (D)
2. Murphy, Morgan (D)
3. Russo, Martin A. (D)
4. Derwinski, Edward J. (R)
5. Kluczynski, John C. (D)
6. Hyde, Henry J. (R)
7. Collins, Cardiss (D)
8. Rostenkowski, Dan (D)
9. Yates, Sidney R. (D)
10. Mikva, Abner J. (D)
11. Annunzio, Frank (D)
12. Crane, Philip M. (R)
13. McClory, Robert (R)
14. Erlenborn, J. N. (R)
15. Hall, Tim L. (D)
16. Anderson, John B. (R)
17. O'Brien, G. M. (R)
18. Michel, Robert H. (R)
19. Railsback, Thomas F. (R)
20. Findley, Paul (R)
21. Madigan, E. R. (R)
22. Shipley, George E. (D)
23. Price, Melvin (D)
24. Simon, Paul (D)
Ind.—1. Madden, Ray J. (D)
2. Fithian, Floyd J. (D)
3. Brademas, John (D)
4. Roush, J. Edward (D)
5. Hillis, Elwood H. (R)
6. Evans, David W. (D)
7. Myers, John (R)
8. Hayes, Philip H. (D)
9. Hamilton, L. H. (D)
10. Sharp, Philip R. (D)
11. Jacobs, Andrew, Jr. (D)
Iowa—1. Mezvinsky, E. (D)
2. Blouin, Michael T. (D)
3. Grassley, Charles E. (R)
4. Smith, Neal (D)
5. Harkin, Tom (D)
6. Bedell, Berkley (D)
Kan.—1. Sebelius, Keith G. (R)
2. Keys, Martha E. (D)
3. Winn, Larry, Jr. (R)
4. Shriver, Garner E. (R)
5. Skubitz, Joseph (R)
Ky.—1. Hubbard, Carroll, Jr. (D)
2. Natcher, William H. (D)
3. Mazzoli, Romano L. (D)
4. Snyder, Gene (R)
5. Carter, Tim L. (R)
6. Breckinridge, J. B. (D)
7. Perkins, Carl D. (D)
La.—1. Hébert, F. Edward (D)
2. Boggs, Lindy (D)
3. Treen, David C. (R)
4. Waggonner, Joe D., Jr. (D)
5. Passman, Otto E. (D)
6. Moore, W. Henson, III (R)
7. Breaux, John B. (D)
8. Long, Gillis W. (D)
Me.—1. Emery, David F. (R)
2. Cohen, W. S. (R)
Md.—1. Bauman, Robert E. (R)
2. Long, Clarence D. (D)
3. Sarbanes, Paul S. (D)
4. Holt, Marjorie S. (R)
5. Spellman, Gladys N. (D)
6. Byron, Goodloe E. (D)
7. Mitchell, Parren J. (D)
8. Gude, Gilbert (R)
Mass.—1. Conte, Silvio O. (R)
2. Boland, Edward P. (D)
3. Early, Joseph D. (D)

4. Drinan, Robert F. (D)
5. Tsongas, Paul E. (D)
6. Harrington, M. J. (D)
7. Macdonald, Torbert H. (D)
8. O'Neill, Thomas P., Jr. (D)
9. Moakley, John J. (D)
10. Heckler, Margaret (R)
11. Burke, James A. (D)
12. Studds, Gerry E. (D)
Mich.—1. Conyers, John, Jr. (D)
2. Esch, Marvin (R)
3. Brown, Garry E. (R)
4. Hutchinson, Edward (R)
5. Vander Veen, R. F. (D)
6. Carr, Bob (D)
7. Riegle, D. W., Jr. (D)
8. Traxler, Bob (D)
9. Vander Jagt, Guy (R)
10. Cederberg, Elford A. (R)
11. Ruppe, Philip (R)
12. O'Hara, James G. (D)
13. Diggs, Charles C., Jr. (D)
14. Nedzi, Lucien N. (D)
15. Ford, W. D. (D)
16. Dingell, John D. (D)
17. Brodhead, William M. (D)
18. Blanchard, James J. (D)
19. Broomfield, William S. (R)
Minn.—1. Quie, Albert H. (R)
2. Hagedorn, Tom (R)
3. Frenzel, William (R)
4. Karth, Joseph E. (D)
5. Fraser, Donald M. (D)
6. Nolan, Richard (D)
7. Bergland, Bob S. (D)
8. Oberstar, James L. (D)
Miss.—1. Whitten, Jamie L. (D)
2. Bowen, D. R. (D)
3. Montgomery, G. V. (D)
4. Cochran, Thad (R)
5. Lott, Trent (R)
Mo.—1. Clay, William (D)
2. Symington, James W. (D)
3. Sullivan, Leonor K. (D)
4. Randall, William J. (D)
5. Bolling, Richard (D)
6. Litton, Jerry (D)
7. Taylor, Gene (R)
8. Ichord, Richard H. (D)
9. Hungate, W. L. (D)
10. Burlison, Bill D. (D)
Mont.—1. Baucus, Max S. (D)
2. Melcher, John (D)
Neb.—1. Thone, Charles (R)
2. McCollister, John Y. (R)
3. Smith, Virginia (R)
Nev.—Santini, James (D)
N.H.—1. D'Amours, Norman E. (D)
2. Cleveland, James C. (R)
N.J.—1. Florio, James J. (D)
2. Hughes, William J. (D)
3. Howard, J. J. (D)
4. Thompson, Frank, Jr. (D)
5. Fenwick, Millicent (R)
6. Forsythe, Edwin B. (R)
7. Maguire, Andrew (D)
8. Roe, Robert A. (D)
9. Helstoski, Henry (D)
10. Rodino, Peter W., Jr. (D)
11. Minish, Joseph G. (D)
12. Rinaldo, M. J. (R)
13. Meyner, Helen S. (D)
14. Daniels, Dominick V. (D)
15. Patten, Edward J. (D)
N.M.—1. Lujan, Manuel, Jr. (R)
2. Runnels, Harold L. (D)
N.Y.—1. Pike, Otis G. (D)
2. Downey, Thomas J. (D)
3. Ambro, Jerome A., Jr. (D)
4. Lent, Norman F. (R)
5. Wydler, John W. (R)
6. Wolff, L. L. (D)
7. Addabbo, Joseph P. (D)
8. Rosenthal, Benjamin S. (D)
9. Delaney, James J. (D)
10. Biaggi, Mario (D)
11. Scheuer, James H. (D)

12. Chisholm, Shirley (D)
13. Solarz, Stephen J. (D)
14. Richmond, Frederick W. (D)
15. Zeferetti, Leo C. (D)
16. Holtzman, Elizabeth (D)
17. Murphy, John M. (D)
18. Koch, Edward I. (D)
19. Rangel, Charles B. (D)
20. Abzug, Bella (D)
21. Badillo, Herman (D)
22. Bingham, J. B. (D)
23. Peyser, Peter A. (R)
24. Ottinger, Richard L. (D)
25. Fish, Hamilton, Jr. (R)
26. Gilman, B. A. (R)
27. McHugh, Matthew F. (D)
28. Stratton, Samuel S. (D)
29. Pattison, Edward W. (D)
30. McEwen, Robert (R)
31. Mitchell, D. J. (R)
32. Hanley, James M. (D)
33. Walsh, W. F. (R)
34. Horton, Frank J. (R)
35. Conable, B., Jr. (R)
36. LaFalce, John J. (D)
37. Nowak, Henry J. (D)
38. Kemp, Jack F. (R)
39. Hastings, James F. (R)
N.C.—1. Jones, Walter B. (D)
2. Fountain, L. H. (D)
3. Henderson, David N. (D)
4. Andrews, Ike F. (D)
5. Neal, Stephen L. (D)
6. Preyer, L. R. (D)
7. Rose, C. G., III (D)
8. Hefner, Bill (D)
9. Martin, J. G. (R)
10. Broyhill, James T. (R)
11. Taylor, Roy A. (D)
N.D.—Andrews, Mark (R)
Ohio—1. Gradison, Willis D. (R)
2. Clancy, Donald D. (R)
3. Whalen, Charles W., Jr. (R)
4. Guyer, Tennyson (R)
5. Latta, Delbert L. (R)
6. Harsha, William H., Jr. (R)
7. Brown, Clarence J., Jr. (R)
8. Kindness, Thomas N. (R)
9. Ashley, Thomas L. (D)
10. Miller, Clarence E. (R)
11. Stanton, John W. (R)
12. Devine, Samuel L. (R)
13. Mosher, Charles A. (R)
14. Seiberling, John F., Jr. (D)
15. Wylie, Chalmers P. (R)
16. Regula, R. S. (R)
17. Ashbrook, John M. (R)
18. Hays, Wayne L. (D)
19. Carney, Charles J. (D)
20. Stanton, James V. (D)
21. Stokes, Louis (D)
22. Vanik, Charles A. (D)
23. Mottl, Ronald M. (D)
Okla.—1. Jones, James R. (D)
2. Risenhoover, Ted (D)
3. Albert, Carl (D)
4. Steed, Tom (D)
5. Jarman, John (D)
6. English, Glenn (D)
Ore.—1. AuCoin, Les (D)
2. Ullman, Al (D)
3. Duncan, Robert (D)
4. Weaver, James (D)
Penn.—1. Barrett, William A. (D)
2. Nix, Robert N. C. (D)
3. Green, William J., III (D)
4. Eilberg, Joshua (D)
5. Schulze, Richard T. (R)
6. Yatron, Gus (D)
7. Edgar, Robert W. (D)
8. Biester, E. G., Jr. (R)
9. Shuster, E. G. (R)
10. McDade, Joseph M. (R)
11. Flood, Daniel J. (D)
12. Murtha, John P. (D)
13. Coughlin, R. L. (R)
14. Moorhead, William S. (D)

15. Rooney, Fred B. (D)
16. Eshleman, Edwin D. (R)
17. Schneebeli, Herman T. (R)
18. Heinz, H. John, III (R)
19. Goodling, William F. (R)
20. Gaydos, Joseph (D)
21. Dent, John H. (D)
22. Morgan, Thomas E. (D)
23. Johnson, Albert W. (R)
24. Vigorito, J. P. (D)
25. Myers, Gary A. (R)
R.I.—1. St. Germain, Fernand (D)
2. Beard, Edward P. (D)
S.C.—1. Davis, Mendel (D)
2. Spence, Floyd D. (R)
3. Derrick, Butler C., Jr. (D)
4. Mann, James B. (D)
5. Holland, Kenneth L. (D)
6. Jenrette, John W., Jr. (D)
S.D.—1. Pressler, Larry L. (R)
2. Abdnor, James (R)
Tenn.—1. Quillen, James H. (R)
2. Duncan, John J. (R)
3. Lloyd, Marilyn (D)
4. Evins, Joseph L. (D)
5. Fulton, Richard (D)
6. Beard, R. L., Jr. (R)
7. Jones, Edward (D)
8. Ford, Harold E. (D)
Tex.—1. Patman, Wright (D)
2. Wilson, Charles (D)
3. Collins, James M. (R)
4. Roberts, Ray (D)
5. Steelman, Alan (R)
6. Teague, Olin E. (D)
7. Archer, William R. (R)
8. Eckhardt, Robert C. (D)
9. Brooks, Jack (D)
10. Pickle, J. J. (D)
11. Poage, W. R. (D)
12. Wright, James C., Jr. (D)
13. Hightower, Jack (D)
14. Young, John (D)
15. de la Garza, E. (D)
16. White, Richard C. (D)
17. Burleson, Omar (D)
18. Jordan, Barbara C. (D)
19. Mahon, George (D)
20. Gonzalez, Henry B. (D)
21. Krueger, Robert (D)
22. Casey, Robert R. (D)
23. Kazen, Abraham, Jr. (D)
24. Milford, Dale (D)
Utah—1. McKay, Koln G. (D)
2. Howe, Allan Turner (D)
Vt.—Jeffords, James M. (R)
Va.—1. Downing, Thomas N. (D)
2. Whitehurst, G. W. (R)
3. Satterfield, D. E., III (D)
4. Daniel, R. W. (R)
5. Daniel, W. C. (D)
6. Butler, M. C. (R)
7. Robinson, James K. (R)
8. Harris, Herbert E. (D)
9. Wampler, William C. (R)
10. Fisher, Joseph L. (D)
Wash.—1. Pritchard, Joel (R)
2. Meeds, Lloyd (D)
3. Bonker, Don (D)
4. McCormack, Mike (D)
5. Foley, Thomas S. (D)
6. Hicks, Floyd V. (D)
7. Adams, B. (D)
W.Va.—1. Mollohan, R. H. (D)
2. Staggers, Harley O. (D)
3. Slack, John M., Jr. (D)
4. Hechler, Ken (D)
Wis.—1. Aspin, Leslie (D)
2. Kastenmeier, Robert W. (D)
3. Baldus, Alvin J. (D)
4. Zablocki, Clement J. (D)
5. Reuss, Henry S. (D)
6. Steiger, William A. (R)
7. Obey, David R. (D)
8. Cornell, Robert J. (D)
9. Kasten, Robert W. (R)
Wyo.—Roncalio, Teno (D)

United States Executive, 1974

Position	Name	Sworn in
President	Richard M. Nixon	Jan. 20, 1969
	Gerald R. Ford*	Aug. 9, 1974
Vice-President	Gerald R. Ford*	Dec. 6, 1973
	Nelson A. Rockefeller	Dec. 19, 1974
Secretary of State	Henry A. Kissinger	Sept. 22, 1973
Secretary of the Treasury	George P. Shultz	June 12, 1972
	William E. Simon	May 8, 1974
Secretary of Defense	James R. Schlesinger	July 2, 1973
Secretary of the Army	Howard H. Callaway	May 15, 1973
Secretary of the Navy	John W. Warner	May 4, 1972
	J. William Middendorf II	June 10, 1974
Secretary of the Air Force	John L. McLucas	July 19, 1973
Attorney General	William B. Saxbe	Jan. 4, 1974
Secretary of the Interior	Rogers C. B. Morton	Jan. 29, 1971
Secretary of Agriculture	Earl L. Butz	Dec. 2, 1971
Secretary of Commerce	Frederick B. Dent	Feb. 2, 1973
Secretary of Labor	Peter J. Brennan	Feb. 2, 1973
Secretary of Health, Education, and Welfare	Caspar W. Weinberger	Feb. 12, 1973
Secretary of Housing and Urban Development	James T. Lynn	Feb. 2, 1973
Secretary of Transportation	Claude S. Brinegar	Feb. 2, 1973

*Succeeded to the presidency.

United States Supreme Court

Title and name	Appointed
Chief Justice of the United States	
Warren E. Burger	1969
Associate Justices	
William O. Douglas	1939
William J. Brennan, Jr.	1956
Potter Stewart	1958
Byron R. White	1962
Thurgood Marshall	1967
Harry A. Blackmun	1970
Lewis F. Powell, Jr.	1972
William H. Rehnquist	1972

acclaimed. Several commentators said that the new president had chosen the best-qualified man available.

Ford's surprise announcement that he was pardoning Nixon for all federal crimes he may have committed as president brought an abrupt end to the period of good feeling that had begun with Nixon's resignation. Characterizing the Nixon family's ordeal as "an American tragedy," Ford said, "It can go on and on, or someone must write 'The End' to it. I have concluded that only I can do that. And if I can, I must." Nixon issued a statement accepting the pardon and expressing regret that he had been "wrong in not acting more decisively and more forthrightly in dealing with Watergate." The White House also announced September 8 that the Ford administration had concluded an agreement with Nixon giving him title to his presidential papers and tape recordings but guaranteeing that they would be kept intact and available for court use for at least three years.

News of the pardon and the agreement on Nixon's papers and tapes brought forth expressions of shock and outrage. Many persons believed that it was a miscarriage of justice to allow Nixon to escape possible criminal prosecution while some of his former aides were in prison for Watergate-related crimes and others were under indictment for similar offenses. The pardon was also characterized as an insult to the painstaking work of the House Judiciary Committee in preparing the articles of impeachment. In some quarters, it was contrasted unfavourably with Ford's offer, made shortly after he took office, of limited clemency for Vietnam draft evaders and deserters. Some went so far as to speculate that the pardon was part of a "deal" made by Ford and Nixon prior to the latter's resignation.

Although the furor eventually subsided, Ford's standing with the public and in the press appeared to have suffered lasting damage. The president's judgment on subsequent matters was called into question time and again. If he was criticized for acting impulsively and without consultation on the pardon, he was also faulted for excessive caution in restaffing the White House and the Cabinet with people of his choosing. His relations with Congress deteriorated as he vetoed 18 bills in his first five months in office; 4 of the vetoes were overridden. And he came under fire for campaigning extensively for Republican congressional candidates instead of concentrating on economic problems in Washington.

The president's economic policies came in for particular criticism. After conducting a televised economic "summit conference" at the White House, Ford

continued on page 719

UNITED STATES

Education. (1973–74) Primary, pupils 35,100,-000, teachers 1,246,000; secondary and vocational, pupils 15,510,000, teachers 1,069,000; higher (including teacher training colleges), students 8,370,000, teaching staff 620,000.

Finance. Monetary unit: U.S. dollar, with (Sept. 16, 1974) a free rate of U.S. $2.31 to £1 sterling. Gold, SDRs, and foreign exchange, official: (June 1974) $13,940,000,000; (June 1973) $13,830,000,000. Federal budget (1974–75 est.): revenue $295 billion; expenditure $304.5 billion. Gross national product: (1973) $1,289,100,000,-000; (1972) $1,155,200,000,000. Money supply: (May 1974) $260.2 billion; (May 1973) $245.6 billion. Cost of living (1970 = 100): (June 1974) 126; (June 1973) 114.

Foreign Trade. (1973) Imports $73,199,000,-000; exports (excluding military aid of $516 million) $70,798,000,000. Import sources: Canada 25%; Japan 14%; West Germany 8%; U.K. 5%. Export destinations: Canada 21%; Japan 12%; West Germany 5%; U.K. 5%. Main exports: machinery 24%; cereals 12% (wheat 6%); motor vehicles 9%; chemicals 8%; aircraft 6%. Tourism (1973): visitors 14.8 million; gross receipts U.S. $3,968,000,000.

Transport and Communications. Roads (1972) 3,786,713 mi. (including 36,021 mi. highways). Motor vehicles in use (1973): passenger 101,237,000; commercial (including buses) 23,-201,000. Railways (1973): 218,024 mi.; traffic (class I only) 9,298,000,000 passenger-mi., freight 846,800,000,000 short ton-mi. Air traffic (1973): 161,957,000,000 passenger-mi. (including internal services 126,317,000,000 passenger-mi.); freight 4,370,000,000 short ton-mi. (including internal services 2,454,000,000 short ton-mi.). Inland waterways freight traffic (1972) 338,-693,000,000 short ton-mi. (including 108,939,-000,000 short ton-mi. on Great Lakes system and 158,453,000,000 short ton-mi. on Mississippi River system). Shipping (1973): merchant vessels 100 gross tons and over 4,063; gross tonnage 14,912,432. Ships entered (including Great Lakes international traffic; 1972) vessels totaling 218,-716,000 net registered tons; goods loaded (1973) 273,493,000 short tons, unloaded 457,771,000 short tons. Telephones (Jan. 1973) 131,606,000. Radio receivers (Dec. 1972) 354 million. Television receivers (Dec. 1972) 99 million.

Agriculture. Production (in 000; metric tons; 1973; 1972 in parentheses): corn 143,344 (141,-568); wheat 46,567 (42,045); oats 9,636 (10,-044); barley 9,244 (9,221); rye 671 (741); rice 4,210 (3,875); sorghum 23,790 (20,556); soybeans 42,634 (34,581); dry beans 740 (817); dry peas c. 104 (122); peanuts 1,564 (1,485); potatoes 13,545 (13,429); sweet potatoes 561 (565); onions c. 1,301 (1,263); tomatoes c. 6,472 (6,151); sugar, raw value c. 5,400 (5,828); apples 2,747 (2,644); pears 657 (554); oranges 9,026 (7,689); grapefruit 2,414 (2,380); lemons 788 (615); wine c. 1,460 (c. 1,080); raisins 195 (95); sunflower seed c. 300 (c. 287); linseed 418 (353); tobacco 802 (793); cotton, lint 2,822 (2,983); butter 418 (500); cheese 2,063 (2,043); eggs 3,927 (4,123); beef and veal 9,813 (10,266); pork 5,784 (6,183); softwood timber (cu.m.; 1972) 272,300, (1971) 254,000; hardwood timber (cu.m.; 1972) 83,400, (1971) 80,300; fish catch (1972) 2,650, (1971) 2,793. Livestock (in 000; Jan. 1973): cattle 121,990; sheep 17,724; pigs 61,502; horses c. 8,000; chickens 412,000.

Industry. Index of production (1970 =100): (1973) 118, (1972) 108; mining (1973) 101, (1972) 99; manufacturing (1973) 119, (1972) 108; electricity, gas, and water (1973) 119, (1972) 112; construction (1973) 115, (1972) 115. Unemployment: (1973) 5%; (1972) 5.6%. Fuel and power (in metric tons; 1973): coal 523,104; lignite 13,363; crude oil 453,174; natural gas (cu.m.) 643,260,000; manufactured gas (cu.m.) 27,639,000; electricity (kw-hr.; 1972) 1,853,390,000. Production (in 000; metric tons; 1973): iron ore (55–60% metal content) 88,800; pig iron 91,811; crude steel 136,462; cement (shipments) 74,167; newsprint 3,098; petroleum products 573,779; sulfuric acid 28,652; caustic soda 9,689; fertilizers (nutrient content; 1972–73) nitrogenous 8,472, phosphate 5,640, potash 2,432; plastics and resins (1972) 8,894; synthetic rubber 2,623; passenger cars (units) 9,657; commercial vehicles (units) 2,980. Merchant vessels launched (100 gross tons and over; 1973) 869,000 gross tons. New dwelling units started (1973) 2,058,000.

IMPEACHMENT OF A PRESIDENT

By Bruce L. Felknor

On Aug. 9, 1974, Richard M. Nixon resigned as president of the United States of America. He alone, among the 36 men to have held the presidency, was driven from that high office by Art. II, Sec. 4 of the U.S. Constitution.

The fact that Nixon resigned before the full House of Representatives could act on the three articles of impeachment recommended by its Judiciary Committee in no way alters the fact that it was the process that forced him out. The House would have impeached him by an overwhelming margin and he realized this even before new evidence revealed that he had deceived his own defense counsel and chief defenders about his involvement in Watergate. After those revelations, conviction by the necessary two-thirds majority of the Senate shifted from likelihood to virtual certainty. But before those last steps—formal impeachment by the whole House, the public spectacle of a trial before Senate and nation, and the degradation of conviction—the president chose what in effect was a plea of nolo contendere, no contest, and resigned. In this step, too, he was the first.

Resignation has resolved earlier impeachment cases, however. Thirteen times the House has voted articles of impeachment against various federal officers. These have led to six acquittals, four convictions, two resignations, and one expulsion. The expulsion involved a member of the Senate in 1797.

Origins and Meaning. Impeachment found its way into law in England in the 14th century, where it was used intermittently until 1806. In 1787 it was built into the U.S. Constitution. Its purpose was to make possible the punishment of a guilty president (or other federal official), whose lesser accomplices would be brought to justice in ordinary courts of law. At the same time, the process would allow for acquittal if the accused were adjudged guilty by less than the overwhelming margin of 2–1. Benjamin Franklin reminded the Constitutional Convention that prior to the adoption of impeachment, whenever a first magistrate was brought to justice, "recourse was had to assassination in which he was not only deprived of his life but of the opportunity of vindicating his character." James Madison saw the need to defend the community "against the incapacity, negligence or perfidy of the chief magistrate." The convention agreed by a vote of 8–2 that the executive be removable on impeachment, with only Massachusetts and South Carolina dissenting.

The idea of impeachment for incapacity was omitted from the final drafts of the Constitution, and incapacity itself is really only dealt with there in the 25th Amendment, ratified in 1967. It was under this amendment that Nixon named Gerald Ford to succeed the disgraced Spiro Agnew when he was forced to resign as vice-president in 1973, but it also provides for orderly succession if a president is gravely ill or otherwise incapable of discharging his responsibilities.

The roots of the word impeachment are in the Latin *impedi-*

Bruce L. Felknor is a board member and former executive director of the Fair Campaign Practices Committee. The author of Dirty Politics (1966), *numerous articles on political ethics and campaign tactics, he has devoted much thought to the significance of the entire Watergate affair and its place in U.S. history.*

care, "to fetter," and not in the Latin *peccare*, "to sin." It comes to English through a Middle French word meaning "hinder." Thus its connotation is closer to "impede" than to "peccable" or "peccadillo." To the founders of the Constitution, it meant both punishment and suspension or displacement, "degradation from office," in Gouverneur Morris' term.

Article II, Section 4: The President, Vice President and all civil Officers of the United States, shall be removed from Office on Impeachment for, and Conviction of, Treason, Bribery, or other high Crimes and Misdemeanors.

The meanings of treason and bribery are clear enough; what then are "high crimes and misdemeanors?" One constitutional lawyer has said that a collection of unanswered traffic tickets would amount to "high misdemeanors" if the U.S. Senate said it did. When Gerald Ford was serving in the House of Representatives, he led a pious and vain effort to impeach Supreme Court Justice William O. Douglas for allowing some of his writings to be published in a magazine Ford considered pornographic. At that time he declared that "An impeachable offense is whatever a majority of the House of Representatives considers it to be at a given moment in history."

The Johnson-Nixon Comparison. "Strict constructionists"—notably the defenders of presidents fighting impeachment—argue that high crimes and misdemeanours must be indictable offenses—explicit violations of law. This was the case with Nixon's defenders as it had been with those of Pres. Andrew Johnson 106 years before. The 11 articles of impeachment against Johnson attempted to identify specific acts as high crimes (two) and misdemeanours (nine), each article ending with some such stipulation as "did then and there commit and was guilty of a high misdemeanor in office." Although the argument about what constituted high crimes and misdemeanours raged across the country as well as in Congress, no consensus ever developed.

Some of Nixon's last-ditch defenders have argued that the Congress with its top-heavy Democratic majority was nothing but a lynch mob, determined to drive him from office at all costs. A review of the history of the 40th Congress, which impeached Johnson and barely acquitted him, is instructive in this respect.

Most historians have romanticized the role of Andrew Johnson as victim, with the radical Republicans in the House as villains. The fact is incontrovertible, however, that the Republicans enjoyed massive dominance in the Congress that impeached and tried Andrew Johnson. The 17th president was a Tennessee Democrat who was elected vice-president under the Republican Lincoln in 1864, and who served all but the first six weeks of Lincoln's second term. All seats in both houses of Congress apportioned to the 11 Confederate states were vacant during the Civil War, and when the Johnson impeachment came to issue before the 40th Congress in 1867 and 1868, only Tennessee had been readmitted to the Union. Thus in the House, 51 normally Democratic votes were vacant seats, as were 20 in the Senate. Thus the Republicans had a "veto-proof Congress," with 74% of the votes in the House and 78% in the Senate. By contrast, in the 93rd Congress, which forced Richard Nixon to resign, Democrats controlled the House with only 57% and the Senate with 58%, margins that are trifling by comparison.

There are a few parallels between the two cases, separated by slightly more than a century in time. Although Lincoln and Johnson had won the 1864 election with 55% of the popular vote, the Tennessee Democrat did not inherit even the modest popularity that the murdered Lincoln had gained. From the start his relations with Congress had been difficult and his foot-dragging and outright interference in the Reconstruction course set by Congress made him enemies by the dozen.

Nixon, who had gained reelection with a historic landslide, was nevertheless personally unpopular, the beneficiary in 1972 of a massive resistance to his opponent rather than a personal or political endorsement for himself. The arrogance of his principal aides reduced his congressional defenders.

In the case of Johnson, his sympathetic support for Southern leaders so recently rebels became increasingly apparent. This, and his manifest distaste for the radical Republicans' program of enfranchising and otherwise aiding Southern blacks, moved the press to step up editorial demands that he be impeached. The roster of newspapers thus assailing Johnson included many that had previously supported him, such as the *Chicago Tribune*.

In the Nixon impeachment, as the president's innocence of ordering or leading the cover-up of Watergate and related excesses became more and more problematical, public support dwindled fast. First, there was damaging testimony before the Senate Watergate committee, then incriminating tape transcripts, and finally the evidence presented to the House Judiciary Committee. The totality of all available information painted a dismaying picture of complicity and deceit. As this happened the moderate and conservative press that had held out hope for his exoneration deserted him and began demanding his impeachment —again including, as 106 years earlier, the *Chicago Tribune*.

Although the party alignment against Nixon was much less heavily weighted than the hostile imbalance that faced Johnson, the GOP ranks of the 40th Congress were split much more deeply than the split existing between Southern and Northern Democrats on which some of Nixon's supporters sought to rely. The radical Republicans in the Congress of 1867–68 were counterbalanced almost evenly on key Reconstruction issues by their conservative Republican fellows. Then, as in 1974, economic and other problems impinged on the impeachment question: a severe post-Civil War recession and sharp controversy over monetary policy.

However, the actions for which Johnson was impeached had been not only public but flamboyant. The Congress had legislated its program for reconstructing Southern society, giving the blacks meaningful freedom, and uniting a country shattered by civil war; the president had impeded, delayed, and countermanded. Congress enfranchised blacks and sent Union troops to oversee their voting; the president named Southern politicians as governors and changed military orders; he fired Republican postmasters and named Democrats in their stead, and threatened more of the same in order to garner local support for his programs. The Congress legislated the Tenure of Office Act, requiring Senate approval for the dismissal of any presidential appointee who had to be confirmed by the Senate. It later became apparent that the act was unconstitutional, but Johnson both observed it and scorned it, striking no consistent pattern. Finally he fired his secretary of war, an act of defiance provoking the ultimate collision.

In the Nixon case all the transgressions had been secret. The president's men had engaged in a host of unlawful actions to ensure what was already certain: that he be elected not narrowly but by a landslide. They had, in effect, set aside the operation of the Constitution and laws as they related to adversaries of the president—whether political campaign opponents, or just detractors, or even suspected traitors against whom the law seemed to find no effective sanctions. The original actions on behalf of the president had been covert; then they had been disguised and covered up; finally it became apparent that the cover-up, clearly involving obstruction of justice and a variety of illegal actions, had been participated in, and even led, by the president of the United States.

Here was the difference: secret abuse of the law by Nixon and his men, flagrant rejection of the law by Johnson. Libertarians among the Republican conservatives of 1868 hesitated to join the vengeful radical throng, and although most senators voted "guilty" against Johnson, he was spared because one man, Edmund Ross of Kansas, voted with the Democrats.

The same kind of legislators—libertarians among 1974 Republicans—were first stunned, then outraged, by the abuse of civil liberties on behalf of a Republican president, who then urged on a conspiracy to cover its own tracks. Republicans gamely insisted on his innocence, and then, as they realized they had been deceived, decided to vote to impeach.

Defenders of Nixon who continued to see him as innocent, as conspired against and traduced by the press, argued that the House Judiciary Committee had been weighted against the president, and that the whole excursion had really been a hanging party. But by comparison with the only other presidential impeachment, the 1974 "Affaire Nixon" was a very model of comportment, of discreet conduct and determination to be fair. A scant handful of Democrats on the Judiciary panel—notably Jerome Waldie of California, Robert Drinan of Massachusetts, and Elizabeth Holtzman of New York, and occasionally Charles Rangel of New York and John Conyers of Michigan—revealed constant animus and fiery rhetorical flights against the iniquity of the president. Most Democrats, however, seemed subdued and uncheered by the prospects.

In the Johnson impeachment, bias was evident everywhere. In the House the radical Republicans who had successfully pressed for impeachment were exultant in their declarations. One saw the Johnson administration as "an illustration of the depth to which political and official perfidy can descend." Such florid proclamations embarrassed the conservative Republicans, one of whom wrote to his wife, "They are determined to ruin the Republican party." Like others, he was much dismayed by Andrew Johnson who, he wrote, "*does* continue to do the most provoking things. If he isn't impeached it won't be his fault."

When Johnson's trial actually took place in the Senate it was presided over, by constitutional mandate, by the chief justice of the United States, Salmon P. Chase—who had let it be known to one leading Democrat that if Andrew Johnson were denied the Democratic presidential nomination later in 1868, he would be willing to accept it.

Under the succession laws then in force, an impeached Johnson would be succeeded, there being no vice-president, by the president pro tempore of the Senate, Benjamin F. Wade—who sat in the Senate during the trial and voted for impeachment. He came within one vote of becoming president himself. The prospect was not lost on conservative Republicans who mistrusted him; more than one observed that but for Wade's obnoxious character Johnson would have been convicted. Sen. David T. Patterson of Tennessee, Johnson's son-in-law, also took part in the trial—and voted for acquittal. Senator Ross—who has been immortalized as the courageous Kansan who cast the crucial vote against conviction—was a conservative Republican who shortly thereafter switched his alignment to Democratic.

Portent for the Future. If the Johnson impeachment left no precedents to be emulated in future exercises of that awesome responsibility, it did leave some horrible examples of conduct the future might shun. And these were indeed shunned during the Nixon impeachment proceedings. In 1974 lamentations were heard among the more partisan Democrats and other antagonists of the former president, that he had been allowed to resign and had thus escaped the actual mill of impeachment. This line of reasoning argues that he was not suitably punished. The hue and cry escalated again when Gerald Ford subsequently granted Nixon a full and complete pardon for any crimes he may have committed during his tenure in office. "Suitable punishment," of course, is a subjective judgment. It is not difficult to imagine that the disgrace of being forced from the presidency of the United States was, of itself, harsh and sufficient punishment on a man who long looked wistfully toward the history books. Consideration must also be given the U.S. Constitution's concern for protecting the republic from the miscreant and his coadjutors, which the founders put coequal with punishment. Again, that concern is met equally well by forced resignation.

As for justice, "Shall any man be above Justice?" George Mason of Virginia asked his fellows in the Constitutional Convention in 1787. "Shall the man who has practised corruption & by that means procured his appointment in the first instance be suffered to escape punishment, by repeating his guilt?" The impeachment process answers "No" quite convincingly, and it should serve to warn future holders of the presidency that impeachment is not some relic of the past or historical curiosity but, rather, a part of the U.S. Constitution—one that still works.

continued from page 716

presented his anti-inflation program to a joint session of Congress on October 8. His economic package contained few mandatory features, relying instead on appeals for the "total mobilization" of persons motivated by "self-discipline" and exhibiting "voluntary restraint." It also called for creation of a board to develop a national energy policy, a cut in foreign oil imports by one million barrels a day, a 5% surtax on families earning more than $15,000 a year and on corporations, and measures to help the depressed housing industry.

The president's package met a cool reception in Congress, but by year's end its fate appeared to have become academic. Technically, the country had been in recession since early spring, and in late fall the decline threatened to become precipitous. Unemployment, fed by massive layoffs in the hard-hit automobile industry, reached 7% in December, leading both economists and politicians to identify recession, rather than inflation, as the most immediate economic problem. It was widely believed that the president would present to the new Congress measures designed to stimulate the economy, probably including a tax cut. At the same time, high oil prices continued to threaten the balance of payments. The president had consistently rejected recommendations for higher gas taxes to discourage consumption, but some combination of tariffs and excise taxes on crude oil was said to be under consideration.

Ford's nomination of Rockefeller to be vice-president encountered unexpected difficulty in Congress, centring largely on the question of whether the former New York governor had improperly used his great wealth to further his political career. The nomination was finally confirmed in late December, and Rockefeller was sworn in December 19. In other high-level administrative changes, Roy Ash resigned as director of the powerful Office of Management and Budget, and the president named James T. Lynn, secretary of housing and urban development, as his successor; Secretary of Transportation Claude S. Brinegar resigned, effective early in 1975; and Attorney General William Saxbe was named ambassador to India.

Watergate Trial. Far from being laid to rest by Ford's pardon of Nixon, Watergate entered the public consciousness again when the trial of five of the seven former Nixon aides indicted March 1 opened October 1 in U.S. District Court in Washington, D.C. (Colson had pleaded guilty to obstruction of justice and Strachan had been separated from the trial.) Although he was not physically present, Nixon soon emerged as a central figure as tapes of conversations between him and his aides were introduced as evidence and played in the courtroom.

One of the defendants, Ehrlichman, insisted that Nixon's testimony was vital to his defense. Nixon, however, was hospitalized in Long Beach, Calif., on September 23, suffering from phlebitis of his left leg, an ailment that had bothered him when he visited the Soviet Union and the Middle East during the summer. Nixon's physician reported that a blood clot had been found in the former president's right lung but that the prognosis was for "a very good chance of recovery." Readmitted to the hospital on October 23 because of complications in his phlebitis condition, Nixon went into life-endangering medical shock after surgery on October 29 and remained in critical condition for some time. A team of three court-appointed physi-

U.S. Representative Wilbur D. Mills (Dem., Ark.), powerful chairman of the House Ways and Means Committee, appeared in a Boston burlesque theatre with performer Fanne Foxe. Following an incident in Washington, D.C., in which the two were in a vehicle stopped by the police, Mills's trip to Boston led to his resignation from the chairmanship of the committee under pressure in December.

cians who examined him concluded that appearing as a witness would endanger his health; Judge Sirica subsequently ruled that his testimony was not essential and that the trial should proceed without him.

The jury's verdict was delivered New Year's Day. Parkinson, a marginal figure, was acquitted, but the other four defendants were found guilty on all counts. It was expected that the verdicts would be appealed. Earlier, in another trial, Ehrlichman had been found guilty in connection with the burglary of a psychiatrist's office by White House investigative personnel attempting to find damaging material about Vietnam war dissident Daniel Ellsberg.

Election Results. As expected, Watergate and the twin spectres of inflation and recession played important roles in the November elections, which saw the Democrats score impressive gains at all levels of government. The Democrats gained 43 seats in the House, for a total of 291; 3 seats in the Senate, for a total of 61; and 4 additional governorships, for a total of 36. The 94th Congress was expected to be considerably more liberal than the 93rd, not only because of the Democratic gains but because of a leftward shift within the Republican delegations. Most of the defeated Republican incumbents were conservatives.

The elections propelled a number of Democrats into positions of prominence within their party. Chief among them were Edmund G. Brown, Jr., the governor-elect of California, and Hugh Carey, the governor-elect of New York. Ella Grasso of Connecticut became the first woman to win a governorship without having succeeded her husband in the office. The Democrats newly elected to the Senate included Gary Hart (Colo.), manager of Sen. George McGovern's presidential campaign in 1972; Dale Bumpers, the governor of Arkansas; and John Glenn (Ohio), the first U.S. astronaut to orbit the earth. The turnover in the House was especially heavy, with 92 new representatives elected and 40 incumbents defeated. The Republican losers included four members of the House Judiciary Committee who had voted against all five articles of impeachment against Nixon.

Democratic successes in the elections contributed

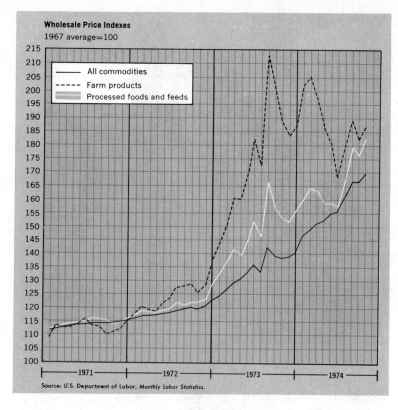

Wholesale Price Indexes
1967 average=100

— All commodities
‑ ‑ Farm products
▒ Processed foods and feeds

1971 1972 1973 1974

Source: U.S. Department of Labor, Monthly Labor Statistics.

to the atmosphere of cordiality that permeated the party's charter conference in Kansas City, Mo., in early December. Regulars and "new forces," who had torn the party apart in 1972, composed their differences and adopted the first major party charter in U.S. history. On the troublesome question of minority representation, it was agreed that "affirmative action" would be taken to involve minority groups but mandatory quotas for national convention delegations were banned.

Pres. Gerald Ford's amnesty program for draft evaders and deserters attracted this group of men seeking a second chance at Camp Atterbury, Indiana, in November.

Congressional Action. Although Congress failed to complete action on a number of key bills, including tax reform, national health insurance, and a consumer protection agency, it did approve several important pieces of legislation in 1974. A campaign financing law

WIDE WORLD

was enacted in response to concern over the campaign-spending violations that came to light during the Watergate scandal. The new law set limits on candidate contributions and expenditures, provided public financing for presidential races, and created a commission to enforce the law. Another Watergate legacy, the new mood of congressional assertiveness, was reflected in a bill establishing new procedures for congressional involvement in federal budget-making and providing for the release of congressionally appropriated funds impounded by the president.

In other action, Congress authorized $11.8 billion for mass-transit programs in the fiscal years 1975–80. For the first time, federal funds (almost $4 billion) would be used to help pay for the daily operating expenses of transit systems. To ensure that private pension funds would contain enough money to pay out benefits, Congress passed legislation setting forth minimum funding standards and established a federally operated insurance corporation to guarantee payment of benefits in the event of a bankruptcy. One of the most controversial measures signed into law in 1974 was a bill establishing an independent corporation to provide legal services for the poor.

Legislation to give the president broad authority to negotiate to reduce trade barriers, approved in late 1973 by the House but bottled up throughout the year in the Senate, was passed in late December. (*See* COMMERCIAL AND TRADE POLICIES.) Action on the bill had been delayed by a controversy over whether most-favoured-nation treatment should be extended to the U.S.S.R. while it restricted emigration of dissidents, especially Jews wishing to go to Israel. In October Sen. Henry Jackson (Dem., Wash.) announced that the Soviets had agreed to permit more Jews to leave, but this was denied in a later Soviet statement. As passed, the bill provided for trade concessions to Communist countries not restricting emigration.

Meeting early in December, the Democrats in the House of Representatives, including those newly elected, voted several major changes in the way the House conducts its business. In a move to undercut the seniority system, the chairman of a major committee was barred from serving at the same time as chairman of another major committee. The power of the speaker of the House was increased by allowing him to nominate Democrats to the Rules Committee. Also, the Ways and Means Committee was stripped of its power to fill Democratic vacancies on other committees, a move probably influenced by the personal difficulties encountered late in the year by longtime Ways and Means chairman Wilbur Mills.

Economic problems seemed likely to preoccupy the 94th Congress when it convened in January. Several committee chairmen announced plans to investigate allegations, made late in the year by the *New York Times,* that the CIA had illegally conducted clandestine activities within the U.S.

Foreign Affairs. Both President Nixon and President Ford engaged in an unusual amount of high-level diplomacy in 1974. In one of the most ambitious foreign trips ever undertaken by a U.S. president, Nixon visited five Middle Eastern countries and the Soviet Union in June and July. The Middle Eastern portion of the trip began two weeks after Secretary of State Henry Kissinger (*see* BIOGRAPHY) had persuaded Israel and Syria to sign an agreement providing for a cease-fire, a separation of their forces on the Golan Heights, and the exchange of prisoners captured in the October 1973 war. For its part, the U.S. agreed to conduct aerial reconnaissance to assure implementation of the agreement and to support Israeli retaliation for any Palestinian commando attacks.

Because of the agreement, Nixon received a hero's welcome in the Middle East. At the end of a three-day stay in Egypt, his first stop, he and Egyptian Pres. Anwar as-Sadat signed an agreement under which the U.S. would sell nuclear reactors and fuel to Egypt. Other parts of the agreement outlined general principles of bilateral relations and stressed cooperation to achieve a peaceful resolution of the Arab-Israeli dispute. From Egypt, Nixon proceeded to Saudi Arabia, Syria, Israel, and Jordan. This portion of the president's journey was highlighted by a joint announcement in Damascus of resumption of U.S.-Syrian diplomatic relations and by Nixon's pledge in Jerusalem of long-term military and economic aid to Israel and the promise to that country of nuclear technology for peaceful purposes.

Returning to the United States for a week, Nixon then flew to the Soviet Union for talks with Soviet Communist Party General Secretary Leonid I. Brezhnev. The two leaders signed a number of limited documents on nuclear relations July 3, the last day of Nixon's visit, but none constituted the hoped-for breakthrough toward permanent agreements on limiting offensive nuclear weapons.

Ford embarked on his first overseas trip as president when he traveled to Japan on November 18. He thus became the first U.S. president to visit that country. Although Ford's visit did not result in any substantive agreements, Kissinger said that it had achieved "the optimum of what one had hoped for"—a display of friendship and candid discussion that could pave the way for more definitive accords in the future.

After a brief stopover in Seoul, where he met with South Korean Pres. Park Chung Hee, Ford flew to Vladivostok to confer with Brezhnev. The U.S. and Soviet leaders reached tentative agreement to limit the numbers of all offensive strategic nuclear weapons and delivery systems through 1985. (*See* DEFENSE.)

In mid-December Ford journeyed to the French island of Martinique for talks with French Pres. Valéry Giscard d'Estaing. The joint communiqué indicated an improvement in relations between the two countries, especially with regard to cooperation on energy matters. (RICHARD L. WORSNOP)

Developments in the States. Ethics and energy were at centre stage among events in the 50 states during 1974, both stemming from apparent failure of leadership in Washington. As inflation and unemployment moved upward nationwide, states responded with economy in budget-making and the second consecutive year of level tax rates. Concern for quality of life in the various states was reflected in a continued strong push for new land use regulation legislation and environmental protection bills.

Regular legislative sessions were held in 43 states during 1974, and special sessions in 8. In addition, state legislative elections were completed in 44 states, and referenda on a wide variety of questions were held in 32 states.

Finance. For the second straight year, most state legislatures were successful in holding the line or even reducing taxes. Nonetheless, state budgets continued to grow as business expansion and inflation caused a 15% boost in general revenue from state income, sales, and other taxes. In addition, the infusion of revenue-sharing funds from the federal government, plus income from higher taxes imposed in the 1969–72

period, helped relieve pressure on state treasuries. A survey by the Tax Foundation revealed that 14 states initiated statutory tax reductions totaling about $685 million annually, while 9 other states passed $335 million in tax hikes during the year. As in 1973, legislators enacted a variety of measures aimed at equalizing assessment burdens and reducing the impact on persons hard hit by inflation.

Ethics. Reacting to general disillusionment with government generated by the Watergate scandal, state legislatures passed an unprecedented number of ethics, disclosure, open meeting, and campaign finance bills in 1974. The new laws had in common an overwhelming trend toward increasing the information available to citizens about public officials.

Many campaign finance reforms were mandated, usually requiring disclosure of contributors and limiting amounts that could legally be collected and spent. By the end of 1974, at least eight states had provided for partial public financing of elections, and seven of these permitted taxpayers to contribute to political campaigns through a checkoff system on their state income tax returns. In New Jersey, which did not have a state income tax, the state treasurer was authorized to give two dollars to gubernatorial candidates for every dollar over $40,000 raised privately.

Laws requiring candidates or officeholders to disclose personal finances and potential conflicts of interest were passed by 14 states. State employees in Michigan were brought under an ethics code. New Jersey ordered financial disclosure for lobbyists.

Energy. Responding to a perceived lack of leadership from Washington, state governments moved on

The letters "WIN" on the football behind which Pres. Gerald Ford was seated at a dinner in Cleveland, O., in October represent "Whip Inflation Now." The slogan was promoted by Ford in an earlier address on the state of the economy and the acronym appeared on buttons and other decorations during the latter part of the year.

WIDE WORLD

In honour of the 200th anniversary of the first U.S. Congress, governors and delegates from the 13 original states convened in Carpenters Hall, Philadelphia, on September 5.

several levels to deal with the energy crisis that confronted the nation during late 1973 and early 1974. An odd-even gas plan, allowing motorists to purchase fuel only on alternate days depending on their license numbers, was first proposed by Oregon Gov. Tom McCall; later, 24 other states adopted the proposal as a gas conservation and distribution aid. Attorneys general from 30 states banded together to furnish aid to the federal government in pressing an antitrust suit against major oil companies. The officials noted that individual suits by the states would largely duplicate the federal effort and would be exceedingly costly. Indeed, each of the law enforcement officers promised to donate resources, especially legal and clerical help, to the Federal Trade Commission for pursuit of a 1973 lawsuit against eight major oil firms.

Among moves to seek alternative sources of energy, Tennessee appropriated $10 million to study conversion of solid wastes into fuel, and Colorado and Idaho passed new laws outlining development of geothermal resources. New Mexico became the first state to lease land for geothermal energy exploration.

(DAVID CAMERON BECKWITH)

See also Defense; Race Relations.

[973.A]

ENCYCLOPÆDIA BRITANNICA FILMS. *Heritage in Black* (1969); *The Pacific West* (1969); *The Rise of Labor* (1969); *The South: Roots of the Urban Crisis* (1969); *Chicano from the Southwest* (1970); *The Industrial Worker* (1970); *Linda and Billy Ray from Appalachia* (1970); *The Mississippi System—Waterway of Commerce* (1970); *The Presidency—Search for a Candidate* (1970); *The Rise of Big Business* (1970); *The Rise of the American City* (1970); *The Great Lakes* (1971); *Jesse from Mississippi* (1971); *Johnny from Fort Apache* (1971); *The Progressive Era* (1971); *Valley Forge* (1971); *The Shot Heard Round the World* (1972); *Yorktown* (1972); *The Boston Tea Party* (1972); *An Essay on War* (1973); *United States Supreme Court: Guardian of the Constitution* (2nd ed., 1973); *United States Congress: Of, By and For the People* (2nd ed., 1973); *President of the United States: Too Much Power?* (1973).

Upper Volta

A republic of West Africa, Upper Volta is bordered by Mali, Niger, Dahomey, Togo, Ghana, and Ivory Coast. Area: 105,870 sq.mi. (274,200 sq.km.). Pop. (1973 est.): 5,737,000. Cap. and largest city: Ouagadougou (pop., 1970 est., 110,000). Language: French

UPPER VOLTA

Education. (1970–71) Primary, pupils 105,706, teachers (including preprimary) 2,389; secondary, pupils 3,010, teachers 474; vocational, pupils 1,577, teachers 139; teacher training, students 337; higher, students 183, teaching staff 30.

Finance. Monetary unit: CFA franc, with (Sept. 16, 1974) a parity of CFA Fr. 50 to the French franc (free rate of CFA Fr. 240.50 = U.S. $1; CFA Fr. 556.50 = £1 sterling). Budget (1973 est.): revenue CFA Fr. 11,726,000,000; expenditure CFA Fr. 9,525,-000,000.

Foreign Trade. (1972) Imports CFA Fr. 15,310,-000,000; exports CFA Fr. 5,140,000,000. Import sources: France 46%; Ivory Coast 17%; West Germany 5%. Export destinations: Ivory Coast 46%; France 19%; Italy 7%; Ghana 5%; Mali 5%. Main exports: livestock 41%; cotton 20%; peanuts 7%; sesame seed 5%.

(official). Religion: animist; Muslim and Christian minorities. President in 1974, Gen. Sangoulé Lamizana; premiers, Gérard Kango Ouedraogo and, from February 8, General Lamizana.

Upper Volta continued to be one of the countries hard hit by the drought in the Sahel region. (*See* AGRICULTURE AND FOOD SUPPLIES: *Special Report.*) Tuareg refugees from the drought-stricken regions complained of the treatment they were receiving from Mali, Niger, and Upper Volta, which they alleged wished to use the drought to exterminate them. The famine resulting from the drought was stated by the Red Cross to be worse in 1974 than in 1973. In May the International Development Association approved a $2.5 million credit to Upper Volta as a country affected by the drought.

President Lamizana, backed by the Army, dismissed Premier Ouedraogo, suspended the constitution, and dissolved the National Assembly on Feb. 8, 1974. He asserted that political factionalism had produced a critical impasse in parliamentary life and corruption in the administration and that, because of the drought, the country's situation was catastrophic. In his new Cabinet Lamizana became premier and minister of justice; nine army officers and four civilians occupied the other posts. In May Lamizana suppressed the existing political parties in favour of a one-party state under a party of his own creation, the Mouvement pour le Renouveau (Movement for Renewal). Freedom of the press and of trade unionism was guaranteed, he said, and new political and administrative structures would be developed locally.

UN Secretary-General Kurt Waldheim (third from right) observes procedures at a food distribution point in northern Upper Volta.

THOMAS A. JOHNSON—THE NEW YORK TIMES

On December 17 tension arose between Upper Volta and Mali as a result of border skirmishes, for which each country blamed the other. A joint Mali–Upper Volta commission had already met amicably on September 4 to discuss the disputed frontier area of Ouladan, a dispute still unsettled after 13 years (the area, having permanent water, is vital to nomads in the dry season).

The European Development Fund in February approved a loan of CFA Fr. 90 million for asphalting a 58-km. (37½ mi.) stretch of road from Nianguédi to the Togolese border, and in May approved CFA Fr. 900 million to build a technical school in Ouagadougou. In September France offered CFA Fr. 786.5 million to subsidize drought relief and the construction and establishment of Ouagadougou University. On July 31 an agreement was signed with a Japanese company to exploit the Tambao manganese deposits jointly.   (R. M. GOODWIN)

[978.E.4.a.i]

Uruguay

A republic of South America, Uruguay is on the Atlantic Ocean and is bounded by Brazil and Argentina. Area: 68,536 sq.mi. (177,508 sq.km.). Pop. (1973 est.): 2,992,000, including white 89%; mestizo 10%. Cap. and largest city: Montevideo (pop., 1972 est., 1,459,200). Language: Spanish. Religion: mainly Roman Catholic. President in 1974, Juan María Bordaberry.

The progressive militarization of the government, which had begun in earnest in June 1973 when President Bordaberry dissolved Congress and began to rule by decree, proceeded apace in 1974. In fact, Uruguay's long tradition of democracy had been doomed since the Army's original show of strength in February 1973 and the subsequent establishment of the National Security Council. The process somewhat resembled a military coup in slow motion, with the president remaining in office while other civilian members of the government were gradually removed by the military. In December 1973 the new situation had been ratified by the establishment of a 25-member Council of State with the task of legitimizing the actions of the executive branch. This allowed a start to be made on implementation of the policy proposals put forward by the president and his military advisers at their conference the previous August. Rumours that Bordaberry himself would be removed on the anniversary of the Army's *pronunciamiento* of February 1973 proved unfounded. He remained in office, partly by skillful political maneuvers of his own and partly, perhaps, because the military was content with its already substantial stake in the leadership and saw in Bordaberry a potential scapegoat should its policies fail.

During the year the military extended its control from a mere handful of functions, such as transport, communications, and police, to most of the country's major institutions. As part of a series of changes in the governmental structure, Bordaberry reinforced the Central Planning and Budget Office with the participation of military advisers. He also created an Economic and Social Council, comprised of the joint chiefs of staff, among others, which would advise the government. Indeed, the decree establishing the coun-cil referred to the armed forces as forming part of the executive branch of government. At the end of July military officers were put in charge of the major state-owned enterprises, including the power and fuel monopolies and the Central Bank. The process seemed to be nearly complete when, in September, President Bordaberry replied to a petition signed by the country's most prominent civilian political leaders, many of them former colleagues, calling for the restoration of Congress and of civil and political liberties. Flanked by leaders of the armed forces, Bordaberry announced in an address to the nation that a return to parliamentary government was no longer possible and that a new constitution was in preparation.

In keeping with the emphasis placed on private enterprise at the 1973 policy conference, a law was passed permitting foreign investments in all sectors of the economy provided they were in the national interest. Government authorization was required in certain strategic industries, but the conditions were generally regarded as liberal. However, they seemed unlikely to stimulate investment. Foreign confidence was at a low ebb, and the law was known to be unpopular with certain hard-liners among the military.

The external economic position in 1973 showed a considerable improvement over previous years. Export earnings rose 62% to $319.2 million, largely as a result of higher world prices for traditional exports, especially wool. A somewhat lower growth rate for imports resulted in a trade surplus of $24.2 million, as against $10.2 million in 1972.

URUGUAY

Education. (1971) Primary, pupils 366,756, teachers 13,435; secondary, pupils 138,422, teachers 8,154; vocational, pupils 35,856, teachers 2,910; teacher training, students 8,347, teachers 341; higher (1968), students 18,650, teaching staff 2,201.

Finance. Monetary unit: peso, with (Sept. 16, 1974) a commercial rate of 1,310 pesos to U.S. $1 (3,025 pesos = £1 sterling). Gold, SDRs, and foreign exchange, official: (May 1974) U.S. $208 million; (May 1973) U.S. $208 million. Budget (1973 actual): revenue 370,160,000,000 pesos; expenditure 406.4 billion pesos. Gross domestic product: (1972) 1,230,300,000 pesos; (1971) 735.7 billion pesos. Money supply: (June 1972) 154,674,000,000 pesos; (June 1971) 104,531,000,000 pesos. Cost of living (Montevideo: 1970 = 100): (Dec. 1973) 513; (Dec. 1972) 290.

Foreign Trade. (1973) Imports U.S. $284.8 million; exports U.S. $321.5 million. Import sources: Brazil 19%; Argentina 15%; U.S. 10%; West Germany 8%; Kuwait 7%; U.K. 6%. Export destinations: West Germany 13%; France 12%; Spain 11%; U.K. 7%; Italy 7%; The Netherlands 6%; Brazil 5%. Main exports: meat 40%; wool 30%; hides and skins 8%.

Transport and Communications. Roads (1973) 49,634 km. Motor vehicles in use (1973): passenger 220,000; commercial (including buses) 80,000. Railways (1972) 2,976 km. Air traffic (1972): 27,320,000 passenger-km.; freight 147,000 net ton-km. Shipping (1973): merchant vessels 100 gross tons and over 38; gross tonnage 142,664. Telephones (Dec. 1972) 241,000. Radio receivers (Dec. 1972) 1.8 million. Television receivers (Dec. 1972) 300,000.

Agriculture. Production (in 000; metric tons; 1973; 1972 in parentheses): wheat c. 400 (187); oats c. 59 (59); corn 229 (141); potatoes (1972) 106, (1971) 150; sweet potatoes (1972) c. 72, (1971) c. 74; rice (1972) 128, (1971) 122; sorghum 225 (57); linseed 29 (43); sunflower seed 91 (60); sugar, raw value (1972) 85, (1971) c. 67; oranges (1972) c. 62, (1971) c. 60; wine (1972) c. 90, (1971) c. 85; wool 33 (32); beef and veal (1972) c. 287, (1971) c. 281. Livestock (in 000; May 1973): sheep 15,902; pigs c. 470; cattle (1972) 9,309; horses c. 410; chickens (1972) c. 6,500.

Industry. Production (in 000; metric tons; 1972): cement 460; crude steel 13; petroleum products 1,560; electricity (excluding most industrial production; kw-hr.; 1971) 2,289,000.

The domestic economy fared less well, however. The real growth rate in 1973 amounted to only about 1%, making the 4% envisaged in the development plan for 1974 seem more than a little optimistic. Inflation, which had been reduced from 94.7% in 1972 to 77.5% in 1973, nevertheless remained a serious problem. Moreover, the restrictive stance adopted by traditional importers of Uruguayan beef and the skyrocketing price of oil supplies were expected to administer a severe setback to the country's external economic position.　(ANNE PARSONS) [974.F.2]

Vatican City State

This independent sovereignty is surrounded by but not part of Rome. As a state with territorial limits, it is properly distinguished from the Holy See, which constitutes the worldwide administrative and legislative body for the Roman Catholic Church. The area of Vatican City is 108.7 ac. (44 ha.). Pop. (1973): 722. As sovereign pontiff, Paul VI is the chief of state. Vatican City is administered by a pontifical commission of five cardinals, of which the secretary of state, Jean Cardinal Villot, is president.

The fourth Synod of Bishops in October examined problems of evangelical work in the contemporary world. It provided an opportunity for the African, Asian, and Latin-American bishops to claim closer identification with local usages and customs for their churches, while respecting unity with Rome. Pope Paul, in a closing speech, stated his opposition to any divergence in theology.

In foreign relations, the Holy See appointed a nuncio to Havana, Cuba, in place of a chargé d'affaires; ambassadors from the new Chilean regime and later from Portugal's new regime were accepted. A start toward diplomatic relations with Poland was made with the appointment of officials responsible for church affairs to that country's embassy in Italy. (*See* POLAND.) Meanwhile, a Czechoslovak delegation visited Rome to discuss relations with the Vatican. The dialogue with Spain to work out a concordat to replace that of 1953 continued. The Spanish foreign minister, Pedro Cortina Mauri, discussed the matter in July at the Vatican with his counterpart, Msgr. Agostino Casaroli. In February the pope received an official visit from Pres. Luis Echeverría Alvarez of Mexico.

Bloodshed in Ireland and the Middle East gave the

Pope Paul VI celebrates mass in the Sistine Chapel in September with 80 bishops from the U.S. who had convened in Rome for a month of prayer and study.

pope concern, as he showed in a speech to the cardinals on his June feast day. Shortly afterward, on the occasion of the 25th anniversary of the establishment of the pontifical commission for aid to Palestine, Paul VI gave his support to the "legitimate aspirations" of Palestinian refugees. Sergio Cardinal Pignedoli, president of the Secretariat for Non-Christians, visited King Faisal of Saudi Arabia in June, and the pope welcomed a delegation of Saudi Arabian ulamas (Muslim theologians) during the autumn. At almost the same time, the pope set up two commissions, one for relations with Jews and the other for relations with Islam. U.S. Secretary of State Henry Kissinger visited the pope in July and again in November.

The pope's health caused some concern in the spring and again in July, when papal audiences were suspended. In September, however, he was able to travel more than 60 mi. from Rome by helicopter to Aquino, to celebrate the seventh centenary of St. Thomas Aquinas, and in October he took part in all the sessions of the synod. On Christmas Eve the pope inaugurated the 1975 Holy Year by opening a door to St. Peter's Basilica, walled up since the last Holy Year in 1950.　(MAX BERGERRE)

See also Religion.

Venezuela

A republic of northern South America, Venezuela is bounded by Colombia, Brazil, Guyana, and the Caribbean Sea. Area: 352,144 sq.mi. (912,050 sq.km.). Pop. (1973 est.): 11,519,600, including mestizo 69%; white 20%; Negro 9%; Indian 2%. Cap. and largest city: Caracas (pop., 1973 est., 1,987,800). Language: Spanish. Religion: predominantly Roman Catholic. Presidents in 1974, Rafael Caldera and, from March 12, Carlos Andrés Pérez.

In the presidential and congressional elections, held Dec. 9, 1973, Carlos Andrés Pérez (*see* BIOGRAPHY) of the opposition Acción Democrática (AD) received 49% of the vote, as against 37% for his main opponent, Lorenzo Fernández of the ruling Comité de Organización Política Electoral Independiente (COPEI). AD also elected 29 senators and 102 deputies, as compared with 14 senators and 64 deputies for COPEI, thus assuring AD of a majority government after the minority term of the outgoing COPEI. Pérez was duly installed as president on March 12, 1974.

Foremost among the advantages of the new administration were the huge sums being received as oil income, averaging $800 million a month and giving AD the funds to finance its many plans. The underlying concern in drafting the government's policy was that social problems could become so severe that an ineffective democratic government would simply be overwhelmed and fall victim to a populist regime. Thus, the government undertook to expand the economic and social content of the political framework to include "the large part of Venezuelans who live under conditions of extreme poverty."

Ten days after being sworn into office, Pérez launched his attack on inflation, decreeing a 90-day freeze at mid-January price levels for basic consumer goods and services. At the same time, he expanded jobs and raised health standards by requiring that all establishments serving the public should have full-time restroom attendants. A similar decree, issued April 28, ordered employment of elevator operators for all public buildings, again on the theory of improving services while creating new jobs for unskilled workers. On May 1 President Pérez asked Congress for extraordinary powers to issue economic and financial measures, including across-the-board wage and salary increases, state takeover of the iron-ore and petroleum industries, and increased taxation on the latter sector. Following the announcement, Pérez ordered a 90-day freeze on dismissals when labour unions claimed that workers were being laid off in large numbers.

However, if allowed to circulate in the economy, oil income represented potential disaster for any anti-inflationary action by the government. The government, therefore, decided that 50% of oil revenue would be put into a fund and used for the development of industry and agriculture at home and for investment abroad in safe foreign securities and in other Latin-American nations until solid projects became available for local investment. Furthermore, Venezuela committed itself to a $500 million fiduciary fund in the Inter-American Development Bank, $540 million to the International Monetary Fund's oil relief fund, a $60 million loan for the Andean Development Corporation, and $35 million for the Caribbean Development Bank.

VENEZUELA
Education. (1971–72) Primary (including preprimary), pupils 1,918,655, teachers 54,387; secondary and vocational, pupils 564,167, teachers 15,665; teacher training (1970–71), students 17,429, teachers 1,199; higher (including 8 universities), students 99,745, teaching staff 9,105.
Finance. Monetary unit: bolívar, with (Sept. 16, 1974) an official selling rate of 4.30 bolivares to U.S. $1 (free rate of 9.83 bolivares = £1 sterling). Gold, SDRs, and foreign exchange, central bank: (June 1974) U.S. $4,474,000,000; (June 1973) U.S. $1,731,-000,000. Budget (1973 actual): revenue 13,517,000,-000 bolivares; expenditure 13,423,000,000 bolivares. Gross national product: (1972) 57,660,000,000 bolivares; (1971) 51,680,000,000 bolivares. Money supply: (Feb. 1974) 11,991,000,000 bolivares; (Feb. 1973) 9,364,000,000 bolivares. Cost of living (Caracas; 1970 = 100): (June 1974) 116; (June 1973) 110.
Foreign Trade. (1972) Imports 10,717,000,000 bolivares; exports 16,340,000,000 bolivares. Import sources: U.S. 39%; West Germany 9%; Japan 8%; Italy 5%; U.K. 5%. Export destinations: U.S. 25%; Netherlands Antilles c. 18%; Canada 10%. Main exports crude oil and petroleum products 93%.
Transport and Communications. Roads (1972) 44,278 km. (including 586 km. expressways). Motor vehicles in use (1971): passenger 778,600; commercial 256,100. Railways (1970): 470 km.; traffic 36 million passenger-km., freight 13 million net ton-km. Air traffic (1973): 1,740,000,000 passenger-km.; freight 77.1 million net ton-km. Shipping (1973): merchant vessels 100 gross tons and over 137; gross tonnage 478,643. Telephones (Dec. 1972) 474,000. Radio receivers (Dec. 1972) 2 million. Television receivers (Dec. 1972) 980,000.
Agriculture. Production (in 000; metric tons; 1973; 1972 in parentheses): corn c. 700 (c. 567); rice c. 250 (226); sesame c. 74 (59); yams (1972) c. 97, (1971) 99; potatoes (1972) c. 118, (1971) 115; cassava (1972) c. 320, (1971) 323; sugar, raw value c. 523 (c. 528); dry beans c. 60 (c. 58); tomatoes c. 72 (c. 72); cocoa c. 19 (17); bananas (1972) c. 988, (1971) 989; oranges (1972) c. 192, (1971) 192; coffee c. 69 (40); tobacco c. 12 (13); cotton, lint c. 18 (20); beef and veal (1972) c. 195, (1971) c. 193. Livestock (in 000; 1972–73): cattle c. 8,780; pigs c. 1,591; sheep 99; horses (1971–72) 432; asses c. 520; poultry (1971–72) 20,295.
Industry. Production (in 000; metric tons; 1973): crude oil 176,331; natural gas (cu.m.; 1972) 9,468,-000; petroleum products (1972) 57,968; iron ore (64% metal content) 22,154; cement (1971) 2,508; gold (troy oz.; 1972) 20; diamonds (metric carats; 1972) 456; electricity (kw-hr.; 1972) 14,656,000.

The government was ambitious to adjust the distribution both of income and to some extent of economic power, thereby transforming the structure of the economy and substituting "a society of producers in place of a society of consumers," to quote the new president's phrase. To help achieve these aims, the Central Bank was to be nationalized. Two major mining enterprises, subsidiaries of U.S. Steel and Bethlehem Steel, were also to be nationalized as of Jan. 1, 1975. In a related move, Venezuela sponsored an Organization of Iron Exporting Countries to embrace Australia, Brazil, Canada, Liberia, Sweden, and India. In addition, the Andean Group's Decision No. 24 (see LATIN-AMERICAN AFFAIRS) was adopted; this measure reserved electric power generation, radio and television broadcasting, Spanish language publication, local transport, advertising, and department stores to ownership by Venezuelan nationals. The foreign enterprises that currently predominated in those sectors were required to sell 80% of their capital within three years. It also seemed likely that the production side of foreign oil operations would be bought out in 1975, though not their international marketing role.

All these takeovers, however, were dwarfed by the scale of oil revenues—the republic's official reserves rose from $2,420,000,000 in December 1973 to $4,718,000,000 by August 1974. The National Development Fund, under the administration of Carlos Guillermo Rangel, received its first endowment of $1.9 billion in August, and this was increased to $3 billion in October; within a year the fund would total $7.5 billion, even though average oil production would fall to three million barrels daily in 1975.

Early signs indicated that high priority was to be given to "downstream investments," capitalizing on Venezuela's new state-owned extractive industries. A tanker fleet was to be built; seven 60,000-ton tankers would be bought at a cost of $200 million by mid-1975. Over the following decade, the state-owned tanker company would build up its fleet to 21–25 tankers, capable of transporting about half the nation's planned output of oil. Similarly, the state steel corporation planned to expand output to 5 million tons from 1.2 million tons through investment of $1.4 billion. Hydroelectric and petrochemical projects were to receive massive investments from the National Development Fund. For the internal economy, funds were set up to encourage investment in agriculture, construction, and industry. Incentives for the establishment of industry in the interior were provided and further development of the Caracas area was banned.

On December 29 Venezuela and Cuba signed an agreement to renew diplomatic relations, broken since 1961. (MICHAEL WOOLLER)

[974.C.1]

Veterinary Science

A major achievement in animal disease control was recorded in May 1974 when Texas became the 50th state in the U.S. to be declared free of hog cholera (swine fever). The event marked the culmination of a 12-year comprehensive state-federal eradication program. A reservoir of the highly contagious virus had been present in many states for more than a century, and a basic step in eradication was reversal of the established concept that vaccination is essential for prevention of the disease. Even with wide-scale vaccination, about 5,000 herds had been affected annually

U.S.S.R.:
see Union of Soviet Socialist Republics

Utilities, Public:
see Cooperatives; Energy; Industrial Production and Technology; Transportation

before the program began, with death losses exceeding 50% in some areas. It was estimated that since 1900 the disease had cost hog producers in excess of $3 billion, or more than 30 times the total cost of the 12-year eradication program.

Swine vesicular disease (SVD) continued to appear in Great Britain, following the first outbreak in 1973, and the cost of the control-by-slaughter program in 1974 was estimated at about £2 million. Doubts concerning the program's effectiveness led some animal health officials to consider vaccination. Since SVD cannot be distinguished clinically from foot-and-mouth disease (FMD) in swine, and there is no cross-immunity, control of one would be complicated by vaccination for the other. Vaccination for FMD was practiced in numerous European countries, where the disease had been a major problem for many years, but control in Britain (as in the U.S.) had always been by slaughter. An outbreak in Brittany during early 1974 was the worst France had experienced for 30 years.

Reports appeared in the popular media suggesting an association between feline leukemia and leukemia in humans. The stories were based largely on the earlier demonstration that feline leukemia virus (FeLV) would multiply in cultures of human tissue cells and on reports that FeLV had been found in a high proportion of cats in households where human cases of leukemia had been diagnosed. One report appearing in the *American Journal of Public Health* in 1972 indicated the presence of FeLV in leukemic persons, but subsequent investigations failed to confirm any association with the disease in cats.

In some areas veterinarians reported a large increase in the number of cases of leukemia and related diseases in cats during the past few years, but this could be attributed in part to greater awareness of the disease and to the recent development of a fluorescent antibody (FA) test for the virus. The FA test could detect FeLV in many healthy cats, and it was inevitable that some FA-positive animals would be found in households where leukemic persons lived. This put many veterinarians in the uncomfortable position of weighing a recommendation to have such cats destroyed, for public health reasons, against the obvious reluctance of owners to do so.

Brutus, a 179-lb. Siberian tiger, sleeps peacefully prior to surgery for cataracts in both eyes at the University of Illinois Eye and Ear Infirmary. A new operative procedure requiring only one tiny incision per eye was used, but Brutus will need eyedrops each day for some time.

This giraffe at the Windsor Safari Park, Berkshire, Eng., suffers from arthritis, for which acupuncture has been prescribed. Needles are electrically activated by the attending veterinarian.

According to a 1974 editorial in the *New England Journal of Medicine*, despite the widespread prevalence of the virus in cats, "there is yet no definitive evidence for linking cats with human cancer." This confirmed the earlier conclusions reached by a panel of veterinary experts and gave support to the more rational recommendation that cats with clinical signs of leukemia (which would soon die anyway) be humanely destroyed and that FA-positive but healthy animals be examined at intervals.

A National Conference on the Ecology of the Surplus Dog and Cat Problem was convened in Chicago in May. Its recommendations, for better control of unwanted animals and wider application of various birth-control methods, affirmed those proposed by veterinary associations and animal control agencies during the preceding decade. By late 1974 the Los Angeles municipal spay and neuter clinics, instituted in 1971, had been credited with having effected a substantial reduction in the number of unwanted animals in the Los Angeles area.

In 1973 the long-established use of diethylstilbestrol (DES) for promoting growth of beef cattle had been banned by the U.S. Food and Drug Administration because of the presumed risk of cancer from hormone residues in meat from such animals. No human case had ever been reported as being due to this cause, however, and in 1974 the ban was lifted pending further investigation. Meanwhile, the usefulness of various nonestrogenic feed additives and implants was being studied.

The outlook for relieving the shortage of veterinarians in the U.S. within a few years was considerably improved by the planned opening of schools in Louisiana (1974) and Florida (1975) and announcements of the funding of new schools in Tennessee, Virginia, Mississippi, and New England. Several existing schools also planned to increase their enrollments.   (J. F. SMITHCORS)

[353.C]

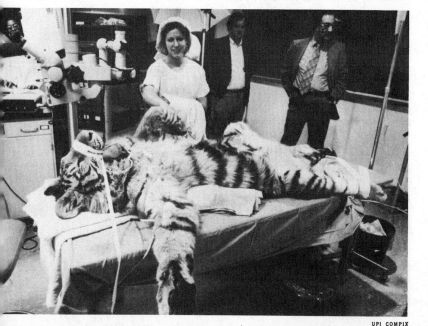

UPI COMPIX

Vietnam

A country comprising the easternmost part of the Indochinese Peninsula, Vietnam was divided de facto into two republics in July 1954.

Republic of Vietnam (South Vietnam). This is bordered by North Vietnam (along the 17th parallel), the South China Sea, Cambodia, and Laos. Area: 67,293 sq.mi. (174,289 sq.km.). Pop. (1974 est.): 19,582,100. Cap. and largest city: Saigon (metro. area pop., 1973 est., 3,805,-900). Language: Vietnamese. Religion: Buddhist; pagan; Confucian; Christian. President in 1974, Nguyen Van Thieu; premier, Tran Thien Khiem. The Provisional Revolutionary Government claimed legitimacy as one of two administrations pending resolution of the country's political future through elections.

Unexpectedly intense political strife throughout 1974 added to the vexing problems of South Vietnam, which was tottering between war and peace. President Thieu seemed firmly entrenched in power at the beginning of the year. His opposition was scattered and uncoordinated. In January the overwhelmingly pro-Thieu National Assembly approved a constitutional amendment permitting the president to run for a third term in 1975 and extending the term of office from four to five years.

Thieu was, however, mindful of growing agitation over widespread self-enrichment by government personnel. As he noted in a January 23 speech, "The first step to cleansing society will be to clean the administration, the Army's ranks, the cadres, the policy, from top to bottom."

The corruption issue provided the rallying point for diverse anti-Thieu groups during subsequent months, but the overall condition of the country also made the Thieu regime susceptible to antigovernment pressures. South Vietnam was faced with crushing inflation while at the same time contending with Communist military actions within its borders. A drastically reduced supply of U.S. military and economic aid contributed to the government's inability to cope with the burdens of restoring social, economic, and military stability.

Corruption charges against Thieu himself, not those under him in the government and the military, grew to the point where the presidential palace was under unprecedented political attack. Misuse of power, it was alleged, resulted in great financial gains for Thieu and members of his immediate family.

Thieu responded to the campaign against him by charging that only "Communists and people working for the Communists" were agitating for his removal. He denied corruption charges in a nationwide address on October 1. He was, nonetheless, conciliatory, offering to liberalize restrictive press laws and to root out corruption. In a dramatic gesture, he offered to resign "if the entire people and Army no longer have confidence in me."

Thieu's opponents were quick to reject the president's offers of liberalization and promises of reform. Repressive police measures to block antigovernment demonstrations in Saigon, Danang, and Hue seemed to cement the opposition into a common front. Suicides by fire and church-led demonstrations that became violent reminded many of the instability that had preceded the overthrow of Pres. Ngo Dinh Diem in 1963.

During October, Thieu attempted to neutralize some of the opposition by removing four members of the Cabinet (including his cousin, Hoang Duc Nha, who as minister of information was widely detested for his arrogant treatment of dissidents), dismissing 377 army officers on charges of corruption, and ousting three of the country's four military region commanders. There was, however, no indication that the opposition would be mollified by these actions, as they sensed that Thieu had possibly become expendable to his once-ardent supporters in the Army and to politicians who might hope to preserve their own positions by surviving a complete overhaul of the government. There were some who believed that Thieu could survive only by assuming complete dictatorial powers or by reducing himself to a figurehead.

To a great extent, Thieu was hurt by his inability to obtain U.S. aid. While the U.S. administration had requested $750 million in economic and $1.6 billion in military assistance for South Vietnam, a Congress wary of Southeast Asian involvements pared the requests to $400 million and $700 million. This affected South Vietnam's ability to meet inflationary problems and to respond to Communist military moves.

Military initiatives by Communist forces in the spring produced a series of defensive withdrawals by government troops and paved the way for more disruptive attacks in July. Bolstered by Soviet-built

The heavy toll of war continues in South Vietnam. A child who lost his leg in earlier action is witness to new air strikes against Viet Cong positions in the distance.

WIDE WORLD

tanks, Communist forces penetrated to within 16 mi. of Saigon itself. The midyear Communist thrusts raised government casualty figures to levels almost identical with those suffered at the height of the war in the late 1960s and early 1970s. According to the government, an average of 1,313 of its troops were killed each month. Intensified Communist attacks began in December; by year's end six district capitals had fallen into Communist hands, and the provincial capital of Phuoc Binh in Phuoc Long Province was under attack.

It was clear the four-nation International Commission of Control and Supervision was unable to enforce a peace of any kind. Hobbled by restraints growing out of required unanimity of action and purpose, the Indonesian, Iranian, Hungarian, and Polish force played no role in effecting compliance with the cease-fire agreement from either side.

A long-standing dispute between South Vietnam and China appeared to have been resolved by force in January when Chinese military forces occupied the Paracel (or Hsisha) Islands. The archipelago in the South China Sea is about 200 mi. from both China and Vietnam, and claims to it antedated the current regimes in both countries. Three outposts had been established on the Paracels by the South Vietnamese. They were quickly overrun by Peking's units after China declared it had "indisputable" rights over the

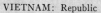

A Vietnamese woman weeps amid the ruins of her former home near the village of Bien Hoa, northeast of Saigon.

Paracels and other islands along its eastern shores.

It was believed that the dispute over the Paracels reached the level of action because of possible offshore oil and gas deposits in the region. During 1974 two exploratory wells, 190 mi. and 214 mi. S of Vung Tau, gave promise of significant petroleum and natural gas development.

South Vietnam was in need of an economic boost if it was to escape further deterioration. Although money earmarked for defense was reduced from 64 to 56% of total budget expenditures, net costs were adversely affected by inflationary pressures that showed no signs of abating. For the average South Vietnamese, who suffered a 65% climb in prices during 1973, the prospect for 1974 was inflationary growth exceeding 100%. Unemployment, at the same time, had soared, reaching 50% levels in some areas.

Democratic Republic of Vietnam (North Vietnam). This is bordered by China, the Gulf of Tonkin, the South China Sea, South Vietnam, and Laos. Area: 63,360 sq.mi. (164,103 sq.km.). Pop. (1973 est.): 22,481,000. Cap. and largest city: Hanoi (pop., 1970 est., 1,348,000). Language: Vietnamese. Religion: Buddhist; pagan; Confucian; Christian. Secretary of the Vietnam Workers (Communist) Party in 1974, Le Duan; president, Ton Duc Thang; premier, Pham Van Dong.

North Vietnam's leadership announced economic reconstruction as the primary goal of the country in 1974 and 1975. Le Duan, first secretary of the ruling Vietnam Workers (Communist) Party, said, "The war has rolled back our originally underdeveloped economy . . . to where it was more than ten years ago."

The task of rebuilding North Vietnam's industrial, transportation, and agricultural bases as the priority task represented a significant change from the previously announced main national purpose, which had been the reunification of Vietnam through military means. While North Vietnam was still hobbled with resource-draining commitments in South Vietnam, the level of involvement was reduced somewhat from the period of full-scale war.

Of immediate concern to North Vietnam's leadership as the year began was agricultural output, which

VIETNAM: Republic

Education: (1970–71) Primary, pupils 2,718,036, teachers 49,194; secondary, pupils 711,240, teachers 23,305; vocational, pupils 30,851, teachers 927; teacher training, students 4,943, teachers 104; higher, students 56,608.

Finance. Monetary unit: piastre, with (Sept. 16, 1974) a free rate of 650 piastres to U.S. $1 (1,530 piastres = £1 sterling). Gold, SDRs, and foreign exchange, central bank: (Jan. 1974) U.S. $171 million; (Jan. 1973) U.S. $229 million. Budget (1972 est.): revenue 328.5 billion piastres; expenditure 365.9 billion piastres. Gross domestic product: (1972) 1,127,000,000,000 piastres; (1971) 956 billion piastres. Money supply: (March 1974) 290.9 billion piastres; (March 1973) 236,170,000,000 piastres. Cost of living (Saigon; 1970 = 100): (June 1974) 327; (June 1973) 197.

Foreign Trade. (1972) Imports 233,245,000,000 piastres; exports 5,467,000,-000 piastres. Import sources: U.S. 41%; Japan 18%; Singapore 8%; Taiwan 7%; France 7%. Export destinations: Japan 30%; Hong Kong 25%; France 19%; Singapore 6%. Main exports: fish 29%; rubber 28%.

Transport and Communications. Roads (1970) 20,917 km. Motor vehicles in use (1971): passenger 58,400; commercial (including buses) 29,200. Railways (1973): c. 680 km.; traffic 170 million passenger-km., freight 1.3 million net ton-km. Air traffic (1973): 390 million passenger-km.; freight 4,060,000 net ton-km. Navigable waterways (1973) c. 4,500 km. Telephones (Dec. 1972) 43,-000. Radio receivers (Dec. 1970) 2.2 million. Television receivers (Dec. 1972) 500,000.

Agriculture. Production (in 000; metric tons; 1973; 1972 in parentheses): rice c. 6,500 (6,384); sweet potatoes (1972) c. 225, (1971) 230; cassava (1972) c. 275, (1971) 270; peanuts (1972) c. 39, (1971) 37; rubber c. 23 (c. 20); copra c. 23 (c. 20); tea c. 5 (5); coffee c. 4 (4); fish catch (1972) 678, (1971) 587. Livestock (in 000; 1972–73): buffalo 501; cattle 853; pigs 4,275; goats 38; chickens 23,250; ducks 18,170.

Industry. Production (in 000; metric tons; 1973): cement 265; salt (1971) 134; cotton yarn 10; woven cotton fabrics (m.; 1972) 43,000; electricity (excluding most industrial production; kw-hr.; 1972) 1,483,000.

VIETNAM: Democratic Republic

Education. (1966–67) Primary and secondary, pupils 4,517,600, teachers 86,495; vocational, pupils 101,880, teachers 4,194; higher (including University of Hanoi), students (1970) c. 72,000, teaching staff (1966–67) 5,004.

Finance and Trade. Monetary unit: dong, with (Sept. 16, 1974) an official exchange rate of 2.35 dong to U.S. $1 (nominal rate of 5.62 dong = £1 sterling). Budget (foreign aid est.; 1971) c. 5 billion dong. Foreign trade (1965): imports c. 530 million dong (1972 est., excluding China, c. 650 million dong); exports c. 290 million dong (1972 est., excluding China, c. 150 million dong). Main import sources: U.S.S.R. c. 40%; China c. 25%; East Germany c. 9%; Czechoslovakia c. 8%; Poland c. 6%. Main export destinations: China c. 40%; U.S.S.R. c. 25%; Japan c. 9%; Czechoslovakia c. 6%; East Germany c. 5%.

Transport. Roads (1972) c. 13,500 km. Railways (1972) c. 780 km.

Agriculture. Production (in 000; metric tons; 1972; 1971 in parentheses): rice c. 4,600 (c. 4,600); corn c. 220 (c. 230); sweet potatoes c. 860 (c. 850); cassava c. 780 (c. 700); peanuts c. 37 (c. 40); tea c. 3 (c. 3); tobacco c. 4 (c. 4). Livestock (in 000; 1971–72): buffalo c. 1,700; cattle c. 880; pigs c. 7,000; horses c. 60; chickens c. 28,000; ducks c. 18,000.

Industry. Production (in 000; metric tons; 1972): coal c. 3,000; phosphate rock (oxide content; 1971) c. 1,145; salt c. 150; cement c. 500; cotton fabrics (m.; 1964) 105,200; paper (1964) 19; electricity (kw-hr.; 1964) 548,000.

was critically reduced because of the 1973–74 winter drought, subsequent typhoon damage, and destructive flooding. In all, 170,000 ha. of rice land were totally lost, and yields were substantially reduced from an additional 300,000 ha. The unanticipated reductions in rice production severely altered supply needs, and it was estimated that North Vietnam would be required to import substantial quantities of food.

Devastating raids by U.S. planes at the height of the war, and most notably just prior to the 1973 cease-fire, crippled North Vietnam's industrial facilities. More than half of the country's factories were totally destroyed. Consequently, Hanoi announced that 85% of the 1974 budget earmarked for construction would be spent on projects associated with basic production.

Capital was a limiting factor in the reconstruction program. The Communist nations (primarily the Soviet Union and China) were providing North Vietnam with an equivalent of $1.2 billion in economic aid, but sufficient funds were not available for meeting many high-priority needs. North Vietnam had anticipated fulfillment of the U.S. pledge of $2.5 billion in economic aid. However, in the face of what were considered continuing violations of the cease-fire agreement, the U.S. Congress refused to provide any economic development funds to Hanoi.

Crucial to North Vietnam's long-term economic rehabilitation would be the attitude it adopted toward reunification. By maintaining large numbers of forces in South Vietnam, as well as in Laos and Cambodia, Hanoi was straining its economic and manpower resources severely. (ROBERT GORALSKI)

See also Defense.
[976.B.4.a–d]

Western Samoa

A constitutional monarchy and member of the Commonwealth of Nations, Western Samoa is an island group in the South Pacific Ocean, about 1,600 mi. E of New Zealand and 2,200 mi. S of Hawaii. Area: 1,133 sq.mi. (2,934 sq.km.), with two major islands, Savai'i (662 sq.mi.) and Upolu (435 sq.mi.), and seven smaller islands. Pop. (1974 est.): 155,000. Cap. and largest city: Apia (pop., 1971, 30,266). Language: Samoan and English. Religion (1971): Congregational 51%, Roman Catholic 22%, Methodist 16%, others 11%. Head of state (*O le Ao o le Malo*) in 1974, Malietoa Tanumafili II; prime minister, Fiame Mata'afa Faumuina Mulinu'u II.

In 1973–74 the government pursued conservative

WESTERN SAMOA
Education. (1972) Primary, pupils 29,467, teachers 978; secondary, pupils 12,088, teachers 289; vocational, pupils 99, teachers 14; teacher training, students 242, teachers 18; higher (1970), students 114, teaching staff 24.
Finance and Trade. Monetary unit: Western Samoan dollar (tala), with (Sept. 16, 1974) a par value of WS$0.60 to U.S. $1 (free rate of WS$1.38 = £1 sterling). Budget (1971 est.): revenue WS$6,478,-000; expenditure WS$6,518,000. Foreign trade (1972): imports WS$13,640,000; exports WS$4 million. Import sources: New Zealand 31%; Australia 20%; Japan 12%; U.K. 10%; U.S. 8%. Export destinations: New Zealand 33%; West Germany 25%; The Netherlands 20%; U.S. 9%. Main exports: copra 45%; cocoa 28%; bananas 12%.

economic policies, cutting back on services and trying to boost the agricultural sector after setbacks caused by hurricane and disease damage since the mid-1960s. In a stringent budget some previously approved projects were canceled. Higher returns from agricultural exports in 1973–74 reflected high world prices and increased production of some commodities. Aid from New Zealand (for rebuilding Apia's hospital), from the Asian Development Bank (for modernizing communications), and from Japanese investment brought some activity.

There were no political parties, but differences over economic policies caused some polarization between the cautious and those who argued that the country was not realizing its full capacity for overseas borrowing and consequent development. Steep rises in the prices of imported consumer items added to voter dissatisfaction. The parliamentary "opposition," mainly younger, well-educated members, unsuccessfully tried to bring about a change of government in December 1973. (BARRIE KEITH MACDONALD)
[977.A.3]

Words and Meanings, New

A new object in the cosmos, thought to be a quasar embedded in a galaxy, was christened **lacertid** when it was discovered independently by French and American researchers early in 1974. The first **earth resources satellite** was made available to geophysicists for registering seasonal changes by means of a **four-channel scanner** capable of remote **multispectral sensing.** Geophysicists differentiated the **cryosphere** (permanently frozen land) from the *lithosphere* (earth's rock crust) and the *hydrosphere* (earth's waters). The **Earthwatch monitoring system** began to operate as part of the UN Environment Program, and the law of the sea was the theme of the Caracas, Venezuela, conference at which an **exclusive economic zone** (EEZ) of 200 mi. was proposed (though not yet accepted) for coastal states.

In public transportation the **maxi-taxi,** like the **minibus,** was a "people-moving" contraption halfway between an omnibus and a private automobile. For **intercity** communication, experiments were made with the **mag-lev** (magnetically levitated) high-speed train. Other devices tested with some promise of success were the **minitram** and the **cabtrack.**

At sea, a special type of container system known as **bacat** (barge aboard catamaran) began to function across the North Sea between Middlesbrough, Eng., and Rotterdam, Neth.

Luxury hotels in African nature reserves were named **safari lodges,** from which tourists could view wildlife from a sort of reverse zoo with animals at large and humans enclosed. In the transmission of heat to towns and cities, **telethermics** made rapid advances and **pipe-in-pipe** was the term applied to the system whereby fluid-bearing tubes were encased in protective pressure-tight tubes. In the sudden worldwide drive to conserve energy and materials, **recycling** became the keyword. Aircraft noise was reduced by furnishing certain types of planes with a **retrofit hushkit.**

The **cyclonet,** a French invention, proved to be neater and quicker than dispersants in clearing oil slicks from the surface of the sea. Another subtle invention, made at Teddington, Eng., was the **verisign,** an electronic device for verifying signatures and thus safeguarding checks and credit cards against fraud. A more sinister invention was the **electro-thanator,** an apparatus for electrocuting unwanted dogs. **Chemoreception** was adopted as an umbrella term to cover those two primary senses of taste and smell, which, unlike sight, hearing, and touch, depend entirely upon chemical stimuli. Another blanket term was **robotics,** the science of **robotism,** mechanical men, or automata. **Biocybernetics** covered all those horrendous and devastating techniques that manipulate and transform the human personality. In language teaching some linguists made an important distinction between **mainstream speech** and standard language. They resuscitated **lexicometrics** to indicate "controlled vocabulary" and coined **prespeech** to signify lip movements made by young children before they enunciate meaningful words.

Throughout the year acronyms multiplied so rapidly that it was not easy to keep track of them. The prize award should probably go to the U.S. National Aeronautics and Space Administration (NASA) for concocting **ALADDIN** (Atmospheric Layering and Density Distribution of Ions and Neutrals) for an ambitious investigation into the intricacies of the ionosphere. Some acronyms, like **Quango** (quasi-nongovernment organization) and the jocular **HIO** (highly important occasion), were probably too frivolous to last.

Many new compounds gained currency because they were brief; for instance, **multicausal,** shorter than "attributable to many causes." The Greek-Latin hybrid **ethnoscience** and the Greek compound **technoeconomics** came into use to label a new departure in comparative anthropology and a new phase in the assessment of wealth resulting from technological research and development. The Greek-Latin hybrid **technostructure** had been created by J. K. Galbraith to denote the hierarchy of experts controlling technology in a society, whereas the Latin-Greek hybrid **socioecology** was concerned with the influence of the environment upon social grouping. So great was the deference paid to consensus that people began to talk seriously about **consensocracy.** The term **guest-worker** became fashionable as an obvious translation of German *Gastarbeiter.* As petroleum-rich third world countries accumulated **petrodollars** paid for their high-priced oil, the very poor less developed countries were relegated to the **fourth world.**

A semantic twist was given to the epithet *unsocial* when the phrase **unsocial hours** came to signify "hours outside usual working times," whereas **paranormal,** "beyond the range of normal experience," enlarged its semantic sphere and embraced the *abnormal, supernatural,* and *metaphysical.* **Simplistic** became fashionable on both sides of the Atlantic. It signified not merely simple but affectedly oversimplified. **Simplism** implied deliberate disregard of complexities and complications. **Scientism** became a favourite abstraction in those quarters where it was held that techniques valid in the natural sciences should be applied unconditionally to all fields of inquiry.

Some vogue words, to be sure, added nothing to linguistic clarity or strength. **Innovative,** for example, was often merely a pretentious substitute for new, **traumatic** for damaging, and **monolithic** for massive. Similarly, **cost-effectiveness** sounded more impressive than "value for money," and **species-specific,** a botanical term meaning "unique to its species," lost all precision. **Threshold payments** and **fringe benefits** were worn threadbare in industrial bargaining. **Coun-**

terinflationary measures, whether *deflationary* or *reflationary,* proved unavailing against the demon of inflation, although **monetarists,** both **neo-Keynesian** and **Friedmanist,** seemed to be everywhere **thick on the ground.** Were we all gradually edging toward a restructured society? The blurring of distinctions between the working and middle classes was branded as **embourgeoisement** by some and as **bourgeoisification** by others.

From the transcripts of former president Richard Nixon's taped conversations, published in the U.S. in connection with the Watergate affair, came **stonewalling,** "offering total resistance" (in this case to investigations of the scandal); **stroking,** borrowed from transactional analysis, where it means to support or reward, but used by Nixon and his aides in a manipulative sense; and **expletive deleted** (meaning precisely that), which gained currency as a catchphrase from the frequency with which it appeared in the version of the transcripts released by the White House.

Nuke, also spelled **newk,** short for "nuclear test," was one of the slang monosyllables that rose in status. Another was **yen,** "longing"; but, oddly enough, no one knew whether it was merely a debasement of *yearn* or an importation from the Far East (Cantonese *yan,* Mandarin *yin*). The designation *Middle East* continued to be used somewhat loosely throughout the year. If Cyprus was said to be in the Middle East, where on earth was the Near East?

(SIMEON POTTER)

[441.C.2.e; 442.B.4]

Yemen, People's Democratic Republic of

A people's republic in the southern coastal region of the Arabian Peninsula, Yemen (Aden) is bordered by Yemen (San'a'), Saudi Arabia, and Oman. Area: 111,-074 sq.mi. (287,680 sq.km.). Pop. (1973): 1,590,275.

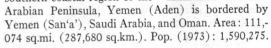

YEMEN, PEOPLE'S DEMOCRATIC REPUBLIC OF
Education. (1970–71) Primary, pupils 134,522, teachers 4,316; secondary, pupils 16,631, teachers 769; vocational, pupils 952, teachers 142; teacher training, students 386, teachers 32; higher, students 91, teaching staff 42.

Finance and Trade. Monetary unit: Yemen dinar, with (Sept. 16, 1974) an official rate of 0.35 dinar to U.S. $1 (free rate of 0.80 dinar = £1 sterling). Budget (1972–73 actual): revenue 12,050,000 dinars; expenditure 21,680,000 dinars. Foreign trade (1971): imports 64.9 million dinars; exports 43.1 million dinars. Import sources: Iran 12%; Kuwait 12%; Japan 11%; Iraq 9%; U.K. 8%. Export destinations: U.K. 12%; Yemen (San'a') 10%; South Africa 10%; Australia 9%; Japan 9%; Thailand 6%. Main export petroleum products 74%.

Transport. Roads (1972) *c.* 4,500 km. (mainly tracks; including *c.* 1,000 km. with improved surface). Motor vehicles in use (1971): passenger 13,000; commercial (including buses) 3,900. There are no railways. Ships entered (1971) vessels totaling 6,598,000 net registered tons; goods loaded 3,322,000 metric tons, unloaded 4,286,000 metric tons.

Agriculture. Production (in 000; metric tons; 1972; 1971 in parentheses): millet and sorghum *c.* 77 (*c.* 75); wheat *c.* 14 (*c.* 13); dates *c.* 8 (*c.* 8); cotton, lint *c.* 5 (6); fish catch 123 (118). Livestock (in 000; 1972–73): cattle *c.* 94; sheep *c.* 225; goats *c.* 885; camels *c.* 40.

Industry. Production (in 000; metric tons; 1972): salt 75; petroleum products (1971) 3,505; electricity (kw-hr.) 139,000.

World Bank:
see Development, Economic and Social

World Council of Churches:
see Religion

Yachting:
see Sailing

Cap. and largest city: Aden (pop., 1973, 132,517). Language: Arabic. Religion: Muslim. Chairman of the Presidential Council in 1974, Salem Ali Rubayyi; prime minister, Ali Nasir Muhammad Husani.

In 1974 the left-wing regime of the People's Democratic Republic of Yemen continued its revolutionary path, supporting the Dhofari rebels in Oman and maintaining close relations with the Communist states. At the same time it made some tentative steps toward a reconciliation with Saudi Arabia and the Persian Gulf states and expanded its ties with Egypt. After the Arab summit meeting in Rabat, Morocco, on October 26–30, the government denied reports that it had agreed to lease Perim Island—which controls the Bab el-Mandeb, the southern entrance to the Red Sea—to Egypt, but it insisted that it would carry its full share of the Arab defense effort.

In the first months of the year, the government continued discussions in San'a' with the Yemen Arab Republic concerning the political and economic union between the two countries agreed upon in 1971. However, this seemed to be ruled out after the June 13 military takeover in San'a', which increased the influence of Saudi Arabia in the Yemen Arab Republic. In September the exiled former Aden chief minister, Abdel Kawi al-Makkawi, claimed that one million South Yemenis had fled the country since the ruling National Liberation Front took power in 1967.

Aden continued to rely heavily on foreign aid for its five-year development plan (1974–79). It received loans or gifts from international banks and funds from Libya, Iraq, and Czechoslovakia. UN relief was provided for the northern areas, which had been stricken by drought since 1970. During 1974 the government took an important step toward establishing a secular state with a new law limiting each man to one wife and making 16 the minimum age of marriage for girls and 20 years the maximum age difference between marriage partners. (PETER MANSFIELD)

[978.B.4.b]

Yemen Arab Republic

A republic situated in the southwestern coastal region of the Arabian Peninsula, Yemen (San'a') is bounded by Yemen (Aden), Saudi Arabia, and the Rea Sea. Area: 77,-200 sq.mi. (200,000 sq.km.). Pop. (1973 est.): 6,217,000. Cap. and largest city: San'a' (pop., 1973 est., 124,000). Language: Arabic. Religion: Muslim. President in 1974, Qadi Abdul Rahman al-Iryani and, from June 13, chairman of the Command Council, Col. Ibrahim al-Hamidi; premiers, Abdullah al-Hagri, from March 3 Hassan Makki, and, from June 22, Mohsin al-Aini.

Despite a military coup in 1974, the Yemen Arab Republic continued to be ruled by a coalition of varied elements with a general inclination toward Saudi Arabia and the West. In January, March, and April, the committee for inter-Yemen unity met in San'a', and government leaders repeatedly expressed support for the principle of unity of the two Yemens.

After reports that Abdullah al-Hagri was unwell, Hassan Makki formed a new government on March 3, with the former Adeni leader Abdullah Asnag as foreign minister. In May Makki headed a top-level delegation to Saudi Arabia and the Persian Gulf states and returned with promises of increased aid. On June 13 a military junta headed by Col. Ibrahim al-Hamidi seized power in a bloodless coup and suspended the constitution and 159-man Consultative Council; the newly formed National Yemeni Union was dissolved. A provisional constitution gave the new Command Council wide executive and legislative powers for 6 months, extended in October to 12 months.

The new leaders claimed that the previous system had become unworkable because of the prolonged feud between President Iryani and the Consultative Council. The deposed president was treated with respect by the Command Council and left for Syria on June 18. The Command Council undertook to root out corruption and inefficiency in the administration and the Army, in which lieutenant colonel was made the highest rank. Although the new regime laid emphasis on friendship with Saudi Arabia and all prospects of unity with the left-wing People's Democratic Republic of Yemen were thought to have been postponed indefinitely, some younger radical elements were included in the new government formed by Mohsin al-Aini on June 22. In October Mohsin al-Aini joined the Command Council. (PETER MANSFIELD)

[978.B.4.b]

Col. Ibrahim al-Hamidi led a military coup that overthrew the Yemen (San'a') government in June.

YEMEN, ARAB REPUBLIC

Education. (1972–73) Primary, pupils 154,607, teachers 4,053; secondary, pupils 9,573, teachers 544; vocational, pupils 374, teachers 50; teacher training, students 939, teaching staff (1965–66) 5; higher, students 439, teaching staff 41.

Finance and Trade. Monetary unit: riyal, with (Sept. 16, 1974) an official rate of 4.575 riyals to U.S. $1 (free rate of 10.50 riyals = £1 sterling). Budget (1972–73 est.): revenue 199 million riyals; expenditure 271 million riyals. Foreign trade (1972): imports 376.2 million riyals; exports 20.1 million riyals. Import sources: Australia 13%; Yemen (Aden) 11%; Japan 10%; West Germany 7%; France 7%; Saudi Arabia 6%; U.K. 5%. Export destinations: China 38%; Yemen (Aden) 21%; Saudi Arabia 11%; U.S.S.R. 9%; Italy 5%. Main exports: cotton 36%; coffee 27%; hides and skins 16%; kat 5%.

Agriculture. Production (in 000; metric tons; 1973; 1972 in parentheses): sorghum c. 1,000 (1,020); wheat c. 30 (c. 32); dates c. 60 (c. 60); coffee c. 5 (c. 5); cotton, lint (1972) c. 1, (1971) 5. Livestock (in 000; March 1972): cattle c. 1,400; sheep c. 3,751; goats c. 8,849; camels c. 60.

Yugoslavia

A federal socialist republic, Yugoslavia is bordered by Italy, Austria, Hungary, Romania, Bulgaria, Greece, and Albania. Area: 98,766 sq.mi. (255,804 sq.km.). Pop. (1974 est.): 21,101,000. Cap. and largest city: Belgrade (pop., 1971, 746,105). Language: Serbo-Croatian, Slovenian, and Macedonian. Religion (1953): Orthodox 41.4%; Roman Catholic 31.8%; Muslim 12.3%. President of the republic for life and president of the League of Communists in 1974, Marshal Tito (Josip Broz); president of the Federal Executive Council (premier), Dzemal Bijedic.

The country's fourth constitution since World War II was promulgated on Feb. 21, 1974. While maintaining a single-party Communist government, it considerably modified the legislative system, replacing the 620-member, five-chambered Federal Assembly by two houses—a Federal Chamber of 220 delegates and a Chamber of Republics and Provinces of 88 delegates. The State Presidency, the supreme organ, was reduced from 23 members to 9.

Yiddish Literature: see Literature

President of the Chamber of Nations of the Yugoslav Federal Assembly Mika Spiljak (second from right) reads the proclamation of the new Yugoslav constitution to assembled officials and dignitaries in Belgrade on February 21.

the chief of staff of the Soviet Army, Gen. Viktor Kulikov, went on as planned in September, and in November President Tito paid a visit to East Germany. But the Yugoslav press strongly emphasized the short visit paid to Belgrade on November 4 by U.S. Secretary of State Henry Kissinger. At the same time Yugoslavia sought to strengthen its links with the third world countries of Africa and Asia. President Tito visited India, Nepal, Sri Lanka, and Syria in January and February. A meeting of nine nonaligned countries was held in Belgrade in September. In the same month, Prime Minister Sirimavo Bandaranaike of Sri Lanka visited Yugoslavia. During the spring Yugoslavia quarreled with Italy over the status of the so-called Zones A and B in the Trieste area that the two countries annexed with the wartime Allies' approval in 1954. In October there was a quarrel with Austria over the position of the Croat and Slovene minorities in Austria.

A slight shift away from the policy of close collaboration with the U.S.S.R. and a sharp deterioration of the country's economic position were the main features of 1974. The internal political situation continued to be uncertain, reflecting the ambiguity of Soviet intentions toward Yugoslavia. In April Yugoslav security services discovered and arrested a group of "Cominformist" (pro-Soviet) Communists who had held a secret party "congress" at Bar, Montenegro, but the news of their arrest was delayed until September 12. On September 20 it was announced that 32 members of the "illegal Cominformist" group had been tried and given sentences ranging from one to 14 years. Warsaw Pact forces' maneuvers in Hungary at the end of September were followed by Yugoslav military exercises close to the borders of Hungary and Bulgaria.

Yugoslavia's relations with China improved perceptibly. In June a Yugoslav parliamentary delegation visited China, and in October a Chinese trade delegation visited Yugoslavia. At the preparatory meeting for a European Communist conference in Warsaw on October 16–19, Yugoslavia strongly resisted Soviet attempts to use the conference as an anti-Chinese platform in the world Communist movement. Visits by the Soviet deputy prime minister, Vladimir Novikov, and

Relations with other Western countries were friendly, although rapport with the EEC was troubled by the Community's ban on non-EEC beef imports. President Tito visited West Germany at the end of June, and during his visit a $300 million West German development loan for Yugoslavia was announced. In October Tito visited Denmark. In August the U.S. firm of Westinghouse was awarded a contract to build Yugoslavia's first nuclear power station at Krsko in Slovenia. An agreement with Czechoslovakia and Hungary to build the Adria pipeline from Omisalj on the Adriatic to Bratislava in Slovakia was signed on February 12.

The dinar was devalued by 7% at the end of October. Yugoslavia's trade gap was expected to reach $3.5 billion by the end of the year. Despite the increased value of workers' remittances from West Germany, foreign exchange earnings did not rise as rapidly in 1974 as in 1973, and the country's balance of payments deficit was estimated at $720 million at the end of 1974. By September about 100,000 Yugoslav workers had returned from the West owing to growing unemployment there. The number of Yugoslavia's own unemployed was 450,000. Yugoslavia had a record wheat harvest of 6.3 million tons, but heavy floods in northern Croatia and Serbia in October destroyed much of the corn (maize) and sugar-beet crops. Inflation reached a level of about 30%.

YUGOSLAVIA

Education. (1972–73) Primary, pupils 2,856,491, teachers 123,860; secondary, pupils 193,275, teachers 9,508; vocational, pupils 499,087, teachers 8,969; teacher training, students 10,174, teachers 710; higher (including 9 universities), students 328,536, teaching staff 19,197.

Finance. Monetary unit: dinar, with (following the devaluation of Oct. 31, 1974) a free rate of 17.27 dinars to U.S. $1 (free rate of 40.29 dinars = £1 sterling). Gold, SDRs, and foreign exchange, central bank: (June 1974) U.S. $1,160,000,000; (June 1973) U.S. $1,039,000,000. Budget (1972 actual): revenue 39,630,000,000 dinars; expenditure 38,671,000,000 dinars. Gross material product: (1972) 245 billion dinars; (1971) 204 billion dinars. Money supply: (March 1974) 86.1 billion dinars; (March 1973) 61.7 billion dinars. Cost of living (1970 = 100): (June 1974) 199; (June 1973) 168.

Foreign Trade. (1973) Imports 76,689,000,000 dinars; exports 48,494,000,000 dinars. Import sources: West Germany 19%; Italy 12%; U.S.S.R. 9%; Austria 5%. Export destinations: Italy 16%; U.S.S.R. 14%; West Germany 11%; U.S. 8%. Main exports: machinery 13%; transport equipment 12%; nonferrous metals 9%; meat 7%; iron and steel 6%; chemicals 6%;

timber 6%; clothing 5%; textile yarns and fabrics 5%. Tourism (1972): visitors 5,139,700; gross receipts U.S. $460 million.

Transport and Communications. Roads (1973) 96,157 km. Motor vehicles in use (1973): passenger 999,540; commercial (including buses) 248,300. Railways: (1972) 10,417 km.; traffic (1973) 10,441,000,000 passenger-km., freight 20,361,000,000 net ton-km. Air traffic (1973): 1,258,000,000 passenger-km.; freight 8.6 million net ton-km. Shipping (1973): merchant vessels 100 gross tons and over 382; gross tonnage 1,667,183. Telephones (Dec. 1972) 911,000. Radio licenses (Dec. 1972) 3,556,000. Television licenses (Dec. 1972) 2,354,000.

Agriculture. Production (in 000; metric tons; 1973; 1972 in parentheses): wheat 4,703 (4,844); barley 540 (487); oats 275 (260); rye 125 (120); corn 7,800 (7,940); potatoes c. 2,700 (2,406); sunflower seed c. 440 (277); sugar, raw value c. 455 (390); dry beans c. 153 (153); onions c. 247 (243); tomatoes c. 374 (368); plums (1972) 1,059, (1971) 817; apples (1972) 316, (1971) 327; pears (1972) 95, (1971) 112; figs (1972) c. 22, (1971) 18; wine c. 700 (626); tobacco c. 62 (62); beef

and veal (1972) c. 290, (1971) 263; pork (1972) c. 385, (1971) 384; timber (cu.m.; 1972) 13,700, (1971) 16,900; fish catch (1972) 49, (1971) 50. Livestock (in 000; Jan. 1973): cattle 5,366; sheep 7,774; pigs 6,342; horses 964; poultry 49,206.

Industry. Fuel and power (in 000; metric tons; 1973): coal 577; lignite 31,873; crude oil 3,392; natural gas (cu.m.) 1,328,000; manufactured gas (cu.m.) 155,000; electricity (kw-hr.) 35,037,000. Production (in 000; metric tons; 1973): cement 6,206; iron ore (35% metal content) 4,670; pig iron 2,114; crude steel 2,673; bauxite 2,169; antimony ore (metal content; 1972) 2; chrome ore (oxide content; 1972) 10; manganese ore (metal content; 1971) 5.7; magnesite (1972) 422; aluminum 85; copper 138; lead 97; zinc 55; gold (troy oz.; 1972) 137; silver (troy oz.; 1972) 3,570; petroleum products (1972) 7,850; sulfuric acid 952; cotton yarn 103; wool yarn 42; rayon, etc., filament yarns and fibres (1972) 64; nylon, etc., filament yarns and fibres (1972) 15; wood pulp (1972) 552; newsprint 76; other paper (1972) 591. Merchant vessels launched (100 gross tons and over; 1973) 612,000 gross tons.

The most important political event of 1974 was the tenth congress of the Yugoslav League of Communists in Belgrade on May 27–30. The congress elected Tito (who on May 16 had been elected president of the republic for life by the two chambers constituting the Assembly of the Federation) party leader "with an unlimited mandate." The congress also adopted new party statutes that emphasized party discipline and gave greater powers to the central party bodies, especially to the Presidium's 12-man Executive Committee in place of the existing 9-man Executive Bureau. The number of generals and army officers in the Central Committee and other leading party bodies increased perceptibly. A general was appointed minister of the interior in July, and another became federal prosecutor. Edvard Kardelj (*see* Biography), one of Tito's closest associates and a member of the State Presidency, and Stane Dolanc, secretary of the League of Communists' new Executive Committee, were probably the two most powerful figures in Yugoslav politics after Tito.

Relations between church and state deteriorated as a result of the stepping up of the indoctrination of schoolchildren and students. In September a liberal Marxist professor and five students were each given ten months' imprisonment in Ljubljana, and dissident author Mihajlo Mihajlov was arrested in October. A group of alleged Croat nationalists was put on trial in Zadar, Croatia. Two young British plane spotters, who had been accused of espionage and sentenced to five years each in 1973, were released and sent home on November 15. (K. F. CVIIC)

[972.B.3.d]

Zaire

A republic of equatorial Africa, Zaire is bounded by the Central African Republic, Sudan, Uganda, Rwanda, Burundi, Tanzania, Zambia, Angola, Congo, and the Atlantic Ocean. Area: 905,365 sq.mi. (2,344,885 sq.km.). Pop. (1974 est.): 24,222,000. Cap. and largest city: Kinshasa (pop., 1973 est., 1,798,576). Language: French; Bantu dialects. Religion: animist approximately 50%; Christian 43%. President in 1974, Mobutu Sese Seko.

On Nov. 30, 1973, President Mobutu announced that foreign-owned agricultural land was to be nationalized and that foreign-owned mining companies would be required to hand over 50% or more of their equity to the government. Many companies were affected by this order, including Lonrho and Unilever. The government also began to work on plans to make possible the refining of copper in Zaire rather than in Europe. Mobutu banned Asian, Greek, and Portuguese traders from living or doing business in five of the country's provinces. Portuguese observers and also Zairians criticized the ban on the ground that government officers were corruptly acquiring foreign-owned properties for their own families. The Greek government was also concerned about some of its nationals who had been robbed of their possessions and forced into refugee camps. The governor of the Central Bank of Zaire insisted, however, that the new arrangements did not affect Zaire's attachment to the idea of a mixed economy and that the changes were not intended to get rid of the guarantees offered to foreign investors.

ZAIRE

Education. (1970–71) Primary, pupils 3,088,011, teachers 70,000; secondary, pupils 253,234, teachers 11,755; vocational (1969–70), pupils 33,985, teachers 3,515; teacher training (1969–70), students 34,532, teachers 2,643; higher, students 12,363, teaching staff 1,386.

Finance. Monetary unit: zaire, with (Sept. 16, 1974) an official exchange rate of 0.50 zaire to U.S. $1 (free rate of 1.16 zaires = £1 sterling). Gold, SDRs, and foreign exchange, central bank: (June 1974) U.S. $246.6 million; (June 1973) U.S. $114,730,000. Budget (1972 actual): revenue 305.5 million zaires; expenditure 426.1 million zaires. Gross national product: (1972) 1,342,900,000 zaires; (1971) 1,244,-800,000 zaires. Money supply: (Dec. 1973) 283,350,-000 zaires; (Dec. 1972) 227,680,000 zaires. Cost of living (Kinshasa; 1970 = 100): (March 1974) 188; (March 1973) 151.

Foreign Trade. (1970) Imports 266.5 million zaires; exports 367.7 million zaires. Import sources: Belgium-Luxembourg 24%; U.S. 11%; West Germany 10%; France 8%; U.K. 7%; Japan 7%; Italy 5%. Export destinations: Belgium-Luxembourg 43%; Italy 11%; U.K. 7%; France 7%. Main exports: copper 67%; diamonds 6%; coffee 5%.

Transport and Communications. Roads (1973) c. 145,000 km. (including 69,347 km. main regional roads). Motor vehicles in use: passenger (1972) 81,-384; commercial 54,350. Railways: (1972) 5,174 km.; traffic (1971) 751 million passenger-km., freight 2,482,000,000 net ton-km. Air traffic (1972): 524 million passenger-km.; freight 19.8 million net ton-km. Shipping (1973): merchant vessels 100 gross tons and over 9; gross tonnage 38,966. Inland waterways (including Zaire [Congo] River; 1973) c. 13,700 km. Telephones (Dec. 1972) 42,000. Radio receivers (Dec. 1972) 100,000. Television receivers (Dec. 1971) 7,100.

Agriculture. Production (in 000; metric tons; 1973; 1972 in parentheses): rice 227 (206); corn (1972) c. 350, (1971) 306; sweet potatoes (1972) c. 360, (1971) c. 360; cassava (1972) c. 10,500, (1971) c. 10,500; peanuts c. 190 (c. 180); dry peas c. 80 (c. 80); palm kernels c. 110 (c. 105); palm oil c. 190 (c. 180); coffee c. 79 (c. 83); sugar, raw value c. 60 (c. 39); rubber c. 40 (c. 40); cotton, lint c. 24 (c. 20); timber (cu.m.; 1972) 14,700, (1971) 14,300; fish catch (1971) 124, (1970) 137. Livestock (in 000; Dec. 1972): cattle c. 980; sheep c. 720; goats c. 2,100; pigs c. 550.

Industry. Production (in 000; metric tons; 1972): coal 123; copper 300; tin 1.4; zinc 67; manganese ore (metal content) 196; gold (troy oz.) 139; silver (troy oz.) 2,100; diamonds (metric carats) 13,381; electricity (kw-hr.) 3,842,000.

At the same time, compensation for nationalization would only apply to large-scale industries and agricultural land.

The search for offshore oil proved extremely expensive, but it was hoped that some return would begin to be seen by the middle of 1975. At a conference of the leading copper-producing countries held in Lusaka,

Pres. Mobutu Sese Seko introduces George Foreman and Muhammad Ali at opening ceremonies in Kinshasa prior to their world heavyweight championship fight. Ali subsequently won the match.

WIDE WORLD

Zambia, in June 1974, representatives of Zaire joined with the other delegates in severely criticizing the system under which copper prices were fixed by the London Metal Exchange. Encouraged by the actions of oil-producing countries, the conference set out to make plans to enable copper-producing countries to fix prices. (*See* COMMODITY TRADE: *Special Report.*)

Relations with Belgium became strained early in the year over the publication of a highly critical biography of President Mobutu by a Belgian lawyer. Later in the year the situation improved with the arrival of a new Belgian envoy in Kinshasa. Potentially more serious over the long term were Portuguese fears that Zairian forces might unite with Holden Roberto's Angolan guerrilla movement, with an eye, perhaps, on the oil resources of the Cabinda enclave. Portuguese border defenses were strengthened, but no action ensued on the part of the Zairian government although it was thought that Mobutu was anxious to abandon the moderate role he had played for the previous ten years and emerge as a leader of the more militant African nationalists. The president congratulated Frelimo on its successes in Mozambique after the military coup in Portugal, and he joined with Sudan's President Gaafar Nimeiry in criticizing the Organization of African Unity for failing to unite the various guerrilla movements in Angola.

With encouragement from Mobutu, the promoters of the boxing match between George Foreman and Muhammad Ali for the heavyweight championship of the world successfully staged it in Kinshasa. (*See* BOXING.)

Trading figures for 1973 showed a number of promising developments. Exports to Japan had quadrupled over the 1972 figures to show a total value of $81.2 million, while the corresponding figure for imports was only $59.9 million. Trade with Britain had followed a similar if less striking pattern. In 1974 Zaire received an offer from Japan for a loan of $112 million toward construction of a railway between Banana and Matadi. (KENNETH INGHAM)

[978.E.7.a.i]

MARC & EVELYNE BERNHEIM—RAPHO GUILLUMETTE

A worker prepares spools of copper wire for shipment at a Zambian cable manufacturing plant.

which had alleged that he had sent people out of the country to train to overthrow the government.

Zambia's economic situation seemed promising, though there remained obstacles to be overcome. Negotiations took place early in 1974 with a view to increasing the export of copper to China, which had first begun when the government took control of the copper mines in 1970, and in February Kaunda paid a goodwill visit to China. As a result of technical de-

---

Zambia

A republic and a member of the Commonwealth of Nations, Zambia is bounded by Tanzania, Malawi, Mozambique, Rhodesia, South West Africa, Angola, and Zaire. Area: 290,586 sq.mi. (752,614 sq.km.). Pop. (1974 est.): 4,751,000, about 99% of whom are Africans. Cap. and largest city: Lusaka (pop., 1974 est., 415,000). Language: English and Bantu. Religion: predominantly animist. President in 1974, Kenneth Kaunda; prime minister, Mainza Chona.

President Kaunda's personal success in being elected to a third five-year term in December 1973 was clouded by the defeat of three of his leading ministers in the general election and by the poor turnout (39%) of voters. However, the meeting of the United National Independence Party national council in April 1974 produced a vigorous exchange of views, suggesting that the unity for which Kaunda had striven and in search of which he had banned opposition parties was beginning to be felt. Previously, criticism of government policy had tended too readily to deteriorate into hostility and bitter opposition, often along tribal lines. In March, Simon Kapwepwe, the former vice-president, won a libel suit against the state-owned radio and television service and two newspapers,

ZAMBIA

Education. (1973) Primary, pupils 777,873, teachers 16,491; secondary, pupils 60,051; vocational, pupils 1,871; secondary and vocational, teachers 2,779; teacher training, students 2,186, teachers 164; higher, students 1,934, teaching staff 214.

Finance. Monetary unit: kwacha, with (Sept. 16, 1974) a par value of 0.64 kwacha to U.S. $1 (free rate of 1.49 kwachas = £1 sterling). Gold and foreign exchange, official: (March 1974) U.S. $219.2 million; (March 1973) U.S. $195 million. Budget (1974 est.): revenue 499.7 million kwachas; expenditure 436 million kwachas. Gross domestic product: (1972) 1,217,-000,000 kwachas; (1971) 1,106,000,000 kwachas. Cost of living (1970 = 100): (Feb. 1974) 126; (Feb. 1973) 114.

Foreign Trade. (1973) Imports 393.7 million kwachas; exports 742 million kwachas. Import sources (1972): U.K. 24%; South Africa 15%; Japan 10%; U.S. 9%; Italy 5%; West Germany 5%. Export destinations (1972): Japan 20%; U.K. 20%; Italy 12%; France 9%; West Germany 8%; Brazil 6%. Main export copper 94%.

Transport and Communications. Roads (1972) 34,963 km. Motor vehicles in use: passenger (1972) 64,000; commercial 40,000. Railways (1972) 1,297 km. (excluding the new 1,860-km. Tanzam railway linking Zambia with Dar es Salaam in Tanzania). Air traffic (1973): 340 million passenger-km.; freight 16,-370,000 net ton-km. Telephones (Dec. 1972) 58,000. Radio receivers (Dec. 1972) 100,000. Television receivers (Dec. 1972) 20,000.

Agriculture. Production (in 000; metric tons; 1973; 1972 in parentheses): corn *c.* 355 (612); cassava (1972) *c.* 145, (1971) *c.* 145; millet *c.* 63 (*c.* 63); sorghum *c.* 140 (*c.* 188); peanuts (1972) *c.* 100, (1971) *c.* 103; sugar, raw value *c.* 54 (*c.* 50); tobacco *c.* 6 (6). Livestock (in 000; 1972–73): cattle *c.* 1,700; sheep *c.* 30; goats *c.* 195; pigs *c.* 115; chickens (1971–72) *c.* 7,000.

Industry. Production (in 000; metric tons; 1973): coal 940; copper 638; lead 25; zinc 53; electricity (kw-hr.) 3,420,000.

velopments by the Nchanga copper mines group, the output of copper in the future was likely to be greatly increased and the cost of production would be relatively low. At a conference of copper-producing countries in Lusaka in June, delegates criticized the system under which prices were fixed by the London Metal Exchange, and discussed plans to enable the copper-producing countries to fix prices. (*See* COMMODITY TRADE: *Special Report*.)

Inadequate transport facilities resulted in the pileup of imported goods intended for Zambia at the docks in Dar es Salaam, Tanzania, early in the year. Metal goods rusted in the heavy rains, while perishable goods, including food, deteriorated in the heat. One section of the new Tanzam railway, from Dar es Salaam to the northern Zambian border, was brought into operation in April ahead of schedule to try to reduce the backlog. While the railway might produce an immediate improvement in the import situation, its long-term benefits to Zambia were expected to lie primarily in providing a new outlet for raw materials that would not depend on the cooperation of ideologically opposed neighbouring states.

Probably the most important development in foreign affairs was the change of government in Mozambique. In May Kaunda called upon the new military government in Portugal to grant independence to Mozambique and Angola, and in September, at his initiative, Frelimo leaders and the Portuguese foreign minister, Mário Soares, met in Lusaka. There, final details were arranged for Frelimo's participation in an interim government in Mozambique. In December Kaunda was host to meetings that led to an agreement between Ian Smith's regime and black leaders in Rhodesia. (*See* RHODESIA.)   (KENNETH INGHAM)

[978.E.8.b.iii]

Zoos and Botanical Gardens

Zoos. During 1974 even greater stress was being placed on conservation of animals in the wild and the breeding of animals in zoos. Officially listed as endangered were some 290 species and subspecies of mammals, 340 birds, 180 reptiles and amphibians, and 90 fish. It was hoped that the Convention on International Trade in Endangered Species of Wild Fauna and Flora, adopted in 1973 and so far signed by 39 nations, would help the endangered animals in their natural habitat and give zoos even more inducement to form captive breeding groups. Many zoos throughout the world now operated loan programs whereby single animals were sent to other zoos to form breeding pairs.

Probably the greatest contribution to conservation that zoos could make was to breed endangered animals in such numbers that they could be returned to the wild state. One of the most successful of such conservation programs had been started over 20 years earlier at the Wildfowl Trust in Great Britain. At that time only 42 Hawaiian geese (nene) remained in the wild state and three of these were sent to the trust for breeding purposes. Since then the trust had reared over 820, returned 200 geese to Hawaii, and had loaned 180 birds to other zoos for breeding purposes. The Wildfowl Trust, with a surplus of Hawaiian geese, was allowing some to fly at liberty throughout their grounds and also offered some for sale to other zoos. Other notable breeding successes with endangered species had been the European bison and the Père David's deer, both of which were extinct in the wild. Whipsnade Park in England had even sent some Père David's deer to their native China.

Other organizations were also setting up breeding programs, and zoos could learn a great deal from the research undertaken. Cornell University had set up a captive breeding program for the peregrine falcon, virtually exterminated in North America as a result of exposure to toxic chemicals. In 1974, 20 peregrines were reared, so that it would be possible to start the release program sooner than expected.

The recording of a new first breeding was becoming increasingly difficult but the Point Defiance Aquarium, Tacoma, Wash., recorded the first captive propagation of sea otters. All zoos were now striving to attain second generation captive breeding, and the National Zoological Park, Washington, D.C., recorded this with golden marmosets—a species in danger of extinction. Also at Washington, a bald eagle was hatched; only three others had ever been bred of this now uncommon species, which is the emblem of the U.S. At the Toledo (O.) Zoo the first chimpanzee birth

This lioness is one of several kinds of African animals that freely roam in Lion Country Safari, a zoo in Ashland, Va., through which visitors can drive.

Zanzibar:
see Tanzania

Zinc:
see Mining and
   Quarrying

Zoology:
see Life Sciences

PICTORIAL PARADE

Chia-Chia and Ching-Ching, pandas given to the London Zoo by China, rest comfortably in their new quarters.

from artificial insemination was recorded. The Jersey Zoo, Channel Islands, bred two lowland gorillas which were being hand-reared and could be observed on closed-circuit television. An Andean condor was bred at Yokohama (Jap.) City Zoo, and Chester Zoo in England had a record bird-breeding year with many rarities, including a first red-headed laughing thrush.

Red-fronted macaws were captured alive in Bolivia for the first time. This species is found in a very restricted area and is hunted by the natives, so ten were taken into captivity to form a breeding nucleus. West Berlin Zoo received two vulturine parrots from New Guinea, a species that could only be seen at two other zoos in the world. Giant pandas always form a great attraction, and a pair were received at the London Zoo as a gift from the Chinese government.

A large number of new buildings were erected. The Bronx (N.Y.) Zoo was constructing a new five-acre South American exhibit and the National Zoological Park was enlarging its giant panda enclosures. The Twycross (Eng.) Zoo opened a new orangutan house. Under construction at West Berlin was the most advanced carnivore house in Europe and a new tropical house. The Chester Zoo constructed new moated enclosures for antelope including the Arabian gazelle, a species virtually exterminated in the wild. Perhaps the height of luxury was reached at the Philadelphia Zoo where carpets were fitted in the public part of three of the animal houses. But even such sumptuousness did not satisfy a group of several hundred activist animal lovers, who demonstrated in New York in November demanding the immediate shutdown of Central Park and Prospect Park zoos and the eventual closing of zoos in general.   (G. S. MOTTERSHEAD)

Botanical Gardens. A new feature of the New York Botanical Garden was the Junkin Memorial Limestone Garden, opened May 23, 1974. Constructed of huge limestone blocks and landscaped with a cascade and pools, it formed an ideal habitat for plants loving alkaline conditions. About 75 mi. away from New York City, but under the same direction, the Cary Arboretum reported rapid development in its third year.

At the Missouri Botanical Garden 1974 saw the initial ground-breaking ceremony for the new Japanese garden. Plans for this three-year, ten-acre project included an enlarged lake and other major features.

The new horticultural unit at the Santa Barbara (Calif.) Botanic Garden had a large greenhouse with Saran shading and automatically controlled cooling and heating, as well as other facilities.

At the Royal Botanic Gardens, Kew, Eng., several special collections received particular attention. The Oleaceae, *Escallonia, Buddleia,* and grass collections were replanned, extended, and replanted. Dutch elm disease continued to exact a toll and an injection program using the fungicide Lignasan had encouraging results. Hazel coppice plantings were made in the Queen's Cottage grounds and the Queen's Garden was extended around the front of Kew Palace. Part of the ferneries was landscaped for *Selaginella* plantings. At Wakehurst Place a new bog garden was part of the project for conserving wetland species.

The world trend toward specialist gardens as satellites of larger institutions was exemplified by the National Botanic Gardens of South Africa, where extensive collections of species of the particular region were being represented in each garden. At the central Kirstenbosch Gardens work on the Proteaceae garden was being completed. The *Leucadendron* species were reported to be flowering and the grassed pathways were doing very well. Rocky outcrops were placed in the *Erica* garden where the lawns were extended and the broad connecting approaches were graded prior to being grassed.

The Dunedin (N.Z.) Botanical Garden, one of the world's numerous municipal gardens, reported an increase in their remarkable collection of *Rhododendron* species in cultivation. In gardens with high alkalinity, however, the cultivation of acid-loving plants poses a problem. For example, at the Geneva botanic garden the construction of the rhododendron massif entailed the excavation of soil to a depth of one metre and filling with Jura peat. Lateral seepage of alkaline water was avoided by lining the sides of the depression with plastic sheet, while allowing free drainage through the floor. Feeding once annually with a proprietary manure was found to be adequate to maintain plant health and maximum flowering.

The two gardens in the Canary Islands were expanding. Planting had taken place on the 40-ha. extension to the Jardín Canario, Gran Canaria, which since 1951 had specialized in endemic Canary Islands species. The other extension was taking place on Tenerife where the historic Jardín de Aclimatación (founded in 1788) specialized in exotic plants introduced by early travelers.

Reorganization of research at the National Botanical Gardens, Lucknow, India, placed all projects under seven well-defined areas of research. Among these were the introduction, consideration, and documentation of germ plasm; medicinal and aromatic plants; and other ornamental and economic species. Large collections of roses, *Bougainvillaea, Sansevieria,* and especially of *Chrysanthemum* had been built up since the gardens had been declared a national repository for these cultivars.

Donetsk Botanical Garden, Ukraine, U.S.S.R., was opened to the public in 1974, after nine years of preparation. The garden was situated in an industrial zone with huge waste dumps from mining operations, and the difficult substratum created problems of selection of suitable species of acacia and rose to consolidate the soil.   (FRANK N. HEPPER)

[355.C.6]

ENCYCLOPÆDIA BRITANNICA FILMS. *Zoo's-Eye View: Dawn to Dark* (1973).

CONTRIBUTORS

Names of contributors to the Britannica Book of the Year *with the articles written by them.*
The arrangement is alphabetical by last name.

AARSDAL, STENER. Economic Editor, *Børsen*, Copenhagen.
Denmark

ACCARDO, JOSEPH J. Washington Columnist.
Energy (*in part*)

AGRELLA, JOSEPH C. Turf Editor, *Chicago Sun-Times*. Author of *Ten Commandments for Professional Handicapping*.
Horse Racing (*in part*)

AGUS, JACOB B. Visiting Professor of Modern Jewish Philosophy, Dropsie University, Philadelphia, Pa. Author of *The Evolution of Jewish Thought; Dialogue and Tradition*.
Religion (*in part*)

ALLABY, MICHAEL. Free-lance Writer and Lecturer. Author of *The Eco-Activists; Who Will Eat?; A Blueprint for Survival*.
Environment (*in part*)

ALLAN, J. A. Lecturer in Geography, School of Oriental and African Studies, University of London.
Libya

ALLEN, V. L. Professor of the Sociology of Industrial Society, University of Leeds, Eng. Author of *Power in Trade Unions; Trade Union Leadership; Trade Unions and the Government; Militant Trade Unionism; International Bibliography of Trade Unionism; Sociology of Industrial Relations*.
Industrial Relations

ALSTON, REX. Broadcaster and Journalist. Author of *Taking the Air; Over to Rex Alston; Test Commentary; Watching Cricket*.
Cricket

ANTONINI, GUSTAVO ARTHUR. Associate Professor, Center for Latin American Studies, University of Florida.
Dominican Republic

ARCHIBALD, JOHN J. Writer, *St. Louis Post-Dispatch*. Author of *Bowling for Boys and Girls*.
Bowling and Lawn Bowls (*in part*)

ARMSTRONG, A. G. Lecturer, Department of Economics, University of Bristol, Eng.
Investment, International; Trade, International

ARNOLD, BRUCE. Free-lance Journalist and Writer, Dublin.
Ireland

ARRINGTON, LEONARD JAMES. Church Historian, Church of Jesus Christ of Latter-day Saints. Author of *Great Basin Kingdom: An Economic History of the Latter-day Saints*.
Religion (*in part*)

ASTROM, ERIC A. Executive Assistant to the President, The Ontario Jockey Club; Director, National Association of Canadian Race Tracks.
Horse Racing (*in part*)

AYTON, CYRIL J. Editor, *Motorcycle Sport*, London.
Motor Sports (*in part*)

BARROS, SALVADOR. Literary Critic, *Visión*. Lecturer in Latin American Literature, University of Mexico.
Literature (*in part*)

BASS, HOWARD. Journalist and Broadcaster. Editor, *Winter Sports*, 1948–69; Winter Sports Correspondent, *Daily Telegraph*, London; *Christian Science Monitor*, Boston; *Canadian Skater*, Vancouver; *Skate*, London; *Skating*, Boston; *Ski Racing*, Denver; *Sportsworld*, London. Author of *The Sense in Sport; This Skating Age; The Magic of Skiing; International Encyclopaedia of Winter Sports; Let's Go Skating*.
Biography (*in part*); Hockey (*in part*); Ice Skating; Skiing

BEALL, JOHN VALENTINE. Business Development Engineer. Author of sections 1 and 34, *Mining Engineering Handbook*. Frequent Contributor to *Mining Engineering*, New York.
Mining and Quarrying (*in part*)

BEATTY, J. R. Senior Research Associate, B. F. Goodrich Research Center, Brecksville, O.
Industrial Production and Technology (*in part*)

BECKWITH, DAVID CAMERON. Correspondent, *Time* magazine, Washington, D.C.
United States (*in part*)

BEDDOES, R. H. Sports Columnist, *Toronto Globe and Mail*.
Hockey (*in part*)

BELTRÁN, WILLIAM. Senior Economic Research Officer, Lloyds Bank International, London.
Latin-American Affairs

BERGERRE, MAX. Correspondent ANSA for Vatican Affairs, Rome.
Vatican City State

BERGSTEIN, STANLEY F. Executive Secretary, Harness Tracks of America Inc.; Vice-President, United States Trotting Association.
Horse Racing (*in part*)

BICKELHAUPT, DAVID L. Professor of Insurance, College of Administrative Science, Ohio State University. Author of *Transition to Multiple-Line Insurance Companies; General Insurance* (9th ed.).
Insurance

BILEFIELD, LIONEL. Technical Journalist.
Industrial Production and Technology (*in part*)

BLYTH, ALAN. Music Critic, London.
Music (*in part*)

BODDY, WILLIAM C. Editor, *Motor Sport*. Full Member, Guild of Motoring Writers. Author of *The Story of Brooklands; The 200 Mile Race; The World's Land Speed Record; Continental Sports Cars; The Sports Car Pocketbook; The Bugatti Story; History of Montlhéry; Vintage Years of the Morgan Three-wheeler*.
Motor Sports (*in part*)

BOLT, PETER H. Secretary, British Committee, World Methodist Council. Author of *A Way of Loving*.
Religion (*in part*)

BOONSTRA, DICK. Assistant Professor, Department of Political Science, Free University, Amsterdam.
Netherlands, The

BOOTH, JOHN NICHOLLS. Unitarian Universalist clergyman. Co-founder, Japan Free Religious Association. Author of *The Quest for Preaching Power; Introducing Unitarian Universalism*.
Religion (*in part*)

BOSWALL, JEFFERY. Producer of Sound and Television Programs, British Broadcasting Corporation Natural History Unit, Bristol, Eng.
Life Sciences (*in part*)

BOYLE, C. L. Lieutenant Colonel, R.A. (retd.). Chairman, Survival Service Commission, International Union for Conservation of Nature and Natural Resources, 1958–63; Secretary, Fauna Preservation Society, London, 1950–63.
Environment (*in part*)

BRACKMAN, ARNOLD C. Author of *Indonesian Communism: A History; Southeast Asia's Second Front: The Power Struggle in the Malay Archipelago; The Communist Collapse in Indonesia*.
Indonesia

BRADY, LUTHER WELDON, JR. Professor and Chairman, Department of Radiation Therapy and Nuclear Medicine, Hahnemann Medical College and Hospital, Philadelphia. Contributor to *Clinical Dynamic Function Studies with Radionuclides; New Techniques in Tumor Localization and Radioimmunoassay*.
Health and Disease (*in part*)

BRAIDWOOD, ROBERT J. Professor of Old World Prehistory, the Oriental Institute and the Department of Anthropology, the University of Chicago.
Archaeology (*in part*)

BRAZEE, RUTLAGE J. Senior Seismologist, Solid Earth Data Services Division, D62, NOAA, Boulder, Colo.
Earth Sciences (*in part*)

BRICKHOUSE, JACK. Vice-President and Manager of Sports, WGN Continental Broadcasting Company.
Baseball (*in part*)

BRIERRE, ANNIE. Literary Critic, *La Croix Histoire Pour Tous; France-Culture; France-U.S.A.* Author of *Ninon de Lenclos*.
Literature (*in part*)

BURDIN, JOEL L. Associate Director, American Association of Colleges for Teacher Education; Secretary, Associated Organizations for Teacher Education; Editor, *Journal of Teacher Education*, Washington, D.C. Author of *A Reader's Guide to the Comprehensive Models for Preparing Elementary Teachers*. Co-author of *Elementary School Curriculum and Instruction*.
Education (*in part*)

BURKE, DONALD P. Executive Editor, *Chemical Week*.
Industrial Production and Technology (*in part*)

BURKS, ARDATH W. Professor and Associate Vice-President for Academic Affairs, Rutgers University, New Brunswick, N.J. Author of *The Government of Japan; East Asia: China, Korea, Japan.*
Japan

BUSHONG, ALLEN D. Associate Professor of Geography, University of South Carolina.
El Salvador; Honduras

BUTLER, DAVID RICHARD. Publications Officer, Institution of Gas Engineers, London.
Energy (*in part*)

BUTLER, FRANK. Sports Editor, *News of the World,* London. Author of *A History of Boxing in Britain.*
Boxing

BYRNE, DON. Associate Editor, *Traffic World Magazine,* Washington, D.C.
Telecommunications (*in part*)

CALASCIONE. JOHN. Press and Publications Officer, International Organization of Consumers Unions, The Hague, Neth.
Consumerism (*in part*)

CALHOUN, DAVID R. Editor, Encyclopædia Britannica, Yearbooks.
Biography (*in part*); Consumerism (*in part*)

CAMPBELL, H. C. Chief Librarian, Toronto Public Library, Toronto. Author of *Public Libraries in the Urban Metropolitan Setting.*
Literature (*in part*)

CARSANIGA, GIOVANNI. Reader in Italian, University of Sussex, Eng.
Literature (*in part*)

CASEMENT, RICHARD. Transport Correspondent, *The Economist,* London. Author of *Urban Traffic: Policies in Congestion.*
Transportation (*in part*)

CASSIDY, VICTOR M. Writer and editor, currently at work on a biography of Wyndham Lewis.
Biography (*in part*)

CHALMEY, LUCIEN. Adviser, Union Internationale des Producteurs et Distributeurs d'Énergie Électrique, Paris.
Energy (*in part*)

CHAPMAN, KENNETH F. Editor, *Stamp Collecting;* Philatelic Correspondent, *The Times,* London. Author of *Good Stamp Collecting; Commonwealth Stamp Collecting.*
Philately and Numismatics (*in part*)

CHAPMAN, ROBIN. Senior Economic Research Officer, Lloyds Bank International, London.
Cuba; Mexico

CHAPPELL, DUNCAN. Director, Law and Justice Study Center, Battelle Memorial Institute, Seattle, Washington. Co-author of *The Police and the Public in Australia and New Zealand; The Australian Criminal Justice System.*
Crime and Law Enforcement (*in part*)

CHAUSSIN. ROBERT. Government Civil Engineer, SETRA (Service d'études Techniques des Routes et Autoroutes), Bagneux, France.
Engineering Projects (*in part*)

CHU, HUNG-TI. Expert in Far Eastern Affairs. UN Area Specialist and Chief of Asia-Africa Section and Trusteeship Council Section, 1946–67; Professor of Government, Texas Tech. University, Lubbock, 1968–69.
China; Taiwan

CLIFTON, DONALD F. Professor of Metallurgy, University of Idaho.
Metallurgy

CLOUD, STANLEY WILLS. Washington, D.C., Correspondent, *Time* magazine.
Biography (*in part*)

COGLE, T. C. J. Editor, *Electrical Review,* London.
Industrial Production and Technology (*in part*)

COLLINS, LESLIE JOHN DUDLEY. Lecturer in Bulgarian History, University of London.
Cyprus

COOTE, JAMES. Athletics Correspondent, The *Daily Telegraph,* London. Author of *Olympic Report 1968; The Olympics 1972; A Picture History of the Olympics.*
Track and Field Sports (*in part*)

COPELAND, JAMES C. Associate Professor, Department of Microbiology, Ohio State University.
Life Sciences (*in part*)

COSTIN, STANLEY H. British Correspondent, *Australian Tailor and Menswear* and *Herrenjournal International.* Former President, Men's Fashion Writers International.
Fashion and Dress (*in part*)

CRATER, RUFUS W. Chief Correspondent, *Broadcasting,* New York City.
Television and Radio (*in part*)

CROSSLAND, NORMAN. Bonn Correspondent, *The Guardian,* London, and British Broadcasting Corporation.
Biography (*in part*); German Democratic Republic; Germany, Federal Republic of

CVIIC, K. F. Leader Writer and East European Specialist, *The Economist,* London.
Biography (*in part*); Czechoslovakia; Yugoslavia

DAIFUKU, HIROSHI, Chief, Sites and Monuments Division, UNESCO, Paris.
Historic Preservation

DAUME, DAPHNE. Editor, Encyclopædia Britannica, Yearbooks.
Biography (*in part*)

DAVID, TUDOR. Managing Editor, *Education,* London.
Education (*in part*)

DAVIS, DONALD A. Editor, *Drug & Cosmetic Industry,* New York. Contributor to *The Science and Technology of Aerosol Packaging.*
Industrial Production and Technology (*in part*)

DAWBER, ALFRED. Textile consultant in all aspects of textile production. Specialized writer on textile, engineering, and electrical subjects.
Industrial Production and Technology (*in part*)

d'ECA, RAUL. Formerly Fulbright Visiting Lecturer on American History, University of Minas Gerais, Belo Horizonte, Braz. Co-author of *Latin American History.*
Brazil

DECRAENE, PHILIPPE. Member of editorial staff, *Le Monde,* Paris. Editor in Chief, *Revue française d'Études politiques africaines.* Author of *Le Panafricanisme; Tableau des Partis Politiques Africains.*
Cameroon; Central African Republic; Chad; Congo; Dahomey; Dependent States (*in part*); Ivory Coast

de la BARRE, KENNETH. Director, Montreal Office, Arctic Institute of North America.
Arctic Regions

DEMPSEY, GEOFFREY. Fellow of Institute of Practitioners in Advertising, J. Walter Thompson Co. Ltd., London.
Advertising (*in part*)

DENNERSTEIN, R. J. M. Free-lance Writer, Jerusalem.
Biography (*in part*)

DE PUY, NORMAN R. Senior Minister, First Baptist Church of Dearborn, Mich.; formerly Executive Director, Division of Communication, American Baptist Churches, USA, Valley Forge, Pa. Author of *The Bible Alive.*
Religion (*in part*)

DILLARD, DUDLEY. Professor and Chairman, Department of Economics, University of Maryland. Author of *The Economics of John Maynard Keynes; Economic Development of the North Atlantic Community.*
Economics

DIRNBACHER, ELFRIEDE. Austrian Civil Servant.
Austria; Biography (*in part*)

EDLIN, HERBERT L. Publications Officer, Forestry Commission of Great Britain. Author of *Trees, Woods and Man; Wayside and Woodland Trees; Man and Plants; What Wood Is That?; Guide to Tree Planting and Cultivation.* Co-author of *Atlas of Plant Life; The World of Trees.*
Environment (*in part*)

EDWARDS, JOHN. Research Fellow, University of Leeds, Eng. Author of *Social Patterns in Birmingham.*
Housing

EISENBERG, WARREN W. Administrative Assistant to Rep. H. John Heinz III, Washington, D.C.
Populations and Areas

ENGELS, JAN R. Editor, *Vooruitgang* (Quarterly of the Belgian Party for Freedom and Progress), Brussels.
Belgium; Biography (*in part*)

EWART, W. D. Editor and Director, *Fairplay International Shipping Weekly,* London. Author of *Marine Engines; Atomic Submarines; Hydrofoils and Hovercraft; Building a Ship.* Editor of *World Atlas of Shipping.*
Industrial Production and Technology (*in part*); Transportation (*in part*)

FARR, D. M. L. Professor of History, Carleton University, Ottawa. Author of *The Colonial Office and Canada, 1867–1887; Two Democracies; The Canadian Experience.*
Canada

FAULKNER, D. J. Fellow, Mount Stromlo and Siding Spring Observatory, Australian National University, Canberra. Contributor to various scientific journals.
Astronomy

FENDELL, ROBERT J. New York Editor, *Automotive News.* Automobile Columnist for *Gentleman's Quarterly.* President Emeritus, International Motor Press Association. Co-author, *Encyclopedia of Motor Racing Greats.*
Motor Sports (*in part*)

FERRIER, R. W. Group Historian,
British Petroleum, London.
Energy (*in part*)

FIDDICK, PETER, Features Editor,
The Guardian, London.
Publishing (*in part*)

FIRTH, DAVID GEORGE. Editor, *The
Friend*, London ; formerly Editor, *Quaker
Monthly*, London.
Religion (*in part*)

FOWELL, R. J. Lecturer, Department
of Mining Engineering, University of
Newcastle upon Tyne, Eng.
Energy (*in part*)

FRANCO, JEAN. Professor of Spanish
and Portuguese, Stanford University.
Author of *The Modern Culture of Latin
America ; An Introduction to Spanish-
American Literature*.
Literature (*in part*)

FRANKLIN, HAROLD. Editor, *English
Bridge Quarterly*. Bridge Correspondent,
Yorkshire Post ; Yorkshire Evening Post.
Broadcaster. Author of *Best of Bridge on
the Air*.
Contract Bridge

FREDRICKSON, DAVID A. Associate
Professor of Anthropology, Sonoma State
College, Rohnert Park, Calif.
Archaeology (*in part*)

FRIDOVICH, IRWIN. Professor of
Biochemistry, Duke University Medical
Center, Durham, N.C.
Life Sciences (*in part*)

FRIEDLY, ROBERT L. Director,
Office of Communication, Christian Church
(Disciples of Christ), Indianapolis, Ind.
Religion (*in part*)

FRIEDMAN, IRVING S. Senior
International Policy Adviser, First
National City Bank of New York, and
formerly Economic Adviser to the
President of the World Bank and
Department Director of the International
Monetary Fund. Author of *Inflation: A
World-Wide Disaster ; Exchange Controls
and the International Monetary System ;
U.S. Foreign Economic Policy*.
Development, Economic and Social

FROST, DAVID. Rugby Union
Correspondent, *The Guardian*, London.
Football (*in part*)

FROST, J. WILLIAM. Associate Professor
of Religion and Director, Friends
Historical Library, Swarthmore (Penn.)
College. Author of *The Quaker Family
in Colonial America*.
Religion (*in part*)

FULLER, M. F. Lecturer in Economic
and Social Statistics, Darwin College,
University of Kent at Canterbury, Eng.
Income, National

GADDUM, PETER W. Chairman,
H. T. Gaddum and Company Ltd.,
Silk Merchants, Macclesfield,
Cheshire, Eng. President, International
Silk Association, Lyons. Author of
Silk—How and Where It Is Produced.
Industrial Production and Technology
   (*in part*)

GALVANO, FABIO. Special
Correspondent, *Gazzetta del Popolo*,
Turin, Italy.
Italy

GANADO, ALBERT. Lawyer, Malta.
Malta

GEORGE, T. J. S. World Population
Year Secretariat, United Nations, New
York. Author of *Krishna Menon: A
Biography ; Lee Kuan Yew's Singapore*.
Biography (*in part*) ; Cambodia; Korea; Laos;
   Southeast Asian Affairs; Thailand

GINZBERG, ELI. A. Barton Hepburn
Professor of Economics and Director,
Conservation of Human Resources,
Columbia University. Author of *Men,
Money and Medicine ; Urban Health
Services: The Case of New York*.
Health and Disease (*in part*)

GJESTER, FAY. Oslo Correspondent,
Financial Times, London.
Norway

GLIKSON, PAUL. Secretary, Division of
Jewish Demography and Statistics,
Institute of Contemporary Jewry, the
Hebrew University of Jerusalem, Israel.
Religion (*in part*)

GODWIN, MORGAN. W. Assistant
Secretary, American Radio Relay
League, Newington, Conn.
Television and Radio (*in part*)

GOLLAND, B. L. General Secretary,
the General Assembly of Unitarian and
Free Christian Churches, London.
Religion (*in part*)

GOLOMBEK, HARRY. British Chess
Champion, 1947, 1949, and 1955.
Chess Correspondent, *The Times* and
Observer, London. Author of *Penguin
Handbook on the Game of Chess ;
Modern Opening Chess Strategy*.
Biography (*in part*) ; Chess

GOODWIN, R. M. Free-lance Writer,
London.
Gabon; Guinea; Horse Racing (*in part*) ;
   Malagasy Republic; Mali; Mauritania;
   Niger; Senegal; Togo; Upper Volta

GORALSKI, ROBERT. NBC News
Washington Correspondent.
Vietnam

GOULD, DONALD W. Medical
Correspondent, *The New Statesman*,
London.
Drug Abuse (*in part*) ; Health and
   Disease (*in part*)

GOULD, ROWLAND. Free-lance Writer.
Biography (*in part*)

GRAHAM, JARLATH JOHN. Editor,
Advertising Age.
Advertising (*in part*)

GRAY, LYNDA. News Editor, *B & T
Weekly*, Sydney, Austr.
Television and Radio (*in part*)

GREEN, BENNY. Jazz Critic, *Observer*,
London ; Record Reviewer, British Broad-
casting Corporation. Author of *The
Reluctant Art ; Blame It on My Youth ;
58 Minutes to London ; Jazz Decade ;
Drums in My Ears*. Contributor to
Encyclopedia of Jazz.
Music (*in part*)

GRIFFITHS, A. R. G. Senior Lecturer
in History, Flinders University of South
Australia.
Australia; Biography (*in part*) ; Nauru

GROVE, ROBERT D. Former Director,
Division of Vital Statistics, U.S.
Public Health Service. Co-author of *Vital
Statistics Rates in the United States,
1900–1940 ; Vital Statistics Rates in
the United States, 1940–1960*.
Demography

HACHTEN, WILLIAM A. Professor,
School of Journalism and Mass
Communication, University of Wisconsin,
Madison.
Publishing (*in part*)

HARRIES, DAVID A. Director, Kinnear
Moodie (1973) Ltd., Peterborough, Eng.
Engineering Projects (*in part*)

HARRIS, LEONARD R. Director of
Projects for Subsidiaries, the *New York
Times*.
Publishing (*in part*)

HASEGAWA, RYUSAKU. Editor,
TBS-Britannica Co., Ltd., Tokyo.
Biography (*in part*)

HATHAWAY, RICHARD O. Teaching
Faculty, History and International Studies,
Goddard College, Plainfield, Vt.
Pacifism and Nonviolent Movements

HAWKLAND, WILLIAM D. Professor
of Law, University of Illinois.
Author of *Sales Under Uniform
Commercial Code ; Cases on Bills and
Notes ; Commercial Paper ; Transactional
Guide of the Uniform Commercial Code ;
Cases on Sales and Security*.
Law (*in part*)

HAWLEY, H. B. Consultant, Human
Nutrition and Food Science,
Sherborne, Eng.
Food Processing (*in part*)

HEAP, JOHN ARNFIELD. Former
member of the British Antarctic Survey.
Antarctica

HEBBLETHWAITE, PETER. Deputy
Editor, *Frontier*, Cambridge, Eng. Author
of *Bernanos ; The Council Fathers and
Atheism ; Understanding the Synod*.
Editor of *Faith in Question ; Talking
with Unbelievers*.
Biography (*in part*) ; Religion (*in part*)

HENDERSHOTT, MYRL C. Associate
Professor of Oceanography,
Scripps Institution of Oceanography,
La Jolla, Calif.
Earth Sciences (*in part*)

HEPPER, FRANK N. Principal Scientific
Officer, Herbarium, Royal Botanic
Gardens, Kew, Eng. Co-author of
Plant Collectors in West Africa.
Editor of *Flora of West Tropical Africa*
(vol. ii and iii).
Zoos and Botanical Gardens (*in part*)

HOCKLEY, G. C. Senior Lecturer,
Department of Economics, University
College, Cardiff, Wales. Author of
Monetary Policy and Public Finance.
Co-author of *The Wealth of the Nation:
The Balance Sheet of the United Kingdom,
1957–61*.
Taxation (*in part*)

HODGSON, ROBERT D. The Geographer,
U.S. Department of State, Washington,
D.C. Author of *The Changing Map
of Africa*.
Andorra; Liechtenstein; Luxembourg; Monaco;
San Marino

HOLLANDS, R. L. Hockey Correspondent,
the *Daily Telegraph*, London. Co-author
of *Hockey*.
Hockey (*in part*)

HOLZ, ERNEST W. National Chief
Secretary and Colonel, Salvation Army,
U.S.A.
Religion (*in part*)

HOPE, THOMAS WALKER. President
and Publisher, Hope Reports, Inc.,
Rochester, N.Y. Author of *Hope Reports
AV-USA 1972 ; Hope Reports Education &
Media 1972*.
Motion Pictures (*in part*)

HORN, PATRICE DAILY. Editor,
Behavior Today ; Senior Editor,
Psychology Today, Del Mar, Calif.
Behavioural Sciences

HOTZ, LOUIS. Former editorial writer,
the *Johannesburg* (S.Af.) *Star*. Co-author
and contributor to *The Jews in
South Africa: A History*.
Biography (*in part*) ; South Africa

HUGHES, TERENCE. Director of Publications, International Broadcast Institute, London.
Television and Radio (*in part*)

HUNNINGS, NEVILLE MARCH. General Editor, Common Law Reports Ltd., London. Editor of *Common Market Law Reports, European Law Digest*, and *Eurolaw Commercial Intelligence*. Author of *Film Censors and the Law*. Co-editor of *Legal Problems of an Enlarged European Community*.
Law (*in part*)

HURTIG, SERGE. Secretary General, Fondation Nationale des Sciences Politiques; Professor, Paris Institute of Political Studies. Former Secretary-General, International Political Science Association.
Political Science

INGHAM, KENNETH. Professor of History, University of Bristol, Eng. Author of *Reformers in India; A History of East Africa*.
Dependent States (*in part*); Guinea-Bissau; Kenya; Malawi; Rhodesia; Tanzania; Uganda; Zaire; Zambia

ISSA (INTERNATIONAL SOCIAL SECURITY ASSOCIATION), Geneva.
Social and Welfare Services (*in part*)

ITU (INTERNATIONAL TELECOMMUNICATION UNION), Geneva.
Telecommunications (*in part*)

IULA. Research staff, International Union of Local Authorities, The Hague, Neth.
Cities and Urban Affairs

JACKSON, D. A. S. Research Officer, Department of Applied Economics, University of Cambridge; Fellow of St. Catharine's College, Cambridge.
Employment, Wages, and Hours

JARDINE, ADRIAN. Company Director and Public Relations Consultant. Secretary, Guild of Yachting Writers.
Sailing

JASPERT, W. PINCUS. Technical editorial consultant. European Editor, North American Publishing Company, Philadelphia, Pa. Member, Society of Photographic Scientists and Engineers. Editor of *Encyclopaedia of Type Faces*.
Industrial Production and Technology (*in part*)

JOHN, LAURIE. Producer, Science and Features Department, British Broadcasting Corporation, London.
Telecommunications (*in part*)

JONES, C. M. Editor, *World Bowls; Lawn Tennis*. Author of *Winning Bowls; How to Become a Champion;* numerous books on tennis. Co-author of *Tackle Bowls My Way; Bryant on Bowls*.
Bowling and Lawn Bowls (*in part*)

JONES, W. GLYN. Professor of Scandinavian Studies, University of Newcastle upon Tyne, Eng. Author of *Johannes Jørgensens modne år; Johannes Jørgensen; Denmark; William Heinesen; Færø og kosmos*.
Literature (*in part*)

JOSEPH, LOU. Manager of Media Relations, Bureau of Public Information, American Dental Association. Author of *Allergy—Facts and Fallacies*.
Health and Disease (*in part*)

KAAN, FREDERIK H. Secretary of the Department of Cooperation and Witness, World Alliance of Reformed Churches (Presbyterian and Congregational), Geneva. Author of *Pilgrim Praise* (hymns).
Religion (*in part*)

KAPLANSKY, IRVING. George Herbert Mead Distinguished Service Professor, Department of Mathematics, the University of Chicago.
Mathematics

KATZ, WILLIAM A. Professor, School of Library Science, State University of New York. Author of *Magazines for Libraries; Introduction to Reference Work*.
Publishing (*in part*)

KELLEHER, JOHN A. Editor, *The Dominion*, Wellington, N.Z.
Biography (*in part*); New Zealand

KENT, LOTTE. Editor, *Cooperative News Service*, International Cooperative Alliance, London.
Cooperatives

KERR, J. A. Senior Lecturer, University of Birmingham, Eng.
Chemistry (*in part*)

KERRIGAN, ANTHONY. Editor and translator of *Selected Works* of Miguel de Unamuno (10 vol.). Author of *At the Front Door of the Atlantic*. Editor and Translator of works of Jorge Luis Borges.
Literature (*in part*)

KILLHEFFER, JOHN V. Associate Editor, *Encyclopædia Britannica*.
Chemistry (*in part*)

KILLIN, ORLAND B. Professor of Industrial Education and Technology, Eastern Washington State College.
Industrial Production and Technology (*in part*)

KILNER, PETER. Editor, *Arab Report and Record*, London.
Algeria; Biography (*in part*); Morocco; Sudan

KIMCHE, JON. Expert on Middle East Affairs, *Evening Standard*, London. Author of *There Could Have Been Peace: The Untold Story of Why We Failed with Palestine and Again with Israel*.
Israel

KIND, JOSHUA B. Associate Professor of Art History, Northern Illinois University. Author of *Rouault*.
Museums (*in part*)

KIRKHAM, FRANCES. Information Officer, British Non-Ferrous Metals Federation, Birmingham, Eng.
Argentina; Peru

KITAGAWA, JOSEPH M. Professor of History of Religions and Dean of the Divinity School, the University of Chicago. Author of *Religions of the East; Religion in Japanese History*.
Religion (*in part*)

KLARE, HUGH J. Member of Parole Board for England and Wales; Member of the Council, International Penal and Penitentiary Foundations. Secretary, Howard League for Penal Reform 1950–71. Author of *People in Prison*.
Prisons and Penology

KLAUSLER, ALFRED P. Editor at Large, *Christian Century*, Chicago; Religion Editor, Westinghouse Broadcasting Company. Author of *Censorship, Obscenity and Sex; Growth in Worship*. Co-editor of *The Journalist's Prayer Book*.
Religion (*in part*)

KNECHT, JEAN. Former Assistant Foreign Editor, *Le Monde*, Paris; Former Permanent Correspondent in Washington and Vice-President of the Association de la Presse Diplomatique Française.
France

KNEESHAW, JOHN. Economist, Bank for International Settlements, Basel, Switz.
Money and Banking

KNORR, N. H. President, Watch Tower Bible and Tract Society of Pennsylvania.
Religion (*in part*)

KOPPER, PHILIP. Free-lance Writer, Washington, D.C.
Biography (*in part*); Nobel Prizes

KOVAN, RICHARD W. Features Editor, *Nuclear Engineering International*, London.
Industrial Production and Technology (*in part*)

KRADER, BARBARA. Past President, Society for Ethnomusicology; Executive Secretary, International Folk Music Council, London, 1965–66.
Music (*in part*)

KRIZ, MIROSLAV A. Vice-President, First National City Bank, New York City, 1958–73; Federal Reserve Bank of New York, 1945–58; Economic and Financial Department of the Secretariat of the League of Nations, 1936–45.
Economy, World; Exchange and Payments, International

KUBITSCHEK, H. E. Senior Biophysicist, Division of Biological and Medical Research, Argonne National Laboratory. Author of *Introduction to Research with Continuous Cultures*.
Life Sciences (*in part*)

LEGUM, COLIN. Associate Editor and Commonwealth Correspondent, *Observer*, London. Author of *Must We Lose Africa?; Congo Disaster*. Editor of *Africa Contemporary Record*.
African Affairs; Biography (*in part*)

LEIFER, MICHAEL. Reader in International Relations, London School of Economics and Political Science. Author of *Dilemmas of Statehood in Southeast Asia*.
Malaysia; Singapore

LENNOX-KERR, PETER. Editor and Publisher, *Textile Manufacturer*, Manchester. Author of *Index to Man-Made Fibres of the World; The World Fibres Book*. Editor of *Nonwovens '71*.
Industrial Production and Technology (*in part*)

LINFORD, AARON. Editor of *Redemption Tidings*, weekly official organ of Assemblies of God in Great Britain and Ireland. Author of *Will the Church Go Through the Tribulation?; A Course of Study in Spiritual Gifts; The Baptism in the Holy Spirit; Living like Angels; Fabulously Rich; Divine Retribution*.
Religion (*in part*)

LITTELL, FRANKLIN H. Professor, Department of Religion, Temple University, Philadelphia, Pa. Co-editor of *Weltkirchenlexikon*.
Religion (*in part*)

LULING, VIRGINIA R. Social Anthropologist.
Somalia

LUSTIG, LAWRENCE K. Managing Editor, Encyclopædia Britannica, Yearbooks.
Biography (*in part*)

MacDONALD, BARRIE KEITH. Lecturer in History, Massey University, Palmerston North, N.Z. Author of several articles on the history and politics of Pacific islands.
Fiji; Tonga; Western Samoa

MacDONALD, M. C. Director, Econtel Research Ltd., London. Editor, *World Series; Business Cycle Series*.
Agriculture and Food Supplies (*in part*) Transportation (*in part*)

MACDONALD, TREVOR J. Manager, International Affairs, British Steel Corporation.
Industrial Production and Technology (*in part*)

McMANUS, IRENE. Associate Editor, *American Forests*, Washington, D.C.
Forestry

McMURRIN, STERLING M. Ericksen Distinguished Professor and Dean of the Graduate School, University of Utah. Co-author of *A History of Philosophy*.
Philosophy

MALLETT, H. M. F. Editor, *Weekly Wool Chart*, Bradford, Eng.
Industrial Production and Technology (*in part*)

MANGO, ANDREW. Orientalist and Broadcaster.
Biography (*in part*); Turkey

MANSFIELD, PETER. Formerly Middle East Correspondent, *Sunday Times*, London. Free-lance Writer on Middle East affairs.
Bahrain; Biography (*in part*); Egypt; Iraq; Jordan; Kuwait; Lebanon; Middle Eastern Affairs; Oman; Qatar; Saudi Arabia; Syria; United Arab Emirates; Yemen, People's Democratic Republic of; Yemen Arab Republic

MARCELLO, ALDO. Civil Engineer.
Engineering Projects (*in part*)

MARCUS, IRVING H. Publisher, *Wine Publications*; Columnist, *Wines and Vines*. Author of *Dictionary of Wine Terms; Lines About Wines; How to Test and Improve Your Wine Judging Ability*.
Alcoholic Beverages (*in part*)

MARSHALL, J. G. SCOTT. Horticultural Consultant.
Gardening (*in part*)

MARTENHOFF, JIM. Boating Editor, *Miami* (Fla.) *Herald*. Author of *How to Buy a Better Boat; Handbook of Skin and Scuba Diving*.
Motor Sports (*in part*)

MATSUBARA, MASAKI. Director of Planning, *Zaikai* magazine, Tokyo.
Biography (*in part*)

MATTHÍASSON, BJÖRN. Iceland Correspondent, *Financial Times*, London.
Iceland

MAUDE, N. F. Consultant Editor, *British Journal of Photography*; *Photo Trader*. Editor, *Photographic Processor*. Author of *Take Better Photos; Choosing a Camera*.
Photography

MAURON, PAUL. Director, International Vine and Wine Office, Paris.
Alcoholic Beverages (*in part*)

MAZIE, DAVID M. Associate of Carl T. Rowan, syndicated columnist. Free-lance Writer.
Social and Welfare Services (*in part*)

MERMEL, T. W. Consulting Engineer; formerly Assistant to Commissioner for Scientific Affairs, Bureau of Reclamation, U.S. Department of the Interior, Washington, D.C. Chairman, Committee on World Register of Dams, International Commission on Large Dams. Author of *Register of Dams in the United States*.
Engineering Projects (*in part*)

MEYENDORFF, JOHN. Professor of Church History and Patristics, St. Vladimir's Seminary; Professor of History, Fordham University, New York City; Lecturer in Eastern Orthodoxy, Union Theological Seminary, New York.
Religion (*in part*)

MILES, PETER W. Chairman, Department of Entomology, University of Adelaide, Austr.
Life Sciences (*in part*)

MILLARD, R. S. Deputy Director, Transport and Road Research Laboratory, Department of the Environment, Crowthorne, Berkshire, Eng.
Engineering Projects (*in part*)

MILLER, WILLIAM B. Manager, Department of History, United Presbyterian Church, U.S.A.
Religion (*in part*)

MILLIKIN, SANDRA. Architectural Historian.
Architecture; Art Exhibitions

MINNES, GORDON. Secretary, Canadian Pulp and Paper Association.
Industrial Production and Technology (*in part*)

MITCHELL, K. K. Lecturer, Department of Physical Education, Leeds University. Hon. General Secretary, Amateur Basket Ball Association.
Basketball (*in part*)

MODEAN, ERIK W. Director, News Bureau, Lutheran Council in the U.S.A.
Religion (*in part*)

MODIANO, MARIO. Athens Correspondent, *The Times*, London.
Greece

MORGAN, HAZEL. Production Assistant (Sleevenotes and Covers), E.M.I. Records Ltd., London.
Music (*in part*)

MORRISON, DONALD MATHER. Staff Writer, *Time* magazine, New York.
Publishing (*in part*)

MORTIMER, MOLLY. Commonwealth Correspondent, *The Spectator*, London. Author of *Trusteeship in Practice; Kenya*.
Botswana; Burundi; Commonwealth of Nations; Dependent States (*in part*); Gambia, The; Ghana; Lesotho; Maldives; Mauritius; Nigeria; Rwanda; Sierra Leone; Swaziland

MOSS, ROBERT V. President, United Church of Christ, New York City; President, American Association of Theological Schools, 1966–68. Author of *The Life of Paul; We Believe; As Paul Sees Christ*.
Religion (*in part*)

MOTTERSHEAD, G. S. Director-Secretary, Chester Zoo, Chester, Eng.
Zoos and Botanical Gardens (*in part*)

MULLINS, STEPHANIE. Historian.
Biography (*in part*)

NARBOROUGH, COLIN. Reuters Correspondent, Helsinki, Fin.
Finland

NATOLI, SALVATORE J. Educational Affairs Director, Association of American Geographers. Co-author of *Dictionary of Basic Geography*.
Geography

NAYLOR, ERNEST. Professor of Marine Biology, University of Liverpool; Director, Marine Biological Laboratory, Port Erin, Isle of Man. Author of *British Marine Isopods*.
Life Sciences (*in part*)

NEILL, JOHN. Chief Chemical Engineer, Submerged Combustion Ltd. Author of Climbers' Club Guides; *Cwm Silyn and Tremadoc, Snowdon South*; Alpine Club Guide: *Selected Climbs in the Pennine Alps*.
Mountaineering

NELSON, BERT. Editor and Publisher, *Track and Field News*.
Track and Field Sports (*in part*)

NETSCHERT, BRUCE C. Vice-President, National Economic Research Associates, Inc., Washington, D.C. Author of *The Future Supply of Oil and Gas*. Co-author of *Energy in the American Economy: 1850–1975*.
Energy (*in part*)

NEWMAN, PHILIP L. Associate Professor of Anthropology, University of California at Los Angeles. Author of *Knowing the Gururumba*.
Anthropology

NOEL, H. S. Managing Editor, *World Fishing*, London.
Fisheries (*in part*)

NORMAN, GERALDINE. Saleroom Correspondent, *The Times*, London. Author of *The Sale of Works of Art*.
Art Sales

NOVALES, RONALD R. Professor of Biological Sciences, Northwestern University, Evanston, Ill. Chairman, Division of Comparative Endocrinology, The American Society of Zoologists.
Life Sciences (*in part*)

NOVICK, JULIUS. Associate Professor of Literature, State University of New York at Purchase. Drama Critic for the *Village Voice* and *The Humanist*. Contributor to *The Nation*; the *New York Times*. Author of *Beyond Broadway: The Quest for Permanent Theatres*.
Theatre (*in part*)

NOVOSTI. Novosti Press Agency, Moscow.
Literature (*in part*)

O'LEARY, JEREMIAH A. State Department Correspondent, *Washington* (D.C.) *Evening Star-News*. Author of *Dominican Action—1965; Panama: Canal Issues and Treaty Talks—1967*.
Biography (*in part*); Chile

OSBORNE, KEITH. Editor, *Rowing*, 1961–63. Hon. Editor, *British Rowing Almanack*, 1961– .
Rowing

OSTERBIND, CARTER C. Director, Bureau of Economic and Business Research, University of Florida. Editor, *Feasible Planning for Social Change in the Field of Aging*.
Engineering Projects (*in part*); Industrial Production and Technology (*in part*)

PAKEMAN, SIDNEY A. Historian. Author of *Ceylon*.
Sri Lanka.

PALMER, S. B. Lecturer, Department of Applied Physics, University of Hull, Eng.
Physics

PANIĆ, MILIVOJE. Chief Economist, National Economic Development Office, London.
Prices

PARGAS, RAFAEL. Free-lance Writer, Washington, D.C.
Philippines

PARKER, SANDY. Fur Editor, *Women's Wear Daily.*
Furs

PARNELL, COLIN. Editor, *Wine and Spirit Trade International,* London.
Alcoholic Beverages (*in part*)

PARSONS, ANNE. Economic Research Officer, Lloyds Bank International, London.
Ecuador; Paraguay; Uruguay

PATTEN, GEORGE P. Professor of Geography, Ohio State University.
Nicaragua

PATTERSON, SHEILA. Research Associate, Department of Anthropology, University College, London. Author of *Colour and Culture in South Africa; The Last Trek; Dark Strangers; Immigrants in Industry.*
Bahamas, The; Barbados; Dependent States (*in part*); Grenada; Guyana; Jamaica; Migration, International; Race Relations (*in part*); Trinidad and Tobago.

PEARCE, JOAN. Research Officer, Economics Department, Lloyds Bank International, London. Editor of *Latin America: A Broader World Role.*
Biography (*in part*); Colombia; Costa Rica; Guatemala; Spain

PENFOLD, ROBIN C. Public relations executive, Carl Byoir and Associates Ltd., London. Author of *A Journalist's Guide to Plastics.*
Industrial Production and Technology (*in part*)

PETERSON, VIRGIL W. Executive Director, Chicago Crime Commission, 1942–70. Author of *Gambling—Should It Be Legalized?; Barbarians in Our Midst.*
Crime and Law Enforcement (*in part*)

PETHERICK, KARIN. Crown Princess Louise Lecturer in Swedish, University College, London.
Literature (*in part*)

PETTIGREW, THOMAS F. Professor of Social Psychology, Harvard University. Author of *A Profile of the Negro American; Racially Separate or Together?; Racial Discrimination in the United States.*
Race Relations (*in part*)

PFEFFER, IRVING. Professor of Insurance and Finance, College of Business, Virginia Polytechnic Institute and State University. Author of *Insurance and Economic Theory; The Financing of Small Business; Perspectives on Insurance.*
Stock Exchanges (*in part*)

PHILLIPS, D. K. R. Former Secretary-General, Association of Track and Field Statisticians. Contributor, *Sportsworld.* Editor, *World Sports Olympic Games Report.* Co-compiler of *Guinness Book of Olympic Records; Sportsworld International Athletics Annual.*
Sporting Record

PICK, OTTO. Professor of International Relations, University of Surrey, Guildford, Eng. Director, Atlantic Information Centre for Teachers, London.
Union of Soviet Socialist Republics

PIERCE, FRANCIS S. Editor, Consumers Digest, Inc., Chicago. Contributor to *Encyclopædia Britannica.*
Biography (*in part*); Government Finance

PLATT, MAURICE. Consulting Engineer. Former Director of Engineering, Vauxhall Motors, Ltd. Author of *Elements of Automobile Engineering.*
Industrial Production and Technology (*in part*)

PLOTKIN, FREDERICK S. Associate Professor of English and Philosophy, Chairman, Department of English, Stern College, Yeshiva University, New York. Author of *Milton's Inward Jerusalem; Faith and Reason; Judaism and Tragic Theology.*
Literature (*in part*)

POLLACK, GERALD A. Senior Economic Adviser, Exxon Corporation. Author of *Perspectives on the U.S. International Financial Position.*
Profits

POTTER, SIMEON. Emeritus Professor of English Language and Philology, University of Liverpool, Eng. Author of *Our Language; Language in the Modern World; Modern Linguistics; Changing English.*
Words and Meanings, New

PRAG, DEREK. Business Consultant and Free-lance Journalist. Director, London Information Office of the European Communities, 1965–73. Co-author of *Businessman's Guide to the Common Market.*
European Unity

PRASAD, H. Y. SHARADA. Director of Information, Prime Minister's Secretariat, New Delhi, India.
Biography (*in part*); India

PREIL, GABRIEL. Writer. Hebrew and Yiddish poet. Author of *Israeli Poetry in Peace and War; Nof Shemesh Ukhfor* ("Landscape of Sun and Frost"); *Ner Mul Kokhavim* ("Candle Against the Stars"); *Mapat Erev* ("Map of Evening"); *Lieder* ("Poems"); *Haesh Vehadmama* ("The Fire and the Silence"); *Mitoch Zeman Venof* ("Of Time and Place").
Literature (*in part*)

RANGER, ROBERT J. Assistant Professor, Department of Political Science, St. Francis Xavier University, Antigonish, Nova Scotia.
Defense

RAVEN, VIVIAN. Managing Editor, *Tobacco,* London.
Industrial Production and Technology (*in part*)

RAY, G. F. Senior Research Fellow, National Institute of Economic and Social Research, London.
Industrial Production and Technology (*in part*)

READ, HARRY. Director, Salvation Army International Information Services, London.
Religion (*in part*)

RECKERT, STEPHEN. Camoens Professor of Portuguese, King's College, University of London. Author of *Do cancioneiro de amigo; Gil Vicente: espíritu y letra.*
Literature (*in part*)

REIBSTEIN, JOAN NATALIE. Free-lance Writer and Editor. Former Staff Writer, *Encyclopædia Britannica.*
Biography (*in part*)

REICHELDERFER, FRANCIS W. Aeronautical and Marine Meteorology Consultant. Former Chief, Weather Bureau, U.S. Department of Commerce, Washington, D.C.
Earth Sciences (*in part*)

REID, J. H. Lecturer in German, University of Nottingham, Eng. Author of *Heinrich Böll: Withdrawal and Re-emergence.* Co-author of *Critical Strategies: German Fiction in the 20th Century.*
Literature (*in part*)

REYNOLDS, ARTHUR GUY. Formerly Registrar and Professor of Church History, Emmanuel College, Toronto.
Religion (*in part*)

RILEY, WALLACE B. Computers Editor, *Electronics* magazine.
Computers

ROBBINS, FRANCES G. Environmental Policy Division, Congressional Research Service, Library of Congress.
Agriculture and Food Supplies (*in part*)

ROBERTS, R. L. Editorial Consultant, *Church Times,* London.
Religion (*in part*)

ROBINSON, DAVID. Film Critic, *The Times,* London. Author of *Buster Keaton; Hollywood in the Twenties; The Great Funnies—A History of Screen Comedy; A History of World Cinema.*
Motion Pictures (*in part*)

RODERICK, JOHN P. Foreign Correspondent in Tokyo, Associated Press. Author of *What You Should Know About China.*
Biography (*in part*)

ROSENWALD, ALAN K. Chairman, Department of Psychology, Illinois State Psychiatric Institute, Chicago.
Health and Disease (*in part*)

RYBCZYNSKI, T. M. Chief Economist and Director, Lazard Securities Ltd., London.
Savings and Investment

SAEKI, SHOICHI. Professor, College of General Education, University of Tokyo.
Literature (*in part*)

SAINT-AMOUR, ROBERT. Professor, Department of Literary Studies, University of Quebec at Montreal. Author of various articles on literary topics.
Literature (*in part*)

SANDON, HAROLD. Former Professor of Zoology, University of Khartoum, Sudan. Author of *The Protozoan Fauna of the Soil; The Food of Protozoa; An Illustrated Guide to the Fresh-Water Fishes of the Sudan; Essays on Protozoology.*
Life Sciences (*in part*)

SARAHETE, YRJÖ. Secretary, Fédération Internationale des Quilleurs, Helsinki, Fin.
Bowling and Lawn Bowls (*in part*)

SCHMITT, TILMAN. Brewery Engineer. Editor of *Brauwelt; Brauwissenschaft,* Nürnberg, W.Ger.
Alcoholic Beverages (*in part*)

SCHOENFIELD, ALBERT. Editor, *Swimming World.*
Swimming

SCHULIAN, JOHN. Reporter, the *Baltimore Evening Sun.*
Basketball (*in part*); Football (*in part*)

SCOTT, BYRON THORPE. Assistant Professor of Journalism, College of Communication, Ohio University.
Health and Disease (*in part*)

SERGEANT, HOWARD. Lecturer and Writer. Editor of *Outposts*, Walton-on-Thames, Eng. Author of *The Cumberland Wordsworth; Tradition in the Making of Modern Poetry*.
Literature (*in part*)

SHACKLEFORD, PETER. Research Adviser, World Tourism Organization (WTO), Geneva.
Tourism

SHARPE, MITCHELL R. Science Writer. Author of *Living in Space: The Environment of the Astronaut; Yuri Gagarin, First Man in Space; Satellites and Probes: The Development of Unmanned Space Flight; "It Is I, Seagull": The Life of Valentina Tereshkova*. Co-author of *Applied Astronautics; Basic Astronautics; Dividends from Space*.
Space Exploration

SHAW, T. R. Commander, Royal Navy. Member, British Cave Research Association.
Speleology

SHERMAN, HARVEY R. Environmental Policy Division, Congressional Research Service, Library of Congress.
Agriculture and Food Supplies (*in part*)

SHIH, C. CHUNG-TSE. Senior Adviser on Trade Negotiations, United Nations Conference on Trade and Development (UNCTAD), Switzerland.
Commercial and Trade Policies

SHOREY, JOHN C. Lecturer in Economics, University College, Cardiff, Wales.
Marketing and Merchandising

SIMPSON, NOEL. Managing Director, Sydney Bloodstock Proprietary Ltd., Sydney, Austr.
Horse Racing (*in part*)

SKELDING, FRANK H. Manager, Market Research, Fluor Utah, Inc.
Energy (*in part*); Mining and Quarrying (*in part*)

SMEDLEY, GLENN B. Governor, American Numismatic Association.
Philately and Numismatics (*in part*)

SMITH, DAN THROOP. Professor Emeritus, Harvard University; Senior Research Fellow, Hoover Institution, Stanford (Calif.) University; Director, Cambridge Research Institute; Former Deputy to Secretary of the Treasury; Former President, National Tax Association and Tax Institute of America. Author of *Federal Tax Reform; Tax Factors in Business Decisions*.
Taxation (*in part*)

SMITH, R. W. Provost, Callison College, University of the Pacific, Stockton, Calif.
Religion (*in part*)

SMITHCORS, J. F. Editor, American Veterinary Publications, Inc., Santa Barbara, Calif. Author of *Evolution of the Veterinary Art; The American Veterinary Profession*.
Veterinary Science

SMOGORZEWSKI, K. M. Writer on contemporary history. Founder and Editor, *Free Europe*, London. Author of *The United States and Great Britain; Poland's Access to the Sea*.
Albania; Biography (*in part*); Bulgaria; Hungary; Mongolia; Poland; Romania; Soviet Bloc Economies

STACKS, JOHN F. Washington, D.C., Bureau News Editor, *Time* magazine. Author of *Stripping: The Surface Mining of America*.
Biography (*in part*)

STAERK, MELANIE. Member, Swiss National Commission for UNESCO (Information).
Switzerland

STAMLER, JEREMIAH. Professor and Chairman, Department of Community Health and Preventive Medicine, and Dingman Professor of Cardiology, Northwestern University Medical School, Chicago. Author of *Lectures on Preventive Cardiology; Your Heart Has Nine Lives*.
Health and Disease (*in part*)

STANTON, LEONARD. Professor of Radiation Therapy and Nuclear Medicine, Hahnemann Medical College and Hospital, Philadelphia. Author of *Basic Medical Radiation Physics*; chapters in *Physics of Diagnostic Radiology*.
Health and Disease (*in part*)

STARKMAN, MOSHE. Essayist in Yiddish and Hebrew; Bibliographer. Former President, Yiddish P.E.N. Club; New York Editor, *Hemshekh Anthology of American Yiddish Poetry*. Associate Editor, *Lexicon of Yiddish Literature*. Contributor, *Jewish Daily Forward*, New York.
Literature (*in part*)

STEVENSON, TOM. Garden Columnist, *Baltimore News American; Washington Post;* Washington Post-Los Angeles Times News Service. Author of *Pruning Guide for Trees, Shrubs and Vines; Lawn Guide; Gardening for the Beginner*.
Gardening (*in part*)

STOKES, J. BUROUGHS. Manager, Committees on Publication, The First Church of Christ, Scientist, Boston.
Religion (*in part*)

STØVERUD, TORBJØRN. W. P. Ker Senior Lecturer in Norwegian, University College, London.
Literature (*in part*)

SWEETINBURGH, THELMA. Paris Fashion Correspondent for *International Textiles* (Amsterdam) and the British Wool Textile Industry.
Fashion and Dress (*in part*)

SWIFT, RICHARD N. Professor of Politics, New York University, New York City. Author of *International Law: Current and Classic*.
United Nations

SYNAN, VINSON. Division Chairman, Emmanuel College, Franklin Springs, Ga.; General Secretary, Pentecostal Holiness Church; President, Society for Pentecostal Studies. Author of *The Holiness-Pentecostal Movement; The Old Time Power*.
Religion (*in part*)

TAISHOFF, SOL. Chairman and Editor, *Broadcasting*, Washington, D.C.
Television and Radio (*in part*)

TATTERSALL, ARTHUR. Textile Trade Expert and Statistician, Manchester, Eng.
Industrial Production and Technology (*in part*)

TAYLOR, WINSTON H. Director, Washington Office, United Methodist Communications. Author of *Angels Don't Need Public Relations; Ending Racial Segregation in the Methodist Church; Toward an Inclusive Church*.
Religion (*in part*)

TERRY, WALTER. Dance Critic, *Saturday Review* magazine, New York. Author of *The Dance in America; The Ballet Companion; Miss Ruth: The "More Living Life" of Ruth St. Denis*.
Dance (*in part*)

THOMAS, HARFORD. City Editor, *The Guardian*, London.
Biography (*in part*); United Kingdom

THOMPSON, ANTHONY. European Linguist, College of Librarianship, Aberystwyth, Wales. General Secretary, International Federation of Library Associations, 1962–70. Author of *Vocabularium Bibliothecarii; Library Buildings of Britain and Europe*.
Libraries

THOMSON, RONALD WILLIAM. Former Assistant General Secretary, Baptist Union of Great Britain and Ireland. Author of *Heroes of the Baptist Church; William Carey; The Service of Our Lives; A Pocket History of the Baptists*.
Religion (*in part*)

TINGAY, LANCE. Lawn Tennis Correspondent, the *Daily Telegraph*, London.
Tennis

TRAIN, CHRISTOPHER JOHN. Assistant Secretary, Probation and After Care Department, Home Office, London.
Drug Abuse (*in part*)

TRIGG, ROBERT H. Senior Economic Adviser and Manager, Institutional Research, New York Stock Exchange.
Stock Exchanges (*in part*)

TRILLING, OSSIA. Vice-President, International Association of Theatre Critics. Co-editor and contributor, *International Theatre*. Contributor, BBC, the *Financial Times*, London.
Biography (*in part*); Theatre (*in part*)

TSUJIMOTO, ICHIRO. Public Relations Officer, Nippon Hoso Kyokai (Japan Broadcasting Corp.), Tokyo.
Television and Radio (*in part*)

TYPE, MICHAEL. Head of Permanent Secretariat, European Broadcasting Union, Geneva.
Television and Radio (*in part*)

UNHCR. The Office of the United Nations High Commissioner for Refugees, Geneva.
Refugees

UNNY, GOVINDAN. Agence France-Presse Special Correspondent for India, Nepal, and Ceylon.
Bangladesh; Bhutan; Burma; Dependent States (*in part*); Nepal

URQUHART, NORMAN R. Assistant Vice-President, in charge of Commodity Section, Economics Department, First National City Bank, New York City.
Commodity Trade

van PRAAG, JACK H. Chairman, National Badminton News Committee, American Badminton Association, Pasadena, Calif. Author of numerous articles on badminton.
Biography (*in part*)

VIANSSON-PONTÉ, PIERRE. Editorial Adviser and Leader Writer, *Le Monde*, Paris. Author of *Les Gaullistes; The King and His Court; Les Politiques; Histoire de la République Gaullienne*.
Biography (*in part*)

VIELVOYE, ROGER. Industrial Journalist, London.
Transportation (*in part*)

VILLAÇA, ANTONIO CARLOS. Editor, *Jornal Do Brasil*, Rio de Janeiro.
Literature (*in part*)

WADLEY, J. B. Writer and Broadcaster on cycling. Author of *Tour de France 1970, 1971,* and *1973; Old Roads and New.*
Cycling

WARD-THOMAS, P. A. Golf Correspondent, *The Guardian,* London.
Golf

WAY, DIANE LOIS. Archivist, Anglican Diocese of Toronto, Can.
Biography (*in part*)

WEBB, W. L. Literary Editor, *The Guardian,* London and Manchester.
Literature (*in part*)

WEBSTER, PETER L. Assistant Professor, Department of Botany, University of Massachusetts, Amherst.
Life Sciences (*in part*)

WEEDEN, CYRIL. Assistant Director, Glass Manufacturers' Federation, London.
Industrial Production and Technology (*in part*)

WEIGEL, J. TIMOTHY. Sports Columnist, the *Chicago Daily News.* Author of *The Buckeyes.*
Biography (*in part*)

WHITE, A. A. Editor, *Toys International,* London.
Games and Toys

WILE, JULIUS. Senior Vice-President, Julius Wile Sons & Co., Inc., New York City. Vice-President, New England Distillers, Inc., Teterboro, N.J. Chairman, Table Wine Committee, National Association of Alcoholic Beverage Importers, Inc. Lecturer on wines, School of Hotel Administration, Cornell University.
Alcoholic Beverages (*in part*)

WILLIAMS, BRIAN. Free-lance Writer, London.
Television and Radio (*in part*)

WILLIAMS, DAVID L. Associate Professor of Government, Ohio University.
Communist Movement

WILLIAMS, L. F. RUSHBROOK. Fellow of All Souls College, Oxford University, 1914–21; Professor of Modern Indian History, Allahabad, India, 1914–19. Author of *The State of Pakistan; What About India?; Kutch in History and Legend.* Editor of *Handbook to India, Pakistan, Bangladesh, Nepal, and Sri Lanka* and *Sufi Studies East and West.*
Afghanistan; Iran; Pakistan

WILLIAMS, PETER. Editor, *Dance and Dancers,* London.
Dance (*in part*)

WILLIAMSON, TREVOR. Chief Sports subeditor, the *Daily Telegraph,* London.
Biography (*in part*); Football (*in part*)

WILSON, ALAN. Associate Editor, *Scanorama,* Bromma, Swed.
Sweden

WILSON, J. TUZO. Professor of Geophysics, University of Toronto, Ontario. Director General, Ontario Science Center, Don Mills, Ont. Author of *Continents Adrift.* Co-author of *Physics and Geology.*
Geology

WILSON, MICHAEL. Technical Editor, *Flight International,* London. Free-lance Writer.
Industrial Production and Technology (*in part*)

WISE, CONRAD. Chief, Division of Standards, Research and Museums, UNESCO, Paris.
Museums (*in part*)

WOOD, KENNETH H. Editor, *The Advent Review and Sabbath Herald.* Author of *Meditations for Moderns; Relevant Religions.* Co-author of *His Initials Were F. D. N.*
Religion (*in part*)

WOOLLER, MICHAEL. Economic Research Officer, Lloyds Bank International, London.
Biography (*in part*); Bolivia; Haiti; Portugal; Venezuela

WOOLLEY, DAVID. Editor, *Airports International,* London.
Transportation (*in part*)

WORSNOP, RICHARD L. Writer, Editorial Research Reports, Washington, D.C.
Liberia; United States (*in part*)

WRIGHT, ALMON R. Retired Senior Historian, U.S. Department of State.
Panama

YOLLES, STANLEY F., M.D. Professor and Chairman, Department of Psychiatry and Behavioral Science, School of Medicine, Health Sciences Center, State University of New York at Stony Brook.
Drug Abuse (*in part*)

YOUNG, M. NORVEL. Chancellor, Pepperdine University, Malibu, Calif. Editor of *Twentieth Century Christian; Power for Today.* Author of *Churches of Today.*
Religion (*in part*)

ZIMMERMAN, DONNA. Free-lance Writer.
Biography (*in part*)

Index

The black type entries are article headings in the *Book of the Year*. These black type article entries do not show page notations because they are to be found in their alphabetical position in the body of the book. They show the dates of the issues of the *Book of the Year* in which the articles appear. For example "Archaeology 75, 74, 73" indicates that the article "Archaeology" is to be found in the 1975, 1974, and 1973 *Book of the Year*.

The light type headings that are indented under black type article headings refer to material elsewhere in the text related to the subject under which they are listed. The light type headings that are not indented refer to information in the text not given a special article. Biographies and obituaries are listed as cross references to the articles "*Biography*" and "*Obituaries*" for the year in which they appear. References to illustrations are preceded by the abbreviation "il."

All headings, whether consisting of a single word or more, are treated for the purpose of alphabetization as single complete headings. Names beginning with "Mc" and "Mac" are alphabetized as "Mac"; "St." is treated as "Saint." All references below show the exact quarter of the page by means of the letters *a, b, c* and *d,* signifying, respectively, the upper and lower halves of the first column and the upper and lower halves of the second column. Exceptions to this rule are tables, illustrations, and references from biographies and the articles "*Energy*" and "*Industrial Production and Technology.*"

F

U